GAIN
STALLIO

STALLIONS FOR 2004

In England	**CADEAUX GENEREUX**	
	Fee for 2004: £20,000 O	
	FANTASTIC LIGHT 199_ ...y – Jood	
	Fee for 2004: £30,000 October 1st SLF	
	GREEN DESERT 1983 by Danzig – Foreign Courier	
	Fee for 2004: £85,000 October 1st	
	ROYAL APPLAUSE 1993 by Waajib – Flying Melody	
	Fee for 2004: £15,000 October 1st	
NEW FOR 2004	**STORMING HOME** 1998 by Machiavellian – Try To Catch Me	
	Fee for 2004: £10,000 SLF	
	ZILZAL 1986 by Nureyev – French Charmer	
	Fee for 2004: £5,000 October 1st	
In Ireland	**DILSHAAN** 1998 by Darshaan – Avila	
	Fee for 2004: €6,000 October 1st	
	KEY OF LUCK 1991 by Chief's Crown – Balbonella	
	Fee for 2004: €25,000 October 1st	
NEW FOR 2004	**KRIS KIN** 2000 by Kris S – Angel In My Heart	
	Fee for 2004: €8,000 October 1st	
In USA	**ELUSIVE QUALITY** 1993 by Gone West – Touch of Greatness	
	Fee for 2004: $50,000 October 1st	
	LABEEB 1992 by Lear Fan – Lady Blackfoot	
	Fee for 2004: $7,500 October 1st	
	QUIET AMERICAN 1986 by Fappiano – Demure	
	Fee for 2004: $35,000 Live Foal October 1st	
	RAHY 1985 by Blushing Groom – Glorious Song	
	Fee for 2004: $80,000 Live Foal September 1st	
	SHADEED 1982 by Nijinsky – Continual	
	Fee for 2004: $2,500 Live Foal October 1st	
In Canada	**ASCOT KNIGHT** 1984 by Danzig – Bambee T.T.	
	Fee for 2004: $6,500 (Canadian) Live Foal	

Enquiries to:
M.H. Goodbody,
Gainsborough Stud, Woolton Hill,
Newbury, Berkshire RG20 9TE
T: (01635) 253273
F: (01635) 254690
E: office@gainsborough-stud.com
W: www.gainsborough-equine.com

or Allen Kershaw,
Gainsborough Farm,
7200 Steele Road, Versailles,
Kentucky 40383, USA
T: (859) 873 8918
F: (859) 873 2462
E: info@gainsboroughfarm.com
W: www.gainsboroughfarm.com

STALLIONS FOR 2004

AGE, WEIGHT & DISTANCE TABLE

Timeform's scale of weight-for-age for the flat

Dist	Age	Jan 1-16	Jan 17-31	Feb 1-16	Feb 17-28	Mar 1-16	Mar 17-31	Apr 1-16	Apr 17-30	May 1-16	May 17-31	June 1-16	June 17-30
5f	4	10—0	10—0	10—0	10—0	10—0	10—0	10—0	10—0	10—0	10—0	10—0	10—0
	3	9—5	9—5	9—6	9—7	9—7	9—8	9—8	9—9	9—9	9-10	9-10	9-11
	2						8—0	8—1	8—3	8—4	8—5	8—6	8—7
6f	4	10—0	10—0	10—0	10—0	10—0	10—0	10—0	10—0	10—0	10—0	10—0	10—0
	3	9—2	9—3	9—4	9—5	9—5	9—6	9—7	9—7	9—8	9—8	9—9	9—9
	2									8—0	8—2	8—3	8—4
7f	4	9-13	9-13	10—0	10—0	10—0	10—0	10—0	10—0	10—0	10—0	10—0	10—0
	3	9—0	9—1	9—2	9—3	9—4	9—4	9—5	9—6	9—6	9—7	9—8	9—8
	2											7-13	8—1
1m	4	9-13	9-13	9-13	9-13	10—0	10—0	10—0	10—0	10—0	10—0	10—0	10—0
	3	8-12	8-13	9—0	9—1	9—2	9—2	9—3	9—4	9—5	9—5	9—6	9—7
	2												
9f	4	9-12	9-12	9-12	9-13	9-13	9-13	9-13	10—0	10—0	10—0	10—0	10—0
	3	8-10	8-11	8-12	8-13	9—0	9—1	9—2	9—2	9—3	9—4	9—5	9—5
	2												
1¼m	4	9-11	9-12	9-12	9-12	9-13	9-13	9-13	9-13	9-13	10—0	10—0	10—0
	3	8—8	8—9	8-10	8-11	8-12	8-13	9—0	9—1	9—2	9—2	9—3	9—4
	2												
11f	4	9-10	9-11	9-11	9-12	9-12	9-12	9-13	9-13	9-13	9-13	9-13	10—0
	3	8—6	8—7	8—8	8—9	8-10	8-11	8-12	8-13	9—0	9—1	9—2	9—2
1½m	4	9-10	9-10	9-10	9-11	9-11	9-12	9-12	9-12	9-13	9-13	9-13	9-13
	3	8—4	8—5	8—6	8—7	8—8	8—9	8-10	8-11	8-12	8-13	9—0	9—1
13f	4	9—9	9—9	9-10	9-10	9-11	9-11	9-11	9-12	9-12	9-12	9-13	9-13
	3	8—2	8—3	8—4	8—5	8—7	8—8	8—9	8-10	8-11	8-12	8-13	9—0
1¾m	4	9—8	9—8	9—9	9—9	9-10	9-10	9-11	9-11	9-12	9-12	9-12	9-13
	3	8—0	8—2	8—3	8—4	8—5	8—6	8—7	8—8	8—9	8-10	8-11	8-12
15f	4	9—7	9—8	9—8	9—9	9—9	9-10	9-10	9-11	9-11	9-11	9-12	9-12
	3	7-13	8—0	8—1	8—2	8—4	8—5	8—6	8—7	8—8	8—9	8-10	8-11
2m	4	9—6	9—7	9—7	9—8	9—9	9—9	9-10	9-10	9-11	9-11	9-11	9-12
	3	7-11	7-12	7-13	8—1	8—2	8—3	8—4	8—5	8—6	8—7	8—8	8—9
2¼m	4	9—5	9—5	9—6	9—7	9—7	9—8	9—9	9—9	9-10	9-10	9-10	9-11
	3	7—8	7—9	7-11	7-12	7-13	8—0	8—2	8—3	8—4	8—5	8—6	8—7
2½m	4	9—3	9—4	9—5	9—6	9—6	9—7	9—7	9—8	9—9	9—9	9-10	9-10
	3	7—5	7—7	7—8	7—9	7-11	7-12	7-13	8—1	8—2	8—3	8—4	8—5

For 5-y-o's and older, use 10-0 in all cases
Race distances in the above tables are shown only at 1 furlong intervals.
For races over odd distances, the nearest distance shown in the table should be used:
thus for races of 1m to 1m 109 yards, use the table weights for 1m;
for 1m 110 yards to 1m 219 yards use the 9f table

**The age, weight and distance table covering July to December
appears on the end paper at the back of the book**

RACEHORSES OF 2003

Price £70.00

A TIMEFORM PUBLICATION

CONTENTS

The age, weight and distance tables, for use in applying the ratings in races involving horses of different ages, appear on the end papers at the front and back of the book

Compiled and produced by

G. Greetham (Director), C. S. Williams (Managing Editor & Handicapper), J. Ingles (Essays & Editor for pedigrees & 'Top Horses Abroad'), E. K. Wilkinson (Essays & Editor), M. S. Rigg (Essays & Editor), S. D. Rowlands (Handicapper & Short Commentaries), G. J. North, S. Molyneux (Handicappers), G. J. McGibbon (Handicapper & Essays), P. Morrell, J. Early, M. J. Dwyer (Essays), R. J. O'Brien, J. A. Todd (Short Commentaries), S. Wright (pedigrees, database updates), G. Crowther, G. Johnstone (proof checking), M. Hall, D. Holdsworth, W. Muncaster, A-M. Stevens, R. Todd, C. Wright (Production)

© **Portway Press Limited 2004**   ISBN 1 901570 41 X

Racehorses of 2003

Introduction

The turf season opened with the country at war in Iraq, as Anglo American-led action to vanquish terrorists and confront rogue states developing 'weapons of mass destruction' was begun in the aftermath of the atrocities of September 11th 2001. Although the invasion of Iraq was expedited quickly, it will not be so easy to eliminate the terrorist threat. A progress report of sorts was provided by the unprecedented scale of the security operation mounted for a state visit in the autumn by the American president, dubbed the 'invisible visitor' by sections of the British media. For racing, however, the watchword in 2003 was 'business as usual'. The Dubai World Cup meeting, international racing's richest one-day programme, went ahead with fighting taking place only eight hundred miles away. The essay on **Moon Ballad**, who won the eighth Dubai World Cup, describes the effects of the war on the build-up. Further afield, an outbreak of the deadly illness SARS in the Far East did affect international racing, resulting in the cancellation of the first leg of the World Series in Singapore, while there were no runners from Britain in what then became the first leg, the Queen Elizabeth II Cup at Sha Tin in April. Closer to home, a spreading outbreak of equine flu at Newmarket caused concern for a time in the spring.

Two of horseracing's own modern-day 'superpowers' the Maktoum family's Godolphin operation and Coolmore's racing arm Ballydoyle encountered plenty of resistance in 2003 as they tried to maintain their superiority. After a flying start at the World Cup, Godolphin's international campaign faltered somewhat, as outlined in the write-up on **Sulamani** who eventually provided the team's much awaited, one hundredth Group/Grade 1 winner courtesy of the stewards in the Arlington Million. **Dubai Destination**'s triumph in the newly-elevated Queen Anne Stakes at Royal Ascot was Godolphin's only success in the twenty-

'The show must go on'—the world's richest race the Dubai World Cup took place in a subdued atmosphere

Racecourse attendances topped six million in 2003, helped by a notably warm and dry summer; Australian star Choisir thrilled record crowds at Royal Ascot

nine Group 1s in Britain, while **Mezzo Soprano** was the only three-year-old to contribute to the nine Group/Grade 1 winners worldwide.

Godolphin's trainer Saeed bin Suroor, four times champion, finished outside the top ten in the trainers' table in Britain for the first time since Godolphin's inception, though he headed the list of the most successful British-based trainers overseas for the sixth year in succession, as British challengers enjoyed their best year abroad since 1997, a haul of one hundred and four winners contributing to overall earnings of £10,745,396, according to figures produced by the International Racing Bureau. British-based trainers saddled a record seven hundred and twenty-nine foreign runners, an indication of the continuing internationalisation of racing. Ballydoyle's trainer Aidan O'Brien, champion in Britain in the two previous years, was down to eighth in 2003, his Group 1 victories coming in the Lockinge with **Hawk Wing**, the highest rated horse of the year (the essay provides an insight into Timeform's handicapping methods), and in the St Leger with **Brian Boru**, ridden by Jamie Spencer who takes over from thirteen-times Irish champion Michael Kinane as Ballydoyle's number one in 2004 when the stable has plenty to look forward to, housing two colts at the forefront of the ante-post betting for the Two Thousand Guineas in **One Cool Cat** and for the Derby in once-raced **Yeats**.

O'Brien's domination of domestic Irish racing continued with a sixth trainers' championship and victories in six of the ten Irish Group 1s, most notably with **High Chaparral** in a strong field for the Irish Champion Stakes. High Chaparral went on to record a second successive victory in the Breeders' Cup Turf, dead-heating with locally-trained Johar, and providing O'Brien (who saddled over a hundred runners outside Ireland) with one of seven overseas victories which helped him to earn £2,588,874 abroad, £800,000 or so more than the figure that put Saeed bin Suroor at the top of the British table for overseas earnings. Irish trainers had a good year at home—**Indian Haven** was the only overseas raider to win a Group 1—and internationally. Dermot Weld landed the Two Thousand Guineas at Newmarket with **Refuse To Bend** and big races in North America (outlined in the summary on **Dimitrova**), in addition to saddling **Vinnie Roe** for his third win in the Irish St Leger, and training the very promising two-year-old **Grey Swallow**. Michael Kinane will be riding

4

for John Oxx in 2004 but the Oxx-trained Irish Derby winner **Alamshar**, who went on to win the King George VI and Queen Elizabeth Stakes, is now at stud in Japan, having been sold by his owner the Aga Khan, for whom he was a fifth Irish Derby winner. The Aga Khan also had his fifth Prix du Jockey Club and third Prix de l'Arc de Triomphe victory with **Dalakhani**. The reviews of Alamshar and Dalakhani provide an historical insight into the Aga Khan's successful racing and bloodstock empire.

Irish-trained Group 1 winners in Britain are familiar, but the success of Australian-trained **Choisir** in the Golden Jubilee Stakes was the first by a challenger from the southern hemisphere in Britain. One of several runners from outside Europe attracted to Royal Ascot, Choisir also won the King's Stand Stakes on the opening day and was the first horse for twenty years to record two successes at Royal Ascot in the same year. Choisir saw a little over three minutes action during his short stay—he was also second in the July Cup—but he left a tremendous impression. The attendances over the five days of Royal Ascot totalled 306,174, up slightly on the previous year. Other courses posted buoyant figures too, including York whose three-day August meeting attracted record crowds of 83,560 (York is to stage the Royal meeting in 2005 when Ascot undergoes major rebuilding). Attendances at British racecourses topped six million in 2003, a modern-day record, helped by a long, dry summer which was compared to Britain's record hot summer of 1976. The British weather is a topic of endless fascination, its unpredictability illustrated on August 10th, the hottest day. While temperatures in Kent reached 101.3F (the highest ever recorded in Britain) and roads melted in Essex, trees and power lines crashed down and homes were flooded in severe storms in the North East (where Redcar's race meeting had to be abandoned).

On the domestic racing scene, Sir Michael Stoute was champion trainer for the seventh time, with record earnings, his first-three prize money of £3,608,776 topping Aidan O'Brien's 2001 total. Stoute's stable-jockey Kieren Fallon won his sixth championship with 221 winners (his fourth double century) and first-three prize money of £5,053,055 which was also a new high. Stoute and Fallon won Europe's richest race, the Derby, with **Kris Kin** whose wide-ranging essay examines, among other things, the way the race is promoted and covered on television nowadays. Stoute and Fallon also teamed up for Group 1 victories with **Russian Rhythm** (One Thousand Guineas, Coronation Stakes and Nassau Stakes), **Islington** (Yorkshire Oaks) and the two-year-old **Red Bloom** (Fillies' Mile). Islington also provided the pair with a notable overseas success, becoming the first British-trained winner of a Breeders' Cup race staged in California. Islington has now been retired but Russian Rhythm stays in training and her connections will have a wider range of opportunities following an overhaul of the pattern system as it relates to fillies and mares. Providing more Group 1 opportunities for the top older fillies may, however, prove a mixed blessing. Islington and Russian Rhythm both added to the competitiveness of races in which they took on the colts, as did other fillies, including the French-trained quartet **Bright Sky**, **Etoile Montante**, **Nebraska Tornado** and the Breeders' Cup Mile winner **Six Perfections**. The pattern changes are outlined in the entry on Russian Rhythm, with other aspects covered under **Buy The Sport**, **Macadamia** and Dimitrova. Fallon's six domestic Group 1 victories for Freemason Lodge were supplemented by another on the Paul Cole-trained **Mr Dinos** in the Gold Cup, in which he beat the ever-popular **Persian Punch** who won three of the season's other major Cup races, the Goodwood Cup, the Doncaster Cup and the Jockey Club Cup. Persian Punch became the first British-trained gelding to win more than £1m in total prize money and also became the joint-oldest winner of a European

5

David Nicholls leads out one of his twelve runners in the Stewards' Cup consolation race at Goodwood

pattern race, an achievement also equalled later by the sprinter **Repertory**. Two other trainers' records are worth recording: eighty-four-year-old Paddy Mullins became the oldest trainer in living memory to saddle a major European classic winner when **Vintage Tipple** won the Irish Oaks, and David Nicholls set a record for the most runners in one race with twelve of the twenty-one that lined up for the consolation race for the Stewards' Cup at Goodwood (the race was won by a former inmate of the stable).

The only other horse to win three British Group 1 races, apart from Russian Rhythm, was the tough and versatile top-class five-year-old **Falbrav** who won the Coral-Eclipse, the Juddmonte International and the Queen Elizabeth II Stakes. The first two races formed part of the British Horseracing Board's much vaunted Summer Triple Crown/Grand Slam, one of the topics discussed in the essay. Taking up foreign challenges is becoming part and parcel of a top European horse's year and Falbrav ran on three different continents and in five different countries, crowning a memorable campaign with victory over another ex-Italian performer, Champion Stakes winner **Rakti**, in the Hong Kong Cup. The three top older horses in Italy in 2003, Sunstrach, Salselon and Maktub, will be racing for British stables in 2004. Britain's top older horses were a good collection, also including the Marcus Tregoning-trained Arc runner-up **Mubtaker** and Prince of Wales's Stakes winner **Nayef**. Tregoning also trained the St Leger runner-up **High Accolade** who won the King Edward VII Stakes to supplement Nayef's Royal Ascot victory. The St Leger third **Phoenix Reach** went on to win the Canadian International to crown a fine first season for Andrew Balding, who took over at Kingsclere from his father. Balding also saddled **Casual Look** to win the Oaks, though she was lucky with Irish One Thousand Guineas winner **Yesterday** failing to obtain a clear run for much of the straight. Casual Look was the lowest rated winner of the Oaks for nearly forty years and Yesterday's stable-companion **L'Ancresse** put up the best performance of the year by a three-year-old filly over middle distances when second to Islington in the Breeders' Cup Filly & Mare Turf.

When a horse makes a successful transition from handicap to pattern company, there always seems an underlying assumption that it has shown significantly improved form in doing so. The form of the big handicaps is often stronger than is generally appreciated, as the commentary on Wokingham dead-heater **Fayr Jag** points out. Macadamia didn't have to step up on her Royal Hunt Cup form to win a pattern race next time, and **Patavellian** had to improve only a few pounds on his Stewards' Cup performance to take the Prix de l'Abbaye de Longchamp on his next outing. The same applied to John Smith's Cup winner **Far Lane** whose late-season victories in pattern and listed company at Newmarket helped Khalid Abdulla to become leading owner in Britain for the first time. Abdulla's Juddmonte Farms breeding operation had

Khalid Abdulla was leading owner in Britain for the first time

Mick Channon trained the most winners and finished third in the trainers' prize money table

a magnificent year internationally and its achievements are set out in the extended entry on champion sprinter **Oasis Dream**, the best horse to carry the Abdulla colours in Europe in the latest season. French-trained **American Post**, who was supplemented to win the Racing Post Trophy, and **Three Valleys** were the pick of the Abdulla two-year-olds on form. The latter was the first horse to lose a Group 1 race in Britain through failing a dope test since the Aga Khan's Aliysa was stripped of the 1989 Oaks (Godolphin's Noverre was disqualified in the Poule d'Essai des Poulains in 2001 in similar circumstances). Three Valleys tested positive after the Middle Park Stakes for clenbuterol, a fairly routine treatment for horses with breathing problems or congested lungs.

There was precious little between the top two-year-olds, the most highly rated being French-trained **Bago** who maintained his unbeaten record when spreadeagling the field in the Criterium International, a race inaugurated in 2001 and won previously by Act One and Dalakhani. For strength in depth among the two-year-olds the stable of Mark Johnston took some beating. Johnston stopped writing his trenchant weekly column for the *Racing Post* just before Royal Ascot, following a difference of opinion over the paper's campaign for a better deal for stable staff. The timing was unfortunate since Johnston was very much the man in the news with five winners at the Royal meeting, including the two-year-olds **Attraction**—the season's highest rated juvenile filly—**Pearl of Love** and **Russian Valour**. The stable also housed the Vintage Stakes and Champagne Stakes winner **Lucky Story**. Johnston reached a century of winners for the tenth consecutive season and finished second in the trainers' prize money table, one place ahead of Mick Channon who pipped Johnston by five winners (144 to 139) in the race to saddle most winners. Ten of Channon's wins came courtesy of the outstandingly tough **Misternando**,

7

while **Zafeen** (St James's Palace Stakes) and another particularly resilient performer **Imperial Dancer** (Premio Roma) provided the stable with Group 1 victories at home and abroad. Zafeen has joined Godolphin, as has the Jeremy Noseda-trained Cheveley Park winner **Carry On Katie** and **Bayeux**, the highest rated two-year-old trained by David Loder who reversed his decision to retire at the end of the season and will be a public trainer in 2004 with Irish-based Johnny Murtagh set to ride regularly for his yard. Bayeux went down by a neck to subsequent Dewhurst winner **Milk It Mick** in the Somerville Tattersall Stakes at Newmarket. Milk It Mick, the highest rated two-year-old colt in Britain, started the season in maiden auction company and won the Dewhurst—from Three Valleys—on his twelfth outing.

Milk It Mick's multi-millionaire owner Paul Dixon was prominent among those who tried to orchestrate a campaign to boycott low-value races in the autumn, following the suspension for the last four months of the year of guaranteed minimum values for races. The Levy Board announced a £6m cut from its planned contribution to prize money for that period, following a shortfall in the estimated levy yield for 2002/3. The Levy Board originally set a target of £50m for its allocation to prize money during the year but its revised total of £43.9m was still more than ten per cent above the Levy Board's prize money contribution of the previous year; at the same time as the cut was announced, the Levy Board set its prize money allocation for 2004 at £48m, representing a nine per cent year-on-year increase on the revised figure for the current year. For the Racehorse Owners' Association, the autumn cuts reportedly amounted to 'brutal carnage'. The owners' boycott barely got off the ground. One protest involved reducing a race at Sedgefield to two runners, while another led to wholesale withdrawals at an all-weather meeting at Wolverhampton. Owners referred to purses of £2,750 as 'an insult', but the 'fair deal for stable staff' campaign had revealed that it would take some stable hands three months to earn that amount, while the Levy Board subsidy itself, which makes up just under half of the entire prize money fund, is raised from ordinary betting shop customers.

Owners weren't the only ones to show militancy in 2003. The jockeys were at loggerheads with the Jockey Club over regulations restricting the use of mobile phones during meetings. The proposed restrictions, advised after a review of security by the Jockey Club, had followed evidence, given in a court case, that former jockeys had admitted passing 'information' from the weighing

The Jockey Club's attempt to impose restrictions on the use of mobile phones in the weighing room led to the first abandonment of a race meeting in Britain because of strike action within the sport

room before races. The row over the restrictions came to a head with the boycotting of a meeting at Sandown in September, forcing the first-ever abandonment as a result of strike action within racing. The new rules were eventually modified to lessen the inconvenience to jockeys who seemed eventually to accept the need to co-operate, in the wider interests of bolstering the integrity of the sport, which had been portrayed as corrupt in two slanted investigative BBC television programmes the year before.

If the storms involving action by owners and jockeys were arguably of the teacup variety, the one hanging over racing as a result of a long-running investigation by the Office of Fair Trading is set to have much wider ramifications. The leading bookmakers and the British Horseracing Board may both come to regret that they did not follow the schoolboy adage that it is always better to sort out playground disputes yourself than to go running to teacher. By originally lodging complaints with the OFT about uncompetitive activities and abuse of monopoly power, they set in motion something that could not be stopped. At the time, the BHB and the bookmakers were involved in seemingly-interminable arguments, latterly over the price of pre-race data, such as runners and riders, and pictures for betting shops. The BHB had been at daggers drawn with the major bookmakers since BHB chairman Peter Savill's first year in office in 1998 when Savill had claimed the bookmakers could 'afford an extra £80m without passing it on to the punter.' The BHB began championing 'spectator-friendly' fixtures as a way of compensating for money it was not getting—but felt it was entitled to—through the levy. 'The bookies won't like more racing on Sundays and in the evenings . . . I'd rather racing gained and the bookies lost,' was the stated view of the BHB chairman.

The changing mood has been brought about by the Government's decision in 2001 to replace betting tax with a tax on bookmakers' gross profits. An agreement made between the off-course bookmakers and the BHB in 2002 links bookmakers' payments towards the funding of racing to their profits from British racing. This has led to a situation where the sport's governing body now has a vested interest in seeing bookmakers' profits maximised. Both William Hill and the Ladbroke Group announced record turnover and record profits for the first half of 2003, but almost all the growth in profits from betting was accounted for by non-racing products. The face of High Street betting is changing, with football (win singles now allowed) and fixed-odds betting terminals (in particular the game of virtual roulette) now providing rival attractions to the traditional horse and dog racing. An incessant supply of virtual racing from Portman Park and Steepledowns, virtual greyhound racing, and balls with numbers on them, have also brought something of the feeling of a betting arcade to many shops. Faced with paying tax on their British horseracing profits, it is understandable that the bookmakers should have looked to promote other betting opportunities (nearly all of them more profitable than racing anyway). Betting on horse racing now accounts for only just over 60% of all off-course betting with bookmakers, and contributes less than half of total profits.

The abolition of betting tax made betting on shorter-priced horses more attractive and, with much of the subsequent extra betting coming on such horses, bookmakers have experienced a decline in their overall margins on horse racing, which in turn led to the shortfall in the forecast levy yield and the subsequent cut in prize money that so angered owners. The continuing growth in the popularity and success of person-to-person betting exchanges was also cited by bookmakers and the BHB as a reason for the levy shortfall. Hills and Ladbrokes have led the way in blaming the exchanges for the fall in bookmakers' margins, while the BHB, all too predictably, has joined in the attempt to discredit the betting exchanges, not only blaming them for the 'hole' in racing's finances, but claiming they are a threat to racing's integrity. 'Betting exchanges have for the first time enfranchised thirty million people in Britain to make money out of horses losing races, whereas previously there were only 3,791, the number of on- and off-course bookmakers with permits,' said BHB chairman Peter Savill, amid claims that the exchanges were being used by money-launderers and international crime syndicates. Concerns over the regulation of the exchanges, and in particular about the laying of bets by individuals who do not hold bookmakers' permits, were aired fully to the Government. The Minister of Gambling, Lord McIntosh, rejected the claims, telling the bookmakers that the Government had listened to the arguments but did not agree with any of them. These included claims by the Association of British Bookmakers that there were 'stories almost every day of horses drifting in the market after being laid to lose on the exchanges.' Betting exchanges, which provide the opportunity to trade at better odds than those offered by traditional bookmakers, are also taxed and levied on their gross profits (the major bookmakers wanted the Government to impose a further tax on the profits made by those who 'act as bookmakers' by laying on the exchanges). The largest of the exchanges, Betfair, told the parliamentary committee on the new Gambling Bill that less than one per cent of its customers—which included registered bookmakers—were making more than £15,000 a year. The perception that layers made more money than backers was not true, while claims that the introduction of exchanges had exacerbated corruption—one journalist labelled them 'a charter for cheats'—were refuted. Betfair told the committee that, in 2003, no fewer than 1,700 *winners* had more than doubled in price, including one horse which had drifted from 7/1 to 80/1. All customers on Betfair, which has been transparent in its dealings over security with racing's regulatory body the Jockey Club, have to sign away their rights to confidentiality.

The edge that the betting exchanges provide for most customers usually lies in backing horses to win rather than to lose, but it is true that the exchanges opened up a new way—potentially at least—to benefit from a horse losing. Comprehensive camera patrol facilities and stronger deterrents had seemed to make 'non-triers' a less pressing issue in recent years for the authorities. On the evidence of the latest season, however, cases where the only reasonable interpretation of events seen on the course was that a horse was a 'non-trier' did seem more prevalent, at times at least. Even more worryingly, some could be interpreted more seriously than as simply cases of horses being brought along 'quietly' for another day. The authorities are, however, arguably barking up the wrong tree by monitoring movements on the betting exchanges. 'Drifters' are by no means necessarily 'non-triers', as Betfair's statistics indicate, and in strong betting races movement would not be pronounced for relatively short-priced horses coming into races in top form whose chances are there for all to see beforehand. The Jockey Club should instead, perhaps, be asking itself whether it has sufficient numbers of good stewards and supporting officials, an issue that it needs to address anyway given the scale of increase in the number of fixtures envisaged over the next few years.

In the new era of co-operation between the BHB and the bookmakers, the BHB is falling over itself to provide more 'betting opportunities' to bolster British racing's market share in the betting shops and to meet the bookmakers' needs for reliably available, all-year-round racing. The BHB's long-term vision is that there will be '363 days of the year with racing from 11 am until 10 pm, with more floodlit racing.' More floodlit racing means more all-weather tracks and Newbury, Sedgefield, Newmarket, Kempton and a new course—the first for over seventy-five years—at Great Leighs in Essex are among those gearing up. A BHB review team came up with seventy-six recommendations in a blueprint for British racing which was unveiled at the end of April. The proposals included the much expanded fixture list and the creation of a three-tier system of premier (the most prestigious and valuable meetings), national and regional racing, with bigger prize money differentials between the types. Regional racing was introduced on an experimental basis at the start of 2004, when the poorest Flat horses started running in races for as little as £1,500. The seventy extra meetings created for the experiment contributed to a record fixture list of 1,341 meetings for 2004, with an unbroken sequence (except for Good Friday) of 320 days' racing between February 2nd and December 18th, and only nine blank days out of 366. There are plenty who think this is not the right course.

The BHB's blueprint appeared shortly after the Office of Fair Trading issued a 'rule 14 notice' concluding that 'aspects of the BHB's and Jockey Club's Rules and Orders infringe the 1998 Competition Act.' By limiting the freedom of racecourses, through controlling the allocation of fixtures, the types of races staged at them and the prize money offered, the BHB was abusing a monopoly position, as it was by being the sole supplier of data such as runners, riders and weights. The notice raised questions about whether the BHB blueprint would ever be implemented. In theory, there seemed likely to be nothing stopping individual tracks from racing when, and as often, as they wanted; individual groups like Arena Leisure and Northern Racing, for example, would be able to negotiate their own deals with the big bookmakers to provide racing, threatening the future of some of the smaller tracks. The BHB's undiplomatic riposte was that 'the OFT has fundamentally misunderstood how and why British racing operates as it does.'

The BHB did, however, propose, in the wake of the OFT report, the transfer of its commercial activities, notably the sale of media rights, to a new body—British Horseracing Enterprises—consisting mainly of owners and racecourses. However, the Jockey Club described allowing racecourses and owners to dictate fixture and prize money policy as potentially 'a disaster for the sport' in that it would deliver control to the betting industry which is 'no longer run by racing men but by accountants.' The dangers to quality Flat racing, and to jump racing in general, became a burning issue among critics of the OFT's stance; it was feared that the bookmakers would cherry-pick the fixtures they wanted (all-weather with guaranteed fields) and shun those which

While the deliberations of the Office of Fair Trading cast a shadow over racing, the restrictive conditions of the newly-instituted Grey Horse Handicap (exclusively for greys) at Newmarket in August caused comment; the BHB insisted that Newmarket staged a similar race for which horses registered as greys were ineligible!

yielded the lowest turnover or profit. The Jockey Club's subsidiary Racecourse Holdings Trust, which includes two of the courses building all-weather tracks, Newmarket and Kempton, was the only racecourse grouping to attack the OFT's findings (Arena, for example, had told the OFT that it would like to stage up to 303 additional fixtures at its three all-weather tracks).

Some of the critics took the argument against the OFT to the extreme, but it was hard to disagree, in essence, with the logic of the OFT's findings. The BHB has exercised its power widely and rigidly over racecourses, using it for example: to control the balance between Flat, all-weather and jumping (a free market would shift more emphasis to the Flat, in particular the all-weather); to prevent racecourses that wanted to stage Saturday evening meetings from doing so in 2000; to prevent racecourses within fifty miles of each other from staging simultaneous meetings; to undermine plans for a new racecourse at London City, which was reportedly offered only ten fixtures, being told it would have to 'buy' any others; and to prevent some notably successful racecourses, including Ascot, from staging more meetings. By interfering with the forces of supply and demand, the BHB, and the Jockey Club before it, have not only protected 'lame duck' courses from the effects of a free market, but have also stifled the entrepreneurial talents of British racing's best racecourse managements. Why should the BHB alone, for example, determine the content of race programmes, or dictate how prize money is allocated across different types of races? One thing the OFT made clear was that racecourses would have to be given greater choice, that successful ones would have to be allowed to expand and that supporting the existing fifty-nine courses at the expense of outside investment was no longer acceptable.

For much of the year, the BHB and, to a lesser extent, the Jockey Club engaged the OFT in procedural, legal argument, rather than in trying to address the OFT's concerns over anti-competitive behaviour. This frustrated the Minister of Sport, Richard Caborn, who, by the end of the year, announced that he had decided to summon the chairman of the BHB, the senior steward of the Jockey Club (Julian Richmond-Watson), the president of the Racehorse Owners Association (Chris Deuters) and the chairman of the Racecourse Association (Keith Brown) to obtain assurances 'that the racing industry is doing all it can to offer realistic options for the OFT to consider.' There had seemingly been some unease within the Government about the effects on the BHB's ability to provide effective leadership if the OFT's reforms were implemented in full (the BHB was established in 1993 after a House of Commons report had called for racing to have 'strong and unified commercial leadership [through the creation of] a powerful and competent single body to speak for and manage the industry'). It takes something of a miracle to get agreement on anything among racing's main sectional interests, so finding a unified proposal to present to the OFT—particularly over the sale of media rights—presents an enormous challenge. But it is the only way the OFT is likely to be persuaded from delivering a doctrinaire final verdict, expected in the first half of 2004.

The OFT was also involved in continuing plans for the sale of the Tote. It opposed the idea that a newly-privatised Tote—which might be sold to a racing trust—should be granted an exclusive pool betting licence for seven years. This was deemed 'anti-competitive' by the OFT and the Treasury supported that view, suggesting an exclusive licence should be issued only for two years. When the abolition of the Horserace Totalisator Board and the proposed sale of its assets was dealt with in Parliament, the bill—effectively nationalising the Tote so it can be sold off—did not specify that it should be sold to a racing trust, nor did it make clear the basis on which the price would be determined, while the length of any exclusive licence was fixed at seven years only by way of a late amendment at the bill's report stage. The future of the Levy Board, whose life has been extended again, until 2006, was also covered by the bill.

The Tote's commercial decision to cut its deductions to punters earlier in the year inadvertently led to another tricky situation for racing's rulers. The ten-year £307m media rights deal with attheraces, which was already looking doomed as a result of OFT intervention, was threatened with being revoked by the television consortium at the end of the year when the gross profit margins of the Tote, which attheraces uses for its pool betting, fell below a level stipulated in the contract. The scenario had echoes of the collapse of the ITV Digital deal which threw a number of clubs in the Football League into financial crisis. The original valuation of the attheraces contract was founded on the notion that associated interactive and internet betting would prove a goldmine. There is now speculation that, to have any hope of making its business profitable, attheraces may need to renegotiate the deal—possibly separately with the different racecourse groupings to avoid OFT scrutiny—at a total of around £180m. The forty-nine participating racecourses had already collectively received about £100m by the end of 2003. If the deal—also covering terrestrial TV rights—is renegotiated at the figure being suggested, it will be a blow to Peter Savill who regards the restructuring of the contract in June 2001 as one of his most satisfying achievements as BHB chairman, a role he is set to relinquish in June 2004.

The most significant figure to relinquish his role in 2003 was eleven-times champion jockey Pat Eddery who retired at the end of the turf season. His

handling of Derby runner-up **The Great Gatsby** at Epsom was one of the rides of the season and he also won Group 1s on **Reel Buddy**, in whose essay his career is summarised, and on **Balmont** who was awarded the Middle Park. The achievements of owner-breeder Jean-Luc Lagardere, one of the most influential figures in French racing, are covered in the essay on **Clodovil**, who carried his colours to victory in the Poule d'Essai des Poulains a few weeks after his death. As usual, the horses highlighted in bold in this introduction are among those with extended entries. Consistency of thought, style and presentation has always been the hallmark of Timeform's select team of essay writers. The approach gives *Racehorses* the cohesion that has enabled it to establish an unrivalled reputation over the years as *the* definitive record of the *whole* racing year. Nowadays that remit extends well beyond the shores of the British Isles. Timeform ratings are used round the world and the 'Top Horses Abroad' section provides Timeform

Pat Eddery weighs in
after his final ride in Britain on Gamut
at Doncaster in November

ratings for the leading horses in Ireland, France, Germany, Italy, Scandinavia, the UAE, North America, Japan, Hong Kong and Australia/New Zealand.

February 2004

2003 STATISTICS

The following tables show the leading owners, trainers, jockeys, sires of winners and horses on the Flat in Britain during 2003 (Jan 1–Dec 31). The prize-money statistics, compiled by *Timeform*, relate to first-three prize money and win-money. Win money was traditionally used to decide the trainers' championship until, in 1994, the BHB and the National Trainers' Federation established a championship decided by total prize-money as determined by *Racing Post*. The jockeys' championship has traditionally been decided by the number of winners ridden during the year, though since 1997 the Jockeys' Association has recognised a championship that runs for the turf season (Mar–Nov).

	OWNERS (1,2,3 earnings)	Horses	Indiv'l Wnrs	Races Won	Runs	%	Stakes £
1	Mr K. Abdulla	119	56	78	357	21.8	1,735,745
2	Mr Hamdan Al Maktoum	160	79	103	524	19.6	1,591,611
3	Cheveley Park Stud	72	33	48	237	20.2	1,324,142
4	Sheikh Mohammed	116	67	96	366	26.2	1,305,078
5	Mr Saeed Suhail	17	10	17	57	29.8	1,171,227
6	Godolphin	47	21	23	98	23.4	903,691
7	H. H. Aga Khan	14	9	15	51	29.4	853,246
8	Mrs John Magnier	10	4	4	18	22.2	829,907
9	Scuderia Rencati Srl	4	2	5	20	25.0	700,236
10	Mr J. C. Smith	29	13	23	179	12.8	523,733
11	Mr Saeed Manana	16	8	15	120	12.5	510,479
12	Exors of the late Lord Weinstock	15	9	14	50	28.0	499,611

	OWNERS (win-money, £½m+)	Horses	Indiv'l Wnrs	Races Won	Runs	%	Stakes £
1	Mr K. Abdulla	119	56	78	357	21.8	1,221,520
2	Mr Hamdan Al Maktoum	160	79	103	524	19.6	1,125,869
3	Cheveley Park Stud	72	33	48	237	20.2	1,023,304
4	Mr Saeed Suhail	17	10	17	57	29.8	1,018,581
5	Sheikh Mohammed	116	67	96	366	26.2	834,230
6	Scuderia Rencati Srl	4	2	5	20	25.0	698,401
7	H. H. Aga Khan	14	9	15	51	29.4	581,887
8	Godolphin	47	21	23	98	23.4	529,433

	TRAINERS (1,2,3 earnings)	Horses	Indiv'l Wnrs	Races Won	Runs	%	Stakes £
1	Sir Michael Stoute	155	83	115	482	23.8	3,608,776
2	M. Johnston	168	84	139	758	18.3	1,910,956
3	M. R. Channon	170	85	144	1136	12.6	1,855,922
4	R. Hannon	200	82	122	1032	11.8	1,571,095
5	B. W. Hills	165	79	107	640	16.7	1,373,307
6	J. H. M. Gosden	131	57	72	391	18.4	1,313,286
7	M. P. Tregoning	75	34	56	260	21.5	1,312,178
8	A. P. O'Brien, Ireland	36	6	6	58	10.3	1,145,392
9	L. M. Cumani	64	30	57	268	21.2	1,101,180
10	A. M. Balding	103	37	54	521	10.3	1,080,126
11	T. D. Easterby	134	40	58	829	6.9	1,065,012
12	D. R. Loder	72	44	70	225	31.1	1,025,977

TRAINERS (win-money, £1m+)	Horses	Indiv'l Wnrs	Races Won	Runs	%	Stakes £
1 Sir Michael Stoute	155	83	115	482	23.8	2,760,771
2 M. Johnston	168	84	139	758	18.3	1,410,780
3 M. R. Channon	170	85	144	1136	12.6	1,174,800
4 R. Hannon	200	82	122	1032	11.8	1,028,956
5 L. M. Cumani	64	30	57	268	21.2	1,009,176

TRAINERS (with 100+ winners)	Horses	Indiv'l Wnrs	Races Won	2nd	3rd	Runs	%
1 M. R. Channon	170	85	144	124	151	1136	12.6
2 M. Johnston	168	84	139	105	72	758	18.3
3 R. Hannon	200	82	122	118	101	1032	11.8
4 Sir Michael Stoute	155	83	115	74	68	482	23.8
5 B. W. Hills	165	79	107	72	76	640	16.7

JOCKEYS (by winners)	1st	2nd	3rd	Unpl	Total Mts	%
1 K. Fallon	221	164	142	528	1055	20.9
2 D. Holland	157	136	109	588	990	15.8
3 K. Darley	125	114	98	531	868	14.4
4 R. Hughes	121	88	80	462	751	16.1
5 A. Culhane	112	106	89	555	862	12.9
6 Dane O'Neill	110	109	111	688	1018	10.8
7 S. Drowne	109	104	99	710	1022	10.6
8 E. Ahern	107	103	90	552	852	12.5
9 J. P. Spencer	102	96	62	337	597	17.0
10 S. Sanders	101	106	90	563	860	11.7
11 L. Dettori	101	90	62	242	495	20.4
12 R. Winston	93	80	85	654	912	10.1

Note: K. Fallon was leading jockey in the turf season with 208 winners

JOCKEYS (1,2,3 earnings)	Races Won	Rides	%	Stakes £
1 K. Fallon	221	1055	20.9	5,053,055
2 D. Holland	157	990	15.8	2,984,073
3 L. Dettori	101	495	20.4	2,622,766
4 R. Hughes	121	751	16.1	1,943,335
5 Pat Eddery	78	624	12.5	1,941,308
6 Martin Dwyer	90	789	11.4	1,845,845
7 J. P. Spencer	102	597	17.0	1,743,762
8 K. Darley	125	868	14.4	1,726,366
9 P. Robinson	70	486	14.4	1,443,900
10 E. Ahern	107	852	12.5	1,321,931
11 R. Hills	75	374	20.0	1,279,133
12 Dane O'Neill	110	1018	10.8	1,265,087

JOCKEYS (win-money, £1m+)	Races Won	Rides	%	Stakes £
1 K. Fallon	221	1055	20.9	3,700,808
2 D. Holland	157	990	15.8	2,165,610
3 L. Dettori	101	495	20.4	1,711,521
4 R. Hughes	121	751	16.1	1,346,122
5 Martin Dwyer	90	789	11.4	1,277,942
6 J. P. Spencer	102	597	17.0	1,216,033

		1st	2nd	3rd	Unpl	Total Mts	%
7	Pat Eddery		78	624	12.5		1,165,796
8	K. Darley		125	868	14.4		1,087,319
9	P. Robinson		70	486	14.4		1,019,458

APPRENTICES (by winners)

		1st	2nd	3rd	Unpl	Total Mts	%
1	R. L. Moore	59	66	58	444	627	9.4
2	S. Hitchcott	45	31	30	216	322	13.9
3	D. Allan	43	56	59	400	558	7.7
4	Lisa Jones	43	32	46	397	518	8.3

SIRES OF WINNERS (1,2,3 earnings)

		Races Won	Runs	%	Stakes £
1	Sadler's Wells (by Northern Dancer)	54	355	15.2	1,823,440
2	Kris S (by Roberto)	15	63	23.8	1,278,813
3	Green Desert (by Danzig)	50	392	12.7	1,067,285
4	Cadeaux Genereux (by Young Generation)	60	514	11.6	912,482
5	Kingmambo (by Mr Prospector)	26	146	17.8	908,386
6	Indian Ridge (by Ahonoora)	57	464	12.2	892,539
7	Danehill (by Danzig)	65	489	13.2	890,558
8	Grand Lodge (by Chief's Crown)	60	532	11.2	888,009
9	Royal Applause (by Waajib)	58	488	11.8	859,433
10	Selkirk (by Sharpen Up)	56	377	14.8	848,663
11	Machiavellian (by Mr Prospector)	61	390	15.6	785,800
12	Night Shift (by Northern Dancer)	64	718	8.9	775,665

SIRES OF WINNERS (win-money)

		Horses	Indiv'l Wnrs	Races Won	Stakes £
1	Kris S (by Roberto)	13	8	15	1,129,335
2	Sadler's Wells (by Northern Dancer)	116	39	54	1,000,196
3	Green Desert (by Danzig)	75	33	50	772,207
4	Kingmambo (by Mr Prospector)	42	14	26	739,816
5	Fairy King (by Northern Dancer)	8	3	5	680,941
6	Cadeaux Genereux (by Young Generation)	105	34	60	679,948
7	Indian Ridge (by Ahonoora)	79	37	57	629,774
8	Royal Applause (by Waajib)	83	32	58	592,850
9	Danehill (by Danzig)	104	40	65	587,770
10	Grand Lodge (by Chief's Crown)	108	34	60	586,539
11	Machiavellian (by Mr Prospector)	77	40	61	559,599
12	Night Shift (by Northern Dancer)	100	42	64	530,790

LEADING HORSES (1,2,3 earnings)

		Races Won	Runs	Stakes £
1	Kris Kin 3 ch.c. Kris S – Angel In My Heart	2	3	978,500
2	Falbrav 5 b.h. Fairy King – Gift of The Night	3	5	669,900
3	Alamshar 3 b.c. Key of Luck – Alaiyda	1	3	596,700
4	Russian Rhythm 3 ch.f. Kingmambo – Balistroika	3	5	529,700
5	Nayef 5 b.h. Gulch – Height of Fashion	1	5	335,000
6	Oasis Dream 3 b.c. Green Desert – Hope	2	4	325,900
7	The Great Gatsby 3 b.c. Sadler's Wells – Ionian Sea	0	1	323,400
8	Rakti 4 b.c. Polish Precedent – Ragera	1	2	309,000
9	Warrsan 5 b.h. Caerleon – Lucayan Princess	3	5	291,800
10	Choisir 4 ch.c. Danehill Dancer – Great Selection	2	3	281,200
11	High Accolade 3 b.c. Mark of Esteem – Generous Lady	4	9	277,635
12	Brian Boru 3 b.c. Sadler's Wells – Eva Luna	1	3	273,000

HORSE OF THE YEAR
JOINT-BEST MIDDLE DISTANCE HORSE
RATED AT 133

FALBRAV

BEST TWO-YEAR-OLD FILLY RATED AT 118
ATTRACTION
BEST TWO-YEAR-OLD COLT RATED AT 121p
BAGO
BEST THREE-YEAR-OLD FILLY RATED AT 124
SIX PERFECTIONS
BEST THREE-YEAR-OLD COLTS
JOINT-BEST MIDDLE-DISTANCE HORSES
RATED AT 133

ALAMSHAR
DALAKHANI

BEST OLDER FEMALE RATED AT 124
ISLINGTON
BEST OLDER MALE/BEST MILER
RATED AT 136
HAWK WING
BEST SPRINTER RATED AT 129
OASIS DREAM
BEST STAYER RATED AT 125
VINNIE ROE
BEST PERFORMANCES IN A HANDICAP IN BRITAIN
IMPERIAL DANCER
ran to 120
when winning Littlewoods Bet Direct Summer Stakes at Goodwood
PATAVELLIAN
ran to 120
when winning Vodafone Stewards' Cup at Goodwood
BEST PERFORMANCE ON ALL-WEATHER IN BRITAIN
PARASOL
ran to 117
when winning Littlewoods Bet Direct Winter Derby at Lingfield

THE TIMEFORM 'TOP HUNDRED'

Here are listed the 'Top 100' two-year-olds, three-year-olds and older horses in the annual. Fillies and mares are denoted by (f).

2 YEAR OLDS

121p	Bago
120	Milk It Mick
119p	Lucky Story
119	Three Valleys
118p	American Post
118p	One Cool Cat
118	Attraction (f)
118	Whipper
117	Balmont
116p	Grey Swallow
116p	Majestic Missile
116	Bayeux
115p	Bachelor Duke
115p	Diamond Green
115+	Haafhd
115	Fokine
115	Holborn
115	Russian Valour
114	Auditorium
114	Colossus
114	Kheleyf
114	Troubadour
113p	Denebola (f)
113p	Imperial Stride
113	Fantastic View
113	Much Faster (f)
113	Nevisian Lad
113	Voix du Nord
113	Wathab
112p	Magritte
112	Grand Reward
112	Green Noon (f)
112	Peak To Creek
112	Pearl of Love
111p	Apsis
111p	Snow Ridge
111	Byron
111	Chineur
111	Howick Falls
111	Spirit of Desert
110p	Latice
110p	Pastoral Pursuits
110p	Red Bloom (f)
110	Cape Fear
110	Simplex
109p	Carry On Katie (f)
109p	Duke of Venice
109	Azarole
109	Barbajuan
109	Moscow Ballet
109	Mutahayya
109	Old Deuteronomy
109	Rule of Law
109	Top Seed
108p	Azamour

108p	Boogie Street
108	Charming Prince
108	Majestic Desert (f)
108	Tahreeb
108	The Mighty Tiger
107p	Punctilious (f)
107p	Sundrop (f)
107	Nyramba (f)
107	Relaxed Gesture
107	Sabbeeh
106p	Cairns (f)
106p	Mikado
106	Carrizo Creek
106	Celtic Cat
106	China Eyes (f)
106	Leicester Square
106	Mokabra
105p	Kinnaird (f)
105p	Necklace (f)
105p	Secret Charm (f)
105p	Top Romance (f)
105	Antonius Pius
105	Blue Tomato
105	Brunel
105	Catstar (f)
105	Gwaihir
105	Matloob
105	Orcadian
104p	Cobra
104p	Nero's Return
104p	Rum Shot
104p	Spotlight (f)
104	Diospyros Blue
104	Mac Love
104	Moonlight Man
104	Needles And Pins (f)
104	Psychiatrist
104	Silca's Gift (f)
104	Tashkil
103P	Malevitch
103p	Badminton (f)
103p	Chester Le Street
103p	Josephus
103p	Venturi
103	Cartography
103	Happy Crusader
103	Kings Point
103	Malaica (f)
103	Nights Cross
103	Parkview Love
103	Privy Seal

3 YEAR OLDS

133	Alamshar
133	Dalakhani
129	Oasis Dream

126	Kalaman
126	Kris Kin
125	Somnus
125	Vespone
124	Brian Boru
124	Ikhtyar
124	Magistretti
124	Refuse To Bend
124	Six Perfections (f)
124	Trade Fair
123	Dai Jin
123	L'Ancresse (f)
123	Nebraska Tornado (f)
123	Roosevelt
123	Russian Rhythm (f)
123	Zafeen
122p	Doyen
122p	Phoenix Reach
122	High Accolade
122	Powerscourt
121	Super Celebre
120	Airwave (f)
120	The Great Gatsby
120	Weightless
119	Arakan
119	Baron's Pit
119	Dimitrova (f)
119	Etoile Montante (f)
119	Indian Haven
119	Le Vie dei Colori
119	Martillo
119	Membership
119	Ocean Silk (f)
119	Sabre d'Argent
119	Spanish Sun (f)
119	Yesterday (f)
118p	Leporello
118	Big Bad Bob
118	Muqbil
118	Norse Dancer
118	Pleasure Place (f)
118	Soviet Song (f)
118	Tarjman
117	Balestrini
117	Checkit
117	Hawk Flyer
117	Hold That Tiger
117	Kalabar
117	Maharib
117	Mezzo Soprano (f)
117	Mingun
117	Musical Chimes (f)
117	Policy Maker
117	Ransom O'War
117	Vintage Tipple (f)
117	Westmoreland Road

116	Alberto Giacometti	126	Ipi Tombe (f)	118	Loxias
116	Avonbridge	126	Nayyir	118	Maktub
116	Clodovil	126	Rakti	118	Martaline
116	Deportivo	126	Silent Witness	118	Nysaean
116	Itnab (f)	125	Lohengrin	118	Passing Glance
116	Lateen Sails	125	Storming Home	118	Polar Ben
116	Look Honey	125	Telegnosis	118	Polish Summer
116	Maiden Tower (f)	125	Vinnie Roe	118	Princely Venture
116	Rimrod	124	Ange Gabriel	118	Priors Lodge
116	Stormont	124	Islington (f)	118	Razkalla
115p	Salsalino	124	Leadership	118	Reel Buddy
115+	Lago d'Orta	124	Mr Dinos	118	Royal Millennium
115	Behkara (f)	124	Patavellian	118	Salselon
115	Catcher In The Rye	124	Special Kaldoun	118	Systematic
115	Delsarte	123	Asian Heights	118	Twilight Blues
115	France	123	Bollin Eric	118	Where Or When
115	Hilbre Island	123	Fair Mix	117	Alcazar
115	Monsieur Bond	123	Imperial Dancer	117	Altieri
115	Prince Tum Tum	122	Mamool	117	Ashdown Express
115	Songlark	122	Tillerman	117	Beauchamp Pilot
115	Statue of Liberty	121	Aquarelliste (f)	117	Blatant
115	Tantina (f)	121	Black Sam Bellamy	117	Border Subject
115	Tashkandi	121	Carnival Dancer	117	Dandoun
115	Tout Seul	121	Ekraar	117	Epalo
115	Vallee Enchantee (f)	121	Gamut	117	Feet So Fast
114p	Persian Majesty	121	Highest	117	Firebolt
114	Buy The Sport	121	Kaieteur	117	Highdown
114	Casual Look (f)	121	Millenary	117	Pablo
114	Devious Boy	121	Next Desert	117	Porlezza (f)
114	Dubai Success	121	Olden Times	117	Rawyaan
114	Dunhill Star	121	Paolini	117	Right Approach
114	Etesaal	121	Warrsan	117	State City
114	Hoh Buzzard (f)	121	Westerner	117	With Reason
114	Middlemarch	120	Bright Sky (f)	117d	Pugin
114	Osorio	120	Dano-Mast		
114	Striking Ambition	120	Desert Deer		
114	Summitville (f)	120	Far Lane		
113+	Tiber	120	Just James		
113	Discreet Brief (f)	120	My Risk		
113	Fidelite (f)	120	Persian Punch		
113	Hawksbill	120	The Tatling		
113	Howle Hill	120	The Trader		
113	Hurricane Alan	120	Victory Moon		
113	Miss Emma (f)	120§	Grandera		
113	Moments of Joy (f)	119	Darasim		
113	Private Charter	119	First Charter		
113d	Tuning Fork	119	Indian Creek		
		119	In Time's Eye		

OLDER HORSES

136	Hawk Wing	119	Jardines Lookout	
133	Candy Ride	119	Parasol	
133	Falbrav	119	Short Pause	
132	High Chaparral	119	Sights On Gold	
132	Mineshaft	119	Sunstrach	
132	Mubtaker	119	Zipping	
132	Symboli Kris S	118	Acclamation	
131	Moon Ballad	118	Ana Marie (f)	
128	Domedriver	118	Aolus	
128	Nayef	118	Bandari	
128	Sulamani	118	Compton Bolter	
127	Dubai Destination	118	Danger Over	
126	Choisir	118	Execute	
		118	Firebreak	

conclusions can be drawn with fair certainty, we have drawn them; if it is a matter of probability or possibility we have put it that way, being careful not to say the one when we mean the other; and where real conclusions are not to be drawn, we have been content to state the facts. Furthermore, when we say that a horse *may* not be suited by firm going, we do not expect it to be treated as though we had said the horse *is not* suited by firm going. In short, both in our thinking and in the setting out of our views we have aimed at precision.

THE FORM SUMMARIES

The form summary enclosed in the brackets lists each horse's performances on the Flat during the past year in chronological sequence, showing, for each race, the distance, the state of the going and the horse's placing at the finish.

The distance of each race is given in furlongs, fractional distances being expressed in the decimal notation to the nearest tenth of a furlong. The prefix 'a' signifies a race on an artificial surface (except for 'f' for fibresand at Southwell and Wolverhampton, and 'p' for polytrack at Lingfield).

The going is symbolised as follows: f=firm (turf) or fast (artificial surface); m=good to firm, or standard to fast (artificial surface); g=good (turf) or standard (artificial surface); d=good to soft/dead, or standard to slow (artificial surface); s=soft (turf) or slow, sloppy, muddy or wet (artificial surface); v=heavy.

Placings are indicated, up to sixth place, by the use of superior figures, an asterisk being used to denote a win.

Thus [2003 81: 10s* 12f³ 11.7g f11g² Sep 7] signifies that the horse was rated 81 the previous year (if there is no rating it indicates that the horse did not appear in 'Racehorses' for that year). In 2003 it ran four times, winning over 10 furlongs on soft going first time out, then finishing third over 12 furlongs on firm going, then out of the first six over 11.7 furlongs on good going, then second over 11 furlongs on standard going on a fibresand track. The date of its last run was September 7.

Included in the pedigree details are the highest Timeform Annual ratings during their racing careers of the sires, dams and sires of dams of all horses, where the information is available.

Where sale prices are considered relevant F denotes the price as a foal, Y the price as a yearling, 2-y-o as a two-year-old, and so on. These are given in guineas unless prefixed by IR (Irish guineas), $ (American dollars), € (euros) or accompanied by francs (French francs). Other currencies are converted approximately into guineas or pounds sterling at the prevailing exchange rate. Sales mentioned towards the end of the commentaries refer to those after the horse's final outing.

THE RATING SYMBOLS

The following may be attached to, or appear instead of, a rating:-

p   likely to improve.

P   capable of *much* better form.

+   the horse may be better than we have rated it.

d   the horse appears to have deteriorated, and might no longer be capable of running to the rating given.

§   unreliable (for temperamental or other reasons).

§§   so temperamentally unsatisfactory as not to be worth a rating.

?   the horse's rating is suspect. If used without a rating the symbol implies that the horse can't be assessed with confidence, or, if used in the in-season Timeform publications, that the horse is out of form.

RACEHORSES OF 2003

Horse	Commentary	Rating

AAHGOWANGOWAN (IRE)   4 b.f. Tagula (IRE) 116 – Cabcharge Princess (IRE) **66**
64 (Rambo Dancer (CAN) 107) [2003 73: 6.1g 5g 5d³ 5g 5g³ 5m 5g* 5d 5m² 6g³ 5g Oct
22] sturdy filly: poor mover: fair handicapper: won at Hamilton in July: probably best at
5f: acts on any turf going, not discredited on fibresand: tried visored: tongue tied in 2003:
usually races prominently. *M. Dods*

ABACO SUNSET   2 ch.f. (Feb 14) Bahamian Bounty 116 – Thicket 87 (Wolfhound **58**
(USA) 126) [2003 5m Jul 14] 3,600F, 10,000Y: first foal: dam, 5f winner, ran only at 2
yrs: 50/1, eighth of 14 in maiden at Windsor. *C. G. Cox*

ABAJANY   9 b.g. Akarad (FR) 130 – Miss Ivory Coast (USA) (Sir Ivor 135) [2003 70, **–**
a62: 10.2m⁶ 10.2g 10d Aug 18] sturdy gelding: fair performer at 8 yrs: showed little in
2003: tried visored. *R. J. Baker*

ABANINETOES (IRE)   3 b.f. General Monash (USA) 107 – Gilly-G (IRE) (Tenby **–**
125) [2003 59: p5g p6g p5g 5.7f 7f f7g f8g Nov 24] little form in 2003: tried blinkered.
P. D. Evans

ABBAJABBA   7 b.g. Barrys Gamble 102 – Bo' Babbity 75 (Strong Gale 116) [2003 **95**
103: 6f⁴ 6g 6m 6f 6m 6g 6s 6d⁶ Nov 8] quite good-topped gelding: has a round action:
useful performer: good sixth in listed race at Doncaster final start: best at 5f/6f: acts on
good to firm ground, all wins on good or softer: usually waited with. *C. W. Fairhurst*

ABBALEVA   4 b.f. Shaddad (USA) 75 – Bo' Babbity 75 (Strong Gale 116) [2003 60, **–**
a48: p7g f9.4s Jan 31] leggy filly: modest performer at 3 yrs: well held in 2003, reportedly
lame final start: blinkered in 2003. *C. W. Fairhurst*

ABBEYGATE   2 b.c. (Feb 10) Unfuwain (USA) 131 – Ayunli 81 (Chief Singer 131) **62**
[2003 8.1d 10g p10g⁶ Nov 29] strong colt: fourth foal: half-brother to fairly useful 2001
2-y-o 5f winner Ayzal (by Zilzal) and US 9f winner Helms Deep (by Royal Applause):
dam 8.5f to 15.5f winner: best effort (modest form) when sixth to Pukka in maiden at
Lingfield: should stay 1½m. *T. Keddy*

ABBEY'S VALENTINE   3 b.c. My Best Valentine 122 – My Abbey 77 (Hadeer 118) **–**
[2003 5m Aug 16] close-coupled colt: first foal: dam 5f winner, including at 2 yrs: well
beaten in maiden at Ripon. *M. Mullineaux*

ABBIEJO (IRE)   6 b.m. Blues Traveller (IRE) 119 – Chesham Lady (IRE) (Fayruz **–**
116) [2003 –: 8.1d May 26] no sign of ability. *G. Fierro*

A BEETOO (IRE)   3 b.f. Bahhare (USA) 122 – Sonya's Pearl (IRE) (Conquering Hero **63**
(USA) 116) [2003 58: p7g² p10g⁴ p10g⁶ p8g² p8g⁶ p6g⁵ p7g Dec 29] modest maiden:
best form at 7f/1m: acts on polytrack, unraced on turf: sometimes slowly away. *J. R. Best*

ABELARD (IRE)   2 b.g. (Mar 3) Fasliyev (USA) 120 – Half-Hitch (USA) 88 (Diesis **66**
133) [2003 5m³ 5.1m³ 5m³ Sep 17] €45,000Y: smallish gelding: second foal: half-brother
to Spanish 2002 2-y-o 5.5f winner Hecterine (by Hector Protector): dam, 2-y-o 6f winner,
out of very smart miler Marling: fair form when third in maidens: made most at Beverley
final start: likely to stay 6f. *R. A. Fahey*

ABELLABRIG   3 b.f. Puissance 110 – Rare Indigo 80 (Timeless Times (USA) 99) **–**
[2003 6f 6m⁶ f6g Oct 20] 15,000Y: second foal: sister to 2001 2-y-o 5f winner Lady
Ansell: dam, 5f winner, ran only at 2 yrs: soundly beaten in maidens. *A. Berry*

ABERCORN (IRE)   4 b.g. Woodborough (USA) 112 – Ravensdale Rose (IRE) (Henbit **–**
(USA) 130) [2003 57, a68: f5g f7g f6g Feb 24] smallish, well-made gelding: modest
performer: well held in 2003: often blinkered. *J. L. Spearing*

ABERKEEN   8 ch.g. Keen 116 – Miss Aboyne 64 (Lochnager 132) [2003 66: f8s⁵ **43**
f11s⁶ f11s 8.3d⁶ 11.8g f11g Jun 19] workmanlike gelding: poor performer: stays 1¼m:
acts on firm going, soft and fibresand: visored (well beaten) once: sometimes slowly
away: held up: has found little. *Jedd O'Keeffe*

A BID IN TIME (IRE) 2 b.f. (Mar 22) Danetime (IRE) 121 – Bidni (IRE) (Mael- **54**
strom Lake 118) [2003 f5g 5m⁶ 5.1g⁴ f5s 5d* 5f⁵ 5m 6g p7g 5g 5m 5.2s Oct 29] 7,000Y:
leggy, good-topped filly: first foal: dam lightly-raced half-sister to useful Irish/US
performer up to 1¼m Inchacooley: modest performer: won seller at Beverley in May:
some respectable efforts in nurseries after: should stay 6f: acts on good to soft going,
good to firm and fibresand. *D. Shaw*

ABILITY 4 b.g. Alflora (IRE) 120 – Beatle Song 70 (Song 132) [2003 68: p7g 9.7g **52**
10m Apr 14] well-made gelding: fair maiden at 3 yrs: modest in 2003: should stay at least
1¼m: acts on soft and good to firm going: sold £10,000. *C. E. Brittain*

ABINGTON ANGEL 2 ch.f. (Apr 23) Machiavellian (USA) 123 – Band (USA) **78**
(Northern Dancer) [2003 6m³ 7m² 7m⁶ p7g⁶ p8g Nov 18] 160,000Y: close-coupled,
good-quartered filly: has a quick action: closely related to winner in USA by Seeking The
Gold and half-sister to several winners, including 1995 2-y-o 5f/6f winner Applaud (by
Rahy) and 1¼m winner Glam Rock (by Nashwan), both useful: dam maiden out of high-
class sprinter Swingtime, later successful in graded stakes up to 9f in USA: maiden:
placed at Newmarket and Newbury, best efforts: stays 1m: tongue tied last 2 starts.
B. J. Meehan

A BIT OF FUN 2 ch.g. (Mar 14) Unfuwain (USA) 131 – Horseshoe Reef 88 (Mill Reef **–**
(USA) 141) [2003 6m 6m 6m Aug 30] 26,000Y: useful-looking gelding: half-brother to
several winners, including useful 6f (at 2 yrs)/7f winner Reefs Sis (by Muhtarram) and
fairly useful 11.5f winner Slipper (by Suave Dancer): dam 1¼m winner: no form in
maidens: looked difficult ride final start. *T. D. Barron*

ABLAJ (IRE) 2 ch.g. (Mar 10) Horse Chestnut (SAF) 119 – Passe Passe (USA) 78 **66**
(Lear Fan (USA) 130) [2003 6m⁴ 7m 7s Nov 3] 100,000Y: sturdy gelding: first foal: dam,
maiden (should have stayed further than 1½m), out of half-sister to high-class Fanmore
(stayed 1¼m) and very smart Labeeb (best at 1m/9f): fair form at best in maidens: hung
left when well beaten final start. *E. A. L. Dunlop*

ABLE BAKER CHARLIE (IRE) 4 b.g. Sri Pekan (USA) 117 – Lavezzola (IRE) **100 p**
(Salmon Leap (USA) 131) [2003 88: 10d 10d 10m² 10g⁵ 9m* 8m* 9m Oct 4] useful-
looking gelding: useful performer: continued to progress in 2003, and won handicap at
Newbury and minor event at Ascot (beat Reyadi by 1½ lengths) in August: shaped better
than result suggests when tenth of 34 to Chivalry in Cambridgeshire at Newmarket final
start, short of room 2f out: at least as effective at 1m as 1¼m: acts on polytrack, good to
firm and good to soft ground: has worn crossed noseband: sometimes edges right: type to
do better still in 2004. *J. R. Fanshawe*

ABLE MIND 3 b.g. Mind Games 121 – Chlo-Jo 65 (Belmez (USA) 131) [2003 71: **79**
6g² 7d² 7f³ 7.6g² f8.5g³ 7m³ Oct 21] rather leggy, lengthy gelding: fair maiden: best
efforts when runner-up: probably best at 6f/7f: acts on good to firm and good to soft
ground: hung left fourth start: sold 11,000 gns. *W. J. Haggas*

ABNOBA (USA) 3 b.f. Celtic Swing 138 – Zakousky (USA) (Arazi (USA) 135) [2003 **–**
8.1s 7m Jul 2] 16,500Y: first foal: dam, French 2-y-o 1m winner, out of very smart French
1½m performer Zartota: well held, including in seller: sent to Sweden. *W. Jarvis*

ABOUSTAR 3 b.g. Abou Zouz (USA) 109 – Three Star Rated (IRE) 79 (Pips Pride **–**
117) [2003 –: 7s 7m Oct 25] tall, leggy gelding: no form: tried in cheekpieces. *M. Brittain*

ABOU ZULU 3 ch.g. Abou Zouz (USA) 109 – Mary From Dunlow 49 (Nicholas Bill **–**
125) [2003 58d: 10.1d 7f 8f 9.3m 7.5m 9f⁶ 7m Sep 9] good-topped gelding: disappointing
maiden: sometimes blinkered. *H. A. McWilliams*

ABOVE BOARD 8 b.g. Night Shift (USA) – Bundled Up (USA) (Sharpen Up 127) **–**
[2003 –, a53: f5g⁵ f6g f6g f5s f6g f5s Dec 27] smallish, robust gelding: poor performer:
effective at 5f/6f: acts on fibresand: tried blinkered/in cheekpieces: often tongue tied.
R. F. Marvin

ABOVE THE CUT (USA) 11 ch.g. Topsider (USA) – Placer Queen (Habitat 134) **–**
[2003 –: 16.4m Jul 10] fair hurdler: lightly raced and no recent form on Flat.
C. P. Morlock

ABRACADABJAR 5 b.g. Royal Abjar (USA) 121 – Celt Song (IRE) (Unfuwain **–**
(USA) 131) [2003 –: p12g p12g p16g f11g p13g 11.9m Oct 2] short-backed gelding: of
little account. *Miss Z. C. Davison*

ABRAXAS 5 b.g. Emperor Jones (USA) 119 – Snipe Hall 93 (Crofthall 110) [2003 48, **45**
a58: 6g p5g 5m 5m 5g 5m 5m f5g² f5s⁶ Dec 31] modest maiden on all-weather, poor on **a61**

turf: stays 6f: acts on all-weather and good to firm going: tried blinkered/in cheekpieces: inconsistent. *J. Akehurst*

ABROGATE (IRE) 2 b.g. (Mar 27) Revoque (IRE) 122 – Czarina's Sister (Soviet   **51**
Lad (USA)) [2003 f6g 5.9d⁵ 7d 7m³ 8m 10f f8s³ Dec 13] 8,000Y: good-topped gelding: first foal: dam, lightly-raced maiden, out of half-sister to Cheveley Park winner Pass The Peace: modest maiden: stays 1m: acts on fibresand, good to firm and good to soft going. *P. C. Haslam*

ABSENT FRIENDS 6 b.g. Rock City 120 – Green Supreme (Primo Dominie 121)   **108**
[2003 96: 5f 5m 5v⁶ 5g⁴ 5f 6m 5f* 5.1m⁵ 5m⁴ 5.1m* 5d⁶ 5d² 5m⁵ 5m 5m Oct 25] strong, lengthy gelding: impresses in appearance: useful performer: better than ever in 2003, winning handicap at Doncaster in June and minor event at Nottingham (by ¾ length from Dubaian Gift) in August: best at 5f: acts on firm and good to soft going: sometimes early to post (withdrawn after unseating rider and running loose once): sometimes slowly away/hangs left: usually races prominently. *J. Balding*

ABSINTHER 6 b.g. Presidium 124 – Heavenly Queen (Scottish Reel 123) [2003 66:   **56**
f12g p12g p12g 10m⁴ 12m⁵ 12.1d 11.6m* 11.6g⁴ 12m⁴ 9.9m 12m 10m Oct 23] good-bodied gelding: modest handicapper: won at Windsor in July: stays 1½m: acts on fibresand, firm and soft ground: visored once earlier in career: has run well when sweating: waited with. *M. R. Bosley*

ABSOLUTELY FAB (IRE) 2 ch.f. (Jan 18) Entrepreneur 123 – Hamama (USA)   **–**
(Majestic Light (USA)) [2003 p5g 5f 6m 7.5m 6.1d Jul 26] €5,500Y: lengthy, good-bodied filly: sixth foal: half-sister to winner in Turkey by Wolfhound: dam, third at 7f in Ireland, half-sister to 1000 Guineas winner Quick As Lightning: no form in minor events/maidens. *Mrs C. A. Dunnett*

ABSOLUTELY SOAKED (IRE) 2 b.f. (Apr 21) Alhaarth (IRE) 126 – Vasilopoula   **62**
(IRE) (Kenmare (FR) 125) [2003 7g³ 7.9m Sep 3] IR 9,000F, 12,000 2-y-o: smallish filly: second foal: dam twice-raced daughter of Nassau Stakes winner Mamaluna: green, modest form in maidens at Yarmouth and York. *Dr J. D. Scargill*

ABSOLUTELYTHEBEST (IRE) 2 b.c. (Apr 16) Anabaa (USA) 130 – Recherchee   **64 p**
(Rainbow Quest (USA) 134) [2003 7m 8.3m p10g⁴ Nov 29] 120,000Y: rangy colt: eighth foal: closely related to useful 5f (at 2 yrs) to 1m (in France) winner Recondite and 1¼m/1½m winner Freedom Quest (both by Polish Patriot) and half-brother to 5-y-o Celtic Star: dam unraced: best effort in maidens final start, first start since leaving Sir Michael Stoute) when staying-on fourth at Lingfield: will stay at least 1½m: open to progress. *E. A. L. Dunlop*

ABSOLUTE PLEASURE 2 br.f. (Apr 18) Polar Falcon (USA) 126 – Soluce 98   **52**
(Junius (USA) 124) [2003 7.1m f8g⁴ 10m Oct 22] 6,000F, €27,000Y, resold 21,000Y: compact filly: sister to 2 winners, including fair 7f/1m winner Polar Lady, and half-sister to numerous winners, including smart 5f (at 2 yrs)/6f winner Splice (by Sharpo), herself dam of smart sprinter Feet So Fast: dam Irish 7f winner: modest form at best in maidens/seller: stays 1m: tongue tied on debut. *G. C. Bravery*

ABSOLUTE UTOPIA (USA) 10 b.g. Mr Prospector (USA) – Magic Gleam (USA)   **63**
122 (Danzig (USA)) [2003 58, a66: p10g* p10g⁶ p10g³ p10g² 10.2m* 9.7m* 10.2f p10g   **a69**
p10g* p10g 10.2m² 10d³ 10.9m² p10g* 10.9m p10g* Dec 30] tall gelding: hobdayed/had soft palate operation early in career: fair on all-weather, modest on turf: had good season and won handicap, 2 sellers and a selling handicap at Lingfield, seller at Bath and handicap at Folkestone: effective at 1¼m/1½m: acts on polytrack, firm and good to soft ground (well held both starts on soft): tried blinkered earlier in career: usually held up. *J. L. Spearing*

ABUELOS 4 b.g. Sabrehill (USA) 120 – Miss Oasis 54 (Green Desert (USA) 127)   **–**
[2003 68: p7g p7g p7g 7m 8.1m 7g f6g 7f⁵ 7g 8m Oct 23] smallish, well-made gelding: poor performer nowadays: should stay 1m: acts on polytrack, probably on any turf going: tried in cheekpieces: held up. *S. Dow*

ABUNAWWAS (IRE) 3 b.c. In The Wings 128 – Copper Creek 78 (Habitat 134) [2003   **110**
100: 7d² 7d⁴ 8d 7d* 6f⁴ Aug 10] IR 320,000Y: sturdy colt: half-brother to several winners, notably 5f/6f performer Tipsy Creek (by Dayjur) and 6f (at 2 yrs) to 9f (in UAE) winner Wathik (by Ogygian), both smart: dam, 6f winner, from good family: smart performer: won maiden at Galway at 2 yrs: best effort when winning Eircom Ballycorus Stakes at Leopardstown in June by 1½ lengths from One More Round: fair fourth to

Bonus in Phoenix Sprint Stakes at the Curragh final start: best effort at 7f: acts on soft going. *K. Prendergast, Ireland*

ABUNDANT   3 b.f. Zafonic (USA) 130 – Glorious (Nashwan (USA) 135) [2003 96: 7g⁴ Oct 11] lengthy, useful-looking filly: useful performer: has run only 3 times: won minor event at Yarmouth at 2 yrs: respectable fourth to Chic in listed race at Ascot only start in 2003, flicking tail under pressure: should stay 1m: acts on soft ground: hung markedly left second 2-y-o outing. *J. R. Fanshawe*   **91 +**

ACADEMY BRIEF (IRE)   3 b.g. Brief Truce (USA) 126 – Stylish Academy (IRE) (Royal Academy (USA) 130) [2003 68: f11g³ p10g p12g f8s 10m³ 9.7m² 11.6m 10.2f⁶ 10g⁶ 10.2m 8f⁶ Oct 17] modest maiden: stays 11f: acts on fibresand and firm going: tried in cheekpieces and visor: races up with pace. *J. W. Mullins*   **58**

ACADEMY (IRE)   8 ch.g. Archway (IRE) 115 – Dream Academy (Town And Country 124) [2003 71, a45+: 14.1g³ 14.1m 16.2m 16g⁵ 16m² 16.2m⁵ 17.1m² 16.1m² 16.2f 17.1m² 18m⁴ p16g Nov 26] close-coupled gelding: fair handicapper on turf, modest on all-weather: effective at 1¾m to 19f: acts on firm going and fibresand: held up. *Andrew Turnell*   **68 a52**

A C AZURE (IRE)   5 br.g. Dolphin Street (FR) 125 – Kelvedon (General Assembly (USA)) [2003 –: p7g 10.5f 6.5f³ 8m⁴ 6d 9f³ 6m⁴ 8.5d 8m Oct 30] poor maiden: left P. Mooney in Ireland after final 4-y-o start and Mrs L. Jewell after reappearance: stays 9f: acts on fibresand and firm ground: often blinkered: tongue tied last 4 outings. *W. A. Murphy, Ireland*   **46**

ACCA LARENTIA (IRE)   2 gr.f. (Apr 15) Titus Livius (FR) 115 – Daisy Grey 46 (Nordance (USA)) [2003 5g 7m 7m⁶ 7m² Oct 17] 6,000Y, 10,000 2-y-o: leggy, close-coupled filly: fluent mover: sixth foal: half-sister to 2 winners abroad, including French 15f winner Rafeef (by Salse): dam, 7f seller winner, half-sister to dam of Lochsong: modest maiden: second in claimer at Redcar: should stay 1m. *R. M. Whitaker*   **60**

ACCELERATION (IRE)   3 b.g. Groom Dancer (USA) 128 – Overdrive 99 (Shirley Heights 130) [2003 –p: 14.1m² 14.1m³ f12g³ 17.2m* f16.2g⁶ 16g 16.1m⁴ 18m Oct 20] big gelding: fair handicapper: won at Carlisle in June: generally disappointing after: best at 2m+: acts on good to firm ground: blinkered last 2 starts: ungenuine: sold 20,000 gns. *Sir Mark Prescott*   **69 §**

ACCENTOR (IRE)   3 ch.f. Bluebird (USA) 125 – Law Review (IRE) 63 (Case Law 113) [2003 57: p6g 8g 12d 12f⁴ 12d 10m Oct 1] workmanlike filly: poor maiden at 3 yrs: left J. Noseda after reappearance: stays 1½m: acts on firm ground and polytrack: tried visored/blinkered. *M. J. P. O'Brien, Ireland*   **46**

ACCEPTING   6 b.g. Mtoto 134 – D'Azy 91 (Persian Bold 123) [2003 –: f16.2g 14.1g 17.1m* 18m Oct 20] close-coupled gelding: modest handicapper: 25/1-winner at Pontefract in October: stays 17f: acts on good to firm and good to soft going (well held on soft): wore cheekpieces last 2 starts: sometimes hangs: unreliable. *J. Mackie*   **62 §**

ACCLAMATION   4 b.c. Royal Applause 124 – Princess Athena 119 (Ahonoora 122) [2003 114: 5m³ 5f² 6m 6m* 5m³ 6m* 6f* 5s⁴ 5m⁵ Dec 14]   **118**

Patience had its reward for veteran Devon trainer Gerald Cottrell in the latest season. Since first taking out a licence in 1971, Cottrell has plied his trade with largely modest horses and a string averaging fewer than twenty. Before Acclamation won the £200000 St Leger Yearling Stakes at Doncaster as a two-year-old, the highlights of Cottrell's career had probably been the Portland Handicap victory of Roman Prose and dead-heats in two other big sprint handicaps, with Governor General in the William Hill Trophy and with Young Inca in the Bovis Stakes at Ascot. Readers might also recall prolific minor winners Cape Pigeon and Conspicuous, among others. Governor General was transferred from Cottrell to David Elsworth after his three-year-old days and developed into a pattern performer, coming closest to achieving a victory in such company when runner-up in the Diadem, the Duke of York and the King's Stand. The Diadem and the King's Stand—both at Ascot, which Cottrell describes as his favourite course—featured on Acclamation's programme in the latest season, and he achieved a first pattern win for himself and for his trainer when successful in the Millennium & Copthorne Hotels Diadem in September.

Millennium & Copthorne Hotels Diadem Stakes, Ascot—Acclamation battles on well to beat Polar Way (blaze) and Lochridge; Ashdown Express (left) finishes fast for fourth

Acclamation was off the course for over twelve months after winning the St Leger Yearling Stakes, reportedly beset by training problems including persistent mucus in his lungs. Cottrell got him back on the course for two races at the end of his three-year-old season and he ran very well to finish third in the Diadem and in a listed event at Newmarket. With no penalties to carry, the lightly-raced Acclamation looked just the type to pick up a minor pattern race as a four-year-old, especially as there seemed a dearth of high-class sprinters around. But, after a creditable third to Airwave in the Temple Stakes at Sandown, Acclamation was thrown in at the deep end. Starting at 16/1, he showed improved form to split 25/1 Australian challenger Choisir and Oasis Dream in a big field for the King's Stand, finishing very strongly after being checked in the stand-side group when travelling well over a furlong out. Acclamation couldn't repeat the form in the July Cup at Newmarket, where he finished down the field as Oasis Dream turned the tables on Choisir. Dropped in class, Acclamation had to settle for a share of the spoils with Chookie Heiton in a well-contested minor event at Doncaster before again running really well to finish third to Oasis Dream in Britain's only Group 1 race over five furlongs, the Nunthorpe at York. Kept on the go, odds-on Acclamation narrowly won a listed event at Goodwood in September from Torosay Spring before contesting an up-to-scratch renewal of the Diadem. There might have been a touch of fortune in Acclamation's victory in that a number of those held up at Ascot, notably the favourite Airwave, met trouble in running. Normally held up himself, Acclamation—ridden for the first time by Frankie Dettori—was in the first three throughout and battled on well to beat the also-prominent pair Polar Way and Lochridge by three quarters of a length and a neck. Eight days later, Acclamation raced prominently again in the Prix de l'Abbaye at Longchamp and was just run out of a place behind Patavellian, The Trader and The Tatling as British-trained challengers dominated. The partnership which owned Acclamation, the spokesman for whom had also been associated with Young Inca, sold the horse to Rathbarry Stud in Ireland (where he will stand at €10,000, October 1st terms, in 2004) and he ran in new ownership in the Hong Kong Sprint at Sha Tin in December when fifth to Silent Witness, turning the tables from the Abbaye on The Trader and The Tatling.

The lengthy, attractive Acclamation, a grand sort who really took the eye before his races, is by the Middle Park and Haydock Sprint Cup winner Royal Applause, a young sire who is making a name for himself, particularly with his sprinting two-year-olds. Acclamation turned out to be a bargain at the 33,000 guineas he cost at Doncaster's St Leger Yearling Sales, at which the latest offspring of the smart sprinter Princess Athena, a filly by Efisio, broke Doncaster's twenty-one-year-old record price for a filly when knocked down for 120,000 guineas in the latest season. A daughter of the Irish six-furlong winner Shopping Wise, Princess Athena gained her most important success in the Queen Mary Stakes as a two-year-old but trained on well, her best effort coming when second in the King George

Mr Liam Cashman's "Acclamation"

Acclamation (b.c. 1999)	Royal Applause (b 1993)	Waajib (b 1983)	Try My Best / Coryana
		Flying Melody (b 1979)	Auction Ring / Whispering Star
	Princess Athena (b 1985)	Ahonoora (ch 1975)	Lorenzaccio / Helen Nichols
		Shopping Wise (b 1965)	Floribunda / Sea Melody

Stakes at Goodwood on her only outing as a four-year-old. She has bred three other winners including the useful six- and seven-furlong performer Waypoint (by Cadeaux Genereux). Waypoint is the dam of Prix Robert Papin winner Never A Doubt, who was also runner-up in the Queen Mary. In keeping with his pedigree, Acclamation was best at five and six furlongs. He acted on firm and soft going. *L. G. Cottrell*

ACE CLUB 2 ch.g. (Apr 14) Indian Rocket 115 – Presently 48 (Cadeaux Genereux 131) [2003 5m² 5g* Sep 28] 28,000Y: angular gelding: fifth foal: half-brother to 2 winners, including 3-y-o Brioso: dam, 5f winner, half-sister to smart sprinter Sizzling Melody: favourite, won maiden at Musselburgh cosily by length from Champagne Cracker, getting on top final 1f: will stay 6f: open to progress. *W. J. Haggas* **74 p**

ACE COMING 2 b.g. (Mar 3) First Trump 118 – Tarry 65 (Salse (USA) 128) [2003 5g² 5.1f⁴ 6d² 7.2f³ 6g⁴ 7m² 8.1g 8m 7.9f Oct 9] sparely-made gelding: third foal: dam, 7f (at 2 yrs) and 1¾m winner, also won over hurdles: fair maiden: left Mrs L. Stubbs after third start: ran poorly in nurseries last 3: should stay at least 1m: acts on firm and good to soft going: blinkered (ran creditably) sixth outing. *D. Eddy* **68 d**

acts on soft and good to firm going, probably on firm: sometimes slowly away: best held up. *J. Cullinan*

AEGEAN LINE   3 b.f. Bijou d'Inde 127 – Load Line (High Line 125) [2003 72: 8.3g 8.3m⁶ 7m⁵ 8.3m⁵ 7d⁵ 7f⁶ Aug 27] modest performer: best form at 6f/7f: acts on soft and good to firm ground: free-going sort. *R. Hannon*   **63**

AEGEAN MAGIC   3 b.f. Wolfhound (USA) 126 – Sayulita 67 (Habitat 134) [2003 71: p5g⁶ f6g 6m⁵ 6.1g 6f⁵ 6g* 6g* 6m 6m⁵ 7m 7m Sep 25] lengthy filly: fair performer: won maiden at Salisbury and handicap at Lingfield in July: stays 6f: acts on all-weather, firm and soft ground: below form in cheekpieces on reappearance. *R. Hannon*   **76**

AEGEAN MIST   3 ch.f. Prince Sabo 123 – Dizzydaisy 57 (Sharpo 132) [2003 63, a–: f8.5g⁴ p8g⁵ f9.4g⁵ 7g⁴ 8.3g 7m 8.2m f8.5s⁵ 11.6m Jul 14] little form at 3 yrs. *P. Howling*   **–**

AESCULUS (USA)   2 b. or br.f. (Mar 19) Horse Chestnut (SAF) 119 – Crafty Buzz (USA) (Crafty Prospector (USA)) [2003 7g 6.1d⁵ p6g* Nov 18] tall, lengthy filly: has scope: fluent mover: fourth foal: half-sister to 3-y-o Blackwater Fever and a winner in USA by St Jovite: dam minor 2-y-o stakes winner up to 6f in USA: fair form in maidens: best effort when winning at Lingfield by 1½ lengths from Muktasb, dictating pace: should stay 7f: type to do better still at 3 yrs. *L. M. Cumani*   **71 p**

AFAAN (IRE)   10 ch.h. Cadeaux Genereux 131 – Rawaabe (USA) 87 (Nureyev (USA) 131) [2003 74: f5s 5f 5d 5m 5m 5d 5m 5.2m² 5m 5f Aug 21] big horse: poor mover: modest performer nowadays: best at 5f: acts on fibresand, firm and soft ground: wears headgear: tried tongue tied: has hung right: races prominently. *R. F. Marvin*   **61**

AFADAN (IRE)   5 br.g. Royal Academy (USA) 130 – Afasara (IRE) (Shardari 134) [2003 93: p12g p12g⁴ p12g³ p12g 12g 14m 14g p12g Dec 17] rangy gelding: fairly useful handicapper: stays 1¾m: acts on polytrack, raced mainly on good ground or softer on turf: sometimes tongue tied earlier in career: has started slowly: none too genuine. *J. R. Jenkins*   **87**

AFEEF (USA)   4 br.g. Dayjur (USA) 137 – Jah (USA) (Relaunch (USA)) [2003 68: 9g 10m Jul 28] good-topped gelding: fair maiden handicapper, very lightly raced: well held in 2003: tried tongue tied. *R. T. Phillips*   **–**

AFRICAN DAWN   5 b.g. Spectrum (IRE) 126 – Lamu Lady (IRE) 70 (Lomond (USA) 128) [2003 f11s⁴ 14.4d p13g² f12g² Apr 28] leggy gelding: fair performer: left P. Webber after third start: stays 1¾m: acts on all-weather and firm going: wears tongue tie: sold £2,000. *N. P. Littmoden*   **72**

AFRICAN SAHARA (USA)   4 br.c. El Gran Senor (USA) 136 – Able Money (USA) (Distinctive (USA)) [2003 82: p8g⁴ p8g² f9.4g* p10g³ 8g⁵ 8.3g⁵ 9.2g⁶ 8f² 9m* 8g 9g⁴ 8d 8m⁵ 9m* 8m² 8.1d* 8.5g 8m 8m² 8.9f² 9g⁶ Oct 25] close-coupled, good-topped colt: fairly useful performer: won maiden at Wolverhampton in March (trained until after next start by G. Chung), minor events at Redcar in July and Sandown in July and Sandown (dead-heated with Impeller) in August and handicap at Sandown later in August: effective at 1m/easy 1¼m: acts on all-weather, firm and good to firm ground: usually tongue tied: has worn crossed noseband: tough and genuine. *Miss D. Mountain*   **90**

AFRICAN SPUR (IRE)   3 b.g. Flying Spur (AUS) – African Bloom (African Sky 124) [2003 73: 5.3f⁵ 5m² 6.1m 5.3d* 6m 6m 6g³ 6m 5f⁴ 7f² 8m p7g 5m f6g f7s Dec 13] deep-girthed gelding: fairly useful handicapper: won at Brighton in May: effective at 5f to easy 7f: acts on fibresand, firm and soft ground: effective blinkered or not: none too consistent. *P. A. Blockley*   **84 a74**

AFRICAN STAR   2 b.c. (Apr 5) Mtoto 134 – Pass The Rose (IRE) (Thatching 131) [2003 7d f7g⁵ Nov 25] 42,000F: workmanlike colt: fourth foal: half-brother to 1999 2-y-o 6f seller winner Methodist (by Rainbows For Life) and 3-y-o Pascali: dam unraced half-sister to Cheveley Park winner Pass The Peace, herself dam of Cheveley Park winner Embassy and smart performer up to 1¼m Tarfshi (by Mtoto): modest form in maidens at Doncaster (raced freely) and Southwell: will stay 1m. *Mrs A. J. Perrett*   **58**

AFTER ALL (IRE)   2 gr.f. (Apr 11) Desert Story (IRE) 115 – All Ashore (Nureyev (USA) 131) [2003 p6g 5m² 5g³ 5g⁵ p5g⁵ p6g² p6g⁶ Dec 29] half-sister to 3 winners, including Irish 1991 2-y-o 7f winner Almante (by Ahonoora), later good winner in Hong Kong: dam, ran twice, close relation to smart Irish 1991 2-y-o El Prado and half-sister to high-class 1¼m performer Entitled: modest maiden: second at Musselburgh and Lingfield: bred to stay 1m: blinkered final start: weak finisher. *G. A. Butler*   **64**

AFTER SHOCK (IRE)   5 ch.g. Grand Lodge (USA) 125 – Fancy Boots (IRE) 62 (Salt Dome (USA)) [2003 83: 6g 5d 10m 7m f5s f6g Jun 30] ex-Irish gelding: fairly useful   **–**

handicapper in 2002, winning at Cork: well held in 2003 (including in sellers), leaving G. Stack after second start: effective at 5f/6f: acts on fibresand and good to soft ground: tried blinkered/visored. *E. J. O'Neill*

AFTER THE SHOW   2 b.c. (Apr 8) Royal Applause 124 – Tango Teaser (Shareef   **71** Dancer (USA) 135) [2003 6.1d⁶ 6m 6m⁴ 6m p6g⁵ 5.2s* Oct 29] useful-looking colt: has scope: third foal: half-brother to 2 winning sprinters, including 3-y-o Westmead Tango: dam, well held both starts, out of smart 7f/1m winner Ever Genial: fair performer: won nursery at Yarmouth by neck from Foursquare, hanging left: barely stays 6f: acts on polytrack, good to firm and soft going. *J. R. Jenkins*

AGGI MAC   2 b.f. (Mar 12) Defacto (USA) – Giffoine 79 (Timeless Times (USA)   **43** 99) [2003 p5g⁶ 5f⁶ 6f 6m² 5g 6m³ 7m 6g³ 6d 6m 6m⁵ Oct 20] 1,600Y: close-coupled, good-topped filly: first foal: dam, 2-y-o 5f winner, sister to useful 5f winner Aurigny: poor maiden: stays 6f, probably not 7f: acts on good to firm ground and polytrack. *N. Bycroft*

AGILIS (IRE)   3 b.g. Titus Livius (FR) 115 – Green Life 63 (Green Desert (USA) 127)   **88** [2003 89: p7g⁴ p10g p8g⁵ 8f p7g p7g p8g⁴ p8g⁶ Dec 30] fairly useful performer: best at 7f/1m: acts on polytrack, well beaten on turf. *Jamie Poulton*

AGINCOURT WARRIOR   4 b.c. Distant Relative 128 – Careful (IRE) 59 (Distinctly   **65 d** North (USA) 115) [2003 –: p6g f8.5g p7g 8m⁵ 7m 7m 5.7g 7g Jun 3] good-topped colt: fair performer: little form after reappearance: stays 1m: acts on polytrack and good to firm ground: tried blinkered/visored: sold 3,000 gns. *J. M. P. Eustace*

AGUILA LOCO (IRE)   4 ch.g. Eagle Eyed (USA) 111 – Go Likecrazy 51 (Dowsing   **43** (USA) 124) [2003 64: 5m 5g 5g 5g 5m 5m f5s Dec 27] smallish, good-topped gelding: poor handicapper: left E. Alston 700 gns before final start: best at 5f: acts on firm going, good to soft and fibresand: tried blinkered (raced freely)/in cheekpieces: edgy sort: sometimes slowly away: usually races prominently. *M. C. Chapman*

AGUILERA   2 ch.f. (Mar 31) Wolfhound (USA) 126 – Mockingbird 64 (Sharpo 132)   **–** [2003 8g 7m Oct 12] 8,000Y: lengthy filly: fourth foal: half-sister to 5f/6f winner Ridicule (by Piccolo): dam 2-y-o 6f winner: well beaten in maidens at Ripon and Newcastle. *M. Dods*

AILINCALA (IRE)   5 b.m. Pursuit of Love 124 – Diabaig 76 (Precocious 126) [2003   **94** 71: 8m³ 8.1m² 8m* 8.1m⁶ 8f* 8f* 8m* 10f⁴ 8f Sep 27] lengthy mare: fairly useful performer: much improved in 2003, winning 4 handicaps at Brighton between May and August: good fourth to Dawnus in listed event there penultimate start: barely stays 1¼m: acts on firm going, good to soft and polytrack: sometimes slowly away: held up: tough and consistent. *C. F. Wall*

AIMEE'S DELIGHT   3 b.f. Robellino (USA) 127 – Lloc 79 (Absalom 128) [2003   **85** 76: 7g 7.5f 7.1m* 6d 7g³ 8.2m* 8m Jul 19] strong filly: fairly useful handicapper: won at Warwick in May and Nottingham in June: stays 1m: acts on fibresand and good to firm ground, seemingly not on softer than good. *J. G. Given*

AIMING   3 br.f. Highest Honor (FR) 124 – Sweeping 104 (Indian King (USA) 128)   **76** [2003 73: 8.1m³ 7g 7g⁶ 8f² 8.3m 8.1m² 8.3m Sep 29] fair maiden handicapper: stays 1m: raced only on good going or firmer: usually races prominently: sold 30,000 gns. *R. Hannon*

AINTNECESSARILYSO   5 ch.g. So Factual (USA) 120 – Ovideo 58 (Domynsky   **51** 110) [2003 58: 5g 5.3m⁵ 5m⁶ 5.3m⁵ 5m 5m 5f 5m³ 5.7f 5.3f p6g⁵ f6g⁴ f5s⁶ f5s⁵ Dec 31] workmanlike gelding: has a quick action: modest handicapper: left J. M. Bradley after tenth start: best at 5f/6f: acts on all-weather, firm and soft ground: tried in blinkers/cheekpieces. *N. E. Berry*

AIR ADAIR (USA)   3 ch.f. Storm Cat (USA) – Beyrouth (USA) (Alleged (USA) 138)   **?** [2003 93: 8d 7m⁵ 9g⁶ Oct 7] leggy, useful-looking filly: fairly useful performer, lightly raced: in lead when ducking out through tapes and unseating rider 2f out in listed race at Compiegne in May: raced freely in blinkers when last of 5 in minor event at Leicester next time: left J. Gosden and off 4 months, respectable effort in allowance race at Delaware final outing: stays 9f: unraced on extremes of going: possibly temperamental. *J. E. Sheppard, USA*

AIREDALE LAD (IRE)   2 b.g. (Apr 18) Charnwood Forest (IRE) 125 – Tamarsiya   **–** (USA) (Shahrastani (USA) 135) [2003 6m Jun 10] €10,000Y: half-brother to several winners, including Irish 1m winner Headfort Rose (by Desert Style): dam unraced: tailed off in maiden at Redcar. *J. R. Norton*

AIRGUSTA (IRE)   2 b.c. (Apr 20) Danehill Dancer (IRE) 117 – Ministerial Model **66**
(IRE) 94 (Shalford (IRE) 124§) [2003 6g 6d p7g Oct 8] IR 4,500F, €72,000Y: second
foal: dam, Irish 7f/1m winner, also won over hurdles: easily best effort in maidens (fair
form) when ninth at Lingfield final start: will probably stay 1m. *C. R. Egerton*

AIR MAIL   6 b.g. Night Shift (USA) – Wizardry 83 (Shirley Heights 130) [2003 56, **–**
a100: f8s² f8s f7s f6s f7s f8.5g⁶ f8.5s Mar 8] leggy gelding: fairly useful handicapper on **a93**
all-weather, modest on turf: well below form last 4 starts: stays 8.5f: acts on any turf
going and fibresand, below form on polytrack: tried blinkered/visored/in cheekpieces.
Mrs N. Macauley

AIR OF ESTEEM   7 b.g. Forzando 122 – Shadow Bird 70 (Martinmas 128) [2003 52: **59**
f8s⁴ f8s³ f7g* f8g⁵ p8g f8g* 7m² 8g 7g 8m² f8s 8m f8s⁴ f8.5g⁵ f8g⁵ f8g³ Dec 19] smallish
gelding: modest performer: won seller at Wolverhampton in January and claimer at
Southwell in March: left D. Nicholls after thirteenth start: best at 7f/1m: acts on fibresand
(forced strong pace only start on polytrack), good to firm and good to soft going: tried
visored, not in 2003. *Ian Emmerson*

AIRWAVE   3 b.f. Air Express (IRE) 125 – Kangra Valley 56 (Indian Ridge 123) **120**
[2003 114p: 5m* 6f² 6m³ 6d³ 6f⁶ 5s Oct 5]
     'You can give weight but you can't give start' is an adage with a fair amount
of truth to it. Ground conceded at the start or in the early part of a race has to be
made up sooner or later—and the later it is left the more likely it is that most of the
runners will be travelling at or near their top speed. On turf, more energy is nearly
always expended in making up five lengths in the closing stages of a race than is
saved by conceding the same distance in the first half furlong or so. Airwave
overcame the loss of five or six lengths to record a most striking performance in the
Tripleprint Temple Stakes on her reappearance at Sandown in May. Furthermore,
Airwave was the only Group 1 winner among the seven runners in the Group 2
event and shouldered a 7-lb penalty for her success in the previous year's Cheveley
Park Stakes. Airwave's two-year-old career marked her as a sprinter purely and
simply. She showed a splendid turn of foot to beat Russian Rhythm in a race with a
steady early pace at Newmarket on her first outing in pattern company, after which
connections quickly dispelled any notion that Airwave might be tried in one of
the Guineas trials. Despite the presence in the Temple line-up of the trail-blazing
Repertory, the pace was not strong and Airwave recovered her lost ground in the
middle part of the race. She was back on the bridle approaching the final furlong
and quickened right away once Dane O'Neill opened her out inside the final
furlong. Airwave had three lengths to spare over Repertory at the line, with
Acclamation a neck further back in third.
     Considering Airwave had not come in her coat at Sandown, where she also
spoiled her appearance by sweating, there seemed reason to regard her Temple
Stakes performance as that of a potentially top-class sprinting filly. She was the first
three-year-old to win the Temple since Dayjur and Mind Games in the 'nineties,
and neither of them had had to carry a Group 1 penalty. Little went right for
Airwave afterwards, however, and she failed to get her head in front again in five

Tripleprint Temple Stakes, Sandown—
Airwave overcomes a very slow start to win impressively from Repertory and Acclamation (spots)

starts. All may not be lost, though, since Airwave remains in training with a four-year-old career more straightforward to plan, without a Group 1 penalty. The choice for Airwave's connections at Royal Ascot in the latest season was to saddle her under her Group 1 penalty in the Group 2 King's Stand Stakes over the Temple distance of five furlongs, or run her in the Group 1 Golden Jubilee Stakes over the Cheveley Park distance of six. The Temple Stakes demonstrated that Airwave's forte was speed but she didn't get the opportunity to race at the minimum trip again until October. Starting 11/8 favourite in a strong line-up for the Golden Jubilee Stakes, Airwave weaved her way through the seventeen-runner field to have every chance but went down by half a length, tending to edge right throughout the final furlong, to Australian-trained Choisir, who had already made history by winning the King's Stand on the opening day of the meeting.

Airwave finished behind Choisir again in the July Cup at Newmarket, the pair filling the places behind Oasis Dream; ridden by Kieren Fallon because O'Neill was suspended, Airwave didn't enjoy the clearest of runs and finished well to be beaten a length and a half and a neck. Contracting a lung infection afterwards, Airwave was off the course for two months, the five-furlong Nunthorpe at York going by without her. She was seen next in the Sprint Cup at Haydock in September, her trainer fearing she had 'lost a lot of fitness'. Airwave came a creditable third to Somnus and Oasis Dream. Reverting to Group 2 company in the Diadem Stakes at Ascot later in the month, Airwave was the only penalised runner, carrying an extra 4 lb for her Temple Stakes victory (wins before the current season not counting). She should have won, her rider having to extricate her after she became hemmed in, and eventually being forced to bring her to the wide outside to obtain a clear run (earning himself a two-day suspension in the process for causing interference). Airwave finished with a flourish but had too much to do, beaten around two lengths into sixth behind Acclamation. Seeking compensation a week later in the Prix de l'Abbaye at Longchamp, a race that looked tailor-made for her, Airwave again encountered trouble in running, being shuffled back in the field at around halfway and never looking likely to recover, coming home only eleventh of nineteen. Provided she trains on, there are certainly more good sprints to be won with Airwave, though her style of coming from behind, often accentuated by a tendency to start tardily (she is usually blanketed for stall entry), means she is always likely to need everything to fall right for her in a big field.

Airwave (b.f. 2000)	Air Express (IRE) (b 1994)	Salse (b 1985)	Topsider
			Carnival Princess
		Ibtisamm (ch 1981)	Caucasus
			Lorgnette
	Kangra Valley (ch 1991)	Indian Ridge (ch 1985)	Ahonoora
			Hillbrow
		Thorner Lane (b 1985)	Tina's Pet
			Spinner

Airwave, a rangy, good sort, is by the miler Air Express, who had only a short-lived career at stud. Airwave's dam the modest sprinter Kangra Valley, who gained her only victory in a five-furlong maiden as a two-year-old, has bred several other minor sprint winners; her unraced two-year-old Soundwave (by Prince Sabo) is with Airwave's trainer. Airwave has won on soft going but her very best form has been shown on good to firm or firmer, conditions which place the emphasis on speed. She will always be best at five and six furlongs. *H. Candy*

AISLE   6 b.g. Arazi (USA) 135 – Chancel (USA) 60 (Al Nasr (FR) 126) [2003 42: f12g⁶ f16.2g⁶ 16d May 2] small gelding: little form in 2003: often wears blinkers/tongue tie/cheekpieces: tends to carry head awkwardly/edge left. *L. R. James*   –

AITANA   3 b.f. Slip Anchor 136 – Tsungani 64 (Cure The Blues (USA)) [2003 10g 8m 7d⁶ 10d Jun 23] has a round action: closely related to 5-y-o Achilles Sun and half-sister to 2 winners, including fairly useful 8.5f to 15.4f winner Ayunli (by Chief Singer): dam 2-y-o 6f winner: modest maiden: should stay at least 1¼m. *S. C. Williams*   61

AJWAA (IRE)   5 ch.g. Mujtahid (USA) 118 – Nouvelle Star (AUS) (Luskin Star (AUS)) [2003 60§: 8.1m* 7f* 7.1m⁶ 9.1g 8f 8m 8.2f Oct 1] smallish, sturdy gelding: fair handicapper: won at Chepstow (seller) and Yarmouth in July: stays 1m: acts on firm and soft going: tried blinkered/visored: sometimes slowly away: unreliable. *J. G. M. O'Shea*   69 §

AKEBONO (IRE) 7 ch.g. Case Law 113 – Elanmatina (IRE) 77 (Burslem 123) [2003 **46**
53: 8m⁵ 8f⁵ p12g 8.1m Jul 4] poor performer: brought down final start: stayed 1¼m:
acted on polytrack, heavy and good to firm going: sometimes blinkered earlier in career:
sometimes found little: dead. *Mrs S. A. Liddiard*

AKEYDAH (IRE) 3 ch.f. Selkirk (USA) 129 – Abeyr 106 (Unfuwain (USA) 131) **70**
[2003 8.2m³ 7g⁵ May 21] big, lengthy filly: third foal: half-sister to useful 7f winner
Raheibb (by Lion Cavern) and fairly useful 6f winner (including at 2 yrs) Aldafra (by
Spectrum): dam 7f/1m winner: fair form in maidens at Nottingham and Goodwood: stays
1m: sold 7,500 gns. *D. R. Loder*

AKIMBO (USA) 2 b.c. (Apr 1) Kingmambo (USA) 125 – All At Sea (USA) 124 **96 p**
(Riverman (USA) 131) [2003 7m² Aug 16] close-coupled, attractive colt: seventh living
foal: closely related to 2 winners, including useful 1m winner Insinuate (by Mr Prospector), and half-brother to useful 6f/7f winner (including at 2 yrs) Imroz (by Nureyev)
and fairly useful 1m winner Stormy Channel (by Storm Cat): dam won Prix du Moulin
and Musidora Stakes and runner-up in Oaks: odds on but coltish and green, head second
of 11 to Mukafeh in maiden at Newbury, dictating pace and clear of remainder: will stay
at least 1m: should improve, and sure to win a race or 2. *H. R. A. Cecil*

AKRITAS 2 b.c. (Feb 11) Polish Precedent (USA) 131 – Dazzling Heights 99 (Shirley **83**
Heights 130) [2003 8m* 9g 10g 10g Nov 1] 52,000Y: quite good-topped, useful-looking colt:
closely related to useful 6f (at 2 yrs) to 1m winner Mauri Moon (by Green Desert) and
half-brother to several winners, including useful French performer around 1¼m All
Glory (by Alzao): dam 7f (at 2 yrs) and 11f (in France) winner: fairly useful form when
winning maiden at Newmarket in September in good style: ran as if amiss in Prix de
Conde at Longchamp (hung badly left) and listed race at Newmarket: should be suited by
1¼m/1½m. *P. F. I. Cole*

AKRMINA 3 ch.f. Zafonic (USA) 130 – Pastorale 91 (Nureyev (USA) 131) [2003 **74**
75p: 7m² 8.1m³ 10.3m 8m³ 7m* 7m⁶ 6m Sep 18] good-topped filly: fair performer: won
maiden at Folkestone in July: effective at 7f/1m: raced only on good to firm ground:
has worn cheekpieces/crossed noseband: reportedly in season fourth start: usually races
prominently. *M. A. Jarvis*

AKSHAR (IRE) 4 b.c. Danehill (USA) 126 – Akilara (IRE) 87 (Kahyasi 130) [2003 **113**
95p: 8m* 10.1m* 10f³ 10.4m* 8.9m³ 9m Oct 4] good-bodied colt: carries plenty of condition: smart performer: won minor event at Goodwood in May and handicaps at Epsom in
June and York (beat Howle Hill by ¾ length) in August: close third to Naheef in Strensall
Stakes at York penultimate start: raced freely when below form in Cambridgeshire at

Vodafone Newbury Handicap, Epsom—
the progressive Akshar overhauls front-running Danelor (right); Pagan Dance takes third

Newmarket final one: effective at 1m to 10.5f: raced only on ground firmer than good: sold 170,000 gns. *Sir Michael Stoute*

AL AALI 5 b.h. Lahib (USA) 129 – Maraatib (IRE) 93 (Green Desert (USA) 127) **91** [2003 92: 7d 7.1m³ 7g⁵ 6m² 6g Jun 30] good-bodied, quite attractive horse: fairly useful performer, lightly raced: beaten head by Nivernais (pair clear) in handicap at Salisbury: ran as though amiss final start: effective at 6f/7f: acts on good to firm going. *A. G. Newcombe*

ALAARED (USA) 3 b.c. King of Kings (IRE) 125 – Celtic Loot (USA) (Irish River **87** (FR) 131) [2003 8m⁶ 10m⁴ 9.9f² 12g² 12m* 14.1f⁴ Sep 15] $150,000F, $310,000Y: useful-looking colt: has no off eye: seventh foal: half-brother to several winners by El Gran Senor, including 7f (including in France/Germany) winner Don Bosio and 1m (at 2 yrs) to 10.5f winner Himself (both useful): dam minor winner at 1m in USA at 4 yrs: fairly useful performer: won maiden at Newmarket in August: good fourth in handicap at Redcar final start: stays 1¾m, at least with emphasis on speed: raced only on good ground or firmer: tends to wander/carry head awkwardly: sold 13,000 gns. *J. L. Dunlop*

ALABASTRINE 3 gr.f. Green Desert (USA) 127 – Alruccaba 83 (Crystal Palace **56** (FR) 132) [2003 7m² 8m⁴ f7s⁶ 8f Oct 17] rather leggy, quite good-topped filly: half-sister to several winners, including very smart 1¼m filly Last Second (by Alzao), 6f/7f winner at 2 yrs, smart 1¼m to 2¼m winner Alleluia (by Caerleon) and to dams of Alborada, Quarter Moon and Yesterday: dam 2-y-o 6f winner: modest maiden: clearly best effort on debut: should stay at least 1m: visored last 2 starts: looks difficult ride. *Sir Mark Prescott*

ALAFDAL (USA) 3 b. or br.c. Gone West (USA) – Aqaarid (USA) 116 (Nashwan **70** (USA) 135) [2003 8m⁶ 10.1m² 10.1m 10m 10m Oct 14] leggy colt: third foal: closely related to 2000 2-y-o 1m winner Elmonjed (by Gulch), later 7f winner in UAE: dam, won Fillies' Mile and second in 1000 Guineas, from very good family: fair maiden: ran as if amiss last 3 starts: stays 1¼m: sold 10,000 gns. *J. L. Dunlop*

ALAFZAR (IRE) 5 b.g. Green Desert (USA) 127 – Alasana (IRE) (Darshaan 133) **69** [2003 84: a6.5f 8m a8f a6.5f 7f 8g 7g 7m 8f 7g⁴ 7m 7m 8f 7m⁴ 8d Nov 7] lengthy gelding: fair handicapper nowadays: well beaten in UAE first 5 starts (left R. Beckett after second outing, S. Seemar after fifth): mostly creditable efforts back in Britain: best form at 7f/ 1m: acts on polytrack, firm and good to soft going: tried visored: usually tongue tied nowadays. *P. D. Evans*

ALALOOF (USA) 2 b.f. (Mar 18) Swain (IRE) 134 – Alattrah (USA) (Shadeed (USA) **68** 135) [2003 8.2m⁶ 8m 8.2f⁵ Sep 30] smallish, well-made filly: first foal: dam unraced sister to 1000 Guineas winner Shadayid: best effort in maidens (fair form) when never-nearer fifth at Nottingham: will be suited. *J. L. Dunlop*

ALAMOUNA (IRE) 3 ch.f. Indian Ridge 123 – Alasana (IRE) (Darshaan 133) [2003 **85** 10m 10g⁵ 9m³ 10m* 10m⁶ 10.1m Sep 17] sturdy filly: fourth living foal: half-sister to smart 7f (at 2 yrs) and 1m winner Alasha (by Barathea) who stayed 1¼m and 5-y-o Alafzar: dam, French 1m/9f winner, half-sister to high-class French 1½m performer Altayan: fairly useful performer: won maiden at Brighton in July: stiff tasks in handicaps after: will stay 1½m: raced only on good/good to firm ground. *Sir Michael Stoute*

ALAMSHAR (IRE) 3 b.c. Key of Luck (USA) 126 – Alaiyda (USA) 84 (Shah- **133** rastani (USA) 135) [2003 112p: 10m² 10g* 12m³ 12m* 12d* 10f⁴ 10m⁶ Oct 18]
    The winners of Britain's two most prestigious races over a mile and a half, the Derby and the King George VI and Queen Elizabeth Stakes, continue to be a particularly attractive target for the rich Japanese studs. Seven of the Derby winners in the 'nineties, including Generous and Lammtarra (both of whom also won the King George) were exported to Japan. Generous, Erhaab and the 1992 Derby winner Dr Devious—now in Italy—were subsequently returned to Britain and Ireland, while King George winner Pentire will be available to German breeders in 2004. But Lammtarra and Opera House, the other King George winner since Generous to have gone to Japan, look to be on a one-way ticket. They have now been joined by Alamshar, who, after finishing third in the Derby, went on to win the Budweiser Irish Derby and King George VI and Queen Elizabeth Diamond Stakes.
    Alamshar was one of two top-class middle-distance three-year-old colts to race for the Aga Khan in the latest season. The king's ransom paid for the horse by the Japanese was not disclosed, but the owner's decision to 'take advantage of a commercial opportunity that presented itself' is unlikely to be one that he will lose much sleep over. The Aga Khan also enjoyed tremendous success with Alamshar's

French-trained contemporary Dalakhani, who won the Prix du Jockey Club and the Prix de l'Arc de Triomphe. Dalakhani has been retired to the Aga's Gilltown Stud, where he will stand alongside his celebrated half-brother Daylami, winner of seven Group/Grade 1 events including a King George and now off to a good start at stud, and Sinndar, the Derby, Irish Derby and Arc winner of 2000, who will have his first runners in 2004. More than most who have reaped the benefits of selling to Japan, the Aga Khan can be counted on to reinvest the money from the sale of Alamshar into European bloodstock. Operating entirely outside the commercial market, he has built up one of the most successful private breeding undertakings in Europe, the current edition of his stud book listing some two hundred and thirty-nine broodmares, who supply his requirements as an owner. The importance of maintaining the quality of the stud's mares is paramount for the Aga Khan. 'I don't want to diminish the importance of a Dalakhani, an Alamshar or a Sinndar, who bring in the biggest returns from an economic viewpoint,' he said after the latest Arc, 'but if I go ten years without winning a major pattern race with a filly, my stud is dead. Keeping up the quality of the broodmares is the cornerstone of its success.'

The 1996 King George winner Pentire, the last one bought by the Japanese before Alamshar, was the fortieth colt to win what quickly became established, after its inauguration at Ascot in 1951, as Britain's most important championship event for three-year-olds and upwards. Strategically placed towards the end of July, its profile provided an opportunity for the high-class older middle-distance horses still in training to test the mettle of the best representatives of the classic generation in a true championship race on weight-for-age terms. The fact that the fifty-two runnings before the latest edition resulted in twenty-six victories apiece for the two age groups supports the view that the King George has achieved its main objective of intensifying competition for the top middle-distance three-year-olds. The King George's roll of honour contains the names of some of the last half century's finest thoroughbreds, but outstanding racecourse success has not guaranteed outstanding performance at stud for winners of the race. Interestingly, only four of the forty colts to win the King George up to 1996 have gone on to head the sires' list in Britain. Aureole was twice leading sire in the 'sixties but that achievement couldn't secure him the same lasting influence as the three other champion sires to come

Derrinstown Stud Derby Trial Stakes, Leopardstown—Alamshar has to work hard to peg back The Great Gatsby (rails); Brian Boru and Napper Tandy (left) come third and fourth

Budweiser Irish Derby, the Curragh—a 1,2 for the Aga Khan as Alamshar
and Dalakhani (noseband) pull clear; Roosevelt, one of six Ballydoyle representatives, is next to finish

from the race, Ribot, Nijinsky and Mill Reef. Of the other King George winners, Busted, who built up a good record at stud, and The Minstrel, who sired the winners of more than fifty European pattern races, deserve an honourable mention; but, by and large, the winners of the race have, collectively, performed little better than the average for the stallion population at large. Among the Derby and King George winners exported in fairly recent times to Japan, the 1993 Derby winner Commander In Chief—now becoming established as a 'top ten' sire—has probably been the most significant loss to British and Irish breeding, though Opera House has sired a champion in T. M. Opera O, and Lammtarra has made a reasonable start and may yet make his mark. Commander In Chief followed his own sire, the 1986 King George winner Dancing Brave, in being exported to Japan.

Alamshar started second favourite for the Derby behind Two Thousand Guineas winner Refuse To Bend after an unlucky defeat in the Ballysax Stakes at Leopardstown in April and a scrambled victory in the Derrinstown Stud Derby Trial over the same course in May, a trial won by the three previous Derby winners, Sinndar, Galileo and High Chaparral, each of whom had followed up in the Irish Derby. At Epsom, Alamshar stayed on from a position in the middle of the field, tending to edge to his right under pressure entering the final furlong, and was beaten a length and a short head by Kris Kin and The Great Gatsby. The connections of Kris Kin opted not to supplement him for the Curragh, so the horse didn't run again before the King George. However, both The Great Gatsby and Alamshar lined up for the Irish Derby, the former one of six representatives for Ballydoyle. Most attention was focused on the odds-on, unbeaten Prix du Jockey Club winner Dalakhani in the Aga Khan's familiar 'green, red epaulets', Alamshar wearing the 'green, chocolate hoops' made famous by the Aga Khan's grandfather but now used for second strings. Alamshar's participation was put in doubt in the days before the race with the recurrence of a muscular problem in his back, which had troubled him, along with an abscess on a hoof, before the Derby Trial at Leopardstown. Alamshar started 4/1 second favourite at the Curragh on the day, with 6/1-shot The Great Gatsby the only other runner sent off at shorter than 12/1.

With the Ballydoyle colts High Country and Handel setting a blistering gallop, Dalakhani found himself in a very different sort of race from those he had been contesting in France, where finishing speed had been the deciding factor. The Irish Derby turned into a thorough test with the field soon well strung out, Dalakhani racing in third, some way off the leaders but well clear of the main pack in which Alamshar was to the fore. Alamshar was produced with a smooth run to draw up to Dalakhani after that horse was left in front early in the straight. There was a good duel over the last two furlongs before the hard-ridden Alamshar finally asserted in the last hundred yards to win by half a length, Dalakhani finishing three and a half lengths in front of the first Ballydoyle representative Roosevelt, a 150/1-shot who was two and a half lengths ahead of fourth-placed Brian Boru, with The Great Gatsby and Powerscourt, a further three lengths and three quarters of a length away, giving Ballydoyle third, fourth, fifth and sixth. Alamshar's victory provided his owner with his fifth Irish Derby winner—following Shergar, Shahrastani and Kahyasi in the 'eighties and Sinndar—and it can't be long before the Aga Khan follows the first two inductees, Vincent O'Brien (trainer of six winners) and Lester Piggott (who rode five), into the newly-instituted Irish Derby Hall of Fame.

Some expressed surprise that the Aga Khan ran Alamshar and Dalakhani against each other in the Irish Derby. If Alamshar had won at Epsom it might have been a very different story, but the owner clearly felt the horse deserved another shot at a Derby. It was announced immediately after the Irish Derby, however, that the pair would not meet again, Alamshar—'a horse for the summer'—being aimed at the King George VI and Queen Elizabeth Stakes and Dalakhani—'a horse more for the autumn'—at the Prix de l'Arc de Triomphe. Alamshar's performance at the Curragh represented a significant improvement on his Epsom third, and he was at shorter odds than Kris Kin throughout the ante-post betting on the King George, favourite in most books. Early indications were anything but encouraging for the chances of the leading three-year-olds in the King George when the five runners representing the classic crop in the Coral-Eclipse at Sandown managed only ninth, tenth, eleventh, twelfth and thirteenth behind the five-year-olds Falbrav and Nayef. The only three-year-old in the Princess of Wales's Stakes at the Newmarket July meeting, the King Edward VII Stakes winner High Accolade, finished last of six to six-year-old Millenary. Nayef started 3/1 favourite in a field of twelve for the King George on the day, with Kris Kin at 7/2, the previous year's Prix du Jockey Club winner and Arc runner-up Sulamani at 9/2, Alamshar at 13/2, Falbrav and South African challenger Victory Moon at 12/1, Coronation Cup winner Warrsan at 14/1, and Millenary and the previous year's St Leger winner Bollin Eric at 16/1, 25/1 bar. The Hardwicke winner Indian Creek was withdrawn on the morning of the race after overnight rain, while a vet's certificate was produced for the third three-year-old among the final declarations, the Dante winner Magistretti who had met a lot of trouble in the Derby before finishing runner-up in the Grand Prix de Paris.

Alamshar's drifting in the market on the day could be put down to the perception that the overnight change in the going to good to soft (it had been good to firm for the Irish Derby) was against him. Ascot was the first time Alamshar had encountered ground on the soft side of good since beating Brian Boru narrowly in the Beresford Stakes at the Curragh to end his two-year-old campaign with two wins out of two and earn a prominent position in the winter betting on the Derby, for which he was a supplementary entry in April (Dalakhani was an original entry). The more testing ground had seemed to suit Alamshar in the Beresford, and his performance in the Irish Derby confirmed finally what had been suspected since the Beresford: that stamina was his strong suit. Alamshar's connections had reportedly doubted his stamina to some degree early in the latest season, and he had been ridden fairly conservatively at Epsom. Johnny Murtagh, who rode him in all his

King George VI and Queen Elizabeth Diamond Stakes, Ascot—
after stealing a march off the turn, Alamshar is never in the slightest danger;
Sulamani is a clear second ahead of Kris Kin (right), Bollin Eric (centre) and Falbrav

races, had him well placed all the way in the King George, tactics that paid off when, despite the presence of a pacemaker for Nayef, the gallop turned out to be only fair. Alamshar made first run for home turning into the straight, quickly drawing clear when rousted along. Out of the pack eventually came Sulamani, who had been settled halfway down the field, and Kris Kin, not best placed at least five lengths behind Alamshar beginning the run up from Swinley Bottom, then forced wide round the home turn. Neither ever looked like pegging back Alamshar, who was still running on strongly at the finish where he had three and a half lengths—only eight King George winners have won by a bigger margin—to spare over Sulamani, with a further two lengths back to Kris Kin, who stayed on to beat Bollin Eric by half a length for third. Falbrav gave away ground by racing next to the outer rail on the bend approaching Swinley Bottom, his rider thinking the going might be slightly firmer there. He was below form in fifth, ahead of Warrsan, Nayef and Millenary. As in the finish of the Irish Derby, the experienced Murtagh deserved tremendous credit for his riding of Alamshar, which illustrated that it is usually an advantage to be up with the leaders in a race that is not truly run, the main disadvantage of such tactics for a jockey being that he cannot see what is happening behind him.

Dettori on Sulamani and Darley on Bollin Eric were among those left to rue the relatively steady pace in King George post-race interviews. Darley claimed that the muddling pace had detracted from the race. 'They slowed it down in front to a crawl and many of us just had to sit and suffer . . . it turned into a three-furlong sprint and was not an honest race.' Except for the 1997 edition run under very testing conditions, only Opera House (on good to soft) has returned a slower winning time for the race in its past fifteen runnings. But Alamshar's was a top-class effort, representing a little improvement on the form of his Irish Derby victory. Of the eleven before Alamshar to complete the Irish Derby/King George double, all had also contested the Derby at Epsom, reaching a place at least. Nijinsky, Grundy, The Minstrel, Troy, Shergar, Generous and Galileo completed the treble, while Ballymoss, Meadow Court and St Jovite came second at Epsom, and Ragusa third. Alamshar improved nearly a stone in the seven-week period between Epsom and Ascot, illustrating, as his trainer said, that 'handicappers improve and there is no reason why the good horses shouldn't do the same.'

The fortunes of Alamshar waned after the King George, as did those of his jockey. Murtagh's career has been punctuated by weight worries. A niggling back injury, suffered when falling from a two-year-old before the start of a race at Royal Ascot, made it hard for him to keep up the jogging which had become part of the regime for controlling his weight. Matters came to a head on the second Sunday in August when he was forced to give up mounts in two pattern races at the Curragh because he couldn't make the weight of 8-11. He took a break from riding—initially announcing that he was to miss the rest of the year—but was back to ride Alamshar (carrying 8-11) in the Irish Champion Stakes at Leopardstown in early-September. Alamshar found the step back to a mile and a quarter against him, unable to quicken in the straight and managing only fourth, albeit beaten under two lengths, to High Chaparral. Alamshar remained ready to run in the Prix de l'Arc de Triomphe, in the event of anything untoward happening to Dalakhani, and was also said at one time to have the Canadian International at Woodbine on his agenda. In the end, he made his final racecourse appearance, again over a mile and a quarter, in the Champion Stakes at Newmarket where, starting favourite, he signed off in disappointing fashion, managing only sixth to Rakti, ridden prominently but swept readily aside when the race began in earnest. His rider's long association with the Oxx stable, including other highlights such as the career of Sinndar, ended with the announcement in November that Michael Kinane was taking over after leaving Ballydoyle. Murtagh has said that he will be seen more in Britain where he is set to ride for David Loder.

The quick-actioned Alamshar, dwarfed by the majority of his rivals in the paddock before the Champion Stakes, is no great physical specimen, being on the small side. He is a product of one of the Aga Khan's long-established families descended from the legendary Mumtaz Mahal, bought for the Aga Khan's grandfather as a yearling at Doncaster in 1922. Renowned as 'the fastest filly in the annals of the turf', Mumtaz Mahal produced nine foals, seven of them winners, and three of her daughters also became distinguished broodmares. They were Mah Mahal (dam of Mahmoud), Mumtaz Begum (dam of Nasrullah) and the unraced Rustom Mahal (dam of Abernant). Alamshar is descended from Mah Mahal, through Mah Iran (dam of Migoli), Mah Behar (also a sister to Star of Iran, the dam of Petite Etoile), Nucciolina (grandam of Nishapour and Nassipour, and in recent times fourth dam of Alborada and the sisters Quarter Moon and Yesterday), and then, as illustrated in the tabulated pedigree, Alannya (a smart racemare and dam of nine winners), the 1989 Oaks 'winner' Aliysa (eventually disqualified after a long-running saga) and the only filly produced by Aliysa, the fairly useful racemare Alaiyda, who was trained by Oxx. Alaiyda was one of only four foals produced by Aliysa, all of which won, including the smart Desert Story, successful in the Horris Hill at two and the Craven at three and now at stud. Alaiyda ran five times, gaining her only success in a mile and a quarter maiden at Roscommon, but she stayed well, finishing a good third in the Leopardstown November Handicap over two miles.

Alamshar (IRE) (b.c. 2000)	Key of Luck (USA) (b 1991)	Chief's Crown (b 1982)	Danzig
			Six Crowns
		Balbonella (b or br 1984)	Gay Mecene
			Bamieres
	Alaiyda (USA) (ch 1991)	Shahrastani (ch 1983)	Nijinsky
			Shademah
		Aliysa (b 1986)	Darshaan
			Alannya

As with Sinndar's dam, another Oxx inmate Sinntara, who was successful at up to two miles with the Irish Cesarewitch among her wins, Alaiyda's career at stud has followed a familiar pattern for one of the Aga Khan's mares. Like Sinntara,

H.H. Aga Khan's "Alamshar"

Alaiyda is the product of a home-bred sire and dam, and, also like Sinntara, she visited eight different stallions in her first eight seasons at stud. Alaiyda's pedigree—by a Derby winner out of a first-past-the-post in the Oaks—didn't guarantee visits to the top stallions. She has been covered by sires with a wide variety of racing and pedigree profiles, none of them particularly fashionable or commercial at the time. Again in common with Sinntara, Alaiyda, who has had only one other winner in the fairly useful middle-distance filly Alaya (by Ela-Mana-Mou), has produced a notable classic horse by a stallion son of American-raced Chief's Crown, a tough and consistent racehorse whose eight Grade 1 wins included the Breeders' Cup Juvenile and the Travers Stakes. Chief's Crown was also placed in the three legs of the American triple crown, the Kentucky Derby, the Preakness and the Belmont, and, as a sire, did fairly well with his European runners, who include Derby winner Erhaab and Sinndar's sire Grand Lodge. The Chief's Crown stallion Key of Luck had a similar profile as a racehorse to Grand Lodge, in that he was an early-maturing horse, winning the Prix d'Arenberg over five furlongs as a two-year-old, and, as with the mating of Grand Lodge and Sinntara, was probably seen by the Aga Khan as a means of introducing a degree of speed to a dam who stayed well. Key of Luck, a close relative of champion sprinter Anabaa (by Chief's Crown's sire Danzig), missed his three-year-old season through injury but then carried on racing—on and off—until he was six, gaining a memorable twenty-length victory at the age of five in the Dubai Duty Free over a mile and a quarter on dirt at Nad Al Sheba. Retired to stud in Ireland, Key of Luck covered Alaiyda in his second season when his fee was only IR 3,500 guineas. Grand Lodge stood at IR 9,000 guineas when he sired Sinndar, who, along with Alamshar and others including top miler Sendawar (by Priolo when his fee was IR 3,000 guineas), have reaped rewards for the Aga Khan's policy with outside stallions. 'With the prices asked for top-of-the-line stallions having become prohibitive, breeding decisions which may have seemed to many to be unwise or unconventional have represented the key to our survival and have shown some promising results,' he said. Key of Luck's fee, which rose steeply to €12,500 in 2003, will be €25,000 in 2004, largely as a result of Alamshar's achievements, although he was also represented in the latest season by the smart sprinter Miss Emma. The genuine Alamshar showed better form at a mile and a half than at a mile and a quarter. He acted on firm and good to soft going. *J. Oxx, Ireland*

ALAM (USA) 4 b.g. Silver Hawk (USA) 123 – Ghashtah (USA) (Nijinsky (CAN) 138) [2003 75: 13d Sep 29] fair maiden: well held only outing in 2003: should stay 1½m: raced only on going softer than good: winning hurdler. *P. Monteith* —

ALASIL (USA) 3 b.c. Swain (IRE) 134 – Asl (USA) 114 (Caro 133) [2003 89: 10m 10f⁶ 11.9m⁶ 12m⁴ 11.8m Oct 13] good-topped colt: fairly useful handicapper: good fourth at Newmarket penultimate start: folded tamely final one: stays 1½m: raced only on good going or firmer: sold 41,000 gns, joined Mrs N. Smith. *J. L. Dunlop* **93**

ALASTAIR SMELLIE 7 ch.g. Sabrehill (USA) 120 – Reel Foyle (USA) 77 (Irish River (FR) 131) [2003 63§, a50§: f6g f5g 5m³ 6f Aug 2] good-topped gelding: modest performer: best at 5f/6f: acts on polytrack, firm and soft going: usually visored nowadays: sometimes slowly away (refused to race once): flashes tail: unreliable. *S. L. Keightley* **55 §**
a– §

AL AWWAM 4 b.g. Machiavellian (USA) 123 – Just A Mirage 76 (Green Desert (USA) 127) [2003 –: 14.1d 10d 7.1m⁵ 8.1m 8m f9.4g⁶ Nov 1] big, useful-looking gelding: poor maiden: left W. M. Brisbourne after fifth start: stays 1m: acts on good to firm ground: tongue tied last 2 starts (reportedly had breathing problem on debut). *J. W. Unett* **47 +**

AL AZHAR 9 b.g. Alzao (USA) 117 – Upend 120 (Main Reef 126) [2003 79, a63: 12g⁴ 12g⁵ 11.1d³ May 16] well-made gelding: has reportedly had knee trouble: fair performer: stays 1½m: acts on fibresand, heavy and good to firm going: sometimes starts slowly: usually patiently ridden. *M. Dods* **79**

ALBADI 2 b.c. (Feb 11) Green Desert (USA) 127 – Lyrist 77 (Cozzene (USA)) [2003 7s Oct 29] €35,000Y: first foal: dam, 1¼m/1½m winner, out of half-sister to Irish 2000 Guineas winner Prince of Birds: 25/1, slowly away and well held in maiden at Yarmouth. *C. E. Brittain* —

ALBANOVA 4 gr.f. Alzao (USA) 117 – Alouette 105 (Darshaan 133) [2003 113: 11.9v* 12m 12d² 15.5s⁶ Oct 26] tall, rather leggy, close-coupled filly: smart performer: **113**

landed odds in listed event at Haydock in May by 8 lengths from Prompt Payment: best subsequent effort when creditable 1¼ lengths second to Mamool in Preis von Europa at Cologne: blinkered, pulled hard early stages when sixth in Prix Royal-Oak at Longchamp final start: stays 1½m: has run creditably on good to firm ground, but gives impression ideally suited by good or softer (acts on heavy): usually waited with. *Sir Mark Prescott*

ALBANOV (IRE) 3 b.c. Sadler's Wells (USA) 132 – Love For Ever (IRE) (Darshaan **104** 133) [2003 83: 12g³ 11.9d² 12.1d* 14g³ 14g⁴ 15d⁵ 15.5d² 15s² Nov 22] quite good-topped colt: useful performer: won maiden at Chepstow in May: blinkered, improved efforts when second to Le Carre in listed races at Saint-Cloud (beaten 3 lengths) and Fontainebleau (beaten 4 lengths) last 2 starts: stays 15.5f: acts on heavy and good to firm going: usually races prominently: reliable. *J. L. Dunlop*

ALBANY (IRE) 3 ch.g. Alhaarth (IRE) 126 – Tochar Ban (USA) 83 (Assert 134) **89** [2003 76: 8m 10g⁵ 9.9d⁴ 12.1m⁴ 11.9f³ 11.9m* 12.3m⁴ 14m* Aug 8] strong gelding: fairly useful handicapper: dictated pace when winning at Haydock in July and August: stays 1¾m: acts on firm and soft ground: sold 57,000 gns, joined J. Howard Johnson. *Mrs J. R. Ramsden*

ALBASHOOSH 5 b.g. Cadeaux Genereux 131 – Annona (USA) 72 (Diesis 133) **91 d** [2003 95: 8m 6m 6d 7g 7m 6f 8m² 7g⁶ 7f⁶ 7.2g⁴ 8m⁴ 7.2f³ 7.9m 8m 8g 7m6 Oct 12] quite good-topped gelding: fairly useful handicapper at best in 2003: effective at 6f to easy 1m: acts on firm and soft going: blinkered/visored 3 times, racing freely on each occasion (successful once): usually waited with: sold 10,000 gns. *J. S. Goldie*

ALBA STELLA 3 b. or gr.f. Nashwan (USA) 135 – Alouette 105 (Darshaan 133) **92** [2003 70p: 12.4m* 12m* 12m³ 12m 14.1s Oct 29] leggy, unfurnished filly: fairly useful performer: landed odds in handicaps at Newcastle and Folkestone in August: below form in listed races last 2 starts: stayed 12.4f: acted on good to firm ground: stud. *Sir Mark Prescott*

ALBAVILLA 3 b.f. Spectrum (IRE) 126 – Lydia Maria 70 (Dancing Brave (USA) **70** 140) [2003 69p: 8m⁵ 9.9m⁵ 10f⁶ Jun 25] rangy, good sort: fair maiden: stays 1¼m: acts on soft and good to firm ground. *P. W. Harris*

AL BEEDAA (USA) 2 ch.f. (Apr 11) Swain (IRE) 134 – Histoire (FR) (Riverman **75** (USA) 131) [2003 7m 8.2f³ Sep 30] strong, short-backed filly: half-sister to several winners, notably high-class 7f (at 2 yrs) to 1½m (Derby) winner Erhaab (by Chief's Crown) and smart 7f (at 2 yrs) and 1¼m winner Oumaldaaya (by Nureyev): dam French 10.5f winner: better effort in maidens (fair form) when 7½ lengths third to Deraasaat at Nottingham: will be suited by at least 1½m. *J. L. Dunlop*

ALBERICH (IRE) 8 b.g. Night Shift (USA) – Tetradonna (IRE) 102 (Teenoso (USA) **85** 135) [2003 93: f16.2g⁶ Mar 8] sturdy gelding: good mover: has reportedly had knee problem: fairly useful performer: effective at 1½m, barely stays 21f: acts on fibresand and probably any turf going: usually races up with pace: sometimes hangs: game: sold 8,500 gns. *A. G. Newcombe*

ALBERTINE 3 b.f. Bahhare (USA) 122 – Rosa Royale 61 (Arazi (USA) 135) [2003 **–** p8g Apr 9] 12,000Y: first foal: dam, maiden who stayed 1½m, out of smart 1m to 10.5f performer Gussy Marlowe: tailed off in maiden at Lingfield. *C. F. Wall*

ALBERTO GIACOMETTI (IRE) 3 b.c. Sadler's Wells (USA) 132 – Sweeten Up **116** 76 (Shirley Heights 130) [2003 111p: 10m³ 10.5g³ 12m 10g⁶ 10f 10f Dec 29] sturdy, close-coupled colt: fluent mover: smart performer: won Criterium de Saint-Cloud at 2 yrs: third to Ballestrini in Ballysax Stakes at Leopardstown and to Dalakhani in Prix Lupin at Longchamp (best effort, beaten 1¾ lengths) first 2 starts: just respectable efforts at best after, leaving A. O'Brien, Ireland, after fourth outing: beaten under 2 lengths when tenth of 13 to Sweet Return in Hollywood Derby on penultimate start: should stay 1½m (twelfth of 20 in Derby at Epsom when tried): possibly best on good ground or softer. *L. De Seroux, USA*

ALBINUS 2 gr.c. (Feb 4) Selkirk (USA) 129 – Alouette 105 (Darshaan 133) [2003 8.2d **69 p** p8g³ Dec 10] big, good sort: sixth foal: half-brother to several winners, including very smart 7f (at 2 yrs) and 1¼m (dual Champion Stakes) winner Alborada and 4-y-o Albanova (both by Alzao): dam, Irish 1m (at 2 yrs) and 1½m winner, sister to dam of Quarter Moon and Yesterday and half-sister to very smart 1¼m winner Last Second and smart stayer Alleluia: better effort in maidens (fair form) when third to Jake The Snake at Lingfield, green and never nearer: will stay at least 1¼m: should improve. *A. M. Balding*

ALBUHERA (IRE) 5 b.g. Desert Style (IRE) 121 – Morning Welcome (IRE) (Be My **105** Guest (USA) 126) [2003 8g 10m⁴ 8.9f³ 10f 10g⁵ 10.4f 9.9g 8g 10.5m Aug 9] lengthy, good sort: smart handicapper at 3 yrs: missed 2002 after reportedly fracturing a hind pedal bone: useful in 2003, creditable efforts third and fifth starts, third to Krugerrand at York on first occasion: stays 1¼m: well beaten last 4 outings: yet to race on heavy going, acts on any other: blinkered last 2 starts: usually races prominently: joined P. Nicholls, and useful form over hurdles. *M. Johnston*

ALBURACK 5 b.g. Rock City 120 – Suzannah's Song (Song 132) [2003 42: 7m Oct 25] leggy gelding: poor maiden: stays 6f: acts on good to firm and good to soft going: tried blinkered. *G. G. Margarson* —

ALBURY HEATH 3 b.g. Mistertopogigo (IRE) 118 – Walsham Witch 61 (Music Maestro 119) [2003 57?: p8g p6g5 p6g 6m 8.2m Oct 28] good-bodied gelding: poor maiden: probably best at 5f/6f: raced only on polytrack/good to firm ground: tried visored. *T. M. Jones* —

ALCAZAR (IRE) 8 b.g. Alzao (USA) 117 – Sahara Breeze 85 (Ela-Mana-Mou 132) [2003 14.1g* 16.2g* 20m 15.5s2 12d4 Nov 8] **117**

Alcazar has had a remarkable career. Unraced at two, he was successful in four races for John Dunlop as a three-year-old, including the listed Serlby Stakes at Doncaster, but then problems began. According to his current trainer, Alcazar has suffered a stress fracture of his pelvis at least three times, a broken bone in a hind leg and two serious tendon strains. Between 1999 and the current season, Alcazar got to the racecourse just once, in a handicap at Newmarket in September 2001, which he won at 25/1 after being with his new trainer for only four months. If that was a notable training feat, Morrison's achievement in again bringing back Alcazar in 2003 deserves even more credit. Not only did Alcazar stay sound enough to put in five appearances, he also returned very nearly as good as in his three-year-old days. After beating Darasim in the listed 'Further Flight' Stakes at Nottingham in April, Alcazar passed the post first by a neck at Ascot in the Bovis Homes Sagaro Stakes later in the month, only for the stewards to demote him after Alcazar's jockey Michael Fenton caught Savannah Bay in the face with his whip in the closing stages. Connections appealed and just over two weeks later Alcazar was reinstated, giving Morrison his first pattern-race success.

Alcazar missed the Henry II Stakes at Sandown at the end of May reportedly because of the firmish ground, but conditions were similar for the Gold Cup at Royal Ascot. Starting at 25/1, he seemed in the process of running respectably before tiring markedly halfway up the straight and trailing in last of the twelve runners. It looked as if his old problems might have returned. However, there was no serious injury this time and, after another absence, Alcazar came back to form in the Prix Royal-Oak at Longchamp in October, staying on well to finish two and a half lengths second to Westerner, with the favourite, Vinnie Roe, back in fourth place. Alcazar probably needs further than a mile and a half nowadays, at least when conditions aren't testing, and he should stay beyond two miles. He acts on soft and good to firm going, though it seems unlikely he will be risked on firmish going in future. *H. Morrison*

Bovis Homes Sagaro Stakes, Ascot—Alcazar keeps on gamely
while Savannah Bay reacts to being struck by the winning rider's whip

Princess Elizabeth Stakes (sponsored by Vodafone), Epsom—
the genuine Aldora gains her fourth win of the season; Londonnetdotcom (blaze) finishes second

ALCHEMIST MASTER   4 b.g. Machiavellian (USA) 123 – Gussy Marlowe 118 **55**
(Final Straw 127) [2003 53+, a79: p8g⁴ f8s* f8.5g⁴ 8m 7.9m 7.5d 6g Oct 14] leggy, quite **a85 +**
good-topped gelding: fairly useful handicapper on all-weather, modest on turf: won at
Southwell in February: stays 1m: acts on all-weather. *R. M. Whitaker*

ALCHEMYSTIC (IRE)   3 b.g. In The Wings 128 – Kama Tashoof 72 (Mtoto 134) **70 §**
[2003 –p: p10g p10g* p10g³ 11.6d 12s 10m³ 12m³ 13.8m Sep 9] good-topped gelding:
fairly useful performer on all-weather, fair on turf: won maiden at Lingfield in February:
probably best short of 1½m: acts on polytrack and good to firm ground: blinkered last 2
starts: ungenuine: sold 15,000 gns, joined G. L. Moore, won juvenile hurdle in December.
Mrs A. J. Perrett

ALCHERA   2 b.c. (Apr 23) Mind Games 121 – Kind of Shy 61 (Kind of Hush 118) **77**
[2003 5f⁶ 5g⁶ 5.7m⁵ 7g 5m² 6g* 6m Oct 4] 16,000Y: quite attractive colt: shows a quick
action: closely related to several winners by Puissance, including 5f to 7.6f winner
Corunna and 7f winner Kai One, both fairly useful, and half-brother to 1995 2-y-o 6f
seller winner My Kind (by Mon Tresor): dam maiden who stayed 1m: fair performer:
won nursery at Epsom in September: stays 6f, possibly not 7f: acts on good to firm going:
blinkered last 3 starts: often races prominently. *R. F. Johnson Houghton*

ALDERNEY RACE (USA)   2 ch.c. (Feb 1) Seeking The Gold (USA) – Oyster **89 p**
Catcher (IRE) 105 (Bluebird (USA) 125) [2003 6g⁴ Oct 24] tall colt: first foal: dam,
Irish 6f winner, half-sister to smart Irish 7f winner (including Moyglare Stud Stakes)
Sequoyah, out of sister to dam of high-class sprinter/miler Dolphin Street and Irish 2000
Guineas winner Saffron Walden: 12/1 and better for race, 2 lengths fourth of 19 to So Will
I in maiden at Newbury, slowly away and staying on well, not unduly punished: likely to
stay 1m: should improve and win races. *R. Charlton*

ALDER PARK   3 b.g. Alderbrook 120 – Melody Park 104 (Music Boy 124) [2003 68:   **–**
12f⁶ 12g 8m 10m 7m 6f Jul 16] workmanlike gelding: modest maiden at 2 yrs: little solid
form in 2003. *J. G. Given*

ALDORA   4 ch.f. Magic Ring (IRE) 115 – Sharp Top 62 (Sharpo 132) [2003 99: 8g*   **109**
p7g² 9d* 10.4m³ 8m* 8.5m* Jun 6] leggy, good-topped filly: useful performer: in
excellent form in first half of year, winning handicap at Doncaster in March and listed
races at Newmarket and Goodwood in May and Epsom in June: beat Londonnetdotcom
by 1½ lengths at Epsom (struck into on off-fore): effective at 7f to easy 10.4f: acts on
good to firm going, good to soft and polytrack: genuine and consistent: stays in training.
M. J. Ryan

ALEJANDRO BARRERAS   3 b.g. Royal Applause 124 – Andbell (Trojan Fen 118)   **–**
[2003 10g Jul 8] ninth foal: half-brother to 6-y-o Willoughby's Boy and a winner in
Norway by Mango Express: dam of little account: well beaten in maiden at Pontefract.
B. Hanbury

ALEKHINE (IRE)   2 b.g. (May 1) Soviet Star (USA) 128 – Alriyaah 73 (Shareef **86 p**
Dancer (USA) 135) [2003 7m* 8d⁶ Nov 7] €80,000Y: strong, lengthy gelding: half-
brother to several winners, including 7f winner Catz (by Catrail, later successful in USA)
and 5f winner Magic Star (by Revoque), both fairly useful in Ireland: dam 2-y-o 5f

winner: green, won maiden at Doncaster in October by ½ length from West Country: only sixth in minor event on softer going at same course: should stay 1m: likely to make useful 3-y-o. *P. W. Harris*

ALERON (IRE) 5 b.h. Sadler's Wells (USA) 132 – High Hawk 124 (Shirley Heights 130) [2003 68, a–: f16s⁵ f12s* f11s⁶ f11g⁴ 13.8m² 14m* 12m² 12.3m³ 13d³ 12.1g 11.9f 11.9m 11.9m 13.1m³ 11.9d³ f14.8g⁴ 13.8d³ 16.5d⁴ Nov 8] quite good-topped horse: fairly useful handicapper on turf, fair on all-weather: won at Southwell in February and Musselburgh in April: effective at 1½m, barely stays 2m: acts on dirt/fibresand, good to firm and good to soft ground: sometimes visored, not in 2003: tried tongue tied: has hung/found little. *J. J. Quinn* **85 a68**

ALESSANDRO SEVERO 4 gr.g. Brief Truce (USA) 126 – Altaia (FR) 90 (Sicyos (USA) 126) [2003 71, a84: p10g p12g* p12g 10.3m⁴ 12g 10.2g 10.3m 10m 10.3d Sep 24] leggy gelding: fairly useful handicapper on all-weather, fair on turf: won at Lingfield in January: below form last 5 starts: stays 1½m: acts on all-weather, good to firm and good to soft going: usually blinkered, has worn cheekpieces: often slowly away: looks difficult ride: sold 3,400 gns. *N. P. Littmoden* **71 a89**

ALETHEA GEE 5 b.m. Sure Blade (USA) 130 – Star Flower (Star Appeal 133) [2003 8.1m Jul 24] eighth foal: half-sister to 1½m winners Country Orchid (by Town And Country) and Elusive Star (by Ardross): dam, maiden, out of half-sister to Gold Cup winner Shangamuzo: last in maiden at Sandown. *John Berry* **–**

ALEXANDER ANAPOLIS (IRE) 3 b.f. Spectrum (IRE) 126 – Pirouette 114 (Sadler's Wells (USA) 132) [2003 94?: 7.5d⁴ 8d⁵ 7s 7m⁵ 10s³ 10g 10d 8.5v² 8g 9m⁶ 10g⁶ f12s* Dec 6] IR 47,000Y: eighth foal: half-sister to winners in Japan by Woodman and Dehere: dam, Irish 7f winner, half-sister to very smart sprinter Ballad Rock: fair performer: left K. Prendergast in Ireland, not at best to win maiden at Wolverhampton in December by 2 lengths from Exit To Heaven, carrying head awkwardly: stays 1½m: acts on heavy going and fibresand. *N. A. Callaghan* **79**

ALEXANDER BALLET 4 b.f. Mind Games 121 – Dayville (USA) 86 (Dayjur (USA) 137) [2003 72: 5g 5.1s 6m Jun 5] 66,000Y: leggy, ex-Irish filly: first foal: dam, 6f winner (including at 2 yrs), half-sister to smart filly up to 1¼m Spanish Fern out of sister to Irish 1000 Guineas winner Al Bahathri: fair performer for M. Grassick in 2002, winning maiden at Bellewstown: only modest at 4 yrs: effective at 5f/6f: acts on firm ground. *T. D. Easterby* **57 d**

ALEXANDER CHARLOTE (IRE) 2 b.f. (Apr 11) Titus Livius (FR) 115 – Sabaniya (FR) (Lashkari 128) [2003 6m⁵ 7m 6.1f³ 6m² 6.1d³ Nov 8] €110,000Y: good-topped filly: fourth foal: half-sister to fairly useful 2000 2-y-o 5f winner Chaguaramas (by Mujadil): dam, Irish bumper winner, half-sister to high-class French 1¼m/1½m winner Sadjiyd and to grandam of Sinndar: fair maiden: second at Redcar: probably stays 7f: acts on good to firm going: took strong hold/carried head awkwardly final start. *B. W. Hills* **77**

ALEXANDER PRINCE (IRE) 3 b.g. Desert Prince (IRE) 130 – National Ballet (Shareef Dancer (USA) 135) [2003 73: 10g⁶ 10m 8g May 20] strong, compact gelding: fair maiden: barely stayed 1¼m: acted on polytrack: dead. *Lady Herries* **71**

ALEXANDER STAR (IRE) 5 b. or br.m. Inzar (USA) 112 – Business Centre (IRE) 58 (Digamist (USA) 110) [2003 –: 6m 6.1g 5.1f⁵ 5m² 5g 5m* 5m Jul 25] smallish, workmanlike mare: modest performer: second run in 2 days, dead-heated with Blackheath in handicap at Carlisle in July: stays 6f: effective at 5f/6f: acts on good to firm ground: tried blinkered/visored/tongue tied: none too consistent. *P. J. McBride* **58**

ALFANO (IRE) 5 b.g. Priolo (USA) 127 – Sartigila 67 (Efisio 120) [2003 70: 10d p12g* 11.9d⁴ Sep 26] quite good-topped gelding: fair handicapper: won amateur event at Lingfield in June: stays 1½m: acts on polytrack, soft and good to firm ground: occasionally visored/tongue tied in 2001: wore cheekpieces final 4-y-o start: sold £1,100. *E. L. James* **70**

ALFELMA (IRE) 3 ch.f. Case Law 113 – Billie Grey 72 (Chilibang 120) [2003 –: 5.1m³ 6m 5m f6f Jul 25] seemed to show modest form when never-dangerous third to Cape Royal in maiden at Nottingham: well held otherwise. *P. R. Wood* **57**

ALFIE LEE (IRE) 6 ch.g. Case Law 113 – Nordic Living (IRE) 53 (Nordico (USA)) [2003 46+: 5m 5m 5g 5m 5f 5m 5f⁴ 6d 5g Nov 5] compact, well-made gelding: unimpressive mover: modest handicapper: raced mainly at 5f: acts on firm going and fibresand: tried in blinkers/cheekpieces: tongue tied nowadays. *D. A. Nolan* **50**

ALFONSO 2 ch.c. (Mar 7) Efisio 120 – Winnebago 63 (Kris 135) [2003 6g 6g⁴ Oct 31] quite good-topped colt: third foal: brother to 4-y-o Pablo and 3-y-o San Antonio: **71 p**

dam, 13f winner, half-sister to very smart Apache (stayed 13f): better effort in maidens (fair form) when 5¾ lengths fourth to Caveral at Newmarket: will be suited by 7f/1m: should progress. *B. W. Hills*

ALFRED SISLEY 3 b.g. Royal Applause 124 – Dalu (IRE) 72 (Dancing Brave (USA) 140) [2003 63p: 8.2g 7.1m* 7.1m 7d 6f⁴ 7m⁶ 6f⁴ 8.5s 7v 6.5g 6m Aug 30] fair handicapper: won at Warwick in April: left P. Cole after seventh start: soundly beaten for new stable: stays 7f: acts on firm ground and fibresand: tried blinkered/in cheekpieces: free-going sort: has found little. *S. J. Mahon, Ireland* **69 d**

ALHAURIN 4 ch.g. Classic Cliche (IRE) 128 – Fairey Firefly 64 (Hallgate 127) [2003 10.4f Oct 9] second foal: dam 6f winner: well held in bumpers: tailed off in claimer at York. *Miss J. A. Camacho* **–**

ALHESN (USA) 8 b. or br.g. Woodman (USA) 126 – Deceit Princess (CAN) (Vice Regent (CAN)) [2003 32, a44: f16g Jan 9] angular gelding: poor handicapper: stays 2m: acts on fibresand and firm going, possibly not on softer than good: tried visored/tongue tied/in cheekpieces: sometimes slowly away: usually soon off bridle. *C. N. Allen* **–**

ALIABAD (IRE) 8 b. or br.g. Doyoun 124 – Alannya (FR) (Relko 136) [2003 –: 16.2d 10.2g f12g 16m Sep 19] little form in 2003: tried visored/blinkered. *J. G. M. O'Shea* **–**

ALIBA (IRE) 2 ch.g. (Mar 4) Ali-Royal (IRE) 127 – Kiba (IRE) (Tirol 127) [2003 6g³ 5m⁵ 5.9d⁴ Jul 30] €12,000Y: first foal: dam, fourth at 1m at 3 yrs only start, grand-daughter of Oaks second Bonnie Isle: modest form in maidens: third at Hamilton: should stay 1m. *B. Smart* **62**

ALIBONGO (CZE) 2 ch.c. (Mar 26) Dara Monarch 128 – Alvilde 70 (Alzao (USA) 117) [2003 5m⁶ 6d 6g⁶ f5g⁶ 5m 7m Aug 22] close-coupled colt: second known foal: dam 5f winner in Slovakia: poor maiden: stays 6f: acts on good to soft ground. *R. Bastiman* **43**

ALI CAN (IRE) 4 b.g. Ali-Royal (IRE) 127 – Desert Native 42 (Formidable (USA) 125) [2003 65: p10g⁵ f9.4g³ f12g⁴ f12g⁵ a10g⁴ a12g* a10g² 12g a10g⁶ a10g⁶ a12g a8g a15g⁴ a12g* a12g² Dec 30] modest performer: sold from A. Jarvis 1,000 gns after fourth outing: won handicap at Taby in May and minor event there in November: seems to stay 15f: acts on dirt/all-weather and good to firm going: effective visored or not. *Catherina Wenell, Sweden* **61**

ALICE BLACKTHORN 2 b.f. (May 4) Forzando 122 – Owdbetts (IRE) 69 (High Estate 127) [2003 6m 6g 6.1m⁴ 6m⁴ 6f⁵ 6m* 6d Nov 4] 8,500Y: leggy, rather unfurnished filly: fourth foal: half-sister to 5-y-o Ratio: dam 7f (including at 2 yrs) and 1¼m winner: fair performer: won maiden at Pontefract in October: should stay 7f: acts on good to firm ground. *B. Smart* **70**

ALICE BRAND (IRE) 5 b.m. Nucleon (USA) 94 – Tormented (USA) (Alleged (USA) 138) [2003 74?: 8.2g⁴ 6m 6.9d³ f8g f7g Dec 16] IR 3,000Y: ex-Irish mare: third living foal: sister to useful Irish 6f and 1m winner Anna Elise: dam lightly-raced maiden: modest maiden: trained by J. Flynn in 2002: effective at 6f to 1m: acts on soft and good to firm going, well held on fibresand. *G. M. Moore* **56 a–**

ALI D 5 b.g. Alhijaz 122 – Doppio 62 (Dublin Taxi) [2003 f7s² f7g⁵ f7g⁶ f8.5g 8.2s² 8m 8m⁴ 8.1g 10.5m* 10m⁴ 10d 10.4m Sep 3] sturdy gelding: fair handicapper: won at Haydock in July: stays 10.5f: acts on fibresand, soft and good to firm ground: usually wears cheekpieces: held up. *Mrs N. Macauley* **68**

ALI DEO 2 ch.c. (Mar 8) Ali-Royal (IRE) 127 – Lady In Colour (IRE) 71 (Cadeaux Genereux 131) [2003 7m 6m Oct 16] good-topped colt: first foal: dam, second at 1¼m only start, half-sister to very smart French 1¼m/1½m (Prix Vermeille) winner Pearly Shells: better effort at Newmarket (fair form) when eighth in maiden on debut: will be suited by at least 1m. *W. J. Haggas* **79**

ALIGATOU 4 b.g. Distant Relative 128 – Follow The Stars 86 (Sparkler 130) [2003 –: f7g Jan 28] disappointing maiden: tried in blinkers and cheekpieces. *Mrs L. Stubbs* **–**

AL IHTITHAR (IRE) 3 b.f. Barathea (IRE) 127 – Azyaa 101 (Kris 135) [2003 98p: 10g⁵ 8.1g 10m* 10.3d* Nov 7] good-topped filly: useful performer: improved to win listed events at Newmarket in October and Doncaster in November: beat Russian Society by head in latter: stayed 10.3f: acted on soft and good to firm going: visits Daylami. *B. W. Hills* **106**

ALINDA (IRE) 2 b.f. (Apr 23) Revoque (IRE) 122 – Gratclo 65 (Belfort (FR) 89) [2003 6d f6s* Oct 21] 30,000Y: rather leggy, lengthy filly: half-sister to several winners, including useful 1996 2-y-o 6f (July Stakes) winner Rich Ground (by Common Grounds) and 6-y-o Bandanna: dam 6f (including at 2 yrs)/7f winner: better effort in maidens (fair **69 p**

form) when winning at Southwell by ¾ length from Pick of The Crop, racing prominently: likely to stay 7f: should progress. *P. W. Harris*

ALI PASHA   4 b.g. Ali-Royal (IRE) 127 – Edge of Darkness 62 (Vaigly Great 127)   **45 d**
[2003 53: f9.4g 11.8m⁴ 10.2g³ 11.7f 8m 11.9m 10m Oct 23] poor maiden: left D. Burchell before well held last 2 starts: stays 1½m: acts on all-weather, raced only on good going or firmer on turf: has found little. *M. D. I. Usher*

ALI'S OASIS   2 b.g. (Apr 2) Ali-Royal (IRE) 127 – Miss Walsh (Distant Relative 128)   **58 d**
[2003 5m* 5m⁵ 5d⁴ 6g⁶ 5f 5m 6m 7.1m Oct 25] 2,500Y, resold 6,500Y: smallish gelding: fourth foal: dam lightly-raced maiden: modest performer: won maiden at Musselburgh in April: ran poorly in nurseries/sellers last 4 starts: stays 6f: acts on good to firm ground: tried blinkered: sold 1,600 gns, sent to Macau. *B. Smart*

A LITTLE BIT YARIE   2 b.g. (Mar 24) Paris House 123 – Slipperose 72 (Persepolis   **81**
(FR) 127) [2003 5g³ 5d* 5m² 5f³ Jun 18] 13,000Y: tall gelding: ninth foal: half-brother to 8-y-o Yorkies Boy (formerly smart): dam 11.5f winner: fairly useful performer: won maiden at Hamilton in May: best effort when second in minor event at Redcar: likely to prove best at 5f/6f: acts on good to firm and good to soft ground: tends to hang: gelded. *K. R. Burke*

ALI ZANDRA   2 b.f. (Apr 1) Prince Sabo 123 – Priceless Fantasy (Dunbeath (USA)   **–**
127) [2003 5m f5s May 12] second foal: dam 9f to 11f winner: last in maiden/claimer. *Julian Poulton*

ALIZARIN (IRE)   4 b.f. Tagula (IRE) 116 – Persian Empress (IRE) 51 (Persian Bold   **–**
123) [2003 –: 6m May 12] disappointing maiden: tried blinkered. *R. E. Barr*

ALIZAR (IRE)   2 b.f. (Jan 28) Rahy (USA) 115 – Capua (USA) (Private Terms (USA))   **58**
[2003 5g 5m⁶ 5f 5m f5g 7.1m⁴ 7m⁴ 8f 6g⁶ f5g³ f6s⁶ f5g* f6s⁶ f6g⁵ f6g³ Dec 26]   **a61**
€8,000Y: unfurnished filly: first foal: dam unraced, out of half-sister to high-class French performer up to 9f Magical Wonder: modest performer: won 2 sellers at Southwell in December: effective at 5f to easy 7f: acts on fibresand and good to firm ground: tried in cheekpieces: edgy sort. *M. J. Polglase*

AL JADEED (USA)   3 b.c. Coronado's Quest (USA) 130 – Aljawza (USA) 86 (River-   **107**
man (USA) 131) [2003 109: 8g³ 9m² 9m Oct 18] close-coupled, quite attractive colt: has a quick action: useful performer: won Royal Lodge Stakes at Ascot at 2 yrs: creditable 3 lengths third of 4 to Heretic in minor event at Doncaster on reappearance in July: below form after, tailed off in Darley Stakes at Newmarket final start: stays 1m: raced only on good going or firmer: has raced freely/worn crossed noseband. *J. H. M. Gosden*

ALJARD (USA)   5 ch.g. Gilded Time (USA) – Diaspora (USA) (Vice Regent (CAN))   **–**
[2003 59, a69: f8g 8g 8.1m Aug 8] lengthy gelding: fair handicapper in 2002: well beaten in 2003: tried blinkered/tongue tied. *Mrs S. J. Smith*

ALJAZEERA (USA)   3 b.f. Swain (IRE) 134 – Matiya (IRE) 116 (Alzao (USA) 117)   **91**
[2003 84: 7g 7m⁵ 7g⁴ 7.1m² 8m⁴ 9.9m⁶ 10m⁶ 7d Oct 4] close-coupled filly: fairly useful handicapper: mostly creditable efforts in 2003: free-going sort, probably best short of 1¼m: yet to race on extremes of going: tongue tied: sometimes flashes tail: sold 41,000 gns. *B. Hanbury*

ALJOMAR   4 b.g. College Chapel 122 – Running For You (FR) (Pampabird 124)   **44**
[2003 45: f8s f6g⁴ f7g⁴ f7g⁵ 7m f7g 8f⁶ 7f⁴ 8g 7g 8d 8m 6f⁴ 7f f11g Dec 19] leggy gelding: poor maiden: stays 8.5f: acts on fibresand and firm ground: tried in cheekpieces: none too consistent. *R. E. Barr*

AL JOUDHA (FR)   2 b.f. (Mar 4) Green Desert (USA) 127 – Palacegate Episode   **–**
(IRE) 111 (Drumalis 125) [2003 5m⁵ 5.6f Jun 29] €80,000Y: leggy filly: fourth foal: closely related to smart Scandinavian sprinter King Quantas (by Danehill) and half-sister to 3-y-o Gilded Edge: dam 5f winner, including at 2 yrs: well held in maidens at Warwick and Doncaster: sold 12,000 gns. *M. R. Channon*

ALKAADHEM   3 b.c. Green Desert (USA) 127 – Balalaika 108 (Sadler's Wells   **106 p**
(USA) 132) [2003 8.1m* 7m² 7g* Jul 31] 200,000Y: strong, quite attractive colt: second foal: half-brother to useful 1m/1¼m winner Lookalike (by Rainbow Quest): dam, 9f winner who stayed 1½m, sister to high-class 1¼m performer Stagecraft from excellent family of Opera House and Kayf Tara: useful form: won maiden at Warwick and minor event at Goodwood (by length from Digital) in July: creditable 1¾ lengths second to Meshaheer in minor event at Newbury in between: effective at 7f/1m: open to further improvement. *M. P. Tregoning*

ALKAASED (USA)   3 b.c. Kingmambo (USA) 125 – Chesa Plana (Niniski (USA)   **103**
125) [2003 87p: 11.5g² 12.3g* 14m² 11.8m² Oct 13] big, strong, good-bodied colt:

unimpressive mover: useful performer: landed odds in maiden at Ripon in August: good second in handicaps at Newmarket (beaten length by Ten Carat) and Leicester (short-headed by Dovedon Hero) last 2 starts: at least as effective at 1½m as 1¾m: raced only on good/good to firm ground: sold 42,000 gns, joined L. Cumani. *Sir Michael Stoute*

ALKA INTERNATIONAL 11 b.g. Northern State (USA) 91 – Cachucha (Gay Fandango (USA) 132) [2003 p16g Dec 2] workmanlike gelding: fair hurdler: lightly-raced maiden on Flat. *Mrs P. Townsley* –

ALLA CAPPELLA (IRE) 3 ch.f. College Chapel 122 – Keiko 76 (Generous (IRE) 139) [2003 64: 6.1m 6.1d⁵ 6m 6d 8.3g Aug 10] close-coupled, unfurnished filly: modest maiden: best form at 5f/6f: acts on good to soft ground and polytrack: sold £1,300 later in August. *C. F. Wall* **64**

ALL BUSINESS 4 b.f. Entrepreneur 123 – Belle Esprit (Warning 136) [2003 92: 12.1g 12m 12g⁵ Jul 17] leggy, angular filly: fairly useful performer at 3 yrs for J. Noseda: fair form at best in 2003: stays 14.8f: acts on polytrack and good to firm going, showed promise on soft: has wandered/carried head awkwardly. *Jedd O'Keeffe* **72 ?**

ALL DIAMONDS (IRE) 2 ch.c. (Mar 11) Priolo (USA) 127 – Afisiak 60 (Efisio 120) [2003 8.3d⁵ 8.2m⁶ Oct 28] good-bodied colt: second foal: dam 2-y-o 5f winner: better effort in maidens (modest form) when sixth at Nottingham, no extra late on: likely to prove best up to 1m: open to progress. *J. G. Given* **62 p**

ALLEGEDLY (IRE) 2 br.f. (May 10) Alhaarth (IRE) 126 – Society Ball 72 (Law Society (USA) 130) [2003 5g⁵ 6.1m² 7.1f² 7m* Jul 23] 12,000Y: workmanlike filly: has a fluent, rather round action: half-sister to useful 1m winner Keld (by Lion Cavern) and Italian 7f (at 2 yrs) and 10.5f winner by Ezzoud: dam 1½m winner (also won over hurdles) out of sister to dam of Zafonic: fair performer: won nursery at Catterick, leading halfway: should stay at least 1m: sent to USA. *P. C. Haslam* **71**

ALLEGRINA (IRE) 3 b.f. Barathea (IRE) 127 – Pianola (USA) 76 (Diesis 133) [2003 70p: 7m* 10m⁴ 8.1g 8m⁵ f8.5g⁶ f8s Dec 13] lengthy filly: fair performer: landed odds in maiden at Thirsk in June: should stay 1¼m: raced only on good/good to firm ground on turf, well held on fibresand: tried visored/blinkered: none too consistent. *K. A. Ryan* **69**

ALL EMBRACING (IRE) 3 b.f. Night Shift (USA) – Rispoto 58 (Mtoto 134) [2003 7g 7m* 8.1g 6m⁴ 7g⁵ 7.1m 7g⁴ 7m 6g Oct 6] IR 36,000F, 20,000Y: strong, close-coupled filly: fifth foal: half-sister to 3 winners, including 4-y-o Highdown and fairly useful Irish 9f winner Sweet Surrender (by Pennekamp): dam, 1½m winner, half-sister to smart performer up to 1¾m Jahafil: fairly useful performer: won maiden at Yarmouth in June: well below form 3 of last 4 starts: best form at 7f: raced only on good/good to firm ground: usually waited with, and ran poorly when making running sixth start: sold 85,000 gns. *G. C. Bravery* **82**

ALLENWOOD 3 b.g. Inchinor 119 – Bumpkin 108 (Free State 125) [2003 60§: p5g² f5g² 6m⁶ 5m⁶ 6m⁵ 6m 7m⁴ 7m f5s Jul 14] modest maiden: effective at 5f to 7f: acts on good to firm ground and all-weather: wears blinkers/visor/cheekpieces: ungenuine. *D. J. S. Cosgrove* **56 §**

ALLERGY 3 b.f. Alzao (USA) 117 – Rash Gift 78 (Cadeaux Genereux 131) [2003 99: 11.4m⁶ 14g⁶ 11.9m⁶ 14.1s Oct 29] smallish, close-coupled filly: useful performer: clearly best effort in listed races in 2003 when 4½ lengths sixth to Moments of Joy at Goodwood second outing: stays 1¾m: acts on soft ground, below form on good to firm: usually races prominently: sold 24,000 gns. *R. Charlton* **99**

ALLERTON BOY 4 ch.g. Beveled (USA) – Darakah 78 (Doulab (USA) 115) [2003 61: 5.7f 5m⁴ 5.3m 5m 5.1m 5.5m 8f 5m Sep 24] modest maiden handicapper: well below form after second start, including in blinkers: free-going sort, probably best at 5f: acts on firm ground. *R. J. Hodges* **64 d**

ALLEZ MOUSSON 5 b.g. Hernando (FR) 127 – Rynechra 102 (Blakeney 126) [2003 76: 18g⁶ 15.9m 17.5m³ 16m Oct 28] tall, leggy gelding: fair handicapper: best at 2m+: acts on soft and good to firm going: tried blinkered: often soon off bridle. *A. Bailey* **67**

ALLIED VICTORY (USA) 3 b.c. Red Ransom (USA) – Coral Dance (FR) 111 (Green Dancer (USA) 132) [2003 85: 10g⁵ 10s³ 9.5d² 8v 10d³ 10d² 8g³ 10.5d 8m³ 10d² 10s⁴ Nov 3] unlucky-looking, ex-Irish colt: closely related to 2 winners by Lear Fan, including useful French/UAE 1¼m/1½m performer Shaal, and half-brother to several winners, notably 2000 Guineas winner Pennekamp (by Bering), Irish 2000 Guineas winner Black Minnaloushe (by Storm Cat) and very smart French/US 1¼m to 1¾m winner Nasr El Arab (by Al Nasr): dam, French 2-y-o 1m winner, later successful in **81**

USA: fairly useful maiden: left J. Bolger 37,000 gns after sixth start: effective at 1m/1¼m: acts on firm and soft going, well beaten on heavy. *E. J. Alston*

ALLINJIM (IRE) 4 b.g. Turtle Island (IRE) 123 – Bounayya (USA) (Al Nasr (FR) 126) [2003 93: 12m 13.9m 14m* 12.3m 14.6g 13.1m⁶ 14d Sep 27] big, good-bodied gelding: fairly useful handicapper: won at Haydock in June: amiss on same course final start: stays 15f: acts on any going: wore cheekpieces in 2003: has worn crossed noseband: races prominently. *J. A. Glover* **91**

ALLODARLIN (IRE) 2 b.f. (Apr 16) Cape Cross (IRE) 129 – Sharp Circle (IRE) 83 (Sure Blade (USA) 130) [2003 8.3g⁵ 6m 6g f7s⁶ p8g Nov 22] €21,000Y, 9,000 2-y-o: leggy, quite good-topped filly: half-sister to 1996 2-y-o 7f seller winner Compact Disc (by Royal Academy): dam, 1m winner (better at 11.5f) half-sister to very smart sprinter Greenland Park: modest maiden: best effort on debut: probably better at 1m than shorter. *P. F. I. Cole* **60**

ALL ON MY OWN (USA) 8 ch.g. Unbridled (USA) 128 – Some For All (USA) (One For All (USA)) [2003 50: f8s⁵ f8.5s f8g f12g 9.2g⁵ 12m⁵ 9.9m 12d f16g Nov 19] close-coupled, workmanlike gelding: poor maiden: effective at 9f (given test) to 2m: acts on heavy going, good to firm and fibresand: usually blinkered, tried in visor/cheekpieces: usually slowly away. *I. W. McInnes* **44**

ALL QUIET 2 b.f. (Mar 31) Piccolo 121 – War Shanty 66 (Warrshan (USA) 117) [2003 6m 7f 7.5m Sep 17] leggy filly: second foal: dam lightly-raced half-sister to very smart sprinter Bold Edge: fair form in maidens: bred to prove best up to 1m. *R. Hannon* **70**

ALL'S NOT LOST 4 b.f. Binary Star (USA) – Flo's Choice (IRE) 35 (Dancing Dissident (USA) 119) [2003 –: 7d 8m Apr 22] good-bodied filly: well held in maidens. *Don Enrico Incisa* **–**

ALL THE MORE (IRE) 2 b.f. (Mar 8) Ali-Royal (IRE) 127 – Koukla Mou (Keen 116) [2003 5g⁴ 5m 6f 5g³ 5.2m 6m² 6m⁵ 5d³ 5.1f³ 5m³ 6g Oct 13] €8,000Y: sturdy filly: first foal: dam unraced: fair maiden: possibly amiss final start: effective at 5f/6f: acts on firm and good to soft going: sold 4,500 gns, sent to Belgium. *Mrs P. N. Dutfield* **77**

ALLY MAKBUL 3 b.f. Makbul 104 – Clarice Orsini (Common Grounds 118) [2003 53: 9.7m⁵ 9.7m³ 10m 8g f6g* f6g f6g p7g Dec 10] modest performer: won claimer at Wolverhampton in November: probably best up to 1m: acts on polytrack, raced only on good ground or firmer on turf. *J. R. Best* **61**

ALLY MCBEAL (IRE) 4 b.f. Ali-Royal (IRE) 127 – Vian (USA) (Far Out East (USA)) [2003 40: 6f⁴ 8m 7m f8.5g⁵ 9.9m f8.5s⁵ Sep 6] leggy filly: modest maiden: best effort on reappearance: stays 6f, not 8.5f: raced only on fibresand/good ground or firmer: blinkered 2 of last 3 starts. *J. G. Given* **55**

ALMANAC (IRE) 2 b.c. (May 14) Desert Style (IRE) 121 – Share The Vision (Vision (USA)) [2003 6.1d Nov 6] 3,500Y, £1,800 2-y-o: half-brother to several winners, including 5-y-o Homelife: dam unraced: 100/1, slowly away and always behind in maiden at Nottingham. *B. P. J. Baugh* **–**

ALMARA 3 b.f. Wolfhound (USA) 126 – Alacrity 62 (Alzao (USA) 117) [2003 59: 5m 6d 8f 5.7f Oct 12] modest maiden: well beaten in 2003, including in cheekpieces. *Miss K. B. Boutflower* **–**

ALMAVIVA (IRE) 3 b.f. Grand Lodge (USA) 125 – Kafayef (USA) 46 (Secreto (USA) 128) [2003 90p: 8.1g⁶ 12m⁵ Aug 3] leggy filly: fairly useful performer: best effort when sixth to Favourable Terms in listed event at Sandown in July: should stay 1¼m: raced only on good/good to firm ground. *J. Noseda* **93**

ALMAYDAN 5 b.g. Marju (IRE) 127 – Cunning 118 (Bustino 136) [2003 94: 16.2m 14v⁶ 14f⁶ 14g Jul 3] strong, good-bodied gelding: fair handicapper: barely stays 2½m: acts on firm and good to soft going: carries head awkwardly: often makes running. *R. Lee* **78 ?**

ALMEIDA (IRE) 5 b.m. Sadler's Wells (USA) 132 – Benning (USA) 68 (Manila (USA)) [2003 63: 14.1m⁵ 16.2m Aug 25] IR 150,000Y: quite good-topped, ex-Irish mare: first foal: dam, maiden who stayed 1½m, closely related to smart French winner up to 1¼m Beccari, and half-sister to Grand Criterium winner Treizieme and Gold Cup second Eastern Mystic: modest maiden: well held in handicaps in 2003: stays 1½m: acts on soft ground: tried blinkered: often tongue tied. *John Berry* **–**

ALMIZAN (IRE) 3 b.c. Darshaan 133 – Bint Albaadiya (USA) 108 (Woodman (USA) 126) [2003 11m⁴ 12g⁴ 12m⁴ 14g* 13.9m 15m* 14m⁵ 16g⁶ 16g⁴ Nov 5] leggy, angular colt: first foal: dam, 6f (including at 2 yrs) winner who probably stayed 7f, out of smart miler Pixie Erin, herself half-sister to high-class performer up to 1¼m Star Pastures: useful performer: won maiden at Thirsk in May and handicaps at Goodwood (awarded **96**

race) in July and Ayr in September: barely stays 2m: raced only on good/good to firm going: often races prominently. *M. R. Channon*

ALMOND BEACH   3 ch.g. Hector Protector (USA) 124 – Dancing Spirit (IRE) 72   – (Ahonoora 122) [2003 78: 8f⁵ 9m 7m p7g Aug 20] lengthy gelding: fair maiden at 2 yrs: well held in 2003, including in blinkers. *B. J. Meehan*

ALMOND MOUSSE (FR)   4 b.f. Exit To Nowhere (USA) 122 – Missy Dancer   **109** (Shareef Dancer (USA) 135) [2003 108: a10g³ 12.5g 8d³ 8g² 8g 8g⁴ 10s⁴ 8g 10d³ 8d⁵ 10d 10d⁴ 8m³ 8m 8s Nov 1] 260,000 francs Y: leggy, quite good-topped filly: second foal: half-sister to fairly useful French 9f/1¼m winner Highway Mouse (by Mtoto): dam, Swiss 1½m winner, half-sister to smart French performer up to 1½m Mousse Glacee: useful performer: won 3 races in 2002, including listed race at Saint-Cloud: several creditable efforts in 2003, including when beaten nose by Salselon in Prix Edmond Blanc at Saint-Cloud fourth start, third to Vangelis in Grand Prix de Vichy ninth outing and 1½ lengths third to Echoes In Eternity in Sun Chariot Stakes at Newmarket thirteenth one: effective at 1m to 11f: acts on heavy and good to firm going: tough. *R. Collet, France*

ALMOND WILLOW (IRE)   2 b.f. (Mar 25) Alhaarth (IRE) 126 – Miss Willow   **69** Bend (USA) (Willow Hour) [2003 6m 6m⁶ 7.9m 8.3g³ 8s⁶ f8.5g* Nov 17] €20,000Y, 36,000 2-y-o: good-topped filly: fluent mover: half-sister to several winners, including 5f/6f winner (including at 2 yrs) Willow Dale (by Danehill) and 5f winner Groovy Willow (by Night Shift), both fairly useful: dam winning sprinter in USA: fair performer: won maiden at Wolverhampton by 1¼ lengths from Hawkit: stays 8.5f: acts on fibresand, soft and good to firm ground: flashed tail last 2 starts. *J. Noseda*

ALMOST FAMOUS (IRE)   4 ch.c. Grand Lodge (USA) 125 – Smouldering (IRE)   **99** (Caerleon (USA) 132) [2003 105: 10g⁵ 8.7m⁵ 8m 10f² 8m 9m Oct 4] 44,000F, 210,000Y: strong, compact colt: fifth foal: half-brother to 2 winning sprinters, including 1999 2-y-o 6f winner Camp Fire (by Lahib): dam, ran once, half-sister to Irish 2000 Guineas winner Flash of Steel: useful performer: won 2 handicaps and a minor event in 2002: mostly respectable efforts in 2003: hampered after 4f and soon tailed off in Cambridgeshire at Newmarket final start: stays 1¼m: acts on firm and soft going: usually blinkered prior to 2003. *J. S. Bolger, Ireland*

ALMOST ROYAL (IRE)   2 b.f. (Mar 16) Princely Heir (IRE) 111 – A Little While   – (Millfontaine 114) [2003 6m 6d 6g f5g f6g Nov 21] €5,000Y: half-sister to French 1997 2-y-o 6f winner Small But Sharp (by Conquering Hero): dam unraced: little sign of ability in maidens/sellers. *R. M. Beckett*

ALMOST WELCOME   2 b.c. (May 8) First Trump 118 – Choral Sundown 81 (Night   **55 ?** Shift (USA)) [2003 6m 5g 7g p10g Nov 29] 18,000Y: good-bodied colt: half-brother to several winners, including smart 2000 2-y-o 7f/1m winner Snowstorm (by Environment Friend), later 11f winner in Hong Kong, and useful 1m to 1½m winner Celestial Welcome (by Most Welcome): dam effective at 1m to 1½m: modest maiden: form only at 1¼m. *S. Dow*

ALMOTAWAG   3 ch.g. Abou Zouz (USA) 109 – As Mustard (Keen 116) [2003 60p: – f6g⁶ p5g Jan 11] lengthy, good-bodied gelding: modest maiden: well held in 2003. *Mrs L. Stubbs*

AL MUALLIM (USA)   9 b.g. Theatrical 128 – Gerri N Jo Go (USA) (Top Command   **45** (USA)) [2003 74, a57: p6g² p6g⁶ p6g⁶ p6g p7g p7g* 7f 7m 7m 7g 7f 6m p7g Dec 10]   **a57** compact gelding: modest performer on all-weather, poor on turf: won claimer at Lingfield in March: best at 6f/7f: acts on polytrack, firm and soft going: tongue tied: often slowly away: sometimes edgy/races freely: best held up. *Andrew Reid*

ALMURAAD (IRE)   2 b.c. (Apr 11) Machiavellian (USA) 123 – Wellspring (IRE) 88   **100 p** (Caerleon (USA) 132) [2003 7m* 8f⁶ Sep 27] 420,000Y: angular, good-bodied colt: third foal: half-brother to a 7f winner in Hong Kong by Cadeaux Genereux: dam, 6f winner, sister to very smart sprinter/miler Caerwent and half-sister to very smart miler Marling, out of Marwell: won maiden at Leicester in September: still green, useful form when 5 lengths sixth of 10 to Snow Ridge in Royal Lodge Stakes at Ascot, forced wide: not sure to stay much beyond 1m: has scope to do better at 3 yrs. *Sir Michael Stoute*

ALMUTASADER   3 b.c. Sadler's Wells (USA) 132 – Dreamawhile 85 (Known Fact   **95** (USA) 135) [2003 61: 11.8m* 12.3g* 14m* 14.6g⁴ Sep 12] big, good-topped colt: useful handicapper: improved at 3 yrs, winning at Leicester in May and at Ripon and Sandown (beat Flamenco Bride by 2 lengths) in July: creditable fourth to Shabernak in Mallard Stakes at Doncaster final start: will stay 2m: acts on good to firm going. *J. L. Dunlop*

ALNAJA (USA)   4 b.g. Woodman (USA) 126 – Cursory Look (USA) (Nijinsky (CAN)   **82 p** 138) [2003 10m⁶ 10m 10.3m³ 12d² 14.4m³ 14d* Sep 27] 82,000Y: sixth foal: half-brother to fairly useful 1½m winner Glance (by Ela-Mana-Mou): dam, ran once in Ireland, from family of Hernando: fairly useful form: best effort when winning handicap at Haydock in September by head from Duke of Earl (pair clear), getting on top close home despite carrying head high: will probably stay 2m: best efforts on ground softer than good: lightly raced, and open to further improvement. *W. J. Haggas*

ALNASREYA (IRE) 3 b.f. Machiavellian (USA) 123 – Littlewick (IRE) 49 (Green **80** Desert (USA) 127) [2003 8m* 8m⁵ 8.1m Sep 17] 215,000F, 500,000Y: fourth living foal: half-sister to Chilean Grade 1 11f winner Fontanella Borghese (by Roy): dam lightly-raced half-sister to dam of very smart 7f/1m performer Rebecca Sharp (by Machiavellian): fairly useful form: landed odds in maiden at Newmarket in May: wandered and found little next time: off 3 months before final outing: raced only at 1m on good to firm going: visits Royal Applause. *Sir Michael Stoute*

ALPEN WOLF (IRE) 8 ch.g. Wolfhound (USA) 126 – Oatfield 69 (Great Nephew **78** 126) [2003 82, a76: 6m 6m 5f 6.1m⁵ 5.3m² 5.3m² 6m 6g 5.3f² 5.3f² 5.3m² 5.3f⁴ 5m² 5m³ 5.3f² 6m⁵ 5d Nov 7] sturdy, rather dipped-backed gelding: fair handicapper: runner-up 7 times in 2003, 6 times at Brighton: effective at 5f/6f: acts on all-weather, best on good going or firmer on turf: tried visored/blinkered: usually races prominently: tough and consistent. *W. R. Muir*

ALPHA APACHE (IRE) 3 b.g. Primo Dominie 121 – Apache Squaw 54 (Be My **–** Guest (USA) 126) [2003 f8g f7s Feb 4] 5,500Y: sixth foal: half-brother to 6-y-o Geronimo and a winner in Italy by Distant Relative: dam, middle-distance maiden, half-sister to very smart middle-distance performer Apache: well beaten in maidens at Southwell. *M. W. Easterby*

ALPHABAR (IRE) 3 ch.g. Bahhare (USA) 122 – Happy Flower 63 (Unfuwain **–** (USA) 131) [2003 8.1s 7.5m 12.1m⁴ 6.9m 11g Jul 26] 12,500Y: good-topped gelding: second foal: dam lightly-raced Irish maiden: well held in maidens/seller: tried blinkered: has looked reluctant. *T. D. Easterby*

ALPHA NOBLE (GER) 6 b.g. Lando (GER) 128 – Alpha (GER) (Frontal 122) **–** [2003 12m Aug 25] ex-German gelding: useful performer: won maiden at Frankfurt at 4 yrs and minor events at Mulheim and Neuss in 2002: left P. Rau, well held in amateur handicap at Epsom only 6-y-o start: fell fatally over hurdles following month: stayed 1½m: acted on good to soft going. *Miss Venetia Williams*

ALPHA ZETA 2 b.c. (Mar 29) Primo Dominie 121 – Preening 62 (Persian Bold 123) **–** [2003 6.1d Nov 6] stocky colt: brother to 1998 2-y-o 5f winner Alpha and half-brother to 6f winner White Cliffs (by Bluebird): dam, 1½m winner, half-sister to smart 7f/1m winner Hadeer: 66/1 and very backward, slowly away and always well behind in maiden at Nottingham. *C. W. Thornton*

ALPHECCA (USA) 2 b.c. (Jan 29) Kingmambo (USA) 125 – Limbo (USA) (A P **– p** Indy (USA) 131) [2003 7m Aug 22] close-coupled, quite good-topped colt: first foal: dam, lightly-raced French maiden, half-sister to very smart 1984 Irish 2-y-o Gold Crest and US Grade 1 1¼m winner Scoot, out of Canadian Oaks winner Northernette, herself sister to Storm Bird: 10/1, burly and green, slowly away and always behind in maiden at Newmarket: likely to do better. *Sir Michael Stoute*

ALPINE HIDEAWAY (IRE) 10 b.g. Tirol 127 – Arbour (USA) 76 (Graustark) **51** [2003 46: 7.5m 8s⁶ 8.5m* 8m⁴ 8.9m Sep 7] good-topped gelding: modest performer: won claimer at Beverley in August: effective at 1m to 1¼m: acts on any turf going and fibresand: tried blinkered/visored/in cheekpieces: none too consistent. *J. S. Wainwright*

ALPINE RACER (IRE) 4 b.g. Lake Coniston (IRE) 131 – Cut No Ice 97 (Great **–** Nephew 126) [2003 64d: f12s 12m 13.8m Jul 9] leggy, lengthy gelding: modest maiden: well beaten in 2003: tried blinkered/visored/in cheekpieces: sold £2,000. *R. E. Barr*

ALPINE SPECIAL (IRE) 2 gr.g. (Mar 1) Orpen (USA) 116 – Halomix (Linamix **71** (FR) 127) [2003 5m 6m² 6m 7g³ 8m² 8m* 8m Oct 20] IR 7,500F, 12,000Y: good-topped gelding: first foal: dam French 1½m winner: fair performer: won 4-runner maiden at Musselburgh in September: will stay 1¼m. *P. C. Haslam*

ALQAAYID 2 b.c. (Apr 10) Machiavellian (USA) 123 – One So Wonderful 121 **71 §** (Nashwan (USA) 135) [2003 6m 7m⁶ 8m 8m Oct 16] 450,000Y: sturdy, useful-looking colt: fluent mover: first foal: dam 7f (at 2 yrs) to 1¼m (Juddmonte International Stakes) winner: fair form when sixth in maiden at Newmarket: showed little otherwise: pulled hard/found little in blinkers final start: probably ungenuine. *M. P. Tregoning*

ALRABAB 3 ch.f. Nashwan (USA) 135 – Jamrat Jumairah (IRE) 91 (Polar Falcon **108** (USA) 126) [2003 10m* 8m³ 10g* 12f* 11.8f* 10.3d⁴ Nov 7] strong filly: second foal:

closely related to 4-y-o Haripur: dam, 1m winner, half-sister to very smart miler Waajib: progressed into useful performer, winning maiden at Sandown, handicaps at Ripon and Goodwood (beat Jasmick by 3 lengths) and 3-runner minor event at Leicester (unextended to lands odds) between August and October: not discredited when never-nearer fourth to Al Ihtithar in listed race at Doncaster final start: will stay 1¾m: acts on firm and good to soft ground: waited with: tends to hang. *M. P. Tregoning*

ALRAFID (IRE)   4 ch.c. Halling (USA) 133 – Ginger Tree (USA) 86 (Dayjur (USA)   **93**
137) [2003 82: p10g 8g 8g 9g* 8.1d 9m⁶ 10g² 9g² p10g⁴ p10g² p10g⁶ Dec 10] rather unfurnished colt: has a round action: fairly useful handicapper: creditable efforts last 5 starts: stays 1¼m: acts on polytrack, soft and good to firm going: has been slowly away/taken good hold: usually held up. *G. L. Moore*

AL RAJIBA (USA)   3 ch.f. Diesis 133 – Nymphea (USA) (General Assembly (USA))   **70**
[2003 10m⁵ 10s⁶ 7m⁶ 10.1g 7f² 8m* 8.5d Oct 4] $100,000Y: useful-looking filly: fifth foal: half-sister to winners in USA by Green Dancer and Storm Bird: dam, stakes-placed winner in USA, half-sister to smart French/US performer up to 1¼m Taffeta And Tulle: fair performer: landed odds in maiden at Musselburgh in September: stays 1m: acts on firm ground, below form on softer than good. *C. E. Brittain*

ALRIDA (IRE)   4 b.g. Ali-Royal (IRE) 127 – Ride Bold (USA) (J O Tobin (USA)   **86 d**
130) [2003 93: 16m⁶ 16m⁵ 16.1d⁶ 14.6m 16.1m 14m⁵ 11.5g Sep 16] leggy gelding: fairly useful handicapper at best: stays 2m: acts on any going: tried in cheekpieces: held up: sold 30,000 gns. *W. Jarvis*

ALSAFI (USA)   4 b.g. Red Ransom (USA) – Altair (USA) (Alydar (USA)) [2003 91:   **–**
7m 8m 6d Aug 1] rangy gelding: fairly useful form when winning maiden at Windsor at 3 yrs on debut: little form since, including in visor: stays 8.3f: acts on good to firm going. *J. Noseda*

AL'S ALIBI   10 b.g. Alzao (USA) 117 – Lady Kris (IRE) (Kris 135) [2003 58: f12g³   **52**
p13g⁴ f12g² 12m f14.8g⁶ f12s³ 10.3g f12s⁴ 11.6m p12g f11g² Dec 3] smallish, sturdy gelding: shows knee action: modest performer: best at 11f to 1¾m: acts on good to firm going, soft and all-weather. *W. R. Muir*

ALSHAWAMEQ (IRE)   2 b.g. (Apr 21) Green Desert (USA) 127 – Azdihaar (USA)   **81**
81 (Mr Prospector (USA)) [2003 7m⁶ 8m* 8.2m⁵ Oct 22] tall, leggy gelding: fifth foal: half-brother to 3 winners, including useful French 1999 2-y-o 6.5f winner Sand Pigeon (by Lammtarra) and 3-y-o Maghanim: dam, 7f winner, half-sister to 1000 Guineas winner Shadayid and smart performer up to 7f Fath: fairly useful form: won maiden at Salisbury in October by 3 lengths from In Deep: fifth in minor event at Nottingham, slowly away and racing freely: not sure to stay much beyond 1m: blinkered last 2 starts: tends to wander/carry head awkwardly. *J. L. Dunlop*

AL SHUUA   2 b.f. (May 5) Lomitas 129 – Sephala (USA) (Mr Prospector (USA))   **67**
[2003 7m³ 7.1m⁶ Sep 8] leggy filly: sixth foal: half-sister to UAE 9f winner Septette (by Indian Ridge) and winner in Spain by Warning: dam, French 2-y-o 7f/1m winner, sister to smart French/US performer up to 9f Sha Tha and to dam of One Cool Cat: better effort in maidens (fair form) when third at Folkestone: should stay at least 1¼m: edged left latter start. *C. E. Brittain*

AL SIFAAT   2 ch.f. (Jan 28) Unfuwain (USA) 131 – Almurooj 54 (Zafonic (USA) 130)   **88 p**
[2003 6m² 6m* Sep 1] lengthy, rather dipped-backed filly: second foal: closely related to 3-y-o Judhoor: dam, ran 4 times (best effort at 6f), half-sister to smart 7f performer Munir out of Irish 1000 Guineas winner Al Bahathri: fairly useful form: won maiden at Leicester, dictating pace: better effort when second to Bay Tree in similar event at Newbury, hanging left: should stay 7f: open to improvement. *Saeed bin Suroor*

ALSYATI   5 ch.g. Salse (USA) 128 – Rubbiyati 56 (Cadeaux Genereux 131) [2003 62:   **53**
p10g⁵ f9.4s³ f8.5g⁵ 10d 10.1g⁶ 10.3g 10m 9.7g 10.9m⁴ p12g Oct 3] quite attractive gelding: modest handicapper: effective at 1m to 11.5f: acts on soft going, firm and all-weather: tried blinkered/tongue tied: sold 5,000 gns. *C. E. Brittain*

ALTARES   2 b.c. (May 12) Alhaarth (IRE) 126 – Reach The Wind (USA) (Relaunch   **–**
(USA)) [2003 7m 7m 7g f8s Dec 13] 8,500 2-y-o: small colt: eighth foal: half-brother to 3 winners, including 6f winner Thundergod (by Torrential): dam, Irish 6f winner (including at 2 yrs), half-sister to useful sprinter Ozone Friendly: well held in maidens/nursery: tends to be slowly away. *P. Howling*

ALTAY   6 b.g. Erins Isle 121 – Aliuska (IRE) 70 (Fijar Tango (FR) 127) [2003 83:   **86**
p13g* p12g* p12g⁶ Jan 25] tall gelding: has a round action: fairly useful handicapper: better than ever when winning twice at Lingfield in January (originally disqualified on

first occasion, but reinstated on appeal): effective at 1¼m to 13f: acts on firm going, soft and polytrack: usually races prominently: fairly useful hurdler, successful in valuable handicap at Haydock in May. *R. A. Fahey*

ALTIERI 5 ch.h. Selkirk (USA) 129 – Minya (USA) (Blushing Groom (FR) 131) [2003 **117** 117: 9g* 8m* 10g³ 8m 10d² Nov 16] smart performer: won minor event at Milan in March and listed race at Rome in April: respectable 2¼ lengths third to Rakti in Premio Presidente della Repubblica at Rome in May and back to best when 3 lengths second to Imperial Dancer in Premio Roma there final outing: best at 1m/1¼m: acts on heavy and good to firm ground. *V. Caruso, Italy*

ALTITUDE DANCER (IRE) 3 b.g. Sadler's Wells (USA) 132 – Height of Passion **67** (Shirley Heights 130) [2003 67?: f12s f12g⁵ 14.1m 14.1m* 14g³ 16.2m³ 16d* 14.4g 17.5m⁵ 16.1m³ Oct 1] smallish gelding: fair handicapper: left M. Johnston after third start: won at Redcar (maiden event) in May and Thirsk in August: stays 17.5f: acts on good to firm and good to soft ground: well held only try in blinkers: usually held up. *B. Ellison*

AL TURF (IRE) 3 ch.c. Alhaarth (IRE) 126 – Petomi 75 (Presidium 124) [2003 101: **101** p7g⁶ p8g⁵ 7d² 8g⁶ 8g² 8g 8d 8.5f⁶ Oct 22] rather leggy, useful-looking colt: useful performer: best efforts at 3 yrs when runner-up in Tetrarch Stakes (beaten ¾ length by France) and Goffs International Stakes (beaten length by Sea Dart), both at the Curragh: well held in listed race at Goodwood (visored and sweating), Prix Quincey at Deauville (final outing for R. Hannon) and allowance race at Delaware last 3 starts: stays 1m: acts on soft going: below form in cheekpieces: often makes running. *H. G. Motion, USA*

ALUMNI NEWS (USA) 3 b.c. Belong To Me (USA) – Private Status (USA) (Alydar **77** (USA)) [2003 77p: 8m* 11m 10.1s Oct 29] fairly useful performer: made all in maiden at Salisbury in August: ran as if amiss in handicap at Newbury (well-backed favourite) and minor event at Yarmouth after: stays 1¼m: acts on polytrack and good to firm going: sent to USA. *J. H. M. Gosden*

ALUMNUS 3 ch.g. Primo Dominie 121 – Katyushka (IRE) 73 (Soviet Star (USA) **59** 128) [2003 60: 6m⁵ 7m⁵ 6d 6m Aug 25] workmanlike gelding: fair maiden: well below form last 2 starts: stays 7f: acts on good to firm ground: free-going sort. *C. A. Horgan*

ALVARO (IRE) 6 ch.g. Priolo (USA) 127 – Gezalle (Shareef Dancer (USA) 135) **–** [2003 34: 19.1m Jun 21] strong gelding: winning hurdler: poor maiden on Flat: stays 2m: acts on good to firm and good to soft going: tried blinkered. *D. J. Wintle*

ALWAYS BELIEVE (USA) 7 b.g. Carr de Naskra (USA) – Wonder Mar (USA) (Fire **–** Dancer (USA)) [2003 –: p6g p6g p8g p8g³ p10g p8g⁶ 8m 8.2m Jun 14] modest performer **a56** nowadays: stays 1m: acts on dirt and polytrack, no form on turf: tried blinkered/tongue tied: reportedly bled from nose only 6-y-o start. *M. R. Bosley*

ALWAYS DARING 4 b.f. Atraf 116 – Steamy Windows § (Dominion 123) [2003 –: **–** 7d Sep 20] no longer of much account: tried blinkered. *C. J. Teague*

ALWAYS ESTEEMED (IRE) 3 b.g. Mark of Esteem (IRE) 137 – Always Far **104 d** (USA) (Alydar (USA)) [2003 8m* 8.1m² 8.1m 10.3m⁴ 10m 8g 8m 10m Oct 4] 800,000 francs Y: big, strong, lengthy, good sort: has plenty of scope: fifth foal: half-brother to fairly useful 2000 2-y-o 7f winner Ashlinn (by Ashkalani) and French 1½m winner Arlina (by Polish Precedent): dam unraced daughter of 1000 Guineas winner Fairy Foot-steps: useful performer at best: won maiden at Ripon in April: placed in minor events at Sandown (beaten 5 lengths by Ikhtyar) and Doncaster next 2 starts: well held last 4 outings: probably best around 1m: raced only on good/good to firm going: blinkered (looked far from keen) penultimate start. *G. Wragg*

ALWAYS FIRST 2 b.c. (Mar 29) Barathea (IRE) 127 – Pink Cristal 113 (Dilum (USA) **102 P** 115) [2003 7.1m* Aug 13] 200,000Y: first foal: dam, 7f/1m winner, half-sister to smart performer up to 1¼m Crystal Hearted: 11/2, won 6-runner minor event at Sandown by neck from Mutahayya, taking while to find stride but staying on well under hands and heels to lead close home: will stay at least 1¼m: open to considerable improvement, and sure to do well as 3-y-o. *Sir Michael Stoute*

ALWAYS FLYING (USA) 2 ch.g. (May 15) Fly So Free (USA) 122 – Dubiously **70** (USA) (Jolie Jo (USA)) [2003 5g³ f6g 5m⁶ 7.5m² 7m⁵ 7g 8m³ 8d⁵ f8.5g⁵ Nov 1] 5,000Y: leggy, quite good-topped gelding: brother to 2 winners abroad and half-brother to several winners, including 3-y-o Town Called Malice: dam, 2-y-o 6f/6.5f winner in USA: fair maiden: second at Beverley: stays 1m: acts on good to firm and good to soft ground: blinkered (ran poorly) sixth start: races prominently. *M. Johnston*

ALYOUSUFEYA (IRE) 2 ch.f. (Feb 26) Kingmambo (USA) 125 – Musicale (USA) **75** 109 (The Minstrel (CAN) 135) [2003 6m 7g⁴ Nov 1] €320,000Y: close-coupled filly:

eighth foal: closely related to US 7f to 8.5f winner Belasco (by Gone West) and half-sister to 2 winners, including fairly useful 1999 2-y-o 1m winner Colonial Rule (by Pleasant Colony): dam, 6f/7f winner at 2 yrs and successful in Fred Darling Stakes, out of half-sister to high-class sprinter Committed: fair form in maidens at Newbury and Newmarket (disputed lead long way when fourth to Si Si Amiga): likely to prove best up to 1m. *J. L. Dunlop*

AMALFI COAST   4 b.g. Emperor Jones (USA) 119 – Legend's Daughter (USA)   **53 ?** (Alleged (USA) 138) [2003 14.1f⁵ 9.3m⁴ 10m⁴ 12m 10.1g Oct 22] 4,000F, 6,600Y: tall gelding: fourth foal: closely related to UAE 1m to 1¼m winner Descendent (by Hamas): dam, Italian 11f winner, half-sister to 2000 Guineas fourth State Performer: seemingly modest maiden: raced only on good ground or firmer: unseated rider leaving stall final start. *W. S. Cunningham*

AMALIANBURG   3 b.f. Hector Protector (USA) 124 – Ayodhya (IRE) (Astronef   **76** 116) [2003 –p: 10d⁴ 11.9m² 11.8m* 14m 10v⁵ 10.5v Dec 4] strong, well-made filly: fair performer: landed odds in maiden at Leicester in September: left H. Cecil after next start: stays 1½m: acts on good to firm and good to soft ground. *N. Clement, France*

AMAMUS   3 b.f. Zafonic (USA) 130 – Princess Sadie 86 (Shavian 125) [2003 8.1s³   **62 ?** 8.1m³ 7.1g⁵ 10d f8.5s Sep 6] tall, lengthy filly: third living foal: half-sister to 5-y-o Attorney: dam, 5f winner at 2 yrs, out of half-sister to dam of 1000 Guineas winner Ameerat: seemingly modest maiden: ran as if amiss last 2 starts: effective at 7f/1m: acts on soft and good to firm ground. *M. A. Jarvis*

AMANDA'S LAD (IRE)   3 b.g. Danetime (IRE) 121 – Art Duo 86 (Artaius (USA)   **52 §** 129) [2003 61, a–: f6g f5s⁶ f5g⁵ f5s p5g⁶ p5g⁴ 5m⁶ 5m 5f⁵ 5f⁵ 7f 6m 6g⁵ 5m 6m 5m 6d 5f 5m 6m³ f6g Dec 9] tall gelding: modest maiden: best at 5f/6f: acts on firm going, good to soft and all-weather: tried blinkered: often races prominently: unreliable. *M. C. Chapman*

AMANDUS (USA)   3 b.g. Danehill (USA) 126 – Affection Affirmed (USA) (Affirmed   **100** (USA)) [2003 95: a8f p10g² f9.4g* 9m⁴ Aug 24] good-topped gelding: useful performer: well held in maiden at Nad Al Sheba for Saeed bin Suroor on reappearance: returned to former trainer: won maiden at Wolverhampton in August: best effort when fourth to Zabaglione in handicap at Goodwood final start, dictating pace: probably best short of 1¼m: acts on all-weather, raced only on good ground or firmer on turf: visored since debut: races prominently: sometimes looks none too resolute. *D. R. Loder*

AMANPURI (GER)   5 br.g. Fairy King (USA) – Aratika (FR) (Zino 127) [2003 8s 8d   **–** f12s f12g Nov 10] ex-German gelding: fifth living foal: won maiden at 3 yrs and handicap at 4 yrs, both at Munich, for W. Figge: showed little in 2003, leaving D. Weld in Ireland 15,000 gns after second start: stays 11f: acts on soft going: tried blinkered. *Miss Gay Kelleway*

AMARAKU   4 b.g. Kylian (USA) – Shernborne (Kalaglow 132) [2003 58: 10.9m   **–** Jun 22] modest maiden: well held only 4-y-o start: should stay at least 1½m: acts on polytrack. *A. L. Forbes*

AMARANTH (IRE)   7 b.g. Mujadil (USA) 119 – Zoes Delight (IRE) (Hatim (USA)   **74 d** 121) [2003 87: f7s p8g⁴ p8g 7g 7m⁵ 7m 7m 7f 6m 7f⁴ 7g⁵ 6.9m 6f Aug 22] tall, quite good-topped gelding: fair performer at best in 2003: effective at 6f to easy 8.5f: successful on good ground, best efforts on good or firmer/all-weather: tongue tied: usually races prominently: none too consistent: sent to Spain. *D. Carroll*

AMAR (CZE)   2 ch.c. (Mar 27) Beccari (USA) 112 – Autumn (FR) 55 (Rainbow   **–** Quest (USA) 134) [2003 7m⁴ 7s⁶ 7d Sep 10] good-topped colt: second foal: half-brother to 2-y-o 7f winner in Czech Republic by Keen: dam, lightly-raced maiden in Britain (later successful at 1¼m in Czech Republic): last in minor events. *R. Bastiman*

AMARETTO EXPRESS (IRE)   4 b.g. Blues Traveller (IRE) 119 – Cappuchino   **– §** (IRE) 59 (Roi Danzig (USA)) [2003 –§: 8m 6m 6f 6m Sep 6] useful-looking gelding: temperamental maiden: tried blinkered and in cheekpieces. *R. E. Barr*

AMBER FOX (IRE)   2 b.f. (Mar 2) Foxhound (USA) 103 – Paradable (IRE) 82 (Elbio   **57** 125) [2003 5m⁴ 5d⁵ 5f⁶ 6m 6d 6m⁴ Oct 20] €10,000Y: first foal: dam Irish 6f winner: modest maiden: barely stays 6f: acts on good to firm and good to soft ground. *A. Berry*

AMBER LEGEND   2 b.f. (Feb 27) Fraam 114 – Abstone Queen 66 (Presidium 124)   **58** [2003 f5g* 5m⁶ 6m² 5g² 6g⁶ f5g 5f² 6m Sep 2] leggy filly: third foal: dam 6f (including at 2 yrs)/7f winner: modest performer: won maiden at Southwell in March: second in sellers/claimer after: stays 6f: acts on fibresand, probably on firm going: ran badly in blinkers sixth start: none too consistent. *J. G. Given*

AMBER NECTAR TWO 3 b.g. Bluegrass Prince (IRE) 110 – Another Batchworth –
72 (Beveled (USA)) [2003 –: 5s 6g 7f Sep 26] little form: left E. Wheeler after second
start: tried blinkered. *D. Loughnane, Ireland*

AMBER'S BLUFF 4 b.f. Mind Games 121 – Amber Mill 96 (Doulab (USA) 115) **70 d**
[2003 80: 5d 6m 5m Jun 19] tall filly: just fair handicapper: raced only at 5f/6f: acts on
polytrack and good to firm going, probably on good to soft: blinkered last 6 starts: has
carried head awkwardly: sometimes slowly away. *T. D. Easterby*

AMBERSONG 5 ch.g. Hernando (FR) 127 – Stygian (USA) 73 (Irish River (FR) 131) **59**
[2003 60: f9.4g f12g 8.1m 10.2m 9.9m f12s* 14.1m⁴ f14.8g² f12g² f12g Dec 22] strong,
angular gelding: modest performer: left I. Williams after second start: won selling
handicap at Wolverhampton in September: stays 14.8f: acts on good to firm ground and
fibresand: tried visored, not in 2003: sometimes slowly away. *A. W. Carroll*

AMBITIOUS ANNIE 4 b.f. Most Welcome 131 – Pasja (IRE) (Posen (USA)) [2003 **48**
49: f16.2g⁵ 10g f14.8g* f16g² f16g⁴ f12g² Dec 22] big filly: poor handicapper: won
apprentice race at Wolverhampton in August: stays 2m: acts on fibresand, good to firm
and soft ground. *R. Hollinshead*

AMBONNAY 3 ch.f. Ashkalani (IRE) 128 – Babycham Sparkle 80 (So Blessed 130) **89**
[2003 83p: 6m⁵ 6g 7.1m 6f³ 6m Sep 26] sturdy filly: has a quick action: fairly useful
performer: best effort when third to Marker in minor event at Kempton: probably best at
5f/6f: raced on good going or firmer. *Mrs A. J. Perrett*

AMBROSINE 3 ch.f. Nashwan (USA) 135 – Tularosa (In The Wings 128) [2003 67: **81**
10m⁶ 12.6m⁶ 10m⁴ 10f³ 10d* 11.9m* 12m³ Aug 13] rather sparely-made, plain filly:
fairly useful performer: won handicap at Windsor in June and minor event at Brighton
in July: effective at 1¼m to 12.6f: acts on firm and good to soft going: usually races
prominently: consistent. *Mrs A. J. Perrett*

AMBUSHED (IRE) 7 b.g. Indian Ridge 123 – Surprise Move (IRE) (Simply Great **70**
(FR) 122) [2003 76: 8.3d⁴ 10g² 10m 10.9g³ 12.1g Sep 1] fair handicapper: stays 1¼m:
acts on fibresand and any turf going: tried blinkered earlier in career: held up, and best
in well-run race. *P. Monteith*

AMELIA (IRE) 5 b.m. General Monash (USA) 107 – Rose Tint (IRE) (Salse (USA) **57**
128) [2003 54: p6g³ p6g³ p7g⁶ p6g 6.1m⁵ 5.7f* 6m 6m⁴ f6g⁶ f6g f6g² Dec 26] neat
mare: has a short action: modest handicapper: won at Bath in June: left J. Cullinan after
eighth start, A. Reid after ninth: best around 6f: acts on firm ground, good to soft and all-
weather: edgy sort: races prominently: sometimes hangs. *W. M. Brisbourne*

AMERAS (IRE) 5 b.m. Hamas (IRE) 125§ – Amerindian 84 (Commanche Run 133) **– §**
[2003 –§: 6.9d Jul 30] lightly raced and no recent form: tried visored/tongue tied.
Miss S. E. Forster

AMERICA AMERICA (USA) 2 ch.f. (Feb 23) Mister Baileys 123 – Gal of Mine **93**
(USA) (Mining (USA)) [2003 a3f* a3f² 5m 6m⁵ 5s² 5.1m³ 6m² 7.1m² 8m² 8f³ 8f³ a8.5f²
8f* 9f a7f⁵ a8.5f* a8.5f Dec 5] $5,000Y: strong filly: first foal: dam unraced: fairly useful
performer: won maiden at Gulfstream in April, allowance race at Keeneland in October
and valuable non-graded event at Sam Houston Park in November: several good efforts
in Europe during summer, including when second in listed races at Hamburg (short-
headed by Aristaios), Newbury (went down by ¾ length to Venables), Sandown (beaten 5
lengths by Lucky Pipit) and Salisbury (3 lengths behind Sgt Pepper, 4 ran) fifth, seventh,
eighth and ninth outings: stays 8.5f: acts on dirt, firm and soft going: blinkered tenth start:
tongue tied last 3 outings in Europe: tough (raced in 4 different countries). *F. Mourier,
USA*

AMERICAN COUSIN 8 b.g. Distant Relative 128 – Zelda (USA) (Sharpen Up 127) **65**
[2003 77, a?: 5.9g 5g 5g 5m⁴ 5m* 6m 5m⁵ 5m 5m⁴ 6g 6f⁴ 5m* 5m⁴ 5m Oct 1] sturdy
gelding: fair performer: won claimer at Hamilton in June and handicap at Beverley in
September: best at 5f: acts on any going: tried blinkered, not for long time: sometimes
slowly away: often held up: none too consistent. *D. Nicholls*

AMERICAN DUKE (USA) 2 b.g. (Mar 20) Cryptoclearance (USA) – Prologue **73**
(USA) (Theatrical 128) [2003 6d⁴ 7.1m⁴ 6g 5.2s Oct 29] $20,000Y, 19,000 2-y-o:
leggy, useful-looking gelding: second foal: dam unraced: fair maiden: fourth at Windsor and Warwick: barely stays 7f: acts on good to firm going: slowly away final start.
B. J. Meehan

AMERICAN EMBASSY (USA) 3 b.c. Quiet American (USA) – Foreign Courier **46**
(USA) (Sir Ivor 135) [2003 –: 8m 8d 10m 10.1d Oct 4] good-bodied colt: poor form: left
E. Dunlop 14,000 gns after third start: tried tongue tied. *P. W. D'Arcy*

Prix Jean-Luc Lagardere (Grand Criterium), Longchamp—American Post wins in good style;
Charming Prince is second, ahead of Newton and Tycoon (rail), the latter pair both demoted

AMERICAN POST   2 br.c. (Feb 3) Bering 136 – Wells Fargo (Sadler's Wells   **118 p**
(USA) 132) [2003 6d² 7m* 7s* 8m* Oct 25]

    The practice of supplementing horses for races is becoming almost commonplace, with thirteen instances in Britain in Group 1 events in the latest season. The fact that three of these additions won—Kris Kin in the Derby, Falbrav in the Queen Elizabeth II Stakes and American Post in the Racing Post Trophy—will do nothing to discourage the tendency, though it is to be doubted whether the motives for supplementing will often match those of Khalid Abdulla with American Post, at a cost of £17,500. One of the principal aims was to confirm his position on top of the Flat owners' table, which he led by more than £100,000. American Post's victory at Doncaster, worth £151,500, seemed to put the title beyond doubt, though the disqualification of Three Valleys in the Middle Park Stakes and Tillerman (from second) in the Queen Anne Stakes—combined earnings almost exactly the same as American Post's—raised the possibility for a time of Abdulla's being pipped. It was the first time he had been leading owner in Britain.

    It was just as well for the Racing Post Trophy that American Post and another runner Fantastic View were added to the field, since, following the withdrawal with veterinary certificates of Cape Fear (also supplemented) and Mikado, only four lined up, the smallest field since 1995. This for a race which had had one hundred and twenty-two entries. American Post was a rare French challenger, the first for nearly twenty years, the shortfall presumably explained by the presence in the French calendar of appropriate alternatives, plus a general wariness by leading trainers there to cross the Channel, compared to the enthusiasm shown by some of their British- and Irish-based counterparts. American Post had won two of his three previous starts, displaying form that resulted in his going off 6/5-on favourite. Apparently late into training—he reportedly didn't arrive at his trainer's yard until May—American Post lost a newcomers race at Deauville by a short head to Ximb, but then won a minor event at Longchamp in September comfortably before being stepped up in class in the Prix Jean-Luc Lagardere, formerly the Grand Criterium, on Arc day (the race renamed in honour of leading owner-breeder Lagardere, president of France Galop from 1995 until his death aged seventy-five following a

Racing Post Trophy, Doncaster—American Post becomes the first to achieve the
Grand Criterium/Racing Post double, quickening away from Fantastic View, Magritte (blaze) and Tahreeb

Mr K. Abdulla's "American Post"

hip operation in March). The withdrawal of Diamond Green, the likely favourite, because of the going, left only six runners at Longchamp, none of them a pattern winner. Charming Prince, runner-up to Diamond Green previously in the Prix La Rochette, was favourite in a tight market ahead of the coupled O'Brien runners, Acropolis, Newton and Tycoon, followed by Ximb and American Post, the outsider of the field at 7/2. Those odds looked far from tempting given the way American Post behaved beforehand, requiring two handlers in the preliminaries and rearing up persistently at the start, giving his rider Richard Hughes an uncomfortable time.

American Post showed equal exuberance, though properly directed this time, once the race was under way, travelling strongly from the off, leading on the bridle early in the straight and quickening away to win by four lengths from the favourite. Ximb did not have a clear run owing to the waywardness of Acropolis but, even with better luck, he would not have troubled the winner. Although not a strong renewal of what is widely regarded as France's top two-year-old prize, the Lagardere showed that American Post was clearly a promising colt. Given the strength of the opposition at Doncaster he was a worthy favourite. Fantastic View had won two stakes races, notably the Autumn Stakes at Ascot; Magrítte, trying to give Aidan O'Brien his fifth win in the race in seven years, had landed a maiden race easily at Tipperary; and Tahreeb had put up his best effort when third in the Mill Reef. American Post looked the part at Doncaster and behaved much better than at Longchamp, while still giving the impression he is a nervous type, with speed the dominant characteristic in his make-up. Waited with as Magritte led, American Post showed good acceleration to move to the front a furlong out and, despite carrying his head high and edging right, had no difficulty holding Fantastic View by a length and three quarters.

		Arctic Tern	Sea Bird II
	Bering	(ch 1973)	Bubbling Beauty
	(ch 1983)	Beaune	Lyphard
American Post		(ch 1974)	Barbra
(br.c. Feb 3, 2001)		Sadler's Wells	Northern Dancer
	Wells Fargo	(b 1981)	Fairy Bridge
	(b 1996)	Cruising Height	Shirley Heights
		(b 1987)	Nomadic Pleasure

Soon after the Racing Post Trophy, Criquette Head-Maarek, whose father Alec had saddled the last French-trained winner of the race with Green Dancer in 1974, said that American Post would probably not be sent for the Two Thousand Guineas. His owner apparently prefers the idea of contesting the Poule d'Essai des Poulains, which Green Dancer won but in which Abdulla has so far drawn a blank. American Post should have improvement in him and would appear to hold a major chance in that race, as he would in the Two Thousand Guineas if there were to be a change of plan. It may be a different matter altogether as regards the Derby, for which American Post was quoted at odds between 7/1 and 10/1 at the time of writing. Unless maturity brings a more restrained approach, his temperament is likely to count against his chances of staying a mile and a half. On the face of it, he is bred to get the trip, with a Prix du Jockey Club winner and Arc second as his sire, and a mare by Sadler's Wells from a stout family as his dam. However, Bering has not been a thoroughgoing influence for stamina at stud, with most of his eleven other Group 1 and Group 2 scorers, including Guineas winner Pennekamp, gaining their main victories at up to a mile. American Post is the first and only foal out of the unraced Wells Fargo, who died in 2002. Two of Wells Fargo's siblings showed well-above-average ability, namely smart stayer Corradini and High And Low, who earned a rating of 120 after winning the Cheshire Oaks and coming second in the Yorkshire Oaks and St Leger. Their dam and American Post's grandam, Cruising Height, who scored over an extended ten and twelve furlongs and was runner-up in the Lancashire Oaks, is a sister to Northumberland Plate winner Highflying and a half-sister to the Park Hill winner Trampship from the family of top performers Paulista and High Top. There are not that many modern families with more stamina, but suffice it to say that American Post, who acts on soft and good to firm going, looks as if he will prove best at up to a mile and a quarter. American Post is a strong, good-topped individual who really took the eye when we photographed him, even though it was fairly late in the year. *Mme C. Head-Maarek, France*

AMETHYST ROCK 5 b.g. Rock Hopper 124 – Kind Lady 56 (Kind of Hush 118) **41** [2003 10m 10m 10.3m 10m⁶ 14.1f Aug 26] 3,500 3-y-o: smallish, strong gelding: sixth foal: half-brother to 3 winners, including 6-y-o Kind Emperor: dam 2-y-o 6f seller winner who probably stayed 1½m: poor maiden: stays 1¼m: raced only on going firmer than good. *P. L. Gilligan*

AMEYRAH (IRE) 2 b. or b.f. (Mar 26) In The Wings 128 – Alfaaselah (GER) 97 **59** (Dancing Brave (USA) 140) [2003 8g p8g Nov 13] quite good-topped filly: third foal: half-sister to useful 5f (at 2 yrs) to 7f winner Historic Treble (by Lycius) and French winner up to 15f Benhabeebi (by Bin Ajwaad): dam, 7f (at 2 yrs) to 9.5f (in Germany) winner, from family of Urban Sea and Galileo: modest form in maidens at Newbury and Lingfield: should be suited by at least 1¼m. *M. R. Channon*

AMID THE CHAOS (IRE) 3 ch.c. Nashwan (USA) 135 – Celebrity Style (USA) **95** 96 (Seeking The Gold (USA)) [2003 10g 9.5d⁴ 16.2f 10g* Oct 6] strong colt: second foal: dam, Irish 7f and 9f winner, out of close relative to US Grade 1 9f winner Chain Bracelet: useful performer: best effort when eighth to Shanty Star in Queen's Vase at Royal Ascot third start: won maiden at Roscommon in October: seems to stay 2m: acts on firm ground: sold €180,000. *D. K. Weld, Ireland*

AMIE 3 b.f. Northern Amethyst 99 – Break Point (Reference Point 139) [2003 –: p10g **–** p10g Feb 19] little form. *Mrs A. J. Perrett*

AMIGO (IRE) 5 b.g. Spectrum (IRE) 126 – Eleanor Antoinette (IRE) (Double **88** Schwartz 128) [2003 89: p16g⁴ p12g⁴ p13g 11.6g⁶ Apr 7] tall, close-coupled gelding: fairly useful handicapper: stays easy 2m: acts on all-weather, soft and good to firm going: blinkered (raced freely) once: hung left final 4-y-o start: usually waited with. *P. Mitchell*

AMIR ZAMAN 5 ch.g. Salse (USA) 128 – Colorvista (Shirley Heights 130) [2003 **67** 73: p16g* p16g⁶ 14.4d 16m³ f16.2g 13.3m 14.1m⁶ p16g⁶ f12s* f12s* p12g³ Nov 2] big, **a82**

strong, lengthy gelding: fairly useful handicapper on all-weather, fair on turf: won at Lingfield in January and twice at Southwell in October: effective at 1½m to 2m: acts on all-weather, firm and good to soft ground: usually races prominently. *J. R. Jenkins*

AMMENAYR (IRE) 3 b.g. Entrepreneur 123 – Katiyfa (Auction Ring (USA) 123) **85** [2003 f8.5g⁶ 7g* 8.1m 7m⁵ p8g Dec 30] IR 60,000Y: medium-sized, lengthy gelding: half-brother to several winners, including smart Irish 1½m/1¾m winner Katiykha (by Darshaan) and 6-y-o Katiypour: dam French 1m/1¼m winner: fairly useful performer: won maiden at Newmarket in April: should stay 1m: probably acts on polytrack, raced only on good ground or firmer on turf. *T. G. Mills*

AMNESTY 4 ch.g. Salse (USA) 128 – Amaranthus (Shirley Heights 130) [2003 68: **74** 8.2s⁵ 7.1g³ 8.3g² 7f 8.3g 8.3g³ 8.2m Oct 22] lengthy gelding: fair maiden handicapper: probably acts on soft and good to firm going: has raced freely: sold 8,000 gns. *H. Candy*

AMONG DREAMS 2 ch.f. (Mar 6) Among Men (USA) 124 – Russell Creek 80 **67** (Sandy Creek 123) [2003 6g* 5d⁵ f7g³ Nov 14] big, workmanlike filly: seventh foal: half-sister to 3 winners, including 1996 2-y-o 5f seller winner Assumpta (by Superpower): dam, 1m winner, out of half-sister to very smart 1m/1¼m performer Jellaby: fair form: 50/1-winner of claimer at Haydock in July, then left A. Newcombe: raced freely when third in nursery at Wolverhampton: barely stays 7f: acts on fibresand. *J. A. Osborne*

AMONG FRIENDS (IRE) 3 b.g. Among Men (USA) 124 – Anita's Contessa (IRE) **75** 68 (Anita's Prince 126) [2003 75: 6m 5.1m³ 6m⁶ Jul 31] leggy, good-topped gelding: fair performer: effective at 5f/6f: raced only on polytrack and good to firm ground. *B. Palling*

AMONGST AMIGOS (IRE) 2 b.c. (Apr 30) Imperial Ballet (IRE) 110 – Red Lory **–** 87 (Bay Express 132) [2003 5.3m⁵ 6g 6g Jul 28] €23,000Y: half-brother to several winners, including 6-y-o Amoras and useful French/US sprinter Cyrano Storme (by Cyrano de Bergerac): dam 2-y-o 5f winner: well held in maidens/seller. *G. C. Bravery*

A MONK SWIMMING (IRE) 2 br.g. (Mar 9) Among Men (USA) 124 – Sea Magic **–** (IRE) 85 (Distinctly North (USA) 115) [2003 5m 6f⁶ 6.1d Nov 6] tall, workmanlike gelding: second foal: dam 5f winner at 2 yrs who stayed 7f: well held in maidens. *John Berry*

AMORAS (IRE) 6 b.m. Hamas (IRE) 125§ – Red Lory 87 (Bay Express 132) [2003 **81** 81: 8.5m² 8.3d* 8g 9g⁵ 8.5m² 8.3g 8m p8g p8g² Nov 22] good-bodied mare: fairly useful handicapper: won at Hamilton in May: raced mainly around 1m: acts on any turf going and polytrack: usually held up: sold 12,000 gns. *J. W. Hills*

AMPOULE 4 b.g. Zamindar (USA) 116 – Diamond Park (IRE) 91 (Alzao (USA) 117) **77** [2003 53: p10g² p12g² f12g* f12s p12g* 12m⁵ 14.4g⁶ 13.9m 14.1m⁵ 12m³ 12m⁶ 10.5m³ 11.9f* 11.9m 11.9m⁴ 14m² 11.5g² Sep 16] big, good-topped gelding: fair performer: won maiden at Wolverhampton in February, minor event at Lingfield in March and handicap at Brighton in August: stays 14.4f: acts on all-weather, raced only on good going or firmer on turf: visored last 5 starts: tends to idle. *C. E. Brittain*

AMRITSAR 6 ch.g. Indian Ridge 123 – Trying For Gold (USA) 103 (Northern Baby **–** (CAN) 127) [2003 –: f9.4g Jul 19] modest maiden at 4 yrs: no form since. *K. G. Wingrove*

AMUNDSEN (USA) 3 b.g. Gone West (USA) – Aunt Anne (USA) (Deputy Minister **48** (CAN)) [2003 84p: 11.8m 12.3d⁵ 15.8m⁶ f12g³ 16.2g Aug 25] lengthy gelding: fairly useful at 2 yrs: only poor form in 2003, leaving M. Johnston after second start: stayed 1½m: acted on firm going and fibresand: blinkered last 2 starts: dead. *J. Jay*

AMUSED 4 ch.f. Prince Sabo 123 – Indigo 86 (Primo Dominie 121) [2003 73: 5d 6m⁵ **78** 7.2m² 6d* 6g⁵ 6f⁶ Jul 12] short-backed filly: fair handicapper: won at Pontefract in June: effective at 6f/7f: acts on firm and good to soft going: visored last 3 outings: sometimes slowly away: consistent. *R. A. Fahey*

AMWELL BRAVE 2 b.c. (Apr 23) Pyramus (USA) 78 – Passage Creeping (IRE) 75 **71** (Persian Bold 123) [2003 6m 6m⁵ 6f f6s 8s³ p8g⁴ f8s⁵ Dec 13] second foal: half-brother to winner abroad by Theatrical Charmer: dam, maiden, stayed 1¼m: fair maiden: much better at 1m than 6f, and should stay 1¼m: acts on all-weather and soft ground: tried visored. *J. R. Jenkins*

ANACAPRI 3 b.f. Barathea (IRE) 127 – Dancerette (Groom Dancer (USA) 128) **–** [2003 10.1m Oct 12] 20,000F, 20,000Y: close-coupled filly: first foal: dam, French 11f winner, granddaughter of smart French 1½m performer Contradictive: always behind in maiden at Newcastle. *W. S. Cunningham*

ANAK PEKAN 3 ch.g. In The Wings 128 – Trefoil (FR) (Blakeney 126) [2003 –p: **94 p** 10g 11.1m 12g² 14m² 14.1f* 14.4g² 16g² 16.5d² Nov 8] stocky gelding: fairly useful handicapper: improved throughout 2003, winning at Yarmouth in August: good efforts when runner-up last 3 starts, to Ponderon at Doncaster final one: will stay beyond 2m: acts on firm and good to soft ground: reportedly had breathing problem third start: type to do better still at 4 yrs. *M. A. Jarvis*

ANALOGY (IRE) 3 ch.g. Bahhare (USA) 122 – Anna Comnena (IRE) 71 (Shareef **70**
Dancer (USA) 135) [2003 7m 7m 9.2m⁵ 11.9m² 13.1m* 11.9m² 12m² 16g Jul 28] IR 120,000Y: half-brother to several winners, including 5-y-o Sadlers Wings and useful 1¼m winner who stayed 12.5f Abyaan (by Ela-Mana-Mou): dam, maiden who should have stayed 1½m, half-sister to dams of very smart performers Annus Mirabilis (at 9f to 1½m) and Annaba (around 1½m): fair handicapper: won apprentice event at Ayr in June: stays 13f, seemingly not 2m: raced only on good/good to firm ground: tongue tied last 4 starts: tends to wander/carry head high: sold 27,000 gns, joined C. Mann, and fairly useful form over hurdles. *Sir Mark Prescott*

ANALYZE (FR) 5 b.g. Anabaa (USA) 130 – Bramosia (Forzando 122) [2003 79: **82**
p10g⁶ p10g⁶ 10g² 10m 10.1m* 10m² 10m² 10m 10m⁶ 10m³ 10m⁴ 10.3m³ 10.2f 10.1g⁴ 10.1m³ 10m³ 10.2g³ 10f* 10g⁵ 10.1g p10g⁶ Nov 29] smallish, workmanlike gelding: fairly useful handicapper: won at Newcastle in April and Ayr in August: left M. Channon before final start: best around 1¼m: acts on firm ground, good to soft and polytrack: often held up: tough. *B. G. Powell*

ANA MARIE (FR) 4 b.f. Anabaa (USA) 130 – Marie de Ken (FR) 110 (Kendor (FR) **118**
122) [2003 118: 10g* 10.5d⁵ 12g⁴ 12g⁵ 9.9g² 10s⁵ 11f 12d Nov 30] close-coupled, useful-looking filly: smart performer: won Prix d'Harcourt at Longchamp in March by short neck from Fair Mix: creditable efforts after when 4½ lengths sixth (promoted a place) to Ange Gabriel in Grand Prix de Saint-Cloud and neck second to Russian Rhythm in Nassau Stakes at Goodwood: below form last 3 outings, in Prix de l'Opera at Longchamp, Queen Elizabeth II Commemorative Cup at Kyoto and Japan Cup at Tokyo: stays 1½m: acts on good to firm and good to soft going, probably on heavy. *P. H. Demercastel, France*

ANANI (USA) 3 b.c. Miswaki (USA) 124 – Mystery Rays (USA) 122 (Nijinsky **110**
(CAN) 138) [2003 85p: 8m* 9g² 10.1m³ 12f⁴¹ 10.4f⁵ 10g* 10g 10.8s² Nov 2] lengthy colt: smart performer: won maiden at Ascot in March and listed race at Le Lion d'Angers (by head from Weightless) in September: good efforts when fourth to High Accolade in King Edward VII Stakes at Royal Ascot and ½-length second to Royal Fantasy in Frankfurt Trophy at Frankfurt final start: stays 1½m: acts on firm and soft going: carries head awkwardly. *E. A. L. Dunlop*

ANATOM 2 ch.f. (Apr 28) Komaite (USA) – Zamarra 59 (Clantime 101) [2003 5.3f **–**
5.7m f5s 5m⁶ p6g⁶ f5g Dec 15] 3,500Y: third foal: half-sister to 3-y-o Double Assembly: dam, lightly-raced maiden at 2 yrs, best at 5f: probably of little account. *M. Quinn*

ANA WINTA (FR) 3 b.g. Anabaa (USA) 130 – Steeple (Selkirk (USA) 129) [2003 **63**
7m⁵ 7m 6m⁴ 6m⁵ Sep 3] 120,000Y: first foal: dam, French 9.2f winner, closely related to smart performers around 1m Soprano and Enharmonic from good family: fair maiden: better at 6f than 7f: raced only on good to firm going: blinkered (ran creditably) final start. *J. W. Payne*

ANCHORSHOLME 3 b.g. Fleetwood (IRE) 107 – Loch Clair (IRE) 53 (Lomond **69 ?**
(USA) 128) [2003 10m⁶ 11.8m 10m 11.9d Sep 26] 6,000Y: angular gelding: fifth foal: half-brother to fairly useful 1¼m winner Agony Aunt (by Formidable) and 5-y-o Magic Charm: dam, lightly-raced maiden, half-sister to smart middle-distance performer Wind In Her Hair, the family of Nashwan, Unfuwain and Nayef: fair form when sixth in maiden at Newbury on debut: well held after: should be suited by 1½m+: sold 14,000 gns. *J. L. Dunlop*

ANCIENT WORLD (USA) 3 br.c. Spinning World (USA) 130 – Headline (Machia- **112 p**
vellian (USA) 123) [2003 8d⁴ 8d⁴ 8.5g* 8s* Oct 9] third foal: half-brother to smart US 1m and (Grade 1) 1½m winner Jilbab (by A P Indy): dam unraced half-sister to US Grade 1 2-y-o 1m winner Saratoga Six and William Hill Futurity winner Dunbeath: progressive form in minor events, winning at Longchamp in September and October, both in good style: smooth headway to lead 1½f out and just pushed clear when beating Shakanndi by 5 lengths on latter occasion: raced only around 1m: has good turn of foot: joined Godolphin: already smart, and type to hold his own in better company in 2004. *A. Fabre, France*

ANDEAN 2 b.c. (Mar 7) Singspiel (IRE) 133 – Anna Matrushka (Mill Reef (USA) **82 p**
141) [2003 7m⁶ Jul 8] quite attractive colt: closely related to very smart 1¼m/1½m winner Annaba and 3-y-o Annambo (both by In The Wings), and half-brother to several at least useful winners, including 11.5f to 14.6f winner Anna of Saxony (by Ela-Mana-

Mou) and French/UAE 1½m and 15f winner Pozarica (by Rainbow Quest), both smart: dam unraced close relation to dam of very smart performer up to 1½m Annus Mirabilis: favourite, 2¾ lengths sixth of 13 to Josephus in maiden at Newmarket, unable to quicken: will be suited by 1¼m/1½m: sure to do better. *D. R. Loder*

ANDREYEV (IRE)   9 ch.g. Presidium 124 – Missish (Mummy's Pet 125) [2003 –: – 6m 6d 7g 8m 7g 7.2g 8m 8f 7.2g⁵ 7.2g⁵ 7m 9.1m 8g Sep 28] tall gelding: one-time smart performer: very much on the downgrade: tried in headgear. *J. S. Goldie*

ANDROMACHE   4 ch.f. Hector Protector (USA) 124 – South Sea Bubble (IRE) 75   **61** (Bustino 136) [2003 66: 10m⁴ 9.9m⁴ 12.3g⁴ 13.1f⁴ 12m⁶ Sep 12] rather leggy, lengthy filly: modest maiden handicapper: barely stays 13f: acts on firm and good to soft going. *G. B. Balding*

AND TOTO TOO   3 br.f. Averti (IRE) 117 – Divina Mia 66 (Dowsing (USA) 124)   **79** [2003 69: p8g f7g² p8g² f8.5g² f7g² p7g⁵ f9.4g³ p8g 7m f7g* f8.5s⁴ 7g⁵ 6.1d* 6m³ 6m 6f* 6d³ 7m³ 7m³ 7m* 6d³ 7.1m 6.1m³ 7f⁶ 7f 6m³ 7.1m* f7g⁵ 7m³ 8g⁵ p7g* f7s⁵ Dec 31] fair performer: had a good season, winning handicaps at Wolverhampton in April, Chepstow in May, Salisbury in June and Lingfield in December, and minor events at Lingfield in July and Chepstow in September: effective at 6f to easy 8.5f: acts on all-weather, firm and soft going: blinkered/visored in 2003: sometimes slowly away: usually waited with: tough. *P. D. Evans*

ANDURIL   2 ch.c. (Jan 27) Kris 135 – Attribute 69 (Warning 136) [2003 6m p7g⁴ p8g⁵   **70** Nov 2] 2,500F, 15,000Y: workmanlike colt: fourth foal: half-brother to 8.5f winner Reasoning (by Selkirk): dam maiden out of half-sister to Xaar, a very good family: fair form in maidens: will need to settle to stay beyond 1m. *J. M. P. Eustace*

ANDY'S ELECTIVE   6 b.g. Democratic (USA) 101 – English Mint 66 (Jalmood   **45 §** (USA) 126) [2003 56§: p7g 10.2f 7d 8f 7g⁶ 7m⁵ 7m⁵ 7m Sep 16] poor handicapper nowadays: stays 1m: acts on firm and soft ground, probably on polytrack: tried in visor/cheekpieces: often races prominently: unreliable. *J. R. Jenkins*

ANECDOTE   3 ch.f. Zamindar (USA) 116 – Rainy Sky (Rainbow Quest (USA) 134)   – [2003 11.7f⁵ p8g Oct 8] 3,500 3-y-o: third living foal: dam, French 1½m winner, sister to smart French winner up to 1½m Bonash and half-sister to dam of 3-y-o Nebraska Tornado and 4-y-o Burning Sun: well held in maiden/seller. *P. D. Evans*

ANEMOS (IRE)   8 ch.g. Be My Guest (USA) 126 – Frendly Persuasion (General   **54** Assembly (USA)) [2003 56: f9.4g³ f8.5g* p8g³ f8.5s³ 9.7m⁵ 10.9m³ 9.7m³ 10m³ 7d⁶ 9m⁶   **a63** 8.1m f8.5g² 9f 8.1m⁵ f9.4g⁵ 8m⁶ p10g p10g p10g Dec 29] tall gelding: modest handi-capper, better on all-weather than turf: won at Wolverhampton in February: effective at 7f to 11f: acts on firm ground, soft and all-weather: tried visored/blinkered/hooded/tongue tied. *P. W. D'Arcy*

ANGE GABRIEL (FR)   5 gr.h. Kaldounevees (FR) 118 – Mount Gable (Head   **124** For Heights 125) [2003 124: 12g² 12g* 12g* 12m* 12s 12d Nov 30]

Racegoers never got the chance to see Ange Gabriel on a British racecourse. Plans to run him in the Coronation Cup and the King George VI and Queen Eliza-beth Stakes in the latest season were shelved, and at the end of the year it was announced that he had been retired to his owner/breeders' Haras du Mesnil, his fee set at €6,000, with the October 1st concession. Ange Gabriel wouldn't have been up to beating Alamshar in the King George, but a reproduction of his best form would have been good enough to have taken care of Warrsan and company at Epsom. He was a very smart performer, and a thoroughly genuine and reliable one too, the winner of twelve of his twenty-one starts and getting on for £1.5m in prize money.

The last six of Ange Gabriel's victories were gained in pattern company and included the two most recent runnings of France's most important all-aged middle-distance event of the summer, the Grand Prix de Saint-Cloud, his other success at Group 1 level coming in the Hong Kong Vase at Sha Tin on his final outing in 2002. Long-distance travel was evidently no hardship to Ange Gabriel. After Hong Kong, he was sent to Nad Al Sheba in March and ran right up to his best in finishing second to Sulamani, beaten three quarters of a length, in the Dubai Sheema Classic. On his return to France he proceeded to win three races in succession, starting at odds on for two of those, the Grand Prix de Chantilly and the Prix Foy Gray d'Albion Barriere at Longchamp, both of which he won from Martaline, but faced a stiffer task in between in the Grand Prix de Saint-Cloud. Disappointingly, the field

Grand Prix de Saint-Cloud—almost a re-run of the previous year, as Ange Gabriel wins from Polish Summer (third right); Millstreet (rail, demoted) and Loxias (blinkers) are next

of nine contained no three-year-olds, and with Sulamani failing to give his running it turned out to be at best no more than an average renewal. Sulamani, coupled for betting purposes with his pacemaker Millstreet, started at odds on with Ange Gabriel next in the betting at 2/1, unlike in the previous year's edition when Ange Gabriel had been the outsider of six. There was a moment when Millstreet, who had quickened a couple of lengths clear off the turn, looked as though he might make all, but Ange Gabriel collared him inside the final furlong and went on to win by a length and a half from Polish Summer, also runner-up twelve months earlier. Ange Gabriel was below form on his last two outings, the Prix de l'Arc de Triomphe and Japan Cup, reportedly sustaining a bump on a fetlock joint in the latter. The ground wasn't ideal for him on either occasion. Ange Gabriel has won on good to soft and soft, but he has put up his best performances on good and good to firm.

		Kaldoun (gr 1975)	Caro
	Kaldounevees (FR) (gr 1991)		Katana
		Safaroa (b 1978)	Satingo
Ange Gabriel (FR) (gr.h. 1998)			Traverse Afar
		Head For Heights (b 1981)	Shirley Heights
	Mount Gable (b 1986)		Vivante
		Cupids Hill (b 1977)	Sallust
			Sweet J

The Haras du Mesnil belongs to Henri and Antonia Devin and is also the home of Ange Gabriel's sire Kaldounevees, a smart performer at a mile to eleven furlongs. Ange Gabriel is the fourth foal of Mount Gable, who was unraced as a two-year-old but ran twenty-six times in France up to the age of five, winning twice at around a mile and three furlongs and proving effective at up to a mile and seven. Mount Gable's third foal Dubayotte (by Turgeon) won over an extended mile and a half in France in 2002. Though Mount Gable's family is not particularly distinguished, she is out of a half-sister to the very smart miler of the 'seventies Ardoon. Ange Gabriel, a rather leggy, quite good-topped individual, was best at a mile and a half. He shouldn't fail at stud to begin with through lack of patronage, with the Devins reported to be sending some of their best mares to him. *E. Libaud, France*

ANGEL ANNIE   3 b.f. Alzao (USA) 117 – Pure (Slip Anchor 136) [2003 80: p6g⁵ p6g   **65** f8g 7m⁵ 10.1m⁵ 7d 8g 6m p6g 7g* 7m 7.6g 7g 10m⁵ 5.3f 6m 8m Oct 2] close-coupled filly: fair performer: left B. Hills 6,800 gns after second start: won minor event at Lingfield in June: headstrong, but stays 7f: acts on polytrack, good to firm and good to soft ground: has edged left: usually races prominently: inconsistent: sold 5,000 gns. *J. A. Gilbert*

ANGELICA GARNETT   3 ch.f. Desert Story (IRE) 115 – Vanessa Bell (IRE)   **–** (Lahib (USA) 129) [2003 64: 7m 6s 8f Sep 2] rather leggy filly: fluent mover: modest maiden at 2 yrs: well held in 2003, leaving R. Charlton 2,000 gns after second start: tried in cheekpieces/blinkers. *T. E. Powell*

ANGEL ISA (IRE)   3 b.f. Fayruz 116 – Isa (Dance In Time (CAN)) [2003 53, a59:   **58** f6g f6g⁶ 5m 7.1f* 6.9m 7d⁶ 7m Oct 13] quite attractive filly: modest handicapper: won at Musselburgh in August despite wandering: stays 7f: acts on fibresand and firm going, below form on good to soft. *R. A. Fahey*

65

ANGEL MAID 2 b.f. (May 11) Forzando 122 – Esilam 62 (Frimley Park 109) [2003 –
6m 6g 6g Oct 24] sturdy filly: sister to 3-y-o Formalise and half-sister to several winners,
including 8-y-o Pure Coincidence (formerly useful): dam, 2-y-o 5f winner in Britain, won
up to 1m in Italy: well held in maidens. *G. B. Balding*

ANGELO'S PRIDE 2 ch.c. (Feb 18) Young Ern 120 – Considerable Charm 51 **55**
(Charmer 123) [2003 f6g Nov 1] third foal: dam, maiden (second at 7f), half-sister to
useful performer up to 8.5f Neither Nor: 20/1 and green, seventh of 13 in maiden at
Wolverhampton, slowly away and not knocked about: should do better. *J. A. Osborne*

ANGELS VENTURE 7 ch.g. Unfuwain (USA) 131 – City of Angels (Woodman **59**
(USA) 126) [2003 68: 11m 12g p12g⁶ Jun 3] close-coupled gelding: modest handicapper:
stays 1½m: acts on soft going, good to firm and polytrack: tried visored: usually tongue
tied prior to 2003: sometimes hangs left: fair hurdler. *J. R. Jenkins*

ANGELUS DOMINI (IRE) 4 b.f. Blues Traveller (IRE) 119 – Lyphards Goddess –
(IRE) (Lyphard's Special (USA) 122) [2003 54: f6g 11m 10.2m 7g Jul 28] leggy filly:
modest maiden at best: well beaten in 2003. *B. A. McMahon*

ANGIE'S DOUBLE 3 ch.f. Double Trigger (IRE) 123 – Arch Angel (IRE) 55 (Arch- –
way (IRE) 115) [2003 –: 10.2m May 30] unfurnished filly: little form. *D. J. S. ffrench
Davis*

ANGLO SAXON (USA) 3 br.c. Seeking The Gold (USA) – Anna Palariva (IRE) **89 p**
108 (Caerleon (USA) 132) [2003 7.5d* 8.1g 8m* Aug 5] useful-looking colt: first foal:
dam, won Prix d'Aumale (raced only at 1m at 2 yrs), daughter of smart 11.5f to 14.6f
winner Anna of Saxony, herself half-sister to very smart 1¼m/1½m performer Annaba:
fairly useful form: won maiden at Beverley in May and handicap at Bath in August,
beating Zeuss by ¾ length in latter: reportedly had breathing problem when below form
in between: should stay at least 1¼m: looks capable of better still. *D. R. Loder*

ANICAFLASH 2 b.f. (Apr 10) Cayman Kai (IRE) 114 – Sharp Top 62 (Sharpo 132) –
[2003 8m 8d Oct 14] leggy, lengthy filly: half-sister to several winners, including smart
1m to 10.5f winner Polar Red (by Polar Falcon) and 4-y-o Aldora: dam 1½m and 2m
winner, also successful over hurdles: slowly away and always behind in maidens at
Newcastle and Ayr (looked wayward). *M. Dods*

ANIMAL CRACKER 5 gr.m. Primo Dominie 121 – Child Star (FR) 58 (Bellypha **50**
130) [2003 52d: 7m f6g⁵ 6m May 5] close-coupled, workmanlike mare: modest
performer: best at 5f/6f: acts on soft going, good to firm and fibresand: tried blinkered/
tongue tied: none too consistent. *J. Balding*

ANIMAL LOVER (IRE) 3 b.f. Danehill Dancer (IRE) 117 – Trojan Honey (Trojan **55**
Fen 117) [2003 –: 11.9d 10d* 10d 8m 8.5s⁴ f9g 7v* 7.5g 9f 8.5d 8d f7g Nov 21] seventh
foal: half-sister to German 1m winner Treaty of Rome (by Rhoman Rule): dam Irish
maiden: modest handicapper: won at Clonmel in June and Galway in July: well held after,
including an all-weather debut at Wolverhampton final start: stays 1¼m: acts on heavy
going: tried tongue tied. *T. Hogan, Ireland*

ANISETTE 2 b.f. (Mar 20) Abou Zouz (USA) 109 – Natural Gold (USA) (Gold **57**
Meridian (USA) 112) [2003 f6g² Nov 29] second foal: dam Italian 7.5f winner: 14/1 and
green, short-headed by Sable 'n Silk in maiden at Wolverhampton, leading much of final
1f. *Julian Poulton*

ANNA ALMOST 5 b.m. Tragic Role (USA) – Princess Hotpot (IRE) (King's Ride –
88) [2003 f12g Mar 3] second foal: dam winning hurdler/chaser: poor maiden hurdler:
well beaten in maiden at Wolverhampton. *T. Wall*

ANNABEL LEE (UAE) 2 ch.f. (Feb 11) Halling (USA) 133 – Sheet Music (IRE) **61**
(Sadler's Wells (USA) 132) [2003 6g⁴ 6g⁵ f7g Aug 2] leggy filly: first foal: dam unraced
out of half-sister to College Chapel: green, won maiden at Hamilton in July: well beaten
in minor event/nursery: should stay at least 7f: sold 1,600 gns. *M. Johnston*

ANNAKITA 3 b.f. Unfuwain (USA) 131 – Cuban Reef 54 (Dowsing (USA) 124) –
[2003 10d 10g 8.3m p12g f12s⁶ f12g Dec 22] second foal: dam 7f and 1¼m winner: little
form. *W. J. Musson*

ANNAMBO 3 ch.c. In The Wings 128 – Anna Matrushka (Mill Reef (USA) 141) **93**
[2003 82p: 12f* 12.3d² 12.6f 16.2f 11.7f* 14g 13.9m Aug 21] useful-looking colt: fairly useful
performer: won maiden at Thirsk in April and minor event at Bath in July: probably stays
1¾m (failed to stay 2m in Queens Vase at Royal Ascot): acts on firm and good to soft
ground: visored last 4 outings: has carried head awkwardly/flashed tail. *D. R. Loder*

ANNA PANNA   2 b.f. (Feb 4) Piccolo 121 – Miss Laetitia (IRE) (Entitled 126) [2003   **55 p**
f7s³ Dec 31] 1,600Y: fourth living foal: half-sister to 1¼m seller winner Diletia (by
Dilum): dam of little account: 20/1, 8 lengths third to Denver in maiden at Wolverhampton, starting slowly, racing wide and not unduly knocked about: should improve.
H. Candy

ANNA WALHAAN (IRE)   4 b.g. Green Desert (USA) 127 – Queen's Music (USA)   **88**
66 (Dixieland Band (USA)) [2003 95: f8.5s 8.1m 8g⁴ 8.3g⁴ 8.5m³ 8m 8f⁶ 8.5d⁴ 8m² 8.5g
8m⁵ Sep 16] close-coupled, deep-bodied gelding: fairly useful handicapper: in frame 5
times in 2003: left M. Channon after eighth start: stays 8.5f: acts on firm going, possibly
not on good to soft: sometimes visored, not since reappearance. *Ian Williams*

ANNEKA   3 b.f. Among Men (USA) 124 – Treasure Hunt (Hadeer 118) [2003 43: 9d   **–**
7m 8.5m Jul 15] lengthy filly: poor maiden at 2 yrs: well held in 2003, leaving Miss
S. Hall after reappearance. *C. W. Thornton*

ANNIE HARVEY   2 ch.f. (Apr 30) Fleetwood (IRE) 107 – Resemblance (State   **75**
Diplomacy (USA)) [2003 6d⁵ 7d* 8m⁴ 6m³ 7d Nov 8] 500Y: close-coupled, good-topped
filly: second foal: dam, tailed off only start, out of half-sister to useful 7f/1m performer
Peculiarity: fair performer: won maiden at Thirsk in August: good third in sales race at
Doncaster, easily best effort after: should stay 1m (saddle slipped and lost weight cloth
when tried): acts on good to firm and good to soft going. *B. Smart*

ANNIE MILLER (IRE)   2 b.f. (Feb 7) Night Shift (USA) – Lost Dream (Niniski   **67**
(USA) 125) [2003 5m⁵ 5.1f³ p7g 6m⁵ Sep 22] rather leggy filly: fourth foal: dam, ran
twice, half-sister to smart 1983 2-y-o sprinter Rocket Alert: fair maiden: third at Bath:
likely to prove best at 5f/6f. *M. J. Wallace*

ANNIJAZ   6 b.m. Alhijaz 122 – Figment 75 (Posse (USA) 130) [2003 57, a49: 5.7m²   **64**
6g* 5.7f⁴ 8m* 8m 7m* 5.5f 8f 8.1m⁶ 7.1g Sep 11] sparely-made mare: modest handicapper: won at Yarmouth in May and at Redcar and Doncaster in June: effective at 5.7f to
1m: acts on fibresand and any turf going: held up. *J. M. Bradley*

ANNISHIRANI   3 b.f. Shaamit (IRE) 127 – Silent Miracle (IRE) 80 (Night Shift   **82**
(USA)) [2003 8g³ 9.2f² p8g² p7g* p10g* p8g⁴ Nov 22] first foal: dam 6f winner: fairly
useful performer: won maiden at Lingfield in October and handicap there in November:
effective at 7f to 1¼m: acts on polytrack, raced only on good going or firmer on turf:
free-going sort: difficult at stall and found little second start: hung right for second win.
G. A. Butler

ANNIVERSARY GUEST (IRE)   4 b. or br.f. Desert King (IRE) 129 – Polynesian   **42**
Goddess (IRE) (Salmon Leap (USA) 131) [2003 54: 15m 16.2m⁴ 16g⁵ 17.1m 14.1m⁶
12.6m 17.2f³ 17.1m 18m⁵ Oct 20] close-coupled filly: poor maiden handicapper:
stays 2¼m: acts on firm going: usually held up: sometimes races freely/finds little.
Mrs Lucinda Featherstone

ANN'S FLYER   3 b.f. Cool Jazz 116 – Spice And Sugar 65 (Chilibang 120) [2003 57§:   **– §**
7f Jun 6] modest maiden at 2 yrs: well beaten only 3-y-o start: often blinkered: unreliable.
P. A. Blockley

ANN SUMMERS TWO (USA)   2 b.f. (Mar 9) Elusive Quality (USA) – Lakeland   **85**
(USA) (Alleged (USA) 138) [2003 5m⁶ 5m⁴ 5g⁶ 6g² 5m³ 6g² 7d⁵ 7g² 6m² Sep 23]
$10,000F, $50,000Y: good-bodied filly: second foal: dam unraced out of half-sister to
Erhaab: fairly useful maiden: in frame in varied races, including Queen Mary Stakes at
Royal Ascot (fourth to Attraction) and nurseries: stays easy 7f: acts on good to firm
going: blinkered (ran respectably) sixth start: sent to USA. *B. J. Meehan*

ANOTHER ASPECT (IRE)   4 b.g. Inzar (USA) 112 – The Aspecto Girl (IRE) 53   **–**
(Alzao (USA) 117) [2003 –: 14.4g p16g May 17] little form since 2001. *J. Cullinan*

ANOTHER BOTTLE (IRE)   2 b.c. (May 11) Cape Cross (IRE) 129 – Aster Aweke   **74**
(IRE) 87 (Alzao (USA) 117) [2003 6m 7m³ 8g³ Sep 27] IR 1,200F, 10,000Y: round-
barrelled colt: fifth foal: half-brother to 3-y-o Say What You See: dam, Irish 9f winner,
half-sister to smart performer up to 1½m in Ireland/USA Baba Karam: fair form in
maidens: third at Doncaster and Ripon: will be suited by 1¼m/1½m. *T. P. Tate*

ANOTHER CHOICE (IRE)   2 ch.c. (Feb 1) Be My Guest (USA) 126 – Gipsy Rose   **66**
Lee (IRE) 100 (Marju (IRE) 127) [2003 7m 8m⁶ 8m 6m 7d Nov 8] 17,500Y, 30,000
2-y-o: good-topped colt: first foal: dam 2-y-o 5f/6f winner: fair maiden: stays 1m: acts on
good to firm going: tongue tied after debut. *N. P. Littmoden*

ANOTHER CON (IRE)   2 b.f. (Mar 23) Lake Coniston (IRE) 131 – Sweet Unison   **55**
(USA) (One For All (USA)) [2003 p8g⁶ p8g³ Dec 20] €4,500Y: half-sister to 2 winners

in Germany by Waajib, including useful winner up to 1½m Bad Bertrich: dam unraced: modest form at Lingfield in maiden/minor event (third to Boxgrove): should stay 1¼m. *Mrs P. N. Dutfield*

ANOTHER DEAL (FR)   4 ch.g. Barathea (IRE) 127 – Mill Rainbow (FR) (Rainbow   **71 ?**
Quest (USA) 134) [2003 8.1d⁶ 7m 11.7f³ 7g 11.8g⁴ 11.7f Aug 17] workmanlike gelding: second foal: dam, French 10.5f winner, out of half-sister to Prix Jacques le Marois winner Miss Satamixa: fair maiden: seemingly best effort third start: should prove best at 1¼m/ 1½m: acts on firm ground, probably good to soft. *R. J. Hodges*

ANOTHER EXPLETIVE   2 b.f. (Apr 25) Wizard King 122 – French Project (IRE)   **43**
84 (Project Manager 111) [2003 f7g 6m 5.1m 5g f7g⁴ Oct 20] third foal: dam, maiden who stayed 1½m, winning hurdler: poor maiden: probably stays 7f: acts on good to firm going. *J. White*

ANOTHER FAUX PAS (IRE)   2 b.f. (Mar 21) Slip Anchor 136 – Pirie (USA)   **–**
(Green Dancer (USA) 132) [2003 7f Jun 25] €11,000Y: second foal: dam unraced out of half-sister to dam of Irish Oaks winner Wemyss Bight: last of 7 in maiden at Kempton. *R. Hannon*

ANOTHER GLIMPSE   5 b.g. Rudimentary (USA) 118 – Running Glimpse (IRE)   **75**
84 (Runnett 125) [2003 80: p6g⁶ p7g³ p6g² p6g² p5g⁵ p7g⁵ 6m 5g⁶ 7f⁵ 5m Jul 23] strong,   **a80**
close-coupled gelding: fairly useful handicapper on all-weather, fair on turf: best at 6f/ easy 7f: acts on firm ground and polytrack: usually tongue tied: sometimes races freely/ wanders: reliable. *Miss B. Sanders*

ANOTHER SECRET   5 b.m. Efisio 120 – Secrets of Honour (Belmez (USA) 131)   **55**
[2003 86: 8m 10m 8g 8g 8g 8d⁶ 8.2d p10g p10g⁴ Dec 20] sturdy mare: fairly useful handicapper for R. Hannon at 4 yrs: only modest in 2003, leaving J. M. Bradley after fifth start: stays 1¼m: acts on polytrack, soft and good to firm going: tried in blinkers/ cheekpieces. *G. L. Moore*

ANOTHER VICTIM   9 ch.g. Beveled (USA) – Ragtime Rose (Ragstone 128) [2003   **53**
65: 5g 5m Jun 26] leggy gelding: modest handicapper: best at 5f/6f: has form on good to firm ground, but all wins on good or softer (acts on heavy): has hung left/flashed tail: none too consistent. *M. R. Bosley*

ANOUSA (IRE)   2 b.c. (Apr 29) Intikhab (USA) 135 – Annaletta 89 (Belmez (USA)   **81**
131) [2003 7m² 7f⁵ 7m 8m* Oct 1] €80,000Y: strong, stocky colt: second foal: half-brother to 3-y-o Prince Nureyev: dam French 1½m winner from family of very smart performer up to 1½m Annus Mirabilis: fairly useful performer: won maiden at Newcastle by length from Tyzack, early reminders but finishing strongly: likely to be suited by 1¼m/1½m: moved poorly to post when last on third start. *P. Howling*

ANQOOD (IRE)   3 ch.f. Elmaamul (USA) 125 – Mayaasa (USA) 70 (Lyphard (USA)   **82**
132) [2003 6m 7.6m* 8.5m Jul 31] quite good-topped filly: fifth foal: half-sister to 3 winners by Lahib, including 6f winner Fatwa and 6f (at 2 yrs) and 1m winner Hirasah, both useful: dam, 1½m winner, closely related to high-class miler Maroof and to dam of Desert King: clearly best effort (fairly useful form) when making all in maiden at Chester in July: should stay at least 1m: raced only on good to firm ground: sold 25,000 gns. *B. Hanbury*

ANSWERED PROMISE (FR)   4 gr.g. Highest Honor (FR) 124 – Answered Prayer   **61**
(Green Desert (USA) 127) [2003 75: 9m 10.1m 8f 8m 9.2g* 8.3m 8m* 8m f8g p10g Dec 20] strong, short-backed gelding: has a quick action: modest performer: trained by J. Czerpak third/fourth starts: won claimers at Hamilton and Newcastle in August: left I. Semple after eighth start: stays 9f: acts on soft going, good to firm and all-weather: usually races prominently: none too consistent. *A. W. Carroll*

ANTEDILUVIAN   2 b.f. (May 4) Air Express (IRE) 125 – Divina Mia 66 (Dowsing   **91 p**
(USA) 124) [2003 7m* Oct 4] 30,000Y: big, well-made filly: has scope: fifth foal: half-sister to 3 winners, including useful 2001 2-y-o 6f winner Mine Host (by Elmaamul), later successful at 9f/1¼m in Hong Kong, and 3-y-o And Toto Too: dam, 2-y-o 6f winner who stayed 11f, out of useful half-sister to Shirley Heights: 20/1, won 12-runner maiden at Redcar by 6 lengths from Mystical Girl, slowly away but leading over 1f out and pushed clear: will stay 1m: sold 150,000 gns: should make a useful 3-y-o. *J. G. Given*

ANTHEMION (IRE)   6 ch.g. Night Shift (USA) – New Sensitive (Wattlefield 117)   **70**
[2003 8m⁴ 8.3d 8g⁶ 9.2g⁶ 8f⁵ 8.3m² 9.3d 9.2m 8.3g 7.9m² 8m⁵ Sep 15] good-topped gelding: fair performer: missed 2001 and 2002: stays 1m: acts on fibresand, firm and good to soft going. *Mrs J. C. McGregor*

AOL

ANTHONY ROYLE 5 ch.g. King's Signet (USA) 110 – La Thuile 46 (Statoblest –
120) [2003 48: f6g Mar 22] sparely-made gelding: poor maiden: well beaten only 5-y-o
start: tried blinkered. *A. Berry*

ANTHOS (GER) 2 b.f. (Jan 25) Big Shuffle (USA) 122 – Anemoni (GER) (Motley **91**
(USA) 123) [2003 6g² 6d⁶ 6m* 6f⁴ Sep 4] €22,000Y: rather leggy, lengthy filly: second
foal: half-sister to German 1m winner Amanka (by Dashing Blade): dam German 6.5f to
1¼m winner (including at 1m at 2 yrs): fairly useful performer: edged left when winning
maiden at Brighton in August: good 2¾ lengths fourth to Nyramba in listed event at
Salisbury, racing freely and reportedly finishing lame: will need to settle to stay beyond
6f: acts on firm going. *J. R. Fanshawe*

ANTICIPATING 3 b.g. Polish Precedent (USA) 131 – D'Azy 91 (Persian Bold 123) **93**
[2003 68p: 12f³ 12.1m* 14.6m² 16m 12f² 12g* 12d⁴ 13.9m⁶ 13.3m Sep 20] rather
lengthy, good-topped gelding: fairly useful performer: won maiden at Beverley in April
and handicap at Salisbury in July: good fourth to No Refuge in Tote Gold Trophy at
Goodwood next time: should stay beyond 14.6f (saddle slipped at 2m): acts on firm and
good to soft going, some promise on soft. *A. M. Balding*

ANTON DE LOOKA (IRE) 3 b.g. Sesaro (USA) 81 – Regal Fanfare (IRE) 94 –
(Taufan (USA) 119) [2003 –: 10g⁶ 12m Aug 5] little form. *R. F. Fisher*

ANTONIO CANOVA 7 ch.g. Komaite (USA) – Joan's Venture (Beldale Flutter –
(USA) 130) [2003 89: 7g Nov 1] stocky gelding: useful handicapper at 5 yrs: lightly raced
since and well beaten only start in 2003. *Bob Jones*

ANTONIUS PIUS (USA) 2 b.c. (Apr 23) Danzig (USA) – Catchascatchcan 122 **105**
(Pursuit of Love 124) [2003 7d⁵ 6m* 7m Oct 18] $1,500,000Y: close-coupled colt: first
foal: dam won all 4 starts (at around 1½m), including Yorkshire Oaks: useful form:
landed odds in 3-runner maiden at Gowran in May and Anheuser Busch Railway Stakes
at the Curragh (comfortably, by ½ length from Spanish Ace) in June: raced freely but far
from discredited when eleventh of 12 in Dewhurst Stakes at Newmarket: should stay 1m.
A. P. O'Brien, Ireland

ANTONY EBENEEZER 4 ch.c. Hurricane Sky (AUS) – Captivating (IRE) 63 **49**
(Wolfhound (USA) 126) [2003 50, a42: f12s² f12g* f11s⁴ f16.2g² 10.9m² 14.1m f14.8s
11.5g 11.8g 12.6f⁴ 11.6m 14.1m Aug 24] leggy colt: modest handicapper: won amateur
race at Southwell in January: effective at 11f to 2m: acts on fibresand and firm going,
seemingly not on softer than good: tongue tied last 3 outings: sometimes carries head
awkwardly: none too consistent. *C. R. Dore*

ANUVASTEEL 2 gr.c. (Mar 18) Vettori (IRE) 119 – Mrs Gray 61 (Red Sunset 120) **84**
[2003 6g 6m 6m⁵ 7d* 8m⁵ 8.3g 6g p7g⁵ p8g* p7g³ p8g² Dec 20] 42,000Y: leggy, quite
good-topped colt: half-brother to several winners, including useful 2002 2-y-o 5f
to 7f winner Steelaninch (by Inchinor), later 1m minor stakes winner in USA: dam
2-y-o 7f winner: fairly useful performer: won maiden at Epsom in July and nursery at
Lingfield in December: stays 1m: acts on polytrack, good to firm and good to soft going.
N. A. Callaghan

ANYAAS (IRE) 3 b.f. Green Desert (USA) 127 – Anwaar (IRE) 90 (Machiavellian **99**
(USA) 123) [2003 a7.5f* a8f⁴ 8g p8g Nov 2] third foal: dam, Irish 2-y-o 1m winner,
granddaughter of Coronation Stakes winner Kesar Queen: useful form: won maiden at
Nad Al Sheba in February: fourth to Mezzo Soprano in UAE 1000 Guineas there next
time: best effort when eighth to Musical Chimes in Poule d'Essai des Pouliches at
Longchamp third start: off 5½ months, slowly away after reportedly hitting head on stall
when well held in listed event at Lingfield final outing: stays 1m. *Saeed bin Suroor*

ANYHOW (IRE) 6 b.m. Distant Relative 128 – Fast Chick 93 (Henbit (USA) 130) **71**
[2003 75: p10g f9.4g³ f8g p10g 8m⁴ 10g p10g 10.3m⁴ 11.6g⁴ 8.2m³ 9.7f 11.6g* p12g
p10g² 11.6g 10m 10.9m* 10.9m⁶ 9.9m* p12g* p12g⁴ 10d Nov 6] angular mare: fair
handicapper: had a good 2003, winning at Windsor in June, Warwick (claiming event,
claimed from A. Reid £8,000) in September and at Salisbury (apprentices) and Lingfield
in October: effective at 1¼m/1½m: acts on all-weather, firm and soft going: usually held
up: sometimes wanders: tough. *Miss K. M. George*

AOLUS (GER) 4 b.c. Winged Love (IRE) 121 – Asuma (GER) (Surumu (GER)) [2003 **118**
11s² 11g* 11g* 11g* 12d Jul 27] first foal: dam German 9.5f winner: smart performer:
unbeaten at 3 yrs in maiden at Gelsenkirchen (off 6 months afterwards) and minor events
at Krefeld and Frankfurt (both by wide margins): improved in 2003, winning Grosser
Preis der Bremer Wirtschaft (by 1¼ lengths from Epalo) in April and Gerling-Preis (by
1½ lengths from Levirat) in May, both at Cologne, and Idee Hansa-Preis at Hamburg (by

69

length from Epalo) in June: pulled up lame final outing: stays 1½m: acts on heavy going. *A. Schutz, Germany*

A ONE (IRE)   4 b.g. Alzao (USA) 117 – Anita's Contessa (IRE) 68 (Anita's Prince **60**
126) [2003 65, a–: 8.2g³ 7d 7g 8.3m 7m f7g Nov 19] rather leggy gelding: modest **a–**
performer: well held after reappearance: stays 1m: acts on any turf going (below form on
all-weather): sometimes early to post: none too reliable. *B. Palling*

AONINCH   3 ch.f. Inchinor 119 – Willowbank 66 (Gay Fandango (USA) 132) [2003 **72**
61: 7g 7m 10d³ 10m 11.7m* 12.6m* 10g³ Oct 28] lengthy filly: fair performer: improved
in second half of year, winning handicap at Bath in August and minor event at Warwick
in September: free-going sort, but stays 12.6f: acts on firm and good to soft ground: held
up. *Mrs P. N. Dutfield*

APACHE POINT (IRE)   6 ch.g. Indian Ridge 123 – Ausherra (USA) 106 (Diesis **73**
133) [2003 68: 7m³ 8m⁴ 9m* 9.2g⁴ 8f³ 8.1g² 8.3m* 8.2g³ 9.2m 7.9m 10m 8m 9m² 8.2d⁴
Nov 6] rather leggy gelding: fair performer: won handicap at Redcar in May and minor
event at Hamilton in July: stays 9f: acts on any ground: has been early to post: sometimes
races freely: usually held up. *N. Tinkler*

APACHE QUEEN   3 b.f. Pennekamp (USA) 130 – Croeso Cynnes 70 (Most Welcome **56**
131) [2003 6g May 4] 10,000Y: second foal: dam, 5f and (including at 2 yrs) 6f winner:
16/1 and green, seventh of 17 to Desert Opal in maiden at Salisbury. *A. M. Balding*

APADI (USA)   7 ch.g. Diesis 133 – Ixtapa (USA) (Chief's Crown (USA)) [2003 –:   **–**
f11g f7g 10m Sep 18] lightly raced and no recent form on Flat: won over hurdles in June.
M. C. Chapman

APERITIF   2 ch.g. (Mar 30) Pivotal 124 – Art Deco Lady 51 (Master Willie 129) [2003 **74 p**
6.1m⁶ 5.1m⁶ p5g³ Nov 12] 27,000Y, 70,000 2-y-o: strong, good sort: third foal: dam,
maiden, stayed 1¾m: fair form in maidens: beaten 2 short heads by Darting at Lingfield
final start: should stay at least 6f: type to make a better 3-y-o. *W. J. Haggas*

APEX   2 ch.c. (Apr 9) Efisio 120 – Royal Loft 105 (Homing 130) [2003 6g⁴ 6m⁴ 5m³ **74**
6m³ 6m³ 6m 6g³ 7d Nov 8] 15,000Y: leggy, angular colt: has a short, round action:
half-brother to several winners, including fairly useful Irish 7f (including at 2 yrs) and 9f
winner Sir Slaves (by Salse) and 3-y-o Flying Express: dam 6f/7f winner who stayed 1m:
fair maiden: in frame 6 times, including in nursery: should stay 7f: acts on good to firm
going: reportedly had sore shins second start: sometimes finds little. *E. A. L. Dunlop*

APEX STAR (USA)   3 ch.c. Diesis 133 – Imroz (USA) 99 (Nureyev (USA) 131) **69**
[2003 95p: 9m⁶ 10m 7g 8m⁵ 8.5d Oct 4] smallish, sturdy colt: shows knee action: useful
at 2 yrs, just fair in 2003: should stay 1m: unraced on extremes of going: tried tongue tied:
often races freely: sold 14,000 gns, sent to Denmark. *H. R. A. Cecil*

APHRA BENN (IRE)   4 b.f. In The Wings 128 – Aigue 96 (High Top 131) [2003 67: **64**
p10g 11.8g³ 12g 11.6g⁶ Jun 30] rangy filly: modest maiden handicapper: stays 1½m:
acts on soft going, well held both starts on all-weather: often slowly away: carries head
awkwardly: sold 12,000 gns. *G. Wragg*

APOLLO GEE (IRE)   2 b.g. (Apr 6) Spectrum (IRE) 126 – Suspiria (IRE) 87 (Glen- **68**
stal (USA) 118) [2003 6g 6m³ 6g Oct 13] 6,200F: sixth foal: closely related to 1999 2-y-o
7f winner Gin Oclock (by Bin Ajwaad) and half-brother to winner in Turkey by Anshan:
dam, 5f winner in Italy at 2 yrs, half-sister to smart miler Ventiquattrofogli: best effort
(fair form) when third in maiden at Lingfield: will probably stay 7f. *B. J. Meehan*

APOLLONIUS (IRE)   6 ch.h. Nucleon (USA) 94 – Warthill Whispers 59 (Grey   **–**
Desire 115) [2003 53: f7s Jan 16] fair performer at best in Ireland: well held both starts in
Britain: tried tongue tied. *G. M. Moore*

APOLLO VICTORIA (FR)   6 b.g. Sadler's Wells (USA) 132 – Dame Solitaire   **–**
(CAN) (Halo (USA)) [2003 p10g Mar 15] close-coupled, good-topped gelding: useful
for A. O'Brien in 2000: tailed off in listed race at Lingfield on belated comeback: tried
visored/blinkered. *B. G. Powell*

APPALACHIAN TRAIL (IRE)   2 b.c. (Apr 6) Indian Ridge 123 – Karinski (USA) **78**
(Palace Music (USA) 129) [2003 7.1f 7m⁵ Jul 11] €50,000Y: useful-looking colt: fifth
foal: half-brother to 3 fairly useful winners, including 1999 2-y-o 6f winner Pekanski (by
Sri Pekan) and 3-y-o Makulu: dam unraced: better effort in maidens (fair form) when fifth
of 11 at York: should stay 1m: sold 18,000 gns. *J. H. M. Gosden*

APPETINA   2 b.f. (Mar 23) Perugino (USA) 84 – Tina Heights 79 (Shirley Heights **76**
130) [2003 6m² 7.2g³ 6.5m 8d³ Oct 14] 30,000Y: tall, quite good-topped filly: has a
fluent, round action: second foal: half-sister to 3-y-o Summitville: dam, 1¼m winner on

only start, half-sister to useful stayer Life of Riley: fair maiden: placed at Redcar and twice at Ayr: should stay at least 1¼m: acts on good to firm and good to soft ground. *J. G. Given*

APPLEACRE   4 b.f. Polar Falcon (USA) 126 – Absaloute Service 96 (Absalom 128)   **94 d**
[2003 86: f12g* p12g5 f12g4 14.6m p12g Nov 13] strong, useful-looking filly: fairly useful handicapper: won at Wolverhampton in January: left H. Cyzer and off 8 months before well held last 2 starts: stays 1½m: acts on all-weather, soft and good to firm going: races prominently. *B. R. Johnson*

APPROACH   3 gr.f. Darshaan 133 – Last Second (IRE) 121 (Alzao (USA) 117) [2003   **105**
101p: 10m* 12g4 14g 9.5f2 12d Nov 15] well-made filly: useful performer: reportedly fractured pelvis final 2-y-o start: landed odds in listed race at Newbury in June: blinkered, best effort when 4 lengths fourth of 6 to High Praise in Prix de Malleret at Saint-Cloud, carrying head awkwardly: 7¼ lengths second to Bien Nicole in Grade 2 WinStar Galaxy Stakes at Keeneland penultimate outing, final one for Sir Mark Prescott: stays 1½m: yet to race on soft/heavy going, probably acts on any other: free-going sort: has worn crossed noseband/had 2 handlers. *H. G. Motion, USA*

APPROVAL   4 b.c. Royal Applause 124 – Gentle Persuasion 95 (Bustino 136) [2003   **95**
105: 7m4 7.1g Aug 25] tall, lengthy colt: useful performer: easily better effort in 2003 on first start: barely stays 7f: acts on good to firm and good to soft going: tried blinkered: carries head high. *R. Hannon*

APRIL MISS (FR)   3 bl.f. Averti (IRE) 117 – Lady of Jakarta (USA) (Procida (USA)   **–**
129) [2003 7m 8.1m 8g f7g Jun 9] 1,000Y: fourth foal: dam, French 1m winner, half-sister to dam of Sulamani and Dream Well: well held in maidens: tried in cheekpieces. *John Allen*

APRIL STOCK   8 ch.m. Beveled (USA) – Stockline (Capricorn Line 111) [2003 95:   **97**
p13g 12m* p13g 9.9g2 14g 10f6 10m Sep 20] leggy mare: useful handicapper: came from long way back to win at Epsom in April: career-best effort when head second to Imperial Dancer at Goodwood 3 months later: best at 1¼m/1½m: acts on polytrack and on any turf ground: usually tongue tied: held up: reportedly in foal to Dr Fong. *G. A. Butler*

APSIS   2 b.c. (Mar 12) Barathea (IRE) 127 – Apogee 113 (Shirley Heights 130)   **111 p**
[2003 8g* 8g* Oct 14]
American Post and Three Valleys were the pick of the two-year-olds who raced in Khalid Abdulla's colours in Europe in 2003, but Apsis wasn't all that far behind them and, as the least experienced of this trio, is probably open to the most improvement as a three-year-old. Apsis had just two runs in his first season, both over a mile, accounting for three rivals in a slowly-run newcomers race at Long-champ in September and following up in good style in the far more competitive Prix Thomas Bryon at Saint-Cloud the following month. The Group 3 Thomas Bryon attracted six runners including two others who had also been successful on their previous starts, Always King in a listed event at the same course and Gwaihir, the only contender trained outside France, in a similar race at Deauville. Apsis, who started at odds on, broke best and led through the very early stages, then raced in third as Gwaihir led from Always King. Apsis was still travelling well when moving through to challenge early in the straight and, when shaken up around two furlongs out, quickly took command, showing signs of inexperience after hitting the front but continuing to draw clear. At the line Apsis had three lengths to spare over Gwaihir and there was a further length and a half back to third-placed Always

Prix Thomas Bryon, Saint-Cloud—Apsis wins easily from Gwaihir (visor) and Always King

King, with the other three well beaten off. Apsis showed plenty of speed, but judged on his pedigree he will almost certainly need further than a mile to be seen to best advantage at three and is likely to stay a mile and a half.

Apsis (b.c. Mar 12, 2001)	Barathea (IRE) (b 1990)	Sadler's Wells (b 1981)	Northern Dancer
			Fairy Bridge
		Brocade (b 1981)	Habitat
			Canton Silk
	Apogee (b 1990)	Shirley Heights (b 1975)	Mill Reef
			Hardiemina
		Bourbon Girl (b 1984)	Ile de Bourbon
			Fleet Girl

Barathea, the sire of Apsis, was best at a mile but plenty of his offspring stay much further than he did and the average distance of races won by his offspring aged three or more over the past four seasons is almost a mile and a quarter. Apogee, the dam, was a smart performer who stayed a mile and a half, winning the Prix du Royaumont at that trip, as did one of her five previous foals Dance Routine (by Sadler's Wells), who is closely related to Apsis. Dance Routine, also successful in the Prix de Royallieu, is a sister to one useful French performer at around a mile and a half in Light Ballet, and half-sister to another in Space Quest (by Rainbow Quest). Apogee is one of several winners produced by Bourbon Girl, runner-up in both the Oaks and the Irish Oaks. They include the Grand Prix de Chantilly winner Daring Miss, and the six-year-old Bourgeois, who showed useful form at a mile and a half and much further in the latest season. The next dam Fleet Girl, raced only at three, was a wide-margin winner at nine furlongs and a mile and a half on consecutive days at Tramore. Apsis looks a good prospect and, along with American Post and Three Valleys to name just two others, will give his owner a strong hand in the 2004 European classics. *A. Fabre, France*

AQRIBAA (IRE) 5 b. or br.g. Pennekamp (USA) 130 – Karayb (IRE) 93 (Last Tycoon 131) [2003 –: 9m 8.5m* 8.9m 8.5m 9.9d Sep 23] lengthy, angular gelding: only form (modest) in 2003 when winning amateur handicap at Beverley in August, edging right: best around 1m: acts on good to firm and good to soft ground: tried blinkered: unreliable. *A. J. Lockwood* **57 §**

AQUALUNG 2 b.c. (Mar 3) Desert King (IRE) 129 – Aquarelle (Kenmare (FR) 125) [2003 7m⁴ Jul 11] tall, good-topped colt: third foal: half-brother to fairly useful French 6f to 1m (including at 2 yrs) winner Coastline (by Night Shift): dam, useful French 2-y-o 1m winner, out of close relative to St Leger winner Toulon: 10/1, 8 lengths fourth of 11 in maiden at York, strong hold to post and racing freely: bred to stay at least 1m: should improve if all is well. *B. W. Hills* **78 p**

AQUA PURA (GER) 4 b.c. Acatenango (GER) 127 – Actraphane (Shareef Dancer (USA) 135) [2003 ?: f14.8s⁵ Sep 20] ex-German colt: fair winner for A. Trybuhl in 2002: well held both Flat starts in Britain: tried blinkered. *B. J. Curley* **–**

AQUARELLISTE (FR) 5 b.m. Danehill (USA) 126 – Agathe (USA) 114 (Manila (USA)) [2003 121: 10s* a10f Mar 29] big, strong, rather plain mare: good walker: very smart performer: won Prix Exbury at Saint-Cloud in March by 5 lengths from Caesarion, clear inside final 1f: well held on dirt debut in Dubai World Cup later in March: effective at 1¼m to 1½m: acted on soft and good to firm going: covered by Sadler's Wells. *E. Lellouche, France* **121**

AQUIFORM 3 ch.f. Cadeaux Genereux 131 – Aquarelle (Kenmare (FR) 125) [2003 7g Aug 10] 3,000 3-y-o: second foal: half-sister to fairly useful French 6f to 1m (including at 2 yrs) winner Coastline (by Night Shift): dam, useful French 2-y-o 1m winner, out of close relative to St Leger winner Toulon: 33/1 and green, eleventh of 19 in seller at Leicester. *K. A. Morgan* **–**

ARABIAN KNIGHT (IRE) 3 ch.g. Fayruz 116 – Cheerful Knight (IRE) (Mac's Imp (USA) 116) [2003 69, a61: f5g f5s⁴ p5g² f5s³ p5g* p5g² p5g³ 5m³ p5g⁴ 6m 5.7m* 5.7m 7.1g 5.1m⁶ Jul 24] close-coupled gelding: modest performer: won maiden at Lingfield in February and claimer at Bath (claimed from A. Berry £9,000) in May: stays 5.7f: acts on soft going, good to firm and all-weather: effective blinkered/visored or not: tends to hang left: races lazily: ungenuine. *R. J. Hodges* **64 §**

ARABIAN MOON (IRE) 7 ch.h. Barathea (IRE) 127 – Excellent Alibi (USA) (Exceller (USA) 129) [2003 91: p12g 20m 10.1m⁶ 13.3m Jul 19] leggy, quite good-topped horse: easy mover: fair at best in 2003: stays 21f: acts on polytrack, best turf efforts on good going or firmer: usually held up: often finds little: won 2 novice chases in August. *S. Dow*

ARABIE   5 b.g. Polish Precedent (USA) 131 – Always Friendly 111 (High Line 125)   **95**
[2003 112: 12f 10.3f⁵ Jun 29] lengthy, angular gelding: smart performer in 2002: just useful form in 2 handicaps for new yard in 2003, finding little in latter: best form around 1¼m: yet to race on heavy going, acts on any other: free-going sort. *M. Johnston*

ARABIN   4 b.g. Bin Ajwaad (IRE) 119 – Just Julia (Natroun (FR) 128) [2003 52: p7g   **–**
f7g f5s Feb 27] leggy, quite good-topped gelding: modest maiden at best: well beaten in 2003. *J. M. P. Eustace*

ARAF   4 b.g. Millkom 124 – Euphyllia 70 (Superpower 113) [2003 54: f12s 8.5m 6.9m   **37**
10f 8m Sep 18] just poor form in 2003: tried in cheekpieces/blinkers. *N. Wilson*

ARAGLIN   4 b.g. Sadler's Wells (USA) 132 – River Cara (USA) 86 (Irish River (FR)   **–**
131) [2003 –§: f16s Feb 4] useful-looking gelding: fair winner at 2 yrs: well held since: often blinkered: won maiden hurdle in October. *Miss S. J. Wilton*

ARAGON DANCER   2 b.g. (Apr 10) Aragon 118 – Jambo 68 (Rambo Dancer (CAN)   **–**
107) [2003 6d 6g 8.5g⁶ Sep 10] 1,200Y, resold 1,400Y: fourth foal: dam 7f (at 2 yrs)/1m winner: well beaten in maidens. *T. M. Jones*

ARAGON'S BOY   3 ch.g. Aragon 118 – Fancier Bit (Lion Cavern (USA) 117) [2003   **75**
6m 7f⁵ 8.1m⁴ Jul 24] first foal: dam unraced out of useful close relation to top-class French/US 1m/9f winner Thrill Show: best effort (fair form) in maidens when fourth to Gift Horse at Sandown: stays 1m. *H. Candy*

ARAKAN (USA)   3 br.c. Nureyev (USA) 131 – Far Across (Common Grounds 118)   **119**
[2003 91p: 8.1m* 8g² 7m* 7m² 7g² 8m⁶ 7m³ Oct 18] good-topped, attractive colt: smart performer: won maiden at Warwick in April and handicap at York in May: placed after in Jersey Stakes at Royal Ascot (2½ lengths second to Membership), Lennox Stakes at

Niarchos Family's "Arakan"

Goodwood (unlucky head second to Nayyir, persistently short of room and finishing very strongly) and Challenge Stakes at Newmarket (¾-length third to Just James): effective at 7f/1m: raced only on good/good to firm going: usually waited with: below form when sweating sixth start. *Sir Michael Stoute*

ARAMUS (CHI) 6 b.h. Royal Danzig (USA) – Anysha (CHI) (Baalbek (CHI)) [2003 **114** 113: 5g⁴ 5.8m* 6s²ᵈ 6.8g⁶ a6g*ᵈⁱˢ 5.8g* a6g* Sep 28] big, leggy ex-Chilean horse: smart performer: winner of 10 of his 15 starts in native country: won 3 listed races in Scandinavia and Polar Million Cup at Ovrevoll in 2002: respectable fourth to Needwood Blade in Palace House Stakes at Newmarket on reappearance: won listed races at Taby in June and Jagersro (disqualified/failed dope test) in August, and Lambada Taby Open Sprint Championship (by short head from Musadif) and handicap at Jagersro in September: effective at 5f to 6.8f: acts on soft, good to firm going and dirt: speedy. *F. Castro, Sweden*

ARBIE (CAN) 4 b.g. Mountain Cat (USA) – Empress of Love (USA) (Czaravich **–** (USA)) [2003 –: p10g 10m 9.7g Sep 1] maiden handicapper: no form since 2 yrs: has worn cheekpieces/visor. *Mrs L. C. Jewell*

ARCALIS 3 gr.g. Lear Fan (USA) 130 – Aristocratique 71 (Cadeaux Genereux 131) **100 p** [2003 72: 8m 12g⁴ 12.1d⁵ 10m* 10m* 10m³ 10.3g² 10.3m⁴ 10f* 10.3g² Sep 13] tall, quite good-topped gelding: useful handicapper: won at Leicester and Pontefract in June and Newmarket in August: very good short-head second of 18 to Tug of Love at Doncaster final start: effective at 1¼m/1½m: acts on firm and good to soft ground: usually waited with: capable of better still. *Mrs J. R. Ramsden*

ARC EL CIEL (ARG) 5 b.g. Fitzcarraldo (ARG) – Ardoise (USA) (Diamond Pros- **–** pect (USA) 126) [2003 65: 7f2g* 7f7s* 7f7g* 7f7g³ 8.5s² 8.5g³ 8.3d p8g 7f7s* 7f7g⁶ 7f7s² **a82** Dec 31] fairly useful performer: won 2 sellers (left B. R. Millman after first one) in January, handicap in February and minor event (after 6-month absence) in December, all at Wolverhampton: effective at 6f (given test) to 8.5f: acts on fibresand: visored earlier in career, and final start (ran well): game. *Mrs S. A. Liddiard*

ARC EN CIEL 5 b.g. Rainbow Quest (USA) 134 – Nadia Nerina (CAN) 82 (Northern **–** Dancer) [2003 –: p10g Dec 29] useful-looking gelding: fairly useful handicapper at 3 yrs: lightly raced and well held since: tried visored/tongue tied. *G. L. Moore*

ARCHDUKE FERDINAND (FR) 5 ch.g. Dernier Empereur (USA) 125 – Lady **97** Norcliffe (USA) (Norcliffe (CAN)) [2003 111d: 18.7m 16.2m⁵ 13.9m² 16.2f⁴ 18m 16g Nov 5] strong, close-coupled gelding: useful handicapper nowadays: creditable efforts in 2003 only on second to fourth starts, including when in frame at York and Ascot: best form at 2m+: well held only run on heavy going: acts on any other: has worn cheekpieces: often races freely. *P. F. I. Cole*

ARCHERFIELD (IRE) 2 ch.f. (Apr 27) Docksider (USA) 124 – Willow River **64** (CAN) 66 (Vice Regent (CAN)) [2003 p7g 7m 6g⁵ 7.1g⁵ Nov 5] €30,000Y: close-coupled filly: second foal: dam third at 7f: modest maiden: should stay 1m: raced freely final start. *J. W. Hills*

ARCHIE BABE (IRE) 7 ch.g. Archway (IRE) 115 – Frensham Manor (Le Johnstan **74** 123) [2003 62§: f14g 12g* 10.1d⁴ 12.4g 11.9g⁴ 12g* 11.2g 11.1g⁴ 13.1d 10m 10s Nov 3] workmanlike gelding: fair handicapper: won at Doncaster (apprentices) in March and Pontefract in May: effective at 1¼m/1½m: below form on firm going, acts on any other turf and fibresand: usually held up. *J. J. Quinn*

ARCHIRONDEL 5 b.g. Bin Ajwaad (IRE) 119 – Penang Rose (NZ) (Kingdom Bay **70** (NZ)) [2003 76: 8f⁴ 8.3d 8m 10.3m 10m 9.7m⁵ 10f⁵ 10m⁶ 10.9m 10.9m³ 11.7f Oct 12] smallish gelding: fair handicapper: best at 1m/1¼m: acts on firm ground, probably not on softer than good: has raced freely/finished weakly: usually held up: sold 7,800 gns. *John Berry*

ARCHMAIL (USA) 3 br.c. Arch (USA) 127 – Crafty Nan (USA) (Crafty Prospector **68 ?** (USA)) [2003 10m⁵ 10m 10m⁴ Aug 14] $35,000F, $100,000Y: strong, well-made colt: half-brother to several winners, including smart 1995 2-y-o 5f/5.5f winner Lucky Lionel and fairly useful 7f winner Rushmore (both by Mt Livermore): dam unraced: easily best effort in maidens when slow-starting fifth at Leicester: possibly amiss after: sold 8,000 gns. *J. H. M. Gosden*

ARCHON (IRE) 6 ch.g. Archway (IRE) 115 – Lindas Delight 54 (Batshoof 122) [2003 **47** 51, a60: p8g² p8g⁴ p7g⁶ p8g⁶ 10.9m⁶ f8.5g 8m Jun 2] strong gelding: modest performer **a64** on all-weather, poor on turf: probably best at 1m/1¼m nowadays: acts on all-weather and good to firm ground: tongue tied earlier in career: sometimes looks less than keen. *Mrs P. N. Dutfield*

ARCTIC BLUE 3 b.g. Polar Prince (IRE) 117 – Miss Sarajane 74 (Skyliner 117) [2003 –
67, a–: 8g 14.1m 11.6d 14.1m Jul 2] modest maiden at 2 yrs: well held in 2003.
J. S. Moore

ARCTIC BURST (USA) 3 b.g. Royal Academy (USA) 130 – Polar Bird 111 (Thatch- **85**
ing 131) [2003 95: 6g* 7m Jun 28] strong, lengthy gelding: has scope: has a quick, fluent
action: fairly useful performer, lightly raced: landed odds in maiden at Pontefract in May:
only eighth in handicap at Chester following month: effective at 6f/7f: raced on good/
good to firm ground: tongue tied in 2003: sold 16,000 gns in August, joined D. Shaw.
B. W. Hills

ARCTIC DESERT 3 b.g. Desert Prince (IRE) 130 – Thamud (IRE) (Lahib (USA) **100**
129) [2003 77p: p7g* 8f⁵ 7g 7g 7d⁴ 7m³ 6m⁵ 7f² Oct 11] big, good-topped gelding:
impresses in appearance and has plenty of scope: useful performer: impressive winner of
maiden at Lingfield in April: good efforts 3 of last 4 starts, length second to Naahy in
handicap at York final one: free-going sort, but stays 7f: acts on polytrack, firm and good
to soft going: tried tongue tied. *A. M. Balding*

ARCTIC FALCON (IRE) 4 b.f. Polar Falcon (USA) 126 – Chandni (IRE) (Ahonoora –
122) [2003 64: p6g f6g Jan 21] rather angular filly: modest performer: well held in 2003:
should stay 7f: acts on good to firm going and fibresand. *S. L. Keightley*

ARCTIC QUEEN 2 br.f. (Apr 2) Linamix (FR) 127 – Thamud (IRE) (Lahib (USA) –
129) [2003 f8g Dec 19] second foal: half-sister to 3-y-o Arctic Desert: dam, unraced, out
of sister to top-class 1½m performer Celestial Storm and half-sister to Ribblesdale winner
Thawakib, latter dam of Sakhee: 20/1, well beaten in maiden at Southwell, starting very
slowly. *A. M. Balding*

ARDENT LADY 3 b.f. Alhaarth (IRE) 126 – Arvika (FR) (Baillamont (USA) 124) **79**
[2003 67: 8m⁵ 7g 9.3m* 9m² 9f⁶ Jul 2] quite attractive filly: fair handicapper: won at
Carlisle in June: had heels clipped and eased final outing: will stay 1¼m: raced only on
good ground or firmer. *E. A. L. Dunlop*

ARDGOWAN 6 b.g. Ardkinglass 114 – Final Fling 49 (Last Tycoon 131) [2003 f11s –
f14.8g Feb 1] of little account: tried visored. *I. Semple*

ARDKEEL LASS (IRE) 2 ch.f. (May 8) Fumo di Londra (IRE) 108 – Wot-A-Noise **67**
(IRE) (Petorius 117) [2003 5.1m³ 5.1m² 5.1g³ 6g 5d⁶ Oct 4] €2,000Y: second foal: sister
to winner in Greece: dam unraced: fair performer: won seller at Chepstow (sold from
B. Palling 27,000 gns) in June by 8 lengths: mostly creditable efforts in minor events/
nurseries after: needs to settle to stay 6f: races prominently. *D. K. Ivory*

ARDWELSHIN (FR) 5 b.g. Ajdayt (USA) 87 – Reem Dubai (IRE) 63 (Nashwan **54 d**
(USA) 135) [2003 58: p10g p12g⁶ 10.2f⁴ 10.9m 9.7m 10.2m 9m 8f 8.1m 7g Jul 26]
ex-Irish gelding: modest handicapper: won twice in 2002: lost his form after third start
and left B. Powell after penultimate outing: barely stays 1½m: acts on polytrack and firm
going: usually wears headgear: sold 2,200 gns (privately). *Mrs P. Townsley*

AREEB (IRE) 3 b.f. Emarati (USA) 74 – Racing Brenda 72 (Faustus (USA) 118) **38**
[2003 42: 5m 5.1f⁴ 5m 5.1m 5m May 14] lengthy filly: poor maiden: best at 5f: acts on
fibresand and good to firm ground: visored in 2003. *J. D. Czerpak*

ARE YOU THERE 2 b.f. (May 12) Presidium 124 – Scoffera 63 (Scottish Reel 123) **64 d**
[2003 5m³ f5g* 5m* 5f 6g 8m f6g f5g⁶ f6g Dec 15] 3,300Y: rather leggy, workmanlike
filly: fifth foal: dam, 1m/1¼m winner (also won over hurdles), half-sister to useful
sprinter Bid For Blue: modest performer: won maiden at Southwell and claimer at
Beverley in April: well below form last 5 starts, including in visor/blinkers: should stay
6f: acts on fibresand and good to firm going. *T. D. Barron*

ARFABEAT 3 ch.f. Abou Zouz (USA) 109 – Sans Egale (FR) (Lashkari 128) [2003 –
40: p8g Jan 7] poor maiden: should stay at least 1m: has carried head high. *J. S. Moore*

ARFINNIT (IRE) 2 b.g. (Feb 26) College Chapel 122 – Tidal Reach (USA) 68 (Kris **84**
S (USA)) [2003 5m 5s³ 6g⁶ 6f⁵ 6g* 7d⁶ 6m³ 6f 8.1g 6d Sep 10] IR 13,000F, 33,000Y:
good-topped gelding: has a quick action: fourth foal: half-brother to useful 2000 2-y-o 5f
to 1m winner Innit (by Distinctly North), later US Grade 2 1¼m winner, and 1999 2-y-o
5f winner Step Ahead (by Shalford): dam 2-y-o 1m winner who stayed 10.5f: fairly useful
performer: won nursery at Ayr in July: creditable effort after only when third in similar
event at Haydock: should stay 7f: acts on firm going: visored final start. *M. R. Channon*

ARGAMIA (GER) 7 b.m. Orfano (GER) – Arkona (GER) 108 (Aspros (GER)) [2003 **55**
59: 14.1m³ 12m 14.6m Jun 28] tall, angular mare: modest handicapper: effective at 1½m

(given test) to 2m: acts on fibresand, heavy and good to firm going: blinkered 3 times at 4 yrs: usually held up. *P. J. McBride*

ARGENT 2 b.c. (Jan 29) Barathea (IRE) 127 – Red Tiara (USA) 60 (Mr Prospector (USA)) [2003 5d³ 6d⁵ f7g⁵ f7g Aug 8] 30,000Y: first foal: dam, disappointing maiden, closely related to very smart Japanese sprinter Meiner Love out of 1000 Guineas runner-up Heart of Joy: modest maiden: will probably stay 1m: tongue tied last 2 outings. *D. Carroll* **55**

ARGENT FACILE (IRE) 6 b.g. Midhish 109 – Rosinish (IRE) (Lomond (USA) 128) [2003 6m 5g 6m Aug 8] lengthy, quite attractive gelding: one-time fairly useful performer: unraced in 2002, no form in 2003: well held only try in blinkers: sometimes tongue tied: tends to carry head high/hang. *H. J. Collingridge* **–**

ARGENTUM 2 b.g. (May 4) Sillery (USA) 122 – Frustration 108 (Salse (USA) 128) [2003 8m 8.2m Oct 28] big, plain gelding: half-brother to 1¼m winner Star Protector (by Hector Protector): dam, 1¼m winner, half-sister to US Grade 1 9f winner Mister Wonderful: well held in maidens at Newmarket (signs of ability after missing break) and Nottingham. *Lady Herries* **–**

ARGONAUT 3 ch.g. Rainbow Quest (USA) 134 – Chief Bee 89 (Chief's Crown (USA)) [2003 10m³ 10f* Jun 14] 200,000Y: good-bodied gelding: third foal: brother to smart 1½m winner Beekeeper and half-brother to useful winner around 1m in Scandinavia Cabriac (by Machiavellian): dam, 9f to 14.6f winner, sister to Racing Post Trophy winner Be My Chief from family of high-class miler Shavian and Gold Cup winner Paean: landed odds in 10-runner maiden at Sandown (fairly useful form) in June by 3 lengths from Skelligs Rock, still seeming green but just pushed out to go clear from 2f out: subsequently gelded: should stay 1½m: looked open to considerable improvement. *Sir Michael Stoute* **86 p**

ARICOVAIR (IRE) 3 ch.g. Desert Prince (IRE) 130 – Linoise (FR) 108 (Caerwent 123) [2003 8g 10m p10g May 24] 11,500Y: heavy-bodied gelding: first foal: dam French sprinter: well held in maidens: tongue tied final start. *Mrs A. J. Bowlby* **–**

ARIES (GER) 3 ch.f. Big Shuffle (USA) 122 – Auenlust (GER) (Surumu (GER)) [2003 79: 8.1m³ 6.1m² 7f f7s 6m Sep 18] lengthy, workmanlike filly: fair handicapper: stays 7f: acts on firm and soft going: visored last 2 outings, slowly away on penultimate. *M. J. Wallace* **76**

ARIZONA (IRE) 5 b.g. Sadler's Wells (USA) 132 – Marie de Beaujeu (FR) 108 (Kenmare (FR) 125) [2003 12.3m Apr 2] strong gelding: no form. *B. S. Rothwell* **–**

ARJAY 5 b.g. Shaamit (IRE) 127 – Jenny's Call (Petong 126) [2003 86: 8.1g 9.9m² 10g⁴ 11.9m 10.1m 8m 8.2m Oct 22] tall, rather leggy gelding: just fair performer in 2003: effective at 7f to 1¼m: acts on heavy and good to firm going: blinkered last 3 starts at 4 yrs: none too reliable. *Andrew Turnell* **65**

ARK ADMIRAL 4 b.g. Inchinor 119 – Kelimutu 58 (Top Ville 129) [2003 89: 10g⁶ 10d 10m 10m 10m Jul 28] good-bodied gelding: fairly useful performer in 2002: well below form in 2003: tried blinkered: free-going type. *B. J. Meehan* **68 d**

ARKHOLME 2 b.g. (Feb 8) Robellino (USA) 127 – Free Spirit (IRE) (Caerleon (USA) 132) [2003 7.5m⁴ 8.1d* Sep 27] useful-looking gelding: second foal: half-brother to 3-y-o Perfect Love: dam unraced: fairly useful form: won maiden at Haydock by short head from Asiatic, getting up close home: will be suited by 1¼m/1½m: open to progress. *W. J. Haggas* **81 p**

ARMADA GROVE 3 ch.f. Fleetwood (IRE) 107 – Wannaplantatree 72 (Niniski (USA) 125) [2003 75: p7g p8g f7g⁶ Feb 14] leggy, unfurnished filly: fair performer at 2 yrs: well held in handicaps in 2003: visored final start. *A. P. Jarvis* **–**

ARMAGNAC 5 b.g. Young Ern 120 – Arianna Aldini (Habitat 134) [2003 96: 6g 6m 5g 6g 6m* 6f 6g⁴ 6g⁶ 6f Jul 12] tall, good-topped gelding: unimpressive mover: fairly useful handicapper: won at Haydock in June: stays 6f: yet to race on heavy going, acts on any other (unsuitable trip run on all-weather): tried in cheekpieces: occasionally slowly away/pulls hard. *M. A. Buckley* **89**

ARMENTIERES 2 b.f. (Mar 9) Robellino (USA) 127 – Perfect Poppy 73 (Shareef Dancer (USA) 135) [2003 6g⁶ f7f³ f6g 7.1m⁶ 8f³ 8m 10f 8.2m* 8d⁴ f8.5g³ p8g⁵ f8g³ f8.5s Dec 31] deep-girthed filly: third foal: dam 1½m winner: modest performer: left J. Eustace after second start: won seller at Nottingham in October: should be suited by 1¼m/1½m: acts on all-weather, firm and good to soft going: blinkered last 6 starts: unreliable. *J. L. Spearing* **59 §**
a55 §

ARMS ACROSSTHESEA 4 b.g. Namaqualand (USA) – Zolica 60 (Beveled (USA)) – [2003 70: 10.1m 9.3g 7.9m 7.1f 12m⁶ 10g 6.9m 8m Sep 18] leggy gelding: fair handicapper at 3 yrs: no form in 2003: tried in headgear. *F. P. Murtagh*

ARNBI DANCER 4 b.g. Presidium 124 – Travel Myth 66§ (Bairn (USA) 126) [2003 – 63: f6s² f6g³ f7g⁴ f6g 6d 6f f7s² Sep 6] good-topped gelding: fair performer on all- **a66** weather: likely to prove best at 6f/7f: acts on fibresand, little form on turf: wore cheek-pieces penultimate start: sometimes wanders/looks less than keen. *P. C. Haslam*

AROGANT PRINCE 6 ch.g. Aragon 118 – Versaillesprincess (Legend of France **73 d** (USA) 124) [2003 72, a86: f6g f5g⁵ 5m³ 5m³ 6m⁶ 6d⁵ 6m⁴ 5m f7s 6m⁵ 5.2m⁶ f6s f6s² 6.1f 5d Nov 4] smallish gelding: fair handicapper: steadily regressed in 2003: left I. Semple after seventh start, A. Carroll after ninth and Mrs N. Macauley after fourteenth: effective at 5f to easy 7f: acts on any turf going and fibresand: sometimes wears blinkers/cheek-pieces. *I. Semple*

AROUSHA (USA) 3 ch.g. King of Kings (IRE) 125 – Hushi (USA) (Riverman (USA) – 131) [2003 71: 8g p10g⁶ May 24] useful-looking gelding: form (fair) from 3 runs in maidens only on debut: dead. *E. A. L. Dunlop*

ARPEGGIO 8 b.g. Polar Falcon (USA) 126 – Hilly 96 (Town Crier 119) [2003 80, a?: **80** f8g* f8g² f7s f9.4g² p10g³ p10g f8.5g² 8.5m³ 8.2d² 8.3g 10m² 8m³ 9.2m⁴ 9m³ Sep 15] **a84** good-topped gelding: had a useful handicapper: fairly useful handicapper: won at Southwell in January: was effective at 1m/easy 1¼m: acted on all-weather, firm and soft going: blinkered once: dead. *D. Nicholls*

ARRAN 3 ch.c. Selkirk 129 – Humble Pie 92 (Known Fact (USA) 135) [2003 – 8.2f p8g p7g p6g Nov 13] 140,000F, £2,800 3-y-o: sturdy colt: brother to untrustworthy 7f/1m winner Rimatara, closely related to smart sprinter Leap For Joy (by Sharpo), and half-brother to 3 winners, including 4-y-o Pie High: dam, 2-y-o 6f winner, half-sister to very smart 6f/7f performer College Chapel: well held in maidens: unseated rider leaving stall on debut. *H. J. Collingridge*

ARRAN SCOUT (IRE) 2 b.g. (Feb 21) Piccolo 121 – Evie Hone (IRE) 69 (Royal **74** Academy (USA) 130) [2003 8m 8d⁴ Nov 7] 8,500Y: big, strong gelding: first foal: dam, lightly-raced maiden (virtually refused to race final outing), half-sister to US Grade 2 1m/ 9f winner Uncharted Haven: easily better effort in maidens (fair form) when 1½ lengths fourth of 24 to Hello It's Me at Doncaster: likely to stay 1¼m. *Mrs L. Stubbs*

ARRESTING 3 b.g. Hector Protector (USA) 124 – Misbelief 107 (Shirley Heights **86 +** 130) [2003 9d³ 10d² 12g² 11.1g² Sep 27] 11,500Y: leggy, useful-looking gelding: third foal: half-brother to Italian 7.5f winner by Polar Falcon: dam 1¼m to 1¾m winner: fairly useful form in maidens: good second to Phoenix Reach at Newbury penultimate start: will stay 1¾m: stumbled on bend at Ripon final start: may still be capable of better. *J. R. Fanshawe*

ARRGATT (IRE) 2 gr.c. (Feb 21) Intikhab (USA) 135 – Nuit Chaud (USA) (Wood- **– p** man (USA) 126) [2003 7m Oct 3] 60,000Y: lengthy colt: third foal: half-brother to winner in USA (including at 2 yrs) by Fastness: dam, ran twice in USA, half-sister to dam of Danehill Dancer: 16/1 and green, well held in 23-runner maiden at Newmarket, slowly away: should do better. *M. A. Jarvis*

ARROW 4 b.g. Pivotal 124 – Cremets 94 (Mummy's Pet 125) [2003 57p: 8.3d 8m Jun – 20] big gelding: modest maiden, lightly raced: well held in handicaps in 2003: should stay 1m: blinkered final start. *R. A. Fahey*

ARRY DASH 3 b.g. Fraam 114 – Miletrian Cares (IRE) 67 (Hamas (IRE) 125§) [2003 **92** 79: f8g* p10g² 9d 8.3g* 8.1m⁵ Apr 25] small gelding: fairly useful performer: won minor event at Southwell in January and handicap at Windsor (flicked tail) in April: stays 1¼m: acts on all-weather and good to soft going. *M. R. Channon*

ARTE ET LABORE (IRE) 3 b.f. Raphane (USA) 102 – Bouffant (High Top 131) **46 §** [2003 58, a48: 7m 8.2d 8d⁶ 6.9f² 7.1f 8.5m 8.1m 10m⁴ Aug 30] lengthy filly: poor maiden **a– §** handicapper: probably stays easy 1¼m: acts on firm going, good to soft and fibresand: blinkered final start: sometimes slowly away: unreliable. *K. A. Ryan*

ART EXPERT (FR) 5 b.g. Pursuit of Love 124 – Celtic Wing (Midyan (USA) 124) **– §** [2003 50d: f16s⁵ f16.2g⁵ 21.6m Apr 14] sturdy gelding: disappointing maiden: usually wears headgear: carries head high: unreliable. *Mrs N. Macauley*

ARTHUR PENDRAGON 3 b.g. Botanic (USA) – Blue Room 70 (Gorytus (USA) **49 §** 132) [2003 65p: p8g⁴ 8f Mar 31] best effort in maidens only run at 2 yrs: has refused to enter stall, and unseated (reared as stall opened) second outing: bred to stay 1¼m: one to treat with caution. *B. W. Hills*

ARTHURS KINGDOM (IRE)   7 b.g. Roi Danzig (USA) – Merrie Moment (IRE)   – (Taufan (USA) 119) [2003 40: f16s Feb 13] tall, angular gelding: poor maiden handicapper: stays 1¾m: acts on good to firm ground, good to soft and fibresand: sometimes visored: wore cheekpieces (well held) only run in 2003: successful over hurdles in March. *Miss Kate Milligan*

ARTIC REASON (IRE)   4 b.g. Perugino (USA) 84 – Vendetta Valentino (USA)   – (Bering 136) [2003 55: p10g Jan 18] IR 10,000Y: first foal: dam, German 1¼m winner, half-sister to Criterium de Saint-Cloud winner Magistros lightly-raced maiden: sold €3,200 in February. *Declan Gillespie, Ireland*

ARTIE   4 b.g. Whittingham (IRE) 104 – Calamanco 71 (Clantime 101) [2003 99: 5.1m   **88** 5m 5v 6f⁵ 5m³ 5f 6m² 6m 5m⁶ 5s³ 5d Nov 7] big, good-topped gelding: fairly useful handicapper nowadays: best efforts of season when placed at Newcastle on fifth start and Ripon on seventh: effective at 5f/easy 6f: probably acts on any going: usually races up with pace. *T. D. Easterby*

ARTIFACT   5 b.m. So Factual (USA) 120 – Ancient Secret (Warrshan (USA) 117)   – [2003 –, a73d: f8s Jan 14] tall, lengthy mare: one-time fair handicapper: no form since early in 2002: tried blinkered: held up. *J. A. Pickering*

ARTISIA (IRE)   3 ch.f. Peintre Celebre (USA) 137 – Almaaseh (IRE) 63 (Dancing   – Brave (USA) 140) [2003 –: 8f² 7m Aug 18] well beaten in minor event and 2 maidens. *W. R. Muir*

ARTISTICIMPRESSION (IRE)   2 b.c. (Feb 8) Rainbow Quest (USA) 134 – Entice   **70** (FR) 111 (Selkirk (USA) 129) [2003 7m 7m⁶ Sep 17] good-bodied colt: third foal: half-brother to fairly useful 2002 French 2-y-o 5.5f winner Energetic Star (by Anabaa): dam, 7f (at 2 yrs) to 1¼m winner, out of half-sister to dam of top-class Japanese 1m/1¼m winner Agnes Digital: better effort in maidens (fair form) when 5¾ lengths sixth to Eden Rock at Yarmouth, racing freely: should be suited by 1¼m/1½m. *E. A. L. Dunlop*

ARTISTIC LAD   3 ch.c. Peintre Celebre (USA) 137 – Maid For The Hills 101 (Indian   – Ridge 123) [2003 87p: 10g Jul 4] lengthy colt: won maiden at Leicester on only run at 2 yrs: well held in listed race at Sandown, only outing in 2003: should stay 1¼m. *Sir Michael Stoute*

ARTISTIC STYLE   3 b.c. Anabaa (USA) 130 – Fine Detail (IRE) 93 (Shirley Heights   **84 ?** 130) [2003 8g³ 8g 5.5d² 8m² 10d³ Oct 14] ex-French colt: third foal: half-brother to fairly useful 7f winner Fine Arts (by Cadeaux Genereux): dam, 1½m winner on only start, half-sister to French performer up to 12.5f De Quest and US Grade 1 9f/1¼m winner Wandesta, both very smart: fairly useful form when placed in newcomers event at Longchamp and minor event at Deauville first/third starts: left Mme C. Head-Maarek, better effort in Britain (just fair form) when third to Shouette in maiden at Ayr final outing: probably stays 1¼m: unraced on extremes of going. *B. Ellison*

ARTISTRY   3 b.f. Night Shift (USA) – Arriving 105 (Most Welcome 131) [2003 54,   **64** a64: 10m³ 10f³ 10m³ 10.3g⁵ 10.3m⁵ 9f³ 9m⁴ 10m⁵ 10m⁴ 8g Oct 31] sturdy, lengthy filly: modest maiden: below form last 3 starts: stays 1¼m: acts on polytrack and firm going. *P. Howling*

ARTISTS LICENCE   2 gr.g. (Feb 20) Linamix (FR) 127 – Once Upon A Time 77   **– p** (Teenoso (USA) 135) [2003 p7g 8g Oct 25] sixth living foal: half-brother to 3 winners, including smart winner up to 1½m Arabian Story (by Sharrood) and fairly useful 1¼m winner Island Story (by Shirley Heights), who both stayed 2m: dam, 8.5f (at 2 yrs) and 1½m winner, sister to smart 1¼m performer Starlet: backward, signs of ability in maidens at Lingfield and Newbury: likely to do better at 1¼m+. *R. Charlton*

ART TRADER (USA)   2 b.c. (Mar 14) Arch (USA) 127 – Math (USA) (Devil's Bag   **95 p** (USA)) [2003 8m* 8d⁴ Nov 7] $130,000Y: big, good-topped colt: has a quick action: sixth foal: half-brother to 3 winners, including US Grade 3-placed winner It All Adds Up (by Our Emblem): dam, minor winner in US, out of half-sister to smart miler Emperor Jones and William Hill Futurity winner Bakharoff: useful form when winning maiden at Newmarket in October by neck from Buckeye Wonder (pair clear), travelling well and getting up near finish: only fourth in minor event at Doncaster on softer going: likely to stay 1¼m: type to train on well. *Mrs A. J. Perrett*

ARTZOLA (IRE)   3 b.f. Alzao (USA) 117 – Polistatic 53 (Free State 125) [2003 8.3m   – 8m⁵ p7g Oct 27] good-bodied filly: seventh foal: half-sister to 1¼m winner Regal Gallery (by Royal Academy): dam, 11f and 1½m winner, sister to Ebor winner Western Dancer: well held in maidens. *C. A. Horgan*

ARUNDEL (IRE)   3 b.c. Sadler's Wells (USA) 132 – Luna Blue (FR) (Cure The Blues (USA)) [2003 89p: 10g* 14m² 14m⁶ Aug 24] 6,500,000 francs Y: brother to useful French 1½m/12.5f winner Luna Sacra and half-brother to several winners abroad, notably very smart French/US 1½m performer Luazur (by Bikala): dam, French 11f winner, half-sister to Linamix: smart form: won maiden at the Curragh in April: ran well when ¾-length second to Maharib in Curragh Cup nearly 2 months later, despite wandering/tending to hang: disappointing in listed race at Fairyhouse final start: will stay 2m: sold only 9,000 gns, sent to UAE. *A. P. O'Brien, Ireland*   **110**

ARZOO (IRE)   3 b.c. Bahhare (USA) 122 – Ishtiyak 80 (Green Desert (USA) 127) [2003 83: 6m⁴ 6m³ 6g 8m⁴ 8g⁵ 8.1m* 10m⁴ 8m³ 7m* 8m* 8.1d 7f Oct 11] good-topped colt: useful performer: won minor events at Sandown in July and Yarmouth in September and handicap at Musselburgh (beat Bravo Dancer 3½ lengths) later in September: pulled up final start: was effective at 7f/1m: acted on good to firm going: was usually held up: dead. *L. M. Cumani*   **104**

ASALEEB   2 b.f. (Mar 28) Alhaarth (IRE) 126 – Gharam (USA) 108 (Green Dancer (USA) 132) [2003 7g³ 8m² Oct 24] lengthy, good-topped filly: half-sister to several winners, including smart 1¼m winner who stayed 2½m Shaya (by Nashwan) and useful 1997 2-y-o 7f winner Elshamms (by Zafonic): dam, 2-y-o 6f winner, third in Poule d'Essai des Pouliches and Ribblesdale Stakes: fair form in maidens at Newmarket and Doncaster (rallied when 2 lengths second of 22 to Jath): will be suited by 1¼m/1½m: open to progress. *A. C. Stewart*   **79 p**

ASBO   3 b.f. Abou Zouz (USA) 109 – Star 83 (Most Welcome 131) [2003 66: 6.1m 5s May 19] leggy, workmanlike filly: fair form, lightly raced: ran respectably in handicap final start: not certain to stay beyond 6f: slowly away both 2-y-o starts: reportedly hung on reappearance. *Dr J. D. Scargill*   **54**

ASCARI   7 br.g. Presidium 124 – Ping Pong 65 (Petong 126) [2003 71, a64: 12.6m 10g⁶ Aug 10] strong gelding: fair handicapper at best: well held both starts in 2003: tried visored/blinkered earlier in career. *A. L. Forbes*   **–**

ASCERTAIN (IRE)   2 ch.g. (Apr 18) Intikhab (USA) 135 – Self Assured (IRE) 97 (Ahonoora 122) [2003 7d p8g* Nov 26] €42,000Y: fifth foal: half-brother to 3-y-o Miss Assertive: dam, 2-y-o 7f winner and second in May Hill Stakes, out of half-sister to very smart sprinter Sayyaf: much better effort in maidens (fair form) when 40/1-winner of 12-runner event at Lingfield, beating Kali 1¼ lengths: stays 1m. *N. P. Littmoden*   **79**

ASHDOWN EXPRESS (IRE)   4 ch.g. Ashkalani (IRE) 128 – Indian Express 61 (Indian Ridge 123) [2003 112: 6g³ 6m 6g² 6f² 6g⁴ 6m² 6m* 7m³ 7d⁵ 6f⁴ 6m* 6d Nov 8] sturdy, lengthy gelding: smart performer: won minor event at Yarmouth in August and Bentinck Stakes at Newmarket in October, latter by ½ length from Royal Millennium: mostly at least respectable efforts otherwise in 2003, including when placed in 4 listed races and in Hungerford Stakes at Newbury: raced freely, and probably better at 6f than 7f: acts on firm and good to soft going: blinkered final 3-y-o start: sweated first 2 outings: has worn crossed noseband/been early to post: consistent. *C. F. Wall*   **117**

Bentinck Stakes, Newmarket—Ashdown Express gains his first pattern-race victory;
Royal Millennium (No.10), Colonel Cotton (far side) and The Tatling come next

ASHFIELD   2 ch.f. (Feb 4) Zilzal (USA) 137 – Ninaki (USA) (Miswaki (USA) 124)   **67**
[2003 7m² 7g⁴ Sep 1] leggy, close-coupled filly: first foal: dam, French 12.5f winner from
3 starts, half-sister to smart French winner up to 12.5f Fabulous Hostess: better effort in
maidens (fair form) when second to Mandobi at Newmarket: bred to stay at least 1m:
raced freely/wandered latter start. *J. M. P. Eustace*

ASH LADDIE (IRE)   3 ch.g. Ashkalani (IRE) 128 – Lady Ellen 67 (Horage 124) [2003   **60**
56: 6f 7.9m⁵ 7.1f Aug 21] lengthy, useful-looking gelding: modest form, lightly raced:
stiff task in handicap (became unbalanced) final start. *E. J. Alston*

ASHLEIGH BAKER (IRE)   8 b. or br.m. Don't Forget Me 127 – Gayla Orchestra   **–**
(Lord Gayle (USA) 124) [2003 59, a–: 13g Jun 12] leggy, angular mare: modest
handicapper on turf: well held only outing in 2003: effective at 1¼m (given good test) to
easy 2m: acts on any turf going, well held on fibresand in 1998: usually
waited with: none too consistent. *A. Bailey*

ASH MOON (IRE)   5 ch.m. General Monash (USA) 107 – Jarmar Moon (Unfuwain   **69**
(USA) 131) [2003 90d: 8.3d p10g 10g² 11.6g 10m⁴ 11.9f Jun 14] lengthy, leggy mare:
fair handicapper: probably best at 1¼m/easy 1½m: acts on soft going, good to firm and
polytrack: blinkered (ran creditably) once: sometimes slowly away/races freely/wanders.
W. J. Musson

ASHSTANZA   2 gr.g. (Feb 14) Ashkalani (IRE) 128 – Poetry In Motion (IRE) 76 (Bal-   **60**
lad Rock 122) [2003 6m p7g⁴ Oct 30] 12,000F, 45,000Y: smallish, well-made gelding:
first foal: dam, 5f winner, out of smart performer up to 1m Nasseem: better effort in
maidens (modest form) when fourth to Bravo Maestro at Lingfield: likely to prove best
up to 1m. *M. A. Jarvis*

ASHTAROUTE (USA)   3 b.f. Holy Bull (USA) 134 – Beating The Buzz (IRE) 96   **60 ?**
(Bluebird (USA) 125) [2003 10g⁴ 9.9m⁴ 11.5f³ f12s 12m 12d⁵ f12g Nov 24] $42,000Y,
3,000 3-y-o: second foal: half-sister to winner in USA by Gulch: dam Irish 6f winner
(including at 2 yrs): modest maiden: stays 1½m: tends to wander/carry head awkwardly.
M. C. Chapman

ASHTORETH (IRE)   4 ch.f. Ashkalani (IRE) 128 – Sally Chase 101 (Sallust 134)   **–**
[2003 52: f8.5s Mar 31] good-bodied filly: modest maiden: stays 1m: acts on good to firm
going and polytrack. *D. McCain*

ASHTREE BELLE   4 b.f. Up And At 'em 109 – Paris Babe 94 (Teenoso (USA) 135)   **84**
[2003 75: 6.1g f6s f7g⁶ f7g* 7m⁵ 7g* f7s⁵ f7g² f7g² p7g⁴ p6g f7g* f7s⁴ Dec 13] fairly
useful handicapper: won at Wolverhampton in June, Newbury in July and Wolverhampton in November: stays 7f: acts on good to firm going, good to soft and all-weather:
sometimes slowly away: consistent. *D. Haydn Jones*

ASHVILLE LAD   6 b.g. Bigstone (IRE) 126 – Hooray Lady 92 (Ahonoora 122) [2003   **54**
51: f8.5s² Feb 28] strong gelding: modest maiden handicapper: effective at 8.5f to 1¼m:
acts on fibresand and firm going: usually blinkered/visored (not on only start in 2003):
tongue tied. *B. A. McMahon*

ASHWAAQ (USA)   2 b.f. (May 3) Gone West (USA) – Wasnah (USA) 96 (Nijinsky   **81 p**
(CAN) 138) [2003 7g⁴ Nov 1] big, good-topped filly: has scope: closely related to 2
winners, including very smart 1996 2-y-o 7f winner who stayed 1¼m Bahhare (by Woodman) and half-sister to 2 winners by Riverman, notably high-class 6f (at 2 yrs) and 1m
winner who stayed 10.4f Bahri: dam, maiden (should have stayed 1½m), half-sister to
dam of Breeders' Cup Distaff winner Ajina: 12/1, 4½ lengths fourth of 18 to Damsel in
maiden at Newmarket, slowly away and not unduly punished: should stay at least 1m:
sure to improve and win a race or 2. *J. L. Dunlop*

ASIAN HEIGHTS   5 b.h. Hernando (FR) 127 – Miss Rinjani 83 (Shirley Heights   **123**
130) [2003 116: 12m² 13.4m* May 8]
    Asian Heights, like the three-wheeled wagon in the comic song, somehow
manages to keep rolling along. Beset by leg problems over the years, he has been
restricted to a mere eight appearances in four seasons' racing, and it says much for
the skill of his trainer that Asian Heights has developed into a very smart performer
and won five races, two of them pattern events. Yet another setback meant that
Asian Heights's latest season ended in early-May, but it is expected that he will
return to action in 2004. Asian Heights is well capable of winning more good races
over a mile and a half or more, and it is to be hoped that he stays sound enough for
long enough to make the most of the opportunities that will be available to him.
    Asian Heights, having won a maiden at Lingfield on his sole start at two
years, was in the Derby picture after winning the Predominate Stakes at Goodwood

betfair.com Ormonde Stakes, Chester—
Asian Heights sees out the longer trip well, ahead of Compton Bolter and Razkalla

on his second outing at three, but split a pastern in his final workout before Epsom, not only having to miss that race but also the remainder of the season. With the injury requiring an operation, during which two screws were inserted, Asian Heights's racing career looked in the balance, yet one year after the Predominate he returned to win another listed race, at Windsor. Not that his troubles were behind him. Asian Heights reportedly suffered an infected hock shortly after Windsor and was then off the course for over three months. Once again he made a successful return, this time in the September Stakes at Kempton, putting up a performance which encouraged connections to let him take his chance in the Prix de l'Arc de Triomphe. For whatever reason, Asian Heights ran a lacklustre race at Longchamp, trailing throughout following a slow start, but that has been his only disappointing run to date. He showed himself better than ever when reappearing in the latest season in the Dubai Irish Village Stakes (John Porter) at Newbury in April, failing by only a short head to peg back Warrsan, who was receiving 3 lb; and he went one better in another Group 3 race, the betfair.com Ormonde Stakes, at Chester the following month. Asian Heights, sensibly ridden close to a steady early pace in the Ormonde Stakes, collared the leader Compton Bolter inside the final furlong and went on to beat him by a length and a quarter. He was giving both his owner and trainer a third successive win in this event, his half-brother St Expedit (by Sadler's Wells) having captured the two previous runnings. Incidentally, in between those two victories, St Expedit also fractured a pastern and had a couple of screws inserted.

Asian Heights (b.h. 1998)	Hernando (FR) (b 1990)	Niniski (b 1976)	Nijinsky
			Virginia Hills
		Whakilyric (b 1984)	Miswaki
			Lyrism
	Miss Rinjani (b 1991)	Shirley Heights (b 1975)	Mill Reef
			Hardiemma
		Miss Kuta Beach (ch 1981)	Bold Lad
			Miss Bali

Asian Heights is by the Prix du Jockey Club winner Hernando, responsible for two who have emulated him in that race, Holding Court and Sulamani. Asian Heights was bred by his owner, as were the first three dams on the bottom line of his pedigree, all of whom won races in Mr Pearce's familiar dark blue and white silks. Miss Rinjani gained her only success in a seven-furlong maiden at two, though she did show fairly useful form at up to a mile and a half at three. Miss Kuta Beach was also fairly useful, at up to a mile and a quarter, while Miss Bali was a useful winner over a mile and a half. Asian Heights is the third foal and third winner produced by Miss Rinjani, following Miss Amanpuri (by Alzao), a fairly useful filly who won over seven furlongs and stayed a mile and a quarter, and St Expedit. The extended thirteen furlongs of the Ormonde Stakes is the longest trip Asian Heights has encountered so far, and, though he may stay a bit further, it's likely that he will be kept to distances around a mile and a half—the Hardwicke Stakes at

Royal Ascot was the race he would have contested after Chester but for going lame just a few days beforehand. Asian Heights has shown his best form, and won three races, on good to firm ground, but that is not to say such a surface is essential. On the only occasions that Asian Heights has encountered ground softer than good he was successful, including on heavy on his debut. A leggy, quite attractive individual with a quick action, Asian Heights carries his head awkwardly but seems genuine enough, and is certainly consistent. He is usually held up. *G. Wragg*

ASIAN PERSUASION (IRE) 4 gr.g. Danehill Dancer (IRE) 117 – Kaitlin (IRE) — (Salmon Leap (USA) 131) [2003 56: f12g f14.8s Mar 31] rather leggy, workmanlike gelding: modest maiden: well held in 2003: seems to stay easy 1¼m: acts on good to firm going and all-weather: has worn cheekpieces. *B. A. Pearce*

ASIATIC 2 ch.c. (Mar 31) Lomitas 129 – Potri Pe (ARG) (Potrillazo (ARG)) [2003 **81 p** 8.1d² 7.2d⁴ 8.2m* Oct 28] lengthy, angular colt: half-brother to several winners, including Derby Italiano winner Mukhalif (by Caerleon), 7f winner at 2 yrs, and useful UAE 1m winner Parhelion (by Southern Halo): dam Argentinian Grade 1 winner: in frame in maidens at Haydock and Ayr before winning similar event at Nottingham comfortably by 3 lengths from Ma Yahab, making all: should make useful 3-y-o at 1¼m+. *M. Johnston*

ASIA WINDS (IRE) 2 ch.f. (Apr 6) Machiavellian (USA) 123 – Ascot Cyclone (USA) **95** 93 (Rahy (USA) 115) [2003 6m 5.1f* 5m⁴ 7m* 7g* 6.5d⁵ 7m⁵ Oct 4] close-coupled filly: second foal: half-sister to 3-y-o Fancy Lady: dam, 5.7f (at 2 yrs) and 7f winner, half-sister to smart performer up to 1¼m Magellan out of 1000 Guineas runner-up Dabaweyaa: useful performer: won maiden at Bath in July and nurseries at Newbury and Chester in August: creditable fifth in nurseries at Doncaster and Newmarket after: will probably stay 1m: acts on firm and good to soft going. *B. W. Hills*

ASKARIYAH (USA) 3 b.f. Kris S (USA) – Awaamir 102 (Green Desert (USA) 127) **48** [2003 –: p8g f8.5g f8g 10f³ 11g 13d 12m 12f 13m⁴ 12f Aug 30] sturdy filly: poor maiden handicapper: left G. Margarson after third start: stays 13f: acts on firm ground: tried blinkered, tongue tied nowadays. *T. Hogan, Ireland*

ASKHAM (USA) 5 b.h. El Gran Senor (USA) 136 – Konvincha (USA) (Cormorant **97** (USA)) [2003 112: 10m⁵ 8g⁴ 7.9m 9f³ 8.5f* Oct 25] good-topped horse: smart performer at 3 and 4 yrs: below form for J. Given first 3 starts in 2003, then off 5 months: won allowance race at Laurel in October: stays 1¼m: acts on firm going: often takes good hold (much too free third outing). *M. W. Dickinson, USA*

ASK THE CLERK (IRE) 2 b.g. (Mar 7) Turtle Island (IRE) 123 – Some Fun (Wol- **74** verlife 115) [2003 5d⁵ 6s⁴ 6v⁵ 8m² 7m⁶ 6g⁴ 6m³ 7d 7f³ p5g Nov 12] €10,000Y: ex-Irish gelding: fifth foal: half-brother to useful Irish 6f winner (including at 2 yrs) Jimmy The Greek (by Tenby), later successful in Hong Kong: dam winning sprinter in Ireland: fair maiden: in frame 5 times: left P. Prendergast after ninth start: stays 1m: acts on any turf ground, probably on polytrack: effective blinkered or not. *H. J. Collingridge*

ASK THE DRIVER 2 b.g. (Feb 9) Ashkalani (IRE) 128 – Tithcar 67 (Cadeaux Gene- **51** reux 131) [2003 6m f8.5s⁵ 6d Sep 26] €26,000Y: lengthy gelding: third foal: half-brother to 3-y-o Chetak: dam, maiden who stayed 7f, half-sister to 7-y-o Zindabad: modest form in maidens/minor event: seems to stay 8.5f: slowly away first 2 starts. *D. J. S. ffrench Davis*

ASSIGNATION 3 b.g. Compton Place 125 – Hug Me 96 (Shareef Dancer (USA) 135) **52** [2003 82?: 7m 6.1m 7.1m 7m 10.2g 10m 8.3g Oct 13] strong, well-made gelding: modest maiden: probably stays 1¼m: acts on good to soft ground, probably on good to firm: tried visored: sold £1,700. *B. R. Millman*

ASSOON 4 b.c. Ezzoud (IRE) 126 – Handy Dancer 87 (Green God 128) [2003 18f² **64** 14m³ Aug 8] half-brother to several winners, including smart 1m to 1½m winner Karinga Bay (by Ardross) and useful 1½m and 2m winner Roll A Dollar (by Spin of A Coin): dam 1¼m winner: won bumper in July: modest form in maidens at Warwick and Lingfield (looked unsuited by marked drop in trip): stays 2¼m. *G. L. Moore*

ASSRAAR 3 b.f. Cadeaux Genereux 131 – Possessive Dancer 118 (Shareef Dancer — (USA) 135) [2003 86p: 8.1d Sep 27] fairly useful winner at 2 yrs: well held in handicap on only outing in 2003 (looked less than keen): should stay 1m. *A. C. Stewart*

ASTAFORT (FR) 4 ch.g. Kendor (FR) 122 – Tres Chic (USA) (Northern Fashion — (USA) 114) [2003 –: 16.1d Mar 24] close-coupled gelding: no form. *A. C. Whillans*

ASTARAMONGSTTHEM (IRE)   2 b.g. (Mar 24) Among Men (USA) 124 – Astu- **62**
riana (Julio Mariner 127) [2003 6d⁵ Jun 23] €7,800Y: half-brother to several winners,
including 5f winner (including at 2 yrs) Twice In Bundoran (by Bold Arrangement) and
1½m winner Spirit of Tenby (by Tenby): dam lightly raced: fifth of 16 in maiden at
Windsor: withdrawn after rearing in stall in July: dead. *P. D. Evans*

ASTLE (IRE)   5 ch.g. Spectrum (IRE) 126 – Very Sophisticated (USA) (Affirmed **–**
(USA)) [2003 –, a66d: f9.4s May 12] big gelding: fairly useful performer at 3 yrs: very
much on the downgrade: blinkered first 6 starts in 2002. *Mrs N. Macauley*

ASTORMYDAYISCOMING   5 b.g. Alhaatmi – Valentine Song 63 (Pas de Seul **–**
133) [2003 37: 12.6m 16.5m Jul 10] lengthy gelding: blinkered/tongue tied, no form in
2003. *G. F. Bridgwater*

ASTRAC (IRE)   12 b.g. Nordico (USA) – Shirleen (Daring Display (USA) 129) [2003 **58**
62: p7g 7.1d 7g 7.5d⁵ 6.9m³ 6f 7f* 5.7f* 7m⁵ Oct 13] sturdy gelding: modest performer:
won seller at Brighton and handicap at Bath in September: stays 7.5f: acts on firm going,
soft and fibresand: tried blinkered: none too consistent. *Mrs A. L. M. King*

ASTRAL PRINCE   5 ch.g. Efisio 120 – Val d'Erica 119 (Ashmore (FR) 125) [2003 **53 §**
64§: 12.3m f8.5g⁶ 8g⁶ Oct 22] strong gelding: modest handicapper: left A. Crook after
first start: stays 1¼m: acts on fibresand and good to firm going: sometimes blinkered:
tongue tied final start: has taken good hold: not one to trust. *Mrs K. Walton*

ASTROCHARM (IRE)   4 b.f. Charnwood Forest (IRE) 125 – Charm The Stars (Roi **85**
Danzig (USA)) [2003 99: 8g 8g 9g⁶ 8m³ 8m 8m² 10f 8m³ 10m 10.4f 10.1m⁴ 12g p12g
Nov 22] leggy filly: has a round action: fairly useful handicapper: stays 1¼m: acts on
firm and good to soft ground: blinkered last 3 outings. *M. H. Tompkins*

ASTROMANCER (USA)   3 b. or br.f. Silver Hawk (USA) 123 – Colour Dance **62**
(Rainbow Quest (USA) 134) [2003 62p: 11.8m 14g 10.9g 12g⁵ f11s p13g² p16g⁴ p16g⁴
Dec 2] rather leggy filly: modest maiden handicapper: stays 2m: acts on polytrack,
unraced on extremes of going on turf. *M. H. Tompkins*

ASTRONAUT   6 b.g. Sri Pekan (USA) 117 – Wild Abandon (USA) (Graustark) [2003 **47**
f12g f8.5g⁶ f9.4s⁶ 10.2m f12s Jun 21] useful-looking gelding: poor handicapper nowadays: should stay easy 1½m: acts on fibresand, good to firm and good to soft going: tried
in headgear: has refused to race over hurdles, though successful in August (sold 6,000
gns, and joined M. Pipe). *A. E. Jones*

ASTYANAX (IRE)   3 b.c. Hector Protector (USA) 124 – Craigmill 85 (Slip Anchor **81**
136) [2003 –p: f12g* 12.6m³ 14.1m² 16.2m⁴ 14.1m* Aug 6] lengthy colt: fairly useful
handicapper: won at Southwell in May and ladies event at Yarmouth in August: stays 2m:
acts on fibresand and good to firm going. *Sir Mark Prescott*

ASWAN (IRE)   5 ch.g. Ashkalani (IRE) 128 – Ghariba 112 (Final Straw 127) [2003 **78**
81: p7g⁴ p8g⁵ p7g 10g³ 8m⁴ 9.9f⁴ 10m Apr 26] sturdy gelding: fair handicapper: left
T. Etherington after third start: barely stays 1¼m: acts on firm going and polytrack: tried
blinkered: tongue tied (ran poorly) final start: often races freely and has carried head high/
found little. *S. R. Bowring*

ATAHUELPA   3 b.g. Hernando (FR) 127 – Certain Story (Known Fact (USA) 135) **90**
[2003 89: 8m⁴ 8.1g³ 9m* 9.9m Aug 23] compact gelding: fairly useful performer: won
claimer at Newbury in August: stays 9f: acts on fibresand, soft and good to firm ground:
races prominently: joined M. Harris. *P. F. I. Cole*

ATAVUS   6 b.h. Distant Relative 128 – Elysian 94 (Northfields (USA)) [2003 107: 8g⁴ **104**
7g⁶ 8.3d² 8.5m 7m⁵ 7g 6.5g 7.1g³ 7d 6g* 6m 7m⁴ Oct 25] sturdy horse: poor mover:
useful performer: won minor event at Yarmouth in September: ran creditably earlier in
year when in frame in listed races at Doncaster and Windsor (1½ lengths second to Right
Approach) and minor event at Chepstow: effective at 6f to 1m: acts on firm and good to
soft going: blinkered (well held) once: sometimes slowly away: has edged right: best
when able to lead: none too consistent. *G. G. Margarson*

A TEEN   5 ch.h. Presidium 124 – Very Good (Noalto 120) [2003 –§, a57§: f5g p6g² p7g **73**
6m⁴ 5m 5g⁴ 6m 6m² 6m 6d* 6m³ 6d 6m⁵ 5m 6m⁵ 5d 5.7f⁶ 6.1f⁵ 6g⁶ 6.1m* p7g p7g p6g **a58**
Dec 30] fair handicapper on turf, modest on all-weather: won at Lingfield in July and
Nottingham in October: effective at 5f, barely at 7f: acts on firm ground, good to soft and
all-weather: tried blinkered, not in 2003: has carried head high. *P. Howling*

ATHBOY   2 ch.c. (Feb 26) Entrepreneur 123 – Glorious (Nashwan (USA) 135) [2003 **55**
p7g⁶ f8s Oct 7] 6,000F, 12,000Y, 15,000 2-y-o: third foal: half-brother to 3-y-o Abundant:

dam unraced half-sister to smart miler Killer Instinct from family of Opera House and Kayf Tara: modest form in minor event at Lingfield: well beaten next time. *D. Mullarkey*

ATHEER (USA) 3 b.f. Lear Fan (USA) 130 – Rhumba Rage (USA) (Nureyev (USA) 131) [2003 72: f8.5s 8g⁵ 8.2m* 8m⁴ 8d 7m⁶ 7m Oct 17] smallish filly: fair handicapper: won at Nottingham in June: stays 1m: unraced on extremes of going on turf: visored/blinkered 4 of last 5 starts: found little sixth start. *E. A. L. Dunlop*   **74**

ATHENIAN 4 b.g. Distant Relative 128 – Confection (Formidable (USA) 125) [2003 84: 10m² 10g² 10m 8.9f 10.3f* 9.9g⁵ 10.5m Aug 9] leggy gelding: useful handicapper: won at Doncaster in June: stayed 1¼m: acted on all-weather, firm and soft going: was tough and game: dead. *D. Morris*   **95**

ATHOLLBROSE (USA) 2 b.g. (Apr 2) Mister Baileys 123 – Knightly Cut Up (USA) (Gold Crest (USA) 120) [2003 f5g⁴ 5g 7m Sep 6] 8,000Y: useful-looking gelding: unimpressive mover: second foal: dam ran once in USA: modest form in maidens: fourth at Southwell: should stay beyond 5f. *T. D. Easterby*   **57**

ATLANTIC ACE 6 b.g. First Trump 118 – Risalah (Marju (IRE) 127) [2003 101: 8g 8m⁶ 8g 7.9m 8.5d⁵ 8m 8f 10g⁵ 9m 8m* 8g 8.2m⁵ Oct 28] good-topped gelding: useful performer: won minor event at Pontefract in September, despite missing break: effective at 7f to 9f: best form on good ground or firmer: tried in cheekpieces: usually held up: found little ninth start. *B. Smart*   **95**

ATLANTIC BREEZE 2 br.f. (Feb 12) Deploy 131 – Atlantic Air (Air Trooper 115) [2003 f6s⁴ f8g* f8s Dec 27] quite good-topped filly: half-sister to several winners, including 6f winner Count Calypso (by King's Signet) and 7f (including at 2 yrs)/1m winner Mullitover (by Interrex), both fairly useful: dam Italian 1¼m winner: fair form: won maiden at Southwell in December: stiff task and well beaten in nursery there final start: should be suited by 1¼m/1½m. *Mrs N. Macauley*   **65**

ATLANTIC CITY 2 ch.g. (May 7) First Trump 118 – Pleasuring 68 (Good Times (ITY)) [2003 7m⁶ 8m² 8m² Oct 17] 20,000Y: quite good-topped, attractive gelding: sixth foal: half-brother to 3 winners by Reprimand, including 5-y-o Suggestive and useful French 6f to 9f (including at 2 yrs) winner Rashbag: dam sprint maiden: fair form in maidens: favourite, looked none too keen when second at Musselburgh and Redcar: not sure to stay beyond 1m. *W. J. Haggas*   **71**

ATLANTIC QUEST (USA) 4 b. or br.g. Woodman (USA) 126 – Pleasant Pat (USA) (Pleasant Colony (USA)) [2003 89: p10g⁵ 8.3g 8.1g 10d 8g* 8.1m² 8m 9.1f* 10.5g⁴ 8f² 10.3m 8g⁶ 9m 10.3d 8g⁴ 8m* 8m Oct 25] rather leggy, close-coupled gelding: fairly useful performer: won minor event at Musselburgh in May, handicap at Ayr in June and (having been claimed from M. Johnston £25,000 after ninth start) handicap at Redcar in October: stays easy 1¼m: acts on polytrack, firm and good to soft going: often visored: wore cheekpieces last 2 starts: tends to wander/carry head high: none too consistent. *G. A. Harker*   **90**

ATLANTIC SKY 3 b.f. Bishop of Cashel 122 – Naval Dispatch (Slip Anchor 136) [2003 10.2g 10f 10f⁵ 10d 10f⁴ Aug 27] first foal: dam, 6f/1m winner in Norway, out of half-sister to dam of very smart 7f/1m winner Decorated Hero: well held, including in seller. *H. Morrison*   **–**

ATLANTIC TERN 2 b.c. (May 3) Atraf 116 – Great Tern 59 (Simply Great (FR) 122) [2003 8.2d p8g Dec 20] second foal: dam 1¾m winner: well held in maiden/minor event. *N. M. Babbage*   **–**

Vodafone 'Dash' Rated Stakes (Handicap), Epsom—a career-best effort from Atlantic Viking, who is followed home, left to right, by Damalis, Repertory and Bishops Court

Buckingham Palace Stakes (Handicap), Royal Ascot—the winner Attache and runner-up Hurricane Floyd (right) are separated almost by the width of the course

ATLANTIC VIKING (IRE)   8 b.g. Danehill (USA) 126 – Hi Bettina 96 (Henbit (USA) 130) [2003 101: 5f⁶ 5m² 5g 5m* 6f 5m⁵ 5d 5m⁶ 5.6d Sep 10] well-made gelding: useful handicapper: won listed Vodafone 'Dash' Rated Stakes at Epsom in June by 1¼ lengths from Damalis: ran creditably penultimate start: best at 5f/easy 6f: below form on heavy going, acts on any other: sometimes blinkered earlier in career, visored (stumbled early) final start: often races prominently: sometimes wanders. *D. Nicholls*   **103**

ATRACTIVE GIRL   4 ch.f. Atraf 116 – Harold's Girl (FR) (Northfields (USA)) [2003 f9.4g Jan 17] poor maiden: tried blinkered. *J. L. Spearing*   **–**

ATTACCA   2 b.c. (Apr 8) Piccolo 121 – Jubilee Place (IRE) 76 (Prince Sabo 123) [2003 7m 6m 6m² 6m* Oct 20] 6,500F, 5,000Y: tall, quite good-topped colt: fourth foal: half-brother to 3-y-o Linden's Lady and winner in Italy by So Factual: dam 2-y-o 6f winner: fair form in maidens: won 10-runner event at Pontefract by 1½ lengths from Whistful, making all and veering right late on: should stay 7f: wore cheekpieces last 2 starts. *J. R. Weymes*   **78**

ATTACHE   5 ch.g. Wolfhound (USA) 126 – Royal Passion 78 (Ahonoora 122) [2003 105: 7m* 6g⁵ 7.1m⁵ 7f* 7g 7m⁵ 7.1g* 8.1d³ 7f Sep 27] strong, lengthy gelding: smart performer: won handicaps at Newmarket in April and Royal Ascot (best effort, beat Hurricane Floyd ½ length in 27-runner event) in June, and minor event at Chepstow (beat Audience 1½ lengths) in August: below form last 2 starts: probably best around 7f: best recent form on good going or firmer: blinkered (raced too freely) once: sometimes early to post: usually tracks pace: joined I. Mohammed in UAE. *M. A. Jarvis*   **113**

ATTACK   7 gr.g. Sabrehill (USA) 120 – Butsova 93 (Formidable (USA) 125) [2003 73: p16g p12g⁴ p13g⁵ 12g 15m 14.1m Apr 21] lengthy, workmanlike gelding: fair maiden handicapper: stays 13f: acts on good to soft going and polytrack: tried blinkered: often tongue tied: joined P. Hobbs, well beaten in 2 outings over fences, sold 4,800 gns. *Mrs A. L. M. King*   **65 ?**

ATTACK MINDED   2 ch.g. (Mar 31) Timeless Times (USA) 99 – French Ginger 66 (Most Welcome 131) [2003 6m Jul 10] 1,500Y: first foal: dam 7f winner: 100/1 and backward, tailed off in maiden at Doncaster, looking difficult ride. *L. R. James*   **–**

ATTILA THE HUN   4 b.g. Piccolo 121 – Katya (IRE) 93 (Dancing Dissident (USA) 119) [2003 –: 7m 6m 8m 7f 5m f6g f6g Dec 19] little form. *F. Watson*   **–**

ATTORNEY   5 ch.g. Wolfhound (USA) 126 – Princess Sadie 86 (Shavian 125) [2003 74d, a71d: f6s⁶ f6g f5s* f5g f5g⁴ f5s f5s³ f6g² p5g f6g f5g f6s 5m f6g⁵ 5g 5.1s 5g f5g⁶ 5m 6m⁴ 5m 6m² 6m⁶ 6m 6m 5d³ 5m 5m f5s 5.1g 6m f6g³ f7g f6g f6g f6g⁴ Dec 26] tall, quite good-topped gelding: modest handicapper: won at Wolverhampton in January: regressed steadily after: effective at 5f/6f: acts on soft going, good to firm and fibresand: tried blinkered, usually visored: usually gets behind: sometimes wanders. *D. Shaw*   **62 d**

ATTORNEY GENERAL (IRE)   4 b.g. Sadler's Wells (USA) 132 – Her Ladyship 119 (Polish Precedent (USA) 131) [2003 93: 11.6g Apr 7] angular gelding: fairly useful winner at 3 yrs: well held only Flat outing in 2003: will be suited by 1¾m+: successful over hurdles in November. *J. A. B. Old*   **–**

ATTRACTION   2 b.f. (Feb 19) Efisio 120 – Flirtation (Pursuit of Love 124) [2003 5.1g* 5g* 5m* 5m* 6m* Jul 8]   **118**

Attraction involves drawing power, and the filly of that name showed a full measure of the quality in a season regrettably curtailed by a serious injury. Her crushing victories in the Queen Mary Stakes and the Cherry Hinton Stakes were the best performances by any of her age and sex in Europe, and almost a match for the best the colts could manage. Not bad for a filly whose owner, according to Mark

Queen Mary Stakes, Royal Ascot—Attraction produces the best performance in this race for many years; Catstar is clear of the rest in second

Johnston, gave him the relatively modest brief of 'winning a race and then getting black type'.

The Duke of Roxburghe's requirements were soon fulfilled as, by the end of May, Attraction had won minor events at Nottingham and Thirsk, beating a field including three previous winners in the latter, and the listed Hilary Needler Trophy at Beverley, where she forged clear in the final two furlongs to defeat Tolzey eased by two and a half lengths. Attraction's hallmark was electrifying speed and, after overcoming a slight injury scare when she stumbled and went down on her knees on the gallops, grazing a foreleg, she repeated the dose with interest in the Queen Mary Stakes at Royal Ascot. Favourite in a field of fourteen, with only Leicester winner Catstar at shorter than 10/1 among her rivals, she was soon in front and had the others floundering in the final two furlongs. She trounced Catstar by three lengths with Majestic Desert five lengths back in third. Even North American-trained filly America America, a winner over three furlongs earlier in the season, was unable to go the early pace, but there was no hint of Attraction's stopping at the finish, which suggested six furlongs would probably be within her compass. The test of that came in the Chippenham Lodge Stud Cherry Hinton Stakes at the Newmarket July meeting, where Attraction started at 7/4-on to beat seven rivals, giving 3 lb all round. All but one of the seven had won, second favourite Pearl Grey in a listed event, but none of them could cope with Attraction, whose success provided one of the most abiding memories of the season. Squeezed out leaving the stalls, she had to be waited with and was caught briefly in a pocket towards the far rail with a couple of furlongs to go. Once a gap appeared, Attraction accelerated in an instant, led a furlong out and drew clear in breathtaking style with her rider just waving his whip. The winning margin over Pearl Grey was five lengths, with Birthday Suit a length away third.

Attraction's performance in the Cherry Hinton was an excellent display by a juvenile filly at that particular stage of the season—her timefigure, the equivalent to a timerating of 118 and marginally better than the figure she had recorded at Royal Ascot, confirms as much. In fact, the only fillies in the last couple of decades to have been rated more highly by the end of July were Ma Biche, rated 120 in 1982 on the strength of her success against the colts in the Prix Robert Papin, and Circus Ring, rated 122 in 1981 after landing the Princess Margaret Stakes by ten lengths. In 1986 Forest Flower (who ended the season with a rating of 127) was 116 at the same stage of her career. There was every reason to anticipate Attraction's adding to her reputation, just as Circus Ring (Lowther Stakes) and Ma Biche and

Chippenham Lodge Stud Cherry Hinton Stakes, Newmarket—another trouncing for her rivals as Attraction is even more impressive; Pearl Grey is her nearest pursuer

Forest Flower (Cheveley Park Stakes) had done. Races mentioned as targets after Newmarket were the Prix Robert Papin, Lowther Stakes and Nunthorpe Stakes, then the Prix Morny, but she missed all of these, suffering an overreach while swimming. Bony changes in her knees, revealed by precautionary x-rays, gave cause for concern. The final straw came when Attraction cracked a pedal bone in her near-hind foot towards the end of September, when being prepared for the Cheveley Park.

Attraction (b.f. Feb 19, 2001)	Efisio (b 1982)	Formidable (b 1975)	Forli
			Native Partner
		Eldoret (b 1976)	High Top
			Bamburi
	Flirtation (b 1994)	Pursuit of Love (b 1989)	Groom Dancer
			Dance Quest
		Eastern Shore (ch 1979)	Sun Prince
			Land Ho

Attraction is hardly bred in the purple but that is not to say her sire Efisio has an indifferent record. He was best at seven furlongs to a mile, winning the Challenge Stakes and Premio Emilio Turati among other races and, with the exception of Prix Vermeille winner Pearly Shells, all his best progeny—Hever Golf Rose, Le Vie dei Colori, Pips Pride and Tomba—have shone at up to a mile, with Hever Golf Rose best at the minimum trip. Attraction is the second foal of Flirtation. The first, Aunty Mary (by Common Grounds), was a sprinter successful over five furlongs at two, while the most recent addition to the family is a yearling colt by Inchinor who fetched 230,000 guineas at Tattersalls October Sales. Flirtation ran just once and is out of Eastern Shore, who stayed a mile and a half and has foaled four winners, notably Carmita, successful in a listed race over a mile and a half in the French Provinces and third in the Group 2 Prix de Royallieu. Eastern Shore is a half-sister to the grandam of the very smart Lord of Men, whose biggest victory came in the Prix de la Salamandre; this is also the family of top miler Sonic Lady. The pedigree suggests Attraction, quite a good-topped filly who has raced only on good or good to firm going, should stay a mile, but her style of racing suggests otherwise. Providing she makes a full recovery from her injury and stays sound—a potential problem given her setbacks in the second half of the year and the less-than-perfect conformation of her forelegs (reportedly the reason she wasn't sent to the sales as a yearling)—her best prospects of adding a Group 1 race to her tally appear to lie, not in the classics, but in the top sprints, which have the added advantage of coming later in the season should she require more time. At her best Attraction, who has an ungainly action, would undoubtedly be a force to reckon with in the top races over five and six furlongs. *M. Johnston*

ATTUNE 2 ch.f. (Feb 10) Singspiel (IRE) 133 – Arriving 105 (Most Welcome 131) **64 p**
[2003 7m⁴ Aug 28] second foal: dam 1¼m to 11.4f winner: 6/1 and green, 5½ lengths fourth of 13 to Mango Mischief in maiden at Salisbury: will be suited by 1¼m/1½m: should improve. *B. J. Meehan*

A TWO (IRE) 4 b.f. Ali-Royal (IRE) 127 – Rainelle (Rainbow Quest (USA) 134) **–**
[2003 56: f14.8s 11.8g f16g f11s Dec 13] modest performer: showed nothing in 2003 (reportedly had breathing problem on reappearance). *B. Palling*

AUDACIOUS PRINCE (IRE) 3 b.c. Desert Prince (IRE) 130 – Sheer Audacity **103**
(Troy 137) [2003 91p: 8g² 10m* 7m Dec 14] useful form: 1½ lengths second to Milla-fonic in minor event at Ayr in May prior to making all in listed race at Saint-Cloud following month, holding on by a neck from Ridaar: left Sir Mark Prescott and renamed Winning Kevin, tailed off at Sha Tin final start: tends to race freely and not sure to stay beyond 1¼m: raced only on good/good to firm going. *A. T. Millard, Hong Kong*

AUDIENCE 3 b.g. Zilzal (USA) 137 – Only Yours 113 (Aragon 118) [2003 85p: 8g **103**
9m 8d 7.1g² 8g² 7m⁶ Oct 4] big, good-topped gelding: useful performer, lightly raced: good second in minor events at Chepstow (beaten 1½ lengths by Attache) and Doncaster (went down by 3½ lengths to Checkit): below form in listed race at Redcar final start, finding little: may prove best short of 1m: yet to race on extremes of going: blinkered last 4 starts: took good hold fifth start: sold 48,000 gns. *W. J. Haggas*

AUDITORIUM 2 b.c. (Mar 30) Royal Applause 124 – Degree 81 (Warning 136) **114**
[2003 6m 6m* 6g* 7g² 6m³ Oct 3] 115,000Y: sturdy, useful-looking colt: third foal: brother to smart 5f/6f (at 2 yrs) and 1m winner Mister Cosmi: dam 1m winner at 4 yrs:

smart performer: won maiden at Pontefract and listed race at Ripon (beat Peak To Creek comfortably by 1½ lengths) in August: good neck second to Lucky Story in Champagne Stakes at Doncaster and 1½ lengths fourth (promoted to third) behind disqualified Three Valleys in Middle Park Stakes at Newmarket: stays 7f: acts on good to firm going: coltish before early starts, more settled for last 2: tends to be soon off bridle. *Sir Michael Stoute*

AUGUSTINE 2 b.c. (Apr 7) Machiavellian (USA) 123 – Crown of Light 112 (Mtoto 134) [2003 6m⁵ May 31] close-coupled colt: second foal: half-brother to 3-y-o Balkan Knight: dam, 7f (at 2 yrs) and 11.5f winner, also third in Oaks: evens, fifth of 9 to Old Deuteronomy in maiden at Newmarket, not clear run but finishing well: bred to be suited by 1¼m/1½m. *D. R. Loder*   **72**

AUNT DORIS 6 b.m. Distant Relative 128 – Nevis 61 (Connaught 130) [2003 44: f6g Nov 24] poor handicapper: well held only 6-y-o start: often visored. *Paul Johnson*   **–**

AUNT HILDA 4 b.f. Distant Relative 128 – Aloha Jane (USA) 57 (Hawaii) [2003 69: 10.9m 8.1m 9f 10.2m⁵ 7g Aug 10] small filly: fair maiden at best: poor form in 2003: stays 11.7f: acts on firm and good to soft going: free-going sort: often blinkered. *M. F. Harris*   **36**

AUNT RITA (IRE) 3 ch.f. Grand Lodge (USA) 125 – Dance Alone (USA) (Monteverdi 129) [2003 78: 8g 6f⁵ 7m⁴ 7.1m³ 8.3d 10g⁵ 12f Oct 12] rather leggy, useful-looking filly: fairly useful handicapper: below form after third start: likely to prove best up to 1m: acts on firm ground: tends to race freely/carry head high: sold 31,000 gns. *M. L. W. Bell*   **81**

AUNTY LIL (USA) 3 b. or br.f. Swain (IRE) 134 – Singular Broad (USA) (Broad Brush (USA)) [2003 p10g 10m 8.3g⁶ f9.4g Nov 1] first foal: dam US 2-y-o 8.5f winner, out of half-sister to high-class miler Shaadi: well held in maidens: unseated/ran loose in paddock before second outing. *P. R. Chamings*   **–**

AUNTY NINA (IRE) 3 b.f. Mujadil (USA) 119 – Nobodys Child (IRE) (Jareer (USA) 115) [2003 p6g Jan 29] fourth living foal: half-sister to Irish 1½m winner Chestnut Falls (by River Falls), and winner in Germany by Persian Bold: dam lightly raced in Ireland: 33/1, broke down in seller at Lingfield. *J. S. Moore*   **–**

AURELIA (IRE) 2 b.f. (May 6) Rainbow Quest (USA) 134 – Fern 100 (Shirley Heights 130) [2003 8m⁶ 8f³ 10.2f* 10m⁴ Oct 13] 45,000Y: sturdy filly: half-sister to several winners, including 5-y-o Dance On The Top and 4-y-o Dimple Chad: dam, 1½m winner, half-sister to Oaks second Shamshir: fair form: won maiden at Bath in September, hanging fire briefly in front: found little when creditable fourth to Cohn Blue in minor event at Leicester: will stay at least 1½m: slowly away third 3 starts: tail swisher. *Sir Mark Prescott*   **78**

AUROVILLE 2 b.c. (Apr 30) Cadeaux Genereux 131 – Silent Tribute (IRE) 104 (Lion Cavern (USA) 117) [2003 7m 7m⁵ 7m Sep 17] 42,000Y: leggy, workmanlike colt: second foal: dam, ran only at 2 yrs when 6f and 1m (Italian listed race) winner, out of useful half-sister to Middle Park winner Balla Cove: fair form in maidens: fifth at Yarmouth: will probably stay 1m. *M. L. W. Bell*   **66**

AUTHORITY (IRE) 3 b.g. Bluebird (USA) 125 – Persian Tapestry 70 (Tap On Wood 130) [2003 7m² 7m⁴ Jul 19] 125,000F, 140,000Y: rangy, good sort: brother to useful 2000 2-y-o 5f/6f winner Triple Blue and half-brother to 2 winners, including 5f winner Need You Badly (by Robellino): dam, 1¼m winner, half-sister to top-class sprinter Lake Coniston: fair form in frame in maidens at Newmarket: will stay 1m: sold 11,000 gns, and gelded. *W. J. Haggas*   **75**

AUTUMN FANTASY (USA) 4 b. or br.c. Lear Fan (USA) 130 – Autumn Glory (USA) (Graustark) [2003 87: f16.2g 12g 12.3m 13.9m 11.9f 14.6m Jun 28] good-topped colt: fairly useful handicapper at 3 yrs: well held for new trainer in 2003: tongue tied last 2 starts. *B. Ellison*   **–**

AUTUMN FLYER (IRE) 2 ch.g. (Feb 19) Salse (USA) 128 – Autumn Fall (USA) (Sanglamore (USA) 126) [2003 7m 7m p7g Oct 15] IR 25,000F, €75,000Y: fourth foal: half-brother to winner in Greece by Marju: dam unraced: fair form at best in maidens: raced freely second start: wandered final one: should stay 1m. *C. G. Cox*   **66**

AUTUMN GLORY (IRE) 3 b.c. Charnwood Forest (IRE) 125 – Archipova (IRE) (Ela-Mana-Mou 132) [2003 8g* 7m⁴ 7.1m Oct 25] 12,000F, 62,000Y: good-topped, rather leggy colt: first foal: dam, Italian 1½m/15f winner, sister to useful performer up to 12.5f Abyaan and half-sister to 5-y-o Sadlers Wings: fairly useful form: won maiden at Leicester in March: off 6 months, better effort after when 5¼ lengths fourth to Fantasy Believer in minor event at Newcastle: bred to be suited by further than 1m: slowly away final outing. *G. Wragg*   **89**

AUTUMN PEARL   2 b.f. (Jan 25) Orpen (USA) 116 – Cyclone Flyer 67 (College   **82 p**
Chapel 122) [2003 5g* 6g⁵ p5g* Oct 30] 35,000Y: lengthy, rather unfurnished filly:
unimpressive mover: first foal: dam, 5f winner, half-sister to very smart sprinter Bolshoi:
won maiden at Sandown in June and minor event at Lingfield (by 1¾ lengths from
Trotters Bottom, making most and edging right) in October: likely to prove best at 5f/easy
6f: should make a useful 3-y-o. *M. A. Jarvis*

AVEIRO (IRE)   7 b.g. Darshaan 133 – Avila 76 (Ajdal (USA) 130) [2003 63d, a66d: **41**
f14.8s⁴ 11.9f³ 11.5m 11.9m 16.2m⁶ 12m 10m³ p13g f12g⁴ f11g* f12g⁴ f12g Dec 26] big   **a48**
gelding: poor handicapper: left C. Morlock after fourth start: won claimer at Southwell
in December: effective at 11.5f to easy 2m: acts on all-weather, firm and soft ground:
usually blinkered, tried visored/in cheekpieces: usually races prominently: none too
consistent. *B. G. Powell*

A VENDRE (FR)   4 b.g. Kendor (FR) 122 – Waaria (Shareef Dancer (USA) 135)   **–**
[2003 67: 10.2m Apr 29] leggy gelding: fair maiden: last in seller (visored) only Flat run
in 2003: barely stays 1¼m: acts on good to firm going: also tried blinkered (pulled hard
first occasion). *M. C. Pipe*

AVENING   3 br.c. Averti (IRE) 117 – Dependable (Formidable (USA) 125) [2003 95:   **91 d**
5m 6m 7g 6g 6d Nov 9] useful-looking colt: fairly useful performer: well below form
after reappearance: effective at 5f/6f: acts on firm going, probably on heavy: went right
leaving stall (tongue tied) fourth 2-y-o start. *R. Hannon*

AVENLEA   2 b.c. (Apr 18) Averti (IRE) 117 – Cloudslea (USA) (Chief's Crown   **–**
(USA)) [2003 5g Jun 2] half-brother to 7f/1m winner Picture Puzzle (by Royal Academy)
and a winner in Turkey by Tirol: dam French 10.5f winner: green, last of 7 in minor event
at Windsor, slowly away. *R. Hannon*

AVENTURA (IRE)   3 b.c. Sri Pekan (USA) 117 – La Belle Katherine (USA) (Lyphard   **95 ?**
(USA) 132) [2003 83: p6g³ p8g* 7g 7.5m⁵ 7g² 7m 6d³ 6.1d⁵ 7g⁵ 7m⁶ 7.5m³ 8m⁵ 8.9m⁴
8.1d³ f7g Oct 16] sturdy, close-coupled colt: useful performer: won claimer at Lingfield
(left M. Jarvis) in February: mostly creditable efforts after, seemingly very good third to
Desert Opal in handicap at Haydock penultimate start: shaped as if amiss final outing:
effective at 6f to easy 9f: acts on polytrack, good to firm and good to soft going:
free-going sort. *M. J. Polglase*

AVERAMI   2 b.f. (Feb 25) Averti (IRE) 117 – Friend For Life 64 (Lahib (USA) 129)   **68**
[2003 6.1d p5g⁶ p5g⁵ p6g⁴ Dec 29] leggy filly: first foal: dam, maiden (should have
stayed 1¼m), out of useful half-sister to Shirley Heights: fair maiden: best effort when
fifth to Treasure Cay in minor event at Lingfield: should stay at least 6f. *A. M. Balding*

AVERLLINE   2 b.f. (Apr 19) Averti (IRE) 117 – Spring Sunrise 59 (Robellino (USA)   **74**
127) [2003 5.1g 6m 6.1m³ 6g 7g 6m³ 6.1m³ 6m² 7m² 6d* 5.1d Nov 6] second foal: dam
2-y-o 6f/7f winner: fair performer: won maiden at Brighton in October: possibly amiss
final start: barely stays 7f: acts on good to firm and good to soft going. *B. De Haan*

AVERSHAM   3 b.c. Averti (IRE) 117 – Vavona 60 (Ballad Rock 122) [2003 90: 6m⁴   **101**
5f⁵ 7g³ 7m⁴ 6v 6g⁴ 7f 7m⁴ 7m⁴ 7f² 6g³ 6d Nov 9] strong, close-coupled colt: useful
performer: best efforts when fourth in handicaps at York (to Arakan) and Newmarket
(behind Royal Storm) on fourth/ninth starts: also in frame in minor events and a listed
race (at Redcar): effective at 6f/7f: acts on firm and soft going (below form on heavy).
R. Hannon

A VERY GOOD YEAR (IRE)   3 b.c. Indian Ridge 123 – Ma N'Ieme Biche (USA)   **100**
(Key To The Kingdom (USA)) [2003 77p: p7g³ 7m* 7m p6g² 6m* 6m² Sep 26] big,
strong colt: has plenty of scope: improved into a useful performer: won maiden at
Salisbury in June and handicap at Kempton in September, latter by 1¼ lengths from Texas
Gold: good second to Mazepa in handicap at Ascot final start, despite meeting trouble:
likely to prove best at 5f/6f: acts on polytrack, good to firm and good to soft going:
free-going sort: sent to Hong Kong, where renamed Whatabob. *T. G. Mills*

AVESA   3 b.f. Averti (IRE) 117 – Andalish 82 (Polish Precedent (USA) 131) [2003 59:   **–**
5g 8f 9.2m⁶ 10.9g 7.1f 9.2d Sep 29] smallish filly: modest maiden at 2 yrs for R. Hannon:
well beaten in 2003: tried blinkered. *D. A. Nolan*

AVESOMEOFTHAT (IRE)   2 b.g. (Apr 27) Lahib (USA) 129 – Lacinia 107 (Groom   **74**
Dancer (USA) 128) [2003 8.3g⁴ 8f⁵ 8f² 8.3g Oct 13] €13,000Y: fourth foal: brother to
3-y-o Maxilla: dam Irish 6f (at 2 yrs) and 11f winner: fair maiden: second at Bath:
possibly amiss final outing: will stay 1¼m: slowly away first 2 starts. *Mrs P. N. Dutfield*

AVESSIA   2 b.f. (Mar 18) Averti (IRE) 117 – Alessia 91 (Caerleon (USA) 132) [2003   **– p**
6g Oct 31] leggy filly: fourth foal: sister to 3-y-o Avonbridge and half-sister to 5-y-o

Patavellian: dam, 2-y-o 7f winner who stayed 1¼m, sister to Park Hill Stakes winner Casey: 14/1 and green, not knocked about when well held in maiden at Newmarket: should do better. *R. Charlton*

AVID SPELL (USA) 2 b.c. (Mar 8) Expelled (USA) 116 – Deep Magic (USA) (Gone West (USA)) [2003 5.1g² 6m² 6d* 5f⁴ 8g a6f a6g⁶ Dec 26] small, good-bodied colt: second foal: dam, ran 3 times, half-sister to dams of very smart US Grade 1 1¼m winner Skimming and 1000 Guineas winner Wince: fairly useful performer: won minor event at Brighton in May: blinkered, respectable effort next time (final one for R. Charlton): below form in allowance races/claimer for new trainer: likely to prove best at 5f/6f: acts on good to firm and good to soft ground. *M. L. Rouck, USA* **80**

AVIT (IRE) 3 ch.f. General Monash (USA) 107 – Breakfast Boogie 59 (Sizzling Melody 117) [2003 p6g 6m⁵ 5g 6m 5m 7m Jul 2] IR 1,000F: compact filly: fourth foal: half-sister to a winner in Turkey by Petong: dam, 5f winner, sister to useful 5f winner Major Quality: modest maiden: may prove best at 5f/6f. *P. L. Gilligan* **52**

AVONBRIDGE 3 b.c. Averti (IRE) 117 – Alessia 91 (Caerleon (USA) 132) [2003 104p: 6g² 6m² 6f* 6.5g³ 6s⁴ 6f³ Sep 13] strong, angular, good-topped colt: smart performer: did well physically and improved in 2003: won listed race at Salisbury in June by length from Ashdown Express: good length third to Porlezza in Prix Maurice de Gheest at Deauville next time: below best after in Prix de Meautry at Deauville and Ridgewood Pearl Stakes (third to Fayr Jag) at the Curragh: raced only around 6f: acts on firm going, possibly not on soft. *R. Charlton* **116**

AVONDALE LAD (IRE) 3 ch.g. Titus Livius (FR) 115 – Skinity (Rarity 129) [2003 68: 6.1m 6g 6m 6d f6s 6m² f6g³ 7.5m⁴ 7.2g⁴ 5.9m⁶ f7s f6g Nov 14] sturdy, close-coupled gelding: modest performer: left K. Ryan after ninth start: barely stays 7f: acts on fibresand, yet to race on extremes of going on turf: often wears cheekpieces: free-going sort. *M. Dods* **54**

Mr D. J. Deer's "Avonbridge"

John Roarty Memorial Scurry Handicap, the Curragh—Avorado (nearest camera)
repeats his 2001 success in this valuable handicap; Cool Cousin is second

AVONLOCH   2 b.g. (Mar 4) Averti (IRE) 117 – Loch Fyne 70 (Ardkinglass 114) [2003   **68**
5.2m 5m³ Jun 4] smallish gelding: first foal: dam, sprint maiden, half-sister to useful
sprinter Lennox Lewis: better effort in maidens (fair form) when third at Kempton, still
green: should stay 6f. *R. Hannon*

AVORADO (IRE)   5 b.g. Royal Academy (USA) 130 – Voronova (IRE) 71 (Sadler's   **114**
Wells (USA) 132) [2003 100: 8d³ 6g* 8d⁵ 8d² 6.3m* 7g* 8m⁴ 6d 8g² Nov 8] tall, attractive gelding: smart performer: better than ever in 2003: successful at the Curragh in
handicaps in April and June (latter valuable event by neck from Cool Cousin) and
Emirates Airline Minstrel Stakes (beat D'Anjou ¾ length) in July: good 1½ lengths
second to Major Title in handicap at Leopardstown final start: effective at 6f to 9f: acts on
good to firm and good to soft ground: usually blinkered before 2003: held up. *J. S. Bolger,
Ireland*

AWAKE   6 ch.g. First Trump 118 – Pluvial 90 (Habat 127) [2003 93: 5g⁵ 5.1m⁶ 5.1g⁵ 5g   **88**
5s Nov 3] strong, smallish gelding: fairly useful performer: mainly respectable efforts
prior to shaping as though amiss final start: effective at 5f/6f: acts on good to firm and
heavy going: tried visored (not discredited): slowly away penultimate start: sometimes
early to post. *D. Nicholls*

AWARDING   3 ch.g. Mark of Esteem (IRE) 137 – Monaiya (Shareef Dancer (USA)   **84**
135) [2003 82p: 5m² 6m⁴ 6m 5f⁴ 5f⁵ 6m⁶ 5m⁵ p6g p7g⁶ Dec 29] good-topped gelding:
fairly useful handicapper: mostly creditable efforts in 2003: probably best at 5f: acts on
polytrack and firm going: sometimes tongue tied: tends to carry head high: sometimes
slowly away. *R. F. Johnson Houghton*

AWEIGH   3 b.f. Polar Falcon (USA) 126 – Shore Line 107 (High Line 125) [2003   **–**
f8.5g⁵ Apr 28] sister to fairly useful 1¾m winner Special, closely related to very smart
7f/1m performer in Britain/USA Soviet Line (by Soviet Star), and half-sister to several
winners, including useful 1¼m/1½m winner South Shore (by Caerleon): dam, 7f winner
at 2 yrs and fourth in Oaks, sister to Park Hill winner Quay Line: weak 6/1-shot, well-
beaten fifth to Telemachus in maiden at Wolverhampton, slowly away and running green.
Sir Mark Prescott

AWESOME LOVE (USA)   2 br.c. (Feb 28) Awesome Again (CAN) 133 – Circus   **75 p**
Toons (USA) (Wild Again (USA)) [2003 6f^2 Jul 14] $135,000F: third foal: half-brother
to 4-y-o Love Regardless: dam minor 6f/8.5f stakes winner in USA: 5/2 and green,
short-head second in maiden at Ayr, slowly away: should stay 1m: likely to improve if all
is well. *M. Johnston*

A WOMAN IN LOVE   4 gr.f. Muhtarram (USA) 125 – Ma Lumiere (FR) (Niniski   **68**
(USA) 125) [2003 69: p7g p7g 6m^4 5.3m 7m 7g 8.5m^4 7m* 6m 7m 7f^3 7g^5 6g^4 8m^2 p6g^5
p7g^6 p7g^4 p7g Dec 6] angular filly: fair handicapper: won at Lingfield in August:
effective at 6f to 1m: acts on polytrack, raced only on good ground or firmer on turf: often
slowly away: free-going sort. *Miss B. Sanders*

AXIS   2 b.c. (Apr 22) Pivotal 124 – Bollin Victoria 51 (Jalmood (USA) 126) [2003 6d 5d   **98**
5m* 6m^2 6d^3 Sep 10] 27,000Y: tall colt: half-brother to several winners, including fairly
useful 1999 2-y-o 5f winner First Blood (by Rambo Dancer) and 4-y-o Bullfighter: dam,
ran only at 2 yrs, third at 7f: useful performer: won maiden at Hamilton in July: placed in
nursery at York (second to Blue Tomato) and sales race at Doncaster (excellent third to
Cape Fear): stays 6f: acts on good to firm and good to soft going: sent to Hong Kong,
where renamed Classic Solo. *T. D. Barron*

AYUN (USA)   3 ch.f. Swain (IRE) 134 – Oumaldaaya (USA) 111 (Nureyev (USA)   **99**
131) [2003 83: 8f* 8m^4 10m^4 11.7f^2 10.1d* 10m* Aug 4] close-coupled, sparely-made
filly: fluent mover: useful performer: won maiden at Bath in March, minor event at
Epsom in July and handicap at Ripon (beat Chief Yeoman by 2 lengths) in August: best at
1¼m/easy 11.7f: unraced on soft/heavy going, acted on any other: raced up with pace:
reliable: visits Sakhee. *J. L. Dunlop*

AZAMOUR (IRE)   2 b.c. (Mar 8) Night Shift (USA) – Asmara (USA) 109 (Lear   **108 p**
Fan (USA) 130) [2003 7f* 8d* Oct 12]
    The Juddmonte Beresford Stakes, run over a mile at the Curragh in October,
was won for a second successive season by a colt owned and bred by the Aga Khan,
trained by John Oxx and ridden by Johnny Murtagh; and Azamour, like Alamshar
before him, had also won a maiden on his only previous start. That is where the
similarities between the two will probably end. Even if Azamour develops into a
top-class three-year-old he is unlikely to have the stamina required to win races
such as the Irish Derby and the King George as Alamshar did. Alamshar's pedigree
pointed to his being well suited by a mile and a half, while Azamour's suggests that
he is not certain to get much beyond a mile, a view with which his trainer concurs.
'This horse is a great athlete and I'd say he's probably a miler,' said Oxx after the
Beresford. Azamour, having justified favouritism in good style at the Curragh in

Juddmonte Beresford Stakes, the Curragh—
Azamour gets the better of a good battle with Relaxed Gesture (blaze)

September, also headed the market in the six-runner Beresford, though not by much. He was sent off at 6/4 with another once-raced winner of a maiden Five Dynasties, one of three Aidan O'Brien-trained runners, at 13/8. Next in the betting came Relaxed Gesture, also the winner of a maiden on his previous start and representing the Dermot Weld stable. It was Relaxed Gesture who dictated the pace, pressed by Azamour, and they soon put distance between themselves and their rivals when the race began in earnest early in the straight. The pair were involved in a good battle from that point, Azamour still showing signs of inexperience but finding enough to edge ahead near the line and win by a neck. Azamour's form was a little below that shown by Alamshar when narrowly accounting for Brian Boru in this event, which had been upgraded from Group 3 to Group 2 in the interim, but there is little doubt that Azamour is open to a fair amount of improvement.

Azamour (IRE) (b.c. Mar 8, 2001)	Night Shift (USA) (b 1980)	Northern Dancer (b 1961)	Nearctic
			Natalma
		Ciboulette (b 1961)	Chop Chop
			Windy Answer
	Asmara (USA) (b 1993)	Lear Fan (b 1981)	Roberto
			Wac
		Anaza (b 1986)	Darshaan
			Azaarika

Azamour is the fourth foal and fourth winner of the useful Asmara who, like all of her offspring, was trained by Oxx, winning a seven-furlong maiden at Roscommon for him at two and a listed event over a mile and a quarter at Leopardstown at three. Asmara's first foal Arameen (by Halling) showed fairly useful form over seven furlongs and a mile, her second Ahsanabad (by Muhtarram), showed

H.H. Aga Khan's "Azamour"

useful form at up to a mile and a quarter and her third Arawan (by Entrepreneur), a fairly useful winner over seven furlongs in the latest season, stays a mile. Azamour's grandam Anaza, a useful winner of two races over a mile in France at two, her only season to race, is responsible for numerous winners apart from Asmara, the pick of them the very smart Astarabad, winner of the Prix d'Harcourt and Prix Ganay. The next dam Azaarika won over nine and a half and eleven furlongs in minor company at four. Azamour's sire Night Shift gained his sole success over six furlongs, and while he has been responsible for some good winners at a mile and a half it has to be said that, for the most part, his offspring tend towards speed and precocity. *J. Oxx, Ireland*

AZAROLE (IRE)   2 b.c. (Jan 29) Alzao (USA) 117 – Cashew 80 (Sharrood (USA) **109**
124) [2003 6m² 6m* 6g* 7g⁴ 7m⁴ Oct 2] strong colt: fourth foal: half-brother to 3 winners, including 4-y-o Macadamia and smart winner up to 1m (including in Scandinavia and at 5f/6f at 2 yrs) Pistachio (by Unblest): dam 1m winner: useful performer: won maiden at Newmarket in July and minor event at Windsor (hung right) in August: good fourth in Champagne Stakes won by Lucky Story at Doncaster and Somerville Tattersall Stakes won by Milk It Mick at Newmarket, beaten just over 2 lengths both times: will probably stay 1m. *J. R. Fanshawe*

AZOLLA   2 b.f. (Jan 13) Cadeaux Genereux 131 – Frond 85 (Alzao (USA) 117) [2003 **73**
6g⁴ 7g² 7m³ 6g⁵ 6d² Sep 29] second foal: dam, 7f winner (ran only at 2 yrs), out of useful 1½m winner Fern, herself half-sister to Oaks runner-up Shamshir: fair maiden: second at Yarmouth and Hamilton (nursery): will stay 1m: best effort on good to soft going: sold 12,000 gns, sent to Sweden *L. M. Cumani*

AZREME   3 ch.c. Unfuwain (USA) 131 – Mariette 35 (Blushing Scribe (USA) 107) **75**
[2003 71: f6s² 8.2g⁶ 7d* f7g 7g p7g f9.4s⁶ Dec 6] well-made colt: fair performer: well **a68**
held after winning handicap at Lingfield in May: stays 1m: acts on all-weather and good to soft ground, unraced on firmer than good: often visored. *P. W. D'Arcy*

AZUR (IRE)   6 b.m. Brief Truce (USA) 126 – Bayadere (USA) 61 (Green Dancer **76**
(USA) 132) [2003 70: 10m³ 13.1g³ 12m⁴ 11.9f⁵ 11.8m² 11.5m² 12m² 12.6m* 11.9m 17.2f² 17.1m⁴ 14.1m³ 14.6m⁴ Oct 24] quite good-topped mare: fair handicapper: won at Warwick in August: remained in form: effective at 1¼m, and seems to stay 17f: acts on firm and good to soft going, below form both starts on soft: usually blinkered/visored nowadays: held up: genuine. *Mrs A. L. M. King*

B

BAAWRAH   2 ch.c. (May 17) Cadeaux Genereux 131 – Kronengold (USA) (Golden **76**
Act (USA)) [2003 6g 8.2m⁶ f9.4g³ p10g² Nov 22] strong, workmanlike colt: sixth foal: half-brother to German 10.5f winner Aneefah (by Unfuwain): dam, German 9f to 11f winner (placed in 1½m Group 3), half-sister to smart middle-distance performer Komtur: fair form in maidens: placed at Wolverhampton and Lingfield: stays 1¼m: acts on all-weather. *M. R. Channon*

BABA MIA   3 b.f. Gothenberg (IRE) 117 – Kagram Queen 64 (Prince Ragusa 96) **–**
[2003 –: 10m 8m 11g 15.8m 7d⁶ Sep 20] leggy filly: little form: left I. McInnes after second start, J. Wainwright after fourth. *P. T. Midgley*

BABODANA   3 ch.c. Bahamian Bounty 116 – Daanat Nawal (Machiavellian (USA) **105**
123) [2003 97: 6v⁴ 7g 7g 8g⁴ 8d² 8g* p10g Nov 22] good-topped colt: has scope: useful performer: best effort when winning listed event at Newmarket in November by 1½ lengths from Checkit, racing alone near stand rail: stays 1m: raced only on good going or softer on turf, badly hampered on polytrack at Lingfield final outing: slowly away/soon off bridle third outing. *M. H. Tompkins*

BABOOSH (IRE)   2 b.f. (Feb 24) Marju (IRE) 127 – Slipper 94 (Suave Dancer (USA) **78 p**
136) [2003 7.5m² Sep 17] leggy filly: second foal: half-sister to useful French 1m (at 2 yrs) and 10.5f winner Cartier Opera (by Zilzal): dam 1½m winner: 20/1, 1½ lengths second of 11 to Spring Goddess in maiden at Beverley: will be suited by 1¼m/1½m: should improve. *J. R. Fanshawe*

BABOUSHKA (IRE)   2 b.f. (Apr 11) Soviet Star (USA) 128 – Kabayil 75 (Dancing **62 p**
Brave (USA) 140) [2003 7g 7s⁴ Nov 3] workmanlike filly: fifth foal: half-sister to useful

7f to 2m winner Dancing Bay (by Suave Dancer) and 4-y-o Kasamba: dam 1¼m winner and fairly useful hurdler: better effort in maidens (modest form) when fourth to Zeitgeist at Redcar, possibly still needing race: will stay 1¼m, probably 1½m: open to improvement. *C. G. Cox*

BABY BARRY   6 b.g. Komaite (USA) – Malcesine (IRE) 46 (Auction Ring (USA)   **65 §**
123) [2003 82: 6g 6m 6m 5.9g 6g⁵ 6m⁶ f6g³ 6m 6.1f f6s⁴ p6g² f6g³ f7g f6g Dec 9]
good-topped gelding: fair handicapper: effective at 6f/easy 7f: acts on all-weather and firm going, possibly not on softer than good: tried blinkered, usually visored: often leads: sometimes hangs: unreliable. *Mrs G. S. Rees*

BACHELOR DUKE (USA)   2 b.c. (Mar 11) Miswaki (USA) 124 – Gossamer   **115 p**
(USA) (Seattle Slew (USA)) [2003 7m³ 7m³ 7m⁴ Oct 18]
        Another name can be added to the list of smart performers the Duke of Devonshire has had in training with James Toller over the years, even though the horse in question, Bachelor Duke, has run just three times and is still a maiden. Bachelor Duke has already shown himself of a similar standard to such as Duck Row, Emperor Fountain, Lord of The Field and Teapot Row, and with further improvement likely he could eventually prove himself as good as his connections' 1997 July Cup winner Compton Place. A promising third in a maiden at Yarmouth in September on his debut, Bachelor Duke finished in the frame in two pattern races won by Milk It Mick at Newmarket the following month, starting at 25/1 both times. In the Group 3 Somerville Tattersall Stakes, Bachelor Duke took third place, beaten a neck and the same by Milk It Mick and Bayeux, waited with before improving well against the far rail to challenge in the final furlong. Bachelor Duke was also settled off the pace in the Dewhurst Stakes, and stayed on strongly to finish fourth, beaten a length and a half, with Three Valleys and Haafhd coming between him and the winner on this occasion.

	Miswaki (USA) (ch 1978)	Mr Prospector (b 1970)	Raise A Native
Bachelor Duke (USA)			Gold Digger
(b.c. Mar 11, 2001)		Hopespringseternal (ch 1971)	Buckpasser
			Rose Bower
	Gossamer (USA) (b 1991)	Seattle Slew (b or br 1974)	Bold Reasoning
			My Charmer
		Lisaleen (ch 1982)	Northern Dancer
			Lisadell

        Bachelor Duke, raced only at seven furlongs, will be suited by a step up to a mile and possibly more. The fourth foal of American-raced Gossamer (not to be confused with the 2002 Irish One Thousand Guineas winner of the same name), who won twice at around a mile, he is closely related to Translucid (by Woodman), a useful winner at up to a mile and a half and also a fairly useful winner over hurdles. Gossamer is from an excellent family. Her dam Lisaleen, a useful winner at seven furlongs and a mile in Ireland, is closely related to the 1993 Irish Two Thousand Guineas runner-up Fatherland and smart sprinter Yeats, the latter also a successful sire in Australia. Lisadell won the Coronation Stakes and is a sister to the top-class sprinter/miler Thatch and half-sister to the Irish Derby and St Leger second King Pellinore and the disqualified July Cup winner Marinsky. Bachelor Duke, a €125,000 yearling, is a big, good-topped colt with plenty of scope. His three races all took place on good to firm ground. *J. A. R. Toller*

BACHELOR OF ARTS   2 b.c. (Jan 30) Stravinsky (USA) 133 – Wannabe Grand   **96**
(IRE) 116 (Danehill (USA) 126) [2003 5g² 5.1m* 5f⁵ 5g⁴ 5.2g² 5g⁶ Aug 26] 52,000Y:
well-made colt: first foal: dam Cherry Hinton/Cheveley Park winner and runner-up in 1000 Guineas: useful performer: won maiden at Chester in June: in frame after in listed race at Sandown (lost shoe when fourth to Fortunately) and minor event at Yarmouth (very good second to Traytonic): ran poorly final start: likely to prove best at 5f/6f: very best efforts on good going: blinkered/visored after debut: sold 35,000 gns. *D. R. Loder*

BACHELORS PAD   9 b.g. Pursuit of Love 124 – Note Book 94 (Mummy's Pet 125)   **–**
[2003 –: 12.3g Aug 29] leggy gelding: of little account on Flat nowadays: tried blinkered. *Miss S. J. Wilton*

BACHELOR'S TONIC (IRE)   5 b.g. Fayruz 116 – Dance Alone (USA) (Monte-   **–**
verdi 129) [2003 f9.4g Dec 22] no worthwhile form in bumpers: slowly away and always behind in claimer at Wolverhampton. *K. A. Morgan*

Sheikh Marwan Al Maktoum's "Badminton"

BACK AT DE FRONT (IRE) 2 b.f. (Jan 25) Cape Cross (IRE) 129 – Bold Fashion **70**
(FR) (Nashwan (USA) 135) [2003 5m 6f* 6g* f5g⁵ p5g f6g⁴ Dec 26] 4,500Y: lengthy
filly: fourth foal: dam, French 10.5f winner, sister to useful French 1m/9f performer Irish
Fashion: fair performer: won seller at York in June and nursery at Kempton (then left
R. Hannon) in July: below form last 2 starts: should stay 1m: acts on firm going and
fibresand. *N. E. Berry*

BACK IN ACTION 3 b.c. Hector Protector (USA) 124 – Lucca (Sure Blade (USA) –
130) [2003 85p: p8g⁵ 8m p12g p12g Nov 29] leggy colt: fairly useful form on second
start at 2 yrs for D. Arbuthnot: well held in 2003: blinkered (raced too freely) final outing:
tongue tied. *M. A. Magnusson*

BACK IN FASHION 2 b.f. (Mar 5) Puissance 110 – Spring Collection (Tina's Pet –
121) [2003 f8g 8.2m Oct 28] 1,000Y: third foal: dam unraced: tailed off/pulled up in
sellers. *J. Mackie*

BACK IN SPIRIT 3 ch.g. Primo Dominie 121 – Pusey Street Girl 87 (Gildoran 123) –
[2003 76d: f6g 7.9d Jul 30] well-grown gelding: fair winner at 2 yrs: no form since: tried
tongue tied. *B. A. McMahon*

BACKLASH 2 b.f. (Apr 2) Fraam 114 – Mezza Luna (Distant Relative 128) [2003 p6g –
Dec 2] first foal: dam well beaten only outing: 50/1, slowly away and soon behind in
minor event at Lingfield. *A. W. Carroll*

BACKOFTHENET 2 b.c. (Apr 25) Timeless Times (USA) 99 – Nuthatch (IRE) 36 **56**
(Thatching 131) [2003 5m 5m² 5m² 6m⁵ 5f³ Aug 21] 4,000Y: smallish, good-bodied colt:
third foal: brother to 5f (at 2 yrs) and 1m winner Algunas Veces: dam, maiden, should
have stayed 1m: modest maiden: placed in claimer/seller: likely to prove best at 5f/6f:
wore cheekpieces final start. *K. R. Burke*

BACKWELL (USA) 3 b.g. Allied Forces (USA) 123 – Shehazahome (USA) (Known **88 ?**
Fact (USA) 135) [2003 89: 8g 8m f8.5s* 8m⁵ 7m⁶ 10m* 10d² 10.5d⁶ Sep 26] workman-

96

like gelding: fairly useful performer: won maiden at Wolverhampton in June and claimer at Newmarket in July: stays 1¼m: acts on heavy and good to firm going: wore cheek-pieces last 4 outings: tricky ride: usually forces pace: sold 22,000 gns. *M. A. Jarvis*

BADHBH (IRE) 2 ch.f. (Feb 25) Deploy 131 – Painted Desert 89 (Green Desert (USA) **55** 127) [2003 6g 6d⁶ 7f³ p7g⁵ 8f⁴ 8m 10m⁶ 8m Oct 21] IR 7,500F, 26,000Y: sparely-made filly: fifth foal: half-sister to 4-y-o Plateau and to winner in Malaysia by Zafonic: dam, 2-y-o 5.7f winner, out of sister to Lowther winner Kingscote: modest maiden: stays 1¼m: acts on polytrack, firm and good to soft going: tongue tied after debut. *G. C. Bravery*

BAD INTENTIONS (IRE) 3 b.f. Victory Note (USA) 120 – Fallacy (Selkirk (USA) **76** 129) [2003 76: 7m⁵ 6g³ 6m 5f 6m⁵ 5g⁶ 7f⁵ 6m 8.1d Sep 26] tall, leggy filly: fair handicapper: left G. Chung after second start, Miss D. Mountain after fifth: races freely, and probably best at 6f/7f: acts on firm and soft going: has been mounted on track/early to post: sold 10,000 gns. *G. A. Harker*

BADMINTON 2 b.f. (Feb 23) Zieten (USA) 118 – Badawi (USA) 103 (Diesis 133) **103 p** [2003 6m* 6m² 6m³ Oct 2] useful-looking filly: closely related to 2 winners by Green Desert, including 7f winner Balfour, later successful at 1m/9f in Scandinavia, and half-sister to 3 winners, including 4-y-o Rafferty: dam 1m/9f winner: won maiden at Doncaster in June: useful form behind Carry On Katie in Lowther Stakes at York (2 lengths second) and Cheveley Park Stakes at Newmarket (beaten 1¾ lengths), keeping on well both times: will be suited by 7f/1m: joined Godolphin: likely to make a smart 3-y-o. *C. E. Brittain*

BADOU 3 b.g. Averti (IRE) 117 – Bint Albadou (IRE) 91 (Green Desert (USA) 127) **55** [2003 59: p6g* p5g p6g p6g⁶ p7g⁵ 7g 8g 6d 8m² 8f⁴ p7g p8g p7g Dec 17] good-topped **a59** gelding: modest performer: mostly well held after winning claimer at Lingfield (claimed from G. Butler £8,000) in January: stays 1m: acts on soft going, good to firm and poly-track: best efforts in visor: sometimes slowly away. *L. Montague Hall*

BADRINATH (IRE) 9 b.g. Imperial Frontier (USA) 112 – Badedra (Kings Lake **–** (USA) 133) [2003 54, a58: 11.5m p10g Dec 30] quite good-topped gelding: modest performer: trained in Spain last five 8-y-o starts before returning to former trainer: well beaten in 2003. *H. J. Collingridge*

BADR (USA) 2 b.c. (Feb 26) Theatrical 128 – Bejat (USA) (Mr Prospector (USA)) **67 p** [2003 8.3g² 8d Sep 10] $90,000Y: rangy, good sort: unfurnished at 2 yrs: seventh foal: brother to minor stakes winner in USA and half-brother to 3 winners abroad: dam unraced half-sister to US Grade 1 2-y-o 8.5f winner One of A Klein: fair form when second in maiden at Hamilton: sweated when well held in similar event at Doncaster month later: will be suited by 1¼m/1½m: type to do better at 3 yrs. *M. Johnston*

BAFFLE 2 b.f. (Jan 28) Selkirk (USA) 129 – Elude (Slip Anchor 136) [2003 7m 7m² **76** 7.5m⁶ Sep 17] sturdy, workmanlike filly: first foal: dam unraced close relation to smart 1¼m performer Perpendicular out of half-sister to Kris, Diesis and Presidium: fair form in maidens: best effort when staying-on second at Newmarket: likely to be suited by 1¼m/1½m. *J. L. Dunlop*

BAGAN (FR) 4 b.c. Rainbow Quest (USA) 134 – Maid of Erin (USA) (Irish River **96** (FR) 131) [2003 77: 10m² 10m 9.9g 11.9m* 12g⁵ Sep 13] big, good-topped, attractive colt: useful handicapper: 50/1-winner at York in August by length from Trust Rule: stays 1½m: acts on good to firm going, probably on soft: free-going sort: best efforts held up: reportedly lost action third start. *H. R. A. Cecil*

BAGO (FR) 2 b. or br.c. (Feb 3) Nashwan (USA) 135 – Moonlight's Box (USA) **121 p** (Nureyev (USA) 131) [2003 8g* 8d* 8g* 8s* Nov 1]

The Criterium International, inaugurated in 2001 and run at Saint-Cloud in early-November, has quickly established itself as a significant pointer to some of the following season's top races. In that respect, it has proved considerably more successful than the latter years of the Grand Criterium at Longchamp, which it replaced as France's Group 1 race for two-year-old colts over a mile. Both the first two winners, Act One and Dalakhani, maintained unbeaten records in the Criterium International, each looking fine prospects for the following season, and neither disappointed. The latest winner Bago is also unbeaten and looks every bit as good as that pair did at the same stage. Indeed, his form can already be rated better. Act One's victory had been gained by a neck (over future Poule d'Essai des Poulains winner Landseer), and Dalakhani's by half a length, but Bago spreadeagled his field, winning impressively by six lengths. The winning margin, of course, is not

Criterium International, Saint-Cloud—Bago looks a high-class performer in the making as he spreadeagles the opposition; the British-trained Top Speed beats the rest convincingly

enough in itself for him to be rated superior to that pair, but, on our reading of the form, he gets the nod as Europe's top two-year-old. In a year when no two-year-old colt stood out, Bago's win was certainly the most decisive by a juvenile in a Group 1 contest.

The Criterium International might not have drawn the strongest field— Bago's reputation was already such that he must have scared off some potential rivals—but no-one could argue with the international nature of its line-up. Bago started at 5/2-on (coupled with a pacemaker, Alnitak), with Joursanvault, whom Bago had already beaten in an earlier encounter, at 28/10 second favourite and the only other French-trained runner. The foreign challengers in betting order were: the Aidan O'Brien-trained Acropolis, who had finished last in the Grand Criterium; the German maiden Marabout Directa, placed in listed/pattern company in his own country; a rare Russian challenger, Brief Floyed, who had had his limitations exposed in the Gran Criterium at Milan; and the Mick Channon-trained Top Seed, who, despite starting the outsider of the field, had some of the best form on offer among Bago's rivals.

Beforehand at least, it would have come as no surprise if Bago had not had to better his earlier form to stay unbeaten in the Criterium International, but it turned out to be an informative contest. Alnitak set off in his pacemaking role but was quickly joined by the three long-shots, whilst the riders of Bago, Joursanvault and Acropolis were content to bide their time some ten lengths behind the leading quartet. By the home turn the field had regrouped, Bago in particular moving smoothly up to the leaders. Once into the straight, however, the riders went their separate ways in search of the best ground in the soft conditions. Joursanvault was the only one to stay on the far side, saving ground, whilst Bago tracked Top Seed as that pair turned in widest of all to come down the stand side. The remainder were strung out across the centre of the course, but it was soon clear that Bago was travelling best of all. Passing the hard-ridden Top Seed over a furlong out, Bago forged clear inside the last. Acropolis could only stay on at one pace to be beaten a total of ten lengths in third, with the rest toiling further back at wide intervals. Anyone making hard and fast judgements based on the official times returned on French races should be wary (the accuracy, or otherwise, of French race-times is a subject discussed in the past, including in Imperial Beauty's essay in *Racehorses of 2001*), but for what it's worth Bago's win was achieved in a faster time than the other mile races on the same card, notably a listed race for three-year-old fillies and the Group 3 Prix Perth.

Bago's three earlier victories had earned him rave reviews in some quarters, but, whilst he won nicely each time, showing progressive form, it was not until Saint-Cloud that he really justified them. The main impression formed in his first two starts was that he would benefit from the experience. On his debut at Deauville in August against ten other newcomers he had taken a long time to settle and then shown signs of greenness before quickening decisively for a two-length win. He still looked as if he had a bit to learn when accounting for the much more experienced Joursanvault by the same margin in a minor event at Longchamp the following month. It was his third win, again at Longchamp, in the Prix des Chenes later in September (a race that Dalakhani had also won on the way to the Criterium International) which showed Bago was heading towards the top. Again there was nothing spectacular about his victory but he did it comfortably, pulled out from behind the favourite Valixir, himself unbeaten in two starts, to win by a length and a half. Third was Happy Crusader, who had shown useful form in nurseries in Britain, while fourth was Voix du Nord who went on to win the Criterium de Saint-Cloud over a mile and a quarter a week after Bago's success there.

		Blushing Groom	Red God
	Nashwan (USA)	(ch 1974)	Runaway Bride
	(ch 1986)	Height of Fashion	Bustino
Bago (FR)		(b 1979)	Highclere
(b. or br.c. Feb 3, 2001)		Nureyev	Northern Dancer
	Moonlight's Box (USA)	(b 1977)	Special
	(b 1996)	Coup de Genie	Mr Prospector
		(b 1991)	Coup de Folie

Whilst Bago's three-year-old prospects look excellent, it is less straightforward to predict what direction his second season will take. Act One and Dalakhani both had pedigrees which pointed to campaigns geared towards the top mile and a

Niarchos Family's "Bago"

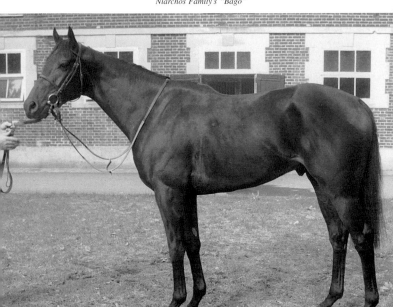

half races. Bago's stamina is less certain. The vast majority of Nashwan's three-year-old winners in Britain in recent seasons have come at between a mile and a quarter and a mile and a half, which gives some encouragement for Bago's staying further, as does the fact that he saw out the mile at Saint-Cloud really well, his first start in testing conditions at the trip. Bago is the first foal of an unraced mare Moonlight's Box, but for the most part Bago's family has enjoyed most success at around a mile. At least to start with, it seems that Bago's three-year-old campaign will continue at a mile, but will he contest the Two Thousand Guineas or the Poule d'Essai des Poulains? Connections have not committed him to either race, but the odds of 16/1 quoted immediately after the International would look attractive if he is given the opportunity to emulate his sire at Newmarket. Trainer Jonathan Pease's visitors to Britain are few and far between, his last runner here being Moon Driver, who disappointed when favourite for the 1999 Cheveley Park Stakes. However, Pease is no stranger to success outside France, with two Breeders' Cup winners, Tikkanen and Spinning World, to his name. The latter, incidentally, won the Irish Two Thousand Guineas after contesting the French equivalent.

The latest season was a significant one for French-trained two-year-olds as they managed to win all five of the Group 1 races confined to their age group in France. The last time this happened was 1993 when Bago's own grandam Coup de Genie played a leading role in keeping them all at home by winning both the Prix Morny and Prix de la Salamandre. She started joint favourite for the One Thousand Guineas the following season and finished just a short head and a neck behind the winner Las Meninas. Four years earlier, Coup de Genie's full brother Machiavellian had also been sent to Newmarket after winning the Morny and Salamandre and finished second to Tirol as Two Thousand Guineas favourite. Their dam, Coup de Folie (out of a half-sister to Northern Dancer), who won the Prix d'Aumale and finished third in the Marcel Boussac, also bred two other milers of note, the very smart Exit To Nowhere, who was a later developer than most in this family, peaking as a four-year-old when successful in the Prix Jacques le Marois, and the smart Hydro Calido, second in the Poule d'Essai des Pouliches. Coup de Genie's own record at stud is starting to rival that of her dam. Details of her offspring can be found in the essay on her daughter Denebola, winner of the Prix Marcel Boussac and another with genuine classic prospects for the Niarchos family in 2004. *J. E. Pease, France*

BAG 'O' NAILS (IRE) 2 b.c. (Mar 21) Desert Prince (IRE) 130 – Dulcinea 73 **– p** (Selkirk (USA) 129) [2003 7m Sep 23] big, good sort: third foal: half-brother to useful 7f winner Hideaway Heroine (by Hernando): dam, 7f/1m winner, half-sister to smart French performer up to 1¼m Amato out of smart winner up to 10.5f Ahohoney: 10/1, well held in 17-runner maiden at Newmarket, racing freely before hanging left/carrying head awkwardly: should do better. *H. J. Cyzer*

BAHAMA BELLE 2 b.f. (Feb 1) Bahamian Bounty 116 – Barque Bleue (USA) **63** (Steinlen 127) [2003 5f 5m 6m 6g Oct 6] 1,800Y: workmanlike filly: fourth foal: dam unraced half-sister to very smart French performer up to 1m Bon Vent: modest maiden: best effort third start: will probably stay 7f. *H. S. Howe*

BAHAMA REEF (IRE) 2 b.g. (Feb 19) Sri Pekan (USA) 117 – Caribbean Dancer **72** 71 (Shareef Dancer (USA) 135) [2003 5g⁴ 5.1m² 6g 6m² 5m 7g⁶ 8m⁴ 7m 8g Sep 22] 15,500Y: angular gelding: second foal: dam, lightly-raced 1m winner, from family of Needle Gun, Luso and 5-y-o Warrsan: fair maiden: second at Bath and Brighton: barely stays 1m: ran badly in visor last 2 starts. *B. Gubby*

BAHAMIAN BELLE 3 b.f. Bahamian Bounty 116 – Marjorie's Memory (IRE) 76 **61** (Fairy King (USA)) [2003 62: f5g⁶ 5.1m⁶ 5g⁴ 5m⁵ 5m⁵ f5g⁶ 5m⁵ 5f² 5m³ 5m⁴ 5g f7g⁵ **a52** Nov 10] good-topped filly: modest maiden: best form at 5f: raced only on good ground or firmer on turf, below form on fibresand: usually blinkered of late, tried in cheekpieces: races freely. *J. Balding*

BAHAMIAN BREEZE 2 b.g. (Apr 7) Piccolo 121 – Norgabie 94 (Northfields (USA)) **78** [2003 5.2f² 5f* 6m⁶ Aug 19] 55,000Y: robust gelding: fifth foal: closely related to fairly useful 1998 2-y-o 6f winner No Warning (by Warning), later successful at 6.5f in Germany, and half-brother to 1995 2-y-o 5f winner Nostoi (by Rock City): dam best at 6f: fair form: won maiden at Thirsk in August: respectable sixth to Blue Tomato in nursery at York: likely to prove best at 5f/6f. *J. Noseda*

BAHAMIAN HEIR (IRE)   4 b.c. Lake Coniston (IRE) 131 – Bally Souza (IRE) 87   **48**
(Alzao (USA) 117) [2003 50: f12s⁴ f11g⁵ f11g f12s Feb 27] lengthy colt: fluent mover:
poor maiden: left D. Nicholls after third start (blinkered): stays 11f: acts on good to firm
going and fibresand: usually races prominently. *N. Wilson*

BAHAMIAN PIRATE (USA)   8 ch.g. Housebuster (USA) – Shining Through (USA)   **113**
(Deputy Minister (CAN)) [2003 120: 5g² 6m 6g² 5f 5g⁴ 6m⁵ 5m⁴ 5g⁶ 5m 5s⁶ Oct 5] sturdy
gelding: smart performer: hasn't won since 2001, but ran creditably at 8 yrs when length
second to Needwood Blade in Palace House Stakes on reappearance, fifth to Oasis Dream
in July Cup, also at Newmarket, and when sixth to Patavellian in Prix de l'Abbaye at
Longchamp on final outing: best at 5f/6f: acts on soft and good to firm ground: sometimes
slowly away: usually held up: none too consistent. *D. Nicholls*

BAHIANO (IRE)   2 ch.c. (Mar 16) Barathea (IRE) 127 – Trystero (Shareef Dancer   **73 p**
(USA) 135) [2003 7d⁶ f7s² Dec 31] 25,000Y: half-brother to useful 6f (at 2 yrs) to 1m
winner Cadeaux Tryst (by Cadeaux Genereux) and to a winner abroad by Groom Dancer:
dam unraced half-sister to smart 7f/1m performer Fraam: better effort in maidens (fair
form) when 2 lengths second to Denver at Wolverhampton, not knocked about: should
stay 1m: open to progress. *C. E. Brittain*

B A HIGHFLYER   3 b.g. Compton Place 125 – Primulette 82 (Mummy's Pet 125)   **71**
[2003 85: 6m 6g 6s⁶ 6m 7m⁵ 6g³ 6m³ 6m⁴ 6m² 6m⁴ 8.1m 7m 6m⁵ 7g 7m 6g f6g² 7m² 6d*
7d⁶ Nov 4] good-bodied gelding: has a quick action: fair handicapper: won at Brighton in
October: effective at 6f/7f: acts on all-weather, firm and soft going: occasionally visored.
M. R. Channon

BAHITA (IRE)   3 b.f. Bahhare (USA) 122 – Bolshoi Star 65§ (Soviet Star (USA) 128)   **33**
[2003 64: f7g⁵ f7g⁵ f5g⁶ Apr 25] modest maiden at 2 yrs: well held in 2003. *E. J. Alston*

BAHLINO (IRE)   3 gr.g. Bahhare (USA) 122 – Azulino (IRE) (Bluebird (USA) 125)   **85**
[2003 56: 7g 9m² 9.9d² 11m* 12.1m* 12m³ p12g² 12s³ 12g⁴ 11.6m² 11.8m⁴ Oct 13]
good-bodied gelding: fairly useful handicapper: won at Redcar in May and Beverley in
June: stays 1½m: acts on polytrack, soft and good to firm going: ran creditably only try
in cheekpieces: has hung left: consistent: sold 75,000 gns, joined J. Howard Johnson.
W. Jarvis

BAHRQUEEN (USA)   4 b.f. Bahri (USA) 125 – April In Kentucky (USA) (Palace   **84**
Music (USA) 129) [2003 78: 7.1m² 12f² 9f* 9f⁴ 11m³ 12m⁶ Aug 24] quite attractive filly:
has a quick action: fairly useful performer: in frame 10 of 11 outings: won handicap at
Kempton in June: effective at 9f to 1½m: acts on firm and good to soft going: races
prominently: reliable. *D. R. C. Elsworth*

BAILAORA (IRE)   2 b.c. (Feb 14) Shinko Forest (IRE) – Tart (FR) 76 (Warning 136)   **81**
[2003 7g⁴ 7g⁴ 7m⁴ 7.1d³ 8d 7f² Oct 12] 10,500Y: good-bodied colt: third foal: half-
brother to German winner around 11f Twingo (by Bigstone): dam 1¼m and 11.5f winner:
fairly useful maiden: blinkered, good second in nursery at Goodwood, though found little
in front: should stay 1m: acts on firm and good to soft going. *B. W. Duke*

BAILEYS DANCER   2 b.f. (Apr 12) Groom Dancer (USA) 128 – Darshay (FR) 87   **90**
(Darshaan 133) [2003 5m⁵ 8.3g* 8.1g*⁷ 8m⁴ 8g Nov 1] sparely-made filly: has a quick
action: half-sister to 3 winners, including useful 1m (at 2 yrs)/1¼m winner Deal Fair (by
Grand Lodge), later successful in Germany, and 5-y-o Francis Flute: dam, 2-y-o maiden,
later 9f winner in Belgium: fairly useful performer: won maiden at Hamilton in August
and nursery at Haydock in September: good 6 lengths fourth to Fantastic View at Goodwood, better effort in listed events after: should stay 1¼m: often races up with pace.
M. Johnston

BAILEYS IMPERIAL (USA)   3 b.g. Imperial Ballet (IRE) 110 – Ms Deborah Ann   **–**
(USA) (Shenadoah River (USA)) [2003 7m⁶ 8g 7m 8.2m 8f Jun 25] IR 16,000Y: brother
to a winner in USA and half-brother to several winners in USA, including minor stakes
winner by Silent Review: dam 1m winner in USA: little form, including in blinkers: sold
3,000 gns in July. *M. Johnston*

BAILIEBOROUGH (IRE)   4 b.g. Charnwood Forest (IRE) 125 – Sherannda (USA)   **75 §**
(Trempolino (USA) 135) [2003 80: 7m 6.9m 7m⁵ 6.9m 7g² 7.1m⁵ 8.5m² 8m 7m* 7m
7m 7.2m 7.1g Sep 28] quite good-topped gelding: fair performer: won minor event at
Folkestone in August: best at 7f/1m: acts on good to firm and good to soft going: visored
(ran respectably) once: often slowly away: usually held up: has hung left: unreliable.
D. Nicholls

BAINESSE   4 b.f. Hernando (FR) 127 – Aeolina (FR) 60 (Kaldoun (FR) 122) [2003 –:   **–**
9.2d 10d 14f Jun 16] good-topped filly: no form. *C. W. Thornton*

BAJAN DESERT 4 ch.g. Zamindar (USA) 116 – Bajan Rose 89 (Dashing Blade 117) –
[2003 51: f7g p7g f7s Feb 6] modest maiden at 2 yrs: well held in 2003: tried tongue tied.
M. Blanshard

BAJAN STORM 2 ch.c. (Mar 29) First Trump 118 – Bajan Rose 89 (Dashing Blade 62
117) [2003 5m³ 6m 6g⁵ 5m f6f⁴ f7g² f7g⁶ 7m f7s³ f6s² f6s f6g Nov 10] 12,500Y: leggy
colt: third foal: half-brother to 3-y-o Ivy Moon: dam, 5f/6f winner (including at 2 yrs),
half-sister to smart sprinter Rambling Bear: modest maiden: second in nursery/claimer:
stays easy 7f: acts on fibresand and good to firm going: blinkered (ran poorly) final start:
none too consistent. *M. Blanshard*

BAKER OF OZ 2 b.c. (May 11) Pursuit of Love 124 – Moorish Idol 90 (Aragon 118) 75
[2003 7m² 8m² 8.5g⁴ 8.3m⁶ f7g Nov 28] 16,000Y: strong, close-coupled colt: half-
brother to several winners, including useful Scandinavian performer up to 1½m Duty
Time (by Night Shift), 7f/1m winner in Britain at 2 yrs, and 3-y-o Interceptor: dam 2-y-o
6f winner who probably stayed 1m: fair maiden: second at Salisbury and Goodwood: well
below form after: stays 1m: acts on good to firm going. *R. Hannon*

BAKERS DOZEN 3 ch.g. Whittingham (IRE) 104 – Blue Empress (Blue Cashmere –
129) [2003 p8g f9.4g Feb 21] half-brother to several winners, including 1m/1¼m seller
winner Miami Blues (by Palm Track): dam showed no ability: well beaten in maidens.
P. D. Evans

BAKHTYAR 2 gr.g. (Mar 29) Daylami (IRE) 138 – Gentilesse 81 (Generous (IRE) 64 p
139) [2003 p8g 8.2m 7s⁵ Nov 3] 54,000Y: leggy, quite good-topped gelding: third foal:
dam, won at 1¼m only start, out of smart French winner around 1m As You Desire Me:
modest form in maidens: type to do better in handicaps at 1¼m/1½m. *R. Charlton*

BALAKHERI (IRE) 4 b.c. Theatrical 128 – Balanka (IRE) 116 (Alzao (USA) 117) 111
[2003 121: 12d⁶ 13.9m 12g³ 12f Jun 21] good-bodied, quite attractive colt: very smart
performer in 2002, winning King Edward VII Stakes: easily best effort in 2003 (smart
form) when 4 lengths third to Ange Gabriel in Grand Prix de Chantilly third start: should
stay 1¾m: yet to race on heavy going, acts on any other: tried visored: has carried head
awkwardly: none too reliable. *Sir Michael Stoute*

BALAKIREF 4 b.g. Royal Applause 124 – Pluck 80 (Never So Bold 135) [2003 82: 73 d
6g 6m 6m 7g² 7.2g 6m 6g 7.2g 7g f6s Oct 7] quite attractive gelding: fair performer: well
below form last 4 starts: best at 6f/7f: acts on firm going, soft and fibresand: tried visored:
sometimes slowly away. *M. Dods*

BALALAIKA TUNE (IRE) 4 b.f. Lure (USA) 131 – Bohemienne (USA) (Polish 38
Navy (USA)) [2003 8f 8m⁵ 12g⁵ f7g Dec 16] ex-French filly: fourth foal: half-sister to
French 1997 2-y-o 1m winner Bandit d'Honneur (by Pistolet Bleu): dam unraced: fairly
useful form at 3 yrs for E. Lellouche: poor form in Britain. *W. Storey*

BALDOUR (IRE) 4 b.g. Green Desert (USA) 127 – Baldemara (FR) (Sanglamore 90
(USA) 126) [2003 92d: 7m³ 7m³ 7.1f³ 8m* 8d 7.2f² 8.3g⁶ 7.2m 7m² 7.1m Oct 25] good-
topped gelding: fairly useful handicapper: reportedly struck into himself when winning at
Brighton in July: first home on far side at Newcastle penultimate outing: effective at 7f/
1m: acts on firm going, below form on softer than good: effective visored or not: sold
19,000 gns. *E. A. L. Dunlop*

BALEARIC STAR (IRE) 2 b.c. (Apr 7) Night Shift (USA) – La Menorquina (USA) 73
65 (Woodman (USA) 126) [2003 7m⁶ 6m 6g 7f 8.3g Oct 13] IR 28,000F, 16,000Y: strong,
close-coupled colt: second foal: dam, won at 2m and over hurdles, half-sister to smart
Irish 1¼m/1½m performer His Excellence: fair maiden: best efforts first and third starts:
should stay at least 1m. *B. R. Millman*

BALERNO 4 b.g. Machiavellian (USA) 123 – Balabina (USA) 110 (Nijinsky (CAN) 58
138) [2003 68: p10g⁴ 12g 11.5m p10g f8g⁴ f8.5g⁵ 10.1m 7.1d 7m p8g⁵ 10.1g³ p10g
p10g Dec 29] close-coupled gelding: modest maiden handicapper: left S. Williams after
ninth start: stays 1¼m: acts on all-weather, good to firm and good to soft going: tried in
headgear. *R. Ingram*

BALESTRINI (IRE) 3 b.c. Danehill (USA) 126 – Welsh Love (Ela-Mana-Mou 132) 117
[2003 81: 10m* 10.5g⁴ 12m⁵ 10g Jul 5] IR 2,100,000Y: big, good-topped colt: half-
brother to several winners, including very smart miler (including Grand Criterium at 2
yrs) Second Empire (by Fairy King) and smart performers up to 1¼m Ihtiram (by Royal
Academy) and Ajhiba (by Barathea): dam, Irish 1½m winner, half-sister to dam of
Salsabil and Marju: smart performer: 33/1, won P. W. McGrath Memorial Ballysax
Stakes at Leopardstown in April by ½ length from Alamshar (made all): sweating, ran
well when 3¼ lengths fifth of 20 to Kris Kin in Derby at Epsom: respectable fourth to

Dalakhani in Prix Lupin at Longchamp, but only tenth in Eclipse Stakes at Sandown on other starts: effective at 1¼m/1½m: acts on good to firm going: has worn crossed noseband: sent to USA, joined N. Drysdale. *A. P. O'Brien, Ireland*

BALIN'S SWORD (IRE) 3 b.c. Spectrum (IRE) 126 – Green Delight (IRE) (Green **108** Desert (USA) 127) [2003 93: 8m* 8m² 8m⁵ 8g³ 8.5f²ᵈ 9g⁵ 8d Oct 19] useful performer: won handicap at Newbury (reared leaving stall, beat El Coto ¾ length) in April: good efforts next 3 starts, notably when narrowly-beaten third to King's Drama in Prix de la Jonchere at Chantilly: left B. Meehan and off 3 months, below form in allowance races in US last 3 outings: stays 9f: acts on firm going. *J. R. Fisher, USA*

BALI ROYAL 5 b.m. King's Signet (USA) 110 – Baligay 84 (Balidar 133) [2003 104: **111** 5.1g 5.2m³ 5m 5.1m⁵ 5m³ 5v 5g⁵ 5f² 5m⁴ 5g² 5m² 5g* 5m² 5m⁴ Oct 16] strong, good-quartered mare: smart performer, better than ever at 5 yrs: left J. M. Bradley after tenth start: won listed event at Hamilton in September by short head from Dominica: beaten 3 short heads in handicap at Newmarket final start: best at 5f: acts on firm ground, soft and fibresand: has been early to post/mounted on track: sometimes carries head awkwardly: front runner: tough. *M. S. Saunders*

BALI-STAR 8 b.g. Alnasr Alwasheek 117 – Baligay 84 (Balidar 133) [2003 60: 6g² **53** p6g 5m⁵ 6.1m 5.7g 5f⁴ 5.1f 5.1m⁵ 5d 5m f6g⁵ Dec 9] modest performer: effective at 5f/ 6f: acts on all-weather, firm and good to soft going: tried blinkered: often races handily: none too consistent. *R. J. Hodges*

BALKAN KNIGHT 3 b.c. Selkirk (USA) 129 – Crown of Light 112 (Mtoto 134) **88** [2003 79: 10m* Sep 17] fair sort: fairly useful form: off 14 months, beat Jubilee Treat by neck in handicap at Sandown only 3-y-o start: stays 1¼m: acts on good to firm and good to soft ground: visored last 2 starts. *D. R. Loder*

BALLARE (IRE) 4 b.g. Barathea (IRE) 127 – Raindancing (IRE) 94 (Tirol 127) [2003 **56** 56: 10.1g⁴ 10.2g 8m² 8.2f f8g Nov 19] good-topped gelding: modest maiden handicapper: best at 1m/1¼m: acts on good to firm ground. *Bob Jones*

BALLASILLA 8 b.m. Puissance 110 – Darussalam 78 (Tina's Pet 121) [2003 8.1m **–** 5m Sep 1] poor maiden handicapper: off 4 years, soundly beaten in 2003. *B. Palling*

BALLERINA BELLE (IRE) 3 b.f. Zafonic (USA) 130 – Bayadere (USA) 61 (Green **67** Dancer (USA) 132) [2003 p8g³ p8g³ Jan 29] fifth living foal: half-sister to 3 winners, including useful 1m to 1½m winner Bryony Brind (by Kris) and 6-y-o Azur: dam staying maiden: fair form in maidens at Lingfield: will stay 1¼m: sold 4,500 gns in December. *J. R. Fanshawe*

BALLET RUSE 2 ch.f. (Mar 9) Rainbow Quest (USA) 134 – El Opera (IRE) 100 **– p** (Sadler's Wells (USA) 132) [2003 7g 7s 7d Nov 7] leggy, quite good-topped filly: fourth foal: sister to fairly useful 1¼m winner Rainshine and closely related to ungenuine 1½m winner Dafne (by Nashwan): dam, 7f winner who stayed 1¼m well, closely related to smart sprinter Pharaoh's Delight: well held in maidens: likely to do better at 1¼m+. *Sir Mark Prescott*

BALL GAMES 5 b.g. Mind Games 121 – Deb's Ball 70 (Glenstal (USA) 118) [2003 **–** 58: 9.2g 8.3m Aug 19] rather leggy, close-coupled gelding: modest maiden at best: well held in sellers in 2003: tried visored. *James Moffatt*

BALLINGER RIDGE 4 b.g. Sabrehill (USA) 120 – Branston Ridge (Indian Ridge **79** 123) [2003 77: 8.3m² 8d 9.9m 8f 8.3m⁶ 8.3g³ Oct 13] good-topped gelding: fair maiden handicapper: stays easy 1¼m: acts on good to firm going, seemingly not on softer than good: takes good hold, and often makes running. *A. M. Balding*

BALLIN ROUGE 2 ch.f. (Apr 29) Dr Fong (USA) 128 – Bogus John (CAN) (Blush- **–** ing John (USA) 120) [2003 5m 7m Oct 1] 9,000Y: strong filly: fifth foal: half-sister to 3 winners, including 5-y-o Blushing Spur: dam unraced: well held in maidens at Beverley and Newcastle. *T. J. Fitzgerald*

BALL KING (IRE) 5 ch.g. Ball Park (NZ) – Firey Encounter (IRE) (Kris 135) [2003 **58** 74: p7g 8.3g³ 7f² Apr 10] rather sparely-made gelding: fair performer: placed in sellers in 2003: probably best at 7f/1m: acts on polytrack, soft and good to firm ground: tried blinkered: wears tongue tie: sometimes finds little. *P. J. Makin*

BALLYBORO (IRE) 2 b.f. (Feb 21) Entrepreneur 123 – Tathkara (USA) (Alydar **57 p** (USA)) [2003 8.5m⁵ Aug 24] IR 31,000F, €35,000Y: close-coupled filly: second foal: dam unraced sister to US Grade 1 9f winner Talinum: 9/4, fifth of 12 in maiden at Beverley, slowly away and green: likely to do better. *M. J. Wallace*

BALLYBUNION (IRE)   4 ch.g. Entrepreneur 123 – Clarentia 111 (Ballad Rock 122)   **76**
[2003 68: 6m⁶ 7f 5m 6m 6m 6f* 5.9f⁵ 6m 5m² 6f 5m* 6g⁶ 5m³ 5.7f² 6m⁶ 6f* 5d 5m Sep
17] strong gelding: fair performer: won handicaps at Catterick in June and Folkestone
in July and minor event at Catterick in August: effective at 5f/6f: acts on firm going,
probably on polytrack: tried visored/tongue tied: reluctant to race/very slowly away third
3-y-o start: sometimes races freely. *D. Nicholls*

BALLYGRIFFIN KID   3 gr.g. Komaite (USA) – Ballygriffin Belle (Another Realm   **50**
118) [2003 65: 6g 8.2d 8m⁵ 6f⁶ 6f³ Aug 12] just modest maiden at 3 yrs: should stay 7f:
acts on firm ground: often races up with pace. *T. P. McGovern*

BALLY HALL (IRE)   3 b.c. Saddlers' Hall (IRE) 126 – Sally Rose 92 (Sallust 134)   **81**
[2003 –p: f8.5s⁵ 10m* 9.9d 10f* 10g* 11m³ᵈ 12.1g⁵ 10s⁴ Aug 28] strong, close-coupled
colt: fairly useful performer: won handicap at Nottingham in April and minor event at
Brighton and handicap at Nottingham (easily) in June: best efforts around 1¼m: acts on
firm and soft going: usually tongue tied: hung right sixth start: sometimes finds little.
G. A. Butler

BALLYHURRY (USA)   6 b.g. Rubiano (USA) – Balakhna (FR) (Tyrant (USA)) [2003   **83**
60: 8m* 8m⁶ 8.3d 7.1m² 7.2g* 7.2f² 7.1f* 7.2g⁵ 7.1m* 7g³ 7m 7.2m* 7.1g⁵ 7.1m⁴ Oct 25]
angular gelding: fairly useful handicapper: better than ever in 2003, winning at Musselburgh (3) and Ayr (2) between April and September: effective at 7f/1m: acts on firm and
soft going: successful in blinkers earlier in career: usually held up: reliable. *J. S. Goldie*

BALLYKEATING   2 b.c. (Apr 4) Danzero (AUS) – Pearly River 72 (Elegant Air 119)   **95**
[2003 5g* 6m 6d 5d² 6m 7g³ Oct 11] 20,000Y: tall colt: fifth foal: half-brother to
3-y-o River Falcon, 1999 2-y-o 7f winner Another Pearl (by Ezzoud) and 6f/7f winner
Rumbunctious (by Charnwood Forest): dam, 7f (at 2 yrs) and 1½m winner, out of half-
sister to Roseate Tern and Ibn Bey: useful performer: won maiden at Redcar in July: good
placed efforts in minor events at Beverley (second to Cartography) and Ascot (third to
Oriental Warrior): stays 7f: acts on good to soft going: tends to sweat: sometimes carries
head awkwardly: sent to Hong Kong, joined D. Hill and renamed Don Felipe.
N. A. Callaghan

BALMACARA   4 b.f. Lake Coniston (IRE) 131 – Diabaig 76 (Precocious 126) [2003   **57**
53: p8g² p8g p7g 7m 8m⁵ 7.9m 7m² 7g 7m 6m 6m 7f⁵ p7g⁵ p8g⁴ Dec 6] lengthy, angular
filly: modest maiden: stays 1m: acts on polytrack and firm going: tried blinkered, wore
cheekpieces last 5 starts. *Miss K. B. Boutflower*

BALMONT (USA)   2 b.c. (Mar 11) Stravinsky (USA) 133 – Aldebaran Light   **117**
(USA) (Seattle Slew (USA)) [2003 6m² 6m* 6m* 6m* 6m* 7m Oct 18]
        When Balmont was awarded the Middle Park Stakes at an inquiry after the
turn of the year, he became the sixth horse in the past fifty years to have achieved
the Gimcrack/Middle Park double. Crocket, Petingo, Steel Heart, Stalker and Royal

Scottish Equitable Gimcrack Stakes, York—Balmont and Fokine (spotted cap) fight it out;
Byron (star on cap) passes the post in third place, but is demoted

*Shadwell Stud Middle Park Stakes, Newmarket—Balmont finishes second
to Three Valleys (white sleeves) but is later awarded the race on technical grounds;
Holborn (star on cap), Auditorium (sash) and Whipper (far right) are the next to finish*

Applause all passed the post first in both races but, although Balmont managed to do so at York, he had to settle for second behind Three Valleys at Newmarket, seemingly beaten on merit, only to become the chief beneficiary when Three Valleys failed a drugs test. Balmont is rated lower than any of the previous winners of the double, so could find things tough as a three-year-old, especially as he will be burdened with a Group 1 penalty when racing at a lower level. Still, he's a genuine colt and will surely have a more successful second season than either Stalker or Royal Applause did. The former showed very little in three runs, while the latter gained his only success when landing the odds unimpressively in a minor event, though Royal Applause did recapture his best form as a four-year-old, winning four races including the Cork And Orrery Stakes and the Haydock Park Sprint Cup, and is now making a name for himself at stud.

The Two Thousand Guineas will be Balmont's first major objective in the next season, but given the speed he showed at two, when all but one of his races were at six furlongs, he seems unlikely to be so effective at a mile. A most promising second to Byron at Newmarket on his debut, Balmont landed the odds easily in a maiden at Doncaster and a minor event at Newmarket on his next two starts, making the running both times and looking more than ready for the step up to pattern company. The Scottish Equitable Gimcrack Stakes at York in August provided Balmont with a far sterner test. All eight of his rivals were winners, and they included the Aidan O'Brien-trained Grand Reward, who had created a highly favourable impression on his only start, and Majestic Missile, the latter upped in trip after completing a hat-trick in the Molecomb Stakes; while Byron, third in the July Stakes following his defeat of Balmont, was again in opposition. Grand Reward went off favourite, with Balmont, who also came in for good support, next in the betting. Pat Eddery once again elected to make the running on Balmont, the other leading contenders all being waited with, and his mount travelled strongly, pressed by Fokine. Sent for home around two furlongs out, Balmont edged left but found plenty for pressure and held on by a head from Fokine, the pair just over a length ahead of Byron and Grand Reward whose third and fourth placings were subsequently reversed.

Balmont and Fokine met again in the Shadwell Stud Middle Park Stakes at Newmarket in October, the pair among a dozen entries in what was an up-to-standard renewal of one of the most significant races for juveniles. The impressive Coventry Stakes winner Three Valleys started favourite despite a defeat on his previous start, when he was found to have had mucus in his lungs, and Grand Reward, one of four O'Brien runners, and recent Doncaster winner Kheleyf were also preferred to 8/1-shot Balmont in the betting. Whipper, winner of the Prix Morny on his previous outing and the only French challenger in the field, was sent off at 16/1. Balmont was ridden with restraint this time, sensibly so given that two of the O'Brien runners went off too fast, the pair largely ignored. He again

Mr Sanford R. Robertson's "Balmont"

Balmont (USA) (b.c. Mar 11, 2001)	Stravinsky (USA) (b 1996)	Nureyev (b 1977)	Northern Dancer Special
		Fire The Groom (b 1987)	Blushing Groom Prospector's Fire
	Aldebaran Light (USA) (b 1996)	Seattle Slew (b or br 1974)	Bold Reasoning My Charmer
		Altair (b 1991)	Alydar Stellar Odyssey

impressed with the manner in which he travelled, and also with the speed he showed to get into a challenging position after two furlongs out, at which point Three Valleys and Holborn came through to dispute the lead. Three Valleys soon took Holborn's measure and ran on strongly to hold on by three quarters of a length from Balmont, who in turn finished half a length ahead of Holborn, this trio followed closely by Auditorium, Whipper and Grand Reward, who were all nearest at the finish. Fokine finished eighth. So far, Balmont hadn't stopped improving, but he was below both his Gimcrack and Middle Park form when tried at seven furlongs on his final start, in the Dewhurst Stakes at Newmarket. He did come through to have a chance after being waited with but could do no more in the final furlong and finished seventh behind Milk It Mick, about two and a half lengths behind second-placed Three Valleys. It was reported that Balmont returned slightly lame, having popped an abscess on the heel of his near-fore.

It appears likely that Balmont will be given the opportunity to prove himself in North America as well as in Britain in the next season. In his speech at the Gimcrack dinner Balmont's American owner Sanford Robertson made reference to the significantly lower prize money on offer in Britain compared to the States, going on to say that 'I will keep a horse like Balmont in England as long as I can, primarily for his chance at classic success, but at some point it may be more desirable and more profitable, to bring him home.' Mr Robertson, however, was otherwise full of praise for racing in Britain, and in reference to the disqualification of Three Valleys said: 'This gives me the perfect chance to applaud your staunch medication rules, compared to our often too lax and many-times abused rules in America.'

Balmont, bred by his owner, is the first foal of Aldebaran Light, who won three races at around a mile in the States. The next dam Altair, a daughter of a half-sister to the Kentucky Derby winner Cannonade, has bred two other winners. One of those, Blazonry, was a fairly useful winning two-year-old for Balmont's owner/trainer in 2002 and won a Grade 2 event in the States in the latest season. While his dam's side of the pedigree suggests that Balmont should stay beyond six furlongs, the fact that he is by Stravinsky makes it less likely. Stravinsky was a sprinter, and a top-class one at that, winner of the July Cup and Nunthorpe Stakes. Balmont is one of thirteen individual winners in Britain from Stravinsky's very successful first crop, the quality of which can be judged by its individual median Timeform rating of 83, the highest by a first-season sire in 2003. Balmont, a tall, leggy, quite good-topped colt, has raced only on good to firm ground. *J. Noseda*

BALTIC BLAZER (IRE)   3 b.g. Polish Precedent (USA) 131 – Pine Needle 89 (Kris   **78 p** 135) [2003 8.1d² 8.3g* Oct 13] 13,000Y: sturdy gelding: third foal: half-brother to 5-y-o Dumaran: dam, 1m (at 2 yrs) to 1¾m winner, closely related to useful middle-distance stayer Nibbs Point, herself dam of 8-y-o Border Arrow: fair form in maidens: favourite, still looked green when winning at Windsor in October by ½ length from Margery Daw: should stay beyond 1m: remains capable of better. *P. W. Harris*

BALTIC BREEZE (USA)   3 b.f. Labeeb 124 – Blue Grass Baby (USA) (Icecapade   **55** (USA)) [2003 70: p7g p8g 10s 6.5f⁶ 7g 7g Aug 10] smallish filly: just modest maiden at 3 yrs: left R. Hannon after second start: probably stays 7f: tried tongue tied/in cheekpieces. *W. Durkan, Ireland*

BALTIC KING   3 b.c. Danetime (IRE) 121 – Lindfield Belle (IRE) 78 (Fairy King   **112** (USA)) [2003 87: 6m* 5f² 6m² 5d 5m⁴ 5.6d³ 5f* 5g 6m Oct 17] lengthy colt: smart performer: won minor event at Leicester in May and handicap at Ascot (best effort, showed good turn of foot to beat Salviati 2½ lengths) in September: eased after being badly hampered in Bentinck Stakes at Newmarket final start: effective at 5f/6f: acts on firm and good to soft going: usually tongue tied: has worn crossed noseband: usually waited with. *H. Morrison*

BALTIC WAVE   2 b.g. (Jan 25) Polish Precedent (USA) 131 – Flourish (Selkirk (USA)   **93** 129) [2003 5m* 5m² 6g* 6g⁴ 6g⁴ Aug 10] 16,000Y: good-topped gelding: has scope: first foal: dam unraced half-sister to useful 1¼m performer Forthwith: fairly useful performer: won maiden at Ripon in April and minor event at Doncaster in July: creditable fourth in nursery at Newmarket and minor event at Windsor: should be suited by 7f/1m. *T. D. Barron*

BALWEARIE (IRE)   2 b.g. (Feb 24) Sesaro (USA) 81 – Eight Mile Rock 76 (Dom-   **64** inion 123) [2003 6g 6f⁴ 5m⁴ 7.1m² 8.3g⁵ 6m⁴ Sep 18] IR 6,000F, 16,000Y: half-brother to several winners, including unreliable 1m (at 2 yrs) to 1¾m winner World Express (by Jareer) and useful French 9f and 1½m winner Macruby (by High Estate): dam 7f winner: modest maiden: second at Musselburgh: ran well in cheekpieces final start: stays 7f: acts on good to firm going. *Miss L. A. Perratt*

BAND   3 b.g. Band On The Run 102 – Little Tich (Great Nephew 126) [2003 7g⁶ 7.1f²   **82 d** 7m⁶ 8.1v³ 8m 8.1m³ 10.4m⁶ 8.1d Sep 26] 500F: strong, close-coupled gelding: half-brother to 6f winner Swinging Tich (by Swing Easy): dam unraced: fairly useful maiden: good third to Jazz Messenger in Silver Bowl (Handicap) at Haydock fourth start: well below form after: stays 1m: acts on any ground: sweating fifth/final outings. *B. A. McMahon*

BANDANNA   6 gr.m. Bandmaster (USA) 97 – Gratclo 65 (Belfort (FR) 89) [2003 98:   **91** 6g 6g 6g⁶ 5g⁵ 5.7f³ 5.5f⁴ 6g Jul 25] big, close-coupled mare: fairly useful performer: effective at 5f/6f: acts on any going: has taken good hold: usually waited with: tough and consistent: reportedly in foal to Averti. *R. J. Hodges*

BANDARI (IRE)   4 b.c. Alhaarth (IRE) 126 – Miss Audimar (USA) (Mr Leader   **118** (USA)) [2003 123: 12d⁴ 12m⁴ 12f⁴ 12m² Jul 8] angular colt: smart performer: creditable efforts when fourth to Warrsan in Coronation Cup at Epsom on second start and 1½ lengths second to Millenary in Princess of Wales's Stakes at Newmarket: probably stays 1¾m: acts on soft and good to firm going: nervy sort, has been late into paddock/reluctant at stall: has run well when sweating: usually races prominently, below form when held up third start. *M. Johnston*

BANDBOX (IRE)   8 ch.g. Imperial Frontier (USA) 112 – Dublah (USA) (Private   **42**
Account (USA)) [2003 63: 6m 7m 7f p10g⁶ 10.9m 10m Oct 23] small, strong gelding:
poor handicapper nowadays: stays 7f: acts on fibresand, firm and soft going: tried
visored/blinkered/tongue tied: none too consistent. *I. A. Wood*

BANDINI (SAF)   3 bl.g. Zafonic (USA) 130 – Estime (FR) 70 (Caerleon (USA) 132)
[2003 p6g Dec 17] 800 3-y-o: first foal: dam, lightly-raced maiden, half-sister to useful   **–**
winner up to 1m in Britain/UAE Man Howa: 20/1, disputed lead 4f when well held in
maiden at Lingfield. *P. D. Evans*

BANDIT QUEEN   3 b.f. Desert Prince (IRE) 130 – Wildwood Flower 107 (Distant   **88**
Relative 128) [2003 90: 6g⁵ 5m 5f 6m* 6m⁶ 6.1g⁵ 6m p6g Nov 2] leggy filly: fairly useful
performer: won minor event at Kempton in July: stays 6f: acts on good to firm and good
to soft ground: blinkered (ran poorly on all-weather debut) final start: usually races
prominently. *M. A. Jarvis*

BAND OF LOVE   4 b.f. Pursuit of Love 124 – Dixie Favor (USA) 82 (Dixieland Band   **–**
(USA)) [2003 67d: f8g 8.5f 8f Jun 16] quite good-topped filly: fair maiden at best at 3
yrs: well held in 2003, leaving Miss J. Camacho after second start: stayed 1¼m: tried in
cheekpieces: dead. *R. Ingram*

BANDOLINA   3 b.f. Most Welcome 131 – Choral Sundown 81 (Night Shift (USA))   **–**
[2003 –: 10m 9.2d May 9] little form. *I. Semple*

BANDOS   3 ch.g. Cayman Kai (IRE) 114 – Lekuti (Le Coq d'Or 101) [2003 57: 7.2m*   **84**
7.2f* 6d 7m² 8f² 7.2m Sep 20] lengthy gelding: fairly useful performer: won minor event
in June and handicap in July, both at Ayr: good efforts in handicaps last 3 starts: barely
stays 1m: acts on firm and soft ground: tongue tied: has raced freely. *I. Semple*

BANGALORE   7 ch.g. Sanglamore (USA) 126 – Ajuga (USA) 102 (The Minstrel   **108**
(CAN) 135) [2003 112: 12.3m² 13.3m 16.4m May 26] big, lengthy gelding: poor mover:
useful performer: had tendon trouble in 2001: unlucky neck second to Windermere in
minor event at Ripon on reappearance: well beaten in listed race at Newbury and Henry
II Stakes at Sandown (reportedly strained tendon) after: best form around 2m: acts on any
going: sometimes bandaged in front: races prominently: game. *Mrs A. J. Perrett*

BANG IN TUNE   3 b.f. Victory Note (USA) 120 – Canlubang (Mujtahid (USA) 118)   **–**
[2003 63: f7g² f6g³ f5s² f7s³ f5g³ f6g f6s³ 6m f6g³ 7m f6s⁴ f5s f5s⁶ f8.5f f7g f7s Oct 21]   **a50**
unfurnished filly: modest maiden: in frame 8 times at Wolverhampton/Southwell in 2003:
seems to stay 8.5f: acts on fibresand, best turf efforts on good/good to soft ground: tried
blinkered, wears cheekpieces nowadays: has carried head high: often races up with pace.
J. O'Reilly

BANJAXED   4 b.f. Prince Sabo 123 – Classic Fan (USA) (Lear Fan (USA) 130) [2003   **–**
–: p7g f8s f5g Jan 18] little form: tried blinkered. *Mrs S. A. Liddiard*

BANJO BAY (IRE)   5 b.g. Common Grounds 118 – Thirlmere (Cadeaux Genereux   **95**
131) [2003 100: 7m 7g 6g* 6f 6g 7.6m 7d Sep 11] close-coupled gelding: useful handicapper: clearly best 5-y-o effort when winning at Goodwood in May: ran badly last 2
starts: probably best at 6f/7f: acts on firm and soft going: often slowly away: got worked
up prior to reappearance: unseated rider leaving stall second start: none too reliable: sold
20,000 gns. *J. G. Given*

BANK ON HIM   8 b.g. Elmaamul (USA) 125 – Feather Flower 74 (Relkino 131)   **–**
[2003 53, a81: p10g⁴ p10g² p10g² p8g* p8g* p8g³ p10g p10g 8g Jul 4] modest performer   **a64**
nowadays: won 2 sellers at Lingfield in February, claimed from A. Reid 11,000 gns after
second: best at 1m/1¼m: acts on good to firm going, good to soft and all-weather: sometimes races freely/hangs left. *C. Weedon*

BANNERS FLYING (IRE)   3 ch.c. Zafonic (USA) 130 – Banafsajee (USA) 107   **78**
(Pleasant Colony (USA)) [2003 8.2g² 10.2g⁴ 10.3m⁵ Jun 28] big, angular colt: first foal:
dam, French 1m to 10.5f winner, half-sister to smart 1m/9f performer Slip Stream: fair
form in maidens, best effort on debut: should stay 1¼m: raced only on good ground or
firmer. *B. W. Hills*

BANNINGHAM BLAZE   3 b.f. Averti (IRE) 117 – Ma Pavlova (USA) 102 (Irish   **67**
River (FR) 131) [2003 48: f8g f8s f7s f8s⁴ p7g p7g p12g⁵ 12m⁴ 10m⁵ 12.1f* 10.9m² 12g²
14.1m 12.1d⁴ 11.8m² 11.8m 11m² p12g* p12g p12g 10m 12.1m Sep 17] close-coupled,
good-topped filly: fair handicapper: left D. Shaw after sixth outing: won at Beverley
in April and Lingfield in July: stays 1½m (well below form at 1¾m): acts on firm going,
good to soft and polytrack: visored: held up: tough. *C. R. Dore*

BANNISTER   5 ch.g. Inchinor 119 – Shall We Run 59 (Hotfoot 126) [2003 –: 6m f5g   **66**
6m 5m⁴ 6f² 5.9f³ 6m³ 5g⁴ 5m 5g² 5.9d 6m 5f* 7m 6f Sep 15] useful-looking gelding: has
a quick action: fair handicapper: first success since 2 yrs at Catterick in August: best at 5f
to 7f: acts on firm ground: tried blinkered/visored/tongue tied. *D. Nicholls*

BANUTAN (IRE)   3 b.f. Charnwood Forest (IRE) 125 – Banariya (USA) 82 (Lear Fan   **73 d**
(USA) 130) [2003 71: 7d 6s 7f 7d⁴ 7f² 7m³ 7.5g 7g⁶ 7m 8m f8g p8g Dec 2] IR 3,000Y:
third foal: dam Irish 1½m winner: fair maiden handicapper: left M. Halford, Ireland, after
eighth start: below form after: stays 7f, probably not 1m: acts on firm ground: tried
visored. *K. R. Burke*

BARABELLA (IRE)   2 gr.f. (Apr 7) Barathea (IRE) 127 – Thatchabella (IRE)   **65**
(Thatching 131) [2003 5.7m⁴ 7m⁴ 7.1g⁴ 8m Sep 25] 15,000Y: second foal: dam unraced
out of close relation to smart Irish 1991 2-y-o El Prado and half-sister to high-class 1¼m
performer Entitled: fair maiden: slowly away when last in nursery final start: should stay
1m. *R. J. Hodges*

BARALINKA (IRE)   4 b.f. Barathea (IRE) 127 – Kalinka (IRE) 88 (Soviet Star   **89**
(USA) 128) [2003 93: 6m 6g 6d⁴ 6m⁵ 6m 6m 6m 6m 6f Oct 10] well-made filly: fairly
useful performer: below form last 5 starts: best at 5f/6f: acted on fibresand, firm and soft
going: tried tongue tied/blinkered: stud. *P. F. I. Cole*

BARALOTI (IRE)   3 b.f. Barathea (IRE) 127 – Charlotte Corday 105 (Kris 135)   **71**
[2003 58p: 8m² 8.3d³ p8g⁴ 8g Oct 31] fair maiden: should stay beyond 1m: acts on good
to firm and good to soft ground: visored (ran poorly) final start: hung left (reportedly
finished lame) penultimate one. *J. H. M. Gosden*

BARATHEA BLAZER   4 b.g. Barathea (IRE) 127 – Empty Purse (Pennine Walk   **107**
120) [2003 109: 14.1g⁴ 12m 12.3m³ 13.3m 15m* 11.8m³ 16.1g 12.5g 13.4m⁴ 14.6g Sep
12] sturdy, good-bodied gelding: useful performer: won listed race at Chantilly (by short
head from Windermere) in June: good third to Razkalla in similar event at Leicester next
time: stays 15f: acts on soft and good to firm ground: usually races prominently: gelded
after final start. *P. W. Harris*

BARBAJUAN (IRE)   2 b.c. (Jan 29) Danehill Dancer (IRE) 117 – Courtier (Saddlers'   **109**
Hall (IRE) 126) [2003 5g* 6m* 6f⁴ 7m⁵ 7.1d* 7f⁴ 8m³ Oct 19] IR 6,200F, 54,000Y: good-
topped colt: has a round action: first foal: dam unraced out of half-sister to very smart
1984 staying 2-y-o Khozaam: useful performer: won maiden at Lingfield and minor event

Iveco Daily Solario Stakes, Sandown—
Barbajuan is given an enterprising ride by Darryll Holland to beat Milk It Mick and Matloob (right)

at Kempton in May and Iveco Daily Solario Stakes at Sandown (enterprisingly ridden when beating Milk It Mick ½ length) in August: creditable efforts in National Stakes at the Curragh (3¼ lengths fourth to One Cool Cat) and Gran Criterium at Milan (1¼ lengths third to Pearl of Love) last 2 starts: stays 1m: acts on firm and good to soft going: races prominently. *N. A. Callaghan*

BARBILYRIFLE (IRE) 2 b.g. (Feb 25) Indian Rocket 115 – Age of Elegance (Troy 137) [2003 5d 5.2m³ 5.1f* 5f 5.2m 6m 7g Oct 24] €18,000Y: good-topped gelding: half-brother to several winners, including useful 6f (at 2 yrs) to 1¼m (in Italy) winner Sheer Precocity (by Precocious) and 1¼m to 1¾m winner Netta Rufina (by Night Shift): dam French 1½m winner: fair performer: won maiden at Bath in June: showed little after, including in nurseries: should stay 6f: acts on firm ground: sometimes wears cheekpieces: usually races prominently: cocked jaw penultimate start: ungenuine. *H. Morrison* **73 §**

BARG 2 b.c. (Mar 19) Perugino (USA) 84 – Dramatic Mood (Jalmood (USA) 126) [2003 6m Jun 6] 48,000Y: quite good-topped colt: closely related to 1m winner Drama Premiere (by Emarati) and half-brother to 3 winners, including useful 6f/7f winner (including at 2 yrs) Merlin's Ring (by Magic Ring), later successful up to 9f in USA: dam unraced: better for race, behind in maiden at Haydock: sold 1,800 gns, sent to Sweden. *M. R. Channon* **–**

BARGAIN HUNT (IRE) 2 b.g. (Jan 21) Foxhound (USA) 103 – Atisayin (USA) (Al Nasr (FR) 126) [2003 5d 6d 6f 5f 7m⁵ 5m⁴ 6m 6f⁶ 7m 8m⁶ 7d⁴ 6g 7.1m³ Oct 25] 7,000F, €6,000Y, resold 2,000Y: quite good-topped gelding: fifth foal: half-brother to a winner in Japan by Bin Ajwaad: dam, poor maiden, half-sister to dam of Derby winner Benny The Dip: modest maiden: good third in seller at Musselburgh: stays 7f: acts on good to firm going: wore visor/cheekpieces 7 of last 8 starts: often races prominently: sometimes hangs right. *W. Storey* **54**

BARITONE 9 b.g. Midyan (USA) 124 – Zinzi (Song 132) [2003 –, a63: f6s f5s Jan 11] close-coupled gelding: fair handicapper at best: well beaten in 2003: tried blinkered/visored. *J. Balding* **–**

BARKING MAD (USA) 5 b. or br.g. Dayjur (USA) 137 – Avian Assembly (USA) (General Assembly (USA)) [2003 96: 7.1m 7g 10g² 10m* 10.4f 10m* 9.9m 10f³ 10.3d⁵ 8m Oct 17] sturdy, lengthy gelding: fairly useful performer: won handicaps at Windsor in June and Newmarket in July: stays 1¼m: acts on firm and good to soft going, probably on polytrack: edgy sort: has run well when sweating: often races freely/makes running. *M. L. W. Bell* **92**

BARMAN (USA) 4 ch.g. Atticus (USA) 121 – Blue Tip (FR) 117 (Tip Moss (FR)) [2003 93: 10g 10d⁴ 13d 12g 10.5g 11m 12d* 12m⁶ 11.7f³ 12m⁴ 11.9f² 12m² 11.9f⁵ 12m* Oct 17] big, quite good-topped gelding: fairly useful performer: won claimers at Salisbury in July and Newmarket in October: stays 1½m: acts on firm going, soft and polytrack: tried blinkered/in cheekpieces: usually tongue tied: free-going sort: has edged right/carried head awkwardly: has reportedly had breathing problems: none too resolute. *P. F. I. Cole* **89**

BARNEY MCALL (IRE) 3 b.g. Grand Lodge (USA) 125 – Persian Song 45 (Persian Bold 123) [2003 84+: 10.3g⁵ 10.5f³ 10d* 10g* 10.1m 9.9g Aug 1] leggy, quite attractive gelding: fairly useful performer: won minor event at Windsor in April and handicap on same course (beat Famous Grouse 2 lengths) in May, edging left both times: well below form after: stays 10.5f: acts on any going: wore cheekpieces last 3 starts. *Mrs A. J. Perrett* **92**

BARNEYS LYRIC 3 ch.g. Hector Protector (USA) 124 – Anchorage (IRE) 86 (Slip Anchor 136) [2003 12g⁵ 12.1d⁶ 12g Jul 3] 20,000Y: well-made gelding: sixth foal: half-brother to 3 winners, including 1997 2-y-o 7f winner Red Leggings (by Shareef Dancer) and 2m winner Lord Alaska (by Sir Harry Lewis), both fairly useful: dam 1½m winner: fair form in maidens: will stay 1¾m: joined N. Twiston-Davies, and won 2 juvenile hurdles in October. *R. Charlton* **68**

BAR OF SILVER (IRE) 3 ch.g. Bahhare (USA) 122 – Shaping Up (USA) 89 (Storm Bird (CAN) 134) [2003 50p: f7g⁴ f7g³ f8s⁴ 7m² 7s 8m² 10.9f⁵ 10.2m 10.2f⁵ f8.5g Nov 15] modest maiden: claimed from J. Osborne sixth start: stays 1m: acts on good to firm going and fibresand: tried in cheekpieces. *R. Brotherton* **61**

BAROLO 4 b.g. Danehill (USA) 126 – Lydia Maria 70 (Dancing Brave (USA) 140) [2003 84p: 8.3g⁴ 10m 10d* 12g³ 12m* 13.9f* 13.9f⁴ Jul 12] strong, close-coupled gelding: useful handicapper: won at Newmarket (twice) in May and York in June, beating Mamcazma by ½ length on latter course: should stay 2m: acts on firm and good to soft going: usually waited with. *P. W. Harris* **106**

J. T. & K. M. Thomas' "Baron's Pit"

BARON RHODES 2 b.f. (Mar 29) Presidium 124 – Superstream (Superpower 113) **68**
[2003 5m 5d³ 5m⁴ 5m³ 5m³ 5d* 5m⁶ f5s 5d⁴ 5m² Oct 25] lengthy, unfurnished filly: fourth
foal: half-sister to 5-y-o Tommy Smith: dam unraced: fair performer: sweating, won
maiden at Thirsk in August: good efforts in frame in minor event at Beverley and nursery
at Musselburgh last 2 starts: likely to prove best at 5f: acts on good to firm and good to
soft going. *J. S. Wainwright*

BARON'S PIT 3 gr.c. Night Shift (USA) – Incendio (Siberian Express (USA) 125) **119**
[2003 107: 7m² 6g³ 6f³ 7g 6f 7m Oct 18] big, well-made colt: type to carry condition:
smart performer: placed in listed Free Handicap at Newmarket (2½ lengths second to
Indian Haven), listed race at Ascot (2¼ lengths third to Striking Ambition) and Golden
Jubilee Stakes at Royal Ascot (swished tail beforehand, finished well when 1½ lengths
third to Choisir, best effort): just fair efforts in Diadem Stakes at Ascot and Challenge
Stakes at Newmarket last 2 outings: probably better at 6f than 7f: raced only on good
going or firmer. *R. Hannon*

BARONS SPY (IRE) 2 b.c. (Feb 6) Danzero (AUS) – Princess Accord (USA) 115 **66**
(D'Accord (USA)) [2003 6g 7d Nov 7] 20,000Y: lengthy colt: half-brother to several
winners, including useful 9f winner Darcy (by Miswaki): dam, 6f (at 2 yrs) to 9f winner,
sister to smart US 1994 2-y-o Montreal Red: tongue tied, fair form in mid-division in
maidens at Newbury and Doncaster: should stay 1m. *A. W. Carroll*

BAROUCHE 2 b.g. (Apr 25) Danehill (USA) 126 – Barbarella (Bering 136) [2003 7s **–**
Oct 29] second foal: closely related to fairly useful Irish 5f winner Barbaresque (by Green
Desert): dam unraced half-sister to very smart French sprinter Balbonella, herself dam of
Anabaa: 16/1, well held in maiden at Yarmouth: sold 1,200 gns. *E. A. L. Dunlop*

BARRANTES 6 b.m. Distant Relative 128 – Try The Duchess 99 (Try My Best (USA) **90**
130) [2003 73: 7m² 5.7g⁴ 5g² 6m² 6m² 5g* 5m⁴ 6f* 6.5m 5m³ 5m 5d⁴ 5.2m⁴ 6g² 6m³
5g⁶ 6m 5f p10g Dec 10] fairly useful performer: won handicaps at Lingfield in June
and Kempton in July: seemingly best effort when close third to Fayr Jag in listed race at
Newmarket fifteenth start: best at 5f/6f: acts on firm and good to soft ground: races up
with pace: tough. *Miss S. West*

BARRAS (IRE) 2 b.g. (May 11) Raphane (USA) 102 – Lady Fleetsin (IRE) (Double **57**
Schwartz 128) [2003 5m 5f 5m⁴ 6d⁴ 6f⁵ 5g³ f7g² 5m* Jul 9] IR 3,000F, 8,000Y: close-
coupled gelding: second foal: half-brother to 6f (including at 2 yrs) to 1m (in UAE)
winner Cable Media Boy (by Great Commotion): dam unraced: modest performer: won
seller at Catterick: likely to prove best at 5f/6f: acts on fibresand, good to firm and good
to soft ground: wore cheekpieces after second start: sold 9,000 gns in August, joined
Gay Kelleway. *R. F. Fisher*

BARRESBO 9 br.g. Barrys Gamble 102 – Bo' Babbity 75 (Strong Gale 116) [2003 **–**
21.6m Apr 14] strong, lengthy gelding: poor handicapper: well held only outing in 2003:
tried visored/blinkered: dead. *A. C. Whillans*

BARRISSIMO (IRE) 3 b.g. Night Shift (USA) – Belle de Cadix (IRE) 82 (Law **97 ?**
Society (USA) 130) [2003 94p: 10m³ 11.6g⁵ Aug 23] strong, good-bodied gelding: has a
quick action: useful performer, lightly raced: seemingly easily better effort at 3 yrs when
3 lengths third of 4 to Bonecrusher in minor event at Newmarket: stays 1¼m: acts on soft
and good to firm ground. *W. J. Musson*

BARROSA 4 b.f. Sabrehill (USA) 120 – Shehana (USA) 86 (The Minstrel (CAN) 135) **–**
[2003 –: 10.2g 8.1m Aug 14] leggy filly: little form since 2 yrs. *Miss K. M. George*

BARRY ISLAND 4 b.g. Turtle Island (IRE) 123 – Pine Ridge 80 (High Top 131) **85**
[2003 89: 12g 11.6g⁶ 10f³ 9.9f⁶ 10d 12m⁴ Oct 17] good-topped gelding: fairly useful
handicapper: should stay at least 1½m: acts on polytrack and firm going: held up.
D. R. C. Elsworth

BARTON FLOWER 2 br.f. (Mar 5) Danzero (AUS) – Iota 83 (Niniski (USA) 125) **– p**
[2003 7.9m 7.5m Sep 17] 15,500Y: leggy filly: fourth foal: dam 14.6f to 2m winner:
backward, signs of a little ability in maidens at York and Beverley: will probably do better
at 1¼m+. *M. W. Easterby*

BARTON SANDS (IRE) 6 b.g. Tenby 125 – Hetty Green (Bay Express 132) [2003 **70**
72?: 10m 10m⁴ 12m⁶ 11.8m 10.9m* 10.9m 10.3d Sep 24] neat gelding: fair performer:
won seller at Warwick in August: barely stays 1½m: acts on firm and good to soft ground,
well beaten on dead/heavy: tried visored/blinkered, tongue tied last 3 starts: none too
consistent. *M. C. Pipe*

BARZAK (IRE) 3 b.c. Barathea (IRE) 127 – Zakuska 96 (Zafonic (USA) 130) [2003 **74**
80p: 8m⁶ 8g f7g 7g 7d 7d f8g* f8g f8g f8s⁵ Dec 27] sturdy colt: fair handicapper: won at
Southwell in November: below form after: stays 1m: acts on good to soft ground and
fibresand: tried tongue tied, including at Southwell: wore cheekpieces last 2 starts.
S. R. Bowring

BASBOUSATE NADIA 4 b.f. Wolfhound (USA) 126 – Sarabah (IRE) 83 (Ela- **–**
Mana-Mou 132) [2003 68: 6g 7m⁶ 7d 6m Jun 7] tall, good-topped filly: fairly useful at
best: well held in 2003. *W. R. Muir*

BASHEERA 3 ch.f. Bahhare (USA) 122 – Samheh (USA) 62 (Private Account **– §**
(USA)) [2003 46: 10m 7m Apr 23] strong, compact filly: poor maiden: blinkered (very
slowly away) once: untrustworthy. *E. J. Alston*

BASINET 5 b.g. Alzao (USA) 117 – Valiancy 87 (Grundy 137) [2003 72: f8g⁴ f9.4s⁴ **72**
p8g⁶ f8.5s 8f⁶ 8.1m³ 8m 9m 8.3m* 7.9f⁵ 8.1g⁴ 8g⁶ 9.1g⁵ 10.1m 8.2d⁶ Nov 6] strong
gelding: fair handicapper: won at Windsor in June: stays 9f: acts on good to firm ground,
soft and all-weather: has worn cheekpieces: has been slowly away: sometimes takes
strong hold/carries head high: usually held up. *J. J. Quinn*

BATAILLEY 3 ch.f. First Trump 118 – Phantom Ring 62 (Magic Ring (IRE) 115) **52**
[2003 64: 6g 5.9m 7m² 8.1m Jul 4] modest maiden: stays 7f: acts on soft and good to firm
going: blinkered (ran poorly) final start: inconsistent. *Mrs H. Dalton*

BATCHWORTH BREEZE 5 ch.m. Beveled (USA) – Batchworth Dancer 67 (Balla- **–**
cashtal (CAN)) [2003 –: 6g 5.7f 5.1m Jul 24] no form: tried blinkered. *E. A. Wheeler*

BATCHWORTH LOCK 5 b.g. Beveled (USA) – Treasurebound 63 (Beldale **–**
Flutter (USA) 130) [2003 –: 7g 6m Sep 29] of little account. *E. A. Wheeler*

112

BATCHWORTH PARK   3 b.f. Young Ern 120 – Treasurebound 63 (Beldale Flutter –
(USA) 130) [2003 p7g p7g p6g 8.3g 5.3d 6g Jun 3] half-sister to useful but unruly 5f/6f
(latter at 2 yrs) winner Batchworth Belle (by Interrex) and 5f winner Batchworth Bound
(by Ballacashtal): dam third at 6f at 4 yrs: little form: tried blinkered. *E. A. Wheeler*

BATHWICK BILL (USA)   2 ch.c. (May 23) Stravinsky (USA) 133 – Special Park **85**
(USA) (Trempolino (USA) 135) [2003 5m⁶ 5g⁴ 5.1f* 6g* 7d⁵ 6.1m³ 6d Sep 10] 29,000Y:
workmanlike colt: second foal: half-brother to 3-y-o Colourful Lady: dam, French 1m/9f
winner, half-sister to US Grade 3 1m winner Wasatch: fairly useful performer: won minor
event at Bath in June and nursery at Lingfield (edged right) in July: third in nursery at
Chepstow, only creditable effort after: likely to prove best at 5f/6f: acts on firm going:
blinkered final start. *B. R. Millman*

BATHWICK BRUCE (IRE)   5 b.g. College Chapel 122 – Naivity (IRE) 72 (Auction **77**
Ring (USA) 123) [2003 84: p10g 10g³ 10m 10m³ 10m⁶ 8m 8f 8d p8g p8g⁴ Oct 27]
good-topped gelding: fair handicapper: stays 1¼m: acts on polytrack, soft and good to
firm going. *B. R. Millman*

BATHWICK DREAM   6 b.m. Tragic Role (USA) – Trina 37 (Malaspina 118) [2003 –
f12g Nov 28] modest performer at 4 yrs: well beaten in seller only outing since.
B. R. Millman

BATISTE   3 b.c. Barathea (IRE) 127 – Mill Line 71 (Mill Reef (USA) 141) [2003 8g –
10.5v⁵ 10g 12g p16g Oct 15] 50,000Y: strong, compact colt: half-brother to several
winners, notably very smart Irish/Yorkshire Oaks winner Pure Grain (by Polish Precedent), 7f winner at 2 yrs: dam, 14.6f winner, out of Park Hill winner Quay Line: little form.
P. W. Harris

BATOOL (USA)   4 b.f. Bahri (USA) 125 – Mrs Paddy (USA) (Woodman (USA) 126) –
[2003 69: 7.9f Jun 15] big, useful-looking filly: fair maiden, lightly raced: well beaten
only 4-y-o start. *D. Nicholls*

BATSWING   8 b.g. Batshoof 122 – Magic Milly 60 (Simply Great (FR) 122) [2003 –
f11s Jan 14] quite good-topped gelding: fairly useful handicapper at best: wearing cheekpieces, well held only 8-y-o start: tried blinkered at 2 yrs. *B. Ellison*

BATTLE BACK (BEL)   2 b.f. (May 22) Pursuit of Love 124 – Batalya (BEL) –
(Boulou) [2003 7g f7g Dec 12] well-made filly: half-sister to several winners, including
useful French performer up to 15f Battle Green (by Pharly): dam won 6 races in Belgium:
well held in maidens. *S. C. Williams*

BATTLE CHANT (USA)   3 b.g. Coronado's Quest (USA) 130 – Appointed One **105**
(USA) (Danzig (USA)) [2003 104p: 8m⁵ 10.4m 8.5m⁴ 7m 8g³ 8.2d Nov 6] rangy gelding:
useful performer: best efforts in 2003 when fifth in Craven Stakes at Newmarket,
seventh (beaten 3¼ lengths behind Magistretti) in Dante Stakes at York and fourth
(beaten 3½ lengths by Gateman) in Diomed Stakes at Epsom first 3 starts: found little
final outing: probably best around 1m: yet to race on extremes of going: tried tongue tied.
E. A. L. Dunlop

BATTLE WARNING   8 b.g. Warning 136 – Royal Ballet (IRE) (Sadler's Wells (USA) **75**
132) [2003 75: 16m 17.1m² 17.1m³ 18m Jun 22] well-made gelding: fair handicapper:
reportedly lame final start: stays 2¼m: acts on soft going, firm and fibresand: useful
hurdler. *P. Bowen*

BATTO   3 b.g. Slip Anchor 136 – Frog 84 (Akarad (FR) 130) [2003 –: 10m 14m 12g **53**
12m⁴ 14.1f Aug 26] rangy gelding: modest maiden: should stay at least 1¾m: raced only
on good ground or firmer on turf. *W. J. Haggas*

BATUSHKA (IRE)   3 b.f. Spectrum (IRE) 126 – Ustka 60 (Lomond (USA) 128) [2003 –
8.3s 12f⁵ 12g Sep 11] well-made filly: sixth living foal: half-sister to several winners,
including smart 1¼m to 15f winner Travelmate (by Persian Bold) and 7-y-o Kuster: dam,
7f winner, closely related to useful middle-distance performer Adam Smith and smart
middle-distance stayer Braashee: well held in maidens: sold from J. Gosden 16,000 gns
after debut. *T. Stack, Ireland*

BAYADERE (GER)   3 b.f. Lavirco (GER) 125 – Brangane (IRE) (Anita's Prince 126) **93**
[2003 10.3m³ 10.1m Sep 17] leggy, lengthy ex-German filly: second foal: half-sister to
smart German 1¼m winner Belcore (by Saumarez): dam German 5f (at 2 yrs) to 9.5f
winner (also won Czech and Slovak Guineas): fairly useful performer: won maiden at
Bremen at 2 yrs when trained by A. Wohler: creditable third to Ekraar in minor event at
Doncaster on reappearance: soundly beaten in listed event at Yarmouth 3 months later:
stays 1¼m: acts on soft and good to firm ground. *Sir Michael Stoute*

BAYCHEVELLE (IRE) 2 ch.f. (Feb 6) Bahamian Bounty 116 – Phantom Ring 62 **55**
(Magic Ring (IRE) 115) [2003 6.1f Sep 30] workmanlike filly: second foal: dam 5f
winner: 100/1, ninth of 15 in maiden at Nottingham, slowly away: bred to prove best
short of 1m. *Mrs H. Dalton*

BAYEUX (USA) 2 b.c. (Apr 8) Red Ransom (USA) – Elizabeth Bay (USA) 116 **116**
(Mr Prospector (USA)) [2003 6g* 7m 7m² Oct 2]
    After five years in charge of Godolphin's two-year-old academy David
Loder is moving across Newmarket to the historic Egerton Stud, next to the July
course, from where he'll be operating as a public trainer once again. Loder's final
year with Godolphin was his most successful and compensated for a particularly
disappointing 2002, when only ten of the hundred or so blue-blooded juveniles in
his care managed to win a race, recording a mere fourteen victories between them.
In the latest season, with the two-year-old division now augmented by a strong team
of older horses, Loder was responsible for forty-four individual winners of seventy
races in Britain worth over £700,000, with win and place prize money topping the
million mark. The two-year-olds who made the most significant contributions
included the Mill Reef Stakes winner Byron, the Flying Childers Stakes winner
Howick Falls and Sutters Fort, successful in the valuable Irish Breeders Foal Levy
Stakes. Yet the one who ended up being the highest rated of the Loder juveniles,
namely Bayeux, managed to win only one race worth £4,901.
    Bayeux's victory came first time out, when he landed the odds narrowly in
a thirteen-runner maiden at Goodwood in May. It was a race which worked out
well, with the runner-up Gwaihir and the third-placed Carrizo Creek two of four in
the field to go on and win their next start. Bayeux was sent off joint favourite to
do the same when stepped up to Group 3 company on his next appearance, in the
Superlative Stakes at Newmarket, but, tried in a tongue strap, he managed to beat
only one of his eight rivals, dropping away tamely in the last two furlongs. A
breathing problem was said to have been the reason for Bayeux's disappointing
display, and he was given a three-month break. Another Group 3 contest at Newmarket, the Somerville Tattersall Stakes, was chosen for Bayeux's return and,
having reportedly impressed in his work in the run-up to it, he started a well-backed
favourite to account for seven rivals. Without the tongue strap, Bayeux put his
previous effort well behind him in just failing to justify the strong support.
Recovering from a slowish start to track the pace, Bayeux took up the running over
two furlongs out and was collared only near the line by Milk It Mick, who beat
Bayeux a neck, with the same distance back to third-placed Bachelor Duke.
Bayeux's performance was made to look even better sixteen days later when, over
the same course and distance, Milk It Mick and Bachelor Duke finished first and
fourth respectively in the Dewhurst Stakes. Bayeux, who should be seen to even
better advantage when stepped up to a mile or more, seems likely to win pattern
races for Godolphin at three.

		Roberto	Hail To Reason
	Red Ransom (USA)	(b 1969)	Bramalea
	(b 1987)	Arabia	Damascus
Bayeux (USA)		(b 1977)	Christmas Wind
(b.c. Apr 8, 2001)		Mr Prospector	Raise A Native
	Elizabeth Bay (USA)	(b 1970)	Gold Digger
	(b 1990)	Life At The Top	Seattle Slew
		(b 1983)	See You At The Top

    Red Ransom, the sire of Bayeux, has been imported from the States to stand
at Dalham Hall following an exceptional 2003 season, the highlight of which was
the Oaks success of Casual Look. The dam Elizabeth Bay, who stayed nine furlongs
and was trained by Andre Fabre for most of her career, won both her starts at two,
showed smart form at three when in the frame in six of her seven starts, including a
neck second in the Coronation Stakes, and was successful in the States as a
four-year-old. Elizabeth Bay's two foals prior to Bayeux, both by Danzig, were also
winners. Jahaam, who stays a mile, won a maiden for Loder at two years and has
been successful in the States since, while Dunnes River won a maiden over a mile
at three, her only start. Bayeux's grandam Life At The Top, from the same family as
Bold Forbes, Saratoga Six and Dunbeath, was a high-class filly in the States,

successful in Grade 1 events over nine furlongs and a mile and a quarter. Bayeux, a lengthy, attractive colt who very much takes the eye, has raced on good and good to firm ground to date. *D. R. Loder*

BAYHIRR 2 b.c. (Mar 10) Selkirk (USA) 129 – Pass The Peace 116 (Alzao (USA) 117) – p [2003 7g Nov 1] rangy colt: has scope: half-brother to several winners, notably 1997 Cheveley Park Stakes winner Embassy (by Cadeaux Genereux) and 7f (at 2 yrs) to 1¼m winner Tarfshi (by Mtoto), both smart: dam won Cheveley Park and second in Poule d'Essai des Pouliches: 11/2 and very green, slowly away and considerably handled when seventh of 13 in maiden at Newmarket: sure to do better. *M. A. Jarvis*

BAYLAW STAR 2 b.c. (Apr 4) Case Law 113 – Caisson 67 (Shaadi (USA) 126) [2003 78 5m² 5m* 5m⁶ 5f² 5g* 6g⁶ 5m* 5f⁴ 6g³ 6d 6m 5.2s³ Oct 29] 500Y: sturdy, close-coupled colt: fourth foal: half-brother to 6f winner I'm Sophie (by Shalford): dam lightly raced: fair performer: won maiden at Hamilton in April, claimer there in June and nursery at Musselburgh in July: left T. D. Barron prior to penultimate start: ran creditably final one: effective at 5f/6f: unraced on heavy going, acts on any other: visored (ran creditably) eighth outing: often races prominently: sometimes drifts right. *J. Balding*

BAY OF ISLANDS 11 b.g. Jupiter Island 126 – Lawyer's Wave (USA) (Advocator) 95 [2003 96: 16m 18.7m 16.2m* Jun 5] strong gelding: fluent mover: useful performer: won 6 races during career, including Northumberland Plate at Newcastle in 2000 and handicap at Haydock in June, latter by 2 lengths from Rahwaan: struck into second start: stayed 2¼m: acted on firm and good to soft going: usually visored: usually tracked leaders: found to have suffered hairline fracture of a splint bone after Haydock, and reportedly retired. *D. Morris*

BAYONET 7 b.m. Then Again 126 – Lambay 88 (Lorenzaccio 130) [2003 –: 7m 7g 45 7m 7m 7f 6m Jul 12] deep-girthed mare: poor handicapper: effective at 6f/7f: acts on good to firm ground: tried blinkered and in cheekpieces. *Jane Southcombe*

BAY SOLITAIRE 2 b.g. (Mar 29) Charnwood Forest (IRE) 125 – Golden Wings – (USA) (Devil's Bag (USA)) [2003 7.9m 7.5m 8g Sep 27] 14,000Y: tall, angular gelding: second foal: dam useful French 10.5f winner: well held in maidens. *T. D. Easterby*

BAYTOWN FLYER 3 ch.f. Whittingham (IRE) 104 – The Fernhill Flyer (IRE) 71 – (Red Sunset 120) [2003 66: f7g 6.1g⁶ 8.2m 7m 8.2d⁶ 6m 8f 7m 8m 7m f6g Nov 14] smallish filly: fair performer at 2 yrs: well held in 2003, leaving C. Kellett after ninth start: tried blinkered/in cheekpieces. *J. Balding*

BAYTOWN SHAMROCK (IRE) 2 b.f. (Mar 21) First Trump 118 – Siana Springs 51 § (IRE) 59 (Emarati (USA) 74) [2003 p5g 5.1f³ 5.3f 5.3f² 5m⁵ 5.1m 5.1m⁶ 5d² 5m³ p5g² 5m 7m 5.1f³ 5m⁶ 5m⁶ 5.1m⁵ 5g 5.7f⁴ 5.3m f5g Oct 4] €800Y: compact filly: first foal: dam, 2-y-o 5f seller winner: modest maiden: usually runs in sellers: will prove best at 5f: acts on polytrack, firm and good to soft going: visored (ran poorly) final start: sometimes gives trouble stall: no battler. *P. S. McEntee*

BAY TREE (IRE) 2 b.f. (Apr 12) Daylami (IRE) 138 – My Branch 111 (Distant Rela- 100 tive 128) [2003 6m* 7m* 8s 7m Oct 18] small, quite attractive filly: fourth foal: half-sister to 3 winners, including 3-y-o Tante Rose and fairly useful 7f winner Future Flight (by Polar Falcon): dam, 5f (at 2 yrs) to 7f winner, also third in Irish 1000 Guineas: useful form: won maiden at Newbury and listed race at Newmarket (best effort, beat Qasirah by 1¼ lengths) in August: behind in Prix Marcel Boussac at Longchamp (travelled strongly long way) and Rockfel Stakes at Newmarket: stays 7f: joined D. Loder, 450,000 gns. *B. W. Hills*

BEACH PARTY (IRE) 2 b.f. (Apr 2) Danzero (AUS) – Shore Lark (USA) (Storm 58 Bird (CAN) 134) [2003 6g 6m⁵ Oct 17] 42,000F: sturdy filly: third foal: half-sister to 4-y-o Lake Verdi and a winner in Greece by Sri Pekan: dam unraced half-sister to smart performers Tipsy Creek (5f/6f) and Wathik (1m/9f, in UAE): modest form in maidens at Windsor and Redcar (possibly still needed race): bred to prove best up to 1m. *M. L. W. Bell*

BEACON BLUE (IRE) 2 ch.f. (May 11) Peintre Celebre (USA) 137 – Catch The 68 Blues (IRE) 115 (Bluebird (USA) 125) [2003 6m⁵ 6m 8d⁵ 8s⁵ Nov 3] €55,000Y: leggy, lengthy filly: third foal: half-sister to useful 7f winner Beacon Wood (by Wood-man): dam Irish 5f (including Ballyogan Stakes) and 7f winner: fair maiden: ran creditably in nursery final start: likely to stay 1¼m: acts on soft ground. *M. Johnston*

BEACON OF LIGHT (IRE) 5 b.m. Lake Coniston (IRE) 131 – Deydarika (IRE) – (Kahyasi 130) [2003 –: 12d Sep 20] quite good-topped mare: little form on Flat: winning selling hurdler. *Ferdy Murphy*

BEADY (IRE) 4 b.g. Eagle Eyed (USA) 111 – Tales of Wisdom 70 (Rousillon (USA) **73**
133) [2003 72: f11s⁵ f12s* f12g* f14s⁴ f12g² f12g⁵ 13.8m 12g Nov 5] good-topped
gelding: fair handicapper: won apprentice and amateur events at Southwell in January:
stays 1¾m: acts on fibresand, soft and good to firm going: often races freely: held up.
B. Smart

BEAMISH PRINCE 4 ch.g. Bijou d'Inde 127 – Unconditional Love (IRE) 104 **66 §**
(Polish Patriot (USA) 128) [2003 71: a9f 12m a12f 12m 8m³ 7.9f 7.9f 9.2g³ 9.2g³ Jul 24]
close-coupled gelding: fair performer: raced in UAE first 4 starts: stays 1¼m: raced only
on good going or firmer on turf, has run respectably on dirt: blinkered last 3 starts: none
too consistent: ungenuine. *M. Johnston*

BEAMSLEY BEACON 2 ch.g. (Apr 10) Wolfhound (USA) 126 – Petindia 65 (Pet- **62**
ong 126) [2003 5d⁵ f6g⁶ f6g² 8m 6g Oct 13] 2,000F, 5,000Y: sturdy gelding: fourth foal:
dam 2-y-o 7f seller winner: modest maiden: second at Southwell: last in nurseries after:
best efforts at 6f on fibresand. *G. M. Moore*

BEAT THE HEAT (IRE) 5 b.g. Salse (USA) 128 – Summer Trysting (USA) 83 **89**
(Alleged (USA) 138) [2003 89: f11s² f12g 12m 11.9f Oct 9] lengthy gelding: fairly useful
handicapper: stays 1½m: acts on fibresand and any turf going: blinkered 4 times in 2001:
wandered on reappearance, folded tamely next time: won twice over hurdles in autumn.
Jedd O'Keeffe

BEAT TIME 4 ro.f. Lion Cavern (USA) 117 – Brilliant Timing (USA) (The Minstrel **– §**
(CAN) 135) [2003 78§: 8.5f 6m 5m Jun 24] lengthy, angular filly: fair performer at 3 yrs:
well held in 2003: ungenuine. *M. W. Easterby*

BEAU ARTISTE 3 ch.g. Peintre Celebre (USA) 137 – Belle Esprit (Warning 136) **73 §**
[2003 81: 8g³ 10m² 10.3m³ 10m² 10.1d 9m³ 12g² 11.8m⁶ p12g Oct 27] leggy gelding: fair
maiden: stays easy 1½m: acts on soft going, good to firm and polytrack: tried blinkered:
ungenuine: sold 16,000 gns. *Jedd O'Keeffe*

BEAUCETTE (USA) 3 br.f. Mr Prospector (USA) – Mackie (USA) (Summer Squall **76**
(USA)) [2003 73p: 8.2g³ 7f² 8.1m³ 9.7m² 9.2d⁶ Sep 29] quite good-topped filly: fair
maiden: stays 9.7f: acts on firm ground: visored (found little) final start: sent to USA. *Sir
Michael Stoute*

BEAUCHAMP MAGIC 8 b.g. Northern Park (USA) 107 – Beauchamp Buzz 85 **54**
(High Top 131) [2003 57: f14.8g p16g² f16.2g Feb 3] good-bodied gelding: modest
performer: stays 2m: acts on all-weather and firm ground: tried blinkered/visored/tongue
tied earlier in career: usually held up: none too consistent. *K. R. Burke*

BEAUCHAMP PILOT 5 ch.g. Inchinor 119 – Beauchamp Image 79 (Midyan (USA) **117**
124) [2003 118: a10f³ 8f 8f² 10g Aug 16] big, rather leggy gelding: smart performer:
good third to Grandera in Maktoum Challenge (Round III) at Nad Al Sheba on reappearance (reportedly suffered injury afterwards): respectable ¾-length second to Tillerman in
Silver Trophy at Ascot third start: well beaten in Arlington Million final one: best at 1m
to 1¼m: acts on firm going, good to soft and polytrack: has worn crossed noseband/been
bandaged in front: usually waited with, but made running last 2 starts. *G. A. Butler*

BEAUCHAMP RIBBON 3 b.f. Vettori (IRE) 119 – Beauchamp Kate 61 (Petoski **75 §**
135) [2003 –p: 7m⁵ 10m² 8.1m² 9.9d 8.1m⁵ 11.7f* 10f* 10.2m* 11m³ 10g 10f³ p8g
Oct 27] smallish, sturdy filly: fair performer: won sellers at Bath and Brighton in August
and handicap at Chepstow in September: stays 11.7f: acts on firm ground, below form
on good to soft/polytrack: sometimes tongue tied, blinkered of late: has worn crossed
noseband: has given trouble in preliminaries/been slowly away: ungenuine: sold £1,300.
G. A. Butler

BEAUCHAMP ROSE 3 ch.f. Pharly (FR) 130 – Beauchamp Cactus 86 (Niniski **81**
(USA) 125) [2003 –p: 8g³ 10f² 10m² p12g Jun 28] fairly useful maiden: broke leg at
Lingfield in June: stayed 1¼m: acted on firm going: dead. *G. A. Butler*

BEAUCHAMP SPARK 2 ch.g. (Mar 3) Pharly (FR) 130 – Beauchamp Buzz 85 (High **–**
Top 131) [2003 f9.4g Nov 15] half-brother to useful 1½m winner Beauchamp Jade (by
Kalaglow) and 8-y-o Beauchamp Magic: dam, maiden who stayed 1m, half-sister to very
smart 1½m performer Beauchamp Hero: 66/1, soundly beaten in maiden at Wolverhampton, starting slowly. *A. P. Jones*

BEAUCHAMP SUN 2 b.f. (Mar 4) Pharly (FR) 130 – Beauchamp Jade 105 (Kalaglow **– p**
132) [2003 6g Oct 24] leggy, quite good-topped filly: second foal: half-sister to 1½m
winner (difficult at start) Beauchamp Quiz (by Inchinor): dam, 1½m winner, out of
half-sister to very smart 1½m winner Beauchamp Hero: 33/1, well beaten in maiden at
Newbury: should do better at 1½m+. *G. A. Butler*

BEAUCHAMP SURPRISE   2 ch.f. (Feb 16) Pharly (FR) 130 – Beauchamp Image   – p
79 (Midyan (USA) 124) [2003 7g 6d f8.5g Nov 28] good-topped filly: has scope: fifth
foal: half-sister to 5-y-o Beauchamp Pilot: dam, Irish 9f winner, half-sister to useful
performer up to 15f Beauchamp Express: backward, not knocked about when well held
in maidens: should do better at 1¼m+. *G. A. Butler*

BEAU JAZZ   2 br.c. (Mar 3) Merdon Melody 98 – Ichor 52 (Primo Dominie 121)   **61**
[2003 6m 6g 6m 7m³ 6.1m⁶ 6f 6g p5g⁵ 5.1d⁶ Nov 6] 500Y: strong colt: fourth foal: dam,
maiden, ran only at 5f at 2 yrs: modest maiden: effective at 5f/easy 6f: acts on polytrack,
firm and good to soft going. *W. de Best-Turner*

BEAU SAUVAGE   5 b.g. Wolfhound (USA) 126 – Maestrale (Top Ville 129) [2003   – §
54: f8g 7.5m f8.5g⁶ 7m 8d⁶ 7m Aug 15] lengthy gelding: modest handicapper at 4 yrs:
well held in 2003: sometimes blinkered: very slowly away last 4 starts, twice looking
reluctant to race: one to leave alone. *M. W. Easterby*

BEAUSEJOUR (USA)   5 ch.m. Diesis 133 – Libeccio (NZ) (Danzatore (CAN) 120)   **39**
[2003 42: f8s⁵ p8g 8.5d⁵ Jul 3] rather sparely-made mare: poor maiden: stays 9.7f: acts on
good to firm going, good to soft and fibresand: tried in headgear. *B. G. Powell*

BEAUTEOUS (IRE)   4 ch.g. Tagula (IRE) 116 – Beauty Appeal (USA) (Shadeed   **74**
(USA) 135) [2003 66d: f7s f6g 7.1d* 5.9g 7.1m⁶ 7f 7.2f⁴ 8.9m* 7.1f⁵ 7m⁶ 6.9m 7.2g²   **a–**
7.1m 7g⁴ 7.2m 7m Oct 18] tall gelding: fair handicapper on turf: won at Musselburgh in
May and Carlisle in June: will prove best at 7f/1m: acts on firm and good to soft ground,
little form on fibresand: has wandered/flicked tail: makes running/races prominently.
A. Berry

BEAUTIFUL NOISE   2 b.f. (Mar 10) Piccolo 121 – Mrs Moonlight (Ajdal (USA)   **67 p**
130) [2003 7m 8m⁵ 8m 8s⁶ Oct 29] tall filly: has scope: seventh foal: closely related to
smart 7f (at 2 yrs)/1m winner Soviet Flash (by Warning) and half-sister to 1m winner in
Japan by Machiavellian: dam unraced half-sister to 1½m performer Jupiter Island and
1983 2-y-o Precocious, both high class: fair form in maidens, shaping better than result
most starts: likely to prove best short of 1m: type to make her mark in handicaps as 3-y-o.
D. Morris

BEAUTIFULTOMMORROW   4 ch.f. Pursuit of Love 124 – Bella Domani (Cadeaux Genereux 131) [2003 –: f8s Jan 10] small, strong, angular filly: lightly raced and no
form since 2 yrs: tried visored. *K. R. Burke*

BEAUTY OF DREAMS   2 b.f. (Apr 11) Russian Revival (USA) 125 – Giggleswick   **70**
Girl 67 (Full Extent (USA) 113) [2003 6m² 6m² 6m⁴ 5d* 5m⁵ 7g Sep 13] leggy, close-
coupled filly: fourth foal: half-sister to 5-y-o Blakeshall Boy: dam 5f and (at 2 yrs) 6f
winner: fair performer: won maiden at Beverley in July: effective at 5f/6f: acts on good to
firm and good to soft ground: slowly away final start: usually races prominently:
sometimes wanders. *M. R. Channon*

BEAUVRAI   3 b.g. Bahamian Bounty 116 – Lets Be Fair 94 (Efisio 120) [2003 93p: **84**
5.5m 5f 5m 5f 5d Jul 5] close-coupled gelding: fairly useful handicapper: shaped well
first/third starts (lame in between): ran as though amiss last 2 outings: effective at 5f/6f:
acts on good to firm ground and all-weather. *J. J. Quinn*

BEAU WEST   2 b.f. (Apr 8) The West (USA) 107 – Total Truth (Reesh 117) [2003   **62**
8.2d⁵ f8.5g⁶ Nov 17] £1,000Y: sixth foal: half-sister to 6f winner in Hong Kong by
Distant Relative: dam ran 4 times: better effort in maidens (modest form) when fifth at
Nottingham: not certain to stay beyond 1m. *S. Kirk*

BEAVER DIVA   2 b.f. (Apr 17) Bishop of Cashel 122 – Beaver Skin Hunter (Ballacashtal (CAN)) [2003 5d May 3] 800Y: eighth foal: half-sister to winner in Greece by
Distant Relative: dam winner in Belgium, including at 2 yrs: 20/1, very slowly away and
always tailed off in maiden at Haydock. *W. M. Brisbourne*

BEBOPSKIDDLY   2 b.c. (Apr 24) Robellino (USA) 127 – Adarama (IRE) (Persian   **63**
Bold 123) [2003 8.3g p7g 8.1g Sep 11] 5,000F, 8,000Y: third foal: half-brother to 1½m
winner Strath Fillan (by Dolphin Street): dam Italian 2-y-o 7f winner: best effort (modest
form) when seventh in maiden at Chepstow final start: should be suited by 1¼m/1½m.
B. G. Powell

BECKON   7 ch.m. Beveled (USA) – Carolynchristensen 58 (Sweet Revenge 129)   –
[2003 44, a60: 8f 10.1f 12m Jul 31] leggy, lengthy mare: modest at best, well held in
2003: tried visored. *P. A. Blockley*

BEDAZZLED   3 b.f. Wolfhound (USA) 126 – Glowing Jade 75 (Kalaglow 132) [2003   –
61: 5m p7g f7g Nov 21] modest maiden at 2 yrs: well held first 2 outings in 2003:
collapsed and died at Wolverhampton in November (blinkered). *J. A. Glover*

BEE

BEECHES STAR (IRE) 3 b.f. Lake Coniston (IRE) 131 – Eleonora d'Arborea 78 – (Prince Sabo 123) [2003 60, a–: p7g f6g 8.1m 6.1d 7f 6.1m 5.1m Jul 24] lengthy filly: modest maiden at 2 yrs: well held in 2003: tried in headgear: somewhat wayward. *R. Brotherton*

BEECHY BANK (IRE) 5 b.m. Shareef Dancer (USA) 135 – Neptunalia 70 (Slip **78** Anchor 136) [2003 57: 12.1d⁴ 11.6g³ 14.1m* Jul 12] fair performer, lightly raced: won handicap at Nottingham in July: should stay 2m: unraced on extremes of going on turf: tried blinkered. *Mrs Mary Hambro*

BEE DEES LEGACY 2 b.c. (Mar 4) Atraf 116 – Bee Dee Dancer (Ballacashtal – (CAN)) [2003 8.3g Aug 10] 9,200Y: eighth foal: half-brother to 3 winners, including 4-y-o Didnt Tell My Wife: dam well beaten only start: 33/1, last of 14 in maiden at Windsor. *C. Weedon*

BEE HEALTH BOY 10 b.g. Superpower 113 – Rekindle 70 (Relkino 131) [2003 55: **58 d** 8.5f³ 8g² 7g* 7g 8m 10.5m⁵ 8m 8m 9.1d 8g Oct 22] lengthy, good-topped gelding: modest performer: won apprentice claimer at Newcastle in May: below form after: effective at 7f to 8.5f: acts on any turf ground (well beaten in 3 runs on fibresand): effective blinkered or not, tried in cheekpieces: has run well when sweating: has pulled hard: usually races prominently. *R. A. Fahey*

BEEJAY 2 b.f. (Mar 26) Piccolo 121 – Letluce 92 (Aragon 118) [2003 5g³ p5g* Apr 1] **66** first living foal: dam 2-y-o 7f winner: fair form when justifying favouritism in maiden at Lingfield by short head: should stay at least 6f. *P. F. I. Cole*

BEE J GEE 5 b.g. Dilum (USA) 115 – Sound Check 62 (Formidable (USA) 125) – [2003 –: p8g 10m 10m f12s Jul 14] maiden handicapper: no form since at 2 yrs: tried visored/in cheekpieces. *Mrs Lydia Pearce*

BEE MINOR 2 b.f. (Mar 31) Barathea (IRE) 127 – Bee Off (IRE) 59 (Wolfhound **73** (USA) 126) [2003 5.2m⁴ 6g² 5g⁶ 6m⁵ 6g³ 7.1d⁵ 6.5d 6.5m Sep 26] IR 30,000F, 33,000Y: workmanlike filly: second foal: dam, Irish maiden who stayed 7f, half-sister to Nell Gwyn winner Thrilling Day: fair maiden: placed at Lingfield and Windsor (nursery): should stay 1m: acts on good to soft going, probably on good to firm. *R. Hannon*

BEENABOUTABIT 5 b.m. Komaite (USA) – Tassagh Bridge (IRE) (Double Schwartz – 128) [2003 51: 7g 7f 10m Aug 20] angular mare: modest maiden at best: well held in 2003, leaving R. Ingram after reappearance: tried in headgear. *Mrs L. C. Jewell*

BEERSHEBA 3 b.f. Thowra (FR) – Hymn Book (IRE) 65 (Darshaan 133) [2003 –: p8g – 10d Jun 23] lightly raced and no form: left B. Johnson after reappearance. *G. L. Moore*

BEETLE BUG 3 br.f. Robellino (USA) 127 – Special Beat 65 (Bustino 136) [2003 **49** –p: 9.7g⁵ 10m f12g 12.1d 16.2m 16.2g p13g Dec 29] workmanlike filly: poor maiden handicapper: barely stays 2m: yet to race on extremes of going. *A. M. Hales*

BEFORE DAWN (IRE) 3 gr.g. Mujadil (USA) 119 – Nirvavita (FR) (Highest Honor – (FR) 124) [2003 74: f6g⁶ p7g 8.1m May 5] 15,000Y: third foal: half-brother to 2001 2-y-o 1m winner Full House (by King's Theatre): dam French 1m winner out of half-sister to very smart French 7f/1m performer Nikos: fair maiden for D. Weld in Ireland at 2 yrs (effective at 6f/7f, acted on soft and good to firm going): no form in 2003: tried blinkered/ visored. *J. D. Czerpak*

BEGIN THE BEGUINE (IRE) 3 b.f. Peintre Celebre (USA) 137 – Beguine (USA) **72** 77 (Green Dancer (USA) 132) [2003 8.1m⁶ 10f 10m* 10m 10.5d Sep 27] 160,000Y: lengthy filly: second foal: half-sister to fairly useful Irish 2001 2-y-o 5f/7f winner Master Papa (by Key of Luck): dam, lightly-raced maiden (form on only 2-y-o outing), half-sister to Grand Lodge: easily best effort (fair form) when winning maiden at Pontefract in July: well held in handicaps after: should stay 1½m: sold 85,000 gns. *W. Jarvis*

BEHAN 4 ch.g. Rainbows For Life (CAN) – With Finesse (Be My Guest (USA) 126) **44** [2003 59: f8g f12g f8.5g 10.1m⁴ 11.8m 12m³ 17.1m 11.9m 12m⁶ f11g Dec 3] smallish, sturdy gelding: poor performer nowadays: left G. M. Moore after fourth start: best form up to 1¼m: acts on fibresand, firm and good to soft ground: usually blinkered/visored. *A. Crook*

BEHKARA (IRE) 3 b.f. Kris 135 – Behera 129 (Mill Reef (USA) 141) [2003 11g⁴ **115** 14g³ 15g* 12g* 15d* 15.5s³ Oct 26] half-sister to 3 winners, including 1¼m winner Behra (by Grand Lodge) and French stayer Bayrika (by Kahyasi), both useful: dam, won Prix Saint-Alary and second in Prix de l'Arc de Triomphe, would have stayed beyond 1½m: smart performer: won minor event at Deauville in August, listed race at Saint-Cloud in September and Prix Hubert de Chaudenay Casino Barriere de Menton at

H.H. Aga Khan's "Behkara"

Longchamp (by 1½ lengths from Risk Seeker) in October: improved again when keeping-on 3½ lengths third to Westerner in Prix Royal-Oak at Longchamp: stays 15f well: acts on soft ground. *A. de Royer Dupre, France*

BELINDA   6 ch.m. Mizoram (USA) 105 – Mountain Dew (Pharly (FR) 130) [2003 –, a58d: f12s⁶ f12g* f12g² f12s⁶ p12g p12g⁶ f14.8s* 12.1d Jul 25] modest handicapper: blind in one eye: won at Wolverhampton in January and July: barely stays 14.8f: acts on fibresand (probably on polytrack), little recent form on turf: tongue tied last 2 starts: tends to carry head awkwardly. *K. Bell*   **–** **a64**

BELISCO (USA)   2 b.c. (Mar 28) Royal Academy (USA) 130 – A Mean Fit (USA) (Fit To Fight (USA)) [2003 7m⁵ 8s Oct 29] $85,000Y: lengthy, useful-looking colt: fourth foal: half-brother to winners in USA by Wild Again and Holy Bull: dam Canadian 9f winner: better effort in maidens (fair form) when slow-starting fifth at Leicester: should stay 1m. *Mrs A. J. Perrett*   **70**

BELLA BAMBINA   3 b.f. Turtle Island (IRE) 123 – Lady Eurolink 55 (Kala Shikari 125) [2003 7m 8.2g p10g⁴ p12g Sep 3] tall, leggy filly: sister to 7-y-o Eurolink Zante and half-sister to 3 winners, including useful 1¼m/1½m winner Duke of Eurolink (by Jupiter Island): dam 1m winner: poor maiden: seemed not to stay 1½m: joined M. Pipe. *J. L. Dunlop*   **45**

BELLA BEGUINE   4 b.f. Komaite (USA) – On The Record 72 (Record Token 128) [2003 67, a71: f7s 5m⁵ 6m 6.1g 6f⁴ 6m³ 6m⁵ 5g 6f³ 6m² 5m² 5m⁵ f6s³ 6m f6s* 6g 6.1m f7g² f8.5g f7g² Nov 14] workmanlike filly: fair handicapper: won at Southwell in October: effective at 5f to 7f: acts on soft going, good to firm and fibresand: effective blinkered/visored: usually races up with pace. *A. Bailey*   **65** **a78**

BELLA BIANCA (IRE)   3 b.f. Barathea (IRE) 127 – Alarme Belle 105 (Warning 136) [2003 78: 6d Jun 30] lengthy, useful-looking filly: has a quick action: fair performer, lightly raced: well held only run in 2003: should stay 7f: acts on firm and good to soft ground: hung markedly right once at 2 yrs. *R. Hannon*   **–**

119

BELLA BOY ZEE (IRE)   2 b.f. (Apr 12) Anita's Prince 126 – Waikiki (GER) (Zam-   **62**
pano (GER)) [2003 5g f5g³ 5m* 5m² 5m* 6d² 5m* 5g³ 5m³ 5.1g 6m 6g 5.1d Nov 6]
€1,200Y: workmanlike filly: third foal: dam German 1¼m/11f winner: modest performer: won maiden at Warwick in April (left P. McEntee after next outing) and claimers
at Thirsk (left P. Blockley after next start) and Leicester (for D. Nicholls) in May: trained
eighth start only by A. Reid: effective at 5f/6f: acts on good to firm going: visored (ran
respectably) final start: rejoined P. Blockley. *R. Wilman*

BELLA CASTANA   3 ch.f. Efisio 120 – Simple Logic 73 (Aragon 118) [2003 –: 8.2g   **–**
7g p7g Oct 27] leggy, close-coupled filly: second foal: dam 2-y-o 6f winner: well held in
maidens: slowly away first 2 outings. *A. Charlton*

BELLAGIO PRINCESS   2 ch.f. (Mar 5) Kris 135 – Forest Call 67 (Wolfhound (USA)   **58**
126) [2003 5m 6m³ p7g 8m Sep 16] workmanlike filly: first foal: dam, maiden, effective
at 5f to 1m, out of sister to smart miler Inchmurrin: modest maiden: third at Catterick: no
form after: should stay 1m. *A. M. Balding*

BELLA PAVLINA   5 ch.m. Sure Blade (USA) 130 – Pab's Choice 61 (Telsmoss 91)   **34**
[2003 48: f12g³ f8g⁶ Dec 8] poor maiden: stays 1½m: acts on fibresand, soft and firm
going. *W. M. Brisbourne*

BELLA TUTRICE (IRE)   2 b.f. (Apr 4) Woodborough (USA) 112 – Institutrice   **78**
(IRE) 87 (College Chapel 122) [2003 5g³ 5g² 5g² 5d² 5m* 5m³ 6f 5g² 5d p5g Oct 30]
€6,500Y: small, good-bodied filly: first foal: dam, Irish maiden who seemed to stay
1¼m, half-sister to useful Irish performer up to 1½m Cheviot Amble, herself dam of
smart 1¼m/1½m performer Amalia: fair performer: won maiden at Musselburgh in May:
placed in listed event at Beverley (6 lengths third to Attraction) and minor contest at
Windsor after: left I. Wood before well held last 2 starts: best at 5f: acts on good to firm
and good to soft going. *John A. Harris*

BELL BOTTOM BLUES   3 b.f. Whittingham (IRE) 104 – Bella Coola 50 (Northern   **48**
State (USA) 91) [2003 59: 7m 7.1g⁶ 8f⁶ 8m Jul 23] just poor maiden at 3 yrs: stays 1m:
raced only on good ground or firmer on turf. *C. G. Cox*

BELLE BLEU   3 b.f. Bluegrass Prince (IRE) 110 – Hello Lady (Wolverlife 115) [2003   **–**
–: 10.3m p12g Sep 3] leggy filly: well beaten in maidens. *M. R. Bosley*

BELLE DU JOUR (AUS)   6 b.m. Dehere (USA) 121 – Delightful Belle (NZ) (Bal-   **112**
merino (NZ) 133) [2003 6d² 6g* a6f⁴ 6d⁴ 5m² 6f Jun 21] rather leggy, workmanlike
ex-Australian mare: very smart performer at best (rated 120) in native country, winner of
9 races, including Group 1 Golden Slipper in 2000 and 21-runner Group 1 Rosemount
Estate Newmarket Handicap at Flemington in March by ¾ length from Bel Esprit
(Choisir sixth): left C. Conners after next start, best effort for new stable (smart form)
when neck second of 5 to Miss Anabaa in Ballyogan Stakes at Cork penultimate start:
sweating freely and unimpressive in appearance, well held in Golden Jubilee Stakes at
Royal Ascot (reportedly struck into) final outing: stayed 6f: acted on good to firm and
good to soft going: usually blinkered: to visit Sadler's Wells. *D. K. Weld, Ireland*

BELLESOEUR   3 ch.f. Whittingham (IRE) 104 – Trina's Pet 65 (Efisio 120) [2003 –:   **–**
9.7g⁶ 10m⁵ 11.5g f12s 12m⁶ 14.1s³ Oct 29] has shown little, including in seller.
P. Howling

BELLS BEACH (IRE)   5 ch.m. General Monash (USA) 107 – Clifton Beach (Auction   **55**
Ring (USA) 123) [2003 60, a–: f6g⁵ f6g⁶ f6g 5.7m³ 5.3m 5.7f 5m⁴ 5.3m Jul 6] strong,   **a43**
close-coupled mare: modest on turf, poor on all-weather: raced mainly at 5f/6f: acts on
good to firm going, good to soft and fibresand: sometimes slowly away: won £700.
A. G. Newcombe

BELLS BOY'S   4 b.g. Mind Games 121 – Millie's Lady (IRE) (Common Grounds   **43**
118) [2003 56: 6m 6m⁵ f6g f6g⁵ Dec 9] workmanlike gelding: poor maiden nowadays:
left A. Dickman after second start: barely stays 6f: acts on firm ground and fibresand:
often races prominently: tried in cheekpieces. *K. A. Ryan*

BELT AND BRACES   2 b.g. (May 5) Merdon Melody 98 – Dutyful 78 (Bold Owl   **–**
101) [2003 5m 6m 6m f8g Dec 8] 2,000Y: lengthy, useful-looking gelding: fifth foal:
brother to winner in Italy: dam winner up to 2m: no form, including in seller. *C. Smith*

BELTANE   5 b.g. Magic Ring (IRE) 115 – Sally's Trust (IRE) 51 (Classic Secret (USA)   **–**
91) [2003 –: 10d Oct 31] probably of little account nowadays. *W. de Best-Turner*

BELUGA BAY   4 b.g. Millkom 124 – Bellyphax (Bellypha 130) [2003 86: 8d³ 7m²   **94**
8.5d⁴ 8.1d 7m* 8m* Oct 17] sturdy gelding: unimpressive mover: fairly useful performer: suffered minor fracture at 3 yrs: improved form when winning handicaps at Newbury

(hung markedly left) in September and Newmarket (quickened in good style to lead close home when beating Impeller a head) in October: stays 8.5f: acts on soft and good to firm going: lightly raced. *J. R. Fanshawe*

BE MY ALIBI (IRE)   2 ch.f. (May 6) Daggers Drawn (USA) 114 – Join The Party   **56 d** (Be My Guest (USA) 126) [2003 5m⁵ 5d³ f6g⁴ 6g 7f⁵ 5.1d f8.5g f8g Dec 8] €1,200Y: quite good-topped filly: sixth foal: dam lightly-raced Irish 2-y-o 5f winner: modest maiden: third at Hamilton: soundly beaten last 3 starts: stays 6f: acts on good to soft ground and fibresand: sold £850. *J. S. Moore*

BE MY TINKER   5 ch.m. Be My Chief (USA) 122 – Tinkerbird 76 (Music Boy 124)   **49** [2003 75: 5m 6.1d 5m 6m 7m 5.5f⁶ 5m 6m Aug 11] lengthy mare: fair handicapper at 4 yrs: only poor form in 2003: best at 5f/6f: acts on all-weather and firm going: blinkered once as 3-y-o: usually races prominently. *M. A. Buckley*

BENBAUN (IRE)   2 b.c. (Feb 21) Stravinsky (USA) 133 – Escape To Victory (Salse   **85** (USA) 128) [2003 7.1f 7s⁴ 7.5m 5.1g* 6g⁶ 5f* 5d² 5g Oct 11] 14,000Y: useful-looking colt: second foal: dam, Italian 2-y-o 7f winner, half-sister to high-class 1m/1¼m performer Hawksley Hill: fairly useful performer: won nurseries at Chepstow in August and Redcar (by 5 lengths) in September: creditable ninth in Cornwallis Stakes at Ascot final start: likely to prove best at 5f: acts on firm and good to soft ground: visored last 5 outings: races prominently: sometimes edges left. *M. J. Wallace*

BENDARSHAAN   3 b.c. Darshaan 133 – Calypso Run (Lycius (USA) 124) [2003   **84** 8m² 10m² 11.5g³ 12.1d² 12.3f³ Jun 18] 100,000Y: close-coupled, attractive colt: third foal: brother to French 1½m winner Newtown: dam, ran once, from very good middle-distance family: fairly useful maiden: placed all starts: stays 1½m: acts on good to firm and good to soft ground, probably unsuited by firm (odds on) final start: sent to UAE. *E. A. L. Dunlop*

BENEFACTOR (IRE)   3 b.c. Hector Protector (USA) 124 – Beneficiary 69 (Jalmood   **–** (USA) 126) [2003 –: 9d 7.5d May 20] good-topped colt: well beaten in maidens. *M. W. Easterby*

BENEKING   3 b. or br.g. Wizard King 122 – Gagajulu 75 (Al Hareb (USA) 123) [2003   **80 d** 73: p7g⁴ 7g⁵ 6m 7g² 7m³ 8m⁵ 6.1m⁵ 7m² 7.1m⁶ p7g 7.1m⁴ p7g p6g f6g Nov 25] rather leggy gelding: fairly useful maiden handicapper at best: effective at 6f, should stay 1m: acts on good to firm going and polytrack: tried blinkered (reportedly lost action)/in cheekpieces: none too consistent. *J. Gallagher*

BENEVENTA   3 b.f. Most Welcome 131 – Dara Dee 87 (Dara Monarch 128) [2003   **100** 8f² 10f* 10d* 10m* 10.1m* 10.1m³ 12d⁴ 10m Oct 16] 3,500F: tall, leggy filly: still on weak side: sixth foal: sister to fairly useful 1¼m winner Beneventus and half-sister to 2 winners, including fairly useful 1¼m winner Hernandita (by Hernando): dam 7f/1m winner: useful performer: won maiden at Kempton, handicaps at Ascot and Newmarket and minor event at Yarmouth (beat Putra Kuantan by 2½ lengths in 3-runner event) in July/August: creditable efforts in frame in listed races at Yarmouth and Saint-Cloud next 2 starts, ran poorly in similar company at Newmarket final outing: stays 1½m: acts on firm and good to soft going: edged left fourth outing. *J. L. Dunlop*

BEN HUR   4 b.g. Zafonic (USA) 130 – Gayane 125 (Nureyev (USA) 131) [2003 65:   **72** 9.3g² 9m⁶ 10.3m³ 10m⁴ 9.1f⁴ 7.9m² 8.1m³ 8.3g² f8.5s* 8.3d 8.2m p8g⁵ 8d Nov 7] lengthy gelding: fair handicapper: won maiden on all-weather debut at Wolverhampton in September: effective at 1m to 1¼m: acts on fibresand, firm and soft going (yet to race on heavy): tried in cheekpieces, including for win: has been early to post/troublesome at stall/slowly away: tends to race freely: has carried head awkwardly: often races prominently. *W. M. Brisbourne*

BENJAMIN (IRE)   5 b.g. Night Shift (USA) – Best Academy (USA) (Roberto (USA)   **48 +** 131) [2003 –: 8f³ f8.5s 8g 8f⁶ 8.1m 8.1m 8.1m³ 13.1f⁶ Aug 22] poor maiden handicapper: stays 1m: acts on firm going: tongue tied. *Jane Southcombe*

BEN KENOBI   5 ch.g. Accondy (IRE) 79 – Nour El Sahar (USA) (Sagace (FR) 135)   **55 §** [2003 –: f9.4g f9.4s 12.6m⁴ 12.6f* 12.1g 12m Oct 6] well-made gelding: modest performer: won handicap at Warwick in July: folded both starts after: stays 12.6f: acts on firm ground. *Mrs P. Ford*

BEN LOMAND   3 ch.g. Inchinor 119 – Benjarong 50 (Sharpo 132) [2003 82: 7g 8m   **82** 8g 6m* 6m⁴ 6d* 6m² 6g 6m 7g Nov 1] good-bodied gelding: fairly useful performer: won minor event at Brighton in May and handicap at Windsor in June: ran poorly in handicaps last 3 starts: best efforts at 6f: acts on good to firm and good to soft ground. *B. W. Duke*

BENNY THE BALL (USA)   2 b. or br.c. (May 14) Benny The Dip (USA) 127 – **86 p**
Heloise (USA) (Forty Niner (USA)) [2003 6m⁴ p7g² 10g⁶ f7g* Nov 25] $6,000Y, 8,000
2-y-o: big, good-bodied colt: has scope: fourth living foal: half-brother to 3 winners in
USA, including minor stakes winner Padlock (by Boundary): dam 6.5f to 1m winner in
USA: fairly useful form: landed odds comfortably in maiden at Southwell: good sixth
in listed event at Newmarket, weakening having forced pace: should stay 1¼m: acts on
all-weather: type to train on well. *N. P. Littmoden*

BENNY THE VICE (USA)   4 ch.g. Benny The Dip (USA) 127 – Vice On Ice (USA)   –
(Vice Regent (CAN)) [2003 71d: f16s⁵ Jan 1] tall, rangy gelding: fair performer at best:
has shown little since early 2002: has worn headgear. *Mrs A. Duffield*

BENTLEY'S BALL (USA)   2 b. or br.c. (Mar 11) Stravinsky (USA) 133 – Slide By   **93**
83 (Aragon 118) [2003 6g⁶ 5g³ 5f* 6g* 6f⁴ 7f³ 6m² Oct 17] $50,000F: rather leggy,
quite good-topped colt: third foal: dam, Irish 2-y-o 7f winner, half-sister to very smart
performer up to 13f Water Jump: fairly useful performer: won maiden at Sandown in June
and nursery at Newmarket in August: creditable efforts in nurseries after, particularly
when second at Newmarket: stays 7f: acts on firm ground. *R. Hannon*

BENVOLIO   6 br.g. Cidrax (FR) – Miss Capulet (Commanche Run 133) [2003 12m   –
f12g Aug 15] small gelding: little sign of ability. *P. L. Clinton*

BERESFORD BOY   2 b.c. (May 2) Easycall 115 – Devils Dirge 68 (Song 132) [2003   **53**
5.1m p6g⁶ Nov 18] close-coupled colt: closely related to 2 winners by Forzando, notably
smart sprinter Superior Premium, and half-brother to 2 winners by Phountzi: dam maiden
who probably stayed 7f: modest form in maidens: not sure to stay beyond 6f. *D. K. Ivory*

BERGAMO   7 b.g. Robellino (USA) 127 – Pretty Thing 83 (Star Appeal 133) [2003   **54**
41, a–: f14s⁵ f16g⁶ f16s² f16.2g² f16.2g Mar 3] small, compact gelding: fluent mover:
modest handicapper: won at Southwell in January: stays easy 2m: acts on fibresand, firm
and soft going: usually wears headgear: sometimes looks less than keen. *B. Ellison*

BERGERAC PIE   4 b.f. Cyrano de Bergerac 120 – Foxtrot Pie 77 (Shernazar 131)   –
[2003 67: 10g Apr 29] smallish filly: fair maiden at 3 yrs: soundly beaten only run in
2003. *R. Hollinshead*

BERKELEY HALL   6 b.m. Saddlers' Hall (IRE) 126 – Serious Affair (Valiyar 129)   **54**
[2003 59, a–: 7m 7m⁵ 8.2m² 8.1m⁶ 8.1m Jul 11] stocky mare: modest performer: effective   **a–**
at 6f to 1m: acts on firm and good to soft going, well held on all-weather: usually
blinkered/wears cheekpieces. *R. Lee*

BERKELEY HEIGHTS   3 b.f. Hector Protector (USA) 124 – Dancing Heights   –
(IRE) 80 (High Estate 127) [2003 73: 8.5m⁵ 8.5m 10g f12g⁶ f11g⁵ Dec 16] sturdy filly:
fair maiden at 2 yrs: well held in 2003: tried blinkered. *B. Smart*

BERNARD   3 b.g. Nashwan (USA) 135 – Tabyan (USA) 68 (Topsider (USA)) [2003   **71**
8m 10d 10.5v⁴ 14m⁴ 14g² 14.1m³ Aug 14] big, good-topped gelding: seventh foal:
half-brother to smart 1m to 1¼m winner Cap Juluca and 1½m winner in Italy (both by
Mtoto): dam 6f winner: fair maiden handicapper: stays 1¾m: acts on good to firm ground,
probably on heavy: ran in snatches and flashed tail final outing: sold £4,500. *R. Charlton*

BERNINI (IRE)   3 b.g. Grand Lodge (USA) 125 – Alsahah (IRE) (Unfuwain (USA)   **?**
131) [2003 –: f12g* f11.8m 11.9m 11.6d Jun 23] big, deep-girthed gelding: fair form: won   **a75**
maiden at Southwell (ran in snatches) in March: well held on turf other 4 starts: will stay
at least 1¾m. *M. L. W. Bell*

BERRY RACER (IRE)   2 ch.f. (Apr 18) Titus Livius (FR) 115 – Opening Day (Day   **53 ?**
Is Done 115) [2003 5m 6.1m 5.7f³ 5.1f 6.1m⁵ Oct 22] €5,000Y, 13,000 2-y-o: good-
bodied filly: half-sister to several winners, including fairly useful 5f and (including at 2
yrs) 6f winner Norwegian Blue (by Mac's Imp) and 7f winner Moonstone (by Statoblest):
dam Irish 1m winner: seemed to show modest form when third in maiden at Bath: poor
otherwise: bred to prove best up to 1m. *R. J. Smith*

BERTIE BUCKS   3 br.g. Charmer 123 – Dolly Mixture (Midyan (USA) 124) [2003 –:   –
8m 7m 9.9m Jul 21] leggy, workmanlike gelding: little form. *J. Hetherton*

BERTOCELLI   2 ch.c. (Feb 12) Vettori (IRE) 119 – Dame Jude 76 (Dilum (USA)   **76**
115) [2003 5.1g⁵ 6m⁵ 7m 8.1m⁶ 7f* 7d Nov 8] compact colt: first foal: dam best at 2 yrs
when 5f winner: fair performer: won nursery at Leicester in October by neck from Disco
Diva, making most: last in similar event at Doncaster final start: seems best at 7f: acts on
firm going. *G. G. Margarson*

BESSEMER (JPN)   2 b.c. (Mar 18) Carnegie (IRE) 129 – Chalna (IRE) 83 (Darshaan   **92**
133) [2003 5m³ 6g* 7m Aug 15] rangy colt: second foal: dam, Irish 1½m winner, half-

sister to high-class French winner up to 10.5f Creator out of Coronation Stakes winner Chalon: fairly useful form: landed odds in maiden at Ayr in August easily by 7 lengths, making all: last of 8 in listed race at Newbury, veering left: bred to be well suited by 1¼m/ 1½m: wayward, and may benefit from headgear. *M. Johnston*

BEST BEFORE (IRE) 3 b.g. Mujadil (USA) 119 – Miss Margate (IRE) 60 (Don't **70 §** Forget Me 127) [2003 6m² 5g⁵ 5.2m² 6g² f6g⁴ 6m² 7.1g 6m⁶ f8.5g⁵ Dec 26] 20,000 2-y-o: workmanlike gelding: first foal: dam, Irish maiden who stayed 2m, half-sister to smart performer up to 2m Shambo: fair maiden: well below form last 5 starts, leaving J. Osborne 19,000 gns and gelded before final one: should be suited by 7f+: raced only on good/good to firm going on turf, well below form on fibresand: tried blinkered: has hung/ found little: one to treat with some caution. *P. D. Evans*

BEST BE GOING (IRE) 3 b.g. Danehill (USA) 126 – Bye Bold Aileen (IRE) (Warn- **88 p** ing 136) [2003 8m³ 8f⁴ 8.1d⁵ 8f* Oct 12] IR 65,000Y: sturdy, close-coupled gelding: second foal: brother to 4-y-o Concubine: dam, Irish maiden (seemed to stay 1¼m), half-sister to 2 useful performers up to 1¼m: fairly useful maiden: best effort when winning handicap at Goodwood in October by 2½ lengths from Exzilarating: will probably stay 1¼m: acts on firm going: lightly raced, and probably capable of better still. *P. W. Harris*

BEST BOND 6 ch.g. Cadeaux Genereux 131 – My Darlingdaughter (Night Shift **43** (USA)) [2003 52+: p6g 6g³ 6m Apr 15] lengthy gelding: poor handicapper nowadays: best at 6f/7f: acts on all-weather, good to firm and soft going: tried blinkered/in cheek-pieces, usually visored: has started slowly/looked no easy ride. *N. P. Littmoden*

BEST DESERT (IRE) 2 b.g. (Mar 3) Desert Style (IRE) 121 – La Alla Wa Asa (IRE) **65** 60 (Alzao (USA) 117) [2003 5m³ 5m⁵ 5m⁶ 7g 7m² Oct 3] €14,000Y, 21,000 2-y-o: fifth foal: half-brother to 1999 2-y-o winner in Sweden by Common Grounds: dam, ran twice, sister to smart performer up to 1¼m Aldbourne: fair maiden: good second in nursery at Lingfield: should stay 1m. *J. R. Best*

BEST FLIGHT 3 gr.g. Sheikh Albadou 128 – Bustling Nelly 94 (Bustino 136) [2003 **78 p** p7g f7g³ 7d⁴ f8.5s* Sep 20] half-brother to several winners, notably very smart middle-distance stayer Busy Flight (by Pharly) and fairly useful 1½m winner Shareef (by Shareef Dancer): dam, 1½m winner, half-sister to Further Flight: fair form: much more impressive than bare result indicates when winning maiden handicap at Wolverhampton in September by length from Coronado Forest: stays 8.5f: acts on fibresand: capable of better still, and well up to winning more handicaps. *B. W. Hills*

BEST FORCE 2 b.f. (Apr 3) Compton Place 125 – Bestemor 60 (Selkirk (USA) 129) **– p** [2003 6m⁵ 6g 6.1d Nov 6] neat filly: third foal: half-sister to 4-y-o Best Lead: dam maiden who stayed 1m: signs of ability, not knocked about, in maidens: likely to do better in handicaps at up to 1m. *G. A. Butler*

BEST LEAD 4 b.g. Distant Relative 128 – Bestemor 60 (Selkirk (USA) 129) [2003 –: **58** f6g 5m 5g 5.9f 6f f6g⁶ f5s⁵ Dec 27] leggy gelding: fairly useful at 2 yrs for G. Butler: lightly raced and modest at best since: likely to prove best at 5f/easy 6f: acts on firm and soft going, probably on fibresand: tried visored/blinkered: has carried head awkwardly/ hung right. *Ian Emmerson*

BEST PORT (IRE) 7 b.g. Be My Guest (USA) 126 – Portree 82 (Slip Anchor 136) **63** [2003 68: 12m 16g⁴ 12.1m³ 16.2m⁴ 16g⁴ 14.1m³ 14.1f³ 15.9d 14.1m⁵ 14.1m⁴ Oct 17] lightly-made gelding: modest handicapper nowadays: best at 1¾m/2m: acts on firm going, good to soft and fibresand: held up: often finds little. *J. Parkes*

BESTSELLER 3 ch.f. Selkirk (USA) 129 – Top Shop 75 (Nashwan (USA) 135) **–** [2003 10m Jul 8] angular, good-topped filly: third foal: half-sister to fairly useful 7f winner Up Market (by Mark of Esteem): dam, 1½m winner, half-sister to King Edward VII Stakes winner Private Tender: 50/1, very green and burly when well behind in maiden at Newmarket: subsequently found to be lame: sold 3,500 gns. *E. A. L. Dunlop*

BESTWILLINTHEWORLD 3 b.c. Winning Gallery 94 – Earthly Pleasure 58 **–** (Music Boy 124) [2003 11.5g 12m 11.8m 10f Oct 1] close-coupled colt: fifth living foal: dam maiden who stayed 1½m: no sign of ability: tried in cheekpieces. *T. T. Clement*

BE SWIFT 4 ch.g. Millkom 124 – Conwy (Rock City 120) [2003 50: p13g⁶ 18m 12.6m **–** Sep 20] smallish, deep-girthed gelding: modest maiden: well held in 2003, leaving S. Dow after reappearance. *A. J. Chamberlain*

BETHANYS BOY (IRE) 2 ch.g. (May 3) Docksider (USA) 124 – Daymoon (USA) **81** (Dayjur (USA) 137) [2003 5d⁴ 6g⁴ 6m⁶ 6g⁴ 6m 7.2m⁴ 6m 8s² f7g⁵ f8s* Dec 13] €18,000Y, 16,000 2-y-o: close-coupled gelding: second foal: dam, French maiden, closely related to smart 1m/1¼m performer Masterful: fairly useful performer: won maiden at Southwell by 3½ lengths from Carriacou: should stay 1¼m: acts on soft ground and fibresand. *B. Ellison*

BETTALATETHANNEVER (IRE) 2 ch.g. (Apr 25) Titus Livius (FR) 115 – Sham- **85**
bodia (IRE) (Petardia 113) [2003 p6g p6g⁶ p7g* Dec 17] €7,000Y, 20,000 2-y-o: second
foal: dam unraced out of sister to smart performer up to 2m Shambo: progressed with
each outing, fairly useful form when landing gamble in minor event at Lingfield by head
from Queenstown (pair clear): should stay 1m: slowly away first 2 starts. *S. Dow*

BETTER GAMBLE 4 b.g. Bluegrass Prince (IRE) 110 – Come To Good (Swing **– §**
Easy (USA) 126) [2003 50§, a–§: f12g Jan 21] poor maiden: blinkered 4 of last 5 outings:
unreliable. *R. M. Flower*

BETTERGETGONE 4 b.f. Bettergeton 97 – Impromptu Melody (IRE) (Mac's Imp **–**
(USA) 116) [2003 7g f8.5g Nov 17] leggy filly: little worthwhile form: left B. Leavy after
reappearance: tried visored/blinkered/tongue tied. *W. Clay*

BETTER OFF 5 ch.g. Bettergeton 97 – Miami Pride 48 (Miami Springs 121) [2003 –, **–**
a75: f7s f7g⁵ f7s* f7g* f7g f8g f7g f7g f9.4g Dec 22] strong gelding: poor mover: fairly **a85 d**
useful performer: won minor event at Southwell in February and handicap at Wolverhampton (idled) in March: lost form completely after: effective at 6f to 1m: acts on
fibresand, no form on turf: usually wears cheekpieces/visor: sometimes slowly away/
slow to warm up. *Mrs N. Macauley*

BETTER PAL 4 ch.g. Prince Sabo 123 – Rattle Along 80 (Tap On Wood 130) [2003 **64 d**
78: 7g⁶ 7m 7.5m 9.9m 12f f7g f8g Nov 24] good-bodied gelding: modest maiden handicapper nowadays: well held after reappearance: stays 1m, probably not 1¼m: acts on soft
and good to firm going: blinkered once: sometimes slowly away/wanders. *P. R. Wood*

BETTERWARE BOY 3 ch.g. Barathea (IRE) 127 – Crystal Drop 101 (Cadeaux **68**
Genereux 131) [2003 10m⁵ 10g⁴ p10g⁵ Dec 6] IR 48,000Y: second foal: dam, French 1m
winner who stayed 11f, out of close relation to Irish 1000 Guineas winner Ensconse: fair
form in maidens: sold £4,500 and left Mrs A. Perrett after second start: has started slowly/
raced freely. *P. M. Phelan*

BETTY'S PRIDE 4 b.f. Lion Cavern (USA) 117 – Final Verdict (IRE) (Law Society **62 §**
(USA) 130) [2003 89: 5g 5f 5f⁶ 5m 5f Aug 20] leggy, quite good-topped filly: fairly
useful performer 2002: only modest form in 2003, leaving A. Berry after third start:
best at 5f: acts on firm ground: sometimes takes good hold/carries head awkwardly: one
to treat with caution. *M. Dods*

BETTY STOGS (IRE) 2 b.f. (Jan 30) Perugino (USA) 84 – Marabela (IRE) 79 (Sher- **81**
nazar 131) [2003 7g 7m⁶ 7m* 7g Oct 25] sturdy filly: first living foal: dam, 1m winner
from 4 starts, out of half-sister to smart French performers Madaiyn (stayed 1¾m) and
Malakim (stayed 1½m): fairly useful performer: won maiden at Leicester in October: on
edge/going in coat, creditable seventh in listed event at Newbury final start: will stay 1m:
refused to enter stall intended second outing. *N. A. Gaselee*

BETTYS TRIBUTE 2 ch.f. (May 6) Daggers Drawn (USA) 114 – Cavatina 72 (Chief **66**
Singer 131) [2003 5.1m f7g* f7g⁴ p7g² 7g⁴ 8m⁴ Oct 21] 2,500Y: sturdy filly: fourth
foal: dam, 6f/7.5f winner, out of half-sister to high-class sprinter Mummy's Pet: fair
performer: won seller at Wolverhampton in June: ran well in nurseries at Lingfield and
Yarmouth fourth and fifth starts: stays 7f, probably not 1m: acts on all-weather: usually
races prominently: sold 16,500 gns, sent to USA. *C. A. Dwyer*

BEVELLER 4 ch.g. Beveled (USA) – Kairover 50 (Smackover 107) [2003 –: 11.1d **61**
8m³ 7.5d 7.6m⁴ 7.1m² 7m f7s⁴ f6g² Nov 19] rangy gelding: modest maiden: free-going
sort, at least as effective at 6f as 7f: acts on fibresand and good to firm ground: sometimes
slowly away. *W. M. Brisbourne*

BEVERLEY MACCA 5 ch.m. Piccolo 121 – Kangra Valley 56 (Indian Ridge 123) **61**
[2003 70, a66: p5g⁵ Jan 18] small, compact mare: unimpressive mover: fair performer at
4 yrs: below form only outing 2003: best at 5f: possibly unsuited by soft/heavy going,
acts on any other turf/all-weather: sometimes edges right: runs the odd poor race: often
leads: sold 25,000 gns. *A. Berry*

BEVIER 9 b.g. Nashwan (USA) 135 – Bevel (USA) (Mr Prospector (USA)) [2003 –: **53**
f9.4s* f16.2g f9.4s 11.8g 12.6m⁴ 12.6f Jul 10] leggy gelding: modest handicapper: won
at Wolverhampton (edged left) in February: effective at 9f, probably stays 1½m: acts on
fibresand and good to firm ground: blinkered (raced freely) once. *T. Wall*

BE WISE GIRL 2 ch.f. (Mar 25) Fleetwood (IRE) 107 – Zabelina (USA) 57 (Diesis **49**
133) [2003 7.1m f8s³ Oct 7] 4,500Y: workmanlike filly: sixth foal: half-sister to 3

winners, including 4-y-o Millennium King: dam, maiden who stayed 1m, half-sister to US Grade 1 1¼m winner Dance Teacher: better effort in maidens (poor form) when third at Southwell: likely to stay 1¼m: looks difficult ride. *J. G. Given*

BEYOND CALCULATION (USA)   9 ch.g. Geiger Counter (USA) – Placer Queen **83** (Habitat 134) [2003 81, a70: 5g 5.7f⁵ 5m² 5f³ 5.3m⁴ 5m 5m 5f⁶ 5m 5f⁶ 5.7f 5m 6g Oct 13] **a–** sturdy gelding: fairly useful handicapper on turf: effective at 5f/6f: acts on all-weather, firm and good to soft going: very slowly away and tailed off final start. *J. M. Bradley*

BEYOND THE CLOUDS (IRE)   7 b.g. Midhish 109 – Tongabezi (IRE) 75 (Sher- **97** nazar 131) [2003 90: 5g⁴ 5f⁵ 6d 5d⁶ 5g² 6m 5f⁶ 5m² 5f⁶ 5d 5m 5d² 6m 5d 5.6d 5d³ 6f 5m 5m Oct 25] big gelding: useful handicapper: good efforts when runner-up in valuable events at Newcastle and Ascot (beaten ¾ length by Salviati) eighth/twelfth outings, and when third in minor event at Beverley in September: best at 5f (all wins)/easy 6f: acts on any going except soft/heavy: tried visored (not since 2000): sometimes restless in stall, and has been slowly away: usually races prominently. *J. S. Wainwright*

BEYOND THE POLE (USA)   5 b.g. Ghazi (USA) – North of Sunset (USA) (North- **71** ern Baby (CAN) 127) [2003 91: p12g p13g² p12g² p16g⁴ 14.4d f16.2s p12g p13g Nov 12] $8,000Y: half-brother to several winners abroad, including German 11f winner Nassem (by Irish River): dam, French maiden, half-sister to US Grade 2 6f winner Salt Dome: fair handicapper: trained by D. Weld in Ireland (fairly useful) in 2002: first past post in amateur event at Lingfield (demoted having bumped runner-up Mostarsil) third start: stays easy 2m: acts on firm going, soft and polytrack: tried blinkered. *B. R. Johnson*

BEZANT (IRE)   3 ch.f. Zamindar (USA) 116 – Foresta Verde (USA) 46 (Green Forest **51 ?** (USA) 134) [2003 –: 7m⁵ 8m³ May 14] fifth foal: dam sprint maiden: seemingly modest form, lightly raced: stays 1m: acts on good to firm going. *C. B. B. Booth*

BHANOYI (IRE)   4 ch.g. Perugino (USA) 84 – Bourgeonette 81 (Mummy's Pet **–** 125) [2003 –: p12g 14.1m 10m 14.1s Oct 29] little sign of ability: tried visored. *Mrs C. A. Dunnett*

BHUTAN (IRE)   8 b.g. Polish Patriot (USA) 128 – Bustinetta 89 (Bustino 136) [2003 **70** 58: f11g² f12s² f12g² f12g* f11g⁴ f12g* f16.2g⁵ p12g* f11g³ p12g Mar 28] lengthy gelding: fair handicapper: won at Wolverhampton (twice) and Lingfield (amateurs) in February: effective at 11f to 17.5f: acts on any turf going and all-weather: visored (below form) once: held up, and often finds little. *G. L. Moore*

BIBLE BOX (IRE)   5 b.m. Bin Ajwaad (IRE) 119 – Addie Pray (IRE) 68 (Great **93** Commotion (USA) 123) [2003 86: 8g* 8m⁴ 8m Jun 28] workmanlike mare: fairly useful performer: won handicap at Leicester in May: good fourth to Macadamia in listed race at Pontefract next time: best efforts on good/good to firm going: raced too freely final start. *Mrs Lydia Pearce*

BID FOR FAME (USA)   6 b. or br.g. Quest For Fame 127 – Shroud (USA) (Vaguely **97** Noble 140) [2003 91: 16m² 20m 16.1m 16.2m⁶ f16g² f14g* Dec 9] leggy, lengthy, quite attractive gelding: has a quick, rather round action: useful handicapper: left N. Henderson prior to winning at Southwell in December by 5 lengths from Victory Quest: stays 2m: acts on fibresand, best turf efforts on good going or firmer: blinkered (ran poorly) once at 4 yrs: has won when sweating. *N. Tinkler*

BID SPOTTER (IRE)   4 b.g. Eagle Eyed (USA) 111 – Bebe Auction (IRE) (Auction **–** Ring (USA) 123) [2003 57: f12g f12g f14g Dec 12] modest handicapper at best: well held in 2003: tried visored. *Mrs Lucinda Featherstone*

BIEN GOOD   2 b.f. (Mar 12) Bien Bien (USA) 125 – Southern Sky 89 (Comedy Star **–** (USA) 121) [2003 7s Nov 3] half-sister to 3 winners, including fairly useful 1993 2-y-o 6f winner Southern Ridge (by Indian Ridge) and 4-y-o Celtic Romance: dam 7f/1m winner: 25/1 and backward, tailed off in maiden at Redcar. *D. Nicholls*

BIENHEUREUX   2 b.g. (Mar 24) Bien Bien (USA) 125 – Rochea 67 (Rock City 120) **48 +** [2003 7m 5g Aug 26] 5,000Y: workmanlike gelding: second foal: dam, maiden (effective at 6f to 1¼m), half-sister to smart 6f performer Gorse: poor form in seller at Newmarket (slowly away, not knocked about) and maiden at Ripon: likely to be suited by at least 1m. *W. J. Musson*

BIENVENUE   2 ch.f. (Apr 18) Bien Bien (USA) 125 – Mossy Rose 78 (King of Spain **67 p** 121) [2003 p8g² p8g³ p8g⁵ Dec 10] half-sister to fairly useful winner around 1½m/1¾m Browning (by Warshaan): dam 6f and 1m winner: fair form in maidens at Lingfield: not knocked about final start: will stay at least 1¼m: remains open to improvement. *M. P. Tregoning*

Windflower Overseas Holdings Inc's "Big Bad Bob"

BIGALOTHEGIGALO (IRE)   3 b.g. Desert Story (IRE) 115 – Noble Clare (IRE)   **97 +**
(The Noble Player (USA) 126) [2003 81p: 7g² 7g 7m² 7g Oct 11] big gelding: useful
form: best efforts when runner-up in handicaps at Doncaster and York (split Arakan and
New Seeker): left J. Quinn, renamed Master Gigolo and off 5 months before final outing:
stays 7f: yet to race on extremes of going. *J. Moore, Hong Kong*

BIG BAD BOB (IRE)   3 br.c. Bob Back (USA) 124 – Fantasy Girl (IRE) 55 (Marju   **118**
(IRE) 127) [2003 110p: 10.3m² 12f 10.5m* 10g* 10g* 10g Sep 21] medium-sized, rather
leggy colt: smart performer: 2 lengths second of 4 to Kris Kin in Dee Stakes at Chester on
reappearance: successful in minor event at Haydock (by 11 lengths), listed race at
Deauville and Furstenberg-Rennen at Baden-Baden (clear 2f out, pushed out to beat
Senex ¾ length) in July/August: set too strong a pace when last in Euro-Cup at Frankfurt
final outing (reportedly dismounted afterwards): best around 1¼m (dropped away in
straight when last in King Edward VII Stakes at Royal Ascot at 1½m): acts on good to
firm going (probably on firm), yet to race on softer than good: drifted badly left second
2-y-o start, jinked badly first turn at Chester. *J. L. Dunlop*

BIG BAD BURT   2 ch.c. (Feb 6) Efisio 120 – Mountain Bluebird (USA) 79 (Clever   **61 p**
Trick (USA)) [2003 p6g⁶ 7g p5g Nov 12] 65,000Y: brother to 4-y-o Waxwing and
half-brother to several winners, including useful stayer Anchor Clever (by Slip Anchor):
dam 1m winner: modest form in maidens: left J. Noseda 14,000 gns before final start
(slowly away): should stay 1m: type to do better. *M. J. Wallace*

BIG BERTHA   5 ch.m. Dancing Spree (USA) – Bertrade 75 (Homeboy 114) [2003 77:   **75**
8g⁵ 10g 9.3f⁴ p12g* 14m⁶ p12g⁶ p12g² p13g³ Dec 6] strong mare: fair handicapper: won
at Lingfield in July: stays easy 1½m: acts on polytrack, best turf effort on good going.
John Berry

BIG BRADFORD 2 b.g. (Jan 17) Tamure (IRE) 125 – Heather Honey (Insan (USA) **89**
119) [2003 5.1m² 6.1d² 5m* 7m⁶ 5.1m⁴ 6m³ 6f² 6m⁴ p6g² p7g Nov 12] 3,000Y: sturdy
gelding: has a quick, fluent action: fifth foal: half-brother to 2001 2-y-o 5f/6f seller winner Dusty Bankes (by Greensmith): dam unraced: fairly useful performer: won maiden at
Carlisle in June: in frame, mostly running creditably, in varied events after, including
Two-Year-Old Trophy at Redcar (fourth to Peak To Creek) eighth start: barely stays 7f:
acts on polytrack, firm and good to soft going: blinkered last 4 outings. *E. L. James*

BIG CHEESE (IRE) 3 b.c. Danetime (IRE) 121 – Pat Said No (IRE) 59 (Last Tycoon –
131) [2003 8g 8m 11.6m Jul 14] smallish colt: second foal: half-brother to 7f seller
winner Bueno Vida (by Petardia): dam, second at 5f at 2 yrs, half-sister to useful stayer El
Conquistador: well held, including in seller. *D. J. S. Cosgrove*

BIG LUCIANO (USA) 3 b.c. Pleasant Colony (USA) – Fast Tipper (USA) (Exceller **80 +**
(USA) 129) [2003 81p: f8g² p7g⁵ 8.8g² 8g* 7.5g* a8.8g* 10g 11m³ 7d² a8g* 7.5g* Dec
14] fairly useful performer: left M. Johnston after second start: in fine form in amateur
events for new stable, winning seller at Cosma e Damiano, handicaps at Naples and Cor-
ridonia, minor event at Rome, and handicap at Pisa between June and December: seems
best around 7f/1m: acts on all-weather/sand, well held only start on soft. *F. Boccardelli,
Italy*

BIG MOMENT 5 ch.g. Be My Guest (USA) 126 – Petralona (USA) (Alleged (USA) **102**
138) [2003 104: 12m⁴ 18.7m² 16.1g 14g⁴ 18.7m⁴ 18m Oct 18] leggy, quite attractive
gelding: has a short, round action: useful handicapper: very good ½-length second to
Hugs Dancer in Chester Cup on second start: didn't get run of things and creditable efforts
next 3 outings: stays 18.7f: acts on firm and good to soft going: sweated profusely (bit
below form) fourth 4-y-o start: usually waited with: useful hurdler. *Mrs A. J. Perrett*

BIG PEE TEE 3 gr.g. Petong 126 – Duchess of Ferrara (IRE) 52 (Fairy King (USA)) –
[2003 45: f8g 5m Mar 26] good-topped gelding: poor maiden: well held in 2003: tried
visored (looked none too keen)/blinkered. *K. A. Ryan*

BIG SMOKE (IRE) 3 gr.g. Perugino (USA) 84 – Lightning Bug (Prince Bee 128) **84**
[2003 81: 9g 10m 10g³ 8.1f² 8g 8m³ 8.1m 10g Oct 6] rather leggy gelding: fairly useful
performer: ran poorly last 2 starts: stays 1¼m: acts on firm and good to soft going:
occasionally blinkered: carries head high/finds little: sold 18,000 gns, joined J. Howard
Johnson. *B. J. Meehan*

BIG TOM (IRE) 2 ch.c. (Mar 6) Cadeaux Genereux 131 – Zilayah (USA) 79 (Zilzal **67**
(USA) 137) [2003 5m⁴ 5.9d² 6.1m⁵ 5m 5g⁴ Sep 28] €25,000Y, 25,000 2-y-o: sturdy colt:
fifth foal: half-brother to fairly useful French 1m/9f winner Billowing Sail (by Bering):
dam, 2-y-o 7f winner, half-sister to smart French stayer Molesnes and to dam of very
smart French sprinter Cherokee Rose: fair maiden: second at Carlisle: below form
last 2 starts: should stay 7f: acts on good to firm and good to soft ground: usually races
prominently. *D. Carroll*

BIJAN (IRE) 5 b.m. Mukaddamah (USA) 125 – Alkariyh (USA) 79 (Alydar (USA)) **44**
[2003 60d: f6s f7g f7s f7g³ f6s⁶ 6m 5m⁴ 6.1m f6g⁵ Nov 24] leggy mare: poor handicapper
nowadays: effective at 5f to easy 7f: acts on fibresand, good to firm and good to soft
going: visored once. *R. Hollinshead*

BIJOU DANCER 3 ch.g. Bijou d'Inde 127 – Dancing Diana 82 (Raga Navarro (ITY) **55**
119) [2003 –: 6g 6.1m 5.1m⁵ 7g⁶ 7.1g Jun 13] medium-sized gelding: modest maiden:
should prove best at 6f: acts on good to firm going. *R. Hannon*

BIJOUX (USA) 3 ch.f. King of Kings (IRE) 125 – Golden Wreath (USA) (Majestic **72**
Light (USA)) [2003 84: 9.9m⁴ 12.1g³ 9.9f⁴ 8.1m⁴ 10m⁶ 8s⁵ 10.1d² Oct 4] leggy, quite
good-topped filly: fair maiden: stays 1½m: acts on firm and good to soft ground: has
wandered: sold 10,000 gns. *R. Hannon*

BILL BENNETT (FR) 2 b.g. (Feb 20) Bishop of Cashel 122 – Concert (Polar Falcon **70**
(USA) 126) [2003 7f⁶ 7m 8f³ 10d³ f9.4g² p10g f9.4g* Dec 22] first foal: dam unraced **a74**
close relation to useful performer up to 1¼m Rudimental: fair performer: won maiden at
Wolverhampton by 4 lengths: stays 1¼m: acts on fibresand, firm and good to soft going:
blinkered/tongue tied second start: pulled hard second/sixth outings. *J. Jay*

BILLIARD 2 ch.f. (Feb 10) Kirkwall 118 – Ivorine (USA) (Blushing Groom (FR) 131) **73**
[2003 7.1m 8m* 8s Nov 3] deep-girthed filly: seventh foal: half-sister to useful 6f (at 2
yrs) to 8.5f (US Grade 3 event) winner Marine (by Marju) and 9.4f to 11f winner Generate
(by Generous): dam, French 11f winner, out of Poule d'Essai des Pouliches and Arc
winner Ivanjica: easily best effort (fair form) when winning maiden at Brighton in
October: should stay 1¼m: sold 18,000 gns, sent to USA. *R. Charlton*

BILL MIDDLETON (USA)   3 b. or br.g. K O Punch (USA) – Coin (USA) (Lemhi **48**
Gold (USA) 123) [2003 70: f11g⁶ p10g⁶ p8g f7g 7m p12g Oct 3] poor maiden: visored
last 4 starts. *D. Shaw*

BILLY ALLEN (IRE)   2 b.c. (Mar 31) Night Shift (USA) – Daintree (IRE) 66 (Tirol **88**
127) [2003 5.1g⁵ 5m⁴ 7.1m² 7m* 7f² 7g⁴ 8.2m² 8.1g⁴ 7.1m⁴ 7m⁴ 6m⁶ Oct 25] 21,000Y:
leggy, useful-looking colt: first foal: dam, 1m winner, half-sister to 6-y-o The Tatling:
fairly useful performer: won maiden at Brighton in July: in frame, mostly running creditably, in minor events/nurseries after: barely stays 1m: acts on firm going: sometimes
edgy: sold 30,000 gns. *R. Hannon*

BILLY BATHWICK (IRE)   6 ch.g. Fayruz 116 – Cut It Fine (USA) (Big Spruce **68**
(USA)) [2003 60: f12s f9.4g 11.5g⁴ 12g² 10.9m³ 9.9m* 12f* 12g 11.6m⁴ 11.6g⁴ 11.6g⁶ **a–**
11m⁵ 12m⁵ 11.7f³ Oct 12] smallish, close-coupled gelding: fair handicapper on turf: left
Dr J. Naylor after second start: won at Beverley and Musselburgh in June: stays easy
1½m: acts on firm and soft going, and fibresand: tried blinkered earlier in career, wore
cheekpieces (ran creditably) penultimate start. *I. A. Wood*

BILLY WHIP TOP (IRE)   2 ch.g. (Jan 31) Titus Livius (FR) 115 – Poker Dice (Primo **61 §**
Dominie 121) [2003 5m³ 5f f5g³ 5s⁴ 5.1m³ 5.1m⁶ 5.1m 5g 5f 6m Oct 6] 10,000Y: **a75 §**
smallish, sturdy gelding: first foal: dam unraced daughter of Flying Childers Stakes
winner Poker Chip: fair maiden on all-weather, modest on turf: likely to prove best at 5f/
6f: acts on fibresand, good to firm and soft ground: blinkered last 6 starts: sometimes
wanders: ungenuine: sold 1,500 gns and gelded. *T. D. Easterby*

BILLY WHISTLER   2 ch.c. (May 10) Dancing Spree (USA) – Polar Refrain 59 (Polar **–**
Falcon (USA) 126) [2003 5g Oct 28] first foal: dam 1m winner: 66/1, tailed off in maiden
at Redcar. *J. Balding*

BINANTI   3 b.g. Bin Ajwaad (IRE) 119 – Princess Rosananti (IRE) (Shareef Dancer **95**
(USA) 135) [2003 100: 7g 7g 8m 8g⁴ 7.1f² 7g 7.1m* 8m⁴ 7m Sep 19] smallish, useful-
looking gelding: useful performer: ridden more patiently than usual when winning
handicap at Sandown in August by ¾ length from Contractor: stays 1m: acts on fibresand,
raced only on good going or firmer on turf. *P. R. Chamings*

BINARY FILE (USA)   5 b.h. Nureyev (USA) 131 – Binary 109 (Rainbow Quest **113**
(USA) 134) [2003 115: 8.2m² 10f⁶ 10m⁴ 8g⁴ 8m 8d⁵ Aug 29] deep-girthed horse: has a
round action: smart performer: creditable efforts in 2003 only when 6 lengths second to
Dubai Destination in minor event at Nottingham and fourth of 7 to Mubtaker in listed
event at Newbury first/third starts: effective at 1m/1¼m: raced mostly on good ground or
firmer: has been tongue tied/worn crossed noseband (formerly free-going sort): sold
18,000 gns in December. *J. H. M. Gosden*

BINNION BAY (IRE)   2 b.g. (Apr 29) Fasliyev (USA) 120 – Literary 79 (Woodman **84**
(USA) 126) [2003 5g³ 5g* 6g p7g Nov 12] 15,000Y: tall, useful-looking gelding: third
foal: half-brother to Italian 6f (at 2 yrs) and 1m winner Bod Entrewood (by Entrepreneur):
dam, 1m winner, out of half-sister to Middle Park winner Lycius: fairly useful form: won
maiden at Goodwood in May: off 5 months, ran poorly after: should stay 7f. *R. Hannon*

BINT ALHAARTH (IRE)   3 b.f. Alhaarth (IRE) 126 – Idle Fancy 79 (Mujtahid **78**
(USA) 118) [2003 74: 8m⁶ 8.1m 8.1d* 10d⁶ Oct 13] leggy filly: fair performer: won
maiden at Haydock (under pressure by halfway) in September, good sixth in handicap
next time: stays 1¼m: acts on firm and good to soft going: sold 3,000 gns. *B. W. Hills*

BINT MAKBUL   4 b.f. Makbul 104 – Victoria Sioux 54 (Ron's Victory (USA) 129) **65**
[2003 a9f⁴ a8f⁶ a7f 6m³ 7.1g² 6f³ f7g8* p7g⁴ Dec 6] first foal: dam sprint maiden: fair
handicapper: left J. Sadler in UAE after third start: won at Wolverhampton in November:
effective at 6f to 9f: acts on dirt, all-weather and good to firm ground: tried blinkered.
R. Hannon

BINT ROYAL (IRE)   5 ch.m. Royal Abjar (USA) 121 – Living Legend (USA) **69**
(Septieme Ciel (USA) 123) [2003 67, a78: p7g 7m f7g³ 7m⁴ 6g² f6g² f7g² 6m⁶ f7g 7m⁴ **a76**
6d⁶ 7g* 7.6m⁶ 7d 8.3d⁶ 7m² 7f 6m f7s* f6s Oct 21] close-coupled, workmanlike mare:
fair handicapper: won at Yarmouth in July and Southwell in September: effective at 6f to
1m: acts on firm going, good to soft and all-weather: tried visored/blinkered, usually
wears cheekpieces nowadays. *Miss V. Haigh*

BI POLAR   3 b.g. Polar Falcon (USA) 126 – Doctor Bid (USA) (Spectacular Bid **89**
(USA)) [2003 80: p6g⁵ 7m* 7d 8m 6.5m 7m⁶ f7g 7g² 7d Nov 8] useful-looking gelding:
fairly useful performer: reportedly split pastern final 2-y-o start: won maiden at Kempton
in April, edging right: very good ½-length second to Penelewey in handicap at New-

market penultimate start: at least as good at 7f as 1m: acts on soft and good to firm ground. *D. R. C. Elsworth*

BIRCHWOOD SUN 13 b.g. Bluebird (USA) 125 – Shapely Test (USA) (Elocutionist (USA)) [2003 48: 6d 7m May 1] compact gelding: poor mover: poor performer: effective at 6f (given test) to 1m: acts on any going: blinkered/visored: comes from behind. *M. Dods* **45**

BIRIKINA 2 b.f. (Mar 22) Atraf 116 – Fizzy Fiona (Efisio 120) [2003 5d* 5d³ 6g⁶ 5f² 6f⁶ 5g* 6g 5f⁶ 5m 5m 6d 5m 6m f6g Nov 10] close-coupled filly: third foal: half-sister to 3-y-o Frascati: dam unraced: fair performer: won maiden in May and minor event in July, both at Hamilton: ran poorly last 5 starts: should stay 6f: acts on firm and good to soft ground: tried in cheekpieces. *A. Berry* **75 d**

BIRTHDAY SUIT (IRE) 2 ch.f. (Feb 26) Daylami (IRE) 138 – Wanton 106 (Kris 135) [2003 5m* 5m* 6m³ Jul 8] strong filly: half-sister to several winners, including Irish 1000 Guineas winner Classic Park (by Robellino) and fairly useful performer around 7f Cashmere (by Barathea): dam, sprinter (best at 2 yrs), half-sister to smart sprinter Easy Option: won maiden at York in May and minor event at Beverley in June: fairly useful form when 6 lengths third of 8 to Attraction in Cherry Hinton Stakes at Newmarket, edging right: suffered injury on gallops after: should stay 7f. *T. D. Easterby* **94**

BIRTH OF THE BLUES 7 ch.g. Efisio 120 – Great Steps 88 (Vaigly Great 127) [2003 52: p10g 10.2m⁴ 11.9m 11.9m⁶ 12m* 11.9m⁴ 12m 11.6m² 12.1d⁵ 11.6m⁶ 11.9f Aug 7] lengthy, angular gelding: poor handicapper: won amateur event at Salisbury in June: stays 1½m: acts on any turf going: tried visored/blinkered at 4 yrs. *A. Charlton* **48**

BISCAR TWO (IRE) 2 b.g. (Apr 21) Daggers Drawn (USA) 114 – Thoughtful Kate 64 (Rock Hopper 124) [2003 8g 8m f8.5g Nov 17] €9,000Y: leggy gelding: third foal: dam, maiden who stayed 1½m, half-sister to 4-y-o Captain Rio: well held in maidens: slowly away first 2 starts. *R. M. Whitaker* **–**

BISH BASH BOSH (IRE) 2 b.f. (Feb 27) Bien Bien (USA) 125 – Eurolink Virago (Charmer 123) [2003 f5g 5g f5g⁶ 7m 5.1f⁴ 6m Oct 20] €7,000Y, €32,000 2-y-o: close-coupled filly: fifth foal: half-sister to 3 winners, including fairly useful 9f winner Eurolink Rooster (by Turtle Island): dam unraced half-sister to smart 7f/1m performer Eurolink Thunder: poor maiden: sent to France. *M. F. Harris* **36**

BISHOPRIC 3 b.g. Bishop of Cashel 122 – Nisha (Nishapour (FR) 125) [2003 8g⁴ 8.1d* May 26] lengthy gelding: sixth foal: half-brother to 1m winner Snow And Ice (by Chilibang): dam, lightly-raced maiden, out of half-sister to high-class sprinter New Model: fairly useful form: won maiden at Chepstow in May by 9 lengths from Khanjar, held up: shade mulish at stall on debut: seemed likely to improve. *H. Candy* **81 +**

BISHOPS BOUNCE 2 b.c. (Mar 10) Bishop of Cashel 122 – Heights of Love 51 (Persian Heights 129) [2003 f6g⁶ 5.9d⁶ 7m 6m 6m 6d² f6s 6m 6g Oct 28] 800F: small, plain colt: fourth foal: dam, headstrong maiden, best effort at 5f at 2 yrs: fair maiden: second at Catterick: showed little after: stays 6f: acts on good to soft going: sometimes early to post: often races prominently: sold 600 gns. *G. M. Moore* **73 d**

BISHOPS COURT 9 ch.g. Clantime 101 – Indigo 86 (Primo Dominie 121) [2003 116: 6g⁴ 5m⁶ 5m⁴ 5.1m* 5g⁵ 5d³ Sep 11] big, good-quartered gelding: usually looks really well: smart performer: reportedly sustained hairline fracture of pelvis final 7-y-o start: as good as ever when winning listed event at Chester (for second successive year) in July, beating Dragon Flyer a length: ran at least respectably all other starts in 2003, third to Dubaian Gift in similar race at Doncaster final one: speedy, and best at 5f: acts on any going: tongue tied in 2000: usually bandaged nowadays: has edged left/idled: held up. *Mrs J. R. Ramsden* **112**

BISHOPS FINGER 3 b.g. Bishop of Cashel 122 – Bit of A Tart (Distant Relative 128) [2003 –, a61: p10g p10g⁴ p8g³ p8g⁵ p8g p8g³ 11.6g 10.3g p10g* p12g 10m⁶ p12g Oct 27] fair performer on all-weather, modest on turf: best effort when winning minor event at Lingfield in July: no form after: stays 1¼m: acts on all-weather, unraced on extremes of going on turf: blinkered/visored: sometimes slowly away: has looked none too keen: not one to trust implicitly. *Jamie Poulton* **52 a68**

BISHOP'S LAKE 3 b.f. Lake Coniston (IRE) 131 – Clincher Club 77 (Polish Patriot (USA) 128) [2003 87d: 5m 6.1f 6m Aug 7] angular filly: fairly useful performer at best at 2 yrs: little form in 2003: sold 10,000 gns in December. *M. G. Quinlan* **–**

BISHOPSTONE MAN 6 b.g. Piccolo 121 – Auntie Gladys 49 (Great Nephew 126) [2003 75, a–: 8m⁵ 7m 7.1g⁵ 7.5m* 7g³ 8.5m⁴ 8.2m² 7.9m² 8.3m⁴ 8.2m Oct 22] well-made gelding: fairly useful handicapper on turf: won at Beverley in June: mostly creditable **83 a–**

efforts after: best at 7f/1m: acts on firm and soft going, and fibresand: effective visored or not: sometimes pulls hard and has worn crossed noseband: has hung: apprentice ridden: consistent. *H. Candy*

BISHOP TO ACTRESS 2 ch.f. (Mar 13) Paris House 123 – Chess Mistress (USA) **54** 59 (Run The Gantlet (USA)) [2003 7.1m⁴ f6g⁵ 5g³ 6m⁶ 7.1m⁶ f6s Oct 21] 1,500Y: leggy filly: fifth foal: half-sister to 1½m winners Buzz The Agent (by Prince Sabo) and Comanche Queen (by Totem): dam 1½m winner in France: modest maiden: third at Ripon: below form after: stays 6f: acts on fibresand. *M. J. Polglase*

BITHNAH 4 b.f. Halling (USA) 133 – Najmat Alshemaal (IRE) 98 (Dancing Brave **–** (USA) 140) [2003 48: 10d May 23] poor form: should be suited by 1¼m+. *C. R. Dore*

BITTER SWEET 7 gr.m. Deploy 131 – Julia Flyte 91 (Drone (USA)) [2003 59: 9.7m **59** 9m 8m⁶ 9.7f* 9g³ 9.9d* 9.7m⁶ 10m 10m 10m Aug 20] lengthy, angular mare: modest handicapper: won at Folkestone (for second successive year) in June and Beverley in July: probably best around 1¼m nowadays: acts on firm and soft going: sometimes visored in 2000: held up: sold 4,200 gns. *J. L. Spearing*

BLACK FALCON (IRE) 3 ch.c. In The Wings 128 – Muwasim (USA) (Meadow- **97 §** lake (USA)) [2003 10.3g³ 10.1m* 12g⁴ 10.4f* 10m 9.9g 12.3m⁵ 12m Aug 27] rather leggy, quite attractive colt: first foal: dam unraced half-sister to US minor stakes winner and Grade 3 6f runner-up Robin de Nest: useful performer at best: won maiden at Newcastle in April and handicap at York in June: below form after, including in visor final start: should stay 1½m: acts on firm going: often slowly away: ungenuine, and needs treating with caution: sold 16,000 gns. *M. R. Channon*

BLACKHEATH (IRE) 7 ch.g. Common Grounds 118 – Queen Caroline (USA) 67 **91** (Chief's Crown (USA)) [2003 72: 6.1g 5m* 6m² 5m⁶ 5.7g² 6m⁵ 6m² 5m⁴ 6f⁶ 5m⁶ 5m* 6g² 6g 6m⁵ 6m 5d* 6m 6m² 5d³ Sep 27] barrel-shaped gelding: type to carry condition: fluent mover: fairly useful performer: won minor event at Folkestone in April and handicaps at Carlisle (dead-heated) in July and Haydock in September: good placed efforts in handicaps last 2 starts: best at 5f/easy 6f: acts on firm and good to soft going: tried blinkered/tongue tied: sometimes reluctant stall/slowly away: usually waited with: tough. *D. Nicholls*

BLACK LEGEND (IRE) 4 b.g. Marju (IRE) 127 – Lamping (Warning 136) [2003 **–** 62: 11.7m May 6] ex-Irish gelding: second foal: dam unraced half-sister to smart US Grade 2 8.5f winner Didina from family of Xaar: unraced at 2 yrs: modest maiden at 3 yrs (trained by C. O'Brien), best effort when blinkered final start: well held only outing in 2003: should stay 1½m: raced mainly on good going or softer (acts on heavy). *R. Lee*

BLACKMAIL (USA) 5 b.g. Twining (USA) 120 – Black Penny (USA) (Private **68** Account (USA)) [2003 90: p8g p10g⁶ p10g* p10g⁴ p10g⁵ p10g² 10g 10.1m⁵ 11.9f 12m **a87** 8m Sep 12] sturdy gelding: fairly useful handicapper on all-weather, fair on turf: won at Lingfield in February: stays 1¼m: acts on polytrack and good to firm ground: tried tongue tied/visored, blinkered nowadays. *Miss B. Sanders*

BLACKMOLL (IRE) 2 b.f. (May 16) Desert Story (IRE) 115 – Sanctuary Cove **42** (Habitat 134) [2003 5g⁴ 5.1f 5m⁵ 6.1d⁴ 7m 6m⁵ 7m Oct 17] €4,000Y: small filly: half-sister to 3 winners, including 7-y-o Bundy and 1¼m seller winner Hiding Place (by Saddlers' Hall): dam Irish maiden: poor maiden: stays 6f: acts on good to soft going: visored penultimate start. *P. D. Evans*

BLACK OVAL 2 b.f. (Apr 30) Royal Applause 124 – Corniche Quest (IRE) 74 (Salt **78 d** Dome (USA)) [2003 5f* 5m³ 6g 6.5m 7m 6g⁶ 6g 6d⁶ Nov 4] 48,000Y: quite good-topped filly: third foal: half-sister to 2001 2-y-o 5f seller winner Blakeshall (by Piccolo) and 3-y-o Blakeshall Quest: dam 5f to 1m winner: fair performer: won maiden at Salisbury in June: disappointed after next start, mostly in nurseries: likely to prove best at 5f/6f: acts on firm ground. *M. R. Channon*

BLACK PAGODA (IRE) 4 b.g. Spectrum (IRE) 126 – Melodrama 102 (Busted **–** 134) [2003 –: 11.1d 7.2g 9f⁶ 10.9m 9f 8m 7.2g Jul 22] ex-Irish gelding: fair form in maidens at 2 yrs for A. O'Brien: little form since: tried blinkered/in cheekpieces. *P. Monteith*

BLACKPOOL BEAU 3 b.g. Danetime (IRE) 121 – Blackpool Belle 70 (The Brian- **56** stan 128) [2003 76: 5m⁴ 6f⁵ May 30] close-coupled, quite good-topped colt: just modest maiden at 3 yrs: may prove best at 5f: acts on good to soft ground. *K. A. Ryan*

BLACK RAINBOW (IRE) 5 br.m. Definite Article 121 – Inonder 31 (Belfort (FR) **–** 89) [2003 p13g Feb 5] 4,000Y: fourth foal: half-sister to 3 winners by Common Grounds, including 1997 2-y-o 5f to 7.5f winner Chips and 6f (at 2 yrs)/7f winner Aretino, both fairly useful: dam poor maiden: modest form in bumpers: well held over hurdles, and on Flat debut in Lingfield maiden: sold 4,800 gns. *T. J. Etherington*

BLACK SAM BELLAMY (IRE)   4 b.c. Sadler's Wells (USA) 132 – Urban Sea **121**
(USA) 126 (Miswaki (USA) 124) [2003 117: 10g* 10.5d 10.5d* 12m³ 20m 10g⁵
12g² 12s⁶ 12m⁴ Oct 19]
　　　　　The decision to keep Black Sam Bellamy in training as a four-year-old, with a view to furthering his stallion credentials, was vindicated when he ran away with the Tattersalls Gold Cup at the Curragh in May. Black Sam Bellamy had the pedigree—he is a brother to King George and dual Derby winner Galileo—and was already a Group 1 winner, having won the Gran Premio del Jockey Club at Milan on his final outing in 2002, but his form as a three-year-old had been only smart at best. Shortly after the Tattersalls Gold Cup Black Sam Bellamy was sold for an undisclosed sum to the German stud Gestut Fahrhof, where he will stand in 2004 at a fee of €7,500, live foal.
　　　　　Black Sam Bellamy had won three of his eleven starts prior to the Tattersalls Gold Cup. Unsuccessful on his three outings as a two-year-old, when he finished third in the Criterium de Saint-Cloud, Black Sam Bellamy won twice at three, a win in a Curragh maiden on his reappearance his only victory before Milan. He made a winning return in the latest season, making all in an eight-runner listed event at Leopardstown in March, which was followed by a poor effort when second favourite for the Prix Ganay at Longchamp the following month, finishing last of nine to Fair Mix. Black Sam Bellamy bounced back in the Tattersalls Gold Cup four weeks later, starting fourth in the betting in an eight-runner race. Overlooking his Prix Ganay running, Black Sam Bellamy still needed to improve on his best form to win at the Curragh, and, in a weakish renewal, he did so in striking fashion. Once sent into the lead early in the straight he quickly opened up a gap and galloped on strongly to win by eight lengths from the Godolphin-owned Highdown, with Narrative a further length and a half back in third. Black Sam Bellamy repeated the form when a close third of nine to Warrsan in the Coronation Cup at Epsom, leading from three furlongs out and rallying splendidly after being headed inside the last furlong. The best of five subsequent efforts was a half-length second of eight to Mamool in the Grosser Bugatti Preis (formerly known as the Grosser Preis von Baden) at Baden-Baden in September, though he was also a respectable sixth behind Dalakhani in the Arc.

Black Sam Bellamy (IRE) (b.c. 1999)	Sadler's Wells (USA) (b 1981)	Northern Dancer (b 1961)	Nearctic Natalma
		Fairy Bridge (b 1975)	Bold Reason Special
	Urban Sea (USA) (ch 1989)	Miswaki (ch 1978)	Mr Prospector Hopespringseternal
		Allegretta (ch 1978)	Lombard Anatevka

　　　　　The big, strong, close-coupled Black Sam Bellamy, who has a round, choppy action, should have plenty of appeal to German breeders. Not only is he from one of the most successful families of recent years, but his family is also German. His grandam Allegretta is a half-sister to the German Group 2 winners

Tattersalls Gold Cup, the Curragh—Black Sam Bellamy is a runaway winner

in the 'eighties Anno and Anatas, out of the German-bred broodmare Anatevka. Allegretta's useful exploits on the racecourse were outshone by her outstanding career as a broodmare. A two-year-old winner over a mile and over nine furlongs, and second in the Lingfield Oaks Trial, Allegretta later foaled both Black Sam Bellamy's Arc-winning dam Urban Sea and the Two Thousand Guineas winner King's Best. She is also the grandam of Prix du Jockey Club winner Anabaa Blue and the Deutschland-Preis winner Anzillero. Urban Sea had three foals before Black Sam Bellamy. As well as the top-class Galileo, Urban Sea has also been represented by the smart pair Urban Ocean and Melikah, the latter third in the Oaks and second in the Irish Oaks in 2000. Black Sam Bellamy has an unraced brother and sister, the year-younger Atticus and the 2003 two-year-old All Too Beautiful, both in training at Ballydoyle. All Too Beautiful had set a new European record for a filly foal when sold for 1,100,000 guineas at Tattersalls in December 2001. Urban Sea also has a yearling by Giant's Causeway and visited Sadler's Wells again in 2002. Black Sam Bellamy, who wore a crossed noseband and raced prominently, was best at a mile and a quarter and a mile and a half (he failed to stay on two occasions, including in the Gold Cup, when he was raced over further). He never encountered firm going, but acted on any other. *A. P. O'Brien, Ireland*

BLACK STRIPE GEM 2 ch.f. (Apr 18) Precious Metal 106 – Just Like You (Sand- – hurst Prince 128) [2003 5m Apr 23] leggy filly: second foal: dam well beaten: unseated rider at start and again leaving stall in seller at Catterick. *M. Todhunter*

BLACK SWAN (IRE) 3 b.g. Nashwan (USA) 135 – Sea Spray (IRE) 101 (Royal – Academy (USA) 130) [2003 –p: 12.1g⁵ 10g Oct 6] lengthy gelding: well held in 3 maidens. *G. A. Ham*

BLACKTHORN 4 ch.g. Deploy 131 – Balliasta (USA) (Lyphard (USA) 132) [2003 **74** 85d: 10.1d⁶ 9.9f³ 11m 12.3m 10g³ 12.1g 12.1m* 12.1g⁵ 12m² 12.1m 13.1m 12m² Oct 18] strong, compact gelding: has a fluent, round action: fair performer: won claimer at Beverley in June: stays 1½m, at least when conditions aren't testing: acts on firm and soft going: tried in cheekpieces: sometimes on toes/races freely. *R. A. Fahey*

BLACKWATER ANGEL (USA) 3 b.f. Kingmambo (USA) 125 – Zephyr (CAN) **61** (His Majesty (USA)) [2003 79: 9.9m 10g⁵ Jul 8] tall, leggy, angular filly: fair performer at 2 yrs, only modest in 2003: best form at 1m: acts on firm going: raced freely final start: sent to USA. *J. L. Dunlop*

BLACKWATER FEVER (USA) 3 b.c. Irish River (FR) 131 – Crafty Buzz (USA) **66** (Crafty Prospector (USA)) [2003 69p: 10.1m³ 10.5d 10m⁶ 12d 10g* Jul 7] good-topped colt: has scope: fair performer: failed to impress with attitude when winning seller at Ripon (blinkered) in July: stays 1¼m: acts on good to firm ground, below form both starts on good to soft: sold 15,000 gns later in July. *M. Johnston*

BLADE'S DANCER 3 b.g. Komaite (USA) – Banningham Blade 94 (Sure Blade – (USA) 130) [2003 63: f6s Sep 2] plain gelding: modest maiden at 2 yrs: blinkered, well held only outing in 2003: got loose before start/withdrawn intended reappearance. *D. Shaw*

BLADE'S DAUGHTER 2 gr.f. (Mar 10) Paris House 123 – Banningham Blade 94 – (Sure Blade (USA) 130) [2003 5g 6m 5m Sep 17] leggy, quite good-topped filly: second foal: dam best at 2 yrs when 5f winner: well held in maidens. *K. A. Ryan*

BLADE'S EDGE 2 b.c. (Apr 14) Daggers Drawn (USA) 114 – Hayhurst (Sandhurst **73** Prince 128) [2003 6f³ 7.2d 6f⁴ Oct 27] leggy, close-coupled colt: half-brother to Irish 9f winner River Hopper (by River Falls) and 7f/1m winner in Italy by Classic Secret: dam, staying maiden on Flat, won over hurdles in Ireland: easily best effort in maidens (fair form) when third to Nero's Return at York: not knocked about final start: should stay at least 7f. *A. Bailey*

BLAEBERRY 2 b.f. (Jan 26) Kirkwall 118 – Top Berry 87 (High Top 131) [2003 7g **61** 8d Nov 7] lengthy, quite good-topped filly: half-sister to several winners, including useful 7f (at 2 yrs) and 1m winner Derryquin (by Lion Cavern) and 3-y-o Parknasilla: dam 1m winner: better effort in maidens (modest form) when eighth at Doncaster latter start: will stay at least 1¼m. *P. L. Gilligan*

BLAINA 3 ch.f. Compton Place 125 – Miss Silca Key 102 (Welsh Saint 126) [2003 **76 §** 8f 7f³ 8s² 7m² 8.1d⁶ f7g Nov 21] 20,000Y: big, lengthy filly: half-sister to several at least useful winners, including smart 5f (including at 2 yrs)/6f winner Central City (by

132

Midyan) and winner up to 1m Consigliere (by Caerleon): dam won Jersey Stakes: fair maiden: stays 1m: best effort on soft ground: temperamental. *D. R. C. Elsworth*

BLAISE CASTLE (USA)   3 b.f. Irish River (FR) 131 – Castellina (USA) (Danzig   **95**
Connection (USA)) [2003 94p: 8f 10m 6d³ 7s 8s⁴ 7s² Nov 14] strong, quite attractive
filly: useful form: creditable efforts last 3 starts, stiff task in Prix de la Foret at Longchamp (ninth of 10), then fourth to Peinture Rose in listed race at Saint-Cloud and 4
lengths second to Great News in similar event at Maisons-Laffitte, making running each
time: stays 1m: acts on soft going: has been heavily bandaged on fore joints. *G. A. Butler*

BLAISE WOOD (USA)   2 b.g. (Apr 7) Woodman (USA) 126 – Castellina (USA)   **61**
(Danzig Connection (USA)) [2003 7.1g⁶ Jul 4] good-topped gelding: fourth foal: half-
brother to 3-y-o Blaise Castle and 4-y-o Castle River: dam, US 8.5f winner, half-sister to
smart US Grade 1 1¼m winner Chelsey Flower: 14/1 and backward, slowly away when
sixth of 7 in maiden at Sandown. *R. Hannon*

BLAKESET   8 ch.g. Midyan (USA) 124 – Penset (Red Sunset 120) [2003 f7g⁶ f6g²   **67**
f7g* f6g* 6g* 6g f6g* Dec 15] sturdy gelding: fair performer: ran for a variety of trainers   **a79 +**
in USA in 2001 and 2002: won sellers at Wolverhampton in April and Southwell in May,
amateur handicap at Hamilton in June and handicap at Southwell in December: best at 6f/
7f: acts on fibresand/dirt, good to firm and good to soft going: tried tongue tied earlier in
career: effective with/without blinkers/visor: races prominently. *T. D. Barron*

BLAKESEVEN   3 b.g. Forzando 122 – Up And Going (FR) (Never So Bold 135)   **60**
[2003 73: p7g p6g³ 6g 6g 6.1m 5g 6d 8m⁴ p7g Dec 30] modest maiden handicapper:
should be at least as effective at 7f as 1m: acts on good to firm going and polytrack: tends
to race freely. *W. J. Musson*

BLAKESHALL BOY   5 b.g. Piccolo 121 – Giggleswick Girl 67 (Full Extent (USA)   **64 +**
113) [2003 82: 5.1m⁶ 5m 5m 6g 6g p6g⁴ p7g⁴ Nov 13] rather leggy, quite attractive
gelding: fairly useful handicapper in 2002, just modest nowadays: effective at 5f to 7f:
acts on firm ground, soft and polytrack: tried visored (ran respectably): reportedly had
breathing problem once at 3 yrs: hangs left: usually held up. *R. Lee*

BLAKESHALL GIRL   3 ch.f. Piccolo 121 – Giggleswick Girl 67 (Full Extent   **64 d**
(USA) 113) [2003 6m³ 6m 6m 6d 6.1m Jun 16] workmanlike filly: third foal: sister to
5-y-o Blakeshall Boy: dam 5f and (at 2 yrs) 6f winner: easily best effort (modest form) on
debut. *J. L. Spearing*

BLAKESHALL QUEST   3 b.f. Piccolo 121 – Corniche Quest (IRE) 74 (Salt Dome   **63**
(USA)) [2003 38: f7g² f6s* f7s² 6g⁶ f6g* 6.1d p7g f7g f6g f6g f6g Dec 26] fairly useful   **a78**
performer on all-weather, modest on turf: left M. Channon after reappearance: won
maiden at Wolverhampton in February and handicap at Southwell in May: below form
after: stays easy 7f: acts on fibresand, probably on good to soft ground. *R. Brotherton*

BLANCO (IRE)   3 ch.g. First Trump 118 – Balance The Books 75 (Elmaamul (USA)   **62**
125) [2003 f8s⁴ p8g⁵ 10.3g⁶ 10m* 8.2m* 8.3d³ 8m⁶ f8.5g³ 8f⁵ 9.3m³ 8f⁵ 7.1m⁶ Aug 14]
IR 11,500F, IR 18,000Y: lengthy gelding: first foal: dam 2-y-o 5f winner: modest performer: won seller at Southwell in March and handicap at Nottingham in April: effective
at 7f to 9.3f: acts on polytrack and firm going, probably on good to soft. *M. J. Wallace*

BLANDYS (IRE)   3 b.f. Dolphin Street (FR) 125 – Bodfaridistinction (IRE) 77   **43**
(Distinctly North (USA) 115) [2003 51: f7g³ f7g⁴ f5s³ f6g* f6g 5.3m 6s f5g³ f7s Oct 21]   **a53**
workmanlike filly: modest on all-weather, poor on turf: won handicap at Southwell in
March: barely stays 7f: acts on all-weather: usually blinkered. *J. White*

BLATANT   4 ch.c. Machiavellian (USA) 123 – Negligent 118 (Ahonoora 122) [2003   **117**
114: 8.3d³ 8.5m⁵ 8f⁵ 8d 8d 8f⁴ 8m² Oct 12] lengthy colt: smart performer: unraced at 2
yrs: acted as pacemaker in Group 1 events third to sixth starts in 2003, running well when
5¾ lengths fourth of 8 to Falbrav in Queen Elizabeth II Stakes at Ascot: best effort when
½-length second to Le Vie dei Colori in Premio Vittorio di Capua at Milan final start:
stays 1m: acts on firm and good to soft going: tongue tied all starts, visored last 5: joined
I. Mohammed in UAE. *Saeed bin Suroor*

BLAU GRAU (GER)   6 b.g. Neshad (USA) 108 – Belle Orfana (GER) (Orfano (GER))   **50**
[2003 f8s* f8g f9.4g⁵ 9.2m 12m May 8] first foal: dam German 7.8f winner: won maiden
and 3 handicaps in Germany in 2001: only placing in handicaps in 2002 when third at
Cologne: modest form when winning seller at Southwell in January on British debut
(claimed from H. Hiller 6,000 gns): well held subsequently, leaving R. Wilman after third
start: stays 8.5f: acts on heavy going, good to firm and fibresand/sand: usually blinkered.
P. A. Blockley

133

BLAZEAWAY (USA) 3 b. or br.g. Hansel (USA) – Alessia's Song (USA) (Air Forbes **69**
Won (USA)) [2003 75: a8f⁵ a8f⁵ 9.1g 10m³ 11.9m 8.5g Jul 17] rather leggy, lengthy
gelding: fair maiden: well below form in handicaps last 2 starts: stays 1¼m: acts on good
to firm ground (looked ill at ease on firm once at 2 yrs). *M. Johnston*

BLAZE OF COLOUR 2 ch.f. (Feb 18) Rainbow Quest (USA) 134 – Hawait Al Barr **– p**
100 (Green Desert (USA) 127) [2003 8m Oct 24] good-bodied filly: sixth foal: half-sister
to 1m (at 2 yrs)/9f winner Equity Princess (by Warning) and French 6f winner Blue
Dream (by Cadeaux Genereux), both useful: dam, 1½m to 2m winner, half-sister to dam
of Kentucky Derby/Preakness Stakes winner Real Quiet: 50/1, burly and green (swished
tail repeatedly in paddock), never-dangerous twelfth of 22 in maiden at Doncaster: bred
to be suited by at least 1½m: should do better. *Sir Michael Stoute*

BLAZING MOMENT 3 ch.g. Timeless Times (USA) 99 – Kabella (Kabour 80) **–**
[2003 –: 5d 5m f6g 7.5m 8g⁴ 12.1m Jul 29] strong gelding: little form. *R. Bastiman*

BLAZING SADDLES (IRE) 4 b.g. Sadler's Wells (USA) 132 – Dalawara (IRE) **–**
(Top Ville 129) [2003 –: 13.3m p12g Jun 3] rather leggy, workmanlike gelding: has a
round action: disappointing maiden: visored last 2 starts. *P. R. Hedger*

BLAZING THE TRAIL (IRE) 3 ch.g. Indian Ridge 123 – Divine Pursuit 69 (Kris **73**
135) [2003 7m 10d 12g³ 12d Aug 1] IR 20,000Y: third foal: half-brother to winner in
USA by Marju: dam, maiden who stayed 8.5f, sister to smart French sprinter Divine
Danse and half-sister to very smart sprinter/miler Pursuit of Love: fair form: easily best
effort when third in maiden at Kempton: stays 1½m: blinkered (tailed off) final start:
tends to carry head high. *J. W. Hills*

BLAZING THUNDER 3 b.c. Zafonic (USA) 130 – Bright Spells (USA) (Alleged **107 ?**
(USA) 138) [2003 94p: 7.1m* 7m 8g 9m³ 8d³ Oct 13] leggy, good-topped colt: has a
quick, unimpressive action: useful form: won 3-runner minor event at Haydock in June
by 1¾ lengths from Terfel: disappointing in Jersey Stakes at Royal Ascot (appeared to
lose action) and listed event at Goodwood next 2 starts: appeared to run well when third
to Putra Pekan in muddling minor event at Newbury penultimate start, but just respectable effort behind Makhlab in similar race at Ayr final outing: stays easy 9f: acts on good
to firm and good to soft going: sold 32,000 gns. *J. H. M. Gosden*

BLENHEIM TERRACE 10 b.g. Rambo Dancer (CAN) 107 – Boulevard Girl 80 **51**
(Nicholas Bill 125) [2003 51: 16m 16d⁵ 13.8f* 14.1m³ Jun 21] sturdy gelding: modest
handicapper: won at Catterick in May: effective at 1½m to 2m: best recent efforts on good
ground or firmer: reportedly had breathing problem once at 9 yrs. *W. H. Tinning*

BLESSED PLACE 3 ch.g. Compton Place 125 – Cathedra (So Blessed 130) [2003 **69**
47: p5g³ f6g² p6g⁵ p5g³ p5g² p5g* 5.1f² 5.1m² 5.3m³ 5s⁵ 5m 5m 5m⁵ 5g Aug 10] leggy
gelding: fair handicapper: won at Lingfield in March: stays 6f: acts on all-weather, firm
and soft going: wore cheekpieces fourth start: usually races prominently. *Jean-Rene
Auvray*

BLESS 'EM ALL 2 b.f. (Mar 25) Orpen (USA) 116 – Edgeaway 70 (Ajdal (USA) **–**
130) [2003 p8g Nov 26] fifth foal: half-sister to fairly useful 1m winner (including at 2
yrs) Hayes Way (by Lahib) and 4-y-o Fact O' The Matter: dam 7f winner: 50/1, soundly
beaten in maiden at Lingfield: sold £400. *M. Blanshard*

BLESS HER 3 b.f. Piccolo 121 – Bliss (IRE) 75 (Statoblest 120) [2003 55: f6g 5m 7m **42**
5.1m May 30] poor maiden at 3 yrs: stays 6f: acts on firm and soft ground, well beaten
both starts on all-weather: tried blinkered. *Mrs P. N. Dutfield*

BLESSINGINDISGUISE 10 b.g. Kala Shikari 125 – Blowing Bubbles 72 (Native **57**
Admiral (USA)) [2003 67d: 6m² 5.1s 6f³ 5m 5f⁵ 5m⁴ 5m⁴ 5m⁶ 5m⁶ 5m 5m² 5f² 5m²
5g⁴ f6g Nov 25] strong gelding: modest handicapper nowadays: effective at 5f/easy 6f:
possibly unsuited by soft/heavy going, acts on any other turf: blinkered: often gives
trouble at stall: races prominently. *M. W. Easterby*

BLOEMFONTAIN (IRE) 2 b.f. (Jan 26) Cape Cross (IRE) 129 – Carotene (CAN) **71**
(Great Nephew 126) [2003 6m⁴ 6m² 6d* Sep 20] strong filly: closely related to German
winner around 7f Cartwheel (by Green Desert) and half-sister to several winners,
including useful 7f (in UAE)/1m winner Teshami (by Diesis): dam, champion Canadian
filly, won up to 1½m: fair form in maidens: second at Newcastle before landing odds
unimpressively in maiden at Catterick: should stay at least 1m. *M. Johnston*

BLOFELD 2 b.g. (Apr 24) Royal Applause 124 – Bliss (IRE) 75 (Statoblest 120) [2003 **70**
5.2m 5m⁶ 6m 6m f6s³ p7g⁵ f6g* f6g* Dec 19] 54,000Y: good-bodied gelding: second
foal: dam, 2-y-o 5f winner, half-sister to useful 1998 2-y-o 6f/7f winner Smittenby: fair

performer: won 2 nurseries at Southwell in December: likely to prove best at 5f/6f: acts on fibresand, some promise on turf. *W. Jarvis*

BLONDE EN BLONDE (IRE)   3 ch.f. Hamas (IRE) 125§ – Hulm (IRE) 79   **57** (Mujtahid (USA) 118) [2003 54: p5g f6g* f6g* f6g* f7g² f5s f7s⁴ f7g³ f8.5g 7d 6.9m*   **a74** 7.9f⁶ f7s² f7g² f7g f7g³ f7g⁵ f7s³ f6g⁴ Dec 26] good-bodied filly: fair on all-weather, modest on turf: won claimer at Wolverhampton in January, handicaps there and at Southwell in February, and claimer at Carlisle in August: seems best at 6f/7f: acts on fibresand, soft and probably firm going: has been slowly away: sometimes edges left: tail flasher. *N. P. Littmoden*

BLONDE STREAK (USA)   3 ch.f. Dumaani (USA) 115 – Katiba (USA) 99 (Gulch   **87** (USA)) [2003 76: 8.2g* 8m 8d* 8m³ 8m² 8.1d 10m⁴ Oct 22] tall filly: fairly useful performer: won maiden at Nottingham in June and handicap at Thirsk in August: will prove best short of 1¼m: unraced on extremes of going: looked less than keen second start. *T. D. Barron*

BLOOMING LUCKY (IRE)   4 b.f. Lucky Guest 109 – Persian Flower (Persian   **–** Heights 129) [2003 40: f7s f9.4g p8g Feb 19] no form in 2003: tried blinkered. *J. A. Osborne*

BLOSSOM WHISPERS   6 b.m. Ezzoud (IRE) 126 – Springs Welcome 86 (Blakeney   **–** 126) [2003 46: 16.1d Mar 24] good-bodied mare: poor maiden nowadays: well held only Flat run in 2003: stays 2¼m: acts on good to firm going, good to soft and fibresand: tried blinkered. *Mrs M. Reveley*

BLOWING AWAY (IRE)   9 b. or br.m. Last Tycoon 131 – Taken By Force (Persian   **–** Bold 123) [2003 36, a–: 21.6m Apr 14] leggy mare: poor performer: stays 2m: probably acts on any turf going/all-weather: sometimes visored: sometimes slowly away. *Julian Poulton*

BLUE A FUSE (IRE)   3 b.f. Bluebird (USA) 125 – Gleaming Heather (USA) 61 (Irish   **–** River (FR) 131) [2003 –: 7d Mar 24] well beaten in 2 maidens. *M. Brittain*

BLUEBERRY JIM   2 ch.g. (Jun 4) First Trump 118 – Short And Sharp 88 (Sharpen   **–** Up 127) [2003 5.1g 6m⁶ 6g 6m 6d Sep 26] 2,200Y: small gelding: half-brother to several winners, including useful 6f (at 2 yrs) to 7.5f winner Golden Fortune (by Forzando): dam, placed at 6f/7f, ran only at 2 yrs: little form, including in seller. *T. H. Caldwell*

BLUEBERRY RHYME   4 b.g. Alhijaz 122 – Irenic 64 (Mummy's Pet 125) [2003   **73 §** 69§: f5g³ f5g⁴ f5g² f5g³ Dec 22] good-topped gelding: fair maiden: best at 5f/easy 6f: acts on soft ground and fibresand: usually visored: has found little: moody and can't be trusted. *P. J. Makin*

BLUE BIJOU   3 b.g. Bijou d'Inde 127 – Jucea 77 (Bluebird (USA) 125) [2003 6g Jun   **–** 21] second foal: dam 5f and 5.7f winner: 11/2 from 50/1, slowly away and reportedly finished lame in maiden at Lingfield. *T. T. Clement*

BLUEBIRD SPIRIT   3 ch.f. Bluebird (USA) 125 – My Lewicia (IRE) 100 (Taufan   **68** (USA) 119) [2003 60: 8.3g⁵ 10m² 12.1m Jun 4] medium-sized, workmanlike filly: fair maiden, lightly raced: second in handicap at Redcar: stays 1¼m: unraced on extremes of going: sold 3,000 gns. *P. W. Harris*

BLUEBOK   2 ch.c. (Feb 28) Indian Ridge 123 – Blue Sirocco (Bluebird (USA) 125)   **68** [2003 6g⁵ Jun 28] 150,000Y: compact colt: first foal: dam, ran once at 3 yrs, half-sister to 1¼m to 15f winner Khamaseen and 1m to 13f winner Azzilfi, both smart: joint favourite, fifth of 8 in maiden at Newcastle, slowly away and green: should stay at least 1m. *D. R. Loder*

BLUE BOUNTY (IRE)   3 b.f. Blues Traveller (IRE) 119 – Cwm Deri (IRE) (Alzao   **–** (USA) 117) [2003 55: 6g 8.3d May 12] modest maiden at 2 yrs: well held in handicaps in 2003: dead. *J. Akehurst*

BLUE CIRCLE   3 b.c. Whittingham (IRE) 104 – Reshift 94 (Night Shift (USA)) [2003   **–** –: f6g p5g f6g⁵ f6g f6s² 6d⁶ 5d 5m 7m f8.5s⁶ 5g f6g f7g f6g f5g f6g Dec 26] smallish, heavy-topped colt: little form: usually blinkered, tried in cheekpieces. *M. Mullineaux*

BLUE DAZE   2 b.f. (Mar 19) Danzero (AUS) – Sparkling (Kris 135) [2003 5m 6.1m*   **75** Jun 14] 16,000F, 16,500Y: second foal: half-sister to 1m winner in Spain by Groom Dancer: dam unraced close relative to smart performer up to 1¼m Port Lucaya out of half-sister to Oaks winner Diminuendo: clearly better effort in maidens (fair form) when winning 11-runner race at Nottingham, leading halfway and flicking tail: should stay 1m. *R. Hannon*

BLUE EMPEROR (IRE)   2 b.c. (Feb 15) Groom Dancer (USA) 128 – Bague Bleue   **64**
(IRE) (Last Tycoon 131) [2003 5g³ f5g⁴ 5m⁶ Apr 22] 3,500F, 7,800Y, resold €10,000Y:
leggy, quite good-topped colt: brother to winning sprinter abroad, closely related to 1996
French 2-y-o 6f winner Luminosity (by Sillery) and half-brother to 2 winners in France/
Germany by Selkirk: dam, French 2-y-o 6f winner, sister to high-class 7f to 1¼m winner
Bigstone: easily best effort in maidens (modest form) when third at Doncaster: should
stay 6f: tongue tied final start. *P. A. Blockley*

BLUE EMPIRE (IRE)   2 b.g. (Mar 21) Second Empire (IRE) 124 – Paleria (USA)   **76**
77 (Zilzal (USA) 137) [2003 6m f8s* 8s f8s² f7g* Dec 16] 15,000Y: compact gelding:
first foal: dam 2-y-o 6f winner (stayed 1m): fair performer: won claimer at Southwell in
September and nursery at same course in December: stays 1m: acts on fibresand, some
promise on turf: sometimes slowly away. *P. C. Haslam*

BLUEFIELD (IRE)   2 b.c. (Feb 17) Second Empire (IRE) 124 – Imco Reverie (IRE)   **77 p**
(Grand Lodge (USA) 125) [2003 7m 8g³ Oct 25] 9,000Y: tall, leggy colt: first foal: dam
Italian 2-y-o 9f winner: better effort in maidens (fair form) when 9½ lengths third to
Salford City at Newbury, racing prominently: should stay at least 1¼m: open to further
improvement. *R. F. Johnson Houghton*

BLUE GALLERY (IRE)   2 b.f. (May 7) Bluebird (USA) 125 – Lovely Deise (IRE)   **57**
46 (Tate Gallery (USA) 117) [2003 f5g⁴ f6g* f6g³ 7m 6g Aug 26] IR 4,000F, €10,000Y:
quite good-topped filly: sixth foal: half-sister to fairly useful Irish 1¾m/2m winner
Dyrick Daybreak (by Ali-Royal): dam lightly-raced maiden: modest performer: won
seller at Wolverhampton in May: should stay at least 1m: acts on fibresand: blinkered
final start. *P. A. Blockley*

BLUEGRASS BEAU   3 ch.g. Bluegrass Prince (IRE) 110 – Blushing Belle 74 (Local   **66**
Suitor (USA) 128) [2003 79: 10m 8.3g 11.6d⁶ 8m 8.3m³ 10.9m⁶ p12g 9.7m⁵ 12g 10.9m
f14.8g Oct 20] rather leggy, workmanlike gelding: fair performer: left I. Wood after
fourth start: ran creditably after only on next outing: should stay at least 1¼m: acts on
firm and good to soft going: tried in cheekpieces: edged markedly left third start.
B. G. Powell

BLUEGRASS BOY   3 b.g. Bluegrass Prince (IRE) 110 – Honey Mill 67 (Milford   **73**
119) [2003 80: 10m 10m² 9.9m⁵ p10g³ p12g p10g Dec 29] angular gelding: fair maiden:
stays 1¼m: acts on good to firm going and polytrack. *G. B. Balding*

BLUEGRASS STAMPEDE   2 ch.c. (Feb 25) Bluegrass Prince (IRE) 110 – Sylvaner   **–**
(IRE) (Montelimar (USA) 122) [2003 5m⁶ May 26] fifth foal: brother to winner in
Greece: dam Irish maiden half-sister to useful sprinter Sizzling Saga: 25/1, last in claimer
at Leicester. *J. D. Czerpak*

BLUE HILLS   2 br.g. (Mar 9) Vettori (IRE) 119 – Slow Jazz (USA) 106 (Chief's Crown   **74**
(USA)) [2003 7m 8.3g⁵ 8.3d² Sep 29] 12,000Y: tall gelding: weak at 2 yrs: sixth foal:
half-brother to useful Italian 5f (at 2 yrs) to 1m winner Mister Cavern (by Lion Cavern)
and fairly useful 6f (at 2 yrs) and 1m winner Mellow Jazz (by Lycius): dam, French 6f (at
2 yrs) to 1m winner, closely related to smart 6f/7f performers Zieten and Blue Duster:
clearly best effort in maidens (fair form) when staying-on second at Hamilton: will stay
1¼m. *M. Johnston*

BLUE JAVA   2 ch.c. (Apr 24) Bluegrass Prince (IRE) 110 – Java Bay (Statoblest 120)   **66**
[2003 8g f8g⁴ p8g Dec 10] smallish colt: third foal: dam, signs of only a little ability,
half-sister to useful 7f performer Captain Holly: best effort (fair form) when eighth
to Jake The Snake in maiden at Lingfield final start: not sure to stay beyond 1m.
H. Morrison

BLUE KNIGHT (IRE)   4 ch.g. Bluebird (USA) 125 – Fer de Lance (IRE) (Diesis   **78**
133) [2003 89: 6m 6m 6m 6m² 6m⁶ 6m 6m Jul 10] big, lengthy gelding: fair handicapper:
reportedly underwent a soft palate operation after final start: effective at 5f to 7f: acts on
all-weather and good to firm ground, probably on soft. *A. P. Jarvis*

BLUE LEADER (IRE)   4 b.g. Cadeaux Genereux 131 – Blue Duster (USA) 118   **78 ?**
(Danzig (USA)) [2003 86: 7.1m 10m May 16] rangy gelding: fairly useful performer at 3
yrs: appeared to run respectably first of 2 starts on Flat in 2003: better at 1¼m than 1m:
acts on good to firm and good to soft going: carries head awkwardly: wore cheekpieces in
2003: gelded, and successful over hurdles in October. *G. Brown*

BLUE MAEVE   3 b.g. Blue Ocean (USA) 87 – Louisville Belle (IRE) 71 (Ahonoora   **45**
122) [2003 f7s 10s f6g f6g⁶ Dec 9] 2,200F: second foal: dam 6f/7f winner who stayed
1m: poor form in maidens/handicap: should stay 7f. *J. Hetherton*

BLUE MARINER 3 b.c. Marju (IRE) 127 – Mazarine Blue 65 (Bellypha 130) [2003 —
81p: f8g Dec 9] promising second on sole 2-y-o start in maiden at Leicester: well held in
similar event at Southwell (slowly away) 16 months later. *P. W. Harris*

BLUE MONDAY 2 b.c. (Feb 14) Darshaan 133 – Lunda (IRE) 60 (Soviet Star (USA) **100 p**
128) [2003 8m 7.9f* 8d* Nov 7] 125,000Y: good-bodied colt: fourth foal: brother to
3-y-o Lundy's Lane and half-brother to 7f winner Jakarta (by Machiavellian) and 1m/
1¼m winner Dancing Tsar (by Salse): dam, maiden, half-sister to several at least smart
performers, including 1½m performer Luso and 5-y-o Warrsan: useful form: won maiden
at York in October and minor event at Doncaster (got up close home to beat Kingdom
Come a neck) in November: will be suited by 1¼m+: should do better still as 3-y-o.
R. Charlton

BLUE MOON HITMAN (IRE) 2 ch.c. (Apr 27) Blue Ocean (USA) 87 – Miss **56**
Kookaburra (IRE) 44 (Namaqualand (USA)) [2003 6d 5m⁵ 5g⁵ 5f⁵ 5m² 5m³ 5m² 5.1m²
5m³ 5f⁴ 5m⁵ 5.1d⁴ f5g⁶ f5g³ f5s⁶ Dec 27] €4,500Y: small colt: first foal: dam Irish
maiden: modest maiden: should stay 6f: acts on fibresand, good to firm and good to soft
ground: wore cheekpieces sixth start: usually races prominently: sometimes hangs left.
A. Berry

BLUE MUEMONIC 3 b.g. Bluegrass Prince (IRE) 110 – Forget To Remindme 51 —
(Forzando 122) [2003 45: p8g Jan 7] poor maiden: stays 9.4f: acts on good to soft going,
good to firm and all-weather: tried in cheekpieces/blinkers. *J. S. Moore*

BLUE MYST 3 b.f. Blue Ocean (USA) 87 – Broom Isle 74 (Damister (USA) 123) **60**
[2003 –: 10m 12g 9.9d³ 12m 10.1g f11s⁶ 10.9d Oct 13] good-topped filly: modest
maiden: below form last 4 starts: should stay 1½m: acts on good to firm and good to soft
ground. *G. A. Swinbank*

BLUE MYSTIQUE 4 b.f. Whittingham (IRE) 104 – Gold And Blue (IRE) (Bluebird **55**
(USA) 125) [2003 65: f7g f8.5g³ f7g f6g⁴ f8.5g⁶ 7m 8m Jun 2] modest handicapper: left
N. Littmoden after fifth start: stays 8.5f: acts on fibresand and good to firm going: tried in
headgear: none too consistent. *M. Mullineaux*

BLUE PATRICK 3 gr.g. Wizard King 122 – Great Intent (Aragon 118) [2003 87: 8m⁴ **92**
8m 8m* 8m⁶ p10g p8g Dec 20] rather leggy gelding: fluent mover: fairly useful performer: won claimer at Ascot in July: stays 1m: raced only on ground firmer than good on
turf, well held on polytrack. *J. M. P. Eustace*

BLUE PLANET (IRE) 5 b.g. Bluebird (USA) 125 – Millie Musique (Miller's Mate **63 ?**
116) [2003 88: p12g 14g Jun 5] big, good-topped gelding: fairly useful handicapper at
best: only modest nowadays: stays easy 1½m: yet to race on heavy ground, acts on any
other turf and polytrack: sometimes slowly away. *P. G. Murphy*

BLUE POWER (IRE) 2 b.c. (Apr 18) Zieten (USA) 118 – La Miserable (USA) **67**
(Miswaki (USA) 124) [2003 6d 7m f6s⁴ f6g⁴ f5g² f5g* f5g³ Dec 22] IR 7,000F, 6,000Y:
well-made colt: sixth foal: half-brother to French 1997 2-y-o 6f winner Azelna (by
Tropular): dam twice-raced half-sister to smart stayer Always Aloof: fair performer: best
effort when winning nursery at Southwell in December: will prove best at 5f/6f: acts on
fibresand. *K. R. Burke*

BLUE QUIVER (IRE) 3 b.c. Bluebird (USA) 125 – Paradise Forum 78 (Prince Sabo **57**
123) [2003 8.3g p7g⁶ Oct 27] sixth foal: dam 2-y-o 5f winner: better effort in maidens
(modest form) when 6 lengths sixth to Leoballero at Lingfield final outing, taking strong
hold: slowly away both outings. *C. A. Horgan*

BLUE REIGNS 5 b.g. Whittingham (IRE) 104 – Gold And Blue (IRE) (Bluebird —
(USA) 125) [2003 65: p7g Jan 25] tall, useful-looking gelding: has a quick action: fairly
useful handicapper in 2001, fair form at best since: well held only run in 2003: best at 5f/
6f: acts on good to firm going, good to soft and fibresand: tried blinkered. *J. W. Unett*

BLUE RONDO (IRE) 3 b.g. Hernando (FR) 127 – Blueberry Walk (Green Desert **64**
(USA) 127) [2003 –: p8g⁴ p10g 12.6m p10g f12s Dec 27] modest maiden: left
R. Charlton 17,000 gns after third outing: stays 1¼m: raced only on all-weather/good to
firm going: blinkered first 3 starts in 2003: ran loose before second outing. *Ian Williams*

BLUE SAVANNA 3 ch.g. Bluegrass Prince (IRE) 110 – Dusk In Daytona 64 (Beveled **55**
(USA)) [2003 65: f12g 14m 11.6d 10.9m⁴ 10f 10m 10m² 9.7g⁶ 11f⁶ p10g³ Dec 30]
modest maiden: stays 1¼m: acts on all-weather and good to firm ground: tried in cheek-
pieces/blinkers last 4 starts: has raced freely: inconsistent. *J. G. Portman*

BLUE SKY THINKING (IRE) 4 b.g. Danehill Dancer (IRE) 117 – Lauretta Blue **104 +**
(IRE) (Bluebird (USA) 125) [2003 102p: 8m 8m* 8.9m⁶ 7m³ 8.2d³ p10g⁴ Nov 22] tall,

rather leggy gelding: useful performer: won minor event at Thirsk in August by ¾ length from Zingari: good efforts last 3 starts, particularly when fourth to Compton Bolter in listed event at Lingfield final one: stays 1¼m: acts on polytrack, yet to race on extremes of going: has been bandaged in front. *K. R. Burke*

BLUES OVER (IRE) 2 b.f. (Feb 17) Sri Pekan (USA) 117 – Crystal Blue (IRE) (Bluebird (USA) 125) [2003 f8g p6g Dec 20] €4,500Y: first foal: dam, ran once in Ireland, half-sister to useful Irish performer up to 1m Sedulous: well held in sellers. *W. J. Musson* —

BLUE SPINNAKER (IRE) 4 b.g. Bluebird (USA) 125 – Suedoise (Kris 135) [2003 6g² 6m³ 5m* 6f³ 7f² 7d⁴ 8.1m* 7.9m⁴ 10m 9m 7.9f⁴ Oct 10] 420,000 francs Y: sturdy gelding: first foal: dam, French 2-y-o 1m winner on only start, half-sister to high-class 1½m performer Wagon Master: useful performer: well held only run for J. Hammond in France in 2002: won maiden at Doncaster in June and handicap at Haydock in August: good fourth to Calcutta in handicap at York final outing: should stay beyond 1m: acts on firm ground, well below form only run on good to soft. *M. W. Easterby* 97 +

BLUES PRINCESS 3 b.f. Bluebird (USA) 125 – Queen Shirley (IRE) (Fairy King (USA)) [2003 70: 5m 5d 6m 6.1f Sep 30] smallish, sturdy filly: fair performer: will prove best at 5f/6f: acts on good to firm and good to soft ground: blinkered (ran creditably) once at 2 yrs: none too consistent. *R. A. Fahey* 66

BLUE STAR 7 b.g. Whittingham (IRE) 104 – Gold And Blue (IRE) (Bluebird (USA) 125) [2003 79, a93: 7.1g 7.9m 8g⁵ 8g³ 12.3m² 10.5m³ 10.5m⁴ 11.9m 15.9m⁵ 11.9f⁵ 15.9d Sep 24] strong, rangy gelding: usually impressed in appearance: fair handicapper on turf (fairly useful on all-weather when last ran in 2002): mostly creditable efforts in 2003 prior to pulled up final outing: stayed 1½m: acted on fibresand/dirt, firm and soft going: usually visored/blinkered: tended to be fractious stall/slowly away: was often held up: dead. *M. Mullineaux* 79 a–

BLUESTONE 4 ch.c. Bluebird (USA) 125 – Romoosh 69 (Formidable (USA) 125) [2003 –: 7m Sep 9] lengthy colt: well held in 3 maidens, off 17 months before final one: sold 3,000 gns, sent to Pakistan. *G. Wragg* —

BLUE STREAK (IRE) 6 ch.g. Bluebird (USA) 125 – Fleet Amour (USA) (Afleet (CAN)) [2003 58: p12g 10.9m 10m⁵ 11.9m⁵ 11.9f² 11.9f² 12m Sep 12] tall, rangy gelding: modest performer: probably best at 1¼m/easy 1½m: acts on firm going, good to soft and polytrack: tried in headgear: winning hurdler. *G. L. Moore* 56

BLUE SYMPHONY 3 b.f. Darshaan 133 – Blue Duster (USA) 118 (Danzig (USA)) [2003 57: 10m² p10g² 10m³ 10f² 10m 10.9m 10m* 9.7m⁵ Aug 11] smallish, quite good-topped filly: fair performer: best effort when winning apprentice maiden handicap at Brighton in August: stays 1¼m: acts on firm ground and polytrack: carries head awkwardly and looks none too keen. *E. A. L. Dunlop* 73

BLUE TOMATO 2 b.c. (Feb 9) Orpen (USA) 116 – Ocean Grove (IRE) 84 (Fairy King (USA)) [2003 5.2m⁴ 6f* 6g* 6m* 6m⁵ 6d 6f³ Oct 11] 21,000F, 50,000Y: lengthy, useful-looking colt: has scope: usually looks well: third foal: half-brother to 3-y-o On The Brink and 2000 2-y-o 5f winner Night Gypsy (by Mind Games): dam 2-y-o 6f winner who stayed 1m: useful performer: won maiden in July and nurseries at Goodwood and York (came from well back) in August: creditable fifth in Mill Reef Stakes at Newbury and third in listed event at York (carried head awkwardly): should stay 7f: acts on firm ground: tends to be soon off bridle. *P. F. I. Cole* 105

BLUETORIA 2 b.f. (Apr 27) Vettori (IRE) 119 – Blue Birds Fly 78 (Rainbow Quest (USA) 134) [2003 6.1m Jul 12] 15,000Y: sixth foal: half-sister to 3 winners, including fairly useful 2-y-o 5f winners Strange Destiny (in 2000, by Mujadil) and For Old Times Sake (in 1996, by Efisio): dam 1¼m winner: 16/1, slowly away and very green when tailed off in maiden at Nottingham. *J. A. Glover* —

BLUE TROJAN (IRE) 3 b.g. Inzar (USA) 112 – Roman Heights (IRE) (Head For Heights 125) [2003 80: p7g f8.5g⁵ 7m 9.9f 7.1d² 8d* p7g 8m³ f9.4g 8f* 8d⁵ f8.5g⁶ p8g⁴ p10g⁴ Dec 29] neat gelding: fairly useful handicapper on turf, fair on all-weather: won at Leicester in July and October: stays 1¼m: acts on firm going, good to soft and all-weather: sometimes edges left. *S. Kirk* 88 a76

BLUE VENTURE (IRE) 3 ch.g. Alhaarth (IRE) 126 – September Tide (IRE) 58 (Thatching 131) [2003 74: f8g⁴ f7s³ f7s³ 7.5m 8m Jun 20] good-bodied gelding: fair maiden at 2 yrs: just modest form over longer trips in 2003: stays 6f: acts on firm going and fibresand: tried in cheekpieces: won juvenile hurdle in July. *P. C. Haslam* 59

BLUE VIKING (IRE)   2 b.c. (Jan 8) Danetime (IRE) 121 – Jenny Spinner (IRE) 58   –
(Bluebird (USA) 125) [2003 7f^4 Jul 16] 4,000Y: first foal: dam, lightly-raced Irish
maiden, out of useful Irish miler Run To Jenny: 14/1, remote fourth of 5 in minor event at
Catterick. *J. R. Weymes*

BLUE WATER   3 b.f. Shaamit (IRE) 127 – November Song (Scorpio (FR) 127) [2003   **45**
42: f8.5g f11s f12s^5 f12g^6 f12g f12g^2 f12g^3 12g f14.8g^6 14.1m^3 f12g 14g^6 16.2m Jul 19]
quite good-topped filly: poor maiden: should stay 2m: acts on fibresand, raced only on
good ground or firmer on turf: wears cheekpieces nowadays. *M. Mullineaux*

BLUNHAM   3 b.g. Danzig Connection (USA) – Relatively Sharp 86 (Sharpen Up 127)   **61**
[2003 67: 7g 7.5m 6m^4 6m^6 7m* 6m 7m f8g f6g f8g f5s Dec 27] tall, rather leggy gelding: **a–**
modest performer on turf: left C. Fairhurst prior to winning maiden at Catterick in
September: well held after: stays 1m: unraced on extremes of going on turf, well beaten
on fibresand: tried blinkered. *M. C. Chapman*

BLUSHING GRENADIER (IRE)   11 ch.g. Salt Dome (USA) – La Duse 66 (Junius   –
(USA) 124) [2003 53: f6g f6g f7s Feb 6] leggy gelding: one-time fair performer: soundly
beaten in sellers/claimer in 2003: usually blinkered, tried visored. *S. R. Bowring*

BLUSHING PRINCE (IRE)   5 b.g. Priolo (USA) 127 – Eliade (IRE) 82 (Flash of   **51 §**
Steel 120) [2003 –, a80: f9.4g f9.4g* f9.4g f9.4s* f9.4g^3 10.9m^5 9.2g^6 f9.4g^3 f8.5g^3 **a71 §**
10.9m^6 f9.4g Oct 4] fair on all-weather, modest on turf: won sellers at Wolverhampton in
February and April: stays 10.9f: acts on fibresand and good to firm going: usually tongue
tied: sometimes looks none too keen: unreliable: modest hurdler. *Mrs L. Stubbs*

BLUSHING SPUR   5 b.g. Flying Spur (AUS) – Bogus John (CAN) (Blushing John   **57**
(USA) 120) [2003 76, a81: f6g^2 f6g* f6s^4 f6s^2 p7g^3 p6g 6g^4 f7g 7m 5g f6g 7m Jul 31]   **a63**
tall gelding: modest performer: won claimer at Wolverhampton in February: left D. Shaw
after fourth start: effective at 6f/7f: acts on all-weather, good to firm and heavy going:
wears headgear: sometimes slowly away/looks none too hearty. *A. Charlton*

BLYTHE KNIGHT (IRE)   3 ch.c. Selkirk (USA) 129 – Blushing Barada (USA) 53   **108**
(Blushing Groom (FR) 131) [2003 82p: 10.3g* 10.4m^5 10m* 12m^5 10m 10.5m^4 9.9m^3
10m Sep 20] quite good-topped colt: has a round action: useful performer: won maiden at
Doncaster in March and 3-runner minor event at Pontefract in June: some creditable
efforts in handicaps after, including when fifth to Fantastic Love in King George V Stakes
at Royal Ascot and when third to Spuradich in quite valuable event at Beverley: effective
at 1¼m/1½m: raced only on good ground or firmer: travels strongly, and sometimes finds
little. *E. A. L. Dunlop*

BLYTHE SPIRIT   4 b.g. Bahamian Bounty 116 – Lithe Spirit (IRE) 74 (Dancing   **88**
Dissident (USA) 119) [2003 89: 6g 7g^6 7.1m 8m* 7f 8f^4 7f 7.2g 7.2g^5 7d 6f^4 7.1m^5 Oct
25] lengthy, unfurnished gelding: fairly useful performer: won handicap at Newcastle in
June: respectable efforts at best: effective at 6f to 1m: acts on firm and soft ground:
tried blinkered/in cheekpieces: possibly temperamental. *R. A. Fahey*

BOANERGES (IRE)   6 br.g. Caerleon (USA) 132 – Sea Siren 68 (Slip Anchor 136)   **74 d**
[2003 94: 5m 5g 5d 5g 5m 5f 5m 5.1d^5 Jul 25] smallish, strong gelding: fair handicapper
at best in 2003: effective at 5f/sharp 6f: acts on firm and good to soft going: visored
once at 2 yrs: sometimes early to post (bolted and withdrawn once): usually held up.
J. M. Bradley

BOATER   9 b.g. Batshoof 122 – Velvet Beret (IRE) (Dominion 123) [2003 58§: 10.2f   **– §**
Mar 31] well-made gelding: modest handicapper: well held only outing in 2003: stays
12.6f: acts on firm and soft ground: tried blinkered: ungenuine. *R. J. Baker*

BOAVISTA (IRE)   3 b.f. Fayruz 116 – Florissa (FR) (Persepolis (FR) 127) [2003 65:   **61**
5m^6 f6g^4 5d^4 6m^3 6m 5m^3 5m^2 6m^2 6m^4 6m^3 Oct 17] small, angular filly: modest maiden
handicapper: stays 6f: acts on firm ground: sold 7,000 gns. *T. D. Easterby*

BOBANVI   5 b.m. Timeless Times (USA) 99 – Bobanlyn (IRE) 76 (Dance of Life   **29**
(USA) [2003 –: f14g 14f^6 17.2m^4 15.8m^5 16.2m Aug 14] small mare: bad maiden: stays
17f: acts on fibresand, heavy and good to firm going: tried blinkered, wore cheekpieces
in 2003: poor hurdler. *J. S. Wainwright*

BOBBY KENNARD   4 b.g. Bobinski 115 – Midnight Break 78 (Night Shift (USA))   **85**
[2003 76: f16s* f16.2g f16s^2 Feb 27] fairly useful handicapper: won at Southwell in
January: good second there final outing: stays 2m: acts on all-weather: reportedly lost
action penultimate start: carries head awkwardly. *J. A. Osborne*

BOBERING   3 b.g. Bob's Return (IRE) 123 – Ring The Rafters (Batshoof 122) [2003   –
8.1m Sep 8] strong, close-coupled gelding: first foal: dam no form: 66/1, slowly away
and tailed off in maiden at Warwick. *B. P. J. Baugh*

BOB'S BUZZ 3 ch.g. Zilzal (USA) 137 – Aethra (USA) 89 (Trempolino (USA) 135) **77**
[2003 –: 7m³ 5g* 7f* 7m Sep 20] strong, close-coupled gelding: fair form, lightly raced:
won maiden at Newcastle (slowly away) in July and handicap at Yarmouth (well-backed
favourite) in August: slowly away and pulled too hard final outing: stays 7f: raced only
on good ground or firmer: unseated rider before start on reappearance: may still do better.
S. C. Williams

BOB'S GONE (IRE) 5 ch.g. Eurobus – Bob's Girl (IRE) 43 (Bob Back (USA) 124) **–**
[2003 –: f12g Feb 7] IR 4,000Y: ex-Irish gelding: fourth foal: half-brother to Irish 6f
winner Ponda Rosa (by Case Law): dam poor maiden: fair performer: won maiden at
Roscommon in 2001: well held on sole Flat outing each of last 2 seasons, leaving Miss
F. Crowley before reappearance: stays 2m: acts on good to firm and good to soft ground:
fair hurdler. *R. J. Smith*

BOBSLEIGH 4 b.g. Robellino (USA) 127 – Do Run Run 75 (Commanche Run 133) **88**
[2003 87: 14.1g⁴ 16m² 20m 16.1m³ 21d 16m³ 16.2f 16f⁴ 18m Oct 18] leggy, useful-
looking gelding: fairly useful handicapper: mostly creditable efforts in 2003: stays 2½m:
acts on firm and good to soft going: carried head awkwardly and appeared to bite winner
sixth 3-y-o start: has run well when edgy. *Mrs A. J. Perrett*

BOB'S SHERIE 4 b.f. Bob's Return (IRE) 123 – Sheraton Girl 49 (Mon Tresor 113) **–**
[2003 –: f12s f14.8g Feb 1] no sign of ability, including in seller. *W. M. Brisbourne*

BOCACCIO (IRE) 5 b.g. Brief Truce (USA) 126 – Idara 109 (Top Ville 129) [2003 **80**
88: p10g⁶ f8.5g⁶ 8.3g 8g May 21] fairly useful handicapper: won at Limerick and
Leopardstown in 2002 for M. Grassick in Ireland: respectable effort in 2003 only on
reappearance: stays 1¼m: acts on soft ground and polytrack: usually blinkered: sold
2,000 gns. *R. Ingram*

BODFARI PRIDE (IRE) 8 b.g. Pips Pride 117 – Renata's Ring (IRE) (Auction Ring **66**
(USA) 123) [2003 82d: f7g⁶ f7g 6m² 7m* f7g 6d³ 7g⁵ 7.2g³ 6g² 6m⁵ 7.2f⁵ 6g 7.6m 6m
7m Jul 23] strong, lengthy gelding: poor mover: one-time fairly useful performer, fair at
best in 2003: won seller at Southwell in April: was effective at 5f to easy 7.6f: acted on
soft going, good to firm and fibresand: blinkered (well held) once: dead. *A. Bailey*

BODFARI ROSE 4 ch.f. Indian Ridge 123 – Royale Rose (FR) 75 (Bering 136) [2003 **–**
62: f16.2g⁴ 14m Apr 10] modest maiden at 3 yrs: showed nothing in 2 runs in 2003
(reportedly broke blood vessel on reappearance): tried in cheekpieces. *A. Bailey*

BODILLA (IRE) 3 b.f. Mujadil (USA) 119 – Shambodia (IRE) (Petardia 113) [2003 **–**
6m May 10] leggy filly: first foal: dam unraced out of sister to smart performer up to
2m Shambo: 33/1 and backward, eleventh of 18 in maiden at Thirsk: withdrawn after
unseating rider and bolting next intended outing. *T. D. Easterby*

BOGUS BALLET 4 ch.f. Halling (USA) 133 – Classic Ballet (FR) 75 (Fabulous **–**
Dancer (USA) 124) [2003 53d: p7g f9.4g p7g 5.7f⁶ p7g 5.7m May 6] small filly:
disappointing maiden. *D. Burchell*

BOHOLA FLYER (IRE) 2 b.f. (Feb 19) Barathea (IRE) 127 – Sharp Catch (IRE) 98 **75**
(Common Grounds 118) [2003 7m 6.5m 6d² Nov 8] 120,000Y: first foal: dam, Irish 5f
(at 2 yrs) and 1m winner, half-sister to smart sprinter Catch The Blues: fair form: neck
second to Miss Langkawi in maiden at Doncaster: should stay 1m. *R. Hannon*

BOING BOING (IRE) 3 b.g. King's Theatre (IRE) 128 – Limerick Princess (IRE) **63**
68 (Polish Patriot (USA) 128) [2003 69?: p8g⁶ 10.3g 8f³ 8.2s 8.3g 7m⁵ 8.2g f8.5s 7m*
Sep 22] modest performer: won seller at Leicester (sold 8,500 gns) in September: stays
1m, possibly not 1¼m: acts on firm going and polytrack (below form both starts on
fibresand): visored penultimate outing: usually races prominently: joined Miss S. Wilton.
J. W. Hills

BOISDALE (IRE) 5 b.g. Common Grounds 118 – Alstomeria 61 (Petoski 135) [2003 **64 d**
60: 6m⁵ f6g* 6m⁵ 7m² f6g 5m⁶ 6f⁶ f6g* f7g f6s f7s⁶ f6s f6g f6g f6g Dec 19] workmanlike
gelding: modest performer: won amateur claimer in April and minor event in June, both
at Southwell: effective at 6f/7f: acts on fibresand, soft and good to firm ground: tried
tongue tied: none too consistent. *D. Nicholls*

BOJANGLES (IRE) 4 b.g. Danehill (USA) 126 – Itching (IRE) (Thatching 131) **–**
[2003 89: 10.9m 10.5m 14.8m⁴ 10g⁵ f9.4g 10.9m Aug 25] deep-girthed gelding: type to
carry plenty of condition: fairly useful form in second of 2 maidens for H. Cecil at 3 yrs:
sold 1,000 gns and off 11 months, well held in 2003, including in seller: wore cheekpieces
final start. *R. Brotherton*

BOLD AMUSEMENT   13 ch.g. Never So Bold 135 – Hysterical 68 (High Top 131)   **50**
[2003 59: 10.1m⁶ 9.2g² 10.1m Aug 15] strong gelding: modest performer: effective at 9f
to 1½m: acts on firm and good to soft going, probably not on softer nowadays: tried in
blinkers/cheekpieces: sometimes races freely/wanders. *W. S. Cunningham*

BOLD BLADE   2 b.g. (Apr 6) Sure Blade (USA) 130 – Golden Ciel (USA) (Septieme   **71**
Ciel (USA) 123) [2003 5f⁶ 6m f7s f7g⁴ f8s* f8s³ Dec 27] 2,800Y: good-bodied gelding:
second foal: dam 2-y-o sprint winner in Italy: fair performer: best efforts in blinkers last 3
starts, winning nursery at Southwell in December by 6 lengths: stays 1m: acts on fibresand. *B. Smart*

BOLD EFFORT (FR)   11 b.g. Bold Arrangement 127 – Malham Tarn (Riverman   **– §**
(USA) 131) [2003 –§: p6g 6.1g 5.7g f5g 5.7f⁶ 6m 6m 5.7m f7g f8g Nov 25] good-
quartered, dipped-backed gelding: poor mover: still fairly useful in 2001, little form
since: usually wears headgear: best left alone. *K. O. Cunningham-Brown*

BOLD EWAR (IRE)   6 ch.g. Persian Bold 123 – Hot Curry (USA) (Sharpen Up 127)   **82**
[2003 71: p13g⁶ p13g⁵ f16.2g 14.1g* 17.1m² 16m⁶ f14.8s* f16.2g⁴ 17.1m⁴ 15.9d 14.1m²   **a68**
p16g⁵ Oct 15] close-coupled gelding: easy mover: fairly useful handicapper on turf, fair
on all-weather: won at Nottingham in March and Wolverhampton in May: stayed 17f:
acted on all-weather, firm and good to soft going: usually blinkered but not after third
6-y-o start: tried tongue tied: sometimes carried head awkwardly/ran in snatches:
inconsistent: dead. *C. E. Brittain*

BOLD JOE (IRE)   2 b.c. (Feb 16) Singspiel (IRE) 133 – Wavy Up (IRE) (Brustolon   **71**
117) [2003 6m 8m 8.1m 8.3m 8m 10d² p8g⁵ Nov 18] 50,000 2-y-o: smallish colt: first
foal: dam, French 8.5f winner, half-sister to smart performer up to 1m Wavy Run: fair
maiden: stayed 1¼m: acted on polytrack, good to firm and good to soft going: sometimes
slowly away: dead. *P. Mitchell*

BOLD RIDGE (IRE)   3 b.g. Indian Ridge 123 – Cutting Ground (IRE) 85 (Common   **57 ?**
Grounds 118) [2003 p10g p10g Dec 30] second foal: brother to 4-y-o Cut Ridge: dam,
Irish 9f winner, half-sister to useful 1m/1¼m winner Stone Ridge (by Indian Ridge): well
held in maidens at Lingfield. *S. Kirk*

BOLD SHOUT (IRE)   2 b.c. (May 8) Alzao (USA) 117 – Bye Bold Aileen (IRE)   **–**
(Warning 136) [2003 8.3g p7g 8.3g Oct 13] €15,000Y: third foal: half-brother to 4-y-o
Concubine and 3-y-o Best Be Going: dam, Irish maiden who seemed to stay 1¼m: little
sign of ability, including in seller. *R. F. Johnson Houghton*

BOLD TRUMP   2 b.g. (Mar 6) First Trump 118 – Blue Nile (IRE) 70 (Bluebird (USA)   **–**
125) [2003 7g Jul 3] 3,400F, 6,000Y: leggy gelding: fifth foal: half-brother to 5-y-o Gone
Too Far and a winner in Greece by Lion Cavern: dam, 1¼m winner, half-sister to smart
1¼m performer Revelation: 50/1, last of 15 in maiden at Newbury. *Jean-Rene Auvray*

BOLD WOLF   2 b.c. (Apr 7) Wolfhound (USA) 126 – Rambold 72 (Rambo Dancer   **52**
(CAN) 107) [2003 6.1m 6d 6g 6m 5.1f² 5m Oct 25] first foal: dam 6f winner, including at
2 yrs: modest maiden: made most when good second in nursery at Bath: likely to prove
best at 5f/6f: acts on firm ground: tongue tied after debut. *P. W. Harris*

BOLEYN CASTLE (USA)   6 ch.g. River Special (USA) – Dance Skirt (CAN)   **103**
(Caucasus (USA) 127) [2003 119: 5m³ 5f 5g 5d 5m 5f 5d Oct 4] strong, compact gelding:
smart performer at 5 yrs: just useful form when third to Peruvian Chief in listed event at
Kempton on reappearance: well held after: best at 5f: acts on firm and soft ground:
visored fifth outing: has been early to post/shown reluctance at stall: usually ridden by
claimer R. Miles: often tries to dominate: inconsistent: sold 15,000 gns. *T. G. Mills*

BOLHAM LADY   5 b.m. Timeless Times (USA) 99 – Stratford Lady 48 (Touching   **–**
Wood (USA) 127) [2003 –: f6g f5g Feb 14] compact mare: modest performer at 3 yrs,
well beaten since: tried in cheekpieces, usually blinkered. *J. Balding*

BOLLIN ANNABEL   2 b.f. (Jun 8) King's Theatre (IRE) 128 – Bollin Magdalene 55   **– p**
(Teenoso (USA) 135) [2003 8.1d Sep 27] good-bodied filly: has scope: fifth foal: half-
sister to useful 1¼m/1½m winner Bollin Nellie (by Rock Hopper) and 5-y-o Bollin
Thomas: dam, staying maiden on Flat, winner over hurdles: 50/1, green and better for
race, not knocked about when ninth of 14 in maiden at Haydock: type to do better at
1¼m+ at 3 yrs. *T. D. Easterby*

BOLLIN EDWARD   4 b.g. Timeless Times (USA) 99 – Bollin Harriet (Lochnager   **81 d**
132) [2003 75: 6m² 6d 6m 6g⁴ 6g³ 6m 6f 7.5d 6g 6.1m Oct 28] good-bodied gelding:
fairly useful handicapper: well below form after sixth start: will prove best at 5f/6f: acts
on good to firm and good to soft going, below form on soft: effective visored or not, tried
blinkered. *T. D. Easterby*

Weatherbys Insurance Lonsdale Stakes, York—
Bollin Eric has taken the measure of Cover Up, Zindabad (visor) and Persian Punch

BOLLIN ERIC   4 b.c. Shaamit (IRE) 127 – Bollin Zola 90 (Alzao (USA) 117)   **123**
[2003 125: 12m⁴ 13.9m³ 12f² 12m⁴ 12d⁴ 15.9m* 14f⁴ 12s Oct 5]

The 1997 St Leger winner Silver Patriarch has been joined at the National Stud by Bollin Eric, who won the final classic in 2002, £2,500 the fee for both horses. Silver Patriarch increased his standing in two seasons' racing following his victory at Doncaster, continuing to show high-class form raced mainly at around a mile and a half and winning three races including the Coronation Cup and Gran Premio del Jockey Club, both Group 1 events. It can't be said that Bollin Eric enhanced his reputation in his final season, but he did it little harm either. Bollin Eric was given plenty of opportunities to show what he could do at a mile and a half, and while he had several creditable efforts to his name at the trip his only win came when stepped up to two miles, in the Weatherbys Insurance Lonsdale Stakes at York in August.

Bollin Eric had finished in the frame on all five of his starts in the latest season prior to the Lonsdale, his two best efforts coming at Ascot. Bollin Eric successfully conceded weight to all except one of his eight rivals in the Hardwicke Stakes at the Royal meeting, looking the likely winner when driven ahead a furlong out, but collared close home and beaten a neck by Indian Creek, the pair clear. In the King George VI and Queen Elizabeth Stakes a month later, Bollin Eric was found wanting for speed in a muddling race, though he did keep on willingly to take fourth, six lengths behind the winner Alamshar. There was nothing of Alamshar's calibre to contend with when Bollin Eric turned up at York, though his Group 1 penalty again meant that he had to give weight to all of his rivals in the Group 3 Lonsdale Stakes there, including Boreas and Cover Up who had finished first and second respectively in the previous year's edition. Doubts were expressed as to how effective Bollin Eric would be at the longer trip given that he tended to race freely but, fitted with a crossed noseband for the first time, he settled well under restraint, and was also helped by Persian Punch not setting his usual strong pace, which counted against the out-and-out stayers. Bollin Eric, who looked in excellent shape and was sent off the clear favourite, travelled strongly and produced much the best finishing speed, quickening to the front over a furlong out and winning comfortably by two lengths from Cover Up, who just got the better of Zindabad in the battle for the minor placings. It was one of the best winning performances in the Lonsdale in recent times, and in terms of form was almost on a par with Bollin Eric's St Leger win. He couldn't match it on his next start when fourth to Vinnie Roe in the Irish St Leger at the Curragh, for which he started favourite; and he was some way below his best in the Prix de l'Arc de Triomphe at Longchamp on his final appearance, finishing eighth to Dalakhani. Bollin Eric had coped well enough with good to soft going in the King George, but was possibly unsuited by the even softer surface at Longchamp. The ground was good or firmer for all his other starts, and he acted on firm.

Bollin Eric (b.c. 1999)	Shaamit (IRE) (b 1993)	Mtoto (b 1983)	Busted
			Amazer
		Shomoose (b 1985)	Habitat
			Epithet
	Bollin Zola (b 1986)	Alzao (b 1980)	Lyphard
			Lady Rebecca
		Sauntry (br 1982)	Ballad Rock
			Crestia

Bollin Eric is the eighth foal of the fairly useful Bollin Zola, who was successful at up to seven and a half furlongs, and her fourth winner, following on from the smart sprinter Bollin Joanne (by Damister), the fairly useful miler Bollin Terry (by Terimon) and the fair sprinter Bollin Ann (by Anshan). Sauntry, the grandam of Bollin Eric, was unraced, but the great grandam Crestia won over six furlongs at two years. Bollin Eric, a big, strong, good sort who usually impressed in appearance, is a good walker, and he has a short, round action. Effective at a mile and a half to two miles, he raced most genuinely and was notably consistent, the Arc the only occasion he finished out of the first four in eighteen starts. Silver Patriarch's first crop reached racing age in the latest season but none was successful. If his offspring are to make their mark it will more than likely be as handicappers over distances of a mile and a half and more, or as jumpers, and similar remarks apply to Bollin Eric who is much the best horse sired by the now-deceased Derby winner Shaamit. Shaamit himself began his stud career at the National Stud, and Bollin Eric was foaled there. *T. D. Easterby*

BOLLIN JANET 3 b.f. Sheikh Albadou 128 – Bollin Emily 82 (Lochnager 132) [2003 **83** 78p: 6m 5d 5f⁴ 6g* 6m⁵ 5m 5s Nov 3] strong, well-made filly: fairly useful performer: won handicap at Haydock in July: disappointing after: will prove best at 5f/6f: acts on firm going, probably on good to soft. *T. D. Easterby*

BOLLIN JEANNIE 3 b.f. Royal Applause 124 – Bollin Joanne 118 (Damister **62** (USA) 123) [2003 74: 6d 6s 5m⁴ 5.9m⁵ 8g 6m⁴ 6g Oct 22] smallish, compact filly: has a quick action: fair performer: below form last 3 starts: stays 6f: acts on good to firm and good to soft ground: tried blinkered. *T. D. Easterby*

BOLLIN THOMAS 5 b.g. Alhijaz 122 – Bollin Magdalene 55 (Teenoso (USA) 135) **89** [2003 88: 13d 14v 13.9f⁶ 14.6m* 16.1m 14.8m³ Jul 19] close-coupled, workmanlike gelding: fairly useful handicapper: won at Doncaster in June: effective at 1½m to 2m: acts on any ground. *T. D. Easterby*

BOLSHEVIK (IRE) 2 b.g. (Jan 30) Fasliyev (USA) 120 – Cheviot Amble (IRE) 105 **– p** (Pennine Walk 120) [2003 5m 6m⁶ Aug 6] IR 24,000F, 16,000Y: good-topped gelding: half-brother to smart 1m to 10.4f winner Amalia (by Danehill): dam Irish 6f to 1¼m winner: not given hard time when well held in maidens at Beverley and Pontefract: should do better. *T. D. Easterby*

BOLSHOI BALLET 5 b.g. Dancing Spree (USA) – Broom Isle 74 (Damister (USA) **76** 123) [2003 71: 14.1g f12g⁴ f14.8g Oct 20] quite good-topped gelding: fair performer: winning hurdler: ran creditably in 2003 only when fourth in handicap at Southwell: probably stays 2m: acts on heavy going, good to firm and fibresand: found little last 2 starts. *J. Mackie*

BOMB ALASKA 8 br.g. Polar Falcon (USA) 126 – So True 116 (So Blessed 130) **82 +** [2003 7d⁴ Mar 22] big, rangy gelding: useful performer in 2000: disappointing in 2001: 50/1, only Flat outing since when fourth in handicap at Kempton, carrying head awkwardly: stays 1¼m: acts on good to firm and heavy ground: reportedly had wind operation after final 5-y-o start. *G. B. Balding*

BO MCGINTY (IRE) 2 ch.g. (May 12) Fayruz 116 – Georges Park Lady (IRE) (Tirol **83** 127) [2003 5m³ 5f 5m* Aug 4] €1,500Y, resold €6,000Y: good-topped gelding: third foal: dam unraced: fairly useful form: won maiden at Carlisle, briefly hanging right: best effort when third in minor event at Beverley in June: should stay 6f: very slowly away second appearance. *R. A. Fahey*

BON AMI (IRE) 7 b.g. Paris House 123 – Felin Special (Lyphard's Special (USA) **82** 122) [2003 84: f6s p7g⁶ f7g⁴ 7.1m² 6m 7.1m Apr 21] rather leggy gelding: fluent mover: fairly useful performer: was better at 7f than 6f latterly: acted on any turf going and all-weather: was effective blinkered/visored or not: sometimes edged left/carried head high: was usually held up: dead. *A. Berry*

BOND BECKS (IRE)   3 ch.g. Tagula (IRE) 116 – At Amal (IRE) (Astronef 116)   **96**
[2003 101: 8g 6m³ 5f⁴ 6m⁴ 6g 5m⁶ 5m⁵ 5d Sep 23] big, lengthy gelding: has scope: useful
performer: ran creditably in 2003 on second to sixth starts: likely to prove best at bare 5f:
acts on firm going: headstrong: carried head awkwardly second outing. *B. Smart*

BOND BOY   6 b.g. Piccolo 121 – Arabellajill 97 (Aragon 118) [2003 103: 6f³ 6g⁶ 6d²   **102**
5m 6d f5g Nov 19] useful performer: best efforts in 2003 when placed in handicap
at York (third to Fayr Jag) and minor event at Hamilton (neck second to Tom Tun):
best at 5f/6f: acts on any turf going, needed experience on fibresand final start: genuine.
B. Smart

BOND BROOKLYN   2 b.c. (Mar 25) Mind Games 121 – Crystal Sand (GER) (For-   **67**
zando 122) [2003 6m 6m⁵ 5m⁵ 6g² f6s³ 6g⁵ f6g³ f6g³ f7g Nov 28] 18,000Y: good-bodied
colt: third foal: brother to useful 2002 2-y-o 6f winner Cumbrian Venture: dam unraced:
fair maiden: will prove best at 5f/6f: acts on fibresand, best turf efforts on good going:
blinkered/visored last 6 outings, possibly amiss final one. *B. Smart*

BOND DIAMOND   6 gr.g. Prince Sabo 123 – Alsiba 68 (Northfields (USA)) [2003   **86**
83: 8.3g* 8.1g 8g⁴ 8m 8m⁴ 7f 8m 8m³ 8g⁴ Sep 22] strong, lengthy gelding: fairly useful
handicapper: won at Windsor in April: mostly creditable efforts after: stays easy 1¼m:
acts on firm going, good to soft and all-weather: sometimes wears crossed noseband/
carries head awkwardly: usually held up: sold 17,000 gns. *P. R. Webber*

BOND DOMINGO   4 b.g. Mind Games 121 – Antonia's Folly 64 (Music Boy 124)   **?**
[2003 76d: f8s f8s⁶ f6g f6g 6d 5m 6f f6g Dec 9] strong, well-made gelding: just modest   **a50 §**
performer at best in 2003: best at 5f: acts on fibresand and heavy going: usually blinkered,
tried visored: sometimes hangs left: unreliable. *B. Smart*

BONDI (FR)   3 b.f. Sillery (USA) 122 – Biscay 67 (Unfuwain (USA) 131) [2003 –:   **–**
8.5m 6.1m 7.6g⁵ p7g Oct 27] leggy filly: little form. *A. M. Balding*

BOND JOVI (IRE)   4 b.g. Danehill Dancer (IRE) 117 – Vieux Carre (Pas de Seul   **–**
133) [2003 –: f8s Jan 1] smallish gelding: fair performer at 2 yrs, little form since: tried
blinkered: looks difficult ride. *B. Smart*

BOND MAY DAY   3 b.f. Among Men (USA) 124 – State Romance 67 (Free State   **79**
125) [2003 68: f7s⁶ f8g³ 10m² 10m² 12f* 12.1f² f12g⁴ 11m 11m 9.9m* 12m⁶ 9.9m Aug
24] angular filly: fair performer: won minor event at Thirsk in April and handicap at
Beverley in July: has won at 1½m, but may prove best at 1¼m: acts on fibresand, raced
only on good going or firmer on turf: has reared leaving stall. *B. Smart*

BOND MILLENNIUM   5 ch.g. Piccolo 121 – Farmer's Pet 90 (Sharrood (USA)   **69**
124) [2003 79, a81+: 8.2g⁵ 10.1m⁶ 8.3d 7.9f* 8m³ 8m⁵ 8.5m² 6.9m⁵ 9.2m⁴ 7.9m⁶ 8.5m   **a71**
10.1m² 10g⁴ f8g⁵ f9.4g⁵ Dec 26] sturdy gelding: just fair performer in 2003: won minor
event at Carlisle in June: effective at 1m/1¼m: acts on firm going, soft and all-weather:
waited with: has raced freely/found little, but is consistent. *B. Smart*

BOND MIRAGE   5 b.g. Primo Dominie 121 – Arabellajill 97 (Aragon 118) [2003 –,   **–**
a56: f8g³ 8g f8.5g May 23] modest performer, lightly raced: ran creditably in 2003 only   **a57**
in claimer on reappearance: unlikely to stay beyond 1m: acts on fibresand. *B. Smart*

BOND MOONLIGHT   2 ch.g. (Mar 4) Danehill Dancer (IRE) 117 – Interregnum   **68**
(Interrex (CAN)) [2003 f8s⁴ 8.1d f8s⁴ Oct 7] 8,000Y: good-topped gelding: first foal: dam
of no account: easily best effort in maidens (fair form) at Southwell on debut: not sure to
stay much beyond 1m. *B. Smart*

BOND PLAYBOY   3 b.g. Piccolo 121 – Highest Ever (FR) (Highest Honor (FR) 124)   **–**
[2003 87: f6g⁶ f6g² 5.5m 5.1m 6d 6s f6g* f5g² Dec 9] good-bodied gelding: useful handi-   **a97**
capper: ran well last 2 starts, winning at Wolverhampton in November: should prove best
at 5f/6f: acts on fibresand, good to firm and good to soft going: tried blinkered at 2 yrs:
usually races prominently: possibly temperamental. *B. Smart*

BOND ROMEO (IRE)   2 ch.g. (Apr 12) Titus Livius (FR) 115 – At Amal (IRE)   **75**
(Astronef 116) [2003 5g 5f⁵ 5d⁵ 5f⁵ 5m 5g² f5g Nov 21] lengthy gelding: fourth foal:
half-brother to 3-y-o Bond Becks and a winner in Holland by Rainbows For Life: dam
unraced: fair maiden: easily best effort when second to Great Fox at Redcar: will need to
settle to stay beyond 5f: sometimes hangs left. *B. Smart*

BOND ROYALE   3 ch.f. Piccolo 121 – Passiflora 75 (Night Shift (USA)) [2003 73,   **88**
a89: f6g³ 6m 6.1m 6f 6d f6g⁴ p6g Nov 26] strong, close-coupled filly: fairly useful
performer: stays 6f: acts on fibresand and good to firm going: inconsistent. *B. Smart*

BOND SHAKIRA 2 ch.f. (Feb 25) Daggers Drawn (USA) 114 – Cinnamon Lady 77 – (Emarati (USA) 74) [2003 5g⁵ Jul 26] 44,000Y: first foal: dam 7f winner: 11/2, last in maiden at Redcar, taking good hold and stumbling. *B. Smart*

BOND SOLITAIRE 3 ch.f. Atraf 116 – Laena 72 (Roman Warrior 132) [2003 66p: – 8m 7g 6m 6g f7s f7g Nov 19] big, close-coupled filly: fair form only outing at 2 yrs: little show in 2003. *B. Smart*

BOND STASIA (IRE) 3 b.f. Mukaddamah (USA) 125 – Idrak 68 (Young Generation – 129) [2003 54: 5g May 24] lengthy filly: modest form in 2 runs at 2 yrs: well held only outing in 2003. *B. Smart*

BONECRUSHER 4 b.g. Revoque (IRE) 122 – Eurolink Mischief 84 (Be My Chief **109** (USA) 122) [2003 110: 10g⁴ a10f⁶ 10g⁴ 10m* 10.3g⁴ 9m Oct 4] strong gelding: useful performer: left Saeed bin Suroor after second start: won 4-runner minor event at Newmarket in August by 2½ lengths from Gallant Hero: creditable fourth to Rawyaan in minor event at Doncaster and ran respectably in Cambridgeshire at Newmarket (fourteenth to Chivalry) last 2 starts: stays 10.5f: acts on soft and good to firm going, below form on dirt: visored last 3 outings: edgy sort, sometimes early to post. *D. R. Loder*

BONELLA (IRE) 5 gr.m. Eagle Eyed (USA) 111 – Mettlesome (Lomond (USA) 128) – [2003 55: 11.6g 10m Aug 9] tall mare: modest handicapper at best: never dangerous both outings in 2003: stays 1½m: acts on soft and good to firm going: sometimes races freely. *W. J. Musson*

BONITO 5 ch.g. Pivotal 124 – Bonita 57 (Primo Dominie 121) [2003 69, a62: p7g f6g⁶ **62** 7m² 7m⁶ 6g⁶ f7g 7.5d² 6.9m⁴ 7m⁶ Oct 13] modest performer: has won at 1m, may prove best around 7f: acts on any turf going and on fibresand: has worn cheekpieces/visor: has started slowly/hung left. *P. C. Haslam*

BONJOUR BOND (IRE) 2 ro.g. (Apr 8) Portrait Gallery (IRE) 110 – Musical **63** Essence 65 (Song 132) [2003 8.5m⁴ 8.1d 8.2d Nov 6] 17,000 2-y-o: leggy gelding: half-brother to several winners, including 3-y-o Monsieur Bond and 5-y-o Up Tempo: dam third at 1m: modest form in maidens: moved poorly to post when fourth at Beverley: will probably stay 1¼m. *B. Smart*

BONJOUR DIRECTA (GER) 3 ch.c. Monsun (GER) 124 – Bonarda (GER) (Aca- – tenango (GER) 127) [2003 8d 10d 8.5g⁶ 8.9g 10.9d⁶ 13.9f⁵ 10.5d f11s Dec 13] second foal: dam unraced: well held in maidens/handicaps in Germany and on British debut in claimer at Southwell. *T. H. Hansen, Germany*

BONKERS 3 ch.f. Efisio 120 – Flourishing (IRE) 85 (Trojan Fen 118) [2003 63: f5g **57 +** 8d 6d 5m f6g⁵ 6g² 5f³ 5g³ 6g* a7.5g³ 6g³ 5g 7d* Nov 22] good-bodied filly: modest performer: sold from T. Easterby 4,500 gns after fifth start: won minor event in September and claimer in November, both at Ostend: stays 7.5f: acts on fibresand and dirt, firm and good to soft ground. *G. Heymans, Belgium*

BONNE DE FLEUR 2 b.f. (May 8) Whittingham (IRE) 104 – L'Estable Fleurie **80** (IRE) 76 (Common Grounds 118) [2003 5m³ 5m* 6.1m* 6m² 6f³ 6.1m² Oct 22] £400Y: small, strong filly: second foal: dam 7f winner: fairly useful performer: won maiden at Beverley in July and nursery at Nottingham in August: good placed efforts after, hanging left in front in minor event at Nottingham final start: will probably stay 7f. *B. Smart*

BONNIE LAD (IRE) 4 b.g. Tagula (IRE) 116 – Sabonis (USA) 68 (The Minstrel – (CAN) 135) [2003 56: 5m 5m 5g Jun 12] rather leggy, useful-looking gelding: maiden: no form in 2003: tried blinkered/in cheekpieces: often slowly away. *A. Berry*

BONNY RUAN 4 b.f. So Factual (USA) 120 – Sans Diablo (IRE) (Mac's Imp (USA) **63 d** 116) [2003 81: 5m 5.7m⁵ 5.7g 5.7f 5.7f³ f5s² f6g³ f6g 5m f5s* 5.1g Sep 11] tall, leggy **a56** filly: fair handicapper: won at Southwell in September: effective at 5f/6f: acts on good to firm ground and fibresand: sometimes blinkered, visored at Southwell. *D. Haydn Jones*

BONSAI (IRE) 2 b.f. (Jan 25) Woodman (USA) 126 – Karakia (IRE) 101 (Sadler's – Wells (USA) 132) [2003 6g Oct 6] 40,000Y, 52,000 2-y-o: first foal: dam, 9f/1¼m winner: 25/1 and better for race, well held in maiden at Windsor. *R. T. Phillips*

BONTADINI 4 b.g. Emarati (USA) 74 – Kintail 76 (Kris 135) [2003 –, a70: f8s p10g² – 10.2f 10.1g f8g f8g 14.1s f8.5g Nov 29] good-topped gelding: fair performer on **a70 d** all-weather: good second in handicap at Lingfield in February: no form after: stays 1¼m: acts on all-weather: tried visored. *D. Morris*

Tote Scoop6 Sprint (Handicap), Lingfield—
the first valuable sprint handicap of the season for three-year-olds;
Bonus completes his hat-trick with Move It and Hit's Only Money (white nose) filling the places

BONUS (IRE) 3 b.c. Cadeaux Genereux 131 – Khamseh 85 (Thatching 131) [2003 **110**
78: 6g³ 6g² 6m* 6g* 6m* 6m² 6m⁵ 6f* 5m⁵ Aug 31] big, strong, angular colt: smart
performer: vastly improved in 2003, winning maiden at Newmarket in April, handicaps
at Salisbury and Lingfield (beat Move It 2 lengths in Tote Scoop6 Sprint) in May and
Phoenix Sprint Stakes at the Curragh (beat Sun Slash 1½ lengths) in August: just
respectable fifth to Deportivo in Flying Five on last-named course final outing: should
prove at least as effective at 5f as 6f: acts on firm going: often lethargic in preliminaries:
usually races up with pace: edged right on fifth outing. *R. Hannon*

BOOGIE MAGIC 3 b.f. Wizard King 122 – Dalby Dancer 71 (Bustiki) [2003 8.2g **65**
8.2m 8.3s⁴ 8d p10g Dec 17] 2,000Y, 4,000 2-y-o: good-topped filly: seventh living
foal: half-sister to 3 winners, including useful 7.5f to 1¼m winner Yabint El Sultan (by
Safawan): dam won up to 2m: fair maiden: well held in handicaps last 2 starts: stays 1m:
acts on soft ground. *C. N. Allen*

BOOGIE STREET 2 b.c. (Mar 13) Compton Place 125 – Tart And A Half 83 (Distant **108 p**
Relative 128) [2003 6g⁵ 5m* 6g³ 5g⁴ 5m* Sep 18] 19,000F, 40,000Y: big, lengthy,
good-topped colt: has scope: third foal: dam 2-y-o 5f winner who stayed 7f: won maiden
at Sandown (by 8 lengths) in August and listed race at Ayr (by 1½ lengths from Nights
Cross, making all) in September: respectable fourth to Howick Falls in Flying Childers
Stakes at Doncaster: probably best at 5f: tongue tied last 2 outings: type to make a smart
3-y-o. *R. Hannon*

BOOKIESINDEXDOTCOM 2 b.f. (Mar 12) Great Dane (IRE) 122 – Fifth Emerald **63**
54 (Formidable (USA) 125) [2003 5m 6g⁵ 7m³ 7g⁴ 7m p7g⁶ 5.7f⁴ f6g³ f6s² f6g² f6g² Nov
17] sparely-made filly: second foal: half-sister to 3-y-o Goodbye Mr Bond: dam,
1m winner, out of close relation to smart middle-distance filly Valley of Gold: modest
maiden: stays easy 7f: acts on all-weather and good to firm going: visored/blinkered after
second outing: often races prominently/looks none too keen. *J. R. Jenkins*

BOOK MATCHED 2 b.g. (Mar 28) Efisio 120 – Princess Latifa 63 (Wolfhound (USA) **69 p**
126) [2003 7s 6d f7g³ Nov 25] 10,000Y: leggy gelding: first foal: dam lightly-raced
maiden who stayed 7f: best effort in maidens (fair form) when third to Benny The Ball at
Southwell, late headway: should stay 1m: open to progress. *B. Smart*

BOOM OR BUST (IRE) 4 ch.g. Entrepreneur 123 – Classic Affair (USA) 66 (Trem- **54**
polino (USA) 135) [2003 58: f12g³ f9.4s p12g 8.1m⁵ 11.6m³ 11.7f² 10.9m 16m Sep 19]
unfurnished gelding: modest performer: seems to stay 1¾m, not 2m: acts on fibresand
and probably any turf going: sometimes visored/blinkered: usually wears cheekpieces
nowadays: held up: sometimes looks none too keen. *Miss K. M. George*

BOON COMPANION 4 b.g. Sure Blade (USA) 130 – Pea Green 98 (Try My Best –
(USA) 130) [2003 p5g 6g 11.6g p12g Sep 3] 15,000Y: half-brother to several winners,
including fairly useful middle-distance stayer The Green Grey (by Environment Friend)
and 6-y-o Sussex Lad: dam, 2-y-o 5f winner who probably stayed 1m, grandam of smart
sprinter Sampower Star: little sign of ability. *John Berry*

BOOZY DOUZ 3 ch.f. Abou Zouz (USA) 109 – Ackcontent (USA) (Key To Content –
(USA)) [2003 –: p8g Jan 7] no form. *H. S. Howe*

BOPPYS BABE 2 ch.f. (May 5) Clan of Roses – Joara (FR) (Radetzky 123) [2003 5d –
6m 5d 5m 7m Oct 1] leggy filly: fifth reported foal: dam, lightly raced on Flat, winning
hurdler: little form, including in sellers. *J. S. Wainwright*

BOPPYS PRINCESS 2 b.f. (Mar 21) Wizard King 122 – Laurel Queen (IRE) 76 **38**
(Viking (USA)) [2003 5m 6m⁵ 6f 7.5d⁶ 8.5m 7m 7m 6m Oct 24] 800Y: quite good-topped
filly: fourth foal: dam prolific 6f to 8.5f winner: poor maiden: visored final start.
J. S. Wainwright

Highclere Thoroughbred Racing VII's "Bonus"

BORDER ARROW   8 ch.g. Selkirk (USA) 129 – Nibbs Point (IRE) 107 (Sure Blade **110 §**
(USA) 130) [2003 116§: 10s³ 10g 10g⁵ May 3] big, lengthy gelding: has a markedly
round action: has reportedly had leg problems: smart performer: best effort in 3 runs in
2003 when creditable third to Aquarelliste in Prix Exbury at Saint-Cloud on reappearance: effective at 1¼m/1½m: acts on heavy and good to firm going, well below form on
polytrack: sometimes visored, wore cheekpieces on reappearance and final outing:
played up in preliminaries when tongue tied first 2 starts in 2002: tends to sweat:
sometimes slowly away/soon off bridle: not one to trust. *A. M. Balding*

BORDER ARTIST   4 ch.g. Selkirk (USA) 129 – Aunt Tate (Tate Gallery (USA) 117) **74**
[2003 69, a61: f7g⁴ 6m⁴ 8m² 7.1d* 6m 7.1m* 7.2g⁶ 6m 6.9m⁴ 6m 7f³ 6m* 7.5m* 7m⁶ 8d **a54**
7.5m 7.9m 7.9m Sep 7] well-made gelding: fair handicapper on turf, modest on
all-weather: won at Musselburgh (2) in May and Epsom and Beverley in July: effective at
6f to 1m: acts on polytrack, firm and good to soft going: blinkered (slowly away) once:
usually waited with. *D. Nicholls*

BORDER CASTLE   2 b.c. (Feb 20) Grand Lodge (USA) 125 – Tempting Prospect 95 **82 p**
(Shirley Heights 130) [2003 7g⁴ 8.3m⁴ 8.2m* Oct 28] deep-girthed colt: has scope:
second foal: half-brother to 3-y-o Promotion: dam, 2-y-o 1m winner who stayed 1½m,
half-sister to smart performer up to 13f Phantom Gold, herself dam of Oaks runner-up
Flight of Fancy: landed odds in 10-runner maiden at Nottingham comfortably by 4
lengths from Show No Fear, leading over 1f out: will be suited by 1¼m/1½m: should
make a useful 3-y-o. *Sir Michael Stoute*

BORDER EDGE   5 b.g. Beveled (USA) – Seymour Ann (Krayyan 117) [2003 63, **95**
a61: p7g* p7g⁴ p7g* p7g p7g³ p8g⁵ p8g 8g 8m* 8g⁴ 8.3g* 8m⁴ 7f² 8.5m² 8d 8m³ 8g² 7m
8m* 8f 7d* 6m² 8g p7g p8g Dec 30] useful performer: much improved in 2003, winning
handicaps at Lingfield in January and February, Bath in May and Windsor in June, and
minor events at Salisbury in September and Epsom in October: best at 6f to 1m: acts on

147

firm ground, good to soft and all-weather: usually blinkered/visored: effective making running or held up: pulled hard 2 of last 3 starts: tough and reliable. *J. J. Bridger*

BORDER MUSIC 2 b.g. (Feb 23) Selkirk (USA) 129 – Mara River 86 (Efisio 120) **83 p** [2003 8m³ 8g⁶ p8g* Nov 2] tall, good-topped gelding: third foal: dam 6f to 1m winner: fairly useful form in maidens: won 10-runner event at Lingfield comfortably by 1½ lengths from Odiham: likely to stay 1¼m: type to progress further. *A. M. Balding*

BORDER RUN 6 b.g. Missed Flight 123 – Edraianthus 78 (Windjammer (USA)) **–** [2003 f12s Jan 10] well-made gelding: fair maiden at 3 yrs: of little account over jumps nowadays and tailed off on Flat return: blinkered twice. *M. Mullineaux*

BORDER SUBJECT 6 b.g. Selkirk (USA) 129 – Topicality (USA) (Topsider (USA)) **117** [2003 117: 7m⁶ 6g⁴ 6m* 6f 6g Jul 5] big, strong gelding: reportedly suffers from breathing problem: smart performer: good fourth to The Tatling in handicap at Newmarket prior to winning similar event at York in May by ¾ length from same rival: well below form after in Wokingham at Royal Ascot and minor event at Haydock: has won at 1m, but very best form at 6f and should prove effective at 5f: acts on good to soft and good to firm going: sometimes tongue tied earlier in career: has won when edgy: free-going front runner. *R. Charlton*

BORDER TALE 3 b.g. Selkirk (USA) 129 – Likely Story (IRE) 94 (Night Shift (USA)) **87** [2003 61: 12m² 12.3m² 12g³ 11.6d* 11.6s⁴ 12g² 12.1g³ 11.9f⁶ 12.3m* 11m² 10.3m⁵ 10g⁴ Aug 1] strong gelding: fairly useful handicapper: won at Windsor in May and Chester in June: stays 12.3f: acts on soft ground, good to firm and fibresand: tried visored/tongue tied at 2 yrs: joined C. Weedon. *M. L. W. Bell*

BORDER TERRIER (IRE) 5 b.g. Balnibarbi 95 – Ring Side (IRE) (Alzao (USA)) **65** 117 [2003 f7g 10.1m² 9.9m 10.1m⁵ 10d 10.1g* 12g Nov 5] fair performer: unraced in 2001 and 2002: first success in handicap at Newcastle in October: reportedly finished lame final outing: stays 1¼m: acts on soft and good to firm going: inconsistent. *M. D. Hammond*

BOREAL (GER) 5 ch.h. Java Gold (USA) – Britannia (GER) (Tarim) [2003 126: 12g **–** Mar 29] stocky horse: high-class performer at best: won Deutsches Derby at Hamburg in 2001 and Coronation Cup at Epsom in 2002: well below best subsequently in Group 1 events, including when last in Dubai Sheema Classic at Nad Al Sheba only 5-y-o start: stayed 1½m well: acted on heavy going, seemingly not on good to firm: to stand at Gestut Ammerland, Germany, fee €6,000, Oct 1st. *P. Schiergen, Germany*

BOREAS 8 b.g. In The Wings 128 – Reamur 68 (Top Ville 129) [2003 119: 12d⁵ 16.4m⁵ **109** 16g⁴ 15.9m⁶ Aug 19] leggy gelding: good mover with a long stride: just useful form in 2003, beaten favourite in Henry II Stakes at Sandown behind Mr Dinos and Goodwood Cup behind Persian Punch second/third starts: sustained tendon injury final outing: probably needs further than 1½m nowadays, and stays 2¼m: acts on any going: best held up. *L. M. Cumani*

BORI MIROV (IRE) 5 ch.h. Carroll House 132 – Borj Kadija (FR) (Fabulous **80 ?** Dancer (USA) 124) [2003 p10g 8s³ 8g³ 9g* 8.5g 8g 10d* 8.5d⁶ 9.5g² 9.8s 9s⁶ 10.5s a11.5g⁶ Dec 29] first foal: dam German 7.5f winner: fair performer: well related at Lingfield on reappearance, only outing for H. Collingridge: won handicap at Baden-Baden in May and claimer at Deauville (claimed from Frau A. Bodenhagen €16,666) in August: stays 11f: acts on soft ground. *A. Fracas, France*

BORIS THE SPIDER 2 b.g. (May 4) Makbul 104 – Try Vickers (USA) 72 (Fuzz- **64 ?** buster (USA)) [2003 6m 6g 6m 6m Oct 1] 3,000Y: big, workmanlike gelding: half-brother to several winners, including 1½m winner Hurgill Dancer (by Rambo Dancer) and 5f/6f (latter including at 2 yrs) winner Nordico Dancer (by Nordico): dam, maiden, stayed 1¼m: modest maiden: possibly flattered when seeming to run best race penultimate start: should stay 7f: hung final outing. *M. D. Hammond*

BORN IN AMERICA (USA) 2 b.c. (Feb 10) Danzig (USA) – Flying Fairy 79 **86** (Bustino 136) [2003 6d⁴ 5m* 6f 5g⁶ 6m 6m Oct 3] $575,000Y: good-bodied colt: has a quick action: closely related to 2 winners, notably top-class 6f (at 2 yrs) to 1m winner Desert Prince (by Green Desert), and half-brother to 2 winners, including useful Irish 2002 5-y-o 5f/6f winner Ontario (by Storm Cat): dam, maiden who stayed 1½m, out of 1000 Guineas winner Fairy Footsteps: fairly useful performer: won maiden at Tipperary in July: acted as pacemaker when last 3 times in Group races after: should stay 6f: acts on good to firm ground: sent to Macau. *A. P. O'Brien, Ireland*

BORN SPECIAL 4 b.g. Bluebird (USA) 125 – Dixie Eyes Blazing (USA) 56 (Gone **–** West (USA)) [2003 –: f8.5g 7g May 5] modest maiden at 2 yrs: lightly raced and well held since. *P. C. Haslam*

BORODIN 2 gr.c. (Apr 12) Linamix (FR) 127 – Lady of Jakarta (USA) (Procida (USA) **58 p**
129) [2003 p8g Oct 15] fifth foal: dam, French 1m winner, half-sister to dam of Sulamani
and Dream Well: 12/1, very slowly away when ninth of 12 in maiden at Lingfield, getting
hang of things late on: should do better. *G. A. Butler*

BORODINSKY 2 b.c. (Feb 12) Magic Ring (IRE) 115 – Valldemosa 81 (Music Boy **–**
124) [2003 6m 5g 6d Nov 8] 20,000Y: heavy-topped colt: eighth foal: half-brother to 3
winners, including 5-y-o Ragamuffin and 1m winner Swoosh (by Absalom): dam, 5f
winner, including at 2 yrs: well held in maidens: reportedly finished lame final outing.
A. Berry

BOROUGHSET BOY (IRE) 3 b. or br.g. Woodborough (USA) 112 – Alpine Sunset **53**
(Auction Ring (USA) 123) [2003 61, a64: 6m 7m⁶ 6m⁶ 5g⁵ 7f Jul 16] good-bodied
gelding: modest maiden: stays 6f: acts on fibresand, raced only on good ground or firmer
on turf: has worn cheekpieces last 3 starts: sold 1,800 gns. *J. R. Weymes*

BORREGO (IRE) 3 b.c. Green Desert (USA) 127 – Pripet (USA) 86 (Alleged (USA) **85 p**
138) [2003 10.3m 7.5m 7.1m 10.3m⁴ 9.7m 8m² 8.1m* 8f* 7m² Sep 20] good-bodied colt:
brother to useful 1997 2-y-o 5.5f (Prix Robert Papin)/6f winner Greenlander and 2001
2-y-o 6f winner Yaselda, and half-brother to 1¾m winner Priluki (by Lycius): dam, 2m
winner, sister to 1000 Guineas/Oaks winner Midway Lady: fairly useful handicapper:
won at Haydock in August and Salisbury (edging right) in September: very good neck
second at Newbury (soon off bridle) final start: will prove best at 7f/1m: raced only on
going firmer than good: likely to improve further. *C. E. Brittain*

BORU BORU (IRE) 4 b.g. Bluebird (USA) 125 – Tudor Loom (Sallust 134) [2003 **–**
69: 7.1g 8m f8.5g 8.1m Jul 4] fair performer at best: well held in handicaps in 2003:
visored last time: sometimes slowly away. *P. D. Evans*

BORZOI MAESTRO 2 ch.g. (Feb 20) Wolfhound (USA) 126 – Ashkernazy (IRE) **81**
60 (Salt Dome (USA)) [2003 5g⁵ 5.2m⁶ 5g³ 5.1m f5g² f5g* 5m* f6f* 6.1m⁴ 5f⁴ 5.1g³ 5m
5m⁴ p6g 6m Oct 24] 2,600Y: small gelding: first foal: dam 5f winner, including at 2 yrs:
fairly useful performer: won seller at Wolverhampton and nurseries at Lingfield and
Wolverhampton in July: creditable efforts when in frame in nurseries after: will probably
prove best at 5f: acts on fibresand and firm going: usually wears cheekpieces: front
runner. *J. L. Spearing*

BOSCO (IRE) 2 br.c. (Mar 28) Petardia 113 – Classic Goddess (IRE) (Classic Secret **65**
(USA) 91) [2003 6g⁶ 8.3m 8f⁵ Oct 17] €16,000Y: brother to 2 winners abroad and
half-brother to 3 winners, including fairly useful 2000 2-y-o 6f winner Blue Goddess (by
Blues Traveller): dam unraced: best effort (fair form) when seventh in maiden at
Windsor: should stay 1¼m. *R. Hannon*

BOSHAM MILL 5 ch.g. Nashwan (USA) 135 – Mill On The Floss 117 (Mill Reef **96 §**
(USA) 141) [2003 115§: 16m Apr 19] tall, close-coupled gelding: fluent mover: smart
performer at best: mainly well held in pattern company in 2002 for G. Wragg: useful form
when mid-division in handicap at Kempton only run in 2003: stays 2¼m: acts on soft and
good to firm going: usually sweating/on edge: sometimes flashes tail/goes in snatches:
untrustworthy: fairly useful hurdler (now with J. O'Neill). *Ian Williams*

BOSPHORUS 4 b.g. Polish Precedent (USA) 131 – Ancara 109 (Dancing Brave **56**
(USA) 140) [2003 f12s³ f12g 10m 10.9m 12.6f⁴ f16.2f³ f14.8g² f16.2g³ 13.1f² f12s⁵ Sep
20] 3,000 2-y-o: strong gelding: third foal: half-brother to fairly useful 1¼m winners
Anamore (by Sanglamore) and Monolith (by Bigstone): dam French 1¼m/1½m winner:
modest maiden handicapper: may prove best at 1½m/1¾m: acts on fibresand, raced only
on going firmer than good on turf: visored last 6 starts. *D. G. Bridgwater*

BOSS MAN (IRE) 3 b.g. Entrepreneur 123 – Triste Oeil (USA) 103 (Raise A Cup **– §**
(USA)) [2003 –p: 10m⁶ 12.1m 17.2m 10m Aug 30] well-made gelding: well held all
starts: tried blinkered: one to treat with caution. *T. D. Easterby*

BOSTON LODGE 3 ch.g. Grand Lodge (USA) 125 – Ffestiniog (IRE) 96 (Efisio **98**
120) [2003 91: 9m³ 8m² 7.6m⁴ 9g 8m 8m² 8m³ 8m² 8m⁴ 8m* Oct 6] well-made, close-
coupled gelding: useful performer: mostly creditable efforts in 2003, winning claimer
at Pontefract (by 2½ lengths from Four Jays, claimed £60,000) in October: runner-up
earlier in handicaps at Ripon and Newmarket and minor event at Salisbury: will prove
best up to 9f: acts on polytrack and good to firm going, showed promise on heavy: game.
P. F. I. Cole

BOSWORTH DIXIE (IRE) 3 b.f. Turtle Island (IRE) 123 – Alice En Ballade (Tap **–**
On Wood 130) [2003 –: 6m⁶ Aug 13] lengthy filly: has a quick action: little sign of ability.
J. Gallagher

BOTANICAL (USA)   2 b.c. (Jan 25) Seeking The Gold (USA) – Satin Flower (USA)   **97**
115 (Shadeed (USA) 135) [2003 6m* 6f² 7m 6g⁴ Aug 25] well-made colt: good walker:
has a quick action: sixth living foal: brother to smart 1998 2-y-o 6f (Middle Park) winner
Lujain, closely related to fairly useful 2001 2-y-o 5f winner Deceptor (by Machiavellian),
and half-brother to smart 7f (at 2 yrs) winner Lilium (by Nashwan): dam, won
Jersey Stakes and second in US Grade 1 9f event, half-sister to US Grade 1 1¼m winner
Martial Law: useful performer: won maiden at York in May by ½ length from Pearl of
Love: creditable efforts in Coventry Stakes at Royal Ascot (8 lengths second to Three
Valleys) and listed race at Ripon (visored when last of 4 to Auditorium): reportedly had
breathing problem penultimate start: should stay 7f: joined Saeed bin Suroor. *D. R. Loder*

BOTTOM DRAWER   3 b.g. My Best Valentine 122 – Little Egret 74 (Carwhite 127)   **–**
[2003 9m f12s Sep 26] 2,000Y: half-brother to untrustworthy 2000 2-y-o 6f winner
Captain Gibson (by Beveled): dam Italian 1¼m/11f winner: well beaten in maidens.
D. J. S. ffrench Davis

BOUDICA (IRE)   4 b.f. Alhaarth (IRE) 126 – Supportive (IRE) (Nashamaa 113) [2003   **–**
–: f6g Jan 3] lengthy filly: well held all starts. *D. W. P. Arbuthnot*

BOULE D'OR (IRE)   2 b.c. (Mar 22) Croco Rouge (IRE) 126 – Saffron Crocus 83   **84**
(Shareef Dancer (USA) 135) [2003 7g* 7g³ 7.9f 8m Oct 16] €62,000Y, 10,000 2-y-o: tall,
quite good-topped colt: good walker: closely related to useful Irish 6.5f (at 2 yrs) to 1¼m
winner Saffron Dancer (by Bin Ajwaad) and half-brother to 3 winners, including useful
1½m to 2m winner Knockholt (by Be My Chief): dam Irish 1½m/13f winner: fairly useful
performer: won maiden at Leicester in August: raced freely when below form in nurseries
last 2 starts: bred to be suited by 1¼m+. *R. Ingram*

BOULTON   3 b.c. Syrtos 106 – Penny Dip 86 (Cadeaux Genereux 131) [2003 7m 10.2g   **–**
8.1g Sep 11] 1,600F: fourth foal: dam 6f winner: well beaten in sellers. *B. N. Doran*

BOUMAHOU (IRE)   3 b.c. Desert Story (IRE) 115 – Kilbride Lass (IRE) (Lahib   **66**
(USA) 129) [2003 9m⁶ 12g⁴ p13g⁴ 10.3m Oct 24] IR 12,500F: sturdy colt: second foal:
half-brother to 4-y-o Consensus: dam unraced half-sister to 3-y-o Phoenix Reach out of
half-sister to Arc winner Carroll House: reportedly had a bone infection after injuring a
leg as a foal: modest maiden: barely stays 13f. *A. P. Jarvis*

BOUNCER   2 ch.g. (Mar 31) Night Shift (USA) – Blugem (FR) (Bluebird (USA) 125)   **–**
[2003 5.1m⁶ 6.1g 6m⁶ p8g Nov 22] 12,000Y: first foal: dam unraced: no form, including
in seller: left R. Hannon after third start. *W. R. Muir*

BOUNCING BOWDLER   5 b.g. Mujadil (USA) 119 – Prima Volta 80 (Primo   **90**
Dominie 121) [2003 109: a7f a8f⁶ a8f 7m⁵ 7.1f 7g 8f³ 7.2g⁴ 9.2g² 8f 5m Sep 21] rather
leggy, quite good-topped gelding: has a quick action: fairly useful performer nowadays:
claimed from M. Johnston £20,500 after ninth outing: stays 1m: acts on firm and soft
going: blinkered last 6 outings: usually races up with pace: inconsistent. *S. J. Mahon,
Ireland*

BOUND   5 b.g. Kris 135 – Tender Moment (IRE) 78 (Caerleon (USA) 132) [2003 12m   **–**
Apr 16] big, workmanlike gelding: fairly useful on all-weather, fair on turf at 2 yrs:
tongue tied, reportedly choked only 3-y-o start, final outing for B. Hills: fair handicap
hurdler nowadays, well held on Flat return: should stay at least 1¼m: acts on fibresand
and soft going, probably on good to firm. *Mrs L. Wadham*

BOUNDLESS PROSPECT (USA)   4 b.g. Boundary (USA) 117 – Cape (USA) (Mr   **82**
Prospector (USA)) [2003 95: 8.1g 8g 8m⁵ 8f⁵ 8.5m 9g Aug 2] good-bodied gelding: fairly
useful handicapper: just respectable efforts at best in 2003: stays 7.6f: acts on firm and
good to soft going: visored final start: races freely. *J. W. Hills*

BOURBONNAIS (IRE)   3 b.c. Singspiel (IRE) 133 – Rose Bourbon (USA) (Wood-   **107**
man (USA) 126) [2003 104p: a8f³ a10f³ 8g May 11] angular, good-bodied colt: useful
performer: ran well when 1¾ lengths third to Victory Moon in UAE 2000 Guineas at Nad
Al Sheba on reappearance: just respectable efforts since in UAE Derby then (fifth to same
rival) and Poule d'Essai des Poulains at Longchamp (eighth to Clodovil): probably stays
1¼m: acts on dirt, yet to race on extremes of going on turf: has had tongue tied: left
Godolphin, and sent to USA. *Saeed bin Suroor*

BOURGAINVILLE   5 b.g. Pivotal 124 – Petonica (IRE) 77 (Petoski 135) [2003 110:   **114**
p10g⁴ 8g⁵ 10m³ 10g² 12g⁴ 10m⁵ 10f⁵ 10.4f 10g² 8.9m⁶ Sep 3] tall, close-coupled gelding:
usually looks well: has a long, rather round stride: smart performer: best efforts when
neck second in Gordon Richards Stakes at Sandown (won by Indian Creek) and Winter
Hill Stakes at Windsor (won by Leporello): stays 1¼m: yet to race on heavy going, acts
on any other turf and polytrack: sometimes races freely. *A. M. Balding*

BOURGEOIS 6 ch.g. Sanglamore (USA) 126 – Bourbon Girl 116 (Ile de Bourbon **107**
(USA) 133) [2003 103: 14f* 18.7m⁵ 12.1d² 16.1g 13.9f³ 13.9m 13.4m³ 14.6g⁵ 13d Sep
29] strong, deep-girthed gelding: useful handicapper: won at Haydock in April: ran well
in Chester Cup (fifth to Hugs Dancer) and listed event at Hamilton (second to Compton
Bolter) next 2 starts: mostly respectable efforts after: effective at 1½m to easy 19f: acts
on firm and good to soft going: tried blinkered, visored sixth/seventh starts: probably best
held up. *T. D. Easterby*

BOWING 3 b.g. Desert Prince (IRE) 130 – Introducing 78 (Mtoto 134) [2003 82p: 9g³ **89 §**
11g² 12m 12g⁴ 10m² 10m³ Aug 14] leggy, lengthy gelding: fairly useful maiden: should
stay 1½m: acts on firm and soft ground: wore cheekpieces (looked none too keen)
final outing: free to post third start: one to be wary of: sold 20,000 gns, and gelded.
J. H. M. Gosden

BOWLEGS BILLY 3 gr.g. Raphane (USA) 102 – Swallow Bay 54 (Penmarric (USA) **61**
111) [2003 5d² 5m⁵ f7g 6.1f 5g Oct 13] leggy gelding: half-brother to several winners,
including 2000 2-y-o 6f/7f winner Chaweng Beach (by Chaddleworth): dam, 2-y-o 6f
winner, barely stayed 1¼m: modest maiden: reportedly suffered sore shins second start
and no form after: may prove best at 5f: acts on good to firm and good to soft going:
hung left throughout final outing. *J. Balding*

BOWLING ALONG 2 b.f. (Mar 31) The West (USA) 107 – Bystrouska (Gorytus **59**
(USA) 132) [2003 5f 6d 6f* 6f⁴ 5g⁴ 5m³ 7d² 6.1f⁵ 7m³ 6m 6d Nov 4] 1,000Y: leggy,
rather unfurnished filly: fourth foal: half-sister to fairly useful 6f (including at 2 yrs)/7f
winner Charlie Sillett (by Handsome Sailor) and winner in Belgium by Green Ruby: dam
ran once: modest performer: won seller at Catterick in May: mostly creditable efforts,
including in nurseries, after: stays easy 7f: acts on firm and good to soft ground: visored
(ran to form) eighth outing: sometimes slowly away/carries head awkwardly: usually
races prominently. *M. E. Sowersby*

BOWMAN (USA) 4 b.c. Irish River (FR) 131 – Cherokee Rose (IRE) 122 (Dancing **110**
Brave (USA) 140) [2003 117: 8m* 8m Aug 14] quite good-topped colt: smart performer:
left A. Fabre after final 3-y-o outing: off 9 months, won listed race at Goodwood in June
by head from Passing Glance: ran poorly in similar event at Salisbury only subsequent
start: stays 1m: raced only on good going or firmer after debut: held up, and has taken
good hold: left Godolphin. *Saeed bin Suroor*

BOW RIVER GOLD 3 b.f. Rainbow Quest (USA) 134 – Lady Blackfoot 108 (Prince **–**
Tenderfoot (USA) 126) [2003 8.1m 8m⁴ 6m Sep 6] 60,000Y: half-sister to numerous
winners, including high-class US performer up to 1¼m Fanmore and very smart
1m/9f performer in France/US Labeeb (both by Lear Fan), and to smart 1m/9f winner
Alrassaam (by Zafonic): dam Irish sprinter: well held in maidens, losing all chance by
swerving left as stall opened final outing: sold 48,000 gns. *J. G. Given*

BOW SPRIT 3 ch.g. Fleetwood (IRE) 107 – Longwood Lady 56 (Rudimentary (USA) **54**
118) [2003 p8g⁶ p10g 8g³ 6.1m 7.9g May 9] workmanlike gelding: first foal: dam, ran 4
times at 3 yrs, out of half-sister to smart dam of high-class miler Sonic Lady: best effort
(modest form) on third outing. *M. R. Channon*

BOWSTRING (IRE) 2 b.f. (May 25) Sadler's Wells (USA) 132 – Cantanta 74 (Top **– p**
Ville 129) [2003 8.1d Sep 27] lengthy, sturdy filly: closely related to Tailfeather (stayed
15f, by In The Wings) and 1999 2-y-o 1m winner Welcome (by Be My Guest), and
half-sister to 1¼m/1½m winner Cantilever (by Sanglamore), all useful in France: dam,
2m winner, sister to Irish Oaks winner Princess Pati and half-sister to high-class
middle-distance performer Seymour Hicks: 8/1, better for race and green, well held in
maiden at Haydock, not given hard time: should be suited by 1½m+: likely to do better.
J. H. M. Gosden

BOXGROVE (FR) 2 gr.g. (Apr 15) Trempolino (USA) 135 – Little Emily 48 (Zafonic **75**
(USA) 130) [2003 p8g³ p8g⁶ p8g* Dec 20] second foal: half-brother to French 2002 2-y-o
1m winner Fireworks (by Kendor): dam lightly-raced daughter of Norfolk Stakes winner
Petillante: fair form: won minor event at Lingfield by short head from Freak Occurence:
will stay at least 1¼m. *C. E. Brittain*

BRADLEY MY BOY (IRE) 7 ch.g. Treasure Hunter 78 – Clonaslee Baby (Konigs- **55**
see) [2003 65: 13.8f 16m 12.1m³ 12.1g⁵ 11.9m⁴ 16m 11.9m Sep 4] bumper winner for
M. Pipe in 2001: modest performer on Flat: best around 1½m: acts on good to firm
ground. *Mrs A. M. Naughton*

BRADY BOYS (USA) 6 b.g. Cozzene (USA) – Elvia (USA) (Roberto (USA) 131) **47**
[2003 54: f12g³ f12s⁶ Jul 11] strong, lengthy gelding: poor maiden: should stay 1¾m:

acts on fibresand, form on turf only on heavy/soft going: tried blinkered/visored. *J. G. M. O'Shea*

BRAIN BOX (IRE) 3 ch.g. Entrepreneur 123 – Alcadia (IRE) 91 (Thatching 131) **60** [2003 67: 11.9m 11m 10m Jun 9] well-made gelding: modest maiden handicapper: should stay 1¼m: acts on firm going. *T. D. Easterby*

BRAIN TEASER 3 b.f. Mind Games 121 – Salacious (Sallust 134) [2003 –: 6m⁵ 7g – 6g f6s 8f Jun 25] smallish filly: little form: blinkered last 2 starts. *B. J. Meehan*

BRAMANTINO (IRE) 3 b.g. Perugino (USA) 84 – Headrest (Habitat 134) [2003 – 61: 7.1m 8.2m 10m May 9] strong, lengthy gelding: has scope: modest maiden at 2 yrs: well held in 2003: tried blinkered. *R. A. Fahey*

BRAMLEY DANCER 4 b.g. Suave Dancer (USA) 136 – Hailgaf 61 (Raja Baba – (USA)) [2003 52: 10m 10.1m 16.4m Aug 13] modest maiden handicapper: soundly beaten in 2003: tried visored/blinkered/tongue tied. *Miss B. Sanders*

BRANDY COVE 6 b.g. Lugana Beach 116 – Tender Moment (IRE) 78 (Caerleon – (USA) 132) [2003 –, a65: f8g³ f8g* f8g³ f8s² f8g* 8m f8g⁴ f8g⁵ f8s² f8s³ Dec 27] tall **a74** gelding: fair performer: won handicap at Southwell (idled) in January and minor event there in April: best efforts at 1m: acts on fibresand, little recent form on turf: hung left/ flashed tail sixth outing: usually waited with. *B. Smart*

BRANDYWINE BAY (IRE) 3 b.f. Mujadil (USA) 119 – Ned's Contessa (IRE) 48 **49** (Persian Heights 129) [2003 –: f7g³ f7g f8.5g f7g f6s⁵ f5g 5.5f⁵ 6m⁴ 6m³ 7f⁵ 8f³ 8m⁵ 8m f7g⁴ Nov 10] poor maiden handicapper: left W. Muir after second outing, D. ffrench Davis after sixth: stays 1m: raced only on fibresand/good going or firmer on turf: tried blinkered/tongue tied, wears cheekpieces nowadays: sometimes slowly away. *A. P. Jones*

BRANSTON MELODY 2 b.f. (Mar 28) Sri Pekan (USA) 117 – Food of Love 109 **56 d** (Music Boy 124) [2003 5.1m 5m² f5s⁶ 5.1m 5m³ 5m⁵ 7m Aug 15] 14,000Y: strong, close-coupled filly: sixth living foal: half-sister to 3 fairly useful winners, including 5f winner (including at 2 yrs) Price of Passion (by Dolphin Street) and 4-y-o Tough Love: dam 5f winner, including at 2 yrs: modest maiden: second at Musselburgh: deteriorated after: possibly best at 5f: tends to wander: ungenuine. *J. G. Given*

BRANSTON NELL 4 b.f. Classic Cliche (IRE) 128 – Indefinite Article (IRE) (Indian **63 d** Ridge 123) [2003 63: f16.2g² f16s 15.8m* 17.1m 10.9m Sep 8] smallish filly: modest performer: below form after reappearance, though still won seller at Catterick in August: stays easy 2m: acts on firm going and fibresand: visored final start. *I. A. Wood*

BRANSTON TIGER 4 b.c. Mark of Esteem (IRE) 137 – Tuxford Hideaway 102 **85** (Cawston's Clown 113) [2003 80: f7g⁴ 6m⁶ 6d* 6g 5d⁵ 6m f6s⁴ Oct 21] rangy colt: fairly useful performer: won handicap at Thirsk in May: respectable efforts at best: effective at 5f to 7f: acts on all-weather, firm and soft going: joined G. A. Swinbank. *J. G. Given*

BRANTWOOD (IRE) 3 b.c. Lake Coniston (IRE) 131 – Angelic Sounds (IRE) (The **89 d** Noble Player (USA) 126) [2003 87: 5f 7.6m⁵ 6d⁶ 6v³ 6f 6m⁵ 5d 8.2d 8.1m⁵ 6.1g f6g 5m Oct 18] angular, quite good-topped colt: fairly useful handicapper: well below form after sixth start: barely stays 7.6f: acts on heavy and good to firm going: blinkered (bolted before start) once. *B. A. McMahon*

BRAVE BURT (IRE) 6 ch.g. Pips Pride 117 – Friendly Song 48 (Song 132) [2003 **91** 93: 5g 5m⁴ 5v 5m 5f 5m* 5d³ Oct 4] good-topped gelding: fairly useful handicapper: won at Ayr in September: good third at Epsom final start: best at 5f: acts on firm and good to soft going: usually leads: game. *D. Nicholls*

BRAVE CALL (USA) 3 ch.c. Theatrical 128 – Darya (USA) (Gulch (USA)) [2003 **95** 82p: 8m⁴ 8m 10m³ 10m* Oct 22] strong colt: useful performer: reportedly returned home with a viral problem after second start and subsequently off 3½ months: good efforts both outings after, winning handicap at Nottingham in October by ¾ length from Mister Arjay: stays 1¼m: acts on soft going, good to firm and polytrack: started slowly final outing: sold 110,000 gns, sent to USA. *J. W. Hills*

BRAVE CHIEF 2 ch.c. (Mar 3) Komaite (USA) – Victoria Sioux 54 (Ron's Victory **55** (USA) [2003 6m f6g f5s² Dec 27] strong, lengthy colt: third foal: half-brother to 4-y-o Bint Makbul: dam sprint maiden: first form (modest) when second to Smart Starprincess in seller at Southwell: should stay 6f. *J. A. Pickering*

BRAVE DANE (IRE) 5 b.g. Danehill (USA) 126 – Nuriva (USA) 100 (Woodman **62** (USA) 126) [2003 62: 10.9m⁵ 11.5m³ 11.7m⁵ 10m 8d Nov 7] lengthy, angular gelding: just modest performer nowadays: left J. Spearing after fourth start: stays 11.7f: acts on heavy and good to firm ground: tried blinkered: usually held up. *A. W. Carroll*

BRAVE DOMINIE 3 b.f. Primo Dominie 121 – Red Embers 64 (Saddlers' Hall (IRE) **36** 126) [2003 46: p10g⁶ f7s⁴ f6g p7g p7g 5.1f⁶ f6g 10m 8g May 28] poor maiden: left I. Wood after seventh start: should stay 1m: acts on all-weather, well held on turf: tried visored. *C. R. Dore*

BRAVE KNIGHT 6 b.g. Presidium 124 – Agnes Jane (Sweet Monday 122) [2003 48: – 12.1m 12m 12m⁶ 10m⁶ Sep 18] big, lengthy gelding: little form in 2003: blinkered final start: has looked temperamental. *N. Bycroft*

BRAVE PROTECTOR 3 ch.g. Hector Protector (USA) 124 – Brave Revival 93 – (Dancing Brave (USA) 140) [2003 11.6m p8g Oct 8] 8,000F, 12,000Y, 700 3-y-o: fourth foal: half-brother to fairly useful 2000 2-y-o 6f winner Bravado (by Zafonic) and 1999 2-y-o 7f winner Vigour (by Lion Cavern): dam, 1m winner (including at 2 yrs) who stayed 1¼m, half-sister to very smart sprinter Pivotal: tailed off in claimer/seller: tried in cheekpieces. *A. P. Jones*

BRAVO DANCER 3 ch.f. Acatenango (GER) 127 – Nijoodh (Selkirk (USA) 129) **87** [2003 83: 10.2m³ 8g* 8m 8m² 8m⁶ 8.9f 10.3m* 14.1s p10g² Nov 12] rangy, rather unfurnished filly: fairly useful performer: won maiden at Newcastle in June and handicap at Doncaster in October: should stay 1½m: acts on polytrack, firm and good to soft ground: edgy sort: mulish to post/ran badly third start. *M. R. Channon*

BRAVO MAESTRO (USA) 2 b.c. (Feb 19) Stravinsky (USA) 133 – Amaranthus **95 p** (USA) (Kingmambo (USA) 125) [2003 6m p7g* p7g* Nov 12] $260,000F, 65,000Y: tall, leggy colt: second foal: dam unraced half-sister to smart performer up to 1½m Falak out of sister to Prix du Cadran winner Chief Contender: useful form: won maiden at Lingfield (gambled on, by 6 lengths from Star of Light) in October and nursery there (beat Pregnant Pause by 2½ lengths) in November, quickening well both times: stays 7f: should progress further. *D. W. P. Arbuthnot*

BRAVURA 5 ch.g. Never So Bold 135 – Sylvan Song (Song 132) [2003 –, a69: p10g **46** p10g p10g³ p8g³ p10g* f8g p8g² p10g³ 10m⁵ Jul 7] fair handicapper on all-weather, poor **a70** on turf: won at Lingfield (second consecutive win in race) in February: best at 1m/1¼m: acts on polytrack and good to firm ground, little form on fibresand: effective blinkered or not. *G. L. Moore*

BRAZILIAN TERRACE 3 ch.f. Zilzal (USA) 137 – Elaine's Honor (USA) (Chief's **84** Crown (USA)) [2003 77: 8m⁶ 7m 8g* 8g⁵ 8.2m² 8.1f 8m² 8m⁵ 8m³ 8.3g⁶ 8m* 8g⁵ 9g Oct 25] sparely-made filly: fairly useful handicapper: won at Yarmouth in May and Thirsk in September: better at 1m than shorter (raced too freely at 9f): acts on good to firm and good to soft ground: sometimes slowly away. *M. L. W. Bell*

BREAD OF HEAVEN 2 b.f. (Jan 19) Machiavellian (USA) 123 – Khubza 86 (Green **79 p** Desert (USA) 127) [2003 6g³ 6m² 6m² 6m* Oct 17] strong, heavy-topped filly: fifth foal: half-sister to 6f (at 2 yrs) to smart 8.5f winner Trans Island, useful 1999 2-y-o 7f winner Nothing Daunted and 4-y-o Welsh Diva (all by Selkirk): dam, 7f winner, half-sister to smart performers Barrow Creek (at 6f to 1m in Germany) and Last Resort (7f): fair form: won maiden at Redcar comfortably by ¾ length from Alexander Charlote: will stay 7f, probably 1m: went right leaving stall/flashed tail third start: type to train on as a 3-y-o. *Mrs A. J. Perrett*

BREATHING SUN (IRE) 2 b.c. (Feb 11) Bahhare (USA) 122 – Zapata (IRE) 77 **79** (Thatching 131) [2003 p5g 6m³ 7m 8m* 8d* Sep 11] IR 11,000F, 12,500Y: strong colt: third foal: half-brother to fairly useful Irish 2002 2-y-o 7f winner Imazulutoo (by Marju) and winner in Italy by Spectrum: dam, Irish maiden, stayed 7f: fair performer: won nurseries at Ripon in August and Doncaster (tongue tied, beat Overdrawn by ¾ length) in September, coming from off pace: should stay 1¼m: acts on good to firm and good to soft ground: often slowly away. *W. J. Musson*

BREATHTAKING VIEW (USA) 7 b.g. Country Pine (USA) – Lituya Bay (USA) – (Empery (USA) 128) [2003 –: p12g Jan 30] formerly smart in UAE: well held in 3 Flat starts in Britain: stays 1½m: acts on firm going and dirt: tried visored: modest hurdler. *G. Prodromou*

BRECONGILL LAD 11 b.g. Clantime 101 – Chikala 81 (Pitskelly 122) [2003 64: **68** 6m 5m 5.9f 6.1m 6f* 5m 6m² 5m* 5m 5f³ 7m² 6f 6g⁴ 6.1f Sep 30] tall, good-topped gelding: fair performer nowadays: left Mrs M. Reveley and returned to former trainer after third outing: won handicaps at Thirsk (ladies selling event, first success for nearly 3 years) and Pontefract in August: effective at 5f to 7f: acts on firm and soft going: tried blinkered/visored earlier in career: has raced freely/hung/carried head high/idled. *D. Nicholls*

153

BREEZER 3 b.g. Forzando 122 – Lady Lacey 66 (Kampala 120) [2003 –: 8g⁵ 8.1d⁵ 9g **65**
8d Nov 7] fair maiden, lightly raced: stays 9f: raced only on good/good to soft ground:
unseated rider and ran loose to post on debut. *G. B. Balding*

BREEZIT (USA) 2 b.f. (Mar 4) Stravinsky (USA) 133 – Sharka 97 (Shareef Dancer **61**
(USA) 135) [2003 5m⁴ 5.1m⁴ 5.1g 7.1m⁶ 6m* 6.1m 8m⁶ 7m 5f³ 5g 6m Oct 6] €55,000Y:
angular filly: has a quick action: eighth foal: half-sister to French 1998 2-y-o 1m winner
Jaskini (by Lion Cavern) and Irish 1m winner Sharavati (by Nashwan), both fairly useful:
dam 1m (at 2 yrs) and 8.5f winner: modest performer: won claimer at Brighton (left
M. Channon) in July: just 2 respectable efforts in nurseries after: probably stays easy 1m:
acts on firm going: wore cheekpieces sixth start, blinkers eighth to tenth. *S. R. Bowring*

BRESSBEE (USA) 5 ch.g. Twining (USA) 120 – Bressay (USA) (Nureyev (USA) **60**
131) [2003 65, a81: f9.4g⁴ f9.4s* a10g* 10.2f f8.5s 10.4m 8.2d³ f8.5g f9.4g Nov 29] **a84**
close-coupled gelding: fairly useful handicapper on all-weather, modest on turf: won at
Wolverhampton in January and Grosser Preis von St Moritz (on snow, reportedly suffered
quarter-crack) in February: below form after: stays 1¼m: acts on fibresand and any turf
going: visored/blinkered: often races up with pace: sold £10,500. *J. W. Unett*

BRETTON 2 b.g. (Apr 15) Polar Prince (IRE) 117 – Understudy 60 (In The Wings **48**
128) [2003 5.9d 7g⁶ 8.1f⁵ 10f f9.4g f7g⁵ f9.4g⁴ f8.5s⁴ Dec 31] 9,500Y: small, close-
coupled gelding: third foal: half-brother to 4-y-o Castle Ring: dam, placed at 1¼m, half-
sister to smart performer up to 1½m Pipsted: poor maiden: should stay at least 1m: acts
on fibresand: wore cheekpieces/blinkers last 4 starts. *R. Hollinshead*

BREUDDWYD LYN 5 br.g. Awesome 73 – Royal Resort 57 (King of Spain 121) **42**
[2003 42: f9.4g p12g⁴ f12s Feb 28] poor maiden: stays 1½m: raced only on all-weather.
D. Burchell

BREVITY 8 b.g. Tenby 125 – Rive (USA) (Riverman (USA) 131) [2003 106: f6s 6g **85 d**
6m 6m⁵ 6d 6m 6m 6m 5.7f 8f⁵ 6m⁶ 6m 5.3f⁶ 5.7f 6f⁴ 8f 7.1g Sep 11] big, strong gelding:
useful at best: regressed in 2003: effective at stiff 5f to easy 7f: acts on fibresand, best turf
efforts on good going or firmer: sometimes wears headgear/carries head awkwardly: one
to treat with caution: sold 3,600 gns. *J. M. Bradley*

BRIAN BORU 3 b.c. Sadler's Wells (USA) 132 – Eva Luna (USA) 114 (Alleged **124**
(USA) 138) [2003 117p: 10g³ 12m 12m⁴ 11.9m² 14.6g* 12d³ Oct 19]
Quick learners in sport tend to be labelled 'naturals', but, even for the more
gifted jockeys, it is only experience that enables them to reach their full potential.
Tactically, in particular, young jockeys tend to start with a blank sheet of paper.
Jamie Spencer is widely seen as having more potential than most young riders.
Poised and outwardly confident, he can be inclined to 'exhibitionism' in a finish
but, unlike many riders who tend not to digress much from a 'stock' ride once they
find one that brings a steady flow of winners, Spencer has already shown a willing-
ness to spread his wings tactically, sometimes bringing public criticism. His on-off
association with Ballydoyle in the last two seasons, when he was also courted by
the Godolphin operation, led to prolonged speculation about his future, and that
of Ballydoyle's stable-jockey Michael Kinane. Spencer's first big chance to prove
himself for Ballydoyle in a British classic ended in defeat on red-hot favourite
Hawk Wing in the Two Thousand Guineas in 2002. Shunned for a period by the
yard, Spencer was given the chance to redeem himself on favourite Brian Boru in
the St Leger in 2003.
Brian Boru became clear favourite for the Seabiscuit St Leger once doubts
emerged over the participation of his stable-companion Powerscourt. With Hawk
Flyer fatally injured on the gallops in the week of the race and Salsalino lame overnight, eleven took on Brian Boru. Heading his market rivals at 13/2 was Westmoreland Road, winner of three of his four starts as a three-year-old. The filly Moments
of Joy, unbeaten in two starts, including a listed event at Goodwood, came next at
7/1. Phoenix Reach and High Accolade, first and second in the Gordon Stakes,
were both at 8/1, with improving Maharib at 9/1 and Oaks third Summitville at
16/1. Brian Boru had disputed ante-post favouritism with Powerscourt after the pair
dominated the finish of one of the traditional St Leger trials, the Great Voltigeur at
York, where he'd gone down by a neck to his stable-companion. Brian Boru reportedly thrived in his work afterwards and, with Powerscourt running a close third to
Vinnie Roe in the Irish St Leger at the Curragh minutes before the off at Doncaster,
Brian Boru was backed down to 5/4. Spencer settled Brian Boru in rear as outsider

Gold Medallist made the running. Straightening for home as the field began to bunch, Spencer kept Brian Boru wide, and was the last rider still sitting confidently when he became pocketed briefly as High Accolade made his move on his outside. Under two furlongs out, Spencer produced Brian Boru and he and High Accolade drew upsides Maharib, the race still in the balance. Spencer, using his whip in his left hand as Brian Boru hung towards High Accolade as the pair drew away, drove Brian Boru out to win by a length and a quarter. Phoenix Reach, who had been short of room on the inside, finished a length and a half further back in third, Maharib fourth and Moments of Joy fifth, the rest well beaten off. An emotional Spencer reacted to his victory by standing up in his irons and blowing a kiss to the sky in memory of his long-standing friend Kieran Kelly, who had died as the result of a fall over jumps the previous month. Spencer's St Leger ride drew widespread praise, chiefly for the way he had held his nerve. One interesting postscript to the race was that Spencer, having only his second St Leger mount, had discussed the pace of the race during the contest with the veteran Pat Eddery, who was having his last. 'I said to Pat we were going too quick,' said Spencer. 'Too fast son,' Eddery had reportedly replied. Sections of the media also interpreted the St Leger as being run at a furious gallop, but terms applied to pace tend to be superficial and rather too subjective. Races are often labelled as being strongly run when the gallop has, in fact, taken some while to pick up. The mere sight of a field soon being strung out, as it was in the Leger, doesn't automatically mean the gallop is strong throughout, which it needs to be if the word strong is to be applied reasonably. It is our experience that races run at a genuinely strong gallop are few and far between. Tactically, the style of British racing nowadays is very much a game of cat and mouse. Few riders' 'stock' approach is to make the running, and this often leads to races turning into a test of finishing speed. Not uncommonly, the first three in the Leger were all horses equally effective at a mile and a half.

Seabiscuit St Leger Stakes, Doncaster—the favourite Brian Boru has finally taken the measure of High Accolade (right) as Phoenix Reach (stars on sleeves) finds his stride after being short of room; Maharib (striped cap) is fourth and Moments of Joy (second left) fifth

A jockey, of course, doesn't always decide tactics. Trainers and owners, agents and mentors often have an influence. From what was said in public, Aidan O'Brien's influence on Spencer's approach to the race at Doncaster seemed minimal, perhaps surprisingly so, and the timing of the discussion between them about tactics might have raised a few eyebrows too. 'Jamie told me as we were walking out that he was going to drop him out,' O'Brien told the media. Either way, Spencer rewarded O'Brien's faith, and it was announced late in the season that he would replace Kinane as stable jockey at Ballydoyle, with Kinane moving to John Oxx and Johnny Murtagh leaving Oxx to ride freelance. Inevitably, the move drew further comparison between Spencer and Lester Piggott, a Ballydoyle jockey in the days of Vincent O'Brien. Like Piggott, Spencer was born into a racing family—his late father George trained the 1963 Champion Hurdle winner—and he was set on being a jockey from an early age. He rode work for trainer Liam Browne in Ireland in his school holidays at thirteen, partnered his first winner at fifteen and was still only seventeen when winning the Irish One Thousand Guineas on Tarascon in 1998, being champion apprentice there the following season. Like Piggott, Spencer has also had brushes with authority and also turned his hand briefly to National Hunt racing, winning bances over hurdles and being successful in the bumper at the Cheltenham Festival in 2002. Spencer rode a hundred winners on the Flat for the first time in 2001 after joining Luca Cumani. He passed the landmark again in 2003, but, at twenty-three, is a lot younger and is less experienced in major races than Piggott had been when he first linked up with Ballydoyle, by which time he had ridden eight English classic winners, including three in the Derby.

Spencer's first success in a British classic after disappointments on Hawk Wing and Gossamer, on whom he won the Irish One Thousand Guineas after she had also been a beaten favourite at Newmarket, naturally brought an upsurge in confidence. He rode thirty winners in Britain and Ireland subsequently before leaving for Hong Kong in November (from where he returned early to concentrate on his new job at Ballydoyle), deploying a wide range of tactics. Spencer's tactics never varied on the occasions he rode Brian Boru, arguably to some cost. Brian Boru was no match for Alamshar and Dalakhani when the pair first teamed up in the Irish Derby at the Curragh, starting at 12/1 and finishing a never-dangerous fourth, beaten two and a half lengths by stable-companion Roosevelt for third, six and a half lengths in all. At York next time, Brian Boru was set a great deal to do in the Great Voltigeur, making up five or six lengths in a short space of time in the straight before going down narrowly in a race run at only a fair gallop. Brian Boru was again asked to come from well behind when dropped back to a mile and a half after the St Leger in the Canadian International at Woodbine. Switched wide in the shortish straight, Brian Boru couldn't confirm Doncaster placings with Phoenix Reach, going down by three quarters of a length and a head in third, looking to hang fire a little as he came to challenge.

Spencer teamed up with Brian Boru only after the Derby. Winner of the Racing Post Trophy on his final start at two, when far from the finished article physically, Brian Boru was as short as 3/1 with one major bookmaker for Epsom in the early spring. He was left out of the Ballysax Stakes at Leopardstown in April in error, and made his reappearance instead the following month in the Derrinstown Stud Derby Trial, but he could finish only third to Alamshar, conceding 5 lb all round. The performance saw his Derby odds lengthened, but Brian Boru was supported again for Epsom after his trainer declared himself far from despondent afterwards. O'Brien's remarks on the race, made at a stable visit by a handful of journalists after Leopardstown, were taken by some as suggesting Brian Boru hadn't run on his merits and led to the authorities looking again. O'Brien was rightly exonerated by the Turf Club. In a nutshell, Brian Boru simply didn't look quick enough at Leopardstown, where he was given several sharp reminders, and he didn't impress as a likely winner at Epsom under anything but testing conditions. Brian Boru went off third favourite for the Derby at 9/2, but, perfectly positioned by Kinane, looked in trouble rounding Tattenham Corner and was eased right up in the straight, finishing sixteenth. He was fitted with a tongue strap subsequently.

Brian Boru's efforts after Epsom suggest he would have been good enough to reach a place in what turned out to be an ordinary Derby, had he been at his best on the day. Like most recent St Leger winners, Brian Boru isn't short of speed for a mile and a half and, though he will need to improve to be up to winning the very best races at four, physically he is the type to develop. It is conceivable that Brian Boru may be given a crack at the Gold Cup, as was the stable's Black Sam Bellamy in 2003, but he is unlikely to be at his best over such a very long distance in a well-run race.

Brian Boru (b.c. 2000)	Sadler's Wells (USA) (b 1981)	Northern Dancer (b 1961)	Nearctic Natalma
		Fairy Bridge (b 1975)	Bold Reason Special
	Eva Luna (USA) (b 1992)	Alleged (b 1974)	Hoist The Flag Princess Pout
		Media Luna (b 1981)	Star Appeal Sounion

Brian Boru is a product of a recently-instituted foal-sharing scheme between Coolmore and Khalid Abdulla's Juddmonte Farms, involving Sadler's Wells, a collaboration of empires which also produced Powerscourt. Brian Boru's dam Eva Luna was bred by Juddmonte Farms and won the Park Hill at Doncaster in her first season to race as a four-year-old when trained by Henry Cecil. Her first foal, the Rainbow Quest filly Moon Search, made into a smart performer for Andre Fabre in 2003, winning a listed race over a mile and a quarter at Longchamp in May and the Prix de Royallieu over a mile and a half at Longchamp in October, though she had fortune on her side in the latter, the jockey on runner-up Whortleberry easing off prematurely. Eva Luna's dam Media Luna was beaten only a neck in the Oaks at 66/1 before becoming unpredictable, and she was a half-sister to Suni,

Mrs John Magnier's "Brian Boru"

another placed in the Oaks. Apart from Brian Boru's dam, Media Luna has also produced the Ebor runner-up Media Star and the graded-stakes placed Rougeur, dam of the Kentucky Oaks winner Flute. Eva Luna's latest foal of racing age, the filly Soviet Moon, a sister to Brian Boru, was unraced in 2003 and there is a yearling sister. Brian Boru was the second British classic winner of the season for his sire Sadler's Wells. Brian Boru and Two Thousand Guineas winner Refuse To Bend couldn't do enough, however, to see Sadler's Wells past Kris Kin's sire Kris S in win-money in Britain in 2003, but, along with the likes of High Chaparral and Islington, they helped him equal Highflyer's record of thirteen consecutive Anglo-Irish sires' championships. Yesterday gave Sadler's Wells a classic winner in Ireland with her success in the One Thousand Guineas. The angular, good-topped Brian Boru, who shows a fluent, rather round action, is unraced on heavy or firm ground, but he acts on any other. His head carriage is generally a little awkward, though that's not unusual with the Sadler's Wells connection, and he has swished his tail in the paddock, tending to sweat at Doncaster. *A. P. O'Brien, Ireland*

BRIAN POTTER   2 b.g. (Mar 21) Pursuit of Love 124 – Elora Gorge (IRE) (High   – Estate 127) [2003 6g⁶ 5m 6d⁶ 7s⁵ 6m Aug 16] 800F, 1,000Y: lengthy, unfurnished gelding: second foal: dam unraced out of half-sister to high-class 1¼m performer Timarida: well held in minor events. *A. Berry*

BRIAR (CZE)   4 b.c. House Rules (USA) – Bright Angel (AUT) (Antuco (GER))   – [2003 f12g Nov 24] Czech-bred colt: placed once from 4 starts in Czech Republic at 2/3 yrs: winning hurdler for current stable: always behind in maiden at Southwell. *M. Pitman*

BRIAREUS   3 ch.g. Halling (USA) 133 – Lower The Tone (IRE) 74 (Phone Trick   **85** (USA)) [2003 77p: 8m⁴ 10g* 9.9g⁵ 9.9g 10m³ 12m² 14.4g⁴ Sep 6] big, rather leggy gelding: fairly useful performer: landed odds in maiden at Windsor in April: creditable efforts last 3 starts: stays 1¾m: raced on good/good to firm going: races prominently. *A. M. Balding*

BRIDAL WHITE   7 b.m. Robellino (USA) 127 – Alwatar (USA) 64 (Caerleon (USA)   – 132) [2003 p7g 5.1g Apr 1] tall mare: no form since 1999: tried blinkered. *M. Wigham*

BRIDEWELL (USA)   4 b.g. Woodman (USA) 126 – La Alleged (USA) (Alleged   – (USA) 138) [2003 66: 12m 12g 12m 12d f12s Dec 6] neat gelding: has a round action: fair maiden handicapper at best: well held since first start 2002: tried visored: very slowly away second start. *F. Watson*

BRIDGE PAL   3 ch.f. First Trump 118 – White Domino 67 (Sharpen Up 127) [2003   **67** 70p: p6g p7g f8s² 8m⁴ 10m² 10m³ 11.8m⁴ 12m² 14m 12g Nov 5] sturdy, close-coupled filly: fair maiden handicapper: stays 1½m: acts on fibresand and good to firm going: has hung/looked none too keen. *W. Jarvis*

BRIDGEWATER BOYS   2 b.g. (Feb 1) Atraf 116 – Dunloe (IRE) 54 (Shaadi (USA)   **58** 126) [2003 5m⁴ f5g 5m⁵ 6d⁴ 6f² 5m³ 5m 6m² 5m⁵ 5g⁶ f6g² f6g* f6g⁵ Dec 12] 1,500Y: **a69** lengthy gelding: has scope: fourth foal: half-brother to French/Belgian 7f to 9f winner Dulcification (by So Factual): dam 1m winner: fair on all-weather, modest on turf: left J. Weymes after fifth start: second in seller/nurseries before winning maiden at Wolverhampton in November: stays 6f: acts on firm ground and fibresand: blinkered/visored last 9 starts: veered right sixth outing. *K. A. Ryan*

BRIEF CONTACT (IRE)   5 b.g. Brief Truce (USA) 126 – Incommunicado (IRE)   – (Sadler's Wells (USA) 132) [2003 p12g 16f Oct 12] maiden: well held in 2003: tried blinkered. *Jamie Poulton*

BRIEF GOODBYE   3 b.g. Slip Anchor 136 – Queen of Silk (IRE) 93 (Brief Truce   **80** (USA) 126) [2003 72: 6f 7.9g⁴ 9.2d 8f* 7.9f⁶ 10.3g⁶ 8.1m³ Sep 22] fairly useful handicapper: won apprentice event at Salisbury in June: stays 1m: acts on firm ground: sometimes races freely. *John Berry*

BRIERY MEC   8 b.g. Ron's Victory (USA) 129 – Briery Fille 81 (Sayyaf 121) [2003   – 53, a57: f12s p12g 13.3m 10m Jul 21] tall gelding: modest handicapper: well held in 2003: effective at 1¼m/easy 1½m: acts on soft going, good to firm and polytrack: has worn cheekpieces: has raced freely. *H. J. Collingridge*

BRIGADORE   4 b.g. Magic Ring (IRE) 115 – Music Mistress (IRE) 55 (Classic Music   **81** (USA)) [2003 86: 6m 5g 5.1m 5g 5g 5m⁵ 5f⁴ 5m⁵ 5m⁴ 5f* 5d³ 6m 6m³ 6g 5f 5.1m 5m Oct 1] small, good-quartered gelding: fairly useful handicapper: won at Ayr in July: barely stays easy 6f: acts on firm and good to soft going: races prominently. *J. R. Weymes*

BRIGHT EAGLE (IRE)   3 ch.g. Eagle Eyed (USA) 111 – Lumiere (USA) (Northjet   **62**
136) [2003 p7g 10g 10d p10g^5 10.9m^3 10.9m^2 10d^3 12m^6 14.1f^5 p16g^5 12.6m Sep 20]
8,000F, 240,000 francs Y: eighth foal: half-brother to 2 winners abroad, including useful
Italian sprinter Bella Michela (by Superpower): dam French 9.5f winner: modest maiden:
stays 1¾m: acts on firm and good to soft ground: tailed off in blinkers. *C. F. Wall*

BRIGHT FIRE (IRE)   2 b.f. (Apr 19) Daggers Drawn (USA) 114 – Jarmar Moon   **52**
(Unfuwain (USA) 131) [2003 6d 5m^6 Jul 24] 13,000Y: fifth foal: half-sister to 5-y-o Ash
Moon: dam lightly raced: better effort in maidens (modest form) when sixth at Sandown:
slowly away both times: should stay at least 6f. *W. J. Musson*

BRIGHT GREEN   4 b.g. Green Desert (USA) 127 – Shining High 90 (Shirley   **–**
Heights 130) [2003 85: 10d p10g Dec 10] workmanlike gelding: fairly useful at 3 yrs for
E. Dunlop: well held in 2003: stays 1¼m: raced mainly on going firmer than good (well
below form on soft). *J. A. B. Old*

BRIGHT SKY (IRE)   4 ch.f. Wolfhound (USA) 126 – Bright Moon (USA) 123   **120**
(Alysheba (USA)) [2003 124: 9.3g^2 8d* 8g^3 10s^3 12f^6 10m^4 Dec 14]
         Bright Sky's four-year-old campaign took a very different route to the one
envisaged for her at the start of the year. Her decisive four-length win in the Prix de
l'Opera at Longchamp the previous autumn left many wondering how she might
have fared in the Arc on the same afternoon, and connections had given every
indication that the Arc would be her main target in 2003. But, a year on, it was again
the Opera rather than the Arc that was Bright Sky's chosen engagement on the first
Sunday in October and, more surprisingly, it was as a miler that Bright Sky enjoyed
the most success earlier in the season.
         To an extent, connections' hands were forced in campaigning Bright Sky
over shorter trips as there are few opportunities in France for older fillies at a mile
and a quarter or more, a situation which is to be remedied as part of a shake-up in
the European pattern for fillies and mares in 2004. But ground conditions were also
a factor in her programme. Possible appearances in Britain in the Prince of Wales's
Stakes and the Eclipse Stakes had to be shelved when it was deemed that conditions
were too firm. Despite winning twice on heavy going as a two-year-old, Bright Sky
had not exactly been held back by less testing conditions—she ran exclusively on
good ground or firmer—in her three-year-old season when she'd proved herself the
best of her age and sex in France, winning the Prix de Diane (on good to firm) as
well as the Opera. But her connections were convinced that Bright Sky needed it
softer, and, with no other opportunities available, they took her chance in the Prix
d'Astarte at Deauville in August on good to soft going, her first start over a mile
since her two-year-old days.
         Bright Sky might have been expected to be the main attraction in most races
she turned up in, certainly a Group 2 event confined to fillies, but this was also the
contest that Six Perfections' connections had chosen to get her season back on track
after her luckless spring campaign. With Musical Chimes and Diacada, the winners
of the French and German equivalents of the One Thousand Guineas, also in the
field, plus Acago, who had been unlucky in the Pouliches and had since won the
Prix Chloe very easily, this was a particularly well-contested renewal. Passing
halfway Bright Sky looked poorly placed, not because she was having trouble
going the pace, but because she was hemmed in against the rail in the middle of the
tightly-grouped field of twelve. But, approaching the final furlong, Bright Sky was
on the heels of Six Perfections, and when that filly went to the front Bright Sky had
room to follow her through before wearing her down near the line to win by a neck.
The Italian filly Marbye pipped Acago for third, a length and a half back, with the
proximity of some just useful fillies behind them restricting the view that could be
taken of the bare form.
         Whilst Six Perfections was turned out a fortnight later to win the Prix
Jacques le Marois, Bright Sky was kept for the following month's Prix du Moulin
at Longchamp. Starting favourite in a field of fourteen which included seven other
Group 1 winners, Bright Sky ran creditably to be beaten a length and half into third
behind the latest Prix de Diane winner Nebraska Tornado. Bright Sky would have
been suited by more of a test, staying on after initially failing to quicken when the
pace increased. With less than a month to go, the Arc was still an option for Bright
Sky despite her rather unorthodox preparation. Unorthodox, but not unique, as

Helissio had finished second in the Moulin for Bright Sky's trainer Elie Lellouche prior to his bid for a second Arc win in 1997. Ultimately though, it was the three-year-old colt Policy Maker who carried the Wildenstein colours in the Arc, with Bright Sky starting odds on in her bid to win a second Prix de l'Opera. For the second year running, Bright Sky looked as well as any horse we saw at Longchamp that afternoon, but on this occasion her well-being belied the performance in the race. Although she nosed ahead briefly over a furlong out, Bright Sky was unable to produce the same turn of speed as twelve months earlier and tired close home to be beaten a head and a neck behind Zee Zee Top and Yesterday. Conditions were the softest Bright Sky had encountered since her two-year-old days and, to our eyes at least, if not to those of her connections, would seem a valid excuse. Bright Sky's rider reported that she had run a flat race, and even suggested that she might have been in season.

Like her three-year-old campaign, Bright Sky's four-year-old season ended outside Europe. The Breeders' Cup had been ruled out for her in 2002 on the grounds that it came too soon after Longchamp for a three-year-old, but there were no such qualms about her participation this time round. The only question now was which of the Breeders' Cup races she would contest. The answer was perhaps the least expected of the three options. Her chosen engagement in the Turf over a mile and a half looked the toughest task of the three, if only because it meant a third meeting with Falbrav. Their first two clashes had gone Falbrav's way. Bright Sky had finished a long way behind him in the previous season's Japan Cup and she had gone down by a length and half when favourite for her reappearance in the Prix d'Ispahan at Longchamp in May. Starting as one of the outsiders at Santa Anita, Bright Sky managed only sixth of the nine runners. Her final outing, in the Hong Kong Cup at Sha Tin, brought yet another meeting with Falbrav, and while the return to a mile and a quarter was in Bright Sky's favour, and she ran close to her best, her effort was only good enough to see her into fourth place behind Falbrav, who was also back over his ideal trip.

Bright Sky's dam Bright Moon also remained in training as a four-year-old, though she was given her chance in the Arc for the second year running. As a three-year-old she had finished towards the rear after meeting trouble in running but a year later got to within a length of Carnegie in finishing fifth, despite sustaining a fetlock injury. Even if the Prix de l'Opera had been a Group 1 prize and run over a mile and a quarter in Bright Moon's day, it is unlikely that it would have lured her away from the Arc. She was much more of a staying type than Bright Sky, her wins including successive victories in the Prix de Pomone at Deauville over an extended thirteen furlongs. Further details of Bright Sky's pedigree appeared in last year's Annual. Since then her three-year-old half-sister Blue Icon (by Peintre Celebre) has reached the track, winning on her debut at Maisons-Laffitte over eleven furlongs but failing to reach the frame in listed company thereafter. Bright Moon's unraced two-year-old of 2003 is named Boukhara and, being by Rainbow Quest, is likely to need at least a mile and quarter, while Bright Moon's 2002 produce is a colt by Loup Solitaire named Bulgakov.

Prix d'Astarte, Deauville—two very smart fillies fight out the finish;
Bright Sky (noseband) wears down Six Perfections, with Marbye (left) and Acago (right) third and fourth

Bright Sky (IRE)
(ch.f. 1999)

	Wolfhound (USA) (ch 1989)	Nureyev (b 1977)	Northern Dancer / Special
		Lassie Dear (b 1974)	Buckpasser / Gay Missile
	Bright Moon (USA) (ch 1990)	Alysheba (b 1984)	Alydar / Bel Sheba
		Bonshamile (b 1983)	Ile de Bourbon / Narration

Bright Sky is a lengthy filly, as was her dam, and, whilst no longer an unfurnished type, is not so strongly made as Bright Moon. Her best form was at up to a mile and a quarter and, despite those wins in the mud at two, her very best efforts came on good or good to firm going. Bright Sky reportedly begins her stud career with a visit to A P Indy in 2004, an interesting choice of stallion given that he is out of a half-sister to Bright Sky's own sire Wolfhound. *E. Lellouche, France*

BRIGHT SPANGLE (IRE) 4 ch.f. General Monash (USA) 107 – No Shame 56 (Formidable (USA) 125) [2003 55, a61: f14.8g f11g f12s⁵ f12s Sep 6] sturdy filly: just poor form in 2003: stays easy 1½m: acts on heavy going, good to firm and all-weather: tried visored: none too consistent. *B. Palling* — a46 ?

BRIGHT SPARK (IRE) 6 b.g. Sri Pekan (USA) 117 – Exciting (Mill Reef (USA) 141) [2003 58: 9.7m 7m May 23] tall gelding: one-time fairly useful: well held in 2003: tried visored: usually very slowly away. *S. Dow* — §

BRIGHT SUN (IRE) 2 b.c. (May 12) Desert Sun 120 – Kealbra Lady (Petong 126) [2003 6m⁵ 6d² 6.1m* 6m 6m Oct 17] IR 10,000F: useful-looking colt: fourth foal: half-brother to 5-y-o Vendome: dam, of little account, half-sister to smart 6f/7f performer Prince Ferdinand: fairly useful performer: good second in maiden at Newmarket before justifying favouritism in similar event at Nottingham in August, making all and hanging left: should stay 7f: acts on good to firm and good to soft ground: found little final start: sold 36,000 gns. *W. Jarvis* — 88

BRILLIANT RED 10 b.g. Royal Academy (USA) 130 – Red Comes Up (USA) (Blushing Groom (FR) 131) [2003 103: p10g² p12g³ p10g⁵ p10g 10m⁶ 10.1m 12m³ 10g 12m⁴ 10m³ 10m² 10g⁴ 10m⁴ p12g p10g p10g³ Dec 10] tall, lengthy gelding: has a long stride: useful on all-weather, fairly useful on turf: best efforts in 2003 when placed in handicaps at Lingfield on first 2 starts, beaten head by Kirovski on first occasion: stays easy 1½m: acts on firm going, soft and polytrack: sometimes visored: tongue tied: often slowly away: tends to carry head awkwardly/race lazily. *Jamie Poulton* — 92 a101

BRILLIANTRIO 5 ch.m. Selkirk (USA) 129 – Loucoum (FR) 93 (Iron Duke (FR) 122) [2003 71: 7m³ f8g⁵ 7m 8f⁵ 10.2g 8f* 8f 10.4f 9m⁶ f7g⁵ f8g f7g⁵ Dec 16] big, workmanlike mare: fair on turf, poor on all-weather: won seller at Thirsk (sold from J. O'Shea 7,000 gns) in June: stays 1¼m: acts on fibresand, firm and good to soft going: tried visored/blinkered/tongue tied: bucked and unseated rider leaving stall seventh start: none too genuine. *M. C. Chapman* — 65 a49

BRILLIANT WATERS 3 ch.g. Mark of Esteem (IRE) 137 – Faraway Waters 102 (Pharly (FR) 130) [2003 7d f6g⁶ 6d 6m p7g Nov 18] second foal: dam, 2-y-o 6f winner who probably stayed 1½m, out of sister to dam of Tenby: modest form in maidens second/third starts: best efforts at 6f: reportedly broke blood vessel final start. *D. W. P. Arbuthnot* — 55

BRILLYANT DANCER 5 b.m. Environment Friend 128 – Brillyant Glen (IRE) (Glenstal (USA) 118) [2003 7m 10.1m 8g 8m 9.2m 9m⁴ Aug 6] poor maiden: stays 1¼m: acts on firm going. *Mrs A. Duffield* — –

BRIMSTONE (IRE) 8 ch.g. Ballad Rock 122 – Blazing Glory (IRE) (Glow (USA)) [2003 –: 6m Jul 2] tall, good-topped gelding: no longer of much account: usually visored, tried blinkered. *P. L. Gilligan* — –

BRINDISI 2 b.f. (Feb 21) Dr Fong (USA) 128 – Genoa 96 (Zafonic (USA) 130) [2003 7.1m² Sep 8] lengthy filly: has scope: second foal: half-sister to 3-y-o Fellow Ship: dam, possibly temperamental 11.5f winner (in match), granddaughter of Oaks winner Bireme: 10/3, 1½ lengths second of 15 to Spotlight in maiden at Warwick, running on well after slow start: will stay at least 1m: should improve. *B. W. Hills* — 75 p

BRIOS BOY 3 ch.g. My Best Valentine 122 – Rose Elegance 83 (Bairn (USA) 126) [2003 –: 6f 6.9m⁶ 7.1f f12g Dec 22] little form: left R. Bastiman after third start: tried in cheekpieces. *G. A. Harker* — –

BRIOSO (IRE) 3 b.g. Victory Note (USA) 120 – Presently 48 (Cadeaux Genereux 131) [2003 –: 6.1g 7g f6g² f5s* 5g f6g* f6g f5g p6g f5g Nov 28] compact gelding: modest — a62

161

handicapper: won at Wolverhampton in June and July: effective at 5f/6f: form only on fibresand: blinkered (out of form) final start: often races up with pace. *J. M. P. Eustace*

BRISSCOLA   3 ch.f. First Trump 118 – Princess Dancer (Alzao (USA) 117) [2003 52: –
10m f8g 8f 7.1f 8m Aug 25] smallish filly: maiden: no form in 2003. *C. B. B. Booth*

BROADWAY BLUES   3 b.f. Broadway Flyer (USA) 121 – Nashville Blues (IRE) 94   **51**
(Try My Best (USA) 130) [2003 –: 10g⁵ 10m⁶ p12g p16g Sep 3] modest maiden: stays
1¼m: raced only on good/good to firm ground on turf: sold 900 gns. *J. W. Hills*

BROADWAY SCORE (USA)   5 b.h. Theatrical 128 – Brocaro (USA) (Mr Prospector   **105 §**
(USA)) [2003 108: 8g 10m² 10m* 10.1m 10g 9.9g 13.4m 10g Oct 11] good-bodied horse:
shows plenty of knee action: useful handicapper: won quite valuable event at Kempton in
April by ½ length from Goblet of Fire: well below form last 3 starts: effective at 1m to
10.5f: acts on good to firm going: has shown reluctance at stall: has reportedly been
treated for a vertebra problem: often forces pace: inconsistent: sold 25,000 gns. *J. W. Hills*

BRONX BOMBER   5 ch.g. Prince Sabo 123 – Super Yankee (IRE) (Superlative 118)   **43**
[2003 –: 12m⁶ f12g 10m Aug 15] leggy gelding: poor maiden: stays 1½m: acts on good
to firm ground: tried tongue tied. *Dr J. D. Scargill*

BROOKLANDS LODGE (USA)   2 ch.f. (Mar 27) Grand Lodge (USA) 125 –   **67 p**
Princess Dixieland (USA) (Dixieland Band (USA)) [2003 6g⁴ 7m⁵ 8m Oct 24] €19,000Y:
strong filly: seventh foal: sister to useful Irish 1½m winner Piranesi and half-sister
to 2 winners, including 8-y-o Rafters Music: dam fairly useful Irish 7f (at 2 yrs) and
1¼m winner: fair form in maidens: left I. Wood after fourth at Newmarket: hampered
final start: should be suited by 1¼m/1½m: joined P. Blockley: open to improvement.
John A. Harris

BROOKLANDS TIME (IRE)   2 b.f. (Apr 20) Danetime (IRE) 121 – Lute And Lyre   **63**
(IRE) 96 (The Noble Player (USA) 126) [2003 5m⁴ f5s³ f5g³ May 4] €20,000Y: rather
leggy filly: half-sister to several winners, including 1994 2-y-o 7f winner Travelling Lite
(by Blues Traveller) and Irish 5f (at 2 yrs) and 1m winner Cat Belling (by Catrail), both
fairly useful: dam Irish 5f (including at 2 yrs) winner: modest form in maidens: should
stay 6f. *I. A. Wood*

BROOKLYN'S GOLD (USA)   8 b.g. Seeking The Gold (USA) – Brooklyn's Dance   **84**
(FR) 119 (Shirley Heights 130) [2003 10g⁴ 10g Oct 25] ex-French gelding: useful performer at 3 yrs when awarded listed race at Longchamp: sold from Mme C. Head-Maarek
280,000 francs after final Flat start in 2000: fairly useful form over hurdles since, and
similar level in handicap at Windsor on first of 2 starts on Flat in 2003: stays 10.5f: acts
on heavy and good to firm ground. *Ian Williams*

BROTHER CADFAEL   2 ch.g. (Apr 21) So Factual (USA) 120 – High Habit 79   **47**
(Slip Anchor 136) [2003 5g⁵ f7g³ 6g f6f 7m f8g⁴ f7g⁵ f8.5s⁶ Dec 31] strong gelding:
eighth foal: half-brother to fairly useful 6f winner Alegria (by Night Shift) and winner up
to 13f in Scandinavia by Robellino: dam, second at 11.5f, half-sister to smart sprinter
Blue Siren: poor maiden: left J. Eustace after third start: stays 8.5f: acts on fibresand: tried
in cheekpieces: often races prominently. *John A. Harris*

BROTHER KIT   3 b.g. Bishop of Cashel 122 – Fabulous Night (FR) (Fabulous   –
Dancer (USA) 124) [2003 –: p8g p7g Mar 4] well held in maidens at Lingfield: wore
cheekpieces final start: dead. *Dr J. D. Scargill*

BROUGH SUPREME   2 b.g. (Jan 25) Sayaarr (USA) – Loriner's Lady (Saddlers'   **61 p**
Hall (IRE) 126) [2003 8.2d Nov 6] rangy, good sort: has plenty of scope: third foal: dam
unraced: 9/1 and better for race, ninth of 17 in maiden at Nottingham, not knocked about:
will be suited by 1¼m+: sure to do better. *H. Morrison*

BROUGHTON BOUNTY   2 b.f. (Mar 20) Bahamian Bounty 116 – Sleave Silk (IRE)   **68**
58 (Unfuwain (USA) 131) [2003 6g 6m⁶ 7m³ 7m⁵ Aug 8] good-topped filly: first foal:
dam 1½m and 2m winner: fair maiden: third at Leicester: ran poorly in nursery final start:
should stay at least 1m. *W. J. Musson*

BROUGHTON KNOWS   6 b.g. Most Welcome 131 – Broughtons Pet (IRE) (Cyrano   **46 §**
de Bergerac 120) [2003 f11g f8.5g f16.2g* f16.2g⁴ 12g f14g⁴ f16.2g³ f16.2s⁶ f12g² Dec
22] tall gelding: poor handicapper: won at Wolverhampton in February: stays 2m: acts on
fibresand and soft going: tried blinkered: has been slowly away: sometimes races freely/
finds little: carries head high: needs treating with caution. *W. J. Musson*

BROUGHTON MELODY   4 ch.f. Alhijaz 122 – Broughton Singer (IRE) 61 (Com-   –
mon Grounds 118) [2003 f11g⁶ Dec 3] unfurnished filly: well held in maidens/claimer,
off 2 years before reappearance. *W. J. Musson*

BROUGHTONS MILL   8 gr.g. Ron's Victory (USA) 129 – Sandra's Desire (Grey   –
Desire 115) [2003 47: 12m 10.1m May 14] poor maiden at 7 yrs: no form in 2003: seems
to stay 12.5f: acts on soft going: tried blinkered/in cheekpieces. *Mrs A. M. Naughton*

BROUGHTON SPIRIT   3 b.f. Bishop of Cashel 122 – Rainy Day Song 61 (Persian   **56**
Bold 123) [2003 41: f8s* 10m* 10m* p10g 10m 10d⁶ 12g 10g Aug 25] modest
handicapper: won at Southwell in February, March and April: stays 1¼m: acts on fibresand (possibly not polytrack), good to firm and good to soft going: sold 5,000 gns.
W. J. Musson

BROUGHTON ZEST   4 b.f. Colonel Collins (USA) 122 – Broughtons Relish (Nom-   **71 §**
ination 125) [2003 69§: p10g⁴ p10g p12g⁶ p16g⁶ 12g² 16m* 12m² 17.1m 9.9m Apr 24]
smallish filly: fair handicapper: won at Musselburgh in March: reportedly lame final
start: effective at 1¼m to 2m: acts on firm going, good to soft and polytrack, no form on
fibresand: sometimes reluctant to go to start: unseated leaving stall once at 3 yrs: held up:
ungenuine. *J. R. Best*

BROWN DRAGON   2 ch.g. (Mar 4) Primo Dominie 121 – Cole Slaw (Absalom 128)   –
[2003 6m 6d Sep 26] 36,000Y: workmanlike gelding: fifth living foal: half-brother to 3
winners, including 1998 2-y-o 5f winner Ivory's Promise and 1999 2-y-o 6f winner Coley
(both by Pursuit of Love): dam unraced: well held in maidens at Windsor and Haydock.
D. Haydn Jones

BROWN HOLLY   5 br.g. So Factual (USA) 120 – Scarlett Holly 81 (Red Sunset 120)   –
[2003 51: f14.8g Jan 17] modest maiden: well held only outing in 2003: stays 9.4f: acts
on fibresand, no form on turf. *H. E. Haynes*

BRUNEL (IRE)   2 b.c. (Mar 2) Marju (IRE) 127 – Castlerahan (IRE) (Thatching 131)   **105**
[2003 6g² 7m² 7m* 7m* 7m⁵ Oct 2] IR 40,000F, €230,000Y: angular, good-topped colt: fourth
foal: dam unraced out of half-sister to smart 7f/1m performer Hadeer: useful performer:
won maiden at Salisbury in September by 9 lengths from Settlement Craic, quickening
clear over 1f out: sweating, creditable 4 lengths fifth to Milk It Mick in Somerville
Tattersall Stakes at Newmarket: likely to stay 1m: races prominently. *W. J. Haggas*

BRUNSTON CASTLE   3 b.g. Hector Protector (USA) 124 – Villella (Sadler's Wells   **60**
(USA) 132) [2003 10g 10g 10m 12m 12.1m* 12g⁵ Jul 4] 28,000Y: seventh living foal:
half-brother to French 10.5f/11.5f winner Periwinkle (by Bering): dam unraced out of
smart performer up to 1½m Ghaiya, herself sister to US Grade 1 9f/1¼m winner Fiesta
Gal: modest performer: won 3-runner maiden at Chepstow in June: slowly away and
never going pace in handicap final start: likely to stay 1¾m: raced only on good/good to
firm ground: tongue tied last 3 starts. *B. R. Millman*

BRYANO DE BERGERAC   4 b.c. Cyrano de Bergerac 120 – Cow Pastures (Homing   **63**
130) [2003 80: 7m 6m 6m 6m 5m 5g³ 5m 5d 6m Sep 8] big colt: fairly useful handicapper
in 2002, only modest form in 2003: probably stayed easy 6f: acted on firm and good to
soft going: wore cheekpieces/blinkers last 2 starts: was often slowly away: sometimes
hung left: dead. *J. J. Quinn*

BUALADHBOS (IRE)   4 b.g. Royal Applause 124 – Goodnight Girl (IRE) (Alzao   –
(USA) 117) [2003 61: p10g f11g f12g 11.6g 10.9m Jul 4] good-topped gelding: modest
maiden handicapper at best: well held in 2003 (slowly away 4 of 5 starts). *F. Jordan*

BUBBLE UP (IRE)   4 b.f. Nicolotte 118 – Mousseux (IRE) (Jareer (USA) 115) [2003   – §
75: 7m Mar 29] sturdy filly: maiden handicapper, fair form at best: well held only run
in 2003 (refused to enter stalls twice): stayed 8.2f: acted on good to soft going: dead.
J. G. Portman

BUBBLING FUN   2 b.f. (Mar 10) Marju (IRE) 127 – Blushing Barada (USA) 53   **?**
(Blushing Groom (FR) 131) [2003 8m 7m² Oct 17] big, quite good-topped filly: fifth
foal: half-sister to several winners, including 12.5f to 2m winner Bid Me Welcome (by
Alzao) and 3-y-o Blythe Knight: dam maiden half-sister to Irish St Leger winner Authaal:
signs of only a little ability at Newmarket in maiden and match. *E. A. L. Dunlop*

BUCHANAN STREET (IRE)   2 b.c. (May 1) Barathea (IRE) 127 – Please Believe   **?**
Me 93 (Try My Best (USA) 130) [2003 7m 6m² 6d f8s⁶ Dec 11] strong, close-coupled
colt: half-brother to several winners, including useful 5f (at 2 yrs)/6f winner Autumnal
(by Indian Ridge) and 3-y-o Mazepa: dam 2-y-o 5f winner: signs of only a little ability
(beaten 12 lengths by Balmont in 4-runner minor event at Newmarket second start):
blinkered/tongue tied final start. *N. A. Callaghan*

BUCKENHAM STONE   4 ch.f. Wing Park 104 – Walk That Walk 61 (Hadeer 118)   –
[2003 p7g p7g Dec 10] second foal: dam 2-y-o 5f winner: well held in maiden/seller at
Lingfield. *Mrs Lydia Pearce*

BUC

BUCKEYE WONDER (USA) 2 b.c. (Feb 1) Silver Hawk (USA) 123 – Ameriflora **94**
(USA) (Danzig (USA)) [2003 8m² 8m⁴ Oct 17] well-grown, close-coupled colt: has
round action: fifth foal: brother to high-class Japanese performer up to 12.5f Grass
Wonder and smart US Grade 1 9f winner Wonder Again and half-brother to 2 winners in
USA: dam unraced sister to US Grade 1 9f winner Tribulation, dam of smart winner up to
11f Coshocton (by Silver Hawk): fairly useful form: in frame in maidens at Newmarket
won by Art Trader (beaten neck) and Lunar Exit (only fourth when favourite), taking
good hold both times: bred to be well suited by 1¼m/1½m, though needs to settle better.
M. A. Jarvis

BUCKLE IN BABY (USA) 4 ch.f. Buckhar (USA) 120 – Alzabella (USA) (Top **–**
Command (USA)) [2003 5f⁵ 5m 6m Aug 2] half-sister to fairly useful Irish 1½m winner
The Cute Won (by Defensive Play) and several winners in USA: dam minor stakes-placed
winner in USA: raced mainly in claimers in USA in 2002 for W. Murty, winning at
Oaklawn and Great Lakes Downs (twice): held in minor events/claimer in Britain:
best efforts in USA at 5.5f on dirt. *Mrs A. M. Naughton*

BUCKS 6 b.g. Slip Anchor 136 – Alligram (USA) 61 (Alysheba (USA)) [2003 79d: **81**
11.9m³ 16m⁵ p12g² f12g* p16g² f14g⁵ Dec 15] quite good-topped gelding: fairly useful
performer: won maiden at Southwell in November: good second in amateur handicap at
Lingfield following month: effective at 1½m to 2m: acts on all-weather, firm and soft
ground: has carried head awkwardly. *D. K. Ivory*

BUDE 4 gr.g. Environment Friend 128 – Gay Da Cheen (IRE) (Tenby 125) [2003 –: **–**
12.6m Jul 4] small gelding: disappointing maiden on Flat: tried blinkered: poor winning
hurdler. *S. A. Brookshaw*

BUDELLI (IRE) 6 b.g. Elbio 125 – Eves Temptation (IRE) (Glenstal (USA) 118) **101**
[2003 100: 6m 6g 6g⁴ 6m³ 6g 6f 6g⁶ 6.1m³ 6m⁴ 6g³ 6g 6m* 6g 6m⁴ 6m 6m² 6m⁵ 5.6d 6m
6m 5g³ 5m 6m 6g Oct 24] strong gelding: useful handicapper: won at Ripon in August by
2½ lengths from Artie: some creditable efforts after: effective at 5f/6f: acts on any going:
effective visored or not: usually ridden by apprentice: hung right fourteenth outing,
sometimes edges left: tough. *M. R. Channon*

BUD THE WISER 3 ch.g. Forzando 122 – Short And Sharp 88 (Sharpen Up 127) **48**
[2003 –: p8g 7m p8g 10m 10m⁶ 10g 11g² 12g 11m 11.5g⁴ 11f 11.5m⁵ Oct 21]
workmanlike gelding: poor maiden: left G. Chung after third start: stays 11.5f: raced
mainly on good ground or firmer on turf: tongue tied: tried in cheekpieces: inconsistent.
Miss D. Mountain

BUGALOO BAND (USA) 6 b.m. Dixieland Band (USA) – Bugaloo (USA) (Forty **46**
Niner (USA)) [2003 45: 5m⁵ 5.7m 6g⁴ 5.7f 6m Jun 12] ex-Irish mare: first foal: dam
unraced: poor maiden: trained until latest season by F. Keogh: seemed to go amiss final
start: effective at 6f/7f: acts on good to firm ground: visored last 3 starts. *J. R. Jenkins*

BUGINARUG 3 b.g. Paris House 123 – Sweeten Gale 55 (On Your Mark 125) [2003 **42**
9d 6f 6m 5f 5g⁶ 5m⁵ 5m 5m Sep 8] fourth reported foal: dam third at 5f at 2 yrs: poor
maiden: will probably prove best at 5f. *H. A. McWilliams*

BUGLE CALL 3 b.g. Zamindar (USA) 116 – Petillante 101 (Petong 126) [2003 6g **58**
8g⁶ 10.2g f9.4s 8g 8d⁵ 7g f7s p7g f7g f12g Nov 28] tall gelding: seventh foal: half-brother **a–**
to fairly useful 1m winner Lady Georgia (by Arazi): dam won Norfolk Stakes but failed
to train on: modest maiden: stays 1m: raced only on good/good to soft going on turf, no
form on all-weather: possibly temperamental. *K. O. Cunningham-Brown*

BUKIT FRASER (IRE) 2 b.c. (Apr 27) Sri Pekan (USA) 117 – London Pride (USA) **79 p**
106 (Lear Fan (USA) 130) [2003 7g³ 8m⁴ Sep 5] leggy, quite good-topped colt: seventh
foal: brother to 2000 2-y-o 7f winner Pekan's Pride and half-brother to German 1m
winner Bremen Rose (by Shadeed): dam 1m winner and third in Fred Darling Stakes only
outings in Britain (also ran 3 times in USA): fair form in frame in maidens at Newbury
and Kempton (fourth to Resplendent One): likely to stay 1¼m: open to improvement.
P. F. I. Cole

BULAWAYO 6 b.g. Prince Sabo 123 – Ra Ra Girl 77 (Shack (USA) 118) [2003 –, **66**
a78§: f7g⁴ f6g³ f7s³ f7g³ f7g⁵ f7g⁵ f7g 6m* 6f 7m³ 7m⁶ f7g² f7g² p7g f7g³ f7g Dec 16]
strong gelding: fair performer: won claimer at Haydock in August: left B. McMahon after
thirteenth start: effective at 6f/7f: acts on fibresand, good to firm and good to soft going:
tried visored: races up with pace: formerly none too reliable. *Andrew Reid*

BULGARIA MOON 3 ch.g. Groom Dancer (USA) 128 – Gai Bulga 110 (Kris 135) **–**
[2003 –: 10m 12f Jul 16] big gelding: little form: tried tongue tied. *C. Grant*

BULLFIGHTER 4 b.g. Makbul 104 – Bollin Victoria 51 (Jalmood (USA) 126) [2003 **67**
62: p6g⁶ f6g* p6g 6g p6g³ p6g f6g Mar 22] smallish, robust gelding: fair handicapper:

164

won at Wolverhampton in January: probably best at 6f: acts on soft going, good to firm and all-weather: often wears blinkers/cheekpieces: sometimes slowly away: sent to Spain. *N. P. Littmoden*

BUMBLEFLY   3 b.g. Petong 126 – Doppio 62 (Dublin Taxi) [2003 –: f6g Jan 27] little – form: has hung left: visored (looked wayward) only run in 2003. *Jamie Poulton*

BUMPTIOUS   2 b.c. (Feb 6) Mister Baileys 123 – Gleam of Light (IRE) 81 (Danehill   **73** (USA) 126) [2003 8m³ 8m⁴ 8d⁶ Nov 7] 30,000F, 26,000Y: fifth foal: half-brother to useful 2000 2-y-o 7f winner Gleaming Blade (by Diesis) and 4-y-o Opening Ceremony: dam, 7.5f winner, out of half-sister to 2000 Guineas winner Don't Forget Me: fair form in maidens: in frame at Yarmouth and Musselburgh: will stay 1¼m. *M. H. Tompkins*

BUNDABERG   3 b.c. Komaite (USA) – Lizzy Cantle 52 (Homing 130) [2003 f7g   – 7.1m⁵ Aug 25] sixth foal: half-brother to 6f winner Dryad (by Risk Me): dam 7f winner: slowly away when well held in maidens at Wolverhampton and Warwick: withdrawn after unseating rider and bolting to post intended second outing. *P. W. Hiatt*

BUNDY   7 b.g. Ezzoud (IRE) 126 – Sanctuary Cove (Habitat 134) [2003 72: 6d 5.9g 6d*   **74** 7g 6g 6g⁴ 6g 7m⁶ 6m* 7.2m⁴ 7m⁵ 6g Oct 22] smallish, leggy gelding: fair handicapper: won at Hamilton (apprentice event) in May and Newcastle in September: stays 7f: acts on heavy and good to firm going, below form on fibresand: blinkered once at 3 yrs: often races prominently. *M. Dods*

BUNINO VEN   2 gr.c. (Apr 18) Silver Patriarch (IRE) 125 – Plaything 69 (High Top   – 131) [2003 8m 8m 6g Oct 6] good-bodied colt: half-brother to 3 winners, including fairly useful 1½m and 2m winner Little Acorn (by Unfuwain): dam lightly-raced 1m winner: last in maidens. *S. C. Williams*

BUNNY HUG BRIDE   3 b.f. Groom Dancer (USA) 128 – Tender Moment (IRE) 78   – (Caerleon (USA) 132) [2003 –: 7m 10m 14.1m f9.4s Jun 21] quite good-topped filly: little form. *J. G. Given*

BUNYAH (IRE)   2 ch.f. (Apr 26) Distant View (USA) 126 – Miss Mistletoes (IRE) 89   **65 p** (The Minstrel (CAN) 135) [2003 7d Nov 7] €160,000Y: quite attractive filly: seventh foal: closely related to 3 winners, including smart 7f (at 2 yrs) to 1½m winner Hattab (by Woodman) and useful 2002 2-y-o 7f winner Governor Brown (by Kingmambo), and half-sister to fairly useful Irish 1998 2-y-o 1m winner Faddad (by Irish River): dam, Irish 7f and 9f winner, out of half-sister to Le Moss and Levmoss: 12/1 and green, hampered when tenth of 18 to Divine Gift in maiden at Doncaster: will stay at least 1m: should do better. *E. A. L. Dunlop*

BUON AMICI   2 b.f. (Mar 28) Pivotal 124 – Supreme Rose 95 (Frimley Park 109)   – [2003 6d Sep 26] 26,000Y: unfurnished filly: half-sister to several winners, including smart Rambling Bear (by Sharrood) and fairly useful Bajan Rose (by Dashing Blade), both 5f/6f winners (including at 2 yrs): dam sprinter: 20/1 and better for race, well held in maiden at Haydock, starting slowly: sold 3,000 gns. *K. R. Burke*

BURDEROP   3 b.f. Sheikh Albadou 128 – Grace Browning 84 (Forzando 122) [2003   **45** 55: p7g 6m 6f 6.1m 7f⁶ Jul 21] poor maiden: not sure to stay much beyond 6f. *R. M. Beckett*

BURGHMUIR (IRE)   3 ch.f. Cadeaux Genereux 131 – Luana 101 (Shaadi (USA)   – 126) [2003 –: 8f 9.2d 10d Oct 14] well held in maidens/handicap: left Miss L. Perratt after reappearance. *I. Semple*

BURGUNDY   6 b.g. Lycius (USA) 124 – Decant 68 (Rousillon (USA) 133) [2003 96§,   **79 §** a98§: p10g p10g p10g 10m 10.1m 11.9m 10m 10.1m³ 10.1m 11.9f³ 10.1g p8g* p12g⁵ p10g p8g* p10g Dec 27] smallish gelding: fair performer nowadays: won seller (left S. Dow 7,400 gns) in October and claimer in December, both at Lingfield: effective at 1m to 1½m: acts on polytrack, soft and good to firm ground: wore cheekpieces first 3 starts in 2003, usually visored: often slowly away: sometimes wanders/finishes weakly: temperamental. *P. Mitchell*

BURKEES GRAW (IRE)   2 ch.g. (Feb 27) Fayruz 116 – Dancing Willma (IRE)   **67 d** (Dancing Dissident (USA) 119) [2003 5m⁴ 5.1m f5g⁶ 6f² 5m* 6g 5f 5m⁵ 5m³ f7g f5s Dec 27] sturdy gelding: first foal: dam unraced: fair performer: left P. D. Evans before making all in 4-runner claimer at Ayr in June: below form after, looking less than keen: stays 6f: acts on firm going: tried visored/blinkered. *D. Nicholls*

BURLEY FIREBRAND   3 b.c. Bahamian Bounty 116 – Vallauris 94 (Faustus (USA)   **67** 118) [2003 58: 7m 8.2g³ 9m* 9.3m² 10m f12s² f11s Sep 26] quite good-topped colt: fair handicapper: won at Musselburgh in July: stays 1½m: acts on good to firm going and fibresand. *J. G. Given*

BURLEY FLAME   2 b.g. (Feb 23) Marju (IRE) 127 – Tarsa 81 (Ballad Rock 122)   **60 p**
[2003 8.2d Nov 6] 31,000F, 42,000Y: sturdy, angular gelding: half-brother to several
winners, including useful 7f (at 2 yrs in Ireland) and 1m (in USA) winner Churchland (by
Kylian) and fairly useful Irish 6f/7f winner Antrim Coast (by Mujtahid): dam, 6f winner,
later successful in Italy: 33/1 and better for race, ninth of 16 in maiden at Nottingham:
should improve. *J. G. Given*

BURLINGTON PLACE   2 b.g. (Mar 12) Compton Place 125 – Wandering Stranger   **68**
69 (Petong 126) [2003 6m 6.1m⁴ p8g p6g² p6g⁴ f6g⁶ Dec 12] 16,500Y, 10,500 2-y-o:
fifth foal: half-brother to 7f/1m winner Leofric (by Alhijaz) and 6-y-o Stepastray: dam 6f
winner: fair maiden: second at Lingfield: should prove best at 5f/6f: acts on polytrack and
good to firm going. *S. Kirk*

BURMA   3 b.f. Sri Pekan (USA) 117 – Bunting 102 (Shaadi (USA) 126) [2003 10m   **67**
10d³ 10m⁵ 8.1m⁵ 9m Aug 20] very big, lengthy filly: fourth foal: half-sister to 3 winners,
including 1m (at 2 yrs) and 1¼m winner Mot Juste (by Mtoto) and 4-y-o Parasol, both
smart: dam, 1m (at 2 yrs)/1¼m winner, also third in Oaks d'Italia: fair maiden: will stay
1½m: unraced on extremes of going: visored (ran creditably, though slowly away and
looked none too keen) penultimate start: tailed off as if amiss final outing: sold 13,000
gns in December. *E. A. L. Dunlop*

BURNING MOON   2 b.c. (Feb 17) Bering 136 – Triple Green 69 (Green Desert (USA)   **75 p**
127) [2003 7m⁵ 8m Sep 5] leggy, useful-looking colt: first foal: dam maiden who stayed
1m, half-sister to smart 1¼m/1½m performer Talented and to dam of 6-y-o Three Points:
fair form in maidens at Newmarket and Kempton (still green and not knocked about): will
probably stay 1¼m: open to further improvement. *J. Noseda*

BURNING SUN (USA)   4 b.c. Danzig (USA) – Media Nox 98 (Lycius (USA) 124)   **113**
[2003 119: 10.3m³ 10.5d⁵ 10g⁵ Jul 4] good-topped colt: smart performer: creditable
¾-length third of 6 to Parasol in listed event at Chester on reappearance, finishing well
having been short of room: better effort after when respectable fifth to Ikhtyar in similar

Mr K. Abdulla's "Burning Sun"

race at Sandown final outing: stays 1¼m: acts on firm and good to soft ground: flashed tail when winning listed event at Royal Ascot at 3 yrs: sent to USA. *H. R. A. Cecil*

BURNT COPPER (IRE) 3 b.g. College Chapel 122 – Try My Rosie 93 (Try My   **65**
Best (USA) 130) [2003 67: p7g⁶ p8g³ p10g p10g 6m 7m⁶ p10g⁴ p10g 7g⁵ p10g 8m⁴ 12m²
16.4m⁵ 12m Sep 12] leggy, quite good-topped gelding: fair maiden handicapper: stays
1½m, not 2m: acts on polytrack, raced only on good going or firmer on turf: tried in
cheekpieces (raced freely): sometimes slowly away: none too consistent. *J. R. Best*

BURRY BRAVE 4 b.g. Presidium 124 – Keep Mum 63 (Mummy's Pet 125) [2003 –:   **–**
5g 5m⁶ 5g 6g Jul 11] small gelding: little form: tried blinkered. *J. S. Goldie*

BURTON GOLD 3 b.f. Master Willie 129 – Misowni (Niniski (USA) 125) [2003   **–**
9.9m May 15] ninth foal: half-sister to 1m winner Coral Island (by Charmer) and 7f/1m
winner Jalmaid (by Jalmood): dam unraced half-sister to very smart middle-distance
stayer Bustomi: 25/1, always behind in maiden at Salisbury. *H. Morrison*

BURY ST EDMUNDS (USA) 3 br.c. Swain (IRE) 134 – Vibrant (Machiavellian   **98**
(USA) 123) [2003 10m⁴ 9m* 10.1m³ 8g⁶ Sep 12] 40,000Y: close-coupled colt: first foal:
dam unraced out of high-class 5f to 1m performer Vilikaia: useful form: won maiden at
Newbury (beat Manama Rose 2½ lengths) in August: seemingly ran well when 2¾
lengths last of 3 to Beneventa in minor event at Yarmouth next time: stayed 1¼m: dead.
J. R. Fanshawe

BUSCADOR (USA) 4 ch.g. Crafty Prospector (USA) – Fairway Flag (USA) (Fairway   **58**
Phantom (USA)) [2003 7g 10.1m³ 9.1f 10s³ 10.5g⁶ f9.4g* f9.4f* 8.2g f9.4g⁶ f9.4s* Dec   **a78**
6] fair on all-weather, modest on turf: won seller and handicap in July and handicap in
December, all at Wolverhampton: effective at 9f/1¼m: acts on fibresand, good to firm
and soft ground: races prominently: none too consistent. *W. M. Brisbourne*

BUSH CAT (USA) 3 b.f. Kingmambo (USA) 125 – Arbusha (USA) 103 (Danzig   **93**
(USA)) [2003 87: 8m 7.5m⁶ 11.4m⁴ 10m⁵ 10.1m 10.1g⁵ 12m⁵ 9.7m⁶ Aug 11] smallish,
quite attractive filly: fairly useful performer: best efforts in listed races third/fourth starts,
fourth to Hammiya at Chester, then fifth to Sun On The Sea at Newbury: stays 11.4f:
raced on good ground or firmer on turf: tried in cheekpieces (raced freely): tongue tied
(very slowly away) final outing: one to treat with some caution. *C. E. Brittain*

BUSHIE BILL 5 ch.g. Captain Webster 69 – Mistress Royal 74 (Royalty 130) [2003   **58**
p12g⁶ Oct 8] fair maiden in 4 races at 3 yrs: modest form only run on Flat since: will stay
1¾m+: yet to race on extremes of going: has been slowly away. *P. R. Hedger*

BUSINESS 4 br.c. Bluegrass Prince (IRE) 110 – Dancing Doll (USA) (Buckfinder   **–**
(USA)) [2003 –: f9.4s f8.5g Mar 3] no sign of ability: tried blinkered/visored. *G. A. Ham*

BUSINESS MATTERS (IRE) 3 b.f. Desert Style (IRE) 121 – Hear Me (Simply   **63 ?**
Great (FR) 122) [2003 73: 6m⁴ 8.5m 10.2m 6m⁵ 9m 8.3m³ 6d 8.1m 8m Sep 18] IR
4,000F, IR 5,000Y: half-sister to several winners, including Irish 1995 2-y-o 7f winner
General Allgood (by Soviet Lad): dam Irish 7f/9f winner: fair maiden for K. Prendergast
in Ireland in 2002: clearly best effort at 3 yrs on sixth start: ran next time only for
Mrs L. Stubbs before rejoining former trainer: stays 1m: acts on firm and soft going:
sometimes slowly away: reportedly bled penultimate start. *J. C. Fox*

BUSINESS MIND 2 b.g. (May 11) Mind Games 121 – Business Woman (Primo   **39**
Dominie 121) [2003 5d 5m⁴ 7m Aug 1] 3,000Y: angular gelding: first foal: dam little sign
of ability: best effort (poor form) when fourth in claimer at Beverley: should stay 6f.
M. W. Easterby

BUSINESS TRAVELLER (IRE) 3 ch.g. Titus Livius (FR) 115 – Dancing Venus   **47**
61 (Pursuit of Love 124) [2003 –: 10.1m⁵ 11.1d 14g⁵ 16.2m⁴ 16g Aug 1] strong,
close-coupled gelding: poor maiden handicapper: stays 2m: acts on good to firm going.
G. A. Swinbank

BUSTAN (IRE) 4 b.c. Darshaan 133 – Dazzlingly Radiant 81 (Try My Best (USA)   **110**
130) [2003 116: 10.3m⁴ 10.9m⁴ 10g² Oct 31] strong, compact colt: reportedly had chip
removed from joint at 2 yrs: smart performer: best effort in 2003 when 1½ lengths second
to Far Lane in listed race at Newmarket: stays 1½m: raced only on good ground or firmer:
raced freely/edged left on reappearance. *M. P. Tregoning*

BUSTED FLUSH (IRE) 2 b.g. (Feb 24) Desert Sun 120 – Gold Stamp (Golden Act   **69**
(USA)) [2003 5g⁵ 5m⁵ f5s³ 5m⁵ f6g⁶ 7m² 6m* 6m* 6m² 5d a7.5g 6d Sep 3] 5,000Y:
sixth foal: half-brother to 1m (at 2 yrs) to 1¼m winner Philatelic Lady (by Pips Pride)
and Irish 7f winner Woodstamp (by Woodborough), both fairly useful: dam unraced: fair
performer: won sellers at Thirsk and Newcastle in June: left J. Osborne after next start

and seemed to run well in claimers first 2 starts for new stable: seems to stay 7.5f: acts on good to firm going and fibresand/all-weather at Deauville: blinkered fifth to tenth outings: races prominently. *A. Hermans, Belgium*

BUSTLING RIO (IRE) 7 b.g. Up And At 'em 109 – Une Venitienne (FR) (Green **72** Dancer (USA) 132) 2003 72: f16s² 18g 17.1m 17.1m³ 17.1m* 18m⁵ 16f⁶ 16.5m Jul 10] big, good-topped gelding: fair handicapper: won at Pontefract in June: stays 2¼m well: acts on fibresand, best turf efforts on good going or firmer: tried in cheekpieces: held up, and tends to idle/hang in front. *P. C. Haslam*

BUSTYERBUBBLE 3 b.f. Sri Pekan (USA) 117 – South Sea Bubble (IRE) 75 **–** (Bustino 136) [2003 10m Oct 13] third foal: dam, 1¼m winner, out of useful sprinter Night At Sea: 20/1, tailed off in seller at Leicester. *C. N. Kellett*

BUTHAINA (IRE) 3 b.f. Bahhare (USA) 122 – Haddeyah (USA) 68 (Dayjur (USA) **71** 137) [2003 –: 7g³ 8m* Apr 22] leggy filly: fair form in maidens: best effort when close third at Leicester on reappearance: dead-heated with Swift Alchemist at Newcastle next time: stays 1m: unraced on extremes of going: sold 12,500 gns in July. *J. L. Dunlop*

BUTRINTO 9 ch.g. Anshan 119 – Bay Bay 101 (Bay Express 132) [2003 53, a59: **48** p10g p10g* p8g p8g 10m 10d 8f⁶ 10.3g⁵ p10g p10g 7g 10m Aug 8] tall, strong gelding: **a54** good mover: modest on all-weather, poor on turf: won seller at Lingfield in January: effective at 7f, probably at easy 1¼m: acts on any turf going/all-weather: tried blinkered/visored earlier in career: sometimes slowly away: free-going sort: often carries head high: inconsistent. *B. R. Johnson*

BUY ON THE RED 2 b.c. (Feb 25) Komaite (USA) – Red Rosein 97 (Red Sunset **71** 120) [2003 p6g⁴ 5.1m² 6d⁴ Nov 8] 16,000Y: tall, quite good-topped colt: sixth foal: brother to 5-y-o Proud Boast and half-brother to 2 winners, including unreliable 7f/1m winner Young Rosein (by Distant Relative): dam, tough sprinter, won Wokingham: fair form in maidens: second at Nottingham: bred to prove best at 5f/6f. *W. R. Muir*

BUY THE SPORT (USA) 3 b.f. Devil's Bag (USA) – Final Accord (USA) **98 +** (D'Accord (USA)) [2003 97: p8g* 8g⁶ 10.4m⁵ 8m⁵ a9f* a9f³ a9f⁵ Oct 25] **a114**
British-trained winners of Grade 1 races on dirt in the States were beginning to look an endangered species, at least in terms of those actually based in Britain, until Brian Meehan's Buy The Sport landed the Gazelle Handicap at Belmont Park in September. Since Sheikh Albadou's victory in the Breeders' Cup Sprint at Churchill Downs for Alex Scott in 1991, only the Saeed bin Suroor-trained trio of Street Cry (Stephen Foster Handicap), Jilbab (Coaching Club American Oaks) and Imperial Gesture (Gazelle Handicap and Beldame Stakes) had achieved the feat, though they were based in America in 2002 when the successes were gained. In fact, after French-trained Arcangues caused a 133/1 surprise in the Breeders' Cup Classic in 1993, there was an eight-year wait for the next European-trained Grade 1 winner on dirt in North America, Aidan O'Brien's Johannesburg in the Breeders' Cup Juvenile in 2001. Dermot Weld's 1990 Belmont Stakes winner Go And Go and Francois Boutin's 1991 Breeders' Cup Juvenile winner Arazi were the only other European-trained winners of Grade 1 races on dirt in North America in the 'nineties.

River Keen, The Deputy, Skimming, Aldebaran and Mineshaft are recent examples of horses who have shown plenty of improvement to win at the highest level on dirt in North America after being transferred from a British stable. Another to have done so is Sarava, who, after showing only fair form at best in two-year-old maidens for Meehan in Britain in 2001, was transferred to Ken McPeek in the States, where he landed the Belmont Stakes the following season. Meehan was still listed as the trainer of Buy The Sport for her tilt at the Gazelle Handicap, though she was given time to acclimatize at Bobby Barbara's stable at Belmont, having been purchased privately by American Peter Minikes to race in the name of Georgica Stable after finishing fifth in the Falmouth Stakes at Newmarket. Minikes had reportedly tried to buy her prior to the Breeders' Cup in 2002 but the sale had fallen through. Among Buy The Sport's seven opponents at Belmont were Grade 1 winners Island Fashion, Lady Tak and Spoken Fur, all of whom were conceding the 48/1-shot Buy The Sport 8 lb or 9 lb. In a strongly-run race, favourite Lady Tak cruised to the front on the home turn with her rider sitting motionless and went about five lengths clear when shaken up over a furlong out. From then on, however, the complexion of the race changed completely, Lady Tak weakening dramatically

Gazelle Handicap, Belmont Park—the Brian Meehan-trained Buy The Sport (nearest camera) springs a surprise in America; she stays on too strongly for Lady Tak (right) and Spoken Fur

and Buy The Sport, who had looked beaten around three furlongs out, keeping on up the middle of the track under Pat Day to get on top near the finish and defeat Lady Tak by half a length, with Spoken Fur a nose back in third. The bare result may flatter Buy The Sport somewhat, but her connections' shrewd placing yielded a Grade 1 prize worth over £94,000, with Buy The Sport needing to show only smart form. Buy The Sport showed comparable form in Britain just once, on her only run on an artificial surface, making all under a well-judged ride from Darryll Holland in a listed race at Lingfield on her reappearance, beating subsequent Jersey Stakes winner Membership by two lengths. Buy The Sport had just useful form on turf, in between her Lingfield win and the Falmouth Stakes finishing out of the frame in the Premio Regina Elena in Rome and the Musidora Stakes at York, carrying her head awkwardly as she weakened in the latter. As a two-year-old, she had idled in front when a well-backed winner of a three-runner minor event at Windsor on her debut before finishing fourth in the Princess Margaret, Prestige Stakes and May Hill Stakes. After the Gazelle, Buy The Sport continued her career for Barbara and, though failing to emulate Imperial Gesture in completing the Gazelle-Beldame double, she wasn't discredited in that race, beaten nine and a quarter lengths by Sightseek, who also finished in front of her when she came fifth behind Adoration in the Breeders' Cup Distaff at Santa Anita on her final start.

New York-bred Buy The Sport was sold for 82,000 dollars as a yearling, then bought by Meehan for 155,000 dollars as a two-year-old in training at the Calder 'breeze-up' sale in Miami, the same venue where he had purchased Sarava. Looking at her American pedigree, it's hardly surprising that Buy The Sport showed a much greater propensity for racing on dirt and polytrack than on turf, though her sire Devil's Bag, the champion two-year-old colt in the States in 1983, has proved capable of siring high-class horses on turf, his progeny including the Japanese-trained Prix Jacques le Marois winner Taiki Shuttle. Buy The Sport's dam

BUZ

			Halo	Hail To Reason
	Devil's Bag (USA)	(b or br 1969)	Cosmah
	(b 1981)	Ballade	Herbager
Buy The Sport (USA)		(b or br 1972)	Miss Swapsco
(b.f. 2000)		D'Accord	Secretariat
	Final Accord (USA)	(b 1979)	Fanfreluche
	(ch 1989)	Adelaide's Lament	Mr Leader
		(b 1975)	Warfingers

Final Accord won one race over eight and a half furlongs. All five of her foals to have raced have won, four of them stakes winners, the others being Try N Sue (by Sir Harry Lewis), Winter Dreams (by Distinctive Pro) and Haggs Castle (by Husband). Final Accord is also responsible for an unraced two-year-old colt by Belong To Me and a yearling filly by Peaks And Valleys. Even though there will be an increase in opportunities for good older fillies and mares in Europe in 2004 (more of which can be found in the essays on Russian Rhythm, Dimitrova and Macadamia), it is likely that Buy The Sport would have been found wanting in top pattern company on this side of the Atlantic. Valuable graded handicaps in the States are likely to continue to offer a better option for horses with a similar profile to Buy The Sport. The heavy-topped Buy The Sport stays nine furlongs and has raced only on good and good to firm going on turf. *R. Barbara, USA*

BUZ KIRI (USA)   5 b.g. Gulch (USA) – White Corners (USA) (Caro 133) [2003 46: f16s p12g6 15m6 16m 11.9m6 14.1m 12.1g3 10.2g 13.1f 12.1d4 11.9m6 Oct 2] smallish, sturdy gelding: poor maiden handicapper: effective at 1½m to 2m: acts on fibresand, firm and good to soft going: tried blinkered/visored/tongue tied: usually held up. *A. W. Carroll*   **42**

BUZZ BUZZ   2 b.f. (May 4) Mtoto 134 – Abuzz 101 (Absalom 128) [2003 6m 6m2 7f 8m4 8d Sep 11] lengthy, useful-looking filly: half-sister to several winners, including useful 5f (at 2 yrs)/6f winner World Premier (by Shareef Dancer), 4-y-o Shiny and 5-y-o Shush: dam 5f (at 2 yrs) and 7f winner, half-sister to dam of very smart miler Revoque: fair maiden: second in minor event at Pontefract: stays 1m: form only on good to firm going. *C. E. Brittain*   **67**

BY ALL MEN (IRE)   3 b.g. Among Men (USA) 124 – Bellinzona (Northfields (USA)) [2003 –: p8g f11g f12s Dec 13] good-topped gelding: little form: left N. Graham and off 10 months after reappearance. *P. A. Blockley*   **–**

BY DEFINITION (IRE)   5 gr. or b.m. Definite Article 121 – Miss Goodbody (Castle Keep 121) [2003 34: f8s 10.2g 8.1m Aug 14] rather sparely-made mare: poor maiden: no form in 2003: tried blinkered/in cheekpieces. *J. M. Bradley*   **–**

BY FAR (FR)   5 b.h. Machiavellian (USA) 123 – Makri 65 (Night Shift (USA)) [2003 103: 8g3 7m 8g 8d2 Sep 29] leggy horse: useful performer, lightly raced: placed in minor event at Lyon Parilly and apprentice race at Compiegne (2½ lengths second to Shy Mail) in 2003: well held in between in handicaps at Newmarket (Bunbury Cup) and Deauville (listed contest): stays 1m: very best form on good going or softer: has been tongue tied. *J. E. Hammond, France*   **95**

Dubai Duty Free Mill Reef Stakes, Newbury—Byron shows a good turn of foot;
his closest pursuers, from left to right, are Grand Reward, Tahreeb, Holborn and Blue Tomato

BYGONE DAYS 2 ch.g. (Apr 13) Desert King (IRE) 129 – May Light 62 (Midyan **74 p**
(USA) 124) [2003 6d 5m² Oct 3] 32,000Y: fifth foal: half-brother to fairly useful 1998
2-y-o 1m winner Trio (by Cyrano de Bergerac): dam, maiden who stayed 7f, half-sister to
smart middle-distance stayer Torus: better effort in maidens (fair form) when second to
Green Manalishi at Lingfield, showing plenty of speed: bred to stay 1m: open to progress.
W. J. Haggas

BY HEC 3 ch.g. Hector Protector (USA) 124 – Dancing Wolf (IRE) 76 (Wolfhound **–**
(USA) 126) [2003 57: 10m 8g f12g 14g 10.9g⁵ Jul 21] modest maiden at 2 yrs: well held
in 2003: tried in cheekpieces. *M. Dods*

BYINCHKA 3 br.g. Inchinor 119 – Bystrouska (Gorytus (USA) 132) [2003 –: p7g 7m **52**
f9.4s 8m⁶ 10m 11.9m⁴ p12g Nov 12] close-coupled gelding: modest maiden: stays easy
1½m: acts on good to firm going: tried blinkered. *S. L. Keightley*

BYO (IRE) 5 gr.g. Paris House 123 – Navan Royal (IRE) 61 (Dominion Royale 112) **75**
[2003 67, a⁷/4: p5g² f5g⁴ p5g⁶ p5g⁴ 5.7f* 5.3f³ 5m² 5g³ 5.7g 5m⁶ 5.7f² 5.7f⁴ 5.1m⁴ 5.7m³
5.2m 5.5m* 5.7f² 5m² 5.3f⁴ 6m p7g p6g⁴ p5g⁴ p6g⁴ Dec 30] smallish, workmanlike
gelding: fair performer: won minor event at Bath in March and handicap at Warwick in
August: best at 5f/easy 6f: acts on all-weather and any turf going: consistent. *M. Quinn*

BYRON 2 b.c. (Apr 5) Green Desert (USA) 127 – Gay Gallanta (USA) 112 (Woodman **111**
(USA) 126) [2003 6m* 6m³ 6m⁴ 6m* Sep 19] quite attractive colt: good mover: fifth foal:
closely related to 3-y-o Gallivant and half-brother to 4-y-o Gallant Hero and fairly useful
9f winner Gallant (by Rainbow Quest): dam, Queen Mary/Cheveley Park winner, half-
sister to very smart Irish performer up to 1¼m Sportsworld from family of A P Indy and
Wolfhound: smart form: won maiden at Newmarket in June and Dubai Duty Free Mill
Reef Stakes at Newbury in September, latter by ¾ length from Grand Reward, quickening

Sheikh Mohammed's "Byron"

to lead over 1f out then wandering: good third to Nevisian Lad in July Stakes at Newmarket and to Balmont in Gimcrack Stakes at York (beaten just over a length, demoted after causing interference): travels strongly, and will prove best at 5f/6f: joined Saeed bin Suroor. *D. R. Loder*

C

CABARET QUEST   7 ch.g. Pursuit of Love 124 – Cabaret Artiste (Shareef Dancer (USA) 135) [2003 –: 10g Apr 30] strong gelding: no form after 2001: tried blinkered/tongue tied: dead. *R. C. Guest* —

CABEZA DE VACA   3 ch.g. Lahib (USA) 129 – Norbella (Nordico (USA)) [2003 80: 7m³ 8m² 7f² 8g⁵ 9v a6.5g a6.5g³ Dec 29] sturdy, close-coupled gelding: fair maiden: left M. Johnston after third start: stays easy 1m: acts on firm and good to soft ground and on all-weather at Deauville: tried blinkered/visored: none too resolute. *Stal Ecobo, Belgium*   **76**

CACHE CREEK (IRE)   5 b.m. Marju (IRE) 127 – Tongue River (USA) (Riverman (USA) 131) [2003 79: 6g 8.5s* 10d* 8m² 8.5s⁴ 7d⁵ 8f⁶ 10f⁵ 9m 9.5m³ 8m⁵ 8g Nov 8] IR 38,000Y: lengthy mare: first foal: dam unraced half-sister to smart Irish performer up to 1½m Tursanah: useful performer: won handicaps at Killarney in May and Navan in June: good third to Livadiya in listed race at Gowran tenth start: stays 1¼m: acts on firm and soft going: stumbled and unseated rider after 4f in Cambridgeshire at Newmarket ninth outing. *P. Hughes, Ireland*   **96**

CADEAU SPECIALE   3 b.f. Cadeaux Genereux 131 – Pat Or Else 72 (Alzao (USA) 117) [2003 f6g⁶ f6g³ f6g 7g f8.5s Sep 20] third foal: half-sister to 1996 2-y-o 6f/7f seller winner Run Lucy Run (by Risk Me) and 1½m winner Salvem (by Salse): dam, staying maiden, half-sister to Classic Cliche and My Emma: modest maiden: should stay 7f: raced only on fibresand/good ground. *R. Guest*   **54**

CADEAUX DES MAGES   3 b.g. Cadeaux Genereux 131 – On Tiptoes 107 (Shareef Dancer (USA) 135) [2003 7.1m* 8m⁶ 8.1d² Sep 26] deep-girthed gelding: seventh foal: brother to useful 6f (including at 2 yrs)/7f winner Caballero and half-brother to 3 winners, including 6-y-o Currency: dam, 5f (including Queen Mary Stakes) winner, from family of high-class miler Wassl: fairly useful form: 33/1-winner of maiden at Haydock in June: 66/1 after 3-month absence, clearly best effort when ½-length second to Sarraaf in handicap there final start, slowly away, then finishing strongly: should stay beyond 1m: capable of better still, and should win more races. *J. G. Given*   **93 p**

CADEAUX ROUGE (IRE)   2 ch.f. (Feb 17) Croco Rouge (IRE) 126 – Gift of Glory (FR) (Niniski (USA) 125) [2003 7.1f⁵ 7.1g⁵ 7.1m⁶ 8f Sep 8] €10,500Y: leggy filly: sixth foal: closely related to 4-y-o Zahunda and half-sister to 3 winners, including French 11.5f winner Seixo Branco (by Saddlers' Hall): dam, French maiden, closely related to smart French 1m/1¼m performer Garden Rose: modest maiden: ran poorly in nursery final start: should be suited by 1¼m+. *Mrs P. N. Dutfield*   **63**

CADRAVEL   4 b.g. Cadeaux Genereux 131 – Space Travel (Dancing Dissident (USA) 119) [2003 49: p7g 7m May 26] sturdy gelding: little form: tried blinkered. *J. Gallagher* —

CADWALLADER (USA)   3 ch.g. Kingmambo (USA) 125 – Light On Your Feet (USA) (Nijinsky (CAN) 138) [2003 f12g 11.8m³ 12f⁵ 12.6m p12g Nov 26] $50,000Y: good-topped gelding: fourth foal: brother to winner in Japan and half-brother to US minor stakes winner Reflect The Music (by A P Indy): dam, winner in US, daughter of Prix Marcel Boussac winner Play It Safe: poor maiden: left M. Johnston £3,800 after fourth start (reportedly had breathing problem): raced only around 1½m: tongue tied final outing. *P. Burgoyne*   **49**

CAERNOMORE   5 b.g. Caerleon (USA) 132 – Nuryana 107 (Nureyev (USA) 131) [2003 –, a51: f12s f12g f8.5g⁵ f9.4g Feb 15] poor maiden: stays 1¼m: acts on all-weather: tried blinkered. *P. C. Haslam*   **–**
a37

CAERPHILLY GAL   3 b.f. Averti (IRE) 117 – Noble Lustre (USA) 71 (Lyphard's Wish (FR) 124) [2003 57: p7g p5g p6g 6d 5f 7m³ 8m⁵ 7.1m* 7f³ 7m 7m⁴ 7m Oct 24] modest handicapper: won at Chepstow in August: best form at 7f: acts on firm and good to soft ground: free-going front runner. *P. L. Gilligan*   **63**

CAESAREAN HUNTER (USA) 4 ch.g. Jade Hunter (USA) – Grey Fay (USA) **71** (Grey Dawn II 132) [2003 75: p13g³ f11g* f12g³ 11.8g 12m 14.1f² 16.4m 11.6m p16g* **a85** 14.1m⁵ Oct 1] big gelding: fairly useful handicapper on all-weather, fair on turf: won at Southwell in January and Lingfield: stays 2m: acts on all-weather and firm ground: sold 31,000 gns. *S. Kirk*

CAFE AMERICANO 3 b.g. Labeeb 124 – Coffee Ice 92 (Primo Dominie 121) [2003 **56** 72: 8m p8g⁶ 7m 6m⁵ 8f 10m 7f Oct 27] modest maiden: stays 1m: raced only on good going or firmer on turf: tried visored: free-going sort. *D. W. P. Arbuthnot*

CAFE CONCERTO (USA) 3 b.f. Trempolino (USA) 135 – Charmie Carmie (USA) – (Lyphard (USA) 132) [2003 –: 12m⁵ 12m⁴ 8f Sep 2] little form. *M. L. W. Bell*

CAHAN (IRE) 4 b.f. Up And At 'em 109 – Global Princess (USA) (Transworld (USA) – 121) [2003 –: 10m 10m Jun 12] close-coupled filly: of little account: tried in cheekpieces. *S. L. Keightley*

CAIRNS (UAE) 2 b.f. (Apr 5) Cadeaux Genereux 131 – Tanami 111 (Green Desert **106 p** (USA) 127) [2003 6m* 7m* Oct 18]
The Owen Brown Rockfel Stakes has an impressive record for revealing fillies that go on to take high rank at three, with classic winners Musical Bliss, Valentine Waltz, Wince, Lahan, Ameerat, Imagine, Casual Look and Yesterday all having run in the Newmarket race. Significantly, not all of them won and none ran to a rating higher than 112, the mark achieved by Musical Bliss in 1988. Cairns, a leggy, attractive individual who came from last to first to land the spoils, has a similar profile and there's no denying she looks a filly with a future. Owing to what her trainer described as 'a few little setbacks', she was not seen out until September, when she appeared in an eleven-runner maiden at Salisbury. Cairns looked green in the preliminaries but not once they got under way, showing plenty of speed to track the leaders before going on inside the final furlong and accounting for The Jobber by a length. This was not a good enough performance to make Cairns prominent in the betting for the ten-runner Rockfel at Newmarket in October. She was a 12/1 shot, with five at shorter odds, only one of whom, Prestige Stakes winner Grace-fully, had scored in pattern company. Favourite was Snow Goose, successful on her last three starts, the latest a nursery at Newmarket. Tarot Card and Bay Tree, both recently beaten in Group 1 company, came next, followed by Gracefully and Surf The Net, the latter winner of a Newmarket maiden in June on her only appearance.

Owen Brown Rockfel Stakes, Newmarket—the UAE-bred Cairns looks a smart performer in the making as she ends the winning sequence of Snow Goose (No.7); Kelucia is third

CAI

Held up on the rail after a slightly tardy start, Cairns had to be switched outside over a furlong out and quickened decisively to cut down front-runner Snow Goose and forge clear for a length and a half victory with listed-placed Kelucia a neck away third.

		Young Generation (b 1976)	Balidar
	Cadeaux Genereux (ch 1985)		Brig O'Doon
		Smarten Up (ch 1975)	Sharpen Up
Cairns (UAE) (b.f. Apr 5, 2001)			L'Anguissola
		Green Desert (b 1983)	Danzig
	Tanami (br 1992)		Foreign Courier
		Propensity (br 1984)	Habitat
			Kalamac

Horses with the (UAE) suffix are appearing more regularly on race cards, though they are still not a major force numerically, with only around fifty foaled in the Emirates each year. Campsie Fells, successful in the Prix Vanteaux, Joel Stakes winner Splendid Era and Cairns have gained the most notable successes, though Middle Park Stakes promoted second Holborn and Cedarberg have also shown above-average ability. The theory behind the arrangement, according to a spokesman for Sheikh Mohammed's Darley operation, is that the Sheikh 'wants to return thoroughbred breeding to its roots. He wants to do the unusual thing. It's getting pleasure from doing the creative thing—that typifies the man.' Doing the unusual thing did not extend to leaving Cairns with Mick Channon, because she has now joined Godolphin. Granted the anticipated improvement, it is a fair bet she will be aimed initially at the One Thousand Guineas, together with Carry On Katie and Punctilious in the same ownership. However, even if she proves good enough there

Sheikh Mohammed's "Cairns"

is no certainty that a mile will suit Cairns, for all that she seems pretty relaxed when racing. Her sire Cadeaux Genereux, a champion sprinter, is essentially an influence for speed. The dam of Cairns, Tanami, is by one speed influence in Green Desert out of a two-year-old five-furlong winner by another speed influence in Habitat. Tanami showed form at seven furlongs but put up easily her best effort over six when making the running and going down only by half a length to Gay Gallanta in the Cheveley Park Stakes. Cairns, Tanami's fourth foal, is a half-sister to two winners over sprint distances—Machynleth (by Machiavellian), successful over five at two, and Tangram (by Indian Ridge), who picked up two races over six in Dubai as a three-year-old. *M. R. Channon*

CAITLAND 4 b.f. Puissance 110 – Lorlanne (Bustino 136) [2003 45: 9.2m[6] 14m 10.9m 9f 16m 12m 9m[6] Sep 15] unfurnished filly: poor maiden: stays 1m: acts on any ground: tried in cheekpieces/visor: ungenuine. *R. Allan* **31 §**

CAKE IT EASY (IRE) 3 ch.f. Kendor (FR) 122 – Diese Memory (USA) (Diesis 133) [2003 71: 12.1d[2] 11.9s* May 23] leggy, quite good-topped filly: fair performer: won maiden at Haydock in May: likely to prove best at 1¼m/1½m: acts on soft going, firm and fibresand: front runner. *M. Johnston* **71**

CALA (FR) 3 b.f. Desert Prince (IRE) 130 – Badawi (USA) 103 (Diesis 133) [2003 58: p7g[3] p7g* 6.1m* 7g[2] 8g[4] 8f[5] 7.1g 6m Oct 2] lengthy filly: useful performer: won handicap at Lingfield in March and minor event at Warwick in April: best efforts when 2 lengths second to Khulood in Nell Gwyn Stakes at Newmarket and 5¾ lengths fourth to Golden Nepi in Premio Regina Elena at Rome: off 4 months, below form last 3 starts: stays 1m: acts on polytrack and good to firm going: sent to USA. *C. E. Brittain* **98**

CALAMINT 4 gr.g. Kaldoun (FR) 122 – Coigach 110 (Niniski (USA) 125) [2003 73: 10d May 16] close-coupled, good-topped gelding: fair maiden at best: soundly beaten only 4-y-o start: tried visored/tongue tied. *K. C. Bailey* **–**

CALAMINTHA 3 b.f. Mtoto 134 – Calendula 75 (Be My Guest (USA) 126) [2003 –: 8g[5] 8f 11.8m[3] 13.8m[5] 14.1m 14.1s* Oct 29] fair performer: won seller at Yarmouth in October by 20 lengths: should stay 2m: acts on soft and good to firm ground: sold 13,200 gns, joined M. Pipe, won juvenile hurdle in November. *R. M. Beckett* **66**

CALARA HILLS 2 ch.f. (Apr 29) Bluegrass Prince (IRE) 110 – Atlantic Line (Capricorn Line 111) [2003 6g 8.1d f8.5g[6] Nov 1] 900F, 800Y: leggy filly: sixth foal: half-sister to 2 winners, including 1¼m to 2m winner Thrower (by Thowra): dam unraced: best effort in maidens (modest form) when sixth at Wolverhampton: will be suited by 1¼m+. *W. M. Brisbourne* **51**

CALBRAE (IRE) 3 b.f. Indian Ridge 123 – Willow Dale (IRE) 89 (Danehill (USA) 126) [2003 83: p5g[2] p5g[2] 5m Apr 25] good-quartered filly: fairly useful maiden: stayed 6f: acted on polytrack, firm and good to soft going: sometimes hung right: dead. *D. R. C. Elsworth* **84**

CALCAR (IRE) 3 b.g. Flying Spur (AUS) – Poscimur (IRE) (Prince Rupert (FR) 121) [2003 58: 10m p10g 13.1g[2] f12g 16.2d[5] 10m 12d f12g[5] f16g f11g Dec 15] tall gelding: modest maiden: left J. Hills after fifth start: stays 13f: acts on fibresand and good to soft ground: tried visored: none too consistent. *Mrs S. Lamyman* **54**

CALCULAITE 2 b.g. (Mar 26) Komaite (USA) – Miss Calculate 67 (Mummy's Game 120) [2003 f6g f8.5g f8g Dec 8] fifth foal: brother to 5-y-o Sandles and 3-y-o Playtime Blue: dam 6f/7f winner, including at 2 yrs: modest form at best in maidens: should prove best up to 1m. *Mrs G. S. Rees* **51 ?**

CALCULUS (IRE) 3 b.c. Barathea (IRE) 127 – Mood Swings (IRE) 77 (Shirley Heights 130) [2003 8m Jul 10] IR 130,000Y: rather leggy, attractive colt: third foal: half-brother to 5-y-o Hurricane Floyd and 5f winner Psychic (by Alhaarth): dam 2-y-o 6f winner: 25/1, 9½ lengths eighth of 13 to Crail in maiden at Doncaster, not knocked about having been hampered twice: looked sure to improve. *J. Nicol* **50**

CALCUTTA 7 b.h. Indian Ridge 123 – Echoing 93 (Formidable (USA) 125) [2003 112: 7g[6] a8f[3] a8f[6] a8g 8.1m[5] 8m[3] 8.1g 8m[6] 8g 8m[5] 7.9m[5] 7g[4] 8g[5] 8m[3] 8f* 7f[3] 7.9f* 8m[4] Oct 17] smallish, sturdy horse: carries condition: useful performer: raced in UAE for P. Rudkin first 4 starts: won minor event at Bath (for second successive year, 3 ran) in September and handicap at York (beat Flighty Fellow ½ length) in October: also ran well when in frame in between and on final start: best at 7f/1m: acts on dirt, firm and good to soft going: tried blinkered: sometimes swishes tail/looks less than keen, and usually produced late. *B. W. Hills* **109**

CALDY DANCER (IRE)   2 ch.f. (Feb 9) Soviet Star (USA) 128 – Smile Awhile   **97**
(USA) (Woodman (USA) 126) [2003 5f* 5.1m* 5m 5m 6g⁵ 7f² 7m⁵ Aug 24] 1,600F,
€7,500Y: useful-looking filly: has a quick action: third foal: half-sister to 3-y-o Just One
Smile and winner in Japan by Lure: dam, ran once, sister to useful performer up to 1½m
Gypsy Passion: useful performer: won maiden at Haydock in April and minor event at
Chester in May: left A. Berry after fourth outing: good length second to Necklace in
Debutante Stakes at the Curragh, easily best effort after: stays 7f: acts on firm going.
M. R. Channon

CALEDONIAN (IRE)   2 b.c. (Apr 20) Soviet Star (USA) 128 – Supercal 106 (Envi-   **78**
ronment Friend 128) [2003 7g p7g* p8g Dec 20] 30,000Y: quite good-topped colt: first
foal: dam 6f (including at 2 yrs)/7f winner (fair form) when winning minor event at
Lingfield in November by head from Mister Saif, leading close home: reportedly
made a noise when well beaten final start: should stay 1m. *D. R. C. Elsworth*

CALENDAR GIRL (IRE)   3 b.f. Revoque (IRE) 122 – March Fourteenth (USA) 61   **55**
(Tricky Creek (USA)) [2003 5m³ 6m⁵ f6g p6g Dec 2] 3,000Y: second foal: dam, ran 3
times, half-sister to useful performers Green Ruby (sprinter) and Zero Watt (stayer) and
to dam of Poule d'Essai des Pouliches winner Ta Rib: modest maiden: will be suited by
7f+: slowly away on debut. *P. J. Makin*

CALIBAN (IRE)   5 ch.g. Rainbows For Life (CAN) – Amour Toujours (IRE) (Law   **60**
Society (USA) 130) [2003 49: f16g⁵ f16.2g* f12g⁴ f14.8s⁵ 15m⁵ f14.8s May 12] lengthy
gelding: modest handicapper: won at Wolverhampton in March: stays 2m: acts on fibresand and good to firm going: usually visored in 2001. *Ian Williams*

CALIBRE (USA)   3 b.c. Lear Fan (USA) 130 – Carya (USA) (Northern Dancer)   **103 ?**
[2003 95p: 10m⁵ 12g² May 3] big, strong, well-made colt: useful form: seemingly better
effort in minor events in spring when 7 lengths second of 4 to Westmoreland Road at
Newmarket, finding little/hanging right: stays 1½m: raced only on good/good to firm
going: carried head high only start in 2002: has worn crossed noseband: blanketed for
stall entry/pulled hard on reappearance. *J. H. M. Gosden*

CALIFET (FR)   5 b.h. Freedom Cry 132 – Sally's Room (FR) (Kendor (FR) 122)   **–**
[2003 126: a10f 12g Mar 29] sparely-made horse: developed into a high-class performer
(good fourth in Arc) at 4 yrs for G. Cherel in France: tongue tied, ran poorly in Maktoum
Challenge (Round III) and Dubai Sheema Classic (pulled hard early) at Nad Al Sheba in
March: stays 1½m: acts on heavy and good to firm going: left Godolphin, and sent to
USA. *Saeed bin Suroor*

CALIFORNIAN   3 ch.c. Zafonic (USA) 130 – Asterita 103 (Rainbow Quest (USA)   **110**
134) [2003 77: p10g* p10g* p10g³ 9d* 8.5f 9.5g² 10g 9f⁵ 10f Nov 30] tall, quite attractive colt: smart performer: much improved in 2003, winning handicap and minor event
at Lingfield in January and (having left G. Butler after third start) non-graded event at
Keeneland in April: good neck second to Evolving Tactics in Grade 2 American Derby at
Arlington in July: never a threat after in Secretariat Stakes there, Grade 2 Oak Tree Derby
at Santa Anita (last of 5) and Hollywood Derby, though wasn't discredited in last 2:
effective at 9f and will stay 1½m: acts on polytrack, firm and soft going: tried visored:
less than straightforward. *K. Mulhall, USA*

CALIWAG (IRE)   7 b.g. Lahib (USA) 129 – Mitsubishi Style (Try My Best (USA)   **45**
130) [2003 63d: p10g⁴ p10g⁶ p12g² 12m Sep 24] poor maiden: tried blinkered/tongue
tied. *Jamie Poulton*

CALLIGRAPHY   3 ch.f. Kris 135 – Ink Pot (USA) 73 (Green Dancer (USA) 132)   **79**
[2003 73p: 7.1m³ 8.3m 7f* 8.1m Aug 7] well-made filly: fair performer: won 4-runner
maiden at Yarmouth in July: in cheekpieces and upset in stall, last in handicap final start:
should stay 1m: raced only on ground firmer than good. *W. J. Haggas*

CALL ME SUNSHINE   3 b.f. Robellino (USA) 127 – Kirana (Niniski (USA) 125)   **71**
[2003 78, a72: p8g⁵ 9.2d⁴ 8d 10g² Jul 5] compact filly: fair maiden: stays 1¼m: acts on   **a?**
good to firm going, good to soft and polytrack: tried in cheekpieces. *P. C. Haslam*

CALL OF THE WILD   3 ch.g. Wolfhound (USA) 126 – Biba (IRE) (Superlative 118)   **62**
[2003 66: 7g 8.5m³ 9.2d⁵ 8.5m⁶ 7.9f 9m³ 9.3m⁴ 10.9g⁶ Aug 1] lengthy gelding: modest
maiden handicapper: stays 9f: acts on firm and soft ground: tried in cheekpieces.
R. A. Fahey

CALL THE MARK (IRE)   4 b.g. Goldmark (USA) 113 – Shalerina (USA) (Shalford   **–**
(IRE) 124§) [2003 –, a64: p7g p6g³ f7g⁵ f8g f7g 7g Mar 27] smallish, sturdy gelding: **a48**

poor maiden: left P. Mitchell after second start: effective at 6f to 1m: acts on all-weather: tried tongue tied: sold 700 gns. *C. N. Kellett*

CAL MAC 4 b.g. Botanic (USA) – Shifting Mist 76 (Night Shift (USA)) [2003 94: **92 §** 8.1m* 7.6m 8m⁶ 8f³ 8m⁶ 7g 8m 8g³ 8m⁴ Oct 25] smallish, quite good-topped gelding: has a quick action: fairly useful handicapper: best effort in 2003 when winning apprentice event at Warwick in May: stays 8.5f: acts on fibresand and firm going: visored seventh start: usually held up: ungenuine: sold 7,000 gns. *H. Morrison*

CALOMERIA 2 b.f. (Mar 17) Groom Dancer (USA) 128 – Calendula 75 (Be My **– p** Guest (USA) 126) [2003 p7g 7g Nov 1] big, close-coupled filly: third foal: half-sister to 3-y-o Calamintha: dam, 1¼m/1½m winner, out of smart middle-distance stayer Sesame, herself half-sister to Gold Cup winner Celeric: well held in maidens at Lingfield and Newmarket: type to do better at 1¼m+. *R. M. Beckett*

CALONNOG (IRE) 3 ch.f. Peintre Celebre (USA) 137 – Meadow Spirit (USA) **68 p** (Chief's Crown (USA)) [2003 10s⁵ Nov 3] 230,000Y: sturdy filly: fifth foal: half-sister to 2 winners by Sunshine Forever, notably very smart Irish 1½m/1¾m performer Sunshine Street: dam, ran once in US, half-sister to US Grade 1 1¼m winner Dawn's Curtsey: 25/1 and green, fifth of 13 to Grooms Affection in maiden at Redcar, slowly away: will be suited by 1½m+: should improve. *H. R. A. Cecil*

CALUSA LADY (IRE) 3 ch.f. Titus Livius (FR) 115 – Solas Abu (IRE) 82 (Red **66** Sunset 120) [2003 65: 6.1d⁴ 6f⁴ 6m⁶ 6g p6g p7g p7g⁵ Dec 6] smallish, lengthy filly: fair maiden: effective at 6f/easy 7f: acts on polytrack, firm and soft going: tried tongue tied/visored. *G. B. Balding*

CAMADERRY (IRE) 5 ch.g. Dr Devious (IRE) 127 – Rathvindon 93 (Realm 129) **–** [2003 69: 10g 10g Jul 22] strong gelding: fair maiden at best: soundly beaten both 5-y-o starts: tried blinkered/visored. *Mrs A. M. Naughton*

CAMARADERIE 7 b.g. Most Welcome 131 – Secret Valentine 71 (Wollow 132) **–** [2003 58: f12g Feb 14] leggy, workmanlike gelding: modest performer at best: well beaten only start on Flat at 7 yrs: sometimes blinkered: winning hurdler. *A. G. Juckes*

CAMBERLEY (IRE) 6 b.g. Sri Pekan (USA) 117 – Nsx 74 (Roi Danzig (USA)) [2003 **98** –: 7m* 7f 7g² 7g 7m* 7m³ 7m² Oct 1] rangy gelding: good mover: useful performer: won minor event in June and handicap (beat Royal Storm ½ length) in August, both at Goodwood: good second to Fantasy Believer in minor event at Newcastle final start: best at 7f: acts on firm and good to soft going: blinkered 3 times at 4 yrs: has worn crossed noseband: free-going sort: best held up: sometimes looks none too resolute. *P. F. I. Cole*

CAMELOT 4 br.g. Machiavellian (USA) 123 – Bombazine (IRE) 97 (Generous (IRE) **98** 139) [2003 91: 8m 7.9m² 8m* 8.1f* 7.9f⁶ Oct 10] well-made gelding: useful handicapper: won at Redcar in August and Haydock (best effort, beat Summer View 1½ lengths) in September: best form around 1m on going firmer than good: races prominently: sold 55,000 gns, joined G. Butler. *L. M. Cumani*

CAMEO COOLER 4 ch.g. Inchinor 119 – Mystique Smile 78 (Music Boy 124) [2003 **–** 41: 7.1f Jun 16] good-topped gelding: poor maiden: well held only 4-y-o outing: blinkered last 5 starts. *Miss L. A. Perratt*

CAMEO ROLE (GER) 3 b.f. Acatenango (GER) 127 – Coyaima (GER) 100 (Night **72** Shift (USA)) [2003 78: 8.3g* 8.1g 9d 7g Oct 11] fair performer: won maiden at Windsor in April: not discredited next time, but well beaten in listed events last 2 starts: free-going sort, but should stay beyond 1m: acts on good to firm going. *C. F. Wall*

CAMEROSA 7 b.g. Risk Me (FR) 127 – High Heather (Shirley Heights 130) [2003 **–** f12g f16.2g⁴ f16s Feb 13] of little account: tried blinkered. *A. D. Smith*

CAMILLE PISSARRO (USA) 3 b.g. Red Ransom (USA) – Serenity 98 (Selkirk **99** (USA) 129) [2003 78: f8.5g* 8m³ 8.1m⁶ 10.4m² 10.4f⁶ 9.7m² 9m⁵ 10.5d⁵ 8.1d 8m⁵ 8.2m³ Oct 28] big, strong, lengthy gelding: useful performer: won maiden at Wolverhampton in March: best effort when ½-length second to Etesaal in handicap at York fourth start: free-going sort, but stays 10.4f: acts on fibresand and good to firm ground: blinkered (ran poorly) ninth start: sold 55,000 gns, joined D. Wintle. *P. F. I. Cole*

CAMLET 3 b.f. Green Desert (USA) 127 – Brocade 121 (Habitat 134) [2003 94p: 6m **90** 6g² 5m 6.1m* 6m 6m Aug 17] strong, angular filly: fairly useful performer: won 2-runner minor event at Chepstow in June: below form in Summer Stakes at York and listed event at Pontefract after: stays 7f: raced only on good/good to firm going: often early to post: reportedly distressed on reappearance: free-going sort. *L. M. Cumani*

CAMPANINI   3 ch.g. Singspiel (IRE) 133 – Fiddle-Dee-Dee (IRE) (Mujtahid (USA) 118) [2003 8.1m 10.9m 11.5g⁵ 8.3m 8d a12g Dec 9] 37,000F, 47,000Y: first foal: dam unraced half-sister to smart performer up to 10.5f Dartrey: modest maiden: sold from M. Channon 3,200 gns after fifth start: stays 11f. *N. Minner, France*   **55 ?**

CAMPBELLS LAD   2 b.c. (Mar 17) Mind Games 121 – T O O Mamma's (IRE) 50 (Classic Secret (USA) 91) [2003 6m 6g⁵ 6d⁴ 6m Oct 12] 2,000Y: big, strong colt: fourth foal: dam, 9.4f and 11f winner (also successful over hurdles), half-sister to useful sprinter Whittingham: mostly well held in maidens/selling nursery. *A. Berry*   **–**

CAMP COMMANDER (IRE)   4 gr.c. Pennekamp (USA) 130 – Khalatara (IRE) (Kalaglow 132) [2003 92: 7m 7g* 7.9m³ 8m² 7m 7g 8g 7.9m 7f p7g³ p7g⁴ Dec 29] rather leggy colt: fluent mover: smart handicapper on turf, useful on all-weather: won Sony Victoria Cup at Ascot in April by ¾ length from Selective: excellent second to Maca-damia in Hunt Cup at Royal Ascot fourth start: not discredited last 3 outings: will prove better at 1m/9f than 7f: acts on polytrack, firm and soft going: tongue tied: often slowly away: waited with. *C. E. Brittain*   **110 a102**

CAMROSE   2 ch.c. (Feb 27) Zafonic (USA) 130 – Tularosa (In The Wings 128) [2003 7.1g⁴ 7.1m³ 8m² 8.5g* Sep 10] good-bodied colt: has scope: second living foal: half-brother to 3-y-o Ambrosine: dam, French 11f winner, half-sister to top-class 1m to 1½m performer Most Welcome out of very smart performer up to 1¼m Topsy, herself half-sister to Teenoso: fairly useful performer: justified favouritism in maiden at Epsom by head from Prime Powered: should be suited by 1¼m/1½m: carries head high. *J. L. Dunlop*   **89**

CAMZO (USA)   5 ch.g. Diesis 133 – Cary Grove (USA) (Theatrical 128) [2003 80: 12m 14.1f⁴ 14.4f 12g⁶ 14.1m⁵ 14.1m 14.1m³ p16g⁴ Oct 15] compact gelding: fair handicapper: best effort in 2003 when winning at Lingfield in October: stays easy 2m: acts on polytrack and firm going: tried visored: no easy ride. *P. W. Harris*   **79**

CANADA   5 b.g. Ezzoud (IRE) 126 – Chancel (USA) 60 (Al Nasr (FR) 126) [2003 18.7m 14m 12f⁴ 11.9g⁶ 13.9m 12m² 12d Nov 8] tall, leggy gelding: useful handicapper: slowly away when good second to Eastern Breeze at Newmarket: stays 1½m: acts on any going: tried visored, including last 2 starts: free-going sort: usually races prominently: none too consistent. *M. C. Pipe*   **99**

CANADIAN STORM   2 gr.c. (Apr 14) With Approval (CAN) – Sheer Gold (USA) (Cutlass (USA)) [2003 6g 7d⁵ p7g Oct 30] 62,000Y: close-coupled colt: sixth foal: half-brother to smart 5f/6f winner San Salvador (by Dayjur), later successful in UAE: dam stakes-placed winner up to 1¼m in USA: best effort in maidens (fair form) when fifth at Chester, pulling hard: likely to stay 1m. *M. H. Tompkins*   **70**

CANATRICE (IRE)   3 gr.f. Brief Truce (USA) 126 – Cantata (IRE) (Saddlers' Hall (IRE) 126) [2003 –: 10m⁵ 11m⁴ 11.9m³ p12g⁴ 11.6m² 14.1d 11.5s* p12g 10d Oct 31] modest performer: left W. Musson after reappearance: won seller at Lingfield in August, then left B. Johnson: stays 1½m: acts on polytrack, soft and good to firm going: wore visor/cheekpieces last 5 starts: sometimes slowly away/wanders. *T. D. McCarthy*   **57**

CAN CAN FLYER (IRE)   2 ch.c. (Apr 16) In The Wings 128 – Can Can Lady 82 (Anshan 119) [2003 8d f9.4g f8g⁶ Dec 8] third foal: half-brother to 4-y-o Robbie Can Can: dam 6f (at 2 yrs) to 9f winner: best effort in maidens (modest form) when tenth of 24 at Doncaster on debut: should be suited by 1¼m/1½m. *M. Johnston*   **62**

CANDELABRA   3 br.f. Grand Lodge (USA) 125 – Chatterberry 67 (Aragon 118) [2003 72: 7.1m⁷ 7g⁶ 7m* 7.1m 7m Sep 20] fairly useful performer: won maiden at Warwick in April and handicap at Yarmouth (by 5 lengths) in August: should stay 1m: acts on good to firm going: sometimes slowly away: sold 90,000 gns. *Sir Michael Stoute*   **94**

CANDLERIGGS (IRE)   7 ch.g. Indian Ridge 123 – Ridge Pool (IRE) 74 (Bluebird (USA) 125) [2003 93: 5f⁵ 6g 6m⁶ 5g⁵ 6m Jun 21] smallish, sturdy, lengthy gelding: impresses in appearance: poor mover: fairly useful handicapper: best at stiff 5f/6f: acts on good to firm and good to soft ground. *D. Nicholls*   **81**

CANDY ANCHOR (FR)   4 b.f. Slip Anchor 136 – Kandavu 87 (Safawan 118) [2003 50: p12g 11.6m 10m³ p12g 12f⁶ Jun 27] lengthy filly: poor maiden: stays 1½m: acts on polytrack, firm and good to soft going: blinkered in 2003: tongue tied last 3 starts. *Andrew Reid*   **38**

CANDY RIDE (ARG)   4 b.c. Ride The Rails (USA) 116 – Candy Girl (ARG) (Candy   **133**
Stripes (USA) 115) [2003 a8.5f* 9f* a10f* Aug 24] brother to a winner in USA and half-
brother to 3 winners in Argentina: dam unraced sister to Argentinian Grade 1 winner City
West: top-class ex-Argentinian-trained performer: unbeaten in 6 races, namely maiden at
Hipodromo Argentino (by 12 lengths) and 2 Grade 1 events at San Isidro (both by 8
lengths, then left R. Lopez for reported $900,000) in 2002, optional claimer and Grade 2
American Handicap, both at Hollywood (latter by ¾ length from Special Ring), and
Pacific Classic at Del Mar: created huge impression when beating Medaglia d'Oro by 3¼
lengths in last-named event, tracking runner-up closely, challenging travelling clearly the
better 2f out and shaken up to go clear (broke track record): put away for season after:
will prove as effective back at 9f as 1¼m: acts on firm going and on dirt. *R. L. McAnally,
USA*

CA NE FAIT RIEN (IRE)   7 gr.g. Denel (FR) 126 – Fairytale-Ending (Sweet Story   **–**
122) [2003 f12s Sep 26] 8,000 5-y-o: seventh foal: dam poor novice hurdler: tailed off in
maiden at Southwell. *N. M. Babbage*

CANLIS   4 b.c. Halling (USA) 133 – Fajjoura (IRE) 84 (Fairy King (USA)) [2003 55:   **42**
8m 8g 8m 9.1d Oct 14] unfurnished colt: has a quick action: poor maiden: stays 1m:
blinkered (ran as if amiss) final start: sometimes slowly away/edges left. *K. A. Ryan*

CANNI THINKAAR (IRE)   2 b.g. (Feb 26) Alhaarth (IRE) 126 – Cannikin (IRE)   **72**
82 (Lahib (USA) 129) [2003 7g 8.1m⁴ 8m 10f⁶ Sep 30] 27,000Y: angular gelding: second
living foal: half-brother to 3-y-o Icannshift: dam, Irish 2-y-o 6f winner, half-sister to
useful Irish performer up to 1½m Tout A Coup: fair maiden: wandered when fourth at
Sandown: should stay 1¼m. *P. W. Harris*

CANNON FIRE (FR)   2 ch.c. (Feb 14) Grand Lodge (USA) 125 – Muirfield (FR)   **76**
(Crystal Glitters (USA) 127) [2003 7.1m⁵ 8.3g⁴ 8.1g² 8.3g³ 10.2f³ 8f³ Oct 24]
€130,000Y: half-brother to several winners, including useful 1998 2-y-o 5f/5.5f (in
France) winner Zirconi (by Zieten) and French winner up to 10.5f Crasy Deb (by Exit To
Nowhere): dam French 1½m winner: fair maiden: placed last 4 starts: will be suited by at
least 1½m: acts on firm going: consistent. *M. R. Channon*

CANOSA (IRE)   3 gr.f. Catrail (USA) 123 – Abergwrle (Absalom 128) [2003 53: 6g   **43**
6m⁶ 5d 6.9f 5m 5m 5m 5m² 5m⁶ 5m⁴ Sep 1] leggy filly: poor maiden: best form at 5f: acts
on soft and good to firm going: sometimes awkward leaving stall/looks no easy ride.
E. J. Alston

CANOVAS KINGDOM   5 ch.g. Aragon 118 – Joan's Venture (Beldale Flutter (USA)   **45**
130) [2003 61: 8.2s 8.1m 9m 6.1g 6m 7m Aug 6] strong, lengthy gelding: has a round
action: poor maiden handicapper: stays 1m: acts on firm and good to soft going: edgy
sort: sometimes carries head awkwardly. *Bob Jones*

CAN'T BUY ME LOVE   4 ch.f. Bijou d'Inde 127 – Addicted To Love 73 (Touching   **64**
Wood (USA) 127) [2003 67: f12s p10g 8.5v 7.5g* 9f³ 7.5g 8f 10m 7m Oct 11] tall
filly: fair handicapper: left B. Meehan after second start: won at Tipperary in August:
stays 9f: acts on firm going and polytrack: tried blinkered: none too genuine. *L. Young,
Ireland*

CANTEMERLE (IRE)   3 b.f. Bluebird (USA) 125 – Legally Delicious 67 (Law   **67 d**
Society (USA) 130) [2003 10.5d³ 11.9s² 10s 10m 10.5d 10d 12d³ f12g⁵ f16.2s Dec 6]
17,000Y: strong filly: fourth foal: half-sister to fairly useful Irish 6f winner Turtles
Reprisal (by Turtle Island): dam 1m winner: fair maiden: best efforts first 2 starts: stays
1½m: acts on soft ground: blinkered last 3 outings (looked temperamental final one).
W. M. Brisbourne

CANTERLOUPE (IRE)   5 b.m. Wolfhound (USA) 126 – Missed Again 84 (High   **89**
Top 131) [2003 98: 6d 6m 6g⁶ 6m⁵ 6m³ 6m³ 6f p6g⁵ f6g* f6g⁶ Dec 15] quite good-
topped mare: fairly useful handicapper: won at Wolverhampton in November: stays 6f:
acts on all-weather, good to firm and good to soft going: sometimes last/steadily to post.
P. J. Makin

CANTORIS   3 b.g. Unfuwain (USA) 131 – Choir Mistress (Chief Singer 131) [2003   **65**
10m² 11.1m 12g⁴ 12.1d⁶ 11.9d 12m⁵ Oct 18] 26,000Y: strong gelding: sixth foal: brother
to useful 1998 2-y-o 7f winner Choirgirl and half-brother to 4-y-o Chorist and 7f (at 2 yrs)
to 2m winner Operatic (by Goofalik): dam unraced half-sister to smart middle-distance
stayer Sacrament: fair maiden: stays 1½m: unraced on extremes of going: sold 4,000 gns.
M. Johnston

£200000 St Leger Yearling Stakes, Doncaster—one of Europe's most valuable two-year-old races goes to the favourite Cape Fear, who beats Psychiatrist, Axis and Valjarv

CANTRIP   3 b.f. Celtic Swing 138 – Circe 73 (Main Reef 126) [2003 60p: p10g 10g 11.6d 11.8m* 14.1m² 12.3m⁴ 12m² 13.8m⁶ 14.1m⁶ p13g Dec 29] sparely-made filly: fair handicapper: won at Lingfield in May: below form last 3 outings, leaving R. Beckett 9,000 gns after penultimate one: stays 1¾m: acts on good to firm going: tried tongue tied: often makes running. *Miss B. Sanders*   **74 a?**

CAPAL GARMON (IRE)   5 b.g. Caerleon (USA) 132 – Elevate 98 (Ela-Mana-Mou 132) [2003 106?: 10g 13.3m May 17] lengthy gelding: smart performer at 3 yrs (needed oxygen after winning Jockey Club Stakes at Newmarket): well held in 2003: tried tongue tied: has worn crossed noseband. *J. H. M. Gosden*   **–**

CAPE COAST (IRE)   6 b.g. Common Grounds 118 – Strike It Rich (FR) 88 (Rheingold 137) [2003 43: f6g 6m⁴ 6f 6m 7g 6m Aug 19] poor performer: stays 7f: acts on fibresand, heavy and good to firm going: tried blinkered/visored. *P. D. Evans*   **46 d**

CAPE FEAR   2 b.c. (Feb 22) Cape Cross (IRE) 129 – Only In Dreams 78 (Polar Falcon (USA) 126) [2003 5g* 6m³ 6m² 6m⁵ 6d* 7m Oct 18] 22,000Y: lengthy colt: second foal: half-brother to 3-y-o If I Can Dream: dam, 2-y-o 7f winner, stayed 1m: smart performer: won maiden at Kempton in May and £200000 St Leger Yearling Stakes at Doncaster in September, storming home to beat Psychiatrist ¾ length in latter: length second to Nevisian Lad in July Stakes at Newmarket: also ran well when unplaced in Gimcrack Stakes at York and Dewhurst Stakes at Newmarket: stays 7f: acts on good to firm and good to soft going: game and consistent. *B. J. Meehan*   **110**

CAPE FIZZ   2 b.f. (Apr 12) Efisio 120 – Cape Siren (Warning 136) [2003 6m Jul 16] first foal: dam, no form, half-sister to useful performer up to 1½m Raiwand: unseated/ got loose prior to well held in maiden at Kempton, very slowly away: sold 1,000 gns. *Miss G. Browne*   **–**

CAPER   3 b.g. Salse (USA) 128 – Spinning Mouse 65 (Bustino 136) [2003 –: 10.9m 14.1m⁶ 14g Jul 4] smallish, good-topped gelding: modest maiden: stays 1¾m: raced only on good/good to firm ground. *W. M. Brisbourne*   **51**

CAPE ROYAL   3 b.g. Prince Sabo 123 – Indigo 86 (Primo Dominie 121) [2003 55: 6g² 5.1m* 5f 5.1m² 5g² 5m Aug 20] good-bodied gelding: fairly useful performer: won maiden at Nottingham in June, hanging left: good second after in handicaps at Chester   **90**

180

and Goodwood: likely to prove best at bare 5f: raced on good ground or firmer: free-going sort. *Mrs J. R. Ramsden*

CAPE ST VINCENT 3 gr.c. Paris House 123 – Cape Merino 103 (Clantime 101) [2003 6.1m⁴ f6g² f6f* 6m² 5f p6g² f7g⁴ Oct 20] second foal: half-brother to 7f winner Cape of Good Hope (by Inchinor), later very smart 5f/7f winner in Hong Kong: dam 5f/6f winner, including at 2 yrs: fair form: won maiden at Wolverhampton (drifted right) in July: stays 7f: acts on all-weather, raced only on ground firmer than good on turf: often slowly away: lightly raced, and open to improvement. *H. Morrison* **78 p**

CAPE TIA (IRE) 2 b.f. (Mar 1) Cape Cross (IRE) 129 – Granza (FR) (Saumarez 132) [2003 p6g Dec 6] €18,000Y: third foal: dam, French 1½m winner, out of half-sister to smart French 2-y-o 5f winner Greenway: 25/1, slowly away and always behind in maiden at Lingfield. *R. A. Fahey* **–**

CAPETOWN GIRL 2 b.f. (Feb 3) Danzero (AUS) – Cavernista 75 (Lion Cavern (USA) 117) [2003 6m³ 6.1m 6d² 6.5d 7m² f7s⁵ Oct 21] 12,500Y: lengthy filly: first foal: dam, lightly-raced maiden, half-sister to smart stayer Give Notice: fair maiden: second at Thirsk and Newcastle: will stay 1m: acts on good to firm and good to soft going. *K. R. Burke* **71**

CAPE TOWN (IRE) 6 gr.h. Desert Style (IRE) 121 – Rossaldene 79 (Mummy's Pet 125) [2003 111d: 8g 8g⁵ 10g³ 10m* May 28] leggy, quite good-topped horse: just useful performer: won 4-runner minor event at Newbury in May by length from Leo's Lucky-man: third to Carnival Dancer in minor event at Newmarket previous start: effective at 1m/1¼m: yet to race on heavy going, acts on any other: effective blinkered or not: tends to edge left. *R. Hannon* **104**

Kennet Valley Thoroughbreds II's "Cape Fear"

CAPE TRAFALGAR (IRE)   2 b.f. (Feb 17) Cape Cross (IRE) 129 – West Escape   **88 d**
95 (Gone West (USA)) [2003 5d⁴ f5g² 6g⁵ 6m³ 6m* 6m³ 5m* 5m* 5f* 5.1g⁴ 5.2m 6.1g³
6f 6m⁵ 6m 6m 5.2s Oct 29] €25,000Y: small, quite attractive filly: first foal: dam, 1m
winner, granddaughter of Prix de Diane winner Escaline: fairly useful performer: won
maiden at Goodwood in June and nurseries at Haydock and Leicester in July and Thirsk
in August: respectable efforts at best after: effective at 5f/6f: acts on firm ground, showed
promise on fibresand: sometimes fractious at/rears in stall (blindfold usually left on until
last possible moment): sold 10,000 gns, sent to USA. *J. A. Osborne*

CAPE VINCENT   2 b.c. (Feb 10) Cape Cross (IRE) 129 – Samhat Mtoto 64 (Mtoto   **92 p**
134) [2003 7.1d 8d³ Sep 10] 90,000F, 90,000Y: strong, lengthy colt: third foal: dam, won
at 11f in Spain, half-sister to dam of 1000 Guineas winner Ameerat: highly promising
debut, and less than month later 2 lengths third of 17 to Mutawassel in maiden at Doncaster (taken steadily to post): should stay 1¼m: useful prospect, sure to win a race or 2.
J. H. M. Gosden

CAP FERRAT   3 b.c. Robellino (USA) 127 – Trick (IRE) 76 (Shirley Heights 130)   **84**
[2003 88+: 8.1m⁴ 7.9m 8f⁶ 10.5g* 14g 12m 12m² 10g 11.8m* 12m⁵ Oct 17] quite attractive colt: fairly useful performer: won claimers at Haydock in July and Leicester in
October: stays 11.8f: raced only on good ground or firmer: none too genuine: sold 19,000
gns. *R. Hannon*

CAPITAL ACCESS   4 b.g. Efisio 120 – Thilda (IRE) (Roi Danzig (USA)) [2003 72§:   **47 d**
5g f6g f5s⁵ f6g 6m May 5] lengthy, well-made gelding: on downgrade and just poor form
in 2003: stays easy 7f: acts on good to firm going, soft and polytrack: usually blinkered:
often slowly away: one to treat with caution. *B. J. Meehan*

CAPITANO CORELLI (IRE)   4 b.c. Sadler's Wells (USA) 132 – Ahead 113   **105**
(Shirley Heights 130) [2003 95p: 11.9m⁵ 14g 12m* 11g² 12d Nov 8] very big, rangy colt:
useful performer: won handicap at Ascot (dictated pace/edged left) in August by ¾ length
from Sergeant Cecil: easily better effort after when good 5 lengths second of 6 to Maktub
in Premio Federico Tesio at Milan: should stay 1¾m: acts on soft and good to firm going:
tongue tied 2 of last 3 outings: usually races prominently. *P. F. I. Cole*

CAPLAW SONG   2 ch.f. (Feb 21) Opening Verse (USA) 126 – Mary From Dunlow   **42**
49 (Nicholas Bill 125) [2003 6d⁵ 6f⁴ 6m 7m f7f f5g 7.1m f6g Nov 21] quite good-topped
filly: half-sister to 6f (at 2 yrs) to 1m winner Smokey From Caplaw (by Sizzling Melody)
and winner in Scandinavia by Clantime: dam 2-y-o 5f winner: poor maiden: raced only in
sellers: stays 6f: acts on firm and good to soft going. *A. Berry*

CAPPED FOR VICTORY (USA)   2 b.c. (May 14) Red Ransom (USA) – Nazoo   **102**
(IRE) 99 (Nijinsky (CAN) 138) [2003 7.1m² 7m³ 8m² Sep 18] big, good-topped colt:
half-brother to several winners, including smart French 1¼m winner (including at 2 yrs)
Nadia and useful 1½m winner Sunray Superstar (both by Nashwan): dam, 2-y-o 6f/7f
winner, from very good family: useful form when third to Rule of Law (beaten 2 necks)
in listed race at York: odds on, raced too freely when second in maiden at Yarmouth final
start: should stay 1m: capable of winning races. *Sir Michael Stoute*

CAPRICCIO (IRE)   6 gr.g. Robellino (USA) 127 – Yamamah 54 (Siberian Express   **56**
(USA) 125) [2003 75: 12.1g 13g⁴ 16m⁴ Sep 15] modest maiden, lightly raced: stays 2m:
acts on soft ground, probably good to firm: visored last 2 starts. *Mrs S. C. Bradburne*

CAPRICHO (IRE)   6 gr.g. Lake Coniston (IRE) 131 – Star Spectacle (Spectacular   **116**
Bid (USA)) [2003 111: 7m 6g* 6f⁴ 6s* 7g⁴ 7s Oct 12] tall, leggy, useful-looking gelding:
smart performer, better than ever in 2003: awarded handicap at Newmarket (beaten short
head by The Tatling) in May and won Holsten-Trophy at Hamburg (beat disqualified
Aramus a neck) in July: good fourth to dead-heaters Fayr Jag and Ratio in Wokingham
Handicap (won race in 2002) at Royal Ascot in between: last of 10 in Prix de la Foret at
Longchamp final start: effective at 6f/7f: acts on firm and soft going: has been bandaged
hind joints: has gone freely to post: game and reliable. *J. Akehurst*

CAPRICIOUS   4 ch.f. Primo Dominie 121 – Megan's Flight 74 (Welsh Pageant 132)   **77**
[2003 69: 12m* Apr 4] tall filly: fair performer: won handicap at Folkestone in April:
should stay beyond 1½m: raced only on good/good to firm ground. *Lady Herries*

CAPTAIN BECKER (IRE)   2 b.c. (May 17) Cape Cross (IRE) 129 – Zifta (USA)   **– p**
82 (Zilzal (USA) 137) [2003 7.1g Nov 5] fourth foal: half-brother to 3-y-o Ground Zero
and a winner in Sweden by Alzao: dam 5f and 7f winner: 5/1, last of 10 in maiden at
Musselburgh, prominent nearly 5f: should do better. *M. Johnston*

CAPTAIN CLIPPER 3 b.g. Royal Applause 124 – Collide 102 (High Line 125) **79**
[2003 70p: 8g⁶ 8m³ 12.3d³ 10m⁵ 8m⁵ 9.9m* 10.1g Sep 11] good-bodied gelding: fair
performer: won maiden at Beverley in August: stays 1¼m: yet to race on extremes of
going. *D. Nicholls*

CAPTAIN CLOUDY 3 b.g. Whittingham (IRE) 104 – Money Supply (Brigadier **69**
Gerard 144) [2003 70: 5s³ 6d 6m p7g 6m⁴ 5m 6d p6g Nov 29] leggy, good-topped
gelding: fair maiden handicapper: left G. Balding after third start: should stay 7f: acts on
soft and good to firm ground: tried visored. *M. Madgwick*

CAPTAIN DARLING (IRE) 3 b.g. Pennekamp (USA) 130 – Gale Warning (IRE) **72**
(Last Tycoon 131) [2003 66p: 7.5d⁵ 6m³ 7f⁴ 7g* 8d⁵ 7f⁴ 7g⁵ 10f p10g⁴ f8g⁵ f7g⁴
p7g³ Dec 30] big gelding: fair handicapper: won at Lingfield in July: effective at 7f to
easy 1¼m: acts on firm ground and all-weather: tried in cheekpieces (including for win)/
tongue tied: sometimes slowly away: sometimes races freely. *R. M. H. Cowell*

CAPTAIN GINGER 3 ch.g. Muhtarram (USA) 125 – Brand (Shareef Dancer (USA) **76 ?**
135) [2003 85: 7g 6f 7g³ 8m⁴ 7m p8g f11g Dec 15] angular gelding: fair performer: left
A. Balding after fifth start: stays easy 1m: raced only on good going or firmer on turf:
often tongue tied: usually races prominently. *H. Morrison*

CAPTAIN HARDY (IRE) 3 b.g. Victory Note (USA) 120 – Airey Fairy (IRE) (Alzao **83**
(USA) 117) [2003 73: f6g² p7g f6g* p6g⁵ 7m⁶ 6m⁶ 6m² 6.1m⁶ 7m² 7g 8.1m* 8.1m⁴
10d⁴ 8m³ 8.5d⁶ 10m⁴ Oct 14] strong, compact gelding: fairly useful handicapper: won at
Wolverhampton in January and Chepstow in July: stays 1¼m: acts on all-weather and
good to firm going: sometimes edges left: sold 16,000 gns, joined G. Brown. *S. Kirk*

CAPTAIN MARRYAT 2 ch.g. (May 7) Inchinor 119 – Finlaggan 83 (Be My Chief **– p**
(USA) 122) [2003 8d Nov 7] 20,000Y: useful-looking gelding: fifth foal: half-brother to
3 winners, including 5-y-o Needwood Blade and useful German performer up to 1¼m
Australian Dreams (by Magic Ring): dam 11f to 2m winner: 12/1, well held in 24-runner
maiden at Doncaster: type to do better. *P. W. Harris*

CAPTAIN RIO 4 ch.c. Pivotal 124 – Beloved Visitor (USA) 83 (Miswaki (USA) 124) **115**
[2003 122: 6d² 5m⁴ 5f Jun 17] strong, good-topped colt: just smart performer in 2003:
reportedly chipped bone in knee third outing in 2002: left R. Whitaker after final 3-y-o
start: 4 lengths second to Miss Emma in Greenlands Stakes at the Curragh on reappearance: best 4-y-o effort when fourth to Porlezza in Prix du Gros-Chene at Chantilly: only
seventh to Choisir in King's Stand Stakes at Royal Ascot final outing: best at 5f/6f: had
form on good to firm going, best efforts on ground softer than good (below form on dirt
first 2 starts in 2002): usually raced prominently/travelled strongly: to stand at Ballyhane
Stud, Co Carlow, Ireland, fee €5,000, Oct 1st. *D. Nicholls*

CAPTAIN SAIF 3 b.c. Compton Place 125 – Bahawir Pour (USA) (Green Dancer **95**
(USA) 132) [2003 105p: 8m⁵ 8m⁶ 8g⁶ 7g³ 6f⁵ Aug 17] tall, leggy colt: useful performer:
respectable efforts in listed races/minor events first 4 starts at 3 yrs: stays 1m: raced only
on good going or firmer: blinkered second outing: carries head high. *R. Hannon*

CAPTAIN SENSIBLE 3 ch.g. Pivotal 124 – Il Doria (IRE) 66 (Mac's Imp (USA) 116) **42**
[2003 6g 8m 5g 6m 5m Sep 6] 22,000Y: good-topped gelding: second foal: dam, sprint
maiden, half-sister to smart 5f performer Palacegate Episode: poor maiden: likely to
prove best at 5f/6f. *D. Nicholls*

CAPTAIN VENTI 4 br.g. Ventiquattrofogli (IRE) 118 – Lady Liza 69 (Air Trooper **88**
115) [2003 95: 8g 8m 7.6m 8.1s 8.3g² 8.9f Jun 14] robust gelding: just fairly useful
handicapper in 2003, easily best effort on penultimate start: stays 8.5f: acts on heavy and
good to firm going. *J. J. Quinn*

CAPULETTE (IRE) 3 b.f. Grand Lodge (USA) 125 – Malabarista (FR) (Assert 134) **82**
[2003 81: 10.5f⁵ 12.3m 10.3m 8m² 8m* 8m⁶ 8.1m³ 7f² 7m³ 8m* 8.1m⁶ Sep 17] good-
bodied filly: fairly useful performer: won claimers at Newmarket in June and Kempton in
September: best at 1m to 10.5f: raced only on going firmer than good: tried in cheekpieces: often makes running: sold 23,000 gns, sent to USA. *W. Jarvis*

CAQUI D'OR (IRE) 5 b.g. Danehill (USA) 126 – Ghaiya (USA) 110 (Alleged (USA) **–**
138) [2003 90: 14g 16.2d 14d 16g Oct 31] sturdy, angular gelding: lightly-raced
handicapper, fairly useful at best: well held in 2003: blinkered last 2 outings. *J. L. Dunlop*

CARA BELLA 2 ch.f. (Apr 8) Seeking The Gold (USA) – Cherokee Rose (IRE) 122 **74**
(Dancing Brave (USA) 140) [2003 6m⁴ May 13] fifth foal: half-sister to 4-y-o Bowman

and to French 9f winner Moyesii (by Diesis): dam, 6f (Haydock Park Sprint Cup)/7f winner, out of half-sister to smart winner up to 2½m (Prix du Cadran) Molesnes: 7/1, fair form when fourth of 8 in minor event at York, not unduly knocked about: should stay 1m. *D. R. Loder*

CARACAL (IRE) 2 b.c. (Apr 9) Desert Style (IRE) 121 – Telemania (IRE) 87 (Mujtahid (USA) 118) [2003 6m Aug 27] 26,000Y: third foal: dam 2-y-o 6f winner (stayed 1m): 14/1, well held in maiden at Ascot, slowly away: dead. *P. J. Makin* —

CARACARA (IRE) 2 ch.f. (Apr 30) Nashwan (USA) 135 – Vivid Imagination (USA) (Raise A Man (USA)) [2003 7g² 7.5m* 8d Sep 11] tall, angular filly: easy mover with round action: eighth foal: closely related to winner in USA by Rahy and half-sister to 3-y-o Ketan and 7f winner Stormy Voyage (by Storm Bird): dam, US 5f to (Grade 3 event) 1m winner at 2 yrs, half-sister to multiple US Grade 1 winner up to 9f Serena's Song, herself dam of Coronation Stakes winner Sophisticat: landed odds in maiden at Beverley in August by 3½ lengths from Cohn Blue, making all: well held in May Hill Stakes at Doncaster: should stay at least 1m: acts on good to firm going: likely to make useful 3-y-o. *M. Johnston* **88 p**

CARA FANTASY (IRE) 3 b.f. Sadler's Wells (USA) 132 – Gay Fantasy (Troy 137) [2003 75p: 11.8m* 12g⁶ 12m⁶ 11.8g* Jul 5] rather leggy, lengthy filly: fairly useful performer: won maiden in April and handicap in July, both at Leicester: should stay 1¾m: acts on firm going. *J. L. Dunlop* **81**

CARDINAL VENTURE (IRE) 5 b.g. Bishop of Cashel 122 – Phoenix Venture (IRE) 69 (Thatching 131) [2003 86: 6g 7g²* 7g 7m 8m³ 7.1g⁵ 7.2g³ 8f² 7d² 8m 8g f8.5g* f8.5g* f8g* Dec 3] tall, close-coupled gelding: useful handicapper: better than ever at 5 yrs, winning at Thirsk in May, Wolverhampton (2) in November and Southwell (beat Te Quiero ½ length) in December: effective at 7f to 8.5f: acts on fibresand, firm and good to soft going: tried in cheekpieces/blinkers (raced freely): front runner: tough. *K. A. Ryan* **96 a103**

CARD TABLE 2 ch.f. (Mar 29) First Trump 118 – Murray Grey 53 (Be My Chief (USA) 122) [2003 7.2f⁵ 7m 7m Oct 17] 500Y: close-coupled filly: second foal: dam 1m winner: well held in maidens/claimer. *J. R. Weymes* —

CARENAGE (IRE) 3 b.f. Alzao (USA) 117 – Key Change (IRE) 117 (Darshaan 133) [2003 80p: 10m³ 12m* 12.3m Aug 30] smallish, strong filly: has a round action: fairly useful performer: easily landed odds in maiden at Kempton in August: will stay 1¾m: acts on soft and good to firm ground: sold 75,000 gns in December. *J. L. Dunlop* **83**

CARENS HERO (IRE) 6 ch.g. Petardia 113 – Clear Glade (Vitiges (FR) 132) [2003 –, a54d: f8s Jan 1] big, strong gelding: poor performer: well beaten in seller only start in 2003: tried blinkered/in cheekpieces. *R. Brotherton* —

CARGO 4 b.g. Emarati (USA) 74 – Portvasco 90 (Sharpo 132) [2003 67: p5g p6g⁵ p6g f5g p6g⁵ 6m 6m 5m 5m p7g p6g⁵ Dec 30] angular gelding: modest performer: effective at 5f to easy 7f: acts on firm ground, good to soft and all-weather: sometimes races freely/finds little. *H. J. Collingridge* **63**

CARIBBEAN BLUE 2 b.f. (Feb 23) First Trump 118 – Something Blue (Petong 126) [2003 6m⁶ 6m 6f Oct 10] 24,000Y: rather leggy filly: third foal: half-sister to 3-y-o Steel Blue and 4-y-o Yorkshire Blue: dam, useful winner, half-sister to useful sprinter Blues Indigo and to dam of 9-y-o Bishops Court: best effort in maidens (modest form) when sixth at Thirsk: not sure to stay much beyond 6f. *R. M. Whitaker* **61**

CARIBBEAN CORAL 4 ch.g. Brief Truce (USA) 126 – Caribbean Star 81 (Soviet Star (USA) 128) [2003 96: 6m 5g* 5g⁶ 5f 5d 5d 5.1d 5m* 5m² Oct 16] strong, good sort: useful handicapper: won at Sandown in June and Newcastle (beat Wicked Uncle a neck) in October: good short-head second to Smart Predator at Newmarket final start: effective at 5f/6f: yet to race on soft/heavy going, acts on any other: waited with: sold 45,000 gns. *C. F. Wall* **96**

CARIBBEAN MAN 3 b.g. Hector Protector (USA) 124 – Caribbean Star 81 (Soviet Star (USA) 128) [2003 8g 7g 7.5m 8.1m Sep 22] useful-looking gelding: second foal: half-brother to 4-y-o Caribbean Coral: dam, 7f winner, half-sister to smart miler Caribbean Monarch: ran as though something amiss after, leaving Sir Michael Stoute prior to final one. *B. J. Llewellyn* **71 d**

CARIBBEAN SUN (IRE) 3 b.c. Grand Lodge (USA) 125 – Carranita (IRE) 111 (Anita's Prince 126) [2003 –: 8.1s 10m Jul 7] little form. *B. Palling* —

CARINI 2 b.f. (Apr 2) Vettori (IRE) 119 – Secret Waters 100 (Pharly (FR) 130) [2003 7m* 8.2m* Oct 22] 2,000Y: smallish, sparely-made filly: seventh foal: half-sister to 9f **97 p**

to 13f winner (including in France) Gargalhada Final (by Sabrehill) and winner abroad by Fleetwood: dam, 12.5f to 1¾m winner, half-sister to dam of Tenby: won maiden at Salisbury in August and minor event at Nottingham in October, useful form when making all to beat Fancy Foxtrot by 4 lengths in latter: should be well suited by 1¼m/1½m: open to further progress. *H. Candy*

CARINO AMOURE 2 ch.f. (Mar 14) Pursuit of Love 124 – Pretty Pollyanna (General **66** Assembly (USA)) [2003 7m 7m Oct 13] 20,000Y: big, deep-girthed filly: half-sister to several winners, including useful 1m (including at 2 yrs) winner Peculiarity (by Perpendicular) and 7f to 1¼m winner Polly Peculiar (by Squill): dam unraced: better effort in maidens (fair form) when seventh at Leicester: dead. *C. G. Cox*

CARK 5 b.g. Farfelu 103 – Precious Girl 76 (Precious Metal 106) [2003 66, a61: f5s⁵ **56 §** f5g 5m 5s⁴ 5g⁴ 5m* 5m 5m 5m³ 5.1m⁴ f5s 5m 5m f5g⁴ f6g f5s Dec 27] sturdy gelding: **a47 §** modest performer: left I. Semple after second start: won claimer at Newcastle (claimed from M. Todhunter) in June: best at 5f: acts on any turf going and fibresand: tried visored/ in cheekpieces in 2002: sometimes idles/wanders: races prominently: unreliable. *J. Balding*

CARLA MOON 2 b.f. (Mar 13) Desert Prince (IRE) 130 – Khambani (IRE) 80 **68 ?** (Royal Academy (USA) 130) [2003 6m⁶ 6d 6d Sep 26] 30,000Y: well-made filly: fifth foal: dam, Irish 6.5f winner, half-sister to top-class middle-distance performer Celestial Storm and Ribblesdale winner Thawakib, herself dam of Sakhee: easily best effort in maidens (seemingly fair form) when sixth in slowly-run contest at Newmarket: should stay 1m. *C. F. Wall*

CARLBURG (IRE) 2 b.g. (Feb 27) Barathea (IRE) 127 – Ichnusa 83 (Bay Express **75** 132) [2003 6m 6f 7.1g² 7g 7.1m Sep 8] 27,000Y: smallish, close-coupled gelding: sixth foal: half-brother to 3 winners, including 6f winner Maid O'Cannie and 6f and 1m winner Sartigila (both by Efisio): dam, 7f winner, seemed to stay 9f: fair maiden: easily best effort when second at Sandown: should stay 1m. *C. E. Brittain*

CARLTON (IRE) 9 ch.g. Thatching 131 – Hooray Lady 92 (Ahonoora 122) [2003 **76** 84, a78: f7g⁵ f7s⁵ f6g* f6s⁴ f6s³ 6d* 6m* 6d 5f⁵ f8g⁵ 6d 6g 7m Oct 12] sturdy gelding: **a69** fair performer: won claimers at Southwell, Newcastle and Doncaster in first half of 2003: best at 6f/7f: acts on fibresand and any turf going: usually blinkered at 4/5 yrs, tried visored. *J. J. Quinn*

CARMEN JONES 3 b.f. Zamindar (USA) 116 – Sipsi Fach 100 (Prince Sabo 123) **–** [2003 –: 10m 9.1m 12f 12.1m Jul 29] angular filly: little form. *J. Hetherton*

CARMINE SILK (IRE) 2 b.c. (Feb 3) Barathea (IRE) 127 – Scarlet Plume 103 **70** (Warning 136) [2003 7g 7m Jul 19] leggy colt: third foal: half-brother to 2001 2-y-o 6f winner Scarlet Ribbons (by Anabaa): dam, 2-y-o 1m (including Italian Group 3) winner, out of Oaks winner Circus Plume: fair form when ninth at Newbury on first start in maidens: dead. *J. L. Dunlop*

CARNAGE (IRE) 6 b.g. Catrail (USA) 123 – Caranina (USA) 85 (Caro 133) [2003 **46** 57: f14g f12s⁶ Jan 16] tall, leggy gelding: poor handicapper nowadays, lightly raced: stays 2m: acts on fibresand, soft and good to firm ground. *C. Drew*

CARNIVAL DANCER 5 b.h. Sadler's Wells (USA) 132 – Red Carnival (USA) **121** 109 (Mr Prospector (USA)) [2003 116: 10g⁵ 10g* 9.3g³ 10d* 10m² 10d* 9.8d 10m² Oct 18]

Further pattern-race victories had seemed assured for Carnival Dancer following his impressive performance in the 2001 Scottish Classic at Ayr, but he then lost his way and failed to make even the first three in five subsequent appearances for Sir Michael Stoute. A drop in class not only helped end Carnival Dancer's losing run—he justified favouritism in a minor event at Newmarket in May on his second start for his new yard—but it probably did his confidence good too. Returned to pattern company afterwards, Carnival Dancer recaptured the very smart form he had shown at Ayr and won La Coupe at Longchamp and the Prix Gontaut-Biron at Deauville.

Carnival Dancer was ridden on both occasions by Olivier Peslier, who had also been on board when Carnival Dancer finished fifth to Nayef in the 2001 Champion Stakes. The tactics employed by Peslier that day reportedly didn't please connections, who said he had ignored instructions and given the horse too much to do. They would surely have nothing but praise for his handling of Carnival Dancer at Longchamp and Deauville, though. Apparently considered to be most effective

Prix Gontaut-Biron, Deauville—Carnival Dancer wins his second French pattern race of the year at the chief expense of Without Connexion (left) and Sunstrach (second left)

held up for a late run, Carnival Dancer quickened to lead well inside the final furlong in La Coupe, having had to wait for a gap, when beating Naheef half a length; and he hit the front at around the same point when scoring by the same margin from Without Connexion in the Gontaut-Biron. Carnival Dancer also had some good placed efforts to his name, including when third to Falbrav in the Prix d'Ispahan at Longchamp and second to both Mingun, beaten a head, in the Meld Stakes at Leopardstown and to Rakti in the Champion Stakes at Newmarket. It was Carnival Dancer's third successive appearance in the Champion—he'd finished fourth to Storming Home in the 2002 renewal—and he belied odds of 33/1 in going down by two lengths to Rakti, keeping on well having had to barge his way through somewhat. There won't be a fourth Champion Stakes for Carnival Dancer. Owned by the Cheveley Park Stud, he has now taken up stallion duties there at a fee of £4,000, October 1st.

Carnival Dancer (b.h. 1998)	Sadler's Wells (USA) (b 1981)	Northern Dancer (b 1961)	Nearctic
			Natalma
		Fairy Bridge (b 1975)	Bold Reason
			Special
	Red Carnival (USA) (b 1992)	Mr Prospector (b 1970)	Raise A Native
			Gold Digger
		Seaside Attraction (b 1987)	Seattle Slew
			Kamar

Carnival Dancer should make a fair amount of appeal to breeders as, apart from his undoubted ability, he also looks the part, being a lengthy, good-topped individual, and has an admirable pedigree. By Sadler's Wells, Carnival Dancer is the first foal of Red Carnival, a 750,000-dollar yearling who showed useful form when trained by Sir Michael Stoute for the same connections. The winner of both her starts as a two-year-old, including the Cherry Hinton Stakes, Red Carnival was placed in all three of her races the following season, notably when third in the Challenge Stakes, before failing to give her running in two starts as a four-year-old. A sister to Golden Attraction, a leading two-year-old filly in the States in 1995, and half-sister to the 1998 Florida Derby winner Cape Town, Red Carnival is a daughter of the Kentucky Oaks winner Seaside Attraction. Seaside Attraction is closely related to another Oaks winner, Gorgeous, who won the Hollywood version the same year as she won the Grade 1 Ashland Stakes and finished second in the Breeders' Cup Distaff; Seaside Attraction is also a half-sister to the Queen's Plate winner and 1984 champion Canadian three-year-old Key To The Moon and the Stoute-trained Princess Margaret winner Hiaam. Both their dam Kamar and grandam Square Angel won the Canadian Oaks and were champions in Canada, and are now the grandams of Fantastic Light and Swain respectively. Red Carnival's second and third foals have also won races for the Cheveley Park Stud/Stoute combination, Funfair (by Singspiel) showing himself a smart miler in the latest

Cheveley Park Stud's "Carnival Dancer"

season, and Desert Lord proving a fairly useful two-year-old over six and seven furlongs in 2002. Carnival Dancer, who did the bulk of his racing at around a mile and a quarter, put up his best performances early in his career on good to soft going, but there is no doubt that he was just as effective on good to firm. *Mrs A. J. Perrett*

CARNT SPELL 2 b.g. (Apr 29) Wizard King 122 – Forever Shineing 62 (Glint of Gold 128) [2003 8.1d f8s 7g Oct 28] 8,000Y: well-made gelding: fifth foal: half-brother to 4-y-o Treasure Trail: dam, 1½m winner, half-sister to very smart sprinter Crews Hill and to dam of Classic Cliche and My Emma: no promise in maidens/minor event. *Ms Deborah J. Evans* –

CAROLINA MORNING (IRE) 3 gr.f. Entrepreneur 123 – Caroline Lady (JPN) (Caro 133) [2003 8.2m p12g Nov 29] 25,000F, 5,000Y: seventh foal: half-sister to 3 winners, including 6-y-o Forest Heath: dam French 1½m winner: green, well held in maidens. *H. J. Collingridge* –

CAROLINE'S ROSE 5 bl. or br.m. Fraam 114 – Just Rosie (Sula Bula 109) [2003 –: p10g Dec 30] no form. *A. P. Jones* –

CAROLLAN (IRE) 4 b.f. Marju (IRE) 127 – Caroline Lady (JPN) (Caro 133) [2003 68: p7g f7g Jun 25] fair maiden at 3 yrs: well held in handicaps in 2003. *R. Guest* –

CAROLOU'S COURT 2 b.f. (Feb 19) Vettori (IRE) 119 – Glascoed (Adbass (USA) 102) [2003 6m 6g⁵ 6.1m 7m⁶ 6m⁵ 5.3m Oct 2] first foal: dam unraced half-sister to useful 1997 2-y-o 5f winner Mugello: modest maiden: visored, last in seller final start: stays 6f. *A. P. Jarvis* 64

CAROLS CHOICE 6 ch.m. Emarati (USA) 74 – Lucky Song 91 (Lucky Wednesday –
124) [2003 –, a63: f5g⁶ f6g⁶ f5s f5g⁵ f5s⁴ f5g² f5g⁵ f5g⁴ f6g f5s f7g⁶ f6g³ f5g f6g f6g f6g **a56 d**
Dec 26] modest performer: left D. Haydn Jones after reappearance: best at 5f: acts on
firm and good to soft going, raced only on fibresand in 2003: tried in headgear: sometimes swishes tail: usually races prominently: none too consistent. *A. Sadik*

CARONTE (IRE) 3 b.g. Sesaro (USA) 81 – Go Likecrazy 51 (Dowsing (USA) 124) **54**
[2003 63: f6g⁶ f5s f6g f5s⁶ f8s² f8g f6g 5m 7m⁴ 7.5f⁶ 8.2m⁶ 6m 8.2d f6g⁶ 5m 7.5m Aug
24] sturdy gelding: modest maiden: stays 1m: acts on fibresand, firm and good to soft
going: effective blinkered or not, has worn cheekpieces: often tongue tied. *S. R. Bowring*

CAROUBIER (IRE) 3 ch.g. Woodborough (USA) 112 – Patsy Grimes 95 (Beveled **75**
(USA)) [2003 60: f8.5g* f8g* f9.4g² p10g f8.5s³ p8g² f8g* f8g* 8m 8.2m 8f* 8m⁵ **a84**
8g 10m² f11s² f9.4s⁴ Dec 31] fairly useful on all-weather, fair on turf: won seller at
Wolverhampton, handicap and 2 claimers (left J. Osborne after latter) at Southwell and
apprentice handicap at Salisbury in first half of 2003: left H. Cyzer after fourteenth start,
claimed from I. Williams £10,000 fifteenth: effective at 1m to 11f: acts on all-weather
and firm going: usually held up. *T. D. Barron*

CARPET LOVER (IRE) 3 b.f. Fayruz 116 – Bold As Love (Lomond (USA) 128) **46**
[2003 5.1m Apr 21] IR 60,000F: stocky filly: fourth foal: half-sister to 3 winners, including smart sprinter Misty Eyed (by Paris House) and fairly useful 1999 2-y-o 5f winner
Travesty of Law (by Case Law): dam unraced: 20/1 and better for race, eighth of 14 to
Excalinor in maiden at Nottingham. *Mrs P. N. Dutfield*

CARRIACOU 2 b.f. (May 7) Mark of Esteem (IRE) 137 – Cockatoo Island 99 (High **85**
Top 131) [2003 6m⁵ 8d² 8.1d² 10g f8g f8s² Dec 13] rather leggy, useful-looking filly: **a69**
half-sister to several winners, including useful 1¾m winner Collier Bay (also won
Champion Hurdle, by Green Desert), 3-y-o Complete Circle and 4-y-o Young Collier:
dam 1½m to 14.8f winner: fairly useful maiden on turf, fair on all-weather: second at
Newmarket, Haydock and Southwell: should stay 1¼m: acts on fibresand and good to
soft going: sometimes races freely. *P. W. D'Arcy*

CARRIZO CREEK (IRE) 2 b.c. (Apr 14) Charnwood Forest (IRE) 125 – Violet **106**
Spring (IRE) 32 (Exactly Sharp (USA) 121) [2003 6g³ 6m* 6.3g* 6g* 6s⁵ Aug 31]
€42,000Y: useful-looking colt: first foal: dam, Irish 2m winner, out of sister to top-class
sprinter Balidar: useful performer: won maiden at Brighton in May, Goffs Challenge at
the Curragh (edged right) in June and Four Star Sales Richmond Stakes at Goodwood
(beat Old Deuteronomy ½ length) in July: below form when fifth to Whipper in Prix
Morny at Deauville: should stay 7f. *B. J. Meehan*

CARROWDORE (IRE) 3 b.c. Danehill (USA) 126 – Euromill (Shirley Heights **85**
130) [2003 77: p10g³ 10.3g³ 11.6d⁵ 10m 10m 9.9m⁶ 8m⁶ 10m² 8.5m³ 9m³ 8.5d⁴ p10g⁵
p8g² p10g² p10g Nov 29] small, strong, well-made colt: fairly useful handicapper:
runner-up 3 times in 2003: effective at 1m, and should stay 1½m: acts on firm ground and
polytrack: tried in cheekpieces. *R. Hannon*

*Four Star Sales Richmond Stakes, Goodwood—Carrizo Creek improves again to complete a hat-trick;
Old Deuteronomy is next, followed by Cedarberg (white sleeves), Venables,
Cop Hill Lad (No.3) and Fokine (No.4)*

Mr J. S. Threadwell's "Carrizo Creek"

CARRY ON DOC 2 b.c. (Mar 6) Dr Devious (IRE) 127 – Florentynna Bay 61 (Aragon **74**
118) [2003 7m⁵ 7m³ 7m⁵ 7.1m⁵ Sep 20] 26,000Y: compact colt: half-brother to several
winners, including smart 1m winner Sunstreak (by Primo Dominie) and fairly useful 5f
(at 2 yrs) to 7f winner Albert The Bear (by Puissance): dam, 2-y-o 5f winner, half-sister
to smart sprinter Superpower: fair maiden: ran creditably in nursery final start: likely to
stay 1m. *J. W. Hills*

CARRY ON KATIE (USA) 2 br.f. (Jan 14) Fasliyev (USA) 120 – Dinka Raja **109 p**
(USA) (Woodman (USA) 126) [2003 6g* 6m* 6m* Oct 2]
    Fasliyev's position at the top of the European first-season sires' table by
numbers of winners—from more than seventy runners he had thirty-four winners,
equalling the northern hemisphere record set by North American sire End Sweep in
1998—was predictable if not exactly a foregone conclusion. His position at the top
of the overall juvenile earnings table, with more than £900,000 in win and place
prize money, was less so, allowing for the fact that he had as many runners as any
sire. A well-bred and precocious individual in his short-lived racing days, Fasliyev
was retired to stud because of injury at the end of a two-year-old campaign that
saw him win all his five starts, highlighted by the Phoenix Stakes and Prix Morny.
Benefiting from all the marketing expertise for which Coolmore Stud is well
known, he covered one hundred and forty-two mares in his first book, getting one
hundred and eleven foals. Producing seven stakes winners, headed by Carry On
Katie (Lowther Stakes, Cheveley Park Stakes), Much Faster (Prix Robert Papin,
second Prix Morny), Russian Valour (Norfolk Stakes) and Kings Point (Superlative
Stakes) gave him an excellent start, one which bodes well for the rest of his career.
Inevitably, success has had a major impact on his fee. Having stood at IR 25,000

189

Peugeot Lowther Stakes, York—after all but bolting to post,
Carry On Katie comes home in much better style, completing the Gimcrack/Lowther double
for trainer Jeremy Noseda; Badminton (light colours) and Dunloskin come next

guineas when he retired and in 2001, his fee then dropped to €20,000 in 2003, but
will be €75,000 in 2004. Swings and roundabouts on the grand scale.

Carry On Katie was not the best of her generation—Attraction's form in
landing the Cherry Hinton Stakes was some way ahead of hers in the Cheveley
Park—but she is an admirable filly and should have improvement in her. Her
racecourse debut in a six-runner maiden event at Ascot in July was eye-catching
both for her behaviour beforehand and for the way she won. Edgy and nervy in the
preliminaries, she was taken very steadily to post by Darryll Holland, who was
fined for delaying the start. Carry On Katie showed a strong desire to get on with
things in the race as well, taking a good hold in front and drawing away easily in
the closing stages to score by twelve lengths despite looking green. Sold for an
undisclosed sum soon afterwards, she reappeared in the Peugeot Lowther Stakes at
York in August, in which only four of her eight rivals started at shorter than 25/1.
Silca's Gift, emphatic winner of a listed race at Royal Ascot, was a heavily-backed
favourite as Carry On Katie drifted alarmingly out to 3/1, but if the way the market
moved was a reflection of worries about Carry On Katie's well-being, someone
must have got their wires crossed. Once again nervy beforehand, Carry On Katie
was taken down early and all but bolted, but she showed more restraint once the
race was under way, albeit still racing freely at the head of affairs. In complete
command from over a furlong out, she beat Doncaster maiden Badminton
by two lengths with Dunloskin, runner-up in a Goodwood maiden, third. Silca's
Gift finished last. Frankie Dettori, Carry On Katie's rider at York, called her 'hot
and spicy' with good reason, and it was obvious that the filly needed to calm down

Sky Bet Cheveley Park Stakes, Newmarket—Carry On Katie doesn't get so worked up beforehand
and maintains her unbeaten record, holding off Majestic Desert (striped sleeves), with Badminton third

if she was to fulfil her potential. Signs of this came at Newmarket in the Sky Bet Cheveley Park Stakes in early-October. Attraction was an absentee through injury but the nine other runners promised to provide Carry On Katie, who started a strong favourite, with a proper test, including as they did Much Faster, sales race winners Majestic Desert and Nyramba, Badminton again, Flying Childers Stakes runner-up China Eyes (also by Fasliyev) and Ruby Rocket, successful in the Firth of Clyde Stakes. Although taken to post early again, Carry On Katie was much less edgy this time, and settled better while still showing her usual speed. Having got the better of Ruby Rocket from the Dip, Carry On Katie battled on genuinely to hold the late challenge of Majestic Desert by a short head with Badminton third, a length and three quarters away. Much Faster ran well below form in ninth.

Carry On Katie (USA) (br.f. Jan 14, 2001)	Fasliyev (USA) (b 1997)	Nureyev (b 1977)	Northern Dancer
			Special
		Mr P'S Princess (b 1993)	Mr Prospector
			Anne Campbell
	Dinka Raja (USA) (br 1995)	Woodman (ch 1983)	Mr Prospector
			Playmate
		Miss Profile (b 1990)	Sadler's Wells
			Katie May

It was all Piccadilly to a pineapple that Carry On Katie would join Godolphin at the end of the season, since after the Cheveley Park her owner's brother

Mr Mohammed Rashid's "Carry On Katie"

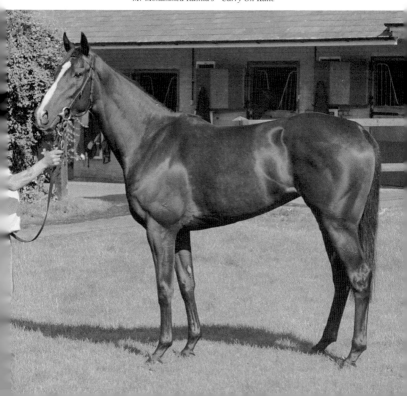

said: 'Sheikh Mohammed supports us, advises us and advised us to buy this filly. She'll spend the winter in Dubai but what happens next year will be up to (my brother) and Sheikh Mohammed. We take his opinion.' At the end of October Carry On Katie was duly confirmed a Godolphin filly, a blow for her trainer Jeremy Noseda, a former Godolphin team member who had already lost the highly promising (and much lauded) filly Park Accord to a fatal injury in September. However, Noseda is to train some of Darley Stud's two-year-olds in 2004. Carry On Katie will doubtless be trained for the One Thousand Guineas but, even allowing that a little more maturity might make her more tractable, she does not race as though she will be suited by a mile. Her pedigree is not conclusive on the matter. Fasliyev, unraced at three and with only juveniles to represent him, is something of an unknown quantity, but he had speed and most of his progeny have followed in his footsteps. Having said that, two of his stakes winners, Kings Point and Sgt Pepper, have won at seven furlongs and a mile respectively. The dam Dinka Raja won a minor event at a mile at Toulouse in France as a three-year-old on the first of her only two starts and was out of a half-sister to very smart fillies Grise Mine and Kostroma, who won Group/Grade 1 races at around a mile and a quarter. Carry On Katie's third dam, useful seven furlongs and mile winner Katie May, was a daughter of champion juvenile filly Cawston's Pride. Dinka Raja fetched 100,000 guineas at Tattersalls December Sales in 1999 when carrying a colt by Peintre Celebre who has won in the States. Carry On Katie, a good-topped filly, was well bought for €100,000 at Deauville as a yearling, around fifty per cent more than the average for Fasliyev's seventy-one yearlings sold at auction in 2002. Carry On Katie has raced only on good or good to firm going. *J. Noseda*

CARRY THE FIRE (USA) 3 ch.c. Smoke Glacken (USA) 120 – Vibrant Future (USA) (Vigors (USA)) [2003 p7g p10g p10g Mar 26] $32,000Y: sixth foal: half-brother to winners in USA by Apalachee and Lord Avie: dam won 10 times up to 9f in US, including up to 6f at 2 yrs: slowly away and soundly beaten in maidens. *M. J. Roberts* —

CARTE NOIRE 2 b.f. (Jan 24) Revoque (IRE) 122 – Coffee Cream 87 (Common Grounds 118) [2003 6m⁶ 7m 8m³ 8s Nov 3] workmanlike filly: first foal: dam, 7f (at 2 yrs)/1m winner, out of half-sister to dam of Racing Post Trophy and 2000 Guineas runner-up Even Top: fair maiden: got run of race when third at Goodwood, best effort: stays 1m: acts on good to firm ground: hung markedly left second start. *J. G. Portman* 65

CARTE SAUVAGE (USA) 2 gr. or ro.c. (Feb 19) Kris S (USA) – See You (USA) (Gulch (USA)) [2003 7.1m⁴ 7.2g* 8m² 8m³ 10g³ Nov 1] $25,000Y: close-coupled, good-topped colt: has a quick action: third foal: half-brother to winner in USA by Academy Award: dam, US 2-y-o 5f/6f winner, out of half-sister to US 2-y-o Grade 1 1m winner Eastern Echo: useful performer: won maiden at Ayr in July: good third in listed events at Pontefract (sweated) and Newmarket (beaten 1¾ lengths by Fun And Games): will stay at least 1½m: races prominently: game. *M. Johnston* 98

CARTOGRAPHY (IRE) 2 b.c. (Mar 27) Zafonic (USA) 130 – Sans Escale (USA) (Diesis 133) [2003 5.6f* 6m³ 5d* 5g Oct 11] 60,000Y: useful-looking colt: has scope: second foal: closely related to useful 1m winner West Escape (by Gone West) and half-brother to 2 winners, including fairly useful 2001 2-y-o 7f winner Sequin (by Green Desert): dam, French 11f winner, out of Prix de Diane winner Escaline: useful performer: won maiden at Doncaster in June and minor event at Beverley (by 3 lengths from Ballykeating) in September: raced alone when good 2¼ lengths third to Pastoral Pursuits in Sirenia Stakes at Kempton: hung right when below form in Cornwallis Stakes at Ascot: will stay 7f: acts on firm and good to soft going: joined Godolphin. *M. A. Jarvis* 103

CARTRONAGEERAGHLAD (IRE) 2 b.c. (Apr 27) Mujadil (USA) 119 – Night Scent (IRE) 85 (Scenic 128) [2003 6m f6g* 6f f7g⁶ 8s⁴ 7d* p7g⁶ f8s Dec 13] €50,000Y: sturdy colt: second foal: half-brother to useful Italian 7f to 10.5f (including at 2 yrs) winner Fielding (by Ali-Royal): dam, Irish 1m/9f winner, half-sister to smart Irish sprinter Bradawn Breever: fairly useful performer: won maiden at Southwell in June and nursery at Doncaster (best effort, beat Mrs Moh 2½ lengths) in November: should stay 1m: acts on all-weather and good to soft ground: blinkered (made running) last 3 starts: reportedly lame final outing. *J. A. Osborne* 83

CASANTELLA 2 b.f. (May 3) Atraf 116 – Ramajana (USA) (Shadeed (USA) 135) [2003 6m⁶ 7m 6g 7m f8.5g f7g f7g³ f9.4g⁶ Dec 22] 1,200Y: workmanlike filly: fourth foal: half-sister to 3 winners, including 4-y-o Dilys and 3-y-o Lady Natilda: dam 6f 47 (at 2 yrs) and 1m winner in Germany: poor maiden: left M. Wigham after fourth start, M. Quinlan after sixth: stays 7f: acts on fibresand: tried blinkered/visored. *M. J. Polglase*

CASARABONELA   3 b.f. Magic Ring (IRE) 115 – Carmenoura (IRE) (Carmelite   –
House (USA) 118) [2003 p6g 8.3g Apr 14] third foal: half-sister to 4-y-o Sebring: dam maiden granddaughter of Irish 1000 Guineas winner Royal Danseuse: well held in 2 maidens. *T. E. Powell*

CASE HISTORY   3 br.g. Case Law 113 – Brigadore Gold 51 (Petong 126) [2003 –:   –
8m Oct 2] maiden: well held only 3-y-o outing. *J. J. Bridger*

CASH   5 b.g. Bishop of Cashel 122 – Ballad Island 83 (Ballad Rock 122) [2003 68, a83:   –
f5s f6s f5g f5s^3 f5g f5g 5g f6g f5g f6g f5g^5 f6g f5g* f6g^6 f5s^4 Dec 31] angular gelding: **a75**
fair handicapper: won at Southwell in December: best at 5f/easy 6f: acts on fibresand, good to firm and good to soft ground: wore cheekpieces last 3 starts: none too reliable. *Paul Johnson*

CASHEL MEAD   3 b.f. Bishop of Cashel 122 – Island Mead 86 (Pharly (FR) 130)   **88**
[2003 89: 7g 7d 8.1d f6g^6 f6g^2 f6g^3 Dec 15] leggy filly: fairly useful handicapper: best 3-y-o efforts when placed at Wolverhampton (slowly away) and Southwell last 2 starts: should stay 7f: acts on fibresand, raced only on good going or softer on turf. *J. L. Spearing*

CASHEMA (IRE)   2 b.f. (Jan 25) Cape Cross (IRE) 129 – Miss Shema (USA) 81   –
(Gulch (USA)) [2003 7g 7m 7.9m Sep 3] €9,000Y: leggy, lengthy filly: first foal: dam 7f winner: little sign of ability in maidens. *Mrs P. N. Dutfield*

CASHNEEM (IRE)   5 b.g. Case Law 113 – Haanem 64 (Mtoto 134) [2003 72: 6.1d   **67**
7f 6m 6m 7.1m^4 8m* 7.9m^4 7.1g* 7.5d 8m Oct 4] strong gelding: fair handicapper: won at Redcar in August and Chepstow in September: stays 1m: acts on soft and good to firm ground: free-going sort. *W. M. Brisbourne*

CASPIAN DUSK   2 b.g. (Apr 10) Up And At 'em 109 – Caspian Morn 63 (Lugana   **42**
Beach 116) [2003 5.3m^4 6.1g 7m^6 Jun 24] second foal: half-brother to 11f/1½m winner Precaster (by Factual): dam 6f winner: poor form at best in maidens/claimer. *W. G. M. Turner*

CASSANOS (IRE)   2 b.c. (Apr 26) Ali-Royal (IRE) 127 – I'm Your Girl (Shavian 125)   **56**
[2003 6m 7.9m f7s f8s Dec 13] 15,000 2-y-o: rather leggy colt: fourth foal: half-brother to winners in Italy by Among Men (7f at 2 yrs) and Definite Article (up to 10.5f): dam unraced: modest form in maidens: should stay at least 1m. *Miss Gay Kelleway*

CASSE-NOISETTE (IRE)   5 b.m. Brief Truce (USA) 126 – Highdrive (Ballymore   –
123) [2003 12.1d 7f 10f Aug 27] of no account: tried blinkered/tongue tied. *Miss Z. C. Davison*

CASSIODORUS   2 ch.g. (Mar 4) Efisio 120 – Chicodove 91 (In The Wings 128) [2003   –
7.2f 8.1d Sep 27] compact gelding: first foal: dam 11f/1½m winner: slowly away and last in maidens at Ayr and Haydock (visored). *E. A. L. Dunlop*

CASSIS (USA)   3 b.f. Red Ransom (USA) – Minstress (USA) (The Minstrel (CAN)   **106**
135) [2003 103: 7m 10.4m* 10.5g^5 8f^4 9.9g^6 9f^4 10f Sep 28] strong, compact filly: useful performer: won Tattersalls Musidora Stakes at York in May by length from Geminiani: mostly creditable efforts after, including when 3 lengths fifth to Nebraska Tornado in Prix de Diane at Chantilly and 1¼ lengths fourth to Dessert in Del Mar Oaks (final outing for J. Noseda) then 7¼ lengths seventh of 8 to Tates Creek in Yellow Ribbon Stakes at Santa Anita last 2 starts: stays 10.5f: acts on firm going, good to soft and polytrack: has been bandaged behind: races freely. *Kathy Walsh, USA*

CASTAGNA (USA)   2 ch.f. (Mar 20) Horse Chestnut (SAF) 119 – Thrilling Day 112   – p
(Groom Dancer (USA) 128) [2003 8.1d Sep 27] lengthy filly: third foal: half-sister to fairly useful 2001 2-y-o 6f winner In Space (by Sky Classic): dam, 6f (at 2 yrs) to 8.5f (US Grade 3) winner, also won Nell Gwyn Stakes: 7/1, eighth of 14 in maiden at Haydock: likely to do better. *H. R. A. Cecil*

CASTAIGNE (FR)   4 ch.f. Pivotal 124 – Storm Warning 117 (Tumble Wind (USA))   **70 §**
[2003 73: 6g^5 7m 7m 7m^4 7m 8g^4 8f^4 7d^4 8g^6 8m^4 8.1m^5 9.9m 8f^6 8m 8.1m^2 8f^4 f8g p7g p10g^2 p10g Dec 17] workmanlike filly: fair maiden: effective at 7f to easy 1¼m: yet to race on soft/heavy going, acts on any other turf and polytrack: tried in cheekpieces/blinkers/tongue tie: sometimes slowly away/races freely: ungenuine. *B. W. Duke*

CASTAWAY QUEEN (IRE)   4 ch.f. Selkirk (USA) 129 – Surfing 71 (Grundy 137)   **70**
[2003 76: 8.5m p10g 8.3m^5 10f^3 10g^3 9f^5 10.2m^2 9g 10m^5 10f^6 10m^2 10f Sep 30] strong, close-coupled filly: fair maiden: stays easy 1¼m: acts on firm and good to soft going: tried in cheekpieces. *W. R. Muir*

CAS

CAST IRON 4 b.g. Efisio 120 – Misellina (FR) 57 (Polish Precedent (USA) 131) [2003 –
–, a65: p10g f9.4s p8g Feb 19] fair performer at best: well beaten all 3 starts in 2003:
often blinkered/visored: tried in cheekpieces. *J. R. Boyle*

CASTLEBRIDGE 6 b.g. Batshoof 122 – Super Sisters (AUS) (Call Report (USA)) – §
[2003 49§, a–§: 12m Jun 10] neat gelding: poor handicapper: soundly beaten only 6-y-o
start: usually visored/blinkered: *K. R. Burke*

CASTLE FROME (IRE) 4 b.g. Spectrum (IRE) 126 – Vendimia 60 (Dominion 123) 47 ?
[2003 8.1d 10m 9.9f⁵ f8.5s 8.3g 7m⁶ 8f Sep 8] IR 20,000Y: second foal: half-brother to
winner in Italy by Tagula: dam lightly-raced half-sister to 5-y-o Salim Toto: poor maiden:
stays easy 1¼m: acts on firm going: sometimes races freely. *Miss K. B. Boutflower*

CASTLE RING 4 b.g. Sri Pekan (USA) 117 – Understudy 60 (In The Wings 128) 54
[2003 53, a51: f12s f9.4s⁵ 10g 10g f12s 9.9m 9.9m* 10.9m 10m 12m Oct 6] strong
gelding: modest performer: won apprentice maiden handicap at Beverley in August:
stays 1½m: acts on soft ground, firm and fibresand: tried blinkered, sometimes wears
cheekpieces. *R. Hollinshead*

CASTLE RIVER (USA) 4 b.g. Irish River (FR) 131 – Castellina (USA) (Danzig 56 ?
Connection (USA)) [2003 84: 8m 8g 8.1m 10g 10f 10.1m² 9.9m Oct 1] close-coupled
gelding: modest performer nowadays: stays 1¼m: acts on firm and good to soft going:
very slowly away final start: tends to race freely: sometimes finds little: winning hurdler.
B. G. Powell

CASTLESHANE (IRE) 6 b.g. Kris 135 – Ahbab (IRE) 81 (Ajdal (USA) 130) [2003 100
90: 10g 11.6g 10m⁴ 10.3m 10f* 10m* 10.5m² 10g* 10.5m 12m 10.3d 10m 10.4f Oct 10]
big, strong gelding: useful handicapper: won at Ripon and Redcar (within 4 days) in June
and Kempton in July: stays 1½m: acts on any going: blinkered (raced freely) twice at 4
yrs: usually forces pace: game. *S. Gollings*

CASTLETON 2 b.c. (Feb 25) Cape Cross (IRE) 129 – Craigmill 85 (Slip Anchor 136) 99
[2003 6f³ 7d⁴ Jul 30] 12,000Y: close-coupled colt: fifth foal: half-brother to 3 winners,
including useful German performer up to 1½m Fleurie Domaine (by Unfuwain) and
3-y-o Astyanax: dam, 2-y-o 7f winner, half-sister to Park Hill winner Coigach and smart
performer up to 1¾m Applecross (latter dam of Craigsteel and Invermark): very green
when close third to Blue Tomato in maiden at York: useful form when 5¼ lengths fourth
to Lucky Story in Vintage Stakes at Goodwood, leading until over 2f out: will stay 1m:
capable of winning races. *H. J. Cyzer*

CASUAL FAME (USA) 5 b.h. Quest For Fame 127 – Never A Care (USA) 88 –
(Roberto (USA) 131) [2003 12g p10g 11.6m 16.2d Jul 25] good-topped horse: third foal:
dam 2-y-o 7f winner who stayed 1¼m: won 9f maiden at Le Croise-Laroche and 1m
listed race at Lyon Parilly at 2 yrs: left M. Zilber in France 6,500 gns before well held in
2003, including in seller: sold £3,300. *M. Quinn*

CASUAL LOOK (USA) 3 b.f. Red Ransom (USA) – Style Setter (USA) (Manila 114
(USA)) [2003 107: 8g⁶ 12g* 12g³ 11.9m 12m 9f³ 8.5d⁵ Nov 15]
An old racing saying has it that 'fillies are remembered for their best
performances, colts for their worst.' Neither Derby winner Kris Kin nor Oaks
winner Casual Look won again after Epsom, but there's no doubt whose reputation
suffered the most. Five defeats after the Vodafone Oaks made not a scrap of difference to Casual Look's stud value or prospects. She will, however, go down as a
substandard Oaks winner—the lowest rated winner of the race since Long Look
(112) in 1965—and a lucky one too. The favourite Yesterday couldn't get a clear
run and finished very strongly after being checked and switched in the closing
stages. Casual Look herself didn't get her head in front until well inside the final
furlong and deserved plenty of credit for responding gamely under pressure in the
home straight after being close up from the start. She held off Yesterday by a neck
with Summitville half a length away in third. The fact that the first eight were
covered by five lengths suggested at the time that the latest Oaks was far from a
vintage renewal. Further confirmation was forthcoming when, among the principals, only sixth-placed Hanami—who had finished ahead of the first three when
fifth in the One Thousand Guineas—and eighth-placed Thingmebob managed to
win a race afterwards. Fourth-placed Inchberry, a 100/1-shot, came only sixth in the
Ribblesdale at Royal Ascot on her next start and ended the season beaten in a
maiden at Musselburgh. Casual Look, who started at 10/1, provided a first classic
winner for Andrew Balding, who smoothly took over the reins at Kingsclere from

194

Vodafone Oaks, Epsom—Casual Look (left) provides Andrew Balding with his first classic winner in his first season of training; Yesterday (white face) is an unlucky second, ahead of Summitville (second left), Inchberry (striped sleeves) and Hi Dubai

his father Ian in the latest season. The stable landed a treble on Oaks day when Passing Glance won one of the valuable handicaps and Rimrod the Surrey Stakes. Casual Look's jockey Martin Dwyer, who started at Kingsclere at the age of fifteen, also had three winners on Oaks day, Passing Glance and Casual Look following Aldora in the opening Princess Elizabeth Stakes.

Casual Look won only one other race in her career, a maiden at Bath as a two-year-old, when she developed into a useful performer, finishing runner-up in the Fillies' Mile at Ascot and the Rockfel Stakes at Newmarket on her last two starts. She was a 50/1-shot when reappearing in the One Thousand Guineas, in which she was far from discredited in sixth, staying on well. Casual Look was kept at a mile and a half for her three races in Europe after the Oaks. She found a couple too good for her in the Irish Oaks in Vintage Tipple, who had been sidelined with a hairline fracture since her reappearance over seven furlongs in April, and L'Ancresse, who had been pulled up in the Oaks after being checked and losing her action; fourth-placed Yesterday, a short-priced favourite to gain compensation for her defeat at Epsom, finished behind Casual Look in a classic for the third time. Casual Look had a slight setback, pricking her foot, in the build-up to the Yorkshire Oaks, though whether it was enough to account for a disappointing performance, in which she beat only one home, is debatable. Another below-form run followed in the Prix Vermeille at Longchamp, where Casual Look was unable to sustain her effort after being rushed into the lead five furlongs out, eventually fading into eighth behind Mezzo Soprano (Yesterday a close second). Casual Look raced for her breeder William Farish III, the United States ambassador to London, and was returned to North America for an autumn campaign. She was still in Balding's care when a good third to Film Maker and Maiden Tower in the Queen Elizabeth II Challenge Cup, a Group 1 event over nine furlongs at Keeneland, but her retirement was announced when she managed only fifth behind the former Michael Bell-trained Hoh Buzzard in the Grade 2 Mrs Revere Stakes at Churchill Downs in mid-November.

Casual Look is by Roberto's son Red Ransom (another son of Roberto, Kris S, sired the Derby winner), whose arrival in Europe for the 2004 breeding season was trumpeted by a glossy brochure entitled 'Red hot', which, in a master-stroke of timing by Darley's marketing team, arrived by post on August 10th, the day that Britain sizzled on the hottest day since records began, the temperature reaching 101.3F (38.5C) at Brogdale, near Faversham in Kent. Previously based at Vinery in Kentucky and shuttled to Australia, Red Ransom, who had only a brief racing career, will stand at Dalham Hall Stud, Newmarket, at a fee of £35,000, with the October 1st concession, his fee reflecting a fairly good overall stud record and an exceptional year with his British-based runners—'the Red Army'—in 2003. Eight of his nine three-year-old runners were successful (with only one of them rated below 95), as were five of his ten two-year-olds, while Ekraar and Ransom o'War

Mr W. S. Farish III's "Casual Look"

Casual Look (USA) (b.f. 2000)	Red Ransom (USA) (b 1987)	Roberto (b 1969)	Hail To Reason Bramalea
		Arabia (b 1977)	Damascus Christmas Wind
	Style Setter (USA) (ch 1990)	Manila (b 1983)	Lyphard Dona Ysidra
		Charleston Rag (ch 1982)	General Assembly Music Ville

provided him with other Group 1 winners in Europe. The average distance of races won by Red Ransom's European runners at three and upwards is just over nine furlongs and there was conjecture before Epsom about whether Casual Look was bred to get the Oaks trip. Her dam Style Setter was a winning miler in the States and, to a previous mating with Red Ransom, had produced the smart French filly Shabby Chic, who had been successful at up to a mile and a quarter, the longest distance she had tackled. Style Setter had also had winners in North America, Racket Club (by Alysheba) and American Style (by Quiet American), neither winning at much beyond a mile. Charleston Rag, the dam of Style Setter, won the Grade 1 Frizette Stakes over a mile as a two-year-old but injury cut short her three-year-old career; she was bred for stamina, by Travers Stakes winner General Assembly out of Irish Oaks fifth Music Ville, a close relative of Irish Derby and King George winner Meadow Court. Style Setter's latest foal to reach the racecourse, the Gone West two-year-old colt Saville Row, showed fairly useful form for Andre Fabre in France, winning a newcomers event at Chantilly and a minor event at Deauville. The big, leggy Casual Look, who acted on firm going

196

and only once encountered ground softer than good (on her final start), begins her career as a broodmare with a visit to Mineshaft, who carried the Farish colours with distinction in the States in the latest season. *N. J. Howard, USA*

CATALINI 2 ch.c. (Apr 2) Seeking The Gold (USA) – Calando (USA) 110 (Storm Cat (USA)) [2003 7g⁵ 7m⁵ 7m³ 7s⁶ 7d³ Nov 7] small, quite attractive colt: first foal: dam, 2-y-o 7f/1m (May Hill Stakes) winner, out of Oaks winner and St Leger second Diminuendo: fairly useful maiden: third twice at Doncaster, best effort on first occasion: should be suited by 1¼m/1½m: acts on good to firm ground. *M. R. Channon* — **84**

CATCHER IN THE RYE (IRE) 3 b.c. Danehill (USA) – Truly A Dream (IRE) 116 (Darshaan 133) [2003 105: 8g* 8g² May 11] 4,900,000 francs Y: fourth foal: half-brother to French 2000 2-y-o 1m winner Truly Yours (by Barathea) and 2001 2-y-o 7f winner Indian Dreamer (by Indian Ridge), later 5.5f winner in UAE: dam, won Prix de Royaumont and E P Taylor Stakes, half-sister to smart stayer Wareed: smart form: won maiden at Leopardstown in March: plenty of improvement and unlucky not to have gone closer still when length second to Clodovil in Poule d'Essai des Poulains at Longchamp in May, still last 1f out and running on strongly once switched: would have stayed beyond 1m: looked sure to improve again, but reported in June to have suffered serious leg injury on gallops: to stand at Castlehyde Stud, Co Cork, Ireland, fee €4,000, Oct 1st. *A. P. O'Brien, Ireland* — **115**

CATCHTHEBATCH 7 b.g. Beveled (USA) – Batchworth Dancer 67 (Ballacashtal (CAN)) [2003 54, a76: 5g⁶ 5.1m 5.5m⁵ f5s 5.1g² 5m f5g f5g f5g f6s⁶ f6g³ f5g f5s Dec 31] lengthy, sparely-made gelding: modest performer: effective at 5f/easy 6f: acts on all-weather and good to firm going: tried blinkered: sometimes slowly away: usually races prominently: none too consistent. *E. A. Wheeler* — **55**

CATCH THE CAT (IRE) 4 b.g. Catrail (USA) 123 – Tongabezi (IRE) 75 (Shernazar 131) [2003 65: 6m 5g f7g 5m³ 5m³ 5g² 5m* 5m⁶ 5m⁴ 5m f5s⁵ 5g* 5m 5m 5m⁵ 5s⁶ 5d f6g⁵ f5g Dec 12] well-made gelding: fair handicapper on turf, modest on all-weather: won at Beverley in July and Doncaster in September: best at 5f: acts on fibresand, good to firm and soft ground: wears headgear: sometimes slowly away: often races prominently. *J. S. Wainwright* — **74** **a54**

CATCH THE FOX 3 b.g. Fraam 114 – Versaillesprincess (Legend of France (USA) 124) [2003 49: 9g 8.3g 7m 8f⁵ 8.5g Jul 17] leggy, workmanlike gelding: poor maiden handicapper: stays easy 1m: acts on firm and soft ground: difficult ride. *J. J. Bridger* — **48 ?**

CATCH THE WIND 2 b.f. (Mar 6) Bahamian Bounty 116 – Tinkerbird 76 (Music Boy 124) [2003 5d³ 5m* 6f⁴ 6g Jul 26] 9,000Y: sturdy, lengthy filly: half-sister to several winners, including 5f/6f winner Bataleur (by Midyan) and 5-y-o Be My Tinker: dam sprinting half-sister to useful Irish 1½m to 2m performer Quinze: fairly useful performer: made all in maiden at Pontefract in June: hampered when creditable 10½ lengths fourth to Silca's Gift in listed race at Royal Ascot: stiff task final start: stays 6f: acts on firm ground. *I. A. Wood* — **81**

CATEEL BAY 5 ch.m. Most Welcome 131 – Calachuchi 74 (Martinmas 128) [2003 –: 14.1d Jul 26] lightly raced and of little account. *H. Alexander* — **–**

CATERHAM COMMON 4 b.g. Common Grounds 118 – Pennine Pink (IRE) 72 (Pennine Walk 120) [2003 54: f8g f8s f7s⁶ f8g 7.1f 12.1g 5.9d 6f Aug 29] smallish, sturdy gelding: unimpressive mover: no form in 2003: sometimes blinkered. *D. W. Chapman* — **–**

CATHERINE HOWARD 2 b.f. (Mar 26) Kingmambo (USA) 125 – Darling Flame (USA) 101 (Capote (USA)) [2003 6g* May 24] third foal: half-sister to smart French 7f winner Bezrin (by Danzig) and fairly useful Irish 7.5f winner Flamelet (by Theatrical): dam, 6f (at 2 yrs)/7f winner, half-sister to smart 7f/1m performer Heart Lake out of US Grade 1 8.5f winner My Darling One: favourite, fair form when winning 7-runner maiden at Lingfield, slowly away and green: injured pedal bone after: should stay at least 7f. *M. R. Channon* — **74**

CATHY PEE 2 ch.f. (Mar 30) Groom Dancer (USA) 128 – Stormswept (USA) 74 (Storm Bird (CAN) 134) [2003 5m 6m 6m⁵ Aug 23] workmanlike filly: seventh foal: half-sister to 3 winners, including 1m winner Amico (by Efisio) and 4-y-o Michaels Dream: dam, 2-y-o 5f winner, closely related to Colonel Collins, Lit de Justice and Commander Collins: well beaten in maidens. *J. Hetherton* — **–**

CATHY RUAN 3 bl.f. Robellino (USA) 127 – Q Factor 90 (Tragic Role (USA)) [2003 –: f6g Jun 9] little form. *D. Haydn Jones* — **–**

CATIE DASH 2 ch.f. (May 10) Daggers Drawn (USA) 114 – Papita (IRE) 77 (Law **83** Society (USA) 130) [2003 5.1g² 5m² 5.1f* 5g⁵ 5.1f* Oct 12] £1,000Y: second foal: half-sister to 3-y-o Summer Lightning: dam 2-y-o 6f winner who stayed 1¼m: fairly useful performer: won maiden in September and nursery in October, both at Bath: should prove best at 5f/easy 6f: acts on firm going: started slowly first 2 outings. *R. M. Beckett*

CATMINT 3 b.f. Piccolo 121 – Kitty Kitty Cancan 73 (Warrshan (USA) 117) [2003 **85 d** 84: 5.1g⁴ 6m 5f 6m Jul 16] rather leggy filly: fairly useful performer: form in 2003 only on reappearance: should stay 6f: raced only on good ground or firmer. *Mrs P. N. Dutfield*

CAT ONA HIGH (USA) 3 ch.g. Tabasco Cat (USA) 126 – Uforia (USA) (Zilzal **108** (USA) 137) [2003 101p: 8m⁴ 10.4m 8m⁶ 8g² 9m⁴ Sep 12] good-topped gelding: useful performer: struck into in Dante Stakes at York second outing and off 3 months: best efforts on last 2 starts, in frame under top weight in handicaps at Ripon (beaten ¾ length by Fremen) and Goodwood (length fourth to Impeller): stays 9f: acts on good to firm going: sent to Hong Kong, where renamed Kingfield. *Mrs A. J. Perrett*

CATSTAR (USA) 2 br.f. (Jan 25) Storm Cat (USA) – Advancing Star (USA) 115 **105** (Soviet Star (USA) 128) [2003 5m* 5m² Jun 18] lengthy, rather unfurnished filly: second foal: sister to winner in USA: dam, smart US 5.5f and 6.5f Grade 3 winner, stayed 8.5f: green, landed odds in 4-runner maiden at Leicester in May: useful form when 3 lengths second to Attraction in Queen Mary Stakes at Royal Ascot, never far away and pulling 5 lengths clear of rest: will stay at least 6f: joined Saeed bin Suroor. *D. R. Loder*

CAT'S WHISKERS 4 b.g. Catrail (USA) 123 – Haut Volee (Top Ville 129) [2003 **98** 92: 8g 8m⁵ 8g² 10m² 8.9f 10.4f 7.6m 10.3g Sep 13] leggy gelding: useful handicapper: good second at Thirsk and Redcar (beaten ¾ length by Hazim in Zetland Gold Cup) in May: effective at 1m/1¼m: acts on soft and good to firm going: has been early to post/blanketed for stall entry. *M. W. Easterby*

Sheikh Mohammed's "Catstar"

CAUGHT IN THE DARK 3 b.f. Night Shift (USA) – Captive Heart (Conquistador **89**
Cielo (USA)) [2003 85: 5.5m⁵ 6.1m³ 6.1d² 6m 6f² 6m 6m* 5.1f⁵ 6g Sep 22] lengthy
filly: fairly useful performer: made all at Epsom in July: free-going sort, should prove as
effective at 5f as 6f: acts on firm and soft ground: blinkered (well beaten) final start: races
prominently: sold 8,500 gns, sent to USA. *J. L. Dunlop*

CAUGHT OUT 3 b.g. Ordway (USA) 117 – Catch (USA) (Blushing Groom (FR) **–**
131) [2003 63: 8g 7.1m³ 8m 6m 7f 7.1f⁵ 7.2g 6m⁶ 6m 8m 8m⁵ 7.5m 7.2f⁵ 8m 8g 6m⁶ 8m
8d⁶ Oct 13] sparely-made gelding: modest at 2 yrs: little solid form in 2003. *A. Berry*

CAUSE CELEBRE (IRE) 2 gr.f. (Feb 12) Peintre Celebre (USA) 137 – Madame **79**
Belga (USA) (Al Nasr (FR) 126) [2003 7m 8m³ 8.2f² 7.9f⁴ Oct 11] 20,000Y: leggy,
unfurnished filly: has a quick action: sixth foal: closely related to French 9f winner
Spinning Lady (by Spinning World) and half-sister to winners in USA by Carson City
and Silver Hawk: dam unraced close relative of top-class French miler Bellypha: fair
maiden: second at Nottingham, best effort: will be suited by 1¼m/1½m. *B. W. Hills*

CAUSTIC WIT (IRE) 5 b.g. Cadeaux Genereux 123 – Baldemosa (FR) (Lead On **58 d**
Time (USA) 123) [2003 ?: 6g 5g 5g f5s³ f5g f6g³ f6g Nov 25] leggy, quite good-topped
gelding: useful at 2 yrs: reportedly fractured pelvis at 3 yrs: modest in 2003: best at 5f/6f:
acts on fibresand and good to firm going. *M. S. Saunders*

CAUTIOUS 3 gr.g. Petong 126 – Kind of Shy 61 (Kind of Hush 118) [2003 59: 6g 7m⁵ **51**
7m Jul 2] close-coupled, quite good-topped gelding: modest maiden, lightly raced:
stays 7f: acts on good to firm and good to soft ground: wore cheekpieces last 2 starts.
R. M. Beckett

CAVERAL 2 ch.f. (Mar 29) Ashkalani (IRE) 128 – Melting Gold (USA) 108 (Cadeaux **82 p**
Genereux 131) [2003 6g³ 6g* Oct 31] €16,000Y: fifth foal: half-sister to French 9f winner Gold Venture (by Indian Ridge) and French 10.5f winner Golden Days (by Mark of
Esteem): dam French 2-y-o 7f winner out of half-sister to 2000 Guineas winner Shadeed:
confirmed promise when winning maiden at Newmarket by 3 lengths from Fun To Ride,
making most despite hanging left: will be suited by at least 1m: should make a useful
3-y-o. *R. Hannon*

CAVERSFIELD 8 ch.g. Tina's Pet 121 – Canoodle 66 (Warpath 113) [2003 55§, **– §**
a59§: f7g⁴ f7s f7g p7g Jan 22] workmanlike gelding: poor performer: was best at 7f/1m: **a46 §**
acted on fibresand, firm and soft ground: tried visored: usually blinkered: unreliable:
dead. *J. M. Bradley*

CAYENNE 2 b.f. (Apr 4) Fraam 114 – Katya (IRE) 93 (Dancing Dissident (USA) 119) **–**
[2003 5.7f 5.7m 7m 5.1m Aug 5] third living foal: half-sister to winner in Jersey
by Piccolo: dam 5f (at 2 yrs) and 6f winner: little sign of ability, including in sellers.
M. R. Channon

CAYMAN BREEZE 3 b.g. Danzig (USA) – Lady Thynn (FR) (Crystal Glitters (USA) **74**
127) [2003 78: 6m³ 6.1g 6g⁵ 6m² 6m² 6f* 8m f6g 7s p7g³ p7g p7g Dec 30] smallish,
sturdy gelding: fair performer: won maiden at Catterick in August: left E. Dunlop 8,000
gns after ninth start: stays easy 7f: acts on polytrack, raced mainly on good going or
firmer on turf: has carried head awkwardly. *S. Dow*

CAYMAN MISCHIEF 3 b.f. Cayman Kai (IRE) 114 – Tribal Mischief 61 (Be My **–**
Chief (USA) 122) [2003 f7s 5d Nov 4] first foal: dam 2-y-o 5f winner: well held in seller/
claimer. *James Moffatt*

CAYMAN SUNRISE (IRE) 3 gr.f. Peintre Celebre (USA) 137 – Sum (USA) (Spec- **68**
tacular Bid (USA)) [2003 7.5m³ 8.1d⁴ 9.9m⁴ 8.2m² p10g⁶ p7g⁶ Dec 29] leggy filly: half-
sister to several winners abroad, including useful French 10.5f winner Magical Hawk (by
Silver Hawk): dam, US Grade 3 9f winner, half-sister to smart miler Emperor Jones and
William Hill Futurity winner Bakharoff: fair maiden: stays 1¼m: acts on polytrack,
unraced on extremes of going on turf: reportedly returned home jarred up after debut.
E. A. L. Dunlop

CAZISA STAR (USA) 2 ch.f. (Mar 13) Mister Baileys 123 – Placer Queen (Habitat **63**
134) [2003 7.6m 8.1f³ 7m⁶ Sep 22] rather leggy, close-coupled filly: half-sister to several
winners, including 9-y-o Beyond Calculation and 4-y-o Triplemoon: dam won up to 1¼m
in Canada: modest form in maidens: should stay 1m. *P. W. Harris*

CD EUROPE (IRE) 5 ch.g. Royal Academy (USA) 130 – Woodland Orchid (IRE) **100**
64 (Woodman (USA) 126) [2003 91: f5s 6m 6m* 5m⁴ 6d 5g 6f² 6g 6m² 6m 6f² 6s*
Nov 3] lengthy gelding: carries little condition: has reportedly had sinus problems: useful
handicapper: found guilty under non-triers rule on reappearance: won at Hamilton in
April and Redcar (beat Steel Blue 1¼ lengths) in November: best at 6f: acts on firm and

soft going (well held on heavy once): wore cheekpieces last 2 starts: reared as stall opened fifth outing: held up. *K. A. Ryan*

CD FLYER (IRE) 6 ch.g. Grand Lodge (USA) 125 – Pretext (Polish Precedent (USA) **94** 131) [2003 85: p6g⁴ 6m⁵ 6m² 6g³ 6d⁵ 6d 6m³ 5.7f⁴ 6g* 6m* 6m Sep 19] lengthy, angular gelding: good walker: fairly useful handicapper: won at Haydock in July and Goodwood (career-best effort, beat Fantasy Believer 1¼ lengths) in August: best at 6f: acts on any turf going and polytrack: sometimes hangs: held up: tough and reliable: sold 24,000 gns. *M. R. Channon*

CEAD MILE FAILTE 8 ch.g. Most Welcome 131 – Avionne 59 (Derrylin 115) [2003 **–** 46: f12g f16.2g f12g f12g Feb 21] poor performer: well beaten in 2003: tried in cheekpieces. *B. J. Llewellyn*

CEASAR (IRE) 2 b.g. (Feb 18) Orpen (USA) 116 – Fen Princess (IRE) 72 (Trojan **63 d** Fen 118) [2003 6m⁶ 6g² 6f 7.5m⁶ 8d f8g f7g⁴ Dec 16] workmanlike gelding: half-brother to 3 winners, including useful 9f to 15f winner Fiori (by Anshan): dam 15f winner at 4 yrs: modest maiden: second at Hamilton: showed little after, including in nurseries: should stay at least 1m. *P. C. Haslam*

CEDARBERG (UAE) 2 b.c. (Feb 26) Cape Cross (IRE) 129 – Crinolette (IRE) **102** (Sadler's Wells (USA) 132) [2003 6d² 6m² 6.1m* 6g³ Jul 29] strong, lengthy colt: has a quick action: third foal: dam, once-raced half-sister to very smart Irish 6f/7f performer Desert Style, from family of Barathea: useful performer: second in maiden at the Curragh and listed race at Epsom (sweating/good hold to post) prior to landing odds in maiden at Chepstow in July, making all: good third, beaten under a length by Carrizo Creek, in Richmond Stakes at Goodwood: should stay 7f: acts on good to firm going, probably on good to soft: joined Godolphin. *M. R. Channon*

CEDAR GROVE 6 b.g. Shirley Heights 130 – Trojan Desert 97 (Troy 137) [2003 **44 §** 54§: f16g⁶ f12s f14g³ f16.2s⁴ 16d² f14.8g 13.1m⁴ 14.1m 14.1d² 16d Aug 11] good-topped gelding: poor maiden: stays easy 2m: acts on fibresand, good to firm and good to soft going: tried tongue tied, wore cheekpieces in 2003: unreliable: sold 2,000 gns. *John A. Harris*

CEDAR MASTER (IRE) 6 b.g. Soviet Lad (USA) – Samriah (IRE) (Wassl 125) **82** [2003 74: 15.4m² 16m 20m 16m⁵ 15.4m Jul 28] quite attractive gelding: fairly useful handicapper: best effort at 6 yrs when second at Folkestone in April: left R. O'Sullivan after second start: stays 2m: acts on polytrack, firm and good to soft going, probably soft: tends to hang: none too consistent: winning hurdler. *J. R. Boyle*

CEDAR RANGERS (USA) 5 b.g. Anabaa (USA) 130 – Chelsea (USA) (Miswaki **60 §** (USA) 124) [2003 65d: p7g⁴ p10g p8g p8g p7g Feb 26] rather leggy gelding: modest performer: stays 1m: acts on polytrack and good to firm going: wore blinkers/cheekpieces in 2003: unreliable. *R. J. O'Sullivan*

CEEPIO (IRE) 5 b.g. Pennekamp (USA) 130 – Boranwood (IRE) (Exhibitioner 111) **107** [2003 100: 7d* 6g 7m² 7m² 7f Sep 27] lengthy, good-topped gelding: has a quick action: useful performer: won handicap at Kempton in March: good efforts after when runner-up in minor event at Leicester and handicap at Goodwood: effective at 6f/7f: acts on soft and good to firm going: races freely/prominently: sold 17,000 gns, sent to USA. *T. G. Mills*

CEFIRA (USA) 2 b.f. (Mar 19) Distant View (USA) 126 – Bold Jessie (Never So **63** Bold 135) [2003 6m Jul 10] useful-looking filly: closely related to 6f (at 2 yrs)/7f winner Jentzen and 5f/6f (including at 2 yrs) winner Abou Zouz (both useful and by Miswaki), and half-sister to 2 winners: dam, Irish 2-y-o 6f winner, half-sister to sprinters Prince Sabo (very smart) and Millyant (smart): 20/1, eleventh of 12 in maiden at Newmarket, racing freely. *M. H. Tompkins*

CELADON (IRE) 2 b.c. (Mar 24) Fasliyev (USA) 120 – Dancing Drop 103 (Green **70** Desert (IRE) 127) [2003 5d⁴ 5m³ 5f⁵ f6g Nov 29] €75,000Y: third foal: half-brother to useful German 6f (including at 2 yrs)/6.5f winner Davignon (by Highest Honor): dam 2-y-o 6f winner who stayed 1m: fair maiden: never-dangerous third at Lingfield: slowly away last 2 starts, leaving J. Noseda before final one: should stay 6f. *N. P. Littmoden*

CELESTIA 3 b.f. Anabaa (USA) 130 – Divine Quest 81 (Kris 135) [2003 81: 7g 8g **72** May 4] quite attractive filly: has a round action: useful performer at 2 yrs: just fair form early in 2003: races freely, and likely to prove best up to 7f: raced on good going or firmer: sold 13,000 gns in December. *J. L. Dunlop*

CELLARMASTER (IRE) 2 ch.g. (Mar 7) Alhaarth (IRE) 126 – Cheeky Weeky **73 p** (Cadeaux Genereux 131) [2003 7.5m³ 8m⁵ f8.5s² Sep 20] IR 28,000F, 32,000Y: angular, useful-looking gelding: second foal: dam, French maiden who stayed 1½m, out of close relative to smart 1990 2-y-o sprinter Mujadil and half-sister to high-class 1½m performer Fruits of Love: fair form in maidens: late headway when second at Wolverhampton: will be suited by 1¼m/1½m: slowly away first 2 starts: open to improvement. *A. C. Stewart*

CELLINO 2 b.f. (Mar 8) Robellino (USA) 127 – Celandine 80 (Warning 136) [2003 **56** 5m 6f 5m⁵ 5m Sep 9] smallish filly: first foal: dam 5.7f (at 2 yrs) and 7f winner: modest maiden: should stay at least 6f. *Andrew Turnell*

CELLO 2 gr.c. (May 15) Pivotal 124 – Raffelina (USA) (Carson City (USA)) [2003 6f⁶ **78** 6m³ 7m⁵ p7g⁵ Oct 30] 25,000Y: big, good-topped colt: has scope: third foal: half-brother to 4-y-o Prima Stella and winner in Greece by Magic Ring: dam unraced: fair maiden: third at Goodwood: needs to settle to stay 1m: acts on good to firm going. *R. Hannon*

CELTIC BLAZE (IRE) 4 b.f. Charente River (IRE) 67 – Firdaunt (Tanfirion 110) **67** [2003 69: f12g² f12g⁶ 13.8m* 14m³ 14.1g 16.2m⁶ 12.1m Aug 24] close-coupled filly: fifth living foal: dam Irish 1½m winner: fair handicapper: trained by S. Fahey in Ireland at 2/3 yrs: won at Catterick in March: stays 1¾m: acts on firm ground and fibresand. *B. S. Rothwell*

CELTIC CAT (IRE) 2 b.c. (Feb 22) Danehill (USA) 126 – Golden Cat (USA) 102 **106** (Storm Cat (USA)) [2003 5g* 7m² 7f⁶ Sep 14] 220,000Y: sturdy, lengthy colt: second foal: dam, Irish 1m winner (stayed 1¼m), half-sister to useful Irish 1½m winner Bowmore out of Irish St Leger winner Eurobird: landed odds in maiden at Cork in July: useful form when neck second to Rule of Law in listed race at York (still green, finished strongly) and sixth of 8 to stable-companion One Cool Cat in National Stakes at the Curragh: will stay 1m. *A. P. O'Brien, Ireland*

CELTIC CHARMER 4 b.g. Celtic Swing 138 – Hamsah (IRE) 86 (Green Desert **–** (USA) 127) [2003 –: f12s f8s Jan 10] quite good-topped gelding: little form. *R. Craggs*

CELTIC HEROINE (IRE) 2 ch.f. (Apr 29) Hernando (FR) 127 – Celtic Fling 77 **83** (Lion Cavern (USA) 117) [2003 7m⁵ p7g* 7g⁵ p7g⁴ f8s* Dec 13] sturdy filly: first foal: dam, 1m winner, closely related to Racing Post Trophy and Prix du Jockey Club winner Celtic Swing: fairly useful performer: won maiden at Lingfield in October and nursery at Southwell (beat Blue Empire a short head) in December: should be suited by 1¼m/1½m: acts on all-weather, better turf effort on good going. *M. A. Jarvis*

CELTIC LEGEND 5 b.m. Celtic Swing 138 – No Reprieve (NZ) (Deputy Governor **–** (USA) 123) [2003 –: f6g Apr 7] leggy, plain mare: no form. *Paul Johnson*

CELTIC MILL 5 b.g. Celtic Swing 138 – Madam Millie 99 (Milford 119) [2003 82, **98** a90: 7m⁴ 6g* 6m* 7d² 6m⁴ 6m 7g³ 6d 6m* 7f⁴ 7.1m Oct 25] tall gelding: useful performer: won handicaps at Pontefract and Hamilton in July, and apprentice minor event at Catterick in October: good fourth in handicap at York penultimate start: best at 6f/7f: acts on fibresand, firm and good to soft going: front runner: game. *D. W. Barker*

CELTIC ROMANCE 4 b.f. Celtic Swing 138 – Southern Sky 89 (Comedy Star **–** (USA) 121) [2003 –: 6g 7f 8m 10s Jun 30] sparely-made filly: lightly raced and little form since 2001. *D. Nicholls*

CELTIC ROVER 5 b.g. Celtic Swing 138 – Lady Sabo 69 (Prince Sabo 123) [2003 **– §** 39§: f6g⁵ f7g 6m 6m May 12] plain gelding: poor maiden: stays 6f: tried blinkered: temperamental. *C. R. Dore*

CELTIC SAPPHIRE (FR) 3 b.f. Celtic Swing 138 – Smart 'n Noble (USA) (Smarten **71** (USA)) [2003 89: 10.4m 11.9m 7.9f⁵ 8.5m³ 9m⁴ 11.9m² 9.9m³ 14.1m³ 12.1m 10g 12d⁶ Nov 4] tall filly: just fair maiden in 2003: stays easy 1¾m: acts on good to firm and good to soft ground. *T. D. Easterby*

CELTIC SOLITUDE (IRE) 2 b.f. (May 6) Celtic Swing 138 – Smart 'n Noble **–** (USA) (Smarten (USA)) [2003 8g⁶ f7g Nov 25] fourth foal: sister to smart performer up to 1¼m Celtic Silence, 6f/7f winner at 2 yrs: dam won 12 races in USA, including Grade 2 7f event: well held in maidens at Musselburgh (slowly away/raced freely) and Southwell. *M. Johnston*

CELTIC STAR (IRE) 5 b.g. Celtic Swing 138 – Recherchee (Rainbow Quest (USA) **67** 134) [2003 12.1d* 12.1g* 12m⁶ Aug 25] tall gelding: fair handicapper: missed 2002: won at Chepstow in July (amateur event, edged left) and August (idled): stays 1½m: acts on good to soft ground: tried visored: fair hurdler. *Nick Williams*

CELTIC STYLE 4 b.g. Celtic Swing 138 – Stylish Rose (IRE) 65 (Don't Forget Me **84** 127) [2003 89: 12g 12m 12m² 14.6m⁴ 15.8m³ 14.8m⁶ 14m⁴ 14f³ Aug 21] very tall, leggy gelding: fairly useful handicapper: barely stayed 15.8f: acted on good to firm and good to soft going: sometimes carried head awkwardly: dead. *M. Johnston*

CELTIC TED   5 b.g. Celtic Swing 138 – Careful Dancer (Gorytus (USA) 132) [2003 **–** –: 12g f9.4s Apr 12] angular gelding: well held, including in sellers. *P. Butler*

CELTIC THATCHER   5 b.g. Celtic Swing 138 – Native Thatch (IRE) 47 (Thatching **–** 131) [2003 –, a100d: f7s Jan 16] formerly useful on all-weather, modest on turf: well beaten only 5-y-o start: tried in cheekpieces, usually visored. *N. P. Littmoden*

CELTIC THUNDER   2 b.g. (Mar 19) Mind Games 121 – Lake Mistassiu 86 (Tina's **86 p** Pet 121) [2003 5g⁴ 5m3 5m* 5m² 5m⁴ 6f⁶ Oct 10] 6,500Y: good-topped gelding: seventh foal: half-brother to 7f (at 2 yrs) to 11f winner Santiburi Girl (by Casteddu): dam 5f winner, including at 2 yrs: won maiden at Beverley in July: good efforts in nurseries after, despite not always lasting home: will prove best at 5f/easy 6f: acts on firm going: has scope to make a useful 3-y-o. *T. J. Etherington*

CELTIC TRUTH (USA)   3 b. or br.f. Known Fact (USA) 135 – Caithness (USA) **90** (Roberto (USA) 131) [2003 8f 10m* 10f* 10.5d⁴ 11.6m⁵ 12f⁵ Oct 12] seventh living foal: sister to useful 1997 2-y-o 7f winner Blue Gentian and half-sister to 2 winners, including useful French 10.5f winner (stayed 15f) Stromness (by Trempolino): dam, French 11f winner, half-sister to very smart performer around 7f Condrillac: fairly useful performer: won maiden at Windsor in July and handicap at Brighton (4 ran) in August: stays 1½m: acts on firm and good to soft going: front runner: sold 27,000 gns. *R. Charlton*

CENTRAL COMMAND   3 b.g. Cadeaux Genereux 131 – Possessive Artiste 73 **53 ?** (Shareef Dancer (USA) 135) [2003 8.3g⁴ 8.3d 11.5g 7m Oct 21] third foal: half-brother to useful 1m to 1¼m winner in Hong Kong Blue Stitch (by Selkirk): dam, 11.5f winner, sister to smart Irish/Italian Oaks winner Possessive Dancer: modest maiden: stays 8.3f: wore cheekpieces third start: sold 2,500 gns. *D. J. Daly*

CEOL NA SRAIDE (IRE)   4 b.f. King's Theatre (IRE) 128 – My Lady's Key (USA) **80 d** (Key To The Mint (USA)) [2003 86: 14g 10g 12m⁶ 10s⁶ 12d 10f⁵ 11.9g 10m 10.5d 10s Nov 3] quite good-topped filly: half-sister to several winners, including fairly useful Irish 1¼m to 1¾m winner Panchita (by Erins Isle): dam, unraced, from family of Danehill: fairly useful performer: won maiden at Roscommon in 2002: left J. Bolger, Ireland, after fifth start: below form after first start in Britain: stays 1½m: acts on soft and good to firm ground: tried blinkered. *B. S. Rothwell*

CEREZO (USA)   2 b.g. (Feb 19) Cherokee Run (USA) 122 – Dahshah 77 (Mujtahid **56** (USA) 118) [2003 5g⁶ 5d p7g 8s³ 8s⁵ f8g Oct 16] 10,000Y: tall, leggy gelding: looked weak at 2 yrs: first foal: dam, 1m winner, half-sister to smart performer up to 1m in Britain/UAE Asaal: modest maiden: third in maiden at Southwell: stays 1m: acts on fibresand: ran badly in visor final start: sent to Spain. *S. L. Keightley*

CERTA CITO   3 b.f. Mind Games 121 – Bollin Dorothy 73 (Rambo Dancer (CAN) **64** 107) [2003 6m* 6g³ f6s f6g Nov 24] big, good-topped filly: second foal: dam 7f winner: **a–** reportedly suffered from sore shins at 2 yrs: modest performer: won maiden at Catterick in March: off over 5 months (reportedly chipped bone in knee and underwent operation) after second start: raced only at 6f: no form on fibresand. *T. D. Easterby*

CERTAIN JUSTICE (USA)   5 gr.g. Lit de Justice (USA) 125 – Pure Misk 55 (Rain- **95** bow Quest (USA) 134) [2003 103: 8g 7m⁵ 7.6m 8g⁶ 8g f8.5g⁴ p7g Nov 22] rather leggy gelding: useful handicapper: best effort in 2003 when fifth to Kareeb at Newmarket: stays 1m: acts on soft and good to firm going: tried blinkered, including when successful. *P. F. I. Cole*

CERULEAN ROSE   4 ch.f. Bluegrass Prince (IRE) 110 – Elegant Rose 72 (Noalto **77** 120) [2003 –: 8.1m 5.7f³ 5g 5g* 5.1d* 5d* 5.1m* 5m* 5.7f³ 6m⁵ Sep 13] workmanlike filly: progressed into fair handicapper in 2003 and won 5 races in succession, at Don-caster (apprentices), Chepstow and Goodwood in July and Bath and Newmarket in August: effective at 5f/easy 6f: act on firm and good to soft going: tried blinkered/tongue tied at 3 yrs. *A. W. Carroll*

CESARE BORGIA (IRE)   3 ch.c. Dr Devious (IRE) 127 – Prospering 50 (Prince **47 ?** Sabo 123) [2003 60, a–: f7g⁴ f8.5g f7g f7g 9.9m 8.3d 7m⁶ 8g⁵ 8g 7m 8m⁶ 9.2m⁵ 10.5m⁴ 10g⁶ 8.1m Aug 7] smallish, strong colt: poor maiden. *A. Berry*

CEZZARO (IRE)   5 ch.g. Ashkalani (IRE) 128 – Sept Roses (USA) (Septieme Ciel **51** (USA) 123) [2003 49: f12s 7m 12m⁵ 10.1m 8g 8f² 12.6f² 11.8m⁶ 9.2g* 8.5m 10m⁴ 10f **a–** Sep 15] compact gelding: fluent mover: modest performer: won seller at Hamilton in July: stays 12.6f: acts on any ground: tried visored/in cheekpieces: often races promin-ently: none too consistent. *S. R. Bowring*

CHAAYID (IRE) 2 br.c. (May 10) Grand Lodge (USA) 125 – Shiny Waters (USA) – (Irish River (FR) 131) [2003 7m 7m 8m Oct 17] 30,000Y: rather leggy, close-coupled colt: third foal: half-brother to 7.5f winner in Italy by Danehill: dam unraced out of US Grade 1 1¼m winner Spit Curl: well held in maidens at Newmarket: sold 6,000 gns. *J. L. Dunlop*

CHABIBI 4 br.f. Mark of Esteem (IRE) 137 – Nunsharpa 87 (Sharpo 132) [2003 57:   **56**
f7g 7.5g* f8g⁴ f8g² Dec 19] leggy, quite good-topped filly: modest performer: left T. Caldwell after reappearance and Frau A. Bodenhagen after winning maiden at Baden-Baden in May: in frame in minor event/handicap at Southwell last 2 starts: stays 10.5f: acts on fibresand, firm and good to soft ground. *T. H. Hansen, Germany*

CHAFFINCH (USA) 3 b.f. Lear Fan (USA) 130 – Chain Fern (USA) (Blushing   **87**
Groom (FR) 131) [2003 88p: 10m⁶ 11g 11.7f* 12g⁶ 10g Sep 6] close-coupled filly: easy mover: fairly useful performer: won minor event at Bath in June: below form in handicaps after: stayed 11.7f: raced only on good going or firmer: tried visored: stud. *R. Charlton*

CHAIN OF HOPE (IRE) 2 ch.g. (Apr 12) Shinko Forest (IRE) – Fleeting Smile   **57**
(IRE) (Bluebird (USA) 125) [2003 6d 6g 6g⁶ Sep 10] 4,500F, 4,200Y: lengthy gelding: first foal: dam unraced: modest form in maidens: slowly away and not knocked about final start: should stay 7f. *D. E. Cantillon*

CHAIRMAN BOBBY 5 ch.g. Clantime 101 – Formidable Liz 66 (Formidable (USA)   **76**
125) [2003 49, a61: 6m³ 6m 5g* 5.9f* 6m² 6g² 7m³ 5m² 5f² 5m³ 5g 5m⁶ 5f² Oct 10] smallish, sturdy gelding: fair performer: won handicaps at Hamilton (maiden) and Carlisle within 4 days in June: best at 5f/6f: acts on fibresand, soft and firm going: carries head awkwardly: often races prominently: reliable. *D. W. Barker*

CHAI WALLA 4 ch.g. In The Wings 128 – Carmita (Caerleon (USA) 132) [2003   **100**
96: 12m* 14m May 22] leggy, lengthy gelding: useful handicapper, lightly raced (has reportedly had foot problems): won at Newmarket in April by 1¼ lengths from Shami, idling: hung right when well held following month: suffered tendon injury after: should stay 1¾m: acts on soft and good to firm going. *H. R. A. Cecil*

CHAKA ZULU 6 b.g. Muhtarram (USA) 125 – Muttahayej (USA) (El Gran Senor   **65**
(USA) 136) [2003 60: 12m³ 16f³ 16m 12.3g² 10.9m 13.8m² 12g² f14.8g⁴ Nov 14] sturdy gelding: fair on turf, modest on all-weather: stays 14.8f: acts on firm ground and fibresand: tried visored/tongue tied in 2001: usually waited with. *A. C. Whillans*

CHALOM (IRE) 5 b.g. Mujadil (USA) 119 – The Poachers Lady (IRE) (Salmon   –
Leap (USA) 131) [2003 8g Apr 30] strong, lengthy gelding: fairly useful handicapper, lightly raced: missed 2002: well held only 5-y-o start. *B. J. Meehan*

CHAMBRAY (IRE) 2 b.f. (Mar 29) Barathea (IRE) 127 – Spurned (USA) 91 (Robel-   **– p**
lino (USA) 127) [2003 8.1g⁵ Aug 25] half-sister to several winners, including 7f and (at 2 yrs) 1m winner Hidden Meadow and 7f (at 2 yrs) to 1½m winner Scorned (both smart and by Selkirk) and 4-y-o Passing Glance: dam 2-y-o 7f winner who stayed 1¼m: 10/1, well-beaten fifth of 11 in maiden at Chepstow, never dangerous and not knocked about: should do better. *A. M. Balding*

CHAMPAGNE CRACKER 2 ch.f. (Apr 17) Up And At 'em 109 – Kiveton Komet   **65**
71 (Precocious 126) [2003 5f³ 6f⁵ 5m² 5f⁶ 5g² 5m² Oct 7] 1,000Y: seventh foal: half-sister to fairly useful 6f winner Mister Superb (by Superlative) and 1m seller winner Waltz Time (by Rambo Dancer): dam sprinter: fair maiden: second at Musselburgh (twice) and Catterick: will prove best at 5f/easy 6f: acts on good to firm going. *Miss L. A. Perratt*

CHAMPAGNE RIDER 7 b.g. Presidium 124 – Petitesse 55 (Petong 126) [2003 81d,   –
a90d: f7g³ f7g f7g f6g f7s f9.4g f7g f7g f8g⁵ 8.2d f7g f8g f6g Dec 9] leggy, angular   **a53 d**
gelding: fairly useful performer at best: severely on the downgrade: tried blinkered/visored: irresolute. *D. Shaw*

CHAMPAIN SANDS (IRE) 4 b.g. Green Desert (USA) 127 – Grecian Bride (IRE)   **70 d**
(Groom Dancer (USA) 128) [2003 63?: 10.2f³ 10m 8.3d² 9g 10.1m 8f 8f p8g⁶ 11.5m² Oct 21] smallish gelding: fair maiden handicapper: left P. Harris after third start and below form after: stays 11.5f: acts on all-weather, firm and good to soft ground: tried visored/blinkered/tongue tied: reportedly lost action sixth outing: sold 5,000 gns. *J. R. Boyle*

CHAMPION LION (IRE) 4 b.g. Sadler's Wells (USA) 132 – Honey Bun 51   **88**
(Unfuwain (USA) 131) [2003 89: 11.9g 12d 14m³ 12g 12m 16g⁵ 12d Nov 8] strong, close-coupled gelding: fluent mover: fairly useful handicapper: creditable effort after reappearance only when third at Haydock in August: barely stays 1¾m: acts on soft and good to firm going. *M. R. Channon*

CHANCE FOR ROMANCE 2 ch.f. (Jan 8) Entrepreneur 123 – My First Romance **75 +**
61 (Danehill (USA) 126) [2003 5.1f 5f² 5.7f* 5g 6m⁶ 6.5m 6m⁵ 6g Oct 31] 120,000Y:
strong filly: fifth foal: half-sister to several useful sprinters, including Queen Mary
winners Romantic Myth (in 2000, by Mind Games) and 3-y-o Romantic Liason: dam ran
twice: fair performer: won maiden at Bath in July: stiff tasks after, seeming to run very
well when sixth in Lowther Stakes at York: likely to prove best at 5f/6f: acts on firm
going: wore cheekpieces final start. *W. R. Muir*

CHANCELLOR (IRE) 5 ch.h. Halling (USA) 133 – Isticanna (USA) 96 (Far North **114**
(CAN) 120) [2003 118: 10.5d⁴ 10.5d⁶ 9.8d⁴ Oct 4] strong, lengthy horse: smart performer: creditable efforts in 2003 when fourth in Prix Ganay (beaten 4 lengths by Fair
Mix) and Prix Dollar (beaten 2 lengths by Weightless) at Longchamp: rare poor effort in
Tattersalls Gold Cup at the Curragh in between: best around 1¼m: below form on firm
going, acts on any other: wore cheekpieces last 2 starts: game and consistent: changed
hands 110,000 gns. *B. W. Hills*

CHANDELIER 3 ch.g. Sabrehill (USA) 120 – La Noisette (Rock Hopper 124) [2003 **60**
59: f8g³ p8g* p8g³ p8g p8g⁵ 11.6g 8.1m 7m⁶ 8f Jun 25] modest handicapper: won
apprentice event at Lingfield in January: likely to prove best at 7f/1m: acts on polytrack
and good to firm ground: sometimes slowly away. *M. S. Saunders*

CHANFRON 2 ch.g. (Feb 22) Double Trigger (IRE) 123 – Mhargaidh Nua (Thowra **64**
(FR)) [2003 7m 8.3g³ 8m⁶ 10f Sep 30] £2,200Y: lengthy gelding: fourth foal: dam
unraced: modest maiden: third at Windsor: races freely, but should stay 1¼m: best effort
on good ground: races prominently. *B. R. Millman*

CHANGARI (USA) 2 b.f. (Jan 30) Gulch (USA) – Danzari 111 (Arazi (USA) 135) **90**
[2003 5m* 6m² 6m⁵ 6f⁵ Sep 4] leggy filly: first foal: dam, French 2-y-o 5f winner, out of
close relative of smart miler Zaizafon, herself dam of Zafonic: fairly useful performer:
won maiden at Warwick in June: creditable second in minor event at Windsor and fifth in
listed race at Salisbury: likely to prove best at 5f/6f: saddle reportedly slipped when
below form penultimate start. *R. Charlton*

CHANGE OF HEART (IRE) 3 b.f. Revoque (IRE) 122 – Heart of India (IRE) (Try **–**
My Best (USA) 130) [2003 59?: 7.5d Jul 4] unfurnished filly: modest maiden in 2002:
well beaten in seller only 3-y-o start. *T. D. Easterby*

CHANGE OF IMAGE 5 b.m. Spectrum (IRE) 126 – Reveuse du Soir (Vision **–**
(USA)) [2003 56d: 12g 12f⁵ 12m⁴ 12.1g 16.2m Jul 19] smallish mare: poor handicapper
nowadays: stays 1½m: acts on firm and good to soft going: wore cheekpieces 6 of last 7
starts: broke out of stall intended third outing. *J. R. Weymes*

CHANGE PARTNERS (IRE) 3 ch.f. Hernando (FR) 127 – Favorable Exchange **79**
(USA) (Exceller (USA) 129) [2003 74p: 8f³ p12g³ 9.9m² 10m² 12d* 12v Nov 19] fair
performer: won maiden at Catterick in November easily: stays easy 1½m: acts on firm
and good to soft ground (very stiff task on heavy final outing). *R. Charlton*

CHANTERELLE (IRE) 2 ch.f. (May 6) Indian Ridge 123 – Chantereine (USA) **86 p**
(Trempolino (USA) 135) [2003 6m⁴ 6d* Sep 26] 70,000Y: lengthy filly: third foal:
half-sister to French 1m winners Chanteline (useful, by Danehill) and Pochettino (by
Barathea): dam, French 9f winner, half-sister to dam of Kentucky Derby/Belmont Stakes
winner Thunder Gulch out of Irish Oaks winner Shoot A Line: best effort in maidens
(fairly useful form) when winning at Haydock by head from First Candlelight, making
all: should stay 1m: open to progress. *J. L. Dunlop*

CHANTEUSE 3 b.f. Rudimentary (USA) 118 – Enchanting Melody 71 (Chief Singer **60 d**
131) [2003 7.5d⁶ 7.5m⁴ 8m² 8.1g 7m 8d f8g Dec 8] big, good-topped filly: fifth foal:
half-sister to 8.5f winner Nunthorpe (by Mystiko) and 2 winners in Italy: dam maiden
who should have stayed 1m: modest maiden: easily best effort on second outing, left
J. Glover 700 gns after sixth one: stays 7.5f: acts on good to firm going: tried visored.
D. W. Chapman

CHANTILLY GOLD (USA) 4 ch.f. Mutakddim (USA) 112 – Bouffant (USA) (Aly- **–**
dar (USA)) [2003 53: 5.7m 8m 8f 8f 7g 8.1m Aug 14] unfurnished filly: disappointing
maiden; wore cheekpieces last 3 starts. *J. M. Bradley*

CHANTILLY SUNSET (IRE) 2 b.f. (Apr 22) General Monash (USA) 107 – Alpine **–**
Sunset (Auction Ring (USA) 123) [2003 5m Jul 7] €7,500 2-y-o: half-sister to 3 winners,
including fairly useful 1991 2-y-o 5f/6f winner Afif (by Midyan) and 4-y-o Woodland
Blaze: dam unraced half-sister to very smart sprinter Cyrano de Bergerac: 33/1, tailed off
in maiden at Musselburgh. *A. Berry*

CHANTRESS 3 b.f. Peintre Celebre (USA) 137 – Up Anchor (IRE) 114 (Slip Anchor **99**
136) [2003 8g² 9.3f* 12g⁴ 10.3g* 10.3g³ Sep 13] leggy, lengthy filly: sixth foal: half-
sister to 3 winners, including smart performer up to 1½m Red Sea (by Barathea),
Coventry Stakes winner at 2 yrs, and useful 7f to 1½m winner Sailing (by Arazi): dam 1m
(at 2 yrs) to 12.5f (St Simon Stakes) winner: useful performer, lightly raced: won maiden
at Carlisle in June and handicap at Chester (beat Not Amused 2 lengths) in August:
further improvement when close third to Tug of Love in handicap at Doncaster: should
stay 1½m: raced only on good ground or firmer: often races prominently: sold 140,000
gns in December, joined Mrs J. Ramsden. *M. Johnston*

CHANTRY FALLS (IRE) 3 br.g. Mukaddamah (USA) 125 – Woodie Dancer (USA) **52**
(Green Dancer (USA) 132) [2003 –: 7m² 7f³ 7.9d 7f² 6f⁵ 7m 8m⁶ 7m³ Oct 13] tall
gelding: modest maiden: stays 7f: acts on firm ground, below form on softer than good:
tried tongue tied. *J. R. Weymes*

CHAPEL ROYALE (IRE) 6 gr.g. College Chapel 122 – Merci Royale (Fairy King **68**
(USA)) [2003 75, a66: 8.3d 8.1s 8m 8.1g 8m⁶ 9.1g⁶ Aug 1] tall gelding: fair handicapper: **a–**
stays easy 9f: acts on fibresand, soft (probably on heavy) and good to firm going: usually
tongue tied: comes from off pace: sold 5,000 gns. *Jedd O'Keeffe*

CHAPLIN 2 b.c. (Mar 16) Groom Dancer (USA) 128 – Princess Borghese (USA) 82 **– p**
(Nijinsky (CAN) 138) [2003 7m Sep 23] rangy colt: has plenty of scope: sixth foal: dam,
10.5f winner, from very good family of Sanglamore: 5/1, went well long way when
eleventh of 17 in maiden at Newmarket: should be suited by 1¼m/1½m: type to do better.
B. W. Hills

CHAPTER HOUSE (USA) 4 b.g. Pulpit (USA) 117 – Lilian Bayliss (IRE) 100 **–**
(Sadler's Wells (USA) 132) [2003 81: 6g May 24] tall, quite attractive gelding: fairly
useful performer at 3 yrs: well held only start in 2003: tried visored: sold 20,000 gns.
D. Nicholls

CHARA 2 ch.f. (Mar 26) Deploy 131 – Subtle One (IRE) (Polish Patriot (USA) 128) **65**
[2003 6g⁴ 7g p10g⁴ f8g⁵ Dec 19] close-coupled filly: third foal: dam, lightly-raced
maiden, half-sister to very smart performer up to 2m Manhattan Cafe and smart winner
up to 11f Air Smap, both in Japan: fair maiden: fourth at Windsor and Lingfield: should
stay at least 1½m. *J. R. Jenkins*

CHARGE 7 gr.g. Petong 126 – Madam Petoski 61 (Petoski 135) [2003 57§, a72§: p6g **– §**
Jan 8] fair performer at best: tongue tied for first time since 2001, reportedly lame when
well held only 7-y-o start: blinkered twice: sold 1,300 gns. *Mrs L. Stubbs*

CHARIOT (IRE) 2 ch.c. (Apr 15) Titus Livius (FR) 115 – Battle Queen 85 (Kind of **64**
Hush 118) [2003 5.2m 6f⁶ f7g⁴ 7.1m 8m³ f8s² Dec 13] €100,000Y: sturdy colt: half-
brother to several winners, including useful 2001 2-y-o 6f winner Advance Party (by
Mujadil) and useful 7f/1m winner Celebration Town (by Case Law) who became
untrustworthy: dam best as 6f/7f: modest maiden: placed in nurseries, leaving B. Hills in
between: stays 1m: acts on fibresand. *M. R. Bosley*

CHARIOTS OF BLUE 2 ch.g. (Feb 11) Bluebird (USA) 125 – Boadicea's Chariot **–**
(Commanche Run 133) [2003 6.1g 8.3g Aug 10] 20,000F: fifth foal: half-brother to
useful 1999 2-y-o 7f winner Agrippina (by Timeless Times): dam, Irish 1½m winner,
later winner over hurdles: well beaten in maidens. *W. G. M. Turner*

CHARLES SPENCELAYH (IRE) 7 b.g. Tenby 125 – Legit (IRE) (Runnett 125) **–**
[2003 79, a66: f14.8g⁵ Jan 17] fair performer at best: cheekpieces, well beaten in seller
only outing in 2003: dead. *J. G. M. O'Shea*

CHARLEY FARLEY 4 ch.g. Bluegrass Prince (IRE) 110 – Miss Copyforce (Aragon **–**
118) [2003 55, a–: p7g Jan 4] big, lengthy gelding: modest maiden at best: soundly beaten
only 4-y-o start: blinkered last 4 outings. *E. A. Wheeler*

CHARLIE BEAR 2 ch.c. (Apr 22) Bahamian Bounty 116 – Abi 84 (Chief's Crown **70 p**
(USA)) [2003 7.1g⁵ 6m 6g Oct 13] tall colt: second foal: dam, 1¼m winner, closely
related to smart German miler Royal Dragon: fair form in maidens: hampered final start:
should stay 1m: type to do better at 3 yrs. *E. A. L. Dunlop*

CHARLIE GOLF (IRE) 3 b.g. Cadeaux Genereux 131 – Keepers Dawn (IRE) 103 **54**
(Alzao (USA) 117) [2003 –: p10g³ f9.4g p12g⁵ 12m Mar 27] modest maiden: blinkered,
looked reluctant and pulled up on turf debut final start: should stay 1½m: acts on polytrack: tried in cheekpieces. *J. W. Hills*

CHARLIEISMYDARLING 2 b.g. (Mar 7) Mind Games 121 – Blessed Lass (HOL) **58**
(Good Times (ITY)) [2003 f6s⁴ p6g f6g⁵ f5g⁶ f5g Dec 15] 3,000Y: fourth foal: half-

brother to a winner in Turkey by Classic Cliche: dam ran a few times in Holland: modest maiden: should prove best at 5f/6f: awkward leaving stalls last 2 starts, and looked reluctant final one. *J. A. Osborne*

CHARLIE PARKES   5 ch.g. Pursuit of Love 124 – Lucky Parkes 108 (Full Extent **95** (USA) 113) [2003 92: 5f* 5m⁴ 5f⁵ 5f 5m 5.1m 5m 5f Oct 10] strong, lengthy gelding: useful performer: won minor event at Thirsk in April: best effort in handicaps after when close fourth at York: best at 5f: acts on firm going: has had 2 handlers: often forces pace. *E. J. Alston*

CHARLIES BRIDE (IRE)   8 b. or br.m. Rich Charlie 117 – Nordic Bride (IRE)   **–** (Nordico (USA)) [2003 7.9m 8m Jul 7] small mare: fair handicapper at 3/4 yrs: well beaten only starts since: often blinkered. *M. A. Barnes*

CHARLIE TANGO (IRE)   2 b.g. (May 1) Desert Prince (IRE) 130 – Precedence   **72** (IRE) 88 (Polish Precedent (USA) 131) [2003 7g⁵ 6m 7.6g³ 8d Sep 11] €130,000Y: leggy gelding: first foal: dam, Irish maiden who stayed 9f, out of smart 1¼m performer Braiswick: fair maiden: third of 5 in minor event at Chester, best effort: not knocked about final start: should stay 1m. *M. R. Channon*

CHARLOTTEBUTTERFLY   3 b.f. Millkom 124 – Tee Gee Jay 63 (Northern Tem-   **63** pest (USA) 120) [2003 5m⁵ 6g³ 7m⁴ 6m³ p6g 5m³ 6m⁵ f6s³ Sep 2] good-topped filly: third foal: dam, 2-y-o 6f winner, became irresolute: fair maiden: effective at 5f to 7f: acts on fibresand, raced only on good/good to firm ground on turf. *T. T. Clement*

CHARLOTTE VALE   2 ch.f. (Apr 23) Pivotal 124 – Drying Grass Moon 66 (Be My   **60** Chief (USA) 122) [2003 5m⁴ 6g² 7d⁴ 6g⁶ Aug 26] leggy, plain filly: first foal: dam ran 3 times: modest maiden: second at Hamilton: should stay 7f: acts on good to firm going. *M. D. Hammond*

CHARMANTE FEMME   5 b.m. Bin Ajwaad (IRE) 119 – Charmante Dame (FR)   **51** (Bellypha 130) [2003 53: 15m⁵ 12f⁴ 14g* 14g 11.9m³ p13g⁶ p16g Dec 2] modest handi-capper: won apprentice event at Cork in July: left P. Flynn in Ireland 10,000 gns after fifth start: below form, swishing tail, both starts back in Britain: stays 1¾m: acts on soft and good to firm going. *P. D. Evans*

CHARMATIC (IRE)   2 br.f. (Apr 10) Charnwood Forest (IRE) 125 – Instamatic 97   **– p** (Night Shift (USA)) [2003 6d 7s Nov 3] €44,000Y: strong, lengthy filly: second foal: dam, Irish maiden who stayed 1m, closely related to 7-y-o Dano-Mast: signs of a little ability in maidens at Leicester and Redcar (tongue tied, wandered): should stay 1m: likely to do better. *J. A. Glover*

CHARMAWAY   5 b.g. Charmer 123 – Dismiss 95 (Daring March 116) [2003 –: p7g   **–** p8g Feb 12] tall, rather leggy gelding: disappointing maiden. *C. E. Brittain*

CHARMING ADMIRAL (IRE)   10 b.g. Shareef Dancer (USA) 135 – Lilac Charm   **–** 87 (Bustino 136) [2003 16d May 28] workmanlike gelding: carries plenty of condition: modest chaser nowadays: unraced on Flat in 2002: well beaten only 10-y-o outing on Flat: visored/blinkered. *Mrs A. Duffield*

CHARMING PRINCE (IRE)   2 b.c. (Jan 20) Barathea (IRE) 127 – Most Charming   **108** (FR) (Darshaan 133) [2003 7g* 7d* 7d² 7s² Oct 5] strong, good-topped colt: third foal: half-brother to fairly useful 2001 2-y-o 6f winner Perfect Fun (by Marju): dam, French 2-y-o 1m winner, granddaughter of Cheveley Park/1000 Guineas winner Ma Biche: useful form: won minor event at Maisons-Laffitte in July and listed race at Vichy (by neck from Northerner) in August: progressed again at Longchamp when second to Diamond Green in Prix La Rochette (kept on well from rear, beaten 2½ lengths) and American Post in Prix Jean-Luc Lagardere (made most, beaten 4 lengths): bred to stay 1m: acts on soft ground. *A. Fabre, France*

CHARNOCK BATES ONE (IRE)   2 b.f. (Apr 23) Desert Sun 120 – Fleetwood   **64** Fancy (Taufan (USA) 119) [2003 6v⁴ 6.1m⁵ 7.5m³ 7m³ 8m⁵ 8m⁴ Sep 13] IR 14,000F, €22,000Y: angular filly: has a quick action: half-sister to several winners, including fairly useful 6f (at 2 yrs) to 1m winner Al Fahda (by Be My Chief) and 1993 2-y-o 7f winner Western Fleet (by Westheriter): dam, Irish 2-y-o 5f winner, later won up to 9f in USA: modest maiden: third at Beverley and Catterick (nursery): stays 1m. *T. D. Easterby*

CHARNWOOD STREET (IRE)   4 b.g. Charnwood Forest (IRE) 125 – La Vigie   **56 d** (King of Clubs 124) [2003 69d: f16s⁴ f16.2g⁴ f16s⁶ p16g f14.8g⁵ f16g Nov 19] leggy gelding: modest handicapper: well held last 4 starts: stays 2m: acts on good to soft going and fibresand: often visored: none too consistent. *D. Shaw*

CHASE THE BLUES (IRE) 6 b.g. Blues Traveller (IRE) 119 – Highdrive (Bally- –
more 123) [2003 –: f12s f14.8g Feb 1] lightly-raced maiden: well held both starts in 2003:
tried in headgear. *R. Wilman*

CHASE THE RAINBOW 2 gr.f. (Apr 10) Danzig Connection (USA) – Delta Tempo 57
(IRE) (Bluebird (USA) 125) [2003 5m⁵ 7m* 6g f7g f7g² Nov 24] third foal: half-sister to
5-y-o Paso Doble: dam unraced out of half-sister to Mill Reef Stakes winner Showbrook:
modest performer: won maiden at Catterick in October: should stay 1m: acts on fibresand
and good to firm going. *M. Johnston*

CHATEAU NICOL 4 b.g. Distant Relative 128 – Glensara (Petoski 135) [2003 ?: 79
8.1g 8g⁶ 7m⁵ 7.1g 7g⁶ p8g³ 8.2m p7g p7g p8g p7g* p7g* p7g p8g Dec 20] fair performer:
won handicap and minor event at Lingfield in November: stays 1m: acts on all-weather
and good to firm going, yet to race on softer than good: visored/blinkered after
reappearance: pulled hard/hung left tenth start. *B. G. Powell*

CHATIFA (IRE) 3 ch.f. Titus Livius (FR) 115 – Lagrion (USA) 68 (Diesis 133) [2003 83
8m² 7f⁴ 8m* 7g Oct 11] IR 11,000F, IR 380,000Y: well-made, useful-looking filly: sixth
foal: half-sister to 3 winners, notably high-class 2001 2-y-o 5f/6f winner Queen's Logic
(by Grand Lodge): dam, Irish maiden who stayed 1½m, sister to Middle Park second Pure
Genius: reportedly had a splint freeze-fired: fairly useful form: won maiden at Salisbury
in September by 7 lengths: ran as if amiss in listed event at Ascot final start: stayed 1m:
raced only on good going or firmer: stud. *M. P. Tregoning*

CHAUVINISM (IRE) 2 b.g. (Mar 24) Danetime (IRE) 121 – Ceannanas (IRE) 77 92 p
(Magical Wonder (USA) 125) [2003 6m* 6m² Oct 1] €50,000Y: close-coupled, work-
manlike gelding: second foal: dam, Irish maiden, stayed 1m: won maiden at Ayr in
September: improved when 1¼ lengths second of 5 to Millbag in minor event at
Salisbury, racing freely/carrying head awkwardly: should stay 7f: sent to Hong Kong,
where renamed Special King Prawn: open to improvement. *N. P. Littmoden*

CHECKIT (IRE) 3 br.c. Mukaddamah (USA) 125 – Collected (IRE) (Taufan (USA) 117
119) [2003 102: 8.5g³ 8g 7.1g⁴ 8.1d⁴ 8g* 8d⁴ 9m³ 9m³ 8g² 8d Nov 16] well-made colt:
has a quick, fluent action: smart performer: off nearly 4 months after reportedly throwing
a splint in 2000 Guineas at Newmarket second start: won minor event at Doncaster in
September by 3½ lengths from Audience: best efforts when third to Chivalry in
Cambridgeshire (beaten 2 lengths when appearing to excel himself) at Newmarket and to
Far Lane in Darley Stakes (beaten ¾ length) on same course after: stays 9f: yet to race on
heavy going, acts on any other: tends to wander. *M. R. Channon*

CHEEKY GIRL 3 b.f. College Chapel 122 – Merry Rous 66 (Rousillon (USA) 133) 71
[2003 62: f8g 7m 12m* 14.1m⁴ 12.1d 11.8m² 12.1m² 12f* 12.3g³ 12m⁵ 12m⁴ 12.1m⁴
14.1f⁵ 12m* Oct 18] leggy, quite good-topped filly: fair performer: won seller at Pontefract in April, handicap at Thirsk in June and apprentice claimer at Catterick in October:
barely stays 1¾m: acts on firm going: sold 10,000 gns. *T. D. Easterby*

CHEEKY LAD 3 b.g. Bering 136 – Cheeky Charm (USA) 56 (Nureyev (USA) 131) –
[2003 –: 6g May 4] strong, lengthy gelding: well beaten in 2 maidens. *B. W. Hills*

CHEESE 'N BISCUITS 3 b.f. Spectrum (IRE) 126 – Bint Shihama (USA) 78 94
(Cadeaux Genereux 131) [2003 p7g p7g* p8g p7g p8g⁶ 7d 7m⁵ 7f7g⁵ p6g⁴ 9g p7g³ p7g³
p7g* p7g³ 6v⁵ Nov 19] second foal: half-sister to winner in Greece by Sabrehill: dam, 7f
winner (stayed 1m), out of sister to 1000 Guineas winner Sayyedati and half-sister to
high-class 1¼m/1½m winner Golden Snake: fairly useful performer: won maiden in
February and, having left C. Cyzer 19,000 gns after ninth start, handicap in October, both
at Lingfield: good efforts last 2 starts, including in listed event at Maisons-Laffitte (fifth
to Soave): should stay 1m: acts on polytrack, heavy going and good to firm. *G. L. Moore*

CHELSEA BLUE (ITY) 5 ch.m. Barathea (IRE) 127 – Indigo Blue (IRE) 56 (Blue- 52
bird (USA) 125) [2003 59, a–: 5m⁴ 6m Sep 18] big, strong mare: modest maiden
handicapper, lightly raced: stays 6f: raced only on good going or firmer on turf: wore
cheekpieces both 5-y-o starts, finding little in latter. *J. W. Payne*

CHEMICALREACTION 3 b.g. Definite Article 121 – Ewar Snowflake (Snow 51 ?
Chief (USA)) [2003 f7g f8.5g f8.5s 13.1m 12f 8.1m⁴ 9.9m⁴ 10m⁶ Sep 4] 2,000Y, resold
IR 6,500Y: second foal: dam, no form, out of Norfolk Stakes winner Petillante: modest
form at best in maidens/handicaps: blinkered last 3 starts. *R. A. Fahey*

CHERINE (IRE) 4 b.f. Robellino (USA) 127 – Escrime (USA) 92 (Sharpen Up 127) 46
[2003 f7s* f8g⁵ f12s f9.4s⁴ p10g⁵ f8g Mar 20] good-topped filly: poor handicapper: ran
in Germany in 2002 for H. Blume: won at Southwell in February: should stay 9f: acts on
fibresand, probably on polytrack: tried blinkered/visored/in cheekpieces. *N. P. Littmoden*

CHERISHED NUMBER 4 b.g. King's Signet (USA) 110 – Pretty Average 40 (Sky-liner 117) [2003 84, a79: 8m 8g⁵ 8.3d* 8.1s³ 10g⁴ 8m* 7.9m⁶ 9.2m³ 8.3g⁴ 8m 8m f8.5g⁴ Nov 10] workmanlike gelding: fairly useful on turf, fair on all-weather: won handicap at Hamilton in May and minor event at Ayr (short-headed Albashoosh) in June: stays 9f: acts on any turf going and fibresand: tried in cheekpieces. *I. Semple*   **92 a64**

CHEROKEE BAY 3 b.f. Primo Dominie 121 – Me Cherokee 48 (Persian Bold 123) [2003 83: p10g⁶ 9m 8.1g f7g 8m p8g 10m³ Sep 29] good-topped filly: fair performer: left P. D'Arcy and below form after reappearance: stays 9f: acts on soft and good to firm ground: sold 6,000 gns. *J. A. Osborne*   **70 d**

CHEROKEE NATION 2 br.c. (May 1) Emperor Jones (USA) 119 – Me Cherokee 48 (Persian Bold 123) [2003 6m f5s f6s⁶ Oct 21] 12,000Y: tall colt: fourth foal: half-brother to 3-y-o Cherokee Bay: dam, poor maiden who stayed 1½m, half-sister to smart middle-distance stayer Apache: modest form in maidens: not knocked about final start: should stay 1m: pulled hard/hung left on debut. *P. W. D'Arcy*   **52**

CHERUBIM (JPN) 2 ch.f. (Feb 16) Sunday Silence (USA) – Curly Angel (JPN) (Judge Angelucci (USA)) [2003 6m³ 7g² Jul 3] compact, attractive filly: fourth known foal: sister to Japanese stakes winner Egao O Misete and half-sister to winner in Japan by Tony Bin: dam Japanese maiden, half-sister to smart Japanese middle-distance performer Air Groove: better effort (fair form) when second in maiden at Yarmouth, still green: made running both starts: should stay at least 1m. *D. R. Loder*   **79**

CHESNUT CRACKER 3 ch.f. Compton Place 125 – Triple Tricks (IRE) 70 (Royal Academy (USA) 130) [2003 –: f5s⁴ 7s⁶ 5m f7g Nov 19] tall, lengthy filly: little form: tried tongue tied. *P. C. Haslam*   **–**

CHESNUT RIPPLE 4 ch.f. Cosmonaut – Shaft of Sunlight 58 (Sparkler 130) [2003 64: 10d² 10g⁶ 9.9m 10f⁴ 11.9g 10m⁶ 12.3m⁶ f8g² f8g⁵ Dec 15] strong filly: fair maiden: regressed after reappearance: left R. Whitaker 5,000 gns after seventh start: barely stays 1½m: acts on fibresand, good to firm and soft going: tried visored: sometimes gives trouble at stall/takes strong hold/hangs left. *D. Shaw*   **71 d**

CHESTER LE STREET (USA) 2 b.c. (Apr 14) Horse Chestnut (SAF) 119 – Evening Primrose (USA) (Dayjur (USA) 137) [2003 6d⁴ 7.2f* 7m² Jul 10] $185,000Y: big, well-made colt: has scope: fourth foal: half-brother to 2 winners in USA, notably smart sprinter/miler Great Notion (by Elusive Quality): dam unraced half-sister to US Grade 1 9f winner Talinum and to dam of smart performer up to 1½m Simeon: landed odds in maiden at Ayr in June by 7 lengths: much improved and useful form when head second to Kings Point in Superlative Stakes at Newmarket, making most but edging right late on: will stay 1m: joined Godolphin: type to do better still at 3 yrs if all is well. *M. Johnston*   **103 p**

CHESTER PARK 5 ch.g. King's Signet (USA) 110 – Good Skills 57 (Bustino 136) [2003 7.1g Aug 7] fourth foal: dam, headstrong maiden, bred to stay 1½m: well beaten in maiden at Chepstow. *K. Bishop*   **–**

CHETAK (IRE) 3 ch.f. Halling (USA) 133 – Tithcar 67 (Cadeaux Genereux 131) [2003 77: 8m* 8m 8.1g² 9d⁴ 8g³ p7g² p8g⁶ Nov 22] smallish, rather leggy, plain filly: useful performer: won maiden at Bath in May: best effort in handicaps after when second to Cheese 'n Biscuits at Lingfield (hung left) penultimate start: effective at 7f to easy 9f: acts on polytrack, good to firm and good to soft ground: free-going sort: usually waited with: sold 32,000 gns. *B. W. Hills*   **96**

CHEVERAK FOREST (IRE) 2 ch.g. (Mar 4) Shinko Forest (IRE) – Meranie Girl (IRE) 52 (Mujadil (USA) 119) [2003 5.3f³ 5.3m³ 5m⁴ 6d⁴ 6g⁴ 7g⁵ 6m 7m⁶ 7m⁵ 6g* 7m 7.5m⁵ 6m⁵ f6s³ 6m* 7m⁵ 7d Nov 8] 23,000Y: smallish gelding: first foal: dam, maiden best at 5f at 2 yrs, out of sister to very smart sprinter Hever Golf Rose: fair performer: won claimer at Newcastle in May, seller at Ripon in August and selling nursery at Newcastle (left M. Channon) in October: likely to stay 1m: acts on fibresand, good to firm and good to soft going: visored fourteenth outing. *Don Enrico Incisa*   **70**

CHEVIN 4 ch.f. Danzig Connection (USA) – Starr Danias (USA) (Sensitive Prince (USA)) [2003 53: 12.4m 12g 14.1f* 10.9m* 12m⁵ 12f⁴ 12m⁵ 16d Aug 11] sparely-made filly: modest handicapper: won at Carlisle and Warwick on consecutive days in June: effective at 11f to 2m: acts on firm ground: free-going sort. *R. A. Fahey*   **55**

CHEVRONNE 3 b.g. Compton Place 125 – Maria Isabella (FR) (Young Generation 129) [2003 –: 8g³ 8m³ 8d p8g³ p12g⁵ p12g Nov 18] compact gelding: fair maiden: seems to stay easy 1½m: acts on polytrack and good to firm ground. *L. G. Cottrell*   **75**

CHEYENNE CHIEF 4 b.g. Be My Chief (USA) 122 – Cartuccia (IRE) (Doyoun 124) [2003 52, a58: 16.1d Mar 24] leggy gelding: modest maiden at best: cheekpieces and tongue strap, well beaten only 4-y-o start: tried visored/blinkered at 3 yrs. *G. M. Moore* —

CHEYENNE DAWN 3 ch.f. The West (USA) 107 – Miss Lear (Lear Fan (USA) 130) [2003 –: f5s 7f 7d Jul 30] lightly raced and little form. *W. G. M. Turner* —

CHIASSO (USA) 3 ch.f. Woodman (USA) 126 – Qirmazi (USA) 113 (Riverman (USA) 131) [2003 8g⁴ 8g 9.3g 8.2m⁴ f9.4g f8g Dec 3] smallish ex-French filly: sister to fairly useful 1m to 1¼m (in France) winner Quinwood, closely related to 6-y-o Quito, and half-sister to several winners, including useful French 7f (at 2 yrs) to 1m winner Quarter Note (by Danehill): dam, French 6f (at 2 yrs) and 9f winner, third in Prix Saint-Alary: modest maiden: left H-A. Pantall after third start: stays 1m: tried blinkered in France. *H. Morrison* 58

CHIC 3 ch.f. Machiavellian (USA) 123 – Exclusive 115 (Polar Falcon (USA) 126) [2003 75: 7m⁵ 8m* 8f³ 7m⁶ 7d² 7g* Oct 11] lengthy filly: useful performer: won maiden at Chester in May, handicap at Kempton in June and listed race at Ascot (beat dead-heaters Starbeck and Duty Paid 2 lengths) in October: effective at 7f/1m: acts on good to soft going, probably on firm: slowly away fourth/fifth outings. *Sir Michael Stoute* 104

CHICAGO BOND (USA) 2 b.f. (May 3) Real Quiet (USA) 131 – Shariyfa (FR) (Zayyani 119) [2003 6m⁵ 5m⁴ 6m³ 7m⁶ 8m Oct 20] $10,000Y: leggy, rather sparely-made filly: has a quick action: third foal: half-sister to winners abroad by Eagle Eyed and Dixieland Band: dam unraced half-sister to smart French performer up to 1½m Sherarda and to dam of high-class French miler Sendawar: modest maiden: third at Thirsk: should stay 7f. *B. Smart* 64

CHICA (IRE) 2 gr.f. (Mar 23) Spectrum (IRE) 126 – Wild Rose of York 64 (Unfuwain (USA) 131) [2003 6m 7f 7m Jul 6] £18,000Y: leggy filly: third foal: dam, 1m and 1¼m winner (also winning hurdler): well held in maidens: very slowly away final outing. *J. A. Osborne* —

CHICKADO (IRE) 2 b.f. (Apr 8) Mujadil (USA) 119 – Arcevia (IRE) 85 (Archway (IRE) 115) [2003 5.1m 6.1d 5f⁶ f6g* f5g³ Nov 21] €20,000Y: angular filly: second foal: dam 11f winner: fair performer: won maiden at Wolverhampton (edged right) in November: should prove best at 5f/6f: usually races prominently. *D. Haydn Jones* 69

CHICKASAW TRAIL 5 ch.m. Be My Chief (USA) 122 – Maraschino 53 (Lycius (USA) 124) [2003 52, a33: 12.1m 10.2m 10.9m 7m f8g Dec 8] small mare: poor maiden: effective at 7f, barely at 1½m: acts on firm going, soft and fibresand. *R. Hollinshead* 39 a–

CHICO GUAPO (IRE) 3 b.g. Sesaro (USA) 81 – Summer Queen 80 (Robellino (USA) 127) [2003 65, a75: p5g⁵ p5g* 5d 6g 5m* 5m² 5.1m² 5m 5f⁴ 5m⁴ 5.1m* 5g 5d* 5m⁵ Aug 23] compact gelding: fairly useful performer: won maiden at Lingfield in February and handicaps at Catterick in April, Chester in July and Thirsk in August: best at bare 5f: acts on all-weather, good to firm and good to soft ground: wore cheekpieces after third start: free-going front runner. *J. A. Glover* 82

CHIEF YEOMAN 3 b.g. Machiavellian (USA) 123 – Step Aloft 87 (Shirley Heights 130) [2003 83p: 7g* 8g³ 10.1m 12m 10m² Aug 4] close-coupled, quite good-topped gelding: useful performer: won maiden at Lingfield in May: best effort in handicaps after when second to Ayun at Ripon: should stay 1½m (too free in visor when tried): raced only on good/good to firm going: wore cheekpieces third start: sold 21,000 gns, joined Venetia Williams, won juvenile hurdle in October. *Sir Michael Stoute* 95

CHIFFON 3 b.f. Polish Precedent (USA) 131 – Photo Call 73 (Chief Singer 131) [2003 64: 7.1f* 10.2g⁵ 8.1m Jun 6] quite good-topped filly: fair performer: won maiden at Haydock in April: should stay 1m: form only on firm ground: unreliable. *B. J. Meehan* 70 §

CHIGORIN 2 b.g. (Mar 14) Pivotal 124 – Belle Vue 78 (Petong 126) [2003 7m 6g³ Oct 13] 27,000Y, 34,000 2-y-o: second foal: half-brother to 6f/7f winner (including at 2 yrs) It Was Meant To Be (by Distant Relative): dam, 6f winner from 2 starts at 2 yrs, out of half-sister to Forzando: fair form in maidens at Yarmouth (green) and Windsor, strong-finishing third to Fiddle Me Blue in latter, having had to wait for run: likely to prove best short of 1m: open to improvement. *J. M. P. Eustace* 70 p

CHILI PEPPER 6 b.m. Chilibang 120 – Game Germaine (Mummy's Game 120) [2003 33: f8s f11g 9.9m 7m Jul 9] poor handicapper: no form in 2003: usually blinkered. *P. R. Wood* —

CHIMALI (IRE) 2 b.g. (Jan 28) Foxhound (USA) 103 – Mari-Ela (IRE) 60 (River **69 p**
Falls 113) [2003 6m⁴ Aug 6] €150,000Y: second foal: dam, 2-y-o 7f seller winner, half-
sister to useful performer up to 1m Scarteen Fox (by Foxhound): 7/1, fourth of 13 in
maiden at Newcastle, isolated in centre: should improve. *J. Nicol*

CHIMES EIGHT 2 b.f. (Apr 20) Octagonal (NZ) 126 – Bell Toll 87 (High Line 125) **40**
[2003 f7g f7s Dec 31] half-sister to several winners, including 5f (at 2 yrs) to 1m winner
Prince Babar (by Fairy King) and 1m (at 2 yrs) to 11.5f (in France) winner Warning Order
(by Warrshan), both useful: dam, 2-y-o 7f/1m winner, sister to dam of Prix Jean Prat
winner Suances: poor form in maidens at Southwell and Wolverhampton. *R. A. Fahey*

CHIMICHANGA (IRE) 3 b.g. Fayruz 116 – Lindas Delight 54 (Batshoof 122) [2003 **–**
43: f5g 5m May 19] tall, quite good-topped gelding: poor maiden at 2 yrs: well held in
2003: tried visored/blinkered: seems temperamental. *M. J. Polglase*

CHINA BEAUTY 3 b.f. Slip Anchor 136 – Tasseled (USA) (Tate Gallery (USA) 117) **64**
[2003 8.3d⁵ 9.3m² 8d a12g² a11.5g⁴ Dec 23] closely related to 2 winners by Deploy,
including useful 8.5f (at 2 yrs) and 1½m winner Deploy Venture, and half-sister to 3
winners: dam, ran 3 times in USA, closely related to dam of Rock of Gibraltar out of
half-sister to Riverman: modest performer: in frame in maiden at Carlisle (final start for
J. Noseda) and 2 apprentice minor events at Deauville: bred to be suited by 1½m: slowly
away both starts in Britain. *Mme M. Bollack-Badel, France*

CHINA EYES (IRE) 2 b.f. (May 17) Fasliyev (USA) 120 – Limpopo 49 (Green **106**
Desert (USA) 127) [2003 5.2m⁵ 5m² 5m* 5g² 6m⁶ Oct 2] €100,000Y: quite good-topped
filly: half-sister to several winners, including very smart 5f (including at 2 yrs)/6f winner
Pipalong (by Pips Pride), useful 1999 2-y-o 6f to 7f winner Out of Africa (by Common
Grounds) and 4-y-o Corton: dam makes out of smart Irish 7f to 8.5f winner Grey
Goddess: useful performer: won maiden at Windsor in July by 6 lengths: very good
¾-length second to Howick Falls in Flying Childers Stakes at Doncaster next time:
travelled well long way when only sixth in Cheveley Park Stakes at Newmarket: probably
best at 5f. *B. W. Hills*

CHINEUR (FR) 2 b.c. (Apr 17) Fasliyev (USA) 120 – Wardara 107 (Sharpo 132) **111**
[2003 6g² 6d³ 5d* 6s² 6s* Nov 12] €63,000Y: third foal: half-brother to 4-y-o Dark
Charm: dam 5f/6f winner: smart performer: won listed races at Maisons-Laffitte (by 2½
lengths from Olonella) in October and Saint-Cloud (by 2 lengths from Raffelberger) in
November: 2½ lengths second to Whipper in Criterium de Maisons-Laffitte penultimate
outing: likely to prove best at 5f/6f: acts on soft ground. *M. Delzangles, France*

CHINKARA 3 ch.g. Desert Prince (IRE) 130 – You Make Me Real (USA) (Give Me **96**
Strength (USA)) [2003 80: 10.3g⁴ p10g* 10m⁴ 9g* 9g* 8m Jul 10] strong, good-bodied
gelding: type to carry condition: useful performer: won maiden at Lingfield in March and
handicaps at Kempton and Goodwood (valuable event, by ¾ length from Anani) in May:
stays 1¼m: acts on polytrack, raced only on good ground or firmer on turf: sometimes
early to post: races freely: reliable. *B. J. Meehan*

Tote Trifecta Stakes (Handicap), Goodwood—
Chinkara shows improved form to take this £40,000 prize from Anani

Tote Cambridgeshire (Handicap), Newmarket—another notable training success for Sir Mark Prescott as Chivalry defies an eleven-month absence; Adiemus (No.24), Checkit (far side), Lady Bear (visored, towards far side) and Far Lane (No.1) are next home

CHINSOLA (IRE) 2 ch.c. (Feb 10) Inchinor 119 – Skerray 71 (Soviet Star (USA) 128) [2003 5.1f⁴ 6.1g² p5g* 7f* 7d* 7m² 7.1d⁴ 6.3m⁴ 7g Oct 24] 25,000Y: quite good-topped colt: first foal: dam, lightly-raced maiden, half-sister to smart performer up to 1m Ardkinglass: useful performer: won maiden at Lingfield and 2 minor events (second of them by 7 lengths) at Ascot in July: creditable efforts in minor event at Ascot and Solario Stakes at Sandown (fourth to Barbajuan) next 2 starts: will stay 1m: acts on polytrack, firm and good to soft going. *R. Hannon* **101**

CHIQITITA (IRE) 2 b.f. (Mar 29) Saddlers' Hall (IRE) 126 – Funny Cut (IRE) (Sure Blade (USA) 130) [2003 f5g⁶ 6.1g 6m 5.6f⁴ 7f⁶ 6g⁶ 7m 10f Sep 30] 1,800Y: smallish filly: third foal: half-sister to 3-y-o Landing Strip and winner in Sweden by Malvernico: dam Swedish 1m/1¼m winner: modest maiden: form only on fourth and sixth starts: left M. Wigham and edgy, raced freely final one: should stay at least 7f. *M. G. Quinlan* **59**

CHIRU (IRE) 3 b.f. Entrepreneur 123 – Formulate 119 (Reform 132) [2003 66: 7.5d 10.5f⁴ 12g⁶ 10m 12f⁶ 14m⁴ 12.5m⁴ p13g Dec 29] half-sister to several winners, notably Oaks winner Shahtoush (by Alzao) and Oaks runner-up Game Plan (by Darshaan): dam won Fillies' Mile: fair maiden: left Mrs J. Harrington, Ireland, 74,000 gns in December, well held at Lingfield only subsequent start: stays 1¾m: acts on firm ground. *B. J. Meehan* **73**

CHISPA 5 b.m. Imperial Frontier (USA) 112 – Digamist Girl (IRE) (Digamist (USA) 110) [2003 87, a74: 6d³ f6g⁵ f5s³ 6.1g 6d² 6s* 5s 5g 5g 5m⁵ 6g³ 5g f6g² f6g* f5g f6g Dec 15] lengthy mare: poor mover: fair performer: won claimer at Windsor in May and handicap at Southwell (edged left) in December: best at 5f/6f: acts on fibresand, firm and soft going: tried blinkered: has flashed tail: reportedly bled from nose seventh outing: usually races prominently. *K. R. Burke* **70**

CHIVALRY 4 b.g. Mark of Esteem (IRE) 137 – Gai Bulga 110 (Kris 135) [2003 95: 9m* Oct 4] big, lengthy gelding: made good physical progress from 3 to 4 yrs: useful performer: first race for almost a year, won Tote Cambridgeshire at Newmarket in October by short head from Adiemus, quickening to lead 2f out and edging right: barely stays testing 1¼m: yet to race on heavy going, acts on any other: has raced freely/carried head awkwardly: joined J. Howard Johnson 170,000 gns, won over hurdles in November: should improve further on Flat. *Sir Mark Prescott* **102 p**

CHIVITE (IRE) 4 b.g. Alhaarth (IRE) 126 – Laura Margaret (Persian Bold 123) [2003 81: p13g Jan 8] well-made gelding: fair maiden: probably stays 1¾m: acts on soft going: visored only 4-y-o start: fair winning hurdler for P. Hobbs. *K. R. Burke* **68**

CHOCOLATE BOY (IRE) 4 b.g. Dolphin Street (FR) 125 – Kawther (Tap On Wood 130) [2003 51: p8g p10g Dec 30] poor maiden: probably stays easy 1¼m: acts on polytrack, yet to race on extremes of going on turf. *G. L. Moore* **43**

CHOISIR (AUS)   4 ch.c. Danehill Dancer (IRE) 117 – Great Selection (AUS)   **126**
(Lunchtime 123) [2003 5g* 5.5d³ 7g 6g⁶ 5f* 6f* 6m² Jul 10]

He had just three races in Britain, spread over little more than three weeks, and saw not much more than three minutes action, but few overseas-trained horses can have made so great an impression in such a short stay as the Australian sprinter Choisir. There have been better foreign visitors, and he wasn't the season's champion sprinter, but when the time came for his stallion career, the promoters had no shortage of advertising material. Choisir's victory in the King's Stand Stakes made him the first Australian-trained horse to win in Britain, and when he won Royal Ascot's other big sprint, the Golden Jubilee Stakes, four days later, he earned himself another entry in the record books.

Royal Ascot has long drawn Irish and French runners but, until recently, has never been deliberately promoted as an international meeting in the same way as more recent creations such as the Dubai World Cup and the Hong Kong International meeting. Unlike those events, Royal Ascot is not reliant on top foreign horses taking on the locals to make the occasion, but with championship events over a range of distances there is considerable potential for the Royal meeting to become a major international festival. The Ascot authority will reap the rewards of its drive to draw competitors from all over the world, particularly once the racecourse's redevelopment has been completed. Choisir's successes made the headlines but he was just one of several runners from outside Europe who contributed to what must have been the most cosmopolitan Royal Ascot so far. Apart from Choisir, other competitors from outside Europe included: the American sprinter Morluc, twice runner-up in the Hong Kong Sprint; one of Hong Kong's leading sprinters Firebolt; the South African-trained UAE 2000 Guineas/Derby winner Victory Moon; and the Dubai-trained UAE Oaks runner-up Desert Glow.

Choisir's connections had given some warning of what to expect from their charge. 'He's a monster of a horse—like a Brahma bull—and Johnny Murtagh will feel the power. I expect him to be hard to catch at Ascot.' The words of Shannon Perry, assistant to his father Paul, trainer of Choisir, were easy to dismiss as fighting talk beforehand and racegoers at Ascot could have been forgiven for leaving Choisir out of their calculations, even if he did have Group 1 form in his own country. Reproducing it halfway round the world was a tall order, and on top of that he had to give weight away in the King's Stand to all bar one of his nineteen rivals, with the addition of a penalty for his Group 1 success in Australia earlier in the year. Sticking with the more familiar names in the field, punters made the previous year's top two-year-old Oasis Dream the 6/1 favourite despite the fact that he was making his reappearance after taking time to come to hand during the spring. Olivia Grace, who had put up a smart effort when winning a handicap over the King's Stand course and distance the previous autumn was next in the betting at 9/1, ahead of the first two home from the previous year, Dominica and Continent, and the latter's stable-companion Captain Rio, on 10/1.

Choisir certainly stood out in the preliminaries in terms of physique, even in a field of top sprinters. He made an immediate impression once the race was

King's Stand Stakes, Royal Ascot—Australian-trained Choisir proves more than a match for some of the best sprinters in Europe; Acclamation (spots) finishes strongly for second ahead of Oasis Dream

under way as well. Equipped with a white bridle and black eyeshields or 'pacifiers', Choisir was soon going strongly in the lead near the stand rail with Hong Kong's Firebolt the only one able to go with him through the early stages. Approaching the last two furlongs, Firebolt had been seen off, and Choisir had the race sewn up when quickening clear against the stand rail over a furlong out. The significance of what Choisir was about to accomplish was not lost on BBC TV's Australian-born commentator Jim McGrath whose impartiality momentarily went out of the commentary box window with the words 'the Aussie's gonna do it!' as Choisir drew clear. Feeling the strain close home, Choisir had a length to spare over the strong-finishing Acclamation, who had been checked over a furlong out, with Oasis Dream third and Dominica, also making her reappearance, fourth.

Very few Australasian horses had been campaigned in Europe before Choisir, and only the Prix de l'Arc de Triomphe had served as a big enough incentive to entice the few who did make the trip. The New Zealand-bred Balmerino had been the outstanding three-year-old in Australasia in 1975/6 and joined John Dunlop for a crack at the 1977 Arc following a four-race campaign in California. After winning the Valdoe Stakes at Goodwood in a canter on his European debut, he found only Alleged too good at Longchamp, passing horse after horse in the straight and finishing full of running. Balmerino lost the Gran Premio del Jockey Club at Milan in the stewards' room later that autumn, and, although he finished second in the Eclipse the following year, he failed to recapture his top-class form as a six-year-old. Seven years after Balmerino's attempt, it was the turn of another former champion Australian three-year-old Strawberry Road, who finished fifth to Sagace in the Arc. The winner of Australia's most important weight-for-age event the Cox Plate, Strawberry Road was accompanied by a private trainer, John Nicholls, for his European campaign and was warmed up for the Arc with a couple of runs at Baden-Baden, winning the Grosser Preis there. Strawberry Road's globe-trotting also took in the Washington International (in which he came third), Breeders' Cup Turf (fourth) and the Japan Cup (seventh), and, trained by Patrick Biancone in France at six, he won the Grand Prix de Saint-Cloud and was beaten a neck by Pebbles in a second attempt at the Breeders' Cup Turf. The most recent challenger for the Arc from Australia was Nothin' Leica Dane who finished well held in the 1997 renewal. Runner-up in the 1995 Melbourne Cup, his best effort in four starts for John Hammond in France came when second in the Prix Foy at Longchamp.

Coincidentally, Choisir was not the only Australian horse to race in Europe in the latest season, though Belle du Jour had left her Australian handler for the stables of Dermot Weld for her European campaign. Like Choisir, she was a good sprinter in Australia (the pair had already met earlier in the season) and lined up as one of Choisir's sixteen rivals in the Golden Jubilee Stakes, four days after the King's Stand. Choisir was treated with a good deal more public respect this time, though such had been his tremendous show of speed earlier in the week that there had to be a doubt about his seeing out the extra furlong of the Golden Jubilee. He also faced a potentially stronger rival than any in the King's Stand, in the form of the impressive Temple Stakes winner Airwave, who was sent off 11/8 favourite. Choisir was next in the betting at 13/2 along with the previous year's winner Malhub, the remainder starting at 10/1 or longer. Choisir was drawn high this time, well away from what had widely been regarded as the 'favoured' stand rail. The result of the Wokingham Handicap, the following race, was to show that there was no great advantage to be had on any part of the track but, with connections fearing that Choisir had 'drawn the bad alley' as they put it, Murtagh gradually tacked Choisir across the course, so that with over a furlong to run he was in the same position as he had been in the King's Stand, hard up against the stand rail. Choisir's early speed had enabled him to make the manoeuvre successfully and, although he had to work harder this time, Choisir kept on gamely under pressure to run out a half-length winner from the slow-starting Airwave, with rank outsider Baron's Pit filling third place another length behind.

It was time to get the record books out again. Winning two races at the Royal meeting in the same year was a relatively common achievement in the late-nineteenth century, but in recent times few horses have been asked to run twice at the meeting, and dual winners have become considerably rarer. The last dual winner before Choisir was the Irish mare Stanerra, who won the Prince of Wales's Stakes and the Hardwicke Stakes twenty years previously. The only others since the Second World War were the stayers Trelawny and Mountain Cross, who both won the Ascot Stakes and the Queen Alexandra Stakes, Trelawny achieving the feat twice, in 1962 and 1963. The more specific double of winning both of Royal Ascot's top sprints in the same year had last been achieved in 1920 by the mare Diadem, later remembered in the Group 2 sprint run at Ascot's September meeting. However, Diadem's wins were gained in very different circumstances to Choisir's. For a start, the two races were run on consecutive days in Diadem's era as they were for most years right up until 1999, the King's Stand being run on the Friday, the day after what was then known as the All-Aged Stakes. Choisir beat a total of thirty-five rivals to complete his double, whereas Diadem had a single opponent in the All-Aged Stakes and nine in the King's Stand. She won the latter race, incidentally, by four lengths under 10-7, giving the runner-up two stone! In addition, prior to the All-Aged Stakes, Diadem had walked over the same afternoon to win the Rous Memorial.

Some records last longer than others, and one that was broken very quickly was Choisir's new fastest time for the six furlongs at Ascot which he held for little more than half an hour. Previously set by Shalford in the same race (then the Cork And Orrery) in 1992, Choisir set a new mark of 1m 12.23sec, only for the dead-heaters Fayr Jag and Ratio to shave off another five hundredths of a second in the Wokingham. As that suggests, conditions on the final day of the meeting were extremely firm, bordering on hard in fact, which accounted for the majority of the half-dozen non-runners in the Golden Jubilee Stakes.

With his mission accomplished more successfully than could reasonably have been expected, Choisir originally looked all set for a return to Australia. He did hold an entry in the July Cup, though his stable explained that 'he was never meant to go for it and he was only put in the race because it closed while we were over'. However, quarantine for return to Australia could not begin until July 18th. 'I think we'll push on and run at Newmarket' said Paul Perry. 'He's just marking time at the moment, so he might as well.' Choisir was now creating a deal of interest, both in Australia, where the July Cup was broadcast live, and in Britain. At Newmarket, Australian visitors were admitted at half price on July Cup day. Choisir started favourite this time, having beaten the majority of his opponents in one or other of his Royal Ascot races, among them his main market rivals Airwave and Oasis Dream. The decision to let Choisir take his chance resulted in one of the races of the season, and the reports which made mention of Choisir's 'failure' to emulate Diadem's record (she had gone on to win the July Cup following her Royal Ascot treble) were churlish in the extreme. For one thing, Diadem had won her July Cup with another walk-over! Choisir may have met with his first defeat in Britain, but there was little sense of failure in going down to Oasis Dream, who had clearly benefited from his reappearance three weeks earlier. Drawn next to the far rail,

Golden Jubilee Stakes, Royal Ascot—Choisir completes an historic double; Airwave is second and Baron's Pit third

Choisir was a couple of lengths clear in a matter of strides leaving the stalls and, whilst Oasis Dream pressed him from two out, Choisir did not go down without a fight, finally giving best close home to be beaten a length and a half. It was only a matter of days later that the announcement came that Choisir had been sold and would be retired to stud.

As a promoter of Australian racing abroad, Choisir's achievements drew comparisons with those of Australia's horse of the twentieth century Phar Lap. The winner of thirty-seven of his fifty-one races, fourteen of them on the trot as a four-year-old (including the Melbourne Cup under 9-12), the New Zealand-bred Phar Lap gained his most famous victory on his first venture abroad—and in what turned out to be his final race—in the Agua Caliente Handicap at Tijuana in Mexico in 1932. Overcoming a heel injury and a lack of experience on dirt, not to mention being shipped across the Pacific to San Francisco and a four-hundred-mile road journey across the Mexican border, Phar Lap won the 50,000-dollar race, worth more than £10,000 at the prevailing rate of exchange. Phar Lap had been due to continue his career in North America, but within a fortnight of his win he was dead, seemingly as a result of 'his picking some poisonous vegetation' as the *Bloodstock Breeders' Review* phrased it. 'The death of Phar Lap was regarded almost as a national calamity,' it went on. 'The magnificent career of this exceptional racehorse ended at its zenith. He has left behind him an immortal reputation, and was universally regarded as the greatest racehorse ever bred in Australia [*sic*], and, in fact must have been one of the world's best racehorses.'

It was fairly straightforward to get a good idea of how Choisir compared with the best sprinters in Britain, but how had he been measuring up against his rivals in Australia before being sent abroad? The *Racehorses* Annuals have included ratings for the best horses in Australasia since 1998, and in *Racehorses of 2002* Choisir had a rating of 124, making him the joint-third-best three-year-old in his part of the world in 2002, just a pound behind the top two, Bel Esprit (also a sprinter) and Helenus. The International Classifications for 2002, on the other hand, had seriously underestimated Choisir and the Australian sprinters in general, his rating of 110 being the same as that awarded to the likes of Bishops Court, Smokin Beau, Dominica, Polar Way and Twilight Blues in Britain, all of them some way removed from the very best sprinters in Europe. Choisir showed plenty of ability from early on in his career, but his headstrong nature, which was almost to the point of waywardness it seemed, prevented him from realising his potential fully. Choisir was placed in all three legs of Australia's juvenile triple crown in 2002, but the remarks in his form summary on each race tell their own story: Golden Slipper ('jumped awkwardly'), Sires Produce Stakes ('raced erratically'), Champagne Stakes ('pulled hard'). The last of those races was over a mile but, when put back to sprinting late in the year over the straight track at Flemington, it soon became clear that Choisir would emerge as a leading sprinter. He was demoted to third after passing the post first in the Group 3 L'Oreal Plate, gaining compensation five days later with a victory over top older sprinters Falvelon, the aforementioned Belle du Jour, and Spinning Hill in the Group 2 Emirates Stakes. Falvelon went on to finish third in the Hong Kong Sprint, a race which he had won for the two previous years.

Choisir resumed in 2003 with four runs in Group 1 company before being sent to Britain. He reappeared at Flemington in February with a victory over Spinning Hill again in the five-furlong Lightning Stakes and was considered an unlucky loser after suffering interference when a close third in the Oakleigh Plate over an extra half furlong at Caulfield a fortnight later. Choisir's next two outings did not see him at his best, however, and he managed only seventh in the Futurity Stakes at Caulfield over seven furlongs, and sixth of twenty-one to Belle du Jour back at Flemington over six in the A$1m Newmarket Handicap a week later. Despite showing some of the best sprinting form in Australia, Choisir was voted only third-best behind the Futurity winner Yell and the mare Spinning Hill in the Australian Racing Writers' Association's poll to determine the country's top sprinter of 2002/3, though he did receive an award for being Champion International Performer.

Even after taking into account the now-annual European raid on the Melbourne Cup, the traffic in racehorses moving between the two hemispheres is tiny compared to the number of stallions who shuttle to Australasia. Choisir's grandsire Danehill has been much the most successful to date, with a string of sires' championships in Australia to his name. Although he died in the spring, Danehill leaves a legacy of more than sixty sons currently at stud in Australia, some of them, including Choisir's sire Danehill Dancer, based for the other half of the year in the northern hemisphere. Danehill Dancer's owners Coolmore won the battle to secure Choisir as a stallion shortly after the July Cup, and he has already started in his new career in New South Wales at a fee of A$30,250. His fee in Ireland has been set at €15,000. Having proved himself in Group 1 company in both Europe and Australia, he should not lack support from breeders on either continent. The female side of Choisir's pedigree is more modest. Costing A$55,000 as a yearling, Choisir is the fourth and final foal out of his dam Great Selection, who died in 2001. Great Selection's other winners are also sprinters, though the filly Supermarket (by Zephyr Zip) and Choisir's gelded brother Danny Dancer have won only in minor company. Great Selection won over six furlongs in Australia as a two-year-old and was by the 1972 Dewhurst winner Lunchtime, who, in pre-shuttling days, was sent to Australia on a one-way ticket after disappointing as a three-year-old. Choisir's grandam Pensive Mood won four small races in Australia but was out of a mare, Staid, who performed in better company, finishing fourth in the AJC Oaks.

Choisir (AUS) (ch.c. 1999)	Danehill Dancer (IRE) (b 1993)	Danehill (b 1986)	Danzig / Razyana
		Mira Adonde (b or br 1986)	Sharpen Up / Lettre d'Amour
	Great Selection (AUS) (ch 1990)	Lunchtime (ch 1970)	Silly Season / Great Occasion
		Pensive Mood (ch 1983)	Biscay / Staid

Mr T. W. Wallace & Partners' "Choisir"

The stocky, robust Choisir was every inch a sprinter in build, perhaps not everyone's idea of a model physical specimen but impressive all the same. His tendency to sweat, the fact that he was taken steadily to post, and his wearing of a pacifier (a mesh covering the eyes, the use of which is commonplace in Australia and Asia) were all indicative of his still rather headstrong tendencies. Channelled in the right direction, that side of his nature made him a most effective front runner. Choisir had form at a mile but sprinting was his game. He had a fluent, easy action and went well on firm ground. The top sprints that Choisir did not contest were very much the poorer without him. In particular, his presence would have enlivened what turned out to be a very one-sided Nunthorpe at York, where the five furlongs on a flat track would surely have been right up Choisir's street. *Paul Perry, Australia*

CHOOKIE HEITON (IRE) 5 br.g. Fumo di Londra (IRE) 108 – Royal Wolff (Prince **112** Tenderfoot (USA) 126) [2003 113: 6g 6g 6m 6m* 7m Aug 16] strong, lengthy gelding: smart performer: better than ever when dead-heating with Acclamation in minor event at Doncaster in August, leading well over 1f out and joined final stride: tailed off in Hungerford Stakes at Newbury final start: effective at 5f/6f: acts on firm and good to soft going: has been bandaged in front: game. *I. Semple*

CHORAL CHIMES (JPN) 3 b.f. Sunday Silence (USA) – Polent (Polish Precedent **72** (USA) 131) [2003 82p: 12m* 12m⁵ 11.8m⁶ May 10] leggy filly: fair performer: won maiden at Folkestone in April: blinkered, took good hold/found little in listed event at Lingfield final start: will stay 1¾m: raced only on good to firm ground: hung left second outing: sent to Australia. *D. R. Loder*

CHORIST 4 ch.f. Pivotal 124 – Choir Mistress (Chief Singer 131) [2003 108: 10.4m² **114 +** 10.1g* 10.2d* 11.9m 10f* 12g³ Oct 11] big, angular filly: smart performer: better than ever at 4 yrs, winning listed race at Newcastle (by head from Monturani) in June, Oakgrove Stud Golden Daffodil Stakes at Chepstow (by 2½ lengths from Favourable Terms) in July and Irish National Stud Blandford Stakes at the Curragh (beat Place Rouge 4 lengths) in September: stays 1¼m: acts on soft (yet to race on heavy) and firm going: usually races prominently: tough and game. *W. J. Haggas*

CHORISTAR 2 ch.g. (Apr 12) Inchinor 119 – Star Tulip 99 (Night Shift (USA)) [2003 **60** 5m 7g⁶ 6g Oct 13] fourth foal: closely related to fairly useful 6f (at 2 yrs) to 1½m winner Indian Sun (by Indian Ridge) and half-brother to 5-y-o Texas Gold: dam 6f winner, including at 2 yrs: modest form on first 2 starts in maidens: likely to stay 1m. *W. R. Muir*

CHORUS 6 b.m. Bandmaster (USA) 97 – Name That Tune 40 (Fayruz 116) [2003 70§, **63 §** a54§: f6g³ p6g f6g³ f6s² f6s⁴ 6m² 6.1g 6m 5.7f f6s* f6g² f6g⁶ f6g⁴ 6m f6s⁶ Sep 6] neat mare: modest handicapper: won at Wolverhampton in June: effective at 6f/7f: ran poorly on heavy going, acts on any other turf and fibresand: tried blinkered/in cheekpieces, usually visored: has reared leaving stall/swerved right under pressure: untrustworthy. *B. R. Millman*

CHORUS BEAUTY 2 b.f. (Mar 27) Royal Applause 124 – Happy Lady (FR) 72 **64 p** (Cadeaux Genereux 131) [2003 p6g p6g* Dec 29] 16,000Y: first foal: dam, maiden (stayed 1m), half-sister to smart performer up to 2m Rainbow Ways: easily better effort in maidens at Lingfield (modest form) when winning 10-runner event by 1½ lengths from Mugeba, leading 1f out: should stay 7f: likely to improve further. *G. Wragg*

CHOTO MATE (IRE) 7 ch.g. Brief Truce (USA) 126 – Greatest Pleasure (Be My **88** Guest (USA) 126) [2003 89: p8g⁶ p8g² p7g 7m Jul 31] useful-looking gelding: poor mover (reportedly suffered from knee chips at 3 yrs): fairly useful performer: form at 7 yrs (including in claimer) only when second in handicap at Lingfield: effective at 7f/1m: acts on polytrack (well held on fibresand), firm and good to soft going: difficult ride. *S. Kirk*

CHRISTINA SANCHEZ (USA) 3 gr.f. El Prado (IRE) 119 – Cope's Light (USA) **59 +** (Copelan (USA)) [2003 –p: f8.5g f6g³ f7s³ f6g 7.9d a8.5f² a8g* Dec 18] lengthy filly: modest performer: left Sir Mark Prescott after fifth outing: won maiden at Penn National in December: stays 1m: acts on fibresand/dirt, little form on turf: blinkered/visored after reappearance. *H. G. Motion, USA*

CHRISTINA'S DREAM 2 b.f. (Feb 13) Spectrum (IRE) 126 – Christine Daae 74 **74 p** (Sadler's Wells (USA) 132) [2003 6m³ 6m³ 6g⁴ Oct 6] well-made filly: half-sister to several winners, including smart sprinter To The Roof (by Thatching) and useful 5f (at 2 yrs) and 1m winner Risque Lady (by Kenmare): dam 1¼m winner: fair form in maidens:

third at Newbury (shaped very well) and Salisbury: should stay at least 1m: early to post final start: type to do well in handicaps as 3-y-o. *P. W. Harris*

CHRISTMAS TRUCE (IRE)　4 b.g. Brief Truce (USA) 126 – Superflash (Superlative 118) [2003 84: f14s⁶ 12m 11.9m³ 13d⁵ 12.1g f12g² 12.6m 16.5m 11.6g 12m 11.9d p12g Oct 3] good-topped gelding: fairly useful performer: well below form after being claimed from M. Tompkins sixth outing: stays 13f: acts on all-weather, good to firm and heavy going: tried visored/in cheekpieces: sometimes slowly away/races moodily: none too consistent. *Ian Williams*　**78 d**

CHUBBES　2 b.g. (Jan 31) Kris 135 – St Radegund 85 (Green Desert (USA) 127) [2003 6g 6m⁵ 6g 7m 7m⁶ 8.3g* 7d⁴ p8g² f7g³ p8g Dec 2] first foal: dam, 7f winner from 2 starts, out of 1000 Guineas and Sussex Stakes winner On The House: fair performer: won seller at Windsor (left R. Charlton 24,500 gns) in October: creditable efforts in nurseries after when fourth at Doncaster and second at Lingfield: effective at 7f/1m: acts on polytrack and good to soft going: visored last 5 starts. *M. C. Pipe*　**79**

CIACOLE　2 b.f. (Apr 16) Primo Dominie 121 – Dance On A Cloud (USA) 76 (Capote (USA)) [2003 6m⁶ 6f⁵ 7m⁴ f5g Dec 9] fourth foal: half-sister to fairly useful 1½m winner Dardanus (by Komaite): dam, 2-y-o 7f winner who probably stayed 9f, out of US Grade 1 9f winner Sharp Dance: fair maiden: fourth at Folkestone, then left Mrs A. Perrett: should stay 1m. *S. C. Williams*　**68**

CICATRICE　2 ch.c. (Mar 21) Wolfhound (USA) 126 – Capricious Lady (IRE) (Capricorn Line 111) [2003 p7g Nov 18] sixth foal: half-brother to 1996 2-y-o 7f winner Buzzby (by Buzzards Bay) and winner (including at 2 yrs) in Italy by Beveled: dam in frame in bumpers: 40/1, missed break when well beaten in claimer at Lingfield. *A. Charlton*　**–**

CIEL　3 b.f. Rainbow Quest (USA) 134 – River Cara (USA) 86 (Irish River (FR) 131) [2003 78p: 11.8m 9f⁶ 10g⁴ 12m² 12m Aug 27] leggy filly: fairly useful handicapper, lightly raced: best effort when second at Salisbury: stays 1½m: raced only on good ground or firmer: sold 18,000 gns. *M. L. W. Bell*　**85**

CILL DROICHEAD (IRE)　3 b.c. Entrepreneur 123 – Havinia (Habitat 134) [2003 74: p10g⁵ p10g* p8g⁵ p10g⁶ 10d p10g* 10m⁴ 11.9m² 12m 12f 10m⁴ 10.1d⁵ 10g² 11.7f 10.3g⁶ 12m⁶ 11.6g Oct 6] leggy colt: fairly useful performer: won handicaps at Lingfield in February and May: stays easy 1½m: acts on polytrack and firm going, probably on good to soft: tried blinkered: sometimes takes strong hold/carries head high/finishes weakly: none too consistent: sold 26,000 gns. *E. J. O'Neill*　**90**

CIMYLA (IRE)　2 b.c. (Jan 22) Lomitas 129 – Coyaima (GER) 100 (Night Shift (USA)) [2003 7m⁴ p8g* Oct 15] 20,000Y: good-topped colt: third foal: half-brother to 3-y-o Cameo Role and a winner in Germany by Platini: dam, German 7f (at 2 yrs) and 1m (listed) winner, half-sister to smart German middle-distance performer Concepcion: fair form: promising debut, and less than month later won 12-runner maiden at Lingfield by 1¼ lengths from Cutting Crew, leading over 1f out: will be suited by 1¼m/1½m: open to progress. *C. F. Wall*　**78 p**

CINNAMON RIDGE (IRE)　2 b.g. (Feb 21) Indian Ridge 123 – Savoury 67 (Salse (USA) 128) [2003 6m 6d Jul 30] IR 65,000F, €80,000Y: big, good-bodied gelding: has scope: first foal: dam, disappointing maiden, out of half-sister to dam of Domedriver (by Indian Ridge): backward, behind in maidens at Newbury and Leicester (early speed): should do better. *B. J. Meehan*　**– p**

CIRCASSIAN (IRE)　2 b.g. (Mar 11) Groom Dancer (USA) 128 – Daraliya (IRE) (Kahyasi 130) [2003 f8s 7.1g 7.1m 7.9f Oct 10] 48,000Y: big, lengthy gelding: first foal: dam, French 12.5f winner, half-sister to several useful winners in France, out of smart Prix Minerve winner Daralinsha: signs of ability when well held in maidens: should do better at 1¼m+. *Sir Mark Prescott*　**– p**

CIRCUIT DANCER (IRE)　3 b.g. Mujadil (USA) 119 – Trysinger (IRE) (Try My Best (USA) 130) [2003 81: 6m⁶ 6.1m⁶ 6d⁵ 6f 6f² 6g 6m* 6d² 6m² 6m³ 6.1g* 7f⁶ Oct 11] tall gelding: fairly useful handicapper: won at Haydock (edged left) in July and Chester in August: stays 6f: acts on firm and good to soft going: sometimes slowly away (reared as stall opened on sixth outing), races prominently otherwise. *A. Berry*　**92**

CIRCUS MAXIMUS (USA)　6 b.g. Pleasant Colony (USA) – Crockadore (USA) 102 (Nijinsky (CAN) 138) [2003 61+: 12g⁵ p16g 14.1m² 16g Jul 28] fair performer: won maiden at Tralee in 2000: left D. Weld, Ireland, after only 5-y-o outing: stays 2m: acts on firm going, soft and polytrack: tried in cheekpieces, usually blinkered: ungenuine: won 2-finisher novice chase in October. *Ian Williams*　**65 §**

CITA VERDA (FR) 5 b.m. Take Risks (FR) 116 – Mossita (FR) (Tip Moss (FR)) [2003 **79**
–: 10.1d* 12m⁴ 10d Oct 13] heavy-bodied mare: fairly useful hurdler: fair handicapper
on Flat, lightly raced: won at Newcastle in March: stays 1½m: acts on good to firm and
heavy ground. *P. Monteith*

CITRINE (IRE) 5 ch.m. Selkirk (USA) 129 – Classic Coral (USA) (Seattle Dancer **–**
(USA) 119) [2003 81: 16m Apr 19] tall, leggy mare: fairly useful handicapper at best:
tailed off only 5-y-o outing: tried visored. *C. F. Wall*

CITRINE SPIRIT (IRE) 2 gr.f. (Feb 10) Soviet Star (USA) 128 – Casessa (USA) **– p**
(Caro 133) [2003 7g Nov 1] €90,000Y: sturdy filly: sixth foal: closely related to 4-y-o
Temple of Artemis and half-sister to several winners, including 7.5f (at 2 yrs) to 9.4f
winner New Century (by Manila) and 1½m winner Smart Play (by Sovereign Dancer),
both early: dam maiden half-sister to 1000 Guineas winner Musical Bliss: 10/1, twelfth
of 17 in maiden at Newmarket, showing up well long way: will do better. *J. H. M. Gosden*

CITRUS MAGIC 6 b.g. Cosmonaut – Up All Night 56 (Green Desert (USA) 127) **46 §**
[2003 54§: f14s f12s⁴ p13g⁵ f16s f14g⁶ Mar 11] poor maiden: stays 2m: acts on soft and
good to firm going, raced only on all-weather at 5/6 yrs: tried visored, usually blinkered:
unreliable. *K. Bell*

CITY AFFAIR 2 b.g. (Apr 5) Inchinor 119 – Aldevonie 75 (Green Desert (USA) 127) **63**
[2003 6g³ 5.9d 5m⁵ 8m 7m 7m³ f8g p6g⁵ Dec 29] 27,000Y: third living foal: half-brother
to 2000 2-y-o 5f winner Nashira (by Prince Sabo) and 3-y-o Victory Vee: dam, second at
1m at 2 yrs from 2 starts, would have stayed 1¼m: modest maiden: left Sir Mark Prescott
after sixth start: should stay 1m: acts on good to firm going and polytrack: blinkered fifth
to seventh outings. *Mrs L. C. Jewell*

CITY FLITE 3 b.f. Magic King (IRE) 115 – Lady Mabel 34 (Inchinor 119) [2003 43d: **–**
5m 5f 5f Jun 30] little form: tried visored. *P. Monteith*

CITY FLYER 6 br.g. Night Shift (USA) – Al Guswa 98 (Shernazar 131) [2003 53, **–**
a67: f8g f8.5g f9.4g⁵ f9.4s f9.4g May 19] leggy, good-topped gelding: poor performer:
stays 1¼m: acts on good to firm going and fibresand: tried visored/tongue tied: tends to
carry head awkwardly. *Miss J. Feilden*

CITY GENERAL (IRE) 2 ch.g. (Mar 12) General Monash (USA) 107 – Astra (IRE) **62**
(Glenstal (USA) 118) [2003 5.1m 6.1d³ 7m² 7m* 7g³ 7m³ 7m⁴ 7g 8m⁶ f7g² p6g⁵ f8g f8g
Dec 8] €7,000Y: workmanlike gelding: seventh foal: half-brother to 1998 2-y-o 6f winner
Montague Tigg (by Common Grounds) and winner in Italy by College Chapel: dam Irish
middle-distance maiden: modest performer: won seller at Yarmouth in June: stays 7f: acts
on all-weather and good to firm going: wore cheekpieces 8 of last 9 starts: often races
prominently: none too consistent. *J. S. Moore*

CITY PALACE 2 ch.c. (Apr 23) Grand Lodge (USA) 125 – Ajuga (USA) 102 (The **74 p**
Minstrel (CAN) 135) [2003 6g⁶ Oct 24] strong colt: half-brother to several winners,
including 7-y-o Bangalore and smart 1m/1¼m winner Prolix (by Kris): dam, 6f (at 2 yrs)
and 7f winner, out of Irish 1000 Guineas and Champion Stakes winner Cairn Rouge: 7/1
and better for race, 4½ lengths sixth of 18 to Warrad in maiden at Newbury, slowly away
and not knocked about: will stay at least 1m: should do better. *B. W. Hills*

CLANN A COUGAR 3 ch.g. Bahamian Bounty 116 – Move Darling (Rock City 120) **78**
[2003 77: 7.6g⁶ 7d³ 8m 7.6g 7m⁶ 7g⁴ 7.1m⁴ 7f 7m⁴ Sep 1] leggy, useful-looking gelding:
has a quick action: fair performer: stays 7.6f: acts on soft and good to firm going: tried in
cheekpieces. *I. A. Wood*

CLAPTRAP 3 b.c. Royal Applause 124 – Stardyn (Star Appeal 133) [2003 –: f9.4g³ **55**
f12g² 11.5m³ f12g² f9.4s³ 13f³ f16.2g⁴ 12.6f⁶ f12s f12g f14.8g* f14g⁵ Dec 12] fair on all- **a65**
weather, modest on turf: heavily eased and collared post when short-headed in handicap
at Southwell fourth start: won claimer at Wolverhampton (claimed from J. Osborne
£6,000) in November: stays 14.8f: acts on fibresand, raced only on ground firmer than
good on turf: refused to enter stall seventh intended outing. *R. Brotherton*

CLARADOTNET 3 b.f. Sri Pekan (USA) 117 – Lypharitissima (FR) (Lightning (FR) **82**
129) [2003 10m² 11.7f* 10.5d Sep 26] 17,000Y: half-sister to 3 winners, including 9f/
1¼m winner Generous Diana and 7f to 8.5f winner One Dinar (both fairly useful, by
Generous): dam unraced sister to Prix de Diane winner Lypharita: fairly useful form: won
maiden at Bath in September, idling: stays 11.7f: acts on firm going, probably on good to
soft. *H. R. A. Cecil*

CLARICE STARLING 5 b.m. Saddlers' Hall (IRE) 126 – Uncharted Waters 68 **–**
(Celestial Storm (USA) 132) [2003 52: f16s p13g Feb 1] strong mare: poor maiden: stays
1½m. *C. A. Cyzer*

CLARINCH CLAYMORE 7 b.g. Sabrehill (USA) 120 – Salu 65 (Ardross 134) **80**
[2003 90: 16g³ 14v⁵ 11.9g 16.2m* 16.2m 14g 14d 13.1d⁴ 16g⁶ Nov 5] smallish, good-
bodied gelding: fairly useful handicapper: won at Beverley in July: effective at 13f to 2m:
acts on heavy going, good to firm and fibresand: has raced freely: held up. *J. M. Jefferson*

CLARISSE 4 b.f. Salse (USA) 128 – Celia Brady 62 (Last Tycoon 131) [2003 76: **82**
11.7m* 12.1d³ 10m⁴ 11.9g 12d³ 10g³ 12m⁵ 11.6g⁴ 10.1m² 12g Oct 31] angular filly:
fairly useful handicapper: reportedly injured pelvis at 3 yrs: won at Bath in April: mostly
creditable efforts after: stays 1½m: acts on firm and good to soft going: blinkered last 2
outings. *H. Candy*

CLASSICAL DANCER 2 ch.f. (Feb 28) Dr Fong (USA) 128 – Gorgeous Dancer **86 p**
(IRE) (Nordico (USA)) [2003 6m³ Aug 3] fifth living foal: half-sister to 3 at least useful
winners, notably 5-y-o Imperial Dancer: dam, Irish 1m winner who stayed 1¾m, out of
half-sister to Irish Oaks winner Give Thanks: 13/2, 2 lengths third of 13 to Bay Tree in
maiden at Newbury, running on well despite carrying head to one side: will stay at least
1m: sure to do better if all is well. *H. Candy*

CLASSICAL SONG (IRE) 3 b.f. Fayruz 116 – Dieci Anno (IRE) 72 (Classic Music **57 d**
(USA)) [2003 69: 7.5f 8.3d 8g 6f³ 6f 7g 7g 7m⁶ 8m 8g Oct 22] modest maiden: below
best after fourth outing: stays 7f: acts on polytrack and firm ground: tried in cheekpieces/
blinkers: sometimes awkward leaving stall: sold 3,000 gns. *P. W. Harris*

CLASSICAL WALTZ (IRE) 5 ch.m. In The Wings 128 – Fascination Waltz 83 (Shy **–**
Groom (USA)) [2003 –: p12g Jul 9] poor maiden at 3 yrs: lightly raced and no form since.
J. J. Sheehan

CLASSIC EVENT (IRE) 2 ch.c. (Mar 2) Croco Rouge (IRE) 126 – Delta Town **62**
(USA) (Sanglamore (USA) 126) [2003 7m 7d³ 7m⁵ 8s Nov 3] 18,000Y: tall, close-
coupled colt: has short, choppy action: fourth foal: half-brother to 3-y-o Kentucky Blue:
dam French maiden daughter of smart French performer up to 1¼m Daeltown: modest
maiden: third at Newcastle: ran creditably in nursery final start: should be suited by 1¼m/
1½m: acts on good ground. *T. D. Easterby*

CLASSIC EXAMPLE 4 ch.c. Mark of Esteem (IRE) 137 – Classic Form (IRE) 58 **–**
(Alzao (USA) 117) [2003 82, a68: 12g 10g⁶ 11m 12f Jun 6] fairly useful maiden at 3 yrs:
well held in 2003: tried in cheekpieces: dead. *Miss S. J. Wilton*

CLASSIC MILLENNIUM 5 b.m. Midyan (USA) 124 – Classic Colleen (IRE) 79 **72**
(Sadler's Wells (USA) 132) [2003 58: 11.7m 13.1g* 14g⁴ 14f 14.4f* 12m* 14.4m² 12s5 **a?**
11.9f⁴ 12m 11.9f* 14.6m⁵ p13g⁵ Nov 12] small, lightly-made mare: fair handicapper:
better than ever at 5 yrs, winning at Bath in May, Kempton and Pontefract in July and
York (apprentices) in October: stays 14.4f: acts on firm going, soft and polytrack: tried
blinkered: sometimes slowly away: held up: tough. *W. J. Musson*

CLASSIC QUARTET 3 b.f. Classic Cliche (IRE) 128 – Carolside 108 (Music Maes- **52 ?**
tro 119) [2003 12f⁴ 10m 12d 11.9s⁴ 12.1m 12.3g⁵ Aug 29] 600Y: leggy filly: half-sister to
several winners, including useful 1m/9f winner Eton Lad (by Never So Bold): dam 2-y-o
5f winner who didn't progress: seemingly modest performer: virtually ran out on bend
third start: tried in cheekpieces. *Mrs L. Williamson*

CLASSIC ROLE 4 b.g. Tragic Role (USA) – Clare Island 108 (Connaught 130) **84**
[2003 83: 14.4d⁵ 11.6g 12.3m 12g² 13.3m 12f⁴ 10m* 10m 10.3m 10s p10g f11g³ p10g **a79**
Dec 10] sparely-made gelding: fairly useful handicapper on turf, fair on all-weather:
best effort in 2003 when winning at Windsor in July: effective at 1¼m/1½m: acts on
all-weather, firm and soft going: often carries head awkwardly. *R. Ingram*

CLASSIC VISION 3 b.f. Classic Cliche (IRE) 128 – Orient 106 (Bay Express 132) **57**
[2003 8g⁵ f8.5s³ Jun 13] closely related to smart 7f/1m performer Yeast (by Salse) and
half-sister to several winners, notably 5-y-o Orientor: dam sprinter: better effort in
maidens (modest form) on debut. *W. J. Haggas*

CLASSY LASSIE (IRE) 3 ch.f. Goldmark (USA) 113 – Okay Baby (IRE) 67 (Trea- **70**
sure Kay 114) [2003 61: 6m* 6d 6m 7m 6g⁵ Aug 25] fair handicapper: easily best effort
when winning at Redcar in June: should stay 7f: acts on good to firm and good to soft
ground. *G. A. Swinbank*

CLASSY TIMES 2 b.g. (Jan 26) Mind Games 121 – Gay Ming 50 (Gay Meadow 52) **–**
[2003 5m 7m Jun 10] 3,000Y: close-coupled gelding: fifth foal: half-brother to winner in
Greece by Forzando: dam 1¼m winner who stayed 2m: well held in minor event and
seller at Redcar. *J. S. Wainwright*

CLAUDIA'S PEARL   3 ch.f. Deploy 131 – Triple Zee (USA) (Zilzal (USA) 137)   **59**
[2003 10m 10f 10f⁶ 12g³ Aug 2] workmanlike filly: second foal: half-sister to useful 2000
2-y-o 7f winner Cauvery (by Exit To Nowhere): dam unraced: modest maiden: stays
1½m. *P. W. Harris*

CLEARING SKY (IRE)   2 gr.f. (Feb 23) Exploit (USA) 117 – Litchfield Hills (USA)   **56**
(Relaunch (USA)) [2003 p6g p5g Nov 22] 13,000Y: first foal: dam, winner in USA, out
of half-sister to dam of Croco Rouge: better effort in maidens at Lingfield (modest form)
when eighth of 9 latter start, missing break. *Miss Z. C. Davison*

CLEARLY TOUGH (IRE)   2 b.g. (Apr 24) Indian Rocket 115 – Pharmacy 80 (Mtoto   **43**
134) [2003 5g⁵ 5f⁶ 5f 5.9m⁶ 6d 6m⁵ 7.1m Oct 25] 4,500 2-y-o: close-coupled gelding:
fourth foal: half-brother to a winner in Italy by Danetime: dam, 6f (at 2 yrs) and 7f winner,
half-sister to 5-y-o Adiemus: poor maiden: stays 6f: acts on firm ground: blinkered/
visored 4 of last 5 starts: sometimes slowly away/hangs. *I. Semple*

CLEAVER   2 ch.c. (May 27) Kris 135 – Much Too Risky 87 (Bustino 136) [2003 7s   **– p**
Oct 29] half-brother to several winners, including very smart 7f (at 2 yrs) to 1½m winner
Little Rock (by Warning) and smart 1m to 13.5f winner Whitewater Affair (by Machiavellian): dam 2-y-o 7f/1m winner: 28/1, well held in maiden at Yarmouth, pulling hard:
should do better. *W. Jarvis*

CLEVELAND WAY   3 b.g. Forzando 122 – Fallal (IRE) 47 (Fayruz 116) [2003 59:   **55**
5m⁵ 8m 7m 5d⁵ 5.9m² 5.9m 5f⁴ 5m f6g f6g Dec 9] good-topped gelding: modest maiden:
best at 5f/6f: acts on firm going and fibresand: visored/blinkered after second start:
usually races up with pace: none too consistent. *D. Carroll*

CLEVER CLOGS   3 ch.f. Nashwan (USA) 135 – High Standard 83 (Kris 135) [2003   **96**
72p: 9m³ 11.8m² 12m* 14.8m 11.6m³ 11.8m* 11.8m³ 12g⁶ 12d Nov 8] big, lengthy filly:
useful performer: won maiden at Pontefract in June and minor event at York in October,
both in small fields: good efforts next 2 starts, including when third to Dovedon Hero in
handicap at Leicester: probably stays 14.8f: acts on firm ground: has run well when
sweating. *E. A. L. Dunlop*

CLIFDEN (IRE)   2 ch.c. (Feb 21) Gold Away (IRE) 125 – Romora (FR) (Sillery (USA)   **101**
122) [2003 5.2m* 6.1d³ 6d² 6g* 6f* 6d⁶ Aug 22] 8,000Y: first foal: dam unraced granddaughter of high-class French performer up to 12.5f Riverqueen: useful performer: won
maiden at Yarmouth in April, minor event at Ayr in May and Premio Primi Passi at Milan
(beat Golden Pivotal 4 lengths) in June: changed hands 170,000 gns, then only sixth in
Prix de Cabourg at Deauville: should stay 7f: acts on firm ground: often races up with
pace: sent to UAE, joined M. Al Kurdi. *M. J. Wallace*

CLIMATE (IRE)   4 ch.g. Catrail (USA) 123 – Burishki 49 (Chilibang 120) [2003 93:   **93 §**
8m 8.1g 8g³ 7f⁴ 8f⁴ 8.1g 8d 8m 8.3g⁵ 7m 8f 10g³ p10g Nov 29] strong, compact gelding:
fairly useful handicapper: creditable efforts at 4 yrs when in frame: left R. Hannon 17,000
gns after twelfth start: effective at 7f to 1¼m: acts on polytrack, soft and firm going:
effective blinkered or not: carries head awkwardly: none too genuine. *J. R. Boyle*

CLIPPERTON   4 b.g. Mister Baileys 123 – Theresita (GER) (Surumu (GER)) [2003   **83**
87: 10m⁴ 10m⁵ 10.3m May 5] leggy gelding: had a fluent, round action: fairly useful
handicapper: stayed 1¼m: acted on firm and good to soft going: dead. *A. M. Balding*

CLODOVIL (IRE)   3 gr.c. Danehill (USA) 126 – Clodora (FR) 113 (Linamix (FR)   **116**
127) [2003 8g* 8d* 8g* 8f⁵ 8d 8g⁵ Sep 7]
      The grey silks with pink cap of Jean-Luc Lagardère have been as familiar
as any on the racecourses of France for many years; and even after his death in
March they continued in the spotlight, with the Poule d'Essai des Poulains winner
Clodovil one of those to carry them under the Lagardère Family banner. A major
industrialist in Europe, Lagardère was one of the most influential and respected
figures in French racing, not only as an owner and breeder but also as head of
France Galop from 1995 until his death. The Grand Criterium, run at Longchamp
on Arc day, has been renamed in his honour. Those grey and pink colours were
famous long before they were purchased by Lagardère, along with the Haras
d'Ouilly, from the Dupre family in 1986, having been carried with distinction by
such as the 1963 Derby winner Relko and the 1965 Prix du Jockey Club winner
Reliance. Lagardère, at that time, was already the owner of the Haras du Val Henry
and had enjoyed a fair amount of success as an owner/breeder, but nothing compared to what was to follow. In 1988 Resless Kara gave Lagardère his first Group 1
victory, in the Prix de Diane, and other home-breds went on to provide him with

*Gainsborough Poule d'Essai des Poulains, Longchamp—Clodovil extends his unbeaten run to five;
Catcher In The Rye (far right) finishes really strongly to take second,
with Krataios (stars) third and France (blinkers) fourth*

further big-race winners, most notably Sagamix, who in 1998, won the Prix de l'Arc de Triomphe. Before Sagamix there were such as the Val Henry's outstanding stallion Linamix, who also won the Poule d'Essai des Poulains, the Prix Jacques le Marois winner Miss Satamixa and the Prix Saint-Alary winner Luna Wells. Also in 1998, Fragrant Mix won the Grand Prix de Saint-Cloud, and since then there have been victories for Slickly in the Grand Prix de Paris, Amilynx in two consecutive runnings of the Prix Royal-Oak and Vahorimix in the Poule d'Essai des Poulains and Prix Jacques le Marois, both on disqualifications. Lagardere, who also bred the 1992 Prix du Jockey Club winner Polytain, whom he also owned until the horse changed hands a few months before the race after winning a claimer, was the leading breeder in France on nine occasions.

At the time of his owner's death, Clodovil had yet to reappear in his second season, having won a newcomers race over four and a half furlongs and a minor event over six, both at Saint-Cloud, on his only outings in his first. Raced only at a mile as a three-year-old, Clodovil was still unbeaten when he turned up at Longchamp in May for the Gainsborough Poule d'Essai des Poulains, having won a minor event and the Prix de Fontainebleau at the same venue in the interim. He was sent off favourite to account for nine rivals, of whom only the Prix Morny winner Elusive City had been successful in a Group 1 contest, that horse one of six trained outside France. Aidan O'Brien was responsible for three of those, his Dalcassian effectively acting as pacemaker. Clodovil had arguably profited from an O'Brien-trained rival Tomahawk meeting trouble in running in the Fontainebleau and it was a similar story again. This time it was Catcher In The Rye who failed to get a clear run, although Clodovil himself didn't get the smoothest of passages in the straight after being settled in mid-division on the rail. Clodovil did work his way to the front over a furlong out, however, where Catcher In The Rye was still last, and he ran on well to hold the latter's very strong finish by a length, the pair providing their sire Danehill, who had also been responsible for the 2002 winner Landseer, with first and second just a day before he died (more detail on Danehill can be found in the essay on Westerner). It looked a below-standard Poulains at the time and nothing that happened subsequently suggested otherwise, with sixth-placed Sign of The Wolf, successful in the Group 3 Prix Andre Baboin at Lyon Parilly, the only one to win during the remainder of the season, though the second and third didn't run again. Clodovil failed even to make the frame in three subsequent starts, though he did run respectably when fifth to Zafeen in the St James's Palace Stakes at Royal Ascot and to Nebraska Tornado in the Prix du Moulin at Longchamp. A smart miler, though no better than that, Clodovil has been retired and is to stand at the Rathasker Stud in Ireland at a fee of €12,000, with the October 1st concession.

Clodovil is the second foal of Clodora, who in terms of racecourse merit wasn't that much inferior to her offspring. Clodora was also trained by Andre Fabre and raced only as a three-year-old, when she won three races, including a listed event over a mile at Deauville and the Prix de l'Opera over an extended nine furlongs at Longchamp. Clodora, by Linamix, is out of the useful Cloche d'Or, who did most of her racing at six and seven furlongs. Cloche d'Or gained her only win in the Princess Margaret Stakes at Ascot, but finished in the frame on several

222

Famille Lagardere's "Clodovil"

		Danzig	Northern Dancer
Clodovil (IRE) (gr.c. 2000)	Danehill (USA) (b 1986)	(b 1977)	Pas de Nom
		Razyana (b 1981)	His Majesty
			Spring Adieu
	Clodora (FR) (gr 1994)	Linamix (gr 1987)	Mendez
			Lunadix
		Cloche d'Or (b 1988)	Good Times
			Chrysicabana

occasions, including in the Lowther and Nell Gwyn Stakes. She was bought by Lagardere for 37,000 guineas at the 1991 December Sales. Clodovil's great gran-dam Chrysicabana gained her sole victory in a ten-furlong minor event at Windsor, starting at 50/1. Clodovil, a smallish, strong, lengthy colt, raced only on good ground or softer apart from at Ascot. *A. Fabre, France*

CLOG DANCE (USA)   2 b.f. (Feb 16) Woodman (USA) 126 – Royal Fandango   **72**
(USA) (Slew O' Gold (USA)) [2003 7f 7m 8d p7g² f9.4g* Nov 15] leggy filly: fourth
foal: half-sister to winner in US by Rahy: dam French 1½m winner: fair performer:
won maiden at Wolverhampton, hanging right: likely to be suited by 1¼m/1½m: acts on all-
weather and good to firm going: sold 20,000 gns. *J. H. M. Gosden*

CLOSE FISTED   2 b.c. (Jan 27) Forzando 122 – Not So Generous (IRE) 68 (Fayruz   **58**
116) [2003 5g 5f f5g 5f Sep 15] 13,000Y: compact colt: fourth living foal: half-brother to
4-y-o Neptune's Gift: dam 5f winner, including at 2 yrs: modest maiden: best effort on
debut: will need to settle to stay beyond 5f. *B. A. McMahon*

CLOUD CATCHER (IRE)   2 br.f. (Jan 26) Charnwood Forest (IRE) 125 – Notley   **–**
Park 71 (Wolfhound (USA) 126) [2003 5g Mar 22] €12,000Y: second foal: half-sister to

223

3-y-o Mulan Princess: dam, maiden who stayed 7.5f, half-sister to smart sprinter Notley: last of 14 in maiden at Doncaster, slowly away and hanging left. *P. S. McEntee*

CLOUD DANCER   4 b. or br.f. Bishop of Cashel 122 – Summer Pageant 81 (Chief's Crown (USA)) [2003 86: 8.1d 8m³ 8m 8m⁶ 7m² 7f 7m³ f7g³ f7g* f6g Dec 15] leggy filly: fairly useful performer: won claimer at Southwell (claimed from D. Coakley £14,000) in December: best at 7f/1m: acts on fibresand and good to firm going, probably on good to soft. *K. A. Ryan*   **84**

CLOUDINGSWELL   2 b.f. (Feb 3) Cloudings (IRE) 112 – L'Ancressaan 67 (Dalsaan 125) [2003 6m 7m⁴ p7g³ 8m 8.3g 7m⁶ Oct 23] close-coupled filly: sixth foal: half-sister to fairly useful 1m/1¼m winner Komreyev Dancer (by Komaite) and 7f winner Mr Cospector (by Cosmonaut): dam 2-y-o 6f winner: fair maiden: third at Lingfield: should stay 1m: acts on polytrack and good to firm going. *I. A. Wood*   **69**

CLOUDLESS (USA)   3 b. or br.f. Lord Avie (USA) – Summer Retreat (USA) 78 (Gone West (USA)) [2003 5.5g 6.5g⁶ 7d f7s⁴ f8.5s f6g³ 5d f6g f5g* f5s⁵ Dec 31] third foal: half-sister to 4-y-o Summer Recluse: dam, 7f winner who stayed 1m, sister to smart sprinter Western Approach and half-sister to very smart US Grade 1 9f/1¼m winner Tinners Way: fair performer: left M. Zilber, France, 5,000 gns after third start: won maiden at Wolverhampton in December: had form up to 1m in France, but likely to prove best at 5f/6f: acts on fibresand, raced only on good going or softer (acts on heavy) on turf: tried tongue tied. *J. W. Unett*   **75**

CLUB OASIS   2 b.f. (Mar 6) Forzando 122 – Tatouma (USA) 79 (The Minstrel (CAN) 135) [2003 7.5m⁵ 7.5m³ Aug 14] 1,200Y: leggy filly: half-sister to fairly useful 1994 2-y-o 7f winner Trimming (by Thatching) and winner up to 1m in Germany by Dowsing: dam 2-y-o 5f/6f winner: well-beaten last in minor events at Beverley: very stirred up before latter start. *M. E. Sowersby*   **–**

COAT OF HONOUR (USA)   3 gr.g. Mark of Esteem (IRE) 137 – Ballymac Girl 63 (Niniski (USA) 125) [2003 69: 8g² 8.5m⁵ 10m* 10m* 11.9g³ 10.5d² Sep 26] lengthy gelding: progressed into useful handicapper in 2003, winning at Pontefract in June and Brighton in July: excellent neck second to Fabulous Jet at Haydock final start, idling after moving easily into lead: likely to prove best at 1¼m/1½m: yet to race on extremes of going: often blinkered: free-going sort: type to improve again at 4 yrs. *Sir Mark Prescott*   **101 p**

COBALT BLUE (IRE)   2 b.g. (Feb 19) Bluebird (USA) 125 – Amy Hunter (USA) (Jade Hunter (USA)) [2003 6m 6g 6g 6d Nov 4] 40,000F, 62,000Y: tall gelding: first foal: dam 6f winner in USA: modest maiden: seemed to run best race third start: should stay 7f. *W. J. Haggas*   **58**

COBRA (IRE)   2 b.c. (Mar 9) Sadler's Wells (USA) 132 – Puck's Castle 92 (Shirley Heights 130) [2003 8m³ 8m* Oct 27] €825,000Y: fourth foal: half-brother to useful 5f winner (including at 2 yrs) Emerald Peace (by Green Desert): dam, 1m winner (ran only at 2 yrs), half-sister to Cheveley Park winner Embassy out of Cheveley Park winner Pass The Peace: useful form when landing odds in 12-runner maiden at Leopardstown easily by 6 lengths from Market Watcher, leading over 1f out: likely to be suited by 1¼m/1½m: should make his mark in stronger company as 3-y-o. *A. P. O'Brien, Ireland*   **104 p**

COCKNEY BOSS (IRE)   4 b.g. General Monash (USA) 107 – Cockney Ground (IRE) (Common Grounds 118) [2003 60?: p7g 7g Mar 27] tall, angular gelding: poor mover: headstrong maiden: well held both 4-y-o starts. *B. R. Millman*   **–**

COCO LOCO   6 b.m. Bin Ajwaad (IRE) 119 – Mainly Me 76 (Huntingdale 132) [2003 83: f16s³ p16g f16s 18g⁴ 14.1s 16.1d³ 17.1m Jun 1] tall, workmanlike mare: fair handicapper: stays 2¼m: acts on fibresand (probably on polytrack), good to firm and heavy going: slowly away last 2 starts (wore cheekpieces penultimate one): unreliable. *Mrs Lydia Pearce*   **74 §**

COCONUT COOKIE   2 ch.f. (Mar 4) Bahamian Bounty 116 – Spicy Manner (USA) (Cryptoclearance (USA)) [2003 6m² 7f 6.5m Sep 26] 17,000F, 10,000Y: first foal: dam unraced half-sister to very smart miler Allied Forces out of half-sister to dam of Kentucky Derby winner Real Quiet: fair form in maidens at Windsor and Salisbury: stiff task final start: will probably stay 1m. *R. Hannon*   **68**

COCONUT PENANG (IRE)   3 b.c. Night Shift (USA) – Play With Fire (FR) (Priolo (USA) 127) [2003 98: 6g⁶ 6v² 5f³ 6m⁶ 6m³ 6s⁵ 6m Sep 26] deep-girthed colt: useful performer: best efforts when placed in listed rated stakes at Haydock (½-length second to The Kiddykid), handicap at Royal Ascot (third to Deportivo) and valuable event at Ascot (neck third to Move It): effective at 5f/6f: acts on any going: effective ridden up with pace or held up. *B. R. Millman*   **103**

COCO REEF 2 b.f. (Feb 12) Kingsinger (IRE) 94 – Highland Blue 55 (Never So Bold **64**
135) [2003 5.1m f5g³ f6g³ f5s Sep 2] £1,000Y: first foal: dam, ran 3 times, half-sister
to 8-y-o Lord Kintyre: modest maiden: probably better at 6f than 5f: acts on fibresand.
B. Palling

COCTAIL LADY (IRE) 3 ch.f. Piccolo 121 – Last Ambition (IRE) 29 (Cadeaux **– §**
Genereux 131) [2003 –§, a61§: p5g p7g⁶ p7g f7s 7g 6g 7f 10f p16g Dec 2] rather leggy, **a53 d**
workmanlike filly: modest maiden: stays easy 7f: acts on all-weather, no form on turf:
often visored at 2 yrs, tried in hood/tongue tie/cheekpieces: difficult ride: untrustworthy.
B. W. Duke

CODY 4 ch.g. Zilzal (USA) 137 – Ibtihaj (USA) 97 (Raja Baba (USA)) [2003 54: **52**
10.2m 14.1d⁴ 11.7f Oct 12] good-topped gelding: modest maiden: stays 1¾m: acts on
good to soft going: tried visored. *G. A. Ham*

COFFEE TIME (IRE) 4 b.f. Efisio 120 – Petula 103 (Petong 126) [2003 80§: p7g² **65 §**
p6g⁶ p6g³ p8g⁴ p6g 5.7m⁶ 5.1s 5g⁶ 5g⁵ 5f⁶ 5m 6f 6m 5m⁴ 5m Jul 23] quite good-topped
filly: fair maiden handicapper: effective at 5f to 1m: acts on firm going, good to soft
and polytrack: tried in cheekpieces, usually blinkered: held up: thoroughly ungenuine.
D. J. S. ffrench Davis

COHN BLUE (IRE) 2 b.c. (Mar 20) Bluebird (USA) 125 – Kates Choice (IRE) 86 **99**
(Taufan (USA) 119) [2003 7.5m² 8.1g* 10m* 10g² 10d Nov 8] IR 25,000F, €55,000Y:
rather leggy, useful-looking colt: fourth foal: dam Irish 8.5f winner: useful performer:
won maiden at Chepstow in August and minor event at Leicester in October: good 1½
lengths second to Fun And Games in listed event at Newmarket, tying up only near finish:
race possibly came too soon when last of 10 in Criterium de Saint-Cloud week later: stays
1¼m. *Mrs A. J. Perrett*

COLD CLIMATE 8 b.g. Pursuit of Love 124 – Sharpthorne (USA) 91 (Sharpen Up **64**
127) [2003 73: 7m 7g 7.1g⁶ 6d³ 6m 6m 6m⁴ 6m 7m⁵ 6m* 7s⁵ p7g² p7g* Dec 6] lengthy **a73**
gelding: fair handicapper on all-weather, modest on turf: won at Yarmouth in September
and Lingfield in December: effective at 6f/easy 7f: acts on polytrack and any turf going:
sometimes visored: usually held up. *Bob Jones*

COLD TURKEY 3 b.g. Polar Falcon (USA) 126 – South Rock 102 (Rock City 120) **89**
[2003 67: p8g⁶ p8g⁵ 10f 10g* 11.6m⁴ 11.6g² 12m² 12m f12s 11f* p12g* p13g* p12g*
p13g² Dec 6] leggy gelding: improved into fairly useful performer: won claimer at
Leicester (left W. Jarvis) in July, claimer at Goodwood and handicap at Lingfield (idled)
in October, then apprentice handicap and amateur handicap at Lingfield in November:
also ran well in handicap final start: stays easy 13f: acts on polytrack and firm going,
possibly not on soft: sometimes slowly away: free-going sort. *G. L. Moore*

COLEMANSTOWN 3 b.g. Charnwood Forest (IRE) 125 – Arme Fatale (IRE) **81**
(Trempolino (USA) 135) [2003 75: 7d* 7m⁴ 8s 8g 7.2m 6f⁵ 7.1m⁶ Oct 25] 17,000Y:
second foal: half-brother to a winner in Italy by Lion Cavern: dam French 1m winner:
fairly useful performer: won handicap at the Curragh in March: left D. Weld, Ireland,
20,000 gns after fourth start: best effort in Britain on penultimate start: stays 7f: acts on
firm and good to soft going. *B. Ellison*

COLEORTON PRINCE (IRE) 2 b.g. (Mar 10) Paris House 123 – Tayovullin (IRE) **37**
65 (Shalford (IRE) 124§) [2003 f5g 5f 7m 6f f5g f6g Dec 15] 9,500Y: close-coupled
gelding: first foal: dam, 7f winner, out of half-sister to Irish St Leger and Melbourne
Cup winner Vintage Crop: poor maiden: stays 7f: tried in cheekpieces: none too genuine.
K. A. Ryan

COLISAY 4 b.g. Entrepreneur 123 – La Sorrela (IRE) (Cadeaux Genereux 131) [2003 **112**
103+: 8g⁴ 8.1g² 8.1m* 8m Jun 18] sturdy gelding: smart handicapper: won at Sandown in
May by 1½ lengths from Duke of Modena: good efforts in frame at Doncaster (Lincoln,
fourth to Pablo) and Sandown (neck second to Duke of Modena): tenth in Hunt Cup at
Royal Ascot final start, finishing well from poor position on unfavoured side (returned
injured): stays 1m: acts on good to firm and good to soft going: wandered for both wins in
2002. *A. C. Stewart*

COLLEGE CITY (IRE) 4 b.g. College Chapel 122 – Polish Crack (IRE) (Polish **–**
Patriot (USA) 128) [2003 –: 16.1d Mar 24] strong gelding: poor maiden: well held only
4-y-o start: tried blinkered/visored. *R. C. Guest*

COLLEGE DELINQUENT (IRE) 4 br.g. College Chapel 122 – St Cyr Aty (IRE) **60**
(Ela-Mana-Mou 132) [2003 75?: p8g* p8g⁶ p10g p8g⁴ 8.3d⁵ 10m p8g p8g³ p8g³ p10g **a76**
p8g³ Dec 2] quite good-topped gelding: fair on all-weather, modest on turf: won maiden

at Lingfield in January: stays 1m: acts on polytrack, firm and soft going: often blinkered at 3 yrs: tongue tied in 2003. *K. Bell*

COLLEGE FUND GIRL (IRE) 3 b.f. Kahyasi 130 – Pearl Kite (USA) 106§ (Silver **76** Hawk (USA) 123) [2003 p10g p12g* 12g Oct 31] IR 16,500F, 15,000Y: fifth foal: half-sister to 3 at least smart winners, including 4-y-o Highest and 5-y-o Nayyir: dam, 2-y-o 1m winner who stayed 1¾m, not one to trust: fair form when winning maiden at Lingfield in September: ran poorly in handicap at Newmarket 7 weeks later: will be suited by 1¾m+: sold 82,000 gns. *G. A. Butler*

COLLEGE HIPPIE 4 b.f. Cosmonaut – Eccentric Dancer 47 (Rambo Dancer (CAN) **64** 107) [2003 67: 5m 5d 5d 5.5f² 5m 5m⁴ 5.1g 5m f6s 6m 5g⁴ 5g f5g⁶ f5s Dec 27] plain, **a49** angular filly: modest on turf, poor on all-weather: best at 5f: acts on fibresand, firm and soft ground: often races prominently. *J. F. Coupland*

COLLEGE MAID (IRE) 6 b.m. College Chapel 122 – Maid of Mourne (Fairy King **66** (USA)) [2003 68: 5m 5m⁴ 5m⁴ 6m 6m 5m 6d 5d⁵ 5g* 6d³ 5g 5g 5m* 6g 5g⁴ 5m 5f 6g 5g 6g 6m 5m³ 6f 6m³ 6f 6g 5g⁶ Nov 5] sturdy mare: fair handicapper: won at Ayr in May and Musselburgh in June: best at 5f/6f: probably acts on any going: tried in cheekpieces, often blinkered: has been mulish in paddock: has edged right: effective held up or ridden prominently: tough. *J. S. Goldie*

COLLEGE QUEEN 5 b.m. Lugana Beach 116 – Eccentric Dancer 47 (Rambo Dancer **74** (CAN) 107) [2003 68: 6.1g 6g³ 6m 6m 5m 6d 6m³ 6m 6m* 6.1m* 5m³ 5.1g 6.1m⁵ 5.1d⁵ 5m⁴ 6.1m 6.1m 5d Nov 7] strong mare: fair handicapper: won at Folkestone (for second successive year) and Nottingham in August: effective at 5f/6f: acts on fibresand, good to firm and good to soft going: tried tongue tied, blinkered last 9 starts: front runner/races prominently. *S. Gollings*

COLLEGE ROCK 6 ch.g. Rock Hopper 124 – Sea Aura 89 (Roi Soleil 125) [2003 **77** 79, a–: 7m⁴ 7m³ 8m 7f³ Aug 7] small, sturdy gelding: fair handicapper: probably best at **a–** 7f/1m: acts on fibresand, probably on any turf going: tried blinkered, usually visored prior to 2003. *A. G. Newcombe*

COLLEGE SONG 3 b.g. College Chapel 122 – Celt Song (IRE) (Unfuwain (USA) **–** 131) [2003 49: f5s 5.1m Apr 29] smallish, good-topped gelding: lightly-raced maiden: slowly away and well beaten in 2003: tried tongue tied. *G. A. Butler*

COLLEGE STAR 5 b.g. Lugana Beach 116 – Alis Princess (Sayf El Arab (USA) **–** 127) [2003 –, a32: f8s f7s⁴ f8g f9.4s⁶ f8s⁵ 9.9m 8m 8f 7m 8.5m 10f f8g f8g Dec 19] tall **a32** gelding: poor maiden: tried visored/blinkered. *J. F. Coupland*

COLLEGE TIME (IRE) 2 b.g. (Mar 10) Danetime (IRE) 121 – Respectful (IRE) **80** (College Chapel 122) [2003 8.3g f6g² f6g⁵ Nov 1] 8,500Y: small, good-quartered geld- ing: first foal: dam unraced half-sister to useful Scandinavian performer up to 8.5f Senador: easily best effort in maidens (fairly useful form) when short-headed at South- well: not knocked about final start: should stay 7f. *P. A. Blockley*

COLLIER HILL 5 ch.g. Dr Devious (IRE) 127 – Polar Queen 76 (Polish Precedent **103** (USA) 131) [2003 91: 13d* 11.9g* 11.9m⁶ 12d 13d³ 13.1d 16g³ Nov 5] strong gelding: poor mover: useful performer: improved again at 5 yrs, winning handicaps at Hamilton in

bet365 Old Newton Cup (Handicap), Haydock—
Collier Hill beats Royal Ascot winner Waverley, Counsel's Opinion (No.5) and Manoubi

May and Haydock (bet365 Old Newton Cup by ½ length from Waverley, idled) in July: good third to Misternando in listed race at Musselburgh final start: stays easy 2m: acts on soft going, not on firmer than good: usually waited with. *G. A. Swinbank*

COLLOSEUM 2 b.g. (Mar 27) Piccolo 121 – Trig Point (Rudimentary (USA) 118) **60**
[2003 6g⁵ 7.1g⁶ Nov 5] good-topped gelding: first foal: dam unraced half-sister to useful performer up to 1½m Clever Cliche out of sister to Height of Fashion, herself dam of Nashwan, Unfuwain and 5-y-o Nayef: green, modest form in maidens at Newcastle and Musselburgh (pulled hard): needs to settle to stay beyond 7f. *T. J. Etherington*

COLNE VALLEY AMY 6 b.m. Mizoram (USA) 105 – Panchellita (USA) 78 (Pancho –
Villa (USA)) [2003 60, a–: f8.5g 8m⁶ 10d May 23] tall mare: poor handicapper: stays 1¼m: acts on firm going, good to soft and all-weather: tried blinkered. *G. L. Moore*

COLONEL COTTON (IRE) 4 b.g. Royal Applause 124 – Cutpurse Moll 76 (Green **115**
Desert (USA) 127) [2003 95, a66: 5m 6g 5m² 6g⁶ 5g 5f 5g² 5f⁴ 5d⁵ 6g³ 5.6d⁵ 5f 5m* 6m³ 6d Nov 8] good-topped gelding: smart performer: much improved form when winning listed event at Newmarket in October by ½ length from Bali Royal: even better effort when ½-length third to Ashdown Express in Bentinck Stakes on same course penultimate start: effective at 5f/6f: acts on soft and firm going: effective blinkered/visored or not: has worn crossed noseband: waited with: difficult ride. *N. A. Callaghan*

COLONEL TELFORD 3 br.g. Emperor Fountain 112 – Petaz (Petong 126) [2003 –
46: 12.1m⁶ 10g 7.5m 5m 5m 6m Sep 6] of little account. *M. E. Sowersby*

COLONNADE 4 b.f. Blushing Flame (USA) 109 – White Palace 80 (Shirley Heights **59 ?**
130) [2003 –: f11s³ f16s⁶ f12s 14.1m 13.8m Oct 18] lengthy filly: modest maiden, lightly raced: left D. Nicholls after third start: stays 2m: acts on firm going and fibresand. *C. Grant*

COLOPHONY (USA) 3 ch.g. Distant View (USA) 126 – Private Line (USA) 105 **83**
(Private Account (USA)) [2003 7.9f³ 8g² 10.5m* 10g⁶ Aug 10] big, strong gelding: third foal: brother to 1¼m winner Conclude and half-brother to French 7f to 10.5f winner Dance Dress (by Nureyev), both useful: dam, half (at 2 yrs) to 8.5f (in USA) winner, half-sister to Prix de la Salamandre second Most Precious (dam of smart 1m to 1½m performer Matiara): fairly useful form: won maiden at Haydock in July: stays 10.5f: tongue tied last 3 starts: sold 9,000 gns in October, gelded, joined K. Morgan. *H. R. A. Cecil*

COLOSSUS (IRE) 2 b.c. (Apr 27) Danehill (USA) 126 – Mira Adonde (USA) (Shar- **114**
pen Up 127) [2003 5d* 5.5d² 6s 6f* 6.3m⁶ 6m 6m* Oct 19] sturdy colt: brother to 3 winners, including smart performer up to 7f Danehill Dancer (6f/7f winner at 2 yrs) and useful 6f/7f winner Plaisir d'Amour, and half-brother to 2 winners, including useful Irish 9f/1¼m winner Adonesque (by Sadler's Wells): dam ran once: smart performer: won maiden at the Curragh in March (off 4 months after, reportedly pulled muscle), listed event there in September (awarded race, having been short-headed by Castledale) and valuable nursery at Naas in October: excellent effort (giving upwards of 18 lb all round) when beating Sheltingham 2½ lengths in last-named: creditable second to Much Faster in Prix Robert Papin at Maisons-Laffitte (beaten 3 lengths) and ninth to disqualified Three Valleys in Middle Park Stakes at Newmarket: likely to stay 7f: acts on firm and good to soft going (ran badly on soft). *A. P. O'Brien, Ireland*

COLOUR CODE (IRE) 2 b.c. (Apr 24) Spectrum (IRE) 126 – Viendra Nur (USA) **72**
(Nureyev (USA) 131) [2003 f6g² f7g Nov 25] €22,000Y: closely related to Italian 6f/7.5f (including at 2 yrs) winner Bies (by Bin Ajwaad) and half-brother to several winners in Italy: dam placed twice in Italy out of smart 1¼m performer Viendra: much better effort in maidens (fair form) when second to Pompey Blue at Wolverhampton, missing break/ carrying head awkwardly: should stay 7f. *M. P. Tregoning*

COLOURFUL LADY (USA) 3 b.f. Quest For Fame 127 – Special Park (USA) **70**
(Trempolino (USA) 135) [2003 66: 8f 8.2g⁴ 10m² 10m 10.1g³ 9.9m⁶ 12m² 11.9d 12m 16m p10g Nov 26] compact filly: fair handicapper: stays 1½m: acts on good to firm and good to soft ground: tried in cheekpieces. *P. W. Harris*

COLOURFUL LIFE (IRE) 7 ch.g. Rainbows For Life (CAN) – Rasmara 94§ (Kala- **77**
glow 132) [2003 –: p12g⁴ 12.4g² 16.5d Nov 8] big, workmanlike gelding: fairly useful hurdler: fair maiden on Flat: will be suited by 1¾m+: raced only on good going or softer on turf. *Mrs M. Reveley*

COLOUR SERGEANT (USA) 5 ch.g. Candy Stripes (USA) 115 – Princess Afleet **46**
(USA) (Afleet (CAN)) [2003 50, a–: 7.9m 7d 7m³ 8m 7f⁵ f7s Sep 26] smallish, lengthy gelding: poor maiden: left Don Enrico Incisa after reappearance: stays 8.5f: acts on fibresand, soft and firm going: tried visored, tongue tied last 5 outings. *N. Tinkler*

227

COLOUR WHEEL   2 ch.c. (Mar 28) Spectrum (IRE) 126 – Risanda (Kris 135) [2003 **89 p**
6m 7g* 7.2m² 7m² Oct 1] good-bodied colt: sixth foal: half-brother to fairly useful
winners around 1¼m Andalish (by Polish Precedent) and Lease (by Lycius): dam
unraced half-sister to Cheveley Park winner Prophecy out of Lancashire Oaks winner
Andaleeb: won maiden at Folkestone in September: good second in minor events at Ayr
and Salisbury (beaten ¾ length by Kingsword): will stay 1m: should make a useful 3-y-o.
R. Charlton

COLUMBINE (IRE)   5 b.m. Pivotal 124 – Heart of India (IRE) (Try My Best (USA) **66**
130) [2003 60: f5g³ 5m* 5m² 5m⁶ 5.7m⁴ 5d 5g 5m³ 6m 5m³ 5m² 5f⁵ 6d 5g³ 6d⁶ 5.1m²
5f³ 5m³ 5m* 5.1d⁴ 6.1f⁴ 6g 5g Nov 5] lengthy, useful-looking mare: good walker: fair
handicapper: won at Musselburgh in March and Folkestone in August: best at 5f/6f: acts
on firm going, soft and fibresand: tried blinkered/in cheekpieces: usually slowly away:
tough. *A. Berry*

COLWAY RITZ   9 b.g. Rudimentary (USA) 118 – Million Heiress (Auction Ring **73 ?**
(USA) 123) [2003 70: 12.4m² 12g³ 10d 13.8f⁵ 11.9d 12m⁶ 11.9f 10.1m 13.8m⁴ 10.1g²
10g² Oct 28] big, strong gelding: good mover: fair performer: effective at 1¼m to 13.8f:
acts on any going except soft/heavy: tried blinkered, wore cheekpieces most starts at
9 yrs: usually held up. *W. Storey*

COMANCHE QUEEN   6 ch.m. Totem (USA) 118 – Chess Mistress (USA) 59 (Run **–**
The Gantlet (USA)) [2003 45: 9.9m Jun 19] close-coupled mare: poor handicapper: well
beaten only start in 2003: tried blinkered. *J. S. Wainwright*

COMANCHE WOMAN   3 b.f. Distinctly North (USA) 115 – Possibility 59 (Robel- **–**
lino (USA) 127) [2003 10.2m f11g 11.7f⁴ p12g Nov 26] fourth foal: half-sister to 4-y-o
Polish Corridor and winner in Switzerland by Dancing Spree: dam 7f winner: well beaten
in maidens/claimers, seeming ill at ease on firm ground third start. *K. O. Cunningham-
Brown*

COME AWAY WITH ME (IRE)   3 b.f. Machiavellian (USA) 123 – Vert Val (USA) **55 p**
103 (Septieme Ciel (USA) 123) [2003 8m 7f* f6g² Jul 11] 160,000Y: second foal: half-
sister to French 7f (at 2 yrs) and 1m winner Seattle Bird (by Bering): dam, French
6.5f to 9f (at 2 yrs) winner, out of half-sister to Green Dancer and to dam of Alhaarth:
modest form: won maiden at Thirsk in June: best effort when second in handicap at
Wolverhampton, missing break/still looking green: stays 7f: should improve further, if all
is well. *M. A. Buckley*

COME ON PATSY   2 ch.f. (Feb 16) Compton Place 125 – Royal Roulette 77 (Risk **43**
Me (FR) 127) [2003 5g⁶ 6g 5m⁵ 6g f5g Jul 11] 8,000Y: plain filly: first foal: dam 1m to
2m winner: poor maiden: wore cheekpieces final start: sometimes pulls hard. *J. S. Moore*

COMERAINCOMESHINE (IRE)   2 ch.f. (Feb 9) Night Shift (USA) – Future Past **61**
(USA) (Super Concorde (USA) 128) [2003 7m p6g³ p7g Nov 29] 120,000Y: sturdy filly:
sister to useful 1¼m winner Just In Time and half-sister to several winners, notably 4-y-o
Where Or When and smart 1¼m and 1½m winner All The Way (by Shirley Heights):
dam, won up to 9f in USA, out of half-sister to dam of Blushing Groom: best effort
(modest form) when third to Kabreet in maiden at Lingfield, staying on strongly: should
stay at least 7f: slowly away and possibly amiss on debut. *T. G. Mills*

COME WHAT JULY (IRE)   2 b.c. (Apr 12) Indian Rocket 115 – Persian Sally (IRE) **68**
(Persian Bold 123) [2003 6m⁵ 6m⁵ 5m 7m² 6m f7g² f8g³ Dec 8] IR 6,500F, €32,000Y:
compact colt: third foal: half-brother to 3-y-o Jimmy Byrne and useful Italian winner up
to 1m Mr Picchio (by Cois Na Tine): dam unraced: fair maiden: best efforts when placed
at Wolverhampton (nursery) and Southwell last 2 starts: stays 1m: blinkered last 4
outings. *R. Guest*

COMFORTABLE CALL   5 ch.g. Nashwan (USA) 135 – High Standard 83 (Kris 135) **–**
[2003 16f Jun 30] strong gelding: fair maiden at 3 yrs: tongue tied, no encouragement
only start on Flat since. *H. Alexander*

COMFY (USA)   4 b.c. Lear Fan (USA) 130 – Souplesse (USA) (Majestic Light (USA)) **116**
[2003 7m* 10g 9m³ Aug 6] strong, good sort: good mover: smart performer: missed 2002
due to leg injury: won minor event at Leicester in May by ½ length from Ceepio: early to
post, best effort when never-nearer seventh to Falbrav in Eclipse Stakes at Sandown: odds
on, only third to Lundy's Lane in minor event at Kempton final start: stays 1¼m: unraced
on extremes of going. *Sir Michael Stoute*

COMIC GENIUS   2 b.f. (Apr 14) Comic Strip (USA) 115 – Itsy Bitsy Betsy (USA) **46**
(Beau Genius (CAN)) [2003 f6s⁴ f8s⁶ f8s f7g⁶ f8.5s² Dec 31] 6,000Y: first foal: dam 6f

winner in USA: poor maiden: second in seller at Wolverhampton: stays 8.5f: visored third/final starts. *D. Haydn Jones*

COMIC TALES 2 b.g. (Feb 13) Mind Games 121 – Glorious Aragon 88 (Aragon 118) [2003 6.1d Nov 6] fourth foal: half-brother to 6f to 9f winner in Spain by Petong: dam 5f winner who stayed 6f: 50/1 and backward, slowly away and always behind in maiden at Nottingham. *M. Mullineaux*

COMIC TIMES 3 b.f. Puissance 110 – Glorious Aragon 88 (Aragon 118) [2003 –: – 6m 5g May 24] well beaten in maidens. *M. Mullineaux*

COMING AGAIN (IRE) 2 b.c. (Apr 14) Rainbow Quest (USA) 134 – Hagwah **91 p** (USA) 109 (Dancing Brave (USA) 140) [2003 6g² Oct 24] quite good-topped colt: fourth foal: half-brother to 3-y-o Trust Rule and winner abroad by Machiavellian: dam, 1m to 1½m winner, half-sister to very smart performer up to 11f Sarafan: 50/1 and better for race, 1½ lengths second of 19 to So Will I in maiden at Newbury, always prominent: bred to be suited by 1¼m+: should improve and win races. *B. W. Hills*

COMING HOME 2 ch.f. (Feb 16) Vettori (IRE) 119 – Bonne Etoile 94 (Diesis 133) **– p** [2003 7m Aug 28] 52,000F, 50,000Y: third foal: half-sister to French 13f winner Xanthus (by Hector Protector): dam, 1m/1¼m winner, out of smart middle-distance stayer/US Grade 1 1¼m winner Bonne Ile: 8/1, seventh of 13 in maiden at Salisbury, tracking leaders until 2f out: should be suited by 1¼m/1½m: sold 6,500 gns: will probably do better. *Sir Michael Stoute*

COMMANCHE WIND (IRE) 8 b.g. Commanche Run 133 – Delko (Decent Fellow – 114) [2003 42: 16m Jul 7] poor maiden: well beaten only 8-y-o outing. *E. W. Tuer*

COMMANDER BOND 2 b.g. (Feb 25) Piccolo 121 – Lonesome 60 (Night Shift **74 p** (USA)) [2003 6m 7m 6m⁴ Oct 1] 24,000Y: well-made gelding: first foal: dam, lightly-raced maiden, sister to high-class 1m to 1½m performer In The Groove and half-sister to dam of very smart sprinter Harmonic Way: easily best effort in maidens (fair form) when fourth at Newcastle, prominent long way: likely to prove best at 5f/6f: type to do better in handicaps as 3-y-o. *B. Smart*

COMMANDER FLIP (IRE) 3 ch.g. In Command (IRE) 114 – Boldabsa 96 (Persian **57** Bold 123) [2003 7.1g 11.8m² 10m³ 10f Oct 1] IR 2,000Y: tall, leggy, close-coupled gelding: half-brother to several winners, including 7-y-o Downland and 1994 2-y-o 5f/6f winner Painted Madam (both useful, by Common Grounds): dam Irish 9f/1¼m winner: modest maiden: stumbled badly final start: stays 1½m. *R. Hollinshead*

COMMANDING 4 ch.g. Pennekamp (USA) 130 – Lady Joyce (FR) (Galetto (FR) **91** 118) [2003 93: 8m⁵ 8m 8f 8m⁶ 7m Oct 25] strong gelding: fairly useful performer: well below form in claimer at Doncaster final start: free-going sort, barely stays 1¼m: acts on firm going, possibly not on softer than good: tongue tied: sometimes finds little: sold 16,000 gns. *Mrs A. J. Perrett*

COMMANDO SCOTT (IRE) 2 b.g. (Mar 16) Danetime (IRE) 121 – Faye 79 **78** (Monsanto (FR) 121) [2003 5m⁵ 6m³ 6g⁴ 6m Oct 4] IR 11,500F, 8,000Y: good-topped gelding: half-brother to several winners, including useful Irish 1m/9f winner Wray (by Sharp Victor) and 4-y-o Duke of Earl: dam, 2-y-o 6f winner, later successful in USA: fair maiden: fourth in sales race at Doncaster penultimate start, hanging left: likely to stay 7f. *A. Berry*

COMMEMORATION DAY (IRE) 2 b.g. (May 7) Daylami (IRE) 138 – Bequeath **66** (USA) (Lyphard (USA) 132) [2003 8m⁶ 7m Oct 24] €110,000Y: strong, compact gelding: has fluent, round action: half-brother to several winners, including very smart 7f/1m performer Decorated Hero (by Warning) and useful 7f winner Mubrik (by Lahib): dam French 9f winner: fair form in maidens at Pontefract and Doncaster: subsequently gelded: should be suited by at least 1¼m. *J. G. Given*

COMMISSAR (IRE) 4 b.g. Common Grounds 118 – Trescalini (IRE) (Sadler's – Wells (USA) 132) [2003 78: p12g Jan 15] fair performer, lightly raced: folded tamely/again carried head awkwardly only outing in 2003: tongue tied last 2 starts in 2002 (reportedly had breathing problem on debut): dead. *J. J. Bridger*

COMMISSION (USA) 3 ch.c. Gulch (USA) – Accountable Lady (USA) (The Min- **102** strel (CAN) 135) [2003 100p: 8.1m³ 10.2m³ 7g 7m⁴ 8g⁶ 9.9m⁶ Aug 23] useful performer: mostly creditable efforts at 3 yrs, including when fourth to Patavellian in Bunbury Cup at Newmarket: unseated rider (saddle slipped) in final 1f at Newcastle previous outing: stays easy 1¼m: raced only on good/good to firm going: blinkered final start, tongue tied other outings at 3 yrs: sent to USA. *G. A. Butler*

COMMITMENT LECTURE 3 b.f. Komaite (USA) – Hurtleberry (IRE) 87 (Tirol **64**
127) [2003 52: 6f f7g 6g 7m² 8d* 8.5m⁶ 8g⁴ 8d² 8.1m 10.9d Oct 13] smallish filly: modest
handicapper: won at Newcastle in May: stays 1m: acts on good to firm and good to soft
going: usually held up. *M. Dods*

COMMONDINI (IRE) 4 b.f. Common Grounds 118 – Windini (Windjammer (USA)) **51**
[2003 50: 10.9m 9.7m Apr 15] well-made filly: modest maiden: stays easy 1¼m: acts on
firm going, good to soft and polytrack: tried tongue tied/blinkered. *P. W. Harris*

COMMON THOUGHT (IRE) 4 b.g. Common Grounds 118 – Zuhal 67 (Busted **54**
134) [2003 81: 7m 7f 8m 9m 7.5m 7.5m 8m 7m Aug 5] quite attractive gelding: just
modest handicapper in 2003: stayed 1m: best form on going firmer than good: tried in
cheekpieces: dead. *J. J. Quinn*

COMMON WORLD (USA) 4 ch.c. Spinning World (USA) 130 – Spenderella (FR) **106**
(Common Grounds 118) [2003 112: a8f 7m³ 8.5m⁶ Jun 7] rather leggy, quite attractive
colt: just useful performer at 4 yrs: third to Comfy in minor event at Leicester: stays 1¼m:
acts on soft and good to firm going, well beaten in prestige race on dirt at Nad Al Sheba
on reappearance: heavily bandaged in front final start: has hung/carried head awkwardly/
found little: sometimes slowly away. *G. A. Butler*

COMPANION 5 b.m. Most Welcome 131 – Benazir 91 (High Top 131) [2003 –, a75d: **–**
f12g f8.5s⁴ p10g* p10g⁵ p10g³ 10.1g p10g Sep 9] tall, good-topped mare: modest per- **a62**
former: won seller at Lingfield in March: reportedly had breathing problem penultimate
outing, then left J. Poulton: stays easy 1¼m: acts on all-weather, lightly raced and no form
on turf since 2001: tried visored/tongue tied: sometimes slowly away. *Miss Gay Kelleway*

COMPASSION (IRE) 2 b.f. (Apr 15) Alhaarth (IRE) 126 – Titania (Fairy King **62**
(USA)) [2003 5d 5.1g⁴ 5m 6m² 6m⁵ 6g⁴ 5m⁴ 6d⁵ f6g Nov 10] €27,000Y: rather leggy
filly: second foal: half-sister to Swedish 2002 2-y-o 5f/6f winner by Primo Dominie: dam
unraced half-sister to 2 useful winners: modest maiden: left R. Hannon after second in
seller at Windsor: likely to prove best at 5f/6f: acts on good to firm going, tailed off on
fibresand. *Miss L. A. Perratt*

COMPETITOR 2 b.c. (Feb 25) Danzero (AUS) – Ceanothus (IRE) 61 (Bluebird **72**
(USA) 125) [2003 8m* p8g Dec 20] 17,000F: third foal: half-brother to 4-y-o Prince
Hector: dam, maiden who stayed 1½m, half-sister to smart 9f/1¼m winner Golden Wells:
fair form when winning maiden at Redcar in October: left Mrs A. Perrett 15,000 gns, well
held in minor event at Lingfield: will probably stay 1¼m. *J. Akehurst*

COMPLETE CIRCLE 3 ch.f. Vettori (IRE) 119 – Cockatoo Island 99 (High Top **78**
131) [2003 70p: f9.4g* 10.5g⁶ 12.3m 11.6s 12m 8g⁴ p8g⁵ 10d⁵ p12g f16g⁴ Dec 3] lengthy, **a86**
leggy filly: fairly useful on all-weather, fair on turf: won maiden at Wolverhampton in
February: good fifth to Tadris in listed event at Lingfield seventh outing: stays easy 1½m:
acts on all-weather and good to firm ground: tried visored: sold 17,000 gns. *P. W. D'Arcy*

COMPLICATION 3 b.f. Compton Place 125 – Hard Task 82 (Formidable (USA) **74**
125) [2003 7d 7m 6m³ 5m* 6m* 6m6 5.1m³ Oct 28] 10,500Y: smallish, sturdy
filly: fourth foal: half-sister to 5-y-o Gryffindor: dam, 1½m winner, half-sister to smart
middle-distance stayer Midnight Legend and 5-y-o Vicious Knight: fair performer: won
maiden at Thirsk in September: stays 6f: acts on good to firm ground: blinkered last 7
outings. *J. A. R. Toller*

COMPOS MENTIS 3 b.g. Bijou d'Inde 127 – Red Cloud (IRE) 61 (Taufan (USA) **–**
119) [2003 78: 8g 8m p12g f8g Nov 25] leggy gelding: fair maiden at 2 yrs: well beaten
in 2003, in blinkers final start. *D. Morris*

COMPTON ALICE 3 ch.f. Compton Place 125 – Secret Circle (Magic Ring (IRE) **–**
115) [2003 58: f5g⁵ 6g 6g Jul 11] modest maiden at 2 yrs: well held in 2003.
N. P. Littmoden

COMPTON ARROW (IRE) 7 b.g. Petardia 113 – Impressive Lady 98 (Mr Fluoro- **71**
carbon 126) [2003 71: 7m 6m⁵ 7m 7m² 6m⁶ 6m⁴ 6m⁴ 6.9m 7m* 6g f7g Nov 14] big, rangy
gelding: has a quick action: fair handicapper: won at Catterick (hung left) in October: best
at 6f/7f: acts on soft going, good to firm and fibresand: tried blinkered/visored, sometimes tongue tied: often slowly away. *D. Nicholls*

COMPTON AVIATOR 7 ch.g. First Trump 118 – Rifada 103 (Ela-Mana-Mou 132) **65**
[2003 75d: p10g⁵ p12g p12g² p12g⁶ 9.7m⁵ 8g 11.5g 10.1g 12f* 12m⁵ 11.6m³ 11.6g⁵ 12m³
11.9m 12m² 12m⁴ p12g⁴ Oct 8] lengthy gelding: fair handicapper: won in Jersey in June:
best at 1¼m to easy 1½m: acts on good to firm going, good to soft and polytrack: tongue
tied: tried blinkered: held up: consistent. *A. W. Carroll*

betfair.com Rated Stakes (Handicap) (Chester), Chester—jockey Eddie Ahern completes a treble on the day as Compton Bolter puts up a smart performance under top weight to beat Supremacy

COMPTON BANKER (IRE) 6 br.g. Distinctly North (USA) 115 – Mary Hinge 100 (Dowsing (USA) 124) [2003 98: p6g³ p7g p5g p7g p5g³ 5m 5.1m 5.1g 5d 5.7f⁵ 5m 6g p7g⁴ p7g* p6g* p7g⁵ Dec 29] small, strong gelding: fairly useful handicapper: won at Lingfield in November and December: stays easy 7f: acts on firm going and polytrack: tried blinkered/in cheekpieces, effective visored or not: sometimes rears stall/slowly away: held up. *G. A. Butler* **91**

COMPTON BAY 3 b.g. Compton Place 125 – Silver Sun 83 (Green Desert (USA) 127) [2003 46: f7g Jan 28] leggy, plain gelding: poor form at 2 yrs: well held only start in 2003. *M. Brittain* **–**

COMPTON BOLTER (IRE) 6 b.g. Red Sunset 120 – Milk And Honey 102 (So Blessed 130) [2003 108: p10g⁶ p12g p10g⁵ 10m² 12m³ 12.3m⁴ 13.4m² 12.1d* 16.4m⁶ 12f 12g⁵ 13.4m* 11m* 12f² 12m² 12g p10g* Nov 22] smallish gelding: has a quick action: smart performer: reportedly suffered knee injury in 2002: won listed rated stakes at Hamilton in May and Chester (beat Supremacy by 1½ lengths) in August and listed races at Newbury (by a neck from Researched) in September and Lingfield (third success in race, beat Grand Passion a short head) in November: also ran well when length second to Ekraar in listed race at Newmarket fifteenth start: stays easy 13.4f: acts on dirt/ polytrack, firm and good to soft going: blinkered (in USA) once as 3-y-o, visored second 6-y-o start: has worn crossed noseband: tried tongue tied earlier in career: often races prominently: tough. *G. A. Butler* **118**

COMPTON CHICK (IRE) 5 b.m. Dolphin Street (FR) 125 – Cecina 100 (Welsh Saint 126) [2003 –: 16f Oct 12] modest maiden at 3 yrs: lightly raced and well held on Flat since: tried tongue tied/in cheekpieces. *J. W. Mullins* **–**

COMPTON COMMANDER 5 ch.g. Barathea (IRE) 127 – Triode (USA) 105 (Sharpen Up 127) [2003 94§: p12g* p12g p12g 10.3m May 6] useful-looking gelding: fairly useful handicapper: won at Lingfield in January by neck from High Hope: acts on any turf going and polytrack: tried blinkered, often visored: carries head awkwardly: ungenuine: joined I. Williams. *G. A. Butler* **94 §**

COMPTON DICTATOR 4 b.g. Shareef Dancer (USA) 135 – Princess Pati 124 (Top Ville 129) [2003 p7g⁶ 10.9m 11.5m 9.7m 7f Sep 2] leggy, useful-looking gelding: poor **48 §**

231

maiden: should be suited by 1¼m+: tried tongue tied/visored: thoroughly ungenuine: sold £900. *G. A. Butler*

COMPTON DRAGON (USA)   4 ch.g. Woodman (USA) 126 – Vilikaia (USA) 125 (Nureyev (USA) 131) [2003 109: 8g⁴ 8.9g 8.5m 8m⁵ 7g 6g 6m 7m 7.1m Oct 25] compact gelding: useful performer: not discredited in listed race and Jebel Hatta at Nad Al Sheba first 2 starts: below form back in Britain, leaving G. Butler after sixth outing: stays 1m: acts on polytrack and good to firm going: tried blinkered/in cheekpieces: edgy sort: sometimes slowly away. *D. Nicholls*   **106 d**

COMPTON DRAKE   4 b.g. Mark of Esteem (IRE) 137 – Reprocolor 114 (Jimmy Reppin 131) [2003 –p: p7g² 10.2f⁵ 14.1m⁴ 9f 9.7g⁵ 8m 10m² 12g* p10g* f9.4g* Dec 26] fair handicapper: won at Musselburgh and Lingfield in November and Wolverhampton in December: effective at 1¼m/1½m: acts on good to firm going and all-weather: tried blinkered/tongue tied. *G. A. Butler*   **75**

COMPTON DYNAMO   4 b.g. Wolfhound (USA) 126 – Asteroid Field (USA) 123 (Forli (ARG)) [2003 101: 6m 6g 6g 5g 6m* 6f⁵ 6m 6g 6g 6f³ 6m⁴ 6m 6m⁵ 6f⁶ p6g Nov 2] rather leggy gelding: useful handicapper: won at Windsor in June by 1¼ lengths from Barrantes: mostly at least respectable efforts after: effective at 5f/6f: acts on polytrack, firm and good to soft ground: free-going sort: held up. *W. J. Musson*   **96**

COMPTON EAGLE   3 b.g. Zafonic (USA) 130 – Gayane 125 (Nureyev (USA) 131) [2003 7m Jun 12] 25,000Y: rangy gelding: has scope: brother to 4-y-o Ben Hur and half-brother to 3 winners, including useful 1m winner Maramba (by Rainbow Quest): dam, 6f/7f winner, half-sister to Sun Chariot winner Ristna from family of Oh So Sharp: 14/1 and green, eighth of 10 to Tree Peony in maiden at Newbury. *G. A. Butler*   **60**

COMPTON EARL   3 ch.c. Efisio 120 – Bay Bay 101 (Bay Express 132) [2003 6m 8.1m 6m⁵ 6f* 7.1g Sep 11] IR 40,000Y: strong colt: brother to 4-y-o My Bayard and half-brother to several winners, including useful 5f/6f winner Boast (by Most Welcome): dam 7.6f winner: fair performer: won maiden at Ayr in August: should prove best at 5f/6f: acts on firm going: tongue tied 4 of 5 starts: has been slowly away. *G. A. Butler*   **66**

COMPTON ECLAIRE (IRE)   3 ch.f. Lycius (USA) 124 – Baylands Sunshine (IRE) (Classic Secret (USA) 91) [2003 p5g 5.1m 6.1g 8m⁵ 9.2m⁶ p12g² 14.1m* 11.9f² p16g⁶ 12m⁴ p12g p12g* p12g f12g³ p13g⁴ Dec 29] IR 8,500Y: good-topped filly: second foal: half-sister to Irish 9f to 13f winner Mount George (by Greensmith): dam unraced half-sister to high-class sprinter Anita's Prince: fair on turf, modest on all-weather: won handicap at Redcar in August and claimer at Lingfield (slowly away) in November: stays 1¾m: acts on all-weather, raced only on good ground or firmer on turf: usually blinkered/visored. *G. A. Butler*   **66 a61**

COMPTON ECLIPSE   3 ch.g. Singspiel (IRE) 133 – Fatah Flare (USA) 121 (Alydar (USA)) [2003 –: f8.5s 7.1m⁶ 8d² 7f* 8.2g⁵ 7.9f* 10g⁴ 8m 8f³ 10.1g 8f² 7m* 7.1g 7m Oct 17] leggy gelding: fairly useful handicapper: won at Brighton and Carlisle in June and at Newbury in September: well below form last 2 starts, bandaged in front final one: gelded after: likely to prove best at 7f/1m: acts on firm ground: tongue tied fourth to eighth 3-y-o starts, blinkered after: sometimes carries head high. *G. A. Butler*   **87**

COMPTON EMERALD (IRE)   3 ch.f. Bluebird (USA) 125 – Cheviot Amble (IRE) 105 (Pennine Walk 120) [2003 77: 7m 8g 10f³ 11f⁴ 11g⁶ p8g Dec 6] fair maiden: should stay 1½m: acts on firm going and polytrack: tried blinkered/visored: none too reliable. *G. A. Butler*   **71**

COMPTON EMPEROR   3 b.c. Bijou d'Inde 127 – Princess Tara 85 (Prince Sabo 123) [2003 85p: p7g 7d⁵ 8g* 7g 8m⁶ 8m 7g⁶ 9g 7g Oct 28] smallish, useful-looking colt: fairly useful handicapper: won at Newmarket in May: best effort after when sixth of 29 to New Seeker in Britannia Stakes at Royal Ascot fifth start: effective at 7f/1m: acts on soft and good to firm ground: tried visored/blinkered/tongue tied: ungenuine. *G. A. Butler*   **89 §**

COMPTON EXPERT (IRE)   3 b.g. Cadeaux Genereux 131 – Samira 94 (Rainbow Quest (USA) 134) [2003 p7g⁵ p12g⁶ 8.1d⁶ Sep 26] 27,000Y: well-made gelding: second foal: dam, Irish 1½m winner, half-sister to smart 1½m filly Cunning: modest form in maidens: should stay at least 1m. *G. A. Butler*   **62**

COMPTON FAIR   3 b.f. Compton Place 125 – Fair Dominion 107 (Dominion 123) [2003 8m 10d 8.2g 12m Aug 1] smallish filly: half-sister to several winners, including winners around 1m Mornings Minion (fairly useful, by Polar Falcon) and 8-y-o Dom Shadeed: dam, 1m/1¼m performer, later successful in USA: no form in maidens/handicap (blinkered). *J. D. Bethell*   **–**

COMPTON MICKY 2 ch.c. (Apr 8) Compton Place 125 – Nunthorpe 79 (Mystiko –
(USA) 124) [2003 6d Nov 8] strong, workmanlike colt: first foal: dam 8.5f winner: 66/1,
last of 13 in maiden at Doncaster, slowly away. *J. Balding*

COMPTON PLUME 3 ch.g. Compton Place 125 – Brockton Flame 72 (Emarati **56**
(USA) 74) [2003 –: f6g⁶ f9.4g 7m⁵ 6f 5m³ 6m 7f 5m³ 5g⁴ 6m⁴ 6m⁴ 6f² 5m² 5m 6m² 5g⁶
Oct 13] strong, lengthy gelding: modest maiden: left M. Easterby after twelfth start: stays
6f: acts on firm ground: blinkered/visored after second outing. *W. H. Tinning*

COMPTON PRINCESS 3 b.f. Compton Place 125 – Curlew Calling (IRE) 51 **49**
(Pennine Walk 120) [2003 40: f6g 7m³ 7m 5.9m³ 7m⁴ 6.9f 6m 7m 5m 8.2f Sep 30] poor
maiden: stays easy 1m: acts on firm going: tried visored. *Mrs A. Duffield*

COMPTON'S ELEVEN 2 gr.g. (Mar 27) Compton Place 125 – Princess Tara 85 **92**
(Prince Sabo 123) [2003 6d⁵ 5.2f* 6m* 6m 6m 5m³ 6m³ Oct 21] 24,000F, 90,000Y:
good-topped gelding: half-brother to several winners, including useful 1998 2-y-o 5f/6f
winner El Tango (by Risk Me) and 3-y-o Compton Emperor: dam, 6f (at 2 yrs) and 1m
winner, half-sister to high-class French sprinter Kind Music: fairly useful performer: won
maiden at Yarmouth in August and nursery at Goodwood in September: creditable third
in minor events at Catterick and Yarmouth (not look keen): stays 6f: acts on firm ground.
M. R. Channon

COMPTON STAR 3 ch.g. Compton Place 125 – Darakah 78 (Doulab (USA) 115) –
[2003 –: 7.1m 5.7m 5.1m 8f Jun 25] little form. *R. J. Hodges*

COMTAKE DOT COM (IRE) 2 b.f. (Apr 7) Tagula (IRE) 116 – Be Prepared (IRE) –
(Be My Guest (USA) 126) [2003 5m⁵ 6m⁴ 7.1m 5f Sep 5] 12,000Y: fourth foal: half-sister
to 3-y-o Countess Elton and 5-y-o Look First: dam unraced: well held in maidens/seller:
blinkered second start, then left A. Berry. *S. A. Brookshaw*

COMTESSE NOIRE (CAN) 4 b.f. Woodman (USA) 126 – Faux Pas (IRE) 63 **58**
(Sadler's Wells (USA) 132) [2003 61: f9.4g³ f12g³ f9.4s³ 11.8g² 11.8m⁵ p12g⁴ p16g⁴
10.2m³ 12.1m 11.6g³ Aug 11] angular filly: modest maiden handicapper: effective at 9.4f,
barely at 1½m: acts on soft ground, good to firm and all-weather: sometimes swishes tail/
carries head high/edges left: consistent. *A. M. Balding*

CONCER ETO 4 ch.g. Sabrehill (USA) 120 – Drudwen (Sayf El Arab (USA) 127) **82**
[2003 72: 8g 8m³ 7m 8f* 7g² 7f 8g Sep 22] fairly useful handicapper: best effort when
winning at Yarmouth in August: effective at 7f to 1¼m: acts on fibresand, firm and good
to soft ground: tongue tied (ran poorly) once, wore cheekpieces other outings at 4 yrs.
S. C. Williams

CONCERT HALL (USA) 2 b.f. (Feb 2) Stravinsky (USA) 133 – Proflare (USA) **76**
101 (Mr Prospector (USA)) [2003 7m³ 8m³ 8.2d³ Nov 6] leggy filly: half-sister to several
winners, including miler Apple of Kent (by Kris S) and 6f (at 2 yrs in France) to 1m (in
USA) winner War Zone (by Danzig), both smart: dam French 1m (at 2 yrs) and 9f winner:
fair form when third in maidens at Brighton (2) and Nottingham, appearing to lose action/
hang fire on latter course final start: not certain to stay beyond 1m. *Mrs A. J. Perrett*

CONCHONITA 3 b.f. Bishop of Cashel 122 – Cactus Road (FR) (Iron Duke (FR) **37**
122) [2003 –: f8.5s³ f8.5g⁶ 10.2m 10m⁶ 11.6m⁶ f8.5g² f11g⁶ Dec 19] poor maiden: stays **a49**
8.5f: acts on fibresand. *B. Palling*

CONCUBINE (IRE) 4 b.f. Danehill (USA) 126 – Bye Bold Aileen (IRE) (Warning **74**
136) [2003 76, a54: 7m 7m² 7m² 7d⁴ 7f 6m³ 7f 7g Sep 11] close-coupled filly: has a quick **a–**
action: fair handicapper: stays 7f: acts on good to firm and good to soft going. *J. R. Boyle*

CONDOLEEZZA (USA) 3 gr.f. Cozzene (USA) – Rosabella 97 (Niniski (USA) **76**
125) [2003 78: 10g 11.6s⁶ 14g 12.1g² 14f⁶ 16g Oct 31] rather leggy, close-coupled filly:
fair performer: won maiden at Goodwood in October: pulled up soon after start final outing: should stay 2m: acts on firm and soft ground: usually races prominently. *J. L. Dunlop*

CONFUZED 3 b.g. Pivotal 124 – Times of Times (IRE) 78 (Distinctly North (USA) –
115) [2003 –: 6g Sep 16] well beaten in minor event/maiden 13 months apart, getting
loose before start in latter. *Andrew Reid*

CONFUZION (IRE) 2 b.f. (Jan 27) Inzar (USA) 112 – Fernlea (USA) (Sir Ivor 135) –
[2003 p7g 8.2m f8g Nov 25] 4,000 2-y-o: sixth foal: half-sister to 1m winner Buddeliea
(by Pivotal) and 6f winner Hopeful Henry (by Cadeaux Genereux): dam, lightly-raced
Irish sprint maiden, second in listed race: signs of only a little ability, including in seller:
wore cheekpieces final start. *A. P. Jones*

CONISTON BAY (IRE)   3 b.f. Lake Coniston (IRE) 131 – Mary Ellen Best (IRE) 64   –
(Danehill (USA) 126) [2003 55: 9.3m 6m Aug 7] close-coupled, angular filly: modest
maiden at 2 yrs: well held in 2003. *E. J. Alston*

CONNECT   6 b.g. Petong 126 – Natchez Trace 52 (Commanche Run 133) [2003 92,   **95**
a–: p5g³ p5g⁴ p6g* p6g³ 5g⁶ 6m 5g⁴ 5.1g 5g 5f* 5.1m² 5g⁴ 5f² 5m³ 5.6d 5.2g⁶ 5f 5g
5m⁶ Oct 16] strong, lengthy gelding: unimpressive mover: useful on turf, fairly useful on
all-weather: won minor event at Lingfield in February and handicap at York in June: good
placed efforts 3 of next 4 starts: effective at 5f/easy 6f: acts on firm going, good to soft and
all-weather: tried visored, usually blinkered: sometimes hangs: held up. *M. H. Tompkins*

CONQUERING LOVE (IRE)   5 b.g. Pursuit of Love 124 – Susquehanna Days   **89**
(USA) 68 (Chief's Crown (USA)) [2003 74: 14m² 12g* 12m² 11.9f⁴ 12.3m* 12f* 11.9m
Aug 19] quite good-topped gelding: fairly useful performer: won
handicaps at Musselburgh (idled) in May and Ripon in July and minor event at Thirsk
(beat Promotion a neck, 3 ran) in August: effective at 1½m/1¾m: best form on good
going or firmer: consistent. *B. Ellison*

CONSENSUS (IRE)   4 b.f. Common Grounds 118 – Kilbride Lass (IRE) (Lahib (USA)   **89**
129) [2003 86: 6g⁵ 6m 5m* 5.1m 6d 6g 5m 6s⁶ f5g p6g Dec 6] leggy filly: unimpressive   **a–**
mover: fairly useful handicapper: won at Newcastle in April: yet to race
on heavy ground, acts on any other: none too consistent. *M. Brittain*

CONSIDINE (USA)   2 b.c. (Jan 30) Romanov (IRE) 119 – Libeccio (NZ) (Danzatore   **61**
(CAN) 120) [2003 6m f6g⁴ f6s⁵ Oct 21] $15,000Y: big, workmanlike colt: sixth foal:
half-brother to 8.5f winner Hollow Haze (by Woodman): dam unraced daughter of half-
sister to Generous and Imagine: modest form in maidens: fourth at Wolverhampton:
should be suited by 1¼m+: slowly away first 2 starts. *J. M. P. Eustace*

CONSIGNIA (IRE)   4 ch.f. Definite Article 121 – Coppelia (IRE) (Mac's Imp (USA)   **55**
116) [2003 66: f6s 5.7m 5.7g f7g 6m 6.1m 7f³ 7m³ 6f 7f³ 8f* 7f 8d f8.5g* f7g p8g⁶ f8g
Dec 19] lengthy filly: modest performer: won sellers at Bath (handicap) in September and
Wolverhampton in November: stays 8.5f: acts on firm going, good to soft and fibresand:
tried tongue tied, usually blinkered/visored: sometimes races freely: none too consistent.
D. Haydn Jones

CONSTABLE BURTON   2 b.g. (Mar 23) Foxhound (USA) 103 – Actress 73 (Known   –
Fact (USA) 135) [2003 7.2m 6m 6g Oct 22] 5,500F, 2,200Y: big, workmanlike gelding:
seventh foal: half-brother to 3 winners, including 5f (at 2 yrs) to 7f winner La Dolce Vita
(by Mazilier): dam 7f winner: well held in maidens. *Mrs A. Duffield*

CONSTANTINE   3 gr.g. Linamix (FR) 127 – Speremm (IRE) (Sadler's Wells (USA)   **80**
132) [2003 85p: 8m 10.4m 8g⁶ 10m⁵ 11m 10g 14m² 14.4m* 14g 16f Sep 30] leggy
gelding: fairly useful handicapper: won at Newcastle in August: stays 14.4f, probably
not 2m: raced only on good ground or firmer: sold 26,000 gns, joined G. L. Moore.
J. S. Goldie

CONTACT DANCER (IRE)   4 b.g. Sadler's Wells (USA) 132 – Rain Queen (Rain-   **96 ?**
bow Quest (USA) 134) [2003 92p: 14.1s⁵ 15s⁶ Nov 22] leggy gelding: useful performer,
lightly raced: better effort in 2003 (6 months apart) when sixth to Le Carre in listed race
at Fontainebleau, possibly flattered: stays 2¼m: successful on good to firm going, best
efforts on softer than good (acts on heavy): wandered final 3-y-o start. *J. L. Dunlop*

CONTAGIOUS   2 ch.f. (Apr 12) Polar Falcon (USA) 126 – Rash (Pursuit of Love 124)   **72 p**
[2003 6m² f6g² Oct 16] useful-looking filly: third foal: sister to fairly useful 1m winner
Loveleaves and half-sister to 2002 2-y-o 5f winner Foolhardy (by Primo Dominie): dam
unraced half-sister to useful 2-y-o sprinters Maid For Walking and Maid For The Hills:
fair form when second in maidens at Yarmouth and Southwell (tied up and caught near
finish): likely to prove best at 5f/6f: sold 36,000 gns, sent to USA: open to improvement.
W. J. Haggas

CONTINENT   6 ch.g. Lake Coniston (IRE) 131 – Krisia (Kris 135) [2003 123: 5f 6f   **115 §**
6m⁶ 5m 6d Sep 6] angular gelding: very smart at 5 yrs, winning July Cup at Newmarket
and Prix de l'Abbaye de Longchamp: best effort in 2003 (smart form) when sixth to Oasis
Dream in July Cup: lost all chance with very slow starts when last in Nunthorpe Stakes at
York and Sprint Cup at Haydock (visored) after: best at 5f/6f: acts on firm and soft
ground: often tongue tied: has run well when sweating: held up: unreliable. *D. Nicholls*

CONTRABAND   5 b.g. Red Ransom (USA) – Shortfall 103 (Last Tycoon 131) [2003   **102**
99: 13.9m⁵ 12m² Oct 16] big, good-topped gelding: useful handicapper, lightly raced: off
10 months, good fifth to Saint Alebe in Ebor at York on reappearance: steadily to post,
raced too freely at Newmarket latter 5-y-o start: will prove best at 1½m/1¾m: yet to race

on soft/heavy going, acts on any other: free-going sort: joined M. Pipe 64,000 gns: useful form over hurdles, won 3 times in November/December. *W. J. Haggas*

CONTRACT 4 b.g. Entrepreneur 123 – Ispahan 85 (Rusticaro (FR) 124) [2003 100: 8g 7g 7m⁵ 8.3g Aug 23] leggy, quite attractive gelding: unimpressive mover: fairly useful handicapper: best effort in 2003 when fifth to Pomfret Lad at Newbury, edging left: stays 7f: acts on good to soft and good to firm going: blinkered (raced too freely) final outing: sold 8,000 gns, sent to Italy. *Mrs A. J. Perrett* **89**

CONTRACTOR 3 gr.c. Spectrum (IRE) 126 – Karsiyaka (IRE) (Kahyasi 130) [2003 85p: 7g² 8m² 8m 7.1m* 7g² 7.1m² 8m² 7m⁴ Sep 23] lengthy colt: useful performer: won handicap at Sandown (idled) in July: good efforts all starts after, fourth to Three Graces in minor event at Newmarket final one: effective at 7f/1m: acts on polytrack, raced only on good/good to firm going on turf: sold 58,000 gns, sent to USA. *T. G. Mills* **99**

CONTRARY MARY 8 b.m. Mujadil (USA) 119 – Love Street 62 (Mummy's Pet 125) [2003 84: 6g³ 7m³ 7g 6m⁵ 7d 7s 7d p7g Nov 18] smallish, lightly-made mare: fair handicapper: won at Folkestone in March: effective at 6f/7f: acts on heavy and good to firm going: sometimes looks difficult ride (best held up). *J. Akehurst* **74**

CONUNDRUM (IRE) 5 ch.g. Dr Devious (IRE) 127 – Wasabi (IRE) (Polar Falcon (USA) 126) [2003 83, a63: 7.1m Apr 10] fairly useful handicapper at 4 yrs: well beaten only start in 2003: often tongue tied: has twice failed stalls tests and banned from Flat racing from stalls until January 2004. *D. W. Chapman* **–**

CONVENT GIRL (IRE) 3 b.f. Bishop of Cashel 122 – Right To The Top (Nashwan (USA) 135) [2003 85: 8m 9.9g 9g 10m³ 9.9f⁴ 8m* 8m 8g* 8m² 9m³ 8.1m* 8f² 9m⁶ Oct 4] big filly: poor walker: useful performer: won handicap at Salisbury and minor event at Kempton in July, and handicap at Sandown (beat Dicharachera 3 lengths) in September: good second to Tadris in listed rated stakes at Ascot penultimate start: respectable sixth to Chivalry in Cambridgeshire at Newmarket final outing: best at 1m/9f: acts on firm going: waited with. *Mrs P. N. Dutfield* **107**

CONVEX (USA) 3 b.c. Nureyev (USA) 131 – Conical 63 (Zafonic (USA) 130) [2003 81: 8g 8m 7m⁶ 7m 7g⁴ 7f⁵ 7m⁵ 6m⁶ 7.1m* Sep 20] neat colt: fair performer: won claimer at Warwick (claimed £10,000) in September: barely stays 1m: acts on good to firm and good to soft ground: tried in visor/cheekpieces, blinkered last 2 starts: free-going sort: sent to UAE. *R. Guest* **74**

CONVINCE (USA) 2 ch.g. (May 4) Mt Livermore (USA) – Conical 63 (Zafonic (USA) 130) [2003 6m³ 6m² 6g* 5m 6m⁴ Oct 21] tall, close-coupled gelding: second foal: half-brother to 3-y-o Convex: dam, maiden in Britain/USA, half-sister to good middle-distance trio Turners Hill, Wandesta and De Quest: useful performer: won maiden at Windsor in August by 2½ lengths from Ann Summers Two, making all: respectable efforts in listed event/minor race after: needs to settle to stay beyond 6f: carries head awkwardly: sold 29,000 gns and gelded. *Sir Michael Stoute* **95**

COODEN BEACH (IRE) 3 b.f. Peintre Celebre (USA) 137 – Joyful (IRE) 71 (Green Desert (USA) 127) [2003 –p: 8.2m⁴ 8m 7m 9.7f 8m³ 8f² Sep 29] leggy filly: modest maiden: should stay 1¼m: acts on firm going: tried tongue tied. *M. L. W. Bell* **56**

COOL ALIBI 3 b.f. Distinctly North (USA) 115 – Alis Princess (Sayf El Arab (USA) 127) [2003 –: 6m Apr 3] well beaten in maidens/seller. *J. F. Coupland* **–**

COOL BALLERINA (IRE) 4 b.f. Danehill Dancer (IRE) 117 – Arctic Ford (FR) 85 (Arctic Tern (USA) 126) [2003 72: f5g 6.1g p8g 7m 6m 8f 6m Aug 30] IR 10,000Y: half-sister to several winners, including useful 1995 Irish 2-y-o 6f winner No Animosity (by Ajraas): dam 7f winner: fair maiden for D. Weld in Ireland at 2/3 yrs: little show in 2003, leaving Mrs S. Liddiard after fifth start: tried blinkered: ran out final outing. *D. G. McArdle, Ireland* **–**

COOL BART 3 ch.g. Cool Jazz 116 – Margaretrose Anna 58 (Handsome Sailor 125) [2003 –: f7g 5.7m May 6] lengthy gelding: no sign of ability: tried visored. *B. P. J. Baugh* **–**

COOL BATHWICK (IRE) 4 b.g. Entrepreneur 123 – Tarafa 93 (Akarad (FR) 130) [2003 79, a67: f11g 12.6m p13g Dec 29] useful-looking gelding: fair maiden: well below form in 2003, leaving E. O'Neill/off 8½ months after reappearance: stays 1½m: acts on firm and good to soft going: tried visored. *B. R. Millman* **–**

COOLBYTHEPOOL 3 b.c. Bijou d'Inde 127 – Alchi (USA) 112 (Alleged (USA) 138) [2003 –: f9.4g* f9.4g* p10g⁵ 12m⁵ 10.9g² 12.1m* 12.1m³ 12.3m* 12f 11m 13g* 13m* 14g 12.1g² 13.9m 11.9f³ 13.1m⁵ Sep 20] leggy colt: progressed into fairly useful handicapper at 3 yrs, winning at Wolverhampton (2), Beverley, Ripon and Hamilton (2) **88**

between January and July: good efforts 3 of last 4 starts: stays 13f: acts on firm ground and all-weather: usually races prominently: sold 20,000 gns. *M. Johnston*

COOLFORE JADE (IRE)   3 ch.f. Mukaddamah (USA) 125 – Cashel Princess (IRE)   **69** 91 (Fayruz 116) [2003 6g 10.5f* 8m⁴ 12m f7g p10g⁴ p13g⁵ Dec 29] IR 10,500Y: leggy filly: third foal: dam Irish 9f/1¼m winner: fair performer: won maiden at Down Royal in June, then left E. Lynam, Ireland: left M. Wallace 5,000 gns after fourth start: probably stays 13f (raced freely at trip): acts on firm ground and polytrack. *N. E. Berry*

COOLING OFF (IRE)   6 b.m. Brief Truce (USA) 126 – Lovers' Parlour 83 (Beldale   **– §** Flutter (USA) 130) [2003 63: 11.6g p12g Jul 9] good-topped mare: modest maiden: well beaten in handicaps both 6-y-o starts: tried blinkered/visored. *J. R. Jenkins*

COOL SILK (IRE)   2 ch.c. (Apr 25) Polar Falcon (USA) 126 – Lady Barrister (Law   **58 §** Society (USA) 130) [2003 5f 5m 7m 7.5d 7m⁴ 7m 8f Aug 22] 13,000Y: leggy, lengthy colt: brother to 3 winners, including 3-y-o Legality, and half-brother to several winners, including fairly useful 1m winner (in Italy) who stayed 1¾m Edipo Re (by Slip Anchor): dam unraced: modest maiden: stays 7f: acts on good to firm going: swerved and unseated fourth start: slowly away in blinkers next 2: temperamental. *T. D. Easterby*

COOL SINGER   5 b.g. Sea Raven (IRE) 75 – Clean Singer 42 (Chief Singer 131) [2003   **–** 53: f7g f11s⁴ f12g⁵ f9.4s Feb 17] close-coupled, quite good-topped gelding: modest maiden: stays 11f: acts on fibresand and good to soft going. *Jedd O'Keeffe*

COOL SPICE   6 b.m. Karinga Bay 116 – Cool Run 87 (Deep Run 119) [2003 89: 12f   **88** 11.6g* 13.3m 12.3g⁶ Aug 29] good-bodied mare: fairly useful handicapper: won amateur event at Windsor in August by 2½ lengths from Saxe-Coburg: stays 13f: acts on soft and good to firm going. *P. J. Hobbs*

COOL TEMPER   7 b.g. Magic Ring (IRE) 115 – Ovideo 58 (Domynsky 110) [2003   **79** 62, a85: 8.3m* 8m* 7.9m 8.1g* 8.1d⁴ 8d f8g³ f8g³ f9.4s⁶ Dec 31] sturdy gelding: fairly   **a85** useful handicapper on all-weather, fair on turf: won at Windsor (edged right), Newmarket and Chepstow (last 2 ladies races) in summer: best efforts when third at Southwell after: effective at 1m/easy 1¼m: acts on fibresand and any turf going: sometimes tongue tied: often held up. *P. F. I. Cole*

COOZINHA (IRE)   3 b.f. Lake Coniston (IRE) 131 – Desert Palace (Green Desert   **–** (USA) 127) [2003 –: p5g 6m⁶ 6f 5f 5m 5m⁶ Aug 4] little form: tried visored. *J. A. Glover*

COP HILL LAD   2 ch.c. (Jan 29) Atraf 116 – Crofters Ceilidh 101 (Scottish Reel 123)   **102** [2003 5.1g* 5g² 6g* 6m⁵ 5.2m² 6g⁵ 6d 6m⁶ 6m⁵ Oct 4] 25,000Y: well-made colt: third foal: dam, 5f winner (including at 2 yrs), half-sister to 8-y-o Lord Kintyre: useful performer: won maiden at Nottingham in April and minor event at Pontefract in May: ran creditably after when beaten second in Super Sprint at Newbury, fifth in Richmond Stakes at Goodwood (on sixth start) and sixth in Mill Reef Stakes at Newbury: moved poorly to post when below form final appearance: stays 6f: acts on good to firm going: sold 140,000 gns. *B. R. Millman*

COPPERFIELDS LASS   4 b.f. Millkom 124 – Salvezza (IRE) 97 (Superpower 113)   **–** [2003 63: 6g f8.5g 7m⁶ 7f 8m Oct 23] poor maiden: left Mrs L. Pearce after reappearance: should stay 1¼m: acts on good to firm and good to soft ground: tried visored. *W. G. M. Turner*

COPPINGTON FLYER (IRE)   3 ch.f. Eagle Eyed (USA) 111 – Miss Flite (IRE)   **75** (Law Society (USA) 130) [2003 73, a57: p7g* p7g³ p6g⁴ p7g² p7g⁵ p7g² 7m 8.1m 7m*   **a68** 7g 7g³ 7m⁴ 7f 7g 7m⁵ 7g⁶ 8.3g 7m p7g p8g p7g p7g Dec 6] smallish, strong filly: fair handicapper: won at Lingfield in January and Folkestone in May: effective at 6f/7f: acts on firm going and all-weather: blinkered final start: sometimes looks none too keen. *B. W. Duke*

COPPLESTONE (IRE)   7 b.g. Second Set (IRE) 127 – Queen of The Brush (Averof   **49 §** 123) [2003 64d: 14f² 12f⁶ 14.1d⁵ 12.4m⁶ 15.8m⁵ Oct 7] tall gelding: poor handicapper: stays 2m: acts on fibresand, firm and good to soft going: tried visored/tongue tied/in cheekpieces. *W. Storey*

COQUETERIA (USA)   2 b.f. (Apr 2) Cozzene (USA) – Miss Waikiki (USA) (Miss   **83 p** waki (USA) 124) [2003 6m 6m⁴ 7m⁴ 7g* Oct 24] $80,000Y: tall, leggy filly: half-sister to several winners in USA: dam, won in USA at 2 yrs, half-sister to smart 1¼m performer Husyan and to dam of 6-y-o Mubtaker: fairly useful form: won nursery at Newbury by ½ length from English Rocket, leading over 1f out and carrying head high/idling: bred to stay at least 1m: raced freely second start: open to improvement. *G. Wragg*

COQUETRY (USA) 3 b.f. Distant View (USA) 126 – Souplesse (USA) (Majestic –
Light (USA)) [2003 88: 6g Jun 2] leggy, quite attractive filly: fairly useful form at 2
yrs: well held (reportedly finished distressed) only outing in 2003: sold 85,000 gns in
December. *Sir Michael Stoute*

CORACLE KING 3 b.g. Compton Place 125 – Dicentra (Rambo Dancer (CAN) 107) 74
[2003 74: 5d 5f⁴ 5.1m³ 6g* 6m 6m⁵ 6m⁵ 7g³ 6.8m⁴ 5d 5.5g⁶ 6.3g³ 6d⁴ 6d 7g⁴ 7v 6s 6.8d²
a6.5g Dec 9] good-topped gelding: fair performer: won minor event at Thirsk in May:
sold from J. Quinn 10,000 gns after seventh start: in frame in varied company for new
stable: best form at 6f/7f: acts on firm and good to soft ground, below form on all-
weather: tried in cheekpieces. *C. Boutin, France*

CORA (IRE) 2 b.f. (Apr 7) Machiavellian (USA) 123 – Mythical Creek (USA) (Pleas- – p
ant Tap (USA)) [2003 8s p8g Nov 13] third foal: half-sister to 4-y-o Fiddlers Creek: dam,
won in Italy at 2 yrs, half-sister to dam of smart Irish/Hong Kong performer up to 1¼m
Johann Cruyff and 3-y-o Spartacus, out of sister to US Grade 1 winners De La Rose (9f)
and Upper Nile (1¼m): signs of a little ability in maidens at Yarmouth and Lingfield:
likely to do better. *L. M. Cumani*

CORANGLAIS 3 ch.g. Piccolo 121 – Antonia's Folly 64 (Music Boy 124) [2003 79: 82
6f 5.1m⁵ 6g* 6g⁶ 7m² 7m 7g⁵ 7f Aug 23] compact gelding: good walker: fairly useful performer: won maiden at Pontefract in April: stays easy 7f: acts on good to firm and good to
soft ground, below form on firm (including in blinkers): sold 7,500 gns. *T. D. Easterby*

CORBEL (USA) 3 b.f. Diesis 133 – Corsini 88 (Machiavellian (USA) 123) [2003 77: 65
7m³ Jun 12] angular filly: fair form in 3 maidens: should stay at least 1m: acts on firm
ground: sold 5,000 gns in December. *Sir Michael Stoute*

CORDIAL (IRE) 3 gr.g. Charnwood Forest (IRE) 125 – Moon Festival 74 (Be My 80
Guest (USA) 126) [2003 56p: 10m* 10m³ 12g Jul 4] big, lengthy gelding: fairly useful
handicapper: won at Redcar in June: raced freely, best effort next time: stays 1¼m (forced
too strong a pace over 1½m): acts on good to firm ground, some promise on all-weather.
Sir Mark Prescott

CORISA (IRE) 3 ch.f. Be My Guest (USA) 126 – Unalaska (IRE) 65 (High Estate –
127) [2003 –: p10g Mar 15] smallish filly: unimpressive mover: behind in maidens 5
months apart, looking difficult ride and virtually pulled up in latter. *B. R. Millman*

CORK HARBOUR (FR) 7 ch.g. Grand Lodge (USA) 125 – Irish Sea 66 (Irish River 66
(FR) 131) [2003 81: 8.3g 8.5m 11.7m⁴ 11.5g⁴ 12m 15m 12.6f² 12.1g⁶ 12.6m Aug 25]
strong gelding: fair handicapper: stays 12.6f: acts on polytrack, firm and soft going: tried
visored, usually blinkered: races prominently: none too consistent: won over hurdles in
October. *P. Bowen*

CORMORANT WHARF (IRE) 3 b.c. Alzao (USA) 117 – Mercy Bien (IRE) 63 –
(Be My Guest (USA) 126) [2003 79p: 6f Jun 25] fairly useful form: tongue tied, well held
only 3-y-o start: should stay at least 7f: acts on soft and good to firm going: sold 4,000
gns in October. *P. J. Makin*

CORNELIUS 6 b.g. Baratheaa (IRE) 127 – Rainbow Mountain 71 (Rainbow Quest 108
(USA) 134) [2003 115: 8g 8.2m³ 8.1g 8g 8s⁴ 8.2d* p10g Nov 22] tall, good-topped
gelding: has an unimpressive, rather round action: useful performer: won minor event at
Nottingham in November by short head from Danger Over: best effort in 2003 when
seventh to Putra Pekan in Tote Scoop6 Handicap at Sandown third start: effective at 1m/
1¼m: acts on heavy and good to firm going: has been bandaged behind: usually races
prominently: tends to carry head high. *P. F. I. Cole*

CORNISH GOLD 2 b.f. (Feb 2) Slip Anchor 136 – Sans Diablo (IRE) (Mac's Imp 65
(USA) 116) [2003 6m p7g 6d⁵ 7g⁶ Nov 25] workmanlike filly: fourth foal: half-sister to
4-y-o Bonny Ruan: dam unraced: fair maiden: best effort when fifth at Doncaster: should
stay at least 7f: acts on good to soft going. *D. Haydn Jones*

CORNWALLIS 2 b.c. (May 10) Forzando 122 – Up And Going (FR) (Never So Bold 60
135) [2003 f6g p6g⁶ Dec 29] 20,000Y: eighth foal: brother to smart 5f/6f winner (including at 2 yrs) Easycall and half-brother to 2 winners abroad: dam unraced half-sister to
useful sprinter Up And At 'em (by Forzando): still green, better effort in maidens (modest
form) when never-nearer sixth to Chorus Beauty at Lingfield: slowly away on debut: bred
to prove best at 5f/6f. *R. Guest*

CORONADO FOREST (USA) 4 b.g. Spinning World (USA) 130 – Desert Jewel 71
(USA) (Caerleon (USA) 132) [2003 81: p8g² p8g p8g³ 8.5m p8g p8g p7g f8.5s² f8.5s²
p8g⁶ f8s f7g⁶ p10g Dec 10] $210,000F: first foal: dam unraced sister to smart French
performer up to 1m Psychobabble and closely related to very smart performer up to 1½m

in France/USA Louis Cyphre: fair maiden: trained in 2002 by D. Wachman, Ireland: will prove best up to 8.5f: acts on all-weather and firm ground: races prominently. *M. R. Hoad*

CORPS DE BALLET (IRE) 2 b.f. (Mar 11) Fasliyev (USA) 120 – Dwell (USA) 96 **85** (Habitat 134) [2003 6m⁵ 6m⁴ 6m³ 5.1m* Oct 28] close-coupled filly: half-sister to several winners, including very smart 5f and (including at 2 yrs) 7f winner Misraah (by Lure) and useful Italian performer up to 1¼m Doowaley (by Sadler's Wells): dam 1m winner: fairly useful performer: landed odds in maiden at Nottingham by 5 lengths from Buy On The Red, leading over 1f out: likely to prove best at 5f/6f: races prominently. *J. L. Dunlop*

CORRIDOR CREEPER (FR) 6 ch.g. Polish Precedent (USA) 131 – Sonia Rose **102** (USA) (Superbity (USA)) [2003 91: 5.1g² 5g² 5f² 5f² 5m 5d³ 5m⁵ 5m³ 5m* 5.6d² 5.2g² 6m 5f 5m Oct 25] useful-looking gelding: useful handicapper: won at Epsom in August: good second after to Halmahera in Portland at Doncaster and to Palawan at Yarmouth (unlucky): best at 5f: acts on firm and good to soft ground: tried blinkered/tongue tied, wore cheekpieces after reappearance: sometimes finds little: usually races handily: consistent. *J. M. Bradley*

CORRYONG 2 ch.f. (Mar 29) Wolfhound (USA) 126 – Easy Risk (Risk Me (FR) 127) **–** [2003 5d May 4] third foal: dam tailed off only start: 50/1, slowly away and always behind in Hamilton maiden. *B. Mactaggart*

CORSICAN NATIVE (USA) 2 b.c. (Feb 18) Lear Fan (USA) 130 – Corsini 88 **79 p** (Machiavellian (USA) 123) [2003 7s³ Oct 29] second foal: dam, 2-y-o 7f winner, out of close relative to dam of Zafonic: 6/1, 6½ lengths third of 14 to Crystal Curling in maiden at Yarmouth, not given unduly hard time: will stay at least 1m: sure to improve. *Mrs A. J. Perrett*

CORTON DENHAM 2 ch.c. (Mar 18) Wolfhound (USA) 126 – Wigit (Safawan 118) **–** [2003 p8g Dec 20] third foal: closely related to 1¼m winner Sayit (by Sayaarr): dam unraced: 50/1, always behind in minor event at Lingfield. *G. P. Enright*

CORTON (IRE) 4 b. or gr.g. Definite Article 121 – Limpopo 49 (Green Desert (USA) **90** 127) [2003 –: 10m 11.9m² 13.9m 12m² 12.3m⁵ 13.3m Aug 15] strong gelding: fairly useful handicapper: best effort in 2003 when second to Double Obsession at Ascot fourth start: stays 1½m: acts on good to firm going: often races prominently. *P. F. I. Cole*

CORYLUS (USA) 2 b.f. (Jan 23) Kingmambo (USA) 125 – Pennygown 91 (Rainbow **–** Quest (USA) 134) [2003 7m 8.2f 7m 8d f7g Nov 14] leggy, close-coupled filly: first foal: dam, 1½m winner on only start, half-sister to very smart pair Craigsteel (best at 1½m/ 1¾m) and Invermark (stays 2½m): little sign of ability in maidens/nurseries: may do better at 1½m+. *Sir Mark Prescott*

COSABAWN (IRE) 3 b.f. Barathea (IRE) 127 – Riyda 101 (Be My Guest (USA) 126) **57 +** [2003 8.2g⁶ 8g 10f⁵ 11.6d⁶ Jun 23] IR 145,000Y: strong, heavy-bodied filly: half-sister to several winners, including 1½m winner Ridaiyma (by Kahyasi): dam, 1m/1¼m winner, half-sister to smart Irish performer up to 1¾m Rayseka: modest form in maidens: stays 1¼m: acts on firm ground. *L. M. Cumani*

COSMIC CASE 8 b.m. Casteddu 111 – La Fontainova (IRE) (Lafontaine (USA) 117) **58** [2003 62: 14m 13d 12m² 16g⁵ 14f* 11.9f⁵ 15.9m⁵ 14.4m³ 14.1m 12g Nov 5] angular mare: modest handicapper: won apprentice event at Musselburgh in June: barely stays 2m: acts on any going: tried visored at 2/5yrs: held up: tough. *J. S. Goldie*

COSMIC ROYALE (IRE) 3 ch.f. Pennekamp (USA) 130 – Windmill Princess 55 **–** (Gorytus (USA) 132) [2003 p6g 7m⁶ 8.3d 6d Jul 19] IR 10,500Y: leggy filly: half-sister to several winners, including useful 6f (at 2 yrs) to 1m (in USA) winner Cosmic Prince (by Teenoso): dam, placed at 1m and 11f, out of half-sister to Derby winners Blakeney and Morston: signs of some ability. *T. P. McGovern*

COSMIC SONG 6 b.m. Cosmonaut – Hotaria 68 (Sizzling Melody 117) [2003 45: **–** f8s⁴ f8g Feb 11] big mare: poor performer: little encouragement both 6-y-o starts. *R. M. Whitaker*

COSMOCRAT 5 b.g. Cosmonaut – Bella Coola 50 (Northern State (USA) 91) [2003 **57 ?** 65+: 10g Apr 1] modest performer, lightly raced: stays 1¼m: acts on soft ground: sold 8,000 gns in May: joined R. Stronge and won over hurdles in November. *C. G. Cox*

COSTA DEL SOL (IRE) 2 ch.g. (Mar 7) General Monash (USA) 107 – L'Harmonie **55** (USA) (Bering 136) [2003 5.1g⁶ f5s⁶ f6g⁴ 6g⁴ 7m⁵ f5g³ 5g³ 6f² 6g³ 6f⁴ 6m⁴ 5.3m² 6g 6d⁶ p6g p8g p6g⁵ Dec 20] IR 4,000F, 7,000Y: good-topped gelding: third foal: half-brother to Italian 2001 2-y-o 5f winner by Woodborough: dam French maiden: modest maiden: left

D. Ivory after eleventh outing: stays 6f: acts on fibresand and firm going: tried blinkered/visored. *J. J. Bridger*

COTEBROOK 4 ch.g. First Trump 118 – Chantelys 52 (Ballacashtal (CAN)) [2003 65, a53: f11s⁴ f12s Feb 27] angular gelding: poor maiden: barely stays 1¾m: acts on fibresand and soft ground: tried in cheekpieces: sometimes races freely. *J. M. Jefferson* — a45 ?

COTE SOLEIL 6 ch.g. Inchinor 119 – Sunshine Coast 86 (Posse (USA) 130) [2003 65: f8g⁶ 9f⁶ 8.1g f9.4g Oct 4] smallish gelding: modest handicapper: best at 1m/6f: acts on any turf going, probably on fibresand: tried blinkered/visored: usually raced prominently. *C. R. Egerton* — 59

COTOSOL 2 b.g. (Apr 6) Forzando 122 – Emerald Dream (IRE) 47 (Vision (USA)) [2003 5g 5m⁵ 5m² f5g* 6.1d⁴ 5f⁵ 6d⁴ 6g f6f⁶ 6.1m³ 6m² 7m³ 7g 7m² 7d⁶ Nov 8] 4,500Y, resold 8,500Y: strong, lengthy gelding: third foal: dam maiden who stayed 1¼m: fair performer: won maiden at Southwell in May: several creditable efforts after, including when placed in nurseries: stays 7f: acts on fibresand, good to firm and good to soft going: often races prominently. *B. A. McMahon* — 77

COTTAM GRANGE 3 b.c. River Falls 113 – Karminski 70 (Pitskelly 122) [2003 60: 12m⁶ 9.9m 12.1m 8.5m 9.9m⁶ 14.1m⁵ f16.2s⁴ Dec 6] unfurnished colt: poor maiden: stays easy 2m: acts on fibresand, unraced on extremes of going on turf. *M. W. Easterby* — 47

COTTINGHAM (IRE) 2 b.c. (Feb 22) Perugino (USA) 84 – Stately Princess 70 (Robellino (USA) 127) [2003 5g⁵ 6m⁵ 5m⁴ 7m² 7m⁴ 6m 7.9f f8g f8g⁴ f8s Dec 27] 9,000F, 9,100Y: workmanlike colt: second foal: dam 5f (at 2 yrs) and 6f winner: fair maiden: second in nursery at Catterick: left C. Fairhurst after next start then below form: stays 7f: acts on good to firm ground and fibresand. *M. C. Chapman* — 70

COTTON EYED JOE (IRE) 2 b.c. (Apr 9) Indian Rocket 115 – Cwm Deri (IRE) (Alzao (USA) 117) [2003 5g 5d⁵ 5m⁶ 7m 7d Sep 20] €9,500Y: good-bodied colt: half-brother to several winners, including 1995 2-y-o 6f winner Kossolian (by Emarati) and 1½m winner Chocstaw (by Mtoto): dam unraced: well held, including in seller: sold 500 gns. *A. Berry* —

COTTON HOUSE (IRE) 6 b.m. Mujadil (USA) 119 – Romanovna (Mummy's Pet 125) [2003 101: 6.1s⁶ 5m⁵ 6m 6g 5g Jul 5] lengthy, useful-looking mare: unimpressive mover: useful performer: good efforts in listed race at Nottingham and Temple Stakes at Sandown (5½ lengths fifth to Airwave) first 2 starts: best at 5f/6f: acts on any turf going and polytrack: none too consistent: reportedly in foal to Tobougg. *M. R. Channon* — 100

COULD SHE BE MAGIC (IRE) 2 b.f. (Apr 7) Titus Livius (FR) 115 – Ponteilla (FR) (Arctic Tern (USA) 126) [2003 5f 5g f6g³ 6g⁵ 7d f7g* Nov 24] €7,000Y: close-coupled, workmanlike filly: first foal: dam third at 1m in France at 2 yrs: modest on all-weather, poor on turf: won seller at Southwell (gambled on) in November, making most: stays 7f: acts on fibresand, firm and good to soft going. *T. D. Easterby* — 42 a58

COULTERS CANDY 5 ch.g. Clantime 101 – Heldigvis 63 (Hot Grove 128) [2003 7.1f Jun 16] maiden hurdler: well held in claimer at Musselburgh only start on Flat. *A. C. Whillans* —

COUNSEL'S OPINION (IRE) 6 ch.g. Rudimentary (USA) 118 – Fairy Fortune 78 (Rainbow Quest (USA) 134) [2003 101: 10m 10g³ 12g* 12f 11.9g³ 12g 12g 10m* 10g* 10g Oct 31] big gelding: smart performer: better than ever in 2003, winning handicap at Newbury in May, minor event at Ascot in September and handicap at Ascot (beat unlucky Navado a length) in October: respectable seventh in listed event at Newmarket final start: effective at 1¼m/1½m: acts on fibresand, soft and good to firm going: has worn crossed noseband: sometimes early to post/slowly away: usually waited with: game and reliable. *C. F. Wall* — 111

COUNT COUGAR (USA) 3 b.g. Sir Cat (USA) 118 – Gold Script (USA) (Seeking The Gold (USA)) [2003 73: 5m⁴ 5f³ 5f 5d 5g⁶ 5f f5s f5g* f5g Dec 16] sturdy gelding: poor walker and mover: fair performer: back to best to win handicap at Southwell in October: left T. D. Barron 7,000 gns after: best at 5f: acts on fibresand, firm and soft ground: tried blinkered. *S. P. Griffiths* — 73

COUNT DAVANTI 4 b.g. Puissance 110 – I'm Playing (Primo Dominie 121) [2003 –: 5.1m 5g 10.5m Aug 7] sparely-made gelding: little form: tried blinkered. *M. Mullineaux* —

COUNT DRACULA 2 b.c. (Apr 15) Dracula (AUS) – Chipaya 116 (Northern Prospect (USA)) [2003 6m p7g² p7g Oct 30] 13,000F, 42,000Y: close-coupled colt: fifth foal: half-brother to fairly useful 1½m winner Aymara (by Darshaan): dam 6f (at 2 yrs) and 1m — 74 winner who later won in USA: clearly best effort in maidens (fair form) when second at Lingfield: should stay 1m. *A. M. Balding*

COUNTESS ELTON (IRE) 3 ch.f. Mukaddamah (USA) 125 – Be Prepared (IRE) – §
(Be My Guest (USA) 126) [2003 57§, a41§: 5.9m 8m 7.5m 8g 11g Oct 28] tall, leggy filly: modest and unreliable winner at 2 yrs: well held in 2003, leaving K. Ryan after second start. *R. E. Barr*

COUNTESS KIRI 5 b.m. Opera Ghost 91 – Ballagh Countess (King's Ride 88) –
[2003 18f Jul 19] first foal: dam winning hurdler/chaser: modest form in bumpers: slowly away and showed little in maiden at Warwick on Flat debut. *P. Bowen*

COUNTESS MILETRIAN (IRE) 4 b.f. Barathea (IRE) 127 – Sweet Alma 67 –
(Alzao (USA) 117) [2003 86: 10m 9g⁶ Jul 3] smallish, workmanlike filly: fairly useful handicapper in 2002: well held both 4-y-o starts: stays 1¼m: unraced on heavy going, acts on any other turf and polytrack. *M. R. Channon*

COUNT ON US 3 ch.g. Danehill Dancer (IRE) 117 – Capricious Lady (IRE) (Capri- –
corn Line 111) [2003 –: p7g 8m⁶ Jul 6] no form: left A. Charlton after reappearance. *Miss E. C. Lavelle*

COUNTRY REEL (USA) 3 b.c. Danzig (USA) – Country Belle (USA) 108 (Seattle **110**
Slew (USA)) [2003 109: 6g² 6m 6m⁵ Oct 17] strong, lengthy colt: fluent mover: smart performer, lightly raced: good efforts at 3 yrs when short-headed by Orientor in Chipchase Stakes at Newcastle and when 2½ lengths fifth to Ashdown Express in Bentinck Stakes at Newmarket: should stay 7f: acts on firm ground, probably on good to soft: tongue tied in 2003. *Saeed bin Suroor*

COUNTRYWIDE DANCER (IRE) 3 b.f. Danehill Dancer (IRE) 117 – Meadow –
Grass (IRE) (Thatching 131) [2003 61: 6f⁴ 8m⁶ Sep 18] tall, useful-looking filly: modest performer at 2 yrs: well held in 2003: tried blinkered. *A. Berry*

COUNTRYWIDE FLYER (IRE) 2 b.g. (Apr 24) Revoque (IRE) 122 – Unbidden **76**
Melody (USA) (Chieftain) [2003 5m 5f f7g⁴ 7.5d⁴ 7m² 8f² f8.5s² 8m³ 7f⁴ f8s² f8g* **a82**
f8g* f8s⁴ Dec 27] €7,000Y: strong gelding: half-brother to numerous winners, including useful 11f winner (stayed 21f) Greenhope (by Definite Article) and 7f/1m winner Great Melody (by Pips Pride): dam ran twice in USA: fairly useful on all-weather, fair on turf: won seller in October (by 16 lengths, sold from A. Berry £19,500) and minor event in November (beat Queenstown a neck, wandering), both at Southwell: stays 8.5f: acts on firm ground and fibresand: often races prominently: reliable. *T. D. Barron*

COUNTRYWIDE GIRL (IRE) 4 ch.f. Catrail (USA) 123 – Polish Saga 59 (Polish –
Patriot (USA) 128) [2003 –: f7g 6m 6.1m 6m Aug 8] leggy, quite good-topped filly: poor performer: no form in 2003 (unseated rider leaving stall final start). *A. Berry*

COUNTRYWIDE STAR (IRE) 5 ch.g. Common Grounds 118 – Silver Slipper 67 –
(Indian Ridge 123) [2003 54: f8s f8s f12g Jan 23] sturdy gelding: has a round action: modest performer: no form at 5 yrs: tried visored. *C. N. Kellett*

COUNT WALEWSKI 3 b.g. Polish Precedent (USA) 131 – Classic Beauty (IRE) 65 **75**
(Fairy King (USA)) [2003 74: 8m 8.3d² 8.2m² 8m* 8f Oct 12] good-bodied gelding: fair performer: won maiden at Brighton in October: reportedly lame final start: stays 1m: acts on good to firm and good to soft going: free-going sort: sold 13,000 gns. *J. L. Dunlop*

COUNTYKAT (IRE) 3 b.g. Woodborough (USA) 112 – Kitty Kildare (USA) 68 **84**
(Seattle Dancer (USA) 119) [2003 92: 9m⁵ 8g⁵ 10m³ 8.9f⁶ f8.5g³ f8g Dec 3] lengthy gelding: fairly useful performer: operated on for twisted gut after final 2-y-o start: stays easy 1¼m: acts on fibresand/dirt, raced only on good going or firmer on turf: effective visored or not: sometimes carries head high. *K. R. Burke*

COUP DE CHANCE (IRE) 3 ch.f. Ashkalani (IRE) 128 – Tout A Coup (IRE) 105 **94**
(Ela-Mana-Mou 132) [2003 10g⁴ 10s³ 9.5d⁶ 12v² 12m* 11d⁴ 11f* 10m 12g* 12d 12d⁴ 11.9f* 11.9m* Oct 23] IR 34,000Y: second foal: half-sister to 2003 Irish 2-y-o 7f winner Dame Facile (by Entrepreneur): dam Irish 7f (at 2 yrs) to 1½m winner: useful performer: won maiden at Tramore/in May, claimers at Limerick in June and Naas (claimed from K. Prendergast €25,000) in July and 2 handicaps at Brighton (apprentices) in October: stays 1½m: probably acts on any ground: usually blinkered: free-going sort: has idled badly. *P. A. Blockley*

COUPLET 2 b.f. (Mar 20) Trempolino (USA) 135 – Coigach 110 (Niniski (USA) 125) **66**
[2003 8.2m³ 7.5m Sep 17] smallish, close-coupled filly: fifth foal: half-sister to useful 1½m winner Motto (by Mtoto) and fairly useful 1999 2-y-o 7f winner Aston Mara (by Bering): dam 1m (at 2 yrs) to 14.6f (Park Hill) winner from good staying family: better

effort in maidens (fair form) when third at Nottingham: will be suited by 1¼m+: sold 5,200 gns, sent to Hungary. *H. R. A. Cecil*

COURAGEOUS DUKE (USA)   4 b.c. Spinning World (USA) 130 – Araadh (USA)   **105**
70 (Blushing Groom (FR) 131) [2003 94: p10g 8g 8m 10m* 10g² 10.4f⁴ 10d 12m⁶ 9m
Oct 4] close-coupled, quite good-topped colt: useful handicapper: won at Newmarket
in June: good efforts in frame at Sandown (head second to Nuit Sombre) and York
(finished well when fourth to Far Lane in John Smith's Cup) next 2 starts: below form in
Cambridgeshire at Newmarket final outing: stays 1¼m, not quite 1½m: acts on firm
ground. *J. Noseda*

COURANT D'AIR (IRE)   2 b.g. (Mar 3) Indian Rocket 115 – Red River Rose (IRE)   **52**
51 (Red Sunset 120) [2003 5d⁴ 5g f6s 5.9m Sep 4] 9,500Y, 16,500 2-y-o: second foal:
third foal: half-brother to 7f winner Hi Red (by Atraf): dam 2-y-o 6f winner who stayed
1m: modest maiden: showed little after debut: should stay 6f: wandered final start.
P. C. Haslam

COURT ALLIANCE   4 ch.g. Alhijaz 122 – Fairfields Cone (Celtic Cone 116) [2003   **51**
–: 16m 14.1d⁵ 13.3m* 15.8m 16m⁶ Oct 28] modest handicapper, lightly raced: won at
Newbury in May: stays 2m: acts on good to firm ground. *R. J. Price*

COURT CHANCELLOR   2 b.c. (Mar 6) Primo Dominie 121 – Welcome Home 55   **–**
(Most Welcome 131) [2003 6m 8.1m 7m Oct 1] 5,500Y: smallish colt: third foal: dam,
1½m winner, half-sister to smart sprinter Two Clubs: well held in maidens/minor event.
P. Mitchell

COURTELIMORR   3 b.f. Defacto (USA) – Auntie Fay (IRE) (Fayruz 116) [2003 –:   **28**
10g 7f 8m⁵ 9.9d Jul 4] bad maiden: wore visor/cheekpieces last 3 starts. *B. S. Rothwell*

COURT MASTERPIECE   3 b.c. Polish Precedent (USA) 131 – Easy Option (IRE)   **112**
115 (Prince Sabo 123) [2003 95p: 6m⁴ 7g² 8m³ 7m 8g* Aug 2] lengthy, angular colt:
smart performer: won listed event at Goodwood in August by length from Hurricane
Alan: earlier ran well in handicaps at Epsom (short-head second to Tarjman) and Royal
Ascot (close third to New Seeker in Britannia Stakes): effective at 7f/1m: raced only on
good/good to firm going: slowly away first 2 starts in 2003. *E. A. L. Dunlop*

COURT MUSIC (IRE)   4 b. or br.f. Revoque (IRE) 122 – Lute And Lyre (IRE) 96   **–**
(The Noble Player (USA) 126) [2003 60: 6d 6.9d 7m 8g f6g f8g Dec 12] rather leggy,
angular filly: modest performer: well held in 2003: tried blinkered/visored/in cheekpieces. *R. E. Barr*

COURT OF APPEAL   6 ch.g. Bering 136 – Hiawatha's Song (USA) (Chief's Crown   **80**
(USA)) [2003 84: f12g² 10.3g 12.3m* 11.9f 10m⁴ 10m⁶ 12m⁴ 11.9f 13.8d² f12g⁴ f14g³
f12s⁴ Dec 27] lengthy gelding: fairly useful handicapper: won at Chester in May: effective at 1¼m to easy 1¾m: acts on any turf going and fibresand: tongue tied: often races
prominently: consistent. *B. Ellison*

COURT ONE   5 b.g. Shareef Dancer (USA) 135 – Fairfields Cone (Celtic Cone 116)   **44**
[2003 39: f14.8g p12g 13.3m 19.1m⁶ 16.2d⁴ 16.2f² 16.2m⁶ 14.1d 17.1m 16.2m Aug 25]
small, leggy gelding: shows knee action: poor maiden handicapper: stays 2m: acts on
firm ground: tried visored: sometimes slowly away. *R. J. Price*

COURT SHAREEF   8 b.g. Shareef Dancer (USA) 135 – Fairfields Cone (Celtic Cone   **98**
116) [2003 101: 12g³ 14.1g⁵ 13.9m 13.4m⁶ 18m Oct 18] small gelding: useful performer:
good efforts at 8 yrs when third to Razkalla in minor event at Doncaster and fifth to
Alcazar in listed race at Nottingham: effective at 1½m to 2m: yet to race on heavy going,
acts on any other: bandaged behind final start: usually held up. *R. J. Price*

COURTYARD   2 b.f. (May 18) Halling (USA) 133 – Jubilee Trail 82 (Shareef Dancer   **70 p**
(USA) 135) [2003 8g⁶ Oct 25] leggy, quite good-topped filly: half-sister to several
winners, including 7f (including at 2 yrs) to 1m winner Peace Envoy and French 1m
winner Jubilation (by Zamindar), both useful: dam, 10.4f winner, half-sister to Park Hill
winner Rejuvenate: 9/1, 3 lengths sixth of 17 to Rave Reviews in maiden at Newbury,
soon plenty to do and keeping on not knocked about: will be suited by 1¼m: sure to
improve. *J. H. M. Gosden*

COUSTOU   3 b.g. In Command (IRE) 114 – Carranza (IRE) (Lead On Time   **81**
(USA) 123) [2003 83: 8.1g 7g 8m 8g⁵ Aug 10] lengthy, good-topped gelding: fairly
useful performer: best effort at 3 yrs on reappearance: stays 1m: raced only on good/good
to firm going: tried in cheekpieces, blinkered (dropped out tamely having set strong pace)
final start. *M. A. Jarvis*

Queen Alexandra Stakes, Royal Ascot—Cover Up gains a second successive win in the race;
Tamiami Trail and Double Honour follow him home

COVENTINA (IRE) 2 gr.f. (Apr 14) Daylami (IRE) 138 – Lady of The Lake 104 **90**
(Caerleon (USA) 132) [2003 7f⁵ 7m³ 8.1g* 8.3g Oct 13] third foal: half-sister to 3-y-o
Largo: dam, 2m/17f winner, out of smart performer up to 9f Llyn Gwynant: fairly useful
performer: justified favouritism comfortably in maiden at Chepstow in August: never
dangerous when only twelfth in nursery: will be suited by 1¼m+. *J. L. Dunlop*

COVER UP (IRE) 6 b.g. Machiavellian (USA) 123 – Sought Out (IRE) 119 (Rainbow **114**
Quest (USA) 134) [2003 112: 18.7m⁶ 22.2f* 16.4g² 15.9m² Aug 19] close-coupled, quite
good-topped gelding: smart performer: won Queen Alexandra Stakes at Royal Ascot (for
second year running, beat Tamiami Trail 1¼ lengths) in June, idling/flashing tail: good
second in listed race at Sandown (short-headed by Persian Punch) and Lonsdale Stakes at
York (beaten 2 lengths by Bollin Eric): reportedly suffered suspensory injury after: stays
2¾m: acts on firm and good to soft going, probably on heavy: visored once at 3 yrs: has
raced lazily: patiently ridden. *Sir Michael Stoute*

COWBOY (IRE) 3 b.c. Unfuwain (USA) 131 – Wynona (IRE) 89 (Cyrano de Bergerac –
120) [2003 10g 10m 10m⁴ 14.1m 14.1m Jun 12] 9,500Y: angular colt: fourth foal: half-
brother to winners in Sweden and Spain (by Dilum and Bluebird): dam, 2-y-o 7f winner
who stayed 1¼m: little form: looked reluctant early on penultimate start. *G. C. Bravery*

COWBOYS AND ANGELS 6 b.g. Bin Ajwaad (IRE) 119 – Halimah 56 (Be My –
Guest (USA) 126) [2003 63, a71: f7g p7g p7g p7g f7g f8g⁶ f8.5s Mar 31] modest performer: stays 8.5f: acts on any turf going/all-weather: tried visored, sometimes blinkered/
tongue tied. *Mrs Lydia Pearce*

COXMOORE (IRE) 2 b.g. (Mar 29) Among Men (USA) 124 – Esh Sham (USA) **84 p**
(Damascus (USA)) [2003 6g* 7.5m* Aug 14] €5,800Y: tall, useful-looking gelding: half-
brother to 3 winners, including Italian 7f/1m winner by Storm Bird: dam ran once: fairly
useful form: won maiden at Newcastle in July and minor event at Beverley (3 ran) in
August, racing freely/drifting left in latter: should stay 1m: sent to Hong Kong, where
renamed Peaceful Star: should improve further. *J. J. Quinn*

COY (IRE) 2 b.f. (Mar 5) Danehill (USA) 126 – Demure (Machiavellian (USA) 123 **88 p**
[2003 6m 6g* Oct 22] €380,000Y: leggy, unfurnished filly: second foal: dam unraced
half-sister to very smart 6f/7f performer Diffident: better effort in maidens when winning
at Newcastle by 3 lengths from Fun To Ride, quickening to lead over 1f out: should stay
7f: useful prospect. *Sir Michael Stoute*

CRACKA SHAKOON 2 ch.f. (Mar 2) First Trump 118 – Natural Key 74 (Safawan –
118) [2003 5.1m 6.1d Nov 6] 600Y: small filly: third foal: dam 5f/6f winner: well held in
maidens at Nottingham. *R. Hollinshead*

CRACKING BLADE 6 b.g. Sure Blade (USA) 130 – Norstock 52 (Norwick (USA) –
125) [2003 11.5s Aug 28] second foal: dam, 2m winner, prolific winning jumper: no form
in bumpers: well beaten in seller at Lingfield. *J. White*

CRACKING ROSIE (IRE) 2 b.f. (May 5) Alzao (USA) 117 – Crystal Land (Kris **68 p**
135) [2003 6g⁵ p8g* Oct 27] €6,000Y, 25,000 2-y-o: good-topped filly: half-sister to 9.4f
winner Crystal Gold (by Arazi) and 1¼m winner King's Crown (by Lead On Time), both
fairly useful: dam lightly-raced sister to Prix Saint-Alary winner Fitnah: better effort in
maidens (fair form) when winning at Lingfield by length from Suave Quartet, making
most: should be suited by 1¼m/1½m: sent to USA: open to progress. *J. Noseda*

CRACKLEANDO 2 ch.c. (Mar 20) Forzando 122 – Crackling 57 (Electric 126) **59** [2003 p8g p10g f9.4g Dec 22] 8,500Y, resold 16,000Y: third foal: half-brother to 5.7f (at 2 yrs) to 1¼m winner Crackle (by Anshan) and Irish 2001 2-y-o 5f winner Lets Try Again (by Emarati): dam 9f and 1½m winner who stayed 2m: modest form at best in maidens: should stay 1½m. *N. P. Littmoden*

CRAFTY CALLING (USA) 3 b.c. Crafty Prospector (USA) – Glorious Calling **101** (USA) (Nijinsky (CAN) 138) [2003 100p: 6m³ 7g 7.1g* 7g 7g⁵ 7.6g⁴ Aug 28] tall, quite attractive colt: useful performer: won handicap at Sandown in July by neck from Tizzy May: creditable fifth to El Coto in handicap at Leicester: stays 7f: unraced on extremes of going: tongue tied final outing: races prominently. *P. F. I. Cole*

CRAFTY FANCY (IRE) 2 ch.f. (Apr 6) Intikhab (USA) 135 – Idle Fancy 79 (Muj- **90** tahid (USA) 118) [2003 5.1m³ 5d* 5s* 5m 6m⁶ 5.2m⁵ 6f⁶ 5m⁵ 6g⁵ Oct 31] 14,000Y: leggy, quite good-topped filly: third foal: half-sister to 5-y-o Idle Power and 3-y-o Bint Alhaarth: dam, Irish 1m winner, half-sister to dam of smart 1½m performer Ela Athena: fairly useful performer: won maiden in April and minor event (beat Russian Valour by neck) in May, both at Windsor: creditable efforts after only in Cherry Hinton Stakes at Newmarket and listed contest at Newbury on fifth/sixth starts: should stay 7f: acts on soft and good to firm ground. *D. J. S. ffrench Davis*

CRAFTY POLITICIAN (USA) 6 ch.h. Supremo (USA) 116 – Sauve Qui Peut **64 d** (CAN) (Cerf Volant (CAN)) [2003 a5.5g² 6.5s² 6.5g 5.5m* 6.5g³ 7g* 5.5d 6f⁴ 8d 7.1m 7g p7g p7g p10g Dec 30] $7,700Y: ex-German trained horse: half-brother to numerous winners in USA: dam lightly-raced maiden in USA: won 2 races in USA at 3 yrs, handi- cap at Mannheim at 5 yrs and claimers at Le Croise-Laroche and Longchamp in April/ May 2003: modest form in Britain, leaving C. Von Der Recke, Germany, after eighth start: stays 7f: acts on soft going, good to firm and dirt: sometimes blinkered, tried tongue tied. *G. L. Moore*

CRAIC SA CEILI (IRE) 3 b.f. Danehill Dancer (IRE) 117 – Fay's Song (IRE) 84 **82 +** (Fayruz 116) [2003 83: 8.1m⁵ 7.1m 7g⁴ 8.1g⁵ f7g Oct 20] leggy filly: fairly useful handi- capper: sweating, clearly best effort in 2003 on third outing: effective at 7f/1m: acts on good to firm ground, only win on soft. *M. S. Saunders*

CRAIL 3 b.g. Vettori (IRE) 119 – Tendency 77 (Ballad Rock 122) [2003 70p: p8g 10d **79** 8m* 8g Jul 24] workmanlike gelding: fair performer: won maiden at Doncaster in July: stays 1m: acts on soft and good to firm ground: found little final start. *C. F. Wall*

CRAIOVA (IRE) 4 b.c. Turtle Island (IRE) 123 – Velvet Appeal (IRE) 101 (Petorius **100** 117) [2003 85: p7g³ 7d* 7.1m* 7g 7.1g* 8d² 7d⁵ 8g Nov 1] strong, lengthy, attractive colt: has a quick action: useful performer: won maiden at Newcastle in March, minor event at Warwick in May and handicap at Haydock in July: best effort in handicaps after when second to Gilded Dancer at Ascot: effective at 7f/1m: acts on good to firm and good to soft going, found little/carried head awkwardly on polytrack on reappearance. *B. W. Hills*

CRANACHAN 2 b.f. (Jan 16) Selkirk (USA) 129 – Baked Alaska 93 (Green Desert **80** (USA) 127) [2003 7m⁴ 7f 8.1d Sep 27] quite good-topped filly: third foal: half-sister to Italian 1¼m winner Stacomud (by Machiavellian): dam 2-y-o 6f winner: fairly useful form when fourth in maiden at Newmarket: reportedly had breathing problems when running badly in similar events after: should stay 1m. *J. H. M. Gosden*

CRATHORNE (IRE) 3 b.g. Alzao (USA) 117 – Shirley Blue (IRE) (Shirley Heights **93** 130) [2003 85: 10.3g 12.3m⁵ 12.3m² 10.1m 12.3m² 14g 11.9m⁴ 11.9m⁵ 10m 11.9f³ 12m Oct 25] deep-girthed gelding: fairly useful handicapper: best efforts on fifth and seventh starts: stays 1½m: acts on firm and soft ground: wore cheekpieces last 3 outings: none too consistent. *J. D. Bethell*

CREDENZA MOMENT 5 b.g. Pyramus (USA) 78 – Mystoski 35 (Petoski 135) **–** [2003 –: p12g Feb 25] sparely-made gelding: poor maiden: well held only 5-y-o outing: tried blinkered/visored. *M. Madgwick*

CREED (IRE) 3 ch.g. Entrepreneur 123 – Ardent Range (IRE) (Archway (IRE) 115) **59** [2003 –: 10.1m⁴ 12g⁶ 14m⁴ 14.1m 12.1m⁵ 17.2m⁶ Jun 25] strong, workmanlike gelding: modest maiden: stays 1¾m: raced only on good/good to firm ground. *R. A. Fahey*

CREG NY SHEE 4 b.g. Anabaa (USA) 130 – Cos I Do (IRE) (Double Schwartz 128) **–** [2003 –: p8g p10g 9g Aug 6] little form: left P. D. Evans after second start: blinkered/ tongue tied final outing. *W. A. Murphy, Ireland*

CRESKELD (IRE) 4 b.g. Sri Pekan (USA) 117 – Pizzazz 47 (Unfuwain (USA) 131) **87** [2003 75, a87: f8.5g* f8.5s² 8g 8.3d 7.5m 8.5d⁶ 7.5m⁴ 8.2g⁵ 7.9m³ 7.5d* 7g 7d Nov 4] **a96**

sparely-made gelding: useful handicapper on all-weather, fairly useful on turf: won at Wolverhampton (by length from Marlo) in February and Beverley (by 3½ lengths from Qualitair Wings) in September: well held last 2 starts: stays 8.5f: acts on all-weather, soft and good to firm going. *B. Smart*

CRESSEX KATIE 4 b.f. Komaite (USA) – Kakisa 81 (Forlorn River 124) [2003 61: f6g² p6g f5s p7g 6m* 5.7m* 5.7g* 6m 6m⁶ 5.7f⁴ f6s f5g Dec 12] fair handicapper on turf, modest on all-weather: much improved when winning at Brighton and Bath (twice, beat Blackheath ¾ length latter occasion) in May: below form after, leaving J. Cullinan prior to final start (left off): best around 6f: acts on soft going, good to firm and all-weather: sometimes slowly away. *J. R. Best* **76 a61**

CRESTA DANCE 3 ch.f. Hector Protector (USA) 124 – Red Hot Dancer (USA) (Seattle Dancer (USA) 119) [2003 12m⁵ 12g⁴ 18f⁵ Jul 19] 7,500Y: fourth foal: half-sister to winner in USA by Technology: dam, placed in USA, half-sister to dam of Poule d'Essai des Pouliches winner Ta Rib: modest form in maidens: should stay beyond 1½m (seemed not to stay 2¼m). *Mrs Lydia Pearce* **53**

CRETAN GIFT 12 ch.g. Cadeaux Genereux 131 – Caro's Niece (USA) 86 (Caro 133) [2003 6s p6g⁵ f5g p6g Dec 20] lengthy gelding: smart at best: missed 2002: fairly useful at 12 yrs: stays 7f: acts on all-weather, firm and soft going: visored/blinkered: tends to start slowly/get behind. *N. P. Littmoden* **85**

CREWES MISS ISLE 2 b.f. (Mar 2) Makbul 104 – Riviere Rouge (Forzando 122) [2003 f5g⁴ 5f⁵ 5g² 6m* 6f⁵ 7g⁶ 6f⁴ 6m² f6g Nov 10] 5,000Y: smallish filly: fourth foal: half-sister to winner in Italy by Weldnaas: dam, ran 4 times, out of half-sister to smart performer up to 1½m Florid: fair performer: won seller at Thirsk in June, then left K. Ryan: left J. Harris after running creditably penultimate start: stays 6f: acts on firm going and fibresand. *A. G. Newcombe* **75**

CRIMSON DANCER 3 b.f. Groom Dancer (USA) 128 – Crimson Rosella 54 (Polar Falcon (USA) 126) [2003 –: 8m 8.5s* 8.5g* 10m⁴ 10g⁵ f9.4f² f12g² 10m* 10m⁶ 10g* 10m³ Oct 14] quite good-topped filly: fairly useful handicapper: won at Wolverhampton (2) in May, Leicester in September and Windsor in October: barely stays 1½m: acts on fibresand and good to firm ground: sometimes slowly away/raced freely: held up: sold 27,000 gns, joined Miss S. Wilton. *W. J. Haggas* **84**

CRIMSON SILK 3 ch.g. Forzando 122 – Sylhall (Sharpo 132) [2003 101: 6g³ 6.1m 6d⁶ 6d³ Nov 8] sturdy gelding: useful performer: best efforts when third in minor event at Haydock (to Somnus) and listed race at Doncaster (3½ lengths behind Steenberg): raced around 6f: acts on good to firm and good to soft going: seemed not to handle course at Chester second outing. *D. Haydn Jones* **103**

CRIMSON TOPAZ 3 b.f. Hernando (FR) 127 – Bronzewing 103 (Beldale Flutter (USA) 130) [2003 10g⁶ 11.1d* May 9] tall, unfurnished filly: half-sister to several winners, including smart 7f (at 2 yrs) and 1¼m winner Merry Merlin (by Polar Falcon) and 4-y-o Dusky Warbler: dam 6f and 1m winner: won maiden at Hamilton (swished tail) in May: should stay 1½m. *M. L. W. Bell* **75**

CRIPSEY BROOK 5 ch.g. Lycius (USA) 124 – Duwon (IRE) 55 (Polish Precedent (USA) 131) [2003 71: 10.1m* 10.1m² 10m* 10.1m* 10.5m* 10.1d⁶ 10.3m⁵ 10.5m* 10g* 10.3d³ 10m³ 10.4f Oct 10] tall gelding: progressed into useful performer at 5 yrs, winning claimer at Newcastle in May, handicap at Nottingham and minor event at Newcastle in June, and handicaps at Haydock (2) and Ripon (beat Prairie Wolf 1½ lengths) in July/August: stays 10.5f: acts on firm and good to soft going: free-going sort: tough and genuine. *Don Enrico Incisa* **95**

CRISPIN GIRL (IRE) 2 ch.f. (Mar 3) General Monash (USA) 107 – Penultimate Cress (IRE) (My Generation 111) [2003 6.1d 6g⁴ 6m 6d⁵ f7g 6g 5g 5.1d p5g p6g Dec 20] €8,000Y: smallish filly: fifth foal: sister to 5f (at 2 yrs) to 1m winner Dancing Penny and fairly useful 2002 2-y-o 6f to 1m winner Rutters Renegade: dam unraced: modest maiden: stays 6f: acts on polytrack and good to soft ground. *J. L. Spearing* **57**

CRISPIN HOUSE 3 b.f. Inchinor 119 – Ayr Classic 74 (Local Suitor (USA) 128) [2003 8.2g f12g 6g 6m 10.9m Jun 22] 3,000Y, £500 2-y-o: half-sister to 3 winners, including 1999 2-y-o 5f winner Able Ayr (by Formidable) and 7f to 8.5f winner (including 1m winner at 2 yrs) People Direct (by Ron's Victory): dam 2-y-o 5f/6f winner: no form. *R. J. Price* **–**

CRITICAL STAGE (IRE) 4 b.g. King's Theatre (IRE) 128 – Zandaka (FR) (Doyoun 124) [2003 62: p10g f11g* f11s* f12s² f11s³ f12g³ 13.8m⁵ 13d 16.2m 10.3d 9g³ 10d³ f8g⁵ Dec 12] sturdy gelding: fair handicapper: won at Southwell in January and February: **69 a74**

stays 1½m: acts on fibresand, good to firm and good to soft ground: usually held up. *John Berry*

CROCIERA (IRE)   2 b.c. (Apr 21) Croco Rouge (IRE) 126 – Ombry Girl (IRE)   **– p**
(Distinctly North (USA) 115) [2003 8m 7g Nov 1] IR 10,000F, 15,000Y: lengthy, good-topped colt: first foal: dam, Italian 7f to 1¼m winner, out of half-sister to smart performer up to 7f Superlative: signs of a little ability in Newmarket maidens: likely to do better at 1¼m/1½m. *M. H. Tompkins*

CROCODILE DUNDEE (IRE)   2 b.c. (Mar 26) Croco Rouge (IRE) 126 – Miss   **90**
Salsa Dancer 64 (Salse (USA) 128) [2003 p7g* 7g p7g⁵ Nov 29] 30,000F, €35,000 2-y-o: sturdy, close-coupled colt: second foal: dam, 1m winner, out of close relation to Norfolk Stakes winner Magic Mirror: fairly useful form: won maiden at Lingfield in October by 1½ lengths from Benny The Ball: last of 9 in Horris Hill Stakes at Newbury following week, better effort after: should stay at least 1¼m: sent to France. *Jamie Poulton*

CROESO CROESO   5 b.m. Most Welcome 131 – Croeso-I-Cymru 96 (Welsh Captain   **100**
113) [2003 100: 5.1m* 5g⁶ 6f⁴ 6m 5d⁴ 6.1m⁴ 5m 5g Sep 1] sturdy, deep-bodied mare: useful performer: won listed race at Bath in April by head from Dragon Flyer: mostly creditable efforts in handicaps/listed races after: effective at 5f/6f: acts on firm and good to soft going: sometimes early to post/starts slowly: held up: genuine. *J. L. Spearing*

CROIX DE GUERRE (IRE)   3 gr.g. Highest Honor (FR) 124 – Esclava (USA)   **59 §**
(Nureyev (USA) 131) [2003 7g 8m p10g 10m* 10f⁵ 12m⁵ 12f³ 10m² Oct 2] IR 120,000Y: tall gelding: fifth foal: half-brother to 3 winners in Japan: dam, third in France at 1¼m, daughter of Prix de Diane winner Escaline: modest handicapper: won at Brighton in July: stays easy 1½m: raced only on good ground or firmer on turf: tried blinkered: wayward: sold 18,000 gns. *Sir Mark Prescott*

CROSBY DONJOHN   6 ch.g. Magic Ring (IRE) 115 – Ovideo 58 (Domynsky 110)   **44 §**
[2003 52§: f8s 8m 10.1m⁵ 9.2g 9f 8f 9.2g 8m 9.2g 9f⁵ 10m⁴ Sep 25] good-bodied gelding: has a round action: poor performer: stays 1¼m: acts on firm going, good to soft and fibresand: wears blinkers/cheekpieces: unreliable. *J. R. Weymes*

CROSBY JUBILEE (IRE)   2 b.g. (Feb 4) Shinko Forest (IRE) – Quicksand (IRE)   **–**
(Lycius (USA) 124) [2003 6m Oct 1] neat gelding: first foal: dam ran twice (once in a bumper) in Ireland: 50/1, last of 15 in maiden at Newcastle, slowly away. *J. R. Weymes*

CROSBY ROCKER   5 b.m. Rock Hopper 124 – Mary Macblain 49 (Damister (USA)   **–**
123) [2003 11.8m⁶ 8g 8g 11m 7m Sep 9] of little account: tried in cheekpieces. *John A. Harris*

CROSS ASH (IRE)   3 ch.g. Ashkalani (IRE) 128 – Priorite (IRE) 85 (Kenmare (FR)   **81**
125) [2003 6f 7.1f⁵ 7f* 7m 7d Sep 11] IR 8,000Y: strong, workmanlike gelding: second foal: dam lightly-raced Irish 2-y-o 7f winner: fairly useful performer: won maiden at Catterick in May: should stay 1m: acts on firm ground. *R. Hollinshead*

CROSSED WIRE   5 ch.m. Lycius (USA) 124 – Maze Garden (USA) (Riverman   **–**
(USA) 131) [2003 77: 12m p16g 16g f14g Nov 24] fair handicapper in 2002: well held at 5 yrs: tried visored. *Miss J. Feilden*

CROWN AGENT (IRE)   3 b.g. Mukaddamah (USA) 125 – Supreme Crown (USA)   **78**
(Chief's Crown (USA)) [2003 67: 10g 11.6g 12.6m² 11.6s² 11.8m May 27] fair maiden handicapper: stumbled and unseated rider final outing: stays 12.6f: acts on soft and good to firm going. *A. M. Balding*

CROWN CITY (USA)   3 b.f. Coronado's Quest (USA) 130 – Trisha Brown (USA)   **56**
(Theatrical 128) [2003 –p: 7m 7g⁶ 6g 8.1m⁶ f8.5g 8m Oct 12] sturdy filly: modest maiden: left M. Jarvis after third start: stays 1m: acts on good to firm ground: tongue tied last 3 outings. *B. P. J. Baugh*

CROWN COUNSEL   3 b.c. Machiavellian (USA) 123 – Confidante (USA) 95 (Dayjur   **91**
(USA) 137) [2003 85p: 7m* 7g⁴ Apr 15] strong, close-coupled colt: fairly useful form: won maiden at Folkestone in April: good fourth in handicap at Newmarket: would have stayed 1m: dead. *Mrs A. J. Perrett*

CROWNFIELD   4 b.g. Blushing Flame (USA) 109 – Chief Island 62 (Be My Chief   **80**
(USA) 122) [2003 14.1m* May 26] tall, leggy gelding: fairly useful form: missed 2002: improved effort when winning handicap at Redcar only start on Flat in 2003, beating Joely Green a length: stays 1¾m: raced only on ground firmer than good. *Mrs M. Reveley*

CROW WOOD   4 b.g. Halling 133 – Play With Me (IRE) 73 (Alzao (USA) 117)   **98**
[2003 80: 10.3m* 10m³ 10.5m* 8.9f 10g* 10.1g³ 10m 10g⁵ Oct 11] strong, close-coupled

gelding: useful performer: better than ever at 4 yrs, winning handicaps at Doncaster in May and Haydock in June, and minor event at Ayr (beat Wunderwood 2½ lengths) in August: stays 10.5f: acts on fibresand, soft and firm going: sometimes races freely: hung right last 2 starts: usually ridden prominently. *J. G. Given*

CROZON 3 ch.f. Peintre Celebre (USA) 137 – Armorique (IRE) (Top Ville 129) [2003 **68** 10.2f* 10g Oct 12] sixth foal: half-sister to useful 6f (at 2 yrs) to 7.5f winner (including in Italy) Darwin and fairly useful 7f winner Camaret (both by Danehill): dam, French 1½m winner, half-sister to several good middle-distance performers out of Irish 1000 Guineas winner Arctique Royale: easily better effort (fair form) when winning 4-runner maiden at Bath in September: should stay 1½m. *J. H. M. Gosden*

CRUISE DIRECTOR 3 b.g. Zilzal (USA) 137 – Briggsmaid 70 (Elegant Air 119) **88 +** [2003 68: p7g⁵ p8g* p8g³ p10g² 10.3g² 11.6d* p10g Nov 13] heavy-topped gelding: progressed into fairly useful handicapper in first half of 2003, winning at Lingfield in February and Windsor in April: stays 11.6f: acts on polytrack, raced only on good/good to soft going on turf. *W. J. Musson*

CRUNCHY (IRE) 5 ch.g. Common Grounds 118 – Credit Crunch (IRE) 51 (Caerleon – (USA) 132) [2003 51: f11g* f12g⁵ f11s* f11g³ 10.5m f11g Nov 25] fair handicapper on **a77** all-weather, modest on turf: won at Southwell in January (amateur event) and February: ran as if amiss last 2 starts (reportedly had breathing problem penultimate one): stays 11f: acts on fibresand, good to firm and soft going: tongue tied. *B. Ellison*

CRUSOE (IRE) 6 b.g. Turtle Island (IRE) 123 – Self Reliance 72 (Never So Bold – 135) [2003 73d: f8s² f7s* f8g f7s f7g⁶ f7g⁵ f7g³ f8.5s* f8.5g f7g³ f8g* f8.5g f9.4g⁴ f9.4s² **a76** f8g* f8.5g f8g³ f8g f8.5g* 8.3m f7g⁵ f9.4f³ f8.5g⁵ f11g f8g⁴ f9.4s⁴ f8g Dec 12] small gelding: fair performer: won maiden/claimer/handicap at Southwell and 2 handicaps at Wolverhampton (amateur event latterly) in first half of 2003: stays 9.4f: acts on soft ground and fibresand: tried in cheekpieces, often blinkered: none too consistent. *A. Sadik*

CRUSTY LILY 7 gr.m. Whittingham (IRE) 104 – Miss Crusty 45 (Belfort (FR) 89) – [2003 46: f5s f6s 5m 5m 5.7m 6g May 16] smallish, lengthy mare: well held in 2003. *P. D. Evans*

CRUZSPIEL 3 br.c. Singspiel (IRE) 133 – Allespagne (USA) (Trempolino (USA) 135) **106** [2003 10g 10m* 12.3m⁴ 12d⁴ 16.2f³ 14g³ 14m* 15d⁶ Oct 4] 80,000Y: quite good-topped colt: third foal: half-brother to 1½m winner Larousse (by Unfuwain): dam useful French 1½m/1¾m winner: useful performer: won handicaps at Leopardstown in April and listed race at Fairyhouse (made most and held on gamely to beat Golly Gosh a short head) in August: better effort in Britain when 1½ lengths third to Shanty Star in Queen's Vase at Royal Ascot fifth start: possibly something amiss when last in Prix Hubert de Chaudenay at Longchamp final outing: stays 2m: acts on firm and good to soft going: blinkered 4 of last 5 starts: genuine. *J. Oxx, Ireland*

CRYFIELD 6 b.g. Efisio 120 – Ciboure 74 (Norwick (USA) 125) [2003 74: 8.2g 8m⁴ **76** 8m⁵ 8m* 7.5m⁶ 7g⁶ 8.3g³ 7.5m 7m⁶ 7.5d f8s⁵ Oct 21] good-bodied gelding: fair handicapper: won at Leicester in June: mostly respectable efforts after: stays 8.5f: acts on any turf going and fibresand: sometimes visored prior to 2003: free-going sort. *N. Tinkler*

CRYPTOGAM 3 b.f. Zamindar (USA) 116 – Moss (Alzao (USA) 117) [2003 73p: **69 d** 8.1m² 8g 8m 7.1m 12.1m 10f⁴ 10.1m⁴ 8.2m Oct 28] smallish filly: fair maiden: left Mrs A. Perrett after second start: well beaten after: should stay 1¼m: raced only on good ground or firmer. *M. E. Sowersby*

CRYSTAL CASTLE (USA) 5 b.g. Gilded Time (USA) – Wayage (USA) (Mr Pros- **107** pector (USA)) [2003 120: a6f⁴ a6f 6s³ 6f 6s Oct 31] good-topped gelding: very smart performer in 2002: just useful form at 5 yrs, fourth to Conroy in Group 3 event at Nad Al Sheba on reappearance and (after sustaining injury) third to Blanche in Prix de Meautry at Deauville third start: only tenth when attempting repeat win in Diadem Stakes at Ascot next outing: effective at 6f/7f: acts on soft and good to firm going. *J. E. Hammond, France*

CRYSTAL CHOIR 3 b.f. Singspiel (IRE) 133 – Crystal Ring (IRE) 83 (Kris 135) – [2003 10s Nov 3] 50,000Y: rangy filly: eighth foal: half-sister to several winners, including useful 1m/1¼m winner Lizzey Letti (by Grand Lodge) and smart German 1¼m/1½m performer Catella (by Generous): dam, untrustworthy 1m winner, half-sister to Diamond Shoal and Glint of Gold: 7/1, well beaten in maiden at Redcar. *R. Charlton*

CRYSTAL COLLEEN (IRE) 3 gr.f. Desert King (IRE) 129 – Silver Kristal 81 **42** (Kris 135) [2003 57: f8g³ f8s⁵ 6.9f⁵ 8m⁴ 9m⁶ 8s 8m Aug 6] small filly: poor maiden: barely stays 1m: acts on fibresand, firm and soft going: free-going sort. *R. Guest*

246

CRYSTAL CURLING (IRE)   2 ch.f. (Apr 30) Peintre Celebre (USA) 137 – State **88 p**
Crystal (IRE) 114 (High Estate 127) [2003 6.1f^2 7s* Oct 29] quite attractive filly: fifth
living foal: half-sister to fairly useful 1¼m winner True Crystal (by Sadler's Wells) and
3-y-o Time Crystal: dam, 7f (at 2 yrs) and 1½m (Lancashire Oaks) winner, half-sister to
Fillies' Mile winner Crystal Music and smart middle-distance stayer Tchaikovsky: better
effort in maidens (fairly useful form) when winning at Yarmouth comfortably by 3
lengths from Flamboyant Lad, quite free before leading over 2f out: bred to stay at least
1½m: unimpressive to post and bandaged off-hind joint on debut: open to further
improvement. *B. W. Hills*

CRYSTAL (IRE)   2 b.f. (Apr 28) Danehill (USA) 126 – Solar Crystal (IRE) 110 (Alzao **85 p**
(USA) 117) [2003 8g Nov 1] 475,000Y: well-made filly: fourth foal: half-sister to useful
2000 2-y-o 7f winner Lunar Crystal (by Shirley Heights): dam, 2-y-o 6f and 1m (May
Hill) winner who should have stayed 1½m, half-sister to Fillies' Mile winner Crystal
Music and smart middle-distance stayer Tchaikovsky: 25/1, 7½ lengths eighth of 12 to
Spotlight in listed event at Newmarket, green but staying on: should stay 1¼m: open to
improvement. *B. J. Meehan*

CRYSTAL SEAS   3 ch.f. Zamindar (USA) 116 – Abi 84 (Chief's Crown (USA)) **47**
[2003 7d 8m^4 f7g^6 10m^5 7m Oct 17] first foal: dam, 1¼m winner, closely related to smart
German miler Royal Dragon: poor maiden: left E. Dunlop 6,500 gns after debut: stays
1m: acts on good to firm ground. *M. W. Easterby*

CRYSTAL STAR   3 ch.f. Mark of Esteem (IRE) 137 – Crystal Cavern (USA) 89 (Be **100**
My Guest (USA) 126) [2003 99p: 7m^2 8g 7g 7d Sep 11] close-coupled, sparely-made
filly: useful performer: 1¼ lengths second to Tante Rose in Dubai Duty Free Stakes (Fred
Darling) at Newbury: well held in Poule d'Essai des Pouliches at Longchamp and 2 listed
events after: should stay 1m: acts on firm and soft ground: tail swisher. *Sir Michael Stoute*

CRYSTAL THEATRE (IRE)   3 b.f. King's Theatre (IRE) 128 – Solar Crystal (IRE) **72**
110 (Alzao (USA) 117) [2003 10d^2 10.2m^4 12.3g^2 p12g Sep 9] close-coupled filly: third
foal: half-sister to useful 2000 2-y-o 7f winner Lunar Crystal (by Shirley Heights): dam,
2-y-o 6f and 1m (May Hill) winner who should have stayed 1½m, half-sister to Fillies'
Mile winner Crystal Music and smart middle-distance stayer Tchaikovsky: fair maiden:
best effort when short-headed by Desert Quest at Windsor on debut: stays 1½m: acts
on good to soft going, took strong hold when well beaten on polytrack final start.
H. R. A. Cecil

CTESIPHON (USA)   2 b.f. (Mar 27) Arch (USA) 127 – Beautiful Bedouin (USA) **55**
(His Majesty (USA)) [2003 7s f9.4g^3 Dec 22] quite good-topped filly: half-sister to
several winners, notably smart 1m/1¼m winner Wandering Star (by Red Ransom): dam
unraced half-sister to Silver Hawk: modest form in maidens: third at Wolverhampton:
likely to be suited by 1¼m/1½m. *J. G. Given*

CUBAPESKY   3 b.f. Fleetwood (IRE) 107 – Robert's Daughter (Robellino (USA) **–**
127) [2003 –: f8g Jan 4] little worthwhile form: visored only 3-y-o start. *E. J. O'Neill*

CUCHI   3 b.f. Danzig Connection (USA) – Classic Faster (IRE) (Running Steps (USA) **–**
79) [2003 –: p5g 5m 5.1m 5.3m 5.7f 8f Oct 17] no sign of ability. *K. O. Cunningham-
Brown*

CUDDLES (FR)   4 b.f. Anabaa (USA) 130 – Palomelle (FR) 112 (Moulin 103) [2003 **78**
73, a92: p8g p12g 9m^6 9.9m 9f^3 p10g^5 10.2d^4 9d^3 10f^3 8.3g^4 10g^5 10s Nov 3] leggy filly: **a87**
fairly useful on all-weather, fair on turf: stays 1¼m: acts on any turf going and polytrack:
sometimes in visor/cheekpieces: none too genuine. *C. E. Brittain*

CULCABOCK (IRE)   3 b.g. Unfuwain (USA) 131 – Evidently (IRE) (Slip Anchor **57**
136) [2003 73p: 11f 6.5f 12g^6 11g^2 12.4m^5 9.2g^6 10.9d Oct 13] IR 2,600Y: first foal: dam
1¼m winner in France, from family of Shiva and Limnos: fair form when winning
maiden at Bellewstown latter 2-y-o outing: left J. Crowley, Ireland, after fourth 3-y-o
start: below form in seller/claimers after: stays 11f: form only on good/good to firm
going: won over hurdles in November. *P. Monteith*

CULMINATE   6 ch.g. Afzal 83 – Straw Blade 66 (Final Straw 127) [2003 –: 7g^6 10m **–**
10m 8.1g 7.1m Sep 22] of little account. *J. E. Long*

CUMBRIAN CRYSTAL   4 b.f. Mind Games 121 – Crystal Sand (GER) (Forzando **–**
122) [2003 –: 6.1g 6f 6m 7m May 10] unfurnished filly: modest maiden, lightly raced:
should stay 7f: acts on soft going: tried blinkered. *T. D. Easterby*

CUMBRIAN PRINCESS   6 gr.m. Mtoto 134 – Cumbrian Melody 83 (Petong 126) **36**
[2003 63: f9.4g f6g 7.1m 8g 7m f8g f8g^5 Dec 19] leggy, sparely-made mare: poor

handicapper: stays 9.4f: acts on fibresand, soft and good to firm going: tried blinkered: none too reliable. *M. Blanshard*

CUMWHITTON   4 b.f. Jumbo Hirt (USA) 90§ – Dominance (Dominion 123) [2003 16m⁶ 18m Oct 20] leggy filly: no sign of ability. *R. A. Fahey*   –

CUPOLA   2 b.c. (Mar 16) Fasliyev (USA) 120 – Spring Mood (FR) (Nashwan (USA) 135) [2003 5g⁴ 6m³ 5m² 5f⁴ a8f³ a6f* Dec 26] 15,000Y: well-grown, lengthy colt: first foal: dam unraced out of half-sister to very smart French 1¼m performer Gunboat Diplomacy: fairly useful performer: left P. D'Arcy and off 6 months after fourth start (visored): won maiden at Jebel Ali in December: stays 6f: acts on dirt and firm going: tends to race freely. *M. Al Kurdi, UAE*   88

CURATE (USA)   4 ch.g. Unfuwain (USA) 131 – Carniola 104 (Rainbow Quest (USA) 134) [2003 f16g f12g f12s f8g 12.3m⁴ 12.4m 10m⁴ 10.1m May 14] leggy, quite good-topped gelding: poor maiden: stays 12.4f: acts on good to firm ground: often tongue tied. *J. Parkes*   49

CURFEW   4 b.f. Marju (IRE) 127 – Twilight Patrol 96 (Robellino (USA) 127) [2003 101: 7m⁵ 6f 5f⁵ Jul 12] useful handicapper: good close fifth to Strathclyde at Ascot final start, slowly away: effective at 5f to 7f: acts on firm going: tried tongue tied: free-going sort (has been early and quietly to post): held up. *J. R. Fanshawe*   102

CURLEW RIVER (IRE)   3 b.g. Alhaarth (IRE) 126 – Sudden Interest (FR) (Highest Honor (FR) 124) [2003 –: 10.3m⁶ 10g² 9m² 12g 12g* 12s⁵ 11.6m Sep 29] workmanlike gelding: fairly useful performer: won maiden at Kempton in July: good fifth to Adopted Hero in handicap at Ascot next time: pulled up amiss final start: stays 1½m: acts on soft and good to firm ground. *D. R. C. Elsworth*   84

CURRAGH GOLD (IRE)   3 b.f. Flying Spur (AUS) – Go Indigo (IRE) 67 (Cyrano de Bergerac 120) [2003 60: p10g f7s⁶ f7s* f7g³ 8.3g f11s Sep 26] IR 6,000Y: fourth foal: half-sister to fairly useful 7f (at 2 yrs) and 1¾m winner Estival Park (by Elbio): dam Irish 5f winner: modest performer: trained by K. Prendergast in Ireland in 2002: won seller at Southwell in February, idling: should stay 1m: acts on fibresand: sometimes blinkered, tried in cheekpieces. *Mrs P. N. Dutfield*   52

CURRENCY   6 b.g. Sri Pekan (USA) 117 – On Tiptoes 107 (Shareef Dancer (USA) 135) [2003 90: 5f* 6g 6d 6f 6g 6g⁵ 6m 6m³ 6m⁶ 6m 5f⁶ p6g⁶ 5d f6g Nov 17] sturdy gelding: fairly useful handicapper: reportedly split a cannon bone in 2002: won at Salisbury in June: effective at 5f/6f: best on good going or firmer: has been heavily bandaged in front: none too consistent. *J. M. Bradley*   85

CURZON LODGE (IRE)   3 ch.g. Grand Lodge (USA) 125 – Curzon Street 70 (Night Shift (USA)) [2003 7g May 9] second foal: dam, maiden who stayed 1½m (not one to trust implicitly), sister to high-class 1m to 1½m winner In The Groove: well held in maiden at Lingfield. *A. J. Lidderdale*   –

CUSCO (IRE)   2 ch.f. (Feb 14) Titus Livius (FR) 115 – John's Ballad (IRE) (Ballad Rock 122) [2003 7g³ 8.1m* 7m³ 7m 8g⁵ Nov 1] IR 5,000F, €42,000Y: sturdy, close-coupled filly: fifth foal: half-sister to 6-y-o Peruvian Chief and Irish 5f winner Black Paddy (by Mujadil): dam unraced out of half-sister to Dewhurst winner Monteverdi: fairly useful performer: won maiden at Sandown in August by 6 lengths: good third to Silk Fan in minor event at Newbury next time: respectable efforts in listed events last 2 starts: not sure to stay beyond 1m. *R. Hannon*   91

CUSIN   7 ch.g. Arazi (USA) 135 – Fairy Tern 109 (Mill Reef (USA) 141) [2003 10m Jun 20] close-coupled, angular gelding: has a short action: fair performer at best: missed 2002: well held in claimer only 7-y-o outing: blinkered once, tongue tied last 8 starts. *M. E. Sowersby*   –

CUSP   3 b.f. Pivotal 124 – Bambolona 108 (Bustino 136) [2003 9.2d 12g 12.4g³ 16.1m Oct 1] tall, unfurnished filly: half-sister to several winners, including fairly useful 6f to 9f winner Miss Haggis and winner around 1¼m Scottish Bambi (both by Scottish Reel): dam 2-y-o 6f winner: well beaten in maidens/handicap. *C. W. Thornton*   –

CUT AND DRIED   2 ch.g. (Jan 19) Daggers Drawn (USA) 114 – Apple Sauce 70 (Prince Sabo 123) [2003 5f⁴ p5g⁶ 5d⁶ 6m 5g Sep 27] 34,000Y: sturdy gelding: first foal: dam, 5f winner, half-sister to smart sprinter Sizzling Melody: modest maiden: will prove best at 5f/6f: acts on firm ground and polytrack: tends to race freely. *W. Jarvis*   60

CUTE CAIT   2 b.f. (Apr 28) Atraf 116 – Clunk Click 72 (Star Appeal 133) [2003 5d⁶ 5m² 6m* 7.1m³ 7.5d⁵ 6g 7m 8f Aug 22] 2,500Y: close-coupled filly: half-sister to numerous winners, including French 1990 2-y-o 6f winner Touch And Love (by Green Desert) and 6f (at 2 yrs)/7f winner Crazy Paving (by Danehill), both useful: dam, maiden, stayed   53

1½m: modest performer: won seller at Haydock in June: stays 6f: acts on good to firm going: none too consistent. *Mrs L. Stubbs*

CUT RATE (USA) 5 ch.g. Diesis 133 – Itsamazing (USA) 85 (The Minstrel (CAN) 135) [2003 80: p10g p8g² p8g 8.1g³ p8g⁴ p8g p8g Jul 2] quite good-topped gelding: fair performer: effective at 1m to 1½m: acts on all-weather and good to soft going: tried tongue tied: inconsistent: sold 3,500 gns. *K. Bell*   **73 §**

CUT RIDGE (IRE) 4 b.f. Indian Ridge 123 – Cutting Ground (IRE) 85 (Common Grounds 118) [2003 60: 6m 6m 6m 5d 5g⁴ 5d³ 6m⁴ 6m* 5m⁵ 5m 7d² 6m Oct 13] lengthy filly: modest performer: won maiden handicap at Ripon in July: stays 7f: acts on good to firm and good to soft going: tried in cheekpieces: none too consistent. *J. S. Wainwright*   **57**

CUTTING CREW (USA) 2 ch.c. (Mar 10) Diesis 133 – Poppy Carew (IRE) 110 (Danehill (USA) 126) [2003 7.1m⁴ 8d p8g² Oct 15] rather unfurnished colt: third foal: half-brother to 1m/1¼m winner Mad Carew (by Rahy): dam 7f (at 2 yrs) to 1½m winner: fairly useful form when fourth of 6 in minor event at Sandown: below that level in maidens at Doncaster and Lingfield (edged right): should stay at least 1m. *P. W. Harris*   **88**

CYBER CINDERS 3 ch.f. Cayman Kai (IRE) 114 – Petticoat Rule (Stanford 121§) [2003 52: 5g 5g 5g Nov 5] modest maiden at 2 yrs: refused to race last 2 outings in 2003, in blinkers final one: banned from racing on Flat and over jumps. *Miss L. A. Perratt*   **§§**

CYCLONE CONNIE 5 ch.m. Dr Devious (IRE) 127 – Cutpurse Moll 76 (Green Desert (USA) 127) [2003 92: 6m 5.1m Apr 29] smallish, sturdy mare: unimpressive mover: fairly useful performer at best: well held both 5-y-o starts (reportedly bled from nose on latter). *C. A. Cyzer*   **–**

CYCLONIC STORM 4 b.f. Catrail (USA) 123 – Wheeler's Wonder (IRE) 43 (Sure Blade (USA) 130) [2003 76: 8.3d² 9m 9.2g* 9.3f² 9.2g³ 10m 10.3g 10.5d 10g Oct 28] rather leggy filly: fair handicapper: won at Hamilton in June: should stay 1¼m: acts on firm and soft going: wore cheekpieces last 3 starts. *R. A. Fahey*   **78**

CYFRWYS (IRE) 2 b.f. (Mar 4) Foxhound (USA) 103 – Divine Elegance (IRE) (College Chapel 122) [2003 5.7m⁴ 6d² 6m⁵ 6g² p7g⁴ Oct 30] IR 1,600F: close-coupled filly: third foal: half-sister to 1m winner in Spain by Petardia: dam unraced: fairly useful maiden: second at Leicester and Windsor: will need to settle to stay 7f: acts on good to soft going, showed up well long way but reportedly finished lame on polytrack. *B. Palling*   **80**

CZARINA WALTZ 4 b.f. Emperor Jones (USA) 119 – Ballerina Bay 75 (Myjinski (USA)) [2003 75, a83: 10d² 10d³ 10.3m* 9g³ 10m⁵ p10g* 9m 10.1s⁴ p10g Nov 22] good-topped filly: useful performer: better than ever at 4 yrs, winning handicaps in May and July (slowly away, beat Anyhow 2 lengths), both at Lingfield: best around 1¼m: acts on polytrack and good to firm going, probably on soft: tends to race freely: sometimes slowly away: waited with. *C. F. Wall*   **96**

CZARS PRINCESS (IRE) 2 b.f. (May 6) Soviet Star (USA) 128 – Pearl Shell (USA) (Bering 136) [2003 6f 6m 7m p7g Nov 18] €10,000Y, 4,500 2-y-o: tall, leggy filly: fourth foal: half-sister to useful 7f winner Pearly Gates and 3-y-o Oysterfed (both by Night Shift): dam, French 1½m winner, out of top-class middle-distance performer Paulista: modest maiden: races freely, and barely stays 7f. *G. L. Moore*   **51**

CZAR WARS 8 b.g. Warrshan (USA) 117 – Dutch Czarina 45 (Prince Sabo 123) [2003 72d, a81d: f6g³ f5g³ f7s² f7g³ f6g* f6g⁶ f6g* f6s⁵ f6g³ 7m f6g 6d³ f5s* 6g f6g⁵ f6g* f6s² f6s* f6s³ f6s Oct 21] sturdy gelding: fair on all-weather, modest on turf: won minor event and handicap at Southwell in January/February, sellers at Wolverhampton in June/August, and handicap at Wolverhampton in September: effective at 5f, barely at 7f: acts on fibresand, firm and soft going: tried tongue tied/in cheekpieces, usually blinkered: sometimes drifts left. *J. Balding*   **62 a74**

D

DABUS 8 b.g. Kris 135 – Licorne 93 (Sadler's Wells (USA) 132) [2003 45: 12m 12f 10s⁶ 11.6m 12m⁶ 10m Sep 18] small, stocky gelding: useful at 3 yrs: just poor since and well held at 8 yrs. *M. C. Chapman*   **–**

D'ACCORD 6 ch.g. Beveled (USA) – National Time (USA) (Lord Avie (USA)) [2003 70, a77: f6s p6g³ 5m 6.1m* 6m 6m* May 29] tall gelding: fairly useful handicapper: won at Nottingham (apprentices) and Goodwood in May: best at 5f/6f: below form on firm going, acts on any other turf/all-weather: tried visored/blinkered earlier in career: often races prominently: sometimes wanders. *S. Kirk*   **74**

DAFFODIL GIRL 4 ch.f. Vettori (IRE) 119 – Top Treat (USA) 101 (Topsider (USA))   –
[2003 –: f8.5g Feb 15] plain filly: modest maiden at 2 yrs: no form since: tried in blinkers/
cheekpieces. *B. Palling*

DAFFODILLY 2 ch.f. (Apr 3) Dr Fong (USA) 128 – Daffodil Fields (Try My Best   **64**
(USA) 130) [2003 5s⁶ 6m 6m 7g⁵ Sep 16] neat filly: half-sister to several winners, including 3-y-o Naahy: dam, Irish maiden, from family of Environment Friend: modest maiden:
still green when fifth in nursery: stays 7f: acts on good to firm ground. *M. A. Jarvis*

DAGGERS CANYON 2 ch.g. (May 19) Daggers Drawn (USA) 114 – Chipewyas   **63**
(FR) (Bering 136) [2003 7d p8g⁵ f7g⁴ f7s Dec 31] second foal: dam unraced: modest
maiden: stays easy 1m: pulled hard second start, possibly amiss final one. *Julian Poulton*

DAGOLA (IRE) 2 b.g. (May 13) Daggers Drawn (USA) 114 – Diabola (USA) (Devil's   **53**
Bag (USA)) [2003 5d 6m 6.1m 7m Oct 3] IR 12,000F, €18,000Y: fifth foal: half-brother
to 3 winners, including fairly useful Irish 7f/1m winner Silverware (by Mukaddamah):
dam, French 9f and 11f winner, half-sister to Poule d'Essai des Poulains runner-up Noble
Minstrel: modest maiden: should stay 7f. *C. G. Cox*

DAHLIDYA 8 b.m. Midyan (USA) 124 – Dahlawise (IRE) 76 (Caerleon (USA) 132)   –
[2003 –, a48: f6s⁵ f6g³ f7s⁶ f8g f7s Feb 20] angular mare: poor handicapper: best at 6f/7f: **a45 §**
acts on fibresand, good to firm and good to soft going: tried blinkered: often very slowly
away: unreliable. *R. Wilman*

DAI JIN 3 b.c. Peintre Celebre (USA) 137 – Dawlah 91 (Shirley Heights 130)   **123**
[2003 8.5d² 11g² 11g* 12d* 12g* 12s Oct 5]

Andreas Schutz failed in his bid to train the first, second and third in the
Deutsches Derby for the third time in the past four seasons, though he still saddled
four of the first five home! Samum and Next Desert, who led home a clean sweep
of the placings for Schutz in 2000 and 2002 respectively, had suffered only one
defeat between them in their build-up to the race, and both justified favouritism in
clear-cut style. Dai Jin, on the other hand, had lost more races than he won prior to
the latest renewal at Hamburg in July, but he ended the season rated a better horse
than Next Desert and only 3 lb inferior to Samum at the same stage of his career.

Dai Jin was successful in a national listed race at Dortmund on the second
of his two outings as a two-year-old, but could finish only second in listed races on
his first couple of starts as a three-year-old. The first indication that Dai Jin could
be a leading Deutsches Derby candidate came less than a month before the race, in
the Oppenheim-Union-Rennen at Cologne. Schutz's unbeaten Storm Trooper was
widely expected to cement his position as the leading contender for the Deutsches
Derby, as Next Desert had in the race the year before, but it was Dai Jin, apparently
the stable's third string, who landed the spoils by a neck from North Lodge, Storm
Trooper beating one home. Success in the main trial wasn't enough to secure
favouritism for Dai Jin in the Deutsches Derby, for which total prize money was a
new record at around the equivalent of £400,000. The only British-trained representative, Godolphin's New South Wales, started favourite ahead of Dai Jin and
stable-companion Next Gina, the winner of the Preis der Diana and a half-sister to

*BMW Deutsches Derby, Hamburg—trainer Andreas Schutz dominates with a 1,3,4,5
as Dai Jin gives him his fourth win in the last six runnings of the race;
the ex-Mark Johnston-trained Ransom o'War (right) is second with Storm Trooper clear of the others*

Credit Suisse Private Banking-Pokal, Cologne—Dai Jin gets the better of stable-companion Next Desert (left) in a clash of the 2002 and 2003 German Derby winners; Warrsan is third

Next Desert. Schutz was responsible for five of the twenty runners, his others being Akihito, Cherub and Storm Trooper. Dai Jin raced lazily for much of the way, something which became customary for him. He was still being pushed along well off the pace over half a mile out but stayed on strongly up the centre of the track to win by a length and a quarter. Runner-up, Ransom o'War, vastly improved since being transferred from Mark Johnston's stable to that of Erika Mader after his final two-year-old outing, was the only horse not trained by Schutz to make the frame. Storm Trooper, who led early in the straight, finished third, with Next Gina fourth and Akihito fifth; New South Wales finished tailed-off last.

Dai Jin's best performance—one that confirms that he is up to the standard of other recent winners of the Deutsches Derby—came in the Credit Suisse Private Banking-Pokal at Cologne in August, the Derby form having already received a boost when Ransom o'War defeated a field containing Godolphin and Ballydoyle raiders in the Grosser Dallmayr-Preis at Munich. Dai Jin's four rivals in the Pokal were all older horses, and included Next Desert, Coronation Cup winner Warrsan and 2001 Pokal winner Sabiango. Dai Jin was off the bridle from the start, and still adrift two thirds of the way through the race, but he once again responded really well in the straight, leading over a furlong out and beating Next Desert by two and a half lengths, with Warrsan two lengths back in third. Dai Jin received 12 lb weight-for-age from each of his rivals (he'd have got only 10 lb in Britain) but it was still a very smart effort. Olivier Peslier, who rode Dai Jin from the Deutsches Derby onwards, reportedly remarked after the Pokal that he had never ridden such a good horse who was so lazy, adding 'you have to push him from start to finish'. Dai Jin wasn't discredited when seventh to Dalakhani in the Arc on his final outing, but it was announced in the week after the race that he had returned with a pulled tendon. He was retired and will stand at Gestut Zoppenbroich, Germany, at a fee of €7,500.

			Nureyev	Northern Dancer
	Peintre Celebre (USA)		(b 1977)	Special
	(ch 1994)		Peinture Bleue	Alydar
Dai Jin			(ch 1987)	Petroluese
(b.c. 2000)			Shirley Heights	Mill Reef
	Dawlah		(b 1975)	Hardiemma
	(b 1992)		Urjwan	Seattle Slew
			(b 1984)	White Star Line

Dai Jin was the seventeenth Deutsches Derby winner to be bred by Germany's oldest privately-owned stud, Gestut Schlenderhan, though the last to carry their colours to victory was Stuyvesant back in 1976. Dai Jin's dam Dawlah was acquired by Schlenderhan for 160,000 guineas at the 1997 December Sales, so the sale of Dai Jin for DM 95,000 (about £29,500) at the BBAG yearling sale and

251

the subsequent sale of Dawlah for only DM 57,000 (about £18,000) when in foal to Monsun represented a disappointing return. However, the concept of a commercial market for the breeding and selling of yearlings has been appreciated only relatively recently in Germany, and it is encouraging for German racing as a whole that, while the likes of Schlenderhan still race many of their home-bred stock, they are moving more into the commercial sphere in being increasingly prepared to send well-bred yearlings to the sales. Dawlah ran nine times, her only success coming as a three-year-old in a maiden at Doncaster over a mile and a quarter. She seemed to stay two and a quarter miles and was a half-sister to Jiyush and Historic, smart stayers on the Flat and over hurdles respectively. Historic isn't the only smart hurdler in the family as grandam Urjwan is a half-sister to Prix de Pomone winner Whitehaven, the dam of Tote Gold Trophy winner Copeland, who won the Swiss Derby in his days on the Flat. Urjwan is also a half-sister to the dams of Oaks d'Italia winner Valley of Gold and Moyglare Stud Stakes winner Preseli, while great grandam White Star Line won three Grade 1 races in the States, including the Kentucky Oaks. Dai Jin is Dawlah's third living foal but her only one to have made the racecourse so far. Her yearling colt by Monsun was led out unsold at the 2003 BBAG sale at €130,000. Dai Jin stayed a mile and a half well and would probably have stayed further. He raced only on good going or softer and was an unimpressive mover, something which wasn't lost on Schutz, who reportedly warned Peslier before the Deutsches Derby: 'Think of the worst-galloping horse you've sat on—this one is worse.' *A. Schutz, Germany*

DAIMAJIN (IRE)   4 b.g. Dr Devious (IRE) 127 – Arrow Field (USA) (Sunshine Forever (USA)) [2003 83, a75+: p10g 7m 7m p8g 8g 8f 10m Oct 20] unfurnished gelding: fair handicapper: left B. Powell after reappearance: stays 1¼m: acts on soft and good to firm ground, probably on polytrack: blinkered (ran creditably) twice at 3 yrs: sold 3,200 gns. *D. W. P. Arbuthnot*   **76 a—**

DAINTREE AFFAIR (IRE)   3 b.g. Charnwood Forest (IRE) 125 – Madam Loving 99 (Vaigly Great 127) [2003 68: p5g f5g³ p5g³ f5g* 5f f5g f5s⁵ f5g³ Dec 16] fair handicapper: won at Southwell in April: will prove best at 5f/6f: acts on firm ground and all-weather: headstrong. *K. R. Burke*   **66**

DAISYCUTTER   3 ch.f. Zafonic (USA) 130 – Ingozi 91 (Warning 136) [2003 62: 8m⁵ 10m⁵ p12g Nov 12] lengthy filly: modest maiden, lightly raced: stays 1¼m: raced only on good/good to firm ground on turf, below form on polytrack: slowly away on reappearance. *G. Wragg*   **57**

DAKHIRA   5 b.m. Emperor Jones (USA) 119 – Fakhira (IRE) 83 (Jareer (USA) 115) [2003 –: p10g 10.2m Apr 29] disappointing maiden. *D. R. C. Elsworth*   **–**

DAKOTA BLACKHILLS   2 b.c. (May 25) Singspiel (IRE) 133 – Lady Blackfoot 108 (Prince Tenderfoot (USA) 126) [2003 7d² Nov 7] 7,000 2-y-o: quite attractive colt: half-brother to numerous winners, including high-class US performer up to 1¼m Fanmore and very smart 1m/9f performer in France/US Labeeb (both by Lear Fan), and to smart 1m/9f winner Alrassaam (by Zafonic): dam Irish sprinter: 50/1 and green, ½-length second of 18 to Divine Gift (pair clear) in maiden at Doncaster, slowly away and running on well: likely to stay 1¼m: should improve and win a race or 2. *J. G. Given*   **88 p**

DALAKHANI (IRE)   3 gr.c. Darshaan 133 – Daltawa (IRE) (Miswaki (USA) 124) [2003 116p: 10.5d* 10.5g* 12m* 12m² 12m* 12s* Oct 5]   **133**

Three-year-olds have a significantly better overall record in the Prix de l'Arc de Triomphe—thirty-three victories in fifty-five runnings since the race was raised sharply in value in 1949—than they do in 'Britain's Arc', the King George VI and Queen Elizabeth Stakes. Given that French-trained colts have provided the lion's share of the Arc successes for the classic generation with twenty victories (six French-trained fillies and seven overseas-trained colts make up the number), it is surprising that Dalakhani is only the fifth Prix du Jockey Club winner on the Arc's roll of honour in the period under review. In the fifty-three runnings of the King George—the Arc's main challenger as Europe's most important weight-for-age championship—the three-year-old winners collectively are ahead of the older horses only by one. Epsom Derby winners have accounted for thirteen of the twenty-seven three-year-old successes (two other Derby winners have won the King George as four-year-olds). The contrast attests, for one thing, to the fact that more often than not the Derby is harder to win than its French counterpart, Epsom winners also enjoying the better record in the Irish Derby in which they have come out on top in the four most recent meetings at the Curragh between winners of the respective races, in 1988, 1991, 1993 and 2000.

The latest winner of the Prix du Jockey Club, Dalakhani, suffered the only reverse of his nine-race career in the Irish Derby, though that narrow defeat—at the hands of the same owner's Alamshar, who went on to win the King George—can hardly be labelled a blemish on his record. There have been only half a dozen more highly rated French-trained Prix du Jockey Club winners since Sassafras became the first, in 1970, to land the Jockey Club/Arc double after the Second World War. There was another long gap before the feat was achieved again. In fact, no French-trained classic colt of any description managed to win the Arc again for seventeen years. Trempolino stopped the rot, winning in record time in 1987; he had gone down narrowly in a driving finish to the Prix du Jockey Club, won incidentally by Natroun, the most recent winner of that race for the Aga Khan before Dalakhani. The 'nineties saw the Jockey Club/Arc double completed three times: in 1991 by Suave Dancer (who, like Dalakhani, was beaten in the Irish Derby—though by a better horse than Alamshar in Generous); in 1997 by Peintre Celebre (who contested the Grand Prix de Paris rather than the Irish Derby on his next start); and in 1999 by Montjeu (who followed up a four-length victory at Chantilly with a five-length one in the Irish Derby, slamming the Epsom second and third). Dalakhani was a most impressive winner of the Prix du Jockey Club, but his Arc-winning performance, showing the best form of his career, was generally the subject of exaggerated plaudits. Beating the 33/1-shot Mubtaker by three quarters of a length, pushed out firmly to the line, puts Dalakhani in the category of an average Arc winner, judged strictly on the result, not an outstanding one. His performance fell short of those of Suave Dancer, Peintre Celebre and Montjeu, though that is not to denigrate Dalakhani. Along with 1996 winner Helissio and 2001 winner Sakhee, that particular trio are the best Arc winners of the past seventeen years, since Dancing Brave put up one of the finest performances in our experience to beat a notably strong and most representative field in 1986.

The fields for the Prix de l'Arc de Triomphe traditionally tended to be big, usually with between twenty to thirty runners, but since the mid-'eighties fields of twenty or more have become much rarer. There were eighteen runners in Peintre Celebre's year and seventeen in Sakhee's year, the largest in the last nine runnings, which have also seen fields of ten in 2000—the smallest since the race was elevated to worldwide importance—and thirteen in the latest edition. Only twelve lined up in 1950, when Tantieme gained the first of his two victories, and eleven in Trempolino's year. Dalakhani (coupled with his pacemaker) started favourite on the pari-mutuel ahead of the four-year-old High Chaparral (coupled with stable-companion Black Sam Bellamy), winner of the Derby at both Epsom and the Curragh and also successful as a three-year-old in the Breeders' Cup Turf. High Chaparral's reappearance in the latest season had been delayed until August

Prix Lupin, Longchamp—Dalakhani lands the odds with the minimum of fuss from Super Celebre and the Ballydoyle pair Alberto Giacometti and Balestrini

Prix du Jockey Club, Chantilly—
Dalakhani provides a third French classic winner of the year for jockey Christophe Soumillon,
who taunts Dominique Boeuf in the closing stages as Super Celebre is runner-up again

by a shoulder injury, but he had been successful on both his outings, most recently in a strong field for the Irish Champion Stakes at Leopardstown. High Chaparral's only defeat in six races as a three-year-old had been when third in the Arc after an interrupted preparation. The previous year's Prix du Jockey Club winner and Arc runner-up Sulamani bypassed Longchamp, leaving Godolphin—successful in the two previous editions with Marienbard and Sakhee—without a representative. Also fairly conspicuous by their absence were the likes of Eclipse and Juddmonte International winner Falbrav, the high-class Nayef and the top four-year-old filly Islington (fifth in the Arc in 2002 but now given more time before a second tilt at the Breeders' Cup Filly & Mare Turf). Sulamani, in America in the autumn being prepared for the Breeders' Cup, had come second in the King George to Alamshar, who also missed Longchamp, having been ready to run if anything befell Dalakhani. The latest crop of classic middle-distance fillies was substandard, but it was still unusual that there were no fillies at all in the line-up, three-year-old fillies having finished second and third in 2000, through Egyptband and Volvoreta, and provided the runner-up in 2001 with Aquarelliste (also sixth in 2002). Too many good horses were missing from the latest Arc but Dalakhani and High Chaparral did face two other Derby winners, both from the current classic crop. Epsom winner Kris Kin had come third in the King George but Dalakhani had beaten him convincingly in the Prix Niel, three weeks before the Arc. The other Derby winner was Dai Jin, successful in the German equivalent before beating the 2002 Deutsches Derby winner Next Desert in the Pokal at Cologne. Apart from Dalakhani's pacemaker Diyapour, there were two other three-year-olds in the line-up, the progressive French-trained pair Doyen (runner-up in the Prix Niel) and Policy Maker, both stepping up to Group 1 company for the first time. The seven older horses also included a six-year-old, the dual Geoffrey Freer Stakes winner Mubtaker, and two five-year-olds, Vinnie Roe, the winner of three successive Irish St Legers, and Ange Gabriel, twice successful in the Grand Prix de Saint-Cloud. The field was completed by the four-year-olds Black Sam Bellamy (tenth in 2002 and the latest Tattersalls Gold Cup winner, whose dam Urban Sea won the 1993 Arc), Bollin Eric (the 2002 St Leger winner and fourth behind Vinnie Roe at the Curragh on his latest start) and Kris Kin's pacemaker First Charter.

The anticipated duel between Dalakhani and High Chaparral at Longchamp failed to materialise, High Chaparral soon in trouble when asked to close rounding the home turn and able only to keep on at one pace for third. By contrast, the confidently-ridden Dalakhani, dropped in from his draw on the wide outside, showed a fine turn of foot to cut down his rivals in the home straight, depriving the always-prominent Mubtaker of the lead about a furlong out and, despite edging left when pushed along, staying on to win by three quarters of a length, with five lengths back to an obviously below-form High Chaparral. Doyen was the second three-year-old home, a length and a half behind High Chaparral, with Vinnie Roe and Black Sam Bellamy not discredited in fifth and sixth; Dai Jin stayed on past tiring horses for seventh, while Kris Kin, already struggling to keep up when hampered by Doyen before the home turn, beat only the pacemakers.

Dalakhani provided his owner with a third Arc victory, following the filly Akiyda in 1982 and Irish-trained Sinndar in 2000. It was the first Arc win, after a long wait, for Alain de Royer Dupre, who succeeded Akiyda's trainer Francois Mathet in charge of the Aga Khan's horses in France, and for the exciting young Belgian jockey Christophe Soumillon, labelled 'the new Yves Saint-Martin' by the French media. Soumillon, who first rose to prominence when winning the Prix du Jockey Club on Anabaa Blue in 2001, enjoyed a magnificent year in France, becoming champion jockey for the first time with a record 207 victories. One of the highlights came at Longchamp on the second Sunday in May, when a four-timer included a classic double for Andre Fabre on Clodovil (Poule d'Essai des Poulains) and Musical Chimes (Poule d'Essai des Pouliches) and a victory on Dalakhani in the Group 1 Prix Lupin.

Dalakhani's win in the second running of the Criterium International at Saint-Cloud, his third in a row, had established him as much the best two-year-old colt in France and he maintained his unbeaten record when odds-on for the Prix Greffulhe on his reappearance at Longchamp in April. Dalakhani's participation in the Prix Lupin, in doubt for a time after connections warned he would not be risked on firmish going, provided an informative clash with Super Celebre, who had looked a good prospect in another of the early Prix du Jockey Club trials, the Prix Noailles. Dalakhani came through his stiffest test at up to that time with the minimum of fuss, travelling well and just being pushed along, after taking the lead approaching the final furlong, to hold the challenge of Super Celebre by a length, with the Ballydoyle pair Alberto Giacometti and Balestrini third and fourth. There was no overseas challenge for the Prix du Jockey Club at Chantilly, which attracted only seven runners, the smallest field since the same number ran in Suave Dancer's year and only the fourth single-figure line-up in over half a century. Dalakhani stretched his unbeaten run to six with a comfortable two-length victory over Super Celebre, whose jockey had to endure the sight of Soumillon on the winner gesturing to him in the closing stages to 'come and catch me'.

Soumillon's victories on Dalakhani came to be accompanied by a one-finger salute as the pair crossed the line, but the aura of invincibility surrounding Dalakhani was dented by his defeat in the Irish Derby, after which connections gave him a summer break. The Ballydoyle pacemakers made it a searching test at the Curragh—a very different type of race from those Dalakhani had been contesting in France—and stamina, rather than finishing speed, was the deciding factor. Dalakhani, a 7/4-on shot, probably raced more prominently than ideal for a horse with his turn of foot. Soumillon had him in third, some way behind the pacemakers but clear of the main pack, and was left in front early in the straight, presumably much earlier than planned. Dalakhani went down by half a length after a good battle over the last two furlongs with Alamshar, Soumillon noticeably only going for his whip as a last resort as Alamshar began to assert inside the final furlong. Dalakhani's trainer summed up the performance succinctly: 'My horse has run a good race but he raced like a leader and he is not a leader.' The owner was more circumspect: 'It is very unusual for an owner to have two top-class horses in the same year. They had

Prix Niel Casino Barriere d'Enghien-Les-Bains, Longchamp—Dalakhani warms up for the Arc; the progressive Doyen is second with Kris Kin third

Prix de l'Arc de Triomphe Lucien Barriere, Longchamp—Dalakhani is pushed out to beat Mubtaker; they are clear of High Chaparral and Doyen (right)

to meet some time and the decision was vindicated in that they finished first and second.' The tributes paid by the Aga Khan after the Arc made it clear, however, that he regarded Dalakhani more highly. 'He has got to be the outstanding horse of his generation over all distances and all goings. I have always said it is difficult to make comparisons between champions but Dalakhani, such a beautiful mover, has a concentration of unusual talent.' The genuine and consistent Dalakhani was effective on going ranging from heavy to good to firm. Usually held up to use his finishing speed, he possessed a telling turn of foot for a horse who stayed a mile and a half and would almost certainly have been capable of winning more top races at around a mile and a quarter had connections wished to campaign him at around that distance. In that respect, it was perhaps a little disappointing that the Aga Khan maintained the tradition with Dalakhani of retiring his top middle-distance three-year-olds to stud. Attitudes have been changing and the successes as four-year-olds of major Derby winners such as Montjeu, High Chaparral and Sulamani in recent seasons will hopefully provide encouragement to a few more owners to keep classic winners in training. There would have been a wide variety of targets available as a four-year-old for a horse of Dalakhani's versatility.

Dalakhani is no great physical specimen, being quite attractive but rather finely made. He was the fifth winner of the Prix du Jockey Club for his owner-breeder, who has also won the Irish Derby five times and the Epsom Derby on four occasions, with ten individual colts. Shergar, Shahrastani, Kahyasi and Alamshar all descended from families that the present Aga Khan inherited from his father and grandfather. Top Ville, Mouktar and Natroun, three of the Aga Khan's Prix du Jockey Club winners, came from mares acquired in the 'seventies with the purchase of much of the bloodstock belonging to the leading French owner-breeder Mme Francois Dupre, for whom Mathet trained at the time. Darshaan, winner of the 1984 Prix du Jockey Club (from Sadler's Wells and Rainbow Quest), Sinndar and Dalakhani all descend from mares acquired when the bloodstock of French textile tycoon Marcel Boussac was also dispersed in the 'seventies. Boussac was a dominant owner-breeder for decades, nineteen times leading owner in France and its leading breeder on seventeen occasions; he won virtually everything that was worth winning on the turf in Britain—where he was leading owner and breeder in 1950 and 1951—as well as France, his domestic record including six Arcs and twelve Prix du Jockey Clubs, the last of them with Acamas in 1978, not long after which the Boussac bloodstock interests were acquired for a sum reportedly between 8.1m and 9.7m dollars. Among the first big dividends was Akiyda (out of Licata the dam of Acamas), with whom the Aga Khan qualified for the winning breeder's prize, as well as the owner's prize, after her Arc success.

Home-bred Darshaan, the sire of Dalakhani, traces back on the dam's side to the celebrated Boussac mare Tourzima, whom the Aga Khan describes as his 'rock, just as Mumtaz Mahal was for my grandfather.' Tourzima's daughters Corejada (Cheveley Park, Poule d'Essai des Pouliches and Irish Oaks), Gloriana and Albanilla (the fourth dam of Darshaan) all made names for themselves at stud, while Sinndar is descended from another of Tourzima's daughters Bielka. Darshaan, who died in 2001, has been an influence for stamina at stud; his other notable successes in the latest season included the Prix Vermeille winner Mezzo Soprano, the Breeders' Cup Filly & Mare Turf runner-up L'Ancresse and the Moyglare Stud Stakes winner Necklace. Darshaan's influence will be long-lasting as his status as a broodmare sire continues to grow, Breeders' Cup winners High Chaparral and Islington, and Irish One Thousand Guineas winner Yesterday, being among the winners out of Darshaan mares in the latest season. Like Darshaan, Dalakhani's dam the Miswaki mare Daltawa, a winner at a mile and a quarter as a two-year-old and over ten a half furlongs (in listed company) at three, comes from a Boussac family. This one is founded on the Prix du Conseil Municipal winner Astana, who has twenty-one descendants among the two hundred and thirty-nine broodmares listed in the current edition of the Aga Khan's stud book. Among the daughters of Astana were Crepellana, the last of five Prix de Diane winners for Boussac, and Dalakhani's fourth dam Rose Ness (dam of St James's Palace runner-up Raykour), while the family also includes Behera (Prix Saint-Alary, second in the Arc), who, along with her pattern-winning (Prix Berteux) daughter Bayrika and

Dalakhani (IRE) (gr.c. 2000)	Darshaan (br 1981)	Shirley Heights (b 1975)	Mill Reef
			Hardiemma
		Delsy (br 1972)	Abdos
			Kelty
	Daltawa (IRE) (gr 1989)	Miswaki (ch 1978)	Mr Prospector
			Hopespringseternal
		Damana (gr 1981)	Crystal Palace
			Denia

H.H. Aga Khan's "Dalakhani"

Dalakhani's dam and her own winning daughter Daltaiyma, is among the Aga Khan's current broodmare band.

The Aga Khan describes the breeding of thoroughbreds as 'a game of chess with nature', but the decision to send Daltawa to Darshaan was one of the more obvious moves. Daltawa's first foal the Doyoun colt Daylami had just added the Tattersalls Gold Cup, the Coral-Eclipse and the Man o' War Stakes as a four-year-old to a classic success in the Poule d'Essai des Poulains. Daltawa's second foal Daymarti (by Caerleon) had finished second in the most recent renewal of the Prix Lupin but had ended the season still a maiden and looking of doubtful temperament (he eventually won a listed race in the Provinces as a four-year-old before being sent to race in Singapore). Daltawa had also twice been returned to Two Thousand Guineas winner and Derby third Doyoun—producing Daltaiyma and being barren—but Doyoun was then sold to Turkey. Doyoun was a son of Mill Reef, a strong influence for stamina. Darshaan, a grandson of Mill Reef, provided an obvious alternative stallion for Daltawa. The combined achievements of Daylami, who raced for Godolphin after his three-year-old days and added the Coronation Cup, the King George, the Irish Champion Stakes and the Breeders' Cup Turf to his record at five, and of Dalakhani make Daltawa probably the most-prized of the Aga Khan's current mares. She was sent to Sadler's Wells after foaling Dalakhani and produced a filly, now named Dalataya and as yet unraced; not covered in 2001, she had a filly foal by Doyoun's son Kalanisi in 2003. Although the average winning distance of races won by progeny of the Mr Prospector stallion Miswaki in Europe is only a little over a mile, Daltawa's family has plenty of stamina on the dam's side, her dam the mile-and-three-quarter winner Damana (weeded out of the Aga Khan's studs in the mid-'nineties), her grandam Denia and Rose Ness all being by winners of the Derby or the Prix du Jockey Club. Dalakhani begins his stud career at Gilltown in Ireland at a fee of €45,000 (October 1st terms), alongside Daylami whose first crop gave him a good start in 2003. With Darshaan's last crop reaching the racecourse in 2004, Dalakhani is assured of a full opportunity to prove himself his rightful heir. *A. de Royer Dupre, France*

DALARAM (IRE)   3 b.g. Sadler's Wells (USA) 132 – Dalara (IRE) 114 (Doyoun **107**
124) [2003 85: 10.4m 11.9d* 11.9m* 16.2f 14.8m⁵ 13.9m* 14m⁵ Oct 2] lengthy, useful-looking gelding: very good mover: useful performer: won maiden at Brighton in May and handicaps at Haydock in June and York (best effort, beat Archduke Ferdinand by 1¼ lengths) in September: stays 2m: acts on firm and good to soft going: tongue tied first 5 starts in 2003: has worn crossed noseband: has run well when sweating: quirky: sold 67,000 gns, joined J. Howard Johnson, and gelded. *Sir Michael Stoute*

DALBLAIR (IRE)   4 b.g. Lake Coniston (IRE) 131 – Cartagena Lady (IRE) (Prince **72**
Rupert (FR) 121) [2003 78: 10m 12g⁴ 12m 12m 9.9d 12.3m⁴ 16g 11.9d Sep 26] rather leggy gelding: fluent mover: fair handicapper: stays 1½m: acts on firm and soft going: tried in headgear: often races prominently: none too reliable. *J. A. Glover*

DALIDA   2 ch.f. (Apr 21) Pursuit of Love 124 – Debutante Days 83 (Dominion 123) **59**
[2003 7d f7g Nov 25] 18,000Y: second foal: dam, 1¼m/1½m winner, also useful hurdler: better effort in maidens (modest form) when eighth at Doncaster on debut (backward and slowly away): will stay at least 1m. *P. C. Haslam*

DALISAY (IRE)   2 b.f. (May 3) Sadler's Wells (USA) 132 – Dabiliya (Vayrann 133)   **– p**
[2003 7m Oct 3] 340,000Y: rangy filly: has scope: closely related to useful Irish 1¼m winner Dabaya (by In The Wings), who stayed 1¾m and half-sister to several winners, including useful Irish performer up to 1¾m Dabtia (by Shirley Heights): dam unraced half-sister to Darshaan: 10/1 and very green, well held in maiden at Newmarket: will be suited by 1¼m+: should do better. *Sir Michael Stoute*

DALLAAH   2 b.f. (Mar 11) Green Desert (USA) 127 – Saeedah 75 (Bustino 136) [2003 **94**
6g* 5g³ 5.2m 6m⁶ Sep 20] leggy, close-coupled filly: fluent mover: second foal: dam twice-raced sister to smart performer up to 1¼m Bulaxie and half-sister to very smart performer up to 1½m Zimzalabim: fairly useful performer: won maiden at Lingfield in July: good 3½ lengths third to Majestic Missile in Molecomb Stakes at Goodwood: ran poorly in listed events last 2 starts: likely to prove best at 5f/6f: races prominently. *M. A. Jarvis*

DALYAN (IRE)   6 b.g. Turtle Island (IRE) 123 – Salette 110 (Sallust 134) [2003 9.9m   **–**
16.2m Aug 14] tall, workmanlike gelding: maiden handicapper: off 2 years, well held in 2003. *A. J. Lockwood*

DAMACHIDA (IRE) 4 ch.g. Mukaddamah (USA) 125 – Lady Loire 94 (Wolverlife **98**
115) [2003 a6.8g* 6s 6.8g 9g⁶ 7m 6f a6g* Oct 28] IR 6,800F, IR 12,000Y: half-brother to
1¼m/1½m winner Rock The Barney (by Coquelin): dam Irish 7f/1m winner, including at
2 yrs: useful performer at best: runner-up in Norsk 2000 Guineas/Derby at Ovrevoll in
2002: successful at Taby in handicap in April and minor event in October: well held in
Supreme Stakes at Goodwood and handicap at York (wandered in blinkers) fifth/sixth
outings: seems best up to 7f: acts on good to firm ground, all 4 wins on dirt: has had
tongue tied. *T. Langvad, Sweden*

DAMALIS (IRE) 7 b.m. Mukaddamah (USA) 125 – Art Age (Artaius (USA) 129) **99**
[2003 95: 5.1m* 5m² 5.3m Jun 29] lengthy, sturdy mare: in foal to Polish Precedent:
useful performer: won handicap at Chester (fifth course success) in May by 1¼ lengths
from Little Edward, making all: much better effort after when good second to Atlantic
Viking in listed rated stakes at Epsom next time: best at 5f/6f: acts on firm and soft going:
tried tongue tied: sometimes edgy/pulls hard/carries head awkwardly: has run poorly
when sweating. *E. J. Alston*

DAMASK DANCER (IRE) 4 b.g. Barathea (IRE) 127 – Polish Rhythm (IRE) 77 **55**
(Polish Patriot (USA) 128) [2003 54: p7g⁵ p7g⁵ 9.7m p10g f12s Sep 20] modest maiden:
left F. Murphy after reappearance: should stay 1¼m: acts on polytrack, below form only
run on turf: blinkered last 4 starts. *J. A. Supple*

DAME BLANCHE (IRE) 3 ch.f. Be My Guest (USA) 126 – Streetcar (IRE) 69 (In **67**
The Wings 128) [2003 8.3s 10m⁶ 10m⁶ 8m³ Aug 5] IR 18,500Y: compact filly: first
foal: dam, lightly raced at 2 yrs in Ireland, half-sister to smart but untrustworthy 6f to 1m
winner Intimate Guest (by Be My Guest): fair maiden: should be suited by 1¼m: acts on
good to firm ground: slowly away final outing. *C. F. Wall*

DAME DE NOCHE 3 b.f. Lion Cavern (USA) 117 – Goodnight Kiss 109 (Night **102**
Shift (USA)) [2003 84: 8.2g* 7m 8m³ 8m³ 8m 7.2g* 7g* 7m 7f³ 7g 7.1m Oct 25] work-
manlike filly: useful performer: won maiden at Nottingham in April and minor event at
Ayr and handicap at Goodwood in July: excellent third of 25 to Master Robbie in Tote
Trifecta Handicap at Ascot after: effective at 7f/1m: acts on firm going, shaped with
promise on good to soft on debut: has flashed tail: races prominently. *J. G. Given*

DAME EDNA (FR) 3 b.f. Octagonal (NZ) 126 – Mohave Desert (USA) (Diesis 133) **–**
[2003 8.3g 8.2m Oct 28] 100,000 francs Y: rather leggy filly: third living foal: half-sister
to winner in Belgium by Ganges: dam French 1¼m winner: well held in maidens at
Windsor and Nottingham. *Miss S. West*

DAME MARGARET 3 ch.f. Elmaamul (USA) 125 – Pomorie (IRE) 67§ (Be My **49**
Guest (USA) 126) [2003 46: 10d⁴ 12g 10.2m² 9.7g 12m⁶ p13g³ Nov 12] poor maiden
handicapper: stays 13f: acts on polytrack, good to firm and good to soft going: tends to
race freely: inconsistent. *M. L. W. Bell*

DAME NOVA (IRE) 2 b.f. (Mar 4) Definite Article 121 – Red Note (Rusticaro (FR) **–**
124) [2003 6m 7.9m 7m Oct 12] 15,000Y: tall, quite good-topped filly: half-sister to
several winners, including useful 1m winner Kuwait Dawn (by Pips Pride) and 5-y-o Sir
Francis: dam lightly raced in Ireland: well held in maidens. *P. C. Haslam*

DAMI (USA) 2 b.f. (Jan 28) Dynaformer (USA) – Trampoli (USA) 115 (Trempolino **70**
(USA) 135) [2003 7g⁴ 7m⁴ 7f 7m Oct 4] $80,000Y: fifth foal: closely
related to fairly useful 10.5f winner (stayed 2m) First Officer (by Lear Fan) and half-
sister to 2 winners, including 2001 2-y-o 1m winner Risker (by Gone West): dam, 1¼m/
1½m winner in France/USA, half-sister to very smart middle-distance performers Roi
Normand and Luth Dancer: fair maiden: fourth at Yarmouth and Folkestone: looked none
too keen in nursery final start: should be suited by 1¼m/1½m. *C. E. Brittain*

DAMSEL 2 b.f. (Apr 8) Danzero (AUS) – Rensaler (USA) (Stop The Music (USA)) **92 p**
[2003 8m⁵ 7.1m³ 7g* Nov 1] tall, quite good-topped filly: half-sister to numerous
winners, including 1989 2-y-o 6f winner Jovial (by Northern Jove), later Grade 1 9f
winner in USA, useful winner around 1¼m Silence Reigns (by Saddlers' Hall) and 4-y-o
Tour de Force: dam won around 1m in USA: easily best effort in maidens when winning
18-runner event at Newmarket by ½ length from Sydney Star, making most and rallying
well: should stay at least 1m: useful prospect. *J. H. M. Gosden*

DANAAN PRINCE (IRE) 3 ch.c. Danehill Dancer (IRE) 117 – Classic Queen (IRE) **71**
(Classic Secret (USA) 91) [2003 74: 7m⁶ 7.1m⁶ 8m⁶ 7m 7g 10m⁴ 10m Jul 28] lengthy
colt: fair maiden handicapper: stays 1¼m: acts on polytrack and good to firm ground:
sometimes slowly away. *R. Hannon*

DANAKIL   8 b.g. Warning 136 – Danilova (USA) (Lyphard (USA) 132) [2003 90: p12g   **88** p12g⁶ p12g 12m⁴ 12g⁵ 12g 14m 12m⁴ 12m³ p13g Dec 6] small gelding: unimpressive mover: fairly useful handicapper: should stay 1¾m: acts on all-weather, firm and soft going: visored (below par) once: usually held up: sometimes hangs: consistent. *S. Dow*

DANAKIM   6 b.g. Emarati (USA) 74 – Kangra Valley 56 (Indian Ridge 123) [2003   **43** 64d: 5m 6m 5m 5m 6m 5.3m 6f 5f 5m 5m⁵ 6m 5m⁶ 6f Aug 22] lengthy, good-quartered gelding: poor performer: best at 5f/6f: probably acts on any turf going, well beaten on fibresand: tried blinkered: has been early to post/refused to enter stall. *J. R. Weymes*

DANCE CLASS (IRE)   3 b.f. Desert Prince (IRE) 130 – Dance Ahead 81 (Shareef   **50** Dancer (USA) 135) [2003 58: 7m 5.7m 6f 8f⁶ 6m⁶ 6g 7f Sep 27] strong filly: modest maiden handicapper: left Mrs P. N. Dutfield after third outing: best form at 6f: acts on good to firm going: tried in cheekpieces. *P. Hughes, Ireland*

DANCEHALL DARCY   4 ch.f. Bahamian Bounty 116 – Dancing Chimes (London   **–** Bells (CAN) 109) [2003 49: p5g 6g⁴ 5m⁶ 5m Aug 6] poor maiden: showed little at 4 yrs: should prove best at 5f/6f: tried in blinkers/cheekpieces: sometimes takes good hold. *A. Charlton*

DANCE IN THE DAY (IRE)   5 b.g. Caerleon (USA) 132 – One To One (Shirley   **70** Heights 130) [2003 81: 16m 16.2m⁶ 14v May 24] strong gelding: unimpressive mover: fairly useful handicapper at 3 yrs/4 yrs, just fair form in 2003: best form at 1½m/1¾m: acted on any going: often held up: dead. *E. J. Alston*

DANCE IN THE SUN   3 b.f. Halling (USA) 133 – Sunny Davis (USA) 71 (Alydar   **91** (USA)) [2003 74: p8g² 9.7g* 9.9m⁵ 9f² p12g⁴ p10g* 10.5s Nov 25] lengthy filly: fairly useful performer: won maiden at Folkestone in March and handicap at Lingfield in November: well held in listed race at Saint-Cloud final start: best around 1¼m: acts on polytrack and firm going: consistent. *Mrs A. J. Perrett*

DANCE LIGHT (IRE)   4 b.f. Lycius (USA) 124 – Embracing 91 (Reference Point   **–** 139) [2003 73: 14.1m 16g⁶ p16g f14g Dec 12] angular filly: fair performer at 3 yrs: well beaten in 2003. *T. T. Clement*

DANCE OF LIFE   4 b.f. Shareef Dancer (USA) 135 – Regan (USA) 60 (Lear Fan   **–** (USA) 130) [2003 –: 11.5g Jul 3] rather leggy, good-topped filly: little form on Flat: tried blinkered. *S. Gollings*

DANCE ON THE TOP   5 ch.g. Caerleon (USA) 132 – Fern 100 (Shirley Heights   **87** 130) [2003 95d: p8g* 10.1m 8g 8g 8m⁴ 8.3g³ 8g² 8f Oct 12] close-coupled, good-topped gelding: poor mover: fairly useful handicapper: won at Lingfield in March: has form at 1½m, may prove best around 1m: acts on polytrack and firm going: visored (below form) once at 4 yrs: has pulled hard. *J. R. Boyle*

DANCE PARTY (IRE)   3 b.f. Charnwood Forest (IRE) 125 – Society Ball 72 (Law   **67** Society (USA) 130) [2003 7g 8m⁴ 8.3m³ 8.5m⁴ 8.1m f9.4g Oct 4] good-topped filly: half-sister to useful 1m winner Keld (by Lion Cavern) and winner up to 10.5f in Italy by Ezzoud: dam, 1½m winner, out of sister to dam of Zafonic: fair maiden: will be suited by 1¼m+: raced only on good/good to firm ground on turf (slowly away on all-weather debut). *A. M. Balding*

DANCER POLISH (POL)   5 b.g. Professional (IRE) 73 – Doloreska (POL) (Who   **–** Knows 114) [2003 56: f12s f14.8g Nov 14] Polish-bred gelding: modest form in Britain (raced only on fibresand): well held in 2003. *A. Sadik*

DANCE SOLO   2 b.f. (Feb 21) Sadler's Wells (USA) 132 – Obsessive (USA) 102   **66** (Seeking The Gold (USA)) [2003 7m 7.5m³ 8m⁴ Oct 23] rather leggy filly: fourth foal: sister to 3-y-o Double Obsession and half-sister to 4-y-o Medallist and 5-y-o Spy Master (fairly useful 6f winner at 2 yrs): dam, 2-y-o 6f winner who stayed 10.4f, out of half-sister to smart performer up to 1½m Beyton: fair form in maidens: will be suited by 1¼m+: sold 15,000 gns, joined U. Ostmann, Germany. *Sir Michael Stoute*

DANCES WITH ANGELS (IRE)   3 b.f. Mukaddamah (USA) 125 – Lady of Leisure   **46** (USA) 76 (Diesis 133) [2003 53: p10g f8.5s 12m⁵ 10.9m 10.2f⁴ 9.9d⁴ 12f⁴ 12m 10m Aug 20] poor maiden handicapper: stays 1½m: acts on firm and good to soft going: tried in cheekpieces. *Mrs A. L. M. King*

DANCES WITH RIVERS   4 b.f. River Falls 113 – Make Merry (IRE) (Dunbeath   **53** (USA) 127) [2003 10.9m⁶ Jun 22] second foal: dam unraced: well held in bumper for Mrs M. Reveley: 100/1 and apprentice ridden, sixth to Strategy in maiden at Warwick. *R. A. Fahey*

DANCE TO MY TUNE 2 b.f. (May 6) Halling (USA) 133 – Stolen Melody 74 **58**
(Robellino (USA) 127) [2003 5m³ 6m³ 7.5m⁴ 6g 6f⁶ 6m 6f⁶ Oct 10] big, workmanlike
filly: third foal: dam 2-y-o 6f winner: modest maiden: stays 6f: acts on firm going:
wandered/flashed tail fifth start: visored (ran respectably) final outing. *M. E. Sowersby*

DANCING-ALONE 11 ch.g. Adbass (USA) 102 – Lady Alone 59 (Mr Fluorocarbon **–**
126) [2003 f12s Feb 18] modest performer, very lightly raced: well held only start since
1999: has worn bandages/tongue strap. *D. Mullarkey*

DANCING BEAR 2 b.c. (Apr 16) Groom Dancer (USA) 128 – Sickle Moon (Shirley **–**
Heights 130) [2003 10g Nov 1] well-made colt: half-brother to 4-y-o Oldenway and
German 1m winner Misty Moon (by Polar Falcon): dam unraced: 50/1 and better for race,
well held in listed event at Newmarket. *Julian Poulton*

DANCING FOREST (IRE) 3 br.g. Charnwood Forest (IRE) 125 – Fauna (IRE) 65 **69**
(Taufan (USA) 119) [2003 72: f5g³ f6g⁵ f7s p7g* p7g³ p8g* 7g 8.3g⁵ 9m⁵ 8.3d 7m 8.1m **a75**
p7g 10s² 8f 10.2m p7g p7g p7g Dec 30] fair performer: won claimer in February and
handicap in March, both at Lingfield: effective at 7f to 1¼m: acts on soft going, good to
firm and polytrack: sometimes slowly away: has raced freely. *D. K. Ivory*

DANCINGINTHESTREET 3 b.g. Groom Dancer (USA) 128 – Usk The Way 72 **90**
(Caerleon (USA) 132) [2003 79: 8g 10.5s⁴ 12m³ 14.1f⁴ 15.8m² 14m 16.2m² 16m*
15.9m³ Aug 30] close-coupled gelding: fairly useful performer: won handicap at Thirsk
in August: will stay beyond 2m: acts on firm ground: usually races prominently: sold
2,500 gns. *J. G. Given*

DANCING KEY 3 ch.f. Halling (USA) 133 – Fleet Key (Afleet (CAN)) [2003 74: **–**
f8g⁵ 10m 8m⁵ Jun 20] fair form on debut at 2 yrs: little form since: sold 4,000 gns early in
July, sent to Pakistan. *B. W. Hills*

DANCING KING (IRE) 7 b.g. Fairy King (USA) – Zariysha (IRE) (Darshaan 133) **58**
[2003 65?: 7.6g 7m 8.2m⁴ 8.2m* 8.1m⁵ 7.9m 8d⁴ 8.3m 8.5g 8m f8g Dec 19] lengthy **a–**
gelding: modest handicapper: won selling event at Nottingham in June: stays 1m: acts on
firm and good to soft going: often races prominently. *P. W. Hiatt*

DANCING LILY 6 ch.m. Clantime 101 – Sun Follower (Relkino 131) [2003 26, a37: **–**
8f 9g 7f 8g 10m 8.1m Aug 14] bad maiden: sometimes races freely/hangs. *J. J. Bridger*

DANCING LYRA 2 b.c. (Mar 5) Alzao (USA) 117 – Badaayer (USA) 105 (Silver **85**
Hawk (USA) 123) [2003 6g 6g³ 7m 7m Jul 10] €31,000Y: compact colt: first foal: dam
1m/1¼m winner who stayed 1½m: fairly useful maiden: best effort when never-nearer
seventh in listed race at Royal Ascot third start: ran poorly final outing: should be suited
by 1¼m/1½m. *J. W. Hills*

DANCING MO (IRE) 2 b.f. (Apr 22) Danehill Dancer (IRE) 117 – Honey Bee **50**
(Alnasr Alwasheek 117) [2003 5m*5m 5.1f³ 5g³ 5.1f⁶ 5.1m f5g Oct 4] €8,000Y: second
foal: dam lightly-raced maiden: modest maiden: likely to prove best at 5f/6f: acts on firm
going: wore cheekpieces sixth outing: possibly temperamental. *J. L. Spearing*

DANCING MYSTERY 9 b.g. Beveled (USA) – Batchworth Dancer 67 (Ballacashtal **97**
(CAN)) [2003 102, a107: 5.1g⁵ 5.2m⁶ 6m⁵ 6g 6f 5f 5m 5f³ 5.5f⁵ 5g 5.1f² 5.1m⁵ 5.2g 5s
5d* f5g³ f5g³ Dec 9] close-coupled gelding: useful performer: won handicap at Doncaster
in November by 2½ lengths from Steel Blue: good efforts after: best at 5f: acts on all-
weather and any turf ground: blinkered again nowadays: has spoilt chance by rearing in
stall (broke out and withdrawn in May): races prominently. *E. A. Wheeler*

DANCING NELLY 3 b.f. Shareef Dancer (USA) 135 – Silent Witness (Inchinor 119) **52**
[2003 48: f9.4s 6g³ 7f 6d Jul 25] leggy, unfurnished filly: modest maiden: should stay 1m.
B. W. Hills

DANCING NUGGET (USA) 3 b.f. Seeking The Gold (USA) – Shalimar Garden **67**
(IRE) 89 (Caerleon (USA) 132) [2003 66p: 7g⁴ 7.5m⁵ 7g 10.2m⁴ 11.9m³ 12m³ 10m³
10.2m⁶ 10.2f⁴ Oct 12] close-coupled filly: fair maiden handicapper: stays easy 1½m:
raced only on polytrack and going or firmer: sold 36,000 gns. *J. W. Hills*

DANCING PEARL 5 ch.m. Dancing Spree (USA) – Elegant Rose 72 (Noalto 120) **–**
[2003 –: f12g⁵ Feb 24] modest winning hurdler: no form in 2 maidens on Flat. *C. J. Price*

DANCING PHANTOM 8 b.g. Darshaan 133 – Dancing Prize (IRE) 99 (Sadler's **83**
Wells (USA) 132) [2003 105: 12g f12g⁶ 11.9m⁵ 13.1d² 11g* Oct 28] quite attractive
gelding: has a quick action: just fairly useful form for new trainer in 2003: made all in
claimer at Redcar in October: stays 13f: acts on heavy and good to firm going: tried
visored: sometimes edgy/on toes, reportedly bolted before start on reappearance: free-
going sort. *James Moffatt*

DANCING PRINCE (IRE) 2 b.c. (Feb 14) Imperial Ballet (IRE) 110 – Eastern Aura –
(IRE) 49 (Ahonoora 122) [2003 p6g 6m 5m⁵ Oct 3] IR 15,000F, 23,000Y: quite attractive
colt: sixth foal: closely related to a winner in Norway by Scenic and half-brother to 2
other winners abroad: dam poor maiden: little sign of ability in maidens: visored final
start: headstrong. *A. P. Jarvis*

DANCING RIDGE (IRE) 6 b.g. Ridgewood Ben 113 – May We Dance (IRE) 57 –
(Dance of Life (USA)) [2003 52: 5.1d f6g Nov 19] good-topped gelding: modest maiden:
well held in 2003: tried visored/in cheekpieces. *A. Senior*

DANCING TASSEL 4 b.f. Most Welcome 131 – Delicious 51 (Dominion 123) [2003 –
–: f12s p10g Jan 30] unfurnished filly: lightly raced and no form. *D. Morris*

DANCING TILLY 5 b.m. Dancing Spree (USA) – L'Ancressaan 67 (Dalsaan 125) **38**
[2003 41: 9.9m 11.5g 13.8f 10m⁶ 8.5m⁵ 8m³ 8m 10f⁶ Sep 15] leggy mare: poor maiden
handicapper: seems to stay 1¼m: acts on firm ground: has run creditably in cheekpieces:
hard ride. *R. A. Fahey*

DANCLARE (USA) 2 ch.f. (May 10) Stravinsky (USA) 133 – Beyond Temptation **82 p**
(USA) (Sunny's Halo (CAN)) [2003 6m⁴ 6m² 7m* 8s Oct 5] good-topped filly: seventh
foal: half-sister to winner in Italy by Prospect Bay: dam maiden sister to US Grade 1 8.5f
winner Race The Wild Wind, herself dam of very smart 6f/7f performer King Charle-
magne and 4-y-o Meshaheer: fairly useful form: landed odds in maiden at Kempton in
September by 1¼ lengths from Hunter's Valley, making most: tailed off in Prix Marcel
Boussac at Longchamp (swished tail in paddock): stays 7f: has scope to do better at 3 yrs.
J. H. M. Gosden

DANDOUCE 2 b.f. (Mar 2) Danzero (AUS) – Douce Maison (IRE) 67 (Fools Holme **70**
(USA)) [2003 5.1m⁴ p5g² p6g³ Dec 2] 16,000Y: lengthy filly: fifth foal: half-sister to
3 winners, including useful German miler Montestefano (by Emperor Jones) and 3-y-o
Zariano: dam 1m winner who stayed 1½m: best effort (fair form) when length third to
Missus Links in minor event at Lingfield: stays 6f: visored first 2 starts. *S. L. Keightley*

DANDOUN 5 b.h. Halling (USA) 133 – Moneefa 73 (Darshaan 133) [2003 114: 8g* **117**
8g* 9.3g 8g 8d Oct 4] useful-looking horse: has a quick, unimpressive action: smart
performer: successful in listed race at Doncaster (for second year running, beat With
Reason 4 lengths) in March and Prix du Muguet at Saint-Cloud (beat Domedriver, who
gave 7 lb, short neck) in May: below form after at Longchamp in Prix d'Ispahan (then off
3½ months), Prix du Moulin and Prix Daniel Wildenstein: stays 9f: acts on soft and good
to firm going: has worn crossed noseband: often edgy: takes strong hold: stays in training.
J. L. Dunlop

DANDY JIM 2 b.c. (Feb 8) Dashing Blade 117 – Madam Trilby (Grundy 137) [2003 –
f6g f6g f6g⁶ Dec 26] 2,800 2-y-o: half-brother to several winners, including 9-y-o Sharp
Hat, useful at best: dam ran once: little sign of ability in claimers/seller (slowly away).
D. W. Chapman

DANEBANK (IRE) 3 b.g. Danehill (USA) 126 – Snow Bank (IRE) (Law Society **63**
(USA) 130) [2003 64: 11.8m 10m⁵ 9.9f⁶ 8m 10f⁶ 12m⁴ 12.6m⁶ Oct 27] close-
coupled gelding: modest maiden: stays 1½m: raced only on ground firmer than good on
turf: visored (found little) 2 of last 3 starts: sold 11,000 gns. *J. W. Hills*

DANECARE (IRE) 3 b.c. Danetime (IRE) 121 – Nordic Flavour (IRE) 84 (Nordico **94**
(USA)) [2003 79: 7m 5.8s⁶ 6s* 6v⁶ 6m* 6.3m 6m Aug 23] small colt: second foal: dam
Irish 1¼m winner: fairly useful performer: won handicaps at Naas in May and Cork in
June: below form in listed stakes at Haydock in between (raced freely): best around
6f: acts on soft and good to firm ground. *James G. Burns, Ireland*

DANEFONIQUE (IRE) 2 b.f. (Jan 3) Danetime (IRE) 121 – Umlaut (Zafonic (USA) **55**
130) [2003 5g⁵ 5m⁵ 6m 7.1f³ f8s 7m⁵ 8m Oct 20] 6,000Y: strong, workmanlike filly: first
foal: dam unraced out of sister to Shirley Heights: modest maiden: third at Musselburgh:
stays 7f: acts on firm going. *D. Carroll*

DANEHILL LAD (IRE) 3 b.g. Danehill (USA) 126 – River Missy (USA) (Riverman **62 ?**
(USA) 131) [2003 –: p10g⁵ p10g² 11.6d 9g 10.2g⁴ 10m 10d 10d p12g² p12g² p12g² p13g² **a77**
p12g⁶ Dec 17] leggy, plain gelding: fair maiden on turf, modest on turf: left S. Dow after
ninth start: should stay 1¾m: acts on polytrack. *T. Keddy*

DANEHILL MISS (IRE) 3 b.f. Danehill Dancer (IRE) 117 – Persian Flower (Persian –
Heights 129) [2003 50: 5.9m 6g 6m 14f Oct 2] neat, angular filly: well held after debut:
left T. Easterby 2,500 gns after reappearance. *Joseph Crowley, Ireland*

DANEHILL STROLLER (IRE) 3 b.g. Danetime (IRE) 121 – Tuft Hill 92 (Grundy **98**
137) [2003 86: 6m⁵ 6m⁶ 6g² 6m² 6g* 6m 6m* 6m² 6m⁴ 6m³ Oct 1] angular gelding:
useful performer: won handicap at Doncaster in July and minor event at Newcastle (beat
Manaar a neck) in August: creditable efforts last 3 starts: effective at 5f/6f: acts on good
to firm going, good to soft and polytrack: wore cheekpieces last 7 starts: pulled hard early
penultimate start: usually held up. *R. M. Beckett*

DANEHURST 5 b.m. Danehill (USA) 126 – Miswaki Belle (USA) 73 (Miswaki (USA) **106**
124) [2003 118: 6g 6.1d* 5s 6s Oct 31] small, barrel-shaped mare: just useful performer
in 2003: off nearly 4 months, won listed race at Chester in September by neck from
Golden Nun: never on terms in Prix de l'Abbaye de Longchamp and Prix de Seine-
et-Oise at Maisons-Laffitte after: effective at 5f/6f: has won on good to firm going and
fibresand, races mainly on good or softer nowadays: blinkered. *Sir Mark Prescott*

DANELOR (IRE) 5 b.g. Danehill (USA) 126 – Formulate 119 (Reform 132) [2003 **96**
90: 8m⁴ 10.1m² 10.1m² 10.4f Jul 12] sturdy, good-bodied gelding: useful handicapper:
good efforts when in frame in Spring Cup at Newbury and quite valuable events at
Epsom, second to Akshar penultimate start: stays 1¼m: yet to race on soft/heavy going,
acts on any other: free-going sort, and usually races prominently: bandaged in front final
outing. *R. A. Fahey*

DANESMEAD (IRE) 2 b.c. (Mar 15) Danehill Dancer (IRE) 117 – Indian Honey **98**
(Indian King (USA) 128) [2003 5g² 5m⁴ 5d² 6m* 6.3g² 5.2m³ 6m³ 6m³ Aug 16]
€32,000Y: rather leggy, useful-looking colt: half-brother to several winners, including
4-y-o Good Girl: dam unraced: useful performer: landed odds in maiden at Doncaster in
June: placed in sales races at the Curragh (second to Carrizo Creek) and Newbury (third
to If Paradise) fifth/sixth starts: good third in minor event at Ripon final outing: should
stay 7f: acts on good to firm and good to soft going. *T. D. Easterby*

DANESTAT 4 b.f. Danehill Dancer (IRE) 117 – Statuette 57 (Statoblest 120) [2003 f5s **–**
Apr 12] second foal: dam, 5f seller winner, ran only at 2 yrs: 40/1 and blinkered, tailed off
in Wolverhampton claimer. *B. Palling*

DANESWOOD 4 b.g. Be My Chief (USA) 122 – Floria Tosca § (Petong 126) [2003 **– §**
54§: f9.4g Jan 24] modest performer: tailed off only start 2003 (all-weather debut): sometimes blinkered/visored: ungenuine: sold 2,000 gns. *K. F. Clutterbuck*

DANETIME LADY 3 b.f. Danetime (IRE) 121 – Hawattef (IRE) (Mujtahid **60**
(USA) 118) [2003 69: f8.5g f5g 9g⁶ 9f Aug 17] IR 2,500Y: first foal: dam unraced: modest maiden: well held at Wolverhampton first 2 starts: stays 9f. *John A. Quinn, Ireland*

DANGER BIRD (IRE) 3 ch.f. Eagle Eyed (USA) 111 – Danger Ahead (Mill Reef **42**
(USA) 141) [2003 51, a54: f7g³ f8.5s² f8.5s 5m 7m⁵ f7g³ f8g⁵ f8.5g² Dec 26] leggy filly: **a55**
modest maiden: stays easy 8.5f: acts on fibresand, raced only on ground firmer than good
on turf: sometimes races freely: none too consistent. *R. Hollinshead*

DANGEROUS BEANS 3 b.g. Bluegrass Prince (IRE) 110 – A Little Hot (Petong **65**
126) [2003 p10g⁵ f12g⁶ p12g 10.9m 16g 8f² 10d* f8g p12g⁴ Nov 26] fifth foal: dam
sprint maiden: fair performer: won handicap at Brighton in October: stays 1½m: acts on
polytrack, firm and good to soft going: refused to enter stall final intended outing. *S. Kirk*

DANGEROUS DAVE 4 b.g. Superpower 113 – Lovely Lilly (Arrasas (USA) 100) **–**
[2003 –: p7g p8g f6g Jan 27] well held in maidens/seller. *Jamie Poulton*

DANGEROUSLY GOOD 5 b.g. Shareef Dancer (USA) 135 – Ecologically Kind **74**
(Alleged (USA) 138) [2003 12.3m⁶ 14.1g⁵ 12g a12g⁶ a12s³ Nov 23] leggy gelding:
fair performer: won at Mijas and San Sebastian (Copa de Oro) in 2002: best effort in
handicaps on return to Britain second 5-y-o start: looked reluctant next time, then
left R. C. Guest: trained next start only by G. Bindella, then rejoined 2002 trainer: stays
1¾m: acts on heavy going, good to firm and sand: wore headgear in Britain: held up.
J. H. Brown, Spain

DANGER OVER 6 b.h. Warning 136 – Danilova (USA) (Lyphard (USA) 132) [2003 **118**
115: 6m⁶ 5m⁴ 6g³ 7g³ 7g 7g⁴ 6d⁵ 7m³ 8g 8.2d² Nov 6] compact, useful-looking ex-French
horse: smart performer: as good as ever for new stable, winning minor event at Kempton
in April by 1½ lengths from The Tatling: good efforts when third to Orientor in Chipchase
Stakes at Newcastle and New Seeker in Tote International Handicap at Ascot (hung right)
third/fourth starts: below form after, short-headed by Cornelius in minor event at
Nottingham final outing: effective at 6f to 1m:· acts on good to soft and good to firm
going: blinkered (below form) final 5-y-o start: has worn crossed noseband. *J. A. Osborne*

DANIELLE'S LAD 7 b.g. Emarati (USA) 74 – Cactus Road (FR) (Iron Duke (FR) **80**
122) [2003 92, a–: f7g³ f6s p8g f8.5g² f7g² f7g² 7d f8.5s³ 7.1m p7g f6s f7g³ f7s p7g **a86**

f8.5g⁵ Dec 26] strong gelding: fairly useful handicapper: probably needs further than 6f nowadays, and stays easy 8.5f: acts on fibresand, heavy and good to firm going: blinkered: often early to post: has raced freely/edged right. *B. Palling*

DANIFAH (IRE) 2 b.f. (May 8) Perugino (USA) 84 – Afifah 66 (Nashwan (USA) **69 d** 135) [2003 5g⁵ 5g³ 5m³ 5.1m 6g 5g² 5.1f² 5m* 5g 5.1m 5m⁵ 5.1g* 5.1g 6.1m 5m 5.1m 5m 5.1f Oct 12] €3,500Y: leggy, close-coupled filly: fourth foal: closely related to 5-y-o Only One Legend and half-sister to 7f (at 2 yrs) to 9f winner in Italy by Bigstone: dam, ran once, out of half-sister to top-class sprinter Marwell, herself dam of Marling: fair performer: won maiden at Warwick in June and nursery at Chepstow in August: mostly well below form after: stays 6f: acts on firm going: blinkered fifth outing: probably ungenuine. *P. D. Evans*

DANI RIDGE (IRE) 5 b.m. Indian Ridge 123 – Daniella Drive (USA) (Shelter Half **92** (USA)) [2003 92d: 6m⁴ 6d* 7m 6m 7g 6.1d p6g³ 6d Nov 8] good-topped mare: fairly useful handicapper: ran at Ripon in May: good third at Lingfield penultimate start: effective at 6f/7f: acts on any turf going and polytrack. *E. J. Alston*

DANISH DECORUM (IRE) 4 ch.g. Danehill Dancer (IRE) 117 – Dignified Air **88 d** (FR) 70 (Wolver Hollow 126) [2003 86: 10g² 10.9m 10m 12f Jun 25] tall gelding: fairly useful handicapper: below form after reappearance: seems to stay 1½m: acts on firm going: sold 9,000 gns, joined Evan Williams. *C. G. Cox*

DANISH MONARCH 2 b.g. (Feb 1) Great Dane (IRE) 122 – Moly 64 (Inchinor **79** 119) [2003 6g² 6m⁶ 7g² 7.5m² 7m⁴ Oct 2] 14,000Y: leggy gelding: first foal: dam, ran 3 times (should have stayed 1½m), half-sister to smart performer up to 1½m Don Miche-letto: fair maiden: second at Salisbury, Folkestone and Beverley: should stay 1m: sold 14,000 gns. *J. L. Dunlop*

D'ANJOU 6 b.g. Marju (IRE) 127 – Rose de Thai (USA) 99 (Lear Fan (USA) 130) **113** [2003 113: 8m⁵ 7g² 8m⁶ 6m⁴ 7f* 7.5m* Oct 5] smart performer: as good as ever when winning handicap at Leopardstown in September by ¾ length from One More Round: also ran well in 2003 when ¾-length second to Avorado in Minstrel Stakes at the Curragh on second start: very best efforts at 6f/7f: acts on firm and good to soft going: blinkered once. *J. Oxx, Ireland*

DANNY LEAHY (FR) 3 b.c. Danehill (USA) 126 – Paloma Bay (IRE) 92 (Alzao **69** (USA) 117) [2003 7m³ 9d⁶ 10m⁴ 10m f12s⁵ f8g³ Oct 16] 900,000 francs Y: strong, good-bodied colt: third foal: half-brother to 4-y-o Spectroscope: dam, 2-y-o 6f winner who stayed 1m, out of sister to smart Irish sprinter Rustic Amber: fair maiden: stays 1¼m: acts on good to firm ground and fibresand: sold 13,000 gns. *J. G. Given*

DANO-MAST 7 b.h. Unfuwain (USA) 131 – Camera Girl (Kalaglow 132) [2003 120: **120** 12g 12d* 12g³ 10m 10m Dec 14] lengthy, attractive horse: very smart performer: report-edly took time to recover from below-form reappearance in Dubai Sheema Classic at Nad Al Sheba but as good as ever when winning Scandinavian Open Championship at Copenhagen in August by 2½ lengths from Parthe: creditable 2½ lengths third to Mamool in Grosser Bugatti Preis at Baden-Baden next time, but well held in Champion Stakes at Newmarket and Hong Kong Cup at Sha Tin last 2 starts: effective at 9f to 1½m: acts on soft and good to firm going. *F. Poulsen, Denmark*

DANTE'S DEVINE (IRE) 2 b.g. (Jan 19) Ashkalani (IRE) 128 – Basilea (FR) **66** (Frere Basile (FR) 129) [2003 7d 7.2d 8.2m⁵ f8g⁵ Dec 8] 8,500F, 6,000Y: strong, angular gelding: half-brother to several winners, including smart French sprinter Pont-Aven (by Try My Best), now dam of Sainte Marine and Josr Algarhoud, and useful French performer up to 1m Albacora (by Fairy King): dam, French maiden (stayed 1½m), half-sister to smart French sprinter Bold Apparel: fair maiden: best effort when fifth at Nottingham penultimate start: should stay 1¼m: acts on good to firm going. *A. Bailey*

DANUM 3 b.c. Perpendicular 119 – Maid of Essex 66 (Bustino 136) [2003 10.3m⁴ **59** 8.1s⁶ 8.1m⁵ 10.3m⁶ f8g f12s⁵ f11g⁶ Dec 15] strong, deep-girthed colt: seventh foal: half-brother to 3 winners abroad: dam 1m winner: modest maiden: probably stays 1½m: acts on good to firm ground, soft and fibresand: tried in cheekpieces. *R. Hollinshead*

DANZIG PRINCE 4 b.g. Danzig Connection (USA) – Lovely Greek Lady (Ela- **–** Mana-Mou 132) [2003 f12g⁶ f12s f12g 14.1d 16m Jun 10] 700F: lengthy gelding: sixth reported foal: half-brother to 1½m to 2m winner Indiana Princess (by Warrshan) and winner abroad by Alleging: dam unraced: no form, leaving J. Given after third start: wore cheekpieces final outing. *K. A. Morgan*

DANZIG RIVER (IRE) 2 b.c. (Feb 16) Green Desert (USA) 127 – Sahara Breeze **95** 85 (Ela-Mana-Mou 132) [2003 7.1g 7.2g⁴ 6d⁶ 5.7f* 6m* 6f⁵ Oct 10] €50,000Y: good-bodied colt: half-brother to 3 winners, including 8-y-o Alcazar and smart French 1m (including Prix Marcel Boussac at 2 yrs) winner Lady of Chad (by Last Tycoon): dam, maiden who stayed 1m, half-sister to Fillies' Mile winner Ivanka: useful performer: won nurseries at Bath in September and Newmarket (beat Free Trip 2½ lengths) in October: ran respectably final start: should stay 7f: acts on firm going. *B. W. Hills*

DANZIG'S HEIRESS   2 b.f. (Apr 8) Danzig Connection (USA) – Zielana Gora (Polish Precedent (USA) 131) [2003 8m 7.1g Nov 5] leggy filly: first foal: dam, no sign of ability, half-sister to smart performers Mon Tresor (up to 7f) and Montendre (sprinter): well held in maidens. *J. G. Given*   –

DANZIG TWISTER   3 b.f. Danzig Connection (USA) – Early Gales (Precocious 126) [2003 f7s 8m Oct 6] 500Y: fifth living foal: half-sister to 2 winners, notably one-time smart 6f (including at 2 yrs) to 1m winner Nigrasine (by Mon Tresor): dam lightly-raced maiden: soundly beaten in maidens at Southwell and Pontefract. *C. J. Teague*

DAPHNE'S DOLL (IRE)   8 b.m. Polish Patriot (USA) 128 – Helietta 78 (Tyrnavos 129) [2003 42, a–: p7g 10.2m³ 11.9m⁶ 9m 10m 8g 10m 11.6m 8m 10m 16m 16m Sep 25] big mare: poor handicapper: barely stays 1½m: acts on polytrack, good to firm and heavy going, well held both runs on fibresand: tried visored/in cheekpieces. *Dr J. R. J. Naylor*   **38 a–**

DARA MAC   4 b.g. Presidium 124 – Nishara (Nishapour (FR) 125) [2003 60: 8m 9m 7m³ 8f 7.9f⁶ 7.5d⁴ 7m 8d² 8.3m 8m 8m⁵ Sep 18] modest maiden: stays 8.5f: acts on firm and good to soft ground: tried blinkered, sometimes wears cheekpieces: sometimes starts slowly. *N. Bycroft*   **58**

DARASIM (IRE)   5 b.g. Kahyasi 130 – Dararita (IRE) (Halo (USA)) [2003 113: 12g⁴ 14.1g² 15.5d⁴ 16.4m 11.8m⁴ 12m⁴ 14g* 12g³ 15d* 15.5m* 20s³ 15.5s Oct 26]   **119**
Royal Rebel might have been out for the season but his stable still managed to pick up a couple of long-distance pattern races thanks to Darasim, a gelding who proved himself not far behind the dual Gold Cup winner in terms of ability and just about as difficult to predict. Midway through the latest campaign Darasim looked to be going completely the wrong way temperamentally, his performance in a listed race at Newmarket on his sixth start showing him at his worst. Slowly away, Darasim looked reluctant throughout and trailed home last of four behind Razkalla. Yet he returned from a month off to win three of his next four starts, including the Group 2 Prix Kergorlay at Deauville and the Group 3 Prix Gladiateur Royal Thalasso Barriere at Longchamp.

Darasim's enthusiasm was rekindled at Goodwood at the end of July when, under top weight in the ladbrokes.com Prestige Stakes, a valuable handicap in which he had finished second twelve months earlier, Darasim had his fourteen rivals well strung out at the line, where he had three and a half lengths to spare over his nearest pursuer Romany Prince. Darasim didn't travel with the same fluency and could finish only third behind Researched in the listed Glorious Rated Stakes (Handicap) at the same venue three days later, shaping as though a mile and a half is barely far enough for him nowadays. The step back up in trip, to distances just short of two miles in the Prix Kergorlay and Prix Gladiateur, brought out the best in Darasim, who also benefited from being allowed to dictate the pace in each contest. Westerner finished second in both, Darasim beating him by three lengths in the

ladbrokes.com Prestige Stakes (Handicap), Goodwood—
Darasim defies top weight to win from Romany Prince and Shabernak

*Prix Gladiateur Royal Thalasso Barriere, Longchamp—Darasim dictates matters;
Westerner is second ahead of Soreze (rail) and Prompt Payment*

former and by two lengths in the latter. It was a very different story when the pair met on soft ground in two races at Longchamp in October. Westerner won both of them, with Darasim finishing eleven lengths behind him in third in the Prix du Cadran and trailing home last of fourteen in the Prix Royal-Oak. Darasim wasn't disgraced in the former, as a distance of two and a half miles is almost certainly too far for him, especially when conditions are testing; he had seemed barely to stay two and a quarter miles when third in the previous season's Doncaster Cup. In the Royal-Oak, however, Darasim showed that he is still not one to trust implicitly, finding nothing in the straight after being taken on for the lead.

		Ile de Bourbon	Nijinsky
	Kahyasi	(br 1975)	Roseliere
	(b 1985)	Kadissya	Blushing Groom
Darasim (IRE)		(b 1979)	Kalkeen
(b.g. 1998)		Halo	Hail To Reason
	Dararita (IRE)	(b or br 1969)	Cosmah
	(b 1991)	Darara	Top Ville
		(b 1983)	Delsy

Darasim was bred by the Aga Khan, and raced in his colours when with John Oxx in Ireland in 2001, winning two of his four starts. He had three runs for his present stable that year, winning the Mallard Handicap at Doncaster on the second of them. Joe Fanning rode Darasim on his first five appearances in Britain, winning twice on him, but he didn't partner him again until winning on him at Goodwood in July. Fanning, who enjoyed his most successful year to date with eighty-four winners, kept the mount and played no small part in Darasim's triumphs at Deauville and Longchamp, riding very well-judged races in front. Darasim is the third foal of Dararita, who is also responsible for a couple of fairly useful Aga Khan fillies in Darariyna (by Shirley Heights), a winner over a mile and a half and an extended thirteen furlongs, and Darabela (by Desert King), successful in a seven-furlong maiden at Leopardstown for John Oxx in April, as well as the winning selling hurdler Darak (by Doyoun). Dararita, a winner at around a mile and a half in France, is a half-sister to several at least smart performers at distances of a mile and a half and more. They include the Prix Maurice de Nieuil winner Darazari, later successful in a Group 1 in Australia, the Prix du Jockey Club third Rhagaas, the King Edward VII Stakes runner-up Kilimanjaro and the four-year-old River Dancer, a winner in Hong Kong in the latest season having won the Prix La Force in 2002, when known as Diaghilev and trained by Aidan O'Brien. Darasim's grandam Darara, a half-sister to Darshaan, won the Prix Vermeille. Darasim, a lengthy, quite good-topped gelding, acts on firm and good to soft ground. He wore blinkers on four occasions early on in his career, winning twice in them, but has been visored on all but one of his starts since successful without headgear on his four-year-old reappearance. *M. Johnston*

266

DARCIE MIA 2 ch.f. (Feb 17) Polar Falcon (USA) 126 – Marie La Rose (FR) (Night **40**
Shift (USA)) [2003 7m f8s f6s 7d f6g Nov 19] 3,000Y: rather leggy filly: half-sister to 1m
(at 2 yrs) and 1¼m winner Contemporary Art (by Blushing Flame) and to winner up to
1½m Danni La Rose (by Lycius), both in France: dam French 1¼m winner: poor maiden:
should stay 1m: tried blinkered. *J. R. Weymes*

DARE 8 b.g. Beveled (USA) – Run Amber Run (Run The Gantlet (USA)) [2003 f14g **–**
Apr 4] leggy gelding: fair performer in 2001: out of sorts over hurdles prior to well held
on Flat return: often blinkered/visored: tongue tied last 2 starts: tends to carry head high.
R. Lee

DARE TO RUN 3 b.f. Presidium 124 – Kabs Twist (Kabour 80) [2003 –: f8.5g Jan 13] **–**
well held in maiden/sellers: visored (seemed reluctant to race early) final start. *J. O'Reilly*

DARING AFFAIR 2 b.f. (Mar 27) Bien Bien (USA) 125 – Daring Destiny 113 (Daring **65**
March 116) [2003 6g 7.1f⁴ 6d⁴ f7g⁵ f6g² p7g⁶ Dec 27] good-topped filly: second foal:
dam 6f/7f winner: fair maiden: good second in nursery at Southwell in December: probably best at 6f: acts on all-weather and good to soft ground. *K. R. Burke*

DARING AIM 2 b.f. (Mar 8) Daylami (IRE) 138 – Phantom Gold 119 (Machiavellian **80 P**
(USA) 123) [2003 7m⁴ Sep 5] leggy, useful-looking filly: fourth foal: half-sister to Oaks
runner-up Flight of Fancy (by Sadler's Wells), 7f winner at 2 yrs, and useful 2002 2-y-o
7f winner Desert Star (by Green Desert): dam, 1m (at 2 yrs) to 13f winner, from good
middle-distance family: 16/1 and green, 3¼ lengths fourth of 7 to Park Accord in minor
event at Kempton, slowly away and flashing tail before running on under hands and heels:
had 2 handlers/got worked up beforehand: will be well suited by 1¼m/1½m: should
improve considerably and win races. *Sir Michael Stoute*

DARING CONNECTION 3 b.f. Danzig Connection (USA) – Daring Destiny 113 **–**
(Daring March 116) [2003 –: 7f 8f Jun 18] leggy filly: little sign of ability: upset in stall
and withdrawn once at 2 yrs. *K. R. Burke*

DARING NEWS 8 b.g. Risk Me (FR) 127 – Hot Sunday Sport 42 (Star Appeal 133) **–**
[2003 f12s Feb 17] rangy gelding: poor maiden: very lightly raced and no form since
1998: tried blinkered: possibly ungenuine. *O. O'Neill*

DARK CHAMPION 3 b.g. Abou Zouz (USA) 109 – Hazy Kay (IRE) 77 (Treasure **67**
Kay 114) [2003 71: 7f 6g⁵ 5g² 5m³ 6f³ 5m² 5g³ 6g⁴ f6g⁴ p6g f6s⁵ Dec 27] good-topped **a57**
gelding: fair maiden on turf, modest on all-weather: effective at 5f to 7f: acts on fibresand
and good to firm ground, probably on soft: has raced freely. *Jedd O'Keeffe*

DARK CHARM (FR) 4 b.g. Anabaa (USA) 130 – Wardara 107 (Sharpo 132) [2003 **100**
104: 7g⁵ 7m² 7.1g 7m⁴ 7f 6g Oct 24] tall, quite good-topped gelding: useful handicapper:
creditable efforts in frame at Newbury second/fourth starts: effective at 6f/7f: acts on
polytrack, soft and firm going: troublesome to post on reappearance: has been blanketed
for stall entry: races freely: sold 55,000 gns. *A. M. Balding*

DARK CUT (IRE) 3 b.g. Ali-Royal (IRE) 127 – Prima Nox (Sabrehill (USA) 120) **60**
[2003 –: 9.2d² 9.2d* 8.3m 8.1m Sep 22] modest performer: won handicap at Hamilton in
May: no form after, leaving Mrs A. Naughton before final start: will stay 1¼m: acts on
good to soft going. *A. Charlton*

DARK DAY BLUES (IRE) 2 ch.c. (Mar 22) Night Shift (USA) – Tavildara (IRE) **73**
(Kahyasi 130) [2003 6m³ 6m² 6.1m 6m⁶ 6d² 7f³ 7g Oct 24] €9,000Y, 30,000 2-y-o:
workmanlike colt: first foal: dam unraced out of half-sister to Dante winner Torjoun: fair
maiden: will stay 1m: acts on firm and good to soft ground. *R. Hannon*

DARK DOLORES 5 b.m. Inchinor 119 – Pingin (Corvaro (USA) 124) [2003 49: **47**
f8s f8.5g⁶ 7g⁵ 8g 8m 8.5d⁶ 10.1f² f12s 11.9m 10m⁵ p12g⁶ Nov 13] poor maiden: left **a37**
N. Littmoden after sixth start: seems best around 1¼m: acts on firm and good to soft
ground: none too consistent. *J. R. Boyle*

DARK EMPRESS (IRE) 2 br.f. (Feb 24) Second Empire (IRE) 124 – Good Refer- **92**
ence (IRE) 84 (Reference Point 139) [2003 6m² 7.1f* 7.1m⁵ 7m⁵ 8f³ 6.5m 6m⁵ Oct 17]
5,000Y: quite attractive filly: fourth foal: half-sister to fairly useful but untrustworthy 7f
(including at 2 yrs) winner Schnitzel (by Tirol) and 5-y-o The Fairy Flag: dam 7f (at 2
yrs) and 1m winner: fairly useful performer: won minor event at Warwick in July:
creditable efforts after only in listed race and nursery (wore cheekpieces) at Newmarket
on fourth and final starts: stays 7f: no easy ride. *R. M. Beckett*

DARK RAIDER (IRE) 2 br. or gr.f. (Feb 8) Definite Article 121 – Lady Shikari **77 ?**
(Kala Shikari 125) [2003 7g 7.1g Nov 5] half-sister to fairly useful 1999 2-y-o 6f (in
Ireland) winner Harry's Game (by Emperor Jones): dam unraced: seemed to show fair

form when eighth of 12 in steadily-run listed event at Newbury: well beaten in maiden at Musselburgh 11 days later. *A. P. Jones*

DARK SHADOWS   8 b.g. Machiavellian (USA) 123 – Instant Desire (USA) 86   **45** (Northern Dancer) [2003 –: 12.4g 13g Jun 12] big, good-topped gelding: has a high knee action: poor handicapper nowadays. *W. Storey*

DARK SHAH (IRE)   3 b.g. Night Shift (USA) – Shanjah (Darshaan 133) [2003 74:   **77 §** 6m⁶ 7d⁶ 8m⁴ 7.9f 8d 7g Sep 16] smallish, sturdy gelding: fair performer: has been tubed: below form last 3 starts: effective at 7f/1m: acts on soft and good to firm ground: often tongue tied: has carried head high/found little: took little interest final start: one to treat with caution. *A. M. Balding*

DARK SKYE (IRE)   2 br.f. (Feb 9) Idris (IRE) 118 – Bobby's Dream 53 (Reference   **52** Point 139) [2003 6g⁵ 7m² 7g⁶ 7m⁵ Sep 4] second foal: dam staying maiden out of half-sister to King Edward VII Stakes winner Head For Heights: modest maiden: left M. Tompkins before second in claimer at Thirsk: stayed 7f: dead. *D. Shaw*

DARK VICTOR (IRE)   7 b.g. Cadeaux Genereux 131 – Dimmer 108 (Kalaglow 132)   **–** [2003 69, a–: f8s Jan 14] leggy, workmanlike gelding: one-time fair handicapper: well below form last 7 starts: sometimes blinkered/visored. *D. Shaw*

DARKWOOD BEACH (IRE)   4 b.g. Darkwood Bay (USA) 82 – Call of The Night   **–** (IRE) 72 (Night Shift (USA)) [2003 f12g Feb 10] fourth foal: half-brother to winner in Belgium by Rock City: dam 1m winner who should have been suited by at least 1¼m: 33/1, tailed off in maiden at Wolverhampton: sold 1,200 gns. *S. Kirk*

DARLA (IRE)   2 b.f. (Feb 11) Night Shift (USA) – Darbela (IRE) 102 (Doyoun 124)   **73** [2003 5m⁴ 5m² 5.1g³ 6.5m p5g⁶ Oct 30] 32,000Y: close-coupled filly: first foal: dam, Irish 1½m and 2m winner (also won over hurdles), half-sister to Prix de Diane and Prix Vermeille winner Daryaba (by Night Shift): fair maiden: should stay at least 7f: acts on good to firm going. *J. W. Payne*

DARMAGI (IRE)   3 b.f. Desert King (IRE) 129 – Safe Care (IRE) (Caerleon (USA)   **80 +** 132) [2003 77p: 9m² 10.3m³ 10.9m² 10g³ 12d 12d Nov 4] strong filly: fairly useful maiden: stays 1½m: acts on heavy and good to firm ground: has worn cheekpieces, blinkered (well below form) final start: has looked none too keen. *Mrs A. J. Perrett*

DARN GOOD   2 ch.c. (Mar 22) Bien Bien (USA) 125 – Thimbalina 63 (Salmon Leap   **73** (USA) 131) [2003 6m 7.1f⁴ 7f⁵ 7m³ 8f⁶ 10.2f⁴ 8.3g⁵ p8g p10g Nov 29] big, quite good-topped colt: seventh foal: half-brother to 1½m and 16.5f winner Saint Albert (by Keen) and winner in Greece by Most Welcome: dam, 1¼m/1½m winner, from family of Halling: fair maiden: third in nursery at Goodwood: stays 1¼m: acts on firm going, some promise on polytrack. *R. Hannon*

DARSALAM (IRE)   2 ch.c. (Apr 24) Desert King (IRE) 129 – Moonsilk (Solinus   **–** 130) [2003 10m 10m Oct 13] €65,000Y: big, strong colt: has scope: half-brother to several winners, notably very smart but untrustworthy St Leger winner Moonax (by Caerleon): dam, placed at 9f in France, half-sister to 1000 Guineas winner Nocturnal Spree: very green, tailed off in maiden and minor event: sold 6,500 gns. *M. Johnston*

DARTING (USA)   2 b.f. (May 4) Sahm (USA) 112 – Mur Taasha (USA) 108 (River-   **78** man (USA) 131) [2003 6m³ 7g³ p5g* Nov 12] $27,000Y, 20,000 2-y-o: attractive filly: sixth foal: closely related to smart 1998 2-y-o 7f winner Iftitah (by Gone West) and useful 1m to 1¼m (including in UAE) winner Mahroos (by Kingmambo): dam, 7f/1m winner, out of smart 7f winner Linda's Magic: fair form: won maiden at Lingfield by short head from Dandouce: likely to prove best up to 7f. *G. A. Butler*

DARZAO (IRE)   3 b.f. Alzao (USA) 117 – Arctic Maid (IRE) 72 (Darshaan 133)   **–** [2003 –: 11.9m⁵ 10g⁶ Aug 10] angular filly: last in maidens: withdrawn after playing up at start on intended reappearance. *E. J. O'Neill*

DASAR   3 ch.f. Catrail (USA) 123 – Rising of The Moon (IRE) 82 (Warning 136) [2003   **58** 69: 8.2g 6g⁶ 7m 7g 6m 7m 7m f7g f8g f7g⁶ Dec 16] close-coupled filly: modest handi-capper: stays 7f: raced on good/good to firm going on turf. *M. Brittain*

DASH FOR COVER (IRE)   3 b.g. Sesaro (USA) 81 – Raindancing (IRE) 94 (Tirol   **75** 127) [2003 81: 8.1d³ 7m³ 8m 7g 7m* Aug 14] compact gelding: fair performer: won maiden at Salisbury in August: stays 7f: acts on good to firm and good to soft ground. *R. Hannon*

DASH FOR GLORY   4 ch.g. Bluegrass Prince (IRE) 110 – Rekindled Flame (IRE)   **53** (Kings Lake (USA) 133) [2003 65: 8.2g 10m 10.1g 10.2g 9g 12.6f 14.1d Jul 25] leggy gelding: modest maiden handicapper: mostly well held in 2003: stays 1¼m: acts on good to firm going and polytrack: tongue tied fourth/fifth starts. *M. Blanshard*

DASHING DANE 3 b.c. Danehill (USA) 126 – Baldemara (FR) (Sanglamore (USA) **58**
126) [2003 p8g⁴ Oct 8] second foal: closely related to 4-y-o Baldour: dam unraced
half-sister to very smart French filly up to 1m Balbonella, herself dam of top-class
sprinter Anabaa: 20/1, some promise when fourth to Miss Pebbles in maiden at Lingfield,
seeming green and not knocked about once held: joined D. Chapman 5,500 gns.
E. A. L. Dunlop

DASHING GENT 3 ch.g. Prince Sabo 123 – Sistabelle (Bellypha 130) [2003 51: 10g –
8.1d 7g Jun 3] poor maiden: well held in 2003: tried blinkered. *M. S. Saunders*

DASHING STEVE 4 b.g. Danzig Connection (USA) – Blazing Sunset 55 (Blazing **27**
Saddles (AUS)) [2003 44: f8s f8s⁴ f6g 5.7f 7f f9.4g Jul 19] bad maiden: left M. Hammond
after third start: tried visored. *Mrs A. M. Thorpe*

DASH OF GINGER (IRE) 2 ch.f. (Apr 28) General Monash (USA) 107 – Kingdom –
Pearl 57 (Statoblest 120) [2003 6m 7.5m f8g Oct 16] 5,500Y: workmanlike filly: third
foal: half-sister to 3-y-o Unicorn Reward and winner in Belgium by Woodborough: dam,
1½m winner: little sign of ability in maidens/seller: trained first 2 starts by Julian Poulton.
J. G. Given

DASH OF MAGIC 5 b.m. Magic Ring (IRE) 115 – Praglia (IRE) 64 (Darshaan 133) **52**
[2003 57: f12g* f11g² 11.8m⁴ f12g 9.9m* 12m⁴ 12.1d* 12.1g 12.1m⁴ f12s f14g f14g Dec **a46**
12] leggy, quite good-topped mare: modest handicapper on turf, poor on all-weather: won
at Southwell in January and Beverley in June (apprentices) and July (dead-heated): stays
1½m: acts on fibresand, firm and good to soft ground: tried blinkered/visored: has been
slowly away/looked none too keen. *J. Hetherton*

DAUNTED (IRE) 7 b.g. Priolo (USA) 127 – Dauntess (Formidable (USA) 125) [2003 **?**
–, a65: f14g⁴ Dec 12] quite good-topped gelding: fair handicapper: ran respectably **a65**
only 7-y-o outing: stays 2m: acts on fibresand, little form on turf since 1999: formerly
blinkered: usually held up: carries head awkwardly. *P. A. Blockley*

DAVE BEST (IRE) 3 b.c. Marju (IRE) 127 – Tajanama (IRE) 52 (Gorytus (USA) – §
132) [2003 64d: 6f 5m Jun 23] small, sparely-made colt: disappointing maiden: twice
blinkered: virtually refused to race on reappearance: reluctant to post next time: one to
leave alone. *A. Berry*

DAVE (IRE) 2 b.g. (Feb 15) Danzero (AUS) – Paradise News 51 (Sure Blade (USA) **64 ?**
130) [2003 5g 5g 5.1f⁵ 5m Oct 25] IR 27,000F, 20,000Y, 10,000 2-y-o: lengthy gelding:
fourth foal: half-brother to 5f winners abroad by Ezzoud (at 2 yrs) and Pivotal: dam, 5f
winner at 2 yrs, half-sister to useful performer up to 1½m Musetta: modest maiden:
seemingly best effort when last of 5 at Nottingham: likely to prove best at 5f/6f. *J. R. Best*

DAVID'S GIRL 2 b.f. (Mar 17) Royal Applause 124 – Cheer (Efisio 120) [2003 6d⁵ **54 d**
7m⁴ 8m 8.2m⁶ p8g f8g f9.4g⁵ Dec 22] leggy filly: first foal: dam, unraced half-sister to
5-y-o Canada, out of half-sister to winner up to 10.5f Church Parade and to middle-
distance stayer Castle Rising, both smart: modest maiden: best effort on debut: should
stay 1m. *D. Morris*

DAVIDS MARK 3 b.g. Polar Prince (IRE) 117 – Star of Flanders (Puissance 110) **64**
[2003 p6g p7g p6g* f6g⁶ 6g⁵ 6m³ 5.3m⁵ 6m⁵ 6g⁶ 6g 6m³ 6m⁵ 5.3f p6g³ p7g
Nov 2] 1,800 2-y-o: second foal: dam unraced: modest performer: won seller at Lingfield
in February and handicap at Folkestone in March: effective at 5f/6f: acts on polytrack
and good to firm going: tried visored/in cheekpieces (not discredited) 4 of last 5 starts:
sometimes slowly away. *J. R. Jenkins*

DAVOS 3 gr.g. Wolfhound (USA) 126 – Misty Goddess (IRE) 63 (Godswalk (USA) –
130) [2003 38, a161: p6g⁴ f7s⁵ f7s⁴ f7g⁴ f6g⁴ 5.9m 7g f6g f7s Oct 21] strong, stocky **a53**
gelding: modest performer on all-weather: well below form last 4 starts: finds 6f on sharp
side and stays 8.5f: acts on all-weather and good to firm going: tends to be slowly away
(unruly and withdrawn once at 2 yrs): sold 4,000 gns. *N. P. Littmoden*

DAVY LEESE 3 b.g. Overbury (IRE) 116 – Mac's Type (IRE) (Mac's Imp (USA) 116) –
[2003 47: 6g 8d 8s 7.9d 5.9m Aug 4] no longer of much account: tried in cheekpieces.
W. Storey

DAWAARR (IRE) 3 ch.c. Indian Ridge 123 – Zarawa (IRE) (Kahyasi 130) [2003 8g **82**
8m⁴ 10g² p12g* a10f a10f Dec 18] 130,000Y: medium-sized, quite attractive colt: first
foal: dam, ran once in France at 3 yrs, half-sister to smart French 7f/1m winner Zarannda:
fairly useful form: won maiden at Lingfield (dead-heated) in July: left M. Jarvis and off 4
months before penultimate start: barely stays 1½m: acts on polytrack: raced only on good
going or firmer on turf: reportedly suffered from sore shins after second outing. *A. Smith,
UAE*

DAWARI (IRE) 5 b.g. In The Wings 128 – Dawala (IRE) (Lashkari 128) [2003 101: ?
a12g^2 a12g a10.5g^5 a12g^6 15g^4 14g 18m Oct 18] close-coupled, attractive gelding: useful
performer at best: only placed effort in 2003 when second in minor event at Mijas on
reappearance: well held in Cesarewitch at Newmarket final start: stays 1½m: acts on soft
going, seemed ill at ease on firm: has worn net muzzle/visor: has flashed tail/been slowly
away/looked none too keen. *P. Haley, Spain*

DAWN AIR (USA) 2 b.f. (Apr 26) Diesis 133 – Midnight Air (USA) 111 (Green –
Dancer (USA) 132) [2003 7g Nov 1] half-sister to several winners, including smart 7f (at
2 yrs) to 1½m winner Midnight Line (by Kris S) and 3-y-o Westerly Air: dam won May
Hill Stakes and first past post in Fillies' Mile: 25/1, well held in maiden at Newmarket.
D. J. Daly

DAWN DUEL (IRE) 2 b.f. (Apr 28) Daggers Drawn (USA) 114 – Dawn's Folly (IRE) –
47 (Bluebird (USA) 125) [2003 6g Jul 31] 11,000Y: third foal: half-sister to fairly useful
2002 2-y-o 6f/7f winner Love Is Blind (by Ali-Royal) and 5f winner (including at 2 yrs)
Red Eagle (by Eagle Eyed): dam Irish maiden (probably stayed 7f) out of half-sister to
high-class miler Be My Guest: 66/1, well held in maiden at Newcastle. *B. Smart*

DAWN INVASION (IRE) 4 b.c. Common Grounds 118 – Princess of Zurich (IRE) 115
(Law Society (USA) 130) [2003 111: 12g 14m^4 12m* Oct 16] quite good-topped colt:
smart performer: off nearly a year before reappearance: best effort when winning handicap at Newmarket in October under top weight by 1½ lengths from Trust Rule: well held
in listed race at Goodwood previous outing: stays easy 1¾m: yet to race on extremes of
going: sweated first 2 starts: sometimes carries head awkwardly: sold 65,000 gns.
Mrs A. J. Perrett

DAWN PIPER (USA) 3 b.g. Desert Prince (IRE) 130 – June Moon (IRE) (Sadler's 87
Wells (USA) 132) [2003 8.5m^3 7m^2 May 5] $400,000Y: compact gelding: sixth foal:
half-brother to several winners, including smart milers Pacino and Dupont (both by
Zafonic): dam unraced daughter of 1000 Guineas runner-up and smart sprinter Kerrera:
fairly useful form: placed in maidens at Beverley and Doncaster (neck second to San
Antonio, soon niggled along but every chance): gelded after: may prove best around 1m:
has worn crossed noseband. *D. R. Loder*

DAWN SURPRISE (USA) 2 b.f. (Mar 2) Theatrical 128 – Lignify (ARG) (Con- 78 p
fidential Talk (USA)) [2003 8m^3 Oct 24] quite attractive filly: first foal: dam Argentinian
12.5f Group 1 winner at 4 yrs: 2/1 but very green, 2½ lengths third of 22 to Jath in maiden
at Doncaster, staying on: will be well suited by 1¼m/1½m: sure to improve, and should
win a race or 2. *Saeed bin Suroor*

DAWNUS (IRE) 3 b.f. Night Shift (USA) – Dame's Violet (IRE) (Groom Dancer 103
(USA) 128) [2003 7m^2 8.2g^2 8m^2 8.1m* 10g* 12m^4 10f* 10.1m Sep 17] IR 110,000Y:
leggy, quite attractive filly: first living foal: dam, French 1m winner, closely related to
high-class 1½m performer Wagon Master: useful performer: won maiden at Chepstow in
June, minor event at Pontefract in July and listed rated stakes at Brighton (beat In A Silent
Way by head) in August: always behind in listed event at Yarmouth final outing: probably
better at 1¼m than 1½m: raced only on good going or firmer (acts on firm): tongue tied
first 3 starts: usually wears crossed noseband. *H. R. A. Cecil*

DA WOLF (IRE) 5 ch.g. Wolfhound (USA) 126 – Lady Joyce (FR) (Galetto (FR) 39
118) [2003 51: f6s f5g^4 f7s 6m 6m May 5] strong gelding: modest form at best: showed
little at 5 yrs: has worn blinkers, visored last 2 starts. *D. Nicholls*

DAY DIESIS (USA) 3 ch.f. Diesis 133 – Bird of Time (IRE) 75 (Persian Bold 123) 51
[2003 8m 10.5d^5 9.9m 9.1g^6 8.5d 11v Nov 22] 42,000Y: unfurnished filly: third living
foal: half-sister to winners in USA by Conte di Savoya: dam, 7f to 8.3f winner, half-sister
to smart Italian 1¼m to 1½m winner Redipuglia: modest maiden at best: sold from
M. Channon following fourth start: last in Germany after: stays 1¼m. *K. Davies,
Netherlands*

DAYDREAM DANCER 2 gr.f. (Mar 26) Daylami (IRE) 138 – Dancing Wolf (IRE) –
76 (Wolfhound (USA) 126) [2003 6m 8.3g 6.1f Sep 30] 8,000Y: close-coupled filly:
second foal: dam, maiden effective at 7f/1m, half-sister to useful dam of smart performer
up to 1¼m Monturani: signs of only a little ability in maidens. *C. G. Cox*

DAY FORT (IRE) 3 b.c. Tagula (IRE) 116 – Young Affair (IRE) (Mukaddamah (USA) 104
125) [2003 7m^5 8g* 9f* 10m^3 11g Dec 21] 42,000F, 80,000Y: lengthy colt: first foal: dam
unraced: reportedly had knee injury at 2 yrs: useful form: won maiden at Bath in May and
handicap at Sandown in June: good 1½ lengths third to Leporello in handicap at Newmarket next time: left M. Tregoning and off 5½ months, well below form final outing:
stays 1¼m: raced only on good ground or firmer. *A. Smith, UAE*

DAYGLOW DANCER   5 b.g. Fraam 114 – Fading (Pharly (FR) 130) [2003 95, **82** a103: 8.1g 7.6m 8g 8.1s 7.1g* 7f³ 7m 7g³ 7f 7.2g³ 7d⁶ 7.6m Aug 3] rather sparely-made **a–** gelding: useful handicapper when last ran on all-weather, fairly useful on turf: won at Chepstow in June: effective at 7f to 8.5f: acts on any turf going and fibresand: usually races up with pace. *M. R. Channon*

DAY ONE   2 ch.c. (Jan 13) Daylami (IRE) 138 – Myself 110 (Nashwan (USA) 135) **60 p** [2003 p8g Nov 26] fourth foal: half-brother to useful 2000 2-y-o 6f winner Ghayth (by Sadler's Wells) and 3-y-o Ego: dam, 6f (at 2 yrs) and 7f (Nell Gwyn Stakes) winner, half-sister to smart 5f to 7f performer Bluebook out of smart Queen Mary winner Pushy: 12/1 and green, 4½ lengths seventh to Messe de Minuit in maiden at Lingfield, racing freely: should improve. *G. Wragg*

DAYS OF GRACE   8 gr.m. Wolfhound (USA) 126 – Inshirah (USA) 90 (Caro 133) **62** [2003 65: p7g f6g⁵ f6s⁵ p6g f7g Mar 20] lengthy mare: modest handicapper: effective at stiff 5f to easy 7f: acts on firm going, soft and all-weather: blinkered twice, visored nowadays: usually races prominently. *L. Montague Hall*

DAYTIME GIRL (IRE)   2 gr.f. (Feb 9) Daylami (IRE) 138 – Snoozeandyoulose **77 p** (IRE) 73 (Scenic 128) [2003 7m⁵ 8.1d* Sep 27] 60,000F, 75,000Y: sturdy filly: fourth foal: half-brother to smart sprinter Thrifty Trio: fair form in maidens, winning 14-runner event at Haydock by ½ length from Carriacou, carrying head high before leading close home: should stay 1¼m: open to progress. *B. W. Hills*

DAY TO REMEMBER   2 gr.c. (Apr 9) Daylami (IRE) 138 – Miss Universe (IRE) 99 **77 p** (Warning 136) [2003 7.5m⁴ 7.1m³ Sep 20] 50,000Y: small, quite attractive colt: first foal: dam, 2-y-o 6f winner, out of half-sister to smart but untrustworthy performer up to 1¼m Intimate Guest: better effort in maidens (fair form) when third at Warwick: likely to be suited by at least 1¼m: open to progress. *A. C. Stewart*

DAZZLING BAY   3 b.g. Mind Games 121 – Adorable Cherub (USA) 58 (Halo **107** (USA)) [2003 73§: 5d 6m² 6m* 6f* 6f* 6m 6m² 6m 6d⁶ Sep 29] big, rather leggy gelding: has a round action: useful handicapper: much improved to win at Newmarket in May and York (William Hill Trophy, beat Stormont by 4 lengths) and Ripon (landed odds by 5 lengths from Circuit Dancer) in June: also good neck second to Royal Beacon at Newmarket after: stays 6f: has won on soft going, but best efforts on good to firm/firm: blinkered once at 2 yrs: difficult ride, ducked markedly right at York. *T. D. Easterby*

DAZZLING RIO (IRE)   4 b.g. Ashkalani (IRE) 128 – Dazzling Fire (IRE) 78 (Blue- **–** bird (USA) 125) [2003 58: f16.2g⁶ 10g Jul 8] strong, sturdy gelding: modest handicapper at 3 yrs: well held both starts at 4 yrs, leaving P. Haslam after reappearance. *Miss Kate Milligan*

William Hill Trophy (Handicap), York—a near-record crowd of 30,799 for Timeform Charity Day sees Dazzling Bay win with plenty to spare over Stormont; the day raised £229,403, the second-highest total in its 33-year history

DBEST (IRE) 3 b.g. Woodborough (USA) 112 – Leopard Lily (IRE) (Belmez (USA) **73**
131) [2003 –: 7d 6f 9.5m² 10f* 8.5s* 8.5d⁴ 10g 10m 8.5d Sep 10] IR 7,000F, IR 5,000Y:
second foal: dam unraced out of smart May Hill Stakes winner Bright Crocus: fair
performer: well beaten in maiden at Thirsk second start: won handicaps at Clonmel in
June and Galway in July: stays 1¼m: acts on firm and soft going: wore cheekpieces final
outing. *Ms J. Morgan, Ireland*

DEAR SIR (IRE) 3 ch.g. Among Men (USA) 124 – Deerussa (IRE) (Jareer (USA) **58**
115) [2003 9.7m 14.1m⁵ p12g 12m² 13.1f⁶ Sep 8] fourth foal: half-brother to fairly useful
2000 2-y-o 5f winner Secret Index (by Nicolotte) and winner in Italy by Archway: dam
unraced: modest maiden handicapper: stays easy 13f. *Mrs P. N. Dutfield*

DEBANDY BOY 3 b.g. Timeless Times (USA) 99 – Judys Girl (IRE) (Simply Great **–**
(FR) 122) [2003 –: 9.9m May 10] sturdy gelding: little form: tried visored. *J. S. Wainwright*

DEBBIE 4 b.f. Deploy 131 – Elita (Sharpo 132) [2003 61?: f12g³ p10g⁶ 10g 11.6g 10m³ **66**
10m* 10m* 10m³ 9.9m* Oct 1] close-coupled filly: fair handicapper: won at Newmarket
and Lingfield in August: best form around 1¼m: acts on soft and good to firm going:
tends to race freely, and ideally suited by well-run races: sold 16,000 gns. *I. A. Wood*

DECELERATE 3 ch.c. Polar Falcon (USA) 126 – Speed To Lead (IRE) 90 (Darshaan **60**
133) [2003 58: p10g* p10g³ p10g³ p10g³ p12g* f16g Dec 16] well-made colt:
modest performer: won claimers in January and November (left I. Wood £6,000), both at
Lingfield: stays easy 1½m: acts on all-weather and good to firm ground: has wandered/
carried head high. *A. Charlton*

DECISIVE 4 b.g. Alhaarth (IRE) 126 – Alys 107 (Blakeney 126) [2003 72: p16g* **82**
16m* 18g² 20m 16.2d 16.1m* Aug 9] well-made gelding: fairly useful handicapper:
further improvement in 2003, winning at Lingfield (apprentices) in March, Kempton in
May and Newmarket in August: stays 2½m: acts on polytrack and good to firm going:
often makes running. *P. R. Webber*

DECO LADY 3 ch.f. Wolfhound (USA) 126 – Art Deco Lady 51 (Master Willie 129) **62 d**
[2003 65: 6m 6d⁵ 6.1m 8.3m f9.4g f7g⁵ f8.5g⁶ f8.5g Nov 17] lengthy filly: modest maiden **a–**
handicapper: below form after second start: stays 6f: acts on firm and good to soft going,
below form on all-weather: tried visored. *P. D. Evans*

DECO STAR (IRE) 4 b.g. Dolphin Street (FR) 125 – Ecco Mi (IRE) (Priolo (USA) **–**
127) [2003 57, a60: f12g⁴ f12s³ f12g* f12g⁵ Feb 1] modest handicapper: won selling **a60**
event at Wolverhampton in January: stays 1½m: acts on firm going and fibresand: visored
last 5 starts. *I. A. Wood*

DEE DEE GIRL (IRE) 2 b.f. (Mar 25) Primo Dominie 121 – Chapel Lawn (Generous **60**
(IRE) 139) [2003 6d 7m 6m 7m* p7g Nov 18] 18,000Y: rather leggy filly: second foal:
dam unraced half-sister to 6f performer Halland Park Girl out of 2-y-o 7f winner Katsina,
both useful: modest performer: won claimer at Redcar in October, only form: not sure to
stay beyond 7f. *R. Hannon*

DEEKAZZ (IRE) 4 b.f. Definite Article 121 – Lyric Junction (IRE) (Classic Secret **41**
(USA) 91) [2003 49: f8g f8.5g⁴ f9.4s f9.4s⁶ Feb 28] lengthy, angular filly: poor maiden
handicapper: stays 1¼m: acts on fibresand, best turf efforts on good going or firmer: often
blinkered/visored. *K. A. Ryan*

DEEPER IN DEBT 5 ch.g. Piccolo 121 – Harold's Girl (FR) (Northfields (USA)) **79**
[2003 88: f8.5g³ 8.3g 8.3m 8f 9g 10m 8m³ 8f* 8m* p8g² Nov 12] fairly useful performer:
won handicap at Bath and minor event at Brighton in October: stays easy 1¼m: acts on
all-weather, firm and soft going: tried blinkered/tongue tied: usually races prominently.
J. Akehurst

DEEWAAR (IRE) 3 b.g. Ashkalani (IRE) 128 – Chandni (IRE) (Ahonoora 122) [2003 **53 §**
–: f9.4g p10g² p12g p10g 10f⁵ 10.9m³ 10m² 9.9m 11.9m 10m Aug 15] workmanlike
gelding: modest maiden: well held last 3 starts: stays easy 11f: acts on firm going and
polytrack: tried visored/in cheekpieces: wayward (has tried to run out) and not to be
trusted. *J. S. Moore*

DEFANA 2 b.g. (Mar 5) Defacto (USA) – Thalya (Crofthall 110) [2003 5m 6d⁶ 7m⁵ **48**
7.5d³ Jul 5] 3,200Y: leggy gelding: fifth foal: half-brother to 5-y-o Fairgame Man: dam
never ran: poor maiden: ran in claimers/sellers: stays 7.5f. *M. Dods*

DEFIANCE 8 b.g. Warning 136 – Princess Athena 119 (Ahonoora 122) [2003 38§: **– §**
5.1d 5.7f Aug 17] tall gelding: poor maiden: well beaten in 2003: blinkered: unreliable.
A. P. James

DEFINING   4 b.g. Definite Article 121 – Gooseberry Pie 63 (Green Desert (USA) 127)   **98**
[2003 101p: 13.4m 11.6m^2 14g 12m^3 Aug 16] lengthy gelding: useful performer: creditable efforts at 4 yrs in 4-runner minor events at Windsor (head second to Largo) and
Newmarket (third to Westmoreland Road): stays 1½m: acts on polytrack and good to firm
going, shaped with promise on fibresand at 2 yrs. *J. R. Fanshawe*

DEFINITE FLASH (IRE)   5 b.m. Definite Article 121 – Superflash (Superlative   **–**
118) [2003 –: f14g Apr 4] maiden: no form since 2001: tried visored. *M. Wellings*

DEFINITE GUEST (IRE)   5 gr.g. Definite Article 121 – Nicea (IRE) 90 (Dominion   **89**
123) [2003 84: 7d^5 8m 7.6m^5 p8g^3 7.9m^2 7.9m* 8m* 9.9g^3 7.6m^5 10m^6 8f^5 Sep 28] leggy
gelding: fairly useful handicapper: won at York and Newbury in July: stays 1¼m: acts on
firm and good to soft going, well held on soft/heavy: blinkered once: tends to wander:
held up. *R. A. Fahey*

DEFINITELY SPECIAL (IRE)   5 b.m. Definite Article 121 – Legit (IRE) (Runnett   **43**
125) [2003 50: p7g f7s p7g^4 p7g^4 8m 8f^3 8m 7g^6 6m 8.1m 8m p7g p7g Dec 29] modest   **a51**
maiden on all-weather, poor on turf: left J. M. Bradley after eleventh start: best form at 7f/
1m: acts on polytrack, raced only on good going or firmer on turf. *N. E. Berry*

DEFINITE RETURN (IRE)   5 ch.m. Definite Article 121 – Keen Note 69 (Sharpo   **–**
132) [2003 f9.4g Feb 7] little form: tried tongue tied. *D. J. Wintle*

DEIGN TO DANCE (IRE)   2 b.f. (Feb 7) Danetime (IRE) 121 – Lady Montekin   **75**
(Montekin 125) [2003 5s 6.1m 5.7m^2 6m^6 6m^2 7m Oct 4] €16,000Y: strong filly: half-
sister to fairly useful 1998 2-y-o 5f winner Open Secret (by Mac's Imp) and winners
abroad by Classic Secret and Contract Law: dam, Irish maiden, third at 7f: fair maiden:
second at Bath and Goodwood: stays 6f: acts on good to firm going. *J. G. Portman*

DELAWARE TRAIL   4 b.g. Catrail (USA) 123 – Dilwara (IRE) (Lashkari 128) [2003   **47**
–: 8m^6 12m 10.1m 7m 8m^6 Sep 8] big, leggy gelding: poor maiden: stays 1m: acts on
good to firm ground. *J. S. Wainwright*

DELCIENNE   2 b.f. (Mar 25) Golden Heights 82 – Delciana (IRE) 61 (Danehill (USA)   **53**
126) [2003 7m 6m^4 6m 8.3g p8g^2 f7g Nov 24] first foal: dam maiden who stayed 11f:
modest maiden: stays 1m: acts on polytrack and good to firm going: got very worked up
on intended debut. *G. G. Margarson*

DELEGATE   10 ch.g. Polish Precedent (USA) 131 – Dangora (USA) 98 (Sovereign   **74**
Dancer (USA)) [2003 86: 5f 5m 5m 5m 5.3f* 5.3f^5 5.1m^2 5m^3 5m^3 5m Oct 4] lengthy
gelding: poor mover: fair handicapper: won at Brighton in August: best around 5f: acts
on any turf going: sometimes slowly away/hangs: usually held up. *N. A. Callaghan*

DELHAM (IRE)   3 ch.c. Machiavellian (USA) 123 – Matila (IRE) 98 (Persian Bold   **57**
123) [2003 67?: f8.5g^4 p12g^3 12m^5 f14g 10.9m^4 f12g^5 14.1m^3 10m 12.1d^3 12.1m^6 f12g^6
14g 12m^4 16.2m^2 14m^5 11.9m^5 16d^4 Aug 11] tall, leggy colt: modest maiden handicapper: stays 2m: acts on firm going, good to soft and all-weather: tried visored: generally
gives his running. *J. D. Czerpak*

DELICHON   3 b.f. Bluebird (USA) 125 – Summer Style (IRE) 70 (Indian   **–**
Ridge 123) [2003 p6g p7g^6 p8g f6g f6g 7m^5 6m May 8] 36,000Y: first foal: dam, second
at 9f in Ireland, sister to very smart performer up to 1½m Definite Article: little form:
tried in cheekpieces: has looked temperamental. *G. L. Moore*

DELIGHTFUL GIFT   3 b.f. Cadeaux Genereux 131 – Delightful Chime (IRE) 79   **48**
(Alzao (USA) 117) [2003 6m 6.1g 6f^6 7s^4 7g Jul 31] 1,200Y: leggy, close-coupled filly:
fourth foal: dam, Irish 2-y-o 1m winner, sister to Cheveley Park/Moyglare Stud winner
Capricciosa: poor maiden: best effort at 7f. *M. Brittain*

DELIGHTFULLY   2 b.f. (Mar 8) Definite Article 121 – Kingpin Delight (Emarati   **61**
(USA) 74) [2003 6m Jul 18] 3,500F, 10,000Y: third foal: half-sister to useful Irish 2002
2-y-o 6f winner (stays 1m) Dixie Evans (by Efisio) and a winner in Greece by Formidable: dam unraced: 50/1, late headway when eighth of 13 in maiden at Newbury: suffered
setback after: will stay at least 1m. *B. W. Hills*

DELLAGIO (IRE)   2 b.c. (May 6) Fasliyev (USA) 120 – Lady Ounavarra (IRE)   **81**
(Simply Great (FR) 122) [2003 6g 5f* 6f Jun 17] €24,000Y, 50,000 2-y-o: good-bodied
colt: has quick action: half-brother to winners abroad by Danehill and King's Theatre:
dam, useful performer up to 1½m in Italy, also 1m winner in Ireland at 2 yrs: fairly useful
form when winning 5-runner maiden at York: last of 13 in Coventry Stakes at Royal
Ascot (took strong hold to post) 4 days later: needs to settle to stay 6f: races prominently:
joined C. Dwyer. *D. Nicholls*

DEL MAR SUNSET 4 b.g. Unfuwain (USA) 131 – City of Angels (Woodman (USA) 126) [2003 67, a93: f8.5g² f8.5g* f8.5s 8.5m 8d 8.3g⁴ 10g³ 8m² 10f² 8d f8.5g f8g f9.4s³ Dec 31] tall, rather leggy gelding: fairly useful handicapper on all-weather, fair on turf: won at Wolverhampton in February: stays 1¼m: acts on all-weather, and firm going: tried blinkered/tongue tied: often races prominently: game. *W. J. Haggas* — **78 a93**

DELSARTE (USA) 3 b.c. Theatrical 128 – Delauncy (Machiavellian (USA) 123) [2003 10m* 10d* 12f² 10g 10g³ 11.9m⁴ Aug 19] $200,000F, $170,000Y: tall colt: has scope: first foal: dam, useful French 2-y-o 1m winner who stayed 1¼m, daughter of Park Hill winner Casey: smart performer: won maiden at Leicester in April and listed race at Newmarket (still green when beating Wilful by 5 lengths) in May: also ran creditably when second to High Accolade (beaten 2 lengths) in King Edward VII Stakes at Royal Ascot and third to Princely Venture (beaten length) in Scottish Derby at Ayr: effective at 1¼m/1½m: acts on firm and good to soft going: joined Godolphin. *M. Johnston* — **115**

DELTA FLYER (IRE) 4 b.g. Zafonic (USA) 130 – Pacy (USA) (Manila (USA)) [2003 8.1m 7.1g f7s⁴ f8s Oct 7] 880,000 francs Y: second foal: half-brother to French 11f winner Black Streets (by King's Theatre): dam unraced half-sister to dam of Peintre Celebre out of half-sister to Pawneese: modest form at best in maidens/handicap: should stay at least 1m: sold 5,000 gns. *W. R. Muir* — **60 ?**

DELTA FORCE 4 b.g. High Kicker (USA) – Maedaley 45 (Charmer 123) [2003 f7g⁵ f5s f6g f5g³ 6d 5m 6m⁶ 7f³ 5g⁵ f7g⁶ f6g f11g³ f12g* Dec 26] first foal: dam, maiden, should have stayed at least 1m: modest performer: left D. Shaw after eleventh start: won seller at Wolverhampton in December: stays 1½m: acts on firm ground and fibresand. *P. A. Blockley* — **55**

DELTA LADY 2 b.f. (Mar 25) River Falls 113 – Compton Lady (USA) 100 (Sovereign **45**
Dancer (USA)) [2003 5g 5m 7m³ 7m⁴ 7.5d² f7f⁶ 6m 7m Oct 17] 2,200Y: leggy filly:
sister to Scandinavian 5.5f/6f winner Diamond Falls and half-sister to 1m/1¼m winner in
Scandinavia by Slip Anchor: dam 7f (at 2 yrs) and 1½m winner: poor maiden: stays 7.5f:
acts on good to firm and good to soft ground, some promise on fibresand: blinkered (ran
respectably) fourth start. *C. W. Fairhurst*

DELUSION 2 b.f. (Feb 26) Hennessy (USA) 122 – Another Fantasy (IRE) 103 (Dane- **65**
hill (USA) 126) [2003 6m³ 6.1m² 6d 5m⁴ 6.5d 6f⁴ 6m Oct 6] small, strong filly: first foal:
dam, 5f/6f winner at 2 yrs who probably stayed 1¼m (became disappointing), out of sister
to Italian Group 1 1¼m winner Stufida (grandam of Pivotal): fair maiden: should stay 7f:
acts on firm ground, possibly not good to soft. *T. D. Easterby*

DEMI BOUTEILLE 2 b.f. (Mar 22) Wolfhound (USA) 126 – Tattinger 85 (Prince **47**
Sabo 123) [2003 5.1m 5g 5d⁴ 6f May 31] 3,500Y: small, compact filly: second foal: dam
6f winner: poor maiden: will stay 6f: acts on good to firm and good to soft going. *Mrs
J. R. Ramsden*

DEMOLITION MOLLY 2 b.f. (Apr 20) Rudimentary (USA) 118 – Persian Fortune **75**
53 (Forzando 122) [2003 5m 5.6f⁵ 5g* 5.1m⁵ 5m 5f⁵ f5g⁴ Dec 9] close-coupled filly:
second foal: dam 2-y-o 5f seller winner: fair performer: made all in maiden at Ripon in
July: not discredited in nurseries last 2 starts: will prove best at 5f/easy 6f: acts on firm
going and fibresand: races prominently. *R. F. Marvin*

DEMONSTRATE (USA) 5 ch.h. Storm Bird (CAN) 134 – Substance (USA) (Diesis **112**
133) [2003 112: 8g³ 6g* 7g⁴ Jun 22] well-made horse: has a quick action: smart performer: as good as ever in 2003 winning listed event at Windsor in May by ¾ length
from Ashdown Express: respectable fourth to Lucky Strike in Prix de la Porte Maillot at

Mr K. Abdulla's "Demonstrate"

Longchamp: best form at 6f/7f: raced only on good going or firmer: sold only 16,000 gns in December. *J. H. M. Gosden*

DENEBOLA (USA) 2 br.f. (Apr 6) Storm Cat (USA) – Coup de Genie (USA) 114   **113 p** (Mr Prospector (USA)) [2003 5.5d⁴ 6d* 6s³ 8s* Oct 5]

Take two, as they say in the film industry. One year after a filly owned by the Niarchos family and trained by Pascal Bary had won the Prix Marcel Boussac, another hit the bullseye. Denebola did not win so readily as Six Perfections and she will have her work cut out emulating the Breeders' Cup Mile winner, but she is superbly bred and looks as good a classic prospect as any among the French-trained fillies. Her chance in the One Thousand Guineas will certainly have to be respected should Bary decide to run her—he was non-committal after her success—not least because, unlike several of the others in the ante-post lists, she will have no difficulty getting the trip.

Taking the market as a guide, Denebola was not expected to win any of the three pattern races she contested after a debut fourth in a minor event at Deauville in July, since she started at around 9/1 for all of them. She won the Prix de Cabourg, at Deauville again in August, by half a length from Bonaire but then found six furlongs too sharp, even in testing conditions, in the Prix Morny on the same course later in the month. Held up, Denebola stayed on strongly after being switched over a furlong out and very nearly caught her stable-companion Much Faster, two lengths behind the winner Whipper. A longer trip looked in order and Denebola received it in the Prix Marcel Boussac-Criterium des Pouliches Royal Barriere Deauville at Longchamp in October. This appeared not to be a vintage renewal, but it was certainly competitive with sixteen runners, including three other pattern winners in Necklace (Debutante Stakes and Moyglare Stud Stakes), Green Noon (Prix d'Aumale) and Green Swallow (Prix du Calvados), plus three challengers from Britain led by listed Sweet Solera Stakes winner Bay Tree, along with highly-regarded French filly Bright Abundance, an impressive scorer at Saint-Cloud. Confidently ridden and soon travelling strongly, Denebola had at least eight in front of her with two furlongs left but showed a good turn of foot to join issue soon afterwards. Despite needing firmish handling, she was always doing enough to repel Green Noon's persistent challenge and passed the post a short neck to the good with Tulipe Royale two lengths away third and Green Swallow fourth. Necklace ran below her best, but there is no reason to doubt the form and the promise the winner showed; although Bary said that Denebola is a bit odd and can get excited, there was no sign of that at Longchamp.

By winning the Prix de Cabourg, Denebola was continuing a family tradition, as her dam Coup de Genie and year-older half-sister Loving Kindness (by Seattle Slew) had both preceded her. Coup de Genie went on to land the Prix Morny and Prix de la Salamandre before running third in the One Thousand Guineas. Besides Loving Kindness, who disappointed in a prestige race at Nad Al Sheba in

Prix Marcel Boussac–Criterium des Pouliches Royal Barriere Deauville, Longchamp—
Denebola (white face) puts herself right in the Guineas picture;
Green Noon is a game second ahead of Tulipe Royale and Green Swallow (noseband)

Niarchos Family's "Denebola"

Denebola (USA) (br.f. Apr 6, 2001)	Storm Cat (USA) (b or br 1983)	Storm Bird (b 1978)	Northern Dancer South Ocean
		Terlingua (ch 1976)	Secretariat Crimson Saint
	Coup de Genie (USA) (b 1991)	Mr Prospector (b 1970)	Raise A Native Gold Digger
		Coup de Folie (b 1982)	Halo Raise The Standard

February and a non-graded event at Aqueduct in November, she has produced two stakes winners in America by A P Indy—Snake Mountain notched three Grade 3 races at around nine furlongs; and Glia won a non-graded stakes at the same trip and was beaten a neck in a Grade 2 after being pattern-placed as a two-year-old and then winning the Prix Imprudence in France. To put icing on the cake, Coup de Genie's 1996 foal, the unraced Nureyev filly Moonlight's Box, has produced the latest Criterium International victor Bago. This is a splendid family, albeit one whose members, as often as not, are better at two than three. Coup de Genie—a sparely-made individual, unlike the close-coupled, quite good-topped Denebola—is a sister to a couple of pattern winners, namely champion juvenile and first-rate sire Machiavellian and Ocean of Wisdom, successful in the Prix La Rochette. Her half-brother Exit To Nowhere was a high-class miler while one of her half-sisters Salchow has foaled Grand Criterium winner Way of Light and another, Prix d'Astarte winner Hydro Calido, has produced a Group 2 winner in Japan. Coup de Genie's dam Coup de Folie won the Prix d'Aumale, also at two. With Storm Cat as her sire, Denebola, who has raced only on good to soft or soft going, is not certain to be suited by further than a mile. *P. Bary, France*

DENISE BEST (IRE)   5 ch.m. Goldmark (USA) 113 – Titchwell Lass 57 (Lead On **63**
Time (USA) 123) [2003 45: f8.5g 12.1d⁵ 7m 10m* Oct 20] modest handicapper: left Miss
K. George after second start: won at Pontefract in October: stays 1½m: acts on fibresand,
good to firm and heavy going: tried in cheekpieces/blinkers: sometimes slowly away.
M. Johnston

DENMARK (IRE)   4 b.g. Danehill (USA) 126 – Shamarra (FR) (Zayyani 119) [2003   **–**
74: 8.3g 10d 10.2f p8g Sep 3] tall, good sort: fair performer, lightly raced: well held in
2003: sold 1,800 gns. *P. G. Murphy*

DENNIS OUR MENACE   5 b.g. Piccolo 121 – Free On Board 73 (Free State 125)   **67**
[2003 82, a86: p8g p8g⁵ p8g³ p8g 8g 8.2d⁵ 8.3g⁶ 8f Sep 4] sturdy gelding: fairly useful on   **a81**
all-weather, fair on turf: was best around 1m: acted on soft going, firm and all-weather:
was tried in cheekpieces: dead. *S. Dow*

DEN'S-JOY   7 b.m. Archway (IRE) 115 – Bonvin (Taufan (USA) 119) [2003 72, a82:   **75 d**
f8s f9.4g 8m³ 8.3d 10d* 8.3g 10g 8.3g 9f 8.3g⁴ 10m 10m 8f 10.1g f9.4g 10g 9m⁵ f9.4g⁶   **a65**
Nov 15] close-coupled mare: fair performer: won minor event at Windsor in May: best at
1m/1¼m: acts on fibresand, firm and good to soft going (probably on soft): tried visored/
in cheekpieces: sometimes slowly away: usually held up. *Miss D. A. McHale*

DENVER (IRE)   2 b.c. (Jan 12) Danehill (USA) 126 – Born Beautiful (USA) (Silver   **78**
Deputy (CAN)) [2003 5s⁴ 8.5g² 7.5m⁵ f8g² f7s* Dec 31] €770,000Y: first foal: dam
unraced half-sister to dam of Cheveley Park winner Pas de Reponse and Poule d'Essai
des Poulains winner Green Tune, an excellent family: fair performer: left A. O'Brien
30,000 gns after third start: blinkered, won maiden at Wolverhampton in December:
should stay 1¼m: acts on fibresand and soft ground. *B. J. Meehan*

DEPORTIVO   3 b.c. Night Shift (USA) – Valencia 79 (Kenmare (FR) 125) [2003 107:   **116**
5m⁶ 5f* 5.3m* 5.1m 5m* 5m Dec 14] big, well-made colt: has plenty of scope: smart
performer: successful in 6 of his 9 starts, including 26-runner Balmoral Handicap at
Royal Ascot (top weight, by 2 lengths from Baltic King), listed race at the Curragh (by
1½ lengths from Osterhase) later in June and Big Shuffle Flying Five on latter course
(beat Daganya 1½ lengths) in August: off 3½ months, last in Hong Kong Sprint at Sha
Tin final outing: at least as effective at 5f as 6f: acts on firm and good to soft going: races
prominently: reportedly pulled a shoe off and said to have been unsuited by track at
Chester fourth outing: genuine. *R. Charlton*

DERAASAAT   2 ch.f. (Feb 28) Nashwan (USA) 135 – Nafhaat (USA) 91 (Roberto   **92 p**
(USA) 131) [2003 7.5m 8.2f* Sep 30] sturdy filly: has a powerful, round action: sister to
4-y-o winner Wahchi (useful 1m winner at 2 yrs), closely related to smart 1¼m to 14.6f
winner Ranin (by Unfuwain), and half-sister to several winners, including 7f/1m winner
Ghalib (by Soviet Star) and 7f winner Qhazeenah (by Marju), both useful: dam, 1½m
winner, out of sister to US Grade 1 1¼m winner Sisterhood: justified favouritism in
9-runner maiden at Nottingham, making all to beat Seeking A Way 6 lengths: will be
suited by 1¼m/1½m: useful prospect at least. *E. A. L. Dunlop*

DERRICHE (IRE)   2 ch.f. (Apr 11) Ali-Royal (IRE) 127 – Royal Daughter (High Top   **54**
131) [2003 7m 7.1f⁵ f7f⁴ 7m⁴ 7.9m f8s Sep 26] €8,000Y: half-sister to several winners,
including 1990 2-y-o 6f winner Love of The Arts (by Tate Gallery) and 1m to 1½m
winner Admirals Place (by Perugino): dam third at 1½m: modest maiden: should stay
1m: acts on fibresand and firm going: visored first 2 starts: twice slowly away: sent to
Denmark. *I. A. Wood*

*Balmoral Handicap, Royal Ascot—Deportivo defies top weight in this competitive handicap
for three-year-olds; behind him come Baltic King, Coconut Penang (rail), Awarding and Telepathic*

Mr K. Abdulla's "Deportivo"

DERWENT (USA) 4 b.g. Distant View (USA) 126 – Nothing Sweeter (USA) (Darby   –
Creek Road (USA)) [2003 94: 10m 10m³ Jun 22] rangy gelding: has a quick action: fairly
useful at 3 yrs: ran as though amiss in 2003: usually blinkered (wasn't last start): went
freely to post/refused to settle final 3-y-o outing. *J. D. Bethell*

DES 3 b.g. Timeless Times (USA) 99 – Song's Best (Never So Bold 135) [2003 66d: 5m   **59**
6m³ 5.9m 6m Jun 17] well-made gelding: modest maiden: stayed easy 6f: acted on firm
going: tried in cheekpieces: dead. *J. J. Quinn*

DESERT ARC (IRE) 5 b.g. Spectrum (IRE) 126 – Bint Albadou (IRE) 91 (Green   **65**
Desert (USA) 127) [2003 8.5m⁴ 6g⁶ 6m⁶ 6g 6g Oct 22] third foal: half-brother to French
1½m winner Pibale (by Mujtahid) and 6f winner Badou (by Averti): dam Irish 2-y-o 6f
winner out of very smart filly up to 1¼m Cistus: ran in 2 bumpers for J. O'Neill: fair form
at best: will be suited by further than 6f (bred to stay at least 1¼m): raced only on good/
good to firm ground: sold 7,000 gns. *A. M. Balding*

DESERT BATTLE (IRE) 2 ch.g. (Feb 22) Desert Sun 120 – Papal (Selkirk (USA)   **69**
129) [2003 6m³ 6m⁴ 7m 7g 7m Oct 1] IR 5,000F, €28,000Y: rangy, workmanlike gelding:
first foal: dam unraced: fair maiden: should stay at least 7f. *M. Blanshard*

DESERT BEAU (IRE) 2 b.g. (Mar 6) Desert Style (IRE) 121 – Miss Siham (IRE) 59   **60**
(Green Forest (USA) 134) [2003 6m 6.1m⁵ 6g f7g p8g⁶ Nov 22] €20,000Y: smallish,
robust gelding: fourth foal: closely related to 3-y-o Tamarella and half-brother to 2001
2-y-o 5f winner Addo (by Mujadil): dam 5f winner, including at 2 yrs: modest maiden:
should prove best at 5f/6f: tried visored. *Mrs P. N. Dutfield*

DESERT CRISTAL (IRE) 2 ch.f. (Mar 20) Desert King (IRE) 129 – Damiana (IRE)   **82**
(Thatching 131) [2003 6d² 7f⁵ Sep 4] €14,000Y: first foal: dam, French maiden who
stayed 1m, sister to useful French 1m winner Dirca: better effort in maidens (fairly useful
form) when 1¼ lengths second of 18 to Moss Vale at Windsor: hung right both starts:
should stay at least 1m. *J. R. Boyle*

279

Bet attheraces Mile, Sandown—
Desert Deer justifies strong support in the betting, producing a career-best effort to win from Smirk

DESERT DAISY (IRE)   2 gr.f. (Apr 3) Desert Prince (IRE) 130 – Pomponette (USA)   **67**
(Rahy (USA) 115) [2003 7g² 6m² 7m⁶ 6g Oct 28] rather leggy, useful-looking filly: first
foal: dam unraced half-sister to smart sprinter Blue Goblin: fair maiden: second at
Newmarket and Thirsk: likely to prove best up to 7f. *I. A. Wood*

DESERT DANCE (IRE)   3 b.g. Desert Story (IRE) 115 – Cindy's Star (IRE) 68   **73**
(Dancing Dissident (USA) 119) [2003 –p: 8m⁴ 8.3g³ 8m 8m Oct 25] leggy, rather
unfurnished gelding: below form when fourth in maiden at Newmarket on reappearance:
below that after, markedly so in handicaps last 2 starts: stays 1m: raced only on good/
good to firm ground. *G. Wragg*

DESERT DEER   5 ch.h. Cadeaux Genereux 131 – Tuxford Hideaway 102 (Cawston's   **120**
Clown 113) [2003 118: 9m² 8.1g* 8f Jun 17] big, strong horse: very smart performer:
winner of 7 of 13 starts: better than ever when beating Smirk by 2½ lengths in Bet attheraces Mile at Sandown in April: refused to enter stall for Lockinge Stakes at Newbury
intended next outing, and ran poorly (seemed to race moodily) in Queen Anne Stakes at
Royal Ascot final start: effective at 1m/1¼m: raced only on good going or firmer since
debut: also shade mulish stall on 4-y-o reappearance: front runner. *M. Johnston*

DESERT DESTINY   3 b.g. Desert Prince (IRE) 130 – High Savannah 77 (Rousillon   **109**
(USA) 133) [2003 97: 7m* 8g⁵ 8d 7m⁵ 7m⁴ Aug 21] leggy, useful-looking gelding: useful
performer: won minor event at Newmarket in April: mostly creditable efforts after, fifth
to Clodovil in Poule d'Essai des Poulains at Longchamp (beaten 3½ lengths) and to
Membership in Jersey Stakes at Royal Ascot (swished tail, reluctant to go to post and
found less than seemed likely), and fourth to Vanderlin in listed event at York (visored):
stays 1m: acts on good to firm going: coltish last 2 starts, and subsequently gelded: joined
Saeed bin Suroor. *D. R. Loder*

DESERT DIPLOMAT (IRE)   2 br.g. (Mar 22) Machiavellian (USA) 123 – Desert   **71 p**
Beauty (IRE) 103 (Green Desert (USA) 127) [2003 7m 7m⁴ 7s Oct 29] big, good-bodied
gelding: has scope: second foal: dam, 7f/1m winner, half-sister to very smart 1¼m
performer Greek Dance and 4-y-o Islington: best effort in maidens (fair form) when
fourth at Leicester: will be suited by 1m/1¼m: ran poorly on soft going: reportedly had
sore mouth on debut: type to make his mark in handicaps at 3 yrs. *Sir Michael Stoute*

DESERT DREAMER (IRE)   2 b.g. (Feb 12) Green Desert (USA) 127 – Follow   **98**
That Dream 90 (Darshaan 133) [2003 6g⁴ 7g* 7m⁵ 6m⁴ 6.1m² 7d Sep 10] good-topped
gelding: first foal: dam, 1½m winner who stayed 14.6f, half-sister to high-class 1¼m/
1½m performer Storming Home: useful performer: won maiden at Newbury in July:
good efforts in frame in minor events at Ripon and Chester (2 lengths second of 4 to
Soonest) after: barely stays 7f: acts on good to firm ground. *B. W. Hills*

DESERT FLAME   3 b.g. Desert Prince (IRE) 130 – Paradise Soul (USA) 82 (Dyna-   **51**
former (USA)) [2003 80: 9d 8f² 11.6d 8f 10.9m p10g Jul 16] modest maiden: bred to
be suited by 1¼m/1½m: acts on firm going: tried visored/blinkered: looked increasingly
temperamental. *A. M. Balding*

DESERT FORTUNE (IRE)   3 ch.g. Desert Prince (IRE) 130 – Fairy Fortune 78   **55 §**
(Rainbow Quest (USA) 134) [2003 67: 10.3g 8d 8.3m⁶ 10.2m³ 10m 10f 8f Sep 29]
heavy-topped gelding: modest maiden: left M. Johnston after third start: stays 1¼m: acts
on good to firm going: tried blinkered: probably ungenuine: sold 2,500 gns. *M. J. Wallace*

DESERT FURY   6 b.g. Warning 136 – Number One Spot 71 (Reference Point 139)   **74 d**
[2003 86, a76: f7s² f7g⁵ f7s⁶ f7g⁶ 7m 7m³ 8.3d 10d 8.3g f8.5g f8.5s⁵ 7d 6m 7s Oct 29]
small gelding: fair performer: mostly well below form in second half of year: barely stays
8.5f: acts on soft going, good to firm and fibresand: tried in cheekpieces (ran poorly):
sometimes slowly away. *R. Bastiman*

DESERT GLOW (IRE)   3 b.f. Machiavellian (USA) 123 – Alumisiyah (USA) 93   **?**
(Danzig (USA)) [2003 75: a7.5f³ a8f a7.5f⁵ a8f⁴ a9f² 10m a8.5f a11f⁵ Dec 12] IR   **a95 ?**
42,000Y: workmanlike filly: second foal: dam, 5.3f (at 2 yrs) and 6f winner, closely
related to useful 2-y-o 5f/6f (Cherry Hinton) winner Asfurah: fair form when placed in
minor event/maiden at Cork for E. Lynam at 2 yrs: ran to similar level in UAE early in
year before seeming to show useful form when second to Danuta in UAE Oaks in April:
heavily bandaged in front, well held in listed race at Royal Ascot next time: off 5½
months, well below best back in maiden company in UAE last 2 starts: stays 9f: acts on
dirt, raced only on good/good to firm going on turf. *S. Seemar, UAE*

DESERT HEAT   5 b.h. Green Desert (USA) 127 – Lypharitissima (FR) (Lightning   **62**
(FR) 129) [2003 90: 10f⁶ 8.2f⁴ p7g f12g f12s⁴ Dec 6] sturdy, good-bodied horse: modest
maiden nowadays: left H. Cecil 5,000 gns after third start: barely stays 1½m: acts on
fibresand, good to soft and probably good to firm ground. *I. Semple*

DESERT IMAGE (IRE)   2 b.c. (Apr 15) Desert King (IRE) 129 – Identical (IRE)   **70**
(Machiavellian (USA) 123) [2003 6d f8s³ f8.5s³ f7g Nov 14] second foal: half-brother to
3-y-o Repeat: dam unraced half-sister to smart 7f/1m performer Darnay: fair maiden:
barely stays 8.5f: acts on fibresand, some promise on turf. *A. J. Lidderdale*

DESERT ISLAND DISC   6 b.m. Turtle Island (IRE) 123 – Distant Music (Darshaan   **84**
133) [2003 70: 10.2f² 10m 11.7m⁴ 11.9m 10m 10m³ 12f⁶ 12f 9f² 10g² 10m⁴ 12g* 12m*
12m³ 10d³ 10g⁶ 13.3m⁶ 12g 11.9m³ p12g Nov 2] fairly useful performer: won handicaps
at Kempton (apprentices) in July and Salisbury in August: effective at 1¼m/1½m: acts on
any turf going: sometimes races freely: tough, game and consistent. *J. J. Bridger*

Mr Jaber Abdullah's "Desert Deer"

DESERT LIGHT (IRE) 2 b.c. (Mar 15) Desert Sun 120 – Nacote (IRE) (Mtoto 134) **46**
[2003 f5s f6g f6s f5g f5g f8s f7g⁶ f8.5s Dec 31] 11,500 2-y-o: smallish, sturdy colt: half-
brother to fairly useful Irish 2002 2-y-o 6f winner Sineogron (by Lycius) and a winner in
Italy by Namaqualand: dam unraced daughter of smart French performer up to 10.5f
Nadina: poor maiden: stays 7f: tried visored. *D. Shaw*

DESERT LOCH (IRE) 3 b.f. Desert King (IRE) 129 – Kinlochewe 102 (Old Vic **42**
136) [2003 56: f12g 9.9m 12.1d 12.1m 9.3m 10g⁴ 12.1m⁴ 9.9m 10m Aug 30] sturdy,
close-coupled filly: poor handicapper nowadays: stays 1½m: acts on firm and good to
soft going: tongue tied. *N. Tinkler*

DESERT OPAL 3 ch.c. Cadeaux Genereux 131 – Nullarbor (Green Desert (USA) **105**
127) [2003 –p: 7m 6g⁴ 7g⁴ 8.1g² 8g⁴ 8.1d⁴ 8g Nov 1] sturdy colt: progressed into useful
performer, winning maiden at Salisbury in May and handicaps at Newbury in July and
Haydock (beat Flighty Fellow a length, tended to hang left) in September: ran poorly at
Newmarket final start: will prove best up to 1m: acts on good to soft going, yet to race on
extremes. *J. H. M. Gosden*

DESERT QUEST (IRE) 3 b.g. Rainbow Quest (USA) 134 – Jumilla (USA) 100 (El **102**
Gran Senor (USA) 136) [2003 77P: 10d* 12g⁴ 12m⁶ 10g* Oct 13] rather leggy gelding:
useful performer: won maiden at Windsor in April and handicap on same course (beat
Alrafid a head edging left near finish) in October: hung under pressure previous outing:
stays 1½m: acts on good to firm ground: visored last 2 starts. *Sir Michael Stoute*

DESERT QUILL (IRE) 3 ch.f. In The Wings 128 – Aljood 111 (Kris 135) [2003 –: **53 ?**
8.1m⁵ p10g 8.3g 10f 11.6g 12m³ 11f Oct 12] probably modest maiden: seems to stay
1½m: acts on good to firm going: sold 5,500 gns. *D. R. C. Elsworth*

DESERT REIGN 2 ch.c. (Apr 7) Desert King (IRE) 129 – Moondance (Siberian **68**
Express (USA) 125) [2003 6g 7m 8m Oct 17] 32,000Y: workmanlike colt: second foal:
dam unraced half-sister to top-class French performer up to 1½m Freedom Cry: best
effort (fair form) when seventh in maiden at Goodwood on debut: suffered minor fracture
next start: raced freely final one: should stay at least 1m. *A. P. Jarvis*

DESERT ROCK (IRE) 3 b.g. Desert Style (IRE) 121 – Olympic Rock (IRE) (Ballad **–**
Rock 122) [2003 62: 7g 8.1m Aug 14] modest form at 2 yrs: well held in 2003. *N. Tinkler*

DESERT ROYAL (IRE) 4 ch.g. Ali-Royal (IRE) 127 – Hajat 64 (Mujtahid (USA) **48 d**
118) [2003 62d: f7g 7m⁶ 8.5f 5s 6f 6f Aug 22] leggy, sparely-made gelding: one-time fair
performer: very much on downgrade: sometimes blinkered. *A. Bailey*

DESERT ROYALTY (IRE) 3 b.f. Alhaarth (IRE) 126 – Buraida 64 (Balidar 133) **94**
[2003 69: 8.3d* 9m⁶ 10m² 9f⁵ 10m* 9.7m³ 12g* 10m² 12f³ Oct 12] close-coupled, good-
bodied filly: fairly useful handicapper: won at Windsor in May, Brighton in August
and Epsom in September: creditable efforts at Ayr (unlucky) and Goodwood after: stays
1½m: acts on firm and good to soft going: free-going sort. *E. A. L. Dunlop*

DESERT SPA (USA) 8 b.g. Sheikh Albadou 128 – Healing Waters (USA) (Temper- **–**
ence Hill (USA)) [2003 –, a78: f12g f12g p13g p8g⁶ p12g p12g f13g Aug 15] workman- **a41**
like gelding: has round action: only poor nowadays: best at 1¼m/1½m: acts on fibresand
(all 10 wins on it, including 6 in 2002): tried blinkered: has looked none too keen. *Andrew
Reid*

DESERT SPIRIT (IRE) 3 b.g. Desert Style (IRE) 121 – Lady Bennington (Hot **93**
Grove 128) [2003 73: p7g* p6g⁴ p6g* p10g* Feb 8] quite good-topped gelding: fairly
useful performer: progressed well at Lingfield, winning 3 handicaps in January/February:
stays easy 1¼m: acts on polytrack, yet to race on extremes of going on turf: free-going
sort: withdrawn (gave trouble start) once: sent to USA. *J. R. Best*

DESERT TOMMY 2 b.g. (Feb 24) Desert King (IRE) 129 – Flambera (FR) (Akarad **–**
(FR) 130) [2003 7m Sep 17] 65,000F, 52,000Y: half-brother to several winners, including
very smart US performer up to 9f Jumron (by Sharpo) and fairly useful 2001 2-y-o 6f
winner (stayed 10.5f) Far Pavilions (by Halling): dam French 1¼m winner: 33/1 and very
green, soon detached in maiden at Yarmouth. *T. G. Mills*

DESERT VALENTINE 8 b.g. Midyan (USA) 124 – Mo Ceri 63 (Kampala 120) [2003 **43**
56: 12m 12.1d p12g Nov 2] tall, lengthy gelding: has high knee action: only poor form in
2003: probably best at 1¼m/1½m: acts on heavy and good to firm going: has started
slowly/found little: tends to race freely. *L. G. Cottrell*

DESIGNER CITY (IRE) 2 b.f. (Feb 14) Mujadil (USA) 119 – Carnickian (IRE) (Sri **60 §**
Pekan (USA) 117) [2003 5d 5m⁵ f5s⁵ f6g³ f6s 5.1m⁶ f5g⁴ 5m⁴ 6m⁶ f6s⁶ f5g Nov 14]
€5,000Y: leggy filly: first foal: dam, ran once in Ireland, half-sister to useful 1997 2-y-o

5f winner Diligence: modest maiden: stays 6f: acts on fibresand and good to firm ground: reportedly finished lame fifth start: unreliable. *A. Berry*

DESIGN PERFECTION (USA)   3 b.f. Diesis 133 – Bella Ballerina 90 (Sadler's Wells (USA) 132) [2003 10m* 10d³ Sep 2] rather leggy, attractive filly: third foal: dam, 9f winner, sister to high-class 1¼m performer Stagecraft from family of Opera House and Kayf Tara: 6/5 favourite, bandaged behind, won 4-runner maiden at Newbury in August: better effort (useful form) when ½-length third to Actrice in listed race at Longchamp, tending to hang then leading briefly over 1f out: would probably have stayed 1½m: stud. *J. H. M. Gosden*   **105**

DESIRES DESTINY   5 b.m. Grey Desire 115 – Tanoda 77 (Tyrnavos 129) [2003 9.9d⁶ 10d⁶ 7.5m f8g Dec 15] third foal: dam 5f (at 2 yrs) to 1½m winner: poor maiden: stays 1¼m. *M. Brittain*   **47**

DESPERATE DAN   2 b.c. (Mar 17) Danzero (AUS) – Alzianah 102 (Alzao (USA) 117) [2003 p6g* 6d 6g² Sep 27] 40,000Y: quite good-topped colt: half-brother to several winners, including fairly useful 5f (including at 2 yrs) winner Leozian (by Lion Cavern), 3-y-o Voluptuous and 4-y-o Patientes Virtis: dam 5f/6f performer (including at 2 yrs): won maiden at Lingfield in August: best effort when second of 6 to Philharmonic in minor event at Ripon, taking good hold early and seeming ill at ease on undulations: likely to prove best at 5f/6f: should make a useful handicapper at 3 yrs. *J. A. Osborne*   **92 p**

DESRAYA (IRE)   6 b.g. Desert Style (IRE) 121 – Madaraya (USA) (Shahrastani (USA) 135) [2003 76: 6m 6m³ 5m³ 5.9f 6g 6m 6m 7g Aug 28] strong, lengthy gelding: fair performer: best at 5f (given test)/6f: yet to race on heavy ground, acts on any other turf: often blinkered/visored, also tried in cheekpieces: sometimes drifts left: reportedly broke blood vessel second start. *K. A. Ryan*   **70**

DESTINATION DUBAI (USA)   2 br.c. (Mar 27) Kingmambo (USA) 125 – Mysterial (USA) (Alleged (USA) 138) [2003 8d² 8m² Sep 25] $1,500,000Y: tall, close-coupled colt: third foal: brother to 4-y-o Dubai Destination: dam, ran twice, half-sister to very smart Japanese performers Agnes World (sprinter) and Hishi Akebono (sprinter/miler): useful form when short-headed by Mutawassel in 17-runner maiden at Doncaster, travelling strongly: 5/2-on when only second of 9 to Maraahel in similar event at Pontefract 15 days later, carrying head to one side, tending to hang and off bridle some way out: not sure to stay much beyond 1m: 2 handlers/wore crossed noseband both starts: joined Saeed bin Suroor. *D. R. Loder*   **97**

DESTINY STAR   2 b.f. (Mar 17) Forzando 122 – Troia (IRE) 54 (Last Tycoon 131) [2003 6m 6m a6g a8g⁵ a6s a8g Nov 9] 600Y: tall, leggy filly: first foal: dam, lightly-raced maiden, half-sister to smart performer up to 1½m Ela-Aristokrati: no form, including in seller: left Miss V. Haigh after second start. *M. Lundgren, Spain*   **–**

DESTRUCTIVE (USA)   5 b. or br.g. Dehere (USA) 121 – Respectability (USA) (His Majesty (USA)) [2003 –: f16s Feb 6] rangy gelding: modest maiden at 3 yrs, no form since: tried visored. *J. Mackie*   **–**

DETAILED (IRE)   2 b.c. (Apr 13) Alhaarth (IRE) 126 – Arab Scimetar (IRE) (Sure Blade (USA) 130) [2003 7m⁴ 7m² 7.1m⁴ 8m⁴ Sep 24] IR 26,000F, €70,000Y: rather leggy colt: half-brother to 3 winners, including 7-y-o Mitcham: dam unraced: fair maiden: second at Lingfield: should stay 1m. *R. Hannon*   **74**

DETONATEUR (FR)   5 b.g. Pistolet Bleu (IRE) 133 – Soviet Princess (IRE) (Soviet Lad (USA)) [2003 p12g⁶ Feb 1] first foal: dam 7f (at 2 yrs) to 1½m winner on Flat in France: placed in two 10.5f minor events at Saint-Cloud for Mme M. Bollack-Badel in 2001: apparently modest form in maiden at Lingfield. *Ian Williams*   **64 ?**

DEVANT (NZ)   3 b.f. Zabeel (NZ) – Frenetic (NZ) (Truly Vain (AUS)) [2003 79: 8m* 8.5m⁶ 10.1m 7m* 7g 8m⁶ 8f 10.1s⁵ Oct 29] quite good-topped filly: useful performer: won handicaps at Yarmouth in April and Newmarket (short-headed Zietory) in July: below form after: effective at 7f/1m: acts on good to firm and good to soft going: none too consistent. *M. A. Jarvis*   **98**

DEVIL MOON (IRE)   2 b.c. (Apr 28) Danehill (USA) 126 – Moon Drop 103 (Dominion 123) [2003 5g² 5d* 6m⁶ 7d³ 6f⁴ Aug 10] €400,000Y: good-bodied colt: closely related to useful 1996 2-y-o 6f winner Dancing Drop (by Green Desert) and half-brother to several winners, including useful 5f (at 2 yrs) to 7f winner Moon King (by Cadeaux Genereux): dam, best at 6f, half-sister to dam of smart 7f/1m performer Fa-Eq: useful performer: won maiden at Tipperary in April: good efforts when 4¼ lengths third to Lucky Story in Vintage Stakes at Goodwood and 4¾ lengths fourth to One Cool Cat in   **101**

Phoenix Stakes at the Curragh (short to post) last 2 starts: stays 7f: acts on firm and good to soft going: sent to Hong Kong, joined J. Size. *A. P. O'Brien, Ireland*

DEVIL'S BITE   2 ch.c. (Mar 28) Dracula (AUS) – Niggle 65 (Night Shift (USA)) [2003   **78** 6m⁶ 6m⁵ 6m⁶ 7.2d² 8m Oct 24] strong, workmanlike colt: has a round action: second living foal: half-brother to fairly useful 1999 2-y-o 5f winner Punctuate (by Distant Relative): dam ran twice: fair maiden: second at Ayr: should stay 1m: acts on good to firm and good to soft going. *B. W. Hills*

DEVIL'S TEARDROP   3 ch.g. Hernando (FR) 127 – River Divine (USA) 59 (Irish   **60** River (FR) 131) [2003 67, a71: 8g 8g⁵ May 16] just modest form second 3-y-o start: should stay at least 1m: acts on fibresand and good to firm ground: effective blinkered or not: gelded, then sold 7,000 gns in October. *D. J. S. Cosgrove*

DEVINE LIGHT (IRE)   3 b.f. Spectrum (IRE) 126 – Siskin (IRE) (Royal Academy   **64 ?** (USA) 130) [2003 66: p7g⁴ p10g 8.1m 8.3d 8g f8.5g 8f⁵ 7g 9m* Oct 25] leggy filly: modest performer: left A. Jarvis, 100/1-winner of maiden at Musselburgh in October: likely to stay 1¼m: raced mainly on good ground or firmer on turf: visored (below form) fifth to eighth starts: probably none too genuine. *B. Mactaggart*

DEVIOUS AYERS (IRE)   2 b.g. (Apr 11) Dr Devious (IRE) 127 – Yulara (IRE) 99   **62 p** (Night Shift (USA)) [2003 p6g³ Dec 29] 17,500Y: first foal: dam 7f winner out of half-sister to Vintage Crop: 6/1, 2¾ lengths third of 10 to Chorus Beauty in maiden at Lingfield, held up after slow start and going on well at finish: should improve. *G. A. Butler*

DEVIOUS BOY   3 br.g. Dr Devious (IRE) 127 – Oh Hebe (IRE) 74 (Night Shift (USA))   **114** [2003 99: p7g³ p10g³ 8f* 8.5f² 9f² 9f* a8f Dec 26] small, good-bodied gelding: smart performer: creditable third to Desert Spirit in handicap at Lingfield on reappearance: left P. Haslam after next start: improved in US, winning non-graded stakes at Del Mar in July and Grade 2 Oak Tree Derby at Santa Anita in October, latter gamely by a head from Sweet Return: runner-up in Grade 3/2 events at Del Mar in between: stays 9f, probably not 1¼m: acts on polytrack, firm and soft going. *Kathy Walsh, USA*

DEVIOUS PADDY (IRE)   3 b.g. Dr Devious (IRE) 127 – Night Arcade (IRE) 77   **75** (Night Shift (USA)) [2003 8.5d² 10s 12.5f⁶ 10g³ 9m f8g⁵ Dec 3] first foal: dam, second at 7f in Ireland (lightly raced), out of half-sister to smart miler Yeast: fair maiden: left M. Halford in Ireland after fifth start: stays 1¼m: acts on good to soft going, well below form on fibresand debut. *N. Tinkler*

DEVISE (IRE)   4 b.g. Hamas (IRE) 125§ – Soreze (IRE) 102 (Gallic League 119) [2003   **81** –: f5g 5g 5g* 6m 5m³ 5m⁶ 5m 6g Aug 1] smallish, close-coupled gelding: fairly useful handicapper: won at Windsor in June: should stay 6f: acts on good to firm and good to soft ground. *M. S. Saunders*

DEVITO (FR)   2 ch.c. (Apr 18) Trempolino (USA) 135 – Snowy (FR) (Wollow 132)   **–** [2003 f8s Sep 2] €9,000Y, €16,000 2-y-o: half-brother to numerous winners in France, including listed 9.5f/1¼m winner Snow House (by Vacarme), herself dam of smart French/US performer up to 11f Snow Polina (by Trempolino): dam French 11f winner: 33/1, last of 9 in maiden at Southwell. *M. F. Harris*

DEVOLUTION (IRE)   5 b.g. Distinctly North (USA) 115 – Election Special 78 (Chief   **83** Singer 131) [2003 82, a88: f9.4g 10g 10d³ Jul 30] angular gelding: fluent mover: fairly useful handicapper: won at Leicester in July: stays 1¼m: acts on polytrack, best turf efforts on ground softer than good: sometimes slowly away: refused to race once at 3 yrs: sold 2,600 gns in November. *J. M. P. Eustace*

DEVON FLAME   4 b.g. Whittingham (IRE) 104 – Uae Flame (IRE) (Polish Precedent   **72** (USA) 131) [2003 –: 8.1d⁴ 6.1g* 6m* 6m* Jul 17] fair handicapper, lightly raced: progressed well in 2003, winning at Chepstow (maiden event) in June, and Windsor and Leicester in July: likely to prove best at 5f/6f: acts on good to firm ground: looked wayward last two 3-y-o starts: usually races prominently. *R. J. Hodges*

DEVON MAID   4 ch.f. Fraam 114 – Sharp Dance 41 (Dance of Life (USA)) [2003 p7g   **–** Dec 29] first foal: dam, maiden on Flat, winning hurdler: well held in bumper, and in maiden at Lingfield. *R. J. Hodges*

DEXILEOS (IRE)   4 b.g. Danehill (USA) 126 – Theano (IRE) 114 (Thatching 131)   **75** [2003 79: 8.3g 8.2s⁴ 7m f8g 8d Aug 1] close-coupled ex-Irish gelding: first foal: dam, Irish 6f to 9f winner, out of half-sister to smart middle-distance stayer Demophilos: fair maiden: sold from C. O'Brien 15,000 gns after final 3-y-o start: stays 1m: acts on soft and good to firm going: visored/sweating final start. *A. D. W. Pinder*

DHABYAN (USA) 3 b.c. Silver Hawk (USA) 123 – Fleur de Nuit (USA) (Woodman **102**
(USA) 126) [2003 103+: 8g⁵ 10.4m⁶ May 13] good-topped colt: useful performer, lightly
raced: much better effort in 2003 when creditable sixth to Etesaal in handicap at York:
suffered injury after: races freely, but stays 1¼m: acts on firm ground: stays in training.
B. Hanbury

DHAKHIRAH (IRE) 3 b.f. Sadler's Wells (USA) 132 – Good Luck Charm (USA) **77**
(Caro 133) [2003 10m 10.5d 8m² 8.1g³ 9.9m² p8g⁶ Nov 12] IR 280,000Y: good-bodied,
quite attractive filly: sister to Irish 1m winner Star of Jupiter and half-sister to 2 winners
abroad: dam unraced half-sister to 2000 Guineas winner King of Kings (by Sadler's
Wells): fair maiden: should stay further than 1¼m: yet to race on extremes of going on
turf, some promise on polytrack: sold 42,000 gns. *A. C. Stewart*

DHEHDAAH 2 b.c. (Mar 31) Alhaarth (IRE) 126 – Carina Clare (Slip Anchor 136) **62**
[2003 8m⁶ 8.1m 7d Nov 7] 38,000Y: angular colt: fourth foal: dam unraced close relation to useful stayer Clare Heights: modest form in maidens: likely to stay at least 1½m.
N. A. Graham

DIACADA (GER) 3 b.f. Cadeaux Genereux 131 – Diasprina (GER) (Aspros (GER)) **108**
[2003 8g* 8f 8d 8d³ 8m 8d Nov 16] useful-looking filly: half-sister to several winners in
Germany, including useful 5f (at 2 yrs) to 7f winner Desidera (by Shaadi): dam German
2-y-o 5f to 1m winner: useful performer: won national listed race at Mulheim at 2 yrs and
Henkel-Rennen at Dusseldorf (by 1¼ lengths from White Rose) in May: ran well when
¾-length third to Peppercorn in Grosse Europa Meile at Cologne in September: well held
other outings in 2003, including in Coronation Stakes at Royal Ascot second start: stayed
1m: acted on good to soft going: blinkered final start: stud. *H. Blume, Germany*

DIAGON ALLEY (IRE) 3 ro.g. Petong 126 – Mubadara (IRE) 80 (Lahib (USA) **–**
129) [2003 –: 7.9f 7g 8.1m 8.1m Aug 14] close-coupled gelding: well held, including in
claimer. *K. W. Hogg, Isle of Man*

DIALING TONE (USA) 3 b.f. Distant View (USA) 126 – Call Account (USA) **–**
(Private Account (USA)) [2003 100: 7.1m 8f Aug 17] leggy, useful-looking filly: useful
form at 2 yrs: off 8 months, well held in listed events at Warwick and Bath in 2003: stayed
7f: acted on good to firm going: stud. *Sir Michael Stoute*

DIAL SQUARE 2 b.g. (Apr 29) Bluegrass Prince (IRE) 110 – Honey Mill 67 (Milford **–**
119) [2003 7s f6g Nov 10] 800Y: seventh foal: half-brother to 2 winners, including 5f and
7f winner Erinvale (by Mon Tresor): dam maiden who should have stayed 1m: well held
in maidens at Yarmouth and Wolverhampton. *P. Howling*

DIAMOND DARREN (IRE) 4 ch.g. Dolphin Street (FR) 125 – Deerussa (IRE) **–**
(Jareer (USA) 115) [2003 48: f12g 12.4m Apr 21] leggy, close-coupled gelding: poor
maiden handicapper: well held in 2003: usually visored/blinkered at 2 yrs: difficult ride.
R. D. E. Woodhouse

DIAMOND DECORUM (IRE) 7 ch.g. Fayruz 116 – Astra Adastra (Mount Hagen **42**
(FR) 127) [2003 56: 6m 6m⁵ 7d May 23] leggy, workmanlike gelding: fluent mover:
poor performer: best at 6f/easy 7f: acts on firm and soft going: tried visored/tongue tied:
sometimes races freely/carries head awkwardly/hangs right. *J. Hetherton*

DIAMOND DREAMER 2 b.f. (Feb 26) Loup Solitaire (USA) 117 – Wakeful Night **54**
(FR) (Linamix (FR) 127) [2003 7.9m 7m⁶ 8.3g⁶ Oct 13] 8,500Y: rather leggy filly:
second foal: dam, second at 10.5f in France, out of half-sister to smart French performers
up to 1½m Walk On Mix and Walking Around: modest form in maidens/seller: likely to
be suited by 1¼m/1½m: refused to enter stall 3 days after final outing. *M. G. Quinlan*

DIAMOND GEORGE (IRE) 2 b.g. (Apr 8) Sri Pekan (USA) 117 – Golden Choice **65**
(Midyan (USA) 124) [2003 6g² 7.1m⁶ 6m⁶ Sep 7] €7,000Y: close-coupled gelding: third
foal: half-brother to 3-y-o Titian Flame: dam unraced half-sister to smart 1½m/13f performer Phantom Gold, herself dam of Oaks second Flight of Fancy: best effort in maidens
(fair form) when second at Lingfield: sweated final start: should stay 7f. *John Berry*

DIAMOND GIRL 3 b.f. Mind Games 121 – Its All Relative 90 (Distant Relative 128) **–**
[2003 60: 5d 6m Jun 17] modest maiden handicapper: well beaten in 2003: raced only at
5f/6f: acts on firm and good to soft ground: tried blinkered: slowly away on reappearance.
T. D. Easterby

DIAMOND GREEN (ARG) 5 ch.g. Roy (USA) – Diamond Ring (ARG) (El Basco **–**
(USA)) [2003 64, a72: f9.4g⁵ f8.5g* f8.5g⁶ f8.5g* f8.5s* 8.1m May 27] useful handi- **a95**
capper on all-weather, modest on turf: won at Wolverhampton in January (amateurs),
March and April: stays 9.4f: acts on fibresand and good to firm going: visored: has raced
freely/looked none too keen: sent to Macau. *B. R. Millman*

DIAMOND GREEN (FR)   2 b.c. (Apr 7) Green Desert (USA) 127 – Diamonaka   **115 p**
(FR) 105 (Akarad (FR) 130) [2003 7d* 7g* 7d* Sep 11]

The withdrawal of Diamond Green from the Prix Jean-Luc Lagardere at Longchamp on Arc day after conditions turned soft was disappointing in more ways than one. On a personal level for his connections, it meant missing out on a first-rate chance of winning the race, formerly the Grand Criterium, which had been renamed in honour of the colt's late owner/breeder who died in March. More generally, it prevented Diamond Green from contesting what would almost certainly have been the most informative race of his career to date, following three impressive wins which had made him one of the most exciting prospects among a good crop of French two-year-olds. With talk of his contesting the Dewhurst instead also coming to nothing, Diamond Green remains something of an unknown quantity, but his opportunity to make his mark at the top level looks merely to have been delayed.

Diamond Green's career began with a couple of easy wins at Deauville in the summer. He started with a five-length success against nine other newcomers in July, drawing clear in the closing stages in fine style under just hands and heels from his rider. The runner-up was also to prove himself one of the better two-year-old colts in France by the end of the season, albeit over longer trips, Voix du Nord going on to win the Criterium de Saint-Cloud. Diamond Green's debut had come on the round course at Deauville but his win there in a minor event the following month came in a rather muddling five-runner race on the straight course. Held up on the rail initially, Diamond Green was switched to make his challenge and again just had to be pushed out in the closing stages to win with something in hand by two and a half lengths.

Diamond Green earned his place as would-be favourite for the Prix Jean-Luc Lagardere by completing his hat-trick in the main trial for that race, the Prix La Rochette, run over the same course and distance at Longchamp in September. Among his six rivals were the pair who had chased him home at Deauville the time before, Xapoteco and Charmo, but it was stable-companion Charming Prince, also unbeaten in two starts (including a listed race at Vichy), who was regarded as his chief rival. Diamond Green came through his biggest test yet with another easy victory to land the odds, travelling well in fourth and quickly putting the issue beyond doubt when moving up smoothly to lead over a furlong out. Charming Prince came from a long way back to claim second place, two and a half lengths behind the winner, just ahead of Ershaad, the winner of his only previous start.

Prix La Rochette, Longchamp—
Diamond Green looks a very smart performer in the making as he remains unbeaten;
Charming Prince (third right) is about to take second place off Ershaad (striped cap)

There was a three-length break to the rest. In Diamond Green's absence, Charming Prince was sent off favourite for the Prix Jean-Luc Lagardere, in which he improved on his Rochette form under a more enterprising ride but proved no match for four-length winner American Post.

Diamond Green (FR) (b.c. Apr 7, 2001)	Green Desert (USA) (b 1983)	Danzig (b 1977)	Northern Dancer Pas de Nom
		Foreign Courier (b 1979)	Sir Ivor Courtly Dee
	Diamonaka (FR) (gr 1990)	Akarad (b or br 1978)	Labus Licata
		Diamond Seal (gr 1984)	Persian Bold Panserina

Diamond Green keeps up his dam's fine record at stud by becoming her seventh winner from as many foals. Five of Diamonaka's first six winners were by Linamix, the sire who has become synonymous with Jean-Luc Lagardere's success as a breeder. Pick of the Linamix quintet are the fillies Diamilina and Diamonixa. Diamilina showed very smart form, going down by a short neck to Aquarelliste in the Prix Vermeille after wins in the Prix de Malleret and Prix de la Nonette. First foal Diamonixa had looked a really good prospect after winning her first two starts, notably the Prix Cleopatre by eight lengths, but subsequently met with a fatal accident at home. By Green Desert, Diamond Green is not bred to stay so well as his Linamix half-sisters, though it is worth noting that the result of Diamonaka's mating with another sprinter Cadeaux Genereux was Diamond Gift who won over fifteen furlongs in handicap company at Cagnes-sur-Mer in the latest season. Diamonaka was a useful filly who won a minor event at Evry before finishing second in two pattern races at a mile and a half, the Prix de Royaumont and Prix de Malleret. Her half-sisters include a trio of middle-distance pattern winners, Diamond Mix (Prix Greffulhe), Diamond Dance (Prix Penelope) and in the latest season Diasilixa (Prix de Royaumont). Diamond Green's grandam Diamond Seal won three races in Ireland with John Oxx, including a listed event over a mile and a half at Phoenix Park, but she was well beaten in the Irish Oaks when trying to emulate her own grandam Pampalina, who won the Curragh classic in 1967. Success in good company over middle distances therefore runs deep in this family, but one of its best members does have a profile a bit more in keeping with Diamond Green's. Pampapaul, a half-brother to Diamond Green's once-raced great grandam Panserina, won the Irish Two Thousand Guineas, having also been a leading two-year-old when his wins included the National Stakes. A mile will be well within Diamond Green's range as a three-year-old and he may stay a bit further, though he is essentially a speedier type than most of his relatives, with a good turn of foot. Spared that run in the mud at Longchamp, Diamond Green raced only on good or good to soft ground at two and, if in any way typical of his sire's stock, will not be at all inconvenienced by firmer conditions. *A. Fabre, France*

DIAMOND HOLLY (IRE)   2 b.f. (Apr 29) Imperial Ballet (IRE) 110 – Common   –
Bond (IRE) 76 (Common Grounds 118) [2003 5.1m 6.1d 5.1m Jun 23] €5,500Y: small
filly: half-sister to Irish 2000 2-y-o 5f winner Millenium Love (by Great Commotion)
and fairly useful Irish 2001 2-y-o 6f winner Jassas (by Desert Style): dam Irish 2-y-o 5f
winner: well held in maidens/seller. *P. D. Evans*

DIAMOND JOBE (IRE)   4 ch.g. College Chapel 122 – Dazzling Maid (IRE) 64 (Tate   –
Gallery (USA) 117) [2003 51: f8s f9.4g 8g May 23] angular gelding: poor maiden:
soundly beaten in 2003. *J. Hetherton*

DIAMOND JOSHUA (IRE)   5 b.g. Mujadil (USA) 119 – Elminya (IRE) (Sure Blade   –
(USA) 130) [2003 –: 17.1m Apr 8] workmanlike gelding: no longer seems of much
account: tried blinkered/tongue tied. *M. E. Sowersby*

DIAMOND MAXINE (IRE)   3 b.f. Turtle Island (IRE) 123 – Kawther (Tap On Wood   – §
130) [2003 61d: 8.1m Sep 22] lengthy filly: no form since second 2-y-o start: refused to
race on debut: needs treating with caution. *John Berry*

DIAMOND MAX (IRE)   5 b.g. Nicolotte 118 – Kawther (Tap On Wood 130) [2003   **96**
107, a114: f8s³ f8.5s⁴ f8.5s 8g 6m 6g⁶ 9.2m² 8.1d* 8.3g 6g* 8f 7.6m 7d⁵ f8.5g Nov 17]
angular gelding: useful performer: won minor event at Chepstow in May and handicap at

Windsor in June: barely stays 9f: acts on fibresand, best turf efforts on good ground or softer (acts on heavy): tried visored. *P. D. Evans*

DIAMOND MICK 3 ch.g. Pivotal 124 – Miss Poll Flinders (Swing Easy (USA) 126) **69** [2003 72: 8.2g 11.8m 8.3g⁵ 8.2m³ 10m² 11.6m⁴ 10.1m 10g Oct 28] big, good-topped gelding: fair maiden handicapper: stays 1¼m: acts on good to firm ground, unraced on soft/heavy: tried in cheekpieces, blinkered last 6 starts. *G. G. Margarson*

DIAMOND ORCHID (IRE) 3 gr.f. Victory Note (USA) 120 – Olivia's Pride (IRE) **57** (Digamist (USA) 110) [2003 75: 8g 6f f7g p8g 12s 6m 10m⁶ 9.1d² Oct 14] strong filly: modest performer nowadays: left D. Carroll after third start: stays 9f: best on going softer than good: tried visored: has wandered/carried head awkwardly: races freely. *P. D. Evans*

DIAMOND RACKET 3 b.g. Cyrano de Bergerac 120 – Reina 24 (Homeboy 114) **–** [2003 60, a57: f8g f6g f5g f6g⁶ f6g⁶ 5m 6g 6m f5s 5m 6m Sep 16] good-topped gelding: modest at 2 yrs: well held in 2003: tried visored, usually blinkered. *D. W. Chapman*

DIAMOND RIBBY (IRE) 2 br.f. (Mar 2) Desert Sun 120 – Kathleen's Dream (USA) **–** (Last Tycoon 131) [2003 7.1m Sep 22] €5,000Y: third foal: half-sister to useful French 2002 2-y-o 6f winner Castor Troy (by Ali-Royal): dam unraced: 50/1, slowly away when well held in maiden at Chepstow. *P. D. Evans*

DIAMOND RIGHT 3 b.f. Robellino (USA) 127 – Petrikov (IRE) (In The Wings 128) **–** [2003 –: p12g Sep 9] good-bodied filly: tailed off in maidens. *M. Wigham*

DIAMOND RING 4 b.f. Magic Ring (IRE) 115 – Reticent Bride (IRE) 71 (Shy Groom **58** (USA)) [2003 73: f6g p6g f12g 6.1g 5m 5g 6m³ 5m⁶ 5m 5g⁵ 5m³ 5.1d⁶ 5.5m Aug 25] quite good-topped filly: modest handicapper nowadays: best at 5f/6f: acts on good to firm and good to soft going: tried visored. *Mrs J. Candlish*

DIAMOND SHANNON (IRE) 2 b.f. (Mar 16) Petorius 117 – Balgren (IRE) (Ballad **47 p** Rock 122) [2003 6m² Sep 3] €6,000Y: third foal: sister to fairly useful Irish 7f winner The Block Monster: dam unraced: 7/1, 2½ lengths second of 16 to Mouseman in seller at Lingfield, taking good hold: likely to stay 7f: should improve. *D. Carroll*

DIAMONDS RED RUBY 2 b.f. (Mar 21) Factual (USA) 108 – Dispol Diamond 72 **–** (Sharpo 132) [2003 5d 5m Jul 15] 500Y: small, heavy-bodied filly: first foal: dam 7f/1m winner: last in maidens. *J. S. Wainwright*

DIAMONDS WILL DO (IRE) 6 b.m. Bigstone (IRE) 126 – Clear Ability (IRE) 81 **62** (Be My Guest (USA) 126) [2003 68: 12m² 16m Oct 28] ex-Irish mare: first foal: dam Irish 1½m/hurdles winner: modest maiden, lightly raced on Flat: left M. O'Brien 12,000 gns after 5 yrs: stays 13f: acts on soft and good to firm ground. *Miss Venetia Williams*

DIAMOND WAY (USA) 2 ch.c. (Mar 3) Boundary (USA) 117 – Discover Silver **60** (USA) (Valid Appeal (USA)) [2003 7m 6g p6g Oct 3] $37,000F, 57,000Y: second foal: half-brother to a winner in USA by Skip Away: dam 5.5f (at 2 yrs) to 1m winner in USA: modest form in maidens: should stay 1m: changed ownership 15,000 gns. *D. R. Loder*

DIAPHANOUS 5 b.m. Beveled (USA) – Sharp Venita 84 (Sharp Edge 123) [2003 46+: **52** p6g f5s⁵ p5g⁴ 6g 5g³ 5.3m² 5g 5f³ 5.1f 5m 5m⁶ 5m⁴ f5g⁴ Dec 22] sturdy mare: modest maiden: best at 5f: acts on all-weather and any turf ground: usually blinkered: very slowly away seventh outing: headstrong front runner. *E. A. Wheeler*

DIBBLE'S BARN 3 b.f. Thowra (FR) – Colette's Choice (IRE) (Alzao (USA) 117) **–** [2003 10.9m Aug 25] first foal: dam, unraced on Flat, winning selling hurdler: slowly away and tailed off in seller at Warwick. *R. J. Hodges*

DICHARACHERA 3 b.f. Mark of Esteem (IRE) 137 – Al Persian (IRE) (Persian Bold **91** 123) [2003 9m⁴ 8m³ 10d³ 8.1d* 8.1m² 8f 8m³ Oct 14] leggy filly: third foal: half-sister to Spanish 1m to 10.5f winner by Suave Dancer: dam, winner in Spain at 3/4 yrs, half-sister to high-class performer up to 1½m Legal Case: fairly useful performer: won maiden at Sandown in August: good second in handicap at same course next time: stays 1¼m: acts on good to firm and good to soft ground: has hinted at temperament. *H. R. A. Cecil*

DICKIE DEADEYE 6 b.g. Distant Relative 128 – Accuracy 83 (Gunner B 126) [2003 **65** 67: 10m 9f p10g⁵ p10g Dec 20] fair handicapper, lightly raced nowadays: will stay at least 1½m: acts on polytrack, goes well on ground softer than good. *G. B. Balding*

DICK THE TAXI 9 b.g. Karlinsky (USA) – Another Galaxy (Anita's Prince **81** 126) [2003 74: f12s⁵ f12g² f12g* f12s⁵ 10d² Nov 6] big, good-topped gelding: fairly useful handicapper on Flat, lightly raced: won amateur event at Wolverhampton (has good record there) in February: stays 1½m, seemingly not 2m: acts on all-weather (successful over hurdles on heavy ground): has carried head high: consistent. *R. J. Smith*

DIDIFON 8 b.g. Zafonic (USA) 130 – Didicoy (USA) 104 (Danzig (USA)) [2003 –: – 12.1m 17.1m Aug 17] strong, good sort: fairly useful performer in 1999 but lightly raced and little form on Flat since: stays 11.5f: acts on good to soft going: wore cheekpieces last 2 starts: winning jumper. *C. W. Fairhurst*

DIDNT TELL MY WIFE 4 ch.g. Aragon 118 – Bee Dee Dancer (Ballacashtal **76** (CAN)) [2003 66: p8g f8.5s p7g 7m 7m* 7g² 7g 8m⁴ 8s* 8m 8.2d² p8g* Nov 12] unfurnished gelding: fair handicapper: won at Lingfield (ladies event) in May, Thirsk (apprentice event) in July and Lingfield in November: stays 1m: acts on all-weather, soft and good to firm going: blinkered (very slowly away) once: sometimes edges left/races freely. *C. F. Wall*

DIDOE 4 br.f. Son Pardo 107 – My Diamond Ring 65 (Sparkling Boy 110) [2003 48: **57** p7g f8s p8g⁶ f7g p7g f6g⁵ f7g⁴ f7g 7m³ 10f 8f³ 8f³ 10.2f³ 7m Oct 14] easy filly: modest **a46 ?** maiden handicapper on turf, poor on all-weather: stays easy 1¼m: acts on firm going and polytrack: has been slowly away. *P. W. Hiatt*

DIEQUEST (USA) 2 ch.c. (May 22) Diesis 133 – Nuance (IRE) 70 (Rainbow Quest – (USA) 134) [2003 6m Jul 28] 10,000 2-y-o: second foal: dam, ran twice, half-sister to 3-y-o Indian Haven and dam of very smart 1½m/13f winner High Pitched: 66/1, very slowly away when well held in maiden at Windsor. *Jamie Poulton*

DIFFERENTIAL (USA) 6 b. or br.g. Known Fact (USA) 135 – Talk About Home **84** (USA) (Elocutionist (USA)) [2003 –: f8g f7g* 7m f7g* 7f* 6.9m 8g⁶ 7g 7m* Aug 15] small, sturdy gelding: fairly useful performer: won claimer/handicap at Southwell and 2 handicaps at Catterick between February and August: stays 7f: acts on all-weather, raced only on good ground or firmer on turf: sometimes early to post: often slowly away: sometimes races freely. *B. Smart*

DIGDAGA (USA) 4 b. or br.f. Machiavellian (USA) 123 – Baaderah (IRE) 102 (Cad- – eaux Genereux 131) [2003 54d: f8s f11s f12s Feb 6] disappointing maiden: often tongue tied (has reportedly had breathing problems): tried blinkered. *Mrs S. Lamyman*

DIGGER (IRE) 4 ch.g. Danzig Connection (USA) – Baliana 75 (Midyan (USA) 124) **71** [2003 63, a75: p7g p7g p7g⁴ f7g³ f8.5g³ f8g⁴ 7m f9.4s² 10d f12g³ 12.3m* 12.6m³ f16.2g² **a80** 16.2d 14.1m f16.2g² f16.2g⁵ f11g² f12g³ f14g⁶ Dec 9] big, workmanlike gelding: fairly useful handicapper on all-weather, fair on turf: left G. Balding after third start: won ladies event at Ripon in June: stays easy 2m, at least as effective at shorter: acts on good to firm going, good to soft and fibresand: usually wears headgear: usually tongue tied: withdrawn having unseated and bolted to post intended fifth outing: free-going sort. *Miss Gay Kelleway*

DIGITAL 6 ch.g. Safawan 118 – Heavenly Goddess (Soviet Star (USA) 128) [2003 **103** 97: 7d 7g⁵ 7.6g* 7g² 7m⁶ 7f 7.1g² 7m 7g² 7.6m 7m⁴ 7.6m² 7m* 7m⁶ 7f 7m 7m² Oct 25] workmanlike gelding: useful performer: won minor event at Lingfield in May and handicap at Goodwood (beat Ceepio 1¾ lengths) in September: good second to Polar Way in minor event at Doncaster final start: effective at 7f/1m: acts on any going: has carried head awkwardly/raced freely: usually waited with. *M. R. Channon*

DIGNIFIED 3 b.f. Entrepreneur 123 – Awtaar (USA) 67 (Lyphard (USA) 132) [2003 – –: 8g 10g f12g 14.1m p12g 7m 10m⁵ Aug 15] of little account: tried visored. *Mrs C. A. Dunnett*

DIL 8 b.g. Primo Dominie 121 – Swellegant 84 (Midyan (USA) 124) [2003 –, a74: f6s⁵ – f6s f6g f6g* f6s f7g f6s⁶ f6g³ f6s⁶ f7g 6.1m 7g f6s⁶ f6g f6s f7g f6g³ Dec 26] lengthy, **a67 d** good-topped gelding: fair performer: won claimer at Southwell in January: effective at 5f/6f: acts on fibresand, lightly raced and little form on turf since 1999: sometimes visored earlier in career: tried tongue tied/in cheekpieces: sometimes wears net muzzle to post: unreliable. *Mrs N. Macauley*

DILEER (IRE) 4 b.g. Barathea (IRE) 127 – Stay Sharpe (USA) (Sharpen Up 127) **92** [2003 86: 10.4m⁶ 10g* 12f 10.5m 10.1m⁵ 11.9f² 12m Oct 25] close-coupled gelding: fairly useful performer: landed odds in maiden at Ayr in May: creditable efforts after only on fifth/sixth starts: stays 1½m, at least with emphasis on speed: raced only on good going or firmer: sold 30,000 gns, joined D. Wintle. *L. M. Cumani*

DILIGENT LAD 3 b.g. Secret Appeal – Mohibbah (USA) 86 (Conquistador Cielo **– §** (USA)) [2003 –: 12f Apr 12] tall, angular gelding: well held in maidens/minor event: looked very hard ride only outing in 2003. *D. W. Barker*

DILIZA 4 b.f. Dilum (USA) 115 – Little White Lies 78 (Runnett 125) [2003 65: 8.3g **59** 8.1m 9m 8.3m⁴ 8g⁵ 8m³ 8m² 8.5g 8g⁵ 8m Sep 24] good-bodied filly: modest handicapper: stays 1m: acts on firm and good to soft going: sometimes slowly away: none too consistent. *G. B. Balding*

DILSAA   6 ch.g. Night Shift (USA) – Llia 94 (Shirley Heights 130) [2003 45: 10.9m⁵   **35**
Jun 20] strong, lengthy gelding: poor performer: stays 1¾m: acts on soft going, firm and
fibresand: tried blinkered: sometimes races freely: won over hurdles in August/October.
K. A. Ryan

DILYS   4 b.f. Efisio 120 – Ramajana (USA) (Shadeed (USA) 135) [2003 75d: 6.1g 8g   **58 d**
7m 7g f6g p7g⁴ Dec 17] smallish, sturdy filly: modest handicapper: barely stays easy
1m: acts on heavy and good to firm going, probably on polytrack: visored (well held)
penultimate start: often races prominently: not one to trust implicitly. *W. S. Kittow*

DIMITROVA (USA)   3 b.f. Swain (IRE) 134 – The Caretaker 113 (Caerleon   **119**
(USA) 132) [2003 87: 8g* 7m* 8d³ 10f* 9g² 10f* 10f Oct 25]
        Dimitrova is the latest performer from the Dermot Weld stable to illustrate
the massive dividends that can accrue from an enterprising approach. The Phileas
Fogg of Irish training has long been renowned for his successful international
raids, with hard cash one of the attractions, as is illustrated by the amount of prize
money Dimitrova earned when winning the very valuable, but ungraded, American
Oaks at Hollywood in July and the Grade 1 Flower Bowl Invitational Stakes at
Belmont Park in September. Dimitrova's four outings in the States, which also
included a second in the Grade 1 Garden City Breeders' Cup Handicap at Belmont
Park, yielded around £580,000 for connections. Compare Dimitrova's campaign
with that of Yesterday, behind whom Dimitrova finished third in the Irish One
Thousand Guineas at the Curragh in May. Yesterday's win and place prize money
for her efforts in Europe amounted to around £250,000 less than that achieved by
Dimitrova in the States. It's not only good-class European fillies and mares that

Flower Bowl Invitational Stakes, Belmont—
Dimitrova gains her second win in the States as she beats the German-trained Walzerkoenigin

can be found lucrative opportunities in the States. Another Weld horse, Evolving Tactics, was sent over to Arlington in July and completed a notable victory for his trainer in the Grade 2 American Derby. The best performance by Evolving Tactics in a race in Europe had been his third in a listed contest at Royal Ascot, upon which he did not need to improve to pick up the equivalent of around £92,000 at Arlington. Weld is not alone in targeting races outside the Breeders' Cup programme in North America in recent years. Alec Stewart sent out Mutamam to win the Canadian International in 2001 with Aidan O'Brien (Ballingarry) and Andrew Balding (Phoenix Reach) repeating the feat in 2002 and 2003 respectively. European challengers are not short of potentially lucrative opportunities—there were 460 graded races staged in the States in 2003 and levels of prize money are considerably higher than in Europe. Despite the alterations to the European pattern system for 2004, including the expansion of opportunities for good fillies and mares to race against their own sex (more about which can be found in the essays on Russian Rhythm and Macadamia), the transfer of Dimitrova to Neil Drysdale in the United States clearly makes more sense from a financial point of view. She seems sure to add more valuable wins as a four-year-old.

Dimitrova made the frame in maidens at Tralee and Navan as a two-year-old before winning a maiden in March and a listed race in April (the latter by a head from L'Ancresse) on her first two starts at three, both at Leopardstown. Dimitrova improved again when third, beaten three quarters of a length, in the Irish Guineas before being sent across the Atlantic for her four-race campaign. Starting off in the fourteen-runner American Oaks, Dimitrova made the perfect start by beating Sand Springs comfortably by two lengths. The American Oaks was being run for only the second time, and as such was ineligible for official status (American races qualify for grading only when they have been staged twice under virtually the same non-restrictive conditions); the race has been awarded Grade 1 status for 2004. Dimitrova ran creditably when four lengths second of eight to Indy Five Hundred in the Garden City Handicap two months later, particularly as she conceded 9 lb to the winner. The seven-runner Flower Bowl Invitational followed later in September with Dimitrova running on well to beat the German challenger Walzerkoenigin by a length. On her final outing, Dimitrova disappointed in the Breeders' Cup Filly & Mare Turf at Santa Anita, trailing in last. Incidentally, Walzerkoenigin, who finished third in the Falmouth Stakes at Newmarket on her second outing, ran three times in North America without winning, but still earned the equivalent of around £120,000 for her efforts.

Dimitrova (USA) (b.f. 2000)	Swain (IRE) (b 1992)	Nashwan (b 1986)	Blushing Groom
			Height of Fashion
		Love Smitten (b 1981)	Key To The Mint
			Square Angel
	The Caretaker (b 1987)	Caerleon (b 1980)	Nijinsky
			Foreseer
		Go Feather Go (b 1972)	Go Marching
			Feather Bed

When the time comes, Dimitrova will be a valuable breeding proposition. She is a half-sister to the St Leger and Coronation Cup winner Mutafaweq, the only other winner out of The Caretaker, Dimitrova being her fifth living produce. The Caretaker was also trained by Weld, and he was as conscious of making the most of her earnings potential as he was with Dimitrova. The Caretaker won four listed races in Ireland (two each as a two- and three-year-old), most notably the extremely valuable sales race the Cartier Million at Phoenix Park, which was worth IR £500,000 to the winner. The Caretaker, who raced without success in the States, was a daughter of Irish five-furlong two-year-old winner Go Feather Go. Dimitrova is by promising American-based sire Swain, who is also the sire of Muqbil. The strong, lengthy Dimitrova stays a mile and a quarter; she acts on firm and good to soft going. *D. K. Weld, Ireland*

DIMPLE CHAD 4 b.g. Sadler's Wells (USA) 132 – Fern 100 (Shirley Heights 130) –
[2003 93: 13.9f Jul 12] rather leggy, quite good-topped gelding: fairly useful performer at 3 yrs: off 12 months, well held in listed rated stakes only run in 2003: should be suited by at least 1½m: acts on good to firm and good to soft ground: sold 7,500 gns in October, joined M. Todhunter. *L. M. Cumani*

ACMC Park Hill Stakes, Doncaster—Discreet Brief slams her rivals; Floreeda is second

DINGLEY LASS   3 ch.f. Fleetwood (IRE) 107 – Riverine (Risk Me (FR) 127) [2003 –
10f p12g Jul 23] third foal: half-sister to 4-y-o Pango: dam, ran twice, out of half-sister to
Yorkshire Oaks winner Hellenic, herself dam of Greek Dance and Islington: behind in
maidens at Kempton and Lingfield. *H. Morrison*

DINOFELIS   5 b.g. Rainbow Quest (USA) 134 – Revonda (IRE) (Sadler's Wells   **46**
(USA) 132) [2003 52: 12.3m⁶ 11.1m² 12.1g 12m⁶ 12.1m 12.1g Sep 1] quite attractive
gelding: poor handicapper: should stay 2m: acts on firm and good to soft ground: has
pulled hard: sometimes slowly away: usually held up: successful over hurdles in October.
W. M. Brisbourne

DIORAMA (GER)   8 b.m. Bakharoff (USA) 130 – Dosha (FR) (Sharpman) [2003   –
f16s Feb 4] fifth foal: half-sister to smart French performer up to 1½m Sharp Counsel
(by Leading Counsel): dam winner at around 9f in France: won over 9f in Germany at
3 yrs: well held in handicap at Southwell only Flat run in 2003: poor winning hurdler.
L. A. Dace

DIOSYPROS BLUE (IRE)   2 b.c. (Mar 8) Bluebird (USA) 125 – Calamander (IRE)   **104**
69 (Alzao (USA) 117) [2003 7m 6m⁵ 6m* 6f* 6m* 6m² 6m⁶ Oct 4] 20,000Y: leggy, quite
attractive colt: second foal: dam, Irish 1m winner, half-sister to useful 1m winner Lady
Miletrian: useful performer: won maiden at Ripon and nurseries at Newmarket and
Ascot, all in August: good 2 lengths second to Pastoral Pursuits in Sirenia Stakes at
Kempton: will stay 1m: acts on firm going: takes while to warm to task: sold 230,000 gns,
joined L. Ho in Hong Kong. *J. A. Osborne*

DIRECT BEARING (IRE)   6 b.g. Polish Precedent (USA) 131 – Uncertain Affair   **98**
(IRE) 79 (Darshaan 133) [2003 100: 18.7m 12g⁴ 16f³ 18m⁴ 16g³ Nov 8] good-topped
gelding: useful handicapper, lightly raced on Flat: ran at least respectably in 2003, including seventh in Chester Cup (visored) and fourth to Landing Light in Cesarewitch at
Newmarket: effective at 1½m to 2¼m: acts on firm and good to soft going: tongue tied
third outing: won on chasing debut in December. *D. K. Weld, Ireland*

DIRECT REACTION (IRE)   6 b.g. College Chapel 122 – Mary's Way (GR) 78   –
(Night Shift (USA)) [2003 39, a54: p7g f9.4g f16.2g⁵ Feb 3] lengthy gelding: poor
handicapper: usually wears headgear/tongue tie. *Miss Gay Kelleway*

DISABUSE   3 ch.g. Fleetwood (IRE) 107 – Agony Aunt 81 (Formidable (USA) 125)   **56**
[2003 10d 11.8m 12g 7.1m² 8.1m⁶ f8g⁶ Nov 24] 6,000Y: strong, workmanlike gelding:
second foal: half-brother to fairly useful 6f winner Cool Tune (by Piccolo): dam, 1¼m
winner, out of half-sister to Oaks second Wind In Her Hair: modest maiden: probably
stays 1m: acts on good to firm going. *S. C. Williams*

DISCO DIVA   2 ch.f. (Mar 29) Spectrum (IRE) 126 – Compact Disc (IRE) 48 (Royal   **71**
Academy (USA) 130) [2003 6g⁶ 5m⁴ 5m³ 5.7m⁶ 5.1m 6m* 6m⁵ 7f² Oct 27] 4,000Y:
third living foal: half-sister to 5-y-o Single Track Mind and 4-y-o Turibius: dam, 2-y-o 7f
winner, out of half-sister to very smart sprinter Greenland Park: fair performer: won

nursery at Leicester in September: good second to Bertocelli in similar event there: stays 7f: acts on firm going: sometimes races freely. *M. Blanshard*

DISCOED   3 b.f. Distinctly North (USA) 115 – Lunar Music 67 (Komaite (USA)) – [2003 38: f11g f7g⁶ f6g Jan 24] lengthy, angular filly: no form in 2003. *M. J. Polglase*

DISCREET BRIEF (IRE)   3 b.f. Darshaan 133 – Quiet Counsel (IRE) 81 (Law   113 Society (USA) 130) [2003 86p: 10.1m* 11g³ 12f² 14.8m² 14g² 14.6d* 14s⁴ Oct 5] big, good-topped filly: smart performer: won maiden at Newcastle in April and ACMC Park Hill Stakes at Doncaster (improved effort, travelled strongly before quickening clear final 2f to beat Floreeda 7 lengths) in September: favourite, below-form fourth to Royal Fantasy in Deutsches St Leger at Dortmund final outing: stayed 1¾m: acted on firm and good to soft going: reliable: stud. *J. L. Dunlop*

DISCREET GIRL   4 b.f. Mistertopogigo (IRE) 118 – Pillow Talk (IRE) 60 (Taufan – (USA) 119) [2003 f6g 9.9d 8f Jun 26] second foal: dam 8.5f winner: no form, including in sellers. *Mrs S. Lamyman*

DISENGAGE (USA)   2 gr. or ro.c. (Apr 11) Runaway Groom (CAN) – Teeming   78 p Shore (USA) 110 (L'Emigrant (USA) 129) [2003 p7g⁴ 7m³ 7.1g* p7g Dec 10] $26,000Y: eighth foal: half-brother to 3 winners, including smart Irish 6f winner Conormara (by Carr de Naskra) and fairly useful 5f (at 2 yrs) to 1¼m winner Spirito Libro (by Lear Fan): dam sprinter: fair form: won maiden at Musselburgh in November: ran creditably in nursery final start: free-going sort, and may prove best at 6f/7f: acts on polytrack, better turf effort on good going: open to progress. *G. A. Butler*

DISGRACE   3 b.g. Distinctly North (USA) 115 – Ace Girl 58 (Stanford 121§) [2003 – –: 7f 9.3m Jun 25] no form in maidens/seller. *A. Berry*

Mrs Sonia Rogers' "Discreet Brief"

DISKO BAY (IRE) 3 b.f. Charnwood Forest (IRE) 125 – Mermaid Beach (Slew O' **51 ?**
Gold (USA)) [2003 p10g p10g 7m⁴ 8.2m 8f Jun 15] IR 2,500F, 10,500Y: fourth foal:
half-sister to winners abroad by Marju and Primo Dominie: dam, Italian 7f winner, half-
sister to useful middle-distance stayer Haleakala: seemingly modest maiden: should stay
at least 1m. *A. M. Balding*

DISPOL EVITA 4 ch.f. Presidium 124 – She's A Breeze 35 (Crofthall 110) [2003 **56 §**
56§, a65§: p10g p8g 10m 9m 10m* 10m* 10m 10.1m⁴ 10f⁴ 10.2m 10.1m⁶ 10m⁵ 10f³ **a59 §**
10m⁵ p10g p8g² p10g Dec 17] rather leggy, close-coupled filly: modest performer: won
seller and claimer at Brighton in June: left A. Reid after fifteenth start: stays easy 1½m:
acts on all-weather and firm going: tried in cheekpieces/blinkers: often slowly away/
looks more too keen (refused to race once at 2 yrs): spoilt chance by swerving left
thirteenth start. *Jamie Poulton*

DISPOL KATIE 2 ch.f. (Apr 28) Komaite (USA) – Twilight Time (Aragon 118) [2003 **88**
5f³ 5g² 5m* 5f³ 5m* 6.5d 5g² 6m² Oct 24] 3,000Y: tall filly: fifth foal: half-sister to
several winners, including 3-y-o Paradise Eve: dam unraced: fairly useful performer:
won maiden at Carlisle (hung left) in July and nursery at Beverley in August: good second
in nursery at Ripon and sales race at Doncaster (short-headed by Enchantment, who
raced on other side of track) last 2 starts: should prove best at 5f/6f: acts on firm going.
T. D. Barron

DISPOL PETO 3 gr.g. Petong 126 – Plie 75 (Superlative 118) [2003 67: f5s f7s* f8.5s⁴ **67**
7m⁵ 8g 7m May 14] strong, good-quartered gelding: fair performer: won claimer at
Southwell in February, final start T. D. Barron: barely stays 8.5f: acts on soft going,
good to firm and fibresand: tried blinkered, wore cheekpieces last 5 starts: usually races
prominently: none too genuine. *Ian Emmerson*

DISPOL VELETA 2 b.f. (Mar 18) Makbul 104 – Foxtrot Pie 77 (Shernazar 131) [2003 **–**
5m Jul 9] 1,800Y: half-sister to 1999 2-y-o 6f/7f winner Dispol Jazz and 1m/9f winner
Dispol Foxtrot (both by Alhijaz): dam, maiden, should have been best at 1½m+: 4/1,
slowly away and very green when behind in seller at Catterick. *T. D. Barron*

DISTANT CONNECTION (IRE) 2 b.c. (Feb 21) Cadeaux Genereux 131 – Night **79**
Owl 73 (Night Shift (USA)) [2003 8m 8m⁴ 8m⁵ 7.9f 7g³ Oct 24] 26,000Y: good-topped
colt: second foal: dam, headstrong maiden who stayed 6f, half-sister to useful 1½m/1¾m
winner Lord Jim and smart French performer up to 10.5f Audacieuse: fair maiden: good
third of 19 to Coqueteria in nursery at Newbury: should stay 1m: best effort on good
going. *A. P. Jarvis*

DISTANT COUNTRY (USA) 4 b.g. Distant View (USA) 126 – Memsahb (USA) **82**
(Restless Native) [2003 a8g³ a8g 8m 8g 7m³ 7m⁴ 7f* 8m 7m* 7g⁴ Oct 28] $37,000F,
$45,000Y: tall, good-topped ex-French gelding: seventh foal: half-brother to several min-
or winners in US: dam multiple winner in US: fairly useful performer: left J. Hammond
in France after fourth start: won maiden at Redcar in September and claimer at Doncaster
in October: effective at 7f/1m: acts on firm ground: best efforts in cheekpieces: usually
waited with: sold 13,000 gns. *Mrs J. R. Ramsden*

DISTANT COUSIN 6 b.g. Distant Relative 128 – Tinaca (USA) (Manila (USA)) **72**
[2003 89: 10m 12g 12m 12m³ 14.6m³ 14.1m² 12g² 12.3m² 12.3m² 11.9m⁵ 14.6m⁶ Oct
24] quite good-topped gelding: fairly useful handicapper on all-weather, fair on turf:
effective at 1½m to 14.6f: acts on soft going, good to firm and all-weather: wears visor:
will probably prove best with exaggerated waiting tactics. *M. A. Buckley*

DISTANT DIVA 4 b.f. Distant Relative 128 – Miss Poll Flinders (Swing Easy (USA) **54**
126) [2003 63: 5m 5m⁵ 6m 5m⁶ 5m Jun 19] good-topped filly: good walker: fairly useful
at 2 yrs, just modest form since: effective at 5f/6f: acts on soft and good to firm going.
D. Nicholls

DISTANT KING 10 b.g. Distant Relative 128 – Lindfield Belle (IRE) 78 (Fairy King **–**
(USA)) [2003 –: 6g⁶ 5m⁵ 6m Aug 8] no longer of much account. *G. P. Kelly*

DISTANT LIGHT 3 b.f. Groom Dancer (USA) 128 – Warning Star 104 (Warning 136) **50 ?**
[2003 57p: 8m 7m f6g⁶ p7g Oct 27] lengthy, unfurnished filly: modest maiden: may
prove best short of 7f: raced only on all-weather and good to firm ground. *M. S. Saunders*

DISTANT PROSPECT (IRE) 6 b.g. Namaqualand (USA) – Ukraine's Affair (USA) **100**
(The Minstrel (CAN) 135) [2003 102: 16.2g 16.1g 14.6g³ 18m 16.5d³ Nov 8] useful
handicapper: at least respectable efforts in 2003, including when third twice at Doncaster,
and when seventh to Landing Light in Cesarewitch (won race in 2001) at Newmarket in
between: effective at 2m to 2½m: acts on any turf going, though all wins on good or

softer: has run well when sweating: held up: genuine and consistent: fairly useful winner over hurdles in December. *A. M. Balding*

DISTANT SCENE (USA) 5 b.g. Distant View (USA) 126 – Dangora (USA) 98 (Sovereign Dancer (USA)) [2003 63d: p6g² p6g⁴ 6g 7f Apr 10] tall gelding: modest maiden: probably best at 6f: acts on polytrack and good to firm going: sometimes blinkered/hooded: has looked none too genuine. *T. D. McCarthy* **64 d**

DISTANT SKY (USA) 6 ch.g. Distant View (USA) 126 – Nijinsky Star (USA) (Nijinsky (CAN) 138) [2003 68: p16g Jan 22] lengthy, useful-looking gelding: maiden: well held only Flat outing of 2003: sometimes blinkered/wore cheekpieces: dead. *P. Mitchell*

DISTANT STORM 10 ch.g. Pharly (FR) 130 – Candle In The Wind 90 (Thatching 131) [2003 43§: 21.6m Apr 14] robust gelding: poor handicapper: well held only Flat outing of 2003: blinkered/visored: usually tongue tied: free-going sort. *B. J. Llewellyn* **– §**

DISTANT TIMES 2 b.c. (Apr 18) Orpen (USA) 116 – Simply Times (USA) 64 (Dodge (USA)) [2003 6m⁴ 6g³ 6m² 6m² 6m³ Sep 8] big, lengthy colt: has scope: fourth foal: half-brother to 3-y-o Majestic Times, 4-y-o Welsh Emperor and 5-y-o Forever Times: dam twice at 2 yrs: fair maiden: second at Newcastle and Ripon: likely to stay 7f: blinkered (ran respectably) final start. *T. D. Easterby* **76**

DISTINCTION (IRE) 4 b.g. Danehill (USA) 126 – Ivy Leaf (IRE) 76 (Nureyev (USA) 131) [2003 108: 14m³ 16.2f⁴ 13.9m 14.1f* 12f⁵ Sep 28] big, strong, good sort: smart performer: won minor event at Salisbury in September by ¾ length from Scott's View: seemed unsuited by drop in trip/false pace when fifth to Jagger in Seabiscuit Handicap at Ascot final outing: stays 1¾m: acts on firm going, probably on good to soft: has wandered/raced freely. *Sir Michael Stoute* **112**

DISTINCTIVE DANCER (IRE) 5 b. or br.h. Distinctly North (USA) 115 – Resiusa (ITY) (Niniski (USA) 125) [2003 –: p10g f14s 12m Sep 12] no form. *I. A. Wood* **–**

DISTINCTIVE DREAM (IRE) 9 b.g. Distinctly North (USA) 115 – Green Side (USA) 37 (Green Dancer (USA) 132) [2003 55§, a48§: f6g³ f6g⁶ f7s⁶ f6s² Feb 27] strong, lengthy gelding: modest performer: effective at 6f to 1m: acts on any turf going and fibresand: usually wears headgear: sometimes slowly away: moody. *A. Bailey* **55 §**

DISTINCTLYSPLENDID 3 b.g. Distinctly North (USA) 115 – Shelley Marie 67 (Gunner B 126) [2003 –: p8g 9.9m 11m 8f 7.1f p10g⁶ 10.2m⁴ 11.5s f8.5g f7g p12g p10g Dec 30] close-coupled gelding: modest maiden: below form after reappearance: stays 1¼m: acts on polytrack and firm ground: tried blinkered: has looked headstrong. *I. A. Wood* **54 d**

DISTINCTLYTHEBEST 3 b.c. Distinctly North (USA) 115 – Euphyllia 70 (Superpower 113) [2003 6m May 26] 800Y: third foal: half-brother to 4-y-o Araf: dam 7f winner: 150/1, always behind in maiden at Redcar. *F. Watson* **–**

DIUM MAC 2 b.g. (May 26) Presidium 124 – Efipetite 54 (Efisio 120) [2003 7m² 6m⁴ Oct 24] 1,500Y: leggy gelding: third foal: brother to 5-y-o Efidium and 3-y-o Efimac: dam 1m winner: fair form in maiden at Newcastle (second to Vademecum) and sales race at Doncaster (fourth to Enchantment): should stay 1m. *N. Bycroft* **75**

DIVA DANCER 3 ch.f. Dr Devious (IRE) 127 – Catina 102 (Nureyev (USA) 131) [2003 42: 10.1m 8.2m Oct 28] sturdy filly: poor form only start at 2 yrs: well held in 2003. *J. Hetherton* **–**

DIVA MARIA 4 b.f. Kris 135 – May Light 62 (Midyan (USA) 124) [2003 56: 7g f7s 7m Aug 8] modest maiden at 3 yrs: well held in 2003. *R. F. Johnson Houghton* **–**

DIVERSIFICATION 2 ch.f. (May 8) Piccolo 121 – Atan's Gem (USA) (Sharpen Up 127) [2003 6g 5m⁵ Jul 9] 1,000Y: fifth living foal: half-sister to winners abroad by Rudimentary and Night Shift: dam no form: well held in claimer/seller. *P. D. Evans* **–**

DIVINE GIFT 2 b.c. (Mar 26) Groom Dancer (USA) 128 – Child's Play (USA) (Sharpen Up 127) [2003 6m² 7m 7.2d² 7d* Nov 7] 45,000Y: good-topped colt: has a quick action: half-brother to smart 7f (at 2 yrs) to 1¼m winner Sharp Play (by Robellino) and 6-y-o Pax: dam, French 10.5f winner, out of half-sister to Precocious and Jupiter Island: left 1 Noseda after second start: won maiden at Doncaster cosily by ½ length from Dakota Blackhills, always prominent: should stay 1m: acts on good to soft ground, probably on good to firm: should make useful handicapper at 3 yrs. *M. A. Jarvis* **89 p**

DIVINE SPIRIT 2 b.g. (Feb 21) Foxhound (USA) 103 – Vocation (IRE) 74 (Royal Academy (USA) 130) [2003 5m⁴ 6m⁵ 5m⁴ 5m³ 6g 5m⁴ 6g⁴ 6m⁴ 5f² 5f* 6g⁶ 5m* Sep 15] 8,500Y, resold 23,000Y: leggy gelding: first foal: dam, 2-y-o 7f winner, sister to useful **84**

performer up to 1m Caviar Royale: fairly useful performer: won maiden at Catterick in August and nursery at Musselburgh in September: should prove best at 5f/easy 6f: acts on firm going: wore cheekpieces last 4 outings: races up with pace. *M. Dods*

DIVORCE ACTION (IRE)   7 b.g. Common Grounds 118 – Overdue Reaction (Be – §
My Guest (USA) 126) [2003 –§: 9.9d Sep 23] sturdy gelding: temperamental handicapper: reluctant to race only 6-y-o start. *S. R. Bowring*

DIVULGE (USA)   6 b.g. Diesis 133 – Avira (Dancing Brave (USA) 140) [2003 73:   –
12.3m Jun 19] sturdy gelding: fair performer at best: probably best around 1m: acts on polytrack and good to firm going: wore cheekpieces (well held) only Flat run in 2003. *A. Crook*

DIXIE DANCING   4 ch.f. Greensmith 121 – Daylight Dreams 77 (Indian Ridge 123)   65
[2003 75: 7m⁵ p7g p7g³ p7g Oct 30] sturdy filly: fair performer: stays easy 1m: acts on good to firm going and polytrack: free-going sort, usually held up. *C. A. Cyzer*

DI YOUNG   3 b.f. Hernando (FR) 127 – Mo Chos Chle 80 (Indian Ridge 123) [2003   63
62p: p8g p10g⁵ p10g 10.9f 11.7f 11.9f⁵ Aug 27] modest maiden: should stay 1½m: acts on polytrack. *J. W. Hills*

DIZZY IN THE HEAD   4 b.g. Mind Games 121 – Giddy 60 (Polar Falcon (USA)   81 §
126) [2003 79: 5m⁵ 6.1d* 6f⁵ 6m⁶ 6m 5g 6g Oct 22] leggy gelding: fair performer: won minor event at Nottingham in May: effective at 5f/6f: acts on any ground: usually visored/blinkered: very slowly away final outing: has looked none too keen/tends to hang markedly: front runner: unreliable. *J. O'Reilly*

DMITRI   3 b.g. Emperor Jones (USA) 119 – Shining Cloud 73 (Indian Ridge 123)   90
[2003 81: 7g 7.9m² 8g 8f⁴ 8.2d 7m⁴ 10f⁵ 8.9f 8f² Oct 27] lengthy gelding: fairly useful handicapper: best effort on second outing: stays 1m: acts on firm and good to soft going: visored (raced too freely) fifth start: often leads: inconsistent. *M. L. W. Bell*

DOBERMAN (IRE)   8 br.g. Dilum (USA) 115 – Switch Blade (IRE) 60 (Robellino   45
(USA) 127) [2003 48, a66: f9.4g³ f8.5g⁶ f12g⁶ 10.2m 10.2m⁴ 8.5m Aug 14] rangy gelding: poor performer: left W. M. Brisbourne after fourth start: probably best at 1m/easy 1¼m: acts on fibresand, firm and soft going: usually wears headgear: tried tongue tied: usually races prominently: sometimes looks none too resolute. *P. D. Evans*

DO BUY ME (IRE)   3 b.f. First Trump 118 – Reticent Bride (IRE) 71 (Shy Groom   –
(USA)) [2003 f7g⁴ 6.1m⁶ 8m Jul 23] 7,500Y: smallish filly: half-sister to several winners, including fairly useful 6f winner Barnacla (by Bluebird) and 4-y-o Diamond Ring: dam, Irish 6f winner, sister to Lowther winner Miss Demure: little form. *W. J. Haggas*

DOCDUCKOUT   3 b.g. Bluegrass Prince (IRE) 110 – Fayre Holly (IRE) 57 (Fayruz   56
116) [2003 59: p7g f7g* f9.4g⁶ f7s Feb 13] modest performer: won seller at Southwell (drifted right) in January: well beaten after: stays 7f: acts on fibresand: wore cheekpieces final outing: sold 5,000 gns in October. *J. M. P. Eustace*

DOCKLANDS BABYGIRL   2 b.f. (Apr 30) Polar Falcon (USA) 126 – Anytime   61
Baby 56 (Bairn (USA) 126) [2003 6.1m³ 6g⁴ 5.7m⁶ Aug 5] 9,000Y: first foal: half-sister to 2000 2-y-o 5f selling winner Acorn Catcher (by Emarati) and 4-y-o Online Investor: dam 5f winner: modest form in maidens: third at Nottingham: needs to settle to stay beyond 6f: sold 3,000 gns. *N. P. Littmoden*

DOCKLANDS BLUE (IRE)   2 ch.f. (Mar 22) Cadeaux Genereux 131 – Copious   57
(IRE) (Generous (IRE) 139) [2003 f6g6 f5g³ p6g Dec 29] 5,000Y, 12,000 2-y-o: second foal: half-sister to fairly useful Irish performer up to 1½m Fluirseach (by In The Wings), 7f winner at 2 yrs: dam unraced half-sister to dam of high-class miler Landseer and 3-y-o Ikhtyar: best effort in maidens (modest form) when third at Wolverhampton: will stay 6f. *N. P. Littmoden*

DOCKLANDS BRIAN   2 ch.g. (Feb 8) First Trump 118 – Mystique (Mystiko (USA)   54 d
124) [2003 6m 6f 7m⁵ 6g 7m⁵ 7m 8m f7s Oct 21] 7,000F, 6,500Y: robust gelding: second foal: dam unraced half-sister to smart winner up to 1m Bahamian Bandit (by First Trump): modest maiden: ran badly last 3 starts: stays 7f: acts on good to firm going: slowly away first 4 outings. *P. S. McEntee*

DOCKLANDS MAXIMUS (IRE)   3 ch.g. Danehill Dancer (IRE) 117 – Thats Luck   84
(IRE) (Posen (USA)) [2003 83: 8g⁶ 8.1v⁵ 7m⁴ 8.1m⁶ 7.1g⁴ 7m a6g Dec 26] workmanlike gelding: fairly useful handicapper: left N. Littmoden after fifth start: likely to prove best at 1m: acts on polytrack and any turf going: free-going sort: consistent in Britain: renamed Determination, below form both starts for new stable. *I. W. Allan, Hong Kong*

DOCKLANDS PRINCESS (IRE) 3 ch.f. Desert Prince (IRE) 130 – Alamiya (IRE) – (Doyoun 124) [2003 56: p10g 12.1g Jul 24] modest maiden at 2 yrs: well held in 2003. *M. H. Tompkins*

DOCKLANDS PRINCE (USA) 3 ch.g. Distant View (USA) 126 – Texas Trophy – (USA) (Deerhound (USA) 64) [2003 7m p10g Jul 19] $28,000F, IR 16,000Y: first foal: dam ran twice in USA: last in maiden and seller. *N. P. Littmoden*

DOCKSIDE STORY (IRE) 2 b.g. (Mar 16) Docksider (USA) 124 – Fiction 59 – (Dominion 123) [2003 5m 6g 5f⁶ 7m Oct 17] 6,000Y: leggy, close-coupled gelding: seventh foal: half-brother to 3 winners, including 1999 2-y-o 5f winner Palmstead Belle (by Wolfhound): dam 2-y-o 5f winner: soundly beaten in maidens/claimers: sold 600 gns. *A. Berry*

DOCTORATE 2 b.c. (Feb 11) Dr Fong (USA) 128 – Aunt Tate (Tate Gallery (USA) **67** 117) [2003 6m⁴ May 31] 52,000Y: angular colt: fifth foal: half-brother to 3 winners, including fairly useful 2002 2-y-o 7f winner Lodge Keeper (by Grand Lodge) and French 12.5f winner Devious Aunty (by Dr Devious): dam, ran twice, out of smart French 1¼m winner Aunty: 12/1, fourth of 9 to Old Deuteronomy in slowly-run maiden at Newmarket: should stay at least 1m. *E. A. L. Dunlop*

DOCTOR DENNIS (IRE) 6 b.g. Last Tycoon 131 – Noble Lustre (USA) 71 **61 d** (Lyphard's Wish (FR) 124) [2003 68: p6g⁵ f6s p7g 7m f6g 6s⁴ p6g f7g³ f6g⁶ 6f⁵ 6.1m 6m⁴ 6m 6g 7s⁴ f6g⁴ f6g⁴ f7g⁶ Dec 16] good-bodied gelding: modest performer: effective at 6f/7f: acts on firm going, soft and all-weather: usually wears headgear: none too consistent. *Mrs Lydia Pearce*

DOCTORED 2 ch.g. (Mar 21) Dr Devious (IRE) 127 – Polygueza (FR) 78 (Be My **59 §** Guest (USA) 126) [2003 f7g⁵ f7g² 7.1f⁵ 8d⁶ p7g 7m² 7.5m 8.3g² f8g³ Oct 16] 8,000Y: strong, workmanlike gelding: fourth foal: half-brother to winner around 7f in Italy by Barathea: dam, Irish 7f winner, half-sister to useful Irish miler Lepoushka: modest maiden: placed 4 times, including in sellers/nursery: stays 1m: acts on fibresand and good to firm ground: blinkered last 5 starts, tongue tied last 4: unreliable. *B. J. Meehan*

DOCTOR ONE 2 ch.g. (Mar 5) Dr Fong (USA) 128 – City of Angels (Woodman **82** (USA) 126) [2003 7.9m* Sep 3] 16,000Y: quite good-topped gelding: sixth foal: half-brother to 3 winners, including 4-y-o Del Mar Sunset and fairly useful 1¼m winner Charmer Venture (by Zilzal): dam unraced: 100/1, won 19-runner maiden at York by ½ length from Florida Heart, leading final 1f: should stay 1¼m: sent to Hong Kong, joined D. Hill and renamed Super Catcher. *M. Dods*

DOCTOR PRICE 2 ch.g. (Apr 8) Wolfhound (USA) 126 – Water Pixie (IRE) (Dance **?** of Life (USA)) [2003 5.1m³ 5.8m³ 5.8g* 8d² a8g* Dec 14] 3,000Y: fifth foal: half-brother to 1m winner Pix Me Up (by Up And At 'em): dam unraced: third in seller at Nottingham (claimed from K. Ryan £6,000) on debut: won minor events at Taby in September and Dos Hermanas (by 12 lengths) in December: stays 1m. *C. Bjorling, Spain*

DOCTOR SPIN (IRE) 7 b.g. Namaqualand (USA) – Madam Loving 99 (Vaigly **59** Great 127) [2003 94: 6d 7m² 6f³ May 30] tall gelding: smart performer at best, just modest in 2003: best at 5f/6f: acted on firm going, below form on soft: tried blinkered: edgy sort: sometimes found little: dead. *D. Nicholls*

DOCTRINE 2 b.f. (Jan 29) Barathea (IRE) 127 – Auspicious 103 (Shirley Heights **97** 130) [2003 6m⁶ 8.2m² 8m* 7m* 8g⁶ Oct 21] well-made filly: first foal: dam, 1¼m winner who stayed 1½m, sister to smart middle-distance stayer Sacrament: useful performer: won maiden at Yarmouth in September and nursery at Catterick (comfortably at odds on) in October: good sixth, beaten about 4 lengths by Via Milano, in Prix des Reservoirs at Deauville final start: will stay 1¼m, probably 1½m. *J. H. M. Gosden*

DOC WATSON (FR) 3 ch.c. Dr Devious (IRE) 127 – Blinding (IRE) (High Top 131) **90** [2003 87: 8m⁵ p8g* 9m² Apr 21] big, strong colt: fairly useful performer: won maiden at Lingfield in April on all-weather debut: good second in handicap at Kempton later in month: will need to become more tractable to stay 1¼m: acts on polytrack, raced only on good/good to firm going on turf: consistent: sent to USA. *R. Hannon*

DODGER (IRE) 3 b.g. Among Men (USA) 124 – Hazy Image (Ahonoora 122) [2003 – –: p6g p10g 10m⁶ 7m⁴ 6m 5.3m 12m⁴ Aug 21] small, well-made gelding: of little account: tried blinkered/visored. *Jamie Poulton*

DODONA 5 b.m. Lahib (USA) 129 – Dukrame 76 (Top Ville 129) [2003 64: 9.7f³ 10f³ **73** 9.7m² 10m² 8m⁶ 9.7g* 10.9m* Sep 20] fair handicapper: won at Folkestone and Warwick in September: stays 10.9f: acts on soft and good to firm going: tried blinkered: sometimes starts slowly/hangs: free-going sort. *T. D. McCarthy*

DOLCE PICCATA 2 ch.f. (Mar 18) Piccolo 121 – Highland Rhapsody (IRE) 78 (Kris **88** 135) [2003 p5g⁴ 5m² 5m² 5.1m² 5g⁴ f5g² 5.1m³ 5.2m 5m* 5.2m³ 6.1g² Aug 28] 16,000Y: workmanlike filly: fourth foal: half-sister to fairly useful 5f winner (including at 2 yrs) Muja Farewell (by Mujtahid) and 3-y-o Super Song: dam, 6f winner, should have stayed 1m: fairly useful performer: won maiden at Musselburgh in July: very good 3 lengths third to Needles And Pins in listed race at Newbury next time: probably best at 5f: acts on good to firm going, probably on fibresand: blinkered third and fifth starts. *B. J. Meehan*

DOLLAR KING (IRE) 5 b.g. Ela-Mana-Mou 132 – Summerhill (Habitat 134) [2003 **–** 72?: 10g Mar 27] lengthy, angular gelding: fair handicapper at best at 4 yrs: well held only outing in 2003: tried visored: dead. *B. J. Llewellyn*

DOLLAR LAW 7 ch.g. Selkirk (USA) 129 – Western Heights (Shirley Heights 130) **–** [2003 72, a–: f11g Jan 21] leggy, short-backed gelding: fair handicapper in 2002: well held only start on Flat in 2003 (won over hurdles in March): tongue tied nowadays: has been taken steadily/alone to post: has hung left: raced freely. *R. J. Price*

DOLLY WOTNOT (IRE) 2 b.f. (May 16) Desert King (IRE) 129 – Riding School **65** (IRE) (Royal Academy (USA) 130) [2003 7.5m 8.2m⁴ 8m⁴ f9.4g⁵ Nov 15] 21,000Y: leggy, sparely-made filly: first living foal: dam, third at 1½m in France, half-sister to William Hill Futurity winner Emmson (stayed 1½m): fair maiden: fourth at Nottingham and Yarmouth: should be suited by 1¼m/1½m: below form on fibresand. *N. P. Littmoden*

DOLPHINELLE (IRE) 7 b.g. Dolphin Street (FR) 125 – Mamie's Joy (Prince Ten- **– §** derfoot (USA) 126) [2003 41§, a55§: p8g p10g p10g p7g⁵ p8g p8g p7g⁵ p7g³ p10g⁵ Dec **a55 §** 30] sturdy gelding: modest on all-weather, poor on turf: stays 1¼m: below form on heavy going, probably acts on any other turf/all-weather: often blinkered/visored: tends to race lazily: untrustworthy. *Jamie Poulton*

DOLZAGO 3 b.g. Pursuit of Love 124 – Doctor's Glory (USA) 91 (Elmaamul (USA) **50** 125) [2003 59p: 8m 8m 10m 12.1g⁵ p12g⁵ Sep 3] good-bodied gelding: modest maiden, lightly raced: stays 1½m: acts on good to soft going, probably on polytrack: sold 8,000 gns in November. *P. W. Harris*

DOMBEYA (IRE) 3 b.f. Danehill (USA) 126 – The Faraway Tree 113 (Suave Dancer **66** (USA) 136) [2003 8.1m⁴ 12.3g³ 10s Nov 3] lengthy filly: first foal: dam, 6f (at 2 yrs) and 1¾m winner, half-sister to very smart 9f/1¼m performer Sasuru: fair form when fourth to Rossiya in maiden at Sandown: failed to progress: will probably prove best short of 1½m. *J. H. M. Gosden*

DOMEDRIVER (IRE) 5 b.h. Indian Ridge 123 – Napoli 108 (Baillamont **128** (USA) 124) [2003 128: 8g² 8m⁴ 8g⁵ 8d² 8g Sep 7]
The winner of the 2002 Breeders' Cup Mile Domedriver failed to add to that success as a five-year-old, but that shouldn't be held against him as he embarks on a stud career. Domedriver's high-class performance at Arlington, when bringing to an end Rock of Gibraltar's Group 1-winning spree, didn't get the recognition it deserved at the time and he ran right up to that form in the latest season, going close to recording a second top-level success. Domedriver went down only by a short neck to Six Perfections, also owned by the Niarchos family, in the twelve-runner Prix Jacques le Marois in August, a race in which Domedriver had also finished second—to Banks Hill—twelve months previously. Domedriver was held up as usual at Deauville, and came through to hold every chance, keeping on well inside the final furlong but just unable to get past his more handily-ridden stablemate. Domedriver returned to his best at Deauville after a couple of disappointing efforts since a short-neck second of ten, coming out best at the weights, to Dandoun in the Prix du Muguet at Saint-Cloud in May on his reappearance. Domedriver ran disappointingly in both the Lockinge Stakes and the Prix Messidor. The trainer put Domedriver's performance at Newbury down to the fact that he was unsuited by racing without any cover in the six-runner field, though it was difficult to envisage circumstances in which Domedriver would have got near the spectacular eleven-length winner Hawk Wing that day. Domedriver seemed to be presented with an excellent opportunity in the Group 3 Prix Messidor, in which he didn't have to shoulder a penalty for his Breeders' Cup win. He should have fared better at Deauville than fifth of ten, albeit beaten only around a length, behind Special Kaldoun, despite the extenuating circumstances of being poorly placed once the race began in earnest after a muddling pace and of not getting much room when making his effort. Things did not fall Domedriver's way either in the Prix du Moulin at Long-

champ in early-September on his final outing. Six Perfections was missing but the field was fairly representative of the season's top milers—Hawk Wing had been retired the previous month. Most of the jockeys seemed intent on riding waiting races, resulting in no more than a fair pace which told against Domedriver, who was doubly unfortunate in also being short of room from under two furlongs out; in the end Domedriver finished full of running in seventh of fourteen, beaten just over five lengths by the winner Nebraska Tornado.

Domedriver (IRE) (b.h. 1998)	Indian Ridge (ch 1985)	Ahonoora (ch 1975)	Lorenzaccio
			Helen Nichols
		Hillbrow (ch 1975)	Swing Easy
			Golden City
	Napoli (b 1991)	Baillamont (b 1982)	Blushing Groom
			Lodeve
		Bella Senora (b 1984)	Northern Dancer
			Sex Appeal

Domedriver will stand at Lanwades Stud in Newmarket, where, if the stud's record with its other stallions is anything to go by, he will achieve success. His fee is £12,000, October 1st terms. The stallions currently resident at Lanwades—Hernando, Selkirk and Zilzal—have each sired European classic winners. The success achieved with Hernando and Selkirk in particular (the pair were responsible for the 2003 Group 1 winners Sulamani, Leadership and Red Bloom) is made more noteworthy by the fact that neither has the kind of fashionable pedigree associated with the modern notion of the ideal commercial stallion. In some respects, Domedriver, whose pedigree was covered in detail in *Racehorses of 2002*, conforms to the Hernando/Selkirk model. He is by the prolific Indian Ridge, who has yet to make a name for himself as a sire of sires, though time is still very much on his side. The best horse sired by a son of Indian Ridge is the triple Irish St Leger winner Vinnie Roe, who is by Irish Derby runner-up Definite Article. That particular father and son buck the general trend, as Indian Ridge, who did not stay a mile himself,

Niarchos Family's "Domedriver"

has, as his own pedigree suggested would be the case, been predominantly an influence for speed at stud.

Domedriver is out of the useful French mile- to mile-and-a-quarter winner Napoli, who stayed a mile and a half. Napoli is out of Bella Senora, a sister to El Gran Senor and Try My Best. A medium-sized, quite attractive horse, best at a mile and possessed of a good turn of foot, Domedriver acted on soft and good to firm going. *P. Bary, France*

DOMENICO (IRE) 5 b.g. Sadler's Wells (USA) 132 – Russian Ballet (USA) (Nijinsky (CAN) 138) [2003 89: 16.2m⁶ 15m 22.2f 16.2m² Jul 15] strong, close-coupled gelding: fairly useful performer: probably stays 2½m: acts on soft and good to firm ground: blinkered (well beaten) once at 3 yrs: winning hurdler. *J. R. Jenkins* **82**

DOMESTICA (IRE) 2 b.f. (Apr 5) Robellino (USA) 127 – Pictina (Petong 126) [2003 7d Nov 7] first living foal: dam unraced out of sister to very smart miler Dominion: 25/1, well beaten in maiden at Doncaster. *A. M. Balding* **–**

DOMINAITE 5 b.g. Komaite (USA) – Fairy Kingdom (Prince Sabo 123) [2003 6g Jul 8] lengthy, angular gelding: fairly useful performer at 2 yrs for M. Easterby: last in handicap (found to be sore) only run since. *G. P. Kelly* **–**

DOMINICA 4 ch.f. Alhaarth (IRE) 126 – Dominio (IRE) 99 (Dominion 123) [2003 115: 5f⁴ 5m⁴ 5g² 5s Oct 5] smallish filly: smart performer in 2002, successful in King's Stand Stakes at Royal Ascot: respectable efforts first 3 starts in 2003 when fourth to Choisir in same race and to Oasis Dream in Nunthorpe Stakes at York, and short-head second to Bali Royal in listed event at Hamilton (odds on): visored, well beaten in Prix de l'Abbaye at Longchamp final outing: best at 5f: acts on firm and good to soft ground: races prominently: has flashed tail but is genuine. *M. P. Tregoning* **109**

DOMINION PRINCE 5 b.g. First Trump 118 – Lammastide 93 (Martinmas 128) [2003 –: p16g f12s Feb 18] tall, good-topped gelding: maiden: no form since 2000: tried tongue tied. *D. Mullarkey* **–**

DOMINION ROSE (USA) 4 b. or br.f. Spinning World (USA) 130 – Louju (USA) (Silver Hawk (USA) 123) [2003 65d: f7g* 7.2m⁶ 7m Jun 28] rather leggy, unfurnished filly: had a short, round action: modest handicapper: won at Southwell in June: effective at 7f on all-weather, probably stayed 1¼m: acted on good to firm going, good to soft and fibresand: reportedly in foal. *W. R. Muir* **55**

DOMIRATI 3 b.g. Emarati (USA) 74 – Julia Domna (Dominion 123) [2003 74p: p5g* 5f³ 6.1m² 5m³ 5g 5m² 5m² 6g³ 6m⁴ Oct 1] angular gelding: fairly useful handicapper: won at Lingfield in April: effective at 5f/easy 6f: raced only on all-weather and good ground or firmer: has been early to post/had 2 handlers: races prominently: reliable. *R. Charlton* **85**

DOMQUISTA D'OR 6 b.g. Superpower 113 – Gild The Lily 83 (Ile de Bourbon (USA) 133) [2003 –: f12g f12s⁶ f12g⁶ f12g Mar 3] strong, lengthy gelding: poor maiden: probably stayed 11f: acted on soft ground and fibresand: tried blinkered/visored: dead. *G. A. Ham* **–**

DOM SHADEED 8 b.g. Shadeed (USA) 135 – Fair Dominion 107 (Dominion 123) [2003 49: p13g⁴ p13g p13g³ f14.8g p12g 11.7f Oct 12] tall gelding: modest performer nowadays: should stay 1¾m: acts on all-weather, soft and good to firm going: blinkered (well held) once, also tried in cheekpieces. *R. J. Baker* **–** **a54**

DONA MARIA 3 b.f. Titus Livius (FR) 115 – Distant Isle (IRE) (Bluebird (USA) 125) [2003 53: f8g⁵ f6s 6m Apr 3] modest maiden at 2 yrs: stiff tasks and last all starts in 2003: stays 6f. *A. Berry* **–**

DON ARGENTO 2 gr.c. (Feb 12) Sri Pekan (USA) 117 – Grey Galava 64 (Generous (IRE) 139) [2003 6.1m 6.1m 7.1m Sep 22] 15,000Y: workmanlike colt: third foal: half-brother to 3-y-o Millagros and winner in Germany by Mukaddamah: dam 1¾m winner: well held in maidens: pulled hard second start. *Mrs A. J. Bowlby* **–**

DONASTRELA (IRE) 2 b.f. (Feb 25) Tagula (IRE) 116 – David's Star (Welsh Saint 126) [2003 p8g Nov 13] €1,800Y: half-sister to useful Irish 8.5f winner Beamish Boy (by Mujtahid) and fairly useful 7f to 1¼m winner Golconda (by Lahib): dam lightly raced: 33/1, well held in maiden at Lingfield, slowly away. *A. M. Balding* **–**

DONATELLO PRIMO (IRE) 4 ch.g. Entrepreneur 123 – Mystical River (USA) (Riverman (USA) 131) [2003 78: 7g 7m 7m⁵ 7m p8g 6.5m Jul 11] strong gelding: fair handicapper: effective at 5f and seems to stay 7f: acts on all-weather and good to firm **70**

going, probably on heavy: has worn cheekpieces last 5 starts: has started slowly: sold £1,500. *Miss A. M. Newton-Smith*

DONEGAL DANCER (IRE)   3 ch.g. Spectrum (IRE) 126 – Unfuwaanah 74 (Unfu- **80** wain (USA) 131) [2003 78: 8f* 9g⁶ 8f⁵ 8g 8g³ 7f 8m⁶ 8f⁶ 7.5d 6.5d⁶ 7.5m Dec 20] tall gelding: fairly useful handicapper: won at Brighton in April: sold from B. Hills 10,000 gns after eighth start: barely stays 9f: unraced on heavy going, acts on any other turf (below form on polytrack). *A. Feligioni, Italy*

DONEGAL SHORE (IRE)   4 b.c. Mujadil (USA) 119 – Distant Shore (IRE) 71   **–** (Jareer (USA) 115) [2003 90: p12g f8.5g 12m⁶ 8.2f f14.8g Oct 20] rather leggy colt: formerly useful: reportedly had breathing problem final 3-y-o start and no longer of much account: tried tongue tied. *Mrs J. Candlish*

DON FAYRUZ (IRE)   11 b.g. Fayruz 116 – Gobolino (Don 128) [2003 64: 8.2m 8.1m   **–** 8.1m Jul 11] good-topped gelding: little form in 2003. *Mrs A. J. Bowlby*

DON FERNANDO   4 b.c. Zilzal (USA) 137 – Teulada (USA) 61 (Riverman (USA)   **90** 131) [2003 93: 20m 16.1g 16.2d 18m Oct 18] tall, good-topped colt: fairly useful handi-capper: creditable seventh in Ascot Stakes at Royal Ascot on reappearance: below form after: stays 2½m, but doesn't need thorough test of stamina: acts on firm going, possibly not on soft: visored once at 3 yrs: has worn crossed noseband: useful hurdler. *M. C. Pipe*

DONIZETTI (IRE)   3 b.c. Deputy Minister (CAN) – Festival Song (USA) 87 (Irish   **84** River (FR) 131) [2003 91: 7g 7m 6m 7m 6f Oct 10] quite useful-topped colt: fairly useful performer: best effort in 2003 when seventh in handicap at Newbury penultimate start: likely to prove best at 6f/7f: raced only on good ground or firmer on turf: sold 23,000 gns, sent to USA. *R. Charlton*

DONNA ANNA   4 b.f. Be My Chief (USA) 122 – Countess Olivia 80 (Prince Tender-   **–** foot (USA) 126) [2003 –: p12g p12g Feb 15] no form: tried blinkered. *C. F. Wall*

DONNA'S DOUBLE   8 ch.g. Weldnaas (USA) 112 – Shadha 57 (Shirley Heights 130)   **71** [2003 88, a–: 10.1d 8m 10d 10.4f⁶ 10m 10.1m³ 8m 9.3d³ 10.3m 9.1m⁵ 8.3d³ 10m⁴ 10.4f   **a–** 10m⁵ 10g⁵ 12g⁵ Nov 5] smallish, workmanlike gelding: just a fair performer nowadays: best at 1m/1¼m: acts on firm and soft going, some promise on fibresand: tried blinkered, usually wears cheekpieces nowadays: sometimes carries head awkwardly/finds little: usually held up. *D. Eddy*

DONNA VITA   2 b.f. (May 23) Vettori (IRE) 119 – Soolaimon (IRE) 71 (Shareef   **78 p** Dancer (USA) 135) [2003 p7g* 8s Oct 5] angular filly: fourth foal: half-sister to useful 1m (at 2 yrs) and 1¼m (in USA) winner Reduit (by Lion Cavern) and 4-y-o Sentinel: dam, maiden who should have stayed 1½m, half-sister to smart French performer up to 10.5f Audacieuse and useful stayer Lord Jim: fair form when winning 11-runner maiden at Lingfield in September by 1½ lengths from Ice Dragon, quickening well to lead final 1f: always behind in Prix Marcel Boussac at Longchamp: will be suited by 1¼m/1½m: open to improvement. *G. A. Butler*

DONNY BOWLING   3 b.f. Sesaro (USA) 81 – Breakfast Creek 63 (Hallgate 127)   **49** [2003 58: 5m 5m 7.5m³ 8s⁶ 8.5m 7.5m 8m 13.8d³ 12m Oct 7] leggy, lengthy filly: poor performer: stays 7.5m: acts on firm and soft going. *M. E. Sowersby*

DONT CALL ME DEREK   2 b.g. (Mar 29) Sri Pekan (USA) 117 – Cultural Role 95   **74 p** (Night Shift (USA)) [2003 5.1m p5g⁴ Nov 22] 3,600Y, resold 5,000Y: big, workmanlike gelding: second foal: half-brother to fairly useful Irish 1m winner Diplomatic Gamble (by Big Shuffle): dam Irish 2-y-o 7f winner: better effort in maidens (fair form) when eye-catching fourth to Intriguing Glimpse at Lingfield, again starting slowly and finish-ing well not knocked about (rated winner): bred to stay at least 6f: capable of better still. *S. C. Williams*

DONT LET GO   2 b.f. (Jan 18) Danzero (AUS) – Il Doria (IRE) 66 (Mac's Imp (USA)   **–** 116) [2003 p5g p6g Dec 20] 3,000Y: third foal: dam, sprint maiden, half-sister to smart 5f performer Palacegate Episode: well held in minor event/seller at Lingfield. *C. R. Dore*

DON'T MATTER   3 b.f. Petong 126 – Cool Run 87 (Deep Run 119) [2003 60: 8g   **–** f8.5g Jun 6] modest maiden at 2 yrs: well held in 2003. *B. Palling*

DON'T SIOUX ME (IRE)   5 b.g. Sadler's Wells¶(USA) 132 – Commanche Belle 74   **–** (Shirley Heights 130) [2003 100: 14f⁴ Jun 29] deep-girthed gelding: useful performer for H. Cecil at 3/4 yrs: sold 8,000 gns, won over hurdles before and after tailed off in minor event at Goodwood on return to Flat: tried tongue tied: has given trouble in preliminaries. *C. R. Dore*

DONTSTOPTHEMUSIC (IRE) 2 b.f. (Jan 24) Night Shift (USA) – Sevi's Choice **79** (USA) (Sir Ivor 135) [2003 6m⁵ 5m² 5m³ 5.1g* 6m 5.1g² 6f 6.5d Sep 10] 70,000F, €120,000Y: first foal: dam German 1¼m winner: fair performer: made all in maiden at Nottingham: creditable second in nursery at Chepstow later in August: stays 6f: acts on firm going: visored last 3 outings: sold 13,000 gns, sent to USA. *M. R. Channon*

DONT TALK SHOP (IRE) 4 b.g. Desert Style (IRE) 121 – Madam Loving 99 **–** (Vaigly Great 127) [2003 51d: f6g³ f6s⁶ f6g Mar 13] half-brother to several winners, including 7-y-o Doctor Spin: dam 5f/6f winner, best at 2 yrs: poor maiden on balance: trained in 2002 by M. Halford in Ireland: stays 6f: acts on good to firm going and fibresand: tried blinkered/tongue tied as 3-y-o. *N. P. Littmoden*

DON'T TELL ROSEY 3 b.g. Barathea (IRE) 127 – Patsy Western 81 (Precocious **80** 126) [2003 71: 6m 6.1g 5s⁶ 5.1g² 5f² 5f* 5f Jul 9] compact gelding: fairly useful per-former: won maiden at Folkestone in June (reportedly finished distressed final start, subsequently gelded): raced only at 5f/6f: acts on firm and soft going: has looked difficult ride (ran out second 2-y-o start). *M. Blanshard*

DON'T WORRY MIKE 9 ch.g. Forzando 122 – Hat Hill (Roan Rocket 128) [2003 **–** –: f9.4g Feb 7] leggy, workmanlike gelding: of little account nowadays. *G. F. Bridgwater*

DOOHULLA (USA) 2 ch.f. (Mar 13) Stravinsky (USA) 133 – Viva Zapata (USA) 116 **87** (Affirmed (USA)) [2003 6m³ 6m⁵ p6g* 6g³ Oct 31] 45,000Y: tall filly: closely related to 2 winners, including useful French/UAE performer up to 1m Viva Nureyev (by Nureyev) and half-sister to several winners, including useful 1¼m winner Mexican Hawk (by Silver Hawk): dam French sprinter: fairly useful performer: won minor event at Lingfield: about 4¼ lengths third of 7 to Dowager in listed event at Newmarket later in October: not sure to stay much beyond 6f: acts on polytrack, best turf effort on good going: blinkered last 2 starts: tends to carry head high. *G. A. Butler*

DORA CORBINO 3 b.f. Superpower 113 – Smartie Lee 66 (Dominion 123) [2003 –: **50 ?** 8.1m⁵ 12g⁶ 10m Oct 22] quite good-topped filly: form (seemingly modest) only in maiden on reappearance: probably stays 1m. *R. Hollinshead*

DORCHESTER 6 b.g. Primo Dominie 121 – Penthouse Lady (Last Tycoon 131) [2003 **83** 85: 6m 6m⁴ 6f⁴ 6f 6m* 6m³ 6g 7g⁵ p7g³ Nov 13] good-topped gelding: fairly useful handicapper: won at Newmarket in July: effective at 6f/7f: acts on firm going, soft and all-weather: blinkered once at 3 yrs: tends to edge right. *W. J. Musson*

DORINGO 2 b.c. (Apr 7) Prince Sabo 123 – Mistral's Dance (Shareef Dancer (USA) **–** 135) [2003 6d Nov 8] 7,500Y: leggy, sparely-made colt: brother to 6f (at 2 yrs)/7f winner Cruise and 1m winner Brocketeer and half-brother to 2 winners by Risk Me, including fairly useful 5f (at 2 yrs) to 11.6f winner Queen's Pageant: dam, maiden, best at 7f: 20/1, behind in Doncaster maiden. *J. L. Spearing*

DORISIMA (FR) 2 ch.f. (Feb 8) Mark of Esteem (IRE) 137 – Suhaad 111 (Unfuwain **–** (USA) 131) [2003 7.2m Sep 19] €16,000Y: first foal: dam 1¼m/1½m winner: 40/1 and green, well beaten in maiden at Ayr. *D. Nicholls*

DORIS SOUTER (IRE) 3 b. or br.f. Desert Story (IRE) 115 – Hope And Glory (USA) **81** 87 (Well Decorated (USA)) [2003 65d: p7g⁴ 9m⁴ p8g² 11.8m⁶ 10m* 10d² 9.7m³ 10m* 10g⁵ 10.2g³ Sep 11] well-grown, close-coupled filly: fairly useful handicapper: won at Windsor in June and Newbury in August: should stay beyond 1¼m: acts on good to firm ground, good to soft and polytrack: usually races prominently: consistent. *R. Hannon*

DORMY TWO (IRE) 3 b.f. Eagle Eyed (USA) 111 – Tartan Lady (IRE) 88 (Taufan **57** (USA) 119) [2003 10g³ 11.7f⁴ 10g Oct 6] IR 8,000Y: good-topped filly: fourth foal: half-sister to fairly useful 1999 2-y-o 1m winner Scotty Guest (by Distinctly North) and Irish 1¼m winner Lady For Life (by Rainbows For Life): dam 7f winner (at 2 yrs) and 9f winner in Ireland: modest form in maidens first 2 starts: probably stays 1¼m: raced only on good ground or firmer: weakened quickly having made running last 2 starts: sold 3,200 gns. *Mrs P. N. Dutfield*

DOROTHY'S FRIEND 3 b.g. Grand Lodge (USA) 125 – Isle of Flame (Shirley **90 p** Heights 130) [2003 64: 10.2g⁵ 11.9f* 14.4g* 16.1m* Sep 8] useful-looking gelding: fairly useful handicapper: won at Brighton, Kempton and Newcastle (by 6 lengths despite swerving left under whip) within 7 days in September: stays 2m: acts on firm ground: probably capable of better still. *R. Charlton*

DOROTHYS SWIFT (IRE) 3 b.f. Petardia 113 – Verica (USA) (Diesis 133) [2003 **–** 62: f5g⁴ f7g 6m 6m 8g 10m Jun 24] leggy filly: modest maiden at 2 yrs: little form in 2003, leaving G. Chung after fourth start: has been slowly away: wore cheekpieces last 3 starts. *Miss D. Mountain*

DOTTIE DIGGER (IRE)   4 b.f. Catrail (USA) 123 – Hint-Of-Romance (IRE) 86   –
(Treasure Kay 114) [2003 63, a–: 9m Apr 10] heavy-topped filly: modest maiden: tailed
off only Flat run in 2003: tried in headgear: won over hurdles in November. *Miss Lucinda
V. Russell*

DOUBLE ASSEMBLY   3 ch.f. Presidium 124 – Zamarra 59 (Clantime 101) [2003   **62 d**
74: f6g4 f5s p6g 6f 6m 6m Aug 20] good-topped filly: poor mover: modest handicapper:
below form after reappearance: likely to prove best at 5f/easy 6f: unraced on heavy going,
acts on any other turf and on fibresand. *J. R. Best*

DOUBLE BLADE   8 b.g. Kris 135 – Sesame 117 (Derrylin 115) [2003 67: 12.3m4   **54**
12.4m 11.9m6 16m4 14.1m 14.1m4 Aug 9] big, angular gelding: modest handicapper:
mostly below form in 2003: effective at 9f to 2m: acts on firm going, good to soft and
polytrack: blinkered (ran poorly) once at 3 yrs: best with waiting tactics: has started
slowly/pulled hard/found little: carries head high: successful over hurdles in September
(joined N. Wilson £7,000)/October. *Mrs M. Reveley*

DOUBLE BREW   5 ch.g. Primo Dominie 121 – Boozy 111 (Absalom 128) [2003 58,   **56**
a60: f5g2 f6g5 p5g f6g f6g p6g2 p7g p6g Mar 5] good-topped gelding: modest performer:
effective at 5f to easy 7f: acts on all-weather, firm and good to soft going: tried blinkered (below form): usually wears cheekpieces: carries head high, and sometimes a weak
finisher: none too reliable. *J. L. Spearing*

DOUBLE DEMON   3 ch.c. Double Eclipse (IRE) 122 – Stately Favour 59 (Statoblest   **– §**
120) [2003 –: p10g p10g f9.4g Feb 1] leggy, workmanlike colt: little sign of ability, unseating rider (tried to run out) penultimate start: one to treat with caution. *B. R. Millman*

DOUBLE HELIX   4 b.g. Marju (IRE) 127 – Totham 84 (Shernazar 131) [2003 72:   **49**
8m5 9.9m 8m Sep 6] good-topped gelding: reportedly suffered series of setbacks in 2001:
poor maiden nowadays: best form at 7f on good to soft/soft going: visored last 2 starts
at 3 yrs: raced freely and looked none too keen): has pulled hard/carried
head awkwardly. *M. E. Sowersby*

DOUBLE HONOUR (FR)   5 gr.g. Highest Honor (FR) 124 – Silver Cobra (USA)   **106**
(Silver Hawk (USA) 123) [2003 116: 22.2f3 16.2f Jul 12] leggy, close-coupled gelding:
not a good walker: has a round action: smart performer at best: respectable third to Cover
Up in minor event at Royal Ascot on reappearance: ran poorly in handicap subsequent
start: stays 2¾m: has form on firm going, possibly ideally suited by good or softer:
usually races prominently. *P. J. Hobbs*

DOUBLE M   6 ch.h. First Trump 118 – Girton Degree 41 (Balliol 125) [2003 56, a64:   **57**
p6g p6g4 p6g5 p6g3 p7g6 p6g5 p7g5 p6g 5m4 5g6 5m 5m2 5m4 5.7f4 6d2 5m6 5g3d 5.7f4
5d 7f 5m 5.3f Oct 17] modest handicapper: effective at 5f to easy 7f: acts on all-weather,
firm and good to soft ground: tried blinkered, usually visored. *Mrs L. Richards*

DOUBLE MYSTERY (FR)   3 ch.g. Starborough 126 – Chene de Coeur (FR)   **62**
(Comrade In Arms 123) [2003 81p: p10g5 p12g3 8m 10.2m 12m 9.9f5 8m p8g p12g6 8m
11f Oct 12] smallish, lengthy gelding: disappointing maiden: free-going sort, and may
prove best up to 1¼m: acts on firm ground, probably on soft: tried blinkered: races
prominently: sold 6,000 gns. *Jamie Poulton*

DOUBLE OBSESSION   3 b.c. Sadler's Wells (USA) 132 – Obsessive (USA) 102   **102**
(Seeking The Gold (USA)) [2003 85p: 12.3m5 11m5 12m5 12m6 12m* 12d* 12d 12m2
13.4m 12f 12m Oct 25] compact colt: useful handicapper: won twice (wandered first
occasion) at Ascot in July: ran well after only when second to High Action at Pontefract:
should stay 1¾m: acts on good to firm and good to soft ground: effective blinkered or not,
visored final outing: usually races prominently: none too reliable. *M. Johnston*

DOUBLE OSCAR (IRE)   10 ch.g. Royal Academy (USA) 130 – Broadway Rosie   **57**
101 (Absalom 128) [2003 60, a63: f6g f6g p6g6 p6g Feb 26] good-bodied gelding:
modest handicapper nowadays: best at 5f/6f: acts on firm going, soft and fibresand:
usually blinkered/visored: has had tongue tied: sometimes slowly away: usually held up.
D. Nicholls

DOUBLE RANSOM   4 b.g. Bahamian Bounty 116 – Secrets of Honour (Belmez   **64**
(USA) 131) [2003 68: 10.1d 10m 9.2g 10g 8.2d3 p10g2 Dec 20] lengthy, good-topped
gelding: modest handicapper: effective at 1m (given thorough test), probably stays easy
1¼m: acts on heavy ground and polytrack, well held on fibresand: often blinkered.
Mrs L. Stubbs

DOUBLE SPEY   4 b.g. Atraf 116 – Yankee Special 60 (Bold Lad (IRE) 133) [2003 –:   **50**
f8s 10.1d 9m6 14.1m 17.2m Jun 25] workmanlike gelding: modest maiden handicapper:

effective at 9f and seems to stay 1¾m: acts on firm and good to soft going: has looked difficult ride. *P. C. Haslam*

DOUBLE TURN 3 ch.g. Double Trigger (IRE) 123 – Its My Turn 80 (Palm Track 122) –
[2003 12m⁵ Jun 22] lengthy, angular gelding: half-brother to several winners, including 1½m winner Prince Nicholas (by Midyan): dam miler: 9/2 and backward, soundly beaten in maiden at Pontefract. *J. G. Given*

DOUBLE VODKA (IRE) 2 b. or br.c. (Jan 14) Russian Revival (USA) 125 – Silius **65**
(Junius (USA) 124) [2003 6g⁶ 7m 7m³ 8m⁵ Sep 19] €43,000Y: leggy colt: fifth foal: half-brother to useful Irish sprinter Dairine's Delight (by Fairy King): dam, Irish 1m/9.5f winner, half-sister to dam of Racing Post Trophy winner Seattle Rhyme: fair maiden: third at Newcastle: stays 1m. *M. Dods*

DOUGLAS (IRE) 2 br.c. (Feb 25) Marju (IRE) 127 – Keylock (USA) 65 (Diesis 133) **73**
[2003 6m 7m* 7m⁴ 8m 7m⁴ 8m 7f Oct 27] IR 14,500F, €13,500Y: leggy, sparely-made colt: third foal: half-brother to 8.5f winner in Sweden by Charnwood Forest: dam 1¾m winner: fair performer: won seller at Newmarket in August: stayed 7f: wore cheekpieces fourth outing, visored, brought down final one: tended to wander/carry head high: dead. *R. Hannon*

DOVEDON HERO 3 ch.g. Millkom 124 – Hot Topic (IRE) (Desse Zenny (USA)) **88**
[2003 8.2g² 10.2f* 10g⁴ 10f 11.9m³ 12g³ 14m 11.8m* 12m⁶ Oct 25] 2,500Y: sturdy, close-coupled gelding: second foal: half-brother to winner in Italy by Glory of Dancer: dam no sign of ability: fairly useful performer: won maiden at Bath in July and handicap at Leicester in October: stays 1½m, raced freely at 1¾m: raced only on good ground or firmer (acts on firm): blinkered last 2 starts: usually held up. *P. J. McBride*

DOVE TREE (FR) 3 b.f. Charnwood Forest (IRE) 125 – Quaver (USA) 74 (The Min- **93**
strel (CAN) 135) [2003 80: 8.2d* 7.1f* 7m Jul 8] quite good-topped filly: fairly useful performer: successful in minor events at Nottingham in May and Sandown in June: below form in handicap at Newmarket (headstrong to post and in race) final start: effective at 7f/1m: acts on firm and good to soft going (below form on soft): races prominently. *H. Candy*

DOWAGER 2 b.f. (Mar 19) Groom Dancer (USA) 128 – Rose Noble (USA) 62 (Vagu- **99**
ely Noble 140) [2003 6m 7f* 7.1m⁶ 6f² 7m⁴ 7g⁶ 6g* Oct 31] leggy, useful-looking filly: seventh foal: sister to 8-y-o Dower House and half-sister to 3-y-o Zither: dam, 11.5f winner, half-sister to high-class performer up to 1¼m Grand Lodge: useful performer: won maiden at Kempton in June and listed race at Newmarket (by 1¼ lengths from Kunda) in October: also in frame in listed events at Salisbury and Newmarket: effective at 6f/7f: acts on firm going: often races up with pace. *R. Hannon*

DOWER HOUSE 8 ch.g. Groom Dancer (USA) 128 – Rose Noble (USA) 62 (Vaguely **90**
Noble 140) [2003 –: p8g⁵ p10g p10g⁶ 10g² 10.3d 10d³ p10g* p10g Dec 2] lengthy, rather leggy gelding: has a fluent, round action: fairly useful handicapper: won apprentice event at Lingfield in November: best around 1¼m: acts on polytrack and firm going, probably on soft: tongue tied both 6-y-o outings: takes good hold. *Andrew Turnell*

DOWHATJEN 4 b.f. Desert Style (IRE) 121 – Cupid Miss (Anita's Prince 126) [2003 **86**
82: 7m³ 7m⁴ 6f 6.5m 7d² 8.5m³ 7m⁵ 8.3g² 7m² 7f² 7d 7.2m 7d⁵ 7m Oct 12] lengthy filly: fairly useful performer: effective at 7f/1m: yet to race on heavy going, acts on any other: front runner: none too consistent. *M. R. Channon*

DOWNING STREET (IRE) 2 b.c. (Mar 24) Sadler's Wells (USA) 132 – Photo- **66 p**
graphie (USA) (Trempolino (USA) 135) [2003 8.1m⁵ 8m⁴ 8m Oct 14] 40,000Y, resold 120,000Y: big, quite good-topped colt: second foal: dam, French maiden, sister to Marcel Boussac winner Juvenia and closely related to very smart French 1m/9f performer In Extremis: fair form in maidens, twice not knocked about: type to do better in handicaps at 1¼m/1½m. *A. M. Balding*

DOWNLAND (IRE) 7 b.g. Common Grounds 118 – Boldabsa 96 (Persian Bold 123) **61 §**
[2003 74§: 6d 6d⁶ 6m 5m 7s Oct 29] tall, good sort: only modest handicapper nowadays: effective at 6f to 1m: has won on good to firm going, goes well on soft/heavy: blinkered 3 times at 4 yrs: sometimes early to post/mounted on track: inconsistent. *N. Tinkler*

DOWN MEMORY LANE 3 b.c. Pursuit of Love 124 – Sirene Bleu Marine (USA) **85**
(Secreto (USA) 128) [2003 84p: p8g² p8g* 10g⁴ 10.4m 10.5s³ 11.9m⁶ 10.3m⁶ 9.2m* Jul 17] good-bodied colt: has scope: fairly useful performer: won maiden at Lingfield in January and claimer at Hamilton in July: stays 1¼m: acts on polytrack, heavy and good to firm ground: has taken good hold: sent to UAE, joined C. Wroe. *B. W. Hills*

DOWNTHEREFORDANCIN (IRE) 3 b.g. Groom Dancer (USA) 128 – Merlin's **71**
Fancy 62 (Caerleon (USA) 132) [2003 58, a51: p7g⁴ f7g p6g⁶ p7g² p7g² p12g² 11m*
11.9m⁴ 11.6d* Jun 23] fair performer: claimed from S. Kirk £6,000 prior to winning
selling handicap at Goodwood (sold from S. Dow 12,000 gns) in May: best effort when
winning minor event at Windsor in June: stays easy 1½m: acts on heavy going, good to
firm and all-weather: blinkered (not discredited) once at 2 yrs: fair hurdler. *M. C. Pipe*

DOWNTIME (IRE) 3 ch.g. Perugino (USA) 84 – Razana (IRE) 71 (Kahyasi 130) **66**
[2003 –p: 7m³ 7.9g 10m* 10.3m² 11.6m Jul 28] workmanlike gelding: had a quick action:
fair handicapper: won at Leicester in June: stayed 1¼m: acted on good to firm going:
dead. *J. R. Fanshawe*

DOWN TO THE WOODS (USA) 5 ch.g. Woodman (USA) 126 – Riviera Wonder **68 §**
(USA) (Batonnier (USA)) [2003 83§: p10g f9.4s³ p10g f8.5g f12g⁵ 10g 8f 9m 8m⁶ f8.5g
8.2m 14f⁴ 16g Sep 28] tall, angular gelding: good mover: just a fair performer nowadays:
barely stays 1¼m: acts on firm going, soft and fibresand: often blinkered/visored/tongue
tied: sometimes slowly away: has hung left/found little: unpredictable. *M. J. Polglase*

DOYEN (IRE) 3 b.c. Sadler's Wells (USA) 132 – Moon Cactus 118 (Kris 135) **122 p**
[2003 12g* 12d* 12g* 12m² 12s⁴ Oct 5]
With Sulamani remaining in training, Godolphin is assured of at least one
top-class mile-and-a-half performer in its team in 2004, and if Doyen continues to
progress at the same rate as he did when trained by Andre Fabre it won't be long
before it is two. Carrying the colours of Sheikh Mohammed, Doyen finished fourth
in the Prix de l'Arc de Triomphe at Longchamp in October, just twelve months after
failing to make the frame on his only start at two, in a newcomers race at Maisons-
Laffitte.
Doyen made five appearances in the latest season, all over a mile and a half,
stepped up in class each time. He was successful on the first three occasions, in a
minor event at Saint-Cloud, a listed race at Lyon-Parilly and the Prix du Lys at
Longchamp. The last-named, which Doyen's connections had won the previous
year with Morozov, attracted just four runners but all had won their previous starts.
The favourite Policy Maker had made it two from two when winning a minor event
at Saint-Cloud, Doyen's stable-companion Mosogno had won a minor event at
Maisons-Laffitte on the second of his two starts, while Jazz Sweep had won a listed
race at La Teste. Doyen was ridden for the first time by Dettori, who also partnered
him subsequently, and made his rivals look ordinary, held up in last place before
sweeping through on the outside in the straight to lead over a furlong out and draw
clear to beat Policy Maker by four lengths. After a summer break in readiness for
an autumn campaign, Doyen returned to take on Dalakhani and Kris Kin in the Prix
Niel, also at Longchamp. In the meantime his performance in the Prix du Lys had
been made to look even better, Policy Maker winning a listed race and being
awarded the Grand Prix de Deauville. Doyen looked in very good shape while
giving the impression the race would put him spot on for the Arc, and he showed
that he, too, was still on the upgrade by splitting the two Derby winners. Again
dropped out last before making good headway in the straight, Doyen proved the
only danger to the length-and-a-half winner Dalakhani in the closing stages, not
knocked about when unable to find extra towards the finish. Doyen did go on to
show a bit more improvement in the Arc, even though he finished just over seven
lengths behind Dalakhani. Along with Policy Maker, he was the least experienced
runner in the field, and he betrayed signs of that by edging right under pressure in
the straight, having been slightly hampered by one of the pacemakers approaching
the home turn. The tall, rangy Doyen still looked rather a shell of a horse beforehand, and there seems little doubt that he is going to be capable of even better as he
matures further.
Doyen has already lived up to his distinguished pedigree. By Sadler's
Wells, he is the seventh foal of the Prix de Diane second Moon Cactus and a brother
to three winners, notably the 1995 Oaks winner Moonshell and the very smart
Hatha Anna, the latter a good fourth in the 2002 Gold Cup. Moon Cactus, a hard
puller who won twice over seven furlongs at two and the mile-and-a-quarter Lupe
Stakes on her reappearance at three, has also produced Ocean of Storms (by Arazi),
a smart winner at up to fifteen furlongs in France in 1998 and successful several
times since in the United Arab Emirates, and Avionic (by In The Wings), a seven-

Sheikh Mohammed's "Doyen"

		Northern Dancer (b 1961)	Nearctic Natalma
	Sadler's Wells (USA) (b 1981)	Fairy Bridge (b 1975)	Bold Reason Special
Doyen (IRE) (b.c. 2000)		Kris (ch 1976)	Sharpen Up Doubly Sure
	Moon Cactus (b 1987)	Lady Moon (b 1980)	Mill Reef Moonlight Night

furlong winner in the UAE in the latest season. There is also plenty of stamina further back in Doyen's pedigree. His grandam Lady Moon won three times at around a mile and a half and is out of the Musidora winner and Oaks third Moonlight Night. Moonlight Night, a half-sister to the Cumberland Lodge and St Simon Stakes winner Main Reef, comes from a fine family, being a daughter of Lovely Light, a half-sister, among others, to Picture Light (the dam of Welsh Pageant and Photo Flash), Chandelier (the dam of Crocket) and Crystal Palace (the dam of Royal Palace, Prince Consort and Selhurst, and the grandam of Light Cavalry and Fairy Footsteps). Lady Moon was carrying Moon Cactus when Sheikh Mohammed paid 600,000 guineas for her at the dispersal of Jim Joel's Childwick Bury bloodstock at the December Sales in 1986. Doyen showed himself effective on good to firm ground and he seemed to cope well enough with the very soft ground on which the Arc was run. Unusually for a horse trained by Andre Fabre, Doyen was equipped with a sheepskin noseband, one of the very few others we can recall being Lycius, runner-up in the 1991 Two Thousand Guineas. *A. Fabre, France*

306

DRAGON FLYER (IRE)   4 b.f. Tagula (IRE) 116 – Noble Rocket (Reprimand 122)   **105**
[2003 103: p5g 5.2m⁵ 5.1m² 5m³ 5g² 5m⁵ 5.1m² 5g² 5d 5.2m³ 5s 6m Oct 16] small,
sturdy filly: useful performer: best efforts in 2003 when placed in listed/pattern company,
beaten neck when second to The Tatling in King George Stakes at Goodwood and 1½
lengths when third to Ratio in World Trophy at Newbury eighth/tenth starts: speedy, and
best at 5f: yet to race on heavy going, acts on any other: often races prominently: game.
M. Quinn

DRAMA KING   11 b.g. Tragic Role (USA) – Consistent Queen 55 (Queen's Hussar   –
124) [2003 –: 21.6m Apr 14] sturdy gelding: no form after early-2001: often blinkered.
B. J. Llewellyn

DRAMATIC QUEST   6 b.g. Zafonic (USA) 130 – Ultra Finesse (USA) 107 (Rahy   **77**
(USA) 115) [2003 –: f16s p12g² p12g² 12g⁴ May 24] rangy gelding: fair performer: stays
1½m: acts on good to firm going and polytrack: usually wears cheekpieces nowadays.
Ian Williams

DRAMRAIRE MIST   4 gr.f. Darshaan 133 – Marie Dora (FR) 86 (Kendor (FR) 122)   –
[2003 73, a49: f12g Feb 10] fair maiden on turf, poor on all-weather: well held only
outing in 2003. *B. J. Meehan*

DR CERULLO   2 b.c. (Feb 4) Dr Fong (USA) 128 – Precocious Miss (USA) 88 (Diesis   **75**
133) [2003 5.1m² 5.7m⁶ p8g³ 7f7g p8g² 7f9.4g* Dec 22] 26,000Y: first foal: dam, lightly-raced
2-y-o 6f winner, out of sister to Green Desert: fair performer: trained by A. Lidderdale
until after third start: won maiden at Wolverhampton by 6 lengths from Unintentional:
will stay at least 1¼m: acts on all-weather and good to firm ground: slowly away penultimate start. *C. Tinkler*

DREAM FALCON   3 br.g. Polar Falcon (USA) 126 – Pip's Dream 52 (Glint of Gold   –
128) [2003 –: 13.1f 8f Sep 29] little form. *R. J. Hodges*

DREAMIE BATTLE   5 br.m. Makbul 104 – Highland Rossie 67 (Pablond 93) [2003   –
–: f12s Jan 14] leggy, quite good-topped mare: little form since 2001: wore cheekpieces
(slowly away) on reappearance. *R. Hollinshead*

DREAMING DIVA   4 ch.f. Whittingham (IRE) 104 – Any Dream (IRE) 81 (Shernazar   –
131) [2003 –: p8g p10g 10.3g p10g Mar 26] strong, lengthy filly: fair winner at 2 yrs:
little form since. *J. C. Fox*

DREAMING OF YOU (IRE)   2 b.f. (Apr 23) Spectrum (IRE) 126 – Gay Hellene   **– p**
111 (Ela-Mana-Mou 132) [2003 7m Oct 13] tall filly: closely related to 2 winners by
Rainbow Quest, including fairly useful 1¼m/11f winner Greek Gold and half-sister to
several winners, including 8-y-o Landing Light: dam, 1¼m/1½m winner, from family
of Pilsudski: 9/1, very green when behind in maiden at Leicester: should do better.
Sir Michael Stoute

DREAMING WATERS   2 ch.f. (Feb 16) Groom Dancer (USA) 128 – Faraway   **62**
Waters 102 (Pharly (FR) 130) [2003 7g⁶ 6g 6g Oct 24] 3,000Y: third foal: own 2-y-o 6f
winner who probably stayed 1½m, out of sister to smart performer up to 14.6f Shining
Water, herself dam of Tenby: modest form in maidens: will be suited by 1¼m/1½m.
R. F. Johnson Houghton

DREAM KING (IRE)   3 b.g. Petardia 113 – Barinia (Corvaro (USA) 124) [2003 –:   –
12m⁶ 10m 12.6m f12g 8m 7d⁵ 8m 8f 8.5g⁵ 8.2m 7m⁶ Oct 13] close-coupled gelding: little
form: tried blinkered: has looked temperamental. *M. J. Polglase*

DREAM MAGIC   5 b.g. Magic Ring (IRE) 115 – Pip's Dream 52 (Glint of Gold 128)   **92**
[2003 89: p10g³ p10g² p12g³ p10g f11g⁶ 10g* 10.4m 10m⁵ 9m³ 10g 10f 9g⁴ 8.2d⁴ Nov 6]
big, good-topped gelding: fairly useful handicapper: won at Nottingham in March:
good effort in minor event there final start: stays easy 1½m: acts on firm ground, soft and
polytrack: tough: sold 20,000 gns. *M. J. Ryan*

DREAM OF DUBAI (IRE)   2 b.f. (Feb 6) Vettori (IRE) 119 – Immortelle (Arazi   **60**
(USA) 135) [2003 p6g p7g⁵ Sep 9] 21,000Y: first foal: dam unraced half-sister to several
at least smart winners, including Poule d'Essai des Pouliches winner Danseuse du Soir:
modest form in maidens at Lingfield: slowly away on debut: will stay at least 1m.
P. Mitchell

DREAM SCENE (IRE)   2 b.f. (Jan 31) Sadler's Wells (USA) 132 – Highest Accolade   **69 p**
71 (Shirley Heights 130) [2003 7m⁴ Jul 18] close-coupled filly: second foal: sister to
3-y-o Urowells: dam, 1¼m winner from 3 starts, out of half-sister to Awaasif (also dam of
Snow Bride and grandam of Lammtarra), the family of Bosra Sham and Hector Protector:

favourite but backward, 3½ lengths fourth of 18 to Qasirah in maiden at Newbury, not knocked about: should be suited by at least 1¼m: seems sure to do better. *J. H. M. Gosden*

DREAMS FORGOTTEN (IRE) 3 b.f. Victory Note (USA) 120 – Sevens Are Wild **63** 40 (Petorius 117) [2003 58: 7m³ 8.3d² 8g 7m Jun 10] modest maiden handicapper: free-going sort, likely to prove best up to easy 1m: acts on good to firm ground, good to soft and fibresand. *S. Kirk*

DREAMS UNITED 2 br.f. (Mar 15) Dancing Spree (USA) – Kaliala (FR) (Pharly **39** (FR) 130) [2003 6g 7m⁵ 8.1g Aug 25] half-sister to 1m seller winner Chauvelin (by Durgam) and 2 winners abroad: dam French 1m winner: best effort (poor form) when fifth in claimer at Thirsk: should stay 1m. *A. G. Newcombe*

DREAM VALLEY (IRE) 2 b.f. (Feb 22) Sadler's Wells (USA) 132 – Vallee Des **– p** Reves (USA) (Kingmambo (USA) 125) [2003 7g 6d Nov 8] leggy, lengthy filly: second foal: dam unraced half-sister to very smart French performers Vetheuil (miler) and Verveine (up to 1½m): behind in maidens at Newmarket and Doncaster: should do better at 1¼m+. *B. W. Hills*

DREAM WITH ME (FR) 6 b.g. Johann Quatz (FR) 120 – Midnight Ride (FR) (Fast **–** Topaze (USA) 128) [2003 12m Oct 3] lengthy, quite attractive gelding: useful performer at 4 yrs: well held in handicap only Flat outing since: should be as effective at 1¼m as 1½m: acts on soft ground. *M. C. Pipe*

DRESS PEARL 2 b.f. (Mar 24) Atraf 116 – Dress Design (IRE) 84 (Brief Truce **77 d** (USA) 126) [2003 5m 5d² 5m⁶ 6v² 6m 6m⁶ f5g 7m⁶ 7g 6d f6g f7g Dec 16] workmanlike filly: second foal: half-sister to Italian 5f/6f winner Green Target (by Catrail): dam, Irish 2-y-o 5f winner, granddaughter of 1000 Guineas winner Mrs McArdy: fair maiden: second twice at Haydock, only form: stays 6f: acts on heavy going. *A. Berry*

DR FOX (IRE) 2 b.g. (Mar 21) Foxhound (USA) 103 – Eleonora d'Arborea 78 (Prince **60** Sabo 123) [2003 5m⁵ 5g 6m 7m 6f⁵ 8m 6m⁵ Oct 6] 2,500F, 5,000Y: short-backed gelding: third foal: half-brother to 4-y-o Leonora Truce: dam 6f winner, ran only at 2 yrs: modest maiden: below form in nurseries last 2 starts, blinkered final one: should stay 7f: acts on firm going. *N. P. Littmoden*

DRIZZLE 2 ch.c. (Mar 25) Hector Protector (USA) 124 – Rainy Sky (Rainbow Quest **67** (USA) 134) [2003 8m³ f8.5g f8g³ Dec 8] fourth living foal: dam, French 1½m winner, sister to smart French winner up to 1½m Bonash and half-sister to dam of 3-y-o Neb-raska Tornado and 4-y-o Burning Sun: fair form in maidens: third at Redcar (then left Mrs A. Perrett 22,000 gns) and Southwell: will stay 1¼m: slowly away second outing. *J. W. Unett*

DR JULIAN (IRE) 3 b.g. Sesaro (USA) 81 – Toda 53 (Absalom 128) [2003 58: f7g **53 §** p8g³ f8.5g³ f8g⁶ 11.9m³ 10.5m⁵ 7m f7g f8.5g⁴ 9.9m³ 12f⁴ 13.8m² 15.8d 16.1m 14.1m 12m⁵ 12m 12d f12s Dec 13] sturdy, close-coupled gelding: modest maiden handicapper: left J. Osborne after fourth start: stays 13.8f: acts on all-weather and firm ground: tried in blinkers/visor/cheekpieces: tends to edge left: ungenuine. *Miss A. Stokell*

DR RAJ 4 ch.g. In The Wings 128 – Tawaaded (IRE) 91 (Nashwan (USA) 135) [2003 **–** 10.2g Jun 5] 1,500Y: second foal: half-brother to 5-y-o Sahaat: dam, 7f winner who stayed 1m, from family of Singspiel (by In The Wings): poor form in bumpers: 100/1, well held in maiden at Chepstow, racing freely after slow start. *B. A. McMahon*

DR SHARP (IRE) 3 ch.g. Dr Devious (IRE) 127 – Stoned Imaculate (IRE) 73 (Durgam **75** (USA)) [2003 64: 12g 12.3d* 11.1g* 12.1g⁴ Jul 1] good-topped gelding: fair performer: won handicap at Ripon in May and minor event at Hamilton in June: stays 1½m: acts on soft ground: front runner. *T. P. Tate*

DR SYNN 2 br.c. (Apr 12) Danzero (AUS) – Our Shirley 84 (Shirley Heights 130) [2003 **69 p** 6d⁶ Nov 8] good-topped colt: half-brother to several winners, including 7-y-o Gentleman Venture and fairly useful 5f (at 2 yrs) to 16.4f winner Pearl Venture (by Salse): dam 1¼m winner: 25/1 and better for race, 3 lengths sixth of 14 to Miss Langkawi in maiden at Doncaster, staying on: should stay at least 1m: open to improvement. *J. Akehurst*

DR THONG 2 ch.c. (May 3) Dr Fong (USA) 128 – Always On My Mind 91 (Distant **74 P** Relative 128) [2003 7m⁵ Sep 23] 40,000Y: tall, good-topped colt: has scope: second foal: dam, 6f winner, half-sister to 5-y-o Red Carpet: 25/1, 5½ lengths fifth of 17 to Primus Inter Pares in maiden at Newmarket, travelling strongly long way and merely pushed out late on having been short of room: will probably stay 1m: open to considerable improve-ment, and should win races as a 3-y-o. *P. F. I. Cole*

DRUID   2 b.g. (Apr 18) Magic Ring (IRE) 115 – Country Spirit (Sayf El Arab (USA)   **51**
127) [2003 f6g 6g⁶ f8.5g⁵ Nov 14] 13,500Y: sixth foal: brother to 5f (at 2 yrs) and 1m
winner Millennium Magic and half-brother to 3-y-o Semenovskii: dam unraced: first
form (modest) when fifth in claimer at Wolverhampton. *P. C. Haslam*

DRURY LANE (IRE)   3 b. or br.c. Royal Applause 124 – Ghost Tree (IRE) 88 (Caer-   **85**
leon (USA) 132) [2003 84: 8m 7d 6m 6.1m* 6f⁵ p6g 6m³ 6d 7g 7.1m Sep 20] rather
unfurnished colt: fairly useful handicapper: won at Nottingham in June: well below form
last 3 starts: best at 6f/7f: acts on firm going: blinkered 6 outings prior to tried in
cheekpieces final one: sold 6,000 gns, joined D. Chapman. *B. W. Hills*

DRY WIT (IRE)   2 b.f. (Mar 18) Desert Prince (IRE) 130 – Nawasib (IRE) 94 (Warning   **68**
136) [2003 7.1f² 7d⁴ 7m² 8m⁶ 7m Oct 7] €35,000Y: smallish filly: third foal: dam, 1¼m
winner in Ireland, half-sister to Azzilfi (stayed 1¾m) and Khamaseen (should have stayed
further than 2m), both smart: fair maiden: second at Warwick and Thirsk: ran poorly final
start: probably stays 1m: acts on firm going. *R. M. Beckett*

DUBAIAN DUEL   2 b.f. (Mar 15) Daggers Drawn (USA) 114 – River's Rising (FR)   **86 +**
88 (Mendez (FR) 128) [2003 6m 7.5m* 7g² 7m³ 6.5m² Sep 26] 2,000Y: quite good-
topped filly: half-sister to several winners, including fairly useful 1996 2-y-o 7f winner
Mudflap (by Slip Anchor), 4-y-o Grey Pearl and 3-y-o Haze Babybear: dam 1m winner:
fairly useful performer: won maiden at Beverley in June: placed in nursery and Prestige
Stakes (2½ lengths third of 6 to Gracefully, possibly somewhat flattered) at Goodwood
and sales race at Ascot (second of 30 to Nyramba): barely stays 7.5f: usually races in clear
lead: sold 105,000 gns, joined L. Lewis in USA. *A. M. Balding*

DUBAIAN GIFT   4 b.g. Bahamian Bounty 116 – Hot Lavender (CAN) 67 (Shadeed   **115**
(USA) 135) [2003 86: 5f 5m 5g* 5g* 5m 5.1m 5m² 5.1m² 5d* 5.2m⁶ Sep 20] smallish
gelding: smart performer: much improved again in 2003, winning handicaps at Lingfield
and Windsor in May, and listed race at Doncaster (by 2½ lengths from Fire Up The Band)
in September: below form in World Trophy won by Ratio at Newbury final start: speedy,
and best at bare 5f: yet to race on soft/heavy going, acts on any other turf and all-weather:
has been early to post: often forces pace. *A. M. Balding*

DUBAIAN MIST   2 b.f. (Apr 27) Docksider (USA) 124 – Robellino Miss (USA)   **55**
(Robellino (USA) 127) [2003 5d p8g⁵ Dec 20] 12,000Y: closely related to useful 1999
2-y-o 7f winner Decision Maid and 1m winner Be Decisive (both by Diesis), and
half-sister to several winners, including 3-y-o Miss Ivanhoe (by Selkirk): dam, won up to
9f in USA, out of close relation to high-class sprinter Silver Fling: modest form when
eighth of 19 in maiden at Windsor, slowly away: not knocked about in minor event at
Lingfield 8 months later: bred to stay 1m. *A. M. Balding*

DUBAI DESTINATION (USA)   4 b.c. Kingmambo (USA) 125 – Mysterial   **127**
(USA) (Alleged (USA) 138) [2003 119: 8.2m* 8f* 8d⁵ 8f Sep 27]
          The memory of Dubai Destination's victory over Rock of Gibraltar as a
two-year-old in the Champagne Stakes at Doncaster remains vivid. Dropped out
last and seemingly set with plenty to do, he produced an impressive burst of speed
to win in most decisive style, trouncing a horse who afterwards won the Grand
Criterium and the Dewhurst. While that horse, Rock of Gibraltar, went on the
following season to extend his winning sequence to seven Group 1 races, Dubai
Destination made it to the racecourse only once, when second in the Predominate
Stakes at Goodwood. A ligament problem had kept him off the course after the
Champagne and his three-year-old campaign was delayed because of a bruised foot
in mid-March. Another injury—this time to his near-fore—came to light after the
Predominate and eventually led to Dubai Destination's being returned early to
Dubai. Godolphin's faith in the seemingly rather fragile Dubai Destination and
their perseverance paid off when he returned to the track as a four-year-old to show
his true colours again in the Queen Anne Stakes. Unfortunately, it turned out to be
only a brief sighting. In two more outings after the Queen Anne, in the Prix Jacques
le Marios at Deauville and the Queen Elizabeth II Stakes at Ascot, Dubai Destination ran nowhere near his Royal Ascot form, looking a shadow of his real self when
last of eight in the latter.
          A considerable home reputation had led to the name of Dubai Destination,
the second-highest-priced yearling colt of his year at 1,500,000 dollars, being alter-
ed from Copernican before the horse set foot on a racecourse. Dubai Millennium's
outstanding potential had been marked in a similar way when his name was

changed as a youngster from Yaazer. Dubai Destination had been left in the Judd-monte International at York, only two days after the Jacques le Marois, at the final declaration stage, and the intention, so it was said, was that he would have taken up the engagement had he won at Deauville. Such high expectations arose from Dubai Destination's splendid performance in the Queen Anne, which for the first time was a Group 1 contest. Warmed up in a four-runner conditions event at Nottingham in early-June, when he beat Binary File impressively by six lengths, Dubai Destination was having only the sixth start of his career at Royal Ascot. All eyes were on the odds-on Hawk Wing, who had won the Lockinge Stakes by eleven lengths from Where Or When. The latter, along with another Lockinge runner Tillerman, also took the field in the Queen Anne. Dubai Destination started second favourite and, with Hawk Wing running no sort of a race, unleashed a good turn of foot after being patiently ridden, winning by four lengths and three quarters of a length from Tillerman (disqualified some months later on a technicality) and Right Approach, with Where Or When fourth and Hawk Wing only seventh of the ten runners. Dubai Destination gave Godolphin and trainer Saeed bin Suroor their fifth Queen Anne winner in eight years, following Charnwood Forest, Allied Forces, Intikhab and Cape Cross at the end of the 'nineties (the three renewals in the interim had all fallen to the Stoute stable). With the current classic crop of miling colts looking fairly ordinary, Dubai Destination seemed set for further successes, though connections bypassed the next obvious target, the Sussex Stakes at Goodwood (where they were represented by Moon Ballad). When Dubai Destination was next seen out in Britain—in the Queen Elizabeth II Stakes—his appearance was accompanied by stories of impressive home work in the build-up to Ascot. Starting third favourite behind Falbrav and Russian Rhythm, Dubai Destination turned in a most disappointing effort, in trouble rounding the home turn and soon a spent force.

		Mr Prospector (b 1970)	Raise A Native Gold Digger
Dubai Destination (USA) (b.c. 1999)	Kingmambo (USA) (b 1990)		
		Miesque (b 1984)	Nureyev Pasadoble
	Mysterial (USA) (b or br 1994)	Alleged (b 1974)	Hoist The Flag Princess Pout
		Mysteries (b 1986)	Seattle Slew Phydilla

The rangy, quite attractive Dubai Destination is by the high-class miler Kingmambo, the only living American-based stallion to feature in the top twenty sires in Britain and Ireland in the latest season. Responsible for a Group 1 winner in Golden Jubilee Stakes victor Malhub at Royal Ascot in 2002, Kingmambo had two Group 1 winners at the latest Royal meeting, Dubai Destination being followed by One Thousand Guineas winner Russian Rhythm in the Coronation Stakes. Dubai Destination is the first foal of twice-raced Mysterial, who was also represented on the racecourse in the latest season in Britain by Dubai Destination's two-year-old full brother, Destination Dubai (another seven-figure yearling purchase, who showed useful form when runner-up in a maiden at Doncaster before being beaten at odds on at Pontefract). The grandam Mysteries didn't win a race but came third in the Musidora Stakes. She has done very well at stud, producing the Prix de l'Abbaye and July Cup winner Agnes World and his Japanese-trained compatriot the very smart sprinter-miler Hishi Akebono, as well as the stakes-winning North

Godolphin's "Dubai Destination"

American filly My Sea Castles. Dubai Destination's great grandam Phydilla was a high-class miler and a half-sister to Royal Suzuka, another leading performer in Japan, and to the Irish Derby runner-up Observation Post. Dubai Destination showed his best form at a mile and acted on good to soft going (which he encountered in the Champagne Stakes) and firm. Tried in a crossed noseband and tongue strap, he also tended to flash his tail. A fine turn of foot was the hallmark of his best performances. He will be standing at Dalham Hall Stud, Newmarket, in 2004 at a fee of £25,000 with a special live foal concession. *Saeed bin Suroor*

DUBAI DREAMS 3 b.g. Marju (IRE) 127 – Arndilly 75 (Robellino (USA) 127) **75**
[2003 71§: f11s* p10g⁴ 10.3g 8.2g⁴ 7.5f² 9.9m² 8g 8.5m⁵ 10m⁵ 12m⁴ 16.2m⁶ 10f 10.4f 8.2d f8g f12g* f14g⁴ f12s Dec 27] close-coupled gelding: unimpressive mover: fair handicapper: won at Southwell in February and (apprentice event) December: effective at 7.5f to 1½m: acts on firm going, good to soft and all-weather: often blinkered/visored: has raced freely: often races up with pace/finishes weakly. *M. J. Polglase*

DUBAI PRINCE (IRE) 4 b.g. Anita's Prince 126 – Balqis (USA) 93 (Advocator) **62 §**
[2003 –§: 12m 12m 8.3g 10.1m⁴ Aug 15] fair maiden at 2 yrs: no show over hurdles in Ireland prior to just modest form in 2003: probably stayed 1½m: veered left and unseated leaving stall/refused to race last 2 starts at 3 yrs: was one to avoid: dead. *M. J. Wallace*

DUBAI SEVEN STARS 5 ch.m. Suave Dancer (USA) 136 – Her Honour 94 (Teenoso **83 §**
(USA) 135) [2003 89: 16m 20m 16.1m 18f* 16.4m⁵ 16m² 16m⁶ 16.2f 16f 18m Oct 18] leggy, workmanlike mare: fairly useful performer: won maiden at Warwick in July: stays 2¼m: acts on firm and soft going: visored last 7 outings: held up: ungenuine. *M. C. Pipe*

DUBAI SUCCESS 3 b.c. Sadler's Wells (USA) 132 – Crystal Spray 75 (Beldale Flutter **114**
(USA) 130) [2003 10d* 12g 11.9m⁵ 12g* 12g³ Oct 25] 750,000Y: lengthy, quite attrac-

311

tive colt: has a quick action: brother to smart 7f (at 2 yrs) and 1¼m winner who stayed
1½m Tchaikovsky, closely related to smart 2000 2-y-o 7f and 1m (Fillies' Mile) winner
Crystal Music (by Nureyev), and half-brother to 3 winners, including 7f (at 2 yrs) and
1½m winner State Crystal (by High Estate) and 1995 2-y-o 6f and 1m (May Hill Stakes)
winner Solar Crystal (by Alzao), both smart: dam Irish 1¾m winner from good family:
smart performer: in training with Saeed bin Suroor prior to successful debut in maiden at
Ripon in May: further improvement when winning listed race at Doncaster in September
by 2½ lengths from Wareed: creditable 4 lengths third to Imperial Dancer in St Simon
Stakes at Newbury final outing: stays 1½m: yet to race on extremes of going. *B. W. Hills*

DUBAI TOWER (USA)   3 b.c. Imperial Ballet (IRE) 110 – Multimara (USA) (Arctic   **75**
Tern (USA) 126) [2003 f7g⁴ p6g f7s³ f8.5s* f9.4g⁴ 9.9m⁴ 9.2d² 10m* May 12] $30,000Y:
close-coupled colt: brother to smart 5f/6f (latter including at 2 yrs) winner Imperial
Beauty and to 5-y-o King's Ballet, and half-brother to 2 winners abroad: dam, placed
in USA, half-sister to May Hill Stakes winner Midnight Air: fair handicapper: won at
Wolverhampton in February and Redcar in May: stays 1¼m: acts on fibresand, good to
firm and good to soft going: usually races prominently: sold 5,000 gns. *M. Johnston*

DUB DASH (USA)   3 b.g. Siphon (BRZ) 130 – Thesky'sthelimit (USA) (Northern   **77**
Prospect (USA)) [2003 p12g f12s* Dec 13] second foal: dam winning sprinter in USA:
easily better effort in maidens (fair form) when winning at Southwell in December by 5
lengths from Exit To Heaven: slowly away on debut. *S. C. Williams*

DUBLIN (IRE)   3 b.c. Carson City (USA) – Lustre (USA) 90 (Halo (USA)) [2003   **105**
107: a8f a8f* Mar 20] quite attractive colt: useful performer: successful 3 times at 2 yrs
(when trained by D. Loder), including Vintage Stakes at Goodwood: below form in UAE
2000 Guineas on reappearance, then won minor event at Nad Al Sheba in March by ¼
length from Al Saqaar: should be suited by 1m+: raced only on good going or firmer on
turf, and acts on dirt: effective with or without visor: has worn tongue tie/crossed noseband: left Godolphin. *Saeed bin Suroor*

DUBOIS   2 b.c. (Feb 24) Sadler's Wells (USA) 132 – Dazzle 116 (Gone West (USA))   **81**
[2003 7m² 8.3m⁵ Sep 29] third foal: half-brother to 2001 2-y-o 6f winner Wish (by Danehill) and fairly useful 2002 2-y-o 7f winner Rainbow Queen (by Rainbow Quest): dam,
best at 2 yrs when 5f/6f winner, later 7f winner and third in 1000 Guineas: fairly useful
form in maidens at Yarmouth (second to Eden Rock, marginally better effort) and
Windsor: not sure to stay beyond 1m: joined Saeed bin Suroor. *D. R. Loder*

DUBONAI (IRE)   3 ch.c. Peintre Celebre (USA) 137 – Web of Intrigue 66 (Machia-   **62**
vellian (USA) 123) [2003 69: 8g⁴ 10m 9.9m 11.9m³ 12.4m² 10m³ 9.9d Sep 23] leggy
colt: modest maiden: stays 1½m: acts on good to firm going and polytrack: reportedly
had breathing problems second/third starts, tried tongue tied after. *Andrew Turnell*

DUBROVSKY   3 ch.g. Hector Protector (USA) 124 – Reuval 102 (Sharpen Up 127)   **90**
[2003 90p: 8m 8m³ 8m Aug 17] lengthy gelding: fairly useful performer, lightly raced:
best effort in handicaps in 2003 when third at Newmarket: stays 1m: raced only on good
to firm ground: wandered/found little final outing: subsequently gelded. *J. R. Fanshawe*

DUCK EGG BLUE (IRE)   4 b.g. Flying Spur (AUS) – Trojan Treasure (Trojan Fen   **–**
118) [2003 p8g p7g p7g Feb 25] €2,000 3-y-o: half-brother to winner in Italy by Scenic:
dam ran once: well held in maidens at Lingfield. *Edward Butler, Ireland*

DUCK ROW (USA)   8 ch.g. Diesis 133 – Sunny Moment (USA) (Roberto (USA)   **113**
131) [2003 116: 8f⁴ 8g²* 7m⁴ 8.9m⁴ 8d⁴ 8g Nov 1] sturdy, close-coupled gelding: smart
performer: reportedly slightly lame early in year and not seen out until July: won minor
event at Newmarket (by short head from Shamrock City) in August: best effort after when
good fourth to With Reason in Hungerford Stakes at Newbury next start: probably best at
1m/9f: acts on firm and good to soft going, below form on soft: waited with: genuine.
J. A. R. Toller

DUC'S DREAM   5 b.g. Bay Tern (USA) 86 – Kala's Image 55 (Kala Shikari 125) [2003   **71**
–, a73: f11s³ f11g⁶ f11g 10g⁵ 10.1g³ f12g² p10g⁶ 12d² 12g² 14.1m³ 11.5g* 11.9d⁶ 12m³
16m f11g p12g Dec 17] leggy gelding: fair handicapper: won at Yarmouth in September:
effective at 1¼m to 1¾m: acts on heavy going, good to firm and fibresand, probably on
polytrack: tried blinkered/visored: consistent. *D. Morris*

DUDIE   4 b.f. Pebble Powder – Valise 52 (Salse (USA) 128) [2003 6m Sep 2] second   **–**
foal: dam, sprint maiden, half-sister to useful performer up to 1½m Billy Bushwacker:
80/1, slowly away and carried head high when tailed off in claimer at Yarmouth. *Mrs
C. A. Dunnett*

DUE DILIGENCE (IRE) 4 ch.g. Entrepreneur 123 – Kerry Project (IRE) 79 (Project **65 d**
Manager 111) [2003 65: 7g 8m⁴ 8s 8g⁴ 8m 7m 8m 10m f8s Oct 21] angular gelding: third
foal: half-brother to Irish 9f winner Kerry Isle (by Erins Isle): dam Irish 2-y-o 6f winner:
fair handicapper: won at Listowel and Leopardstown in 2002: left J. Bolger 10,000 gns
after fourth outing then below form all starts in Britain: stays 1m: acts on firm and good
to soft going (well beaten on soft): tried blinkered (pulled hard). *C. W. Fairhurst*

DUELLING BANJOS 4 ch.g. Most Welcome 131 – Khadino (Relkino 131) [2003 **77**
80, a59: p8g* 8g 8.2d⁴ p8g⁶ 8m 8.3g 9g 8g 8.2d* Nov 6] fair handicapper: won at **a72**
Lingfield in March and Nottingham in November: should stay 1¼m: best efforts on
ground softer than good and all-weather: raced freely/carried head awkwardly once at 3
yrs. *J. Akehurst*

DUE RESPECT (IRE) 3 b.g. Danehill (USA) 126 – Stylish (Anshan 119) [2003 91: **85**
8.1m 7.1m⁵ 10m⁶ 7.6m Aug 30] lengthy, quite attractive gelding: type to carry condition:
has scope: fairly useful performer: headstrong, and not sure to stay beyond 7f: raced only
on good ground or firmer: often early to post: races prominently: has looked ungenuine,
including final start: subsequently gelded. *R. Hannon*

DUESCALS (USA) 3 b.f. Danzig (USA) – Vue (USA) (Mr Prospector (USA)) [2003 **68**
–p: 8m² 10.2f² p10g Oct 15] big, lengthy filly: fair maiden, lightly raced: likely to prove
best short of 1¼m: sent to USA. *J. H. M. Gosden*

DUE TO ME 3 gr.f. Compton Place 125 – Always Lucky 71 (Absalom 128) [2003 58: **50**
5.3f⁴ 6m 6f Oct 12] modest maiden: well held after reappearance: stays 6f: acts on good
to firm and good to soft going: tried in blinkers: has carried head high. *G. L. Moore*

DUGDALE 3 b.g. Vettori (IRE) 119 – Coigach 110 (Niniski (USA) 125) [2003 71: **66**
13.8m⁴ 12s 11.1m⁴ 15.8d p12g Oct 3] fair maiden: stays 11f: acts on fibresand and good
to firm going, well held both starts on softer than good: blinkered final outing: sold 9,000
gns. *Sir Mark Prescott*

DUGGAN'S DILEMMA (IRE) 2 b.g. (Feb 5) Lake Coniston (IRE) 131 – Miss Iron- **44**
wood (Junius (USA) 124) [2003 5m 5m⁵ 6f f6g Aug 7] IR 1,000F, 3,900Y: leggy gelding:
seventh foal: half-brother to 3 winners, including 2000 2-y-o 6f winner Milliken Park (by
Fumo di Londra): dam maiden half-sister to US Grade 1 winners Anka Germania (1½m)
and Mourjane (1¼m): poor maiden: should stay 6f. *Ian Emmerson*

DUKE OF EARL (IRE) 4 ch.g. Ali-Royal (IRE) 127 – Faye 79 (Monsanto (FR) 121) **95**
[2003 91: 21d 14g 14d² Sep 27] useful-looking gelding: useful handicapper: good
head second to Alnaja (pair clear) at Haydock final start: effective at 1¼m (given a
test) to 1¾m (well beaten over 21f): acts on any going: tough: winning hurdler: sent to
USA. *S. Kirk*

DUKE OF MODENA 6 ch.g. Salse (USA) 128 – Palace Street (USA) 103 (Secreto **100**
(USA) 128) [2003 103: 8m 8.1g* 8g³ 8.1m² 8m 8m⁴ 8m 8g Nov 1] sturdy gelding: fairly
useful handicapper: won at Sandown (for second successive year) in April: good placed
efforts at Kempton and Sandown next 2 starts: well below form last 3 outings: effective
at 7f/1m: acts on heavy and good to firm going: has been bandaged: usually held up.
G. B. Balding

DUKE OF VENICE (USA) 2 b.c. (Mar 25) Theatrical 128 – Rihan (USA) 84 (Dayjur **109 p**
(USA) 137) [2003 6m³ 8.1m* 7m Oct 18] $75,000F, $300,000Y: tall, rather unfurnished
colt: has scope: second foal: dam, 2-y-o 6f winner, out of Breeders' Cup Juvenile Fillies
runner-up Sweet Roberta: very green on debut: landed odds in 11-runner maiden at
Sandown in September most impressively by 13 lengths from Fahlawi, making nearly all
and storming clear: 13/2, about 6 lengths tenth of 12 to Milk It Mick in Dewhurst Stakes
at Newmarket, not knocked about having helped force good pace: will stay at least 1¼m:
upset stall debut, edgy at Newmarket: joined Godolphin: likely to make his mark in good
company as 3-y-o. *M. Johnston*

DUKE'S VIEW (IRE) 2 b.g. (Apr 19) Sadler's Wells (USA) 132 – Igreja (ARG) 101 **69**
(Southern Halo (USA)) [2003 7m 7m 7d⁶ Nov 7] €170,000Y: good-topped gelding:
second foal: dam, 5f to 1m winner in South Africa (including Group 1 event), ran 3
times in Britain: fair form in maidens: sixth to Divine Gift at Doncaster: should stay 1m.
Mrs A. J. Perrett

DULCE DE LECHE 2 b.g. (Apr 15) Cayman Kai (IRE) 114 – Give Us A Treat (Cree **60**
Song 99) [2003 7m 5m Jun 16] 3,000F, 3,200Y, 11,000 2-y-o: sturdy gelding: fifth foal:
brother to 3-y-o Whippasnapper: dam, maiden who should have stayed 1m, half-sister
to US Grade 3 6.5f winner Imperial Star: better effort (well backed in seller on debut)

when tenth in maiden at Windsor, showing modest form: needs to settle to stay 7f.
S. C. Williams

DUMARAN (IRE)   5 b.g. Be My Chief (USA) 122 – Pine Needle 89 (Kris 135) [2003   **104**
106: 8g⁶ 10.1m 8.3d⁵ 8.5m 8f 10m⁴ 9m 10g³ Oct 25] rather leggy gelding: useful handicapper: some creditable efforts in 2003, including third to Pagan Sky at Newbury final
outing: effective at 7f (given a test), and stays 1¼m: best efforts on good going or softer,
possibly unsuited by firm fifth start (carried head high): visored (ran poorly) penultimate
outing: has pulled hard: sold 22,000 gns. *A. M. Balding*

DUMFRIES   2 ch.g. (Jan 29) Selkirk (USA) 129 – Pat Or Else 72 (Alzao (USA) 117)   **82 p**
[2003 6g 8m³ 10m* Oct 6] 180,000Y: big, good-bodied gelding: fourth foal: half-brother
to fairly useful 1½m winner Saluem (by Salse) and 1996 2-y-o 6f/7f seller winner Run
Lucy Run (by Risk Me): dam, staying maiden, half-sister to St Leger/Gold Cup winner
Classic Cliche and Yorkshire Oaks/Prix Vermeille winner My Emma: fairly useful form
in maidens: third at Goodwood prior to winning 12-runner event at Pontefract by length
from Fanling Lady, leading close home: will be suited by 1½m+: likely to make a useful
3-y-o. *J. H. M. Gosden*

DUMNONI   2 b.f. (Apr 14) Titus Livius (FR) 115 – Lamees (USA) (Lomond (USA)   **84**
128) [2003 p7g³ 7m⁶ p7g³ f7g* Nov 15] leggy filly: half-sister to several winners, including smart 7f (at 2 yrs) and 1¼m winner Francesco Guardi and useful 7f (at 2 yrs) and
1¼m winner Lomberto, both by Robellino: dam unraced: fairly useful performer: easily
best effort when winning 10-runner maiden at Wolverhampton in November by 8 lengths:
will stay 1m: hung left second start. *Julian Poulton*

DUNASKIN (IRE)   3 b.g. Bahhare (USA) 122 – Mirwara (IRE) (Darshaan 133) [2003   **95**
68: 10.3g⁶ 10m* 12f² 9.9m* 10.4m 8d* 9.9g 9.9m⁵ 9m 12m⁵ 10g³ Sep 27] smallish,
workmanlike gelding: useful handicapper: won at Ripon (twice) and Beverley in the
spring: good efforts last 2 starts, third to Alrabab at Ripon final one: probably stays 1½m:
acts on good to firm and good to soft ground: hangs right (proved virtually unrideable on
fifth start), and all 3 wins on right-handed tracks: front runner. *D. Eddy*

DUNCANBIL (IRE)   2 b.f. (Apr 1) Turtle Island (IRE) 123 – Saintly Guest (What A   **57**
Guest 119) [2003 6m⁶ 6g 7.1f⁵ 7m 6g 7s⁶ f7g⁶ Dec 8] €2,800Y: workmanlike filly:
half-sister to several winners, including useful 5f/6f winner (latter including at 2 yrs)
Benzoe (by Taufan) and fairly useful 5f to 7f winner Shalstayholy (by Shalford): dam
lightly-raced French maiden: modest maiden: should stay 1m: acts on good to firm and
soft ground, probably on fibresand. *R. F. Fisher*

DUNCAN DOCK (USA)   4 ch.g. Rakeen (USA) 99 – Smailer (USA) (Smarten
(USA)) [2003 97p: 10.3m 10m⁶ 10d 9g Oct 25] big, useful-looking gelding: won both   **57**
outings on fibresand at Southwell at 3 yrs, showing useful form: well held on turf in 2003
(twice slowly away): visored final start: sold 18,000 gns. *W. J. Haggas*

DUNDONALD   4 ch.g. Magic Ring (IRE) 115 – Cal Norma's Lady (IRE) 87 (Lyphard's   **49 §**
Special 122) [2003 67§, a71§: f6g f8.5g² f7g 7m 7m 10.1m 8.1m f8.5s 7m⁴ 6.9m   **a59 §**
Aug 18] big, leggy gelding: modest performer: left I. Semple after third start, P. Niven after
sixth: stays 8.5f: acts on good to firm ground and fibresand: wears visor/cheekpieces:
often finds little: not to be trusted. *J. D. Czerpak*

DUNDRY   2 b.g. (Jan 17) Bin Ajwaad (IRE) 119 – China's Pearl (Shirley Heights 130)   **68 p**
[2003 7g Jul 3] good-topped gelding: fourth foal: dam of little account: 40/1 and better
for race, twelfth of 15 in maiden at Newbury, slowly away and short of room: should stay
1m. *R. Hannon*

DUNEDIN RASCAL   6 b.g. Piccolo 121 – Thorner Lane 86 (Tina's Pet 121) [2003 66,   **–**
a77: p7g p6g* f6g⁴ p6g p6g 6s 5g 6m 5g 5m p7g f6g⁴ p6g p5g Dec 20] smallish gelding: **a80**
fairly useful handicapper on all-weather, poor on turf: won at Lingfield in January:
effective at 5f to easy 7f: acts on any turf going/all-weather: blinkered nowadays: held up.
E. A. Wheeler

DUNE SAFARI (IRE)   4 br.f. Key of Luck (USA) 126 – Zafaaf 105 (Kris 135) [2003   **–**
63?: 10m 7m f8.5f Jul 25] tall filly: modest form at 3 yrs, well beaten at 4 yrs. *M. A. Allen*

DUNHILL STAR (IRE)   3 b.c. Danehill (USA) 126 – Sueboog (IRE) 109 (Darshaan   **114**
133) [2003 80p: 9d* 9m² 10.4m³ 12m 10m⁵ Jul 19] well-made, quite attractive colt: smart
performer: won minor event at Kempton in March: good efforts behind Magistretti in
listed race at Newmarket (head second) and Dante Stakes at York (1¾ lengths third) next
2 starts: well beaten in Derby at Epsom, then fair fifth to Mubtaker in listed event at
Newbury: should stay 1½m: winner (at 2 yrs) on polytrack, unraced on extremes of going
on turf: has carried head awkwardly. *B. W. Hills*

314

DUNLEA DANCER   2 b.g. (Mar 23) Groom Dancer (USA) 128 – Be My Lass (IRE)   **52**
(Be My Guest (USA) 126) [2003 5d⁵ 6m 6f⁵ 6g 8m Oct 20] 11,000Y: close-coupled
gelding: half-brother to several winners, including useful 7f winner Qazween (by Primo
Dominie) and fairly useful 1½m winner My Lass (by Elmaamul): dam, French 11f winner, half-sister to smart middle-distance performers Bonne Ile and Ile de Nisky: modest
maiden: form only on third and fourth starts: should stay at least 1¼m. *M. Johnston*

DUNLOSKIN   2 b.f. (Apr 21) Selkirk (USA) 129 – Dalinda (USA) (Nureyev (USA)   **100**
131) [2003 6d² 6m³ 6.5m⁵ Sep 26] 56,000Y: strong filly: third foal: half-sister to fairly
useful 1m winners Savonarola (in UAE, by Machiavellian) and New Deal (in France, by
Rainbow Quest): dam, French 8.5f winner, out of US Grade 3 6.5f winner Daloma: useful
maiden: placed at Goodwood and York, easily best effort when 3 lengths third to Carry
On Katie in Lowther Stakes on latter course (swished tail in paddock): first home stand
side when fifth of 30 to Nyramba in sales race at Ascot: bred to stay beyond 6f, but races
freely: joined Godolphin: sure to win a race or 2. *M. A. Jarvis*

DUNMIDOE   3 b.f. Case Law 113 – Rion River (IRE) (Taufan (USA) 119) [2003 62?:   **–**
6g p10g 11.6m 8m 10.1m⁵ 8.1m 7g Sep 16] leggy filly: little form at 3 yrs: tried in cheekpieces. *C. Drew*

DUNN ALMU (IRE)   6 br.g. Hamas (IRE) 125§ – Art Age (Artaius (USA) 129) [2003   **48**
42: p7g p12g Feb 25] poor maiden: better effort in handicaps at Lingfield in 2003 on
reappearance: stays 1¼m: acts on polytrack: often blinkered. *Edward Butler, Ireland*

Mr Mohamed Obaida's "Dunhill Star"

DUNN DEAL (IRE) 3 b.g. Revoque (IRE) 122 – Buddy And Soda (IRE) 75 (Imperial **66 §**
Frontier (USA) 112) [2003 74: 5f⁶ 5m⁵ 5.7m⁴ 5s 5f⁶ 5m⁶ 5m Sep 13] smallish, sturdy
gelding: fair performer: best at 5f: acts on firm and soft going: tried tongue tied:
sometimes wanders: untrustworthy. *W. M. Brisbourne*

DUNNETT AGAIN (IRE) 2 b.c. (May 5) Petardia 113 – Pat Said No (IRE) 59 (Last **59 d**
Tycoon 131) [2003 5g 5.1g⁴ 5.2m 6g 6m 6.1m f6g p6g f6s f6g Nov 1] €7,500Y: leggy
colt: third foal: brother to 7f seller winner Bueno Vida: dam, second at 5f at 2 yrs, half-
sister to useful stayer El Conquistador: modest maiden: lost his form: should stay 7f: acts
on good to firm going: signs of temperament. *Mrs C. A. Dunnett*

DUO LEONI 3 ch.f. Vettori (IRE) 119 – La Dolce Vita 76 (Mazilier (USA) 107) [2003 **71**
8f⁶ 7f² 7m³ 7f³ 7.9f 7m² 7d* 8m⁵ p7g f7g² f6g Dec 9] second foal: dam 5f (at 2 yrs) and
7f winner: fair performer: won maiden at Catterick in September: likely to prove best
at 6f/7f: acts on firm going, good to soft and all-weather. *R. M. Beckett*

DUPONT 4 b.c. Zafonic (USA) 130 – June Moon (IRE) (Sadler's Wells (USA) 132) **104**
[2003 115: 8.1g 8.5m 8g³ 8m⁵ Sep 25] quite good-topped colt: has a short, round
action: smart performer at 3 yrs: only useful in 2003, best effort when third to Scapolo
in Otto Wolff-Meile at Cologne third start: best around 1m: acts on good to firm going
and polytrack: visored (not discredited) penultimate start, wore cheekpieces (folded)
final one: has worn crossed noseband: sometimes wanders under pressure: sent to South
Africa. *W. J. Haggas*

DU PRE 2 b.f. (Feb 27) Singspiel (IRE) 133 – Child Prodigy (IRE) 87 (Ballad Rock **65**
122) [2003 6m³ 6m Jul 10] 42,000Y: smallish, compact filly: half-sister to fairly useful
2002 2-y-o 8.5f winner Menuhin (by Royal Academy): dam, 6f (at 2 yrs) and 1m (in
USA) winner, half-sister to very smart 1¼m/1½m performer Kutub: fair form in
maidens at Newmarket: third of 5 in slowly-run race: should be suited by 1¼m/1½m.
Mrs A. J. Perrett

DURAID (IRE) 11 ch.g. Irish River (FR) 131 – Fateful Princess (USA) 95 (Vaguely –
Noble 140) [2003 70: 8m 8d 8m 7.9f Jun 15] workmanlike gelding: has a round action:
fair handicapper in 2002: soundly beaten in 2003: visored once. *C. Grant*

DURKAR STAR (IRE) 5 b.g. Bin Ajwaad (IRE) 119 – Faith Alone 85 (Safawan 118) –
[2003 –: 6m May 5] no form. *M. C. Chapman*

DUSK DANCER (FR) 3 b.g. Groom Dancer (USA) 128 – Nightitude 93 (Night Shift **67**
(USA)) [2003 8g⁴ 8m Mar 29] 32,000Y: rangy, angular gelding: fifth foal: half-brother to
useful Italian 7f/1m performer Golden Cavern (by Lion Cavern): dam, 2-y-o 5f winner,
became one to treat with caution: modest form in maidens at Doncaster and Ascot
(reportedly had breathing problem): subsequently gelded. *B. J. Meehan*

DUSKY WARBLER 4 br.g. Ezzoud (IRE) 126 – Bronzewing 103 (Beldale Flutter **110**
(USA) 130) [2003 106: 14.1g³ 13s⁵ 12.1d³ 16.2m³ 16.4g³ 18d² 14.6d⁵ Nov 7] big, leggy
gelding: smart performer: mostly good efforts in 2003, including when placed behind
Persian Punch in listed race at Sandown (1½ lengths third) and Doncaster Cup (7 lengths
second) fifth/sixth outings: disappointing final start: stays 2¼m: acts on heavy and good
to firm going: carried head high fifth appearance. *M. L. W. Bell*

DUST COVER 3 b.c. Desert Story (IRE) 115 – Convenience (IRE) (Ela-Mana-Mou **107**
132) [2003 80p: 8m³ 10m⁴ 10m⁵ Jun 19] close-coupled, useful-looking colt: useful
performer: best efforts in listed races at Kempton (1¾ lengths third to Prince Tum Tum)
and Royal Ascot (3¼ lengths fifth to Persian Majesty): stays 1¼m: raced only on good/
good to firm going: sent to USA. *P. J. Makin*

DUST GODDESS 3 ch.f. Hector Protector (USA) 124 – Galaxie Dust (USA) 86 **72**
(Blushing Groom (FR) 131) [2003 7g² 8.3s⁶ 8g⁴ 10d Jun 23] well-made filly: half-sister
to several winners, including 7f to 1½m winner Dust Dancer (by Suave Dancer), 7f (at 2
yrs) and 1¼m winner Bulaxie (by Bustino), both smart, and very smart middle-distance
performer Zimzalabim (by Damister): dam 2-y-o 6f winner: fair form: best effort on
debut: should stay 1¼m: has carried head awkwardly/edged right: slowly away final
outing. *E. A. L. Dunlop*

DUSTY DAZZLER (IRE) 3 ch.f. Titus Livius (FR) 115 – Satinette 109 (Shirley **93**
Heights 130) [2003 91: p5g* p5g⁵ 5m³ 5.1m 6d 5f 5.1m⁴ 6f² 6m p6g² Dec 20] strong, **a102**
lengthy filly: has scope: useful handicapper on all-weather, fairly useful on turf: won at
Lingfield in February: very good 1¼ lengths second to Law Breaker there final start: best
at 5f/easy 6f: acts on firm ground and polytrack (below form on fibresand): tends to hang
right. *W. G. M. Turner*

Sheikh Marwan Al Maktoum's "Dutch Gold"

DUSTY WUGG (IRE) 4 b.f. General Monash (USA) 107 – Welsh Berry (USA) (Sir **59**
Ivor 135) [2003 64d: f7g f7g2 f7g f7s 6f4 7d Sep 20] leggy filly: has a quick action:
modest maiden: stays 7f: acts on soft going, firm and fibresand: tried blinkered (ran well
first occasion)/visored/in cheekpieces: often slowly away. *A. Dickman*

DUTCH GOLD (USA) 3 ch.c. Lahib (USA) 129 – Crimson Conquest (USA) 85 **112**
(Diesis 133) [2003 89: p10g* 10m3 8m2 12.3m* 12m6 10g 11.9m 12.5s6 Aug 31] good-
topped colt: has plenty of scope: smart performer: won maiden at Lingfield in March and
4-runner Victor Chandler Chester Vase (by 6 lengths from Summerland, dictating pace)
in May: creditable 7¼ lengths sixth to Kris Kin in Derby at Epsom next time, but well
held after in Eclipse Stakes at Sandown, Great Voltigeur Stakes at York (tongue tied) and
Grand Prix de Deauville: stays 1½m: acts on polytrack and good to firm going, possibly
not on soft: has flashed tail: often races prominently. *C. E. Brittain*

DUTY PAID (IRE) 3 b.f. Barathea (IRE) 127 – Local Custom (IRE) (Be My Native **98**
(USA) 122) [2003 99+: 8g 7g3 8f6 8.1g 7g6 6m 7g2 6m p8g4 p8g5 Nov 22] big, lengthy,
rather unfurnished filly: useful performer: in frame in 3 listed events in 2003, including
1½ lengths third to Rimrod at Epsom (despite appearing not to handle track) and equal
2-length second to Chic at Ascot: best form at 7f/1m: acts on soft and good to firm going,
probably on firm/polytrack: usually bandaged behind: has raced freely: none too
consistent. *D. R. C. Elsworth*

DVINSKY (USA) 2 b.c. (Feb 4) Stravinsky (USA) 133 – Festive Season (USA) **92 p**
(Lypheor 118) [2003 6m6 6m* Sep 12] €200,000Y: compact colt: half-brother to several
winners, including 1995 2-y-o 1m winner D'Naan (by Royal Academy): dam, ran twice,
half-sister to Prix Marcel Boussac winner Mary Linoa: better effort in maidens when
winning 8-runner event at Goodwood (gave bit of trouble start) by 3½ lengths from

317

Mahmoom, leading halfway and quickening away final 1f: will probably stay 7f: should make a useful 3-y-o. *G. A. Butler*

DYNAMO MINSK (IRE) 4 b.f. Polish Precedent (USA) 131 – Blazing Glory (IRE) – (Glow (USA)) [2003 62: f8g Jan 21] big, lengthy filly: modest maiden: well held only run in 2003: tried tongue tied. *John A. Harris*

E

EACHY PEACHY (IRE) 4 ch.f. Perugino (USA) 84 – Miss Big John (IRE) (Martin John) [2003 54: p13g³ p13g p13g⁵ 11.9m p12g 16.4m² 11.6m⁵ 14.1d³ 14f⁶ Aug 21] rather leggy filly: poor maiden: stays easy 2m: acts on good to firm going, good to soft and all-weather: often slowly away/carries head high. *J. R. Best* — 46

EAGER ANGEL (IRE) 5 b.m. Up And At 'em 109 – Seanee Squaw (Indian Ridge 123) [2003 –, a39: f5g³ f6g f6g f5s² f5s f6s 5.1m⁶ f5s 5d f7g f6g⁶ f6g³ f5g Dec 22] small, good-quartered mare: poor maiden: stays 6f: acts on fibresand and firm going: sometimes wears blinkers/cheekpieces/tongue tie. *R. F. Marvin* — 48

EAGLES IN THE WIND (IRE) 3 ch.f. Eagle Eyed (USA) 111 – Quiver Tree 68 – (Lion Cavern (USA) 117) [2003 7.5m 7.6g⁶ 12g 8m⁴ Oct 14] 7,000Y: strong filly: first foal: dam French 8.5f winner: no sign of ability. *A. Berry*

EAGLE'S LANDING 5 b.m. Eagle Eyed (USA) 111 – Anchorage (IRE) 86 (Slip Anchor 136) [2003 p10g f8g f12s⁵ p12g f11g⁵ f14g* 14.1m⁶ f12g⁶ f14.8s³ f16.2g f14.8g* 13.8f³ May 31] poor handicapper: trained in Spain by P. Haley in 2002: won at Southwell in April and Wolverhampton in May: stays 14.8f: acts on sand/fibresand and firm going: tried in cheekpieces. *D. K. Ivory* — 49

EAGLES VIEW (IRE) 3 b.f. Eagle Eyed (USA) 111 – Rock On (IRE) (Ballad Rock 122) [2003 59: 8.2m 7m⁴ 6m 8.3g 8f⁶ 8f⁴ 7f² 7g 8m 6m 6m 7m² 7.1m⁶ 8f 7m Oct 13] sturdy, close-coupled filly: modest maiden: best around 7f: acts on firm ground: tried blinkered, usually visored nowadays: has been slowly away (got very upset in stall final outing): races freely. *Mrs P. N. Dutfield* — 63

EAGLET (IRE) 5 b.g. Eagle Eyed (USA) 111 – Justice System (USA) 57 (Criminal Type (USA)) [2003 62?: 7d 8m 11.9m 14m⁵ Sep 13] small, sparely-made gelding: poor maiden: stays 1m: acts on firm going: tried blinkered. *Miss V. Scott* — 45

EARLSFIELD RAIDER 3 ch.g. Double Trigger (IRE) 123 – Harlequin Walk (IRE) 57 (Pennine Walk 120) [2003 10d⁶ 10.3m 10m 10g⁴ 11.9f p12g Oct 30] leggy gelding: first foal: dam, 1m to 1½m winner (also successful over hurdles), half-sister to useful 2000 2-y-o sprinter Bram Stoker: modest maiden on Flat: left R. O'Sullivan after third start: stays 1¼m: acts on good to soft going: won over hurdles in November. *G. L. Moore* — 62

EARLSTON 3 ch.g. Fleetwood (IRE) 107 – Mystique Smile 78 (Music Boy 124) [2003 67: 7m³ 9.2d³ 8d⁵ 8.1m⁶ 8m⁶ 7.2f² 7g² 6m⁴ 7.2m 8.3d 7m Oct 25] leggy gelding: fair handicapper: effective at 7f/1m: acts on firm and soft ground: wore cheekpieces (saddle reportedly slipped) eighth start: often slowly away: has raced freely (found little final start): sold 5,000 gns. *J. S. Goldie* — 73

EASIBET DOT NET 3 gr.g. Atraf 116 – Silvery 67 (Petong 126) [2003 8m 7g 9.2d⁴ 12g⁴ 10.9m³ 10.9g² 12g³ f12g² f12g* f14.8s⁵ Dec 31] 3,000F, 3,700Y: tall gelding: first foal: dam 1¼m winner: fair handicapper: won at Wolverhampton in November, idling: effective at 1¼m/1½m: acts on fibresand, good to firm and good to soft going: wore cheekpieces last 4 starts: often slowly away: carries head high: has run in snatches. *I. Semple* — 72

EASILY AVERTED (IRE) 2 b.c. (Apr 25) Averti (IRE) 117 – Altishaan (Darshaan 133) [2003 7m⁶ 6m 6g² 5.1m⁴ 6m* p6g³ 5.2s f6g p5g⁶ Dec 17] €85,000Y: sturdy, close-coupled colt: second foal: dam unraced out of useful half-sister to disqualified Oaks winner Aliysa, herself grandam of Alamshar: fair performer: won nursery at Brighton in October: will prove best at 5f/easy 6f: acts on polytrack and good to firm ground: often races up with pace. *J. A. Osborne* — 72

EASTBOROUGH (IRE) 4 b.g. Woodborough (USA) 112 – Easter Girl (Efisio 120) [2003 77, a88: p8g⁶ Dec 20] close-coupled, quite good-topped gelding: fair performer: off 15 months, not knocked about in minor event at Lingfield only outing in 2003: best form at 1¼m/1½m: acts on all-weather, good to firm and good to soft going: tried blinkered: held up. *B. G. Powell* — 72 +

EAST CAPE 6 b.g. Bering 136 – Reine de Danse (USA) 78 (Nureyev (USA) 131) [2003 **53** 64: 12.4m 11m 12g⁶ 10.4f 12.1d⁶ 11.1m⁶ 10.1m³ 10f⁴ f12s⁴ f11g⁵ f12s Dec 27] leggy, useful-looking gelding: modest handicapper: effective at 1¼m/1½m: acts on any turf going and fibresand: tried visored. *Don Enrico Incisa*

EASTERN BLUE (IRE) 4 ch.f. Be My Guest (USA) 126 – Stifen (Burslem 123) **62** [2003 68: 6d⁵ p7g⁶ 6.1g* 6.1m 6d 6m 7m 6d⁴ 6m⁵ 6m 6f 6m⁶ f6g² f6g² Dec 9] sturdy filly: modest handicapper: won at Nottingham in April: stays 6f: acts on fibresand (some promise on polytrack), firm and good to soft ground: tried in cheekpieces/blinkers: has found little. *Mrs L. Stubbs*

EASTERN BREEZE (IRE) 5 b.g. Sri Pekan (USA) 117 – Elegant Bloom (IRE) 84 **103** (Be My Guest (USA) 126) [2003 100: p10g⁴ p10g⁴ f8.5s³ 12g³ 10.4m 12m³ 10.1m³ 12m* 12g⁶ 12d⁶ p10g⁶ Nov 22] leggy, quite good-topped gelding: useful performer: won handicap at Newmarket in October by 3 lengths from Canada: very stiff task, far from discredited when sixth to Imperial Dancer in St Simon Stakes at Newbury next time: stays 1½m: acts on good to firm going, soft and all-weather: edgy sort (tends to sweat), sometimes early to post: raced too freely fourth/fifth starts. *P. W. D'Arcy*

EASTERN DAGGER 3 b.c. Kris 135 – Shehana (USA) 86 (The Minstrel (CAN) **78 d** 135) [2003 72p: p8g⁴ f7g* 7.1m 8m* 7g⁵ 8.2g 7m⁴ 8m f8.5g⁶ 8m Sep 12] leggy colt: fair performer: won maiden at Wolverhampton in February and claimer at Leicester (left M. Johnston) in May: below form last 5 starts, leaving Mrs N. Macauley after second of them: stays 1m: acts on good to firm ground and all-weather: tried visored. *R. Wilman*

EASTERN FAITH 2 ch.g. (Feb 27) Perugino (USA) 84 – Bright Fountain (IRE) 47 **60** (Cadeaux Genereux 131) [2003 5g 6g⁴ 7d 7f f7s⁵ Oct 21] 800Y: good-topped gelding: second foal: dam lightly-raced daughter of useful stayer High Fountain: modest maiden: stays 7f: acts on good to soft ground, probably on fibresand. *Mrs L. Stubbs*

EASTERN GATE 3 b.g. Elmaamul (USA) 125 – Redgrave Design 77 (Nebbiolo 125) **–** [2003 –: 7m Apr 23] little form. *Miss A. Stokell*

EASTERN HOPE (IRE) 4 b.g. Danehill Dancer (IRE) 117 – Hope And Glory (USA) **76** 87 (Well Decorated (USA)) [2003 84: 8.5d 8.5d⁵ 8d 7g⁶ 7g Nov 1] tall, good-topped gelding: fair handicapper: effective at 7f/1m: acts on good to firm and good to soft going: has run well in blinkers: sometimes races freely/wanders. *Mrs L. Stubbs*

EASTERNKING 4 ch.f. Sabrehill (USA) 120 – Kshessinskaya 99 (Hadeer 118) [2003 **–** –: 12.1d Sep 23] smallish, sturdy filly: little form: tried in cheekpieces. *J. S. Wainwright*

EASTERN MAGENTA (IRE) 3 b.g. Turtle Island (IRE) 123 – Blue Heights (IRE) **–** (Persian Heights 129) [2003 86: 6d 6s 7m 7d Nov 8] rather unfurnished gelding: fairly useful performer at 2 yrs: well held in 2003. *Mrs L. Stubbs*

EASTERN PEARL 2 ch.f. (Mar 25) Wolfhound (USA) 126 – Wild Humour (IRE) **75** 60 (Fayruz 116) [2003 5m⁶ 5m 5m 5m² 5f² 5d* 5g 5g Oct 11] 4,500Y: leggy, lengthy filly: fifth foal: dam lightly-raced maiden (ran only at 2 yrs): fair performer: won nursery at Sandown in August: sweating, seemed to run creditably when ninth in Flying Childers Stakes at Doncaster next time: likely to prove best at 5f/6f: acts on good to soft going. *Mrs L. Stubbs*

EASTERN ROYAL 4 b.g. Royal Applause 124 – Kentfield (Busted 134) [2003 52: f8s **–** 7g 7.2g Jul 22] leggy gelding: modest performer at 3 yrs: well held in 2003. *Mrs L. Stubbs*

EASTERN SCARLET (IRE) 3 b.g. Woodborough (USA) 112 – Cuddles (IRE) 89 **52 §** (Taufan (USA) 119) [2003 73: 7m 6m 7f 9.3m³ 12d⁵ 10g⁵ 10.1m⁵ Aug 6] good-bodied gelding: fair performer at 2 yrs: modest in 2003: stays 9.3f: acts on good to firm going: wore cheekpieces last 2 starts: often very slowly away: ungenuine. *Mrs L. Stubbs*

EASTERN TRUMPETER 7 b.h. First Trump 118 – Oriental Air (IRE) 56 (Taufan **72 d** (USA) 119) [2003 85: 5g 5m 5d 5g 5f 5m 5g⁵ 5m⁵ 5m⁶ 5m f5g 5.3m⁴ f6s 6m 5m 5.3f Oct 17] compact horse: fair handicapper: left J. M. Bradley after eleventh start: effective at 5f/6f: acts on fibresand, firm and soft going: reportedly had breathing problem fifth outing and mostly tongue tied after: has given trouble at stall: has been slowly away: usually half-hour: unreliable. *H. J. Cyzer*

EASTER OGIL (IRE) 8 ch.g. Pips Pride 117 – Piney Pass (Persian Bold 123) [2003 **67** 66, a64: p7g* p7g³ p8g* p7g* p8g* p8g* p8g p8g p10g 9.7m⁴ 8.5g* 11.8g⁴ 11.6g³ **a77** 8m p13g⁶ p10g⁴ p12g² p13g² Dec 29] lengthy, good-topped gelding: unimpressive mover: fair performer: won minor event/claimer (for A. Balding), 2 handicaps/seller (for M. Wallace), all at Lingfield in January/February, and in Jersey in May: effective at 7f, barely at 13f: acts on all-weather and any turf going: effective visored or not: tried in cheekpieces: sometimes soon off bridle: tough and consistent. *Jane Southcombe*

EASTER PARADE   3 b.f. Entrepreneur 123 – Starlet 119 (Teenoso (USA) 135) [2003 **78**
68p: 8g 12.1d* 14.1f* 14.4f 13.3m⁴ Jul 19] smallish, leggy filly: fair handicapper: won at
Chepstow in May and Salisbury in June: stays 1¾m: acts on firm and good to soft ground:
sold 15,000 gns in December. *R. Charlton*

EAST FLARES   3 ch.g. Environment Friend 128 – Ijada Bianca (Absalom 128) [2003 **66 ?**
–: 8.2m⁶ 10f* 11.8m Oct 13] close-coupled, rather unfurnished gelding: fair form, lightly
raced: dictated steady pace when winning maiden at Nottingham in October: stiff task,
tailed off in handicap final start: stays 1¼m: raced only on good to firm/firm going on
turf. *J. W. Unett*

EAST RIDING   3 b.f. Gothenberg (IRE) 117 – Bettynouche 69 (Midyan (USA) 124) **55**
[2003 74: 6.1g 9.2d 6d 5.9m⁶ f7g 7m² 7m 6m 7.1f⁵ Aug 21] tall, leggy filly: modest handicapper: left M. Johnston 600 gns after sixth start: stays 7f: acts on any ground: carried
head awkwardly final start. *Miss A. Stokell*

EAST TYCOON (IRE)   4 ch.g. Bigstone (IRE) 126 – Princesse Sharpo (USA) (Trem- **–**
polino (USA) 135) [2003 101: 10.3g Sep 13] IR 6,000Y: tall gelding: third foal: dam
French maiden: useful form at 3 yrs, winning maiden at Fairyhouse: left M. Grassick in
Ireland: well held only Flat outing in 2003: stays 1¼m: raced only on good/good to firm
ground on Flat: fairly useful hurdler. *Jonjo O'Neill*

EASTWELL VIOLET   3 b.f. Danzig Connection (USA) – Kinchenjunga 67 (Dar- **49**
shaan 133) [2003 p8g p10g⁴ p12g⁴ 11.6d 12m⁶ Jul 10] fourth foal: half-sister to 9.7f to
2¼m winner Eastwell Hall (by Saddlers' Hall): dam, second at 1m on only 2-y-o start but
showed nothing afterwards: poor maiden: ran wide on bends at Folkestone final start:
should stay beyond 1½m. *S. Dow*

EASY BREEZE   3 b.g. Paley Prince (USA) 110 – Hawthorns Alice (Stan Flashman **–**
72) [2003 f7g p6g f8.5g Nov 29] second foal: dam unraced: no sign of ability in maidens/
seller. *J. M. Bradley*

EASY RIDER (IRE)   3 b.g. Blues Traveller (IRE) 119 – Curie Express (IRE) 65 (Fay- **61**
ruz 116) [2003 65: p8g² p7g² f8.5s⁶ p7g 6m³ 5.9m⁴ 8g 7f² 7g⁴ Aug 10] modest maiden:
probably best at 6f/7f: acts on good to firm ground, soft and all-weather: tongue tied last
5 starts: sold 6,700 gns, sent to France. *E. L. James*

EAU PURE (FR)   6 b.m. Epervier Bleu 131 – Eau de Nuit (Kings Lake (USA) 133) **–**
[2003 p8g Apr 5] seventh foal: half-sister to 2 winners, including fairly useful French
winner around 1½m Esamix (by Linamix): dam, 7f/1m winner, half-sister to dam of smart
sprinter Titus Livius: maiden on Flat at 3/4 yrs in France before winning over fences in
2001 (subsequently left J. Barbe): well held on British debut. *B. A. Pearce*

EBORACUM (IRE)   2 b.f. (Apr 25) Alzao (USA) 117 – Fire of London 78 (Shirley **63**
Heights 130) [2003 6m⁴ 6m⁵ 8g² 8s Nov 3] 7,000Y: good-topped filly: has scope: fourth
foal: dam, second at 1¼m, sister to useful winner up to 1¼m Spitfire: modest maiden:
second at Ripon: ran respectably in nursery final start: should stay 1¼m. *T. D. Easterby*

EBORACUM LADY (USA)   3 b.f. Lure (USA) 131 – Konvincha (USA) (Cormorant **58 ?**
(USA)) [2003 10s 9m³ 8m⁴ 12.4g⁶ Oct 22] $22,000F, $35,000Y: big, plain filly: fourth

foal: half-sister to 5-y-o Askham: dam, won up to 9f in USA, half-sister to US Grade 2 7f winner Lottsa Talc: easily best effort in maidens (modest form) on second outing: stays 9f, possibly not 12.4f: acts on good to firm ground. *J. D. Bethell*

ECCENTRIC 2 ch.g. (Mar 19) Most Welcome 131 – Sure Care 62 (Caerleon (USA) –
132) [2003 7m Sep 17] £15,000Y: fourth foal: brother to useful 5f (at 2 yrs) to 7f winner Deceitful and half-brother to 3-y-o Willheconquertoo: dam 13f winner: 100/1 and green, slowly away when last of 15 in maiden at Yarmouth. *Andrew Reid*

ECHOES IN ETERNITY (IRE) 3 b.f. Spinning World (USA) 130 – Magnificent **111**
Style (USA) 107 (Silver Hawk (USA) 123) [2003 98P: 10.4m 9.9m³ 8.1d 10.1m* 8m* Oct 4] lengthy filly: smart performer, lightly raced: trained by J. Gosden in 2002: suffered injury on reappearance and off 3 months: confirmed 2-y-o promise when winning listed race at Yarmouth in September and Peugeot Sun Chariot Stakes at Newmarket in October, latter by a neck from Macadamia, disputing before quickening ahead over 2f out and holding on well: stays 1¼m: acts on good to firm going: stays in training. *Saeed bin Suroor*

E C TOO 3 b.f. Sheikh Albadou 128 – Scarlett Holly 81 (Red Sunset 120) [2003 62: **61**
6m⁶ f7g 5.3m⁴ 5.3d⁴ 5.7m⁶ 6.1m 6f Jun 27] lengthy filly: modest maiden handicapper: bred to prove best up to 7f: acts on good to firm and good to soft going: blinkered (ran as if amiss) final start: temperament under suspicion. *J. L. Spearing*

ECUADOR (IRE) 3 ch.g. Among Men (USA) 124 – Christle Mill (Pas de Seul 133) –
[2003 –: 4f 10.2m⁶ 13.1f Sep 8] good-topped gelding: little form: unseated rider and bolted to post once at 2 yrs. *J. G. M. O'Shea*

EDDIES JEWEL 3 b.g. Presidium 124 – Superstream (Superpower 113) [2003 –: 5g **51 ?**
5m 8m 7d³ 8m f7g Nov 10] strong gelding: seemingly modest form at best in maidens: stays 7f: acts on good to soft going: wore cheekpieces/visor last 4 starts. *J. S. Wainwright*

EDDU 5 ch.g. Casteddu 111 – Cabra (Red Sunset 120) [2003 61: p10g² p13g² p10g Feb **74**
8] big, lengthy gelding: fair performer: stayed easy 13f: acted on firm going and polytrack: dead. *W. M. Brisbourne*

EDEN ROCK (IRE) 2 b.c. (Jan 4) Danehill (USA) 126 – Marlene-D 57 (Selkirk **84 P**
(USA) 129) [2003 7m⁶ 7m* Sep 17] €700,000Y: big, good-bodied colt: has plenty of scope: first foal: dam, Irish 9f winner, half-sister to useful French sprinter Kerulen and smart stayer Arden: confirmed considerable promise of debut when justifying favouritism in 15-runner maiden at Yarmouth by 1¼ lengths from Dubois, soon leading, quickening 2f out and just pushed out, carrying head high: will stay 1m: has good deal of potential, and seems sure to do well at 3 yrs. *Sir Michael Stoute*

EDE'S 3 ch.g. Bijou d'Inde 127 – Ballagarrow Girl 66 (North Stoke 130) [2003 47: 7m⁶ **50**
12m⁵ Jul 10] lengthy gelding: modest maiden, lightly raced: should stay 1m, probably not 1½m. *W. G. M. Turner*

EDGEHILL (IRE) 2 b.c. (Apr 5) Ali-Royal (IRE) 127 – Elfin Queen (IRE) 64 (Fairy **60**
King (USA)) [2003 p7g 6d Nov 8] IR 24,000F, 22,000Y: tall colt: third foal: half-brother to winner in Greece by Dolphin Street: dam, sprint maiden, half-sister to smart 7f/1m performer Tempting Fate: modest form when seventh in maidens at Lingfield and Doncaster, slowly away: will stay 1m. *C. R. Egerton*

EDIFICE (JPN) 7 ch.g. Carroll House 132 – Moon Tosho (JPN) (Steel Heart 128) –
[2003 46: 10g 11m 14.1m 11.9m 8m 10.1m Jun 27] smallish, sturdy gelding: little form in 2003: tried in headgear: sometimes looks none too keen. *B. Ellison*

EDMO YEWKAY (IRE) 3 b. or br.g. Sri Pekan (USA) 117 – Mannequin (IRE) 79 **78**
(In The Wings 128) [2003 80: 10.4f 12.3m⁵ 12.3g⁴ 10m 9.9m 10g⁶ 10s Nov 3] rangy gelding: has a round action: fair performer: stays easy 1½m: acts on any going: effective blinkered or not: won over hurdles in November. *T. D. Easterby*

EDUCATING RITA 3 b.f. Emarati (USA) 74 – Charnwood Queen 61 (Cadeaux **64**
Genereux 131) [2003 5g* 5m Jun 9] 6,500Y: third foal: sister to 5-y-o Greenwood: dam, 6f winner, half-sister to smart 7f/1m performer Sunstreak: 50/1, made all in maiden at Doncaster to win by length from Hiccups, edging left: tailed off in minor event at Windsor following month, hanging left. *M. A. Buckley*

EDWARD'S BROTHER 3 b.g. Wolfhound (USA) 126 – Dolly Bevan 53 (Another **55**
Realm 118) [2003 55: p6g³ p8g 7g 6f⁴ 6f 7g³ 8m 7m 8f Oct 17] modest maiden: stays 7f: acts on polytrack and firm ground: tried blinkered: sold 2,000 gns. *M. Wigham*

EEZAA GEEZER (IRE) 2 b. or br.c. (Apr 9) Lahib (USA) 129 – Baylands Sunshine **73**
(IRE) (Classic Secret (USA) 91) [2003 6m 5f⁴ 5m⁵ 6m⁵ 7m* 7.1d⁴ 7g⁵ Sep 13] €38,000Y:

close-coupled colt: third foal: half-brother to 3-y-o Compton Eclaire and Irish 9f to 13f winner Mount George (by Greensmith): dam unraced half-sister to high-class sprinter Anita's Prince: fair performer: won claimer at Salisbury in August: stayed 7f: acted on firm and good to soft going: dead. *R. Hannon*

EFFECTIVE 3 ch.g. Bahamian Bounty 116 – Efficacy 62 (Efisio 120) [2003 68: p7g f6g² p6g² f6g* f6g⁴ 6g 6m 6g² 7d f7g f6g Nov 11] lengthy gelding: fair performer: won maiden at Wolverhampton in February: stays 6f: acts on all-weather, unraced on extremes of going on turf. *A. P. Jarvis* **65 a76**

EFFERVESCE (IRE) 5 b.m. Sri Pekan (USA) 117 – Arctic Winter (CAN) (Briartic (CAN)) [2003 80: p7g³ p8g 7m 6m³ 6m* 6m 7.1m³ 6m 6d 6g 6g* 6m⁵ 6.1m⁵ 7d Sep 11] strong mare: fairly useful performer: won handicap at Leicester in April and minor event at Doncaster in July: was effective from 5f to easy 1m: acted on good to firm going, good to soft and all-weather: ran well when sweating/edgy: held up: dead. *M. A. Buckley* **87**

EFFIE GRAY 4 b.f. Sri Pekan (USA) 117 – Rose Bouquet 78 (General Assembly (USA)) [2003 71d: 13g⁵ 12.1g⁶ Jul 24] short-backed, workmanlike filly: just a modest maiden nowadays: stays 1½m: acts on firm and soft going: tried visored: sold 1,200 gns. *P. Monteith* **53 ?**

EFIDIUM 5 b.g. Presidium 124 – Efipetite 54 (Efisio 120) [2003 55: 5m 8m* 7m* 5.9g 7g* 7f⁴ 5.9f 7m² 6.9m⁶ 8m⁵ 6.9m* 8s⁴ 8f⁶ 8m 7.5m 7m 7m⁴ 7m⁶ Sep 17] small gelding: fair performer: better than ever in 2003, winning ladies handicap at Ripon, seller at Redcar, apprentice handicap at Doncaster and handicap at Carlisle: best at 6f to easy 1m: acts on firm going, good to soft and fibresand: usually blinkered earlier in career: sometimes slowly away/edges right: ridden by claimer Suzanne France nowadays. *N. Bycroft* **76**

EFIMAC 3 b.f. Presidium 124 – Efipetite 54 (Efisio 120) [2003 53: p6g⁵ f7g f8g⁵ p7g p7g Mar 5] small, plain filly: poor performer: stays easy 7f: acts on all-weather, raced on good/good to firm going on turf. *N. Bycroft* **49**

EFINEW (IRE) 2 b.c. (Apr 1) Efisio 120 – Silly Mid-On (Midyan (USA) 124) [2003 7m 7g⁴ 6m Sep 7] 14,000Y: close-coupled colt: second foal: dam once-raced half-sister to smart 1¼m to 2m winner Sarangani: easily best effort in maidens (fair form) when fourth at Yarmouth: should stay 1m: tongue tied last 2 outings: sold 8,500 gns. *M. G. Quinlan* **70**

EFRHINA (IRE) 3 ch.f. Woodman (USA) 126 – Eshq Albahr (USA) (Riverman (USA) 131) [2003 7m 8.1d 10.2f² Oct 12] useful-looking filly: first foal: dam unraced half-sister to useful 1m/1¼m performer Dayflower out of half-sister to smart 7f winner Weldnaas: modest form in maidens: stays easy 1¼m: acts on firm and good to soft ground: sold 11,000 gns. *A. C. Stewart* **63**

EGO 3 b.f. Green Desert (USA) 127 – Myself 110 (Nashwan (USA) 135) [2003 107: 7g⁵ 6m³ 5g⁶ 5.1m³ 5g⁵ 6.1d Sep 24] tall, lengthy, quite attractive filly: just fairly useful performer in 2003, looking none too keen: free-going sort, and will probably prove best at 5f/6f: raced mainly on good going or firmer (tailed off on good to soft): blinkered last 3 starts: attitude under suspicion. *G. Wragg* **93**

EGO TRIP 2 b.c. (Apr 9) Deploy 131 – Boulevard Rouge (USA) 71 (Red Ransom (USA)) [2003 5m 6m³ 6m⁶ 8m 7g 6m 8m Oct 20] close-coupled colt: first foal: dam maiden who barely stayed 11f: modest maiden: third at Catterick: ran poorly in nurseries last 2 starts: should stay at least 1m. *M. W. Easterby* **60**

EHAB (IRE) 4 b.g. Cadeaux Genereux 131 – Dernier Cri 63 (Slip Anchor 136) [2003 73: f9.4s* f8.5g² 7g 7g f9.4g⁴ 7m 8m f7s Sep 26] fair performer: regressed after winning maiden at Wolverhampton in January: stays 1¼m: acts on all-weather, yet to race on extremes of going on turf: sold 7,500 gns. *P. J. Makin* **73 d**

EI EI 8 b.g. North Briton 67 – Branitska (Mummy's Pet 125) [2003 12m Sep 16] no longer of much account on Flat but is a useful chaser: tried blinkered. *M. C. Chapman* **–**

EIGHT ELLINGTON (IRE) 2 b.g. (Mar 29) Ali-Royal (IRE) 127 – Where's Charlotte 53 (Sure Blade (USA) 130) [2003 6.1g³ 6m⁴ 6m f5s 6g 7g Oct 24] €8,500Y, resold 8,000Y: quite well-topped gelding: first foal: dam sprint maiden: modest maiden: third at Chepstow: below form after next start: should stay 7f: sold 1,000 gns, and gelded. *R. F. Johnson Houghton* **59**

EIGHT (IRE) 7 ch.g. Thatching 131 – Up To You (Sallust 134) [2003 61, a46: f11g p12g² 12.1d² 10.9m 11g Oct 28] workmanlike gelding: modest on turf, poor on all-weather: stays 1¾m: acts on polytrack (well held on fibresand), firm and good to soft going: often visored/blinkered early in career. *C. G. Cox* **57 a45**

Gran Premio del Jockey Club, Milan—
Ekraar gains a first Group 1 victory at the age of six; Maktub is second

EIGHT TRUMPS   3 ch.g. First Trump 118 – Misty Silks 81 (Scottish Reel 123) [2003 –: 10.1d f12g⁵ 9m f11s Sep 26] strong gelding: little form: has looked wayward. *P. R. Wood*

EIGHT WOODS (IRE)   5 ch.g. Woods of Windsor (USA) – Cd Super Targeting (IRE) 62 (Polish Patriot (USA) 128) [2003 –: f12g⁶ f9.4g⁶ f9.4g³ Mar 1] fairly useful in Ireland at 2/3 yrs: only fair nowadays: stays 1½m: acts on fibresand and any turf going. *T. D. Barron*   **69**

EJAY   4 b.f. Emperor Jones (USA) 119 – Lough Erne 83 (Never So Bold 135) [2003 p8g p7g f6g⁶ Dec 9] poor maiden: well held at 4 yrs. *Julian Poulton*   **–**

EKRAAR (USA)   6 b.h. Red Ransom (USA) – Sacahuista (USA) (Raja Baba (USA)) [2003 121: 12g3 10.3m* 10m 12m* 12m* Oct 19] well-made horse: good walker: very smart performer: left Saeed bin Suroor before reappearance, and returned to former trainer: creditable 4 lengths third to Sulamani in Dubai Sheema Classic at Nad Al Sheba, then won minor event at Doncaster in June, listed race at Newmarket (by length from Compton Bolter) and Gran Premio del Jockey Club at Milan (by 2 lengths from Maktub), last 2 in October: was effective at 1¼m/1½m: acted on firm and soft going, just respectable efforts on dirt: sometimes blinkered/visored/tongue tied: game: to stand at Allevamento di Besnate, Italy, fee €7,000. *M. P. Tregoning*   **121**

ELA AGORI MOU (IRE)   6 ch.g. Ela-Mana-Mou 132 – La Courant (USA) (Little Current (USA)) [2003 12.4m 12.4g 16.1d 16d 16g 14.1m 14.1m Oct 17] fair bumper performer: little form on Flat in 2003: tried in cheekpieces. *D. Eddy*   **–**

ELA D'ARGENT (IRE)   4 b.f. Ela-Mana-Mou 132 – Petite-D-Argent 91 (Noalto 120) [2003 66: 11.7m² 11.7m 13.1g⁵ May 19] angular, quite good-topped filly: fair handicapper: stays 13f: acts on soft and good to firm ground: has been tongue tied: has started slowly. *M. C. Pipe*   **74**

ELA FIGURA   3 ch.f. The West (USA) 107 – Chili Bouchier (USA) (Stop The Music (USA)) [2003 56: 5.1m 6m 5.1g⁴ 6m 5f 5.1m⁴ 5m 5g³ 5m³ 5d³ 5.7f² 5m 6.1f 5.7f² 6d Oct 31] good-topped filly: modest maiden: stays 5.7f: acts on firm ground, good to soft and all-weather: sometimes visored. *A. W. Carroll*   **63**

ELA JAY   4 b.f. Double Eclipse (IRE) 122 – Papirusa (IRE) (Pennine Walk 120) [2003 61: 14.1d² 16d⁶ 16.2m 16m⁶ 16m Sep 19] modest maiden handicapper: well held after re-   **57**

323

appearance: stays 2¼m: acts on firm going, good to soft and polytrack: blinkered (found little) last 2 starts: got upset in stall and withdrawn on intended reappearance: one to treat with caution: successful over hurdles in November. *H. Morrison*

ELA PAPAROUNA   2 b.f. (Apr 3) Vettori (IRE) 119 – Pretty Poppy 67 (Song 132)   **74**
[2003 6m⁵ 6g⁴ 6f³ Oct 27] €60,000Y: sturdy filly: half-sister to several winning sprinters, notably high-class 5f performer Kyllachy (by Pivotal): dam 2-y-o 5f winner who stayed 7.6f: fair form in maidens: in frame at Windsor and Leicester (odds on, slowly away): likely to prove best at 5f/6f. *H. Candy*

ELA RE   4 ch.g. Sabrehill (USA) 120 – Lucia Tarditi (FR) (Crystal Glitters (USA) 127)   **–**
[2003 58: p12g Mar 4] strong gelding: has a round action: modest maiden: well held on all-weather debut, only Flat run in 2003: successful twice over hurdles after: barely stays testing 1¼m: acts on soft going. *C. R. Dore*

EL COTO   3 b.c. Forzando 122 – Thatcherella 80 (Thatching 131) [2003 85: 7g* 8m²   **106**
8m 8m³ 8m⁶ 7g* 7.9m 10.5d³ 8g 10m⁴ Oct 25] smallish, good-topped colt: useful handicapper: won at Doncaster in March and Leicester (by 1½ lengths from Into The Breeze) in August: ran creditably after when third to Fabulous Jet at Haydock: effective at 7f, and probably stays 10.5f: acts on soft and good to firm going. *B. A. McMahon*

ELECTRIQUE (IRE)   3 b.g. Elmaamul (USA) 125 – Majmu (USA) 105 (Al Nasr   **88**
(FR) 126) [2003 65: 10.2f³ 10m³ 10m² 8f² 10.4m* Sep 7] leggy, quite good-topped gelding: fairly useful performer: won maiden at York in September, despite edging left: effective at 1m/1¼m: acts on firm going and fibresand: free-going sort: usually races prominently. *J. A. Osborne*

ELEGANT GRACIE (IRE)   3 ch.f. Desert Prince (IRE) 130 – Elegant Fragrant (IRE)   **59**
(Be My Guest (USA) 126) [2003 p10g p10g p10g³ Dec 30] 19,000F, 9,000Y: fourth foal: dam unraced out of smart Cork And Orrery Stakes winner Sweet Mint: modest form in maidens at Lingfield: should prove at least as effective at 1m as 1¼m: very slowly away second outing. *R. Guest*

ELEGANT SHADOW   3 ch.f. Grand Lodge (USA) 125 – White Shadow (IRE) 87   **74**
(Last Tycoon 131) [2003 83p: 7f² 7.6m³ 8.2m Oct 28] good-topped filly: has scope: fair maiden: found little and well below best last 2 starts: will probably stay 1m: acts on firm and good to soft ground: sold 10,000 gns. *R. Charlton*

ELEONOR SYMPSON   4 b.f. Cadeaux Genereux 131 – Anne Bonny 105 (Ajdal   **–**
(USA) 130) [2003 50: 8.1m 7g May 28] modest maiden at 3 yrs: no form 2003: wore cheekpieces last 3 starts. *R. M. H. Cowell*

ELFHELM (IRE)   3 b.c. Perugino (USA) 84 – Symphony (IRE) (Cyrano de Bergerac   **79**
120) [2003 76: p8g² Jan 30] fair maiden, lightly raced: second at Lingfield, only run in 2003: stays 8.5f: acts on all-weather: carried head high final 2-y-o start: sent to Hong Kong. *Edward Butler, Ireland*

EL GRAN HOMBRE (USA)   7 ch.g. El Gran Senor (USA) 136 – Conquistress   **–**
(USA) (Conquistador Cielo (USA)) [2003 f7g Jan 2] leggy, close-coupled gelding: seems of little account nowadays. *R. Bastiman*

EL HAMRA (IRE)   5 gr.g. Royal Abjar (USA) 121 – Cherlinoa (FR) (Crystal Palace   **–**
(FR) 132) [2003 –, a77d: p8g Mar 26] small, strong gelding: fair handicapper on all-weather at best: on downgrade: tried blinkered/visored. *M. J. Haynes*

ELHEBA (IRE)   4 b. or br.g. Elbio 125 – Fireheba (ITY) (Fire of Life (USA) 113)   **–**
[2003 –, a82: f9.4g f9.4g⁴ f8.5s⁴ p12g f9.4g f12g p12g Nov 13] big, leggy gelding: fair   **a72 d**
performer: well below form last 4 starts, leaving R. Wilman after first of them: effective at 1m to easy 1¼m: acts on all-weather and soft going: blinkered/visored. *M. Wigham*

ELIDORE   3 b.f. Danetime (IRE) 121 – Beveled Edge 60 (Beveled (USA)) [2003 95:   **80**
7m³ 7m 8.1m f7g Oct 16] rangy filly: fairly useful performer at 2 yrs: below form in 2003: stays easy 7f (pulled hard over 1m): acts on any turf going: usually races prominently. *B. Palling*

ELIIPOP   5 b.g. First Trump 118 – Hasty Key (USA) (Key To The Mint (USA)) [2003   **62**
–: f12g² f14s⁵ f14.8s⁶ Sep 20] fair maiden at 3 yrs: just modest since: stays 1½m: acts on fibresand and firm ground. *R. J. Price*

ELITISTA (FR)   2 gr.f. (Jan 25) Linamix (FR) 127 – Elacata (GER) 111 (Acatenango   **49**
(GER) 127) [2003 6g 7m⁵ p8g⁵ f8.5g⁵ Nov 17] 5,000Y: rather unfurnished filly: sixth foal: half-sister to winner in Sweden by Java Gold and winner in Germany by Law Society: dam, German 7f (at 2 yrs) to 10.5f winner, half-sister to German St Leger winner Elsurimo: poor maiden: needs to settle to stay beyond 1m: best effort on polytrack. *E. J. O'Neill*

ELLA CARISA 4 b.f. Elmaamul (USA) 125 – Salty Girl (IRE) 70 (Scenic 128) [2003 –
52: f16s f16.2g p13g 17.2f 16.2d⁵ 16g Oct 24] leggy filly: modest maiden at 3 yrs: well
held in 2003. *A. Charlton*

ELLA FALLS (IRE) 8 ch.m. Dancing Dissident (USA) 119 – Over Swing (FR) 46
(Saint Cyrien (FR) 128) [2003 43: 14.1m⁴ 14.1m⁵ 16.5m⁵ f16.2s Dec 6] leggy mare: poor a–
handicapper: stays 2m: acts on firm going, good to soft and fibresand: tried blinkered.
Mrs H. Dalton

ELLAMYTE 3 b.f. Elmaamul (USA) 125 – Deanta In Eirinn (Red Sunset 120) [2003 58
75: 6m 5f 6m 6d 5m⁵ 6.1m³ 6.1f 5.7f³ p6g 7g Nov 14] leggy filly: modest performer
nowadays: claimed from H. Morrison £6,000 after eighth start: effective at 5f/6f: acts on
firm and good to soft going: blinkered/visored last 6 starts: sometimes wanders: has
flashed tail. *D. G. Bridgwater*

EL LAOOB (USA) 3 b.f. Red Ransom (USA) – Ajfan (USA) 112 (Woodman (USA) 95
126) [2003 7d³ 8g⁶ 10m⁎ 10.1g⁴ 12m² 12.5g⁶ Aug 26] good-bodied filly: fifth foal: half-
sister to smart 5f/6f winner in Britain/UAE Mutamayyaz (by Nureyev) and to fairly
useful 1997 2-y-o 7f winner Elsurur (by Storm Cat): dam, 7f (at 2 yrs)/1m winner who
was third in 1000 Guineas, half-sister to smart performer up to 14.6f Minds Music: useful
performer: won maiden at Newbury in June: ran well when 1¼ lengths second to Floreeda
in listed race there and when sixth to Whortleberry in Prix Minerve at Deauville last 2
starts: stays 1½m: unraced on extremes of going: sold 110,000 gns in December, sent to
USA. *J. H. M. Gosden*

ELLA'S WISH (IRE) 3 ch.f. Bluebird (USA) 125 – Red Rita (IRE) 97§ (Kefaah 60
(USA) 124) [2003 8.2m p10g⁴ 8.1m p10g p12g Nov 29] 80,000Y: lengthy filly: fourth
foal: half-sister to smart 6f (at 2 yrs) to 1¼m winner Foodbroker Fancy (by Halling) and
useful 6f winner (including at 2 yrs) Femme Fatale (by Fairy King): dam untrustworthy
6f winner: modest maiden: well held last 3 starts: stays 1¼m: acts on polytrack: blinkered
final outing. *J. H. M. Gosden*

ELLEN MOONEY 4 ch.f. Efisio 120 – Budby 72 (Rock City 120) [2003 83: 8g 7.6m 79
8g 8.1g 8g 8.3d² f8s⁎ 8g⁵ 8d f8g² Dec 8] workmanlike filly: poor walker: fair handicapper: won at Southwell in October: barely stays 10.5f: acts on good to firm ground, soft
and fibresand: wore cheekpieces last 6 starts: sometimes slowly away. *B. Smart*

ELLENS ACADEMY (IRE) 8 b.g. Royal Academy (USA) 130 – Lady Ellen 67 85
(Horage 124) [2003 103: 6d⁵ 6m 5v 6m 6g 5m⁶ 7d 6m 6m⁶ 6f⁎ 5m³ 6f⁎ Oct 10] big,
useful-looking gelding: impresses in appearance: smart at 6 yrs: reportedly sustained
small fracture final start in 2002, and just fairly useful nowadays: won apprentice
handicap at Redcar in September and minor event at York in October: best at 5f (given
stiff track)/6f: acts on fibresand and firm going, probably on soft: occasionally blinkered:
sometimes slowly away/wanders: reportedly resents whip, and usually ridden with hands
and heels nowadays. *E. J. Alston*

ELLENS LAD (IRE) 9 b.g. Polish Patriot (USA) 128 – Lady Ellen 67 (Horage 124) 77
[2003 98: 5d f5g f6s⁎ Dec 6] sturdy, strong-quartered gelding: just fair form in 2003, won
claimer at Wolverhampton in December: best at 5f/easy 6f: probably acts on any going:
blinkered 5 of last 6 starts: usually held up. *W. J. Musson*

ELLEN'S ROCK 5 b.m. Rock Hopper 124 – Hellene (Dominion 123) [2003 f6g Jun –
9] 600Y: half-sister to 6f winner Sideloader Special (by Song) and 5f winner D'Marti (by
Emarati): dam unraced: well beaten in bumper, and maiden at Southwell. *Paul Johnson*

ELLE ROYAL (IRE) 4 br.f. Ali-Royal (IRE) 127 – Silvretta (IRE) 73 (Tirol 127) –
[2003 –: 11.9m May 14] leggy, light-bodied filly: fair maiden at 2 yrs: little form since.
T. P. McGovern

ELLINA 2 b.f. (Mar 28) Robellino (USA) 127 – Native Flair 87 (Be My Native (USA) –
122) [2003 7m 8d Nov 7] workmanlike filly: half-sister to several winners, including 1m/
1¼m winner Holy Smoke (by Statoblest) and 1m (at 2 yrs) to 1¾m winner Nosey Native
(by Cyrano de Bergerac), both fairly useful: dam 1¼m/1½m winner: well held in maidens
at Newmarket and Doncaster (signs of ability). *Mrs Lydia Pearce*

ELLIOT'S CHOICE (IRE) 2 b.c. (Apr 25) Foxhound (USA) 103 – Indian City 57 64
(Lahib (USA) 129) [2003 5g 5f³ 5m 5m² 5m Jul 4] €9,000Y: close-coupled, useful-
looking colt: first foal: dam 2-y-o 6f winner: modest maiden: likely to prove best at 5f:
acts on firm going: looked none too keen final start. *D. Carroll*

ELLOVAMUL 3 b.f. Elmaamul (USA) 125 – Multi-Sofft 30 (Northern State (USA) 62
91) [2003 54: 9.3m⁴ 10m 9.9d f12g⁶ 10m⁎ 11.5g⁎ 10.2m⁵ f11s⁴ 11.9f⁵ Oct 17] small,
workmanlike filly: modest performer: won apprentice selling handicap at Ripon in

325

August and claimer at Yarmouth (took good hold/edged right) in September: should stay 1½m: acts on fibresand and good to firm ground: tried blinkered at 2 yrs. *W. M. Brisbourne*

ELLWAY HEIGHTS   6 b.g. Shirley Heights 130 – Amina 80 (Brigadier Gerard 144)   **61**
[2003 –: 14.1d 12.1g* 11.9m* 12m* 12m 12m² 11.9f Oct 9] angular gelding: modest handicapper: won at Hamilton (apprentices), Carlisle and Goodwood (amateurs) in September: should stay 1¾m: acts on firm ground: saddle slipped fifth start. *W. M. Brisbourne*

EL MAGNIFICO   2 b.g. (Apr 30) Forzando 122 – Princess Poquito (Hard Fought 125)   **53**
[2003 7.1m p6g f6g⁶ Oct 16] 10,000Y: workmanlike gelding: closely related to 4-y-o Queensberry and half-brother to several winners, including 1990 2-y-o 1m winner Magic Box (by Magic Ring): dam unraced: modest form in maidens: best effort second start: should stay at least 7f. *P. D. Cundell*

EL MISTI   4 b.f. Elmaamul (USA) 125 – Sherrington 56 (Thatching 131) [2003 47d: **– §**
f6g f5g⁶ f5s⁶ Feb 17] quite good-topped filly: untrustworthy maiden: tried blinkered/in cheekpieces. *K. R. Burke*

ELOQUENT SILENCE   3 ch.f. Nashwan (USA) 135 – Flower Girl 108 (Pharly (FR)   **64**
130) [2003 72p: 10m 10m⁵ 12.1m Jun 11] big, quite good-topped filly: fair performer at 2 yrs: only modest form in handicaps in 2003: best form at 1m: acts on polytrack, unraced on extremes of going on turf. *B. W. Hills*

EL PALMAR   2 b.g. (Apr 23) Case Law 113 – Aybeegirl 66 (Mazilier (USA) 107)   **65**
[2003 5m⁶ 5m² Aug 4] 2,500Y: second foal: dam 2-y-o 5f winner: better effort in maidens (fair form) when staying-on second of 9 at Carlisle: should stay 6f. *T. D. Barron*

EL PEDRO   4 b.g. Piccolo 121 – Standard Rose 52 (Ile de Bourbon (USA) 133) [2003   **57 d**
51, a65: f8.5g⁵ f12g⁵ 12g 11m² 11.7m³ 10m 10d 10.1g 10.2g³ 10.2m 10.3g³ 8.1m 11.6m*   **a63 d**
10.2m 12d⁵ 10.2g⁴ 10.1m⁵ 11.7f⁵ 10.9m⁶ 9.7g 10f⁵ 10m⁴ f9.4g f8g f12g⁵ Dec 26] tall gelding: modest performer: won seller at Windsor in July: left M. Channon after twenty-first start: stays easy 1½m: acts on firm going, good to soft and fibresand: sometimes visored: has dropped away tamely. *N. E. Berry*

EL RAYMONDO   4 b.g. Night Shift (USA) – Alaraby (IRE) 77 (Caerleon (USA)   **55**
132) [2003 58: p7g p8g² p7g f8.5g p7g⁶ 8.3g Apr 7] modest performer: stays 1m: acts on polytrack: sometimes blinkered. *M. Blanshard*

ELSHADI (IRE)   2 b.c. (Mar 26) Cape Cross (IRE) 129 – Rispoto 58 (Mtoto 134) [2003   **98**
8.5m* 8m* 8g⁴ Oct 11] 130,000Y: quite good-topped colt: fluent mover: half-brother to several winners, including 4-y-o Highdown and 3-y-o All Embracing: dam, 1½m winner, half-sister to smart performer up 1¾m Jahafil: useful form: won maiden at Beverley (wandered) in August and minor event at Newbury (beat Let The Lion Roar by 2½ lengths, making all) in September: ran as though amiss final start: should be suited by 1¼m/1½m: blinkered all starts. *M. P. Tregoning*

ELSIE B   3 gr.f. First Trump 118 – Evening Falls 82 (Beveled (USA)) [2003 –: f7g f8g   **–**
Jan 28] small filly: little sign of ability. *P. Howling*

ELSINORA   2 b.f. (Apr 16) Great Dane (IRE) 122 – Deanta In Eirinn (Red Sunset 120)   **57**
[2003 6m 5.7m³ 6.1m 6m Oct 16] workmanlike filly: half-sister to numerous winners, including 1997 Irish 2-y-o 5f winner Welcome Sunset (by Most Welcome) and 2000 2-y-o 5f winner Flowing Rio (by First Trump): dam ran once at 2 yrs: modest maiden: likely to stay 7f. *H. Morrison*

ELUCIDATE   4 ch.f. Elmaamul (USA) 125 – Speed To Lead (IRE) 90 (Darshaan 133)   **–**
[2003: f8s p7g f9.4s f8.5g 11m 7m⁶ 10g 8m Jun 2] tall, angular filly: modest at best: well held in 2003. *C. R. Dore*

ELUSIVE CITY (USA)   3 b.c. Elusive Quality (USA) – Star of Paris (USA) (Dayjur   **101**
(USA) 137) [2003 117: 7m⁵ 8g 5f⁶ Jun 17] strong, compact, attractive colt: smart performer at 2 yrs, winner of Prix Morny at Deauville and third in Middle Park Stakes at Newmarket (reportedly returned with sore shins): just useful form in 2003, back to suitable trip when only sixth to Choisir in King's Stand Stakes at Royal Ascot final start (tongue tied and sweating, carried head awkwardly): likely to prove best at 5f/6f (pulled hard in Poule d'Essai des Poulains at 1m): acts on polytrack, raced only on good or firmer going on turf: proved troublesome in preliminaries at 2 yrs: sent to USA, joined R. Mandella. *G. A. Butler*

ELUSIVE DREAM   2 b.c. (Mar 23) Rainbow Quest (USA) 134 – Dance A Dream   **58 p**
115 (Sadler's Wells (USA) 132) [2003 7s 8.2d f7g p10g Nov 29] rangy, useful-looking colt: has scope: third reported foal: dam, 1m (at 2 yrs) and 11.4f winner who was second

in Oaks, sister to 2000 Guineas winner Entrepreneur and half-sister to Coronation Stakes winner Exclusive: modest form in maidens: will be suited by 1¼m+: should do better at 3 yrs. *Sir Mark Prescott*

ELUSIVE KITTY (USA) 2 b.f. (Jan 18) Elusive Quality (USA) – Al Fahda 93 (Be **69** My Chief (USA) 122) [2003 6m⁵ p8g² p6g⁵ p7g⁵ Dec 29] 20,000Y: smallish, lightly-made filly: first foal: dam 6f (at 2 yrs) to 1m winner: fair maiden: second at Lingfield: stays 1m. *G. A. Butler*

ELVINA 2 b.f. (Apr 15) Mark of Esteem (IRE) 137 – Pharaoh's Joy 66 (Robellino **43 p** (USA) 127) [2003 f5g⁴ Dec 15] third foal: dam, 5f/6f winner (latter at 2 yrs), out of half-sister to very smart stayer Band: well backed, 8½ lengths fourth to Scottish Exile in maiden at Southwell, not unduly punished: should improve. *A. G. Newcombe*

ELVINGTON BOY 6 ch.g. Emarati (USA) 74 – Catherines Well 99 (Junius (USA) **72** 124) [2003 92: 5f⁶ 5g 5m 5m Sep 18] quite good-topped gelding: only fair form in 2003: effective at 5f/easy 6f: acts on firm going, possibly not on soft: tried visored/tongue tied: normally fast starter. *M. W. Easterby*

EMARADIA 2 ch.f. (Apr 14) Emarati (USA) 74 – Rewardia (IRE) 66 (Petardia 113) **55 §** [2003 5g f5g³ f5g f5s² 5.1m⁴ 5m⁵ 5.1f² 5m* 5.1m⁴ f5g² 5m 6m⁵ 5g⁶ f5g² f6g³ p6g⁴ f5g⁵ f5g⁴ f6g² f6g² Dec 26] 1,200Y: leggy, good-topped filly: second foal: dam, maiden, probably stayed 1¼m: modest performer: won claimer at Folkestone in July: mostly creditable efforts after: effective at 5f/6f: acts on all-weather and firm going: effective visored/blinkered or not: sometimes gives trouble at start (has bolted and been with-drawn): races prominently: sometimes wanders: ungenuine. *P. D. Evans*

EMARATI'S IMAGE 5 b.g. Emarati (USA) 74 – Choir's Image 53 (Lochnager 132) **–** [2003 46: f6s³ 5.1g f5g⁴ 5.1s 7f f6g Jun 19] big, good-topped gelding: modest performer **a53** on all-weather: best at 5f/6f: acts on soft going and fibresand: sold 2,000 gns. *J. O'Reilly*

EMBASSY LORD 2 b.g. (Feb 1) Mind Games 121 – Keen Melody (USA) 60 (Sharpen **64** Up 127) [2003 6.1d 6g⁶ f6s⁵ 6m⁴ 7f⁶ 6g² f6g² 6f* 7m⁵ f6s f6g Nov 10] 11,000Y: leggy gelding: seventh living foal: half-brother to 9-y-o Mutasawwar and 1995 2-y-o 7f winner Rock Sharp (by Rock City): dam, maiden, stayed 1m: modest performer: made all in claimer at Yarmouth in August: left B. Meehan 6,800 gns after tenth start: will prove best at 5f/6f: acts on firm ground and fibresand: blinkered last 7 outings: free-going sort: sometimes hangs/finds little. *J. O'Reilly*

EMBASSY SWEETS (USA) 2 b.f. (Apr 16) Affirmed (USA) – Leaveemlaughing **–** (USA) (Dynaformer (USA)) [2003 p6g p8g Dec 10] $45,000Y: first foal: dam US 7f (at 2 yrs) to 8.5f winner: well held in minor event/maiden at Lingfield. *F. I. Cole*

EMBER DAYS 4 gr.f. Reprimand 122 – Evening Falls 82 (Beveled (USA)) [2003 **?** 76: 8g p8g⁵ p10g⁵ p10g² p10g² Dec 17] tall, unfurnished filly: modest handicapper on **a63** all-weather: stays easy 1¼m: acts on polytrack and soft going. *J. L. Spearing*

EMERALD FIRE 4 b.f. Pivotal 124 – Four-Legged Friend 101 (Aragon 118) [2003 **83** 86: p6g* p7g 6d⁶ 7.1m 6m³ 6d p6g p6g p6g⁵ Dec 6] small, leggy filly: fairly useful handicapper: won at Lingfield in March: effective at 5f (given test)/6f: acts on polytrack, good to firm and heavy going: visored last 2 starts. *A. M. Balding*

EMERALD MIST (IRE) 4 b.f. Sacrament 118 – Jade's Gem (Sulaafah (USA) 119) **–** [2003 –: 12m 16.2m Jun 16] smallish, good-topped filly: little form: tried visored. *G. B. Balding*

EMERALD SPIRIT (IRE) 2 br.f. (Feb 9) Key of Luck (USA) 126 – Watch Me **–** (IRE) 106 (Green Desert (USA) 127) [2003 5m Jul 14] third foal: half-sister to fairly useful Irish 2001 2-y-o 5f winner Church Cross (by Cadeaux Genereux): dam 6f winner: 16/1 and backward, well held in maiden at Windsor: sold 2,000 gns, sent to Serbia. *M. R. Channon*

EMERGING STAR (IRE) 3 b.g. Desert Style (IRE) 121 – Feather Star (Soviet Star **78** (USA) 128) [2003 74: 10.3g 10m³ 12.3m 9.9d⁵ 10m 10m* 10.1m 10m Oct 4] leggy, quite good-topped gelding: fair performer: left Mrs J. Ramsden after third start: won 4-runner minor event at Ripon (idled markedly) in June: stays 1¼m: acts on good to firm and good to soft going: wore cheekpieces last 3 starts. *G. M. Moore*

EMHALA (IRE) 2 ch.f. (Apr 4) Docksider (USA) 124 – Adarika (Kings Lake (USA) **–** 133) [2003 f6g Jun 9] €6,000Y: half-sister to several winners, including 6-y-o King's Mill and smart 9f Prix Chloe winner Adaiyka (by Doyoun): dam unraced: 25/1, tailed off in maiden at Southwell. *P. A. Blockley*

EMIGRATE 4 b.f. Emarati (USA) 74 – Fly South (Polar Falcon (USA) 126) [2003 65d: f7s³ p6g f5s⁴ f5s⁴ 5.1m Aug 5] angular filly: poor maiden nowadays: may prove best around 6f: acts on fibresand, little form on turf: visored/tongue tied final start. *P. J. Makin*   **– a47**

EMILY DEE 4 b.f. Classic Cliche (IRE) 128 – Alpi Dora (Valiyar 129) [2003 –: 6.1g 6m 10.2g² 12.1m³ 9.9m Aug 23] quite good-topped filly: poor maiden nowadays: should stay 1½m: tried blinkered/in cheekpieces. *J. M. Bradley*   **41**

EMILYS DAWN 2 b.f. (Apr 15) Komaite (USA) – Spice And Sugar 65 (Chilibang 120) [2003 p6g p8g p6g⁶ f7g Dec 12] 4,000Y: fourth foal: dam 6f (at 2 yrs) and 1½m winner: form in maidens (modest) only when sixth at Lingfield: twice slowly away. *D. K. Ivory*   **54**

EMINENT AURA (USA) 2 ch.f. (Feb 21) Charismatic (USA) 127 – Perfectly Clear (USA) (Woodman (USA) 126) [2003 5f 5m Apr 23] strong filly: first foal: dam 1m to 9f winner in USA: last in claimer/seller. *A. Dickman*   **–**

E MINOR (IRE) 4 b.f. Blushing Flame (USA) 109 – Watch The Clock 93 (Mtoto 134) [2003 78, a86: 15m³ 14.1g 14v 16.2m⁴ 14.6m⁵ 15m 16.2m⁴ 16m⁴ 16f 16m f16.2g⁶ Nov 17] rather leggy, lengthy filly: fair handicapper, below form after reappearance, including on fibresand debut: stays 2m: acts on polytrack (quite useful form on surface at 3 yrs), good to firm and good to soft going: usually held up. *T. Wall*   **77 d a59**

EMMEFFAICH (IRE) 2 ch.f. (Apr 6) Foxhound (USA) 103 – Shalstayholy (IRE) 84 (Shalford (IRE) 124§) [2003 7m 7m⁴ 7f⁵ 7.5m⁴ f8s 8.3g Oct 13] £900Y: smallish, compact filly: second foal: dam 5f to 7f winner: modest maiden: well beaten last 2 starts: should stay 1m: acts on firm going. *J. G. Portman*   **54**

EMMERVALE 4 b.f. Emarati (USA) 74 – Raintree Venture (Good Times (ITY)) [2003 62: 7m f7g 5.3m⁵ 6m 6f* 6f 6m³ 7f⁶ 7d* 6m f8s Oct 21] angular, unfurnished filly: modest handicapper: won at Brighton (NH jockeys maiden event) in July and Catterick in September: stays easy 7f: acts on firm and soft going (yet to race on heavy): visored last 9 starts: often races prominently. *R. M. H. Cowell*   **59**

EMPEROR CAT (IRE) 2 b.g. (Mar 28) Desert Story (IRE) 115 – Catfoot Lane 50 (Batshoof 122) [2003 5.1m 5m 6g⁵ 7m⁶ 6m³ 5m⁴ 5m⁴ 5.1m³ 6m⁶ 5f* 6f⁶ 6m f5g* 5.1f 7m⁵ Oct 18] IR 5,000F, 5,000Y: close-coupled gelding: second foal: dam 1m seller winner: modest performer: won sellers at Musselburgh in August and Wolverhampton in October: probably best at 5f/easy 6f: acts on fibresand and firm going: blinkered second to fourth outings: none too consistent. *P. A. Blockley*   **60**

EMPERORS LOT 3 b.f. Emperor Jones (USA) 119 – Westering 54 (Auction Ring (USA) 123) [2003 –: 8g 8m 8.1m f8.5g Jul 11] workmanlike filly: little sign of ability. *M. Wellings*   **–**

EMPEROR STAR 3 b.f. Emperor Jones (USA) 119 – Blu Tamantara (USA) (Miswaki (USA) 124) [2003 67: p8g p10g f7g² f8.5s⁵ 7m 10g 10s⁶ Sep 7] leggy, quite good-topped filly: modest maiden: sold from T. Mills 6,500 gns after fifth start: effective at 7f/1m: acts on all-weather. *C. Alonso, Spain*   **62**

EMPEROR'S WELL 4 ch.g. First Trump 118 – Catherines Well 99 (Junius (USA) 124) [2003 48: 6m 7.5m 8d 8.5m² 8m 10f⁴ 8m* 9.9d⁴ f8g⁶ Oct 16] well-made gelding: modest performer: won selling handicap at Pontefract in September: likely to prove best around 1m: acts on good to firm going and probably fibresand: visored final 3-y-o start, blinkered last 6 outings: sometimes slowly away: hung markedly right final start: races prominently. *M. W. Easterby*   **64**

EMPIRE PARK 8 b.g. Tragic Role (USA) – Millaine 69 (Formidable (USA) 125) [2003 60: 21.6m Apr 14] leggy, workmanlike gelding: one-time fair performer, lightly raced on Flat in recent seasons/well held in cheekpieces only Flat outing in 2003: probably stayed 1¾m: acted on good to firm going, probably on soft: was sometimes blinkered: dead. *C. R. Egerton*   **–**

EMPRESS JOSEPHINE 3 b.f. Emperor Jones (USA) 119 – Valmaranda (USA) (Sir Ivor 135) [2003 55: p7g p5g⁴ 5m 5m 6.1m f5g* f5s² f5g⁴ f6g² f5g⁴ Dec 12] modest handicapper: won at Southwell in June: probably best at 5f: acts on fibresand: visored last 5 outings. *J. R. Jenkins*   **60**

EMRAN (USA) 3 b.c. Silver Hawk (USA) 123 – Indihash (USA) 81 (Gulch (USA)) [2003 88p: 11m⁶ 8m* 8m 10m Jul 9] rather lengthy, good-topped colt: useful handicapper: clearly best effort when winning at Newmarket in May by 1¼ lengths from Star Sensation: better at 1m than further: acts on soft and good to firm going: sent to UAE, joined M. Al Muhairi. *E. A. L. Dunlop*   **99**

EMTEE 3 b.g. Hector Protector (USA) 124 – Moneefa 73 (Darshaan 133) [2003 8g 8g May 26] quite good-topped gelding: fourth foal: half-brother to 5-y-o Dandoun and 4-y-o Zyzania: dam 1¼m winner: well held in maidens at Newbury and Leicester: bandaged fore joints. *J. L. Dunlop* —

EMTEYAZ 5 b.h. Mark of Esteem (IRE) 137 – Najmat Alshemaal (IRE) 98 (Dancing Brave (USA) 140) [2003 a10f* a10f³ a8f⁴ a10f* 16g 8m 10.5m a10f⁴ 11g⁶ Dec 21] strong, close-coupled horse: left A. Stewart in 2001: has since won 5 races in UAE (also disqualified once) and vastly improved in 2003 (useful form): successful in handicaps at Nad Al Sheba in January and March, latter a prestige event by ¼ length from Elghani: off 4 months, ran creditably on same course penultimate start: showed little in Britain sixth/seventh (raced freely) outings: has won at 1½m, seems best at 1¼m nowadays: acts on good to firm going and dirt: blinkered. *A. Smith, UAE* **89 a101**

EMTILAAK 2 b.c. (Mar 23) Marju (IRE) 127 – Just A Mirage 76 (Green Desert (USA) 127) [2003 7m 6m² 6m³ Oct 16] big, good-topped colt: has scope: has a quick action: brother to 6-y-o Sawwaah and half-brother to 7f winners Kahal (very smart) and Doomna (useful), both by Machiavellian: dam maiden who stayed 1m: fairly useful form in maidens at Newmarket: placed behind Mahmoom and Phantom Wind: free-going sort, likely to prove best at 5f/6f. *B. Hanbury* **81**

ENCHANTED 4 b.f. Magic Ring (IRE) 115 – Snugfit Annie 49 (Midyan (USA) 124) [2003 7m³ 6g⁶ 6f 7m 7g 6m⁶ 8f 7m⁴ 6m⁶ 7f³ Oct 27] quite good-topped filly: useful performer: some creditably efforts in 2003, including when sixth in listed events at Windsor (to Demonstrate) and Newmarket (to Frizzante) on second/penultimate starts, and when fourth in handicap at Newmarket eighth outing: effective at 6f/7f: raced only on good going or firmer: tongue tied first 5 outings in 2003: usually waited with: has run creditably when sweating. *G. G. Margarson* **96**

ENCHANTED PRINCESS 3 b.f. Royal Applause 124 – Hawayah (IRE) 68 (Shareef Dancer (USA) 135) [2003 7m 8.3m* Jul 28] 84,000Y: well-made filly: sister to useful 7f/1m winner Bishr and half-sister to 3 winners, including 1½m winner Showpiece (by Selkirk): dam 2-y-o 7f winner out of Nell Gwyn winner Ghariba, herself half-sister to smart performer up to 2m Braashee: fair form: won maiden at Windsor in July by ¾ length from Photofit, all out: stays 1m. *J. H. M. Gosden* **73**

ENCHANTMENT 2 b.f. (Apr 22) Compton Place 125 – Tharwa (IRE) 63 (Last Tycoon 131) [2003 5m 5m* 5m⁶ 6.5m 6m* Oct 24] 4,000Y: third foal: half-sister to fairly useful 6f/7f winner Nisr (by Grand Lodge): dam, 5f (at 2 yrs)/6f winner, half-sister to dam of very smart 7f to 9f winner Bin Rosie: fairly useful performer: won maiden at Carlisle (made all) in September and sales race at Doncaster (beat Dispol Katie a short head, clear on far side most of way) in October: will prove best at 5f/6f. *I. A. Wood* **88**

ENCORE ROYALE 3 b.f. Royal Applause 124 – Verbena (IRE) (Don't Forget Me 127) [2003 56p: 7m⁵ 7g 7m 8f² 8g⁵ 10d 10.2g 8m Sep 18] medium-sized, quite attractive filly: modest maiden handicapper: stays 1m: acts on firm ground: very slowly away final outing: free-going sort: sold 4,000 gns. *P. W. Harris* **63**

ENCOUNTER 7 br.g. Primo Dominie 121 – Dancing Spirit (IRE) 72 (Ahonoora 122) [2003 61, a–: 7m⁴ 8m⁵ 7.1d 8m* 7g⁶ 8m 8.3g 8m³ 7.5m⁵ 7m 9.2g² 8d⁴ 8.1m 9.2m² 10g⁴ 10.4m 8.5m⁶ 8.2f⁵ 10.1m 8.2m Oct 22] lengthy gelding: modest handicapper: won at Redcar in May: effective at 7f to easy 1¼m: probably acts on any turf going, little form on fibresand: sometimes slowly away: usually held up. *J. Hetherton* **60 a–**

ENDLESS HALL 7 b.h. Saddlers' Hall (IRE) 126 – Endless Joy 90 (Law Society (USA) 130) [2003 10g 9.9m³ May 22] strong, medium-sized horse: had a quick action: high-class performer at best, successful in Gran Premio di Milano in 2000 and Singapore Airlines International Cup at Kranji in 2001: missed 2002 (reportedly had suspensory/sesamoid problem): better effort in 2003 (just useful form) when 3 lengths third to Island House in listed race at Goodwood: stays 1¼m/1½m: acts on soft going, but best on firmer than good: usually front runner: to stand at Razza Ascagnano, Italy, fee €3,500. *L. M. Cumani* **106 ?**

ENDLESS SUMMER 5 b.g. Zafonic (USA) 130 – Well Away (IRE) (Sadler's Wells (USA) 132) [2003 6g⁵ 6g 6f 6m⁴ 5.6d 6f 5d⁴ Nov 4] small, sturdy, attractive gelding: good walker: smart performer for J. Gosden at 2 yrs: missed 2001 and below best in 2 optional claimers in USA in 2002 for R. Frankel: fairly useful on balance of form in 2003: free-going sort, and is probably best at 6f: acts on firm and good to soft going: has carried head awkwardly: broke blood vessel third/sixth starts. *K. A. Ryan* **100 d**

ENFORD PRINCESS 2 b.f. (Mar 10) Pivotal 124 – Expectation (IRE) 59 (Night Shift (USA)) [2003 6g* 6g* 6m 6.5m Sep 26] 30,000Y: well-made filly: third foal: half- **86**

sister to 3-y-o Polly Plunkett: dam, sprint maiden, granddaughter of Irish 1000 Guineas winner Front Row: fairly useful performer: won maiden at Newmarket and minor event at Windsor in May: below form in listed race at Newmarket and sales race at Ascot: should stay 7f. *R. Hannon*

ENGLISH ROCKET (IRE) 2 b.c. (Jan 31) Indian Rocket 115 – Golden Charm (IRE) 63 (Common Grounds 118) [2003 6m f6g² 7g⁵ f6g³ 7g² 7d³ Nov 8] 10,000Y: first foal: dam, 2-y-o 6f winner, half-sister to useful Italian/US performer up to 11f Clefairy: fair maiden: placed 4 times, including in nurseries: should stay 1m: acts on fibresand and good to soft going. *D. J. S. ffrench Davis*   **75**

ENGULFED (USA) 3 b.f. Gulch (USA) – Storm Dove (USA) 108 (Storm Bird (CAN) 134) [2003 72: p8g Feb 1] fair form when third in maiden (slowly away) on debut at 2 yrs: found little both starts since. *W. Jarvis*   **–**

ENJOY THE BUZZ 4 b.c. Prince of Birds (USA) 121 – Abaklea (IRE) (Doyoun 124) [2003 –: f6g f6g 6m² f5g Nov 28] small, sturdy colt: left J. Pickering and off 9 months, only form (poor) when second in maiden at Redcar: stays 6f: acts on good to firm ground. *J. M. Bradley*   **47**

ENRAPTURE (USA) 2 b.f. (Feb 22) Lear Fan (USA) 130 – Cheviot Hills (USA) (Gulch (USA)) [2003 7m⁵ Aug 16] sturdy filly: first foal: dam, French 9f/1¼m winner, half-sister to smart British/US performer up to 8.5f Fantastic Fellow (by Lear Fan) out of half-sister to Henbit: 12/1, fifth of 12 to Red Bloom in maiden at Newmarket, looking and running as if in need of race: should stay at least 1m: will do better. *Mrs A. J. Perrett*   **80 p**

ENSEMBLE 3 b.g. Polish Precedent (USA) 131 – Full Orchestra 83 (Shirley Heights 130) [2003 –: 12.1m 12.1m Jun 11] strong, useful-looking gelding: of no account: tried blinkered. *M. W. Easterby*   **–**

ENTRAP (USA) 4 b.f. Phone Trick (USA) – Mystic Lure 70 (Green Desert (USA) 127) [2003 106: 7m² 6m³ 6m Jul 11] big, rangy filly: useful performer at 3 yrs: suffered injury to near-hind ankle and off nearly a year: respectable efforts in listed races at Lingfield (second to Presto Vento) and Haydock (third to Topkamp) first 2 starts in 2003: sweating, found little in Summer Stakes at York final outing: best form at 6f: raced only on good going or firmer: wore crossed noseband last 2 outings: has raced freely. *W. J. Haggas*   **98**

ENVIRONMENTALIST 4 b.c. Danehill (USA) 126 – Way O'Gold (USA) (Slew O' Gold (USA)) [2003 72: 8g 8.3m 8m⁶ Sep 22] quite good-topped colt: has a quick action: fair maiden at 3 yrs: soundly beaten in 2003 (reportedly had breathing problem penultimate start): should stay 1¼m. *M. A. Jarvis*   **–**

ENVIRONMENT AUDIT 4 ch.g. Kris 135 – Bold And Beautiful 105 (Bold Lad (IRE) 133) [2003 84: p12g Feb 8] rather leggy gelding: fairly useful at 3 yrs: well held on return to Flat: effective at 1¼m/1½m: acts on firm and good to soft going. *J. R. Jenkins*   **–**

EOZ (IRE) 3 b.f. Sadler's Wells (USA) 132 – Greek Moon (IRE) (Shirley Heights 130) [2003 68p: 9d² p12g⁴ p12g² f12g* 10.5d f12g² p12g Oct 27] good-bodied filly: fairly useful handicapper: won at Wolverhampton in August: good second there penultimate start: should stay 1¾m: acts on all-weather, raced only on good/good to soft ground on turf. *M. A. Jarvis*   **86**

EPALO (GER) 4 b.c. Lando (GER) 128 – Evening Kiss (Kris 135) [2003 11g² 10d* 11g* 11g² 10g² 12g² Sep 13] closely related to 2 winners in Germany by Acatenango, including useful stayer Evening Storm, and half-brother to useful German 1¼m/1½m performer Evening Breeze (by Surumu): dam, French 1m to 10.5f winner, half-sister to very smart French 1m/1¼m performer Splendid Moment: smart performer: improved at 4 yrs, winning listed race at Munich (by 8 lengths) in May and Grosser Mercedes-Benz-Preis at Baden-Baden (made all, beat Salve Regina 3½ lengths) in June: runner-up all other starts, in Grosser Preis der Bremer Wirtschaft at Cologne (went down by 1¼ lengths to Aolus), Hansa-Preis at Hamburg (beaten length by Aolus), Grosser Dallmayr-Preis at Munich (dead-heated, 1¼ lengths behind Ransom o'War) and Bosphorus Cup at Veliefendi (beaten length by Grand Ekinoks): has won at 1¾m but best form at 1¼m/1½m: acts on dirt and good to soft ground (well beaten on heavy). *A. Schutz, Germany*   **117**

EPAMINONDAS (USA) 2 ch.c. (May 15) Miswaki (USA) 124 – Nora Nova (USA) (Green Dancer (USA) 132) [2003 6g 6g⁵ 7g³ Nov 1] $30,000F, €110,000Y: sturdy colt: fourth foal: half-brother to winner in USA by Runaway Groom: dam, 1m winner in USA, sister to smart French/US 1m performer Bistro Garden: easily best effort in maidens (fairly useful form) when ½-length third of 13 to Hezaam at Newmarket, always up with pace and carried right near finish: will probably stay 1m. *R. Hannon*   **82**

EPHESUS 3 b.c. Efisio 120 – Composition 82 (Wolfhound (USA) 126) [2003 75p: p7g⁵ p8g* p10g* p10g³ f8.5s² f9.4g² 9.9g f7g* 8g³ 7g³ f7s Sep 6] fairly useful performer: **90**

won maiden and handicap (then left J. Noseda 25,000 gns) at Lingfield in January and handicap at Wolverhampton in June: said to have pulled muscles in back final start: effective at 7f to 1¼m: acts on all-weather, raced only on good ground on turf: usually visored, tried in cheekpieces. *Miss Gay Kelleway*

EQUUS (IRE)   2 b.c. (Mar 25) Desert Style (IRE) 121 – Iolanta (IRE) 77 (Danehill   **69** (USA) 126) [2003 8.1m⁵ 8m p8g Oct 27] IR 5,000F, 20,000Y: well-made colt: third foal: dam, second at 7f (at 2 yrs) to 8.5f, out of half-sister to smart 1995 2-y-o 6f winner Kahir Almaydan: easily best effort in maidens (fair form) when fifth at Sandown: not sure to stay beyond 1m: soon off bridle: sold 1,800 gns. *R. Hannon*

ERMINE GREY   2 gr.g. (Mar 13) Wolfhound (USA) 126 – Impulsive Decision (IRE)   **70** 71 (Nomination 125) [2003 f6g 6m⁶ 7m⁵ f8s* 6g f7g* f7g⁶ Nov 28] 20,000Y: rather leggy   **a82** gelding: second foal: dam 6f (at 2 yrs) and 1m winner: fairly useful on all-weather, fair on turf: won maiden at Southwell in September and nursery at Wolverhampton in November: stays 1m: acts on fibresand, best turf effort on good to firm going: blinkered/visored last 4 starts. *D. Haydn Jones*

ERRACHT   5 gr.m. Emarati (USA) 74 – Port Na Blath (On Your Mark 125) [2003 64,   **73** a54: f5g p5g³ f5g* f5s f5g* f5g 5m* 5m 5m 5.3m⁵ 5g⁴ 5.7f³ 5.3m⁵ 5m³ 5.1m* 5.1m³   **a62** 5.3m⁶ 5.3f² 5.3f f5g³ f5s Dec 31] lengthy mare: fair on turf, modest on all-weather: won sellers at Wolverhampton (2), handicap at Musselburgh and claimer at Bath: effective at 5f/6f: acts on any turf going and all-weather: often forces pace: sometimes carries head awkwardly: consistent. *K. R. Burke*

ERROL   4 ch.g. Dancing Spree (USA) – Primo Panache (Primo Dominie 121) [2003   **41 d** f9.4s⁴ f8.5s f11g f8g 10m 11.9m 12.3m 14.1d 15.8m Aug 5] sturdy gelding: second foal: dam no form: poor maiden. *J. F. Coupland*

ERSAAL (USA)   3 ch.g. Gulch (USA) – Madame Secretary (USA) (Secretariat (USA))   **60** [2003 70: 10m f12s⁶ f12g⁵ 16m f12g³ f8g f11g f12s Dec 27] good-topped gelding: just modest maiden at 3 yrs, leaving E. Dunlop 8,000 gns after reappearance: stays easy 1½m: raced only on fibresand and good/good to firm ground: blinkered (well held) final start. *J. Jay*

ERTE   2 ch.g. (Jan 24) Vettori (IRE) 119 – Cragreen (Green Desert (USA) 127) [2003   **68** 7m⁴ 8.1g 7.2f³ 7.1m⁴ 6m 7f⁶ Oct 12] 65,000Y: leggy, useful-looking gelding: first foal: dam, Italian 2-y-o 7f winner, out of Italian Group 2 7f winner Croda Alta: fair maiden: third at Ayr: stays 7f: acts on firm going: none too consistent. *M. R. Channon*

ERUPT   10 b.g. Beveled (USA) – Sparklingsovereign 53 (Sparkler 130) [2003 56§,   **56 §** a–§: 10.1d³ 10.1m 8g 10.1m 12.1d 9.1d⁶ 11g Oct 28] plain, leggy gelding: moderate   **a– §** performer: below form after reappearance: stays 1¼m: acts on any going: tried blinkered/ visored/tongue tied: sometimes slowly away: moody. *M. Brittain*

ESATTO   4 b.g. Puissance 110 – Stoneydale 83 (Tickled Pink 114) [2003 90: 5f 7g 6d   **83** 7.1m⁶ 5.5f 7.1m 5.3m* 5m² 5d 6g⁵ 5f 5.3f⁶ 6m³ f6g⁵ Nov 17] big, quite good-topped gelding: fairly useful handicapper on turf, fair on all-weather: won at Brighton (for second successive year) in August: acts on firm going, soft and all-weather: tried in headgear: usually tongue tied: sometimes slowly away: has edged right. *P. A. Blockley*

ESCALADE   6 b.g. Green Desert (USA) 127 – Sans Escale (USA) (Diesis 133) [2003   **66** 76, a63: f11g³ f11g f11g 10.3m⁵ 10.1m² 10m 9.2g³ 10m 9.2m 10f⁴ 10m² 10m 10m 9g⁴ f9.4g⁵   **a61** p10g Dec 20] small, compact gelding: fair handicapper on turf, modest on all-weather: effective at 8.5f to 11f: acts on any turf going: tried in cheekpieces: often races freely: sometimes finds little/wanders, and usually held up. *W. M. Brisbourne*

ESCAYOLA (IRE)   3 b.g. Revoque (IRE) 122 – First Fling (IRE) 63 (Last Tycoon   **99 p** 131) [2003 62: f8.5g⁵ 12g 16.2g* 14.1m* 17.5m* 16.1m² 16f* 16g* Nov 5] good-topped gelding: useful handicapper: progressed extremely well in 2003, winning at Chepstow in August, Yarmouth and Ayr in September, Goodwood (NH jockeys race) in October and (having been sold for 105,000 gns) Musselburgh (beat Overstrand readily by 3 lengths) in November: stays 17.5f: acts on firm ground, showed promise on soft on debut: visored/ blinkered last 6 starts: sometimes races freely: tends to hang left: usually waited with: likely to improve further. *W. J. Haggas*

ESENIN   4 b.g. Danehill (USA) 126 – Boojum 101 (Mujtahid (USA) 118) [2003 79§:   **– §** p7g 6m f7g 11.9m 10g May 26] strong, lengthy gelding: one-time fairly useful 6f winner: has become most disappointing: tried blinkered/visored. *D. G. Bridgwater*

ESPADA (IRE)   7 b.g. Mukaddamah (USA) 125 – Folk Song (CAN) (The Minstrel   **92 d** (CAN) 135) [2003 94: p7g⁶ 8.3g* 7g 7.6m p8g p7g² Dec 17] smallish, strong gelding: fairly useful performer: easily best effort in 2003 when winning minor event at Windsor in April: reportedly suffered injury and off 7 months before last 2 starts: effective at 6f (given test) to 1m: acts on any turf going, probably on polytrack: visored once: has raced freely/hung left/found little: often makes running. *J. A. Osborne*

ESPERANCE (IRE) 3 ch.g. Bluebird (USA) 125 – Dioscorea (IRE) (Pharly (FR) 130) **68** [2003 73: 7g 7d 11.8m 11.1g² 10g p10g⁴ p13g p10g p10g p13g Dec 29] good-topped gelding: fair maiden: left M. Tompkins after fifth start: takes good hold, but stays 11f: acts on soft ground and polytrack: tried in cheekpieces. *J. Akehurst*

ESPLANADE 3 b.f. Danehill (USA) 126 – Atropa (USA) 84 (Vaguely Noble 140) **77** [2003 8m³ 10d² 10g³ 10.2f* 8.9f Oct 11] lengthy filly: sister to useful French/US 6f (at 2 yrs)/1m winner Kithira and half-sister to smart French 1¼m/1½m winner Tenuous (by Generous) and useful French performer up to 15f Welsh Run (by Caerleon): dam maiden who stayed 1½m: fair performer: landed odds in 4-runner maiden at Bath in September: raced too freely in handicap final start: stayed 1¼m: acted on firm and good to soft going: stud. *Sir Michael Stoute*

ESPRESSO TIME (IRE) 3 b.g. Danetime (IRE) 121 – Cappuchino (IRE) 59 (Roi **73** Danzig (USA)) [2003 70d: 6g³ 7m² 6m³ 7g⁶ 7f⁵ f6s⁴ p7g f7s³ f6s⁵ Oct 7] leggy, quite **a62** good-topped gelding: fair maiden: stays 7f: acts on good to firm ground, soft and fibresand: sold 12,500 gns. *S. L. Keightley*

ESSAY BABY (FR) 3 b.f. Saumarez 132 – Easter Baby (Derrylin 115) [2003 57: f12g **55** 8.3d⁴ 8.3g 10d p12g 8.1m⁵ 8g Oct 31] modest maiden handicapper: should be suited by 1¼m+: acts on polytrack, good to firm and good to soft going: blinkered last 2 starts. *P. D. Cundell*

ESSEQUIBO (IRE) 3 b.g. Spectrum (IRE) 126 – Far From Home 73 (Habitat 134) **55 d** [2003 58: f7s* p7g⁵ p7g p7g 7g f11s Sep 26] tall gelding: modest performer: won claimer at Southwell (left B. Meehan) in January: left N. Littmoden after fourth start, soundly beaten subsequent starts: stays 7f: acts on all-weather: sometimes blinkered/visored: sometimes wanders: sold 800 gns. *M. J. Polglase*

ESSEX (IRE) 3 b.c. Sadler's Wells (USA) 132 – Knight's Baroness 116 (Rainbow **78** Quest (USA) 134) [2003 10m⁴ 12g² 12m⁶ 10d Oct 14] 460,000Y: half-brother to several winners, including very smart 1¼m/1½m winner Riyadian (by Polish Precedent) and useful 1m (at 2 yrs) and 1½m winner Wales (by Caerleon): dam won Irish Oaks: fair form in maidens: found little last 2 starts: will stay 1¾m: sold 8,000 gns. *Sir Michael Stoute*

ESSEX STAR (IRE) 2 b.f. (Mar 30) Revoque (IRE) 122 – Touch of White 77 (Song **61** 132) [2003 6m 6m 6m 6m Oct 6] lengthy filly: fifth reported foal: half-sister to 4-y-o Tychy: dam 5f performer: modest maiden: form only on second start: should stay 7f. *Miss J. Feilden*

ESSEX STREET (IRE) 6 b.g. Dolphin Street (FR) 125 – Filet Mignon (USA) (Top- **42** sider (USA)) [2003 50: f6s⁶ 7f⁵ f6g⁵ f6g Jan 27] poor maiden: effective at 5f to 7f: acts on fibresand, good and good to firm going: usually wears headgear: tried in tongue tie. *D. Shaw*

ESSNAAD (USA) 3 b.c. Swain (IRE) 134 – Shfoug (USA) 106 (Sheikh Albadou 128) **84** [2003 79p: 12m³ 12d⁴ 12.6m* 14g 13.3m⁴ 15.9m⁶ 13.3m Sep 20] lengthy, quite attractive colt: fairly useful performer: easy task to win maiden at Warwick in June: good efforts in handicaps fifth/sixth starts: probably stays 2m: sold 18,000 gns. *B. W. Hills*

ESTABELLA (IRE) 6 ch.m. Mujtahid (USA) 118 – Lady In Green (Shareef Dancer **–** (USA) 135) [2003 –: f12s f12g Jan 17] fair handicapper at best: no form since 2001. *M. Wellings*

ESTABLISHED 6 gr.g. Not In Doubt (USA) 101 – Copper Trader 53 (Faustus (USA) **–** 118) [2003 49: f16.2g² f16.2g f16.2g Feb 21] smallish, strong gelding: well held in 2003: tried blinkered: sometimes reluctant stall/races lazily. *J. R. Best*

ESTABLISHMENT 6 b.g. Muhtarram (USA) 125 – Uncharted Waters 68 (Celestial **90** Storm (USA) 132) [2003 88, a–: 16.2m² 16m 14g⁵ 20m⁴ 22.2f⁵ 16.1m 16f² 18m 16g* **a–** 16.5d⁵ Nov 8] smallish, workmanlike gelding: fairly useful handicapper: won at New-market in October: best at 2m to 2½m nowadays: acts on polytrack, firm and soft going (well beaten on heavy): blinkered (below form) once: has run well when sweating: sometimes races freely: usually held up. *C. A. Cyzer*

ESTEBAN 3 b.g. Groom Dancer (USA) 128 – Ellie Ardensky 100 (Slip Anchor 136) **58** [2003 57p: 8.5m 8d 10m⁴ 10.9g⁵ 12.4m Aug 25] tall, unfurnished gelding: modest maiden handicapper: stays 11f: acts on good to firm going and fibresand. *J. J. Quinn*

ESTEEMED LADY (IRE) 2 b.f. (Mar 12) Mark of Esteem (IRE) 137 – Bareily **96 p** (USA) (Lyphard (USA) 132) [2003 6m³ 6.5m⁴ Sep 26] 110,000Y: close-coupled, well-made filly: half-sister to 3-y-o Revenue: dam, unraced close relation to Prix de Diane second Baya, out of sister to Triptych: in frame in maiden at Leicester and sales race at Ascot: useful form and caught the eye when 4¼ lengths fourth of 30 to Nyramba in latter, going on well at line: should stay 1m: open to progress, and sure to win races as 3-y-o. *Sir Michael Stoute*

ESTI AB (IRE)   2 b.c. (May 25) Danehill (USA) 126 – Bintalshaati 95 (Kris 135) **85**
[2003 7m 8m 8g² 7.9f³ 7g Oct 24] lengthy, good-topped colt: fifth foal: half-brother to fairly useful 1¼m winner Munadil (by Nashwan): dam, 1m winner, out of half-sister to Kentucky Derby winner Winning Colors: fairly useful maiden: placed at Kempton (best effort) and York (nursery): found little final start: stays 1m. *M. P. Tregoning*

ESTIHLAL   2 b.f. (Apr 2) Green Desert (USA) 127 – Ta Rib (USA) 116 (Mr Prospector   **– p**
(USA)) [2003 7g⁶ 6.1d Nov 6] leggy filly: fourth foal: half-sister to 3-y-o Khaizarana and 11f winner Mawaheb (by Nashwan), both fairly useful: dam 7f and 1m (Poule d'Essai des Pouliches) winner: well beaten but showed promise in maidens at Newcastle and Nottingham (good speed): will do better. *E. A. L. Dunlop*

ESTILHAAM (USA)   2 b.f. (Feb 27) Gulch (USA) – Mamlakah (IRE) 104 (Unfuwain   **– p**
(USA) 131) [2003 7m⁵ Sep 19] tall filly: fourth foal: sister to fairly useful Irish 7f/1m winner Al Mamaaliq and half-sister to 3-y-o Nayzak: dam 2-y-o 7f/1m (May Hill Stakes) winner: 8/1 and better for race, 10 lengths fifth of 8 to Silk Fan in minor event at Newbury: should stay 1m: likely to do better. *Sir Michael Stoute*

ESTILO   3 b.g. Deploy 131 – Vilcabamba (USA) (Green Dancer (USA) 132) [2003 –:   **–**
p12g f11s p12g f12g Apr 7] of little account. *R. M. Flower*

ESTIMADA   3 ch.f. Mark of Esteem (IRE) 137 – Gisarne (USA) 104 (Diesis 133) [2003   **64**
11.5f² Aug 26] fifth foal: half-sister to 2m winner Hastate (by Persian Bold): dam 1¼m winner who stayed 1½m: 1¼ lengths second of 4 to Rich Affair in maiden at Yarmouth, not given unduly hard time when held, only outing. *H. R. A. Cecil*

ESTIMATE   3 b.f. Mark of Esteem (IRE) 137 – Mistle Thrush (USA) 90 (Storm Bird   **69**
(CAN) 134) [2003 82p: 8.1m⁶ 8.5m³ 10m³ 7g 8f 10m² 12.1m⁶ 10m² 10.1d⁶ p10g⁴ Nov 12] tall, unfurnished filly: fair maiden: should stay 1½m: acts on good to firm ground: visored last 6 outings, looking none too keen final one: sold 3,000 gns. *C. E. Brittain*

ESTIMATION   3 b.f. Mark of Esteem (IRE) 137 – Mohican Girl 112 (Dancing Brave   **78**
(USA) 140) [2003 56: p8g³ 8.2g³ 10g f8.5g 9f 7m 6m p8g² f8.5s⁴ 8m⁴ 8m² f8s* 8g* p10g³ f8g⁶ f8g⁵ f8s* Dec 27] tall, lengthy filly: fair handicapper: won at Southwell and Newmarket (apprentices) in October and Southwell in December: stays 1m: raced only on all-weather/good ground or firmer on turf: tried in cheekpieces, visored fifth to seventh starts: sometimes races freely. *R. M. H. Cowell*

ESTRELLA LEVANTE   3 ch.g. Abou Zouz (USA) 109 – Star of Modena (IRE)   **69**
(Waajib 121) [2003 75: 7m p8g⁵ f8.5g 7m⁴ 7m 8.5d f6g⁵ p8g⁵ Dec 6] tall, leggy gelding: **a53**
fair maiden on turf, modest on all-weather: stays 1m: acts on all-weather and good to firm ground: sometimes wears cheekpieces/blinkers: sold £3,300. *G. L. Moore*

ETCHING (USA)   3 b.f. Groom Dancer (USA) 128 – Eternity 77 (Suave Dancer (USA)   **71**
136) [2003 p8g⁶ f8.5s 9.7m⁶ 12f² 12m³ 16.2m³ 16g² 16.2g² 16.2m² 16m* 17.1m Oct 6] first foal: dam, 11f/1½m winner, half-sister to May Hill Stakes/Fillies' Mile winner Tessla: fair handicapper: won at Nottingham in September: should stay beyond 2m: raced only on good going or firmer on turf (well beaten on fibresand). *J. R. Fanshawe*

ETERNAL BEAUTY (USA)   3 b.f. Zafonic (USA) 130 – Strawberry Roan (IRE)   **63**
113 (Sadler's Wells (USA) 132) [2003 8d 5.5g⁶ 6m Sep 6] second foal: dam Irish 1m/9f winner (including at 2 yrs), sister to Oaks winner Imagine and half-sister to Generous: fair form in minor events at Longchamp and Dieppe in June, when trained by J. Hammond in France: well held in maiden at Thirsk on British debut. *M. J. Wallace*

ETERNAL BLOOM   5 b.m. Reprimand 122 – Forever Roses 70 (Forzando 122)   **–**
[2003 –: f8g f7s 5d May 22] poor maiden handicapper: well held since 2 yrs. *M. Brittain*

ETERNAL DANCER (USA)   2 b.c. (May 4) Royal Academy (USA) 130 – Tara   **–**
Roma (USA) (Lyphard (USA) 132) [2003 7m 8.2m Oct 28] $35,000Y: strong, compact colt: fourth foal: half-brother to 2 winners in USA, including smart Grade 1 9f winner Serra Lake (by Seattle Slew): dam US Grade 2 1¼m winner: last in maidens at Leicester and Nottingham, weakening quickly both times. *M. Johnston*

ETESAAL (USA)   3 br.c. Danzig (USA) – Electric Society (IRE) 107 (Law Society   **114**
(USA) 130) [2003 77: f8.5s* 10.4m* 12m⁴ 10.4f² Jul 12] good-bodied colt: quickly progressed into a smart performer, winning maiden at Wolverhampton in April and

handicap at York (by ½ length from Camille Pissarro) in May: good efforts in handicaps after when 4 lengths fourth to Fantastic Love in King George V Stakes at Royal Ascot and ½-length second to Far Lane in John Smith's Cup at York: effective at 1¼m/1½m: acts on firm ground and fibresand: has worn crossed noseband/had 2 handlers: joined Saeed bin Suroor. *D. R. Loder*

ETHOS   3 b.g. Emarati (USA) 74 – Leprechaun Lady 57 (Royal Blend 117) [2003 64: 10f 8.2m 10m 8.2d May 16] rather leggy gelding: modest maiden at 2 yrs: well held in handicaps in 2003: tried in blinkers/cheekpieces: sometimes races freely. *B. R. Millman*   –

ETMAAM   2 b.c. (Mar 3) Intikhab (USA) 135 – Sudeley 65 (Dancing Brave (USA) 140) [2003 6m⁴ Sep 25] €60,000Y: sturdy colt: sixth living foal: half-brother to useful Irish 2000 2-y-o 7f winner Katherine Seymour (by Green Desert), later winner in USA: dam, 11.5f winner, half-sister to Coronation Cup winner Quiet Fling from very good family: 20/1 and very green, 5¾ lengths fourth of 11 to Granato in maiden at Pontefract, slowly away, still plenty to do 2f out and finishing strongly: should stay 1m: sure to improve considerably and will win races. *M. Johnston*   **74 P**

ETOILE MONTANTE (USA)   3 ch.f. Miswaki (USA) 124 – Willstar (USA) (Nureyev (USA) 131) [2003 115p: 8d⁴ 8g³ 8d* 6.5g² 7g* 7s* 8f Nov 30]   **119**

Etoile Montante ended her two-year-old season as the second-best juvenile filly in France, finishing five lengths clear of the remainder when second to Six Perfections in an above average renewal of the Prix Marcel Boussac. She would have been good enough to win most recent runnings of that race, and, as *Racehorses of 2002* pointed out, she ended her season with a higher rating than any of the four fillies who had won the Marcel Boussac for Criquette Head-Maarek in the 'nineties. Whilst Etoile Montante's three-year-old season lacked the high-profile successes of Six Perfections, she too had a Group 1 success to her name by the end of the year.

With Six Perfections aimed at the One Thousand Guineas at Newmarket and the Curragh, Etoile Montante looked the most likely beneficiary from her absence from the Poule d'Essai des Pouliches. Etoile Montante started favourite at Longchamp after finishing a close fourth to Maiden Tower in the main trial, the Prix de la Grotte, over the same course and distance three weeks earlier. She had evidently benefited from her reappearance, but could secure only third in the Pouliches, beaten a length and a short neck behind Musical Chimes and Maiden Tower, racing prominently as usual and running on, though tending to edge left in the straight. Now with two Group 1 placings to her name, but only a couple of wins in minor company, Etoile Montante took a marked drop in class to contest a listed race, again over a mile, at Compiegne later in May. She had to work a lot harder than expected, though she did have to give weight away all round and had a couple of fillies behind her who themselves proved up to winning pattern races later in the season when stepped up in trip, runner-up State of Art and fourth-placed Visorama.

Etoile Montante's own future lay over distances short of a mile. After a mid-season break, she reappeared at Deauville in August and took on sprinters for the first time in the Prix Maurice de Gheest. She ran at least as well as ever, shaping as though the extended six furlongs was a minimum for her and putting in her best work close home to pip Avonbridge for second, a length behind the older filly Porlezza. Back in listed company, and over a slightly longer trip, Etoile Montante

Prix de la Foret, Longchamp—the middle leg of a five-timer on the card for jockey Olivier Peslier as Etoile Montante pulls away from Royal Millennium (rail), Saratan (visor) and Intercontinental

made all the running in the seven-furlong Prix du Pin at Longchamp in September and won by two lengths from Star Valley, running a sound trial for the Prix de la Foret there three weeks later. Etoile Montante faced nine rivals in the Foret, six of them trained in Britain, including the 2001 winner Mount Abu, Park Stakes winner Polar Ben, Holsten-Trophy winner Capricho and Jersey Stakes third Rimrod. Etoile Montante was given most to do by the outsider of the British party, Royal Millennium, who swept into the lead over a furlong out, just as Olivier Peslier was about to pull Etoile Montante out from behind the One Thousand Guineas third Intercontinental. Now with a couple of lengths to make up on Royal Millennium, Etoile Montante responded well, overhauling him inside the final furlong to win by a length and a half, with the same distance to Saratan, who finished well for third. Mount Abu, who made most of the running, fared best of the other British runners in sixth. Etoile Montante was her trainer's fifth winner of this Group 1 prize, following Ma Biche in 1983, Septieme Ciel and Occupandiste in the 'nineties, and Dedication in 2002. Peslier also had a five-timer to celebrate, accomplished on an afternoon when he also rode three seconds on the eight-race card!

			Raise A Native
		Mr Prospector	Gold Digger
	Miswaki (USA)	(b 1970)	
	(ch 1978)	Hopespringseternal	Buckpasser
Etoile Montante (USA)		(ch 1971)	Rose Bower
(ch.f. 2000)			Northern Dancer
		Nureyev	Special
	Willstar (USA)	(b 1977)	
	(ch 1993)	Nijinsky Star	Nijinsky
		(b 1980)	Chris Evert

Whilst Etoile Montante was doing her bit towards Khalid Abdulla's bid for an owners' championship in France—which he eventually won very narrowly from the Aga Khan—a couple of her relatives were making a sizeable contribution to

Mr K. Abdulla's "Etoile Montante"

Juddmonte Farms' Eclipse Award-winning season in the United States. The fillies in question were Sightseek and Tates Creek, both daughters of Viviana, a full sister to Etoile Montante's dam Willstar. Between them, the half-sisters won six Grade 1 races in 2003. Four-year-old Sightseek made into a high-class performer on dirt, while the year-older Tates Creek showed smart form on turf, avenging Etoile Montante's defeat in the Pouliches by beating the winner of that race Musical Chimes in the Yellow Ribbon Stakes at Santa Anita. A slightly more distant relative who made a name for himself in the latest season was the runaway winner of the Japan Cup, Tap Dance City, a great grandson of Etoile Montante's fourth dam Miss Carmie. There is little to add to the other details of Etoile Montante's relatives which were covered in last year's Annual, except to say that her two-year-old close relative Spacecraft, by Sightseek's sire Distant View, was in training with Criquette Head-Maarek but did not race. Etoile Montante's future also lies in the States, and she made her debut there in November, running the first poor race of her career when finishing well held in the Matriarch Stakes at Hollywood won by another Khalid Abdulla filly Heat Haze (from Musical Chimes and Dedication). She subsequently joined Heat Haze, Sightseek and Tates Creek in the care of Bobby Frankel. Although Etoile Montante's very best effort in Europe came at seven furlongs, she does stay a mile. The strong, close-coupled Etoile Montante acts on soft and good to firm ground, and, if she thrives in the States, perhaps she'll be among Six Perfections' opponents should that filly return to defend her Breeders' Cup Mile crown. *Mme C. Head-Maarek, France*

ETOILE SOLITAIRE (USA) 3 gr.g. Lit de Justice (USA) 125 – Cydalia (USA) 109 (Cresta Rider (USA) 124) [2003 72: p6g⁶ 6g⁴ 6m* 7g⁴ 7m 7g² 8d f7g² Oct 16] big, strong, lengthy gelding: fair performer: won maiden at Brighton in May: good second in handicap at Southwell final start: barely stays 7f: acts on good to firm ground and fibresand: wore cheekpieces last 3 starts: has been led to post/edged left: refused to enter stall second intended outing: sold 11,000 gns. *M. A. Jarvis* **72 a80**

ETON (GER) 7 ch.g. Suave Dancer (USA) 136 – Ermione (Surumu (GER)) [2003 88: 12g 10.1m 10d 11.1d⁴ 10.1m⁶ 9.9m 10m² 10.1m⁵ 9.9d 11.9m² 10m 9.9m⁵ 12m³ 12.1m³ 12m* 11.9m Sep 3] strong, close-coupled gelding: fair handicapper: won amateur event at Epsom in August (said to have bled from nose final start): stays 1½m: best recent form on good going or firmer (acts on firm): tried blinkered earlier in career. *D. Nicholls* **78**

ETTRICK WATER 4 ch.g. Selkirk (USA) 129 – Sadly Sober (IRE) 70 (Roi Danzig (USA)) [2003 87: 10d 10m⁵ 7.2m* 8m⁴ 7f² 8f* 8.3g* 8f³ Sep 28] strong gelding: useful performer: won maiden at Ayr in June and handicaps at Bath in August and Hamilton in September: effective at 7f to 1¼m: acts on soft and firm going: usually visored/blinkered nowadays: ridden prominently nowadays. *L. M. Cumani* **96**

EUCALYPTUS (IRE) 6 ch.g. Mujtahid (USA) 118 – Imprecise 64 (Polish Precedent (USA) 131) [2003 59: p8g p7g⁶ p8g Jan 30] big, lengthy gelding: poor mover: modest performer: likely to prove best short of 1¼m: acts on polytrack, soft and good to firm going: often visored, wore cheekpieces last 2 outings: weak finisher. *S. Dow* **54**

EUGENIE 2 ch.f. (Jan 28) Primo Dominie 121 – Misty Goddess (IRE) 63 (Godswalk (USA) 130) [2003 6d p6g Nov 18] good-topped filly: sixth foal: half-sister to 3 winners, including 3-y-o Davos and 4-y-o Love In The Mist: dam 7f (at 2 yrs) to 11f winner: well held in maidens at Haydock (slowly away) and Lingfield. *R. Hannon* **–**

EUIPPE 2 b.f. (Apr 30) Air Express (IRE) 125 – Myth 89 (Troy 137) [2003 7m⁴ 7.1m⁵ 8.2f⁶ Sep 30] tall, rather leggy filly: half-sister to several winners, including 5-y-o Vicious Knight and smart 1m (including at 2 yrs) to 1¾m winner Midnight Legend (by Night Shift): dam 1½m/13f winner: modest form in maidens: should stay at least 1m. *J. G. Given* **64**

EUJANE (IRE) 3 b.f. Alzao (USA) 117 – Tribal Rite 95 (Be My Native (USA) 122) [2003 8.1m⁵ 7.1m⁵ 7m 10d 10.9f⁵ 8g⁶ Oct 31] IR 23,000Y: half-sister to several winners, including useful 1997 2-y-o 6f and 1m winner Silent Tribute (by Lion Cavern) and 1½m winner Danesrath (by Danehill): dam Irish 6f (at 2 yrs) to 1¼m winner: modest maiden: below form after second start: should be suited by 1¼m+: acts on good to firm ground. *M. L. W. Bell* **56**

EUNICE CHOICE 2 b.g. (Apr 20) College Chapel 122 – Aquiletta 67 (Bairn (USA) 126) [2003 6m p7g Oct 8] 6,500F, 5,000Y: fourth foal: half-brother to 6-y-o Tick Tock: dam, maiden, effective at 6f/7f: last in maidens at Epsom and Lingfield. *M. J. Haynes* **–**

EURO IMPORT   5 ch.g. Imp Society (USA) – Upper Club (IRE) 59 (Taufan (USA)   –
119) [2003 12d Nov 4] leggy gelding: no form. *P. D. Niven*

EUROLINK ARTEMIS   6 b.m. Common Grounds 118 – Taiga 69 (Northfields   **63 d**
(USA)) [2003 68, a64: f8g f9.4g² f8g² f8.5g⁴ f9.4g⁴ f8.5s f12g³ f8g f8g⁶ 10g² f9.4s 10g
f9.4g f12g f9.4g f8g Dec 8] useful-looking mare: modest handicapper: left Julian Poulton
after twelfth start: stays easy 1½m: acts on soft going, good to firm and all-weather: tried
blinkered, usually wears cheekpieces. *Miss Gay Kelleway*

EUROLINK ZANTE (IRE)   7 b.g. Turtle Island (IRE) 123 – Lady Eurolink 55 (Kala   **63**
Shikari 125) [2003 77: p8g 8.3d⁶ 7m 7m 7m⁶ 7s 8.2d⁶ p8g Dec 6] modest handicapper
nowadays: stays 1m: acts on soft and good to firm going, probably on polytrack: usually
held up: tried in cheekpieces. *T. D. McCarthy*

EUROLIS (FR)   4 gr.f. Highest Honor (FR) 124 – Eidothea (GER) (Teotepec) [2003   –
14g Aug 2] half-sister to several winners, including smart French winners up to 15f
Epaphos and Eurynome (both by Acatenango): dam unraced: raced in French Provinces
in 2002, winning maiden at Jallais: sold from D. Sepulchre 9,500 gns before tailed off in
listed event at Goodwood only start at 4 yrs: stays 1½m: raced only on good going or
softer: has been blinkered, including for win. *T. T. Clement*

EURO ROUTE (IRE)   2 b.g. (Jan 4) Desert Style (IRE) 121 – Fresh Look (IRE) 64   **79**
(Alzao (USA) 117) [2003 7v 6.3g⁵ 5g⁵ 7m 6m* 6m⁴ 6m⁴ Oct 19] €8,000Y: fourth foal:
half-brother to 4-y-o Tuscarora: dam 11.5f winner: fair performer: won maiden at Ballinrobe in August: creditable fourth in nurseries: last at Ascot fourth start: should stay 7f:
acts on good to firm going. *Edgar Byrne, Ireland*

EURO VENTURE   8 b.g. Prince Sabo 123 – Brave Advance (USA) 98 (Bold Laddie   **47**
(USA)) [2003 56: f7g f6g² f7s⁵ f6g 7f 7g Apr 10] sturdy gelding: modest nowadays: left
R. Wilman after fourth start: probably best at 5f/6f: unraced on heavy going, acts on any
other turf and fibresand: blinkered/visored last 4 starts. *P. A. Blockley*

EVA JEAN   2 b.f. (Apr 17) Singspiel (IRE) 133 – Go For Red (IRE) (Thatching 131)   **– p**
[2003 8g Oct 25] smallish filly: sixth foal: half-sister to useful 1m (at 2 yrs) to 1½m
winner Primary Colours and 1¼m winner Pinot Noir (both by Saddlers' Hall): dam
unraced: 16/1, eleventh of 17 in maiden at Newbury: likely to do better. *H. Morrison*

EVALUATOR (IRE)   2 b.c. (Mar 7) Ela-Mana-Mou 132 – Summerhill (Habitat 134)   **70**
[2003 p7g³ p8g⁶ Nov 13] €39,000Y: useful-looking colt: brother to 6-y-o Mana-Mou Bay
and 9f winner Dollar King and half-brother to 2 winners: dam Irish 6f winner: better
effort in maidens at Lingfield when 8½ lengths third to Bravo Maestro: should stay 1m.
T. G. Mills

EVANGELIST (IRE)   3 b.f. Namaqualand (USA) – Errazuriz (IRE) 94 (Classic Music   **57 d**
(USA)) [2003 68d: f5g f6g f6s 5d² 5.7m⁵ 6m f5s⁶ 7.2m f6g⁴ 6m⁴ 6m 5.9m 6m 6m 5.7f
f6g Dec 9] quite attractive filly: has a quick action: modest performer: well below form
last 6 starts: stays 6f: acts on firm going, good to soft and fibresand: tried in cheekpieces/
blinkered: ungenuine. *A. Berry*

EVA PERON (IRE)   3 b.f. Alzao (USA) 117 – High Flying Adored (IRE) 85 (In The   **68 §**
Wings 128) [2003 79: 12.3m 8.1d 8.3g p10g 8.3g⁶ 9m⁶ f8s 10m 9g Oct 24] small, sparely-
made filly: fair performer: little impact in handicaps in 2003: likely to prove best at 1m/
1¼m: acts on fibresand and good to firm going: ungenuine: sold 1,000 gns. *H. Morrison*

EVEN EASIER   2 gr.f. (Mar 28) Petong 126 – Comme Ca (Cyrano de Bergerac 120)   **60**
[2003 5d 5m p5g⁴ 6m* 7m² 6m⁶ Jul 17] 6,500Y: first foal: dam unraced: modest performer: won claimer at Brighton in June: ran well next time: stays 7f: acts on good to firm
ground: wore cheekpieces last 3 starts. *G. L. Moore*

EVEN HOTTER   2 b.f. (Apr 2) Desert Style (IRE) 121 – Level Pegging (IRE) 48   –
(Common Grounds 118) [2003 6g Jun 30] first foal: dam, ran twice at 2 yrs, sister to smart
5f performer Flanders: 33/1, well held in maiden at Windsor. *D. W. P. Arbuthnot*

EVENING ENCORE   3 b.f. Kris 135 – Eveningperformance 121 (Night Shift (USA))   **69**
[2003 8m⁵ 7.1g* 6m 7m Sep 9] good-bodied filly: first foal: dam, 5f performer, out of
half-sister to 2000 Guineas winner Tirol: fair performer: won maiden at Chepstow in
August: well held in handicaps after: better form at 7f than 1m, and should prove effective
at 6f: raced only on good/good to firm ground: sent to USA. *H. Candy*

EVENING FRAGRANCE   2 gr.g. (Mar 11) Bluegrass Prince (IRE) 110 – Evening   –
Falls 82 (Beveled (USA)) [2003 p6g f8g f7g f8.5s Dec 31] 7,000Y: fifth foal: half-brother
to 1m winner Ember Days (by Reprimand) and 7f (at 2 yrs) to 11f (in France) winner
Chimney Dust (by Pelder): dam sprinter: last in maidens/seller: blinkered last 3 starts.
G. C. H. Chung

EVENING POST 3 b.g. Petong 126 – Nevis 61 (Connaught 130) [2003 –: p7g⁵ p7g – §
6g 7m 5.7m 7m f8.5g 8f 10m 11.7f 12m Jul 10] little form: usually wears headgear: has
missed break badly (reluctant to race second outing): one to leave alone. *J. R. Boyle*

EVENING PRESS 4 b.f. River Falls 113 – Shiny Kay 65 (Star Appeal 133) [2003 42: –
7m 10g 7.2m 8s Jul 25] good-topped filly: poor maiden handicapper: well beaten in 2003:
ran badly in blinkers and visor. *T. J. Etherington*

EVENTUAIL (ARG) 5 b.g. Candy Stripes (USA) 115 – Evidenciable (ARG) (Equal- 113
ize (USA)) [2003 10g⁵ 8.9g⁴ 8g⁶ 8d 8.9m² 9m⁶ Sep 20] workmanlike Argentinian-bred
gelding: smart performer: won 5 races in South Africa in 2002, notably Group 1 Sunday
Tribune South African Guineas at Greyville and Group 1 Summer Cup at Turffontein:
good fourth to Ipi Tombe in Dubai Duty Free at Nad Al Sheba second outing at 5 yrs
(final one for G. Woodruff, South Africa): best effort in Europe when head second to
Naheef in Strensall Stakes at York: stays 1¼m: acts on good to firm going. *W. J. Haggas*

EVER CHEERFUL 2 b.g. (Feb 22) Atraf 116 – Big Story 50 (Cadeaux Genereux 131) 68
[2003 5g⁴ 5m² 5f² 5.1m² f5g² 7g 5.1f³ f5s⁴ f6s³ p7g⁴ p7g⁶ Nov 29] 6,000Y: workmanlike
gelding: fluent mover: fifth foal: half-brother to 1998 2-y-o 6f winner (probably stayed
1¾m) Scoop (by Scenic): dam ran twice: fair maiden: in frame 9 of 11 starts: stays 7f:
acts on all-weather and firm going: hung right penultimate outing. *W. G. M. Turner*

EVEREST (IRE) 6 ch.g. Indian Ridge 123 – Reine d'Beaute 97 (Caerleon (USA) 94
132) [2003 75: p8g⁵ 8m⁵ 8.1g* 8g* 8.5m 8m² 8m³ 7.6m 8m 9m Oct 4] strong, deep-
girthed gelding: useful handicapper: won at Sandown and Ascot in April: well backed,
shaped encouragingly, not getting run of race, when never-nearer seventh to Chivalry
in Cambridgeshire at Newmarket final start: best at 1m/9f: acts on any turf going and
polytrack, probably on fibresand: has wandered: often races freely: held up. *B. Ellison*

EVERY NOTE COUNTS 3 b.c. Bluegrass Prince (IRE) 110 – Miss Mirror 77 (Magic 84
Mirror 105) [2003 77: f6g⁴ p7g⁴ 8.3g p10g² 10.4f² 12f⁴ 10.5g² 11.9m⁴ 10d⁵ 10m² 10.4f
Oct 9] leggy colt: fairly useful performer: stays 1½m: acts on all-weather, firm and soft
ground: races up with pace: game and reliable: sold 22,000 gns. *W. Jarvis*

Mr & Mrs L. Jaffee's "Eventuail"

EVES WOOD 2 ch.f. (Mar 4) Fleetwood (IRE) 107 – Maesteg (Reprimand 122) [2003 6.1m f8s 8.3g Oct 13] first foal: dam no form: well held in maidens/seller. *J. G. Portman* —

EVEZIO RUFO 11 b.g. Blakeney 126 – Empress Corina 74 (Free State 125) [2003 –§, a55§: f11g f12g f16.2g² f16.2g f16.2g Mar 3] neat gelding: poor handicapper nowadays: effective at 1½m to 2m: acts on firm ground (though very lightly raced on turf) and fibresand: blinkered/visored: has hung: no easy ride: unreliable. *N. P. Littmoden* – §
a46 §

EVOLUTION BABY (IRE) 3 b.g. Inzar (USA) 112 – Go Flightline (IRE) 63 (Common Grounds 118) [2003 80: p8g³ p7g⁶ f6g³ f6g³ f7g⁴ 7f⁶ 6d Jul 23] fairly useful performer on all-weather: in frame at Lingfield and Wolverhampton (3 times): effective at 6f to 1m: acts on all-weather, little form on turf: wore cheekpieces third/fourth starts. *John A. Quinn, Ireland* –
a80

EVOLVING TACTICS (IRE) 3 b.c. Machiavellian (USA) 123 – Token Gesture (IRE) 113 (Alzao (USA) 117) [2003 85: 8g³ 8m* 8d 10m³ 9.5g* 10g⁶ Aug 16] leggy, quite good-topped colt: second foal: half-brother to 1m/1½m winner Turn of Phrase (by Cadeaux Genereux): dam, Irish 7f (at 2 yrs) and 1½m winner, half-sister to US Grade 2 9f winner Wait Till Monday: useful performer: won maiden at Cork in April and Grade 2 American Derby at Arlington in July, latter by neck from Californian: also ran creditably in listed race at Royal Ascot (2¾ lengths third to Persian Majesty) and Secretariat Stakes at Arlington (blinkered, 7 lengths sixth to Kicken Kris) fourth/final outings: stays 1¼m: unraced on extremes of going. *D. K. Weld, Ireland* 107

EXALTED (IRE) 10 b.g. High Estate 127 – Heavenward (USA) (Conquistador Cielo (USA)) [2003 66: 13d 13d⁴ 13.1g* 13f⁴ 15g² 14.1d² 14.1f 16.1m Sep 8] good-topped gelding: has round action: fair performer: won minor event at Ayr in May: effective at 1½m/1¾m, possibly not 2m: acts on soft and good to firm ground. *T. A. K. Cuthbert* 66

EXCALINOR 3 br.c. Inchinor 119 – Noble Story 61 (Last Tycoon 131) [2003 61p: p5g⁴ 5.1m* 6m* 7.1g⁵ 7g⁵ p7g Oct 13] quite good-topped colt: fairly useful performer: won maiden at Nottingham in April and handicap at Goodwood in June: best at 5f/6f: acts on good to firm ground. *P. F. I. Cole* 83

EXCELLENTO (USA) 3 ch.c. Rahy (USA) 115 – Golden Opinion (USA) 127 (Slew O' Gold (USA)) [2003 82p: 8m* 7g* 8d* 8.1g³ Jul 5] strong, useful-looking colt: quickly made into a useful performer: landed odds in maiden at Ripon in April and minor events at Newmarket and Thirsk in May: very good 3 lengths third to Putra Pekan in Tote Scoop6 Stakes (Handicap) at Sandown final start: will prove best at 7f/1m: acts on good to firm and good to soft ground: has worn crossed noseband: joined Saeed bin Suroor: capable of better still, and should win more races. *D. R. Loder* 108 p

EXCELSIUS (IRE) 3 ch.c. Dr Devious (IRE) 127 – Folgore (USA) 83 (Irish River (FR) 131) [2003 101: 9m³ 11g 8g³ 8s³ 8g 8s* Nov 21] leggy colt: smart performer: won listed race at Saint-Cloud in November by 2½ lengths from Maxwell, driven ahead final 2f: third in similar events at Newmarket, Goodwood (to Court Masterpiece) and Longchamp earlier: tends to race freely and best around 1m: goes well on soft ground: lost action on reappearance, pulled hard and ran as if amiss next time. *J. L. Dunlop* 110

EXCLUSIVE AIR (USA) 4 ch.g. Affirmed (USA) – Lac Dessert (USA) 91 (Lac Ouimet (USA)) [2003 69, a72: f8s⁴ f8g⁶ f11g⁵ f11s⁶ f12g* p13g f12g⁴ 10m 9.3g f12g f8g f12g⁶ 12m Jul 31] smallish, good-topped gelding: fair performer: won minor event at Southwell in February: stays 1½m: acts on fibresand and firm going: tried blinkered/in cheekpieces: often tongue tied: sold 4,000 gns. *T. D. Barron* –
a67

EXCLUSIVE DANIELLE 2 ch.f. (Mar 24) Thunder Gulch (USA) 129 – Hasta (USA) (Theatrical 128) [2003 7g³ Oct 22] rather leggy filly: second foal: dam 7f/8.5f winner in USA: 9/1, 3½ lengths third of 15 to First Candlelight in maiden at Newcastle, keeping on not knocked about: refused to enter stall on intended debut: should stay at least 1m: likely to improve. *B. W. Hills* 73 p

EXECUTE (FR) 6 ch.h. Suave Dancer (USA) 136 – She's My Lovely (Sharpo 132) [2003 117: 10g⁶ 10.5d² 9.3g⁵ 9.8d³ 8s² 10d⁶ Nov 16] smart performer: has reportedly suffered from knee problems: best effort when second in Prix Ganay at Longchamp for second year running, beaten 2½ lengths by Fair Mix, keeping on after getting no daylight in rear: ran respectably afterwards when third to Weightless (beaten 2 lengths) in Prix Dollar at Longchamp and short-neck second to My Risk in Prix Perth at Saint-Cloud in autumn: has won at 1½m but best around 1¼m: acts on heavy and good to firm ground: held up. *J. E. Hammond, France* 118

EXECUTIVE CHOICE (IRE) 9 b.g. Don't Forget Me 127 – Shadia (USA) 53 (Naskra (USA)) [2003 46: 13.8f May 30] small gelding: poor performer: well held only start in 2003: tried blinkered: usually tongue tied. *J. R. Weymes* –

EXIT TO HEAVEN 3 ch.f. Exit To Nowhere (USA) 122 – Shona (USA) 60 (Lyphard **64** (USA) 132) [2003 63: 8f³ 10.2m p10g 11.8g⁶ 16g p12g p8g f12s² f12s² f12g⁵ Dec 22] fair maiden: left J. Dunlop 4,000 gns after seventh start: should stay 1¾m: acts on fibresand, raced only on good going or firmer on turf: often races prominently. *Miss Gay Kelleway*

EX MILL LADY 2 br.f. (Feb 6) Bishop of Cashel 122 – Hickleton Lady (IRE) 64 **51** (Kala Shikari 125) [2003 p6g⁵ Dec 6] fourth foal: half-sister to 3 winners, including 1m winner Pleasure Dome (by Most Welcome) and 6f (at 2 yrs) and 1¼m winner En Grisaille (by Mystiko): dam 7f/1m winner: 100/1, 3½ lengths fifth to La Landonne in maiden at Lingfield, not knocked about: should stay at least 7f. *John Berry*

EXODOUS (ARG) 7 ch.g. Equalize (USA) – Empire Glory (ARG) (Good Manners – (USA)) [2003 –: 12m Jun 20] well held on Flat in Britain: winning hurdler. *J. A. B. Old*

EXPECTED BONUS (USA) 4 b. or br.g. Kris S (USA) – Nidd (USA) 112 (Known – Fact (USA) 135) [2003 93: p12g p12g p12g 16g 16.1m 12.3m 10.2g Aug 25] lengthy gelding: poor walker: useful at best: no form in 2003: blinkered fourth start. *S. C. Williams*

EXPERTISE 3 ch.f. Selkirk (USA) 129 – Bacinella (USA) (El Gran Senor (USA) **65** 136) [2003 69: 11.6d 10m 8f 9.9d Jul 4] useful-looking filly: fair maiden: creditable effort in handicaps in 2003 only on second start: probably stays 1¼m: acts on good to firm and good to soft ground: visored penultimate outing: sold 13,500 gns, sent to Belgium. *E. A. L. Dunlop*

EXPLODE 6 b.g. Zafonic (USA) 130 – Didicoy (USA) 104 (Danzig (USA)) [2003 –: **57 §** 8.1s 10.5m 10.1m⁸ 8.2d³ 9.3d⁵ 9f 10.1m 8.1d 8m 8m 8.2d Nov 6] useful at 3 yrs, modest nowadays: stays 1¼m: best efforts on softer than good: unreliable. *Miss L. C. Siddall*

EXPLORING (IRE) 4 br.g. Charnwood Forest (IRE) 125 – Caribbean Quest (IRE) **64** (Rainbow Quest (USA) 134) [2003 75: f8.5g⁵ f7g p8g 10.3g f8.5g⁴ Mar 24] close-coupled, useful-looking gelding: unimpressive mover: modest performer: stays 1¼m: acts on good to firm going, probably on all-weather: tongue tied penultimate start. *John A. Quinn, Ireland*

EXPRESSIONIST 3 b.c. Peintre Celebre (USA) 137 – Pato 90 (High Top 131) [2003 – 12g Jul 3] leggy, quite good-topped colt: half-brother to several winners, notably high-class 1½m to 2½m performer Classic Cliche (by Salse) and Yorkshire Oaks/Prix Vermeille winner My Emma (by Marju): dam 7f (at 2 yrs) and 1¼m winner: 33/1, went amiss in maiden at Newbury, pulled up lame after passing line: dead. *R. Guest*

EXQUISITE AFFAIR 3 b.f. Alzao (USA) 117 – Excellent Alibi (USA) (Exceller **78** (USA) 129) [2003 8m 10m 12f³ 12s 12m⁶ 17.2f* 16f Oct 12] leggy filly: closely related to smart stayer Witness Box (by Lyphard) and half-sister to several winners, including 7-y-o Arabian Moon: dam, French 1¼m to 1½m winner, closely related to Dahlia: fair performer: won handicap at Bath in September: stays easy 17f: acts on firm going, below form only start on soft: sold 10,000 gns. *J. L. Dunlop*

EXTEMPORISE (IRE) 3 ch.c. Indian Ridge 123 – No Rehearsal (FR) (Baillamont **47 ?** (USA) 124) [2003 f6g 8.3g⁵ 5m Aug 23] 220,000Y, £4,200 3-y-o: stoutly bred: seventh foal: half-brother to smart 7f (at 2 yrs) and 1½m winner Jelani (by Darshaan) and useful French sprinter Lever To Heaven (by Bluebird): dam, French 8.5f to 1¼m winner, out of half-sister to Miesque: poor form in maidens. *J. D. S. Cosgrove*

EXTERIOR (USA) 2 ch.c. (Apr 28) Distant View (USA) 126 – Alvernia (USA) **75 p** (Alydar (USA)) [2003 7g³ Sep 1] sixth foal: half-brother to useful 1m winner Verbose (by Storm Bird): dam, US 8.5f/9f winner, half-sister to dam of Poule d'Essai des Pouliches winner Matiara: 5/4, 2 lengths third of 8 to Stevedore in maiden at Folkestone, slowly away: will stay 1m: sure to improve. *Mrs A. J. Perrett*

EXTINGUISHER 4 ch.g. Zamindar (USA) 116 – Xaymara (USA) (Sanglamore **83** (USA) 126) [2003 92: 5g 6m 6d 6g 6m 7d Sep 11] strong gelding: useful in France at 2 yrs: fairly useful handicapper nowadays: well held last 2 starts: stays 7f: raced mainly on good going or softer. *D. Nicholls*

EXTRA COVER (IRE) 2 b.g. (Jan 24) Danehill Dancer (IRE) 117 – Ballycurrane **74 p** (IRE) (Elbio 125) [2003 8d⁵ Nov 7] IR 28,000F, 67,000Y: unfurnished gelding: second foal: unraced half-sister to smart Italian performer up to 1½m Toto Le Moko: 25/1 and green, 1¾ lengths fifth of 24 to Hello It's Me in maiden at Doncaster, hanging left: not sure to stay much beyond 1m: should do better. *R. Charlton*

EXTRA GEAR (USA) 3 ch.c. Diesis 133 – Petiteness (USA) (Chief's Crown (USA)) **71 +** [2003 80: p10g³ Jan 25] fair maiden, lightly raced: placed 3 times at Lingfield: stays 1¼m: acts on polytrack: visored only outing of 2003: has reared leaving stall/edged left: sent to USA. *G. A. Butler*

EXZILARATING 3 ch.c. Zilzal (USA) 137 – Personal Best (IRE) (Kris 135) [2003 **76**
77: 7m 8m 7m⁵ 8f 8f⁴ 10.2m 8m³ 8f² 7m² p7g² Oct 27] tall, rather leggy colt: fair maiden:
best at 7f/1m: acts on polytrack and firm ground, well held on soft: tongue tied last 6
outings: tends to sweat/race freely: reportedly had breathing problem on reappearance:
often makes running: sold 7,500 gns. *R. F. Johnson Houghton*

EYECATCHER 6 b.g. Green Desert (USA) 127 – Reuval 102 (Sharpen Up 127) [2003 **102**
100: p7g² Mar 15] heavy-topped gelding: useful handicapper: good short-head second to
Lygeton Lad at Lingfield (looked likely winner when challenging) only run in 2003: will
prove better at 6f than 7f and should be effective at 5f: acts on polytrack, firm and good to
soft ground: sometimes starts slowly (refused to enter stall once at 5 yrs), and usually held
up. *J. R. Fanshawe*

EYES DONT LIE (IRE) 5 b.g. Namaqualand (USA) – Avidal Park 68 (Horage 124) **38 §**
[2003 –§: 16m⁶ 14m⁶ 16d 11.1d 9.2d 8g 16f⁵ 16m⁶ 12m² 12.1g Sep 1] poor maiden: stays
2m: acts on good to firm ground: tried in headgear/tongue tie: untrustworthy. *D. A. Nolan*

EYES TO THE RIGHT (IRE) 4 ch.g. Eagle Eyed (USA) 111 – Capable Kate (IRE) **–**
(Alzao (USA) 117) [2003 61: f11g p10g f12s⁵ f9.4g Jan 27] sturdy gelding: modest at
best: showed little in 2003: visored once: tried tongue tied: has started slowly/wandered.
P. S. McEntee

EYES WIDE OPEN 5 b.m. Fraam 114 – Dreamtime Quest (Blakeney 126) [2003 44: **44 d**
f8s⁴ f7s f16s f8.5g⁶ f7g 8f Jun 16] well-made mare: poor maiden: stays 1m: acts on good
to firm going, good to soft and fibresand. *P. F. I. Cole*

EYRE O PLAIN JANE 3 ch.f. Wolfhound (USA) 126 – Pushkinia (FR) 95 (Pharly **–**
(FR) 130) [2003 49, a52: f7g f7g Jan 23] close-coupled filly: modest maiden at 2 yrs: well
held in 2003. *P. C. Haslam*

EZZ ELKHEIL 4 b.g. Bering 136 – Numidie (FR) (Baillamont (USA) 124) [2003 85: **85 §**
8.1g 10d 10m 10.1m² 12d* 12m 14g 11.5g⁵ 12m Sep 24] tall, useful-looking gelding:
fairly useful performer: won handicap at Newmarket in August: stays 1½m: acts on firm
and good to soft going: virtually refused to race on reappearance, reluctant to set off sixth
start: ungenuine. *J. W. Payne*

F

FAAYEJ (IRE) 3 b.c. Sadler's Wells (USA) 132 – Russian Ballet (USA) (Nijinsky **76**
(CAN) 138) [2003 10m⁵ 12.4g² 9.9m* Aug 24] 750,000Y: leggy, attractive colt: brother
to fairly useful 12.5f winner in Ireland Domenico and half-brother to several winners by
Woodman, notably very smart Irish 1¼m to 1¾m winner (also second in Irish Derby) Dr
Johnson: dam twice-raced close relation to Try My Best and El Gran Senor, an excellent
family: fair form: landed odds in maiden at Beverley in August by head, making all: stays
1½m: raced freely/hung on debut. *Sir Michael Stoute*

FABRANESE 3 b.f. Dr Devious (IRE) 127 – Babsy Babe 94 (Polish Patriot (USA) **–**
128) [2003 10.5m⁵ 12m⁴ Aug 9] 1,000Y: second foal: dam winner at 5f (at 2 yrs) and 6f:
well beaten in maidens. *P. Howling*

FABRIAN 5 b.g. Danehill (USA) 126 – Dockage (CAN) (Riverman (USA) 131) [2003 **73 d**
92?: p7g f6g 7m 6m 6m³ 6.1f p7g 8.2d⁵ f7g⁵ p8g⁴ p10g Dec 20] ex-French gelding: fair
maiden: on the downgrade: stays 7f: acts on all-weather, good to firm and good to soft
ground. *D. W. P. Arbuthnot*

FABUCO (IRE) 2 b.f. (Apr 28) Mujadil (USA) 119 – Beechwood (USA) (Blushing **67**
Groom (FR) 131) [2003 5m³ 5m⁶ 5m⁵ 5g⁴ 5m 5.1f* f5s⁶ 5m 5.1f⁵ 6m Oct 25] 25,000Y:
small, sturdy filly: sister to 3 winners, including useful 2-y-o 5f winners Connemara (in
1996) and Presentation (in 1999), and half-sister to 2 winners: dam French 11f winner:
fair performer: made all in maiden at Bath in August: will prove best at 5f/6f: acts on
fibresand and firm going: wore cheekpieces (very stiff task) final start. *S. L. Keightley*

FABULOSO 2 b.f. (Mar 10) Dr Fong (USA) 128 – Shafir (IRE) 68 (Shaadi (USA) 126) **52 ?**
[2003 p5g⁵ 5d 6m 6m p7g 8.2f Sep 30] leggy, lengthy filly: fifth foal: half-sister to
winners in Italy by Petong and Spain by Alhijaz: dam 2-y-o 5f winner: best effort in
maidens (seemingly modest form) when seventh at Nottingham final start: stays 1m:
sometimes slowly away. *S. L. Keightley*

FABULOUS JET (FR) 3 ch.g. Starborough 126 – Jetty (FR) (Fabulous Dancer (USA) **105**
124) [2003 82: 8g² 9g² 10.1d* 12m 12g 10.1d* 10m⁵ 10.5d* 10m 10.5d* Sep 26] close-

coupled gelding: unimpressive mover: useful performer: won maiden in May and minor event in July, both at Newcastle, and 2 handicaps at Haydock in September: beat Coat of Honour by a neck for final success: effective at 9f to 1½m: has form on good to firm going, best efforts on softer than good: sometimes races freely: tough: sold 60,000 gns, joined Venetia Williams. *M. R. Channon*

FACE THE LIMELIGHT (IRE) 4 b.g. Quest For Fame 127 – Miss Boniface 112 **79** (Tap On Wood 130) [2003 76: 9.7m* 10m⁵ 10g⁵ 12.6m 10f⁵ 10m Oct 20] leggy, quite good-topped gelding: fair handicapper: won at Folkestone in April: stays 11.6f: acts on fibresand and any turf going: usually held up: sometimes flicks tail under pressure: sold 10,000 gns. *H. Morrison*

FACING THE FACTS 2 ch.g. (Mar 15) Defacto (USA) – Sassy Lady (IRE) 63 (Brief – Truce (USA) 126) [2003 f6g May 19] 800Y: first foal: dam, maiden, form only at 6f at 2 yrs: 16/1, well beaten in seller at Wolverhampton. *C. A. Dwyer*

FACTOR FIFTEEN 4 gr.g. Hector Protector (USA) 124 – Catch The Sun (Kalaglow **86** 132) [2003 81: 16g⁴ 14.1s⁶ 10m* 9.9m² 10m² 12m³ 9.9m 10d⁴ 10m⁶ 10m⁶ Oct 4] big, strong gelding: fairly useful handicapper: won at Sandown in May: good placed efforts next 4 starts: probably best around 1¼m: acts on good to firm and good to soft going: tried visored: free-going sort: has flashed tail/carried head high: consistent: sold 48,000 gns, joined J. Howard Johnson. *E. A. L. Dunlop*

FACTORSFORVALUE 3 b.f. Entrepreneur 123 – Jeanne Avril 99 (Music Boy 124) – [2003 –: 9d 8f Jun 18] small, compact filly: no form. *Ronald Thompson*

FACT O' THE MATTER 4 b.g. So Factual (USA) 120 – Edgeaway 70 (Ajdal (USA) **64** 130) [2003 65: f7s f7g⁴ p7g⁶ f7g⁵ 8g f7g⁵ Jun 6] leggy, close-coupled gelding: modest handicapper: effective at 7f, barely stays 9.4f: acts on heavy going, good to firm and all-weather: blinkered once at 2 yrs. *M. Blanshard*

FACTUAL LAD 5 b.g. So Factual (USA) 120 – Surprise Surprise 91 (Robellino (USA) **75** 127) [2003 73: f8.5g³ p10g² f8.5g⁴ 10.1m⁵ 9.7m* 10f* 10m Aug 18] close-coupled, workmanlike gelding: poor mover: fair handicapper: won at Folkestone in July and Brighton in August: effective at 1m/1¼m: acts on firm going, good to soft and all-weather: tried blinkered/in cheekpieces: front runner. *B. R. Millman*

FADEELA (IRE) 2 ch.f. (Feb 5) Desert King (IRE) 129 – Gift Box (IRE) 63§ (Jareer **75** (USA) 115) [2003 f8.5s⁴ f8s f7s² 7d⁵ f7g² f7g* p7g Dec 10] third living foal: dam temperamental maiden half-sister to smart 6f/7f performer Danehill Dancer: fair performer: won nursery at Wolverhampton in November: stays 7f: acts on fibresand, some promise only run on turf. *P. W. D'Arcy*

FAHLAWI (IRE) 2 gr.c. (Feb 18) Daylami (IRE) 138 – Dancing Sea (USA) 80 (Storm **85** Cat (USA)) [2003 7m⁴ 8.1m² Sep 17] 120,000Y: lengthy colt: first foal: dam, maiden (raced only at 7f/1m), half-sister to Pennekamp and Black Minnaloushe: fairly useful form in maidens at Newbury and Sandown, when beaten 13 lengths by Duke of Venice in latter: likely to stay 1¼m. *B. W. Hills*

FAILED TO HIT 10 b.g. Warrshan (USA) 117 – Missed Again 84 (High Top 131) – [2003 –, a68: f14.8g* f12g⁴ f12g⁵ f12g⁶ Dec 26] lengthy gelding: modest performer: **a56** successful 14 times at Wolverhampton, including seller in January: effective at 1½m to 15f: acts on fibresand, lightly raced and little recent form on turf: blinkered/visored: often forces pace. *N. P. Littmoden*

FAILTE (IRE) 5 b.g. Most Welcome 131 – Esh Sham (USA) (Damascus (USA)) [2003 – –: 11.5g 8.3m 11.9m Jun 12] lightly raced and little form: tried visored/in cheekpieces. *L. A. Dace*

FAIR COMPTON 2 b.f. (Mar 6) Compton Place 125 – Fair Eleanor (Saritamer (USA) **60** 130) [2003 5m 6.1m⁴ Jun 14] 9,500Y: half-sister to several winners, including fairly useful 2000 2-y-o 5f/6f winner Imperial Measure (by Inchinor) and 1¼m winner Nicolai (by Piccolo): dam maiden who stayed 1m: better effort in maidens (modest form) when slow-starting fourth at Nottingham: likely to stay 7f. *R. Hannon*

FAIRFAX FLICKER (IRE) 3 b.f. Sri Pekan (USA) 117 – Charwelton 78 (Indian – Ridge 123) [2003 –: f8.5g 11.8m Jun 2] lightly-raced maiden: no form. *C. R. Egerton*

FAIRGAME MAN 5 ch.g. Clantime 101 – Thalya (Crofthall 110) [2003 79: 6m 5m **68** 5g 6g³ 5m⁵ 6f² 5.1m⁴ 6g 5m 5f 5.1m³ f6g 5m 5m 6f 6.9m Sep 4] strong gelding: fair handicapper: well held last 5 starts: best at 5f/6f: acts on firm going, below form on fibresand: tried in cheekpieces: sold 3,800 gns. *A. Berry*

FAIRLIE 2 b.f. (Apr 2) Halling (USA) 133 – Fairy Flax (IRE) 97 (Dancing Brave (USA) **70**
140) [2003 6m^4 6m* 6g 7m^4 7m^6 Aug 6] lengthy, useful-looking filly: half-sister to 3
winners, including fairly useful 1¼m winner Fairywings (by Kris) and 5f to 1m winner
Caution (by Warning): dam, 6f winner, half-sister to smart performer up to 9f Hoy: fair
performer: won maiden at Pontefract in June: respectable efforts in nurseries last 2 starts:
should stay 1m. *Mrs J. R. Ramsden*

FAIRLY HIGH (IRE) 3 b.f. Sri Pekan (USA) 117 – Ecco Mi (IRE) (Priolo (USA) **59**
127) [2003 66: f8.5g^5 f8s p10g^6 12.6m 11.6d^5 f12g^5 May 23] big, strong filly: modest **a45**
performer: acts on fibresand, soft and good to firm going: none too
consistent: sold 600 gns. *P. G. Murphy*

FAIRLY WILD (USA) 2 ch.f. (May 4) Forest Wildcat (USA) 120 – Markham Fair **65**
(CAN) (Woodman (USA) 126) [2003 5.2f^5 5m^3 6m f5s^4 6.1m 6.1m Sep 19] leggy, close-
coupled filly: closely related to a winner in USA by Storm Boot and half-sister to 3
winners abroad: dam Irish 7f winner: fair maiden: fourth in nursery at Southwell, best
effort: should stay 6f: sold 11,000 gns, sent to Saudi Arabia. *M. J. Wallace*

FAIR MIX (IRE) 5 gr.h. Linamix (FR) 127 – Fairlee Wild (USA) (Wild Again **123**
(USA)) [2003 119: 10s^5 10g^2 10.5d* 12g^6 10d^5 12m^5 Dec 14]
Getting a working spacecraft to Mars has proved frustratingly difficult so
far. Contact on the martian surface with Europe's first Mars probe, Beagle 2, built
in Britain at an estimated cost of around £40m, was lost following its descent in
late-December. Expensive failures in racing are commonplace, with horses costing
large sums often unable to live up to the hopes held for them. On the other side of
the coin, however, races at the top level are won by horses purchased for relatively
modest sums, for whom lofty ambitions were not originally held. Take Fair Mix,
for example, bought as a prospective jumper out of Andre Fabre's stable for
265,555 francs after landing a Saint-Cloud claimer in December 2001. Less than
seventeen months later, Fair Mix ran out a clear-cut winner of the Group 1 Prix
Ganay at Longchamp. Training racehorses may not be rocket science, but the
improvement Fair Mix showed after joining Marcel Rolland was nothing short of
astronomical.
Fair Mix, owned by the French racing magazine *Week-End*, was still plying
his trade in handicaps, winning at Longchamp in April and May, at the
time Aquarelliste landed the Ganay in 2002. By the end of his four-year-old season, Fair
Mix had progressed into a smart performer, gaining further successes in a listed
race at Deauville and La Coupe de Maisons-Laffitte, as well as finishing eighth to
Marienbard in the Arc. Fair Mix managed only fifth to Aquarelliste in the Prix
Exbury at Saint-Cloud on his reappearance, but shaped much more encourag-

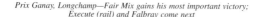

Prix Ganay, Longchamp—Fair Mix gains his most important victory;
Execute (rail) and Falbrav come next

ingly in the Prix d'Harcourt at Longchamp next time, when just touched off by Ana Marie. Fair Mix's Harcourt conqueror reopposed in the Ganay, along with Valentino, Secret Singer and Execute, who had finished third, fourth and sixth respectively in the Harcourt. They were joined by Chancellor and three horses who had been successful at Group 1 level in 2002, Falbrav, Kaieteur and Black Sam Bellamy, the last-named fresh from a winning reappearance in a listed event at Leopardstown. Black Sam Bellamy set a sound pace, pressed by Chancellor, with Fair Mix travelling noticeably strongly just behind. Fair Mix was shaken up to lead over a furlong out and went clear in the closing stages to win by two and a half lengths, Execute pipping Falbrav to finish runner-up for the second year in succession. The form represented a career-best effort by Fair Mix, who underwent an operation to remove a chip in his near-fore knee after the Ganay and wasn't seen out again for almost six months. He was unable to repeat his Ganay form in three starts on his return, though wasn't discredited when fifth to Vallee Enchantee in the Hong Kong Vase on his final outing, staying on as well as anything after being switched to the outside in the straight.

		Mendez	Bellypha
Fair Mix (IRE) (gr.h. 1998)	Linamix (FR) (gr 1987)	(gr 1981)	Miss Carina
		Lunadix (gr 1975)	Breton
			Lutine
	Fairlee Wild (USA) (b 1988)	Wild Again (b or br 1980)	Icecapade
			Bushel-N-Peck
		Raise Me (b or br 1979)	Mr Prospector
			Leave Me

Bred and originally owned by Jean-Luc Lagardere (about whom more can be found in the essay on Clodovil), Fair Mix is the fourth foal of Fairlee Wild, a winner of six races between six furlongs and eight and a half furlongs in the States. Fairlee Wild has bred two other winners by Linamix in Fairlee Mixa and Fairly Grey, who were in training with Andre Fabre, winning as juveniles and showing useful form at up to a mile. Fairly Grey is the dam of Fairly Ransom, who won three

Ecurie Week-End's "Fair Mix"

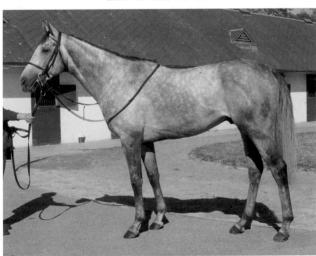

344

times in France (including a listed race on the same card as the Prix d'Harcourt) and showed smart form after being transferred to the States, winning the Grade 2 Del Mar Derby in September. Fairlee Wild's other foal to have made the racecourse is Farlee Hill (by Danehill), who showed fairly useful form in 2003, winning over eight and a half furlongs at Longchamp a week before Fair Mix's Ganay success. The grandam Raise Me won once at two in the States and bred two winners besides Fairlee Wild, including Old Road, a modest chaser in the 'nineties. Fairlee Wild, who also has a yearling colt by Barathea, was sold to a Turkish owner for 70,000 guineas in late-2002 and was due to have been covered by Linamix again in 2003. The well-made Fair Mix stays twelve and a half furlongs and acts on heavy and good to firm going. *M. Rolland, France*

FAIRMORNING (IRE)   4 b.g. Ridgewood Ben 113 – The Bratpack (IRE) (Mister   **47**
Majestic 122) [2003 –: f9.4g⁶ f12g⁵ f12g⁵ f14.8s⁴ f16g⁴ f12g³ Dec 26] smallish, good-topped gelding: poor maiden: stays 2m: acts on fibresand. *J. W. Unett*

FAIR SHAKE (IRE)   3 b.g. Sheikh Albadou 128 – Shamrock Fair (IRE) 77 (Shavian   **71**
125) [2003 60: p5g⁴ f5g 5d* 5f⁵ 6m 6g 6d* 6g 6g⁶ 7m 7d Nov 4] close-coupled gelding: fair handicapper: won at Newcastle (20/1) in March and Hamilton (50/1) in May: effective at 5f/6f: acts on firm and good to soft ground, probably on polytrack: sometimes slowly away. *D. Eddy*

FAIR SPIN   3 ch.g. Pivotal 124 – Frankie Fair (IRE) 73 (Red Sunset 120) [2003 6f 5f 5m   **81 d**
5v 6m 6f⁴ 6g 6g 8.1d Sep 26] 11,500Y: smallish, sturdy, close-coupled gelding: first foal: dam 7f/1m winner: fairly useful performer at best: won minor event at Milan at 2 yrs, when also runner-up in listed race on same course (subsequently left M. Quinlan 30,000 gns): regressed after reappearance: should stay 7f: acts on any ground. *M. D. Hammond*

FAIRY MONARCH (IRE)   4 b.g. Ali-Royal (IRE) 127 – Cookawara (IRE) (Fairy   **56 §**
King (USA)) [2003 84d: 9.9f 10.1m 10.1m⁶ 9.9m 10m 8.5m⁵ 8f 7.9m 8.9m 8m Sep 18] neat gelding: modest performer nowadays: left I. McInnes after third outing, J. Wainwright after sixth: stays 1m: yet to race on heavy going, acts on any other: tried blinkered, wore cheekpieces last 7 starts: tried tongue tied: looks difficult ride. *P. T. Midgley*

FAIRY WIND (GER)   6 b.h. Dashing Blade 117 – Fairy Bluebird 66 (Be My Guest   **71**
(USA) 126) [2003 p10g f9.4g f12g⁶ p13g 14.1g 14.1g 14.1m f12s² f12g Nov 21] ex-   **a55**
German horse: half-brother to several winners, including useful 1m to 1½m winner Fair Warning (by Warning), who stays 1½m: dam, maiden, stayed 1¼m: fairly useful winner in Germany/France in 2002 when trained by A. Schutz: fair form on turf in Britain, modest on all-weather: stays 1¾m: acts on all-weather and heavy going: tried blinkered/visored. *B. J. Curley*

FAITES VOS JEUX   2 b.f. (Feb 20) Foxhound (USA) 103 – Desert Bloom (FR) (Last   **56**
Tycoon 131) [2003 5.1m⁶ 5.1m⁶ 5g⁴ 6m⁴ f6g³ f6g Nov 17] lengthy filly: second foal: dam second at 7.5f in France: modest maiden: third at Wolverhampton, best effort: likely to prove best at 5f/6f: acts on fibresand: has given plenty of trouble at stalls (withdrawn once). *C. N. Kellett*

FAITHFUL WARRIOR (USA)   5 ch.g. Diesis 133 – Dabaweyaa 118 (Shareef   **102**
Dancer (USA) 135) [2003 94: 8m² 10.1m 7.6m⁴ 8m 8f 7.9m* 8m 8g² 7.9m Aug 21] good-topped gelding: useful handicapper: ended long losing run when beating Nuit Sombre by 1¾ lengths at York in July: good 1¼ lengths second of 21 to Lady Bear in valuable event at Goodwood eighth start: free-going sort, probably best at 7f/1m: acts on firm and good to soft going: has worn crossed noseband: edgy type, sometimes early/steadily to post: waited with: none too reliable. *B. W. Hills*

FALBRAV (IRE)   5 b.h. Fairy King (USA) – Gift of The Night (USA) (Slewpy   **133**
(USA)) [2003 125: 10.5d³ 9.3g* 10m⁵ 10g* 12d⁵ 10.4m* 10f² 8f* 12f³ 10m*
Dec 14]
         There aren't many uncharted frontiers left. The celebrations in 2003 to mark the fiftieth anniversary of the conquest of Everest, once the most daunting challenge on earth, provided a reminder of how things move on. Men had trekked to the poles, crossed the major deserts and circumnavigated the globe, but the world's highest peak had been insurmountable. The expedition that succeeded in 1953 was the tenth British attempt in just over thirty years and it took seven weeks from base camp before Hillary and his sherpa Tenzing finally reached the summit on May 29th. It was a further four days before news of the ascent got back to civilisation,

British newspapers carrying the story on June 2nd, the day of Queen Elizabeth's coronation. It was a crowning summer for sport in Britain too. England's cricketers won the Ashes for the first time since the 'bodyline' tour of 1932/3; the FA Cup produced the 'Matthews final', one of the most dramatic ever played; eighteen-year-old Maureen Connolly won Wimbledon for the second time on her way to a 'grand slam' of the world's four major titles; Ben Hogan, having won the Masters and the US Open earlier in the year, produced near-flawless golf to win the Open; Roger Bannister, who had to hold down a job while training, lowered the British mile record on his way to becoming the first man to break the four-minute barrier the following year; and, in racing, after twenty-seven attempts Gordon Richards, knighted in the coronation honours, at last won the Derby.

'Tis distance lends enchantment to the view, but just how good were those achievements and performances of fifty years ago compared to those of today? Since Hillary and Tenzing, there have been over 1,600 successful ascents of Everest and in 2003 a thirty-six-year-old sherpa climbed it in ten hours and fifty-six minutes. But has Hillary's and Tenzing's pioneering climb been diminished by subsequent events? Not judged by the way it was feted again in 2003. The same might be said of Bannister's time for the mile which would now be bettered routinely in training by the present generation of professional middle-distance runners. It is possible to argue that Ben Hogan would have been a match for Tiger Woods and company, given the same modern equipment, and that 'Little Mo' Connolly would have coped with the power of the Williams sisters. Which brings us to Gordon Richards' Derby winner Pinza. *Racehorses of 1953* felt justified in writing of Pinza, who won the Derby by four lengths and the King George VI and Queen Elizabeth Stakes comfortably by three, that he was 'unquestionably the best three-year-old of 1953'. The victory of French-trained Worden II in the second running of the Washington International was recorded prominently but *Racehorses* effectively ignored anything else that happened in 1953 on the racetracks outside Europe. When the millennium prompted racing historians Randall and Morris to write *A Century of Champions* in conjunction with Timeform, Pinza appeared at number 42 in the authors' 'World Top 200'. At number 13 was the leading North American three-year-old of 1953 Native Dancer, who won two legs of the Triple Crown, the Preakness and the Belmont, and was beaten a head in the other, the Kentucky Derby, which turned out to be his only defeat in ten starts as a three-year-old and his only one in a twenty-two race career. But Native Dancer's achievements as a three-year-old weren't enough to earn him America's Horse of the Year crown in 1953, which went to the four-year-old Tom Fool (world number 53), who dominated his own division, winning ten out of ten in the season. A bruised foot sustained by Native Dancer put paid to a possible meeting with Tom Fool, while the fact that both raced on dirt and that international racing was only in its infancy virtually ruled out any chance of meaningful contemporary comparisons with Europe's best turf performers.

Fifty years on, the concept of a recognised world champion in racing is not so out of place. The inauguration of the million-dollar World Series championship, decided by points gained in a dozen or so of the world's top middle-distances races, received the full support of the Godolphin battalions in particular and provided further valuable momentum to international racing, the seeds of which were sewn back in 1952 with the inauguration of the Washington International on grass. That event became the most important international target for some of the leading European-trained middle-distance horses until the Breeders' Cup was introduced in 1984, since when prestigious international races have sprung up in other countries, the Dubai World Cup and richly-endowed Cups in places like Singapore, Japan and Hong Kong among them. Taking up foreign challenges is becoming almost part and parcel of a top European middle-distance horse's campaign. The first winner of the World Series, Daylami in 1999, ran on three continents and in five different countries that year, while Fantastic Light, who won the Series twice and became the first horse in British racing history to pass the £4m mark in total prize money, was equally widely travelled, his twelve career victories also recorded on three continents and in five different countries. The 2002 World Series winner Grandera clocked up even more miles than Daylami and Fantastic Light; in a campaign beginning in February and ending in December he contested eight races in six

Prix d'Ispahan, Longchamp—in a downpour, Falbrav gets off the mark for the season; Bright Sky, Carnival Dancer and Bernebeau (right) follow him home

different countries, again visiting three continents (though Australasia instead of America in his case).

Falbrav's season was not formulated with the World Series in mind, but his remarkable campaign in 2003 established him as one of the toughest, soundest and most versatile top horses of the modern era. He too ran on three continents and in five different countries in the latest season, racing more often than Daylami, Fantastic Light or Grandera, contesting ten races, all of Group 1 status, and showing top-class form at a mile, a mile and a quarter and over an easy mile and a half. His trainer's claim, made immediately after Falbrav was unluckily beaten by High Chaparral in the Irish Champion, that Falbrav 'was definitely the best horse anywhere in the world' was widely reported at the time. Luca Cumani subsequently said he made the remark 'in a moment of desperation' and qualified it after Falbrav's next victory, when dropped back to a mile in the Queen Elizabeth II Stakes, to 'the best horse in the world on grass between a mile and a mile and a quarter'. Leaving the long-since-retired Hawk Wing out of the argument, few could have disagreed with the assessment after Falbrav rounded off a most memorable season in tremendous style in the Hong Kong Cup over a mile and a quarter at Sha Tin in mid-December. It was his fifth victory of the year, all gained at a mile to a mile and a quarter, and, in an above-average renewal, he recorded a performance close to his best to win by two lengths from the other British-trained challenger, Champion Stakes winner Rakti, who repeated his Newmarket form. Odds-on Falbrav, reunited with Frankie Dettori for the first time since their victory in the 2002 Japan Cup, soon had the race won once he was produced to lead a furlong out after being held up as usual. In third was the smart Hong Kong performer Elegant Fashion, second in the Queen Elizabeth II Cup over the same course and distance earlier in the year, while French-trained Bright Sky came fourth in the field of fourteen.

Falbrav beat Bright Sky by a length and a half when recording the first of his Group 1 victories as a five-year-old in the Prix d'Ispahan at Longchamp in May. Falbrav had joined Cumani's stable at the start of the year after a reported fall-out between the owners and Falbrav's previous trainer Luciano d'Auria, for whom Falbrav had made up into a high-class performer. Runner-up in the Derby Italiano (which Rakti won the following year), Falbrav was much improved as a four-year-old, when he won two Group 1 events in Italy, the Premio Presidente della Repubblica and Gran Premio di Milano, as well as the Japan Cup (he was ninth in the Prix de l'Arc). The Japan Cup was run over eleven furlongs, instead of the traditional mile and a half, following a temporary switch of venue; the two Italian Group 1s were over a mile and a quarter and a mile and a half respectively. One common factor with all three races was that they were run on going firmer than good, conditions which suited Falbrav very well, and which prevailed widely on Britain's racecourses during the second half of one of the warmest and driest summers on record. Falbrav didn't really begin to achieve recognition as a worthy contender for Horse of the Year honours—an award he richly deserved in the end—until the second half of the season. His Prix d'Ispahan victory, which followed a creditable third on going softer than ideal in the Prix Ganay, was followed by defeat at Royal Ascot, where he managed only fifth to Nayef in the Prince of Wales's Stakes. Falbrav was bumped leaving the stalls and also found himself short of room inside the final furlong, so it seemed best to forgive him, even though he finished seven and a half lengths behind the winner after being eased near the finish.

The Prince of Wales's had been chosen for Falbrav in preference to a much more lucrative target in Japan, connections reportedly keen to tackle the British Horseracing Board's much vaunted Summer Triple Crown/Grand Slam. To win the £1m bonus associated with the first, a winner of the Derby, Oaks, Coronation Cup or Prince of Wales's Stakes had to go on to take both the Eclipse and the King George VI and Queen Elizabeth Stakes; a fourth success in the International Stakes at York would earn the additional £4m bonus for the so-called 'grand slam'. Before the Coral-Eclipse, however, the BHB was facing the embarrassing possibility that none of the qualified contenders from the 'first round' would take up the challenge. The concept of linking some of Britain's top summer events arose from fears about the competition to British domestic racing arising from the growth in number of valuable international races. However, the mere prospect of achieving eligibility for large bonuses was never, in itself, going to have any influence on the number of individual runners from the top European stables in the 'first round' events. Owners and trainers run their horses where they think they have the best chance of winning. The same general rule applied to the qualified contenders once they were identified. Epsom winners Kris Kin, Casual Look and Warrsan were all quickly ruled out of the Eclipse, while Nayef was at first reported 'likely' to miss the race. Connections of Nayef had a change of heart closer to the event—the lure of the bonus reportedly playing no part—and Nayef started 6/4 favourite in the second-biggest field in the history of the Eclipse. The fifteen-strong line-up included Falbrav and two others who had finished ahead of him at Royal Ascot, third-placed Islington and fourth-placed Olden Times, as well as the Prince of Wales's sixth and seventh Kaieteur and Grandera. The older horses dominated the Eclipse, Falbrav showing that his Prince of Wales's running hadn't done him justice by turning the tables on Nayef, Islington and Olden Times. Ridden for the first time by Darryll Holland, who kept the mount until the Hong Kong Cup, Falbrav moved well on the heels of the leaders and never looked like being caught after quickening clear impressively two furlongs out. Nayef was bumped by the Godolphin pacemaker Narrative—whose rider received

Coral-Eclipse Stakes, Sandown—Falbrav holds off Nayef, Kaieteur (right) and Olden Times (noseband)

Juddmonte International Stakes, York—a top-class display as Falbrav has a good deal more to spare over Nayef (rail) this time; Magistretti splits the pair, and Mingun finishes fourth

a five-day suspension for his actions—as he was starting his run and Falbrav held him off by three quarters of a length, with Kaieteur and Olden Times third and fourth, Islington sixth and Grandera eighth. The five three-year-olds who contested the event, which provides the first major clash of the generations, finished ninth, tenth, eleventh, twelfth and thirteenth, beating only Nayef's pacemaker Izdiham and Narrative.

Nayef's defeat brought to a premature end the BHB scheme that had been designed to 'identify a true champion which will be an asset to the British breed', an idea that was nonsense anyway. The BHB's marketing effort now began to focus on the ancillary BHB Middle Distance Championship, in which points were awarded on a sliding scale to the first six in each of the scheme's seven qualifying events, the horse with the most points earning £250,000. Further potential embarrassment could have been caused if the BHB's championship had been won—as was possible under the points-scoring system—by a horse who had succeeded in none of the qualifying races. But Falbrav's connections were keen to scoop the bonus, Cumani explaining that 'the £250,000 offered is in line with winning a Group 1 race, and it is encouragement for the owner to upgrade.' Cumani said that the existence of the championship influenced connections to run Falbrav next in the King George VI and Queen Elizabeth Stakes at Ascot. The style of Falbrav's Eclipse victory cast doubts on how effective he might be back at a stiff mile and a half on prevailing good to soft going and up against very much tougher opposition than he had faced when beating Narrative over the trip in the Gran Premio di Milano. Falbrav raced wide for much of the way at Ascot, his rider forfeiting ground in search of better going next to the outer rail along the bend approaching Swinley Bottom. After tacking across to rejoin the main body of the field before the home turn, Falbrav finished fifth of twelve, his challenge petering out halfway up the straight. He was beaten nine lengths by the winner Alamshar, but was far from disgraced under the circumstances in a field which, incidentally, contained three of the four 'first round' BHB series winners, Kris Kin (third), Warrsan (sixth) and Nayef (seventh).

Falbrav and Nayef met for the fourth time during the season in the Juddmonte International at York in August, though the fact that the so-called 'middle distance championship' was at stake, with Nayef holding a narrow lead over Falbrav, generated very little extra publicity. Three runners dominated the betting, the unlucky St James's Palace runner-up Kalaman starting favourite at 15/8, with Falbrav at 5/2 and Nayef at 3/1. Neither Kalaman, who failed by a long way to repeat his Royal Ascot form, nor Nayef, who had won the previous year's International, produced his best, which made Falbrav's job easier on the day. That said, it would be hard to imagine either beating Falbrav, even if they had been in top form. Falbrav travelled strongly from the start and swept past Nayef into the lead over two furlongs out, again displaying a decisive turn of foot. Four lengths clear at one point inside the final furlong, the impressive Falbrav won by two from the staying-on Magistretti, with Nayef a further length and three quarters away in third. Connections intimated that part of the BHB's bonus would be used to pay for an entry in the Breeders' Cup at Santa Anita, for which Falbrav needed to be supplemented (at an eventual cost of 180,000 dollars). Falbrav's long-term future lay in Japan, a half-share in him having been purchased earlier in the season by leading Japanese owner-breeder Teruya Yoshida, but there were still two more races to be tackled in Europe. The first of them was the Irish Champion Stakes at Leopardstown in early-September, one of the best-contested races of the European year. King George winner Alamshar was a short-priced favourite, but also in the line-up was the dual Derby winner and Breeders' Cup Turf winner High Chaparral, whose reappearance had been delayed until August because of a shoulder injury, the Dubai World Cup winner Moon Ballad, Islington and Irish Oaks winner Vintage Tipple. High Chaparral beat Falbrav by a neck, with the keeping-on Islington a head away third and Alamshar only fourth, but if Falbrav had enjoyed better fortune the result might well have been different. Travelling best of all but squeezed for room throughout most of the last two and a half furlongs, Falbrav obtained a run against the rail all too late, well inside the final furlong, and was just unable to peg back the winner. Holland lodged an objection to High Chaparral for taking his ground and intimidating Falbrav in the last half furlong, the stewards calling an inquiry which also looked into possible interference caused by Falbrav to Moon Ballad. The head-on camera showed that, although High Chaparral came off a true line in the closing stages, there was no contact with Falbrav, who appeared to have just enough room (though Holland was unable to use his whip). After fairly lengthy deliberations, the stewards allowed the result to stand, though that wasn't the end of the matter. Falbrav's connections lodged an appeal to the Irish Turf Club.

The choice for Falbrav's final race in Britain—the Queen Elizabeth II Stakes over a mile at Ascot—came as a welcome surprise. Top trainers are fond of espousing versatility as a virtue in a leading racehorse. The modern-day Derby winner who 'could win a July Cup' remains a mythical creature, however, and few top horses actually have their versatility tested over so wide a range of distances as Falbrav. The Queen Elizabeth II Stakes, sponsored by NetJets, was Falbrav's first run over a mile since his two-year-old days but he started 6/4 favourite after being supplemented at a cost of £25,000. What was set to be the biggest field in the history of the race was reduced to eight after six were withdrawn because of the very firm going. Aidan O'Brien, who withdrew four of his Group 1 contenders on the day, was one trainer who described the course as having 'hard patches'; a total of twenty runners were pulled out because of the conditions, which saw the two-year-old time record for the Old Mile lowered twice during the afternoon and a new all-aged record for the seven-furlong course. The lightning-fast conditions made the Queen Elizabeth II Stakes very much a test of speed. Falbrav passed with flying colours, beating his main rival, One Thousand Guineas winner Russian Rhythm, to the punch when depriving the Godolphin pacemaker Blatant of the lead early in the straight and winning convincingly by a long-looking two lengths, Russian Rhythm never looking likely to trouble him but coming out clear second-best, a length and a quarter ahead of Tillerman, third in the race for the second year in succession. The fact that Godolphin's main challenger Dubai Destination failed to do himself justice, trailing in last, and the proximity of 100/1-shot Blatant, a further two and a half lengths back in fourth, initially cast doubts on the value of the bare form, though the latter subsequently paid the form a compliment by finishing runner-up

Queen Elizabeth II Stakes (sponsored by NetJets), Ascot—
Falbrav proves his versatility, dropped back in trip; he has quickened clear of Russian Rhythm,
Tillerman (rail), Blatant (visor) and Soviet Song

Hong Kong Cup, Sha Tin—Falbrav ends a marvellous career in style; Rakti is second

in the Premio Vittorio di Capua. The race, however, served to underline Falbrav's many sterling qualities, his performance reflecting great credit on his connections, whose decision to run enabled Falbrav to demonstrate, what his trainer had always claimed, that he possessed the speed and acceleration of a top-class miler.

From a mile at Ascot, it was back to a mile and a half at Santa Anita. Connections deliberated for some time about whether to tackle the Breeders' Cup Classic over a mile and a quarter on dirt, but that would have been Falbrav's first run on an artificial surface and a supplementary entry would have cost 360,000 dollars, twice as much as for the Breeders' Cup Turf. The Mile, it seems, was never seriously considered. The tight turns and relatively short straight at Santa Anita, coupled with the prevailing firm going, made the Breeders' Cup Turf as much of a test of speed as almost any race over a mile and a half can be. If Falbrav was going to take on top-class mile-and-a-half performers, Santa Anita was the place to do it. Breeders' Cup week saw the appeal over the Irish Champion Stakes turned down by the Irish Turf Club after a three-hour hearing, which added extra spice to the Breeders' Cup Turf, in which Falbrav renewed rivalry with High Chaparral, a four-horse European-trained challenge completed by Sulamani and Bright Sky. The race produced a tremendous finish, High Chaparral dead-heating with locally-trained Johar, the pair a head in front of Falbrav, with the first three five and a half lengths and upwards clear of the rest. The form was top class and Falbrav was caught close home after taking up the running over a furlong out. The perception was that Falbrav just failed to get home, though to argue that the Breeders' Cup Turf showed that he didn't stay a mile and a half in top company was arguably stretching a point. By our reckoning, Falbrav's form at Santa Anita was no more than 2 lb or 3 lb below his best at shorter distances. High Chaparral had now pipped Falbrav twice in important races and he did so again when taking the latest World Series by virtue of his victories in those two events and a third place in another designated race, the Prix de l'Arc de Triomphe. Falbrav's victory in the Hong Kong Cup, the final leg in the 2003 series, coupled with points collected in the King George, Irish Champion and Breeders' Cup Turf, left him one short of High Chaparral's total, though the championship didn't enjoy anything like the same profile as in previous years. Without a sponsor there was no bonus, the series being run 'solely for prestige', in the words of the organisers, who were on hand to present the trophy at Sha Tin.

The strong, heavy-bodied Falbrav—the type to carry plenty of condition—usually impressed in appearance and was a splendid mover. His sire Fairy King ran only once and owed his chance at stud mainly to the fact that he was a brother to Sadler's Wells. As a sire, however, Fairy King, who died in 1999, took more after his three-parts brother Nureyev, becoming known mainly for endowing his progeny with speed rather than stamina. The average distance of races won by Fairy King's offspring at three years and upwards has been around a mile. Top-class mile-and-a-half winners were the exception, though Oath gave him a Derby winner and Helissio a five-length Arc winner. Like Helissio, Falbrav is out of a mare by the now-deceased Slewpy, the American Grade 1 winner who finished down the field

Scuderia Rencati Srl's "Falbrav"

	Fairy King (USA) (b 1982)	Northern Dancer (b 1961)	Neartic Natalma
		Fairy Bridge (b 1975)	Bold Reason Special
Falbrav (IRE) (b.h. 1998)			
	Gift of The Night (USA) (b 1990)	Slewpy (b or br 1980)	Seattle Slew Rare Bouquet
		Little Nana (ch 1975)	Lithiot Nenana Road

when ambitiously sent over for the 1983 Derby. Slewpy made his name as a sire of sprinters and milers on dirt, so with Fairy King as his sire and Slewpy as his maternal grandsire, Falbrav certainly seemed bred more for speed than stamina (as, by the same token, had Helissio). Falbrav's dam Gift of The Night—one of only two broodmares by Slewpy based in Ireland the year after Helissio's Arc win—was from a French family and won over seven and a half furlongs as a two-year-old before becoming temperamental, refusing to race in the Prix de Conde. She was retired after finishing last on her only run at three, but her three foals before Falbrav were all successful in Italy. Fanofadiga (by Alzao) won at up to a mile and a half, Fiur (by Grand Lodge) at nine furlongs and Fafinta (by Indian Ridge) at up to a mile and a quarter. Gift of The Night was barren for three years after producing Falbrav but has a yearling colt (named Falpiase) by Montjeu. Falbrav's grandam Little Nana was notably tough, winning seven of her fourteen starts as a two-year-old and, after being unsuccessful in an even busier campaign at three, returning better than ever at four, when she won three times at around a mile and a quarter, once in listed company at Deauville. Further back on the distaff side, Falbrav's great grandam

352

Nenana Road was a winning half-sister to Poule d'Essai des Pouliches winner La Sarre, Prix du Conseil and Hialeah Turf Cup winner Carteret and Prix d'Astarte winner Begrolles.

With Group 1 victories in five countries—Italy, Japan, France, Britain and Hong Kong—Falbrav's merit has been widely advertised. He was already acknowledged, before the latest season, as the best horse trained in Italy since the 1988 Arc winner Tony Bin. But his achievements in the latest season were a revelation, reflecting tremendous credit on those who worked with him, particularly trainer Luca Cumani. In the late-'eighties, jokes were made about Cumani's first lot causing traffic chaos in Newmarket. His string was on the way to reaching two hundred at its peak before, in Cumani's words, he 'was put down a rung or two in the Sheikh Mohammed operation with the birth of Godolphin and other factors.' Cumani enjoyed his best season in 1990 when sending out 109 winners and finishing second to Henry Cecil in the trainers' table. Top miler Markofdistinction was the stable's best horse that year. The Aga Khan, for whom Cumani saddled Derby/Irish Derby winner Kahyasi, withdrew his horses from Britain for four years up to 1996 in the aftermath of the disqualification of 1989 Oaks winner Aliysa. One of the chief sufferers of the Aga Khan's boycott, Cumani had his partnership with the Aga terminated altogether in 1999 when thirty horses were removed from the yard following the disqualification of two of the owner's horses in twelve months for failing dope tests. Cumani had saddled a second Derby winner, High-Rise, the previous year, but, apart from him, Irish Two Thousand Guineas winner Barathea, who went on to win the Breeders' Cup Mile, was the stable's only other classic winner in the 'nineties. It is a tribute to Falbrav that Cumani said of him: 'I have never trained a horse as good as this and I'll be very lucky if I ever train another one as good.' Falbrav begins his stud career at the Shadai Stallion Station at a fee of four million yen (around £21,250), and he'll also shuttle to Australia for the southern hemisphere breeding season in a deal with Arrowfield Stud. *L. M. Cumani*

FALCON GEORGIE   4 b.f. Sri Pekan (USA) 117 – Georgia Stephens (USA) 64 (The Minstrel (CAN) 135) [2003 –: p12g Jan 7] neat filly: of little account. *Miss B. Sanders*   –

FALCON HILL   4 b.g. Polar Falcon (USA) 126 – Branston Jewel (IRE) 95 (Prince Sabo 123) [2003 108d: a6.5f a6f a6f⁵ a8f a6.5f a7f⁶ a6f 7d 7m Oct 25] good-topped gelding: useful at best at 3 yrs: disappointing in 2003 (raced in UAE first 7 starts): stays 6f: has form on firm going, very best efforts on soft/heavy: tried blinkered: sold 12,000 gns. *M. Johnston*   83 ?

FALCON ON THE HILL (USA)   3 b.g. Southern Halo (USA) – Inca Empress (USA) (Sovereign Dancer (USA)) [2003 75: 10m⁴ 11m a8.6g* a8.6g⁵ a11g³ a12g⁶ a8g* Nov 16] heavy-topped gelding: fair performer at best: sold from M. Johnston 11,000 gns after second start: won minor events at Jagersro in August and Taby in November: stays 11f: acts on dirt, best turf effort on good ground. *J. Tandari, Sweden*   ?

FALL IN LINE   3 gr.g. Linamix (FR) 127 – Shortfall 103 (Last Tycoon 131) [2003 f9.4g³ 8.2m⁴ f12s³ Sep 26] 62,000Y: big, good-topped gelding: has plenty of scope: third foal: half-brother to 4-y-o Parachute and 5-y-o Contraband; dam, 1¼m/1½m performer who later won in USA, out of St Simon Stakes winner Upend from family of high-class stayer Royal Gait: fair form in maidens, best work closing stages each time: will stay 1¾m: reluctant/fractious in stall on debut: almost certainly capable of better, and type to do well in handicaps. *Sir Mark Prescott*   66 p

FAME   3 ch.c. Northern Amethyst 99 – First Sapphire (Simply Great (FR) 122) [2003 10m⁴ 12g³ 10g² Oct 6] tall, lengthy, angular colt: fourth foal: brother to useful 1¼m winner Rolling Stone and half-brother to fairly useful 11.6f winner First Impression (by Saddlers' Hall): dam of no account: fairly useful form: best effort in maidens when third of 14 to Phoenix Reach at Newbury second start: off 3 months and dropped in trip, raced too freely next time: stays 1½m. *Mrs A. J. Perrett*   83

FAMILIAR AFFAIR   2 b.g. (May 3) Intikhab (USA) – Familiar (USA) 96 (Diesis 133) [2003 7m* 7g⁴ Oct 28] 15,000Y, 6,500 2-y-o: leggy, close-coupled gelding: has a rather round action: half-brother to several winners, including 1¼m winner Manorson (by Desert King) and 7.5f (at 2 yrs) and 1¼m winner Esyoueffcee (by Alzao), both useful: dam, 1m winner, half-sister to Oaks runner-up All At Sea: won maiden at Thirsk in September by neck from Jarvo: fairly useful form when 6¾ lengths fourth of 7 to La Coruna in minor event at Redcar: will probably stay 1m. *B. Smart*   81

King George V Stakes (Handicap), Royal Ascot—
Fantastic Love, having passed virtually the whole field in the straight, just hangs on from Salsalino (left);
behind them come Lodger, Etesaal (No.3), Blythe Knight (right) and Double Obsession

FAMILY FOLLY   3 b.g. Green Horizon – Dry Land 84 (Nonoalco (USA) 131) [2003   –
7g 7m May 8] half-brother to several winners, including 7f winner Trojan Desert (by
Troy) and 1m winner River's Rising (by Mendez), both fairly useful: dam 5f winner: well
beaten in seller/claimer. *J. Nicol*

FAMOUS GROUSE   3 b.g. Selkirk (USA) 129 – Shoot Clear 111 (Bay Express 132)   **110**
[2003 96p: 10g² 12m 9.9g² 9m Oct 4] quite attractive gelding: smart performer: best
effort when ½-length second to Tiber in quite valuable handicap at Goodwood third start:
mid-division in Cambridgeshire at Newmarket final one: has taken good hold, but should
stay beyond 1¼m: acts on soft and good to firm ground. *R. Charlton*

FANCY AFFAIR   3 b.f. Kris 135 – Mafatin (IRE) 74 (Sadler's Wells (USA) 132)   **74**
[2003 10m⁵ 12.1g³ Sep 11] strong, lengthy filly: fifth foal: half-sister to a winner in
Poland by Bahri: dam, 1¼m winner, half-sister to 1000 Guineas winner Fairy Footsteps
and St Leger winner Light Cavalry: fair form in maidens at Newbury (raced freely) and
Chepstow (carried head high): stays 1½m: sold 1,400 gns. *H. R. A. Cecil*

FANCY FOXTROT   2 b.c. (Mar 18) Danehill Dancer (IRE) 117 – Smooth Princess   **94**
(IRE) 63 (Roi Danzig (USA)) [2003 6g 6m² 6f⁵ 7f² 7f³ 8.2m² p8g⁶ Nov 2] 34,000F,
115,000Y: rangy, good sort: has a rather round action: second foal: dam 2-y-o 7f seller
winner: fairly useful maiden: good fifth in Coventry Stakes at Royal Ascot: pulled hard/
flashed tail final start: stays 1m: acts on firm going. *B. J. Meehan*

FANCY LADY   3 ch.f. Cadeaux Genereux 131 – Ascot Cyclone (USA) 93 (Rahy   **99**
(USA) 115) [2003 99: 7m⁶ 6.1s 6m⁴ 5f 6m 5.6d 6m 6m Oct 16] angular, quite attractive
filly: fluent mover: useful handicapper: best effort at 3 yrs when seventh to Halmahera in
Portland at Doncaster sixth start: probably best around 6f: acts on soft and good to firm
going: usually races prominently. *B. W. Hills*

FANLING LADY   2 gr.f. (Mar 16) Highest Honor (FR) 124 – Pain Perdu (IRE) (Waajib   **75**
121) [2003 6g⁶ 7f³ 7f 8.1g³ 8d 8m³ 10m² Oct 6] 22,000Y: close-coupled filly: second
foal: half-sister to 3-y-o Sister Bluebird: dam, French 1¼m winner, half-sister to smart
French miler Fine Fellow: fair maiden: second at Pontefract: should stay at least 1½m:
acts on firm going. *A. P. Jarvis*

FANNY'S FANCY   3 b.f. Groom Dancer (USA) 128 – Fanny's Choice (IRE) 90 (Fairy   **99 p**
King (USA)) [2003 74p: p6g* p6g* 6.1d⁴ p6g³ Oct 16] sturdy, good-quartered filly: useful
form: won maiden in April and handicap in July, both at Lingfield: good efforts in frame
in listed races at Chester and Newmarket (close third to Frizzante) last 2 starts: will prove
best at 5f/6f: acts on polytrack, unraced on extremes of going on turf: lightly raced, and
probably capable of better still. *C. F. Wall*

FANTASIZE   3 ch.f. Groom Dancer (USA) 128 – Belle Et Deluree (USA) (The Minstrel   **99**
(CAN) 135) [2003 8p: 8g* 8m³ 8f⁵ 9.9m⁵ Aug 13] big, angular filly: useful performer:
won listed race at Ascot in April: good efforts when ¾-length third to Aldora in similar
event at Goodwood and when fifth to Russian Rhythm in Coronation Stakes at Royal
Ascot next 2 starts: should stay 1¼m (below form when tried): acts on firm ground. *Sir
Michael Stoute*

FANTASMIC RIVER (IRE)   3 ch.f. Magic Ring (IRE) 115 – River Maiden (USA)   –
(Riverman (USA) 131) [2003 8g 8.2g⁶ f8g Dec 9] 1,200 2-y-o: good-topped filly: fourth

foal: half-sister to Irish 9f winner Zaidaan (by Ezzoud): dam French 2-y-o 6f winner: well held in maidens. *B. Smart*

FANTASTIC LOVE (USA)   3 b.c. Peintre Celebre (USA) 137 – Moon Flower (IRE) **110 p**
95 (Sadler's Wells (USA) 132) [2003 8m² 8m² 11.1m* 11.6g² 12m* Jun 19] $50,000Y:
quite good-topped colt: second foal: half-brother to a winner in Japan by Spectrum:
dam, Irish 1m (at 2 yrs) and 1¼m winner, closely related to top-class sprinter/miler Last
Tycoon and smart sprinter Astronef, a good family: progressive form in first half of
season: made all to land odds in maiden at Hamilton in April: clearly best effort when
winning King George V Stakes (Handicap) at Royal Ascot by short head from Salsalino,
held up after slow start then staying on strongly to lead 1f out: will stay 1¾m: raced
only on good/good to firm ground: joined Godolphin: already smart, and should improve
further and win more races. *M. Johnston*

FANTASTICO (IRE)   3 b.f. Bahhare (USA) 122 – Minatina (IRE) 78 (Ela-Mana- **71**
Mou 132) [2003 74: 11.6s 11.9d⁴ 14m⁶ 11.6d⁶ p12g³ 16.2m⁵ 16g⁶ 12m* 14.1m⁴ 11.9f³
11.9f Oct 9] good-topped filly: fair handicapper: won at Folkestone in August: left S. Kirk
before final start: effective at 1½m to 2m: acts on all-weather, firm and soft ground.
Mrs K. Walton

FANTASTIC VIEW (USA)   2 ch.c. (Apr 15) Distant View (USA) 126 – Promptly **113**
(IRE) 88 (Lead On Time (USA) 123) [2003 7g* 8f² 8m* 8g* 8m² Oct 25] 35,000 2-y-o:
smallish, sturdy colt: third foal: half-brother to fairly useful 2002 2-y-o 6f/7f winner To
The Rescue (by Cozzene): dam, 6f and (US minor stakes) 1m winner, out of Nell Gwyn
winner Ghariba, herself half-sister to smart stayer Braashee: smart performer: won
maiden at Ascot in July, listed race at Goodwood in September and Tom McGee Autumn
Stakes at Ascot (by 4 lengths from Menokee, travelling strongly and leading over 1f out)
in October: good 1¾ lengths second of 4 to American Post in Racing Post Trophy at
Doncaster on final start: not sure to stay beyond 1m: acts on firm going: game. *R. Hannon*

Mr Malih L. Al Basti's "Fantastic View"

FANTASTIC WORLD (FR)   4 b.g. Spinning World (USA) 130 – Fanjica (IRE) 115   –
(Law Society (USA) 130) [2003 10m f6g* f7s 5d a6.5g* Dec 23] close-coupled gelding: **a71 +**
first foal: dam, 7.5f (at 2 yrs) to 1½m (Lancashire Oaks) winner, also successful in
USA: fair form: won maiden at Wolverhampton in June and (having left S. Dow after next
start) claimer at Deauville in December: should stay at least 7f: form only on all-weather.
P. Laloum, France

FANTASY BELIEVER   5 b.g. Sure Blade (USA) 130 – Delicious 51 (Dominion   **102**
123) [2003 99d: 6m 6g 6m 6d* 6f² 6g² 6g* 6m 6m² 5.6d 6m⁴ 7m* Oct 1] sturdy gelding:
useful performer: returned to best in 2003, winning handicaps at Ayr in May and Ascot in
July and minor event at Newcastle (beat Camberley by 1¼ lengths) in October: effective
at 6f/7f: acts on any going: has worn near-side pricker and hung/carried head awkwardly:
effective ridden prominently or held up. *J. J. Quinn*

FANTASY CRUSADER   4 ch.g. Beveled (USA) – Cranfield Charger (Northern State   **58**
(USA) 91) [2003 –: f8.5s 10d 8.2d 8f² 7m 10.3g² 10f⁶ 10.5m 9.7m³ 10m* 12m 9.7g 11.5g
9.9d Sep 23] modest handicapper: won at Lingfield in August: stays 1¼m: acts on firm
ground: usually wears cheekpieces/tongue strap: has raced freely/looked none too keen.
J. A. Gilbert

FARAWAY ECHO   2 gr.f. (Feb 5) Second Empire (IRE) 124 – Salalah 62 (Lion Cavern   **60**
(USA) 117) [2003 6g⁵ 6.1m 6m Sep 1] 13,000Y: rather leggy filly: first foal: dam, 7f
winner, half-sister to useful 1995 sprinting 2-y-o Flying Squaw: easily best effort in
maidens (modest form) when fifth at Windsor: should stay 7f. *M. L. W. Bell*

FARAWAY JOHN (IRE)   5 b.g. Farhaan 77 – Indiana Dancer (Hallgate 127) [2003   –
48: f11g 12g May 24] poor handicapper: no show in 2003: tried in cheekpieces.
G. P. Enright

FARAWAY LADY   3 b.f. Alzao (USA) 117 – Eurolinka (IRE) (Tirol 127) [2003 8.3g   **87**
8.2g 8.2m 8m 10.9m 16.2m* 16g* 17.1m* 16g² 16.2m* 16m² 16f² 13.9f⁶ Oct 11] close-
coupled, good-bodied filly: first foal: dam unraced half-sister to useful 1½m performer
Duke of Eurolink: made into fairly useful handicapper: won at Beverley (maiden event)
and Yarmouth (left clear when Misternando unseated rider final 1f) in July, Pontefract in
August and Warwick (apprentices) in September: should stay 2¼m: raced only on good
ground or firmer: has hung right/been slowly away, but seems genuine. *L. M. Cumani*

FARAWAY LOOK (USA)   6 br.g. Distant View (USA) 126 – Summer Trip (USA)   **67**
117 (L'Emigrant (USA) 129) [2003 –, a76: f8s⁵ f11s⁴ f11g⁴ f9.4g² f8.5g⁴ 10g⁶ 10g³ f8.5s⁵   **a74**
12m⁵ f11g³ f8s⁴ Dec 13] good-bodied gelding: fair handicapper: in frame 7 times in 2003:
effective at 9.4f to 1½m: acts on fibresand, best turf efforts on good/good to firm going:
tried visored/in cheekpieces: sometimes carries head high. *J. G. M. O'Shea*

‹   **FAREHAM**   5 b.m. Komaite (USA) – Lizzy Cantle 52 (Homing 130) [2003 f12g⁶ Mar   – §
24] no form and looks temperamental: tried blinkered/visored: one to leave alone.
Mrs N. Macauley

FAREWELL GIFT   2 b.c. (Apr 15) Cadeaux Genereux 131 – Daring Ditty (Daring   **98**
March 116) [2003 6g² 6m 6d Jul 25] 75,000Y: good-topped colt: half-brother to 3
winners, notably sprinters Bold Edge (very smart) and Brave Edge (useful), both by
Beveled: dam twice-raced daughter of useful sprinter Dawn Ditty: second to Grand
Reward in maiden at Newbury before useful form when 5¼ lengths last of 8 to Nevisian
Lad in July Stakes at Newmarket: ran poorly at odds on final start: bred to prove best at
5f/6f. *R. Hannon*

FAREWELL TO ARMS   2 ch.f. (Jan 30) Efisio 120 – Blow Me A Kiss 72 (Kris 135)   **80**
[2003 5g² 5m* 5.1m² 6f 6.5f⁵ Nov 7] smallish, workmanlike filly: first foal: dam, maiden
who stayed 1¼m, out of half-sister to very smart middle-distance colt Apache: fairly
useful performer: won maiden at Pontefract in April: left B. Hills and off 4½ months
before final outing: should stay at least 6f. *Jenine Sahadi, USA*

FAR FOR LULU   2 ch.f. (May 12) Farfelu 103 – Shady Habitat (Sharpo 132) [2003   **41**
p5g f6g⁵ 5.1m⁴ 6f⁵ f7f 7m Aug 21] £1,200Y: second foal: dam unraced half-sister to
smart Italian 9f winner Big Reef: poor maiden: form only at 5f on good to firm going.
W. R. Muir

FAR LANE (USA)   4 b.c. Lear Fan (USA) 130 – Pattimech (USA) (Nureyev   **120**
(USA) 131) [2003 108: 10.4m³ 10.4f* 10.5m² 10.3g³ 9.9m³ 9m⁵ 9m* 10g* Oct 31]
          A win in a Doncaster maiden in March was scant reward for Far Lane's
efforts in 2002. In eight subsequent runs in handicaps, he did nothing but progress,
ending his campaign with a second to Beauchamp Pilot in the Cambridgeshire,

faring easily the best of those who raced in the group towards the stand side (the next home in the group was the 2003 Cambridgeshire winner Chivalry). Far Lane didn't have the run of the race in the 2002 Cambridgeshire, but he enjoyed a slice of fortune in the John Smith's Cup at York in the latest season when gaining a deserved big-race prize. Returned to York for the John Smith's after running close to form when third to Researched in a competitive handicap on the same course two months earlier, Far Lane showed improved form to beat Etesaal by half a length, producing one of the handicap performances of the season. His jockey that day, Michael Hills, had intended to have him prominent but, after missing the break, he held him up, a change that arguably contributed to victory, those who raced up with the pace in a strongly-run affair all finishing well beaten.

Far Lane's performance in the John Smith's suggested he would be up to making his mark in pattern company, a step taken in the Rose of Lancaster Stakes at Haydock. Starting a short-priced favourite in a field of five, Far Lane made the running but was collared late by the unexposed Sabre d'Argent. Far Lane then turned in a couple of below-par efforts, finishing third to Rawyaan when odds-on in a minor event at Doncaster and filling the same position behind Imtiyaz in a listed race at Goodwood. Reverting to handicap company for a second crack at the Cambridgeshire, Far Lane faced a stiff task off a mark of 110, 19 lb higher than the previous year, and he put up a creditable effort to finish fifth. His trainer was tempted to send him to Australia for the Caulfield Cup, but, with Khalid Abdulla in with a good chance of becoming leading owner in Britain for the first time, Far Lane stayed to lend a hand in winning the title. Far Lane's next appearance came over the Cambridgeshire course and distance in the Darley Stakes, which Far Lane won to give him his first success in pattern company, making the running and responding well to pressure to beat Pawn Broker by half a length. Penalised 7 lb for that success, Far Lane repeated the form when beating Bustan by a length and a half in the listed James Seymour Stakes at Newmarket's next meeting, after which he was sold in a private deal, remaining in training with Barry Hills. Far Lane will have to improve if he is to make his mark in better races in the next season, but there

John Smith's Cup (Handicap), York—
Far Lane (left) and Etesaal have the finish to themselves; Persian Lightning is third

are plenty of opportunities for him at listed and minor pattern level and, given that the Caulfield Cup came under consideration, he may be campaigned internationally. Though his trainer said after the John Smith's Cup that he sees no reason why Far Lane shouldn't stay a mile and a half, he is a free-going sort for whom nine furlongs to a mile and a quarter is probably the optimum distance.

	Lear Fan (USA) (b 1981)	Roberto (b 1969)	Hail To Reason
			Bramalea
		Wac (b 1969)	Lt Stevens
Far Lane (USA) (b.c. 1999)			Belthazar
	Pattimech (USA) (b 1989)	Nureyev (b 1977)	Northern Dancer
			Special
		My Nord (b 1973)	Vent du Nord
			My Alison

Juddmonte Farms had another fine year but Far Lane is one horse who carried the Abdulla colours that was not home bred. Bred by Airlie Stud in Ireland, Far Lane changed hands as a yearling at the Goffs Orby Sale for IR 75,000 guineas. Far Lane is the sixth foal of Pattimech and much the best. He is a half-brother to four winners, including the fairly useful miler Riverina (by Irish River) and My Personal Space (by Rahy), a two-year-old winner in the latest season. Pattimech was a winner in America at six and a half furlongs and is a sister to the American Grade 1 nine-furlong winner Annoconnor and a half-sister to the Grand Prix de Paris and Melbourne Cup winner At Talaq (also runner-up in the Caulfield Cup, incidentally), and to the dam of the smart sprinter Munjiz. A strong, rangy, good sort, Far Lane, who has been fitted with a net muzzle but usually wears a crossed noseband nowadays, is not a straightforward ride as he tends to hang under pressure, though he has done nothing to suggest he is anything but genuine and largely consistent. He has yet to race on heavy going but acts on any other. *B. W. Hills*

FARMERS MARKET 2 ch.c. (Apr 19) Mark of Esteem (IRE) 137 – La Fazenda (Warning 136) [2003 8.1g Sep 11] 22,000Y: second foal: dam unraced daughter of smart Spanish filly (won Spanish 1000 Guineas/Oaks) Teresa: 50/1, tailed off in maiden at Chepstow. *M. C. Pipe* —

FAR NOTE (USA) 5 ch.g. Distant View (USA) 126 – Descant (USA) (Nureyev (USA) 131) [2003 –: 6m² 5m⁶ 5m⁶ 6m⁴ 5g* 6f 6m⁴ 6g² f6g* f7s Dec 13] sturdy, well-made gelding: fair handicapper: won at Haydock in July and Southwell in November: effective at 5f/6f: acts on fibresand, good to firm and good to soft going: tried in cheekpieces, blinkered last 5 starts. *S. R. Bowring* **70**

FARQAD (USA) 4 b.c. Danzig (USA) – Futuh (USA) 95 (Diesis 133) [2003 a6f 8m³ 7m 7g 7m 6m⁵ Sep 13] robust, good-bodied colt: useful performer: missed 2002: left Saeed bin Suroor after reappearance: best effort when third to Bowman in listed event at Goodwood second start: stays 1m: acts on good to firm ground: reared and unseated rider leaving stall third start: sent to Serbia. *M. P. Tregoning* **106 ?**

FARRIERS CHARM 2 b.f. (Mar 27) In Command (IRE) 114 – Carn Maire 83 (Northern Prospect (USA)) [2003 6g⁶ 5.7f⁴ 7m⁴ Oct 23] half-sister to several winners, including fairly useful 1999 2-y-o 5f winner Passion Flower (by Forzando) and 6f winner Maple Burl (by Dominion): dam 2-y-o 5f winner: easily best effort (modest form) in maiden at Bath second start: likely to prove best at 5f/6f. *D. J. Coakley* **58**

FAR STORM (USA) 3 ch.g. Smart Strike (CAN) 121 – Kadeena 76 (Never So Bold 135) [2003 61p: p12g 12m³ 11.6g Apr 14] tall gelding: modest maiden: stays 1½m: acts on good to firm and good to soft ground: tried visored: has raced freely/carried head awkwardly. *A. M. Balding* **58**

FAST AND NEAT (IRE) 7 ch.g. Soviet Lad (USA) – Stop The Cavalry (Relko 136) [2003 –: 11.9m⁵ 11.9m⁵ 16g* 14.1m³ 16.5m 14.1m³ 16d Aug 11] leggy gelding: modest performer: 33/1-winner of minor event at Nottingham in June: stays easy 2m: acts on good to firm going: front runner. *R. Guest* **60**

FAST CINDY (USA) 4 b.f. Fastness (IRE) 127 – Forever Cindy (ARG) (Forever Sparkle (USA)) [2003 73: 15m² 15.9m f16.2g f16.2s f14.8s Dec 31] tall, sparely-made filly: fair handicapper: below form after reappearance, leaving P. Cole 4,000 gns after next start: stays 2m: acts on firm and good to soft ground (well held on all-weather): usually held up. *J. W. Unett* **74 d**

FAST FOIL (IRE) 5 b.m. Lahib (USA) 129 – Fast Chick 93 (Henbit (USA) 130) **88**
[2003 78: f11g⁵ 11.6g⁵ 12m 11.7m 11.9v⁴ 10.3m² 10.5m⁴ 12f⁴ 9.9f* 10.2m² 10.3m³
10m³ 10m⁶ 10g³ 12m⁴ Aug 3] sparely-made mare: fairly useful handicapper: won at
Salisbury in June: fourth in listed race at Newbury final start: stays easy 1½m: acts on any
going and all-weather: sometimes slowly away: usually held up: tough and consistent.
M. R. Channon

FAST FORWARD FRED 12 gr.g. Sharrood (USA) 124 – Sun Street 73 (Ile de Bour- **52**
bon (USA) 133) [2003 52, a48: 16.4m Jul 10] big, lengthy gelding: shows knee action: **a–**
modest handicapper on turf, poor on all-weather: stays 2¼m: acts on firm ground and
polytrack. *L. Montague Hall*

FAST HEART 2 b.c. (Apr 26) Fasliyev (USA) 120 – Heart of India (IRE) (Try My **98**
Best (USA) 130) [2003 6m 5m⁶ 5m* 5m³ 5.1g* 5g 6m 5g³ Oct 11] 26,000Y: good-bodied
colt: fifth foal: half-brother to 2 winners, including useful Irish 6f winner (including at
2 yrs) King of Russia (by Common Grounds): dam unraced half-sister to very smart
sprinter Bolshoi: useful performer: won maiden at Haydock and nursery at Chester in
August: good 5¼ lengths third to Majestic Missile in Cornwallis Stakes at Ascot final
start: probably best at 5f: acts on good to firm going: usually tongue tied: often held up.
B. J. Meehan

FATAL FLAW (USA) 6 b.g. Hansel (USA) – Fateful (USA) 90 (Topsider (USA)) **65**
[2003 f11g⁵ p10g f12g f16s⁵ f12g* p12g p13g⁶ Mar 1] fair performer: trained by
C. Boutin in France until 2001: missed 2002: won seller at Wolverhampton in February:
stays 1½m: acts on all-weather and soft going: usually tongue tied. *D. Shaw*

FATAYAAT (IRE) 2 b.f. (Apr 17) Machiavellian (USA) 123 – Maraatib (IRE) 93 **65 p**
(Green Desert (USA) 127) [2003 6g Oct 24] small filly: closely related to 2 winners by
Lycius, including useful 5f/6f winner (including at 2 yrs) Khasayl, and half-sister to
several winners, including 3-y-o Muwajaha: dam 5f (including at 2 yrs)/6f winner: 5/1,
eighth of 18 in maiden at Newbury, starting slowly: will probably do better. *B. W. Hills*

FATEHALKHAIR (IRE) 11 ch.g. Kris 135 – Midway Lady (USA) 126 (Alleged **–**
(USA) 138) [2003 77, a–: f16s⁶ 13.8m Mar 26] leggy, angular gelding: fairly useful
jumper: fair handicapper on Flat at best: well held in 2003: tried visored. *B. Ellison*

FATIK (USA) 3 br.c. Gone West (USA) – Muhbubh (USA) 108 (Blushing Groom **88**
(FR) 131) [2003 94p: 7.9m² 7m² 7.1g⁴ Jul 3] neat, attractive colt: fairly useful maiden:
best 3-y-o effort when 2 lengths second at York on reappearance: races freely and should
prove best up to 7f: unraced on extremes of ground: has edged right: twice upset in stall:
sent to USA. *M. P. Tregoning*

FATTAAN (IRE) 3 b.g. Danehill (USA) 126 – Bintalshaati 95 (Kris 135) [2003 –: 8g **64**
10.2g⁵ 8f 8g⁶ f9.4g Nov 1] compact gelding: modest maiden: sold out of M. Tregoning's
stable 6,500 gns after fourth start: won juvenile hurdle in September for P. Hobbs: well
beaten on return to Flat final start: stays 1¼m: sometimes slowly away. *J. G. M. O'Shea*

FAVIA 4 b.f. Mujadil (USA) 119 – Gustavia (IRE) 89 (Red Sunset 120) [2003 68: p7g⁴ **61**
f8s p7g⁶ p8g Feb 12] smallish, good-bodied filly: modest maiden: stays 7f: acts on polytrack. *W. J. Haggas*

FAVORISIO 6 br.g. Efisio 120 – Dixie Favor (USA) 82 (Dixieland Band (USA)) **62 §**
[2003 70§: f14.8g* f12s⁵ f14g² f12g* f14.8s³ f12g³ f14.8s⁵ f14.8g³ f14.8g f16.2g²
Aug 15] robust gelding: modest performer: won sellers at Wolverhampton in February
and Southwell in March: stays 2m: acts on fibresand and good to firm going: wears
visor/cheekpieces: sometimes slowly away: sometimes hangs: untrustworthy. *Miss
J. A. Camacho*

FAVOUR 3 b.f. Gothenberg (IRE) 117 – Prejudice 83 (Young Generation 129) [2003 **82 +**
78p: 6.1m⁶ 6m⁵ 7m 6.1m⁶ 6m* 5m 6m² 6g² 7g³ Nov 1] leggy, quite good-topped filly:
fairly useful handicapper: won at Thirsk in September: good placed efforts last 3 starts:
effective at 6f/7f: unraced on extremes of going: carried head high/wandered fourth start:
races freely. *Mrs J. R. Ramsden*

FAVOURABLE TERMS 3 b.f. Selkirk (USA) 129 – Fatefully (USA) 110 (Private **110**
Account (USA)) [2003 7g² 8.1g* 10.2d² 8f* 8m⁵ Oct 4] sturdy filly: second foal:
half-sister to useful 6.5f (in USA at 2 yrs) to 1¼m (in UAE) winner Opportunist (by
Machiavellian): dam 7f/1m winner who probably stayed 1¼m: smart performer: won
maiden at Goodwood in May, listed race at Sandown (edgy) in July and betfair.com
Matron Stakes at Leopardstown (beat Perfect Touch by neck) in September: respectable
2½ lengths second to Chorist in Daffodil Stakes at Chepstow in between: below form in

Maktoum Al Maktoum's "Favourable Terms"

Sun Chariot Stakes at Newmarket final start, slowly away and edging right: barely stays 1¼m: acts on firm and good to soft going: stays in training. *Sir Michael Stoute*

FAX TO SOOTY 4 b.g. Factual (USA) 108 – Saltina (Bustino 136) [2003 55: 7m Aug 28] lengthy gelding: modest handicapper: well beaten only 4-y-o start: usually visored/blinkered. *M. R. Bosley* –

FAYR FIRENZE (IRE) 2 b.c. (Mar 26) Fayruz 116 – Shillay (Lomond (USA) 128) [2003 f6s 7m f6g 6m f6g⁶ f5g⁵ f6g⁶ Nov 21] IR 6,500F, 4,800Y, 8,000 2-y-o: half-brother to fairly useful 1998 2-y-o 7f winner Gold Rush (by Namaqualand) and 1¼m winner Princely Affair (by Prince Sabo): dam French 1¼m/11f winner: modest maiden: stays 6f: acts on fibresand: blinkered last 4 outings. *M. F. Harris* 56

FAYR JAG (IRE) 4 b.g. Fayruz 116 – Lominda (IRE) 80 (Lomond (USA) 128) [2003 106: 5f² 6m³ 6m* 6f* 6f* 6g 6m* 6d⁵ 6f* 6f 6m Oct 17] 115
The latest renewal of the Wokingham Stakes at Royal Ascot demonstrated that there is often little or nothing between the form shown by the principals in the top handicaps and some pattern races, which is not altogether surprising considering some of the prize money on offer in the respective races. Dead-heaters Fayr Jag and Ratio both lowered the six-furlong course record that had been set little more than half an hour earlier by Choisir in the Group 1 Golden Jubilee Stakes. Fayr Jag went on to get the better of subsequent Haydock Sprint Cup winner Somnus in a six-runner listed event at Newmarket in August before taking the twelve-runner Group 3 Ridgewood Pearl Stakes at the Curragh in September by a head from Hanabad, while Ratio won the Group 3 Dubai International Airport World Trophy at Newbury in September. The Tatling, third at Royal Ascot, landed the King George Stakes at Goodwood and finished runner-up to Oasis Dream in the Nunthorpe; fourth-placed Capricho won the Group 3 Holsten-Trophy at Hamburg; fifth

Wokingham Stakes (Handicap), Royal Ascot—
Fayr Jag, whose bit has slipped, is joined on the line by French-trained Ratio (far side);
the pair are followed by The Tatling, Capricho (grey) and Patavellian (far side)

home, Patavellian made remarkable progress to win his three subsequent starts, notably the Prix de l'Abbaye at Longchamp, whilst even sixth-placed Torosay Spring also went on to pattern success, taking the Group 3 Summer Stakes at York.

Fayr Jag had won only three of his thirteen starts before the latest season, a maiden at Thirsk as a two-year-old and handicaps at Ripon and Newmarket at three, but he had shown himself to be a useful and progressive performer. Fayr Jag continued to improve as a four-year-old, placed efforts in a minor event at Beverley and rated stakes at York being followed by a hat-trick of wins in June, including the Wokingham. As a consequence of his successes in rated stakes at Pontefract and York, Fayr Jag ran off his highest ever mark at Royal Ascot. He improved again and was distinctly unfortunate not to win outright, bursting clear of the stand-side group a furlong out and looking sure to prevail, albeit narrowly, until his jockey had to stop riding close home when the bit slipped out of Fayr Jag's mouth. Ratio, in front of those on the far rail, got up in the last stride to force the dead-heat. Fayr Jag's wins at Newmarket and the Curragh came, respectively, after a creditable eighth to Patavellian in the Stewards' Cup at Goodwood and a respectable fifth to Somnus in the Sprint Cup at Haydock. Fayr Jag had mixed fortunes on his last two starts, a below-par effort in the Diadem Stakes at Ascot being followed by the unseating of his rider after stumbling when still in contention just inside the final furlong in the Bentinck Stakes won by Ashdown Express at Newmarket. The close-coupled Fayr Jag is the best progeny of both his sire Fayruz and his dam Lominda. Lominda was a fairly useful two-year-old six-furlong winner who was herself out of the useful

Hopeful Stakes, Newmarket—Fayr Jag just holds off stable-companion Somnus;
third-placed Barrantes is virtually obscured by the winner, while Revenue is fourth

FAY

Mr Jonathan Gill's "Fayr Jag"

Irish two-year-old seven-and-a-half furlong winner Olinda. Best at six furlongs and effective on firm and good to soft going (possibly not on soft), the game and consistent Fayr Jag usually races just off the pace. *T. D. Easterby*

FAYRWAY RHYTHM (IRE) 6 b.g. Fayruz 116 – The Way She Moves (North Stoke **44**
130) [2003 f12g f12g 11.9m 16m 14.1f⁵ f14g Dec 12] strong gelding: fairly useful in 2000 for M. Jarvis: just poor form in 2003: seems to stay 2m: acts on soft going, good to firm and fibresand: tried in visor, cheekpieces and tongue strap. *Ian Emmerson*

FAYRZ PLEASE (IRE) 2 ch.g. (Feb 12) Fayruz 116 – Castlelue (IRE) (Tremblant **56**
112) [2003 6d f5g³ Dec 15] €7,800Y, 6,000 2-y-o: second foal: dam unraced: much better effort in maidens (modest form) when third at Southwell: likely to prove best at 5f/6f. *M. C. Chapman*

FEARBY CROSS (IRE) 7 b.g. Unblest 117 – Two Magpies 43 (Doulab (USA) 115) **76**
[2003 83: 6.1d 6m 6m⁶ 7m* 7f⁵ 6d* 6m⁴ 6f⁴ 6g p7g p7g Nov 18] strong gelding: poor mover: fair handicapper: won at Newmarket in June (apprentices) and August: effective at 6f/7f: acts on soft and firm going, and on polytrack: blinkered once at 3 yrs: has swished tail/carried head awkwardly: usually held up. *W. J. Musson*

FEAST OF ROMANCE 6 b.g. Pursuit of Love 124 – June Fayre (Sagaro 133) [2003 **–**
56+, a68: f6g⁴ f7g p8g⁶ f6s p7g⁵ p6g f7g p7g² p7g 7m f7g⁴ f7s³ᵈ f7g f7s² f6g 6d f6g² 7f **a59**
f7s³ f8.5g³ p7g⁶ Dec 17] sturdy gelding: modest performer: effective at 6f/7f: acts on all-weather, well beaten on turf in 2003: tried blinkered early in career, has worn cheekpieces: none too consistent. *P. Howling*

FEATHER BOA (IRE) 3 b.f. Sri Pekan (USA) 117 – Dancing Feather 72 (Suave **77**
Dancer (USA) 136) [2003 81: 6g 6d 7m 7m 7m⁵ 8g² 8.1m⁴ 8.5m 8.3g⁵ 9m³ 10m 8.1d 8.3m p10g p8g Nov 12] leggy, close-coupled filly: fair handicapper: stays 9f: acts on polytrack and firm ground, below form on soft: usually waited with. *M. Blanshard*

FEED THE METER (IRE) 3 b.f. Desert King (IRE) 129 – Watch The Clock 93 **–**
(Mtoto 134) [2003 70p: 8g May 4] big, good-bodied filly: fair form at 2 yrs: well beaten only 3-y-o start. *G. C. H. Chung*

FEEL GOOD FACTOR 3 b.g. Singspiel (IRE) 133 – Colorspin (FR) 118 (High Top **74** 131) [2003 10.1m⁴ 10.4m⁴ 12g³ 10g Oct 6] tall, leggy, good-topped gelding: half-brother to several winners, notably 7f (at 2 yrs) to 1½m winner Opera House and 1¼m to 2½m winner Kayf Tara (both top class by Sadler's Wells) and 4-y-o Zee Zee Top: dam, won Irish Oaks, half-sister to Bella Colora and Cezanne: fair maiden: stays 1½m: raced only on good/good to firm ground: has raced freely. *L. M. Cumani*

FEELING BLUE 4 b.f. Missed Flight 123 – Blues Indigo 103 (Music Boy 124) [2003 **51** 60+: 5m⁶ 5m Oct 4] leggy, angular filly: has a splayed action: modest handicapper: best at 5f: unraced on extremes of going: sometimes slowly away: often races prominently. *B. N. Pollock*

FEEL THE PRIDE (IRE) 5 b.m. Persian Bold 123 – Nordic Pride (Horage 124) **–** [2003 79: 12m Aug 24] IR 30,000Y: workmanlike ex-Irish mare: sister to useful Irish 7f (at 2 yrs) to 1¼m winner Identify and half-sister to Irish 1997 2-y-o 6f winner Taispeain (by Petorius): dam Irish 2-y-o 6f winner: fair handicapper: won at Tipperary in 2002: left J. Bolger €34,000, well held only Flat outing in Britain: stays 1¾m: acts on soft ground: tried blinkered: fairly useful hurdler. *Jonjo O'Neill*

FEET SO FAST 4 ch.g. Pivotal 124 – Splice 114 (Sharpo 132) [2003 119: 6g³ 7g* **117** 6g* 6m May 13] lengthy gelding: smart performer: won listed races at Abu Dhabi (by nose from Royal Tryst) and Nad Al Sheba (beat Firebreak by ¼ length) in January for S. Seemar: tongue tied, below form in Duke of York Stakes only outing back in Britain: effective at 6f/7f: acts on good to soft going: tried visored: usually races prominently: left Godolphin. *Saeed bin Suroor*

FEISTY FLORA (IRE) 2 b.f. (Mar 23) Petardia 113 – Highland Crumpet 46 (First **–** Trump 118) [2003 5m 6f⁴ 6m 7.5m f5g 6m Oct 20] €5,000Y: sturdy filly: second foal: half-sister to 2002 2-y-o 5f winner Highness (by Titus Livius): dam, sprint maiden (ran only at 2 yrs), half-sister to Middle Park winner Stalker: little form, including in sellers: visored last 2 starts. *A. M. Balding*

FEIZOR (IRE) 3 ch.f. Titus Livius (FR) 115 – Blues Queen 85 (Lahib (USA) 129) **42 §** [2003 53d: 5m 6d 9.3m 9f 10g³ f12s 11g 10.9d Oct 13] angular filly: poor maiden: stays 1¼m: raced mainly on good ground or firmer on turf, below form on fibresand: tried blinkered: ungenuine. *R. F. Fisher*

FELICITY (IRE) 3 b.f. Selkirk (USA) 129 – Las Flores (IRE) 102 (Sadler's Wells **106** (USA) 132) [2003 65p: 10m³ 10g³ 10m² 10f³ 10g* 10d³ 12d⁵ 10.3d³ 10.5s⁵ Nov 25] big, close-coupled filly: useful performer: landed odds in maiden at Windsor in August: best effort when length third to State of Art in Prix de la Nonette at Deauville next time: ran just respectably in listed races after, 1½ lengths third to Al Ihtithar at Doncaster on penultimate one: takes strong hold, and probably better at 1¼m than 1½m: best efforts on ground softer than good. *J. H. M. Gosden*

FELIDAE (USA) 3 ch.c. Storm Cat (USA) – Colcon (USA) (Pleasant Colony (USA)) **–** [2003 8m 10d f8.5g⁵ f11g Dec 15] $900,000Y, £4,800 3-y-o: close-coupled colt: first foal: dam, US Grade 3 winner at 1m to 9f, half-sister to dual 1¼m US Grade 1 winner Flying Continental: little form: twice slowly away. *M. Brittain*

FELIX HOLT (IRE) 3 b.g. Woodborough (USA) 112 – In The Mind (IRE) (Taufan **–** (USA) 119) [2003 –: 14.1s⁴ f12g Nov 28] no form: tried blinkered. *J. R. Best*

FELLOW SHIP 3 b.g. Elmaamul (USA) 125 – Genoa 96 (Zafonic (USA) 130) [2003 **83 §** 83§: 7m* 7.6m 7g⁵ p6g³ 7m⁴ p7g 8.1g³ 11m⁵ p8g Dec 30] close-coupled gelding: fairly useful performer: won maiden at Folkestone in April: claimed from G. Butler £7,500 seventh start: effective at 6f to 1¼m, probably at 11f: acts on firm ground and polytrack: often tongue tied, tried in cheekpieces/blinkers: sometimes pulls hard/finds little: usually held up: temperamental. *P. Butler*

FELONY (IRE) 8 ch.g. Pharly (FR) 130 – Scales of Justice 85 (Final Straw 127) **–** [2003 f16.2g Feb 7] poor maiden: well held only Flat outing since 1999: usually tongue tied. *L. P. Grassick*

FEN GYPSY 5 b.g. Nashwan (USA) 135 – Didicoy (USA) 104 (Danzig (USA)) [2003 **73** –: 6g³ 8.2s* 7m² 7.9f² 7.9m 8.1g* 10.3m⁶ 7g 8.2m 10d Nov 6] good-topped gelding: fair handicapper: won at Nottingham (apprentices) in May and Haydock in July: effective at 1m/1¼m: acts on firm and soft ground: tried blinkered/tongue tied: often front runner. *P. D. Evans*

FENWICKS PRIDE (IRE) 5 b.g. Imperial Frontier (USA) 112 – Stunt Girl (IRE) **–** (Thatching 131) [2003 65, a–: 6g Oct 14] strong, lengthy gelding: fair handicapper: well held on belated reappearance: tried visored. *R. A. Fahey*

FERNERY 3 b.f. Danehill (USA) 126 – Fern 100 (Shirley Heights 130) [2003 8g 8.3s³ **78**
10s* Jun 30] strong, angular filly: half-sister to several winners, including useful 7f (at 2
yrs) and 1m winner On The Top (by Caerleon) and fairly useful 1997 2-y-o 7f winner
Frond (by Alzao): dam, 1½m winner, half-sister to Oaks second Shamshir: best effort in
maidens (fair form) when winning at Pontefract in June by 1¾ lengths from Phi Beta
Kappa: will stay 1½m: raced only on good ground or softer. *L. M. Cumani*

FERNWORTHY 3 ch.g. Sheikh Albadou 128 – Daring Damsel (Daring March 116) **–**
[2003 7m p8g 6f Oct 12] fifth foal: dam, ran once in Britain, later won in Belgium: well
beaten in maidens. *Jamie Poulton*

FESTIVE AFFAIR 5 b.g. Mujadil (USA) 119 – Christmas Kiss 82 (Taufan (USA) **–**
119) [2003 57: f6g* f6s⁶ f6g⁴ f6f f6g Dec 9] modest performer: has reportedly had 3 **a56**
wind operations: won seller at Southwell in January: raced mainly at 6f: acts on fibresand
and heavy going: tried tongue tied: reportedly bled once at 4 yrs. *B. Smart*

FESTOR 3 ch.g. Paris House 123 – Miami Dolphin 85 (Derrylin 115) [2003 –: 5g 8m **–**
7d Sep 20] well beaten in maidens: unseated rider at start on reappearance. *A. Berry*

FEU DUTY (IRE) 2 b.f. (Feb 23) Fayruz 116 – Fire Reply (IRE) (Royal Academy **64**
(USA) 130) [2003 f5g 5g 5m* 5m Oct 25] IR 2,500F, 6,000Y: workmanlike filly: first
foal: dam German 6f winner: modest performer: made all in 5-runner maiden at Musselburgh in September: well beaten in nursery final start: should prove best at 5f/6f.
T. J. Etherington

FFYNNON GOLD 6 b.m. Beveled (USA) – Sparklingsovereign 53 (Sparkler 130) **59**
[2003 68: 7g 7m⁴ 6m⁴ 7m 7m 5.5f⁴ 7m³ Jul 31] modest performer: raced mainly at
6f/7f: acts on fibresand, firm and soft going: sometimes slowly away: has pulled hard.
B. J. Llewellyn

FIAMMA ROYALE (IRE) 5 b.m. Fumo di Londra (IRE) 108 – Ariadne 79 (Bustino **69**
136) [2003 63, a68: f6g² f6g³ f6g² f5g f6g⁵ 5.7m f6s⁵ 5m² 5d 5.1m⁵ 5m p6g f5g Dec 12]
leggy, quite good-topped mare: fair handicapper: effective at 5f/6f: acts on any turf going/
all-weather: sometimes carries head high/finds little: tried in cheekpieces: usually races
up with pace. *M. S. Saunders*

FICTIONAL 2 b.c. (Mar 8) Fraam 114 – Manon Lescaut 56 (Then Again 126) [2003 **80 p**
6m² 5.9d 6m³ 6m* 6m³ 6g² Oct 25] 4,500F, 7,000Y: sturdy colt: sixth foal: half-brother
to winner in Greece by Magic Ring: dam staying maiden: fairly useful performer: won
maiden at Catterick in September: good efforts in nurseries at Newmarket and Newbury
(neck second of 17 to Milly Waters) after: may prove best at 5f/6f: acts on good to firm
ground: races prominently: type to do well in handicaps as 3-y-o. *B. A. McMahon*

FIDDLE ME BLUE 2 ch.f. (Jan 19) Bluebird (USA) 125 – Fiddle-Dee-Dee (IRE) **77 p**
(Mujtahid (USA) 118) [2003 6d³ 6g* Oct 13] 46,000Y: strong filly: second foal: dam
unraced half-sister to smart performer who stayed 10.5f Dartrey: showed promise on
debut then landed odds by neck from Speedbird in 13-runner maiden at Windsor, pulling
hard and just pushed out after quickening 1f out: may well prove best at 5f/6f: should
make a fairly useful handicapper. *H. Morrison*

*Prix Saint-Alary, Longchamp—Fidelite overturns the favourite Hi Dubai;
Arvada (rail) and Campsie Fells are third and fourth*

FIDDLERS CREEK (IRE) 4 b.g. Danehill (USA) 126 – Mythical Creek (USA) **70**
(Pleasant Tap (USA)) [2003 75p: p12g² p12g⁴ 12.1g 9.2m³ 12.3m⁶ 16g Nov 5] quite **a82**
good-topped gelding: fairly useful handicapper on all-weather, fair on turf: stays 1½m:
acts on all-weather, good to firm and soft ground: has worn cheekpieces. *R. Allan*

FIDDLERS FORD (IRE) 2 b.g. (Apr 10) Sadler's Wells (USA) 132 – Old Domes- **–**
day Book 93 (High Top 131) [2003 7m Aug 8] 65,000F, €500,000Y: good-bodied
gelding: has scope: closely related to 6f winner Midnight Shift (by Night Shift) and
half-brother to several winners, notably very smart sprinter Owington (by Green Desert):
dam 10.4f winner: 14/1 and visored, slowly away and went in snatches when thirteenth of
18 in maiden at Newmarket: subsequently gelded. *J. Noseda*

FIDDLERS REACH (CAN) 3 ch.g. Kingmambo (USA) 125 – Tiny Decision (USA) **101**
(Ogygian (USA)) [2003 101: p7g³ 7m⁶ 6g⁴ 6m⁵ 7g 5m⁶ Dec 20] lengthy, useful-ooking
gelding: has a quick action: useful performer: sixth to Muqbil in Greenham Stakes at
Newbury on second start and fourth (beaten 3½ lengths) to Striking Ambition in listed
race at Ascot on third: ran poorly last 2 outings in Britain: left B. Meehan and renamed
Expectations before final start: stays 7f: acts on polytrack, firm and soft going: tried
blinkered: has found little. *B. K. Ng, Hong Kong*

FIDDLES MUSIC 2 b.f. (Jan 19) Fraam 114 – Fiddles Delight 45 (Colmore Row **–**
111) [2003 6m Sep 3] second foal: dam little form: 20/1, eighth of 16 in seller at Lingfield.
M. R. Channon

FIDELIS SEMPER (IRE) 3 b.f. College Chapel 122 – Reflection Time (IRE) **46 d**
(Fayruz 116) [2003 –: 5m⁴ f5g 5d 5g 5m 5m 7m 8m Oct 6] smallish, strong filly: poor
maiden: below form after reappearance: best at 5f: acts on good to firm going: tried
blinkered. *T. J. Etherington*

FIDELITE (IRE) 3 ch.f. In The Wings 128 – Onereuse (Sanglamore (USA) 126) **113**
[2003 10g* 9.3d⁴ 10g* 10.5g 12m³ 12g Oct 19] strong, good-topped filly: second foal:
closely related to French 11f winner Amour Multiple (by Poliglote): dam French maiden

Wertheimer et Frere's "Fidelite"

half-sister to Irish Derby winner Winged Love (by In The Wings): smart performer: won minor event at Longchamp in March and Prix Saint-Alary there (by 2 lengths from Hi Dubai) in May: disappointing in Prix de Diane at Chantilly next time but ran well when 3¼ lengths third to Mezzo Soprano in Prix Vermeille at Longchamp on penultimate start: below form in Prix du Conseil de Paris at Longchamp final outing: stays 1½m: acts on good to firm going. *Mme C. Head-Maarek, France*

FIELD SPARK 3 b.g. Sillery (USA) 122 – On The Top (High Top 131) [2003 60: **68** 12m* 11.6g³ 12g⁵ 14.1m⁵ 12.1d² 11m⁴ 11.8m³ 11.8m⁵ 12.6f 16g⁴ 12.1m⁶ 16m⁶ 12m* 13.8m⁶ Oct 18] good-bodied gelding: fair handicapper: won at Catterick in March and October: effective at 1½m to 2m: acts on good to firm and good to soft ground: tried visored, wore cheekpieces 5 of last 6 starts: free-going sort, usually held up. *J. A. Glover*

FIENNES (USA) 5 b. or br.g. Dayjur (USA) 137 – Artic Strech (USA) (Arctic Tern (USA) 126) [2003 53, a63: f6s 6m f6g⁵ f6g² f6g⁶ f5s³ Dec 27] small, sparely-made gelding: **a47** poor performer: effective at 5f to easy 7f: acts on good to firm ground and fibresand: tried in headgear. *Mrs N. Macauley*

FIFE AND DRUM (USA) 6 b. or br.g. Rahy (USA) 115 – Fife (IRE) 95 (Lomond **69** (USA) 128) [2003 72: 10m⁶ 10.3g p10g 10.1f* 11.9f³ 10.9m⁴ p10g² 8m² p8g² p10g p10g p13g Dec 29] smallish gelding: fair performer: won seller at Yarmouth in July: claimed from J. Akehurst £5,500 after ninth outing: unseated rider leaving stalls next time: best at 1m/1¼m: acts on polytrack, best turf efforts on good going or firmer: tried blinkered, often wears cheekpieces: usually races prominently. *Miss J. Feilden*

FIFTH COLUMN (USA) 2 b.g. (May 8) Allied Forces (USA) 123 – Miff (USA) **– p** (Beau Genius (CAN)) [2003 8m Sep 23] compact, attractive gelding: second foal: dam unraced: favourite but very green, well held in maiden at Newmarket: likely to do better. *J. R. Fanshawe*

FIFTH EDITION 7 b.m. Rock Hopper 124 – Glossary (Reference Point 139) [2003 **58** 62: 11.8g⁴ 12d⁵ 16m² Jul 31] modest handicapper: won apprentice event at Leicester in May: stays 2m: acts on firm and soft going: usually held up. *R. Guest*

FIGHT THE FEELING 5 ch.g. Beveled (USA) – Alvecote Lady 50 (Touching **66** Wood (USA) 127) [2003 66: f12s* f12g⁴ f12g f9.4s⁴ f12g 12.1d* 13m³ 12g⁵ f14.8s³ f12s f12g* f9.4g⁶ Dec 26] angular gelding: fair handicapper: won at Southwell in January, Beverley (dead-heated) in July and Wolverhampton in November: barely stays 2m: acts on heavy going, good to firm and fibresand: visored last 2 starts: consistent. *J. W. Unett*

FIGHT YOUR CORNER 4 b.c. Muhtarram (USA) 125 – Dame Ashfield 90 (Grundy **114** 137) [2003 111: 12g⁵ 13.3m² 20m Jun 19] tall, angular, useful-looking colt: fluent mover: smart performer: fractured hind cannon bone when fifth in Derby at Epsom final 3-y-o outing (left M. Johnston after): right back to best when ¾-length second to Gamut in listed race at Newbury in May: took good hold to post (also fly leaping) and in race when always behind in Gold Cup at Royal Ascot: suffered from serious ligament injury after: should stay at least 2m: acts on firm and good to soft going: soon off bridle/carried head awkwardly on 3-y-o reappearance: stays in training. *Saeed bin Suroor*

FIG LEAF (FR) 4 b.f. Distant Relative 128 – Shady Leaf (IRE) 56 (Glint of Gold **58** 128) [2003 75: p7g f8g⁵ Jan 21] tall, useful-looking filly: fair performer: below form in 2003: usually blinkered/visored: races prominently. *P. W. D'Arcy*

FIGURA 5 b.m. Rudimentary (USA) 118 – Dream Baby (Master Willie 129) [2003 64: **79 d** p10g* p10g p10g* p12g⁴ p10g⁵ p10g² p12g² p10g* 10g 11.9m³ 10d 9m 10f³ p12g 10m³ 10m 10m 8.5g Sep 10] big, leggy mare: fair handicapper on all-weather, modest on turf: won at Lingfield in January, February and April: effective at 1¼m to 1½m: acts on polytrack and firm going, no form on softer than good: usually held up: sold 5,800 gns. *R. Ingram*

FILLE DE ROI 3 b.f. Desert King (IRE) 129 – Western Heights (Shirley Heights 130) **–** [2003 –: 7m 8m 8.1m Jun 6] close-coupled filly: little form. *Jedd O'Keeffe*

FILLIEMOU (IRE) 2 gr.f. (Mar 10) Goldmark (USA) 113 – St Louis Lady 71 (Absa- **65** lom 128) [2003 5m 5s⁴ 6g⁴ 8.1g 8m⁴ 7m 7g Oct 24] quite good-topped filly: fourth foal: half-sister to 3-y-o Twentytwosilver: dam 7f winner: fair maiden: stays easy 1m: acts on soft and good to firm going: sometimes mounted on track/swerves leaving stall. *A. W. Carroll*

FINAL DIVIDEND (IRE) 7 b.g. Second Set (IRE) 127 – Prime Interest (IRE) **61** (Kings Lake (USA) 133) [2003 74: 10.3g p12g 11.9m* 12.3m⁶ 11.5g⁵ p12g⁵ f12s 10d⁶ p13g⁴ p16g³ Nov 26] close-coupled gelding: modest performer: won ladies minor event at Brighton in June: effective at 1½m to easy 2m: acts on soft and firm going, probably better on polytrack than fibresand: tried in cheekpieces: often amateur ridden. *J. M. P. Eustace*

FINAL FAZE   4 ch.f. Chaddleworth (IRE) 103 – Fine Fettle (Final Straw 127) [2003   –
59: p10g 8.2s May 17] lengthy filly: modest maiden: well held in 2003: tried tongue tied.
D. J. Coakley

FINAL LAP   7 b.g. Batshoof 122 – Lap of Honour 100 (Final Straw 127) [2003 –:   –
17.2f f12s f12g Dec 22] of little account nowadays. *S. T. Lewis*

FINAL VIEW (FR)   4 b.g. Distant View (USA) 126 – Unafurtivalagrima (USA) (Quest   –
For Fame 127) [2003 f12g 14m⁵ f12g Nov 28] 550,000 francs Y: first foal: dam, US
maiden, granddaughter of Oaks winner Monade: fairly useful form in France at 3 yrs
(ran twice) for M. Zilber: well held in Britain, leaving T. Wall after reappearance: tried
blinkered. *N. P. Littmoden*

FINANCIAL FUTURE   3 b.g. Barathea (IRE) 127 – In Perpetuity 90 (Great Nephew   **103 +**
126) [2003 89: 9d² 10g³ 10g² 11.5g² 11.9m* 12g* 12d Jul 30] strong, close-coupled
gelding: useful performer: won maiden at Haydock (by 8 lengths from Trust Rule) and
Davidoff Swiss Derby at Frauenfeld (by ¾ length from Lyndaar), both in June: below
form in Tote Gold Trophy (Handicap) at Goodwood final start: gelded after: stays 1½m:
acts on good to firm and good to soft going: usually races prominently. *M. Johnston*

FINDERS KEEPERS   2 b.g. (Feb 11) Selkirk (USA) 129 – La Nuit Rose (FR) 109   **87**
(Rainbow Quest (USA) 134) [2003 6m³ 6d² 6m Aug 20] tall, rangy gelding: has scope:
second foal: half-brother to 3-y-o Finger of Fate: dam, 2-y-o 7f winner, out of Prix de
Diane winner Caerlina: fairly useful form in maidens when placed at Newbury and Goodwood (6 lengths second to Tahreeb): raced much too freely final start: needs to settle to
stay beyond 6f. *E. A. L. Dunlop*

FINE FRENZY (IRE)   3 b.f. Great Commotion (USA) 123 – Fine Project (IRE) 92   **53**
(Project Manager 111) [2003 68d: p7g⁵ p8g⁶ p7g⁵ p7g 7m 6f⁵ 7m² 6.9m 7g³ 7f⁶ 7g⁴ 7m
Oct 14] rather leggy, useful-looking filly: fluent mover: modest performer: stays 7f: acts
on good to firm going and polytrack: visored (pulled hard) sixth start, wore cheekpieces
next 4 outings. *J. W. Hills*

FINE PALETTE   3 ch.c. Peintre Celebre (USA) 137 – Filly Mignonne (IRE) (Nashwan   **79 p**
(USA) 135) [2003 10s² Nov 3] 22,000 3-y-o: big, strong, gelded colt: third foal:
half-brother to fairly useful 7f (including at 2 yrs) winner Sauce Tartar (by Salse): dam,
lightly-raced maiden, from family of Warning and Rainbow Quest: 7/2, ¾-length second
to Grooms Affection in maiden at Redcar, leading from 2f out until final 100 yds: should
improve. *H. R. A. Cecil*

FINE SILVER (IRE)   2 gr.c. (Mar 4) Intikhab (USA) 135 – Petula 103 (Petong 126)   **83**
[2003 5g² 5m² 5.7f* 7f⁴ 8.3g⁶ Oct 13] €65,000Y: angular, quite good-topped colt: fifth
foal: half-brother to 3 winners, including 5-y-o Middleton Grey: dam 2-y-o 5f/6f winner:
fairly useful performer: won 2-runner maiden at Bath in June: creditable fourth in nursery
at Ascot: stays 7f: acts on firm going: tends to hang right. *P. F. I. Cole*

FINGAL NIGHTS (IRE)   4 ch.f. Night Shift (USA) – Advantageous (Top Ville 129)   **81**
[2003 76: 7m⁵ 6d⁴ p10g⁴ 9.3d⁶ 8.1m³ 8.3g³ 7f 8m⁴ 8.3m 8m Oct 4] IR 27,000Y: stocky
filly: sixth foal: dam lightly-raced half-sister to smart miler Luzum: fairly useful performer: trained at 2 and 3 yrs in Ireland by E. Lynam, winning twice: best efforts in
handicaps in Britain when third at Chepstow and Windsor: stays easy 1¼m: acts on
polytrack, good to soft and good to firm going. *E. J. O'Neill*

FINGER OF FATE   3 br.c. Machiavellian (USA) 123 – La Nuit Rose (FR) 109 (Rain-   –
bow Quest (USA) 134) [2003 87: 8g⁶ 8m 7.6m 7m 6f⁶ 6g Jun 28] sparely-made colt:
fairly useful at 2 yrs for Sir Michael Stoute: little form in 2003: wore cheekpieces last 2
starts: free-going sort. *I. Semple*

FINIANS GOLD   2 b.c. (Mar 20) Fasliyev (USA) 120 – Belle Esprit (Warning 136)   **58 d**
[2003 5d⁵ 5m⁴ 5m 5m f5g Nov 21] third foal: half-brother to 4-y-o All Business: dam,
unraced sister to smart performer up to 1¼m Torch Rouge, from family of Opera House
and Kayf Tara: modest maiden: showed little last 3 starts, leaving J. O'Keeffe before final
one: should stay at least 6f. *J. G. M. O'Shea*

FINISHED ARTICLE (IRE)   6 b.g. Indian Ridge 123 – Summer Fashion 84 (Moore-   **104**
style 137) [2003 100: 8g 8m 10g⁶ 8g⁵ 8m 8m⁵ 8f² 8d* 8m⁵ 9m² 8f² 8m 8g⁴ Nov 1]
workmanlike gelding: useful handicapper: won at Goodwood in July by head from
Haripur: career-best effort when neck second to Pagan Prince at Ascot eleventh start: best
at 1m/1¼m: acts on firm and good to soft going: usually held up. *D. R. C. Elsworth*

FINMAR   5 b.g. Efisio 120 – Patiala (IRE) (Nashwan (USA) 135) [2003 64: 9m⁶ 8m   **65 §**
8m 9m* 8m 7.9m⁴ 9f³ 9.1f² 7.9f² 9.2g⁵ 8g⁴ 9.2g⁶ 8.3m Aug 19] strong gelding: fair
performer: won apprentice handicap at Redcar in May: stays 9f: acts on firm and good to

soft going, well held on fibresand: usually wears cheekpieces: sometimes slowly away: has looked none too keen: unreliable. *Miss L. A. Perratt*

FINNFOREST (IRE)   3 ch.g. Eagle Eyed (USA) 111 – Stockrose (Horage 124) [2003 **59** 61: 8m 7m 6g 7m 8.1m⁴ 8.1f 10m² 9.9m⁵ Aug 23] well-made gelding: modest maiden handicapper: stays 1¼m: raced only on good ground or firmer: tried blinkered: races prominently. *Mrs A. J. Bowlby*

FINNINGLEY CONNOR   3 b.g. Cosmonaut – Arroganza 62 (Crofthall 110) [2003 **–** 68: 6g 8.2d f6g Dec 9] rather leggy, lengthy gelding: fair performer at 2 yrs: soundly beaten in 2003. *Ronald Thompson*

FIORE DI BOSCO (IRE)   2 b.f. (Apr 18) Charnwood Forest (IRE) 125 – Carabine **79** (USA) (Dehere (USA) 121) [2003 f5g* 5m² 5g² 5m 6m* 6g³ 6m 6d 7m² Oct 7] 1,000Y: tall, rangy filly: first foal: dam, ran 4 times, half-sister to 2000 Guineas winner Mystiko: fair performer: won maiden at Southwell in April and nursery at Leicester in July: good second in nursery at Catterick final start: stays easy 7f: acts on fibresand and good to firm ground: none too consistent. *T. D. Barron*

FIREBELLY   2 b.f. (Mar 31) Nicolotte 118 – Desert Delight (IRE) (Green Desert **86** (USA) 127) [2003 6m* 6g³ 6.1g* 7.5m* Jul 6] 8,500F: smallish, sturdy filly: fifth foal: half-sister to 3 winners, including fairly useful 1999 2-y-o winner Alphilda (by Ezzoud): dam unraced half-sister to May Hill winner Intimate Guest: fairly useful performer: won maiden at Redcar in May, minor event at Chepstow in June and listed race at Milan (by 2½ lengths from Looking Back) in July: suffered injury after: will stay at least 1m. *M. J. Wallace*

FIREBIRD RISING (USA)   2 b.f. (Apr 29) Stravinsky (USA) 133 – Capable (USA) **66** (Capote (USA)) [2003 5m³ May 15] $28,000Y: tall, lengthy filly: fourth foal: half-sister to fairly useful Irish 2000 2-y-o 7f winner Crown Capers (by Chief's Crown): dam, winner in USA, half-sister to smart performer up to 1¼m Young Senor: joint favourite, fair form when third of 6 in maiden at York, carrying head awkwardly: gave some trouble at start. *T. D. Barron*

FIREBOLT (IRE)   5 b.g. Flying Spur (AUS) – Musianica 92 (Music Boy 124) [2003 **117** 120: 5m² 5g² 6m³ 5f 5g³ 5m³ 5m⁴ Dec 14] strong, good-bodied gelding: type to carry condition: smart performer: trained by M. Tompkins at 3 yrs when known as Volata: won twice at Sha Tin in 2002, including Centenary Sprint Cup, and good 1½ lengths second to All Thrills Too in Hong Kong Sprint there final 4-y-o outing: in frame all starts on same course in 2003, including when 2¾ lengths fourth to Silent Witness in Hong Kong Sprint on final outing: below-form ninth to Choisir in King's Stand Stakes at Royal Ascot fourth start: effective at 5f/6f: acts on firm and good to soft going: often blinkered. *I. W. Allan, Hong Kong*

Godolphin Mile, Nad Al Sheba—Firebreak shows himself just as good on dirt as on turf; the previous year's winner Grey Memo (off picture) finishes well to take second place, in front of Estimraar and Cayoke (rail)

Godolphin's "Firebreak"

FIREBREAK   4 b.c. Charnwood Forest (IRE) 125 – Breakaway 98 (Song 132) [2003   **118**
118: 6g² a8f* 6f 7g 8m⁵ Dec 14] smallish, leggy, quite attractive colt: smart performer:
good ¼-length second to Feet So Fast in listed event at Nad Al Sheba in January: won
Godolphin Mile at Nad Al Sheba in March by ¾ length from Grey Memo: well held in
Golden Jubilee Stakes at Royal Ascot and Lennox Stakes at Goodwood next 2 starts, but
back to form after break when 1½ lengths fifth to Lucky Owners in Hong Kong Mile at
Sha Tin final start: effective at 6f to 1m: acts on dirt, firm and soft going. *Saeed bin Suroor*

FIREBURST   4 ch.f. Spectrum (IRE) 126 – Explosiva (USA) 88§ (Explodent (USA))   –
[2003 –: f12s f8g⁶ Jan 28] little form: has worn cheekpieces: sold 21,000 gns.
T. J. Naughton

FIRE CAT   4 ch.g. Beveled (USA) – Noble Soul 67 (Sayf El Arab (USA) 127) [2003 –:   **58**
7m² f7s² 6f⁵ p7g f6g f5g Dec 12] modest maiden: stays 7f: acts on all-weather and good to
firm ground: bolted before start and withdrawn on intended reappearance (subsequently
gelded). *A. P. Jones*

FIRE DOME (IRE)   11 ch.g. Salt Dome (USA) – Penny Habit (Habitat 134) [2003   **72**
90, a–: 6s³ 6d⁴ p7g Nov 13] rangy gelding: just fair form in 2003: best at 6f on good going
or softer: tried blinkered/visored/tongue tied: usually held up. *Andrew Reid*

FIRE IN ICE   4 b.f. Missed Flight 123 – Boulabas (IRE) 66 (Nashamaa 113) [2003 –:   –
f8s f9.4g 10m Apr 26] leggy, close-coupled filly: little form: banned from racing after
temperamental displays over hurdles. *B. P. J. Baugh*

FIRE ME (CZE)   3 ch.f. Beccari (USA) 112 – Fantasy Friend (USA) (Elmaamul (USA)   –
125) [2003 8.3g 10.2m f12g⁶ May 23] first known foal: dam won Czech and Slovak
Oaks: placed twice in Czech Republic at 2 yrs: well beaten in Britain. *A. G. Newcombe*

FIRE MOON (IRE)   4 b.g. Royal Applause 124 – Welwyn 92 (Welsh Saint 126)   –
[2003 55: f12s f6g Jan 21] smallish, well-made gelding: has a quick action: modest
maiden: well held in 2003: sometimes blinkered. *S. R. Bowring*

369

*Ladbrokes Handicap, Newmarket—Fire Up The Band is a clear-cut winner of this competitive event;
Irish-trained Perfect Touch (No.11) and Cd Flyer (No.30) fill the places;
Prince of Blues is the riderless horse*

FIRESTONE (GER)   6 b.g. Dictator's Song (USA) – Fatinizza (IRE) (Niniski (USA) **63**
125) [2003 75: p10g³ Jan 25] tall, leggy gelding: fair performer at best in Britain: stayed
11.6f: acted on polytrack, good to soft and good to firm ground: tried blinkered/tongue
tied: dead. *A. W. Carroll*

FIRE UP THE BAND   4 b.c. Prince Sabo 123 – Green Supreme (Primo Dominie **116**
121) [2003 103p: 6g³ 6m* 6g* 6g² 6m 5d² 6m³ Sep 20] lengthy, good-topped colt: smart
handicapper: won at Ascot (by 1¼ lengths from Strathclyde) in March and Newmarket
(justified favouritism in 30-runner race, by 2½ lengths from Perfect Touch) in May: best
efforts when second to Patavellian in Stewards' Cup at Goodwood fourth start and
narrowly-beaten third to Quito in Ayr Gold Cup: winner at easy 7f, probably best at 5f/6f:
acts on firm going, good to soft and polytrack: game. *D. Nicholls*

FIREWIRE   5 b.g. Blushing Flame (USA) 109 – Bay Risk (Risk Me (FR) 127) [2003 **71**
72d: 8.3m⁵ 9g² 8g* 8.3g² 8.1d 8.5g 8.3m Sep 29] smallish, workmanlike gelding: fair
handicapper: won at Kempton in July: has form at 7f to 1½m, races mainly around 1m
nowadays: acts on good to firm going, well held on softer than good and polytrack: has
been slowly away/reluctant to race: usually waited with. *Miss B. Sanders*

FIREWORK   5 b.g. Primo Dominie 121 – Prancing 98 (Prince Sabo 123) [2003 71d: **72**
f6g⁴ f6s³ p6g 7f⁴ 6m f6g 6m* 5.7f* 6d³ 6m* 5.3f³ 6m⁴ 5.7f² 6g Oct 6] quite attractive
gelding: good walker: fair performer: won sellers at Wolverhampton, Leicester and
Bath, and handicap at Lingfield: effective at 5f to easy 7f: acts on firm going, soft and
fibresand: tried blinkered/visored: wore cheekpieces last 8 starts: usually races up with
pace. *J. Akehurst*

FIREWORKS (FR)   3 gr.g. Kendor (FR) 122 – Little Emily 48 (Zafonic (USA) 130) **60**
[2003 a6.5g⁵ a6.5g⁶ 7v 9m 7m 9m⁶ Aug 15] 380,000 francs Y: leggy ex-French gelding:
first foal: dam lightly-raced daughter of Norfolk Stakes winner Petillante: fairly useful at
best, winning maiden at Fontainebleau at 2 yrs: just modest form early in 2003, then left
J. Pease, France after fourth start: well beaten in 2 claimers in Britain: stays 1m: acts on
heavy ground. *K. O. Cunningham-Brown*

FIROZI   4 b.f. Forzando 122 – Lambast 70 (Relkino 131) [2003 63: 8f 7m 6.9m⁴ 8s⁵ 8g **54**
10.1m² 7.9f² 10f³ Aug 29] smallish, workmanlike filly: modest handicapper: stays 1¼m:
acts on firm going, probably on soft: tried blinkered/in cheekpieces. *R. A. Fahey*

FIRST ACORN   2 b.f. (Jan 28) Petong 126 – Mimining 83 (Tower Walk 130) [2003 **43**
5m 5g⁵ 6m 6g 5.9d 8.2m⁴ 5.9m 5f f8s⁶ f8g 7g Dec 16] close-coupled filly: sixth foal:
half-sister to 9.4f and 1½m winner Wellcome Inn (by Most Welcome): dam sprinter: poor
maiden: stays 1m: acts on fibresand, best turf efforts on good going: wore cheekpieces
last 5 starts. *G. M. Moore*

FIRST BALLOT (IRE)   7 b.g. Perugino (USA) 84 – Election Special 78 (Chief Singer **107**
131) [2003 110: 16m⁴ 16.2g⁴ 13.3m⁶ 22.2f⁴ 14f³ 12m³ 12g 14.1f⁵ 12m⁵ Oct 3] tall, good-
topped gelding: useful performer: reportedly had wind operation before reappearance:
best efforts in 2003 when fourth at Kempton (handicap) and Ascot (Group 3 event)
first 2 starts, and when third in minor events at Goodwood and Newmarket: finds
1½m a bare minimum, and stays 2½m: acts on firm and good to soft going: tried in
cheekpieces: usually races up with pace: sometimes runs in snatches: none too consistent.
D. R. C. Elsworth

FIRST BASE   4 ch.g. First Trump 118 – Rose Music 86 (Luthier 126) [2003 –: 14.1m   **–**
12m 8.5m Aug 13] quite good-topped gelding: no longer of any account: tried in cheekpieces. *R. E. Barr*

FIRST CANDLELIGHT   2 b.f. (Apr 14) First Trump 118 – No Candles Tonight 74   **82 p**
(Star Appeal 133) [2003 6d² 7g* Oct 22] quite good-topped filly: third living foal: dam,
1¼m/11f winner, half-sister to smart performer up to 1½m Starstreak: fairly useful form:
confirmed debut promise when winning 15-runner maiden at Newcastle by 3½ lengths
from Telefonica, pulling way to front: should stay at least 1m, though needs to settle:
should progress. *J. G. Given*

FIRST CELEBRATION   3 ch.f. Cadeaux Genereux 131 – Loving Claim (USA) 110   **76**
(Hansel (USA)) [2003 a7.5f a8f⁶ 7f⁵ 10m* Aug 30] sturdy, close-coupled filly: first foal:
dam, French 2-y-o 1m winner (including Prix Marcel Boussac) who later stayed 1¼m,
half-sister to smart July Stakes winner City On A Hill: fair form: trained first 2 starts in
UAE by J. Wickham: best effort when winning maiden at Ripon in August by 1½ lengths
from Gold Bar, making virtually all: stays 1¼m: raced only on ground firmer than good
on turf: sent to Australia. *B. W. Hills*

FIRST CENTURION   2 b.c. (Feb 23) Peintre Celebre (USA) 137 – Valley of Hope   **68 p**
(USA) (Riverman (USA) 131) [2003 p7g⁶ Oct 8] €30,000Y: fifth foal: brother to fairly
useful 1m winner Reyadi and half-brother to 9.6f winner Nicola Bella and 7f (at 2 yrs)
and 1¼m winner Sister Bella (both useful in Ireland, by Sadler's Wells): dam unraced
half-sister to Mill Reef Stakes winner Vacarme and Prix Jacques le Marois winner Vin de
France: 10/1, 4½ lengths sixth of 15 to Celtic Heroine in maiden at Lingfield, finishing
strongly after running green in rear: will stay at least 1m: sure to improve. *J. W. Hills*

FIRST CHARTER   4 b.c. Polish Precedent (USA) 131 – By Charter 104 (Shirley   **119**
Heights 130) [2003 113: 12m³ 12m* 14m* 12g² 12s Oct 5] lengthy, quite attractive colt:
smart performer: better than ever in 2003, winning minor event at Newmarket (by neck
from Putra Sandhurst) in July and listed race at Goodwood (for second successive year,
by 2½ lengths from Scott's View) in August: 5 lengths second to Mubtaker in September
Stakes at Kempton: should stay 2m: acts on good to firm going, probably on good to soft
(acted as pacemaker in Prix de l'Arc de Triomphe on soft). *Sir Michael Stoute*

FIRST CLASS LADY   3 ch.f. Lion Cavern (USA) 117 – Tino-Ella 73 (Bustino 136)   **51**
[2003 p10g p10g⁶ 8.3g 11m 10m⁴ 11.5m⁶ Oct 21] 1,500Y: half-sister to 3 winners,
including fairly useful 1997 2-y-o 7f winner Absolutely Sparklin (by Midyan) and 1¾m
winner Doddington Flyer (by Distant Relative): dam 1¼m winner: modest maiden: stays
1¼m: raced only on polytrack and good ground or firmer. *P. Mitchell*

FIRST DAWN   2 ch.f. (Apr 19) Dr Fong (USA) 128 – Delight of Dawn 74 (Never So   **68**
Bold 135) [2003 7f 7m⁶ Sep 22] leggy filly: first foal: dam 6f (at 2 yrs) to 1m winner:
better effort in maidens (fair form) when seventh at Salisbury: should stay 1m.
M. R. Channon

FIRST EAGLE   4 b.g. Hector Protector (USA) 124 – Merlin's Fancy 62 (Caerleon   **–**
(USA) 132) [2003 –, a62: f12g f12s f12g³ f9.4g² Nov 1] modest maiden: barely stays   **a54**
1½m: acts on all-weather, no form on turf: tried in headgear. *Mrs N. Macauley*

FIRST ECLIPSE (IRE)   2 b.f. (Jan 9) Fayruz 116 – Naked Poser (IRE) 83 (Night Shift   **66 d**
(USA)) [2003 6m 5f* 5g⁵ 5g⁴ 5f⁶ 5m 5.1d Nov 6] 26,000Y: good-topped filly: second
foal: half-sister to 2001 2-y-o 6f winner Twenty Seven (by Efisio): dam, 2-y-o 6f winner,
half-sister to 7-y-o Damalis: fair performer: won maiden at Musselburgh in June: below
form in nurseries last 4 starts: likely to prove best at 5f/easy 6f: acts on firm ground:
blinkered (slowly away) penultimate appearance: often races up with pace. *J. Balding*

*March Stakes, Goodwood—First Charter wins the race for the second year in succession,
landing the odds from Scott's View; Romany Prince is third*

FIRST FOOTING   3 ch.g. Inchinor 119 – Laleston 73 (Junius (USA) 124) [2003 77:   –
6g 6d⁵ 8.2m f8.5g 8.3m Sep 29] smallish gelding: fair winner at 2 yrs: well beaten in
2003, pulled up final start. *M. L. W. Bell*

FIRST FORTUNE   3 br.g. Primo Dominie 121 – Jeewan 82 (Touching Wood (USA)   –
127) [2003 49: 8m 11.5g May 16] poor maiden at 3 yrs: well held in 2003. *P. W. Harris*

FIRST MAITE   10 b.g. Komaite (USA) – Marina Plata (Julio Mariner 127) [2003 81,   **66**
a85: f7g f7g f7g⁴ 7m 8.1m 6.1d 8g³ 9m⁵ f8g² 8m⁴ f8g³ f8g² 8.5d³ 8m 9.2g⁴ 6m⁶ 7.5m⁴   **a79**
10.4m⁴ 7m 8.5m⁵ 9.9d³ 10.1m 10.1g⁶ f8g f8s² Dec 27] tall, lengthy gelding: has a round
action: fair handicapper, better on all-weather than turf: effective at 6f to 1¼m: acts on
fibresand, soft and good to firm going: tried blinkered/visored/tongue tied: occasionally
slowly away/hangs. *S. R. Bowring*

FIRST NOTE (USA)   2 ch.c. (Apr 4) Pioneering (USA) – Angelic Note (USA) 90 (The   **79**
Minstrel (CAN) 135) [2003 p6g 7.1m⁵ 8m² Sep 23] 30,000Y: tall, leggy colt: closely
related to useful 2001 2-y-o 7f/1m winner Angelus Sunset (by Numerous) and half-
brother to 3 winners in USA: dam, 2-y-o 7f winner, half-sister to smart performer up to 9f
Satin Flower, herself dam of Middle Park winner Lujain: easily best effort (fair form)
when 1½ lengths second of 17 to Akritas in maiden at Newmarket, taking good hold up
with pace: not sure to stay much beyond 1m: sent to USA. *B. J. Meehan*

FIRST OF MAY   2 b.f. (Mar 16) Halling (USA) 133 – Finger of Light 89 (Green Desert   **60 p**
(USA) 127) [2003 7g Nov 1] 38,000Y: unfurnished filly: fifth foal: half-sister to 3-y-o
The Local and fairly useful Italian 5f (at 2 yrs) to 7f winner Far Hope (by Barathea):
dam 2-y-o 6f winner out of Lowther winner Circus Ring: 12/1, ninth of 17 in maiden at
Newmarket, slowly away and green: will stay at least 1m: should do better. *M. A. Jarvis*

FIRST ORDAINED (IRE)   4 b.g. Mujadil (USA) 119 – Ordinate (Nashwan (USA)   –
135) [2003 63: p8g 8m 10m f9.4s 10g 11.6m p12g p10g Jul 9] sturdy, lengthy gelding:
modest maiden: well held in 2003: tried visored. *A. D. W. Pinder*

FIRST ORDER   2 b.g. (Mar 24) Primo Dominie 121 – Unconditional Love (IRE) 104   **99**
(Polish Patriot (USA) 128) [2003 6m³ 5f* 5d² 5f* 5.1m* 5.2g³ Jul 28] 32,000Y: quite
good-topped gelding: third foal: half-brother to 4-y-o Beamish Prince: dam 5f (at 2 yrs)
and 1¼m winner: useful performer: won minor event at Ripon in June and nursery at
York and minor event at Bath (by neck from Oro Verde) in July: found little final start:
gelded after: will prove best at 5f/6f: acts on firm ground: tends to swish tail. *Sir Mark
Prescott*

FIRST PRESSURE   3 b.g. Double Trigger (IRE) 123 – Princesse Lyphard 36 (Keen   **60**
116) [2003 71: 11.6g 14m 12m⁴ p12g f16g⁶ p16g Nov 26] modest maiden handicapper:
left J. Mullins after third start: stays 1½m: acts on soft and good to firm ground: tried in
cheekpieces. *D. R. C. Elsworth*

FIRST TARF   2 ch.f. (Mar 29) Primo Dominie 121 – Tarf (USA) 92 (Diesis 133) [2003   –
5m⁶ Aug 13] third foal: dam, 2-y-o 5f winner, half-sister to Queen Mary Stakes winner
Nadwah out of useful sprinter Tadwin: 33/1, well held in maiden at Sandown.
G. L. Moore

FISBY   2 ch.c. (Mar 27) Efisio 120 – Trilby 72 (In The Wings 128) [2003 6m Jun 12]   –
15,000Y: sturdy colt: third foal: dam, 1½m and 2m winner (also successful over hurdles),
out of half-sister to Teenoso: 66/1 and backward, always behind after slow start in maiden
at Newbury. *S. Kirk*

FISHER'S DREAM   2 b.g. (Apr 26) Groom Dancer (USA) 128 – Cremets 94   **55**
(Mummy's Pet 125) [2003 5m 6d 7m 7.5d f6g⁶ f5g⁴ f6g² f6g⁶ f5s⁴ Dec 27] leggy, angular
gelding: half-brother to 3 winners, including smart Italian performer up to 15f My Irish
(by Assert) and 1m winner Sejaal (by Persian Heights): dam, 6f (at 2 yrs) and 7f winner,
sister to high-class sprinter Runnett: modest maiden: in frame in sellers: stays 6f: acts on
fibresand: visored 6 of last 7 starts. *J. R. Norton*

FISHLAKE FLYER (IRE)   2 b.f. (Feb 4) Desert Style (IRE) 121 – Millitrix 82   **76 §**
(Doyoun 124) [2003 5g² 5m² 5d² 5.2m 5m⁴ 5m³ 5f² Aug 27] 15,000Y: lengthy, useful-
looking filly: first foal: dam, ran 4 times (second at 7f at 2 yrs), half-sister to 5-y-o
Royal Millennium out of half-sister to Croco Rouge, a very good family: fair maiden: in
frame 6 of 7 starts: likely to prove best at 5f/easy 6f: best effort on good to soft going:
temperamental. *J. G. Given*

FISIO THERAPY   3 b.g. Efisio 120 – Corn Lily 78 (Aragon 118) [2003 8m⁶ 8.1s*   **90**
9.9m⁴ 10m³ 10.1d³ 10.5m⁵ Jul 13] smallish, good-topped gelding: sixth foal: dam,
effective at 1½m/1¾m, also successful over hurdles: fairly useful performer: won maiden
at Haydock in May: in frame in 2 handicaps and minor event after: stays 1¼m: acts on

soft and good to firm ground, though seemed ill at ease on latter final start: wandered third outing. *M. Johnston*

FISSION 2 ch.f. (Feb 2) Efisio 120 – Area Girl 76 (Jareer (USA) 115) [2003 5m⁴ f5g⁴ f6g* 6g⁴ 5m⁵ f6g* f5g³ Dec 9] lengthy filly: sister to useful 6f (including at 2 yrs)/7f winner Flying Officer and half-sister to several winners, including fairly useful 2000 2-y-o 5f/6f winner Clarion (by First Trump), later winner up to 1m abroad: dam 2-y-o 5f winner: fair performer: won maiden at Southwell in June and claimer at Wolverhampton (then left Sir Mark Prescott) in August: good third in nursery at Southwell: should prove best at 5f/6f: acts on fibresand and good to firm going: blinkered last 5 starts: often races up with pace. *J. A. Osborne* **68 a77**

FITTING GUEST (IRE) 2 ch.c. (Mar 11) Grand Lodge (USA) 125 – Sarah-Clare 67 (Reach 122) [2003 8.2m⁴ 8.2d Nov 6] 260,000F, 160,000Y: fourth foal: half-brother to smart 6f/7f performer Nice One Clare (by Mukaddamah) and 5f winner La Belle Clare (by Paris House): dam 1m/1¼m winner: modest form in maidens at Nottingham: hung right on debut: pulled hard next time: needs to settle to stay beyond 1m. *G. G. Margarson* **64**

FITTLEWORTH (IRE) 3 gr.f. Bijou d'Inde 127 – Remany 66 (Bellypha 130) [2003 51: 11m⁶ 10m 10.9f³ 12.1m⁵ Jul 29] poor maiden: stays 11f: acts on fibresand, firm and good to soft going: races prominently. *W. G. M. Turner* **47**

FIT TO FLY (IRE) 2 b.c. (Apr 20) Lahib (USA) 129 – Maid of Mourne (Fairy King (USA)) [2003 6g 6m⁵ 6.3g Jun 27] IR 7,500F, €17,000Y: quite attractive colt: half-brother to several winners, including 3-y-o Young Mr Grace and 6-y-o College Maid: dam Irish 2-y-o 6f winner: green, fair form in maidens first 2 starts: tailed off in sales race at the Curragh: should stay 7f. *S. Kirk* **72**

FITZ THE BILL (IRE) 3 b.f. Mon Tresor 113 – In The Sky (IRE) 70 (Imp Society (USA)) [2003 7m 6g⁶ 8m 7m f6g Dec 9] first foal: dam, maiden, stayed 8.5f: little form. *N. B. King* **–**

FITZWARREN 2 b.g. (May 11) Presidium 124 – Coney Hills 35 (Beverley Boy 99) [2003 5f² 5m 5m² 5f³ 5f* 5m⁶ 6.1m 5m 5m⁴ 6m⁴ 6m 6g² Oct 28] small gelding: second foal: dam, maiden, stayed 7f: fair performer: won maiden at Carlisle in June: good second in nursery at Redcar final start: stays 6f: tongue tied sixth to ninth starts: visored last 2: sometimes slowly away: often races up with pace. *N. Bycroft* **72**

FIVE GOLD (IRE) 2 b.c. (Feb 5) Desert Prince (IRE) 130 – Ceide Dancer (IRE) 79 (Alzao (USA) 117) [2003 6g 6m⁶ f8s² 8m⁴ f8s* 7g Oct 24] €22,000Y: workmanlike colt: fifth foal: half-brother to fairly useful 7f winner Prairie Dunes and winner in Italy (both by Indian Ridge): dam, 8.5f winner, half-sister to smart winner up to 7f (including Haydock Park Sprint Cup) Lavinia Fontana: fair performer: landed odds in maiden at Southwell in October: not sure to stay much beyond 1m: acts on fibresand and good to firm going. *B. R. Millman* **75**

FIVEOCLOCK EXPRESS (IRE) 3 gr.g. Woodborough (USA) 112 – Brooks Masquerade (Absalom 128) [2003 79: 7.1m³ 7d 6f³ 7g³ 6m p7g 7m² f7s* 8m³ 7.1g 8m Oct 17] deep-girthed gelding: useful handicapper on all-weather, fairly useful on turf: left J. Fanshawe after third start: best effort when winning at Wolverhampton (by 8 lengths from Blonde En Blonde) in September: well below form last 2 outings: effective at 7f/1m: acts on firm going and fibresand, probably on polytrack: visored last 4 outings: sometimes slowly away: sold 25,000 gns, joined Gay Kelleway. *C. A. Dwyer* **92 a100**

FIVE YEARS ON (IRE) 2 b.g. (Feb 17) Desert Sun 120 – Snowspin 75 (Carwhite 127) [2003 5.1m p5g² f5g⁴ Dec 19] 24,000Y: good-topped gelding: fifth foal: half-brother to 3 winners abroad: dam, 1½m winner who stayed 2m (later successful abroad), half-sister to smart performer up to 1½m Gulland: best effort in maidens (fair form) when ¾-length second to Intriguing Glimpse at Lingfield: awkward leaving stall when beaten favourite final start: will be suited by 6f+: open to progress. *W. J. Haggas* **68 p**

FIZZY LADY 2 b.f. (Feb 22) Efisio 120 – The Frog Lady (IRE) 52 (Al Hareb (USA) 123) [2003 6g⁵ 6.1d⁴ Nov 6] small, sturdy filly: fourth foal: half-sister to useful 2000 2-y-o 6f winner Piccolo Player (by Piccolo) and 1999 2-y-o 7f winner The Frog Queen (by Bin Ajwaad): dam, maiden, best form at 1¼m/1½m: fair form in maidens at Newbury and Nottingham (bandaged hind joints and unimpressive to post): will stay 7f, probably 1m. *B. W. Hills* **70**

FIZZY LIZZY 3 b.f. Cool Jazz 116 – Formidable Liz 66 (Formidable (USA) 125) [2003 54: 6g 5m⁶ 5m⁴ 6g⁴ 5d 5m 6g⁵ 6m 6m 6f 6.1m Sep 19] dipped-backed filly: modest maiden handicapper: effective at 5f/6f: acts on good to firm going: none too consistent. *Jedd O'Keeffe* **52 d**

FLAKE 3 ch.g. Zilzal (USA) 137 – Impatiente (USA) (Vaguely Noble 140) [2003 72: –
9.2d 7m 10.5m Aug 7] smallish, close-coupled gelding: fair performer: well held in
handicaps in 2003, leaving G. M. Moore after reappearance. *Mrs S. J. Smith*

FLAK JACKET 8 b.g. Magic Ring (IRE) 115 – Vaula 49 (Henbit (USA) 130) [2003 **77**
88: 6m 5d 5m⁴ 5d 6g⁵ 6m 5.5m Aug 25] strong gelding: impresses in appearance: just fair
handicapper in 2003: best at 5f/6f: acts on firm and soft going: blinkered once: usually
tongue tied: reportedly bled second start: often races prominently: sometimes hangs right.
D. Nicholls

FLAMBE 5 b.g. Whittingham (IRE) 104 – Uae Flame (IRE) (Polish Precedent (USA) –
131) [2003 65, a72: 8f 8m f8g⁴ Nov 24] good-topped gelding: modest handicapper: stays **a56**
9.4f: acts on fibresand and firm ground: tried tongue tied. *P. C. Haslam*

FLAMBOYANT LAD 2 ch.c. (Mar 25) Nashwan (USA) 135 – Cheeky Charm (USA) **86 p**
56 (Nureyev (USA) 131) [2003 7s² Oct 29] half-brother to useful French 10.5f winner
Calling Card (by Bering) and fairly useful 6f (at 2 yrs) to 1m (in Sweden) winner Golden
Miracle (by Cadeaux Genereux): dam, ran twice, close relation to smart middle-distance
colts Mohaajir and Theatrical Charmer out of sister to Dahlia: 16/1, 3 lengths second of
14 to stable-companion Crystal Curling in maiden at Yarmouth, travelling comfortably
and pulling clear of remainder under hands and heels: likely to be suited by 1¼m/1½m:
sure to improve and win a race or 2. *B. W. Hills*

FLAMENCA (USA) 4 b.f. Diesis 133 – Highland Ceilidh (IRE) 100 (Scottish Reel –
123) [2003 49: f12g⁵ f12g Dec 22] sturdy filly: poor maiden: well held in 2003, leaving
R. Allan after reappearance. *Mrs L. B. Normile*

FLAMENCO BRIDE 3 b.f. Hernando (FR) 127 – Premier Night 102 (Old Vic 136) **79**
[2003 –p: 10f 14.1m* 14m² 14m³ 12m⁴ 11.6g⁵ 16g 16.5d Nov 8] good-topped filly: fair
performer: won maiden at Salisbury in July: good efforts next 4 starts: should stay at least
2m: acts on good to firm ground. *D. R. C. Elsworth*

FLAME OF ZARA 4 ch.f. Blushing Flame (USA) 109 – Sierra Madrona (USA) **60 ?**
(Woodman (USA) 126) [2003 12g 12.1d⁴ 12f⁶ 14.1m Oct 4] second foal: dam ungenuine
3m hurdle winner: fairly useful form in bumpers: modest maiden on Flat: should stay
1¾m. *Mrs M. Reveley*

FLAME PHOENIX (USA) 4 b.g. Quest For Fame 127 – Kingscote 118 (Kings **77**
Lake (USA) 133) [2003 10.2g³ 11.5g³ Jul 3] 5,000 3-y-o: closely related to Poule d'Essai
des Poulains second Rainbow Corner (by Rainbow Quest) and half-brother to several
winners, including smart 6f/7f performer Welcome Friend (by Kingmambo): dam won
Lowther Stakes: fairly useful bumper winner: fair form in maidens at Chepstow and
Yarmouth: should stay 1½m. *P. R. Webber*

FLAME PRINCESS 3 ch.f. Bluegrass Prince (IRE) 110 – Rekindled Flame (IRE) –
(Kings Lake (USA) 133) [2003 41: f6g p7g f7s p8g 7m 8m⁵ 7m⁵ 7f 7m Sep 22] maiden:
little form in 2003. *J. R. Boyle*

FLAME QUEEN 2 b.f. (Apr 22) The West (USA) 107 – Red Cloud (IRE) 61 (Taufan **73**
(USA) 119) [2003 7g 6m 6f² Oct 27] leggy filly: fifth foal: dam, maiden who stayed 7f
and sometimes looked none too keen, half-sister to 6-y-o Cape Town: best effort in
maidens (fair form) when neck second of 9 to Oasis Star at Leicester: should stay 7f.
Miss K. B. Boutflower

FLAME ROYALE (IRE) 4 ch.f. Ali-Royal (IRE) 127 – Paradise Forum 78 (Prince –
Sabo 123) [2003 10.3m 8.3s 9m⁶ p12g 12g 8m 14.1m Oct 1] workmanlike filly: fifth
foal: dam 2-y-o 5f winner: little form: twice slowly away: wore cheekpieces last 2 starts.
C. A. Horgan

FLAMING SPIRIT 4 b.f. Blushing Flame (USA) 109 – Fair Test 95 (Fair Season 120) – §
[2003 78§: f11s Jan 14] lengthy filly: fair handicapper: well beaten only 4-y-o start:
unreliable. *J. S. Moore*

FLAMJICA (USA) 2 ch.f. (Apr 30) Real Quiet (USA) 131 – Fiamma (IRE) 97 (Irish **81 ?**
River (FR) 131) [2003 8m³ 8g⁵ Oct 11] $11,000Y, 27,000 2-y-o: leggy filly: first foal:
dam, 2-y-o 7f winner in Italy and winner up to 1½m in USA, half-sister to smart
performer up to 13.5f Fanjica: promising third in maiden at Newmarket: seemed to show
fairly useful form when last of 5 to Fantastic View in Autumn Stakes at Ascot: should be
suited by 1¼m/1½m. *J. A. R. Toller*

FLAPDOODLE 5 b.m. Superpower 113 – My Concordia 58 (Belfort (FR) 89) [2003 **63**
60, a51: p6g 5.7f 5.3m* 5.1m 5m 5g² 5.3f 5m⁶ 5.1g³ 5m 5f⁵ 5g Oct 22] modest handicapper: won at Brighton in June: best at 5f: acts on fibresand, firm and good to soft going:
sometimes blinkered: has hung: races prominently. *A. W. Carroll*

374

FLARAN 3 b.g. Emarati (USA) 74 – Fragrance (Mtoto 134) [2003 58: 7f 8.1f 6m* 5m⁵ **67** 6g 6d⁴ Oct 31] smallish, rather dipped–backed gelding: fair handicapper: won at Haydock in August: best at 5f/6f: acts on good to firm ground. *A. C. Stewart*

FLASHING BLADE 3 b.f. Inchinor 119 – Finlaggan 83 (Be My Chief (USA) 122) **90 ?** [2003 7g 7m 6g⁵ Oct 31] 20,000Y: good-topped filly: type to carry condition: fourth foal: half-sister to 3 winners, including 5-y-o Needwood Blade and useful German performer up to 1¼m Australian Dreams (by Magic Ring): dam 11f to 2m winner: fairly useful maiden: 66/1, seemingly best effort when eighth to Tante Rose in Dubai Duty Free Stakes (Fred Darling) at Newbury second start: free-going sort, likely to prove best at 6f/7f: raced only on good/good to firm ground. *B. A. McMahon*

FLASH OF GOLD 3 b.f. Darshaan 133 – Trying For Gold (USA) 103 (Northern **76** Baby (CAN) 127) [2003 73P: 9.9m⁶ 11.9f² 12m⁴ 11.7f² p13g⁵ Oct 3] tall, lengthy filly: fair maiden: raced only on good ground or firmer on turf, below form (in cheekpieces) on polytrack. *Sir Michael Stoute*

FLASH RAM 2 b.c. (Feb 2) Mind Games 121 – Just A Gem (Superlative 118) [2003 **64** 5f³ 5m³ 5d³ May 17] 7,000Y: lengthy colt: third foal: dam unraced sister to Oaks winner Pearl Angel: modest form in maidens: blinkered final start: suffered sore shins after: will stay 6f. *T. D. Easterby*

FLAT STANLEY 4 b.g. Celtic Swing 138 – Cool Grey 49 (Absalom 128) [2003 –: **41** f12g⁴ f16.2g⁶ f12g² 14.1g f14g 10g⁴ 9.9m May 10] workmanlike gelding: modest maiden **a51** on all-weather, poor on turf: stays 1½m: acts on fibresand and good to soft ground: tried in cheekpieces: none too consistent. *R. Bastiman*

FLEET ANCHOR 2 b.c. (Mar 30) Fleetwood (IRE) 107 – Upping The Tempo (Dun- **67** beath (USA) 127) [2003 6g⁵ 6g Oct 24] fifth foal: half-brother to 3-y-o Hey Presto and winner in Turkey by Forzando: dam unraced half-sister to useful sprinter Up And At 'em: better effort in maidens (fair form) when fifth at Windsor: not sure to stay much beyond 6f. *J. M. Bradley*

FLEETFOOT MAC 2 b.g. (Mar 21) Fleetwood (IRE) 107 – Desert Flower (Green **61** Desert (USA) 127) [2003 6m 7.1m f7g 10m⁶ Oct 22] compact gelding: first foal: dam unraced sister to smart 1991 2-y-o 5f winner Magic Ring: modest maiden: sweating, sixth at Nottingham, best effort: likely to stay at least 1½m. *P. D. Evans*

FLEETING MOON 3 ch.f. Fleetwood (IRE) 107 – Aunt Judy (Great Nephew 126) **– p** [2003 p8g Apr 9] 10,000Y: half-sister to several winners, including useful 6f and 7.5f winner Golden Dragon (by Piccolo): dam, well beaten, out of Oaks winner Juliette Marny: very slowly away in maiden at Lingfield: should improve. *A. M. Balding*

FLEET OF LIGHT 4 b.f. Spectrum (IRE) 126 – Fleet Amour (USA) (Afleet (CAN)) **94** [2003 8.3s 7g² 7.5m* 8m² 8m⁵ 10m* Jul 24] good-topped filly: third foal: half-sister to fairly useful 7f winner Affaire Royale (by Royal Academy) and 6-y-o Blue Streak: dam, ran 4 times in USA, closely related to US Grade 1 1m winner Quiet American: fairly useful performer: won maiden at Beverley in June and handicap at Sandown in July, best effort when beating Sky Quest by 1½ lengths in latter: stays 1¼m: acts on good to firm going: reportedly in foal to Muhtarram. *J. R. Fanshawe*

FLEETWOOD BAY 3 b.g. Fleetwood (IRE) 107 – Caviar And Candy 47 (Soviet **76** Star (USA) 128) [2003 85: 7g 6m 6d 6g 5.7m² 6d Jun 23] smallish, workmanlike gelding: has a round action: fair performer: effective at 5.7f to 7f: acts on polytrack, soft and good to firm going: usually races prominently. *B. R. Millman*

FLETCHER 9 b.g. Salse (USA) 128 – Ballet Classique (USA) 84 (Sadler's Wells **49** (USA) 132) [2003 68, a–: 12m 11.7m 12g⁶ 11.9m² 12m 11.9f⁴ Aug 12] useful-looking **a–** gelding: easy mover: poor handicapper nowadays: effective at 1½m to 2m: possibly unsuited by heavy going, acts on any other: tried visored/in cheekpieces: sometimes looks none too keen. *H. Morrison*

FLIGHT COMMANDER (IRE) 3 b.g. In The Wings 128 – Lucrezia (IRE) 89 **65** (Machiavellian (USA) 123) [2003 11.9m⁵ 12g⁵ Jul 8] 8,500 2-y-o: first foal: dam, 1½m and 12.5f winner, half-sister to St Leger runner-up Air Marshall (by In The Wings): modest form when fifth in maidens at Haydock and Pontefract: should be suited by 1¾m+. *I. Semple*

FLIGHT OF EAGLES (IRE) 4 gr.g. Paris House 123 – Wisdom To Know (Bay **52** Express 132) [2003 –: 5m 6f⁵ 5m⁶ 6m Oct 17] tall, leggy gelding: modest maiden: probably best at 5f: sometimes tongue tied: sold 500 gns. *A. Berry*

FLIGHT OF ESTEEM 3 b.g. Mark of Esteem (IRE) 137 – Miss Up N Go (Gorytus **99** (USA) 132) [2003 79: p10g² p10g* 10m⁵ 12g 9.9m² 9.9f² 10g* 10m* 10.3g³ 12m*

11.9m⁴ 12f³ 12m Oct 16] lengthy, quite good-topped gelding: useful performer: won maiden at Lingfield in January and handicaps at Sandown and Newmarket (awarded race) in July and Newmarket (beat Prins Willem a length) in August: stays 1½m: acts on polytrack, raced only on good going or firmer on turf: has flashed tail: carries head awkwardly: races prominently: tough and consistent. *P. W. Harris*

FLIGHT TIMES   5 b.g. Timeless Times (USA) 99 – Petite Elite 47 (Anfield 117)   – [2003 –: f7s f7s Jan 16] no form. *N. Bycroft*

FLIGHT TO TUSCANY   5 b.m. Bonny Scot (IRE) 119 – Tuscan Butterfly (Beldale   **44 ?** Flutter (USA) 130) [2003 32: 8m³ 10f 8.1g⁵ 8.1m 9.9m 10.9m Aug 25] poor maiden: effective at 1m to 1½m: raced mainly on good going or firmer: has worn blinkers/cheekpieces last 6 outings: carries head awkwardly. *J. M. Bradley*

FLIGHTY FELLOW (IRE)   3 ch.g. Flying Spur (AUS) – Al Theraab (USA) 81   **101** (Roberto (USA) 131) [2003 82: 7.5m 7.6m 8g⁶ 8.5m² 8m 8.5d* 8m³ 9.9g 8m* 10.3g⁴ 8g³ 8.1d² 7.9f² Oct 10] tall, quite good-topped gelding: has scope: useful handicapper: won at Beverley in July and Pontefract in August: good placed efforts last 3 starts, including when second at Haydock (beaten length by Desert Opal) and York (went down by ½ length to Calcutta): effective at 1m to easy 10.3f: acts on firm and soft ground: blinkered last 8 starts: has been edgy/slowly away/wandered: ridden for both 3-y-o successes by S. Sanders. *T. D. Easterby*

FLIGHTY MAC   3 gr.f. Paris House 123 – Stilvella (Camden Town 125) [2003 41:   – f6g 5m 5m 6m 7.5m 10m Aug 30] maiden: little form in 2003. *N. Bycroft*

FLINT RIVER   5 b.g. Red Ransom (USA) – She's All Class (USA) (Rahy (USA) 115)   **83** [2003 75: p7g² p7g⁶ f8.5g* f8.5g* f8.5g* 8g 7m* 7.1f² 7f 6g p6g² f7g* p7g Nov 22]   **a93** close-coupled gelding: fairly useful performer: left S. Kirk after second start: revitalized for new stable, winning minor event and 2 handicaps at Wolverhampton and handicaps at Brighton (dead-heated) and Wolverhampton (career-best effort): effective at 6f to 1m: acts on firm going and all-weather: tried blinkered, not in 2003: has run well when sweating. *H. Morrison*

FLIPANDO (IRE)   2 b.g. (Apr 25) Sri Pekan (USA) 117 – Magic Touch (Fairy King   **79** (USA)) [2003 5f³ 6m* 6m Oct 4] €50,000Y: tall gelding: second foal: half-brother to winner in Italy by Royal Applause: dam unraced half-sister to smart performer up to 7f Sharp Prod: fair form: confirmed debut promise when winning maiden at Newcastle in September: unimpressive to post, pulled hard when held in Two-Year-Old Trophy at Redcar: likely to prove best at 5f/6f. *T. D. Barron*

FLIP FLOP AND FLY (IRE)   2 b.c. (Mar 25) Woodborough (USA) 112 – Angelus   **94** Chimes 80 (Northfields (USA)) [2003 6.1g 6g* 6m³ 6f 6d Sep 10] 14,500Y, 14,500 2-y-o: strong, sturdy colt: brother to fairly useful 6f (at 2 yrs) and 1m winner Stroke of Six and half-brother to several winners, notably smart 6f (at 2 yrs) to 1¼m performer Revelation (by Thatching): dam won at 1½m at 4 yrs in Ireland: fairly useful performer: won maiden at Newcastle in June: good length third of 6 to Venables in listed event at Newbury, only other form: should stay 7f: acts on good to firm going: hung left first 2 starts. *S. Kirk*

FLOPPIE DISK   3 b.f. Magic Ring (IRE) 115 – Floppie (FR) (Law Society (USA)   **77 d** 130) [2003 82: 5.1m 5d 5m³ 5m 5.3m⁶ 5.1m 5.5f⁶ 5g 5d³ 5.1m 5m 5f f5g Nov 28] small, strong-quartered filly: fair handicapper: well below form last 4 starts: best at bare 5f: acts on firm and good to soft ground: races up with pace. *J. A. Pickering*

FLOREEDA   3 b. or gr.f. Linamix (FR) 127 – La Sky (IRE) 107 (Law Society (USA)   **104** 130) [2003 75p: 10m³ 10g² 10m⁶ 11.5g* 12m* 12.5g⁴ 14.6d² 12m⁵ 14.1s⁶ Oct 29] leggy, close-coupled filly: useful performer: won maiden at Yarmouth in July and listed race at Newbury (beat El Laoob by 1¼ lengths) in August: good 7 lengths second to Discreet Brief in Park Hill Stakes at Doncaster seventh start: stays 14.6f: acts on good to firm and good to soft ground: has worn crossed noseband: front runner. *H. R. A. Cecil*

FLORENZAR (IRE)   5 b.m. Inzar (USA) 112 – Nurse Tyra (USA) (Dr Blum (USA))   **58** [2003 47+: 10m 10m² 10m⁶ 11.5s² 14.1m Oct 1] modest maiden: claimed from Miss S. West £6,000 fourth start: stays 11.5f: acts on soft and good to firm ground. *P. D. Evans*

FLORETTE   3 ch.f. Fleetwood (IRE) 107 – Antum 56 (Hittite Glory 125) [2003 –: 7d   – 7g Sep 16] no form: tried blinkered. *D. Morris*

FLORIAN   5 b.g. Young Ern 120 – Murmuring 69 (Kind of Hush 118) [2003 –, a63:   **74** p8g p7g² f7g⁴ p8g* 8m* p8g³ p7g³ Oct 30] fair performer: left P. Mitchell 6,500 gns after second start: improved and won handicaps at Lingfield in May and Kempton (apprentices) in August: effective at 7f/1m (worth another try at 6f): acts on all-weather and good to firm going (lightly raced on turf): often makes running. *T. G. Mills*

FLORIDA HEART 2 ch.f. (Jan 28) First Trump 118 – Miami Dancer (USA) (Seattle **75**
Dancer (USA) 119) [2003 6m^4 6m 7g^5 7m^4 8m^2 7.9m^2 8m* Sep 19] 5,500F, €16,000Y:
rather leggy, quite good-topped filly: fourth foal: half-sister to 1½m winner Crossways
(by Mister Baileys) and winner in USA by Ruhlmann: dam won up to 9f in USA: fair
performer: second in maidens before winning nursery at Ayr: stays 1m: acts on good to
firm going: consistent. *A. M. Balding*

FLORIDA (IRE) 5 b.m. Sri Pekan (USA) 117 – Florinda (CAN) (Vice Regent (CAN)) **32**
[2003 43: p16g f14.8g^3 13.8f 17.2f f14.8g^3 f16.2g^5 15.8m^4 16.2m f14s^6 Sep 2] smallish **a40**
mare: poor performer: stays 2m: acts on fibresand, soft and firm going: often blinkered.
I. A. Wood

FLOTTA 4 ch.g. Elmaamul (USA) 125 – Heavenly Goddess (Soviet Star (USA) 128) **93**
[2003 78: p13g^3 12m^3 14.1g^2 p12g^6 12m^3 12m^3 10g^4 10.3g 12g* 13.9f^2 14.6m* 12d Nov
8] big, plain gelding: fairly useful performer: won maiden at Musselburgh in September
and handicap at Doncaster in October, beating Gralmano by ¾ length in latter: stays
14.6f: acts on polytrack and firm ground: usually held up. *M. R. Channon*

FLOW BEAU 6 b.m. Mtoto 134 – Radiance (FR) 115 (Blakeney 126) [2003 54: 10.9m **–**
10.1m 10.9m 10m 9m Jul 6] poor performer: well held in 2003: tried blinkered, visored
and in cheekpieces: sent to France. *J. O'Reilly*

FLOWER BREEZE (USA) 3 ch.f. Rahy (USA) 115 – Now Showing (USA) (Golden **55**
Act (USA)) [2003 75: 7g 7.5f 8d^4 12.1m 8.2m 9.9m^5 f8.5g Jul 11] quite attractive filly:
modest maiden: probably stays 1¼m: raced mainly on good going or firmer: sometimes
slowly away. *M. W. Easterby*

FLOWERDRUM (USA) 3 b.f. Mister Baileys 123 – Norelands (USA) (Irish River **90 p**
(FR) 131) [2003 64: 8g* 8g* p7g^6 f7g* Oct 16] tall filly: progressive form: won maiden
at Leicester in May and handicaps at Pontefract (idled) in July and Southwell in
October: beat Etoile Solitaire by 2½ lengths at Southwell: effective at 7f/1m: acts on all-
weather, raced only on good ground or firmer on turf: useful performer in the making.
W. J. Haggas

FLOWNAWAY 4 b.g. Polar Falcon (USA) 126 – No More Rosies 74 (Warpath 113) **101**
[2003 86: p16g* p13g^2 16.2m* 18.7m 14m* 14g 12m^5 13.9m 16.2f^3 18m Oct 18] strong
gelding: has a quick action: useful handicapper: won at Lingfield in February, Ascot in
March and Goodwood in May: creditable third of 4 to Supremacy in listed race at Ascot
ninth start: stays 2m: acts on all-weather, raced only on good ground or firmer on turf:
usually tracks leaders: sold privately, joined J. Howard Johnson. *W. Jarvis*

FLUR NA H ALBA 4 b.g. Atraf 116 – Tyrian Belle 77 (Enchantment 115) [2003 91§: **91 §**
6m^4 6g^3 6d 7.2f* 7.2g^6 8.1m^2 7g 7.1g 7m Oct 12] smallish, strong gelding: fairly useful
handicapper: won at Ayr in June: effective at 6f to 1m: acts on firm and soft ground:
sometimes wears blinkers/cheekpieces: usually races prominently: unreliable. *I. Semple*

FLYING ADORED 2 b.f. (Apr 7) Polar Falcon (USA) 126 – Shining High 90 (Shirley **74**
Heights 130) [2003 6m 6m^4 7m Oct 13] quite good-topped filly: fourth foal: half-sister to
4-y-o Bright Green: dam, 2m winner, half-sister to useful miler Polar Boy: fair form in
maidens: fourth at Goodwood: raced freely final start: should stay at least 7f. *J. L. Dunlop*

FLYING BANTAM (IRE) 2 b.g. (Mar 5) Fayruz 116 – Natural Pearl (Petong 126) **76**
[2003 5f^2 5d^2 6m^5 6g 5g^3 Sep 28] IR 8,200F, 14,000Y: small, well-made gelding: first
foal: dam, little sign of ability, half-sister to useful sprinter Amazing Bay: fair maiden:
second at Carlisle and Beverley: likely to prove best at 5f/easy 6f: acts on firm and good
to soft ground: refused to enter stall intended third outing. *R. A. Fahey*

FLYING EDGE (IRE) 3 b.g. Flying Spur (AUS) – Day Is Dawning (IRE) (Green **68**
Forest (USA) 134) [2003 70d: 7.1m 5m 6g 6m^6 5g^6 5.9m^2 6m* 5.9m^5 7f* 7m^6 7m Oct
17] close-coupled gelding: fair handicapper: won at Hamilton in July and Catterick in
August: stays 7f: acts on firm and soft ground: tried blinkered. *E. J. Alston*

FLYING EXPRESS 3 ch.c. Air Express (IRE) 125 – Royal Loft 105 (Homing 130) **98**
[2003 94p: 6f^6 6m 7m^6 7f^4 7d^4 Nov 8] lengthy, good-topped colt: useful handicapper:
fourth at York and Doncaster (behind Tahirah in apprentice race) last 2 starts: stays 7f:
raced only on good ground or firmer. *B. W. Hills*

FLYING FAISAL (USA) 5 b.h. Alydeed (CAN) 120 – Peaceful Silence (USA) **60**
(Proper Reality (USA)) [2003 59, a54: f6s^2 p7g^6 f7s f5s f6s^4 f6g f6g 6m* 6m 6.1m 7m^5 **a54**
6m^6 6.1g 6d 6m Jul 23] sturdy horse: modest performer: won apprentice handicap at
Folkestone in April: effective at 5f to easy 7f: acts on good to soft going, good to firm and
fibresand: tried in headgear/tongue tie: none too consistent. *J. M. Bradley*

FLY

FLYING PATRIARCH   2 gr.c. (Apr 7) Silver Patriarch (IRE) 125 – Flying Wind 51   –
(Forzando 122) [2003 8.1m 10d p10g Nov 29] fifth foal: half-brother to 6f winner Master
Luke (by Contract Law) and 7f winner My Emily (by King's Signet): dam, maiden who
stayed 1m, half-sister to smart 1m to 1½m performer Karinga Bay: well held in maidens:
blinkered last 2 starts. *G. L. Moore*

FLYING PHIN (IRE)   6 ch.g. Dolphin Street (FR) 125 – Robin Red Breast 74 (Red   –
Alert 127) [2003 f11s f12g Mar 20] well held, including when blinkered in seller.
B. Hanbury

FLYING RIBOT (USA)   3 b.c. Exclusive Ribot (USA) – Flying Starlet (USA) (Flying   –
Paster (USA)) [2003 61: 8.2m⁶ 10m f8.5g 8f⁶ 8m Sep 18] modest maiden handicapper:
stays 1m: acts on firm going: usually races prominently: none too consistent: sold 1,700
gns, sent to Denmark. *B. W. Hills*

FLYING ROMANCE (IRE)   5 b.m. Flying Spur (AUS) – State Romance 67 (Free   –
State 125) [2003 68, a54: f12s⁶ f12g Jan 17] small, angular mare: fair handicapper: well
held in 2003: tried visored: sold 5,600 gns. *P. D. Evans*

FLYING SPIRIT (IRE)   4 b.g. Flying Spur (AUS) – All Laughter (Vision (USA))   **67**
[2003 78: p10g 8.2g 12m² 11.9m* 11.9m* 11.9m² 12.3m³ 12m* 10f 11.9f² Aug 7] quite
good-topped gelding: fair performer: won seller (left M. Tompkins) and ladies claimer at
Brighton in May and apprentice handicap at Epsom (carried head awkwardly) in July:
stays 1½m: acts on firm and good to soft going (well held on polytrack): tried visored/
blinkered, wore cheekpieces last 2 starts: has raced freely/looked difficult ride: races
prominently: fairly useful form over hurdles. *G. L. Moore*

FLYING SPUD   2 ch.g. (Feb 7) Fraam 114 – Lorcanjo 36 (Hallgate 127) [2003 f6g f6g   –
Aug 15] 4,000Y: second foal: dam, third at 1½m on Flat, poor/unreliable winning hurdler:
little sign of ability in claimer (slowly away) and maiden at Wolverhampton: withdrawn
after getting upset in stall shortly after final outing. *J. L. Spearing*

FLYING TACKLE   5 ch.g. First Trump 118 – Frighten The Life (Kings Lake (USA)   **59**
133) [2003 67: 5g 5g 5g 5m³ 6m² 6f⁵ 6f 6m 5m³ Sep 25] strong, lengthy gelding: modest
handicapper: left J. Wainwright after third start: best at 5f/6f: acts on good to firm and
heavy going: tried blinkered/visored, wore cheekpieces last 6 starts: has wandered.
M. Dods

FLYING TREATY (USA)   6 br.h. You And I (USA) 118 – Cherie's Hope (USA)   **83**
(Flying Paster (USA)) [2003 –, a94: f8s* f8g² f8s* f7s* f8.5s p12g f8.5s 8g 7m⁴ 7m   **a100**
7.1m³ 7.6m 7.1m 8g⁴ 7.9f Oct 10] useful-looking horse: has reportedly been hobdayed/
had soft palate operation: useful on all-weather, fairly useful on turf: won 2 handicaps and
minor event at Southwell in January: beat Loyal Tycoon a length on last occasion: best
efforts at 7f/1m: acts on good to firm ground, better form on fibresand than polytrack:
tried visored: usually races prominently. *Miss A. Stokell*

FLYING WANDA   3 b.f. Alzao (USA) 117 – Royal York 75 (Bustino 136) [2003 87p: **104**
11.8m 10m² 11.9g² 14g⁴ 11.9m* 12m³ 14m⁴ 14.1s Oct 29] close-coupled, quite good-
topped filly: easy mover: useful performer: best efforts when placed in Lancashire Oaks
at Haydock (5 lengths second to Place Rouge) third start and listed race at Ascot (2¾
lengths third to My Renee) sixth one: stays 1¾m: raced mainly on good/good to firm
going: visored (well held) final outing: usually waited with. *J. Noseda*

FLY KICKER   6 ch.g. High Kicker (USA) – Double Birthday (Cavo Doro 124) [2003   **40**
–: 17.2m 15g⁶ 13.8m⁴ Aug 5] poor maiden handicapper: stays 1¾m: acts on good to firm
going: wore cheekpieces in 2003: winning hurdler. *W. Storey*

FLY MORE   6 ch.g. Lycius (USA) 124 – Double River (USA) (Irish River (FR) 131)   **87**
[2003 76: 5m 5.1s³ 5m* 5g⁴ 5m² 5m⁶ 6.1m² 5g* 6g⁴ 5m 5.5f² 5m⁴ 5d 5.2m* 5.2m³ 6f 6m
6m 6m 5f 5d Nov 7] very big, lengthy gelding: fairly useful handicapper: won at Goodwood (apprentices) in May, Newcastle in June and Newbury in August: effective at 5f/6f:
acts on firm and soft going: has folded/drifted left. *J. M. Bradley*

FLYOFF (IRE)   6 b.g. Mtoto 134 – Flyleaf (FR) (Persian Bold 123) [2003 –: f12s   **53**
11.8m* 11.5f* 14.4m⁶ 12m⁴ Aug 20] modest performer: won claimer at Leicester (100/1)
and handicap at Yarmouth in July: stays 1½m: acts on firm ground: has been blinkered,
visored last 4 starts: makes running. *K. A. Morgan*

FLYOVER   6 b.m. Presidium 124 – Flash-By (Ilium 121) [2003 11.9m 12m Jun 10]   –
poor performer: well held in 2003: tried blinkered/visored. *J. C. Fox*

FOGGIELOAN   3 b.f. Cyrano de Bergerac 120 – Sea Mist (IRE) 53 (Shalford (IRE)   –
124§) [2003 8.3m 8.3d⁶ 8.2f f8.5g Nov 15] sturdy filly: second foal: dam maiden who
stayed 7f: little form. *C. G. Cox*

Mr R. E. Sangster's "Fokine"

FOKINE (USA)   2 b.c. (Apr 18) Royal Academy (USA) 130 – Polar Bird 111 (Thatching 131) [2003 6m* 6g⁶ 6m² 6m Oct 3] sturdy, lengthy colt: seventh foal: brother to 3-y-o Arctic Burst and half-brother to 2 winners, including smart 1996 2-y-o 5.5f (Prix Robert Papin)/6f winner Ocean Ridge (by Storm Bird): dam sprinter: smart performer: won minor event at Newmarket in July: very good head second to Balmont in Gimcrack Stakes at York: respectable eighth in Middle Park Stakes at Newmarket: may stay 7f, probably not 1m: hung right at Goodwood second outing. *B. W. Hills*   **115**

FOLEY MILLENNIUM (IRE)   5 ch.g. Tagula (IRE) 116 – Inshirah (USA) 90 (Caro 133) [2003 –: f5g⁶ f5s Feb 17] tall, lengthy gelding: lightly raced and modest nowadays: raced mainly at 5f: ran as if amiss final start. *M. Quinn*   **54**

FOLEY PRINCE   2 b.g. (Mar 21) Makbul 104 – Princess Foley (IRE) 64 (Forest Wind (USA) 111) [2003 5.7m 6m⁵ 6m 6g³ 7.5m 7.1m³ 7d 7f⁵ 8.3g* 8m⁴ 7f⁶ Oct 27] lengthy gelding: first foal: dam, sprint maiden, half-sister to useful 2000 2-y-o sprinter Bram Stoker: fair performer: left W. Turner after fourth start: made all in nursery at Windsor in October: stays 1m: best effort on good going: sometimes edgy/races freely. *D. Flood*   **71**

FOLIO (IRE)   3 b.g. Perugino (USA) 84 – Bayleaf 104 (Efisio 120) [2003 99: 6g 6g³ 6f 6m 7g 8.1d Sep 27] rather leggy, useful-looking performer: stays 7f: acts on firm going, possibly not on softer than good. *W. J. Musson*   **87**

FOLLOW ME   7 ch.g. Keen 116 – Fairlead 57 (Slip Anchor 136) [2003 21.6m Apr 14] modest performer in 1999: wearing cheekpieces, well beaten on only Flat outing since. *F. P. Murtagh*   **–**

FONTHILL ROAD (IRE)   3 ch.g. Royal Abjar (USA) 121 – Hannah Huxtable (IRE) (Master Willie 129) [2003 f6g* 5m* 6m⁶ 6s* f7g² Jun 27] IR 6,400Y: strong gelding: third living foal: dam unraced half-sister to dam of smart sprinter Passion For Life: fair performer: won maiden at Southwell and minor event at Catterick in March and handicap at Haydock in May: likely to prove best short of 7f: acts on fibresand, soft and good to firm ground. *R. A. Fahey*   **78**

379

FOODBROKER FOUNDER 3 ch.g. Groom Dancer (USA) 128 – Nemea (USA) 97 **112**
(The Minstrel (CAN) 135) [2003 84: 9m* 11.8m⁵ 10.1m 10m² 10g 9.9g Aug 1] good-
bodied gelding: smart performer: won handicap at Kempton in April: vastly improved
form when neck second to Persian Majesty in listed event at Royal Ascot, finishing well:
well held both starts after, and gelded: should stay 1½m: acts on firm and good to soft
ground: often races prominently. *D. R. C. Elsworth*

FOOLISH GIFT (FR) 3 b.f. Barathea (IRE) 127 – Fancy Wrap (Kris 135) [2003 –: **53**
12.1d 12.6m² 12g⁶ f12g³ 12m f12s Sep 6] modest maiden handicapper: stays 1½m: acts
on fibresand, unraced on extremes of going on turf. *W. R. Muir*

FOOLISH THOUGHT (IRE) 3 b.g. Green Desert (USA) 127 – Trusted Partner **69**
(USA) 114 (Affirmed (USA)) [2003 83, a?: f6g 6g f6g p7g⁴ p8g p7g⁴ p7g Dec 6] ex-Irish
gelding: fair sort: closely related to very smart Irish performer up to 9f Dress To Thrill
(by Danehill) and half-brother to several winners, including 1½m winner Blend of Pace
and 1½m/1¾m winner Archive Footage (both useful in Ireland, by Sadler's Wells): dam
won Irish 1000 Guineas: fairly useful form for D. Weld at 2 yrs: fair at best in Britain:
stays 7f: raced only on all-weather and good/good to firm ground: tried tongue tied:
usually races prominently. *R. A. Fahey*

FOOL ON THE HILL 6 b.g. Reprimand 122 – Stock Hill Lass 87 (Air Trooper 115) **88**
[2003 90: 12g 11.6g* 12m⁵ 10g⁶ 12d 10m⁴ 10d 13.3m 11.6g Oct 6] workmanlike gelding:
fairly useful handicapper: won at Windsor in May: stays easy 1½m: acts on any going:
effective visored or not: sold 20,000 gns, joined P. Hobbs. *L. G. Cottrell*

FOOLS ENTIRE 2 ch.g. (May 7) Fraam 114 – Poly Blue (IRE) 82 (Thatching 131) **73**
[2003 7f² 7m³ 7d 7.1m² 7g⁴ 8m³ 7m 6m 7f p6g* p6g³ p7g² p7g² Dec 17] 5,400Y, resold
14,000Y: tall, leggy gelding: second foal: dam, 2-y-o 6f winner, out of half-sister to dual
Gold Cup winner Sadeem: fair performer: won seller at Lingfield (left M. Channon) in
November: stays 7f: acts on firm going and polytrack: wore cheekpieces final start:
sometimes looks none too keen. *J. A. Gilbert*

FOOTBALL CRAZY (IRE) 4 b.g. Mujadil (USA) 119 – Schonbein (IRE) 60 **95**
(Persian Heights 129) [2003 101: 10m 10g⁵ 8.3d³ 10g* 10f 10.5g³ 10.1m* 12m³ 9.2g³
9.1m² 10.4f 10.1s Oct 29] lengthy, quite good-topped gelding: useful performer: won
handicap at Ayr in May and claimer at Yarmouth (left N. Callaghan) in August: stays
1½m: acts on soft and good to firm going: sweated (ran badly) on reappearance: has hung
left: usually races up with pace: none too reliable: sold 11,000 gns, joined P. Bowen.
S. Gollings

FOOT FAULT (IRE) 2 b.f. (Mar 15) Danehill (USA) 126 – Mockery (Nashwan **59**
(USA) 135) [2003 7m 7m p6g⁴ f6g⁶ Dec 19] €160,000Y: second foal: closely related to
3-y-o Tease: dam, 10.5f and 15f winner in France, out of half-sister to smart
middle-distance fillies Braiswick and Percy's Lass: modest maiden: left M. Channon
after second start: should stay at least 7f: acts on polytrack. *N. A. Callaghan*

FORBEARING (IRE) 6 b.g. Bering 136 – For Example (USA) 66 (Northern Baby **83**
(CAN) 127) [2003 93: 12g 10.1m 10.4f* 10.3m 11.9m* 12d⁶ 12m* 10.4f Oct 9] good-
topped gelding: carries plenty of condition: smart in 2000: missed 2001: fairly useful
nowadays: won claimers at York in June, Carlisle in July and Catterick (claimed from Sir
Mark Prescott £15,000) in August: stays 1½m: acts on firm going, good to soft and
fibresand: tends to race freely: winning hurdler. *M. C. Pipe*

FORCEFUL 3 b.f. Forzando 122 – Instinction (Never So Bold 135) [2003 49: p6g Feb **–**
12] rather leggy filly: poor maiden: well held only 3-y-o start. *J. G. Portman*

FORCE OF NATURE (USA) 3 b.f. Sadler's Wells (USA) 132 – Yashmak (USA) **83**
118 (Danzig (USA)) [2003 10f² Jun 25] second foal: dam, 6f (at 2 yrs) to 1½m (Ribblesdale Stakes) winner, half-sister to Warning, Commander In Chief and Deploy: 5/1, 3
lengths second of 16 to Uraib in maiden at Kempton, staying on: will stay 1½m: looked
likely to improve. *H. R. A. Cecil*

FOREIGN AFFAIRS 5 ch.h. Hernando (FR) 127 – Entente Cordiale (USA) (Affir- **107**
med (USA)) [2003 114: 12d⁴ 10f 12g⁴ 12m² 14m Nov 3] good-topped horse:
just useful performer in 2003: won listed race at La Teste in September by nose from
Mont Rocher: effective at 1¼m to 1¾m: acts on good to firm going and fibresand: ran in
snatches second start, blinkered (ran creditably) on third. *Sir Mark Prescott*

FOREIGN EDITOR 7 ch.g. Magic Ring (IRE) 115 – True Precision 84 (Presidium **–**
124) [2003 –, a75: f7s⁵ p7g f6s f6s 7m 7m May 10] workmanlike gelding: fair performer: **a69 d**
well below form after reappearance: stays easy 1m: acts on all-weather and good to firm
going: tried visored: often races up with pace. *J. J. Quinn*

FOREST AIR (IRE) 3 br.f. Charnwood Forest (IRE) 125 – Auriga 73 (Belmez (USA) **49**
131) [2003 6.9m⁵ 8g⁵ 6.9m 9f³ 10m 8m Oct 25] 15,000Y: workmanlike filly: third foal:
half-sister to a winner in Czech Republic by Barathea: dam, maiden who should have
stayed beyond 7f, half-sister to smart performer up to 1½m Beldale Star: poor maiden:
stays 9f: raced only on good ground or firmer. *Miss L. A. Perratt*

FOREST DANE 3 b.g. Danetime (IRE) 121 – Forest Maid (Thatching 131) [2003 6.1g **66**
5.2m 6m⁶ 5m⁴ Jul 23] 1,000F: smallish, good-topped gelding: second foal: dam unraced
out of half-sister to high-class 7f to 9f performer Indian Lodge: fair maiden: raced only at
5f/6f on good/good to firm ground. *J. Cullinan*

FOREST HEATH (IRE) 6 gr.g. Common Grounds 118 – Caroline Lady (JPN) (Caro **– §**
133) [2003 75d: p10g Jan 8] quite good-topped gelding: fair handicapper: wearing cheekpieces, well held only 6-y-o start: tried blinkered/visored/tongue tied: temperamental.
H. J. Collingridge

FOREST PRIZE 4 b.f. Charnwood Forest (IRE) 125 – Midnight's Reward 84 (Night **61 §**
Shift (USA)) [2003 75§: 10.3g 8.2g 7m 7f⁵ 8m Jun 10] leggy filly: modest performer:
effective at 7f to 1¼m: acts on soft and firm ground: tried blinkered: unreliable.
T. D. Easterby

FOREST QUEEN 6 b.m. Risk Me (FR) 127 – Grey Cree 64 (Creetown 123) [2003 –: **–**
f9.4g 8m Aug 25] poor maiden. *A. Berry*

FOREST RAIL (IRE) 3 b.f. Catrail (USA) 123 – Forest Heights 81 (Slip Anchor **43 §**
136) [2003 66: f5s⁶ f7s⁴ Feb 20] fair performer at 2 yrs, just poor in 2003: best at 5f: acts
on all-weather (below form only run on turf): tried blinkered: makes running: has refused
to enter stall several times, and banned from Flat racing from stalls until April 2004.
R. Wilman

FOREST TUNE (IRE) 5 b.g. Charnwood Forest (IRE) 125 – Swift Chorus (Music **69**
Boy 124) [2003 70, a83: p12g 11m⁶ 10d* 10m f12g⁶ Oct 4] well-made, attractive gelding: **a74**
fair handicapper: won at Brighton in May: stays 1¼m: acts on soft going, good to firm
and fibresand, probably on polytrack: tried blinkered/tongue tied. *B. Hanbury*

FORETOLD (IRE) 3 b.g. Darshaan 133 – For Example (USA) 66 (Northern Baby **77**
(CAN) 127) [2003 –p: p10g³ 8m⁶ 9.1g⁴ p12g² 9f⁶ Oct 14] fair maiden: best effort on
handicap debut fourth start, then left J. Noseda: stays 1½m: acts on polytrack: wore
cheekpieces/blinkers last 2 starts: temperament under suspicion. *J. E.Sheppard, USA*

FOREVER FANTASY (IRE) 2 b.g. (Feb 18) Daylami (IRE) 138 – Gay Fantasy **– p**
(Troy 137) [2003 7g 8.1g 8.2m³ 8d⁶ Oct 31] half-brother to numerous winners, including
1¾m and 2¼m winner Fantasy Hill (by Danehill) and 1m to 1½m winner Son of Sharp
Shot (by Sharp Shot), both useful: dam unraced: signs of ability in maidens/nursery, not
at all knocked about in latter: likely to do better at 1¼m+. *J. L. Dunlop*

FOREVER LOVED 4 ch.f. Deploy 131 – Truly Madly Deeply (Most Welcome 131) **86**
[2003 84: p12g 14.1g² 14.1s⁴ 13.3m³ 14g* 18.7m Aug 3] heavy-topped filly: fairly useful
handicapper: won at Haydock in July by ½ length from Tom Paddington: seems to stay
18.7f: acts on all-weather, good to firm and soft going: game and reliable. *D. Haydn Jones*

FOREVER MY LORD 5 b.g. Be My Chief (USA) 122 – In Love Again (IRE) 86 **64**
(Prince Rupert (FR) 121) [2003 57: p12g³ 10.3g* 16.4m⁴ p16g² 14m⁴ 15.4m⁴ 12.1g⁴ **a57**
14.1m² 14f* 12m² 15.9m 14.1m p13g⁴ f14g³ p16g Nov 26] good-bodied gelding: modest
handicapper: won at Lingfield (apprentice event) in July and Musselburgh in August:
effective at 1¼m, and stays easy 2m: acts on all-weather, soft and firm ground: tried
blinkered/tongue tied: often slowly away: effective making running or held up: reliable.
J. R. Best

FOREVER PHOENIX 3 b.f. Shareef Dancer (USA) 135 – With Care 78 (Warning **76**
136) [2003 8g⁴ 7.5m² 7f f8.5g* Dec 26] strong, lengthy filly: third foal: half-sister to
5-y-o On Guard: dam 7f winner: fair performer: left J. Fanshawe, won maiden at
Wolverhampton in December: bred to be suited by 1¼m+. *R. M. H. Cowell*

FOREVER TIMES 5 b.m. So Factual (USA) 120 – Simply Times (USA) 64 (Dodge **90**
(USA)) [2003 97: 6f 6g 6f³ 6m* 6m³ 6m 7g⁵ 6m 6m 6m⁵ 7f⁵ Oct 9] neat mare: unimpressive mover: fairly useful handicapper: reportedly visited Agnes World in spring, but
didn't get in foal: won at Newmarket in July: effective at 6f/7f: acts on any turf going,
well beaten only run on fibresand: tough. *T. D. Easterby*

FOR FREEDOM (IRE) 3 b.f. King of Kings (IRE) 125 – Louju (USA) (Silver Hawk **59**
(USA) 123) [2003 78: 7m⁵ 7m⁴ 7m² 9f⁶ 8s a8g² Nov 16] angular filly: modest maiden in
2003, leaving B. Hills 6,500 gns after second start: probably stays 1m: acts on good to
firm and good to soft going. *Alex Vanderhaeghen, Belgium*

FORGE VALLEY LADY 4 ch.f. Hamas (IRE) 125§ – Salul (Soviet Star (USA) 128) **64** [2003 69: p7g p7g f7s p7g 6m² 7m 7f⁴ 8m⁵ 7m 7.1d⁴ 8.3d³ 8.3d² May 16] workmanlike filly: fair handicapper: stayed 1m: acted on all-weather, firm and soft going: tried in headgear: sometimes raced freely: dead. *D. Carroll*

FORMALISE 3 b.g. Forzando 122 – Esilam 62 (Frimley Park 109) [2003 85: 6m 6m **77** 5f⁴ 6g 6m⁵ 6m 5m⁶ 5f Sep 4] good-topped gelding: fair handicapper: effective at 5f/6f: acts on firm ground: has worn cheekpieces: often races prominently: none too reliable. *G. B. Balding*

FORMERIC 7 ch.g. Formidable (USA) 125 – Irish Limerick 89 (Try My Best (USA) **–** 130) [2003 62: 6.1m 6m 6m 6g 6f f6g f8g Dec 19] big, workmanlike gelding: modest performer: well held in handicaps in 2003: usually visored/blinkered. *Miss L. C. Siddall*

FORMIDABLE STELLA 7 b.m. Formidable (USA) 125 – Stellajoe 39 (Le Dauphin **–** 73) [2003 –: p10g Apr 1] no sign of ability. *Miss Z. C. Davison*

FORREST GUMP 3 ch.g. Zilzal (USA) 137 – Mish Mish (Groom Dancer (USA) **–** 128) [2003 f7s 8m Oct 6] IR 22,000Y, 600 3-y-o: third foal: brother to German 1m winner Morcotto and half-brother to a winner in Norway by Hernando: dam, French 1m/9f winner, out of half-sister to Petoski: well beaten in maidens: tried visored/blinkered. *C. J. Teague*

FORSYTHIA 3 b.f. Most Welcome 131 – No More Rosies 74 (Warpath 113) [2003 **63** 10d 12m² 11.1g 13.8d Nov 4] leggy filly: half-sister to several winners, including 4-y-o Flownaway and 1990 2-y-o 7f winner who stayed 15f Beachy Head (by Damister): dam 1¼m winner: modest maiden: should stay 1¾m: acts on good to firm ground. *Mrs K. Walton*

FORT 2 ch.g. (Mar 4) Dr Fong (USA) 128 – Chief's Quest (USA) (Chief's Crown **89** (USA)) [2003 7m* 7.1m³ Sep 17] 52,000Y: rather leggy gelding: half-brother to several winners, including fairly useful 6f (at 2 yrs) to 1m winner Rich In Love (by Alzao) and 7f winner Reservation (by Common Grounds): dam, French 8.5f winner, half-sister to Prix de la Salamandre winner Noblequest and to dam of Pursuit of Love: fairly useful form: won maiden at Epsom in August: better effort when 5¼ lengths third of 5 to Tashkil in minor event at Sandown, leading briefly over 1f out: gelded after: will stay at least 1m. *M. Johnston*

FORT CHURCHILL (IRE) 2 b.g. (Jan 16) Barathea (IRE) 127 – Brisighella (IRE) **–** (Al Hareb (USA) 123) [2003 7s 7g Nov 1] 43,000Y: fifth foal: brother to useful 2002 2-y-o 6f winner Winisk River and half-brother to 2000 2-y-o 6f winner Grove Dancer (by Reprimand): dam Italian 5f (at 2 yrs) to 1m winner: well held in maidens at Yarmouth (slowly away) and Newmarket. *M. H. Tompkins*

FORT DIGNITY (USA) 2 b.c. (Feb 6) Seeking The Gold (USA) – Kitza (IRE) 113 **93 p** (Danehill (USA) 126) [2003 7m* Aug 6] first foal: dam, Irish 6f (at 2 yrs) and 1m winner (later won in USA), half-sister to smart sprinter Marouble: favourite but very green, won 6-runner minor event at Yarmouth by 1¾ lengths from Sew'n'so Character, soon off bridle after slow start before switched and getting on top under hands and heels: will stay 1m: should make a useful 3-y-o at least. *Sir Michael Stoute*

FORTHRIGHT 2 b.g. (Feb 24) Cadeaux Genereux 131 – Forthwith 104 (Midyan **85** (USA) 124) [2003 6g² 7m* 7m⁶ 7d 8m⁶ 10g Nov 1] tall, good sort: has scope: fourth foal: half-brother to smart 1½m winner (stayed 2m) Time Zone (by Shirley Heights) and 5-y-o Sinjaree: dam 7f (at 2 yrs) and 1¼m winner: fairly useful performer: won maiden at Newmarket in June: ran creditably in pattern races/listed event next 3 starts: stays 1m: acts on good to firm and good to soft ground: wore cheekpieces penultimate start. *C. E. Brittain*

FORTINO 2 ch.c. (Apr 24) Abou Zouz (USA) 109 – Blazing Sunset 55 (Blazing **–** Saddles (AUS)) [2003 5m 5m 5g 5m Jun 23] 2,400Y: workmanlike colt: seventh foal: half-brother to 2000 2-y-o 5f seller winner Light Evidence (by Factual): dam 5f and (at 2 yrs) 6f winner: no form: visored in seller final start. *M. D. Hammond*

FORT MCHENRY (IRE) 3 b.g. Danehill (IRE) 117 – Griqualand (Con- **76** naught 130) [2003 78: 7d 7g 7m⁶ 8m 7g⁴ 7g* 5d* 5.2g 6g Oct 6] big, strong, lengthy gelding: fair performer: won amateur minor event at Redcar (wore cheekpieces) in July and handicap at Sandown in August, making virtually all each time: effective at 5f to 7f: unraced on extremes of going. *N. A. Callaghan*

FORT SAUMAREZ 4 b.g. Magic Ring (IRE) 115 – Rocquaine Bay 47 (Morston (FR) **–** 125) [2003 10m 10.2g Jun 5] second foal: dam 1½m winner: well beaten in maidens. *Mrs L. Richards*

FORTUNA MEA　3 b.f. Mon Tresor 113 – Veni Vici (IRE) (Namaqualand (USA))　**41**
[2003 44, a54: 9.3m 12.3m⁶ 10.3m 10.1g 10m 9.1d Oct 14] angular filly: just poor form　**a–**
in 2003. *W. M. Brisbourne*

FORTUNATE DAVE (USA)　4 b.g. Lear Fan (USA) 130 – Lady Ameriflora (USA)　**62**
(Lord Avie (USA)) [2003 72: f12s⁵ f14.8g Oct 20] leggy, quite good-topped gelding: poor
mover: modest handicapper: stays 1¾m: acts on all-weather, good to firm and good to
soft going. *Ian Williams*

FORTUNATELY　2 b.f. (Mar 8) Forzando 122 – Lucky Dip 68 (Tirol 127) [2003 f5g⁴　**95**
5f² 5m* f5s* 5.1g² 5g* 5m³ 5g* 6g 5g⁵ 6g⁵ Aug 10] 1,000Y: close-coupled filly: half-
sister to 3-y-o Wittily: dam 5f winner: useful performer: won seller at Catterick in
April, claimer at Wolverhampton (claimed from A. Berry £10,000) in May, minor event
at Windsor in June and listed race at Sandown (beat Prince of Denmark by 1½ lengths) in
July: ran badly final start: will prove best at 5f/easy 6f: acts on fibresand and good to firm
going: sometimes early to post/wanders: game. *P. D. Evans*

FORTUNATELY MINE　2 b.f. (Feb 13) Dancing Spree (USA) – Fortuitious (IRE)　**–**
42 (Polish Patriot (USA) 128) [2003 f5g⁵ 5.1m f6g May 19] 500Y: second foal: dam
maiden who stayed 1m: no form in sellers/maiden. *A. G. Newcombe*

FORTUNE ISLAND (IRE)　4 b.g. Turtle Island (IRE) 123 – Blue Kestrel (IRE) 70　**93**
(Bluebird (USA) 125) [2003 84: 16m* 18.7m 20m Jun 18] good-topped gelding: fairly
useful handicapper: best effort when winning at Kempton in April by 4 lengths from
Prairie Falcon: well held in Chester Cup (raced wide and freely) and Ascot Stakes (wore
crossed noseband, hung right) after: stays 2m: acts on good to firm going and polytrack,
probably on soft. *M. C. Pipe*

FORTUNE POINT (IRE)　5 ch.g. Cadeaux Genereux 131 – Mountains of Mist (IRE)　**71 §**
80 (Shirley Heights 130) [2003 80: 8g⁶ 8m² 10m² 10.5m 7.1d⁶ 8g⁴ 8m Sep 12] strong,
angular gelding: fair performer: left M. Pipe after third start: effective at 7f to 1¼m: acts
on heavy and good to firm going: usually visored/tongue tied: wandered (would have
won otherwise) seventh 4-y-o start: sometimes finds little: one to treat with caution.
A. W. Carroll

FORTUNES FAVOURITE　3 ch.f. Barathea (IRE) 127 – Golden Fortune 102 (For-　**54**
zando 122) [2003 12d f12g⁴ f12s⁵ Dec 13] first foal: dam 6f (at 2 yrs) to 7.5f winner:
modest form in maidens: should stay 1¾m. *G. M. Moore*

FORTY FORTE　7 b.g. Pursuit of Love 124 – Cominna (Dominion 123) [2003 –: f11g　**71 d**
f8.5g* f8s p10g⁴ 10.3g f8.5g f9.4s 10.5m 8.1m f8.5g² f8g Dec 19] fair handicapper: won
amateur event at Wolverhampton in January: best at 1m/1¼m: acts on heavy going, good
to firm and all-weather: has worn cheekpieces: free-going sort: needs to dominate:
inconsistent. *Miss S. J. Wilton*

FOR YOUR EYES ONLY　9 b.g. Pursuit of Love 124 – Rivers Rhapsody 104 (Dom-　**–**
inion 123) [2003 7f 7m Jul 28] one-time smart winner up to 1m: no longer of any account:
usually blinkered. *C. E. Brittain*

FORZACURITY　4 ch.g. Forzando 122 – Nice Lady 65 (Connaught 130) [2003　**– §**
77§: 8.3m 8.3g p7g 8g Oct 28] strong gelding: fair performer: well held on Flat in 2003:
tried in visor and cheekpieces: inconsistent: successful over hurdles in November.
J. L. Spearing

FORZA GLORY　4 ch.f. Forzando 122 – Glory Isle 60 (Hittite Glory 125) [2003 54:　**54**
14.1d Jul 25] modest maiden: well beaten only 4-y-o start. *Miss B. Sanders*

FORZENUFF　2 b.c. (Mar 12) Mujadil (USA) 119 – Sada 74 (Mujtahid (USA) 118)　**68**
[2003 p5g 5m⁵ 5m⁴ 5g⁵ 5.7f* 5.1f⁶ p6g p5g³ Dec 17] 3,500Y, 9,000 2-y-o: small colt:
third foal: dam, sprint maiden, half-sister to useful 6f/7f performer Matila, dam of smart
performer up to 9f Easaar: fair performer: made all in maiden at Bath in September: likely
to prove best at 5f/6f: acts on firm going and polytrack: none too consistent. *J. R. Boyle*

FOSFORITO (FR)　5 b.g. Zieten (USA) 118 – Bardouine (USA) (Northern Baby　**71**
(CAN) 127) [2003 a8g a8g⁵ a8g³ a8g³ 10m⁶ 10f⁶ Sep 30] half-brother to 3 winners in France,
including 7.5f winner Baragouin (by Le Balafre): dam won up to 15f in France: fairly
useful performer at 3/4 yrs in France/Spain (won at Mijas): trained by G. Bindella in
Spain first 3 starts in 2003: fair form in 2 handicaps in Britain: stays 1¼m: acts on sand,
best turf efforts on good ground or softer: tried blinkered. *G. L. Moore*

FOSSGATE　2 ch.g. (Mar 26) Halling (USA) 133 – Peryllys 67 (Warning 136) [2003　**73**
7m 7s⁵ Nov 3] 25,000Y: rangy gelding: fifth foal: half-brother to 3 winners, including
3-y-o Penelewey and 7.5f winner Honest Warning (by Mtoto): dam, maiden who stayed
1m, half-sister to smart sprinter Cragside: better effort in maidens (fair form) when 4
lengths fifth of 15 to Go Padero at Redcar: should stay 1m. *J. D. Bethell*

383

FOU DOUX (FR) 7 b.g. Le Grillon II (FR) – Folie Douce (FR) (Fast (FR)) [2003 – f16g Jan 9] ex-French non-thoroughbred gelding: blinkered, won 1¾m minor event for non-thoroughbreds at Royan in 2000: well held on only Flat outing in Britain. *P. W. Hiatt*

FOURALI 3 b.c. Lion Cavern (USA) 117 – Zobaida (IRE) 77 (Green Desert (USA) – 127) [2003 7.1g Jul 3] good-topped colt: first foal: dam, 7f winner who stayed 8.5f, out of half-sister to Zilzal: 33/1, edgy and green, tailed off in maiden at Haydock: sold 2,000 gns. *A. C. Stewart*

FOUR AMIGOS (USA) 2 b.c. (Apr 13) Southern Halo (USA) – Larentia 58 (Salse **78** (USA) 128) [2003 5f⁵ f5g 5d* 5.2m 6g⁵ 6d 5d* 5m 5.1d² Nov 6] 10,000Y: compact colt: fourth foal: half-brother to 3-y-o Perelandra and 2 winners abroad, including French 10.5f winner Lantana (by Charnwood Forest): dam lightly-raced half-sister to smart sprinter Bahamian Bounty: fair performer: won maiden at Lingfield in May and nursery at Epsom in October: should stay 6f: acts on good to soft ground, possibly not on firmer than good. *J. G. Given*

FOUR CORONA 3 b.f. Perpendicular 119 – Pixel (IRE) (Silver Kite (USA) 111) – [2003 11.1d 11.9m 10.3m⁶ Jun 28] first foal: dam unraced: well beaten in maidens. *W. M. Brisbourne*

FOUR JAYS (IRE) 3 b.g. Alzao (USA) 117 – Paparazzi (IRE) 68 (Shernazar 131) **89 d** [2003 82, a85: 7.6m² 8g 7.1f² 7m 7.5m² 6.1f³ 7.6m 6m⁵ 7f³ 7f p7g 8m² 8f⁶ p10g p8g⁵ p7g p7g⁵ Dec 30] good-bodied gelding: fairly useful performer: below best after third start: stays 1m: acts on all-weather, raced only on good going or firmer on turf: often wears cheekpieces: has looked none too keen. *N. P. Littmoden*

FOUR PENCE (IRE) 2 b.c. (Mar 2) Rainbow Quest (USA) 134 – American Queen **71 p** (FR) (Fairy King (USA)) [2003 8g⁴ 7g Nov 1] €140,000Y: good-bodied colt: first foal: dam, ran 3 times in France, closely related to very smart French middle-distance performer Antheus and half-sister to smart dam of Criterium de Saint-Cloud winner/Prix du Jockey Club runner-up Poliglote: better effort in maidens (fair form) when fourth of 8 to Menokee at Kempton, slowly away and staying on: will be suited by 1¼m/1½m: type to make a better 3-y-o. *B. W. Hills*

FOURSQUARE (IRE) 2 b.c. (Apr 3) Fayruz 116 – Waroonga (IRE) (Brief Truce **86 p** (USA) 126) [2003 6m⁵ 5.1f* 5g 5.2s² Oct 29] 15,000 2-y-o: robust colt: first foal: dam unraced: fairly useful form: won maiden at Nottingham in October: good second to After The Show in nursery at Yarmouth: will prove best at bare 5f: acts on firm and soft going: type to make a useful handicapper at 3 yrs. *J. Mackie*

FOURSWAINBY (IRE) 2 b.g. (Apr 28) Foxhound (USA) 103 – Arena 86 (Sallust – 134) [2003 5g 6d May 16] €5,500Y, 10,000 2-y-o: half-brother to several winners, including 1m/1¼m winner Wakil (by Tate Gallery): dam lightly-raced half-sister to dam of Vintage Crop: little sign of ability in maidens at Carlisle (slowly away) and Hamilton (hung right). *B. Ellison*

FOURTH DIMENSION (IRE) 4 b.c. Entrepreneur 123 – Isle of Spice (USA) 74 **94** (Diesis 133) [2003 88: 12m⁶ 14f³ 14m* 13.3m³ 14.6g 16.2f 18m Oct 18] sturdy colt: fairly useful handicapper: won at Sandown in July by 1½ lengths from Trained Bythe Best: good third at Newbury next time: should stay 2m: best form on ground firmer than good: usually held up: sold 30,000 gns. *A. C. Stewart*

FOVANT 3 ch.f. Night Shift (USA) – Sheppard's Cross 88 (Soviet Star (USA) 128) **74** [2003 78: 6g 7g 6d Nov 8] good-bodied filly: fair performer: stiff task in listed races last 2 starts, visored on final one: stays 7f: acts on soft ground. *M. P. Tregoning*

FOX COVERT (IRE) 2 b.g. (Jan 23) Foxhound (USA) 103 – Serious Contender **72** (IRE) (Tenby 125) [2003 6g 6f³ 6m³ 6g⁶ 6g⁵ 7m³ 6g² 7g³ 6m² 6d³ 6g Oct 13] 10,000Y: workmanlike gelding: second foal: dam unraced: fair maiden: effective at 6f/7f: acts on firm and good to soft going: races prominently: sold 12,000 gns. *D. W. Barker*

FOXDALE LADY 2 b.f. (Feb 18) First Trump 118 – Nordesta (IRE) 72 (Nordico – (USA)) [2003 6d 7m Jun 10] 600Y: close-coupled filly: third foal: dam 2-y-o 5f winner: well held in sellers at Ripon and Redcar. *J. R. Weymes*

FOXEY LOXEY (IRE) 2 b.c. (Apr 27) Foxhound (USA) 103 – Lamp of Phoebus – (USA) (Sunshine Forever (USA)) [2003 5m Jun 1] 1,200Y: close-coupled colt: fifth foal: dam, ran twice, half-sister to smart French performer up to 10.5f Accommodating: behind in maiden at Pontefract, breaking down fatally after line. *W. Storey*

FOXGLOVE 3 b.f. Hernando (FR) 127 – Rynechra 102 (Blakeney 126) [2003 10m⁴ **66** 12m² p12g Sep 3] sister to 5-y-o Allez Mousson, closely related to smart 1m (at 2 yrs) to 14.6f (Park Hill) winner Coigach (by Niniski) and half-sister to 3 winners, including smart 1¼m to 13f winner Applecross (by Glint of Gold), herself dam of Invermark and Craigsteel: dam 1½m winner: fair maiden: best effort on debut: ran poorly final start: should stay at least 1¾m: sent to France. *J. R. Fanshawe*

FOX HOLLOW (IRE) 2 b.c. (Apr 24) Foxhound (USA) 103 – Soignee (Night Shift (USA)) [2003 6m⁶ 7d⁶ 5m⁵ 6m p7g Nov 29] IR 14,500F: workmanlike colt: half-brother to 3 winners, including French 1¼m winner Algarve Sunset (by Sri Pekan) and fairly useful 1m (at 2 yrs) and 9f winner Radar (by Petardia): dam unraced: no form, including in sellers. *M. J. Haynes* —

FOXIES FUTURE (IRE) 2 b.f. (Mar 24) General Monash (USA) 107 – Indescent Blue 63 (Bluebird (USA) 125) [2003 6g f5s⁶ 7m⁶ f6g* 6g f6g⁵ f7g f6g⁴ Dec 19] 5,500Y: leggy, close-coupled filly: fourth foal: half-sister to 2 winners by Woodborough, including fairly useful 7f (at 2 yrs) to 1¾m winner Lapadar: dam maiden who stayed 1m: fair performer: best effort when 33/1-winner of maiden at Southwell in October, getting up near finish: should stay at least 7f: acts on fibresand, some promise on turf: wore cheekpieces sixth start: usually slowly away. *J. R. Weymes* **65**

FOXILLA (IRE) 2 ch.f. (Mar 9) Foxhound (USA) 103 – Lilissa (IRE) (Doyoun 124) [2003 7g 7m 8m Sep 5] 23,000Y: good-bodied filly: half-sister to several at least useful winners, including 7-y-o Livadiya and 1¼m/1½m winner Lidakiya (by Kahyasi): dam, French 9f/10.5f winner, half-sister to smart French filly up to 13.5f Linnga: modest form when seventh in maiden at Goodwood on debut: looked difficult ride both starts after: should stay at least 1m. *D. R. C. Elsworth* **56**

FOXTROTROMEOYANKEE 3 b.g. Tragic Role (USA) – Hope Chest 70 (Kris 135) [2003 56: p10g⁴ p8g p10g p10g⁴ 11m p10g² 11.5f Jul 24] modest maiden: left M. Usher before running well sixth start: should stay 1½m: acts on polytrack, no form on turf: free-going sort. *L. A. Dace* **a61**

FOXTROT TOO (IRE) 2 b.c. (Feb 24) Foxhound (USA) 103 – Dance Desire (IRE) (Caerleon (USA) 132) [2003 6g⁴ 5.1m* 6g 7m⁵ 6m 6g Oct 13] €12,500Y: first foal: dam unraced half-sister to smart but untrustworthy winner up to 1¼m Intimate Guest: fair performer: won 3-runner maiden at Chester in July: well held in nurseries last 2 starts: probably stays 7f: sometimes carries head high. *M. H. Tompkins* **72**

FOX WOOD (IRE) 2 ch.c. (Feb 15) Woodborough (USA) 112 – Fastnet (Forzando 122) [2003 5g f5g³ 7g Aug 10] 9,000Y: close-coupled colt: second living foal: dam well beaten only start: form (modest) only when slow-starting third of 5 in maiden at Southwell: should stay at least 6f: looked ungenuine in blinkers on debut. *B. A. McMahon* **50**

FOXY DIVA (IRE) 2 b.f. (Mar 14) Foxhound (USA) 103 – Quest For Best (USA) 64 (Quest For Fame 127) [2003 6m f5g 6m³ 6g³ 6m⁴ a6g a8g Sep 28] 5,000Y: third foal: half-sister to French 2-y-o winner in Italy by Night Shift: dam, maiden, seemed to stay 1¾m: poor maiden: third in sellers: left Miss V. Haigh after fifth start: stays 6f: acts on good to firm going. *M. Lundgren, Spain* **42**

FRAAMTASTIC 6 b.m. Fraam 114 – Fading (Pharly (FR) 130) [2003 43d, a52d: f7g⁵ p8g f11s⁴ f8g Mar 20] angular mare: poor performer: well held in 2003: often wears visor/cheekpieces. *B. A. Pearce* **a37**

FRAGRANT STAR 2 gr.f. (Apr 16) Soviet Star (USA) 128 – Norfolk Lavender (CAN) 80 (Ascot Knight (CAN) 130) [2003 5d 6g⁴ 6f 6g* 7.1m 6g⁵ Aug 2] 15,000Y: tall, useful-looking filly: fifth foal: half-sister to useful 1m (including at 2 yrs) to 1½m winner Celtic Mission (by Cozzene) and 3-y-o In The Pink: dam, 1m winner (later 8.5f minor stakes winner in USA), out of 1000 Guineas winner Nocturnal Spree: fair performer: won nursery at Pontefract in July: should stay 1m: best effort on good going: often slowly away. *C. E. Brittain* **78**

FRAMBO (IRE) 2 b.f. (Apr 26) Fraam 114 – Wings Awarded 67 (Shareef Dancer (USA) 135) [2003 f5g 5d 7.5m⁷ f8s² f8g⁵ Nov 25] €13,000Y: leggy filly: second foal: sister to 3-y-o Leonor de Soto: dam 1m and 1½m winner: modest maiden: will stay at least 1¼m: acts on fibresand and good to firm going. *J. G. Portman* **53**

FRANCE 3 b.c. Desert Prince (IRE) 130 – Hyperspectra 91 (Rainbow Quest (USA) 134) [2003 101: 8m⁴ 7d⁶ 8g⁴ 8d² 8f 8g³ 10g⁴ 10f⁶ Sep 6] well-made, attractive colt: smart performer: won Rock of Gibraltar EBF Tetrarch Stakes at the Curragh in April by ¾ length from Al Turf: in frame after in Poule d'Essai des Poulains at Longchamp (fourth to Clodovil), Irish 2000 Guineas at the Curragh (clearly best effort, length second to Indian Haven), Goffs International Stakes at the Curragh and Secretariat Stakes at Arlington: best form at 1m: acted on good to firm and good to soft going: usually blinkered/visored **115**

(not last 2 outings): wore crossed noseband: sometimes looked none too keen: to stand at Allevamenti della Berardenga, Italy, fee €6,000. *A. P. O'Brien, Ireland*

FRANCES CANTY (USA) 2 b.f. (Jan 29) Lear Fan (USA) 130 – Beyond The Realm (USA) (Stop The Music (USA)) [2003 7m⁴ 8.3g⁶ p7g Sep 9] $12,000Y: first foal: dam, ran 4 times in France/US, half-sister to smart French performers Glorify (probably stayed 15f) and Doree (1994 2-y-o 5.5f winner): little sign of ability in maidens. *E. J. O'Neill* —

FRANCIS FLUTE 5 b.g. Polar Falcon (USA) 126 – Darshay (FR) 87 (Darshaan 133) [2003 67: 6d 9m⁴ 6.9m⁶ 6d 6g 8m Oct 25] modest performer: effective at 7f to easy 9f: yet to race on extremes of going: headstrong, and often makes running. *B. Mactaggart* 59

FRANCKEN (ITY) 4 ro.g. Petit Loup (USA) 123 – Filicaia 79 (Sallust 134) [2003 42: 10m Apr 26] good-topped gelding: poor maiden, lightly raced: well held only 4-y-o start. *Don Enrico Incisa* —

FRANCPORT 7 b.g. Efisio 120 – Elkie Brooks 82 (Relkino 131) [2003 71d: f6s⁴ p6g f6s* f7s² f6s⁴ Feb 27] big, lengthy gelding: modest nowadays: won seller at Southwell in February: best at 6f/7f: acts on all-weather and any turf going: tried blinkered earlier in career, wore cheekpieces in 2003: sometimes slowly away. *K. A. Ryan* — a64

FRANGIPANI (IRE) 2 b.f. (Apr 9) Sri Pekan (USA) 117 – Sharkashka (IRE) 84 (Shardari 134) [2003 6m³ 7g³ 7.5g⁴ Aug 17] £4,500Y: tall filly: third foal: dam, Irish 1½m winner (also won over hurdles), half-sister to Yorkshire Oaks winner Key Change: fair form: third in minor event at Windsor and maiden at Goodwood, and fourth in listed race at Livorno (Italy): will stay at least 1m. *P. F. I. Cole* 76

FRANKIES WINGS (IRE) 2 b.c. (Mar 12) In The Wings 128 – River Fantasy (USA) (Irish River (FR) 131) [2003 f8s Dec 13] 52,000Y: third living foal: half-brother to 5-y-o Frenchmans Bay: dam, no worthwhile form, half-sister to Norfolk Stakes winner Romeo Romani: 9/2, always behind in maiden at Southwell: should do better. *T. G. Mills* — p

FRANKINCENSE (IRE) 7 gr.g. Paris House 123 – Mistral Wood (USA) (Far North (CAN) 120) [2003 –: 16.2d Jul 5] good-bodied gelding: no longer of any account: tried blinkered. *A. J. Lockwood* —

FRANKLINS GARDENS 3 b.c. Halling (USA) 133 – Woodbeck 90 (Terimon 124) [2003 84p: 10.1m* 11.8m* 12m Jun 7] rather leggy, close-coupled colt: smart performer: won minor event at Epsom (by short head from Gala Sunday) in April and Bet attheraces Derby Trial Stakes at Lingfield (beat Let Me Try Again by ½ length) in May: well beaten in Derby at Epsom final start: stays 1½m: raced only on good/good to firm ground: game. *M. H. Tompkins* 111

Bet attheraces On 0800 083 83 83 Derby Trial Stakes, Lingfield—
Franklins Gardens and Let Me Try Again (left) have pulled a long way clear

FRANKSALOT (IRE) 3 ch.g. Desert Story (IRE) 115 – Rosie's Guest (IRE) (Be My **76**
Guest (USA) 126) [2003 69: 7d 7g⁵ 5f⁵ 6g³ 6m⁴ 6m³ 6d² 7f* 7g² 7m² 8m² Oct 2] well-grown, close-coupled gelding: fair performer: won minor event at Brighton in August:
good second last 3 starts: stays easy 1m: acts on polytrack, firm and good to soft going:
tends to edge left: consistent. *Miss B. Sanders*

FRANKSKIPS 4 b.g. Bishop of Cashel 122 – Kevins Lady (Alzao (USA) 117) [2003 **74**
75: p8g* p8g p8g⁵ 8.1g p10g Dec 10] tall, close-coupled gelding: fair performer: won
maiden at Lingfield in January: effective at 1m/1¼m: acts on polytrack, firm and soft
ground: tried tongue tied: usually races prominently. *Miss B. Sanders*

FRANK SONATA 2 b.c. (Apr 6) Opening Verse (USA) 126 – Megdale (IRE) 74 **93**
(Waajib 121) [2003 7g 7d⁴ 7d⁴ 8f 10g Nov 1] 10,000Y: good-bodied colt: fifth foal: half-brother to 3 winners abroad, including French winner up to 10.5f Peaceful Paradise (by
Turtle Island), also useful 7f winner in Britain at 2 yrs: dam, maiden who probably stayed
1½m, half-sister to very smart miler Alhijaz: fairly useful performer: won maiden at
Newcastle in July by 9 lengths: respectable efforts at best after, including in Royal Lodge
Stakes at Ascot: stays 1m: acts on good to soft ground. *M. G. Quinlan*

FRANK'S QUEST (IRE) 3 b.g. Mujadil (USA) 119 – Questuary (IRE) 63 (Rainbow **62**
Quest (USA) 134) [2003 72: p8g p7g 7s² f8g² f8g⁴ 9.9m⁴ 8d* 7.2m⁴ 8m² 8g 8.5m 8d⁴
10g Aug 25] IR 10,500Y: sturdy gelding: first foal: dam 1m seller winner at 2 yrs: modest
performer: trained by C. Collins in Ireland at 2 yrs and G. Butler on reappearance: won
claimer at Ripon in May: stays 1m: acts on fibresand, firm and good to soft ground.
John A. Harris

FRAN'S FUTURE 3 ch.f. Danzig Connection (USA) – Revoke (USA) 70 (Riverman **–**
(USA) 131) [2003 8.3g 8.1g Sep 11] eighth foal: half-sister to 3 winners, including 4-y-o
Majik and fairly useful 5.5f to 7f winner (including in UAE) First Principle (by Rudi-mentary): dam maiden half-sister to very smart French/US 1½m performer Contested
Bid: well beaten in maiden/seller. *A. G. Newcombe*

FRANTIC ANNIE (IRE) 3 b.f. Among Men 124 – Queen Sigi (IRE) (Fairy **a45**
King (USA)) [2003 63: p7g p5g³ p6g p5g⁵ f5s⁵ p6g⁵ p7g 6g 6.1g Apr 1] workmanlike
filly: poor maiden: barely stays 7f: acts on polytrack and firm ground: tongue tied last 5
starts: has worn net muzzle: sometimes slowly away. *D. W. P. Arbuthnot*

FRASCATI 3 b.f. Emarati (USA) 74 – Fizzy Fiona (Efisio 120) [2003 69, a78: 5d⁵ **81**
5f³ 5f⁶ 5m² 5.1m⁶ 5g² 5g⁶ 5g 5m 5g⁴ f5g² f5g⁵ f5g* Dec 16] robust filly: fairly useful
handicapper: won at Southwell in December: best at 5f: acts on all-weather, firm and
good to soft going: usually races prominently: sometimes flashes tail. *A. Berry*

FRATERNITY 6 b.g. Grand Lodge (USA) 125 – Catawba 98 (Mill Reef (USA) 141) **45**
[2003 a7f a10f⁵ 12m f14.8s⁶ f14.8g⁴ Aug 8] modest handicapper: left C. Wroe (UAE)
after third start: stays 1½m: acts on good to soft going and dirt: inconsistent.
J. A. Pickering

FRAZERS FORTUNE 3 ch.g. Environment Friend 128 – Safidar 83 (Roan Rocket **–**
128) [2003 p12g 8g 8m May 27] half-brother to several winners, including useful 1994
2-y-o 7f winner Anniversarypresent (by Puissance): dam 1m winner: well held in
maidens/claimer. *G. Brown*

FRAZZLED 4 b.g. Greensmith 121 – Time For Tea (IRE) 73 (Imperial Frontier (USA) **73**
112) [2003 85, a87: p8g⁴ p8g p8g p7g p8g⁴ p8g³ p8g³ 8m 7m⁶ 8f a8g a8s a8s Dec 7] **a81**
smallish, close-coupled gelding: fairly useful handicapper on all-weather, fair on turf:
sold from C. Cyzer 17,000 gns after tenth start: seems best at 7f/1m: acts on polytrack,
firm and soft going: none too consistent. *C. Bjorling, Spain*

FREAK OCCURENCE (IRE) 2 b.c. (Apr 3) Stravinsky (USA) 133 – Date Mate **85**
(USA) (Thorn Dance (USA) 107) [2003 7g 7m 6m 8.3g 8m⁴ 8s* p8g* p8g⁴ p8g² f8s Dec
27] 16,000F, 35,000Y: good-topped colt: has a round action: first foal: dam, lightly-raced
US maiden, out of smart French 1¼m winner Doubling Time, herself half-sister to very
smart French 9f/1¼m performer Baillamont: fairly useful performer: won nurseries at
Redcar and Lingfield (visored, beat Chubbes by 1½ lengths) in November: should stay
1¼m: acts on polytrack, good to firm and soft ground. *Miss E. C. Lavelle*

FREDDIE FRECCLES 2 ch.g. (Apr 25) Komaite (USA) – Leprechaun Lady 57 **65**
(Royal Blend 117) [2003 f7s* f8g Nov 24] 9,500Y: lengthy, unfurnished gelding: brother
to 6-y-o Optimaite and half-brother to 3 winners, including 6f (at 2 yrs) to 1¾m winner
Goodbye Millie (by Sayf El Arab): dam winning stayer: edgy, fair form when winning
maiden at Southwell in October by ½ length from She's Our Lass, leading close home:
hampered halfway when well held in minor event there: should stay at least 1m.
J. G. Given

FRED'S FIRST   2 b.g. (May 5) Nomination 125 – Perecapa (IRE) 44 (Archway (IRE)   –
115) [2003 f7g Nov 15] first foal: dam 11f winner: 33/1, well held in maiden at Wolverhampton. *B. Palling*

FREECOM NET (IRE)   5 b.g. Zieten (USA) 118 – Radiance (IRE) 54 (Thatching   –
131) [2003 –, a65: f16s Feb 6] sturdy gelding: fair performer in 2002: blinkered, well
beaten only 5-y-o start. *A. Crook*

FREEDOM BAY   3 b.g. Slip Anchor 136 – Bobbie Dee 93 (Blakeney 126) [2003 12g   –
11.8m 10f 14g 14.1m Oct 1] second foal: dam, maiden who should have stayed 1½m,
also third over hurdles: little form. *Mrs P. N. Dutfield*

FREEDOM NOW (IRE)   5 b.g. Sadler's Wells (USA) 132 – Free At Last 115   **86**
(Shirley Heights 130) [2003 12m³ 10d⁶ 12m⁶ 12m Oct 17] compact gelding: fairly useful
handicapper: trained by J. Pease in France in 2002: effective at 1¼m/1½m: acts on good
to firm and good to soft going: sold 13,000 gns, joined M. Hammond. *J. W. Hills*

FREE FLYING   3 ch.f. Groom Dancer (USA) 128 – Free Guest 125 (Be My Guest   **52**
(USA) 126) [2003 10m 8.1m Jul 4] closely related to 2 winners by Rainbow Quest including smart 1m to 1½m winner Freequent and half-sister to several winners, including
Fillies' Mile winner/Oaks second Shamshir (by Kris): dam won up to 1½m: modest form
in maidens. *L. M. Cumani*

FREEHOLDER   3 ch.f. Zamindar (USA) 116 – Wild Humour (IRE) 60 (Fayruz 116)   –
[2003 37: f8.5g p10g⁵ f8.5g Mar 8] maiden: well held at 3 yrs: tried visored. *A. G. Newcombe*

FREELOADER (IRE)   3 b.g. Revoque (IRE) 122 – Indian Sand (Indian King (USA)   **84**
128) [2003 57: 8m p10g* 8.1f³ 8g³ 8.1m³ 8d³ 10m* 10.4m* 10.2g² 10g⁶ 10.3m Oct 24]
strong, lengthy gelding: fairly useful handicapper: won at Lingfield in May, Nottingham
(wandered) in August and York (apprentices, by 5 lengths) in September: below form last
2 starts: stays 10.4f: acts on all-weather, firm and good to soft going: races freely: often
slowly away. *J. W. Hills*

FREE OPTION (IRE)   8 ch.g. Indian Ridge 123 – Saneena 80 (Kris 135) [2003 92:   **76**
p10g* p10g p8g⁵ 10.3m 8.1m 10m⁵ 10.1m³ 10.3m 8.5m p8g³ p10g p7g* p7g² p8g Dec   **a83**
30] lengthy gelding: fairly useful performer on all-weather, fair on turf: won handicap at
Lingfield in January and seller on same course (left B. Hanbury 6,200 gns) in December:
claimed from G. L. Moore £10,000 after penultimate start: effective at 7f to easy 1¼m:
acts on firm going, good to soft and polytrack: tried blinkered: held up. *W. J. Musson*

FREE TRIP   2 ch.c. (Apr 7) Cadeaux Genereux 131 – Well Away (IRE) (Sadler's Wells   **81**
(USA) 132) [2003 6m 6d* 6.1m* 6m² 7g Oct 24] compact, attractive colt: seventh foal:
half-brother to 5-y-o Endless Summer (smart 6f winner at 2 yrs): dam, French 2-y-o 1m
winner, sister to Dewhurst winner Scenic from excellent family: fairly useful performer:
won maiden at Haydock and nursery at Nottingham in September: good staying-on
second at Newmarket, better effort in nurseries after: should stay 7f: acts on good to firm
and good to soft ground. *J. H. M. Gosden*

FREE WHEELIN (IRE)   3 b.g. Polar Falcon (USA) 126 – Farhana 109 (Fayruz 116)   **93**
[2003 88: 5.5m 6m 6s² 6m 6m 5d 6g Oct 31] lengthy, useful-looking gelding: fairly useful
handicapper: clearly best 3-y-o effort when second at Haydock in May: stays 6f: acts on
soft going and good to firm ground: has been slowly away/raced freely. *W. Jarvis*

FREMEN (USA)   3 ch.c. Rahy (USA) 115 – Northern Trick (USA) 131 (Northern   **102 p**
Dancer) [2003 8.5m² 8.1m 8.3g* 8g* 7f Sep 27] big, lengthy, quite good-topped colt:
closely related to useful French 9f winner Ciel de Feu (by Blushing John) and half-
brother to several winners, including useful Irish 1¼m/1½m winner Yuan (by Miswaki):
dam won Prix de Diane and Prix Vermeille and runner-up in Arc: useful performer, lightly
raced: won maiden at Windsor and handicap at Ripon (beat Cat Ona High by ¾ length,
idling) in August: not discredited when tenth to Master Robbie in Tote Trifecta Handicap
at Ascot final start: probably better at 1m than 7f, and should stay 1¼m: raced only on
good going or firmer: should improve further and win more races. *Sir Michael Stoute*

FRENCH CAT (USA)   5 b. or br.g. Storm Cat (USA) – Shannkara (IRE) (Akarad   –
(FR) 130) [2003 –: f5g 12.6m Sep 20] sturdy, close-coupled gelding: of little account: left
I. McInnes after reappearance: tried blinkered. *G. Fierro*

FRENCH CONNECTION   8 b.g. Tirol 127 – Heaven-Liegh-Grey 90 (Grey Desire   –
115) [2003 –: f12s Feb 6] no longer of any account on Flat: tried blinkered/visored.
B. D. Leavy

FRENCH GIGOLO   3 ch.g. Pursuit of Love 124 – French Mist 71 (Mystiko (USA)   –
124) [2003 77?: 8g 10m 7.6g Jun 21] sturdy gelding: little form. *C. N. Allen*

FRENCH HORN   6 b.g. Fraam 114 – Runcina (Runnett 125) [2003 82?: p10g p10g   **70**
f8g⁶ 8m³ 8.1g 8m 8m 7s Oct 29] workmanlike gelding: fair handicapper: stays
1m: acts on polytrack, best turf efforts on ground softer than good: tried blinkered, wears
cheekpieces nowadays: sold 1,600 gns. *M. J. Ryan*

FRENCHMANS BAY (FR)   5 br.h. Polar Falcon (USA) 126 – River Fantasy (USA)   **113**
(Irish River (FR) 131) [2003 114: p7g⁴ 8.1g⁵ 7d May 22] big, good-topped horse: smart
performer, lightly raced (had knee problems): won minor event at Lingfield (all-weather
debut, beat Aldora short head) in April: respectable fifth to Desert Deer in attheraces Mile
at Sandown next time: below form in Prix du Palais-Royal at Longchamp final outing:
was effective at 7f/1m: acted on good to soft and polytrack: had raced
freely: to stand at Ballintry Stud, Co Meath, Ireland. *R. Charlton*

FRENCHMANS LODGE   3 b.g. Piccolo 121 – St Helena (Monsanto (FR) 121)   **60 d**
[2003 70: p5g³ p5g⁵ 6g 6.1m 6d 8.1g Sep 11] modest maiden: well held last 4 starts: best
form at 5f: acts on polytrack, unraced on extremes of going on turf: often slowly away:
sold £1,400. *D. J. S. ffrench Davis*

FRENCH RISK (IRE)   3 b.c. Entrepreneur 123 – Troyes 81 (Troy 137) [2003 –: p8g   **53**
f9.4g⁴ p10g² 10m 9.9m³ 12.1m⁵ p12g⁵ Jun 28] strong, lengthy colt: modest maiden: stays
1½m: acts on good to firm ground and all-weather: blinkered last 2 starts: sold 5,000 gns.
N. A. Graham

FRENCH TUNE (FR)   5 ch.g. Green Tune (USA) 125 – Guerre de Troie (Risk Me   –
(FR) 127) [2003 –: 12.1m Jul 29] strong gelding: little form in Britain: tried blinkered/
visored. *Miss S. E. Hall*

FREYA ALEX   4 b.f. Makbul 104 – Crissem (IRE) 70 (Thatching 131) [2003 54: 10m   **42**
16d⁴ May 2] workmanlike filly: only poor form in 2003: stays 1½m: acts on fibresand
and good to firm ground: has been slowly away. *G. M. Moore*

FREYA'S DREAM (IRE)   4 b.f. Danehill Dancer (IRE) 117 – Ruwy 77 (Soviet Star   **91**
(USA) 128) [2003 90: 7g³ 7g⁴ 7m 8m* 8m⁴ 7.9m 8g 8.1m 8m 8m Sep 20] rather leggy,
angular filly: fairly useful handicapper: won 4-runner race at Thirsk in June: well below
form last 5 starts: effective at 7f/1m: acts on good to firm going: tried blinkered: sold
17,000 gns. *T. D. Easterby*

FRIAR TUCK   8 ch.g. Inchinor 119 – Jay Gee Ell 78 (Vaigly Great 127) [2003 80: 5m   **68 d**
6d 5g 6m 6g⁵ 6m 6f 6g 5m 6g 5m 6g⁵ 6m 6m 6f³ 6f² 6g 5g Oct 22] leggy, lengthy gelding:
has reportedly had several wind operations: just a modest handicapper nowadays: best at
5f/6f: acts on any going: inconsistent. *Miss L. A. Perratt*

FRIDAY'S TAKINGS   4 ch.g. Beveled (USA) – Pretty Pollyanna (General Assembly   **60**
(USA)) [2003 55, a67+: f8g* f8s² 8m² 8m 8g f8g f8.5g Dec 26] fairly useful handicapper   **a80**
on all-weather, modest on turf: won at Southwell in January: stays 1m: acts on all-
weather, good to soft and good to firm going: blinkered nowadays: usually races up with
pace. *B. Smart*

FRIEDA KAHLO (IRE)   3 ch.f. Indian Ridge 123 – Devil's Bones (USA) (Devil's   **81 §**
Bag (USA)) [2003 78: 7.1m³ 8.3d⁴ 8.3m 8g 10m⁵ 8.1m⁴ 10m 7m⁴ Oct 21] lengthy filly:
fairly useful maiden: stays 8.3f: acts on good to firm and good to soft going: tried
blinkered: has raced freely: ungenuine. *G. Wragg*

FRIENDLY ALLIANCE   7 b.g. Shareef Dancer (USA) 135 – Snow Huntress 80   **52**
(Shirley Heights 130) [2003 58: 16m 13.3m 22.2f 12f 16.4m p16g³ 15.4m⁵ Jul 28] tall,
workmanlike gelding: modest handicapper: effective at 1½m to 2m: acts on firm going,
good to soft and polytrack: blinkered last 4 starts: sometimes hangs left: usually held up.
R. M. Flower

FRIMLEY'S MATTERRY   3 b.c. Bluegrass Prince (IRE) 110 – Lonely Street 93   **54**
(Frimley Park 109) [2003 68: f7g⁵ f6g⁶ p6g³ p6g 6.1m Apr 21] modest maiden: effective
at 6f/7f: acts on all-weather, raced only on good to firm going on turf: tried visored: races
prominently. *A. P. Jarvis*

FRITILLARY   2 b.f. (May 21) Vettori (IRE) 119 – Fetlar (Pharly (FR) 130) [2003 7m   **74**
7g 7.5m* 8f⁵ Sep 8] leggy, useful-looking filly: half-sister to several winners, 3 useful,
including 1994 2-y-o 6f/7f winner Be Mindful (by Warning), later successful in USA,
and 4-y-o Mythic: dam unraced half-sister to Jersey Stakes winner Ardkinglass: fair
performer: made all in maiden at Beverley in July: should stay 1m: acts on good to firm
going, below form on firm. *Sir Mark Prescott*

FRIXOS (IRE) 3 ch.g. Barathea (IRE) 127 – Local Lass 106 (Local Suitor (USA) **56 §**
128) [2003 63: 8m⁵ f9.4g* f12g² 10.2g⁶ 10m 10g 10.2g Sep 11] big gelding: fairly useful **a80 §**
on all-weather, modest on turf: won at Wolverhampton in April: well beaten last 4 starts,
pulled up on third of them: stays easy 1½m: acts on fibresand, heavy and good to firm
ground: tried in cheekpieces/blinkers: ungenuine: joined M. Scudamore. *P. F. I. Cole*

FRIZZANTE 4 b.f. Efisio 120 – Juliet Bravo 61 (Glow (USA)) [2003 75p: 6m* 6m* **106 p**
6g⁴ 6m⁶ 6m* 6m* Oct 16] good-topped filly: useful performer: won handicaps at
Leicester in May and Doncaster in June and handicap and listed race at Newmarket in
October: easily beat Ringmoor Down by neck for third success, and got up near finish to
beat Goldeva by ½ length for final one: good efforts when unfavourably drawn in
Stewards' Cup at Goodwood and Gold Cup at Ayr third/fourth starts: will prove best at
5f/6f: raced only on good going or firmer: has been slowly away, and usually waited with:
open to further improvement, and should win pattern races in 2004. *J. R. Fanshawe*

FROMSONG (IRE) 5 b.g. Fayruz 116 – Lindas Delight 54 (Batshoof 122) [2003 105: **93**
5g 5.1g³ 5.2m 5m 6g* 6f 5g 6g f5g Dec 9] tall, angular gelding: fairly useful performer:
best 5-y-o effort when winning minor event at Windsor in June by ¾ length from Prince
Cyrano: effective at 5f/6f: acts on soft and good to firm going: tongue tied (ran badly)
third 4-y-o start: has worn crossed noseband. *B. R. Millman*

FROM THE NORTH (IRE) 2 ch.f. (Mar 16) Foxhound (USA) 103 – Best Swinger **–**
(IRE) (Ela-Mana-Mou 132) [2003 6d 6m Oct 1] lengthy filly: sister to useful 1999 2-y-o
7f winner Scarteen Fox (later 1m winner in Hong Kong) and half-sister to 2 winners,
including 2001 2-y-o 5f winner Boobala (by General Monash): dam Irish 7f winner: no
show in maidens: soon tailed off and pulled up on debut. *A. Dickman*

FRONTIER 6 b.g. Indian Ridge 123 – Adatiya (IRE) (Shardari 134) [2003 73: 11.6g⁴ **83**
10m² 10g* 10.3m² 10d⁶ 9m 10.3g 11.6g 10d Nov 6] well-made gelding: good walker:
fairly useful handicapper: won at Windsor in June: best around 1¼m: acts on soft and
good to firm ground: sometimes tongue tied: usually races prominently. *B. J. Llewellyn*

FRONT RANK (IRE) 3 b.c. Sadler's Wells (USA) 132 – Alignment (IRE) 98 (Alzao **74**
(USA) 117) [2003 10m p12g f9.4g² f12s² Sep 26] strong, good-bodied colt: first foal:
dam, headstrong maiden (second in Prestige Stakes), half-sister to smart performer up to
14.6f Bonny Scot and to dam of Golan: fair maiden: should stay 1¾m: acts on fibresand:
sold 23,000 gns. *Sir Michael Stoute*

FRUIT OF GLORY 4 b.f. Glory of Dancer 121 – Fresh Fruit Daily 92 (Reprimand **97**
122) [2003 84: 7m* 8.3m² 7g 6m* 7m* 6f* 6m⁶ 5.2g³ 6m³ 5m³ 6g⁵ Oct 24] sturdy,
lengthy filly: useful handicapper: had a good year, winning at Goodwood in June and 3
times at Newmarket in August: best efforts at 5f to 7f: acts on polytrack, soft and firm
ground: has had 2 handlers: usually makes running. *J. R. Jenkins*

FUBOS 2 b.g. (Feb 3) Atraf 116 – Homebeforemidnight (Fools Holme (USA)) [2003 **71**
p7g p7g 8d f8s Dec 13] 500Y, resold 1,100Y: workmanlike gelding: fourth foal: dam
lightly-raced half-sister to smart sprinter Roman Prose: easily best effort in maidens (fair
form) when seventh of 24 at Doncaster third start, leading long way: not sure to stay
beyond 1m: well held on all-weather. *Julian Poulton*

FU FIGHTER 2 b.g. (Feb 3) Unfuwain (USA) 131 – Runelia (Runnett 125) [2003 **69 p**
p7g⁵ p8g⁴ Oct 27] 12,000Y: half-brother to several winners, including useful 1¼m/1½m
winner (including in UAE) Kumatour (by Batshoof): dam, lightly-raced maiden, from
family of Oaks winner Blue Wind: fair form in maidens at Lingfield: staying-on fourth to
Cracking Rosie: will be suited by 1¼m+: open to progress. *J. A. Osborne*

FUJISAWA 2 b.f. (Mar 17) Green Desert (USA) 127 – Fursa (USA) (Mr Prospector **67**
(USA)) [2003 5m³ 6m³ 6f² 5.1f³ Oct 1] angular filly: second foal: dam unraced out of
smart French 1m winner (also second in Prix de Diane) Baya, herself out of sister to Triptych: fair maiden: second at Redcar: should stay 7f: acts on firm going: sold 26,000 gns.
M. R. Channon

FULL EGALITE 7 gr.g. Ezzoud (IRE) 126 – Milva 56 (Jellaby 124) [2003 36: p16g **–**
Mar 5] smallish, sturdy gelding: poor handicapper: well held only 7-y-o start: often
blinkered/visored. *B. A. Pearce*

FULL ENGLISH 4 b.f. Perugino (USA) 84 – Grown At Rowan 75 (Gabitat (IRE) 119) [2003 **–**
f8.5g f12g Nov 24] fourth foal: half-sister to moody 7f winner Twoforten (by Robellino)
and Irish 1¼m winner Wild Zing (by Jupiter Island): dam 7f winner: well held in fibresand maidens. *A. P. Jones*

FULL HOUSE (IRE) 4 br.g. King's Theatre (IRE) 128 – Nirvavita (FR) (Highest **73**
Honor (FR) 124) [2003 75: 13.3m² 14.4f⁴ Jul 9] useful-looking gelding: fair handicapper:

stays 1¾m: acts on polytrack and firm going, possibly not on good to soft: tried blinkered: sometimes races freely. *P. R. Webber*

FULL KWAI MA (IRE)   3 b.c. Night Shift (USA) – So Kind 90 (Kind of Hush 118)   **60**
[2003 62?: 5m³ 5d⁴ May 9] good-bodied colt: has a quick action: modest maiden: should stay 6f: acts on good to firm and good to soft going. *Miss L. A. Perratt*

FULL SPATE   8 ch.g. Unfuwain (USA) 131 – Double River (USA) (Irish River (FR)   **79**
131) [2003 80: 6g⁶ 6m² 6g 6m 6m⁵ 6d 6m 6m⁵ 6m 6f 6m³ 6f² 6g 6f 6d⁶ 6g 6m⁶ 7m 6g⁶ 6g* Oct 13] tall, good-topped gelding: fair handicapper: won at Windsor in October: races mainly at 6f: acts on any going: well beaten in blinkers/cheekpieces: often slowly away, and usually waited with. *J. M. Bradley*

FULL TIME (IRE)   4 b.g. Bigstone (IRE) 126 – Oiche Mhaith 74 (Night Shift (USA))   **–**
[2003 11.1m⁵ f14.8s Jul 14] lightly-raced maiden: well beaten in 2003. *G. A. Swinbank*

FULLY FLEDGED   3 b.f. Fraam 114 – Alarming Motown (Warning 136) [2003 8.3m   **46**
12m³ 11.8m⁵ Sep 1] leggy, plain filly: first foal: dam, ran twice, out of half-sister to top-class sprinter Committed: poor maiden: seems to stay 1½m: raced only on good to firm ground. *G. B. Balding*

FULVIO (USA)   3 b.g. Sword Dance – One Tuff Gal (USA) (Lac Ouimet (USA)) [2003   **76**
64: f7g³ p8g³ f6g* f6g³ p7g³ p8g⁴ p7g* p7g* p7g⁴ 8f² 8.1m 7m 7.1m 6m³ 6m⁶ p6g⁶ 6g⁵ 7m p7g p6g⁴ p6g p7g p7g Dec 30] big gelding: fair performer: won handicaps at Wolver-hampton and Lingfield and claimer at Lingfield (then left S. Williams) early in 2003: effective at 6f to easy 1m: acts on all-weather, firm and good to soft going: occasionally visored. *Jamie Poulton*

FUN AND GAMES (IRE)   2 ch.f. (Mar 14) Rahy (USA) 115 – Sharpwitted 58   **97**
(Sadler's Wells (USA) 132) [2003 5g* 6m⁴ 6m⁶ 7.1m⁴ 8m³ 10g* Nov 1] quite good-topped, rather leggy filly: second foal: dam maiden sister to smart middle-distance stayers Sacho and Savoire Vivre and closely related to dam of St Leger winner Shantou out of Oh So Sharp: useful performer: won maiden at Carlisle in May and listed event at Newmarket (by 1½ lengths from Cohn Blue, staying on to lead final 1f) in November: will stay at least 1½m: acts on good to firm going. *M. R. Channon*

FUNFAIR   4 b.g. Singspiel (IRE) 133 – Red Carnival (USA) 109 (Mr Prospector (USA))   **114**
[2003 106: 7.9m* 8m 8.1g² 7g Jul 26] strong, lengthy gelding: smart handicapper: won listed rated stakes at York in May by 1¼ lengths from With Reason: best effort when ½-length second to Putra Pekan in valuable contest at Sandown: stays 1m: winner on soft ground, best form on good/good to firm: refused to enter stall once at 2 yrs (has been blanketed since): has run well when sweating. *Sir Michael Stoute*

Bank of Scotland Business Banking Hambleton Rated Stakes (Handicap), York—
Funfair edges left as he takes over from With Reason;
Camp Commander (left) and Sahaat are next

FUNFAIR WANE   4 b.g. Unfuwain (USA) 131 – Ivory Bride 86 (Domynsky 110)   **102 ?**
[2003 119: 6g 6f 5m* 5m 6m 6g 6m 7m 6m Sep 20] strong, lengthy gelding: has a long
stride: just a useful performer in 2003: won minor event at Beverley in May by length
from Peruvian Chief: well held most starts after: likely to prove best at 5f/6f: acts on good
to firm and good to soft ground: often edgy: has had 2 handlers/been early to post: has run
well when sweating: none too consistent. *D. Nicholls*

FUNNY VALENTINE (IRE)   5 ch.g. Cadeaux Genereux 131 – Aunt Hester (IRE)   **–**
68 (Caerleon (USA) 132) [2003 –: 6g 5g May 31] lengthy, attractive gelding: smart 5f
performer in 2001: lightly raced and well held since. *T. G. Mills*

FUN TO RIDE   2 ch.f. (Jan 22) Desert Prince (IRE) 130 – Zafaaf 105 (Kris 135) [2003   **80**
6g² 6g² Oct 31] rather leggy filly: fifth foal: closely related to 5f/6f winner Ashover
Amber (by Green Desert) and half-sister to 5f (at 2 yrs) to 9.4f winner Queens Bench
(by Wolfhound), both fairly useful: dam 7f/1m winner: 3 lengths second in maidens at
Newcastle (better effort, fairly useful form) and Newmarket: should stay 7f. *B. W. Hills*

FURAAT (IRE)   3 b.f. Danehill (USA) 126 – Istibshar (USA) 78 (Mr Prospector   **81**
(USA)) [2003 a7.5f⁶ a8f³ 7.6m² 7f* 8f Aug 17] fourth living foal: half-sister to fairly
useful 7f (in UAE) and 1½m winner Mostabshir (by Unfuwain): dam, 6f winner, sister to
US Grade 3 8.5f winner Namaqualand from very good family: fairly useful performer:
trained by Saeed bin Suroor in UAE first 2 starts: won maiden at Thirsk in August: should
stay 1¼m: raced only on dirt and ground firmer than good: sold 21,000 gns in December.
J. H. M. Gosden

FURNITURE FACTORS (IRE)   3 b.g. Magic Ring (IRE) 115 – Make Hay (Nom-   **–**
ination 125) [2003 68: 8m 10m Apr 22] workmanlike gelding: fair maiden: well beaten in
2003, reportedly losing action final start: tried tongue tied. *Ronald Thompson*

FURTHER OUTLOOK (USA)   9 gr.g. Zilzal (USA) 137 – Future Bright (USA)   **76**
(Lyphard's Wish (FR) 124) [2003 100, a77: p6g p7g p10g 6m 6s² 5g 6m Jun 7] big, strong
gelding: carries condition: just a fair performer nowadays: claimed from A. Reid fifth
start: best at 5f/6f: acts on all-weather, good to firm and heavy ground: tried tongue tied:
has been bandaged in front: takes strong hold, and usually races up with pace. *D. K. Ivory*

FUSILLADE (IRE)   3 ch.g. Grand Lodge (USA) 125 – Lili Cup (FR) (Fabulous   **–**
Dancer (USA) 124) [2003 –: 10g 11.5g May 16] sturdy, lengthy gelding: little form in
maidens: has carried head high. *M. A. Jarvis*

FUTOO (IRE)   2 b.g. (Mar 22) Foxhound (USA) 103 – Nicola Wynn 83 (Nicholas Bill   **71**
125) [2003 5m³ 5m⁶ 6.1d³ 6d⁴ 7g 6m* 6.1m 7m⁶ 8d 7d* 8d 7g⁶ Oct 28] IR 27,000F,
42,000Y: tall, useful-looking gelding: seventh foal: half-brother to 7f winner Niki (by
Fairy King) and 1m winner Bold Acre (by Never So Bold): dam, 1½m winner, half-sister
to grandam of Barathea and Gossamer: fair performer: won seller at Ripon in July and
(having left M. Channon after eighth start) nursery at Catterick in September: stays 7f:
acts on good to firm and good to soft going: visored sixth to eighth outings. *G. M. Moore*

FUTURE COUP (USA)   7 b.g. Lord At War (ARG) – Holy Moly (USA) (Halo (USA))   **55**
[2003 55: 10.9m 12.4m⁶ 12.4g 12f² 12.6m⁵ 12m 12f⁴ 12m⁵ 12m⁴ 14.1m 12.1d Sep 23]
lengthy, quite attractive gelding: modest performer: stays 1½m: acts on firm going, good
to soft and fibresand: tried blinkered/visored: waited with: none too consistent: sold 1,800
gns. *J. R. Norton*

FUTURISTIC   3 b.g. Magic Ring (IRE) 115 – Corn Futures 78 (Nomination 125) [2003   **67**
64p: 7m f7g* f7s² f8.5g⁶ 7g f9.4g f8s⁶ Oct 7] quite good-topped gelding: fair performer:
won maiden at Southwell in June: below form last 4 starts: stays 7f: acts on fibresand,
best turf effort on good to soft going: sold 5,200 gns. *J. G. Given*

FUTURO VENCEDOR   3 b.g. Komaite (USA) – Takeall 72 (Another Realm 118)   **–**
[2003 56: 7.9g 10m 8.5m 9.9m 8m Aug 6] big, leggy gelding: maiden: no form in
handicaps in 2003. *M. W. Easterby*

FYODOR (IRE)   2 b.c. (Apr 4) Fasliyev (USA) 120 – Royale Figurine (IRE) 107   **86 p**
(Dominion Royale 112) [2003 6g² 6m³ 5m* 5m² Sep 15] 55,000F: tall, rather leggy,
good-topped colt: closely related to smart French 1¼m/1½m winner Craig's
Falcon (by Polar Falcon) and half-brother to winner in Greece by Most Welcome: dam 5f
(including at 2 yrs) and 6f winner: fairly useful form: won maiden at Pontefract in
August: good neck second in nursery at Musselburgh final start, going on strongly at
finish: should prove as effective at 6f as 5f: open to progress. *W. J. Haggas*

GABANA (IRE)   2 br.f. (Mar 1) Polish Precedent (USA) 131 – Out West (USA) 103   **71**
(Gone West (USA)) [2003 7.1m p7g 8d³ Nov 7] lengthy, rather unfurnished filly: second
foal: dam, 7.5f (at 2 yrs)/1m winner, out of half-sister to US Grade 1 9f winner Wavering
Monarch: easily best effort in maidens (fair form) when ½-length third to Hello It's Me at
Doncaster, travelling well long way: stays 1m: looked reluctant second start. *C. F. Wall*

GABOR   4 b.g. Danzig Connection (USA) – Kiomi 65 (Niniski (USA) 125) [2003 83:   **69**
10m 10m⁴ 10f 11.9m³ 11.8m 11.5m³ 10m² 10f* 10m 10m⁴ 11.9m⁵ p10g p12g Dec 17]
tall gelding: fair performer: won amateur handicap at Brighton in August: stays easy
1½m: acts on good to firm and good to soft ground: tried blinkered: often makes running.
G. L. Moore

GAELIC PRINCESS   3 b.f. Cois Na Tine (IRE) 101 – Berenice (ITY) (Marouble   **91**
116) [2003 88: f5g* 5f³ 5f 5.1m 6m⁵ 6m² 6f⁴ 7f 6m³ 6f Oct 11] good-bodied filly: fairly
useful performer: won claimer at Wolverhampton (claimed from K. Ryan) in March:
best efforts after when third in listed race at Haydock second start and handicap at Ascot
penultimate one: stays 6f, not 7f: acts on fibresand and firm going. *A. G. Newcombe*

GAELIC PROBE (IRE)   9 b.g. Roi Danzig (USA) – Scottish Gaelic (USA) (High-   **–**
land Park (USA)) [2003 f14.8g⁶ Aug 8] fair 13f winner in Ireland in 1997: well held only
Flat outing since: tried blinkered. *R. M. H. Cowell*

GAELIC ROULETTE (IRE)   3 b.f. Turtle Island (IRE) 123 – Money Spinner (USA)   **78**
61 (Teenoso (USA) 135) [2003 8.3g⁵ 8.2m⁶ 8g 10f p12g 12m³ 12m* 12m* 11.9m⁶ 11m⁵
13.9f Oct 11] IR 25,000Y: rather leggy filly: fourth living foal: half-sister to 3 winners,
including fairly useful 1m (at 2 yrs) and 1¾m winner King Spinner (by Mujadil): dam 1m
winner who should have stayed further: fair handicapper: won at Thirsk (edged right) and
Kempton in August: stays 1½m: raced only on good ground or firmer on turf: often
slowly away. *P. W. Harris*

GAIETY GIRL (USA)   2 b.f. (Mar 20) Swain (IRE) 134 – Knoosh (USA) 113 (Storm   **69**
Bird (CAN) 134) [2003 7.5m⁴ 7.5m⁴ 7m³ 8m Oct 25] €36,000Y: rather leggy, quite good-
topped filly: half-sister to 3 winners, including smart 7f to 1¼m winner Nooshman (by
Woodman) and fairly useful 8.5f winner All Our Hope (by Gulch): dam 7f (at 2 yrs) to
1½m winner: fair maiden: should stay at least 1m: races prominently. *T. D. Easterby*

GALA AFFAIR   4 ch.f. Zilzal (USA) 137 – Sally Slade 80 (Dowsing (USA) 124)   **–**
[2003 55+: 6g 5g 5.7f 8.5d Jul 3] poor handicapper: stays 6f: best efforts on good to firm
ground: sold 1,600 gns. *C. A. Cyzer*

GALANDORA   3 b.f. Bijou d'Inde 127 – Jelabna (Jalmood (USA) 126) [2003 54:   **56**
10.2m 11.8m⁴ 11.9m⁵ 11.6d⁵ p12g⁶ 16.2m³ 16.2m⁵ 16g 16.2g⁶ 13.1f³ 14.1m f14.8g Oct
20] close-coupled filly: modest maiden handicapper: stays 2m: acts on polytrack and firm
ground: tongue tied last 7 starts: usually held up. *Dr J. R. J. Naylor*

GALAPAGOS GIRL (IRE)   5 b.m. Turtle Island (IRE) 123 – Shabby Doll 69   **–**
(Northfields (USA)) [2003 –: 7.1d 8.1m Aug 14] fairly useful at 3 yrs: little form since,
including in visor. *J. G. M. O'Shea*

GALA SUNDAY (USA)   3 b.c. Lear Fan (USA) 130 – Sunday Bazaar (USA) (Nureyev   **105**
(USA) 131) [2003 92p: 10m* 10.1m² 10d⁵ 9.2m* 9.9g 9.9m Aug 23] smallish, well-made
colt: useful performer: won maiden at Pontefract in April and minor event at Hamilton in
July: best effort when short-headed by Franklins Gardens in minor event at Epsom second
start: ran poorly last 2 outings, something seemingly amiss on final one: should stay
1½m: unraced on extremes of ground: has worn crossed noseband: sold only 6,500 gns.
B. W. Hills

GALAXY THUNDERBIRD   4 ch.g. Bahamian Bounty 116 – Milva 56 (Jellaby   **57 ?**
124) [2003 61: p10g p8g⁶ p8g p8g p7g Feb 26] strong gelding: modest performer: stays
1m: acts on soft going, good to firm and polytrack: twice very slowly away. *S. Dow*

GALEY RIVER (USA)   4 ch.g. Irish River (FR) 131 – Carefree Kate (USA) (Lyphard   **–**
(USA) 132) [2003 76: 8g 8.2s 10.2m 8.3g 8.3m f8.5g 8g Sep 22] strong, close-coupled
gelding: little form at 4 yrs: left G. L. Moore after fifth start: tried in cheekpieces/blinkers.
J. J. Sheehan

GALFAN   3 ch.g. Atraf 116 – Clunk Click 72 (Star Appeal 133) [2003 49: f12g⁴ f14.8s   **43**
Jul 14] strong gelding: poor maiden: stays 1½m: acts on fibresand. *B. Palling*

GALLANT BOY (IRE) 4 ch.g. Grand Lodge (USA) 125 – Damerela (IRE) (Alzao (USA) 117) [2003 93+: p8g² p10g⁵ p10g* p12g 8g 10m 10g 10.3m⁵ 12g 8.3g 10.1m 8.9f 10m* 10.3f² 10g 10.4f 10.5m³ 10g 10m⁵ 10f 8m⁴ 10.3d⁴ 11.6g* 10.4f 10g 12d p12g⁵ p10g p12g⁵ f9.4s Dec 31] rather leggy, quite good-topped gelding: good walker: easy mover: fairly useful performer: won handicap at Lingfield in February and minor events at Leicester in June and Windsor in October: stays easy 1½m: acts on all-weather, firm and good to soft ground: tried visored: tongue tied: held up: tough. *P. D. Evans* **90 a95**

GALLANT HERO 4 b.g. Rainbow Quest (USA) 134 – Gay Gallanta (USA) 112 (Woodman (USA) 126) [2003 109: 10.3m⁶ 11.6g⁴ 11.8m⁵ 10m² 10.1m⁴ Aug 25] tall, quite good-topped gelding: useful performer: best 4-y-o effort when fourth of 5 to Leadership in listed race at Windsor second start: stays 1½m: raced only on good going or firmer: visored (folded) third start: none too consistent: joined P. Hobbs. *Sir Michael Stoute* **106**

GALLAS (IRE) 2 b.c. (Apr 21) Charnwood Forest (IRE) 125 – Nellie's Away (IRE) 72 (Magical Strike (USA) 114) [2003 6m 6m⁵ 6f⁵ 5m 7m 7.1d Aug 30] €3,000Y: rather leggy, quite good-topped colt: fifth foal: half-brother to winner abroad by Revoque: dam, third at 1½m in Ireland, half-sister to 2000 Guineas winner Tap On Wood: fair maiden: left B. Meehan after third start: well below form after: should stay 7f: acts on good to firm going. *J. S. Wainwright* **69 d**

GALLEON BEACH 6 b.g. Shirley Heights 130 – Music In My Life (IRE) 59 (Law Society (USA) 130) [2003 77: 16.2m 17.2f⁶ Sep 29] sturdy, deep-girthed gelding: one-time useful performer: well held in 2003 (bled both starts): used to be effective blinkered/visored or not: tried tongue tied. *W. M. Brisbourne* **–**

GALLERY BREEZE 4 b.f. Zamindar (USA) 116 – Wantage Park 104 (Pas de Seul 133) [2003 8.3g 6m 6m⁴ 6f* p7g* p7g² p7g Dec 6] leggy filly: fair performer: off 22 months before reappearance: won maiden at Goodwood in October and handicap at Lingfield in November: stays 7f: acts on polytrack, firm and soft ground: tried blinkered: has hung left: sometimes slowly away. *J. L. Spearing* **74**

GALLERY GOD (FR) 7 ch.g. In The Wings 128 – El Fabulous (FR) 111 (Fabulous Dancer (USA) 124) [2003 109: 12.5g* 12.5g⁶ 12m* 12f 12.5g 12g⁴ 10g Oct 11] rangy gelding: has a quick action: useful performer: made all in minor event at Cagnes-sur-Mer in February and handicap at Epsom (beat Zibeline 1¼ lengths) in June: effective at 1½m/1¾m: acts on any going: often sweats/takes good hold: often makes running. *S. Dow* **106**

GALLEY LAW 3 ch.g. Most Welcome 131 – Miss Blitz 83 (Formidable (USA) 125) [2003 10.1m 11.1g f9.4g f12s Dec 13] 4,400Y: sturdy gelding: brother to fairly useful 5f to 7f winner Berge and half-brother to winner in Hong Kong by Alzao: dam 6f winner, including at 2 yrs: well beaten in maidens. *R. Craggs* **–**

GALLIVANT 3 b.f. Danehill (USA) 126 – Gay Gallanta (USA) 112 (Woodman (USA) 126) [2003 88: 6m³ 6m⁴ 6m⁵ 7f 7f³ Oct 11] stocky, good-quartered filly: has a quick, fluent action: fairly useful handicapper: best efforts at Newmarket, Goodwood and York on first, third and final starts: effective at 6f/7f: raced only on good going or firmer: tried visored. *Sir Michael Stoute* **93**

GALORE (IRE) 3 b.f. Desert Style (IRE) 121 – Rend Rover (FR) (Monseigneur (USA) 127) [2003 48: 7m 6m Jun 2] lengthy filly: little form at 3 yrs. *J. M. Bradley* **–**

GALVANISE (USA) 2 b.c. (Feb 7) Run Softly (USA) 114 – Shining Bright 98 (Rainbow Quest (USA) 134) [2003 7m Jul 8] close-coupled, good-topped colt: seventh foal: half-brother to 3 winners, including 3-y-o Spanish Sun and fairly useful 1½m winner Eagle's Cross (by Trempolino): dam, French 1¼m winner, half-sister to smart French middle-distance performers Apogee and Daring Miss: 12/1, better for race and green, not knocked about when seventh of 13 in maiden at Newmarket: should be suited by 1¼m/1½m: will do better. *B. W. Hills* **78 p**

GAME DAME 2 ch.f. (Feb 20) Nashwan (USA) 135 – Gentle Dame 75 (Kris 135) [2003 7f³ 7m³ Sep 16] lengthy, rather sparely-made filly: first foal: dam, 1¼m winner, out of half-sister to Oaks winner Diminuendo: fair form in maidens at Salisbury won by Silk Fan and Brunel: should be suited by 1¼m/1½m. *B. W. Hills* **78**

GAME FLORA 2 b.f. (Apr 11) Mind Games 121 – Breakfast Creek 63 (Hallgate 127) [2003 5f⁴ 5m⁴ 5m⁵ 6m 6m f6g Nov 19] 5,500Y: leggy filly: third foal: half-sister to 3-y-o Donny Bowling: dam 2-y-o 5f winner: modest maiden: below form after second start: likely to prove best at 5f/6f. *M. E. Sowersby* **55 d**

GAME GURU 4 b.g. First Trump 118 – Scarlett Holly 81 (Red Sunset 120) [2003 –, a93: f7s f6s³ f6s³ f6s f7g⁶ f7g f7g f7g³ᵈ f6g³ f7g f8g* Dec 19] leggy, quite good-topped **a71**

gelding: just a fair handicapper nowadays: won at Southwell in December: effective at 6f to 1m: acts on all-weather, yet to race on extremes of going on turf: effective blinkered or not: usually races prominently: none too reliable. *T. D. Barron*

GAMESET'N'MATCH   2 b.g. (Feb 17) Hector Protector (USA) 124 – Tanasie   **71**
(Cadeaux Genereux 131) [2003 5g 5m² 5.1m 6g⁶ 5.1g⁵ Aug 25] 17,000Y: lengthy gelding: first foal: dam, French 1m winner, out of close relative to Most Welcome: fair maiden: hung right but ran creditably in nursery penultimate start: stays 6f: acts on good to firm going: wore blinkers/cheekpieces after debut. *W. G. M. Turner*

GAME TIME   4 b.f. Atraf 116 – Real Popcorn (IRE) 52 (Jareer (USA) 115) [2003 52:   **39**
f9.4g f8g f7g⁴ 7f 10m Aug 20] poor handicapper: stays 9.4f: acts on all-weather, lightly raced on turf: sometimes races freely/carries head high. *A. G. Newcombe*

GAMUT (IRE)   4 b.c. Spectrum (IRE) 126 – Greektown (Ela-Mana-Mou 132)   **121**
[2003 116p: 13.3m* 12m³ 11.6g* 14f² 12d³ Nov 8]

Gamut is probably better known for a race that he lost rather than for those he has won. Odds on to provide Pat Eddery with a winner on his final ride, Gamut turned in his one disappointing effort in nine appearances to date when third to Scott's View in a listed race at Doncaster in November. It is possible that Gamut was unsuited by the good to soft ground—he has raced mainly on good going or firmer and acts on firm—though it is worth noting that he did shape very well on a similar surface when second at Newmarket on his sole start at two. At least his record of never having finished out of the frame remained intact.

Having won at Newbury on his first outing at three, Gamut repeated the feat in the latest season. A well-backed favourite for the ten-runner skybet.com Stakes (Aston Park), Gamut won with something to spare by three quarters of a length from Fight Your Corner, confidently ridden and always on top through the final furlong. He had to work harder to justify favouritism again in a five-runner minor event at Windsor three months later, a race in which he had finished second twelve months earlier. The second favourite Millstreet was allowed to dictate the pace, but Gamut always had him in his sights and found plenty under pressure to lead close home, winning by a head. Gamut also acquitted himself well on his two appearances in pattern company, when two and a half lengths third of six to Millenary in the Princess of Wales's Stakes at Newmarket on his second outing and a length second of six to Vinnie Roe, who was winning the race for the third successive time, in the Irish Field St Leger at the Curragh. Stepped up to a mile and three quarters, Gamut set the pace in the latter event and, although Vinnie Roe had his measure from over a furlong out, he did manage to hold off the challenges of those very smart performers Powerscourt and Bollin Eric.

Gamut (IRE) (b.c. 1999)	Spectrum (IRE) (b 1992)	Rainbow Quest (b 1981)	Blushing Groom I Will Follow
		River Dancer (b 1983)	Irish River Dancing Shadow
	Greektown (ch 1985)	Ela-Mana-Mou (b 1976)	Pitcairn Rose Bertin
		Edinburgh (b 1974)	Charlottown Queen's Castle

skybet.com Stakes (Aston Park), Newbury—Gamut makes a successful return;
Fight Your Corner and Swing Wing are his nearest pursuers

Gamut is the seventh living foal of Greektown, a winner over a mile and a quarter and a mile and a half in France. He is closely related to two winners by Rainbow Quest, the 1998 Geoffrey Freer Stakes winner Multicoloured and Rainbow City, the latter a stable-companion who won a maiden at Salisbury in May; and he is a half-brother to the useful winner at up to ten furlongs Athens Belle (by Groom Dancer). Greektown herself is a half-sister to the Prix du Cadran winner Sought Out, and to the grandam of Golan. Gamut's grandam Edinburgh was a smart performer at around a mile as a two-year-old and later showed she stayed ten and a half furlongs. Gamut, a strong, well-made colt who has a quick but unimpressive action, is usually tongue tied. He was sold privately by the executors of Lord Weinstock prior to Doncaster and is now owned by Gay Smith, who enjoyed a good deal of success with the jumpers who represented her in the 2002/3 season, the Triumph Hurdle winner Spectroscope being one of them. Gamut is more than capable of winning a good race or two for her on the Flat in 2004. *Sir Michael Stoute*

GANDON   6 ch.g. Hernando (FR) 127 – Severine (USA) 65 (Trempolino (USA) 135)   –
[2003 49: f9.4g f16.2g May 19] angular gelding: well beaten in 2003. *P. G. Murphy*

GANESHA   4 b.f. Magic Ring (IRE) 115 – Breed Reference (Reference Point 139)   –
[2003 f8.5s 6.1m Sep 19] good-bodied filly: poor maiden. *J. Balding*

GANYMEDE   2 gr.c. (Apr 5) Daylami (IRE) 138 – Germane 100 (Distant Relative   **77 p**
128) [2003 7m⁶ 7m³ Oct 14] 35,000Y: close-coupled colt: fifth foal: half-brother to useful 1m winner Granted (by Cadeaux Genereux): dam, 2-y-o 7f (Rockfel Stakes) winner, out of half-sister to very smart performer up to 11f Running Stag: better effort in maidens (fair form) when 5 lengths third to Penrith at Leicester: should stay at least 1¼m: open to progress. *M. L. W. Bell*

GARDOR (FR)   5 b.g. Kendor (FR) 122 – Garboesque (Priolo (USA) 127) [2003 55:   –
10.9m Jun 16] angular gelding: maiden: well beaten only 5-y-o start: tried tongue tied. *T. J. Fitzgerald*

GARGOYLE GIRL   6 b.m. Be My Chief (USA) 122 – May Hills Legacy (IRE) 68   **68**
(Be My Guest (USA) 126) [2003 75: 12m 12g⁶ 13g 9.1f 12f² 11.9g³ 12m* 12.1g⁴ 13m² 12.1m 12.1g 14m⁶ 10.9m⁴ 11.9f Oct 9] big, good-topped mare: fair handicapper: won at Musselburgh in July: effective at stiff 1¼m to 2m: acts on firm and good to soft going: tried visored/in cheekpieces: usually waited with. *J. S. Goldie*

GARMOUCHEH (USA)   3 b. or br.f. Silver Hawk (USA) 123 – Flowing (USA) 114   **91**
(El Gran Senor (USA) 136) [2003 99: 7g 10m 10.3g* 10.2g³ 9.9g Aug 1] smallish, sturdy filly: fairly useful performer: won minor event at Doncaster in May: creditable efforts after: will prove best up to 1¼m: acts on firm and soft going. *R. Hannon*

GARNOCK BELLE (IRE)   2 b.f. (Mar 3) Marju (IRE) 127 – Trojan Relation (Trojan   –
Fen 118) [2003 6m⁵ 5m 5m Sep 15] IR 8,000F: half-sister to 3 winners, including fairly useful 6f winner Darren Boy (by Ballad Rock): dam unraced: well held in maidens. *A. Berry*

GARNOCK VENTURE (IRE)   2 b.c. (Apr 26) Mujadil (USA) 119 – Stay Sharpe   **57**
(USA) (Sharpen Up 127) [2003 5f⁶ 7.2f⁶ 7.1m⁵ 7f f7g f7g⁴ f7g³ Dec 16] €32,000Y: brother to fairly useful Irish 2000 2-y-o 7f winner Allez La Classe and useful brother to several winners, including 4-y-o Dileer and useful 1¼m/1½m winner Takamaka Bay (by Unfuwain): dam unraced: modest maiden: blinkered, in frame in nurseries at Southwell: will probably stay 1m: acts on fibresand and firm going. *A. Berry*

GARRIGON   2 b.c. (Mar 13) Hector Protector (USA) 124 – Queen of The Keys 56   **68**
(Royal Academy (USA) 130) [2003 6m 7d² 7m⁶ p7g 7g⁶ 6m² 6g f6g p7g² Dec 29] work-   **a64**
manlike colt: first foal: dam 1¼m winner: fair maiden on turf, modest on all-weather: should stay 1m: acts on polytrack, good to firm and good to soft going: sometimes finds little: none too consistent. *N. P. Littmoden*

GARROS (USA)   3 b.c. Grand Slam (USA) 120 – Affirmatively (USA) (Affirmed   **92 ?**
(USA)) [2003 97p: 10.2m⁵ 10m² Jun 22] big, lengthy colt: fairly useful performer: better 3-y-o effort when fifth to High Accolade in minor event at Bath: should stay 1½m: acts on good to firm ground: often makes running: sold 13,000 gns, sent to USA. *M. Johnston*

GARRYURRA   2 gr.f. (Feb 20) Daylami (IRE) 138 – Tropical 122 (Green Desert   **75 p**
(USA) 127 [2003 7m² 8m⁶ Oct 24] smallish, sturdy filly: fourth foal: half-sister to UAE 7.5f/8.5f winner Tropical Star (by Machiavellian) and useful 7f/1m winner Soft Breeze (by Zafonic): dam, Irish sprinter, half-sister to very smart French miler Shake The Yoke: fair form in maidens at Kempton (second to Solar Power) and Doncaster (hampered twice): likely to stay 1¼m: probably open to progress. *Sir Michael Stoute*

GARSTON STAR 2 ch.g. (Feb 2) Fleetwood (IRE) 107 – Conquista 87 (Aragon 118) **54**
[2003 6.1g 7m⁶ 8m⁵ f8s 8.3g 8.2m 10d⁶ Oct 31] 1,000F, 2,200Y: good-topped gelding:
sixth foal: half-brother to fairly useful 1997 2-y-o 6f winner Cumbrian Caruso (by Primo
Dominie): dam 1m winner: modest maiden: stays 1¼m: acts on good to firm and good to
soft going: sometimes carries head awkwardly. *J. S. Moore*

GARW VALLEY 4 b.f. Mtoto 134 – Morgannwg (IRE) 86 (Simply Great (FR) 122) **–**
[2003 73: p8g 8.2s 10f 14.1f Aug 26] rather leggy filly: fair maiden at 3 yrs: well held in
2003: tried blinkered. *Miss J. Feilden*

GASPARINI (IRE) 2 ch.c. (Feb 20) Docksider (USA) 124 – Tarjou (Marju (IRE) 127) **60**
[2003 6d² May 18] 9,000Y: quite attractive colt: second foal: dam unraced out of half-
sister to Middle Park winner Balla Cove: 12/1, staying-on 13 lengths second to Sabbeeh
in maiden at Ripon: should stay 1m. *T. D. Easterby*

GATE EXPECTATIONS 5 b.m. Alflora (IRE) 120 – Dorazine 77 (Kalaglow 132) **–**
[2003 f12s Jan 10] fourth foal: dam, 7f to 10.5f winner, out of half-sister to St Leger
winner Bruni: soundly beaten in maiden at Southwell. *R. J. Price*

GATEMAN 6 b.g. Owington 123 – Scandalette (Niniski (USA) 125) [2003 117: 7m² **116**
8m³ 8.5m* 8f⁴ 8.1d* 8d³ 8m⁵ Oct 12] big, well-made gelding: smart performer: won
Vodafone Diomed Stakes at Epsom (by 1¼ lengths from Reel Buddy) in June and listed
event at Haydock (by 2½ lengths from Pentecost) in September: creditable third to
Special Kaldoun in Prix Daniel Wildenstein at Longchamp penultimate start: winner at 9f
in USA, probably best at 7f/1m: acts on firm and soft going, well held only outing on dirt:
often front runner: tough and game. *M. Johnston*

GATWICK (IRE) 2 b.c. (Apr 20) Ali-Royal (IRE) 127 – Airport (Warpath 113) [2003 **71 p**
6.1m³ Aug 18] 10,000Y: brother to Irish 7f winner Settle and half-brother to several
winners, including fairly useful Irish 1989 2-y-o 7f winner Hero's Welcome (by Simply
Great), later successful in USA: dam, maiden, sister to Derby fourth Shotgun: 7/1, third
of 19 to Bright Sun in maiden at Nottingham, hanging left: will stay 7f: should improve.
M. R. Channon

Vodafone Diomed Stakes, Epsom—a Derby Day victory for Gateman,
who runs on splendidly ahead of Reel Buddy (left), King of Happiness and Battle Chant (No.10)

Mrs E. Roberts & Nick Roberts' "Geminiani"

GAVROCHE (IRE)   2 b.c. (Feb 21) Docksider (USA) 124 – Regal Revolution 105   **67**
(Hamas (IRE) 125§) [2003 7m⁴ 7m f6g Aug 15] 22,000Y: close-coupled colt: first foal:
dam, 2-y-o 6f winner, didn't train on: clearly best effort in maidens (fair form) when
fourth at Folkestone: should stay 1m. *M. J. Wallace*

GAY BREEZE   10 b.g. Dominion 123 – Judy's Dowry 80 (Dragonara Palace (USA)   **–**
115) [2003 67, a49: f6g Jan 13] compact gelding: fair handicapper in 2002: lost action
and pulled up only 10-y-o start. *P. S. Felgate*

GAYLE STORM (IRE)   2 b.f. (Mar 27) Mujadil (USA) 119 – Mercy Bien (IRE) 63   **59**
(Be My Guest (USA) 126) [2003 f5g⁶ f6g⁵ 6.1m³ 6m⁶ Oct 2] 11,000F: leggy, close-
coupled filly: sixth foal: half-sister to 3-y-o Cormorant Wharf: dam, placed at 7f and 1¼m
in Ireland, half-sister to smart dam of high-class sprinter Malhub: modest maiden: third
at Nottingham: slowly away but ran creditably in nursery final start: should stay 7f.
A. J. Lidderdale

GAZING (USA)   3 b.f. Gulch (USA) – Hidden Dreams (Soviet Star (USA) 128) [2003   **62**
p8g² Mar 15] $100,000Y: third foal: closely related to a winner in Japan by Gone West
and half-sister to a winner in USA by Quiet American: dam, 7.5f winner in France,
half-sister to high-class 1½m performer Assatis: second to Woodland Spirit in maiden at
Lingfield, soon close up after slow start: sold 1,500 gns in December. *M. R. Channon*

GDANSK (IRE)   6 b.g. Pips Pride 117 – Merry Twinkle (Martinmas 128) [2003 90: 5g   **83**
6m 5.1m 5v⁵ 6m 6g² 6g 6g 6m Sep 19] leggy, lengthy gelding: has a round action: fairly
useful handicapper: best at 5f/6f: acts on good to firm and heavy ground: usually slowly
away: has carried head high: none too reliable: sold 4,200 gns. *A. Berry*

398

GEE BEE BOY 9 ch.g. Beveled (USA) – Blue And White (Busted 134) [2003 –: f9.4g f16.2g Feb 7] strong gelding: no longer of any account. *G. F. Bridgwater* —

GEESPOT 4 b.f. Pursuit of Love 124 – My Discovery (IRE) (Imperial Frontier (USA) 112) [2003 48, a54: p7g p7g p7g⁵ 7f 8m Oct 23] small filly: poor performer: stays 7f: acts on soft going, good to firm and all-weather: visored (well beaten) once: none too consistent. *D. J. S. ffrench Davis* **46**

GEKKOACCOUNTDOTCOM (IRE) 4 b.g. Grand Lodge (USA) 125 – House Music (IRE) 89 (Thatching 131) [2003 51?: 7m² 7m 7m 6m 7g 7m Jun 10] poor maiden: stays 1m: acts on good to firm going: tried blinkered. *R. M. Flower* **49 d**

GELLER 2 b.g. (Mar 3) Mind Games 121 – Time To Tango 73 (Timeless Times (USA) 99) [2003 8.3g² 6.1m² 6d 8m⁴ Sep 19] 4,600F, 9,000Y: tall, leggy gelding: second foal: dam 5f/6f winner: fairly useful maiden: in frame at Windsor, Nottingham and Newbury (minor event): not sure to stay much beyond 1m: acts on good to firm and good to soft going. *R. Hannon* **80**

GEM BIEN (USA) 5 b.g. Bien Bien (USA) 125 – Eastern Gem (USA) (Jade Hunter (USA)) [2003 88: 7m 8g* 8.1m⁶ 8.2m⁴ p7g Nov 22] rather leggy, quite attractive gelding: fairly useful handicapper: won at Ayr in July: effective at 1m to 1¼m: acts on soft and good to firm ground, well held on polytrack: tongue tied once at 3 yrs: often makes running: carries head awkwardly/wanders: none too reliable. *Andrew Turnell* **91**

GEMEISTER 3 b.g. Superlative 118 – Enfant du Paradis (IRE) 52 (Shernazar 131) [2003 –: 10m⁵ 9.9m May 10] leggy gelding: no sign of ability. *B. P. J. Baugh* —

GEMI BED (FR) 8 b.g. Double Bed (FR) 121 – Gemia (FR) (King of Macedon 126) [2003 52: f11g⁶ f12g⁶ p12g⁵ p12g* 12g* 12g⁵ p13g³ Dec 29] modest performer: won claimer at Lingfield and handicap at Folkestone in March: effective at 1½m to 2m: acts on polytrack, best turf efforts on good going: wears blinkers. *G. L. Moore* **54**

GEMINIANI (IRE) 3 b.f. King of Kings (IRE) 125 – Tadkiyra (IRE) (Darshaan 133) [2003 106p: 10.4m² 12g 9.9g Aug 2] angular, attractive filly: has a quick action: useful performer: creditable length second to Cassis in Musidora Stakes at York: respectable ninth to Casual Look in Oaks at Epsom following month: unimpressive to post before tailed-off last in Nassau Stakes at Goodwood final outing: probably better at 1¼m than 1½m: raced only on good/good to firm ground: bandaged behind: sold 300,000 gns in December. *B. W. Hills* **102**

GEMINI FUTURE (IRE) 3 b.c. Flying Spur (AUS) – Bianca Cappello (IRE) (Glenstal (USA) 118) [2003 7m 7m⁴ 7f⁴ 6.9m* 9m⁴ Aug 14] 36,000Y: sturdy colt: third foal: half-brother to useful 2000 2-y-o 6f/6.5f (Prix Eclipse) winner Potaro (by Catrail), later successful up to 1¼m in USA: dam, no form, half-sister to smart Irish 7f to 1¼m performer Idris: fairly useful form: landed odds in maiden at Carlisle in July: good fourth in minor event at Sandown final start: may prove best at 7f/1m: raced only on ground firmer than good: sold 18,000 gns. *A. C. Stewart* **81 +**

GEMINI GIRL (IRE) 2 b.f. (Feb 18) Petardia 113 – Miss Sabre (Sabrehill (USA) 120) [2003 5g 5f 5f⁵ 5m³ 5m⁶ 5m⁶ Jul 31] 3,000Y: small filly: first foal: dam unraced out of half-sister to Irish St Leger winner Leading Counsel: modest maiden: should stay 6f: acts on firm going. *M. D. Hammond* **55**

GEMINI LADY 3 b.f. Emperor Fountain 112 – Raunchy Rita (Brigadier Gerard 144) [2003 –: 7.9g⁵ 10m 9m³ 8.1f³ 7.9d³ 8.1m 7.9f⁴ 10m² 12m Oct 7] modest maiden handicapper: stays 1¼m: acts on firm and good to soft ground, well held on fibresand on debut: races freely. *Mrs G. S. Rees* **54**

GEMMA 3 b.f. Petong 126 – Gem 58 (Most Welcome 131) [2003 7m 7f 8.1m⁶ 8.5g 8d f8.5s 10m p12g Nov 26] rather leggy filly: first foal: dam, lightly-raced maiden, sister to useful performers Wilcuma (stayed 2m) and Welville (stayed 8.5f): little form. *P. J. Makin* —

GEMS BOND 3 b.g. Magic Ring (IRE) 115 – Jucinda 58 (Midyan (USA) 124) [2003 86: 7m 8m⁶ 7m 8.1m² 7m² 8m* 8m⁴ 7m 8m* 9g Oct 25] leggy, quite good-topped gelding: fairly useful handicapper: won at Newmarket in July and Ascot (beat Night Kiss ½ length) in September: effective at 7f/1m: acts on good to firm ground: has wandered: sent to UAE. *R. Hannon* **92**

GEMTASTIC 5 b.m. Tagula (IRE) 116 – It's So Easy 63 (Shaadi (USA) 126) [2003 43: f5g⁴ f5g Mar 24] small, sparely-made mare: poor performer: best at 5f/6f: acts on all-weather, firm and good to soft going: sometimes flashes tail. *R. Hollinshead* **40**

GENERAL FEELING (IRE) 2 b.c. (Apr 28) General Monash (USA) 107 – Kama- **67 p**
dara (IRE) (Kahyasi 130) [2003 6.1m³ Sep 8] €9,500Y, 14,500 2-y-o: good-bodied colt:
fourth foal: half-brother to 3 winners abroad, including 10.5f winner in Italy by Distinctly
North: dam unraced: favourite, 1½ lengths third of 10 to Urban Rose in maiden at
Warwick, showing good speed: should improve. *S. Kirk*

GENERAL FLUMPA 2 b.g. (Feb 4) Vettori (IRE) 119 – Macca Luna (IRE) 78 (Kah- **58**
yasi 130) [2003 p8g Oct 27] 18,000Y: first foal: dam, 1m (at 2 yrs) and 1½m winner, out
of half-sister to Park Hill winner Eva Luna, herself dam of St Leger winner Brian Boru:
20/1, seventh of 12 in maiden at Lingfield, slowly away: likely to stay at least 1½m.
C. F. Wall

GENERAL HAWK (IRE) 5 b.g. Distinctly North (USA) 115 – Sabev (USA) (Saber –
Thrust (CAN)) [2003 77: 8g 7.5m Jun 11] rather leggy gelding: fair performer at 4 yrs:
well held in 2003: tried in cheekpieces. *R. A. Fahey*

GENERAL JACKSON 6 ch.g. Cadeaux Genereux 131 – Moidart 90 (Electric 126) –
[2003 –: 15.4m Apr 15] big, good-topped gelding: maiden: no form since 2001: tried
blinkered. *Jane Southcombe*

GENERAL (KSA) 2 b.c. (Jan 14) Wiorno 123 – Cloette 69 (Damister (USA) 123) **68**
[2003 7m p7g Oct 15] good-topped colt: second known foal: dam, 7f winner, half-sister
to smart performer up to 1½m French Fellow: better effort in maidens (fair form) when
seventh at Lingfield final start: will stay 1m: sent to Saudi Arabia. *C. F. Wall*

GENERAL SMITH 4 b.g. Greensmith 121 – Second Call 67 (Kind of Hush 118) **68**
[2003 63: 5.3f⁶ 5m² 5m 5g 5.7g 5g 5m 5g⁵ 5.3m³ 5m* 5m 5m³ 5.1d 5m³ 5.3f⁶ 5.7f³
5.5m² 5.1m⁴ 5m⁶ 5.7f⁵ 5m⁵ Sep 22] fair handicapper: won at Lingfield in June: effective
at 5f/6f: acts on firm going, good to soft and fibresand: often slowly away: tried in cheekpieces: consistent. *J. M. Bradley*

GENEROUS GESTURE (IRE) 2 b.f. (Feb 5) Fasliyev (USA) 120 – Royal Bounty **69**
(IRE) 80 (Generous (IRE) 139) [2003 6m⁶ 6m 6g⁴ Oct 6] €70,000Y: lengthy, quite
good-topped filly: second foal: dam, 7.5f winner (ran only at 2 yrs), out of smart 1¼m/
1½m performer Queen Helen, herself half-sister to smart French stayer Sought Out: fair
form in maidens: raced to Rum Shot at Windsor: should stay 7f. *M. L. W. Bell*

GENEROUS SHARE 3 ch.f. Cadeaux Genereux 131 – Marl 94 (Lycius (USA) 124) –
[2003 62: 6m f7s f7s⁵ p7g f8.5g Nov 17] modest performer at 2 yrs: little form in 2003.
M. S. Saunders

GENEROUS WAYS 8 ch.g. Generous (IRE) 139 – Clara Bow (USA) (Coastal (USA)) – §
[2003 16.2m Jun 16] leggy, quite good-topped gelding: fair handicapper at 6 yrs: tongue
tied, folded only start in 2003: blinkered once: unreliable. *R. Lee*

GENGHIS (IRE) 4 br.g. Persian Bold 123 – Cindy's Baby 36 (Bairn (USA) 126) [2003 **89 +**
83: 10m³ Apr 26] rather leggy gelding: very lightly-raced maiden: best effort (fairly
useful form) when 5¾ lengths third to Delsarte at Leicester only 4-y-o start: stays 1½m:
raced only on ground firmer than good. *P. R. Webber*

GENIAL GENIE 7 b.g. Sizzling Melody 117 – Needwood Sprite 58 (Joshua 129) **62**
[2003 74: 8f 7g⁴ 7f 7.5m p7g f7g Nov 1] good-topped gelding: modest performer:
effective at 7f/1m: acts on fibresand, soft and firm going: tongue tied: sometimes races
freely: tends to hang: none too consistent. *R. Hollinshead*

GENTEEL (IRE) 3 b.f. Titus Livius (FR) 115 – Danseuse Davis (FR) (Glow (USA)) –
[2003 58: 7d 6f Aug 12] workmanlike filly: modest performer at 2 yrs: well beaten in
2003: visored (looked none too keen) once. *P. D. Evans*

GENTLEMAN GEORGE 2 b.c. (Mar 28) Kingsinger (IRE) 94 – Miss Bigwig 84 **50**
(Distinctly North (USA) 115) [2003 5m f5g⁵ f6g f7g Dec 16] 7,500Y: sturdy colt: fourth
foal: half-brother to 2 winning Italian sprinters by Whittingham: dam, 2-y-o winner (ran
only at 5f), half-sister to useful sprinter Ivory's Joy: modest maiden: best effort when fifth
at Wolverhampton: should stay 6f. *D. K. Ivory*

GENTLEMAN VENTURE 7 b.g. Polar Falcon (USA) 126 – Our Shirley 84 (Shirley **85**
Heights 130) [2003 97d: 10d⁴ 12g⁵ 10.1m 11.9g Jul 5] quite attractive gelding: fairly
useful handicapper: effective at 1¼m/1½m: acts on any going: usually a free-going sort,
and often races prominently. *J. Akehurst*

GENTLE RESPONSE 3 b.f. Puissance 110 – Sweet Whisper 63 (Petong 126) [2003 **59**
52d: 5.1m 5.1m⁴ 5g 6.1d 5m² 6.1m 5.9m 5m⁶ 5.7f⁵ 5.1m² 6m 5m 5f 8f Sep 2] good-
bodied filly: modest maiden: left B. McMahon £8,000 after tenth start: best form at 5f:
acts on firm ground: none too consistent. *C. A. Dwyer*

GENUINE JAY GEE (IRE)   2 b.c. (Mar 2) Fasliyev (USA) 120 – Jay Gee (IRE) 93   **49**
(Second Set (IRE) 127) [2003 7m p6g Dec 29] 43,000F: first foal: dam, 2-y-o 6f winner,
became unreliable: poor form in maidens at Yarmouth (disputed early lead) and Lingfield. *G. G. Margarson*

GENUINELY (IRE)   2 b.f. (Feb 3) Entrepreneur 123 – Fearless 53 (Groom Dancer   **–**
(USA) 128) [2003 6m 7g Nov 1] 28,000Y: workmanlike filly: second foal: dam, maiden
who stayed 7f, half-sister to very smart sprinter Pivotal: well beaten in maidens at
Newmarket: started slowly on debut. *W. J. Musson*

GEOFFSTAR   3 b.c. Groom Dancer (USA) 128 – Skuld (Kris 135) [2003 –: p10g⁴   **63 §**
f9.4g 10m³ 8.3g Apr 7] modest maiden: clearly best effort on reappearance: should stay
1½m: acts on polytrack: tried blinkered: probably ungenuine. *T. G. Mills*

GEOGRAPHY (IRE)   3 ch.g. Definite Article 121 – Classic Ring (IRE) 50 (Auction   **52**
Ring (USA) 123) [2003 62: 12m⁶ 11.6g f8.5g³ 8.1m 11.8m 8f 10.9m 12m⁵ Aug 23]
modest maiden handicapper: well below form last 3 starts, sold out of P. Cole's stable
7,000 gns before final one: should stay 1¼m: acts on all-weather, soft and good to firm
going: has worn cheekpieces. *P. Butler*

GEORGE ROMNEY (USA)   4 b.g. Distant View (USA) 126 – Polish Socialite   **47**
(USA) (Polish Navy (USA)) [2003 70: f8.5g p8g⁴ f8.5g⁴ Mar 3] good-bodied gelding:
poor walker: disappointing maiden: stays 8.5f: acts on all-weather and soft going: tried
blinkered/in cheekpieces: often tongue tied. *H. J. Cyzer*

GEORGE STUBBS (USA)   5 b. or br.g. Affirmed (USA) – Mia Duchessa (USA)   **80**
(Nijinsky (CAN) 138) [2003 81: 7m³ 8g 7m⁶ 7m 7.5m³ 7d² 6m³ 5m p7g⁵ p7g⁶ p6g f7g⁶
f11g³ f12g² Dec 19] leggy, quite good-topped gelding: fairly useful handicapper: left
N. Littmoden after twelfth start: effective at 6f, and stays easy 1½m: acts on all-weather,
soft and good to firm going: has found little: often wears blinkers/cheekpieces.
M. J. Polglase

GEORGE THE BEST (IRE)   2 b.g. (Jan 30) Imperial Ballet (IRE) 110 – En Retard   **86**
(IRE) 97 (Petardia 113) [2003 5d² 5m⁵ 5f³ 5d* 6g* 5f 6d 6d Sep 29] 13,500Y: workmanlike gelding: first foal: dam Irish 5f/6f winner: fairly useful performer: won maiden at
Pontefract in June and nursery at Hamilton in July: ran badly last 3 starts, looking
wayward first occasion: stays 6f: best effort on good going. *M. D. Hammond*

GEORGIC BLAZE   9 b.g. Petoski 135 – Pooka 65 (Dominion 123) [2003 14.1d May   **–**
16] workmanlike gelding: poor hurdler: 100/1, pulled up in maiden at Nottingham.
G. A. Ham

GERI ROULETTE   5 b.m. Perpendicular 119 – Clashfern (Smackover 107) [2003   **63**
60?, a52: f14g⁶ f12g f12s² 12m² 12.4m* 10g³ 13g* 11.9g⁶ 12m⁶ 14.1d 10.1g f12g³ f12g   **a51**
Nov 21] good-topped mare: modest handicapper: won at Newcastle in April and Hamilton in June: stays easy 15f: acts on fibresand and good to firm going: usually races up
with pace. *E. J. Alston*

GERONIMO   6 b.g. Efisio 120 – Apache Squaw 54 (Be My Guest (USA) 126) [2003 ?   **–**
, a71: f6g⁴ f6g² f6g³ f5g f6g* f6g f7g f6s f6g⁵ f7g³ f6g⁴ f6g² f6g⁵ f7s⁶ f6g⁶ f7g f5g⁶   **a71**
f6g f7g² f6g Dec 9] sparely-made gelding: fair handicapper: won at Wolverhampton in
February: best at 6f/7f: has form on good to firm ground, raced exclusively on fibresand
in 2003: tried blinkered, often wears cheekpieces nowadays: sometimes slowly away:
often gets behind: none too consistent. *Miss Gay Kelleway*

GETATEM (IRE)   4 b.g. Up And At 'em 109 – Fiaba 66 (Precocious 126) [2003 52:   **40**
5m 6m 7.1d 6m 6d 5g 6f⁴ 5m 6g⁵ 6m 6m 6m 5f Aug 21] small, compact gelding: poor
handicapper: effective at 5f/6f: acts on firm ground: usually blinkered. *Miss L. A. Perratt*

GET STUCK IN (IRE)   7 b.g. Up And At 'em 109 – Shoka (FR) 86 (Kaldoun (FR)   **– §**
122) [2003 85§: 5m Sep 18] leggy, quite attractive gelding: fairly useful sprint handicapper at 6 yrs: wearing cheekpieces, well beaten only start in 2003: blinkered once:
unreliable. *Miss L. A. Perratt*

GET TO THE POINT   2 ch.c. (May 16) Daggers Drawn (USA) 114 – Penny Mint 79   **65**
(Mummy's Game 120) [2003 f5g⁵ 5.3f⁴ 6m 6g 5.1d p6g⁵ f8g Dec 19] 5,000Y: sturdy,
lengthy colt: seventh foal: half-brother to 7f winner (including at 2 yrs) Ron's Pet (by
Ron's Victory) and 7f/1m winner Present Generation (by Cadeaux Genereux), both fairly
useful: dam 2-y-o 6f winner: fair maiden: should stay 7f: acts on fibresand, good to firm
and good to soft going: reared in stall second intended outing. *P. W. D'Arcy*

GHUTAH   9 ch.g. Lycius (USA) 124 – Barada (USA) (Damascus (USA)) [2003 19.1m   **–**
Jun 21] little form on Flat since 1999: tried blinkered/visored. *Mrs A. M. Thorpe*

GIFTED FLAME 4 b.g. Revoque (IRE) 122 – Little Lady Leah (USA) (Shareef **79 §**
Dancer (USA) 135) [2003 78: 8m³ 8m 8g⁴ 10.1m⁵ 8m² 7.9f* 7.9m⁶ 7.5m 9.3d⁴ 9.2g 9m
8m⁶ Sep 16] rangy gelding: fair handicapper: won at Carlisle in June: effective at 7f to
8.5f: acts on firm going, possibly not on softer than good: tried visored, usually wears
cheekpieces nowadays: sometimes slowly away: often races freely: not one to trust.
I. Semple

GIFT HORSE 3 ch.g. Cadeaux Genereux 131 – Careful Dancer (Gorytus (USA) 132) **87**
[2003 8.1m² 8.1m* 8m⁶ Aug 16] 30,000F, 58,000Y: sixth foal: half-brother to several
winners, including 6f/7f winner Peggy Spencer and 7f winner Victorious (latter also
successful sprinter in Sweden, both by Formidable): dam twice-raced half-sister to smart
French performer up to 1½m Darine: fairly useful form: won maiden at Sandown in July
by length from Glamorous Girl: only sixth in handicap at Newmarket final start: not sure
to stay beyond 1m: raced only on good to firm ground. *J. R. Fanshawe*

GIG HARBOR 4 b.g. Efisio 120 – Petonica (IRE) 77 (Petoski 135) [2003 70: p12g* **84**
p12g* p10g2 p12g3 p10g 10m 12m 10d 18m 10g6 p12g2 p10g6 Dec 2] good-bodied colt: **a96**
poor mover: useful handicapper on all-weather, fairly useful on turf: won at Lingfield in
January and February: best at 1¼m/1½m: acts on polytrack, good to firm and good to soft
going. *Miss E. C. Lavelle*

GIKO 9 b.g. Arazi (USA) 135 – Gayane 125 (Nureyev (USA) 131) [2003 46: 14.4d **50**
p12g 12f* 12g* 11.9m 12m⁴ 12.6m* 12m⁶ 11.6g 13.1f² 12m 14.1m Oct 1] leggy gelding:
has a round action: modest handicapper: successful in Jersey in April and May, and won
amateur event at Warwick in July: stays 13f: acts on firm going, soft and fibresand: tried
in blinkers/tongue strap: usually races prominently: inconsistent. *Jane Southcombe*

GILDED COVE 3 b.c. Polar Prince (IRE) 117 – Cloudy Reef 57 (Cragador 110) **78**
[2003 68: f6s⁴ f6s⁵ f5g² f6g² f6s f5g* f5g³ f5g* f5s² f6g³ f6g³ f5s Dec 6] strong
colt: fair performer: won claimers at Wolverhampton and Southwell and 2 handicaps at
Wolverhampton between April and July: effective at 5f/6f: acts on fibresand and good to
firm ground: sometimes slowly away. *R. Hollinshead*

GILDED DANCER 5 b.g. Bishop of Cashel 122 – La Piaf (FR) (Fabulous Dancer **100**
(USA) 124) [2003 90, a55: 8m 8g 7g* 7.6g* 8m* 8d* Jul 27] small, good-bodied gelding:
useful performer: in excellent form in June/July, winning claimer and handicap at Lingfield and handicaps at Newmarket and Ascot: beat Craiova by ½ length at Ascot: stays
1m: acts on good to firm and good to soft going: usually waited with. *W. R. Muir*

GILDED EDGE 3 ch.f. Cadeaux Genereux 131 – Palacegate Episode (IRE) 111 **81**
(Drumalis 125) [2003 94p: 6m 5g Sep 7] lengthy filly: fairly useful performer: won
maiden at Newbury at 2 yrs: below best in 2003 in listed race at Leopardstown and Prix
du Petit Couvert at Longchamp: sent to USA, joined P. Byrne. *J. H. M. Gosden*

GILDEN MAGIC 5 b.g. Magic Ring (IRE) 115 – Have Form (Haveroid 122) [2003 **48**
38: f9.4g f8s* f8.5g² f7g f8g 10m 8m⁴ f8g 8.1m 7.9m 8.5m Aug 14] close-coupled **a55**
gelding: modest handicapper on all-weather, poor on turf: won apprentice maiden event
at Southwell in February: stays 8.5f: acts on heavy going, good to firm and fibresand:
none too consistent. *P. W. Hiatt*

GILLY'S GENERAL (IRE) 3 ch.g. General Monash (USA) 107 – Good Aim (IRE) **49**
(Priolo (USA) 127) [2003 72d: 7.1m f8.5g f6g² f6g 7m⁵ 7f Oct 27] sturdy gelding: just
poor maiden at 3 yrs: stays 7f: acts on fibresand, raced only on good going or firmer on
turf: usually races prominently. *J. W. Unett*

GINGER ICE 3 ch.g. Bahamian Bounty 116 – Sharp Top 62 (Sharpo 132) [2003 70: **–**
10.3g 8.2g 7g f8.5g p7g p8g p10g⁶ Dec 30] tall, leggy gelding: fair maiden at 2 yrs: little
form in 2003: tried in cheekpieces. *G. G. Margarson*

GINGER JACK 3 ch.g. Case Law 113 – Miss Realm 86 (Realm 129) [2003 5f 5m **–**
Aug 16] strong gelding: half-brother to 3 winners, including fairly useful 6f to 7.5f
winner Grey Kingdom (by Grey Desire): dam 2-y-o 5f winner: tailed off in maiden at
Thirsk: put down after breaking both forelegs in similar event at Ripon. *S. P. Griffiths*

GINGKO 6 b.g. Pursuit of Love 124 – Arboretum (IRE) 83 (Green Desert (USA) 127) **69**
[2003 73: f12s² f11g³ f11s* f11g 10d 10m⁶ 10g p12g p12g⁶ f11g⁶ Nov 25] fair handi- **a78**
capper: won at Southwell in February: stays 1½m: acts on all-weather and good to firm
going, seemingly not on softer than good: none too consistent. *P. R. Webber*

GINNER MORRIS 8 b.g. Emarati (USA) 74 – Just Run (IRE) 45 (Runnett 125) [2003 **– §**
56§, a–§: f9.4g 7.9f 8s f11g Dec 16] lengthy gelding: modest handicapper: well beaten in
2003: usually blinkered: unreliable. *J. Hetherton*

GIN 'N' FONIC (IRE) 3 ch.g. Zafonic (USA) 130 – Crepe Ginger (IRE) 67 (Sadler's **69**
Wells (USA) 132) [2003 10m 11.5g⁵ 10m⁶ 11.9m⁴ f12g* 11.5s p16g Sep 3] 185,000Y:
big, workmanlike gelding: first foal: dam, ran 3 times in Ireland, half-sister to dam of
Daylami and Dalakhani: fair performer: left J. Fanshawe after third start: won seller at
Wolverhampton in August: stays 1½m: acts on fibresand and good to firm ground, ran
poorly on soft: wore cheekpieces last 3 starts: usually races prominently: has wandered:
sold 11,500 gns. *H. J. Cyzer*

GINOLIN (IRE) 2 b.c. (Feb 14) Perugino (USA) 84 – Nahlin (Slip Anchor 136) [2003 **–**
6d May 18] 3,000Y: third foal: dam, French maiden, half-sister to useful stayer Warfield
and German 1000 Guineas winner Princess Nana: visored and tongue tied, well held in
seller at Ripon. *D. Carroll*

GIN PALACE (IRE) 5 gr.g. King's Theatre (IRE) 128 – Ikala (Lashkari 128) [2003 **94**
14.4g³ May 5] leggy, sparely-made gelding: fairly useful performer, lightly raced: first
run on Flat since 3 yrs (won over hurdles in between) when good third to Got One Too in
handicap at Kempton: will stay 2m: acts on soft and good to firm going: usually held up.
G. L. Moore

GIOCOMO (IRE) 5 ch.g. Indian Ridge 123 – Karri Valley (USA) (Storm Bird (CAN) **–**
134) [2003 13d May 4] half-brother to several winners, including smart 1¼m/1½m
winner Campo Catino (by Woodman) and useful 1½m winner Trebizond (by Sadler's
Wells): dam, ran once, closely related to smart 7f/1m performer Fatherland: fair maiden
at 3 yrs for C. O'Brien in Ireland: soundly beaten only start in 2003: stays 1½m: acts on
good to firm and good to soft going: joined R. Fahey, won novice chase in November.
P. Monteith

GIOCOSO (USA) 3 b.c. Bahri (USA) 125 – Wing My Chimes (USA) (Flying Paster **91**
(USA)) [2003 80p: 8g² 8.1d* 9f² 8g 8g⁶ 7d Nov 8] quite good-topped colt: fairly useful
performer: won maiden at Chepstow in May: good second in handicap at Sandown next
time: stays 9f: acts on firm and good to soft ground, shaped well on heavy. *B. Palling*

GIRL FRIDAY 5 ch.m. Ajraas (USA) 88 – Miss Nonnie (High Kicker (USA)) [2003 **–**
p7g f6g Feb 3] poor maiden: blinkered, well held in 2003. *D. Shaw*

GIRLS NIGHT OUT 2 b.f. (May 6) Docksider (USA) 124 – Beaucatcher (IRE) 55 **–**
(Thatching 131) [2003 p8g Oct 27] 3,500F: second foal: dam, maiden who stayed 1m:
40/1, slowly away and always behind in maiden at Lingfield. *J. W. Hills*

GIRL WARRIOR (USA) 2 ch.f. (Feb 16) Elusive Quality (USA) – Qhazeenah 101 **76 p**
(Marju (IRE) 127) [2003 7g³ Nov 1] $120,000Y: tall, quite good-topped filly: first
foal: dam, 6.5f (at 2 yrs)/7f winner, half-sister to smart 1¼m to 14.6f winner Ranin: 12/1,
length third of 17 to Si Si Amiga in maiden at Newmarket, held up and finishing well:
will stay 1m: sure to improve. *P. F. I. Cole*

GIRONDE 2 b.c. (Apr 21) Sadler's Wells (USA) 132 – Sarah Georgina 79 (Persian Bold **67 p**
123) [2003 8.2d⁵ Nov 6] 280,000Y: rangy, quite good-topped colt: seventh living foal:
half-brother to 3 winners, including smart French 1m to 10.5f winner Audacieuse (by
Rainbow Quest) and useful 1½m/1¾m winner Lord Jim (by Kahyasi): dam, 2-y-o 6f
winner, half-sister to very smart French performer up to 1m Danseuse du Soir: 7/1, burly
and green, fifth of 16 to Vaughan in maiden at Nottingham, running in snatches and not
knocked about: will be suited by 1¼m+: sure to improve. *Sir Michael Stoute*

GIULIANI 3 b.c. Sadler's Wells (USA) 132 – Anka Germania (Malinowski (USA) **82**
123) [2003 72p: 11.6s* 11.6d² 12.3g⁵ Jul 7] deep-bodied colt: fairly useful handicapper:
won at Windsor in May: good second there next time: will stay at least 1¾m: raced
only on good ground or softer: visored (ran respectably) final start: sold 40,000 gns.
L. M. Cumani

GIUNCHIGLIO 4 ch.g. Millkom 124 – Daffodil Fields (Try My Best (USA) 130) **79**
[2003 73: 10m² 10m 9.9f³ 8.2m⁶ 8.3g⁵ 12m⁶ 10.5f 8m Sep 24] tall gelding: fair maiden
handicapper: below form last 5 starts, including in visor: should stay 1½m: acts on firm
going: sold 7,500 gns. *P. J. Makin*

GIUST IN TEMP (IRE) 4 b.c. Polish Precedent (USA) 131 – Blue Stricks (Bluebird **58 d**
(USA) 125) [2003 59?: p8g5 f9.4g² f9.4s² f9.4g⁶ f8s⁶ f9.4g⁶ 10m 10.9m 9f 8f⁵ 8.1g 9.9m
f12g⁶ f8g⁵ f11g Dec 15] quite attractive colt: modest maiden: below form after third start:
stays 9.4f: best efforts on fibresand. *P. W. Hiatt*

GIVE BACK CALAIS (IRE) 5 b.g. Brief Truce (USA) 126 – Nichodoula 65 (Dou- **–**
lab (USA) 115) [2003 95: p10g 7m 7g Jun 3] compact gelding: useful 7f handicapper at 4
yrs: well beaten in 2003: tried in blinkers/cheekpieces/tongue tie: sent to Switzerland.
P. J. Makin

GIVE HIM CREDIT (USA) 3 b.g. Quiet American (USA) – Meniatarra (USA) 68 **72** (Zilzal (USA) 137) [2003 69: 7m* 6s⁴ 7f 7m 7m⁴ 6m 7m Aug 6] small, sturdy gelding: fair performer: won maiden at Catterick in April: stays 7f: acts on good to firm ground: tried visored/blinkered: reportedly had breathing problem sixth start. *Mrs A. Duffield*

GIVEMETHEMOONLIGHT 4 ch.f. Woodborough (USA) 112 – Rockin' Rosie **57** 59 (Song 132) [2003 62: f8.5g⁴ f9.4g f7g⁵ p8g⁶ 7.1g f8.5g³ p8g² f11g⁴ f8.5g² p7g² Dec 29] sturdy filly: modest maiden: left L. G. Cottrell £6,000 seventh start: stays 8.5f: acts on all-weather, some promise on turf: effective blinkered or not. *Mrs S. A. Liddiard*

GIVEN A CHANCE 2 b.g. (Mar 21) Defacto (USA) – Milly Molly Mango (Mango **37** Express 106) [2003 6g 7m 7m⁶ f8.5g f8g Nov 25] close-coupled gelding: third foal: dam Norwegian 1m winner: poor maiden: stays 7f. *J. G. Given*

GIVERAND 4 b.f. Royal Applause 124 – Petersford Girl (IRE) 84 (Taufan (USA) **48** 119) [2003 –: 8f 7.1g 6m³ f6g Nov 14] poor maiden: stays 6f: acts on good to firm ground. *Miss Jacqueline S. Doyle*

GIVIMANINCH 3 ch.g. Inchinor 119 – Tea And Scandals (USA) (Key To The King- **51** dom (USA)) [2003 56: 5.1m⁶ 6m⁴ 6g⁶ 6.1m 5f 6m 5.7f Oct 21] modest maiden: should stay 7f: acts on good to firm going, probably on soft: has raced freely: found little third outing: sold 4,000 gns, sent to Holland. *D. R. C. Elsworth*

GJOVIC 2 br.c. (Mar 9) Singspiel (IRE) 133 – Photo Call 73 (Chief Singer 131) [2003 **73 p** 7m³ 7m⁴ 8m² Sep 13] seventh foal: half-brother to 5-y-o Johannian and 3-y-o Chiffon: dam, 9f (at 2 yrs) and 11f winner, granddaughter of 1000 Guineas second Photo Flash: fair form in maidens: staying-on second to Thyolo at Goodwood: will be well suited by 1¼m/1½m: open to progress. *B. J. Meehan*

GLADYS AYLWARD 3 b.f. Polar Falcon (USA) 126 – Versami (USA) (Riverman **63 d** (USA) 131) [2003 64: 7g 7.5f 8d³ 7f* 6.9f 7.2g 8d f7s⁴ Oct 21] lengthy, useful-looking filly: modest performer: won claimer at Catterick (claimed from T. Easterby £6,000) in June: well below form after: stays 1m: acts on firm and good to soft ground: tried visored. *A. Crook*

GLAMOROUS GIRL (IRE) 3 b. or br.f. Darshaan 133 – Masharik (IRE) 93 (Caer- **91** leon (USA) 132) [2003 8.1m² 10m² 8f* Aug 23] rangy filly: second foal: dam, 1¼m winner, half-sister to high-class middle-distance stayer Ibn Bey and Yorkshire Oaks winner Roseate Tern: fairly useful form: best effort in maidens when winning 4-runner event at Newmarket in August by 5 lengths from Electrique: should have proved at least as effective at 1¼m as 1m: raced only on ground firmer than good: visits Alhaarth. *M. P. Tregoning*

GLANBEHY (IRE) 3 b.f. General Monash (USA) 107 – Ron's Secret 92 (Efisio 120) **– §** [2003 56: p6g p7g Feb 19] sparely-made filly: modest performer at 2 yrs: well beaten in 2003: tried blinkered/visored: ungenuine. *J. A. Glover*

GLANDORE (IRE) 4 ch.f. Persian Bold 123 – Sheen Falls (IRE) 56 (Prince Rupert **–** (FR) 121) [2003 95: 11.9v 10m 11.8g Jul 5] tall ex-Irish filly: third foal: half-sister to useful Irish 7f (including at 2 yrs) to 9f winner Provosky (by Polish Patriot) and 1¼m/11f winner in Italy by Mujtahid: dam Irish maiden half-sister to smart Irish mare up to 1¼m Noora Abu: fairly useful performer in 2002, winning 11f maiden at Killarney for Miss I. Oakes: showed nothing in 3 runs in 2002 (unseated rider leaving stall first time). *E. J. O'Neill*

GLANMIRE 2 b.c. (Apr 2) Inchinor 119 – Bella Helena (Balidar 133) [2003 6m⁴ 8d **–** 7m Aug 8] 5,000Y: lengthy colt: sixth foal: half-brother to fairly useful 5f (including at 2 yrs) winner Bevelena (by Beveled): dam, Italian sprint winner (tailed off only British outing), out of half-sister to useful 5f performer Up And At 'em: no form: blinkered in seller final start. *N. A. Callaghan*

GLARAMARA 2 b.c. (Mar 31) Nicolotte 118 – Digamist Girl (IRE) (Digamist (USA) **93** 110) [2003 6m 6m* 7.2m³ Sep 19] 11,000Y, 32,000 2-y-o: big, good-topped colt: fourth foal: half-brother to 5-y-o Chispa and 3-y-o Queens Rhapsody: dam winning sprinter in Belgium: fairly useful form: won maiden at York in August: on toes, 1¼ lengths third of 4 to Gold History in minor event at Ayr: will need to settle to stay beyond 7f. *A. Bailey*

GLASS NOTE (IRE) 5 b.m. Spectrum (IRE) 126 – Alice En Ballade (Tap On Wood **–** 130) [2003 67: f7s 10.9m 13.1f Aug 22] fair handicapper in 2002 for T. Stack in Ireland: well beaten at 5 yrs. *S. T. Lewis*

GLEBE GARDEN 2 b.f. (Mar 31) Soviet Star (USA) 128 – Trounce (Barathea (IRE) **86** 127) [2003 6g³ 6g* 6m Jul 8] leggy filly: first foal: dam, French 7f winner, half-sister to smart French/US 1m to 1½m performer Bon Point (by Soviet Star): fairly useful form: won maiden at Windsor in June by 5 lengths from Anthos, making all: bandaged behind, last of 8 in Cherry Hinton Stakes at Newmarket: will probably stay 1m. *M. L. W. Bell*

GLENCAIRN STAR 2 b.c. (May 3) Selkirk (USA) 129 – Bianca Nera 107 (Salse **64** (USA) 128) [2003 7.2m 7.2d⁵ Oct 13] 85,000Y: sturdy, good sort: third foal: half-brother to fairly useful Irish 2001 2-y-o 7f winner Pietra Dura (by Cadeaux Genereux): dam, 2-y-o 5f to 7f (including Lowther and Moyglare Stud Stakes) winner, didn't train on: modest form in maidens at Ayr: needs to settle to stay 1m. *J. S. Goldie*

GLENCOE SOLAS (IRE) 3 ch.f. Night Shift (USA) – Boranwood (IRE) (Exhibi- **77** tioner 111) [2003 61: 6g* 7m⁵ 6.1m⁵ 6.1g 6m* 6f³ 5f⁴ 5m² 5g⁶ 6m² 5d⁵ 5.7f⁶ 6g 6g Oct 6] sturdy filly: half-sister to 3 winners, including 5-y-o Ceepio: dam, Irish 2-y-o 6f winner, half-sister to useful Irish sprinter Wicked Folly: fair performer: trained by D. Gillespie in Ireland at 2 yrs: won maiden at Kempton in March and handicap at Windsor in June: mostly creditable efforts in handicaps after: effective at 5f/6f: acts on firm and good to soft going: wandered and found little seventh outing: usually races up with pace. *S. Kirk*

GLENCOYLE (IRE) 3 b.g. In The Wings 128 – Lucky State (USA) (State Dinner **82** (USA)) [2003 10m³ 12.1m⁵ 10f³ 11m 12.1g* 16f⁴ 11.8m⁵ Oct 13] 21,000Y: well-made gelding: half-brother to several winners, including 1m winner Gold Lance (by Seeking The Gold) and a Brazilian Grade 3 winner by Thunder Gulch: dam, French 1m winner, half-sister to 1000 Guineas winner Ravinella: fairly useful performer: won maiden at Chepstow in September: stays 2m: raced only on good ground or firmer: tried blinkered: sold 40,000 gns, joined N. Henderson and gelded. *A. C. Stewart*

GLENDALE 2 ch.g. (May 1) Opening Verse (USA) 126 – Kayartis 57 (Kaytu 112) **73** [2003 7m 8m 8m 8s Nov 3] big, strong gelding: fourth known foal: dam 1½m to 2m winner: fair maiden: form only when eighth of 20 in maiden at Newmarket third start: will be suited by 1¼m/1½m. *C. A. Dwyer*

GLENHURICH (IRE) 6 b.m. Sri Pekan (USA) 117 – Forli's Treat (USA) (Forli **56** (ARG)) [2003 55: 9m³ 8.3d⁶ 7m³ 6m 8m⁵ 8s² 8g* 8.1m 8m³ 8m 10m 8m Oct 4] lengthy mare: modest handicapper: won at Redcar (wandered markedly, first success) in July: effective at 7f to 9f: acts on firm and good going: tried cheekpieces: sometimes slowly away: usually waited with. *J. S. Goldie*

GLENROCK 6 ch.g. Muhtarram (USA) 125 – Elkie Brooks 82 (Relkino 131) [2003 **63** 73d: f7g f7s 6m 7.6m* 7m 7m f7g f7g Dec 16] quite good-topped gelding: just modest nowadays: clearly best effort in 2003 when 50/1-winner of apprentice handicap at Chester (goes well there) in July: stays 7.6f: acts on any turf going and all-weather: often makes running. *A. Berry*

GLENSHIAN (IRE) 2 ch.g. (Apr 7) Ali-Royal (IRE) 127 – Goodnight Girl (IRE) **–** (Alzao (USA) 117) [2003 6g 7.5m Sep 17] 6,500F, 18,000Y: angular, good-topped gelding: sixth foal: half-brother to 3 winners, including fairly useful 2002 2-y-o 5f winner Patavium Princess (by Titus Livius): dam unraced: last in maidens at Doncaster and Beverley. *R. A. Fahey*

GLEN VALE WALK (IRE) 6 ch.g. Balla Cove 119 – Winter Harvest (Grundy 137) **55** [2003 57: 10m 11m⁵ 12g 10.9m⁴ 10s 10.3m⁴ 10.5m⁴ Jul 19] leggy gelding: modest handicapper: stays 1½m: acts on firm and soft going, probably on fibresand: usually blinkered: has wandered/found little: sometimes slowly away, and usually held up: none too consistent. *Mrs G. S. Rees*

GLENVIEWS POLLY (IRE) 3 b.f. Poliglote 121 – Fun Board (FR) (Saumarez **–** 132) [2003 55, a69: p7g f6g 7.5f f8g⁶ 6m 6.9f Jun 15] leggy filly: modest performer: well held in 2003, leaving N. Littmoden after second start: has worn cheekpieces/visor. *Ian Emmerson*

GLENVIEWS PURCHASE (IRE) 3 b.f. Desert Story (IRE) 115 – Whitethroat **77** (Artaius (USA) 129) [2003 74: 6v 6m 8.3f⁴ 8.5d 7.5g⁶ 11f 10m³ 12m 9.5g 10g Oct 25] close-coupled filly: fair performer: left A. Berry after fourth start: stays 1¼m: acts on good to firm going: edgy on reappearance, missed break next time: wore cheekpieces/ blinkers last 3 starts. *Miss I. T. Oakes, Ireland*

GLESNI 4 gr.f. Key of Luck (USA) 126 – Llwy Bren (Lidhame 109) [2003 p12g Nov **–** 12] half-sister to 10-y-o Rushcutter Bay: dam unraced: 33/1, well held in maiden at Lingfield. *S. C. Williams*

GLIDE 2 ch.g. (Mar 16) In The Wings 128 – Ash Glade (Nashwan (USA) 135) [2003 **72 p** 8f 8.1m⁴ 8m⁵ Oct 14] compact, attractive gelding: fourth foal: half-brother to 4-y-o Magic Glade: dam unraced close relative to 8-y-o Ulundi and half-sister to 1000 Guineas winner Wince: best effort (fair form) when fifth to Muhaymin in maiden at Leicester, again not knocked about: will stay at least 1¼m: type to do better in handicaps as 3-y-o. *R. Charlton*

GLIDING BY 2 ch.f. (Mar 7) Halling (USA) 133 – Waft (USA) 67 (Topsider (USA)) – [2003 f8.5g p8g Nov 26] 5,000Y: third foal: dam, third at 1m, half-sister to dam of St Leger and Coronation Cup winner Silver Patriarch: well held in maidens: should be suited by 1½m+. *P. R. Chamings*

GLIMMER OF LIGHT (IRE) 3 b.g. Marju (IRE) 127 – Church Light 88 (Caerleon **79** (USA) 132) [2003 8g⁴ 8m* 9f⁵ 10g Sep 6] IR 26,000Y: leggy gelding: half-brother to several winners, including useful Irish 7f (at 2 yrs)/9f winner Right Honorable (by Rainbows For Life) and fairly useful Irish 1m winner Imperial Light (by Imp Society): dam 6f (at 2 yrs) and 1m winner who stayed 1¼m: fair form: made all in maiden at Kempton in May: well held both starts after, carrying head high final one: stays 1m: raced on good ground or firmer. *P. W. Harris*

GLIMPSE OF GLORY 3 b.g. Makbul 104 – Bright-One 78 (Electric 126) [2003 7d – 8m 7m 14f 10.9g Aug 1] half-brother to 1¾m/2m winner Albrighton (by Terimon): dam, maiden best at 1m on Flat, winning hurdler: well beaten in maidens/handicaps. *C. W. Thornton*

GLISTENING SILVER 3 b.f. Puissance 110 – Silver Blessings (Statoblest 120) **58 d** [2003 49: 7.1g* 6g 7.1m f8s 7f Oct 27] modest performer: off 12 months prior to winning claimer at Chepstow (edged right) in June: ran as if amiss all starts after: likely to prove best at 6f/7f: acts on good to soft going: front runner. *J. Gallagher*

GLITTER AND GLORY 4 b.g. Classic Cliche (IRE) 128 – Veuve (Tirol 127) [2003 **62 §** 68: p16g³ f12g³ p16g f14g p10g f12g⁴ f14.8g² f14.8g⁵ Jun 6] leggy, close-coupled gelding: has a splayed action: modest maiden: stays 2m: acts on all-weather, lightly raced on turf: virtually ran out third start: blinkered next time: not one to trust: sold 6,500 gns. *C. A. Cyzer*

GLOAMING 5 b.m. Celtic Swing 138 – Kandavu 87 (Safawan 118) [2003 74d: p8g⁴ – § p8g 6.1g 10.9m 7m 6.1g 6d 6m Jun 15] good-topped mare: fair performer at best: well held in 2003: tried blinkered/in cheekpieces: unreliable. *J. Gallagher*

GLOBAL CHALLENGE (IRE) 4 b.g. Sadler's Wells (USA) 132 – Middle Prospect **103** (USA) (Mr Prospector (USA)) [2003 97: 12g* 11.9g 14.6g Sep 12] big, rangy gelding: useful performer, lightly raced: off a year prior to winning minor event at Newmarket in May by ½ length from It's The Limit: well held in handicaps after: should stay 1¾m: unraced on extremes of going: tends to wander. *Sir Michael Stoute*

GLORY AYR 4 b.f. Cool Jazz 116 – Sea-Ayr (IRE) 54 (Magical Wonder (USA) 125) – [2003 –: f5g Jan 4] no sign of ability in 2 starts. *B. Ellison*

GLORY GIRL 3 ch.f. Factual (USA) 108 – Glory Gold 59 (Hittite Glory 125) [2003 **50** f6f⁶ 5g³ 5m Aug 16] half-sister to 1m to 1½m winner Gold Desire (by Grey Desire): dam 6f to 7.5f winner: clearly best effort in maidens (modest form) on second outing: should stay 6f. *M. Brittain*

GLORY QUEST (USA) 6 b.g. Quest For Fame 127 – Sonseri 95 (Prince Tenderfoot **83** (USA) 126) [2003 76: f14s⁴ f12s* f12g⁵ f11s³ f12s³ f16s⁴ f12g² f12g* 14.1g 13d⁶ 11.9d⁵ f12g⁴ f8.5g⁵ f14.8g² f14g² f16g³ f14g⁵ f12g⁵ f14.8s² Dec 31] good-topped gelding: fairly useful handicapper: won at Southwell in January and March: effective at 1½m to 15f: acts on firm going, soft and all-weather: tried visored/blinkered earlier in career, sometimes wears cheekpieces: tough. *Miss Gay Kelleway*

GO BANANAS 2 b.g. (Feb 28) Primo Dominie 121 – Amsicora (Cadeaux Genereux **89** 131) [2003 5d³ 5.1g⁶ 6m* 7m³ 6f⁵ 7g* 7f⁶ Sep 28] 30,000 2-y-o: workmanlike gelding: first foal: dam unraced out of sister to very smart 7f/1m winner Efisio: fairly useful performer: won maiden at Windsor in July and nursery at Doncaster (beat Redwood Rocks by ¾ length) in September: edgy, not discredited final start: stays 7f: acts on firm and good to soft ground. *B. J. Meehan*

GO BETWEEN 2 b.f. (May 7) Daggers Drawn (USA) 114 – Pizzicato 64 (Statoblest **77** 120) [2003 6m⁵ 6d⁴ 5m³ 7m² 6m* 6m Oct 2] 100,000Y: good-topped filly: second foal: half-sister to 3-y-o Wunders Dream: dam, 5f winner, half-sister to smart performers in Britain/Hong Kong Volata (sprinter) and Mensa (up to 1¼m): fair performer: won maiden at Yarmouth in September: barely stays easy 7f: acts on good to firm and good to soft going: often races prominently. *E. A. L. Dunlop*

GOBLET OF FIRE (USA) 4 b.g. Green Desert (USA) 127 – Laurentine (USA) **105** (Private Account (USA)) [2003 105: p10g³ 10m² 10g² 10f 8m 10.1m⁵ 10.3g⁶ 9m Oct 4] good-topped gelding: smart on all-weather, useful on turf: best efforts in 2003 when placed in listed Winter Derby at Lingfield (third to Parasol), quite valuable handicap at Kempton (½-length second to Broadway Score) and handicap at Windsor first 3 starts: stays 10.5f: acts on firm going, good to soft and polytrack: sometimes wears crossed noseband: usually blinkered: races prominently: joined P. Nicholls. *B. J. Meehan*

GOBLIN 2 b.g. (Mar 8) Atraf 116 – Forest Fantasy 61 (Rambo Dancer (CAN) 107) **73** [2003 6g³ 6g² 6m³ 6m⁵ 6g 8m 7g Oct 24] 17,000F, 10,000Y: sturdy, lengthy gelding: has scope: third foal: brother to 3-y-o Sheriff's Deputy and 4-y-o Prince Atraf: dam, 1m/9f winner, closely related to US Grade 3 6.5f winner Imperial Star: fair maiden: should stay 1m: acts on good to firm going: sold 20,000 gns. *R. Hannon*

GO CLASSIC 3 b.f. Classic Cliche (IRE) 128 – Edraianthus 78 (Windjammer (USA)) **67** [2003 10d 10m 10m⁴ 11.6g p13g Dec 6] 8,500F: good-bodied filly: half-sister to useful 1m (in France at 2 yrs)/9f (in USA) winner Esquive (by Safawan) and fairly useful 1993 2-y-o 6f winner Close To Reality (by Dreams To Reality), later winner in USA: dam, maiden, best at 6f: fair maiden: left J. Cullinan and off 5 months before well beaten final start: stays 1¼m: unraced on extremes of going. *A. M. Hales*

GO FOR SUCCESS (USA) 3 b.g. Royal Academy (USA) 130 – Barad (Rainbow **83** Quest (USA) 134) [2003 70: 7g⁵ 10m⁶ 8.1d² 9.9m³ 9.9f 10.2f² a8g* a8g⁵ a8f⁴ a10g Dec 21] unfurnished gelding: fairly useful performer: best effort when third in handicap at Goodwood fourth start: sold from E. Dunlop 27,000 gns after sixth outing: won maiden at Taby in October: stays 1¼m: acts on good to firm and good to soft going, and on dirt: visored (went in snatches) sixth start. *F. Reuterskiold, Sweden*

GO FREE 2 b.g. (Apr 13) Easycall 115 – Miss Traxdata (Absalom 128) [2003 p6g 8g **–** Sep 22] first foal: dam no form: signs of only a little ability in maidens at Lingfield (unseated before start) and Kempton. *J. Cullinan*

GO GO GIRL 3 ch.f. Pivotal 124 – Addicted To Love 73 (Touching Wood (USA) **67** 127) [2003 71: 5.2m⁶ 5g⁵ 6m⁶ 5.1g⁵ 5m³ 6f³] fair maiden: effective at 5f/6f: raced only on good ground or firmer on turf. *L. G. Cottrell*

GO IN GENTLY 2 b.f. (Apr 8) Piccolo 121 – Careful (IRE) 59 (Distinctly North **55** (USA) 115) [2003 5.1m 7m Aug 28] fourth foal: half-sister to 4-y-o Agincourt Warrior: dam, maiden best at 6f at 2 yrs, should have stayed further: better effort in maidens (modest form) when eighth at Salisbury on final start, making most: slowly away on debut: not sure to stay much beyond 7f. *P. C. Ritchens*

GOJO (IRE) 2 b.f. (May 4) Danetime (IRE) 121 – Pretonic 73 (Precocious 126) [2003 **71** 6.1d 6m⁶ 6.1d Nov 6] €2,000Y: sixth foal: half-sister to 2 winners, including Irish 9f winner Caishill (by Dolphin Street): dam 5f to 7f winner: easily best effort in maidens (fair form) when sixth of 19 to Unshooda at Kempton: not sure to stay much beyond 6f: acts on good to firm going. *B. Palling*

GOLANO 3 gr.g. Linamix (FR) 127 – Dimakya (USA) 83 (Dayjur (USA) 137) [2003 **86** 85: p10g³ 12g³ 11g³ 10.9g⁴ 10.5d³ p10g* p12g* p12g Nov 22] rather leggy, quite good-topped gelding: fairly useful handicapper: won twice at Lingfield in October: effective at 1¼m/1½m: acts on polytrack, heavy and good to firm ground: usually waited with. *C. F. Wall*

GOLD BAR (IRE) 3 b.f. Barathea (IRE) 127 – Sun Princess 130 (English Prince 129) **74** [2003 10g 10f 10s³ 12g⁴ 10m² 11.1g⁴ 10g² 12v Nov 19] strong, good-topped filly: closely related to several winners including 4-y-o Princely Venture and high-class 7f (at 2 yrs) and 1¼m winner Prince of Dance (by Sadler's Wells), and half-sister to 3 winners: dam won Oaks and St Leger: fair maiden: should stay 1½m: acts on soft and good to firm ground: ran poorly in blinkers fourth start. *M. P. Tregoning*

GOLD BOND (IRE) 4 b.g. Goldmark (USA) 113 – Mujadil Princess (IRE) (Mujadil **–** (USA) 119) [2003 63: p7g Apr 1] modest performer: won handicap at Goodwood final 3-y-o start: well beaten only outing in 2003. *P. Mitchell*

GOLDBRICKER 3 b.g. Muhtarram (USA) 125 – Sally Slade 80 (Dowsing (USA) **67** 124) [2003 p8g 10m f9.4s 10.3m⁵ 10f³ 10.1m³ 16.2g 11.5g² Sep 16] tall, leggy gelding: third foal: half-brother to 4-y-o Gala Affair and 5-y-o Summer Shades: dam 5f winner, including at 2 yrs: fair maiden: races freely, and probably best short of 1½m: raced only on good going or firmer on turf, well held on all-weather: sold 6,000 gns. *C. A. Cyzer*

GOLD CARD 2 b.g. (Jan 17) First Trump 118 – Fleuve d'Or (IRE) (Last Tycoon 131) **71** [2003 7.2m⁶ 8m³ 8g⁴ Nov 5] 3,000Y: second foal: dam, no form, half-sister to smart performers Showbrook (sprinter) and Smarginato (effective at 1m/1¼m): fair form in maidens: in frame at Musselburgh: should stay 1¼m. *J. R. Weymes*

GOLD DUST WOMAN   2 b.f. (Feb 6) Hector Protector (USA) 124 – Hannalou (FR) **47**
70 (Shareef Dancer (USA) 135) [2003 5m 6g 6g⁵ 7d 7m f7s⁶ Sep 20] 9,000 2-y-o: second
foal: dam, maiden best at 7f, out of sister to dam of Dolphin Street and Saffron Walden:
poor maiden: left A. Berry before final start: stays 7f: acts on good to firm going.
J. Balding

GOLDEN ARUBA   4 ch.g. Golden Lahab (USA) – Clover Girl (Spin of A Coin 88)   **–**
[2003 –: 10.4f 6m Oct 17] well beaten in maidens/claimer. *B. Ellison*

GOLDEN BIFF (IRE)   7 ch.g. Shalford (IRE) 124§ – Capable Kate (IRE) (Alzao   **–**
(USA) 117) [2003 f6s⁵ f8.5s Mar 31] lightly raced and little form since 1999: tried
blinkered/visored/tongue tied. *J. J. Matthias*

GOLDEN BOOT   4 ch.g. Unfuwain (USA) 131 – Sports Delight (Star Appeal 133)   **78**
[2003 f11s⁶ 8m 9.9f⁵ 12.3m⁵ 8.3d³ 12g 11.1g² 13f² 14g 15.9m⁶ 13m 12.3m 12.1m²
12.1m³ 13.1m⁴ 16g³ Sep 28] big, strong gelding: fair handicapper: stays easy 2m: acts on
any turf going (below form only run on fibresand): tried in headgear: has run well when
sweating: very slowly away and hung markedly right under inexperienced apprentice
penultimate start: free-going sort, usually held up. *A. Bailey*

GOLDEN BOUNTY   4 b.c. Bahamian Bounty 116 – Cumbrian Melody 83 (Petong   **96**
126) [2003 101: 5.2m 6m⁶ 5m 5g 5f² 5g 6.1m⁵ 5m 5d 6m Oct 1] good-bodied colt: useful
performer: best effort in 2003 when 1¾ lengths second to Little Edward in minor event at
Sandown: barely stays 6f: acts on firm and good to soft going: sometimes swishes tail in
paddock: inconsistent. *R. Hannon*

GOLDEN BRIEF (IRE)   5 ch.g. Brief Truce (USA) 126 – Tiffany's Case (IRE) 65   **72**
(Thatching 131) [2003 66, a79: p7g* f7s p7g³ p7g² p7g² p7g⁴ 7f* 7m 7m³ 7f 7m 6.9m   **a91**
7.1m Jul 31] strong gelding: fairly useful handicapper on all-weather, fair on turf: won at
Lingfield in January and Thirsk in April: acted at 7f/easy 1m: acted on firm going and
polytrack: usually blinkered/visored: tried tongue tied: held up: dead. *K. R. Burke*

GOLDEN CHALICE (IRE)   4 ch.g. Selkirk (USA) 129 – Special Oasis (Green   **99**
Desert (USA) 127) [2003 98: 8m³ 7g 8g 8g⁵ 7d² p7g Nov 22] rather leggy, close-
coupled gelding: useful handicapper: good 1¾ lengths second of 21 to Tahirah in
apprentice event at Doncaster: best at 7f/1m: acts on good to firm and good to soft going:
races prominently. *A. M. Balding*

GOLDEN CHANCE (IRE)   6 b.g. Unfuwain (USA) 131 – Golden Digger (USA) 66   **55**
(Mr Prospector (USA)) [2003 –§: 8f 11m³ 10g³ 12.4g 13.8f² 16m⁴ 16.5m² Jul 10] sturdy
gelding: modest handicapper: stays 2m: acts on good to firm and good to soft going: sold
1,000 gns. *M. W. Easterby*

GOLDEN DIXIE (USA)   4 ch.g. Dixieland Band (USA) – Beyrouth (USA) (Alleged   **97**
(USA) 138) [2003 99: 6g 6m² 6g⁴ 6m 6m 7f 7m Oct 17] good-bodied gelding: useful
handicapper, lightly raced: best effort in 2003 when ¾-length second to Lochridge at
Newbury in July: effective at 6f/7f: raced only on good going or firmer: sometimes edgy/
slowly away/early to post. *A. M. Balding*

GOLDEN DRIFT   2 ch.f. (Apr 10) Inchinor 119 – Carpet of Leaves (USA) (Green
Forest (USA) 134) [2003 p7g Nov 29] third foal: dam, ran twice in France, half-sister to
smart French performers Glorify (up to 15f) and Doree (sprinting 2-y-o): 25/1, slowly
away and not knocked about when eleventh of 13 in minor event at Lingfield. *G. Wragg*

GOLDEN DUAL   3 b.g. Danehill (USA) 126 – Golden Digger (USA) 66 (Mr Pros-   **72**
pector (USA)) [2003 72p: p7g⁴ 10g³ 10g 10.2f⁴ 12g³ 8.3g⁶ p10g⁵ Dec 30] lengthy,
good-topped gelding: fair maiden: below form last 3 starts, leaving B. Hills 12,000 gns
and gelded before final one: stays 1¼m: acts on polytrack, probably on firm going:
blinkered (gave temperamental display) penultimate outing: not one to trust. *S. Dow*

GOLDEN EMPIRE (USA)   2 br.c. (Apr 2) Red Ransom (USA) – Golden Gorse   **78 p**
(USA) (His Majesty (USA)) [2003 6m³ 7m² Sep 2] $100,000Y: close-coupled colt:
closely related to very smart 1m to 1½m winner Lear Spear (by Lear Fan) and half-
brother to 3 winners, including Irish 2m winner Gleaming Heather (by Irish River): dam,
winning US sprinter, half-sister to smart performers up to 1¼m Lotus Pool and Golden
Larch: fair form in maidens at Pontefract and Yarmouth (raced up with pace when 1¼
lengths second to Top Romance): will stay at least 1m: open to progress. *E. A. L. Dunlop*

GOLDEN FACT (USA)   9 b.g. Known Fact (USA) 135 – Cosmic Sea Queen (USA)   **62**
(Determined Cosmic (USA)) [2003 65: f12g f8.5g 8g* Apr 30] angular, close-coupled
gelding: modest handicapper: trained by R. McGlinchey in Ireland in 2002: won selling
event at Pontefract in April: best at 1m/9f: acts on heavy and good to firm ground, well
held on fibresand: tried blinkered. *B. A. McMahon*

GOLDEN FIELDS (IRE) 3 b.f. Definite Article 121 – Quickstep Queen (FR) **57 d**
(Pampabird 124) [2003 50: p8g p10g 10m⁴ 11.6d 11.1g⁴ p12g 10.9f* 11.6m 11.7f 14.1s²
f16.2g Nov 10] lengthy filly: modest performer: won seller at Warwick (left A. Jarvis
4,800 gns) in July: below form after: stays 11f: acts on firm ground: blinkered/visored last
6 outings: reportedly finished distressed fourth start: has hung left. *A. P. Jones*

GOLDEN GOOSE 2 ch.c. (Feb 19) Pivotal 124 – Desert Ditty 67 (Green Desert **–**
(USA) 127) [2003 6d 7d Sep 10] 142,000 francs F: big, workmanlike colt: sixth living
foal: half-brother to several winners, including French 1996 2-y-o 6f winner Alberelle
and 1m/9f winner Entity (both fairly useful, by Rudimentary): dam 6f winner: well held
in maiden at Newmarket (coltish) and minor event at Doncaster: sold 800 gns, sent to
Belgium. *N. A. Callaghan*

GOLDEN GRACE 2 b.c. (Jan 13) Green Desert (USA) 127 – Chief Bee 89 (Chief's **87 p**
Crown (USA)) [2003 8.1g⁶ 7m³ 7g* Nov 1] 160,000Y: well-made, attractive colt: fourth
foal: half-brother to 3 winners, including 3-y-o Argonaut and smart 1¼m/1½m winner
Beekeeper (by Rainbow Quest): dam, 9f to 14.6f winner, sister to Racing Post Trophy
winner Be My Chief: progressive form in maidens: won 12-runner event at Newmarket
by neck from Silent Hawk, soon off bridle but getting up near finish: should be suited by
at least 1m: likely to make a useful 3-y-o. *E. A. L. Dunlop*

GOLDEN HEART 3 ch.f. Salse (USA) 128 – Lonely Heart 101 (Midyan (USA) 124) **77**
[2003 76: 8f⁵ 7f* 8m⁵ 9m 7f 11f² 8d Oct 31] smallish, workmanlike filly: fair performer:
made all in maiden at Salisbury in June: effective at 7f, and seems to stay 11f: acts on firm
ground, well held on good to soft and polytrack: usually races prominently: has looked
none too genuine. *D. R. C. Elsworth*

GOLDEN ISLAND (IRE) 2 ch.f. (Feb 12) Selkirk (USA) 129 – Daftiyna (IRE) 74 **59 p**
(Darshaan 133) [2003 7g Nov 1] €45,000Y: tall filly: fifth foal: dam, placed up to 9f in
Ireland, daughter of very smart sprinter Dafayna, herself half-sister to 2000 Guineas
winner Doyoun: in need of race, 8 lengths tenth of 17 to Si Si Amiga in maiden
at Newmarket: will stay 1m: should improve. *J. W. Hills*

GOLDEN LARIAT (USA) 4 ch.c. Mr Prospector (USA) – Larrocha (IRE) 116 **91**
(Sadler's Wells (USA) 132) [2003 89: 12g 11.9f 12m* 12m 12m⁵ 12m Oct 3] good-
bodied colt: fairly useful handicapper: won at Newmarket in July: folded last 2 starts:
stays 1½m: raced only on good ground or firmer: usually races prominently: raced freely
second outing: sold 22,000 gns. *Sir Michael Stoute*

GOLDEN NUN 3 b.f. Bishop of Cashel 122 – Amber Mill 96 (Doulab (USA) 115) **105**
[2003 98: p7g 6m² 6.1s⁴ 6v⁵ 6m⁶ 6g 6m² 6.1m 6m 6m 6.1d² 6d³ 6s 6d⁵ Nov 8] angular
filly: useful performer: in frame 5 times in 2003, including when 2 lengths equal-second
to Torosay Spring in Summer Stakes at York seventh start, neck second to Danehurst in
listed race at Chester and close third to Hanabad in listed race at the Curragh: below
form last 2 outings: best form at 6f: acts on firm and soft ground: usually wears blinkers/
cheekpieces: best held up. *T. D. Easterby*

GOLDEN QUEST 2 ch.c. (Jan 21) Rainbow Quest (USA) 134 – Souk (IRE) 98 **– p**
(Ahonoora 122) [2003 8m Oct 25] 27,000Y: brother to useful 1½m winner Seek and half-
brother to several winners, including 1¼m/1½m winners Hazim and Puce (both smart, by
Darshaan): dam, 7f winner (including at 2 yrs), better at 1m: 12/1 again, behind in
maiden at Musselburgh, off bridle by halfway: will be suited by 1¼m+: should do better.
M. Johnston

GOLDEN REMEDY 2 b.f. (Feb 26) Dr Fong (USA) 128 – Golden Daring (IRE) **62**
(Night Shift (USA)) [2003 5g 5m³ 6g³ 6d 6m 7.1m⁶ Oct 25] sturdy filly: third foal: dam,
Italian 2-y-o 6f winner, out of sister to very smart sprinter Ballad Rock: modest maiden:
well below form last 3 starts, though led long way when visored in seller final one: stays
6f: acts on good to firm going. *D. W. Barker*

GOLDEN SAHARA (IRE) 2 b.c. (Mar 3) Green Desert (USA) 127 – Golden Digger **101 p**
(USA) 66 (Mr Prospector (USA)) [2003 6m* 6g² 7f² Oct 9] strong, lengthy, attractive
colt: fourth foal: half-brother to 4-y-o Naheef and 6-y-o Golden Chance: dam, maiden
who failed to progress from only 2-y-o start, sister to dam of Irish Oaks/Nassau Stakes
winner Lailani and half-sister to very smart performers Always Fair (at 7f/1m) and
Faithful Son (up to 1½m): landed odds in maiden at Yarmouth in August: tongue tied,
useful form when second in minor events at Doncaster and York (beaten 1¼ lengths by
Moonlight Man): barely stays 7f: type to train on well. *Saeed bin Suroor*

GOLDEN SILCA 7 ch.m. Inchinor 119 – Silca-Cisa 93 (Hallgate 127) [2003 115: 9d³ **100**
10.4m⁵ May 14] lengthy, sparely-made mare: smart performer at best: just useful form in

listed races in 2003: best at 1m/1¼m: acted on firm and soft going: had won when edgy: was usually held up: reportedly in foal to Selkirk. *M. R. Channon*

GOLDEN SKIIS (IRE) 3 ch.f. Hector Protector (USA) 124 – Ski For Gold 76 **73** (Shirley Heights 130) [2003 68p: 10d 11.5m⁴ 16.2m² 13.8m² Jul 23] sturdy, plain filly: fair maiden: will stay beyond 2m: acts on good to firm ground. *J. L. Dunlop*

GOLDEN SPECTRUM (IRE) 4 ch.g. Spectrum (IRE) 126 – Plessaya (USA) (Nure- – yev (USA) 131) [2003 86, a78: p8g 6g 8m 7m 8g 10g Oct 13] leggy, quite good-topped gelding: fairly useful handicapper at 3 yrs: well held in 2003: has worn blinkers/cheek-pieces/tongue strap: sold 8,500 gns and gelded. *R. Hannon*

GOLDEN WELLS (IRE) 5 b.g. Sadler's Wells (USA) 132 – Golden Bloom (Main **102** Reef 126) [2003 12g⁶ Aug 1] close-coupled, good-topped gelding: smart performer at 3 yrs: unraced in 2002 and gelded: useful form when sixth to Researched in handicap at Goodwood on only 5-y-o start: stayed 1½m: very best efforts on ground softer than good: blinkered last 2 outings: dead. *M. Johnston*

GOLDEVA 4 gr.f. Makbul 104 – Gold Belt (IRE) 61 (Bellypha 130) [2003 102: 6g **99** 7m⁵ 6.1s 6m 6m⁶ 6m⁵ 6.1d⁶ 6m² 6d Nov 8] leggy filly: has a quick action: useful perfor-mer: best effort in 2003 when ½-length second to Frizzante in listed race at Newmarket: best form at 6f: acts on any going: effective ridden prominently or held up. *R. Hollinshead*

GOLD FERVOUR 4 b.g. Mon Tresor 113 – Fervent Fan (IRE) 65 (Soviet **46** Lad (USA)) [2003 –: 7.9m 6m⁵ 7m 6m 6m⁵ Oct 17] quite good-topped gelding: poor maiden: should stay 1m: acts on soft and good to firm ground. *W. M. Brisbourne*

GOLD GUEST 4 ch.g. Vettori (IRE) 119 – Cassilis (IRE) (Persian Bold 123) [2003 **79** 87+: p7g f6g p8g⁶ 9m* 9.2m³ 7m⁵ 8f p8g 7.2g⁴ 8.5m⁶ 7.9m 8g f8.5g⁴ f7g⁴ p10g* Dec 20] leggy gelding: fair performer: won claimer at Musselburgh (claimed from S. Williams £10,000) in March: left J. Hetherton after twelfth start: won handicap at Lingfield in December: stays 1¼m: acts on soft going, good to firm and all-weather: tried visored: often slowly away: has looked none too genuine. *P. D. Evans*

GOLD HISTORY (USA) 2 b.c. (Mar 4) Seeking The Gold (USA) – Battle Hymn **96** (USA) (Danzig (USA)) [2003 7m* 7.2m* 7m Oct 12] $125,000Y: big, attractive colt: third foal: dam, 6f/6.5f winner in US, half-sister to very smart US Grade 2 9f winner (stayed 1½m) Parade Ground: useful form: made all in maiden at Leicester and minor event at Ayr (beat Colour Wheel by 1¼ lengths), both in September: below form in Somerville Tattersall Stakes at Newmarket: likely to be suited by 1¼m/1½m. *M. Johnston*

GOLD MASK (USA) 2 b. or br.c. (Feb 17) Seeking The Gold (USA) – Leo's Gypsy **70 ?** Dancer (USA) (Lee Castelli (USA)) [2003 6m Jul 19] attractive colt: first foal: dam US 7f (at 2 yrs) to 8.5f winner, placed in graded stakes: 9/2, seemingly fair form when seventh of 12 in slowly-run maiden at Newmarket, strong hold before finishing well. *J. H. M. Gosden*

GOLD MEDALLIST 3 ch.g. Zilzal (USA) 137 – Spot Prize (USA) 108 (Seattle **107** Dancer (USA) 119) [2003 81: 10g² 11.1m² 12g* 11m 12m* 16.2f⁵ 14.8m* 12g⁶ 14.6g 14m³ Oct 2] big, strong gelding: useful performer: won maiden at Salisbury in May, handicap at Kempton in June and listed race at Newmarket (beat Discreet Brief by neck) in July: well held in St Leger at Doncaster penultimate start: creditable third to Hilbre Island in listed race at Newmarket final one: stays 2m: acts on firm going, well held on soft: races prominently: consistent. *D. R. C. Elsworth*

GOLD MILLENIUM (IRE) 9 gr.g. Kenmare (FR) 125 – Gold Necklace 86 (Golden – Fleece (USA) 133) [2003 59: p16g⁶ Jan 4] tall gelding: modest handicapper: well held only start in 2003. *C. A. Horgan*

GOLD RING 3 ch.g. Groom Dancer (USA) 128 – Indubitable 87 (Sharpo 132) [2003 **95** 81: 9d⁵ 9.9g³ 11m 12.1d³ 12f 12g⁶ 12s² 13.3m² 12m⁴ 12g⁶ Nov 8] leggy, work-manlike gelding: useful performer: landed odds in maiden at Kempton in September: good third to stablemate Turbo in November Handicap at Doncaster final start: will stay 1¾m: acts on firm and soft going: usually races prominently: tough and consistent. *G. B. Balding*

GOLD RIVIERA (USA) 3 ch.c. Irish River (FR) 131 – Raj Dancer (USA) (Rahy – (USA) 115) [2003 69?: 10g 7g 8f Sep 8] good-bodied colt: maiden: well beaten in 2003. *M. C. Pipe*

GOLFAGENT 5 b.g. Kris 135 – Alusha 88 (Soviet Star (USA) 128) [2003 48: f14.8g – Oct 20] small gelding: poor maiden: soundly beaten only Flat outing in 2003: usually tongue tied. *Miss K. Marks*

GOLLY GOSH (IRE) 4 b.f. Danehill (USA) 126 – Miss Declared (USA) (Alleged **103**
(USA) 138) [2003 79: 12m* 12d⁴ 12.3f 12m 14g⁶ 12m⁵ 14m² 15.5m 12g⁶ Oct 11]
3,000Y: good-topped filly: third foal: dam unraced: useful performer: won handicap at
Leopardstown in April: best effort when short-head second to Cruzspiel in listed race at
Fairyhouse seventh start: wearing cheekpieces, well held in Princess Royal Stakes at
Ascot final outing: should stay 2m: acts on firm and good to soft going: tongue tied fourth
to seventh outings. *M. Halford, Ireland*

GONDOLIN (IRE) 3 b.g. Marju (IRE) 127 – Galletina (IRE) 74 (Persian Heights **92**
129) [2003 80p: p7g⁶ 10d* 10.5s² 12m 11.7f³ 10m⁴ 10m⁵ Oct 4] workmanlike gelding:
fairly useful performer: won maiden at Windsor in May: best effort when fourth to
Pagan Sky in handicap at Pontefract: stays 10.5f, raced freely over further: acts on polytrack, soft and good to firm going: tried tongue tied: has carried head high/wandered.
G. A. Butler

GONE LOCO 2 b.f. (Feb 25) Piccolo 121 – Missed Again 84 (High Top 131) [2003 **–**
6g 5.1g⁶ 6m Sep 5] 2,500Y: compact filly: half-sister to 3 winners, including 5-y-o
Canterloupe and 10-y-o Failed To Hit: dam, 1¼m winner, half-sister to smart performers
Desert Shot (up to 1½m) and Mojave (up to 7f): little sign of ability in minor event/
maidens: carried head awkwardly final start. *H. S. Howe*

GONE'N'DUNNETT (IRE) 4 b.g. Petardia 113 – Skerries Bell 71 (Taufan (USA) **76**
119) [2003 58, a80: p6g⁵ f5s⁵ f6s p6g 5g 6m³ 5g 5m 6m 6m⁵ 5.1m 5.2m² 5.3f² 6m f6s
f6g⁴ f5g* f5g f5s³ Dec 6] strong gelding: fair performer: won handicap at Wolverhampton
in November: best at 5f/6f: acts on all-weather, best turf efforts on good to firm/firm
ground: wears headgear. *Mrs C. A. Dunnett*

GONE TO GROUND 2 ch.g. (Feb 25) Foxhound (USA) 103 – Charlie Girl 70 (Puis- **56**
sance 110) [2003 5m⁴ 5m⁶ 6f³ 6m 6g³ f5g³ 6m⁶ 7m* 6f 7m Aug 15] 10,000Y: quite good-
topped gelding: first foal: dam, 2-y-o 5f winner, out of half-sister to high-class French
1¼m performer Creator: modest performer: won seller at Catterick in July: left K. Ryan,
below form last 2 starts: stays 7f: acts on firm going and fibresand: wore headgear after
second outing: sometimes slowly away/races wide. *R. E. Barr*

GONE TOO FAR 5 b.g. Reprimand 122 – Blue Nile (IRE) 70 (Bluebird (USA) 125) **52**
[2003 63: 14m⁴ 16m 16d³ 16m³ Jul 7] sparely-made gelding: modest performer: stays
easy 2m: acts on firm and good to soft going (well held only outing on fibresand): tried
blinkered/visored: races freely: joined M. Pipe 18,000 gns: fair hurdler. *M. Dods*

GONFILIA (GER) 3 b.f. Big Shuffle (USA) 122 – Gonfalon (Slip Anchor 136) [2003 **107**
96p: a8f² 8g 7g² 8d² 7d⁵ 7g* Oct 17] ex-German filly: useful performer: runner-up in
UAE 1000 Guineas at Nad Al Sheba (beaten 3 lengths by Mezzo Soprano) and listed
races at Goodwood (beaten 1½ lengths by Tantina) and Deauville (short-headed by
Zietory): won listed race at Maisons-Laffitte in October by head from Miss Ivanhoe:
effective at 7f/1m: acts on dirt, raced only on good going or softer on turf: has worn
tongue strap: usually races prominently: to run in UAE early in 2004 before visiting
Halling. *Saeed bin Suroor*

GOOD ARTICLE (IRE) 2 b.c. (Mar 8) Definite Article 121 – Good News (IRE) 61 **–**
(Ajraas (USA) 88) [2003 7.9f 8g Oct 25] sturdy colt: blind in near-side eye: second
known foal: dam lightly-raced 7f winner: soundly beaten in maidens at York and Newbury. *A. P. Jones*

GOODBYE GOLDSTONE 7 b.g. Mtoto 134 – Shareehan (Dancing Brave (USA) **–**
140) [2003 67: 11.9m 11.6g 12d 10.1g Oct 22] sparely-made gelding: fair handicapper:
well held in 2003, leaving T. McGovern after second start. *B. Ellison*

GOODBYE MR BOND 3 b.g. Elmaamul (USA) 125 – Fifth Emerald 54 (Formidable **64**
(USA) 125) [2003 –: 9.2d* 10m 10m 8g⁵ f8.5g³ f9.4g⁴ f8g f8g⁴ Dec 8] strong, lengthy
gelding: modest handicapper: won at Hamilton in May: stays 9f: acts on good to soft
going and fibresand: has wandered. *E. J. Alston*

GOODENOUGH MOVER 7 ch.g. Beveled (USA) – Rekindled Flame (IRE) (Kings **81**
Lake (USA) 133) [2003 92: 7m 7m 7f⁶ 7m 6m³ 7m 6g 6.1m p7g Nov 13] rangy gelding:
fairly useful handicapper: best at 6f/7f: acts on polytrack, soft and firm going: front
runner. *J. S. King*

GOODENOUGH STAR 3 b.f. Stronz (IRE) 62 – Goodenough Girl (Mac's Imp **–**
(USA) 116) [2003 7.1g 8m⁶ 7m 5.7f Oct 12] first foal: dam tailed off all 3 starts: little
form. *J. S. King*

GOOD FORM (IRE) 3 b.g. Danetime (IRE) 121 – Faapette (Runnett 125) [2003 57: **47**
f8g p7g f7g² f9.4s⁶ 5.7m⁶ 8.2d⁵ 5.1m 8f³ 8.1g 7.1m 8f p7g Dec 17] poor maiden: left

R. Beckett after second outing: stays 1m: acts on firm ground, good to soft and all-weather: tried tongue tied: sometimes slowly away: inconsistent. *Miss K. M. George*

GOOD GIRL (IRE)   4 b.f. College Chapel 122 – Indian Honey (Indian King (USA)   **92** 128) [2003 100: 6d 5f 6g 5m* 5d 6g 5m 5d 5d 5d 5m 5d 5d 14d] workmanlike filly: fairly useful handicapper: won at Newmarket in July: best at 5f/6f: acts on good to firm and good to soft going, ran poorly on soft: usually blinkered in 2002, often wore eyeshields in 2003: usually edgy, and sometimes early to post: races up with pace: sold 50,000 gns. *T. D. Easterby*

GOOD HEALTH   3 b.f. Magic Ring (IRE) 115 – Fiddling 82 (Music Boy 124) [2003   **74 ?** 78: 5.1m 6m⁶ 7g⁵ 5d p6g Oct 8] leggy, workmanlike filly: fair performer: best at 5f/6f: acts on firm and soft ground: often forces pace: sold 6,500 gns. *W. J. Haggas*

GOOD LOSER (IRE)   3 b.g. Mujadil (USA) 119 – Cockney Star (IRE) (Camden   **64** Town 125) [2003 67: f7s 8.2g 10m⁴ 12f⁴ 12g 9.9m² 12.1d 10g² 12.4m⁴ 14.1m⁴ Jun 12] close-coupled gelding: modest performer: claimed from D. Nicholls £6,000 eighth start: finished lame final outing: effective at 1¼m to 1¾m: acts on firm ground: usually tongue tied. *C. R. Dore*

GOODLY NEWS (IRE)   7 b.g. Project Manager 111 – Nordic Relation (IRE)   **–** (Nordico (USA)) [2003 11m Apr 22] fair maiden handicapper at 3/4 yrs in Ireland for J. Bolger: well held only Flat outing since: effective blinkered or not. *A. W. Carroll*

GOODNESS GRACIOUS (IRE)   3 b.f. Green Desert (USA) 127 – Trois Graces   **93** (USA) (Alysheba (USA)) [2003 89p: 7m⁴ 10g 8.5m 8f Jun 21] tall, leggy filly: fluent mover: fairly useful performer: good fourth to Tante Rose in Dubai Duty Free Stakes (Fred Darling) at Newbury on reappearance: well held in listed events after, looking reluctant in rated stakes in blinkers final start: should be suited by 1m+: acts on good to firm and good to soft ground: sold 55,000 gns in December. *J. L. Dunlop*

GOOD PENNY (IRE)   2 b.g. (Mar 2) Pennekamp (USA) 130 – The Good Life (IRE)   **84** (Rainbow Quest (USA) 134) [2003 5g² 6g² May 29] 13,000F, 13,500Y: first foal: dam, French 12.5f winner, out of smart French miler Once In My Life: second in maiden at Carlisle and minor event at Ayr (fairly useful form): will stay at least 1m: sent to Hong Kong where renamed Winning Rongrong. *T. P. Tate*

GOOD SHOT   2 b.f. (Apr 10) Mind Games 121 – Penny Hasset 73 (Lochnager 132)   **–** [2003 6d 6m Jun 2] seventh foal: half-sister to fairly useful 1999 2-y-o 5f/6f winner Happy Times (by Timeless Times): dam 5f/6f winner: no form in sellers. *M. W. Easterby*

GOOD TIMING   5 bl.g. Timeless Times (USA) 99 – Fort Vally 58 (Belfort (FR) 89)   **–** [2003 –: f8s Jan 14] lengthy, sparely-made gelding: little form since 2001. *J. J. Quinn*

GOOD TO GO   2 ch.g. (Apr 20) Deploy 131 – Lets Fall In Love (USA) (Northern   **65** Baby (CAN) 127) [2003 5m 6m² 7d 7.5m⁴ 8f* 8m Aug 30] 3,500Y: tall, sturdy gelding: half-brother to 3 winners, including 1996 2-y-o 5f winner Heart Throb (by Statoblest), later 7f winner in Germany, and multiple winner in Italy (mainly around 7f/1m) by Tank's Prospect: dam winning sprinter in USA: fair performer: won claimer at Newcastle in August: slowly away when below form in nursery final start: will stay at least 1¼m: acts on firm ground: sold 4,500 gns, sent to Macau. *P. C. Haslam*

GOOD VIBRATIONS   2 b.f. (Feb 10) Bijou d'Inde 127 – Showcase 68 (Shareef   **54** Dancer (USA) 135) [2003 f5g f7f 6m p8g² Nov 22] first foal: dam, lightly-raced maiden, out of half-sister to smart French maiden miler Culture Vulture, the family of Zilzal and Polish Precedent: modest maiden: form only when second in seller at Lingfield, starting slowly and racing freely: stays 1m: acts on polytrack. *P. F. I. Cole*

GOODWOOD FINESSE (IRE)   2 b.f. (Feb 22) Revoque (IRE) 122 – Key To Paris   **70 p** (ARG) (Profit Key (USA)) [2003 8m⁵ 8g⁵ Oct 25] 25,000Y: lengthy filly: first foal: dam, ran twice in Argentina, half-sister to dam of Arc winner Helissio: fair form in maidens at Newmarket and Newbury, late headway not knocked about both times: will be suited by 1¼m+: sure to do better. *J. L. Dunlop*

GOODWOOD PRINCE   3 b.g. Emperor Jones (USA) 119 – Scarlet Lake 60 (Repri-   **81** mand 122) [2003 84: 7g 6m 7m 6m 6m² 6m² 7g² 6m 6m 7g 7m⁶ 8f p6g p6g p5g⁶ Dec 20]   **a70** smallish, sturdy gelding: fairly useful on turf, fair on all-weather: left J. Dunlop 18,000 gns after twelfth outing: effective at 6f/7f: acts on polytrack, soft and good to firm going: tried in cheekpieces/blinkers: none too consistent. *S. Dow*

GOODWOOD PROMISE   4 b.g. Primo Dominie 121 – Noble Destiny 89 (Dancing   **–** Brave (USA) 140) [2003 53: 7d 6m f5s 6m 6f f8g f6g f5s Dec 27] neat gelding: just poor maiden: well held in 2003, leaving J. M. Bradley after third start: best at 5f/6f: acts on good to soft ground: tried blinkered. *N. E. Berry*

GO PADERO (IRE) 2 ch.c. (Apr 30) Night Shift (USA) – Watch The Clock 93 (Mtoto 134) [2003 7m⁶ 7m⁵ 7s* Nov 3] €32,000Y: big, heavy-topped colt: fourth foal: half-brother to 4-y-o E Minor: dam 2-y-o 6f/7.5f winner who stayed 1¼m: best effort in maidens (fairly useful form) when winning 15-runner event at Redcar readily by 2 lengths from Honest Injun, making all: will be suited by at least 1m: open to improvement. *M. Johnston*   **82 p**

GO POLAR 3 b.f. Polar Falcon (USA) 126 – Twilight Patrol 96 (Robellino (USA) 127) [2003 81: 5.5m 6.1g² 5m* 5m 5g⁵ 6m⁶ 6g⁴ Oct 31] leggy filly: fairly useful performer: won handicap at Newmarket in June: effective at 5f/easy 6f: acts on firm ground: hung right sixth outing. *J. Cullinan*   **89**

GORDONS FRIEND 5 ch.g. Clantime 101 – Auntie Fay (IRE) (Fayruz 116) [2003 47: 8g 7.5m 8f Jun 26] smallish gelding: well held in 2003: tried visored. *B. S. Rothwell*   **–**

GORDY'S JOY 3 b.f. Cloudings (IRE) 112 – Beatle Song 70 (Song 132) [2003 10m 10g⁶ 12.1g⁴ 4,600 3-y-o: half-sister to 1¼m/11.5f winner Adriana (by Tragic Role) and a winner in Italy by Silver Kite: dam 5.7f to 1m winner: well beaten in maidens. *G. A. Ham*   **–**

GO SHEEK (IRE) 3 b.f. Kahyasi 130 – Terrama Sioux (Relkino 131) [2003 55p: f8.5s 10m⁴ 12.1f⁵ 14.1m 12.1m² 12f⁵ 16.2m⁶ 11g Jul 26] leggy filly: poor maiden handicapper: stayed 1½m: acted on firm going: dead. *J. J. Quinn*   **49**

GO SOLO 2 b.c. (Mar 23) Primo Dominie 121 – Taza (Persian Bold 123) [2003 6m 6m² 7m* 8d⁵ 7d* 7.9f⁶ Oct 9] workmanlike colt: has a quick action: fifth foal: half-brother to useful 1999 2-y-o 7f winner who stayed 2m Il Capitano (by Be My Chief) and 1m winner Totem Pole (by Pivotal): dam, no form, half-sister to very smart middle-distance performer Apache: fairly useful performer: won maiden in August and nursery in September (by 1½ lengths from Imperialistic), both at Chester: stays 7f: best effort on good to soft going. *B. W. Hills*   **83**

GOTARAPOFAHAMES (IRE) 5 b.g. Midhish 109 – Quench The Lamp (IRE) (Glow (USA)) [2003 91: f6g 5m⁵ 6d 5g 6.3m 5g 5g 8.5d 6s Sep 19] half-brother to winners abroad by Persian Heights and Don't Forget Me: dam ran 3 times in Ireland: fairly useful performer: won handicaps at Cork at 3/4 yrs: well held in handicap at Wolverhampton on reappearance: not discredited in listed race at Cork next time: below form after: effective at 5f/6f: best on good ground or firmer: usually blinkered: tried in cheekpieces/tongue tie. *N. F. Glynn, Ireland*   **88 d**

GO TECH 3 b.g. Gothenberg (IRE) 117 – Bollin Sophie (Efisio 120) [2003 94: 9m⁵ 7g 7.9m 8.1v 10.4f⁵ Jun 14] rather leggy, useful-looking gelding: shows plenty of knee action: fairly useful handicapper: free-going sort, but stays 10.4f: acts on any going: often races prominently. *T. D. Easterby*   **91**

GOTHIC BAY 3 b.g. Gothenberg (IRE) 117 – Greyhill Lady (Grey Desire 115) [2003 –: 8m Aug 6] lengthy gelding: little sign of ability. *M. W. Easterby*   **–**

GO THUNDER (IRE) 9 b.g. Nordico (USA) – Moving Off (Henbit (USA) 130) [2003 –: 9.2m⁴ Jul 17] no form since 2001: usually tongue tied: tubed. *D. A. Nolan*   **–**

GOT ONE TOO (FR) 6 ch.g. Green Tune (USA) 125 – Gloria Mundi (FR) (Saint Cyrien (FR) 128) [2003 14.1m* 14.4g² 16m³ May 24] big, plain gelding: useful hurdler/chaser: fairly useful handicapper on Flat: won at Nottingham (made running) in April and Kempton (slowly away) in May: stays 2m: acts on soft and good to firm going: blinkered on debut (at 2 yrs): usually tongue tied in 2000. *N. J. Henderson*   **80**

GO TO SHUL 4 b.g. Runnett 125 – Kopjes (Bay Express 132) [2003 f12g Mar 20] 1,700Y: brother to a winner in Denmark: dam poor maiden: soundly beaten in seller at Southwell. *M. W. Easterby*   **–**

GOT TO BE CASH 4 ch.f. Lake Coniston (IRE) 131 – Rasayel (USA) 79§ (Bering 136) [2003 57: 12.4m³ 12.4g 13.1g 11.8g⁵ 11.6g 9.9m² 9.7f⁵ 10.9m⁶ 10.5m 9.9m² 11.7f⁶ 10m Oct 20] strong, lengthy filly: modest maiden handicapper: stays 1½m: acts on firm and soft ground, some promise on fibresand: usually waited with. *W. M. Brisbourne*   **53**

GOTYA 3 b.f. Gothenberg (IRE) 117 – Water Well 96 (Sadler's Wells (USA) 132) [2003 8.5m⁶ Jun 24] angular filly: sixth foal: half-sister to 3 winners, including 10-y-o Soaked and 2000 2-y-o 5f winner Face D Facts (by So Factual): dam, 7.6f winner, half-sister to dam of very smart 1¼m/1½m performer Dark Moondancer out of Soba: tailed off in maiden at Beverley. *T. D. Easterby*   **–**

GO YELLOW 2 b.g. (May 31) Overbury (IRE) 116 – Great Lyth Lass (IRE) 67 (Waajib **76**
121) [2003 7m 7.1m⁶ 6g² 7m⁶ Oct 21] close-coupled gelding: third foal: dam maiden who
regressed after debut: fair maiden: easily best effort when second at Windsor, making
most: likely to prove best at 5f/6f. *P. D. Evans*

GRACE BANKES 2 ch.f. (Feb 5) Efisio 120 – Amaranthus (Shirley Heights 130) **44**
[2003 p5g⁶ 5.1m⁴ 6d May 18] 2,400Y: seventh foal: half-sister to fairly useful 7.5f winner
Acidanthera (by Alzao): dam unraced daughter of smart sprinter Amaranda: poor form in
maiden/sellers: should stay 6f: slowly away last 2 starts. *W. G. M. Turner*

GRACE DARLING 2 b.f. (Apr 7) Botanic (USA) – Light On The Waves 71 (Green- **–**
smith 121) [2003 f7s Sep 20] £400Y: first foal: dam 8.5f (at 2 yrs) to 17f winner: last of 7
in seller at Wolverhampton, failing to handle bends. *Miss E. C. Lavelle*

GRACEFUL AIR (IRE) 2 b.f. (Mar 12) Danzero (AUS) – Samsung Spirit 79 (Stato- **65**
blest 120) [2003 5m³ 5m⁴ 6m⁴ 6g² 6g⁵ 7d 6m³ 7f 7.1g³ Nov 5] workmanlike filly: third
foal: half-sister to 3-y-o Spiritual Air: dam, 6f winner (including at 2 yrs), half-sister to
dam of smart 6f/7f performer Indian Rocket: fair maiden: in frame 6 times, including in
nurseries: stays 7f: acts on good to firm going: wore cheekpieces (ran respectably)
seventh start: tail flasher. *J. R. Weymes*

GRACEFULLY (IRE) 2 b.f. (Mar 27) Orpen (USA) 116 – Lady Taufan (IRE) (Taufan **102**
(USA) 119) [2003 6m* 6m* 7m* 7m⁴ Oct 18] 10,000Y: compact filly: sixth foal: half-
sister to useful 1996 2-y-o 6f winner Speedball (by Waajib) and 1997 2-y-o 5f winner
Golden Strategy (by Statoblest), later successful abroad: dam, Irish maiden, stayed 9f:
useful performer: won maiden at Goodwood in June, minor event at Salisbury in July and
Malaysia Airlines Non Stop Prestige Stakes at Goodwood (beat Ithaca by 2 lengths) in

Thurloe Thoroughbreds VI's "Gracefully"

August: respectable 4¼ lengths fourth to Cairns in Rockfel Stakes at Newmarket: should stay 1m: game: sold privately to race in USA. *S. Kirk*

GRACIA 4 gr.f. Linamix (FR) 127 – Francia 59 (Legend of France (USA) 124) [2003 75+: 9.9m³ 9d⁵ 10m 11.9v⁵ 8m³ 8g³ 8m 8.5m* 10d 8m 8d³ Nov 7] lengthy, angular filly: fair handicapper: won at Epsom in July: effective at 1m to 1¼m: acts on polytrack, good to firm and good to soft going: usually races prominently. *S. C. Williams* **78**

GRACIOUS AIR (USA) 5 b.m. Bahri (USA) 125 – Simply Bell (USA) (Simply Majestic (USA)) [2003 64: 12.3m 9.9m 7.9m 10m 10m⁶ f11g Nov 25] tall, leggy, good-topped mare: poor handicapper nowadays: stays 1½m: acts on firm and good to soft going: tried in cheekpieces. *J. R. Weymes* **46**

GRACIOUS DANCER 3 b.g. Mark of Esteem (IRE) 137 – Gracious Beauty (USA) 67 (Nijinsky (CAN) 138) [2003 –p: p8g⁶ f9.4g² f8.5g* 9m 10.2g Sep 11] fair performer: won maiden at Wolverhampton (edged left) in January: tailed off in handicaps after: should stay 1¼m: acts on fibresand. *J. A. Osborne* **?**
a77

GRADUATION DAY 3 b.f. College Chapel 122 – Golden Ciel (USA) (Septieme Ciel (USA) 123) [2003 69p: 7m 7g³ 7g 8.1m f7s⁶ 8g 7.1d 7.1m 8f⁵ f8s Oct 7] modest maiden handicapper: stays 1m: acts on firm and soft going: tried visored: none too consistent: sold 2,200 gns, sent to Holland. *P. W. Harris* **69 d**

GRADY 4 ch.g. Bluegrass Prince (IRE) 110 – Lady Sabina 61 (Bairn (USA) 126) [2003 60: 11.6g 11.6m 10.9m 10m⁶ 11.6g 10g Oct 6] sturdy gelding: modest maiden: well held in 2003: tried in blinkers/cheekpieces. *Miss Jacqueline S. Doyle* **–**

GRAFFITI GIRL (IRE) 4 b.f. Sadler's Wells (USA) 132 – Maharani (USA) (Red Ransom (USA)) [2003 67d: f12g⁶ f11s 11.7m 9.7f Jun 27] IR 110,000Y: second foal: half-sister to 3-y-o Joe Bear and 5-y-o Lucefer: dam, second at 8.5f in Germany, sister to smart 1994 2-y-o Sri Pekan: maiden: tailed off in form at best at 3 yrs for J. Oxx in Ireland: well held in 2003: tried blinkered. *D. Haydn Jones* **–**

GRAFT 4 b.g. Entrepreneur 123 – Mariakova (USA) 84 (The Minstrel (CAN) 135) [2003 86: 9.9f 8g 10d 12m⁴ 9.9m 10.4f 10s Nov 3] quite good-topped gelding: fair handicapper: mostly well held in 2003: stays 1½m: acts on firm going, soft and polytrack: inconsistent. *M. W. Easterby* **75**

GRAHAM ISLAND 2 b.c. (Feb 6) Acatenango (GER) 127 – Gryada 93 (Shirley Heights 130) [2003 7m 7m⁵ Sep 17] 100,000Y: good-bodied colt: has scope: third foal: brother to useful 1¼m/1½m winner Guaranda and half-brother to smart 7f (at 2 yrs) to 1½m winner Grampian (by Selkirk): dam, 2-y-o 7f/1m winner, closely related to useful stayer Gondolier: clearly better effort in maidens (fair form) when 4 lengths fifth of 15 to Eden Rock at Yarmouth, not unduly knocked about: will be suited by at least 1¼m: should progress. *G. Wragg* **74 p**

GRAIKOS 3 b.c. Rainbow Quest (USA) 134 – Grecian Slipper 102 (Sadler's Wells (USA) 132) [2003 105p: 10.4m⁵ 12m Jun 7] good-topped, attractive ex-French-trained colt: smart performer: creditable efforts for new trainer in 2003 when 3 lengths fifth to Magistretti in Dante Stakes at York and 12½ lengths eighth to Kris Kin in Derby at Epsom (short to post, never better than mid-field): suffered from split pastern after: should be suited by 1½m+: acts on soft and good to firm going: tongue tied in 2003: stays in training. *Saeed bin Suroor* **110**

GRALMANO (IRE) 8 b.g. Scenic 128 – Llangollen (IRE) 87 (Caerleon (USA) 132) [2003 83, a89: p10g f16.2g³ 18g³ 16m* 16g 15f³ 15.9m* 14.6g 14.6m² Oct 24] strong gelding: unimpressive mover: fairly useful handicapper: won at Thirsk in May and Chester (carried head awkwardly) in July: good second to Flotta at Doncaster final start: effective at 1¼m to easy 2¼m: acts on all-weather, firm and good to soft ground: tried visored/blinkered earlier in career: edgy sort: usually races prominently: tough and consistent: useful hurdler/fairly useful chaser. *K. A. Ryan* **94**
a89

GRANATO (GER) 2 b.c. (Mar 7) Cadeaux Genereux 131 – Genevra (IRE) 107 (Danehill (USA) 126) [2003 6m² 6f² 6m* Sep 25] 170,000Y: strong colt: good walker: fluent mover: second foal: dam, German 1m winner, out of half-sister to Ballad Rock: fairly useful form in maidens: second at Pontefract and Newmarket prior to winning 11-runner event on former course by neck from River Treat, taking hold and leading 1f out: will probably stay 7f: has scope to train on. *A. C. Stewart* **89 p**

GRAN CLICQUOT 8 gr.m. Gran Alba (USA) 107 – Tina's Beauty 41 (Tina's Pet 121) [2003 43: 8.1m 10.2m* 10m⁴ 10m⁴ 10.9m⁵ 10.9m 10m Oct 23] modest performer: won seller at Bath in July: raced freely/found little last 2 starts: stays 11f: acts on firm ground: has worn cheekpieces. *G. P. Enright* **54**

GRANDALEA 2 b.f. (Mar 12) Grand Lodge (USA) 125 – Red Azalea 95 (Shirley **81**
Heights 130) [2003 7m p7g² 8.2f³ p7g⁶ Oct 30] tall, heavy-topped filly: fourth foal:
half-sister to winner up to 1¼m in Spain by Polar Falcon: dam, 7f (at 2 yrs) and 1¼m
winner, half-sister to smart 7f/1m performer Red Camellia (dam of 2-y-o Red Bloom)
from family of Ibn Bey and Teleprompter: fairly useful maiden: placed at Lingfield and
Nottingham: found little after forcing pace final start: stays 1m. *Sir Michael Stoute*

GRAND APOLLO 2 ch.f. (Mar 23) Grand Lodge (USA) 125 – Narva (Nashwan **67 p**
(USA) 135) [2003 7m⁶ Aug 22] 46,000Y: quite attractive filly: third foal: half-sister to
3-y-o Pretence: dam unraced half-sister to high-class performer up to 1½m Predappio:
14/1 and green, 4 lengths sixth of 8 to Why Dubai in maiden at Newmarket, good
hold to post and not unduly knocked about: will stay at least 1m: should do better.
J. H. M. Gosden

GRAND CROSS 3 ch.c. Zafonic (USA) 130 – La Papagena (Habitat 134) [2003 8m⁶ **68**
8g 8m 10m Jul 12] big, lengthy, hollow-backed colt: half-brother to several winners,
notably high-class 1m/1¼m performer Grand Lodge (by Chief's Crown): dam unraced:
fair maiden: stayed 1m: slowly away first 2 outings: dead. *W. Jarvis*

GRANDERA (IRE) 5 ch.h. Grand Lodge (USA) 125 – Bordighera (USA) (Alysheba **120 §**
(USA)) [2003 129: a10f* a10f⁴ 10m 10g 12d Jul 26] strong, good-topped horse: fluent
mover: high-class performer in 2002, very smart in 2003: won Maktoum Challenge
(Round III) at Nad Al Sheba in March by ½ length from Grundlefoot: respectable fourth
to Moon Ballad in Dubai World Cup on same course later in month: below form in Prince
of Wales's Stakes at Royal Ascot, Eclipse Stakes at Sandown and King George VI and
Queen Elizabeth Diamond Stakes at Ascot last 3 starts: best efforts at 1¼m: acted on firm
going and dirt: tried blinkered and in cheekpieces: edgy sort: carried head awkwardly:
held up: quirky, and needed treating with some caution: to stand at Yushun Co Stallion
Station, Japan, fee Y2 million. *Saeed bin Suroor*

GRANDE TERRE (IRE) 2 b.f. (Jan 27) Grand Lodge (USA) 125 – Savage (IRE) **71**
98 (Polish Patriot (USA) 128) [2003 7m 7.1m 6.5m Sep 26] IR 38,000F, 38,000Y: leggy,
unfurnished filly: third foal: half-sister to Irish 11f/1½m winner Fascinating (by Desert
King): dam German 5f (at 2 yrs) and 1m winner: fair form in maidens/sales race: will stay
at least 1m. *J. G. Given*

GRAND FOLLY (FR) 3 ch.f. Grand Lodge (USA) 125 – Folmanie (USA) (Blushing **72**
John (USA) 120) [2003 69: 8.2m⁵ 9m² 10f 11.8g 9.9m³ 10g p12g⁴ Nov 29] good-topped
filly: fair maiden: left J. Cullinan after sixth start: stays 1½m: acts on polytrack and firm
ground. *A. M. Hales*

GRAND GIFT 3 br.f. Grand Lodge (USA) 125 – Black Velvet Band (Sadler's Wells **50**
(USA) 132) [2003 –p: 8.3s 10g 10d 9.7m Jul 10] good-topped filly: modest maiden: stays
1¼m: has worn cheekpieces: sold 1,800 gns in December. *M. A. Jarvis*

GRAND HALO (IRE) 3 b.g. Grand Lodge (USA) 125 – Band of Angels (IRE) (Alzao **63**
(USA) 117) [2003 58p: p7g 10m f8.5g 10.9m² 9.7g 12.1m⁴ f11s² f12s⁵ Oct 7] strong,
well-made gelding: modest maiden handicapper: left B. Hills 16,000 gns after fourth
start: stays 1½m: acts on fibresand, good to firm and good to soft ground: visored last 2
starts. *J. J. Sheehan*

GRANDISSIMO (IRE) 2 b.g. (May 2) Grand Lodge (USA) 125 – Tuscaloosa (Robel- **–**
lino (USA) 127) [2003 8m Sep 13] 15,000F, 7,000Y: second foal: dam unraced half-sister
to useful Irish 5f winner Serov: 33/1, slowly away when last of 8 in maiden at Goodwood:
gelded after. *N. P. Littmoden*

GRAND LASS (IRE) 4 b.f. Grand Lodge (USA) 125 – Siskin (IRE) (Royal Academy **73 d**
(USA) 130) [2003 66?: 10m 11.5g² 12m⁶ 11.9g⁴ 12g 11.9m 12.1d² 12m 11g⁴ f11g⁶ Dec
16] compact filly: fair maiden: well below form last 5 starts, leaving A. Stewart £6,000
after second of them: should stay 1¾m: acts on good to firm ground: tried visored.
T. D. Barron

GRANDMA LILY (IRE) 5 b.m. Bigstone (IRE) 126 – Mrs Fisher (IRE) 94 (Salmon **87**
Leap (USA) 131) [2003 –, a71: f6s f5g³ f6s⁴ 6m* 6m 5d* 5m⁴ 5f 5f 5m 5m 6m 6m f6g*
f5g⁵ f6g Dec 15] big, lengthy mare: fairly useful handicapper: won at Southwell in
March, Thirsk in May and Southwell in November: has form up to 9.4f, raced only at 5f/
6f in 2003: acts on fibresand, good to soft and good to firm going: has started slowly/hung
left: reportedly bled once at 4 yrs: often races up with pace. *M. C. Chapman*

GRAND PASSION (IRE) 3 b.g. Grand Lodge (USA) 125 – Lovers' Parlour 83 **110**
(Beldale Flutter (USA) 130) [2003 94: 7g³ 8.1m* 10.4f 8m⁴ 8m* 8d² 9m 8g³ p10g² Nov
22] good-bodied gelding: smart performer: won handicaps at Sandown in April and
Newmarket (beat Boston Lodge a neck) in July: placed in listed events 3 of last 4 starts,

short-headed by Compton Bolter at Lingfield on final one: stays 1¼m: acts on polytrack, good to firm and good to soft going: consistent. *G. Wragg*

GRAND PRAIRIE (SWE)   7 b.g. Prairie (ITY) (Primo Dominie 121)   **?**
[2003 12.3m 12.4g a12g a10.5g⁴ a12g³ a12g a10.5s⁴ a12g³ a12s⁵ Nov 23] Swedish-bred gelding: winner of 12 races in Sweden/Spain: completed 5-timer in minor events at Mijas in 2002: well beaten in Britain for R. C. Guest first 2 starts on return: in frame afterwards in minor events at Mijas and Dos Hermanas (trained until last 2 outings by G. Bindella): stays 1½m: acts on sand. *J. H. Brown, Spain*

GRAND PROMPT   4 ch.g. Grand Lodge (USA) 125 – Prompting 76 (Primo Dominie   **–**
121) [2003 p16g 12m p12g Oct 3] 115,000Y: ex-French gelding: fifth foal: half-brother to 3 winners, including useful German 6f to 1m performer Sharp Domino (by Sharpo): dam, 2-y-o 5f winner (later winning sprinter in Switzerland), half-sister to useful sprinter Sharp Prod: fair maiden: sold from R. Gibson 16,000 gns and gelded after final 3-y-o start: modest and unreliable hurdler for Mrs L. Wadham: well held on return to Flat: stays 1½m: acts on heavy and good to firm ground: tried blinkered/visored. *B. R. Johnson*

GRAND REWARD (USA)   2 b. or br.c. (Feb 10) Storm Cat (USA) – Serena's Song   **112**
(USA) 126 (Rahy (USA) 115) [2003 6g* 6m³ 6m² 6m⁵ Oct 3] angular, good-topped colt: fourth foal: brother to smart 6f (at 2 yrs) and 1m (Coronation Stakes) winner Sophisticat and half-brother to 2 winners in USA, including minor stakes winner by Mr Prospector: dam multiple Grade 1 winner in USA (also second in Breeders' Cup Juvenile Fillies' and Breeders' Cup Distaff) and champion US 3-y-o filly: smart performer: won maiden at Newbury in May: reported in June to have sustained minor shoulder injury: good efforts when fourth (promoted a place) to Balmont in Gimcrack Stakes at York, ¾-length second to Byron in Mill Reef Stakes at Newbury (reported to have pulled a muscle) and 2¼ lengths sixth (promoted to fifth) behind disqualified Three Valleys in Middle Park Stakes at Newmarket: will be suited by 7f/1m: slowly away last 2 outings, fractious stall final one. *A. P. O'Brien, Ireland*

GRAND RICH KING (IRE)   2 b.c. (Mar 8) Grand Lodge (USA) 125 – Richly   **93**
Deserved (IRE) (Kings Lake (USA) 133) [2003 5g⁶ 6.1d² 7.1f* 7m 7m² 8.1d³ Aug 29] IR 27,000F, 85,000Y: sturdy, lengthy colt: brother to fairly useful 2001 2-y-o 7f winner Ridley, later successful in USA, and half-brother to 3 winners, including useful 6f to 1¼m winner Kingsdon (by Brief Truce): dam unraced half-sister to high-class winner up to 1¼m Star Pastures: fairly useful performer: won maiden at Sandown in June: good efforts in nursery at Newmarket and minor event at Sandown (third to Psychiatrist) last 2 starts: stays 1m: acts on firm and good to soft ground: often races up with pace. *B. J. Meehan*

GRAND VIEW   7 ch.g. Grand Lodge (USA) 125 – Hemline 77 (Sharpo 132) [2003   **49**
49, a–: 5m⁵ 5g 5m⁵ 5m 6m 5f 6f Aug 29] poor handicapper: effective at 5f/6f: acts on all-weather, soft and good to firm going: tried blinkered. *T. D. Barron*

GRAND WIZARD   3 b.c. Grand Lodge (USA) 125 – Shouk 94 (Shirley Heights 130)   **68 +**
[2003 10m p12g p10g* Dec 30] 48,000Y: close-coupled, quite good-topped colt: first foal: dam, 10.5f winner, closely-related to smart performer up to 14.6f Puce: fair form: off 5 months and still green, easily best effort in maidens when winning at Lingfield in December by ½ length from Margery Daw: took strong hold on debut, ran in snatches/found little second start. *W. Jarvis*

GRANNY'S PET   9 ch.g. Selkirk (USA) 129 – Patsy Western 81 (Precocious 126)   **106**
[2003 106: f7g³ p7g 7.1m² 7.1d⁵ May 3] angular, close-coupled gelding: has a quick action: useful performer: best 9-y-o effort when length second to Vicious Knight in minor event at Warwick in April: best at 6f/7f: acts on firm going, soft and firesand: tried blinkered earlier in career, has worn cheekpieces: usually held up. *P. F. I. Cole*

GRANSTON (IRE)   2 b. or gr.g. (Apr 24) Revoque (IRE) 122 – Gracious Gretclo 54   **74**
(Common Grounds 118) [2003 5g⁴ 5m³ 5f² 6g 6g⁵ 6m⁵ 7m⁴ 7d 7m* Oct 18] 14,000Y: leggy, quite good-topped gelding: third living foal: half-brother to 3-y-o Malahide Express: dam, maiden who stayed 6f, sister to useful 6f/7f performer Rich Ground: fair performer: won nursery at Catterick by 1¾ lengths from Cotosol, racing freely: stays 7f: acts on firm going: sometimes hangs/flashes tail. *J. D. Bethell*

GRANUAILE O'MALLEY (IRE)   3 b.f. Mark of Esteem (IRE) 137 – Dame Laura   **53**
(IRE) 100 (Royal Academy (USA) 130) [2003 55p: p6g 7m 8g⁶ 5m 7m 7.1m 6g³ f6s Dec 27] modest maiden: left P. Harris after third start, below form subsequently: should stay 7f: raced only on good/good to firm ground on turf. *P. W. D'Arcy*

GRASSLANDIK   7 b.g. Ardkinglass 114 – Sophisticated Baby 39 (Bairn (USA) 126)   **62**
[2003 60, a52: f5g f5g⁶ f5g⁵ 5m⁵ 5m 5m 5m 5m 5m 5m⁶ 5m 5.2m⁵ 5m 5f 6f⁶ 5m 6d   **a49**
5m 5m³ 5g 5g Nov 5] lengthy gelding: modest handicapper on turf, poor on all-weather:

races mainly at 5f: acts on fibresand, good to firm and good to soft going: wears headgear: sometimes looks none too keen: none too consistent. *Miss A. Stokell*

GRAVARDLAX   2 ch.c. (Feb 3) Salse (USA) 128 – Rubbiyati 56 (Cadeaux Genereux **89** 131) [2003 7m⁴ 7m² Oct 3] 17,000Y: leggy colt: good mover: third foal: brother to 5-y-o Alsyati: dam, 1m winner at 4 yrs (only season to race), half-sister to high-class miler Air Express (by Salse): fairly useful form in maidens at Newbury and Newmarket (neck second of 23 to Secret Charm): will stay at least 1m. *B. J. Meehan*

GRAVIA (IRE)   3 b.f. Grape Tree Road 122 – Anafi 95 (Slip Anchor 136) [2003 –p: **66** 8.3m⁵ 8.3m⁵ 10f p10g Nov 2] rather leggy, quite good-topped filly: fair maiden: should stay at least 1¼m: raced only on good ground or firmer on turf. *G. Wragg*

GREAT AS GOLD (IRE)   4 b.g. Goldmark (USA) 113 – Great Land (USA) (Friend's **69** Choice (USA)) [2003 49, a70: f14g² f16s⁴ f16s³ f16s³ 18g⁵ 17.1m⁶ 21.6m² 16.2m f16g³ Nov 19] good-topped gelding: fair handicapper: stays 21.6f: acts on good to firm going and fibresand: effective blinkered or not, wore cheekpieces in 2003: tried tongue tied: usually held up: fairly useful hurdler. *B. Ellison*

GREAT BLASKET (IRE)   2 b.f. (Feb 25) Petardia 113 – Alexander Goddess (IRE) **56** (Alzao (USA) 117) [2003 5d 7m* 7g 7f³ 7m p7g 8m 8.2m⁴ Oct 28] €2,500Y: third foal: dam unraced out of half-sister to US Grade 1 1¼m winner Ida Delia and to dam of very smart US 1m/1¼m performer Victory Speech: modest performer: won seller at Redcar in June: stays 1m: acts on firm going: sometimes slowly away, seeming reluctant to race penultimate outing. *E. J. O'Neill*

GREAT EXHIBITION (USA)   2 b.c. (Feb 11) Gone West (USA) – Touch of Great- **88** ness (USA) (Hero's Honor (USA)) [2003 6m³ 7m² Sep 16] $1,800,000Y: close-coupled, quite attractive colt: brother to US Grade 3 7f/1m winner Elusive Quality and to useful 6f (including at 2 yrs) winner Ghazal, and closely related to several winners, notably smart Irish 1999 2-y-o 5f/6f winner Rossini (by Miswaki): dam unraced half-sister to high-class middle-distance performer Gold And Ivory: fairly useful form in maidens at York and Thirsk (briefly unbalanced when second of 4 to Master David): will probably stay 1m: early to post at Thirsk: joined Saeed bin Suroor. *D. R. Loder*

GREAT FOX (IRE)   2 b.c. (May 12) Foxhound (USA) 103 – Good Enough (IRE) **80** (Simply Great (FR) 122) [2003 6m³ 6m² 5g* Oct 28] big, strong colt: fifth living foal: half-brother to 3 winners, including fairly useful 1¼m winner Compatible (by Ela-Mana-Mou): dam won 7 times in Scandinavia, including Norwegian 1000 Guineas: fairly useful form in maidens: placed at Newmarket (hung markedly both times) prior to justifying favouritism in 17-runner event at Redcar by 1¾ lengths from Bond Romeo, making most: will probably prove best at 5f/6f. *P. L. Gilligan*

GREAT GAME   3 b.g. Indian Ridge 123 – Russian Grace (IRE) (Soviet Star (USA) **–** 128) [2003 79: 6m⁶ 7m 6m f6g Oct 16] useful-looking gelding: fair maiden at 2 yrs: well beaten in 2003, leaving R. Hannon after reappearance: tried in blinkers. *B. S. Rothwell*

GREAT LASS   2 b.f. (Apr 4) Great Dane (IRE) 122 – Impala Lass 81 (Kampala 120) **42** [2003 6d⁶ 5m 7.5d 5m 7m 8m Sep 18] 3,100Y: close-coupled filly: half-sister to several winners, including 5f winner Leaping Charlie (by Puissance) and 1m to 9.4f winner Yeoman Oliver (by Precocious): dam sprinter: poor maiden: tried in cheekpieces/blinkers (slowly away). *M. W. Easterby*

GREAT NEWS   8 b.g. Elmaamul (USA) 125 – Amina 80 (Brigadier Gerard 144) [2003 **58** 76, a–: 8.2d 10.1m 10m 8g Oct 22] tall, angular gelding: fair handicapper: well held in 2003: sold 1,200 gns. *N. Tinkler*

GREAT OVATION (FR)   4 ch.f. Boston Two Step (USA) 107 – Baldiloa (No Lute **–** (FR) 129) [2003 8g 10m Jun 12] ex-French filly: half-sister to French 11.5f to 13.5f winner Baldoranic (by Panoramic): dam, French 2-y-o 1m winner, half-sister to smart French middle-distance performer Oa Baldixe: modest maiden at 3 yrs, for E. Lecoiffier and T. Trapenard: well held in handicaps in Britain. *R. T. Phillips*

GREAT PYRAMID (IRE)   3 b.c. Danehill (USA) 126 – Offshore Boom 96 (Be My **107 d** Guest (USA) 126) [2003 107: 8d⁵ 7d⁵ 10m 8m 8g⁴ Jul 4] small, strong colt: useful performer: 4¼ lengths fifth to Indian Haven in Irish 2000 Guineas at the Curragh on reappearance: disappointing after, including in listed race at Royal Ascot third start: stays 1m: acts on good to soft going: blinkered fourth outing: sent to USA. *A. P. O'Brien, Ireland*

GREAT SCOTT   2 b.g. (Feb 7) Fasliyev (USA) 120 – Arabis 88 (Arazi (USA) 135) **90** [2003 5m² 5s* 5m* 5g⁵ 6g 5m 7.9f⁵ Oct 9] 20,000Y: leggy, lengthy gelding: first foal: dam, 1¼m winner who stayed 13f, closely related to 5-y-o Bosham Mill: fairly useful

GRE (header)

performer: won maiden at Haydock in May and minor event at Beverley in June: respectable efforts in nurseries last 2 starts: probably stays 1m: acts on firm and soft ground. *M. Johnston*

GREAT VIEW (IRE)   4 b.g. Great Commotion (USA) 123 – Tara View (IRE) (Wassl 125) [2003 86d: p10g p10g 8m 7.1d⁴ 7g 8.1m² f8.5g⁴ 10g³ 9.9m 10m* 10f⁵ 10.5f⁵ 10.9m⁴ 12d³ 10m² Oct 14] lengthy gelding: modest handicapper: won ladies race at Newbury in August: effective at 1¼m/1½m: acts on firm going, soft and fibresand: usually blinkered/visored: usually held up: formerly unreliable. *Mrs A. L. M. King*   **64 a50**

GREEK REVIVAL (USA)   3 b.g. Royal Academy (USA) 130 – Las Meninas (IRE) 115 (Glenstal (USA) 118) [2003 105: 7m⁶ 7m 7.1g 7g Jul 31] strong, good-topped, attractive gelding: useful performer at 2 yrs: well held in 2003: tried tongue tied: sold 17,000 gns in August, then gelded. *B. W. Hills*   **–**

GREEK STAR   2 b.g. (May 12) Soviet Star (USA) 128 – Graecia Magna (USA) 109 (Private Account (USA)) [2003 7m Sep 23] big, strong gelding: has plenty of scope: closely related to useful 2001 2-y-o 7f winner Bragadino (by Zilzal) and half-brother to several winners, including 2000 2-y-o 7f winner who stayed 14.6f (second in St Leger) Demophilos (by Dr Devious) and 7f/1m performer Thourios (by Green Desert), both smart: dam 7f (at 2 yrs) and 1½m winner: 6/1 and green, behind in 17-runner maiden at Newmarket, missing break: sold 10,000 gns, and gelded. *Sir Michael Stoute*   **–**

GREENAWAY BAY (USA)   9 ch.g. Green Dancer (USA) 132 – Raise 'n Dance (USA) (Raise A Native) [2003 71d: f8.5s⁴ 10.3g² f8g⁶ 8.3d⁵ 9.3g⁴ f12s* f8.5g 9.9d⁵ f12s³ 9.9d 9.1d⁵ Oct 14] quite good-topped gelding: modest performer: won claimer at Wolverhampton in June: stays easy 1½m: acts on fibresand: has form on any going, but goes well on soft/heavy: usually held up. *J. J. Quinn*   **61**

GREENBOROUGH (IRE)   5 b.g. Dr Devious (IRE) 127 – Port Isaac (USA) 64 (Seattle Song (USA) 130) [2003 46: f12g f9.4g Feb 7] tall gelding: no longer of much account. *Mrs P. Ford*   **–**

GREEN CASKET (IRE)   6 b.g. Green Desert (USA) 127 – Grecian Urn 123 (Ela-Mana-Mou 132) [2003 76: p12g 9.9f 12.1m 12.3m 10m Oct 14] quite good-topped gelding: no longer of any account. *J. A. Glover*   **–**

GREENFIRE (FR)   5 ch.g. Ashkalani (IRE) 128 – Greenvera (USA) (Riverman (USA) 131) [2003 12m Aug 15] 22,000Y, 8,500 3-y-o: fifth foal: half-brother to dual Gold Cup winner Royal Rebel (by Robellino): dam French maiden: third in bumper in July: very slowly away and tailed off in maiden at Catterick. *Mrs Dianne Sayer*   **–**

GREEN GINGER   7 ch.g. Ardkinglass 114 – Bella Maggio (Rakaposhi King 119) [2003 54: 7.9m 10m⁵ 10.9m³ 10.9m 10m⁵ 10.9m⁵ 10m Oct 20] modest performer: stays easy 11f: acts on good to firm going and fibresand: tried visored: has given trouble in preliminaries, and very slowly away second start. *W. M. Brisbourne*   **52**

GREEN GO (GER)   5 ch.g. Secret 'n Classy (CAN) – Green Fee (GER) (Windwurf (GER)) [2003 f12g Jun 27] third foal: half-brother to winners in Germany by Goofalik and Al Nasr: dam 7.5f and 9f winner in Germany: well beaten in claimer at Wolverhampton: modest hurdler/chaser. *A. Sadik*   **–**

GREENHILL SCENE (IRE)   3 gr.f. Victory Note (USA) 120 – Saratoga Scene (USA) (Grey Dawn II 132) [2003 p5g⁵ 7d 7s 7g⁵ 7v⁵ 8f⁵ 10m Oct 1] IR 27,000Y: half-sister to several minor winners abroad: dam lightly raced maiden in USA: poor maiden handicapper: best efforts at 7f: acts on heavy ground, below form on polytrack at Lingfield on debut: tried blinkered. *Takashi Kodama, Ireland*   **48**

GREEN IDEAL   5 b.g. Mark of Esteem (IRE) 137 – Emerald (USA) (El Gran Senor (USA) 136) [2003 p12g 12g 12g May 17] useful at 3 yrs: well held on return to Flat: sold 32,000 gns, joined Ferdy Murphy. *N. J. Henderson*   **–**

GREEN IN BLUE (IRE)   3 b.c. Kahyasi 130 – Sea Mistress (Habitat 134) [2003 10g³ 10g³ 10m* Jul 17] 200,000Y: half-brother to several winners, notably smart Irish 6f to 1m winner Nautical Pet (by Petorius): dam unraced: fairly useful form: won maiden at Leicester in July: will probably stay 1½m: raced only on good going or firmer: sent to Hong Kong, joined S. Woods. *W. J. Haggas*   **84**

GREEN LINE   4 b.g. Green Desert (USA) 127 – Marl 94 (Lycius (USA) 124) [2003 96: 7.6m* 7f 7.9m 8m² 8f² 8f 9f⁵ 8.5f⁴ Nov 29] tall, quite attractive gelding: useful performer: won handicap at Chester (beat Santisima Trinidad ½ length) in May: in frame after in handicap at Ascot (½-length second to Pentecost, final outing for Sir Michael Stoute), non-graded handicap at Del Mar (length second to Designed For Luck) and   **110**

Grade 2 Citation Handicap at Hollywood (3½ lengths fourth to Redattore): effective at 6f to 8.5f: best efforts on going firmer than good: wore cheekpieces (below form) second start: has been bandaged near-hind joint: pulled up amiss third outing. *P. Gallagher, USA*

GREEN MANALISHI 2 b.c. (Mar 27) Green Desert (USA) 127 – Silca-Cisa 93 **83** (Hallgate 127) [2003 5g 5.1g⁵ 5m² 5f² 5m⁵ 5m⁵ 5m* Oct 3] 105,000Y: sturdy colt: sixth foal: closely related to fairly useful 7f winner King Silca (by Emarati) and half-brother to 3 winners, notably 7-y-o Golden Silca: dam 5f winner, including at 2 yrs: fairly useful performer: landed odds in 7-runner maiden at Lingfield by 1¼ lengths from Bygone Days, making most: will prove best at 5f/easy 6f: acts on firm going: tends to carry head awkwardly: consistent. *D. W. P. Arbuthnot*

GREEN 'N' GOLD 3 b.f. Cloudings (IRE) 112 – Fishki 36 (Niniski (USA) 125) **55** [2003 51: f7s³ f8.5g 12m⁴ 12.1f 10g 9.9m 12.1m⁴ 14f 17.2m Jun 25] smallish, sturdy filly: modest maiden handicapper: unable to race in second half of year due to dispute over ownership: stays 1½m: acts on fibresand, firm and good to soft going: well held both starts in cheekpieces. *M. D. Hammond*

GREEN NOON (FR) 2 ch.f. (Jan 30) Green Tune (USA) 125 – Terring (FR) (Bering **112** 136) [2003 7d* 7g* 8m* 8s² Oct 5] 57,000 francs F: leggy filly: first foal: dam ran twice in France: smart performer: won newcomers race at Deauville in July, minor event on same course in August and Prix d'Aumale Casino Barriere de Biarritz at Longchamp (by 1½ lengths from Leila, finishing strongly) in September: best effort when half-short-neck second of 16 to Denebola in Prix Marcel Boussac at Longchamp, tracking pace and rallying gamely: stays 1m: bandaged in front. *C. Lerner, France*

GREEN OCEAN 3 gr.f. Environment Friend 128 – Northern Swinger (Northern State **48** (USA) 91) [2003 8.2g⁵ 8.1m⁵ 10m⁶ Aug 30] 700 2-y-o: smallish filly: fourth reported foal: dam unraced: poor maiden: seems to stay 1¼m. *J. W. Unett*

GREEN RIDGE 2 b.f. (Mar 10) Muhtarram (USA) 125 – Top of The Morning 56 **70** (Keen 116) [2003 5.2m² 5m⁵ 7g f6g⁶ Nov 10] leggy filly: first foal: dam, maiden who stayed 1¼m, half-sister to useful performer up to 1½m Whitefoot: fair maiden: second at Yarmouth: probably stays 7f: acts on fibresand and good to firm going. *P. W. D'Arcy*

GREENSLADES 4 ch.c. Perugino (USA) 84 – Woodfield Rose 41 (Scottish Reel 123) **94** [2003 99p: 6m 6g* 6f 7m⁵ Sep 13] strong, workmanlike colt: good walker: fairly useful handicapper, lightly raced: won at Windsor in August by neck from Barrantes: effective at 6f/7f: acts on soft and good to firm going: usually races prominently. *P. J. Makin*

GREENWICH MEANTIME 3 b.g. Royal Academy (USA) 130 – Shirley Valentine **86** 104 (Shirley Heights 130) [2003 9.9m³ 10.4m² 12g² 12.4g* Oct 22] sturdy gelding: half-brother to several winners, including smart 1¼m to 1¾m winner Memorise (by Lyphard) and 4-y-o Sparkling Water: dam, 1½m winner, sister to Deploy and half-sister to Commander In Chief and Warning: fairly useful performer: made all in maiden at Newcastle in October by 3½ lengths from Colourful Life: should stay 1¾m: raced only on good/good to firm ground: sold 47,000 gns, joined Mrs J. Ramsden and gelded. *H. R. A. Cecil*

Prix d'Aumale Casino Barriere de Biarritz, Longchamp—
Green Noon completes a hat-trick at the chief expense of Leila

GREENWOOD 5 ch.g. Emarati (USA) 74 – Charnwood Queen 61 (Cadeaux Genereux **93**
131) [2003 92: f5s³ f5s⁶ f5g 6g⁶ 6m⁶ 6g* 6m 5g 6m² 5m 6g 6g 6d⁶ 5m² 6m² 6f 6f Oct 11] **a86**
strong, lengthy gelding: fairly useful handicapper: won apprentice race at Windsor in
April: claimed from J. Eustace £15,000 fourteenth start: effective at 5f/6f: acts on fibresand, firm and good to soft going: effective blinkered or not. *P. G. Murphy*

GREENWOOD TREE 3 b.f. Keen 116 – Sublime (Conquering Hero (USA) 116)
[2003 8d 8g 8g 8.1m 10.1m 9f⁴ 10f Sep 15] quite good-topped filly: has a markedly round
action: second foal: dam unraced half-sister to smart 1m/1¼m performer Penny Drops:
no form. *C. W. Thornton*

GREGORIAN (IRE) 6 b.g. Foxhound (USA) 103 – East River (FR) (Arctic Tern **55**
(USA) 126) [2003 83: f12s⁴ 16m* f14.8s⁵ Jul 14] fairly useful winner in Ireland in 2002
(left P. Rothwell 5,000 gns after final start): modest form when winning claimer at
Musselburgh in July: stays 2m: has form on fibresand and good to firm going, very best
efforts on soft: effective blinkered or not. *J. G. M. O'Shea*

GRELE (USA) 2 gr.f. (May 10) Loup Sauvage (USA) 125 – Fiveblushingroses (USA) **–**
(Runaway Groom (CAN)) [2003 5g Aug 26] 5,000Y: close-coupled filly: first foal: dam
winner in USA: 33/1, behind in maiden at Ripon. *R. Hollinshead*

GRETA D'ARGENT (IRE) 3 b.f. Great Commotion (USA) 123 – Petite-D-Argent **103**
91 (Noalto 120) [2003 78: p10g 12.3m³ 10g* 10.4m 10.1m 10.3g* 12d⁵ 9.9g⁶ 10.4m⁵
10f⁵ 12g* 10m 8f Sep 27] small, good-bodied filly: poor mover: useful handicapper: won
at Pontefract in April and at Doncaster in July and September: beat Royal Cavalier 1¼
lengths in last-named: below form last 2 starts: effective at 1¼m/1½m: acts on fibresand
(well beaten on polytrack), good to firm and good to soft going: stumbled leaving stall
fourth outing: usually races prominently. *M. Johnston*

GRETNA 2 ch.f. (Apr 1) Groom Dancer (USA) 128 – Llia 94 (Shirley Heights 130) **64 p**
[2003 7m⁶ Jun 27] fifth foal: half-sister to 3 winners, including 3-y-o Jay Gee's Choice
and useful 7f (at 2 yrs) to 8.5f winner Kootenay (by Selkirk): dam, 2-y-o 7f winner who
stayed 1½m, out of smart performer up to 9f Llyn Gwynant: 7/1 but very green, sixth of 7
in maiden at Goodwood: suffered injury after: will stay at least 1m: should do better.
J. L. Dunlop

GREY ADMIRAL (USA) 2 gr.c. (Jan 31) Cozzene (USA) – Remarkable Style (USA) **69**
99 (Danzig (USA)) [2003 8m 8m p8g Nov 2] $100,000Y: workmanlike colt: first foal:
dam, Irish 6f winner (including at 2 yrs), out of half-sister to US Grade 2 7f and 1¼m
winner American Chance: best effort in maidens (fair form) when ninth of 20 at Newmarket second start: needs to settle to stay beyond 1m: refused to enter stall on intended
debut. *A. M. Balding*

GREY BOY (GER) 2 gr.g. (Feb 20) Medaaly 114 – Grey Perri 103 (Siberian Express **53**
(USA) 125) [2003 p6g Oct 3] €30,000Y: second foal: half-brother to French 7f/1m
winner Grand Perri (by Zieten): dam German 5f winner: 12/1, eighth of 14 in maiden at
Lingfield, never a threat: gelded after. *G. C. Bravery*

GREY CLOUDS 3 gr.f. Cloudings (IRE) 112 – Khalsheva 55 (Shirley Heights 130) **76**
[2003 69: 11m⁶ 10m⁶ 13.1m³ 14g 9.9m² 10.1g* 9.9m* 10m⁴ 10m³ 10.5d Sep 27] tall,
rather leggy, close-coupled filly: fair handicapper: won at Newcastle in July and Beverley
in August: should stay 1½m: acts on good to firm and good to soft ground. *T. D. Easterby*

GREY COSSACK 6 gr.g. Kasakov – Royal Rebeka (Grey Desire 115) [2003 93: 6g **88**
7m 6m 6m 6m 5m* 6g* 6m 6f 7m 7d Nov 8] leggy, good-topped gelding: fairly useful
performer: won handicap at Beverley and (having left I. McInnes) minor event at
Doncaster in May: left J. Wainwright after ninth start: effective at stiff 5f/6f: acts on heavy
and good to firm going: tried visored early in career. *P. T. Midgley*

GREY MEDALLION 3 gr.g. Medaaly 114 – Thevetia 65 (Mummy's Pet 125) [2003 **35**
37: f5g 7g³ 8g² 7f³ 8g⁴ 6.5g⁴ a8.6g 8g⁴ 7g² Oct 4] close-coupled gelding: poor maiden:
left M. Brittain after reappearance: stays 1m. *J-E. Pettersson, Sweden*

GREY ORCHID 2 gr.f. (Feb 22) Opening Verse (USA) 126 – Marjorie's Orchid 49 **–**
(Petong 126) [2003 7g 7.1g Nov 5] 800Y: good-bodied filly: third foal: dam sprint
maiden: well held in maidens. *T. J. Etherington*

GREY PEARL 4 gr.f. Ali-Royal (IRE) 127 – River's Rising (FR) 88 (Mendez (FR) **80**
128) [2003 97: 7m 6m 7.6g⁴ 8g p7g⁵ f7g³ f7s⁴ Dec 31] sturdy filly: useful at 3 yrs, just
fairly useful in 2003: effective at 7f/1m: acts on firm ground and all-weather: tried tongue
tied: usually races prominently. *Miss Gay Kelleway*

GREY SWALLOW (IRE)   2 gr.c. (Feb 19) Daylami (IRE) 138 – Style of Life   **116 p**
(USA) (The Minstrel (CAN) 135) [2003 7s* 7m* Oct 27]
    There is every chance that Dermot Weld and Pat Smullen, the trainer and
jockey of the 2003 Two Thousand Guineas winner Refuse To Bend, will be appearing in the winner's enclosure at Newmarket again after the race's 2004 renewal on
May 1st. At the time of writing, the bookmakers' odds about it happening are no
longer than 6/1, for Weld and Smullen are now associated with a colt who looks an
even better prospect than Refuse To Bend did at the same stage. Grey Swallow, like
Refuse To Bend, contested a maiden and a pattern race on his only starts at two, and
each time he was more impressive than Refuse To Bend had been. He showed better
form than Refuse To Bend in the equivalent races, too, even though the pattern race
won by Grey Swallow was a Group 3 contest whereas Refuse To Bend had been
successful in the Group 1 National Stakes. Grey Swallow still has plenty to prove,
of course, but such was the impression he created in his two starts that it is difficult
not to be very enthusiastic about his prospects.
    Grey Swallow's racing career got off to an inauspicious start. The odds-on
favourite for a maiden at the Curragh at the end of June, he had to be withdrawn
after becoming very upset in the stalls. Referring to the incident after Grey Swallow
had won at Galway a month later, Weld said that 'He was very nearly killed at the
Curragh when he was stuck over the central partition of the stalls for three or four
minutes, and it was not a pretty sight.' Grey Swallow started second favourite
at Galway, with the Aidan O'Brien-trained Rock of Cashel, a brother to Rock of
Gibraltar who had finished third on his only start, at slight odds on. The betting
suggested it was a two-horse race, but it turned out even less competitive than that.
Grey Swallow, clearly none the worse for his previous experience, took over from
the pacesetting Rock of Cashel a furlong out and stormed ten lengths clear. Plans to
run Grey Swallow in either the Dewhurst Stakes or Racing Post Trophy were shel-

Mrs Rochelle Quinn's "Grey Swallow"

ved because the good to firm ground at Newmarket and Doncaster was considered unsuitable, and he was re-routed to Leopardstown for the Killavullan Stakes. The going at Leopardstown was officially good, though the times throughout the card suggested it was indeed firmer than that. Either way, it didn't inconvenience Grey Swallow, who was sent off at odds on to account for three opponents who had shown either fairly useful or useful form. Second favourite was the Ballydoyle representative Newton, who on his previous start had finished six and a half lengths third (demoted to fourth) to American Post in the Prix Jean-Luc Lagardere at Longchamp. Newton, blinkered for the first time, ensured that the race was truly-run and Grey Swallow, held up in third, just had to be nudged along to stay in touch before moving through strongly to lead over a furlong out, quickening clear in a matter of strides when sent about his business. Grey Swallow continued to extend his advantage through the final furlong and was still galloping strongly at the line, which he passed with eight lengths to spare over second-placed Newton. Previous winners of Ireland's final pattern race of the season haven't made too much of a name for themselves as three-year-olds, but that shouldn't worry supporters of Grey Swallow. The race has never had a winner as good, or as promising, as Grey Swallow.

		Doyoun	Mill Reef
	Daylami (IRE)	(b 1985)	Dumba
	(gr 1994)	Daltawa	Miswaki
Grey Swallow (IRE)		(gr 1989)	Damana
(gr.c. Feb 19, 2001)		The Minstrel	Northern Dancer
	Style of Life (USA)	(ch 1974)	Fleur
	(b 1985)	Bubinka	Nashua
		(b 1976)	Stolen Date

Bought as a yearling for 150,000 guineas, Grey Swallow is the ninth live foal of Style of Life and her seventh winner. They also include the useful performers Stylish Ways (by Thatching) and Rustic (by Grand Lodge), both beat up to seven furlongs, and Central Lobby (by Kenmare) and Style For Life (by Law Society), who were useful at up to a mile and a half in France. Style of Life won over six and seven furlongs in Ireland, as did her sister the smart performer Seasonal Pickup. Their dam Bubinka won races in France and Italy, notably the Premio Buontalenta, a Group 3 one-mile contest; and their grandam Stolen Date, from a very good family, was a minor sprint winner in the States. Bubinka is a sister to the smart Stoshka, a winner at up to a mile and a half in France and subsequently successful in the States, and half-sister to Taufan, a very smart performer at up to seven furlongs who has enjoyed a fair amount of success at stud. Grey Swallow is from the first crop of Daylami (which also includes the useful performers Bay Tree and Day Or Night), a top-class and admirably genuine and consistent performer who improved with age and distance. Raced only at a mile at three when he won the Poule d'Essai des Poulains, Daylami was successful in the Eclipse Stakes and Man o' War Stakes the following year and crowned a magnificent five-year-old season with victory in the Breeders' Cup Turf. Daylami stayed a mile and a half well but, with more speed than stamina on the dam's side of his pedigree, we shouldn't be sure that Grey Swallow will prove fully effective at that trip. A mile and a quarter should be well within his compass, though. *D. K. Weld, Ireland*

GRIGORIEV (IRE)   2 br.c. (Feb 1) Petardia 113 – Danz Danz (Efisio 120) [2003 6d **52** 7g³ 7.1m⁵ 8.3g 8.2m Oct 28] 6,000 2-y-o: smallish, sturdy colt: first foal: dam unraced out of half-sister to useful 1½m performer Port Helene: modest maiden: ran poorly in sellers last 2 starts, racing freely in blinkers final one: stays 7f: best effort on good going: sent to Spain. *J. W. Hills*

GRIST MIST (IRE)   2 gr.f. (Feb 14) Imperial Ballet (IRE) 110 – Ard Dauphine (IRE) **58** (Forest Wind (USA) 111) [2003 p8g p8.2d Nov 6] €7,500Y: second foal: dam unraced out of half-sister to Irish 2000 Guineas winner Northern Treasure: modest form in maidens at Lingfield (slowly away) and Nottingham (seventh of 17, possibly flattered). *Mrs P. N. Dutfield*

GRIZEDALE (IRE)   4 ch.g. Lake Coniston (IRE) 131 – Zabeta (Diesis 133) [2003 **104** 100: 7g 7m* 7m 6m 7f² 8g Nov 1] strong gelding: useful handicapper: won 18-runner event at Goodwood in May by ¾ length from Master Robbie: very good 1¼ lengths second of 25 to same horse in Tote Trifecta Stakes at Ascot: best at 7f: acts on any going: tongue tied: has been early to post/worn crossed noseband: free-going sort: usually waited with. *J. Akehurst*

GROOMER 2 b.g. (Apr 15) Fraam 114 – Canadian Capers 70 (Ballacashtal (CAN)) **59**
[2003 6m 6m 7.1g 8m⁵ 10f Sep 30] leggy gelding: fifth foal: dam, 5.7f (at 2 yrs) and 7.6f winner, probably stayed 1¼m: modest maiden: best effort at 6f on good to firm going: dead. *M. R. Channon*

GROOMS AFFECTION 3 b.c. Groom Dancer (USA) 128 – Love And Affection **80 p**
(USA) (Exclusive Era (USA)) [2003 60p: 10d 10s* Nov 3] good-bodied colt: well backed after 5½-month absence, clearly best effort (fairly useful form) when winning maiden at Redcar in November by ¾ length from Fine Palette, coming from rear to lead last 100 yds: will stay 1½m: lightly raced, almost certainly capable of better still, and type to do well in handicaps. *P. W. Harris*

GROUND COMMAND (USA) 2 b.g. (Jan 16) Kingmambo (USA) 125 – Cymbala **63**
(FR) (Assert 134) [2003 6d⁶ 8.1m⁶ Sep 17] close-coupled, quite attractive gelding: third foal: brother to fairly useful 1m (at 2 yrs) and 1½m winner Editor In Chief: dam, US Grade 3 1½m winner, earlier successful in France: modest form in maidens at Haydock and Sandown, slowly away and very green: gelded after: will be suited by 1¼m/1½m: should do better. *C. R. Egerton*

GROUND PATROL 2 b.g. (Feb 5) Ashkalani (IRE) 128 – Good Grounds (USA) **– p**
(Alleged (USA) 138) [2003 p7g Dec 17] 20,000Y: first foal: dam unraced: 25/1 and green, well held but not knocked about in minor event at Lingfield: open to improvement. *A. M. Balding*

GROUNDSWELL (IRE) 7 b.g. Common Grounds 118 – Fuchsia Belle (Vision **47**
(USA)) [2003 –: p16g f12g 16m³ f16.2g Nov 10] small gelding: fair winner in Ireland at 3 yrs: just poor nowadays: stays 2m: acts on soft going, good to firm and fibresand. *Ferdy Murphy*

GROUND ZERO (IRE) 3 b. or br.g. Marju (IRE) 127 – Zifta (USA) 82 (Zilzal (USA) **84**
137) [2003 79: 7g³ 7.5d³ 6m* 6m⁶ 6g 6d* 6g³ 7f⁶ 6g 6f Oct 10] quite good-topped gelding: fairly useful handicapper: won at Newcastle in June and July: below form last 3 starts: best 3-y-o efforts at 6f: acts on soft and good to firm going: blinkered final start: has raced freely: slowly away eighth outing: none too reliable: sold 9,000 gns, sent to Macau. *T. D. Easterby*

GROVE LODGE 6 b.g. Donna's Red – Shanuke (IRE) 56 (Contract Law (USA) 108) **–**
[2003 f7s⁴ f9.4s f8g 9.7g Mar 25] poor maiden: showed little in 2003: tried blinkered/ tongue tied/in cheekpieces. *P. R. Hedger*

GROWLER 2 ch.g. (Jun 9) Foxhound (USA) 103 – Femme Femme (USA) (Lyphard **67**
(USA) 132) [2003 6f 7.1m 6d 7d Nov 8] sturdy gelding: closely related to French 1¼m winner Belle d'Arbois (by Anabaa) and half-brother to several winners in France, including fairly useful 1m (including at 2 yrs) winner Femme Epanouie (by Sillery): dam, French maiden, half-sister to Cheveley Park and 1000 Guineas winner Ma Biche: fair maiden: well below form, including in nursery, last 2 starts: stays 7f: acts on firm ground. *J. L. Dunlop*

GRUFF 4 ch.g. Presidium 124 – Kagram Queen 64 (Prince Ragusa 96) [2003 66: 5m **–**
5m f6g 6.1g 5m 6f 5m Sep 17] sturdy gelding: fair handicapper at 3 yrs: failed to show any form in 2003: left I. McInnes after reappearance, J. Wainwright after fifth start. *P. T. Midgley*

GRUMPYINTMORNING 4 b.g. Magic Ring (IRE) 115 – Grecian Belle 53 (Ilium **60 +**
121) [2003 60p: 8f 8m 7.6g⁴ 7f² 7f 8.3g⁵ 8m⁴ Oct 23] tall gelding: modest maiden: sold out of A. Dickman's stable 10,000 gns after second start: stays 1m: raced only on good ground or firmer. *Mrs P. Townsley*

GRYFFINDOR 5 b.g. Marju (IRE) 127 – Hard Task 82 (Formidable (USA) 125) **97 d**
[2003 8m 8g⁶ 8g 8m Jun 18] strong, sturdy gelding: carries plenty of condition: useful handicapper: missed 2002 due to tendon injury: ninth of 25 to Mystic Man in Spring Cup at Newbury on reappearance: well held all 3 starts after: effective at 1m to 11f: acts on any going: effective blinkered or not: sold 7,000 gns in October. *B. J. Meehan*

GRYNGOLETTE 3 gr.f. Linamix (FR) 127 – Imperial Scholar (IRE) 94 (Royal Acad- **82**
emy (USA) 130) [2003 8.2g 10.3m² 9.9d⁴ 11.7f⁴ 9.9m⁴ 8.5g* 8.1d⁵ 7g⁵ p8g⁴ p7g Oct 30] leggy filly: second foal: dam, maiden (best effort at 7f), out of half-sister to French colts Splendid Moment (very smart at 1m/1¼m) and Grand Chelem (smart 2-y-o 1m

winner): fairly useful performer: landed odds in maiden at Epsom in September, hanging left: creditable efforts in handicaps next 3 starts: best at 1m/1¼m: acts on firm ground, good to soft and polytrack: wears tongue strap/crossed noseband, also blinkered/visored 4 of last 5 starts. *G. A. Butler*

GUARD   3 b.c. Night Shift (USA) – Gaijin 97 (Caerleon (USA) 132) [2003 –: p8g f7g 7g 8f f7g Nov 10] little form: tried tongue tied. *N. P. Littmoden*   –

GUARDED SECRET   6 ch.g. Mystiko (USA) 124 – Fen Dance (IRE) 82 (Trojan Fen 118) [2003 79: 12.3m 14v f12g Jun 9] leggy, angular gelding: one-time fairly useful handicapper: well held in 2003: has pulled hard: usually held up. *J. Mackie*   –

GUARDIAN SPIRIT   4 b.f. Hector Protector (USA) 124 – Amongst The Stars (USA) 107 (Proctor (USA)) [2003 –: 8m Jun 22] rather leggy filly: little form. *H. J. Collingridge*   –

GUILDED FLYER   4 b.g. Emarati (USA) 74 – Mo Ceri 63 (Kampala 120) [2003 69+, a92: 10m* 9g² 10m* 9g⁶ 10d⁵ 10m f12g Oct 4] big, lengthy gelding: fairly useful handicapper: won at Leicester in May and Windsor (by 8 lengths from Florenzar) in July: effective at 9f to easy 1½m: acts on all-weather and good to firm going, probably on good to soft: has wandered: often makes running. *W. S. Kittow*   **89**

GUILD'S DELIGHT (IRE)   4 b.g. College Chapel 122 – Tamburello (IRE) (Roi Danzig (USA)) [2003 59: 9m 7g Jul 3] workmanlike gelding: modest maiden: well held in 2003: blinkered (ran creditably) once: tongue tied/in cheekpieces. *W. S. Kittow*   –

GUILSBOROUGH   8 br.g. Northern Score (USA) – Super Sisters (AUS) (Call Report (USA)) [2003 78: 10g 10.9m 8g 8m Jun 15] close-coupled, workmanlike gelding: fair handicapper in 2002: well held in 2003: visored once as 3-y-o: held up. *D. Haydn Jones*   –

GULF (IRE)   4 ch.g. Persian Bold 123 – Broken Romance (IRE) (Ela-Mana-Mou 132) [2003 101: 16m³ 13.9m⁵ 12m 14f* 16.2f³ 16g⁶ 15d 14.6g⁶ 18m 14.6d⁶ Nov 7] big, strong gelding: useful performer: won minor event at Goodwood in June by 1¼ lengths from King's Consul: best effort when third to Mana d'Argent in handicap at Ascot next time: stays 2m: acts on firm ground: has been slowly away: usually waited with. *D. R. C. Elsworth*   **110**

GUNNHILDR (IRE)   3 ch.f. In Command (IRE) 114 – Queen Canute (IRE) (Aho-noora 122) [2003 7m⁵ 7f 8.3m⁴ p10g p10g f7g Nov 29] 11,000Y: strong filly: sixth foal: half-sister to useful 5.7f (at 2 yrs) and 7.5f winner Royal Quarters (by Common Grounds) and a 7f/1m winner in Germany by Rudimentary: dam, well beaten, half-sister to useful 6f winner King of The East and to dam of 4-y-o Just James: fair maiden: stays easy 1m: raced only on polytrack and ground firmer than good: visored last 2 starts. *P. J. Makin*   **60**

GUN SALUTE   3 b.g. Mark of Esteem (IRE) 137 – Affair of State (IRE) 99 (Tate Gal-lery (USA) 117) [2003 p7g 7m 7g² 7g 8f 6m 6f 7g p7g⁵ p7g p6g* p7g Dec 30] 30,000Y, 4,500 2-y-o: seventh foal: half-brother to several winners, including useful 1¼m/1½m winner Mojalid (by Zafonic): dam 2-y-o 5f/6f winner: modest performer: left B. Pearce after eighth start: won maiden at Lingfield in December: effective at 6f/7f: acts on polytrack: wore cheekpieces last 2 starts. *G. L. Moore*   **61**

GUNS AT DAWN (IRE)   2 b.c. (Apr 25) Daggers Drawn (USA) 114 – Princess Tycoon (IRE) 77 (Last Tycoon 131) [2003 6m Sep 7] IR 5,000F, €10,000Y: rather leggy, useful-looking colt: third foal: dam Irish maiden half-sister to useful sprinter Barrys Gamble: broke leg in maiden at York: dead. *K. R. Burke*   –

GUNS BLAZING   4 b.g. Puissance 110 – Queen of Aragon 76 (Aragon 118) [2003 83d: f5g 6m 5m 5f⁶ f5s 5m 5m* 5.3m* 5.1f⁶ 5m* 6m⁶ 5m⁶ 5d⁵ 5m 5m 5m² 5m 5.2m³ 5f⁵ 5m 5m* 6.1f 5f 5m Oct 20] leggy gelding: fair handicapper: won at Leicester (wandered) in June, Brighton and Haydock in July and Pontefract in September: best around 5f: acts on firm and soft going, little show on fibresand: wears headgear: usually races up with pace, but held up for last win. *Miss V. Haigh*   **68**

GWAIHIR (IRE)   2 b.c. (Apr 5) Cape Cross (IRE) 129 – Twilight Tango (Groom Dancer (USA) 128) [2003 6g² 6m* 6.3g⁶ 7.1m³ 8d* 8g² 8f³ Dec 29] €22,000Y: sturdy colt: second foal: half-brother to useful Irish 2002 2-y-o 5f winner Mombassa (by Mujadil): dam unraced sister to Chester Vase winner Twist And Turn: useful performer: won maiden at Newbury in June and listed race at Deauville (by 1½ lengths from Voix du Nord) in August: creditable 3 lengths second of 6 to Apsis in Prix Thomas Bryon at Saint-Cloud penultimate start: left J. Gosden, below form final outing: stays 1m: acts on good to firm and good to soft going: visored/blinkered last 4 starts: usually front runner. *C. A. Lewis, USA*   **105**

GWAZI 3 b.g. Pennekamp (USA) 130 – Made of Pearl (USA) 107 (Nureyev (USA) 131) –
[2003 7d f8g f8g f8g Dec 15] 17,000Y: half-brother to several winners, including useful 1997
2-y-o 7f winner Flawless (by Warning) and 1½m winner Cultured (by Saint Cyrien): dam
French 7f/1m winner: well held in claimer/maidens: tried visored/tongue tied. *Miss
D. A. McHale*

GWEN JOHN (USA) 2 ch.f. (Feb 11) Peintre Celebre (USA) 137 – River Jig (USA) **68 p**
98 (Irish River (FR) 131) [2003 7.5m⁵ Sep 17] 75,000Y: tall filly: closely related to US
Grade 3 9f winner Ocean Queen (by Zilzal) and half-sister to 3 winners, including useful
5f (Queen Mary Stakes) to 1m (US Grade 2 event) winner Dance Parade (by Gone West):
dam, 9f (at 2 yrs) and 1½m winner: 9/2 and better for race, fifth of 11 to Spring Goddess
in maiden at Beverley, not knocked about: will be suited by 1¼m+: sure to do better.
H. Morrison

GWUNGY 3 b.g. Mind Games 121 – Kinlet Vision (IRE) 56 (Vision (USA)) [2003 8.1m –
10.5d May 3] 800Y: leggy, angular gelding: half-brother to several winners, including
8.5f (at 2 yrs) and 2m winner Samarardo (by Son Pardo): dam, 2-y-o 5f/6f winner, also
successful over hurdles: well beaten in maidens. *W. Jenks*

H

HAAFEL (USA) 6 ch.g. Diesis 133 – Dish Dash 118 (Bustino 136) [2003 68: p16g² **75**
p13g p16g² f16s⁵ p16g³ 14.1g² p16g³ 14g f16.2g Aug 15] fair handicapper: stays 2m:
acts on polytrack (possibly not on fibresand), raced only on good going or softer on turf:
blinkered: takes good hold. *G. L. Moore*

HAAFHD 2 ch.c. (Feb 18) Alhaarth (IRE) 126 – Al Bahathri (USA) 123 (Blushing **115 +**
Groom (FR) 131) [2003 6d* 7m* 7g³ 7m³ Oct 18]
    Year in, year out, it pays to concentrate on good two-year-old form in the
Two Thousand Guineas at Newmarket in May. The last winner rated below 100
by Timeform as a two-year-old was the 1991 winner Mystiko; since then, eight
winners have been rated at least 110 at two, and five at least 115. On that basis alone
Haafhd has to enter Two Thousand Guineas calculations and, as a type likely to do
well in one of the recognised trials, could represent value at his ante-post odds of
33/1 at the time of writing. Haafhd created a very good impression when winning
the Stan James Online Stakes (Washington Singer) at Newbury in August, and still
looked in need of experience on his next two starts, when third in the Champagne
Stakes at Doncaster in September and in the Dewhurst Stakes at Newmarket in
October. Furthermore, Haafhd has the physical scope and pedigree of a horse who
looks sure to train on well, and is with a very experienced trainer whose three-year-
olds are usually well forward in the spring.
    Haafhd made a successful debut in a ten-runner maiden at Newmarket in
August (a race in which the five who followed him home all won next time out,
including the useful Moss Vale). Starting favourite in the eight-runner Washington
Singer next time, Haafhd did not need to be hard driven to run out an impressive
five-length winner from Orcadian. On the strength of his first two wins, Haafhd
started odds on for the Champagne Stakes, but in a steadily-run affair he was unable
to sustain his run after moving smoothly upsides the eventual winner Lucky Story,
beaten just over two lengths. Haafhd again seemed unsuited by a somewhat
muddling early pace in the Dewhurst on his final outing. Racing a bit freely, Haafhd
seemed to be caught flat-footed running down into the Dip but kept on again to
finish a creditable length and a half behind Milk It Mick, whom he had finished in
front of at both Newbury and Doncaster.
    Haafhd is by the young sire Alhaarth, who has already shown himself
capable of getting smart performers. His best to date from three crops of racing age
are the four-year-old Bandari and the three-year-old Phoenix Reach, both having
finished third in the St Leger, with the latter also winning the Canadian International. Interestingly, Haafhd was originally excluded from the Washington Singer
due to Alhaarth's own race record. The race conditions stipulate that the listed event
is for the progeny of stallions that won a race of '1 mile, about 2 furlongs or over';
Alhaarth won over nine furlongs and one hundred and sixty-five yards in the Prix

Mr Hamdan Al Maktoum's "Haafhd"

Haafhd (ch.c. Feb 18, 2001)	Alhaarth (IRE) (b 1993)	Unfuwain (b 1985)	Northern Dancer / Height of Fashion
		Irish Valley (ch 1982)	Irish River / Green Valley
	Al Bahathri (USA) (ch 1982)	Blushing Groom (ch 1974)	Red God / Runaway Bride
		Chain Store (b 1972)	Nodouble / General Store

Dollar at Longchamp. Haafhd was reinstated after a degree of flexibility was used. Not so lucky were the connections of Prince of Dance, who passed the post first in the same race in 1988. A son of Sadler's Wells, Prince of Dance was disqualified as in those days it was restricted to horses whose sires had won over a mile and a half or more. Alhaarth was champion two-year-old in 1995, when he was unbeaten in five races including the Champagne Stakes and the Dewhurst. Haafhd's dam Al Bahathri was a very smart performer who trained on from two to three, winning the Lowther Stakes and going on to success in the Irish One Thousand Guineas. Al Bahathri foaled several at least useful performers before Haafhd, including Munir (by Indian Ridge), winner of the Greenham and Challenge Stakes in 2001 for Haafhd's trainer, and the 1989 two-year-old listed winner Hasbah (by Kris), beaten narrowly in the Nell Gwyn Stakes at three. Both Munir and Hasbah were smart performers. The strong, lengthy Haafhd raced handily on all his starts. Though he won on good to soft going on his debut, he has a fluent action and his two best performances have come on good to firm. Haafhd edged right on his debut and carried his head awkwardly in the Dewhurst, but that should be put down—at least for the time being—to his relative immaturity. Haafhd should stay at least a mile. *B. W. Hills*

HABANERO 2 b.c. (Mar 30) Cadeaux Genereux 131 – Queen of Dance (IRE) (Sadler's **73** Wells (USA) 132) [2003 7g 6d⁶ p7g 8m² 8m² 8.3g* Oct 6] 50,000Y: leggy, quite attractive colt: third living foal: half-brother to French 2000 2-y-o 1m winner Queenliness (by Exit To Nowhere) and 1½m winner Tawoos (by Rainbow Quest), later useful 1m/1¼m winner in Scandinavia: dam won at 7f in France at 2 yrs: fair performer: won 16-runner nursery at Windsor comfortably by 2 lengths from Smoothly Does It: will probably stay 1¼m: acts on good to firm going, showed promise on polytrack: usually races prominently. *R. Hannon*

HABIBTI SARA 3 ch.f. Bijou d'Inde 127 – Cut Velvet (USA) (Northern Dancer) **–** [2003 6m 8.1m 9.9d May 20] 5,000Y: leggy filly: half-sister to several winners, including fairly useful Irish 13f winner Torn Silk (by Top Ville): dam 1m winner in USA: no form in maidens. *J. D. Czerpak*

HABITUAL DANCER 2 b.c. (Feb 7) Groom Dancer (USA) 128 – Pomorie (IRE) **53** 67§ (Be My Guest (USA) 126) [2003 6m 7d 7m Aug 22] 6,200Y: good-bodied colt: fifth foal: half-brother to German 6.5f and 1¼m winner My Little Princess (by Celtic Swing): dam, 1¼m and hurdles winner, became untrustworthy: best effort in maidens (modest form) when seventh of 14 at Pontefract on debut: should stay at least 1m. *Jedd O'Keeffe*

HABITUAL (IRE) 2 b.g. (Apr 14) Kahyasi 130 – Kick The Habit 94 (Habitat 134) **– p** [2003 f6g p7g Oct 8] €44,000Y: ninth foal: half-brother to 3 winners, including useful 7f (at 2 yrs) to 1½m winner Three Green Leaves (by Environment Friend): dam 1¼m winner who became one to leave alone: always behind after slow starts in maidens at Wolverhampton and Lingfield: likely to do better at 1¼m+. *Sir Mark Prescott*

HABSHAN (USA) 3 ch.c. Swain (IRE) 134 – Cambara 97 (Dancing Brave (USA) **79** 140) [2003 9.7m⁵ 8.1d² Sep 26] good-topped colt: sixth foal: half-brother to 4-y-o Samhari and UAE 5f to 7.5f winner Afreet (by Kris): dam, 1m winner, half-sister to smart middle-distance performers Pluralisme, Classic Tale and Singletta: fair form in maidens at Folkestone (raced freely) and Haydock (second to Bint Alhaarth): should stay 1½m: sold 12,000 gns. *M. A. Jarvis*

HADATH (IRE) 6 br.g. Mujtahid (USA) 118 – Al Sylah 118 (Nureyev (USA) 131) **79** [2003 82: 7g² 7d 7d⁵ 7d 7d⁴ 8g² 7s 7d 7f² 8.1d⁶ 7m p8g p8g⁵ p7g³ p8g p7g⁴ p7g Dec 17] lengthy gelding: fair performer: left R. Osborne in Ireland after ninth start: effective at 7f/ 1m: acts on any turf going and polytrack: tried in headgear. *B. G. Powell*

HAGEL 2 b.g. (Apr 30) Mtoto 134 – Loving Legacy 82 (Caerleon (USA) 132) [2003 **–** 7m 6d⁵ 7m Oct 12] 2,200Y: sturdy, close-coupled gelding: sixth foal: dam, disappointing maiden, out of useful 2-y-o 7f/1m performer Tender Loving Care: well held in maidens. *Ian Emmerson*

HAGLEY PARK 4 b.f. Petong 126 – Gi La High 68 (Rich Charlie 117) [2003 52, a69: **57** f5g³ f5g p6g f5g² f5g f5g* f5g⁶ f5s⁴ f5g f5g Dec 12] smallish, workmanlike filly: modest performer: left J. Unett after reappearance: won seller at Wolverhampton in March: best at 5f: acts on firm going, good to soft and all-weather: often forces pace: none too consistent. *M. Quinn*

HAIKAL 6 b.g. Owington 123 – Magic Milly 60 (Simply Great (FR) 122) [2003 56: **–** f12s 16m 16d May 2] modest maiden: well held in 2003: tried blinkered/tongue tied. *E. W. Tuer*

HAILE SELASSIE 3 b.g. Awesome 73 – Lady of The Realm (Prince Daniel (USA)) **63** [2003 63: 8.1m⁶ 8d 10m 11.6d* 10m⁶ f12g³ 10g 10m 10.2m Sep 22] well-made gelding: **a69** fair handicapper on all-weather, modest on turf: won at Windsor in June: ran poorly last 3 starts, hinting at temperament: stays easy 1½m: acts on fibresand, good to soft and good to firm going: sold 15,000 gns. *B. W. Hills*

HAIL THE CHIEF 6 b.h. Be My Chief (USA) 122 – Jade Pet 90 (Petong 126) [2003 **–** a8.5f⁶ a8.5f⁵ 7d Nov 8] rather sparely-made horse: good mover: smart on all-weather, fairly useful on turf at 3/4 yrs for R. Hannon: raced in US in 2002, winning allowance race at Gulfstream and Grade 3/2 handicaps at Sportsman's Park and Hawthorne: well held since, including in Grade 3 handicap and allowance race at Gulfstream early in 2003: left N. O'Callaghan in US, then well beaten only 6-y-o outing in Britain: effective at 1m to 1¼m: acts on soft going, good to firm and dirt/fibresand (also successful on equitrack): races prominently. *D. Nicholls*

HAIL THE KING (USA) 3 gr.g. Allied Forces (USA) 123 – Hail Kris (USA) (Kris **–** S (USA)) [2003 60: 7m 8.1m 9.9m⁶ 10m⁶ f8.5s Sep 6] tall, leggy gelding: little form at 3 yrs: tried blinkered/visored. *R. M. Beckett*

HAITHEM (IRE)   6 b.g. Mtoto 134 – Wukk (IRE) (Glow (USA)) [2003 53§: f8g f8s   – §
f8.5g f8.5g[6] f7g f8.5g f9.4s f8.5g p7g[6] 6g[5] 6.9m 8m 8m f8s Dec 27] close-coupled
gelding: little form in 2003: blinkered once, usually tongue tied: temperamental. *D. Shaw*

HAJEER (IRE)   5 b.g. Darshaan 133 – Simouna (Ela-Mana-Mou 132) [2003 53:   55
f16.2g[3] f16s[3] f14.8g[4] f14.8g[2] f16g[3] f16s[2] f16s* f16.2g[2] f16s[3] f14.8g f16g p16g f16g
f14.8s Dec 31] lengthy, angular gelding: modest handicapper: won at Southwell in February: stays 2m: acts on all-weather, lightly raced and little form on turf: tried in blinkers/
cheekpieces. *P. W. Hiatt*

HAKAM (USA)   4 ch.g. Woodman (USA) 126 – Haniya (IRE) 92 (Caerleon (USA)   57 d
132) [2003 70: 7m 9m 14m[5] 12g[5] 14.1f[3] 14.1m 14.4f 10.2m[3] 11.9f[5] 11.7f Aug 22] small
gelding: just a modest maiden in 2003: stays 1¾m: acts on firm and good to soft going:
tried in cheekpieces: usually held up: no easy ride. *John Berry*

HALABALOO (IRE)   2 b.f. (Jan 21) Intikhab (USA) 135 – Outcry 73 (Caerleon   66 p
(USA) 132) [2003 p6g[3] Nov 18] first foal: dam, maiden who should have stayed at
least 1m, out of half-sister to top-class miler Posse: 11/1 and green, 1¾ lengths third to
Aesculus in maiden at Lingfield: will stay 1m: likely to improve. *G. Wragg*

HALAWANDA (IRE)   3 b.f. Ashkalani (IRE) 128 – Haladiya (IRE) (Darshaan 133)   101
[2003 83p: 10m* 11.4m[2] 12g Jun 6] smallish, quite attractive filly: good walker: useful
performer, lightly raced: won maiden at Newbury in April: easily best effort when 1¼
lengths second to Hammiya in listed event at Chester: well beaten in Oaks at Epsom final
start (led for 1m): should have stayed 1½m: raced only on good/good to firm ground:
stud. *Sir Michael Stoute*

HALAWELLFIN HALA   4 ch.g. Kris 135 – Tegwen (USA) 79 (Nijinsky (CAN)   97
138) [2003 95: 10m 8.1g 8.1m[3] 8m 7m[3] 10g 7m[2] 8m[2] 8m[4] Oct 3] tall, rangy gelding:
useful performer: best efforts when third in handicap at Haydock sixth start, and second
in handicap at Newbury and minor event at Goodwood (beaten ½ length by Muchea):
stays 9.7f: acts on fibresand and good to firm going, probably on soft: has had rope halter
for stall entry: often makes running: sent to USA. *C. E. Brittain*

HALCYON MAGIC   5 b.g. Magic Ring (IRE) 115 – Consistent Queen 55 (Queen's   63
Hussar 124) [2003 74, a–: 7m 7g 8m 8d[5] 8f 7s[6] f8g Nov 24] sturdy gelding: modest   a–
handicapper: stays 1m: acts on firm and good to soft going: usually blinkered: none too
consistent. *Miss J. Feilden*

HALF HUNTER (USA)   3 ch.g. Halory Hunter (USA) 126 – Elegant Wish (USA)   ?
(Lyphard's Wish (FR) 124) [2003 70: f7g[4] f7g a6s[4] a11g* a8.6g[4] 8g a11g[5] a8g a8.6d[2]
a12g[4d] a10f Nov 30] fair performer: sold from T. D. Barron 3,000 gns after second start:
won minor event at Jagersro in May: stays 11f: acts on dirt/fibresand, lightly raced on
turf. *C. Hederud, Sweden*

HALF INCH   3 b.f. Inchinor 119 – Anhaar (Ela-Mana-Mou 132) [2003 65: p8g 8.1m*   68
8g[3] 8m 8.1m[4] 10m 9m 8f 10.2m[2] 10m[4] Oct 2] lengthy filly: fair handicapper: won at Warwick in May: stays 1¼m: acts on good to firm and good to soft going: wore cheekpieces/
visor after reappearance: sometimes looks reluctant: none too consistent. *B. I. Case*

HALICARDIA   2 br.f. (Feb 9) Halling (USA) 133 – Pericardia 60 (Petong 126) [2003   94 p
7f[3] 7m* 7m* Aug 21] 17,000F: sturdy, close-coupled filly: fifth foal: half-sister to 3
winners, including fairly useful 5f/6f winner (latter at 2 yrs) Card Games (by First Trump)
and 4-y-o Noble Nick: dam lightly-raced half-sister to smart 6f/7f performer Prince
Ferdinand: won maiden at Folkestone (hung left) in July and nursery at York (still green,
by 2 lengths from Moulin de Mougins) in August: races quite freely, but will probably
stay 1m: potentially useful. *P. W. Harris*

HALLAND   5 ch.g. Halling (USA) 133 – Northshiel 85 (Northfields (USA)) [2003 8g   –
12g May 4] quite attractive gelding: useful handicapper at 3 yrs: unraced in 2002 (reportedly had another operation on hind joint): well held both 5-y-o starts, in cheekpieces on
latter. *N. P. Littmoden*

HALLAND PARK LAD (IRE)   4 ch.g. Danehill Dancer (IRE) 117 – Lassalia (Sal-   –
lust 134) [2003 64: p12g Feb 25] smallish, sturdy gelding: modest performer: ran as if
amiss only 4-y-o outing. *S. Kirk*

HALLION (IRE)   4 b.g. Halling (USA) 133 – Elisa War (Warning 136) [2003 89: 8g*   97
8m 8g 8m[3] Sep 20] sturdy gelding: useful handicapper: made all at Thirsk in May: best
form around 1m: acted on good to firm and good to soft going: dead. *J. G. Given*

HALMAHERA (IRE)   8 b.g. Petardia 113 – Champagne Girl 67 (Robellino (USA)   107
127) [2003 102: 6f[3] 5.1m[2] 6m 6f 6.3m 7m[2] 6m 6g 6m[6] 5.6d* 5.2m 5m 5g* 6m 6d[4] 6v[4]

Tote Trifecta Portland (Handicap), Doncaster—Halmahera gains a second successive victory in the race;
Corridor Creeper runs him closest, with Baltic King (No.4),
Quito (far rail) and Colonel Cotton (near rail) next

Nov 19] good-topped gelding: has a round action: useful performer: won handicaps at Doncaster (Tote Trifecta Portland for second successive year, beating Corridor Creeper ½ length) in September and Ascot (dead-heated with Speed Cop) in October: effective at 5f to easy 7f: acts on any going: tried visored, blinkered last 5 outings: sometimes slowly away/carries head awkwardly: usually held up, and best with strong pace: tough. *K. A. Ryan.*

HAMAASY   2 b.c. (Feb 28) Machiavellian (USA) 123 – Sakha 109 (Wolfhound (USA)   **71** 126) [2003 6f 7m⁶ 7g 7g Oct 24] quite attractive colt: first foal: dam, 5f/6f winner (latter including at 2 yrs), closely related to very smart French/US performer up to 1½m Volochine: fair maiden: form only at 7f on good to firm going: tongue tied second/final outing: free-going sort: sold 9,000 gns. *J. L. Dunlop*

HAMBLEDEN   6 b.g. Vettori (IRE) 119 – Dalu (IRE) 72 (Dancing Brave (USA) 140)   **109** [2003 103: 14.1g 13.9m² 12m* 12f³ 11.9m² 14g⁵ 11.9m³ 12m* 12f² Sep 28] strong, angular gelding: useful handicapper: won at Thirsk in June and Kempton (beat Wunderwood by 1¼ lengths) in September: good efforts otherwise when placed at York (3) and Ascot (2), runner-up to Jagger on latter course final start: effective at 1½m to 2m: acts on firm going, soft and fibresand: races prominently: tough and consistent. *M. A. Jarvis*

HAMLYN (IRE)   6 gr.g. Lure (USA) 131 – Passamaquoddy (USA) (Drone (USA))   **58** [2003 58, a46: f5s* p6g⁴ f5g⁵ p6g p6g f6g⁴ f5g 6m 5s⁴ 6.5f⁵ 6g 8f 6m 6g⁴ 10m 5m⁶ 6f² Oct 18] good-bodied gelding: modest handicapper: won at Wolverhampton in February: left John A. Quinn in Ireland after eleventh start: probably best at 5f/6f: acts on all-weather, firm and soft going: tried tongue tied, usually wears cheekpieces/blinkers: carries head high. *N. Nelson, Ireland*

HAMMER AND SICKLE (IRE)   6 b.g. Soviet Lad (USA) – Preponderance (IRE)   **50 d** 85 (Cyrano de Bergerac 120) [2003 53, a48: 6.1m 5f 5g 5.3m 5.3m 7f 6m Aug 25] good-topped gelding: modest performer: effective at 5f to 7f: acts on firm going, soft and fibresand: tried visored/tongue tied, sometimes blinkered: finds little. *J. R. Boyle*

HAMMIYA (IRE)   3 b.f. Darshaan 133 – Albacora (IRE) 98 (Fairy King (USA)) [2003   **103** 64p: 8.5m* 11.4m* 12g 11.9g 8.9m⁵ Sep 3] leggy, unfurnished filly: useful performer, lightly raced: won maiden at Beverley in April and listed race at Chester (beat Halawanda 1¼ lengths) in May: well held in Oaks at Epsom and Lancashire Oaks at Haydock next 2 starts: respectable fifth to Naheef in Strensall Stakes at York final outing: stayed 11.4f: raced only on good/good to firm going: free-going sort: visits Machiavellian. *M. P. Tregoning*

HAMMOCK (IRE)   5 b. or br.g. Hamas (IRE) 125§ – Sure Victory (IRE) 75 (Stalker   **– §** 121) [2003 f12g Jan 23] temperamental maiden: tried blinkered/visored. *P. S. McEntee*

HAMPTON LUCY (IRE)   4 b.f. Anabaa (USA) 130 – Riveryev (USA) (Irish River   **–** (FR) 131) [2003 –, a65: f6s⁶ 6m f7g⁵ f6g⁵ f6g Jun 27] strong, lengthy filly: modest handi-   **a61** capper: stays easy 7f: acts on fibresand, no form on turf. *M. A. Buckley*

HAMUNAPTRA 4 ch.g. Alhijaz 122 – Princess Dancer (Alzao (USA) 117) [2003 50: p10g f8.5g Feb 7] stocky gelding: modest maiden: well held both 4-y-o starts: stayed 7f: acted on polytrack and good to firm going: usually blinkered: dead. *M. Wigham*

HANABAD (IRE) 3 b.c. Cadeaux Genereux 131 – Handaza (IRE) 93 (Be My Guest (USA) 126) [2003 107: 7g² 8m² 8m⁴ 7m⁵ 8f* 6f² 5m² 6d* Oct 12] lengthy, angular colt: smart performer: won minor event at Limerick in September and listed race at the Curragh (beat Millybaa a short head) in October: some good efforts otherwise, including when fifth to With Reason in Hungerford Stakes at Newbury and when head second to Fayr Jag in Ridgewood Pearl Stakes at the Curragh sixth start: best at 6f to 1m: acts on firm and soft going: sometimes tongue tied. *J. Oxx, Ireland* — **111**

HANA DEE 2 b.f. (Apr 4) Cadeaux Genereux 131 – Jumairah Sun (IRE) 98 (Scenic 128) [2003 7m 7m³ 7g Oct 22] big, workmanlike filly: sixth foal: sister to 4-y-o Najeebon and half-sister to 2 winners, notably 5-y-o Millennium Force: dam 1¼m winner: best effort in maidens (fair form) when third at Redcar: not knocked about final start: not sure to stay much beyond 7f: type to do better as 3-y-o. *M. R. Channon* — **72 p**

HANAMI 3 b.f. Hernando (FR) 127 – Russian Rose (IRE) 82 (Soviet Lad (USA)) [2003 101p: 8g⁵ 12g⁶ 10m* 12g 8m Oct 4] smallish, quite attractive filly: useful performer: won Audi Pretty Polly Stakes at the Curragh in June by neck from demoted Zee Zee Top: good efforts when 4½ lengths fifth to Russian Rhythm in 1000 Guineas at Newmarket and 4¼ lengths sixth to Casual Look in Oaks at Epsom: last in Irish Oaks at the Curragh (reportedly swallowed tongue) and Sun Chariot Stakes at Newmarket last 2 starts: stays 1½m: acts on soft and good to firm going. *J. A. R. Toller* — **108**

HANCORA (FR) 3 ch.f. Septieme Ciel (USA) 123 – Minaudeuse (USA) (The Minstrel (CAN) 135) [2003 6.1s 7g 4.5m Aug 3] 320,000 francs Y: lengthy filly: fifth foal: half-sister to 3 winners, including fairly useful 1m winner Mount Hesse (by Midyan): dam French 1¼m winner: useful performer at 2 yrs, winning newcomers race at Saint-Cloud and minor event/listed race at Maisons-Laffitte: well held in 2003, including in listed race at Nottingham on reappearance (only outing for Sir Mark Prescott): should stay 6f: raced mainly on good/good to firm ground. *J-C. Rouget, France* — **—**

HAND CHIME 6 ch.g. Clantime 101 – Warning Bell 88 (Bustino 136) [2003 97, a102: f7s³ f6g⁴ 6f⁶ 7d 7d 7g p7g³ Dec 29] angular gelding: useful handicapper on all-weather, fairly useful on turf: ran well when in frame all 3 starts on all-weather in 2003: best at 6f/7f: yet to race on heavy going, acts on any other turf and all-weather: sometimes slowly away: sometimes bandaged off-hind joint. *W. J. Haggas* — **89 a99**

HANDSHAKE 3 ch.g. Most Welcome 131 – Lady Day (FR) (Lightning (FR) 129) [2003 62: 5m 8d 8g⁵ 12.1m Jul 29] lengthy, good-bodied gelding: poor maiden: should stay 1¼m: acts on heavy going. *W. McKeown* — **49**

HANDSOME CROSS (IRE) 2 b.c. (Mar 22) Cape Cross (IRE) 129 – Snap Crackle Pop (IRE) 87 (Statoblest 120) [2003 5m⁴ 6m 6g³ 6.1d² 5m* 5m² 5g³ 5m² Oct 18] strong colt: third foal: half-brother to 2001 2-y-o 6f winner Snip Snap (by Revoque): dam 2-y-o 5f winner: fairly useful performer: won maiden at Folkestone in August: creditable efforts in minor events/nursery after: best at 5f: acts on good to firm ground: races prominently: consistent. *I. A. Wood* — **89**

Audi Pretty Polly Stakes, the Curragh—
Hanami gains handsome reward for creditable efforts in the Guineas and Oaks;
Zee Zee Top (left) is demoted a place after being second past the post, in front of Snippets (No.8)

HANNAMIE (IRE) 3 ch.g. Alhaarth (IRE) 126 – Bold Timing 73 (Never So Bold 135) **55 ?**
[2003 69: p8g 6g² 7.1m 7m⁵ 7m 7m 8m Jul 1] modest maiden: stays 1m: acts on soft **a?**
ground, probably on good to firm: well below form in blinkers/tongue strap last 3 starts.
R. Hannon

HANNIBAL TWO 6 b.g. Rock City 120 – Appealing 49 (Star Appeal 133) [2003 f9.4g **–**
Jan 17] well held in bumper, and in claimer at Wolverhampton. *P. D. Evans*

HANSARD (USA) 3 b.g. Deputy Minister (CAN) – Astoria (ARG) (Logical (USA)) **67**
[2003 7m² Apr 23] $600,000F: quite attractive gelding: sixth foal: half-brother to 2
winners in South America, including Argentinian Grade 1 sprint winner Astrologica (by
Senor Pete): dam Argentinian Grade 2 1m winner: 9/4-on, 2 lengths second in maiden at
Catterick (slowly away): sold 6,000 gns, sent to UAE. *D. R. Loder*

HANS CHRISTIAN (IRE) 3 b.c. Danehill (USA) 126 – Mira Adonde (USA) **75 d**
(Sharpen Up 127) [2003 67: 7.5f* 8g 8d 7m 6m Jun 9] angular colt: fair performer: won
handicap at Beverley in April: poor efforts after, leaving M. Johnston after fourth start:
stays 7.5f: acts on firm ground. *Paul Johnson*

HANTON (IRE) 2 b.f. (Mar 25) Orpen (USA) 116 – Yafford (Warrshan (USA) 117) **51**
[2003 6f* 6g⁵ 6m Oct 2] 6,000Y: fourth foal: dam ran once in Ireland: modest form:
favourite (late jockey change of K. Fallon for claimer), won seller at Brighton in July,
then retained 28,000 gns: ran creditably in nursery final start: needs to settle to stay
beyond 6f: carries head awkwardly/tends to hang. *M. J. Wallace*

HAPPY CRUSADER (IRE) 2 b.c. (Jan 24) Cape Cross (IRE) 129 – Les Hurlants **103**
(IRE) (Barathea (IRE) 127) [2003 5m³ 6.1g³ 5m³ 7g* 8m* 8g³ 10d⁶ Nov 8] IR 35,000F,
55,000Y: well-made colt: first foal: dam French 1½m winner: useful performer: won
nurseries at Goodwood and Newcastle (by ½ length from Red Damson) in August: good
3½ lengths third of 7 to Bago in Prix des Chenes at Longchamp in September: should stay
at least 1¼m: best effort on good going. *P. F. I. Cole*

HAPPY HOLIDAY (IRE) 2 b.c. (May 5) Fasliyev (USA) 120 – Ms Calera (USA) **74**
(Diesis 133) [2003 6m 6m⁴ 6m* 6m 6g⁴ 6g² 7.1m Sep 20] €70,000Y: fourth
foal: half-brother to 4-y-o Kayseri: dam, maiden in USA, half-sister to Irish St Leger winner Authaal: fair performer: won maiden at Haydock in July: creditable second in nursery
at Epsom: will probably prove best at 5f/6f: acts on good to firm going: sometimes slowly
away: often races prominently: sold 16,000 gns. *M. R. Channon*

HAPPY UNION 4 b.g. First Trump 118 – Heights of Love 51 (Persian Heights 129) **–**
[2003 48: 7m May 1] close-coupled gelding: poor maiden: well held only 4-y-o start:
usually visored/blinkered. *K. R. Burke*

HARARE 2 b.g. (Feb 19) Bahhare (USA) 122 – Springs Eternal 69 (Salse (USA) 128) **69**
[2003 6d 6m⁶ 7m³ Jul 2] 10,000Y: workmanlike gelding: first foal: dam, maiden (ran
only at 2 yrs) who stayed 1m, half-sister to useful 1997 2-y-o 6f winner Crazee Mental:
best effort in maidens (fair form) when third at Catterick: should stay 1m: signs of waywardness: sold 1,400 gns. *R. M. Whitaker*

HARB (IRE) 3 b.c. Green Desert (USA) 127 – Ajayib (USA) 84 (Riverman (USA) **99**
131) [2003 100: 6m 7g 8m⁴ 8g² 10g 8m Oct 17] smallish, close-coupled, good-topped
colt: useful handicapper: easily best efforts in 2003 when in frame at Kempton, second to
Ice Palace on latter occasion: stays 1m: yet to race on extremes of going: sent to UAE,
joined D. Watson. *J. L. Dunlop*

HARBOUR BELL 4 b.g. Bal Harbour 113 – Bellara 65 (Thowra (FR)) [2003 60: **51 ?**
p16g⁴ p16g⁵ Mar 5] rather sparely-made gelding: modest performer: stays easy 2m: acts
on firm ground and all-weather: tried blinkered. *J. White*

HARBOUR HOUSE 4 b.g. Distant Relative 128 – Double Flutter 92 (Beldale Flutter **63 d**
(USA) 130) [2003 77d: p5g⁵ 5g 5m⁵ 6m 6f³ 6m 5d 8m 10m 8d p7g² p7g Dec 30] leggy **a50**
gelding: modest performer: stays 7f: acts on polytrack and any turf going: tried blinkered/
visored. *J. J. Bridger*

HARBRIDGE 4 ch.g. Muhtarram (USA) 125 – Beacon (High Top 131) [2003 11.5f⁴ **68**
p12g² p13g⁶ Oct 3] 40,000Y: brother to useful 1¼m and 1¾m winner Maycocks Bay and
half-brother to 3 winners, including useful 1994 2-y-o 7f/1m winner who stayed 1½m
Indian Light (by Be My Chief): dam unraced half-sister to smart performer up to 2½m
Compton Ace out of Irish St Leger winner Mountain Lodge: fair form in maidens: should
stay 1¾m. *J. A. R. Toller*

HARCOURT (USA) 3 b.c. Cozzene (USA) – Ballinamallard (USA) 112 (Tom Rolfe) **99**
[2003 82: 8m³ 10m* 12d Nov 8] rangy colt: useful performer, lightly raced: won handi-

cap at Newmarket in April by 1¾ lengths from Once: 9/1, ran as if amiss in November Handicap at Doncaster 6½ months later: should stay 1½m: yet to race on extremes of going. *P. F. I. Cole*

HARD NOSE (IRE) 3 b.c. Entrepreneur 123 – Cutlers Corner 111 (Sharpen Up 127) **94**
[2003 87p: 7g⁶ 7d² 8m Jun 19] well-made colt: fairly useful handicapper, lightly raced: best effort when 5 lengths second to New Seeker at Newmarket: ran poorly in Britannia Stakes at Royal Ascot final start, carrying head high/tending to hang: should stay 1m: acts on good to soft ground: twice slowly away: sold 16,000 gns. *J. H. M. Gosden*

HARD TO CATCH (IRE) 5 b.g. Namaqualand (USA) – Brook's Dilemma 80 **80**
(Known Fact (USA) 135) [2003 79, a76: 6m 5g 6.1d 5.3m* 5.7f³ 5.3m³ 5m 5d 5.3f⁵ 5f⁵ 5.3f⁵ Aug 27] close-coupled gelding: fairly useful handicapper: won at Brighton in May: effective at 5f to 7f: acts on all-weather, firm and good to soft going: tried visored, usually blinkered. *D. K. Ivory*

HARELDA 3 ch.f. Hector Protector (USA) 124 – Hen Harrier 94 (Polar Falcon (USA) **82**
126) [2003 10f⁴ 12m² Jul 25] second foal: half-sister to 4-y-o King Eider: dam, 7f (at 2 yrs) to 1¼m winner, granddaughter of Oaks winner Circus Plume: better effort in maidens (fairly useful form) when 5 lengths second to Red Fort at Newmarket, not knocked about (returned with injury): should stay 1¾m. *H. Morrison*

HAREWOOD END 5 b.g. Bin Ajwaad (IRE) 119 – Tasseled (USA) (Tate Gallery **–**
(USA) 117) [2003 –: 12.3m 7m 6m 8s 9.2g³ 10f Sep 15] sturdy gelding: of little account nowadays: tried in headgear. *A. Crook*

HARIBINI 3 b. or br.f. Groom Dancer (USA) 134 – Mory Kante (USA) (Icecapade **56**
(USA)) [2003 8g 7m⁵ 7f p10g⁴ 10.1m³ 14.1f 11.8m³ 11.5m Oct 21] half-sister to several winners, including 6-y-o Pagan Prince: dam German 7f/1m winner: modest maiden: stays 1½m: acts on polytrack, raced only on good ground or firmer on turf: blinkered last 2 starts: quirky: sold 1,500 gns. *J. A. R. Toller*

HARIK 9 ch.g. Persian Bold 123 – Yaqut (USA) 77 (Northern Dancer) [2003 –, a85: **47**
p12g p12g⁴ p16g² f16.2g f17.2f⁶ Jun 14] rather leggy gelding: fairly useful handicapper **a85**
on all-weather, poor on turf: stays easy 2m: acts on all-weather and good to firm ground: sometimes visored/tongue tied, blinkered last 3 starts. *G. L. Moore*

HARIPUR 4 b.c. Groom Quest (USA) 134 – Jamrat Jumairah (IRE) 91 (Polar Falcon **75 +**
(USA) 126) [2003 62: p10g³ p10g⁵ 10d⁵ 9m⁴ p8g* p8g* 8d² p7g* p7g* p7g* p7g Dec 29] **a108**
lengthy, quite good-topped colt: progressed into useful performer on all-weather in second half of 2003, winning minor event and claimer in July, and handicaps in August, September and October (beat The Best Yet ½ length), all at Lingfield: reportedly finished lame final outing: best at 7f/1m: acts on polytrack (unraced on fibresand), lightly raced and fair form (may yet to better) on turf: tried tongue tied: races prominently. *Andrew Reid*

HARLEQUIN DANCER 7 b.g. Distant Relative 128 – Proudfoot (IRE) (Shareef **–**
Dancer (USA) 135) [2003 59: 6d 8m 7.9f 7.9f 7d Jul 26] strong, good-topped gelding: modest performer in 2002: no form in 2003: tried in visor/cheekpieces. *B. Mactaggart*

HARLESTONE BAY 4 b.g. Shaamit (IRE) 127 – Harlestone Lake 78 (Riboboy **–**
(USA) 124) [2003 66p: 14.1g 14.1m 17.2f Jun 4] smallish, sturdy gelding: lightly-raced maiden handicapper: showed little in 2003: sold 2,500 gns. *J. L. Dunlop*

HARLESTONE GREY 5 gr.g. Shaamit (IRE) 127 – Harlestone Lake 78 (Riboboy **106 ?**
(USA) 124) [2003 111: 12g³ 15f³ 18.7m² 14m⁵ 18m² Sep 18] tall, lengthy gelding: useful performer: reportedly broke a pedal bone after final 4-y-o start: seemingly best effort in 2003 when second to Sun Bird in handicap at Chester third start: well below form last 2 outings: stays 18.7f: acts on firm and good to soft ground: usually held up. *J. L. Dunlop*

HARLEYBROOK 2 b.c. (Jan 19) Bijou d'Inde 127 – Tous Les Jours (USA) 70 (Day- **41**
jur (USA) 137) [2003 7m f6g 8m⁶ Sep 18] 5,200Y: first foal: dam 7f winner, including at 2 yrs: poor maiden: stays 1m: sold 800 gns, sent to Denmark. *J. G. Given*

HARLOT 3 b.f. Bal Harbour 113 – Queen of The Quorn 53 (Governor General 116) **64**
[2003 57: p6g⁴ p8g⁴ 7m 8f p10g p10g p10g³ Dec 17] modest maiden handicapper: stays easy 1¼m: raced only on polytrack/ground firmer than good: tried in cheekpieces. *John Berry*

HARMONIC (USA) 6 b.m. Shadeed (USA) 135 – Running Melody 86 (Rheingold **45**
137) [2003 56: f8.5g f8s⁴ f8g Mar 20] quite attractive mare: poor maiden: left G. Prod-romou after reappearance: stays 8.5f: acts on fibresand, soft and good to firm going: tried in cheekpieces. *H. J. Collingridge*

HARMONY HALL   9 ch.g. Music Boy 124 – Fleeting Affair 98 (Hotfoot 126) [2003   **51 §**
62§: 8.2m 8.1m⁵ 8.1m⁴ 8.1m⁶ Jul 11] big, lengthy gelding: modest handicapper: probably
best at 7f/1m: acts on firm and good to soft going: visored once: sometimes finds little:
unreliable: won over hurdles in July/August: sold 5,400 gns in October. *J. M. Bradley*

HARMONY ROW   5 ch.h. Barathea (IRE) 127 – Little Change 70 (Grundy 137) [2003   **?**
a10.5g a11g³ 8.5d 7m 8m 10d p10g Sep 9] strong, useful-looking horse: fairly useful
winner at 2 yrs for E. Dunlop: winner in Spain at 3/4 yrs for J. Brown: trained from 2 starts
in 2003 by G. Bindella in Spain: well held back in Britain: left R. C. Guest after fifth start:
stays 1½m: acts on sand: tried in cheekpieces. *G. L. Moore*

HARRIET'S TOUCH (USA)   2 b.f. (Jan 26) Touch Gold (USA) 127 – I'm Harriet   **67**
(USA) (Diesis 133) [2003 6m 7g⁵ Jul 3] $280,000F: angular filly: fourth foal: half-sister
to US Grade 2 8.5f winner Who Did It And Run (by Polish Numbers): dam won once in
USA: better effort in maidens (fair form) when fifth of 6 at Yarmouth: needs to settle to
stay beyond 7f. *M. R. Channon*

HARRISON POINT (USA)   3 b.c. Nureyev (USA) 131 – Maid's Broom (USA)   **84**
(Deputy Minister (CAN)) [2003 8.3m⁶ 8.3g* 8.2m 7m² 8f³ 8m Oct 6] $250,000Y: rangy
colt: sixth foal: half-brother to several winners in North America, including US Grade 2
9.5f winner Tenpins (by Smart Strike): dam, 6f winner in USA, out of half-sister to very
smart 1½m performer Petit Loup and high-class 1¼m performer Ascot Knight: fairly useful performer: won maiden at Windsor in August: best efforts when placed in handicaps
at York (short-headed by King Harson) and Bath (failed to handle bend) in September:
reportedly finished lame final start: stays 1m: raced only on good going or firmer: visored
last 3 starts: carried head high third outing: sold 26,000 gns, joined P. Chapple-Hyam.
J. H. M. Gosden

HARRISON'S FLYER (IRE)   2 b.g. (Mar 16) Imperial Ballet (IRE) 110 – Smart   **69 ?**
Pet 77 (Petong 126) [2003 6m⁴ May 14] IR 15,000F, 27,000Y: good-topped gelding: has
scope: fifth foal: dam, 2-y-o 5f winner, out of half-sister to dam of Lochsong and
Lochangel: 33/1 and better for race, seemingly fair form when 9 lengths fourth of 5 to
Botanical in maiden at York. *R. A. Fahey*

HARRY ANCHOR   3 b.g. Slip Anchor 136 – Subtle One (IRE) (Polish Patriot (USA)   **–**
128) [2003 8g⁵ 10m⁶ 11.6m 7m 10m 10.1m⁶ 10m Sep 29] close-coupled gelding: second
foal: dam, lightly-raced maiden, half-sister to very smart performer up to 2m Manhattan
Cafe and smart winner up to 11f Air Smap, both in Japan: no form: tried visored.
J. R. Jenkins

HARRY'S GAME   6 gr.g. Emperor Jones (USA) 119 – Lady Shikari (Kala Shikari   **–**
125) [2003 59: 8m Apr 14] ex-Irish gelding: fairly useful winner at 2 yrs: on downgrade:
left J. Walsh in Ireland prior to well beaten only 6-y-o start: tried blinkered/tongue tied.
J. J. Matthias

HARRY THE HOOVER (IRE)   3 b.g. Fayruz 116 – Mitsubishi Style (Try My Best   **–**
(USA) 130) [2003 88: 6d f8.5g Nov 29] fairly useful winner at 2 yrs: well held in 2003,
leaving M. Hammond after reappearance. *M. J. Gingell*

HARRY TU   3 b.g. Millkom 124 – Risky Tu 62 (Risk Me (FR) 127) [2003 f7g p10g   **–**
Nov 18] first foal: dam 1m and 1½m winner: well held in maidens. *Miss Gay Kelleway*

HARRY UP   2 ch.c. (Jan 24) Piccolo 121 – Faraway Lass 94 (Distant Relative 128)   **96**
[2003 5.1g³ 5m² 5g* 5f⁶ 5.1m* 5g² 5g⁴ 5m⁶ 5g* 5g 5m⁴ 5g Oct 11] strong colt: first foal:
dam 6f winner: usual performer: won maiden at Lingfield in June, nursery at Chester in
July and minor event at Ripon in August: fourth in Molecomb Stakes at Goodwood
(beaten 3½ lengths by Majestic Missile) and listed contest at Ayr: will prove best at 5f/
easy 6f: acts on good to firm going: often races prominently. *J. G. Given*

HARTSHEAD   4 b.g. Machiavellian (USA) 123 – Zalitzine (USA) 98 (Zilzal (USA)   **70 ?**
137) [2003 11.1m³ 12g 8m⁴ 8.5m⁴ 9m⁶ f12s Dec 13] 7,800 3-y-o: leggy gelding: first
foal: dam, 1m winner, daughter of smart French 7f performer Bitooh: seemingly fair form
in maidens/minor events: stays 11f: has raced freely. *G. A. Swinbank*

HASANPOUR (IRE)   3 b.c. Dr Devious (IRE) 127 – Hasainiya (IRE) 109 (Top Ville   **103 p**
129) [2003 88p: 11m³ 11.1d* 10m 13d* Sep 29] tall, useful-looking colt: has scope:
useful performer, lightly raced: won maiden in May and handicap in September (beat
No Refuge a neck), both at Hamilton: stays 13f: unraced on extremes of going: makes
running: sold 150,000 gns: type to progress further. *Sir Michael Stoute*

HASAYIS   2 b.f. (May 2) Danehill (USA) 126 – Intizaa (USA) 77 (Mr Prospector   **59**
(USA)) [2003 6m 6g Oct 24] sturdy, angular filly: first foal: dam, maiden who stayed 1m,
half-sister to smart 7f to 9f performer Haami out of smart half-sister to Derby winner

Erhaab: modest form in maidens at Yarmouth (slowly away) and Newbury: will stay 1m. *J. L. Dunlop*

HASHID (IRE)   3 b.g. Darshaan 133 – Alkaffeyeh (IRE) (Sadler's Wells (USA) 132)   **84**
[2003 12g⁵ 12m³ Jul 25] big gelding: brother to 4-y-o Tholjanah and half-brother to 3 at least useful winners, including 1½m/1¾m winner Ta-Lim (by Ela-Mana-Mou) and 8.8f (in UAE) to 1½m (in Ireland) winner Mudaa-Eb (by Machiavellian), both smart: dam unraced sister to smart 1½m performer Larrocha and half-sister to Ardross: blinkered, fairly useful form in maidens at Newbury and Newmarket (third to Red Fort), carrying head high in both: sold 15,000 gns in October, joined P. Ritchens. *M. P. Tregoning*

HASINA (IRE)   4 b.f. King's Theatre (IRE) 128 – Smaointeach (IRE) 67 (Green Desert   **–**
(USA) 127) [2003 81, a59: p10g p10g⁴ f9.4s Feb 17] modest maiden: stays 12.5f: acts on   **a59**
firm going, soft and polytrack: tried blinkered. *B. W. Duke*

HASTY HANNAH   2 ch.f. (Feb 4) Pursuit of Love 124 – Tenderetta (Tender King   **–**
123) [2003 6m p6g p8g Oct 27] big filly: sister to temperamental 1m (including at 2 yrs) winner Al Ghabraa and 5.7f winner Pursuit of Gold and half-sister to 2 winners, including 3-y-o Royal Beacon: dam Irish 2-y-o 6f and 1m winner: well beaten in maidens. *M. R. Hoad*

HASTY PRINCE   5 ch.g. Halling (USA) 133 – Sister Sophie (USA) (Effervescing   **90**
(USA)) [2003 101: 12g Sep 13] tall gelding: has a round action: useful handicapper at 4 yrs: respectable eighth at Doncaster only 5-y-o start: stays 1½m: acts on firm and soft going: smart hurdler. *Jonjo O'Neill*

HATCH   2 ch.c. (May 8) Cadeaux Genereux 131 – Footlight Fantasy (USA) 68 (Nureyev   **86 p**
(USA) 131) [2003 7m⁵ 6f⁴ 7.1m² 7f Sep 28] 42,000Y: big, lengthy colt: sixth foal: brother to fairly useful 1999 2-y-o 7f winner Leading Role and half-brother to several winners, including 3-y-o Lindop and 4-y-o Unscrupulous: dam 7f winner out of top-class miler Milligram: strong-finishing second in maiden at Warwick: again caught the eye, never placed to challenge, when favourite in nursery at Ascot final start: should stay 1m: type to make a useful handicapper at 3 yrs. *R. Charlton*

HATCH A PLAN (IRE)   2 b.g. (Feb 27) Vettori (IRE) 119 – Fast Chick 93 (Henbit   **69 p**
(USA) 130) [2003 6m 6m 6g Oct 24] IR 38,000F, €40,000Y: leggy gelding: half-brother to several winners, including smart 6f (at 2 yrs) and 1m winner Missile (by Rock City), later successful in Hong Kong, 6-y-o Anyhow and 5-y-o Fast Foil: dam 9f to 1½m winner: best effort in maidens (fair form) when ninth of 18 at Newbury final start, not at all knocked about: should be suited by at least 1¼m: should progress. *R. M. Beckett*

HATHLEN (IRE)   2 b.c. (Mar 24) Singspiel (IRE) 133 – Kameez (IRE) 72 (Arazi   **77**
(USA) 135) [2003 7m 8m² 9f² 10m³ 8d 8m² 8g² Nov 5] 50,000Y: quite attractive colt: second foal: dam, 11f winner, half-sister to smart performers Kalajana (in France at 10.5f) and Kalabo (up to 1½m) from family of Kahyasi: fair maiden: second 4 times: will stay at least 1½m: acts on firm and good to soft ground: consistent. *M. R. Channon*

HATHRAH (IRE)   2 g.r.f. (Jan 22) Linamix (FR) 127 – Zivania (IRE) 101 (Shernazar   **101 p**
131) [2003 7f⁴ 7g* 8d² 7g² Oct 25] 340,000Y: rangy, rather unfurnished filly: half-sister to several winners, including smart performers up to 1½m Ivan Luis (in Italy, by Lycius) and Zero Problemo (in Germany, by Priolo): dam Irish 1m to 9.5f winner: won maiden at Newmarket in August: useful form when 1¾ lengths second in May Hill Stakes at Doncaster won by Kinnaird and listed event at Newbury (going in coat) won by Secret Charm: will stay 1¼m: acts on firm and good to soft ground: open to progress. *J. L. Dunlop*

HATTINGTON   5 b.g. Polish Precedent (USA) 131 – Ruffle (FR) (High Line 125)   **69**
[2003 70: 12m⁶ 11.9g⁵ 13.8f 12g³ 14m⁶ Aug 8] rather leggy gelding: fair handicapper: ran as if amiss 2 of last 3 starts, in cheekpieces final one: barely stays 14.6f: acts on soft and good to firm going: no easy ride. *M. Todhunter*

HAT TRICK MAN   2 gr.c. (Apr 30) Daylami (IRE) 138 – Silver Kristal 81 (Kris 135)   **61**
[2003 7m p7g Oct 15] 22,000Y: second foal: dam, 7f winner, half-sister to several useful performers, including Irish 1m winner Reina Blanca: modest form in maidens at Newmarket and Lingfield (slowly away): will stay at least 1m. *J. Akehurst*

HAULAGE MAN   5 ch.g. Komaite (USA) – Texita 65 (Young Generation 129) [2003   **73**
79: 8m 5.9f² 7.9m 8m 8f 7m 8m 8m⁴ 6g Oct 22] tall gelding: fair handicapper: effective at 6f to 1m: acts on firm and good to soft going (yet to race on softer): tried in cheekpieces: sometimes slowly away. *D. Eddy*

HAUNT THE ZOO   8 b.m. Komaite (USA) – Merryhill Maid (IRE) 71 (M Double M   **–**
(USA)) [2003 –, a86: f8.5g f8.5s f8.5g f8g f8g f8.5g³ f8.5s³ f8.5f² f8.5g⁵ f9.4g* f8s³ Sep   **a67**

2] tall mare: fair handicapper: won apprentice event at Wolverhampton in August: stays 9.4f: acts on fibresand: held up. *John A. Harris*

HAVANTADOUBT (IRE)   3 ch.f. Desert King (IRE) 129 – Batiba (USA) (Time For   **76** A Change (USA)) [2003 82: 9d 8.3g 10.2m 7.1m 8m 11m* 9.9d⁵ 11.6m³ 11.9f³ 12.3m 11m 11f Oct 12] workmanlike filly: fair handicapper: won at Goodwood in June: barely stays 1½m: acts on firm and good to soft ground: wore cheekpieces/visor last 7 starts: free-going front runner: none too consistent: sold 7,000 gns. *J. G. Portman*

HAVE FAITH (IRE)   2 b.f. (Apr 18) Machiavellian (USA) 123 – Fatefully (USA)   **87** 110 (Private Account (USA)) [2003 7m⁶ 7g² 7m* 7g Sep 13] tall, leggy filly: third foal: sister to useful 6.5f (in USA at 2 yrs) to 1¼m (in UAE) winner Opportunist and half-sister to 3-y-o Favourable Terms: dam 7f/1m winner who probably stayed 1¼m: fairly useful performer: made all in maiden at Folkestone in August: creditable seventh of 22 in nursery at Doncaster, getting going too late: should stay 1m. *B. W. Hills*

HAVE SOME FUN   3 ch.g. Bering 136 – Hilaris (Arazi (USA) 135) [2003 f8g⁶ Dec   **43** 9] second foal: half-brother to 1m winner Dance For Fun (by Anabaa): dam unraced out of half-sister to Arc winner Saumarez: 10/1, some ability when sixth in maiden at Southwell. *P. R. Chamings*

HAVETOAVIT (USA)   2 b.g. (Jan 31) Theatrical 128 – Summer Crush (USA) (Summer Squall (USA)) [2003 7m⁵ 7d⁵ f8s⁴ 7.9f 8m Oct 24] €22,000Y, 21,000 2-y-o: useful-   **64** looking gelding: first foal: dam, lightly-raced US maiden, half-sister to Racing Post Trophy/Dante Stakes winner Saratoga Springs: modest maiden: bred to stay 1¼m, but races freely: acts on fibresand and good to soft ground: races prominently. *J. D. Bethell*

HAVOC   4 b.g. Hurricane Sky (AUS) – Padelia (Thatching 131) [2003 68d: f12s f8g Mar   **–** 13] tall gelding: disappointing maiden: blinkered/tongue tied both 4-y-o starts. *N. Wilson*

HAVVA DANZ   2 b.f. (Mar 28) Danzero (AUS) – Possessive Lady 62 (Dara Monarch   **–** 128) [2003 7d Nov 7] 17,000Y: sixth foal: half-sister to 3 winners, including 4-y-o Protectorate and useful French 1¼m winner Morini (by Unfuwain): dam, 1m winner, half-sister to Irish Oaks winner Possessive Dancer: 20/1 and not fully wound up, well held in maiden at Doncaster. *J. G. Given*

HAWK   5 b.g. A P Jet (USA) – Miss Enjoleur (USA) (L'Enjoleur (CAN)) [2003 87§:   **87 d** f5g² 5m f5g³ f5g 5.1s 5g² 5f 6f 5m 5d 5d 5m* 5f³ 5m p7g⁵ Oct 15] big, good-bodied gelding: fairly useful performer: below best after reappearance, though won claimer at Catterick (left D. Nicholls) in August: best at 5f: acts on all-weather and firm going: tried tongue tied/visored: races prominently: unreliable. *P. R. Chamings*

HAWK FLYER (USA)   3 b.c. Silver Hawk (USA) 123 – Dawn's Curtsey (USA) (Far   **117** North (CAN) 120) [2003 7.9f² 10.3m* 12m* 12g³ 11.9m³ Aug 19] $275,000Y: tall, quite good-topped colt: closely related to a winner in USA by Benny The Dip and half-brother to several winners abroad, including US winner Triumph At Dawn (by Alydar), second in Grade 1 1m event: dam, US Grade 1 1¼m winner, half-sister to dam of very smart Irish/US middle-distance stayer Sunshine Street: smart performer: won maiden at Doncaster in June and minor event at Ascot in July: best efforts when third in Gordon Stakes at Goodwood (beaten ½ length by Phoenix Reach) and Great Voltigeur Stakes at York (3 lengths behind Powerscourt): should have been suited by 1¾m+: raced only on good going or firmer: put down after shattering a pastern on gallops in week before St Leger. *Sir Michael Stoute*

HAWKIT (USA)   2 b.g. (Apr 21) Silver Hawk (USA) 123 – Hey Ghaz (USA) (Ghazi   **72** (USA)) [2003 8g² 7s³ f8.5g² f8.5g² f8s³ f8g³ Dec 19] $32,000Y: rather leggy gelding: first foal: dam 6f winner in USA: fair maiden: placed all starts: stays 8.5f: raced freely second/third outings. *J. A. Osborne*

HAWKLEY   4 ch.g. Arctic Tern (USA) 126 – Last Ambition (IRE) 29 (Cadeaux Genereux 131) [2003 71: f8g Mar 20] lengthy gelding: fair performer in 2002: well beaten only   **–** 4-y-o outing. *P. W. D'Arcy*

HAWKSBILL (USA)   3 ch.c. Silver Hawk (USA) 123 – Binary 109 (Rainbow Quest   **113** (USA) 134) [2003 9m* 10s² 11.6g³ 9.9m⁵ 10g⁴ 10g Oct 31] medium-sized, good-topped colt: has a round action: third foal: half-brother to 5-y-o Binary File: dam 9f/1¼m winner in France/USA, sister to smart 1½m performer Bequeath from very good family: smart performer: won maiden at Goodwood in June: good efforts after in minor event at Ascot (short-head second to Howle Hill) and handicap at Ascot (reared leaving stall when fourth to Counsel's Opinion): below form in listed race at Newmarket final outing: will probably prove best around 1¼m: acts on soft going, probably on good to firm: has worn crossed noseband: free-going sort: joined R. Frankel in USA. *J. H. M. Gosden*

HAWK WING (USA) 4 b.c. Woodman (USA) 126 – La Lorgnette (CAN) (Val de **136** L'Orne (FR) 133) [2003 127: 8m* 8f⁶ Jun 17]

How far is too far? An eleven-length winning margin in a Group 1 race, apparently. Scarcely can a top horse have been so maligned as Hawk Wing during his career, some of the reactions to an all-the-way eleven-length spreadeagling of a field of top older milers in the Lockinge Stakes at Newbury in May bringing to mind a quote from Oscar Wilde that 'the play was a great success, but the audience was a disaster.' It is a truism in sport that reputations are hard to earn and easy to lose, and though Hawk Wing was lauded immediately after Newbury it didn't take long for his detractors to start dismissing the performance, especially after his defeat when odds on for the Queen Anne Stakes. Hawk Wing, who wasn't asked to lead on this occasion, found little and trailed home seventh (promoted to sixth) of ten at Royal Ascot and afterwards was found by the racecourse vet to be lame in front. Further examination revealed a near-fore knee ligament strain, and his racing career came to an end with an announcement in August that the injury had not responded sufficiently for him to be raced again.

The respected bloodstock writer Tony Morris, one of Hawk Wing's fiercest critics, described him, after the announcement of his retirement, as 'a real charlatan if ever there was one . . . an old rogue whose Lockinge victory always looked too good to be true.' To another *Racing Post* correspondent he was 'the discredited Hawk Wing', while *The Sun* quoted an unnamed professional punter as labelling Hawk Wing 'a dog who chucks it in if he doesn't have his own way.' Hawk Wing's Lockinge performance was, for some, too far ahead of any of his other form for the result to be accepted, at least in anything like face value. It was a false result, merely 'early-season' form which some had been carried away with, Hawk Wing had had things very much his own way and it might well have been different if 'the big bully' had been taken on—these were the planks of the argument used to undermine Hawk Wing's Newbury performance. It showed how easy it is to fall into the trap of rationalising the result of a horserace to fit one's preconceptions. Hawk Wing's high head carriage, and the fact that he had won only one race as a three-year-old— the Eclipse—and had been a beaten favourite in four Group 1 races, went a long way to convincing some that he was ungenuine. Ultimately, a good judge should be wary of accepting an explanation which reflects upon a horse's honesty if there is another plausible explanation. It is wisest to regard all racehorses as genuine unless there is convincing evidence to the contrary. In our view, there had been no such convincing evidence where Hawk Wing's three-year-old performances had been concerned. He came an unlucky second to Rock of Gibraltar in the Two Thousand Guineas, just failing with a spectacular late surge; a fine second to High Chaparral in the Derby, over a distance which there was no cast-iron guarantee on pedigree that he would stay; a creditable second in the Irish Champion, in which he was caught in the final stride; and, back at a mile for the first time since the Guineas, was below form in the Queen Elizabeth II Stakes in a race which effectively developed into a sprint. Hawk Wing's three-year-old campaign, interrupted when he was among the sufferers from a coughing virus that affected Ballydoyle's horses in late-summer, had concluded with an abortive tilt at the Breeders' Cup Classic on dirt, the first time in ten starts that he had finished out of the first two.

The massed ranks of Ballydoyle's 2003 classic and championship contenders went on public view in a workout after racing at the Curragh on Sunday March 23rd, the day the stable's first two-year-old runner Colossus won and Ireland's Ballydoyle-trained top-rated two-year-old of 2002 Tomahawk completed a straightforward task on his reappearance. While the members of the media were naturally keen to discuss Ballydoyle's classic plans, there was added interest in Hawk Wing and dual Derby and Breeders' Cup winner High Chaparral, who had both been kept in training. Hawk Wing looked in tremendous shape, seeming to have done well physically over the winter, and worked well over a mile with the useful Sahara Desert, who had acted as a pacemaker for some of the stable's leading lights the previous year. Trainer Aidan O'Brien had said of Hawk Wing, at a similar juncture the previous year, that 'If we have a horse to win the triple crown he is it. He could be anything.' Perhaps Ballydoyle felt, in hindsight, that such a prediction might have grated with some, as might other remarks, such as O'Brien's quote before Hawk Wing ran in the Derby that he 'looks like Nijinsky and has the same great presence,' and the trainer's view that 'Hawk Wing would have no problem coming back to the July Cup.' O'Brien confined himself at the 2003 media briefing to a remark that Hawk Wing's work had been 'exceptional' and that Seamus Heffernan, who had been riding Hawk Wing at home, had been 'sizzling' about him. Some of O'Brien's comments after Hawk Wing's Lockinge victory provided an interesting insight: 'He's a very dangerous type of horse because he can make you say things, as everybody saw last year . . . I've learned you have to be very careful . . . If I blow up a horse too much because I believe it, the horse can pay the penalty.'

O'Brien, it seemed, was resolved to let Hawk Wing's performances as a four-year-old largely speak for themselves, though privately he forecast that 'two televisions will be needed to watch the Lockinge'—one to follow Hawk Wing and the other to pick out the opposition. The prophecy wasn't far out. When the normally trail-blazing Desert Deer was withdrawn after refusing to go into his stall, Michael Kinane decided on a change in his normal riding tactics on Hawk Wing, allowing him to stride along in front from the start and gradually stepping up the tempo. None of his five rivals was ever in the race with him or ever even looked like getting into the race from halfway, all of them toiling in Hawk Wing's wake from fully three furlongs out. Stretching further and further clear through the last furlong, edging right late on, Hawk Wing recorded a majestic victory, which, albeit belatedly, lived up to his home reputation. It was an extraordinary performance, Hawk Wing's Queen Elizabeth II Stakes conqueror Where Or When finishing eight lengths clear of third-placed Olden Times, who had shown himself every bit as good as ever when returning from nearly twelve months on the sidelines to win an up-to-scratch renewal of the Earl of Sefton Stakes at Newmarket on his reappearance. French-trained Domedriver, who had ended Rock of Gibraltar's seven-race sequence of Group 1 victories in the Breeders' Cup Mile, finished a length behind Olden Times in fourth, with Reel Buddy fifth, after racing alone on the stand rail, and Tillerman bringing up the rear. Domedriver's trainer was quick to label the Lockinge a 'messy' race—'with one runner on the stand rail and the others stretched out up the centre, it was no good for Domedriver'—while Where Or When's

Juddmonte Lockinge Stakes, Newbury—a double-page spread required
as Hawk Wing turns this Group 1 race into a spectacularly one-sided affair, making all in a downpour
to win by eleven lengths from Where Or When (right); Olden Times (second right) is third

jockey thought his mount might have been 'a little ring rusty' and John Dunlop, trainer of Olden Times, called it a 'strange race on false ground' (the going was good to firm—officially good—but there was a heavy downpour during the race).

    Group 1 races on the Flat have been won by wider margins than eleven lengths, and a wide-margin victory, even in a top race, does not guarantee the rating of a champion. Turtle Island won the 1994 Irish Two Thousand Guineas by fifteen lengths and Paean the 1987 Gold Cup by the same margin, but both races took place under extreme conditions which accentuated the winner's superiority and neither horse was rated up with the best. It was different with twelve-length Group 1 winners Sun Princess (who beat the colts in the St Leger after setting an Oaks record-winning margin), St Jovite (Irish Derby) and Celtic Swing (Racing Post Trophy), all of whom were outstanding in their sphere. Whatever the complexities of individual races, the task of assessing winners who are made to show the full measure of their superiority over the opposition is more straightforward than assessing those who win seemingly without coming off the bridle. The performances were there in black and white for such greats as Shergar (Derby by ten lengths, Chester Vase by twelve and Sandown Classic Trial by ten), Brigadier Gerard (whose brilliant record included a ten-length win in the Goodwood Mile), Mill Reef (including both the Gimcrack Stakes and Prix Ganay by ten) and, further back, Ribot (including the Premio del Jockey Club by fifteen). It is, however, always as well to keep in mind a horse's overall record. Hawk Wing's overall record does not mark him as one of the great horses, to be ranked alongside the likes of Shergar, Brigadier Gerard, Mill Reef and Ribot, for example. Ribot was unbeaten in sixteen races, Brigadier Gerard was beaten only once in eighteen and Mill Reef only twice in fourteen (Shergar, raced only at two and three, won six out of eight).

    Hawk Wing's performance in the Lockinge created plenty of debate, not least because it raised fundamental issues about how the merit of horses should be assessed. Many appear to think that handicapping is simply a matter of finding a horse which has run to form—a 'yardstick'—and basing the entire assessment of a race on this assumption. Interpreting the Lockinge in this way, using the Timeform ratings of the other runners going into the race, would have provided a figure for Hawk Wing that took him to the top of the scale. There were some who claimed such a figure would have been justified. Form analysis is more sophisticated than

that, though, with a variety of other tools at the disposal of the handicapper. There is wisdom in the old handicapping adage that 'you should rate horses on races, not races on horses'. The accepted way of achieving this is through race standardisation, a method of form analysis that has stood the test of time in all sorts of races for which there is historical data. Race standardisation, using the general level of form of past runnings of a race, or similar races, as a guide, is of particular value when collateral lines of form are unclear, or don't exist at all, for instance in some two-year-old handicapping. Sometimes, however, history is not a reliable guide, because the standard of a race is shown by the figures to fluctuate more widely than usual from one year to another. History is most likely to provide a reliable guide in a race such as the Lockinge, a Group 1 event, which, by definition, attracts a similar type of horse year in, year out. Adjusting, among other things, for the weights carried, the distances between the horses, the overall race times and the size of the fields, the historical race standards produced by Timeform for past runnings of the Lockinge essentially indicated that, given the result of the latest running of the Lockinge, it would be unusual—though not impossible—for the rating of the winner to fall outside the range of 135 to 144.

Time analysis is another important aid to form study. Analysis of overall race times has been used by Timeform down the years, the computations involving sophisticated reference to a vast pool of data. The Timeform computer timefigure for Hawk Wing in the Lockinge Stakes, on a day when heavy rain for about twenty minutes during and after that race and a light wind mostly across the runners complicated matters slightly, was 1.24 fast, equivalent to a timerating of 131. This is the timerating of a top-class Group 1 performance—only Oasis Dream in the Nunthorpe recorded a higher figure in the latest season—though it didn't, in itself, support claims that Hawk Wing was quite so good at Newbury as some literal interpretations suggested. Authoritative sectional timing analysis would have shed more light on the construction of the overall time of the Lockinge, but Newbury has yet to take a leaf out of the go-ahead Newmarket racecourse executive's book and produce accurate electrically-timed sectionals (disappointingly, these have stopped being published in the *Racing Post*, though are still available on request from Newmarket racecourse).

So much for race standards and times, what about collateral form considerations in the Lockinge? The value of Hawk Wing's beating Where Or When by eleven lengths could be questioned at the time, but it can be viewed in a wider context with the benefit of hindsight. Where Or When wasn't quite the same horse in 2003 as in the previous season—his Timeform rating is 6 lb lower—and his presence in second certainly attests to the fact that none of the horses further down the field in the Lockinge ran to form. However, Where Or When still received a significantly bigger beating from Hawk Wing in the Lockinge than from any other horse during the year. Where Or When finished two and three quarter lengths closer to Dubai Destination when fourth (promoted to third) in the Queen Anne, over eight and a half lengths closer to Priors Lodge when fourth in the Celebration Mile, six lengths closer to Nebraska Tornado when sixth in the Moulin and three and a quarter lengths closer to Falbrav when sixth in the Queen Elizabeth. It seems fair to say that it must still have taken a very good horse indeed to beat Where Or When by eleven lengths in the latest season. It is just possible, of course, that Hawk Wing himself was the only horse to give his true running at Newbury and that he did not improve on his previous efforts. Possible, but unlikely, taking everything, including his timefigure, into account. It could, on the other hand, be argued that our assessment of Hawk Wing is conservative, though his rating reflects a single performance and does not define him as the 'champion' of 2003. Other horses over the year, notably Falbrav, achieved a greater number of top-class performances. According to some, not enough 'common sense' is used in deciding end-of-season ratings or rankings. One performance proves nothing, they say, and a horse like Hawk Wing should not be rated ahead of a horse so splendidly consistent as Falbrav. There may be something in the argument—though it is not entirely compelling—that the ratings of top horses who have finished their racing careers should be treated more flexibly. The ratings of a good number of the best horses in an annual like *Racehorses* are, after all, largely of academic, rather than practical value. But handicapping in general could never be conducted in this way. Taking account of such

440

attributes as toughness, consistency and versatility when rating horses would be penalising the very attributes that the critics themselves rightly hold so dear. The connections of horses campaigned honestly and enterprisingly, and raced regularly, would be horrified if they thought these factors were being taken into account in the handicap marks allotted to their horses. Likewise, there would be an outcry if a handicapper took the view that 'one performance proved nothing' and allowed a wide margin winner to go unpenalised while it was given another chance to repeat the form.

Hawk Wing's four-year-old campaign may have ended in humiliating fashion, but it did lead to his trainer revealing after the Queen Anne that Hawk Wing had been found at the end of his three-year-old career to have had 'loads of niggling little problems in his shoulders and quarters.' If such problems had affected him in any of his races, it might be argued that it made his performances as a three-year-old all the more meritorious. 'There was always a danger this could happen,' said O'Brien at Royal Ascot. 'We only had three and a half weeks between Newbury and now, and it just wasn't enough time to go through him with a fine tooth comb, if I'd gone through every hair of his body I'd probably have found something and he wouldn't have turned up today.' It was a pity that Hawk Wing's final season on the track was so short, but his Lockinge performance did at least come close to validating his trainer's opinion of him that he was probably the best horse trained at Ballydoyle since triple crown winner Nijinsky. The dual Prix de l'Arc winner Alleged matched Nijinsky's Timeform rating of 138, while both El Gran Senor and Thatch (who incidentally won a two-runner St James's Palace by

Mrs John Magnier's "Hawk Wing"

fifteen lengths) were rated the same as Hawk Wing. Hawk Wing won Group 1 races at two, three and four, a feat also achieved by High Chaparral. The Lockinge represents clearly the best performance of Hawk Wing's career—it was the best over a mile since Mark of Esteem's in the Queen Elizabeth II Stakes in 1996—and he also showed high-class form at a mile and a quarter and a mile and a half. Hawk Wing acted on good to firm and good to soft going, and ran well below form on his only start on dirt. He was usually waited with and wore a crossed noseband.

Hawk Wing (USA) (b.c. 1999)	Woodman (USA) (ch 1983)	Mr Prospector (b 1970)	Raise A Native
			Gold Digger
		Playmate (ch 1975)	Buckpasser
			Intriguing
	La Lorgnette (CAN) (b 1982)	Val de L'Orne (b 1972)	Val de Loir
			Aglae
		The Temptress (b 1973)	Nijinsky
			La Sevillana

The big, close-coupled Hawk Wing has a fine physique, as his portrait shows, and he was also an impressive mover with a fluent action. Hawk Wing is by the Mr Prospector stallion Woodman, a high-class two-year-old but not seen out after being well beaten on his reappearance at three. Woodman has had a mixed record at stud, the highlights including such as Bosra Sham and Hector Protector and American classic winners Hansel and Timber Country. But Woodman has also earned something of a reputation for siring types who don't always live up to their potential. The lack of resolution shown by some of Woodman's progeny was, incidentally, another factor that probably led to Hawk Wing's courage coming under suspicion in some quarters. Though the average distance of races won by Woodman's offspring in Europe is just over nine furlongs, he has had winners over a wide range of distances; Hansel and Prix Lupin winner Ciro were both successful at a mile and a half in North America and the Irish Derby runner-up Dr Johnson won at a mile and three quarters. Hawk Wing was the last foal of La Lorgnette, whose five victories included the Canadian Oaks and a leg of the Canadian triple crown, the Queen's Plate, against colts over a mile and a quarter; the stoutly-bred La Lorgnette was also runner-up in the mile-and-a-half Prince of Wales Stakes, another leg of Canada's triple crown. Six of La Lorgnette's other foals were winners, the most significant of them another individual by a son of Mr Prospector, the Conquistador Cielo filly Alexandrina, a winning stakes performer in Canada and the dam of Canadian International winner Thornfield. Hawk Wing will have two Epsom Oaks winners, Imagine and Lady Carla, among the mares visiting him in his first season at Coolmore, where he will stand at a fee of €25,000 (October 1st terms). Also in Hawk Wing's first book of mares will be Offshore Boom, the dam of his Two Thousand Guineas conqueror Rock of Gibraltar. *A. P. O'Brien, Ireland*

HAWRIDGE PRINCE 3 b.g. Polar Falcon (USA) 126 – Zahwa 72 (Cadeaux Gene-   **84 p**
reux 131) [2003 7m 8.3m³ 8.3d* 10g² Oct 6] 15,000F, 10,000Y: big, lengthy gelding: third foal: half-brother to smart 1m winner Hero's Journey (by Halling): dam, German 7f/1m winner: progressive form: won maiden at Windsor in August: best effort when second to Crimson Dancer in handicap at same course final start: stays 1¼m: unraced on extremes of going: slowly away second outing: lightly raced, and likely to make a useful performer. *L. G. Cottrell*

HAYHAAT (USA) 3 ch.f. Irish River (FR) 131 – Ball Gown (USA) (Silver Hawk   **77**
(USA) 123) [2003 81: 7.5m³ 10d⁶ 11.1g⁵ 12.4g³ 12d* Nov 4] lengthy, angular filly: fair performer: won maiden at Catterick in November by 8 lengths: stays 12.4f: unraced on extremes of going: sold 33,000 gns. *B. W. Hills*

HAYSTACKS (IRE) 7 b.g. Contract Law (USA) 108 – Florissa (FR) (Persepolis   **–**
(FR) 127) [2003 16.1d 12.4g 14m⁶ 14.1m 16.2d⁶ 17.1m Aug 17] strong, close-coupled gelding: modest handicapper: missed 2002: well held in 2003: often visored: difficult ride. *James Moffatt*

HAZE BABYBEAR 3 b.f. Mujadil (USA) 119 – River's Rising (FR) 88 (Mendez   **64**
(FR) 128) [2003 66: 7m 6.1m 6d f5s³ f6s³ 5d* 5g Jul 24] leggy, unfurnished filly: modest performer: won maiden at Beverley in July: stays easy 6f: acts on fibresand and good to soft going. *R. A. Fahey*

Freephone Stanley Zetland Gold Cup (Handicap), Redcar—
the lightly-raced Hazim wins this valuable event on his handicap debut; Cat's Whiskers is a close second

HAZEWIND 2 gr.g. (Feb 24) Daylami (IRE) 138 – Fragrant Oasis (USA) 113 (Rahy   –
(USA) 115) [2003 7m 7m Sep 23] smallish, stocky gelding: first foal: dam 7f winner,
including at 2 yrs: green, behind in maidens at Newmarket: sold 8,000 gns, then gelded.
E. A. L. Dunlop

HAZIM 4 b.c. Darshaan 133 – Souk (IRE) 98 (Ahonoora 122) [2003 98: 10m* 12f 10.4f   **108 +**
Jul 12] tall, rather leggy colt: useful handicapper, lightly raced: improved form when
winning Zetland Gold Cup at Redcar in May by ¾ length from Cat's Whiskers: met
plenty of trouble when mid-field in Duke of Edinburgh Stakes at Royal Ascot and John
Smith's Cup at York: will stay at least 1½m: acts on firm and good to soft going: tends to
sweat. *Sir Michael Stoute*

HAZY 3 b.f. Vettori (IRE) 119 – Shifting Mist 76 (Night Shift (USA)) [2003 7g^6 7f f6g   –
f6f^5 6m f7s Sep 26] 4,500Y: fifth foal: half-sister to 2 winners, including 4-y-o Cal Mac:
dam 1¼m to 1¾m winner: no form in maidens/handicap: tried in cheekpieces/visor.
R. M. H. Cowell

HAZY MORN 4 gr.f. Cyrano de Bergerac 120 – Hazy Kay (IRE) 77 (Treasure Kay   –
114) [2003 5.3f^6 8f^6 Sep 8] close-coupled filly: modest maiden at 2 yrs, has shown little
since: tried blinkered. *R. J. Hodges*

HAZYVIEW 2 b.c. (Feb 25) Cape Cross (IRE) 129 – Euridice (IRE) 66 (Woodman   **69 p**
(USA) 126) [2003 7m 7m 8m 8m^3 8d* Oct 31] 70,000F, 80,000Y: strong, attractive colt:
poor mover: fifth foal: closely related to German 6f to 1m winner Ewington (by Owington) and half-brother to fairly useful 2000 2-y-o 8.5f winner Dusty Carpet (by Pivotal)
and Irish 2m winner Delphi (by Grand Lodge): dam 1¼m winner who probably stayed
15f: fair performer: won nursery at Brighton by head from Keshya: will stay at least 1¼m:
acts on good to firm and good to soft ground: should progress. *N. A. Callaghan*

HEAD BOY 2 ch.g. (Mar 5) Forzando 122 – Don't Jump (IRE) 71 (Entitled 126) [2003   **58**
6d 6g 6d 6g^5 7m* 7m Oct 23] 12,000F, 14,000Y: fourth foal: dam 1m winner: modest
performer: 40/1, won nursery at Lingfield in October: stays 7f: acts on good to firm
ground. *S. Dow*

HEADLAND (USA) 5 b. or br.g. Distant View (USA) 126 – Fijar Echo (USA) (In   **63 §**
Fijar (USA) 121) [2003 ?, a95: f7s p7g f7g* f7g^2 7m 6m 8g 7m^4 7m p7g f7g f6s f6g^4 f6g*   **a88 d**
Dec 19] well-made gelding: fairly useful on all-weather, modest on turf: won handicap at
Wolverhampton in February and, having left J. Eustace after ninth start, seller at Southwell in December: best at 6f/7f: acts on all-weather and good to firm going: tried tongue
tied, usually visored/blinkered: refused to race fifth outing: has refused to enter stall:
sometimes very slowly away: often makes running: unreliable. *D. W. Chapman*

443

HEAD OF COLLEGE (IRE) 3 ch.c. Ashkalani (IRE) 128 – Ceide Dancer (IRE) –
79 (Alzao (USA) 117) [2003 63: f6g 6m Jul 2] smallish, sturdy colt: modest maiden at 2
yrs: well beaten both 3-y-o starts: tried blinkered/tongue tied. *M. C. Chapman*

HEAD OF STATE 2 b.g. (Feb 8) Primo Dominie 121 – Lets Be Fair 94 (Efisio 120) 53
[2003 5m 5m f5g⁶ f5g* Dec 22] 23,000Y: strong gelding: second foal: half-brother to
3-y-o Beauvrai: dam 2-y-o 5f winner: modest performer: gambled on, easily best effort
when making all in 5-runner nursery at Wolverhampton: will probably prove best at 5f.
R. M. Beckett

HEADS YOUR GRAY 2 gr.g. (Mar 13) Atraf 116 – Port Hedland 43 (Then Again –
126) [2003 6g⁴ 6m 8d Aug 1] 2,500F, 1,500Y: well-grown, workmanlike gelding: third
foal: half-brother to winner in Holland by Puissance: dam little form: signs of only a little
ability in minor event/maidens. *D. Morris*

HEAD TO KERRY (IRE) 3 b.g. Eagle Eyed (USA) 111 – The Poachers Lady (IRE) 77
(Salmon Leap (USA) 131) [2003 –: 11.6g 10m⁵ 11.8m³ 11.9m⁶ f12g² 12m* 14.4g³ 12g⁵
16m* 16f³ Oct 12] lengthy gelding: fair handicapper: progressed well, winning at Goodwood in August (hung left) and September: stays easy 2m: acts on firm going and
fibresand: usually races prominently. *D. J. S. ffrench Davis*

HEALEY (IRE) 5 ch.g. Dr Devious (IRE) 127 – Bean Siamsa (Solinus 130) [2003 49
65d: f11g⁴ f9.4g 10m³ 10s² Jun 30] lengthy, quite good-topped gelding: poor performer:
left C. Dwyer after second start: stays 1½m: acts on any going: tried blinkered/tongue
tied/in cheekpieces: none too consistent. *P. R. Wood*

HEARTBEAT 2 b.f. (Mar 19) Pursuit of Love 124 – Lyrical Bid (USA) 77 (Lyphard –
(USA) 132) [2003 6m f7g⁶ Jun 30] good-bodied filly: third foal: half-sister to winner in
Spain by Primo Dominie: dam, 2-y-o 7.5f winner on only start, half-sister to useful
winner up to 2m On Call: signs of only a little ability in maidens at Redcar and Wolverhampton: sold 1,050 gns in December. *M. A. Jarvis*

HEARTBREAKER (IRE) 3 b.g. In Command (IRE) 114 – No Hard Feelings (IRE) –
86 (Alzao (USA) 117) [2003 –: 7m 16.2m Jul 21] strong gelding: no form. *M. W. Easterby*

HEARTHSTEAD DREAM 2 ch.c. (Feb 12) Dr Fong (USA) 128 – Robin Lane 98 72
(Tenby 125) [2003 6m 6m³ 7.1m² 8s Nov 3] long-backed colt: first foal: dam,
9f to 1½m winner, granddaughter of Criterium des Pouliches winner Hippodamia: fair
maiden: ran badly after absence final start: should stay at least 1m: acts on good to firm
ground: carried head high second start (best effort). *M. Johnston*

HEARTHSTEAD PRIDE 4 ch.g. Dr Devious (IRE) 127 – Western Heights (Shirley 71
Heights 130) [2003 88: 12g⁶ 16m Mar 27] angular gelding: fair handicapper: stayed
easy 14.6f: acted on fibresand, raced only on good/good to firm ground on turf: dead.
M. Johnston

HEART'S DESIRE (IRE) 2 b.f. (Mar 6) Royal Applause 124 – Touch And Love 79 p
(IRE) (Green Desert (USA) 127) [2003 6m⁵ 7s² Oct 29] half-sister to several winners,
including useful French 7f (at 2 yrs) and 1m winner Bashful (by Brief Truce): dam, useful
French sprinter, out of half-sister to top-class miler Sure Blade: better effort in maidens
(fair form) when neck second of 13 to Singing Poet at Yarmouth, strong challenge close
home: should stay 1m: open to improvement. *B. W. Hills*

HEARTS 'N MINDS 3 ch.f. Mark of Esteem (IRE) 137 – Magical Retreat (USA) 100
115 (Sir Ivor 135) [2003 p7g 10m⁵ 10g⁴ 9.9g³ 12g 11.9f³ p12g* Jul 23] tall, leggy filly:
fourth foal: dam, 1¼m winner who stayed 14.8f, second in Yorkshire Oaks at 4 yrs: useful
performer: dead-heated in maiden at Lingfield in July: best efforts when in frame in listed
races at Newmarket (to Hi Dubai) and Goodwood (2¾ lengths third to Ocean Silk) on
third/fourth starts: stayed 1½m: acted on polytrack, best turf efforts on good going: had
awkward head carriage: dead. *C. A. Cyzer*

HEART SPRINGS 3 b.f. Parthian Springs 114 – Metannee 63 (The Brianstan 128) –
[2003 p12g 10g Oct 25] leggy filly: third live foal: dam, maiden who stayed 1¾m, winning hurdler: little form in maidens: slowly away on debut, wandered/flashed tail second
outing. *Dr J. R. J. Naylor*

HEATHYARDSBLESSING (IRE) 6 b.g. Unbless 117 – Noble Nadia (Thatching 53
131) [2003 79d: f6s 5m f5g 5g f7g⁶ f6g² f6g³ Dec 19] quite good-topped gelding: useful
winner at 2 yrs, just modest nowadays: stays 6f: acts on fibresand, firm and good to soft
ground: sometimes carries head awkwardly. *R. Hollinshead*

HEATHYARDS JOY 2 ch.f. (May 14) Komaite (USA) – Heathyards Lady (USA) –
76 (Mining (USA)) [2003 6.1f Oct 1] 1,800Y: third foal: dam 6f to 8.5f winner: 125/1,
last of 7 in minor event at Nottingham. *R. Hollinshead*

HEATHYARDS MATE 6 b.g. Timeless Times (USA) 99 – Quenlyn (Welsh Pageant – 132) [2003 45: f8s f9.4g Jan 17] sturdy, close-coupled gelding: poor performer: well held in cheekpieces/blinkers in 2003. *R. J. Baker*

HEATHYARDS PRIDE 3 b.g. Polar Prince (IRE) 117 – Heathyards Lady (USA) 76 **43 p** (Mining (USA)) [2003 f12s⁴ Dec 13] second foal: dam 6f to 8.5f winner: 33/1 and green, well-beaten fourth of 14 in maiden at Southwell. *R. Hollinshead*

HEATHYARDS SWING 5 b.g. Celtic Swing 138 – Butsova 93 (Formidable (USA) **57 §** 125) [2003 72: 11.8g 12.4g 10d f9.4g⁵ 10m f12g f12s² f11g f12s⁵ f12g² Jun 25] quite good-topped gelding: modest performer: stays 1½m: acts on good to firm going, good to soft and fibresand: tried in cheekpieces/blinkers: ungenuine: sold £2,300. *R. Hollinshead*

HEAVENLY BAY (USA) 3 b.f. Rahy (USA) 115 – Bevel (USA) (Mr Prospector **90** (USA)) [2003 9.7g³ 6m³ 8g² 11.8m³ 10m 12m² 11.9m* 14.6d 12f Oct 12] good-topped filly: sixth living foal: closely related to 9-y-o Bevier: dam, French 1m winner, out of close relative of Ajdal and half-sister to Formidable and to grandam of Arazi and Noverre (by Rahy): fairly useful performer: landed odds in 3-runner maiden at Haydock in August: best efforts when placed in listed events at Ascot and Lingfield (third to Santa Sophia) third/fourth starts: stays 1½m: acts on good to firm ground. *C. E. Brittain*

HEBENUS 4 b.g. Hamas (IRE) 125§ – Stinging Nettle 90 (Sharpen Up 127) [2003 62: **50** 7.1d 6d 6f⁵ 5.9f f6g⁶ 8g 9.2g⁵ 8m² 8.3m⁵ 8m Aug 25] lengthy gelding: modest performer: stays 1m: acts on firm and good to soft going: tried blinkered: sold £3,000. *R. A. Fahey*

HECTIC TINA 4 ch.f. Hector Protector (USA) 124 – Tinashaan (IRE) 100 (Darshaan – 133) [2003 85: 9d May 2] good-topped filly: fair maiden, lightly raced: tailed off in listed race at Newmarket only 4-y-o start. *Jedd O'Keeffe*

HECTOR'S GIRL 3 ch.f. Hector Protector (USA) 124 – Present Imperfect 61 **99** (Cadeaux Genereux 131) [2003 95p: 7g³ 8g 8f⁶ Aug 17] lengthy filly: useful performer, lightly raced: best effort when 2¼ lengths third to Khulood in Nell Gwyn Stakes at Newmarket on reappearance: stays 7f, not 1m (in rear in 1000 Guineas at Newmarket on first occasion, then off 3½ months): best form on good going: edgy/free-going sort. *Sir Michael Stoute*

HECUBA 3 ch.f. Hector Protector (USA) 124 – Ajuga (USA) 102 (The Minstrel (CAN) **93** 135) [2003 79p: 10m* 11.4m⁵ 10m³ 14g 14.1s Oct 29] strong, lengthy filly: fairly useful performer: won maiden at Ripon in April by 10 lengths: well held last 3 starts: stays 11.4f: acts on good to firm ground: often makes running: sold 27,000 gns. *B. W. Hills*

HEFIN 6 ch.g. Red Rainbow 105 – Summer Impressions (USA) 70 (Lyphard (USA) **74** 132) [2003 56: 13.3m² 14g 16f² p16g* 15.4m³ f14.8g p16g³ 16m³ 14.1m* p16g³ p16g* Nov 26] rather sparely-made gelding: fair handicapper: won at Lingfield in July, Salisbury in October and Lingfield in November: stays 2m: acts on firm going, good to soft and polytrack (ran badly on fibresand): usually waited with: consistent. *I. A. Wood*

HEIDELBURG (IRE) 3 b.f. Night Shift (USA) – Solar Attraction (IRE) 60 (Salt **63** Dome (USA)) [2003 76: p6g 5.1d p7g⁴ 7g f7g⁶ 9g p7g⁶ f6g² p8g³ p7g f7g p7g Dec 30] **a74** quite attractive filly: fair handicapper on all-weather, modest on turf: stays 1m: acts on all-weather, yet to race on extremes of going on turf: blinkered (ran poorly) once. *S. Kirk*

HEIR TO BE 4 b.g. Elmaamul (USA) 125 – Princess Genista 108 (Ile de Bourbon **84** (USA) 133) [2003 87p: 16m 14.1g 16.1d* 20m 16.1m 21d⁶ Jul 30] angular gelding: fairly useful handicapper: won at Newcastle in May: stays 2m: best on good going or softer. *J. L. Dunlop*

HEIR TODAY (IRE) 2 b.f. (Jan 4) Princely Heir (IRE) 111 – Ransomed (IRE) (Ballad **69** Rock 122) [2003 5.1f 5g 5.3f² 6m* 6m 6.1m 5m Oct 25] IR 14,000F, €8,000Y: lengthy, good-topped filly: fifth foal: half-sister to Irish 2001 2-y-o 6f winner No Apologies (by Eagle Eyed) and winner in Japan by Be My Guest: dam Irish 1¼m winner: fair performer: won nursery at Kempton in August: likely to prove best at 5f/6f: acts on firm going: best efforts racing prominently: sent to USA. *R. M. Beckett*

HEIR TO THE THRONE (IRE) 2 b.c. (Mar 16) Desert Prince (IRE) 130 – Scan-**82** disk (IRE) 88 (Kenmare (FR) 125) [2003 8m³ 10m² Oct 22] 32,000F, 32,000YY: tall, good-topped colt: second foal: half-brother to winner in Italy by Desert King: dam 7f winner in Italy at 2 yrs: fairly useful form in maidens won by Art Trader at Newmarket and by Uncle Cent at Nottingham, slowly away both times: not sure to stay much beyond 1¼m: sent to USA. *Mrs A. J. Perrett*

HEISSE 3 b.c. Darshaan 133 – Hedera (USA) 90 (Woodman (USA) 126) [2003 12.4m* **101** 10.2m² 12m May 25] sturdy colt: second foal: half-brother to useful French performer up to 11.5f Ivy League (by Doyoun): dam, 2-y-o 7f winner who later stayed 1m, out of

445

Ribblesdale Stakes runner-up Ivrea: useful form: won maiden at Newcastle in April: plenty of improvement when ¾-length second to High Accolade in minor event at Bath, then respectable seventh to Osorio in Derby Italiano at Rome: stays 12.4f. *D. R. Loder*

HEKTIKOS 3 ch.g. Hector Protector (USA) 124 – Green Danube (USA) 92 (Irish River (FR) 131) [2003 70: p13g p13g Nov 12] sturdy, quite attractive gelding: lightly-raced maiden: well held both 3-y-o starts. *S. Dow*

HELDERBERG (USA) 3 b.f. Diesis 133 – Banissa (USA) (Lear Fan (USA) 130) **79** [2003 71p: 10m 10.4m 11m³ 11.5m⁵ 10g 10s 12g 9.2d² 8m² 7m* 10.3d Nov 7] lengthy, good-topped filly: fair performer: won handicap at Redcar in October: effective at 7f to 11f: acts on good to firm ground, probably on heavy: none too reliable: sold 11,500 gns. *C. E. Brittain*

HELEN BRADLEY (IRE) 4 ch.f. Indian Ridge 123 – Touraya (Tap On Wood 130) **–** [2003 81: p8g f8.5g f7g p7g p6g p8g Apr 5] tall, angular filly: fairly useful handicapper at 3 yrs: well held at 4 yrs: wore cheekpieces/blinkers last 4 starts. *N. P. Littmoden*

HELENSBURGH (IRE) 2 ch.c. (Apr 13) Mark of Esteem (IRE) 137 – Port Helene **69** 107 (Troy 137) [2003 9f⁴ 8.3d 10m Oct 22] big, angular colt: sixth living foal: half-brother to 2 winners in France, notably smart winner up to 15f Helen of Spain (by Sadler's Wells): dam, 1m (at 2 yrs) and 1½m winner who was third in Park Hill Stakes, from good family: easily best effort in maidens (fair form) when fourth at Redcar: should stay 1½m: acts on firm going: sold 8,000 gns. *M. Johnston*

HELIBEL (IRE) 2 gr.f. (Apr 20) Pivotal 124 – Boughtbyphone 62 (Warning 136) **73** [2003 6m⁴ 6m⁴ 6d² p5g⁴ Nov 12] IR 8,200F, €21,000Y, 32,000 2-y-o: third foal: half-sister to 4-y-o Pentecost and 3-y-o Stars At Midnight: dam, Irish maiden who stayed 1½m, half-sister to 6-y-o Capricho: fair maiden: second at Brighton: should stay 7f: carries head awkwardly. *Mrs A. J. Perrett*

HELLBENT 4 b.g. Selkirk (USA) 129 – Loure (USA) 66 (Lyphard (USA) 132) [2003 **–** 50: f8g Dec 15] modest maiden: well held only start in 2003. *J. A. Osborne*

HELLO HOLLY 6 b.m. Lake Coniston (IRE) 131 – Amandine (IRE) (Darshaan 133) **44** [2003 12m p13g⁶ p16g⁶ Nov 26] big, lengthy mare: poor handicapper: stays 13f: acts on polytrack and good to firm ground. *Mrs A. L. M. King*

HELLO IT'S ME 2 ch.g. (Jan 30) Deploy 131 – Evening Charm (IRE) (Bering 136) **78 p** [2003 8.1d³ 7.9f³ 8d* Nov 7] compact gelding: first foal: dam, French maiden, grand-daughter of Cheveley Park Stakes and 1000 Guineas winner Ma Biche: fair form in maidens: third at Haydock and York before winning 24-runner event at Doncaster by neck from Market Leader, taking good hold and leading close home: will be suited by 1¼m/1½m: open to progress. *H. J. Collingridge*

HELLO ROBERTO 2 b.f. (Mar 28) Up And At 'em 109 – Hello Hobson's (IRE) 67 **66** (Fayruz 116) [2003 6m 5m* 6.1m f5s³ 6f 6g⁴ 5.1d³ f5g² p5g⁴ Dec 17] quite good-topped **a80** filly: fourth foal: dam 5f/6f winner, including at 2 yrs: fairly useful on all-weather, fair on turf: won claimer at Beverley in July, then left R. Bastiman: good efforts after when in frame, including in nurseries: effective at 5f/6f: acts on all-weather, good to firm and good to soft ground: got upset in stall and ran poorly first/third outings. *M. J. Polglase*

HELM BANK 3 b.c. Wild Again (USA) – Imperial Bailiwick (IRE) 104 (Imperial **112** Frontier (USA) 112) [2003 97p: 10.4m 8.1v 11.9m⁵ 8m² Jun 19] rather leggy, useful-looking colt: smart performer, lightly raced: easily best effort when unlucky neck second to New Seeker in Britannia Handicap at Royal Ascot, short of room and finishing strongly to lead stand-side group near finish: likely to prove best at 1m/1¼m: acts on good to firm ground. *M. Johnston*

HENESEYS LEG 3 b.f. Sure Blade (USA) 130 – Away's Halo (USA) (Sunny's Halo **70** (CAN)) [2003 –: 7m 9.7m⁴ 10m* 9.7m² 11.9f² 12g⁶ 11.9f⁴ p10g⁵ Nov 2] fair handi-capper: won at Brighton in August: barely stays 1½m: acts on polytrack, raced only on good ground or firmer on turf: consistent. *John Berry*

HENGROVE 3 b. or br.f. Fraam 114 – Java Rupiah (IRE) (Hamas (IRE) 125§) [2003 **–** 49: f7g⁶ p6g⁶ 5.1m 5.7f Jun 14] modest maiden at 2 yrs: little form in 2003. *M. S. Saunders*

HENNDEY (IRE) 2 b.c. (Feb 17) Indian Ridge 123 – Del Deya (IRE) 117 (Caerleon **–** (USA) 132) [2003 6g Oct 24] good-bodied colt: second foal: dam, 9f/1¼m (including Pretty Polly Stakes) winner, out of sister to Oaks winner Unite: 9/1 and gone in coat, last of 19 in maiden at Newbury, carrying head awkwardly. *M. A. Jarvis*

HENRY AFRIKA (IRE) 5 b.g. Mujadil (USA) 119 – Floralia 81 (Auction Ring **80** (USA) 123) [2003 81+: 7d 8g f9.4g⁵ Nov 29] IR 20,000Y: fourth living foal: half-brother to 1m winners Dorissio (by Efisio) and Flavinia (in France, by Cadeaux Genereux): dam, 7f/9f winner, half-sister to smart miler Sugarfoot: useful handicapper in 2001 for E. Lynam: lightly raced since: wearing cheekpieces, only form in 2003 when fifth at Wolverhampton on British debut: barely stays 9.4f: acts on good to firm ground and fibresand: tried blinkered. *D. G. McArdle, Ireland*

HENRY HALL (IRE)   7 b.h. Common Grounds 118 – Sovereign Grace (IRE) 101   **103** (Standaan (FR) 118) [2003 97: 5f 5g* 5m⁵ 5m² 5g³ 5f 5f² 5m² 5m⁴ 5.2m³ 5.1m³ 5d⁶ 5d⁵ 5d* 5m³ Oct 25] leggy horse: has a round action: useful handicapper: won at Thirsk in May and Epsom (beat Madrasee a head) in October: good third to Smart Hostess at Doncaster final start: best at 5f: acts on firm and soft going: visored once: usually waited with: tough. *N. Tinkler*

HENRY ISLAND (IRE)   10 ch.g. Sharp Victor (USA) 114 – Monterana 99 (Sallust   **77** 134) [2003 68§: 14.1m 11.7m 11.9m 17.2f⁴ 17.2f² 19.1m* 15m* 16.2f⁴ 21d 16.2m* 16m⁴ 16m⁴ 17.2f⁴ 18m³ Oct 20] workmanlike gelding: good mover: fair handicapper: won at Warwick in June, July and August: stays 19f: acts on fibresand, soft and good to firm going: tends to sweat: waited with: sometimes find little. *Mrs A. J. Bowlby*

HENRY TUN   5 b.g. Chaddleworth (IRE) 103 – B Grade 59 (Lucky Wednesday 124)   **44 §** [2003 42§, a60§: f5g* f5s f5g⁶ f5g f5s² f5g* f5g² 5m 5g 5g⁵ f5g f5s f5g f5g³ f5g⁵ f5g f5g   **a68 §** Dec 16] tall gelding: fair on all-weather, poor on turf: won seller in January and handicap in May, both at Southwell: best at 5f: acts on fibresand and firm going: wears headgear: tried tongue tied: races prominently: unreliable. *J. Balding*

HENRY WINDSOR   3 b.g. Forzando 122 – Ski Baby (Petoski 135) [2003 66: 5d 6m   **59** 6m 5g 5.9m* 7.2m⁶ 7.5m 5.9m 6m* a10.5s⁶ a11g a7s a8g Dec 14] strong, close-coupled gelding: modest performer: won maiden at Carlisle in June and handicap at Folkestone (final start) for N. Tinkler) in August: effective at 5f/6f: acts on good to firm and good to soft going, well held on sand/fibresand: tongue tied last 6 starts in Britain, has worn cheekpieces: none too reliable. *J. Salguero, Spain*

HERACLEA   3 ch.f. Groom Dancer (USA) 128 – Tamassos 67 (Dance In Time   **54** (CAN)) [2003 8g⁵ 7m⁶ 8.1m³ 10.1g Jul 28] compact filly: closely related to fairly useful 1¼m winner Anikitos (by Nashwan) and half-sister to several winners, notably middle-distance performers Posidonas (very smart, by Slip Anchor) and Carry The Flag (smart, by Tenby): dam, 1¼m winner, half-sister to Ile de Chypre: modest maiden: should be suited by 1¼m+: sold 30,000 gns in December. *L. M. Cumani*

HERE COMES TOM   5 b.g. Puissance 110 – Young Holly (Risk Me (FR) 127) [2003   **–** –: p7g Jan 4] of little account: blinkered. *Jamie Poulton*

HERETIC   5 b.g. Bishop of Cashel 122 – Barford Lady 93 (Stanford 121§) [2003 114:   **110** 8.1g⁴ 8g* 8g 8g 8.2d Nov 6] good-bodied gelding: has a short, round action: smart per-former, lightly raced: won 4-runner minor event at Doncaster in July by 1¾ lengths from Salcombe: good fourth to Desert Deer in attheraces Mile at Sandown on reappearance: below form last 2 starts: best around 1m: has form on good to firm going, very best efforts on good or softer (yet to race on heavy). *J. R. Fanshawe*

HERE TO ME   2 ch.f. (Feb 20) Muhtarram (USA) 125 – Away To Me (Exit To   **73** Nowhere (USA) 122) [2003 6g³ 6m² 5m² 6.5m 6.1f³ 8m⁵ 7g 6.1d² Nov 6] 5,000Y: rather leggy, workmanlike filly: third foal: dam unraced: fair maiden: stays 1m: acts on good to soft going, probably on firm. *R. Hannon*

HERMINOE   3 b.f. Rainbow Quest (USA) 134 – Hamasaat (IRE) (Sadler's Wells   **83 ?** (USA) 132) [2003 10.5s⁵ 12g² 12.5g³ 12g⁴ 9.5d* 11m⁶ 14.1s 15s Nov 22] leggy filly: first foal: dam unraced close relation to smart 1¼m winner La Confederation out of Oaks/Irish Oaks winner Unite: fairly useful performer: won maiden at Les Sables-d'Olonne in June, then left H-A. Pantall, France 32,000 gns: stiff tasks in listed events last 3 starts: stays 12.5f: raced mainly on good going or softer. *W. R. Muir*

HERMIONE O REALLY   3 b.f. Overbury (IRE) 116 – Sallyoreally (IRE) 57   **–** (Common Grounds 118) [2003 9.2d 9d 9.3f 5f 6m 7.2g 5.9d 5m Aug 4] close-coupled filly: first foal: dam, maiden, probably stayed 1½m: of no account. *W. Storey*

HERNANDO'S BOY   2 b.g. (Apr 12) Hernando (FR) 127 – Leave At Dawn (Slip   **64 p** Anchor 136) [2003 7m 7m 7d Nov 4] 12,000Y: workmanlike gelding: fifth foal: half-brother to 1m winner Nassau Night (by Bahamian Bounty) and 1m winner in Sweden by Bin Ajwaad: dam unraced out of half-sister to smart miler Trojan Fen: modest form in maidens: seventh at Newcastle and Catterick (not knocked about) last 2 starts: will be suited by 1¼m+: should do better. *Mrs M. Reveley*

William Hill Great St Wilfrid Stakes (Handicap), Ripon—those drawn high dominate as Hidden Dragon (nearer camera) just edges out Undeterred; Mutawaqed and Budelli (visored) also make the frame

HERNE BAY (IRE) 3 b.g. Hernando (FR) 127 – Charita (IRE) 103 (Lycius (USA) 124) [2003 75: f11g* p10g f11s⁵ f12g³ 12m⁵ f12g⁴ 16.2f⁵ 12.6f 14.1d 16.2m* 16.2m⁴ 15.9d Sep 24] angular gelding: modest performer: won maiden at Southwell in January and selling handicap at Beverley (sold from M. Johnston) in August: cheekpieces, well held final start: stays 2m well: acts on fibresand and good to firm ground. *A. Bailey* **64**

HERODOTUS 5 b.g. Zafonic (USA) 130 – Thalestria (FR) 91 (Mill Reef (USA) 141) [2003 106§, a112§: p12g⁵ p10g⁶ p10g p12g f12g 12g⁵ 16m Apr 12] big, good sort: useful handicapper: best 5-y-o effort when fifth to Compton Commander at Lingfield on reappearance: tailed off (reportedly bled) final start: stays easy 1¾m: acts on polytrack, firm and soft going: tried tongue tied/blinkered: inconsistent: sent to France. *C. E. Brittain* **92 § a97 §**

HE'S A ROCKET (IRE) 2 b.c. (Feb 15) Indian Rocket 115 – Dellua (IRE) 69 (Suave Dancer (USA) 136) [2003 5g 5m⁴ 5f⁴ 7m⁵ 7m⁶ 6.1m f7s f6g p6g f6g³ Dec 15] IR 5,000F, €6,500Y: close-coupled colt: first foal: dam 1¼m/1½m winner: modest maiden: effective at 5f/6f: acts on firm going and fibresand: visored (ran creditably) final start: refused to enter stall fourth intended outing. *Mrs C. A. Dunnett* **51**

HESELRIG (IRE) 2 b.g. (Jan 17) Entrepreneur 123 – Castara Beach (IRE) 74 (Danehill (USA) 126) [2003 7.5m⁵ 8.5m 8.1d 10m Oct 6] 5,000F, 31,000Y: lengthy, angular gelding: dam lightly-raced sister to useful 6f/7f winner Hill Hopper and half-sister to smart 1½m performer Water Boatman: modest maiden: best effort on debut: dead. *T. D. Easterby* **59**

HESTHERELAD (IRE) 4 b.g. Definite Article 121 – Unbidden Melody (USA) (Chieftain) [2003 –: 9m f12s 12.4g Oct 22] tall gelding: no form. *C. J. Teague* **–**

HE WHO DARES (IRE) 5 b.g. Distinctly North (USA) 115 – Sea Clover (IRE) 77 (Ela-Mana-Mou 132) [2003 76d: 7m⁴ 6m 7m* 9g 8.2d* p7g² Dec 6] rather leggy, quite good-topped gelding: fair performer: won maiden at Lingfield in September and handicap at Nottingham in November: effective at 7f/1m: acts on polytrack, good to firm and heavy going: often tongue tied in 2002. *A. W. Carroll* **69**

HEY PRESTO 3 b.g. Piccolo 121 – Upping The Tempo (Dunbeath (USA) 127) [2003 74: 6m³ 6.1m 6m* 6m² 6f 6g⁶ 6m 6d 6m⁴ 5m Sep 17] strong, good-topped gelding: usually takes the eye: fairly useful handicapper: won at Salisbury in May: good second at Newmarket next time: stays 6f: acts on firm going: tried blinkered. *C. G. Cox* **88**

HEZAAM (USA) 2 b.c. (Jan 26) Red Ransom (USA) – Ashraakat (USA) 105 (Danzig (USA)) [2003 6m 7g* Nov 1] quite attractive colt: second foal: dam, 6f/7f (latter at 2 yrs) winner, sister to high-class sprinter Elnadim and closely related to very smart 1m/1¼m performer Mehthaaf: better effort in maidens at Newmarket when winning 13-runner event by head from Star Pupil, still green but getting up close home: moved poorly to post/bandaged in front on debut: will stay 1m: useful prospect. *J. L. Dunlop* **84 p**

H HARRISON (IRE) 3 b.g. Eagle Eyed (USA) 111 – Penrose (IRE) 75 (Wolfhound (USA) 126) [2003 79§: 5d 5s 5g⁶ 5f⁵ 5f⁵ 5m⁴ 5f⁵ 5m⁴ 5m⁵ 5m 6f² 5m⁵ 7m* 7m* 7.1g* 7m 7.1m³ Oct 25] useful handicapper: left R. Fisher following eighth start: much improved after, winning at Catterick, Yarmouth (apprentices) and Musselburgh (beat Raphael 3 lengths) in September: creditable third at Musselburgh final start: stays 7f: acts on firm going, good to soft and polytrack: tried in cheekpieces: often hangs left/carries head high. *I. W. McInnes* **95**

HIAWATHA (IRE) 4 b.g. Danehill (USA) 126 – Hi Bettina 96 (Henbit (USA) 130) [2003 94: 8d 8m³ 7g 9s 9.5d 8d 8g² 8g 8m 8g⁴ 8.5d 7f 12g² 8.3d 10s² f9.4g f9.4g* Dec **84**

448

22] IR 190,000Y: brother to 8-y-o Atlantic Viking and useful Italian sprinter Fred Bongusto and half-brother to several winners, including Irish 7f winner La Serina (by Royal Academy): dam Irish sprinter: fairly useful performer: won maiden at Down Royal at 3 yrs and, having left K. Prendergast in Ireland after thirteenth start, claimer at Wolverhampton (well backed, claimed £9,000) in December: stays 1¼m: acts on fibresand, soft and good to firm going: blinkered (well beaten) once: joined T. D. Barron. *I. Semple*

HICCUPS 3 b.g. Polar Prince (IRE) 117 – Simmie's Special 75 (Precocious 126) [2003 **84** 6f⁶ 5.1m² 5m³ 5g² 6.1m 5f* 5f 5m* 5m 6m⁶ 5g³ 5d Sep 27] 3,500Y: tall, quite good-topped gelding: fifth foal: half-brother to 4-y-o Sarrego: dam 5f/6f winner: fairly useful handicapper: won at Carlisle in June and Pontefract in July: will prove best at 5f/6f: acts on firm going, below form on good to soft: wore cheekpieces last 7 outings: refused to enter stall on intended debut: sometimes slowly away/carries head awkwardly: usually waited with. *Mrs J. R. Ramsden*

HICKLETON DREAM 6 b.m. Rambo Dancer (CAN) 107 – Elegant Approach 48 **37** (Prince Ragusa 96) [2003 11.9m⁴ 14m Sep 13] sparely-made mare: poor maiden handicapper: stays 1¾m: acts on good to firm going. *G. A. Swinbank*

HI DARL 2 ch.f. (Mar 27) Wolfhound (USA) 126 – Sugar Token 66 (Record Token **52** 128) [2003 5m⁶ f5s⁴ 6g* May 28] closely related to fairly useful 1995 2-y-o 5f/6f winner Lunar Mist (by Komaite) and half-sister to 5f/6f winner Hershebar (by Stanford): dam 6f/ 7f winner, including at 2 yrs: modest form: favourite, won seller at Yarmouth: stays 6f: tends to carry head awkwardly: sold 3,100 gns. *J. G. Given*

HIDDEN DRAGON (USA) 4 b.g. Danzig (USA) – Summer Home (USA) (Easy **108** Goer (USA)) [2003 106: p7g⁵ 6f* 6m⁴ 5m⁶ 6f 6m³ 6m³ 6m* 5m⁴ 5m 5f 6g Oct 24] big, lengthy gelding: useful performer: won minor event at Thirsk in April by short head from Indian Spark and William Hill Great St Wilfrid Handicap at Ripon in August by head from Undeterred: probably best at 6f: acts on polytrack, firm and good to soft ground: tried blinkered: tends to hang. *P. A. Blockley*

HIDDEN HOPE 2 ch.f. (May 24) Daylami (IRE) 138 – Nuryana 107 (Nureyev (USA) **62 p** 131) [2003 6.1f p7g Oct 15] quite good-topped filly: half-sister to several winners, including very smart 7f/1m winner Rebecca Sharp (by Machiavellian) and smart 1m and 11.5f winner Mystic Knight (by Caerleon): dam 1m winner out of half-sister to 1000 Guineas winner On The House: modest form when eighth in maidens at Nottingham and Lingfield (ran wide): will stay at least 1m: should do better. *G. Wragg*

HIDDEN SMILE (USA) 6 b.m. Twilight Agenda (USA) 126 – Smooth Edge (USA) **37** (Meadowlake (USA)) [2003 –: f11s f9.4g⁶ f8.5g⁵ Mar 3] lengthy mare: just poor form in 2003: tried blinkered/in cheekpieces/tongue tied. *F. Jordan*

HIDDEN SURPRISE 4 b.g. Bin Ajwaad (IRE) 119 – Dawawin (USA) 81 (Dixieland **91** Band (USA)) [2003 89p: p8g³ p10g² Feb 25] fairly useful performer, lightly raced: placed in handicaps at Lingfield both 4-y-o starts: stays easy 1¼m: raced only on all-weather: sent to Singapore. *W. A. O'Gorman*

HI DUBAI 3 ch.f. Rahy (USA) 115 – Jood (USA) 87 (Nijinsky (CAN) 138) [2003 88p: **112** 10g* 10g² 12g⁵ 9.9g⁴ 10s³ Oct 19] big, well-made filly: smart performer: won listed race at Newmarket (beat Hold To Ransom a length) in May: good efforts after in Prix Saint-Alary at Longchamp (2 lengths second to Fidelite), Oaks at Epsom (second favourite, 3¼ lengths fifth to Casual Look) and E. P. Taylor Stakes at Woodbine (close third to Volga): stayed 1½m: acted on soft going, unraced on firmer than good: had been bandaged hind joints: stud. *Saeed bin Suroor*

R. L. Davison Pretty Polly Stakes, Newmarket—
Hi Dubai holds off Hold To Ransom and is promoted to ante-post favouritism for the Oaks

HIGH ACCOLADE 3 b.c. Mark of Esteem (IRE) 137 – Generous Lady 98 (Generous (IRE) 139) [2003 95: 10.2m* 11g* 12f* 12m⁶ 12g² 11.9m⁶ 14.6g² 12f* 12g² Oct 25] **122**

If horses had theme songs, High Accolade's would probably be 'My Way'. A highly successful three-year-old campaign, which included four wins and three seconds from nine starts, one of those seconds in the St Leger, belied High Accolade's approach to the job. He proved far from a straightforward partner for his regular rider Martin Dwyer, carrying his head awkwardly in races and often being off the bridle well before many of those he eventually came through to beat. Happily for connections, High Accolade found an understanding partner in Dwyer, one of the most improved riders around in recent seasons.

Trained at two by Richard Hannon, for whom he showed useful form in winning a maiden at Newbury from four outings over seven furlongs, High Accolade won his first three starts, stepped up in trip, for Marcus Tregoning. Connections declined to supplement him for £90,000 for the Derby after he had taken a minor event at Bath and the listed Predominate Stakes at Goodwood in May, the latter by a length and a half from Unigold. Instead, High Accolade waited for the Group 2 King Edward VII Stakes at Royal Ascot, where he also had to be supplemented— for £12,000. Starting favourite at 5/2 in a field of eight, he began to carry his head awkwardly before the straight but, with his rider keeping a firm hold of him, he quickened well as the field opened up, beating Delsarte going away by two lengths. High Accolade was tried in headgear after finishing last of six in the Princess of Wales's Stakes at Newmarket on his next start. The move did the trick only temporarily. He ran his best race when failing by a short head to catch Phoenix Reach when visored in the Gordon Stakes at Goodwood, conceding the winner 5 lb, but produced a mulish display in blinkers when only sixth in the Great Voltigeur at York.

High Accolade's odds for the St Leger lengthened dramatically after York, but, with the headgear left off, he finished the season with a flourish. Starting at 8/1 at Doncaster, he went down by a length and a quarter to Brian Boru, having every chance in the end after a characteristically quirky display. In a small field for the Cumberland Lodge Stakes at Ascot later in September, High Accolade proved amenable to a change of tactics, making all to beat Compton Bolter most decisively by three lengths. Whatever else, High Accolade was proving to be tough. He looked in fine shape at Ascot on his eighth start since the spring, and again took the eye when underlining his well-being with a second to Imperial Dancer in the St Simon Stakes at Newbury on his final outing. He faced a stiff task under a 5-lb penalty against such an improved older horse and went down by three lengths, more patiently ridden again this time.

High Accolade's dam Generous Lady won four races at a mile and a half and a mile and three quarters in Ireland, having been unraced as a two-year-old, and she was also placed over two miles. A daughter of Northern Blossom, a champion three-year-old filly in Canada in 1983, Generous Lady was bought for 35,000 guineas at Newmarket as a yearling and made 100,000 guineas when returned there

King Edward VII Stakes, Royal Ascot—High Accolade makes it three out of three for his new stable; Delsarte and Summerland (blinkered) are placed

Lady Tennant's "High Accolade"

High Accolade (b.c. 2000)	Mark of Esteem (IRE) (b 1993)	Darshaan (br 1981)	Shirley Heights
			Delsey
		Homage (b 1989)	Ajdal
			Home Love
	Generous Lady (ch 1994)	Generous (ch 1988)	Caerleon
			Doff The Derby
		Northern Blossom (ch 1980)	Snow Knight
			Victorian Heiress

at the end of her racing career. Her only foal prior to High Accolade, the Desert King filly Summer Wine, showed fairly useful form, winning a maiden over a mile and a half on fibresand. Her third foal, a colt by Selkirk, was unraced as a two-year-old in 2003, and her yearling filly, another by Mark of Esteem, was led out unsold at 145,000 guineas at Newmarket in October. The pick of Generous Lady's winning half-brothers was Jape, runner-up in the Chester Vase and winner of the Italian St Leger. Mark of Esteem has made a fair start at stud. Among his other three-year-olds of 2003, Waldmark showed useful form, as did the four-year-old Chivalry in winning the Cambridgeshire. For his part, High Accolade now supersedes One Thousand Guineas winner Ameerat and another smart miler Redback as Mark of Esteem's best produce so far. A smallish, sturdy colt, High Accolade will have to improve again to win most Group 1 races at home in 2004, when he will be penalised in the majority of minor pattern races. Raced only on good ground or firmer, and equally effective at a mile and a half and a mile and three quarters, he is a credit to his trainer. *M. P. Tregoning*

Rogerthorpe Manor Hotel Handicap, Pontefract—High Action gains a narrow victory over Montecristo (far side), completing a treble for Kieren Fallon, who went on to ride three more winners at Yarmouth to make it six on the day

HIGH ACTION (USA) 3 ch.c. Theatrical 128 – Secret Imperatrice (USA) (Secretariat (USA)) [2003 –p: 9.2m² 9.3f² 8m* 10.3g⁴ 12m* 12m* 11.9m 12m⁶ Sep 14] strong, close-coupled colt: useful performer: won maiden at Brighton in July and 2 handicaps at Pontefract (sweated, made all to beat Double Obsession 1½ lengths in latter) in August: acted as pacemaker for Kris Kin and far from discredited when sixth to Dalakhani in Prix Niel at Longchamp final start: likely to stay 1¾m: raced only on good ground or firmer: usually races prominently: sold 52,000 gns, joined I. Williams. *Sir Michael Stoute*   **102**

HIGH AND MIGHTY 8 b.g. Shirley Heights 130 – Air Distingue (USA) 120 (Sir Ivor 135) [2003 96: 18g 16m 18.7m 17.1m⁵ Jun 1] sturdy, angular gelding: good mover: useful handicapper at best: failed to make frame in 2003, though seemingly fairly useful from when eighth in Chester Cup third start: reportedly finished lame final outing: stays 2½m: acts on firm and soft going: visored. *G. Barnett*   **80 ?**

HIGHCAL 6 gr.g. King's Signet (USA) 110 – Guarded Expression 51 (Siberian Express (USA) 125) [2003 52: 12m Aug 5] good-bodied gelding: modest performer in 2002: well held only 6-y-o start: tried blinkered. *Ronald Thompson*   **–**

HIGH CANE (USA) 3 ch.f. Diesis 133 – Aerleon Jane 89 (Caerleon (USA) 132) [2003 7.9f⁶ 8.3m 8.1d³ 8.3g⁶ Oct 13] medium-sized, lengthy filly: first foal: dam 7f and (in USA) 1m winner: best effort in maidens (fair form) when third to Bint Alhaarth at Haydock: stays 1m: acts on good to soft going, shaped as if amiss on firm: blinkered (looked none too keen) final start: sold 4,500 gns. *J. Noseda*   **70**

HIGH CHAPARRAL (IRE) 4 b.c. Sadler's Wells (USA) 132 – Kasora (IRE) (Darshaan 133) [2003 130: 10f* 10f* 12s³ 12f* Oct 25]   **132**

    'California is fine—if you're an orange.' Noel Coward's view of the 'sunshine state', long shared by British and Irish trainers of Breeders' Cup hopes, is in need of revision after the latest season. The heat and the usually hard-baked turf—not to mention the extra travelling and bigger change of time zone—have contributed to California's reputation as a Breeders' Cup graveyard for British hopes in particular. Dancing Brave, Sonic Lady, Barathea and Opera House are among those prominent on a lengthy list of British and Irish disappointments in the Breeders' Cup at its west coast venues, Hollywood Park and Santa Anita. On the most recent occasion the Breeders' Cup had been held at Santa Anita—in 1993—not one of the seven British-trained runners had made the frame, whilst, from a smaller team sent to Hollywood Park in 1997, 40/1-shot Decorated Hero's third in the Mile was the only highlight. French-trained runners had, however, flown the flag successfully for Europe, Lashkari, Last Tycoon, Miesque, Arcangues and Spinning World all successful in Breeders' Cup events on the Californian tracks. The French again supplied their customary winner at Santa Anita at the end of October, with Six Perfections in the Breeders' Cup Mile. But it was just one of three European successes, Islington winning the Breeders' Cup Filly & Mare Turf for Stoute's Newmarket stable and Irish-trained dual Derby winner High Chaparral running a dead-heat in the mile-and-a-half John Deere Breeders' Cup Turf, a race he had also won as a three-year-old when the meeting was held at Arlington. Three European victories at Santa Anita matched the total achieved at Churchill Downs in 1991 (Sheikh Albadou, Arazi and Miss Alleged) and Belmont in 2001 (Banks Hill, Johannesburg and Fantastic Light).

As temperatures approached 100F in the week leading up to the meeting (contributing to some devastating wildfires in parts of California shortly afterwards), reports came through of steps taken to shield the European challengers from the worst effects of the heat. Islington, for example, was being equipped with a hydroweave cooling blanket, similar to a type used for burns victims, and most of the European horses were being worked on the track before the sun had risen properly. Even so, High Chaparral and others in the five-strong Ballydoyle team were reportedly 'awash with sweat' after training. Aidan O'Brien seemed unperturbed, however, saying 'This is beautiful weather . . . we'd always like to have it like this but we don't get it very much in Ireland.' O'Brien's faith in the well-being of his team wasn't misplaced, L'Ancresse and Yesterday filling the places behind Islington, and High Chaparral becoming the first horse to get his name on the winning roll more than once in the Breeders' Cup Turf. The absence of a number of dirt stars from the Breeders' Cup Classic, including Mineshaft, Empire Maker and Candy Ride, threw more of the spotlight than usual on to the Turf. Ex-British Storming Home started favourite after passing the post first on all four of his starts in North America during the year, including the Charles Whittingham Handicap at Hollywood Park and the Clement L. Hirsch Memorial Turf Championship at Santa Anita. He had been demoted to fourth in the Arlington Million, which was awarded to the runner-up Sulamani, who had gone on to win the Turf Classic Invitational at Belmont in September on the way to representing Godolphin in the Breeders' Cup

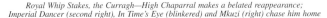

Royal Whip Stakes, the Curragh—High Chaparral makes a belated reappearance;
Imperial Dancer (second right), In Time's Eye (blinkered) and Mkuzi (right) chase him home

Ireland The Food Island Champion Stakes, Leopardstown—in one of the most strongly-contested races of the year High Chaparral holds off the unlucky-in-running Falbrav (rail), with Islington third and Alamshar fourth

Turf. Sulamani's European campaign had included a second in the King George VI and Queen Elizabeth Stakes, but he had missed Europe's other supreme open-aged championship the Prix de l'Arc de Triomphe (in which he was runner-up the year before) in favour of an American preparation at Belmont. Connections regarded the Breeders' Cup as the most important target, as did those involved with Islington, who also bypassed the Arc.

The preparation of Sulamani and Islington indicated a difference in the way some top European horses are campaigned nowadays from the last time the Breeders' Cup was staged at Santa Anita. The Breeders' Cup series was then only just beyond the stage when, in its early years, it was regarded as something of an end-of-season afterthought, particularly for British- and Irish-trained horses (though less so with the French, whose top middle-distance performers tradition-ally had a summer break and had enjoyed a fair amount of success in the big autumn turf races in North America). The two other European-trained 'heavyweights' in the latest Breeders' Cup Turf, High Chaparral and Falbrav, had come first and second in the Irish Champion Stakes at the end of September but had had contrast-ing campaigns. Before their meeting at Leopardstown, High Chaparral had been seen out only once during the season—his reappearance delayed by a shoulder injury—while Falbrav had been on the go from the start, contesting a variety of Group 1 races over distances ranging from just short of nine and a half furlongs to a mile and a half, winning the Prix d'Ispahan, the Coral-Eclipse and the Juddmonte International. Both had run once between the Irish Champion and the Breeders' Cup Turf, High Chaparral coming a below-form third in the Arc and Falbrav dropping back to a mile to win the Queen Elizabeth II Stakes at Ascot. The Prix d'Ispahan runner-up Bright Sky completed the four-strong European challenge, while the American-bred runners also included the previous year's fourth The Tin Man and locally-trained Johar, who had finished second to Storming Home in the Clement L. Hirsch and had a good record at Santa Anita.

Pretty well all American horses race on the diuretic drug lasix—claimed to be beneficial for those who suffer bleeding in their lungs when racing—and some European trainers adopt a 'when in Rome' approach at the Breeders' Cup. It was encouraging, however, to see the majority of the European challengers—including the winners Six Perfections and Islington—running without lasix, which is banned in every other major racing country. The O'Brien fillies L'Ancresse and Yesterday also raced without lasix, but High Chaparral raced on it, as he had the previous year. The pain-masking drug bute, also banned in Europe, is also almost universal in America and it had to be declared at Santa Anita (not a requirement at Arlington). Bute was administered to all the Europeans, in common with all bar one of the non-European-trained runners (ex-British Buy The Sport, who did run on lasix).

Concerns were expressed before the very first Breeders' Cup about the policy on drugs—or 'medication'—but, twenty years on, the Breeders' Cup organisers sadly seem no nearer to coming into line, which detracts from the meeting's claims to being the 'world thoroughbred championships' and a showcase for the sport's biggest stars. Whether lasix or bute aided High Chaparral in the latest Breeders' Cup Turf is impossible to know for certain, but it is interesting that rider Michael Kinane reported after the Arc that the horse had been 'backing off' when he got to work down the sloping approach to the home straight at Longchamp. 'It could be some little thing still in his shoulder that is niggling him,' O'Brien added, though he also blamed the right-handed course at Longchamp, a puzzling explanation given High Chaparral's performances at the Curragh, where his two victories had included the Irish Derby. High Chaparral showed no signs of 'backing off' at Santa Anita, which provided a different test to the previous year. Santa Anita's turns are even tighter than Arlington's—the oval track is only a mile round (nine furlongs at Arlington)—and the firm conditions, which contrasted to the good to soft going of 2002, made the latest Breeders' Cup Turf even more of a test of speed, generally thought to be against High Chaparral, even though the ground had been very firm in the mile-and-a-quarter Irish Champion Stakes. After a good early pace, The Tin Man took it up going into the far turn before Falbrav was sent for home early in the straight, looking the likely winner. High Chaparral had come under pressure on the home turn but, under a very forceful ride from Kinane, he stayed on strongly to catch Falbrav near the finish, only for Johar to get up on the outside to force the dead-heat. The result was not announced for thirteen minutes, the photo-finish showing Falbrav only a head behind the dead-heaters; The Tin Man was five and a half lengths further back in fourth, beaten nearly twice as far by High Chaparral as the previous year, with Sulamani, never a threat after stumbling when hampered on the turn after passing the winning post for the first time, in fifth, Bright Sky sixth and below-form Storming Home seventh. The Breeders' Cup Turf had provided a top-class contest and a tremendous finish, High Chaparral maintaining the fine recent record of the Europeans, who have now won the event five years in a row. European-trained horses have won eight Breeders' Cup races in the last three years, the best performance in any three-year period since the Breeders' Cup's inauguration and a testament to the continuing advances in the training and preparation for international competition.

Falbrav found a mile and a half in tip-top company, even at Santa Anita on firm going, stretching his stamina to its limit, but High Chaparral had been fortunate to beat him in the Ireland The Food Island Champion Stakes at Leopardstown in

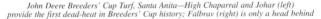

John Deere Breeders' Cup Turf, Santa Anita—High Chaparral and Johar (left)
provide the first dead-heat in Breeders' Cup history; Falbrav (right) is only a head behind

September. High Chaparral's setback in the spring—which some cynics thought might eventually be used as a face-saving device to retire him—kept him off the course until August. He dispelled concerns about whether he had retained his ability with a fine comeback in the Royal Whip Stakes at the Curragh. Shouldering a Group 1 penalty and conceding 7 lb and upwards to his five rivals, High Chaparral won by three quarters of a length and a neck from Imperial Dancer and In Time's Eye, pushed out after jinking right as he took the lead and then idling near the finish. It was the first time High Chaparral had run on very firm going and his performance also confirmed that he was just as effective at a mile and a quarter as at a mile and a half, something that could only be surmised after his three-year-old performances. High Chaparral's Derby-winning performance, bettered only by Generous and Galileo in the past fifteen years, had been recorded under the most testing conditions for a Derby at Epsom since 1983, and conditions had also placed the emphasis on stamina when he followed up at the Curragh. High Chaparral's Breeders' Cup Turf victory at Arlington had shown, however, that he had much more speed than some gave him credit for.

That said, High Chaparral was only third favourite for the Irish Champion Stakes, behind the Irish Derby and King George winner Alamshar and Falbrav. Also in the line-up were the Dubai World Cup winner Moon Ballad, Islington and the Irish Oaks winner Vintage Tipple, the field completed by France, who set a good gallop for High Chaparral. Racing in fourth when beginning his challenge, High Chaparral at first looked to be struggling in the home straight, tending to edge left in behind Moon Ballad, who had been sent on four furlongs out. But, under an inspired ride by Kinane, High Chaparral battled his way to the front a furlong out and stayed on well under continued strong pressure to hold off the persistently short of room Falbrav by a neck, with Islington only a head away. Alamshar, finding the step back in trip against him, finished a further length and a half back in fourth, just in front of Moon Ballad. High Chaparral survived an objection and a stewards' inquiry (and a subsequent appeal) and looked all set to run very well in the Arc, in which he had finished third the previous year after an interrupted preparation. His lacklustre effort in the latest edition, struggling to make ground from the turn into the straight, was one of the few disappointments in his distinguished career. He kept on at one pace to be beaten three quarters of a length and five lengths by Dalakhani and Mubtaker, judged strictly on form the least meritorious performance by High Chaparral since before his two Derby victories. Thankfully, he was given the chance to end his career on a much higher note, connections again proving wrong those who predicted he wouldn't be seen out again. The fighting policy adopted with High Chaparral paid off, as it had with the same owner's other dual Derby winner Montjeu, who was also kept in training at four. High Chaparral's career record was ten victories from thirteen starts, his only defeats coming on his debut and in his two Arcs. He became only the second Epsom Derby winner, after Sir Ivor, to win as a three-year-old in North America, and, with an extra year in training, proved himself to be that very rare bird indeed—an Epsom Derby winner who actually maintained, or even enhanced, his reputation as a four-year-old, something that could probably only be said of Mill Reef, Roberto, Snow Knight (in North America) and Teenoso in the previous thirty years or so.

		Northern Dancer (b 1961)	Nearctic
High Chaparral (IRE) (b.c. 1999)	Sadler's Wells (USA) (b 1981)		Natalma
		Fairy Bridge (b 1975)	Bold Reason
			Special
	Kasora (IRE) (b 1993)	Darshaan (br 1981)	Shirley Heights
			Delsy
		Kozana (br 1982)	Kris
			Koblenza

The angular, good-topped High Chaparral, who had a moderate, quick action, has been retired to Coolmore, where he will stand alongside his sire Sadler's Wells—champion sire in Britain and Ireland for the thirteenth time in 2003—and two other dual Derby winners by Sadler's Wells, Montjeu and Galileo. High Chaparral will stand at a fee of €35,000 (Oct 1st) in 2004, compared to €40,000 for Galileo and €30,000 for Montjeu. Neither Galileo nor Montjeu has yet had runners but both have been well supported by prominent breeders and High Chaparral should also have every chance to prove himself at stud. Sons of Sadler's Wells have something of a mixed record as stallions, with the likes of Old Vic and Saddlers' Hall now covering jumping mares. On the other side of the coin, El Prado was champion sire in North America in 2002, Fort Wood is doing well in South Africa and In The Wings has established himself as the best son of Sadler's Wells so far in Europe. Like High Chaparral, a 270,000-guinea yearling, his dam Kasora went through the Tattersalls sales ring, purchased as an unraced three-year-old at the December Sales from the Aga Khan's studs, also for 270,000 guineas, the third highest-priced filly at the sale. Kasora is a half-sister to Kotama and Khanata, both winners of the One Thousand Guineas Trial at Leopardstown, and to Italian Two Thousand Guineas runner-up Khoraz. Their dam Kozana carried the Aga Khan's colours with distinction, putting up the best performance by a three-year-old filly over middle distances in France in 1985 when third in the Arc; she also won four races that season—two of them in pattern company—at up to a mile and a quarter, and was runner-up in the Prix du Moulin over a mile. High Chaparral's great gran-dam Koblenza, among the bloodstock acquired by the Aga Khan from leading owner-breeder Mme Francois Dupre in the 'seventies, was also one of the best of her sex as a three-year-old in France, winning the Poule d'Essai des Pouliches and finishing second in the Prix Saint-Alary. Koblenza bred several other winners, including the smart stayer Karkour, winner of the Prix du Cadran. High Chaparral's dam is by Darshaan, whose daughters have been responsible for numerous good horses by Sadler's Wells, among them Crimson Tide, Ebadiyla, Election Day, Greek Dance, Milan, Quarter Moon and, in the latest season, Islington and Yesterday. Kasora is the dam of two other winners, Oriental Ben (by Ridgewood

Mr M. Tabor & Mrs John Magnier's "High Chaparral"

Ben), a fairly useful handicapper at his best at up to nine furlongs in Ireland, and the fairly useful two-year-old Treasure The Lady (by Indian Ridge), successful over seven furlongs for John Oxx in Ireland on her debut and third in listed company over a mile on her only other start. The genuine and consistent High Chaparral was effective at a mile and a quarter and at a mile and a half and acted on any going. He tended to idle once in front and was waited with (wore a crossed noseband). A credit to his connections, High Chaparral was given a full opportunity to establish his reputation in championship races on both sides of the Atlantic, a reputation that should stand him in good stead as a stallion. Incidentally, his victories in the Irish Champion and the Breeders' Cup Turf, together with his third in the Arc, enabled High Chaparral to pip Falbrav for a third time in 2003, when he acquired just enough points to win the World Series championship. This is a series and a concept that Ballydoyle has yet to embrace fully, High Chaparral's achievement coming in a year when the series was without a sponsor to put up the customary million-dollar bonus. High Chaparral earned further prestige when named male turf champion for a second time at America's Eclipse awards ceremony in January. *A. P. O'Brien, Ireland*

HIGHCLERE MEMORY (USA) 3 b.f. Cryptoclearance (USA) – Regal State (USA) 122 (Affirmed (USA)) [2003 62: 8.1m 10f⁵ 10m⁵ 11.9f Oct 17] tall, leggy filly: half-sister to Breeders' Cup Classic winner Pleasantly Perfect (by Pleasant Colony): modest maiden: likely to prove best around 1¼m: raced only on good ground or firmer: best form when blinkered: none too genuine: sent to USA. *J. L. Dunlop* **54**

HIGH DIVA 4 b.f. Piccolo 121 – Gifted (Shareef Dancer (USA) 135) [2003 69: p10g⁵ p10g⁵ p13g⁴ p10g 8.3g² 10.2m 10m f8.5g p10g⁶ Dec 30] tall filly: fluent mover: modest maiden: left J. Hills after third start: stays 1¼m: acts on all-weather, raced only on good/good to firm going on turf: tried tongue tied/in cheekpieces: usually held up. *B. R. Johnson* **58**

HIGH DIVING 3 b.c. Barathea (IRE) 127 – High And Low 120 (Rainbow Quest (USA) 134) [2003 76p: 12f² 11.9d³ 12g³ 10g Oct 6] sturdy colt: fairly useful maiden: creditable placed efforts at Thirsk and Brighton (then left B. Hills) first 2 starts: tongue tied, below form last 2 outings: stays 1½m: acts on firm and good to soft going: has raced freely/carried head high. *G. T. Lynch, Ireland* **82**

HIGHDOWN (IRE) 4 b.c. Selkirk (USA) 129 – Rispoto 58 (Mtoto 134) [2003 119: 8.9g⁶ 10.5d² 10g² 10g⁵ 10m² Sep 16] leggy, close-coupled colt: smart performer: best 4-y-o effort when 1¼ lengths equal-second to Ransom o'War in Grosser Dallmayr-Preis at Munich third start: respectable ¾-length second to Gruntled in La Coupe de Maisons-Laffitte final outing: stays 10.5f: acts on firm and good to soft going: visored/tongue tied third/ fourth starts: wears crossed noseband: edgy type: tends to wander. *Saeed bin Suroor* **117**

HIGH DRAMA 6 b.g. In The Wings 128 – Maestrale (Top Ville 129) [2003 44: 15.4m⁵ 16d² 16.2m Aug 25] leggy gelding: poor handicapper: stays 2m: acts on good to firm and good to soft going: blinkered once: held up. *P. Bowen* **42**

HIGH ESTEEM 7 b.g. Common Grounds 118 – Whittle Woods Girl 80 (Emarati (USA) 74) [2003 71: 5.1s⁶ f6g⁸ f6g 5.1d f6s f6g Nov 25] big gelding: fair handicapper on all-weather, modest on turf: won at Wolverhampton in June: effective at 5f to 7f: acts on any turf going and fibresand: often races prominently. *M. A. Buckley* **55 a65**

HIGHEST HONOUR (IRE) 3 b.g. Polish Precedent (USA) 131 – Victoria Cross (USA) (Spectacular Bid (USA)) [2003 –: 8f 5.9m Jun 2] big, workmanlike gelding: little form in maidens: tried blinkered. *A. M. Balding* **–**

HIGHEST (IRE) 4 b.c. Selkirk (USA) 129 – Pearl Kite (USA) 106§ (Silver Hawk (USA) 123) [2003 123: 12g* 12g 12d³ 12m² 12f⁵ Jun 21] big, strong colt: very smart performer: won Group 3 Dubai City of Gold at Nad Al Sheba in March by ¾ length from Grand Ekinoks: best effort of 2003 when ½-length second to Warrsan in Coronation Cup at Epsom penultimate start: visored and grinding teeth, below form in Hardwicke Stakes at Royal Ascot final outing (sustained injury): effective at 1½m to 14.6f: very best form on good or firmer going (yet to race on soft/heavy): stays in training. *Saeed bin Suroor* **121**

HIGHFIELD JEN 4 ch.f. Presidium 124 – Jendorcet 57 (Grey Ghost 98) [2003 –: 10m 16m Jun 10] of no account. *C. W. Fairhurst* **–**

HIGH FINALE 4 b.f. Sure Blade (USA) 130 – High Velocity 53 (Frimley Park 109) [2003 –: 5m Jun 28] leggy, workmanlike filly: fairly useful at 2 yrs: lightly raced and little form in handicaps since: tried visored. *D. K. Ivory* **–**

HIGH FINANCE (IRE)   3 b. or br.f. Entrepreneur 123 – Phylella (Persian Bold 123)   **85**
[2003 68: p8g* f7g⁴ 7g* 7g⁵ 7m* 7m 7m⁴ 7f⁵ 8.1m⁵ Sep 17] rather leggy, useful-looking
filly: fairly useful performer: won maiden at Lingfield in April, minor event at Yarmouth
in May and handicap at Newbury in June: ran well penultimate start: stays easy 1m: acts
on all-weather, raced only on good going or firmer on turf: patiently ridden. *J. W. Hills*

HIGHGATE HILL   3 b.g. Revoque (IRE) 122 – Long View 68 (Persian Bold 123)   **65**
[2003 –p: 7g⁶ 8m⁴ 7.9g 8.5d 8g⁶ 10.1m⁴ p12g⁴ Oct 3] strong, lengthy gelding: fair
maiden: stays easy 1½m: acts on polytrack, unraced on extremes of ground on turf: sold
22,000 gns. *M. H. Tompkins*

HIGH HOPE (FR)   5 ch.h. Lomitas 129 – Highness Lady (GER) (Cagliostro (GER))   **89**
[2003 91: p12g² p12g⁵ 11.6g 12d 11.6g p12g p12g³ Dec 17] leggy horse: fairly useful
performer: stays 15f: acts on polytrack, raced mainly on good going or softer on turf: tried
blinkered. *G. L. Moore*

HIGH JINKS   8 b.g. High Estate 127 – Waffling 68 (Lomond (USA) 128) [2003 48:   **33**
f16g⁵ p16g f16g Dec 16] poor handicapper, lightly raced: stays 2m: acts on fibresand,
raced only on good going or softer on turf: tried in cheekpieces. *R. N. Bevis*

HIGHLAND GAIT   4 ch.f. Most Welcome 131 – Miller's Gait 74§ (Mill Reef (USA)   **63**
141) [2003 61: 7.5m² 8.1g 8m 8.5m³ 7m* 8.1m Aug 8] sturdy filly: easy mover: modest
handicapper: won apprentice maiden event at Thirsk in August: effective at 7f to 1¼m:
acts on good to firm and good to soft ground: tried blinkered: usually races prominently:
none too consistent. *T. D. Easterby*

HIGHLAND GAMES (IRE)   3 b.g. Singspiel (IRE) 133 – Highland Gift (IRE) 95   **89**
(Generous (IRE) 139) [2003 –: 10g⁵ 11.5g* 11.6g* 12m 12d⁶ 10m Sep 25] strong, well-
made gelding: good walker: fairly useful performer: won maiden at Yarmouth and
minor event at Windsor (3 ran, left clear to beat Fantastic Love 3½ lengths), both in May:
respectable efforts in King George V Handicap at Royal Ascot and Tote Gold Trophy
Handicap at Goodwood next 2 starts: will stay 1¾m: yet to race on extremes of going:
sold 32,000 gns, and gelded. *Sir Michael Stoute*

HIGHLAND GOLD (IRE)   6 ch.g. Indian Ridge 123 – Anjuli (Northfields (USA))   **–**
[2003 12.4m 12g May 2] big gelding: fair performer in 2001: well beaten both 6-y-o
outings. *Miss L. A. Perratt*

HIGHLAND REEL   6 ch.g. Selkirk (USA) 129 – Taj Victory 68 (Final Straw 127)   **94 §**
[2003 92: 8g 8m 10d³ 10m³ 8.5m⁶ 8f* 10g 8m 10g 10g Oct 25] leggy gelding: fairly
useful handicapper: won at Salisbury in June by 3 lengths from Joint Statement, edging
right: effective at 1m/1¼m: acts on any going: races freely: unreliable. *D. R. C. Elsworth*

HIGHLAND SHOT   5 b.m. Selkirk (USA) 129 – Optaria 83 (Song 132) [2003 74:   **91**
7m² p8g* 8.5m* 8g 7.1m* 8.5m² 7f 6m² 6m 7m⁵ 7d Sep 11] quite good-topped mare:
progressed into a fairly useful performer at 5 yrs, winning handicap at Lingfield and
minor event at Epsom in April and handicap at Sandown in May: good second at Epsom
and Newmarket after: effective at 6f to easy 8.5f: acts on polytrack, soft and good to firm
going: often pulls hard: waited with: consistent. *A. M. Balding*

HIGHLAND TOFFEE (IRE)   3 ch.g. Miswaki (USA) 124 – Natural Forest (USA)   **–**
(Green Forest (USA) 134) [2003 p7g 7m 7m 11.5m f9.4s 7m Jul 2] IR 33,000Y: seventh
foal: closely related to winner in USA by Prospector's Bid and half-brother to several
winners in USA: dam, winner in USA, half-sister to Dante/Great Voltigeur winner Damister: little form: sold 3,000 gns. *M. L. W. Bell*

HIGHLAND WARRIOR   4 b.c. Makbul 104 – Highland Rowena 59 (Royben 125)   **66**
[2003 78: 8.3d 9.2g 9.1f⁵ 8.1g 8g² 9.1g 9.2m 8m 6g* 6g³ 5g³ Nov 5] big, leggy colt: fair
handicapper: won at Ayr in October: effective at 6f and stays 9f: acts on good to firm and
good to soft going: sometimes slowly away/races freely: waited with. *J. S. Goldie*

HIGHLY LIQUID   3 b.f. Entrepreneur 123 – Premiere Cuvee 109 (Formidable (USA)   **65**
125) [2003 81p: 8.3g² 8.1m⁴ 8.1d p8g Oct 8] good-topped filly: fair maiden, lightly raced:
ran poorly last 2 starts: stays 1m: acts on heavy and good to firm ground: sold 16,000 gns
in December. *W. Jarvis*

HIGHLY PLEASED (USA)   8 b.g. Hansel (USA) – Bint Alfalla (USA) (Nureyev   **–**
(USA) 131) [2003 45: p7g p8g⁶ Jan 15] quite good-topped gelding: little form in 2003.
S. L. Keightley

HIGH POINT (IRE)   5 b.g. Ela-Mana-Mou 132 – Top Lady (IRE) 83 (Shirley Heights   **87**
130) [2003 81: p12g* 14.4d² 16.2m⁵ 14.4g² 14g* 16.1m⁵ 16.2d 12m 18m p12g* Nov 22]
leggy gelding: fairly useful handicapper: won at Lingfield in February, Sandown in June

and Lingfield in November: effective at 1½m to 2m: acts on polytrack, good to firm and good to soft going: held up and usually travels well: tough and reliable. *G. P. Enright*

HIGH POLICY (IRE)   7 ch.g. Machiavellian (USA) 123 – Road To The Top 84   **60**
(Shirley Heights 130) [2003 63, a84: f16.2g⁶ f14s 16.2m² 16d 16g⁶ f14.8g* f14s³ 15.9d   **a73**
f14.8g* f16.2g⁵ f14g⁶ Dec 12] well-made gelding: fair on all-weather, modest on turf:
won apprentice claimer in June and handicap in October, both at Wolverhampton: stays
17f: acts on fibresand and any turf going: visored once at 4 yrs, wears cheekpieces
nowadays: sometimes flashes tail: held up. *R. Hollinshead*

HIGH POWERED (GER)   4 b.f. So Factual (USA) 120 – High Habit 79 (Slip Anchor   **–**
136) [2003 67?: 8m 7m Jul 23] fair maiden: well held both starts at 4 yrs: tried blinkered.
D. W. Thompson

HIGH PRAISE (USA)   3 b.f. Quest For Fame 127 – Stellaria (USA) 98 (Roberto   **111**
(USA) 131) [2003 105: 12g 12g* Jun 29] smallish, quite attractive filly: smart performer,
lightly raced: best effort when winning Prix de Malleret at Saint-Cloud (broke out of stall
beforehand) in June by length from Underwater, making most: took good hold (including
to post) when well beaten in Oaks at Epsom only other 3-y-o start (bandaged hind joints):
stayed 1½m: acted on soft going: stud. *J. H. M. Gosden*

HIGH REACH   3 b.g. Royal Applause 124 – Lady of Limerick (IRE) (Thatching 131)   **98 +**
[2003 –p: p6g³ p7g³ p7g* p8g² 7g² 6.1m⁴ 6m³ 6m* p7g⁴ 6f⁴ Oct 11] strong, compact
gelding: progressed into useful handicapper at 3 yrs, winning at Lingfield (made all) in
February and Ascot in August: not clear run when good fourth to Najeebon at York final
start: probably best at 6f/7f: acts on polytrack and firm going. *T. G. Mills*

Mr K. Abdulla's "High Praise"

HIGH RESERVE 2 b.f. (Mar 15) Dr Fong (USA) 128 – Hyabella 111 (Shirley Heights **71 p**
130) [2003 7m³ 7m⁵ Oct 13] 220,000Y: half-sister to 3 winners, including useful French
2001 2-y-o 6f winner Hothaifah (by Green Desert) and fairly useful 1¼m winner Hyperspectra (by Rainbow Quest): dam, 1m winner, half-sister to high-class 1¼m performer
Stagecraft from excellent family: fair form in maidens at Kempton and Leicester
(travelled well but unable to quicken when fifth to Torcross): will stay 1m, probably
1¼m: open to progress. *J. R. Fanshawe*

HIGH RESOLVE 3 ch.c. Unfuwain (USA) 131 – Asteroid Field (USA) 123 (Forli **69**
(ARG)) [2003 10d 10.5v³ 12f⁵ p12g⁴ 10.1d⁴ Oct 4] 19,000Y: tall, leggy colt: fifth foal:
half-brother to 4-y-o Compton Dynamo: dam 7f (including Challenge Stakes) to 9f (US
Grade 1) winner: fair maiden: stays 1½m: acts on any turf going and polytrack: tongue
tied on debut: sold 1,000 gns. *J. R. Fanshawe*

HIGH RIDGE 4 ch.g. Indian Ridge 123 – Change For A Buck (USA) 83 (Time For A **68**
Change (USA)) [2003 68: 8m⁵ 8m 8.2s 7g³ 7.1g 7.1g 6m³ 6f⁵ 6m³ 6.1f⁶ 6g Oct 13] fair
maiden: effective at 6f to 1¼m: acts on firm and soft going: wore cheekpieces last 6 starts:
none too reliable. *J. M. Bradley*

HIGH SIROCCO 3 ch.g. First Trump 118 – Amid The Stars 61 (Midyan (USA) 124) **–**
[2003 52: 8d 7f Jun 6] tall gelding: modest form at 2 yrs: well held in 2003: tried in
cheekpieces. *D. W. Barker*

HIGH STREET 3 b.g. Mark of Esteem (IRE) 137 – Kentmere (FR) (Galetto (FR) **–**
118) [2003 –: 11g 8f Sep 8] good-topped gelding: signs of only a little ability: tried in
blinkers/cheekpieces. *Mrs Lydia Pearce*

HIGH SWAINSTON 2 ch.g. (Feb 27) The West (USA) 107 – Reamzafonic 46 (Grand **64**
Lodge (USA) 125) [2003 5m 7.5m⁵ 5m⁵ 5m³ 5g Sep 27] 2,800F, 2,600Y: angular, quite
good-topped gelding: first foal: dam, lightly-raced maiden, half-sister to useful Irish
performer up to 9f Hasanat: modest maiden: probably stays 7.5f. *R. Craggs*

HIGH VOLTAGE 2 ch.g. (Feb 9) Wolfhound (USA) 126 – Real Emotion (USA) (El **93**
Prado (IRE) 119) [2003 5m 5m² 6g² 5f* 5m² 6g² 5m 5g² 5m Sep 18] 3,500F, 6,200Y:
good-topped gelding: third foal: half-brother to winner abroad by Millkom: dam 6.5f/7.5f
winner in Italy: fairly useful performer: won maiden at Ayr in June by 7 lengths: second
in 3 minor events after, running creditably at Doncaster on first 2 occasions: likely to
prove best at 5f/easy 6f: wore tongue strap seventh outing: tends to carry head high.
K. R. Burke

HILARIOUS (IRE) 3 b.f. Petorius 117 – Heronwater (IRE) 73 (Ela-Mana-Mou 132) **60**
[2003 63: 8m 8.3g³ 7m 8.1m⁵ 7g 8.3m³ 8.3g⁴ 8f⁴ 9.9m Oct 1] good-topped filly: modest
maiden handicapper: stays 1m: acts on firm and good to soft going: races freely.
B. R. Millman

HILBRE ISLAND 3 b.c. Halling (USA) 133 – Faribole (IRE) 106 (Esprit du Nord **115**
(USA) 126) [2003 99: 10m² 10d⁴ 10.4m⁶ 11g⁶ 13.4m 11m³ 14m* 12g Oct 25] sturdy colt:
fluent mover: smart performer: won listed event at Newmarket in October by 3½ lengths
from Singleton: good close third to Compton Bolter in similar event at Newbury previous
start: will stay 2m: acts on good to firm and good to soft going. *B. J. Meehan*

HILITES (IRE) 2 ch.f. (Apr 8) Desert King (IRE) 129 – Slayjay (IRE) 94 (Mujtahid **85**
(USA) 118) [2003 5g⁴ 5d⁵ 6g 5m⁵ 5g³ 6f 6.3g⁴ 7.1f² 7.1m 5.9d* 6g* 6m 5.7f* 6f 6.5d 6m⁴
Sep 18] €9,000Y: leggy, close-coupled filly: second foal: dam Irish 5f winner: fairly
useful performer: won maiden at Carlisle in July, nursery at Windsor in August and minor
event at Bath later in August: probably stays easy 7f: acts on firm ground, probably on
good to soft. *J. S. Moore*

HILL FARM CLASSIC 3 ch.g. Meqdaam (USA) – Wing of Freedom (Troy 137) **–**
[2003 –: 8.2m 12m Oct 7] rather leggy gelding: little sign of ability. *M. Wellings*

HILL MAGIC 8 br.g. Magic Ring (IRE) 115 – Stock Hill Lass 87 (Air Trooper 115) **73**
[2003 73: 8.3m³ 8.3g⁶ 10m 7m⁵ 8.2m⁶ 8.1g* 8m⁶ p8g⁶ Oct 8] close-coupled, useful-
looking gelding: fair performer: won seller at Chepstow in September: stays 1m: acts on
firm going, good to soft and polytrack: tried in headgear: usually waited with: sold 1,600
gns. *W. S. Kittow*

HILLSIDE GIRL (IRE) 2 b.f. (May 4) Tagula (IRE) 116 – Kunucu (IRE) 94 (Blue- **78**
bird (USA) 125) [2003 5m⁴ 5g* 5g³ 5m⁴ 5f Jun 15] €6,000Y: good-topped filly: third
foal: half-sister to 3-y-o Raccoon: dam 5f winner, including at 2 yrs: fair performer: won
maiden at Newcastle in May: slow-starting fourth in listed event at Beverley after: very
weak in betting, pulled up reportedly lame final start: has since reportedly undergone
surgery to remove chips in a knee: should stay 6f. *A. Berry*

HILLS OF GOLD 4 b.g. Danehill (USA) 126 – Valley of Gold (FR) 117 (Shirley **74** Heights 130) [2003 98: 10m 8g 10d 8m 8.5m⁵ 8.5d 7.5m* 7g* 8.1f⁴ 7m 8g Oct 28] big, lengthy gelding: has a quick, fluent action: fair handicapper: won at Beverley (gambled on) and Chester in August: best at 7f/1m: acts on firm ground: tried tongue tied, reportedly had breathing operation after sixth start. *M. W. Easterby*

HILLS SPITFIRE (IRE) 2 b. or br.c. (Mar 25) Kahyasi 130 – Questina (FR) (Rain- **95 p** bow Quest (USA) 134) [2003 8m² 10g⁴ Nov 1] 38,000Y: lengthy, quite good-topped colt: third foal: half-brother to smart French 9f (at 2 yrs) to 10.5f winner Trumbaka (by In The Wings) and useful French 1m/1¼m winner Arctic Hunt (by Bering): dam French 1¼m winner: short-headed by Lunar Exit in 20-runner maiden at Newmarket: improved (useful form) when 3 lengths fourth to Fun And Games in listed event there, finishing well but too much to do: will stay at least 1½m: slowly away both starts: open to progress, and sure to win a race or 2. *P. W. Harris*

HILLTIME (IRE) 3 b.g. Danetime (IRE) 121 – Ceannanas (IRE) 77 (Magical Wonder – (USA) 125) [2003 61: 8.1d Sep 26] rather unfurnished, quite attractive gelding: modest maiden at 2 yrs: winner over hurdles prior to well beaten only 3-y-o Flat outing: tried visored. *J. J. Quinn*

HILLTOP FANTASY 2 b.f. (Apr 24) Danzig Connection (USA) – Hilltop 45 (Absa- **– p** lom 128) [2003 p7g⁴ Dec 17] first foal: dam, sprint maiden, ran only at 2 yrs: 16/1, 10 lengths fourth of 11 to Bettalatethannever in minor event at Lingfield, not unduly punished: open to improvement. *D. J. Daly*

HILLTOP WARNING 6 b.g. Reprimand 122 – Just Irene 50 (Sagaro 133) [2003 92: **96** 7m 7m* 7m Jul 10] mallish gelding: useful handicapper, lightly raced: easily best effort in 2003 when winning at Newmarket in June by 1½ lengths from Beluga Bay: best around 7f on good/good to firm ground: blinkered once at 3 yrs: held up: no easy ride. *D. J. Daly*

HILLY BE 2 b.f. (Feb 14) Silver Patriarch (IRE) 125 – Lolita (FR) (Hellios (USA)) – [2003 8s Oct 29] first foal: dam French 1½m winner: 66/1, well beaten in maiden at Yarmouth. *J. R. Jenkins*

HILTON PARK (IRE) 4 b.f. Dolphin Street (FR) 125 – Test Case 90 (Busted 134) – [2003 6f 7f f7g Jun 9] leggy filly: little form: tried visored. *J. Balding*

HIP HOP HARRY 3 b.c. First Trump 118 – Rechanit (IRE) (Local Suitor (USA) 128) **84** [2003 8m³ 10m* 10d p10g³ p10g* Dec 10] 16,500Y: sturdy colt: sixth foal: closely related to fairly useful 6f winner Prime Hand (by Primo Dominie), later successful in USA, and half-brother to 2 winners, including fairly useful 1¼m winner Simply Katie (by Most Welcome): dam, won up to 7f in Italy, half-sister to very smart performer up to 1¾m Sapience: fairly useful form: won maiden at Pontefract in September and handicap at Lingfield (by short head) in December: stays 1¼m: acts on good to firm ground and polytrack. *E. A. L. Dunlop*

HIRVINE (FR) 5 ch.g. Snurge 130 – Guadanella (FR) (Guadanini (FR) 125) [2003 **56** 69d: 12m⁵ 14.1d⁴ 16m⁵ 16m³ 15.8m Oct 7] big, strong gelding: modest maiden on Flat: stays 2m: acts on soft and good to firm going: blinkered last 3 starts: sold 14,000 gns, joined P. Bowen: fair form over hurdles. *T. P. Tate*

HISPANIOLA (IRE) 5 ch.m. Barathea (IRE) 127 – Caribbean Quest 90 (Rainbow – Quest (USA) 134) [2003 –: f7g f12g Dec 22] ex-French mare: no form in Britain. *M. W. Easterby*

HITMAN (IRE) 8 b.g. Contract Law (USA) 108 – Loveville (USA) (Assert 134) [2003 – 14.1g May 4] smart at 3 yrs, well held only run on Flat since: fairly useful hurdler/fair chaser. *M. Pitman*

HIT'S ONLY MONEY (IRE) 3 br.g. Hamas (IRE) 125§ – Toordillon (IRE) 69 (Con- **106** tract Law (USA) 108) [2003 6g⁴ 6m* 6m* 6m³ 6m Sep 20] 16,000 2-y-o: work- manlike gelding: second foal: dam Irish 1½m winner: quickly developed into useful performer, winning seller at Leicester and handicaps at Kempton and Ripon (by 4 lengths), all in April: further improvement when 2 lengths third to Bonus in Tote Scoop6 Sprint Handicap at Lingfield next time: off 4 months, well below form in Ayr Gold Cup (Handicap) final start: raced only at 6f on good/good to firm ground. *P. A. Blockley*

HOH BLEU DEE 2 b.c. (Mar 13) Desert Style (IRE) 121 – Ermine (IRE) 86 (Cadeaux **89** Genereux 131) [2003 5.7m* 6m* 7m⁶ 6m⁶ 7g⁶ Oct 11] 40,000Y, 33,000 2-y-o: smallish, well-made colt: first foal: dam, 1m winner, half-sister to very smart 1¼m/1½m winner Border Arrow: fairly useful performer: won maiden at Bath in July and minor event at Ripon in August: below form, including in nursery, last 2 starts: stays 7f. *S. Kirk*

Mr Gary A. Tanaka's "Hoh Buzzard"

HOH BUZZARD (IRE)   3 b.f. Alhaarth (IRE) 126 – Indian Express 61 (Indian Ridge   **114**
123) [2003 79: 9m³ 9g⁴ 8.1g³ 8m* 9d* 9.9m* 10d² 12f⁴ 8.5d* 8.5f⁵ Dec 20] leggy, quite
good-topped filly: smart performer: vastly improved in 2003, winning handicaps at Newmarket in June and Goodwood in July, listed race at Salisbury (beat Quiet Storm ½
length) in August and, having left M. Bell after eighth start, Grade 2 Mrs Revere Stakes
at Churchill Downs (best effort, beat Aud by a neck) in November: creditable ¾-length
second to State of Art in Prix de la Nonette at Deauville on seventh outing: effective at
1m, probably at 1½m: acts on firm and good to soft going: visored/blinkered nowadays:
front runner/races prominently. *B. D. A. Cecil, USA*

HOH INVADER (IRE)   11 b.g. Accordion – Newgate Fairy (Flair Path 122) [2003   **48**
58, a–: 12.4m 10.1m³ May 14] tall gelding: poor maiden: stays 2m: acts on firm going: **a–**
tongue tied both starts in 2003: front runner. *Mrs A. Duffield*

HOH INVESTOR (IRE)   3 b.g. Charnwood Forest (IRE) 125 – Uffizi (IRE) (Royal   **83**
Academy (USA) 130) [2003 79: p7g p7g* p8g⁴ p7g 8m 8g 7g 7.1m³ 7m⁵ 7.1g³ 8.1m⁵ 8m   **a96**
8m⁵ Sep 5] close-coupled, quite good-topped gelding: useful on all-weather, fairly useful
on turf: won minor event at Lingfield in February: effective at 7f/1m: acts on polytrack
and good to firm going: often slowly away: none too consistent: sent to South Korea.
A. M. Balding

463

Sheikh Mohammed's "Holborn"

HOH NELSON 2 b.c. (Apr 13) Halling (USA) 133 – Birsay (Bustino 136) [2003 8m **70 ?**
8m 8.2m Oct 22] strong, angular colt: fourth foal: half-brother to 1¼m/11f winner Yanus
(by Inchinor): dam unraced sister to useful 1½m/1¾m winner Baffin Bay: seemingly best
effort (fair form) when seventh of 8 in minor event at Nottingham final start: should be
well suited by 1¼m+. *H. Morrison*

HOH'S BACK 4 b.g. Royal Applause 124 – Paris Joelle (IRE) (Fairy King (USA)) **76**
[2003 77: f9.4g³ f8.5g² f9.4g⁵ f7g⁶ f8g f8g³ 10.1m⁴ 9m 9.2g⁵ f11g⁶ 10.1m 8m* f8.5s* **a80**
8.5d⁴ f8.5g* 9.2m⁵ p8g 8.5m* 7.5d⁴ 7.1g³ f9.4g f8s² 7m f8g f8.5g Dec 26] well-made
gelding: fairly useful handicapper on all-weather, fair on turf: left S. Kirk after third
start: won at Redcar (apprentices, wandered), Wolverhampton (2) and Beverley between
July/September: effective at 7f to 9.4f: acts on all-weather, soft and good to firm ground:
usually wears cheekpieces: usually races prominently. *Paul Johnson*

HOH VISS 3 b.g. Rudimentary (USA) 118 – Now And Forever (IRE) (Kris 135) [2003 **77**
55p: 10g⁴ 10m⁴ 10m⁵ 11m² 11.7m² 11.5m⁵ p12g⁵ p12g Dec 17] leggy, lengthy gelding:
fair maiden: stays 11.7f: acts on good to firm going, probably on polytrack. *S. Kirk*

HOLBORN (UAE) 2 b.c. (Feb 26) Green Desert (USA) 127 – Court Lane (USA) 81 **115**
(Machiavellian (USA) 123) [2003 5m* 5d⁴ 5f* 6m⁵ 6m⁴ 6m⁴ 6m² Oct 3] close-coupled,
sturdy colt: first foal: dam, 6f (at 2 yrs) and 1m (in France) winner, out of Cherry Hinton
winner Chicarica: smart performer: won maiden at Kempton in April and Windsor Castle
Stakes at Royal Ascot in June: in frame in Sirenia Stakes at Kempton (visored), Mill Reef
Stakes at Newbury and Middle Park Stakes at Newmarket (50/1, best effort when 1¼
lengths third, promoted to second, behind disqualified Three Valleys) after: will probably
stay 7f: acts on firm going, probably on good to soft: joined Godolphin. *M. R. Channon*

HOLD THAT TIGER (USA) 3 b.c. Storm Cat (USA) – Beware of The Cat (USA) **117**
(Caveat (USA)) [2003 117p: 8g 8f⁴ 10g a9f² a10f⁵ Oct 25] big, good-topped colt: smart
performer: won Grand Criterium at Longchamp and third in Breeders' Cup Juvenile at

Arlington at 2 yrs: favourite, never in contention when behind in 2000 Guineas at Newmarket (on toes and had 2 handlers) on reappearance: at least respectable efforts after in St James's Palace Stakes at Royal Ascot (fourth to Zafeen), Woodward Stakes at Belmont (best 3-y-o effort, 4¼ lengths second to Mineshaft) and Breeders' Cup Classic at Santa Anita (fifth to Pleasantly Perfect): effective at 1m/1¼m: acted on dirt, firm and soft ground: wore crossed noseband: reportedly in respiratory distress third 2-y-o start: tended to be slowly away/soon off bridle: to stand at Ashford Stud, USA, fee $15,000. *A. P. O'Brien, Ireland*

HOLD THE LINE   2 b.g. (Apr 9) Titus Livius (FR) 115 – Multi-Sofft 30 (Northern State (USA) 91) [2003 7.5m 7m⁶ f8s² f8.5g p10g⁵ Nov 29] 3,200Y: big gelding: sixth foal: half-brother to 3 winners, including 3-y-o Ellovamul: dam, maiden who probably stayed 1¾m, out of Cheshire Oaks/Lancashire Oaks winner One Over Parr: fair maiden: second at Southwell: will stay at least 1¼m: acts on all-weather, only a little promise on turf: carried head awkwardly fourth start. *W. G. M. Turner*   **72**

HOLD TO RANSOM (USA)   3 b.f. Red Ransom (USA) – Wassifa 95 (Sure Blade (USA) 130) [2003 91: 7g⁴ 10g² 10.4m⁶ 8f* 8m 9f⁵ 8m Oct 4] strong filly: fluent mover: smart performer: best effort at 3 yrs when winning listed rated stakes at Ascot in June by 5 lengths from Sharplaw Venture: respectable fifth to Irish Glora in Grade 2 handicap at Woodbine after: effective at 1m, barely at 1¼m: acts on firm and soft ground: free-going sort: none too consistent: sent to USA. *E. A. L. Dunlop*   **111**

HOLD UP   2 ch.f. (Feb 25) Daggers Drawn (USA) 114 – Select Sale (Auction Ring (USA) 123) [2003 8m Sep 23] rather leggy, attractive filly: half-sister to several winners, notably smart 1½m performer Private Tender (by Shirley Heights): dam unraced half-sister to Ribblesdale Stakes winner Queen Midas: 16/1, tenth of 17 in maiden at Newmarket, racing isolated and not knocked about: should do better. *E. A. L. Dunlop*   **– p**

HO LENG (IRE)   8 ch.g. Statoblest 120 – Indigo Blue (IRE) 56 (Bluebird (USA) 125) [2003 92§: 7.1m 8m⁶ 8.1m 7.2f 7m³ 8m 8m 7.2f⁴ 8m⁴ 8m Sep 20] leggy, lengthy gelding: fairly useful handicapper: stays 1m: best on good going or firmer (acts on firm): often slowly away/rears: unreliable. *Miss L. A. Perratt*   **80 §**

HOLLE BERRY   3 b.f. Petoski 135 – Plectrum 58 (Adonijah 126) [2003 10.1m 11.5s 11.5g 10.1m Sep 17] fourth foal: half-sister to German 1m winner by Mazaad: dam middle-distance maiden: no form in claimers/sellers: refused to enter stall on intended debut. *G. C. H. Chung*

HOLLOW JO   3 b.g. Most Welcome 131 – Sir Hollow (USA) (Sir Ivor 135) [2003 –: 6g² 6m* 7.1f* 5.9m* 6d* 5m² 7m Sep 7] strong, lengthy gelding: fair handicapper: won at Thirsk (ladies), Musselburgh, Carlisle and Windsor in summer: effective at 5f to 7f: acts on firm and good to soft going: tends to wander. *J. R. Jenkins*   **77**

HOLLYBELL   4 b.f. Beveled (USA) – Fayre Holly (IRE) 57 (Fayruz 116) [2003 87§, a67§: p6g p6g 6m Mar 29] leggy filly: fairly useful but unreliable performer at 3 yrs: well held in 2003, in cheekpieces final start. *J. Gallagher*   **– §**

HOLLY HAYES (IRE)   3 b.f. Alzao (USA) 117 – Crystal Land (Kris 135) [2003 10m⁴ 10g⁶ Oct 25] 45,000Y: sturdy, close-coupled filly: seventh foal: half-sister to 9.4f winner Crystal Gold (by Arazi) and 1¼m winner King's Crown (by Lead On Time), both fairly useful: dam French maiden sister to Prix Saint-Alary winner Fitnah: little form in maidens at Newbury: sold 1,200 gns. *H. Candy*   **–**

Sandringham Rated Stakes (Handicap), Royal Ascot—
Hold To Ransom defies top weight on her handicap debut; next to finish are Sharplaw Venture (breastgirth),
Chic (second right) and Secret Formula

HOLLY ROSE 4 b.f. Charnwood Forest (IRE) 125 – Divina Luna 96 (Dowsing (USA) **67 §**
124) [2003 60: 7.9m 8m³ 9.2m⁵ 9.7f⁶ 8m² 9.7m* 8m 10m³ 10m⁴ 10.1m* 9.9m 10m Oct
20] fair performer: won handicap at Folkestone in July and seller at Yarmouth in September: stays 1¼m: acts on polytrack, raced only on good going or firmer on turf: tried
blinkered, wore cheekpieces last 8 starts: temperamental. *D. E. Cantillon*

HOLLY RYDER (USA) 3 ch.f. Spinning World (USA) 130 – Ethyl Mae (USA) **–**
(Woodman (USA) 126) [2003 6g f6g 6g 8m Sep 18] $110,000Y: second foal: half-sister
to winner in USA by Hennessy: dam, won 8.5f minor stakes at 2 yrs in USA, half-sister to
US Grade 2 8.5f winner Mystic Lady: well held in maidens/handicap. *P. F. I. Cole*

HOLLY WALK 2 ch.f. (Feb 22) Dr Fong (USA) 128 – Holly Blue 107 (Bluebird (USA) **46**
125) [2003 7m 7m 8.1g 8m⁴ Sep 18] sturdy filly: first foal: dam 1m winner: poor maiden:
wandered when fourth in nursery at Yarmouth: will stay 1¼m: sold 8,500 gns. *R. Hannon*

HOLLYWOOD HENRY (IRE) 3 b.g. Bahhare (USA) 122 – Takeshi (IRE) 67 **–**
(Cadeaux Genereux 131) [2003 75: 8.3g 9g 8.1f 8.3g 8g 8.5g Sep 10] well-made gelding:
fair maiden at 2 yrs: well held in 2003: tried blinkered. *J. Akehurst*

HOLY ORDERS (IRE) 6 b.g. Unblest 117 – Shadowglow (Shaadi (USA) 126) [2003 **114**
112: 10g² 13s* 12d³ 14d* 13.9m⁶ 12d 16g Nov 4] smallish gelding: smart performer:
won listed race at Navan in April and handicap at Galway in August: very good sixth to
Saint Alebe in Ebor Handicap at York next time: reportedly proved reluctant in work prior
to finishing well beaten in Melbourne Cup (Handicap) at Flemington final outing: stays
2m: acts on heavy and good to firm going: blinkered: held up/travels strongly: usually
ridden by claimer D. Condon. *W. P. Mullins, Ireland*

HOME COMING 5 br.g. Primo Dominie 121 – Carolside 108 (Music Maestro 119) **–**
[2003 –: f8.5s⁶ 6m 7m 6m 6f f7s Sep 26] little form. *P. S. Felgate*

HOME FLEET (USA) 3 ch.c. Gone West (USA) – All At Sea (USA) 124 (Riverman **84**
(USA) 131) [2003 71p: 7g* 8.2d⁴ Jul 26] strong, close-coupled colt: fair performer,
lightly raced: won maiden at Thirsk in May: stays 1m: acts on good to soft ground, probably on polytrack. *H. R. A. Cecil*

HOMELIFE (IRE) 5 b.g. Persian Bold 123 – Share The Vision (Vision (USA)) [2003 **–**
81: 16.1m 14.8m⁵ 14.8m⁵ 12.3m⁶ Aug 30] tall, useful-looking gelding: fairly useful at
best: well held in 2003: has sweated/been slowly away. *P. W. D'Arcy*

HOMERIC TROJAN 3 ch.c. Hector Protector (USA) 124 – Housefull 81 (Habitat **–**
134) [2003 8m 10m 8m Apr 22] tall, quite good-topped colt: has a round action:
eighth foal: half-brother to several winners, including 4-y-o Karminskey Park and
5-y-o Tinian: dam, 1m winner, out of 1000 Guineas winner Full Dress II: well beaten in
maidens. *M. Brittain*

HOMEWARD (IRE) 2 ch.f. (Feb 17) Kris 135 – Home Truth 98 (Known Fact (USA) **– p**
135) [2003 6g Oct 24] sturdy filly: half-sister to several winners, including very smart
6f/7f winner Susu (by Machiavellian) and useful 6f winner Cadeaux Cher (by Cadeaux
Genereux): dam 7f/1m winner: 33/1 and better for race, well held in maiden at Newbury,
never a threat: should stay 1m: likely to do better. *G. A. Butler*

HONEST INJUN 2 b.c. (Apr 24) Efisio 120 – Sioux 76 (Kris 135) [2003 6g 7s² Nov **77 p**
3] third foal: brother to 3-y-o To Wit To Woo: dam 1½m winner: better effort in maidens
(fair form) when 2 lengths second of 15 to Go Padero at Redcar, slowly away: likely to be
suited by 1¼m/1½m: open to progress. *B. W. Hills*

HONEYBOURNE 4 b.f. Sri Pekan (USA) 117 – Peetsie (IRE) (Fairy King (USA)) **55**
[2003 10g 10m 8.1m 7m² Aug 8] first foal: dam, third in bumper (well beten on Flat), out
of half-sister to 1000 Guineas winner One In A Million: modest maiden: may prove best
at 5f/6f: blinkered last 2 starts: sold 800 gns in December. *Mrs Mary Hambro*

HONEY'S GIFT 4 b.f. Terimon 124 – Honeycroft (Crofter (USA) 124) [2003 56: **–**
p12g 12g Mar 25] rather leggy filly: shows knee action: modest maiden: well beaten both
4-y-o outings: tried in cheekpieces. *G. G. Margarson*

HONEYSTREET (IRE) 3 b.f. Woodborough (USA) 112 – Ring of Kerry (IRE) 67 **62**
(Kenmare (FR) 125) [2003 59: p8g 6.1m 7m 7m³ 7.1g 8m 8f* 10m⁵ 8d* 8f⁶ 8.1m 8f Oct
12] sparely-made filly: modest handicapper: won at Bath (seller) in June and Salisbury in
July: stays 1m: acts on firm and good to soft going: wore cheekpieces last 6 outings: held
up: none too consistent. *J. S. Moore*

HONORINE (IRE) 3 b.f. Mark of Esteem (IRE) 137 – Blue Water (USA) 104 (Bering **89**
136) [2003 66: 8f² 8g* 8m² 8m* 8m² 8g⁴ 8.1m³ Sep 17] leggy filly: fairly useful handi-

capper: won at Yarmouth in May and Doncaster in August: stays 1m: raced only on good ground or firmer: held up: consistent. *J. W. Payne*

HONOR ROUGE (IRE) 4 ch.f. Highest Honor (FR) 124 – Ayers Rock (IRE) 95 (In **86** The Wings 128) [2003 96: 10m 12m* 12m⁶ 10f 12m 11.5g Sep 16] good-topped filly: fairly useful handicapper: best effort in 2003 when winning 4-runner event at Salisbury in May by head from Silence Is Golden: stays 1½m: acts on firm ground, possibly not on softer than good: sold 12,000 gns, joined D. Bridgwater. *P. W. Harris*

HONOR'S LAD 4 ch.g. Sabrehill (USA) 120 – Ackcontent (USA) (Key To Content **–** (USA)) [2003 –: f12g p7g f11g Mar 11] angular gelding: little form: tried blinkered/in cheekpieces. *Mrs L. C. Jewell*

HOOPZ 3 gr.f. Linamix (FR) 127 – Pearl Venture 92 (Salse (USA) 128) [2003 70p: 7g **–** 8m⁴ Jun 24] lightly-raced maiden: well held both 3-y-o starts. *Mrs A. J. Perrett*

HO PANG YAU 5 b. or gr.g. Pivotal 124 – La Cabrilla 89 (Carwhite 127) [2003 56: 6g **–** 7.1m 6m 6f Aug 29] close-coupled gelding: modest handicapper at best: well held in 2003: tried blinkered/in cheekpieces. *Miss L. A. Perratt*

HOPE DIAMOND (IRE) 5 ch.g. Bigstone (IRE) 126 – Mujtahida (IRE) 63 (Muj- **46** tahid (USA) 118) [2003 –: 11.9d⁴ a7g 12m Jul 12] poor form: left C. McCarthy, Ireland, after second start. *Mrs J. Candlish*

HOPE SOUND (IRE) 3 b.g. Turtle Island (IRE) 123 – Lucky Pick 69 (Auction Ring **68 ?** (USA) 123) [2003 10.1d² 10g 10m Jul 21] 22,000Y: sixth foal: half-brother to French 7.5f winner Abchere Bissaadak (by Common Grounds) and a winner in Spain by Dancing Dissident: dam, maiden best at 1¼m, sister to very smart 7f/1m performer Lucky Ring: easily best effort in maidens (fair form) when second at Newcastle: not sure to stay beyond 1¼m: slowly away last 2 outings, in visor final one: sold 13,000 gns in October. *J. Noseda*

HORIZON HILL (USA) 3 b.g. Distant View (USA) 126 – Accadia Rocket (USA) **64 d** (Bold Ruckus (USA)) [2003 67p: 7g 7.1m⁵ 7m 8g 8d⁶ 7.5m 5.9m⁴ 6m³ 5g 6m⁶ 7g 8m 7m⁴ Sep 22] rather leggy, lengthy gelding: modest maiden: below form after second outing: effective at 6f/easy 7f: acts on firm and good to soft ground: tried in cheekpieces/blinkers: ungenuine: sold 2,500 gns. *Mrs J. R. Ramsden*

HORIZONTAL (USA) 3 ch.g. Distant View (USA) 126 – Proud Lou (USA) (Proud **59** Clarion) [2003 8m⁵ May 31] closely related to 5-y-o Proud Western and half-brother to several winners, including smart 5.5f (at 2 yrs) to 1m (Poule d'Essai des Pouliches) winner Houseproud (by Riverman) and useful French 7f/1m winner Proud Fact (by Known Fact): dam US Grade 1 2-y-o 1m winner: 20/1 and early to post, fifth to Alnasreya in maiden at Newmarket, carrying head high: sold 9,000 gns. *H. R. A. Cecil*

HORMUZ (IRE) 7 b.g. Hamas (IRE) 125§ – Balqis (USA) 93 (Advocator) [2003 87, **66** a75: f7s 7m f8g 8f⁵ 8m 6d⁴ 6d 10.1m 9m 9f⁴ f8g 8m 7d 8.5m⁶ 7.5m f8s⁴ 10.1m Oct 12] **a56** big, heavy-topped gelding: just fair handicapper on turf, modest on all-weather: stays 9f: acts on all-weather, firm and soft going: tried in cheekpieces: usually front runner: none too consistent. *Paul Johnson*

HORNER (USA) 2 b.c. (Feb 2) Rahy (USA) 115 – Dynashore (CAN) (Dynaformer **79** (USA)) [2003 6m⁴ 7.6g⁴ 7m⁶ Sep 20] $67,000Y: good-bodied colt: second foal: dam 1m/ 9f winner in USA: fair form in maidens at York and Newbury first and final starts: reluctant to post when below form at Chester in between: should stay 1m. *P. F. I. Cole*

HORTON DANCER 6 b.g. Rambo Dancer (USA) 107 – Horton Lady 46 (Midyan **–** (USA) 124) [2003 47, a39: f16g⁶ f16s⁶ Feb 13] close-coupled gelding: poor handicapper: showed little at 6 yrs: tried visored/tongue tied. *I. W. McInnes*

HOTELIERS' DREAM 5 b.m. Reprimand 122 – Pride of Britain (CAN) 67 (Link- **–** age (USA)) [2003 35: 9.9m 11.8m f12s 14.1d Jul 26] of little account: tried visored/ blinkered/tongue tied. *W. S. Kittow*

HOT LIPS PAGE (FR) 2 b.f. (Apr 25) Hamas (IRE) 125§ – Salt Peanuts (IRE) (Salt **72 ?** Dome (USA)) [2003 6m 7m 6m⁵ Oct 4] close-coupled filly: half-sister to several winners in France, including 1m winner Alabamy Sound (by Superlative): dam, won twice in Belgium at 2 yrs, from good staying family: seemingly best effort in maidens (fair form) when fifth at Newmarket, dictating pace: should stay 1m. *R. Hannon*

HOT LOVE 4 b.f. Blushing Flame (USA) 109 – Tiama (IRE) 50 (Last Tycoon 131) **59** [2003 59: f12g² f12g³ f16.2g⁴ f12g 8m 11s May 12] rather leggy, lengthy filly: modest handicapper: left Gay Kelleway after fourth outing: stays 1½m: acts on all-weather and good to soft ground: tried visored, often blinkered: held up. *John J. Walsh, Ireland*

Polypipe Flying Childers Stakes, Doncaster—Howick Falls (left) responds well to beat Pipalong's half-sister China Eyes, Nights Cross (dark colours) and Boogie Street (right)

HOUSE OF BLUES 2 b.c. (Apr 5) Grand Lodge (USA) 125 – Sartigila 67 (Efisio 120) [2003 p8g p8g 8.2d Nov 6] 36,000Y: close-coupled, useful-looking colt: fifth foal: half-brother to 5-y-o Alfano: dam 6f and 1m winner: green, modest form at best in maidens: should stay 1¼m. *J. A. Osborne* **59**

HOUSE OF YORK (USA) 2 b.c. (Apr 22) Seeking The Gold (USA) – Housa Dancer (FR) 109 (Fabulous Dancer (USA) 124) [2003 7m⁶ 7m⁵ 6m Aug 20] second foal: dam, 1m (at 2 yrs)/9f winner in France who later won in USA (where runner-up in Grade 1 9f event), half-sister to very smart Prix Niel winner Housamix: seemingly best effort in maidens (fair form) when fifth of 6 at Doncaster: will stay at least 1m: sold 14,000 gns, sent to Germany. *M. R. Channon* **69 ?**

HOUSEPARTY (IRE) 5 b. or br.g. Grand Lodge (USA) 125 – Special Display (Welsh Pageant 132) [2003 –: 10m 12m Apr 23] good-bodied gelding: fairly useful at 3 yrs: well beaten both starts in 2003. *J. A. B. Old* **–**

HOUT BAY 6 ch.g. Komaite (USA) – Maiden Pool 85 (Sharpen Up 127) [2003 69: f6s p6g⁶ 5g³ 5m⁶ 6m 6m⁵ 5g³ 5m 5g 5g⁶ 5m⁵ 6m 6g Oct 14] big, lengthy gelding: modest handicapper nowadays: best at 5f/easy 6f: acts on good to soft going, firm and all-weather: blinkered (well held) final start: sold 7,000 gns. *Jedd O'Keeffe* **62**

HOV 3 gr.g. Petong 126 – Harifa (Local Suitor (USA) 128) [2003 69p: 7g³ 7.1f³ 6.1m 6g⁴ f7g* f8g* f8g* 8.5d² 10.3g⁵ 8.1d⁴ f7g Oct 16] leggy, quite good-topped gelding: fairly useful performer: won maiden and handicap (beat First Maite 7 lengths) at Southwell in June: stays 8.5f: acts on all-weather and good to soft going: has raced freely. *J. J. Quinn* **88**

HOWABOYS QUEST (USA) 6 b.g. Quest For Fame 127 – Doctor Black (USA) (Family Doctor (USA)) [2003 f12s⁵ 17.2m Jun 25] poor maiden: well held both 6-y-o starts. *Ferdy Murphy* **–**

HOWARDS DREAM (IRE) 5 b.g. King's Theatre (IRE) 128 – Keiko 76 (Generous (IRE) 139) [2003 11.1d 12.1d⁶ 10g³ 13g 14f³ 12m 16f 12.1g* 11.1m⁵ 13m⁴ 12.1g 13g⁵ 14f⁵ 12.1g 14m 10.9m⁶ 13d Sep 29] compact gelding: modest handicapper: won at Hamilton in July: stays 1¾m: acts on firm ground: tried in cheekpieces: usually tongue tied: none too consistent. *D. A. Nolan* **53**

HOWARDS HERO (IRE) 4 gr.g. Paris House 123 – Gold Braisim (IRE) 77 (Jareer (USA) 115) [2003 61: f5s f5g⁴ f5g Mar 11] tall gelding: modest performer: best at 5f: acts on good to firm going, good to soft and fibresand: tried blinkered/visored at 3 yrs. *Paul Johnson* **55**

HOWICK FALLS (USA) 2 br.c. (Feb 1) Stormin Fever (USA) 116 – Hollins (USA) (Roanoke (USA)) [2003 5d* 5f³ 6m 5m* 5g* Sep 13] $29,000F, $70,000Y: good-topped colt: usually looks well: third foal: half-brother to winner in USA by Boone's Mill: dam unraced half-sister to US Grade 3 winner at 7f and 9f Laura's Pistolette: smart performer: won minor event at Newcastle in May, listed race at York (beat If Paradise by 3½ lengths, briefly hanging right) in August and Polypipe Flying Childers Stakes at Doncaster (by ¾ length from China Eyes) in September: free-going sort, probably best at 5f: acts on good to firm ground: visored last 2 starts: bandaged behind penultimate one: joined Saeed bin Suroor. *D. R. Loder* **111**

HOWLE HILL (IRE) 3 b.g. Ali-Royal (IRE) 127 – Grandeur And Grace (USA) 75 (Septieme Ciel (USA) 123) [2003 98: 10m 8g³ 7.9m³ 8m 10s* 10.4m² 11.9m Sep 3] leggy gelding: smart performer: won minor event at Ascot in July by short head from

Hawksbill: good ¾-length second to Akshar in handicap at York next time: stays 10.4f: acts on polytrack, soft and good to firm ground: has worn crossed noseband: tends to sweat: has had 2 handlers/been early to post: reared leaving stall final outing: sometimes races freely: waited with: won juvenile hurdle in November. *A. King*

HOW'S THINGS 3 b.g. Danzig Connection (USA) – Dim Ots 92 (Alhijaz 122) [2003 **78** 62: f7g⁴ f7s⁶ f9.4g⁶ 7m⁴ 8m f9.4g³ f7s* f9.4g* f8g² f8g² f9.4g³ Dec 26] good-topped gelding: fairly useful performer: won seller at Southwell in October and handicap at Wolverhampton in November: effective at 7f to 9.4f: acts on fibresand: tried visored/in cheekpieces: sometimes races freely. *D. Haydn Jones*

HOXNE STAR (IRE) 2 b.g. (May 22) Soviet Star (USA) 128 – Shakanda (IRE) **74 p** (Shernazar 131) [2003 7g* 8f⁴ Aug 22] 20,000Y: eighth foal: half-brother to 3 winners, including smart 7f (at 2 yrs) to 1½m winner The Glow-Worm (by Doyoun) and useful Irish 1¼m and 1¾m winner Deeply (by Darshaan): dam Irish 1½m winner: fair form when winning maiden at Yarmouth in July, leading final 1f: possibly amiss when last in minor event at Newcastle: should stay at least 1m: sold 16,000 gns: probably open to progress. *M. R. Channon*

HSI WANG MU (IRE) 2 ch.f. (Feb 22) Dr Fong (USA) 128 – Oh Hebe (IRE) 74 **50** (Night Shift (USA)) [2003 6g⁴ f5g⁵ 6d 7m³ 8m 8m Oct 21] 25,000Y: second foal: half-sister to 3-y-o Devious Boy: dam, 7f winner, half-sister to 3-y-o Leporello and smart 1¼m/1½m performer Poppy Carew: modest maiden: third in nursery at Redcar: ran badly in similar events after: should stay at least 1m: acts on good to firm going, probably on fibresand: sold 17,500 gns. *G. C. Bravery*

Sheikh Mohammed's "Howick Falls"

Tote Chester Cup (Handicap), Chester—Hugs Dancer responds in typically generous fashion; Big Moment (second left), Knavesmire Omen (third right), Rahwaan (noseband), Bourgeois (rail) and Cover Up (left) are next home

HUB HUB 5 b.g. Polish Precedent (USA) 131 – Ghassanah 73 (Pas de Seul 133) [2003 **45 §** 53: f8s⁶ f7s⁵ f7s⁵ p12g Mar 5] poor maiden: stayed 8.5f: acted on good to firm going, good to soft and fibresand: tried in headgear: unreliable: dead. *W. R. Muir*

HUFFLEPUFF (IRE) 4 b.f. Desert King (IRE) 129 – Circle of Chalk (FR) 74 (Kris **94** 135) [2003 102+: 5.1g⁶ 5.1m⁶ 5m 5f⁵ 6.1m⁴ 5.2m 6m 5d Sep 28] neat filly: useful performer at 3 yrs: just fairly useful in 2003: best at 5f/6f: yet to race on soft/heavy going, acts on any other: often forces pace. *J. L. Dunlop*

HUGE HEART (NZ) 7 b.g. T V Heart Throb (USA) – Christmas Lady (NZ) (Palm **–** Beach (FR) 80) [2003 9.2g Jul 24] 6f winner in New Zealand at 2 yrs: no form over jumps, and showed little only start on Flat in Britain. *W. M. Brisbourne*

HUGH THE MAN (IRE) 4 b.g. Hamas (IRE) 125§ – Run To Jenny 105 (Runnett **58** 125) [2003 56: f7g* p7g f7g f7g² f8.5s* f8.5g² f9.4f⁵ 8d 8m 8.3d f9.4s² f8.5g Dec 26] **a78** close-coupled, good-topped gelding: fair performer at best: won maiden in January and handicap in February, both at Wolverhampton: stays 9.4f: acts on all-weather, lightly raced and modest form on turf: tried visored/in cheekpieces. *N. P. Littmoden*

HUGS DANCER (FR) 6 b.g. Cadeaux Genereux 131 – Embracing 91 (Reference **109** Point 139) [2003 101: 18.7m* 16.4m 16.1g 13.9f* 13.9m 18d³ 12g 16g Nov 4] workmanlike gelding: useful performer: better than ever at 6 yrs, winning Tote Chester Cup (by ½ length from Big Moment) in May and listed event at York (beat Mamcazma 2½ lengths) in July: not discredited last 3 outings, third to Persian Punch in Doncaster Cup, seventh to Mummify in Caulfield Cup (Handicap) and ninth to Makybe Diva in Melbourne Cup (Handicap) at Flemington: effective at 1½m to 21f: acts on firm and good to soft going: tried blinkered/often visored earlier in career: reportedly finished with irregular heartbeat when tailed off in Ebor fifth start: has raced lazily/idled in front: waited with: tough, game and consistent: reportedly sold, and to continue career in Australia with T. McEvoy. *J. G. Given*

HUGWITY 11 ch.g. Cadeaux Genereux 131 – Nuit d'Ete (USA) 90 (Super Concorde **42** (USA) 128) [2003 61: 8m 8m⁴ p10g 11.6m 10.1m⁴ Aug 6] big, good-topped gelding: poor performer nowadays: effective at 1m to easy 1½m: acts on firm going, good to soft and all-weather. *G. C. Bravery*

HUJA (IRE) 3 b.f. Alzao (USA) 117 – Nasanice (IRE) 97 (Nashwan (USA) 135) **–** [2003 102: 7m⁵ May 10] close-coupled filly: has a quick action: useful at 2 yrs (in frame in Prestige Stakes and Fillies' Mile): below form in listed event at Lingfield only 3-y-o start: stays 1m: yet to race on extremes of going: sent to USA. *Sir Michael Stoute*

HULA BALLEW 3 ch.f. Weldnaas (USA) 112 – Ballon 63 (Persian Bold 123) [2003 **70** 60: 10m³ 14.1m 10m 9.1m⁴ 9m² 7.9d* 8m³ 7.9f³ 8f⁶ 8m⁶ Oct 1] smallish filly: fair handicapper: won at Carlisle in July: best around 1m: acts on good to firm and good to soft ground. *M. Dods*

470

HUMDINGER (IRE)   3 b.f. Charnwood Forest (IRE) 125 – High Finish 58 (High **71 d**
Line 125) [2003 60p: p8g p8g 9.9m 11m² 11.6m² 12m* 12f³ 15.4m⁶ f14s* f14g f14g **a66 d**
f12g⁶ f12s Dec 27] fair performer: left D. Coakley after fourth start, M. Pipe after fifth:
won handicap at Folkestone in July and claimer at Southwell (claimed from D. Daly
£10,000) in September: well beaten after: stays 1¾m: acts on fibresand and firm ground.
D. Shaw

HUMID CLIMATE   3 ch.g. Desert King (IRE) 129 – Pontoon 89 (Zafonic (USA) **80**
130) [2003 63p: 10.3m* 11.6g³ 10.3d Sep 10] strong, good-bodied colt: type to carry
condition: fairly useful form: won maiden at Lingfield (took strong hold to post) in May:
well beaten both starts after, hanging badly left penultimate one: stays 1¼m: unraced on
extremes of going: sold 14,000 gns. *Mrs A. J. Perrett*

HUMILITY   2 b.f. (May 5) Polar Falcon (USA) 126 – Rich In Love (IRE) 95 (Alzao **– p**
(USA) 117) [2003 6m Aug 27] first foal: dam 6f (at 2 yrs) to 1m winner out of half-sister
to Prix de la Salamandre winner Noblequest and to dam of Pursuit of Love: 9/1, eleventh
of 16 in maiden at Ascot, slowly away but headway to dispute second before weakening:
sure to do better. *C. A. Cyzer*

HUM (IRE)   2 ch.f. (Apr 22) Cadeaux Genereux 131 – Ensorceleuse (FR) (Fabulous **63**
Dancer (USA) 124) [2003 6m⁶ 7.1m 7.1m Oct 25] €60,000Y: leggy filly: fourth foal:
sister to 2001 2-y-o 1m winner Entretenue and half-sister to 7.5f winner Elitiste (by
Arctic Tern), both in France: dam, French maiden, half-sister to Prix de Diane winner
Escaline: modest form in maidens first 2 starts: well held in seller: should stay 1m: sold
14,000 gns. *A. C. Stewart*

Mr J. G. White's "Hugs Dancer"

Cheveley Park Stud's "Humouresque"

HUMOURESQUE 3 b.f. Pivotal 124 – Miswaki Belle (USA) 73 (Miswaki (USA) **110**
124) [2003 76p: f8g* p10g* p10g* 10.8g⁴ 10.5g* 10.5g* 10g⁶ 12m Jun 19] progressed
into smart performer in first half of 2003, winning maiden at Southwell and handicap at
Lingfield in January, listed events at Cagnes-sur-Mer in February and Saint-Cloud in
March, and Prix Penelope at Saint-Cloud (beat Sweet Folly 1½ lengths) in April: respectable sixth to Fidelite in Prix Saint-Alary at Longchamp next time: dropped out tamely in
Ribblesdale Stakes at Royal Ascot final start: stayed 10.8f: acted on all-weather, raced
mainly on good ground on turf: raced prominently: genuine: visits Linamix. *Sir Mark
Prescott*

HUNTER'S MARK (USA) 3 b.f. Titus Livius (FR) 115 – Manfath (IRE) 65 (Last **48 +**
Tycoon 131) [2003 –p: f7g⁵ 8g 8.1m 12s a8.3f* a8s Nov 28] poor form in Britain: left
J. Hills after third outing: won maiden at Mountaineer Park in November: should stay
1¼m: acts on dirt: blinkered last 3 outings. *J. Fox, USA*

HUNTER'S VALLEY 2 b.f. (Feb 25) Nicolotte 118 – Down The Valley 73 (Kampala **79**
120) [2003 6m 7m⁵ 7m² 7m³ Oct 17] good-bodied filly: half-sister to several winners,
including useful 2001 2-y-o 6f/7f (Rockfel Stakes) winner Distant Valley (by Distant
Relative), later Grade 3 8.5f winner in USA: dam 2-y-o 5f winner who stayed 11f: fair
maiden: second at Kempton: likely to stay 1m. *R. Hannon*

HUNTING LODGE (IRE) 2 ch.c. (Jan 15) Grand Lodge (USA) 125 – Vijaya (USA) **99**
(Lear Fan (USA) 130) [2003 5g* 8.2m* 8m Sep 12] 290,000F: strong colt: third foal:
dam 1m/9f winner in France (later successful in USA): useful form: won minor events at
Newmarket in April and Nottingham (by 4 lengths from Billy Allen) in August: respectable seventh in listed race at Goodwood: will be suited by 1¼m/1½m: visored last 2
starts. *D. R. Loder*

HUNTING PINK 2 b.f. (May 16) Foxhound (USA) 103 – Dancing Bluebell (IRE) 79 **52**
(Bluebird (USA) 125) [2003 6m 7f⁴ 5.7f⁴ 6.1m⁶ 7m³ 10f 8.2m p8g⁴ f8g⁴ Dec 8] close-

472

coupled, good-bodied filly: fourth foal: half-sister to 2000 2-y-o 6f winner Blue Lady (by College Chapel): dam Irish 11f winner: modest maiden: stays 1m: acts on polytrack and firm going: tongue tied (below form) fourth outing. *H. Morrison*

HURRICANE ALAN (IRE)   3 b. or br.c. Mukaddamah (USA) 125 – Bint Al Balad   **113**
(IRE) 63 (Ahonoora 122) [2003 102: 8m* 8g 8f⁶ 7g⁵ 8g² 7m 8m⁵ Aug 23] neat colt: smart performer: won Macau Jockey Club Craven Stakes at Newmarket in April by 1½ lengths from Lundy's Lane: creditable efforts in 2000 Guineas at Newmarket (seventh behind Refuse To Bend), St James's Palace Stakes at Royal Ascot (sixth to Zafeen), Lennox Stakes at Goodwood and listed event at Goodwood (length second to Court Masterpiece) next 4 starts: effective at 7f/1m: raced only on good ground or firmer since debut: got loose in pre-parade ring final intended outing: changed ownership 155,000 gns in October. *R. Hannon*

HURRICANE COAST   4 b.g. Hurricane Sky (AUS) – Tread Carefully 51 (Sharpo   **68 §**
132) [2003 77: 7.5m 7m⁵ 8m 10.5m⁶ 8.2m⁵ 8m 6.9m³ 7m 8d² 8d f7g* f6g² f8.5g³ f6g⁴ f6g⁴ Dec 19] tall gelding: fair performer: left T. Easterby after eighth start: won seller at Southwell (flashed tail) in November: best at 6f to 1m: acts on fibresand, firm and good to soft going: edgy sort: sometimes hangs: carries head awkwardly: temperamental. *P. A. Blockley*

HURRICANE FLOYD (IRE)   5 ch.g. Pennekamp (USA) 130 – Mood Swings   **98 §**
(IRE) 77 (Shirley Heights 130) [2003 104: 8g³ 8.1g 7g 8.5d 7f² 8m 7m 7g 7m³ 7m⁴ 7f 9m 8m³ Oct 17] smallish, sturdy gelding: has a quick action: useful handicapper: several creditable efforts in 2003, including second of 27 to Attache at Royal Ascot fifth start (first run after leaving D. Nicholls): stays 1m: acts on firm ground, probably not on softer than good: usually tongue tied, tried visored: edgy sort: has worn crossed noseband/ear-plugs: usually slowly away, sometimes markedly so: waited with: unreliable. *M. C. Pipe*

Mrs D. M. Wight's "Hurricane Alan"

HURRICANE LILY (IRE) 2 b.f. (Apr 26) Ali-Royal (IRE) 127 – Bint Al Balad **61**
(IRE) 63 (Ahonoora 122) [2003 6m⁴ 6.1d³ 6m 6f⁴ Oct 27] €18,000Y: small filly: fifth
foal: half-sister to 3-y-o Hurricane Alan and 7f winner Eagles High (by Eagle Eyed):
dam, ran twice, sister to Nell Gwyn winner A-To-Z: modest maiden: third at Nottingham:
will probably stay 7f: acts on firm and good to soft ground. *B. J. Meehan*

HURRICANE LOVE (USA) 3 b.f. Quiet American (USA) – Outlasting (USA) **–**
(Seattle Slew (USA)) [2003 –p: 11.4m 7m⁶ Jul 10] leggy, lengthy filly: lightly-raced
maiden: well held both starts at 3 yrs, refusing to settle in Cheshire Oaks at Chester on
reappearance: sent to USA. *B. W. Hills*

HUSKY (POL) 5 b.g. Special Power – Hallo Bambina (POL) (Neman (POL)) [2003 **53**
54: f6s p7g³ 8f 9.7m² 10m 10.1g 8.2m 8m 10f Aug 27] Polish-bred gelding: modest
handicapper: stays 9.7f: acts on all-weather and good to firm going: tried visored/tongue
tied, often wears cheekpieces. *R. M. H. Cowell*

HUWAIDAH 3 b.f. Shareef Dancer (USA) 135 – Romoosh 69 (Formidable (USA) **51**
125) [2003 65p: 10.1m 8.3m⁴ Jun 18] smallish filly: modest maiden, lightly raced: should
be suited by 1m+: unraced on extremes of going. *G. A. Butler*

HYMNS AND ARIAS 2 b.f. (Apr 30) Mtoto 134 – Ewenny 71 (Warrshan (USA) **47**
117) [2003 7m 7m 6m 7.5m* 7m Oct 17] smallish filly: second foal: dam best at 2 yrs
when 5f winner: poor performer: won selling nursery at Beverley in September, then left
M. Bell: no other form: stays 7.5f. *Ronald Thompson*

I

IAMBACK 3 b.f. Perugino (USA) 84 – Smouldering (IRE) (Caerleon (USA) 132) **– §**
[2003 51§: 10m 7m⁶ f6g f8.5g⁶ Dec 26] leggy filly: maiden handicapper: little form in
2003: left M. Quinlan £1,200 and off 8 months prior to final outing: tried blinkered/in
cheekpieces: has looked ungenuine. *Miss Gay Kelleway*

I AM TROUBLE (IRE) 3 b.f. Darnay 117 – Secret Combe (IRE) 81 (Mujadil (USA) **–**
119) [2003 36: f8g p7g Feb 19] compact filly: poor maiden. *J. S. Moore*

IBERUS (GER) 5 b.g. Monsun (GER) 124 – Iberica (GER) (Green Dancer (USA) **?**
132) [2003 107: 13.4m⁶ 8.3d 12g⁵ 12f 10.3m⁵ Jun 28] leggy, angular gelding: seventh
foal: half-brother to winners in Germany by Rainbow Quest and Linamix: dam German
1m/10.5f winner: useful for P. Schiergen in Germany, third in Derby Italiano in 2001 and
listed winner at Cologne and Munich in 2002: disappointing over hurdles early in 2003:
signs of retaining some ability on return to Flat, but little solid form: stays 1½m: acts on
firm and soft going: joined S. Gollings. *M. C. Pipe*

ICANNSHIFT (IRE) 3 b.g. Night Shift (USA) – Cannikin (IRE) 82 (Lahib (USA) **98 d**
129) [2003 96: 7g 7.6m 7g 7.1f 7f 7f 7.1m⁴ 7g 7.1m⁶ p10g p7g Dec 30] small, good-
bodied gelding: useful handicapper: disappointing after reappearance in 2003, leaving
P. Harris 11,000 gns after ninth start: stays 7f: acts on soft and good to firm ground: tried
visored. *S. Dow*

ICE AND FIRE 4 b.g. Cadeaux Genereux 131 – Tanz (IRE) 79 (Sadler's Wells (USA) **63 ?**
132) [2003 10m 8.2d⁶ 7m 8m⁶ 8.1g 7g 10d⁵ Jul 30] quite good-topped gelding: modest
maiden handicapper: stays 1¼m: unraced on extremes of going: tried in blinkers/cheek-
pieces: none too consistent. *G. Barnett*

ICECAP 3 b.f. Polar Falcon (USA) 126 – Warning Light (High Top 131) [2003 72p: **60**
p8g⁴ f8.5g² f8.5s 7.5m⁴ 7f⁴ 7g⁵ 8m⁶ 8m⁶ p7g⁵ p7g p10g p10g² Dec 30] lengthy filly:
modest maiden: left M. Bell after third start, M. Usher after fifth: stays 1¼m: acts on all-
weather and good to firm ground. *P. Butler*

ICE CRACKER 4 b.f. Polar Falcon (USA) 126 – Blessed Honour 77 (Ahonoora 122) **72**
[2003 65: 9.7m 8m p10g 8f² 7m 8.3m³ 8.5m⁶ 8.1m² 8f² 8m* 8.9f Oct 11] lengthy filly:
fair handicapper: won at Goodwood in September: stays 1m: raced only on good ground
or firmer on turf, below form on polytrack: blinkered (ran creditably) once: carries head
awkwardly: sold 33,000 gns. *Mrs A. J. Bowlby*

ICED DIAMOND (IRE) 4 b.g. Petardia 113 – Prime Site (IRE) (Burslem 123) [2003 **60**
71: 7m 5.9g 7g 6m 7.1g 6.1g² 6m⁵ 6m⁶ 6m² 7.1d 6m Aug 9] good-topped gelding: modest

handicapper: left J. M. Bradley after tenth outing: effective at 6f/7f: acts on firm going and polytrack: tried in headgear: often races freely. *W. M. Brisbourne*

ICE DRAGON 2 b.f. (Apr 6) Polar Falcon (USA) 126 – Qilin (IRE) 94 (Second Set **73** (IRE) 127) [2003 7m⁶ p7g² Sep 9] first foal: dam 6f (including at 2 yrs)/7f winner: better effort in maidens (fair form) when 1½ lengths second of 11 to Donna Vita at Lingfield: not sure to stay much beyond 7f. *M. H. Tompkins*

ICE DYNASTY 3 b.f. Polar Prince (IRE) 117 – Yankee Special 60 (Bold Lad (IRE) 133) [2003 9.3f 8.3f⁵ Jun 26] £2,800 2-y-o: half-sister to 6f (at 2 yrs) and 1m winner Langtonian (by Primo Dominie) and French winner up to 11f Soldiers Bay (by Robellino): dam sprint maiden: no sign of ability. *J. S. Wainwright*

ICENASLICE (IRE) 2 b.f. (Feb 22) Fayruz 116 – Come Dancing 48 (Suave Dancer **60** (USA) 136) [2003 7m³ 6m⁴ 7d⁶ Nov 4] €4,000Y: leggy filly: third foal: sister to 3-y-o Uhuru Dawn: dam, disappointing maiden, out of sister to very smart sprinter Primo Dominie: modest form in maidens: third at Newcastle: barely stays 7f. *J. J. Quinn*

ICE PALACE 3 ch.f. Polar Falcon (USA) 126 – White Palace 80 (Shirley Heights 130) **99 +** [2003 83P: 8.1m³ 8.2g* 8g* 8f⁴ 10m Oct 16] tall, leggy filly: useful performer, lightly raced: won maiden at Nottingham in August and handicap at Kempton (beat Harb 1¼ lengths) in September: first home on stand side when fourth to Tadris in listed rated stakes at Ascot: best form at 1m: raced only on good going or firmer. *J. R. Fanshawe*

ICEY RUN 3 b.g. Runnett 125 – Polar Storm (IRE) 76 (Law Society (USA) 130) [2003 **–** 7.1g 8m f12s Sep 26] fifth foal: brother to 5-y-o Run On and Irish 9f winner Lawnett: dam, 6f (at 2 yrs) to 1m winner, half-sister to smart sprinter Polar Bird: soundly beaten in maidens. *D. G. Bridgwater*

ICKLINGHAM (IRE) 3 b.c. Sadler's Wells (USA) 132 – Braiswick 118 (King of **104** Spain 121) [2003 10g 9.5s² 10d² 10s* 16.2f⁶ 14d⁴ Aug 1] quite good-topped colt: seventh foal: brother to fairly useful UAE 11f winner Brampton, closely related to 1¼m winner Prickwillow (by Nureyev), and half-brother to French 2001 2-y-o winner by Polar Falcon: dam, 1m to 11.3f winner: useful performer: won maiden at the Curragh in June: best efforts when sixth in Shanty Star (beaten 4 lengths) in Queen's Vase at Royal Ascot and fourth to Holy Orders in handicap at Galway last 2 outings: stays 2m: acts on firm and soft going: blinkered last 3 starts. *J. Oxx, Ireland*

I CRIED FOR YOU (IRE) 8 b.g. Statoblest 120 – Fall of The Hammer (IRE) **–** (Auction Ring (USA) 123) [2003 106: p10g Mar 15] strong, angular gelding: useful performer at 7 yrs: well held only Flat outing in 2003: tried visored/blinkered earlier in career. *J. G. Given*

IDLE CHATTER 3 b.f. Spectrum (IRE) 126 – Elfin Laughter 76 (Alzao (USA) 117) **–** [2003 –: 8.2d May 16] no form: dead. *M. L. W. Bell*

IDLE POWER (IRE) 5 b. or br.g. Common Grounds 118 – Idle Fancy 79 (Mujtahid **97 d** (USA) 118) [2003 94: 6m² 7g⁶ 6g⁵ 6m 6m 6f 6.5m 6g 7m 6m p7g⁴ 7m 6m p7g Oct 30] rather leggy, close-coupled gelding: useful handicapper: well below form last 3 starts: effective at 6f/7f: acts on firm going, good to soft and polytrack: usually wears blinkers/cheekpieces: free-going sort: unreliable. *J. R. Boyle*

IF 4 b.f. Emperor Jones (USA) 119 – Mighty Flash 81 (Rolfe (USA) 77) [2003 58: 8.3g **–** 7f Oct 27] lightly-raced maiden: no show in 2003. *B. R. Millman*

IF BY CHANCE 5 ch.g. Risk Me (FR) 127 – Out of Harmony 79 (Song 132) [2003 **72** 59§, a67§: f6g⁴ f6g* f7s 6d⁴ f6g* f6s* 6m⁵ f6s f6s 6g* 6.1m f6g⁵ Nov 28] strong, close-coupled gelding: poor mover: fair performer: won sellers at Southwell in January (sold from I. McInnes) and April and handicaps at Wolverhampton in April and Newcastle in October: best at 5f/6f: acts on heavy going, good to firm and fibresand: usually visored/blinkered: reportedly bled seventh start. *R. Craggs*

IFFRAAJ 2 b.c. (Feb 22) Zafonic (USA) 130 – Pastorale 91 (Nureyev (USA) 131) [2003 **88 p** 7.1d³ 7.1m* Sep 20] good-bodied colt: brother to useful 1998 2-y-o 7f winner Kareymah and 3-y-o Akrmina, and half-brother to 3 winners, including useful 1m winner Jathaabeh (by Nashwan): dam, 7f winner from 3 starts, half-sister to Cape Cross and closely related to dam of Diktat, an excellent family: promising third in maiden at Sandown before landing odds in similar event at Warwick by neck from Soulacroix, dictating pace and edging right: should stay 1m: likely to make useful 3-y-o. *M. A. Jarvis*

IFFY 2 b.g. (Apr 2) Orpen (USA) 116 – Hopesay 84 (Warning 136) [2003 7.1m f6g⁵ **58** 5.1m Oct 28] 18,000 2-y-o: workmanlike gelding: third foal: half-brother to 3-y-o Sailing Through and fairly useful 2001 2-y-o 6f winner Road To Justice (by Danehill Dancer):

dam maiden who stayed 6f: modest form in maidens: not knocked about final start: should stay 7f. *P. D. Cundell*

IF I CAN DREAM (IRE)   3 ch.f. Brief Truce (USA) 126 – Only In Dreams 78 (Polar **50** Falcon (USA) 126) [2003 60: p6g f8.5g⁴ f7g³ f8g* 8g² a8g² 7.5g³ 7s³ 8f a8g a8.6g⁶ a6f Nov 25] modest performer: won selling handicap at Southwell in January: sold from B. Meehan 5,200 gns after: stays 1m: acts on firm going and fibresand: sometimes blinkered. *J-E. Pettersson, Sweden*

IF PARADISE   2 b.c. (Apr 10) Compton Place 125 – Sunley Stars (Sallust 134) [2003 **102** 5m³ 5m* 6f⁴ 5.2m* 5g⁶ 5m² 6d 5m⁵ Sep 18] 5,500F, 13,500Y: sturdy, useful-looking colt: closely related to fairly useful 1m (in UAE)/9.4f winner Don Sebastian (by Indian Ridge) and half-brother to 1995 2-y-o 5f winner All She Surveys (by Mazilier): dam, poor maiden, out of sister to high-class sprinter Runnett: useful performer: won maiden at Leicester in May and Weatherbys Super Sprint at Newbury (beat Cop Hill Lad by 1¾ lengths) in July: 3½ lengths second to Howick Falls in listed race at York, best effort after: probably best at 5f: acts on good to firm going: sometimes bandaged in front: often races prominently. *R. Hannon*

IFTIKHAR (USA)   4 b.g. Storm Cat (USA) – Muhbubh (USA) 108 (Blushing Groom **61** (FR) 131) [2003 8.1m 8m² 12m² 12.3g⁴ Aug 25] 9,000 3-y-o: big, strong gelding: half-brother to several winners, including smart 6f (at 2 yrs) and 7f (including Grade 2 event in US) winner Kayrawan (by Mr Prospector): dam won Princess Margaret Stakes: in frame in bumpers: modest form in maidens: stays 1½m: raced only on good/good to firm ground. *W. M. Brisbourne*

I GOT RHYTHM   5 gr.m. Lycius (USA) 124 – Eurythmic 58 (Pharly (FR) 130) [2003 **45** 51: 16m⁶ 16.2m Jul 19] leggy mare: has a round action: poor handicapper: stays 2m: acts on soft going, good to firm and fibresand. *Mrs M. Reveley*

IJTIHAD   3 b. or br.c. Darshaan 133 – Asfurah (USA) 108 (Dayjur (USA) 137) [2003 **80** –: 7m⁶ 7.5m² 9m² 8m² 9.9m² 8.2f² 10.2f* Oct 12] smallish, quite good-topped colt: fairly useful performer: runner-up 5 times in maidens before landing odds in similar event at Bath in October: stays easy 1¼m: acts on firm going: sent to UAE, joined E. Charpy. *M. P. Tregoning*

IKAN (IRE)   3 br.f. Sri Pekan (USA) 117 – Iktidar 80 (Green Desert (USA) 127) [2003 **98** 91: 6d⁴ 6.1s 6v 6f 6m⁶ 5.1m⁴ 5m* 5g³ 5m* 5m² 5g⁴ 5.6d 5g Oct 11] workmanlike filly: unimpressive mover: useful performer: won handicaps at Sandown in July and August: good fourth to Bali Royal in listed race at Hamilton after: best at 5f: acts on firm and soft ground: usually waited with. *N. P. Littmoden*

Weatherbys Super Sprint, Newbury—If Paradise proves well suited by the return to five furlongs, giving his stable a fifth win in the race; Cop Hill Lad (right) is second with Danesmead (No.2) third

Mr Hamdan Al Maktoum's "Ikhtyar"

IKHTYAR (IRE)   3 b.c. Unfuwain (USA) 131 – Sabria (USA) (Miswaki (USA)   **124**
124) [2003 8m³ 8.1m* 8m² 10g* 9.8d Oct 4]

John Gosden's string was slow to come to hand in the latest season and the number of races won by the stable not surprisingly fell some way short of its 2002 total, though, thanks mainly to Oasis Dream, the prize money totals compared favourably. It wasn't until the back end of April that Gosden sent out his first winner on turf, courtesy of a colt who ended up being his trainer's second highest-rated performer of 2003. Ikhtyar, unraced at two and a promising third to Kalaman and Act of Duty in a maiden at Newbury on his debut two weeks earlier, impressed in a five-runner minor event at Sandown in which he quickened clear early in the straight, after dictating in a falsely-run race, to win by five lengths from Always Esteemed.

Ikhtyar then took on Kalaman once again, in the listed Heron Stakes at Kempton, and made a much closer race of it, leading until inside the final furlong and finishing second, beaten a length and a half. Ikhtyar's performance was made to look even better in the light of Kalaman's unlucky second in the St James's Palace Stakes, and Ikhtyar himself gave the Kempton form a further boost when stepped up to a mile and a quarter in the Gala Stakes at Sandown in July. Ridden more patiently this time, Ikhtyar travelled smoothly, as Burning Sun set a sound pace, and produced a most impressive turn of foot after hitting the front two furlongs out, edging right but stretching clear to win by six lengths from stable-companion Royal Stamp. This was a level of performance seen rarely in listed company and Ikhtyar looked sure to win a pattern race before the season was out. Unfortunately, he didn't have the run of the race when his only opportunity came

477

three months later, meeting trouble in the straight in the Prix Dollar at Longchamp and finishing ninth of fourteen behind Weightless.

		Northern Dancer (b 1961)	Nearctic
	Unfuwain (USA) (b 1985)		Natalma
		Height of Fashion (b 1979)	Bustino
Ikhtyar (IRE) (b.c. 2000)			Highclere
		Miswaki (ch 1978)	Mr Prospector
	Sabria (USA) (b 1991)		Hopespringseternal
		Flood (b or br 1983)	Riverman
			Hail Maggie

Ikhtyar, a good-topped, attractive colt who very much takes the eye, fetched 65,000 guineas as a foal and IR 380,000 guineas when sent through the sales ring as a yearling. He is the fourth foal of Sabria, an unraced half-sister to the smart middle-distance performer King Sound, and her fourth winner. Sabria's first foal Ghita (by Zilzal) won at up to nine furlongs in France, her second Sabreon (by Caerleon) was a fairly useful mile-and-a-quarter winner, while her third, the ill-fated Landseer (by Danehill), was a high-class miler, winner of the 2002 Poule d'Essai des Poulains. The next dam Flood won over six furlongs in the States. This is a famous family, that of Triptych, Generous and Imagine, who are all descended from Ikhtyar's fourth dam Margarethen. Ikhtyar, seemingly better at a mile and a quarter than a mile, raced only on good to firm and good ground prior to Longchamp, where it was good to soft. Significantly, connections avoided running him on ground firmer than good after Kempton, and races such as the Irish Champion Stakes and the Queen Elizabeth II Stakes went by without him, though he was among the final declarations for the latter. There is, therefore, a danger that Ikhtyar may not be seen so often if there is another dry summer in 2004, but he is certainly the type to win pattern races if his trainer enjoys a clear run with him. *J. H. M. Gosden.*

IL CAVALIERE   8 b.g. Mtoto 134 – Kalmia (Miller's Mate 116) [2003 70: 16g⁴ Sep 28] good-topped gelding: fair handicapper: stays 2m: acts on firm going, probably on good to soft: usually held up. *Mrs M. Reveley*   **68**

ILE MICHEL   6 b.g. Machiavellian (USA) 123 – Circe's Isle (Be My Guest (USA) 126) [2003 80: 7m* 7m* 8g* 7m⁶ 7m⁶ 7.1m³ 8g² 8.9m* 7f Sep 27] good-topped gelding: useful performer: better than ever in 2003, winning minor event at Folkestone and handicap at Southwell in April, minor event at Musselburgh in May and claimer at York (claimed from Lady Herries £21,000) in September: effective at 7f to 9f: acts on firm ground, below form on softer than good: has hung left/carried head high: reportedly lost action fifth start. *M. C. Pipe*   **98**

ILLEANA (GER)   2 ch.f. (Mar 14) Lomitas 129 – Illyria (IRE) 66 (Nashwan (USA) 135) [2003 7f 8.1g Aug 25] €130,000Y: second foal: closely related to a winner in Greece by Hernando: dam, ran twice in Ireland, half-sister to smart 1½m performer Iscan out of half-sister to Oaks winner Snow Bride, herself dam of Lammtarra: signs of ability in maidens at Kempton and Chepstow: will probably do better at 1¼m+. *W. R. Muir*   **– p**

ILLUSIONIST   5 b.g. Mujtahid (USA) 118 – Merlin's Fancy 62 (Caerleon (USA) 132) [2003 –, a54: 7fs³ 7fs⁴ f8s f8g f7s f7s f8.5s 8f⁵ 10.1f Jul 24] poor performer: best around 7f: acts on firm going, good to soft and fibresand: usually blinkered/visored: ungenuine. *Mrs N. Macauley*   **49 §**

ILLUSIVE GAIT   3 b.g. Cloudings (IRE) 112 – Miller's Gait 74§ (Mill Reef (USA) 141) [2003 10.1d 11.9m 12.1m⁵ Jun 19] closely related to 7f to 2m winner Captain Miller (by Batshoof) and half-brother to 2 winners, including smart stayer Bold Gait (by Persian Bold): dam, ungenuine middle-distance maiden, half-sister to high-class stayer/hurdler Royal Gait: well beaten in maidens. *T. D. Easterby*   **–**

ILLUSIVE (IRE)   6 b.g. Night Shift (USA) – Mirage 60 (Red Sunset 120) [2003 70, a79: p5g p6g⁵ p6g³ p6g p6g⁴ p6g³ p6g² Feb 15] fair handicapper, on a long losing run: best at 5f/6f: acts on firm going, good to soft and all-weather: usually blinkered: sometimes looks none too keen. *M. Wigham*   **72**

ILLUSTRATOR   3 b.c. Sadler's Wells (USA) 132 – Illusory 81 (Kings Lake (USA) 133) [2003 111: 10.4m² 10g* 10g 12s⁶ 10s⁵ Nov 15] smallish, quite good-topped colt: useful performer: 3½ lengths second of 4 to Lateen Sails in listed event at York on reappearance: simple task to win maiden at Windsor in June: creditable effort, though never a   **108**

threat, when eighth to Vespone in Grand Prix de Paris at Longchamp next time: sold from Sir Michael Stoute 55,000 gns, better effort for new stable when respectable fifth to Sarrasin in listed race at Marseilles Borely final start: best around 1¼m: acts on soft and good to firm ground, though gave impression ill at ease on latter at York (tended to edge left): has been fitted with blanket for stall entry. *H.-A. Pantall, France*

ILLUSTRIA 3 b.f. Seeking The Gold (USA) – Noble Rose (IRE) 113 (Caerleon **92** (USA) 132) [2003 92: 7m⁵ 11.4m 7.1m⁴ 8m Jul 9] leggy filly: fairly useful performer: best 3-y-o effort when 4½ lengths fifth to Tante Rose in Dubai Duty Free Stakes (Fred Darling) at Newbury: last in Falmouth Stakes at Newmarket final start: bred to stay at least 1¼m, but races freely: acts on good to firm ground, shaped well on soft: sent to Australia. *M. R. Channon*

ILLUSTRIOUS DUKE 5 b.g. Dancing Spree (USA) – Killick 69 (Slip Anchor 136) **–** [2003 –, a81: f7g f8.5g f8.5g f8s f8.5s⁶ f7g f7g f8.5s f8.5g⁴ 10.5m f7g* f8.5g² f8.5s f9.4g **a61** Aug 15] workmanlike gelding: just a modest handicapper in 2003: won at Southwell in June: effective at 7f to 8.5f: acts on fibresand, little form on turf: has worn cheekpieces: often forces pace: none too reliable. *M. Mullineaux*

ILOVETURTLE (IRE) 3 b.g. Turtle Island (IRE) 123 – Gan Ainm (IRE) 92 (Mujadil **64** (USA) 119) [2003 72d: p8g f8s² p10g f8g⁶ 12m³ f12g⁶ f12g 10g⁴ 12d² 13.9m 12.1m f11s **a60** 15.8m f16g f12s Dec 27] workmanlike gelding: just modest in 2003: left M. Johnston after ninth start: stays 1½m: acts on good to firm going, good to soft and fibresand: blinkered (slowly away/looked difficult ride) third start: none too reliable. *M. C. Chapman*

ILWADOD 2 b.c. (Feb 19) Cadeaux Genereux 131 – Wedoudah (IRE) 80 (Sadler's **–** Wells (USA) 132) [2003 6g 8d f9.4g⁶ Nov 15] lengthy, good-bodied colt: first foal: dam, maiden who stayed 1½m, half-sister to smart US Grade 1 1¼m winner Aube Indienne and smart French performer up to 1½m Mare Nostrum: well held in maidens. *M. R. Channon*

I'M DANCING 2 b.f. (Apr 16) Polish Precedent (USA) 131 – Dancing Heights (IRE) **61** 80 (High Estate 127) [2003 6m 7.5m⁵ 7d³ 7g⁶ 8m Sep 25] 9,000Y: good-topped filly: fifth foal: half-sister to 3 winners, including useful 7f (at 2 yrs) to 9f winner (including in UAE) Bathwick (by Midyan) and 7f winner Last Symphony (by Last Tycoon): dam, 1¼m winner, sister to smart 1½m performer High Baroque: modest maiden: probably stays 1m: acts on good to firm and good to soft going. *T. D. Easterby*

I'M MAGIC 3 ch.f. First Trump 118 – Crystal Magic 92 (Mazilier (USA) 107) [2003 **75** 69: 7m 7m⁴ 6.1m 8d² 8f* 8f 7g Nov 1] rather leggy filly: fair handicapper: won at Brighton in August: stays 1m: acts on firm and good to soft ground: none too consistent. *R. Hannon*

IMNOTALADY 5 ch.m. Shalford (IRE) 124§ – Lissahane Lass (Daring March 116) **62 ?** [2003 p10g p12g⁵ f12s⁴ Feb 17] second known foal: dam, maiden on Flat, won at 2m over hurdles: poor form in bumpers: modest form in maidens: stays 1½m: acts on polytrack. *P. R. Hedger*

I'M NO TIME WASTER 4 ch.f. Timeless Times (USA) 99 – Forbidden Monkey 47 **–** (Gabitat 119) [2003 8.1m f9.4s Jun 21] 4,200Y: half-sister to 5f (at 2 yrs) and 1½m winner Man of The Night (by Clantime): dam, ran only at 2 yrs, placed in sprint sellers: well held in maidens. *Mrs H. Dalton*

IMOYA (IRE) 4 b.f. Desert King (IRE) 129 – Urgent Liaison (IRE) (High Estate 127) **101** [2003 94: 11.6g⁵ 10g 14g⁵ 12v Nov 16] sturdy, close-coupled filly: useful performer: sweating, best effort when fifth to Moments of Joy in listed race at Goodwood third start: barely stays 1¾m: acts on good to firm and heavy going. *B. J. Meehan*

IMPARTIAL 2 b.c. (May 2) Polish Precedent (USA) 131 – Always Friendly 111 (High **72 p** Line 125) [2003 p8g³ Nov 13] 70,000Y: fifth foal: brother to 5-y-o Arabie and closely related to useful Italian 7.5f/1m winner Dane Friendly (by Danehill): dam won Princess Royal Stakes and second in Prix Royal-Oak: 5/1, 2 lengths third to Red Spell in maiden at Lingfield, racing freely: should improve. *P. F. I. Cole*

IMPELLER (IRE) 4 ch.g. Polish Precedent (USA) 131 – Almaaseh (IRE) 63 (Danc- **98** ing Brave (USA) 140) [2003 93: 8m 8.1g⁴ 7.6g³ 8m⁶ 7f 8m² 8m⁴ 8m⁵ 9m* 10g 9m* 10m 9m 8m² 8.2m² Oct 28] tall gelding: useful performer: won minor event at Sandown (dead-heated with African Sahara) in August and handicap at Goodwood in September: short-headed by Janayen in handicap at Nottingham final start: best at 1m/9f: acts on good to firm going: tried blinkered, not in 2003: has raced freely: carries head high: usually waited with. *W. R. Muir*

IMPERATIVE (USA) 3 ch.c. Woodman (USA) 126 – Wandesta 121 (Nashwan (USA) **89 ?** 135) [2003 12d⁵ 8d⁵ 8d f7s 10g Sep 27] third foal: closely related to 7f winner Greek

Dream (by Distant View): dam, 1½m winner and second in 13.5f Prix de Pomone, later champion turf mare (Grade 1 9f/1¼m winner) in USA at 5 yrs: fairly useful maiden: seemed to run creditably first 2 outings: left Mme C. Head-Maarek in France 22,000 gns after next start: well held in handicaps in Britain: seems to stay 1½m: raced only on good going or softer on turf: tried blinkered. *J. W. Unett*

IMPERIAL DANCER   5 b.h. Primo Dominie 121 – Gorgeous Dancer (IRE)   **123**
(Nordico (USA)) [2003 119: 10s⁴ 10g 12m⁵ 10g³ 13.4m⁵ 10.5d 10g⁵ 9.9g* 10f²
12m³ 10.9m* 9.8d⁶ 10m⁴ 12g* 10d* 12m Dec 14]
         Which horse finished only fourth in the Prix Exbury, the first pattern race of
the season in Europe, and went on to win the Premio Roma SIS, the last Group 1
race in Europe in 2003? The answer is Imperial Dancer, who may be some way
behind the very best but has few peers at the top level in terms of toughness and
consistency, and is a great credit to his trainer Mick Channon. The Premio Roma,
which took place in mid-November, was Imperial Dancer's first Group 1 success,
and one he richly deserved. He finished fourth behind Sunstrach in the race in 2002,
and that horse led the home defence again in the latest renewal. Imperial Dancer
was the only British challenger in a ten-strong field, joined by four French raiders
including Fair Mix and Execute, first and second in the Prix Ganay, the first
Group 1 of the season in Europe, in April. Sunstrach took up the running from Quel
del Giaz early in the straight, but Imperial Dancer, held up towards the rear,
produced a strong burst to lead inside the final furlong and win by three lengths
from Altieri, who stayed on to pip Sunstrach for second.
         Trained throughout his career by Channon, Imperial Dancer has been boldly
campaigned since making his debut in the March of his two-year-old season, and,
by the end of 2003, had fifty-two runs under his belt, something almost unheard
of in Europe for a horse competing at the top level. Not only has Imperial Dancer
thrived on a busy schedule, he has been progressive too, earning Timeform ratings
of 103 in 2000, 105 in 2001 and 119 in 2002. Imperial Dancer was raced at up to a
mile at two and three, including when down the field in the Two Thousand Guineas
and the Mehl Mulhens-Rennen, but a step up to a mile and a quarter as a four-year-
old brought further improvement. He was a 33/1-winner of the Rosebery Handicap
on his first attempt at the trip in 2002, then added a listed race at Goodwood, the
Scottish Classic and the Meld Stakes. Imperial Dancer was busier than ever in the
latest season, running sixteen times in all, though his best placing on his first seven
outings—all in pattern races—was third for the second year running in the Gordon
Richards Stakes at Sandown. Dropped back into handicap company in the Littlewoods Bet Direct Summer Stakes at Goodwood in July, Imperial Dancer defied top
weight and a BHB mark of 109 to show that he retained all his ability. Apprentice
Sam Hitchcott's endeavours aboard Imperial Dancer at Goodwood saw him
nominated in some quarters for ride of the season, but that wasn't how we saw it, as
the jockey surely didn't intend to cut it so fine. Hampered and switched to the
outside, Imperial Dancer still had at least eight horses in front of him over a furlong
out, and produced a devastating burst of speed to catch April Stock on the line.

*Premio Roma SIS, Rome—Imperial Dancer gains his first Group 1 success on his fifteenth outing of the
year; he has plenty to spare over two of Italy's top performers, Altieri (noseband) and Sunstrach (left);
Trumbaka (virtually hidden near rail) and the grey Fair Mix are next*

Imperial Dancer won four races in all in 2003, the £11,600 he picked up for taking care of three other at least smart horses, led by Island House, in the listed Doonside Cup at Ayr in September being unreasonably stingy compared to the prizes for some of the handicaps at the meeting. The Tote St Simon Stakes at Newbury the following month was better endowed, and, in a steadily-run race, Imperial Dancer smothered his rivals, leading under two furlongs out and beating the St Leger runner-up High Accolade by three lengths to gain his first success at a mile and a half. Imperial Dancer's best effort in defeat in 2003 came when beaten three quarters of a length by High Chaparral in the Royal Whip Stakes at the Curragh in August, though the winner, giving Imperial Dancer 7 lb, probably wasn't quite at his best on his reappearance. Not surprisingly for one who is held up for a turn of foot, things don't always go smoothly for Imperial Dancer. When fourth to Rakti in the Champion Stakes at Newmarket, for instance, he was short of room before finishing to good effect; he would have bustled up Carnival Dancer for second with better luck. Imperial Dancer was again unlucky in running on his one appearance after the Premio Roma, finishing seventh to Vallee Enchantee in the Hong Kong Vase at Sha Tin in December, dropped in after a slow start in a steadily-run race and being short of room on several occasions in the straight.

Imperial Dancer (b.h. 1998)	Primo Dominie (b 1982)	Dominion (b 1972)	Derring-Do
			Picture Palace
		Swan Ann (ch 1971)	My Swanee
			Anna Barry
	Gorgeous Dancer (IRE) (b 1989)	Nordico (b 1981)	Northern Dancer
			Kennelot
		Simply Gorgeous (ch 1984)	Hello Gorgeous
			Parthica

Sprinters are the stock-in-trade of Imperial Dancer's sire the 1985 King George Stakes winner Primo Dominie, who has now been retired from stud duties. His other notable progeny include First Trump, Perryston View, Romantic Liason and Primo Valentino, but Imperial Dancer is the best horse he has produced so far. Imperial Dancer's dam Gorgeous Dancer has been responsible for two other winners in the useful pair Lafite (by Robellino) and the four-year-old Perfect Storm. Lafite gained her first success at a mile as a three-year-old and won a listed event at York over an extended mile and a quarter the following season, while Perfect Storm, a six-furlong winner at two, showed he stays a mile and a half when runner-up in the November Handicap on his final appearance in 2003. Gorgeous Dancer won a mile maiden at Leopardstown as a three-year-old and was placed at up to a mile and three quarters. Grandam Simply Gorgeous was an unraced half-sister to Irish Oaks winner Give Thanks, the grandam of One Thousand Guineas winner Harayir. The smallish, angular Imperial Dancer has a quick action and is as effective at a mile and a half as at a mile and a quarter, at least when conditions aren't testing, and seemed not to stay an extended thirteen furlongs in the Ormonde Stakes at Chester. He reportedly returned home jarred after the Mehl Mulhens-Rennen, but has since shown his form on both firm and heavy going. Imperial Dancer is still an entire so, as a Group 1 winner, will no doubt be found a place at stud in due course, though he is reportedly to stay in training in 2004, when he can be relied on to win more good prizes. He sometimes carried his head awkwardly earlier in his career, but is as tough and genuine as they come and must be a pleasure to be associated with. *M. R. Channon*

IMPERIAL ECHO (USA) 2 b.g. (Jan 13) Labeeb 124 – Regal Baby (USA) (Northern Baby (CAN) 127) [2003 5m² 6g⁴ 6m² 7.2f* 6g⁴ 5d³ 6m³ Oct 4] $55,000Y: leggy, quite good-topped gelding: half-brother to useful 2000 2-y-o 6f winner Dim Sums (by Repriced) and several winners in USA: dam maiden in USA: fairly useful performer: landed odds in maiden at Ayr in August: creditable third, beaten just over 3 lengths by Peak To Creek, in Two-Year-Old Trophy at Redcar final start, despite slowly away and badly hampered: free-going sort, but stays easy 7f: acts on firm ground: blinkered (respectable effort) penultimate start: hung left fifth one. *T. D. Barron* **88**

IMPERIALISTIC (IRE) 2 b.f. (Apr 17) Imperial Ballet (IRE) 110 – Shefoog 90 (Kefaah (USA) 124) [2003 6m⁵ 6v* 6f 6g⁴ f7g³ f8.5s⁴ 7d² 6d³ Nov 4] 15,000Y: leggy, close-coupled filly: sixth foal: half-sister to fairly useful 9f and 2m winner Makasseb (by **89**

481

Kris) and 1¾m winner Undeniable (by Unfuwain): dam, 7f winner (including at 2 yrs), half-sister to smart winner in Britain/UAE up to 1¼m Murheb: fairly useful performer: won maiden at Haydock in May: placed in nurseries, unlucky (got boxed in) at Catterick final start: stays 7f: acts on fibresand and heavy going: wore cheekpieces penultimate outing: carries head awkwardly/sometimes hangs. *K. R. Burke*

IMPERIAL PRINCESS (IRE)   2 b.f. (Apr 23) Imperial Ballet (IRE) 110 – Rose   –
Tint (IRE) (Salse (USA) 128) [2003 6.1m 6d f5s f6s f8.5g Nov 1] 15,000Y: fourth foal: half-sister to 5-y-o Amelia: dam poor maiden: little form in maidens: visored third start. *D. Haydn Jones*

IMPERIAL ROYALE (IRE)   2 ch.g. (Mar 20) Ali-Royal (IRE) 127 – God Speed   **61**
Her (Pas de Seul 133) [2003 7m 7g⁶ 8.5g³ 7.1m 8.3g 7.1m⁵ 8.2m² Oct 28] IR 10,500F, €38,000Y: leggy gelding: seventh foal: half-brother to several winners, including 10-y-o Sky Dome and fairly useful Irish 7f winner Speed Hill (by Danehill): dam Irish maiden half-sister to smart middle-distance performer Noble Patriarch: modest maiden: should stay 1¼m: acts on good to firm going: hung left fourth start. *M. R. Channon*

IMPERIAL STRIDE   2 b.c. (Mar 11) Indian Ridge 123 – Place de L'Opera 98   **113 p**
(Sadler's Wells (USA) 132) [2003 6g* 7m* 7m⁶ Oct 18]
    Defeat in the Dewhurst isn't necessarily the end of a horse's classic aspirations, and Imperial Stride has a lot going for him as a three-year-old, despite managing only sixth at Newmarket in October. Although unbeaten in two starts prior to Newmarket, where he started at 14/1, Imperial Stride had little in the way of racing experience before the Dewhurst, and it showed. Taking a furlong to settle, he had to be pushed along as the tempo increased, looking green and not getting into full flight until the race was as good as over. Even so, Imperial Stride still managed to show improved form in finishing only a little over two lengths behind the winner Milk It Mick.
    Imperial Stride looked an exciting prospect when making his debut in a six-furlong minor event at Yarmouth in May, when he was his stable's first juvenile runner of the season. Starting odds on, he had only to be shaken up to take control well over a furlong out, beating Forthright by a length and a quarter. Imperial Stride had only one serious rival in his second race, a four-runner minor event at Doncaster in July. There was no mistaking his potential all the same, as he beat the useful White Hawk readily by five lengths, taking time to settle but shaping as though suited by the step up to seven furlongs in the end. A minor problem reportedly kept him off the course until the Dewhurst.

		Ahonoora	Lorenzaccio
Imperial Stride	Indian Ridge	(ch 1975)	Helen Nichols
(b.c. Mar 11, 2001)	(ch 1985)	Hillbrow	Swing Easy
		(ch 1975)	Golden City
	Place de L'Opera	Sadler's Wells	Northern Dancer
	(b 1993)	(or b 1981)	Fairy Bridge
		Madame Dubois	Legend of France
		(ch 1987)	Shadywood

    Imperial Stride, who was bought for 375,000 guineas at Newmarket as a yearling on behalf of King's Best's owner Saeed Suhail, is a brother to the very smart High Pitched. Stamina was the strong suit for High Pitched, who gained his biggest success over a mile and a half in the St Simon Stakes in 2001, when it was run at Newmarket, and he also won the listed Aston Park Stakes at Newbury over an extended thirteen furlongs the following year. At this stage, Imperial Stride looks more likely to take after another son of Indian Ridge, Indian Haven (who finished in the rear in the Dewhurst before winning the Irish Two Thousand Guineas in 2003), to whom Imperial Stride is closely related. Indian Haven's dam Madame Dubois is the grandam of Imperial Stride. Madame Dubois was a very smart performer, winning the Park Hill Stakes and the Prix de Royallieu for Henry Cecil. Place de L'Opera, Imperial Stride's dam, was also trained in a light career by Cecil, winning a maiden and a minor event at around a mile and a half before being placed in a listed event at the same trip. High Pitched was Place de L'Opera's first foal. Her second to race Zero Tolerance (by Nashwan) showed useful form at up to a mile and a quarter as a three-year-old in 2003. Imperial Stride will be suited by a step up to at least a mile. It is asking a lot of him to emulate King's Best, who also finished out of the frame in the Dewhurst but still won the Guineas, though there is surely better to come given Imperial Stride's immaturity at two and his physical scope. A good-bodied, attractive colt, raced only on good ground or firmer, he is one to keep an eye on in the ante-post market in the spring. *Sir Michael Stoute*

IMPERIUM 2 b.g. (Feb 12) Imperial Ballet (IRE) 110 – Partenza (USA) (Red Ransom **79 §** (USA)) [2003 5m 6d³ 5.7m⁴ 6g⁶ 6g² 6m 6m p6g⁴ p7g⁶ Dec 10] second foal: dam unraced out of half-sister to smart French/US filly around 1¼m Aube Indienne: fair maiden: stays 7f: acts on polytrack and good to soft going: blinkered (ran poorly) seventh start: carries head high: has found little: not to be trusted. *B. J. Meehan*

IMPERO 5 b.g. Emperor Jones (USA) 119 – Fight Right (FR) (Crystal Glitters (USA) – 127) [2003 8.1m Jun 21] modest maiden: visored, well beaten only 5-y-o start: tried tongue tied. *C. N. Kellett*

IMPERSONATOR 3 b.g. Zafonic (USA) 130 – Conspiracy 98 (Rudimentary (USA) **90** 118) [2003 94p: 8m 8.1m 9g 9.9g 10d 8.1d⁴ 7g Nov 1] good-bodied gelding: has a long, round stride: fairly useful handicapper: best 3-y-o effort on penultimate start: should stay 1¼m: acts on heavy ground, seemingly not on firmer than good. *J. L. Dunlop*

IMPINDA (IRE) 4 b.f. Idris (IRE) 118 – Last Finale (USA) (Stop The Music (USA)) **54** [2003 10.1m³ 11.1m⁴ 11.1d⁶ 13.1g⁵ 12.4m 13g Jun 12] IR 5,000F, 9,000Y: third foal: sister to a winner in Turkey: dam unraced daughter of multiple US Grade 1 winner Optimistic Gal: modest maiden: stays 1½m: unraced on extremes of going: tongue tied (virtually refused to race) on debut. *P. Monteith*

IMPRESSIVE FLIGHT (IRE) 4 b.f. Flying Spur (AUS) – Certain Impression **95** (USA) (Forli (ARG)) [2003 105p: 6.1s⁵ 6m³ 6m6 Jun 11] lengthy filly: useful performer: respectable fifth to Irresistible in listed race at Nottingham on reappearance: lost chance with awkward start next time: below form in Summer Stakes at York final start: stays 6f: acts on firm and soft going. *T. D. Barron*

IMPRINT (UAE) 2 b.c. (Feb 28) Mark of Esteem (IRE) 137 – Temora (IRE) 90 (Ela- **67** Mana-Mou 132) [2003 5m² 7m Jul 6] fourth foal: half-brother to 3-y-o New South Wales and to fairly useful Irish 9f to 1½m winner Tempter (by In The Wings): dam, 9f (in USA)/ 1¼m winner, sister to very smart 1m/1¼m performer Ela Romara: odds on, fair form when second in maiden at Newcastle: ran as if amiss in similar event at Redcar: should stay at least 1m: sold 9,000 gns. *M. R. Channon*

IMPULSIVE AIR (IRE) 11 b.g. Try My Best (USA) 130 – Tracy's Sundown (Red – § Sunset 120) [2003 44§: 10g 9.9m 10.1m 10m 10m Jun 15] strong gelding: poor per- former: well beaten in 2003: tried visored early in career: untrustworthy. *J. R. Weymes*

IMPULSIVE BID (IRE) 2 b.f. (May 12) Orpen (USA) 116 – Tamburello (IRE) (Roi **67 ?** Danzig (USA)) [2003 5f⁴ 6.1d 6d⁴ Nov 8] 6,500F, 7,500Y, resold 5,000Y: useful-looking filly: third foal: dam, maiden (ran only at 6f and at 2 yrs), half-sister to useful performer up to 9.4f Reported: seemingly best effort in maidens (fair form) when fourth at Don- caster final start, getting run of race: not sure to stay much beyond 6f. *Jedd O'Keeffe*

IMPULSIVO 3 ch.g. Millkom 124 – Joytime (John de Coombe 122) [2003 59p: 8.1m – p13g Oct 3] workmanlike gelding: modest form only 2-y-o start: well held in 2003. *Simon Earle*

IMSHY (IRE) 2 ch.f. (Jan 19) Daggers Drawn (USA) 114 – Paganina (FR) (Galetto **92** (FR) 118) [2003 6g⁴ 7s* 6d* 6.5m⁶ 7s Oct 26] IR 4,000F, 14,000Y: fourth foal: half-sister to 4-y-o Mystic Venture: dam unraced half-sister to smart French 7f performer Philippi: fairly useful performer: won minor events at Compiegne in July and Deauville in August: below form after, though second home on stand side in sales race at Ascot penultimate outing: stays 7f: acts on soft going. *R. Pritchard-Gordon, France*

IMTIHAN (IRE) 4 ch.c. Unfuwain (USA) 131 – Azyaa 101 (Kris 135) [2003 83: 20m – 12d 12m 12.1g 16f Oct 12] good-topped colt: fairly useful handicapper at 3 yrs for B. Hills: well held in 2003: tried in blinkers/cheekpieces. *S. C. Burrough*

IMTIYAZ (USA) 4 ro.c. Woodman (USA) 126 – Shadayid (USA) 122 (Shadeed (USA) **116** 135) [2003 116: a8f* 8.9g 9.3g⁶ 10m³ 9.9m* Sep 24] leggy colt: smart performer: won prestige race at Nad Al Sheba (by 6½ lengths from Mugharreb) in March and listed race at Goodwood (by head from Miss Corniche) in September: creditable third to Mubtaker in listed event at Newbury in between: effective at 1m to 10.4f: acts on dirt, best turf form on ground firmer than good: effective visored or not: usually tongue tied: races prominently/makes running. *Saeed bin Suroor*

IN A SILENT WAY (IRE) 3 b.f. Desert Prince (IRE) 130 – Pray (IRE) (Priolo (USA) **102**
127) [2003 77: 6m 8g² 9f* 10m* 10m 10f² 10.1m² 10m Oct 16] lengthy, useful-looking
filly: useful performer: won handicaps at Kempton and Newbury in July: best efforts
when second after at Brighton (beaten head by Dawnus in listed rated stakes) and
Yarmouth (1½ lengths behind Montmartre in handicap): ran poorly in listed race at Newmarket final outing: stays 1¼m: raced only on good going or firmer: sometimes early to
post: usually waited on. *M. A. Jarvis*

INCA MOON 3 b.f. Sheikh Albadou 128 – Incatinka 63 (Inca Chief (USA)) [2003 58: **55 ?**
f8.5g⁵ f7g² f8.5s⁵ 8.2m⁵ 7m f7g⁶ 8f 10m 7m Oct 14] modest maiden: stays 1m: acts on **a47**
firm and good to soft going: tried visored. *R. Brotherton*

INCH AGAIN 3 ch.c. Inchinor 119 – Spoilt Again 91 (Mummy's Pet 125) [2003 92: **106**
9m* 10m² 11g⁵ 10g⁴ Jul 14] tall, good-topped colt: useful performer: won minor event
at Ripon (beat Mubeen by ½ length, making most) in April: best effort when ½-length
second to Look Honey in Prix Eugene Adam at Maisons-Laffitte final start: should stay
1½m: acts on good to firm ground, tailed off on soft: has hung, but seems genuine: sent to
Hong Kong, where renamed Enchanting. *M. H. Tompkins*

INCHBERRY 3 b.f. Barathea (IRE) 127 – Inchyre 102 (Shirley Heights 130) [2003 **110 ?**
90: 12m² 12g⁴ 12m⁶ 9m³ Oct 25] good-topped filly: seemingly smart maiden: first past
post at Hamilton (disqualified after failing dope test) at 2 yrs: 100/1 when 2½ lengths
fourth to Casual Look in Oaks at Epsom: below form after in Ribblesdale Stakes at Royal
Ascot and (after 4 month absence) maiden at Musselburgh (odds on, took good hold and
found little): stays 1½m: acts on soft and good to firm going: one to treat with caution.
G. A. Butler

INCH BY INCH 4 b.f. Inchinor 119 – Maid Welcome 81 (Mummy's Pet 125) [2003 **65**
58: p7g f6g g6g 5.7m 6m⁴ 5.3m 5.3m⁴ 6f* 6d 6m⁶ 6m² 6m 5.7f 6.1f³ 6m Oct 23]
smallish filly: fair performer: won minor event at Brighton in July: best form at 6f: acts
on firm ground and all-weather: usually blinkered: none too consistent. *P. J. Makin*

INCHCONNEL 2 b.g. (Feb 3) Inchinor 119 – Sharanella (Shareef Dancer (USA) 135) **67**
[2003 7m 7m³ 8.2d Nov 6] 15,000Y: lengthy, good-topped gelding: half-brother to 3
winners, including useful 5f (at 2 yrs) to 1m winner Sonic Boy (by Celestial Storm), later
successful in USA: dam unraced: easily best effort in maidens (fair form) when third at
Newcastle, then left E. Dunlop: should stay 1m. *Bob Jones*

INCHCOONAN 5 b.m. Emperor Jones (USA) 119 – Miss Ivory Coast (USA) (Sir **–**
Ivor 135) [2003 67, a81: f7g⁶ f8.5g⁴ f8g⁵ f7s⁴ f8.5g⁴ p8g² p8g⁴ Apr 5] strong mare: fair **a69**
handicapper: effective at 7f/1m: acts on all-weather and firm going: tried in visor/cheek-
pieces: sometimes races freely: tends to idle. *K. R. Burke*

INCHDURA 5 ch.g. Inchinor 119 – Sunshine Coast 86 (Posse (USA) 130) [2003 105: **78**
7m 8g 7.9m 7g 8.1m 8f 7f Jul 12] quite attractive gelding: useful handicapper in 2002:
mostly well held for new stable in 2003, but shaped well final outing: better form at 7f
than 1m: best form on going firmer than good: sometimes tongue tied earlier in career:
sometimes edgy: usually waited with. *N. Tinkler*

INCHENI (IRE) 2 b.f. (Feb 15) Nashwan (USA) 135 – Inchmurrin 114 (Lomond **71 p**
(USA) 128) [2003 6.1f⁶ p7g* Oct 30] good-bodied filly: sister to smart 1999 2-y-o 7f
winner (stayed 1½m) Inchlonaig and half-sister to several winners, including smart 6f
(at 2 yrs)/7f winner who stayed 1m Inchinor (by Ahonoora) and useful 1m winner who
stayed 1½m Inchyre (by Shirley Heights): dam 5f (at 2 yrs) and 1m winner: fair form:
confirmed promise when landing odds in 10-runner maiden at Lingfield by ½ length from
Princess Alina, idling in front: should be suited by at least 1m: slowly away on debut: will
probably progress. *G. Wragg*

INCH HIGH 5 ch.g. Inchinor 119 – Harrken Heights (IRE) (Belmez (USA) 131) **50 ?**
[2003 –: 6m 6f⁶ 7.2g 7.2g² 6m 8.3m Aug 19] modest maiden: stays 7f. *J. S. Goldie*

INCHING 3 b.f. Inchinor 119 – Tshusick 81 (Dancing Brave (USA) 140) [2003 65: **69 d**
f5s³ f5g² 5m³ 6g 5.1m³ 5m⁶ 5.1g 6g⁴ 6.1f p6g p6g⁶ f6g⁴ f5g⁶ f5g² f6s⁶ Dec 27] fair
maiden: mostly below form after fifth outing: best at 5f/easy 6f: acts on all-weather, raced
on good ground or firmer on turf: tried in visor/cheekpieces/tongue strap. *R. M. H. Cowell*

INCHINNAN 6 b.m. Inchinor 119 – Westering 54 (Auction Ring (USA) 123) [2003 ?: **68**
p10g⁴ p10g⁶ 8g⁵ 10m p8g Sep 3] small mare: fair handicapper: stays 10.5f: has form on
firm going and polytrack: best efforts on soft/heavy. *C. Weedon*

INCH ISLAND (IRE) 3 b.g. Turtle Island (IRE) 123 – Persian Light (IRE) 52 **75**
(Persian Heights 129) [2003 66: 7d² 8g 7.9g* 9.2d³ 7m⁶ 7m f9.4g Oct 20] useful-looking

gelding: fair handicapper: won at Carlisle in May: barely stays 9f: acts on soft and good to firm ground: free-going sort. *J. J. Quinn*

INCHNADAMPH   3 b.g. Inchinor 119 – Pelf (USA) 79 (Al Nasr (FR) 126) [2003 64:   –
8.1g 8.5m f11s Sep 26] modest maiden at 2 yrs: little form in 2003. *T. J. Fitzgerald*

INCHPAST   2 ch.c. (Feb 26) Inchinor 119 – Victor Ludorum (Rainbow Quest (USA)   **67**
134) [2003 7d p8g⁵ f7g Nov 25] 14,500Y: workmanlike colt: first foal: dam unraced sister to useful performer up to 1½m Star Selection out of sister to Teleprompter: clearly best effort in maidens (fair form) when fifth at Lingfield: will stay 1¼m. *M. H. Tompkins*

INCH PERFECT   8 b.g. Inchinor 119 – Scarlet Veil 75 (Tyrnavos 129) [2003 80:   **93**
f11g* f14s* f12g³ Jan 24] tall, good-topped gelding: fairly useful handicapper: won twice at Southwell in January, awarded race on second occasion: stayed 1¾m: acted on any turf going and fibresand: tongue tied once: usually held up: successful over fences in March: dead. *R. A. Fahey*

INCISE   2 ch.f. (Feb 6) Dr Fong (USA) 128 – Pretty Sharp 64 (Interrex (CAN)) [2003   **89**
5.2m³ 5m² 5m 5m* Jul 4] good-topped filly: third foal: half-sister to 4-y-o Twilight Blues: dam maiden (best at 7f at 2 yrs) who became temperamental: fairly useful performer: won maiden at Warwick in July by 5 lengths: good 1½ lengths second, flicking tail, to Russian Valour in listed race at Sandown: likely to prove best at 5f/easy 6f: edgy sort. *B. J. Meehan*

INCISOR   2 b.c. (Feb 17) Dracula (AUS) – Last Night's Fun (IRE) (Law Society (USA)   **55**
130) [2003 8m 8m⁵ 7m⁶ Oct 2] €5,000Y: compact colt: second living foal: dam lightly-raced Irish maiden: modest form in maidens: best effort at 7f. *S. Kirk*

INCLINE (IRE)   4 b.g. Danehill (USA) 126 – Shalwar Kameez (IRE) (Sadler's Wells   **92**
(USA) 132) [2003 89: 8g 8d 7d p7g² p7g² Dec 10] fairly useful handicapper: good second to What-A-Dancer at Lingfield final start: stays 1m: acts on polytrack and heavy going. *T. G. Mills*

INCROYABLE   2 br.f. (Apr 7) Linamix (FR) 127 – Crodelle (IRE) (Formidable (USA)   **– p**
125) [2003 7f 8m 7m 8f⁶ Oct 12] €170,000Y: tall filly: has scope: seventh foal: half-sister to smart 1¼m/1½m winner Ela Athena (by Ezzoud), 4-y-o Shifty and 3-y-o Snow's Ride: dam French 9.5f winner: well held in maidens, not knocked about: likely to do better at 1½m+. *Sir Mark Prescott*

INCURSION   2 b.c. (Apr 26) Inchinor 119 – Morgannwg (IRE) 86 (Simply Great (FR)   **79**
122) [2003 7m 8m⁶ 8g³ Oct 25] 32,000Y: sturdy colt: seventh foal: half-brother to 3 winners, including 5f/6f winner Black Army (by Aragon) and 1½m and 2m winner Welsh Dream (by Mtoto): dam 7f winner: fair form in maidens: third to Rave Reviews at Newbury: likely to stay 1¼m. *A. King*

INDECO (IRE)   2 b.g. (Jan 4) Indian Rocket 115 – Canary Bird (IRE) 59 (Catrail   **48**
(USA) 123) [2003 5.7m 7.9m f8s⁴ f6s Oct 7] IR 4,000F, €4,000Y: compact gelding: first foal: dam, lightly raced in Ireland, half-sister to useful Irish performer up to 1½m Tout A Coup: poor maiden: not sure to stay beyond 1m: best effort on fibresand: sent to Sweden. *Mrs P. N. Dutfield*

IN DEEP   2 b.f. (Feb 21) Deploy 131 – Bobbie Dee 93 (Blakeney 126) [2003 7g⁵ 7m⁵   **80**
8d⁶ 8m² Oct 1] leggy filly: third foal: dam, maiden who should have stayed 1½m, also third over hurdles: fairly useful maiden: sixth to Kinnaird in Maid Army Hill Stakes at Doncaster: will be suited by 1¼m+: best effort on good to soft going. *Mrs P. N. Dutfield*

INDELIBLE   4 br.f. Polar Falcon (USA) 126 – Ink Pot (USA) 73 (Green Dancer (USA)   **– §**
132) [2003 58, a49: f8g f7s 8m May 12] small filly: modest maiden: little form in 2003: unreliable. *J. Hetherton*

INDIANA BLUES   2 ch.f. (Mar 25) Indian Ridge 123 – Blue Siren 113 (Bluebird   **90 p**
(USA) 125) [2003 6f 6m⁴ 6m Oct 2] good-topped filly: third foal: half-sister to 3-y-o Speed Cop: dam, 5f (at 2 yrs) to 7f winner, also first past post in Nunthorpe Stakes: still green, best effort when 6½ lengths eighth of 10 to Carry On Katie in Cheveley Park Stakes at Newmarket final start: should make a useful 3-y-o, probably at 5f/6f. *A. M. Balding*

INDIAN BAZAAR (IRE)   7 ch.g. Indian Ridge 123 – Bazaar Promise 58 (Native   **55**
Bazaar 122) [2003 59: 5m² 5.3m 5m⁵ 5m⁴ 5m³ 5.1f³ 5m⁶ 5g 5.1d³ 5m 5g⁶ 5.2m 5d³ 5.1g*
5.7f⁴ 5m⁵ Sep 24] big, good-topped gelding: modest handicapper: won at Chepstow in September: raced around 5f: acts on firm and soft going, well held on heavy: tried blinkered/in cheekpieces: has edged left: usually races prominently. *J. M. Bradley*

INDIAN BEAT 6 ch.g. Indian Ridge 123 – Rappa Tap Tap (FR) 111 (Tap On Wood 130) [2003 52: 10.2m 17.2f 18m Jul 5] leggy, useful-looking gelding: modest maiden handicapper: soundly beaten in 2003: tried blinkered/visored. *C. L. Popham* –

INDIAN BEAU 2 b.c. (May 12) Indian Rocket 115 – Girl Next Door 58 (Local Suitor (USA) 128) [2003 5m⁴ 7m 6g 6.1m 6m Oct 16] 5,000F, 5,500Y: well-grown, quite good-topped colt: fifth foal: half-brother to 3-y-o Mr Malarkey and unreliable 5f winner Maritun Lad (by Presidium): dam 6f winner, including at 2 yrs: signs of only a little ability in maidens/sales race: wore cheekpieces final start. *N. P. Littmoden* –

INDIAN BLAZE 9 ch.g. Indian Ridge 123 – Odile (Green Dancer (USA) 132) [2003 70§: p10g* p10g* p10g* p10g⁵ p10g³ p10g⁶ p10g p10g⁴ 10m 10d 8.3g³ 8.3m⁴ 8.2g 8.2d p10g p10g Dec 10] workmanlike gelding: fair performer: won seller, claimer (left D. Elsworth) and minor event at Lingfield in January: below form after sixth outing: stays easy 1¼m: acts on any turf going/all-weather: tried blinkered, not in 2003: usually held up: none too reliable. *Andrew Reid* **73 d**

INDIAN CALL 2 ch.c. (Apr 8) Classic Cliche (IRE) 128 – Crees Sqaw (Cree Song 99) [2003 5m 6d 6d⁴ 6m 6m Oct 24] 3,500Y: big colt: first foal: dam well beaten: modest maiden: should stay at least 1m: acts on good to firm and good to soft going. *B. A. McMahon* **64**

INDIAN CREEK 5 br.h. Indian Ridge 123 – Blue Water (USA) 104 (Bering 136) [2003 119: p10g⁴ 10g* 10m³ 12f* 10.4m⁵ 12g³ 12f³ 10m³ 12m Dec 14] **119**

'Champagne for my real friends, real pain for my sham friends.' Day-to-day racing quotes rarely rival those in the wider world, usually tending towards the sycophantic rather than the acidic. Trainers don't often break ranks to snipe at each other openly, but it makes for entertaining reading when they do. David Elsworth produced a strong contender for quote of the year after winning an Epsom sprint with Kathology in April. Referring to the horse's rising handicap mark, he was quoted as saying 'he came down from 90 to 77 after he had spent a year with Mark Johnston and he's back up to 91 now, so perhaps we'd better send him back for another year!' Whether or not Elsworth's remarks were made tongue-in-cheek, they provided a rare illustration of the thirst for recognition among trainers. Reputations ebb and flow, and there is a tendency for volume of winners to over-shadow everything else in the public mind. The veteran Elsworth cannot come close to rivalling Johnston for numbers of winners in an average season, but there have been plenty of highlights in a career which began in the late-'seventies and has seen Elsworth saddle winners of top races under both codes.

It says much for the profile of some of the horses that Elsworth has trained that his part in their success has sometimes been overshadowed. Desert Orchid, Floyd and Rhyme 'N' Reason over jumps, and such as In The Groove and Persian Punch on the Flat have had such colourful careers that they can be discussed at length without mentioning their trainer. Indian Creek is another that has tended to put his trainer in the shade, making a name for himself not so much through his ability but through his quirks. Inclined to sulk in behind in races, his mood can

Hardwicke Stakes, Royal Ascot—
Indian Creek (near side) collars Bollin Eric close home; Zindabad is third

change dramatically if things start to go his way. Indian Creek's victories in the Bet attheraces Gordon Richards Stakes at Sandown and the Hardwicke Stakes at Royal Ascot in 2003 were gained in familiar style. Starting joint favourite at 3/1 in a field of eight at Sandown in April, Indian Creek was slowly away and ran in snatches before quickening well to edge in front late on, beating Bourgainville by a neck, despite carrying his head awkwardly. After finishing only third to Sights On Gold in the Brigadier Gerard Stakes over the same course and distance in May, Indian Creek was stepped up to a mile and a half for the first time in the Hardwicke. In a strong renewal, he started at 14/1, one of the outsiders in a field of nine which included Coronation Cup runner-up Highest and the previous year's St Leger winner Bollin Eric. After again dropping himself out, Indian Creek was still last into the straight. Pulled wide as Zindabad went for home, Indian Creek came with another remarkable run, knuckling down well to collar Bollin Eric close home, beating him a neck in receipt of 5 lb, the pair three lengths clear.

Despite his quirks, Indian Creek can usually be relied on to run his race. He failed to add to his Sandown and Royal Ascot successes in five subsequent starts, but ran at least respectably on each occasion. Even less keen than usual early on when only fifth in the Juddmonte International at York, he was third under a penalty in both the September Stakes at Kempton and the Cumberland Lodge at Ascot. Arguably his best effort in defeat came on his final start in Britain when third to Rakti in the Champion Stakes at Newmarket, where he went down by three and a half lengths in a race in which he had also been third as a three-year-old. Indian Creek's campaign was completed in the Hong Kong Vase at Sha Tin, where he could never really get in a challenge, finishing only ninth though beaten little over

Exors of the late Mr Seymour Cohn's "Indian Creek"

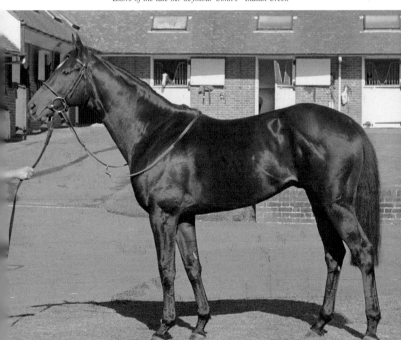

two lengths behind Vallee Enchantee. Before Indian Creek's final outing, the death was announced of his nonagenarian owner Seymour Cohn, whose main racing interests were in New York. Cohn had many graded winners in fifty years owning and breeding, as well as having a long-standing association with British racing. His purple and white check colours with white sleeves were also carried in Europe by the 2000 Prix de la Foret winner Indian Lodge.

Indian Creek (br.h. 1998)	Indian Ridge (ch 1985)	Ahonoora (ch 1975)	Lorenzaccio / Helen Nichols
		Hillbrow (ch 1975)	Swing Easy / Golden City
	Blue Water (USA) (b 1992)	Bering (ch 1983)	Arctic Tern / Beaune
		Shining Water (b 1985)	Riverman / Radiance

Stallions don't necessarily sire horses exactly in their own image and Indian Creek isn't the first pattern winner over middle distances by the King's Stand, Duke of York and Jersey Stakes winner Indian Ridge. Sights On Gold is another by him, as is St Simon Stakes winner High Pitched. Indian Creek's dam Blue Water was useful, winning from a mile to a mile and a half in France and gaining her most important success in a listed race at the latter trip. Her dam Shining Water and her grandam Radiance were also winners in France, at a mile and a quarter and at up to a mile and a half respectively. Radiance is also the grandam of Sun On The Sea, a listed winner in 2003 sold for 250,000 guineas at the December Sales. Indian Creek made 46,000 guineas as a yearling, and was led out unsold at 44,000 guineas when returned to the sales as an unraced two-year-old. His four-year-old half-sister Honorine (by Mark of Esteem) made into a fairly useful handicapper at a mile in the latest season. A smart performer, effective at a mile and a quarter to a mile and a half, Indian Creek has now won nearly £400,000 in prize money. A tall, useful-looking horse, he acts on firm going; his placing in the Champion Stakes as a three-year-old came on good to soft, though connections seemed wary of running him on a similar surface in 2003, withdrawing him on the morning of the King George VI and Queen Elizabeth Stakes after rain. *D. R. C. Elsworth*

INDIAN DREAM (IRE)   3 ch.f. Indian Ridge 123 – Karri Valley (USA) (Storm Bird   **54** (CAN) 134) [2003 8.1m⁵ f9.4g⁶ 10f³ 10g Oct 28] IR 90,000Y: half-sister to several winners, including smart Irish 1¼m/1½m winner Campo Catino (by Woodman) and useful Irish 1½m winner Trebizond (by Sadler's Wells): dam, ran once, closely related to smart 7f/1m performer Fatherland and half-sister to grandam of El Condor Pasa: modest maiden: best effort on debut: should stay 1¼m: sold 35,000 gns in December. *H. R. A. Cecil*

INDIAN EDGE   2 ch.g. (Mar 27) Indian Rocket 115 – Beveled Edge 60 (Beveled   **68** (USA)) [2003 5.1g⁶ 6g⁶ p7g⁶ Oct 30] 25,000Y: good-topped gelding: fifth foal: half-brother to 3-y-o Elidore and useful 6f winner (including at 2 yrs) Bright Edge (by Danehill Dancer): dam 6f winner: best effort in maidens (fair form) at Windsor on second start: not sure to stay much beyond 6f. *B. Palling*

INDIAN HAVEN   3 ch.c. Indian Ridge 123 – Madame Dubois 121 (Legend of   **119** France (USA) 124) [2003 99: 7m* 8g 8d* 8f 10m Oct 18]

Paul D'Arcy surely couldn't have envisaged that his fortunes would take a turn for the better so quickly following his departure from High Havens stables, brought about by a dispute with the yard's owner. Around the time the turf season got under way d'Arcy made the very short journey along Newmarket's Hamilton Road to Green Ridge stables, and within two months of setting up there he had sent out the three-year-old colt Indian Haven to win both the Victor Chandler European Free Handicap and the Entenmann's Irish Two Thousand Guineas.

Indian Haven hadn't looked a potential classic winner as a two-year-old. Highly tried after winning a maiden at Yarmouth on his debut, he failed to make the frame in three further starts, though showing useful form when sixth in the Gimcrack Stakes and fifth in the Champagne Stakes. On his final outing Indian Haven managed to beat only one of fifteen rivals in the Dewhurst Stakes, not long after that making an appearance in the nearby sales ring, where he changed hands

for 95,000 guineas. It was a purchase Indian Haven's three new owners, two of whom reportedly went on to purchase Green Ridge stables, would have no cause to regret. The Free Handicap, in which Indian Haven showed a tremendous turn of foot to win by two and a half lengths from Baron's Pit, was worth over £18,000 to the winner, the Irish Two Thousand Guineas almost £160,000. Indian Haven finished fourteenth of twenty in the Two Thousand Guineas at Newmarket in between those races, and, with four of the horses well in front of him in opposition again, his prospects at the Curragh looked anything but bright, on the face of it. Yet whereas Zafeen (second), Tout Seul (fourth) and Saturn (fifth) all enjoyed a relatively clear run at Newmarket, eighth-placed Tomahawk and Indian Haven had anything but, Indian Haven hampered against the rail inside the final two furlongs when still to be asked for his effort. Once his mount's chance had gone, Indian Haven's rider was quick to accept the situation.

The market certainly suggested that both Indian Haven and Tomahawk would play a much more prominent role at the Curragh. Those who had taken part in the English equivalent occupied five of the first six places in the betting, Tomahawk the favourite at 100/30 with Indian Haven fourth-best at 8/1 in a sixteen-runner field. Whereas many of the field, most notably Tomahawk and Zafeen, failed to do themselves justice, Indian Haven, his trainer's first runner in Ireland, showed just how unlucky he had been at Newmarket. Having to wait for a gap after the field gradually moved across the stand rail in the straight, Indian Haven came through to lead entering the final furlong and ran on well to win by a length from France, with Tout Seul a further two and a half lengths back in third, just ahead of Saturn. The gamble taken to supplement Indian Haven for the race at a cost of €40,000 had paid off handsomely. Indian Haven's performance was just about on a par with that put up by Refuse To Bend at Newmarket, by our reckoning, though the latter's overall form is better. The opportunity for the pair to meet again never came; and whereas Refuse To Bend went on to win the Desmond Stakes, Indian Haven failed by a long way to do himself justice in two subsequent starts, although with valid excuses each time. Reportedly found to be lame after trailing home last of eleven in the St James's Palace Stakes at Royal Ascot, Indian Haven patently failed to stay when stepped up to a mile and a quarter in the Champion Stakes at Newmarket four months later, already beginning to weaken when hampered after two furlongs out.

Indian Haven showed more in the way of stamina than his sire Indian Ridge, who was best at up to seven furlongs, but nothing like so much as his dam, the Park Hill Stakes winner Madame Dubois. Madame Dubois, a thoroughly genuine performer whose five wins, all at three, also included one in the Prix de Royallieu, has proved very successful as a broodmare. Indian Haven is her eighth foal and sixth winner, all of them at least fairly useful. They include Count Dubois (by Zafonic), who was successful in the Group 1 Gran Criterium on his final start at two and is now at stud in South Africa, and Place de L'Opera, a useful performer at a mile and a half and dam of the 2001 St Simon Stakes winner High Pitched and the smart two-year-old Imperial Stride, both of them by Indian Haven's sire Indian Ridge. Both Place de L'Opera and High Pitched were trained by Henry Cecil, and are from a family which served Warren Place extremely well for many years. Indian Haven's grandam Shadywood, who showed useful form at a mile and a quarter and a mile and a half, is a daughter of the Cheshire Oaks winner Milly Moss, herself a sister to the Nassau and Park Hill winner Mil's Bomb. The tall, good-bodied Indian

P. Gleeson, J. Smith and L. Conway's "Indian Haven"

Indian Haven (ch.c. 2000)	Indian Ridge (ch 1985)	Ahonoora (ch 1975)	Lorenzaccio
			Helen Nichols
		Hillbrow (ch 1975)	Swing Easy
			Golden City
	Madame Dubois (ch 1987)	Legend of France (b 1980)	Lyphard
			Lupe
		Shadywood (ch 1982)	Habitat
			Milly Moss

Haven, who fetched 62,000 guineas as a yearling, acts on good to firm and good to soft going, and he is usually waited with. He stays a mile, but will probably prove effective back at six furlongs, a trip he last tried on his second outing as a two-year-old. He will have to prove himself once more when he returns in 2004, but if he can recapture the form he showed at the Curragh another good race should come his way. *P. W. D'Arcy*

INDIAN MAIDEN (IRE) 3 br.f. Indian Ridge 123 – Jinsiyah (USA) 98 (Housebuster (USA)) [2003 68: f6g f6g* f6g* 6.1g* 6m 6.1d6 p6g f6g Nov 17] tall, leggy filly: fair performer: won maiden in January and handicap in March, both at Wolverhampton, and handicap at Nottingham in April: stays 6f: acts on all-weather and good to soft ground, below form on good to firm: sometimes slowly away. *M. S. Saunders* — **75**

INDIAN MUSIC 6 b.g. Indian Ridge 123 – Dagny Juel (USA) 75 (Danzig (USA)) [2003 69d: f6s f7s f8g f9.4s2 f8.5g 7.1d5 f8.5g3 7.1f 8f f8.5g 8m Jul 7] stocky gelding: poor performer: sometimes blinkered/wears cheekpieces: carries head high: unreliable. *A. Berry* — **39 §** / **a45 §**

INDIAN OAK (IRE) 2 b.f. (Feb 24) Indian Rocket 115 – Marathon Maid 82 (Kala-glow 132) [2003 5m5 6m Sep 9] £1,500 2-y-o: first foal: dam, 5f (at 2 yrs) to 1m winner, seemed to stay 1¾m: last in minor event/maiden at Lingfield. *M. P. Muggeridge* — **–**

INDIAN RUM 2 b.g. (Apr 4) Spectrum (IRE) 126 – Apache Squaw 54 (Be My Guest (USA) 126) [2003 6m5 6d f6s Oct 21] good-topped gelding: has scope: seventh foal: — **– p**

490

half-brother to 6-y-o Geronimo and winner in Italy by Distant Relative: dam, middle-distance maiden, half-sister to very smart middle-distance performer Apache: signs of ability in maidens: likely to do better at 1¼m+. *M. W. Easterby*

INDIAN SAPPHIRE   2 ch.f. (Mar 30) Bijou d'Inde 127 – Capriati (USA) 83 (Diesis   –
133) [2003 7.5m 7.2m⁴ 7m f7s Oct 21] 2,000Y: workmanlike filly: eighth foal: sister to a winner in Spain and half-sister to 3 winners, including 1m to 1½m winner As-Is (by Lomond): dam, placed up to 1¼m in Britain, later won up to 9f in USA: well held in maidens/minor event: sold 850 gns. *A. Berry*

INDIAN SHORES   4 b.f. Forzando 122 – Cottonwood 80 (Teenoso (USA) 135) [2003   **66 d**
57: 6f* 5.9f 6g 7m⁶ 8.2d Nov 6] neat filly: fair performer: won maiden at Catterick in May: well held subsequently, leaving B. Smart after second start: brought down final one: best at 5f/6f: acts on firm and good to soft going, ran poorly on fibresand: has been awkward at stall/slowly away: none too consistent. *M. Mullineaux*

INDIAN SOLITAIRE (IRE)   4 b.g. Bigstone (IRE) 126 – Terrama Sioux (Relkino   **81**
131) [2003 91: 10.5f⁵ 11.9m 12m⁶ 11.9f 11.9g 16.2f 11.8m² 12m 14g Sep 6] good-bodied gelding: fairly useful handicapper: not at best in 2003: stays 1¾m: acts on good to firm ground (though may not take repeated racing on it), very best form on good going or softer: blinkered (well held): held up. *R. A. Fahey*

INDIAN SPARK   9 ch.g. Indian Ridge 123 – Annes Gift (Ballymoss 136) [2003 112:   **110**
5g² 5.1g⁴ 6f² 6m 5v* 5f 6g 6m 6f⁶ 6m 5m⁴ 5.6d 6m 6f⁵ 5m 6d Nov 8] close-coupled geld-ing: poor mover (reportedly fractured off-fore joint earlier in career): smart performer: won handicap at Haydock in May by ½ length from Now Look Here: best subsequent effort when fifth to Najeebon in similar event at York fourteenth start: best at 5f/6f: acts on any going: often slow to warm up, and comes from behind: tough. *J. S. Goldie*

INDIAN STEPPES (FR)   4 b.f. Indian Ridge 123 – Ukraine Venture 96 (Slip Anchor   **84**
136) [2003 72: f6g* f7s² f6g⁵ a6g⁵ 6m² 6m² 7f 6m p7g³ Sep 9] angular filly: fairly useful performer: won handicap at Wolverhampton in January: best at 6f/7f: acts on soft going, good to firm and dirt/all-weather: has worn cheekpieces, not in 2003. *Julian Poulton*

INDIAN TRAIL   3 ch.c. Indian Ridge 123 – Take Heart 84 (Electric 126) [2003 80:   **89**
6g³ 7m* 6f* 7.1g 5d Aug 30] strong, useful-looking colt: fairly useful performer: won maiden at Goodwood in May and minor event at Kempton (beat Caught In The Dark by 1½ lengths) in June: ran as if amiss final start: effective at 6f/7f: acts on firm and soft going. *D. R. C. Elsworth*

INDIAN WARRIOR   7 b.g. Be My Chief (USA) 122 – Wanton 106 (Kris 135) [2003   **52**
54: p7g f6g f7g⁵ f6s 7g f6g 7m* 7g 8.1m 6f² 6m⁵ Aug 20] small gelding: modest handi-capper: left W. Musson prior to winning apprentice event at Catterick in July: best at 6f/7f: acts on any turf going/all-weather: tried visored, usually blinkered: tongue tied last 2 starts: has been steadily to post: often starts slowly. *J. Jay*

INDIAN WELCOME   4 ch.g. Most Welcome 131 – Qualitair Ridge (Indian Ridge   **86**
123) [2003 73: 10m 12f⁶ f9.4f p8g* 8.3d⁵ p8g p8g* 10d p10g Nov 13] big gelding: fairly useful performer: won minor event in September and handicap in October, both at Ling-field: best form around 1m: acts on good to firm going, good to soft and polytrack: wore blinkers/cheekpieces last 6 starts: races prominently: none too consistent. *H. Morrison*

INDIGO BAY (IRE)   7 b.g. Royal Academy (USA) 130 – Cape Heights (Shirley   **44 §**
Heights 130) [2003 f12g f11s f12g f12s 10m 10.1m 12g 10m² 12.1m 12.1g² 11.1m⁴ 12m 11.9f 12m 12.1d Sep 23] leggy gelding: poor handicapper: stays 1½m: acts on good to firm ground: tried visored, usually blinkered/tongue tied: often races prominently: unreliable. *R. Bastiman*

INDIVIDUAL TALENTS (USA)   3 ch.f. Distant View (USA) 126 – Indigenous   **77 p**
(USA) 56 (Lyphard (USA) 132) [2003 9.7g 10m 8.3m 10d² 10.1g² 12g⁵ 12d²* 12g³ Oct 31] smallish filly: third living foal: half-sister to fairly useful middle-distance 1¼m winner Twin Logic (by Diesis): dam once-raced close relative to dam of high-class middle-distance performer Muhtarram and half-sister to very smart middle-distance performer St Hilarion: fair form: off 2 months and well backed, won apprentice handicap at Epsom in October: good third to Shamara in similar event at Newmarket final start: stays 1½m: acts on good to soft ground: held up: likely to improve further at 4 yrs. *S. C. Williams*

INDRANI   2 b.f. (Apr 7) Bijou d'Inde 127 – Tea And Scandals (USA) (Key To The   **52**
Kingdom (USA)) [2003 5.2m 5.3f⁶ 5m⁶ 5d⁴ 5f⁵ 6.1f⁶ 6m Oct 24] 1,500Y: unfurnished filly: half-sister to high-class sprinter Ron's Victory (by General Holme) and French 1m and 9.5f winner The Dude (by Owington): dam French 6f winner: modest maiden: should stay at least 6f: acts on good to firm and good to soft ground. *John A. Harris*

INDRAPURA STAR (USA) 3 b.g. Foxhound (USA) 103 – Royal Recall (USA) –
(Native Royalty (USA)) [2003 –: 8g 6g f8.5g Nov 17] well held, including in seller.
Miss J. Feilden

INDULENE (IRE) 3 b.c. Alhaarth (IRE) 126 – Don't Care (IRE) 93 (Nordico (USA)) **63 d**
[2003 62: p6g p8g⁴ p8g f9.4g⁵ f14.8s⁴ f11s 7m Oct 14] modest maiden: well beaten last 3
starts: best effort at 1m: acts on polytrack: tongue tied. *D. Carroll*

INFIDELITY (IRE) 2 b.f. (Mar 7) Bluebird (USA) 125 – Madaniyya (USA) 96 **73**
(Shahrastani (USA) 135) [2003 6g³ 7m⁴ 7m³ 7.5d⁵ 8f⁴ 7.2m⁵ 8.1d⁵ 10f* 8m² 8s Nov 3]
€7,000Y: leggy, lengthy filly: fifth foal: half-sister to fairly useful 1997 2-y-o 7f winner
Madjamila (by Doyoun) and 4-y-o Madalyar: dam Irish 9f/1¼m winner from family of
Slip Anchor: fair performer: left N. Tinkler after fourth start, Don Enrico Incisa after fifth:
won nursery at Nottingham in September: will stay 1½m: acts on firm and good to soft
ground. *A. Bailey*

IN FOR THE CRAIC (IRE) 4 b.g. Our Emblem (USA) 114 – Lucky State (USA) **60**
(State Dinner (USA)) [2003 64: p10g³ f12g² p10g³ p12g⁴ p12g⁴ 10.9m 14.1g May 4]
modest performer: left S. Kirk after third start: stayed 1½m: acted on all-weather and
good to firm going: tended to wander: dead. *P. Butler*

INGLEWOOD 3 ch.g. Fleetwood (IRE) 107 – Preening 62 (Persian Bold 123) [2003 **40**
–: f9.4g f12g 12m⁴ 16.2m Jul 21] poor maiden on Flat: fortunate winner over hurdles in
August. *C. W. Thornton*

INGLIS DREVER 4 b.g. In The Wings 128 – Cormorant Creek 73 (Gorytus (USA) **107**
132) [2003 87: f12g* 12.1g² 12m* 14.8m* 18m Oct 18] good-bodied gelding: useful
handicapper: won at Southwell and Newmarket in June and on latter course (by 1¾
lengths from Trueno) in August: raced freely over longer trip when only eleventh of 36 in
Cesarewitch at Newmarket final start: should stay 2m: acts on polytrack, good to firm and
good to soft ground: sold 110,000 gns, joined J. Howard Johnson, and smart form over
hurdles. *Sir Mark Prescott*

INISTRAHULL ISLAND (IRE) 3 b.g. Flying Spur (AUS) – Dolcezza (FR) **69**
(Lichine (USA) 117) [2003 p7g p8g⁶ 8.5m 7.9f² 10m 7.9d⁵ 8m 7m² 7f⁶ p7g p7g⁴ p7g²
p7g³ Dec 6] seventh foal: half-brother to several winners, including 4-y-o Martin House
and German 9.5f/1¼m winner C'Est Fantastique (by Hernando): dam unraced: fair
maiden handicapper: effective at 7f/1m: acts on polytrack, firm and good to soft ground.
M. H. Tompkins

INITIATIVE 7 ch.g. Arazi (USA) 135 – Dance Quest (FR) 117 (Green Dancer (USA) –
132) [2003 37: 12.1g Jul 11] smallish, leggy gelding: poor performer: well held only
7-y-o start: tried blinkered. *J. Hetherton*

INJAAZ 5 ch.m. Sheikh Albadou 128 – Ferber's Follies (USA) (Saratoga Six (USA)) **91 d**
[2003 99: 5.2m 6g 6d 6m 6f 6m⁴ 6m Sep 13] rangy mare: has a fluent, round action: just a
fairly useful handicapper in 2003, below form after second start: best efforts at 6f: acts on
firm and good to soft going, possibly not on heavy: carries head awkwardly: none too
consistent: sold 100,000 gns in December. *J. L. Dunlop*

IN LOVE 3 b.f. Unfuwain (USA) 131 – Nemesia 111 (Mill Reef (USA) 141) [2003 82p: **91**
10.3m³ 10m* 11.8g³ 12d 13.1d 12g² 12v Nov 19] leggy filly: fairly useful handicapper:
won at Ayr in June: good second to Shamara at Newmarket, finishing strongly: stays
1½m: acts on soft and good to firm going: held up. *E. A. L. Dunlop*

IN LUCK 5 b.m. In The Wings 128 – Lucca (Sure Blade (USA) 130) [2003 72: f12g **68**
11.5m⁶ 9d⁴ 12m⁴ 12m 11.8g⁴ 11.8m⁵ 10.5d 10m⁶ 12g 12d³ f14g Nov 24] lengthy mare: **a–**
unimpressive mover: fair maiden: left C. Brittain after eleventh outing: stays 1½m: acts
on good to firm and good to soft going, below form on all-weather: sometimes pulls hard:
none too genuine. *B. Smart*

INMOM (IRE) 2 b.f. (Mar 2) Barathea (IRE) 127 – Zakuska 96 (Zafonic (USA) 130) **63 ?**
[2003 7m⁵ 8m Sep 9] good-topped filly: second foal: sister to 3-y-o Barzak: dam, 1¼m
winner from 3 starts, closely related to US Grade 1 9f winner Link River: seemingly
modest form when fifth of 6 in maiden at Redcar: reportedly struck into when well held
in similar event at Leicester: should stay at least 1m. *S. R. Bowring*

INNCLASSIC (IRE) 2 b.f. (Mar 3) Stravinsky (USA) 133 – Kyka (USA) (Blushing **72 p**
John (USA) 120) [2003 6g p5g³ Oct 30] €18,000Y: third foal: half-sister to 3-y-o Theatre
Time and winner in USA by Jade Hunter: dam unraced half-sister to Poule d'Essai des
Pouliches winner Madeleine's Dream: better effort (fair form) when third of 8 to Autumn
Pearl in minor event at Lingfield, closing finish: should stay at least 6f: open to progress.
B. J. Meehan

INNOVATION 3 b.f. Salse (USA) 128 – I Will Lead (USA) (Seattle Slew (USA)) [2003 **77**
68p: 9.9m 10m³ 11.7f² 12.1m* 12m Sep 5] tall filly: fair performer: made all in maiden at
Chepstow in August: stays 1½m: acts on firm and good to soft ground: races prominently:
sold 6,500 gns in December. *R. Charlton*

INNSTYLE 2 b.f. (Mar 2) Daggers Drawn (USA) 114 – Tarneem (USA) 87 (Zilzal **74**
(USA) 137) [2003 5m³ 6g³ 5g⁵ 6g² 6f⁶ 6g³ 7.1m⁶ 6.5m 6g³ 5m⁴ 6g⁴ 5.1d Nov 6] 5,500F,
30,000Y: leggy, close-coupled filly: third foal: half-sister to fairly useful 2002 2-y-o 5f
winner Lord of The Inn (by Efisio) and Italian 9.5f to 13.5f winner by Inchinor: dam 1m
winner: fair maiden: in frame 6 times, including in nurseries: effective at 5f to easy 7f:
acts on firm going: blinkered third and last 2 starts: signs of temperament (refused to enter
stall intended seventh outing). *B. J. Meehan*

INSPECTOR BLUE 5 ch.g. Royal Academy (USA) 130 – Blue Siren 113 (Bluebird
(USA) 125) [2003 –: 10.9m 8f 10m Jul 25] leggy, quite good-topped gelding: little form:
tried in cheekpieces. *Miss J. Feilden*

INSPECTOR GENERAL (IRE) 5 b.g. Dilum (USA) 115 – New Generation 91 **59**
(Young Generation 129) [2003 85d: f8g⁵ f8s³ f8s² f8.5g⁴ Jan 20] good-topped gelding:
unimpressive mover: modest performer: stays 10.4f: acts on soft ground, firm and fibresand: blinkered (well held) once: sent to Spain. *T. D. Barron*

INSPECTOR HECTOR (IRE) 3 b.g. Hector Protector (USA) 124 – Sombre Lady **–**
(Sharpen Up 127) [2003 64: 10d p10g 8m 7.1g f9.4g⁵ Jul 11] modest form on final 2-y-o
outing: well held all other starts. *M. Blanshard*

IN SPIRIT (IRE) 5 b.g. Distinctly North (USA) 115 – June Goddess (Junius (USA) **64**
124) [2003 70?: f8.5g 10m⁵ 10d⁵ 12g³ p10g p10g Dec 20] fair handicapper: left D. Cosgrove after fourth start: stays 1½m: acts on firm going and all-weather: tried blinkered/
visored. *B. J. Curley*

INSTANT HIT 4 b.g. Indian Ridge 123 – Pick of The Pops 109 (High Top 131) [2003 **74**
64: f7g p7g f8.5g⁵ f9.4g 8m* 9d 7g⁶ Aug 10] fair performer: trained first 4 starts (all on
all-weather in Britain) in 2003 by John A. Quinn: won handicap at Bellewstown in July
on first start for new stable: stays 1m: acts on good to firm ground: tried tongue tied: wore
cheekpieces on reappearance: has raced freely. *R. P. Burns, Ireland*

INSTINCT 2 b.g. (Mar 17) Zafonic (USA) 130 – Gracious Gift 96 (Cadeaux Genereux **65 p**
131) [2003 6m Aug 30] tall gelding: first foal: dam, 6f/7f winner, half-sister to smart
performer up to 7f Sharp Prod: 12/1 on green, eighth of 19 in maiden at Ripon, racing
freely before hanging right: needs to settle to stay beyond 6f: sold 10,000 gns, then
gelded: should do better. *R. Hannon*

INSTRUCTOR 2 ch.c. (Mar 7) Groom Dancer (USA) 128 – Doctor's Glory (USA) 91 **76**
(Elmaamul (USA) 125) [2003 6m 7m⁴ p7g² Oct 15] 110,000Y: unfurnished colt: easy
mover: third living foal: closely related to useful 7f to 1¼m winner Courting (by Pursuit
of Love): dam, 5f (at 2 yrs)/6f winner, half-sister to useful 1½m to 2m winner On Call:
fair form in maidens: second at Lingfield: should stay 1m. *R. Hannon*

INSUBORDINATE 2 ch.c. (Mar 20) Subordination (USA) 120 – Manila Selection **63**
(USA) (Manila (USA)) [2003 7m f6g⁶ 6m⁴ 6f* 6g 6g 6g⁶ Oct 28] 5,500Y: good-bodied
colt: first foal: dam unraced out of half-sister to very smart performer up to 1¼m in
Britain/USA Montjoy: modest performer: won seller at Redcar (sold from R. Cowell
14,000 gns) in August: should stay 7f: acts on firm going and fibresand: wore cheekpieces
third and fourth starts: signs of temperament (sometimes gives trouble stall/slowly away).
J. S. Goldie

INTEGRATION 3 b.c. Piccolo 121 – Discrimination 72 (Efisio 120) [2003 57: 8.1m **56**
8.1m 7.9f⁵ 10f² 10m 10m⁵ 11.8m³ Sep 1] smallish, quite attractive colt: modest maiden:
stays easy 11.8f: acts on firm going, good to soft and polytrack: usually races prominently: sold 5,200 gns. *P. W. Harris*

INTELLIBET ONE 3 b.f. Compton Place 125 – Safe House 81§ (Lyphard (USA) **68**
132) [2003 74: p6g f5s p5g 5m⁴ 5m 5.7m 6s 5.1m 5f⁴ 5.7f 5m 6m* 5m* 5m² 5g⁴ 6m⁶ 5g² **a–**
5.7f 5d² 5.1m³ 5g 5m 5.1d 6.1m f5g f5g Nov 29] leggy filly: fair handicapper: won at
Catterick and Lingfield in July: effective at 5f/6f: acts on firm going, soft and polytrack:
tried visored: usually races prominently: tough. *P. D. Evans*

INTENSITY 7 b.g. Bigstone (IRE) 126 – Brillante (FR) 118 (Green Dancer (USA) **68**
132) [2003 75: 13s⁶ 12f 10m² 7m f14.8g f12g Dec 3] leggy, useful-looking gelding: fair
handicapper: mostly below form on Flat in 2003, leaving R. Osborne in Ireland after
fourth outing: stays 1½m: acts on firm and good to soft going: held up: winning hurdler.
P. A. Blockley

Mr K. Abdulla's "Intercontinental"

INTERCEPTOR   3 ch.c. Hector Protector (USA) 124 – Moorish Idol 90 (Aragon   **95**
118) [2003 82p: 8.1m² 9g 9.7m³ 11.9m Sep 3] useful-looking colt: useful performer,
lightly raced: best efforts when length second to Grand Passion in handicap at Sandown
and third to Putra Kuantan in minor event at Folkestone: should stay 1½m: raced only on
good/good to firm going: ran in snatches final start. *J. W. Hills*

INTERCESSION   3 ch.f. Bluebird (USA) 125 – Intercede (Pursuit of Love 124) [2003   **90 §**
90p: 8m⁵ 8m⁵ 7.9m 9.9m⁵ 8m⁴ 10m 10m⁵ 14.1m Aug 18] good-bodied filly: fairly useful
performer on her day: creditable fourth to Hoh Buzzard in handicap at Newmarket fifth
start: reluctant to race and pulled up final one: should stay 1¼m: unraced on extremes of
going: blinkered last 2 starts: has carried head high/swished tail in preliminaries/been
reluctant to post: not one to trust. *P. W. Harris*

INTERCONTINENTAL   3 b.f. Danehill (USA) 126 – Hasili (IRE) (Kahyasi 130)   **110**
[2003 105p: 6g* 8g³ 8m³ 7g* 7d² 7s⁴ Oct 12] strong, good-bodied filly: type to carry
plenty of condition: smart performer: won minor event at Maisons-Laffitte in April and
listed race at Deauville (made all, held on by short head from Derrianne) in July: creditable efforts when in frame in 1000 Guineas at Newmarket (2¾ lengths third to Russian
Rhythm, travelling strongly into lead over 1f out but no extra inside last), Prix de Sandringham at Chantilly (3½ lengths third to Maiden Tower), listed race at Maisons-Laffitte
(2 lengths second to Miss Ivanhoe) and Prix de la Foret at Longchamp (3¾ lengths fourth
to Etoile Montante): effective at 1m but races freely, and will prove best at 6f/7f: acts on
soft and good to firm going: to be trained at 4 yrs by R. Frankel in USA. *A. Fabre, France*

INTERNATIONALGUEST (IRE)   4 b.g. Petardia 113 – Banco Solo (Distant Rela-   **91**
tive 128) [2003 100: 10g 8.1s 8m 10.1m³ 10.1s⁶ 12d Nov 8] tall, close-coupled gelding:
fairly useful handicapper: easily best effort in 2003 when third at Yarmouth: stays 1¼m:
acts on heavy and good to firm going: blinkered/visored. *G. G. Margarson*

INTERSTICE   6 b.g. Never So Bold 135 – Mainmast 63 (Bustino 136) [2003 50, a61: **58 +**
f12s* f11g* f11g⁴ f12g² f14s p12g 10.3g³ 12.1d 10.9m f12g f12g f12s Dec 27] fair **a72**
handicapper on all-weather, modest on turf: won twice at Southwell in January: effective
at 1¼m/1½m: acts on soft ground, below form on good to firm: better form on fibresand
than polytrack: usually held up. *A. G. Newcombe*

INTER VISION (USA)   3 b.c. Cryptoclearance (USA) – Fateful (USA) 90 (Topsider **99**
(USA)) [2003 96: 7.6m 6m 5f 5.1m⁶ 6g⁴ 6m⁶ 6m 6g* 6.1g² 7d 7f⁵ 5m⁴ Oct 25] tall colt:
useful handicapper: won at Ripon in August: unlucky not to follow up at Chester next
time: best effort when fourth to Smart Hostess at Doncaster final start, finishing strongly
having been short of room: best at 5f/6f: yet to race on heavy ground, acts on any other:
usually waited with. *A. Dickman*

IN THE GLOAMING (IRE)   3 b.f. Avarice – Katherine Kath (Merdon Melody 98) **–**
[2003 40: 5m 5d 5m May 19] poor maiden: well beaten in 2003. *James Moffatt*

IN THE GREEN   4 b.g. Greensmith 121 – Carn Maire 83 (Northern Prospect (USA)) **47**
[2003 –: 5f 5.1g 5m Sep 24] good-topped gelding: has a short action: poor handicapper:
raced mainly at 5f: acts on firm ground: well held only try in visor. *J. J. Quinn*

IN THE LEATHER (IRE)   2 ch.f. (Feb 5) Dr Devious (IRE) 127 – Bodfari Quarry **–**
92 (Efisio 120) [2003 8.2f Sep 30] good-topped filly: first foal: dam, 5f (at 2 yrs) 1½m
winner, out of half-sister to top-class 1¼m filly Cormorant Wood: 66/1, ran as though
amiss in maiden at Nottingham: sold 3,500 gns. *Mrs J. R. Ramsden*

IN THE PINK (IRE)   3 gr.f. Indian Ridge 123 – Norfolk Lavender (CAN) 80 (Ascot **74**
Knight (CAN) 130) [2003 7m⁵ 7f 8.3m⁵ 7f³ 5m⁵ 7m* Oct 21] IR 92,000Y: close-coupled,
quite good-topped filly: fourth foal: half-sister to useful 1m (at 2 yrs) to 1½m winner
Celtic Mission (by Cozzene): dam, 1m winner (later 8.5f minor stakes winner in USA),
out of 1000 Guineas winner Nocturnal Spree: fair performer: best effort to win maiden at
Yarmouth in October: stays 8.3f: raced only on ground firmer than good. *M. R. Channon*

IN THE STARS (IRE)   5 ch.g. Definite Article 121 – Astronomer Lady (IRE) (Mont- **64 ?**
ekin 125) [2003 68: f12s p12g⁴ 14.4d 11.8g p12g Oct 30] modest maiden handicapper:
stays easy 13f: acts on polytrack, raced only on good/good to soft going on turf.
P. R. Webber

INTIKRAFT (IRE)   2 ch.g. (Apr 17) Intikhab (USA) 135 – Mysistra (FR) (Machia- **76 §**
vellian (USA) 123) [2003 p5g 6g⁶ 6d³ 7m 7.1g 6m 6m f7s⁶ 6f² 6.1d f6g p6g Nov 26] **a52 §**
7,500F, 8,200Y, 7,500 2-y-o: close-coupled gelding: unimpressive mover: fifth foal:
half-brother to Irish 1½m winner Jug of Punch (by In The Wings) and 6f to 1¼m winner
in Italy by Cadeaux Genereux: dam, French 11f winner, out of half-sister to Irish St Leger
winner Dark Lomond: fair maiden on turf, modest on all-weather: barely stays 7f: acts on
firm going, good to soft and fibresand: blinkered/visored last 5 outings: gelded subsequently: ungenuine. *Mrs S. A. Liddiard*

INTIMATE FRIEND (USA)   2 b.f. (Feb 8) Expelled (USA) 116 – Intimate (USA) **85**
(Topsider (USA)) [2003 6m⁴ 7f² 5f⁶ Sep 5] lengthy, rather sparely-made filly: fourth foal:
dam, 6f winner in USA at 4 yrs, half-sister to dam of smart 1998 2-y-o 7f winner Auction
House: easily best effort in maidens (fairly useful form) when fourth to Bay Tree at
Newbury: raced freely/hung left at Brighton next time: should stay 7f. *B. W. Hills*

IN TIME'S EYE   4 b.c. Singspiel (IRE) 133 – Irish Edition (USA) (Alleged (USA) **119**
138) [2003 112: 10.5d⁴ 10f* 10m³ 10f³ 12g Oct 18] tall colt: smart performer: landed

Wolferton Rated Stakes (Handicap), Royal Ascot—the blinkered In Time's Eye lands a gamble;
Persian Lightning runs him closest, and Akshar takes third

gamble in listed Wolferton Rated Stakes at Royal Ascot in June, beating Persian Lightning by neck: creditable third in Meld Stakes at Leopardstown (2¼ lengths behind Mingun) and Royal Whip Stakes at the Curragh (beaten length by High Chaparral, making most) next 2 starts: finished sore when tenth of 18 to Mummify in Caulfield Cup (handicap, top weight) final outing: effective at 1¼m/1½m: acts on firm and good to soft going (promising effort on soft on debut): blinkered last 4 starts. *D. K. Weld, Ireland*

INTITNICE (IRE) 2 b.c. (Apr 25) Danehill Dancer (IRE) 117 – Gathering Place (USA) (Hawaii) [2003 5.1m 6d 6m⁵ 6f⁶ 6m⁴ f5g⁵ 6m² 6.1m 6f² 7m⁵ 6g² 5m 5f⁴ 6m 6m f5g f8g p7g Dec 17] €8,000Y: smallish colt: half-brother to several winners abroad: dam 1m winner in USA: modest maiden: left A. Berry after sixteenth start: barely stays 7f: acts on firm and good to soft ground, well held on all-weather: tried in blinkers/cheek-pieces: none too consistent. *Miss K. M. George*   **52**

INTO THE BLUE (IRE) 4 b.g. Blues Traveller (IRE) 119 – Lux Aeterna (Sandhurst Prince 128) [2003 –: f9.4g Jan 27] tall gelding: no form. *T. M. Jones*   **–**

INTO THE BREEZE (IRE) 3 b.g. Alzao (USA) 117 – Catalane (USA) (Septieme Ciel (USA) 123) [2003 93: 7d 7g² 7g⁶ 7.1f⁵ 7g⁴ 7g² 7.6m⁵ Aug 30] good-bodied gelding: useful handicapper: won at Redcar in July: good efforts last 2 starts, at Leicester (1½ lengths second to El Coto) and Chester (fifth to True Night): stays 7.6f: acts on polytrack, good to firm and good to soft going: usually races prominently. *J. W. Hills*   **103**

INTRICAT 3 ch.g. Bluegrass Prince (IRE) 110 – Noble Soul 67 (Sayf El Arab (USA) 127) [2003 –: p8g⁶ f8s 10.2f 7f⁵ 10.2f² 8g 8.1f⁶ 8m Aug 6] poor maiden handicapper: stays easy 1¼m: acts on firm ground: tried visored. *A. P. Jones*   **42**

INTRICATE WEB (IRE) 7 b.g. Warning 136 – In Anticipation (IRE) 93 (Sadler's Wells (USA) 132) [2003 87, a93: f8.5s⁵ f8.5g⁴ 10g 9.9f² 12.1m⁴ 10d⁴ 10.5m⁵ 12m 10s⁴ f9.4g³ Nov 29] sturdy, angular gelding: fairly useful handicapper: stays 1¼m: acts on fibresand, firm and soft ground: tried blinkered/visored (not in 2003), has run well in cheekpieces: sometimes slowly away: often races lazily nowadays. *E. J. Alston*   **82**

INTRIGUING GLIMPSE 2 b. or br.f. (Jan 27) Piccolo 121 – Running Glimpse (IRE) 84 (Runnett 125) [2003 6g⁶ 6g p5g* p5g* p6g³ Dec 30] fifth foal: half-sister to 5-y-o Another Glimpse and 3-y-o Maureen Ann: dam, 5f (at 2 yrs)/6f winner, half-sister to smart 1¼m/1½m performer Captain Horatius: fair performer: won maiden in November and nursery in December, both at Lingfield: effective at 5f/6f: acts on polytrack, some promise on turf. *Miss B. Sanders*   **72**

INTRODUCING (USA) 3 b.f. Deputy Minister (CAN) – Interim 117 (Sadler's Wells (USA) 132) [2003 81p: 7.2m² 10m³ 9m* 12g⁴ Oct 31] smallish filly: shows knee action: fairly useful performer: landed odds in maiden at Newcastle in August: good fourth to Shamara in handicap at Newmarket final start: stays 1½m: raced only on good/good to firm ground: sent to USA. *B. W. Hills*   **87**

INTRODUCTION 2 b.g. (Apr 3) Opening Verse (USA) 126 – Cartuccia (IRE) (Doyoun 124) [2003 p6g p7g p6g Dec 6] 5,800Y: third foal: half-brother to a winner in Holland by Abou Zouz: dam unraced half-sister to Derby/Irish Derby second City Honours: poor form in seller/claimer/maiden: should be suited by at least 1m. *W. J. Musson*   **47**

IN TUNE 3 b.g. Distinctly North (USA) 115 – Lingering 96 (Kind of Hush 118) [2003 61: p7g⁵ p10g⁵ Jan 15] modest maiden handicapper: best at 7f/1m: acts on polytrack: sometimes slowly away: sold 2,700 gns. *P. Mitchell*   **58**

INVADER 7 b.h. Danehill (USA) 126 – Donya 74 (Mill Reef (USA) 141) [2003 95§, a97§: p7g p10g³ p10g⁴ f8.5s 8m 10.9m⁶ 8g 8m² 8m 8f* p10g⁴ p8g³ Dec 20] big horse: fairly useful handicapper: won at Doncaster in June: acts on 1m/easy 1¼m: acts on firm going, good to soft and all-weather: occasionally blinkered/visored: tried tongue tied: lazy sort, and sometimes finds little: unreliable. *C. E. Brittain*   **90 §**
  a95 §

INVASIAN (IRE) 2 ch.c. (Feb 26) Desert Prince (IRE) 130 – Jarrayan 64 (Machiavellian (USA) 123) [2003 8.3m Sep 29] second foal: half-brother to 3-y-o Lark In The Park: dam, maiden best at 6f at 2 yrs, half-sister to useful UAE sprinter Moonis out of half-sister to smart 1¼m performer Husyan: 14/1, eighth of 12 in maiden at Windsor, disputing lead halfway and not knocked out: not sure to stay beyond 1m: should do better. *H. R. A. Cecil*   **– p**

INVER GOLD 6 ch.h. Arazi (USA) 135 – Mary Martin (Be My Guest (USA) 126) [2003 69, a82: f11s⁵ f12g² f9.4s⁶ 11.7m f14.8g* Jun 6] lengthy horse: poor mover: fair performer on all-weather, modest on turf: won claimer at Wolverhampton (claimed £10,000) in June: stays 14.8f: acts on all-weather, good to firm and good to soft going: often takes while to warm up. *A. G. Newcombe*   **60**
  a79

INVERNESS 3 ch.g. Inchinor 119 – Inimitable 66 (Polish Precedent (USA) 131) [2003 **102**
62p: 8g⁵ 8m* 8m* 8m² 5m 7m Dec 14] lengthy gelding: made into a useful handicapper,
winning at Newmarket in May and Goodwood in June: best effort when head second to
South Atlantic in well-contested event at Newmarket: left J. Fanshawe and off over 4
months before penultimate start: should stay 1¼m: raced only on good/good to firm going
on turf. *Y. O. Wong, Hong Kong*

INVESTMENT AFFAIR (IRE) 3 b.g. Sesaro (USA) 81 – Superb Investment (IRE) **68**
(Hatim (USA) 121) [2003 –p: 7d⁴ 8m 8g* 7m⁶ 8m* 7.9m³ 8m⁶ 8.3m 7.5m 7m Sep 9]
close-coupled, good-topped gelding: fair handicapper: won at Ayr in May and Musselburgh in June: below form last 4 starts: should stay 1¼m: acts on good to firm ground:
races prominently: has wandered: sold 2,000 gns. *M. Johnston*

INVESTMENT FORCE (IRE) 5 b.g. Imperial Frontier (USA) 112 – Superb Invest- **56**
ment (IRE) (Hatim (USA) 121) [2003 f7g f8.5g f7g 9m 6m⁶ 9m 8m³ 7.1g 8.2m 8m 7.5d⁶ **a–**
8.1m⁴ 8m* 7m Aug 5] modest handicapper: made all at Pontefract in July: stays 1m: acts
on good to firm and good to soft ground, not on all-weather: usually visored/blinkered:
sometimes looks none too keen: sold 5,000 gns, joined C. Mann, and won over hurdles in
September. *M. Johnston*

INVICTA 4 b.f. Distant Relative 128 – Blue Zulu (IRE) 94 (Don't Forget Me 127) **76**
[2003 78: p10g⁴ 9.9m 9.5g 10g⁴ 9.5d Oct 31] fair handicapper: left J. Fanshawe 1,500 gns
after second start: stays 10.5f: acts on polytrack, best turf efforts on good going or firmer:
tried tongue tied. *T. J. O'Mara, Ireland*

INVITADO (IRE) 4 ch.g. Be My Guest (USA) 126 – Lady Dulcinea (ARG) (General **–**
(FR)) [2003 –: 12.3m 10.1m 14.1d Jul 26] leggy gelding: little form: tried blinkered/
tongue tied/in cheekpieces. *T. J. Fitzgerald*

INVITATION 5 b.g. Bin Ajwaad (IRE) 119 – On Request (IRE) 53 (Be My Guest **83**
(USA) 126) [2003 85: 10d⁵ 10d 8.1d⁴ 10.1m⁵ 10.1d⁵ 11m 10d Jul 30] angular gelding:
fairly useful handicapper: best around 1¼m: acts on good to firm and heavy ground: tried
in cheekpieces: sometimes races freely/carries head high: usually held up. *A. Charlton*

IN XANADU (IRE) 4 b.g. Persian Bold 123 – Dromoland (Cadeaux Genereux 131) **67 +**
[2003 75: 10g⁴ 9.7m 8m 8g³ 8.3g⁵ 8.5f* 10g³ 7g⁴ 8g⁴ Oct 11] small gelding: fair performer: sold from J. Dunlop 9,000 gns after fifth start: won minor event at Ostend in
August: effective at 1m/1¼m: acts on good to soft and firm going: visored/blinkered most
recent starts in Britain. *Alex Vanderhaeghen, Belgium*

INZABAR (IRE) 2 b.g. (Jan 25) Inzar (USA) 112 – Faypool (IRE) (Fayruz 116) **56**
[2003 5.3f⁵ 6g² 6m⁶ 6.1m 7m² 7m 7m 7.1m Oct 25] €14,000Y: small gelding: third foal:
half-brother to fairly useful 2001 2-y-o 7f winner Mr Blue Sky (by Blues Traveller) and
2002 2-y-o 6f winner Bond Midnight (by Petardia): dam, maiden in Switzerland, half-
sister to smart European Croft Pool: modest maiden: stays 7f: acts on firm going: wore
cheekpieces fourth outing, visored after: sometimes looks difficult ride. *R. M. Beckett*

INZARMOOD (IRE) 5 b.m. Inzar (USA) 112 – Pepilin (Coquelin (USA) 121) [2003 **– §**
46§: f12s f11s Jan 16] neat mare: poor maiden: well beaten in 2003: visored/blinkered:
inconsistent. *K. R. Burke*

IO CALLISTO 2 br.f. (Mar 15) Hector Protector (USA) 124 – Queen Shirley (IRE) **43**
(Fairy King (USA)) [2003 6f⁶ 6m Jul 17] 10,000Y: third foal: half-sister to 3-y-o
Blues Princess: dam unraced: poor form in maidens at Thirsk and Hamilton (wandered).
R. A. Fahey

IONIAN SPRING (IRE) 8 b.g. Ela-Mana-Mou 132 – Well Head (IRE) (Sadler's **93**
Wells (USA) 132) [2003 89: 10.1d⁵ 10m* 10g 10.4m 10m 10.3d⁶ 10m⁵ f12g³ 10g Oct 25]
sturdy gelding: has reportedly suffered from broken blood vessels: fairly useful handicapper: won at Newbury in April: good third at Wolverhampton penultimate start:
effective at 1¼m/easy 1½m: acts on firm going, good to soft and fibresand: sometimes
early to post: tends to edge left: best held up. *C. G. Cox*

IPHIGENIA (IRE) 2 b. or br.f. (Mar 9) Orpen (USA) 116 – Silver Explosive (Rock **60**
Hopper 124) [2003 f5s 6.1g² f5g³ p6g f6g f7g Nov 25] 3,000Y: first foal: dam, ran in 2
Irish bumpers, out of half-sister to very smart 1984 2-y-o Khozaam: modest maiden:
second at Chepstow: will prove best at 5f/easy 6f: best effort on good going, probably
acts on fibresand. *P. W. Hiatt*

IPI TOMBE (ZIM) 5 b.m. Manshood – Carnet de Danse 80 (Dance In Time (CAN)) **126**
[2003 8g* 8.9g* 8.9g* 9f* Jun 28] half-sister to several winners in South Africa: dam
1½m to 1¾m winner in Britain: high-class performer: won 12 of her 14 starts, including
4 out of 5 in Zimbabwe (for N. Peech) and 4 of 5 in South Africa, including Group 1 July

Handicap (changed ownership for reported $750,000 after): continued successful run in UAE/USA after: won listed race in February (by 2¼ lengths from Royal Tryst) and Group 3 Jebel Hatta (by 3¾ lengths from Sights On Gold) and Dubai Duty Free (final outing for M. de Kock, South Africa, by 3 lengths from Paolini) in March, all at Nad Al Sheba: beat Kiss The Devil (rec 7 lb) by ½ length in Grade 3 handicap at Churchill Downs in June: reportedly sustained injury to a leg during work in July and was retired in November after an unsatisfactory bone scan: stayed 11f: acted on firm going: to visit Sadler's Wells. *W. E. Walden, USA*

IPLEDGEALLEGIANCE (USA)   7 b.g. Alleged (USA) 138 – Yafill (USA) 80   **70 d** (Nureyev (USA) 131) [2003 f7g 7m 9m f8g⁵ 8.3g³ 12f² 10.9m* 11.9f 11.5g³ 12.6m⁶ 10g⁴ 12.1m⁶ 12.1m 10f⁵ 10.4m 12m f12s⁴ f12g⁵ f12g⁶ f12g Dec 26] leggy gelding: missed 2001 and 2002: fair handicapper: won at Ayr in June: well below form last 8 starts: stays 1½m: acts on fibresand, firm and soft ground: usually held up. *D. W. Chapman*

IPSA LOQUITUR   3 b.f. Unfuwain (USA) 131 – Plaything 69 (High Top 131) [2003   **63** 69p: p8g⁵ Jan 29] modest form in 2 maidens at Lingfield: not knocked about only 3-y-o start: bred to be well suited by 1¼m+. *S. C. Williams*

IQTE SAAB (USA)   2 b.c. (Mar 27) Bahri (USA) 125 – Shuhrah (USA) 101 (Danzig   **96 p** (USA)) [2003 6m* 7g² Sep 6] rather leggy colt: second foal: dam, 2-y-o 6f winner who stayed 1m, out of half-sister to Lahib: won maiden at Salisbury in August: useful form when 3½ lengths second to Snow Ridge in minor event at Kempton, dictating pace: will stay 1m: open to progress. *J. L. Dunlop*

IRELAND'S EYE (IRE)   8 b.g. Shareef Dancer (USA) 135 – So Romantic (IRE) 97   **–** (Teenoso (USA) 135) [2003 21.6m Apr 14] small gelding: poor maiden handicapper on Flat: well beaten only 8-y-o start: tried visored: fair hurdler. *J. R. Norton*

IRIE RASTA (IRE)   4 ch.g. Desert King (IRE) 129 – Seeds of Doubt (IRE) (Night   **75** Shift (USA)) [2003 81: 15.4m⁶ 14.1g³ 14.1g⁶ 10d³ 11.6g⁴ 12.6m² Jul 4] big, strong gelding: fair handicapper: stays 2m: acts on good to firm and good to soft going: sometimes finds little: none too consistent. *S. Kirk*

IRISH BLADE (IRE)   2 b.c. (Apr 20) Kris 135 – Perle d'Irlande (FR) (Top Ville 129)   **– p** [2003 p8g Nov 26] €65,000Y: seventh foal: half-brother to 3 winners abroad, including French/Spanish winner up to 1½m Pallado (by Bigstone): dam, French 1m (at 2 yrs) and 1¼m winner, half-sister to Prix Marcel Boussac/Vermeille winner Sierra Madre, herself dam of high-class miler Aljabr: 5/1 and green, well held in maiden at Lingfield, starting slowly: should do better. *H. Candy*

IRISH BLESSING (USA)   6 b.g. Ghazi (USA) – Win For Leah (USA) (His Majesty   **–** (USA)) [2003 –: 14.1g⁶ 14.1m Jun 4] sturdy, angular gelding: has shown little since 2000: often blinkered, tongue tied final start (has reportedly had breathing problem). *F. Jordan*

IRISH TYCOON (IRE)   3 ch.g. Entrepreneur 123 – Aoife (IRE) 83 (Thatching 131)   **74** [2003 p7g⁴ p7g² f8.5s 8g⁴ 8.1m 7f² 6.1m 7g 7m⁴ Aug 25] 50,000Y: leggy gelding: first foal: dam, 6f winner, half-sister to 5-y-o Funny Valentine: fair maiden: best form at 7f: acts on polytrack: tried visored, wore cheekpieces last 4 starts: tongue tied last 6: free-going sort: sold 11,500 gns, sent to Holland. *M. A. Magnusson*

IRMA LA DOUCE (IRE)   4 b. or br.f. Elbio 125 – Eves Temptation (IRE) (Glenstal   **58** (USA) 118) [2003 62: 7m 6g 6m 5.7f⁵ 8m 7f 6m 6f³ 7m⁵ 6m² 6f³ 6m 6.9m* 6m 8m Oct 30] neat filly: modest handicapper: won at Carlisle in September: left M. Channon before final start: stays 7f: acts on firm going: usually held up. *M. Halford, Ireland*

IRON TEMPTRESS (IRE)   2 ch.f. (Mar 17) Piccolo 121 – River Divine (USA) 59   **73** (Irish River (FR) 131) [2003 f5g⁵ 5f* 5m² 6m 6m⁴ 5f⁴ 6f³ 7f⁵ 7m² 7g 6d 6m Oct 16] 1,200Y: tall, workmanlike filly: fourth foal: dam ran once: fair performer: won maiden at Beverley in April: some creditable efforts after, including in nursery: stays easy 7f: acts on firm going, some promise on fibresand. *G. M. Moore*

IRON WARRIOR (IRE)   3 b.g. Lear Fan (USA) 130 – Robalana (USA) (Wild Again   **62** (USA)) [2003 58: f11g² f11s⁶ f12g² f12g 12.3m Apr 17] workmanlike gelding: modest maiden: ran poorly last 2 starts: stays 1½m: acts on fibresand: tried in blinkers/cheekpieces. *G. M. Moore*

IRONY (IRE)   4 gr.g. Mujadil (USA) 119 – Cidaris (IRE) (Persian Bold 123) [2003   **98** 105: 7m 6g 6g 7.1f⁵ 8f³ 8m⁶ 8d⁶ 7m 8m* 8.3g⁶ 8.1d³ Aug 29] good-topped gelding: useful handicapper: made all at Kempton in August by 1¾ lengths from Convent Girl: stays easy 1m: acts on firm and good to soft going: tried tongue tied: has worn crossed noseband: often early to post: usually races up with pace. *A. M. Balding*

IROQUOIS CHIEF (USA)   4 b.g. Known Fact (USA) 135 – Celtic Shade (Lomond   –
(USA) 128) [2003 69d: 7m 7g f7s Sep 6] good-topped gelding: on the downgrade, and
well held in 2003: tried visored/tongue tied. *C. N. Kellett*

IRRESISTIBLE   3 b.f. Cadeaux Genereux 131 – Polish Romance (USA) 83 (Danzig   **98**
(USA)) [2003 96: 6.1s* 7d² 6s Aug 31] sturdy, lengthy filly: useful performer: won listed
race at Nottingham in May by short head from Look Here's Carol: good 3½ lengths
second to Perfect Touch in Brownstown Stakes at Leopardstown next time: last in Prix
de Meautry at Deauville final outing: stays 7f: acts on soft and good to firm going:
sometimes bandaged hind joints. *M. L. W. Bell*

IRTAHAL (USA)   3 br.f. Swain (IRE) 134 – Elhasna (USA) 88 (Danzig (USA)) [2003   **94**
7d² 10.4m³ 8m⁴ 8f* 8d⁶ 10.1m Sep 17] close-coupled, quite attractive filly: sixth foal:
half-sister to 1999 2-y-o 5f winner Enaaq (by Bahri) and 2 winners in US by Deputy
Minister: dam, 6f winner, sister to Dayjur and closely related to US Grade 1 9f/1¼m
winner Maplejinsky: fairly useful performer: won 3-runner maiden at Ascot in July by 20
lengths: good efforts earlier when 3½ lengths third to Cassis in Musidora Stakes at York
and fourth to Aldora in listed race at Goodwood: well below form in listed races last 2
starts, dropping out tamely final one: effective at 1m to 10.4f: acted on firm going, shaped
well on good to soft: raced prominently: visits Gulch. *M. P. Tregoning*

ISA'AF (IRE)   4 b.g. Darshaan 133 – Shauna's Honey (IRE) 88 (Danehill (USA) 126)   **61 d**
[2003 61: f12s f12g³ f12g⁵ 12m* 15.4m* 16.2m 14.1s 14.1m 14.1m⁶ 14.1m⁶ p16g 12m²
Sep 16] neat gelding: modest handicapper: won at Pontefract (apprentices) and Folkestone in April: stays 15.4f: acts on fibresand and good to firm going. *P. W. Hiatt*

ISAZ   3 b.c. Elmaamul (USA) 125 – Pretty Poppy 67 (Song 132) [2003 86: 7m⁴ Oct 13]   **?**
strong, good sort: fairly useful form at 2 yrs: reportedly had small problem with hind leg
early in 2003: well below best in maiden at Leicester only outing at 3 yrs: should stay 7f:
unraced on extremes of going. *H. Candy*

I SEE NO SHIPS   3 b.f. Danzig Connection (USA) – Killick 69 (Slip Anchor 136)   –
[2003 f7g 7m 6g May 23] close-coupled filly: third foal: half-sister to 5-y-o Illustrious
Duke: dam 1m and 1½m winner: no sign of ability. *M. Mullineaux*

ISENGARD (USA)   3 b. or br.f. Cobra King (USA) 122 – January Moon (CAN) (Apal-   **76**
achee (USA) 137) [2003 75p: 7g⁵ 6d⁶ 5.1g* 6m² 5f³ p6g Jul 2] fair handicapper: won at
Chepstow in June: effective at 5f/6f: acts on polytrack and good to firm ground: blinkered
(ran poorly) final start. *B. J. Meehan*

ISHELA (IRE)   4 gr.f. Barathea (IRE) 127 – Lalandria (FR) (Highest Honor (FR) 124)   –
[2003 51: 11.1d 11.9m Jun 6] sturdy filly: modest maiden: well beaten in 2003. *A. Berry*

ISIDORE BONHEUR (IRE)   2 b.c. (Mar 18) Mtoto 134 – Way O'Gold (USA) (Slew   **99**
O' Gold (USA)) [2003 7m* 8m⁴ Aug 13] 70,000Y: strong, well-grown, close-coupled
colt: fluent mover: third foal: dam, French maiden, half-sister to 5-y-o Crystal Castle:
useful form when winning 9-runner maiden at Newmarket in July by 1¼ lengths from
Mansfield Park, free to post and in race but quickening to lead final 1f: odds on, ran
as if amiss in listed race at Salisbury (scoped unsatisfactorily after): should stay 1m.
B. W. Hills

ISKANDER   2 b.g. (Apr 24) Danzero (AUS) – Amber Mill 96 (Doulab (USA) 115)   **91**
[2003 5s⁵ 5m² 6f³ 5.2m⁶ 6m* 6d⁵ 7m⁴ Sep 27] 18,000Y: eighth foal: half-brother to 3
winners, including 3-y-o Golden Nun and 4-y-o Amber's Bluff: dam 5f/6f winner, including at 2 yrs: fairly useful performer: won maiden at Hamilton (hung left) in August: good
efforts in sales races fourth and sixth starts: probably best at 5f/6f: acts on good to firm
and good to soft ground: blinkered fourth, fifth and final starts: sometimes slowly away.
K. A. Ryan

ISLA AZUL (IRE)   3 ch.f. Machiavellian (USA) 123 – Nuryana 107 (Nureyev (USA)   **72**
131) [2003 74p: 7m⁴ 8.2m⁵ 9.9f⁶ 10m⁶ 8.3g Aug 23] compact filly: fair maiden: stays
1¼m: raced only on good going or firmer: sent to France. *G. Wragg*

ISLAND HOUSE (IRE)   7 ch.h. Grand Lodge (USA) 125 – Fortitude (IRE) (Last   **115**
Tycoon 131) [2003 118: 10m⁵ 9.9m* 10g⁴ 10.5m⁴ 10g³ 10.9m² Sep 20] tall, quite good-
topped horse: smart performer: won listed race at Goodwood in May by 2½ lengths from
Rawyaan: best efforts after in listed races at Sandown (fourth to Ikhtyar on fourth outing)
and Ayr (½-length second to Imperial Dancer): stays 1½m: acts on any going: has idled/
edged left: usually waited with. *G. Wragg*

ISLAND LADY (IRE)   3 b.f. Hernando (FR) 127 – Prosperous Lady (Prince Tender-   **54**
foot (USA) 126) [2003 –: 10m² 11.1d 10.2f³ p12g Jul 9] sturdy filly: modest maiden:
barely stays 1½m: acts on good to firm going and polytrack. *J. W. Hills*

ISLAND LIGHT 5 b.g. Inchinor 119 – Miss Prism 60 (Niniski (USA) 125) [2003 96: **106**
8g 8m² 10g³ 8m* 8m⁴ 8g² 9m Oct 4] well-made gelding: useful handicapper: improved
again in 2003, winning at Pontefract in June by 3 lengths from Mubeen: good efforts
after when in frame at Ascot (fourth to Pentecost) and Doncaster (2 lengths second to
Muchea): should stay 1¼m: acts on firm and soft going: game: sold 40,000 gns: sent to
USA. *A. C. Stewart*

ISLAND LIGHT (USA) 3 ch.c. Woodman (USA) 126 – Isla Del Rey (USA) 103 **94 §**
(Nureyev (USA) 131) [2003 94p: 8.2d 10.2g* 12m³ 9.7m⁵ 10.1g Sep 10] leggy colt:
fairly useful performer: won minor event at Chepstow in June by 1½ lengths from
Loweswater: well below form last 2 starts: stays 1¼m: acts on firm ground: tried in
cheekpieces: visored (bolted to start and withdrawn) sixth intended outing: not one to
trust: sold 21,000 gns. *E. A. L. Dunlop*

ISLAND RAPTURE 3 b.f. Royal Applause 124 – Gersey (Generous (IRE) 139) [2003 **87**
79: p10g* 9m 9.9f² 10m² 10m³ 9d 10m⁵ 10m⁵ Oct 22] fairly useful performer: won
maiden at Lingfield in February: good efforts after when placed: best up to 1¼m: acts on
polytrack, firm and soft going: usually waited with: sold 27,000 gns. *Mrs A. J. Perrett*

ISLAND SAINT 3 b.g. Efisio 120 – Kembla 59 (Known Fact (USA) 135) [2003 77: **–**
8.2g⁵ 8g Jul 5] neat gelding: fair maiden at 2 yrs: well held in 2003: sold 6,200 gns.
J. L. Dunlop

ISLANDS FAREWELL 3 b.g. Emarati (USA) 74 – Chief Island 62 (Be My Chief **–**
(USA) 122) [2003 8.1d 6m 6m Oct 17] lengthy gelding: third foal: half-brother to 5f (at 2
yrs) to 1¼m winner Celtic Island (by Celtic Swing) and 4-y-o Crownfield: dam ran once:
well held in maidens. *Mrs M. Reveley*

ISLAND SOUND 6 b.g. Turtle Island (IRE) 123 – Ballet 61 (Sharrood (USA) 124) **104**
[2003 –: 10m⁶ 10.1m* 10d 10.1m² 9.9m⁴ 10g⁶ Oct 31] lengthy, angular gelding: has a
round action: useful performer nowadays: won minor event at Epsom in July by 1¾
lengths from Rawzaw: good sixth to Far Lane in listed event at Newmarket final start:
races mainly at 1¼m nowadays: acts on heavy and good to firm going: tried visored/in
cheekpieces: usually front runner. *D. R. C. Elsworth*

ISLAND SPELL 2 b.f. (Mar 1) Singspiel (IRE) 133 – Shifty Mouse 44 (Night Shift **75**
(USA)) [2003 6g 6m 5f³ 6.5m 6f⁶ 5m³ Oct 25] 4,000Y: close-coupled filly: second foal:
half-sister to winner in Hungary by Eagle Eyed: dam, ran twice at 2 yrs, out of sister to
Nassau and Musidora Stakes winner Triple First: fair maiden: should stay at least 1m:
acts on firm going. *C. Grant*

ISLAND STAR (IRE) 3 b.g. Turtle Island (IRE) 123 – Orthorising (Aragon 118) **67 d**
[2003 71: 8f⁴ 8.2g⁶ 8g⁴ f7s 8f f7s p6g⁶ p7g Dec 29] sturdy gelding: fair maiden: well held
last 5 starts, leaving P. Harris cheaply after third of them: races freely, but stays 1m: acts
on polytrack and firm ground: often races prominently. *S. Dow*

ISLAND STREAM (IRE) 4 b.g. Turtle Island (IRE) 123 – Tilbrook (IRE) 78 (Don't **–**
Forget Me 127) [2003 14.1d Jul 25] big gelding: modest maiden at 2 yrs: well held only
4-y-o outing: won twice over hurdles in November. *J. R. Jenkins*

ISLINGTON (IRE) 4 b.f. Sadler's Wells (USA) 132 – Hellenic 125 (Darshaan **124**
133) [2003 123: 10m³ 10g⁶ 11.9m* 10f³ 10f* 12d Nov 30]
One school of thought holds that if at first you don't succeed, give up. Sir
Michael Stoute has resolutely resisted that policy in the Breeders' Cup, saddling
more runners at the meeting over the years—twenty-four—than any other overseas
trainer, with the exception of Andre Fabre and Aidan O'Brien. Stoute suffered his
fair share of Breeders' Cup disappointments before Pilsudski gave him a first
winner at the meeting in the Breeders' Cup Turf in 1996, when he was followed
home by stable-companion Singspiel. The defeats of Shadeed, Sonic Lady and
Zilzal, all in the Mile, were notable setbacks in the 'eighties for Stoute's Breeders'
Cup ambitions, Sonic Lady twice starting favourite and Zilzal starting the shortest-
priced favourite in the early history of the race. Opera House provided another
disappointment in the 1993 Breeders' Cup Turf, but Stoute has gained two more
Breeders' Cup successes since Pilsudski, with Kalanisi in the Turf in 2000 and
with Islington in the Filly & Mare Turf at Santa Anita in the latest season.
Islington's win was the first by a British-trained horse in six Breeders' Cups staged
in California, where only Sonic Lady and Decorated Hero, at Hollywood Park in
1987 and 1997 respectively, had previously earned place money. Stoute's relatively
recent successes probably illustrate, among other things, the benefits of the changes

that have taken place over the years in the approach to international racing, and the preparation for the major targets. Islington, for example, had finished fifth the previous year in the Prix de l'Arc de Triomphe before coming third in the Filly & Mare Turf at Arlington. Connections bypassed the latest Arc because they believed it would enable her to have a smoother preparation for the Breeders' Cup. Her trainer also tackled the problems associated with the heat in California by reportedly treating Islington with a hydroweave blanket, normally used for human burns victims.

Keeping top three-year-old fillies in training is a practice not always blessed with success, and the way Islington's season started hardly boded well for her prospects of adding significantly to a record highlighted by victories in the Nassau Stakes and Yorkshire Oaks, as well as her fifth in the Arc. After an interrupted training programme in the spring due to a foot problem, she missed the Tattersalls Gold Cup because of the good to soft ground and the Brigadier Gerard Stakes because her trainer apparently did not want her contesting a race with a Group 1 penalty. Reappearing in the Prince of Wales's Stakes at Royal Ascot, after what Stoute later admitted was a rushed preparation, Islington wore a crossed noseband and became excitable beforehand, sweating freely, but she still ran creditably, staying on well after being switched to finish over three lengths third to Nayef. Islington sweated up again before the Coral-Eclipse Stakes at Sandown, where, after having every chance two furlongs out, she could find no extra and came home sixth to Falbrav, beaten just over three lengths again. It transpired that Islington came home stiff and sore from Sandown, requiring physiotherapy on her back—the same had happened after the 2002 Oaks—and as a result she missed the King George VI and Queen Elizabeth Stakes and the Nassau Stakes. So with more than half the season gone, Islington had nothing in the bag, but that soon changed.

Odds on for the Aston Upthorpe Yorkshire Oaks, in which she faced seven opponents headed by Oaks winner Casual Look, Irish Oaks runner-up L'Ancresse, Oaks third Summitville and Ribblesdale runner-up Ocean Silk, she gave her supporters little to worry about, tracking the leaders, going on a quarter of a mile out and always doing enough to hold the late challenge of Ocean Silk by a length. Islington was calmer beforehand and became the first to complete successive victories in the Yorkshire Oaks since five-year-old Only Royale in 1994. The Yorkshire Oaks was opened to older fillies and mares in 1991 and Islington's success was the eighth in all in the race for her trainer, for whom one of the other

Aston Upthorpe Yorkshire Oaks, York—Islington wins this Group 1 for the second year in succession; three-year-olds Ocean Silk and Summitville (left) fill the minor placings

Breeders' Cup Filly & Mare Turf, Santa Anita—the first British-trained winner in six Californian runnings of the Breeders' Cup; there's a contrast in styles as Kieren Fallon drives Islington past Edgar Prado-ridden L'Ancresse, with the latter's stable-companion Yesterday (blaze) completing a 1,2,3 for Europe

scorers was Islington's dam Hellenic. With Islington clearly back on track, various races were postulated as targets, including the Arc and the Champion Stakes, but in the event Islington went for the Irish Champion Stakes at Leopardstown. Facing a stiff task, she surpassed herself, running marginally her best race in coming home third, beaten a neck and a head by High Chaparral and the unlucky Falbrav, after galloping on resolutely in the final furlong having been unable to quicken early in the straight.

On her Irish Champion form Islington looked to have a favourite's chance in the Breeders' Cup Filly & Mare Turf at Santa Anita, albeit on a track seemingly plenty tight enough for her if the tactics when third in the previous year's race were repeated; Islington had been held up and never able to launch a challenge. The eleven-strong opposition in the latest edition included virtually all the best North American turf fillies, headed by Heat Haze, Tates Creek, Voodoo Dancer and Megahertz, all Grade 1 winners in the run-up to the race, along with ex-French Musical Chimes (Poule d'Essai des Pouliches). The other European hopes—Dimitrova, Yesterday, L'Ancresse and Mezzo Soprano—all had form at the highest level too. Islington headed the market from Musical Chimes and Tates Creek, and Kieren Fallon, who had come in for a fair bit of criticism from pundits in the States for some of his performances in previous Breeders' Cups, rode a copybook race. Breaking well, Islington lay close to the group of horses pursuing runaway leader Bien Nicole and was driven forcefully to make headway on the home turn. Leading a furlong out, Islington ran on strongly and held off L'Ancresse, running her best race of the season, gamely by a neck. Yesterday was two and a half lengths further away third, providing the Europeans with a rare clean sweep of the places in a Breeders' Cup race—the only other time this has happened was when Swain chased home Pilsudski and Singspiel in the Turf. Islington's victory earned her a prestigious Eclipse award in January as the best female turf performer. Islington did not run anywhere near her best on her final appearance when ninth to all-the-way winner Tap Dance City in the Japan Cup, fading in the straight. The race was run on softer going than usual and Islington lost a shoe as well. She has been retired and visits Rainbow Quest in 2004.

Islington (IRE) (b.f. 1999)	Sadler's Wells (USA) (b 1981)	Northern Dancer (b 1961)	Nearctic
			Natalma
		Fairy Bridge (b 1975)	Bold Reason
			Special
	Hellenic (b 1987)	Darshaan (br 1981)	Shirley Heights
			Delsy
		Grecian Sea (ch 1978)	Homeric
			Sea Venture

Islington's breeding was dealt with fully in *Racehorses of 2002*, and there is not much to add. Her two-year-old sister New Morning (formerly named Greek Flame) showed promise on her only start in a maiden at Ayr in October. Three-year-old Olympienne, who did not race, is also by Sadler's Wells, as is Hellenic's colt foal, and the mare was again tested in foal to the Coolmore stallion last October. Who says repetition is a bad thing? A close-coupled, quite attractive filly with a quick action, Islington was effective at a mile and a quarter to a mile and a half and put up her best efforts on firm or good to firm going. Thoroughly genuine and consistent, she was waited with and often raced freely (she wore a crossed noseband on several occasions, though not after the Eclipse Stakes). *Sir Michael Stoute*

ISOBEL SCARLETT 4 b.f. Emperor Jones (USA) 119 – Key West (FR) (Highest Honor (FR) 124) [2003 55: p7g⁵ p7g p7g Mar 4] modest maiden: stayed 1m: acted on polytrack and good to firm going: dead. *T. D. McCarthy* **57**

ISOLDE'S IDOL 3 ch.f. Night Shift (USA) – Atmospheric Blues (IRE) 91 (Double Schwartz 128) [2003 72: 7m 8.3g 8m Oct 1] smallish, strong filly: fair winner at 2 yrs: well beaten in handicaps in 2003: sold 2,000 gns, sent to Belgium. *C. F. Wall* **–**

ITALIAN AFFAIR 5 ch.m. Fumo di Londra (IRE) 108 – Sergentti (IRE) 76 (Common Grounds 118) [2003 62, a36: f7s f6g⁵ f7g⁴ f6g³ f6g⁴ f7s f8.5g⁴ f8.5g³ 7m 8m 6d⁴ 5m⁶ 6m Jun 15] leggy mare: poor performer: effective at 6f to 8.5f: acts on firm going, good to soft and fibresand: usually races up with pace. *A. Bailey* **49 a45**

ITALIAN MIST (FR) 4 b.g. Forzando 122 – Digamist Girl (IRE) (Digamist (USA) 110) [2003 58d: 6m 5m 6m 7f⁶ 6f² 5.3f 6m 7m⁵ 6g Sep 16] poor maiden: barely stays 7f: acts on firm going and polytrack: tried blinkered/in cheekpieces: carries head awkwardly: untrustworthy. *Julian Poulton* **46 §**

ITCANBEDONE AGAIN (IRE) 4 b.g. Sri Pekan (USA) 117 – Maradata (IRE) 68 (Shardari 134) [2003 71: 8.3m 10m⁶ f12g⁴ Oct 20] tall, good-topped gelding: unimpressive mover: modest performer: probably best around 1¼m: acts on any going: has raced freely. *Ian Williams* **59**

ITCH 8 b.g. Puissance 110 – Panienka (POL) 70 (Dom Racine (FR) 121) [2003 41: f8s Jan 1] good-bodied gelding: poor performer: well beaten only 8-y-o start: tried visored. *R. Bastiman* **–**

ITCHINGTON (IRE) 5 b.h. Royal Academy (USA) 130 – Itching (IRE) (Thatching 131) [2003 10g 12m³ 9.9m⁴ 10f* 10.1m Oct 21] lengthy, angular horse: half-brother to 3 winners, including very smart 1m to 1¼m winner Great Dane (by Danehill) and fairly useful 1996 2-y-o 6f winner Witching Hour (by Alzao): dam unraced half-sister to Croco Rouge and to dam of Ali-Royal, Sleepytime (both by Royal Academy) and Taipan: well held in minor events in French Provinces at 4 yrs for D. Sepulchre: best effort in Britain (fair form) when winning handicap at Nottingham in September: stays 1¼m: raced only on good ground or firmer in Britain: sold 30,000 gns: sent to Spain. *M. P. Tregoning* **75**

I T CONSULTANT 5 b.g. Rock City 120 – Game Germaine (Mummy's Game 120) [2003 60, a53: f9.4g 6d 5m⁶ 5g 6m 5g f6g Nov 14] modest performer: left A. Newcombe after reappearance: best at 5f/6f: acts on fibresand, yet to race on extremes of ground on turf: tried blinkered/tongue tied: inconsistent. *Miss L. A. Perratt* **56 a–**

ITEMISE (USA) 5 b.g. Kris S (USA) – Company Binness (USA) (Seattle Dancer (USA) 119) [2003 87: 12.3m² 10f³ 11.9m³ 14.6g² 14.1s⁴ Oct 29] quite good-topped filly: useful performer: best effort when ¾-length second to Shabernak in Mallard Stakes (Handicap) at Doncaster fourth start, again pulling clear: in frame in listed races at Brighton (rated stakes, beaten 2 heads by Dawnus) and Yarmouth second/final outings: should stay 2m: acts on firm going: sometimes wanders. *M. Johnston* **108**

ITHACA (USA) 2 ch.f. (Jan 17) Distant View (USA) 126 – Reams of Verse (USA) 121 (Nureyev (USA) 131) [2003 7g* 7m² 8f Sep 27] smallish, close-coupled filly: second foal: closely related to fairly useful 2001 2-y-o 6f winner Western Verse (by Gone West): dam, won Fillies' Mile and Oaks, half-sister to high-class 1¼m performer Elmaamul from family of Zafonic: on toes, won maiden at Goodwood in July by 5 lengths: useful form when 2 lengths second to Gracefully in Prestige Stakes on same course and 6½ lengths last of 7 to Red Bloom in Fillies' Mile at Ascot: stays 1m: acts on firm going. *H. R. A. Cecil* **97**

I TINA 7 b.m. Lycius (USA) 124 – Tintomara (IRE) (Niniski (USA) 125) [2003 57§, a53§: 10.2m Jul 24] modest performer: well held only 7-y-o outing: tried visored/blinkered: often spoils chance with slow start. *A. G. Juckes* **– §**

IT MUST BE SPEECH 2 b.c. (May 4) Advise (FR) – Maiden Speech (Pitskelly 122) [2003 7m 8m 7m f9.4g Dec 22] good-bodied colt: first known foal: dam unraced: signs of only a little ability in maidens. *S. L. Keightley* **–**

Princess Royal Willmott Dixon Stakes, Ascot—Itnab gets the better of a sustained duel with Summitville

ITNAB   3 b.f. Green Desert (USA) 127 – Midway Lady (USA) 126 (Alleged (USA)   **116**
138) [2003 76p: 9m* 8.1g⁵ 10d* 12g* Oct 11] good-topped filly: smart performer, lightly
raced: won maiden at Goodwood in May, handicap at Ascot (by ¾ length from Silence Is
Golden) in July and Princess Royal Willmott Dixon Stakes at Ascot (beat Summitville by
length, pair clear) in October: stayed 1½m: acted on good to firm and good to soft going:
raced freely second start: usually held up: visits Kingmambo. *B. Hanbury*

IT'S A BLESSING   2 b.f. (Apr 18) Inchinor 119 – Benedicite (Lomond (USA) 128)   –
[2003 8d Nov 7] 11,000Y: fifth foal: half-sister to useful Irish 1m/1¼m winner Brocheta
(by Hector Protector) and 6f winner Benedictine (by Primo Dominie): dam unraced
half-sister to very smart performer up to 7f College Chapel: 50/1, last of 24 in maiden at
Doncaster. *N. P. Littmoden*

ITSABOY   3 b.g. Wizard King 122 – French Project (IRE) 84 (Project Manager 111)   –
[2003 58: 8.3g 8f Jun 15] modest maiden at 2 yrs: well beaten in 2003. *J. R. Boyle*

ITS ALL EURS (IRE)   3 b.f. Barathea (IRE) 127 – Brief Sentiment (IRE) 96 (Brief   –
Truce (USA) 126) [2003 67: f7g⁵ Jan 17] good-topped filly: fair maiden in 2002: well
held only 3-y-o start. *R. Hannon*

ITS ALL PINK (IRE)   3 gr.f. Victory Note (USA) 120 – Chickamauga (USA) (Wild   –
Again (USA)) [2003 49: p6g f5g Jan 18] small filly: poor maiden at 2 yrs: well beaten in
2003. *D. G. Bridgwater*

ITS A MYSTERY (IRE)   4 b.f. Idris (IRE) 118 – Blue Infanta (Chief Singer 131)   –
[2003 8.3s 7.5m f9.4s 10d Oct 31] IR 3,500Y: tall, workmanlike filly: sister to Swedish
winner up to 21f Mister Painter and half-sister to 6f winner Seanchai (by Treasure Kay):
dam, ran 3 times, half-sister to Lancashire Oaks winner Reprocolor: well beaten in
maidens/handicap. *R. T. Phillips*

ITS A NIGHTMARE (IRE)   3 ch.g. Shahrastani (USA) 135 – Suntan City (IRE)   –
(Salluceva) [2003 11.5g Sep 16] first known foal: dam unraced: 33/1, tailed off in claimer
at Yarmouth. *P. R. Hedger*

IT'S AN OMEN   2 br.c. (Apr 14) Efisio 120 – Another Nightmare (IRE) 59 (Treasure   –
Kay 114) [2003 6g Jul 3] first foal: dam 5f (including at 2 yrs)/6f winner: 16/1 and green,
well beaten in claimer at Haydock. *R. A. Fahey*

ITSANOTHERGIRL   7 b.m. Reprimand 122 – Tasmim 63 (Be My Guest (USA) 126)   –
[2003 67, a–: f12s Jan 2] leggy mare: fair handicapper on turf, little form on all-weather:
well held only 7-y-o start: often blinkered. *M. W. Easterby*

IT'S A WIZARD   3 b.g. Wizard King 122 – Axed Again (Then Again 126) [2003   – §
57§: 5.9m 9.3f Jun 15] leggy gelding: modest maiden at 2 yrs: well beaten in 2003: tried
blinkered: wayward and temperamental. *M. A. Barnes*

IT'S BLUE CHIP   2 b.g. (Mar 18) Polar Falcon (USA) 126 – Bellateena 57 (Nomina-   –
tion 125) [2003 p7g Dec 17] 13,500F, 32,000Y: third foal: half-brother to 6f and 1m
winner in Spain by Emarati: dam 1m/1¼m winner: 20/1, well held in minor event at
Lingfield. *P. W. D'Arcy*

ITSDEDFAST (IRE)   7 ch.g. Lashkari 128 – Amazing Silks 41 (Furry Glen 121)   –
[2003 7d 9m 11.1d 14f 17.2m Jun 25] well-made gelding: won bumper in 2002: well
beaten in maidens/handicaps on Flat. *L. Lungo*

IT'S DEFINITE (IRE)   4 b.g. Definite Article 121 – Taoveret (IRE) (Flash of Steel   **88**
120) [2003 81: p8g p10g p10g p16g* 16m 17.1m* 17.1m 20m³ 14.8m² 21d 18m Oct 18]

504

big, lengthy gelding: fairly useful handicapper: won at Lingfield in May and Pontefract in June: good placed efforts at Royal Ascot (third of 27 to Sindapour in Ascot Stakes) and Newmarket: left A. Jarvis 40,000 gns before final outing: stays 2½m: acts on good to firm going, good to soft and polytrack: tried visored, better form without: usually held up. *P. Bowen*

ITS ECCO BOY   5 ch.g. Clantime 101 – Laena 72 (Roman Warrior 132) [2003 71: f7s p7g³ p7g² p7g p7g³ 6m⁵ 6m 7m⁶ 7g³ 7m³ 7m 6.1m* 6f² 5m⁴ 5.9d² 6m⁴ 6m³ 7f² 7g³ 6g⁶ 7m⁴ 6.1f* 6g³ 6g⁵ 6.1m p7g f7g³ p7g⁶ p7g⁴ p7g Dec 30] tall gelding: fair on turf, modest on all-weather: won seller in July and (having left K. Burke £7,000 after seventeenth start) minor event in September, both at Nottingham: effective at 6f/7f: acts on firm going, good to soft and all-weather: tried visored/in cheekpieces: often races prominently. *P. Howling*   **73 a62**

ITSONLYAGAME   3 b.c. Ali-Royal (IRE) 127 – Mena 58 (Blakeney 126) [2003 62?: 10g⁵ 11.6d⁴ p10g 11.6m⁶ Sep 29] fair maiden: stays 11.6f: acts on firm and good to soft going, well held (raced freely) on polytrack. *R. Ingram*   **68**

IT'S OUR SECRET (IRE)   7 ch.g. Be My Guest (USA) 126 – Lady Dulcinea (ARG) (General (FR)) [2003 79, a70: 8m³ 8g* 7.9m 7m⁵ 8m⁶ 7g⁴ Nov 1] sturdy, lengthy gelding: fairly useful handicapper on turf, fair on all-weather: won at Goodwood in May: effective at 7f to 9f: acts on fibresand, soft and firm going: tried visored, not since 1999: reliable. *M. H. Tompkins*   **82 a–**

IT'S RUMOURED   3 ch.g. Fleetwood (IRE) 107 – Etourdie (USA) (Arctic Tern (USA) 126) [2003 p12g⁶ p12g 12g f12g 11.6d² 11.9m⁵ Jul 1] half-brother to 3 winners, including 4-y-o Toni Alcala: dam unraced: 100/1, easily best effort (fair form) when second in minor event at Windsor: acts on good to soft ground: won juvenile hurdle in August. *Jean-Rene Auvray*   **70 ?**

IT'S THE LIMIT (USA)   4 b.g. Boundary (USA) 117 – Beside (USA) (Sportin' Life (USA)) [2003 100: 12g⁴ 12g² May 24] rangy, good sort: useful performer, lightly raced: creditable ½-length second to Global Challenge in minor event at Newmarket: will stay 1¾m: raced only on good/good to firm ground since debut. *Mrs A. J. Perrett*   **98**

ITS WALLACE JNR   4 b.g. Bedford (USA) 109 – Built In Heaven (Sunley Builds 102) [2003 53?: p12g Feb 25] modest maiden: well held only 4-y-o start: won over hurdles in October. *Miss S. West*   **–**

ITS YOUR BID   5 b.m. Dilum (USA) 115 – By Arrangement (IRE) 60 (Bold Arrangement 127) [2003 53: p16g⁵ 15.4m p16g 17.2f³ 17.2f³ 17.2f² 15.4m² 16.4m³ p16g⁴ 16m³ 16m⁶ 17.2f⁵ 16f Oct 12] modest handicapper: stays 17f: acts on polytrack, firm and good to soft going: often wears headgear: often slowly away: has raced freely: consistent. *S. Woodman*   **56**

IVANIA   3 ch.f. First Trump 118 – Antonia's Choice 73 (Music Boy 124) [2003 81: 5.1m 5m 5.1m 6d² 6.1g Aug 28] good-topped filly: has a quick action: fairly useful performer: clearly best effort at 3 yrs when second in handicap at Thirsk: stays 6f: acts on firm and good to soft ground: inconsistent. *T. D. Easterby*   **81**

IVORY BAY   4 b.g. Piccolo 121 – Fantasy Racing (IRE) 86 (Tirol 127) [2003 55: f8.5s f8g 8g 7g 10.1m 7.9m⁵ f8g 7.5m* 7.9f 7.5m 7.5d 6.9m 8m 8.2m Oct 22] rather leggy gelding: modest handicapper: won at Beverley in June: effective at 7.5f to 1¼m: acts on fibresand and firm going: tried blinkered/in cheekpieces: unreliable: sold 3,000 gns. *J. Hetherton*   **52 §**

IVORY COAST (IRE)   2 b.f. (Mar 17) Cape Cross (IRE) 129 – Ivory League 47 (Last Tycoon 131) [2003 p7g f8.5g p8g⁴ Dec 20] tall, leggy filly: second foal: half-sister to Italian 6f winner Fly Forever (by Compton Place): dam staying maiden: modest form at best in maidens/minor event: unseated rider leaving paddock on debut: should stay 1¼m. *W. R. Muir*   **56**

IVORY LACE   2 b.f. (Apr 21) Atraf 116 – Miriam 59 (Forzando 122) [2003 p5g 5m³ 5.2m³ 5m⁶ 5f* 5f⁵ 5.1m p5g Dec 17] 8,500Y: rather leggy filly: half-sister to several winners, including 3-y-o Park Star and 5-y-o Viewforth: dam 5f winner, including at 2 yrs: fair performer: made all in maiden at Catterick in May: ran poorly after: likely to prove best at 5f: acts on firm going: blinkered in seller penultimate start. *D. K. Ivory*   **70**

IVORY PRINCE (USA)   2 b.g. (May 1) King of Kings (IRE) 125 – Ivory Lane (USA) (Sir Ivor 135) [2003 7.5m 7m 7.5d⁶ 6m f6g f7s 8m Oct 25] $2,500Y, 9,000 2-y-o: smallish gelding: ninth foal: half-brother to French 9f winner by Fairy King and winner in USA by Septieme Ciel: dam, lightly raced in Ireland, sister to Cherry Hinton winner Turkish Treasure: no form, including in claimer: visored last 2 starts. *D. Shaw*   **–**

IVORY VENTURE   3 b.f. Reprimand 122 – Julietta Mia (USA) 72 (Woodman (USA) **57**
126) [2003 54: 5.1f⁵ f5g⁴ f5g p6g Dec 30] modest maiden: should stay 6f: acts on firm
ground, good to soft and fibresand. *D. K. Ivory*

IVY LEAGUE STAR (IRE)   2 b.f. (Apr 10) Sadler's Wells (USA) 132 – Ivy (USA) **59 p**
(Sir Ivor 135) [2003 7g 6d⁶ Nov 8] leggy filly: sister to 2-y-o 7f winners Ivrea (in 1989)
and Iviza (in 1992), both later useful at 1¼m/1½m, and half-sister to 3 winners, notably
smart Oaks d'Italia winner Ivyanna (by Reference Point): dam placed twice at 2 yrs in
USA: modest form in maidens at Newmarket and Doncaster (not knocked about): should
do better at 1¼m/1½m. *B. W. Hills*

IVY MOON   3 b.f. Emperor Jones (USA) 119 – Bajan Rose 89 (Dashing Blade 117) **64**
[2003 8.3g³ 8.2g 8.3s 7f⁶ 7m 7.1m 6m⁶ 7m* 7m 7m³ f8.5g 7f³ f7g Nov 29] leggy filly:
second foal: dam, 5f/6f winner (including at 2 yrs), half-sister to smart sprinter Rambling
Bear: modest performer: won claimer at Leicester in September: sold cheaply from
M. Blanshard after twelfth start: effective at 7f/1m: acts on firm ground, well held on
fibresand: free-going sort: pulls hard: ran out third outing. *B. J. Llewellyn*

I WISH   5 ch.m. Beveled (USA) – Ballystate 71 (Ballacashtal (CAN)) [2003 72: p7g² **73**
5.7m 6m² 7m 7m 6g 7m 6m p7g⁶ p7g* p6g⁴ p7g⁶ Dec 30] tall, leggy mare: fair handicapper: won at Lingfield in November: raced mainly at 6f/7f nowadays: acts on good to
firm going, good to soft and polytrack: tried in cheekpieces: headstrong. *M. Madgwick*

I WISH I KNEW   2 br.g. (Jan 28) Petong 126 – Hoh Dancer 66 (Indian Ridge 123) **57**
[2003 f5s f5g p7g Nov 29] 4,000Y: second foal: dam, disappointing maiden, half-sister to
useful 1987 2-y-o 5f winner Infanta Real: modest form in maidens/minor event: stays 7f.
P. J. Makin

IWO JIMA (IRE)   3 b.c. Desert King (IRE) 129 – Allegheny River (USA) (Lear Fan **73**
(USA) 130) [2003 61: p7g³ p10g² p10g⁶ 10.9m⁴ 10.3m³ 12s⁶ f9.4g 11.1m² Aug 19]
fair maiden: stays 11f: acts on polytrack and good to firm ground: sold 12,500 gns.
N. P. Littmoden

I WON'T DANCE (IRE)   2 b.c. (Feb 13) Marju (IRE) 127 – Carnelly (IRE) 101 **84 p**
(Priolo (USA) 127) [2003 6m 6m* 7m² Oct 14] IR 32,000F, €80,000Y: leggy colt: third
foal: half-brother to 4-y-o Start Over: dam Irish 1½m winner: fairly useful form: won
maiden at Newmarket in September: some improvement when 2½ lengths second of 4 to
Jedburgh in minor event at Leicester: will stay at least 1m: open to progress. *R. Hannon*

IZDIHAM (IRE)   4 ch.c. Nashwan (USA) 135 – Harayir (USA) 119 (Gulch (USA)) **110**
[2003 112: 10g⁴ 10m⁴ 10g 12d 10.5m³ 10.4m 8f² Sep 29] good-bodied colt: smart
performer at best: best efforts in 2003 when fourth at Sandown in Gordon Richards Stakes
(to Indian Creek) and Brigadier Gerard Stakes (2 lengths behind Sights On Gold): acted
as pacemaker on 3 other occasions: odds on, none too keen when neck second of 3 to
Calcutta in minor event at Bath final start: best form at 1¼m: acts on firm and good to soft
going: tried blinkered/visored: sent to UAE, joined P. Rudkin. *M. P. Tregoning*

IZMAIL (IRE)   4 b.g. Bluebird (USA) 125 – My-Lorraine (IRE) 77 (Mac's Imp **79 §**
(USA) 116) [2003 84§: 5g 5f 5f 5f² 5m 5d 6g 5.3f* 5.3m⁵ Aug 18] useful-looking
gelding: just fair performer nowadays: won minor event at Brighton in August: best at 5f/
easy 6f: acts on firm and good to soft going: tried visored: sometimes slowly away/races
freely: unreliable. *D. Nicholls*

IZZA   2 br.f. (Apr 2) Wizard King 122 – Nicholas Mistress 56 (Beveled (USA)) [2003 **–**
7m 7m 6f 7m 6g Oct 22] 800Y: first foal: dam 6f winner: seems of little account. *W. Storey*

J

JABAAR (USA)   5 gr.g. Silver Hawk (USA) 123 – Sierra Madre (FR) 119 (Baillamont **96**
(USA) 124) [2003 106: 10.4m 10.4f⁵ 10f 10.4f 12.3m⁴ 11.7f² 10.3g Sep 13] strong,
lengthy gelding: reportedly suffered stress fracture of pelvis at 3 yrs: useful handicapper:
best effort for new trainer in 2003 when ½-length second to Kuster in ladies race at Bath:
effective at 1¼m/1½m: won maiden on good to soft going, raced on good or firmer
otherwise. *D. Nicholls*

JABULANI (IRE)   4 b.g. Marju (IRE) 127 – Houwara (IRE) (Darshaan 133) [2003 **–**
77d: 8m 9.3g⁵ May 9] tall gelding: fair performer in 2002, slowly away both outings in
2003: sometimes too headstrong. *G. M. Moore*

JACARANDA (IRE) 3 ch.g. Bahhare (USA) 122 – Near Miracle (Be My Guest **86**
(USA) 126) [2003 80: 8.3g 7.1m 7d 7.1m 7m* 7m⁴ 7.6g² 7g⁵ᵈ 7m 7f⁴ 7g 7.1m² f7g⁴ Oct
16] unfurnished gelding: fairly useful handicapper: won at Newbury in June: stays 7f:
acts on firm going and probably fibresand: usually races prominently. *B. J. Meehan*

JACINTO 3 b.g. Komaite (USA) – Times Zando 64 (Forzando 122) [2003 56: 7.1f **–**
10.5d 8.2d 10.5m Jun 7] small, stocky gelding: modest maiden at 2 yrs: well held in 2003.
T. H. Caldwell

JACK DAWSON (IRE) 6 b.g. Persian Bold 123 – Dream of Jenny 73 (Caerleon **81**
(USA) 132) [2003 86: 10.1g² 12d⁴ 16.1m³ 14.8m⁵ 15.9m⁴ 14g Sep 6] neat gelding: fairly
useful handicapper: effective at 13f to easy 2m: seems best on good going or firmer: often
held up: tough and consistent. *John Berry*

JACK DURRANCE (IRE) 3 b.g. Polish Precedent (USA) 131 – Atlantic Desire **79**
(IRE) 100 (Ela-Mana-Mou 132) [2003 –p: 8g⁵ 7m 10.2g* 10.1m 8.3d Sep 29] small,
strong gelding: fair performer, lightly raced: won minor event at Bath in May: last in
handicaps after: will stay 1½m: sold 11,000 gns. *M. Johnston*

JACKIE KIELY 2 ch.g. (Mar 26) Vettori (IRE) 119 – Fudge (Polar Falcon (USA) **–**
126) [2003 7g Sep 11] 18,000F, 12,000Y: second foal: dam unraced half-sister to dam of
very smart Irish Derby runner-up Definite Article: 16/1, seventh of 11 in maiden at
Epsom: should be suited by 1¼m/1½m. *T. G. Mills*

JACKIE'S BABY 7 b.g. Then Again 126 – Guarded Expression 51 (Siberian Express **61**
(USA) 125) [2003 –, a64: f5s 5m 6f⁶ 5.1m 5m 5.3f³ Sep 2] big, good-topped gelding:
modest performer: left J. M. Bradley prior to running well final start (tongue tied): best at
5f: best efforts on fibresand/good going or firmer: tried blinkered: races prominently:
sometimes wanders. *W. G. M. Turner*

JACK OF TRUMPS (IRE) 3 b.c. King's Theatre (IRE) 128 – Queen Caroline (USA) **70 +**
67 (Chief's Crown (USA)) [2003 60: 10.2m³ p10g⁵ Dec 10] strong colt: fair maiden,
lightly raced: probably flattered in minor event at Lingfield final start: stays 1¼m: acts on
polytrack and good to firm going. *G. Wragg*

JACK POINT 2 b.g. (Mar 3) Fraam 114 – Queen's Hat 72 (Cadeaux Genereux 131) **–**
[2003 5m 6g Jul 9] 3,600Y: first foal: dam maiden, best effort at 6f: last in maidens at
Lingfield. *J. J. Bridger*

JACKS DELIGHT 3 b.g. Bettergeton 97 – Impromptu Melody (IRE) (Mac's Imp **–**
(USA) 116) [2003 8m 7.1m Sep 20] fourth foal: half-brother to winners abroad by Suluk
and King's Signet: dam no form: well beaten in maiden/claimer. *Mrs A. L. M. King*

JACK SULLIVAN (USA) 2 ch.c. (Apr 1) Belong To Me (USA) – Provisions (USA) **96**
(Devil's Bag (USA)) [2003 6d⁵ 6g³ p7g² 8d⁶ p7g* 7g⁵ Oct 24] $55,000Y: good-topped
colt: second foal: dam US 6f (including at 2 yrs) to 8.5f winner, including minor stakes:
useful performer: justified favouritism in maiden at Lingfield in October: good 6½
lengths fifth to Peak To Creek in Horris Hill Stakes at Newbury final start: should stay
easy 1m: acts on polytrack, best turf efforts on good going: often races prominently: sold
115,000 gns. *B. J. Meehan*

JACOB (IRE) 2 b.g. (Apr 20) Victory Note (USA) 120 – Persian Mistress (IRE) **62**
(Persian Bold 123) [2003 5f³ 5m⁵ 6d⁵ May 23] IR 7,500F, 12,000Y: compact gelding:
seventh foal: half-brother to Irish 6.5f winner Pip'N Judy (by Pips Pride): dam unraced
half-sister to high-class sprinter Hallgate: modest form in maidens/minor event: likely to
prove best at 5f/6f. *P. A. Blockley*

JACQUI EVANS 2 b.f. (Feb 10) Komaite (USA) – Rudda Flash (General David) **–**
[2003 5m 5f⁵ 6m⁴ Sep 16] strong, lengthy filly: fourth foal: half-brother to 5f winner Jack
To A King (by Nawwar): dam of little account: signs of only a little ability in maidens.
Ronald Thompson

JADAN (IRE) 2 b.g. (Apr 27) Imperial Ballet (IRE) 110 – Sports Post Lady (IRE) 72 **73**
(M Double M (USA)) [2003 6g⁴ 6m⁴ 7m⁵ 6d 5m* Oct 24] IR 8,000F: sturdy gelding:
half-brother to 2 winners abroad, including French sprinter Sports Road (by Common
Grounds): dam best at 5f: fair performer: won maiden at Catterick: stays easy 7f: acts on
good to firm ground. *E. J. Alston*

JADE 3 b.g. Efisio 120 – Nagnagnag (IRE) 103 (Red Sunset 120) [2003 p7g⁴ 8g May **57**
4] sturdy gelding: second foal: dam 5f (at 2 yrs) to 7f winner who stayed 8.5f: better effort
in maidens (modest form) on debut (slowly away): gave trouble stall next time: dead.
Mrs A. J. Perrett

JADEERON 4 b.g. Green Desert (USA) 127 – Rain And Shine (FR) 78 (Rainbow Quest **64** (USA) 134) [2003 64: p10g f8.5g⁶ f9.4g⁵ p12g² f12g² p12g⁴ 11.5m⁵ 11.9m⁴ 11.5g³ 11.5g 11.6g 13.3m⁶ 12.6m f16.2g³ 11.5f² 14.1m* 14.1m⁴ 16m⁴ 16.2f p16g Oct 15] useful-looking gelding: modest handicapper: won at Yarmouth in August: seems to stay 2m: acts on firm going and all-weather: tried blinkered/tongue tied: sometimes wears cheekpieces, including for win: probably best held up and tends to find little. *Miss D. A. McHale*

JADE FOREST (IRE) 3 gr.f. Charnwood Forest (IRE) 125 – Jade Vine (IRE) (Alzao **–** (USA) 117) [2003 –: 10g 12d⁵ 14.1m f12g 12.1m 12f⁶ Aug 27] lengthy filly: little form: wore cheekpieces (ran as if amiss) final start. *B. Smart*

JADE'S PROMISE 4 b.g. Definite Article 121 – Zacinta (USA) (Hawkster (USA)) **63** [2003 71: p13g p10g⁵ f12g⁶ p12g Mar 4] just modest form in 2003: effective at 1¼m to 13f: acts on polytrack. *J. R. Best*

JADE STAR (USA) 3 b.f. Jade Hunter (USA) – Danzig's Girl (USA) (Danzig (USA)) **55** [2003 61: f8g* p8g f7g 10m² f8.5s⁶ 8.3g⁶ 7f 10.1g³ 10.1m² 9m⁵ Aug 20] modest on turf, **a45** poor on all-weather: won seller at Southwell in February: stays 1¼m: acts on fibresand and good to firm going: sometimes wears cheekpieces. *Miss Gay Kelleway*

JAGGED (IRE) 3 b.g. Sesaro (USA) 81 – Latin Mass (Music Boy 124) [2003 p6g⁶ **67** p5g² 6g⁵ 6.1g⁵ 6m 6d³ f7s 6m⁵ 6d 6d⁴ 6g p7g² p7g⁶ f7g³ p7g Nov 29] IR 5,000F, 6,500 2-y-o: workmanlike gelding: fifth foal: half-brother to German 8.5f winner Lisa Marie (by Danehill Dancer): dam, poor maiden, half-sister to smart 7f performer All Systems Go: fair maiden handicapper: stays 7f: acts on good to firm ground, good to soft and all-weather. *K. R. Burke*

JAGGER 3 gr.c. Linamix (FR) 127 – Sweetness Herself 106 (Unfuwain (USA) 131) **109 p** [2003 67p: p5g³ 5f² 9.2d⁴ p10g* 11m⁶ 14g*ᵈⁱˢ 13.9m* 12f* Sep 28] smallish, quite attractive colt: useful handicapper, lightly raced: first past post at Lingfield in June, Goodwood (disqualified after failing dope test) in July, York (Melrose Stakes, by 1¾ lengths from Midas Way) in August and Ascot (Seabiscuit Stakes, by head from Hambleden) in September: stays 1¾m: acts on polytrack, firm and good to soft going: edgy at Ascot, has swished tail through preliminaries and had 2 handlers: held up: should continue to progress. *G. A. Butler*

JAHANGIR 4 b.g. Zamindar (USA) 116 – Imperial Jade 105 (Lochnager 132) [2003 **60 d** 68: p6g⁵ p8g p6g f7g⁴ p7g 5.7g⁵ 5.3m 6f 7f 7m³ 6m Sep 29] close-coupled gelding: modest maiden handicapper at best in 2003: left W. Muir after third start and W. Musson after sixth: should prove at least as effective at 6f as 7f: acts on all-weather and good to firm ground: tried visored/blinkered (below form): sometimes troublesome at stall: free-going sort: none too trustworthy. *B. R. Johnson*

JAILBIRD 2 b.f. (Jan 21) Nicollete 118 – Grace Browning 84 (Forzando 122) [2003 **57** 6.1m⁵ 6g 6f⁵ Oct 27] smallish, sturdy filly: second foal: dam 2-y-o 6f winner: modest form in maidens: will probably stay 7f. *R. M. Beckett*

JAIPUR GAIT 2 b.f. (Mar 15) Thowra (FR) – Dawn Gait (Fearless Action (USA) **–** 116) [2003 6v⁶ 7.5m⁶ Aug 23] close-coupled filly: second foal: dam unraced out of half-sister to top-class hurdler/stayer Royal Gait: well held in maidens at Haydock and Beverley. *T. D. Easterby*

JAIR OHMSFORD (IRE) 4 b.g. Hamas (IRE) 125§ – Harry's Irish Rose (USA) (Sir **68 +** Harry Lewis (USA) 127) [2003 68p: f7g f8.5g⁵ f8g⁴ 10d Nov 6] fair maiden handicapper, lightly raced: should prove best at 1¼m+: raced only on good to soft/soft going on turf, acts on fibresand. *W. J. Musson*

Melrose Rated Stakes (Handicap), York—
Jagger takes centre stage as Midas Way, Wavertree Boy (blaze) and Lodger try to get in on the act

JAKARMI   2 b.g. (Apr 26) Merdon Melody 98 – Lady Ploy 42 (Deploy 131) [2003 **58**
6.1d f8.5g² f8.5g⁶ f8g⁵ f8.5s Dec 31] heavy-topped gelding: first foal: dam little form:
modest maiden: stays 8.5f: acts on fibresand: wandered penultimate start. *B. Palling*

JAKEAL (IRE)   4 b.g. Eagle Eyed (USA) 111 – Karoi (IRE) (Kafu 120) [2003 77: 6m **67**
7m 6.9m³ f7s Sep 26] strong gelding: fair handicapper nowadays: probably best around
7f: acts on firm and good to soft ground: has been awkward leaving stall: has worn severe
bridle. *R. M. Whitaker*

JAKE BLACK (IRE)   3 b.g. Definite Article 121 – Tirhala (IRE) (Chief Singer 131) **57**
[2003 72: 9m⁵ 8m⁶ 10g⁵ 12.1m f12s Oct 7] workmanlike gelding: modest maiden handicapper: stays 1¼m: acts on heavy ground. *J. J. Quinn*

JAKESTER   3 b.c. Lion Cavern (USA) 117 – Torrid Tango (USA) (Green Dancer **90**
(USA) 132) [2003 71: 7m⁴ 7m* 8m 8g² Jul 4] 10,000F, 11,500Y: useful-looking colt:
closely-related to a winner in USA by North Prospect and half-brother to 3 winners,
including Irish 2001 2-y-o 7.8f winner Dancing (by Spectrum), later Grade 2 7f winner in
USA, and 6-y-o Torrid Kentavr: dam, lightly-raced maiden, half-sister to dam of Suave
Dancer: fairly useful performer: won maiden at Gowran in June: good second in minor
event at Limerick final outing: well held in Britannia Handicap at Royal Ascot in
between: stays 1m: acts on good to firm going: sent to USA. *M. Halford, Ireland*

JAKE THE SNAKE (IRE)   2 ch.c. (May 15) Intikhab (USA) 135 – Tilbrook (IRE) **93 p**
78 (Don't Forget Me 127) [2003 p8g* Dec 10] €16,000Y, 16,000 2-y-o: fourth foal:
half-brother to 2000 German 2-y-o 7f winner Directa Irlandia (by Mujadil): dam, 1m
winner, half-sister to smart Irish winner up 7f Bufalino: joint favourite, won 12-runner
maiden at Lingfield by 3 lengths from Secret Place, quickening to lead 2f out: should
progress. *C. N. Allen*

JALOUHAR   3 b.g. Victory Note (USA) 120 – Orient Way (IRE) 61 (Danehill (USA) **67**
126) [2003 67: f6g² 6g³ 6.1m 6d 8g 7f f6g³ f6f² f7g² f7s⁵ 7m f7g⁶ f6g* f6g⁵ Dec 9]
compact gelding: fair performer: claimed from K. Burke £6,000 after eleventh start:
won maiden at Southwell in November: effective at 6f/7f: acts on fibresand and good to
firm going: wore cheekpieces/visor 6 of last 7 outings: usually races prominently.
B. P. J. Baugh

JAMAICAN FLIGHT (USA)   10 b.h. Sunshine Forever (USA) – Kalamona (USA) **61**
(Hawaii) [2003 59d: f16.2g⁴ f16s⁵ f16.2g* f16s⁴ f16.2g* f16.2g² f16.2g 17.1m³ 21.6m* **a55**
16m⁵ 16.2m⁴ f16.2g 17.1m 18m* 15.8m* 16.2m³ 16.1m⁶ 18m⁴ 15.9d⁵ 17.1m Oct 6]
leggy horse: modest handicapper: won at Wolverhampton (2) in February, Pontefract in
April/June and Catterick in July: stays 21f: acts on any turf going/fibresand: tried in visor,
better without: has been too free to post/given trouble start: front runner: tough and game.
Mrs S. Lamyman

JAMES CAIRD (IRE)   3 ch.g. Catrail (USA) 123 – Polish Saga 59 (Polish Patriot **94**
(USA) 128) [2003 7g p7g⁵ p8g² 9.2d 8.1f 7g⁶ 7m⁵ 12m⁵ 10m* 10m* 10m⁶ 10.3m² Oct
24] IR 3,600F, IR 4,000Y: tall, leggy gelding: third foal: brother to 4-y-o Countrywide
Girl and half-brother to winner in Turkey by Persian Bold: dam, maiden best at 6f,
half-sister to smart performer up to 11f Tarawa: fairly useful performer: won apprentice
handicap and apprentice minor event, both at Pontefract in September: unlucky when
very good second in handicap at Doncaster final start: stays 1¼m: acts on fibresand and
firm going: blinkered (below form) seventh outing. *M. H. Tompkins*

JAMES DEE (IRE)   7 b.g. Shalford (IRE) 124§ – Glendale Joy (IRE) (Glenstal (USA) **–**
118) [2003 –: f8.5g f8.5g 7g 5.7f Jun 14] of little account nowadays: wore cheekpieces
last 2 starts: sometimes looks wayward. *Mrs P. Ford*

JAMES DRUMMOND   4 b.g. Shaddad (USA) 75 – Miss Drummond 59 (The Brian- **–**
stan 128) [2003 –: 9.2d 8m⁵ 16m Jul 6] no form. *B. Mactaggart*

JAMES STARK (IRE)   6 b.g. Up And At 'em 109 – June Maid 56 (Junius (USA) 124) **78 §**
[2003 89§, a97§: f6s⁶ p6g⁶ f5g f6g f5g³ f6g 6g p5g* 5.3f 6g⁵ Apr 14] leggy gelding: fairly **a93 §**
useful handicapper: won at Lingfield in March: probably best at 5f/easy 6f: acted on any
turf going/all-weather: tried visored/in cheekpieces, usually blinkered: was unreliable:
dead. *N. P. Littmoden*

JAMESTOWN   6 b.g. Merdon Melody 98 – Thabeh 57 (Shareef Dancer (USA) 135) **66**
[2003 75d: f11s f8g 7g³ 8f 8g 9.7m⁵ 8g* 8m⁵ 9f⁴ 8.5m³ 8m⁵ 8g⁴ 8.2d p8g⁶ f8g³ Dec 19] **a54**
workmanlike, close-coupled gelding: fair performer: won claimer at Pontefract in May:
claimed from C. Smith £8,000 after penultimate start: best at 7f to 9f: acts on all-weather,
firm and soft going: formerly none too reliable. *M. J. Polglase*

JAM

JAM TODAY 3 b.f. Elmaamul (USA) 125 – Sonic Sapphire 67 (Royal Academy (USA) **50**
130) [2003 58: 8.3m⁶ 8.3d⁴ 7m Oct 17] angular, rather unfurnished filly: modest maiden
handicapper: left M. Chapman after second start: stays 1m: unraced on extremes of going:
has pulled hard/hung left: withdrawn after refusing to enter stall third intended outing in
2003. *J. M. Bradley*

JANAYEN (USA) 3 b.f. Zafonic (USA) 130 – Saafeya (IRE) 111 (Sadler's Wells **97 p**
(USA) 132) [2003 9m⁶ 8.3g* 8.2m* Oct 28] sturdy filly: first foal: dam 1m to 10.5f
winner: quickly made into useful performer: won maiden at Windsor and handicap at
Nottingham (easily best effort when beating Impeller by short head despite hanging
left) in October: should prove best around 1m: sold 46,000 gns: should do better still.
M. P. Tregoning

JAN BRUEGHEL (USA) 4 ch.g. Phone Trick (USA) – Sunk (USA) (Polish Navy **–**
(USA) 125) [2003 70d: f7s³ f6g³ f6s* f7g* 7m f6s² f7g⁴ f7g Dec 8] big, strong gelding: fair **a76**
performer: won maiden in February and minor event in March, both at Southwell: stays
easy 7f: acts on fibresand and good to firm going, probably on heavy: sometimes slowly
away. *T. D. Barron*

JANES GEM (IRE) 3 b.f. Among Men (USA) 124 – Kingdom Queen (IRE) 65 **51**
(Night Shift (USA)) [2003 54: f8g³ f8g² 12d⁶ 10.9f⁴ 8s⁵ Jul 25] lengthy filly: modest
performer: stays 8.5f: acts on fibresand, soft and good to firm going: wore cheekpieces
last 4 starts. *A. Bailey*

JANES VALENTINE 3 b.f. My Best Valentine 122 – Jane Herring (Nishapour (FR) **63 d**
125) [2003 74p: p6g⁵ p6g³ p6g p6g² 5.7m 7f² 7m 7g 6f 7m p7g p6g Dec 30] modest
maiden: well below form last 4 starts, leaving J. Boyle £300 before final one: stays 7f:
raced only on polytrack and good ground or firmer on turf: tried in cheekpieces.
J. J. Bridger

JANGO MALFOY (IRE) 2 ch.c. (Apr 9) Russian Revival (USA) 125 – Sialia (IRE) **61**
(Bluebird (USA) 125) [2003 7.5g 10d p10g p7g⁵ p7g Dec 29] sixth foal: half-brother to
2000 2-y-o 6f seller winner Hamasking (by Hamas): dam unraced half-sister to smart 7f/
1m performer Rasa Penang: modest maiden: left M. Grassick in Ireland after debut:
barely stays easy 1¼m: acts on polytrack: blinkered/tongue tied final start. *B. W. Duke*

JANNADAV (IRE) 3 b.f. Barathea (IRE) 127 – Sweet Alma 67 (Alzao (USA) 117) **65**
[2003 72p: f7s⁴ 7.5f⁴ 8.2g Apr 29] rather leggy filly: fair performer, lightly raced: should
be suited by at least 1m: acts on all-weather. *J. A. Osborne*

JANOUEIX (IRE) 4 b.g. Desert King (IRE) 129 – Miniver (IRE) (Mujtahid (USA) **49**
118) [2003 70: 7m⁶ 8m p10g⁵ Jul 9] poor maiden nowadays: stays 1¼m: best efforts on
polytrack: visored once at 3 yrs (found little): sold 800 gns, sent to Italy. *C. R. Egerton*

JAOLINS 2 b.f. (Mar 26) Groom Dancer (USA) 128 – On The Top (High Top 131) **45**
[2003 6m p5g p6g⁶ p7g Nov 18] 2,000Y: leggy filly: closely related to 3-y-o Field Spark
and half-sister to 3 winners, including 1½m winner Top Rank (by Law Society): dam
unraced half-sister to high-class sprinter Double Schwartz: poor maiden: bred to stay at
least 1m. *R. Hannon*

JARDINES LOOKOUT (IRE) 6 b.g. Fourstars Allstar (USA) 122 – Foolish Flight **119**
(IRE) 57 (Fools Holme (USA)) [2003 119: 13.9m⁶ 20m⁴ 16g² 15.9m⁵ 16g³ Nov 4] leggy,
sparely-made gelding: shows knee action: smart performer: in frame in 2003 in Gold
Cup at Royal Ascot (7 lengths fourth to Mr Dinos), Goodwood Cup (brave bid to land
back-to-back renewals, going down by short head to Persian Punch) and Melbourne Cup
(Handicap) at Flemington (4¼ lengths third to Makybe Diva, coming with rare late rally):
needs further than 1¾m and stays 2½m: acts on firm and soft going: got upset in stall on
reappearance: tends to hang. *A. P. Jarvis*

JARJOOR 3 b.c. Alhaarth (IRE) 126 – Neptunalia 70 (Slip Anchor 136) [2003 71: **99**
8.2g* 8.2g* 7.5m² 8m 8.1m³ Aug 7] close-coupled colt: has a quick action: useful handicapper: won at Nottingham in March and April: good third to Three Graces at Haydock
final start: will stay 1¼m: acts on good to firm going: pulled hard penultimate start: sent
to UAE. *M. A. Jarvis*

JARRAAF 3 ch.g. Desert Story (IRE) 115 – Bee Off (IRE) 59 (Wolfhound (USA) 126) **64**
[2003 60: 6.1m 5g 7m f6g² 7.5m⁶ 10d⁵ f8.5g² 8.1m⁴ f8.5g² f8g⁴ f8.5g⁴ Dec 26] good- **a68**
bodied gelding: fair maiden: stays 8.5f: acts on fibresand, good to firm and good to soft
ground. *J. W. Unett*

JARVO 2 b.g. (Apr 27) Pursuit of Love 124 – Pinkie Rose (FR) (Kenmare (FR) 125) **66**
[2003 6m 6m² 7m² 8.3d³ 6m Oct 24] 2,500F, 1,200Y: sturdy gelding: seventh foal:
brother to 1997 2-y-o 7f winner Love Letters: dam French 1½m winner: fair maiden:
stays 1m: acts on good to firm and good to soft going. *N. P. Littmoden*

JASEUR (USA) 10 b.g. Lear Fan (USA) 130 – Spur Wing (USA) (Storm Bird (CAN) – §
134) [2003 16.2d Jul 5] strong gelding: one-time useful handicapper: fair hurdler nowadays: well beaten only Flat run since 2000: usually visored/blinkered: not one to trust.
G. Barnett

JASMICK (IRE) 5 ch.m. Definite Article 121 – Glass Minnow (IRE) 59 (Alzao 94
(USA) 117) [2003 96: 16m⁴ 14.1g 20m 12d 14.8m 13.9m⁵ 13.3m 12f² 16g⁶ 12g Oct 31]
smallish mare: fairly useful handicapper: probably best at 1½m/1¾m: acts on firm and
good to soft going. *H. Morrison*

JASMINE PEARL (IRE) 2 b.f. (Feb 17) King of Kings (IRE) 125 – Tumbleweed 68
Pearl 96 (Aragon 118) [2003 6g⁵ 6m² 6m 6m⁵ f7g⁵ Dec 16] 11,500Y: workmanlike filly:
second foal: dam, 6f winner (including at 2 yrs), half-sister to smart 7f performer Tumbleweed Ridge: fair maiden: second of 5 at Ascot: folded tamely after: will probably stay 7f:
possibly none too genuine. *B. J. Meehan*

JATH 2 b.f. (Apr 5) Bishop of Cashel 122 – Night Trader (USA) (Melyno 130) [2003 84 p
8m* Oct 24] big, leggy filly: fourth foal: half-sister to fairly useful 7f/1m winner Night
Empress (by Emperor Jones): dam, lightly raced, out of sister to Prix de la Salamandre
winner Maximova: 100/1 and green, won 22-runner maiden at Doncaster by 2 lengths
from Asaleeb, slowly away but leading final 1f: not sure to stay much further than 1m:
should improve. *Julian Poulton*

JAVA DAWN (IRE) 3 b.f. Fleetwood (IRE) 107 – Krakatoa (Shirley Heights 130) –
[2003 60: 7m 8.3g 7f Jun 16] modest maiden at 2 yrs: well held in handicaps in 2003:
stays 7f: acts on good to firm going: tried visored: none too genuine. *Miss D. A. McHale*

Ambrose Turnbull Associates' "Jardines Lookout"

JAVELIN 7 ch.g. Generous (IRE) 139 – Moss (Alzao (USA) 117) [2003 70: 10m⁴ **58** 14.4f 14.1d⁴ 12.6m⁵ Aug 25] strong gelding: just modest nowadays: stays 12.6f: acts on firm and good to soft going (some promise on fibresand): fair hurdler. *Ian Williams*

JAWHARI 9 b.g. Lahib (USA) 129 – Lady of The Land 75 (Wollow 132) [2003 88, **81** a80: p6g* 6m 6g 5m⁶ Jul 23] small, sturdy gelding: has a quick action: fairly useful handicapper: successful reappearance for fifth time in career when winning at Lingfield in March: has form at 7.6f, probably ideally suited by 5f/6f: acts on all-weather, good to firm and soft ground: blinkered (raced freely) once: has won for apprentice. *T. G. Mills*

JAWLEYFORD COURT 4 b.f. Moshaajir (USA) 77 – Mrs Jawleyford (USA) 58 **27** (Dixieland Band (USA)) [2003 –: f8s³ Feb 20] lengthy, good-topped filly: bad maiden: should be suited by 1¼m+. *C. Smith*

JAWWALA (USA) 4 b.f. Green Dancer (USA) 132 – Fetch N Carry (USA) (Alleged **69 §** (USA) 138) [2003 75: 14.1g 16f Jun 30] leggy, close-coupled, sparely-made filly: fair handicapper: stays 1¾m: acts on soft going: wore cheekpieces last time: has been slowly away/taken good hold: ungenuine. *J. R. Jenkins*

JAYANJAY 4 b.g. Piccolo 121 – Morica 88 (Moorestyle 137) [2003 83: p6g 5.3f* 5m **88** 6g 6m 6d* 6m⁵ 6g 5m⁴ 5m² 5f 6m 5d⁶ 6m⁶ p6g p6g² Dec 6] close-coupled gelding: fairly useful handicapper: won at Brighton in April and Epsom in July: best at 5f/6f: acts on polytrack, firm and soft going: blinkered fifth start, visored (not discredited) ninth: sometimes slowly away. *Miss B. Sanders*

JAYCEER 4 b.g. Green Desert (USA) 127 – Centaine 109 (Royal Academy (USA) **67** 130) [2003 p8g³ p8g⁴ p7g Feb 25] 74,000F, 40,000Y: third foal: half-brother to German winner up to 9.5f Vicchio (by Cadeaux Genereux): dam won German Oaks: best effort in maidens at Lingfield when fourth: carried head high again and dropped away very tamely final start: should stay 1¼m. *P. W. Harris*

JAY GEE'S CHOICE 3 b.g. Baratea (IRE) 127 – Llia 94 (Shirley Heights 130) **104** [2003 94: 8g 7m⁶ 8.1v 7g⁴ 8m 8g² 8m⁶ 8g 8.2d Nov 6] sturdy, well-made gelding: sort to carry condition: has a quick action: useful performer: ninth in 2000 Guineas at Newmarket on reappearance: in-and-out form, running creditably in handicaps at York, Epsom (fourth to Tarjman) and Newmarket second/fourth/seventh starts and when 1¾ lengths second to Mubeen in minor event at Salisbury: stays 1m: acts on firm and good to soft ground, well held on soft/heavy: usually races prominently. *M. R. Channon*

JAY JAY LASS 3 b.f. Bold Fort 100 – Suelizelle 54 (Carnival Dancer 117) [2003 –: **–** f9.4s f7g p12g Jun 28] of little account. *D. Burchell*

JAZZAAM 4 ch.f. Fraam 114 – Aldwick Colonnade 62 (Kind of Hush 118) [2003 63?: **50** 11.8g⁶ 9m⁵ 8.2m⁶ Jun 14] leggy filly: modest maiden: has form at 1m to 1½m: acts on good to firm going, probably on good to soft. *M. D. I. Usher*

JAZZ MESSENGER (FR) 3 bl.g. Acatenango (GER) 127 – In The Saltmine (FR) **104** (Damister (USA) 123) [2003 67p: 7m* 7.5m³ 8.1v* 10.1m* 10.4f 9m 8.2d⁶ Nov 6] tall, leggy gelding: useful performer: won maiden at Southwell in March, Tote Credit Club Silver Bowl (Handicap) at Haydock (by 6 lengths from Soyuz) in May and valuable handicap at Epsom (by ½ length from Tiber) in June: below form after, including in John Smith's Cup (Handicap) at York (stirred up, helped force strong pace) and in Cambridgeshire at Newmarket: stays 1¼m: acts on heavy and good to firm ground: has been early to post: sweated second outing: races freely. *G. A. Butler*

JAZZ SCENE (IRE) 2 b.c. (Mar 21) Danehill Dancer (IRE) 117 – Dixie Jazz 51 **91 p** (Mtoto 134) [2003 7.1d 6g* 6.3m 6f² Oct 10] IR 3,000F, 30,000Y: rangy colt: first foal: dam maiden who should have stayed 1¼m: won 20-runner sales race at Doncaster in September by neck from Mrs Moh: good length second to Traytonic in nursery at York, finishing strongly: should stay at least 7f: acts on firm ground: tends to be slowly away: likely to make useful 3-y-o handicapper. *M. R. Channon*

JAZZY MILLENNIUM 6 ch.g. Lion Cavern (USA) 117 – Woodcrest 82 (Niniski **65** (USA) 125) [2003 60: p6g p6g p6g⁴ f5g³ 7f* 6m f6g 7m* 5.7f⁵ 7m 6.1f Sep 30] quite attractive gelding: fair performer: won seller in April and handicap in June, both at Brighton (5 of 6 wins there): effective at 5f to easy 7f: well beaten on heavy going, acts on any other turf/all-weather: usually blinkered/visored: reportedly bled seventh outing: races up with pace. *B. R. Millman*

JEANETTE ROMEE 3 b.f. Victory Note (USA) 120 – Latest Flame (IRE) 66 (Last **61** Tycoon 131) [2003 7m 7d 7g 6g 6f⁴ 7m Aug 8] quite good-topped filly: fourth foal: dam 2-y-o 7.5f winner who stayed 1¼m: modest maiden: clearly best effort penultimate outing (slowly away): ran as if amiss final start: should stay 7f: acts on firm ground. *A. Charlton*

JEANNIE WIZ 3 b.f. Wizard King 122 – One For Jeannie 68 (Clantime 101) [2003 54: f7g f6g f6g⁴ f5g⁶ f5g 5.1g Sep 11] strong, lengthy filly: modest maiden at 2 yrs: little form in 2003: blinkered last 4 starts. *A. Bailey* **–**

JEBAL SURAAJ (USA) 3 b.g. Gone West (USA) – Trishyde (USA) 119 (Nureyev (USA) 131) [2003 8m² 9m* 10m* 8m 10m Jul 9] $20,000Y: strong, good-topped gelding: fifth foal: dam, winner in France (including at 1½m) and USA (second in 1¼m Grade 1 event): useful performer: won maiden at Musselburgh in April and handicap at Sandown (beat Tiber by head, edging right) in May: behind in Britannia Handicap at Royal Ascot, then ran creditably when mid-division behind Leporello in handicap at Newmarket: stays 1¼m: raced only on good to firm ground. *M. Johnston* **101**

JEDBURGH 2 b.c. (Jan 24) Selkirk (USA) 129 – Conspiracy 98 (Rudimentary (USA) 118) [2003 7m³ 7m² 7g 7m* 7m* 7m* Oct 14] compact colt: third foal: half-brother to useful 1¼m and 11.6f winner In Disguise (by Nashwan) and 3-y-o Impersonator: dam, 2-y-o 5f winner, closely related to high-class sprinter Gayane out of very smart filly up to 1¼m Roussalka, herself half-sister to Oh So Sharp: fairly useful performer: won nursery at Epsom in August and minor events in small fields at Leicester in September and October (made all, beat I Won't Dance comfortably by 2½ lengths): should stay at least 1m: open to progress. *J. L. Dunlop* **93 p**

JEDEYDD 6 b.g. Shareef Dancer (USA) 135 – Bilad (USA) (Riverman (USA) 131) [2003 90: 6g 6m 6m 8g 7m 7m 8m 5.9f Jun 15] lengthy gelding: fair handicapper: disappointing in 2003: best at 7f/1m: acts on firm ground, probably not on softer than good: wore cheekpieces penultimate start, tongue tied (slowly away) final outing. *M. Dods* **73 d**

JEEPSTAR 3 b.g. Muhtarram (USA) 125 – Jungle Rose 90 (Shirley Heights 130) [2003 66p: 7m³ 7.2f 8d³ 8.1m⁵ 10g* 11.9m² 12m* 10g² 10.4f⁵ 12m³ Oct 25] unfurnished gelding: fairly useful handicapper: won at Ripon in August and Musselburgh in September: at least creditable efforts after: effective at 1¼m/1½m: acts on firm and good to soft ground: has given trouble in preliminaries: races keenly/prominently: game. *T. D. Easterby* **85**

Vodafone Live! Handicap, Epsom—the opening race on Derby Day goes to Jazz Messenger, who wears down Tiber (blinkers) while Anani stays on strongly for third

JELBA 5 b.m. Pursuit of Love 124 – Gold Bracelet § (Golden Fleece (USA) 133) [2003 –
79, a95: f8s⁶ p7g⁴ p8g* p10g p10g Feb 22] tall, quite good-topped mare: useful handi- **a95**
capper on all-weather, fair when last ran on turf: won at Lingfield in February: effective
at 6f to 1m: acts on firm and good to soft going, better form on polytrack than fibresand:
blinkered twice, usually visored: often slowly away: held up, and sometimes finds little:
sold 20,000 gns in December. *N. P. Littmoden*

JELLYHEAD 3 b.c. Distinctly North (USA) 115 – Homebeforemidnight (Fools Holme –
(USA)) [2003 –: 7g 6m 7m Sep 22] well beaten in maidens/sellers. *Mrs S. A. Liddiard*

JENAVIVE 3 b.f. Danzig Connection (USA) – Promise Fulfilled (USA) 90 (Bet Twice **55**
(USA)) [2003 10m⁶ 7m 7m 9.3m⁶ 6.9f³ 8m 9.9d 7.9d 14.1m² 14.1m² 16m 14.1m³ Oct 4]
big, good-bodied filly: half-sister to Danish 11f winner by Timeless Times: dam, 2-y-o 6f
winner, probably stayed 8.5f: modest maiden handicapper: stays 1¾m: acts on firm
ground: races freely: sold 8,000 gns. *T. D. Easterby*

JEROME 2 b.c. (Apr 23) Nicolotte 118 – Mim 39 (Midyan (USA) 124) [2003 5m⁴ 5g⁴ **71**
6f² 5d 6m⁴ 5.9d 7m³ 7.9m⁴ Sep 3] 20,000F, 16,000Y: smallish, sturdy colt: third foal:
dam, little sign of ability, half-sister to smart performers Norton Challenger (at 6f to 1m)
and Young Hal (at 5f/6f): fair maiden: blinkered, ran creditably last 2 starts: not sure to
stay beyond 1m: acts on firm ground. *T. D. Easterby*

JERVAULX FLICKA 4 b.f. Magic Ring (IRE) 115 – Tirolina (IRE) (Thatching 131) –
[2003 41: 6m 8m Jun 20] lengthy filly: poor maiden: tried blinkered. *C. W. Fairhurst*

JESMUND 3 b.f. Bishop of Cashel 122 – Foretell (Tirol 127) [2003 f7g f11g Mar 11] –
second foal: dam unraced out of sister to smart French sprinter Reasonable: well held in
sellers. *Mrs L. C. Jewell*

JESSE SAMUEL 2 ch.c. (Jan 24) First Trump 118 – Miss Kellybell 48 (Kirchner 110) **51**
[2003 5g⁵ 6g⁶ 6m⁶ 5m 5m 6g f6g Oct 16] lengthy colt: second living foal: brother to a
winner in Spain: dam 6f winner: modest maiden: stays 6f: best efforts on good going.
J. R. Jenkins

JESSIE 4 ch.f. Pivotal 124 – Bold Gem 68 (Never So Bold 135) [2003 57: 7g 8g 6.9d⁴ **54**
f8g f8s Dec 13] workmanlike filly: modest performer: seems best around 1m: acts on soft
going, probably on firm. *Don Enrico Incisa*

JESSIE MACDOUGALL 3 br.f. Overbury (IRE) 116 – Miss Crusty 45 (Belfort (FR) **61**
89) [2003 53: 8f³ 16.2g 10.9m 10.2g⁴ 10.2m⁴ Sep 22] leggy filly: modest handicapper:
stays 1¼m: acts on firm and good to soft ground: visored last two 2-y-o starts: hung left
penultimate outing. *P. D. Evans*

JESSINCA 7 b.m. Minshaanshu Amad (USA) 91§ – Noble Soul 67 (Sayf El Arab **53**
(USA) 127) [2003 –: f8g p7g 11.9f⁶ 9.9m 10m⁴ 5.7f f8g* f8g⁶ 9f 8f f9.4g² 10m⁴ 10m⁶
f9.4g⁴ f8g⁶ f8g Nov 24] smallish, sturdy mare: modest handicapper: won at Southwell in
June: barely stays 1¼m: acts on fibresand, recent turf form only on good to firm going:
tried visored: usually waited with. *A. P. Jones*

JEWEL OF INDIA 4 ch.g. Bijou d'Inde 127 – Low Hill (Rousillon (USA) 133) **93**
[2003 93: p10g³ p10g⁵ p10g⁵ 8g Mar 21] leggy, sparely-made gelding: fairly useful performer:
stays easy 1¼m: acts on all-weather and soft going, probably on good to firm: usually
blinkered, though effective without: sometimes slowly away: gelded, won over hurdles
in August/October: subsequently sold 11,000 gns. *P. J. Hobbs*

JEZADIL (IRE) 5 b.m. Mujadil (USA) 119 – Tender Time (Tender King 123) [2003 **51 §**
49: 12.3m* 11m 10.1m² 10g 13.8f* 12f³ 14.1m 12m⁶ 11.6m 12m⁴ 14.1m³ 16.2m Aug 14]
sparely-made mare: modest performer: won selling handicap at Ripon in April and seller
at Catterick in May: stays 13.8f: acts on firm going, soft and fibresand: tried blinkered/in
cheekpieces: often slowly away: often forces pace: sometimes drops out tamely: unreliable. *Mrs L. Stubbs*

JIFFIES FLYER (IRE) 2 ch.f. (Apr 4) Desert Story (IRE) 115 – Moon Dust (Caerleon **53**
(USA) 132) [2003 5m⁴ f6g³ 6f⁵ 7m⁶ 6m⁴ f7g 8f 7m⁶ 6m 7m⁴ Oct 17] close-coupled filly:
fourth foal: half-sister to Scandinavia 1m (at 2 yrs) and 13f winner by Definite Article:
dam unraced: modest maiden: trained first 2 starts by I. Wood: should stay 1m: acts on
firm going and fibresand: visored (below form) eighth outing: possibly none too genuine:
sold 1,500 gns. *D. Carroll*

JILLY WHY (IRE) 2 b.f. (Mar 7) Mujadil (USA) 119 – Ruwy 77 (Soviet Star (USA) **64**
128) [2003 f6g6 6m³ 5f⁴ 7d Sep 24] IR 3,000F, €15,000Y: workmanlike filly: fourth foal:
half-sister to 4-y-o Freya's Dream: dam 1m winner: modest maiden: third at Ripon: stays
6f: acts on firm ground. *Ms Deborah J. Evans*

JIM LAD 3 b.g. Young Ern 120 – Anne's Bank (IRE) 77 (Burslem 123) [2003 –: 8.5g 10d 16.2m 16.2g Aug 25] little form: tried blinkered, usually visored: has looked none too keen. *Dr J. R. J. Naylor* –

JIMMY BYRNE (IRE) 3 ch.g. Red Sunset 120 – Persian Sally (IRE) (Persian Bold 123) [2003 7m 7m* 7m⁵ 8.2d² 10.3g³ 10.2g 8m Oct 6] 3,000F, 3,100Y: workmanlike gelding: second foal: half-brother to useful Italian winner up to 1m Mr Picchio (by Cois Na Tine): dam unraced: fair performer: won maiden at Newmarket (sweating and edgy) in July: stays easy 1¼m: acts on good to firm and good to soft ground. *M. R. Channon* **78**

JIMMY GEE (IRE) 2 b.g. (Feb 15) Efisio 120 – Stica (IRE) (In The Wings 128) [2003 8m² 10m 7m f7g f8g Nov 25] €20,000Y: smallish, quite attractive gelding: second foal: brother to 3-y-o Manx Fizz: dam unraced half-sister to useful Irish winner up to 11f Lacinia: modest maiden: second in seller at Ayr, only form: stays 1m: ungenuine. *D. Nicholls* **58 §**

JIMMY RYAN (IRE) 2 b.c. (Mar 29) Orpen (USA) 116 – Kaysama (FR) (Kenmare (FR) 125) [2003 6.1m* 6m⁴ Oct 17] IR 18,000F, 10,000Y: lengthy, quite good-topped colt: has scope: half-brother to several winners, including Irish 6f winner (including at 2 yrs) Air of Distinction and 1995 2-y-o 6f winner Rabican (both useful and by Distinctly North): dam French sprint winner: fairly useful form: sweating, won maiden at Nottingham in September by 3 lengths, racing freely: good fourth to Russian Ruby in nursery at Newmarket, making most: likely to prove best at 5f/6f: tried to duck out on debut: capable of better. *T. D. McCarthy* **85 p**

JINKSONTHEHOUSE 2 b.f. (May 10) Whittingham (IRE) 104 – Aldwick Colonnade 62 (Kind of Hush 118) [2003 5.1g³ 6m⁵ 5.1f⁵ 6m 7g f6s 8.2m Oct 28] close-coupled filly: half-sister to 6f to 2m winner Coastguards Hero (by Chilibang): dam 1m winner/ winning hurdler: modest maiden on balance: ran badly in seller final start: should stay 7f: acts on firm going. *M. D. I. Usher* **59**

J M W TURNER 4 b.c. Forzando 122 – Noor El Houdah (IRE) 61 (Fayruz 116) [2003 73, a105: f6s⁴ p6g² f6s⁴ f6g⁵ p5g* f7g⁶ 6m 5m⁵ 6g* 6g Jul 8] sturdy colt: useful performer on all-weather, fair on turf: won handicap at Lingfield (beat No Time by short head) in February and minor event at Hamilton in July: effective at 5f to easy 7f: acts on all-weather and firm going: blinkered/visored: best held up. *N. P. Littmoden* **72 a109**

JOB RAGE (IRE) 9 b. or br.g. Yashgan 126 – Snatchingly (Thatch (USA) 136) [2003 39: f16s f16.2g⁶ f12g Feb 21] tall gelding: poor maiden handicapper: tried blinkered: dead. *A. Bailey* –

JOCKS BOY 2 b.g. (Apr 5) Defacto (USA) – Lady Khadija (Nicholas Bill 125) [2003 f6s 6.1d f7g f5g⁵ Dec 3] second foal: dam of no account: poor maiden: probably stays 6f. *P. R. Wood* **49**

JODEEKA 6 ch.m. Fraam 114 – Gold And Blue (IRE) (Bluebird (USA) 125) [2003 84§: p5g* p5g* p5g p6g⁴ 5m 5d⁶ 5m* 5m Aug 13] strong, close-coupled mare: fairly useful handicapper: won at Lingfield in January, Wolverhampton in February, then Pontefract and Beverley in August: best around 5f: acts on good to firm going, good to soft and all-weather: tried visored at 5 yrs: sometimes finds little: in foal to Compton Place. *J. A. Glover* **86**

JODONSTAY 3 b.f. Komaite (USA) – Cliburnel News (IRE) 76 (Horage 124) [2003 –: 5.1m f5g f8g May 1] well beaten in maidens/claimers. *D. Shaw* –

JOE BEAR (IRE) 3 ch.c. Peintre Celebre (USA) 137 – Maharani (USA) (Red Ransom (USA)) [2003 79p: 10m⁶ 9.9m* 10m*ᵈⁱˢ 10g² 9f³ Sep 21] sturdy, quite attractive colt: quickly progressed into a useful performer, first past post in handicaps at Goodwood in June and Newmarket in July, but failed dope test in latter and disqualified: good efforts last 2 starts, 3½ lengths second to Kicken Kris in Secretariat Stakes at Arlington and 2 lengths third to Stroll in Grade 2 Jamaica Handicap at Belmont: stays 1¼m: acts on firm going, yet to race on soft/heavy: likely to improve again at 4 yrs. *P. Mitchell* **109 p**

JOE CHARLIE 2 ch.g. (Mar 24) Daggers Drawn (USA) 114 – La Ballerine 62 (Lafontaine (USA) 117) [2003 6g 7.2m 7.2d Oct 13] IR 10,000Y, 40,000 2-y-o: close-coupled gelding: third reported foal: half-brother to smart 2000 2-y-o 6f winner (stays 1½m) Sunny Glenn (by Rock Hopper): dam 9f and 15f winner: easily best effort in maidens at Ayr (modest form) on debut: should stay 7f. *K. A. Ryan* **53**

JOE LIEBERMAN 2 b.g. (Apr 14) Polish Precedent (USA) 131 – Inchkeith 72 (Reference Point 139) [2003 6d Jun 23] fifth foal: half-brother to 2000 2-y-o 7f winner Swing Band (by Celtic Swing) and German 2001 2-y-o 5f/5.5f winner Ingeburg (by Hector Protector), both fairly useful: dam, 9.4f/1¼m winner who stayed 1½m well, half-sister to **– p**

JOE

smart 6f/7f performer Inchinor out of smart miler Inchmurrin: 14/1 and green, ninth of 16 in maiden at Windsor, slowly away and not knocked about: had knee chip removed after: should do better. *G. B. Balding*

JOELY GREEN 6 b.g. Binary Star (USA) – Comedy Lady 46 (Comedy Star (USA) **60 §**
121) [2003 68, a79: p16g³ p12g⁵ f12g⁵ f12s* p12g f12s² f16.2g⁵ 11.9f⁴ 11.5g 14.1m² **a75 §**
11.9m³ 16m* 19.1m⁵ 14.1m 16.4m³ 16.2d 14.1m⁴ 16.2m³ 16m⁵ Sep 5] tall, workmanlike gelding: fair performer on all-weather, modest on turf: won apprentice handicap at
Wolverhampton in February and claimer at Redcar in June: effective at 1½m, probably
stays 19f: acts on all-weather, raced mainly on good ground or firmer on turf: seems best
blinkered/visored (ran poorly in cheekpieces): sometimes slowly away/wanders: one to
treat with caution. *N. P. Littmoden*

JOEY PERHAPS 2 b.g. (Feb 27) Danzig Connection (USA) – Realms of Gold (USA) **72**
(Gulch (USA)) [2003 5m 6g⁴ 5m⁵ 7m Oct 3] 4,000Y, 10,500 2-y-o: first foal: dam little
form: fair maiden: fourth at Folkestone, only form: needs to settle to stay beyond 6f:
carried head awkwardly third start: sweated on final one. *J. R. Best*

JOHANNIAN 5 b.h. Hernando (FR) 127 – Photo Call 73 (Chief Singer 131) [2003 110:
10g 10d 10m⁵ Sep 26] quite good-topped horse: unimpressive mover: smart performer in
2002: last all outings for new trainer at 5 yrs: tried tongue tied: sometimes bandaged
off-hind. *I. A. Wood*

JOHNNY ALLJAYS (IRE) 2 b.g. (Apr 11) Victory Note (USA) 120 – It's Academic **–**
73 (Royal Academy (USA) 130) [2003 5.2m 5m 7m 8f Sep 8] IR 3,600F, €19,000Y: big
gelding: fifth foal: half-brother to 3 winners, including 4-y-o Strathclyde and 2002 Italian
2-y-o 5f winner Kravitz (by Sri Pekan): dam 6f/7f winner: well held in maidens/nursery.
J. S. Moore

JOHNNY FROM DONNY 2 ch.g. (Mar 18) Young Ern 120 – Polish Lady (IRE) 43 **52 §**
(Posen (USA)) [2003 f5g⁵ f5g 5.1m 5d⁵ 6g 7.5d 7m Jul 23] 500Y, 500 2-y-o: lengthy
gelding: third foal: dam maiden who stayed 7f: modest maiden: form only at 5f on good
to soft going: wore blinkers/cheekpieces last 4 starts: ungenuine. *Ronald Thompson*

JOHNNY PARKES 2 b.g. (Apr 25) Wolfhound (USA) 126 – Lucky Parkes 108 (Full **77**
Extent (USA) 113) [2003 5m² 5m² 5g² 5m² 5f* 6m⁵ Oct 2] strong gelding: fourth foal:
half-brother to fairly useful 2002 2-y-o 5f/6f winner Robinia Parkes (by Robellino) and
5-y-o Charlie Parkes: dam prolific 5f winner: fair performer: landed odds in maiden at
Carlisle in August: no extra late on when creditable fifth in nursery at Newmarket: will
prove best at 5f/easy 6f: acts on firm going: races prominently. *Mrs J. R. Ramsden*

JOHNNY REB 5 b.g. Danehill (USA) 126 – Dixie Eyes Blazing (USA) 56 (Gone **–**
West (USA)) [2003 –: 8m Apr 14] strong gelding: fair handicapper in 2001: well held
since: tried tongue tied. *Mrs S. J. Smith*

JOHN O'GROATS (IRE) 5 b.g. Distinctly North (USA) 115 – Bannons Dream (IRE) **88**
(Thatching 131) [2003 101p: 5g 5f⁴ 6g 6d 6m 5f Jun 13] tall, close-coupled, good-topped
gelding: just fairly useful performer at 5 yrs: effective at 5f/6f: acts on firm and soft going:
held up. *M. Dods*

JOHN'S CHAMP (IRE) 3 b.g. Mujadil (USA) 119 – Big Buyer (USA) 67 (Quest **53**
For Fame 127) [2003 57: p10g⁴ f7g f8g⁶ f9.4g² 11m May 29] modest maiden: seems to
stay 1¼m: acts on all-weather and good to firm going: usually visored. *A. P. Jarvis*

JOHNSON'S POINT 5 ch.m. Sabrehill (USA) 120 – Watership (USA) (Foolish **70**
Pleasure (USA)) [2003 73: 9.9m 11.9g³ 13.9m⁵ 11.8m⁶ 11.9d Sep 26] sturdy mare: fair
handicapper: stays 1¾m: acts on firm and good to soft going: usually blinkered: held up.
M. W. Easterby

JOHNSTON'S DIAMOND (IRE) 5 b.g. Tagula (IRE) 116 – Toshair Flyer 88 **91**
(Ballad Rock 122) [2003 62: f6s* f6g f6s² 6.1g¹* 6m² 6m⁴ 6g⁴ 6g* 6m 5.1d* Sep 24] big,
workmanlike gelding: fairly useful handicapper: won at Southwell in January, Nottingham in March, Newcastle in July and Chester in September: best at 5f/6f: acts on firm
ground, good to soft and fibresand: often leads: consistent. *E. J. Alston*

JOINT DESTINY (IRE) 2 b.f. (Feb 10) Desert Prince (IRE) 130 – Brogan's Well **70 d**
(IRE) (Caerleon (USA) 132) [2003 5m⁵ 6f² 6g² 6m⁵ 6g 6m² 6g³ 6m⁴ p6g Nov 13]
32,000Y: angular, quite good-topped filly: second foal: half-sister to 3-y-o Liquid Form:
dam unraced half-sister to Irish 7f winner Pernilla and Irish stayer Easy To Please, both
useful: fair maiden: below form after third start: left M. Channon after sixth outing,
S. Dow after eighth: should stay 7f: acts on firm going. *G. L. Moore*

516

JOINT STATEMENT 4 b.g. Barathea (IRE) 127 – Gena Ivor (USA) (Sir Ivor 135) **92**
[2003 91: 8m 8.1g⁵ 8g⁶ 8.5m 8f² 8m³ 8m 8f* Aug 2] strong, lengthy gelding: fairly useful
handicapper: won at Thirsk in August: stays 1m: acts on firm going: usually held up:
consistent. *M. R. Channon*

JOKING APART 2 b.f. (Mar 6) Rainbow Quest (USA) 134 – Jood (USA) 87 (Nijinsky **– p**
(CAN) 138) [2003 7d Nov 7] workmanlike filly: seventh foal: closely related to top-class
7f (at 2 yrs) to 1½m winner Fantastic Light (by Rahy) and 3-y-o Hi Dubai and half-sister
to 3 winners, including 6-y-o Westbound Road: dam, third at 7f (at 2 yrs) and 1¼m, her
only starts, out of Canadian Oaks winner Kamar, herself half-sister to dam of Swain: 10/1
and green, never a factor in maiden at Doncaster: likely to do better. *B. W. Hills*

JOLI ERNEST 2 ch.g. (Mar 2) Young Ern 120 – Pip's Dream 52 (Glint of Gold 128) **–**
[2003 5m 7m 5g 6m Sep 3] workmanlike gelding: third foal: half-brother to 5-y-o Dream
Magic: dam 1¼m/1½m winner: no form, including in sellers. *R. J. Hodges*

JOLIZERO 2 br.g. (Apr 23) Danzero (AUS) – Jolis Absent 57 (Primo Dominie 121) **–**
[2003 8.2m 8d f7g Nov 25] big, good-bodied gelding: third foal: half-brother to 5-y-o
Loner: dam, 1½m/1¾m winner, also successful over hurdles: signs of only a little ability
in maidens. *G. G. Margarson*

JOMUS 2 b.g. (Mar 19) Soviet Star (USA) 128 – Oatey 68 (Master Willie 129) [2003 **67**
6g 6m⁴ 5f 6m 5.9m² 7g p7g p8g⁵ Dec 2] 30,000Y: close-coupled, quite good-topped
gelding: first living foal: dam, 5f winner, half-sister to 1½m to 2m performer Hateel and
winner up to 11.5f Munwar, both smart: fair maiden: second in nursery at Carlisle: below
form after, leaving Mrs J. Ramsden following next start: needs to settle to stay beyond 6f:
acts on good to firm going: sometimes slowly away. *L. Montague Hall*

JONALTON (IRE) 4 b.g. Perugino (USA) 84 – Vago Pequeno (IRE) (Posen (USA)) **–**
[2003 47: 10m 14.6m 16.2d 16m f16g Dec 16] angular gelding: poor maiden: well held at
4 yrs. *C. R. Dore*

JONJO 5 b.g. Charnwood Forest (IRE) 125 – Katy-Q (IRE) 58 (Taufan (USA) 119) **–**
[2003 f8.5g Feb 15] good-bodied gelding: well held, including in seller. *B. P. J. Baugh*

JONNY EBENEEZER 4 b.g. Hurricane Sky (AUS) – Leap of Faith (IRE) 65 (North- **86**
iam (USA)) [2003 97: 6g 6g p8g⁴ 6m² 6m² 7d⁴ f6s⁶ 7d⁴ p7g f7g² Nov 19] tall gelding: **a74**
useful in 2002: fairly useful on turf, fair on all-weather in 2003: claimed from I. Wood
after fifth start: effective at 5f to 1m: acts on fibresand, soft and good to firm going: below
form in cheekpieces final start: sometimes awkward leaving stall/wanders: races up with
pace. *R. M. H. Cowell*

JOOLS 5 b.g. Cadeaux Genereux 131 – Madame Crecy (USA) (Al Nasr (FR) 126) **85**
[2003 95?: f6s f7g⁵ 8g 6f⁶ 7m⁴ 8.1d³ 7m 6f* 8.5d* p8g² 10m* 7m⁴ 8.3g* 10g 8.9f Oct 11]
rather leggy gelding: fairly useful performer: won claimers at Folkestone (left P. D. Evans
£9,000) in June, Epsom and Sandown in July and (having been claimed from P. Mitchell
£15,000 after previous start) handicap at Windsor in August: barely stays 1¼m: acts on
firm going, soft and all-weather: visored (not discredited) once: genuine. *D. K. Ivory*

JORDANS ELECT 3 ch.g. Fleetwood (IRE) 107 – Cal Norma's Lady (IRE) 87 **78 ?**
(Lyphard's Special (USA) 122) [2003 –: 8g² 8m³ 8g 9.3f⁴ 9.3m* 12m 10m⁵ 10d 8g Oct
28] tall, rather leggy, useful-looking gelding: fair performer: won maiden at Carlisle in
September: stays 1¼m, will prove at least as effective at 1m/9f: acts on firm ground: tends
to race freely. *I. Semple*

JOSEPHUS (IRE) 2 ch.c. (Jan 26) King of Kings (IRE) 125 – Khulasah (USA) **103 p**
(Affirmed (USA)) [2003 6m⁴ 7m* 7g² Oct 24] €260,000Y: strong, good-bodied colt: has
scope: second foal: half-brother to Irish 1m winner Beautifulballerina (by Nureyev):
dam, US 9f winner, out of close relative to dam of 7-y-o Zindabad: won maiden at Newmarket in July: better for race, further improvement when 3½ lengths second of 9 to Peak
To Creek in Horris Hill Stakes at Newbury: should stay 1m: likely to make smart 3-y-o
and win more races. *R. Charlton*

JOSHUA'S BAY 5 b.g. Karinga Bay 116 – Bonita Blakeney (Baron Blakeney 83) **–**
[2003 22.2f Jun 21] soundly beaten in Queen Alexandra Stakes at Royal Ascot on Flat
debut: fair hurdler, successful in August/October. *J. R. Jenkins*

JOSHUAS BOY (IRE) 3 ch.c. Bahhare (USA) 122 – Broadway Rosie 101 (Absalom **–**
128) [2003 59?: 5m Sep 6] big, strong colt: has scope: little solid form: reportedly treated
for colic early in year. *K. A. Ryan*

JOSHUA'S GOLD (IRE) 2 b.c. (Apr 30) Sesaro (USA) 81 – Lady of The Night (IRE) **54**
54 (Night Shift (USA)) [2003 5m 6m⁶ 5d 7.1m³ 7.5m⁵ 8m⁵ 7d⁵ Sep 20] 2,800Y: sturdy,

close-coupled colt: first foal: dam maiden who stayed 1¼m: modest maiden: third at Musselburgh: stays 7f: acts on good to firm and good to soft going. *D. Carroll*

JOUVERT 3 ch.c. Grand Lodge (USA) 125 – Polygueza (FR) 78 (Be My Guest (USA) **56 ?** 126) [2003 68: 6g 8.3d 6g 8.1m 7m⁵ f8.5g⁶ p7g Dec 17] well-made colt: modest maiden: stays 7f: yet to race on extremes of going on turf, below form on all-weather: tried blinkered/visored. *R. Hannon*

JOYCE'S CHOICE 4 b.g. Mind Games 121 – Madrina 70 (Waajib 121) [2003 60: **56** f6s f6g 5m³ 5m⁵ 5m 5m² 5m 5m⁵ 5m 5m 5m⁵ 5m Oct 20] leggy, unfurnished gelding: modest performer nowadays: often spoilt chance with slow start in 2003: probably best at 5f: acts on firm and soft going: sold 4,600 gns. *A. Berry*

J R STEVENSON (USA) 7 ch.g. Lyphard (USA) 132 – While It Lasts (USA) 78 **93** (Foolish Pleasure (USA)) [2003 92: 8g² 8m 8g 8.5m 8f 8d⁴ p8g² 8d⁶ p10g³ p10g⁵ p10g* Dec 29] strong, close-coupled gelding: has a quick action: fairly useful handicapper: won at Lingfield in December: effective at 1m/1¼m: acts on polytrack, soft and good to firm going: tried visored: held up/often finds trouble. *M. Wigham*

JUAN CARLOS (IRE) 4 ch.g. Ashkalani (IRE) 128 – Mimansa (USA) (El Gran Senor **–** (USA) 136) [2003 –: p10g 11.9m May 30] no form: tried visored/tongue tied. *B. Gubby*

JUBILEE 3 ch.f. Selkirk (USA) 129 – Royal Passion 78 (Ahonoora 122) [2003 65p: **66** 10g 10m 11.9g 10m 10.5m⁶ Aug 7] leggy, angular filly: fair maiden: below form after reappearance: stays 1¼m: unraced on extremes of going: carried head awkwardly final start. *B. J. Meehan*

JUBILEE STREET (IRE) 4 b.g. Dr Devious (IRE) 127 – My Firebird (Rudimentary **57** (USA) 118) [2003 75: 7m 8m 8m 10.3m 7f* 6g⁶ 8s 7m 6m 6f⁵ Sep 15] big gelding: modest performer: won apprentice maiden at Catterick in June: effective at 6f to 1m: acts on firm ground: visored last 2 outings. *D. Nicholls*

JUBILEE TIME 3 b.c. Mark of Esteem (IRE) 137 – Bella Colora 119 (Bellypha 130) **78 p** [2003 8m 10m³ Oct 22] well-made, attractive colt: half-brother to several winners, including high-class 1¼m performer Stagecraft (by Sadler's Wells) and smart 1m winner Hyabella (by Shirley Heights): dam, 6f (at 2 yrs) to 1¼m winner, half-sister to Irish Oaks winner Colorspin, the dam of Opera House, Kayf Tara and 4-y-o Zee Zee Top: easily better effort in maidens (fair form) when length third to Polar Jem at Nottingham, racing very freely and headed final 1f: stays 1¼m: slowly away on debut: will probably do better. *L. M. Cumani*

JUBILEE TREAT (USA) 3 b.f. Seeking The Gold (USA) – Dance Treat (USA) 115 **86** (Nureyev (USA) 131) [2003 7m 8.1m⁴ 8.3s⁵ 10f⁵ 10m* 10m² 10g Oct 13] rather leggy, useful-looking filly: second foal: dam, won La Coupe (1¼m) and Prix de Flore (10.5f), out of half-sister to Derby winner Golden Fleece: fairly useful performer: won handicap at Ripon in August: stays 1¼m: acts on firm going. *G. Wragg*

JUDES LAW 5 gr.m. Contract Law (USA) 108 – Linen Thread (Broxted 120) [2003 **–** 10.2g Aug 7] 820Y: 2,000 3-y-o: eighth foal: dam, twice-raced hurdler, half-sister to top-class staying chaser Brown Chamberlin: well held in 2 bumpers, and seller at Chepstow. *S. C. Burrough*

JUDHOOR 3 b.f. Alhaarth (IRE) 126 – Almurooj 54 (Zafonic (USA) 130) [2003 93: **97** 6m* 5f 6m 6.1d⁵ 6g Oct 24] leggy, close-coupled filly: useful performer: won listed race at Ripon in April by ½ length from Golden Nun: creditable fifth to Danehurst in similar event at Chester penultimate start: stayed 6f: acted on firm and soft going: tended to race freely: visits Swain. *B. W. Hills*

JUFISCEA 4 b.g. Efisio 120 – Jucea 77 (Bluebird (USA) 125) [2003 –: 6m f8.5f f9.4g **–** Aug 15] no form since 2 yrs. *J. L. Spearing*

JULIAN RONJOYLES 3 b.c. Danzig Connection (USA) – Pearl Dawn (IRE) 91 **§§** (Jareer (USA) 115) [2003 7m 6g 7m 8.2g f9.4g 8.1g Sep 11] workmanlike colt: first foal: dam 5f and 1m winner: little form: refused to race penultimate start and refused to set off with rest of field final outing: one to avoid. *I. A. Wood*

JULIETTE (IRE) 3 b.f. Sadler's Wells (USA) 132 – Arutua (USA) (Riverman (USA) **107** 131) [2003 78p: 7d 10.2d⁶ 12f² 12g⁵ 12m* 14.6d⁶ 12d³ Oct 12] quite attractive filly: third foal: closely related to fairly useful 6f winner Farha (by Nureyev) and half-sister to useful Irish 6f (at 2 yrs) and 1m winner Plato (by Lure): dam unraced out of top-class middle-distance mare All Along: useful performer: never-nearer 5¾ lengths fifth to Vintage Tipple in Irish Oaks at the Curragh before winning listed race at Cork in August by length from Kiteflyer: creditable 8½ lengths third to L'Ancresse in listed race at the Curragh final outing: should prove effective at 1¾m (below form in Park Hill Stakes at Doncaster when tried): acts on firm and good to soft going: tongue tied last 4 starts: sold 325,000 gns. *J. Oxx, Ireland*

JUMEIRAH SCARER   2 b.g. (Mar 25) Tagula (IRE) 116 – Mountain Harvest (FR) **64 p**
64§ (Shirley Heights 130) [2003 p7g³ Dec 17] 16,000Y, 33,000 2-y-o: brother to fairly useful 6f (at 2 yrs) to 8.5f winner Takaroa and half-brother to winners in Italy by Sabrehill and Cyrano de Bergerac: dam ungenuine maiden who seemed to stay 1¾m: favourite, 1¾ lengths third to Whitgift Rock in minor event at Lingfield: should progress. *M. R. Channon*

JUMHOOR (IRE)   3 b.c. Bahhare (USA) 122 – West of Eden (Crofter (USA) 124) **77**
[2003 77: 7m² 7d 8f³ 7m* 7.5m⁴ a8f Dec 26] sturdy, attractive colt: fair performer: 16/1-on, won maiden at Thirsk in June: left E. Dunlop before final outing: stays 1m: acts on firm going, well held on good to soft. *E. Charpy, UAE*

JUMMANA (FR)   3 ch.f. Cadeaux Genereux 131 – Forty Belles (USA) (Forty Niner **92**
(USA)) [2003 96p: p8g p7g Nov 22] tall, angular filly: fairly useful form, lightly raced: shaped well in listed event won by Tadris at Lingfield on reappearance: weakened in handicap there following month: likely to prove best up to 7f: raced only on polytrack/ soft ground. *G. A. Butler*

JUNGLE LION   5 ch.g. Lion Cavern (USA) 117 – Star Ridge (USA) (Storm Bird **–**
(CAN) 134) [2003 72: f9.4g⁶ f12s f8.5g⁶ f8g f8.5g Dec 26] lengthy, quite good-topped gelding: fair in 2002: little form in 2003, leaving J. O' Reilly and off 9 months after third start: tried in headgear: tongue tied: has hung left. *John A. Harris*

JUNIKAY (IRE)   9 b.g. Treasure Kay 114 – Junijo (Junius (USA) 124) [2003 71: p10g **61 d**
p16g p13g⁶ p12g⁵ 9.7m Apr 4] workmanlike gelding: just modest performer at best in 2003: stays 13f: acts on soft going, good to firm and polytrack: tried blinkered early in career, wore cheekpieces final start: usually held up. *R. Ingram*

JUNIPER BANKS   2 ch.c. (Mar 9) Night Shift (USA) – Beryl 77 (Bering 136) [2003 **66**
6m 7m⁶ 7.5m 5m⁴ 6g² 6m Sep 18] 39,000Y: good-topped colt: first foal: dam, 1½m winner, out of half-sister to dam of 8-y-o Bahamian Pirate: fair maiden: left E. Dunlop after third outing: hung badly left when second in nursery at Hamilton: stays 6f: acts on good to firm going: tongue tied after debut: wore cheekpieces and got worked up (below form) final start. *Miss A. Stokell*

JUNKANOO   7 ch.g. Generous (IRE) 139 – Lupescu 102 (Dixieland Band (USA)) **–**
[2003 66: 18g Mar 21] strong, good-topped gelding: lightly-raced staying handicapper on Flat: ran as though something amiss only outing in 2003 (has reportedly finished distressed on 3 occasions over hurdles). *Mrs M. Reveley*

JUNOWOT   3 b.f. Cyrano de Bergerac 120 – Aldwick Colonnade 62 (Kind of Hush **–**
118) [2003 8.2g 8.3s 7g Jun 3] smallish, close-coupled filly: fourth foal: half-sister to 6f to 2m winner Coastguards Hero (by Chilibang): dam 1m winner/winning hurdler: no form in maidens/claimer. *M. D. I. Usher*

JURISTICIA (IRE)   3 ch.f. Nashwan (USA) 135 – Jural 108 (Kris 135) [2003 10.1m⁵ **62**
10f² 12g² f12g⁵ Aug 7] unfurnished filly: third foal: half-sister to fairly useful 2000 2-y-o 6f and 7f winner Silk Law (by Barathea): dam, 2-y-o 7f/1m winner who stayed 11f, half-sister to 5-y-o With Reason: modest form in maidens first 3 starts: stays 1½m: raced only on good ground or firmer on turf: carries head high: sold 8,000 gns in December. *M. Johnston*

JUSTAFANCY   5 b.g. Green Desert (USA) 127 – Justsayno (USA) (Dr Blum (USA)) **64 d**
[2003 f7s f6g p7g⁴ p7g p7g 11.9f 11.5m f9.4g May 19] leggy, close-coupled gelding: modest maiden handicapper: well beaten last 3 starts: likely to prove best at 7f/1m: acts on polytrack, soft and good to firm going: blinkered once (ran creditably) at 3 yrs. *Miss J. Feilden*

JUST A FLUKE (IRE)   2 b.c. (Jan 30) Darshaan 133 – Star Profile (IRE) 100 (Sadler's **78 P**
Wells (USA) 132) [2003 7.5m² 7m² Aug 2] lengthy colt: third foal: dam, Irish 2-y-o 6f winner, closely related to smart Irish sprinter Lady Alexander: favourite but very green, fair form in minor event won by Top Seed at Beverley and maiden won by Tashkil at Doncaster (wandered markedly and beaten 1½ lengths): likely to be suited by 1¼m/1½m: looked weak, and very much type to do good deal better as 3-y-o. *M. Johnston*

JUST A GIGOLO   3 b.g. Inchinor 119 – Courtisane (Persepolis (FR) 127) [2003 50: **–**
f6g 6g 8g May 30] neat gelding: poor maiden at 2 yrs: soundly beaten in 2003: wears tongue tie. *N. Tinkler*

JUST A GLIMMER 3 b.f. Bishop of Cashel 122 – Rockin' Rosie 59 (Song 132) [2003 **85** 68, a87: p8g p8g Nov 22] fairly useful performer: better effort in 2003 when respectable seventh to Tadris in listed event at Lingfield on belated reappearance: seems to stay easy 1m: acts on soft going and all-weather: sometimes slowly away. *L. G. Cottrell*

JUSTALORD 5 b.g. King's Signet (USA) 110 – Just Lady 72 (Emarati (USA) 74) **72** [2003 ?, a85: p5g⁵ f5s⁴ f5g* p5g³ p5g³ p5g⁵ 5m 5g³ 5m* 5m⁵ 5.1g² 5f* 5.2m⁵ 5g² 5m **a88** p6g⁶ Dec 20] lengthy gelding: fairly useful handicapper on all-weather, fair on turf: won at Wolverhampton in February, Musselburgh in July and Kempton in August: stays easy 6f: acts on firm ground, soft and all-weather: wears cheekpieces: usually races up with pace/carries head high: consistent. *J. Balding*

JUST A MARTIAN (FR) 3 b.c. Marju (IRE) 127 – Stamatina (Warning 136) [2003 **91** 80: p7g² 8.1m 8f² 8f* 8m⁴ 8g² 8g⁵ 10m⁴ Aug 16] leggy colt: fairly useful handicapper: won at Bath in June: remained in form: stays 1m: acts on polytrack and firm going: waited with: sent to Hong Kong. *W. R. Muir*

JUST A PROMISE (FR) 2 ch.f. (May 3) Grand Lodge (USA) 125 – Jural 108 (Kris – 135) [2003 8.2m Aug 20] fourth foal: half-sister to fairly useful 2000 2-y-o 6f/7f winner Silk Law (by Barathea): dam, 2-y-o 7f/1m winner who stayed 11f, half-sister to 5-y-o With Reason: 12/1 and very green, well held in maiden at Nottingham: sold 8,000 gns. *M. Johnston*

JUSTASTROP (IRE) 2 ch.f. (Mar 8) Daggers Drawn (USA) 114 – Just Blink (IRE) – (Fairy King (USA)) [2003 5.1f⁵ f5g 6f⁶ Jul 15] third foal: dam ran twice at 4 yrs: well held in sellers: dead. *J. S. Moore*

JUST DANCE ME (FR) 2 gr.f. (Apr 4) Linamix (FR) 127 – Reine de La Ciel (USA) – p (Conquistador Cielo (USA)) [2003 7m Oct 13] tall filly: half-sister to several winners, including 5f/6f winner Anthony Mon Amour (by Nicholas): dam, minor US sprint winner, sister to dam of high-class miler Slickly (by Linamix): 33/1, tenth of 13 in maiden at Leicester, green and not knocked about: should do better. *W. J. Haggas*

JUSTE POUR L'AMOUR 3 ch.g. Pharly (FR) 130 – Fontaine Lady 41 (Millfontaine **87** 114) [2003 84: 8.3g 7.6g⁴ 7.1m² 8.1g⁴ 8m⁵ 8g 8m Sep 17] sturdy, workmanlike gelding: fairly useful performer: below form last 2 starts: will probably stay 1¼m: acts on good to firm going: raced freely sixth start. *J. R. Fanshawe*

JUST ERN 4 ch.g. Young Ern 120 – Just Run (IRE) 45 (Runnett 125) [2003 54, a–: f8s – 6m f5g 7g May 5] compact gelding: modest maiden at 2/3 yrs: well held in 2003: sometimes hangs left. *P. C. Haslam*

JUST FILLY (IRE) 2 ch.f. (Mar 1) Woodborough (USA) 112 – Good Aim (IRE) – (Priolo (USA) 127) [2003 p8g Nov 13] €2,000Y: second foal: dam unraced: 100/1, eighth of 12 in maiden at Lingfield, slowly away. *A. P. Jones*

JUST FLY 3 b.g. Efisio 120 – Chrysalis 66 (Soviet Star (USA) 128) [2003 81: p7g⁵ 8.3g **88** 7.1m 7.1m* 7g p7g⁵ p6g p8g⁵ Dec 30] sturdy gelding: fairly useful handicapper: won at Sandown in May: ended year in decent form: best form at 6f/7f: acts on all-weather and good to firm going. *S. Kirk*

JUST JAMES 4 b.g. Spectrum (IRE) 126 – Fairy Flight (IRE) 86 (Fairy King **120** (USA)) [2003 110: 6m² 6f⁵ 7m² 6m 7m* Oct 18]

One of the highest profile lots at the 2002 Autumn Horses In Training Sales at Tattersalls was Just James, the winner of that season's Jersey Stakes at Royal Ascot. He failed to make his reserve of 70,000 guineas, which was surprising given the strength of the market at the sale nowadays due to the increased presence of international buyers. One reason might have been his somewhat mercurial reputation, emanating from a remarkable performance when winning a handicap at Newmarket, where he was detached at halfway, seemingly going nowhere, before finishing with a rare flourish. The view that Just James was an eccentric character was endorsed by his trainer Jeremy Noseda, who said of him 'he does it when he feels like it'.

The first appointment for Just James on his return to Shalfleet stables was with the vet for a gelding operation. He was much more consistent in 2003, running just one below-par race from five starts, in the July Cup at Newmarket. As well as being more consistent, Just James was also an improved performer. His first two starts were over six furlongs, and he ran well when second to Twilight Blues in the Duke of York Stakes at York in May before getting a poor run when fifth to Choisir

Victor Chandler Challenge Stakes, Newmarket—
trouble in behind as Just James hangs left as he strikes the front;
Nayyir (far left) is an unlucky second, with Arakan (second right) finishing third

in the Golden Jubilee Stakes at Royal Ascot. Back at seven in the Criterion Stakes at Newmarket the following month, Just James ran well when second to Trade Fair, beaten four lengths, typically getting behind but running on strongly after the winner had got first run. Given three months off after the July Cup, Just James returned for the Challenge Stakes at Newmarket, starting at 16/1, with the betting dominated by odds-on Trade Fair. Just James was one of the first off the bridle but quickened well when switched to the outside to lead in the final furlong, betraying lingering signs of quirkiness by hanging left and causing plenty of interference on his inside. Just James looked a fortunate winner on the day, as the runner-up Nayyir didn't get in the clear until all too late after being trapped behind a wall of horses over a furlong out, but still produced a very smart performance.

		Spectrum (IRE) (b 1992)	Rainbow Quest (b 1981)	Blushing Groom
Just James (b.g. 1999)				I Will Follow
			River Dancer (b 1983)	Irish River
				Dancing Shadow
		Fairy Flight (IRE) (b 1995)	Fairy King (b 1982)	Northern Dancer
				Fairy Bridge
			Rising Ride (ch 1978)	Red Alert
				Naiad Queen

Just James is to stay in training and, given that his trainer considered the improved form in the Challenge Stakes might have been down to Just James being fresh for the race, he may have even fewer runs in the next season. A strong, compact gelding (not the best of walkers), Just James raced only on good to firm and firm going in the latest season, but won a maiden at Doncaster on soft as a two-year-old. Because of his tendency to get behind, he may be ideally better suited by seven furlongs than six. By the Irish Two Thousand Guineas and Champion Stakes winner Spectrum, Just James is speedily bred on his dam's side. He is the first foal of Fairy Flight, a fairly useful winner over six furlongs as a two-year-old for Charles O'Brien and a sister to the useful sprinter King of The East and a half-sister to fairly useful Irish sprinter Northern Tide. Just James's grandam Rising Tide (a half-sister to the Phoenix Stakes winner King Persian) was a useful two-year-old but didn't train on. Just James capped a good season for his breeder Nancy Ralphs and her Downclose Stud which, from just ten mares, bred the smart sprinter Dubaian Gift, useful miler Pentecost and the useful two-year-old Psychiatrist. *J. Noseda*

JUST JENNIFER 3 b.f. Emperor Jones (USA) 119 – Highest Bid (FR) (Highest Honor **63** (FR) 124) [2003 68: f7s⁵ f7g² f6g⁶ 10m 7m⁶ Jun 26] leggy, quite good-topped filly: modest maiden: stays 7f: acts on fibresand, best turf effort on good going: tried visored/blinkered: sold 1,200 gns in December. *P. W. D'Arcy*

JUST ONE LOOK 2 b.f. (Apr 6) Barathea (IRE) 127 – Western Sal 75 (Salse (USA) 77
128) [2003 6m⁴ 6.1g² 6g* 6g⁴ 6m² 6f⁶ 6m⁵ 7d 7g Oct 24] smallish, quite good-topped
filly: fourth foal: half-sister to 2 winners abroad, including useful German performer up
to 1¾m Western Devil (by Dr Devious): dam 1¼m/1½m winner who stayed 15f: fair performer: won minor event at Haydock in July: creditable efforts after (mostly in nurseries)
until last 2 starts: should stay 7f: acts on firm ground. *M. Blanshard*

JUST ONE SMILE (IRE) 3 b.f. Desert Prince (IRE) 130 – Smile Awhile (USA) 71
(Woodman (USA) 126) [2003 68: 8g 8.3g³ 6.9m³ 7f² 6m* 6.1m⁴ p7g² Nov 13] lengthy,
useful-looking filly: has scope: fair performer: odds on, won maiden at Redcar in
October: good efforts in handicaps after: stays 1m, but may prove best at 5f/6f: acts on
polytrack, raced only on good ground or firmer on turf: has raced freely. *T. D. Easterby*

JUST RED 5 ch.h. Meqdaam (USA) – Orchard Bay 47 (Formidable (USA) 125) [2003 –
10f⁵ f9.4g Nov 1] second foal: dam 2-y-o 5f winner: well held in 2 maidens. *R. Hollins-*
head

JUST SERENADE 4 ch.f. Factual (USA) 108 – Thimbalina 63 (Salmon Leap (USA) 57
131) [2003 66d: f8g² f8g f7g² 8g 8.5g⁴ Jul 11] workmanlike filly: just modest maiden
handicapper at 4 yrs: stays 1m: acts on soft ground, good to firm and fibresand: tried in
headgear: sold 1,700 gns in November. *M. J. Ryan*

JUST TIM (IRE) 2 ch.c. (Jan 13) Inchinor 119 – Simply Sooty 78 (Absalom 128) 76
[2003 7m 7g⁶ 8m p8g² Nov 2] useful-looking colt: sixth foal: brother to smart 6f (at 2 yrs)
to 9f winner Umistim and half-brother to winner in Denmark by First Trump: dam 2-y-o
5f winner: fair maiden: second to King Maximus at Lingfield: stays 1m: acts on polytrack
and good to firm ground. *R. Hannon*

JUST WIZ 7 b.g. Efisio 120 – Jade Pet 90 (Petong 126) [2003 46, a85: f9.4g* f9.4g* 48
p10g f8.5g⁴ f8.5g⁵ f9.4s 10m⁵ f8.5g³ f9.4g² Dec 26] small gelding: fairly useful on all- a79
weather, poor on turf: won 2 claimers at Wolverhampton in January: ran well final start:
stays 9.4f: acts on fibresand, best turf form on good going or firmer: seems effective
blinkered/visored or not: held up. *N. P. Littmoden*

JUWWI 9 ch.g. Mujtahid (USA) 118 – Nouvelle Star (AUS) (Luskin Star (AUS)) 82
[2003 89, a102: f5s p6g f6g f6s f6g f6s⁴ 6g 6m 6g² 6m⁶ 6m 6m³ 6m⁶ 6m 6f⁶ 6g 6f⁶
6g 6m⁵ 5.1d⁴ 6d 5f⁴ 5m 6m 5.1g⁴ 5.7f Sep 15] robust gelding: reportedly split a cannon
bone in 2002: just fairly useful handicapper nowadays: won at Doncaster in May: reportedly broke blood vessel final start: best at 5f/6f: acts on fibresand/any turf going: wore
cheekpieces last 2 outings: usually claimer ridden/slowly away/gets behind: none too
reliable. *J. M. Bradley*

JUYUSH (USA) 11 b.g. Silver Hawk (USA) 123 – Silken Doll (USA) (Chieftain II) 69
[2003 21.6m³ Apr 14] big, strong gelding: fairly useful in 2001: just fair form in handicap
only outing since: stays 21f: acts on firm and soft ground. *P. Bowen*

K

KABIS BOOIE (IRE) 2 ch.c. (Mar 6) Night Shift (USA) – Perfect Welcome (Taufan 77
(USA) 119) [2003 8f² p8g⁴ Oct 27] 10,000Y, 25,000 2-y-o: closely related to useful Irish
6f winner (including at 2 yrs) Immovable Option (by Fairy King) and half-brother to 3
winners, including useful Irish 1m/1¼m winner Leave Me Alone (by Nashwan): dam,
Irish 7f winner, half-sister to high-class miler Chalon from family of Irish Oaks winner
Dance Design: better effort in maidens (fair form) when second to Tree Chopper at Bath:
will stay 1¼m. *H. R. A. Cecil*

KABREET 2 b.c. (Mar 29) Night Shift (USA) – Red Rabbit 86 (Suave Dancer (USA) 79
136) [2003 6g⁵ 6d⁵ 6d³ p6g* p7g p6g* Dec 30] 33,000Y: sturdy colt: second foal: dam,
maiden who stayed 1¼m, out of half-sister to Old Vic: fair performer: won maiden in
November and nursery in December, both at Lingfield: should stay 7f: acts on polytrack
and good to soft going. *E. A. L. Dunlop*

KAFIL (USA) 9 b. or br.g. Housebuster (USA) – Alchaasibiyeh (USA) 85 (Seattle Slew –
(USA)) [2003 –: f9.4s⁵ p7g 6m Jun 27] leggy gelding: no longer of any account: tried
blinkered/visored. *J. J. Bridger*

KAFUWAIN 2 b.c. (Mar 6) Mark of Esteem (IRE) 137 – Anneli Rose 56 (Superlative 83
118) [2003 5g³ 6g 5m 6f* 6g p6g⁵ Oct 15] 50,000Y: tall colt: has a quick action: half-
brother to 3 winners, notably smart 1994 2-y-o 5f/6f winner (including Middle Park

Stakes) Fard (by Reprimand): dam, 6f winner, half-sister to smart sprinter Gallic League: fairly useful performer: won maiden at Ayr in July: ran creditably in minor event at Lingfield final start: not sure to stay much beyond 6f: acts on polytrack and firm going: visored fourth and fifth outings: looks hard ride: sold 17,000 gns. *J. Noseda*

KAGOSHIMA (IRE)   8 b.g. Shirley Heights 130 – Kashteh (IRE) 79 (Green Desert (USA) 127) [2003 –: 16g 16.1m f16g f16g⁶ f16g Dec 16] deep-bodied gelding: just poor form since 2001: usually visored. *J. R. Norton*   **38**

KAHYASI PRINCESS (IRE)   3 b.f. Kahyasi 130 – Dungeon Princess (IRE) 62 (Danehill (USA) 126) [2003 12m³ 12.1m² 11.1d³ 11.1d⁵ 12.3d⁴ 11.9m* f12g 16.2d* 15.9m³ 16.2m* 16.2d* Jul 25] IR 10,500Y: sturdy filly: third foal: half-sister to a winner in Italy by Mtoto: dam, 1m winner, half-sister to dam of Irish performers Rebelline (very smart at 7f to 1¼m) and Quws (smart, stayed 11f): fairly useful performer: won claimer at Carlisle in June and handicaps at Beverley, Haydock and Ascot in July: beat Sindapour by 6 lengths on last-named course: stays 2m: unraced on extremes of going: races prominently. *M. Johnston*   **92**

KAIETEUR (USA)   4 b.c. Marlin (USA) 124 – Strong Embrace (USA) (Regal Embrace (CAN)) [2003 117: 10.5d 10m⁶ 10g³ 10g² 9.9m³ 10m Oct 18]   **121**
    Kaieteur, successful in a Group 1 as a three-year-old, didn't win in the latest season, but ran two very good races in top company and was better than ever. Kaieteur won the Grosser Dallmayr-Preis over a mile and a quarter at Munich in 2002, one of five Group 1 races open to older horses in Germany, having previously been successful in a maiden at Bath and a minor event at Kempton and he finished in the frame in the Classic Trial at Sandown, the King Edward VII Stakes at Royal Ascot and the Prix Eugene Adam at Maisons-Laffitte. His best efforts in 2003 came in the Eclipse Stakes and the Arlington Million. Having been unplaced in the Prix

Mrs Susan McCarthy's "Kaieteur"

Ganay at Longchamp and the Prince of Wales's Stakes at Royal Ascot, Kaieteur defied odds of 100/1 in the Eclipse at Sandown, finishing two and a quarter lengths third to Falbrav and Nayef, keeping on well. Kaieteur repeated the form at Arlington in August when dead-heating for third with Paolini, half a length and head behind Storming Home and Sulamani. Storming Home was demoted to fourth for causing interference when ducking sharply right near the finish and hampering the dead-heaters, who were promoted a place. Kaieteur missed the Irish Champion Stakes after reportedly picking up a slight throat and chest infection, but faced an easier task in the five-runner Select Stakes at Goodwood four weeks after the Arlington Million. However, Kaieteur was unable to justify favouritism and was beaten two necks behind Leporello and Muqbil. But he wasn't discredited on his only other start when seventh, for the second successive year, in the Champion Stakes at Newmarket, where he was staying on when coming off worst in a barging match over two furlongs out with the eventual runner-up Carnival Dancer.

			Sword Dance	Nijinsky
	Marlin (USA)		(b 1984)	Rosa Mundi
	(b 1993)		Syrian Summer	Damascus
Kaieteur (USA)			(b 1984)	Special Warmth
(b.c. 1999)			Regal Embrace	Vice Regent
	Strong Embrace (USA)		(b 1975)	Close Embrace
	(b 1988)		Topper B. Bold	Bold L. B.
			(b 1981)	Break Point

Kaieteur, a big, strong, well-made colt, is the fourth foal out of Strong Embrace, who won eleven of her thirty-five races in the States, including a minor stakes over six furlongs as a two-year-old. She has produced two other winners, Red Reef (by Red Ransom), who won three times in the States, including twice as a two-year-old, and the two-year-old Strong Cat (by Forest Wildcat), who was an impressive winner of a maiden at Santa Anita in December. Both Kaieteur's grandam Topper B. Bold and great grandam Break Point won in minor company. Kaieteur's sire, the genuine and consistent Marlin, won four Grade 1 events, all on turf, including the Arlington Million as a four-year-old before suffering a career-ending injury in a race prior to the 1997 Breeders' Cup. He now stands at the Turkish National Stud.

Kaieteur, who was said to have finished lame in the Champion Stakes, stays in training and has been entered for the Dubai World Cup. While that may prove too tough a task, he is clearly capable of winning in minor pattern company in Britain. Kaieteur is probably best at around a mile and a quarter (he took too strong a hold over a mile and a half) and his best efforts have been on good going or softer, although he has form on firm. He has a tendency to become a bit stirred up in the preliminaries. *B. J. Meehan*

KAIROS (IRE) 3 b.g. Kadeed (IRE) – Oriental Air (IRE) 56 (Taufan (USA) 119) – [2003 8.1d 7.1g 6.1m 7d Jul 30] fifth foal: half-brother to 7-y-o Eastern Trumpeter: dam, 5f winner, half-sister to useful sprinter Sunset Reigns: no form. *J. M. Bradley*

KAISER (IRE) 3 b.g. Barathea (IRE) 127 – Emerald Waters (Kings Lake (USA) 133) **63 ?** [2003 59p: 10d 10m 11.8m⁴ 14.1m Jul 2] quite good-topped gelding: modest maiden: stays 1½m: acts on good to firm ground: visored last 2 starts. *J. R. Fanshawe*

KALABAR 3 b.c. Kahyasi 130 – Imbabala (Zafonic (USA) 130) [2003 10m³ 10g* **117** 10s³ 10g⁴ 10g² 10d* 12g² 12m Dec 14] first foal: dam, French 1m winner, half-sister to dam of 6-y-o Continent out of very smart performer up to 1m Interval: smart performer: won minor event at Maisons-Laffitte in April and Prix Guillaume d'Ornano at Deauville (beat Saturn by short head, leading on line) in August: ran creditably behind Vallee Enchantee last 2 starts, in Prix du Conseil de Paris at Longchamp (½-length second) and Hong Kong Vase at Sha Tin (2¼ lengths eighth): stays 1½m: acts on soft and good to firm going. *P. Bary, France*

KALAMAN (IRE) 3 b.c. Desert Prince (IRE) 130 – Kalamba (IRE) (Green **126** Dancer (USA) 132) [2003 78P: 8m* 8m* 8f² 10.4m 8m² Oct 3]

Four years after Kalanisi won the Heron Stakes at Kempton on his third racecourse appearance, his half-brother Kalaman, also owned by the Aga Khan, achieved the same feat. A training setback kept Kalanisi off the course for the remainder of 1999, so he began his four-year-old career still unbeaten and highly promising. On the other hand Kalaman, who followed his Kempton run with an unlucky second in the St James's Palace Stakes, will start the next season having to prove himself all over again following disappointing performances on his last two starts. Kalanisi more than fulfilled his promise at four—by which time he'd joined Kalaman's trainer Sir Michael Stoute having been with Luca Cumani previously—winning the Queen Anne Stakes, the Champion Stakes and the Breeders' Cup Turf. While it would be too much to expect Kalaman to achieve a similar level of success, he will surely win pattern races if recapturing his best form. Perhaps Kalaman could even emulate Kalanisi by winning the Queen Anne.

Unlike Kalanisi, Kalaman was raced at two, shaping very well when fourth in a maiden at Leicester. After justifying favouritism in a similar event at Newbury on his reappearance, Kalaman went on to do the same in the Pacemaker Heron Stakes, a listed event in which he had six opponents. They included Ikhtyar, who had shown smart form when winning a minor event at Sandown after finishing third to Kalaman at Newbury on his debut, and this pair dominated both the betting and the race itself. The confidently-ridden Kalaman put Ikhtyar firmly in his place once again, quickening in very good style to take the lead entering the final furlong and requiring only hand riding to pull a length and a half clear. Kalaman created such a favourable impression at Kempton that he was sent off favourite once more on his next start, in the St James's Palace Stakes at Royal Ascot, even though he was up against the likes of Clodovil, Indian Haven and Martillo, respective winners of the Poule d'Essai des Poulains, Irish Two Thousand Guineas and Mehl-Mulhens-Rennen. Those who supported Kalaman were unlucky not to collect. Held up, he was twice badly impeded when trying for a run in the penultimate furlong then finished very strongly once in the clear and balanced again, only to find that the

H.H. Aga Khan's "Kalaman"

Two Thousand Guineas runner-up Zafeen had gone beyond recall. Kalaman did extremely well to reduce the margin between them to a length, pulling three lengths clear of third-placed Martillo in the process—his rating assumes that he could have won the race fairly comfortably. It seemed just a matter of time before Kalaman gained a Group 1 success, yet when given another opportunity to do so on his next start, in the International Stakes at York, he managed only seventh of eight behind Falbrav. Sent off favourite yet again, Kalaman was a bit fractious in the stalls and faded after being close enough when the race really began in earnest three furlongs from home, too far out to blame the longer trip alone for his being so far below his best. Nonetheless, the drop back to a mile in the Group 3 Joel Stakes at Newmarket two months later looked to provide Kalaman with a good opportunity to get his campaign back on track, but he was well below form once more and failed to land the odds. Although the race wasn't run to suit Kalaman, held up last of four as Splendid Era set just a steady pace, he did improve readily enough to challenge but didn't help his jockey by hanging right when asked for maximum effort. After promising so much midway through the season, Kalaman ended it under a cloud.

Kalaman (IRE) (b.c. 2000)	Desert Prince (IRE) (b 1995)	Green Desert (b 1983)	Danzig
			Foreign Courier
		Flying Fairy (ch 1983)	Bustino
			Fairy Footsteps
	Kalamba (IRE) (b 1991)	Green Dancer (b 1972)	Nijinsky
			Green Valley
		Kareena (b 1979)	Riverman
			Kermiya

The fifth foal of Kalamba, Kalaman is a half-brother to a couple of winners besides Kalanisi: the fairly useful half-a-mile winner who stayed fifteen furlongs Kalambari (by Kahyasi) and Kalambara (by Bluebird), who was successful over an extended nine furlongs in France. The lightly-raced Kalamba, who was placed in France at up to a mile and a quarter, is a daughter of the smart and thoroughly genuine miler Kareena and granddaughter of the nine-furlong and mile-and-a-quarter winner Kermiya. Kalaman, a well-made, attractive colt, who impresses in appearance, is by Desert Prince, who is much less of an influence for stamina than Kalanisi's sire Doyoun; it is highly unlikely that Kalaman will stay a mile and a half, as Kalanisi did. A mile and a quarter should be within his compass, though, and he is worth another chance at that trip. Raced only on good to firm and firm ground since making his debut on good to soft, Kalaman was withdrawn from the Sussex Stakes on the morning of the race because connections considered the ground—officially good to soft—unsuitable. *Sir Michael Stoute*

KALANI GIRL (IRE)   2 b.f. (Jan 14) Ashkalani (IRE) 128 – Sopran Marida (IRE)   **75** (Darshaan 133) [2003 6g⁵ 5g⁴ 6.3g³ 6m⁴ 7m 7m² 6.5d 7m³ 7m Oct 4] €12,000Y: lengthy, rather unfurnished filly: half-sister to fairly useful 2000 2-y-o 6f winner Millenium Princess (by Eagle Eyed), later successful in USA: dam, Italian 7f and 9f winner, half-sister to useful Italian/US performer up to 1½m Sopran Mariduff: fair maiden: second in nursery at Goodwood: stays 7f: acts on good to firm ground: tongue tied 3 of last 4 starts: sent to USA. *Mrs P. N. Dutfield*

KALANISHA (IRE)   3 ch.c. Ashkalani (IRE) 128 – Camisha (IRE) 82 (Shernazar   **–** 131) [2003 10m 12g 11.1g Sep 27] IR 21,000Y: strong, lengthy colt: brother to 4-y-o Knotty Ash Girl and half-brother to 2 winners in Ireland, including 1½m/1¾m winner Berkeley Bay (by Fit To Fight): dam Irish 11f/1½m winner: well beaten in maidens. *N. A. Graham*

KALARRAM   6 ch.m. Muhtarram (USA) 125 – Kalandariya 78 (Kris 135) [2003 f7g   **–** Jan 20] lightly raced and little form. *T. Wall*

KALI   2 gr.f. (Feb 9) Linamix (FR) 127 – Alkarida (FR) (Akarad (FR) 130) [2003 p8g²   **71 p** Nov 26] first foal: dam French 1m winner: 20/1, 1¼ lengths second of 12 to Ascertain in maiden at Lingfield: will be suited by 1¼m/1½m: should improve. *R. Charlton*

KALISHKA (IRE)   2 b.c. (May 8) Fasliyev (USA) 120 – Andromaque (USA) 111   **66 ?** (Woodman (USA) 126) [2003 5.1m 6m 7m Sep 1] 10,000F, 30,000Y: leggy, angular colt: sixth foal: half-brother to Hong Kong 9f winner Keen Marshal (by Danehill): dam 1m winner and awarded 9f Prix de l'Opera: seemingly best effort in maidens (fair form) when ninth of 13 at Leicester final start, dictating pace: stays 7f. *Andrew Turnell*

KALLISTA'S PRIDE 3 b.f. Puissance 110 – Clan Scotia 47 (Clantime 101) [2003 —
f6g f8.5g Nov 15] 4,000Y: fourth foal: dam 2-y-o 5f winner: well held in maidens at
Wolverhampton. *J. A. Osborne*

KALOU (GER) 5 b.g. Law Society (USA) 130 – Kompetenz (IRE) (Be My Guest **56**
(USA) 126) [2003 87?: f12s⁶ f8g⁵ f14.8s f8g³ Dec 8] only modest form in Britain: stays
11f: acts on fibresand, good to firm and heavy ground: tried blinkered: sometimes slowly
away. *B. J. Curley*

KALUANA COURT 7 b.m. Batshoof 122 – Fairfields Cone (Celtic Cone 116) [2003 **80**
61: 18g³ 14f 15m² 14.8m* 16.2d⁴ 14.8m* 16.1m Aug 9] strong, good-topped mare: fairly
useful handicapper: better than ever in 2003 and won twice at Newmarket in July: stays
17f: best efforts on good/good to firm going: usually held up. *R. J. Price*

KALUSH 2 b.g. (Apr 15) Makbul 104 – The Lady Vanishes (Robin Des Pins (USA) **66**
119) [2003 5g 5f 5g 6d³ 6g 7f² 7m⁶ 8.5m³ 7m³ 7d⁶ Sep 20] 500Y: tall, leggy gelding: third
foal: half-brother to 4-y-o Market Avenue: dam unraced: fair maiden: stays 8.5f: acts on
firm and good to soft ground: often races prominently. *Ronald Thompson*

KAMALA 4 b.f. Priolo (USA) 127 – Fleeting Vision (IRE) 79 (Vision (USA)) [2003 —
68: f16.2g f12s f12g Dec 22] lightly-raced maiden, fair at best: well beaten in 2003:
visored (pulled up) final start. *R. Brotherton*

KAMANDA LAUGH 2 ch.g. (Mar 15) Most Welcome 131 – Kamada (USA) (Blush- **66**
ing Groom (FR) 131) [2003 7m⁶ 6m Aug 27] 7,000F, 6,500Y: strong gelding: half-
brother to numerous winners abroad, including French listed 11.5f winner Kanawar (by
Lashkari): dam French 1¼m winner: better effort in maidens (fair form) when sixth at
Newmarket: raced prominently both starts: should stay at least 1m. *W. Jarvis*

KAMA'S WHEEL 4 ch.f. Magic Ring (IRE) 115 – Tea And Scandals (USA) (Key To **46**
The Kingdom (USA)) [2003 43: f8s f9.4g⁵ f9.4s f8.5g f8s f5s⁶ 8m⁶ 8f 8m⁵ 7f⁴ 7m 7d⁴ᵈ **a–**
8f⁶ 10m Oct 23] workmanlike filly: poor maiden handicapper: stays 1m: acts on firm
ground, good to soft and fibresand: often wears cheekpieces: edgy sort: often slowly
away. *John A. Harris*

KAMENKA 2 ch.f. (Apr 17) Wolfhound (USA) 126 – Aliuska (IRE) 70 (Fijar Tango **66 +**
(FR) 127) [2003 5f⁶ 5m³ 6.5m 6m⁴ f6g⁴ Nov 1] 10,000Y: close-coupled filly: fifth foal:
half-sister to 3 winners, including 4-y-o Perfect Punch and 6-y-o Altay: dam, Irish 5f
winner, ran only at 2 yrs: fair maiden: will probably stay 7f: acts on good to firm ground.
R. A. Fahey

KANGA 4 b.f. Primo Dominie 121 – Princess Zara (Reprimand 122) [2003 59: p7g⁶ **50**
7m⁵ f8.5s 6g⁶ 6m⁵ 5g f6s f8.5g⁶ Jul 11] sparely-made filly: modest maiden handicapper: **a39**
stays 7f: acts on all-weather, good to firm and good to soft ground. *N. P. Littmoden*

KANGARILLA ROAD 4 b.g. Magic Ring (IRE) 115 – Kangra Valley 56 (Indian **78**
Ridge 123) [2003 88p: 5m⁶ 5m 5m May 14] leggy, good-topped gelding: just fair
handicapper at 4 yrs: best at bare 5f: acts on firm ground: sometimes races freely.
Mrs J. R. Ramsden

KANZ WOOD (USA) 7 ch.g. Woodman (USA) 126 – Kanz (USA) 115 (The Minstrel **59**
(CAN) 135) [2003 61, a71: f8s* f8s³ f8s⁴ f7s⁵ 7g³ 7.1g 7.1g f8g p8g f7g Dec 22] strong **a74**
gelding: has reportedly had wind operation: fair handicapper on all-weather, modest
on turf: won at Southwell in January: stays 1m: acts on good to firm going, good to soft
and all-weather: tried tongue tied: sometimes carries head high: none too reliable.
A. W. Carroll

KAPALUA (USA) 3 b.f. King of Kings (IRE) 125 – Numero Privee (USA) (Private —
Account (USA)) [2003 –: 12.3f⁴ Jun 18] well held in maidens. *B. W. Hills*

KAPAROLO (USA) 4 ch.g. El Prado (IRE) 119 – Parliament House (USA) (General **78**
Assembly (USA)) [2003 89: 14.1g⁵ 14v³ 12m 14g⁶ 13.3m⁵ 21d Jul 30] strong gelding:
fair handicapper: below form in cheekpieces last 2 starts: stays 1¾m: acts on soft and
good to firm going: successful over hurdles in October. *Mrs A. J. Perrett*

KARAKUM 4 b.g. Mtoto 134 – Magongo 103 (Be My Chief (USA) 122) [2003 –: 12.1d —
Jul 25] close-coupled gelding: little form since 2 yrs: tried blinkered. *A. J. Chamberlain*

KARAMEA (SWI) 2 gr.f. (Apr 22) Rainbow Quest (USA) 134 – Karapucha (IRE) **76 p**
(Kaldoun (FR) 122) [2003 7m 8m³ Oct 17] leggy, close-coupled filly: first foal: dam
French 2-y-o 7.5f winner from very good family: much better effort (fair form) when
close third of 20 to Lunar Exit in maiden at Newmarket, tending to wander: likely to be
suited by 1¼m/1½m: should progress. *J. L. Dunlop*

KARAOKE (IRE) 3 b.g. Mujadil (USA) 119 – Kayoko (IRE) 74 (Shalford (IRE) **84** 124§) [2003 70: 10m³ 8.2g* 8.1m 10.2g² 9m³ 8m³ 10m* Jun 14] good-bodied gelding: fairly useful performer: won handicap at Nottingham in April and minor event there (beat Desert Royalty by head) in June: effective at 1m/1¼m: acts on good to firm ground and fibresand: reliable. *S. Kirk*

KARAOKE KING 5 ch.h. King's Signet (USA) 110 – Brampton Grace 80 (Tachypous **71** 128) [2003 61: p7g p6g p7g³ f7g² f7g 6g² 6g⁴ 7g² 6.1g³ 5g 6f 6d 6d⁴ 7.1g⁶ 6m* 7.1m⁶ p7g p7g Nov 2] workmanlike horse: fair performer: won apprentice handicap at Salisbury in August: best at 6f/easy 7f: acts on all-weather, good to soft and good to firm ground: often races prominently. *J. E. Long*

KARATHAENA (IRE) 3 b.f. Barathea (IRE) 127 – Dabtara (IRE) 88 (Kahyasi 130) **78 ?** [2003 82: 8g⁵ 9m 8g³ Jul 7] good-bodied filly: fair maiden: best 3-y-o effort when last of 5 in steadily-run listed event at Ascot: should stay 1¼m: acts on soft ground: has raced freely: looked none too keen final start. *J. W. Hills*

KAREEB (FR) 6 b.g. Green Desert (USA) 127 – Braari (USA) 97 (Gulch (USA)) **90** [2003 94: 6g⁴ 6m 7m⁴ 7.1f⁴ 7f 7f* 7g 7m* 7m³ 7f Nov 8] smallish, robust gelding: fairly useful handicapper: won at York in July and Newmarket in August, quickening well to beat Master Robbie 1¾ lengths in latter: better at 7f than 1m: acts on firm and soft going: tried blinkered at 3 yrs: held up: formerly unreliable. *W. J. Musson*

KARJU (IRE) 4 b.g. Marju (IRE) 127 – Karmisymixa (FR) (Linamix (FR) 127) [2003 **62** 55: 8g³ Jun 28] 500,000 francs Y, €3,500 3-y-o: fourth foal: dam unraced sister to useful Kalamisik and half-sister to smart Karmiska, both 1¼m performers in France: won held in maiden at 3 yrs for M. Halford in Ireland: third of 5 in similar event at Newcastle only outing on Flat in 2003: fair hurdler. *M. Todhunter*

KARLI 3 b.f. Superpower 113 – Saraswati 55 (Mansingh (USA) 120) [2003 49: 7m 7m **34** 6f⁶ 7f 8f Jun 18] good-topped filly: poor maiden: stays 7f: acts on firm going, probably on soft. *D. W. Barker*

KARLINIGHT (IRE) 3 b.f. Night Shift (USA) – Karlinaxa (Linamix (FR) 127) [2003 **47 ?** –: f8g³ f7g 8f f6g Apr 28] good-bodied filly: poor maiden: went to Spain. *T. J. Naughton*

KARMA CHAMELIAN (USA) 2 b.f. (Mar 6) Diesis 133 – Wild Rumour (IRE) 89 **–** (Sadler's Wells (USA) 132) [2003 6.1g Jun 5] 22,000Y: fourth foal: dam, 2-y-o 7f winner, closely related to useful Cherry Hinton/Fred Darling winner Musicale out of half-sister to high-class sprinter Committed: 10/1, well held in maiden at Chepstow, slowly away. *J. W. Hills*

KARMINSKEY PARK 4 b.f. Sabrehill (USA) 120 – Housefull 81 (Habitat 134) **71** [2003 71§: p5g* p5g⁶ f5s⁴ p5g² 5m⁴ 6.1g⁴ 5d* 5g⁵ 5d² 5m³ 5g³ 5m 5m 5m⁴ 6g⁴ 5m Oct 20] heavy-bodied filly: fair handicapper: won at Lingfield in January and Newcastle in May: effective at 5f/easy 6f: acts on all-weather, firm and soft going: sometimes flashes tail: usually waited with: consistent. *T. J. Etherington*

KARTUZY (JPN) 3 b.f. Polish Precedent (USA) 131 – Marienbad (FR) (Darshaan **82** 133) [2003 –p: 12d² 11.5m* 12.3m³ 10g³ Aug 10] big, strong, good sort: fairly useful handicapper, lightly raced: won at Yarmouth in June: respectable efforts at Ripon (odds on) and Leicester after: stays 1½m: acts on good to firm and good to soft ground: usually races prominently. *M. A. Jarvis*

KARYON (IRE) 3 b.f. Presidium 124 – Stealthy 73 (Kind of Hush 118) [2003 46: f7g⁶ **40** f8s 8m 8m 10m³ Oct 13] good-topped filly: poor maiden: barely stays 1¼m. *P. C. Haslam*

KASAMBA 4 b.f. Salse (USA) 128 – Kabayil 75 (Dancing Brave (USA) 140) [2003 **–** 80: 10g 8.3d f8.5g f12s Jun 21] quite good-topped filly: fairly useful performer at 3 yrs: well held for new stable in 2003: tried in cheekpieces. *Miss J. A. Camacho*

KASEH (USA) 2 b. or br.c. (Apr 10) Storm Cat (USA) – Magical Allure (USA) 118 **63** (General Meeting (USA)) [2003 6.1m⁴ Sep 19] rather leggy colt: first foal: dam Grade 1 winner at 7f in USA: 7/4-on and tongue tied, fourth of 6 in maiden at Nottingham, finding little: left Godolphin. *Saeed bin Suroor*

KASHMIR SAPPHIRE (IRE) 3 b.g. Bluebird (USA) 125 – Tudor Loom (Sallust **49** 134) [2003 f8.5s 10d 10.5d⁶ 12.1d⁵ p12g⁴ 11.6m 11g⁴ 8m⁶ 11.7f³ f12s Sep 6] IR 22,000Y: lengthy gelding: seventh foal: brother to 3 winners, notably smart Irish/US performer up to 9f Rainbow Blues, 5f/6f winner at 2 yrs, and half-brother to 2 winners: dam third at 7f in Ireland: poor maiden: stays 1½m: acts on firm ground, good to soft and polytrack: blinkered last 4 starts: none too consistent: sent to Denmark. *J. A. Osborne*

KASTHARI (IRE) 4 gr.g. Vettori (IRE) 119 – Karliyka (IRE) (Last Tycoon 131) [2003 **113**
113: 16.4m³ 20m 16m³ Oct 18] tall, lengthy gelding: smart performer, lightly raced:
creditable efforts all starts in 2003, finishing 2¾ lengths third to Mr Dinos in Henry II
Stakes at Sandown, seventh to same horse in Gold Cup at Royal Ascot and length third to
Persian Punch in Jockey Club Cup at Newmarket: probably best short of 2½m: acts on
soft ground, best efforts on good to firm: has edged left, including at Sandown: sold
95,000 gns, joined J. Howard Johnson. *Sir Michael Stoute*

KATAHOLIC 4 b.c. Bluegrass Prince (IRE) 110 – Langton Herring (Nearly A Hand **–**
115) [2003 –: p7g Feb 25] no form: tried blinkered. *G. A. Ham*

KATALI 6 ch.m. Clantime 101 – Portvally (Import 127) [2003 f6g Dec 9] no form. **–**
A. Bailey

KATANO 2 ch.g. (Mar 4) Kris 135 – Flagship 84 (Rainbow Quest (USA) 134) [2003 **74**
7m⁵ Jul 18] close-coupled gelding: second foal: dam, 1¼m winner, sister to smart 1992
2-y-o 7f winner Yawl out of Oaks winner Bireme: fifth of 9 in maiden at Newmarket:
dead. *J. W. Payne*

KATE MAHER (IRE) 4 b.f. Rainbow Quest (USA) 134 – Melodist (USA) 118 (The **–**
Minstrel (CAN) 135) [2003 f12g p8g Feb 22] sister to UAE 1¼m winner Octave and
half-sister to useful Irish 1½m winner Song of The Sword (by Kris) and 1¾m winner
Melodica (by Machiavellian): dam won Italian Oaks and dead-heated in Irish Oaks: well
held in maidens: tried tongue tied. *M. A. Jarvis*

KATHOLOGY (IRE) 6 b.g. College Chapel 122 – Wicken Wonder (IRE) 71 (Distant **96**
Relative 128) [2003 93: p5g 5m* 5.1m 5m 5m⁶ 6f 5g 5d⁵ 5m³ f5g Nov 19] smallish, **a–**
sturdy gelding: useful handicapper: won at Epsom in April by ¾ length from Atlantic
Viking: effective at 5f/6f: acts on soft and good to firm going, some promise on all-
weather: usually races prominently: none too consistent. *D. R. C. Elsworth*

KATIE SAVAGE 3 b.f. Emperor Jones (USA) 119 – Coax Me Molly (USA) (L'Enjol- **–**
eur (CAN)) [2003 10d Jul 26] 2,000F: half-sister to Irish 10.5f winner Softly Softly (by
Lucky Guest) and several winners in USA: dam US 1m to 9f winner: well beaten in
maiden at Nottingham. *J. Mackie*

KATIE'S BATH TIME 2 b.f. (Feb 4) Lugana Beach 116 – Eucharis 41 (Tickled Pink **39**
114) [2003 5d 5g 5m Sep 4] 1,600Y: good-topped filly: sister to 4-y-o Larky's Lob and
half-sister to 3 winners, including 5f winner Chalice (by Governor General): dam maiden
who stayed 1m: poor maiden: should stay 6f. *Ian Emmerson*

KATIE'S ROLE 2 b.f. (Apr 14) Tragic Role (USA) – Mirkan Honey 83 (Ballymore **60**
123) [2003 6m⁶ 6d³ 7m 6m 7d⁴ f8g³ Nov 25] 3,000Y: leggy filly: sister to fairly useful
1¼m winner Lord Pierce and half-sister to several winners, including 5f/6f winner Lee
Artiste (by Tate Gallery) and 1994 2-y-o 6f/7f winner Fleet Hill (by Warrshan), both
useful: dam Irish 2m winner: modest maiden: likely to prove best up to 1m: acts on good
to soft ground, possibly not on good to firm. *Ian Emmerson*

KATIES TIGHT JEANS 9 b.m. Green Adventure (USA) 119 – Haraka Sasa (Town **–**
And Country 124) [2003 –: f6g f8g f9.4s f8.5g 7.1d 8g Jul 30] little form: tried blinkered/
in cheekpieces. *R. E. Peacock*

KATIYPOUR (IRE) 6 ch.g. Be My Guest (USA) 126 – Katiyfa (Auction Ring (USA) **81**
123) [2003 79: p12g f11s² p10g⁶ f9.4s³ f8.5s⁶ 10m 9m² 8m f11g* f12g* 10.1m³ 12g
11.6g⁶ 10.1m* 10.1g³ 10m⁴ 12d⁶ Oct 4] quite attractive gelding: fairly useful performer:
won claimers at Southwell and Wolverhampton (claimed from T. D. Barron) in June and
handicap at Epsom in August: stays easy 1½m: acts on all-weather, best turf efforts on
good ground or firmer: sometimes visored in 2002: sometimes slowly away: has raced
freely: carries head high. *Miss B. Sanders*

KATMANDU 4 b.g. Sadler's Wells (USA) 132 – Kithanga (IRE) 117 (Darshaan 133) **85 +**
[2003 73: 14.1m² 14.1m⁴ 16.1m⁴ Sep 8] tall gelding: fairly useful maiden: should stay
2m: acts on polytrack and good to firm ground: has been slowly away: carried head
awkwardly and found little final start: sold 45,000 gns, joined J. Howard Johnson.
L. M. Cumani

KATY O'HARA 4 b.f. Komaite (USA) – Amy Leigh (IRE) 78 (Imperial Frontier **59 d**
(USA) 112) [2003 –, a76: f6s f6g 5m 6m⁶ 7f 6m f6g 6d 6m Aug 19] good-bodied filly:
modest handicapper: on the downgrade: stays 6f: acts on all-weather and good to firm
going: tried visored. *Miss S. E. Hall*

KATZ PYJAMAS (IRE) 2 b.f. (Apr 24) Fasliyev (USA) 120 – Allepolina (USA) **51 §**
(Trempolino (USA) 135) [2003 5m 5m 5m⁶ 6g⁶ 5m 5f f5s 5m 5m f5g Dec 3] 12,000Y:

leggy, workmanlike filly: fifth foal: half-sister to useful 5f (in Ireland, including at 2 yrs) and 7.5f winner Yorba Linda (by Night Shift): dam unraced half-sister to dam of very smart sprinter Danetime: modest maiden: should prove best at 5f: acts on firm going: blinkered (good effort) eighth start: sometimes slowly away/wanders: inconsistent. *Mrs A. Duffield*

KAVI (IRE) 3 ch.g. Perugino (USA) 84 – Premier Leap (IRE) 56 (Salmon Leap (USA) **61** 131) [2003 64, a70: f8g⁴ f8g³ 9.2d⁶ 10g⁶ 10m⁶ Aug 20] small, strong gelding: modest performer: stays 9f: acts on good to firm going, good to soft and fibresand: won juvenile hurdle in August. *P. C. Haslam*

KAWADER (USA) 3 ch.c. Kingmambo (USA) 125 – Tajannub (USA) 104 (Dixie- **58** land Band (USA)) [2003 7.5m⁶ Jun 11] smallish, sturdy colt: fourth foal: half-brother to 6-y-o Nashaab and a winner in USA by Thunder Gulch: dam 6f (Princess Margaret Stakes at 2 yrs)/7f winner: 16/1 and green, 7 lengths sixth to Fleet of Light in maiden at Beverley: sold 7,500 gns in October. *A. C. Stewart*

KAWAGINO (IRE) 3 b.g. Perugino (USA) 84 – Sharakawa (IRE) (Darshaan 133) **84** [2003 99: 7m⁴ 8g² 7g 8m 8g⁵ 6m⁶ Jul 19] angular, deep-bodied gelding: fairly useful maiden: effective at 7f/easy 1m: unraced on extremes of going: often races prominently. *Mrs P. N. Dutfield*

KAWAKIB (IRE) 2 b.f. (Apr 14) Intikhab (USA) 135 – Haddeyah (USA) 68 (Dayjur **74** (USA) 137) [2003 7m³ 7g⁴ 7m⁶ 8f² 10.2f² Sep 29] fourth foal: half-sister to 3 winners, including fairly useful 2001 2-y-o 1m winner Budoor (by Darshaan) and 3-y-o Buthaina: dam, 6f winner only 2-y-o start, tailed off both 3-y-o outings: fair maiden: should stay 1½m: acts on firm going: sold 22,000 gns. *J. L. Dunlop*

KAYO NOBILE (USA) 3 b. or br.g. Torrential (USA) 117 – Nobile Decretum (USA) **–** (Noble Decree (USA) 127) [2003 –: f12g 8d May 28] no sign of ability: tried blinkered. *T. Keddy*

KAYSERI (IRE) 4 b.c. Alzao (USA) 117 – Ms Calera (USA) (Diesis 133) [2003 107: **103** 10g⁵ 16g* 13.9f⁵ 16g a11f Nov 28] stocky colt: useful performer: won prestige handicap at Nad Al Sheba in April by short head from Celtic Silence: respectable efforts next 2 starts, in listed rated stakes at York (fifth to Hugs Dancer) and Goodwood Cup (raced freely, eighth to Persian Punch): stays 2m: acts on firm and good to soft going: has been bandaged off-hind. *A. Smith, UAE*

KAYSGLORY 4 b.g. Glory of Dancer 121 – Kayartis 57 (Kaytu 112) [2003 12f p12g **–** Jul 23] big, good-topped gelding: second known foal: dam 1½m to 2m winner: tailed off in maidens. *C. A. Dwyer*

KEBREYA (USA) 4 ch.g. Affirmed (USA) – Minifah (USA) 69 (Nureyev (USA) **–** 131) [2003 72: 11.9d f16.2g Nov 10] well-made gelding: modest maiden, lightly raced: well beaten in 2003: tried visored. *R. Ford*

KEDROSS (IRE) 2 ch.f. (Jan 31) King of Kings (IRE) 125 – Nom de Plume (USA) **63** 116 (Nodouble (USA)) [2003 5f⁴ 5d³ 6m⁶ 6g⁴ 6g³ f6f 6g 8.1d Sep 27] €24,000Y: close-coupled filly: half-sister to several winners, including fairly useful 7f winner Pen Point (by Diesis) and 6f winner (including at 2 yrs) Mask Flower (by Dayjur): dam, 1m to 10.5f winner, won Nassau Stakes: modest maiden: left Mrs A. Duffield after second start: should stay 7f: acts on good to soft ground: tends to be slowly away. *R. P. Elliott*

KEELUNG (USA) 2 b.c. (Feb 12) Lear Fan (USA) 130 – Miss Universal (IRE) 107 **66 p** (Lycius (USA) 124) [2003 p8g Nov 2] second foal: dam, maiden in Britain, won US Grade 3 11f event: 11/1, seventh of 10 in maiden at Lingfield, slowly away and racing freely: should be suited by 1¼m/1½m: likely to do better. *M. A. Jarvis*

KEEN HANDS 7 ch.g. Keen 116 – Broken Vow (IRE) (Local Suitor (USA) 128) [2003 **–** –, a74: f7g Jun 9] compact gelding: fair handicapper: wearing cheekpieces, well beaten only 7-y-o start: tried visored. *Mrs N. Macauley*

KEEPERS KNIGHT (IRE) 2 b.c. (Mar 27) Sri Pekan (USA) 117 – Keepers Dawn **62** (IRE) 103 (Alzao (USA) 117) [2003 7m 7m⁵ 7g⁵ Aug 29] 33,000Y: rangy colt: third foal: dam, 2-y-o 6f winner, also second in Fred Darling Stakes: modest form in maidens/claimer: should stay 1¼m. *P. F. I. Cole*

KEEPER'S LODGE (IRE) 2 ch.f. (Apr 24) Grand Lodge (USA) 125 – Gembira **73** (USA) (Alysheba (USA)) [2003 5.1g⁴ 6.1m 6.1g⁵ 6.5d 6d⁴ Sep 26] €11,000Y, 10,000 2-y-o: stocky filly: third foal: closely related to French 1m winner Eolo (by Be My Chief) and half-sister to a winner in France by Bluebird: dam, second at 1m at 2 yrs in France, half-sister to very smart performer up to 1¼m Two Timing: fair maiden: fourth at Nottingham and Haydock: should stay 1m: acts on good to soft going. *B. A. McMahon*

KEEP ON MOVIN' (IRE)   2 b.f. (Mar 20) Danehill Dancer (IRE) 117 – Tormented (USA) (Alleged (USA) 138) [2003 8m 7m⁶ p8g⁵ p8g³ p10g* Nov 29] €28,000Y: tall, rather leggy filly: fifth foal: half-sister to Irish 6f (at 2 yrs) and 1m winner Anna Elise (by Nucleon): dam lightly-raced maiden: fair performer: won maiden at Lingfield, getting up close home: not sure to stay beyond 1¼m: acts on polytrack. *T. G. Mills*   **73**

KEEP THE PEACE (IRE)   5 br.g. Petardia 113 – Eiras Mood 57 (Jalmood (USA) 126) [2003 f9.4s May 12] tall gelding: fair maiden, lightly raced: soundly beaten only 5-y-o start: tried visored. *D. J. Wintle*   **–**

KELBROOK   4 b.g. Unfuwain (USA) 131 – Pidona (Baillamont (USA) 124) [2003 10.5m2 Jul 13] 2,800F, 10,000Y: fourth foal: half-brother to smart 2000 2-y-o 7f winner Tempest (by Zafonic): dam German 1m winner: 12/1, 16 lengths second to Colophony in maiden at Haydock. *A. Bailey*   **45**

KELLS (IRE)   5 b.g. Dilum (USA) 115 – Elizabethan Air 55 (Elegant Air 119) [2003 82, a68: p10g 9g Jul 3] fair handicapper: soundly beaten in 2003. *D. G. Bridgwater*   **–**

KELLY'S TUNE   4 b.f. Alhaarth (IRE) 126 – Roxy Music (IRE) 63 (Song 132) [2003 63d: f6g⁵ Jan 28] smallish, sturdy filly: modest maiden at 3 yrs: well held only 4-y-o start: has worn cheekpieces. *A. P. Jarvis*   **–**

KELPIE (IRE)   4 b.f. Kahyasi 130 – Darrouzett 98 (Darshaan 133) [2003 80: p12g² p10g² p12g p10g p12g* p10g p10g* p10g 10d² 10f⁴ 11.8g² 10.3m⁵ 10m² 10m² 10.5f³ 11m* Sep 19] big, workmanlike filly: fairly useful performer: won handicap in February and minor event in March, both at Lingfield, and handicap at Newbury in September: effective at 1¼m/1½m: acts on polytrack, firm and good to soft going: effective visored or not: usually held up: consistent, though sometimes finds little. *A. M. Balding*   **80 a86**

KELSEAS KOLBY (IRE)   3 b.g. Perugino (USA) 84 – Notre Dame (IRE) (Classic Music (USA)) [2003 64: 6m 6d 8m⁴ f8.5g 8s 8m 7m² 7m* 7m² 8g Oct 22] leggy gelding: fair performer: won selling handicap at Leicester in October: stays 1m: acts on soft and good to firm ground: wore headgear last 6 starts: carries head high. *J. A. Glover*   **66**

KELSEY ROSE   4 b.f. Most Welcome 131 – Duxyana (IRE) (Cyrano de Bergerac 120) [2003 97: f6s p8g⁵ Mar 15] leggy filly: fairly useful performer: stays easy 1m: acts on all-weather, firm and soft going: tried visored: edgy sort: tends to hang right: sold 24,000 gns. *P. D. Evans*   **84**

KELTIC RAINBOW (IRE)   2 b.f. (May 13) Spectrum (IRE) 126 – Secrets of Honour (Belmez (USA) 131) [2003 6d f7s f8.5g³ f8.5g³ Nov 17] leggy filly: fifth foal: half-sister to 4-y-o Double Ransom and 5-y-o Another Secret: dam unraced half-sister to high-class sprinter Mr Brooks and to dam of Middle Park winner First Trump: modest maiden: will be suited by 1¼m+: acts on fibresand. *D. Haydn Jones*   **58**

KELUCIA (IRE)   2 ch.f. (Mar 18) Grand Lodge (USA) 125 – Karachi (SPA) (Zino 127) [2003 7.2g⁶ 7m² 8f* 8.1g² 8m* 7m³ 7m³ 8g⁴ Nov 1] 21,000Y: leggy filly: has scope: third foal: sister to fairly useful Spanish/French 7f/1m winner La Moraleja: dam won 5 races in Spain at 2 yrs: useful performer: won minor events at Newcastle in August and Ayr in September: good third in listed race (to Top Romance) and Rockfel Stakes (beaten 1¾ lengths by Cairns) at Newmarket: should stay 1¼m: acts on firm going: edgy sort (sometimes early to post/flashes tail) but seems genuine. *J. S. Goldie*   **101**

KENLEY LASS (IRE)   3 b.f. Danetime (IRE) 121 – Big Fandango (Bigstone (IRE) 126) [2003 63, a52: p6g⁴ f7s p7g³ p7g³ 6m⁴ 5m⁵ 6.1m⁶ 5.7m 6g 7.1g² 6f⁶ 6g 6.1m 7f 6m 6m⁶ 5m 7g⁵ 6.1m* 5.7f 6d Oct 31] quite attractive filly: modest performer: claimed from Mrs P. Dutfield fourth start: won handicap at Nottingham in September: best around 6f: acts on all-weather and good to firm going, possibly not on softer than good: wore cheekpieces last 6 starts: sometimes slowly away/edges left: none too reliable. *M. D. I. Usher*   **59 a52**

KENNET   8 b.g. Kylian (USA) – Marwell Mitzi 50 (Interrex (CAN)) [2003 61: p13g Feb 12] leggy, plain gelding: one-time fair handicapper: well held only 8-y-o start: tried blinkered/visored. *P. D. Cundell*   **–**

KENNY THE TRUTH (IRE)   4 b.g. Robellino (USA) 127 – Just Blink (IRE) (Fairy King (USA)) [2003 –: f8g f7g f8s² f8g⁴ f8g⁵ 11m 8g 10g f6g Dec 9] robust gelding: modest maiden: left A. Dickman after seventh start: should stay 1¼m: acts on fibresand, no form on turf: has reportedly had breathing problem, and tongue tied final outing. *Mrs J. Candlish*   **– a53**

KENSINGTON (IRE)   2 b.c. (Mar 19) Cape Cross (IRE) 129 – March Star (IRE) 109   **75**
(Mac's Imp (USA) 116) [2003 5d³ 6d³ 5f 6d⁶ 5g⁴ Jul 25] 45,000Y: leggy colt: second
foal: dam 6f winner, including at 2 yrs: fair maiden: third at Tipperary and the Curragh:
hampered at Royal Ascot next time: stays 6f: acts on good to soft ground: bit below form
in blinkers last 2 starts: sold 26,000 gns. *D. K. Weld, Ireland*

KENT   8 b.g. Kylian (USA) – Precious Caroline (IRE) 60 (The Noble Player (USA)   **–**
126) [2003 69, a78: p13g f16s² f16.2g* f16s* f16.2g* 18g 16m f12g⁵ 16g Oct 24] very   **a88**
big gelding: fairly useful handicapper on all-weather, fair on turf: won at Wolverhampton
(2) and Southwell (eighth course success) in February/March: effective at 1½m to 2m:
acted on firm going, good to soft and fibresand: blinkered/visored: usually held up: sometimes ran in snatches/hung/found little: dead. *P. D. Cundell*

KENTMERE (IRE)   2 b.c. (Apr 16) Efisio 120 – Addaya (IRE) (Persian Bold 123)   **72**
[2003 7.2f² 7.1m² 6m⁵ 8d p8g Nov 2] €120,000Y: good-topped colt: fifth foal: brother to
3-y-o Penny Cross and half-brother to 2 winners, notably 5-y-o Priors Lodge: dam, ran
once, out of half-sister to smart 7f/1m performer Hadeer: fair maiden: stays 1m: acts on
firm and good to soft going: tends to look none too genuine. *M. Johnston*

KENTUCKY BLUE (IRE)   3 b.g. Revoque (IRE) 122 – Delta Town (USA) (Sangla-   **93**
more (USA) 126) [2003 90: 8.5m 10.5s* 10.4f⁶ 11.9m³ 9.9m 10.3g⁵ 10.5d⁵ 12d Nov 8]
lengthy, good-topped gelding: fairly useful handicapper: won at Haydock in May: stays
1½m: acts on soft and good to firm going, ran poorly on firm: often races prominently:
won over hurdles in November. *T. D. Easterby*

KENTUCKY BULLET (USA)   7 b.g. Housebuster (USA) – Exactly So (Caro 133)   **38 §**
[2003 –§, a51§: f11g f12g³ f12g* f12g* 11m f12g⁶ f12s* 11.6g 10m⁴ f12g² f12g⁵ Dec 22]   **a56 §**
leggy, angular gelding: modest performer on all-weather, poor on turf: won handicaps at
Southwell and Wolverhampton in March and claimer at Wolverhampton in July: barely
stays 14.8f: acts on fibresand, good to firm and good to soft ground: tried blinkered/
tongue tied earlier in career: ungenuine. *A. G. Newcombe*

KENTUCKY KING (USA)   3 b.g. Tale of The Cat (USA) 113 – Anna's Honor (USA)   **86**
(Alleged (USA) 138) [2003 91p: 8g⁴ May 29] strong, lengthy gelding: fairly useful form
in just 2 races: won maiden at Doncaster at 2 yrs: creditable fourth to Millafonic in minor
event at Ayr, taking strong hold, on return: should stay beyond 1m: sold only 5,500 gns in
October. *M. Johnston*

KEPLER (USA)   4 ch.c. Spinning World (USA) 130 – Perfect Arc (USA) 120 (Brown   **102**
Arc (USA)) [2003 97: p10g f12g* 12m⁴ 12d⁵ May 8] strong colt: useful performer: won
handicap at Wolverhampton in March by 5 lengths from Glory Quest: creditable efforts
in listed races at Longchamp last 2 starts: stayed 1½m: acted on heavy going, good to firm
and all-weather: blinkered (folded) once at 3 yrs: dead. *P. F. I. Cole*

KERALA (IRE)   4 b.f. Mujadil (USA) 119 – Kalisz (IRE) (Polish Precedent (USA)   **–**
131) [2003 –: 6d 6f 6g Apr 30] small filly: no sign of ability: tried tongue tied. *Don Enrico
Incisa*

KERENSAS PRINCE   4 b.g. Rislan (USA) 57 – Skippy (Emarati (USA) 74) [2003   **–**
–: f9.4s 10.2m Apr 29] soundly beaten in sellers. *A. D. Smith*

KERNEL DOWERY (IRE)   3 b.g. Sri Pekan (USA) 117 – Lady Dowery (USA)   **72**
(Manila (USA)) [2003 74: 8f⁴ 10.2m⁵ p10g 10m³ 10m³ 10f² 10.1g 10.2m 10.1m⁴
10d³ Oct 31] fair maiden handicapper: stays 1¼m: acts on polytrack, firm and good to
soft going: often wears cheekpieces: often races prominently: sometimes hangs left.
P. W. Harris

KERRS PINK   2 b.f. (Feb 25) Averti (IRE) 117 – Julietta Mia (USA) 72 (Woodman   **– §**
(USA) 126) [2003 5.1m⁵ 5m 6m⁶ 7.5m 5.3m⁶ f5g Oct 4] 800F, 11,000Y: compact filly:
second foal: dam 2-y-o 7f winner: little form: tried blinkered/in cheekpieces: ungenuine.
Mrs L. Stubbs

KESHENA FALLS (IRE)   3 b.f. Desert Prince (IRE) 130 – Menominee (Soviet Star   **60 ?**
(USA) 128) [2003 7m⁶ 8.3g³ 8.3d 8m 8m⁵ Oct 2] IR 16,000Y: workmanlike filly: fourth
foal: half-sister to smart 1m winner Touch And Fly (by Catrail) and 11f to 1¾m winner
Count de Money (by Last Tycoon): dam unraced half-sister to very smart French middle-
distance stayer Mersey and smart French middle-distance filly Muncie: seemingly
modest form in maidens first 2 starts: well beaten after: stays 1m: unraced on extremes of
ground: sold 6,000 gns. *R. Guest*

KESHYA   2 b.f. (Jan 23) Mtoto 134 – Liberatrice (FR) (Assert 134) [2003 6g 6m 6g⁶   **66**
8d² Oct 31] leggy filly: fourth foal: half-sister to 3-y-o Polka Princess: dam maiden half-
sister to smart French 1989 2-y-o 5.5f winner Zinarelle: fair maiden: second in nursery at

Brighton, carrying head high/edging left under pressure: better at 1m than 6f: best effort on good to soft going. *D. J. Coakley*

KETAN 3 ch.g. Zilzal (USA) 137 – Vivid Imagination (USA) (Raise A Man (USA)) **95** [2003 93: 8.1m 7d 7m 6.1f² 6d⁶ Jul 26] good-topped gelding: fluent mover: useful performer: left M. Johnston after second start: best effort when sixth to Ground Zero in handicap at Newcastle: effective at 6f, barely stays 1m: acts on firm ground, possibly not on good to soft: free-going sort: played up at start and hung left for both wins: sent to Macau. *P. A. Blockley*

KEW 4 b.g. Royal Applause 124 – Cutleaf 81 (Kris 135) [2003 46: p12g p12g 11.9m – 11.6m Jul 14] poor maiden: well held in 2003, leaving J. Bridger £2,100 after third start: tried in headgear. *C. L. Popham*

KEW THE MUSIC 3 b.g. Botanic (USA) – Harmonia (Glint of Gold 128) [2003 **74** p7g⁴ 5.1m 6g⁴ 5m* 6m 6m 7m 6g Oct 6] lengthy gelding: third reported foal: half-brother to 2 winners, including useful 1998 2-y-o 7f winner Thank Heavens (by Theatrical Charmer), later 6f/7f winner in Hong Kong: dam unraced: fair performer: won maiden at Newcastle in May: effective at 5f/6f: raced only on good/good to firm ground on turf. *M. R. Channon*

KEY OF GOLD (IRE) 2 b.c. (Feb 4) Key of Luck (USA) 126 – Damaslin (Camden **78** Town 125) [2003 5m³ 5m f6s* f7g² 6g Oct 13] IR 5,800F, €6,000Y: close-coupled colt: half-brother to 3 winners abroad: dam 2-y-o 7f winner in Ireland: fair performer: made all in maiden at Wolverhampton (gave odd flash of tail) in July: good second in nursery there: will stay 1m: acts on fibresand, some promise on turf. *D. Carroll*

KEY ONEOTHREE (IRE) 3 b.f. Entrepreneur 123 – Wallflower (Polar Falcon **55** (USA) 126) [2003 59: 8m 10m 9.2d³ 8.2d² p12g 11m 12f Jul 16] lengthy, angular filly: modest maiden: claimed from A. Berry third start: stayed 1m, not 1¼m: acted on all-weather and good to soft ground: tried in cheekpieces: dead. *M. Johnston*

KEY PARTNERS (IRE) 2 b.g. (Apr 20) Key of Luck (USA) 126 – Teacher Preacher **74 p** (IRE) 37 (Taufan (USA) 119) [2003 6m⁵ 6f² Oct 10] IR 6,000F, €3,500Y, 6,000 2-y-o: quite good-topped gelding: second foal: dam Irish 7f winner: fair form in maidens at Newmarket (slowly away) and York (10 lengths second to Nero's Return): will be suited by 7f/1m: should progress. *P. A. Blockley*

KHABFAIR 2 b.c. (Mar 10) Intikhab (USA) 135 – Ruby Affair (IRE) 68 (Night Shift **94** (USA)) [2003 6m³ p6g* p6g² Oct 15] good-bodied colt: second foal: dam, second at 7f, half-sister to 2000 Guineas winner Island Sands: fairly useful form: won maiden at Lingfield in October: best effort when second to Doohulla in minor event there, though found little: not sure to stay beyond 6f. *Mrs A. J. Perrett*

KHABIR (USA) 3 br.c. Gulch (USA) – Jafn 104 (Sharpo 132) [2003 86: 7m² 7g 7.1m⁵ **78** a7f Nov 28] good-bodied colt: just fair maiden in 2003: left B. Hanbury before final outing: stays 1m: unraced on extremes of going on turf: blinkered/visored last 2 outings. *D. Watson, UAE*

KHAIZARANA 3 b.f. Alhaarth (IRE) 126 – Ta Rib (USA) 116 (Mr Prospector (USA)) **90** [2003 72p: 7m* 8g³ 10m 10.5d Sep 27] angular good-topped filly: fairly useful performer: won maiden at Newmarket in April: creditable efforts in listed races next 2 starts, 2 lengths third to Fantasize at Ascot on first occasion: stayed 1¼m: unraced on extremes of going: visits Mujahid. *E. A. L. Dunlop*

KHALIDIA (USA) 2 b.c. (Apr 5) Boundary (USA) 117 – Maniches Slew (USA) (Slew **59 p** O' Gold (USA)) [2003 6d Nov 8] $12,000Y, 84,000 2-y-o: good-bodied colt: has scope: third foal: half-brother to winner in USA by Glitterman: dam maiden in USA: 25/1, eighth of 13 in maiden at Doncaster, some late headway not knocked about: will do better. *M. A. Magnusson*

KHALKISSA (USA) 3 b.f. Diesis 133 – Khamsin (USA) (Mr Prospector (USA)) **98** [2003 63p: a8f* 8m* 8s⁶ Nov 1] neat filly: useful performer: won maiden at Nad Al Sheba in March and minor event at Leicester (comfortably beat Vicereine 1½ lengths, making all) in October: below-form sixth of 7 in listed race at Saint-Cloud final start: left Godolphin after: stays 1m: acts on dirt and good to firm ground: has been tongue tied. *Saeed bin Suroor*

KHALYANEE (IRE) 2 b.f. (Mar 26) Prospector J (USA) – Dead End (USA) (Cox's – Ridge (USA)) [2003 6d p7g Aug 28] third known foal: half-sister to a winner in USA by Geiger Counter: dam unraced out of half-sister to US Grade 1 7f winner Mining: well held in maiden at Salisbury and minor event at Lingfield (tongue tied). *L. A. Dace*

KHANJAR (USA)   3 ch.g. Kris S (USA) – Alyssum (USA) (Storm Cat (USA)) [2003   **76**
96+: a8f² 8.1d² May 26] sturdy, attractive gelding: useful in maidens at 2 yrs: below form
in similar events at Nad Al Sheba (only start for Saeed bin Suroor) and Chepstow (odds
on) in 2003: stays 1m. *D. R. Loder*

KHARAK (FR)   4 gr.g. Danehill (USA) 126 – Khariyda (FR) 118 (Shakapour 125)   **–**
[2003 13.1m Sep 20] half-brother to several winners, notably smart French performer up
to 15f Kharizmi (by Lashkari): dam, won around 1¼m (including E. P. Taylor Stakes),
stayed 1½m: ran 4 times in France for A. de Royer Dupre in 2002: tailed off in handicap
on only British outing: blinkered on debut. *Mrs S. C. Bradburne*

KHAYYAM (USA)   5 b.g. Affirmed (USA) – True Celebrity (USA) (Lyphard (USA)   **–**
132) [2003 71d: 8m 8g 11.5g⁶ 10.5m 11.5g Jul 3] well-made gelding: fairly useful at 3 yrs
but has deteriorated markedly: tried in headgear/tongue tie: inconsistent. *S. Gollings*

KHELEYF (USA)   2 br.c. (Jan 11) Green Desert (USA) 127 – Society Lady (USA) 75   **114**
(Mr Prospector (USA)) [2003 5m* 5m² 6g* 6m Oct 3] big, quite good-topped colt: has
scope: brother to smart 1998 2-y-o 5f/6f winner Bint Allayl, closely related to useful 2000
2-y-o 6f winner Nasmatt (by Danehill), and half-brother to 2 winners by Mtoto: dam, ran
4 times at 2 yrs, half-sister to smart US performer up to 8.5f Time Bandit out of champion
Canadian filly La Voyageuse: smart performer: impressive winner of maiden at York in
May and minor event at Doncaster (edgy, beat Golden Sahara 1½ lengths) in September:
odds on when 1¾ lengths second to Russian Valour in Norfolk Stakes at Royal Ascot:
only tenth in Middle Park Stakes at Newmarket: not sure to stay much beyond 6f:
sometimes wears crossed noseband/has 2 handlers: joined Saeed bin Suroor. *D. R. Loder*

KHUCHN (IRE)   7 b.h. Unfuwain (USA) 131 – Stay Sharpe (USA) (Sharpen Up 127)   **39**
[2003 42: 10.1d 12m⁶ 10g Apr 30] strong, good-topped horse: poor handicapper: stays
1½m: acts on fibresand, heavy and good to firm going: has worn tongue strap: often
makes running. *M. Brittain*

Sheikh Ahmed Al Maktoum's "Kheleyf"

KHULOOD (USA) 3 ch.f. Storm Cat (USA) – Elle Seule (USA) 122 (Exclusive **103** Native (USA)) [2003 102p: 7g* 8g 6f 6m² 7d⁶ 6m⁵ Oct 16] tall, leggy filly: most fluent mover with a light action: useful performer: won Shadwell Stud Nell Gwyn Stakes at Newmarket (dictated pace to beat Cala 2 lengths) in April: creditable efforts last 3 starts, 2 lengths second to Torosay Spring in Summer Stakes at York on first of them and fifth to Frizzante in listed race at Newmarket on final one: best form at 6f/7f (well beaten in 1000 Guineas over 1m): acted on firm and good to soft going: carried head awkwardly when disappointing second 2-y-o outing: visits Green Desert. *J. L. Dunlop*

KHUZDAR (IRE) 4 ch.g. Definite Article 121 – Mariyda (IRE) (Vayrann 133) [2003 **72 d** 83: p12g f9.4g p16g 16m⁶ 11.9g 11.5g⁶ 14.1m² 12.6m⁴ 12.1d 14.1m⁴ 11.8m³ 12d⁴ 15.8m³ 11.9f⁴ 16.2m 12.1m 10.9m 12.1d³ 12d⁴ 11.7f* 11.9m⁴ 10d 12g⁶ p12g⁴ f11g Nov 25] fair handicapper: only modest form at best after tenth start, but won at Bath in October: stays 1¾m: acts on polytrack, firm and good to soft going: has been slowly away/carried head awkwardly: none too consistent. *M. R. Channon*

KIBRYAA (USA) 2 ch.c. (Mar 2) Silver Hawk (USA) 123 – Fleur de Nuit (USA) **79** (Woodman (USA) 126) [2003 7m 7m² 7.1m* Sep 13] $50,000F, €280,000Y: good-topped colt: third foal: brother to 3-y-o Dhabyan: dam, US 6f (at 2 yrs) to 9f (Grade 3 event) winner, out of Poule d'Essai des Pouliches winner Pearl Bracelet: fair form in maidens: won at Musselburgh by short head from Kentmere, leading over 1f out: should stay at least 1m. *M. A. Jarvis*

KICKBACK 3 b.g. High Kicker (USA) – Moniques Venture (Midyan (USA) 124) **–** [2003 –: f11s p10g⁶ f7g⁶ 8m p10g Jul 9] little form. *B. A. Pearce*

KID'Z'PLAY (IRE) 7 b.g. Rudimentary (USA) 118 – Saka Saka (Camden Town **73** 125) [2003 72: f12g 10.3g⁴ 12.3m 12.4m 12.1m* 13d³ 11.1d² 12g³ 12.1g⁵ 13f⁶ 12.1g⁴ Jul 24] fair handicapper: won at Hamilton in April: stays 13f: acts on any going: sometimes early to post: usually makes running. *J. S. Goldie*

KIER PARK (IRE) 6 b.h. Foxhound (USA) 103 – Merlannah (IRE) (Shy Groom **107** (USA)) [2003 112: p5g² 5g May 3] tall, quite good-topped horse: useful performer: reportedly split pastern after only 3-y-o outing: length second to Peruvian Chief in minor event at Lingfield on reappearance: reportedly broke blood vessel only subsequent start: effective at 5f to 6.5f: acts on polytrack, soft and good to firm going: has worn cheekpieces: none too consistent. *M. A. Jarvis*

KIKOI (IRE) 3 b.f. Alzao (USA) 117 – Kimono (IRE) (Machiavellian (USA) 123) **–** [2003 –: 7m May 15] well beaten in maiden/claimer. *D. R. C. Elsworth*

KILBRIDE KING (IRE) 8 ch.g. Shalford (IRE) 124§ – Marj (Most Welcome 131) **66** [2003 78: f9.4g p10g p10g p7g p8g⁴ 9.7m Apr 4] fair handicapper: left J. Kiely in Ireland after final 7-y-o start: stays 1¼m: acts on firm ground and polytrack. *I. A. Wood*

KILCULLEN LASS (IRE) 2 ch.f. (Apr 26) Fayruz 116 – Foretell (Tirol 127) [2003 **–** p7g 7m f7g⁶ Oct 20] strong, workmanlike filly: third foal: dam unraced out of sister to smart French sprinter Reasonable: signs of only a little ability in maidens/seller. *P. D. Evans*

KILKENNY CASTLE (IRE) 7 b.g. Grand Lodge (USA) 125 – Shahaamh (IRE) 85 **71** (Reference Point 139) [2003 91: 10g 10d 12g⁵ 10.1d Jul 3] big gelding: just fair form in 2003: stayed 1½m: acted on polytrack, good to firm and good to soft going: held up: dead. *S. Dow*

KILLALA (IRE) 3 b.g. Among Men (USA) 124 – Hat And Gloves (Wolver Hollow **72** 126) [2003 66: 7d⁶ 6.1g⁵ 6f³ 7f* 7g 7m⁴ 7m 7g⁴ 7.1m³ 7m⁶ Oct 25] fair performer: won maiden at Catterick in July: stays 7f: acts on firm and good to soft ground: sold 15,000 gns. *M. H. Tompkins*

KILLER BEE (IRE) 3 b.g. Lake Coniston (IRE) 131 – So Far Away 48 (Robellino **–** (USA) 127) [2003 5g 5m 9.3m Sep 4] IR 4,000F, IR 5,000Y: plain gelding: fourth living foal: dam lightly raced Irish maiden: well held in maidens. *R. A. Fahey*

KILLERBY NICKO 2 ch.g. (Mar 3) Pivotal 124 – Bit of A Tart (Distant Relative **62** 128) [2003 5m 6g Jul 31] 20,000Y: heavy-topped gelding: second foal: half-brother to 3-y-o Bishops Finger: dam unraced: much better effort in maidens (modest form) when eighth at Beverley on debut: should stay at least 6f. *T. D. Easterby*

KILLINALLAN 2 b.f. (Apr 24) Vettori (IRE) 119 – Babycham Sparkle 80 (So Blessed **70 p** 130) [2003 p7g⁵ Oct 30] 20,000Y: lengthy filly: half-sister to several winners, including useful winner around 5f (including at 2 yrs) Deep Finesse (by Reprimand) and 3-y-o

Ambonnay: dam 2-y-o 5f/6f winner: 16/1, fifth of 9 to Zerlina in maiden at Lingfield, running green: will probably stay 1m: should do better. *H. Morrison*

KILLING JOKE 3 b.c. Double Trigger (IRE) 123 – Fleeting Vision (IRE) 79 (Vision (USA)) [2003 73?: 11.1g p16g⁶ 13.8d f16.2s* Dec 6] lengthy colt: fairly useful performer, lightly raced: improved to win handicap at Wolverhampton in December by 11 lengths from Radiant Bride: stays 2m: acts on all-weather and firm ground. *J. G. Given* **80**

KILLING ME SOFTLY 2 b.g. (Apr 10) Kingsinger (IRE) 94 – Slims Lady 59 (Theatrical Charmer 114) [2003 f7g f8.5s* Dec 31] £400Y: first foal: dam, maiden, effective at 1¼m/1½m: much better effort (modest form) when winning seller at Wolverhampton: will stay at least 1¼m: very slowly away on debut. *J. Gallagher* **55**

KILLOCH PLACE (IRE) 2 b.g. (Apr 8) Compton Place 125 – Hibernica (IRE) 69 (Law Society (USA) 130) [2003 5m 6f⁵ 6d 7g Sep 13] 18,000Y: tall, leggy gelding: third foal: half-brother to Italian 2002 2-y-o 1¼m winner Irish Jewel (by Vettori): dam, maiden, should have been suited by further than 1m: signs of only a little ability in maidens/nursery: sold 7,500 gns, then gelded. *J. A. Glover* **–**

KILMEENA LAD 7 b.g. Minshaanshu Amad (USA) 109§ – Kilmeena Glen (Beveled (USA)) [2003 64: p7g p6g p7g Dec 10] good-quartered gelding: fair handicapper: effective at 6f to easy 1m: acts on polytrack and any turf going: tried blinkered: tends to edge left: has run well when sweating. *J. C. Fox* **76**

KILMEENA ROSE 3 ch.f. Compton Place 125 – Kilmeena Glen (Beveled (USA)) [2003 6g 7m 6g Jul 4] unfurnished filly: fourth foal: half-sister to 7-y-o Kilmeena Lad: dam unraced: slowly away and well beaten in maidens at Salisbury. *J. C. Fox* **–**

KILMEENA STAR 5 b.h. So Factual (USA) 120 – Kilmeena Glen (Beveled (USA)) [2003 –: p7g³ 6g 6.1g 6m³ 5.1f 5.7f³ 6f p6g⁶ Dec 2] poor maiden: stays 7f: acts on firm going and polytrack. *J. C. Fox* **43**

KILMINCHY LADY (IRE) 2 b.f. (Mar 1) Cape Cross (IRE) 129 – Lace Flower (Old Vic 136) [2003 7f f8.5g p8g⁶ Dec 20] IR 20,000F, €10,000Y: ex-Irish filly: second foal: half-sister to a winner in Italy by Spectrum: dam, French 10.5f to 13f winner, out of half-sister to very smart French middle-distance stayer Light The Lights: well held in maidens/minor event: trained on debut by D. Weld. *W. R. Muir* **–**

KILMORY 4 b.f. Puissance 110 – Lizzy Cantle 52 (Homing 130) [2003 8.5m 13.1g 10m Jun 24] little form. *J. Cullinan* **–**

KIMOE WARRIOR 5 ch.g. Royal Abjar (USA) 121 – Thewaari (USA) 68 (Eskimo (USA)) [2003 f12g Jan 23] tall, close-coupled gelding: poor maiden on Flat, well held only 5-y-o start: poor winning hurdler. *M. Mullineaux* **–**

KINABALU (IRE) 3 b.g. Danetime (IRE) 121 – Highly Fashionable (IRE) 68 (Polish Precedent (USA) 131) [2003 63: p8g⁵ p10g f9.4g³ f8.5s⁶ p7g⁴ 8.3g* 8.2m Apr 21] lengthy gelding: modest performer: won seller at Windsor in April: stays 8.5f: acts on all-weather, unraced on extremes of going on turf: visored (below form) twice: sold £1,500. *J. S. Moore* **56**

KINBRACE 2 b.f. (Mar 6) Kirkwall 118 – Cache (Bustino 136) [2003 7f 6d⁵ 6m Sep 5] 9,000Y: smallish, close-coupled filly: seventh foal: half-sister to 3 winners, including fairly useful 1½m and 15f winner Swan Hunter (by Sharrood) and 7-y-o Lunar Lord: dam lightly-raced close relative to useful middle-distance performer Black Monday: signs of ability in maidens: tongue tied on debut: should do better at 3 yrs, probably at 1¼m/1½m. *M. P. Tregoning* **– p**

KINCOB (USA) 3 b.f. Kingmambo (USA) 125 – Gossamer (USA) (Seattle Slew (USA)) [2003 63: 8m² 10s Nov 3] leggy filly: just modest form at best in 2003: should stay 1¼m: acts on good to firm ground. *J. Nicol* **55**

KINDA CUTE 2 b.f. (Mar 9) Bahamian Bounty 116 – Feiticeira (USA) 79 (Deposit Ticket (USA)) [2003 6g 7m 7.1m 6m p8g Nov 22] strong filly: first foal: dam, ran 3 times (second at 1m on debut), granddaughter of Breeders' Cup Sprint runner-up Pine Tree Lane: well held, including in seller. *M. Quinn* **–**

KIND EMPEROR 6 br.g. Emperor Jones (USA) 119 – Kind Lady 56 (Kind of Hush 118) [2003 59§: 7m* 10.1g* 7g⁵ 10.1m* 8f⁵ 10.1m Sep 17] leggy, sparely-made gelding: fair performer: raced only at Yarmouth in 2003: won handicaps in April (dead-heated) and May and minor event in August: effective at 7f to 1¼m: acts on firm and soft going (well held on all-weather): visored twice, refusing to race first occasion: tends to hang right: races prominently. *P. L. Gilligan* **69**

KIND (IRE) 2 b.f. (Apr 21) Danehill (USA) 126 – Rainbow Lake 113 (Rainbow Quest (USA) 134) [2003 6m³ 6m⁴ Oct 4] strong, good-topped filly: seventh foal: half-sister to 3 winners, notably 3-y-o Powerscourt and smart 13f/1¾m winner Brimming (by Generous): dam 1¼m/1½m (Lancashire Oaks) winner: favourite, fair form in maidens at Kempton (green) and Newmarket (fourth to Valjarv), slowly away both times: will be suited by at least 1m: likely to do better at 3 yrs. *R. Charlton* — **77 p**

KINDLELIGHT DEBUT 3 b.f. Groom Dancer (USA) 128 – Dancing Debut 83 (Polar Falcon (USA) 126) [2003 71: 8.2g⁴ 7g² 8g² 7m* 7m⁶ 7g² 8.3g³ 7f* 7m p7g Oct 3] smallish filly: fairly useful handicapper: won at Salisbury in June and Newmarket in August: very best efforts at 7f: acts on polytrack and firm ground, unraced on softer than good: usually races prominently. *D. K. Ivory* — **84**

KINDNESS 3 ch.f. Indian Ridge 123 – Kissing Gate (USA) 62 (Easy Goer (USA)) [2003 64: 9.9m 10m⁶ 8g 7g⁵ 7.1d 7m⁵ 8f⁶ 8f p8g 8f³ Oct 17] modest maiden handicapper: should stay 1¼m: acts on firm and soft going. *A. D. W. Pinder* — **60**

KING CARNIVAL (USA) 2 ch.c. (Feb 24) King of Kings (IRE) 125 – Miss Waki Club (USA) (Miswaki (USA) 124) [2003 6g 6g⁵ 6m* 6f* 6g² Aug 10] €160,000Y: close-coupled colt: fourth foal: half-brother to useful French performer up to 1m Six Acts (by Night Shift): dam won in USA: fairly useful performer: won maiden at Haydock in June and nursery at Ascot (by ½ length from Spring Dancer) in July: will probably stay 7f: acts on firm going. *R. Hannon* — **92**

KING CREOLE 4 b.g. Slip Anchor 136 – Myrrh (Salse (USA) 128) [2003 72: 11.7m 12g 13.3m 12.1g 16m 11.9m Oct 2] strong, well-made gelding: fair maiden at 2/3 yrs: well held in 2003. *Ian Williams* — **–**

KING DARSHAAN 3 b.g. Darshaan 133 – Urchin (IRE) (Fairy King (USA)) [2003 74: p10g³ 10g 11m p12g Oct 27] leggy, rather unfurnished gelding: fair maiden: stays 1½m: acts on polytrack, little form on turf: twice slowly away at 2 yrs. *P. R. Hedger* — **? a76**

KING DAVID 4 b.g. Distant Relative 128 – Fleur Rouge 71 (Pharly (FR) 130) [2003 76: f7s⁴ f7s p8g³ 8.1m⁶ 8m³ 8m f8.5g p7g³ p7g f7g Dec 8] well-made gelding: fair performer on all-weather, modest on turf: left J. Osborne 5,200 gns after third start: stays 8.5f: acts on all-weather and firm ground: often races prominently: has raced freely/looked none too keen. *D. Burchell* — **59 a69**

KINGDOM COME (IRE) 2 b.c. (Feb 17) Foxhound (USA) 103 – Garter Royale (IRE) 75 (Garde Royale 120) [2003 5.1m⁶ 6m* 5f 7m⁵ 6m 8.3g² 8m 8d² Nov 7] €18,000Y: sturdy colt: fluent mover: fourth foal: dam, placed at 1¼m to 1¾m in Ireland, closely related to smart Irish performer up to 9f Island Reef: fairly useful performer: made all in maiden at Salisbury in June, hanging left: good second in nursery at Windsor and minor event at Doncaster (run of race when beaten neck by Blue Monday): stays 1m: acts on good to firm and good to soft ground: none too consistent. *S. Kirk* — **93 +**

KING EGBERT (FR) 2 b.c. (Mar 8) Fasliyev (USA) 120 – Exocet (USA) (Deposit Ticket (USA)) [2003 5.6f³ 6g 6d 6m Sep 16] lengthy, good-bodied colt: third foal: half-brother to 4-y-o Shot To Fame and 3-y-o Spinola: dam, sprint winner in USA, out of half-sister to Prix du Cadran winner Molesnes: fair maiden: third at Doncaster, only form: looked none too keen in blinkers final start: not sure to stay much beyond 6f. *J. L. Dunlop* — **66 d**

KING EIDER 4 b. or br.g. Mtoto 134 – Hen Harrier 94 (Polar Falcon (USA) 126) [2003 96: 12m⁵ 13.9m⁶ 16.2f 16g³ Oct 24] smallish, good-topped gelding: useful handicapper: best effort of 2003 when narrowly-beaten third to Misternando at Newbury final start: stays 2m: unraced on heavy going, acts on any other: usually races prominently: sold 42,000 gns, joined N. Henderson. *J. L. Dunlop* — **97**

KINGFISHER EVE (IRE) 5 b.m. Hamas (IRE) 125§ – Houwara (IRE) (Darshaan 133) [2003 8m 12.1d 15.8m Oct 7] big mare: poor maiden. *C. Grant* — **–**

KING FLYER (IRE) 7 b.g. Ezzoud (IRE) 126 – Al Guswa 98 (Shernazar 131) [2003 83, a72: 16g² 16m⁵ 16m⁴ 16m 14f 18m⁴ 16.1m* 16.1m⁴ 14.8m⁶ 13.9m 16m³ 16.2f⁶ Sep 27] leggy, workmanlike gelding: fairly useful handicapper on turf, fair when last ran on all-weather: won at Newmarket in July: finds 1¾m a minimum nowadays, and stays 2¼m: acts on firm and good to soft going: blinkered once: often tongue tied: held up: reliable. *Miss J. Feilden* — **85 a–**

KINGHAM 3 ch.g. Desert Prince (IRE) 130 – Marie de Flandre (FR) 109 (Crystal Palace (FR) 132) [2003 86p: 10s 8m Aug 16] leggy, lengthy gelding: fairly useful winner at 2 yrs: well held for new trainer in 2003 (raced freely second outing). *Mrs Mary Hambro* — **–**

KING HARSON 4 b.g. Greensmith 121 – Safari Park 43 (Absalom 128) [2003 88: 6m **90**
7g 7.1m 6m⁵ 6m 6m 7m* 6m 7m* 7.1g⁶ 7m³ 7g³ 7d* Nov 4] close-coupled, good-bodied
gelding: fairly useful handicapper: won at Newcastle in August, York in September and
Catterick in November, best effort when beating Qualitair Wings by head in last-named:
effective at 6f to 7.5f: acts on any ground: often blinkered/visored: usually races prominently. *J. D. Bethell*

KING HESPERUS (USA) 2 b.c. (May 14) Kingmambo (USA) 125 – Victorica **102**
(USA) (Exbourne (USA) 125) [2003 7m² 6d* 7m³ Jul 10] $330,000Y: smallish, useful-
looking colt: first foal: dam, US 6f (at 2 yrs) to 8.5f (minor stakes) winner, half-sister to
Poule d'Essai des Poulains runner-up Noble Minstrel: useful form: first past post in
maiden at Gowran (demoted for causing interference) and listed race at Leopardstown
(beat Jemmy's Brother by 2½ lengths) in June: creditable 1½ lengths third of 9 to Kings
Point in Superlative Stakes at Newmarket: will probably stay 1m. *A. P. O'Brien, Ireland*

KINGKOHLER (IRE) 4 b.g. King's Theatre (IRE) 128 – Legit (IRE) (Runnett 125) **82 p**
[2003 73: f12g* 11.1d* May 16] IR 24,000Y: seventh foal: half-brother to 1m/9f winner
Champion Lodge (by Sri Pekan), later smart up to 1¾m in USA, and 7-y-o Charles
Spencelayh: dam Irish maiden: fairly useful performer, lightly raced: trained by E. Lynam
in Ireland at 3 yrs: won maiden at Wolverhampton in February and minor event at
Hamilton (by 5 lengths, clearly best effort) in May: stays 1½m: acts on fibresand, raced
only on good or softer ground on turf: open to further improvement. *K. A. Morgan*

KING MAXIMUS (USA) 2 b.g. (May 26) King of Kings (IRE) 125 – Excedent **79 p**
(USA) (Exceller (USA) 129) [2003 8g p8g* Nov 2] $125,000Y: rather leggy, quite attrac-
tive gelding: half-brother to several winners, including smart French 1¼m/1½m winner
Beyond The Waves (by Ocean Crest): dam unraced: confirmed promise when winning
12-runner maiden at Lingfield by 1¼ lengths from Just Tim, getting up late on: will be
suited by 1¼m/1½m: sent to USA: open to progress. *Mrs A. J. Perrett*

KING NICHOLAS (USA) 4 b.g. Nicholas (USA) 111 – Lifetime Honour (USA) **67 d**
(Kingmambo (USA) 125) [2003 68: p7g* f7g 7.5d 8.1m f8s Sep 2] good-topped gelding:
fair handicapper: won at Lingfield in January: left M. Jarvis and off 5 months, well held
after: stays 1m: acts on soft going and all-weather: tried visored/tongue tied. *J. Parkes*

KING OF ADOC 4 ch.g. Dr Devious (IRE) 127 – Urchin (IRE) (Fairy King (USA)) **–**
[2003 –: 6g 7m May 23] poor maiden: no form since 2 yrs: tried in blinkers/cheekpieces.
P. R. Hedger

KING OF CASHEL (IRE) 2 b.c. (Feb 2) King of Kings (IRE) 125 – Jaya (USA) **92**
(Ela-Mana-Mou 132) [2003 7m⁵ 7m³ 8d⁴ 7d* Sep 24] good-bodied colt: first foal: dam,
ran twice in USA, out of half-sister to US Grade 1 1m winner Too Chic: fairly useful
performer: in frame in maidens at Newmarket and Doncaster before landing odds in
similar event at Chester by 1½ lengths from Major Effort, making all but edging right/
carrying head high: stays 1m: acts on good to firm and good to soft going. *R. Hannon*

KING OF DREAMS (IRE) 2 b.c. (Mar 17) Sadler's Wells (USA) 132 – Koniya **79 p**
(IRE) (Doyoun 124) [2003 8m⁴ 7.9f² Oct 11] 150,000Y: rather leggy, quite attractive colt:
first foal: dam, French 15f winner, half-sister to dam of High Chaparral: fair form in
maidens at Pontefract (edged right) and York (head second to Blue Monday): will be
suited by 1¼m+: should progress. *M. Johnston*

KING OF HAPPINESS (USA) 4 ch.c. Spinning World (USA) 130 – Mystery Rays **110**
(USA) 122 (Nijinsky (CAN) 138) [2003 114: 8.9g 8.5m³ 7m³ 8g 8m Aug 14] rather
leggy, good-topped colt: smart performer: creditable third to Gateman in Diomed Stakes
at Epsom and to Trade Fair in Criterion Stakes at Newmarket: poor efforts last 2 starts:
stays 8.5f: raced only on good/good to firm going: tongue tied last 4 outings: has worn
crossed noseband: edgy sort. *Sir Michael Stoute*

KING OF KNIGHT (IRE) 2 gr.g. (Mar 12) Orpen (USA) 116 – Peace Melody (IRE) **65**
69 (Classic Music (USA)) [2003 7m 8m 8s Oct 29] €15,500Y: quite good-topped
gelding: third foal: dam, Irish maiden who stayed 1m, half-sister to National Stakes
winner Manntari: fair form in maidens: best efforts first 2 starts: travelled well long way
final one: not sure to stay much beyond 1m. *G. Prodromou*

KING OF MOMMUR (IRE) 8 b.g. Fairy King (USA) – Monoglow (Kalaglow 132) **–**
[2003 f12s⁵ Jan 10] lengthy, angular gelding: modest maiden nowadays: well held only
Flat outing since 2001, but has won over fences: tried blinkered and in cheekpieces: has
worn tongue strap. *B. G. Powell*

KING OF MUSIC (USA) 2 ch.g. (Feb 20) Jade Hunter (USA) – Hail Roberta (USA) **73**
(Roberto (USA) 131) [2003 7m³ 8m⁵ f6g Nov 10] $7,000Y: rather leggy, angular gelding:

closely related to winner in USA by Allen's Prospect and half-brother to several winners in USA: dam unraced half-sister to very smart French 1¼m/1½m performer Contested Bid: fair form in maidens at Yarmouth (third to Top Romance) and Newmarket (raced freely) first 2 starts: well beaten final outing: not sure to stay much beyond 1m. *G. Prodromou*

KING OF PERU 10 br.g. Inca Chief (USA) – Julie's Star (IRE) 45 (Thatching 131) – [2003 59: 6m 5m Apr 17] tall, leggy gelding: modest performer in 2002: soundly beaten in 2003: effective blinkered/visored or not. *D. Nicholls*

KING OF THE TWEED (IRE) 4 b.g. Robellino (USA) 127 – River Tweed 61 (Selkirk (USA) 129) [2003 f6g f5g⁶ 5d Aug 29] poor maiden, lightly raced: should stay 7f. *J. J. Sheehan* — **47**

KING PRIAM (IRE) 8 b.g. Priolo (USA) 127 – Barinia (Corvaro (USA) 124) [2003 86d: f16g* f14s⁶ f11g³ f12g⁶ f14s⁶ f12s⁶ f12s² f12s⁵ 12g 14.1g f14g 10g 12m 8g 14.1m f12g⁵ f11g⁵ f14.8g⁴ 11.8m 10f f12s Dec 27] sturdy gelding: poor mover: just fair form at best in 2003: won claimer at Southwell in January: stays 2m: acts on any going/all-weather: wears headgear: tried tongue tied: often gets behind: has bled: unreliable. *M. J. Polglase* — **66 d**

KING REVO (IRE) 3 b.g. Revoque (IRE) 122 – Tycoon Aly (IRE) 70 (Last Tycoon 131) [2003 78: p10g² p10g³ 8m⁵ 9.9d 10.5f* 12m⁶ 11.9f p12g⁴ Nov 18] tall, useful-looking gelding: fairly useful handicapper: off 3½ months before winning amateur event at Haydock in September: stays 1½m: acts on polytrack, firm and soft ground: sometimes hangs: won twice over hurdles in December. *P. C. Haslam* — **89**

KING'S BALLET (USA) 5 b.g. Imperial Ballet (IRE) 110 – Multimara (USA) (Arctic Tern (USA) 126) [2003 –: 5m 6m 6s* 5g⁶ 5g 5g 5g 5f 6g 5.1m 5d 5m 5g³ f5g f5g Dec 12] strong, lengthy gelding: fair handicapper: won at Haydock in May: left J. Goldie 5,500 gns after thirteenth start: best at 5f/6f: acts on fibresand and good to firm ground, though all wins on softer than good: tried blinkered/tongue tied. *P. R. Chamings* — **75 d**

KING'S CAPRICE 2 ch.c. (Apr 22) Pursuit of Love 124 – Palace Street (USA) 103 (Secreto (USA) 128) [2003 6m⁵ 6m² 6m³ Oct 1] rather leggy colt: has round action: brother to smart 5f to 7f winner Palace Affair, 6f winner at 2 yrs, and half-brother to several winners, including 3-y-o Marker and 6-y-o Duke of Modena: dam 6f/7f winner: best effort when third of 5 to Millbag in minor event at Salisbury, set plenty to do: will probably prove best up to 7f: likely to make useful 3-y-o, and should win a race or 2. *G. B. Balding* — **91 p**

KINGS COLLEGE BOY 3 b.g. College Chapel 122 – The Kings Daughter 79 (Indian King (USA) 128) [2003 62: 5m⁶ 6g 5d² 6s⁵ 6d 5g² 7.1f 6m² 5m³ 5.1g* 5m 5d⁴ 5.1d² 5m⁶ 5g Oct 13] well-made gelding: fair performer: won minor event at Nottingham in August: best at 5f/6f: acts on soft and good to firm ground: usually blinkered. *R. A. Fahey* — **68**

KING'S CONSUL (USA) 4 b.c. Kingmambo (USA) 125 – Battle Creek Girl (USA) (His Majesty (USA)) [2003 –: 12.3m⁵ 10g⁶ 12m² 12f⁶ 14f² 10.1m⁴ Jul 10] tall, good-topped colt: useful performer: good efforts in handicaps at Thirsk (short-headed by Hambleden) and Royal Ascot (sixth to Waverley) and minor event at Goodwood (second of 4 to Gulf) third to fifth starts: lost action final outing: stayed 1¾m: acted on firm going and dirt: blinkered/visored: wore crossed noseband: usually held up: dead. *D. R. Loder* — **108**

KING'S COUNTY (IRE) 5 b.g. Fairy King (USA) – Kardelle 79 (Kalaglow 132) [2003 10d⁵ 10f⁵ 8m* 8g² Nov 1] strong, good-topped gelding: useful performer: runner-up in 3 Group 1s at 2 yrs and eighth in Poule d'Essai des Poulains at Longchamp at 3 yrs for A. O' Brien in Ireland: well beaten in 6 races for D. Oughton in Hong Kong in 2001/2 (raced under name of Point Grey): won minor event at Newmarket in October: beaten head by Thihn in handicap there following month, finishing strongly: best form around 1m: acts on soft and good to firm going: tried blinkered/visored: has worn dropped noseband: often races freely: has wandered/hung. *L. M. Cumani* — **109**

KING'S CREST 5 b.g. Deploy 131 – Classic Beauty (IRE) 65 (Fairy King (USA)) [2003 78, a–: p12g 12m 12.3m⁶ 12.3m Aug 3] medium-sized gelding: fair handicapper in 2002 but well held in 2003. *R. A. Fahey* — —

KINGSCROSS 5 ch.g. King's Signet (USA) 110 – Calamanco 71 (Clantime 101) [2003 89: 6d 6g 6g 6m⁴ 6g³ 6g 7d 7g Nov 1] strong, good-bodied gelding: fairly useful handicapper: effective at 5f to 6.5f: acts on good to firm and good to soft going, probably on soft: refused to enter stall once in 2002: usually held up. *M. Blanshard* — **83**

KINGSDON (IRE) 6 b.g. Brief Truce (USA) 126 – Richly Deserved (IRE) (Kings **57 d** Lake (USA) 133) [2003 64: 9.9m 10.1m⁴ 10g 10m⁴ 10.1m 10.1g 11g Oct 28] sturdy, useful-looking gelding: modest performer: below form after second start: stays 10.5f: acts on any going: has been blinkered, usually visored/tongue tied: often starts slowly: unreliable. *T. J. Fitzgerald*

KINGS EMPIRE 2 b.g. (Apr 29) Second Empire (IRE) 124 – Dancing Feather 72 **86 p** (Suave Dancer (USA) 136) [2003 8g³ f8s* Oct 7] 13,000Y: sturdy gelding: third foal: half-brother to 3-y-o Feather Boa and useful performer up to 1¼m Feathers Flying (by Royal Applause), 7f winner at 2 yrs: dam, 1m winner who stayed 1½m, half-sister to smart 1¼m performer Spring Oak: confirmed promise when showing fairly useful form to win 13-runner maiden at Southwell by length from Countrywide Flyer, pair well clear: will stay 1¼m: open to progress. *D. Carroll*

KING'S ENVOY (USA) 4 b.g. Royal Academy (USA) 130 – Island of Silver (USA) – 107 (Forty Niner (USA)) [2003 –: 10.9m Sep 18] tall gelding: no form since 2001: tried visored. *Mrs J. C. McGregor*

KING'S IRONBRIDGE (IRE) 5 b.h. King's Theatre (IRE) 128 – Dream Chaser **100 d** 92 (Record Token 128) [2003 106: p7g⁶ 7m⁵ 7g 8.3d⁴ 9.9m⁵ 8.1g 8m 7.1g⁶ Aug 25] tall, good sort: easy mover: just useful at best in 2003: fifth to Attache in handicap at Newmarket second start: deteriorated after: stayed 1m: acted on soft and good to firm going: very slowly away fifth outing, had to be walked to post penultimate one: sometimes raced freely: usually raced prominently: ungenuine: to stand at Ballykisteen Stud, Ireland, fee €1,250. *S. Kirk*

KINGSMAITE 2 b.g. (Mar 5) Komaite (USA) – Antonias Melody 86 (Rambo Dancer **66** (CAN) 107) [2003 6f⁶ 6d 5m³ 6g⁶ 5g⁴ f7g² f8g* f8s² Dec 27] workmanlike gelding: **a79** second foal: dam 6f (including at 2 yrs)/7f winner: fair performer: won maiden at Southwell in December: good second in nursery there final start: stays 1m: acts on fibresand and good to firm ground. *S. R. Bowring*

KING'S MILL (IRE) 6 b.g. Doyoun 124 – Adarika (Kings Lake (USA) 133) [2003 – 105: 10.3m 12g May 24] rangy gelding: useful handicapper at 5 yrs: well held in 2003: sold only £1,000 in December. *N. A. Graham*

KING'S MOUNTAIN (USA) 3 b.g. King of Kings (IRE) 125 – Statistic (USA) (Mr – Prospector (USA)) [2003 83: 11.8m 12.3d⁶ 8m 10.5m Jul 19] close-coupled gelding: fairly useful winner in Ireland at 2 yrs: well held in 2003: tried blinkered. *Mrs A. L. M. King*

KINGS OF ALBION (USA) 3 b.c. King of Kings (IRE) 125 – Akadya (FR) (Akarad – (FR) 130) [2003 –p: 8m 11.6g Apr 14] good-bodied, quite attractive colt: little form. *R. Hannon*

KINGS POINT (IRE) 2 b.c. (Apr 17) Fasliyev (USA) 120 – Rahika Rose 91 **103** (Unfuwain (USA) 131) [2003 5m² 6m⁴ 6f* 7m* 7d⁶ Jul 30] 110,000F, 150,000Y: strong, compact colt: first foal: dam, Irish 7f/1m winner, granddaughter of smart sprinter Rambling Rose: useful performer: won maiden at Goodwood (edged right) in June and Weatherbys Superlative Stakes at Newmarket (beat Chester Le Street by head) in July: respectable sixth of 9 to Lucky Story in Vintage Stakes at Goodwood: will stay 1m: best effort on good to firm going. *R. Hannon*

KING'S PROTECTOR 3 b.c. Hector Protector (USA) 124 – Doliouchka (Saumarez – 132) [2003 88p: 10g 7.9m May 15] rather leggy, lengthy colt: fairly useful form at 2 yrs: well held in handicaps in 2003. *T. D. Easterby*

KINGS ROCK 2 ch.g. (Apr 18) Kris 135 – Both Sides Now (USA) (Topsider (USA)) **66** [2003 7.5m⁵ 8.3g³ 7m⁵ f8s³ 8d Oct 14] 4,200Y, 24,000 2-y-o: rather leggy, useful-looking gelding: has a quick action: closely related to 2001 2-y-o 6f winner Yarrow Bridge (by Selkirk) and half-brother to several winners, including useful 1997 2-y-o 6f/7f (Solario Stakes) winner Little Indian (by Little Missouri) and 6f (at 2 yrs) and 1¼m (in UAE) winner Mukaddar (by Elmaamul): dam placed in USA: fair maiden: will stay 1¼m, probably 1½m: acts on fibresand, good to firm and good to soft going. *K. A. Ryan*

KINGS SQUARE 3 b.g. Bal Harbour 113 – Prime Property (IRE) 60 (Tirol 127) [2003 – 8m 12.1m 8m 12.1m Jun 11] strong, workmanlike gelding: half-brother to 6-y-o Middlethorpe and 1½m winner Property Zone (by Cool Jazz): dam 6f winner: no sign of ability. *M. W. Easterby*

KING'S THOUGHT 4 b.c. King's Theatre (IRE) 128 – Lora's Guest 99 (Be My Guest **105** (USA) 126) [2003 81: p8g* p8g* 8.3g 10d³ 10d* 10.3m⁴ 10.4f 10d³ 10g* 13.4m Aug 30] angular, good-topped colt: useful handicapper: better than ever in 2003, winning at

Lingfield in February and March (minor event), Ripon in May and Newmarket (best effort, beat McBain by 3 lengths) in August: best at 1m/1¼m: acts on polytrack, firm and soft ground: has been bandaged on fore joints: races prominently. *S. Gollings*

KINGSTON GAME 4 b.g. Mind Games 121 – Valmaranda (USA) (Sir Ivor 135) – §
[2003 –§, a55§: f8s f8.5g Mar 24] workmanlike gelding: modest performer: well held in 2003: usually blinkered/visored: unreliable. *Miss K. M. George*

KINGSTON TOWN (USA) 3 ch.g. King of Kings (IRE) 125 – Lady Ferial (FR) 77
(Carwhite 127) [2003 8m⁴ 7m f7g² f8g* Nov 25] leggy, close-coupled gelding: half-brother to several winners in USA: dam, French 11f/11.5f winner, half-sister to dam of Colonel Collins, Commander Collins and Lit de Justice: fair performer: won maiden at Southwell in November by 5 lengths: will stay at least 1¼m: wore blinkers on debut, cheekpieces last 2 starts. *N. P. Littmoden*

KINGSTON WISH (IRE) 4 b.g. Mujadil (USA) 119 – Well Wisher (USA) (Sanglamore (USA) 126) [2003 –: f11g 6m 7m 8g 8m 10f Sep 15] leggy gelding: poor maiden. 40
Ian Emmerson

KINGS TOPIC (USA) 3 ch.g. Kingmambo (USA) 125 – Topicount (USA) (Private –
Account (USA)) [2003 –: 12g May 4] deep-bodied gelding: little sign of ability. *G. Wragg*

KINGSWORD (USA) 2 bl.c. (Feb 22) Dynaformer (USA) – Western Curtsey (USA) 89 p
(Gone West (USA)) [2003 7m⁴ 7m* Oct 1] $200,000Y: tall, close-coupled, useful-looking colt: first foal: dam, 6f winner in USA, daughter of US Grade 1 1¼m winner Dawn's Curtsey: shaped well in maiden at Leicester before justifying favouritism in minor event at Salisbury by ¾ length from Colour Wheel, leading final 1f: will be suited by 1¼m/1½m: should make useful 3-y-o at least. *Sir Michael Stoute*

KING TARA (IRE) 2 b.g. (Mar 18) Foxhound (USA) 103 – Bradwell (IRE) 76 63 d
(Taufan (USA) 119) [2003 5g⁶ 5f⁵ 5g⁶ 7m² 6g⁴ f6f⁵ 6f⁵ 6g⁵ Aug 25] IR 5,000F, €26,000Y: close-coupled, workmanlike gelding: sixth foal: half-brother to 3 winners, including 3-y-o Ryan's Academy: dam 5f winner who probably stayed 7f: modest maiden: regressed after debut: stayed 7f: raced only on good going or firmer on turf: wore cheekpieces final outing: dead. *J. J. Quinn*

KINISKA 2 b.f. (Apr 11) Merdon Melody 98 – Young Whip (Bold Owl 101) [2003 62
p7g⁴ 7d Nov 7] close-coupled filly: sister to 3 winners, notably useful 7f to 1¼m winner Elmhurst Boy: dam unraced: modest form in maidens at Lingfield and Doncaster: will stay 1m. *B. Palling*

KINKOZAN 2 ch.c. (May 15) Peintre Celebre (USA) 137 – Classic Design (Busted –
134) [2003 8m 7g⁶ Nov 1] 25,000Y: quite good-topped colt: half-brother to 3 winners, notably very smart 5f performer Eveningperformance (by Night Shift): dam unraced half-sister to 2000 Guineas winner Tirol: signs of only a little ability in maidens: worked up/reportedly had breathing problem on debut. *N. P. Littmoden*

KINNAIRD (IRE) 2 ch.f. (Feb 27) Dr Devious (IRE) 127 – Ribot's Guest (IRE) (Be 105 p
My Guest (USA) 126) [2003 6g* 6f* 6g⁵ 7s* 7m* 8d* Sep 11] €10,000Y, 8,000 2-y-o: sturdy filly: second foal: dam, ran twice in Italy, half-sister to useful French performer up to 13f Razana: won maiden and minor event at Hamilton in June, minor events at Thirsk in July and Ascot in August and Betdaq May Hill Stakes at Doncaster in September:

Betdaq May Hill Stakes, Doncaster—the genuine and progressive Kinnaird completes a highly successful first season, keeping on too strongly for Hathrah and Lucky Pipit

beat Hathrah by 1¾ lengths for last-named success, leading over 1f out: will stay at least 1¼m: unraced on heavy going, acts on any other: genuine: likely to make a smart 3-y-o. *P. C. Haslam*

KINNESCASH (IRE)   10 ch.g. Persian Heights 129 – Gayla Orchestra (Lord Gayle (USA) 124) [2003 –: 12m Apr 23] small gelding: lightly raced and little form on Flat since 2000. *P. Bowen*   –

KINSMAN (IRE)   6 b.g. Distant Relative 128 – Besito 79 (Wassl 125) [2003 71, a79: p10g p7g⁴ p7g p7g² p7g⁶ 7m 7m⁵ p8g⁵ p8g⁵ 7m p7g p7g⁶ p7g p7g Dec 30] leggy, useful-looking gelding: fair handicapper on all-weather, modest on turf in 2003: effective at 7f to easy 1¼m: acts on firm going, soft and all-weather: tried in headgear and tongue tie: sometimes starts slowly/carries head high: held up. *T. D. McCarthy*   **56 a67**

KINTORE   2 ch.c. (Mar 25) Inchinor 119 – Souadah (USA) (General Holme (USA) 128) [2003 6m 7m 7.2m Sep 19] 16,000Y: quite good-topped colt: closely related to useful 1996 2-y-o 5f winner Blue Ridge (later 1m winner in USA, by Indian Ridge) and half-brother to 3 winners, including 5f (at 2 yrs) to 7f winner Make The Break (by Dominion): dam unraced: well beaten in maidens. *J. S. Goldie*   –

KIRKBY'S TREASURE   5 br.g. Mind Games 121 – Gem of Gold 52 (Jellaby 124) [2003 79: 7m 7m 8.3d 9.3g 7.2g 7.5d³ 8g 7d 5.9d* 6.9m² 6.9f² 6.9m⁶ 7.5d 8m f8.5g⁵ Nov 15] tall, leggy gelding: has a round action: fair performer: won apprentice claimer at Carlisle in July: effective at 6f to 1m: well held on heavy going, acts on any other turf and fibresand: often wears cheekpieces/blinkers: wanders/hangs left: unreliable. *A. Berry*   **67 §**

KIRKHAM ABBEY   3 b.g. Selkirk (USA) 129 – Totham 84 (Shernazar 131) [2003 –: f12g* f12g⁶ 12.1d f9.4s* 9m⁵ f8.5g³ 10m* 10m 10m* 9m* Oct 17] fair handicapper: had a good year, winning at Southwell in April, Wolverhampton in June, Redcar in September and at Brighton and Redcar (edged left and idled) in October: effective at 9f to 1½m: acts on fibresand and good to firm going: wore cheekpieces second start, visored/blinkered after. *M. A. Jarvis*   **74**

KIRKSTONE (IRE)   2 b.g. (Feb 4) Alzao (USA) 117 – Night Mirage (USA) 80 (Silver Hawk (USA) 123) [2003 6g⁶ 7.5m² 7m² 7m² 7m 7f Sep 28] big, good-topped gelding: has scope: second foal: brother to 3-y-o Night Mist: dam 9f winner: fair maiden: below form in nurseries last 2 starts: likely to be suited by 1¼m/1½m: acts on good to firm going: tends to wander/carry head high/flick tail under pressure. *M. Johnston*   **77**

KIRK WYND   3 b.f. Selkirk (USA) 129 – Abbey Strand (USA) 78 (Shadeed (USA) 135) [2003 76: 10.2g* 10m 10g³ 10.5d Sep 26] unfurnished, quite attractive filly: fairly useful performer: won maiden at Chepstow in June: best effort when third in handicap at Windsor: stays 1¼m: acts on firm ground, possibly unsuited by softer than good: hung left/found little support second start: sold 70,000 gns in December. *Sir Michael Stoute*   **88**

KIROVSKI (IRE)   6 b.g. Common Grounds 118 – Nordic Doll (IRE) 71 (Royal Academy (USA) 130) [2003 111: p10g* p10g 10.4m May 15] tall, quite attractive gelding: smart performer: career-best effort when winning handicap at Lingfield in January under top weight by head from Brilliant Red: below form in listed race there next time: finished lame only subsequent outing: effective at 1m/1¼m: acts on firm, soft going and polytrack: usually held up. *P. W. Harris*   **116**

KISMET QUEEN (IRE)   3 b.f. Desert King (IRE) 129 – Kiya (USA) 85 (Dominion 123) [2003 66: f11g⁴ f9.4g 11.1g⁵ f11g 8m f9.4g⁴ Jul 11] leggy, angular filly: disappointing maiden: probably stays 11f: acts on firm going and fibresand: blinkered last 3 starts. *C. W. Thornton*   **50 d**

KISS THE RAIN   3 b.f. Forzando 122 – Devils Dirge 68 (Song 132) [2003 63: 7m f7s 7d² 6d⁶ 7m⁵ 5.7f* 6d f5g³ f5g³ f5s⁴ Dec 31] small filly: modest performer: made all in claimer at Bath (claimed from W. Kittow £6,000) in October: stays 7f: acts on fibresand, firm and soft ground: often visored: often makes running. *R. Brotherton*   **60**

KITEFLYER (IRE)   3 ch.f. In The Wings 128 – Afraah (IRE) (Caerleon (USA) 132) [2003 84: 12g⁴ 12g* 12m² 12m² 11.9m 12f 12.3f³ Sep 27] sturdy filly: first foal: dam unraced daughter of Oaks winner Unite: useful performer: won ladies race at the Curragh in July: best effort when length second to Juliette in listed race at Cork: ridden more patiently than usual when well held in listed race at York fourth start: stays 1½m: acts on firm and good to soft going: sent to Australia. *J. Oxx, Ireland*   **99**

KITLEY   2 b.c. (Apr 1) Muhtarram (USA) 125 – Salsita (Salse (USA) 128) [2003 6g 6m 5m 7m⁴ 7m p7g⁶ 7m⁴ 8m³ Sep 18] 12,000Y: close-coupled colt: fifth foal: half-brother to 2000 2-y-o 7f winner Nun Left (by Bishop of Cashel): dam won 3 times (including at 2   **68**

yrs) in Spain: fair maiden: third in nursery at Yarmouth: free-going sort, but stays 1m: acts on good to firm going, shaped promisingly on polytrack. *B. G. Powell*

KITTYLEE 4 b.f. Bal Harbour 113 – Courtesy Call (Northfields (USA)) [2003 –: p10g Dec 30] of little account on Flat. *M. A. Buckley* —

KITUHWA (USA) 3 br.g. Cherokee Run (USA) 122 – Ruhnke (USA) (Cox's Ridge (USA)) [2003 8m³ 8g 8.1m 10m Aug 16] $150,000Y: rangy gelding: half-brother to several winners in USA: dam, ran once in USA, half-sister to 1998 US Grade 1 2-y-o 8.5f winner One of A Klein: probably fair form when third in maiden at Kempton, wandering: disappointing after: sold 4,000 gns, then gelded. *J. H. M. Gosden* **69 ?**

KNAVESMIRE OMEN 4 b.g. Robellino (USA) 127 – Signs 91 (Risk Me (FR) 127) [2003 100: 14f⁶ 16m³ 18.7m³ 13.9m 20m 16d* 16.2f 21d* 18.7m³ 16.2m Aug 9] sturdy gelding: poor mover: useful performer: won listed race at Hamburg and handicap at Goodwood (made all, beat Positive Profile 5 lengths) in July: stays on any going: blinkered once at 2 yrs: races prominently: tough and very game. *M. Johnston* **105**

KNICKYKNACKIENOO 2 b.g. (Apr 6) Bin Ajwaad (IRE) 119 – Ring Fence 74 (Polar Falcon (USA) 126) [2003 p5g 5.6f⁶ 5.1m⁶ 5m 7d⁴ 8m 7.1d 6g⁶ f8s Dec 13] big, plain gelding: first foal: dam 5f winner from 3 starts: signs of a little ability, including in nursery, but difficult to assess. *T. T. Clement* **?**

KNIGHT ONTHE TILES (IRE) 2 ch.g. (Apr 2) Primo Dominie 121 – Blissful Night (Cadeaux Genereux 131) [2003 5.1g 5g⁵ 5.2m 6.1m⁶ 7m 6f³ 6.1m* 6.1m* 6.1m 5.7f⁵ 6m* 5.2s⁴ 6d* p7g p7g⁶ p5g Dec 17] 12,000F, 16,500Y: smallish gelding: second foal: half-brother to 3-y-o Perfect Night: dam unraced half-sister to smart French middle-distance stayer North Col: fair performer: won nursery at Warwick in August, claimer at Lingfield (then left B. Meehan) in October and nursery at Catterick in November: barely stays easy 7f: acts on firm ground, soft and polytrack: usually blinkered. *J. R. Best* **77 a67**

KNIGHT TO REMEMBER (IRE) 2 ch.g. (Apr 10) Fayruz 116 – Cheerful Knight (IRE) (Mac's Imp (USA) 116) [2003 7.2g 7m f8.5s⁶ f5g f8s Dec 13] €2,500Y, 11,000 2-y-o: workmanlike gelding: third living foal: brother to 3-y-o Arabian Knight: dam Irish maiden: little form. *K. A. Ryan* —

KNOCKDOO (IRE) 10 ch.g. Be My Native (USA) 122 – Ashken (Artaius (USA) 129) [2003 –: 16.1d³ 17.1m 21.6m 16d 13m⁶ 16m² 15g 16m³ Jul 31] poor performer nowadays: stays 21.6f: acts on heavy and good to firm going: tried visored. *J. S. Goldie* **48**

KNOCKEMBACK NELLIE 7 b.m. Forzando 122 – Sea Clover (IRE) 77 (Ela-Mana-Mou 132) [2003 51d: f6g f5g Jan 18] smallish mare: well held in 2003: usually blinkered: tried tongue tied. *J. M. Bradley* **– §**

KNOT IN DOUBT (IRE) 2 b.c. (Apr 30) Woodborough (USA) 112 – In The Mind (IRE) (Taufan (USA) 119) [2003 6g 6m Jun 7] IR 3,500F, 3,800Y: strong, close-coupled colt: third foal: half-brother to Swedish 1m winner by General Monash: dam unraced half-sister to useful 2002 2-y-o sprinter Mister Links: signs of only a little ability in maidens. *J. A. Glover* —

KNOTTY ASH GIRL (IRE) 4 ch.f. Ashkalani (IRE) 128 – Camisha (IRE) 82 (Shernazar 131) [2003 65?: 10.3g 10m 9.9m 12.1d 11.9m 16.2m⁵ 11.9g 12.6f³ 12m 14.1d* Jul 26] smallish, close-coupled filly: modest handicapper: won selling event at Nottingham in July: stays 1¾m: acts on any turf going and fibresand: tried in cheekpieces: blinkered last 5 starts: sold 5,000 gns in October. *B. A. McMahon* **57**

KNOWLE PARK (IRE) 4 br.f. Woodborough (USA) 112 – Nagida 94 (Skyliner 117) [2003 –: f5g Jan 3] well held in maidens/claimer: tried in cheekpieces. *M. S. Saunders* —

KNOWN MANEUVER (USA) 5 b.g. Known Fact (USA) 135 – Northern Maneuver (USA) (Al Nasr (FR) 126) [2003 79d: 10g f16g f14g Dec 9] smallish gelding: well held in 2003: broke out of stall and withdrawn intended reappearance in September. *M. C. Chapman* —

KODIAC 2 b.c. (Apr 28) Danehill (USA) 126 – Rafha 123 (Kris 135) [2003 6m³ Jul 19] smallish, sturdy colt: brother to useful 6f winner (including at 2 yrs) Massarra, closely related to very smart sprinter Invincible Spirit (by Green Desert) and half-brother to several winners, including smart 7.6f (at 2 yrs) to 1¾m winner Sadian (by Shirley Heights): dam 6f (at 2 yrs) to 11.5f winner, including Prix de Diane: 6/1 and better for race, ½-length third of 12 to Oman Gulf in maiden at Newmarket, steadied start and finishing very strongly: took good hold to post/wore crossed noseband: sustained injury after but said to have recovered fully: sure to do better if all remains well. *J. L. Dunlop* **82 p**

KOHIMA (IRE) 3 ch.f. Barathea (IRE) 127 – Albenita (IRE) (Alzao (USA) 117) [2003 – 63: p8g f8g 8.2g 10.9f⁶ Jul 10] modest form only 2-y-o start: well held in 2003: tried tongue tied. *G. C. Bravery*

KOMASH 2 b.f. (Feb 11) Komaite (USA) – Phoenix Princess 65 (Nomination 125) **35** [2003 5d⁶ 6d 7m⁶ 7.1m 6f 5f⁶ 6g 6m Oct 24] 2,200Y: good-topped filly: first foal: dam 6f and 1m winner: poor maiden: sometimes blinkered. *A. Berry*

KOMATI RIVER 4 b.g. Wesaam (USA) 95 – Christening (IRE) (Lahib (USA) 129) **62** [2003 58: p10g⁶ 11.6g² 11.9m⁵ p13g⁶ Dec 29] modest maiden: should stay 1¾m: acts on polytrack, best turf effort on good ground. *J. Akehurst*

KOMENA 5 b.m. Komaite (USA) – Mena 58 (Blakeney 126) [2003 60§: p7g 6m³ 6g **56** 5.7f² 6.1g 6m² 6m³ 7m 6m⁵ f6g² f7g⁴ p7g Dec 17] tall, lengthy mare: modest handicapper: has form at 1m, raced mainly at 6f/7f nowadays: acts on firm going (below form on softer than good) and fibresand: has been edgy/reluctant stall: carries head awkwardly: none too genuine. *J. W. Payne*

KONFUZIUS (GER) 5 b.g. Motley (USA) 123 – Katrina (GER) (Windwurf (GER)) – [2003 14m 9.2m 10.9m 12f Jun 30] trained by H. Blume in Germany in 2002, winning maiden at Neuss: blinkered, no form in Britain. *P. Monteith*

KONICA 4 b.f. Desert King (IRE) 129 – Haboobti (Habitat 134) [2003 55: f8.5g p12g – 12g Mar 25] good-bodied filly: modest maiden: well held in 2003. *Mrs A. L. M. King*

KONKER 8 ch.g. Selkirk (USA) 129 – Helens Dreamgirl 95 (Caerleon (USA) 132) **72** [2003 –: 10s⁶ Nov 3] fairly useful 2m hurdler: fair handicapper on Flat, lightly raced: stays 1½m: acts on heavy ground: usually waited with. *Mrs M. Reveley*

KOODOO 2 gr.c. (May 3) Fasliyev (USA) 120 – Karsiyaka (IRE) (Kahyasi 130) [2003 – 6m 8m 7.9f Oct 11] 36,000 2-y-o: angular colt: second foal: half-brother to 3-y-o Contractor: dam unraced half-sister to dam of smart stayer Kasthari: well held in maidens: looked reluctant final start. *A. Crook*

KOSMIC LADY 6 b.m. Cosmonaut – Ktolo 80 (Tolomeo 127) [2003 56, a43: p8g⁶ – 10d 10.9m Aug 25] strong, lengthy mare: modest at best: well held both starts in 2003: blinkered earlier in career: usually tongue tied: sometimes carries head high. *P. W. Hiatt*

KOTORI (IRE) 4 gr.g. Charnwood Forest (IRE) 125 – La Kermesse (USA) 58 (Storm Bird (CAN) 134) [2003 –: f5g f6g 5.7f 8f f5s² 6m f6g Aug 8] modest maiden: best at **a52** 5f/6f: acts on fibresand, little form on turf: often slowly away: tried in cheekpieces: inconsistent: sold £1,000. *M. S. Saunders*

KOYAANISQATSI 3 ch.g. Selkirk (USA) 129 – Bogus John (CAN) (Blushing John – (USA) 120) [2003 8.3m Jul 28] 700Y: fourth foal: half-brother to 3 winners, including 5-y-o Blushing Spur: dam unraced: 50/1 and reluctant to enter stall, well held in maiden at Windsor. *Jamie Poulton*

KOZANDO 2 ch.g. (Jan 24) Komaite (USA) – Times Zando 64 (Forzando 122) [2003 **74** 6m⁴ 5f⁴ 6g 6m³ 6m* 6.1m² 6g* 7g⁶ 6d⁴ 6f Oct 10] 1,300Y: good-bodied gelding: fifth foal: brother to 6f winners Captain Kozando and Colonel Kozando (former including at 2 yrs): dam 2-y-o 7f/1m winner: fair performer: won nurseries at Haydock in August and Hamilton in September: stays 7f: acts on good to firm ground, ran respectably (though never going well) on good to soft: troublesome at start first 2 outings: usually races prominently: sold 8,000 gns. *Mrs G. S. Rees*

KRIS KIN (USA) 3 ch.c. Kris S (USA) – Angel In My Heart (FR) 119 (Rainbow **126** Quest (USA) 134) [2003 81p: 10.3m* 12m* 12d³ 12m³ 12s Oct 5]
Send in the clowns! It says a lot about the current image of the Derby that to exploit what is left of the race's brand name Epsom has turned to the ringmaster's hardy standby. Despite its assertion that it is attempting to revive the race in the sporting calendar, Epsom now markets the Derby as 'Britain's Biggest Day Out', rather than Europe's richest horserace. It boasts that people from all walks of life flock to the Downs in party mode. The ploy of resorting to cabaret and a themepark atmosphere has seen a revival in the numbers attending the race compared to the 'nineties. Epsom is now able to guarantee a crowd of upwards of 100,000, most gathered on the in-field and many allowed in free. Unfortunately, the repackaging of the event obscures the real nature of Derby Day. Winning the Derby alone may not be nearly so significant as it once was for the breeding industry, but in years such as the first three in the millennium, which featured good renewals won by Sinndar, Galileo and High Chaparral and represented a revival in the race's

fortunes that was largely overlooked, and in ordinary ones such as 2003, the Derby is still an extraordinary race—a thrilling spectacle in which the pick of the season's three-year-olds at the time are put to the test over Britain's most demanding mile-and-a-half course.

The Derby's primary role as a horserace is also showing signs of being overlooked on television. Racing's reputation in some quarters, as a rather insular world which a wider sporting audience finds difficult to relate to, was underlined when the BBC again chose general sports presenter Sue Barker to host its Derby Day edition of *Grandstand*. A show lasting three and a half hours focused mainly on personalities and highlighted the Derby Day experience as the BBC chose to present it, including through the eyes of a stream of minor celebrities. Regular racing anchorwoman Clare Balding was used only in a supporting role. The horses themselves were given scant coverage until close to the race, while the programme only nibbled round the edges of the betting and the most enduring element of Derby Day—the historic course itself. It is the unique character of the course that under-pins the race, part of the attraction of the Derby being the familiarity built up over the years with what it takes to win at Epsom—the type of horse, how it moves, its pedigree, running style, level of form, speed, stamina and temperament. Winning the Derby is not merely a case of a magic wand being waved by a trainer or jockey. Every victory has to be hard-earned and each year brings some new lessons and a reminder of old ones.

The BBC isn't helped in its attempt to give full depth to the story of each Derby, or in building an audience loyal to the event—as it can with the F A Cup, for example—by the scheduling of the trials. The BBC covers only the Blue Riband Trial at Epsom in April and the Predominate Stakes at Goodwood in May, neither

Philip Leverhulme Dee Stakes, Chester—
passed over by stable-jockey Fallon, 20/1-shot Kris Kin has come from last to first;
Big Bad Bob (right), Private Charter (left) and Always Esteemed are the only other runners

of which is usually particularly significant. The validity of some Derby trials came under fire in the latest season because of small fields. Other than the Two Thousand Guineas at Newmarket, and its French and Irish equivalents, only the Dante Stakes at York attracted as many as ten runners among nearly twenty races in April and May which could be expected to attract Derby candidates. The Chester Vase and the Dee Stakes, which took place two days apart at Chester in May, drew only four runners each. The Group 3 Philip Leverhulme Dee Stakes had to be re-opened after only three horses were originally declared. In response, Channel 4 reportedly considered asking for the order of running of the day's races to be rescheduled, while, amid disquiet from bookmaker Victor Chandler (the sponsors of the Vase), Chester's chief executive threatened that one of the long-standing trials could face the axe. Chester has traditionally been seen as good preparation for Derby candidates, but whether the May meeting should still have two trials is open to debate. The Chester Vase over a mile and a half has a counterpart over the same distance at Lingfield, a track likened to Epsom, the Lingfield Trial being run in the latest season only a few days later. Eight of the last ten Derby winners raced as three-year-olds before Epsom, though none of those ran more than twice in the build-up. Interestingly, Ireland has no recognised trial over the full Derby distance yet has produced three of the last four Epsom winners.

The recent domination of the Derby by Irish-trained horses and the apparent strength of the Irish challenge again led to the media virtually cold-shouldering the home trials altogether, except for the Guineas. Too much is sometimes expected in a trial winner on form. Over twenty years on from Shergar's wide-margin wins at Sandown and Chester, before his record-breaking win at Epsom, there is still a 'Shergar syndrome' about middle-distance trials in particular, ignoring the fact that few Derby winners put up a performance before Epsom good enough to win the big race itself. For most, improvement has to be found—often through the test of stamina the Derby provides. Much of the post-race reaction to Kris Kin's win in the Dee Stakes focused on the circumstances surrounding it rather than the perform-ance in the race itself. Reportedly a lazy worker at home, Kris Kin was passed over at Chester by Kieren Fallon, who partnered favourite Big Bad Bob for the Dunlop stable instead, Kris Kin starting at 20/1, the rank outsider.

Derby winners can be hard to spot as two-year-olds, blossoming in the spring of their three-year-old careers. Barely sighted on his debut at Newmarket in October before winning a seven-furlong maiden at Doncaster later in the month, Kris Kin belied his odds at Chester to show smart form, beating Big Bad Bob going away by two lengths under Fergal Lynch. Bookmakers quoted him for Epsom afterwards at 25/1, but there was a lot to like about Kris Kin. A good-topped colt with a powerful, round action, he looked to have done well physically, having appeared on the weak side at two, and though not particularly stoutly bred he shaped as if he would stay the Derby trip. Indeed, had Kris Kin not unseated his rider shortly after the post, the general reaction of most of those watching would have been that he was ready to go round again. Fortunately, Kris Kin and Lynch, who was waving his whip in celebration of his first pattern success when he parted company, came to no harm. Kris Kin had still seemed green on only his third start, off the bridle in rear virtually from the off round the tight turns before storming through late on, and there looked to be more improvement to come. Reaction to Kris Kin's Chester win might have been less subdued had he been entered for Epsom at the time. One of five hundred and thirty-seven entries as a yearling, he was missing from the acceptors as a three-year-old in March, while thirteen of his stable-companions were left in, and connections declined the chance to re-enter him at a cost of £9,000 at the first supplementary stage only a few days before his reappearance. The late-May supplementary stage, which was introduced only in 1998 and will revert to its original cost of £75,000 from £90,000 in 2004, meant that Kris Kin did not miss the Derby, but publicising the Derby immediately after Chester would have been easier had he been an Epsom entry at the time. Perhaps it would be in the Derby's interests, and that of the trials, if in future some of the trials were to carry an automatic entry at Epsom for the winner.

As it was, Kris Kin tiptoed up to Epsom almost unnoticed. Later reportedly described by his trainer as one of the laziest horses he had handled, Kris Kin was said by Fallon, who rode him for the first time in a race in the Derby, to have

*Vodafone Derby Stakes, Epsom—Kris Kin (fifth from right) still has work to do
as The Great Gatsby (rail) and Dutch Gold lead the field round Tattenham Corner;
Balestrini and Alberto Giacometti (rail, partly hidden) come next, while Alamshar is tucked in,
tracking Lundy's Lane (striped cap); Norse Dancer (extreme left) has lots to do*

improved on the gallops since his reappearance. With guaranteed total prize money
of £1,250,000 there was no shortage of Derby runners, despite the low turnouts for
the trials. In fact, two outsiders, Skelligs Rock and Albanov, made history as the
first horses to be eliminated owing to a new safety limit of twenty, the eliminations
being decided by the lowest rated according to the BHB figures. All the same, the
field was the largest since the same number contested Shaamit's Derby in 1996.
Without Dalakhani, and in the absence of a single outstanding candidate on form,
the market was open. Two Thousand Guineas winner Refuse To Bend started favourite at 11/4 to maintain his unbeaten record after a narrow victory at Newmarket.
Alamshar, winner of Ireland's most important preparatory race, the Derrinstown
Stud Derby Trial at Leopardstown, was next best at 4/1. Racing Post Trophy winner
Brian Boru, one of four runners bidding to give Aidan O'Brien an unprecedented
third consecutive Derby success, completed the domination of the market by Irish-
trained horses at 9/2, with his stable-companions Alberto Giacometti, The Great
Gatsby and Balestrini at 12/1, 20/1 and 66/1 respectively. At 16/1, Two Thousand
Guineas third Norse Dancer was preferred to all but Kris Kin among the home trial
winners. Among them, Chester Vase winner Dutch Gold, Dante winner Magistretti
and Shield, successful in the Classic Trial at Sandown, started at 20/1. Franklins
Gardens, successful in the Derby Trial at Lingfield, was at 25/1.

Co-operation between rival television stations has improved to the viewer's
benefit in recent years, and the BBC had clips of some of the major trial winners in
action. Unfortunately, the opportunity to whet the viewer's appetite and allow them
to take sides, was lost by delaying the showing of the clips until the horses had
completed the parade. Derby Day unfolds in stages, which include the various
elements of the preliminaries, and no sooner had the anticipation built with some
excellent close-ups in the paddock, and of the horses on the course, than the flow
was interrupted by the decision to gloss over the runners moving to post. It resulted
in a double own goal. As the runners arrived at the post, the confidence of the BBC
team in Refuse To Bend seemed to be growing. But, what had little made of it was
Refuse To Bend's going too freely to the start. As the runners waited under a strong

547

sun, which made the ground much closer to firm than the official description of good, Kris Kin, who looked in fine shape in the paddock, got a bit warm down the neck and between his legs. Things were hotting up too in the betting ring, where Kris Kin's morning odds of 14/1 contracted to 6/1.

The Derby itself unfolds in stages too—defined by the characteristics of the course. From the stands, the stiffness of the prolonged early climb isn't so apparent—it takes a walk down to the start to appreciate the hundred-foot plus rise fully—but the momentum the runners gain as they race down to and around Tattenham Corner is more obvious. Things happen fast in the straight, which is mostly still downhill, and there's little time to take it all in. Providing commentary on the closing stages of the Derby must be one of the most stressful few seconds in television sport, but two furlongs out in 2003 the BBC's Jim McGrath was right on top of his job. 'Eddery goes for home on The Great Gatsby, Balestrini out after him from Dutch Gold.' And, then a change of tone. 'Here's Kris Kin, Norse Dancer down the outside,' he urged the listener to take note, running the two phrases together. 'The Great Gatsby—falling in a hole with half a furlong to go.' An ambitious call that one, perhaps. If the long-time leader The Great Gatsby was fading, it wasn't by much. Of course, McGrath knew, as did Eddery as he drove The Great Gatsby along, that the Derby course is no poacher's paradise. As the toll of the early hill kicks in hardest, there is one last climb, with the winning post in sight. The commentator was in full cry—'Kris Kin coming at him strongly, Alamshar down the outside.' As they reach the last climb each year in the Derby, the picture seems to slow slightly while the horses fight it out in front of the stands. Only a few yards out, at last there was certainty about the outcome. 'Kris Kin gets to the lead and Kris Kin wins the Derby.' He was the first late-May supplementary entry to do so.

Fallon drew widespread praise for his part in his second Derby success, following Oath in 1999, the latter another winner of the Dee Stakes, incidentally. Sir Michael Stoute, who had also won the race with Shergar in 1981 and Shahrastani in 1986, reportedly called Fallon's effort 'one of the greatest rides you will ever see at Epsom.' BBC Radio '5 Live' got one up on their television counterparts, giving listeners a valuable insight into the race when interviewing Fallon about tactics beforehand. In a programme which also featured one of its team, Luke Harvey, trying out the course on horseback, Fallon told listeners that he would be taking the Piggott route, as he called it, 'four or five back and one off the rail.' So he did, to an extent. But, for Fallon it wasn't all a matter of waiting and pouncing as it had been for Piggott on occasions. From an inside draw, Fallon had to fight for his place once the runners tacked over from the outside after three furlongs or so, a

Vodafone Derby Stakes, Epsom—Kris Kin finds plenty under pressure and overhauls The Great Gatsby, as Alamshar (No.1) stays on for third ahead of Norse Dancer (No.13), Balestrini and Dutch Gold

regular trouble-spot in the race. Once clear of trouble, Kris Kin travelled more smoothly for the most part than he had at Chester, but Fallon had to work on occasions to avoid losing his place as the ground fell away down Tattenham Hill. Turning out of Tattenham Corner, Kris Kin was disputing eighth with Alamshar. At this point, not unusually in the Derby, the leaders were getting away a bit. Briefly, Fallon's heart must have been in his mouth, but then he got a break. Three furlongs out, Brian Boru and Refuse To Bend left a gap right in front of him. Kris Kin was through in a flash and, manoeuvred three horses to his right, began to make ground relentlessly. Galvanising his mount, Fallon saved his whip until Kris Kin was properly balanced again, and, as the pair finally got upsides The Great Gatsby, three right-handed cracks were enough. If anything, Kris Kin was going away at the line.

Bookmakers pronounced the support for Kris Kin as one of the major Derby Day gambles, but the BBC seemed reluctant to develop the theme, giving the betting ring and betting exchanges a wide berth for most of the afternoon. Many in the media tried to put the gamble down to a return to the halcyon days of the race, seeing Fallon as the successor to Piggott's former mantle as 'the housewives' choice'. Television viewing figures hardly lend credence to the idea the gamble was inspired much from outside the usual racing or sporting audience, and it's likely the market was as much catching up with a horse that had waited a long time to get the green light to run, as being gripped by what the media termed the 'Fallon factor'. The BBC reportedly expressed itself as 'far from ecstatic' at viewing figures estimated at 3m for the race, warning that the numbers were a concern for the sport. The figures were also a blow to Epsom's attempt to re-establish the Derby in the nation's consciousness. Steps to promote the race nationally in 2003 included the Derby being written into an episode of the BBC's flagship soap *Eastenders* and a BBC local radio campaign. Epsom announced in 2003 that it had reached agreement with the British Horseracing Board to stage Derby Day on the first Saturday in June for the immediate future, thereby avoiding a direct clash with major sporting events until 2006 at least. As an experiment, the Derby was run later than usual in 2003 at four o'clock, but it might take more drastic measures to revitalise to a significant degree television viewing figures, which are currently only just over half what they were in 1997. With few exceptions nowadays, it seems sporting events need to be shown at the convenience of the viewer if they are to attract the largest audience. If Britain is a tea-on-a-tray society, a tea-time Derby, going off at six o'clock, might be the way forward.

When the 'Pinza' trophy in memory of Sir Gordon Richards' only Derby winner was handed to Kris Kin's owner Saeed Suhail at the presentation, Kieren Fallon was still beaming, as he had been from the moment Kris Kin was led back in. Fallon declared himself a changed man in 2003, a season which began with him announcing he had sought treatment in a clinic for 'alcohol related problems'. As the news leaked out, other riders were backed for the championship, but the race proved the most one-sided for years. Fallon, for whom Kris Kin was a ninth British classic success, and his second of the season following Russian Rhythm, finished more than sixty winners ahead of his nearest pursuer. His total of two hundred and eight successes between March and November gave him his sixth title in a seven-year period interrupted only by a career-threatening shoulder injury in mid-2000. Interestingly, fifty years on, there is quite a bit of Fallon in an appreciation of Sir Gordon's riding style written in the chapter on Pinza, his last Derby ride, in *The History of The Derby Stakes* by Roger Mortimer '. . . Richards was never such a polished horseman as Donoghue, and his style, a dangerous one for lesser men to copy, was unorthodox. In a close finish he seemed to ride not only rather upright, but often sideways, and with a completely loose rein . . . He was invariably in the right place at the critical stage, and above all possessed an overwhelming determination to win . . .' Tactically, Fallon's preferred approach is to sit close up in the pack, as it is with most modern-day riders. The general approach leads to many races being decided by finishing speed. The riding style Fallon has developed lends itself well to such tactics. When gathering his mount, Fallon, who tends to ride on a loose rein in the early stages of a race as well, is inclined to draw both reins as wide as he can in opposite directions, momentarily giving him maximum leverage on the bit, before launching his mount's final effort. In an age when guidelines mean the whip plays less of a part than it used to do in Piggott's era, for example, Fallon is still extremely strong in the saddle, riding with a longer length of stirrup than recently used to be the vogue. In more senses than one, he is very much a jockey for his time.

The somewhat cautious, tactical approach of many modern riders has an impact on the test the Derby provides. The course is only as stiff as the riders ask the horses to make it. If they all agreed to walk the first half mile, for example, the race would be no test of stamina at all. Riders' anxiety to get a good early position means the early stages of the Derby are usually run at a fairly strong pace, but the evidence of the clock does perhaps suggest that the test of stamina set by the Derby has become a little less stiff than it used to be. Kris Kin's official time of 2m 33.35sec has been bettered only by Lammtarra's Derby record set in 1995 and Galileo's time in 2001. The recent run of electrically-recorded times that have bettered Mahmoud's long-standing 1936 hand-timed record of 2m 33.8sec, which Lammtarra broke, contrasts with the impression made by time performance figures of late. Timeform's timefigures, calculated to take account of prevailing conditions, say more about time performance than bare times. Kris Kin's timerating of 119 was respectable, though in common with other recent editions of the Derby a little less than might have been expected looking at the form. The trend represents a contrast to the late-'seventies and 'eighties when a number of winners recorded timefigures some way in advance of the form assessments. The number of horses being bred for speed possibly plays its part in how the Derby is run too. The fewer the horses in the line-up proven at a mile and a half beforehand, or thought likely to be suited by the distance, the more runners will be ridden conservatively—one argument for the continuation of mile-and-a-half trials! It seems that, in terms of the test the race provides, in a changing world, even the winning post in the Derby no longer denotes an entirely fixed point.

Very fast timeratings in the Derby, of course, such as those put up by Troy (145) and Slip Anchor (143), owe much to the fact that those who recorded them were wide-margin winners of the race—horses who dominated their field on the day. No-one could look at the bare form of Kris Kin's length win over The Great Gatsby and say he was anything more than an ordinary winner of the Derby. At the time, Alamshar, beaten a short head for second, had still to develop into the horse he showed himself subsequently, while Refuse To Bend and Brian Boru clearly failed to give anything like their true running. The first five did come clear, however. Among them, The Great Gatsby and Balestrini ran only once more apiece, finishing unplaced. Norse Dancer, who was a length and a half behind Alamshar in fourth, had four more races after Epsom without winning.

Kris Kin also failed to win again after Epsom, joining Erhaab, Shaamit, Benny The Dip, High-Rise and Oath among the last ten Derby winners as being without a subsequent success as a three-year-old. Immediately after Epsom, Kris Kin looked sure to play a bigger part in the second half of the season than he did. He was as inexperienced as any in the field on Derby Day and victory meant he was unbeaten in three starts since his debut. Furthermore, when Kris Kin began his winning run at Epsom he still had a good four lengths to make up and, if any of the principals was better than the bare result, it looked to be him. After Alamshar pipped Dalakhani in the Irish Derby, Kris Kin started second favourite to Nayef at 7/2 for the King George VI and Queen Elizabeth Stakes at Ascot in July, with Alamshar at 13/2. Kris Kin had missed the Irish Derby, for which he would again have had to be supplemented, his trainer reportedly having the course walked and feeling the ground was likely to be too firm. By now, more about Kris Kin's withdrawal from the original Derby entries was emerging. 'That's why he was taken out of the Derby. He had a little problem with his joints,' racing manager Bruce Raymond was reported as saying. Kris Kin, it had also emerged after the Derby, had 'trotted up lame' forty-eight hours before the race, having to have his joints treated with ice. He was reported by his trainer to have had a hard race at Epsom, and connections were still expressing doubts before Ascot about running him on firm ground. As it turned out, morning rain at Ascot left the ground quite testing. Kris Kin looked to have progressed physically again since Epsom, but again warmed up as the preliminaries drew on, and he was in a real lather by the start this time. From a wide draw, he never got in a blow in a race run at a muddling pace, not helping his rider by being off the bridle when poorly positioned in Swinley Bottom. Forced four wide off the turn, as Alamshar went clear, Kris Kin took third from Bollin Eric only near the finish, beaten five and a half lengths by the winner, two lengths by Sulamani for second. It was probably Kris Kin's best effort all the same, and, given the way the race unfolded, it seemed reasonable to expect more from Kris Kin in the autumn.

There was no talk either of the St Leger, or of dropping back to a mile and a quarter, for Kris Kin after Ascot. He was to be trained for the Arc. Taking in the King George and the Arc with a Derby winner has become something shied away from, with most Derby winners aimed at either one or the other. Kris Kin failed to do himself justice in the autumn. He went down by a length and a half and two and a half lengths to Dalakhani and Doyen in the Prix Niel at Longchamp in September, unable to quicken once in the clear after his rider had become involved in a sustained barging match with the eventual fifth, his action looking a little ragged by the end. Kris Kin looked as though he would be better for the race after his break, but he beat only two home in the Arc three weeks later. Kris Kin had his stable-companion First Charter in the race as a pacemaker, and looked fitter than in the Niel, but he was already in trouble on the inside when hampered by Doyen before the home turn, eased right up and finishing one of three tailed off. It was a tame finale.

In the eyes of the breeding world nowadays, the emperor in his suit of new clothes can hide his modesty relatively well compared to a Derby winner without a follow-up win in a major all-aged event. Kris Kin will have to start almost all over again in making his name at stud and will stand at Sheikh Hamdan's Derrinstown Stud in Ireland at €8,000, with the October 1st concession. Bolstered by their subsequent successes in the Arc, King George and Breeders' Cup respectively, Sinndar, Galileo and High Chaparral will stand at €20,000, €40,000 and €35,000 in 2004 (Sinndar and Galileo were more expensive still in 2003 than they will be in 2004). It is a further sign of the times that Group 2 sprint winner Acclamation, retired at the end of 2003, will stand at €10,000. If Kris Kin fails in Europe, there will almost certainly be a place for him at stud in Japan, alongside several Derby winners from the 'nineties. Kris Kin's sire Kris S was represented there in 2003 by Symboli Kris S, Japanese Horse of the Year for each of the last two seasons. Kris S, who died in 2002 at the age of twenty-five, also enjoyed Grade 1 success in America in 2003, when Action This Day took the Breeders' Cup Juvenile and the three-year-old Kicken Kris the Secretariat Stakes on turf. Another Grade 1 win came from the Sword Dancer Handicap winner Whitmore's Conn who also starts stud duties in Ireland in 2004. Kris S sired plenty more good horses in America, including Brocco, Prized, Hollywood Wildcat and Soaring Softly—all winners at the Breeders' Cup as well—and, of his other sons, Arch, Brocco and Prized are now successful sires themselves. Kris S had a truncated career on the racecourse due to a bowed tendon sustained when finishing fourth in the Grade 2 San Felipe Handicap early in his three-year-old season. Winner of two of his three starts as a juvenile and a minor stakes race over nine furlongs on his reappearance at three, Kris S still stood at 5,000 dollars in Florida in his eighth season at stud before his Grade 1 winners eventually raised his fee to around 150,000 dollars. Kris S was even slower to catch on in Europe, where Dr Fong (who has made a promising start to his own stud career) was the first to give a significant boost to his reputation, winning the St James's Palace Stakes in 1998. Kris S's representatives in 2003, which also included the smart Sabre d'Argent and the two-year-old Lucky Story, were enough to see Kris S top the sires' table for win-money in Britain ahead of Sadler's Wells.

Kris Kin completed an Epsom classic double for his grandsire Roberto, also responsible for Casual Look's sire Red Ransom. Derby winners are still a self-perpetuating breed. Roberto was also the grandsire of the 1997 Derby winner Benny The Dip, a son of Silver Hawk, while High-Rise the following year was another in the 'nineties with a Derby winner as his grandsire in Shirley Heights. Kris Kin completes a full set of major European Derby winners bred by the Niarchos family. Hernando carried the colours of Stavros Niarchos in the Prix du Jockey Club in 1993, while Dream Well won for the family at Chantilly and at the Curragh in 1998, two years after Niarchos' death. Dream Well's half-brother Sulamani followed suit for the Niarchos family at Chantilly in 2002. Dream Well remained with his breeders after failing to reach his reserve as a yearling, but Kris Kin was knocked down at Keeneland for 275,000 dollars.

			Hail To Reason
	Kris S (USA)	Roberto	Bramalea
	(b 1977)	(b 1969)	Princequillo
Kris Kin (USA)		Sharp Queen	Bridgework
(ch.c. 2000)		(b 1965)	BlushingGroom
	Angel In My Heart (FR)	Rainbow Quest	I Will Follow
	(ch 1992)	(b 1981)	Lyphard
		Sweetly	Sweet And Lovely II
		(b 1975)	

Kris Kin's grandam Sweetly won a maiden and two allowance races in North America as a three-year-old and was acquired by Niarchos from fellow shipping magnate Ravi Tikkoo after failing to add to those successes in Britain. At stud, Sweetly produced Niarchos' Prix de la Salamandre winner Common Grounds and the useful French seven-furlong and mile winner Lightning Fire. Sent to Rainbow Quest, Sweetly then foaled Kris Kin's dam Angel In My Heart, a smart and consistent performer for John Hammond in France, where she won the Prix de Psyche over a mile and a quarter. Angel In My Heart, who was also successful at a mile, was second at a mile and a half before returning to shorter to finish second in the Prix de l'Opera, as well as the Yellow Ribbon Invitational, the Matriarch Stakes and (as a four-year-old) the Santa Ana Handicap in America. Angel In My Heart's first foal, Venturer (by Gone West), made 400,000 dollars as a yearling, but he

Mr Saeed Suhail's "Kris Kin"

showed only useful form in winning three races over seven furlongs and a mile for John Gosden. Angel In My Heart's second foal, Mimalia (by Silver Hawk), was sent to the Newmarket Sales in December 2002 after being third over a mile and a quarter in France. Sold privately after being led out unsold at 23,000 guineas, she was bought back by the Niarchos family after Kris Kin's Derby victory—no doubt at a handsome profit for the purchaser! Kris Kin's two-year-old half-brother by the Breeders' Cup Sprint winner Cherokee Run made the frame in a couple of maidens in the States in 2003. Named Seyalateralligator, he had been snapped up for $250,000 as a yearling. A high-class colt at his best, Kris Kin proved genuine under pressure, despite his rather indolent nature, and acted on good to firm and good to soft ground, as well as being a winner on soft. *Sir Michael Stoute*

KRISTAL DANCER (IRE) 3 b.f. Charnwood Forest (IRE) 125 – Kristal's Paradise **84** (IRE) 100 (Bluebird (USA) 125) [2003 –p: 7g 8.2g3 10f4 9.9d2 10m6 11.1g* 12g5 Oct 31] rather leggy filly: fairly useful performer: won maiden at Ripon in September: good fifth in handicap at Newmarket: stayed 1½m: acted on firm and good to soft going: stud. *J. L. Dunlop*

KRISTAL FOREST (IRE) 4 b.g. Charnwood Forest (IRE) 125 – Kristal's Paradise **63 d** (IRE) 100 (Bluebird (USA) 125) [2003 77: f12g2 f14s f12g f12s3 12g f12g 9.9m 12g f16g Nov 19] big, rangy gelding: disappointing maiden: stays 12.4f: acts on firm going and fibresand: tried in cheekpieces. *Mrs S. Lamyman*

KRISTAL'S DREAM (IRE) 2 b.f. (May 1) Night Shift (USA) – Kristal's Paradise **77 p** (IRE) 100 (Bluebird (USA) 125) [2003 6.1m5 6g6 6g 7m3 8m* Oct 20] has a round action: fourth foal: half-sister to 3-y-o Kristal Dancer: dam 1¾m/2m winner: fair performer: improved to win nursery at Pontefract by short head from Infidelity, making all: will be suited by 1¼m/1½m: should do better still at 3 yrs. *J. L. Dunlop*

KRISTENSEN 4 ch.g. Kris S (USA) – Papaha (FR) 103 (Green Desert (USA) 127) **93** [2003 85: p12g f16.2g2 13.8m4 10m 16m2 16m2 16g2 20m5 21d5 16.1m6 16g2 18m3 16g3 Nov 5] smallish, sturdy gelding: fairly useful handicapper: particularly good effort when third of 36 to Landing Light in Cesarewitch at Newmarket penultimate start: effective at 1½m to 21f: acts on all-weather, firm and soft ground: wears cheekpieces: usually tracks leaders: consistent. *D. Eddy*

KRISTIANSAND 3 b.c. Halling (USA) 133 – Zonda 100 (Fabulous Dancer (USA) **71** 124) [2003 10g 9m4 10.3m2 9.2m6 7g 9.7m* 8f 10m5 9.1m 8m5 Oct 6] seventh foal: half-brother to several winners, including smart 6f (at 2 yrs) to 1m (in UAE) winner Zoning (by Warning): dam, 5f to 8.5f (in USA) winner, out of half-sister to Oh So Sharp: fair handicapper: won apprentice event at Folkestone in August: stays 1¼m: raced only on good ground or firmer: often leads: sold 9,000 gns. *M. R. Channon*

KRISTOFFERSEN 3 ch.c. Kris 135 – Towaahi (IRE) (Caerleon (USA) 132) [2003 **82** 72p: p8g2 f9.4g4 8f* 8m 10m3 12f5 10g4 p12g3 p13g Dec 6] fairly useful performer: left W. Jarvis prior to winning minor event at Brighton in April: left G. Butler 14,000 gns before final outing: stays 1½m: acts on polytrack, raced only on good ground or firmer on turf: tends to carry head high. *R. M. Stronge*

KRUGERRAND (USA) 4 ch.g. Gulch (USA) – Nasers Pride (USA) (Al Nasr (FR) **92 §** 126) [2003 92: 6g 7g 8.3g6 8.9f* 10g 8m 8d5 8.3g4 9m 8f4 8m Oct 17] big, lengthy geld-ing: fairly useful handicapper: consistent in 2003 and won at York (sweated freely) in June: stays 9f: acts on firm and good to soft going: tongue tied once at 2 yrs: headstrong, and has worn crossed noseband: sometimes slowly away: carries head high, and some-times looks none to keen. *W. J. Musson*

KRYPTON 3 b.g. Kylian (USA) – Tiama (IRE) 50 (Last Tycoon 131) [2003 –: p10g **–** f11s Feb 13] little sign of ability: tried blinkered. *P. D. Cundell*

KSCHESSINKA (USA) 2 br.f. (Apr 24) Nureyev (USA) 131 – Gran Dama (USA) **– p** (Rahy (USA) 115) [2003 6m Oct 4] $210,000Y: sturdy filly: second foal: dam, 6f/6.5f winner in USA, half-sister to useful performers Jarah (best at 1m) and Meshhed (stayed 1¼m): 16/1 and very green, ninth of 10 in maiden at Newmarket: should do better. *W. J. Haggas*

KUFOOF (USA) 3 b.f. Silver Hawk (USA) 123 – Barakat 93 (Bustino 136) [2003 **74** 10d5 Jul 26] half-sister to several winners, including useful 1¼m performer Ta Awun (by Housebuster) and fairly useful 1½m winner Mumaris (by Capote): dam, winner around 1¾m, half-sister to Ibn Bey and Roseate Tern from family of Teleprompter: 25/1, fifth of 10 to Peace in maiden at Nottingham: sold 2,000 gns in December. *A. C. Stewart*

KUKA   2 b.g. (Jan 8) Polar Prince (IRE) 117 – Crissem (IRE) 70 (Thatching 131) [2003   **63**
7d Nov 7] big, rangy gelding: third foal: half-brother to 4-y-o Freya Alex: dam 2-y-o 5f
winner who stayed 7f: 33/1 and better for race, eleventh of 18 in maiden at Doncaster.
R. Hollinshead

KUKINI   2 ch.g. (Apr 12) Presidium 124 – Auntie Fay (IRE) (Fayruz 116) [2003 p5g   **–**
Mar 15] 500Y: third foal: half-brother to 5-y-o Gordons Friend: dam of little account: last
of 10 in minor event at Lingfield: dead. *B. S. Rothwell*

KUMAKAWA   5 ch.g. Dancing Spree (USA) – Maria Cappuccini 70 (Siberian Express   **– §**
(USA) 125) [2003 –§, a60§: f8s⁵ f7g f8s² f8s* f8g⁵ p10g f7g Nov 19] tall gelding: **a52 §**
modest performer: won apprentice claimer at Southwell (left D. Ivory) in January: stays
9.4f: acts on fibresand, very lightly raced on turf nowadays: tried in headgear: has been
edgy/reluctant at stall: difficult ride: unreliable. *E. A. Wheeler*

KUMARI (IRE)   2 b.f. (Feb 25) Desert Story (IRE) 115 – Glow Tina (IRE) (Glow   **48**
(USA)) [2003 p5g⁶ 5.2m⁵ 6.1m 6f f5g f6g Dec 19] IR 5,200F, 4,500Y: close-coupled
filly: fifth foal: half-sister to 2 winners, including fairly useful Irish 2001 2-y-o 6f winner
Golden Glow (by Up And At 'em): dam ran once in Ireland: poor maiden: likely to prove
best at 5f/6f: acts on all-weather and firm going. *W. M. Brisbourne*

KUNDA (IRE)   2 b.f. (Feb 9) Intikhab (USA) 135 – Ustka 60 (Lomond (USA) 128)   **96**
[2003 6m² 6d³ 6m* 7g⁵ 6g² Oct 31] rather leggy filly: half-sister to several winners,
including smart 1¼m to 15f winner Travelmate (by Persian Bold), 7-y-o Kuster and 5-y-o
Team-Mate: dam, 7f winner, closely related to smart middle-distance stayer Braashee:
useful performer: won maiden at Newbury in August: best effort when 1¼ lengths second
of 7 to Dowager in listed event at Newmarket final start, slowly away: should stay at least
1m. *R. Hannon*

KURINGAI   2 b.c. (Jan 31) Royal Applause 124 – Talighta (USA) 62 (Barathea (IRE)   **72**
127) [2003 p5g⁴ 5g p5g³ 5f⁴ 5m³ 5m² 6m² 5.3f* 6g³ 5.2m 6g³ 5f³ 6m³ 6.1m 5.1m² p6g
Dec 30] 3,200Y: smallish, good-bodied colt: first foal: dam Irish sprint maiden: fair performer: made all in maiden at Brighton in June: effective at 5f/6f: acts on polytrack and
firm going: often races prominently: sometimes wanders: tough and reliable. *B. W. Duke*

KUSTER   7 b.g. Indian Ridge 123 – Ustka 60 (Lomond (USA) 128) [2003 89: 10.1m   **97**
10.4m 11.9f³ 11.9g* 12d 11.7f* 11.9f* 12m⁵ Oct 3] good-bodied gelding: unimpressive
mover: useful handicapper: better than ever in 2003, winning at Haydock (apprentices)
in July, Bath (ladies) in August and Haydock (beat Barman ½ length) in September: stays
1½m: acts on firm and soft going: usually blinkered. *L. M. Cumani*

KUSTOM KIT FOR HER   3 b.f. Overbury (IRE) 116 – Antonias Melody 86 (Rambo   **–**
Dancer (CAN) 107) [2003 37: f11g f7g f8s⁵ f6g 10m⁵ f7g⁴ 7f f7g² f8g f6s Dec 27] modest   **a54**
maiden on all-weather: stays 7f: acts on fibresand, little form on turf: blinkered (well
beaten) last 2 starts: usually races prominently. *S. R. Bowring*

KUWAIT THUNDER (IRE)   7 ch.g. Mac's Imp (USA) 116 – Romangoddess (IRE)   **– §**
(Rhoman Rule (USA)) [2003 47§, a43§: f14s f12s 12m Apr 8] quite good-topped gelding: poor handicapper: well beaten in 2003: tried visored/tongue tied. *D. Carroll*

KWAI BABY (USA)   2 gr.f. (Mar 11) Charnwood Forest (IRE) 125 – Roses In The   **–**
Snow (IRE) 101 (Be My Guest (USA) 126) [2003 5g 6g 7g Jun 21] 2,800Y: third foal:
half-sister to a winner in USA by Gulch: dam, 1m winner in Britain and successful at 6f
in USA, out of sister to smart performer up to 1½m Shining Water, herself dam of Tenby:
well beaten in minor events/maiden. *J. J. Bridger*

KYALAMI (IRE)   4 b.g. Kylian (USA) – Nikkicola (USA) (Damascus (USA)) [2003   **–**
–: f16g⁶ f12g Dec 22] fourth foal: half-brother to 4 winners, including Irish 1¼m/
13f winner Feelin' Looser (by Mazaad): dam Irish maiden (stayed 1½m): well beaten
all 6 starts, leaving R. Donohoe in Ireland and off 16 months prior to reappearance.
M. J. Polglase

KYLE OF LOCHALSH   3 gr.g. Vettori (IRE) 119 – Shaieef (IRE) 66 (Shareef Dancer   **64**
(USA) 135) [2003 57: 10g 8m 9g⁵ 9m* 10m 10g³ 10.2m p10g p10g Dec 20] leggy
gelding: modest handicapper: won at Goodwood in May: stays easy 1¼m: raced on good/
good to firm ground on turf, below form on polytrack. *G. G. Margarson*

KYLKENNY   8 b.g. Kylian (USA) – Fashion Flow (Balidar 133) [2003 84: f11s² f11s*   **92**
f11g* f12g³ f11g* 10m⁶ 10m⁴ 12g 11.9f² 10.5m⁴ 12m 11.7f⁵ 12g 12d f12g⁴ Dec 19]
angular, workmanlike gelding: fairly useful performer: better than ever in 2003, winning
minor event and 2 handicaps at Southwell in February/March: short-headed by Sporting
Gesture in ladies handicap at York in June: effective at 1¼m/easy 1½m: acts on fibresand,
firm and good to soft going: tongue tied: sometimes wanders: tough. *H. Morrison*

KYO BID 3 b.g. Endoli (USA) 108 – Hebe (IRE) (Tirol 127) [2003 8m 10m 10.1m⁶ – Apr 22] 500Y: first foal: dam unraced: well beaten in maidens. *M. Brittain*

KYTHIA (IRE) 2 b.f. (Mar 9) Kahyasi 130 – Another Rainbow (IRE) 72§ (Rainbows **73** For Life (CAN)) [2003 7.1m³ 7.5m* 8m⁵ Oct 20] €13,000Y: small filly: first foal: dam, placed up to 1½m and became one to treat with caution, half-sister to Nell Gwyn winner Reunion: fair form: won maiden at Beverley in September, helping force pace: creditable fifth in nursery at Pontefract: should be suited by 1¼m/1½m. *H. Morrison*

L

LAABBIJ (USA) 2 ch.c. (Mar 1) Shuailaan (USA) 122 – United Kingdom (USA) 93 **71 p** (Danzig (USA)) [2003 8g Oct 25] fifth foal: half-brother to fairly useful 1m winner Hakeyma (by Gone West) and to 7f/1m UAE winner Mannjam (by Gulch): dam, 1m (in France) and 1¼m winner, closely related to smart 1¼m winner La Confederation out of Oaks winner Unite: 10/1, 12 lengths seventh of 17 to Salford City in maiden at Newbury: will stay at least 1¼m: should improve. *M. P. Tregoning*

LAAWARIS (USA) 2 b.c. (Apr 15) Souvenir Copy (USA) 113 – Seattle Kat (USA) **78 p** (Seattle Song (USA) 130) [2003 7m* Jun 17] $17,000Y, 65,000 2-y-o: useful-looking colt: fluent mover: eighth foal: closely related to useful 6f (including at 2 yrs) winner Cubism (by Miswaki) and half-brother to 2 winners in USA: dam, won up to 1¼m in USA, sister to Grade 2 9f winner Whadjathink: 4/1 and green, won 9-runner maiden at Thirsk by 1¼ lengths from Whispered Promises, getting on top late on: likely to stay 1m: seems sure to improve. *J. A. Osborne*

LABELLED WITH LOVE 3 ch.g. Zilzal (USA) 137 – Dream Baby (Master Willie – 129) [2003 10m Jul 17] sixth foal: closely related to 3 winners, including 1998 2-y-o 6f winner Dreaming (by Polar Falcon) and 5-y-o Figura, both fairly useful: dam ran once: 66/1, well held in maiden at Leicester, very slowly away. *W. G. M. Turner*

LABRETT 6 b.g. Tragic Role (USA) – Play The Game 70 (Mummy's Game 120) [2003 **92** 84, a82: 7g⁶ 8.3g⁵ 7m* 7f 8m⁴ 8.5m* 7g² 8f³ 10.1m⁴ 7d³ p8g⁶ 9g⁵ p8g* f9.4g f8g⁶ p8g* **a89** Dec 30] good-topped gelding: fairly useful handicapper: won at Brighton in June, Epsom in July and Lingfield in November and December: probably best at 7f to 9f nowadays: acts on all-weather, firm and soft going: effective in headgear or not: sometimes tongue tied: has swished tail: sometimes slowly away: held up: consistent. *Miss Gay Kelleway*

LACONIA (IRE) 2 b.f. (Mar 8) Orpen (USA) 116 – Mislead (IRE) 77 (Distinctly **64** North (USA) 115) [2003 f5g 6g 5.1m³ p5g⁵ f5g Nov 14] IR 5,000F, £5,000Y: big filly: first foal: dam 2-y-o 5f winner: modest maiden: likely to prove best at 5f: best form on polytrack/good to firm going. *J. S. Moore*

LA CORUJERA 3 b.f. Case Law 113 – Aybeegirl 66 (Mazilier (USA) 107) [2003 68: **72 d** 7m² 7m 7f⁵ 6m⁵ 6m 6m⁶ f6g Nov 19] workmanlike filly: fair maiden: well below form last 3 starts: effective at 6f/7f: acts on fibresand, firm and good to soft going: edgy sort, sometimes early to post: sometimes races freely/finds little. *T. D. Barron*

LA CORUNA 2 b.f. (May 8) Deploy 131 – Valencia 79 (Kenmare (FR) 125) [2003 **92 p** 7.6m* 7g* Oct 28] third foal: half-sister to 3-y-o Deportivo and fairly useful 2001 2-y-o 5f winner Irish Vale (by Wolfhound): dam, second at 1m at 2 yrs only start, half-sister to very smart performers Wandesta (up to 13.5f in Britain/USA) and De Quest (up to 12.5f in France): won maiden at Lingfield (slowly away) in August and minor event at Redcar (by 6 lengths from West Highland Way, quickening impressively from front) in October: free-going sort, but likely to stay 1m: useful prospect. *R. Charlton*

LA CUCARACHA 2 b.f. (Mar 26) Piccolo 121 – Peggy Spencer 77 (Formidable **95 +** (USA) 125) [2003 5m* 5.2m* May 16] good-topped filly: fourth foal: half-sister to 2002 2-y-o 6f winner Takes Two To Tango (by Groom Dancer): dam 6f/7f winner: useful form: won maiden at Leicester in April and minor event at Newbury (by 2½ lengths from Ma'soola) in May: suffered injury after, but had recovered by end of season: should stay 6f. *B. W. Hills*

LA DANSEUSE 2 b.f. (Apr 24) Groom Dancer (USA) 128 – Alik (FR) 113 (Targowice **49** (USA) 130) [2003 6m 7.5m⁶ f8s³ p8g⁶ Dec 20] sturdy filly: half-sister to several winners, including smart French 7f to 1¼m performer Goofalik (by Lyphard) and 3-y-o Advent-urist: dam French 1m winner: poor maiden: should stay at least 1¼m. *G. C. Bravery*

LADIES DAY   3 b.f. Robellino (USA) 127 – Fighting Run (Runnett 125) [2003 10d[5]   **69**
12m 10g[5] f9.4g p12g Nov 12] 4,500F, IR 60,000Y: good-topped filly: half-sister to 7.5f   **a–**
winner Croire (by Lomond) and to 3 winners abroad: dam, maiden, from family of
Central Park and Moon Ballad: fair maiden: very stiff task second outing: stays 1¼m:
showed nothing on all-weather, finding hints. *T. G. Mills*

LADIES KNIGHT   3 b.g. Among Men (USA) 124 – Lady Silk 67 (Prince Sabo 123)   **–**
[2003 48: p5g[4] f5g[2] f5s[4] p5g[2] p5g* p5g[5] 5d 5m[4] f6s 5g p6g f5g f5g f5s* Dec 27] leggy,   **a64**
angular gelding: modest performer: won maiden at Lingfield in March and claimer at
Southwell in December: effective at 5f/6f: acts on all-weather: tried visored: restless in
stall and reluctant in race penultimate outing: none too consistent. *D. Shaw*

LA DOLFINA   3 b.f. Pennekamp (USA) 130 – Icecapped 91 (Caerleon (USA) 132)   **94**
[2003 67: 10f[2] 10.2m[4] 10m* 9.3f* 10m[4] 10.3d 8.1d[5] 8.5d* 10m Oct 16] rather leggy,
angular filly: fairly useful handicapper: won at Brighton in May, Carlisle in June and
Epsom in October: not discredited when tenth to Al Ihtithar in listed event at Newmarket
final outing: best up to 1¼m: acts on firm and good to good ground: has been early to post/
raced freely. *H. Morrison*

LADY ALRUNA (IRE)   4 ch.f. Alhaarth (IRE) 126 – In Tranquility (IRE) (Shalford   **61 d**
(IRE) 124§) [2003 68: p6g p6g f6s 6m 7d[5] 7m 8d f6g Nov 14] modest maiden: below
form following reappearance, leaving P. Makin after third start, I. McInnes after fourth:
stays 7f: acts on good to firm ground, good to soft and polytrack: has worn headgear:
probably ungenuine. *P. T. Midgley*

LADY ARNICA   4 b.f. Ezzoud (IRE) 126 – Brand (Shareef Dancer (USA) 135) [2003   **–**
–: 14.1d May 16] lengthy, angular filly: well held in 3 maidens. *A. W. Carroll*

LADY AT LEISURE (IRE)   3 ch.f. Dolphin Street (FR) 125 – In A Hurry (FR) (In   **–**
Fijar (USA) 121) [2003 55, a–: p10g[5] Jan 4] leggy, quite good-topped filly: modest form
at 2 yrs: well held only outing in 2003. *W. G. M. Turner*

LADY BAHIA (IRE)   2 b.f. (Feb 12) Orpen (USA) 116 – Do The Right Thing 71 (Bus-   **69**
ted 134) [2003 f6s 5m 8.1f[2] 7d[4] 6m Oct 20] 5,500Y: big, good-topped filly: unimpressive
mover: third foal: half-sister to 4-y-o Nemo Fugat: dam, 1½m winner, half-sister to useful
2000 2-y-o sprinter Bram Stoker: fair maiden: second at Haydock: stays 1m: acts on firm
and good to soft ground. *R. P. Elliott*

LADY BEAR (IRE)   5 b.m. Grand Lodge (USA) 125 – Boristova (IRE) 79 (Royal   **108**
Academy (USA) 130) [2003 103: 10m[3] 10m[4] 9d[2] 8.3d* 8.5m[6] 8m[6] 8.3f[3] 8.1g* 8g* 7.9m[6]
8.1d* 9m[4] Oct 4] good-topped mare: useful performer: won minor event at Hamilton
in May, and William Hill Mile (Handicap) at Goodwood (by 1¼ lengths from Faithful
Warrior) and listed race at Sandown (beat Zyzania by length), both in August: creditable
fourth to Chivalry in Cambridgeshire at Newmarket final start: effective at 1m/1¼m: acts
on any turf ground and fibresand: usually blinkered/visored: often slowly away/gets
behind: sent to Saudi Arabia. *R. A. Fahey*

LADY BETAMBEAU (IRE)   3 b.f. Grand Lodge (USA) 125 – Boristova (IRE) 79   **–**
(Royal Academy (USA) 130) [2003 63p: 7d 8g 10m May 30] close-coupled filly:
maiden: little form at 3 yrs. *L. M. Cumani*

LADY BIRGITTA   5 b.m. Emperor Jones (USA) 119 – Badiane (USA) (Green Forest   **–**
(USA) 134) [2003 79d, a92d: f8s[2] f7s[4] f8.5g[6] f8.5g[3] f8g Apr 4] angular mare: modest   **a60**
performer nowadays: probably best at 1m/9f: acts on all-weather, good to firm and good
to soft ground: visored (raced too freely) penultimate start: has found little. *K. R. Burke*

*William Hill Mile (Handicap), Goodwood—Lady Bear shows herself better than ever
in accounting for Faithful Warrior (left), Nashaab and Winning Venture*

LADY BLADE (IRE)   2 b.f. (Mar 28) Daggers Drawn (USA) 114 – Singhana (IRE)   **64**
(Mouktar 129) [2003 6m⁶ 7f³ 8g⁶ 8m Oct 20] 10,000Y: tall, angular filly: fifth foal: dam,
Irish 1¾m winner, half-sister to dam of Sinndar: modest maiden: third at Brighton: should
stay 1m: acts on firm going. *B. Hanbury*

LADY BOXER   7 b.m. Komaite (USA) – Lady Broker 54 (Petorius 117) [2003 82?:   **69 d**
f5s 6d 6.1s 6f⁵ 7g 6.1d 6m² Oct 7] close-coupled mare: just fair performer at best in
2003, leaving A. Newcombe after reappearance: effective at 6f to 7.6f: goes well on soft/
heavy ground: sometimes slowly away. *M. Mullineaux*

LADY BROUGHTON (IRE)   2 ch.f. (Feb 6) Grand Lodge (USA) 125 – Veronica   **–**
(Persian Bold 123) [2003 7g Nov 1] 15,500Y: big, workmanlike filly: half-sister to several winners, including 1¼m winner Canford and Irish 1½m winner El Bueno (both useful
and by Caerleon): dam, winner around 1m in USA, half-sister to useful 1m performer
Lady Fairfax: 50/1 and backward, well held in maiden at Newmarket. *W. J. Musson*

LADY CATHERINE   3 ch.f. Bering 136 – Queen Catherine (Machiavellian (USA)   **107**
123) [2003 101p: a8f⁶ 11m² May 18] useful performer: trained by H-A. Pantall in France
at 2 yrs: much the better effort in 2003 when 1¼ lengths second to Meridiana in Oaks
d'Italia at Milan, leading until inside final 1f: stays 11f: acts on soft and good to firm
going, below form on dirt: left Godolphin in October. *Saeed bin Suroor*

LADY CONNIE   2 ch.f. (Mar 25) Atraf 116 – Paris Mist (Paris House 123) [2003 5m   **–**
Apr 23] 1,000Y: small, strong filly: first foal: dam unraced: 12/1, slowly away and well
held in seller at Catterick. *K. A. Ryan*

LADY DOMINATRIX (IRE)   4 b.f. Danehill Dancer (IRE) 117 – Spout House (IRE)   **109**
55 (Flash of Steel 120) [2003 112: 5g 6m 5m⁵ 5f Jun 17] tall, leggy filly: smart performer
at 3 yrs: wearing cheekpieces, easily best effort (useful form) in 2003 when respectable
fifth to Porlezza in Prix du Gros-Chene at Chantilly: found little final outing: effective at
5f/6f: yet to race on heavy going, acts on any other: often makes running: has carried head
awkwardly. *Mrs P. N. Dutfield*

LADY DRUE (IRE)   4 b.f. Darnay 117 – Sharkiyah (IRE) 75 (Polish Precedent (USA)   **–**
131) [2003 –: 11.5g 11.8m 13g Jun 12] little worthwhile form: tried visored. *A. P. Jarvis*

LADY DULCET   3 b.f. Thowra (FR) – Freedom Weekend (USA) (Shahrastani (USA)   **–**
135) [2003 –: f8.5g 12.1d 8.1m⁴ Jun 23] well held in maidens. *D. Burchell*

LADY DUNKIRK (IRE)   2 b.f. (Apr 3) Daggers Drawn (USA) 114 – La Soeur   **57 d**
d'Albert 47 (Puissance 110) [2003 5.7f⁶ 5.3f³ f6g p7g 7g 6m Oct 17] 8,500 2-y-o: first
foal: dam, lightly-raced maiden, half-sister to smart 7f/1m performer Sunstreak: modest
maiden: regressed after third at Brighton: should stay at least 6f. *Mrs Lydia Pearce*

LADY ELLENDUNE   2 b.f. (Mar 3) Piccolo 121 – Eileen's Lady 50 (Mtoto 134)   **43**
[2003 6g 6m 6.1m 6m 6m f8.5g p6g⁶ Dec 20] 1,000Y: smallish filly: first foal: dam,
maiden who stayed 1¾m, out of half-sister to smart middle-distance fillies Braiswick
and Percy's Lass: poor maiden: stays 6f: tried blinkered/in cheekpieces: has been slowly
away/hung right. *D. J. S. ffrench Davis*

LADY ERN   2 b.f. (Apr 23) Young Ern 120 – Just Lady 72 (Emarati (USA) 74) [2003   **44**
f5s⁵ f6g² p5g³ 5m⁶ f5g⁵ 5g⁵ 6m³ 6m Oct 3] third living foal: half-sister to 5-y-o Justalord: **a49**
dam 2-y-o 5f winner: poor maiden: placed in sellers: stays 6f: acts on all-weather and
good to firm ground: tongue tied last 2 starts: sometimes slowly away. *W. G. M. Turner*

LADY FRANPALM (IRE)   3 b.f. Danehill Dancer (IRE) 117 – Be Nimble (Wattle-   **53**
field 117) [2003 50: p5g⁵ 6g⁴ 5m⁴ 6m Sep 3] leggy filly: modest maiden: should stay 7f:
acts on polytrack: raced only on good/good to firm ground on turf. *M. J. Haynes*

LADY GEORGINA   2 gr.f. (Jan 17) Linamix (FR) 127 – Georgia Venture 98 (Shirley   **75**
Heights 130) [2003 7g³ 7m⁴ 7.1m³ 8g 7d Nov 8] small, angular filly: first foal: dam,
1¾m/2m winner, out of half-sister to Kentucky Derby winner Cannonade: fair maiden:
third at Leicester and Warwick: bred to stay at least 1¼m, but races freely: acts on good to
firm going: tongue tied last 3 outings. *J. R. Fanshawe*

LADY GLYDE   3 b.f. Inchinor 119 – Happy And Blessed (IRE) (Prince Sabo 123)   **37**
[2003 45: 7g 7m f9.4g 8g⁶ 11m 10.2f⁵ f12g 10f⁴ 11.9f Aug 7] angular filly: poor maiden
handicapper: stays 1¼m. *A. D. Smith*

LADY HAMILTON   3 ch.f. Double Trigger (IRE) 123 – Crown Flight (Buzzards Bay   **–**
128§) [2003 12m⁵ Sep 9] second reported foal: dam unraced: 50/1, tailed off in maiden at
Catterick. *M. E. Sowersby*

LADY HIBERNIA   3 b.f. Anabaa (USA) 130 – Taj Victory 68 (Final Straw 127) [2003   **–**
p6g 10g 11.1m p8g May 17] seventh foal: half-sister to several winners, including 6-y-o

Highland Reel and 11f winner Pride of The Park (by Marju): dam, 1¼m to 13f winner, half-sister to Gold Cup winner Indian Queen: little form. *J. Noseda*

LADY IN COMMAND (IRE)   3 b.f. In Command (IRE) 114 – Harmer (IRE) 72   –
(Alzao (USA) 117) [2003 p8g 8.3g 7m 7.5m 7d Jul 30] 10,000Y: compact filly: half-sister to 3 winners, including fairly useful 1995 2-y-o 5f winner Amaretto Bay (by Common Grounds), later sprint winner abroad: dam maiden who stayed 7f: no form: tried blinkered/in cheekpieces: has raced freely. *R. M. Beckett*

LADY JUSTICE   3 b.f. Compton Place 125 – Zinzi (Song 132) [2003 67: 5.2m⁵ 5m   **66**
Jun 7] lengthy filly: fair form at best in maidens: may prove best at 5f/6f: acts on good to firm and good to soft ground. *W. Jarvis*

LADY KILLER (IRE)   2 b. or br.f. (Mar 3) Daggers Drawn (USA) 114 – Dee-Lady   **76 d**
93 (Deploy 131) [2003 5g³ 5.1f* 5f* 5g⁶ f5sᵈ 5.1m Sep 22] smallish, quite attractive filly: second foal: dam 2-y-o 5f winner who stayed 1¼m: fair performer: won claimers at Bath in March and Thirsk in April: well held after (twice slowly away) in April: likely to prove best at 5f: acts on firm going. *W. G. M. Turner*

LADY KORRIANDA   2 ch.f. (Feb 27) Dr Fong (USA) 128 – Prima Verde 81 (Leading   **61**
Counsel (USA) 122) [2003 p6g 7d p6g² Dec 6] 2,000Y: third foal: dam 7.5f/1m winner: best effort in maidens (modest form) when second at Lingfield, finishing strongly: will stay at least 7f. *M. J. Wallace*

LADY LAKSHMI   3 ch.f. Bahhare (USA) 122 – Polish Honour (USA) 61 (Danzig   **52**
Connection (USA)) [2003 –: 8.2g 8m 12m³ 12f⁵ 14.1d 12m³ 15.8m Oct 7] sturdy filly: modest maiden handicapper: should stay 1¾m: acts on good to firm ground. *R. Guest*

LADY LAUREATE   5 b.m. Sir Harry Lewis (USA) 127 – Cyrillic 88 (Rock City 120)   **74**
[2003 79: 14.4g 16m 17.2f 16.2f³ 16g⁴ 16m² 16.5d Nov 8] small, sparely-made mare: fair handicapper: stays 17f: acts on firm and soft going: usually held up. *G. C. Bravery*

LADY LENOR   5 b.m. Presidium 124 – Sparkling Roberta 55 (Kind of Hush 118)   **55 d**
[2003 57: 6m 7m² 7.9m 8m⁴ 7.2m⁵ 8g 8g⁵ 8.1m 6f Aug 22] tall mare: modest maiden: below form last 5 starts: stays 7f: acts on fibresand, soft and good to firm going (probably on heavy): wore cheekpieces/blinkers last 8 starts: somewhat wayward. *Mrs G. S. Rees*

LADY LIESEL   3 b.f. Bin Ajwaad (IRE) 119 – Griddle Cake (IRE) 62 (Be My Guest   **54**
(USA) 126) [2003 63, a60: p7g³ p6g 7m⁴ 6g 7m 8f 7m⁶ 7g 6g⁶ 7.1m⁴ 7f⁵ 8f 7m 7m Oct 14] leggy, plain filly: modest maiden handicapper: stays 7f: acts on polytrack and firm ground: has started slowly. *J. J. Bridger*

LADY LINDSAY (IRE)   4 ch.f. Danehill Dancer (IRE) 117 – Jungle Jezebel 107   **100**
(Thatching 131) [2003 105: 8m⁵ 7d 6m² 6f 6s Oct 5] rather leggy, lengthy filly: useful performer: easily best effort in 2003 when 1¾ lengths second to Lochridge in listed event at Pontefract in August: effective at 6f to 1m: acts on good to firm and good to soft ground: blinkered (well held) last 2 starts: held up. *R. Guest*

LADY LLANOVER   3 ch.f. Halling (USA) 133 – Francia 59 (Legend of France   –
(USA) 124) [2003 60: 6.1g 7g f9.4s 9.9d 10.2m Aug 14] workmanlike filly: no form in 2003: tried in visor/cheekpieces. *S. C. Williams*

LADY LUCIA (IRE)   2 b.f. (Jan 21) Royal Applause 124 – Inventive 84 (Sheikh   **51**
Albadou 128) [2003 6m 5g⁴ 7m 7m⁴ 7.5m Sep 17] IR 12,000F, 21,000Y: quite attractive filly: first foal: dam, 5f winner, ran only at 2 yrs: modest maiden: barely stays 7f. *N. A. Callaghan*

LADY LUCINDA   2 b.f. (Mar 6) Muhtarram (USA) 125 – Lady Phyl 67 (Northiam   –
(USA)) [2003 8d Nov 7] big, leggy filly: fourth foal: dam, 2-y-o 6f winner, later successful in Holland: 66/1, well held in maiden at Doncaster. *John A. Harris*

LADY MCNAIR   3 b.f. Sheikh Albadou 128 – Bonita Bee 50 (King of Spain 121)   **86**
[2003 89: 8.1m 8m 8.1m⁴ 11.6m⁴ 10g⁴ 12f⁶ Oct 12] workmanlike filly: fairly useful performer: stays easy 1¼m: acts on good to firm and good to soft ground. *P. D. Cundell*

LADY MIDNIGHT   2 ch.f. (Apr 1) Young Ern 120 – Amathus Glory 76 (Mummy's   –
Pet 125) [2003 f5g⁶ 6m Jul 1] seventh foal: half-sister to 1997 2-y-o 7f seller winner Rock From The Sun (by Rock City) and winner in Greece by Rudimentary: dam 2-y-o 5f winner: well held in seller and claimer. *W. G. M. Turner*

LADY MO   2 b.f. (Apr 30) Young Ern 120 – Just Run (IRE) 45 (Runnett 125) [2003   **58 §**
5d³ 5m⁵ 5m³ 5d⁶ 6m³ 5.1m⁵ 6m* 6.1m⁴ 6f³ 6m⁶ 8.3g 7m⁵ p6g Nov 13] leggy, good-topped filly: seventh foal: half-sister to 3 winners by Emarati, including 1995 2-y-o 5f winner Just Lady: dam ran twice: modest performer: won seller at Lingfield in August, then left W. Turner: stays easy 7f: acts on good to firm and good to soft going: tried tongue tied: often slowly away, sometimes markedly so. *Andrew Reid*

LADY MYTTON 3 ch.f. Lake Coniston (IRE) 131 – The In-Laws (IRE) 90 (Be My 75
Guest (USA) 126) [2003 84+: 7m⁴ Apr 17] lengthy filly: fairly useful winner at 2 yrs: just
fair form only outing in 2003: stays 1m: acts on any going. *A. Bailey*

LADY NATILDA 3 ch.f. First Trump 118 – Ramajana (USA) (Shadeed (USA) 135) 59
[2003 64: f6g⁶ f6g 5.1m 6.1d 5.7m³ f5g f6s⁴ f6g⁵ 8.2d f6g f7g Nov 29] modest handicapper: best at 6f/7f: acts on fibresand and firm ground, probably on good to soft: tried
visored/blinkered. *D. Haydn Jones*

LADY NETBETSPORTS (IRE) 4 b.f. In The Wings 128 – Auntie Maureen (IRE) 75
73 (Roi Danzig (USA)) [2003 74, a–: 10.3g 14.1g⁴ 14.1g⁴ 16.2m 16.1d 17.1m Jun 9] a–
leggy filly: fair maiden handicapper: stays 1¾m: acts on any turf going, below form both
starts on fibresand: tried visored. *B. S. Rothwell*

LADY OASIS (IRE) 2 ch.f. (Mar 2) Desert King (IRE) 129 – Olivia Jane (IRE) (Ela- –
Mana-Mou 132) [2003 5m 6.1g 6m Sep 7] 10,000Y: small filly: eighth foal: half-sister to
7f (at 2 yrs) to 1¼m winner (stayed 15f) King O' The Mana (by Turtle Island) and 1¾m
seller winner Ziggy's Viola (by Roi Danzig): dam unraced half-sister to smart middle-
distance stayer Luchiroverte: well beaten in maidens/minor event. *A. Berry*

LADY OF EMINENCE 3 b. or br.f. Bishop of Cashel 122 – Astrid Gilberto 75 –
(Runnett 125) [2003 8g 8m Jun 27] leggy filly: half-sister to 1¼m seller winner Esperto
and 5f/6f winner Miss Bananas (both by Risk Me): dam 2-y-o 5f/6f winner, also placed
over hurdles: well held in maiden/claimer at Newmarket. *Miss J. Feilden*

LADY OF GDANSK (IRE) 4 ch.f. Danehill Dancer (IRE) 117 – Rebecca's Girl 54
(IRE) (Nashaama 113) [2003 68, a58: p6g p7g f7g 6m 8.3m 9f 7g⁴ 6m 7s f8s Dec 13] a–
big, lengthy filly: modest handicapper: stays 1m: acts on polytrack, soft and good to firm
ground: sometimes front runner: visored (very slowly away) third outing. *H. J. Collingridge*

LADY OF THE LINKS (IRE) 2 b.f. (Feb 14) Desert Style (IRE) 121 – Itkan (IRE) 53
(Marju (IRE) 127) [2003 5m⁵ 5.1m⁴ 5.6f 6m Oct 1] €26,000Y: good-bodied filly: third
foal: half-sister to useful Irish 6f/7f winner Exceptional Paddy (by Common Grounds):
dam lightly-raced half-sister to useful 2-y-o sprinter Painted Madam: modest maiden:
should stay 6f. *N. Tinkler*

LADY ORIANDE 2 b.f. (Feb 18) Makbul 104 – Lady Roxanne 65 (Cyrano de 59
Bergerac 120) [2003 5m May 29] 9,000Y: fourth foal: sister to 3-y-o Striking Ambition
and half-sister to 6f winner Gascon (by Beveled): dam, 5f/6f winner, sister to useful
French/US sprinter Cyrano Storme: 16/1 and green, late headway when ninth of 12 in
maiden at Goodwood: had operation to remove knee chips after. *A. M. Balding*

LADY P 4 b.f. Makbul 104 – Octavia (Sallust 134) [2003 f6g f6s 7m Mar 26] half-sister –
to numerous winners, including 8-y-o Ryefield and 1¼m to 2m winner Kinoko (by
Bairn): dam maiden: no form: unseated leaving stall final outing: sold £1,100. *A. Berry*

LADY PAHIA (IRE) 5 ch.m. Pivotal 124 – Appledorn 99 (Doulab (USA) 115) [2003 72
79: p7g⁵ f8s⁵ p10g² p10g p10g 7m 7g Jul 3] tall, leggy mare: fair handicapper: effective
at 7f to easy 1¼m: acted on firm going, good to soft and polytrack: sometimes hung left:
best held up: in foal to Dr Fong. *A. P. Jarvis*

LADY PAST TIMES 3 b.f. Tragic Role (USA) – Just A Gem (Superlative 118) [2003 51
–: 8.1s 5.9m 7m 10.9f 6.9m 8.1m² 9f² 9m² 10.9d Oct 13] quite good-topped filly: modest
maiden: stays 9f: acts on firm ground: visored last 5 outings: sold 3,400 gns. *E. J. Alston*

LADY PEACHES 2 ch.f. (Mar 13) Bien Bien (USA) 125 – Upper Club (IRE) 59 –
(Taufan (USA) 119) [2003 f6g Jun 25] 1,000Y: third foal: half-sister to a winner in Greece
by Emperor Jones: dam maiden who stayed 9f: 11/1, very slowly away and always rear in
maiden at Southwell. *D. Mullarkey*

LADY PEKAN 4 b.f. Sri Pekan (USA) 117 – Cloudberry 88 (Night Shift (USA)) [2003 69
–: 5.1s 5m 5m² 5m 5g 5f 5.2m⁴ 5f² 5.7f 6g⁵ 5m 6g 6m p6g f5g* f5s⁴ f5s* Dec 31] smallish, strong filly: fair handicapper: left J. Balding after sixth start: won at Wolverhampton
in November (carried head high) and December: best form at 5f: acts on fibresand and
firm ground: effective blinkered/visored or not. *P. S. McEntee*

LADY PERCY 3 ch.f. Double Trigger (IRE) 123 – Dundeelin 46 (Dunbeath (USA) 50
127) [2003 –: 8f⁶ 10.9m 14.1m 10m 7.1g⁴ 8f 10.9f² 8m² 10.2g⁶ 10.2m⁵ 11.7f⁶ Aug 22]
small filly: modest maiden: effective at 7f to easy 11f: acts on firm ground: tried
blinkered/in cheekpieces: sometimes races freely. *B. R. Millman*

LADY PISTE (IRE) 2 b.f. (Mar 1) Ali-Royal (IRE) 127 – Alpine Lady (IRE) (Tirol 67
127) [2003 5d³ 5.1m* 5f⁴ 6m⁵ 5.1m⁵ 6m³ f7g p6g⁴ Dec 20] €5,000Y: leggy filly: second

foal: dam tailed off both starts: fair performer: won maiden at Chester in May: should stay 7f: acts on firm and good to soft ground: tried visored/tongue tied. *P. D. Evans*

LADY PREDOMINANT   2 b.f. (Feb 21) Primo Dominie 121 – Enlisted (IRE) 83   **66 d**
(Sadler's Wells (USA) 132) [2003 5.1g⁴ 5.2m 5.1f⁴ 6m 6m f8g⁵ 6f p6g² p7g Dec 10] sturdy filly: third foal: half-sister to 3-y-o Regimental Dance: dam 1¼m winner: fair maiden: below form after third start, claimed from M. Channon £5,500 penultimate one: should stay at least 7f: acts on firm going, probably on polytrack: visored sixth/seventh starts. *Andrew Reid*

LADY PROTECTOR   4 b.f. Sri Pekan (USA) 117 – Scared (Royal Academy (USA)   **59**
130) [2003 42: f5g f5s 6m⁴ 5m² 5d² 6m 7m 5m f5s 5m⁶ f5g Dec 22] leggy filly: modest   **a44**
maiden handicapper on turf, poor on all-weather: left D. Arbuthnot after second start: left S. R. Bowring before final outing: effective at 5f/6f: acts on fibresand, good to firm and good to soft ground: tried visored/blinkered. *J. Balding*

LADY REDERA (IRE)   2 b.f. (Apr 9) Inzar (USA) 112 – Era 70 (Dalsaan 125) [2003   **55**
7g⁵ 8m⁴ 7m 8m Sep 16] close-coupled filly: half-sister to several winners, including fairly useful 1992 2-y-o 6f/7f winner After The Last (by Infantry) and 3-y-o Ryan's Future: dam scored at 5f at 2 yrs: modest maiden: well beaten in nursery final start: probably stays 1m. *H. S. Howe*

LADY SHOPPER   3 b.f. Merdon Melody 98 – Young Whip (Bold Owl 101) [2003 –:   **–**
p7g 7m p10g 8.5g Jul 17] sturdy, workmanlike filly: well held in maidens/handicap: tongue tied last 2 starts. *S. Dow*

LADYSTGEORGE   4 b.f. Mind Games 121 – Indiahra 76 (Indian Ridge 123) [2003 –:   **–**
f5g 8.2d 7m 7.2m 6m⁴ f6g⁶ Nov 24] bad maiden: sometimes slowly away. *M. Mullineaux*

LADY STRIPES   2 gr.f. (Apr 14) Alzao (USA) 117 – Shamaya (Doyoun 124)   **63**
[2003 6m 6m⁶ 6g Oct 6] €26,000Y: strong filly: third foal: half-sister to 2 winners abroad, including French 1¼m winner King's Show (by King's Theatre): dam, French 9f (at 2 yrs) and 11.5f winner, half-sister to smart Irish stayer Shaiybara: modest form in maidens: should be suited by 1¼m+. *D. Mullarkey*

LADY SUNRISE   4 ch.f. Whittingham (IRE) 104 – Scenic Air (Hadeer 118) [2003   **–**
41: 5.1f 5g 5.1m 6m 7f Sep 2] maiden handicapper: well held in 2003. *Mrs A. L. M. King*

LADY SUNSET (IRE)   2 b.f. (Jan 14) Entrepreneur 123 – Sunset Reigns (IRE) 110   **66**
(Taufan (USA) 119) [2003 5m 5.1m⁵ 5f² 5.6f 5.2m Jul 19] €37,000Y: good-bodied filly: third foal: closely related to Irish 6f winner Errachidia (by King of Kings): dam Irish 5f/6f winner (including at 2 yrs): fair maiden: likely to prove best at 5f/easy 6f. *K. A. Ryan*

LADY TEARAWAY   4 b.f. Arrasas (USA) 100 – Manageress 74 (Mandamus 120)   **–**
[2003 7g 8.3s 10.3m Jul 2] leggy filly: half-sister to 3 winners, including 7f/1m winner Dealers Delight (by Ballacashtal): dam 6f winner at 2 yrs: well held in maidens. *J. E. Long*

LADY TILLY   6 b.m. Puissance 110 – Lady of Itatiba (BEL) (King of Macedon 126)   **–**
[2003 –: 6.9m Aug 4] workmanlike mare: maiden, no longer of much account. *B. Mactaggart*

LADY TRACE (IRE)   2 b.f. (Mar 19) Piccolo 121 – Zelda (USA) (Sharpen Up 127)   **–**
[2003 7m 7g Sep 11] 4,200F, 10,000Y: half-sister to several winners, including 1996 2-y-o 6f winner Spaniards Inn (by Dominion), later 1m/9f winner in Hong Kong, and unreliable 6f winner Robzelda (by Robellino), both fairly useful: dam, ran once, half-sister to Moorestyle: well beaten in maidens at Lingfield and Epsom (slowly away). *S. Dow*

LADYWELL BLAISE (IRE)   6 b.m. Turtle Island (IRE) 123 – Duly Elected (Persian   **54 §**
Bold 123) [2003 57§: 10.2m 7.1m 6m 7m⁴ 7m³ 8m 7m 8g 7m p7g⁶ f5g⁶ Dec 30] sturdy mare: modest handicapper: effective at 6f to easy 1¼m: acts on all-weather, firm and good to soft going: blinkered once: often slowly away: sometimes races freely: unreliable. *J. J. Bridger*

LADY WEST   3 b.f. The West (USA) 107 – Just Run (IRE) 45 (Runnett 125) [2003 55:   **–**
p5g 5m 7g Aug 10] lengthy filly: modest form on debut at 2 yrs: well held since, leaving W. Turner after reappearance. *Dr J. R. J. Naylor*

LADY WURZEL   4 b.f. Dilum (USA) 115 – Fly The Wind 56 (Windjammer (USA))   **–**
[2003 10.2f⁴ Sep 29] second foal: dam, maiden on Flat, winning staying hurdler/chaser: well held in bumper and maiden. *W. S. Kittow*

LADY XANTHIA   2 ch.f. (Apr 22) Bien Bien (USA) 125 – Carmosa (USA) 65   **50**
(Blushing John (USA) 120) [2003 5d 5m p5g⁶ 6m⁶ Jun 2] 2,500Y: third foal: dam placed at 6f to 1m: modest maiden: best effort at 5f on good to soft going: blinkered last 2 starts. *I. A. Wood*

LAFFAH (USA) 8 b.g. Silver Hawk (USA) 123 – Sakiyah (USA) (Secretariat (USA)) – [2003 14.1f⁵ Jun 26] heavy-topped gelding: fair handicapper in 2001: below form over inadequate trip only run since: stays 2½m: acts on firm going: visored once, blinkered last 2 starts: usually tongue tied: has seemed lazy. *G. L. Moore*

LAFI (IRE) 4 ch.g. Indian Ridge 123 – Petal Girl 96 (Caerleon (USA) 132) [2003 80p: **106 p** 7.1f* 8.1g⁴ 7d³ 7.1m* 7f Sep 27] good-topped gelding: useful handicapper, lightly raced: won at Sandown in June and August, pushed out to beat Master Robbie 2½ lengths latter occasion: well held at Ascot final outing: likely to prove best at 7f/1m: acts on firm ground, below par on good to soft: sold 38,000 gns, then gelded: likely to improve further. *A. C. Stewart*

LA FONTEYNE 2 b.f. (Apr 29) Imperial Ballet (IRE) 110 – Baliana 75 (Midyan – (USA) 124) [2003 5g p6g Nov 13] 6,000 2-y-o: sixth foal: half-sister to 3 winners, including 4-y-o Digger and 7f (at 2 yrs)/1m winner Bali Dance (by Rambo Dancer): dam unreliable sprinter: well held in maiden/seller. *C. B. B. Booth*

LAGGAN BAY (IRE) 3 b.g. Alzao (USA) 117 – Green Lucia 116 (Green Dancer **82** (USA) 132) [2003 78: p8g² p10g 10m³ 10.2m 12m⁵ 12g² 11.7f* 11.6m² Jul 14] small gelding: fluent mover: fairly useful handicapper: won maiden event at Bath in July: probably better at 1½m than shorter: acts on firm going, good to soft and polytrack: tried blinkered (raced freely at 2 yrs), visored last 2 starts (slowly away final one): joined J. Fox, and gelded. *R. Hannon*

LAGGAN MINSTREL (IRE) 5 b.g. Mark of Esteem (IRE) 137 – Next Episode – (USA) (Nijinsky (CAN) 138) [2003 92: 8m 8d 8.3g 7g 8f 7d 7f7g p7g f6g Dec 9] tall, close-coupled gelding: fairly useful handicapper at 4 yrs: well held in 2003: tried in cheekpieces/tongue tie: carries head high. *P. W. D'Arcy*

LAGO D'ORTA (IRE) 3 ch.c. Bahhare (USA) 122 – Maelalong (IRE) 77 (Maelstrom **115 +** Lake 118) [2003 86: 7g* 8m 7.6m* 8.1v⁴ 8m* 7.6g* 8g 7.6g* 7m² 9.3g* Oct 19] close-coupled, quite good-topped colt: smart performer: much improved, and had an excellent season, winning handicaps at Leicester in March and Chester in May, minor events at Newmarket in June, Lingfield in July and Chester (by head from Marching Band) in August and listed race at Longchamp (by short neck from Kindjhal) in October: also ran well when 3 lengths second of 5 to Trade Fair in listed race at Newbury: stays 9.3f: acts on heavy and good to firm ground: usually waited with: reliable. *C. G. Cox*

LAGOSTA (SAF) 3 ch.g. Fort Wood (USA) 117 – Rose Wine 91 (Chilibang 120) – [2003 8m 10m 8.2g·10f 11g⁵ Jul 26] quite good-topped gelding: first reported foal: dam Italian 6f (at 2 yrs) to 11f winner: little form: blinkered final start. *W. J. Haggas*

LA GRACE 2 b.f. (Apr 16) Lahib (USA) 129 – Prima Sinfonia 64 (Fairy King (USA)) **63** [2003 6.1d² 7m⁵ 7.1m⁴ 7f⁴ 8g* Sep 27] 2,800Y: close-coupled, rather unfurnished filly: fifth living foal: half-sister to winner in Japan by Tragic Role: dam, ran twice, half-sister to useful Italian stayer London Bank: modest performer: won maiden at Ripon, dictating pace: stays 1m: acts on good to soft going. *R. Hannon*

LAHOB 3 ch.c. First Trump 118 – Mystical Song 68 (Mystiko (USA) 124) [2003 10g **61** 12m³ 13.8m⁶ 10.5m² 11.9m³ 12.3g² 11.8m⁶ Sep 1] 8,000Y: small, strong colt: first foal: dam, form only on sole 2-y-o outing, half-sister to sprinters Prince Sabo (very smart performer) and Millyant (smart): modest maiden: stays 1½m: raced only on good/good to firm ground: wore cheekpieces (well below form) final start. *P. Howling*

LAIDLOW (USA) 3 ch.c. Mt Livermore (USA) – Cato Lady (USA) (Nasty And Bold **101** (USA)) [2003 8g* 7m⁴ 8g⁵ 7.6g³ Aug 28] $50,000F, 28,000Y: rather leggy, quite attractive colt: fifth foal: brother to a winner in USA and half-brother to 3 winners abroad: dam, minor 8.5f stakes winner at 2 yrs in USA: useful form: won maiden at Newmarket in May: seemed to run well when 3¾ lengths fourth to Trade Fair in listed event there next time: creditable efforts last 2 starts, in listed race at Goodwood (fifth to Court Masterpiece) and minor event at Chester (third behind Lago d'Orta, never going well and edging left): stays 1m: has worn crossed noseband/been taken steadily to post: tends to swish tail in paddock: possibly temperamental: sold 20,000 gns, joined M. Chew in USA. *Sir Michael Stoute*

LAIRD DARA MAC 3 b.c. Presidium 124 – Nishara (Nishapour (FR) 125) [2003 – 10.4m 8m⁶ 8.1d Sep 26] 500Y: sturdy colt: third foal: dam, of little account, half-sister to Irish 2000 Guineas winner Dara Monarch: well held in maidens: tried blinkered. *N. Bycroft*

LAIRD OF THE GLEN 2 ch.g. (Mar 9) Muhtarram (USA) 125 – Strath Kitten 36 – (Scottish Reel 123) [2003 5s 6m 7m 7m Aug 15] leggy gelding: fourth foal: dam, maiden, stayed 1¼m: seems of little account. *P. S. McEntee*

LAIS 3 ch.f. Inchinor 119 – Night Transaction 59 (Tina's Pet 121) [2003 –: 7m 7.1f Jun — 30] little sign of ability. *G. C. H. Chung*

LAKATOI 4 b.f. Saddlers' Hall (IRE) 126 – Bireme 127 (Grundy 137) [2003 82d: **65** p12g p10g³ f12g⁴ Mar 3] good-bodied filly: maiden: only fair at best in 2003: stays 13.8f: acts on polytrack, best turf efforts on firm/good to firm going: blinkered (raced freely) last 2 outings. *J. W. Payne*

LAKE DIVA 2 ch.f. (Feb 6) Docksider (USA) 124 – Cutpurse Moll 76 (Green Desert — (USA) 127) [2003 p7g 7d Nov 14] 12,000Y: fourth foal: half-sister to 3 winners, including 4-y-o Colonel Cotton and 5-y-o Cyclone Connie: dam, 7f winner, out of useful 1m/1¼m winner Pretty Pol: well held in maidens at Lingfield and Catterick. *M. J. Wallace*

LAKE EYRE (IRE) 4 b.f. Bluebird (USA) 125 – Pooh Wee 71 (Music Boy 124) **52** [2003 48, a43: 6d f7s⁵ 7m⁴ 6m⁶ f6g f6g³ f5g f6s³ Dec 27] modest maiden: effective at 5f to 7f: acts on good to firm going, good to soft and fibresand: tried visored, not in 2003. *J. Balding*

LAKE GARDA 2 b.c. (Feb 19) Komaite (USA) – Malcesine (IRE) 46 (Auction Ring **83** (USA) 123) [2003 5m² 6m² 5.2m 6d 6m* Sep 16] 19,000Y: good-topped colt: brother to several winners, including 6-y-o Baby Barry and 2000 2-y-o 5f winner Princess Garda: dam 1m seller winner: fairly useful performer: sweating and short to post, landed odds in maiden at Thirsk unimpressively by neck from Momtic: effective at 5f/6f: acts on good to firm and good to soft going. *B. A. McMahon*

LAKEHAVEN LADY 2 b.f. (Mar 25) Abou Zouz (USA) 109 – Sans Egale (FR) — (Lashkari 128) [2003 p8g Oct 27] 8,000Y: second foal: dam, maiden who stayed 1½m, half-sister to smart 1¼m performer Maidment: 50/1, always behind in maiden at Lingfield. *M. G. Quinlan*

LAKELANDS LADY (IRE) 3 ch.f. Woodborough (USA) 112 – Beautyofthepeace **76 d** (IRE) (Exactly Sharp (USA) 121) [2003 67, a85: f7g³ p8g 7.1m⁶ 7g f7g 7d 7d f8s Dec 27] close-coupled, quite good-topped filly: fair performer: off 5 months, well below form last 4 outings: effective at 7f/1m: acts on good to firm ground, soft and fibresand: blinkered (raced freely) sixth start: usually races up with pace. *J. Balding*

LAKE 'O' GOLD 4 ch.f. Karinga Bay 116 – Ginka 57 (Petoski 135) [2003 69: f14.8s⁶ **52** 12m⁵ 16m 11.9m⁵ 12m 16.4m Jul 10] modest maiden: stays 13f: acts on polytrack, probably on good to firm going: sold £1,500. *J. W. Mullins*

LAKESIDE GUY (IRE) 2 b.c. (Mar 2) Revoque (IRE) 122 – Glen of Imaal (IRE) — (Common Grounds 120) [2003 p7g Dec 17] 9,500Y: second living foal: half-brother to 2000 2-y-o 6f seller winner Somers Heath (by Definite Article): dam, Irish maiden, sister to smart 2000 2-y-o Bad As I Wanna Be: 33/1, well held in minor event at Lingfield. *P. S. McEntee*

LAKE VERDI (IRE) 4 ch.g. Lake Coniston (IRE) 131 – Shore Lark (USA) (Storm **70 d** Bird (CAN) 134) [2003 81: 6m 6f 6m 6m 6m⁶ Aug 8] quite good-topped gelding: just a fair handicapper nowadays: well below form after reappearance: stays 7f: acts on firm and good to soft going: often tongue tied, tried blinkered: has been slowly away: temperament under suspicion: sold £2,500. *B. Hanbury*

LAKOTA BRAVE 9 ch.g. Anshan 119 – Pushkinia (FR) 95 (Pharly (FR) 130) [2003 **72** 69, a97: f8.5s⁶ p7g 7m² f9.4g² 8m* 9.9m 10m⁴ 8m³ f7g³ f8.5g* f8.5g² p8g² f9.4s⁵ Dec **a98** 31] leggy, lengthy gelding: useful on all-weather, fair on turf: won claimer at Leicester in June and (having been claimed from N. Littmoden £10,000 after ninth start) handicap at Wolverhampton in November: excellent second in handicap at Wolverhampton next time: seems to stay 9.4f: act on all-weather, raced only on good ground or firmer on turf: tried tongue tied: tends to race freely, and usually held up. *Mrs S. A. Liddiard*

LA LANDONNE 2 b.f. (May 6) Fraam 114 – Le Pin 59 (Persian Bold 123) [2003 **77** p6g³ p8g⁵ p6g* Dec 6] £2,400Y: first foal: dam, maiden bred to stay 1½m, half-sister to very smart 1m/1¼m performer Handsome Ridge: regressive form, but still won maiden at Lingfield in December by neck from Lady Korrianda, despite looking hard ride and idling in front: should stay 1m. *P. M. Phelan*

LALAPAANZI (IRE) 3 b.f. Night Shift (USA) – Sharp Deposit (Sharpo 132) [2003 **62** 57: f5⁵ 6g 6m⁵ 6m⁶ 6m⁶ 5m Sep 13] smallish, quite good-topped filly: modest maiden: stays 6f: raced only on good ground or firmer: tongue tied. *R. M. Beckett*

LA LUNA (IRE) 6 b.m. Gothland (FR) 117 – Diane's Glen (Furry Glen 121) [2003 **57** 18f³ Jul 19] sixth foal: dam Irish hurdler: won bumper in June: 9/2, 8 lengths third to Dubai Seven Stars in maiden at Warwick on Flat debut: modest winner over hurdles in October. *Noel T. Chance*

LA MOULINE (IRE) 3 ch.f. Nashwan (USA) 135 – Lamarque (IRE) (Nureyev (USA) **103** 131) [2003 86p: 10.5f* 11.8m[5] May 10] tall filly: good mover: useful form in just 4 races: well backed but still green and reluctant to post, won 5-runner handicap at Haydock in April by head from Tiber: below-form fifth to Santa Sophia in listed race at Lingfield only subsequent start: stayed 10.5f: acted on firm going: tongue tied in 2003: had had 2 handlers/worn crossed noseband: stud. *G. A. Butler*

LAMPOS (USA) 3 b. or br.g. Southern Halo (USA) – Gone Private (USA) (Private **61** Account (USA)) [2003 67: p8g[4] f8s[6] 8m 10g 9.2d[4] 12.1d 12.1m f12s[3] 16.1m Oct 1] **a51** good-topped gelding: modest maiden handicapper: better on turf than all-weather: left N. Graham after reappearance: stays 1½m: acts on all-weather, yet to race on extremes of going on turf: usually wears headgear: none too consistent. *Miss J. A. Camacho*

LA MUETTE (IRE) 3 b.f. Charnwood Forest (IRE) 125 – Elton Grove (IRE) (Astro- **87 ?** nef 116) [2003 83: 10m[5] 9.9m[3] 10g 12g Oct 31] well-made filly: has scope: fairly useful performer: good fifth in handicap at Sandown on reappearance: dropped away tamely last 2 starts: stays 1¼m: acts on good to firm and good to soft going: sold 9,000 gns. *Mrs A. J. Perrett*

LAMZIG 4 b.g. Danzig Connection (USA) – Lamsonetti 68 (Never So Bold 135) [2003 **–** –: 10g Jul 22] workmanlike gelding: little form: tried visored. *M. Todhunter*

LANA 3 gr.f. Linamix (FR) 127 – Beaming 93 (Mtoto 134) [2003 72: 8g[3] Mar 20] **57** lengthy filly: fair form at 2 yrs: below that on only outing in 2003. *J. G. Given*

L'ANCRESSE (IRE) 3 b.f. Darshaan 133 – Solo de Lune (IRE) (Law Society **123** (USA) 130) [2003 98p: 7m[2] 8g 8d[4] 12g 12g[2] 11.9m[5] 14.6d[4] 12d* 10f[2] Oct 25] Ballydoyle's now-annual raiding party on the Breeders' Cup, sent out to America a week before the meeting, included the surprising addition of the three-year-old filly L'Ancresse who had been 'retired' after winning a well-contested listed event at the Curragh only a week earlier. Her all-the-way victory over the four-year-old Scott's View had come on her eighth start of the season and provided L'Ancresse with her first victory in a campaign which had seen her contest four classics, the One Thousand Guineas and Oaks in both Britain and Ireland. L'Ancresse had put up her best effort when very nearly stealing the Irish Oaks at the Curragh, holding a clear lead for much of the way before being caught by Vintage Tipple. L'Ancresse, a 33/1-shot, had the Epsom Oaks first and second Casual

*Rathbarry Stud's Barathea Finale Stakes, the Curragh—
a well-deserved prize for L'Ancresse, who makes all in this listed race, chased home by Scott's View*

Look and Yesterday behind her in third and fourth that day but it was widely held that the result flattered her. L'Ancresse had finished behind her stable-companion Yesterday in the three earlier classics that the pair had contested, L'Ancresse making the frame behind Yesterday in the Irish One Thousand Guineas before being pulled up at Epsom having been forced to check early on and reportedly lost her action. Seeing that L'Ancresse had managed only fifth behind another Breeders' Cup challenger, the four-year-old Islington in the Yorkshire Oaks, and had then been beaten into fourth in the Park Hill, she looked something of a forlorn hope in the Breeders' Cup Filly & Mare Turf at Santa Anita. Ridden by the American Edgar Prado and racing on bute, but not lasix, L'Ancresse took over on the home turn, after the field had virtually ignored the runaway American-trained leader, and kept on really well. Islington needed most of the length of the home straight to take her measure, L'Ancresse going down by a neck, with Yesterday two and a half lengths away in third. This was, without doubt, L'Ancresse's best effort and also, belatedly, the best performance all season by a three-year-old filly over middle distances.

L'Ancresse (IRE) (b.f. 2000)	Darshaan (br 1981)	Shirley Heights (b 1975)	Mill Reef
			Hardiemma
		Delsy (br 1972)	Abdos
			Kelty
	Solo de Lune (IRE) (b 1990)	Law Society (br 1982)	Alleged
			Bold Bikini
		Truly Special (b 1985)	Caerleon
			Arctique Royale

The leggy, good-topped L'Ancresse, who was trained in Britain as a two-year-old by Roger Charlton, is bred for stamina, by Darshaan out of the French eleven-furlong winner Solo de Lune, a half-sister to the very smart stayer Wareed and the E.P. Taylor Stakes winner Truly A Dream. Solo de Lune has bred several winners, notable among them two other smart performers by Darshaan, the Prix Saint-Alary winner Cerulean Sky, who finished third in the Prix Vermeille, and the stayer Qaatef. L'Ancresse's fourth dam is the 1965 Musidora winner Arctic Melody, also the grandam of Ardross; L'Ancresse's great grandam Arctique Royale won the Moyglare Stud Stakes and the Irish One Thousand Guineas. As well as L'Ancresse's grandam, the Prix de Royaumont winner Truly Special, Arctique Royale bred the very smart French mile-and-a-half performer Modhish and the Irish Oaks runner-up Russian Snows. L'Ancresse, who visits Sadler's Wells, won over a mile and a half (below form when held up in the Park Hill at a mile and three quarters), but raced freely and put up her best effort at a mile and a quarter. A tail flasher, she acted on firm and good to soft going. *A. P. O'Brien, Ireland*

LANDESCENT (IRE) 3 b.g. Grand Lodge (USA) 125 – Traumerei (GER) 70 (Surumu (GER)) [2003 74: p10g⁴ p10g⁶ f9.4g⁵ 8.2g 8f⁶ 9.9m 7.1g 8.3g⁵ 7g⁵ 9m⁴ 8f p8g p12g⁴ p12g² p12g⁶ p16g⁶ p10g Dec 30] smallish, sturdy gelding: fair performer at best: below form after second start: seems to stay easy 1½m: acts on soft going and all-weather: tried blinkered/visored: none too genuine. *M. Quinn* **75 d**

LANDING LIGHT (IRE) 8 b.g. In The Wings 128 – Gay Hellene 111 (Ela-Mana-Mou 132) [2003 13.9m* 20m² 16.1g 18m* Oct 18] sturdy gelding: 1¼m winner in France at 3 yrs for D. Smaga: very smart hurdler since (has failed to impress with attitude): smart form back on Flat (after 4-year break) in 2003, winning handicap at York in May and Tote **115**

Tote Cesarewitch (Handicap), Newmarket—Landing Light (rail) provides Pat Eddery with his first win in the race at the last attempt; Sun Bird (breastgirth, centre) and Kristensen (cheekpieces) are second and third, while the Irish-trained Direct Bearing (noseband, third left) again makes the frame

Cesarewitch at Newmarket (off 3½ months, beat Sun Bird by 2½ lengths) in October: also ran well when second to Sindapour in Ascot Stakes at Royal Ascot: reported in November to have injured near-fore tendon: effective at 1¾m to 2½m: acts on good to firm going. *N. J. Henderson*

LANDING STRIP (IRE) 3 b.g. Dolphin Street (FR) 125 – Funny Cut (IRE) (Sure   **88**
Blade (USA) 130) [2003 70: p5g³ p6g⁴ p7g 6m 5.3d³ 5.3m⁵ 5f* 5f² 6g 6.1f 5f 7m p6g* 5.3f* 6m⁴ p6g⁴ f6g³ f5g⁴ f5g Dec 9] fairly useful handicapper: won at Catterick in June, and Lingfield and Brighton in October: creditable efforts in frame after: effective at 5f/ 6f: acts on firm ground, good to soft and all-weather: tried in cheekpieces: sometimes awkward leaving stall: all 3 wins for claimer F. Ferris: makes running. *J. M. P. Eustace*

LANDINIUM (ITY) 4 b.f. Lando (GER) 128 – Hollywood Girl (Cagliostro (GER))   **103**
[2003 109: 11g² 10g² 10m⁴ 11.9g 11.9m⁵ 12m⁴ 10.5d⁴ 10.3d Nov 7] leggy ex-Italian filly: second foal: half-sister to Italian 9f to 11f winner by Alzao: dam, German 7f to 9.5f winner, half-sister to smart German performer up to 1¾m Hollywood Dream: useful performer: won newcomers race and listed race at Milan at 3 yrs: left V. Valiani after fourth outing in 2003: best effort of year when fourth to Visorama in Prix de Flore at Saint-Cloud penultimate start: at least as effective at 1¼m as 1½m: acts on firm and soft going: edgy and mounted on track fifth outing, wandered final one: has worn crossed noseband/tongue tie. *C. F. Wall*

LAND 'N STARS 3 b.g. Mtoto 134 – Uncharted Waters 68 (Celestial Storm (USA)   **75**
132) [2003 –: 10f⁴ 13.8m² 14f² Oct 12] fair maiden: left H. Cyzer to return to previous trainer prior to good second at Goodwood final start: will be suited by 2m+: raced only on good ground or firmer: sold 20,000 gns. *C. A. Cyzer*

LAND OF FANTASY 4 ch.g. Hernando (FR) 127 – Height of Folly 81 (Shirley   **70 d**
Heights 130) [2003 75: p8g p10g p12g p10g p12g p8g 8.3m f8g 8.1m p8g⁵ 8g 8m Aug 6] close-coupled, quite good-topped gelding: fair performer: below form last 6 starts: should stay 1½m: acts on polytrack: tried visored/blinkered. *D. K. Ivory*

LANDOFHEARTSDESIRE (IRE) 4 b.f. Up And At 'em 109 – Ahonita 90   **55 d**
(Ahonoora 122) [2003 60, a50: 6.1g⁵ 5.9g f7g⁴ 7f f7g 8m⁶ 7m 8g⁶ 8g 6.9d f8g Nov 19] smallish, good-topped filly: modest handicapper at best in 2003: effective at 6f, barely at 1m: acts on fibresand, firm and soft going: wears headgear. *J. S. Wainwright*

LAND OF NOD (IRE) 2 b.f. (Feb 14) Barathea (IRE) 127 – Rafif (USA) 68 (River-   **67 p**
man (USA) 131) [2003 8g p8g Nov 13] 28,000Y: seventh foal: closely related to 5-y-o Rajam and half-sister to fairly useful 1¾m winner Kadir (by Unfuwain): dam, 1¼m winner, out of close relative to Ribblesdale winner Thawakib, herself dam of Sakhee: better effort in maidens (fair form) when 4½ lengths tenth of 17 to Rave Reviews at Newbury on debut: will be suited by 1¼m/1½m: likely to improve. *G. A. Butler*

LAND SUN'S LEGACY (IRE) 2 b.g. (Apr 25) Red Sunset 120 – Almost A Lady   **50**
(IRE) 70 (Entitled 126) [2003 6g⁵ 6d 7s³ 8.5m 7d 7m⁴ 7m⁶ Oct 12] €16,000Y, 6,500 2-y-o: compact gelding: sixth foal: half-brother to useful 2001 2-y-o 6f and 1m winner Henri Lebasque (by Sri Pekan) and 5-y-o Thanks Max: dam, second at 1m at 2 yrs in Ireland, half-sister to very smart 1¼m performer Insatiable: modest maiden: stays 7f: acts on good to firm and soft going: visored/blinkered last 3 starts: tends to get worked up beforehand. *J. S. Wainwright*

LANDUCCI 2 b.c. (Apr 6) Averti (IRE) 117 – Divina Luna 96 (Dowsing (USA) 124)   **70 p**
[2003 7m 7m Oct 3] 3,100F, 18,500Y: big, close-coupled colt: third foal: half-brother to 4-y-o Holly Rose: dam 7f/1m winner: fair form, not knocked about, in maidens at Newmarket: will probably stay 1m: open to improvement. *J. W. Hills*

LANGFORD 3 ch.g. Compton Place 125 – Sharpening 72 (Sharpo 132) [2003 72:   **87**
10.1m² 10g² 10.1m⁴ 10g⁴ 10g² 10m² 10.1m³ 9.7m* 11m³ 8m⁶ Oct 6] well-made gelding: fairly useful performer: won maiden at Folkestone in August: good third in handicap at Newbury penultimate start: stays 11f, but races freely and should be effective at 1m: acts on good to firm going: usually races prominently: consistent. *M. H. Tompkins*

LANOS (POL) 5 ch.g. Special Power – Lubeka (POL) (Milione (FR) 62) [2003 70:   **70**
p13g² f12g³ f12g⁶ p13g* f12g² 13.8m⁶ 14m⁵ 15.4m⁴ p13g⁴ Dec 29] angular gelding: fair handicapper: won at Lingfield in March: stays easy 15.4f: acts on firm ground and all-weather: tried blinkered: tongue tied nowadays: has looked difficult ride. *R. Ford*

LAPADAR (IRE) 4 b. or br.f. Woodborough (USA) 112 – Indescent Blue 63   **–**
(Bluebird (USA) 125) [2003 60, a82: f14s f12g 13.1g⁶ f12s 16g⁵ f16.2g f14g⁵ f14.8g Nov 29] rather leggy filly: fairly useful on all-weather, modest on turf at 3 yrs: well held in 2003: tried in headgear/tongue tie: tried to run out once at 3 yrs. *J. R. Weymes*

LAPDANCING 2 ch.f. (Apr 18) Pursuit of Love 124 – Petrikov (IRE) (In The Wings – 128) [2003 7.2d 8m Oct 25] 3,500F, €10,500Y: third foal: half-sister to winner in Holland by Bishop of Cashel: dam unraced out of sister to 1000 Guineas/Oaks winner Midway Lady: showed nothing in maidens at Ayr and Musselburgh. *Miss L. A. Perratt*

LA PERSIANA 2 gr.f. (Feb 28) Daylami (IRE) 138 – La Papagena (Habitat 134) **73 p** [2003 7m⁴ 7m Oct 13] strong, close-coupled filly: half-sister to several winners, notably high-class 1m/1¼m performer Grand Lodge (by Chief's Crown), Dewhurst winner at 2 yrs, and useful Irish 1m (at 2 yrs) and 1½m winner Sorcerous (by Sadler's Wells): dam unraced: fair form in maidens at Kempton (shaped well) and Leicester: likely to do better at 3 yrs at 1¼m/1½m. *W. Jarvis*

LA PETITE CHINOISE 2 ch.f. (Feb 10) Dr Fong (USA) 128 – Susi Wong (IRE) **68** (Selkirk (USA) 129) [2003 5m³ 5d⁴ 6g 6g⁶ Sep 1] 28,000Y: first foal: dam German 1m winner: fair maiden: third at Warwick: will stay 1m: acts on good to firm and good to soft ground. *R. Guest*

LA PROFESSORESSA (IRE) 2 b.f. (Feb 20) Cadeaux Genereux 131 – Fellwah **67** (IRE) 66 (Sadler's Wells (USA) 132) [2003 6m 7.1g³ 6m 8d 8.3g⁵ Oct 6] €20,000Y: tall filly: third foal: dam once-raced close relative to 2000 Guineas winner Shadeed: fair maiden: ran creditably in nursery final start: free-going sort, but stays 1m: acts on good to soft going. *Mrs P. N. Dutfield*

LA PUCE 2 b.f. (Apr 9) Danzero (AUS) – Verbena (IRE) (Don't Forget Me 127) [2003 **60** 5g³ f5g* 5g⁵ 5g⁴ 6m² 7m³ 7m 6m Oct 17] 4,000Y: tall, leggy filly: second foal: dam French 11f winner: modest performer: won seller at Wolverhampton (sold from M. Wallace 10,000 gns) in March: stays 7f: acts on fibresand and good to firm going: sometimes wears cheekpieces: has been slowly away. *Miss Gay Kelleway*

LARA BAY 3 b.f. Polish Precedent (USA) 131 – Way O'Gold (USA) (Slew O' Gold **64** (USA)) [2003 66: 8g 9.3m⁵ Jun 2] close-coupled, quite attractive filly: modest maiden: should stay 1¼m: raced only on good/good to firm ground. *A. M. Balding*

LARAD (IRE) 2 br.g. (Feb 21) Desert Sun 120 – Glenstal Priory 53 (Glenstal (USA) **53 d** 118) [2003 5g 5g⁵ 6m 6f⁴ Jul 15] 9,000Y: good-bodied gelding: fifth foal: half-brother to 3 winners, including fairly useful 1999 2-y-o 5f winner Duke of Aston (by Shalford): dam 2m/2¼m winner: modest maiden: went wrong way after debut: wore cheekpieces final start. *J. S. Moore*

LARA FALANA 5 b.m. Tagula (IRE) 116 – Victoria Mill 59 (Free State 125) [2003 **78** 71, a65: p10g³ p10g⁵ 9.7g* 9.7m³ 8.5m⁴ 10m* 10g 10.1m 10g⁵ 9m 10g Sep 6] smallish, **a67** good-topped mare: fair performer: won minor event at Folkestone in March and handicap at Kempton in May: stays 1¼m: acts on firm going, good to soft and polytrack: blinkered (folded) once at 4 yrs: has worn tongue tie: races prominently. *Miss B. Sanders*

LARGO (IRE) 3 ch.f. Selkirk (USA) 129 – Lady of The Lake 104 (Caerleon (USA) **94** 132) [2003 83: 11m 12.1g* 11.6m* 12d 12m 14.5g⁵ Oct 19] close-coupled, quite attractive filly: has a short action: useful performer: won maiden at Chepstow in June and minor event at Windsor in July: seemed to run well when fifth to Kirschblute in listed race at Cologne final start: stays 14.5f: acts on good to firm and good to soft going: reared leaving stall/veered right under pressure penultimate 2-y-o outing, saddle slipped fourth appearance at 3 yrs. *J. L. Dunlop*

LARGS 3 ch.f. Sheikh Albadou 128 – Madam Zando 51 (Forzando 122) [2003 –: 5.1m **57** 6.1m⁵ 6m 6m⁶ f7s 6g f6f⁴ 6m⁵ 5m⁵ 5m⁵ 5m² 6m 6m³ f6g⁴ 6d⁵ Oct 31] good-bodied filly: modest maiden handicapper: stays 6f: acts on fibresand, good to firm and good to soft going: tried in cheekpieces. *J. Balding*

LARKING ABOUT (USA) 3 ch.f. Silver Hawk (USA) 123 – Milly Ha Ha 106 **66** (Dancing Brave (USA) 140) [2003 12m⁵ 12m⁴ p13g² 13.8d Nov 4] fifth foal: half-sister to useful 11f winner Jolly Sharp (by Diesis) and fairly useful 1¼m winner Laughing Girl (by Woodman): dam, 1¼m winner who stayed 1¾m, half-sister to smart performer up to 15.5f Bosham Mill and to dam of 4-y-o Scott's View out of smart middle-distance performer Mill On The Floss: fair maiden: well beaten in handicap final start: should stay 1¾m: acts on polytrack: slowly away first 3 outings: sold 10,500 gns. *H. R. A. Cecil*

LARK IN THE PARK (IRE) 3 ch.f. Grand Lodge (USA) 125 – Jarrayan 64 (Machia- **57** vellian (USA) 123) [2003 50: 8m 6.1d 10m 7.6m⁴ 7.9d 8.1m³ 8f* 8f 8f 8.5d⁶ Sep 23] lengthy filly: modest handicapper: won at Bath in August: stays 1m: acts on firm ground: sometimes slowly away: none too consistent. *W. M. Brisbourne*

LARKWING (IRE) 2 b.c. (Mar 2) Ela-Mana-Mou 132 – The Dawn Trader (USA) 70 **70 p** (Naskra (USA)) [2003 7s⁴ Oct 29] IR 11,500F, €160,000Y: fourth foal: brother to 1½m winner Morning Lover and half-brother to winner in Germany by Seattle Dancer: dam, 7f winner, half-sister to smart filly up to 1¼m in Britain/USA Party Cited: 25/1, 10½ lengths fourth of 14 to Crystal Curling in maiden at Yarmouth, slowly away and staying on: bred to be suited by 1¼m/1½m: likely to improve. *G. Wragg*

LARKY'S LOB   4 b.g. Lugana Beach 116 – Eucharis 41 (Tickled Pink 114) [2003 –, a64: f7s³ f6g² f6g² f6s² f6g² f6g³ p7g⁴ f7g³ f7g f6g⁵ 7m 6f f7g f7s⁴ f6g 6f f8.5f 8.5m f8g f6g² Dec 26] leggy, plain gelding: fair performer on all-weather, little form on turf: trained first 5 starts by R. Wilman, sixth by P. Blockley: barely stays easy 1m: acts on all-weather: tried visored/in cheekpieces. *Paul Johnson*   **a65**

LA ROSE   3 b.f. Among Men (USA) 124 – Marie La Rose (FR) (Night Shift (USA)) [2003 –: 7g f12g⁵ f12g⁶ 9.9d⁶ 12.1m² 9.9m f12g Dec 26] small filly: poor maiden handicapper: stays easy 1½m: acts on all-weather and good to firm ground: tried visored: has raced freely. *J. W. Unett*   **42**

LASANGA   4 ch.g. Zamindar (USA) 116 – Shall We Run 59 (Hotfoot 126) [2003 60p: 8.1m³ 8.3g² Aug 11] fairly useful form: best effort in maidens when 1½ lengths second to easy winner Fremen at Windsor, clear until 2f out: probably better at 1m than 1¼m. *Lady Herries*   **85**

LA SCALA (USA)   3 br.f. Theatrical 128 – Estala (Be My Guest (USA) 126) [2003 10g² 10m⁵ 8g* 8m 10.5d Sep 27] leggy, quite good-topped filly: fifth foal: half-sister to useful 7f/1m winner Entail (by Riverman) and 1¼m winner Latest Moment (by Quest For Fame): dam, useful French 2-y-o 9f winner who stayed 10.5f, half-sister to French performers Erudite (smart up to 2m) and Danefair (useful up to 1½m, herself dam of 3-y-o Trade Fair): fairly useful performer: won maiden at Ripon in July: best effort when tenth in handicap at Haydock final outing: effective at 1m/1¼m: free-going sort: joined R. Frankel in USA. *H. R. A. Cecil*   **80**

LAS RAMBLAS (IRE)   6 b.g. Thatching 131 – Raise A Warning 57 (Warning 136) [2003 59: 8.3d 6d 8g 6m 6f⁵ 6g 6m 10g 5m 5f⁶ 6f⁴ 6d Sep 29] compact gelding: poor mover: modest performer: best at 5f/6f: acts on fibresand and any turf going: often wears headgear: usually tongue tied: none too consistent. *D. A. Nolan*   **58**

LASSER LIGHT (IRE)   3 b.g. Inchinor 119 – Light Ray (Rainbow Quest (USA) 134) [2003 7f Jun 29] 10,500Y: third foal: dam third in France at 1m (at 2 yrs)/9f: 33/1, tailed off in maiden at Goodwood. *D. G. Bridgwater*   **–**

LASSITUDE   3 ch.f. Efisio 120 – Lassoo 87 (Caerleon (USA) 132) [2003 58p: 9.2d 10d 12.3g 7.9d 6.9m² 8d Aug 11] workmanlike filly: poor maiden: should stay at least 1m: acts on firm ground: blinkered last 3 outings: sometimes wanders. *C. W. Thornton*   **45**

LAST APPOINTMENT (USA)   3 b.c. Elusive Quality (USA) – Motion In Limine (USA) (Temperence Hill (USA)) [2003 p6g⁴ 7m² 7f* 7d Sep 11] $77,000Y: tall colt: half-brother to several winners in USA: dam 5.5f (at 2 yrs) to 8.5f winner in USA, including minor stakes: fairly useful form: won maiden at Goodwood in June, making all: well beaten in handicap next time: stays 7f: acts on firm ground and polytrack. *J. M. P. Eustace*   **82 +**

LA STELLINA (IRE)   5 b.m. Marju (IRE) 127 – Supportive (IRE) (Nashamaa 113) [2003 85: p7g Jan 18] fairly useful handicapper at best: raced too freely when well held only outing in 2003: wears headgear. *C. A. Dwyer*   **–**

LAST EXHIBIT   5 b.m. Royal Academy (USA) 130 – Noirmant (Dominion 123) [2003 72: p6g⁴ p6g 6m Jun 16] fair handicapper, lightly raced: below form after reappearance: should stay 7f: raced mainly on polytrack. *R. Guest*   **66**

LASTING DELIGHT   2 b.f. (May 3) Robellino (USA) 127 – Last Result (Northern Park (USA) 107) [2003 6.1f f6g⁵ f8.5g* f8s Dec 13] strong, workmanlike filly: first foal: dam, Italian 2-y-o 5.5f to 9.5f winner, half-sister to 5-y-o Foreign Affairs: fair performer: won maiden at Wolverhampton in November: ran as if amiss final start: will be suited by 1¼m+: slowly away first 2 outings. *Sir Mark Prescott*   **69**

LAST QUESTION   4 b.f. Tragic Role (USA) – Question Ali 83 (Petoski 135) [2003 f8g Jan 23] 2,500Y: third foal: half-sister to winner in Spain by Paris House: dam 2-y-o 6f winner: 25/1, slowly away when tailed off in maiden at Southwell. *A. Berry*   **–**

LAST RING   5 br.m. Charmer 123 – Bells of Longwick 92 (Myjinski (USA)) [2003 8m Jun 2] second foal: dam 5f winner: 66/1, tailed off in claimer at Leicester. *P. W. Hiatt*   **–**

LA SYLPHIDE   6 ch.m. Rudimentary (USA) 118 – Primitive Gift 38 (Primitive Rising (USA) 113) [2003 –: 10d 9.2g² 9.2g* 9.2g* 9.2m⁶ 10.5d* 12d Nov 8] workmanlike mare: shows knee action: fairly useful handicapper: better than ever in 2003, winning at Hamilton (2) in July and Haydock in September: stays 1¼m: acts on fibresand and good to soft ground: races prominently. *G. M. Moore*   **84**

LATALOMNE (USA)   9 ch.g. Zilzal (USA) 137 – Sanctuary (Welsh Pageant 132)   **?**
[2003 8g Oct 28] strong gelding: has a powerful, round action: high-class chaser at best:
one-time useful performer on Flat: well held only outing in that sphere since 2000: tried
visored: joined M. Pipe. *B. Ellison*

LATE ARRIVAL   6 b.g. Emperor Jones (USA) 119 – Try Vickers (USA) 72 (Fuzz-   **–**
buster (USA)) [2003 66, a52: f8s⁵ Jan 14] tall gelding: fair handicapper at best: well held
only outing in 2003: visored once, usually blinkered. *M. D. Hammond*

LATE CLAIM (USA)   3 ch.g. King of Kings (IRE) 125 – Irish Flare (USA) (Irish   **91**
River (FR) 131) [2003 83: 8g 10.3g⁵ 12.3m* 12m⁵ 13.1m* 13.1d Oct 14] good-topped
gelding: fairly useful handicapper: won at Chester in August and Ayr (despite carrying
head high) in September: should stay 1¾m: acts on soft and good to firm going: wore
cheekpieces last 2 starts: sold 23,000 gns, joined I. Williams. *B. W. Hills*

LATEEN SAILS   3 ch.c. Elmaamul (USA) 125 – Felucca 94 (Green Desert (USA)   **116**
127) [2003 106P: 8g 10.4m* 10g⁴ 9d* Jul 27] strong, lengthy colt: has a markedly round
action: smart performer: joint second favourite, last of 20 in 2000 Guineas at Newmarket
on reappearance: successful in 4-runner listed race at York (by 3½ lengths from Illustrator) in May and, having finished creditable 2¾ lengths fourth to Vespone in Grand Prix
de Paris at Longchamp, Prix Daphnis at Maisons-Laffitte (easily made all, beat Shakis 5
lengths) in July: suffered injury after: has form at 1¼m, but may prove best at 1m/9f: acts
on firm and good to soft going: stays in training. *Saeed bin Suroor*

LATE OPPOSITION   2 b.c. (Apr 25) Unfuwain (USA) 131 – Hawa (USA) (Wood-   **63**
man (USA) 126) [2003 8d 7m 7.2d⁶ Oct 13] good-bodied colt: first foal: dam unraced
half-sister to useful 1996 2-y-o sprinter Moonshine Girl out of sister to smart 1987 2-y-o
sprinter Digamist: modest form in maidens: not knocked about final start: should stay 1m.
E. A. L. Dunlop

Godolphin's "Lateen Sails"

LATEST EDITION 3 b.f. Charnwood Forest (IRE) 125 – Star of The Future (USA) – 100 (El Gran Senor (USA) 136) [2003 81p: 6g⁶ 7.1f Jun 13] good-topped filly: fairly useful performer at 2 yrs: well held in minor events in 2003 (pulled hard final start): should be suited by 7f+: acts on firm going. *Mrs A. J. Perrett*

LATICE (IRE) 2 ch.f. (Mar 9) Inchinor 119 – Laramie (USA) 63 (Gulch (USA)) [2003 **110 p** 8g* 9g* Oct 19] second foal: dam, ran twice in Ireland, daughter of very smart Prix de Pomone winner Light The Lights: smart form: won newcomers race at Fontainebleau in September and Prix de Conde at Longchamp in October, latter by ½ length from Voix du Nord, quickening to lead final 1f: will stay 1¼m: should improve again. *J-M. Beguigne, France*

LATIF (USA) 2 b.c. (Jan 31) Red Ransom (USA) – Awaamir 102 (Green Desert (USA) **82 p** 127) [2003 7f⁴ Jul 12] third foal: dam, 7f (at 2 yrs)/1m winner, granddaughter of US Grade 1 1¼m winner Castilla: 9/4, 7 lengths fourth of 6 to Chinsola in minor event at Ascot, showing up well until not knocked about late on: should stay 1m: seems sure to improve. *J. H. M. Gosden*

LATIN REVIEW (IRE) 2 ch.f. (Feb 25) Titus Livius (FR) 115 – Law Review (IRE) **87** 63 (Case Law 113) [2003 5d⁴ 5m* 5.2m⁴ 6.1g* 6m Sep 6] 10,000Y: strong, deep-girthed filly: second foal: dam, ran 3 times (best run at 1m), half-sister to top-class sprinter Lake Coniston: fairly useful performer: won maiden at Goodwood in May (pulled muscles and off 3 months after) and minor event at Chester in August: creditable fourth to Needles And Pins in listed race at Newbury in between: reportedly struck into herself final start: likely to prove best at 5f/6f: acts on good to firm going. *A. P. Jarvis*

LAUD KARELIA 4 b.c. Royal Applause 124 – Finlandaise (FR) (Arctic Tern (USA) – 126) [2003 –: 9.9d 14.1d 10.9m Sep 8] smallish, sturdy colt: little form. *A. C. Stewart*

LAUREL DAWN 5 gr.g. Paris House 123 – Madrina 70 (Waajib 121) [2003 81, a85: **64** p5g p5g f5s f5s 5m 5m 5d⁴ 5g⁵ 5g⁵ 5m 5m² 5g⁵ 5m² 5m 5m⁶ 6m⁵ 5f 5.1g f5g² f6g f5g⁴ **a71** f5g* p5g f5s³ Dec 31] leggy, plain gelding: just fair handicapper nowadays: left A. Berry after nineteenth start: won at Southwell in December: best at 5f: acts on firm going, good to soft and all-weather. *I. W. McInnes*

LAURO 3 b.f. Mukaddamah (USA) 125 – Lapu-Lapu 62 (Prince Sabo 123) [2003 71: **82** f7g³ f8.5s² 8.1m* f8.5g² 8f* 10g⁴ Sep 27] strong filly: fairly useful handicapper: won at Haydock in June and Ayr (reluctant at stall) in August: stays 1¼m: acts on fibresand and firm ground. *Miss J. A. Camacho*

LAUTREC (SWI) 3 ch.c. Peintre Celebre (USA) 137 – La Venta (USA) (Drone **69** (USA)) [2003 65: 10m 11m 9m* 10m³ 11m 12.1m Sep 17] good-topped colt: good walker: fair handicapper: won at Redcar in June: should stay beyond 1¼m: raced only on good/good to firm going: sometimes races too freely: sold 14,000 gns. *J. L. Dunlop*

LA VIE EST BELLE 2 b.f. (Feb 5) Makbul 104 – La Belle Vie 73 (Indian King **80** (USA) 128) [2003 5m⁶ 5.1m⁴ 5.1f³ 5m² 5.2m 5.7m* 5f⁶ 6.5d³ 6.1f² 6m Oct 16] leggy filly: sixth foal: sister to 4-y-o Maktavish and half-sister to fairly useful 5f winner Paradise Lane (by Alnasr Alwasheek): dam 6f/7f winner: fairly useful performer: won maiden at Bath in August: good placed efforts in nursery at Doncaster and minor event at Nottingham after: not sure to stay beyond 6.5f: acts on firm and good to soft going: races prominently. *B. R. Millman*

LA VIGNA (IRE) 2 ch.g. (Feb 14) Woodborough (USA) 112 – Bona Fide (Sharpo – 132) [2003 6.1g 6d 8.5m f6s Oct 21] compact gelding: second foal: dam unraced: no form in maidens: visored third start. *Mrs Lucinda Featherstone*

LAVISH TIMES 2 ch.c. (Jan 28) Timeless Times (USA) 99 – Lavernock Lady (Don't **59 §** Forget Me 127) [2003 5g 5m⁵ f5g 5g⁵ 5m 5m* 5m⁵ f6g⁴ 5f f5s 5.1f³ 6m Oct 24] 8,000Y: leggy colt: second foal: brother to 3-y-o Robwillcall: dam no form: modest performer: won seller at Musselburgh in June: likely to be best at 5f/easy 6f: acts on fibresand and firm going: usually blinkered: sometimes hangs left: unreliable. *A. Berry*

LAWAAHEB (IRE) 2 b.c. (May 4) Alhaarth (IRE) 126 – Ajayib (USA) 84 (River- **71** man (USA) 131) [2003 8m 8g⁵ 8m⁶ Oct 14] rangy colt: third foal: half-brother to 3-y-o Harb: dam, 1m winner, half-sister to high-class US performer up to 1¼m Sky Beauty out of close relative of Dayjur: fair form in maidens: will probably stay 1¼m. *J. L. Dunlop*

LAW BREAKER (IRE) 5 ch.g. Case Law 113 – Revelette (Runnett 125) [2003 89, **97** a96: f5s⁵ f6s f6g f6s f6g 6g* 6m 6d f6g⁵ p6g² p6g* Dec 20] leggy gelding: useful handicapper: won at Doncaster in March and Lingfield in December: effective at 5f to easy 7f: acts on soft going, good to firm and all-weather: tried visored/in cheekpieces: sometimes hangs/finds little: usually ridden by apprentice B. Reilly. *J. A. Gilbert*

LAW COMMISSION 13 ch.g. Ela-Mana-Mou 132 – Adjala 89 (Northfields (USA)) – [2003 60: 8m Aug 6] small, sturdy gelding: just modest handicapper in 2002: well held only outing in 2003: sometimes starts slowly/hangs: held up. *J. M. Bradley*

LAWGIVER (IRE) 2 b.c. (Feb 2) Definite Article 121 – Marylou Whitney (USA) (Fappiano (USA)) [2003 7m 8m 7s Nov 3] IR 21,000F, 30,000Y: good-topped colt: has scope: fifth foal: half-brother to 3 winners abroad, including fairly useful Scandinavian winner up to 1½m Reference Lady (by Revoque): dam, placed in USA, out of smart performer up to 1m Top Socialite: well beaten in maidens. *T. J. Fitzgerald*

LAWLESS 3 ch.g. Case Law 113 – Oh My Oh My (Ballacashtal (CAN)) [2003 53: 5m 5g 5m f5s Jul 14] workmanlike gelding: modest form in 2-y-o maidens: well held in 2003, leaving M. Todhunter after third start: likely to prove best at 5f/6f. *James Moffatt*

LAW MAKER 3 b.g. Case Law 113 – Bo' Babbity 75 (Strong Gale 116) [2003 –: 6m 7.1f 6m 6d 6m 5.9m 8s p7g Dec 29] good-topped gelding: little form: left C. Fairhurst prior to final start: tried blinkered. *M. A. Buckley*

LAWOOD (IRE) 3 gr.g. Charnwood Forest (IRE) 125 – La Susiane (Persepolis (FR) **85** 127) [2003 89: p7g² p7g² 8g⁵ 6s 6d⁴ 7m⁵ 7m³ 6d Oct 12] good-topped gelding: has a quick action: fairly useful maiden: runner-up at Lingfield first 2 starts in 2003: best 3-y-o effort when fourth in handicap at the Curragh: effective at 6f to 1m: acts on soft going, good to firm and polytrack: tried in cheekpieces. *Francis Ennis, Ireland*

LAYAN 6 b.m. Puissance 110 – Most Uppitty 69 (Absalom 128) [2003 53§, a34§: 5m – § 5.5f 7d 5.9d⁶ 5m 6f Aug 22] smallish, workmanlike mare: unreliable maiden: little form in 2003. *Miss L. C. Siddall*

LAY DOWN SALLY (IRE) 5 ch.m. General Monash (USA) 107 – Sally Fay (IRE) **56 §** 66 (Fayruz 116) [2003 62: p8g⁵ p6g² p7g p6g p6g³ 5.3f 6f³ 6f f6g² f6g Dec 19] sturdy mare: modest performer: effective at 5f to 7f: acts on all-weather, firm and soft going: tried in cheekpieces, blinkered or not: often slowly away: unreliable. *J. White*

LAZER LASS (IRE) 3 b.f. Ali-Royal (IRE) 127 – Lingdale Lass 60 (Petong 126) [2003 70, a56: p6g p5g⁶ Feb 5] IR 2,000Y: sixth foal: half-sister to 6f (at 2 yrs) and 7f winner Blue Shadow and 6f/1m winner Malaah (both by Pips Pride): dam 2-y-o 6f winner: fair maiden for M. Halford, Ireland, at 2 yrs: well held in sellers in 2003: needs further than 5f, and stays 8.5f: acts on firm and soft ground. *N. P. Littmoden*

LAZZAZ 5 b.g. Muhtarram (USA) 125 – Astern (USA) 67 (Polish Navy (USA)) [2003 **62** –, a55: p10g f9.4g⁶ f11g f9.4s⁴ f8.5g² f9.4s* f12g⁶ f9.4g³ f9.4s* f8.5g² 9.9m² 10d 10.2m³ **a68** 10.5m³ 10.2m³ 11.5g² 11.1m³ 12.1d³ 11.6g 12m² 12.6m² 14.1m f12s* p12g³ 13.8m³ p13g p13g Dec 29] fair handicapper on all-weather, modest on turf: won at Wolverhampton in February, March (amateurs) and September: stays 13.8f: acts on all-weather, soft and good to firm ground: blinkered (ran respectably) once: often leads: reliable. *P. W. Hiatt*

LEADERSHIP 4 b.c. Selkirk (USA) 129 – Louella (USA) (El Gran Senor (USA) **124** 136) [2003 115: 11.6g* 12f* 12d Jul 26]

A rare purchase at the yearling sales in recent times by Khalid Abdulla, Leadership didn't come close to repaying the IR 350,000 guineas paid for him in two seasons' racing in the green, pink and white colours. But the proceeds of his subsequent private sale to Godolphin almost certainly produced a profit. Perhaps, however, Abdulla cashed in too soon on a colt who progressed well as a three-year-old. Leadership maintained his improvement in the latest season and won two of his three starts, including the Group 1 Gran Premio di Milano worth almost £170,000.

Leadership won three races for his original owner, when trained by Sir Michael Stoute, a maiden at Sandown at two and handicaps at Haydock and York at three. The first of those handicap wins came off a BHB mark of 84, the second off one of 102. It was clear from the latter performance that Leadership was ready for a step up in class, and he went close to making it a successful one, finishing a neck second to Asian Heights in the September Stakes at Kempton. Leadership wintered in Dubai following his sale to Godolphin and was having his first race for nine months when making his debut for his new connections in the listed Gala Casinos Berkshire Stakes at Windsor in June. He started odds on to account for four useful rivals and did so comfortably, allowed to coast home in the last half furlong but still winning by a length and three quarters from Potemkin. Three weeks later Leadership was among six who lined up for the Gran Premio di Milano, and one of five

Gran Premio di Milano, Milan—the improved Leadership beats long odds-on Warrsan

who seemed destined for second place at best in a race for which Warrsan, winner of the Coronation Cup on his previous start, was sent off at 5/1-on. Warrsan was the one who had to settle for second, running to form in finishing nine lengths and more clear of the remainder but unable to cope with a much improved Leadership, who lived up to his name by being in front for most of the way. Leadership's progress, and his latest campaign, came to a halt the following month, in the King George VI and Queen Elizabeth Stakes at Ascot, where he shaped as though something had gone amiss when trailing home last of twelve, weakening markedly in the closing stages. It was subsequently found that he had sustained a ligament injury.

		Sharpen Up (ch 1969)	Atan
	Selkirk (USA) (ch 1988)		Rocchetta
		Annie Edge (ch 1980)	Nebbiolo
Leadership (b.c. 1999)			Friendly Court
		El Gran Senor (b 1981)	Northern Dancer
	Louella (USA) (b 1994)		Sex Appeal
		Celtic Loot (ch 1986)	Irish River
			Witwatersrand

Leadership, a well-made, attractive colt who was bandaged on his fore joints at Ascot, is the first foal of Louella, who finished third in a couple of races at around eleven furlongs in France. Louella's second foal Rita Skeater (by Hector Protector) was successful at a mile and a half and a mile and three quarters in Germany in the latest season. A sister to four winners, including the useful mile-and-a-quarter performer Himself and a half-sister to the three-year-old Alaared, Louella is a daughter of one winner in the States in Celtic Loot, and granddaughter of another in Witwatersrand, from the family of Irish Derby winner Sir Harry Lewis. Leadership is effective making the running or held up, and he stays a mile and a half and acts on firm and good to soft going. *Saeed bin Suroor*

LEAHSTAR 4 ch.f. In The Wings 128 – Moondance (Siberian Express (USA) 125) – [2003 –: 11.9m 17.2m 14.1f⁶ 16.1m 15.8d⁵ f16g Dec 16] sturdy filly: no form. *Miss L. C. Siddall*

LEAPING BRAVE (IRE) 2 b.c. (Jan 29) Indian Rocket 115 – Island Heather (IRE) 77 (Salmon Leap (USA) 131) [2003 6d 6.1d⁵ 5.1g³ 6g 6.1m* p6g³ 6m Oct 17] 9,500Y: rather leggy colt: fifth foal: half-brother to 6f winner Somosierra (by Paris House): dam, Irish 6f winner who stayed 9f, out of half-sister to top-class sprinter Bay Express: fair performer: made all in maiden at Chepstow in September: will probably stay 7f: acts on polytrack and good to firm ground. *B. R. Millman* — 77

LEAP YEAR LASS 3 ch.f. Fleetwood (IRE) 107 – Lady Phyl 67 (Northiam (USA)) [2003 7m 8.1m 5.1m⁵ 6.1m 6g Jul 5] 800Y: sturdy filly: third foal: dam, 2-y-o 6f winner, later successful in Holland: little form. *John Allen*

LEARNED LAD (FR) 5 ch.g. Royal Academy (USA) 130 – Blushing Storm (USA) 102 (Blushing Groom (FR) 131) [2003 68, a71: p10g p8g² p10g p10g* 9.7g³ 8.3d 8m³ 9f⁴ 9g 10m² 10m 10m 8m p8g⁵ p10g Dec 10] big gelding: fair handicapper: won at Lingfield in March: effective at 1m, barely at 1½m: acts on polytrack, firm and good to soft going: sometimes races freely: none too reliable. *Jamie Poulton* — 67 a74

LEATHERBACK (IRE) 5 b.g. Turtle Island (IRE) 123 – Phyllode (Pharly (FR) 130) [2003 82: 10g 12g 9.2g 12m 10m² 10m Jul 25] strong, useful-looking gelding: fair handicapper: best around 1¼m: acts on good to firm ground, very best form on soft/heavy: blinkered last 2 outings, visored when refusing to enter stall on intended debut: found little final start: inconsistent. *N. A. Callaghan* — 74

LEAVE TO APPEAL (IRE) 3 b.f. Victory Note (USA) 120 – Justice System (USA) 57 (Criminal Type (USA)) [2003 8m* 8.2d⁵ 8m⁶ 7m⁶ 9d 9m³ 10m² 10.5d⁵ Sep 27] IR 30,000Y: tall, good-topped filly: fourth foal: half-sister to 2001 2-y-o 5f/6f winner Just A Carat (by Distinctly North): dam, Irish maiden, half-sister to very smart 1¼m performer Lear Spear: fairly useful performer: won newcomers event at Newmarket in April: good efforts in handicaps last 2 starts, wandered final one: stays easy 10.5f: yet to race on extremes of going: sold 22,000 gns, sent to USA. *L. M. Cumani* — 85

LEGALIS (USA) 5 ch.g. Gone West (USA) – Loyalize (USA) 105 (Nureyev (USA) 131) [2003 83: 6m 6d 6m f6g⁴ f6g f6s Dec 6] fairly useful handicapper in 2002, just modest in 2003: seems best around 6f: acts on good to soft going, dirt and fibresand: tried in cheekpieces: finished lame third start. *K. A. Ryan* — a62

LEGALITY 3 b.f. Polar Falcon (USA) 126 – Lady Barrister (Law Society (USA) 130) [2003 77: p10g p8g 8.1m⁵ f8.5s 7g 7m f8g p10g⁶ Dec 20] lengthy filly: modest performer: left P. Mitchell after penultimate start: stays 1m: acts on fibresand and good to firm going: tried in cheekpieces. *Julian Poulton* — 63 ?

LEGAL SET (IRE) 7 gr.g. Second Set (IRE) 127 – Tiffany's Case (IRE) 65 (Thatching 131) [2003 84: p6g p6g⁵ p6g² f6s⁶ p7g⁴ 6d² p6g 6m p6g³ 6f 6f³ 6m 6m 7.9m p7g⁶ p6g p6g Dec 30] rather leggy, close-coupled gelding: fair performer: won claimer at Lingfield in February: claimed from K. Burke £8,000 after fifteenth start: has form at 1m, but probably best at 5f to 7f nowadays: acts on any turf going and polytrack (seemingly not fibresand): tried visored/tongue tied: sometimes finds little/looks none too keen: often forces pace: none too consistent. *J. R. Best* — 74

LEGION OF HONOUR (IRE) 4 b.c. Danehill (USA) 126 – Total Chic (USA) (Far North (CAN) 120) [2003 84: 10m 10m 10m Jun 12] leggy colt: fairly useful maiden at 3 yrs for A. O'Brien in Ireland: last all 4 runs in Britain. *Miss S. J. Wilton* —

LE GRAND VIZIER 4 br.g. Doyoun 124 – Just Visiting 85 (Superlative 118) [2003 –: p12g Jan 7] well held in 3 maidens: tried visored. *J. R. Jenkins* —

LEICESTER SQUARE (IRE) 2 ch.c. (Apr 23) Gone West (USA) – Stage Manner 104 (In The Wings 128) [2003 6m* 6.3g² 6m 8f⁴ Sep 27] tall, leggy colt: third foal: dam, French 1¼m/1½m winner, half-sister to Poule d'Essai des Poulains winner Vettori: useful performer: won maiden at Leicester in June: in frame in Anglesey Stakes at the Curragh (beaten 1½ lengths by One Cool Cat) and Royal Lodge Stakes at Ascot (on toes, wandered when fourth to Snow Ridge): stays 1m: acts on firm going: joined Godolphin. *M. Johnston* — 106

LEIGHTON (IRE) 3 b.g. Desert Story (IRE) 115 – Lady Fern (Old Vic 136) [2003 89: 7.9m 8m⁴ 10m³ 9.9m⁴ 10g 10.3m³ Oct 24] tall gelding: fairly useful handicapper: good efforts in frame 3 of last 4 starts: will stay 1½m: raced only on good ground or firmer: tended to hang/carry head awkwardly at 2 yrs. *J. D. Bethell* — 92

LEISURELY WAY 4 b.f. Kris 135 – Arietta's Way (IRE) 71 (Darshaan 133) [2003 **71**
71p: 8.3s* 12g Oct 31] leggy filly: fair performer: only second outing when winning
maiden at Windsor in May by head from Radiant Energy, dictating pace: off 5 months
after: should stay at least 1¼m: raced only on good ground or softer (acts on heavy).
P. R. Chamings

LEITRIM HOUSE 2 ch.c. (Mar 7) Cadeaux Genereux 131 – Lonely Heart 101 (Mid- **92**
yan (USA) 124) [2003 6f* 7g⁶ Sep 12] €60,000Y: quite attractive colt: third foal: half-
brother to 3-y-o Golden Heart and 4-y-o Ace of Hearts: dam 1¼m winner: won maiden at
Newmarket in August by 1¼ lengths from Granato: similar form (fairly useful) when last
behind Lucky Story in Champagne Stakes at Doncaster: will probably stay 1m: sent to
USA. *B. J. Meehan*

LEITRIM ROCK (IRE) 3 b.g. Barathea (IRE) 127 – Kilshanny 70 (Groom Dancer **59 §**
(USA) 128) [2003 83d: f7g f9.4g⁵ f8g² f9.4g⁴ p7g² p8g² 7.1m 8.2m³ 8.1m 8m 10m Sep
29] quite good-topped gelding: modest handicapper: stays 9.4f: acts on all-weather, soft
and good to firm going: tried blinkered/in cheekpieces: often slowly away: ungenuine.
D. W. P. Arbuthnot

LEMAGURUT 3 b.f. Mukaddamah (USA) 125 – Fervent Fan (IRE) 65 (Soviet Lad **60**
(USA)) [2003 61: 8.2m 8.3m 6g³ 6.1f⁵ 7m 6m 7m Oct 14] leggy filly: modest maiden
handicapper: best efforts at 6f: acts on firm ground: sold 1,700 gns. *W. M. Brisbourne*

LEMARATE (USA) 6 b.g. Gulch (USA) – Sayyedati 122 (Shadeed (USA) 135) **–**
[2003 –, a51: f8g f7s f7s 7m⁵ f6g³ f7g 6.1m⁶ 6m 5.9d 16.2m 6f Aug 29] quite attractive
gelding: well held in 2003: often blinkered. *D. W. Chapman*

LE MERIDIEN (IRE) 5 ch.m. Magical Wonder (USA) 125 – Dutch Queen (Aho- **66**
noora 122) [2003 67: 5m 5d⁶ 6m⁴ 5m* 5f⁴ 6d 5m 5m 6m 5m Sep 17] robust mare: fair
handicapper: won at Beverley in June: effective at 5f to 7f: acts on firm and soft going:
sometimes wears visor/tongue tie/cheekpieces. *J. S. Wainwright*

LENNEL 5 b.g. Presidium 124 – Ladykirk 78 (Slip Anchor 136) [2003 68: 9.1f 10.3m⁴ **74**
8.1g 10.9g* 8g⁶ 10m 10.5m* 9.9m* 12m⁴ Aug 15] leggy, close-coupled gelding: fair
performer: won seller at Ayr in July and handicaps at Haydock and Beverley in August:
probably stays 1½m: seems to act on any going: effective blinkered or not: often slowly
away. *A. Bailey*

LENWADE 2 gr.f. (Apr 3) Environment Friend 128 – Branitska (Mummy's Pet 125) **53**
[2003 6m 7m⁶ 7m 8m 10f Sep 30] 2,500F: half-sister to several winners, including smart
1989 2-y-o 6f to 7.5f winner Call To Arms (by North Briton): dam, maiden, from family
of Dominion: modest maiden: should stay at least 1m. *G. G. Margarson*

LEOBALLERO 3 ch.g. Lion Cavern (USA) 117 – Ball Gown 98 (Jalmood (USA) **78**
126) [2003 8m³ 8g⁵ 8g² 8.2g² 8.2f³ p7g* Oct 27] first foal: dam 1m to 1½m winner: fair
performer: won maiden at Lingfield in October, despite hanging left: effective at 7f/1m:
raced only on polytrack/good ground or firmer: tongue tied: free-going sort: carried head
awkwardly fourth outing. *H. J. Collingridge*

LEO BOY (USA) 3 b.c. Danehill (USA) 126 – Leo Girl (USA) 100 (Seattle Slew **87**
(USA)) [2003 79: 7g³ 8g 7d⁵ 10m² 10.3m* 8m⁶ 10g⁵ 10.3m Oct 24] rather leggy, lengthy
colt: fairly useful performer: odds on, made all in maiden at Lingfield in July: stays 1¼m:
acts on good to firm ground: sometimes races freely (failed to handle turn at Nottingham
penultimate start): none too consistent: sold 8,500 gns. *J. L. Dunlop*

LEONARDO DE VINCI (IRE) 3 b.c. Sadler's Wells (USA) 132 – Andromaque **–**
(USA) 111 (Woodman (USA) 126) [2003 70: f9.4g⁶ 7g 10m Apr 2] strong, close-coupled
colt: fair maiden at 2 yrs: well held in 2003. *K. A. Ryan*

LEONORA TRUCE (IRE) 4 b.f. Brief Truce (USA) 126 – Eleonora d'Arborea 78 **–**
(Prince Sabo 123) [2003 –, a60: p8g⁵ f8.5g³ f9.4g³ f9.4g² f9.4s Dec 6] rather leggy filly: **a53**
modest performer: won in Jersey in April: left N. Littmoden and off 7 months before
running badly final outing: barely stays 9.4f: acts on all-weather and good to firm ground:
tried visored/blinkered. *R. P. Elliott*

LEONOR DE SOTO 3 b.f. Fraam 114 – Wings Awarded 67 (Shareef Dancer (USA) **67**
135) [2003 54: 10m 8.2g⁶ 8m* 8.1f* 8.5m⁴ 10f⁶ 8.5m⁶ 8m p8g f8g⁶ p10g⁶ Dec 17]
sparely-made filly: fair performer: won seller at Brighton and handicap at Warwick in
July: left M. Channon after eighth start: stays easy 1¼m: acts on firm ground, soft and
all-weather. *J. R. Best*

LEOPARD CREEK 2 ch.f. (Apr 9) Weldnaas (USA) 112 – Indigo 86 (Primo Dominie **60 p**
121) [2003 5.1f⁴ 5m 5g Oct 28] sister to smart sprinter Astonished and half-sister to

several winning sprinters, including 9-y-o Bishops Court, 4-y-o Amused and 3-y-o Cape Royal: dam 2-y-o 5f winner: modest form, slowly away, in maidens: not at all knocked about final start: will prove best at 5f/6f: should do better. *Mrs J. R. Ramsden*

LEOPARD HUNT (USA) 2 ch.f. (Mar 14) Diesis 133 – Alcando 113 (Alzao (USA) **89** 117) [2003 7m* 7.1m³ 8d Sep 11] small, attractive filly: sister to smart 7f winner (including at 2 yrs) Capistrano Day and half-sister to 3 winners, including 2000 2-y-o 6f winner Bring Plenty (by Southern Halo) and 1m (at 2 yrs) to 1¼m (in UAE) winner Kathir (by Woodman), both useful: dam, 5f (at 2 yrs) to 1¼m winner, also US Grade 1 9f winner at 5 yrs: fairly useful form: won maiden at Goodwood in June: 5¼ lengths third to Lucky Pipit in listed event at Sandown, tending to edge right: only eighth in May Hill Stakes at Doncaster: should stay at least 1m: sent to USA. *J. H. M. Gosden*

LEOPHIN DANCER (USA) 5 b.g. Green Dancer (USA) 132 – Happy Gal (FR) **47** (Habitat 134) [2003 55, a–: f12s⁶ f12s³ f12g³ f14.8g³ f12g 12.6m⁵ 12.6f⁵ 14.1d 15.8m² 16.2m³ 16.2m 13.1f⁵ 15.8d p12g Nov 26] tall, leggy gelding: poor maiden: stays 2m: acts on firm going, good to soft and fibresand: often tongue tied at 4 yrs: free-going sort. *P. W. Hiatt*

LEO'S LUCKYMAN (USA) 4 b. or br.g. Woodman (USA) 126 – Leo's Lucky **107** Lady (USA) (Seattle Slew (USA)) [2003 105: 10m² 10.3m² 10f 10.3f* 10g Jul 4] big, strong, attractive gelding: useful performer: reportedly fractured pelvis in 2002: ran well when placed in minor events in 2003 prior to making all to beat Vintage Premium by 1½ lengths in 2-runner similar event at Doncaster in June: respectable seventh to Ikhtyar in listed race at Sandown final start: stays 1¼m: acts on firm and good to soft going: tried blinkered/tongue tied at 3 yrs: often makes running: withdrawn after breaking out of stall intended final outing: subsequently gelded. *M. Johnston*

LEPORELLO (IRE) 3 b.c. Danehill (USA) 126 – Why So Silent (Mill Reef **118 p** (USA) 141) [2003 7d* 8.1g* 8m³ 10m* 10.5m* 10g* 9.9m* Sep 13]

The names of Leporello and Persian Majesty can be added to a list of the best horses trained by Peter Harris since he took out a licence in 1981, a list which also includes the likes of Katy Nowaitee, Primo Valentino and To The Roof. With Leporello and Persian Majesty having the potential to improve on the smart form they have shown already, future discussion on their trainer's top horses could centre solely on this pair. Persian Majesty, successful on his only start at two, won a listed race at Royal Ascot on his reappearance but had to miss the rest of the season after suffering a small hairline fracture in a knee. Leporello, on the other hand, made seven appearances in what was his first season, and was beaten just once.

Leporello's defeat came on the day after Persian Majesty's Royal Ascot victory. After winning a maiden at Lingfield and a minor contest at Sandown on his first two starts, he was last of three in a slowly-run minor event over a mile. One of the features of Leporello's performances in his subsequent races, all of which took place at around a mile and a quarter, was a fine turn of finishing speed. It was in evidence on his handicap debut when he beat Tiber a short head at Newmarket, and

Stan James Now Online Winter Hill Stakes, Windsor—Leporello (near side) makes a successful transition from handicaps to pattern company, quickening to collar Bourgainville close home; Island House is third

Mrs P. W. Harris' "Leporello"

even more so when he followed up in the valuable Tote Exacta Stakes (Handicap) at Haydock a month later. Leporello was a short-priced favourite in a thirteen-runner field at Haydock, but made up six lengths on the leader Silence Is Golden in the last furlong, after being boxed in for much of the straight, to win by a length. It was a remarkable performance, one which left little doubt that Leporello was ready for another step up in class. When he reappeared two weeks later it was in a Group 3 race, the Stan James Now Online Winter Hill Stakes run at Windsor. His main opponents in the six-runner field looked to be Highdown and Razkalla, but both failed to give their running and it was the front-running Bourgainville who set Leporello most to do. Held up, Leporello was the only one still on the bridle two furlongs out, though boxed in and still with a fair amount of ground to make up on the leader. When a gap appeared, Leporello quickened to collar Bourgainville towards the finish without his rider needing to resort to the whip, winning by a neck but value for a fair bit more. Leporello had a 3-lb penalty to carry when turned out for another Group 3 contest, the Tote Select Stakes at Goodwood, where he had four opponents, including Kaieteur, placed in the Eclipse and Arlington Million on his previous two starts, the Greenham winner Muqbil and Priors Lodge, winner of the Celebration Mile over the same course on his most recent outing. The race was unsatisfactory in that the pace steadied dramatically soon after the start and there was trouble in running, but the quartet still provided an exciting finish, Leporello winning by a neck from Muqbil, with the same distance back to Kaieteur, who in turn was a neck in front of Priors Lodge. Muqbil, persistently short of room in the straight, was arguably unlucky, but Leporello himself received a hefty bump around two furlongs out, and deserves a deal of credit for rallying so well. His performance showed tenacity to be another of his attributes. The Champion Stakes should have been Leporello's next engagement, but he was found to be very stiff on his return from Goodwood and was not seen out again. Leporello will have plenty of opportunities in Group 1 races in the next season. More will be required if he is to be successful in one, of course, but he has good prospects of making the necessary improvement.

Leporello (IRE) (b.c. 2000)	Danehill (USA) (b 1986)	Danzig (b 1977)	Northern Dancer	Pas de Nom
		Razyana (b 1981)	His Majesty	Spring Adieu
	Why So Silent (ch 1986)	Mill Reef (b 1968)	Never Bend	Milan Mill
		Sing Softly (br 1979)	Luthier	Melody Hour

Leporello, who runs in the colours of his trainer's wife, was bred by Peter Harris, as was the colt's unraced dam Why So Silent. The next dam Sing Softly, also owned by Mrs Harris, won the Pretty Polly Stakes and Lancashire Oaks when trained by Henry Cecil. A daughter of the useful two-year-old five-furlong winner Melody Hour, Sing Softly has produced several winners, the Cesarewitch and dual Chester Cup winner Top Cees and the smart Winter Derby winner Supreme Sound among them. Why So Silent had been responsible for six individual winners for the Harris stable even before Leporello came along, the pick of them Leporello's useful sisters Juno Marlowe, best at seven furlongs, and Poppy Carew, who stayed thirteen furlongs. Winning half-sister Oh Hebe is responsible for the three-year-old Devious Boy, who was a smart winner in the States in the latest season. Leporello himself isn't certain to stay much beyond a mile and a quarter. A sturdy colt, he won on good to soft going on his debut but has raced only on good and good to firm since. *P. W. Harris*

LE RUBAN BLEU (IRE) 4 ch.g. Bluebird (USA) 125 – Minervitta (Warrshan (USA) 117) [2003 –: 10.9m 11.9m 14.1m 10m Jul 21] smallish gelding: no form. *H. J. Collingridge* —

LES ARCS (USA) 3 br.c. Arch (USA) 127 – La Sarto (USA) (Cormorant (USA)) [2003 10.2m² 10m* 10.3d Sep 10] $140,000Y: tall, quite good-topped colt: third living foal: half-brother to winner in USA by El Gran Senor: dam, 6f/7f winner in USA, out of half-sister to US Grade 1 winners Desert Wine and Menifee and to dam of Fasliyev: useful performer: landed odds in maiden at Ripon in June impressively by 3 lengths from Beauchamp Rose, eased considerably: favourite, weakened quickly when last in minor event won by Marinas Charm at Doncaster next time: will stay 1½m: sold 32,000 gns. *J. H. M. Gosden* **98**

LESATH (USA) 3 b.g. Mister Baileys 123 – Green Moon (FR) (Shirley Heights 130) [2003 89: 10m* 12m³ 11.7f³ 12m⁶ 12m Oct 16] close-coupled, good-topped gelding: fairly useful performer: won maiden at Southwell in April: good efforts next 2 starts, ran poorly last 2: acts on firm going: hung right second start: sold 22,000 gns. *J. R. Fanshawe* **90**

LESS OF A MYSTERY (USA) 2 b.c. (May 10) Red Ransom (USA) – State Secret (Green Desert (USA) 127) [2003 5d⁴ 5.9m² 6m⁴ 8d³ 8d Oct 14] sturdy, close-coupled colt: first foal: dam, useful French 2-y-o 6.5f winner, half-sister to dams of Storming Home and Poule d'Essai des Pouliches winner Musical Chimes: fair maiden: stays 1m: acts on good to firm and good to soft going: sold 9,500 gns. *M. Johnston* **76**

LE TISS (IRE) 2 b.c. (Apr 15) Croco Rouge (IRE) 126 – Manarah 76 (Marju (IRE) 127) [2003 8.1m 8.1g 8f⁶ 8m* 8m 8g* 8m⁶ 8m² Oct 21] €110,000Y: tall, quite good-topped colt: third foal: dam, Irish 1½m winner, half-sister to smart Irish 1¼m winner Muakaad: fairly useful performer: won nurseries at Salisbury and Musselburgh in September: ran creditably in similar events at Newmarket (failed to handle Dip) and Yarmouth after: will be suited by 1¼m/1½m: acts on good to firm going. *M. R. Channon* **81**

LET IT BE 2 ch.f. (May 16) Entrepreneur 123 – Noble Dane (IRE) 79 (Danehill (USA) 126) [2003 7m 7m 7g Oct 22] 10,000Y: compact filly: second foal: dam, 1m winner at 2 yrs (stayed 1½m), sister to smart but ungenuine winner up to 10.5f Amrak Ajeeb: signs of only a little ability in maidens at Newcastle. *Mrs M. Reveley* —

LET ME TRY AGAIN (IRE) 3 b.g. Sadler's Wells (USA) 132 – Dathiyna (IRE) **110**
(Kris 135) [2003 81: p10g² p12g* 11.6g* 11.8m² 12m 12g⁵ 13.3m⁴ 14.6g Sep 13] good-
bodied gelding: smart performer: won maiden at Lingfield in February and handicap at
Windsor in April: ran well after when ½-length second to Franklins Gardens in Derby
Trial at Lingfield, fifth to Phoenix Reach in Gordon Stakes at Goodwood and fourth to
Mubtaker in Geoffrey Freer Stakes at Newbury: just respectable efforts when seventh in
Derby at Epsom and St Leger at Doncaster: stays 13.3f: acts on polytrack and good to
firm going: visored last 2 outings: tends to sweat/get on edge. *T. G. Mills*

LET'S CELEBRATE 3 b.g. Groom Dancer (USA) 128 – Shimmer 55 (Bustino 136) **–**
[2003 45: f7g 6m 7m 8m 11.9f Aug 7] rather unfurnished gelding: little form at 3 yrs:
tried tongue tied. *C. E. Brittain*

LET'S DANCE AGAIN 2 b.f. (Mar 21) Forzando 122 – Dancing Em 60 (Rambo **52**
Dancer (CAN) 107) [2003 6f⁴ 5g 7d Jul 26] 5,500Y: compact filly: first foal: dam, 7f/1m
winner, half-sister to smart performer up to 8.5f Jo Mell: modest maiden: form only at 6f:
dead. *T. D. Easterby*

LETS GET IT ON (IRE) 2 b.f. (Jan 24) Perugino (USA) 84 – Lets Clic Together **80**
(IRE) 90 (Don't Forget Me 127) [2003 5m* 6g³ 6g⁵ 6.5d 6d² Nov 4] 3,000F: compact
filly: first foal: dam Irish 7f (at 2 yrs) to 1½m winner: fairly useful performer: won
maiden at Ripon in July: free-going sort, likely to prove best at 5f/6f: acts on good to firm
and good to soft ground: carries head high. *J. J. Quinn*

LETSIMPRESS (IRE) 2 b.f. (Feb 24) General Monash (USA) 107 – Vezelay (USA) **80**
(Diesis 133) [2003 5s⁴ 6d* 6g³ 6f⁶ 6f² 6m³ 5m⁵ 5d² 6.5d 6d 8f Nov 28] IR 2,200F,
€3,800Y: leggy, workmanlike filly: third foal: half-sister to 7f winner (including at 2 yrs)
in Italy by Lahib: dam, ran 4 times, half-sister to smart 6f to 1m performer Robellation:
fairly useful performer: won maiden at Ballinrobe in May: third in listed race at Naas next
time, then left D. Gillespie: mostly creditable efforts after, leaving J. Osborne 15,000 gns
before final outing: stays 6.5f: acts on firm and good to soft going. *J. M. Cassidy, USA*

LET'S PARTY (IRE) 3 b.f. Victory Note (USA) 120 – Mashoura (Shareef Dancer **60 d**
(USA) 135) [2003 69: 6g⁶ 6m⁴ 6.1d 7.1g 8m⁶ 8m⁴ 7g f8.5g 10m⁴ 7g 8.2d Nov 6] rather
leggy filly: modest maiden: left R. Hannon after fourth start: well below form last 5 outings, leaving P. McEntee before final one: stays 1m: acts on good to firm and good to soft
going: sometimes tongue tied: carries head high: possibly none too genuine. *P. L. Clinton*

LETS ROLL 2 b.g. (Apr 11) Tamure (IRE) 125 – Miss Petronella (Petoski 135) [2003 **69**
6g 7d² 6m² 8m⁵ 7m* Oct 1] 1,400Y: rather leggy gelding: fifth foal: dam unraced: fair
performer: won maiden at Newcastle by length from Silverhay: stays 1m: acts on good to
firm and good to soft going. *C. W. Thornton*

LET THE LION ROAR 2 b.c. (Feb 27) Sadler's Wells (USA) 132 – Ballerina (IRE) **97 p**
88 (Dancing Brave (USA) 140) [2003 8m* 8m² Sep 19] good-topped colt: has round
action: fifth foal: half-brother to 6-y-o Millenary and smart 1½m winner Head In The
Clouds (by Rainbow Quest): dam, 2-y-o 7f winner, half-sister to Princess Royal winner
Dancing Bloom and smart French performer up to 1m River Dancer, herself dam of
Spectrum: landed odds in maiden at Newmarket in August: coltish, useful form when
staying-on 2½ lengths second of 5 to Elshadi in minor event at Newbury: will be suited
by 1¼m+: soon off bridle both outings: open to further progress. *J. L. Dunlop*

LEVANTINE (IRE) 6 b.g. Sadler's Wells (USA) 132 – Spain Lane (USA) 115 (Seek- **53**
ing The Gold (USA)) [2003 77, a–: 7.2g³ 10.2g 8.1g⁶ 7fg³ f8g³ Nov 24] most modest
nowadays: stays 8.5f: acts on soft going, good to firm, dirt and fibresand: has been
visored, including when successful: wore cheekpieces last 2 starts. *A. G. Newcombe*

LEVELLED 9 b.g. Beveled (USA) – Baino Charm (USA) (Diesis 133) [2003 f6g 6m **–**
f6g Nov 25] angular gelding: useful at best: only win since 1999 in handicap at Jebel Ali
in 2000: off 18 months/left P. Rudkin in UAE, well beaten on return to Britain in 2003:
effective at 5f/6f: acts on dirt/any turf going. *D. W. Chapman*

LE VIE DEI COLORI 3 b.c. Efisio 120 – Mystic Tempo (USA) 76 (El Gran Senor **119**
136) [2003 110: 8g* 8g* 8m* 8m² 8m* Oct 12] workmanlike colt: smart performer, winner of 10 of his 12 starts: successful at Rome at 3 yrs in listed race and Premio
Parioli (beat Prince Kirk and Royal Dignitary by 2½ lengths and ¾ length) in April and
minor event in September: below best when second to Lindholm in listed race at Milan,
but back to form when beating Blatant ½ length in Premio Vittorio di Capua there final
outing: stays 1m: raced only on good ground or firmer: genuine and consistent. *R. Brogi,
Italy*

LEVITATOR 2 b.c. (Apr 25) Sadler's Wells (USA) 132 – Cantilever 107 (Sanglamore **– p**
(USA) 126) [2003 8m Oct 17] quite attractive colt: first foal: dam, French 1¼m/1½m
(Prix de Royaumont) winner, out of sister to Irish Oaks winner Princess Pati: 33/1, in rear
in maiden at Newmarket, travelling strongly before hampered: will do better at 1¼m/
1½m. *Sir Michael Stoute*

LEYAALY 4 ch.f. Night Shift (USA) – Lower The Tone (IRE) 74 (Phone Trick (USA)) **–**
[2003 –: 8.2g 8.5m Apr 23] tailed-off last all 4 starts in maidens. *B. A. Pearce*

LEZARA 2 b.f. (Feb 15) Aragon 118 – Lezayre (Dalsaan 125) [2003 f6s Oct 21] **–**
smallish, close-coupled filly: first known foal: dam well held only start: 50/1, tailed off in
maiden at Southwell, starting very slowly. *M. A. Buckley*

LIAM'S STORY (IRE) 3 gr.g. Desert Story (IRE) 115 – Sweet Class (Rusticaro **–**
(FR) 124) [2003 74: 8g 9.9d May 20] fair maiden at 2 yrs: well held in handicaps in 2003.
K. A. Ryan

LIBERTY 2 b.f. (Feb 22) Singspiel (IRE) 133 – Virtuous 92 (Exit To Nowhere (USA) **71 p**
122) [2003 6m² 6m* Jul 21] leggy, quite good-topped filly: second foal: half-sister to
3-y-o Peace: dam, 2-y-o 1m winner who stayed 11.5f, out of half-sister to 2000 Guineas
winner Entrepreneur: fair form in maidens: landed odds at Windsor, hanging markedly
left: will be suited by 1¼m/1½m: open to progress, all being well. *Sir Michael Stoute*

LIBERTY ROYAL 4 b.g. Ali-Royal (IRE) 127 – Hope Chest 70 (Kris 135) [2003 **85**
91+: 8.3g 8m⁴ 9g p10g p10g p12g Dec 17] fairly useful performer, lightly raced: effective
at 1m/1¼m: raced only on all-weather and good/good to firm ground. *P. J. Makin*

LIBERTY SEEKER (FR) 4 ch.g. Machiavellian (USA) 123 – Samara (IRE) 108 **71 ?**
(Polish Patriot (USA) 128) [2003 77: 10.1d 8.3d 10.1m 8.1d Sep 26] angular gelding: fair
maiden handicapper, lightly raced: seemed to run creditably in 2003 only on third start:
stays 1¼m: acts on soft and good to firm going, some promise on fibresand: won over
hurdles in October. *G. A. Swinbank*

LIBRE 3 b.g. Bahamian Bounty 116 – Premier Blues (FR) 35 (Law Society (USA) 130) **80**
[2003 75: 7g 12.3m 8m 8.2g² 7m³ 9.1g* 10.3m 10m⁴ 7.6m 8f* 8.1m⁴ 8.5d Sep 23] leggy
gelding: fairly useful performer: won maiden at Ayr in May and handicap at Bath in
September: stays 9f: yet to race on heavy going, acts on any other: tried blinkered/tongue
tied, wore cheekpieces fourth to seventh starts: often looks none too keen. *F. Jordan*

LIEUDAY 4 b.g. Atraf 116 – Figment 75 (Posse (USA) 130) [2003 61: 7m 7.9m⁶ f8.5g **58**
7.6m² 8s 7m⁴ᵈ 7m⁵ 7m 6.9m⁵ 7m³ Sep 9] rather leggy gelding: modest maiden: effective
at 6f/7f: acts on soft and good to firm ground, below form both starts on fibresand: tried
visored, usually wears cheekpieces nowadays: slowly away and carried head awkwardly
penultimate start. *W. M. Brisbourne*

LIFE ESTATES 3 b.g. Mark of Esteem (IRE) 137 – Chepstow Vale (USA) 97 (Key To **–**
The Mint (USA)) [2003 –: 7f 6m Jun 17] close-coupled gelding: little form. *T. J. Fitzgerald*

LIFE IS BEAUTIFUL (IRE) 4 b.f. Septieme Ciel (USA) 123 – Palombella (FR) **50 §**
(Groom Dancer (USA) 128) [2003 65: 12.3m 12m f12g 12.1m 10.1m⁶ 11m² 14.1m
12.1dᵃ 12m Oct 6] smallish, sturdy filly: modest performer: won seller at Beverley (for
second year running) in September: stays 1½m: acts on soft and good to firm ground:
sometimes early to post: often beats: unreliable. *W. H. Tinning*

LIFFEY (IRE) 3 br.c. Desert Prince (IRE) 130 – Toujours Irish (USA) (Irish River **88**
(FR) 131) [2003 83p: 7g² Mar 21] strong, lengthy colt: plenty of promise both starts in
maidens: second to Weavers Pride at Doncaster only outing in 2003: may prove best at 7f/
1m: sold 10,000 gns in October. *P. F. I. Cole*

LIFTED WAY 4 b.c. In The Wings 128 – Stack Rock 111 (Ballad Rock 122) [2003 80: **87**
10m⁵ 10m⁶ 8m 8.1m* 8g³ 7m⁵ 7.1m⁴ p7g 8.1m Sep 20] fairly useful performer: won
maiden at Warwick in July: effective at 7f (given bit of a test) to 1¼m: raced only on good
going or firmer on turf, some promise on polytrack penultimate start. *P. R. Chamings*

LI GALLI (USA) 3 b. or br.f. Nureyev (USA) 131 – Redwood Falls (IRE) 107 **–**
(Dancing Brave (USA) 140) [2003 57: p5g⁶ 6g Jul 9] smallish filly: modest form only
start at 2 yrs (raced freely): well held in 2003, leaving G. Butler and off over 4 months
after reappearance. *D. K. Weld, Ireland*

LIGHT BRIGADE 4 b.g. Kris 135 – Mafatin (IRE) 74 (Sadler's Wells (USA) 132) **63**
[2003 –: f11g p12g³ Sep 3] modest maiden: stays 1½m: acts on polytrack, some promise
on good to firm going earlier in career: tried visored. *J. M. P. Eustace*

LIGHTSABRE   3 ch.f. Polar Falcon (USA) 126 – Heavenly Ray (USA) 97 (Rahy **63**
(USA) 115) [2003 55: f6g2 f6g2 f6g5 p8g6 7g Sep 10] modest maiden handicapper: will
need to settle better to stay beyond 6f: raced mainly on all-weather, visored/hung markedly left on turf debut final start: tried in cheekpieces. *Sir Mark Prescott*

LIGHT SCENT (USA)   4 ch.g. Silver Hawk (USA) 123 – Music Lane (USA) (Mis- **95**
waki (USA) 124) [2003 93: 10.1m 11.9m 10m 12m2 12m2 14g6 Jul 4] strong, close-
coupled gelding: useful handicapper: ran well when neck second to Inglis Drever at
Newmarket penultimate start: probably stays 1¾m: acts on soft and good to firm going:
visored last 2 outings in 2002 (raced freely/folded final one): usually races prominently.
J. Akehurst

LIGHT THE DAWN (IRE)   3 ch.f. Indian Ridge 123 – Flaming June (USA) 69   **–**
(Storm Bird (CAN) 134) [2003 p8g Oct 8] IR 130,000Y: third foal: dam, lightly-raced
maiden, half-sister to useful performer up to 1¼m Majmu (dam of high-class miler
Muhtathir): 10/1, seventh of 12 in maiden at Lingfield, soon prominent despite slow start
and not knocked about once held: sold 2,500 gns. *J. H. M. Gosden*

LIGNE D'EAU   2 ch.c. (Mar 16) Cadeaux Genereux 131 – Miss Waterline 77 (Rock **69**
City 120) [2003 6g 7m 6g Oct 31] sturdy, close-coupled colt: second foal: dam, 2-y-o 6f
winner, half-sister to smart sprinters Double Action and Sir Nicholas (latter, by Cadeaux
Genereux, later won up to 1¼m in Hong Kong where known as Red Pepper): best effort
in maidens (fair form) when eighth at Doncaster second start: stays 7f. *P. D. Evans*

LIKELY LADY (IRE)   4 b.f. Revoque (IRE) 122 – Harmer (IRE) 72 (Alzao (USA)   **?**
117) [2003 52, a44: f8s p8g p6g f9.4g f8.5g3 p8g 8.2m Jun 14] quite attractive filly: poor **a37**
nowadays: stays 8.5f: acts on good to soft and all-weather: races
freely: has carried head high/found little. *D. Burchell*

LILAC   4 ch.f. Alhijaz 122 – Fairfield's Breeze (Buckskin (FR) 133) [2003 –: 12.6m **36**
12.1m3 Jul 11] smallish, plain filly: poor maiden. *R. J. Price*

LILARDO   6 b. or br.m. Son Pardo 107 – Jimlil 99 (Nicholas Bill 125) [2003 58: f16.2g   **–**
f12g5 f14g Mar 11] modest winner at 5 yrs: no form in 2003: tongue tied. *B. Palling*

LILIAN   3 b.f. First Trump 118 – Lillibella 64 (Reprimand 122) [2003 60p: p7g p7g 10f **53**
7.1g 8f2 8.5g4 8m6 8f 10m2 10m2 Oct 13] leggy, quite good-topped filly: modest maiden:
stays 1¼m: acts on firm ground and polytrack: visored last 6 outings: sold 5,000 gns.
A. M. Balding

LILLEBROR (GER)   5 b.h. Top Waltz (FR) 119 – Lady Soliciti (GER) (Solicitor (FR)   **–**
121) [2003 10g 12g5 11.6m4 10m 11.9m 15.9d Sep 24] small horse: second foal:
dam German 7.5f winner: winner of 5 races in Germany for H. Groschel: little worthwhile form in Britain: stays 1½m: acts on heavy and good to firm going: tried visored/in
cheekpieces. *B. J. Curley*

LI'L LEES (IRE)   2 ch.g. (Apr 20) Lake Coniston (IRE) 131 – Kayrava (Irish River   **–**
(FR) 131) [2003 7m4 8m 8m Oct 25] €3,500Y: quite good-topped gelding: half-brother
to French 1m winner (including at 2 yrs) Kenavo (by Un Desperado): dam unraced half-
sister to very smart 1¼m performer Kartajana: well beaten in maidens: signs of temperament. *I. Semple*

LILLIES BORDELLO (IRE)   4 b.f. Danehill Dancer (IRE) 117 – Lunulae (Tumble **49**
Wind (USA)) [2003 –: f6g f6g4 f6s5 f6s Feb 17] lengthy, quite good-topped filly: just
poor form in 2003: effective at 5f/6f: acts on good to firm going, good to soft and fibresand: wore cheekpieces/blinkers last 3 starts. *K. A. Ryan*

LILLI MARLANE   3 b.f. Sri Pekan (USA) 117 – Fiveofive (IRE) 61 (Fairy King **82**
(USA)) [2003 7d5 7d 8g2 8.2g* 10m2 10m3 8m3 8m5 8.9f Oct 11] fifth foal: half-sister to
1½m winner Sweet Angeline (by Deploy) and 2001 2-y-o 7f winner My Only Sunshine
(by First Trump): dam 5f (at 2 yrs) and 1m winner: fairly useful handicapper: won at
Nottingham in June: effective at 1m/1¼m: acts on good to firm going. *G. G. Margarson*

LILL'S STAR LAD   5 ch.g. Kasakov – Lady Khadija (Nicholas Bill 125) [2003 –:   **–**
f11g 7f 7m 14.1d Jul 26] no sign of ability. *P. R. Wood*

LILY OF THE GUILD (IRE)   4 ch.f. Lycius (USA) 124 – Secreto Bold (Never So **62**
Bold 135) [2003 65: f7g 8m 7g4 7.1d4 6m4 7.1g6 p7g2 Dec 30] close-coupled filly: modest
handicapper: stays 7f: acts on good to firm going and polytrack: has pulled hard/hung/
swished tail: none too consistent. *W. S. Kittow*

LIMIT DOWN (IRE)   2 b.g. (May 4) Desert Story (IRE) 115 – Princess Raisa (Indian **55**
King (USA) 128) [2003 p6g 6d p5g 7g p7g5 Dec 17] IR 15,000F, 16,000Y: closely
related to fairly useful Irish 7f and 9f winner Indian Desert (by Desert Style) and half-

brother to several winners, including fairly useful 1997 2-y-o 6f winner Distinct Vintage (later 5.5f winner in Norway, by Distinctly North): dam Irish maiden: modest maiden: will stay 1m. *M. J. Wallace*

LIMITED MAGICIAN 2 b.f. (May 2) Wizard King 122 – Pretty Scarce (Handsome – Sailor 125) [2003 8g 6f Oct 10] 2,000Y: workmanlike filly: fourth foal: half-sister to 6-y-o Sergeant Slipper: dam little sign of ability: last in maidens at Ripon and York. *C. Smith*

LINBY LAD (IRE) 3 ch.g. Dolphin Street (FR) 125 – Classic Look (IRE) 58 (Classic – Music (USA)) [2003 75: 8m 8g May 23] useful-looking gelding: fair performer at 2 yrs: well held in handicaps in 2003: will probably stay 1¼m: raced only on good ground or firmer. *J. J. Quinn*

LINCOLN DANCER (IRE) 6 b.g. Turtle Island (IRE) 123 – Double Grange (IRE) **94 d** (Double Schwartz 128) [2003 108: 5g 6m⁶ 7g 6m 6s f5g Dec 9] compact, sturdy, attractive gelding: poor mover: has reportedly had chipped fetlock: just fairly useful handicapper in 2003: off barely 5 months before fourth outing: probably best at 6f/7f: goes well on ground softer than good, well held on all-weather debut final start. *D. Nicholls*

LINDA GREEN 2 b.f. (Jan 17) Victory Note (USA) 120 – Edge of Darkness 62 **61** (Vaigly Great 127) [2003 f5g⁶ 5g⁴ 5g⁴ 5m² 5m f5s³ f5s Sep 26] 1,200Y: rather leggy filly: sixth foal: half-sister to 6f winner (including at 2 yrs) Joint Instruction (by Forzando) and fairly useful 1½m/1¾m winner Salford Flyer (by Pharly): dam 1¼m to 2m winner: modest maiden: ran well when placed: likely to prove best at 5f: acts on fibresand and good to firm ground. *R. Bastiman*

LINDEN'S LADY 3 b.f. Compton Place 125 – Jubilee Place (IRE) 76 (Prince Sabo **82** 123) [2003 79, a–: 7m 6m³ 6m² 6m³ 6f 6m³ 6m² 7f⁴ 6m⁶ 6m⁴ 6g⁴ 6.1g 6m⁵ Sep 16] leggy filly: fairly useful handicapper: stays 6f: acts on firm ground, well beaten on soft/fibresand: tried visored. *J. R. Weymes*

LINDOP 3 ch.c. Nashwan (USA) 135 – Footlight Fantasy (USA) 68 (Nureyev (USA) **89** 131) [2003 8g* May 17] 110,000Y: workmanlike colt: fifth foal: half-brother to 3 winners, including 4-y-o Unscrupulous and useful 1998 2-y-o 6f winner Dominant Dancer (by Primo Dominie): dam 7f winner out of top-class miler Milligram: 6/1 and shade colty, emphatic winner of 18-runner maiden at Newbury in May by 3 lengths from Odabella, steadied leaving stall, weaving through to lead entering final 1f, then drifting left: wore crossed noseband: seemed sure to improve. *J. A. R. Toller*

LINENS FLAME 4 ch.g. Blushing Flame (USA) 109 – Atlantic Air (Air Trooper 115) – [2003 61: p10g p10g 9.7g Mar 25] modest maiden at best: well held in 2003. *B. G. Powell*

LINGO (IRE) 4 b.g. Poliglote 121 – Sea Ring (FR) (Bering 136) [2003 101: 8g 10m* **111 p** 10.1m* Apr 23] strong gelding: smart performer: won minor event at Pontefract and handicap at Epsom (by ½ length from Danelor) in April, carrying head high in latter: probably better at 1¼m than 1½m: acts on soft and good to firm going: held up and has turn of foot: joined Jonjo O'Neill: smart novice hurdler: probably open to further improvement on Flat. *Mrs J. R. Ramsden*

LIN IN GOLD (IRE) 2 b.g. (Mar 7) Second Empire (IRE) 124 – Wasmette (IRE) **80** (Wassl 125) [2003 8f⁵ 8d Nov 7] €13,000Y, 11,500 2-y-o: lengthy gelding: sixth foal: half-brother to 1996 2-y-o 7f seller winner Irish Fiction (by Classic Music) and French 12.5f winner Aqualongo (by Entrepreneur): dam unraced half-sister to very smart middle-distance colt Nisnas: fairly useful form when winning maiden at Brighton in October by length from Little London: sweating/had 2 handlers, well beaten in minor event at Doncaster, pulling hard: needs to settle to stay 1¼m. *P. A. Blockley*

LINNING WINE (IRE) 7 b.g. Scenic 128 – Zallaka (IRE) (Shardari 134) [2003 85, **91** a104: p12g⁴ p10g p10g 10m³ 10m 10.3m² 11.9m 10d 11m p12g p10g p10g² p8g* Dec **a103** 20] lengthy gelding: useful on all-weather, fairly useful on turf: won minor event at Lingfield in December easily by 2½ lengths from Lakota Brave: effective at 1m to 1½m: acts on polytrack, good to firm and good to soft ground: held up, and sometimes finds little. *B. G. Powell*

LIONEL ANDROS 5 b.g. Lion Cavern (USA) 117 – Guyum (Rousillon (USA) 133) **48** [2003 50: f5g 6m⁶ 6m 6m f7g 5g Jun 12] tall, leggy gelding: poor maiden: stays 6f: acts on fibresand, goes well on going firmer than good on turf: tried in headgear: has been slowly away. *K. A. Ryan*

LION GUEST (IRE) 6 ch.g. Lion Cavern (USA) 117 – Decrescendo (IRE) (Polish – Precedent (USA) 131) [2003 15g 12.3m Aug 4] winning hurdler: formerly modest maiden on Flat: well held in 2003: tried blinkered/tongue tied. *Mrs S. C. Bradburne*

LION'S DOMANE 6 b.g. Lion Cavern (USA) 117 – Vilany 87 (Never So Bold 135) **69 d**
[2003 74§, a–§: f7g 7m² 7m 7m* 7.1f* 7.2g 7m 6.9f f7g f6g Dec 9] strong, workmanlike **a– §**
gelding: fair on turf, poor on all-weather: won seller at Thirsk in May and claimer at Musselburgh (hung markedly left) in June: left I. Semple after and little form subsequently:
best around 7f: acts on firm going and fibresand: tried visored and in cheekpieces: wayward (has been equipped with net muzzle): usually leads: unreliable. *A. Berry*

LIPS LION (IRE) 4 ch.c. Lion Cavern (USA) 117 – Glamour Model 78 (Last Tycoon **101 ?**
131) [2003 101: 8g³ 8f⁵ Jul 12] IR 40,000Y: second foal: half-brother to 7f winner Eddys
Lad (by Lahib): dam, Irish 2-y-o 7f winner, half-sister to smart Irish 6f/7f performer
King's College: useful performer: trained by P. Hirschberger at 3 yrs, winning national
listed race at Hoppegarten and second in Group 3 events at Dusseldorf and Bremen: third
to Mr Tango in minor event at Cologne on reappearance: stiff task, seemed to run well
when 4¼ lengths last of 5 to Tillerman in Silver Trophy at Ascot next time: stays 1¼m:
acts on firm and soft ground: consistent. *A. Lowe, Germany*

LIQUIDATE 2 b.g. (May 10) Hector Protector (USA) 124 – Cut And Run (Slip Anchor **58**
136) [2003 7.1g 7m 7.9f⁶ Oct 10] 50,000Y: good-bodied gelding: fifth foal: half-brother
to smart 1½m and 2m winner Ski Run (by Petoski): dam (no form) out of half-sister to
champion US filly Go For Wand: modest form in maidens: will be suited by 1¼m/1½m:
tongue tied first and final starts. *J. W. Hills*

LIQUID FORM (IRE) 3 b.g. Bahhare (USA) 122 – Brogan's Well (IRE) (Caerleon **93**
(USA) 132) [2003 80: 8.1f⁵ 8m⁴ 10.9f⁶ 10m* 10m⁴ 10g 11m* 10.4f³ Oct 10] fairly useful
handicapper: won at Kempton in August and Goodwood in September: best form at 1¼m/
11f: acts on firm ground. *B. Hanbury*

LISA'S LOONEY 4 b.f. Bahamian Bounty 116 – Starfida (Soviet Star (USA) 128) **48**
[2003 42: 6m 6g 6m 6g⁵ 6.1g 6m 6.1m 7m 6m Aug 21] strong, close-coupled filly: poor
maiden: stays 6f: acts on soft and good to firm ground: tried visored: sometimes slowly
away. *Mrs C. A. Dunnett*

LISCOMBE PARK 2 b.f. (Feb 14) Young Ern 120 – Little Park 39 (Cragador 110) **–**
[2003 f8s Sep 2] fourth foal: half-sister to 7f/1m winner in Germany by Wing Park: dam,
maiden, probably stayed 1¼m: 66/1, last of 10 in maiden at Southwell, giving trouble
beforehand. *D. J. Daly*

LISTEN KID (USA) 4 b.g. Royal Academy (USA) 130 – Prosper (USA) (Affirmed **–**
(USA)) [2003 –: 14.1d 11.6g 12m 11.9f 11.5s Aug 28] big, good-topped gelding: no sign
of ability: visored final outing. *Mrs A. J. Bowlby*

LISTEN TO REASON (IRE) 2 b.c. (Mar 31) Mukaddamah (USA) 125 – Tenalist **57**
(IRE) 69 (Tenby 125) [2003 6m⁵ 6m Aug 16] €17,000Y, 12,000 2-y-o: strong, leggy
colt: first foal: dam, Irish 2-y-o 6.5f winner, half-sister to useful 1¼m/1½m winner Prince
Alex: better effort in maidens (modest form) when fifth at Doncaster: hung left at Ripon:
should stay 1m. *J. G. Given*

LITANY 4 b.f. Colonel Collins (USA) 122 – Hymn Book (IRE) 65 (Darshaan 133) **–**
[2003 73: 12g 13.8m 16m Apr 26] leggy filly: unimpressive mover: fair handicapper at 3
yrs: well held in 2003, pulled up reportedly lame final start: tried visored. *John A. Harris*

LITERACY (USA) 3 b.f. Diesis 133 – Tuviah (USA) (Eastern Echo (USA)) [2003 **74**
68: 10.1m⁶ 11.6d⁶ 11.8m⁵ 10.9m* 10m⁴ 10.1g 10f* Oct 1] close-coupled, quite attractive
filly: fair handicapper: won at Warwick in June and Nottingham in October: stays 10.9f:
acts on firm going: sometimes races freely: sold 10,000 gns in December. *C. E. Brittain*

LITEWSKA (IRE) 3 b.f. Mujadil (USA) 119 – Old Tradition (IRE) 76 (Royal **83**
Academy (USA) 130) [2003 86: 6m 6.1d 6m⁴ 5f* 5m 6m* 6g 6m 7m Oct 24] rather leggy,
unfurnished filly: fairly useful performer: won handicap at Sandown in June and minor
event at Windsor in July: well below form last 2 starts: effective at 5f/6f: acts on firm
ground and polytrack: sold 9,000 gns. *R. Hannon*

LITHUANIAN (AUS) 5 br.h. Nureyev (USA) 131 – Doe (USA) (Hansel (USA)) **67**
[2003 78p: p6g* 8.3m Jun 9] fair performer: only second start when winning maiden
at Lingfield in January: last in minor event at Windsor subsequent outing, racing very
freely after slowish start: should stay 1m: clearly not easy to train: sent to South Africa.
W. J. Haggas

LITIGIOUS 6 b.m. Mtoto 134 – Kiomi 65 (Niniski (USA) 125) [2003 –: f8.5g f14.8g **– §**
f9.4g Jul 19] temperamental maiden: sometimes visored. *A. Senior*

LITTLE AMIN 7 b.g. Unfuwain (USA) 131 – Ghassanah 73 (Pas de Seul 133) [2003   **80 §**
85§, a75§: 8.1m 10m⁵ 8.5d⁵ 8.1d May 26] smallish, well-made gelding: has marked knee
action: fairly useful performer: mostly below form in 2003: has won at 1½m, probably
best at 1m/1¼m: acts on fibresand, good to firm and good to soft going: unreliable.
J. D. Czerpak

LITTLE BOB 2 ch.g. (May 20) Zilzal (USA) 137 – Hunters of Brora (IRE) 102 (Sharpo   **–**
132) [2003 7d Nov 7] quite good-topped gelding: second foal: brother to 7f winner Scotland The Brave: dam 7f to 8.5f winner: 25/1 and burly, well held in maiden at Doncaster.
J. D. Bethell

LITTLE BUD 9 br.m. Lord Bud 121 – Sindur (Rolfe (USA) 77) [2003 p12g Nov 12]   **–**
modest hurdler: lightly raced and well held on Flat. *Miss A. M. Newton-Smith*

LITTLE DAISY 5 ch.m. Factual (USA) 108 – Twice In Bundoran (IRE) 70 (Bold   **–**
Arrangement 127) [2003 –: 13.8f f12s Jun 13] of little account. *K. A. Ryan*

LITTLE EDWARD 5 gr.g. King's Signet (USA) 110 – Cedar Lady (Telsmoss 91)   **106**
[2003 101: 6m³ 5.1m² 5g 5f* 6f 5g 5.7f* 5m 5d² 5f² 5f⁵ Sep 28] angular gelding: useful
performer: landed odds in minor events at Sandown in June and Bath in July: very
good short-head second to Serov in handicap at the Curragh penultimate start: stays
5.7f: acts on firm and good to soft going: refused to enter stall once: races prominently.
B. G. Powell

LITTLE ENGLANDER 3 b.g. Piccolo 121 – Anna Karietta 82 (Precocious 126)   **65**
[2003 10m⁶ 10g² 10m⁴ 12.1m Sep 17] half-brother to several winners, including useful
German 6f/7f performer Just Heaven's Gate (by Slip Anchor) and fairly useful 7f winner
Premier Baron (by Primo Dominie): dam 6f/7f winner: fair maiden: likely to prove best
up to 1¼m. *H. Candy*

LITTLE EYE (IRE) 2 b.g. (Mar 16) Groom Dancer (USA) 128 – Beaming 93   **69**
(Mtoto 134) [2003 5m 5m⁶ 5m⁴ 6g 7g 8.3g f6g⁴ f7g² p8g² p7g³ f7s⁴ Dec 31] 8,500F,
26,000Y, 27,000 2-y-o: sturdy, close-coupled gelding: sixth foal: half-brother to French
10.5f/1½m winner Tunnel Topics (by Sri Pekan): dam, 6f (at 2 yrs) and 1m winner, out of
smart 2-y-o sprinter Glancing: fair maiden: second in nurseries at Wolverhampton and
Lingfield: stays 1m: acts on all-weather and good to firm going. *J. R. Best*

LITTLE FLUTE 2 b.c. (Mar 3) Piccolo 121 – Nordic Victory (USA) (Nordico (USA))   **52**
[2003 5m⁴ 5g 7m 6m 7m 6m f8.5g f5g² Dec 22] 5,900F, 11,000Y, 15,000 2-y-o:
smallish, compact colt: first foal: dam sprint winner in US: modest maiden: left C. Cox
1,800 gns before final start: likely to prove best at 5f/6f: acts on fibresand. *T. Keddy*

LITTLE GOOD BAY 3 b.c. Danehill (USA) 126 – Brave Kris (IRE) 104 (Kris 135)   **110**
[2003 79p: 8.3g² 8g⁵ 8g⁴ 7.1f³ 7m* 7g³ 7g* 7f⁶ Sep 27] smallish colt: smart handicapper:
won at Chester in June and August (beat Vanderlin 1½ lengths), slowly away both times:
shaped well when sixth to Master Robbie in Tote Trifecta Stakes at Ascot final start: has
form at 1m, but will probably prove best around 7f: acts on polytrack, raced only on good
going or firmer on turf: visored last 5 starts: has had 2 handlers: sometimes races freely:
has his quirks, but is progressive. *J. H. M. Gosden*

LITTLE JIMBOB 2 b.g. (Feb 23) Desert Story (IRE) 115 – Artistic Licence (High   **71**
Top 131) [2003 5m⁴ 5m³ 5d⁶ 5f⁴ 6g³ 7m² 8m³ 7m⁴ 8m² Sep 13] 8,500F, 10,500Y: close-
coupled gelding: half-brother to several winners, including 3-y-o Riska King: dam
maiden who stayed 1¼m: fair maiden: second in nurseries at Newcastle and Musselburgh: stays 1m: acts on good to firm ground: sometimes early to post. *R. A. Fahey*

LITTLE JOHN 7 b.g. Warrshan (USA) 117 – Silver Venture (USA) (Silver Hawk   **– §**
(USA) 123) [2003 57§: 16d 13.8f 11.9m Jun 2] big, lengthy gelding: maiden handicapper: well held in 2003 (reportedly had breathing problem on reappearance): tried
blinkered/visored: shirker. *Miss L. A. Perratt*

LITTLE LAURA 7 ch.m. Casteddu 111 – At First Sight (He Loves Me 120) [2003   **–**
12.4g⁴ 12.4m Aug 6] 400Y: sister to fair 7f (at 2 yrs) and 1¼m winner Il Destino: dam
unraced: little sign of ability in bumpers/maiden/seller. *K. W. Hogg, Isle of Man*

LITTLE LONDON 2 b.g. (Feb 15) Bahhare (USA) 122 – North Kildare (USA)   **77**
(Northjet 136) [2003 7g 7g³ 7.6m⁵ 8f² Oct 17] useful-looking gelding: seventh foal: half-
brother to 6f (at 2 yrs) and 1¼m winner Flying North (by Distinctly North): dam unraced
half-sister to very smart 1m/9f performer Labeeb and high-class performer up to 1¼m
Fanmore: fair maiden: placed at Epsom (slowly away/hung left) and Brighton: stays 1m:
acts on firm going. *J. L. Dunlop*

LITTLE LOUIS 3 b.g. Defacto (USA) – Naufrage (Main Reef 126) [2003 53, a60: **54**
f7g² p6g f7g⁶ f8g f6g f7s Feb 13] smallish, workmanlike gelding: modest performer: best
at 6f/7f: acts on fibresand, best turf effort on good going: blinkered: often soon off bridle:
sold 650 gns. *P. D. Evans*

LITTLEMISSATTITUDE 4 ch.f. Common Grounds 118 – Last Look (Rainbow **73**
Quest (USA) 134) [2003 75: f8s* f8.5g* f9.4g⁶ f9.4g* f8.5g⁵ p8g a11g² 9.8m a8.6g Aug
10] leggy, sparely-made filly: fair performer: won minor event at Southwell and 2
claimers at Wolverhampton in January/February: claimed from K. Burke £14,000 after
sixth start: finds 1m a bare minimum and stays 11.5f: acts on all-weather, dirt, good to
firm and soft going: has worn cheekpieces: usually visored nowadays. *C. Bjorling,
Sweden*

LITTLE MISS CODY 2 b.f. (Mar 8) Mind Games 121 – Madam Cody (Hot Spark **38**
126) [2003 5m 5d May 20] smallish filly: half-sister to several winners, including fairly
useful 15f winner Mara Askari (by Night Shift) and 1993 2-y-o 5f winner Resonant (by
Forzando): dam second at 7f at 2 yrs in Ireland: poor form in claimer/seller. *T. D. Easterby*

LITTLE MISS TRICKY 4 br.f. Magic Ring (IRE) 115 – Mistook (USA) (Phone
Trick (USA)) [2003 –: p7g p8g p12g p10g Apr 1] seems of little account. *P. Mitchell*

LITTLE NOBBY 4 b.g. Makbul 104 – Simply Style (Bairn (USA) 126) [2003 49: f11s
Jan 1] angular, close-coupled gelding: maiden: well held only start in 2003. *R. Hollinshead*

LITTLE RICHARD (IRE) 4 b.g. Alhaarth (IRE) 126 – Intricacy 65 (Formidable **60 d**
(USA) 125) [2003 59: f16.2g f12g² f14.8g² f12g² f12g³ f12s f12s 16m f12g Nov 21]
small, workmanlike gelding: modest performer: left J. Tuck after fourth start: well below
form last 4 outings: effective at 1½m to 2m: acts on fibresand and good to firm going:
usually wears headgear. *M. Wellings*

LITTLE RIDGE (IRE) 2 b.g. (Mar 29) Charnwood Forest (IRE) 125 – Princess **84 p**
Natalie 78 (Rudimentary (USA) 118) [2003 6m³ 5m⁶ 6g 5m* 5.1d* Nov 6] 5,000Y: close-
coupled, quite attractive gelding: second foal: dam 5f winner (including at 2 yrs): fairly
useful performer: won nurseries at Musselburgh in October and Nottingham (made all to
beat Four Amigos comfortably by 2½ lengths) in November: will prove best at 5f/6f: acts
on good to firm and good to soft ground: progressive. *H. Morrison*

LITTLE ROBS' GIRL 4 ch.f. Cosmonaut – David James' Girl 65 (Faustus (USA) **30**
118) [2003 –: 10g 10.5m⁴ 12.3m 10.5m⁶ 12.3g Aug 29] sparely-made filly: poor maiden:
stays 10.5f: acts on good to firm going: tried in cheekpieces. *M. Mullineaux*

LITTLE SKY 6 gr.m. Terimon 124 – Brown Coast (Oats 126) [2003 14m² f12s p13g **53 ?**
f16.2g Nov 10] sixth foal: dam unraced: seemingly only form when second in maiden at
Lingfield on Flat debut. *D. Mullarkey*

LITTLESTAR (FR) 2 b.c. (Jan 24) Robellino (USA) 127 – Green Charter 77 (Green **57**
Desert (USA) 127) [2003 7m 7g 8m Sep 23] sturdy colt: second reported foal: half-
brother to 2001 2-y-o 7f winner Safe Trip (by Hector Protector): dam, 2-y-o 7f winner,
closely related to 4-y-o First Charter and half-sister to 3-y-o Private Charter: best effort in
maidens (modest form) when seventh of 9 at Folkestone second start: not knocked about
final one: likely to be suited by 1¼m/1½m. *J. L. Dunlop*

LITTLE TASK 5 b.g. Environment Friend 128 – Lucky Thing (Green Desert (USA) **–**
127) [2003 –: 14f⁵ Jun 16] smallish, close-coupled gelding: fair winner at 2 yrs: little Flat
form since: tried blinkered: successful over fences in June. *J. S. Wainwright*

LITTLE TIGER LIVI (IRE) 3 b.f. Namaqualand (USA) – Shahroza (USA) (Sheikh **–**
Albadou 128) [2003 p8g f11s⁵ Feb 20] IR 2,200F, IR 4,200Y: first foal: dam unraced:
well held in maiden (slowly away) and claimer (reared leaving stall/looked difficult ride).
Mrs P. N. Dutfield

LITTLE TOBIAS (IRE) 4 ch.g. Millkom 124 – Barbara Frietchie (IRE) (Try My **61 §**
Best (USA) 130) [2003 54d: 15g* 16d 15.8d* 16m Oct 28] smallish, good-topped gelding: modest handicapper: won at Ayr in July and Catterick in September: stays 15.8f: acts
on firm and good to soft going: ungenuine. *Andrew Turnell*

LITTLETON AMETHYST (IRE) 4 ch.f. Revoque (IRE) 122 – Sept Roses (USA) **?**
(Septieme Ciel (USA) 123) [2003 43: p12g⁴ f12s² f12g³ f16s² f16.2g 12.3m f12g f12g **a49**
f16.2g Aug 15] close-coupled, angular filly: poor maiden handicapper: left T. J. Naughton before penultimate start: barely stays 2m: acts on all-weather and good to firm
ground. *Mrs P. Ford*

LITTLETON ARWEN (USA) 3 b.f. Bahri (USA) 125 – Jathibiyah (USA) 89 (Nure- **93**
yev (USA) 131) [2003 94p: p7g 7m 6g⁵ 7g⁴ 7.1m² 7g Sep 11] rangy filly: has scope: fairly
useful performer: good efforts in listed races at Epsom and Warwick (short-headed by
Tora Bora) on fourth/fifth starts: off 2½ months, ran poorly final start, forcing strong pace
and carrying head high: stays 7f: acts on polytrack and good to firm going: tends to pull
hard/wander: retained 90,000 gns in December. *T. G. Mills*

LITTLETON LIBERTY 2 b.f. (Feb 11) Royal Applause 124 – Lammastide 93 (Mar- **–**
tinmas 128) [2003 5.3f⁴ 5d Apr 28] 8,500F, 17,000Y: sister to ungenuine 2001 2-y-o 6f
seller winner La Perla and half-sister to several winners, including fairly useful 7f winner
Amber Fort (by Indian Ridge): dam, 2-y-o 5f winner, half-sister to 6-y-o Cape Town: well
beaten in maidens: slowly away on debut. *T. J. Naughton*

LITTLETON VALAR (IRE) 3 ch.g. Definite Article 121 – Fresh Look (IRE) 64 **49 §**
(Alzao (USA) 117) [2003 p7g f8.5g⁴ 8m f7g 10g 10m² 13.8m f11s 10m⁶ f8g Dec 8]
9,000Y: third foal: half-brother to 4-y-o Tuscarora: dam 11.5f winner: poor maiden
handicapper: left T. J. Naughton after second start: stays easy 1¼m: tried in cheekpieces:
inconsistent. *J. R. Weymes*

LITTLETON ZEPHIR (USA) 4 b.f. Sandpit (BRZ) 129 – Miss Gorgeous (IRE) 76 **57**
(Damister (USA) 123) [2003 59: f9.4g⁵ f8g⁴ f8g* f9.4s² f8g³ p8g³ f8.5g 11.9m⁶ Jun 12]
sturdy filly: modest handicapper: won at Southwell in February: left T. J. Naughton after
seventh start: best at 1m/1¼m: acts on all-weather: tried in headgear. *Mrs P. Townsley*

LITTLETON ZEUS (IRE) 4 ch.g. Woodborough (USA) 112 – La Fandango (IRE) **–**
51 (Taufan (USA) 119) [2003 45: f7g 10m Jun 20] poor maiden: well held in 2003: tried
visored/in cheekpieces: has looked headstrong. *W. S. Cunningham*

LITTLE TUMBLER 8 b.m. Cyrano de Bergerac 120 – Glass Minnow (IRE) **46**
59 (Alzao (USA) 117) [2003 53: 10m 9f 9f 10f Jul 15] neat mare: poor handicapper:
probably best at 9f/1¼m: acts on firm ground, good to soft and polytrack: sometimes
slowly away. *S. Woodman*

LITTLE VENICE (IRE) 3 b.f. Fumo di Londra (IRE) 108 – Petrine (IRE) (Petorius **85**
117) [2003 71: 7.1m 6.1d³ 7m³ 7.1m* 7g³ 7m* 8m⁶ 7m³ 7f² 7f⁴ 7m Sep 20] fairly useful
performer: won maiden at Warwick in June and handicap at Newmarket (edged left) in
July: best around 7f: acts on firm and good to soft ground: usually races prominently:
consistent. *C. F. Wall*

LITZA 2 gr.f. (Mar 27) Paris House 123 – Strelitza (IRE) 53 (Taufan (USA) 119) [2003 **–**
7m f8s Sep 26] lengthy filly: first foal: dam, maiden who stayed 7f, became one to avoid:
slowly away and well held in seller at Thirsk and claimer at Southwell. *M. W. Easterby*

LITZINSKY 5 b.g. Muhtarram (USA) 125 – Boulevard Girl 80 (Nicholas Bill 125) **–**
[2003 76: 18g 16g⁵ 14.1g 16.1d May 22] rather leggy, lengthy gelding: fair handicapper
at 4 yrs, well held in 2003. *C. B. B. Booth*

LIVADIYA (IRE) 7 b.m. Shernazar 131 – Lilissa (IRE) (Doyoun 124) [2003 98: 8d* **111**
10g⁶ 8d³ 8d* 8d⁴ 8m⁴ 9g* 8f⁶ 8f⁵ 8f² 9.5m* 8m³ 10m* 7g³ Nov 8] first foal: closely related to fairly useful 1¼m winner Lishtar (by Mtoto) and half-sister to 2 winners, including
useful 1¼m/1½m winner Lidakiya (by Kahyasi): dam, French 9f and 10.5f winner, half-
sister to smart French filly up to 13.5f Linnga: smart performer: won handicaps at the
Curragh in March (Irish Lincolnshire, easily by 3½ lengths from Camargue) and May and
Leopardstown (best effort, beat Definate Spectacle a length) in July, and listed races at
Gowran and Leopardstown (by 6 lengths from Royal Devotion) in October: effective at
1m to 1¼m: acts on heavy and good to firm going: held up: tough and genuine. *H. Rogers,
Ireland*

LIVELY FELIX 6 b.g. Presidium 124 – Full of Life 85 (Wolverlife 115) [2003 –: **49 d**
f9.4g⁵ f8.5g² f8.5s³ f7g f11g⁶ f8.5g 6g 12m 10m 10m Sep 19] poor maiden: below form
after third outing, leaving D. Burchell after sixth: stays 8.5f: acts on fibresand and heavy
going: tried visored: usually races up with pace. *D. W. P. Arbuthnot*

LIVELY LADY 7 b.m. Beveled (USA) – In The Papers 87 (Aragon 118) [2003 67§, **54 §**
a–§: 6s 5g 5m 5g Aug 4] sturdy mare: poor mover: modest handicapper nowadays:
effective at 5f/6f: acts on good to firm and heavy going, probably on fibresand: usually
visored/blinkered: sometimes slowly away: usually held up: tends to wander: unreliable.
J. R. Jenkins

LIVING DAYLIGHTS (IRE) 4 b.f. Night Shift (USA) – Shesadelight 67 (Shirley **73**
Heights 130) [2003 56: 11.8g* 14.1g 11.8m* Jun 2] fair handicapper, lightly raced: won
at Leicester in March and June: should stay 1¾m: acts on good to firm ground: reportedly
in foal to Averti. *J. L. Dunlop*

LIVIUS (IRE)   9 b.g. Alzao (USA) 117 – Marie de Beaujeu (FR) 108 (Kenmare (FR)   **55 §**
125) [2003 78d: p10g Jan 8] big gelding: modest performer nowadays: stays 1½m: acts
on all-weather, probably on firm and soft ground: tried blinkered/visored/tongue tied:
usually held up: untrustworthy. *C. A. Dwyer*

LIVY (IRE)   3 ch.g. Titus Livius (FR) 115 – Shalerina (USA) (Shalford (IRE) 124§)   **–**
[2003 51, a77: f5s 5.1g 7g 5.7f p6g f7g f6g Nov 1] useful-looking gelding: fair on
all-weather, modest on turf in 2002: well held in 2003, leaving M. Salaman after
reappearance and I. Wood after fourth start: tried blinkered/tongue tied. *S. Kirk*

LIZHAR (IRE)   2 b.f. (Mar 4) Danetime (IRE) 121 – Amelesa (IRE) 65 (Perugino   **55**
(USA) 84) [2003 f5g³ 5m⁶ 6v 5m⁵ 5g² 6m f6f³ 5f⁵ 6.5d f5s² f6g² f6g³ f6s* 6d⁴ f6g³ f5g⁵   **a73**
Dec 22] IR 2,600F, €4,500Y: compact filly: first foal: dam, maiden (stayed 7f), out of
half-sister to smart miler Luzum: fair on all-weather, modest on turf: won maiden at
Southwell in October: stays 6f: acts on fibresand, good to firm and good to soft ground:
tried in cheekpieces: usually races prominently. *M. J. Polglase*

LLAN ELLI WELLIE   2 ch.g. (May 10) Binary Star (USA) – Runabay (Run The   **–**
Gantlet (USA)) [2003 5.1f⁵ 7.1m Sep 8] 800Y: half-brother to winner up to 9f in Italy by
Indian Ridge: dam French maiden: last in maidens at Bath and Warwick (wore cheek-
pieces). *B. J. Llewellyn*

LOADED GUN   3 ch.g. Highest Honor (FR) 124 – Woodwardia (USA) 93 (El Gran   **–**
Senor (USA) 136) [2003 8f p10g Nov 2] fifth foal: half-brother to 3 winners, including
useful 1¼m/1½m winner Edwardian (by Sanglamore): dam, 2-y-o 1m winner who stayed
11.4f, sister to smart US Grade 1 1¼m winner Spanish Fern: fair maiden who placed in
France at 2 yrs for Mme C. Head-Maarek: in rear in handicaps at Goodwood and
Lingfield (slowly away) in 2003: bred to stay 1¼m. *Miss J. Feilden*

LOBOS (SWI)   4 ch.g. Rainbow Quest (USA) 134 – Lady of Silver (IRE) (Caerleon   **74**
(USA) 132) [2003 74: p7g⁴ p10g³ p7g⁴ p8g p7g⁴ 8.3d 7m 8g 7m 7m 6m 8f* 8.2d p8g*
Dec 2] sparely-made gelding: fair performer: left S. Dow after eleventh start then won
handicaps at Bath (maiden) in September and Lingfield in December: stayed 1m: acted
on polytrack and firm going: dead. *G. L. Moore*

LOCAL POET   2 b.c. (Feb 12) Robellino (USA) 127 – Laugharne (Known Fact   **92 +**
(USA) 135) [2003 6m⁶ 5m² 6m² 6m⁴ Oct 25] 27,000Y: sturdy colt: half-brother to several
winners, including useful sprinter Power Lake (by Formidable) and 7f winner Arctic
Flight (by Polar Falcon): dam ran once: fairly useful maiden: second at Pontefract and
Redcar (beaten head by Peak To Creek in Two-Year-Old Trophy, one of only 2 to race
against far rail): creditable 4½ lengths fourth to Nero's Return in listed race at Doncaster,
bit short of room: not sure to stay much beyond 6f: sure to win a race. *B. A. McMahon*

LOCATOR (IRE)   2 b.c. (Mar 17) Mujadil (USA) 119 – Lifeboat (IRE) (Petorius 117)   **60 p**
[2003 p6g⁵ Nov 18] IR 7,000Y: half-brother to 2 winners in France, including 9.5f winner
Mystara (by Desert Style): dam unraced half-sister to Irish 1000 Guineas winner Miralla:
12/1, 3¼ lengths fifth of 11 to Kabreet in maiden at Lingfield, taking time to settle and
not knocked about: should improve. *J. M. P. Eustace*

LOCHBUIE (IRE)   2 b.c. (May 7) Definite Article 121 – Uncertain Affair (IRE) 79   **73 p**
(Darshaan 133) [2003 6m⁶ 7m⁴ 7m Oct 24] IR 35,000F, €130,000Y: good-bodied colt:
half-brother to several winners in Ireland, including useful 7f (at 2 yrs) and 9f winner
Prize Time (by College Chapel) and 6-y-o Direct Bearing: dam, Irish 1¾m winner, out of
half-sister to dam of Slip Anchor: best effort in maidens (fair form) when staying-on
fourth at Salisbury: mulish at start and never a threat final start: likely to do better in
handicaps at 3 yrs at 1¼m+. *G. Wragg*

LOCH INCH   6 ch.g. Inchinor 119 – Carrie Kool 69 (Prince Sabo 123) [2003 –: 5.7f   **62**
5m 5.7f 5m⁴ 5g 5.7f* 5.2m* 5f 5m* 5f 5.7f 5m Sep 22] smallish gelding: modest handicapper: won at Bath/Yarmouth in August and Leicester in September: best at 5f/6f: acts
on firm going, good to soft and fibresand: usually wears headgear. *J. M. Bradley*

LOCH LAIRD   8 b.g. Beveled (USA) – Daisy Loch (Lochnager 132) [2003 62: p6g 6m²   **62**
7m 7.1g* 8.3m 8m 6m Jul 12] lengthy gelding: modest handicapper: won at Chepstow in
June: best at 6f/7f: acts on firm and soft ground, probably on polytrack: tried visored/
blinkered: has carried head awkwardly/looked difficult ride. *M. Madgwick*

LOCH MAREE   4 b.f. Primo Dominie 121 – Aurora Bay (IRE) (Night Shift (USA))   **–**
[2003 53: f6g Jan 27] angular, quite good-topped filly: modest maiden: barely stays 6f:
best efforts on good ground: usually blinkered. *M. W. Easterby*

Slatch Farm Stud Flying Fillies' Stakes, Pontefract—Lochridge takes the step back up to listed company in her stride; Lady Lindsay and Vita Spericolata (rail) are her nearest pursuers

LOCHRIDGE   4 ch.f. Indian Ridge 123 – Lochsong 129 (Song 132) [2003 96p: 6m⁴ **110** 6g 6f 6m* 7g⁶ 6m* 6m* 6f³ 5s Oct 5] workmanlike, rather unfurnished filly: smart performer: better than ever in 2003, winning handicaps at Newbury and Ascot and listed event at Pontefract (beat Lady Lindsay 1¾ lengths) in July/August: very good length third to Acclamation in Diadem Stakes at Ascot penultimate start: met trouble in Prix de l'Abbaye at Longchamp final outing: better at 6f than 7f: acts on firm going: often makes running. *A. M. Balding*

LOCK INN   4 b.g. Dolphin Street (FR) 125 – Highest Bid (FR) (Highest Honor (FR) **45 d** 124) [2003 56: f12g f14g⁵ f14s f16.2g⁶ p13g f14g f14.8g May 23] poor maiden handicapper: stays 1¾m: acts on all-weather: has worn cheekpieces. *Miss Z. C. Davison*

LOCKSTOCK (IRE)   5 b.g. Inchinor 119 – Risalah (Marju (IRE) 127) [2003 81, **74** a72: 8g 8.1m f7s p7g f7g⁴ f8g* f8g⁴ Dec 12] quite good-topped gelding: fair handicapper: won at Southwell in November: effective at 7f to 9.4f: acts on heavy ground, good to firm and fibresand: sometimes slowly away. *M. S. Saunders*

LOCOMBE HILL (IRE)   7 b.g. Barathea (IRE) 127 – Roberts Pride 62 (Roberto **74** (USA) 131) [2003 83: 7f⁶ 8m 7m 8g⁶ 8m 8.5m 7.5d 8d* f8g f6g Nov 25] very big, rather dipped-backed gelding: fair performer: won ladies handicap at Doncaster in November: best at 7f/1m: acts on good to firm and heavy going, well below form both starts on fibresand: takes good hold: usually races up with pace. *D. Nicholls*

LODGER (FR)   3 ch.c. Grand Lodge (USA) 125 – Light River (USA) (Irish River (FR) **101** 131) [2003 68p: 10g³ 10m² 12m³ 12f² 12.4g* 13.9m⁴ Aug 21] big, good-topped colt: useful performer, lightly raced: landed odds in maiden at Newcastle in July: best efforts when in frame in handicaps, third to Fantastic Love in King George V Stakes at Royal Ascot and fourth to Jagger in Melrose Stakes at York (found little) third/final outings: stays 1¾m: raced only on good ground or firmer: usually held up. *J. Noseda*

LOGIQUE (IRE)   4 b.g. Revoque (IRE) 122 – Logstown (IRE) 98 (Keen 116) [2003 **59** 61: f12g⁵ p12g Feb 25] tall gelding: modest maiden: stays 1½m: acts on good to firm going and fibresand. *C. F. Wall*

LOGISTICAL   3 b.c. Grand Lodge (USA) 125 – Magic Milly 60 (Simply Great (FR) **81** 122) [2003 73: 6g⁵ 7m⁶ 7g* 7m 8m 7m⁵ 7m⁴ 7m⁵ 7m⁶ 7g Nov 1] close-coupled colt: fairly useful performer: won minor event at Leicester (hung left) in July: stays 7f: acts on good to firm ground, probably on soft: sometimes slowly away. *A. D. W. Pinder*

LOGSDAIL   3 b.g. Polish Precedent (USA) 131 – Logic 94 (Slip Anchor 136) [2003 **88** 88: 7g 7g 7.9m⁵ 10.1m 7.1g 8m Jul 8] good-topped gelding: fairly useful handicapper: stays 1m: acts on good to firm and good to soft going: wore cheekpieces last 2 starts: hung left third outing: sold 31,000 gns in July, modest form in juvenile hurdles for P. Hobbs: re-sold 16,000 gns in October, joined G. L. Moore. *Mrs J. R. Ramsden*

LOHENGRIN (JPN)   4 ch.c. Singspiel (IRE) 133 – Carling (FR) 119 (Garde   **125**
Royale 120) [2003 116: 8f² 9d* 8f* 8f³ 8d 8g² 10f 8m³ Dec 14]
Japanese challenges for top races in Europe have become an almost annual
occurrence since the ground-breaking wins of Seeking The Pearl in the Prix
Maurice de Gheest and Taiki Shuttle in the Prix Jacques le Marois at Deauville in
1998. The latest challenge from Japan was a two-pronged raid by the four-year-old
colts Lohengrin and Telegnosis. Their French campaign took in both the Prix
Jacques le Marois and the Prix du Moulin, and while they were not successful, both
went back to Japan with reputations enhanced and place money from two of the
best-contested mile races run in Europe all year. Although the pair were with different stables, both carried the colours of a syndicate operated by Teruya Yoshida's
Shadai Farm which bred both colts.
On their form in Japan, Lohengrin seemingly had the edge over Telegnosis.
Lohengrin had won the Group 2 Nakayama Kinen in March over nine furlongs,
with Telegnosis only eighth, and the pair had finished third and seventh respectively in Japan's top mile race in the first half of the year, the Group 1 Yasuda Kinen
at Tokyo in June. Lohengrin was favourite for the Yasuda Kinen, in which he was
beaten around a length in a race won by the former Hong Kong Cup winner Agnes
Digital. Lohengrin had won another Group 2 event at Hanshin in April on his
previous outing. Telegnosis was a Group 1 winner at three, but his best effort of the
current campaign had come when winning the Group 2 Keio Hai Spring Cup at
Tokyo in May over seven furlongs. In short, both colts were among the leading
milers in Japan, but neither could boast the sort of record which Taiki Shuttle had
brought to Deauville five years earlier. Taiki Shuttle had won nine of his ten races
up until then, including both the Keio Hai Spring Cup and the Yasuda Kinen.
There were contrasting fortunes for the Japanese pair in the two French
races they contested. The well-run Jacques le Marois played to the strengths of the
patiently-ridden Telegnosis, while the more tactical Prix du Moulin favoured the
front-running Lohengrin. The presence of two pacemakers in the Deauville race
meant that Lohengrin was unable to lead, and he ended up paying the price for
chasing Godolphin's pacemaker Blatant. As Lohengrin weakened quickly from the
front rank over a furlong out, the lesser-fancied Telegnosis came through to share
the lead briefly before keeping on stoutly to go down by a short neck and a length
to Six Perfections and Domedriver. Lohengrin ended up beating only the two
pacemakers in the twelve-runner field. Three weeks later the Deauville form was
turned upside down at Longchamp. This time Lohengrin found himself in a race
where none of the others wanted to lead, so that even drawn fourteen of fourteen on
the wide outside, his rider soon had him across to the rail and dictating the pace.
Quickening in the straight, Lohengrin briefly looked like repelling the challenge of
Nebraska Tornado (sixth at Deauville), but was unable to hold her off inside the
final furlong, going down by half a length. Meanwhile, Telegnosis never got into
the argument, finishing last but one. On the evidence of their best efforts in
France—Lohengrin at Longchamp and Telegnosis at Deauville—both colts appear
to be high-class milers, though the pick of their form is a fair bit better than their
earlier efforts in Japan and a good deal better than they achieved back home in
the autumn. Lohengrin finished only thirteenth of eighteen to the top Japanese colt
Symboli Kris S in the ten-furlong Tenno Sho (Autumn) at Tokyo, while Telegnosis
was only fourteenth of eighteen in the Mile Championship at Kyoto. Neither
repeated their best French form when they met again in the Hong Kong Mile,
though Lohengrin again fared the better. Starting at odds on, having been very well
backed on course, Lohengrin was carried wide on the home turn when beaten a
length into third behind the locally-trained pair Lucky Owners and Bowman's
Crossing; Telegnosis was a never-nearer seventh.
Telegnosis and Lohengrin might have been bred in Japan, but there are
familiar names to European readers in the pedigrees of both. Telegnosis is by the
1988 Arc winner Tony Bin, while Lohengrin is by Singspiel, who needs no introduction in Britain and advertised himself to breeders in the Far East when including
the Japan Cup in his haul of top international prizes. Lohengrin's dam Carling will
have been most familiar to French racegoers, as she was one of the leading French
fillies of 1995, when her wins included the Prix de Diane and Prix Vermeille. After
the latter race, she was bought for a reported 5,500,000 francs (around £700,000)

by Teruya Yoshida, and whilst she made little show in either the Arc (finishing ninth and not eighth as was stated in her essay that year) or the Japan Cup that autumn, she fared better for her new owner the following year when successful in the Prix Gontaut-Biron at Deauville. Although beaten a nose in the Poule d'Essai des Pouliches, a mile was on the short side for Carling, but she did contest both the Jacques le Marois and the Moulin during her career. Like her son, she fared much better at Longchamp than Deauville, finishing a good fifth to Ashkalani in the Moulin as a four-year-old, after reportedly sustaining a back injury when last in the Jacques le Marois the previous season. Carling's story was very much a 'rags to riches' one. Her sire Garde Royale has made his name principally as a sire of jumpers, while her dam Corraleja was a near-cripple who didn't make her debut until the age of five, after which she never raced again. Lohengrin is Carling's second foal after a Rainbow Quest colt named Derby County who has so far failed to win in Japan. Carling's sister Garling was also represented in French pattern races in the latest season by her useful daughter Garlinote, who finished fifth in the Poule d'Essai des Pouliches.

Lohengrin (JPN) (ch.c. 1999)	Singspiel (IRE) (b 1992)	In The Wings (b 1986)	Sadler's Wells
			High Hawk
		Glorious Song (b 1976)	Halo
			Ballade
	Carling (FR) (b 1992)	Garde Royale (br 1980)	Mill Reef
			Royal Way
		Corraleja (b 1982)	Carvin
			Darling Dale

Given that both his sire and dam won in top company at a mile and a half, Lohengrin might have been expected to be suited by distances in excess of a mile, though, from what was seen of him in France, his rather free-going style of running provides a good explanation for why he hasn't. That said, Lohengrin did win at up to eleven furlongs among five wins as a three-year-old and finished third at that trip against older horses in that season's Group 1 Takarazuka Kinen. The fifteen furlongs of the Japanese St Leger proved too far for him though, and he finished tailed off in that. Lohengrin has won on dirt and on good to soft going, as well as on the firm ground which normally prevails in Japan. Further details on Telegnosis can be found under his own entry. *M. Ito, Japan*

L'OISEAU D'ARGENT (USA) 4 ch.g. Silver Hawk (USA) 123 – Isla Del Rey (USA) 103 (Nureyev (USA) 131) [2003 107: 7m⁴ 6m³ Aug 2] big, strong, lengthy gelding: useful performer: ran respectably both outings in 2003, 3½ lengths third to dead-heaters Acclamation and Chookie Heiton in minor event at Doncaster: free-going sort, effective at 6f to 1m: raced only on good to firm/firm going: gave trouble at start on reappearance: sent to USA. *Sir Michael Stoute* **102**

LOLA LOLA (IRE) 2 b.f. (Feb 3) Piccolo 121 – French Gift 99 (Cadeaux Genereux 131) [2003 5f 6g 6.1d Nov 6] lengthy filly: fifth foal: half-sister to 3 winners, including 6-y-o Whistler and 5-y-o Pulse: dam, 2-y-o 6f winner, out of high-class sprinter Soba: well left in maidens. *J. L. Dunlop* **–**

LOLANITA 5 b.m. Anita's Prince 126 – Jimlil 99 (Nicholas Bill 125) [2003 42: f8.5g² f9.4s f7g Jun 19] poor maiden: stays 8.5f: raced only on fibresand. *B. Palling* **48**

LOLA'S DESTINY 2 b.f. (Feb 9) Mark of Esteem (IRE) 137 – Kristiana (Kris 135) [2003 6g 7m 7m Aug 6] 11,000F: quite good-topped filly: third foal: half-sister to useful sprinter Rozel: poor form in maidens: should stay 1m. *A. M. Balding* **43**

LOLITA'S GOLD (USA) 4 b.f. Royal Academy (USA) 130 – Shamisen 86 (Diesis 133) [2003 66: p10g p10g 7f⁶ 9f Aug 9] 32,000Y: fourth foal: half-sister to several winners, including 3-y-o Membership: dam, 2-y-o 7f winner, half-sister to smart miler Enharmonic: fair maiden for J. Oxx in Ireland at 3 yrs: little form in 2003, leaving J. Noseda after second outing: stays 1¼m: acts on soft and good to firm going, probably on polytrack: blinkered/visored nowadays. *R. B. Martin, Canada* **–**

LOMAPAMAR 2 b.f. (Apr 1) Nashwan (USA) 135 – Morina (USA) (Lyphard (USA) 132) [2003 7f 8.3m³ 8g Oct 25] leggy filly: sixth foal: half-sister to 3 winners, including very smart 6f (at 2 yrs) to 1½m winner Mons and smart 1¼m winner Inforapenny (both by Deploy): dam, French 11f winner, out of US Grade 1 2-y-o 8.5f winner Arewehaving- **76**

funyet: best effort in maidens (fair form) when staying-on third at Windsor: will be suited by 1¼m+. *Mrs A. J. Perrett*

LOMMEL (UAE) 2 b.c. (Mar 8) Lomitas 129 – Idrica 88 (Rainbow Quest (USA) 134) [2003 6m* p7g⁵ Aug 28] second foal: dam, 1m and 1½m winner, half-sister to smart performer up to 1½m Iscan: fairly useful form when winning minor event at Yarmouth in June by length from Romancero: forced strong pace when only fifth in similar event at Lingfield: bred to be suited by 1¼m/1½m. *D. R. Loder* **84**

LONDOLOZI LAD (IRE) 4 b.g. Ali-Royal (IRE) 127 – Ashdown (Pharly (FR) 130) [2003 40, a49: f8s 8f Jun 26] small gelding: poor handicapper: well held both starts in 2003: tried blinkered. *P. C. Haslam* **–**

LONDON BY NIGHT (USA) 3 br.g. Mt Livermore (USA) – Sheena's Gold (USA) (Fast Gold (USA)) [2003 –: f9.4g⁶ p8g 8m May 27] good-topped gelding: poor maiden, lightly raced. *T. G. Mills* **–**

LONDONER (USA) 5 ch.g. Sky Classic (CAN) – Love And Affection (USA) (Exclusive Era (USA)) [2003 101: 7d 8m 8g 8g 8m 8.5m 8.3g 8.5g 10m 12m p10g⁶ Dec 10] tall gelding: useful at 4 yrs: seemingly fair at best in 2003: effective at 7f, barely at 1½m: yet to race on soft/heavy going, acts on any other turf and probably on polytrack: sometimes tongue tied: weak finisher. *S. Dow* **72 ?**

LONDON MIXTURE 3 b.g. Mind Games 121 – Surrealist (ITY) (Night Shift (USA)) [2003 –: 7f 7f Jul 16] close-coupled gelding: soundly beaten in maidens. *J. D. Bethell* **–**

LONDONNETDOTCOM (IRE) 3 ch.f. Night Shift (USA) – Hopeful Sign (Warning 136) [2003 101: 8g 9.9g⁵ 8.5m² 8f 8.1g³ 8d 7g⁴ 8f* 8.1d⁶ 7d 8f⁶ 8m⁶ 8m Oct 19] big, good-topped filly: useful performer: won listed event at Bath in August by 1½ lengths from Sheppard's Watch: creditable sixth of 10 to Echoes In Eternity in Sun Chariot Stakes at Newmarket penultimate start: stays 8.5f: acts on firm and good to soft going: has found little: usually makes running: tends to run the odd poor race. *M. R. Channon* **100**

LONE PINE 2 b.f. (Mar 17) Sesaro (USA) 81 – North Pine (Import 127) [2003 6d 5m 8.5m 6m Oct 20] 500Y: plain filly: half-sister to several winners, including fairly useful 5f winner (including at 2 yrs) Heaven-Liegh-Grey (by Grey Desire): dam poor half-sister to top-class sprinter Lochnager: seems of little account. *M. E. Sowersby* **–**

LONE PIPER 8 b.g. Warning 136 – Shamisen 86 (Diesis 133) [2003 60: 5m f5g 5m 5m 5.7f 5.7f 5.3f⁵ f5g⁶ Nov 28] small, close-coupled gelding: poor mover: poor handicapper nowadays: successful at 7f, raced mainly at 5f/6f nowadays: acts on fibresand, firm and soft going: tried visored/tongue tied earlier in career: has found little/carried head high: held up. *J. M. Bradley* **47**

LONER 5 b.g. Magic Ring (IRE) 115 – Jolis Absent 57 (Primo Dominie 121) [2003 58, a50: 8.2m⁴ 8.1m* 7g 7m⁴ 7m² 7.5m⁵ 8f 7m Sep 9] strong gelding: modest handicapper: won at Warwick (selling event) in July: effective at 7f/1m: acts on soft and good to firm going, probably on all-weather: blinkered (found little) once at 4 yrs, wore cheekpieces last 4 starts. *M. Wigham* **60 a–**

LONGMEADOWS BOY (IRE) 3 b.g. Victory Note (USA) 120 – Karoi (IRE) (Kafu 120) [2003 58: 7.1f⁴ 9m 8m 8m⁵ 9.3f⁵ 12m⁴ 11.9m³ 11g* 11.9m⁴ Aug 4] workmanlike gelding: modest performer: won maiden seller at Redcar in July: best at 1¼m/1½m: some promise on fibresand, acts on firm and good to soft going: tried in cheekpieces: gave trouble in stall last 2 outings. *A. Berry* **57**

LONG ROADS (IRE) 2 ch.c. (Apr 16) Fayruz 116 – Mystique Air (IRE) 66 (Mujadil (USA) 119) [2003 8.3m Sep 29] IR 7,000f, 26,000Y: second foal: dam 7f and 9f winner: 66/1, last of 12 in maiden at Windsor. *B. R. Millman* **–**

LONG TALL SALLY (IRE) 4 b.f. Danehill Dancer (IRE) 117 – Miss Galwegian (Sandford Lad 133) [2003 71: f6g⁶ p5g p6g p6g⁴ p6g³ p7g 6m* 6m 5m 6m 6m⁴ 6.1m 6m⁵ 6m⁴ 5.7f⁴ 5.7f Sep 15] lengthy, unfurnished filly: fair handicapper: won apprentice race at Goodwood in June: barely stays 7f: acts on polytrack, firm and good to soft ground: wore blinkers/hood last 2 starts: in foal to Bold Edge. *D. W. P. Arbuthnot* **69**

LONG WEEKEND (IRE) 5 b.h. Flying Spur (AUS) – Friday Night (USA) (Trempolino (USA) 135) [2003 52, a56: f8g f6g⁴ f8.5g f6s⁵ f6s 6d 6g 5m 6m 5g 6m* 6m⁴ 6d⁶ 6d Aug 1] sturdy, angular horse: modest handicapper: won apprentice event at Goodwood in June: best form at 6f: acts on all-weather and good to firm going: usually blinkered/visored. *D. Shaw* **54 a–**

589

LOOK EAST   4 b.g. Ezzoud (IRE) 126 – College Night (IRE) 54 (Night Shift (USA))   –
[2003 –: 8m 7g⁶ 8m 7f 7s f12g Nov 28] lengthy gelding: little form: tried visored and in
cheekpieces. *Mrs C. A. Dunnett*

LOOK FIRST (IRE)   5 b.g. Namaqualand (USA) – Be Prepared (IRE) (Be My Guest   87
(USA) 126) [2003 89: p16g* f16.2g⁴ p12g⁵ p16g p13g 16.2m⁴ 16m⁵ 16m⁶ 18g⁵ p16g Jul
16] leggy gelding: fairly useful handicapper: won at Lingfield in January: stayed 17f:
acted on all-weather, firm and soft going: tried visored: was held up: dead. *I. A. Wood*

LOOK HERE NOW   6 gr.g. Ardkinglass 114 – Where's Carol 67 (Anfield 117) [2003   76
79: f6g* 7m⁶ 7m f6g 7m 6.9m³ 7g² 6d⁵ 6m⁴ 7.9m⁴ 8m Sep 16] workmanlike gelding: fair   a79
performer: won claimer at Wolverhampton in March: effective at testing 6f to 1m: acts on
heavy ground, good to firm and fibresand: inconsistent. *B. A. McMahon*

LOOK HERE'S CAROL (IRE)   3 ch.f. Safawan 118 – Where's Carol 67 (Anfield   94
117) [2003 71: 6m² 6m³ 8g 6.1s² 7.1m⁶ 7.1g² 6m 7s* 6.1m 6m 7d 6m⁴ Oct 2] leggy filly:
fairly useful performer: odds on, won maiden (easily) at Thirsk in July: also ran well
when placed in listed races at Ripon and Nottingham (short-head second to Irresistible)
on second/fourth starts and when fourth on handicap debut at Newmarket final outing:
stays 7f: acts on soft and good to firm ground. *B. A. McMahon*

LOOK HONEY (IRE)   3 b.c. Sadler's Wells (USA) 132 – Middle Prospect (USA)   116
(Mr Prospector (USA)) [2003 9s* 10g⁶ 10d* 10g² 10g³ 10g* 12m⁵ 12g⁵ Oct 19] 400,000
francs Y: good-topped colt: brother to 4-y-o Global Challenge and half-brother to winners
in USA by Pleasant Tap and El Raggaas: dam unraced: smart performer: won newcomers
race at Maisons-Laffitte in March, minor event at Longchamp in May and Prix Eugene
Adam at Maisons-Laffitte (kept on gamely to beat Kalabar short neck) in July: best effort
when 2 lengths third to Vespone in Grand Prix de Paris at Longchamp: respectable fifth
to Vallee Enchantee in Prix du Conseil de Paris at Longchamp final start: stays 1½m: acts
on soft ground: has been bandaged in front. *C. Lerner, France*

LOOKING DOWN   3 ch.f. Compton Place 125 – High Stepping (IRE) (Taufan (USA)   87
119) [2003 85: 7.1m⁵ 7.1m⁴ 8m³ 7.1f⁴ 8g 7g 8.3d⁴ 7f p8g³ p7g Dec 17] lengthy filly:
fairly useful performer: stays 1m: acts on polytrack and firm going, probably on soft.
R. Hannon

LOOKING FOR LOVE (IRE)   5 b.m. Tagula (IRE) 116 – Mousseux (IRE) (Jareer   79
(USA) 115) [2003 78: 7m³ 7m⁴ 7g⁵ 7g 7g³ 7s² p7g Nov 18] leggy mare: fair handicapper:
has form at 1¼m, but races mainly around 7f: acts on any turf going, below form both
starts on all-weather: wore cheekpieces last 3 starts: often races prominently: reliable.
J. G. Portman

LOOK NO HANDS   2 ch.f. (Mar 23) Timeless Times (USA) 99 – Belltina 41 (Belfort   –
(FR) 89) [2003 5d Apr 28] 3,000Y: sixth foal: sister to fairly useful 5f (at 2 yrs) to 1m
winner Big Ben and 1995 2-y-o 6f seller winner Ticka Ticka Timing: dam maiden who
stayed 7f: 50/1, slowly away and always behind in Windsor maiden: sold £400 in December. *Mrs S. A. Liddiard*

LOOK NO MORE   2 ch.g. (Mar 31) First Trump 118 – Jadebelle 66 (Beldale Flutter   47
(USA) 130) [2003 5.1f f7s⁵ f8s⁵ 8m⁶ p8g f8.5s Dec 31] half-brother to 3 winning sprinters, including useful 1997 2-y-o 5f/6f winner Prince Foley (by Greensmith): dam 2-y-o
6f winner who stayed 1½m: poor maiden: stays 1m. *W. G. M. Turner*

LOOKS LIKE TROUBLE (IRE)   11 b.g. Zaffaran (USA) 117 – Lavengaddy (Bal-   –
gaddy) [2003 22.2f Jun 21] top-class chaser, winner of Cheltenham Gold Cup in 2000:
lightly raced afterwards (suffered tendon injury): well held in Queen Alexandra Stakes at
Royal Ascot on Flat debut. *Noel T. Chance*

LOOKS THE BUSINESS (IRE)   2 b.g. (Feb 19) Marju (IRE) 127 – Business Centre   67
(IRE) 58 (Digamist (USA) 110) [2003 p7g⁸ 8.1g⁴ 10.2f⁵ Sep 29] €20,000Y, 11,000 2-y-o:
fourth foal: half-brother to 5-y-o Alexander Star: dam, placed at 6.5f in Ireland, from
family of 2000 Guineas winner Doyoun: tongue tied, fair form in minor event/maidens:
gelded after: probably stays 1¼m. *W. G. M. Turner*

LOOP THE LOUP   7 b.g. Petit Loup (USA) 123 – Mithi Al Gamar (USA) 68   86
(Blushing Groom (FR) 131) [2003 87: 20m 14.6m² 16.5d Nov 8] smallish, workmanlike
gelding: fairly useful handicapper: easily best effort in 2003 when second at Doncaster
(won equivalent race in 2002): should stay at least 2m: acts on firm and soft going:
effective blinkered or not: ran in snatches once at 6 yrs: usually held up: useful hurdler.
Mrs M. Reveley

LORD ARTHUR 2 b.g. (May 18) Mind Games 121 – Flower O'Cannie (IRE) 87 –
(Mujadil (USA) 119) [2003 f6g 7d Nov 7] tall, leggy gelding: first foal: dam 6f (at 2 yrs)
to 1½m well held in maidens at Southwell and Doncaster. *M. W. Easterby*

LORD BASKERVILLE 2 b.c. (Mar 17) Wolfhound (USA) 126 – My Dear Watson 59
(Chilibang 120) [2003 6m⁴ 6d 6m³ 6g Jul 31] 8,400Y: leggy colt: fourth foal: dam, ran
twice, half-sister to smart sprinter Sizzling Melody: modest maiden: third at Epsom: will
probably stay 7f: acts on good to firm ground. *M. G. Quinlan*

LORD BREX (FR) 7 gr.g. Saint Estephe (FR) 123 – Light Moon (FR) (Mendez (FR) 54
128) [2003 p13g f16.2s 8.1m 16.2d³ Jul 25] one-time useful winner for F. Doumen in
France: only modest at best in 2003: stays 15f: acts on good to soft ground: usually wears
headgear. *J. G. M. O'Shea*

LORD CHAMBERLAIN 10 b.g. Be My Chief (USA) 122 – Metaphysique (FR) 65
(Law Society (USA) 130) [2003 51: 8.1d 8f⁴ 10f 8.1m³ 10f 7.1d³ 8.2g² 8.1g³ 8f² 8f 7m⁵
8f³ 7.1g⁵ 8m⁴ 8.3m⁵ 9m Oct 17] big gelding: fair handicapper: probably best at 7f/1m
nowadays: acts on any going: blinkered: sometimes slowly away: looks a hard ride
(usually soon off bridle). *J. M. Bradley*

LORD CRISPIN 3 ch.c. Kris 135 – Lamu Lady (IRE) 70 (Lomond (USA) 128) [2003 77
10d 10d⁴ 10.5v² 12m Jun 4] fifth foal: half-brother to 3 winners, including fairly useful
8.5f to 1¼m winner Thekryaati (by Indian Ridge): dam, 2-y-o 7f winner who stayed
1¼m, closely related to high-class miler The Noble Player: clearly best effort when
second in maiden at Haydock (edged right): pulled up subsequent start: carried head high
on debut: dead. *J. H. M. Gosden*

LORD EUROLINK (IRE) 9 b.g. Danehill (USA) 126 – Lady Eurolink 55 (Kala 83
Shikari 125) [2003 91: 10m 10m 9.9m⁶ 9.9d³ 10m⁶ 10m³ 10.4m² 10.9m* Sep 18] strong,
lengthy gelding: fairly useful handicapper: won amateur event at Ayr in September: effective at 1¼m/easy 1½m: acts on fibresand, firm and soft going: usually visored in 2000:
tried tongue tied: often held up. *M. H. Tompkins*

LORD GIZZMO 6 ch.g. Democratic (USA) 101 – Figrant (USA) (L'Emigrant (USA) 50
129) [2003 13.3m 12.6m* 12m³ 11.9f⁵ 13.1f⁵ Aug 22] modest handicapper: missed 2002:
won at Warwick in June: stays 1½m: acts on fibresand and firm ground: races prominently. *J. Cullinan*

LORD GREYSTOKE (IRE) 2 b.c. (Mar 5) Petardia 113 – Jungle Story (IRE) 74 62
(Alzao (USA) 117) [2003 6.1d 7m 7g⁵ 8m 7s⁴ f7g p7g Dec 10] 10,000 2-y-o: good-
bodied colt: first foal: dam, 2-y-o 7f winner, half-sister to 7f/1m performer Lady
Lindsay: modest maiden: well held in nurseries last 2 starts: stays 7f: acts on fibresand,
best turf effort on good going. *C. P. Morlock*

LORD INVINCIBLE 5 b.g. Dancing Spree (USA) – Lady Broker 54 (Petorius 117) –
[2003 –: f6g f12s f8g Mar 13] workmanlike gelding: no longer of any account. *M. Mullineaux*

LORD KINTYRE 8 b.g. Makbul 104 – Highland Rowena 59 (Royben 125) [2003 92
95: p5g⁶ 5m 5.1g³ 5.7f⁶ 5f* 5m 5.1f³ 5.2g Sep 16] good-topped gelding: fairly useful
performer: won handicap at Salisbury in June: raced only at 5f/6f: acts on any turf going
and polytrack: wore cheekpieces last 6 starts: sometimes slowly away. *B. R. Millman*

LORD LAHAR 4 b.g. Fraam 114 – Brigadiers Bird (IRE) (Mujadil (USA) 119) [2003 –
–: p10g p8g Jan 15] well held in 3 maidens. *M. R. Channon*

LORD LAMB 11 gr.g. Dunbeath (USA) 127 – Caroline Lamb 74 (Hotfoot 126) [2003 71
16m 14.1m* 14.4m⁴ Aug 25] tall, good-topped gelding: very lightly raced on Flat
nowadays: fair form in 2003, winning claimer at Redcar in August: stays 2m: acts on
heavy and good to firm going: carries head high and no easy ride. *Mrs M. Reveley*

LORD LINKS (IRE) 2 ch.g. (Feb 9) Daggers Drawn (USA) 114 – Lady From Lime- 84
rick (IRE) 61 (Rainbows For Life (CAN)) [2003 5g⁶ 6m³ 7m 7d⁴ 6d Sep 10] 38,000Y:
strong, workmanlike gelding: second foal: half-brother to fairly useful 2002 2-y-o 7f/1m
winner Pacific Paddy (by Tagula): dam sprint maiden: fairly useful performer: won
maiden at Newmarket in May: creditable efforts in minor events/sales race after: barely
stays 7f: acts on good to firm and good to soft going. *R. Hannon*

LORD MAYOR 2 b.c. (Apr 8) Machiavellian (USA) 123 – Misleading Lady (Warn- 92 p
ing 136) [2003 7m⁶ 7m³ p7g* Oct 8] quite good-topped colt: second foal: dam twice-
raced sister to smart 1½m performer Little Rock and half-sister to smart middle-distance
stayer Whitewater Affair (by Machiavellian): third in maiden at Leicester (tended to
hang) before winning similar event at Lingfield by 1½ lengths from Rydal, racing freely

up with pace: should be suited by 1¼m/1½m: likely to make a useful 3-y-o. *Sir Michael Stoute*

LORD MELBOURNE (IRE)   4 b.g. Lycius (USA) 124 – Adana (IRE) (Classic   **50 §**
Music (USA)) [2003 73: p7g f7g f8.5g⁶ f7g 7f³ 7f⁵ Sep 2] sturdy gelding: modest
performer nowadays: stays 7.6f: acts on firm ground and all-weather: tried blinkered/
in cheekpieces: sometimes takes good hold: tends to carry head high/flick tail: none too
genuine. *J. A. Osborne*

LORD MERLIN (IRE)   4 b.g. Turtle Island (IRE) 123 – My-O-My (IRE) 105   **–**
(Waajib 121) [2003 –: f6g f6g Dec 9] strong gelding: useful at 2 yrs: below form since,
and soundly beaten on all-weather in 2003. *D. Nicholls*

LORDOFENCHANTMENT (IRE)   6 ch.g. Soviet Lad (USA) – Sauvignon (IRE)   **53 §**
63 (Alzao (USA) 117) [2003 61§: 8.5f 7m 7m⁶ 7.2g⁴ 7.5m 7.5d Jul 4] strong gelding:
modest performer: stays 7.5f: acts on heavy and good to firm going: sometimes visored
earlier in career: tongue tied of late: sometimes races freely: untrustworthy. *N. Tinkler*

LORD OF METHLEY   4 gr.g. Zilzal (USA) 137 – Paradise Waters 73 (Celestial   **57**
Storm (USA) 132) [2003 66: f12g⁶ 10m* 8g⁵ 10s⁵ 9.9d 7.5m⁵ 10.1d 8.5m 8d* 8.3m³ 8m⁴
9.9d 10.4f 9m³ f8g⁶ Nov 19] leggy, good-topped gelding: modest performer: won seller
at Ripon in April and selling handicap at Thirsk (flashed tail) in August: effective at 1m/
1¼m: acts on soft and good to firm going, probably on fibresand: sometimes wears headgear. *R. M. Whitaker*

LORD OF THE EAST   4 b.g. Emarati (USA) 74 – Fairy Free (Rousillon (USA) 133)   **73**
[2003 78: p6g p6g 6m 5.7g 5.3m⁴ 6m⁵ 5g 5.3m 5m 7m* 7.1m 6m* 7g 5m 5m⁵ 7m 7m²   **a–**
Oct 25] lengthy gelding: fair performer: won claimers in July (claimed from P. Howling
£8,000) and August (claimed from K. Cunningham-Brown £10,000), both at Epsom (all
4 wins on course): probably needs further than 5f, and stays 7f: acts on firm and soft
ground: tried tongue tied/blinkered (raced too freely)/in cheekpieces (missed break):
hung and flashed tail final outing: usually races prominently. *D. Nicholls*

LORD OF THE SEA (IRE)   2 b.c. (Mar 10) Perugino (USA) 84 – Sea Mistress   **73**
(Habitat 134) [2003 6m 6d⁶ p7g⁵ p7g⁵ Dec 10] 4,000Y: tall, leggy, useful-looking colt:
closely related to 1m seller winner Roi de La Mer (by Fairy King), later successful in
Italy, and half-brother to several winners, notably smart Irish 6f to 1m winner Nautical
Pet (by Petorius): dam unraced: fair maiden: left R. F. Johnson Houghton after third start:
best effort in nursery at Lingfield final one, soon poorly positioned: will probably stay
1m: acts on polytrack. *Jamie Poulton*

LORD PROTECTOR (IRE)   5 b.g. Nicolotte 118 – Scared (Royal Academy (USA)   **105 ?**
130) [2003 103, a93: a8g* 8g a7g² a8g* a12g a8g* 8d⁴ Jul 26] lengthy gelding: useful
performer: won minor events at Mijas in February, Dos Hermanas in May and Mijas
again in June: respectable seventh of 24 to Aldora in handicap at Doncaster second start:
seemed to run well when 1½ lengths fourth to My Risk in listed race at Vichy final start:
effective at 7f/1m: acts on fibresand/sand, soft and good to firm ground: has carried head
awkwardly. *E. J. Creighton, Spain*

LORD TEMUCHIN (IRE)   3 ch.g. Desert Prince (IRE) 130 – Lady Nash 50 (Nash-   **73**
wan (USA) 135) [2003 f8s⁵ p10g² p10g⁶ 7m⁴ 10f⁴ 12m² 10.9d⁴ 11.9m Oct 23] fourth
foal: half-brother to winner in Australia by Marju: dam, headstrong maiden, may have
proved best up to 1m: fair maiden: ran badly last 2 starts: stays 1½m: acts on polytrack
and firm ground: sometimes slowly away: sold 14,500 gns. *M. J. Wallace*

LORD WISHINGWELL (IRE)   2 b.g. (Apr 29) Lake Coniston (IRE) 131 – Spirito   **–**
Libro (USA) 89 (Lear Fan (USA) 130) [2003 6m 6g 7g Nov 1] smallish, workmanlike
gelding: third foal: dam, 5f (at 2 yrs) to 1¼m winner, half-sister to smart Irish 6f winner
Conormara: soundly beaten in maidens at Newmarket (2) and Newbury. *J. S. Wainwright*

LORETO ROSE   4 b.f. Lahib (USA) 129 – Pinkie Rose (FR) (Kenmare (FR) 125)   **76**
[2003 71: p7g⁴ p10g³ p8g⁵ Apr 9] fair maiden: swished tail and found little final start:
stays 1¼m: acts on polytrack (inadequate trip only run on turf). *G. A. Butler*

LORIEN HILL (IRE)   2 b.f. (Mar 12) Danehill (USA) 126 – Lothlorien (USA) 80   **69**
(Woodman (USA) 126) [2003 6m 7d³ p7g⁴ Oct 8] €60,000Y: strong filly: fourth foal:
half-sister to Irish 1½m to 2m winner Miss Devious (by Dr Devious): dam, 1m winner
who stayed 1½m, sister to smart 1¼m/1½m winner Monsajem out of close relative to
Sadler's Wells: fair form in maidens: third at Chester: will stay at least 1m: acts on
polytrack and good to soft ground. *B. W. Hills*

LOST SPIRIT   7 b.g. Strolling Along (USA) – Shoag (USA) (Affirmed (USA)) [2003   **54**
62, a49: p12g⁶ 12g² 12m 12g 11.8g 13m p12g 12.1d 12m⁴ 12m* 12.1m⁴ 12.1g² 12d⁵ 12m   **a36**

Oct 18] strong gelding: modest handicapper on turf, poor on all-weather: won amateur event at Catterick in August: stays 13f: acts on soft going, good to firm and all-weather: tried blinkered: free-going front runner: sometimes drops out tamely: usually claimer ridden. *P. W. Hiatt*

LOTS OF LOVE (USA) 5 b.g. Woodman (USA) 126 – Accountable Lady (USA) **– §** (The Minstrel (CAN) 135) [2003 93, a89: a7.5f⁵ a9f 7g 7.6m 8.3d 7.2g 8.3g Jun 11] lengthy gelding: unimpressive mover: fairly useful handicapper at 4 yrs: well held in UAE during winter, and on return to Britain: blinkered/visored: tends to carry head awkwardly: usually takes a while to warm to task: sold 10,000 gns. *M. Johnston*

LOTTO 2 b.f. (May 9) Nicolotte 118 – Hope Chest 70 (Kris 135) [2003 5.3f³ 6g 6f* **65** 5.7f³ 7m 5.3m* 6m a7g² Nov 16] 3,500Y: rather leggy, workmanlike filly: third foal: half-sister to 4-y-o Liberty Royal: dam, lightly-raced maiden (would have proved best up to 1½m): fair performer: won maiden in July and seller in October, both at Brighton: sold from P. Makin 7,000 gns before final start: stays 7f: acts on firm going and sand: free-going sort. *R. Jurado, Spain*

LOTUS EATER 4 gr.f. Linamix (FR) 127 – La Adrada (Arazi (USA) 135) [2003 –: **–** 12.3m Apr 2] leggy, quite good-topped filly: well beaten in 4 starts: has looked none too keen. *S. C. Williams*

LOUGH BOW (IRE) 5 b.g. Nicolotte 118 – Gale Force Seven (Strong Gale 116) **49** [2003 58: 11.8g 12.1d⁵ f12s Oct 21] quite good-topped gelding: modest handicapper in 2002, poor form in 2003: stays 1½m: acts on soft and good to firm going: visored/blinkered nowadays. *M. W. Easterby*

LOUGHLORIEN (IRE) 4 b.g. Lake Coniston (IRE) 131 – Fey Lady (IRE) (Fairy **66** King (USA)) [2003 70: 5m 5m 6m 5g f6g 6f⁴ 5m* 5m 5g 5m 5m⁴ 5.9d⁵ 5m 6m 5m 6g⁶ Oct 14] close-coupled, good-topped gelding: fair handicapper: won at Beverley in June: effective at 5f/6f: acts on any going: often wears headgear (all wins without): has been slowly away/hung. *K. A. Ryan*

LOUISIADE (IRE) 2 b.g. (Apr 12) Tagula (IRE) 116 – Titchwell Lass 57 (Lead On **74** Time (USA) 123) [2003 5s⁶ 5m* 5m² 6f 5g 6f 6g Oct 28] €13,000Y, 36,000 2-y-o: strong, lengthy gelding: fourth foal: half-brother to 2 winners, including 5-y-o Denise Best: dam 1¼m winner: fair performer: won maiden at Haydock in June: creditable efforts in nurseries on third/sixth starts: stays 6f: acts on firm ground. *T. D. Easterby*

LOUIS NAPOLEON 3 b.c. Indian Ridge 123 – Napoleon's Sister (IRE) 101 (Alzao **80** (USA) 117) [2003 84p: 8.1m 9g 10.1s 12d Nov 8] attractive colt: fairly useful performer, lightly raced: left G. Butler/off 5 months, soundly beaten last 2 starts: should stay at least 1¼m: acts on soft going, probably on good to firm. *Mrs A. J. Perrett*

LOUIS PRIMA 2 gr.c. (Mar 9) Paris House 123 – Chanson d'Amour (IRE) (High **–** Estate 127) [2003 6g⁶ 6m 5f 5f 5g 6g Oct 13] smallish colt: first foal: dam of little account: well beaten in maidens/nurseries: tried in headgear. *Miss L. A. Perratt*

LOU'S WISH 6 b.g. Thatching 131 – Shamaka 53 (Kris 135) [2003 –: 11.1d⁶ May 16] **–** of little account nowadays. *R. E. Barr*

LOVE AFFAIRS (GER) 9 b.g. Konigsstuhl (GER) – Lilac Dance (Fabulous Dancer **–** (USA) 124) [2003 f8.5g Jan 20] German-trained gelding: winner of 12 races, including handicap/claimer at Dortmund and claimer at Compiegne early in 2002: well held in claimer at Wolverhampton only outing in 2003: effective at 7f to 9f: acts on sand and soft ground. *H. W. Hiller, Germany*

LOVE CONNECTION (IRE) 3 b.g. Entrepreneur 123 – Soha (USA) 58 (Dancing **66** Brave (USA) 140) [2003 10g 12d 10g⁴ 10m⁵ 16m⁴ 16m Oct 15] IR 16,000Y: sixth foal: half-brother to 3 winners, notably smart 1m/9f winner Gold Academy (by Royal Academy): dam, second at 1½m, out of Oaks d'Italia winner Paris Royal: fair maiden: left M. Johnston 6,000 gns after debut: stays 2m: acts on good to firm ground: blinkered (well beaten) final start. *S. J. Mahon, Ireland*

LOVED UP 3 b.f. Bin Ajwaad (IRE) 119 – To Love With Love 73 (Cadeaux Genereux **56** 131) [2003 f6g f6g⁵ Jul 11] second foal: dam, 5.3f winner, ran only at 2 yrs: better effort (modest form) when fifth in maiden at Wolverhampton, slowly away. *W. Jarvis*

LOVE EXCELLING (FR) 4 b.f. Polish Precedent (USA) 131 – La Sky (IRE) 107 **–** (Law Society (USA) 130) [2003 10d May 28] angular, deep-girthed filly: sixth foal: half-sister to several winners, notably 1¼m and 1½m (Oaks) winner Love Divine (by Diesis): dam, 1¼m winner (probably stayed 1¾m), closely related to Champion Stakes winner Legal Case: reportedly had pelvis problem in 2002: tailed off in maiden at Ripon (reportedly finished distressed) on only outing. *H. R. A. Cecil*

LOVE GAMES   2 b.f. (Apr 17) Mind Games 121 – Gymcrak Lovebird 84 (Taufan (USA) 119) [2003 6m 7m 7.5d Jul 5] neat filly: half-sister to 2 winning sprinters, including Dominelle (by Domynsky): dam 5f (at 2 yrs) to 1¼m winner: no form in sellers: blinkered final start. *T. D. Easterby*   –

LOVE IN SEATTLE (IRE)   3 b.c. Seattle Slew (USA) – Tamise (USA) 113 (Time For A Change (USA)) [2003 10.3g⁴ 10m² 12g² Apr 15] $70,000Y: big, rangy colt: first foal: dam French 1m to 10.5f (Prix de Flore) winner: favourite, promising efforts in maidens at Doncaster and Leicester (second to Mutajjeb, making running and edging left) first 2 starts: disappointing final start (3 ran): should stay 1½m. *M. Johnston*   **84**

LOVE IN THE MIST   4 gr.f. Pursuit of Love 124 – Misty Goddess (IRE) 63 (Godswalk (USA) 130) [2003 57: f9.4g⁴ Jan 17] modest performer at 3 yrs: off 11 months prior to poor form only start in 2003: stays 1¼m: acts on good to soft going and all-weather: looked less than keen final 3-y-o start. *N. P. Littmoden*   **43**

LOVE IN THE MIST (USA)   2 b.f. (May 2) Silver Hawk (USA) 123 – Fast Nellie (USA) (Ack Ack (USA)) [2003 6m⁴ 7f⁶ 6m⁵ 7f f6g Nov 29] workmanlike filly: half-sister to several winners, including useful Irish 1996 2-y-o sprinter Raphane (by Rahy) and French 9f winner Where's Dave (by Eagle Eyed): dam unraced sister to US Grade 1 8.5f winner Caline: fair maiden: below form last 2 starts: should stay 7f: raced freely second outing. *E. A. L. Dunlop*   **69**

LOVE (IRE)   5 b.g. Royal Academy (USA) 130 – Kentmere (FR) (Galetto (FR) 118) [2003 58, a?: p10g a6g* 5m 7m 6g 8g Sep 17] lengthy, rather leggy gelding: modest performer: form in 2003 only when winning handicap at Laytown in June: effective at 6f to 9f (raced too freely over 1¼m at Lingfield on reappearance, left E. Butler after): acts on sand, best efforts on turf on good going or firmer: often blinkered as 3-y-o: sometimes tongue tied: thoroughly inconsistent: sold €2,800. *R. J. Osborne, Ireland*   **56 §**

LOVEISDANGEROUS   2 b.f. (Feb 10) Pursuit of Love 124 – Brookhead Lady 73 (Petong 126) [2003 5m⁵ 6g⁵ 5m⁴ 5g² 5m* 5m² 6f³ 5m⁵ 5g² 6.1m 6m⁶ Oct 12] 8,200Y, 9,000 2-y-o: rather unfurnished filly: third foal: half-sister to untrustworthy 6f winner Eibh'N Abbie (by Forzando): dam 5f/6f winner, including at 2 yrs: modest performer: won seller at Leicester in July: left N. Tinkler before penultimate start: will prove best at 5f/6f: acts on good to firm going: wore cheekpieces fifth to tenth outings: often races up with pace. *Don Enrico Incisa*   **54**

LOVELLIAN   3 b.f. Machiavellian (USA) 123 – Baby Loves 94 (Sadler's Wells (USA) 132) [2003 8.2m 10m 10.2f⁵ f12g⁴ f9.4g p10g Dec 30] 52,000Y: sturdy filly: fourth foal: sister to fairly useful French 9f to 15f winner Mighty Quinn and closely related to French 9.3f winner Exit To Stage (by Exit To Nowhere): dam 7f (at 2 yrs) and 1¼m winner out of half-sister to Irish St Leger winner Dark Lomond: well held in maidens/handicap: has been slowly away. *B. R. Millman*   –

LOVELY YOU (IRE)   3 b.g. Fayruz 116 – Lovely Me (IRE) 70 (Vision (USA)) [2003 63: p7g 7f Aug 26] modest maiden, lightly raced: well held in handicaps in 2003 (tailed off on latter): stays 6f. *Miss D. A. McHale*   –

LOVE ON REQUEST   3 b.f. Revoque (IRE) 122 – Search For Love (FR) (Groom Dancer (USA) 128) [2003 –p: 7.1m 10g f12g⁴ f12s⁶ 7d⁵ 13d² 9f 12g Sep 25] leggy filly: modest maiden: left J. Given 1,200 gns after fourth start: has form up to 13f, but best effort at 7f: acts on good to soft ground: blinkered/wore cheekpieces last 5 starts: tends to carry head high. *T. G. McCourt, Ireland*   **58 ?**

LOVE REGARDLESS (USA)   4 b. or br.c. Storm Bird (CAN) 134 – Circus Toons (USA) (Wild Again (USA)) [2003 112: a8f 8.1g⁶ 7.1d⁶ May 3] leggy colt: smart at 3 yrs: not at best in 2003, running respectably only when sixth to Desert Deer in Bet attheraces Mile at Sandown on second start: best around 1m: acts on firm and soft ground. *M. Johnston*   **107 ?**

LOVER'S MISSION (FR)   4 ch.f. Jeune Homme (USA) 120 – Tokyo Girl (FR) (Comrade In Arms 123) [2003 –: p7g 8g 7d 9g 7d 7.5g² 7g 7m² 8f Oct 18] fourth reported foal: half-sister to French 10.5f winner Hi Colon (by Nashamaa): dam French 1¼m (at 2 yrs) to 15f winner: fair maiden: stays 1m: acts on good to firm ground, well held on ground softer than good, and on polytrack at Lingfield on reappearance: tried blinkered. *Takashi Kodama, Ireland*   **66**

LOVE'S DESIGN (IRE)   6 b. or br.g. Pursuit of Love 124 – Cephista 61 (Shirley Heights 130) [2003 75, a90d: p10g p10g⁶ p8g⁴ p8g f8.5g* f8g³ f8.5g³ f9.4s⁵ f8.5g Apr   **?
a60**

28] modest performer: won seller at Wolverhampton in March: left Miss J̇. Feilden after seventh start: best at 7f to 8.5f: acts on firm going, good to soft and all-weather: wears headgear: held up: often finds little. *Miss S. J. Wilton*

LOVES REWARD 3 ch.c. Pursuit of Love 124 – Love Returned 94 (Taufan (USA) 119) [2003 7.1f 6g 6m May 10] IR 5,500Y: strong, close-coupled colt: first living foal: dam 5f/6f winner, best at 5f: well held in maidens. *T. D. Easterby* —

LOVES TRAVELLING (IRE) 3 b.g. Blues Traveller (IRE) 119 – Fast Love (IRE) (Second Set (IRE) 127) [2003 63: p8g⁴ p8g⁵ p10g³ 9m⁵ 9.9m 10m⁴ p10g 11.9f* 12.1m* 11.9f² 11.9f³ Oct 17] fairly useful performer: won claimer at Brighton (claimed from J. Hills £8,000) in August and handicap at Beverley in September: ran well after: stays 1½m: acts on polytrack and firm ground: tends to edge left: sold 26,000 gns. *L. M. Cumani* **85**

LOVE THAT BENNY (USA) 3 ch.c. Benny The Dip (USA) 127 – Marie Loves Emma (USA) (Affirmed (USA)) [2003 10m³ 10.1m* 12m 11.6m* 13.1d 16.5d Nov 8] big, rather leggy colt: second foal: dam 1m winner in USA: fairly useful performer: won maiden at Yarmouth in August and handicap at Windsor in September: stays 11.6f: acts on good to firm ground: visored last 3 starts: raced freely penultimate outing: sold 24,000 gns. *J. H. M. Gosden* **91**

LOVE TRIANGLE (IRE) 2 ch.g. (Mar 26) Titus Livius (FR) 115 – Kirsova (Absalom 128) [2003 5g² 5m³ 6m⁵ 6f³ 7g² 7d* 7m⁴ 7.1d⁶ 8m 7f Oct 12] IR 5,600F, 11,000Y, 34,000 2-y-o: smallish, good-topped gelding: half-brother to several winners, including fairly useful winner 6f (at 2 yrs)/7f winner Mujova (by Mujadil) and 9f and 15f winner La Ballerine (by Lafontaine): dam lightly raced: fairly useful performer: won maiden at Galway in August: good fourth at York, best effort in nurseries after: should stay 1m: acts on good to firm and good to soft ground. *D. R. C. Elsworth* **82**

LOW CLOUD 3 b.c. Danehill (USA) 126 – Raincloud (Rainbow Quest (USA) 134) [2003 7m 8.1m* 8.5d⁶ 10m⁶ 8m⁵ 10.1m Sep 17] IR 38,000Y: useful-looking colt: first foal: dam, lightly-raced French 1½m winner, sister to smart performer up to 1¾m Tuning: fairly useful performer: won maiden at Haydock in June: ran well third/fifth starts: should stay 1¼m: acts on good to firm and good to soft ground: sold 18,000 gns. *A. C. Stewart* **83**

LOWE GO 3 b.g. First Trump 118 – Hotel California (IRE) 58 (Last Tycoon 131) [2003 72: 10.3g 11.6g 12.6m⁵ 14g f12g 12d² f14s Sep 2] sparely-made gelding: fair maiden: stays 12.6f: acts on good to firm and good to soft going, probably on soft: wore cheekpieces (below form) final start. *J. G. Portman* **69**

LOWESWATER (USA) 4 b.c. Nureyev (USA) 131 – River Empress (USA) (Riverman (USA) 131) [2003 –: 8m 10.3m² 10m 10.2g² 10m* 9.9g⁴ Jul 29] strong, close-coupled colt: easy mover: useful performer: made all to win 3-runner minor event at Pontefract in June by 11 lengths from Garros: creditable fourth to Imperial Dancer in handicap at Goodwood final start, staying on well despite carrying head to one side: stays 1¼m: raced only on good ground or firmer: has had 2 handlers/been on toes: has worn crossed noseband: sold 10,000 gns in October. *J. H. M. Gosden* **101**

LOXIAS (FR) 4 b.c. Saumarez 132 – Loxandra 76 (Last Tycoon 131) [2003 111: 12.5s* 12g² 12d* 12g³ 12g Sep 7] fourth foal: half-brother to top-class miler Keltos (by Kendor) and useful French 7f/1m winner Iridanos (by Sabrehill): dam 1m winner: smart performer: improved in 2003, winning minor event at Saint-Cloud in March and awarded Prix Jean de Chaudenay there in May (beaten nose by Millenary but carried right): ran well when 2¼ lengths fourth (promoted to third) behind Ange Gabriel in Grand Prix de Saint-Cloud, then below form in Grosser Bugatti Preis at Baden-Baden: stays 12.5f: acts on heavy and good to firm ground: has been blinkered, including last 3 starts. *C. Laffon-Parias, France* **118**

LOYAL (GER) 3 b.g. Bluebird (USA) 125 – La Luganese (Surumu (GER)) [2003 65: 12.1m⁴ 14.1m 14m³ 14.1m² 18m⁶ 12d 12g 12m Oct 16] big, good-topped gelding: fair maiden: left Mrs A. Perrett 18,000 gns after eighth outing: little form after: stays 2¼m: acts on good to firm ground and polytrack, seemingly not on ground softer than good: tongue tied (ran creditably) third to fifth starts. *P. Hughes, Ireland* **72 d**

LOYAL TYCOON (IRE) 5 br.g. Royal Abjar (USA) 121 – Rosy Lydgate 53 (Last Tycoon 131) [2003 87: f6g* f6s* f6s³ f7s² p6g* p7g f6s⁵ 6g 6m² 6m 7g 6d⁶ 6g² 6m³ 6m* 6f 6g⁵ 7m 6g⁵ 6g 5.6d 6m 7f Sep 27] robust, close-coupled gelding: useful performer: won claimer and handicap at Southwell and minor event at Lingfield, all in January, and handicap at Epsom in June: effective at 6f/7f: acts on soft going, good to firm and all- **97**

weather: visored 5 times in 2002: sometimes starts slowly/pulls hard/wanders: usually held up: tough. *D. Nicholls*

LUALUA   2 ch.g. (Apr 26) Presidium 124 – Tawny 81 (Grey Ghost 98) [2003 5m* 5m   **77**
5m⁵ Jun 19] sturdy gelding: seventh living foal: half-brother to 3 winners, including fairly useful 5f (including at 2 yrs) to 7f winner Angel Hill (by King's Signet): dam 2-y-o 5f/6f winner: fair form: won maiden at Musselburgh in May: well beaten after, though showed up long way final start: likely to prove best at 5f. *T. D. Barron*

LUBINAS (IRE)   4 b.g. Grand Lodge (USA) 125 – Liebesgirl (Konigsstuhl (GER))   **?**
[2003 a11.5g² 12g May 3] big ex-Swiss trained gelding: first foal: dam German 2-y-o 7f winner: maiden, in frame several times in Germany, including at Neuss on reappearance (left Frau G. Wenisch after): well beaten at Thirsk on British debut: stays 1½m: acts on sand, raced only on good ground or softer on turf. *F. Jordan*

LUCAYAN BEAUTY (IRE)   2 b.f. (Mar 22) Marju (IRE) 127 – Koumiss (Unfuwain   **80**
(USA) 131) [2003 5m 6g² 6f⁵ 5f² 6d³ 6.1m 7m⁴ 8d 7g³ 8m* 7.9f⁴ 8m Oct 16] €70,000Y: sturdy, lengthy filly: third foal: half-sister to fairly useful 2002 2-y-o 6f winner Black Belt Shopper (by Desert Prince): dam, French maiden who stayed 10.5f, half-sister to smart stayer Arden and useful French sprinter Kerulen: fairly useful performer: left B. Meehan after seventh start (blinkered): won nursery at Pontefract in September: should stay 1¼m: acts on firm going: tends to hang left: sold 20,000 gns, sent to USA. *M. J. Wallace*

LUCAYAN DANCER   3 b.g. Zieten (USA) 118 – Tittle Tattle (IRE) 80 (Soviet Lad   **85 d**
(USA)) [2003 88: 8g 9m⁶ 10.5f² 10.4m 8.1v⁶ 10.1m⁶ 10.4f 11m 10g 10.5m² 9.2g⁶ 10f⁶ 9.2g⁴ 12m 10f³ 10.9d³ 7m⁴ Oct 25] leggy gelding: has a markedly round action: fairly useful performer: below form after sixth outing: stays 1¼m: acts on any ground: wore cheekpieces/blinkers 7 of last 8 starts: sometimes takes strong hold: sold 15,000 gns, and gelded. *J. S. Goldie*

LUCAYAN LEGACY (IRE)   4 b.g. Persian Bold 123 – Catherinofaragon (USA)   **–**
(Chief's Crown (USA)) [2003 –: 8m Apr 8] useful-looking gelding: fairly useful at 2 yrs: well beaten since. *D. Nicholls*

LUCAYAN MELODY (IRE)   3 b.g. Fayruz 116 – Magic Melody 62 (Petong 126)   **55**
[2003 6m 7m³ 6g⁵ May 23] IR 32,000F, 24,000Y: quite attractive gelding: second foal: brother to 6f winner Molly Ellen: dam, maiden best at 6f at 2 yrs, half-sister to useful sprinters Rosselli, Heather Bank and Dancing Music: modest form in maidens: sold 3,500 gns, and gelded. *M. Johnston*

LUCAYAN MONARCH   5 ch.g. Cadeaux Genereux 131 – Flight Soundly (IRE) 78   **73**
(Caerleon (USA) 132) [2003 76: 6m³ p6g* 6m 6m³ 5.9g³ 6m⁶ 7g 6m f7g f8g f8g f8s⁶ f8g⁴ Dec 19] lengthy gelding: fair handicapper: won at Lingfield in April: below form after sixth outing: has won at 9.4f, best form at 6f: acts on all-weather, firm and soft going: tried in cheekpieces: sometimes slowly away. *P. A. Blockley*

LUCEBALL (IRE)   3 b.f. Bluebird (USA) 125 – Mysterious Plans (IRE) (Last Tycoon   **54**
131) [2003 56: 6.1d 6m⁶ 6m⁵ 5g⁵ 6g⁶ 6m 6m⁴ 5m 5f 8d Oct 31] modest maiden handicapper: left E. James after reappearance: stays 6f: acts on good to firm going, well beaten on fibresand: sometimes blinkered: tongue tied final start. *K. J. Condon, Ireland*

LUCEFER (IRE)   5 b.g. Lycius (USA) 124 – Maharani (USA) (Red Ransom (USA))   **55**
[2003 55: 7f 7m 7g⁵ 8.2m 7m⁴ 7g³ 7g⁴ 8m* 8f² Aug 26] leggy gelding: modest handicapper: won apprentice event at Brighton in August: effective at 6f to easy 1m: acts on polytrack, firm and soft ground: tried blinkered at 3 yrs, tongue tied last 7 starts: sometimes carries head high. *G. C. H. Chung*

LUCID DREAMS (IRE)   4 b.g. Sri Pekan (USA) 117 – Scenaria (IRE) (Scenic 128)   **63**
[2003 51: f7g* f7g³ p7g³ 7m f6g⁶ f7g 7m² 7.6m⁵ 7m 7g* 7m² 7m⁴ 6.9m Sep 4] rather leggy, good-topped gelding: modest handicapper: won at Wolverhampton in March and Yarmouth in July: best form at 1m: acts on firm going and all-weather: blinkered first 6 starts in 2003. *M. Wigham*

LUCINDI   3 b.f. Tamure (IRE) 125 – Miss Petronella (Petoski 135) [2003 70: 10.1g⁵   **76**
12.4m² 12.4m⁴ 15m³ 16.1m Oct 1] leggy, lengthy filly: fair maiden handicapper: stays easy 15f: acts on good to firm ground: hung in behind penultimate start, folded tamely final outing. *C. W. Thornton*

LUCIUS VERRUS (USA)   3 b.c. Danzig (USA) – Magic of Life (USA) 118 (Seattle   **55**
Slew (USA)) [2003 f9.4g 5m⁴ p6g² f6s⁴ Dec 27] 17,000 3-y-o: half-brother to several winners, including French 1¼m/1½m winner From Beyond (by Kris) and 2000 2-y-o 6f winner Enthused (by Seeking The Gold), both useful: dam, Mill Reef and Coronation

Stakes winner, from good family: modest form in maidens: may prove better at 7f than 6f: acts on all-weather and good to firm going. *D. Shaw*

LUCKY ARCHER   10 b.g. North Briton 67 – Preobrajenska 93 (Double Form 130)   **72 d**
[2003 74: 8g 9f² 8f⁶ 10.2m 10.2g 8.1m Sep 20] smallish, well-made gelding: fair
handicapper: below form after second start: stays 9f: acts on firm and good to soft going:
blinkered once at 3 yrs: often races up with pace. *Ian Williams*

LUCKY BREAK (IRE)   5 ch.g. Brief Truce (USA) 126 – Paradise Forum 78 (Prince   **–**
Sabo 123) [2003 –, a65: p10g Mar 26] small gelding: maiden: well held only outing in
2003. *C. A. Horgan*

LUCKY DATE (IRE)   3 ch.f. Halling (USA) 133 – Hesperia (Slip Anchor 136) [2003   **91**
81p: 8m² 11.4m 10.1g 8d⁵ 12m⁶ 9m Aug 24] leggy filly: fairly useful performer: below
form after reappearance: should stay beyond 1m: acts on soft and good to firm going:
visored final start: wears crossed noseband: has raced freely. *M. A. Magnusson*

LUCKY HEATHER (IRE)   6 b.m. Soviet Lad (USA) – Idrak 68 (Young Generation   **–**
129) [2003 –: f14.8g Jan 17] probably of little account nowadays. *R. J. Baker*

LUCKY LARGO (IRE)   3 b. or br.g. Key of Luck (USA) 126 – Lingering Melody   **74**
(IRE) 59 (Nordico (USA)) [2003 63: 7d² 7.5d² 9d² 9.5d 8d² 8m Sep 26] IR 31,000Y:
brother to 6f (at 2 yrs) to 8.5f winner B Major, later winner in UAE, and half-brother to 2
winners, notably very smart 5f winner Indian Prince (by Indian Ridge): dam, Irish maiden
who stayed 1m, half-sister to very smart miler Alflora: fair maiden handicapper: left
K. Prendergast/off 4 months before well held on British debut final outing: stays 9f: raced
only on good going or softer prior to final start: blinkered twice. *S. Gollings*

LUCKY LEO   3 b.g. Muhtarram (USA) 125 – Wrong Bride (Reprimand 122) [2003   **75 ?**
70, a–: 8m³ 8.1d 10g Oct 6] lengthy gelding: fair maiden: claimed from M. Channon   **a–**
£10,000 on reappearance: well held in handicaps after: stays 1m: acts on soft and good to
firm ground, well held on all-weather. *Ian Williams*

LUCKY PIPIT   2 b.f. (Feb 26) Key of Luck (USA) 126 – Meadow Pipit (CAN) 113   **102**
(Meadowlake (USA)) [2003 7m 7f* 7.1m* 7f 8d³ Sep 11] leggy filly: third foal: half-
sister to fairly useful 2000 2-y-o 7f winner Paiyda (by Danehill): dam, 7f to 1¼m winner,
out of half-sister to US Grade 1 9f winner Delta Flag: useful performer: made all in
maiden at Kempton and listed race at Sandown (beat America America 5 lengths) in July:
respectable 4¼ lengths third to Kinnaird in May Hill Stakes at Doncaster: should stay 1m:
acts on firm going: edgy sort. *B. W. Hills*

LUCKY ROMANCE   4 b.f. Key of Luck (USA) 126 – In Love Again (IRE) 86   **–**
(Prince Rupert (FR) 121) [2003 61: f6g 6f Jul 21] tall filly: modest maiden at best: well
held in 2003: has looked none too keen. *R. F. Johnson Houghton*

LUCKY STAR   6 b.m. Emarati (USA) 74 – Child Star (FR) 58 (Bellypha 130) [2003   **39**
52, a38: f6g⁶ f5g⁴ f6s f7g f6g 6m 5m 5m f6s² 5m 6f 5m⁵ Aug 15] leggy mare: poor   **a43**
performer: effective at 5f to 8.5f: acts on fibresand, firm and good to soft going: visored
once at 4 yrs: tongue tied penultimate start: usually races prominently. *J. Balding*

LUCKY STORY (USA)   2 br.c. (Feb 1) Kris S (USA) – Spring Flight (USA)   **119 p**
(Miswaki (USA) 124) [2003 6g⁴ 6m* 6d* 7d* 7g* Sep 12]
   The secret of someone's success isn't always obvious. It has become
popular, for example, to attribute the regular sight of a Mark Johnston-trained horse
rallying when the chips are down to an unusually high level of tenacity and fitness
in his horses. At least part of the explanation, however, lies in the way Johnston has
his horses ridden, rather than in any innate extraordinary battling qualities or
fitness. Being in front or near the lead early on is more common with Johnston's
horses than most, and what happens early in a race has a far bigger impact on the
result than is often acknowledged. Those horses held up are generally more
susceptible to pulling, particularly when the pace is steady or muddling. Although
some such horses may improve to challenge, seemingly going strongly, their
finishing efforts can be short-lived, sometimes leading to those that have been
given their heads taking charge again, whether they are notably game or not. Energy
wasted by a horse fighting its rider early on counts against it heavily in a finish.
   Mark Johnston's straightforward approach helped him to a career-best total
of winners in 2003. In the process, Johnston completed a tenth consecutive century,
breaking the previous record set by Henry Cecil, a trainer who encouraged for long
periods similar riding tactics on his horses at the height of his success. Johnston

Veuve Clicquot Vintage Stakes, Goodwood—Lucky Story idles in front but is still too good for
The Mighty Tiger as the pair pull clear of the remainder, headed by Devil Moon (No.4)

reached his landmark century at Glorious Goodwood, where Lucky Story was the
most important of his three winners. Lucky Story's career was only just getting off
the ground as Attraction, Pearl of Love and Russian Valour won two-year-old races
for Johnston at Royal Ascot, but Lucky Story emerged as just about the best of the
stable's crop in the second half of the year, showing himself virtually as good as any
two-year-old trained in Britain. In Royal Ascot week, Lucky Story confirmed the
promise of his debut fourth at Ayr in late-May by landing the odds in a four-runner
maiden on the same course. He took stronger opposition in his stride when again
odds on in the Spindrifter Stakes, a six-furlong minor event at Pontefract later in
June, making light of deteriorating ground to beat Mac The Knife most impressively by six lengths. Lucky Story was again made favourite for the Veuve Clicquot
Vintage Stakes on softish ground at Goodwood in July. In a field of nine, he again
won readily. Stepped up to seven furlongs for the first time, Lucky Story still looked
green as he took over approaching the final two furlongs, pricking his ears in front,
but pulled out extra when challenged to beat The Mighty Tiger by a length and a
quarter.

Lucky Story maintained his winning run in the Champagne Stakes at Doncaster's St Leger meeting. Carrying a 4-lb penalty for Goodwood, he was only
second favourite this time in a field of six, starting at 2/1 behind the unbeaten
Haafhd, who was odds on. Ridden by Darryll Holland in place of Keith Dalgleish
this time, Lucky Story turned in another improved display. With no other rider keen
to go on, Holland sent Lucky Story into the lead. Lucky Story found plenty when
challenged, first by the favourite two furlongs out, then by Auditorium closer to
home, Lucky Story edging away again at the death to win by a neck from Audi-

Champagne Stakes, Doncaster—Lucky Story, awash with sweat, finds plenty to hold off
strong-finishing Auditorium, while Haafhd (striped cap) and Azarole are engaged in their own battle;
Milk It Mick (partially hidden) is fifth

torium with Haafhd two lengths further away. Milk It Mick, who pulled hard early on, faded to be fifth. Lucky Story was the first since Alhaarth in 1995 to complete the Goodwood/Doncaster double, and he would have been a leading fancy to follow in Alhaarth's footsteps by winning the Dewhurst as well had he been able to take his chance. He was second favourite behind Three Valleys when ante-post odds were issued, but connections decided to withdraw him—his trainer reportedly not happy after he had galloped him on the Tuesday before the race. Ironically, given the stable's general approach, there had been talk of Lucky Story having a pacemaker in the Dewhurst. He has shown a tendency to idle in front, notably at Goodwood, and he edged right briefly in the closing stages at Doncaster before knuckling down under strong pressure. Lucky Story is a bit too experienced now for his waywardness to be put down purely to greenness, and seemingly he has his quirks. There is little doubting his gameness all the same and, hopefully, pacemaker or not, he won't be ridden from too far off the early pace in his races as a three-year-old.

Lucky Story (USA) (br.c. Feb 1, 2001)	Kris S (USA) (b 1977)	Roberto (b 1969)	Hail To Reason
			Bramalea
		Sharp Queen (b 1965)	Princequillo
			Bridgework
	Spring Flight (USA) (b 1987)	Miswaki (ch 1978)	Mr Prospector
			Hopespringseternal
		Coco La Investment (b 1975)	Coco La Terreur
			Great Investment

Lucky Story was bought for 95,000 dollars at the Keeneland September Sale in 2002. He is a brother to Dr Fong, who was unbeaten in two races as a juvenile and showed high-class form at three, winning the St James's Palace Stakes and finishing second in the Queen Elizabeth II Stakes. His sire Kris S, who died in 2002, has had most of his success at stud otherwise in the States, though he was also responsible for Kris Kin in 2003. Lucky Story's dam Spring Flight was a minor stakes-winning sprinter-miler in the States, and is a half-sister to non-graded stakes winners. Out of a minor two-year-old sprint winner, Spring Flight has only three other registered foals so far, all minor winners in the States. In between his Ascot efforts, Dr Fong won the Prix Eugene Adam over a mile and a quarter before being returned to the States, where he was second in the Oak Tree Derby over nine furlongs; he was tried in blinkers subsequently. Dr Fong was never tried beyond a mile and a quarter, and Lucky Story is unlikely to stay well enough for the Derby. He will be well suited by a step up from seven furlongs all the same and should stay a mile and a quarter in time. A well-made, quite attractive colt, although calm in the paddock, he was awash with sweat at the start at Doncaster; Dr Fong was prone to sweating too, as are others by Kris S, including Kris Kin. Provided all goes well in the spring, Lucky Story must have a live chance in the Two Thousand Guineas. He has raced on good ground or softer since his maiden win on good to firm. *M. Johnston*

LUCKY VALENTINE 3 b.f. My Best Valentine 122 – Vera's First (IRE) 69 (Exodal (USA)) [2003 55p: p6g p6g³ p5g³ p7g 5.1m³ 5.3m 6m 6m* 6m 6d Oct 31] modest performer: won maiden at Windsor in September: effective at 5f/6f: acts on polytrack, raced mainly on good to firm/firm ground on turf: slowly away sixth outing: tried in cheekpieces/blinkers. *G. L. Moore* **51**

LUCRETIUS 4 b.g. Mind Games 121 – Eastern Ember 85 (Indian King (USA) 128) [2003 p5g 6g⁶ p8g 6.1m May 9] 5,500Y: sixth foal: half-brother to 3 winners, notably smart sprinter Perryston View (by Primo Dominie): dam 5f to 7.5f winner: modest maiden: bred to prove best short of 1m (raced too freely at trip). *D. K. Ivory* **53 ?**

LUFERTON LANE (IRE) 6 b.m. Ela-Mana-Mou 132 – Saddle 'er Up (IRE) (Sadler's Wells (USA) 132) [2003 47: 16.2m 16.1d 16m 12.1m⁶ 12f⁵ 12.1m 14.1m⁶ 12.1m 16.1m 16m Sep 19] ex-Irish mare: fourth foal: dam Irish maiden who stayed 1½m: poor performer: won handicap at Killarney at 5 yrs: left R. Osborne 5,400 gns after final 5-y-o start: well held in 2003. *Don Enrico Incisa* **–**

LUFTIKUS (GER) 6 ch.g. Formidable (USA) 125 – La Paz (GER) (Roi Dagobert 128) [2003 12.1d f12g Aug 15] successful 4 times up to 1½m in Germany, including in minor event at Cologne in 2002 (left C. Von Der Recke after final 5-y-o start): well held in 2003, including in visor final start. *A. G. Hobbs* **–**

LUGTON (IRE) 3 b.g. Mujadil (USA) 119 – Titchwell Lass 57 (Lead On Time (USA) –
123) [2003 f7g⁴ f6g Feb 15] IR 21,000F, 9,500Y: third foal: half-brother to 2 winners,
including 5-y-o Denise Best:: dam 1¼m winner: well held in maidens at Wolverhampton.
J. S. Goldie

LUKE AFTER ME (IRE) 3 b.g. Victory Note (USA) 120 – Summit Talk (Head For   66
Heights 125) [2003 70d: f8g⁶ 7m⁴ 6m 7m 7m Oct 14] angular, good-topped gelding: fair
maiden handicapper: well held last 3 starts: stays 7f: acts on good to firm going, probably
on fibresand. *P. C. Haslam*

LUKE SHARP 2 b.g. (May 7) Muhtarram (USA) 125 – Heaven-Liegh-Grey 90 (Grey   –
Desire 115) [2003 8d 7m 7m Oct 12] 2,000Y: leggy gelding: eighth foal: half-brother to 3
winners, including 1m/9f winner French Connection (by Tirol): dam best at 5f: well
beaten in maidens: blinkered second start. *K. A. Ryan*

LUNAR COLONY (USA) 3 b. or br.f. A P Indy (USA) 131 – Solar Colony (USA)   83
(Pleasant Colony (USA)) [2003 10m² 10g* 14.1s Oct 29] tall filly: first foal: dam, US
8.5f and 9f winner, sister to Breeders' Cup Juvenile Fillies winner Pleasant Stage: fairly
useful form: won maiden at Windsor in October by 1¾ lengths from Fame: tailed off in
listed race at Yarmouth final start: should stay 1½m: sent to USA. *J. H. M. Gosden*

LUNAR EXIT (IRE) 2 gr.g. (Mar 19) Exit To Nowhere (USA) 122 – Moon Magic   95 p
62 (Polish Precedent (USA) 131) [2003 8g³ 8m* 10g⁵ Nov 1] 8,000Y: good-bodied
gelding: sixth foal: half-brother to winner abroad by Be My Chief: dam, ran once,
half-sister to Moon Madness and Sheriff's Star: won maiden at Newmarket in October:
useful form when 3 lengths fifth to Fun And Games in listed event on same course,
staying on well not knocked about: will stay at least 1½m: open to progress. *Lady Herries*

LUNAR LEADER (IRE) 3 b.f. Mujadil (USA) 119 – Moon River (FR) (Groom   78
Dancer (USA) 128) [2003 p7g p7g⁶ 7g⁴ 7.1m⁴ 7m 8.2g f8g⁵ p10g⁵ 8m² 8m* 8m⁴ 9.3m*
8f² 9.3d* 9.7m² 9m 10.1m 9.1m f7g Nov 29] IR 25,000Y: quite good-topped filly: second
foal: dam, third at 2m in France, half-sister to useful dam of 5-y-o Indian Creek: fair performer: claimed from B. Meehan £7,000 on ninth start: won claimer at Ayr in June and
handicap (hung left) and minor event at Carlisle in July: left Mrs L. Stubbs before final
outing: stays easy 1¼m: acts on firm ground, good to soft and polytrack: blinkered (virtually refused to race) sixth outing, wore cheekpieces last 8: has wandered. *M. J. Gingell*

LUNAR LEO 5 b.g. Muhtarram (USA) 125 – Moon Mistress 82 (Storm Cat (USA))   99
[2003 103: p7g 7m³ 7g 7m⁶ 7f 7m⁵ 7.1f⁴ 7.6m 6m 6f² 7g⁶ 7m⁶ Sep 13] sturdy gelding:
useful handicapper: some creditable efforts in 2003, including when fifth to Patavellian
in Bunbury Cup and second to Fruit of Glory, both at Newmarket: best at 6f/7f: acts on
firm ground: sometimes tongue tied: has worn crossed noseband/raced freely/found little:
often early to post, and has been mounted on track. *S. C. Williams*

LUNAR LORD 7 b.g. Elmaamul (USA) 125 – Cache (Bustino 136) [2003 64, a47:   –
f12s⁵ Feb 28] close-coupled gelding: modest on turf, poor on all-weather: well held only
start in 2003. *D. Burchell*

LUNAR RAINBOW (IRE) 4 b.f. Spectrum (IRE) 126 – Brilleaux 73 (Manado 130)   59
[2003 p8g² f9.4g Feb 7] half-sister to several winners, notably very smart 6f (at 2 yrs) to
1¾m winner Bobzao (by Alzao): dam half-sister to useful miler Welsh Flame, herself
grandam of Salsabil and Marju: better effort in maidens when second at Lingfield: will
stay 1¼m. *Sir Mark Prescott*

LUNAR WIND 2 gr.g. (Mar 30) Piccolo 121 – Faraway Moon 61 (Distant Relative   81
128) [2003 5.2m⁴ 6g* 6g 6m⁴ 5m² 5m⁶ 6f 5d⁶ 6m Oct 16] 9,500Y: smallish, lengthy
gelding: first foal: dam, maiden who stayed 1m, out of half-sister to Moon Madness and
Sheriff's Star: fairly useful performer: won maiden at Yarmouth in May: second in
nursery at Leicester: below form after next start: effective at 5f/6f: acts on good to firm
ground: sold 10,000 gns. *M. G. Quinlan*

LUNA TACUMANA (IRE) 3 b.f. Bahhare (USA) 122 – Orange And Blue 50   –
(Prince Sabo 123) [2003 p5g⁶ Feb 15] IR 16,000Y: second foal: half-sister to winner in
Sweden by Royal Abjar: dam 2-y-o 5f winner: 7/2 and tongue tied, fractious in stall and
very slowly away when well held in maiden at Lingfield. *Edward Butler, Ireland*

LUNDY'S LANE (IRE) 3 b.c. Darshaan 133 – Lunda (IRE) 60 (Soviet Star (USA)   108
128) [2003 92p: p8g* p10g* a10f 8m² 8g 12m³ 12m 10g 10.5m² 9m* 8m³ 9m⁴ 9m⁶ p10g
f9.4s Dec 31] lengthy, good-topped colt: useful performer: won maiden and minor event
at Lingfield in January/February, and minor event at Kempton (beat Al Jadeed by 2
lengths) in August: also ran well in Craven Stakes at Newmarket (1½ lengths second to
Hurricane Alan), Derby Italiano at Rome (2¾ lengths third behind Osorio), listed race at

Salisbury (4 lengths third to Passing Glance), minor event at Newbury (equal fourth to Putra Pekan) and Darley Stakes at Newmarket (sixth behind Far Lane): effective at 1m to 1½m: acts on polytrack and dirt, raced only on good/good to firm going on turf: tongue tied tenth to thirteenth starts: reluctant to post and edgy eleventh outing: often makes running. *C. E. Brittain*

LUPINE HOWL   2 b.c. (Feb 3) Wolfhound (USA) 126 – Classic Fan (USA) (Lear   **66**
Fan (USA) 130) [2003 7m 6d 6m⁶ 6d³ f6g 7m⁶ 6d Nov 4] 6,000F, 12,000Y: good-topped colt: third foal: half-brother to useful Irish 6f (at 2 yrs)/7.5f winner Plume Rouge (by Pivotal): dam, maiden, out of Ribblesdale winner Miss Boniface: fair maiden: third at Haydock: below form, including in nurseries, after: ran as if amiss final start: stays 6f, seemingly not 7f: best effort on good to soft going. *B. A. McMahon*

LUVAH GIRL   3 b.f. Alzao (USA) 117 – Girl of My Dreams (IRE) 51 (Marju (IRE)   **99**
127) [2003 110: 6.5g* Feb 28] good-bodied filly: has a quick action: smart performer at 2 yrs, winner of Rockfel Stakes at Newmarket: won non-graded stakes at Santa Anita in February by head from ex-British-trained Katdogawn, only outing in USA: returned to R. Charlton, but reportedly banged her head after rearing over backwards in April: should stay 1m: acts on polytrack, raced only on good/good to firm going on turf: races prominently. *Jenine Sahadi, USA*

LUXI RIVER (USA)   3 b.g. Diesis 133 – Mariella (USA) 106 (Roberto (USA) 131)   **60**
[2003 69: 8f⁶ 12g⁴ Oct 6] big gelding: fair maiden: left N. Graham and off 6 months after reappearance: should prove better at 1¼m+ than shorter. *M. Halford, Ireland*

LUXOR   6 ch.g. Grand Lodge (USA) 125 – Escrime (USA) 92 (Sharpen Up 127) [2003   **–**
60: 10d 10.3m 10m⁶ 10.3m 10.5m 10m⁶ 10.1m 10m 9f 10.4f Oct 10] rangy gelding: fluent mover: modest handicapper in 2002: showed little in 2003: tried in headgear/ tongue tie: headstrong front runner: sometimes flashes tail/finds little. *W. M. Brisbourne*

LUXURY LAUNCH (USA)   2 b.f. (May 18) Seeking The Gold (USA) – Ocean   **– p**
Ridge (USA) 115 (Storm Bird (CAN) 134) [2003 7g⁴ Aug 2] good-topped filly: second foal: dam, 5.5f (Prix Robert Papin)/6f winner at 2 yrs who stayed 1m, out of smart 6f performer Polar Bird: 7/2, well-beaten fourth of 5 in maiden at Newmarket, taking strong hold: likely to do better. *B. W. Hills*

LYCA BALLERINA   2 b.f. (May 1) Marju (IRE) 127 – Lovely Lyca 76 (Night Shift   **76**
(USA) 129) [2003 5g 6g⁴ 6m⁵ 7g⁶ 7g⁴ 8m⁶ 8m³ 7g⁴ Oct 24] 42,000Y: quite attractive filly: fourth foal: half-sister to fairly useful 1m winner Polish Off (by Polish Precedent): dam, 1m and 1½m winner, out of half-sister to Old Vic: fair maiden: raced freely when third in nursery at Newmarket: stays 1m: acts on good to firm going: consistent. *B. W. Hills*

LYCIAN (IRE)   8 b.g. Lycius (USA) 124 – Perfect Time (IRE) (Dance of Life) [2003   **–**
69, a58: p10g p10g f12g f12g⁴ p12g⁶ p12g⁴ 11.8g 12f 11g 14f Aug 18] tall, angular   **a60 d**
gelding: modest performer: left Mrs L. Stubbs after seventh start: well held for new stable: best form at 1m/1¼m, but does seem to stay easy 1½m: acts on all-weather, best turf form on good going or firmer. *Mrs Edwina Finn, Ireland*

LYCIAT SPARKLE (IRE)   5 b.g. Lycius (USA) 124 – Benguiat (FR) (Exceller   **–**
(USA) 129) [2003 36: 10g 10m 8m⁶ 10.5m 7d 8.1g 8.1m Aug 8] angular, close-coupled gelding: maiden handicapper: little form in 2003: headstrong. *R. Ford*

LYDIA'S LOOK (IRE)   6 b.m. Distant View (USA) 126 – Mrs Croesus (USA) (Key   **49**
To The Mint (USA)) [2003 61, a–: p6g 5m⁴ 5g 5m 5m 6d⁵ 5m 6d 5m Aug 6] close-coupled mare: poor handicapper nowadays: effective at 5f/6f: acts on fibresand, firm and soft going: none too reliable. *T. J. Etherington*

LYGETON LAD   5 b.g. Shaamit (IRE) 127 – Smartie Lee 66 (Dominion 123) [2003   **85**
75+, a89: f7g⁴ p8g* p10g⁵ p7g* p8g⁴ f8.5s⁴ p7g* 7d³ p7g⁴ a8.7g 7m 8m⁵ 7m⁵ 8m² 8m   **a112**
f8.5g p7g* p6g p7g* Dec 29] smart handicapper on all-weather, fairly useful on turf: successful 5 times at Lingfield in 2003, best effort when beating The Best Yet by head in December: best at 7f/1m: acts on good to firm and good to soft going, better form on polytrack than fibresand: usually tongue tied: sometimes slowly away: tough, genuine and consistent. *Miss Gay Kelleway*

LYRICAL GIRL (USA)   2 b.f. (Feb 1) Orpen (USA) 116 – Lyric Theatre (USA)   **64**
(Seeking The Gold (USA)) [2003 6g 5.7f² 5.2m 5.1f² 5.7f³ 7m 6g p8g³ f8g* Dec 8] $9,500Y, resold 7,500Y: sturdy filly: third foal: half-sister to winner in Holland by Entrepreneur: dam unraced out of smart 5f performer (best at 2 yrs) Lyric Fantasy: modest performer: left S. Kirk after seventh start: won seller at Southwell: should stay 1¼m: acts on firm going and all-weather. *M. R. Channon*

LYRICAL LADY   2 b.f. (Apr 6) Merdon Melody 98 – Gracious Imp (USA) (Imp   **58** Society (USA)) [2003 6g 6m⁵ p6g⁴ f5g⁶ Dec 15] 10,000Y: well-made filly: third foal: sister to 3-y-o Mesmerised and 4-y-o Sophies Symphony: dam no form: modest form in maidens: probably better at 6f than 5f. *Mrs A. J. Bowlby*

LYRICAL WAY   4 b.g. Vettori (IRE) 119 – Fortunate (Reference Point 139) [2003 62:   **67** p10g 10.2f⁶ 10m 9.9m* 9.7g 10m 9.9m 10m² p10g² p10g² p10g* Dec 20] leggy gelding: fair handicapper: won at Salisbury in August and Lingfield in December: stays 1¼m: acts on polytrack, good to firm and good to soft ground: effective blinkered/visored or not. *P. R. Chamings*

LYRIC MAESTRO   4 b.g. Merdon Melody 98 – Dubitable 59 (Formidable (USA)   **–** 125) [2003 62: 10.9m 11.7m 14.1s May 17] good-bodied gelding: modest maiden: well beaten in handicaps in 2003: tried visored/in cheekpieces. *S. Dow*

LYRIC SOPRANO (IRE)   3 ch.f. Entrepreneur 123 – Lyric Theatre (USA) (Seeking   **–** The Gold (USA)) [2003 8.1m Jun 6] 20,000F, 17,000Y: smallish, plain filly: second foal: sister to winner in Holland: dam unraced daughter of smart sprinter (best at 5f at 2 yrs) Lyric Fantasy: 12/1, eighth in maiden at Haydock: sold 1,000 gns. *M. Johnston*

LYRINGO   9 b.m. Rustingo 94 – Lyricist (Averof 123) [2003 f16g Jan 9] well held in   **–** claimers 19 months apart: tried blinkered: winning hurdler. *B. J. Llewellyn*

LYSANDER'S QUEST (IRE)   5 br.g. King's Theatre (IRE) 128 – Haramayda (FR)   **56** (Doyoun 124) [2003 60: p13g⁴ 14.1g⁵ 11.7m⁶ p16g 13.3m⁵ 13.3m 12d 12.1g 12m Aug 20] tall gelding: modest maiden handicapper: effective at 1½m/1¾m: acts on good to firm going, good to soft and polytrack: visored final start: sometimes slowly away: held up. *L. Montague Hall*

LY'S WEST   3 ch.g. The West (USA) 107 – Lysithea 63 (Imperial Fling (USA) 116)   **–** [2003 –: 6g 5.7m Aug 5] lengthy gelding: well held in maidens/claimer. *W. G. M. Turner*

M

MAALOOF   2 b.c. (Apr 6) A P Indy (USA) 131 – Alabaq (USA) 111 (Riverman (USA)   **81** 131) [2003 7m³ 7m 7m² Oct 14] leggy, quite good-topped colt: first foal: dam, 7f (at 2 yrs) to 1¼m winner, daughter of Salsabil: fairly useful form when placed in maidens at York and Leicester (disputed lead long way when second to Penrith): ran as if amiss in between: will stay 1m. *J. L. Dunlop*

MABEL RILEY (IRE)   3 b.f. Revoque (IRE) 122 – Mystic Dispute (IRE) (Magical   **63 d** Strike (USA) 114) [2003 66: f7g* p8g² f8.5g² f7g 8.1m³ f8.5s 8.3g 7.1g⁵ 8f⁵ 8m⁶ 8m 7d³ 9f⁵ 5.1d p7g f6g f8g Dec 8] modest performer: won seller at Southwell in January: below form after fifth start, claimed from B. Meehan after thirteenth: stays 8.5f: acts on good to firm going and all-weather: tried blinkered/in cheekpieces: sometimes pulls hard/ edges left. *M. A. Buckley*

MAC   3 ch.g. Fleetwood (IRE) 107 – Midnight Break 78 (Night Shift (USA)) [2003 71:   **93** 8.3g 10g⁶ 12m 13.3m⁵ 13.3m⁵ 13.9m⁵ 14g Sep 6] good-bodied gelding: fairly useful handicapper: won at Newbury in July and August (beat Gold Ring by 3 lengths): stays 1¾m: raced only on good/good to firm ground on turf. *M. P. Tregoning*

MACADAMIA (IRE)   4 b.f. Classic Cliche (IRE) 128 – Cashew 80 (Sharrood   **115** (USA) 124) [2003 91: 8m² 8m* 8m* 8m* 9.9g⁵ 8m² 9m Oct 18]

    The financial pressures on an owner of keeping a good-class filly in training after the age of three are nowhere near so great as with a colt of stallion potential. If a filly remains in training her owner forfeits at most the value of one foal. Unlike its American counterpart, the European racing programme has provided only limited opportunities for fillies after the age of three, unless they have been good enough to compete against the colts on weight-for-sex terms. A four-year-old filly in America can have a highly lucrative campaign without taking on the best of the colts. The Horse of The Year in the States in 2002, Azeri, won fourteen of her sixteen career starts, racing only against her own sex. From 2004 there will be more opportunities in Europe following an increase in the number of pattern races open to older fillies. But are the races really worthy of the prestige that is to be bestowed upon them? Take the Stan James Falmouth Stakes, for example, which certainly does not

*Royal Hunt Cup (Handicap), Royal Ascot—the stand-side group provides the first six home;
Macadamia overcomes a 7-lb penalty, beating Camp Commander, Tough Love (No.25), Pentecost,
Morahib (rail) and Unshakable; Norton (No.3) leads home those on the far side*

deserve its upgrading to Group 1, judged on the quality of fields it has attracted over
the years. The latest winner, the four-year-old Macadamia, had to put up no more
than a useful performance to score in an eight-runner line-up that lacked strength in
depth. The runner-up Waldmark, who had anything but a clear run at Newmarket,
and the third, German-trained Walzerkoenigin, failed to win on any of their three
subsequent starts, though the latter enjoyed a financially fruitful late-summer and
autumn campaign in fillies' races in North America.

*Stan James Falmouth Stakes, Newmarket—Macadamia doesn't have to reproduce her Hunt Cup form
to win this Group 2 from Waldmark, German-trained Walzerkoenigin (left) and Nasij (rail)*

MAC

Macadamia was kept in training after showing only fairly useful form at three, her one success coming in a minor event at Newmarket. She showed herself better than ever when beaten a neck by the progressive Akshar in a minor event at Goodwood on her reappearance, a performance which made Macadamia of interest in the Royal Hunt Cup, for which the weights had already been published. Macadamia picked up a 7-lb penalty when routing her rivals in a newly-inaugurated listed race, the Pipalong Stakes, at Pontefract in June, but it wasn't enough to stop her at Royal Ascot. In a typically-competitive renewal of the Royal Hunt Cup, Macadamia quickened clear after two furlongs out and held on in good style to win by a length and three quarters from Camp Commander. When a horse makes a successful transition from handicaps to pattern company, there always seems an underlying assumption that it has achieved the feat by showing improved form. That certainly wasn't so with Macadamia, who didn't have to match her smart Royal Hunt Cup effort to win the Falmouth. Macadamia's best effort in three starts after the Falmouth (on the last of which she lost all chance when badly hampered) came in the Sun Chariot Stakes at Newmarket in early-October, when she went down by a fast-diminishing neck to the three-year-old Echoes In Eternity, showing form on a par with that in the Falmouth.

Macadamia (IRE) (b.f. 1999)	Classic Cliche (IRE) (b 1992)	Salse (b 1985)	Topsider
			Carnival Princess
		Pato (b 1982)	High Top
			Patosky
	Cashew (gr 1991)	Sharrood (ro 1983)	Caro
			Angel Island
		Kashmiri Snow (b 1982)	Shirley Heights
			Two Can Sing

Lord Vestey's "Macadamia"

The lengthy Macadamia is by the St Leger and Gold Cup winner Classic Cliche, who showed himself fully effective at a strongly-run mile and a half when runner-up in the King George VI and Queen Elizabeth Stakes. Macadamia's lightly-raced dam Cashew won a maiden over a mile at Sandown as a three-year-old and is a half-sister to three other winners in Britain, the Stayers' Hurdle winner Karshi, the fairly useful miler Gulmarg and the fair middle-distance handicapper Pickles. Their dam Kashmiri Snow, a fairly useful miler herself, ended up being exported to Turkey, where she has since foaled another three winners. Cashew has done well at stud and was also represented on the racecourse in the latest season by the smart sprinter Pistachio (by Unblest), still plying his trade at the age of seven in Scandinavia, and the useful two-year-old Azarole (by Alzao), successful twice and in the frame in the Champagne Stakes at Doncaster and the Somerville Tattersall at Newmarket. Another of Cashew's offspring, Prime Version (by Primo Dominie), was successful in a six-furlong maiden at Newbury as a two-year-old and later won at up to a mile in Switzerland. The genuine Macadamia, who really thrived as a four-year-old, was effective at a mile and a mile and a quarter and was raced mainly on good going or firmer. She has been retired and visits Red Ransom.
J. R. Fanshawe

MACANILLO (GER) 5 gr.g. Acatenango (GER) 127 – Midday Girl (GER) 99 (Black — Tie Affair 128) [2003 f7s⁴ f9.4s f8.5s Feb 28] trained in 2002 by S. Stokes in Germany, winning maiden at Hanover: well held in handicaps in 2003: stays 1m: raced on good ground or softer on turf: blinkered last 2 starts. *Ian Williams*

MACARONI GOLD (IRE) 3 b.g. Rock Hopper 124 – Strike It Rich (FR) 88 (Rhein- **75** gold 137) [2003 10m⁵ 12.1m 10.1d³ f12s p13g³ f16g* f14g* p16g² Nov 26] IR 24,000F, 5,000Y: unfurnished gelding: half-brother to several winners, including 1m (at 2 yrs) to 11f (Oaks d'Italia) winner Lady Bentley (by Bellypha) and 5-y-o Taras Emperor: dam, Irish 1¼m winner, half-sister to smart stayer Yawa: fair handicapper: won twice at Southwell in November: good second at Lingfield final outing, flashing tail: stays 2m: acts on all-weather, unraced on extremes of going on turf. *W. Jarvis*

MACCHIATO 2 br.f. (Feb 3) Inchinor 119 – Tereyna 58 (Terimon 124) [2003 5g 6m **59** 8.1g⁶ 8m 10f² Sep 30] 9,000Y: leggy filly: second foal: dam, maiden who stayed 15f, half-sister to smart performer up to 1½m Jack Jennings: modest maiden: will stay at least 1½m: acts on firm going. *R. F. Johnson Houghton*

MACEO (GER) 9 ch.g. Acatenango (GER) 127 – Metropolitan Star (USA) 84 (Lyp- **66** hard (USA) 132) [2003 –: 14.1m⁶ Oct 4] good-topped gelding: fair hurdler: lightly raced on Flat nowadays, fair form when sixth in handicap only 9-y-o start: stays 1¾m: acts on soft and good to firm ground. *Mrs M. Reveley*

MA CHERIE 3 b.f. Hernando (FR) 127 – Chere Amie (USA) 75 (Mr Prospector **57** (USA)) [2003 10m⁴ 11.8m 12.1m³ 14g 10.1g⁴ f9.4g⁶ Aug 15] leggy filly: third foal: half-sister to 4-y-o Traveller's Tale: dam, French 1¼m winner, closely related to US Grade 2 7f winner Esteemed Friend: modest maiden: stays 1½m: raced only on good/good to firm ground on turf. *P. W. D'Arcy*

MACHINIST (IRE) 3 br.c. Machiavellian (USA) 123 – Athene (IRE) 83 (Rousillon **88** (USA) 133) [2003 82p: 10g 7g⁴ 8m Aug 9] leggy, useful-looking colt: useful performer: best effort when fourth of 22 to Resonate in ladies handicap at Ascot second start, faring best of those who helped force strong pace: should stay 1m: acts on polytrack, raced only on good/good to firm ground on turf: sold 18,500 gns. *Sir Michael Stoute*

MACHIVENTA 2 b.f. (Apr 16) First Trump 118 – Jomel Amou (IRE) (Ela-Mana- **80** Mou 132) [2003 7m* 8f² 7g* 7m 8m Sep 25] 900Y: sturdy filly: fifth foal: sister to 5f (at 2 yrs) and 1m winner Cautious Joe: dam Irish 1¼m/1½m winner: fairly useful performer: won maiden in July and nursery in September, both at Folkestone: well below form in nurseries after: stays 1m: acts on firm going. *M. G. Quinlan*

MACHRIHANISH 3 b.g. Groom Dancer (USA) 128 – Goodwood Lass (IRE) 71 **– §** (Alzao (USA) 117) [2003 56?: 8m⁶ 9m 9.1g 9.2g Aug 13] quite good-topped gelding: modest maiden at 2 yrs: well beaten in 2003: tried in cheekpieces: twice slowly away, and refused to race final outing. *Miss L. A. Perratt*

MACLEAN 2 b.g. (Feb 11) Machiavellian (USA) 123 – Celtic Cross 100 (Selkirk **80 p** (USA) 129) [2003 7g² Aug 10] first foal: dam, lightly-raced 7f winner, out of half-sister to smart performers Church Parade (won at 6f to 10.5f) and Castle Rising (middle-distance stayer): odds on, very green when 1½ lengths second of 10 to Boule d'Or in maiden at Leicester, slowly away and no extra near finish: subsequently gelded: will stay at least 1m: likely to do better. *Sir Michael Stoute*

MAC LOVE 2 b.g. (Jan 25) Cape Cross (IRE) 129 – My Lass 91 (Elmaamul (USA) **104** 125) [2003 5g6 5.1g2 5m3 5.1m* 5g3 5s6 5m6 5m* 5f* 6g3 5g3 5g6 5s3 6f2 6m3 6m2 Oct 25] 45,000Y: compact gelding: first foal: dam 1½m winner: useful performer: won maiden at Nottingham in April and nurseries at Haydock and Kempton in August: placed in listed events/nursery last 4 starts: stays 6f: acts on firm going: sometimes early to post: tough and consistent: sold 75,000 gns. *M. R. Channon*

MACMILLAN 3 b.g. Machiavellian (USA) 123 – Mill On The Floss 117 (Mill Reef **68** (USA) 141) [2003 10g3 11.8m2 12g3 p16g5 p12g Jul 23] 250,000Y: smallish, good-bodied gelding: half-brother to several winners, including smart but untrustworthy stayer Bosham Mill (by Nashwan): dam 7f (at 2 yrs) and 1½m winner: fair maiden: stays 1½m, seemingly not 2m: tried tongue tied: showed signs of temperament: joined C. Mann, then sold 5,500 gns. *B. J. Meehan*

MACONDO (IRE) 3 b.c. Dr Devious (IRE) 127 – Dreaming Spires 64 (Sadler's **–** Wells (USA) 132) [2003 8m a8g Nov 9] IR 12,000F, IR 7,000Y: half-brother to 3 winners, including 4-y-o Sole Solero: dam soundly beaten after debut: tailed off both starts (left D. Nicholls after debut). *F. Guerra, Spain*

MAC'S ELAN 3 b.c. Darshaan 133 – Elabella (Ela-Mana-Mou 132) [2003 8.3d Aug **–** 18] 6,000Y: half-brother to 3 winners, including useful 5f/6f (latter at 2 yrs) winner Espartero (by Ballad Rock), later 1m winner in USA, and 1½m winner Typographer (by Never So Bold): dam unraced: 16/1, last of 9 in maiden at Windsor. *W. A. O'Gorman*

MAC'S TALISMAN (IRE) 3 ch.c. Hector Protector (USA) 124 – Inherent Magic **75** (IRE) 95 (Magical Wonder (USA) 125) [2003 69p: f6g3 p7g f7g* f7s6 f7g2 6g4 7m 7m4 7g3 6m2 6f p7g f6g3 Oct 16] sturdy colt: fair performer: won maiden at Southwell in January: mostly creditable efforts after: effective at 6f/7f: acts on all-weather, raced only on good ground or firmer on turf: effective blinkered or not: tried tongue tied: has raced freely. *W. A. O'Gorman*

MAC THE KNIFE (IRE) 2 b.c. (Apr 24) Daggers Drawn (USA) 114 – Icefern 88 **80** (Moorestyle 137) [2003 5g* 5.2m2 5g4 5.1g3 6.1g4 6d2 5.2m Jul 19] 21,000Y: compact, well-made colt: half-brother to several winners, including useful 1m winner Iamus (by Most Welcome) and 1997 2-y-o 5f winner Kettlesing (by Mujadil): dam sprinter: fairly useful performer: won maiden at Doncaster in March: in frame in minor events after: reportedly lame final start: will probably prove best at 5f/6f: acts on good to firm and good to soft going: sometimes slowly away/races freely. *R. Hannon*

MADAAR (USA) 4 b.g. Spinning World (USA) 130 – Mur Taasha (USA) 108 (River- **54** man (USA) 131) [2003 66: p10g 7.5m5 8m 8.3g p10g 7m6 8m3 10m3 8.3m 8.1g 8m3 8f 9.1d3 11.5m Oct 21] modest maiden: barely stays 1¼m: acts on firm and good to soft ground: effective visored or not: often slowly away: sold 2,000 gns. *P. D. Evans*

MADAEH (USA) 2 b. or br.f. (Mar 25) Swain (IRE) 134 – Tamgeed (USA) 66 (Wood- **97** man (USA) 126) [2003 7g3 7m* 7m* 7m5 Oct 4] strong filly: first foal: dam, maiden (best effort at 1¼m), out of close relation to Mehthaaf and Elnadim: useful performer: won maiden at Lingfield in July and nursery at Goodwood in August: best effort when 2¾ lengths fifth of 9 to Top Romance in listed race at Newmarket: should be suited by 1¼m/1½m. *J. L. Dunlop*

MADALYAR (IRE) 4 b.g. Darshaan 133 – Madaniyya (USA) 96 (Shahrastani (USA) **–** 135) [2003 90: 10m 11.9m 12m May 30] leggy, angular gelding: fourth foal: half-brother to 1997 2-y-o 7f winner Madjamila (by Doyoun): dam Irish 9f/1¼m winner: fairly useful performer in Ireland at 3 yrs, winning twice: left J. Oxx 50,000 gns, well held in 2003: stays 13f: acts on firm and soft going: effective blinkered or not: has taken strong hold. *Jonjo O'Neill*

MADAME KOMET 2 b.f. (Mar 13) Komaite (USA) – Sky Fighter 43 (Hard Fought **–** 125) [2003 5.1m Apr 21] 800Y: sixth foal: sister to 1996 5-y-o 7f winner Komasta and 7f (at 2 yrs)/1m winner Sandmoor Tartan: dam maiden who stayed 1½m: 25/1, behind in Nottingham seller. *Mrs S. A. Liddiard*

MADAME MARIE (IRE) 3 b.f. Desert King (IRE) 129 – Les Trois Lamas (IRE) **55** (Machiavellian (USA) 123) [2003 63: 9.7g4 8.3d 7.1m 10f 11m3 Jun 27] modest maiden: should stay 1½m: acts on soft going: slowly away last 2 outings. *S. Dow*

MADAME MARJOU (IRE) 3 b.f. Marju (IRE) 127 – Sudeley 65 (Dancing Brave **72** (USA) 140) [2003 10m4 10f5 10f 8m6 10m6 11.1m6 Aug 19] IR 150,000Y: compact, quite attractive filly: fifth living foal: half-sister to useful Irish 2000 2-y-o 7f winner Katherine

Seymour (by Green Desert): dam, 11.5f winner, half-sister to Coronation Cup winner Quiet Fling from very good family: fair maiden: stays 1¼m: swished tail in paddock and early to post fifth start: sold 14,000 gns in December. *M. R. Channon*

MADAME MAXI   9 ch.m. Ron's Victory (USA) 129 – New Pastures (Formidable **66** (USA) 125) [2003 77, a–: 7m 8.3g 8.1g⁴ 8m 8.1m 7d⁶ 8.3g³ 7.1m 8.1d Aug 29] angular mare: shows knee action: fair handicapper: effective at 7f/1m: acts on firm and soft going (no form on fibresand): tried blinkered/visored: often races up with pace. *H. S. Howe*

MADAME MONICA   3 ch.f. Paris House 123 – Merry Molly (Deploy 131) [2003 6f – f7g 7f 10m Aug 30] fifth foal: dam last in seller only start: no form. *Mrs K. Walton*

MADAME ROUX   5 b.m. Rudimentary (USA) 118 – Foreign Mistress (Darshaan 133) – [2003 58d: 5.3f 6m 5m 5g Jul 17] angular mare: maiden: well beaten in 2003. *C. Drew*

MADAMOISELLE JONES   3 b.f. Emperor Jones (USA) 119 – Tiriana (Common **76** Grounds 118) [2003 52: 6g 8.3g³ 8g 9m 7m³ 8.1m* 8.1m³ 8.3m⁴ 8.3g* 8.1m p10g Oct 15] close-coupled filly: fair handicapper: won at Chepstow in June and Windsor in August: stays 1m: acts on soft ground, good to firm and polytrack. *H. S. Howe*

MAD CAREW (USA)   4 ch.g. Rahy (USA) 115 – Poppy Carew (IRE) 110 (Danehill **82** (USA) 126) [2003 –: p10g⁴ p10g* p10g p10g p8g* p8g⁶ 8.5m⁴ 10d p8g² 8m 10.1m 10f 10.1g⁴ 8m* 8f³ 10d² p10g² Nov 29] sturdy gelding: fairly useful performer: won minor event in February and claimer in March, both at Lingfield, and handicap at Goodwood in September: effective at 1m/1¼m: acts on good to firm going, good to soft and polytrack: tried in blinkers and cheekpieces: sometimes hangs/carries head awkwardly. *G. L. Moore*

MADDIE'S A JEM   3 b.f. Emperor Jones (USA) 119 – Royal Orchid (IRE) 74 (Shal- **72** ford (IRE) 124§) [2003 68p: 6g 5g² 5m² 6m* 6m 5d² 6g p6g³ f6g⁴ f6g⁶ p8g Dec 2] deep-girthed filly: fair performer: won maiden at Yarmouth in August: effective at 5f/6f: acts all-weather, soft and good to firm ground: sometimes slowly away, and all but refused to race fifth outing. *J. R. Jenkins*

MADE IN JAPAN (JPN)   3 b.g. Barathea (IRE) 127 – Darrery 98 (Darshaan 133) **88** [2003 82p: 9d 10.2m³ 11m 11.9f³ 11.7f⁶ 14d⁵ p12g² 11.9f² p12g⁶ Oct 27] fairly useful handicapper: mostly creditable efforts in 2003, short-headed at Brighton eighth start: stays easy 1¾m: acts on polytrack, firm and good to soft going: usually tongue tied: ran poorly in cheekpieces: carries head awkwardly: sometimes slowly away: sold 35,000 gns, joined P. Hobbs. *M. A. Magnusson*

MADELINE BASSETT (IRE)   5 b.m. Kahyasi 130 – Impressive Lady 98 (Mr **89** Fluorocarbon 126) [2003 87, a93: p12g a8g 13g 9.8m³ 12s³ 9.8g⁵ a12g a10f* a12f a12g Dec 30] smallish mare: fluent mover: fairly useful performer: sold from G. Butler 6,200 gns after running poorly on reappearance: fifth in listed race at Taby sixth start and won minor event there in November: effective at 1¼m/1½m: acts on soft going, good to firm and dirt/polytrack: tried visored: waited with: has found little. *Madeleine Smith, Sweden*

MADHAHIR (IRE)   3 b.c. Barathea (IRE) 127 – Gharam (USA) 108 (Green Dancer **72** (USA) 132) [2003 8.5m 10f⁶ 12g 12g 14.1m⁴ 11.5g 16.1m⁶ f16.2g² f16.2s Dec 6] good-topped colt: half-brother to several winners, including useful 1997 2-y-o 7f winner Elshamms (by Zafonic) and smart performer up to 2½m Shaya (by Nashwan): dam, 2-y-o 6f winner, third in Poule d'Essai des Pouliches and Ribblesdale Stakes: fair maiden: left A. Stewart 25,000 gns after third start: stays 2m: acts on fibresand, raced only on good going or firmer on turf: has worn cheekpieces. *C. A. Dwyer*

MADIBA   4 b.g. Emperor Jones (USA) 119 – Priluki 65 (Lycius (USA) 124) [2003 81: **70** p16g⁵ 14.4d 16.2m 13.3m 13.3m 12m⁵ 12d f12s⁴ p13g p13g Dec 29] leggy, useful-looking gelding: fair maiden: mostly well held in 2003, leaving S. Dow after seventh start: stays easy 2m: acts on soft going, firm and all-weather: tried visored/blinkered. *P. Howling*

MADIES PRIDE (IRE)   5 b.m. Fayruz 116 – June Lady (Junius (USA) 124) [2003 **56** 58: 5d 5m Jun 2] angular mare: modest handicapper: best at 5f: acted on good to firm and good to soft going: sometimes looked wayward: dead. *J. J. Quinn*

MADISON AVENUE (GER)   6 b.g. Mondrian (GER) 125 – Madly Noble (GER) – (Irish River (FR) 131) [2003 14.1g p16g 12.5s⁴ Oct 14] ex-German gelding: first foal: dam 6f winner in Germany: useful performer at best for C. Von Der Recke, winning 5 times up to 15f: well held in handicaps in 2003: won over hurdles in between. *T. M. Jones*

MAD MAURICE   2 ch.g. (Apr 27) Grand Lodge (USA) 125 – Amarella (FR) (Balleroy **57 p** (USA) 115) [2003 6d Aug 18] 25,000Y: first foal: dam, French 1m/9f winner, half-sister to useful stayer Kristal's Paradise: 12/1, considerately handled when well held in maiden at Windsor: gelded after: will stay at least 1m: likely to do better. *J. Noseda*

MAD MICK MEESON 3 b.g. Whittingham (IRE) 104 – Meeson Times 71 (Enchantment 115) [2003 6g⁴ 7d⁵ 5.2m 5m⁵ 6m 6m⁴ p7g f6g p6g⁴ p7g Dec 29] 20,000Y: third foal: half-brother to fairly useful 2000 2-y-o 5f winner Mise En Scene (by Lugana Beach): dam 5f and (including at 2 yrs) 6f winner: modest maiden: stays easy 7f: acts on polytrack, unraced on extremes of going on turf: tried visored/tongue tied. *G. B. Balding* **63 a51**

MADRASEE 5 b.m. Beveled (USA) – Pendona 72 (Blue Cashmere 129) [2003 79: p6g² p5g² p5g p5g p6g 5m³ 6m 5g 6m⁵ 6m 5d² 5m³ 5.3f* 6m 5d² 6m* Oct 23] fairly useful handicapper on turf, fair on all-weather: better than ever in 2003, winning at Brighton in August and October: effective at 5f/6f: acts on firm going, soft and polytrack: usually races prominently. *L. Montague Hall* **84 a74**

MAEDANCE 3 br.f. Groom Dancer (USA) 128 – Maestrale (Top Ville 129) [2003 73: 8f⁴ 11g 12f³ 12g³ 12g⁴ Jul 30] good-topped filly: fairly useful maiden handicapper: stays 1½m: raced only on good ground or firmer: seems highly-strung and often races freely. *G. B. Balding* **83**

MAFRUZ 4 ch.g. Hamas (IRE) 125§ – Braari (USA) 97 (Gulch (USA)) [2003 75: 8m³ 8.3d⁶ 8d 7m 6.9f⁶ 7.9m Sep 7] good-topped gelding: fair performer: well below form last 3 starts: stays 1m: acts on soft and good to firm going: tried blinkered/in cheekpieces. *R. A. Fahey* **76 d**

MAGANDA (IRE) 2 b.f. (Feb 24) Sadler's Wells (USA) 132 – Minnie Habit (Habitat 134) [2003 8m² 8g Nov 1] neat filly: sister to 2001 2-y-o 9f winner On The Nile and 1m (including at 2 yrs) winner In The Limelight (both useful and in Ireland), closely related to very smart 9f (at 2 yrs) to 1½m winner Kutub (by In The Wings) and half-sister to 2 winners: dam Irish 9f winner: fairly useful form in maiden at Yarmouth (¾-length second to Doctrine, hung left) and listed event at Newmarket (raced freely): bred to be suited by 1¼m/1½m: should do better and win a race or 2. *M. A. Jarvis* **84 p**

MAGARI 2 b.f. (Mar 28) Royal Applause 124 – Thatcher's Era (IRE) 57 (Never So Bold 135) [2003 7m³ Oct 1] lengthy filly: third foal: dam, maiden who stayed 1½m, out of sister to very smart sprinter Primo Dominie: 20/1, 8½ lengths third of 13 to Redwood Rocks in maiden at Newcastle, held up and not knocked about: should stay 1m: sure to progress. *J. G. Given* **59 p**

MAGELTA 6 b.g. Magic Ring (IRE) 115 – Pounelta 91 (Tachypous 128) [2003 61: f9.4g p8g⁴ a10.5g a8g² Aug 23] big, useful-looking gelding: modest performer: left R. Cowell after second outing (wore cheekpieces): stays 1m: acts on good to firm going, good to soft and all-weather: usually tongue tied in Britain, visored (below form) final 5-y-o start. *E. J. Creighton, Spain* **52**

MAGENTA RISING (IRE) 3 ch.f. College Chapel 122 – Fashion Queen (Chilibang 120) [2003 79: f8g³ f8.5g* p10g f9.4g⁶ p7g 8.3g⁵ 7.1m 6.1d 7.1g 6.1m² f7g f9.4g Oct 20] fair performer: won handicap at Wolverhampton in January: below form after, leaving P. D'Arcy 6,500 gns following fifth start: stays 8.5f: acts on fibresand, unraced on extremes of going on turf: tongue tied on debut: none too reliable. *D. Burchell* **79 d**

MAGGIE MAQUETTE 3 ch.f. Atraf 116 – Bronze Maquette (IRE) 66 (Ahonoora 122) [2003 f7g p6g Dec 17] second foal: dam 1¼m winner: well held in maidens. *W. S. Kittow* **–**

MAGGIES CHOICE (IRE) 2 b.f. (May 11) Mujadil (USA) 119 – Big Buyer (USA) 67 (Quest For Fame 127) [2003 5m⁶ 7m⁴ 7m f7f* 7m 7m 7m 8.5g p8g Nov 22] IR 5,200F, 8,000 2-y-o: angular filly: second foal: dam, ran 3 times (should have stayed beyond 1¼m), granddaughter of Irish Oaks winner Regal Exception: modest performer: won seller at Wolverhampton in July: showed nothing after: should stay 1m. *N. P. Littmoden* **53 d**

MAGGIE'S PET 6 b.m. Minshaanshu Amad (USA) 91§ – Run Fast For Gold (Deep Run 119) [2003 57: f11g⁴ 11.5g f8.5s f8s f8g³ f8g⁶ p8g Dec 6] modest maiden: effective at 1m to 11f: acts on fibresand, little form on turf: tried tongue tied. *K. Bell* **? a56**

MAGHANIM 3 b.c. Nashwan (USA) 135 – Azdihaar (USA) 81 (Mr Prospector (USA)) [2003 107: 8m Apr 17] lengthy, quite attractive colt: useful form at 2 yrs: steadily to post, last in Craven Stakes at Newmarket only 3-y-o start: should stay 1m: raced only on good/good to firm going: stays in training. *J. L. Dunlop* **–**

MAGHAS (IRE) 9 ch.g. Lahib (USA) 129 – Rawaabe (USA) 87 (Nureyev (USA) 131) [2003 48: f6g Jan 13] poor performer: well beaten only 9-y-o start: blinkered earlier in career. *J. M. Bradley* **–**

MAGICAL DAY 4 ch.f. Halling (USA) 133 – Ahla 90 (Unfuwain (USA) 131) [2003 – §
54§: f12s Sep 20] rather leggy filly: modest maiden: well held only 4-y-o start: untrustworthy. *W. G. M. Turner*

MAGICAL FIELD 5 ch.m. Deploy 131 – Ash Glade (Nashwan (USA) 135) [2003 59: 57
14.1m⁴ 16m³ Jul 6] big mare: modest maiden handicapper: stays 2m: acts on polytrack
and good to firm ground: usually held up. *Mrs M. Reveley*

MAGICAL FOOL 4 b.g. Magic Ring (IRE) 115 – Vera's First (IRE) 69 (Exodal –
(USA)) [2003 f8s f6g f7s 5m 7f 8f 10.1m 7m Jul 9] compact, workmanlike gelding: little
worthwhile form: tried blinkered/in cheekpieces. *N. Wilson*

MAGICAL GIFT 2 b.f. (May 19) Groom Dancer (USA) 128 – Coffee Ice 92 (Primo 62
Dominie 121) [2003 p8g⁴ p7g⁶ Dec 17] sixth foal: half-sister to winning sprinter in USA
by Twining: dam, 2-y-o 5f winner, later sprint winner in USA: better effort at Lingfield
(modest form) when fourth to Ascertain in maiden, starting slowly: not sure to stay much
beyond 1m. *D. W. P. Arbuthnot*

MAGICALLY 3 ch.f. Ali-Royal (IRE) 127 – Meadmore Magic 68 (Mansingh (USA) –
120) [2003 5f 5m 5m Aug 15] 500Y: fifth foal: half-sister to useful 1996 2-y-o 5f/6f
winner Magical Times (by Timeless Times), later successful in USA, and to 2000 2-y-o
1m winner Chevening Lodge (by Eagle Eyed): dam 2-y-o 5f winner: no form: tried in
cheekpieces. *C. J. Teague*

MAGICAL MIMI 2 b.f. (May 6) Magic Ring (IRE) 115 – Naval Dispatch (Slip 75
Anchor 136) [2003 6m⁵ 6.1f* 6m³ 7g Oct 25] 2,000Y: useful-looking filly: second foal:
dam, 6f and 1m winner in Norway, out of half-sister to dam of very smart 7f/1m winner
Decorated Hero: fair performer: won maiden at Nottingham in September: seemed to run
creditably in listed contest at Newbury final start: should stay 1m. *N. P. Littmoden*

MAGICAL RIVER 6 ch.m. Lahib (USA) 129 – Awtaar (USA) 67 (Lyphard (USA) –
132) [2003 5.7f⁶ 7.1d 6m Aug 11] poor handicapper in 2001: little form at 6 yrs: sometimes slowly away. *I. A. Wood*

MAGIC AMIGO 2 ch.g. (Apr 27) Zilzal (USA) 137 – Emaline (FR) 105 (Empery 75
(USA) 128) [2003 6g 7m⁵ 6g⁴ 6m² 7g Sep 13] 11,000Y: tall, leggy gelding: half-brother
to several winners, including smart 1991 2-y-o 5f winner Magic Ring (by Green Desert)
and 11.5f to 2m winner Monarda (by Pharly): dam French 2-y-o 7f winner: fair maiden:
second of 16 to Soliniki at Ascot, best effort: should stay 1m. *J. R. Jenkins*

MAGIC AMOUR 5 ch.g. Sanglamore (USA) 126 – Rakli 84 (Warning 136) [2003 71
57: 7m³ 7.1g 7m² 7m 7m*⁻ 8.2m*⁻ 7m² 8.1m 8.2f² 8.2d Nov 6] strong, lengthy gelding:
fair handicapper: won at Folkestone in July and Nottingham in August: stays 8.2f: acts on
firm going, well held on softer than good: often makes running. *Ian Williams*

MAGIC ARROW (USA) 7 b.g. Defensive Play (USA) 118 – Magic Blue (USA) –
(Cure The Blues (USA)) [2003 –: f16g f16.2g Feb 7] of little account nowadays: tried
visored. *Ian Emmerson*

MAGIC CHARM 5 b.m. Magic Ring (IRE) 115 – Loch Clair (IRE) 53 (Lomond 47
(USA) 128) [2003 –, a44: f9.4g³ f9.4s⁴ f9.4s f12s⁶ 12f⁵ 10.3g⁶ 11.9f* 11.9f* 12d 10d⁵
Oct 31] angular mare: poor handicapper: won twice at Brighton (first a selling event) in
August: stays 1½m: acts on all-weather and firm ground, below form on softer than good:
often visored/blinkered at 4 yrs: races freely. *A. G. Newcombe*

MAGIC FLIGHT 3 b.f. Lear Fan (USA) 130 – Carpet of Leaves (USA) (Green –
Forest (USA) 134) [2003 10f Jun 25] second foal: dam, ran twice in France, half-sister to
smart French performers Glorify (up to 15f) and Doree (sprinting 2-y-o) and to dams of
Ryafan (by Lear Fan) and Tillerman: 14/1 and very green, always behind in maiden at
Kempton: sold 800 gns in December. *J. G. Given*

MAGIC GLADE 4 b.g. Magic Ring (IRE) 115 – Ash Glade (Nashwan (USA) 135) 81
[2003 98p: p6g f5g Dec 9] useful performer at 3 yrs: well below best both starts for new
stable in 2003: best form at 6f: acts on fibresand, raced only on good going or firmer on
turf. *C. R. Dore*

MAGIC GREY 8 gr.h. Petong 126 – Miss Primula 81 (Dominion 123) [2003 a6g² 7d⁴ ?
7s² 6.5s² 7g² 7s⁵ 6g⁶ f6g⁵ Dec 19] seventh foal: half-brother to 3 winning sprinters,
including useful Tinker Amelia (by Damister): dam sprinter: fairly useful performer at
best: won minor events at Dortmund and Dusseldorf and handicap at Dusseldorf in first
half of 2002: well below best in seller at Southwell final start: stays 7f: acts on heavy
going and sand: usually wears blinkers. *T. H. Hansen, Germany*

MAGIC HANNE   4 ch.f. Magic Ring (IRE) 115 – Sunfleet 59 (Red Sunset 120) [2003   –
55: f7s⁶ f9.4g Feb 14] rather leggy filly: modest maiden: well beaten in 2003: tried in
cheekpieces. *G. C. H. Chung*

MAGIC MAMMA'S TOO   3 b.g. Magic Ring (IRE) 115 – Valona Valley (IRE)   70
(Reprimand 122) [2003 58: f7g² f7s⁴ f6g² f8s³ f7g³ f6g⁴ 8m² 8g³ 7.9g 8m² 7f 8m⁶ 8m⁴ 7g
7.1f³ f8s⁴ f8g³ f8g² f8g² f8g⁶ Dec 19] rather leggy gelding: modest maiden handicapper:
in frame 15 times in 2003: stays 1m: acts on fibresand and firm going: effective with or
without cheekpieces. *T. D. Barron*

MAGIC MISTRESS   4 b.f. Magic Ring (IRE) 115 – Sight'n Sound 63 (Chief Singer   89
131) [2003 79: 8.3d 8m⁴ 9g* 9f⁴ 10m* 10m⁵ 13.3m⁵ 10.5d² 12f⁴ Oct 12] tall filly: fairly
useful handicapper: won at Sandown in June and Ascot in July: best at 1¼m/1½m: acts
on firm and soft ground: often races prominently: reliable: sold 42,000 gns. *S. C. Williams*

MAGIC MUSIC (IRE)   4 b.f. Magic Ring (IRE) 115 – Chiming Melody 71 (Cure   82
The Blues (USA)) [2003 77: 6.1g⁴ 6.1g² 6.1d 6m* 6m* 6d⁴ 6m 6f² Oct 10] good-topped
filly: fairly useful handicapper: won at Leicester and Doncaster in June: raced mainly at
6f: acts on any going: usually races prominently. *Mrs H. Dalton*

MAGIC MYTH (IRE)   3 b.f. Revoque (IRE) 122 – Family At War (USA) 71 (Explod-   80 §
ent (USA)) [2003 81: 5d⁴ 6d 5d 6m 6g 7m⁵ 6d⁵ 7d Nov 8] quite good-topped filly: fairly
useful handicapper: stays 6f: acts on heavy going: tried blinkered/in cheekpieces: has
been slowly away/raced freely: unreliable. *T. D. Easterby*

MAGICO   2 ch.c. (Apr 4) Magic Ring (IRE) 115 – Silken Dalliance 91 (Rambo Dancer   54
(CAN) 107) [2003 6m 5m 6m p7g Dec 10] quite good-topped colt: first foal: dam 6f and
1m winner: modest maiden: should stay at least 7f. *A. M. Balding*

MAGIC RAINBOW   8 b.g. Magic Ring (IRE) 115 – Blues Indigo 103 (Music Boy   74 §
124) [2003 73, a89: p7g² f6g p6g² p7g⁴ 5.7f³ Mar 31] leggy gelding: poor mover: fair
performer: effective at 5f to easy 7f: acted on all-weather, firm and soft going: sometimes
started slowly: wasn't one to trust: dead. *M. L. W. Bell*

MAGIC RED   3 ch.g. Magic Ring (IRE) 115 – Jacquelina (USA) 66 (Private Account   –
(USA)) [2003 71d: p10g 11.8m 8g 8d 10m Aug 20] big, rather leggy gelding: disappointing maiden: tried in headgear. *M. J. Ryan*

MAGIC STING   2 ch.c. (Apr 19) Magic Ring (IRE) 115 – Ground Game 95 (Gildoran   67
123) [2003 7s⁵ Oct 29] 4,000F: first foal: dam 1m (at 2 yrs) and 1¼m winner: 40/1, 7½
lengths fifth of 13 to Singing Poet in maiden at Yarmouth, not knocked about: should stay
1m. *M. L. W. Bell*

MAGIC STONE   3 br.g. Magic Ring (IRE) 115 – Ridgewood Ruby (IRE) 77 (Indian   –
Ridge 123) [2003 –: p6g Apr 5] little form. *A. Charlton*

MAGIC TRICK   4 b.g. Magic Ring (IRE) 115 – Les Amis 70 (Alzao (USA) 117) [2003   –
76: 7.1g 7g 6m Jul 23] big, well-made gelding: fair handicapper at 3 yrs: well beaten in
2003: tried in blinkers/cheekpieces. *Mrs P. N. Dutfield*

MAGIC WARRIOR   3 b.g. Magic Ring (IRE) 115 – Clarista (USA) 67 (Riva Ridge   58
(USA)) [2003 67: 6g⁵ 8.2g p6g p7g⁵ p8g p10g⁵ Dec 20] fair performer on all-weather,   a64
modest on turf: left S. Keightley after second start: best form up to 1m: acts on polytrack,
best effort on turf on good going. *J. C. Fox*

MAGISTRETTI (USA)   3 b.c. Diesis 133 – Ms. Strike Zone (USA) (Deputy   124
Minister (CAN)) [2003 96: 9m* 10.4m* 12m 10g² 10.4m² Aug 19]
Neville Callaghan saddled Michael Tabor's first winner as an owner in a
seller at Haydock in 1975. The quality of horses that Tabor has owned or part
owned, mainly in partnership with the Magniers, has improved markedly since
such humble beginnings, the Tabor colours having been carried to classic victory
and being seen regularly in top races. The majority of horses in which Tabor has an
interest are trained at Ballydoyle, but he has continued to patronise the Callaghan
stable. Danehill Dancer and Danetime, both of whom are by Danehill and are now
sires, were notable performers for the partnership in the 'nineties. Danehill Dancer
was a dual Group 1 winner as a two-year-old, winning the Phoenix Stakes at
Leopardstown and the National Stakes at the Curragh, and Danetime won the
Stewards' Cup at Goodwood before being placed in pattern races, including the
Haydock Park Sprint Cup and the July Cup. In the latest season, Callaghan had the
Tabor three-year-old Magistretti, a horse rated more highly than either Danehill
Dancer or Danetime.

Magistretti was underestimated for much of the season, but Callaghan always held a very high opinion of him and clearly felt vindicated when Magistretti ran second to Falbrav in the Juddmonte International at York on his final start of the year. 'All the doubters can't say much now,' said Callaghan afterwards. The fact that the trainer felt he had to address the 'doubters' shows the pre-conceived notion some in the media have of the profile that a good horse should have. Magistretti was, in fact, beaten on all three of his starts as a two-year-old after his debut, but he showed himself a useful juvenile nonetheless. He blotted his copybook on his final start that year, when stepped up in grade in the Royal Lodge, but clearly couldn't have been right, becoming increasingly on edge during the preliminaries and going too freely both to post and in the race. Magistretti left his two-year-old form well behind when making a winning reappearance in the listed Feilden Stakes at Newmarket in April. More relaxed beforehand and more tractable in the race than at Ascot, Magistretti put up a smart performance to beat Dunhill Star by a head, with eight lengths back to third-placed Excelsius. Magistretti missed his next intended outing in the Classic Trial at Sandown due to a bout of coughing, which came during the time that equine flu was still prevalent in Newmarket. He was saddled instead for the Tote Dante Stakes at York, in which he started at 8/1 with Dunhill Star at the head of the betting at 11/4. Magistretti not only confirmed placings with Dunhill Star at York but beat him by a wider margin, leading close home to beat Tuning Fork by half a length, with the favourite a length and a quarter further back in third.

Traditionally, the Dante is the best of the home trials, over more than a mile, for the Derby but, for a second successive year, the race had little impact on the betting for the race and, like Moon Ballad the winner the previous year, Magistretti went off at 20/1 at Epsom. In a maximum field of twenty, Magistretti got little chance to prove his worth in the Derby, his rider forced to snatch up as the field bunched at the top of the hill resulting in Magistretti being knocked right back to the rear before running on to finish ninth behind Kris Kin. Callaghan kept Magistretti to Group 1 company after the Derby. He showed that he was worth his place in that sphere when second to Vespone, beaten a length and a half, in the Grand Prix de Paris at Longchamp later in the month, shaping a bit better than the

Tote Dante Stakes, York—Magistretti catches Tuning Fork (rail) near the finish;
Dunhill Star (behind winner), Songlark (behind runner-up) and Graikos (left) are next

result, with the winner able to dictate the pace and Magistretti faring much the best of those who came from behind. Withdrawn from the King George VI and Queen Elizabeth Stakes on the morning of the race with a vet's certificate, Magistretti took on the older horses for the first time on his next start in the International at York. In a field of ten and, with Kieren Fallon back on board for the sixth time in nine races, Magistretti produced a very smart performance to finish second to Falbrav, beaten two lengths. Though Magistretti was flattered to finish so close to Falbrav, his timefigure provided confirmation of the merit of the performance. Callaghan promptly announced that Magistretti would be put away for the year. A big, strong colt, with some scope to progress again from three to four, Magistretti will not need to improve much to be a force at the highest level in 2004 at a mile and a quarter and a mile and a half.

Magistretti (USA) (b.c. 2000)	Diesis (ch 1980)	Sharpen Up (ch 1969)	Atan
			Rocchetta
		Doubly Sure (b 1971)	Reliance II
			Soft Angels
	Ms. Strike Zone (USA) (b 1994)	Deputy Minister (b 1979)	Vice Regent
			Mint Copy
		Bat Prospector (b 1987)	Mr Prospector
			Batucada

Magistretti is the second foal of Ms. Strike Zone, and not the first as was stated in *Racehorses of 2002*. He was bought as a foal for 150,000 dollars at the Keeneland Sale and re-sold for IR 170,000 guineas as a yearling at the Goffs Orby & Challenge Sale. Ms. Strike Zone was a winner in America at eight and a half furlongs. Her dam Bat Prospector won at a mile in America and is a sister to the

Mr M. Tabor's "Magistretti"

very smart performer at up to a mile and a half Damister. There are some parallels between Damister and Magistretti. Both won the Dante and ran in the Derby and International at York, Damister finishing third to Slip Anchor in the Derby and filling the same position behind Triptych as a four-year-old in 1986 in the latter. Magistretti's great grandam Batucada was the champion two- and three-year-old in Mexico, winning all eleven of her starts in that country. As a five-year-old, Batucada was transferred to America, where she won five of her twenty-seven starts. Magistretti's wins have come on good to firm and good to soft going, but connections are of the opinion that he is best on ground firmer than good. *N. A. Callaghan*

MAGNETIC POLE 2 b.c. (Mar 5) Machiavellian (USA) 123 – Clear Attraction **88 P**
(USA) (Lear Fan (USA) 130) [2003 8m³ Oct 14] well-made colt: third foal: half-brother to fairly useful 1¼m winner Purple Heather (by Rahy): dam once-raced half-sister to Height of Fashion, the dam of Nashwan, Unfuwain and 5-y-o Nayef: 12/1, 2 lengths third of 11 to Muhaymin in maiden at Leicester, green but going on well at finish under hands and heels: will be well suited by 1¼m/1½m: open to considerable improvement, and sure to win races. *Sir Michael Stoute*

MAGNIFICO 4 b.g. Mark of Esteem (IRE) 137 – Blush Rambler (IRE) (Blushing **–**
Groom (FR) 131) [2003 103: 10f 10m Jul 19] strong, quite attractive gelding: useful performer at 3 yrs: very lightly raced: last in listed races in 2003. *Sir Michael Stoute*

MAGRITTE (IRE) 2 b.c. (Mar 9) Sadler's Wells (USA) 132 – Ionian Sea (Slip **112 p**
Anchor 136) [2003 7.5v* 8m³ Oct 25]
    In an odd way, had he been alive, Rene Magritte might have enjoyed his namesake's defeat in the Racing Post Trophy at Doncaster in October. There would have been little to excite the surrealist Belgian painter in Magritte's appearance in the line-up beforehand. A highly promising, lightly-raced colt, trained by Aidan O'Brien, and already touted as a potential Derby winner, he was trying to follow in the footsteps of his stable-companions High Chaparral and Brian Boru, the winners of the Doncaster race in the two previous years. Nothing to shock or surprise the onlooker there. But, as the race unfolded, all was not quite as it seemed. The pace of the race turned it into a limited test of stamina at the trip. Somewhat unexpectedly, Magritte found himself in a race which apparently didn't suit—like a fish out of water. Now, he was becoming thought provoking!
    Magritte is bred to be a middle-distance stayer and, perhaps because of his immaturity, he wasn't asked to set a more searching gallop at Doncaster. Instead, Magritte was allowed to potter along in front for six furlongs, running green and wandering when finally asked to quicken. In the circumstances, there was no disgrace in going down by three lengths to American Post, finishing a length and a quarter behind second-placed Fantastic View. Magritte drifted from an opening 2/1 to 11/4 in a field of four on good to firm ground at Doncaster. He had gone off at 11/8-on in a maiden at Tipperary over an extended seven furlongs in the mud on his debut in late-July. He revelled in the relative test of stamina that day, winning easily by five lengths. There were few more impressive performances in a maiden all season.

		Northern Dancer	Nearctic
	Sadler's Wells (USA)	(b 1961)	Natalma
	(b 1981)	Fairy Bridge	Bold Reason
Magritte (IRE)		(b 1975)	Special
(b.c. Mar 9, 2001)		Slip Anchor	Shirley Heights
	Ionian Sea	(b 1982)	Sayonara
	(b 1989)	Snow Day	Reliance II
		(b 1978)	Vindaria

    The fortunes of Magritte's dam, Ionian Sea, have turned around since she was sold at Newmarket in 1998 for 45,000 guineas. Her best foal up to that point had been the useful Groom Dancer colt Ithaca, a winner at up to twelve and a half furlongs in France, but matings with Sadler's Wells since have produced Derby runner-up The Great Gatsby as well as Magritte. Sadler's Wells was also responsible for the Derby runner-up Blue Stag and Prix du Jockey Club second Oscar, who were out of Snow Day, the dam of Ionian Sea. It is not surprising that Ionian Sea, a French listed winner by Slip Anchor, and successful at up to a mile and a half, has been a good influence for stamina, and Magritte should get better the further he tackles. An early favourite for the Derby after his debut success, he was as short as 12/1 for Epsom before his defeat at Doncaster, but is more attractively-priced again at the time of writing at around 20/1, and he is bred to get the Leger trip too. A useful-looking colt, still unfurnished, he was far from the finished article at two, still proving green in the preliminaries at Doncaster, and can only do better with time. He looks sure to figure alongside Yeats in his stable's Derby plans in the spring. Incidentally, he showed a short, unimpressive action at Doncaster. *A. P. O'Brien, Ireland*

MAHARIB (IRE)   3 b.c. Alhaarth (IRE) 126 – Diali (USA) 97 (Dayjur (USA) 137)   **117** [2003 7d² 10g² 10s* 12d* 14m* 14.6g⁴ 12d⁵ Oct 12] quite good-topped colt: third foal: dam, Irish 7f winner, closely related to top-class French miler Polish Precedent: smart performer: won maiden at Navan in April and listed race at Limerick (beat Mkuzi 2 lengths) and IAWS Curragh Cup (beat Arundel ¾ length) in June: good 4¾ lengths fourth to Brian Boru in St Leger at Doncaster in September: below form in listed race won by L'Ancresse at the Curragh final start: effective at 1½m/1¾m: acts on soft and good to firm going. *D. K. Weld, Ireland*

MAHASI (USA)   3 ch.c. Woodman (USA) 126 – Lingerie (Shirley Heights 130) [2003   **92** 10g⁴ 10g* 11m⁴ May 17] strong, angular colt: sixth foal: closely related to high-class 8.5f to 10.5f winner Shiva and very smart French 10.5f and 1½m winner Limnos (both by Hector Protector), and half-brother to 2 winners, including useful 7f and (in France) 1m winner Burning Sunset (by Caerleon): dam, French maiden, out of top-class middle-distance filly Northern Trick: fairly useful form: landed odds in maiden at Pontefract in April: well-backed favourite, good fourth to Prince Nureyev in handicap at Newbury final start, racing freely: may prove best around 1¼m. *H. R. A. Cecil*

MAHMOOM   2 ch.c. (Apr 20) Dr Fong (USA) 128 – Rohita (IRE) 94 (Waajib 121)   **94** [2003 6m² 6m* 7m* Oct 17] 170,000Y: strong, attractive colt: sixth foal: half-brother to useful 5f (at 2 yrs) and 7f winner Kalindi and fairly useful 2001 2-y-o 6f winner Addeyll (both by Efisio): dam 2-y-o 5f/6f winner: fairly useful form: landed odds in 13-runner maiden in September and 3-runner minor event (made most and rallied to beat Nephetriti Way by short head) in October, both at Newmarket: should stay 1m. *M. R. Channon*

MAIDEN TOWER   3 b.f. Groom Dancer (USA) 128 – Sawara (Danzig (USA)) [2003   **116** 8g* 8d* 8g² 8m* 9f² 8f Nov 30] second foal: dam unraced close relative to smart 1¼m/ 1½m winner Altamura and half-sister to smart middle-distance stayer Affidavit: smart performer: won listed race at Saint-Cloud in March, Prix de la Grotte at Longchamp in April and Prix de Sandringham at Chantilly (beat Acago 1½ lengths) in June: also ran well when second in Poule d'Essai des Pouliches at Longchamp (beaten a length by Musical Chimes) and Queen Elizabeth II Challenge Cup at Keeneland (lost out by a nose to Film Maker, final outing for H.-A. Pantall, France): behind in Matriarch Stakes at Hollywood final outing: stays easy 9f: acts on heavy and good to firm going: took strong hold to post at Chantilly: front runner: game and consistent. *E. Harty, USA*

MAID FOR A MONARCH   3 b.f. King's Signet (USA) 110 – Regan (USA) 60 (Lear   **–** Fan (USA) 130) [2003 –: p12g⁶ 10m 12d Jun 30] little form. *J. G. Given*

MAID FOR LIFE (IRE)   3 b.f. Entrepreneur 123 – Arandora Star (USA) (Sagace   **66** (FR) 135) [2003 10d 8m⁴ 8.3g⁶ f8.5g⁴ Nov 15] third foal: half-sister to 2 winners in France, including 1m winner Arachne (by Shining Steel): dam, French 1¼m winner, half-sister to very smart Hong Kong 1m/1¼m performer Olympic Express (formerly smart performer in Britain Ecclesiastical): fair maiden: should stay 1¼m: has started slowly/carried head high. *M. J. Wallace*

MAID FOR THE AISLE   3 ch.f. College Chapel 122 – Debutante Days 83 (Domin-   **52** ion 123) [2003 –: 8.5m 8.1m⁶ p10g 9.9m⁶ Jun 19] workmanlike filly: modest maiden: stays 8.5f: raced only on good/good to firm ground on turf: sold 1,200 gns, sent to France. *J. G. Given*

MAID THE CUT   2 ch.f. (May 23) Silver Wizard (USA) 117 – Third Dam (Slip Anchor   **–** 136) [2003 8.2d f8s Dec 13] half-sister to 7f/1m winner Patsy Stone (by Jester): dam no form: soundly beaten in maidens. *A. D. Smith*

MAID TO TREASURE (IRE)   2 b.f. (Apr 1) Rainbow Quest (USA) 134 – Maid For   **77 p** The Hills 101 (Indian Ridge 123) [2003 7g² Nov 1] attractive filly: fourth foal: half-sister to 3 winners, including 3-y-o Artistic Lad and useful 7f (at 2 yrs) and 1¼m winner Maid To Perfection (by Sadler's Wells): dam 2-y-o 6f winner: 12/1, length second of 17 to Si Si

Amiga in maiden at Newmarket, making most: likely to be suited by at least 1¼m: should improve. *J. L. Dunlop*

MAIL THE DESERT (IRE) 3 b.f. Desert Prince (IRE) 130 – Mail Boat (Formidable **110** (USA) 125) [2003 103: 8f³ 8g² 6.5g Aug 10] good-topped filly: smart performer: won Moyglare Stud Stakes at the Curragh at 2 yrs: best effort when 4½ lengths third to Russian Rhythm in Coronation Stakes at Royal Ascot on reappearance: respectable second to Martillo in Grosser Porsche Preis at Hoppegarten, then well held in Prix Maurice de Gheest at Deauville: stayed 1m: acted on firm and soft going: raced prominently: visits Fasliyev. *M. R. Channon*

MAINPOWER (IRE) 3 b.g. Lake Coniston (IRE) 131 – Chipewyas (FR) (Bering **55** 136) [2003 –: p8g Feb 15] twice-raced maiden: modest form when seventh at Lingfield, only outing at 3 yrs. *R. M. Flower*

MAI SCENE 3 ch.f. Among Men (USA) 124 – Scenicris (IRE) 73 (Scenic 128) [2003 **–** –: 7f Jun 6] unfurnished filly: no sign of ability. *G. M. Moore*

MAI TAI (IRE) 8 b.m. Scenic 128 – Oystons Propweekly 74 (Swing Easy (USA) 126) **56** [2003 53: f8s⁴ f11g³ f11s* f12g⁴ f11s³ f12s 12m* 13.8f³ 12f³ 15.8m⁴ Jul 9] good-bodied **a63** mare: modest performer: won sellers at Southwell in January and May: left G. M. Moore after ninth start: stays 13.8f: acts on firm going, soft and fibresand: tried visored/blinkered: usually held up. *R. Hollinshead*

MAJESTIC BAY (IRE) 7 b.g. Unfuwain (USA) 131 – That'll Be The Day (IRE) 68 **–** (Thatching 131) [2003 –: 16m Apr 12] sturdy gelding: winning chaser: well held both Flat runs since 2001: tried blinkered. *J. A. B. Old*

Sheikh Mohammed's "Maiden Tower"

*Tattersalls Breeders Stakes, the Curragh—a 1,2 for British stables
as Majestic Desert (nearer camera) just gets the better of Totally Yours in this valuable sales race*

MAJESTIC DESERT   2 b.f. (Mar 24) Fraam 114 – Calcutta Queen 51 (Night Shift   **108**
(USA)) [2003 5m* 6m² 5m³ 6m* 6m² Oct 2] €15,000Y: leggy filly: has a round action:
fourth foal: dam third at 1m: useful performer: won maiden at Warwick in April and
Tattersalls Breeders Stakes at the Curragh (beat Totally Yours by head) in August: much
improved form when short-head second of 10 to Carry On Katie in Cheveley Park Stakes
at Newmarket final start, finishing strongly: will be suited by 7f/1m. *M. R. Channon*

MAJESTIC HORIZON   3 b.c. Marju (IRE) 127 – Jumairah Sunset 67 (Be My Guest   **92**
(USA) 126) [2003 96p: 8m* 8d⁵ Oct 13] well-made, quite attractive colt: has a quick
action: fairly useful performer: won maiden at Newmarket in July by 1½ lengths from
Chatifa: visored, only fifth of 6 in minor event at Ayr: stays 1m: unraced on extremes of
going: tongue tied in 2003: sent to UAE, and joined A. Al Raihe. *Saeed bin Suroor*

MAJESTIC (IRE)   8 b.g. Belmez (USA) 131 – Noble Lily (USA) (Vaguely Noble   **–**
140) [2003 11.8m Jun 26] useful hurdler: fair performer on Flat, very lightly raced nowadays: well held only 8-y-o start: usually blinkered: has worn tongue strap. *Ian Williams*

MAJESTIC MISSILE (IRE)   2 b.c. (Apr 23) Royal Applause 124 – Tshusick 81   **116 p**
(Dancing Brave (USA) 140) [2003 5m² 5f* 5.1m* 5g* 6m⁶ 6g* Oct 11]
The common perception of the two-year-old sprinter as a 'here today, gone
tomorrow' type of racehorse has some foundation. A good number of leading
two-year-old sprinters fail to train on, the most recent examples including the 2002
Molecomb and Flying Childers winner Wunders Dream and the five-time winner
in 2000 Superstar Leo. On the other side of the coin, however, there have been
plenty of notable examples of good sprinting two-year-olds which have gone on to
pattern-race success at three and beyond. The likes of Paris House, Mind Games,
Acclamation, Oasis Dream and Somnus are a reminder of the foolhardiness of
taking too much notice of generalisations in racing. Majestic Missile may well
become another success story. His performance in the Cornwallis Stakes at Ascot
in October was the best by a two-year-old colt in a British five-furlong race since
Mujadil's in the same contest thirteen years earlier, and there is every reason to
think that, unlike Mujadil, he will train on and show himself even better at three.
      After a very promising second in a Windsor maiden on his debut in June,
Majestic Missile won a five-runner event at Kempton the following month with
plenty in hand from Lucayan Beauty. Majestic Missile again impressed when

Willmott Dixon Cornwallis Stakes, Ascot—
Majestic Missile puts up the best five-furlong performance by a juvenile colt since 1990;
the tough Nights Cross is second, ahead of Fast Heart (diamond on cap)

following up in a six-runner minor event at Chester, beating Nights Cross easily. Stepped up in class on his next outing, Majestic Missile once more had Nights Cross behind in second when recording his third win in July in the nine-runner Betfair Molecomb Stakes at Goodwood, this time winning by a length and three quarters. Plans after his impressive Molecomb success included the Flying Childers Stakes at Doncaster and a tilt at the Prix de l'Abbaye de Longchamp, just as the stable had done with Superstar Leo. As it was, a minor injury before the Flying

Flying Tiger Partnership's "Majestic Missile"

Childers and soft ground at Longchamp (which connections considered unsuitable for him) meant that Majestic Missile met neither engagement. Majestic Missile's last two races came in the Gimcrack Stakes at York in August and in the Cornwallis. Unsuited by the step up to six furlongs in the Gimcrack, Majestic Missile managed only sixth to Balmont—though still showing smart form—before returning to winning ways in fine style at Ascot. Typically racing freely under restraint just behind the leaders, Majestic Missile produced a really good turn of foot approaching the final furlong to win by three and a half lengths, his nearest pursuer once again Nights Cross.

Majestic Missile (IRE) (b.c. Apr 23, 2001)	Royal Applause (b 1993)	Waajib (b 1983)	Try My Best / Coryana
		Flying Melody (b 1979)	Auction Ring / Whispering Star
	Tshusick (b 1991)	Dancing Brave (b 1983)	Lyphard / Navajo Princess
		Infanta Real (ch 1985)	Formidable / Alteza Real

The tall, quite good-topped Majestic Missile has the scope to train on, just as his sire Royal Applause had done. Royal Applause did lose his way somewhat at three, but got back on track as a four-year-old with four wins, including the Sprint Cup at Haydock. Royal Applause has, in general, sired runners of similar aptitude to himself, including the smart four-year-olds Acclamation and Colonel Cotton. Majestic Missile is the fifth foal out of Tshusick. A fairly useful seven-furlong winner on her debut as a three-year-old, Tshusick ran only six times afterwards. She is out of the useful sprinter Infanta Real, while Majestic Missile's great grandam was a half-sister to Forzando, a very smart performer at up to nine furlongs in Britain and the States, and to the smart sprinting filly Lady Constance. Tshusick foaled three winners prior to Majestic Missile, all of them fairly useful, including the sprinter Parisian Elegance (by Zilzal) and the seven-furlong performer Tribal Prince (by Prince Sabo). Majestic Missile was bought for 50,000 guineas at the Tattersalls Breeze Up Sale in April, having fetched 40,000 guineas at the same venue as a foal. Majestic Missile, who has been bandaged on his hind joints and been taken steadily to post, is a sprinter purely and simply and will prove best at five furlongs. He has raced only on good going or firmer. *W. J. Haggas*

MAJESTIC SWING 3 ch.g. Wolfhound (USA) 126 – Royal Girl 67 (Kafu 120) [2003 7.2m⁵ 5m⁴ 6m Jul 2] 8,000Y: good-bodied gelding: fifth foal: half-brother to fairly useful 2001 2-y-o 5f winner Time Royal (by Timeless Times): dam 6f/7f winner: little form. *Miss L. A. Perratt* —

MAJESTIC TIMES (IRE) 3 b.g. Bluebird (USA) 125 – Simply Times (USA) 64 (Dodge (USA)) [2003 79p: 6m³ 8m 6g* 6d⁴ 6m⁵ 6f f7g 6g 6m f7g⁶ 7g Oct 28] fair handicapper on turf, modest on all-weather: highly impressive 5-length winner at Newcastle in May: below form after fifth outing: should stay 7f: best run on good going: tried blinkered: sold 5,000 gns. *T. D. Easterby* **79 a61**

MAJESTIC VISION 2 ch.g. (Apr 30) Desert King (IRE) 129 – Triste Oeil (USA) 103 (Raise A Cup (USA)) [2003 10m³ f9.4g⁴ Nov 15] 10,000Y: close-coupled, quite good-topped gelding: half-brother to several winners, including 7f (at 2 yrs) to 9f winner Right Tune (by Green Desert) and Irish 7f (at 2 yrs) and 11f winner Desert Wish (by Shirley Heights), both fairly useful: dam 7f (at 2 yrs) and 1¼m winner: fair form in maidens: hung away from whip when fourth at Wolverhampton: will be suited by 1½m+. *P. W. Harris* **73**

MAJHOOL 4 b.g. Mark of Esteem (IRE) 137 – Be Peace (USA) (Septieme Ciel (USA) 123) [2003 74: 5d p7g p7g* p7g Nov 13] tall gelding: fair performer: won claimer at Lingfield in October: stays 7f: acts on firm ground and polytrack: sometimes early to post. *G. L. Moore* **77**

MAJHUD (IRE) 3 b.f. Machiavellian (USA) 123 – Winsa (USA) 80 (Riverman (USA) 131) [2003 80: 10m⁴ 11.8m² 12d* 12f 12.3m³ 10.5d Sep 26] leggy, useful-looking filly: fairly useful performer: landed odds in maiden at Thirsk in May, wandering: stayed 1½m: acted on good to firm and good to soft going: visits Linamix. *J. L. Dunlop* **94**

MAJIC DUST 3 b.g. Wizard King 122 – Fuchu 67 (Jupiter Island 126) [2003 p7g p7g Mar 28] third foal: dam 7f winner: well held in maiden/claimer. *J. A. Supple* —

MAJIK   4 ch.g. Pivotal 124 – Revoke (USA) 70 (Riverman (USA) 131) [2003 70: 6.1m   **77**
f6g³ 6m f6g f6s f7s⁴ f6s² f6g³ f6g* f7s³ Dec 13] close-coupled gelding: fair handicapper:
won at Southwell in December: effective at 6f/7f: acts on fibresand, lightly raced (and
well held) on turf in 2003. *D. J. S. ffrench Davis*

MAJLIS (IRE)   6 b.g. Caerleon (USA) 132 – Ploy 87 (Posse (USA) 130) [2003 12g   **74**
12m⁵ 12m 12m f12g² f14g p13g* Dec 29] fair handicapper: trained in Ireland in 2000 by
by K. Prendergast: won at Lingfield in December: should stay 1¾m: acts on good to firm
going and all-weather: usually wears blinkers (including at Lingfield)/cheekpieces: none
too genuine. *R. M. H. Cowell*

MAJOR ATTRACTION   8 gr.g. Major Jacko 78 – My Friend Melody (Sizzling   **63**
Melody 117) [2003 59: 11.5m⁴ 11m³ 11.9m² 11.5g* 11.5g² 12.4m⁶ 12.6f⁵ 12.3m⁵ 11.6g
12.3g⁵ 11.5g 12m Oct 6] sturdy gelding: modest handicapper: won at Yarmouth in May:
stays 13f: acts on fibresand and firm going, not on softer than good: tried blinkered/
visored (not since 2000): sometimes slowly away: held up: tough. *W. M. Brisbourne*

MAJOR BLADE (GER)   5 b.g. Dashing Blade 117 – Misniniski (Niniski (USA) 125)   **64 ?**
[2003 p10g p10g 10.2g⁶ Jun 13] half-brother to winners in Germany by Scenic and Law
Society: dam Irish 2-y-o 1m winner: fairly useful performer in Germany, winning
national listed race at Halle in 2001 (fairly useful form): placed in handicaps most starts
in Germany in 2002 for H. Steinmetz: seemingly modest form at best in handicaps in
Britain: stays 1¼m: acts on good to firm and good to soft going. *B. G. Powell*

MAJORCA   2 b.c. (Mar 24) Green Desert (USA) 127 – Majmu (USA) 105 (Al Nasr   **73 p**
(FR) 126) [2003 6g Oct 24] €400,000Y: good-topped colt: sixth foal: half-brother to
several winners, notably high-class 7f (at 2 yrs) to 1m winner Muhtathir (by Elmaamul)
and useful 7f/1m winner Jawla (by Wolfhound): dam 2-y-o 1m (May Hill Stakes) winner
who stayed 1¼m: 8/1 and better for race, 5 lengths seventh of 18 to Warrad in maiden
at Newbury, not knocked about once fading: will probably stay 1m: likely to do better.
J. H. M. Gosden

MAJOR DANGER   2 b.g. (Feb 8) Marju (IRE) 127 – Threatening 95 (Warning 136)   **81**
[2003 6m 7.1m⁵ f7g³ 7.2f² 7m* 7.5m² 8m Oct 24] €80,000Y: rather leggy gelding: fifth
foal: half-brother to smart 2001 2-y-o 1m (Royal Lodge) winner Mutinyonthebounty (by
Sadler's Wells) and a winner in Hong Kong by Kris: dam, 2-y-o 6f/7f winner who stayed
9f, half-sister to Classic Cliche (St Leger and Gold Cup winner) and My Emma (won
Prix Vermeille and Yorkshire Oaks): fairly useful performer: won nursery at Newcastle in
August: wandered/found little final start: stays 7.5f: acts on good to firm going, some
promise on fibresand: blinkered last 3 outings: sometimes races freely/flashes tail: sold
18,000 gns. *Sir Mark Prescott*

MAJOR EFFORT (USA)   2 b.c. (Feb 12) Rahy (USA) 115 – Tethkar 75 (Machia-   **79 p**
vellian (USA) 123) [2003 7m 7.1m⁵ 7d² Sep 24] good-topped colt: first foal: dam maiden
who should have stayed beyond 1m, out of useful 11.5f winner Munnaya: fair form in
maidens: 1½ lengths second to King of Cashel at Chester: will stay 1m: best effort on
good to soft going: open to progress. *Sir Michael Stoute*

MAJOR PROJECT (IRE)   2 b.g. (Mar 25) General Monash (USA) 107 – Mini Pro-   **–**
ject (IRE) 94 (Project Manager 111) [2003 5m f8s f8g Oct 16] IR 4,000F, 3,200Y: fourth
foal: dam Irish 2-y-o 6f winner who stayed 11f: well held, twice slowly away, in claimers/
seller. *P. C. Haslam*

MAJOR SMILE   2 ch.c. (Mar 21) Wolfhound (USA) 126 – Session 80 (Reform 132)   **–**
[2003 6m 5m Jul 28] 4,000F, 5,500Y: half-brother to several winners, including 1m
winner Shanghai Lady (by Sabrehill) and irresolute 5f winner Somesession (by Prince
Sabo): dam, 7f winner, out of half-sister to high-class 1½m/1¾m performer High Line:
last in minor event/maiden (worked up in stall). *M. R. Channon*

MAJORS MISTRESS   4 b.f. Superpower 113 – Polola 42 (Aragon 118) [2003 9.9m   **–**
p12g 6d Jul 25] half-sister to winner in Italy by Sayf El Arab: dam third over 5f at 2 yrs:
soundly beaten in maidens/seller. *J. C. Fox*

MAJOR SPECULATION (IRE)   3 b.g. Spectrum (IRE) 126 – Pacific Grove 89   **70**
(Persian Bold 123) [2003 85: 7.1f⁶ 10.1d⁶ p7g 8.2f Oct 1] smallish, sturdy gelding: fairly
useful performer at 2 yrs: just fair in 2003: stays 7f: acts on polytrack and good to firm
going: joined M. Pipe, won over hurdles in November. *G. A. Butler*

MAKARIM (IRE)   7 ch.g. Generous (IRE) 139 – Emmaline (USA) (Affirmed (USA))   **76 §**
[2003 80d: f12g³ f12s³ f12g⁶ 14.1m 13.1f⁴ 14.1m p12g f12g⁶ p13g³ Dec 29] tall gelding:
fair handicapper: effective at 1½m to 2m: acts on firm ground and all-weather: sometimes
wears headgear: tends to wander, and is no battler. *M. R. Bosley*

MAKE MY HAY 4 b.g. Bluegrass Prince (IRE) 110 – Shashi (IRE) 79 (Shaadi (USA) **51**
126) [2003 51, a–: 11.9m[6] 10d[4] 10m[3] 11.9m[3] 12g[3] 11.5m[4] 13.1f 11.9m f11g[2] Dec 19]
leggy, sparely-made gelding: modest maiden handicapper: left J. Cullinan before final
start (blinkered): stays 1½m: acts on good to firm and good to soft going: usually held up.
J. White

MAKFOOL (FR) 2 b.c. (Apr 24) Spectrum (IRE) 126 – Abeyr 106 (Unfuwain (USA) **98**
131) [2003 7m[4] 7m[3] 7g[2] 7.2m[3] 7.2d* 8m[2] 7m[4] 8d[3] Nov 7] rather leggy, useful-looking
colt: has a round action: fourth foal: brother to fairly useful 6f winner (including at 2 yrs)
Aldafra and half-brother to useful 7f winner (including in UAE) Raheibb (by Lion Cavern): dam 7f/1m winner: useful performer: won maiden at Ayr in October: good placed
efforts in listed event at Pontefract (½-length second to New Mexican) and minor race at
Doncaster after: stays 1m: acts on good to firm and good to soft going. *M. R. Channon*

MAKHLAB (USA) 3 b.c. Dixieland Band (USA) – Avasand (USA) (Avatar (USA)) **108 +**
[2003 112p: 7m 8d 8d* Oct 13] rangy, good sort: useful performer: well held in Greenham Stakes at Newbury and Irish 2000 Guineas at the Curragh first 2 starts: best 3-y-o
effort when winning minor event at Ayr in October by ½ length from Babodana: stays
1m: has won on good to firm going, but possibly suited by softer than good (acts on soft).
B. W. Hills

MAKILA KING 2 br.g. (Feb 21) Wizard King 122 – Roonah Quay (IRE) (Soviet Lad **88**
(USA)) [2003 5.1m[6] 6m 6d 6m Oct 4] 13,000Y: workmanlike gelding: first foal: dam
little form: fairly useful performer: won maiden at Bath in May: stiff tasks after, seeming
to run creditably in listed race/sales event on first 2 occasions: needs to settle to stay
beyond 6f: looks tricky ride. *A. M. Balding*

MAKING WAVES (IRE) 4 b.f. Danehill (USA) 126 – Wavey 93 (Kris 135) [2003 **–**
70: 7d 10.5f Sep 5] leggy, useful-looking filly: lightly-raced maiden: well beaten in 2003.
Mrs G. S. Rees

MAKTAVISH 4 b.g. Makbul 104 – La Belle Vie 73 (Indian King (USA) 128) [2003 **83**
89: f5s* f5g 5g 5m 5d[5] 5m[5] 5m 5s* f5g f5s Dec 6] close-coupled gelding: fairly useful **a89**
performer: won handicap at Southwell in January and minor event at Redcar in November: best at 5f: acts on fibresand and any turf going: wears cheekpieces: usually races
prominently. *I. Semple*

MAKTUB (ITY) 4 b.c. Love The Groom (USA) 123 – Carmen The Best (IRE) (Waajib **118**
121) [2003 109: 12m* 14m* 11m 14m* 12f[3] 12m* 12m* 11g* 12m[2] 10d 12m Dec 14]
second foal: dam useful Italian performer up to 1¼m: smart performer: successful 6 times
at 3 yrs, last of them St Leger Italiano at Milan: continued in fine form in 2003, winning
minor events at Milan in March/April, Premio Carlo d'Alessio at Rome in May, then
limited handicap, minor event and Premio Federico Tesio (by 5 lengths from Capitano
Corelli) at Milan in July/September/October: ran well when 2 lengths second of 5 to
Ekraar in Gran Premio del Jockey Club at Milan ninth start: in rear in Premio Roma and
Hong Kong Vase at Sha Tin last 2 outings: effective at 1½m to 15f: acts on soft and good
to firm going: has worn tongue tie: reliable: joined M. Jarvis. *B. Grizzetti, Italy*

MAKULU (IRE) 3 b.g. Alzao (USA) 117 – Karinski (USA) (Palace Music (USA) **83**
129) [2003 69: p10g p10g* p10g[2] p10g[5] p10g* p10g[2] p10g* 10m 11.6g[2] 11.6d[3] 11.6m[5]
14g Jul 31] rather leggy, useful-looking gelding: fairly useful performer: won 2 handicaps
and claimer at Lingfield between January and March: soundly beaten first 2 starts: stays
11.6f: acts on polytrack and soft going: tried blinkered. *B. J. Meehan*

MALAAH (IRE) 7 gr.g. Pips Pride 117 – Lingdale Lass 60 (Petong 126) [2003 48, **–**
a61: 7m 6m 6m Aug 16] good-topped gelding: fair at best: well beaten in 2003: blinkered/
visored. *Julian Poulton*

MALAHIDE EXPRESS (IRE) 3 gr.g. Compton Place 125 – Gracious Gretclo 54 **69**
(Common Grounds 118) [2003 76: 5.1m 6m[4] f6s[6] 5m 5m 5.1d f7g 5d[5] f6g[6] f5g[3] f6g[5] f5g
f5s Dec 27] angular gelding: fair performer: left N. Littmoden after fourth start: best at 5f/
6f: acts on all-weather, good to firm and good to soft ground: usually blinkered/wears
cheekpieces: often pulls hard/hangs: often makes running. *M. J. Polglase*

MALAICA (FR) 2 gr.f. (Jan 27) Roi Gironde (IRE) 104 – Carmel (FR) (Highest **103**
Honor (FR) 124) [2003 5d* 5.5s* 6f[3] 6d 8.3d[2] 8s 7g[4] 7s[2] Nov 4] €20,000Y: good-topped
filly: has round action: first foal: dam unraced half-sister to 6-y-o Execute: useful
performer: won maiden at Wissembourg and minor event at Chantilly in May: placed in
listed races at Royal Ascot (8 lengths third to Silca's Gift) and Craon and in Prix Miesque
at Maisons-Laffitte (length second to Dalna): stays 1m: unraced on heavy going, probably
acts on any other. *R. Pritchard-Gordon, France*

MALAK AL MOULOUK (USA) 3 ch.g. King of Kings (IRE) 125 – Honor To Her **67**
(USA) (Sir Ivor 135) [2003 8m⁴ f7s² p8g⁵ Oct 8] $70,000F, 105,000Y: half-brother to
several winners, including useful 1987 French 2-y-o 6.5f/7f winner Savannah's Honor
(by Storm Bird), later stakes winner up to 1½m in USA: dam unraced: fair maiden: better
at 1m+ than shorter. *J. M. P. Eustace*

MALAPROPISM 3 ch.g. Compton Place 125 – Mrs Malaprop 83 (Night Shift (USA)) **93**
[2003 83: 6g 6m 7m 6m⁶ 5.7m* 5f⁴ 6d³ 6g³ 5.1m³ 5.1m² 5g⁴ 6m³ 5m* 5d 6m 5m³ 5g
5m 5g* Nov 5] well-made gelding: fairly useful handicapper: won at Bath in May,
Goodwood in August and Musselburgh (best effort, by neck) in November: free-going
sort, best at 5f: acts on soft and good to firm going: tends to hang/carry head awkwardly: usually races prominently: sometimes rears leaving stall: tough and consistent.
M. R. Channon

MALE-ANA-MOU (IRE) 10 ch.g. Ela-Mana-Mou 132 – Glasson Lady (GER) 108 **–**
(Priamos (GER) 123) [2003 p16g Jan 4] fairly useful handicapper in 1999: tailed off only
start on Flat since. *Jamie Poulton*

MALEVITCH (IRE) 2 b.c. (Feb 16) Exit To Nowhere (USA) 122 – Miss Tahiti **103 P**
(IRE) 114 (Tirol 127) [2003 9s* 10s* Nov 25] fourth foal: half-brother to useful French
performer up to 15f Maximum Security and smart French 1¼m winner Mer de Corail
(both by Sadler's Wells): dam, won Prix Marcel Boussac, placed in Prix de Diane/Prix
Vermeille: won newcomers race at Longchamp in October and minor event at Saint-
Cloud in November: odds on, beat Wild Is The Wind decisively by 2½ lengths in slowly-
run race in latter: will stay at least 1½m: very much the type to make a smart 3-y-o, and
should win races in stronger company. *E. Lellouche, France*

MALEYNA 3 ch.f. Elmaamul (USA) 125 – Tereyna 58 (Terimon 124) [2003 61: 8.2g⁵ **57**
8.3d⁶ 7m 10d 11.7m⁴ 11.7f Aug 22] modest maiden: bred to be suited by 1½m+, but has
raced freely: acts on good to firm and good to soft ground. *R. F. Johnson Houghton*

MALHUB (USA) 5 b. or br.h. Kingmambo (USA) 125 – Arjuzah (IRE) 110 (Ahonoora **113**
122) [2003 126: 6f Jun 21] quite attractive horse: fluent mover: has twice undergone wind
operation: high-class performer in 2002, winning Golden Jubilee Stakes at Royal Ascot:
below best when seventh to Choisir in same event only 5-y-o start, drifting right: best at
5f/6f: acted on firm going: had worn crossed noseband: tongue tied: to stand at Summerhill Stud, South Africa. *J. H. M. Gosden*

MALIN (IRE) 2 b.c. (May 2) Cape Cross (IRE) 129 – Jet Lock (USA) (Crafty Pros- **99 p**
pector (USA)) [2003 7m⁶ 8m* 8m* Sep 25] 13,000Y: workmanlike colt: second foal:
dam, maiden in Ireland/USA, from family of Cheveley Park winner Pas de Reponse:
useful form: won maiden in August and nursery (beat Habanero comfortably by 3½
lengths) in September, both at Goodwood: will stay 1¼m: sold privately, and sent to
USA: open to progress. *J. L. Dunlop*

MALLARD (IRE) 5 b.g. Tagula (IRE) 116 – Frill (Henbit (USA) 130) [2003 67: **69**
f11g⁶ p10g⁶ f7g² f8.5g² f8.5s 7g⁶ f8.5g* 7g f7s* f7g* 7g* 8.3d p8g* Oct 15] good-bodied **a82**
gelding: fairly useful handicapper on all-weather, fair on turf: won at Wolverhampton in
April, July and August, Epsom in September and Lingfield in October: effective at 7f to
8.5f: acts on all-weather, best turf effort on good ground. *J. G. Given*

MALLIA 10 b.g. Statoblest 120 – Pronetta (USA) (Mr Prospector (USA)) [2003 –§, **55 §**
a60§: 6m f6g⁴ 6m⁶ f7g² f7g² f7g f7g 6g² 6m* 5.9d⁴ 6m 6m⁶ Aug 19] lengthy, dipped-backed
gelding: modest performer: won apprentice handicap at Hamilton in July: best at 6f: acts
on any turf going/fibresand: tried in headgear: has started slowly/edged right: held up:
sometimes finds little. *T. D. Barron*

MALLING 2 ch.c. (Mar 31) Halling (USA) 133 – Queens Way (FR) (Zafonic (USA) **–**
130) [2003 8m Oct 14] 16,000Y: leggy colt: second foal: half-brother to winner in Greece
by Polish Precedent: dam unraced out of half-sister to Shergar: 66/1, last of 11 in Leicester maiden. *R. F. Johnson Houghton*

MALMAND (USA) 4 ch.g. Distant View (USA) 126 – Bidski (USA) (Explosive Bid **?**
(USA)) [2003 57: f7g⁶ f8g f9.4g³ f8.5g* f8.5g⁶ f8.5s⁵ 8.3g f8.5g f7g⁵ 8m 10d 7f f8.5g⁵ **a52 §**
f12g f8g Dec 8] compact, quite attractive gelding: modest performer: won seller at
Wolverhampton (wandered) in March: stays 8.5f: acts on soft, good to firm going and
fibresand: tried in headgear: reportedly bled twelfth start. *R. Brotherton*

MALTESE FALCON 3 b.g. Mark of Esteem (IRE) 137 – Crime Ofthecentury 80 **106**
(Pharly (FR) 130) [2003 82p: 6g² 5m³ 5d² 5.1m⁵ Aug 18] useful performer: best efforts
when runner-up in minor event at Haydock (beaten 2½ lengths by Somnus) and listed
race at Deauville (beaten ½ length by Victorieux): tongue tied, ran as though amiss in

minor event at Nottingham final outing: gelded after: will prove at least as effective at 6f as 5f: unraced on extremes of going: races prominently. *P. F. I. Cole*

MALUTI   2 ch.g. (Feb 16) Piccolo 121 – Persian Blue 64 (Persian Bold 123) [2003 6m **52** 7m 6m 5m⁶ Oct 25] small, close-coupled gelding: second foal: dam, maiden, stayed 1½m well: modest maiden: needs to settle to stay 7f. *R. Guest*

MALVERN LIGHT   2 b.f. (Feb 27) Zieten (USA) 118 – Michelle Hicks 92 (Ballad **87 p** Rock 122) [2003 6g⁴ 6.1d* Nov 6] 20,000F, 22,000Y: quite good-topped filly: sixth foal: half-sister to winners in Italy and Turkey, both by Night Shift: dam, 2-y-o 7.5f winner, half-sister to Premio Regina Elena winner Ancestral Dancer: well-backed favourite, won maiden at Nottingham impressively by 5 lengths from Out After Dark, soon in front and eased after clear 1f out: will probably stay 7f: should make a useful 3-y-o. *W. J. Haggas*

MAMA JAFFA (IRE)   3 ch.f. In The Wings 128 – Harir (Kris 135) [2003 58: 11.9s³ **61** 12.4m³ 14g 14.1d f12g⁵ 11.1m⁵ 13.8d* 15.8m² 12m⁴ Oct 18] tall, useful-looking filly: modest performer: won seller at Catterick in September: stays 2m: acts on soft and good to firm ground: visored/blinkered last 4 starts: sold 16,000 gns. *K. R. Burke*

MAMBINA (USA)   2 ch.f. (Feb 4) Kingmambo (USA) 125 – Sonata (Polish Precedent **74** (USA) 131) [2003 7g⁵ p8g Nov 26] $150,000F: compact filly: third foal: dam unraced, sister to dam of 4-y-o Ransom o'War and closely related to smart performers up to 7f Russian Bond and Snaadee: much better effort in maidens (fair form) when never-nearer fifth at Newmarket: should stay 1m. *M. R. Channon*

MAMCAZMA   5 gr.g. Terimon 124 – Merryhill Maid (IRE) 71 (M Double M (USA)) **102** [2003 94: 12g² 13.9m³ 13.9f² 16.1g 13.9f² 12m 13.9m 12m 12m 14.6d² Nov 7] strong, lengthy gelding: useful performer: better than ever: best efforts when second in handicaps at York in June (to Barolo) and July (to Hugs Dancer) and in minor event at Doncaster (beaten head by New South Wales) on third, fifth and final starts: effective at 1½m to 2m: acts on fibresand, soft and firm going: blinkered (below form) once: waited with: sometimes carries head awkwardly. *D. Morris*

MAMEYUKI   4 ch.f. Zafonic (USA) 130 – Musetta (IRE) 107 (Cadeaux Genereux **80 +** 131) [2003 80?: 9d⁶ 7m⁴ 8m 8m 7g⁴ 7.6g³ Jul 16] leggy filly: fairly useful performer: stiff tasks in listed races first 4 starts: stays 7f: acts on good to firm going. *C. E. Brittain*

MAMMAS F·C (IRE)   7 ch.m. Case Law 113 – Wasaif (IRE) 79 (Lomond (USA) **49 §** 128) [2003 64§, a46§: 6m 5m f5g 5.7m 6g 5.7f 5.3m² 5.3m 5.5f 5.7f 5m Jul 23] strong, good-bodied mare: poor handicapper nowadays: mostly well held in 2003: effective at 5f/ 6f: acts on firm going, soft and all-weather: tried in cheekpieces/blinkers: usually held up: unreliable. *J. M. Bradley*

MAMOOL (IRE)   4 b.c. In The Wings 128 – Genovefa (USA) 107 (Woodman **122** (USA) 126) [2003 118: 14g* 13.9m* 20m⁵ 13.3m³ 12g* 12d* 16g Nov 4]

The latest attempt by Godolphin to capture the Melbourne Cup ended in major disappointment. Mamool, their ninth representative in the last six runnings of the race, was sent off favourite but trailed home last of the twenty-three runners and was found to have fractured a sesamoid in his off-hind leg. It was a bad injury but, thankfully, one from which Mamool is expected to make a full recovery, in which case he will be returning to action in 2004. Maybe Mamool will get another chance to show racegoers in Australia just how good he really is. Those who saw him in action in Dubai, Britain and Germany in the latest season would have been left in no doubt that he is a very smart colt.

Mamool won a maiden at Goodwood from four starts as a two-year-old and the Queen's Vase at Royal Ascot from the same number of appearances at three years. He began the latest campaign with a comfortable victory from Pugin in a prestige handicap at Nad Al Sheba in February, after which he was returned to Britain. He reappeared at York in May in the Emirates Airline Yorkshire Cup, a race his connections had won twice in the previous three years with Kayf Tara and Marienbard. Mamool faced seven opponents, among them Bollin Eric, who had had Mamool back in fourth when winning the 2002 St Leger, and Warrsan, who was seeking a hat-trick following victories in the Dubai Irish Village Stakes (John Porter) and the Jockey Club Stakes. Dropped out last in a strongly-run contest, Mamool passed all of his rivals in the straight, the last of those to be collared being Warrsan, who had taken the lead off Bollin Eric over a furlong out. Mamool hit the front close home to win by half a length. As with Kayf Tara and Marienbard, Mamool's next race was the Gold Cup at Royal Ascot. Mamool started favourite

Emirates Airline Yorkshire Cup, York—Mamool provides Saeed bin Suroor with a fifth success in the race in nine years; Warrsan (right) is reeled in close home, while Bollin Eric finishes third

but, like Marienbard, found the two-and-a-half-mile trip too far, finishing fifth behind Mr Dinos, who had finished behind Mamool in both the Queen's Vase and the St Leger. Given a short break after the Gold Cup, Mamool wasn't quite at his best when third to Mubtaker in the Geoffrey Freer Stakes at Newbury in August, but he was certainly back in top form the following month, during which time he contested a couple of mile-and-a-half Group 1 events in Germany.

In the Grosser Bugatti Preis at Baden-Baden, better known as the Grosser Preis von Baden and Germany's most valuable race, Mamool was one of two British challengers, the other being Systematic, who had finished second in the Geoffrey Freer. Ireland was represented by the Tattersalls Gold Cup winner Black Sam Bellamy. The Grosser Preis, the seventh leg of the World Series Racing Championship and a race won by Marienbard on the way to his Arc victory the previous season, attracted eight runners in all. The pick of the three home-trained runners, in the absence of the 2003 Deutsches Derby winner Dai Jin, was Next Desert, who had won that event the previous year, but neither he nor the other German runners was able to make much of an impact in a race run at just a fair pace, set by Black Sam Bellamy. Mamool, who led in the very early stages before being

Grosser Bugatti Preis, Baden-Baden—
Germany's most valuable race (previously known as the Grosser Preis von Baden), in which Mamool gets the better of Black Sam Bellamy (right) with Dano-Mast (left) staying on for third

settled in fourth, made headway wide on the home turn and delivered his challenge as the field came towards the middle of the course in the straight, taking a very narrow advantage well over a furlong out. With Black Sam Bellamy rallying, Mamool's rider Frankie Dettori had to ask his mount for everything and Mamool responded gamely, holding on by half a length. Mamool had a hard race—Dettori received a fine for excessive use of the whip—but showed himself none the worse for it when he returned for the Preis von Europa at Cologne, where he faced a much easier task. Well Made. winner of the event twelve months earlier, was in the field again but wasn't in the same sort of form, and Mamool looked to have something in hand of the four other runners, who included another British challenger in Albanova. Mamool started at 5/2-on and made much of the running this time, with Dettori steering him wide in search of better ground. Well Made took over at around halfway, but Mamool regained the lead two furlongs out and ran on well to win by a length and a quarter from Albanova, who snatched second from Well Made near the line. It was the end of Mamool's European campaign, and he went into quarantine in preparation for his trip to Australia.

Mamool (IRE) (b.c. 1999)	In The Wings (b 1986)	Sadler's Wells (b 1981)	Northern Dancer
			Fairy Bridge
		High Hawk (b 1980)	Shirley Heights
			Sunbittern
	Genovefa (USA) (b 1992)	Woodman (ch 1983)	Mr Prospector
			Playmate
		Reigning Countess (b or br 1982)	Far North
			Countess Fager

Godolphin's "Mamool"

Mamool is the third foal of Genovefa and her third winner, following Ejlaal (by Caerleon), who showed useful form when winning over a mile as a two-year-old in France, and Genova (by Darshaan), who was successful at thirteen furlongs there. Genovefa also showed useful form in France, at up to thirteen and a half furlongs, gaining the second of her two wins in the Prix de Royaumont. She is a close relative or half-sister to several winners, notably the smart fillies Grafin, winner of the Prix de la Nonette, and Miss Turkana, the latter successful in a Grade 3 event in the States. Their dam Reigning Countess was a smart performer at seven furlongs and a mile in the States. Mamool, a good-topped colt, is effective at a mile and a half to two miles, and acts on soft and good to firm going. He has worn a crossed noseband and was tried in a tongue strap at Newbury. *Saeed bin Suroor*

MAMORE GAP (IRE) 5 b.h. General Monash (USA) 107 – Ravensdale Rose (IRE) **81** (Henbit (USA) 130) [2003 80: 8g⁵ 7m* 9g* 9g 9m⁵ 10m Sep 17] smallish, useful-looking horse: fairly useful performer: won claimer at Salisbury in June and apprentice handicap at Newbury in July: effective at 7f to 9f: acts on firm and good to soft ground: found little fifth start. *R. Hannon*

MANAAR (IRE) 3 b.g. Titus Livius (FR) 115 – Zurarah (Siberian Express (USA) 125) **97** [2003 81: p5g³ 5m* 6m² 5m² 6g² 5m Oct 2] good-quartered gelding: useful performer: made all in maiden at Leicester in July: best effort when second to The Trader in minor event there fourth start: effective at 5f/6f: raced only on polytrack and good/good to firm ground: carried head high/hung left on reappearance. *J. Noseda*

MANA D'ARGENT (IRE) 6 b.g. Ela-Mana-Mou 132 – Petite-D-Argent 91 (Noalto **97** 120) [2003 101: 16m 12.1m⁶ 14m 16.2m⁶ 20m⁶ 16.1g 16.2f* 21d⁴ 16.2m³ 12m³ Sep 15] small gelding: good walker: unimpressive mover: useful handicapper: has gained all 5 successes at Ascot, beating Thewhirlingdervish by ¾ length for most recent win in July: good third at Ascot and Musselburgh last 2 starts: effective at 1½m and stays 21f: acts on any turf going and fibresand: sometimes blinkered/visored, not in 2003: held up nowadays: sometimes wanders: tough. *M. Johnston*

MANAMA ROSE (IRE) 3 ch.f. Kris 135 – Top Table 65 (Shirley Heights 130) **97** [2003 7m 10m³ 10.1g⁶ 9m² 10m² 12.3g* 12m⁶ 16.2f² 12g Oct 11] 140,000Y: medium-sized, quite attractive filly: good walker: sixth foal: sister to useful 6f (at 2 yrs) and 1m winner Krispy Knight and half-sister to 1½m winner Parable (by Midyan) and a winner in Denmark by Bering: dam, second at 1½m, half-sister to smart miler Centre Stalls: useful performer: won maiden at Chester in August by 9 lengths: ran well in listed races at Newbury (third, beaten 2 heads by Approach) on second outing and at Ascot on seventh and eighth (length second to Supremacy) starts: well beaten in Princess Royal Stakes on latter course final outing: stays 2m: raced only on good ground or firmer: sometimes blinkered/visored: has worn crossed noseband. *G. A. Butler*

MANA-MOU BAY (IRE) 6 b.g. Ela-Mana-Mou 132 – Summerhill (Habitat 134) **–** [2003 84: 10.1d Mar 24] good-topped gelding: fairly useful performer at best: wearing cheekpieces, well held only Flat outing in 2003: tried visored: won over hurdles in April. *B. Ellison*

MANANIYYA (IRE) 3 ch.f. Ashkalani (IRE) 128 – Madiriya 119 (Diesis 133) [2003 **95** 83p: 8.3g* 10.4m⁴ May 13] good-bodied filly: useful form: landed odds in maiden at Windsor in April: sweating, good 5 lengths fourth to Cassis in Musidora Stakes at York next time, tending to hang: would have stayed 1½m: raced only on good/good to firm ground: stud. *Sir Michael Stoute*

MANA POOLS (IRE) 4 b.f. Brief Truce (USA) 126 – Pipers Pool (IRE) 94 (Mtoto **76** 134) [2003 72: p10g p10g* p10g⁶ 9.9m³ 9.2m² 11.9f 11.9g² p12g 10d⁴ Jul 30] good-topped filly: fair handicapper: won at Lingfield in February: stays 1½m: acts on all-weather, firm and soft ground: tried visored, usually blinkered: has been slowly away: held up. *J. A. Glover*

MANASHIN 3 b.f. Whittingham (IRE) 104 – Montagne 49 (Midyan (USA) 124) [2003 **–** 7.1g 8.2g Aug 1] workmanlike filly: first living foal: dam maiden half-sister to useful German performer up to 11f Turbo Drive: slowly away and well beaten in maidens. *B. Smart*

MAN AT ARMS (IRE) 2 b.c. (Feb 8) Daggers Drawn (USA) 114 – Punta Gorda (IRE) **69** (Roi Danzig (USA)) [2003 6m 7g 7.1m 8m³ Oct 24] IR 39,000F, 60,000Y: well-made colt: second foal: dam, second at 11f in France, half-sister to useful 7f winner Reported:

fair maiden: third in nursery at Doncaster: stays 1m: gave trouble in preliminaries second start. *R. Hannon*

MANCHESTER (IRE) 4 b.g. Danehill Dancer (IRE) 117 – Lils Fairy (Fairy King – (USA)) [2003 p10g Apr 9] 9,500F, IR 20,000Y: fifth foal: half-brother to ungenuine 5f winner Tinker's Surprise (by Cyrano de Bergerac) and Irish 9f and 11f winner Dont You Dare (by Namaqualand): dam unraced: fair maiden for A. O'Brien in Ireland at 2 yrs: tailed off only run on Flat since (no show over hurdles): tried blinkered. *Miss A. M. Newton-Smith*

MAN CRAZY (IRE) 2 b.f. (Apr 20) Foxhound (USA) 103 – Schonbein (IRE) 60 **76** (Persian Heights 129) [2003 5.1m³ 6g³ 6g⁴ 6m² 6m² 7.2f³ 5.7m³ 7m² 6m³ 6.5d p7g Dec 29] €33,000Y: sturdy filly: fourth foal: half-sister to 3 winners, including 4-y-o Football Crazy: dam lightly-raced half-sister to smart Irish sprinter Bradawn Breever: fair maiden: in frame first 9 starts, including in nursery: stays 7f: acts on firm going (blinkered when below form on good to soft): often races prominently. *R. M. Beckett*

MANDARIN SPIRIT (IRE) 3 b.g. Primo Dominie 121 – Lithe Spirit (IRE) 74 **82 +** (Dancing Dissident (USA) 119) [2003 55p: f6g⁵ f8s⁶ 8.2m⁴ 7.1f² 7m* f8.5g* 7.1m 7f⁴ 7g* 7g* 7m 7.1g f7g Oct 20] fairly useful handicapper: won at Catterick (final start for Sir Mark Prescott), Wolverhampton, Folkestone and Epsom between July and September: effective at 7f to 8.5f: raced only on fibresand/good going or firmer: best efforts in blinkers: slowly away last 2 outings: often forces pace. *G. C. H. Chung*

MANDINKA 3 b.g. Distinctly North (USA) 115 – Primo Panache (Primo Dominie – 121) [2003 10d 9.3f 10m 10g 8m⁵ 8g 10f Oct 1] big, good-topped gelding: third foal: dam no form: signs of some ability. *J. F. Coupland*

MANDOBI (IRE) 2 ch.c. (Apr 4) Mark of Esteem (IRE) 137 – Miss Queen (USA) **95** (Miswaki (USA) 124) [2003 6m³ 6m² 7m* 7m² 7m Oct 2] €130,000Y: close-coupled colt: second foal: dam, US 6f winner, half-sister to useful 6f/7f winner Tajannub out of half-sister to Derby third Star of Gdansk: useful performer: won maiden at Newmarket in August by 4 lengths: unlucky short-head second to Overdrawn in nursery at York next time, short of room before finishing strongly: last of 8 in Somerville Tattersall Stakes at Newmarket: should stay 1m. *A. C. Stewart*

MANDOOB 6 b.g. Zafonic (USA) 130 – Thaidah (CAN) 105 (Vice Regent (CAN)) **72** [2003 71, a74: p13g⁵ p12g⁶ p12g³ p12g p13g Dec 6] big, close-coupled gelding: fair handicapper: stays easy 14.8f: acts on all-weather/any turf ground: has worn blinkers/tongue tie. *B. R. Johnson*

MANDOWN 4 b.g. Danehill Dancer (IRE) 117 – Golden Decoy 73 (Decoy Boy 129) **42** [2003 48: p12g⁶ f9.4s⁵ f9.4g Feb 10] poor maiden: stays 9.4f: acts on all-weather. *J. S. Moore*

MANDY'S COLLECTION 4 ch.f. Forzando 122 – Instinction (Never So Bold 135) – [2003 –, a58: f6g f7g Feb 21] maiden: well held in 2003. *A. G. Newcombe*

MAN EATER 3 gr.f. Mark of Esteem (IRE) 137 – Desert Delight (IRE) (Green Desert – (USA) 127) [2003 74: p5g⁶ 5m 5.1g 2g 6s 5m Oct 1] rather leggy filly: fair maiden at 2 yrs: well held in 2003, sold from R. Hannon 13,000 gns after third start: tried blinkered. *T. Cooper, Ireland*

MANE FRAME 8 b.g. Unfuwain (USA) 131 – Moviegoer (Pharly (FR) 130) [2003 **66** –: p16g p16g⁵ Jan 25] rangy gelding: fair handicapper, very lightly raced nowadays: stays 2m: acts on heavy going, good to firm and polytrack. *H. Morrison*

MANGO MISCHIEF (IRE) 2 ch.f. (Mar 21) Desert King (IRE) 129 – Eurolink **84 p** Mischief 84 (By My Chief (USA) 122) [2003 7m* 8g Nov 1] tall, leggy filly: has scope: fourth foal: half-sister to 3 winners, including 4-y-o Bonecrusher and useful 1999 2-y-o 6f/7f winner Eurolink Raindance (by Alzao): dam 1½m winner: fairly useful form: won maiden at Salisbury in August: seemingly some improvement when tenth of 12 in listed event at Newmarket, despite racing too freely: bred to be suited by 1¼m/1½m: open to progress. *J. L. Dunlop*

MANGUS (IRE) 9 b.g. Mac's Imp (USA) 116 – Holly Bird (Runnett 125) [2003 –§, – § a55§: f5g f5s³ f6s⁶ f5g 5m f5g 5.3m⁶ 5m 6m Jul 23] workmanlike gelding: poor handi- **a44 §** capper: raced mainly at 5f: acts on firm going, soft and fibresand: tried tongue tied/in cheekpieces: sometimes starts slowly: not one to trust. *K. O. Cunningham-Brown*

MANICANI (IRE) 5 ch.g. Tagula (IRE) 116 – Pluvia (USA) (Raise A Native) [2003 **72** 82: p7g p6g⁴ p6g p6g⁴ Apr 9] tall, useful-looking gelding: fair handicapper: effective at

6f/7f: acts on polytrack, firm and good to soft going: usually held up: tried tongue tied: has found little. *A. M. Balding*

MANIKATO (USA) 9 b.g. Clever Trick (USA) – Pasampsi (USA) (Crow (FR) 134) **45 d** [2003 49, a43: 11.9f⁵ 9.9m 10m² 10.2m 8g 9.7m⁶ 11.9f⁶ 10f Aug 27] close-coupled **a–** gelding: poor handicapper: below form after third outing: effective at 1¼m/1½m: acts on firm going, good to soft and all-weather: sometimes visored earlier in career. *R. Curtis*

MANIPULATOR (IRE) 2 b.c. (Feb 20) Danehill (USA) 126 – Misallah (IRE) **84** (Shirley Heights 130) [2003 6g⁵ 6m* f7g* 8m⁵ 7.6d³ 8.2m Oct 22] €300,000Y: big, **a95** strong, lengthy colt: has short, unimpressive action: fifth living foal: dam, in frame up to 12.5f in France, closely related to dam of very smart miler Almushtarak: useful on all-weather, fairly useful on turf: won maiden at Hamilton in June and nursery at Wolverhampton (by 4 lengths, despite very slow start) in August: last all starts after: should stay at least 1m: acts on fibresand and good to firm going: possibly temperamental: sold 27,000 gns. *Sir Mark Prescott*

MANNORA 3 b.f. Prince Sabo 123 – Miss Bussell 65 (Sabrehill (USA) 120) [2003 49: **70 ?** 6g⁵ 6.1m⁴ 6m* 7g 6m 6m⁴ 6m³ 6m Sep 18] workmanlike filly: fair performer: easily best effort when winning maiden at Newcastle in June: free-going sort, best at 5f/6f: yet to race on extremes of going. *P. Howling*

MANNTAB (USA) 2 b.c. (Mar 9) Kingmambo (USA) 125 – Saafeya (IRE) 111 **98** (Sadler's Wells (USA) 132) [2003 6f² f7g* 7m⁴ 7.1d⁶ Aug 30] well-made colt: second foal: half-brother to 3-y-o Janayen: dam 1m to 10.5f winner: useful performer: landed odds in maiden at Wolverhampton in June by 7 lengths: good 2 lengths fourth to Kings Point in Superlative Stakes at Newmarket, better effort after: will stay 1m: early to post last 2 starts. *D. R. Loder*

MANNYMAN (IRE) 2 b. or br.f. (Apr 17) Dr Devious (IRE) 127 – Lithe Spirit (IRE) **–** 74 (Dancing Dissident (USA) 119) [2003 6g Oct 31] 7,200Y: workmanlike filly: fourth foal: half-sister to 3 winners, including 3-y-o Mandarin Spirit and 4-y-o Blythe Spirit: dam, maiden (stayed 1m), out of half-sister to smart 7f/1m performers Bog Trotter and Poteen: 50/1 and backward, last of 11 in maiden at Newmarket. *W. Jarvis*

MAN OF LETTERS (UAE) 2 b.c. (Jan 23) Belong To Me (USA) – Personal Busi- **66 p** ness (USA) (Private Account (USA)) [2003 8g⁵ Nov 5] closely related to US Grade 3 7f winner In Conference (by Dayjur) and half-brother to several winners, including useful 6f (in USA at 2 yrs) and 9f (in UAE) winner Expect (by Storm Cat): dam US Grade 1 1¼m winner: 16/1 and green, some late headway when 8 lengths fifth of 6 to Rydal in maiden at Musselburgh: should do better. *M. Johnston*

MANOR FROM HEAVEN 5 ch.m. Most Welcome 131 – Manor Adventure 75 **–** (Smackover 107) [2003 –: f11g Mar 11] leggy mare: little form. *P. T. Dalton*

MANOUBI 4 b.g. Doyoun 124 – Manuetti (IRE) 86 (Sadler's Wells (USA) 132) [2003 **99** 88: 11.9m³ 14m³ 12.1g* 11.9g⁴ 12g Aug 1] good-topped gelding: useful handicapper, lightly raced: won at Hamilton in June by ½ length from Inglis Drever: favourite, best effort when fourth to Collier Hill in Old Newton Cup at Haydock next time: stays 1¾m: yet to race on extremes of going: sweating (below form) final start: sold 52,000 gns, joined Jonjo O'Neill. *Sir Michael Stoute*

MANSFIELD PARK 2 br.f. (Feb 21) Green Desert (USA) 127 – Park Appeal 122 **91 p** (Ahonoora 122) [2003 7m² 7m* Aug 9] good-topped filly: sister to high-class 1m (including at 2 yrs) winner Cape Cross, and half-sister to several winners, including useful French 1½m winner Lord of Appeal (by Sadler's Wells): dam, won Cheveley Park Stakes and 8.5f winner at 4 yrs in USA, half-sister to Desirable and Alydaress and to dam of Russian Rhythm: promising second in maiden at Newmarket before landing odds in 6-runner similar event at Redcar impressively by 7 lengths from Kelucia, soon leading and quickening away under hand riding final 2f: suffered stress fracture to a hind leg after: will stay 1m: joined Saeed bin Suroor: useful prospect. *D. R. Loder*

MAN THE GATE 4 b.g. Elmaamul (USA) 125 – Girl At The Gate 53 (Formidable **71** (USA) 125) [2003 75: p12g⁵ f8g 10m⁵ 12g² 13.3m p10g⁴ 11.8m* 12m 12m p12g⁴ 9g⁵ p10g³ p10g p10g Dec 20] leggy gelding: fair performer: won minor event at Leicester in June: stays 1½m: acts on soft going, good to firm and polytrack. *P. D. Cundell*

MANTILLA 6 b.m. Son Pardo 107 – Well Tried (IRE) 43 (Thatching 131) [2003 f9.4s **–** Feb 28] maiden on Flat: fair hurdler for I. Williams, successful 5 times between August and October. *J. D. Frost*

MANTLES PRIDE 8 b.g. Petong 126 – State Romance 67 (Free State 125) [2003 73: **62 d** 8.3g 8.1g 7m⁶ 7.2g⁶ 7d⁵ 6.9m 9.2g⁴ 8m 8m⁶ 8m⁴ 12m⁵ 9.1d Oct 14] useful-looking gelding: modest performer: below form after third outing: effective at 7f to 1½m: acts on any going: usually visored/blinkered: sometimes slowly away: ungenuine. *M. Dods*

MANX FIZZ 3 b.f. Efisio 120 – Stica (IRE) (In The Wings 128) [2003 55: 8m³ 7.5f **58** 8.2m 9.2d⁵ 8m 8m* 8g³ 10m⁵ 8m⁵ 9f 10m⁵ 10m 9m⁵ 8m 10f⁶ Oct 1] smallish, strong filly: modest handicapper: won at Musselburgh in May: stays 1¼m: acts on heavy and good to firm going: sometimes slowly away: none too consistent: sold 2,500 gns. *J. Hetherton*

MANX MINI 3 b.f. Distinctly North (USA) 115 – Octavia (Sallust 134) [2003 –: 6m **–** 9f 11g Jul 26] little form. *A. Berry*

MANYANA (IRE) 2 b.c. (Feb 23) Alzao (USA) 117 – Sometime (IRE) (Royal **97 p** Academy (USA) 130) [2003 7.1m* Jul 23] 65,000Y: first foal: dam, unraced, sister to Sleepytime and Ali-Royal and half-sister to Taipan, out of half-sister to Croco Rouge: 4/1, won 7-runner maiden at Sandown by short head from Capped For Victory, dictating pace and rallying well: will stay at least 1m: seems sure to do better. *M. P. Tregoning*

MANY THANKS 3 b.f. Octagonal (NZ) 126 – Answered Prayer (Green Desert **73** (USA) 127) [2003 8.2m² 8g⁴ 10m⁴ 8.3g⁴ Oct 13] lengthy, quite good-topped filly: third foal: half-sister to French 1m/10.5f winner Grateful Thanks (by Bering) and 4-y-o Answered Promise: dam, ran once in France, out of Oaks winner Jet Ski Lady: fair maiden: has raced freely, but should stay 1¼m: sold 2,500 gns. *E. A. L. Dunlop*

MARAAHEL (IRE) 2 b.c. (Feb 24) Alzao (USA) 117 – Nasanice (IRE) 97 (Nash- **87 p** wan (USA) 135) [2003 7.1d⁴ 8m* 8m⁴ Oct 20] sturdy colt: has fluent, round action: second foal: brother to 3-y-o Huja: dam Irish 9f winner: won maiden at Pontefract in September readily by ¾ length from Destination Dubai: further improvement when 5½ lengths fourth to New Mexican in listed event on same course: will be suited by 1¼m/1½m: smart prospect. *Sir Michael Stoute*

MARAAKEB (FR) 2 gr.c. (Mar 26) Linamix (FR) 127 – Raheefa (USA) 75 (River- **84 P** man (USA) 131) [2003 7g³ Nov 1] big, useful-looking colt: third foal: half-brother to 4-y-o Rawyaan and useful 7f to 9f winners in Britain/UAE Muthaaber (by Machiavellian): dam, 1¼m winner, granddaughter of US Champion older mare Cascaded (Grade 1 9f winner): favourite, length third of 12 to Golden Grace in maiden at Newmarket, moving well tracking leaders but green off bridle and not subjected to hard time: will be suited by 1¼m/1½m: type to do much better at 3 yrs, and sure to win races. *J. H. M. Gosden*

MARABAR 5 b.m. Sri Pekan (USA) 117 – Erbaya (IRE) (El Gran Senor (USA) 136) **87** [2003 83: 6g³ 6g 6g 6g² 6d⁵ 6m⁵ 6m 7m 7f5g⁵ Nov 21] big, strong mare: fairly useful handicapper: left J. Akehurst after eighth start: effective at 6f/7f: acts on good to firm and good to soft going: tried in cheekpieces. *D. W. Chapman*

MARABELLO 3 b.g. Robellino (USA) 127 – Mara River 86 (Efisio 120) [2003 78d: **64** p7g⁶ 9m 8.3d⁵ p10g⁴ 10g 11.7f⁴ 14.1d 11.7m³ Aug 5] leggy, close-coupled gelding: fair maiden handicapper: stays 11.7f: acts on firm going, good to soft and polytrack: blink-ered/visored last 6 starts: sold 5,000 gns, sent to Spain. *A. M. Balding*

MARAIN (IRE) 3 b.f. Marju (IRE) 127 – Rainstone 57 (Rainbow Quest (USA) 134) **–** [2003 –: 11.6d May 12] sixth foal: sister to useful 1998 2-y-o 5f/6f winner Gipsy Rose Lee and half-sister to 3 winners, including 1m winner Yajtahed (by Mujtahid): dam, placed both starts at 2 yrs (later won in Belgium), half-sister to smart 2-y-o sprinter Magic Ring: no form: trained at 2 yrs in Ireland by P. Hughes. *Mrs P. N. Dutfield*

MARAKABEI 5 ch.m. Hernando (FR) 127 – Kirsten 77 (Kris 135) [2003 72: 14.1g* **98** 12.1g⁶ 14g³ 21d 15.9d 14.1s* Oct 29] smallish mare: useful performer: won handicap at Nottingham in April and listed race at Yarmouth (66/1, beat Mystic Mile by 3½ lengths) in October: best at 1¾m/2m on good going or softer: held up: genuine. *R. Guest*

MARAKASH (IRE) 4 b.g. Ashkalani (IRE) 128 – Marilaya (IRE) 96 (Shernazar 131) **–** [2003 73: 8.3m 8.3g f8.5g p10g Nov 26] fair maiden at best: showed nothing in 2003: tried in cheekpieces. *M. R. Bosley*

MARAVEDI (IRE) 3 ch.f. Hector Protector (USA) 124 – Manuetti (IRE) 86 (Sadler's **–** Wells (USA) 132) [2003 8g p10g 11.9m p12g Jul 2] 12,000 2-y-o: second foal: half-sister to 4-y-o Manoubi: dam, maiden who would have been suited by 1½m, daughter of Prix Saint-Alary winner Rosefinch, herself out of Oh So Sharp: well held in maidens/handicap. *S. L. Keightley*

MARBLE ARCH 7 b.g. Rock Hopper 124 – Mayfair Minx (St Columbus 98) [2003 **91** p12g* 12m 11.9m 12m³ 20m 16.1m⁴ Jul 9] tall, lengthy gelding: very smart hurdler (second in 2002 Champion Hurdle): fairly useful form in first season on Flat in 2003, winning maiden at Lingfield in February: effective at 1½m, barely stays 2½m: acts on polytrack, raced only on good to firm going on turf: wore cheekpieces fourth start: carries head awkwardly: usually held up. *H. Morrison*

MARBLE GARDEN (USA)   2 b. or br.g. (Mar 27) Royal Academy (USA) 130 – Maria de La Luz (Machiavellian (USA) 123) [2003 7m 7m² 7m² 7g Oct 24] close-coupled gelding: first foal: dam, useful French 10.5f winner (also won in USA), out of useful sister to Alzao: fair maiden: second twice at Leicester, including in minor event: raced wide when below form in nursery final start: will stay 1m. *J. R. Fanshawe*   **79**

MARBLE LODGE (IRE)   3 ch.f. Grand Lodge (USA) 125 – Marble Halls (IRE) – (Ballad Rock 122) [2003 –: 8.3g 10m 12.1m f9.4s⁶ Jun 21] small, lengthy filly: no worthwhile form: tried blinkered. *H. Morrison*

MARCH ALONE   4 b.f. Alzao (USA) 117 – I Will Lead (USA) (Seattle Slew (USA)) [2003 58p: p12g³ p12g³ p16g² 10.3g⁶ 13.1g⁶ 11.9m 12m 16.4m Jul 10] fair performer: stays easy 2m: raced only on good/good to firm ground and polytrack: ridden all starts by apprentice/amateur. *Mrs A. J. Perrett*   **60 a67**

MARCH FOR LIBERTY   2 ch.f. (Mar 28) Wolfhound (USA) 126 – Badger Bay (IRE) 67 (Salt Dome (USA)) [2003 f5g 5m⁶ f5g 7m 6m* Sep 2] 2,600Y: fourth foal: dam unreliable maiden who stayed 1m: modest performer: trained by D. Ivory on debut: much improved to win selling nursery at Yarmouth by 5 lengths: stayed 6f: dead. *C. A. Dwyer*   **57**

MARCHING BAND (USA)   3 b.c. Dixieland Band (USA) – More Silver (USA) 90 (Silver Hawk (USA) 123) [2003 101: 7.6g² 7m⁴ 8s Oct 12] smallish, well-made colt: useful performer: best effort when head second to Lago d'Orta in minor event at Chester on reappearance, caught close home: respectable fourth to With Reason in Supreme Stakes at Goodwood next time: probably best short of 1m: acts on good to firm going, well held on soft final outing: sent to USA. *J. H. M. Gosden*   **105**

MARCHING WEST (USA)   2 b.f. (Feb 15) Gone West (USA) – Zaizafon (USA) 119 (The Minstrel (CAN) 135) [2003 5.5d* 5.5d⁴ Jul 27] sister to 3 winners, notably 2000 Guineas winner Zafonic and smart French performer up to 1m Zamindar, closely related to 2 winners in France, including smart 7f winner Shuttle Diplomacy (by Seeking The Gold), and half-sister to 2 winners: dam, 2-y-o 7f winner, half-sister to dam of Elmaamul and Reams of Verse: useful form: won minor event at Deauville in July: favourite, 7¼ lengths fourth of 8 to Much Faster in Prix Robert Papin at Maisons-Laffitte: will stay at least 6f: probably capable of better still. *A. Fabre, France*   **99 p**

MARCUS AURELIUS (IRE)   4 b.g. Alzao (USA) 117 – Kaguyahime (Distant Relative 128) [2003 –: 5m⁴ 5g 6m 5.1s⁴ May 17] strong gelding: fair handicapper: effective at 5f/6f: acted on soft and good to firm going: tried blinkered/tongue tied: dead. *T. D. Barron*   **71**

MARCUS EILE (IRE)   2 b.c. (Feb 20) Daggers Drawn (USA) 114 – Sherannda (USA) (Trempolino (USA) 135) [2003 5d² 5f* 5m* 6m 6f⁴ 7.2f⁴ 7.5m² 8m⁶ p8g³ Dec 20] €14,500Y: sturdy colt: third foal: half-brother to 4-y-o Bailieborough: dam unraced out of half-sister to dam of high-class miler Sendawar: fairly useful performer: won maiden at Beverley and minor event at Newcastle in April: some creditable efforts after: stays easy 1m: acts on firm going and polytrack: wore cheekpieces seventh start, blinkers eighth. *K. R. Burke*   **86**

MARDOOF   3 gr.c. Piccolo 121 – Cumbrian Melody 83 (Petong 126) [2003 79: 5d⁵ 6.1m⁵ 5d 5m 6m a6f² a6f* Dec 12] useful-looking colt: fair handicapper: left M. Channon after fifth outing: won at Jebel Ali in December: effective at 5f/6f: acts on firm going, good to soft and polytrack/dirt: usually ridden up with pace: tongue tied fifth appearance. *A. Smith, UAE*   **79**

MARENGO   9 b.g. Never So Bold 135 – Born To Dance 76 (Dancing Brave (USA) 140) [2003 60, a78: f8s⁶ f8s⁶ f7s f8s f12s f8g⁴ f8g f8g 8g 7.9m f8g f8g f7g 10g⁵ 10.5m 10g 9.9m⁴ 8.9m 10.9m⁶ f12s f8g Dec 8] small gelding: modest performer: mostly well held in 2003, leaving M. Polglase before final outing: stays 11f: acts on fibresand, firm and soft going: tried visored: usually held up: carries head high. *Paul Johnson*   **47 a54 d**

MAREN (USA)   2 b.c. (Mar 7) Gulch (USA) – Fatina 98 (Nashwan (USA) 135) [2003 7m³ 7.1m* Sep 8] angular colt: first foal: dam, 2-y-o 1m winner (ran only twice), sister to smart performer up to 2½m Shaya: confirmed promise when winning 13-runner maiden at Warwick comfortably by 1¼ lengths from Hatton, quickening on over 1f out: will stay 1m, probably 1¼m: useful prospect, should win more races. *A. C. Stewart*   **88 p**

MARE OF WETWANG   5 ch.m. River Falls 113 – Kudos Blue (Elmaamul (USA) 125) [2003 46, a–: f12s Feb 27] sparely-made mare: poor performer: well held only 5-y-o start. *J. D. Bethell*   **–**

MARFOOQ (USA)   3 ch.c. Diesis 133 – Fabulous Fairy (USA) 75 (Alydar (USA))   **86**
[2003 78: 8g 7.5m⁶ 8m³ 8.1m² 10.1m² Aug 13] useful-looking colt: fairly useful maiden:
stays 1m, possibly not 1¼m: raced only on good ground or firmer: sold 18,000 gns.
E. A. L. Dunlop

MARGALITA (IRE)   3 b.f. Sesaro (USA) 81 – Mamma Luigi (IRE) (Classic Music   **86**
(USA)) [2003 a8.5g* a7.5g* 8g³ 7g* 8g³ 8g p8g Dec 20] IR 4,000Y: first foal: dam, ran 3
times, half-sister to Italian Group 2 6f winner Piero Gardino: fairly useful performer: won
maiden in January and minor event in February, both at Neuss, and handicap at Cologne
in May for A. Kleinkorres: left R. Schaaf and off 6 months, well held in minor event at
Lingfield on British debut final outing: stays 8.5f: acts on heavy going and sand: tried
blinkered. *P. Mitchell*

MARGARETS WISH   3 gr.f. Cloudings (IRE) 112 – Gentle Gain 58 (Final Straw   **45**
127) [2003 7g 10.9m 8.1g 10m 10f² 11f f7g Nov 19] sixth living foal: closely related/
half-sister to winners abroad by Batshoof and Keen: dam, maiden, should have been
suited by further than 7f: poor maiden: left Mrs H. Dalton after debut: should stay 1½m:
raced only on good ground or firmer on turf. *T. Wall*

MARGARITA TIME (IRE)   3 ch.f. Grand Lodge (USA) 125 – Brillantina (FR)   **–**
(Crystal Glitters (USA) 127) [2003 –: 9.9m Jun 19] little worthwhile form. *R. A. Fahey*

MARGERY DAW (IRE)   3 b.f. Sri Pekan (USA) 117 – Suyayeb (USA) (The Minstrel   **70**
(CAN) 135) [2003 70p: 8.3g² p10g² p10g⁵ p10g² Dec 30] fair maiden: will prove at least
as effective at 1m as 1¼m: acts on polytrack. *M. P. Tregoning*

MARGHUB (IRE)   4 b.g. Darshaan 133 – Arctique Royale 114 (Royal And Regal   **–**
(USA)) [2003 f12g⁴ 12g⁵ 11.9m p16g Jul 16] 4,200,000 francs Y: rather leggy ex-French
gelding: half-brother to numerous winners, several at least useful, including middle-
distance performers Modhish (very smart) and Russian Snows (smart), both by Sadler's
Wells: dam Irish 1000 Guineas winner: little form, including for J. Hammond in France
at 3 yrs (tried blinkered). *Miss D. A. McHale*

MARGOLD (IRE)   3 ch.f. Goldmark (USA) 113 – Arcevia (IRE) 85 (Archway (IRE)   **56**
115) [2003 67: 10g⁶ 10m 13.8m³ 13.8m³ 12m³ 13.8m f12g⁶ Nov 21] leggy filly: modest
maiden: stays easy 1¾m: unraced on extremes of going on turf. *R. Hollinshead*

MARGOOBA (IRE)   3 ch.f. Selkirk (USA) 129 – Particular Friend 88 (Cadeaux   **69**
Genereux 131) [2003 7m⁴ 7g 6m² 7m Jul 23] IR 100,000Y: workmanlike filly: first foal:
dam, maiden best at 7f at 2 yrs, half-sister to useful 1999 2-y-o sprinter Rowaasi: fair
maiden: best effort on debut: stays 7f: raced only on good/good to firm ground: sold 5,500
gns. *B. Hanbury*

MARIA BONITA (IRE)   2 b.f. (Mar 1) Octagonal (NZ) 126 – Nightitude 93 (Night   **72**
Shift (USA)) [2003 7f 8m³ Sep 23] 21,000F, €26,000Y: close-coupled filly: sixth foal:
half-sister to useful Italian 7f/1m winner (including at 2 yrs) Golden Cavern (by Lion
Cavern): dam, 2-y-o 5f winner, became one to treat with caution: better effort in maidens
(fair form) when third of 11 to Proud Tradition at Newmarket, leading nearly 5f: not sure
to stay much beyond 1m. *R. M. Beckett*

MARIA MARIA (IRE)   2 ch.f. (Feb 16) Among Men (USA) 124 – Yiayia's Girl   **–**
(Smackover 107) [2003 f7g Dec 12] second foal: dam unraced: 50/1, well beaten in
maiden at Southwell. *Mrs N. Macauley*

MARIA VETSERA   2 ch.f. (Feb 6) Selkirk (USA) 129 – Scandalette (Niniski (USA)   **– p**
125) [2003 6m Sep 1] big, lengthy filly: has scope: sixth foal: half-sister to 3 winners,
including 6-y-o Gateman and 7-y-o Surprise Encounter: dam unraced half-sister to high-
class sprinter Polish Patriot: 25/1 and very green, always behind in maiden at Leicester:
will stay at least 1m: should do better. *Sir Mark Prescott*

MARIE LAURENCIN   3 b.f. Peintre Celebre (USA) 137 – Glatisant 104 (Rainbow   **75**
Quest (USA) 134) [2003 10m 12m² May 31] good-topped filly: fourth foal: half-sister to
1998 2-y-o 6f winner Frappe (by Inchinor) and Irish 2m winner Theme Song (by Singspiel), both fairly useful: dam, 2-y-o 6f/7f (Prestige Stakes) winner who became not one
to trust implicitly, daughter of Nassau Stakes winner Dancing Rocks: better effort in
maidens (fair form) when 3½ lengths second to Singleton at Newmarket: stays 1½m: sent
to France. *R. Charlton*

MARINAS CHARM   3 b.f. Zafonic (USA) 130 – Marina Park 112 (Local Suitor   **96**
(USA) 128) [2003 83p: a7.5f⁴ a6f⁴ a7f 7.2g² 7g 9.2g* 8.3d* 9m⁶ 10.3d* 8f Sep 27] small
filly: useful performer: below form in UAE first 3 starts: in good form back in Britain,
winning handicaps at Hamilton and Windsor in August and minor event at Doncaster

(beat Solo Flight a neck) in September: stays 1¼m: acts on heavy going, below form on firmer than good. *M. Johnston*

MARINE CITY (JPN) 2 b.f. (May 25) Carnegie (IRE) 129 – Marienbad (FR) (Dar- **– p**
shaan 133) [2003 7g Nov 1] quite good-topped filly: fifth foal: half-sister to 3 winners, including Arc winner Marienbad (by Caerleon) and 3-y-o Kartuzy: dam French 1m winner, including at 2 yrs: 20/1 and green, well held in maiden at Newmarket: should do better at 1¼m+. *M. A. Jarvis*

MARINO WOOD (IRE) 4 ch.f. Woodpas (USA) 85 – Forgren (IRE) (Thatching 131) **–**
[2003 36, a40: f8s Jan 10] lengthy filly: poor maiden: well held only 4-y-o start: tried blinkered. *C. N. Kellett*

MARITA 2 ch.f. (Mar 14) Dancing Spree (USA) – Maria Cappuccini 70 (Siberian **53**
Express (USA) 125) [2003 f6s⁴ 7m f7f² 7m f7s⁵ f8s f8.5s³ Dec 31] leggy, close-coupled filly: sister to 5-y-o Kumakawa and half-sister to 2 winners, including 7f winner Agent (by Anshan): dam, 5f winner who stayed 7f, half-sister to smart performer up to 7f Marina Park: modest maiden: second in seller at Wolverhampton: below form after: should stay 1¼m: form only on fibresand. *J. G. Given*

MARITIME BLUES 3 b.g. Fleetwood (IRE) 107 – Dixie d'Oats 66 (Alhijaz 122) **78**
[2003 47: 10m p10g⁶ f8.5g* f9.4s² 8m⁵ 10m* 10d* 10g³ 12.4m⁵ 10m⁶ 10f Sep 30] small gelding: fair handicapper: won at Wolverhampton in June and twice at Nottingham in July: ran poorly last 3 starts: stays 1¼m: acts on good to firm going, good to soft and fibresand. *J. G. Given*

MARJURITA (IRE) 4 b.f. Marju (IRE) 127 – Unfuwaanah 74 (Unfuwain (USA) **85**
131) [2003 77: f9.4g* f9.4g* p10g⁴ p10g 8m 8.3d May 9] leggy, lengthy filly: fairly useful handicapper: won at Wolverhampton in January and February: stays 9.4f: acts on firm ground, soft and all-weather. *N. P. Littmoden*

MARK-ANTONY (IRE) 9 ch.g. Phardante (FR) 123 – Judysway (Deep Run 119) **–**
[2003 12.6m⁶ 11.7f⁶ f14.8g 11.6m Jul 21] no form. *A. D. Smith*

MARKER 3 ch.g. Pivotal 124 – Palace Street (USA) 103 (Secreto (USA) 128) [2003 **96**
99: 5.5m 6g⁴ 7g 6g⁴ 6g⁶ 6f* 5d⁶ 5.6d 7f Sep 27] sturdy, close-coupled gelding: useful performer: won minor event at Kempton in August by length from Dusty Dazzler: respectable efforts in handicaps next 2 starts: should stay 7f: acts on firm and good to soft ground: visored (ran creditably) fourth/fifth starts. *G. B. Balding*

MARKET AVENUE 4 b.f. Factual (USA) 108 – The Lady Vanishes (Robin Des Pins **78**
(USA) 119) [2003 68: 8.2g 8m 10m* 10d⁶ 10.3m⁴ 9f* 10g⁵ 10.3m* 10m² 9.9m* 10.3m 10.5m³ 8m⁶ 8m 8m 10.5d 10.1m 8g⁶ Oct 28] lengthy, angular filly: has a quick action: fair performer: won handicaps at Southwell, Musselburgh and Chester and minor event at Beverley between May and July: below form under 7-lb claimer last 5 starts (trainer fined £1,600, apprentice suspended for 10 days and horse banned for 40 days after Jockey Club inquiry into running on final one): best at 9f to 11f: acts on firm and good to soft going: has pulled hard/hung left: waited with. *R. A. Fahey*

MARKET HILL (IRE) 3 b.f. Danehill (USA) 126 – Well Bought (IRE) 35 (Auction **67**
Ring (USA) 123) [2003 8.2g⁶ 8.2m⁴ 8g³ 6m* 7m 7m Sep 25] IR 100,000Y: workmanlike filly: half-sister to smart 2000 2-y-o 1m winner Tamburlaine (by Royal Academy), runner-up in 2000 Guineas: dam, poor maiden, half-sister to smart middle-distance performer Open Day: fair performer: won maiden at Kempton in August, edging left: ran poorly both starts after: effective at 6f to 1m: raced on good/good to firm ground. *S. Kirk*

MARKET LEADER 2 b.f. (May 19) Marju (IRE) 127 – I Will Lead (USA) (Seattle **72**
Slew (USA)) [2003 7.5m⁵ 8m 8d² Nov 7] good-topped filly: fourth foal: half-sister to useful 1¼m winner Stay Behind (by Elmaamul) and 3-y-o Innovation: dam unraced half-sister to Rainbow Quest: easily best effort in maidens (fair form) when neck second of 24 to Hello It's Me at Doncaster: will be suited by 1¼m/1½m. *Mrs A. J. Perrett*

MARKING TIME (IRE) 5 b.g. Goldmark (USA) 113 – Tamarsiya (USA) (Shah- **49**
rastani (USA) 135) [2003 –, a40: f12s⁶ p12g³ f11g* f12g⁶ 12.3m³ Apr 2] smallish **a57**
gelding: modest performer: won seller at Southwell in March: stays 1¾m: acts on good to firm going and fibresand: usually held up: none too consistent. *K. R. Burke*

MARK OF ZORRO (IRE) 3 b.g. Mark of Esteem (IRE) 137 – Sifaara (IRE) (Caer- **86**
leon (USA) 132) [2003 93: 8.1m 10.4m 8g 8m⁵ 8g⁶ 8m³ 8.1m⁶ 10m* 10d⁶ 10m* 10.4f⁶ 10.3m Oct 24] well-made gelding: fairly useful performer: won claimers at Newmarket in August and Leicester in September: stays 1¼m: acts on firm and good to soft ground: often blinkered/visored: sometimes looks difficult ride: joined O. Sherwood. *R. Hannon*

MARKSGOLD (IRE)   2 b.g. (Feb 15) Goldmark (USA) 113 – Lady of Shalott 61   **50**
(Kings Lake (USA) 133) [2003 6d f8.5s p6g Dec 6] IR 1,500F, €3,000Y: half-brother to
several winners, including smart German sprinter Meliksah (by Thatching) and 7f/1m
winner Irrepressible (by Don't Forget Me): dam maiden who stayed 1m: best effort
(modest form) when tenth of 14 in maiden at Lingfield final start: should stay 7f. *K. Bell*

MARK YOUR WAY   3 b.g. Spectrum (IRE) 126 – Titania's Way 91 (Fairy King   **59 ?**
(USA)) [2003 8m⁶ 10.3m 10m Jul 21] 10,000Y: fourth foal: half-brother to a winner in
Greece by Pennekamp: dam 7f/1m winner: modest maiden: clearly best effort on debut:
stays 1m: raced only on good to firm ground: pulled hard second start. *P. R. Chamings*

MARLO   4 b.c. Hector Protector (USA) 124 – Tender Moment (IRE) 78 (Caerleon   **90**
(USA) 132) [2003 86: f8.5g² 7d² 7g 8g 8.1s⁵ 7.1g 8d Jul 27] good-topped colt: useful   **a95**
handicapper: second at Wolverhampton and Kempton first 2 starts, beaten 1¼ lengths by
Ceepio in latter: below form after, tailed off on final outing: stays 8.5f: acts on fibresand,
best turf form on ground softer than good: sold 12,000 gns. *B. W. Hills*

MARMADUKE (IRE)   7 ch.g. Perugino (USA) 84 – Sympathy 77 (Precocious 126)   **63**
[2003 70: f12s⁶ Dec 27] tall gelding: fair handicapper in 2002: off 17 months, respectable
effort only run in 2003: effective at 1½m, seemingly at 2¼m: acts on all-weather and
probably any turf going: tried visored: tends to race freely. *M. Pitman*

MARNIE   6 ch.m. First Trump 118 – Miss Aboyne 64 (Lochnager 132) [2003 63, a66:   **62**
p7g p7g⁶ 8f 8f² 8.3m 8f² 8f 8m⁴ 8m 8.5g 8m Sep 24] sturdy, lengthy mare: modest handi-   **a52**
capper: effective at 7f/1m: acts on firm going, good to soft and polytrack. *J. Akehurst*

MAROMA   5 b.m. First Trump 118 – Madurai 71 (Chilibang 120) [2003 –: 11.6g 10m   **–**
8.1m 10.2m Jul 24] winner 3 times in Czech Republic at 3 yrs: well held in Britain: tried
blinkered. *A. G. Newcombe*

MAROMITO (IRE)   6 b.g. Up And At 'em 109 – Amtico (Bairn (USA) 126) [2003   **65**
84, a–: 5g 5.7f 5.3m 5m f5g Aug 8] well-made gelding: fair handicapper nowadays: best
at bare 5f: acts on firm going, good to soft and fibresand: blinkered last 3 starts: edgy
type: has usually races prominently. *C. R. Dore*

MARON   6 b.g. Puissance 110 – Will Be Bold 79 (Bold Lad (IRE) 133) [2003 –, a56d:
f6g f6g f6g 7g Jul 26] rather leggy gelding: no longer of any account: tried tongue tied/
blinkered/in cheekpieces. *A. Berry*

MAROONED (IRE)   3 ch.f. Definite Article 121 – No Islands (Lomond (USA) 128)   **–**
[2003 50: 9.9m Aug 23] workmanlike filly: modest maiden in 2002: well beaten only
3-y-o start. *J. G. Given*

MARREL   5 b.g. Shareef Dancer (USA) 135 – Upper Caen (High Top 131) [2003 50,   **44**
a55: f14.8g² f12g³ f16.2g³ Feb 7] strong, workmanlike gelding: poor performer: stays
2m: acts on fibresand, best turf efforts on ground firmer than good: often blinkered/visor-
ed: joined D. Burchell £6,000 and won 3 times over hurdles in May/June. *S. L. Keightley*

MARSAD (IRE)   9 ch.g. Fayruz 116 – Broad Haven (IRE) (Be My Guest (USA) 126)   **98**
[2003 102: 7d 6m⁴ 6g⁵ 6g 6g⁵ 6f² 6f 6.5m³ Jul 11] lengthy, good-topped gelding: useful
handicapper: creditable fifth of 30 to Fire Up The Band at Newmarket (had won race
previous 2 years) third start: good third to Master Robbie at Ascot final one: effective at
6f/easy 7f: acts on any going: has run creditably when sweating: consistent. *J. Akehurst*

MARSHAL BOND   5 b.g. Celtic Swing 138 – Arminda (Blakeney 126) [2003 70, a–:   **57 d**
f12g⁵ f11s⁵ f11g 9.9d 12.1m 10.1m 10m 11g Oct 28] workmanlike gelding: fluent mover:
modest handicapper: well below form last 6 starts: stays 1½m: acts on fibresand and any
turf going: tried blinkered: usually races prominently. *B. Smart*

MARSHALLSPARK (IRE)   4 b.g. Fayruz 116 – Lindas Delight 54 (Batshoof 122)   **78**
[2003 78: 7m 7f 5.9g² 6.1d 7g⁴ 7f* 6m³ 7m* 7.2m⁶ 7m 7g Oct 28] sturdy, lengthy gelding:
fair performer: won minor events at Brighton (ladies) in August and Redcar in September: effective at 6f/7f: acts on firm ground, good to soft and fibresand: tried blinkered.
R. A. Fahey

MARSHALL WARNING   3 b.g. Averti (IRE) 117 – Spring Sunrise 59 (Robellino   **–**
(USA) 127) [2003 53: 8f 10m Aug 6] modest maiden at 2 yrs: well held in 2003, including
in blinkers. *B. De Haan*

MARSHMAN (IRE)   4 ch.g. College Chapel 122 – Gold Fly (IRE) (Be My Guest   **99**
(USA) 126) [2003 90, a100: p7g² p7g⁶ 7d 7m⁴ 7g³ 7.1g 7.1m* 7g⁵ 7d³ p7g⁴ Nov 22]
good-topped gelding: useful handicapper: won at Musselburgh in October by ¾ length
from Raphael: effective at 6f/7f: acts on polytrack, firm and soft going: usually waited
with. *M. H. Tompkins*

MARTALINE 4 gr.c. Linamix (FR) 127 – Coraline (Sadler's Wells (USA) 132) [2003 **118**
108: 12g* 12d³ 12g² 14g* 12m² 12f⁴ Sep 28] strong, good-topped colt: has a markedly
round action: first foal: dam, French 12.5f winner, half-sister to Irish Oaks winner
Wemyss Bight (dam of high-class performer up to 1½m Beat Hollow) and to dam of
Oasis Dream and Zenda: smart performer: won minor event at Deauville at 3 yrs:
improved in 2003, winning Prix d'Hedouville at Longchamp (by neck from Loxias) in
April and Prix Maurice de Nieuil at Maisons-Laffitte (by ¾ length from Westerner) in
July: also good second to Ange Gabriel in Grand Prix de Chantilly (beaten 1½ lengths)
and Prix Foy at Longchamp (beaten 2½ lengths): respectable fourth of 5 to High
Accolade in Cumberland Lodge Stakes at Ascot (swished tail in paddock) final start:
stays 15f: probably acts on any going: usually races prominently: consistent. *A. Fabre,
France*

MARTILLO (GER) 3 b.c. Anabaa (USA) 130 – Maltage (USA) (Affirmed (USA)) **119**
[2003 8d* 8g* 8f³ 8g* 8d Aug 17] big, strong colt: third foal: half-brother to German 7f/
1m winner Maegashira (by Owington): dam, ran 3 times in Germany, half-sister to US
Grade 2 2-y-o 8.5f winner Terra Incognita: smart performer: won maiden at Cologne at 2
yrs, listed race at Mulheim in April, Mehl-Mulhens-Rennen at Cologne (beat Royal Price
easily by 6 lengths) in May and Grosser Porsche Preis at Hoppegarten (by 2½ lengths
from Mail The Desert) in July: respectable 4 lengths third to Zafeen in St James's Palace
Stakes at Royal Ascot third start, below form in Prix Jacques le Marois at Deauville final
one: stays 1m: acts on good to soft ground, ran respectably on firm. *R. Suerland, Germany*

MARTIN HOUSE (IRE) 4 b.g. Mujadil (USA) 119 – Dolcezza (FR) (Lichine (USA) **–**
117) [2003 97: 10.5f⁴ 10.3m 10m 11.9m 10m 10.4f Oct 9] tall, leggy gelding: useful
performer at 3 yrs: showed little in 2003: tried visored/tongue tied: often races prominently: sold 8,500 gns. *J. D. Bethell*

MARTIN'S SUNSET 5 ch.g. Royal Academy (USA) 130 – Mainly Sunset (Red **49 §**
Sunset 120) [2003 62§: p12g 14.4g 12f 11.6m⁵ p12g 12d 10f* 10f³ 10d⁶ 9.7g⁴ 10.9m 8m
Oct 23] sparely-made gelding: poor handicapper: won at Brighton in July: stays easy
1½m: acts on firm ground, soft and polytrack: tried in headgear: often soon off bridle: has
found little: unreliable: sold 10,000 gns. *W. R. Muir*

MARTON MERE 7 ch.g. Cadeaux Genereux 131 – Hyatti 74 (Habitat 134) [2003 47: **–**
9.9m⁴ 8.5m Aug 13] angular gelding: poor performer: stiff tasks in 2003. *A. J. Lockwood*

MARWELL'S KRIS (IRE) 7 b.g. Kris 135 – Marwell 133 (Habitat 134) [2003 62: **?**
p6g⁶ 6f* a6g³ a5g* a5g² 5.5d 6f⁴ 5.5g⁶ 5d 6g³ 6g⁴ Oct 25] modest performer: sixth in
selling handicap at Lingfield on reappearance: won minor events at Sterrebeek in April
and May: stays 6f: acts on firm going and dirt/polytrack: has been blinkered. *A. Hermans,
Belgium*

MARY JANE 8 b.m. Tina's Pet 121 – Fair Attempt (IRE) (Try My Best (USA) 130) **68**
[2003 75, a–: 6.1g 5m 5m 5g 5d⁴ 5m² 5m 5m³ 5g 5.1m² 5d⁴ 5.1g⁴ 5m* Aug 22] smallish,
sturdy mare: fair handicapper: won apprentice event at Thirsk (for third successive year)
in August: best at 5f: acted on any turf going and fibresand: tried in blinkers/cheekpieces:
often front runner: tough: in foal to Sugarfoot. *N. Tinkler*

MARY'S BABY 3 b.f. Magic Ring (IRE) 115 – Everdene (Bustino 136) [2003 72: **72**
7m⁴ 6f 8.3m* 8.3m 8.3g² 8.3g⁶ Aug 23] fair performer: won maiden at Windsor in July:
stays 8.3f: acts on soft and good to firm ground. *Mrs A. J. Perrett*

MARY SEA (FR) 3 ch.f. Selkirk (USA) 129 – Mary Astor (FR) (Groom Dancer (USA) **67 ?**
128) [2003 10.5g⁵ 12g 9m⁶ 9g 8m 7f Sep 15] half-sister to a 1m winner in Germany by
Barathea: dam, French 1¼m to 11.5f winner, half-sister to dam of Lit de Justice, Colonel
Collins and Commander Collins: seemingly fair maiden in France for J. Lesbordes:
soundly beaten both starts in Britain: tried blinkered/in cheekpieces. *Mrs K. Walton*

MARYSIENKA 2 b.f. (Mar 18) Primo Dominie 121 – Polish Romance (USA) 83 **78**
(Danzig (USA)) [2003 5m⁴ 5s³ 5.1f⁶ 5m² 6g 5.1g² 5.1g⁶ 5d⁴ Oct 4] 15,000F, €70,000Y:
compact filly: third foal: half-sister to 3-y-o Irresistible: dam 7f winner out of US Grade 1
2-y-o 7f/1m winner Some Romance: fair maiden: second in nurseries: probably best at
5f: acts on good to firm and soft ground: sold 13,500 gns. *R. Hannon*

MASAADER (USA) 3 gr.f. Wild Again (USA) – Futuh (USA) 95 (Diesis 133) [2003 **96**
88: 6m² 6m⁶ 5f 7m³ 6g* Oct 31] compact filly: useful performer: off nearly 4 months,
best effort when winning minor event at Newmarket in October by neck from Pivotal
Point: best at 6f: acted on soft and good to firm going: visits Elnadim. *E. A. L. Dunlop*

MASAFI (IRE) 2 b.c. (Mar 22) Desert King (IRE) 129 – Mrs Fisher (IRE) 94 (Salmon **– p**
Leap (USA) 131) [2003 f6s f6g f6g Nov 10] good-bodied colt: seventh foal: half-brother

to fairly useful 1m (including at 2 yrs) winner Pedro (by Brief Truce) and 5-y-o Grandma Lily: dam 7f winner, including at 2 yrs: green, well held in maidens at Southwell and Wolverhampton (2): will stay at least 7f: likely to do better. *Sir Mark Prescott*

MASJOOR 3 ch.g. Unfuwain (USA) 131 – Mihnah (IRE) 87 (Lahib (USA) 129) [2003 **58**
11.8m 10m³ 11.1g Sep 27] lengthy gelding: first foal: dam, 6f (at 2 yrs) and 1m winner, half-sister to smart performer up to 14.6f Ranin (by Unfuwain): modest form in maidens first 2 starts: tailed off final one: seems to stay 1½m. *N. A. Graham*

MASONRY (IRE) 3 b.g. Grand Lodge (USA) 125 – Tumble (Mtoto 134) [2003 73: –
8.3g⁵ 7m⁴ 10d 7.1m Sep 20] fair maiden at 2 yrs: well below form in 2003: sold 7,500 gns. *P. F. I. Cole*

MA'SOOLA 2 b.f. (Mar 18) Green Desert (USA) 127 – First Waltz (FR) 117 (Green **84**
Dancer (USA) 132) [2003 5.2m² 5m⁵ May 27] quite attractive filly: half-sister to several winners, including useful 1m winners Atlantic Rhapsody (including in Ireland, by Machiavellian) and Gaitero (in France, by Groom Dancer): dam won Prix Morny: fairly useful form when second in minor event at Newbury: broke pastern in listed race at Sandown: dead. *M. R. Channon*

MASSEY 7 br.g. Machiavellian (USA) 123 – Massaraat (USA) (Nureyev (USA) 131) –
[2003 60, a95: f6s* f6g* f6s² 6m f5g f5g p6g Dec 20] big gelding: useful performer on **a103**
all-weather, modest on turf: won minor event at Southwell and handicap at Wolverhampton (by ½ length from dead-heaters Peruvian Chief and Quito), both in February: best at 6f/7f: acts on fibresand and good to firm going: often visored in 2000: game front runner. *T. D. Barron*

MASSOMAH (USA) 3 b.f. Seeking The Gold (USA) – Kerenza (Seattle Dancer **90**
(USA) 119) [2003 10m² 8.1m* May 5] strong, angular filly: third foal: half-sister to useful French 1¼m winner Jomana (by Darshaan): dam, French 11f winner, half-sister to high-class 1984 2-y-o 6f/7f performer Local Suitor, Prix Jean Prat winner Local Talent and to dam of Mark of Esteem: better effort in maidens (fairly useful form) when winning at Warwick in May by 6 lengths from Cryptogam: will stay 1¼m. *D. R. Loder*

MASTER CORBIN 4 b.g. Mind Games 121 – Cafe Solo 51 (Nomination 125) [2003 –
–: 6g Apr 30] sturdy gelding: little form: tried tongue tied. *P. T. Dalton*

MASTER DAVID (USA) 2 ch.c. (Mar 11) Grand Slam (USA) 120 – Nadra (IRE) 61 **101**
(Sadler's Wells (USA) 132) [2003 6m² 7m² 7m* a9f² Nov 29] $100,000 2-y-o: strong, well-made colt: has a quick action: sixth foal: half-brother to useful French 6f (at 2 yrs) to 11f winner Ardent Passion (by Bering) and 3-y-o Tempsford: dam, maiden, out of Yorkshire Oaks and Prix Vermeille winner Bint Pasha: useful performer: won 4-runner maiden at Thirsk in September by 1¼ lengths from Great Exhibition: good 3¾ lengths second of 11 to Read The Footnotes in Grade 2 Remsen Stakes at Aqueduct final start: will stay 1¼m: joined R. Frankel in USA. *B. J. Meehan*

MASTER GATEMAKER 5 b.g. Tragic Role (USA) – Girl At The Gate 53 (Formid- –
able (USA) 125) [2003 12.3m Apr 2] poor maiden on Flat: winning hurdler: tried visored: dead. *R. C. Guest*

MASTERMAN READY 2 b.g. (Apr 27) Unfuwain (USA) 131 – Maria Isabella **53 p**
(FR) (Young Generation 129) [2003 p8g⁶ Oct 27] 14,000F, 8,500Y: brother to useful Italian performer up to 1½m Streisand and useful winner around 1½m Rain In Spain and half-brother to 3 winners: dam French maiden: 10/3, sixth of 11 to The Way We Were in maiden at Lingfield, not knocked about: should be suited by 1¼m/1½m: will do better. *P. W. Harris*

MASTER NIMBUS 3 b.g. Cloudings (IRE) 112 – Miss Charlie 59 (Pharly (FR) 130) –
[2003 67: 6d 7m 5.9m 6m 6m 7g Jul 31] strong, angular gelding: modest maiden handicapper: stays 6f: acts on good to firm ground: inconsistent. *J. J. Quinn*

MASTER PAPA (IRE) 4 br.g. Key of Luck (USA) 126 – Beguine (USA) 77 (Green –
Dancer (USA) 132) [2003 94: 12g⁴ Sep 22] 30,000F, 32,000Y: ex-Irish gelding: first foal: dam, lightly-raced maiden, half-sister to Grand Lodge: fairly useful performer in Ireland at 2 yrs (won twice) and 3 yrs, then left K. Prendergast €52,000: fairly useful form over hurdles: well held only Flat outing in 2003. *N. A. Twiston-Davies*

MASTER PEEWEE 2 ch.c. (May 9) Cigar 68 – Divine Miss-P 90 (Safawan 118) **48**
[2003 5d⁵ p7g 6m⁶ Oct 3] first foal: dam 5f/6f winner: poor form in minor events/claimer: sold £400. *J. Cullinan*

MASTERPOINT 3 ch.g. Mark of Esteem (IRE) 137 – Baize 95 (Efisio 120) [2003 **90**
91: 8.2d⁶ 8g² 8m 8m 8.5m 10.1d⁴ 9.9m 7.5m* 8g* Aug 26] strong gelding: fairly useful

performer: won claimers at Beverley (claimed from M. Johnston £12,000) and Ripon (joined R. Phillips £20,000) within 3 days in August, making most by 4 lengths in latter: stays 1m: acts on firm going: tried blinkered: none too consistent. *B. Smart*

MASTER RATTLE 4 b.g. Sabrehill (USA) 120 – Miss Primula 81 (Dominion 123) **64 §**
[2003 58: f5g⁵ p6g⁶ f6g⁶ p7g* p7g p7g⁵ p8g p7g 7m p7g Dec 30] modest performer: 66/1-winner of maiden at Lingfield in February: stays easy 7f: acts on all-weather and soft ground: has flashed tail: unreliable. *Jane Southcombe*

MASTER ROBBIE 4 b.g. Piccolo 121 – Victoria's Secret (IRE) 70 (Law Society **104** (USA) 130) [2003 91d: 5g 7m² 7f⁵ 8.5m 7m 7m* 7m² 7m* 7m⁵ 7m³ 7.1m* 7f 7d⁵ 6.5m* 7g⁴ 7g 7m² 7.1m² 7m 7.2f* 7m 7f* 7m² 7f* 7m⁶ 7.1m Oct 25] tall, close-coupled gelding: useful performer: had an excellent season, winning handicaps at Salisbury, Newbury, Ascot (2) and York and minor events at Warwick and Ayr between May and October: beat Grizedale by 1¼ lengths in Tote Trifecta Stakes for second success at Ascot: best around 7f: acts on firm going, probably not on softer than good: effective held up or making running: tough and genuine. *M. R. Channon*

MASTER THEO (USA) 2 b.c. (Mar 30) Southern Halo (USA) – Lilian Bayliss (IRE) **72** 100 (Sadler's Wells (USA) 132) [2003 7m³ p8g³ p10g⁵ Nov 29] $27,000Y, 40,000 2-y-o: sturdy colt: half-brother to several winners, including useful 1998 2-y-o 6f to 1m winner Strike A Blow (by Red Ransom) and 7f winner Chapter House (by Pulpit): dam, 7f (at 2 yrs) and 9f winner, sister to smart French sprinter Ernani and half-sister to high-class French miler Phydilla: fair form in maidens: third at Newmarket and Lingfield: needs to settle to stay beyond 1m. *H. J. Collingridge*

MASTER TOMMY (IRE) 3 b.c. Entrepreneur 123 – Dame Rose (IRE) (Machia- **–** vellian (USA) 123) [2003 p7g p7g p7g f8.5g Jun 6] IR 45,000F, IR 25,000Y: second living foal: half-brother to a winner in Turkey by Flying Spur: dam ran 3 times in France: little form. *B. W. Hills*

MASTER T (USA) 4 b.g. Trempolino (USA) 135 – Our Little C (USA) (Marquetry **–** (USA) 121) [2003 66, a73: p10g⁴ p12g p10g 11.5g May 28] sparely-made gelding: fair **a66** performer: stays 1¼m: acts on firm going (below form on softer than good) and poly-track: tried tongue tied. *G. L. Moore*

MASTER WEBB 3 b.c. Whittingham (IRE) 104 – Jackies Webb (Selkirk (USA) 129) **–** [2003 p6g Feb 5] well held in maidens. *Dr J. R. J. Naylor*

MATABELE 3 ch.g. Muhtarram (USA) 125 – Newala 61 (Royal Academy (USA) 130) **–** [2003 ?: 10m f9.4g⁶ 11.5m Oct 21] rather unfurnished gelding: little worthwhile form: left W. Haggas after second start: tried tongue tied/blinkered. *W. J. Musson*

MATERIAL WITNESS (IRE) 6 b.g. Barathea (IRE) 127 – Dial Dream (Gay **95** Mecene (USA) 128) [2003 91: 6d² 6g 7f 6d² 6.1m* 6g 7m Aug 16] angular gelding: useful performer: better than ever in 2003, and won minor event at Chepstow in July by 1¼ lengths from Riva Royale: acts on soft going, firm and polytrack: effective at 6f/7f: tried blinkered/visored, not in 2003: carries head high: races up with pace. *W. R. Muir*

MATHMAGICIAN 4 ch.g. Hector Protector (USA) 124 – Inherent Magic (IRE) 95 **–** (Magical Wonder (USA) 125) [2003 –: f11g³ f8s f12g f12g f16g⁴ f14.8g Feb 1] strong **a45** gelding: poor maiden: stays 11f: form only on fibresand: usually blinkered. *R. F. Marvin*

MATLOOB 2 b.c. (Apr 16) Halling (USA) 133 – Belle Argentine (FR) 113 (Fijar Tango **105** (FR) 127) [2003 6m* 7m* 7.1d³ Aug 30] lengthy, good-topped colt: fourth foal: half-brother to 1m winner Saaryeh (by Royal Academy): dam, French 1m winner (including at 2 yrs) who stayed 10.5f, out of half-sister to high-class French middle-distance performer Lovely Dancer: impressive winner of maiden at Leicester in June and minor event at Newbury in July: best effort (useful form) when 1¾ lengths third of 8 to Bar-bajuan in Solario Stakes at Sandown, no extra after challenging over 1f out: should stay 1m: joined Godolphin. *M. A. Jarvis*

Tote Trifecta Stakes (Handicap), Ascot—the sixth of seven wins during the year for Master Robbie; Grizedale, Dame de Noche (far rail), Mine, Royal Storm and Little Good Bay are next home in a race dominated by those on the far side

MATRIARCHAL 3 ch.f. Presidium 124 – Mayor 86 (Laxton 105) [2003 51: 6.1g 7m **41** 5m⁵ 6m 6m 6.9m 6f⁴ f8g f8g Dec 9] neat filly: poor maiden: probably stays 7f: acts on firm ground: sold tongue tied. *Don Enrico Incisa*

MATT BLANC (IRE) 2 b.c. (Feb 9) Night Shift (USA) – New Tycoon (IRE) (Last **93** Tycoon 131) [2003 6.1g⁴ 6.3g 6g* 6g² 6.1m² 6m* 7d⁵ 6m⁴ Oct 1] IR 23,000F, €52,000Y: lengthy, sturdy colt: has a quick action: half-brother to several winners in USA: dam, won at 8.5f in USA, half-sister to dam of St Leger winner Mutafaweq and 3-y-o Dimitrova: fairly useful performer: won maiden at Salisbury in July and nursery at Ayr (beat Trick Cyclist 3 lengths) in September: respectable fourth of 5 to Millbag in minor event at Salisbury final start, carrying head to one side: should stay 7f: acts on good to firm ground: sold 47,000 gns, sent to USA. *R. Hannon*

MATTHEW MY SON (IRE) 3 ch.g. Lake Coniston (IRE) 131 – Mary Hinge 100 **–** (Dowsing (USA) 124) [2003 6m 9.1d Oct 14] 7,000Y: fourth foal: half-brother to 6-y-o Compton Banker: dam sprinter: well held in maiden/seller. *F. P. Murtagh*

MATTY TUN 4 b.g. Lugana Beach 116 – Barge 59 (Lucky Wednesday 124) [2003 **96** 84: f5s⁶ 5g⁵ 5g³ 5m* 5g* 6s 6d Nov 8] strong gelding: useful handicapper: better than ever in 2003, and won at York (hung right) and Musselburgh (by neck from Salviati) in May: off 5 months and well held on return: probably best at 5f: acts on any turf going and fibresand: tried tongue tied: sometimes slowly away: tends to carry head awkwardly/idle. *J. Balding*

MAUGWENNA 3 b.f. Danehill (USA) 126 – River Abouali (Bluebird (USA) 125) **85** [2003 79: 5m⁴ 6m 6m 5m Sep 17] quite attractive filly: fluent mover: fairly useful performer: best effort when fourth in handicap at Sandown on reappearance: should stay 6f: raced only on good ground or firmer: none too reliable. *J. Noseda*

MAUIRA (IRE) 2 b.f. (May 12) Docksider (USA) 124 – Easy Romance (USA) (North- **?** ern Jove (CAN)) [2003 6m 7g 6m a6.8g³ Dec 30] €7,000Y: workmanlike filly: half-sister to several winners, including Irish 1998 2-y-o 6f/7f winner Storm Cove (by Catrail) and 1m winner Northern Fan (by Lear Fan), both fairly useful: dam won up to 7f in USA: signs of ability in maidens for G. Bravery before third in similar event at Taby: stays 7f. *M. Kahn, Sweden*

MAUNBY RAVER 2 ch.g. (Feb 23) Pivotal 124 – Colleen Liath (Another Realm **65** 118) [2003 5d 7d⁶ 5g⁶ 6m⁴ f6g* f6g² p6g* f7g⁵ Dec 8] 5,500Y: sixth foal: half-brother to winner up to 1½m in Sweden by Efisio: dam unraced half-sister to smart middle-distance stayer Sudden Victory: fair performer: won nurseries at Wolverhampton and Lingfield in November: should stay 7f: acts on all-weather, showed promise on turf. *P. C. Haslam*

MAUNBY ROCKER 3 ch.g. Sheikh Albadou 128 – Bullion 85 (Sabrehill (USA) **60** 120) [2003 73, a64: p10g f8s* f11s² 10.9d⁶ f8g Dec 8] small gelding: modest performer: won handicap at Southwell in February: stays 1m: acts on soft going and fibresand: has worn cheekpieces: sometimes carries head awkwardly: none too consistent. *P. C. Haslam*

MAUNBY ROLLER (IRE) 4 b.g. Flying Spur (AUS) – Brown Foam (Horage 124) **55 d** [2003 62: f8s² f8s* f9.4g⁴ f8s f8.5g³ 12m 9f Aug 22] strong gelding: modest performer: won apprentice claimer at Southwell (left P. Haslam) in January: left R. Wilman after fifth outing, P. Blockley after sixth: stays 9.4f: acts on all-weather, no recent form on turf: wears headgear: carries head awkwardly. *K. A. Morgan*

MAUREEN ANN 3 b.f. Elmaamul (USA) 125 – Running Glimpse (IRE) 84 (Runnett **59** 125) [2003 60?: 10g 8.5m⁵ 7m 7g* 8.5m f8.5g 8.2d p12g Nov 26] modest performer: won handicap at Epsom in July: best form at 7f/1m: acts on good and good to soft going, well held on all-weather: wears hood: sometimes slowly away: has looked hard ride: inconsistent: sold £350. *Miss B. Sanders*

MAWAANI 3 b.f. Indian Ridge 123 – Ginger Tree (USA) 86 (Dayjur (USA) 137) [2003 **70** 8.5m² 7m⁵ 8.1m⁵ Aug 13] quite attractive filly: third foal: half-sister to fairly useful 2000 2-y-o 7f winner Hotaaff (by Arazi) and 4-y-o Alrafid: dam, 2-y-o 6f winner, out of North American Grade 1 1¼m/1½m winner Carotene: fair maiden: may prove best up to 7f: raced only on good to firm ground: found little first 2 starts: sold 6,500 gns in December. *A. C. Stewart*

MAWDSLEY 6 b.m. Piccolo 121 – Legendary Dancer 90 (Shareef Dancer (USA) 135) **–** [2003 f12s f12g Jun 27] no form: tried visored. *A. Senior*

MAWHOOB (USA) 5 gr.g. Dayjur (USA) 137 – Asl (USA) 114 (Caro 133) [2003 –: **– §** f12g* 10g f12s 8m f12s f11g f14g Dec 12] good-bodied gelding: has a round action: **a51 §** modest performer: well held after winning seller at Southwell in June: stays 1½m: acts on firm ground and fibresand: visored: not to be trusted. *Mrs N. Macauley*

MAXILLA (IRE) 3 b. or br.f. Lahib (USA) 129 – Lacinia 107 (Groom Dancer (USA) **77**
128) [2003 68: 8m² p12g⁴ p10g* Dec 6] rangy filly: fair performer: won maiden at
Lingfield in December, making most: best at 1m/1¼m: acts on polytrack and good to firm
ground. *L. M. Cumani*

MAXIMINUS 3 b.g. The West (USA) 107 – Candarela 41 (Damister (USA) 123) [2003 **–**
–: 10g p10g Nov 18] well held in maidens. *M. Madgwick*

MAXIM (IRE) 4 b.g. Zamindar (USA) 116 – Lavanda 60 (Soviet Star (USA) 128) **72 ?**
[2003 49: p5g⁵ 5m Apr 21] lightly-raced maiden, seemed to run easily best race on
reappearance: should stay at least 6f: acts on polytrack: sold only £650. *W. A. O'Gorman*

MAXI'S PRINCESS (IRE) 2 b.f. (Jan 15) Revoque (IRE) 122 – Harmer (IRE) 72 **60**
(Alzao (USA) 117) [2003 5m f6g⁴ 6g 5.1d p5g Nov 22] €2,600Y, resold 2,000Y: ninth
foal: sister to 4-y-o Likely Lady and half-sister to 2 winners, including fairly useful 1995
2-y-o 5f winner Amaretto Bay (by Common Grounds), later sprint winner abroad: dam
maiden who stayed 7f: modest maiden: stays 6f: acts on fibresand, best turf effort on good
going: tongue tied final start. *P. J. Makin*

MAX SCAL (IRE) 2 b.c. (May 11) Danehill Dancer (IRE) 117 – Slightly Latin **79**
(Ahonoora 122) [2003 6m⁶ 9g² 8f⁶ Oct 18] leggy, shallow-girthed colt: has a fluent,
round action: half-brother to 3 winners, including fairly useful 6f winner (including at 2
yrs) Poles Apart (by Distinctly North): dam lightly raced in Ireland: easily best effort in
maidens (fair form) when second at Tipperary: ran at Pontefract on debut: not sure to stay
much beyond 9f. *Mrs A. M. O'Shea, Ireland*

MA YAHAB 2 ch.c. (Apr 16) Dr Fong (USA) 128 – Bay Shade (USA) 90 (Sharpen Up **72 p**
127) [2003 8m 8.2m² 8.2d Nov 6] 105,000Y: good-topped colt: half-brother to several
winners, including 1998 2-y-o 7f winner Forest Shadow (by Sadler's Wells) and 7f (at 2
yrs) and 11.4f winner Abury (by Law Society), both useful: dam, 2-y-o 7f winner, later
won Italian 1m listed event: best effort in maidens (fair form) when second to Asiatic at
Nottingham: good hold and not at all knocked about final start: needs to settle to stay
beyond 1m: probably open to progress. *L. M. Cumani*

MAYBACH 2 gr.c. (Feb 19) Machiavellian (USA) 123 – Capote Line (USA) (Capote **72**
(USA)) [2003 7m⁴ 7.1m³ Sep 13] third foal: half-brother to winners in Norway by Coney-
bury and Entrepreneur: dam, won up to around 9f in Norway, half-sister to 2000 Guineas
winner Mystiko: fair form in maidens at Yarmouth and Musselburgh (third to Kibryaa):
should stay at least 1m: sent to Sweden. *J. Noseda*

MAYBE A LADY 2 b.f. (Apr 21) Woodborough (USA) 112 – Danseuse Davis (FR) **–**
(Glow (USA)) [2003 6g 7m f7g Oct 20] fifth foal: half-sister to fairly useful 5f (at 2 yrs)/
6f winner Polly Mills (by Lugana Beach) and 3-y-o Genteel: dam no form: well held in
maidens/seller. *G. C. H. Chung*

MAYBE BABY (IRE) 4 b.g. Lake Coniston (IRE) 131 – Nadedge (IRE) 78 (Petorius **–**
117) [2003 43: f6g f5s f6g Jan 21] leggy, sparely-made gelding: poor maiden: well held
in 2003: tried visored/in cheekpieces. *D. Carroll*

MAYBE SOMEDAY 2 ch.g. (Mar 10) Dr Fong (USA) 128 – Shicklah (USA) 106 **60**
(The Minstrel (CAN) 135) [2003 5g⁶ 7m f8g² f7g* 8d³ Oct 31] 40,000Y: half-brother to **a74**
numerous winners, including useful 1998 2-y-o 6f (Richmond Stakes) winner Muqtarib
(by Gone West) and 5-y-o Activist: dam 2-y-o 5f/6f winner: fair on all-weather, modest
on turf: left D. Morris after second start: won seller at Wolverhampton in October by 12
lengths, then left H. Cyzer 16,000 gns: creditable third in nursery at Brighton: should stay
1¼m: acts on fibresand and good to soft going. *I. A. Wood*

MAYSIE (IRE) 2 b.f. (Mar 1) Imperial Ballet (IRE) 110 – Mysticism 79 (Mystiko **–**
(USA) 124) [2003 6g 6m p7g 6.1m⁵ 7m Oct 23] 17,000Y: compact filly: first foal: dam 7f
winner: little form, including in nursery. *B. G. Powell*

MAYSTOCK 3 ch.f. Magic Ring (IRE) 115 – Stockline (Capricorn Line 111) [2003 **80**
8.2g 9.7m³ 8m⁵ 9.9f p12g³ f12g⁶ᵈ 11.9d p16g⁴ p13g* p12g⁴ p13g Dec 6] sturdy filly:
seventh living foal: half-sister to 2 winners, including 8-y-o April Stock: dam soundly
beaten: fair handicapper: won apprentice event at Lingfield in November: best short of
2m: acts on polytrack and good to soft going: sometimes visored/tongue tied. *G. A. Butler*

MAYZIN (IRE) 3 b.g. Fayruz 116 – Peep of Day (USA) (Lypheor 118) [2003 66: **60**
f8.5s⁶ 8.2g 6d 7m 8f 10d p7g⁵ p7g⁴ Dec 29] lengthy, angular gelding: modest maiden: left
B. Palling after fifth start: stays 7f: acts on polytrack: best 3-y-o efforts in cheekpieces:
usually races prominently. *R. M. Flower*

MAZEPA (IRE) 3 b.c. Indian Ridge 123 – Please Believe Me 93 (Try My Best (USA) **97**
130) [2003 98: 6.1m 6g 6.1g 6m* 5m 6g Oct 24] rangy, good-topped colt: has a quick

action: useful handicapper: had slipped in weights prior to winning at Ascot in September by 2 lengths from A Very Good Year: good seventh to Royal Millennium at Newbury final start: effective at 5f/6f: acts on polytrack, unraced on extremes of going on turf. *N. A. Callaghan*

MAZRAM 4 b.f. Muhtarram (USA) 125 – Royal Mazi 58 (Kings Lake (USA) 133) – [2003 8.5f Apr 16] fourth foal: dam 2m winner on Flat and ungenuine winning hurdler: well beaten in seller at Beverley. *G. P. Kelly*

MAZUNA (IRE) 2 b.f. (Apr 3) Cape Cross (IRE) 129 – Keswa 94 (Kings Lake (USA) 56 133) [2003 6m 7d⁴ 7.1f⁴ 7g p6g⁶ Oct 3] 17,000Y: neat filly: half-sister to several winners, including untrustworthy 5f (at 2 yrs) to 7f winner Compradore (by Mujtahid) and 6f (at 2 yrs) and 1m winner Nobilissime (by Halling), both fairly useful: dam 1m (at 2 yrs) and 1½m winner from family of Sakhee and Celestial Storm: modest maiden: should stay 1m: acts on polytrack, firm and good to soft going. *C. E. Brittain*

MBOSI (USA) 2 b.c. (Mar 22) Kingmambo (USA) 125 – April Starlight (USA) 94 81 + (Storm Bird (CAN) 134) [2003 8m* 8m⁵ Sep 19] $100,000Y: quite good-topped colt: has short, quick action: first foal: dam, Irish 6f winner (ran only at 2 yrs), out of half-sister to Oaks/Irish Derby winner Balanchine: won maiden at Thirsk in September comfortably by neck from Hathlen: similar form (fairly useful) when last of 5 to Elshadi in minor event at Newbury: should stay 1¼m. *M. Johnston*

MCBAIN (USA) 4 br.c. Lear Fan (USA) 130 – River City Moon (USA) (Riverman 93 (USA) 131) [2003 91: 12m 10.3m 10m³ 10m³ 10.1d² 10g² 10d² 10g 10m Sep 20] leggy colt: fairly useful handicapper: effective at 1¼m/1½m: yet to race on firm going, acts on any other turf and polytrack: sold 26,000 gns. *R. F. Johnson Houghton*

MCGILLYCUDDY REEKS (IRE) 12 b.m. Kefaah (USA) 124 – Kilvarnet 78 63 d (Furry Glen 121) [2003 77d: 10.1d 9.9m⁵ 12.4g³ 10f 12.4f* 12m⁵ 12m 12.3m 12.1m⁵ 11m⁶ 10.1m 12m⁵ Sep 16] small mare: modest handicapper: won at Catterick in June: best at 1¼m/1½m: acts on fibresand and any turf going: tongue tied earlier in career: takes good hold: usually held up. *Don Enrico Incisa*

MCQUEEN (IRE) 3 ch.g. Barathea (IRE) 127 – Bibliotheque (USA) 79 (Woodman 85 (USA) 126) [2003 –p: p10g³ p10g³ 12m² p12g p10g³ f8.5g³ f8g* f8s Dec 13] lengthy gelding: fairly useful performer: claimed from F. J. Houghton £6,000 after third start: best effort when winning handicap at Southwell in November by 8 lengths: best form around 1m: acts on all-weather, raced only on good to firm ground on turf. *Mrs H. Dalton*

MEADAAF (IRE) 2 b.c. (Feb 2) Swain (IRE) 134 – Virgin Hawk (USA) (Silver Hawk 72 (USA) 123) [2003 7m 8d⁴ 7m⁵ Aug 25] €90,000Y: rangy colt: third foal: half-brother to Irish 7f winner Java Lady (by Mt Livermore): dam, lightly-raced US maiden, out of half-sister to top-class 1½m performer Cacoethes: fair form in maidens: best effort on debut: should be suited by 1¼m/1½m. *A. C. Stewart*

MEADOW 2 b.f. (Feb 15) Green Desert (USA) 127 – Marl 94 (Lycius (USA) 124) 70 [2003 5m⁶ 6.1f¹⁸ 6m⁴ Oct 17] quite good-topped filly: fourth foal: sister to 4-y-o Green Line and half-sister to 5-y-o Snow Bunting: dam, 2-y-o 5f winner, best at 6f: fair form in maidens: fourth at Nottingham and Redcar: should stay 7f: sold 15,000 gns. *R. Hannon*

MEADOWS BOY 11 gr.g. Derrylin 115 – What A Coup (Malicious) [2003 f12g⁴ – § 8f⁶ f12g⁵ f16.2s⁶ Apr 12] fair winning hurdler (has refused to race several times): poor performer: not one to trust. *R. Lee*

MEASURE UP 4 ch.g. Inchinor 119 – Victoria Blue (Old Vic 136) [2003 84, a71: 7m 73 d 6m 7.1g 6d⁶ 6m Aug 25] strong, lengthy gelding: maiden handicapper: disappointing in 2003: races freely, but seems to stay 9.4f: acts on all-weather, soft and good to firm going: tried in cheekpieces/blinkers: sometimes carries head awkwardly: successful on hurdling debut in September: sold 7,200 gns. *J. M. Bradley*

MECCA'S MATE 2 gr.f. (Apr 5) Paris House 123 – Clancassie (Clantime 101) [2003 – 5m Aug 4] 3,500Y: third foal: half-sister to 6.5f winner (including at 2 yrs) in Sweden by Presidium: dam well beaten in 3 starts: 66/1, slowly away when last of 9 in maiden at Carlisle. *D. W. Barker*

MEDALLIST 4 b.g. Danehill (USA) 126 – Obsessive (USA) 102 (Seeking The Gold 77 (USA)) [2003 93: f8s f11g 10g⁵ 10.5f³ 11.9g 10.3m³ 10.1d³ 8f Aug 2] lengthy gelding: just fair form in 2003: stays 10.5f: acts on firm and good to soft going: blinkered last 3 starts: sold 10,000 gns. *B. Ellison*

MEDEENA (IRE) 3 b.f. Green Desert (USA) 127 – Tanouma (USA) 114 (Miswaki 95 (USA) 124) [2003 82: 6m* 6m⁶ 6.1s 6g 6m 6m Oct 16] leggy, angular filly: useful performer: disappointed after winning minor event at Leicester in April by ½ length from Look Here's Carol: stayed 6f: acted on good to firm going: sold 115,000 gns in December. *J. L. Dunlop*

MEDKHAN (IRE) 6 ch.g. Lahib (USA) 129 – Safayn (USA) 82 (Lyphard (USA) – 132) [2003 –: 16.2m6 15m6 17.2f4 13.1f Aug 22] poor maiden nowadays: tried blinkered/in cheekpieces. *F. Jordan* —

MEDUSA 3 b.f. Emperor Jones (USA) 119 – Diebiedale 58 (Dominion 123) [2003 –: 6m2 6g3 7g 6m May 26] lengthy filly: fair maiden: placed at Pontefract first 2 starts: well held after: stays 6f: unraced on extremes of going. *D. Morris* **73**

MEELUP (IRE) 3 ch.g. Night Shift (USA) – Centella (IRE) (Thatching 131) [2003 74: 8.3g 7.1m 6m 7.1m 8.1m 8.1m6 7g 7f* f7s p7g p7g Dec 30] sturdy, deep-girthed gelding: unimpressive mover: fair performer: won claimer at Newmarket (claimed from R. Hannon £4,000) in August, hanging left: stays 7f: acts on polytrack, soft and firm going: tried in cheekpieces: usually races prominently: none too reliable. *A. G. Newcombe* **64**

MEGABOND 2 b.g. (Feb 21) Danehill Dancer (IRE) 117 – Apple Peeler (IRE) 56 (Rainbows For Life (CAN)) [2003 5m 6m5 5m2 6m3 7d Nov 8] 5,000Y: lengthy, attractive gelding: first foal: dam, 5f winner, ran only at 2 yrs: modest maiden: second at Carlisle: likely to prove best at 5f/6f. *B. Smart* **64**

MEGAN'S BAY 2 b.f. (Apr 1) Muhtarram (USA) 125 – Beacon (High Top 131) [2003 6f3 Jul 2] 27,000Y: sister to useful 1¼m and 1¾m winner Maycocks Bay and half-sister to 3 winners, including useful 7f/1m winner who stayed 1½m Indian Light (by Be My Chief): dam unraced half-sister to smart performer up to 2½m Compton Ace out of Irish St Leger winner Mountain Lodge: 20/1, 3½ lengths last of 3 to Venables in slowly-run minor event at Kempton: bred to be suited by at least 1¼m: difficult to assess. *R. Charlton* **82 ?**

MEGAN'S MAGIC 3 b.f. Blue Ocean (USA) 87 – Hot Sunday Sport 42 (Star Appeal 133) [2003 10.1m6 9d5 7f5 6.9f4 12f 10.1g2 9.9m3 12.1g4 10m 8m* 10.1m5 7m4 8g2 Oct 31] leggy filly: half-sister to 2 winners by Risk Me, including 1998 2-y-o 7f seller winner Risky Way: dam maiden who stayed 1½m: fair handicapper: won at Pontefract in October: effective at 1m/1¼m: acts on firm ground: usually held up. *W. Storey* **70**

MEGAROLE 4 b.g. Tragic Role (USA) – Our Megan (Puissance 110) [2003 –: 8.2f 8m Oct 12] unfurnished gelding: of no account. *B. P. J. Baugh* —

MEHMAAS 7 b.g. Distant Relative 128 – Guest List 85 (Be My Guest (USA) 126) [2003 72, a66: 8m5 8g2 8.3d 7m 8m5 7.9f 7m 7.5m 8f 8m2 8m 7.5m 7m 8m4 7m5 7.9m 8.5m 7.5d5 8m3 8m5 9m 8.2d f8.5g Nov 29] smallish, sturdy gelding: fair performer: stays 1m: acts on any turf going and fibresand: wears headgear: front runner: unreliable. *R. E. Barr* **72 d**
a– §

MEISSEN 2 ch.f. (Apr 15) Amfortas (IRE) 115 – Musetta (IRE) 107 (Cadeaux Genereux 131) [2003 8m6 7m Oct 4] big, strong, lengthy filly: has scope: fourth foal: half-sister to 4-y-o Mameyuki: dam 7f (at 2 yrs) and 1¼m winner who was fourth in Oaks: fair form when sixth in maiden at Leicester, not knocked about: last of 9 in listed race at Newmarket: likely to do better at 1¼m/1½m. *C. E. Brittain* **68 p**

MEJHAR (IRE) 3 b.c. Desert Prince (IRE) 130 – Factice (USA) 78 (Known Fact (USA) 135) [2003 85: a9g2 a8g2 7g a8g4 a8g6 a8g* a12g* 10m3 12g5 12f 11.5m4 11.5d a10.5s2 a12s* a10g2 Nov 30] IR 44,000Y: fourth foal: half-brother to 3 winners, including Irish 7f winner Festina Famosa (by Priolo): dam Irish 2-y-o 5f winner: fairly useful performer: won maiden at Tipperary at 2 yrs when trained by D. Weld: first past post in minor events at Mijas in March (demoted), June and November, and handicap at Dos Hermanas in May: also eighth of 22 in handicap at Doncaster third start and close third of 20 to Ivowen in similar event at the Curragh eighth outing: stays 1½m: acts on firm and soft ground, and on sand: tried blinkered. *E. J. Creighton, Spain* **86**

MEKURIA (JPN) 2 b.f. (Mar 26) Carnegie (IRE) 129 – Noble Air (IRE) (Lycius (USA) 124) [2003 8.2m2 8.1d4 8d* Oct 14] well-made filly: first known foal: dam, French 1m winner, half-sister to US Grade 1 1¼m winner Sabin and Musidora Stakes winner Fatah Flare: best effort in maidens (fairly useful form) when winning 10-runner event at Ayr by 3 lengths from Mommkin, leading over 2f out: will be suited by 1¼m+: open to progress. *M. Johnston* **84 p**

MELAINA 2 b.f. (Mar 7) Whittingham (IRE) 104 – Oh I Say 74 (Primo Dominie 121) [2003 5m 5m5 6m4 5.1f6 5.1m 7s f5g6 f6g* Nov 21] £400Y: first foal: dam 2-y-o 5f winner: modest performer: left J. M. Bradley after fourth start: cheekpieces, won seller at Wolverhampton: stays 6f: acts on firm ground and fibresand. *M. S. Saunders* **54**

MELFORD RED (IRE) 3 b.g. Sri Pekan (USA) 117 – Sunflower (IRE) (Fairy King – (USA)) [2003 7m 11.8m f7g⁵ Jun 9] 16,000F,12,000 2-y-o: lengthy gelding: first foal: dam unraced: no sign of ability. *R. F. Marvin*

MELINDA'S GIRL 2 b.f. (Mar 29) Intikhab (USA) 135 – Polish Honour (USA) 61 **44** (Danzig Connection (USA)) [2003 5g 5g⁶ 7.5m⁵ 7m Oct 3] 6,000Y: good-topped filly: seventh living foal: half-sister to 2 winners abroad, including 8.5f to 11.5f winner in France/Ireland Salsicaia (by Pursuit of Love): dam ran once: poor maiden: ran as if amiss final start: probably stays 7.5f. *A. P. Jarvis*

MELLINO 3 b.f. Robellino (USA) 127 – Krista 73 (Kris 135) [2003 62: 12f³ 12g 9.9d⁶ **69 §** 8g⁶ 7m 8g² 8.5m² 8g⁶ 8.1m⁶ 8.5d Sep 23] sturdy filly: fair maiden handicapper: effective at 1m to easy 1½m: acts on firm and good to soft ground: tried blinkered: has found little: unreliable: sold 2,500 gns. *T. D. Easterby*

MELMOTT 3 ch.g. Piccolo 121 – Time For Tea (IRE) 73 (Imperial Frontier (USA) – 112) [2003 –: p8g p10g⁶ 7m 8g 6f 8m 7f Jul 21] little form: tried blinkered: has looked none too keen. *C. A. Cyzer*

MELODIAN 8 b.h. Grey Desire 115 – Mere Melody 88 (Dunphy 124) [2003 71d: 8m **71** 9.9d⁶ 9.9d* 10d⁵ 10g⁶ Oct 28] leggy horse: fair handicapper: won at Beverley in September: stays 1¼m: has won on firm ground, best efforts on softer than good: usually blinkered, visored once: often races up with pace. *M. Brittain*

MELODY KING 2 b.g. (Mar 18) Merdon Melody 98 – Retaliator 80 (Rudimentary **70** (USA) 118) [2003 5m⁵ 5.6f² 6m 6.1m 5m³ 6.1m* 6.1m⁴ 7g Aug 29] rather leggy gelding: first foal: dam, 6f (including at 2 yrs)/7f winner, half-sister to useful performer up to 1m Saint Express: fair performer: won nursery at Chepstow in August: ran as if amiss final start: better at 6f than 5f: acts on firm going: visored/blinkered last 4 starts: tends to hang left. *P. D. Evans*

MELODY MASTER (IRE) 3 b.c. Woodborough (USA) 112 – Tabasco Jazz 65 **60** (Salse (USA) 128) [2003 62: p8g p8g* p8g p8g p8g⁴ 8.2g 7g p8g² 8d 8m³ Sep 24] useful- **a67** looking colt: fair handicapper on all-weather, modest on turf: won at Lingfield in January: stays easy 1m: acts on polytrack, raced mainly on good going or firmer on turf: often races prominently: sold £12,000. *M. J. Ryan*

MELODY'S LASS 3 b.f. Danzig Connection (USA) – Keen Melody (USA) 60 – (Sharpen Up 127) [2003 f6g 8.1m 5.7m 5.7f 6.1g Jun 13] 700 2-y-o: workmanlike filly: fifth foal: half-sister to 9-y-o Mutasawwar and 1995 2-y-o 7f winner Rock Sharp (by Rock City): dam, maiden, stayed 1m: no form. *J. M. Bradley*

MELOGRANO (IRE) 3 ch.g. Hector Protector (USA) 124 – Just A Treat (IRE) 47 **50** (Glenstal (USA) 118) [2003 80: f8.5s⁵ 10m 11.6d 10.5m 10m⁶ 12d 11g³ f16.2g⁶ f16.2g Nov 17] modest maiden: stays 11f: acts on heavy ground: inconsistent: sold 6,500 gns. *R. M. Beckett*

MELUSINA (IRE) 3 b.f. Barathea (IRE) 127 – Moon Masquerade (IRE) 69 (Darshaan – 133) [2003 56: 11.6d 14m 19.1m 14.1m⁶ Jul 12] modest maiden at 2 yrs: well held in 2003: tried in cheekpieces: sold 10,000 gns. *Mrs A. J. Perrett*

MEMBERSHIP (USA) 3 ch.c. Belong To Me (USA) – Shamisen 86 (Diesis 133) **119** [2003 103: p7g* p8g² 7m³ 7.1d 6m⁶ 7m² 7m* 6m 7g 7m 7m³ 7m* 7m⁴ Oct 18] strong, lengthy colt: has a quick action: smart performer: won valuable minor event at Lingfield

*Jersey Stakes, Royal Ascot—American Gary Stevens partners Membership to a 20/1 success;
favourite Arakan is second, with (from left to right) Rimrod, Wizard of Noz and
Desert Destiny coming next*

Mr Saeed Manana's "Membership"

(by 1¾ lengths from Our Teddy) in March, Jersey Stakes at Royal Ascot (beat Arakan by 2½ lengths) in June and listed race at Redcar (by a length from Three Graces) in October: good 1¼ lengths fourth to Just James in Challenge Stakes at Newmarket final start: best at 6f/7f: acts on polytrack and firm going, possibly not on good to soft: blinkered once at 2 yrs: free-going sort, best held up. *C. E. Brittain*

MENACING RIO 2 b.g. (Mar 17) Timeless Times (USA) 99 – Marfen (Lochnager 132) [2003 f5g 6g 7m⁵ 6g Aug 25] 3,600Y: good-topped gelding: poor mover: sixth foal: brother to 2 winners, including fairly useful but unreliable 5f/6f winner (latter including at 2 yrs) Ramsey Hope: dam unraced: little sign of ability, including in sellers: visored final start. *P. C. Haslam* –

MENAI STRAIGHTS 2 ch.g. (Apr 22) Alhaarth (IRE) 126 – Kind of Light 83 (Primo Dominie 121) [2003 7d 7m⁵ 8m⁵ 8.2m³ Oct 28] 11,000F, €19,000Y: lengthy, good-topped gelding: second foal: half-brother to winner in Norway by Persian Bold: dam 6f and (at 2 yrs) 7f winner: fair maiden: third to Border Castle at Nottingham: barely stays 1m. *R. F. Fisher* 69

MENEEF (USA) 2 b.c. (Mar 21) Kingmambo (USA) 125 – Black Penny (USA) (Private Account (USA)) [2003 7m⁴ Oct 3] $600,000Y: useful-looking colt: fourth foal: brother to useful Poule d'Essai des Pouliches winner Bluemamba, and half-brother to 5-y-o Blackmail: dam, placed in France, half-sister to Prix Morny winner Orpen out of half-sister to dam of Coup de Genie, Machiavellian and Exit To Nowhere: 8/1, 3 lengths fourth of 23 to Secret Charm in maiden at Newmarket, chasing leaders and not knocked about: will stay 1m, probably 1¼m: sure to do better. *M. P. Tregoning* 82 p

MENFEE (IRE) 2 gr.c. (Apr 24) Linamix (FR) 127 – Wildwood Flower 107 (Distant Relative 128) [2003 6g 6m³ 6m* 7g⁵ 7m 7m³ 8d⁶ Sep 11] 50,000Y: smallish, sturdy colt: third foal: half-brother to 3-y-o Bandit Queen and UAE 7f/7.5f winner Wilde (by Polish Precedent): dam 6f winner (also at 2 yrs), including Ayr Gold Cup: fairly useful per- 89

641

MEN

former: won maiden at Yarmouth in July: creditable third in nursery at Epsom penultimate start: should stay 1m: acts on good to firm going: often slowly away: sent to UAE, joined E. Charpy. *E. A. L. Dunlop*

MENHOUBAH (USA) 2 b.f. (Jan 18) Dixieland Band (USA) – Private Seductress (USA) (Private Account (USA)) [2003 6m* 6m⁴ 6m⁴ 7m⁴ 7m³ 8f⁴ Sep 27] $90,000Y: good-bodied filly: has a quick action: third foal: dam, 6f winner in USA, out of half-sister to top-class miler Posse: useful performer: won maiden at Newmarket in May: in frame in listed races/Cherry Hinton Stakes on same course next 3 starts and (in cheekpieces) in Moyglare Stud Stakes (length third to Necklace) at the Curragh and Fillies' Mile at Ascot on last 2: stays 1m: acts on firm going: sweating/wandered fourth appearance. *C. E. Brittain* **102**

MENOKEE (USA) 2 b.c. (Jan 29) Cherokee Run (USA) 122 – Meniatarra (USA) 68 (Zilzal (USA) 137) [2003 7.1d⁵ 8g* 8g² Oct 11] good-topped colt: second foal: half-brother to 3-y-o Give Him Credit: dam twice-raced half-sister to Lammtarra out of Oaks winner Snow Bride: landed odds in maiden at Kempton in September by 2 lengths from Esti Ab: sweating, went furlong from when 4 lengths second of 5 to Fantastic View in Autumn Stakes at Ascot, off bridle from early stage: will be suited by 1¼m+: type to train on at 3 yrs. *Sir Michael Stoute* **102 p**

MEPHISTO (IRE) 4 b.g. Machiavellian (USA) 123 – Cunning 118 (Bustino 136) [2003 10m³ 10.3m² 12g* 13d⁶ Sep 29] IR 58,000Y: good-bodied gelding: fifth foal: half-brother to 5-y-o Almaydan and winner around 1m in UAE Ejtithaab (by Arazi), both fairly useful: dam won Princess Royal Stakes and second in Prix Vermeille: fairly useful form: won maiden at Pontefract in July: ran well when sixth in handicap at Hamilton, fading: stays 13f: unraced on extremes of going: has taken strong hold. *L. M. Cumani* **87**

MERCERNARY (IRE) 4 b.g. General Monash (USA) 107 – Battle Rage (IRE) (Shernazar 131) [2003 f6g f5g Jan 4] smallish gelding: no sign of ability. *A. Berry* **–**

MERCURIOUS (IRE) 3 ch.f. Grand Lodge (USA) 125 – Rousinette (Rousillon (USA) 133) [2003 48: 10g 10.1g⁶ f11s³ f14g³ f12g⁴ Dec 22] poor maiden handicapper: effective at 1½m/1¾m: acts on fibresand, raced only on good going or softer on turf. *J. Mackie* **48**

MERDIFF 4 b.g. Machiavellian (USA) 123 – Balwa (USA) 101 (Danzig (USA)) [2003 68: 10.5m⁴ 12.3g 10.5f 8f 8.9f³ 8g² 8.2d f8.5g* Nov 15] big gelding: fair performer: tongue tied, won maiden at Wolverhampton in November: probably best around 1m: acts on all-weather and firm ground: usually races prominently. *W. M. Brisbourne* **70**

MERELY A MONARCH 4 b.g. Reprimand 122 – Ruby Princess (IRE) 70 (Mac's Imp (USA) 116) [2003 60: f7s f8s³ f8s f7s 8.3g f8.5g 8f Jun 16] sparely-made gelding: modest performer at best in 2003: stays 1m: acts on fibresand, best turf effort on good going: none too consistent. *I. A. Wood* **56 d**

MERENGUE 3 b.f. Salse (USA) 128 – Swing And Brave (IRE) 70 (Arctic Tern (USA) 126) [2003 –: 8m 9.2d 11.9m Jun 6] smallish, leggy filly: no form: tried in blinkers/cheekpieces. *T. J. Etherington* **–**

MERIDIANA (GER) 3 ch.f. Lomitas 129 – Monbijou (GER) (Dashing Blade 117) [2003 8g* 11m* 10f 12g 12d Nov 15] third foal: half-sister to German 1¼m winners Midnight Express (by Master Willie) and Micana (by Lecroix): dam, German 9.5f/10.5f winner, half-sister to useful German stayer Maitre Levy: useful performer: successful at 2 yrs in maiden at Hamburg and listed race at Baden-Baden: improved in 2003, winning listed race at Cologne in April and Oaks d'Italia at Milan (by 1¼ lengths from Lady Catherine) in May: below form after in American Oaks at Hollywood, Sword Dancer Handicap at Saratoga (left H. Blume, Germany after) and Grade 2 Long Island Handicap at Aqueduct: should stay 1½m: acts on heavy and good to firm going. *C. Clement, USA* **109**

MERLIN'S DANCER 3 b.g. Magic Ring (IRE) 115 – La Piaf (FR) (Fabulous Dancer (USA) 124) [2003 78: 7g⁴ 6m⁵ 6.1g⁶ 6.1m² 6m 6g* 6m* 6g 6g 6g 5d⁴ 6m 5f Sep 4] good-bodied gelding: unimpressive mover: fairly useful performer: won maiden at Lingfield and handicap at Newmarket in June: effective at 5f to 7f: acts on firm and good to soft ground: blinkered (below form) once: free-going sort, best covered up: sold 30,000 gns, and gelded. *W. R. Muir* **84**

MERLIN'S GIFT 3 b.g. Wizard King 122 – Formosanta (USA) (Believe It (USA)) [2003 –: 5m 7d Jul 30] good-bodied gelding: well held in maidens/claimer. *Bob Jones* **–**

MERLINS PRIDE 2 b.f. (May 15) Wizard King 122 – Longden Pride (Superpower 113) [2003 f5g² p5g⁵ 5f⁵ f5s p5g 6f Aug 26] leggy, lengthy, unfurnished filly: second foal: sister to 3-y-o The Wizard Mul: dam unraced: modest maiden: regressed after debut in seller: form only at 5f: visored penultimate start: sometimes slowly away. *P. D. Evans* **53 d**

MERLINS PROFIT 3 b.g. Wizard King 122 – Quick Profit 78 (Formidable (USA) **54** 125) [2003 60: 10.1m 14.1m 12m 9.3m³ Sep 4] rather unfurnished gelding: modest maiden: stays 9.3f: raced only on good/good to firm ground. *M. Todhunter*

MERRYMAKER 3 b.g. Machiavellian (USA) 123 – Wild Pavane (Dancing Brave **70** (USA) 140) [2003 8g 10m⁶ 10.2g 10m 12.3m³ 14m⁴ 14.1f³ 12g³ Sep 1] 230,000Y: angular, rather unfurnished gelding: half-brother to several winners, including useful 7f (at 2 yrs) to 9f winner Apache Star (by Arazi) and 1¼m winner Stately Dancer (by Be My Guest): dam unraced half-sister to dam of Coronation Stakes winner Rebecca Sharp: fair maiden: stays 1¾m: raced only on good going or firmer: tried visored/blinkered: ran in snatches and found little final start: sold 12,500 gns. *Sir Michael Stoute*

MERRYVALE MAN 6 b.g. Rudimentary (USA) 118 – Salu 65 (Ardross 134) [2003 **–** –, a52: f12s f11g f11s f16s Feb 13] leggy gelding: modest handicapper at 5 yrs: little form in 2003: tried blinkered/in cheekpieces. *R. Bastiman*

MERSEY MIRAGE 6 b.g. King's Signet (USA) 110 – Kirriemuir 51 (Lochnager **– §** 132) [2003 68§: 7m Apr 22] neat gelding: fair handicapper: well held only 6-y-o start: tried visored/blinkered: unreliable. *S. J. Magnier*

MERSEY SOUND (IRE) 5 b.g. Ela-Mana-Mou 132 – Coral Sound (IRE) 67 (Glow **77** (USA)) [2003 77: p10g⁴ p12g 13.3m 14.1m 13.3m* 15m³ 14.4f² 13.3m² 14.4m⁴ 13.3m 16m³ 16m² 16.2f* 16g Oct 24] rather leggy, quite attractive gelding: fair handicapper: left D. Elsworth after second start: in good form in 2003, winning at Newbury in June and Ascot in September: stays 2m: acts on firm going and polytrack: tried visored, not in 2003: usually held up: consistent. *S. Kirk*

MESHAHEER (USA) 4 b.c. Nureyev (USA) 131 – Race The Wild Wind (USA) 121 **113** (Sunny's Halo (CAN)) [2003 115: 8g 7d² 7m⁴ 7m* Jul 18] rather unfurnished colt: has a round action: smart performer: beaten length by Saratan in Prix du Palais-Royal at Long-champ: landed odds in minor event at Newbury in July by 1¾ lengths from Alkaadhem: stays 7f: unraced on extremes of going: often tongue tied: has worn crossed noseband/ raced freely. *Saeed bin Suroor*

MESMERIC (IRE) 5 b.g. Sadler's Wells (USA) 132 – Mesmerize (Mill Reef (USA) **101** 141) [2003 111: 12g² 14.1g 12g² 12m⁶ 12g Aug 1] good-topped gelding: useful perform-er: best effort in 2003 when second to Princely Venture in minor event at Goodwood third start: reportedly finished lame next time: should stay 1¾m: yet to race on heavy going, acts on any other: effective blinkered/visored or not: sometimes carries head awkwardly: often held up: sold 17,000 gns. *E. A. L. Dunlop*

MESMERISED 3 b.f. Merdon Melody 98 – Gracious Imp (USA) (Imp Society **57 d** (USA)) [2003 73d: f7g f7s f7s 6m 7f⁴ f6s² 6.9f 7.1f 7.2f 6.9d 6.9m³ 6m 7g 7.5m f7s Oct 21] leggy, workmanlike filly: modest performer at best at 3 yrs: stays 7f: acts on fibre-sand, firm and good to soft ground: tried in cheekpieces: has flashed tail: unreliable. *A. Berry*

MESMERIZING (IRE) 3 b.g. Dr Devious (IRE) 127 – Mesenzana (IRE) (Mac's **55** Imp (USA) 116) [2003 –: 7.1m 7m 9.7m⁵ 10m 8.5m⁵ 8.5d⁵ 8.5m⁶ 8.5d 10m Dec 23] modest maiden: left L. Cumani after fifth start: stays 9.7f: acts on good to firm ground. *R. Brogi, Italy*

MESSE DE MINUIT (IRE) 2 ch.c. (Feb 17) Grand Lodge (USA) 125 – Scrimshaw **76 p** (Selkirk (USA) 129) [2003 7s³ p8g* Nov 26] 26,000F, €115,000Y: compact colt: third foal: dam unraced granddaughter of Arc winner Ivanjica: fair form in maidens: still green when starting at Lingfield by ½ length from Suave Quartet, leading close home: likely to be suited by 1¼m/1½m: capable of better. *R. Charlton*

METICULOUS 5 gr.g. Eagle Eyed (USA) 111 – Careful (IRE) 59 (Distinctly North **–** (USA) 115) [2003 –: 5m Aug 15] leggy, quite good-topped gelding: little form. *M. C. Chapman*

METICULOUS (USA) 5 b. or br.g. Theatrical 128 – Sha Tha (USA) 118 (Mr Pros- **–** pector (USA)) [2003 f11s⁶ Jan 16] fair handicapper (rated 65) in 2002, winning twice over 1¼m at Nad Al Sheba for K. McLaughlin: well held in seller only start in 2003. *M. D. Hammond*

MEXICAN PETE 3 b.g. Atraf 116 – Eskimo Nel (IRE) 75 (Shy Groom (USA)) [2003 **81** 59: 10m⁶ 10.9m* 11.9m² 10.9f² 12g⁴ 10m² 11m* 12m* 11.9f 12d⁵ Sep 20] close-coupled gelding: fairly useful handicapper: won at Warwick in July and at Redcar and Salisbury in August: stays 1½m: acts on firm and good to soft ground, below form only start on polytrack: usually waited with: won juvenile hurdle in October. *P. W. Hiatt*

MEXICAN (USA) 4 b.c. Pine Bluff (USA) – Cuando Quiere (USA) (Affirmed (USA)) **55**
[2003 83: 10.3g 8m 9.9m 8m 9f 8.1g⁵ 10.5m 7m Aug 1] quite attractive colt: just modest
maiden in 2003: stays 1¼m: acts on firm going: tried tongue tied: has found little.
M. D. Hammond

MEZEREON 3 b.f. Alzao (USA) 117 – Blown-Over 41 (Ron's Victory (USA) 129) **60**
[2003 63: 9.3m⁵ f9.4g* f12g⁵ 10.1g 9f* 10.2m Sep 22] quite good-topped filly: modest
performer: won claimers at Wolverhampton in July and Musselburgh (claimed from
J. Given) in August: stays easy 1½m: raced only on fibresand and good ground or firmer:
won juvenile hurdle in October. *D. Carroll*

MEZUZAH 3 b.g. Barathea (IRE) 127 – Mezzogiorno 108 (Unfuwain (USA) 131) **96**
[2003 94p: 8m⁶ 8m³ 12m 9.9g⁴ 10g 10m⁶ Oct 22] lengthy gelding: useful handicapper:
best effort when fourth to Tiber at Goodwood in August: stays 1¼m: acts on heavy and
good to firm going: carries head high: very slowly away final outing (gelded after).
G. Wragg

MEZZO SOPRANO (USA) 3 b.f. Darshaan 133 – Morn of Song (USA) 80 **117**
(Blushing Groom (FR) 131) [2003 a8f* 8g 9.9g² 12m³ 10g³ 11.9m* 12m* 10f
Oct 25]
  How much immediate benefit do Godolphin's principal classic candidates
and older horses gain from their winter in the sun? Sheikh Mohammed's so-called
'Dubai experiment' was hailed as an unqualified success when Balanchine spear-
headed a team of eight sent to Britain for the Newmarket Guineas meeting in 1994,
after being wintered in Dubai. Seven of the eight collected prize money, including
Balanchine, who was touched off in the One Thousand Guineas. The eight Godolphin horses, soon joined by a further half dozen, stayed for the summer with
Balanchine going on to win the Oaks and the Irish Derby. One person not carried
away, however, was Sheikh Mohammed himself. 'Maybe we just had a very good
horse in the first group we brought back to this country,' he said. Subsequent results
have borne out the Sheikh's sensibly cautious approach. The notion that wintering
in a warm climate confers an advantage in the early part of the British season has
become harder to prove than might have seemed likely after that first flush of
success. Perhaps Godolphin has just had a few disappointing crops of three-year-
olds, but the annual round of trials in Dubai for its prospective classic horses, joined
in more recent years by the UAE classics themselves, create a little less interest
than they used to. Lateen Sails won the main colts' trial at Nad Al Sheba on April
4th and became Godolphin's principal Two Thousand Guineas hope, while Mezzo
Soprano, who did not contest the trials, was the main One Thousand Guineas
candidate on the strength of her three-length victory in the UAE One Thousand
Guineas over Gonfilia, who split Hi Dubai and Echoes In Eternity in the main
fillies' trial. Both Lateen Sails and Mezzo Soprano, who won a newcomers race
at Deauville for Andre Fabre on her only two-year-old start, were well backed at
Newmarket, but neither made an impact. Lateen Sails finished last of twenty and
Mezzo Soprano fourteenth of nineteen. Hi Dubai in the Pretty Polly Stakes was the
only winner from Godolphin's seven runners at the meeting (two others picked up
place money).
  Lateen Sails went on to develop into a smart performer and Mezzo Soprano
fared even better, progressing steadily through the season and becoming the only
Godolphin three-year-old to win a Group 1 race in 2003. That victory came in the

Prix Vermeille Fouquet's Barriere, Longchamp—Mezzo Soprano (rail) rallies gamely to thwart Yesterday;
Fidelite (second right) and Vallee Enchantee (No.3) make the frame

gamest fashion in the Prix Vermeille Fouquet's Barriere at Longchamp in September, a race which will be open also to older fillies and mares in 2004. Prominent from the start and taking over early in the straight, Mezzo Soprano rallied in fine style when pressed by Irish One Thousand Guineas winner Yesterday, holding her off by a head with Prix Saint-Alary winner Fidelite and Prix de Pomone winner Vallee Enchantee third and fourth in a less than vintage line-up. Among those down the field was Ocean Silk, who had beaten Mezzo Soprano in the Lupe Stakes at Goodwood and finished ahead of her when the pair came second and third behind Spanish Sun in the Ribblesdale Stakes at Royal Ascot. Mezzo Soprano also turned the tables in the Vermeille on Commercante who had had her back in third when winning the Prix de Psyche at Deauville. Mezzo Soprano had had to wait until the York August meeting to add to her UAE One Thousand Guineas success when taking the Galtres Stakes by a neck from Thingmebob. Mezzo Soprano's only run after the Vermeille was back at a mile and a quarter in the Breeders' Cup Filly & Mare Turf at Santa Anita, where she managed only tenth behind Islington (Yesterday finished third). Mezzo Soprano probably needed a mile and a half to be seen to best advantage by this stage.

Mezzo Soprano (USA) (b.f. 2000)	Darshaan (br 1981)	Shirley Heights (b 1975)	Mill Reef
			Hardiemma
		Delsy (br 1972)	Abdos
			Kelty
	Morn of Song (USA) (b 1988)	Blushing Groom (ch 1974)	Red God
			Runaway Bride
		Glorious Song (b 1976)	Halo
			Ballade

The lengthy Mezzo Soprano, who starts her stud career with a visit to Storm Cat, is impeccably bred. Her successful sire, the now-deceased Darshaan, has also

Godolphin's "Mezzo Soprano"

become one of the most significant sires of broodmares in the modern era, only the daughters of Habitat and Riverman having produced winners of more Group 1 events. Mezzo Soprano's dam Morn of Song won a maiden over seven and a half furlongs at Chester as a three-year-old for the Stoute stable, before winning twice on dirt at up to a mile in the States. Mezzo Soprano is her sixth foal and she hasn't bred another winner (only two of the others reached the track), but she has an illustrious pedigree, being out of the top-class mare Glorious Song, who died in 2003. Glorious Song, purchased privately by Sheikh Mohammed in 1987, was a champion racemare—Horse of the Year in Canada and Champion Older Mare in both Canada and the States—and was an outstanding broodmare, dam of the top-class Singspiel, winner of Group 1 races in four countries, Middle Park runner-up and successful sire Rahy (a brother to Morn of Song) and smart South African performer Rakeen, who has also made a name for himself at stud. Glorious Song was one of eight winners out of Ballade, including two brothers to Glorious Song, Devil's Bag, the top American two-year-old of his year, and Saint Ballado, winner of the Arlington Classic, both of whom became successful sires. Mezzo Suprano, who acted on dirt, soft and good to firm going, usually raced prominently. She had her tongue tied in most of her races after the One Thousand Guineas. *Saeed bin Suroor*

M FOR MAGIC   4 ch.g. First Trump 118 – Celestine 62 (Skyliner 117) [2003 –: 7m 6m³ 7.5m 7m 10m⁵ 10.1m 11m⁴ 9m⁵ Sep 4] useful-looking gelding: poor maiden: seems to stay 11f: acts on good to firm and heavy ground: tried blinkered and in cheekpieces: none too genuine: inconsistent. *C. W. Fairhurst*   **48 §**

MIA FOOL   4 ch.f. Cosmonaut – Young Annabel (USA) 71 (Cahill Road (USA)) [2003 –: p12g Jan 7] well held in maidens. *G. G. Margarson*   **–**

MIAMI EXPLORER   3 b.f. Pennekamp (USA) 130 – Elaine Tully (IRE) 80 (Persian Bold 123) [2003 –: 12.1f⁶ 9.3m 11.9m Jun 12] little form: wayward and unreliable. *H. Morrison*   **– §**

MI AMOR (IRE)   3 b.f. Alzao (USA) 117 – Splicing 82 (Sharpo 132) [2003 7.1m 7g³ 8.3s f8.5g Jul 11] smallish, quite good-topped filly: third foal: half-sister to useful 6f (at 2 yrs) and 1m winner Pairing (by Rudimentary), later successful in Spain, and 4-y-o Sholay: dam, 5f/6f winner, sister to smart sprinter Splice, herself dam of 4-y-o Feet So Fast: poor maiden. *W. J. Haggas*   **47**

MIA'S REFORM   4 b.g. Lugana Beach 116 – Lady Caroline Lamb (IRE) 68 (Contract Law (USA) 108) [2003 51: f6s f5g* f5s f5s f5g 6f f5g 5m 5g Jul 17] smallish gelding: modest on all-weather, poor on turf: well below form after winning seller at Southwell in January, leaving S. R. Bowring after third start: best at bare 5f: acts on fibresand, firm and good to soft ground: blinkered once at 2 yrs: sold 1,000 gns. *Ronald Thompson*   **a54 d**

MI CASTANO (IRE)   4 ch.g. Fayruz 116 – Tadasna (IRE) (Thatching 131) [2003 53: f8s 7m 7m 7g Jun 3] useful-looking gelding: maiden: well below form in 2003: tried blinkered. *N. P. Littmoden*   **–**

MICHABO (IRE)   2 b.g. (Apr 18) Robellino (USA) 127 – Mole Creek 91 (Unfuwain (USA) 131) [2003 6g Jul 26] 50,000Y: strong, good sort: first foal: dam, 11f winner who stayed 1¾m, half-sister to very smart 9f to 1½m performer Terimon: 16/1 and backward, tailed off in newcomers race at Ascot, slowly away and running in snatches: subsequently gelded. *D. R. C. Elsworth*   **–**

MICHAELS DREAM (IRE)   4 b.g. Spectrum (IRE) 126 – Stormswept (USA) 74 (Storm Bird (CAN) 134) [2003 72: f12s⁴ f11g² p12g f12g⁵ 12g 12.3m 12.1m 12m 14.1m 14m 12m³ 14.1m 14.1m Oct 17] smallish gelding: fair handicapper on all-weather, modest on turf: effective at 1¼m to 1¾m: acts on firm going, good to soft and fibresand: usually wears headgear: often races freely. *J. Hetherton*   **50 a71**

MICHELLE MA BELLE (IRE)   3 b.f. Shareef Dancer (USA) 135 – April Magic (Magic Ring (IRE) 115) [2003 90: 6.1d⁶ 7g 6m 6m 6m³ 7.1m³ 6m³ 7g³ 6g⁶ 8.5d⁵ 8f⁵ Oct 12] smallish filly: fairly useful handicapper: best at 6f/7f: acts on firm and soft ground: sometimes races freely: usually waited with. *S. Kirk*   **88**

MICKLEDOR (FR)   3 ch.f. Lake Coniston (IRE) 131 – Shamasiya (FR) (Vayrann 133) [2003 6m 8f 6m⁶ 8s 6.9m 6f³ 7m⁴ Sep 9] 3,000Y: sparely-made filly: half-sister to several winners, including useful 5f (at 2 yrs)/6f winner Rock Symphony and fairly useful 6f and (at 2 yrs) 7f winner Stone of Destiny (both by Ballad Rock): dam French   **49**

1½m winner: poor maiden: stays 7f: acts on firm ground: visored/blinkered after debut. *M. Dods*

MICKLEGATE 2 b.f. (Mar 13) Dracula (AUS) – Primulette 82 (Mummy's Pet 125) **59** [2003 5f 6m⁶ 6m⁴ 7m⁴ 7d³ Nov 4] 8,000Y: quite good-topped filly: half-sister to numerous winners, including 3-y-o B A Highflyer and 7f (at 2 yrs) and 1½m winner Boogy Woogy (by Rock Hopper): dam 5f (at 2 yrs) and 1m winner: modest maiden: third at Catterick: will stay 1m: acts on good to firm and good to soft ground. *J. D. Bethell*

MICKLEHAM MAGIC 3 b.f. Shareef Dancer (USA) 135 – Princess Lily 65 (Blake- – ney 126) [2003 –: p10g Jan 4] 3,000Y: half-sister to several winners, including 8-y-o Risk Free and 1m to 2m winner Royal Roulette (by Risk Me): dam maiden who stayed 1½m: no sign of ability in seller at Southwell in 2002 and claimer at Lingfield. *S. C. Williams*

MICKLEY (IRE) 6 b.g. Ezzoud (IRE) 126 – Dawsha (IRE) 75 (Slip Anchor 136) **74 ?** [2003 83d: p12g⁶ p12g Feb 22] tall, short-backed gelding: just fair handicapper nowadays: barely stays 2m: acts on firm going, good to soft and all-weather: occasionally visored/blinkered: carries head awkwardly: often leads. *P. R. Hedger*

MICKLOW MAGIC 5 b.m. Farfelu 103 – Scotto's Regret (Celtic Cone 116) [2003 – 71: 7m May 12] strong, workmanlike mare: fair handicapper at best: wearing cheekpieces, well beaten only 5-y-o start. *C. Grant*

MICKY THIN 2 br.c. (Apr 28) Prince Sabo 123 – Walsham Witch 61 (Music Maestro **60 d** 119) [2003 5m⁴ 5.3f* 6d⁶ 7g⁴ 7m⁶ 7g⁵ 8.3g Oct 6] 1,800F, 11,000Y: sixth foal: half-brother to 3 winners, including 1999 2-y-o 5f winner Chiko (by Afif): dam 2-y-o 6f winner who probably stayed 2m: modest performer: landed odds in maiden at Brighton in April: ran poorly last 3 starts, blinkered on first 2 occasions: stays 7f: acts on firm going: sold 2,500 gns. *R. Hannon*

MIDAS WAY 3 ch.g. Halling (USA) 133 – Arietta's Way (IRE) 71 (Darshaan 133) **106** [2003 92p: 12.3m⁶ 12f* 14.8m⁶ 14g³ 13.9m² 14.6g Sep 12] rather leggy gelding: useful handicapper: won at Salisbury in June: good efforts next 3 starts, 1¾ lengths second to Jagger in Melrose Rated Stakes (Handicap) at York on third of them: edgy, ran as though amiss in Mallard Handicap at Doncaster final start: should be suited by 2m+: acts on firm and soft going: usually held up. *R. Charlton*

MIDDLEHAM PARK (IRE) 3 b.g. Revoque (IRE) 122 – Snap Crackle Pop (IRE) **68 d** 87 (Statoblest 120) [2003 8m³ 7m² 6m 7.9m f8g⁶ f7g Dec 16] lengthy gelding: second foal: brother to 4-y-o Snip Snap: dam, 2-y-o 5f winner: fair maiden: well below form last 3 starts: stays 1m: raced only on good to firm ground on turf, well beaten on fibresand: twice slowly away. *P. C. Haslam*

MIDDLEHAM ROSE 2 b.f. (Feb 20) Dr Fong (USA) 128 – Shallop 55 (Salse – (USA) 128) [2003 7m 7.9m 7m Oct 17] 7,000Y: tall filly: half-sister to several winners, including 3-y-o Zeusz: dam, untrustworthy maiden, half-sister to smart middle-distance stayer Dry Dock: well held and signs of temperament in maidens/claimer. *P. C. Haslam*

MIDDLEMARCH (IRE) 3 ch.c. Grand Lodge (USA) 125 – Blanche Dubois (Nash- **114** wan (USA) 135) [2003 8m* 8m² 8f³ 10f² 9.8d⁵ 10m 8g* 12d⁶ Nov 8] tall, angular colt: second foal: half-brother to useful 2001 2-y-o 7f winner Lady High Havens (by Bluebird) who stays 1¼m: dam unraced half-sister to 3-y-o Indian Haven and Gran Criterium winner Count Dubois: smart performer: won maiden in June and minor event in October (beat Green Castle 1½ lengths), both at the Curragh: ran well in between when 3 lengths fifth to Weightless in Prix Dollar at Longchamp: left A. O'Brien, Ireland, 100,000 gns before well held in listed race at Doncaster final start: stays 1¼m: acts on firm and good to soft ground: blinkered/visored fifth to seventh starts. *J. S. Goldie*

MIDDLEMISS (IRE) 3 b.f. Midhish 109 – Teresa Deevey 50 (Runnett 125) [2003 –: – 8m⁵ 10m⁵ 11.6m⁵ 10m⁴ Aug 6] little form: tried in cheekpieces. *J. W. Mullins*

MIDDLETHORPE 6 b.g. Noble Patriarch 115 – Prime Property (IRE) 60 (Tirol 127) **74** [2003 77: 12g³ 12.3m³ 14f 11.9d 13.1d⁵ 13.8d⁵ Nov 4] rather sparely-made gelding: poor mover: fair handicapper: stays 13.8f: acts on heavy and good to firm going, below form on firm/fibresand: blinkered: tends to wander. *M. W. Easterby*

MIDDLETON GREY 5 gr.g. Ashkalani (IRE) 128 – Petula 103 (Petong 126) [2003 **74** –, a91: f7g* f6s² f7s⁴ f8.5s f6s³ f7s² f8.5g⁵ f7g² p7g 7m³ 7m⁶ 7.1d f8.5g⁶ f8s⁴ **a97** Dec 27] leggy gelding: useful handicapper on all-weather, fair on turf: won at Wolverhampton in January: left D. Arbuthnot 17,000 gns after twelfth start: effective at 6f to 8.5f: acts on all-weather, unraced on extremes of going on turf: usually wears headgear. *A. G. Newcombe*

MIDGES PRIDE 3 b.g. Puissance 110 – It's All Academic (IRE) 91 (Mazaad 106)   **51**
[2003 58: f6g f5g³ f6g⁴ f8.5g⁴ 6f⁴ 7m 5.9m f7s Sep 6] modest maiden: effective at 5f to 7f:
raced only on fibresand and ground firmer than good: tried visored: none too consistent.
Mrs A. Duffield

MIDMAAR (IRE) 2 b.c. (Mar 19) Cape Cross (IRE) 129 – Khazinat El Dar (USA)   **86**
78 (Slew O' Gold (USA)) [2003 6d⁵ 7d³ 6g* p5g p7g p8g Dec 20] ex-French colt: third
foal: dam, maiden who should have stayed 1m, sister to very smart 1m/1¼m performer
Zaahi: fairly useful performer: won minor event at Maisons-Laffitte in October on final
start for F. Head: well held all 3 outings in Britain: stays 7f. *M. Wigham*

MIDNIGHT BALLARD (USA) 2 b. or br.c. (Mar 20) Mister Baileys 123 – Shadow   **87**
Music (USA) (Shadeed (USA) 135) [2003 6f⁵ 7m³ 7g⁶ Nov 1] 14,000Y: good-topped
colt: second foal: dam lightly-raced close relative to useful 1m winner Balakirev: best
effort in maidens (fairly useful form) when close third of 15 to State Dilemma at Newbury, always close up: off 6 weeks, ran as if just needed final start: should stay 1m.
R. F. Johnson Houghton

MIDNIGHT CHIEF 3 b.g. Bluegrass Prince (IRE) 110 – Midnight Romance (Inca   **51**
Chief (USA)) [2003 53: f9.4g⁵ f8.5g⁴ p7g p8g f7g 10f 7g⁵ 8m May 27] modest maiden:
should stay beyond 1m: acts on fibresand, unraced on ground softer than good: visored
last 3 starts. *A. P. Jarvis*

MIDNIGHT COUP 7 br.g. First Trump 118 – Anhaar (Ela-Mana-Mou 132) [2003   **–**
47: f16s p16g f14.8g 11.9m 16.2m Jun 16] poor handicapper at 6
yrs: well held in 2003: blinkered last 4 starts. *B. G. Powell*

MIDNIGHT CREEK 5 b.g. Tragic Role (USA) – Greek Night Out (IRE) 54 (Ela-   **–**
Mana-Mou 132) [2003 73, a79: 17.1m Apr 8] leggy gelding: fair handicapper at best:
well held only Flat outing in 2003: tried tongue tied/in cheekpieces. *G. A. Swinbank*

MIDNIGHT MAMBO (USA) 3 b.f. Kingmambo (USA) 125 – Witching Hour (FR)   **53 +**
(Fairy King (USA)) [2003 p6g p7g⁵ Dec 29] 58,000Y: first foal: dam, French 1¼m
winner, half-sister to smart French performer up to 1½m Kathmandu: better effort in
maidens (favourite both starts) when fifth at Lingfield, squeezed out at start: may do
better. *R. Guest*

MIDNIGHT PARKES 4 b. or br.g. Polar Falcon (USA) 126 – Summerhill Spruce 70   **80**
(Windjammer (USA)) [2003 87: 6m⁵ 6g 5d 5g³ 6m 6m⁴ 5g⁵ 5m 7m Oct 12] strong,
lengthy gelding: type to carry condition: fairly useful handicapper: left M. Jarvis after
fifth outing: effective at 5f/6f: easily best form on good going or firmer: tried in cheek-
pieces/blinkers: none too consistent. *E. J. Alston*

MIDNIGHT PRINCE 2 b.c. (Mar 8) Dracula (AUS) – Phylian 77 (Glint of Gold   **59**
128) [2003 5m 5g⁴ 6m 7d 6m 7m⁶ Oct 18] 7,000Y: good-topped colt: has scope: fluent
mover: fourth foal: half-brother to 1999 2-y-o 7f seller winner Summertime Joy (by
Muhtarram), later winner abroad: dam 1¼m/1½f winner: modest maiden: below form
after fourth at Ripon: should stay 7f. *M. W. Easterby*

MIDNIGHT SONG (USA) 3 ch.g. Hennessy (USA) 122 – Gratify (USA) (Miswaki   **77**
(USA) 124) [2003 66: 7g 10m² 9.9f² 11.7f⁵ 10.1d³ Oct 18] sturdy gelding: fair maiden:
effective at 1¼m/1½m: acts on firm ground: sold 12,000 gns. *E. A. L. Dunlop*

MIDNIGHT SPECIAL (IRE) 3 b.f. Danetime (IRE) 121 – Daffodil Dale (IRE) 78   **78 d**
(Cyrano de Bergerac 120) [2003 75: p5g 5f* 5f 5m 5.1m 5d 5f 5m Jun 27] angular, quite
good-topped filly: fairly useful handicapper: well held after winning at Thirsk in April:
best at bare 5f: acts on polytrack and firm ground: tried visored: often makes running:
sold 4,000 gns in December. *D. Carroll*

MIDSHIPMAN 5 b.h. Executive Man 119 – Midler (Comedy Star (USA) 121) [2003   **–**
–, a104: p8g Feb 5] good-topped horse: useful performer at 3 and 4 yrs: finished last only
5-y-o start. *M. J. Wallace*

MIDSHIPMAN EASY (USA) 2 ch.g. (Apr 25) Irish River (FR) 131 – Winger 70   **– p**
(In The Wings 128) [2003 8.2m Oct 28] €90,000Y: leggy, attractive gelding: fourth foal:
half-brother to fairly useful Irish 2000 2-y-o 5f winner Warrior Wings (by Indian Ridge)
and Irish 2001 2-y-o 7f winner Goldthroat (by Zafonic): dam, Irish 9f winner, half-sister
to smart 1m winner Killer Instinct, an excellent family: 7/2 and green, well held in maiden
at Nottingham, starting slowly: should do better. *P. W. Harris*

MIDSUMMER 3 ch.f. Kingmambo (USA) 125 – Modena (USA) (Roberto (USA) 131)   **99**
[2003 11.1m* 11.8m² 9.9g⁴ May 21] small, quite attractive filly: half-sister to several
winners, notably high-class 7f (at 2 yrs) to 1¼m (Eclipse) winner Elmaamul (by Diesis)
and very smart 7f (at 2 yrs, when also won Fillies' Mile) to 1½m (Oaks) winner Reams of

Verse (by Nureyev): dam unraced half-sister to smart 7f/1m performer Zaizafon, herself dam of Zafonic: useful performer: won maiden at Kempton in April: good efforts after when second to Santa Sophia (pair clear) in listed race at Lingfield and fourth to Ocean Silk in similar event at Goodwood, hanging left in latter: stayed 1½m: raced only on good/good to firm going: stud. *H. R. A. Cecil*

MIDY'S RISK (FR)   6 gr.g. Take Risks (FR) 116 – Martine Midy (FR) (Lashkari 128)   –
[2003 p13g Apr 1] tall, sparely-made gelding: fair hurdler: maiden on Flat: fairly useful form in 2001: well beaten only 6-y-o start: sold £5,800. *Mrs N. Smith*

MIGHTY PIP (IRE)   7 b.g. Pips Pride 117 – Hard To Stop 77 (Hard Fought 125) [2003   **57**
49: 9.7m 10.2m 10m² 11.9m 10m* 10f 10.9m² 10.9m 9.9m Oct 1] modest performer: won claimer at Brighton in August: stays 11f: acts on heavy going, good to firm and poly-track: tried blinkered/tongue tied: has been slowly away: usually held up. *M. R. Bosley*

MIGRATION   7 b.g. Rainbow Quest (USA) 134 – Armeria (USA) 79 (Northern Dan-   **49**
cer) [2003 f12s⁴ Jun 13] tall gelding: smart winner in 1999: well held in seller only Flat outing since. *M. Pitman*

MIKADO   2 b.c. (Feb 12) Sadler's Wells (USA) 132 – Free At Last 115 (Shirley Heights   **106 p**
130) [2003 9g² 8g* 9g* Nov 8] 450,000Y: sixth foal: brother to 2 winners, including useful 10.5f winner Rosa Parks, and half-brother to 1¼m winner Coretta (by Caerleon), later smart winner up to 1½m in USA, and useful 1¼m winner Trumpet Sound (by Theatrical): dam, 2-y-o 7f winner and fourth in 1000 Guineas (later stakes winner up to 1½m in USA), half-sister to Barathea and Gossamer (both by Sadler's Wells): odds on, won maiden at Listowel in September and listed race at Leopardstown (by 1½ lengths from Tarakala, leading over 1f out) in November: will be suited by 1¼m/1½m: poten-tially smart, and should win more races. *A. P. O'Brien, Ireland*

MIKASA (IRE)   3 b.g. Victory Note (USA) 120 – Resiusa (ITY) (Niniski (USA) 125)   –
[2003 7d 7.1f 6g⁶ 7m 6m f5g Oct 16] IR 7,200F, IR 10,500Y: tall, quite good-topped gelding: half-brother to 3 winners, including 1996 2-y-o 5f/6f winner Robec Girl (by Masterclass): dam Italian 7f (at 2 yrs) to 11f winner: little form. *R. F. Fisher*

MIKATI MAID   2 ch.f. (Apr 14) Piccolo 121 – Dame Helene (USA) (Sir Ivor 135)   **64**
[2003 5.7m 6m² Sep 9] seventh foal: half-sister to fairly useful 1998 2-y-o 7f winner Autocrat (by Polar Falcon), later successful in Austria: dam, no form, out of half-sister to high-class 7f to 9f performer Indian Lodge: better effort in maidens (modest form) when staying-on 4 lengths second of 10 to Sweet Pickle at Lingfield: should stay 7f. *A. P. Jarvis*

MIKES MATE   2 b.g. (May 10) Komaite (USA) – Pitcairn Princess (Capricorn Line   –
111) [2003 f8s Dec 13] 900Y: fifth foal: half-brother to winner up to 10.5f in Italy by Tragic Role: dam tailed off in 2-y-o maidens: 66/1, tailed off in maiden at Southwell, starting very slowly. *C. J. Teague*

MILITAIRE (FR)   5 ch.g. Bering 136 – Moon Review (USA) (Irish River (FR) 131)   –
[2003 10.1m 8m Apr 26] ex-French gelding: fairly useful performer for F. Head at 3 yrs, winning 9f maiden at Compiegne: well held in 2003: sold 15,000 gns. *M. D. Hammond*

MILITARY TWO STEP (IRE)   2 b.g. (Mar 1) General Monash (USA) 107 – Con   **63**
Dancer (Shareef Dancer (USA) 135) [2003 5d⁴ 6d² 6f³ f8s⁵ 6g 6d 7d² Nov 4] 7,000Y: second foal: dam placed in Belgium: modest maiden: stays 7f (raced too freely at 1m): acts on firm and good to soft ground: wore cheekpieces last 2 outings. *K. R. Burke*

MILK AND SULTANA   3 b.f. Millkom 124 – Premier Princess 45 (Hard Fought   **62**
125) [2003 66: f7g* f8.5g³ 10.3m 8.3g f7s 8.1m Sep 22] fair performer: won maiden at   **a67**
Wolverhampton in January: well below form last 3 starts: stays 1m: acts on fibresand, raced only on good ground or firmer on turf. *W. M. Brisbourne*

MILK IT MICK   2 b.c. (Mar 25) Millkom 124 – Lunar Music 67 (Komaite   **120**
(USA)) [2003 5f⁵ 5m* 6g* 7m³ 6f* 6m⁴ 6m⁴ 7m³ 7.1d² 7g⁵ 7m* 7m* Oct 18]
Milk It Mick's first and last starts had just one thing in common—his starting price of 33/1. On April 19th, he failed to break well but still finished fifth of eighteen in a maiden auction event at Haydock. Almost exactly six months later—on his twelfth start—he cut down the colt widely regarded as Britain's top juvenile, Three Valleys, to win the Darley Dewhurst Stakes at Newmarket. Milk It Mick's record was remarkable, yet judged on the 20/1 freely available about him for the Two Thousand Guineas after the Dewhurst, his last performance was viewed with indifference, or even suspicion, by most pundits. Perhaps they didn't believe their own eyes, but, on our reading of the form-book and the stopwatch, Milk It Mick showed himself in the Dewhurst to be the best of the bunch in Britain or

Darley Dewhurst Stakes, Newmarket—33/1-shot Milk It Mick (No.8) provides trainer Jamie Osborne with his first Group 1 success; favourite Three Valleys is second with Haafhd (striped cap) third

Ireland at two—irrespective of what he goes on to achieve, or fails to achieve, at three.

The key to Milk It Mick's improvement came apparently when he encountered the combination of a good pace and waiting tactics. It took a while to work this out, since he was ridden close to the pace in most of his races after his debut, winning a maiden auction at Beverley and minor events at Windsor and Salisbury —on the last-named course at the end of June accounting for five previous winners. The rest of the time Milk It Mick contested listed and pattern events, running consistently without setting the world alight. He put up his best efforts when two lengths fourth to Nevisian Lad in the July Stakes at Newmarket after being ridden more patiently than usual, when third to Haafhd giving weight all round in the Stan James Online Stakes (Washington Singer) at Newbury and when a strong-finishing half-length second to the enterprisingly ridden Barbajuan in the Solario Stakes at Sandown. The level of Milk It Mick's form was just useful, and, in his toughest test, the Champagne at Doncaster, he came only fifth of six to Lucky Story after racing too freely off just a steady pace. Everything changed in the Somerville Tattersall Stakes at Newmarket early in October. Milk It Mick started at 12/1 in a field of eight, with early-season Goodwood winner Bayeux heading the market from Champagne fourth Azarole and Brunel, who had hacked up in a maiden at Salisbury. The gallop was much stronger than at Doncaster and it suited Milk It Mick, who settled better dropped out towards the rear on his trainer's instructions. Quickening impressively from two furlongs out to lead close home, he beat Bayeux and once-raced Bachelor Duke by a neck and the same.

Working on the principle 'nothing ventured, nothing gained', Jamie Osborne brought Milk It Mick back to Newmarket for the Dewhurst two weeks later, without apparently holding great hopes. 'You'd have to be on something to think he could win, but I hope he may be able to stay on into some place money.' The betting public didn't even share Osborne's optimism about place prospects, since only the Aidan O'Brien pacemaker Troubador started at longer odds among the twelve runners. In fact, 33/1 was not a fair reflection of Milk It Mick's prospects. With Lucky Story an absentee after failing to please in his final gallop, only two in the line-up had better public form than Milk It Mick. That put him ahead of promising maiden and minor event winners Duke of Venice, Imperial Stride and Tashkil, his old rival Haafhd, St Leger Yearling Stakes winner Cape Fear, Bachelor

Duke and the O'Brien first string, Railway Stakes winner Antonius Pius. The only runners who had shown better form were the first two past the post in the Middle Park Stakes, the favourite Three Valleys and Balmont. The form of Royal Lodge winner Snow Ridge was on a par with Milk It Mick's. As an added fillip to Milk It Mick's chances, his timefigure in the Somerville Tattersall was equivalent to a rating of 111, while assessment of his sectional times—his figures for the last three furlongs of the race equating to a rating around 118—painted an even rosier picture. Confirmation of the argument put forward in the essay on Lateen Sails a year ago: 'A race-performance time is dictated to some degree by the pace of a race, and may well—and often does—underplay a horse's true ability, particularly if the horse isn't asked to assert until late on. Sectional timing isn't always so limiting.'

The Dewhurst went much the same for Milk It Mick as the Somerville Tattersall. Dropped out towards the rear as Duke of Venice and Troubador led with Snow Ridge and Three Valleys close up, Milk It Mick came with a long run towards the outside to lead with a hundred yards left and kept on gamely to hold Three Valleys' renewed challenge by a head, with Haafhd a length and a quarter away third and Bachelor Duke fourth. The reaction to Milk It Mick's victory was diverting to say the least. With a previous pattern winner coming out on top and the first-past-the-post in a Group 1 finishing second, there seemed no reason to doubt the value of the form, or the winner's ability—his timefigure (upheld by sectional analysis of it) was equivalent to a rating of 119. Suffice to say that while One Cool Cat and Lucky Story probably have more potential as classic colts, Milk It Mick should on no account be left out of calculations for the Two Thousand Guineas, especially at the odds of 20/1 still available at the time of writing. As a point of

Mr Paul J. Dixon's "Milk It Mick"

interest, he is the most-tried juvenile to be top rated in Britain in Timeform's history —the closest to him, Deep Diver, rated 134 in 1971, raced eleven times. Equally, neither Milk It Mick nor Deep Diver was asked to race so often as two-year-olds as some of the giants of the past, including American star of the 'thirties Seabiscuit, subject of a film released in 2003 that was a box-office hit in both America and Britain. Seabiscuit—not a champion as a juvenile, admittedly—ran thirty-five times in his first season, starting in January and finishing in November, getting off the mark only on his eighteenth outing!

Milk It Mick (b.c. Mar 25, 2001)	Millkom (b 1991)	Cyrano de Bergerac (b 1983)	Bold Lad
			Miss St Cyr
		Good Game (b 1984)	Mummy's Game
			Bright Brook
	Lunar Music (b 1994)	Komaite (b 1983)	Nureyev
			Brown Berry
		Lucky Candy (br 1982)	Lucky Wednesday
			Be My Sweet

Milk It Mick's pedigree is nothing like so patrician as that of One Cool Cat, but this has not proved to his detriment so far. A big, good-topped colt with scope, who held his condition well, he is a fine advert for his sire Millkom, in looks as well as toughness and ability. Millkom's record both as a racehorse and sire has been thought-provoking. He was a better racehorse than his pedigree suggested he might be, for, as a son of the sprinter Cyrano de Bergerac he was the exception to that sire's rule on two counts. First, he was high class—Cyrano de Bergerac has had only one other pattern winner Sampower Star—and, secondly, he was suited by middle distances. A twelve-race tally from nineteen starts in France and America included the Grand Prix de Paris, Prix Jean Prat and Man o' War Stakes but injury intervened and, by the time he was retired to the Egerton Stud at Newmarket as a seven-year-old, Millkom was almost a forgotten horse. He covered a total of sixty-three mares in his first two seasons at stud at a fee of £3,500, then only four in his third, one of whom was Milk It Mick's dam Lunar Music. Due to stand at Scarvagh House Stud, Northern Ireland, in 2004 at £3,000, he has sired no other stakes performers. Milk It Mick's dam Lunar Music was no great shakes on the track, picking up three races, two of them sellers, from thirty-four starts. She stayed seven furlongs but her seasonal Timeform ratings of 67, 56, 49 and –, tell their own story. Her unplaced dam Lucky Candy produced five other winners, but the first 'black-type' performer on the catalogue page is Gunner B, a half-brother to the third dam Be My Sweet. Lunar Music has had one other runner, the three-year-old Distinctly North filly Discoed, who was fourth twice from thirteen starts. Discoed went through the sales ring at Doncaster in October but was bought back for 1,400 guineas. The same thing happened to Milk It Mick, who was knocked down to 'cash' for 14,000 guineas and promptly returned to his breeder. His half-sister by Mind Games provoked much more interest at the same venue a year later, topping the sale at 100,000 guineas to a bid from the agent Amanda Skiffington. The filly has gone into training with Osborne. Milk It Mick, who acts on firm and good to soft going, will stay a mile, possibly a shade further. *J. A. Osborne*

MILLAFONIC   3 b.c. Zafonic (USA) 130 – Milligram 130 (Mill Reef (USA) 141)   **97** [2003 8m³ 8g* 8g* 8g⁵ 9m Oct 4] useful-looking colt: ninth foal: half-brother to 7f winner Footlight Fantasy (by Nureyev) and fairly useful 1¼m winner Millennium Dash (by Nashwan): dam, won Queen Elizabeth II Stakes, daughter of 1000 Guineas winner One In A Million: useful performer: won maiden at Kempton and minor event at Ayr (by 1½ lengths from Audacious Prince) in May: reportedly suffered abscess and off 3½ months before fourth start: stiff task in Cambridgeshire at Newmarket final outing: will stay 1¼m: raced only on good/good to firm ground. *L. M. Cumani*

MILLAGROS (IRE)   3 b.f. Pennekamp (USA) 130 – Grey Galava 64 (Generous   **86 +** (IRE) 139) [2003 9m² 11.1d 9.2d² 9.1g⁵ 8.1m 9.2f* 8.3g⁴ 9.2m³ 9.2m⁵ 7.9f* 8.3g 8g⁶ 8d⁴ 8m* 10.3d Nov 7] 5,500Y: good-bodied filly: second foal: half-sister to German 2000 2-y-o 7.5f winner Greese (by Mukaddamah): dam 1¾m winner: fairly useful performer: won maiden at Hamilton in June and handicaps at Carlisle in August and Musselburgh in October: stays 1¼m: acts on firm and good to soft going: went in snatches/wandered seventh start: has hung left: none too consistent. *I. Semple*

Princess of Wales's UAE Equestrian and Racing Federation Stakes, Newmarket—
Millenary, in first-time blinkers, lands the race for the second year in succession; Bandari, Gamut (partly
hidden by runner-up), Bollin Eric (right) and Zindabad are next

MILLBAG (IRE)   2 b. or br.c. (Mar 13) Cape Cross (IRE) 129 – Play With Fire (FR) **98**
(Priolo (USA) 127) [2003 6m³ 5f* 6g³ 6m* 7g³ Oct 24] €110,000Y: good-bodied colt:
has a quick action: second foal: half-brother to 3-y-o Coconut Penang: dam, French 1½m
winner, half-sister to smart performer up to 1½m in France/USA Playact: useful performer: won maiden at Haydock in September and minor event at Salisbury in October:
creditable 5½ lengths third to Peak To Creek in Horris Hill Stakes at Newbury final start:
stays 7f: acts on firm going: usually races up with pace. *M. R. Channon*

MILL BYRE (IRE)   3 b.g. Definite Article 121 – Mummys Best (Bustino 136) [2003 **75 ?**
10d⁴ 10d⁵ 8m May 24] IR 20,000F, IR 130,000Y: fourth foal: half-brother to smart Irish
7f to 9f winner Rush Brook (by Pips Pride): dam, Irish 1¼m winner (and over hurdles),
half-sister to useful Irish 6f/7f winner Quintiliani: easily best effort in maidens (seemingly fair form) on debut: free-going sort, not sure to stay beyond 1¼m: gelded after final
start. *T. G. Mills*

MILLENARY   6 b.h. Rainbow Quest (USA) 134 – Ballerina (IRE) 88 (Dancing Brave **121**
(USA) 140) [2003 121: 12d² 12d² 12m* 12d 12.5s⁴ 16m² Oct 18] leggy, attractive horse:
good walker: fluent mover: very smart performer: first past post in Prix Jean de
Chaudenay at Saint-Cloud (hung right and demoted after beating Loxias a nose) in May
on second start and Princess of Wales's UAE Equestrian and Racing Federation Stakes at
Newmarket (for second year running, beat Bandari 1½ lengths) in July: also ran well
when second in Jockey Club Stakes at Newmarket (beaten 1½ lengths by Warrsan) and
Jockey Club Cup on same course (idled, went down by short head to Persian Punch):
effective at 1½m to 2m: acts on firm and good to soft going, has won on soft: blinkered
third/fourth starts: usually waited with: stays in training. *J. L. Dunlop*

MILL END TEASER   2 b.f. (May 14) Mind Games 121 – Mill End Quest 65 (King's **40**
Signet (USA) 110) [2003 5m 5f 5f 5g⁶ 5m f5s 5m Sep 9] 3,000Y: lengthy, good-topped
filly: first foal: dam 5f (at 2 yrs) and 6f winner: poor maiden: blinkered (ran creditably)
last 2 starts: sometimes looks none too keen. *M. W. Easterby*

MILLENNIUM FORCE   5 b.g. Bin Ajwaad (IRE) 119 – Jumairah Sun (IRE) 98 **115**
(Scenic 128) [2003 113: 7g* 7m³ 7.1d⁴ 7.1m⁴ 7g² 7g³ 7g Jul 26] tall, lengthy gelding:
smart performer: won Castlemartin & La Louviere Studs Gladness Stakes at the Curragh
in April by neck from One More Round: good efforts when close third to Tillerman in
Leicestershire Stakes at Leicester, ½-length second to Lucky Strike in Prix de la Porte
Maillot at Longchamp and ¾-length third to Avorado in Minstrel Stakes at the Curragh:
best at 7f/1m: yet to race on firm going, acts on any other: visored (ran well) once at 3 yrs:
held up: occasionally edges left: reliable. *M. R. Channon*

MILLENNIUM HALL   4 b.g. Saddlers' Hall (IRE) 126 – Millazure (USA) 71 (Day- **66**
jur (USA) 137) [2003 75: 9.9f 8g⁶ 11.1d⁵ 11.1g⁵ 9.2g* 9.1g 9.2m 10.1m⁶ 11.9d Sep 26]
leggy gelding: has a quick action: fair performer: left I. Semple after fourth start: won
handicap at Hamilton in July: stays 11.6f: acts on any ground: has worn cheekpieces.
P. Monteith

MILLENNIUM KING   4 b.g. Piccolo 121 – Zabelina (USA) 57 (Diesis 133) [2003 **49**
74d: 6m f5g 6m 6m³ 7g 5m 6f 6m Aug 20] smallish gelding: poor handicapper: stays 6f:
acts on good to firm ground: wears cheekpieces nowadays. *J. M. Bradley*

MILLFIELDS DREAMS   4 b.g. Dreams End 93 – Millfields Lady 75 (Sayf El Arab **55 ?**
(USA) 127) [2003 8.1m 10.5m⁴ 10.2m 7.1g⁴ 5.7f⁶ 7m 7.1m⁴ Aug 25] modest maiden:

653

likely to prove best at 7f/1m: raced only on good ground or firmer: none too consistent. *R. Brotherton*

MILLIETOM (IRE) 2 b.g. (Apr 15) General Monash (USA) 107 – June Lady (Junius (USA) 124) [2003 f6g f6g f8g Dec 8] €7,000Y, resold €16,000Y: half-brother to several winners, including fairly useful Irish 6f winner Juneson (by Ajraas): dam Irish maiden: no form: tried in blinkers/cheekpieces. *K. A. Ryan*   –

MILLIGAN (FR) 8 b.g. Exit To Nowhere (USA) 122 – Madigan Mill 86 (Mill Reef (USA) 141) [2003 12d Nov 8] quite attractive gelding: smart hurdler: fairly useful handicapper on Flat in 2000: well beaten only outing since. *R. A. Fahey*   –

MILLION PERCENT 4 b.g. Ashkalani (IRE) 128 – Royal Jade 82 (Last Tycoon 131) [2003 89: 5f 6m 6m 6m⁶ 6d⁵ 6.1m* 6g³ 6g* 6d² 6m* 6f⁵ 6m⁴ 6s³ f7g Nov 14] small, strong gelding: fairly useful performer: won minor event at Warwick in June and handicaps at Ayr in July and Newmarket in August: best at 6f/easy 7f: acts on firm ground, soft and polytrack: tried in cheekpieces, better form without: sometimes slowly away. *K. R. Burke*   **91**

MILLKOM ELEGANCE 4 b.f. Millkom 124 – Premier Princess 45 (Hard Fought 125) [2003 49: 8m 8d⁵ 9.9m 10f* Sep 15] small, quite good-topped filly: poor handicapper: blinkered, won selling event at Redcar in September: stays 1¼m: acts on firm and good to soft going. *K. A. Ryan*   **48**

MILLSTREET 4 ch.g. Polish Precedent (USA) 131 – Mill Path (Mill Reef (USA) 141) [2003 112: 14g⁴ 12g⁶ 11.6g² 12g⁵ 16g Nov 4] leggy gelding: smart performer: best efforts in 2003 in Grand Prix de Saint-Cloud (acted as pacemaker and almost certainly flattered, demoted to sixth after third behind Ange Gabriel) and minor event at Windsor (head second to Gamut): well held in Melbourne Cup at Flemington final outing (jarred up after): stays 1½m: acts on firm and good to soft going: tried tongue tied: often makes running. *Saeed bin Suroor*   **111**

MILLYBAA (USA) 3 b.f. Anabaa (USA) 130 – Millyant 114 (Primo Dominie 121) [2003 66p: 6.1g* 6.1s³ 6m 6d² 6s Oct 31] lengthy, quite good-topped filly: useful performer: won maiden at Nottingham in April: best effort when short-head second to Hanabad in listed event at the Curragh fourth start: always behind in Prix de Seine-et-Oise at Maisons-Laffitte final one: raced only at 6f: acts on soft ground. *R. Guest*   **105**

MILLY FLEUR 3 ch.f. Primo Dominie 121 – My Cadeaux 93 (Cadeaux Genereux 131) [2003 60p: 6g² 6d* 6.1m⁴ 6m 7s 7g Nov 1] fair performer: won maiden at Salisbury in July: stays 6f: acts on good to firm and good to soft ground: blinkered (well held) final start. *R. Guest*   **67**

MILLY HATCH 3 b.f. Atraf 116 – Pie Hatch (IRE) 50 (Huntingdale 132) [2003 10.2m 12.1m³ 10m Jul 17] second foal: dam 1½m winner: no worthwhile form: tried visored. *W. S. Kittow*   –

MILLY LAHIB (IRE) 3 b.f. Lahib (USA) 129 – Treadmill (IRE) 51 (High Estate 127) [2003 64: p7g p8g 8.1m 7m 7m 8.1m 8d 8f² 7m 8f⁵ 8f Oct 17] lengthy filly: poor maiden handicapper nowadays: effective at 7f/1m: acts on all-weather and firm going: tried visored: often slowly away, reluctant to race sixth/seventh outings: sometimes leads: one to treat with caution. *D. J. Coakley*   **49 §**

MILLY'S LASS 5 b.m. Mind Games 121 – Millie's Lady (IRE) (Common Grounds 118) [2003 67d: f5s⁴ f5g f5g⁴ 5g 5.5m 5.7f Sep 8] sparely-made mare: poor handicapper: effective at 5f/6f: acts on any turf going and all-weather: usually wears cheekpieces: sometimes starts slowly: inconsistent. *J. M. Bradley*   **39 §**

MILLY WATERS 2 b.f. (Feb 28) Danzero (AUS) – Chilly Waters (Polar Falcon (USA) 126) [2003 5g² f5g² 5m⁴ 5m* 6f 6.5d 6.5m 6m* 6g* Oct 25] tall, leggy filly: second foal: half-sister to winner in Holland by Sabrehill: dam, Italian 1¼m/11f winner, out of half-sister to dam of Oh So Sharp: fairly useful performer: won maiden at Warwick in May and £100000 Tattersalls Autumn Auction Stakes at Newmarket and nursery at Newbury (sweating, led close home to beat Fictional by neck) in October: should stay 7f: acts on fibresand and good to firm ground: game. *W. M. Brisbourne*   **88**

MIMAS GIRL 4 b.f. Samim (USA) 84 – Cocked Hat Girl 47 (Ballacashtal (CAN)) [2003 43: f8s f8g f6g f8g³ f8s f8g⁵ 7m 7f⁴ f7g⁶ Jun 9] poor maiden: effective at 7f/1m: acts on fibresand and firm ground: tried blinkered/tongue tied. *S. R. Bowring*   **43**

MIMIC 3 b.f. Royal Applause 124 – Stripanoora (Ahonoora 122) [2003 63: 7m⁶ 6m 6m⁴ 6g* 5.1g³ 6.1m³ 5f² 5g² 5g⁵ 6m* 6m* 5m⁴ 6f Oct 10] angular filly: fairly useful performer: won handicaps at Lingfield and Yarmouth and minor event at Folkestone   **83**

between June and August: best form at 6f: raced only on good ground or firmer on turf: usually races up with pace: consistent. *R. Guest*

MIND ALERT   2 b.g. (Feb 12) Mind Games 121 – Bombay Sapphire (Be My Chief (USA) 122) [2003 5g⁴ 5m⁴ 5f⁵ 6g² 6g* 6g 6g 6d⁶ Sep 29] 2,000F, 24,000Y: well-grown, good-topped gelding: has scope: third foal: dam, lightly raced, out of smart Italian sprinter Ginny Binny: fair performer: won nursery at Ripon in August: ran poorly after: not sure to stay much beyond 6f: best efforts on good going. *T. D. Easterby*   **73**

MINDANAO   7 b.m. Most Welcome 131 – Salala 83 (Connaught 130) [2003 76: f12g Jan 17] leggy mare: fair handicapper: well held only 7-y-o start: joined L. Lungo, and fairly useful winner over hurdles. *I. Semple*   **–**

MIND BOBBY   3 b.g. Mind Games 121 – Young Holly (Risk Me (FR) 127) [2003 –: 5g 7m Jun 11] no form. *J. Gallagher*   **–**

MINDEROO   5 b.g. Efisio 120 – Mindomica 63 (Dominion 123) [2003 58: f6g f6g p6g² p6g⁵ p6g* p6g⁶ 6.1g 6m 6m 5m 6d Jul 19] quite good-topped gelding: modest performer: won selling handicap at Lingfield in February: left J. M. Bradley after eighth outing: best at 6f: acts on good to soft ground and all-weather: tried in blinkers/cheekpieces/tongue tie: tail flasher, and has found little. *Jamie Poulton*   **49 a59**

MIND PLAY   2 b.f. (May 3) Mind Games 121 – Diplomatist 69 (Dominion 123) [2003 7m 7.1m 8.3g f8g⁶ Oct 16] small filly: fifth foal: half-sister to 3 winners, including 4-y-o Sewmuch Character and 2m winner Mice Design (by Presidium): dam 10.5f/1½m winner: well held in maidens/sellers: blinkered final start. *J. G. Given*   **–**

MINDSET (IRE)   2 b.f. (Mar 19) Vettori (IRE) 119 – Eden (IRE) 88 (Polish Precedent (USA) 131) [2003 7m² 7m³ Jul 28] first foal: dam, 2-y-o 7f winner who should have stayed 1¼m, from family of Middle Park winner Balla Cove: fair form in maidens at Folkestone won by Machiventa and Halicardia: got down in stall and withdrawn in August: should stay at least 1m. *L. M. Cumani*   **78**

MIND THE TIME   2 b.g. (Apr 4) Mind Games 121 – Rare Indigo 80 (Timeless Times (USA) 99) [2003 f8g Dec 19] 12,500Y: third foal: closely related to 2001 2-y-o 5f winner Lady Ansell (by Puissance): dam, 5f winner, ran only at 2 yrs: 50/1, well beaten in maiden at Southwell, starting very slowly. *J. Hetherton*   **–**

MINE BEHIND   3 b.c. Muhtarram (USA) 128 – Arapi (IRE) 89 (Arazi (USA) 135) [2003 7d 6m* 6d⁶ 6g 5g p7g³ p7g² p7g² 8g⁶ 8.2f³ Oct 1] 13,500Y: lengthy colt: second foal: half-brother to Hong Kong 7f/1m winner Kalimantan (by Vettori): dam, 6f winner (ran only at 2 yrs), half-sister to smart performers Pasternak (at 9f/1¼m) and Parthian Springs (up to 1¾m): fairly useful performer: won maiden at Newbury in June: good efforts in handicaps 4 of last 5 starts: stays 1m: acts on polytrack and firm going. *J. R. Best*   **84**

MINE (IRE)   5 b.h. Primo Dominie 121 – Ellebanna 69 (Tina's Pet 121) [2003 99: 8g 7g* 7f³ 7m² 7g 7m³ 7f⁴ 7f 8g⁶ Nov 1] tall, useful-looking horse: smart handicapper: won at Doncaster in May: mostly good efforts after, notably when short-headed by Patavellian in Bunbury Cup at Newmarket (won corresponding event in 2002) and when fourth to Master Robbie in Tote Trifecta Stakes at Ascot (poorly drawn): best around 7f: acts on firm and good to soft going, well below form on heavy: usually visored: waited with. *J. D. Bethell*   **111**

MINELLY   3 b.f. Defacto (USA) – Lady Liza 69 (Air Trooper 115) [2003 42§: 10g Jul 7] small filly: has a markedly round action: poor maiden: well held only 3-y-o start: should stay at least 1m: temperamental. *M. E. Sowersby*   **– §**

MINESHAFT (USA)   4 b. or br.c. A P Indy (USA) 131 – Prospectors Delite (USA) (Mr Prospector (USA)) [2003 109: a8.5f* a8.5f² a9f* a9f* a9.5s* a9f² a10f* a9f* a10f* Sep 27] tall, good-topped colt: trained by J. Gosden in Britain most of 2002: improved into top-class performer for switch to dirt, and enjoyed very successful season in 2003 (voted Horse Of The Year): won non-graded event and Grade 2 handicap at Fair Grounds, Grade 3 event at Keeneland (by 9 lengths), Pimlico Special at Pimlico, Suburban Handicap (beat Volponi impressively by 2¼ lengths), Woodward Stakes (easily, by 4¼ lengths from Hold That Tiger) and Jockey Club Gold Cup (beat Quest impressively by 4¼ lengths), last 3 at Belmont: ran very well when head second to Perfect Drift (who rec. 8 lb) in Stephen Foster Handicap at Churchill Downs sixth outing: was probably best at 9f/1¼m: raced only on good/good to firm going on turf, much better on dirt (was fully effective on a wet track): reported in early-October to have been retired due to an ankle chip, and to stand at Lane's End Stud, Kentucky, fee $100,000. *N. J. Howard, USA*   **132**

MING THE MERCILESS   3 b.g. Hector Protector (USA) 124 – Sundae Girl (USA) –
75 (Green Dancer (USA) 132) [2003 74: 9.9m⁶ 8.2s 11.8m f12g Jun 6] big, strong
gelding: fair maiden: well held in 2003, including in blinkers. *J. G. Given*

MINGUN (USA)   3 b. or br.c. A P Indy (USA) 131 – Miesque (USA) 133 (Nureyev **117**
(USA) 131) [2003 97P: 8v* 8m* 10m* 10.4m⁴ Aug 19] angular, quite good-topped colt:
smart performer: won maiden at Leopardstown in May, listed race at the Curragh (beat
Hanabad by 2½ lengths) in June and Meld Stakes at Leopardstown (by head from
Carnival Dancer) in July: creditable 5¼ lengths fourth to Falbrav in International Stakes
at York: acts on heavy and good to firm ground. *A. P. O'Brien, Ireland*

MINIMUM BID   2 b.f. (Mar 24) First Trump 118 – La Noisette (Rock Hopper 124) **61**
[2003 6g 6m⁶ 5m³ Aug 11] 1,800Y, resold 800Y: fourth foal: half-sister to 3-y-o Chandelier and unreliable 2001 2-y-o 5f seller winner Stalky (by Bahamian Bounty): dam
unraced half-sister to 10-y-o Repertory: modest form in maidens: third at Folkestone:
should stay 6f. *Miss B. Sanders*

MINIRINA   3 b.f. Mistertopogigo (IRE) 118 – Fabulous Rina (FR) (Fabulous Dancer **64 d**
(USA) 124) [2003 65: f5g f5s f5g 5m² 5d³ 5f 5m⁵ 5f⁴ 5m Aug 4] leggy filly: modest
maiden: well below form last 4 starts: raced only at 5f: acts on good to firm going, good
to soft and fibresand: tried blinkered: unreliable. *C. Smith*

MINIVET   8 b.g. Midyan (USA) 124 – Bronzewing 103 (Beldale Flutter (USA) 130) **63**
[2003 10.3m⁶ 9.9m 10.3m 16.1m⁵ 15.8d⁴ Sep 20] workmanlike gelding: fairly useful
handicapper in 2001: missed 2002: modest form on return: effective at 1¼m to 2m: acts
on soft and good to firm going: tried blinkered: usually slowly away: often held up: none
too reliable. *T. D. Easterby*

MINNINA (IRE)   3 ch.f. In The Wings 128 – Cheyenne Spirit 107 (Indian Ridge 123) –
[2003 10s Jun 30] IR 15,000Y: quite good-topped filly: third foal: closely related to fairly
useful 2000 2-y-o 6f winner Alina (by King's Theatre), later 8.5f winner in USA: dam 6f/
7f performer: 33/1, well held in maiden at Pontefract: sold 11,000 gns. *B. Hanbury*

MI ODDS   7 b.g. Sure Blade (USA) 130 – Vado Via 56 (Ardross 134) [2003 –, a94: **55**
f12s* f12s* f12g⁶ f12g f11g⁵ 10.3g⁵ 11m f12g* f11g² f12g⁴ 11.5g* 16.5m 10m⁶ 11.5f⁵ **a99**
10.1m f9.4g* f12s² f11g* f9.4g² f12g* f9.4s² Dec 31] tall gelding: useful on all-weather,
modest on turf: enjoyed very good year, winning claimers at Southwell (2) in February
and Wolverhampton in April and handicaps at Yarmouth (carried head high) in July,
Wolverhampton in October and Southwell in November and December: excellent second
to Nimello in handicap at Wolverhampton final start: effective at 9f to 1½m: acts on
fibresand and good to firm going: tried in cheekpieces, better form without: tough.
Mrs N. Macauley

MIRANT   4 b.c. Danzig Connection (USA) – Ingerence (FR) (Akarad (FR) 130) [2003 –
81: 20m Jun 18] tall, useful-looking colt: fairly useful maiden at 3 yrs: well held (in Ascot
Stakes) only 4-y-o start: fairly useful hurdler. *M. C. Pipe*

MIRASOL PRINCESS   2 ch.f. (Feb 19) Ali-Royal (IRE) 127 – Yanomami (USA) **83**
71 (Slew O' Gold (USA)) [2003 5m* 5g² 5m* 5m 5.2m 5m⁴ 5m* 5m* 6f 6g Oct 25]
10,500Y: smallish filly: second foal: half-sister to 3-y-o Yarrita: dam 6f winner: fairly
useful performer: won maiden at Musselburgh in March, minor event at Redcar in May,
claimer at Haydock (then left K. Ryan) in August and nursery at Windsor in September:
should stay 6f: acts on good to firm going. *D. K. Ivory*

MISAAYEF (USA)   3 b. or br.f. Swain (IRE) 134 – Zakiyya (USA) (Dayjur (USA) **82**
137) [2003 78p: 10m³ 10.5m* 10g Aug 26] rather lengthy, useful-looking filly: fairly
useful performer: long odds on, won maiden at Haydock in August easily: well held in
handicap at Ripon next time: stays 10.5f: raced only on good/good to firm ground: sold
21,000 gns in December. *Sir Michael Stoute*

MISARO (GER)   2 b.g. (Mar 1) Acambaro (GER) 118 – Misniniski (Niniski (USA) **80**
125) [2003 7m³ 10d⁵ 6.1d* Nov 6] €10,000Y: leggy gelding: half-brother to 3 winners
in Germany, including fairly useful 9f winner Major Blade (by Dashing Blade): dam,
Irish 2-y-o 1m winner, stayed 2m: easily best effort (fairly useful form) when winning
16-runner maiden at Nottingham by ¾ length from Here To Me, making most: bred to
stay at least 1¼m. *P. A. Blockley*

MISBEHAVIOUR   4 b.g. Tragic Role (USA) – Exotic Forest 66 (Dominion 123) –
[2003 56: p16g May 17] leggy gelding: modest maiden: well held only Flat outing in
2003: tried visored. *P. Butler*

MIS CHICAF (IRE)   2 b.f. (May 12) Prince Sabo 123 – Champagne Season (USA) **69**
54 (Vaguely Noble 140) [2003 f5g 5m⁵ 5m³ 5m⁵ 6g 5m* Sep 17] €5,200Y, 10,500 2-y-o:

strong, workmanlike filly: seventh foal: sister to useful 7f (at 2 yrs) to 1¼m winner Champagne Prince, later successful in USA, and half-sister to 7f winners Bubbly and Festive (both by Rudimentary): dam ran twice at 2 yrs: fair performer: improved to win maiden at Beverley: should stay 6f. *J. S. Wainwright*

MISCHIEF   7 ch.g. Generous (IRE) 139 – Knight's Baroness 116 (Rainbow Quest (USA) 134) [2003 46§: 9.9m⁶ 12m 13f 16.5m 14.1f* Aug 20] compact gelding: poor performer: won amateur handicap at Carlisle in August: effective at 1½m to easy 2m: acts on fibresand and any turf going: sometimes blinkered/visored: has looked reluctant: unreliable. *K. Bell*   **44 §**

MISCONDUCT   9 gr.m. Risk Me (FR) 127 – Grey Cree 64 (Creetown 123) [2003 14.1m Apr 21] lengthy mare: poor handicapper: well beaten only 9-y-o start. *J. G. Portman*   **–**

MISHALL (USA)   2 ch.c. (Jan 23) Distant View (USA) 126 – Virgin Stanza (USA) (Opening Verse (USA) 126) [2003 7.1f² 7d⁵ Jul 3] 80,000F, 46,000Y: first foal: dam, 8.5f winner in USA, granddaughter of top-class 1m/1¼m performer Rose Bowl: much better effort in maidens (fair form) when always-prominent second at Sandown: will stay 1m. *M. P. Tregoning*   **75**

MISHEAD   5 ch.g. Unfuwain (USA) 131 – Green Jannat (USA) (Alydar (USA)) [2003 –: 16d Aug 11] no form on Flat. *M. C. Chapman*   **–**

MISHKA   5 b.g. Mistertopogigo (IRE) 118 – Walsham Witch 61 (Music Maestro 119) [2003 71, a79: p6g Jan 4] strong, close-coupled gelding: fair performer at best: well beaten only start in 2003: blinkered/visored. *Julian Poulton*   **–**

MISKINA   2 b.f. (May 17) Mark of Esteem (IRE) 137 – Najmat Alshemaal (IRE) 98 (Dancing Brave (USA) 140) [2003 7m 7m² 6d⁴ Oct 31] rather leggy filly: fifth foal: sister to 5-y-o Emteyaz and half-sister to 3-y-o Otototm: dam 1¼m winner who stayed 14.6f: modest form in maidens: should stay at least 1m: sold 9,500 gns. *M. R. Channon*   **57**

MI SOMBRERO   4 ch.f. Factual (USA) 108 – Rose Elegance 83 (Bairn (USA) 126) [2003 –: f8s f7s² f7s⁴ f7s⁵ f7s f7s Feb 18] poor maiden: stays 7f: acts on fibresand: tried in cheekpieces: often slowly away. *D. K. Ivory*   **48**

MISS ADELAIDE (IRE)   2 b.f. (Mar 21) Alzao (USA) 117 – Sweet Adelaide (USA) 98 (The Minstrel (CAN) 135) [2003 7m⁴ 6g³ Oct 24] €40,000Y: smallish, strong, close-coupled filly: half-sister to several winners, including 5f winner Port Augusta (by Tirol) and 1m winner Sweet Trentino (by High Estate): dam, 2-y-o 6f winner, later successful in South Africa: fairly useful form at Newbury in minor event (fourth to Silk Fan) and maiden (third to So Will I): should stay 1m. *B. W. Hills*   **85**

MISS AMAZER   4 b.f. Shaamit (IRE) 127 – Kiss On Time (Lead On Time (USA) 123) [2003 47, a38: 8g 8f⁶ 8.1m Aug 8] compact filly: maiden handicapper: showed little in 2003. *I. A. Wood*   **–**

MISS ANABAA   4 b.f. Anabaa (USA) 130 – Midnight Shift (IRE) 73 (Night Shift (USA)) [2003 85+: 5.5g⁵ 5.5g³ 5g⁵ 5g* 5m* 6s Oct 31] useful performer: won listed race at Naas (by length from Dragon Flyer) and Kerry Group Ballyogan Stakes at Cork (by neck from Belle du Jour) in June: off over 4 months, always behind in Prix de Seine-et-Oise at Maisons-Laffitte final start: should prove as effective at 6f as 5f: won on good to soft going at 3 yrs, best form on good and good to firm: tongue tied for both wins in 2003: usually waited with. *R. Guest*   **107**

MISS ASSERTIVE   3 b.f. Zafonic (USA) 130 – Self Assured (IRE) 97 (Ahonoora 122) [2003 88: p7g 5.5m 7g 7.6m⁶ May 6] leggy, workmanlike filly: fairly useful performer: stays 7.6f: acts on polytrack, firm and soft ground. *N. P. Littmoden*   **81**

MISS BROOKIE   2 br.f. (Mar 18) The West (USA) 107 – Galacia (IRE) 52 (Gallic League 119) [2003 5g⁴ p5g³ 5f* 5m³ 5m² 6d⁵ 5m³ 5m³ 5.1m 5g Aug 23] leggy, quite good-topped filly: second foal: dam, maiden who stayed 6f, also third over hurdles: fair performer: won minor event at Thirsk in April: below form, mostly in claimers/sellers, after: probably best at 5f: acts on firm going: wore cheekpieces/visor seventh to ninth starts: sometimes flashes tail/hangs left: reluctant to race penultimate outing: untrustworthy. *W. G. M. Turner*   **70 d**

MISS CAP FERRAT   3 b.f. Darshaan 133 – Miss Beaulieu 106 (Northfields (USA)) [2003 8m⁶ 9m⁵ Oct 25] tall filly: closely related to fairly useful 1m and (in France) 10.5f winner Riviera Vista (by Shirley Heights) and half-sister to numerous winners, including useful 1m winner Miss Riviera Golf (by Hernando) and 4-y-o Miss Corniche: dam 6f (at 2 yrs) and 1¼m winner: seemingly modest form in maidens at Salisbury (slowly away) and Musselburgh: should stay at least 1¼m. *G. Wragg*   **53 ?**

MISS CELERITY 3 b.f. Compton Place 125 – Film Buff 60 (Midyan (USA) 124) –
[2003 10d 7m⁶ 6m Sep 29] 4,500Y: second foal: half-sister to winner in USA by Robellino: dam, maiden who stayed 1¾m, out of sister to dam of Oaks winner Lady Carla: well
held in maidens. *M. J. Haynes*

MISS CEYLON 3 b.f. Brief Truce (USA) 126 – Five Islands 62 (Bairn (USA) 126) –
[2003 75: 5m 6d 5f⁶ 5f f5g 5m 7.1f⁶ 7m 6d 12.1m 5m 6g 7d Sep 20] angular, close-
coupled filly: fair performer at 2 yrs: well beaten in 2003, including in cheekpieces/visor:
has been reluctant to race and very slowly away last 3 outings. *Miss A. Stokell*

MISS CHAMPERS (IRE) 3 b. or br.f. Grand Lodge (USA) 125 – Katherine Gorge **47**
(USA) (Hansel (USA)) [2003 66, a83: f8.5g⁶ f6s⁴ 7m⁵ 8m⁶ 8m 6m 8.3g f7s⁶ 8.1m f9.4g³ **a75**
f7g f9.4g f7g⁵ f8g* f8g* f7g³ f8g⁵ f8.5g² Dec 26] leggy filly: fair performer on all-
weather, poor on turf: left R. Hannon after fifth start: won handicap and apprentice minor
event at Southwell in December: stays 8.5f: acts on fibresand, best turf form on good to
soft ground. *P. D. Evans*

MISS CHILDREY (IRE) 2 ch.f. (Mar 20) Dr Fong (USA) 128 – Blazing Glory (IRE) **95**
(Glow (USA)) [2003 5d³ 5g* 6g* 5m⁵ 7f 7m 8d⁴ Sep 11] 22,000F, €35,000Y: lengthy
filly: half-sister to several winners, including fairly useful 5f/6f winner La Piazza (by
Polish Patriot): dam Irish 5f winner, including at 2 yrs: useful performer: won maiden at
Cork in April and listed race at Naas in June: highly tried after: creditable 5 lengths fourth
to Kinnaird in May Hill Stakes at Doncaster: barely stays 1m: acts on good to firm and
good to soft going. *Francis Ennis, Ireland*

MISS COMBUSTIBLE (IRE) 3 b.f. Titus Livius (FR) 115 – Highly Motivated 84 –
(Midyan (USA) 124) [2003 7m 6f 9.3f Jun 15] IR 6,000F: smallish filly: second foal:
dam, Irish 2-y-o 7f winner, also won over hurdles: no sign of ability. *A. Berry*

MISS CONCEPT (IRE) 4 b.f. Frimaire – Hard Sweet (Hard Fought 125) [2003 –
f11s⁵ f14.8g⁴ f12g 12.3m Apr 2] little form: has worn cheekpieces. *F. Jordan*

MISS CORANADO 2 b.f. (Apr 10) Piccolo 121 – Sunny Davis (USA) 71 (Alydar **48**
(USA)) [2003 5g⁶ 6d 6m⁴ 7m Jun 10] 4,800F, 8,000Y: smallish, compact filly: closely
related to 2 winners by Warning, including useful 6f (at 2 yrs) to 1m (in Sweden) winner
Warming Trends and half-sister to several winners, including 3-y-o Dance In The Sun:
dam 2-y-o 7f winner: poor maiden: should stay at least 7f. *T. D. Easterby*

MISS CORNICHE 4 b.f. Hernando (FR) 127 – Miss Beaulieu 106 (Northfields **104**
(USA)) [2003 104: 12.3m⁶ 12m³ 11.9m 10d 9.9m² 10m³ 10.5d Oct 27] leggy, useful-
looking filly: useful performer: placed in listed races at Goodwood (head second of 5 to
Imtiyaz) and Newmarket (third to Al Ihtithar) fifth/sixth starts: free-going sort, probably
best short of 1½m: yet to race on firm going, acts on any other: has been bandaged near-
hind. *G. Wragg*

MISSCOSTALOT 3 b.f. Hernando (FR) 127 – Glamour Game 80 (Nashwan (USA) –
135) [2003 11.5g⁶ Jul 3] third living foal: dam, Irish 1¼m winner, also successful over
hurdles (2½m) in Britain: 25/1, tailed off in maiden at Yarmouth. *W. Jarvis*

MISS CROISETTE 4 ch.f. Hernando (FR) 127 – Miss Riviera 103 (Kris 135) [2003 –
69: f16s⁶ Jan 1] strong filly: lightly-raced maiden: well beaten only 4-y-o start. *Mrs
H. Dalton*

MISS ELOISE 2 b.f. (Jan 27) Efisio 120 – Zaima (IRE) 92 (Green Desert (USA) 127) **61**
[2003 6m⁵ 6m 7.5m 6m⁵ 7d² Nov 4] 6,500Y: smallish, stocky filly: third foal: dam, 7f
winner at 2 yrs, out of half-sister to very smart miler Alhijaz: modest maiden: second at
Catterick: should stay 1m: best effort on good to soft going. *T. D. Easterby*

MISS EMMA (IRE) 3 b.f. Key of Luck (USA) 126 – Disregard That (IRE) (Damister **113**
(USA) 123) [2003 90: 6s* 6d* 7d³ 6f Aug 10] IR 18,000Y: fifth foal: half-sister to fairly
useful 1997 2-y-o 5f/5.7f winner Eleventh Duke (by Imperial Frontier) and Irish 1998
2-y-o 1m winner Crosskeys Lass (by Petorius): dam unraced: smart performer: won
maiden at Naas at 2 yrs: much improved first 2 starts on return, winning listed race at
Naas (by head from One Won One) and 5-runner Weatherbys Ireland Greenlands Stakes
at the Curragh (easily, by 4 lengths from Captain Rio) in May: below form in Ballycorus
Stakes at Leopardstown (third to Abunawwas) and Phoenix Sprint Stakes at the Curragh
(pulled hard, found little): best form at 6f: acts on soft going, possibly not on firm: joined
J. Hammond, France. *M. Halford, Ireland*

MISS FARA (FR) 8 ch.m. Galetto (FR) 118 – Faracha (FR) (Kenmare (FR) 125) [2003 **91**
100: 14m 20m 18m Oct 18] leggy, angular mare: useful handicapper in 2002, winning
Cesarewitch: below best in 2003, tenth of 36 in latest running of that race final start: stays
2¼m: acts on firm and good to soft going: held up: sold 30,000 gns. *M. C. Pipe*

MIS

MISS FAYE 3 b. or br.f. Puissance 110 – Bingo Bongo 60 (Petong 126) [2003 –: 7.1m⁴ – 6m⁶ 5.7f⁶ Sep 8] no form. *J. M. Bradley*

MISS GEORGE 5 b.m. Pivotal 124 – Brightside (IRE) 99 (Last Tycoon 131) [2003 **93** 81: p6g⁴ p7g² p6g⁶ p7g² p7g* p7g* p7g* 6m 6m 6g 7.6g⁵ 6m⁶ 5m* 5f 5d 5m⁵ 6m* 6g³ 6f Aug 23] big mare: fairly useful performer: won 2 minor events and a handicap at Lingfield in February/March and minor event and handicap at Windsor in June/July: effective at 5f to 7f: acts on firm going and all-weather: sometimes slowly away/hangs left: has worn cheekpieces, not in 2003: tough and game. *D. K. Ivory*

MISS GLORY BE 5 b.m. Glory of Dancer 121 – Miss Blondie (USA) (Stop The Music **53** (USA)) [2003 64: p10g⁶ f8s² f9.4g² p10g⁶ f7s² p8g⁵ 9.7m f7g* f7g 7m 7g⁵ f8.5g 10m⁶ 8f³ **a68** f8s² f9.4g³ f8g f8g f8.5g⁶ Dec 26] fair handicapper on all-weather, modest on turf: won at Wolverhampton in May: best at 7f to 9.4f: acts on all-weather and firm going: tailed off in visor tenth start, usually wore cheekpieces otherwise in 2003: sometimes carries head awkwardly. *Miss Gay Kelleway*

MISS GRACE 3 ch.f. Atticus (USA) 121 – Jetbeeah (IRE) 95 (Lomond (USA) 128) **64** [2003 68p: p8g³ p10g² p10g* 9.9m³ 10.2g³ 10m⁶ 8g Sep 22] leggy filly: modest performer: landed odds in maiden at Lingfield in March: sold out of B. Hills's stable 21,000 gns after sixth start: stays 1¼m: acts on polytrack, unraced on extremes of going. *J. J. Sheehan*

MISS HOLLY 4 b.f. Makbul 104 – Seraphim (FR) 48 (Lashkari 128) [2003 73: f11g* **85** Jan 4] fairly useful handicapper: won at Southwell in January: should stay 1¾m: acts on good to firm going, good to soft and fibresand. *M. Johnston*

MISS HOOFBEATS 2 b.f. (Feb 21) Unfuwain (USA) 131 – Oiselina (FR) (Linamix – (FR) 127) [2003 7m 7m³ 7m Aug 16] unfurnished filly: second foal: dam, fairly useful French 10.5f winner, sister to useful French 1½m performer Osamixa: well held in maidens at Newmarket. *Miss J. Feilden*

MISSIE 3 ch.f. Compton Place 125 – About Face (Midyan (USA) 124) [2003 –: 7g⁵ **48 ?** 7.2m 7d⁴ 6m⁵ Oct 7] good-topped filly: poor maiden: stays 7f: unraced on extremes of going: unruly at start and withdrawn second intended 2-y-o outing: free-going sort. *G. A. Swinbank*

MISSILE TOE (IRE) 10 b.g. Exactly Sharp (USA) 121 – Debach Dust 64 (Indian **63** King (USA) 128) [2003 66, a–: 10m 10d³ 11.5g³ 10m Jul 18] good-topped gelding: poor **a–** walker: modest handicapper: stays 11.5f: acts on firm and soft going: tried blinkered/visored (not since 1996): pulls hard: usually held up. *D. Morris*

MISS INQUISITIVE 3 b.f. Bijou d'Inde 127 – Forget Me (IRE) (Don't Forget Me – 127) [2003 p7g f7g 10m⁶ 7m 8g 8.2g Jun 23] 1,500F: sixth foal: sister to a winner in USA and half-sister to a winner in Italy by Lear Fan: dam French/Italian 5f (at 2 yrs) to 1m winner: well held, including in sellers. *Mrs C. A. Dunnett*

MISSION AFFIRMED (USA) 2 ch.g. (May 16) Stravinsky (USA) 133 – Affirmed – Legacy (USA) (Affirmed (USA)) [2003 6g⁵ 7g⁵ Oct 28] $20,000Y: good-bodied gelding: third foal: half-brother to winner in USA by Future Storm: dam, 8.5f/9f winner in USA, half-sister to US Grade 2 8.5f/9f winner Bolshoi Boy: signs of just a little ability in minor events at Ripon and Redcar. *T. P. Tate*

MISSION MAN 2 b.c. (Mar 7) Revoque (IRE) 122 – Opopmil (IRE) 68 (Pips Pride **81** 117) [2003 7m 8g² 7g⁴ Nov 1] 5,200Y, 16,000 2-y-o: big, strong colt: has scope: first living foal: dam, maiden best at 5f at 2 yrs, sister to very smart sprinter Pipalong: best effort in maidens (fairly useful form) when head second of 17 to Rave Reviews at Newbury, headed close home: raced freely when respectable fourth to Golden Grace at Newmarket: needs to settle to stay beyond 1m. *R. Hannon*

MISSION TO MARS 4 b.g. Muhtarram (USA) 125 – Ideal Candidate 80 (Celestial **83** Storm (USA) 132) [2003 69§: p12g⁴ f12g* f14.8s 10m 11.5g f12s² p12g* 12g* p12g* p12g* p12g² Nov 18] quite good-topped gelding: fairly useful performer: won maiden at Wolverhampton in March, seller at Lingfield (left C. Cyzer) in June and minor events at Folkestone in September and Lingfield in October (amateurs) and November: ran well final start: stays 1½m: acts on firm going and all-weather: reportedly had breathing problem third start. *P. R. Hedger*

MISS ISSY (IRE) 3 b.f. Victory Note (USA) 120 – Shane's Girl (IRE) (Marktingo) **69** [2003 64: p8g³ f12g 7.1m² 8g 7m⁶ 7m² 7m³ 7.1m⁴ 8g p8g⁴ p7g p7g* p7g Dec 30] lengthy filly: fair performer: claimed from A. Jarvis £10,000 eighth start: won handicap at Lingfield in December: effective at 7f to 8.5f: acts on all-weather, raced only on good

659

ground or firmer on turf: visored last 3 starts: tends to pull hard: sometimes swishes tail. *J. Gallagher*

MISS IVANHOE (IRE) 3 b.f. Selkirk (USA) 129 – Robellino Miss (USA) (Robellino (USA) 127) [2003 8.2g* 10m⁶ 10m⁴ 8.1g² 8d² 7m⁶ 7d* 7g² Oct 17] big, good-topped filly: half-sister to several winners, including 1999 2-y-o 7f winner Decision Maid (by Diesis) and 1998 2-y-o 6f winner Chief Rebel (by Chief's Crown), both useful up to 1m: dam, won up to 9f in USA, out of close relative to high-class sprinter Silver Fling: useful performer: won maiden at Nottingham in April and listed race at Maisons-Laffitte (by 2 lengths from Intercontinental) in September: good head second to Gonfilia in listed race at Maisons-Laffitte final start: best at 7f/1m: acts on good to firm and good to soft going. *G. Wragg* **107 +**

MISS JINGLES 4 b.f. Muhtarram (USA) 125 – Flamingo Times 60 (Good Times (ITY)) [2003 60, a73: f6s f7s p8g² 7m 7.1m⁴ 7m 9m 8.1m p8g⁴ p12g⁵ Jul 9] leggy filly: fair handicapper: stays easy 1½m: acts on good to firm ground and all-weather: sometimes looks none too keen. *J. A. Gilbert* **68**

MISS JUDGED 2 b.f. (Mar 6) Case Law 113 – Marie's Crusader (IRE) (Last Tycoon 131) [2003 6d⁶ 6.1f f5g f6g f6g f6g Dec 15] fourth foal: dam unraced half-sister to smart 1m/1¼m performer Noble Patriarch: poor maiden: fried tongue tied. *A. P. Jones* **46**

MISS JUDGEMENT (IRE) 2 b.f. (Feb 23) Revoque (IRE) 122 – Mugello 96 (Emarati (USA) 74) [2003 5m f6s 5.1m p5g⁶ Nov 22] €13,000Y: second foal: sister to Spanish 1¼m winner: dam 2-y-o 5f winner who didn't train on: modest maiden: best effort at 5f on polytrack. *W. R. Muir* **60**

MISS JULIE JAY (IRE) 2 b.f. (Apr 18) Bahhare (USA) 122 – Gentle Papoose (Commanche Run 133) [2003 6.1m 6m 7m p7g Dec 10] €13,000Y: sixth foal: half-sister to 2 winners, including fairly useful 1998 2-y-o 5f winner Cheyenne Gold (by Anita's Prince), later successful in USA: dam poor Irish maiden: slowly away and well beaten in maidens/nursery: looked reluctant final start. *Noel T. Chance* **–**

MISS KOEN (IRE) 4 b.f. Barathea (IRE) 127 – Fanny Blankers (IRE) (Persian Heights 129) [2003 83: 8.3g⁶ 8.5f 10.2m⁶ 13.1g May 19] third foal: sister to useful Irish 1½m winner (stayed 1¾m) Dutch Harrier and half-sister to winner in Scandinavia by Royal Academy: dam, Irish 2-y-o 7f winner, half-sister to dual Irish St Leger winner Oscar Schindler: fairly useful performer in 2002 (won twice), when trained by K. Prendergast in Ireland: little form in 2003: stays 1½m: acts on soft ground: tried blinkered. *D. L. Williams* **–**

MISS LADY ASH (IRE) 2 b.f. (Apr 22) General Monash (USA) 107 – La Fandango (IRE) 51 (Taufan (USA) 119) [2003 5g⁵ 5.1m f5s Oct 7] €3,000Y: fourth foal: sister to 2002 2-y-o 6f seller winner Ashbourne Lady: dam maiden who stayed 1m: well held in sellers/maiden. *J. S. Moore* **–**

MISS LADYBIRD (USA) 2 b. or br.f. (Mar 26) Labeeb 124 – Bird Dance (CAN) (Storm Bird (CAN) 134) [2003 7d² 7.1m* f8.5s³ 8g³ 8m⁶ Oct 20] 9,000Y: quite good-topped filly: fifth foal: half-sister to winners in USA (by Rhodes) and Australia (by Numerous): dam, maiden in USA, out of sister to King Edward VII Stakes winner Beyton: modest performer: won maiden at Warwick in August: barely stays 8.5f: acts on fibresand, good to firm and good to soft going. *J. G. Given* **64**

MISS LA NAPOULE 2 b.f. (Apr 12) Nashwan (USA) 135 – Miss Riviera 103 (Kris 135) [2003 5s⁵ May 19] useful-looking filly: third foal: half-sister to 3-y-o Super Cannes: dam, 2-y-o 6f winner (later best at 7f/1m), half-sister to useful winners Miss Riviera Golf (at 1m) and Miss Corniche (up to 1¼m): 8/1 and better for race, well-held fifth in maiden at Windsor: sold 3,000 gns, sent to Pakistan. *G. Wragg* **–**

MISS LANGKAWI 2 gr.f. (Mar 16) Daylami (IRE) 138 – Miss Amanpuri 92 (Alzao (USA) 117) [2003 6f³ 6d* Nov 8] rather leggy filly: first foal: dam, 2-y-o 7f winner who stayed 1¼m, half-sister to 5-y-o Asian Heights and smart winner up to 13f St Expedit: fair form in maidens: favourite, won at Doncaster by neck from Bohola Flyer, tacking across from high draw and responding generously to get up near finish: likely to do fair bit better at 1¼m/1½m as 3-y-o. *G. Wragg* **76 p**

MISS LEHMAN 5 ch.m. Beveled (USA) – Lehmans Lot (Oats 126) [2003 9.2d 10.1m⁶ 12d Nov 4] well-made mare: fourth foal: half-sister to 1¾m winner Kilcreggan (by Landyap): dam, placed in bumper, half-sister to smart 1m/1¼m performer Mellottie: well held in maidens. *Mrs M. Reveley* **–**

MISS LYVENNET 2 ch.f. (Apr 16) Then Again 126 – Precious Girl 76 (Precious Metal 106) [2003 5d⁵ 5f⁶ 5g May 9] workmanlike filly: fourth foal: half-sister to 5-y-o **55**

Cark and 3-y-o Rosie's Result: dam 5f/6f winner: modest form in maidens/claimer: hung left final start: likely to prove best at 5f/6f. *M. Todhunter*

MISS MADAME (IRE) 2 b.f. (Apr 17) Cape Cross (IRE) 129 – Cosmic Countess (IRE) 74 (Lahib (USA) 129) [2003 6.1m 6m⁶ 6.5m Sep 26] IR 15,000F, 10,000Y: second foal: dam 2-y-o 6f winner: seemingly best effort (modest form) when front-running sixth in maiden at Yarmouth: should stay 1m. *T. P. McGovern* — **62 ?**

MISS MILLIETANT 2 b.f. (Mar 8) Up And At 'em 109 – Annie Hall (Saddlers' Hall (IRE) 126) [2003 6g p6g Nov 18] compact filly: second foal: dam behind on only start: well beaten in maidens. *L. Montague Hall* — **–**

MISS MIRAGE (IRE) 3 b.f. Alhaarth (IRE) 126 – Mahrah (USA) 89 (Vaguely Noble 140) [2003 7m⁶ 7m⁴ 6f* 7m² 8f 8.5f⁶ Dec 19] 62,000F: leggy filly: closely related to useful Irish 1½m/1¾m winner Hadeb (by Unfuwain) and half-sister to fairly useful 1m winner Mowaadah (by Alzao) and smart 1m to 1¼m winner Fahim (by Green Desert): dam 1m winner: fair performer: won maiden at Ripon in June: ran well in handicap next time: left B. Hills before penultimate outing: stays 7f: raced only on ground firmer than good: blinkered final start: has worn net muzzle. *R. L. Attfield, Canada* — **69**

MISS MIRASOL 3 b.f. Sheikh Albadou 128 – Play The Game 70 (Mummy's Game 120) [2003 92: 6m 7m 7g 6m Aug 16] lengthy, angular filly: fairly useful performer: easily best 3-y-o effort on second start: stays 7f: acts on firm ground: tried in cheekpieces/visor: edgy sort. *K. A. Ryan* — **92 ?**

MISS MYTTON (USA) 2 ch.f. (Feb 2) Mt Livermore (USA) – Sisterella (USA) (Diesis 133) [2003 5.1m⁶ 6d³ f6s⁶ 5m 5.1m³ 5.1m⁵ 6g² 6.1m² 6m 7g⁴ 6m Sep 18] $40,000Y: close-coupled, workmanlike filly: third foal: dam, 9f/1¼m winner in USA, out of Cheveley Park winner Minstrella: fair maiden: below form last 3 starts (blinkered final one): should stay 7f: acts on good to firm and good to soft going: sometimes slowly away. *A. Bailey* — **72**

MISS NOTERIETY 3 b.f. Victory Note (USA) 120 – Mystic Maid (IRE) 62 (Mujtahid (USA) 118) [2003 –: 5m Sep 8] unfurnished filly: well beaten, including in seller. *C. J. Teague* — **–**

MISS OCEAN MONARCH 3 ch.f. Blue Ocean (USA) 87 – Faraway Grey 99 (Absalom 128) [2003 53d: f9.4g 10m 8m⁶ 7m 8d³ 11.1g³ 8f³ 8m² 7.9f⁴ 9m⁴ 10m⁵ 8s³ 7.9d 10.1g⁴ 8m⁴ 10f Oct 1] angular filly: poor handicapper: creditable efforts most starts in 2003: stays 1¼m: acts on firm and soft going: tends to edge left. *D. W. Chapman* — **47**

MISS OPULENCE (IRE) 4 b.f. Kylian (USA) – Oriental Splendour 85 (Runnett 125) [2003 86: 8g 10.5f* 10.3m 8.1s⁴ 10.5m⁶ 10f Jun 18] tall, leggy filly: fairly useful performer: won minor event at Haydock in April: stays easy 10.5f: acts on firm and soft going: sometimes slowly away: looked reluctant final outing. *B. Ellison* — **86**

MISS PEACHES 5 b.m. Emperor Jones (USA) 119 – Dear Person (Rainbow Quest (USA) 134) [2003 –: f8g f7g Jan 28] quite good-topped mare: modest maiden in 2001: well held since. *G. G. Margarson* — **–**

MISS PEBBLES (IRE) 3 ch.f. Lake Coniston (IRE) 131 – Sea of Stone (USA) 71 (Sanglamore (USA) 126) [2003 8.3m² 8s³ 8.1m² p8g* p7g p10g p10g⁵ p10g⁶ Dec 29] sturdy filly: third foal: half-sister to French 9f/1¼m winner Sea of Luck (by Ezzoud): dam, lightly-raced maiden, stayed 1¾m: fair performer: made all in maiden at Lingfield in October: wearing cheekpieces, ran well in handicaps there last 2 starts: stays 1¼m: acts on polytrack, soft and good to firm ground. *B. R. Johnson* — **78**

MISS POPPETS 3 ch.f. Polar Falcon (USA) 126 – Alifandango (IRE) 78 (Alzao (USA) 117) [2003 8f 7f⁵ 7m 6m³ 8.1d 8m⁴ 6f² f6g* Oct 20] 32,000Y: lengthy filly: first foal: dam, 1m winner, half-sister to 6-y-o Trinculo: fair performer on all-weather, modest on turf: won maiden at Wolverhampton in October by 5 lengths from Wainwright: probably better at 6f than further: acts on fibresand, firm and good to soft ground. *D. R. C. Elsworth* — **62 a73**

MISS PORCIA 2 ch.f. (Jan 30) Inchinor 119 – Krista 73 (Kris 135) [2003 7d 7m 8m⁶ f6s Oct 21] 4,500 2-y-o: tall, lengthy, unfurnished filly: second foal: dam 1m winner: little sign of ability, including in listed event: left M. Wigham after third start: tongue tied final one. *M. G. Quinlan* — **–**

MISS PROCURER (IRE) 2 b.f. (Apr 26) Entrepreneur 123 – Kariyh (USA) 96 (Shadeed (USA) 135) [2003 6m⁶ 7m⁵ Aug 21] sturdy filly: second foal: dam 1m winner who stayed 1¼m: seemingly better effort (fair form) when sixth of 8 in minor event at York: should stay at least 7f. *P. F. I. Cole* — **72 ?**

MISS SAMANTHA   5 b.m. Emarati (USA) 74 – Puella Bona 60 (Handsome Sailor **49 ?**
125) [2003 47: f6g f6g⁶ p6g 7m⁵ p7g Apr 9] poor maiden handicapper: effective at 6f/7f:
acts on good to firm ground and all-weather: usually blinkered nowadays. *K. R. Burke*

MISS SANDY CLAWS (IRE)   5 b.m. Catrail (USA) 123 – Arabian Princess (Taufan **43**
(USA) 119) [2003 59: f8.5g⁶ 10g³ 8m⁴ 10s 10s May 18] IR 3,000Y: half-sister to several
winners, including fairly useful 1¼m/1½m winner Master Cooper (by Kahyasi): dam
Irish 2-y-o 7f winner: poor maiden handicapper: stays 1¼m: acts on soft and good to firm
ground, below form on fibresand at Wolverhampton on reappearance: tried blinkered.
E. Tyrrell, Ireland

MISS TILLY   2 b.f. (May 14) Nicolotte 118 – Little White Lies 78 (Runnett 125) [2003   **–**
5d 5d 6m Sep 5] 1,200Y: leggy filly: half-sister to 1m winner Singers Image (by Chief
Singer) and 4-y-o Diliza: dam maiden who stayed 1m: last in maidens. *G. B. Balding*

MISS TRIGGER   3 ch.f. Double Trigger (IRE) 123 – Saint Navarro 77 (Raga Navarro   **–**
(ITY) 119) [2003 –: 12m⁶ Apr 15] well beaten in maidens. *W. R. Muir*

MISS TRINITY   3 b.f. Catrail (USA) 123 – Rosy Sunset (IRE) (Red Sunset 120) [2003 **59**
60, a69: 6.1m 6g⁵ 6g Jun 3] modest maiden: effective at 5f/6f: acts on fibresand and good
to firm going, below form on soft: tried blinkered/in cheekpieces. *C. N. Allen*

MISS TWTI   3 b.f. Ali-Royal (IRE) 127 – Gargren (IRE) (Mujtahid (USA) 118) [2003   **–**
82?: 6g 6g 5f 5m Aug 4] angular filly: fairly useful 5f winner for B. Palling at 2 yrs: well
beaten in 2003, including in blinkers. *B. Smart*

MISSUS LINKS (USA)   2 b.f. (Jan 21) Lure (USA) 131 – Cozisaidso (USA) (Cozzene **69 p**
(USA)) [2003 p6g* Dec 2] 23,000Y: first foal: dam unraced: favourite, won minor event
at Lingfield by ¾ length from Sweetest Revenge, soon prominent and edging ahead final
1f: should stay 7f: open to improvement. *R. Hannon*

MISS VETTORI   4 b.f. Vettori (IRE) 119 – Dahlawise (IRE) 76 (Caerleon (USA) 132)   **–**
[2003 p12g Sep 3] 7,000Y: half-sister to several winners, including 6f winner Denton Lad
(by Prince Sabo) and 1995 2-y-o 7f winner Alfayza (by Danehill): dam 2-y-o 6f winner:
well held in maiden at Lingfield. *G. L. Moore*

MISS WIZZ   3 b.f. Wizard King 122 – Fyas 52 (Sayf El Arab (USA) 127) [2003 55: 6f   **38**
5m 5m 6f 8s 6.9m⁴ 7.5m⁶ 8m Oct 6] lengthy filly: poor maiden: should stay 1m: acts on
good to firm ground: wore cheekpieces last 4 starts. *W. Storey*

MISS WONG ONE (IRE)   3 b.f. Eagle Eyed (USA) 111 – Fakhira (IRE) 83 (Jareer **61**
(USA) 115) [2003 9.5d 12s 10d 7g 7g² 6f f6g³ Dec 9] €1,500 2-y-o: fourth foal: closely
related to 2001 2-y-o 7f and 8.5f winner Offa's Dyke and 7f winner Akhira (both fairly
useful, by Emperor Jones): dam, Irish 2-y-o 5f winner, half-sister to smart 6f/7f performer
Danehill Dancer: modest maiden: best effort when third in 6f handicap at Southwell
(British/all-weather debut) final start: acts on fibresand. *Frederick John Bowles, Ireland*

MISS WOODPIGEON   7 b.m. Landyap (USA) 112 – Pigeon Loft (IRE) 47 (Bellypha   **–**
130) [2003 8.1m 8.1m f7g Oct 4] second foal: dam, maiden, second in seller over hurdles:
fair bumper winner: well held on Flat. *J. D. Frost*

MISS YOU   3 ch.f. Grand Lodge 125 – Miss Queen (USA) (Miswaki (USA) 124)   **66**
[2003 73: p7g² p10g p8g Jan 29] rather unfurnished filly: fair maiden: well held last 2
starts: should stay 1m: acts on firm ground and polytrack: temperament under suspicion:
sold 8,000 gns in December. *N. A. Callaghan*

MISTER ARJAY (USA)   3 b.c. Mister Baileys 123 – Crystal Stepper (USA) (Fred   **86**
Astaire (USA)) [2003 76p: 6.1m⁴ 7m² 7.9m* 7.9m 8g⁴ 9m⁵ 7m³ 8m⁵ 10m² 8d f9.4g Nov
29] smallish, good-bodied colt: fairly useful performer: won handicap at York in May:
left G. Butler 14,000 gns after ninth start: effective at 7f to 1¼m: acts on polytrack and
good to firm ground: tried blinkered: has worn crossed noseband: has hung right: possibly
none too genuine. *B. Ellison*

MISTER BENJI   4 b.g. Catrail (USA) 123 – Katy-Q (IRE) 58 (Taufan (USA) 119)   **69**
[2003 73: 5s 5g 6m f6g³ f6g⁵ f7g⁴ f6s 5m f5g f8g* f7g Dec 16] quite good-topped
gelding: fair handicapper: won amateur event at Southwell in November: effective at
6f to 1m: acts on fibresand, good to firm and good to soft going: tried in headgear.
B. P. J. Baugh

MISTER CLINTON (IRE)   6 ch.g. Lion Cavern (USA) 117 – Thewaari (USA) 68   **62**
(Eskimo (USA)) [2003 67: 7m⁵ 7m³ 8m⁴ 7.1g 6m⁶ 6.1g 7m⁵ 8m 7f⁴ 6d 7g² 8.2g⁶ 7m⁴ 8m²
8f 7m⁴ 10f* 10m 8m p10g p10g Dec 20] tall, lengthy gelding: modest handicapper: ended
long losing run at Brighton in September: stays easy 1¼m: acts on firm going, good to
soft and polytrack: tried visored/blinkered: held up. *D. K. Ivory*

MISTER COMPLETELY (IRE)   2 b.g. (Apr 10) Princely Heir (IRE) 111 – Blue   **52**
Goose (Belmez (USA) 131) [2003 6g 6f³ 6g⁶ p7g⁴ 7m Oct 3] IR 4,700F, €9,000Y, 5,600
2-y-o: third foal: half-brother to Italian 6.5f (at 2 yrs) and 1m winner by Petorius: dam ran
3 times in France: modest maiden: third at Brighton: stays 7f: acts on polytrack, best turf
efforts on good going. *J. R. Best*

MISTER LINKS (IRE)   3 b.c. Flying Spur (AUS) – Lady Anna Livia (Ahonoora   **105**
122) [2003 109: 7m³ 8g May 3] tall, good sort: useful performer: won July Stakes at
Newmarket at 2 yrs: respectable 1¾ lengths third to Muqbil in Greenham Stakes at Newbury on reappearance: pulled hard when eleventh behind Refuse To Bend in 2000
Guineas at Newmarket only subsequent outing: joined Godolphin, but met setback in the
summer: will prove best up to 7f: acts on soft and good to firm going. *R. Hannon*

MISTER MAL (IRE)   7 b.g. Scenic 128 – Fashion Parade (Mount Hagen (FR) 127)   **63**
[2003 86, a74: f6s⁵ 6m⁶ 7.1d⁶ 7g f7g⁶ f7g² f6g⁶ f7s² f8.5f⁴ 8.5m f8g f7g⁵ f6g³ Dec 26]   **a69**
big, strong, lengthy gelding: fair performer: on a long losing run: left R. Fahey before
penultimate start: best at 6f/7f: acts on firm ground, soft and fibresand: tried in blinkers/
cheekpieces: often unruly: free-going sort, usually races prominently. *B. Ellison*

MISTER MAN   3 b.g. Mistertopogigo (IRE) 118 – Louisa Anne 73 (Mummy's Pet   **–**
125) [2003 8.5m 10.5m⁶ Jul 13] 1,800Y: half-brother to 2 winners, including 1988 2-y-o
5f and 7f (including seller) winner Nite Nite Louisa (by Night Shift), later successful in
Italy: dam sprint maiden: tailed off in maidens. *J. S. Wainwright*

MISTER MERLIN (IRE)   2 ch.g. (Mar 12) Titus Livius (FR) 115 – Official Secret   **–**
(Polish Patriot (USA) 128) [2003 5m³ 6m⁵ 5m Jun 1] IR 6,000F, 12,000 2-y-o: sturdy
gelding: fourth foal: half-brother to 1999 2-y-o 6.5f winner Bens Secret (by Ridgewood
Ben) and 1m winner Guby's Star (by Sesaro), both in Ireland: dam unraced: little sign of
ability in minor event/maidens. *M. C. Chapman*

MISTER MONET (IRE)   2 b.c. (Mar 20) Peintre Celebre (USA) 137 – Breyani 101   **92 p**
(Commanche Run 133) [2003 6f³ 7.1g* Jul 4] 62,000Y: strong colt: sixth foal: half-
brother to 3 winners, notably smart Moyglare Stud Stakes/Irish 1000 Guineas winner
Tarascon (by Tirol): dam Irish 11f and 2m winner: fairly useful form in maidens: made all
to land odds in 7-runner race at Sandown: sustained fracture of tibia after: should be
suited by 1¼m+: open to improvement. *M. Johnston*

MISTERNANDO   3 b.c. Hernando (FR) 127 – Mistinguett (IRE) 77 (Doyoun   **109**
124) [2003 12g 14.1d 12.1d 14.1m* 14.1m* 16.2m* 16g 16g* 16.4m* 16.4m*
16g* 16m* 17.5m² 16.2f² 18m⁶ 16g* 16g* Nov 5]
After seventeen starts, ten wins and around thirty-three miles of racing,
Misternando wound up 2003 as one of the most popular and progressive horses
in training. He ended two short of.Madame Jones's post-1900 record of eleven
handicap wins in a year on the Flat. Of the others who have won nine in a season,
the sprinters Chaplins Club (in 1985 and 1988) and Glencroft (also in 1988) are the
only others to have gained all their wins on turf. Misternando capped an outstanding campaign with a typically-determined effort in a six-runner listed event at
Musselburgh, where he beat Scott's View by three quarters of a length. Few outside
his connections could have predicted such remarkable progress after Misternando
recorded three unplaced outings in maiden company. But there was no looking

*Vodafone Group Handicap, Newbury—Misternando gains his ninth success of the year
as he beats Anak Pekan (rail) and King Eider (centre); Promoter is fourth*

*Willie Park Trophy Stakes, Musselburgh—Misternando continues his remarkable progress
by stepping up to listed class, the first such race run at the course;
Scott's View (centre) is second with Collier Hill (left) third*

back after his successful handicap debut off a BHB mark of 48, and at odds of 33/1, at Yarmouth in June. Misternando, who had been unraced at two, went on to win at Yarmouth again, then at Chepstow, Nottingham, Sandown, Folkestone (apprentices), Ripon, Goodwood and—after three defeats—Newbury before Musselburgh. Misternando might well have won nine races in a row had he not swerved and unseated his rider on his seventh start, when leading in the final furlong at Yarmouth in July.

Misternando (b.c. 2000)	Hernando (FR) (b 1990)	Niniski (b 1976)	Nijinsky
			Virginia Hills
		Whakilyric (1984)	Miswaki
			Lyrism
	Mistinguett (IRE) (b 1992)	Doyoun (b 1985)	Mill Reef
			Dumka
		Sidama (b 1982)	Top Ville
			Stoyana

The splendidly tough Misternando started favourite for the Cesarewitch at Newmarket in October, despite being 6 lb out of the handicap and his regular apprentice rider Sam Hitchcott being unable to draw the correct weight, and finished a highly creditable sixth to Landing Light after none too clear a run. If Misternando is seen in handicaps as a four-year-old it will almost certainly be in similarly valuable contests. He is close to minor pattern standard already and will not need to improve much to be winning in such company. By Hernando out of the two-year-old mile winner Mistinguett (later a very smart staying hurdler, the winner of the Grade 1 Cleeve Hurdle at Cheltenham, and herself a close relation to the dam of Sinndar), Misternando is a half-brother to the useful hurdler Mistanoora (by Topanoora). Misternando stays two and a quarter miles and acts on firm ground. He tends to hang and race lazily (often he's the first off the bridle), but there is no doubting his resolution in a finish. Usually held up, Misternando is a tremendous credit to his connections. *M. R. Channon*

MISTER PUTT (USA)   5 b. or br.g. Mister Baileys 123 – Theresita (GER) (Surumu   **69** (GER)) [2003 12m⁶ 11.9m May 3] big, strong gelding: fair maiden handicapper: barely stays 2¼m: acts on firm ground: blinkered in 2003: winning hurdler. *Mrs N. Smith*

MISTER RAMBO   8 b.g. Rambo Dancer (CAN) 107 – Ozra 63 (Red Alert 127)   **75 d** [2003 79: 7m³ f7g 7.2g 7m 7.1f² 7.1f³ 7m 8.5m³ 8.3m² 10.9m Aug 25] strong, lengthy gelding: fair performer: below form last 4 starts: effective at 7f/1m: acts on any going: tried blinkered: usually races up with pace: sometimes finds little. *D. Nicholls*

MISTER RIGHT (IRE)   2 ch.g. (Mar 9) Barathea (IRE) 127 – Broken Spirit (IRE)   **–** (Slip Anchor 136) [2003 6m 6g Oct 24] 34,000F, 36,000Y: lengthy, plain gelding: fourth foal: half-brother to fairly useful Irish 9.5f to 2m winner Ballintry Guest (by Be My Guest) and Irish 6f to 7f winner Detatch (by Thatching): dam unraced: signs of only a little ability in maidens at Newbury: trained on debut by M. Quinn. *K. Bell*

MISTER RUSHBY   3 b.g. Hamas (IRE) 125§ – Final Rush 66 (Final Straw 127)   **– §** [2003 55§, a–§: 6m 5f 7.9d 7g 5.9m 7.1f Aug 21] close-coupled gelding: modest performer at 2 yrs: well beaten in 2003: tried blinkered. *D. W. Chapman*

MISTER SAIF (USA)   2 ch.c. (Feb 1) Miswaki (USA) 124 – Shawgatny (USA) 83   **85** (Danzig Connection (USA)) [2003 6d³ 8m³ 6g* 6m 6m⁶ p6g² p7g² Nov 29] 65,000 2-y-o: rather leggy colt: sixth foal: half-brother to unreliable 1m winner September Harvest (by Mujtahid) and winner in USA by Mt Livermore: dam, Irish 2-y-o 9f winner, sister to very smart 1m/1¼m performer Star of Gdansk: fairly useful performer: made all in maiden at Folkestone in September: effective at 6f to 1m: acts on polytrack, good to firm and good to soft ground: sometimes wanders: usually races prominently. *R. Hannon*

MISTER SWEETS   4 ch.g. Nashwan (USA) 135 – Keyboogie (USA) 97 (Lyphard   **87** (USA) 132) [2003 64: f6g² f6s⁵ f8g³ f7s² f12g⁴ p7g* 6g² 7m* 6d³ 7g 8.5d⁴ 7m³ 8.9f⁵ 8f⁵ 7.9m³ 7g 8d 6m 7.9m Sep 7] lengthy gelding: fairly useful performer: won maiden at Lingfield in February and handicap at Southwell in March: effective at 6f to easy 9f: acts on all-weather, firm and good to soft going: has been slowly away. *M. C. Chapman*

MISTER TRICKSTER (IRE)   2 b.c. (Apr 29) Woodborough (USA) 112 – Tinos   **60** Island (IRE) (Alzao (USA) 117) [2003 7.1m 7.1f⁴ 7.1f⁶ 6.1m⁶ 8.1g⁵ 8d Sep 11] €6,500Y, 11,000 2-y-o: second foal: dam ran 3 times: modest maiden: barely stays 1m: acts on firm going. *R. Dickin*

MISTER TWISTER   2 gr.c. (Feb 20) Mind Games 121 – Its All Relative 90 (Distant   **43** Relative 128) [2003 6.1g 6f 6f³ Jul 15] 9,000Y: quite good-topped colt: second foal: dam, winner at 2 yrs, raced only around 5f: best effort (poor form) when third in seller at Brighton: likely to prove best at 5f/6f. *R. Hannon*

MISTER WATERLINE (IRE)   4 b.g. Mujadil (USA) 119 – Cree's Figurine 63   **–** (Creetown 123) [2003 68d, a72d: 6m Aug 1] leggy, angular gelding: on the downgrade, and well beaten only 4-y-o start: tried blinkered/visored/tongue tied. *P. D. Evans*

MISTRAL SKY   4 b.g. Hurricane Sky (AUS) – Dusk In Daytona 64 (Beveled (USA))   **78** [2003 54: f7s p6g p7g³ p8g² 7g⁴ p8g 7g⁶ 8.3m 7m⁶ 7g* 6m² 7m³ 8m p8g⁴ 7f* p7g* p7g p7g p6g* p6g Dec 2] tall performer: won seller at Leicester in August, claimer on same course (first run after leaving R. Ingram) then minor event and handicap at Lingfield in October/November: effective at 6f to easy 1m: acts on firm going, good to soft and polytrack (tailed off only start on fibresand): tried blinkered, usually visored: tends to wander. *Mrs S. A. Liddiard*

MISTRESS ELLIE   4 b.f. Royal Applause 124 – Ellie Ardensky 100 (Slip Anchor   **–** 136) [2003 63: p10g Jan 8] maiden handicapper: well held only outing in 2003. *J. Nicol*

MISTRESS HOLLIE (IRE)   2 b.f. (Feb 10) Titus Livius (FR) 115 – Soden (IRE) 73   **–** (Mujadil (USA) 119) [2003 8m p8g f8.5g Nov 14] €2,000Y: smallish, strong filly: second foal: half-sister to Italian 2002 2-y-o 5f winner Fisichella (by Starborough): dam 7f (at 2 yrs) to 1½m winner: well held in maidens/claimer: wore cheekpieces last 2 starts. *Mrs P. N. Dutfield*

MISTRESS PAGE   5 b.m. Beveled (USA) – Pallomere 85 (Blue Cashmere 129)   **–** [2003 –: p7g Jan 4] no form: tried blinkered. *E. A. Wheeler*

MISTRESS TWISTER   2 b.f. (Feb 24) Pivotal 124 – Foreign Mistress (Darshaan   **75** 133) [2003 6m 6m³ Oct 17] 9,500Y: leggy, unfurnished filly: half-sister to several winners, including 1997 2-y-o 8.5f selling winner Pink Ticket (by Emarati) and fairly useful 2001 2-y-o 6f winner Lihou Island (by Beveled): dam placed in Italy: better effort in maidens (fair form) when third to Bread of Heaven at Redcar, disputing lead 2f out: should stay 7f. *T. D. Barron*

MISTY DANCER 4 gr.g. Vettori (IRE) 119 – Light Fantastic 66 (Deploy 131) [2003 **82**
73: 10m* 10m 10g³ 10.1g Sep 11] good-topped gelding: has reportedly had sinus problems: fairly useful handicapper: won at Newbury in May: good third at Newmarket: stays
1¼m: unraced on extremes of going: races freely. *Miss Venetia Williams*

MISTY MAN (USA) 5 ch.g. El Gran Senor (USA) 136 – Miasma (USA) 92 (Lear **33**
Fan (USA) 130) [2003 –: 8.2m 8m 10g 11.6g 14.1f f12s⁴ f11g⁴ Dec 16] lengthy, angular
gelding: poor maiden: stays 11f: acts on fibresand: tried tongue tied/visored. *Miss
J. Feilden*

MITCHAM (IRE) 7 br.g. Hamas (IRE) 125§ – Arab Scimetar (IRE) (Sure Blade **98**
(USA) 130) [2003 107: p5g⁵ 6m⁶ 6g⁶ 6g* 6g* 6g Jun 21] strong gelding: usually impresses
in appearance: useful performer: won minor event at Goodwood in May: effective at
5f/6f: acts on firm going, probably on soft: blinkered once as 4-y-o: sometimes finds
little. *T. G. Mills*

MITRASH 3 b.c. Darshaan 133 – L'Ideale (USA) (Alysheba (USA)) [2003 10g⁶ Jun **55**
5] 200,000Y: third living foal: brother to smart 1¼m/11f winner Shagraan and half-
brother to useful 8.5f to 1¼m winner Aegean Dream (by Royal Academy): dam, ran twice
in France, half-sister to high-class French performer up to 1½m Loup Sauvage, a good
family: 7/1, sixth to Stage Shy in maiden at Sandown, slowly away. *B. Hanbury*

MITSUKI 4 b.f. Puissance 110 – Surrealist (ITY) (Night Shift (USA)) [2003 91§: 5f³ **83**
6g 5m 5d 5m* 5f 5m⁴ 5m 6m⁴ 6m 6m⁵ 6m 5g 5m⁴ 5f 5m Oct 20] big filly: fairly useful
handicapper: won at Thirsk in June: effective at 5f/6f: acts on firm going, possibly not on
good to soft: visored (well held) once: tends to get behind, and best with strong pace:
sometimes carries head awkwardly. *J. D. Bethell*

MIXED MARRIAGE (IRE) 5 ch.g. Indian Ridge 123 – Marie de Flandre (FR) 109 **–**
(Crystal Palace (FR) 132) [2003 57: f12s⁶ p13g Feb 12] quite attractive gelding: maiden:
showed little in cheekpieces on Flat in 2003, but won over hurdles: sold £1,300 in
December. *G. L. Moore*

MIX IT UP 2 b.f. (Feb 26) Linamix (FR) 127 – Hawayah (IRE) 68 (Shareef Dancer **– p**
(USA) 135) [2003 p8g Oct 15] 28,000Y: half-sister to several winners, including useful
7f/1m winner Bishr (by Royal Applause), 1½m winner Showpiece (by Selkirk) and 3-y-o
Enchanted Princess: dam 2-y-o 7f winner out of Nell Gwyn winner Ghariba: 50/1, not
knocked about when behind in maiden at Lingfield: should do better. *R. M. Beckett*

MIZHAR (USA) 7 b. or br.g. Dayjur (USA) 137 – Futuh (USA) 95 (Diesis 133) [2003 **70**
84d: f6s f5g f6g⁶ 6m* 6m³ 6.1m² 6.1m² 6m³ 6g 6m Aug 15] sturdy gelding: fair performer:
won seller at Pontefract in April: best at 5f/6f: acts on all-weather, firm and good to soft
going: usually wears headgear: held up. *J. J. Quinn*

MKUZI 4 ch.c. Halling (USA) 133 – African Peace (USA) (Roberto (USA) 131) [2003 **113**
107: 10d² 10.2d* 12d² 10m⁵ 10f⁴ 10f* 10m³ Sep 21] strong, close-coupled colt: half-
brother to several winners, including smart French 6f (at 2 yrs) to 10.5f winner Allitera-
tion (by Polish Precedent): dam, French 1½m winner, out of very smart French performer
up to 13.5f Galla Placidia: smart performer: won handicap at Cork (by ¾ length from
Wensum Dancer) in May and listed race at Leopardstown (beat Middlemarch by ¾
length) in September: ran well when 3 lengths fourth to High Chaparral in Royal Whip
Stakes at the Curragh fifth outing: stays 1½m: acts on firm and good to soft going:
blinkered (ran respectably) final start. *J. Oxx, Ireland*

MOARBAN (IRE) 3 b.c. Bahhare (USA) 122 – Suave Star 48 (Suave Dancer (USA) **84**
136) [2003 87: 8g 7.9m⁶ 11m 8f³ 8.3d² 8.5d⁵ 9m³ 8m² 8.1m² a9f³ a7f a7f Dec 11]
useful-looking colt: has quick action: fairly useful maiden: placed 6 times in 2003: left
M. Channon before below form last 3 starts: best around 1m: acts on firm and good to soft
going: ran creditably in cheekpieces/when sweating: usually tongue tied: has looked less
than keen. *A. Smith, UAE*

MOAYED 4 b.g. Selkirk (USA) 129 – Song of Years (IRE) 89 (Shareef Dancer (USA) **90**
135) [2003 91: p8g* p7g* p8g* p7g⁵ 7.6m p7g Aug 28] fairly useful performer: won
seller and claimer (claimed from B. Johnson £11,000) in January and handicap in
February, all at Lingfield: left C. Dwyer and off nearly 6 months before well beaten last 2
starts, reluctant to race on final one: effective at 7f to 9f: acts on heavy going, good to firm
and polytrack: usually blinkered/tongue tied: slowly away fourth outing: temperament
under suspicion. *N. P. Littmoden*

MOBIL-ONE DOT COM 5 b.g. Magic Ring (IRE) 115 – Not So Generous (IRE) **–**
68 (Fayruz 116) [2003 45: 5g Jun 28] tall gelding: poor maiden handicapper: soundly
beaten only 5-y-o start. *J. S. Goldie*

MOBO-BACO 6 ch.g. Bandmaster (USA) 97 – Darakah 78 (Doulab (USA) 115) [2003 **74**
62: 7g* 8m* 10.9m⁴ 8m⁴ 8f* 8.1g 8f⁴ 8.1d 7.1g 8f³ 8f Oct 12] good-bodied gelding: fair
performer: won seller at Leicester in March and minor events at Pontefract in April and
Bath in June: effective at 7f to 1¼m: acts on fibresand, firm and soft going: has wandered/
raced freely: often races prominently. *R. J. Hodges*

MOCCA (IRE) 2 b.f. (Apr 3) Sri Pekan (USA) 117 – Ewan (IRE) (Indian Ridge 123) **77**
[2003 7g³ 7m⁴ 8.3g* 8m⁵ 10m² Oct 13] €20,000Y: tall filly: third foal: half-sister to
useful 2002 2-y-o 6f winner Cosmo (by Turtle Island): dam unraced out of half-sister to
smart sprinter Ya Malak: fair performer: wandered when winning maiden at Windsor in
August: ran well in nursery/minor event after: will stay at least 1½m. *D. J. Coakley*

MOCHRAS 3 b.f. Mtoto 134 – Natchez Trace 52 (Commanche Run 133) [2003 7.5d **64**
8.3m 8.2g 6m² 6m³ 6m 8m⁵ 8m 6m Oct 13] leggy filly: seventh foal: half-sister to 3
winners, including 1½m winner Be True (by Robellino) and 6-y-o Connect: dam maiden
who should have proved best at 9f+: modest maiden: left B. Smart after debut: stays
1m: acts on good to firm ground: sometimes races freely: sold 3,200 gns. *R. F. Johnson
Houghton*

MODEL FIGURE (USA) 2 b.f. (Feb 13) Distant View (USA) 126 – Sylph (USA) **70**
110 (Alleged (USA) 138) [2003 6g⁴ 6m 6f* Sep 15] half-sister to several winners,
including French 1993 2-y-o 6f and 9f winner Zindari and French/US 1½m winner
Privity (both smart by Private Account): dam, 1¼m/1½m winner, sister to Irish St Leger
winner Leading Counsel: fair form in maidens: tended to wander when winning 6-runner
event at Redcar: will stay at least 1m. *B. W. Hills*

MODEM (IRE) 6 b.g. Midhish 109 – Holy Water (Monseigneur (USA) 127) [2003 **–**
45, a49: f8s f7g³ f7g f6s⁵ f6g Apr 7] sturdy gelding: poor performer: stays 1m: acts on **a49**
soft going, firm and all-weather: tried blinkered, usually visored: successful over hurdles
in October. *D. Shaw*

MODESTY BLAISE (SWE) 3 br.f. Mango Express 106 – Singoalla (IRE) 69 (Alwu- **56**
hush (USA) 121) [2003 7.1f 8.2g Apr 29] rather leggy, workmanlike filly: first foal: dam
6f winner in Sweden: green, modest form when mid-field in maidens at Haydock and
Nottingham. *J. G. Given*

MOFEYDA (IRE) 3 b.f. Mtoto 134 – Princess Haifa (USA) 69 (Mr Prospector (USA)) **70**
[2003 10s⁵ 10m⁴ p12g⁶ Nov 12] tall, quite good-topped filly: fourth foal: sister to UAE 7f
winner Kondoty and half-sister to 11.5f winner Zeyaarah (by Rahy), both fairly useful:
dam, 1m winner (later successful up to 9f in USA), out of sister to Storm Bird: fair
maiden: ran poorly final start: should stay 1½m: sold 12,000 gns. *A. C. Stewart*

MOKABRA (IRE) 2 b.c. (Apr 3) Cape Cross (IRE) 129 – Pacific Grove 89 (Persian **106**
Bold 123) [2003 5g³ 6m* 6g³ 6.3g³ 6m* 6g* 7m⁶ 6s⁵ Oct 31] 90,000F, 80,000Y: smallish
colt: fourth foal: half-brother to 3 winners, including fairly useful 2000 2-y-o 6f winner
Caroline Island (by Catrail) and 3-y-o Major Speculation: dam, 2-y-o 7f/1m winner, half-
sister to useful French performer around 1¼m All Glory: useful performer: won maiden
at Newcastle in May, minor event at Ripon (beat Peak To Creek ¾ length) in August
and Maurice Lacroix Trophy at Baden-Baden (by head from Slawomira) in September:
creditable sixth in Somerville Tattersall Stakes at Newmarket: stays 7f: acts on good to
firm going, ran respectably on soft. *M. R. Channon*

MOLCON (IRE) 2 b.g. (Apr 1) Danetime (IRE) 121 – Wicken Wonder (IRE) 71 **75**
(Distant Relative 128) [2003 5.2f⁶ 5.1m* 5m* 5m⁵ 6m Sep 23] 10,000Y: leggy gelding:
fifth foal: half-brother to 6-y-o Kathology and 3-y-o The Baroness: dam 2-y-o 6f winner:
fair performer: won seller at Bath and nursery at Newmarket in August: probably stays
6f. *N. A. Callaghan*

MOLINIA 2 b.f. (Feb 15) Nicolotte 118 – Themeda 69 (Sure Blade (USA) 130) [2003 **54**
6m⁵ 7m⁵ 6.1d Jul 25] 800Y: workmanlike filly: fifth foal: half-sister to 1½m winner Odyn
Dancer (by Minshaanshu Amad) and 4-y-o Shasta: dam 11f winner: modest form in
maidens: will stay at least 1m. *R. M. Beckett*

MOLLY BE 3 ch.f. First Trump 118 – Broughton Singer (IRE) 61 (Common Grounds **44**
118) [2003 –: p8g⁶ p8g⁶ f9.4g p12g 12g 10m³ Aug 30] poor maiden handicapper: stays
1¼m: acts on polytrack and good to firm ground. *W. J. Musson*

MOLLY MALONE 6 gr.m. Formidable (USA) 125 – Pharland (FR) (Bellypha 130) **–**
[2003 43: f5g f8.5g f5g Mar 24] leggy, workmanlike mare: poor maiden: well held in
2003: tried blinkered/visored. *J. C. Tuck*

MOLLY MOON (IRE) 2 br.f. (Jan 20) Primo Dominie 121 – Snowing 88 (Tate **84**
Gallery (USA) 117) [2003 5m² 5.2m² 5m³ 5m* 5.1m³ 5m* 5.2m⁶ 5g⁴ Aug 26] smallish,

compact filly: fourth foal: half-sister to 5-y-o The Trader: dam Irish 5f winner: fairly useful performer: won maiden in June and minor event in August, both at Lingfield: creditable sixth in listed race at Newbury: likely to prove best at 5f. *M. Blanshard*

MOLLY'S DREAM (IRE) 2 b.f. (Mar 9) Night Shift (USA) – Shirley Blue (IRE) **61** (Shirley Heights 130) [2003 5m 5d 6d³ 7.2f⁵ 7m Aug 6] 20,000F: sturdy, close-coupled filly: third foal: half-sister to 3-y-o Crathorne: dam ran 3 times in France: modest maiden: stayed 7f: acted on firm and good to soft going: dead. *C. W. Thornton*

MOLLYS RAINBOW (IRE) 2 b.f. (Apr 26) Desert Style (IRE) 121 – Rainbow **–** Reliance (Rainbow Quest (USA) 134) [2003 5m Apr 2] €9,000Y: good-topped filly: fourth foal: dam once-raced half-sister to high-class French 7f to 9f performer Procida: backward, last of 10 in Ripon maiden. *K. A. Ryan*

MOLLY'S SECRET 5 b.m. Minshaanshu Amad (USA) 91§ – Secret Miss 55 **58** (Beveled (USA)) [2003 51, a59: p10g⁴ f9.4g⁶ p12g⁵ p12g³ p12g 9.9m 10m* 10.2m⁵ 10.9m² 10.3g 12.1m⁵ 10.1m 10m⁵ 10.2g² 10.9m³ 10.9m 11.7f Oct 12] workmanlike mare: modest handicapper: won apprentice event at Brighton in May: stays easy 1½m: acts on all-weather and good to firm ground: usually wears cheekpieces: free-going sort: sometimes carries head awkwardly. *C. G. Cox*

MOLOTOV 3 b.g. Efisio 120 – Mindomica 63 (Dominion 123) [2003 68: f6g⁵ f6g⁵ **–** f6g³ p7g⁵ f6s⁶ 6m f6g 7m 6m f6s³ f6g f5s 6f 7g 6m Sep 18] fair performer: well below **a69 d** form after fourth outing: claimed from C. Thornton £3,000 after tenth start, and from M. Usher £4,000 after eleventh: stays easy 7f: acts on all-weather, little form on turf: ran poorly only start in blinkers. *I. W. McInnes*

MOMENTOUS JONES 6 b.g. Emperor Jones (USA) 119 – Ivory Moment (USA) **–** (Sir Ivor 135) [2003 52: 17.2f 11.9m Jun 24] leggy gelding: maiden: well held in 2003, including in visor. *M. Madgwick*

MOMENTS I TREASURE (USA) 2 ch.f. (May 4) Mt Livermore (USA) – Munnaya **68** (USA) 101 (Nijinsky (CAN) 138) [2003 8m p8g Nov 2] smallish, workmanlike filly: sixth foal: closely related to useful French 1¼m/11f winner Yaya (by Rahy) and half-sister to 2 winners, including useful French 7f (at 2 yrs)/1m winner Mystic Melody (by Seattle Slew): dam, 11.5f winner out of Princess Margaret winner Hiaam, from out-standing family of Swain and Fantastic Light: better effort in maidens (fair form) when seventh at Doncaster: still green final start: will be suited by 1¼m/1½m. *Sir Michael Stoute*

MOMENTS OF JOY 3 b.f. Darshaan 133 – My Emma 118 (Marju (IRE) 127) [2003 **113** 12f* 14g* 14.6g⁵ Sep 13] big, good-bodied filly: second foal: dam, won Yorkshire Oaks and Prix Vermeille, half-sister to St Leger and Gold Cup winner Classic Cliche: made into a smart performer in only 3 outings: won maiden at Kempton in July and listed event at Goodwood (by ¾ length from Discreet Brief, despite being hampered and still looking green) in August: good 6¼ lengths fifth to Brian Boru in St Leger at Doncaster, every chance 2f out: will stay 2m: raced only on good ground or firmer. *R. Guest*

MOMMKIN 2 b.f. (Jan 27) Royal Academy (USA) 130 – Walimu (IRE) 82 (Top Ville **78** 129) [2003 8.2f⁴ 8d² 8m⁵ Oct 24] big, lengthy, good-topped filly: has plenty of scope: sixth foal: half-sister to 3 winners, including 1000 Guineas winner Ameerat (by Mark of Esteem), 7f winner at 2 yrs, and useful 7.5f/1m winner in UAE Walmooh (by In The Wings): dam 1m to 1½m winner: fair form in maidens: second at Ayr: will probably stay 1¼m. *M. R. Channon*

MOMTIC (IRE) 2 ch.c. (Apr 9) Shinko Forest (IRE) – Uffizi (IRE) (Royal Academy **77** (USA) 130) [2003 6d 5.2f³ 6m² 6g* Oct 13] 15,000F, 34,000Y: well-made colt: third foal: half-brother to 3-y-o Hoh Investor and winner in Italy by Spectrum: dam unraced out of half-sister to Riverman: fair performer: won maiden at Windsor by ¾ length from Sion Hill: will stay 7f: acts on firm going. *W. Jarvis*

MONASH FREEWAY (IRE) 5 ch.h. General Monash (USA) 107 – Pennine Pearl **–** (IRE) (Pennine Walk 120) [2003 13.3m 17.2f 16.2m Jun 16] maiden handicapper: well beaten in 2003: tried blinkered. *Miss Jacqueline S. Doyle*

MONASH GIRL (IRE) 2 b.f. (Apr 15) General Monash (USA) 107 – Maricica **–** (Ahonoora 122) [2003 7f 8.3g Oct 13] €9,000Y, 3,500 2-y-o: half-sister to useful 5f (including at 2 yrs) winner Cortachy Castle (by Pips Pride): dam Irish 1m winner: well held in maiden at Folkestone and seller at Windsor. *B. R. Johnson*

MONASH LADY (IRE) 5 ch.m. General Monash (USA) 107 – Don't Be That Way **–** (IRE) (Dance of Life (USA)) [2003 74d: p10g Jan 8] workmanlike mare: fair handicapper at best: well held only 5-y-o start. *J. S. Moore*

MONDURU 6 b.g. Lion Cavern (USA) 117 – Bint Albadou (IRE) 91 (Green Desert **42**
(USA) 127) [2003 53: f7s⁵ 8.1m 11.6m 10m Aug 6] good-topped gelding: poor maiden
handicapper: stays easy 1¼m: acts on fibresand and any turf going: tried blinkered: sometimes carries head high. *G. L. Moore*

MONEYBAGS (IRE) 3 b.g. Petorius 117 – Creggan Vale Lass (Simply Great (FR) **58**
122) [2003 –: 8g⁶ 8g⁶ 8.1m 8d⁶ 8f Aug 22] modest maiden handicapper: stays 1m: acts on
firm and good to soft ground. *B. Palling*

MONICA GELLER 5 b.m. Komaite (USA) – Rion River (IRE) (Taufan (USA) 119 **63 +**
[2003 60, a52: 10.1g⁵ 8.3g* Aug 23] leggy mare: modest handicapper: won at Windsor in **a–**
August: refused to enter stall intended next outing: should stay 1¼m: acts on all-weather,
soft and good to firm going: tried visored: sometimes slowly away: sold 1,400 gns. *Ian
Williams*

MONKEY OR ME (IRE) 2 b.g. (Mar 10) Sri Pekan (USA) 117 – Ecco Mi (IRE) **–**
(Priolo (USA) 127) [2003 f6g f7g Dec 12] €10,000Y: fifth foal: brother to smart 6f (at 2
yrs) to 1m (in Scandinavia) winner Ecology and 3-y-o Fairly High and half-brother to
4-y-o Deco Star: dam unraced from family of Sun Princess and Saddlers' Hall: well held
in maidens. *P. T. Midgley*

MONKSFORD 4 b.g. Minster Son 130 – Mortify (Prince Sabo 123) [2003 70: f11g **72 §**
10d* 10m 10.2g 10.2m⁵ 10m Jul 7] leggy gelding: fair handicapper: won at Nottingham
in May, carrying head awkwardly: stays 1¼m: acts on firm and good to soft going:
usually races prominently: sometimes wanders: unreliable. *B. J. Llewellyn*

MONKSTON POINT (IRE) 7 b.g. Fayruz 116 – Doon Belle (Ardoon 124) [2003 **100**
111: 6g 7m 6s 7m⁶ 5d⁵ Aug 30] sturdy, good sort: useful performer: best 7-y-o effort
when fifth to Mornin Reserves in handicap at Sandown final start: effective at 5f/6f: has
form on good to firm ground, goes very well on softer than good: visored: has been
bandaged: has been early to post: sold 25,000 gns, sent to UAE. *D. W. P. Arbuthnot*

MON PETIT DIAMANT 3 b.f. Hector Protector (USA) 124 – Desert Girl (Green **–**
Desert (USA) 127) [2003 54: p7g 7d 10m 12.6m⁵ 12f⁵ 10.2f⁶ f12g Nov 24] smallish filly:
little form at 3 yrs: left M. Wigham after sixth start: tried tongue tied. *M. J. Polglase*

MONROE GOLD 3 ch.g. Pivotal 124 – Golden Daring (IRE) (Night Shift (USA)) **40**
[2003 8.2g 8.1m 7m 14.1m 10m 8s² Jul 25] 40,000Y: close-coupled gelding: second foal:
dam, Italian 2-y-o 6f winner, out of sister to very smart sprinter Ballad Rock: poor
maiden: stays 1m: acts on soft ground: visored (best effort) final start. *M. L. W. Bell*

MONSAL DALE (IRE) 4 ch.g. Desert King (IRE) 129 – Zanella (IRE) 87 (Nordico **64**
(USA)) [2003 59: f12s* f12g⁴ f12g⁴ f12g⁴ 11.8g 16m² f14.8s⁴ f16.2g⁶ 18g⁴ 16.2m²
f14.8s³ 16.2m⁵ Sep 8] strong gelding: modest performer: won seller at Southwell in
January: stays 2m: acts on fibresand, unraced on extremes of going on turf: sometimes
races freely: consistent. *B. J. Llewellyn*

MON SECRET (IRE) 5 b.g. General Monash (USA) 107 – Ron's Secret 92 (Efisio **69**
120) [2003 54: f7g* f8g 7m 7f 8.2f 7m* f7g² f7s* f7s³ Dec 31] sparely-made gelding: fair
handicapper: won at Southwell in March, Leicester (apprentices) in October and Southwell in December: best efforts at 7f: acts on all-weather and good to firm ground. *B. Smart*

MONSIEUR BOND (IRE) 3 ch.c. Danehill Dancer (IRE) 117 – Musical Essence **115**
65 (Song 132) [2003 109: 8f³ 8g⁶ 8f 7m* 7g⁶ 7m² 7g* 7m² 6s⁵ Oct 31] close-coupled,
useful-looking colt: smart performer: met trouble in running when good 2¾ lengths sixth
to Refuse To Bend in 2000 Guineas at Newmarket in May: won minor event at Chester in
July and listed race at Epsom (by 2 lengths from Vanderlin) in September: creditable
length second to With Reason in Supreme Stakes at Goodwood eighth start: effective at
7f/1m: acts on good to firm and good to soft going: raced freely and hung right in St
James's Palace Stakes first start: consistent. *B. Smart*

MONTANA 3 b.c. Puissance 110 – Mistral's Dancer (Shareef Dancer (USA) 135) **80 d**
[2003 85?: 6m² 6g² 6.1m³ 6m p6g p7g Nov 29] tall colt: fairly useful maiden: easily best
3-y-o effort when second at Newbury on reappearance: stays 6f: acts on good to firm
ground: ungenuine, and one to avoid. *R. Hannon*

MONTE BIANCO (IRE) 2 b.c. (Apr 10) King of Kings (IRE) 125 – Creme Caramel **79**
(USA) 88 (Septieme Ciel (USA) 123) [2003 6m 6m 6m² 7m* 7f⁵ 8.3g⁴ 7m Oct 25]
30,000Y: rather leggy, close-coupled colt: first foal: dam, 2-y-o 7f winner, half-sister to
smart performer up to 1m Robellation: fair performer: won nursery at Lingfield in September: creditable efforts in similar events next 2 starts: stays 1m: acts on firm going: sold
37,000 gns, sent to USA. *L. M. Cumani*

MONTECASSINO ABBEY (IRE)   4 b.g. Danehill (USA) 126 – Battle Mountain   **83**
(IRE) (Dancing Brave (USA) 140) [2003 84, a93: p8g³ p7g 7m⁵ 8g 7m⁵ 7m May 22]   **a86**
sturdy gelding: fairly useful handicapper: effective at 7f/1m: acts on polytrack, good to
firm and good to soft ground: visored twice (winning once), wears cheekpieces nowadays. *P. W. Harris*

MONTECRISTO   10 br.g. Warning 136 – Sutosky 78 (Great Nephew 126) [2003 84:   **83**
12g³ 11.9g⁵ 11.8m³ 12m² 14m³ Sep 13] leggy, sparely-made gelding: fairly useful handicapper: effective at 1½m to 2m: acts on good to firm going, heavy and fibresand/dirt: held
up: has won twice for lady rider: consistent. *R. Guest*

MONTE MAJOR (IRE)   2 b.g. (Mar 11) Docksider (USA) 124 – Danalia (IRE) 78   **53**
(Danehill (USA) 126) [2003 p8g f8g⁶ Dec 8] 12,000F, 28,000Y: third foal: half-brother to
2002 2-y-o 5f/6f winner Margaret's Fancy (by Ali-Royal) and 5-y-o Mujalia: dam, Irish
2-y-o 5f winner, half-sister to smart middle-distance performer Trakady: better effort in
maidens (modest form) when sixth to Atlantic Breeze at Southwell: should stay 1¼m.
M. A. Jarvis

MONTE MAYOR LAD (IRE)   3 b.g. Sesaro (USA) 81 – Alcalali (USA) 96 (Sep-   **71**
tieme Ciel (USA) 123) [2003 76: f7g⁴ f6g³ f7g³ f6g p6g³ f6g³ f7g⁴ Nov 21] good-bodied
gelding: fair maiden: stays 7f: acts on all-weather, good to firm and good to soft going:
blinkered last 3 starts. *D. Haydn Jones*

MONTESSORI MIO (FR)   4 b.g. Robellino (USA) 127 – Child's Play (USA) (Sharp-   **–**
en Up 127) [2003 61: 13.1m⁶ 17.1m Oct 6] good-topped gelding: maiden handicapper:
well held in cheekpieces both starts in 2003. *R. Ford*

MONTE VERDE (IRE)   3 b.f. Whittingham (IRE) 104 – Anita's Love (IRE) 53   **55**
(Anita's Prince 126) [2003 60: p6g² p7g 5.7g 5.3d⁵ 5.1m* 5.1g⁶ 5.3m 5.7m⁴ f5g p7g Dec
10] smallish filly: modest performer: won claimer at Bath in May: effective at 5f/easy 6f:
acts on polytrack, unraced on extremes of going on turf: usually wears cheekpieces: races
prominently. *B. Palling*

MONTEZ (USA)   4 ch.g. Royal Academy (USA) 130 – Omara (USA) 87 (Storm Cat   **64**
(USA)) [2003 64: 7g 8.3g 6m³ 5m⁶ 6m⁵ 6m 5m Aug 23] strong, good-bodied gelding:
modest maiden: stayed 7f: acted on good to firm going: tried in visor/tongue tie/cheekpieces: dead. *W. M. Brisbourne*

MONTMARTRE (IRE)   3 b.f. Grand Lodge (USA) 125 – French Quarter (Ile de   **98**
Bourbon (USA) 133) [2003 74: 10m 9g 9.2d² 8g⁶ 10.1m⁵ 11.7f⁵ 9.9d² 10.1g* 10m⁴
9m² 10f² 10d³ 10.1m* 12m* 12m Oct 3] tall, angular filly: useful performer: won minor
event at Epsom in July and handicaps at Yarmouth and Ascot (amateurs, beat Diamonds
Will Do 1¾ lengths) in September: stays 1½m: acts on firm and good to soft going,
unraced on soft/heavy: races up with pace: sold 75,000 gns, joined J. Howard Johnson.
N. A. Callaghan

MONTOSARI   4 ch.g. Persian Bold 123 – Sartigila 67 (Efisio 120) [2003 51: 11.5m   **44**
11.9m 13.3m⁴ 14.1f⁶ 12f 12m Jul 10] poor maiden handicapper: stays 13.3f: acts on
all-weather and good to firm ground: inconsistent. *P. Mitchell*

MONTOYA (IRE)   4 b.g. Kylian (USA) – Saborinie 56 (Prince Sabo 123) [2003 71,   **–**
a–: p12g Jan 7] close-coupled gelding: maiden handicapper: well held only 4-y-o start.
P. D. Cundell

MONT ROCHER (FR)   8 gr.g. Caerleon (USA) 132 – Cuixmala (FR) (Highest   **107**
Honor (FR) 124) [2003 110: a10g⁶ 10d 12s² 12g² 10.5d³ 10g Oct 31] big, good-topped
gelding: useful performer nowadays: won listed event at Toulouse in 2002: creditable
efforts in similar events when beaten a nose by Foreign Affairs at La Teste and 1½ lengths
third to Aravis at Strasbourg prior to running just respectably in another listed race won
by Far Lane at Newmarket final start: effective at 1¼m to 15.5f: acts on soft and good
to firm going: has had tongue tied: often blinkered/visored, including last 4 starts.
J. E. Hammond, France

MONTURANI (IRE)   4 b.f. Indian Ridge 123 – Mezzogiorno 108 (Unfuwain (USA)   **108**
131) [2003 112: 8m⁶ 8m² 10.1g² 10.2d³ 8m⁴ 8m² 10.5g² Nov 11] big, good-topped filly:
useful performer: suffered stress fracture of off-hind after final 3-y-o start: best efforts in
2003 when second in listed race at Newcastle (beaten head by Chorist) third start, and in
Premio Sergio Cumani at Milan (beaten ¾ length by Marbye) and Prix Fille de L'Air at
Toulouse (beaten 1½ lengths by Walkamia) last 2: stays 10.5f: yet to race on soft/heavy
going, acts on any other: has worn crossed noseband/had 2 handlers. *G. Wragg*

MOON AT NIGHT 8 gr.g. Pursuit of Love 124 – La Nureyeva (USA) 83 (Nureyev **54**
(USA) 131) [2003 54: f7g Jan 20] leggy gelding: modest handicapper: soundly beaten
only 8-y-o outing: visored (tailed off) once. *Mrs P. Ford*

MOON BALLAD (IRE) 4 ch.c. Singspiel (IRE) 133 – Velvet Moon (IRE) 108 **124**
(Shaadi (USA) 126) [2003 124: a9f* a10f* 10m 8d⁵ 10f⁵ a10f⁵ Sep 27] **a131**
    The eighth running of the Dubai World Cup, the world's richest race
(£2,308,798 to the winner in 2003), went ahead despite the proximity of Dubai to
the war zone in Iraq. Plans for a dozen Japanese runners at Nad Al Sheba were
scrapped and leading American jockeys Gary Stevens and Jerry Bailey were among
those who decided to stay at home, along with thousands of racegoers from Europe,
America, Australia and Japan who cancelled their bookings. The meeting still went
ahead—though without the usual ceremonial opening—and fifteen countries were
represented, including the host nation. Forty-six of the eighty-one runners in the six
races were trained outside the United Arab Emirates, eleven of them in the United
States. Victory Moon and Ipi Tombe, both from the stable of South African Mike de
Kock, were the only overseas winners, while the Maktoums won their own prizes in
the Godolphin Mile (Firebreak), the Dubai Sheema Classic (Sulamani), the Dubai
Golden Shaheen (State City) and the Dubai World Cup itself. Moon Ballad's
runaway victory in the last-named was Godolphin's fourth in the race, following
Almutawakel, Dubai Millennium and Street Cry, while Sheikh Mohammed's
colours were carried to victory by Moon Ballad's sire Singspiel. The three other
runnings have been won by Cigar, Silver Charm and Captain Steve, all challengers
from the United States.
    The eleven-runner field for the latest World Cup lacked strength in depth,
with the North American challenge—comprising Donn Handicap winner Harlan's
Holiday and the fifth in that race Blue Burner—less formidable than usual. The
favourite was British-trained Nayef, winner of the Dubai Sheema Classic after a
late switch from the World Cup twelve months earlier; the two Godolphin flag-
bearers Moon Ballad and Grandera were also preferred to Harlan's Holiday in the
betting, with the French-trained mare Aquarelliste the only other runner at shorter
than 20/1. Nayef, Grandera and Aquarelliste were not fully proven on dirt, but then
both Singspiel and Almutawakel had previously been unraced on an artificial
surface before their World Cup victories. Moon Ballad had won a minor event and
had come fourth on dirt in the UAE Derby as a three-year-old before developing
into a very smart performer on turf in Europe, winning the Dante Stakes at York and
the Select Stakes at Goodwood and also finishing third in the Derby and second
in the Champion Stakes. Frankie Dettori passed up the ride in the Derby and the
Champion, but he partnered Moon Ballad to an easy win in Round II of the
Maktoum Challenge series at Nad Al Sheba on his reappearance in mid-February
and chose him in preference to Grandera in the World Cup.
    Moon Ballad was a revelation in the World Cup, evoking memories of
Dubai Millennium's brilliant victory—over a somewhat stronger field, it must be
said. Dubai Millennium was in front after the first half furlong in his World Cup and
the rest were struggling to keep up before the home straight. Moon Ballad took a
clear advantage before halfway and had his race sewn up early in the straight. Like

*Dubai World Cup, Nad Al Sheba—the world's richest race, in which Moon Ballad is an impressive winner
from US-trained Harlan's Holiday; Nayef (striped cap) is third and Grandera (blaze) fourth*

MOO

Dubai Millennium, he ran on strongly to win unchallenged, the margin of victory five lengths, not quite so far as Dubai Millennium's seven (officially six). The field wasn't stretched so far as in Dubai Millennium's year, when the third-placed horse was six and a half lengths (officially five and a half) behind the runner-up. Harlan's Holiday held off Nayef by a length to finish second behind Moon Ballad, with Grandera a further short head away fourth; Blue Burner came seventh and Aqua-relliste ninth. 'The sky's the limit' was Dettori's post-race assessment of Moon Ballad, who immediately had the Breeders' Cup Classic earmarked as his long-term target. But Moon Ballad failed to win again and didn't take up his Breeders' Cup Classic engagement after trailing in last of five in the Jockey Club Gold Cup at Belmont at the end of September. In the interim he fared respectably in a summer campaign on turf, running poorly behind Nayef in the Prince of Wales's Stakes at Royal Ascot (racing too freely, particularly when harried for the lead by Nayef's pacemaker), then finishing fifth to Reel Buddy in a blanket finish to the Sussex Stakes before running right up to his best turf form—visored for the first time since the Derby—when fifth, beaten around two lengths, behind High Chaparral in the Irish Champion Stakes.

Moon Ballad (IRE) (ch.c. 1999)	Singspiel (IRE) (b 1992)	In The Wings (b 1986)	Sadler's Wells High Hawk
		Glorious Song (b 1976)	Halo Ballade
	Velvet Moon (IRE) (b 1991)	Shaadi (b 1986)	Danzig Unfurled
		Park Special (b 1984)	Relkino Balilla

Godolphin's "Moon Ballad"

The strong, lengthy Moon Ballad, who usually impressed in appearance, has been retired to stud in Japan under the Darley banner, along with Grandera, at the Yushun Co Stallion Station for three million yen with the October 1st concession. Moon Ballad's sire Singspiel also included the Japan Cup among his international successes, while the achievements of Lohengrin and others have promoted him as a stallion to the Japanese audience. Moon Ballad's dam the Lowther Stakes winner Velvet Moon, who was successful at a mile and a quarter as a three-year-old, is a half-sister to Central Park, who won two Group 1 events, including the Derby Italiano, and finished second in the Melbourne Cup carrying the royal blue of Godolphin, and to Lancashire Oaks winner Mellow Park. After the death of her owner, Velvet Moon, in foal to Daylami, fetched 875,000 guineas, the top price for a broodmare at the 2002 December Sales. Sheikh Mohammed was outbid for her but did secure Moon Ballad's useful half-sister Velvet Lady (by Nashwan), in foal to Dr Fong, for 450,000 guineas. Velvet Lady, who won a mile maiden and came sixth in the One Thousand Guineas, is the only other foal out of Velvet Moon to reach the racecourse so far. Velvet Lady's first foal, a filly by Singspiel, is set to start her racing career with Saeed bin Suroor in 2004. Moon Ballad was a top-class performer on dirt at his best, and showed very smart form on turf, acting on firm and good to soft going. He showed the best of his form at around a mile and a quarter. Sometimes visored and usually tongue tied, front-running Moon Ballad had a tendency to edge left under pressure. *Saeed bin Suroor*

MOON EDGE 4 gr.f. Beveled (USA) – Zamoon (Zambrano) [2003 43: p10g p8g⁶ p6g⁵ 7m 8m 8.1m Jul 4] modest maiden handicapper: blinkered, brought down final start: effective at 6f to 1m: raced only on all-weather/good to firm ground. *M. P. Tregoning* **54**

MOON EMPEROR 6 b.g. Emperor Jones (USA) 119 – Sir Hollow (USA) (Sir Ivor 135) [2003 105: p13g* 14.1g 14m⁶ 13.9f⁵ 16.2f⁵ 21d 16.2m Aug 9] tall, close-coupled gelding: useful handicapper: won at Lingfield in March by ¾ length from Flownaway: best effort after when fifth to Mana d'Argent at Ascot fifth start: stays 2m: acts on polytrack, soft and firm going: held up. *J. R. Jenkins* **102**

MOONGLADE (USA) 3 ch.f. Carson City (USA) – Moonshine Girl (USA) 97 (Shadeed (USA) 135) [2003 a7.5f a8f 8.2f f8g f8g Dec 3] second foal: half-sister to 2001 US 2-y-o 5.5f winner Glimmering Bay (by Capote): dam, 2-y-o 5f winner who stayed 7f, out of sister to smart 2-y-o 5f/6f winner Digamist: well beaten in maidens, leaving Saeed bin Suroor 5,000 gns after first 2 starts in UAE: tried visored/tongue tied. *Miss J. Feilden* **–**

MOON JAGUAR (IRE) 3 b.c. Bahhare (USA) 122 – Top of The Form (IRE) 79 (Masterclass (USA) 116) [2003 52: f11g⁵ f9.4g⁴ Feb 3] modest maiden: barely stays 11f: acts on fibresand: sometimes carries head awkwardly: sold 800 gns, sent to Czech Republic. *J. G. Given* **51**

MOON LEGEND (USA) 2 ch.f. (Jan 26) Gulch (USA) – Highland Legend (USA) 93 (Storm Bird (CAN) 134) [2003 6m 6m⁶ Oct 4] $100,000F, 50,000Y: tall, close-coupled filly: sixth foal: sister to winner in USA and half-sister to 2 winners there, including smart performer around 9f Personal Legend (by Awesome Again): dam, 2-y-o 7.5f/1m winner who stayed 11f, out of half-sister to dam of Miesque: better effort in maidens (fair form) when sixth at Newmarket, travelling well long way: should stay 1m: open to progress. *W. Jarvis* **68 p**

MOONLIGHT MAN 2 ch.c. (Mar 2) Night Shift (USA) – Fleeting Rainbow 65 (Rainbow Quest (USA) 134) [2003 6g³ 6m⁴ 6m* 6m* 7f* 6m³ Oct 25] €105,000Y: leggy, quite attractive colt: sixth foal: half-brother to very smart 7f to 10.5f (including at 1m at 2 yrs) winner Rebelline and smart 5f (at 2 yrs) to 11f winner Quws (both in Ireland, by Robellino): dam maiden who should have stayed 1½m: useful performer: won maiden at Kempton in August, nursery at Newmarket in September and minor event at York (made all to beat Golden Sahara by 1¼ lengths) in October: creditable 1½ lengths third to Nero's Return in listed race at Doncaster final start: stays 7f: acts on firm going: sometimes edges left/idles. *R. Hannon* **104**

MOONLIGHT SONG (IRE) 6 b.m. Mujadil (USA) 119 – Model Show (IRE) 82 (Dominion 123) [2003 63, a53: f6g 6.1s 7.2g f7g 7.2m 7.2f 7g 7.2g⁶ 7m Sep 17] modest handicapper in 2002, showed little in 2003: wore cheekpieces last 2 starts. *John A. Harris* **–**

MOONLIGHT TANGO (USA) 2 br.f. (Feb 7) Benny The Dip (USA) 127 – Summer Dance 86 (Sadler's Wells (USA) 132) [2003 7m 8g⁴ Oct 25] leggy, unfurnished filly: third foal: dam, 1m winner, daughter of smart 1m winner Hyabella, herself half-sister **76**

to Stagecraft from family of Opera House and Kayf Tara: fair form in maidens at Newbury, beaten 10 lengths by Salford City when favourite final start: should stay 1¼m. *J. H. M. Gosden*

MOON ROYALE 5 ch.m. Royal Abjar (USA) 121 – Ragged Moon 72 (Raga Navarro (ITY) 119) [2003 45: f8s⁵ f9.4g⁵ f8.5g f8.5g⁴ f8.5g f8g 8f⁶ 7d² 7.9m⁵ 8f 8m Sep 6] close-coupled mare: poor performer: best around 1m: acts on firm ground and fibresand: has worn cheekpieces/visor: none too consistent. *Mrs N. Macauley* **48 a31**

MOONSHINE BEACH 5 b.g. Lugana Beach 116 – Monongelia 98 (Welsh Pageant 132) [2003 73: 11.8m⁶ 18m* 15.4m 17.1m⁵ Aug 17] leggy gelding: fair handicapper, lightly raced: won at Chepstow in July: stays 2¼m: acts on good to firm ground and polytrack: usually held up. *P. W. Hiatt* **71**

MOONSHINE BILL 4 ch.g. Master Willie 129 – Monongelia 98 (Welsh Pageant 132) [2003 f12g 10m 14.1d 10g* 12.1m⁵ 10m² 12m Oct 6] lengthy, workmanlike gelding: half-brother to 3 winners, including 5-y-o Moonshine Beach: dam 1m to 1¼m winner: modest performer: unraced at 2/3 yrs: 50/1-winner of ladies handicap at Pontefract in July: should stay 1½m: unraced on extremes of going on turf. *P. W. Hiatt* **63**

MOON SHOT 7 gr.g. Pistolet Bleu (IRE) 133 – La Luna (USA) (Lyphard (USA) 132) [2003 71: f11g³ Dec 3] good-bodied gelding: fair performer: won handicap at the Curragh in 2002: left M. Cunningham in Ireland before running respectably in claimer at Southwell only 7-y-o start: stays 11.5f: acts on firm going, good to soft and all-weather: tried blinkered/tongue tied. *A. G. Juckes* **66 +**

MOONSPRITE 3 b.f. Seeking The Gold (USA) – Moonshell (IRE) 117 (Sadler's Wells (USA) 132) [2003 82p: 9.9d* 10.3m* 12m 10m Jul 11] lengthy filly: fairly useful performer: won maiden at Beverley in May and minor event at Chester (dictated pace) in June: far from discredited in Ribblesdale Stakes at Royal Ascot third start: reportedly jarred up after well beaten in handicap final one: stays 1½m: acts on soft and good to firm ground: sent to Australia. *E. A. L. Dunlop* **91**

MOONSTONE MYTH (IRE) 2 ch.f. (Feb 25) Night Shift (USA) – Marble Halls (IRE) (Ballad Rock 122) [2003 5g 6m 5.1f⁴ 6m⁶ 7m Sep 9] €23,000Y: close-coupled filly: third foal: half-sister to 4-y-o Waverley: dam twice-raced half-sister to high-class sprinter Hallgate: poor maiden: should stay 7f: acts on firm going. *D. W. P. Arbuthnot* **42**

MOORLAW (IRE) 2 b.c. (Jan 28) Mtoto 134 – Belle Etoile (FR) (Lead On Time (USA) 123) [2003 8d Nov 7] 32,000Y: rather leggy colt: fourth foal: half-brother to fairly useful Irish 1¼m winner Starlight Venture (by Hernando): dam, French 7.5f winner, half-sister to useful French 6f to 1m performer Matin de Printemps: 10/1 and backward, slowly away when well held in maiden at Doncaster. *J. A. Osborne* **–**

MOORS MYTH 2 b.c. (Mar 20) Anabaa (USA) 130 – West Devon (USA) (Gone West (USA)) [2003 7d Nov 7] big, good-topped colt: second living foal: half-brother to 3-y-o Salcombe: dam unraced sister to smart 5f performer Western Approach and half-sister to very smart performer up to 1¼m Tinners Way: 16/1, burly and green, twelfth of 18 in maiden at Doncaster, racing freely and not knocked about: needs to settle to stay beyond 7f: will do better. *B. W. Hills* **67 p**

MOQUI MARBLE (GER) 7 b.g. Petit Loup (USA) 123 – Margo's New Hope (USA) (Cannonade (USA)) [2003 59: f12g⁵ f8.5s³ 8g⁴ 9g 8.5g³ 8s a9g a9g² Dec 28] poor performer: left B. Curley after second start: in frame in minor events after: stays 1¼m: acts on heavy ground and sand/polytrack: tried visored/tongue tied. *Frau J. Roemich, Germany* **?**

MORAG 2 b.f. (Apr 14) Aragon 118 – Minnehaha (Be My Chief (USA) 122) [2003 7g⁵ 7m⁴ 7g 7m* 7m* 6.5m 7m 6m⁵ 7d Nov 8] 1,600Y: first foal: dam unraced half-sister to very smart performer up to 13f Water Jump: fair performer: won maiden at Thirsk in August and nursery at Redcar in September: should stay 1m: acts on good to firm going: tongue tied seventh start. *I. A. Wood* **70**

MORAHIB 5 ch.h. Nashwan (USA) 135 – Irish Valley (USA) (Irish River (FR) 131) [2003 90: 8g* 8m⁵ Jun 18] strong, well-made horse: useful handicapper, very lightly raced: won at Goodwood in May by ¾ length from Namroud: good fifth of 32 to Macadamia in Hunt Cup at Royal Ascot only subsequent outing: best efforts around 1m: acts on good to firm ground: sold 12,000 gns, joined E. J. O'Neill. *M. P. Tregoning* **99**

MOREFINESSE 3 ch.g. Efisio 120 – With Finesse (Be My Guest (USA) 126) [2003 7.5m 7m⁴ 7f⁵ 7g² 7.1f² 8m Sep 18] IR 26,000F: sturdy gelding: second foal: half-brother to 4-y-o Behan: dam unraced: modest maiden handicapper: runner-up at Newcastle and Musselburgh: stays 7f: raced only on good ground or firmer: sold 1,600 gns. *T. D. Easterby* **53**

MORGAN LEWIS (IRE)   2 b.g. (Apr 29) Orpen (USA) 116 – Party Piece (Thatch   **65**
(USA) 136) [2003 5g⁴ 5m 5m Jul 24] 22,000F, 20,000Y: half-brother to several winners,
including fairly useful 5f (at 2 yrs) and 7f (in Ireland) winner Glowing Value (by Glow):
dam Irish maiden: best effort (fair form) when fourth in minor event at Windsor: should
stay 6f. *G. B. Balding*

MORGANS ORCHARD (IRE)   7 ch.g. Forest Wind (USA) 111 – Regina St Cyr   **–**
(IRE) (Doulab (USA) 115) [2003 f12g Apr 28] workmanlike gelding: fair 1½m winner at
5 yrs: well beaten only outing since. *A. G. Newcombe*

MORGAN THE RED   3 ch.g. Presidium 124 – Warning Bell 88 (Bustino 136) [2003   **–**
73: 10m 11g Jul 26] good-topped gelding: fair maiden at 2 yrs: well beaten in 2003.
T. D. Easterby

MORITAT (IRE)   3 b.c. Night Shift (USA) – Aunty Eileen (Ahonoora 122) [2003 –:   **60 ?**
6m 5m² 5.2m 6m⁶ May 30] good-topped colt: modest maiden: form only on second
outing: should stay 6f: tongue tied last 3 starts. *P. S. McEntee*

MORLUC (USA)   7 b.h. Housebuster (USA) – Flashing Eyes (USA) (Time To Explode   **112**
(USA)) [2003 118: 5f² 5s 6f Jun 21] smart performer: runner-up in Hong Kong Sprint at
Sha Tin in 2000 and 2001: reportedly underwent surgery to replace screw in hind leg after
final outing at 6 yrs: stayed on well when beaten head by Fiscally Speaking in Grade 3 Aegon Turf Sprint
Stakes at Churchill Downs on reappearance (had won race in 2001): reportedly suffered a
sesamoid injury when last of 17 in Golden Jubilee Stakes at Royal Ascot final outing: was
best at 5f/6f: raced mostly on turf, but winner on dirt: used to wear blinkers: had been
tongue tied: to stand at Buck Pond Farm, Kentucky, USA, fee $5,000. *R. L. Morse, USA*

MORNING AFTER   3 b.f. Emperor Jones (USA) 119 – Onefortheditch (USA) 79   **82**
(With Approval (CAN)) [2003 84: 7.1m⁴ 8.3m³ Jul 14] fairly useful performer: stays
1m: raced only on good ground or firmer on turf, shaped well on polytrack on debut.
J. R. Fanshawe

MORNING ECHO   3 ch.f. Pivotal 124 – Crofters Ceilidh 101 (Scottish Reel 123)   **–**
[2003 10g Jul 8] second foal: dam, 5f winner (including at 2 yrs), half-sister to 8-y-o Lord
Kintyre: well beaten in maiden at Pontefract: sold 3,500 gns in December. *M. Dods*

MORNING HAWK (USA)   2 b.f. (Mar 29) Silver Hawk (USA) 123 – Dawn Aurora   **51**
(USA) (Night Shift (USA)) [2003 6m 5.7m⁵ 7m 7g 8d Oct 31] €16,000Y: workmanlike
filly: second foal: dam, 5.5f (at 2 yrs in France) and 9f (in UAE) winner, out of close
relative to dam of 4-y-o Mineshaft: modest maiden: should stay at least 7f: acts on good
to firm going. *J. S. Moore*

MORNING LIGHT   3 b.g. Danehill Dancer (IRE) 117 – Edge of Darkness 62 (Vaigly   **–**
Great 127) [2003 –: 13.8d⁵ Sep 20] workmanlike gelding: no sign of ability. *L. R. James*

MORNING SUN   3 b.f. Starborough 126 – Malham Tarn (Riverman (USA) 131)   **–**
[2003 p8g p8g 10g⁶ 10g⁶ 10m⁵ f8.5s 9m 10g f11g Dec 15] workmanlike filly: half-sister
to several winners, including 11-y-o Bold Effort and French 1m winner Lord of The
Manor (by Mark of Esteem), both useful: dam unraced: little form. *K. O. Cunningham-
Brown*

MORNING WARNING (IRE)   2 b.f. (Mar 7) Inzar (USA) 112 – Morning Stroll   **38**
(Tower Walk 130) [2003 5f 5f 6m 5m 6m Oct 12] 10,000Y: half-sister to 3
winners, including 2-y-o 5f winners Million At Dawn (in 1993, by Fayruz) and Red
Ruffian (in 1991, by Red Sunset), latter later useful performer up to 7f in Hong Kong:
dam unraced: poor maiden: left K. Ryan before final start. *J. G. Given*

MORNIN RESERVES   4 b.g. Atraf 116 – Pusey Street Girl 87 (Gildoran 123) [2003   **108**
86: 5v 5g* 5m* 5g³ 5m 5d* 5.2m² Sep 20] tall, angular gelding: useful performer: much
improved in 2003, winning handicaps at Hamilton and Newcastle (Northern Rock
Gosforth Park Cup by 1¾ lengths from Beyond The Clouds) in June and Sandown (wore
cheekpieces, beat Little Edward by 2 lengths) in August: very good 1¼ lengths second to
Ratio in World Trophy at Newbury final start: speedy, and best at 5f: acts on any ground:
usually leads: game. *I. Semple*

MOROZOV (USA)   4 b.c. Sadler's Wells (USA) 132 – High Hawk 124 (Shirley   **115**
Heights 130) [2003 113: 15.5d* 15.5g² 12g 15d Aug 24] brother to several winners,
notably high-class 1½m performer In The Wings, and closely related/half-brother to
several other winners: dam, Ribblesdale and Park Hill Stakes winner, half-sister to dam
of High-Rise: smart performer: won 4 races at 3 yrs, notably Prix du Lys and Prix Hubert
de Chaudenay at Longchamp: in good heart at Longchamp first 2 starts in 2003, winning
Prix de Barbeville in April by 1½ lengths from Clety and neck second to Cut Quartz in
Prix Vicomtesse Vigier: unsatisfactory efforts last 2 outings, swerving and unseating rider

after start in Grand Prix de Chantilly, then last (blinkered) in Prix Kergorlay at Deauville: suited by 15f: acts on soft and good to firm ground: game at 3 yrs: sold 56,000 gns in October, joined C. Allen. *A. Fabre, France*

MORRIS DANCING (USA)   4 b.g. Rahy (USA) 115 – Summer Dance 86 (Sadler's –
Wells (USA) 132) [2003 57d: f8s f11g 8g Apr 30] no longer of any account: tried in tongue strap/cheekpieces. *B. P. J. Baugh*

MORSE (IRE)   2 b.c. (Feb 20) Shinko Forest (IRE) – Auriga 73 (Belmez (USA) 131)   **79**
[2003 5f 6.1d* 6g* 6m 7f⁵ 7m p7g³ 6g³ 6m⁶ Sep 23] 11,000Y: close-coupled colt: fourth foal: half-brother to a winner abroad by Barathea: dam, maiden who should have stayed beyond 7f, half-sister to smart performer up to 1½m Beldale Star: fair performer: won maiden at Nottingham in May and minor event at Windsor in June: stays easy 7f: acts on polytrack, good to firm and good to soft going: races prominently. *J. A. Osborne*

MORSON BOY (USA)   3 b.g. Lear Fan (USA) 130 – Esprit d'Escalier (USA) (Diesis   **110 p**
133) [2003 79p: 12g* 14.6m* 14.1f⁵ 11.9m* Jul 11] tall, leggy gelding: progressed into smart handicapper, winning at Pontefract in April, Doncaster in May and York (beat Hambleden by 3½ lengths, making all) in July: will stay at least 2m: acts on good to firm ground: ungainly galloper, and sometimes wanders: gelded after final start: likeable sort, and should progress further at 4 yrs. *M. Johnston*

MORVERN (IRE)   3 ch.g. Titus Livius (FR) 115 – Scotia Rose (Tap On Wood 130)   **65**
[2003 64?: 8.2g p10g 10m³ 10f⁶ 10.9m p10g 8d 10m⁴ Aug 20] strong gelding: fair maiden: stays 1¼m: acts on good to firm going: tried in visor/cheekpieces: has raced freely. *J. G. Given*

MOSCOW BALLET (IRE)   2 b.c. (Mar 24) Sadler's Wells (USA) 132 – Fire The   **109**
Groom (USA) 115 (Blushing Groom (FR) 131) [2003 7.5g* 8f² 8m⁵ Oct 19] close-coupled, attractive colt: has a quick action: sixth living foal: closely related to 2 winners, notably top-class sprinter Stravinsky (by Nureyev), and half-brother to 2 winners in USA, including Official Flame (by Deputy Minister), also useful 2-y-o 6f winner in Britain: dam, 1m and 9.5f (US Grade 1) winner, half-sister to high-class sprinter Dowsing: won 4-runner minor event at Tipperary in August: useful form when ¾-length second to Snow Ridge in Royal Lodge Stakes at Ascot and fifth to Pearl of Love in Gran Criterium at Milan: likely to stay 1¼m. *A. P. O'Brien, Ireland*

MOSCOW BLUE   2 ch.c. (Mar 25) Soviet Star (USA) 128 – Aquamarine 89 (Shardari   **– p**
134) [2003 7m Aug 8] big, close-coupled colt: sixth living foal: half-brother to 3 winners, including 9f and 1½m winner Marani (by Ashkalani) and French 1996 2-y-o 1m winner Aquarelle (by Kenmare), both useful: dam, 11f winner, closely related to St Leger winner Toulon: 10/1, burly and green, eleventh of 18 in maiden at Newmarket, not knocked about: will stay at least 1m: likely to do better. *J. H. M. Gosden*

MOSCOW EXPRESS (IRE)   11 ch.g. Moscow Society (USA) 110 – Corrielek   **62**
(Menelek 114) [2003 69: 22.2f⁶ 16g 16f⁴ Aug 29] one-time very smart chaser: fairly useful at best on Flat, lightly raced: won handicap at the Curragh only outing in 2002: stiff task, well held in Queen Alexandra Stakes at Royal Ascot on reappearance: stayed 2m: acted on soft going: retired. *Miss F. M. Crowley, Ireland*

MOSCOW (IRE)   4 ch.g. Cadeaux Genereux 131 – Madame Nureyev (USA) (Nure-   –
yev (USA) 131) [2003 –p: 8.1d⁶ 10.2g 8m 8.1g 8f 8f 8f Sep 29] little form: left J. Gosden after third start: visored. *P. D. Evans*

MOSCOW MARY   2 b.f. (Mar 15) Imperial Ballet (IRE) 110 – Baileys Firecat 67   **63**
(Catrail (USA) 123) [2003 5.1m⁶ 5d 6.1d² 6m² 6m⁴ 6m* 5.1m² 7.5d 5m³ 6g² 7m⁴ f6g Dec 26] small, leggy filly: first foal: dam, third at 5f (ran only twice at 2 yrs), should have been well suited by further: modest performer: made all in seller at Windsor in June, then left J. Portman: seems best at 6f: acts on good to firm going, probably good to soft: seemed unsuited by track at Brighton fifth start: often forces pace. *A. G. Newcombe*

MOSCOW TIMES   2 b.c. (Apr 27) Soviet Star (USA) 128 – Bargouzine 67 (Hotfoot   **74**
126) [2003 5.2m⁶ 7m p7g Nov 29] 160,000Y: well-made colt: has scope: closely related to useful German 8.5f/9f winner Murnau (by Rudimentary) and half-brother to several winners, including 9-y-o Muchea: dam, maiden who stayed 1m, half-sister to smart sprinter at 2 yrs As Friendly: best effort (fair form) when tenth in maiden at Newmarket: carried head awkwardly when well held final outing: should stay 1m. *D. R. C. Elsworth*

MOSS VALE (IRE)   2 b.c. (Apr 11) Shinko Forest (IRE) – Wolf Cleugh (IRE) 65 (Last   **99**
Tycoon 131) [2003 6d⁵ 6d* 6m⁶ 5m³ Sep 18] 35,000Y: strong colt: has a quick action: third foal: half-brother to 5-y-o Street Life: dam, lightly-raced maiden, half-sister to smart 6f winner King's College: useful performer: made all in maiden at Windsor in August:

creditable sixth in Sirenia Stakes at Kempton and third (beaten 2½ lengths by Boogie Street) in listed race at Ayr: should prove better at 6f than 5f. *B. W. Hills*

MOSTARSIL (USA)   5 ch.g. Kingmambo (USA) 125 – Naazeq 80 (Nashwan (USA) 135) [2003 58§: p12g* p12g³ 11.8g⁵ 11.9f² 21.6m⁵ 11.7m 11.9m* 12m² 12d* 12g⁴ 12m* 12m⁵ 16m² 16.2f 16f⁶ Oct 12] workmanlike gelding: fair handicapper: won at Lingfield (amateurs, awarded race) in February, Brighton in May, Epsom in July and Goodwood in August: effective at 1½m to 2m: acts on firm going, good to soft and polytrack: tried blinkered: usually wears cheekpieces. *G. L. Moore* **78**

MOST DEFINITELY (IRE)   3 b.g. Definite Article 121 – Unbidden Melody (USA) (Chieftain) [2003 58: 12.3m⁴ f12g 11.9m 14.1m³ 17.2m² 16.2d² 16.2m² 14.4m² 14.1f² Aug 20] leggy gelding: modest maiden handicapper: blinkered, creditable placed efforts last 6 starts: stays 17f: acts on firm and good to soft going, unraced on softer: often finds little. *T. D. Easterby* **64**

MOST-SAUCY   7 br.m. Most Welcome 131 – So Saucy 59 (Teenoso (USA) 135) [2003 66, a78: p10g f8s³ p10g* f9.4g³ p10g p12g⁶ 11m* 11.7m³ p10g⁵ 11.5g 11.6g³ 11.6g* 10m 12f⁵ p10g² 11.6g 12m² 12g* 11.9f⁶ 12m⁴ 10.1m³ 10.1g² 12g 12d 11.9f³ p10g⁵ p12g⁵ f12g⁵ p13g p12g Dec 17] lengthy mare: fairly useful handicapper: won at Lingfield in January, Southwell in April, Windsor in June and Epsom in July, first 2 apprentice events: stays 1½m: acts on firm going, soft and all-weather: usually held up: tough and genuine. *I. A. Wood* **83 a78**

MOTEN SWING   4 b.g. Kris 135 – Lady Bankes (IRE) 69 (Alzao (USA) 117) [2003 85: 7d p8g* 7m 7g⁴ Jul 5] sturdy, good-bodied gelding: fair performer: won minor event at Lingfield (only run on all-weather) in April: stays easy 1m: acts on polytrack and good to firm going, probably on soft: tried blinkered: sold 11,000 gns. *R. Hannon* **78**

MOTHER CORRIGAN (IRE)   7 gr.m. Paris House 123 – Missed Opportunity (IRE) (Exhibitioner 111) [2003 –: f6g³ f7s Feb 1] lengthy, angular mare: poor performer, lightly raced: stays 7f: acts on fibresand and firm ground: often visored/blinkered. *M. Brittain* **46 ?**

MOTIVUS (USA)   2 b.c. (Feb 9) Cherokee Run (USA) 122 – Noble Cause (CAN) (Diesis 133) [2003 6m² 6d⁴ p7g* a8f 8.5f⁶ Nov 29] $22,000Y: compact colt: second foal: dam, 8.5f/9f winner in US, runner-up in 1½m Grade 3 event: improved effort (useful form) to win minor event at Lingfield in August by ½ length from Jack Sullivan, then left G. Butler: well held in Grade 3 at Aqueduct: sixth in non-graded event at Calder: stays 8.5f: acts on polytrack, probably on firm going. *C. Clement, USA* **97**

MOTU (IRE)   2 b.g. (Mar 11) Desert Style (IRE) 121 – Pink Cashmere (IRE) (Polar Falcon (USA) 126) [2003 6d⁴ 6m* 6g Oct 25] 34,000Y: good-topped gelding: fourth foal: half-brother to useful German 2001 2-y-o 6f winner Medina (by Pennekamp) and fairly useful Irish 1999 2-y-o 6f winner Contact (by Grand Lodge): dam unraced half-sister to very smart sprinter Owington: fair form: landed odds in maiden at Ripon in August, flashing tail: favourite, never going well in nursery at Newbury final start: will probably stay 7f. *J. L. Dunlop* **79**

MOUFTARI (USA)   2 b.c. (Jan 28) Miswaki (USA) 124 – Nature's Magic (USA) (Nijinsky (CAN) 138) [2003 7m Aug 22] $200,000Y: well-made colt: fifth foal: brother to very smart 7f (at 2 yrs) and 1m winner Tough Speed, and closely related/half-brother to 2 winners in USA: dam, lightly-raced US maiden, half-sister to US Grade 3 9f winner Stalwars: 33/1, eighth of 15 in maiden at Newmarket, taking strong hold: should stay 1m: type to do better. *B. W. Hills* **68 p**

MOULIN DE MOUGINS (IRE)   2 b.c. (Feb 23) Night Shift (USA) – Sama Veda (IRE) 84 (Rainbow Quest (USA) 134) [2003 5m 6d⁶ 7.5m* 7.5d² 7.2f* 7d* 7m² 8m Aug 25] 19,000Y: robust colt: fourth foal: half-brother to 1¼m seller winner Veda's Rainbow (by Petardia) and Italian 11f winner by Grand Lodge: dam, third at 7f at 2 yrs on only start, out of useful 1m winner Samsova: fairly useful performer: won maiden at Beverley in June, nursery at Ayr in July and minor event at Newmarket (beat Pivotal Guest by neck) in August: ran as if amiss final start: should stay 1m: acts on firm and good to soft going: usually races prominently: sometimes hangs: sold 43,000 gns, sent to USA. *P. C. Haslam* **87**

MOUNT ABU (IRE)   6 b.h. Foxhound (USA) 103 – Twany Angel (Double Form 130) [2003 108: 7d³ 7d⁴ 7s⁶ 7s 6d Nov 16] rather leggy, quite attractive horse: usually took the eye: very smart performer at best, winner of Prix de la Foret at Longchamp in 2001: just useful form since: creditable efforts in Prix du Palais-Royal at Longchamp (third to Saratan), Ballycorus Stakes at Leopardstown (fourth to Abunawwas) and Prix de la Foret at Longchamp (sixth to Etoile Montante) first 3 starts in 2003: best at 6f (given **108**

test)/7f: had form on good to firm going, but all wins on good to soft/soft: often made
running: sold 50,000 gns, and to stand at Sweep Lane Stud, Nurney, Co Kildare, Ireland,
fee €3,500. *J. H. M. Gosden*

MOUNTAIN MEADOW 2 ch.g. (Apr 19) Deploy 131 – Woodwardia (USA) 93 (El   **83 p**
Gran Senor (USA) 136) [2003 8g² Oct 25] sturdy gelding: sixth foal: half-brother to 3
winners, including 1¼m/1½m winner Edwardian (by Sanglamore) and French 6f winner
Kirkwood (by Selkirk), both useful: dam, 2-y-o 1m winner who stayed 11.4f, sister to
smart US Grade 1 1¼m winner Spanish Fern: 50/1, 7 lengths second of 17 to Salford City
in maiden at Newbury, held up and no match for winner late on: will be suited by 1¼m/
1½m: should improve. *Mrs A. J. Perrett*

MOUNT BENGER 3 ch.g. Selkirk (USA) 129 – Vice Vixen (CAN) (Vice Regent   **66**
(CAN)) [2003 73: p6g 10.3g f9.4g Oct 20] leggy gelding: fair maiden, lightly raced: stays
1¼m: raced only on all-weather and good ground. *R. M. Beckett*

MOUNTCHARGE (IRE) 2 b.g. (Apr 4) Intikhab (USA) 135 – Zorilla (Belmez (USA)   **80**
131) [2003 6m 6d⁶ 8m* p8g³ Dec 2] 11,000F: stocky gelding: third foal: half-brother to
3-y-o So Sure: dam French 2-y-o 1m winner: fairly useful performer: won maiden at
Yarmouth in August: good third in nursery at Lingfield: will probably stay 1¼m: acts on
polytrack and good to firm going: very slowly away second outing (gave trouble at start).
C. N. Allen

MOUNT HEATON (IRE) 3 b.f. Among Men (USA) 124 – Dollar Magic (Fairy   **–**
King (USA)) [2003 p8g Jan 30] IR 1,300Y: fifth foal: half-sister to 2 winners abroad by
Lycius: dam twice-raced half-sister to Ebor winner Deposki: 25/1, always behind in
maiden at Lingfield. *E. J. O'Neill*

MOUNT HESSE (FR) 4 ch.g. Midyan (USA) 124 – Minaudeuse (USA) (The Minstrel   **84**
(CAN) 135) [2003 87p: 7m 7.6g⁶ Jun 21] rather leggy gelding: fairly useful performer:
would have stayed 1¼m: acted on firm and soft going: dead. *G. Wragg*

MOUNT HILLABY (IRE) 3 b.f. Mujadil (USA) 119 – Tetradonna (IRE) 102 (Teen-   **67**
oso (USA) 135) [2003 79: 7.5m 8.5m 9.9d 8.1m⁶ 7.5m 6.1f f5g Oct 16] good-topped
filly: fair performer: well below form last 4 starts: seems to stay 1¼m: acts on good to
firm and good to soft ground, probably on fibresand: very slowly away final outing.
M. W. Easterby

MOUNT LOGAN 8 b.h. Shareef Dancer (USA) 135 – Double Entendre 81 (Dominion   **–**
123) [2003 f8g Dec 15] well held in maidens over 3 years apart. *R. Curtis*

MOUNT PEKAN (IRE) 3 b.c. Sri Pekan (USA) 117 – The Highlands (FR) (High   **64 §**
Line 125) [2003 68: 7g 7m 8g⁵ 8d 8g⁴ 7m 9.1m⁵ 9.2g 9.1g 8f Aug 29] leggy colt: modest
maiden handicapper: stays 1m: best efforts on good ground: has raced freely: unreliable.
J. S. Goldie

MOUNTRATH ROCK 6 b.m. Rock Hopper 124 – Point of Law (Law Society   **48 §**
(USA) 130) [2003 38§: 15.4m³ 17.2f⁵ 11.9m⁴ 16.4m⁵ p16g Jul 16] small mare: poor
handicapper: stays 17f: acts on firm going, good to soft and polytrack: usually visored/
blinkered/tongue tied: has been reluctant to race: not one to trust. *Miss B. Sanders*

MOUNT ROYALE (IRE) 5 ch.g. Wolfhound (USA) 126 – Mahabba (USA) 74   **60**
(Elocutionist (USA)) [2003 52: f7g² f7s² f7g² f7s* f7g* f7g⁴ p7g f7g⁵ f6g² 6m³ 7g³ f7g⁴   **a69**
f6g 7f* 6f⁵ Aug 2] close-coupled gelding: has knee action: fair performer on all-weather,
modest on turf: won seller and claimer (then left N. Tinkler) at Southwell in February and
seller at Brighton (left G. L. Moore 6,500 gns) in July: effective at 6f/7f: acts on fibresand
(ran poorly on polytrack), soft and firm going: usually blinkered/visored: tried tongue
tied, not in 2003. *J. A. Osborne*

MOUNTSORREL (IRE) 4 b.g. Charnwood Forest (IRE) 125 – Play The Queen   **–**
(IRE) (King of Clubs 124) [2003 50: f14.8g f8.5g f9.4g 10.9m Jul 4] angular gelding:
poor maiden: well held in 2003: tried in headgear. *T. Wall*

MOUNT SUPERIOR (USA) 7 b.g. Conquistador Cielo (USA) – Zum Solitair (USA)   **43**
(Vice Regent (CAN)) [2003 –: f7g⁶ 7f⁶ Aug 7] poor performer nowadays: stays 7f: tried
blinkered/tongue tied. *P. W. D'Arcy*

MOUNT VETTORE 2 br.g. (May 4) Vettori (IRE) 119 – Honeyspike (IRE) 79   **64 p**
(Chief's Crown (USA)) [2003 5.1m⁵ Oct 28] 10,000Y: strong gelding: sixth foal: brother
to useful 2001 2-y-o 7f winner Dulcet Spear and half-brother to several winners, including fairly useful 2002 2-y-o 7f winner Any Camp (by Hector Protector): dam, Irish
maiden who stayed 1m, half-sister to smart 1¼m winner Casey Tibbs: 25/1 and restless in

stall, fifth of 14 in maiden at Nottingham, getting hang of things late on: will stay at least 1m: should do better. *Mrs J. R. Ramsden*

MOUSEMAN   2 b.c. (Mar 3) Young Ern 120 – Scottish Royal (IRE) (Night Shift   **59**
(USA)) [2003 6m⁶ f7g⁶ 7m³ 6f 7m³ 6m* 6m Oct 3] 500Y, resold 500Y: good-bodied colt:
fourth foal: half-brother to 9.4f seller winner Northern Gold (by Goldmark): dam unraced
out of half-sister to Dancing Brave and Jolypha: modest performer: won seller at Lingfield in September: barely stays 7f: acts on good to firm going: blinkered last 5 starts:
often makes running. *C. N. Kellett*

MOVE IT   3 ch.c. Cadeaux Genereux 131 – Midnight Shift (IRE) 73 (Night Shift (USA))   **107**
[2003 77: 5.1f* 6g* 5m* 6m² 5f 6m* 6m* 6m³ Aug 16] sturdy colt: useful performer:
much improved, winning handicaps at Bath in March, Windsor and Sandown in April
and Newmarket (by length from Baltic King) in July and valuable Shergar Cup Sprint at
Ascot (by neck from Royal Beacon) in August: bit below best final outing: effective at 5f/
6f: acts on firm ground: usually races close to pace: has run well when sweating: reliable:
sent to Hong Kong, and joined T. W. Leung. *R. Charlton*

MOVIE KING (IRE)   4 ch.g. Catrail (USA) 123 – Marilyn (IRE) 72 (Kings Lake   **80**
(USA) 133) [2003 88: p10g p10g* p10g⁶ 10m 10.3m⁴ 11.9m 10g 9m⁴ 10.1m⁵ 10.1m Sep   **a93**
8] workmanlike gelding: fairly useful handicapper: won at Lingfield in February: left
A. Jarvis after eighth outing: best at 1m/1¼m: acts on polytrack and firm going: tried
visored: races up with pace. *S. Gollings*

MOWELGA   9 ch.g. Most Welcome 131 – Galactic Miss 78 (Damister (USA) 123)   **83**
[2003 p12g 12g 12m⁶ 12m⁴ Jun 27] short-backed gelding: fairly useful handicapper,
lightly raced nowadays: free-going sort but stays 1½m: acts on firm and good to soft
going, possibly not on soft: held up and tends to idle. *Lady Herries*

MOYANNA (IRE)   3 b.f. Sri Pekan (USA) 117 – Certain Impression (USA) (Forli   **78 §**
(ARG)) [2003 69: 6f³ 6.1m² 6g 8.2s 8.1m² 7m⁵ 7f² 6m* Oct 7] smallish filly: fair performer: not at best to win maiden at Catterick in October: effective at 6f to 1m: acts on
firm and good to soft ground: has been very slowly away: carries head awkwardly:
ungenuine: sent to USA. *T. D. Barron*

MOYEALA (IRE)   5 b.m. Royal Academy (USA) 130 – Khalsheva 55 (Shirley   **70**
Heights 130) [2003 82d: f8.5g 8m² 8.5g² 8g² 9.6f Aug 13] fair handicapper: well held
only outing on all-weather, at Wolverhampton: stayed 9f: acted on firm going: tried blinkered: dead. *E. Tyrrell, Ireland*

MOYNE PLEASURE (IRE)   5 b.g. Exit To Nowhere (USA) 122 – Ilanga (IRE) 92   **58**
(Common Grounds 118) [2003 79: f11s f8.5g⁶ 10.1d 13d f16.2g² 14.1m 16d² 12f⁴ 13g⁴
13m⁵ f12s Dec 27] small, sparely-made gelding: modest handicapper nowadays: barely
stays 2m: acts on fibresand, firm and soft ground: sometimes looks none too keen. *Paul
Johnson*

MOZZARELLA   3 ch.f. King's Signet (USA) 110 – Martine 68 (Clantime 101) [2003   **–**
–: 5g 5m Sep 8] well held in maidens: tried visored. *Don Enrico Incisa*

MR BELVEDERE   2 b.c. (Feb 16) Royal Applause 124 – Alarming Motown (Warning   **70**
136) [2003 5.1m⁶ 6.1d⁴ 6g² 7g 7m⁵ 7m 7f³ 7d Nov 8] 8,000Y: sturdy colt: second foal:
dam, ran twice, out of half-sister to top-class sprinter Committed: fair maiden: stays 7f:
acts on firm and good to soft ground: blinkered/visored last 3 starts. *R. Hannon*

*Tote Exacta Rated Stakes (Handicap), Newmarket—the much improved Move It
gains his fourth success of the season; Baltic King (far side) and The Kiddykid are placed*

MR BILL 3 ch.g. Cosmonaut – Latch On (IRE) 56 (Dance of Life (USA)) [2003 10m 8g f11g 7.6g Jul 16] second foal: dam Irish maiden: no form: wayward. *Mrs N. Macauley* – §

MR BOUNTIFUL (IRE) 5 b.g. Mukaddamah (USA) 125 – Nawadder 73 (Kris 135) [2003 64+: p7g f7g* f7g* f7g f7g 7m⁴ 7.1d³ 7d 7f f7g 7m³ 7.1f 7m³ 7m 6f² 6m 7m⁶ 7m⁴ p7g* p7g² p7g³ p7g p7g Dec 30] angular gelding: fair performer: won handicap at Wolverhampton in February, minor event at Southwell in March and handicap at Lingfield in November: effective at stiff 5f to 7f: acts on all-weather, soft and firm going: tried in cheekpieces: sometimes slowly away. *M. Dods* 67

MR CHESTNUT TREE 4 b.g. Forzando 122 – Sure Flyer (IRE) (Sure Blade (USA) 130) [2003 –: f5g f9.4g 7d 6m 8m 8f 10.5m 12m 12.1m 10.5f Sep 5] good-topped gelding: little form since 2 yrs: tried visored/in cheekpieces. *Mrs A. M. Naughton* –

MR DAVE 3 b.g. General Monash (USA) 107 – Cavatina 72 (Chief Singer 131) [2003 7d May 17] 23,000F, 33,000Y: third foal: dam 6f/7.5f winner: very slowly away and always behind in maiden at Lingfield: sent to Sweden. *M. A. Jarvis* –

MR DINOS (IRE) 4 b.c. Desert King (IRE) 129 – Spear Dance (Gay Fandango (USA) 132) [2003 117: 16.4m* 20m* 20s⁶ Oct 5] 124

Persian Punch won three of Britain's Cup races—the Goodwood Cup, the Doncaster Cup and the Jockey Club Cup—but was put in his place comprehensively by Mr Dinos in the Gold Cup at Royal Ascot. The Gold Cup has survived more or less in its original form thanks to the Ascot Trustees, who resisted calls in the early-'nineties for a reduction in distance. Underlining its commitment to the race, Ascot has continued to raise its value, the connections of Mr Dinos picking up £145,000 for his victory, nearly twice as much as Westerner earned in the French two-and-a-half-mile Group 1, the Prix du Cadran, and more than the combined total won by Persian Punch at Goodwood, Doncaster and Newmarket. The Gold Cup, once the most important race in Britain for four-year-olds and upwards, continues to be regarded as an anachronism by many, particularly those involved with bloodstock breeding, but it remains a worthy part of the Royal meeting and continues to provide the week's most popular spectacle. The Gold Cup day crowd of 74,792 was, as usual, the biggest of the week and BBC television's Royal Ascot coverage, which attracted an average audience of 1.6m over the five days, peaked at 2m for the Gold Cup. The Gold Cup is the race that matters most for the out-and-out stayers and produced another stirring renewal for racegoers and television viewers alike.

The game, front-running Mr Dinos looked every inch a leading Cup horse in the making as a three-year-old, especially when keeping on strongly to win the Prix Royal-Oak at Longchamp on his final start. He proved a reliable staying three-year-old, his fifth in the St Leger being the only occasion he had failed to reach a place in nine outings, including one as a two-year-old. Looking in magnificent shape on his reappearance, he put himself firmly in the Gold Cup picture when conceding weight all round and defying a Group 1 penalty in a well-contested renewal of the Bonusprint Henry II Stakes at Sandown. With a couple of other front runners in the line-up, Mr Dinos tracked the leaders until quickening well when produced to challenge in the home straight. Leading over two furlongs out, he was soon in control and won, eased by Frankie Dettori, by two and a half lengths from Pole Star, with the lightly-raced Kasthari a neck away third; Persian Punch, successful in the race three times, came fourth and the favourite Boreas fifth.

Bonusprint Henry II Stakes, Sandown—Mr Dinos defies a Group 1 penalty to beat Pole Star (rail), Kasthari, Persian Punch and Boreas in splendid style

Gold Cup, Royal Ascot—another fine display from Mr Dinos; Persian Punch, making his eighth consecutive appearance at Royal Ascot, is second ahead of Pole Star (right)

Boreas was ridden by Kieren Fallon, whose agent, realising Dettori would be claimed by Godolphin in the Gold Cup, quickly snapped up the Royal Ascot ride on Mr Dinos.

The Gold Cup betting was dominated by Dettori's mount, the Yorkshire Cup winner Mamool, and Mr Dinos, who had finished second to Mamool in the Queen's Vase at the meeting twelve months earlier. The pair started at 5/2 and 3/1 respectively, with Godolphin's second string Fight Your Corner next at 8/1, ahead of the Irish-trained Coronation Cup third Black Sam Bellamy at 10/1 and Pole Star and Kasthari at 12/1 (Persian Punch was a 20/1 chance). Royal Rebel, the winner of the two previous Gold Cups, missed the whole of the latest season with a leg injury, while the 2002 runner-up Vinnie Roe was being kept for an autumn campaign after a spell off the course recovering from the effects of a hard-fought fourth under top weight on very firm going in the Melbourne Cup in November. By all accounts, the connections of Mr Dinos had a worrying time in the period before the Gold Cup because of a viral infection which hit the stable, Mr Dinos being kept isolated in a box away from the main yard. On Gold Cup day itself, the trainer expressed fears about the suitability of the prevailing good to firm going (Mr Dinos had won the Prix Royal-Oak on heavy). Reservations were dispelled rounding the home turn as Mr Dinos, who had to be niggled along for much of the race, took over from front-running Persian Punch, who had been really set alight three furlongs out. Mr Dinos forged clear, having the race sewn up well over a furlong out, and won in tremendous style by six lengths, eased a little close home. With fifth-placed Mamool and eighth-placed Black Sam Bellamy patently failing to see out the trip, Mr Dinos probably didn't have to improve much on his splendid effort in the Henry II Stakes to add the Gold Cup to his record. But he still put up a striking performance that ranks him fairly highly among modern-day winners of the race. The resolute Persian Punch held off Pole Star by three quarters of a length for second, with the 2001 Gold Cup third Jardines Lookout a further neck away fourth. Kasthari came seventh, leaving the impression the Gold Cup trip stretched his stamina to its limit, while Fight Your Corner beat only one home in the field of twelve. Unfortunately, Mr Dinos reportedly returned home 'sore' after the Gold Cup and was seen out only once more, when well below form in the Prix du Cadran at Longchamp in October, weakening in the straight. He will, though, be in training again in 2004 with the Gold Cup his principal target.

		Danehill	Danzig
Mr Dinos (IRE) (b.c. 1999)	Desert King (IRE) (b 1994)	(b 1986)	Razyana
		Sabaah	Nureyev
		(ch 1988)	Dish Dash
	Spear Dance (b 1982)	Gay Fandango	Forli
		(ch 1972)	Gay Violin
		Lancette	Double Jump
		(b 1971)	Persian Union

The good-topped Mr Dinos is by Irish Two Thousand Guineas and Derby winner Desert King, a son of the leading international sire (now deceased) Danehill who also enjoyed the distinction of being the paternal grandsire of Choisir (by Danehill Dancer), whose performances at the other end of the distance spectrum in the King's Stand and the Golden Jubilee were also among Royal Ascot's most memorable moments. Desert King now stands in Japan, but with three crops of racing age it seems he is more of an influence for stamina than speed as a sire, the average distance of races won by his three-year-olds in Britain being ten and a half furlongs, and for his older horses just over a mile and three quarters. Apart from Mr Dinos, Lancashire Oaks winner Place Rouge was Desert King's most notable winner in Britain in the latest season and he also sired the Melbourne Cup winner Makybe Diva. Mr Dinos is the last foal of his dam Spear Dance, who won at seven furlongs and a mile at three and is a sister to the Jersey Stakes winner Rasa Penang and a half-sister to the Anglesey Stakes winner Darcy's Thatcher. Their dam the maiden Lancette was a half-sister to the July Stakes and Gimcrack winner Golden Horus, who came fourth in the Two Thousand Guineas. In common with nearly all Gold Cup winners nowadays, Mr Dinos was not bred for extreme distances, though his close relative the smart Risk Material (by Danehill), the best of Spear Dance's other winners, showed form at up to a mile and three quarters. Mr Dinos stays two and a half miles really well. He has yet to race on firm going but acts on any other. *P. F. I. Cole*

MR DIP 3 b.g. Reprimand 122 – Scottish Lady (Dunbeath (USA) 127) [2003 10d 8.1s[5] 7m Jun 10] leggy gelding: half-brother to 6f to 7.6f winner Sharp 'N Smart (by Weldnaas): dam Italian 6f to 7.5f winner: maiden: seemed to show fair form when fifth to Fisio Therapy at Haydock: well beaten both other starts. *A. W. Carroll* **66 ?**

MR DUMBY (IRE) 3 b.c. Sri Pekan (USA) 117 – Lady Windermere (IRE) (Lake Coniston (IRE) 131) [2003 6g[2] 8m 6m Jun 11] IR 32,000F, 60,000 2-y-o: tall, lengthy, good-topped colt: first foal: dam, unraced, half-sister to Moyglare Stud Stakes winner Sequoyah out of sister to dam of Dolphin Street, Saffron Walden and Insight: modest maiden: should stay 1m: looks difficult ride: sold 2,000 gns. *R. Hannon* **61**

MR ED (IRE) 5 ch.g. In The Wings 128 – Center Moriches (IRE) 74 (Magical Wonder (USA) 125) [2003 80: 16.2m 12m 14.1g* 14.1s* 20m 14g[2] 14g[6] 16.1m 12m 14g Sep 6] angular gelding: fairly useful handicapper: won at Salisbury and Nottingham in May: poor efforts last 3 starts, blinkered on final one: effective at 1½m to 2m (raced freely and didn't stay 2½m in Ascot Stakes): acts on soft and good to firm going: sometimes slowly away/wanders: fairly useful hurdler. *P. Bowen* **86**

MR FLEMING 4 b. or br.g. Bin Ajwaad (IRE) 119 – Fabulous Night (FR) (Fabulous Dancer (USA) 124) [2003 56: p8g p7g p12g p10g[4] 11.5m[4] Oct 21] poor maiden: stays 11.5f: raced only on all-weather/good to firm ground: tried blinkered. *Dr J. D. Scargill* **49**

MR FORTYWINKS (IRE) 9 ch.g. Fools Holme (USA) – Dream On 54 (Absalom 128) [2003 70: 16m 13d 16d[5] 16.5m[3] 15g[4] 16m* 17.1m[4] 16.1m 15.9d[6] Sep 24] sparely-made gelding: fair handicapper: won amateur event at Musselburgh in July: stays 17f: acts on fibresand, good to firm and heavy ground: tried tongue tied: tends to sweat: usually races up with pace. *B. Ellison* **67**

MR GISBY (USA) 5 b. or br.g. Chief's Crown (USA) – Double Lock 104 (Home Guard (USA) 129) [2003 64: p16g f14s[2] f14s[2] f16s[3] f12s* f12g Mar 3] lengthy gelding: fairly useful performer: first past post in handicap at Southwell (later demoted, rider his runner-up with whip several times in straight) in January and maiden at Wolverhampton in February: effective at 1½m to 2m: acts on fibresand, raced only on good/good to firm going on turf: usually races prominently: joined Mrs L. Wadham, and won over hurdles in October. *S. C. Williams* **80**

MR HAWKEYE (USA) 4 ch.g. Royal Academy (USA) 130 – Port Plaisance (USA) (Woodman (USA) 126) [2003 69?: 11.9f 16m Apr 22] tall, rather raw-boned gelding: disappointing maiden: tried visored. *Ms A. E. Embiricos* **–**

MR INDEPENDENT (IRE) 2 b.c. (Mar 2) Cadeaux Genereux 131 – Iris May 87 (Brief Truce (USA) 126) [2003 7.2m 8m[3] 6g Oct 13] close-coupled colt: first foal: dam 5f winner, including at 2 yrs: best effort in maidens (fair form) when third at Newcastle: not sure to stay beyond 1m. *E. A. L. Dunlop* **66**

MR JACK DANIELLS (IRE) 2 b.g. (Apr 25) Mujadil (USA) 119 – Neat Shilling (IRE) (Bob Back (USA) 124) [2003 6d 7m* 7g 7m Oct 3] €10,000Y: big gelding: second foal: brother to 3-y-o Tidy: dam unraced sister to useful Irish middle-distance stayer Fill The Bill and half-sister to smart stayer Riddlesdown: fair performer: made all in maiden at Folkestone in August: poor efforts in nurseries after: subsequently gelded: likely to stay 1m. *W. R. Muir* **70**

MR LAMBROS 2 ch.c. (Jan 8) Pivotal 124 – Magical Veil 73 (Majestic Light (USA)) [2003 p6g[3] Nov 22] 36,000F, 88,000Y: sixth living foal: brother to fairly useful 6f winner **78 p**

Uncle Bernon and half-brother to several winners, including fairly useful 1996 2-y-o 1m winner Myrtlebank (by Salse): dam 11.6f winner: 7/1 and green, beaten 2 necks by Petardias Magic in minor event at Lingfield, starting slowly and finishing well: will stay at least 7f: sure to improve. *A. M. Balding*

MR LEAR (USA) 4 b.g. Lear Fan (USA) 130 – Majestic Mae (USA) (Crow (FR) 134)   **82**
[2003 65, a72: f8.5g⁴ 8m⁴ 10.1m³ 10d 10d⁴ 12g* 12m⁵ 11.9f⁶ 13g² 10m* 12.1m² 12.3m* 12.1m 12.3m⁴ 10m Sep 9] sturdy gelding: fairly useful handicapper: won at Musselburgh in May and at Ripon in July and August: effective at 1¼m to 13f: acts on fibresand, good to firm and good to soft ground: makes running: reliable: joined R. Fahey. *T. D. Barron*

MR LEWIN 2 ch.g. (Mar 31) Primo Dominie 121 – Fighting Run (Runnett 125) [2003   **67 p**
6m 7m 7m⁵ Oct 12] 15,000F, 8,000Y: big, workmanlike gelding: half-brother to 7.5f winner Croire (by Lomond) and 3 winners abroad: dam, maiden, from family of Central Park and Moon Ballad: best effort in maidens (fair form) when fifth at Newcastle, still not fully wound up but late headway in unfavoured group: will stay 1m: type to do better in handicaps as 3-y-o. *R. A. Fahey*

MR LOVERMAN (IRE) 3 ch.g. Spectrum (IRE) 126 – Soviet Artic (FR) 84§ (Bering   **– §**
136) [2003 8m 8.1m 8.3m 10.4m 8m f7s Sep 26] strong, sturdy gelding: first reported foal: dam, French 1¼m winner, looked thoroughly mulish on second of 2 starts in Britain: beat only 1 home in 6 races: virtually refused to race in blinkers last 2 outings: one to avoid. *Miss V. Haigh*

MR MALARKEY (IRE) 3 b.g. Pivotal 124 – Girl Next Door 58 (Local Suitor (USA)   **88**
128) [2003 –: 6g 6f* 6.1m* 6m⁵ 6m⁴ 6m² 6m* 6f³ 5m 6m⁴ 6f 5.2g 6g Sep 22] plain gelding: fairly useful performer: won maiden at Thirsk and handicap at Nottingham in April and minor event at Kempton in June: effective at 5f/6f: acts on firm going, yet to race on softer than good: wore cheekpieces on reappearance, usually blinkered/visored after: usually races prominently. *Mrs C. A. Dunnett*

MR MIDASMAN (IRE) 2 b.c. (Feb 3) Entrepreneur 123 – Sifaara (IRE) (Caerleon   **75**
(USA) 132) [2003 6m 6g⁴ 7d* Nov 4] €37,000Y: sturdy colt: second foal: half-brother to 3-y-o Mark of Zorro: dam, ran twice in France at 3 yrs, out of very smart 7f to 9f (US Grade 2 event) winner Royal Touch: fair form in maidens: won at Catterick by 1½ lengths from Miss Eloise, leading final 1f: will stay at least 1m. *R. Hollinshead*

MR MISCHIEF 3 b.g. Millkom 124 – Snow Huntress 80 (Shirley Heights 130) [2003   **72**
82: 10g 8m 10m⁵ 10.9m 10.9d² f14.8g* f11g* Dec 3] leggy gelding: fairly useful perfor-   **a93**
mer on all-weather, fair on turf: won amateur handicap at Wolverhampton in November and claimer at Southwell (odds on) in December: stays 14.8f: acts on fibresand, unraced on extremes of going on turf. *P. C. Haslam*

MR MISCHIEVOUS 2 b.c. (Jan 31) Magic Ring (IRE) 115 – Inya Lake 101 (Whit-   **–**
tingham (IRE) 104) [2003 5m May 26] 10,000Y: first foal: dam 5f (including Molecomb Stakes at 2 yrs) winner: well held in maiden at Leicester: sold 500 gns. *N. P. Littmoden*

MR MOON 2 b.g. (Apr 14) Pursuit of Love 124 – Sound of Sleat (Primo Dominie 121)   **–**
[2003 6m f6g f6g Nov 1] 27,000Y: good-bodied gelding: first foal: dam unraced half-sister to smart French miler Soft Currency: well held in maidens. *M. D. Hammond*

MR PERTEMPS 5 b.g. Primo Dominie 121 – Amber Mill 96 (Doulab (USA) 115)   **63**
[2003 64: f6s³ f6s³ f6s* f5g⁶ 6m f6g Nov 25] tall, lengthy gelding: modest handicapper: won at Southwell in January (idled), February and March: best at 5f/6f: acts on fibresand and soft ground: tried tongue tied: carries head high. *R. A. Fahey*

MR PIANO MAN (IRE) 5 gr.g. Paris House 123 – Winter March (Ballad Rock 122)   **–**
[2003 –: 5.9g 6m May 12] leggy, close-coupled gelding: lightly raced and no recent form. *Mrs A. M. Naughton*

MR SANDANCER 4 b.g. Zafonic (USA) 130 – Um Lardaff (Mill Reef (USA) 141)   **?**
[2003 96: p10g p12g p12g⁵ 8g³ a8s³ 9m a8g⁶ a8g* a10g a8.6g a10g³ a8f² a8g* a8g⁴ Dec 21] strong, attractive gelding: good walker: fair performer at best nowadays: sold from P. Mitchell 4,000 gns after third outing: won minor events at Taby in September and December: stays 1¼m: acts on good to firm going and dirt, possibly not softer than good: tried visored: tongue tied last 2 starts in Britain: has been slowly away. *B. Bjorkman, Sweden*

MRS BOZ 3 b.f. Superpower 113 – Bar None (Rabdan 129) [2003 7m 8m⁶ p10g Nov   **–**
18] second foal: dam unraced: well held in maidens. *A. W. Carroll*

MRS CEE (IRE) 2 b.f. (Apr 23) Orpen (USA) 116 – Cutleaf 81 (Kris 135) [2003 7m*   **71 d**
7.1m 6m⁴ 9m⁴ 10m⁶ Oct 13] 10,000F, €7,000Y: lengthy filly: seventh foal: half-sister

to 3 winners, including fairly useful 1999 2-y-o 1m winner High Cheviot (by Shirley Heights) and 7f (at 2 yrs) and 1½m winner Goodwood Lass (by Alzao): dam, 10.5f winner, half-sister to Ribblesdale winner Strigida: fair performer: won maiden at Milan in June: mostly well beaten in listed race/minor events after. *M. G. Quinlan*

MRS CUBE 4 ch.f. Missed Flight 123 – Norska 67 (Northfields (USA)) [2003 42: 8.1d **42** 7f 6.1g⁶ 8m 7g⁶ 8f Sep 8] well-grown filly: poor maiden: stays 7f: acts on good to firm going: blinkered last 2 starts. *J. M. Bradley*

MRS GEE (IRE) 2 b.f. (Feb 28) Desert Story (IRE) 115 – My Gloria (IRE) (Saint **63** Estephe (FR) 123) [2003 7.6g⁵ 7.9m⁵ 8g⁴ f8g² f8s Dec 27] IR 3,000F, €6,500Y: leggy filly: first foal: dam unraced half-sister to useful stayer Lover's Moon: modest maiden: runner-up at Southwell: will probably stay 1¼m. *R. Hollinshead*

MR SMITHERS JONES 3 br.g. Emperor Jones (USA) 119 – Phylian 77 (Glint of **–** Gold 128) [2003 –: f6g⁵ Feb 15] close-coupled, quite good-topped gelding: well held in maidens. *S. C. Williams*

MRS MOH (IRE) 2 b.f. (Mar 4) Orpen (USA) 116 – My Gray (FR) (Danehill (USA) **85** 126) [2003 f5g* 5.1m⁴ 5m 6g⁴ 6.5d² 6g² 7m 7m³ 7d² Nov 8] IR 14,500F, 13,500Y: sturdy, quite attractive filly: first foal: dam, French maiden, out of half-sister to Prix Royal-Oak winner Mersey: fairly useful performer: won maiden at Southwell in June: mostly good efforts after: stays 7f: acts on fibresand, good to firm and good to soft ground: game. *T. D. Easterby*

MRS PANKHURST 2 b.f. (Mar 12) Selkirk (USA) 129 – Melodist (USA) 118 (The **67** Minstrel (CAN) 135) [2003 7m 8g* 10g Nov 1] leggy filly: closely related to useful Irish 1½m winner Song of The Sword (by Kris) and half-sister to 2 winners, including fairly useful 1¾m winner Melodica (by Machiavellian): dam won Oaks d'Italia and dead-heated in Irish Oaks: fair form: won maiden at Ripon in September, slowly away and getting on top close home: well held in listed event at Newmarket final start: bred to stay at least 1¼m. *B. W. Hills*

MR SPLIFFY (IRE) 4 b.g. Fayruz 116 – Johns Conquerer (IRE) 74 (Conquering **71 §** Hero (USA) 116) [2003 74: 5m 5m 6m 5.3m 5m² 5m 5m⁵ 5m⁴ 5m 5m² 5f⁵ 5.2m 5.1g **a53 §** 5m f5g 5m² 5d f5g f6g f5s⁴ Dec 27] close-coupled gelding: unimpressive mover: fair handicapper on turf, modest on all-weather: best at 5f: acts on fibresand, firm and good to soft ground: tried visored/in cheekpieces: has bolted/been early to post: usually races prominently: unreliable. *K. R. Burke*

MRS PLUM 4 b.f. Emarati (USA) 74 – Aubade (Henbit (USA) 130) [2003 –: f8g Jan **–** 23] fair maiden at 2 yrs but no form since. *I. A. Wood*

MRS POOTERS (IRE) 4 b.f. Petardia 113 – Mrs Hooters (Glint of Gold 128) [2003 **–** 61: p10g p12g Feb 19] modest maiden: well held in 2003, including in cheekpieces. *D. W. P. Arbuthnot*

MRS SHILLING 2 b.f. (Mar 8) Dr Fong (USA) 128 – Papaha (FR) 103 (Green Desert **59 p** (USA) 127) [2003 6m⁶ Oct 16] 35,000Y: useful-looking filly: third foal: closely related to 4-y-o Kristensen: dam 8.5f winner out of half-sister to Old Vic: 16/1 and green, 12 lengths sixth of 12 to Phantom Wind in maiden at Newmarket, not knocked about: took good hold to post: should improve. *J. R. Fanshawe*

MRS SPENCE 2 b.f. (Jun 9) Mind Games 121 – Maid O'Cannie 72 (Efisio 120) [2003 **63** 5d 6m² 7m⁵ Aug 5] tall, leggy filly: fifth foal: half-sister to winner in Belgium by Noble Patriarch: dam 6f winner: modest form in maidens: free-going sort, barely stays 7f. *M. W. Easterby*

MR STROWGER 2 b.c. (Apr 28) Dancing Spree (USA) – Matoaka 72 (Be My Chief **–** (USA) 122) [2003 5d 5g 5d 7g p7g Dec 17] second foal: dam, 1m winner, half-sister to 7-y-o Calcutta: no form: trained first 4 starts by N. Moran in Ireland. *A. Charlton*

MR STYLISH 7 b.g. Mazilier (USA) 107 – Moore Stylish 65 (Moorestyle 137) [2003 **64 §** 68§: f7g f6g f7s² f7g⁴ f7g⁶ f6g² 6m⁶ f7g⁶ 6m f7g f7g⁴ f7g⁴ f7g⁴ f7g f6g Dec 26] lengthy gelding: modest performer: effective at 6f/7f: acts on fibresand and any turf going: usually tongue tied/wears headgear: carries head awkwardly: unreliable. *J. S. Moore*

MR TAMBOURINE MAN (IRE) 2 b.c. (Jan 28) Rainbow Quest (USA) 134 – Girl **82** From Ipanema 106 (Salse (USA) 128) [2003 7m² 7m⁶ 8m* Oct 25] rangy colt: fourth foal: half-brother to 3-y-o Wondrous Joy and winner around 1m Ipanema Beach (by Lion Cavern): dam 7f (at 2 yrs) and 1m winner who stayed 10.5f: fairly useful form in maidens: won 13-runner event at Musselburgh comfortably by 3 lengths from Tytheknot, always to fore: will be suited by 1¼m/1½m. *P. F. I. Cole*

MR TANGERINE (IRE) 2 b.c. (May 12) Fayruz 116 – Mildred Anne (IRE) (Thatch- –
ing 131) [2003 5m 6m Sep 3] €500Y, resold €3,500Y, 15,000 2-y-o: fourth foal: dam
behind in Irish bumper only start: well beaten in maiden (slowly away) and seller at
Lingfield. *M. J. Wallace*

MR TANGO (ARG) 5 b.h. Numerous (USA) – Milonguera Fitz (ARG) (Fitzcarraldo 102
(ARG)) [2003 a10g a9.5g* 8g 8g* 8m⁵ 8g 10g⁶ a8g 10d⁶ a8s³ Dec 7] ex-Argentinian
horse: useful performer: winner of 5 races in native country, and won twice in Spain late
at 4 yrs: had several trainers in 2003, with C. Von Der Recke when winning listed race at
Neuss in February and minor event at Cologne in June and finishing creditable fifth to
Bowman in listed race at Goodwood: trained sixth to eighth outings only by G. L. Moore:
creditable sixth to Sign of The Wolf in Prix Andre Baboin at Lyon Parilly penultimate
start: stays 1¼m: acts on any turf going and on dirt: has worn tongue tie/cheekpieces.
J. H. Brown, Spain

MR UPPITY 4 b.g. Shareef Dancer (USA) 135 – Queenfisher 101 (Scottish Reel 123) 52
[2003 –: p7g f5g³ f5s² f6g⁵ f5g 6m f7s f7g Jun 25] modest maiden: effective at 5f to 7f:
acts on fibresand: wore headgear last 7 outings: none too reliable. *Julian Poulton*

MR VELOCITY (IRE) 3 b.g. Tagula (IRE) 116 – Miss Rusty (IRE) (Mukaddamah 79
(USA) 125) [2003 7f⁶ 7m³ 8.1m³ 8d Nov 7] 25,000Y: compact, quite attractive
colt: first foal: dam 9f winner in Belgium: fair maiden: stays 1m: acts on good to firm
ground. *A. C. Stewart*

MR WHIZZ 6 ch.g. Manhal – Panienka (POL) 70 (Dom Racine (FR) 121) [2003 54: 46
7f⁵ 9.7m 10m⁵ 11.8g 9g 7f 10.9m 10f Sep 2] lengthy gelding: poor handicapper in 2002:
showed little in 2003 (left J. King after fourth start): effective at 7f to 1¼m: acts on any
turf going, some promise on fibresand: tried visored, tongue tied last 2 starts: often races
prominently. *A. P. Jones*

MR WOLF 2 b.c. (Mar 17) Wolfhound (USA) 126 – Madam Millie 99 (Milford 119) 65
[2003 6g 5f⁴ 5m⁵ 6m 6g Oct 13] 9,200Y: sturdy colt: half-brother to several winners, including 5-y-o Celtic Mill and 4-y-o Penny Ha'penny: dam 2-y-o 5f winner: fair maiden:
well beaten in nursery final start: possibly best at 5f: acts on firm going. *D. W. Barker*

MUALAFAH 3 b.f. Indian Ridge 123 – Dalayil (IRE) (Sadler's Wells (USA) 132) 76
[2003 9.9f³ 9m³ 8m⁵ Aug 28] first foal: dam unraced close relative to very smart performer up to 1¼m Alhaarth: fair maiden: possibly amiss final start: may prove best around
1m: sold 5,000 gns in December. *M. P. Tregoning*

MUBEEN (IRE) 3 ch.c. Barathea (IRE) 127 – Fernanda 95 (Be My Chief (USA) 122) 103
[2003 94: 9m² 8d³ 10.4f³ 8m² 8g* 10m² 8g 8g a9f Dec 12] smallish, sturdy colt: useful
performer: won minor event at Salisbury (hung left, beat Jay Gee's Choice by 1¾ lengths)
in July: creditable third (promoted to second) behind disqualified Joe Bear in handicap
at Newmarket next time: left E. Dunlop and off nearly 4 months after seventh outing:
effective at 1m/1¼m: acts on firm going. *E. Charpy, UAE*

MUBTAKER (USA) 6 ch.h. Silver Hawk (USA) 123 – Gazayil (USA) 80 (Irish 132
River (FR) 131) [2003 123: 10m* 13.3m* 12g* 12s² Oct 5]

An improving six-year-old on the Flat is a rare bird. One who achieves the
level of form shown by Mubtaker is rarer still, since his display in running Dalakhani to three quarters of a length in the Prix de l'Arc de Triomphe, five lengths
ahead of High Chaparral and the rest, was the best by any older horse on a European
track over a mile and a half during the season. It was also one of the best by a horse
of his age since *Racehorses* was first published, surpassed in the last thirty years
only by Ardross, rated 134 in 1982 after also finishing runner-up in the Arc, and
Sagaro, rated 133 in 1977 after winning his third Gold Cup. Swain ran to 132 in
1998 when winning the King George VI and Queen Elizabeth Stakes, while those
rated below Mubtaker include Kayf Tara, Lochsong and Vintage Crop. Ardross,
Sagaro and Swain were all multiple Group 1 winners, whereas Mubtaker has yet to
win at that level. Indeed, for various reasons, accidental rather than intentional, the
Arc was his first Group 1 challenge. He remains in training so will have the chance
to put the record straight, provided he keeps his form and remains in good heart.

Keeping his form and being in good heart have been characteristics of
Mubtaker's career, confirmed by his record of eight wins from seventeen starts and
never being out of the first three. A credit to his connections, he is as reliable a horse
as one could wish to find and his record might have been even better with fewer
training troubles, the latest of which occurred when he hurt a joint in his near-hind

while in Dubai over the winter. That kept him off the track in the latest season until July, when he lined up for the listed cantorindex.co.uk Steventon Stakes at Newbury over a mile and a quarter, a trip over which he had not been tried since May 2001 and which looked as if it might be on the sharp side by now. Not a bit of it. Escaping a penalty for his victory in the Group 2 Geoffrey Freer Stakes the previous year, Mubtaker started favourite and benefited from the strong gallop, leading over two furlongs out and staying on well to beat Parasol by a length and a half, putting up a good timefigure in the process. Mubtaker was returned to Newbury the following month for another appearance in the Geoffrey Freer Stakes, sponsored by Stan James. He started at odds on, with doubts about his two principal rivals Systematic and Mamool, the former making his reappearance while the latter had been off for two months. Mubtaker put up a smashing display, leading three furlongs out and beating Systematic by three and a half lengths without being extended.

Another pattern victory followed, and by an even wider margin, under a penalty in the Coral September Stakes at Kempton. It was, however, gained in different style from usual with Mubtaker making the running and taking time to settle. Harried for much of the way by First Charter, he responded really well when driven and forged clear in the final furlong to score by five lengths. Various long-term targets had been mentioned as the season progressed, including the Melbourne Cup and Irish St Leger but, with Mubtaker clearly in the form of his life, connections took the sensible decision to go for broke in the Arc. The soft going seemingly gave cause for concern, and it was only after the trainer had checked conditions once racing got under way that Mubtaker was finally cleared to run. Starting at 33/1—only two of the twelve other runners were at longer odds—Mubtaker did himself proud, given a good ride by Richard Hills. Pegging back the leaders in any type of race tends to be harder work on soft going than on firm, and in such conditions Arc runners sure to stay the trip are best being ridden reasonably close to the pace, even if they possess a turn of finishing speed. Mubtaker tracked the leaders in fourth on the outside, moved ahead rounding the home turn, still going sweetly, and quickened clear of all but Dalakhani, who was obviously going at least as well, if not better. When Mubtaker was headed a furlong out it looked all over, but Mubtaker knuckled down to his task like a Trojan and went down only by three parts of a length. Working on the familiar principle 'first is first, second is nobody', the media tended to ignore Mubtaker in their rush to lavish praise on Dalakhani afterwards. Mubtaker deserved much more credit. He wasn't seen out again though, bypassing all three races mentioned by Tregoning as possible targets, the Canadian International, Japan Cup and Hong Kong Vase.

Mubtaker's pedigree has been dealt with in detail in previous volumes of *Racehorses*, but there are a few items to add. A lengthy horse and an unimpressive mover, he is now the highest rated of his sire Silver Hawk's progeny in Europe, ahead of Mutafaweq (129), Benny The Dip (127), Lady In Silver (127) and Magnificent Star (122). The dam Gazayil had two other runners in Britain during the year and they enjoyed very different fortunes. Three-year-old Spirit of Gold, also by Silver Hawk and an 82,000-dollar yearling, looked the part physically but was

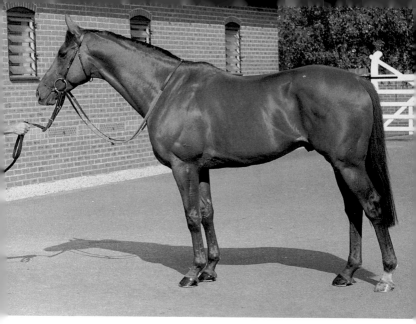

Mr Hamdan Al Maktoum's "Mubtaker"

		Silver Hawk (USA) (b 1979)	Roberto (b 1969)	Hail To Reason Bramalea
Mubtaker (USA) (ch.h. 1997)			Gris Vitesse (gr 1966)	Amerigo Matchiche II
		Gazayil (USA) (ch 1985)	Irish River (ch 1976)	Riverman Irish Star
			Close Comfort (b 1979)	Far North Caterina

well beaten in his two races, and was sold for just 800 guineas to an Italian stable after his debut. Gazayil's two-year-old Tree Chopper (by Woodman), also with Tregoning, similarly had one start in maiden company, at Bath a week after the Arc, but did vastly better, winning readily. If Tree Chopper has half Mubtaker's sterling qualities she will be one to follow. Mubtaker acts on any going and is effective at a mile and a quarter to thirteen furlongs (he would probably stay the trip in the Irish St Leger, but the two miles of the Melbourne Cup would stretch him). By all accounts, Mubtaker's first target as a seven-year-old will be the Dubai Sheema Classic, a race in which he was an intended runner at five before injury intervened. On the evidence of his Arc run, he is plenty good enough to win it. Good luck to him! *M. P. Tregoning*

MUCHACHODELCASTILL (IRE) 2 b.g. (Mar 23) Spectrum (IRE) 126 – Nation-alartgallery (IRE) (Tate Gallery (USA) 117) [2003 5d 6m 6m Aug 30] IR 10,000F, €9,000Y, 10,500 2-y-o: angular, workmanlike gelding: brother to a winner in Italy and half-brother to several winners, including 5f (at 2 yrs)/6f winner Ballina Lad (by Mac's Imp): dam ran 5 times at 2 yrs in Ireland: little sign of ability in maidens: refused to go to post in September. *P. C. Haslam* —

MUCHEA 9 ch.h. Shalford (IRE) 124§ – Bargouzine 67 (Hotfoot 126) [2003 105: 8g 8.9f⁴ 7.9m⁵ 8g⁵ 8m 8m⁴ 8.1d 8.9m² 8g* 8m 8m* 7.9f⁵ 8m⁶ 10g 8g 8.2d⁵ Nov 6] good-topped horse: useful performer: won handicap at Doncaster (for second year running, **103**

687

beat Island Light by 2 lengths) and minor event at Goodwood in September: stays 9f: acts on any going: tried visored, not since 2000: sometimes sweats: has been bandaged: usually held up: tough. *M. R. Channon*

MUCH FASTER (IRE)   2 b.f. (Feb 13) Fasliyev (USA) 120 – Interruption (Zafo- **113**
nic (USA) 130) [2003 5d* 5.5g* 5d* 5.5d* 6s² 6m Oct 2]

  When they leave the blocks in the final of the hundred metres at the 2004 Olympics, the competitors won't try to crowd into one lane as they storm up the track. For a start, the rules forbid it. Furthermore, the momentum and time most of them would lose in doing so would leave the athlete sticking to his lane—in a contest decided by split seconds—with a clear advantage. The lesson seems to be lost on racing. In both sprints and races over longer distances on straight courses it is comparatively rare to see the majority of horses allowed to run in a straight line from start to finish. In some respects horses are different to humans, of course—for one thing, to a extent they need the pace to be judged for them in order to last home. Restraining them too much though, or switching them, brings problems of wasting energy pulling or of giving away ground and also losing momentum.

  The modern style of sprint racing has led to the development of the 'ground bias' theory to try to explain some horses dominating others on straight courses. Is it coincidence, however, that the winners often considered favoured are those which are given their heads soonest or those steered on the straightest course? Much Faster's clear-cut success in the Group 2 Prix Robert Papin at Maisons-Laffitte in late-July is a case in point. After she raced alone up the stand rail, some were inclined to put her performance down to 'ground bias'. With the runners for the preceding sprint handicap having raced on the stand side, most riders shunned the stand rail in the Papin, no doubt believing the ground would be less poached on other parts. Most drawn nearest to the stand side had joined those more towards the centre by halfway. As a result, Much Faster was able to dictate the pace against the rail. She held an advantage over the main group from some way out and drew clear inside the last furlong, beating Colossus by three lengths. The 'ground lobby' then pontificated that the favoured part of the track must be on the stand rail after all!

  Much Faster's victory in the Papin left her unbeaten in four races at around five furlongs. She followed her debut in a newcomers event at Chantilly in May by taking a listed event at Maisons-Laffitte in June, making all both times. Her first success in a pattern race came in the Group 3 Prix du Bois at Deauville in July. Starting at even money in a field of eight, though not dominating this time, she got on top close home to beat Leila by half a length. Much Faster was stepped up to six furlongs for her final two starts. Despite suffering her first defeat, she ran well in the Group 1 Prix Morny at Deauville in August, though, if anything, seeming to be outstayed by Whipper in the soft ground, going down by two lengths after leading two furlongs out. Much Faster's final start of the year came in the Cheveley Park Stakes at Newmarket in early-October. She started second favourite behind Carry On Katie but ran no sort of race, failing to show her customary speed and finishing ninth of ten. It was her first run on ground firmer than good.

  Much Faster, who cost 520,000 francs as a foal, is the first produce of her dam Interruption, who was sold unraced by Juddmonte Farms for 85,000 guineas as a four-year-old in 1999. Interruption is a descendant of the Jock Whitney racing empire, traces of which are to be found in several successful Juddmonte families. Much Faster's grandam Intermission, who won the Cambridgeshire in Whitney's

Prix Robert Papin, Maisons-Laffitte—
Much Faster keeps her unbeaten record, beating the Irish-trained Colossus

Ecurie Jean-Louis Bouchard's "Much Faster"

		Fasliyev (USA) (b 1997)	Nureyev (b 1977)	Northern Dancer Special
Much Faster (IRE) (b.f. Feb 13, 2001)			Mr P'S Princess (b 1993)	Mr Prospector Anne Campbell
		Interruption (ch 1995)	Zafonic (b 1990)	Gone West Zaizafon
			Intermission (ch 1973)	Stage Door Johnny Peace

colours and is a daughter of the fine broodmare Peace, also produced Interval, third in the One Thousand Guineas for Juddmonte behind Miesque in 1987 and grandam of July Cup winner Continent. As a daughter of highly successful first-season sire Fasliyev, also responsible for Carry On Katie amongst others, Much Faster must already be worth a good deal more than was paid for her. Fasliyev was retired through injury after going unbeaten in five races over sprint distances as a two-year-old. The average winning distance of races won by his first crop was under six furlongs and Much Faster is unlikely to stay much beyond that distance, even at three. A strong, good-quartered filly, with the look of a sprinter, British racegoers certainly didn't see the best of her in the Cheveley Park. *P. Bary, France*

MUCHO GUSTO 5 b.g. Casteddu 111 – Heather Honey (Insan (USA) 119) [2003 7m 12m 10m 7.5m f9.4s⁶ 11.5g 11.8g⁵ Aug 10] poor maiden: well held in 2003: tried tongue tied/visored/blinkered. *R. F. Marvin* —

MUCKABELL (IRE) 2 ch.c. (Mar 2) Mukaddamah (USA) 125 – Mystic Belle (IRE) 88 (Thatching 131) [2003 7m a6g² a8g* a8g a8g Dec 14] IR 11,000F, €45,000Y: strong ?

colt: first foal: dam, 7f winner, out of half-sister to dam of smart French/US 6f to 1m performer Chimes Band: tongue tied on debut, when trained by A. Balding: won minor event at Mijas in September: well held after: stays 1m. *E. J. Creighton, Spain*

MUCKY BUSINESS   3 b.g. Lahib (USA) 129 – Berliese (IRE) (High Estate 127)   **59** [2003 68: p10g f11s³ p10g 12.6m May 5] tall gelding: modest maiden: well below form last 2 starts: stays 11f: acts on all-weather: tried visored. *T. G. Mills*

MUDAWIN (IRE)   2 b.g. (Feb 24) Intikhab (USA) 135 – Fida (IRE) (Persian Heights   **73 P** 129) [2003 7d⁵ Nov 7] big, lengthy, good-topped gelding: has plenty of scope: fifth foal: half-brother to useful 6f winner (including at 2 yrs) Maghaarb (by Machiavellian): dam twice-raced close relative of high-class Irish 1m/1¼m winner Kooyonga: 8/1 and very green, 7 lengths fifth of 18 to Divine Gift in maiden at Doncaster, travelling well in rear after slow start and finishing strongly without being at all knocked about: will stay 1m: open to considerable improvement, and sure to win races. *M. P. Tregoning*

MUFFIT (IRE)   4 b.f. Alhaarth (IRE) 126 – Calash (Indian King (USA) 128) [2003   **–** 47: f6g Apr 7] smallish, sturdy filly: poor performer: well beaten only 4-y-o start. *Paul Johnson*

MUFREH (USA)   5 b.g. Dayjur (USA) 137 – Mathkurh (USA) 97 (Riverman (USA)   **–** 131) [2003 67: f6g² f6s² f7g³ f7g* f7g* f8.5s f6g² 6g f6s* f7g² Nov 14] strong, lengthy   **a88** gelding: fairly useful handicapper on all-weather: won at Wolverhampton (2) in March and Southwell in October: effective at 6f/7f: acts on fibresand, lightly raced (and no form) on turf: sometimes slowly away. *A. G. Newcombe*

MUGEBA   2 b.f. (Apr 19) Primo Dominie 121 – Ella Lamees 61 (Statoblest 120) [2003   **60** p6g p6g² Dec 29] second foal: dam, 6f winner, half-sister to smart performer up to 11f Francesco Guardi: better effort in maidens at Lingfield (modest form) when second to Chorus Beauty: not sure to stay much beyond 6f: very slowly away on debut. *W. J. Musson*

MUHAREB (USA)   4 ch.g. Thunder Gulch (USA) 129 – Queen of Spirit (USA)   **106** (Deputy Minister (CAN)) [2003 99: 10m 10.3m⁶ 12m³ 12f 12m³ 13.9m 12f 12m⁴ Oct 16] rather leggy, lengthy gelding: useful handicapper: better than ever in 2003, winning at York (beat Sporting Gesture a length) in May: tongue tied, creditable third to Capitano Corelli at Ascot sixth start: best around 1½m: acts on firm ground, good to soft and all-weather: has run well when sweating: usually races prominently. *C. E. Brittain*

MUHAYMIN (USA)   2 ch.c. (Apr 17) A P Indy (USA) 131 – Shadayid (USA) 122   **89 p** (Shadeed (USA) 135) [2003 7m 7.1g³ 8m* Oct 14] rather leggy, quite attractive colt: half-brother to several winners, including 4-y-o Imtiyaz and useful 1995 2-y-o 6f/7f winner (stayed 1¼m) Bint Shadayid (by Nashwan): dam, won Prix Marcel Boussac and 1000 Guineas, from very good family: easily best effort in maidens when winning 11-runner event at Leicester, getting first run on ½-length second Notable Guest: will probably stay 1¼m: should make a useful 3-y-o. *J. L. Dunlop*

MUJALIA (IRE)   5 b.g. Mujtahid (USA) 118 – Danalia (IRE) 78 (Danehill (USA)   **§§** 126) [2003 11.9m 12m 9f p10g 8m Jul 18] modest performer: soundly beaten all starts in 2003, but refusing to race on reappearance: tried blinkered/tongue tied/in cheekpieces: sometimes slowly away: one to avoid. *P. S. McEntee*

MUJARAD (USA)   3 b.g. King of Kings (IRE) 125 – Happy Result (USA) (Diesis   **85** 133) [2003 81p: 7d 7m* 8m Jun 19] well-made gelding: has a quick action: fairly useful performer: won maiden at Salisbury in June by 3½ lengths from Vandal, making all: ran poorly in Britannia Handicap at Royal Ascot only subsequent outing: should stay 1m: yet to race on extremes of going: visored last 2 starts: sold 28,000 gns, joined S. Mahon in Ireland, and gelded. *J. H. M. Gosden*

MUJKARI (IRE)   7 ch.g. Mujtahid (USA) 118 – Hot Curry (USA) (Sharpen Up 127)   **58** [2003 54§: p8g⁴ p10g p10g⁵ p12g p10g p7g 10.2m⁵ 10.2f 10m⁵ 8m² 7f² 7g⁴ 7.1d* 8.2g⁴ Aug 1] lengthy gelding: modest handicapper: won at Chepstow in July: effective at 7f to 1¼m: acts on firm going, good to soft and all-weather: tried visored, blinkered nowadays: sometimes races moodily. *J. M. Bradley*

MUKAFEH (USA)   2 b.c. (Feb 10) Danzig (USA) – Bint Salsabil (USA) 110 (Nash-   **96 p** wan (USA) 135) [2003 7m* 7d³ Sep 10] angular, well-made colt: fluent mover: has had hocks pin-fired: fourth foal: half-brother to UAE 1m winner Mutawajed (by Gulch) and a winner in USA by Mr Prospector: dam 6f (at 2 yrs, also won Rockfel Stakes) to 1¼m winner, out of Salsabil, a very good family: won maiden at Newbury in August by head from Akimbo: similar form (useful) when 7½ lengths third to Sabbeeh in minor event at Doncaster, not unduly punished once fading: will stay 1m: likely to progress. *J. L. Dunlop*

MUKTASB (USA)   2 b.g. (Apr 24) Bahri (USA) 125 – Maghaarb 104 (Machiavellian **72**
(USA) 123) [2003 6m 6.1d p6g² Nov 18] good-topped gelding: has a quick action: first
foal: dam, 6f winner (including at 2 yrs), out of close relative to high-class filly 1m/
1¼m performer Kooyonga: best effort in maidens (fair form) when 1½ lengths second to
Aesculus at Lingfield: gelded after: should stay 7f, probably 1m. *M. P. Tregoning*

MULABEE (USA)   4 br.g. Gulch (USA) – Shir Dar (FR) (Lead On Time (USA) 123)   **–**
[2003 –: f8s f9.4g f7g p10g 10.2m 7m f7s May 12] useful-looking gelding: fair at 2 yrs
but has shown little since: has worn headgear. *R. Brotherton*

MULAN PRINCESS (IRE)   3 b.f. Mukaddamah (USA) 125 – Notley Park 71 (Wolf- **66 d**
hound (USA) 126) [2003 66: f7g* f7s² f7g³ f7s 7g⁴ 8.1g⁶ 7f 7m 8m Sep 24] leggy filly:
fair performer: won 3-finisher handicap at Southwell in January: left T. J. Naughton after
fifth start: below form after: effective at 7f to 8.5f: acts on fibresand, soft and good to firm
ground: sometimes slowly away. *S. C. Burrough*

MULLER (IRE)   3 gr.g. Bigstone (IRE) 126 – Missie Madam (IRE) (Kenmare (FR)   **–**
125) [2003 –: 9.2d 11.9m Jun 2] no sign of ability. *J. S. Haldane*

MULLION   3 b.g. Reprimand 122 – Royal Jade 82 (Last Tycoon 131) [2003 89: 7m⁶ **86 ?**
6g 7g 8.1g⁵ 8f Jun 14] leggy gelding: good mover: fairly useful performer: stays 1m: acts
on polytrack and good to firm going: visored last 3 starts: none too consistent: sold 2,500
gns. *A. M. Balding*

MULSANNE   5 b.g. Clantime 101 – Prim Lass 65 (Reprimand 122) [2003 –: 6.1m   **–**
8.1m Jul 4] no form. *P. A. Pritchard*

MULTAHAB   4 b. or br.c. Zafonic (USA) 130 – Alumisiyah (USA) 93 (Danzig (USA))   **55**
[2003 p5g² p5g 6g⁵ 5.7f⁵ f5g⁵ Dec 22] 700 3-y-o: first foal: dam, 5f (at 2 yrs)/6f winner,
closely related to useful 1997 2-y-o 5f/6f (Cherry Hinton) winner Asfurah: modest
maiden: left Miss D. McHale and off 9 months before final start: effective at 5f/6f: acts on
all-weather: tried tongue tied. *Miss Gay Kelleway*

MULTAKA (USA)   3 b.f. Gone West (USA) – Wasnah (USA) 96 (Nijinsky (CAN) 138)   **–**
[2003 66p: 8m Apr 26] tall, leggy filly: fair form in 2-y-o maidens: tailed off in handicap
only start in 2003: sold 50,000 gns in December. *J. L. Dunlop*

MULTICOLOUR   3 ch.f. Rainbow Quest (USA) 134 – Raymouna (IRE) (High Top   **58**
131) [2003 64: 9.7g 11.6g⁶ 11.6d 11.6d May 12] angular filly: modest maiden: should
stay 1½m: raced only on good ground or softer on turf: found little last 2 starts. *R. Hannon*

MULTIPLE CHOICE (IRE)   2 ch.c. (Mar 14) Woodborough (USA) 112 – Cosmona   **85**
(Dominion 123) [2003 6g 5g 5f⁴ 5f³ 5.1m⁶ f5g* 6g³ 5m³ 5.1g² 5g 5m f5s⁴ Oct 7] €7,500Y,
17,000 2-y-o: smallish, sturdy colt: third reported foal: dam, won at 9f/1¼m in Ireland at
4 yrs, half-sister to smart sprinter Atall Atall: fairly useful performer: won maiden at
Wolverhampton in July: will prove best at 5f/6f: acts on firm going and fibresand: game
and consistent. *N. P. Littmoden*

MULTISTORE   3 ch.f. Elmaamul (USA) 125 – Superstore (USA) (Blushing Groom   **72 ?**
(FR) 131) [2003 8.1d² 7m³ 6g 8.1m⁴ Sep 8] quite good-topped filly: first foal: half-sister
to French 1m winner Club Card (by Unfuwain) and fairly useful 1¼m winner Voucher
(by Polish Precedent): dam unraced sister to Irish 1000 Guineas winner Al Bahathri: fair
maiden: best efforts first 2 starts: stays 1m: unraced on extremes of going: carries head
awkwardly: has found little: sold 6,500 gns, sent to Bahrain. *R. Charlton*

MUMBLING (IRE)   5 ch.g. Dr Devious (IRE) 127 – Valley Lights (IRE) (Dance of   **82**
Life (USA)) [2003 89: 11.9m 14m 12m* 11.9f 12m² 12g 12m 12m⁶ 11.5g⁶ 11.9f 12m³
14.6m³ p13g Dec 6] strong, lengthy gelding: fairly useful handicapper: won at Thirsk in
June: left M. Tompkins 14,000 gns after twelfth start: effective at 1½m/1¾m: acts on soft
and good to firm going: tried blinkered: effective racing prominently or held up: won over
hurdles in November. *B. G. Powell*

MUNAAFIS (USA)   3 b.c. Storm Cat (USA) – Firdous (Nashwan (USA) 135) [2003   **–**
8g 7m 8.1d Sep 26] has reportedly had wind operation: fourth foal: half-brother to useful
2001 2-y-o 5f winner Izwah (by Bahri): dam, unraced sister/half-sister to 3 smart performers, out of 1000 Guineas, Oaks and Irish Derby winner Salsabil: well held in maidens.
J. L. Dunlop

MUNAAHEJ (IRE)   2 b.c. (Apr 27) Soviet Star (USA) 128 – Azyaa 101 (Kris 135)   **69**
[2003 5.2m 6d⁵ Sep 6] smallish colt: brother to 2 winners, including useful 7f/1m winner
Ihtiraz and half-brother to several winners, including smart 11f to 15f winner Samsaam
(by Sadler's Wells) and 3-y-o Al Ihtithar: dam 7.5f winner from good middle-distance

family: better effort in maidens (fair form) when fifth of 8 at Haydock, hanging left: should stay at least 1m. *B. W. Hills*

MUNAAWASHAT (IRE) 2 b.f. (May 12) Marju (IRE) 127 – Simaat (USA) 72 (Mr **68** Prospector (USA)) [2003 6m² 6g⁶ 6g* Jul 22] close-coupled filly: seventh foal: closely related to winner in Spain by Last Tycoon and half-sister to 3 winners, including useful 7f winner Al Ihsas (by Danehill): dam 1m winner: fair form in maidens: made all at Ayr: should stay 1m: got worked up before disappointing second start. *M. Johnston*

MUNAAWESH (USA) 2 b.c. (Jan 26) Bahri (USA) 125 – Istikbal (USA) (King- **71** mambo (USA) 125) [2003 7.1d 8m⁵ Sep 13] sturdy colt: first foal: dam, ran once, half-sister to smart performer up to 1½m Falak out of sister to Prix du Cadran winner Chief Contender: fair form in maidens at Sandown and Goodwood (front-running fifth): should stay 1¼m. *M. P. Tregoning*

MUNDO RARO 8 b.g. Zafonic (USA) 130 – Star Spectacle (Spectacular Bid (USA)) **–** [2003 45: p16g⁶ Jan 22] robust gelding: poor performer: well held only 8-y-o start: tried blinkered/tongue tied. *R. M. Stronge*

MUNGO DUFF (IRE) 8 b.g. Priolo (USA) 127 – Noble Dust (USA) (Dust Com- **–** mander (USA)) [2003 9m May 1] fair maiden at 4 yrs: tailed off both starts since. *J. Jay*

MUNGO JERRY (GER) 2 b.c. (Feb 10) Tannenkonig (IRE) 111 – Mostly Sure (IRE) **–** (Sure Blade (USA) 130) [2003 7m Oct 24] 3,000Y: fourth foal: half-brother to 3 winners in Germany, including 9f and 11f winner Mr President (by Surako): dam unraced: 40/1 and green, showed little in maiden at Doncaster. *J. G. Given*

MUQARRAR (IRE) 4 ch.c. Alhaarth (IRE) 126 – Narjis (USA) 87 (Blushing Groom **63 ?** (FR) 131) [2003 7.5m 8.1m⁶ 8m⁵ 7m 7.5m 8m f7g⁶ Nov 21] 5,500 3-y-o: workmanlike colt: closely related to 3 winners by Unfuwain, including useful 1994 2-y-o 7f/1m (May Hill) winner Mamlakah and 1996 2-y-o 7f (Chesham Stakes) winner Shamikh, and half-brother to 2 winners: dam 2-y-o 5f winner: seemingly modest maiden: should stay 1¼m: raced only on good to firm ground. *T. J. Fitzgerald*

MUQBIL (USA) 3 ch.c. Swain (IRE) 134 – Istiqlal (USA) (Diesis 133) [2003 106P: **118** 7m* 8g 9.9m² 8m³ 9m⁴ Oct 18] lengthy, quite attractive colt: good walker/mover: smart performer: won Lane's End Greenham Stakes at Newbury in April by 1¼ lengths from Zafeen: off over 4 months, unlucky neck second to Leporello in Select Stakes at Goodwood third start, persistently short of room: not at best in 3 starts at Newmarket otherwise in 2003, including in 2000 Guineas in May and Darley Stakes (drifted right, fourth to Far Lane) in October: stays 1¼m: raced only on ground firmer than good: also hung right at Newmarket final 2-y-o outing. *J. L. Dunlop*

MUQTADI (IRE) 5 b.g. Marju (IRE) 127 – Kadwah (USA) 80 (Mr Prospector (USA)) **59 §** [2003 –: f6g⁶ f6g p6g* p6g p6g⁵ p5g³ p6g 5g 5.3f 5m 5m 6m 6.1m⁴ 6m 5.3m⁶ 6m 6m⁴ 5m 6f⁶ 6g 6.1m² 6f⁴ 5.1m 7g³ 7m 6f 6m 8f 7f² 8m* 8.1g⁴ 8.1m⁶ 8m⁵ 8.3m Sep 29] modest performer: won handicap at Lingfield in January and seller at Thirsk in September: effective at 5f to 1m: acts on firm ground and polytrack, probably on fibresand: usually blinkered: usually slowly away (sometimes markedly so), and held up: unreliable: sold 4,200 gns. *C. R. Dore*

MURAQEB 3 ch.g. Grand Lodge (USA) 125 – Oh So Well (IRE) (Sadler's Wells (USA) **61** 132) [2003 10.4m⁵ 12g⁵ Sep 22] 200,000Y: sturdy gelding: sixth foal: closely related to 1996 2-y-o 6f winner Dances With Dreams and a winner at 1m/8.5f in Scandinavia (both by Be My Chief), and half-brother to very smart 7f (at 2 yrs) to 12.5f winner (including in France/US) Dark Moondancer (by Anshan): dam unraced out of high-class sprinter Soba: well held in maidens: visored/blinkered: sold 7,000 gns. *J. H. M. Gosden*

MURASHAH (USA) 3 ch.c. Storm Cat (USA) – Shadayid (USA) 122 (Shadeed **82 p** (USA) 135) [2003 8.2m* Sep 19] compact colt: half-brother to several winners, including 4-y-o Imtiyaz and useful 1995 2-y-o 6f/7f winner (stayed 1¼m) Bint Shadayid (by Nashwan): dam, won Prix Marcel Boussac and 1000 Guineas, from very good family: 11/8 favourite and tongue tied, made all in maiden at Nottingham in September by 1½ lengths from Count Walewski, giving flash of tail under pressure: wore crossed noseband: should improve. *Saeed bin Suroor*

MURDINGA 4 br.g. Emperor Jones (USA) 119 – Tintinara (Selkirk (USA) 129) [2003 **60** 73: 10s⁴ Jun 30] tall gelding: lightly-raced maiden: just modest form only 4-y-o start: stays 1¼m: acts on good to firm going: sold 11,500 gns. *Lady Herries*

MURTAKEZ 3 b.g. Alhaarth (IRE) 126 – Raaqiyya (USA) (Blushing Groom (FR) **–** 131) [2003 58: p8g 7m 9.9m Aug 13] good-topped gelding: modest maiden at 2 yrs: well beaten in 2003. *S. Dow*

MURZIM   4 b.g. Salse (USA) 128 – Guilty Secret (IRE) 109 (Kris 135) [2003 83: p16g   **83 d**
14.4d* 15m⁴ 14f 14.4g⁵ 16.1d 13.3m 14.6m⁶ 12.6f³ 12.1g Aug 7] angular gelding: fairly
useful handicapper: won at Kempton in March: below form last 5 starts: stays 2m: acts
on polytrack, soft and good to firm going: tried in headgear: usually races prominently.
J. Gallagher

MUSAAYER (USA)   2 br.g. (Apr 26) Erhaab (USA) 127 – Hachiyah (IRE) 91 (Gene-   **72**
rous (IRE) 139) [2003 6m² 7m⁶ 8m 8m Sep 16] small, close-coupled gelding: third foal:
half-brother to 3-y-o Nasij: dam, 1¼m winner, closely related to useful performer up to
1½m Mutawwaj and half-sister to useful performer up to 1m Hiwaya: fair maiden: second
at Leicester: well below form, finding little in visor, in nursery final start: should stay at
least 1m: sold 5,500 gns. *E. A. L. Dunlop*

MUSANID (USA)   3 ch.c. Swain (IRE) 134 – Siyadah (USA) 106 (Mr Prospector   **100**
(USA)) [2003 100: 9d* May 18] good-bodied colt: has a fluent, round action: useful form
in maidens: easily landed odds at Ripon in May: should be suited by 1¼m+: acts on firm
and good to soft ground. *Sir Michael Stoute*

MUSAWAH (USA)   3 b.f. Gulch (USA) – Haniya (IRE) 92 (Caerleon (USA) 132)   **77**
[2003 63p: 7m² 8.1m⁵ 7m 7m³ 8f² 7m* Aug 18] fair performer: won maiden at Brighton
in August: bred to stay further than 1m, but races freely: raced only on ground firmer than
good: carries head awkwardly: sold 48,000 gns in December. *J. L. Dunlop*

MUSCIDA (USA)   2 b.f. (Feb 3) Woodman (USA) 126 – Space Time (FR) (Bering   **89 p**
136) [2003 7m³ 8.2f* Sep 30] 18,000Y: smallish, good-topped filly: first foal: dam, third
over 7f at 2 yrs in France, granddaughter of high-class French 6f/7f performer Proskona:
better effort in maidens when winning 10-runner event at Nottingham by 3 lengths from
Cause Celebre, leading over 1f out: should stay 1¼m: useful prospect. *H. R. A. Cecil*

Mr Hamdan Al Maktoum's "Muqbil"

MUSH (IRE) 6 b.g. Thatching 131 – Petite Jameel (IRE) (Ahonoora 122) [2003 80, **67 d**
a66: p7g² f8.5g³ p8g* p7g² p7g⁴ p8g 8m 8.5m 8d 8.2m 8m Sep 12] quite good-topped
gelding: fair handicapper: won at Lingfield in February: well below form last 6 starts,
pulled up on final one: effective at 7f to 8.5f: acts on firm going, good to soft and all-
weather: sometimes carries head awkwardly. *N. P. Littmoden*

MUSICAL CHIMES (USA) 3 b.f. In Excess 116 – Note Musicale (Sadler's **117**
Wells (USA) 132) [2003 8g⁴ 8d* 8g* 10.5g³ 8d 10f² 10f 8f² Nov 30]
Johnny Murtagh's feat of riding the winners of three consecutive Group 1
races on the same card at Longchamp was emulated by Christophe Soumillon on
French Guineas day in May. Murtagh's treble came at the Arc meeting in 2000, his
victory on Sinndar in the main event sandwiched between those on Namid in the
Prix de l'Abbaye and Petrushka in the Prix de l'Opera. Soumillon, who had also
won the opening race on the card, was successful in the Prix Lupin, the Poule
d'Essai des Poulains and the Poule d'Essai des Pouliches, on Dalakhani, Clodovil
and Musical Chimes respectively. The last two named were both trained by Andre
Fabre, and it was the first time the Poulains/Pouliches double had been achieved by
either a trainer or jockey since 1993, when Francois Boutin and Cash Asmussen
were associated with Kingmambo and Madeleine's Dream. At that time the two
races were run a week apart, but Soumillon was getting the leg up on Musical
Chimes within half an hour of dismounting from Clodovil, his chance seemingly
much less obvious. Whereas Clodovil had started favourite, Musical Chimes was a
12/1-shot, with four of her eleven rivals ahead of her in the betting.
The Gainsborough Poule d'Essai des Pouliches was nothing like so strongly
contested as it might have been, with the connections of both Six Perfections and
Intercontinental opting instead to go for the One Thousand Guineas at Newmarket.
Only one of the field had been successful at pattern level, Maiden Tower having
won the Prix de La Grotte over the same course and distance on her previous start.
She started second favourite, with Etoile Montante, a very good second to Six
Perfections in the Prix Marcel Boussac on her final two-year-old start, going off
favourite. Musical Chimes, who had finished behind three of her opponents when a
promising fourth in a listed event won by Maiden Tower at Saint-Cloud on her
reappearance, hadn't needed to run up to that form to get off the mark, at the
fifth attempt (she'd been demoted after passing the post first in a minor event at
Maisons-Laffitte as a two-year-old), in a minor event run over a mile at Longchamp
next time, which left her still with plenty to find if she was to win the Pouliches. As
in the One Thousand Guineas at Newmarket there was some trouble in running,
with Acago the worst sufferer. Musical Chimes, who had been held up in rear,
looked likely to meet it as Soumillon searched for a way through a wall of horses
over two furlongs out, but she managed to obtain a clear passage after being
switched. Even so, Musical Chimes's prospects didn't look bright, with the front-
running Maiden Tower having gone around two lengths clear, but she stayed on so
strongly that she not only caught the leader well inside the final furlong but had also

Gainsborough Poule d'Essai des Pouliches, Longchamp—
Musical Chimes completes a Group 1 treble on the day for jockey Christophe Soumillon;
Maiden Tower (rail) is second with Etoile Montante and the blinkered Welcome Millenium next

put a length between them by the time the line was reached. Etoile Montante finished a short head further back in third in a race dominated by the home-trained runners, eighth-placed Anyaas the first of the four overseas challengers to finish. Musical Chimes finished her race in a manner which suggested that a mile and a quarter would be within her compass, and three of her four subsequent races were over that distance. She ran respectably enough when third to Nebraska Tornado in the Prix de Diane at Chantilly next time and, following a disappointing effort in the Prix d'Astarte, reproduced her Pouliches form when three quarters of a length second to Tates Creek in the Yellow Ribbon Stakes at Santa Anita two outings later, set a bit to do and taking time to get going before finishing best. Musical Chimes was transferred to Neil Drysdale, and ran easily the better race for her new trainer when beaten a neck by Heat Haze in the Matriarch Stakes at Hollywood on her final outing, leading inside the final furlong, but unable to hold off the winner. Her previous outing had ended in disappointment, tried in blinkers for the only time, in the Breeders' Cup Filly & Mare Turf at Santa Anita, pulling too hard and already weakening when badly hampered on the home turn.

Musical Chimes (USA) (b.f. 2000)	In Excess (b 1987)	Siberian Express (gr 1981)	Caro
			Indian Call
		Kantado (b 1976)	Saulingo
			Vi
	Note Musicale (b 1995)	Sadler's Wells (b 1981)	Northern Dancer
			Fairy Bridge
		It's In The Air (b 1976)	Mr Prospector
			A Wind Is Rising

Musical Chimes, having won back her owner's money in the Pouliches, a race sponsored by Maktoum Al Maktoum's Gainsborough Stud operation, should prove her worth for him as a broodmare when the time comes. As a classic winner

Maktoum Al Maktoum's "Musical Chimes"

from a very good family, she could hardly have much better credentials. Musical Chimes is the first foal of the unraced Note Musicale, who is closely related to the dam of the high-class winner at a mile and a quarter and a half Storming Home, and a daughter of It's In The Air, who was champion two-year-old filly in the United States and winner of sixteen races in all from six furlongs to a mile and a quarter, including five Grade 1s. It's In The Air, whose numerous winning produce include the smart seven-furlong winner Bitooh, is a half-sister to Morning Has Broken, herself the grandam of the Oaks and Irish Derby winner Balanchine and Derby third Romanov. In Excess, the sire of Musical Chimes, showed useful form in Britain before developing into a high-class performer in the States as a four-year-old, winning four Grade 1s at a mile to a mile and a quarter. His best produce is Indian Charlie, winner of the Santa Anita Derby and third in the Kentucky Derby. Musical Chimes, effective from a mile to a mile and a quarter, acts on firm and good to soft going. *N. D. Drysdale, USA*

MUSICAL FAIR 3 b.f. Piccolo 121 – Guarded Expression 51 (Siberian Express 81 (USA) 125) [2003 –: 6g⁶ 6f³ 6g 6.1m* 5.9m³ 5m* 6m² 5f* 6g² 5m 5g* 5m³ 6.1g⁴ 5m Sep 17] sturdy, close-coupled filly: fairly useful handicapper: improved throughout 2003, winning at Warwick in June, Redcar and Catterick in July and Windsor in August: very best form at 5f: acts on firm ground: usually waited with: reliable. *J. A. Glover*

MUSICAL GIFT 3 ch.c. Cadeaux Genereux 131 – Kazoo 108 (Shareef Dancer (USA) 67 135) [2003 p8g² f9.4g² p10g⁴ p12g Nov 12] 52,000F, 120,000Y: fifth living foal: dam, won German 1000 Guineas, from good German family: fair maiden: left D. Loder 23,000 gns after third start: stays 1¼m: raced only on all-weather: races prominently. *C. N. Allen*

MUSICAL HEATH (IRE) 6 b.g. Common Grounds 118 – Song of The Glens 47 (Horage 124) [2003 87d: f7s f8.5g³ 8.3g Apr 7] lengthy, angular gelding: fairly useful handicapper at best: only poor form in 2003: tried tongue tied: usually races prominently. *T. D. Barron*

MUSICAL KEY 3 b.f. Key of Luck (USA) 126 – Musianica 92 (Music Boy 124) [2003 – 71: 5f f6g 6f May 30] close-coupled filly: fair maiden at 2 yrs: well held in handicaps in 2003. *J. G. Given*

MUSICAL LYRICS (USA) 2 b.f. (Mar 27) Quiet American (USA) – Foreign Courier 67 (USA) (Sir Ivor 135) [2003 5f⁴ 6m 6f³ 7m Oct 7] small, sturdy filly: half-sister to several winners, notably high-class sprinter/miler Green Desert (by Danzig) and useful French 1m (at 2 yrs) and 1½m winner Latarmiss (by Sadler's Wells): dam unraced half-sister to top-class US filly Althea: fair maiden: form only when third of 6 at Redcar: should stay 7f. *M. Johnston*

MUSICAL SLEUTH 4 ch.g. Piccolo 121 – My Dear Watson (Chilibang 120) [2003 51 66: f6g 7m 5m 6m⁶ 7d 8m 6.1m Jul 12] workmanlike gelding: modest maiden: stays 7f: acts on soft and good to firm ground: tried blinkered: races freely: none too consistent. *G. C. Bravery*

MUSICAL STAGE (USA) 4 b.g. Theatrical 128 – Changed Tune (USA) (Tunerup – (USA)) [2003 87: 16g Oct 31] $475,000Y: tall, angular ex-Irish gelding: third foal: half-brother to winner in USA by Kris S: dam minor US stakes winner at 6.5f/8.5f: fairly useful performer for D. Weld in 2002, winning a maiden: travelled strongly long way when ninth in handicap at Newmarket only outing in 2003: stays 1½m: acts on soft ground. *P. R. Webber*

MUSIC MAID (IRE) 5 b.m. Inzar (USA) 112 – Richardstown Lass (IRE) (Muscatite 70 122) [2003 58: 8.5m 7m 7g* 7.1m⁵ 7.1g⁴ 7m² 7m⁶ 8g* 8.3m⁴ 7.1d⁵ 8m* 7f* 7m⁵ Sep 16] angular mare: fair handicapper: won at Lingfield in May and at Salisbury in July (apprentices), August and September: effective at 7f to 8.5f: acts on firm going: often slowly away: sometimes races freely/swishes tail/wanders: consistent. *H. S. Howe*

MUSIC MIX (IRE) 2 b.c. (Apr 6) Linamix (FR) 127 – Baldemara (FR) (Sanglamore 64 (USA) 126) [2003 p8g⁴ f7g⁶ f8g⁶ Dec 19] third foal: half-brother to 4-y-o Baldour: dam unraced half-sister to very smart French filly up to 1m Balbonella, herself dam of top-class sprinter Anabaa, high-class 1¼m performer Key of Luck and Poule d'Essai des Pouliches winner Always Loyal: modest form in maidens: not knocked about last 2 starts: should be suited by 1¼m+. *E. A. L. Dunlop*

MUSIOTAL 2 ch.c. (Feb 21) Pivotal 124 – Bemuse 89 (Forzando 122) [2003 6m⁵ 6m – Sep 18] 20,000F, 23,000Y: lengthy, useful-looking colt: second foal: brother to 3-y-o Turn Around: dam, 2-y-o 5f winner (only season to race), half-sister to useful 1996 2-y-o Falkenham: burly, signs of only a little ability in maidens. *J. S. Goldie*

MUSKATSTURM (GER)   4 b.g. Lecroix (GER) 112 – Myrthe (GER) (Konigsstuhl   –
(GER)) [2003 14.1g 12g 16.5d Nov 8] tall, leggy ex-German gelding: third foal: half-
brother to 2 winners in Germany by Dashing Blade: dam 2-y-o 7f winner in Germany:
useful form when successful 4 times for M. Hofer, including in listed race at Hamburg
and Slovak Derby at Bratislava in 2002: fourth in listed event at Nantes final 3-y-o outing:
soundly beaten back on Flat in Britain: stays 1½m: acts on heavy and good to firm going:
usually blinkered. *B. J. Curley*

MUSTAJED   2 b.c. (Apr 25) Alhaarth (IRE) 126 – Jasarah (IRE) 70 (Green Desert   **87**
(USA) 127) [2003 5.2m* May 28] sturdy colt: seventh foal: brother to useful 6f (at 2 yrs)
and 7f (Nell Gwyn) winner Misterah and half-brother to 2 winners, including useful 1998
2-y-o 6f winner Muqtarb (by Cadeaux Genereux): dam, second at 7f, from good middle-
distance family: favourite, won maiden at Newbury comfortably by 1¾ lengths from
Molly Moon: suffered fractured near-hind pastern after: should stay 1m. *M. P. Tregoning*

MUSTANEER (USA)   3 b.c. Gone West (USA) – Market Booster (USA) 117 (Green   **107**
Dancer (USA) 132) [2003 80p: 7m³ 8g⁴ Jul 12] strong, lengthy colt: useful performer,
lightly raced: best effort when 3 lengths third of 5 to Trade Fair in listed event at New-
market in May, finishing well: favourite, only fourth of 5 to Sea Dart in International
Stakes at the Curragh: should stay 1m: acts on soft and good to firm ground. *Sir Michael
Stoute*

MUSTANG ALI (IRE)   2 ch.g. (Apr 28) Ali-Royal (IRE) 127 – Classic Queen (IRE)   **67**
(Classic Secret (USA) 91) [2003 6g⁶ f6s⁵ 7m² 7f² 8m 7m p7g³ Nov 18] €10,500Y: workmanlike gelding: fourth foal: half-brother to 2m winner Blue Hawk (by Prince of Birds):
dam well beaten at 2 yrs in Ireland: fair maiden: should stay 1m: acts on polytrack and
firm going, showed little on fibresand: sometimes soon off bridle. *S. Kirk*

MUSTAWA (USA)   4 b.g. Wild Again (USA) – Tatwij (USA) 94 (Topsider (USA))   –
[2003 –: 8g⁵ 9m⁵ 12f⁶ p10g 7g 10m 10.1m⁶ Sep 17] sturdy, useful-looking gelding: little
form: tried blinkered/in cheekpieces. *Miss D. Mountain*

MUST BE MAGIC   6 b.g. Magic Ring (IRE) 115 – Sequin Lady (Star Appeal 133)   **74**
[2003 64: p10g² p10g² p10g* p10g 8m² 8g p8g⁴ 8m³ 9g* 8d² 9m Aug 30] smallish, good-   **a69**
topped gelding: fair handicapper: won at Lingfield in February and Kempton in July:
effective at 1m/easy 1¼m: acts on soft going, good to firm and polytrack: visored: usually
waited with. *H. J. Collingridge*

MUST BE SO   2 b.f. (Apr 19) So Factual (USA) 120 – Ovideo 58 (Domynsky 110)   **52**
[2003 6m 6m⁴ 6m 5.1d p8g³ p6g* Dec 20] close-coupled filly: sister to 5-y-o Aintnecessarilyso and half-sister to 7-y-o Cool Temper and 6-y-o Crosby Donjohn: dam,
2-y-o 7f winner, half-sister to smart middle-distance performer Captain Horatius: modest
performer: won seller at Lingfield (sold 4,800 gns after): stays 1m: acts on polytrack and
good to firm ground. *D. R. C. Elsworth*

MUTABARI (USA)   9 ch.g. Seeking The Gold (USA) – Cagey Exuberance (USA)   **55 d**
(Exuberant (USA)) [2003 55: f7g* p7g f7g⁶ 7g 7m⁵ f7g⁵ 8f f8.5s f9.4g f8.5f Jul 25] rangy
gelding: modest performer: won handicap at Wolverhampton in March: below form after:
best at 7f to 9f: acts on fibresand and any turf going: sometimes visored earlier in career:
sometimes slowly away: none too consistent. *J. L. Spearing*

MUTABASSIR (IRE)   9 ch.g. Soviet Star (USA) 128 – Anghaam (USA) 80 (Diesis   **63**
133) [2003 63: p7g⁵ f7g⁶ p6g⁶ p7g p6g 7m² 7g⁴ 7m 7m² 8.5m⁶ 7m 6f* 6m Sep 18] modest
performer: won selling handicap at Brighton (goes well there) in August: effective at 6f
to easy 1m: acts on all-weather, best turf form on good going or firmer: sometimes slowly
away. *Andrew Reid*

MUTAFANEN   2 gr.c. (Apr 7) Linamix (FR) 127 – Doomna (IRE) 97 (Machiavellian   **85**
(USA) 123) [2003 7m 7m⁴ 8.1g³ 8m³ 8d* Oct 14] quite good-topped colt: first foal: dam,
lightly-raced 7f winner, sister to very smart 6f/7f performer Kahal: fairly useful performer: won nursery at Ayr by neck from Red Damson, racing prominently: should stay
1¼m: acts on good to firm and good to soft ground: game. *E. A. L. Dunlop*

MUTAHAYYA (IRE)   2 b.c. (Mar 15) Peintre Celebre (USA) 137 – Winsa (USA) 80   **109**
(Riverman (USA) 131) [2003 7f* 7m⁴ 7.1m² 7.6g* 8m² Sep 12] good-topped colt: second
foal: half-brother to 3-y-o Majhud: dam, 1½m winner, sister to high-class miler Bahri and
half-sister to very smart 1996 2-y-o 7f winner Bahhare: useful performer: won maiden at
Salisbury (reportedly finished lame) in June and minor event at Chester (made all) in
August: very good ¾-length second of 8 to Fantastic View in listed race at Goodwood
final start, disputing lead and keeping on, though not striding out well towards finish:
should be well suited by 1¼m/1½m. *J. L. Dunlop*

MUTAJJEB (IRE) 3 b.c. Darshaan 133 – Nightlark (IRE) 85 (Night Shift (USA)) **95 ?**
[2003 67?: 10m* 11g⁴ 16.2f 12g⁵ Aug 2] good-topped, quite attractive colt: fairly useful
performer: won maiden at Leicester in April: best effort when ninth to Shanty Star in
Queen's Vase at Royal Ascot third start: may prove ideally suited by 1½m/1¾m: acts on
firm ground, well held on soft: sold 30,000 gns. *E. A. L. Dunlop*

MUTAMARED (USA) 3 ch.c. Nureyev (USA) 131 – Alydariel (USA) (Alydar **84 ?**
(USA)) [2003 a8f² 7m² 7m⁶ Oct 21] 500,000Y: brother to 3 winners, including smart
French 1m/1¼m winner Jeune Homme and smart French 1¼m winner Dancing Beggar,
closely related to 1991 2-y-o 6f winner Phyliel (by Lyphard), and half-brother to winner
in US by Manila: dam, minor stakes winner around 1m in US, half-sister to Royal
Academy: fair maiden: best effort when second to Parhelion at Nad Al Sheba in February:
odds on at Lingfield next time, found little at Yarmouth final start: stays 1m: tongue tied
last 2 starts: left Godolphin. *Saeed bin Suroor*

MUTARAFAA (USA) 4 b.g. Red Ransom (USA) – Mashaarif (USA) (Mr Prospector **64**
(USA)) [2003 74: f7g f6g⁶ f7s⁶ f7s³ f7g f6g p7g p8g⁶ f8.5g f8g² f8g² f8g* f8.5g*
Dec 26] strong gelding: modest handicapper: won at Southwell and Wolverhampton in
December: effective at 7f to 8.5f: acts on all-weather and good to firm going: visored first
8 starts in 2003. *D. Shaw*

MUTARED (IRE) 5 b.g. Marju (IRE) 127 – Shahaada (USA) 57 (Private Account **83 d**
(USA)) [2003 80, a84: f7s³ f7s⁵ p8g 9f³ 8m 7g 7.9m 10.9m 8d f6g Dec 26] lengthy
gelding: fairly useful handicapper on all-weather, fair on turf: well below form last 6
starts: effective at 6f to 9f: acts on firm ground, soft and fibresand: tried in headgear: often
owner ridden: usually soon off bridle: none too reliable. *N. P. Littmoden*

MUTASAWWAR 9 ch.g. Clantime 101 – Keen Melody (USA) 60 (Sharpen Up 127) **63**
[2003 64: 5g⁴ f5g 5.3f² 5m* 5m² f5g 5.1s² 5s⁵ 5.3m 5m* 5m 5m⁵ 5m 5d 5.3f 6m⁵ 5d⁴ 5f
5.1g Sep 11] lengthy gelding: modest handicapper: won at Ripon (apprentices) in April
and Warwick in June: effective at 5f: acts on any turf going/all-weather: has won in
blinkers, not tried since 1999: often races prominently. *J. M. Bradley*

MUTASSEM (FR) 2 b.c. (Feb 5) Fasliyev (USA) 120 – Fee Eria (FR) (Always Fair **73 p**
(USA) 121) [2003 7m⁶ Oct 24] 82,000F, 150,000Y: workmanlike colt: first foal: dam, ran
twice in France, half-sister to very smart US Grade 1 9f/1½m winner Super Quercus: 16/1
and green, 5 lengths sixth of 16 to Alekhine in maiden at Doncaster, wandering under
pressure: will probably stay 1m: should improve. *E. A. L. Dunlop*

MUTAWAFFER 2 b.c. (Feb 17) Marju (IRE) 127 – Absaar (USA) 76 (Alleged (USA) **102**
138) [2003 6g* 7m⁵ 7.6d* 7g Oct 24] strong, well-made colt: fifth living foal: brother to
2 winners, including smart 6f (including at 2 yrs) winner Munjiz and half-brother to
useful 7f (at 2 yrs) to 9.5f (in UAE) winner Khalas (by Wolfhound): dam, 11f winner,
half-sister to Grand Prix de Paris and Melbourne Cup winner At Talaq: useful performer:
won newcomers race at Ascot (by neck from Brunel) in July and minor event at Chester
(made all to beat Sew'n'so Character by length in 3-runner race) in September: only
eighth in Horris Hill Stakes at Newbury: will stay at least 1m: acts on good to soft going.
B. W. Hills

MUTAWAQED (IRE) 5 ch.g. Zafonic (USA) 130 – Waqood (USA) 75 (Riverman **95**
(USA) 131) [2003 86, a90: p6g* p7g⁶ 6g 6m² 6m³ 6g* 6g 6m³ 6m⁶ 6f³ 6g Oct 25]
heavy-bodied gelding: useful handicapper: won at Lingfield in January and Newcastle
(beat Smart Predator by 3 lengths) in June: good efforts next 4 outings: best at 6f: acts on
all-weather, best efforts on turf on good going or firmer: tried visored/blinkered: often
tongue tied: has been bandaged all round: sometimes slowly away: tends to idle, and best
held up. *M. A. Magnusson*

MUTAWASSEL (USA) 2 b.c. (Jan 24) Kingmambo (USA) 125 – Danzig Darling **97 p**
(CAN) (Danzig (USA)) [2003 7m 8d* Sep 10] 120,000Y: good-topped, quite attractive
colt: has a round action: closely related/half-brother to numerous winners in USA,
including minor stakes winners by Time For A Change and Miswaki: dam won 6f minor
stakes in USA: promising debut, then useful form when winning 17-runner maiden at
Doncaster by short head from Destination Dubai, leading final 1f despite flashing tail: not
sure to stay much beyond 1m: open to progress. *B. W. Hills*

MUTAYAM 3 b.g. Compton Place 125 – Final Shot 91 (Dalsaan 125) [2003 –: 5m⁴ 5d⁶ **42**
5g 5f⁵ 5m² 5f 5g 5f 5g Oct 13] poor maiden on balance: probably best at 5f: acts on firm
ground: tried tongue tied: usually races prominently: none too consistent. *D. A. Nolan*

MUWAJAHA 3 b.f. Night Shift (USA) – Maraatib (IRE) 93 (Green Desert (USA) 127) **73**
[2003 87p: 6m* Apr 8] small, close-coupled filly: fairly useful form: landed odds in

maiden at Pontefract in April only by short head from Medusa, taking good hold: looked likely to prove best at 5f/6f: visits King's Best. *B. W. Hills*

MUYASSIR (IRE)   8 b.g. Brief Truce (USA) 126 – Twine (Thatching 131) [2003 84, a73: p8g⁵ p10g⁶ 8g 8m² 9m⁵ 8.5m 9g 8f³ 8f 8m 8m* 8f p10g Dec 29] deep-bodied gelding: fair handicapper: won at Goodwood in September: effective at 1m/1¼m: acts on firm going and polytrack: tried blinkered/in cheekpieces/tongue tied: none too reliable. *Miss B. Sanders*   **76 a66**

MUY BIEN   2 ch.c. (Apr 20) Daggers Drawn (USA) 114 – Primula Bairn 77 (Bairn (USA) 126) [2003 p5g⁴ 5.2m⁵ f5g² f5g* f5s⁵ 6m 5.1d f6g* p6g⁵ f7g² Dec 8] tall, useful-looking colt: third foal: dam 5f winner: fair performer: won maiden at Wolverhampton (flashed tail/hung left) in May and claimer at Southwell in November: second in nursery on latter course final outing: barely stays 7f: acts on all-weather and good to firm ground: visored last 3 starts. *J. R. Jenkins*   **67 a78**

MY AMERICAN BEAUTY   5 ch.m. Wolfhound (USA) 126 – Hooray Lady 92 (Ahonoora 122) [2003 92: 5f 5m³ 6d 6m 6m 5f* 5g* 5f 6g 5m 5g 5m³ 5.6d 5f⁶ 5g⁴ 5m Oct 16] big, lengthy mare: fairly useful handicapper: won at Hamilton in June and Sandown (beat Colonel Cotton by ¾ length) in July: races mainly at 5f: acts on firm going, below form on softer than good: has been slowly away/reared leaving stall: edgy sort: often races prominently: wore eyeshields last 11 starts: sold 36,000 gns. *T. D. Easterby*   **93**

MYANNABANANA (IRE)   2 ch.c. (Apr 25) Woodborough (USA) 112 – Raging Storm (Horage 124) [2003 7m 6m⁶ 7m 7m f8s⁶ f8s⁶ 8.2m f8.5g* f8g* f8s³ f8s⁵ Dec 27] €2,000Y: quite good-topped colt: half-brother to several winners, including fairly useful 7f (at 2 yrs in Ireland) and 8.5f (in Germany) winner Clewbay Pearl (by Posen): dam Irish 2-y-o 8.5f winner: fair on all-weather, poor on turf: won claimers at Wolverhampton (for P. Howling) and Southwell (for Gay Kelleway) in November: should stay 1¼m: acts on fibresand: visored last 3 outings. *J. R. Weymes*   **44 a66**

MY BAYARD   4 ch.g. Efisio 120 – Bay Bay 101 (Bay Express 132) [2003 61: f8s⁴ f11s² f9.4g² f8.5g² f8.5g² f8s² f8.5s* f8g² f8g²⁷ 7m f8g² 8m Jul 6] fair performer on all-weather, modest on turf: won maiden at Wolverhampton in February: runner-up 8 other times in 2003: effective at 1m to 11f: raced only on fibresand and good to firm ground: tongue tied (below form) once in 2002: tough. *J. O'Reilly*   **63 a76**

MY BROTHER   9 b.g. Lugana Beach 116 – Lucky Love 65 (Mummy's Pet 125) [2003 61§: 6m 5f 6m 6m⁴ 6m 5g 5d⁶ 5.1g 6m 8m Sep 24] poor handicapper: best form at 5f/6f: acts on good to soft ground: usually wears headgear: sometimes starts slowly: untrustworthy. *Dr J. R. J. Naylor*   **48 §**

MY CHICKAWICKA   2 b.f. (Apr 14) Chickawicka (IRE) 97 – Jimlil 99 (Nicholas Bill 125) [2003 7g 6m Oct 3] £700Y: fifth foal: half-sister to 1m seller winner Lilanita (by Anita's Prince) and 6-y-o Lilardo: dam 6f (at 2 yrs) and 1m winner: soundly beaten in maiden at Folkestone and claimer at Lingfield. *S. Kirk*   **–**

MY DAISYCHAIN   3 ch.f. Hector Protector (USA) 124 – Dayville (USA) 86 (Dayjur (USA) 137) [2003 73?: 8g 6f⁶ 6.9f 9.9d* 11.9m⁵ 12m⁵ 9.9m² 12.1m* 9.9m² 12.1g³ 10.5d⁴ Sep 27] lengthy filly: fair handicapper: won at Beverley in July and Hamilton (apprentice race) in August: should stay 1¾m: acts on good to firm and good to soft ground: looked reluctant in blinkers third outing. *M. Johnston*   **79**

MY FAS (USA)   3 b. or br.g. King of Kings (IRE) 125 – Granny Kelly (IRE) 60 (Irish River (FR) 131) [2003 79: 8.5m⁴ 7g⁴ 7m Jul 19] rather leggy, useful-looking gelding: has a quick, fluent action: fair maiden: stays 8.5f: raced only on good going or firmer: tried visored/in cheekpieces. *M. A. Jarvis*   **66**

MY GALLIANO (IRE)   7 b.g. Muharib (USA) 97 – Hogan Stand (Buckskin (FR) 133) [2003 p10g² p12g² p12g² p10g⁶ 10m⁶ 10m 10.1m² 10.1m* 10.1m⁶ Aug 25] fair handicapper: won apprentice event at Epsom in July: effective at 1¼m/1½m: raced only on polytrack/good to firm going: tends to pull hard: often races prominently. *B. G. Powell*   **78**

MY GIRL GEORGIE   2 b.f. (Mar 11) Bin Ajwaad (IRE) 119 – At My Command (IRE) 60 (Barathea (IRE) 127) [2003 5m⁶ 5m 6f Jun 13] leggy, close-coupled filly: first foal: dam maiden who stayed 1m: poor form in claimers/seller: bred to stay 1m: withdrawn last 2 intended outings (broke loose at start on first occasion, reared over at start and jockey refused to take ride second). *M. W. Easterby*   **41**

MY GIRL PEARL (IRE)   3 b.f. Sri Pekan (USA) 117 – Desert Bloom (FR) (Last Tycoon 131) [2003 65: 6.1g⁴ f6g 6m³ 6.1d 7.1g 6.1m 7d⁴ 8.3g f7g Nov 21] angular filly: modest maiden: left J. M. Bradley after eighth start: stays 7f: acts on firm and good to soft ground: tried blinkered: none too consistent. *M. S. Saunders*   **55**

MY HOPE (IRE)   2 b.f. (Apr 10) Danehill (USA) 126 – Lady Elgar (IRE) (Sadler's   **69 p**
Wells (USA) 132) [2003 p7g 7g Nov 1] 250,000Y: tall filly: first foal: dam, well beaten in
France only start, sister to smart Irish performer up to 1½m Desert Fox, out of half-sister
to high-class middle-distance performer Gold And Ivory: better effort in maidens (fair
form) when eighth of 18 to Damsel at Newmarket final start, travelling comfortably long
way and hampered over 1 out: should stay 1m: open to progress. *R. Charlton*

MY JODIE   3 b.f. Bluegrass Prince (IRE) 110 – Sally Green (IRE) 79 (Common   **–**
Grounds 118) [2003 57: 7g⁶ 8d 10f Oct 1] lengthy filly: modest maiden at 2 yrs: little
form in 2003. *M. G. Quinlan*

MY LAST BEAN (IRE)   6 gr.g. Soviet Lad (USA) – Meanz Beanz (High Top 131)   **68**
[2003 76: f12s⁵ f11s⁵ f14s⁴ 12.1m³ 13.8d⁶ Nov 4] fair performer: below form after reappearance: stays 13f: acts on fibresand, soft and good to firm ground: usually blinkered:
races prominently. *B. Smart*

MY LEGAL EAGLE (IRE)   9 b.g. Law Society (USA) 130 – Majestic Nurse 80 (On   **–**
Your Mark 125) [2003 f16.2g⁵ Aug 15] smallish gelding: poor handicapper: well held
on only Flat outing since 2001: occasionally blinkered: won over hurdles in September.
R. J. Price

MY LILLI (IRE)   3 b.f. Marju (IRE) 127 – Tamburello (IRE) (Roi Danzig (USA))   **57 ?**
[2003 p10g⁴ 9m³ p10g 10f p12g p10g Jul 16] 20,000F, 29,000Y: tall, close-coupled filly:
second foal: dam, 2-y-o sprint maiden (only season to race), half-sister to useful performer up to 9.4f Reported: modest maiden: best effort on debut. *P. Mitchell*

MY LINE   6 b.g. Perpendicular 119 – My Desire 88 (Grey Desire 115) [2003 72: 16.1d⁶   **70**
11.9d² Sep 26] lengthy gelding: fair handicapper: will stay beyond 2m: acts on soft going:
has a low head carriage: held up: successful over hurdles in October. *Mrs M. Reveley*

MY LOVELY   5 b.m. Dolphin Street (FR) 125 – My Bonus 79 (Cyrano de Bergerac   **53**
120) [2003 –: 5g⁵ Mar 22] modest performer, very lightly raced: should stay 6f: raced
only on good ground or softer on turf: sold 3,000 gns in December. *D. J. S. Cosgrove*

MY MAITE (IRE)   4 b.g. Komaite (USA) – Mena 58 (Blakeney 126) [2003 70, a73:   **66 d**
p10g³ 9m³ 9.7g⁵ 8.3d 10d 10.1g 12d³ 12.6f⁶ 11.6m 12m 12d⁵ 10m p12g p8g³ p10g⁶   **a77 d**
Nov 26] fair handicapper: below form after second outing: effective at 1¼m/1½m: acts
on good to firm ground, good to soft and polytrack: wears headgear: usually tongue tied:
none too consistent. *R. Ingram*

MY MAN FRIDAY   7 b.g. Lugana Beach 116 – My Ruby Ring 72 (Blushing Scribe   **49 §**
(USA) 107) [2003 54: 8m 7m 5.7f 7m 6.1m⁵ 7f⁵ 7m⁵ 6.9m⁶ 8m 7m 7f Sep 2] poor
performer: effective at 6f/7f: acts on polytrack and any turf going: tried in cheekpieces:
has found little/carried head high: ungenuine. *P. W. Hiatt*

MY MARY LOU (IRE)   3 ch.f. Septieme Ciel (USA) 123 – Kutaisi (IRE) (Soviet   **–**
Star (USA) 128) [2003 10g 7.5m Jun 11] IR 20,000Y: leggy, lengthy filly: third foal: dam
unraced out of smart performer up to 1¼m Mamouna: well beaten in maidens: ran as if
amiss on debut: saddle slipped next time. *J. A. Glover*

MY MATE HENRY   4 ch.g. Pursuit of Love 124 – Gopi 64 (Marju (IRE) 127) [2003   **–**
10f 9m⁶ 12d f12g Nov 24] no form. *T. T. Clement*

MY MELLORS (USA)   3 b.c. Woodman (USA) 126 – Breath Taking (FR) 119 (Nure-   **80**
yev (USA) 131) [2003 66p: 7g² 8m² 9.3f³ 7s² Jul 25] smallish, attractive colt: fairly useful
maiden: placed at Newmarket (2), Carlisle and Thirsk, well below form on last-named
final start: stays 9.3f: acts on firm ground: sold 10,000 gns. *H. R. A. Cecil*

MY MICHELLE   2 b.f. (May 4) Ali-Royal (IRE) 127 – April Magic (Magic Ring (IRE)   **74**
115) [2003 5g⁵ 6m⁵ 6d³ Nov 8] 42,000 2-y-o: leggy, quite good-topped filly: second foal:
half-sister to 3-y-o Michelle Ma Belle: dam unraced: fair form in maidens: third to
Thaminah at Doncaster: will prove best at 5f/6f. *B. Palling*

MYND   3 b.g. Atraf 116 – Prim Lass 65 (Reprimand 122) [2003 65: 6m 6g⁵ f6s p6g 5d³   **68**
p6g⁴ Nov 13] workmanlike gelding: fair maiden: effective at 5f/6f: acts on polytrack and
soft ground, showed promise on fibresand. *R. M. Whitaker*

MY PARIS   2 b.g. (Apr 4) Paris House 123 – My Desire 88 (Grey Desire 115) [2003   **–**
f8s Dec 13] fourth foal: half-brother to 6-y-o My Line: dam, thorough stayer, also
winning hurdler: 40/1 and green, well held in maiden at Southwell. *K. A. Ryan*

MY PENNY (USA)   4 b.f. Gulch (USA) – My Special Song (USA) (Danzig (USA))   **–**
[2003 f8.5g p12g Feb 26] 400,000 francs Y: sixth foal: half-sister to 2 winners by Irish
River, including French 1m winner Divine Devil: dam, French 1m winner, closely related

to dam of Hatoof and half-sister to high-class filly up to 1½m Mrs Penny: poor maiden: left G. Henrot in France before well held in 2003: tried blinkered: covered by Averti, sent to Italy. *E. J. O'Neill*

MY PERSONAL SPACE (USA) 2 ch.f. (Apr 17) Rahy (USA) 115 – Pattimech **80** (USA) (Nureyev (USA) 131) [2003 6m* 7g Oct 25] €57,000Y: smallish, quite good-topped filly: half-sister to several winners, including 4-y-o Far Lane: dam, won up to 7f in USA, half-sister to Grand Prix de Paris/Melbourne Cup winner At Talaq: fairly useful form when winning maiden at Goodwood in May: well held in listed event at Newbury: should stay 7f, probably 1m. *G. A. Butler*

MY PHILOSOPHY 4 gr.g. Green Desert (USA) 127 – Anneli Rose 56 (Superlative **–** 118) [2003 7g 7m 8m Jul 10] 30,000Y: big gelding: sixth foal: half-brother to 3 winners, including smart 1994 2-y-o 5f/6f (latter including Middle Park Stakes) winner Fard (by Reprimand): dam 6f winner: well held in maidens/claimer. *L. A. Dace*

MY PLEDGE (IRE) 8 b.g. Waajib 121 – Pollys Glow (IRE) 91 (Glow (USA)) [2003 **56** 62: p13g 11.6g 12f³ 16.4m 11.6m⁴ 14.1m Aug 14] deep-girthed gelding: modest handi- **a62** capper: should stay 1¾m: acts on polytrack, firm and good to soft going: tried tongue tied/in cheekpieces: often slowly away/races freely. *C. A. Horgan*

MY RAGGEDY MAN 4 b.g. Forzando 122 – Ragged Moon 72 (Raga Navarro **–** (ITY) 119) [2003 102: a7f a7.5f 8.9f 8m 8d 8.9m 9.1m Sep 19] close-coupled gelding: useful handicapper in 2002: well held at 4 yrs, leaving S. Seemar in UAE after second start: tried blinkered/visored/tongue tied: sold 2,500 gns. *D. Nicholls*

MY RENEE (USA) 3 b. or br.f. Kris S (USA) – Mayenne (USA) (Nureyev (USA) **107** 131) [2003 10d³ 12g* 10f⁵ 12m* Sep 26] IR 280,000Y: second foal: half-sister to fairly useful 1m winner Menaggio (by Danehill): dam unraced close relation to Carnegie out of Detroit, both winners of Prix de l'Arc de Triomphe: useful performer: won maiden at Cork in July and listed race at Ascot (best effort, beat Tanaghum by 1½ lengths) in September: stays 1½m: acts on firm going. *M. J. Grassick, Ireland*

MY RETREAT (USA) 6 b.g. Hermitage (USA) – My Jessica Ann (USA) (Native **60 ?** Rythm) [2003 76d: f8s² f8s³ f8s⁶ 7m f7g f8.5g⁶ f8.5s⁴ f9.4g² f9.4f⁴ f9.4g p10g Sep 9] sturdy gelding: modest performer: should stay 1¼m: acts on heavy going and fibresand: tried blinkered/in cheekpieces: usually held up: inconsistent. *G. L. Moore*

MYRIAD 2 ch.f. (Jan 14) Amfortas (IRE) 115 – Spriolo (Priolo (USA) 127) [2003 8m **–** Oct 24] sturdy filly: fourth foal: dam well beaten only start: 100/1, missed break and always behind in 22-runner maiden at Doncaster. *P. Howling*

MY RISK (FR) 4 b.c. Take Risks (FR) 116 – Miss Pat (FR) (Vacarme (USA) 121) **120** [2003 7s* 8g* 7g⁶ 8d* 8d* 8d² 8s* Nov 1] first thoroughbred foal: dam, French 1m (at 2 yrs)/8.5f winner, out of half-sister to dam of smart French performer up to 1½m Mousse Glacee: very smart performer, lightly raced: progressed really well, winning minor event at Saint-Cloud and handicap at Longchamp in March, listed race at Vichy in July, Prix Quincey at Deauville (by length from Star Valley) in August and Prix Perth at Saint-Cloud (rider dropped whip, held on by short neck from Execute) in November: also ran well when 4 lengths second to Special Kaldoun in Prix Daniel Wildenstein at Longchamp penultimate start, keeping on well: stays 1m: acts on heavy going (yet to race on firmer than good): held up. *J-M. Beguigne, France*

MYRTUS 4 ch.g. Double Eclipse (IRE) 122 – My Desire 88 (Grey Desire 115) [2003 **–** –: 12d Nov 4] lengthy gelding: well held in maidens. *Mrs M. Reveley*

MY SHARP GREY 4 gr.f. Tragic Role (USA) – Sharp Anne 74§ (Belfort (FR) 89) **62** [2003 64: p8g 9.7m⁶ 8m⁵ f7g 7.1g⁶ 8.2m 8.1m² 8.1m 8.1g 8f² Sep 8] modest maiden handicapper: effective at 7f to 1¼m: acts on firm going and polytrack: tried blinkered: subsequently won over hurdles for M. Pipe/J. Gallagher. *A. Charlton*

MYSTERI DANCER 5 b.g. Rudimentary (USA) 118 – Mystery Ship 105 (Decoy **–** Boy 129) [2003 79: p10g Jan 18] fair performer in 2002, well held only outing on Flat in 2003: tried visored/in cheekpieces: often takes good hold: joined P. Hobbs, and won over hurdles in August. *R. J. O'Sullivan*

MYSTERINCH 3 b.g. Inchinor 119 – Hakone (IRE) 78 (Alzao (USA) 117) [2003 98: **96** p8g³ Mar 1] good-topped gelding: useful performer: creditable ¾-length third to Pretence in minor event at Lingfield (reportedly sustained minor injury) only 3-y-o start: gelded after: should stay 1¼m: acts on firm going and polytrack. *N. P. Littmoden*

MYSTERIUM 9 gr.g. Mystiko (USA) 124 – Way To Go 69 (Troy 137) [2003 57: **51** 16.2m⁵ 16m 16m⁵ 15.9d 17.1m f16.2g³ f14.8g³ f14.8g³ p16g³ Dec 2] tall, leggy gelding:

modest handicapper: stays 17f: acts on firm going and all-weather: usually visored: sometimes slowly away: held up: sometimes looks none too keen. *N. P. Littmoden*

MYSTERLOVER (IRE) 3 b.g. Night Shift (USA) – Jacaranda City (IRE) 88 (In The Wings 128) [2003 p12g⁴ f12g Mar 24] 16,000Y: second foal: dam, ran once in Ireland, closely related to useful winner up to 13.4f Nassma: modest form when fourth in maiden at Lingfield: pulled up (reportedly had breathing problem) in similar event at Wolverhampton next time. *N. P. Littmoden* **52 ?**

MYSTERY MOUNTAIN 3 b.g. Mistertopogigo (IRE) 118 – Don't Jump (IRE) 71 (Entitled 126) [2003 f5g⁶ f6g⁴ f5s³ 8.2g 7.5f Apr 16] 4,000Y: third foal: dam 1m winner who stayed 1¼m: modest maiden: clearly best effort on second start: should be suited by 7f+: acts on fibresand, well held on turf. *Mrs J. R. Ramsden* **62**

MYSTERY PIPS 3 b.f. Bin Ajwaad (IRE) 119 – Le Shuttle 49 (Presidium 124) [2003 –: f7g f5s f5g 6.1g 5m⁶ 5g 5f f5s 5m³ 5f* 5f⁴ 5m³ 6m⁴ 5m* 5g⁵ Oct 13] modest performer: left A. Berry after third start: made all in seller at Musselburgh in June on final start for A. Senior: best effort when winning handicap at Goodwood in September: effective at 5f/easy 6f: acts on firm ground: usually blinkered/visored: often races prominently: consistent. *N. Tinkler* **57**

MYSTICAL CHARM (IRE) 4 ch.f. Indian Ridge 123 – Manazil (IRE) 98 (Generous (IRE) 139) [2003 –: f8g⁶ f7s 6m 5m⁵ 6.1m* 5.5f 5m Aug 5] lengthy filly: modest performer: left J. Given after second outing: won maiden at Warwick in July: best effort at 6f: raced only on good ground or firmer on turf, below form on fibresand: usually races prominently: sold 800 gns. *D. Nicholls* **53**

MYSTICAL GIRL (USA) 2 ch.f. (Mar 12) Rahy (USA) 115 – Miss Twinkletoes (IRE) (Zafonic (USA) 130) [2003 7m² 7.2d³ 8m Oct 24] €54,000Y: lengthy, good-topped filly: first foal: dam, French 1m winner, half-sister to useful French sprinter Wedding of The Sea: fair form in maidens: not sure to stay beyond 1m. *M. Johnston* **73**

MYSTICAL STAR (FR) 6 b.g. Nicolotte 118 – Addaya (IRE) (Persian Bold 123) [2003 f7s* Sep 26] modest form, twice-raced: returning from 3-year absence, won maiden at Southwell in September: should stay 1m: sold 1,000 gns. *J. J. Sheehan* **61**

MYSTIC FOREST 4 b.g. Charnwood Forest (IRE) 125 – Mystic Beauty (IRE) (Alzao (USA) 117) [2003 81, a84: f16.2g⁵ p16g f14s* p16g f14s³ 14.1s May 17] leggy gelding: fairly useful handicapper: won at Southwell in February: effective at 1¾m/2m: acts on all-weather and soft ground: blinkered/visored last 7 starts: joined C. Mann 12,000 gns, and successful over hurdles in July. *B. J. Meehan* **? a85**

MYSTIC MAN (FR) 5 b.g. Cadeaux Genereux 131 – Shawanni 105 (Shareef Dancer (USA) 135) [2003 84: f7g³ 7m* 8m* 7g⁴ 10m 8.5m Jun 6] strong, angular gelding: made into a useful handicapper, showing good turn of foot to win at Leicester and Newbury (25-runner Bet Direct Spring Cup, by 2 lengths from Faithful Warrior) in April: poorly drawn when good fourth of 28 to Camp Commander in Victoria Cup at Ascot fourth start: best at 7f/1m: acts on fibresand, soft and good to firm going: sometimes tongue tied/ wears crossed noseband: usually held up: tends to race freely: tough and consistent. *K. A. Ryan* **99**

MYSTIC MAYHEM 4 b.f. Danzig Connection (USA) – Mrs Meyrick 42 (Owen Dudley 121) [2003 8m Aug 17] third foal: half-sister to fairly useful 5f/6f winner Clan Chief (by Clantime): dam 13f to 15f winner: well beaten in maiden at Pontefract. *R. Bastiman* **–**

MYSTIC MILE (IRE) 4 gr.f. Sadler's Wells (USA) 132 – Delage (Bellypha 130) [2003 94: 12g³ 13d⁴ 14.1s² 14.6d⁴ 12v Nov 19] big, lengthy filly: unimpressive mover: useful performer: ran creditably all starts in 2003, including in listed events: stays 1¾m: raced only on good going or softer (acts on heavy): consistent. *M. A. Jarvis* **95**

MYSTIC MOON 2 br.f. (Feb 15) First Trump 118 – Misty Moon (Polar Falcon (USA) 126) [2003 p6g Dec 6] 3,700Y: third foal: dam German 8.5f winner: 50/1, always behind in maiden at Lingfield. *J. R. Jenkins* **–**

MYSTIC PROMISE (IRE) 2 g.r.g. (Feb 17) Among Men (USA) 124 – Ivory's Promise 74 (Pursuit of Love 124) [2003 f6g 7m 8m f7s p10g Nov 29] €7,000Y: leggy, lengthy gelding: first foal: dam, 5f winner, ran only at 2 yrs: well beaten in maidens: tried in blinkers/cheekpieces. *Mrs N. Macauley* **–**

MYSTIC VENTURE (IRE) 4 b.g. Woodborough (USA) 112 – Paganina (FR) (Galetto (FR) 118) [2003 48, a62: f7s⁵ f7s f7g 7m Mar 26] smallish, quite good-topped **a42**

NAA

gelding: poor performer: stays 7f: acts on fibresand and good to firm going: tried visored/
in cheekpieces: has been slowly away: often makes running. *K. A. Ryan*

MYSTIC WITCH 4 b.f. Mistertopogigo (IRE) 118 – Walsham Witch 61 (Music Maes- **56**
tro 119) [2003 57: 5m 5g³ 5m 5m 5m Jul 2] smallish filly: modest maiden handicapper:
raced mainly at 5f nowadays: acts on firm ground: often blinkered: reared and unseated
rider leaving stall final outing. *G. A. Swinbank*

MY SUNSHINE (IRE) 2 b.f. (May 14) Alzao (USA) 117 – Sunlit Ride (Ahonoora **62**
122) [2003 7m 7g Jul 31] €55,000Y: smallish filly: half-sister to 3 winners in Italy: dam,
second at 1¼m in Ireland, out of sister to 2000 Guineas winner Bolkonski: modest form
in maidens at Newbury (slowly away) and Goodwood: bred to be suited by 1¼m/1½m.
B. W. Hills

MYTHIC 4 ch.f. Zafonic (USA) 130 – Fetlar (Pharly (FR) 130) [2003 103: 10m⁴ 8m **?**
Jun 9] big, lengthy filly: useful at 3 yrs: long way below form in 2003, including in visor:
stays 1¼m: acts on firm ground: has refused to enter stall/unseated leaving stall (at 3 yrs):
none too reliable. *J. R. Fanshawe*

MYTHICAL AIR (IRE) 2 b.f. (Mar 23) Magic Ring (IRE) 115 – Legendary Dancer **–**
90 (Shareef Dancer (USA) 135) [2003 5m⁶ 6m 6m Oct 24] 8,400Y: tall, close-coupled
filly: sister to 4-y-o Waltzing Wizard and half-sister to 3 winners, including 2m winner
Legend of Love (by Pursuit of Love): dam 1½m winner: no promise in maidens/sales
race. *J. R. Weymes*

MYTHICAL CHARM 4 b.f. Charnwood Forest (IRE) 125 – Triple Tricks (IRE) 70 **63**
(Royal Academy (USA) 130) [2003 63: p13g p10g² p10g* 8.3d p10g⁶ 8.1m 9m 11.6g **a58**
8.3m 7g⁶ 8g⁵ 8m 8g* Sep 22] good-topped filly: modest performer: won seller at Lingfield (sold from B. Johnson 7,000 gns) in April and handicap at Kempton in September:
probably best at 1m/1¼m: acts on all-weather, raced mainly on good/good to firm ground
on turf: tongue tied once as 3-y-o: edged left last 2 starts. *J. J. Bridger*

MYTHICAL KING (IRE) 6 b.g. Fairy King (USA) – Whatcombe (USA) 88 **59**
(Alleged (USA) 138) [2003 67: 11.8g³ 10.2g⁵ 10.9m Jun 16] deep-girthed gelding:
modest handicapper: best at 1¼m/1½m: acts on firm and good to soft going. *R. Lee*

MYTTON'S MAGIC (IRE) 3 br.g. Danetime (IRE) 121 – Maldinion 88 (Dominion **–**
123) [2003 –: 8.1m⁶ 8m 9.1m Sep 19] no form: tried blinkered. *A. Bailey*

MYTTONS MISTAKE 10 b.g. Rambo Dancer (CAN) 107 – Hi-Hunsley 82 (Swing **–**
Easy (USA) 126) [2003 55, a41: f8.5g Jan 20] leggy, workmanlike gelding: modest
handicapper in 2002: well held only 10-y-o start: tried blinkered. *R. J. Baker*

MYTTON'S QUEST (IRE) 3 ch.g. Grand Lodge (USA) 125 – Fleeting Quest (Rain- **–**
bow Quest (USA) 134) [2003 62, a48: f8.5g f7g 7f 7.1f Jun 30] good-bodied gelding:
modest maiden at 2 yrs: well beaten in 2003: tried blinkered/in cheekpieces. *A. Bailey*

MY VALENTINE 4 gr.g. Samim (USA) 84 – Sea Farer Lake 74 (Gairloch 122) [2003 **63 d**
67: f11g f9.4s³ f9.4g² f9.4s³ f8.5s⁴ f8.5g⁵ 8m f8.5g⁵ May 23] modest maiden handicapper: effective at 1m to 9.4f: acts on fibresand, lightly raced on turf: often blinkered:
free-going sort, and tends to find little. *P. R. Chamings*

MY WILD ROVER 3 b.g. Puissance 110 – June Fayre (Sagaro 133) [2003 7m f7g **–**
Jun 9] 1,600Y: half-brother to several winners, including 6-y-o Feast of Romance: dam
ran twice: no form: pulled up (reportedly choked badly) second start. *P. A. Blockley*

MY YORKSHIRE ROSE 3 b.f. Bishop of Cashel 122 – Gloriana 78 (Formidable **–**
(USA) 125) [2003 –: 8.2g 10.1d 8s 8m 9f 13.8m Sep 9] close-coupled filly: little sign of
ability. *T. J. Etherington*

N

NAADDEY 2 b.c. (Apr 11) Seeking The Gold (USA) – Bahr 119 (Generous (IRE) 139) **98**
[2003 7f² 7.5d* 7m² 7m⁵ 8.1d⁴ 8m³ 8.5d⁵ 7m³ Oct 21] neat, attractive colt: second foal:
dam 7f (at 2 yrs) to 1½m (Ribblesdale Stakes) winner, also second in Oaks: useful
performer: landed odds in minor event at Beverley in July: in frame in minor events after,
hanging left and bit below form in visor final start: should stay 1¼m: best efforts on good
to firm going. *M. R. Channon*

NAAHY 3 ch.c. Bahamian Bounty 116 – Daffodil Fields (Try My Best (USA) 130) [2003 **111**
91: p7g 7g* 7g* 7g² 7m 7m⁵ 7g 6m 7f 7f* Oct 11] quite attractive colt: smart performer:

703

won handicaps at Newmarket in April, Goodwood in May and York (beat Arctic Desert a length) in October: creditable short-head second to Rimrod in listed race at Epsom fourth start: well below form in varied company next 5 outings: best at 7f: acts on firm and good to soft ground: has handled left-hand turn poorly at Catterick and Epsom: front runner. *M. R. Channon*

NABOKOV 4 ch.g. Nashwan (USA) 135 – Ninotchka (USA) 110 (Nijinsky (CAN) 138) [2003 –: f16.2g Jan 3] well beaten in maidens/handicap: sold 7,500 gns. *Sir Mark Prescott*   –

NABTAT SAIF 2 b.f. (Mar 15) Compton Place 125 – Bahawir Pour (USA) (Green Dancer (USA) 132) [2003 6m 7g² 5.1m⁴ 7m Aug 30] 2,600F: lengthy filly: third foal: sister to 3-y-o Captain Saif: dam unraced out of half-sister to US Grade 1 winners De La Rose and Upper Nile: fair maiden: second at Goodwood, easily best effort: stays 7f: slowly away/carried head high last 2 starts: sent to UAE, joined D. Watson. *R. Hannon*   70

NADAYEM (USA) 2 ch.f. (Apr 27) Gulch (USA) – Tajannub (USA) 104 (Dixieland Band (USA)) [2003 6.1f⁵ 7m⁴ Oct 13] smallish, quite good-topped filly: fifth foal: closely related to a winner in USA by Thunder Gulch and half-sister to 6-y-o Nashaab: dam 6f (Princess Margaret Stakes at 2 yrs)/7f winner: tongue tied, fair form in maidens at Nottingham and Leicester (fourth to Torcross): will probably stay 1m. *B. Hanbury*   72

NADESZHDA 3 ch.f. Nashwan (USA) 135 – Ninotchka (USA) 110 (Nijinsky (CAN) 138) [2003 –: 12f* 11.9f* f16.2f² Jul 25] fair handicapper, lightly raced: marked improvement to win at Catterick and Brighton (by 7 lengths) in July: long odds-on, second of 4 to Nightwatchman in apprentice event at Wolverhampton final start, almost running out with circuit to go but looking likely winner until tiring inside last: should stay 1¾m: acts on firm ground and fibresand: free-going sort. *Sir Mark Prescott*   83

NADIR 2 b.c. (Mar 3) Pivotal 124 – Amid The Stars 61 (Midyan (USA) 124) [2003 7d³ Nov 7] 11,000Y, 22,000 2-y-o: tall, close-coupled colt: second foal: dam, maiden, out of half-sister to dam of smart fillies Lemon Souffle (stayed 1m) and Caramba (stayed 1¼m): 40/1 and green, 2½ lengths third of 17 to Spring Surprise in maiden at Doncaster: will stay 1m: should improve. *P. Howling*   81 p

NADOUR AL BAHR (IRE) 8 b.g. Be My Guest (USA) 126 – Nona (GER) (Cortez (GER)) [2003 111: 10m 10g⁴ 10g* 10d 10.1m* 12g⁵ 12f⁵ Sep 28] tall, close-coupled gelding: unimpressive mover: smart performer: won handicap at Windsor (by short head from Goblet of Fire) in June and minor event at Epsom (by 1½ lengths from Island Sound) in August: last in September Stakes at Kempton (not discredited behind Mubtaker) and Cumberland Lodge Stakes at Ascot last 2 starts: stays easy 1½m: acts on any going: tailed off in blinkers final 5-y-o start: sometimes slowly away/races freely/wanders: held up: sold 20,000 gns. *T. G. Mills*   110

NAFFERTON GIRL (IRE) 2 b.f. (Feb 23) Orpen (USA) 116 – Petomi 75 (Presidium 124) [2003 5m 7m³ Aug 1] 25,000F, 18,000Y: lengthy filly: fourth foal: half-sister to 3 winners, including 3-y-o Al Turf: dam, 6f/7f winner (latter at 2 yrs), later won in Italy: modest form in maiden at Beverley and claimer (late headway) at Thirsk: will stay 1m. *M. W. Easterby*   51

NAFFERTON HEIGHTS (IRE) 2 b.c. (May 10) Peintre Celebre (USA) 137 – Gold Mist 85 (Darshaan 133) [2003 6m 6m 6m Sep 8] €20,000Y: smallish, leggy colt: second foal: dam, 1¼m and 1¾m winner, sister to useful Irish performer up to 1½m Shandon Lake: well held in maidens: twice slowly away: bred to be suited by 1½m+. *M. W. Easterby*   –

NAFSIKA (USA) 3 b.f. Sky Classic (CAN) – Exotic Beauty (USA) (Java Gold (USA)) [2003 54: 6.1g f6g 8.2m 8.1m 6.1g 10m 9.3m⁶ 8m⁵ 8s Jul 25] lengthy, sturdy filly: poor maiden: stays 1m: raced mainly on good going or firmer: tried blinkered, tongue tied last 5 starts. *B. A. McMahon*   43

NAHANE (IRE) 2 b.c. (Feb 5) Rainbow Quest (USA) 134 – Winona (IRE) 120 (Alzao (USA) 117) [2003 7m 7.2g² 7m² 8m³ 8.3g 5.5f Dec 21] small, quite attractive colt: first foal: dam Irish 7f (at 2 yrs) and 1½m (Irish Oaks) winner: fairly useful maiden: sold from Sir Michael Stoute's stable 20,000 gns before final outing: should be suited by 1¼m/1½m: acts on good to firm going. *M. Chew, USA*   80

NAHEEF (IRE) 4 b.c. Marju (IRE) 127 – Golden Digger (USA) 66 (Mr Prospector (USA)) [2003 117: 10g* 8.9g 8.9g 10d² 10g³ 8.9m* 10g² 9m⁵ Oct 18] unfurnished, quite attractive colt: smart performer: won listed race at Nad Al Sheba in February and sportingoptions.co.uk Strensall Stakes at York (wandered, held on by head from Eventuail) in September: creditable efforts when placed in La Coupe at Longchamp (½-length second   116

Godolphin's "Naheef"

to Carnival Dancer), listed race at Sandown (third to Ikhtyar) and Euro-Cup at Frankfurt (2 lengths second to Fruhlingssturm): effective at 9f/1¼m: yet to race on extremes of going: visored last 3 starts: sometimes tongue tied, including at York: often races prominently. *Saeed bin Suroor*

NAILBITER   4 b.g. Night Shift (USA) – Scylla 50 (Rock City 120) [2003 12.4m⁵ Apr   **60 ?**
21] 24,000Y, 4,500 2-y-o: second foal: dam maiden half-sister to smart sprinter Northern Goddess (by Night Shift): modest maiden hurdler: tongue tied, some ability when fifth in maiden at Newcastle. *Mrs A. Duffield*

NAJAABA (USA)   3 b.f. Bahhare (USA) 122 – Ashbilya (USA) (Nureyev (USA)   **69**
131) [2003 57: 8f f6g⁴ f7g³ f8g* Dec 9] smallish, sturdy filly: modest performer: won maiden at Southwell in December: stays 1m: acts on fibresand, raced only on good going or firmer on turf. *Miss J. Feilden*

NAJ-DE   5 ch.g. Zafonic (USA) 130 – River Jig (USA) 98 (Irish River (FR) 131) [2003   **–**
59d: p8g p7g 10.9m 7g 6m 10m 8f Jun 16] close-coupled gelding: maiden: no form in 2003: tried blinkered/tongue tied. *S. Dow*

NAJEEBON (FR)   4 ch.c. Cadeaux Genereux 131 – Jumairah Sun (IRE) 98 (Scenic   **98**
128) [2003 81: 6m⁵ 6d⁴ 7m² 6m⁵ 7f⁶ 7g⁵ 6m 8d 6m² 6m³ 6m⁶ 6m* 6m 6m 6f* 6g⁴ 6s⁵ 7d Nov 8] lengthy, well-made colt: useful handicapper: won at Pontefract in April, Goodwood in September and York (beat Cd Europe ¾ length) in October: effective at 6f/7f: acts on firm going, probably on soft: tried visored, tongue tied ninth to fourteenth starts: sometimes slowly away/soon off bridle. *M. R. Channon*

NAKOTA   3 ch.f. Emarati (USA) 74 – Naulakha (Bustino 136) [2003 –: 8.1m 7.6g 5.3f   **–**
7m Sep 9] no form: left J. M. Bradley after reappearance: tried blinkered: dead. *J. Gallagher*

NAKWA (IRE)   5 b.g. Namaqualand (USA) – Cajo (IRE) (Tirol 127) [2003 56: f12s³   **61**
f12g⁵ f12g⁴ 10.9m 12.4g* 12m 10m⁴ f12g³ Dec 22] tall gelding: modest handicapper:

won at Newcastle in May: stays 12.4f: acts on fibresand, good to firm and good to soft ground: often slowly away: has reportedly broken blood vessels. *E. J. Alston*

NAMASTE   3 b.f. Alzao (USA) 117 – Bahamian 115 (Mill Reef (USA) 141) [2003   **65** 10g³ 12d² p12g Nov 29] good-topped filly: closely related to Irish Oaks winner Wemyss Bight and to dam of Oasis Dream (both by Dancing Brave) and half-sister to several winners, including 1½m winner New Abbey (by Sadler's Wells): dam 1½m winner who stayed 15f: fair maiden: best effort on debut: stayed 1½m: stud. *H. R. A. Cecil*

NAMED AT DINNER   2 ch.c. (Feb 6) Halling (USA) 133 – Salanka (IRE) 68 (Persian   **75** Heights 129) [2003 7g 8f⁴ 6.1m² 7m² 8.2m⁴ Oct 22] 38,000F, €120,000Y: close-coupled colt: closely related to fairly useful 7f (at 2 yrs) to 1½m winner Kaiapoi (by Elmaamul) and half-brother to 3 winners, including 3-y-o Salinor: dam 1¼m winner: fair maiden: second at Nottingham and Brighton: stays 1m: acts on firm going: often races up with pace: sold 11,000 gns. *B. J. Meehan*

NAMROUD (USA)   4 b.g. Irish River (FR) 131 – Top Line (FR) (Top Ville 129) [2003   **103** 9m³ 8m* 8g² 7m* 6f Jun 21] $85,000/: tall gelding: half-brother to several winners in USA, including 1994 Grade 3 8.5f 2-y-o winner Miss Union Avenue (by Steinlen): dam French 1m winner: reportedly fractured cannon bone at 3 yrs: won maiden at Yarmouth in April and handicap at Chester (beat Nashaab a head) in June: ran as if amiss in Wokingham Handicap at Royal Ascot final start: likely to prove best at 7f/ 1m: acts on good to firm going: sold 26,000 gns. *Sir Michael Stoute*

NANDOO   4 b.f. Forzando 122 – Ascend (IRE) (Glint of Gold 128) [2003 60d: 16.1d   **–** 12.3m 10.1m 13.8f 12m⁶ 12m 12m Aug 15] disappointing maiden on Flat: wore cheek-pieces/blinkers last 6 starts: won over hurdles in September/October. *M. D. Hammond*

NANNA (IRE)   2 b.f. (Mar 3) Danetime (IRE) 121 – Pre Catelan 53 (Polar Falcon   **43** (USA) 126) [2003 f5g f6g Dec 26] €2,400Y, resold €11,000Y: second foal: dam, sprint maiden, half-sister to Middle Park Stakes winner Fard: better effort (poor form) when seventh in maiden at Southwell on debut: should prove best at 5f/6f. *R. Hollinshead*

NANTUCKET SOUND (USA)   2 b.c. (Mar 12) Quiet American (USA) – Anna 97   **68** (Ela-Mana-Mou 132) [2003 7.1g⁶ 8.2m³ p8g⁴ Dec 10] €28,000Y: workmanlike colt: second foal: dam, lightly-raced maiden (third in Musidora Stakes), from family of very smart 1m/1¼m performer Best of The Bests: fair form in maidens: will stay at least 1¼m. *M. C. Pipe*

NAOMI (IRE)   2 br.f. (Jan 28) Polar Falcon (USA) 126 – Duck Over 72 (Warning 136)   **78** [2003 6m⁶ 6d² Nov 8] 7,000Y, 16,000 2-y-o: plain, sparely-made filly: first foal: dam, maiden, who should have stayed 1¼m, half-sister to useful 1¼m winner Maid of Came-lot, from family of smart 7f/1m performer Inchinor: better effort in maidens (fair form) when 2½ lengths second of 13 to Thaminah at Doncaster: will probably stay 1m. *J. Nicol*

NAOMI WILDMAN (USA)   3 b.f. Kingmambo (USA) 125 – Divinite (USA) (Alle-   **–** ged (USA) 138) [2003 10m 10.9m 12g⁵ f14.8g Aug 8] 650,000 francs Y: leggy filly: first foal: dam French 1m winner: well held in maidens/handicap. *W. R. Muir*

NAROOMA   3 b.f. Emperor Jones (USA) 119 – Cassilis (IRE) (Persian Bold 123)   **45** [2003 7g⁴ 7m Jun 2] second foal: half-sister to 4-y-o Gold Guest: dam unraced half-sister to smart German miler Sinyar and to dam of smart performer up to 9f Ventiquattrofogli: poor form on debut: saddle slipped next time. *Lady Herries*

NARRATIVE (IRE)   5 b.h. Sadler's Wells (USA) 132 – Barger (USA) (Riverman   **109** (USA) 131) [2003 117: 12g⁴ 10.5d³ 10g 12g Oct 19] strong, lengthy, good-bodied horse: smart perfomer at 4 yrs: just useful form in 2003, best effort when fourth to Highest in Dubai City of Gold at Nad Al Sheba in March: respectable third to Black Sam Bellamy in Tattersalls Gold Cup at the Curragh, but well held after in Eclipse Stakes at Sandown (acted as pacemaker) and Prix du Conseil de Paris at Longchamp (first race for 3½ months): effective at 1½m/1¾m: yet to race on heavy going, acts on any other turf/dirt: often tongue tied: sweated profusely once at 4 yrs: front runner. *Saeed bin Suroor*

NASHAAB (USA)   6 b.g. Zafonic (USA) 130 – Tajannub (USA) 104 (Dixieland Band   **100** (USA)) [2003 103, a82: 7g 7m 7m² 8m 8f⁵ 8m 7m 8g³ 8.1m⁵ 7.9m 7.6m⁴ 8m² 9m 7.9f 8m   **a81** 8g³ f8.5g p8g⁵ Dec 20] small, quite attractive gelding: useful handicapper on turf, fairly useful on all-weather: some good efforts at 6 yrs, including when third to Lady Bear in William Hill Mile at Goodwood eighth start (final one for R. Beckett): effective at 7f to 9f: acts on fibresand, firm and soft going: effective visored or not: often slowly away: held up: tough. *P. D. Evans*

NASHWAN STAR (IRE)   3 ch.f. Nashwan (USA) 135 – Ibtisamm (USA) 71 (Cau-   **68** casus (USA) 127) [2003 7m³ 10.3m³ 7.5m⁴ 7m⁴ 11.9m³ 11.7f³ 10m³ 10s 12d Nov 4] smallish, workmanlike filly: half-sister to several winners, including high-class miler Air Express (by Salse) and useful 1¼m/1½m winner Aljazzaf (by Mtoto): dam, 1m winner, half-sister to dam of Breeders' Cup Juvenile winner Success Express: fair maiden: stays easy 1½m: acts on firm ground, possibly not on softer than good. *B. W. Hills*

NASIJ (USA) 3 ch.f. Elusive Quality (USA) – Hachiyah (IRE) 91 (Generous (IRE) 139) [2003 101: 8m* 10m⁴ 8f⁶ 8m⁴ 7g 8.1d Aug 30] rather leggy, quite attractive filly: useful performer: won listed race at Kempton in April: good fourth in similar event at Newbury in May and Falmouth Stakes at Newmarket (beaten 3 lengths by Macadamia) in July: effective at 1m to easy 1¼m: acted on good to firm going, below form on good to soft final start: often raced prominently: visits Cape Cross. *E. A. L. Dunlop* **98**

NASSAU STREET 3 gr.g. Bahamian Bounty 116 – Milva 56 (Jellaby 124) [2003 8.3g f9.4g⁴ p12g Nov 29] 5,500Y: brother to 4-y-o Galaxy Thunderbird and half-brother to numerous winners, including fairly useful 6f winner (including at 2 yrs) Milagro (by King of Spain): dam 6f winner: poor maiden. *D. J. S. ffrench Davis* **44**

NASTY NICK 4 gr.g. Petong 126 – Silver Spell 54 (Aragon 118) [2003 –: 7f 9.7m 10m⁴ 6m Aug 16] poor maiden: tried in headgear. *Julian Poulton* **33**

NATALIYA 2 b.f. (Feb 27) Green Desert (USA) 127 – Ninotchka (USA) 110 (Nijinsky (CAN) 138) [2003 6m* 7m³ Aug 9] strong, lengthy filly: fourth foal: half-sister to 3-y-o Nadeszhda: dam, 1½m (including Italian listed race) winner, from family of Nureyev: won maiden at Newbury in July: useful form when 1¼ lengths third of 8 to Bay Tree in listed race at Newmarket, swishing tail in paddock and slowly away: sustained injury after: will stay at least 1m. *J. L. Dunlop* **97**

NATHAN BRITTLES (USA) 3 ch.g. Cat's Career (USA) – Doc's Answer (USA) (Dr Schwartzman (USA)) [2003 54: 5f⁵ 5m² 5f* 5f 5g 5m Oct 1] rangy gelding: fair performer: won maiden at Thirsk in April and handicap at Catterick in May: raced only at 5f: acts on firm ground: races prominently. *T. D. Barron* **77**

NATHAN DETROIT 3 b.c. Entrepreneur 123 – Mainly Sunset (Red Sunset 120) [2003 7s p7s p6g p7g Nov 29] 16,000Y: half-brother to several winners, including fairly useful 5f winner Antonia's Double (by Primo Dominie) and 5-y-o Martin's Sunset: dam lightly-raced half-sister to very smart sprinter Bolshoi: little form: tried blinkered. *P. J. Makin* **–**

NATIONAL PRIDE 3 b.c. Vettori (IRE) 119 – Branston Express (Bay Express 132) [2003 9m² 8m* 9.5f* 9.5f² Oct 22] 26,000F: leggy, useful-looking colt: half-brother to several winning sprinters, including Waltzing Weasel (by Nemorino) and Keramic (by Efisio): dam unraced half-sister to dam of smart sprinter Branston Abby: won maiden at Newcastle (fair form) in September and allowance race at Keeneland in October: beaten a nose in similar event on latter course later in month: stays 9.5f: acts on firm going: flicked tail under pressure on debut. *J. Nicol* **?**

NATIVE TITLE 5 b.g. Pivotal 124 – Bermuda Lily 78 (Dunbeath (USA) 127) [2003 89: 5m 6m* 7f Sep 27] big, close-coupled gelding: has reportedly had wind operation: fairly useful handicapper: 66/1-winner of Tote (Ayr) Silver Cup in September (made reappearance day before), beating Blackheath a neck: last of 25 at Ascot following week: has form at 1m, likely to prove best at 5f/6f: acts on firm and soft going: tried blinkered. *D. Nicholls* **88**

NATIVE TURK (USA) 2 b.c. (Mar 15) Miswaki (USA) 124 – Churn Dat Butter (USA) (Unbridled (USA) 128) [2003 7m Sep 23] $50,000F, $72,000Y: compact colt: fourth foal: half-brother to winner in USA by Lit de Justice: dam, US maiden, half-sister to US Grade 2 8.5f winner Hill Pass: 11/1, eighth of 17 in maiden at Newmarket, slowly away and green: should stay 1m: likely to improve. *J. A. R. Toller* **66 p**

NATMSKY (IRE) 4 b.g. Shadeed (USA) 135 – Cockney Lass 117 (Camden Town 125) [2003 –, a63: f8s f12g f7s Feb 6] quite good-topped gelding: maiden: no form at 4 yrs: tried in headgear. *K. A. Ryan* **–**

NATURAL DANCER 4 b.f. Shareef Dancer (USA) 135 – Naturally Fresh 91 (Thatching 131) [2003 –: f8s f12g 9.7g p10g Mar 26] workmanlike filly: poor mover: little form. *C. N. Allen* **–**

NATURAL GRACE 3 ch.f. Zamindar (USA) 116 – Sharpthorne (USA) 91 (Sharpen Up 127) [2003 f6g Nov 19] 9,000 2-y-o: sister to winner in Greece and half-sister to several winners, including fairly useful 1998 2-y-o 5f winner Thicket (by Wolfhound) and 8-y-o Cold Climate: dam 6f (including at 2 yrs) winner: 33/1, well held in maiden at Southwell. *D. J. Daly* **–**

Courage Best Stakes (Handicap), Newbury—Navado provides apprentice Nicky Mackay with his biggest success; Zabaglione (just off picture to the right) is second ahead of Cripsey Brook (right), Northside Lodge (striped sleeves) and Ionian Spring (dark cap)

NAUGHTY GIRL (IRE) 3 b.f. Dr Devious (IRE) 127 – Mary Magdalene 78 (Night Shift (USA)) [2003 79: 5f 5f⁴ 6m* 6m² 6m⁶ 5d⁵ 6m⁶ p6g Dec 30] smallish, sturdy filly: fair performer: won maiden at Hamilton in July: below form last 2 outings, leaving M. Bell 8,000 gns and off nearly 4 months in between: effective at 5f/6f: acts on good to firm and good to soft going: inconsistent. *P. D. Evans* **79 §**

NAUTICAL 5 ch. or gr.g. Lion Cavern (USA) 117 – Russian Royal (USA) 108 (Nureyev (USA) 131) [2003 10d Jul 30] fair handicapper (rated 72) in 2002, winning at Jebel Ali, Ghantoot and Nad Al Sheba: sold from E. Charpy 30,000 gns after final 4-y-o start: well held only outing in 2003: stays 1¼m: usually tongue tied: tried visored/blinkered. *M. C. Pipe* **–**

NAVADO (USA) 4 b.g. Rainbow Quest (USA) 134 – Miznah (IRE) 102 (Sadler's Wells (USA) 132) [2003 97: 10.3f⁴ 11.9m 10m* 10g² Oct 11] tall, good-bodied gelding: useful handicapper, lightly raced: won Courage Best Stakes at Newbury in September by 1¼ lengths from Zabaglione: further improvement when unlucky second to Counsel's Opinion at Ascot final start, running on strongly from poor position: may prove best at 9f/1¼m: acts on good to firm going: ran as if amiss second outing: usually travels strongly, and effective held up or making running: sold 70,000 gns, joined Jonjo O'Neill. *Sir Michael Stoute* **107**

NAVIASKY (IRE) 8 b. or br.g. Scenic 128 – Black Molly (IRE) (High Top 131) [2003 93§: 7m 7m Jun 10] big, strong gelding: fairly useful at best: refused to race last 4 outings at 7 yrs: very reluctant to race both starts in 2003: banned from racing on Flat and over jumps. *Miss E. C. Lavelle* **§§**

NAWADI 3 ch.f. Machiavellian (USA) 123 – Nawaiet (USA) (Zilzal (USA) 137) [2003 7m³ 8.1d 10.1d* 12g 10.3d Nov 7] leggy filly: fourth foal: sister to very smart 7f (at 2 yrs)/1m winner No Excuse Needed: dam, French 6f winner, half-sister to high-class French middle-distance filly Fitnah out of very smart sprinter Greenland Park: fairly useful performer: won maiden at Epsom in October: stiff tasks last 2 starts, in handicap at Newmarket (far from discredited) and listed race at Doncaster (well held): barely stays 1½m: unraced on extremes of going. *B. W. Hills* **88**

NAWAMEES (IRE) 5 b.h. Darshaan 133 – Truly Generous (IRE) 104 (Generous (IRE) 139) [2003 p12g⁵ p12g² p12g³ 14.1f⁶ Sep 4] 170,000F, 480,000Y: first foal: dam, French 1¼m winner who stayed 12.5f, daughter of Irish 1000 Guineas winner Arctique Royale from family of Prix Saint-Alary winner Cerulean Sky (by Darshaan): fairly useful performer: won maiden at Le Touquet in 2001: left J. Hammond, France, after final 4-y-o start: creditable efforts in handicaps first 3 outings in 2003: should stay 1¾m: acts on polytrack, raced mainly on good/good to soft ground on turf: successful over hurdles in November. *G. L. Moore* **83**

NAWOW 3 b.g. Blushing Flame (USA) 109 – Fair Test 95 (Fair Season 120) [2003 79: p10g³ p10g² 9.9g 11m³ 12m⁶ 11m⁵ 10d 11.6g³ p12g² p12g⁶ Nov 22] tall gelding: fairly useful handicapper: stays 1½m: acts on polytrack and good to firm ground: often makes running: consistent: won over hurdles in December. *P. D. Cundell* **87**

NAYEF (USA)   5 b.h. Gulch (USA) – Height of Fashion (FR) 124 (Bustino 136)   **128**
[2003 129: a10f³ 10m* 10g² 12d 10.4m³ 10m Oct 18]

The latest Coral-Eclipse Stakes, a race which provides the first major clash of the different generations over middle distances, took place on the one-hundredth anniversary of the most famous of all its renewals. The 1903 Eclipse was one of those events for which the description 'race of the century' was not so ill-fitting. The Two Thousand Guineas and Derby winner Rock Sand started favourite, ahead of the supremely tough four-year-old filly Sceptre, who had won four of the five British classics the previous year. The third principal in this epic clash was the four-year-old Ard Patrick, who had won the 1902 Derby (with Sceptre fourth). Rock Sand couldn't live with the four-year-olds, who fought out a close finish which *The Sporting Life* described thus the next day: 'The struggle between the pair was of the most enthralling character, as every stride the mare looked like getting there, but she couldn't.' Ard Patrick triumphed by a neck in a race that was recalled for generations afterwards. Ard Patrick had been sold to Germany before the Eclipse and never ran again, but Sceptre beat Rock Sand for a second time that season in the Jockey Club Stakes, after Rock Sand had won the St Leger to complete the triple crown.

If the 1903 Eclipse lived up to its billing, the same could not quite be said of the 2003 edition. Though the race attracted its second-biggest field ever—the fifteen runners being one short of the record in 1975—the defeat of the favourite Nayef scuppered the British Horseracing Board's expensively-staged inaugural Summer Triple Crown/Grand Slam (which carried £1m and £4m bonuses respectively). Indeed, until Nayef's connections changed their mind—a decision not influenced by the lure of the big bonuses—the organisers were facing the embarrassment of not a single qualified contender lining up for what was only the second leg of a challenge which also included the King George VI and Queen Elizabeth Stakes and the Juddmonte International. The Eclipse is run at a mile and a quarter and doesn't often attract the winners of the Derby, Oaks or Coronation Cup—three of the races nominated by the BHB in a first 'qualifying' round—and the latest winners, Kris Kin, Casual Look and Warrsan, were quickly ruled out of Sandown's showpiece. The fourth qualifying event, the Prince of Wales's Stakes at Royal Ascot over the Eclipse distance, was won by Nayef, who led early in the straight and ran on strongly, despite edging left inside the final furlong, and had two and a half lengths and a length to spare over Rakti and Islington in a good renewal, despite the lack of a challenger from Ireland or France. Further back in fifth was Falbrav, who had been bumped leaving the stalls and then found himself short of room in the final furlong.

Falbrav turned the tables on Nayef in the Eclipse, which was dominated by the older generation, but there was controversy afterwards. Nayef had seemed to benefit from the presence of his own pacemaker at Royal Ascot, where Ekraar, who filled that role, was sent up to harry the free-running favourite Moon Ballad, ensuring he had no respite. But the boot was on the other foot at Sandown, where Nayef was bumped over two furlongs out by Godolphin's pacemaker Narrative, who failed to keep straight as he dropped back. Nayef soon recovered to hold every

Prince of Wales's Stakes, Royal Ascot—Nayef takes one of the 'qualifying' first legs of the BHB's Summer Triple Crown/Grand Slam initiative for middle-distance horses; Rakti and Islington follow him home

chance before going down by three quarters of a length, but Narrative's rider Jamie Spencer received a five-day suspension for improper riding, the implication seeming to be that he had caused interference to Nayef deliberately—something he denied strongly afterwards when making a public apology. The vexed subject of pacemakers proving a hindrance in races and of the use of 'team tactics' was given an airing, though any move to ban the use of pacemakers—who can perform a valuable function when they ensure a truly-run race—seems out of the question. Perhaps stewards should at least be given an option of following the rule in France, where the Ballydoyle horses Newton and Tycoon were demoted after their stable-companion Acropolis had caused interference in the Prix Jean-Luc Lagardere at Longchamp in October. However, such a rule couldn't have been applied satisfactorily in the Eclipse in which Godolphin's first string Grandera managed only eighth.

Nayef and Falbrav were both in their fourth season, tough and much travelled—fine advertisements for the modern thoroughbred—but Nayef's exertions in the Prince of Wales's Stakes and the Eclipse, coming on top of his effort in the Dubai World Cup, seemed, in hindsight, to take their toll on him. When first discussing the pros and cons after Royal Ascot of aiming Nayef at the Eclipse, his trainer had expressed concern that another tough race at Sandown might 'flatten' Nayef for the King George. Nayef had spent all winter in Dubai being trained for the World Cup on dirt—in which he finished third to Moon Ballad, beaten six lengths—and the Prince of Wales's was his first outing of the season in Britain. When he contested the King George VI and Queen Elizabeth Stakes back at Ascot at the end of July, Nayef was having his third big race in the space of five and a half weeks and managed only seventh of twelve. His rider had him perfectly placed, close up in a race run at a rather muddling pace, but he never looked like justifying favouritism after coming under pressure early in the home straight. The jockey

Mr Hamdan Al Maktoum's "Nayef"

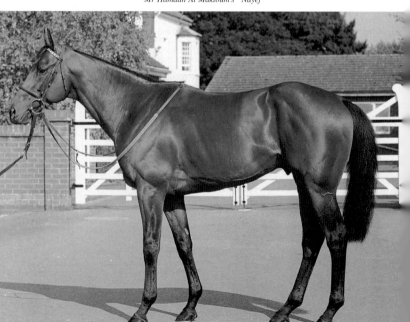

blamed the 'sticky' going but Nayef had plenty of form on soft and heavy. Nayef performed a little better, though still some way below his best (said to have been struck into), when third to Falbrav in the International at York, a race he had won the previous year after going down narrowly to Golan in the King George.

After a two-month absence, Nayef signed off with another below-par effort when only eighth of twelve to Rakti in the Champion Stakes at Newmarket. It was a disappointing end to a fine career in which Nayef had been at or near the top in each of his four seasons to race. Timeform's champion two-year-old, after a crushing victory in the listed Autumn Stakes at Ascot, Nayef went on to win four pattern events as a three-year-old, including the Champion Stakes. The Dubai Sheema Classic and the Juddmonte International provided two more Group 1 victories as a four-year-old, a total brought to four with the Prince of Wales's Stakes in the latest season. Nayef's record of nine wins from twenty starts, and of having finished out of the first three only four times, is further testament to his consistency. He was a resolute galloper, often racing up with the pace, and effective at a mile and a quarter to a mile and a half on going ranging from heavy to good to firm.

		Mr Prospector	Raise A Native
	Gulch (USA)	(b 1970)	Gold Digger
	(b 1984)	Jameela	Rambunctious
Nayef (USA)		(b or br 1976)	Asbury Mary
(b.h. 1998)		Bustino	Busted
	Height of Fashion (FR)	(b 1971)	Ship Yard
	(b 1979)	Highclere	Queen's Hussar
		(b 1971)	Highlight

The rangy Nayef was one of the most imposing horses in training and invariably took the eye before his races. He was a good mover too, with a long stride. The beautifully-bred Nayef was the last foal of Height of Fashion, who died in 2000. Her victories as a two-year-old included the Fillies' Mile at Ascot, after which she became winter favourite for the Oaks. She missed Epsom after struggling to reel in her pacemaker when winning the Lupe Stakes and, wearing blinkers, won the Princess of Wales's Stakes at Newmarket before being purchased from the Queen for over £1 million by Sheikh Hamdan, for whom Height of Fashion disappointed in the King George and the Yorkshire Oaks before being retired. Her magnificent record at stud means she has few rivals as a broodmare. Nayef is one of eight winners bred by Height of Fashion—all rated at least 100—whose second and third foals were Unfuwain (by Northern Dancer) and Nashwan (by Blushing Groom), both top-class racehorses and successful sires. Nayef's sire Gulch was best as a sprinter, gaining his most important victory in the Breeders' Cup Sprint, but Height of Fashion proved a strong influence for stamina, all her winners staying at least a mile and a quarter. Also among them were King Edward VII Stakes runner-up Mukddaam, whom she produced to that outstanding sire of sprinters Danzig, and three fillies by Mr Prospector, Bashayer (runner-up in the Cheshire Oaks), Wijdan and Sarayir, who are among five daughters of Height of Fashion now at stud at Shadwell. Nayef's two most notable half-brothers both died in 2002, Unfuwain due to a neurological condition and Nashwan following complications after a leg operation. Nayef will replace them at Nunnery Stud, Newmarket, in 2004 at a fee of £15,000 with the special live foal concession. *M. P. Tregoning*

NAYYIR   5 ch.g. Indian Ridge 123 – Pearl Kite (USA) 106§ (Silver Hawk (USA)   **126** 123) [2003 125: 6g⁶ 7g* 6.5g 7m² Oct 18]

A case of swings and roundabouts. While Nayyir was fortunate to win a Group 2 race at Goodwood on his second start of the season, he was just as unfortunate not to win a similar event at Newmarket on his final one. For all that Nayyir came out on top in the more valuable of the two races, the financial aspects of his season probably wouldn't have concerned his connections too much. That the gelding was back in rude health just over six months after looking as though he might not survive a serious illness was surely reward enough; that he was once again showing high-class form in pattern races was a bonus.

Unraced until he was four due to a series of niggling problems, Nayyir quickly made up for lost time when he did reach the racecourse, winning five of his ten starts in his first season, including the Diomed Stakes, the Lennox Stakes and

Lennox Stakes, Goodwood—in an event upgraded to Group 2, Nayyir is successful for the second year in a row; Arakan (right) finishes very strongly for second, with Tante Rose (star on cap), Suggestive (far side) and Hurricane Alan (diamonds) close up

the Challenge Stakes. Nayyir's final appearance in 2002 was due to be in the Hong Kong Mile, but he was struck down by a severe form of colitis shortly after arriving there and the road to full recovery was a long one. It was the end of June before Nayyir finally got back onto the racecourse, and he shaped as though in need of the outing in finishing sixth in the Group 3 Chipchase Stakes at Newcastle. That run put Nayyir spot on for his attempt to follow up his previous season's win in Goodwood's Lennox Stakes, which had been upgraded to Group 2 status for the first time. The race attracted a field of thirteen, which included the Jersey Stakes runner-up Arakan and the recent Ascot winner Tillerman, the pair going off joint favourites at 4/1. Nayyir, one of only two carrying a penalty, was next in the betting. The picture of the race changed more than once after the clear early leader Atavus had been largely ignored, but whereas things went very smoothly for Nayyir they went anything but for Arakan. Waited with as usual, Nayyir quickened to lead just inside the final furlong and held on by a head as Arakan finally stormed home after being persistently short of room. Nayyir found himself in the Arakan role in the Challenge Stakes at Newmarket. Still travelling very well but stuck behind a wall of horses entering the final two furlongs, Nayyir finished strongly after being switched right, virtually round the whole field, in the final hundred yards, unfortunately all too late. Nayyir managed to grab second from Arakan but still had half a length to make up on Just James as the line was reached. Nayyir's rating reflects that he would have won with better luck. Perhaps not surprisingly, Nayyir wasn't sent to Hong Kong again, though it does seem likely that he will be competing in Dubai in the early part of 2004, something which had been planned for 2003 until he fell ill.

		Ahonoora (ch 1975)	Lorenzaccio Helen Nichols
Nayyir (ch.g. 1998)	Indian Ridge (ch 1985)	Hillbrow (ch 1975)	Swing Easy Golden City
	Pearl Kite (USA) (b 1991)	Silver Hawk (b 1979)	Roberto Gris Vitesse
		Spur Wing (ch 1984)	Storm Bird Equal Change

Nayyir has won twice over an extended mile but his best performances have been put up at seven furlongs. Given the speed he has shown at the latter trip, there is no reason why he shouldn't be just as effective at slightly shorter, even though he has made the frame only once in four attempts to date, when third in the 2002 Prix Maurice de Gheest over six and a half furlongs at Deauville. He got very warm on a very hot day when only eighth in the latest running of that race, in between Goodwood and Newmarket. Nayyir's sire Indian Ridge was effective at five furlongs and stayed seven, but his dam Pearl Kite showed useful form at up to a mile and three quarters, and her two other notable offspring, the smart Shamaiel (by Lycius) and the very smart Highest (by Selkirk), both stay that far, too. Pearl Kite's fifth foal, College Fund Girl, a three-year-old filly by Kahyasi and stable-companion of

Nayyir, won a mile-and-a-half maiden on polytrack at Lingfield in September. Pearl Kite, who had her share of temperament, as did her close relation the useful stayer Jaseur, is a daughter of Spur Wing, a winner of six races in the States, including a Grade 3 event over nine furlongs. The next dam Equal Change also won in the States and was second in a Grade 1 event there. Nayyir, who wears a crossed noseband, is usually attended by two handlers in the paddock. A lengthy, angular gelding with a round action, he acts on polytrack, soft and good to firm going. Firm ground was the reason for his being withdrawn from both the Golden Jubilee Stakes and Queen Elizabeth II Stakes in the latest season. *G. A. Butler*

NAYZAK (USA) 3 b.f. Silver Hawk (USA) 123 – Mamlakah (IRE) 104 (Unfuwain (USA) 131) [2003 91p: 8.5m Jun 6] fair sort: fairly useful form when winner of 7f maiden only 2-y-o start: favourite, only seventh of 8 to Aldora in listed race at Epsom only outing at 3 yrs, taking good hold (including to post) and edging left: visits Sakhee. *Sir Michael Stoute* –

NAZIMABAD (IRE) 4 b.g. Unfuwain (USA) 131 – Naziriya (FR) (Darshaan 133) [2003 86: p12g p8g p12g 11.9f 12m⁵ 9.9m 9.9d Sep 23] sixth foal: half-brother to 3 winners abroad, including smart US Grade 2 1½m winner Nazirali (by Kahyasi), earlier winner in France: dam, French 10.5f winner, half-sister to Prix du Jockey Club winner Natroun (by J. Oxx in Ireland, winning at Wexford: showed little in 2003 (trained by W. Musson first outing, C. Dwyer next 2): stays 13.5f: acts on good to firm and good to soft ground: sometimes tongue tied: sold 3,400 gns. *Mrs A. Duffield* –

NEAP TIDE 2 br.c. (Jan 28) Zafonic (USA) 130 – Love The Rain (Rainbow Quest (USA) 134) [2003 7g 8g⁶ 7.2d⁴ Oct 13] good-bodied, attractive colt: first foal: dam, 11f winner, sister to smart performer up to 1½m Bonash and half-sister to dam of Burning Sun and Nebraska Tornado: best effort in maidens (fair form) when front-running fourth to Tabadul at Ayr: needs to settle to stay 1m. *J. H. M. Gosden* 75

NEAR DUNLEER (IRE) 8 b.m. Soviet Lad (USA) – Clipper Queen 66 (Balidar 133) [2003 59§: f12g p13g 10s⁶ 13m 12f³ 12g⁵ 12f 12f² 12g² 14m⁵ 12.5m* Oct 30] modest handicapper: trained by J. Fox first 2 outings at 8 yrs only: won at Thurles in October: stays 1¾m: acts on fibresand and any turf going. *M. Hourigan, Ireland* 55 a?

NEARLY A FOOL 5 b.g. Komaite (USA) – Greenway Lady (Prince Daniel (USA)) [2003 74: f7g* p7g f7g f6g p10g p7g* f6g⁶ f8s 7m³ 7m⁵ 8.3m³ Sep 29] close-coupled gelding: fair on turf, modest on all-weather: won seller at Southwell in January and claimer at Lingfield in March: left A. Bailey after seventh start: barely stays 1m: acts on any turf going and all-weather: probably best in blinkers/visor. *G. G. Margarson* 74 a60

NEARLY BEFORE TIME (IRE) 2 b.c. (Jan 1) Orpen (USA) 116 – First Encounter (IRE) 76 (Alzao (USA) 117) [2003 5g 5m 5d f6g* f6f 5f Aug 21] 9,000F, 10,000Y: angular, workmanlike colt: first foal: dam Irish 2-y-o 7f winner: modest performer: won seller at Wolverhampton in June: well below form after, in cheekpieces on final start: stays 6f: acts on fibresand, best turf effort on good to firm going. *A. Berry* 53

NEBRASKA CITY 2 b.g. (Feb 8) Piccolo 121 – Scarlet Veil 75 (Tyrnavos 129) [2003 5g⁵ 5m⁵ 6g 5m⁵ 6m Aug 27] 25,000Y: compact gelding: sixth living foal: half-brother to 3 winners, including 8-y-o Inch Perfect: dam, maiden who stayed 1¼m, half-sister to Mill Reef Stakes winner Red Cross: fair maiden: best form at 5f: wore cheekpieces penultimate start (ran well), visor final one. *B. Gubby* 65

NEBRASKA TORNADO (USA) 3 br.f. Storm Cat (USA) – Media Nox 98 (Lycius (USA) 124) [2003 8s* 10d* 10.5g* 8d⁶ 8g* Sep 7] 123

Four of the five top Group 1-winning three-year-old fillies at around a mile, Six Perfections, Russian Rhythm, Yesterday and Étoile Montante, were far from unknown quantities at the start of the season. The same cannot be said of the final member of the quintet, Nebraska Tornado, who did not make her racecourse debut until May but progressed to end the year with a classic and an open-aged Group 1 prize to her name.

Reportedly Nebraska Tornado did not come in her coat as a juvenile, encouraging her connections to play a waiting game. Success in a newcomers race at Saint-Cloud was followed swiftly by a smooth victory in the listed Prix Melisande at Longchamp, where she impressed when quickening through a gap against the rail. The fact that Andre Fabre thought it worthwhile running her in the Prix de

Prix de Diane Hermes, Chantilly—
Nebraska Tornado gives trainer Andre Fabre his third French classic of the year;
stable-companion Musical Chimes (third right) is third with British-trained Time Ahead splitting the pair

Diane Hermes at Chantilly in June was testament to her potential. Fabre is a master of his profession, with seventeen successive French trainers' titles and more than twenty classics on the scoresheet before the Diane, not to mention five victories in the Prix de l'Arc de Triomphe. He had already won the Poule d'Essai des Poulains with Clodovil and the Poule d'Essai des Pouliches with Musical Chimes, and the latter lined up for the Diane as second favourite behind Prix Saint-Alary winner Fidelite. Nebraska Tornado was fourth favourite at 106/10 in a ten-runner field also including Campsie Fells (Prix Vanteaux) along with British challengers Cassis (Musidora Stakes) and the lightly-raced Time Ahead, winner of a Newmarket maiden. Nebraska Tornado had the reputation of being high-mettled and she displayed signs of stubbornness at the start. She was a model of decorum in the race though, travelling sweetly close to the leader, taking over early in the straight and staying on well under pressure to beat Time Ahead by three quarters of a length with Musical Chimes a length away third.

On balance it did not look a strong renewal of the Diane—only two of the beaten horses subsequently won (one of them, Vallee Enchantee, wasn't the filly then that she became in the second half of the year)—and Nebraska Tornado's standing as a substandard winner seemed to be confirmed in the Prix Jacques le Marois at Deauville in August. She was not one of the market leaders and was

NetJets Prix du Moulin de Longchamp—Nebraska Tornado beats the Japanese-trained Lohengrin (rail),
Bright Sky (noseband), Soviet Song, the grey Clodovil and Where Or When (diamonds)

left behind in the final furlong, finishing six lengths sixth to Six Perfections. Six Perfections bypassed the NetJets Prix du Moulin de Longchamp the following month but Nebraska Tornado's chance still looked far from obvious against such as the favourite Bright Sky, who had defeated Six Perfections in the Prix d'Astarte on her latest start, the Jacques le Marois runner-up Domedriver and Two Thousand Guineas winner Refuse To Bend. Nebraska Tornado was sent off at nearly 15/1 in a field of fourteen also containing Clodovil, Sussex Stakes winner Reel Buddy, Soviet Song and Where Or When. Nebraska Tornado had to be ridden in the paddock and once again wasn't too keen about entering the stalls. Most of the jockeys in the Moulin seemed intent on riding a waiting race. Hiroki Goto on Japanese-trained Lohengrin set a steady pace, tracked by Richard Hughes on Nebraska Tornado and, when the leader quickened the tempo a furlong and a half out, several of the field were caught flat-footed. Nebraska Tornado wasn't one of them, as she caught Lohengrin and gradually asserted to win by half a length as Bright Sky stayed on into third, a length further back. A good performance, and one which suggested Nebraska Tornado would make her presence felt in late-season races. However, despite being pencilled in for the Queen Elizabeth II Stakes at Keeneland, the Breeders' Cup and/or the Champion Stakes, she was not seen out

Nebraska Tornado (USA) (br.f. 2000)	Storm Cat (USA) (b or br 1983)	Storm Bird (b 1978)	Northern Dancer South Ocean
		Terlingua (ch 1976)	Secretariat Crimson Saint
	Media Nox (ch 1993)	Lycius (ch 1988)	Mr Prospector Lypatia
		Sky Love (b 1985)	Nijinsky Gangster of Love

Mr K. Abdulla's "Nebraska Tornado"

again, apparently having started to turn in her coat. She stays in training and a race between her, Six Perfections and Russian Rhythm would be worth going a long way to see.

Nebraska Tornado, yet another top performer sired by Storm Cat, is effective at a mile to ten and half furlongs and has raced only on good going or softer. Details of the distaff side of her pedigree were given in the essay on her half-brother Burning Sun in *Racehorses of 2002* in which Nebraska Tornado was erroneously described as being out of Sky Love. Burning Sun was by Danzig and won the Prix Eugene Adam at three but could not add to his tally as a four-year-old, putting up his best effort when third in a listed event at Chester on the first of three starts. Media Empire (also by Danzig), the two-year-old out of Media Nox, has not run; the mare also has a yearling filly by Lear Fan, a colt foal by Maria's Mon and has since visited Forest Wildcat. Two visits to Danzig, sandwiching one to Storm Cat, followed by Lear Fan, Maria's Mon and Forest Wildcat, may seem an eccentric mating policy but anyone questioning the wisdom of Juddmonte Farms' methods would be advised to hold their counsel. Media Nox, a Group 3 winner (the Prix du Bois) at five furlongs and Grade 2 winner (the Buena Vista Handicap at Santa Anita) at a mile, was the result of her dam Sky Love's visiting Lycius, an ordinary stallion, in the middle of five matings with Rainbow Quest and one with Shirley Heights, far from ordinary stallions. Those six matings produced a Group 2 winner, Bonash, and at least two other useful performers. *A. Fabre, France*

NECKAR VALLEY (IRE)   4 b.g. Desert King (IRE) 129 – Solar Attraction (IRE)   **85**
60 (Salt Dome (USA)) [2003 75: 12m² 10s 13s 9.9d⁴ 11.1m⁵ 9.2m² 10.3m 10.5m⁵ 11.9m⁵ 12g³ 11.6g Oct 6] 27,000Y: lengthy, quite good-topped gelding: third foal: half-brother to 7f winner in Hong Kong by Last Tycoon: dam third at 5f in Ireland at 2 yrs: fairly useful handicapper: won at Fairyhouse at 3 yrs and, having left Declan Gillespie in Ireland after third 4-y-o start, Hamilton in July: ran as if amiss final outing: effective at 9f to 1½m: acts on good to firm and good to soft going, not on soft. *R. A. Fahey*

NECKLACE   2 b.f. (Feb 24) Darshaan 133 – Spinning The Yarn 70 (Barathea (IRE)   **105 p**
127) [2003 6g² 7f* 7m* 8s Oct 5] 600,000Y: rather leggy, close-coupled filly: first foal: dam, ran once, closely related to Kayf Tara and Opera House and half-sister to 4-y-o Zee Zee Top: useful form when length winner of Robert H. Griffin Debutante Stakes (from Caldy Dancer) and Moyglare Stud Stakes (from Red Feather) at the Curragh in August, strong run to lead final 1f both times: never going well in Prix Marcel Boussac at Longchamp final start: should be very well suited by 1¼m/1½m: acts on firm going: likely to make a better 3-y-o. *A. P. O'Brien, Ireland*

Moyglare Stud Stakes, the Curragh—Necklace gives trainer Aidan O'Brien his third success in the race in the last four years; Red Feather (No.9) just gets the better of Menhoubah for second

NEEDLES AND PINS (IRE) 2 b.f. (Apr 30) Fasliyev (USA) 120 – Fairy Contessa **104**
(IRE) 63 (Fairy King (USA)) [2003 5f 5d* 5m² 6g⁶ 5.2m* 5.5d² 5g⁵ Oct 11] smallish
filly: first foal: dam, lightly-raced maiden (stayed 7f), half-sister to Gimcrack winner
River Falls: useful performer: won maiden at Haydock in May and listed race at Newbury
(by 2 lengths from Nyramba) in August: very good short-head second of 4 to Villadolide
in Prix d'Arenberg at Maisons-Laffitte penultimate start: on toes when running poorly
final one: will prove best at 5f/easy 6f: acts on good to firm and good to soft going.
M. L. W. Bell

NEEDWOOD BLADE 5 ch.h. Pivotal 124 – Finlaggan 83 (Be My Chief (USA) **115**
122) [2003 117: 6g⁴ 6g* 5g* 6m 6f 6m 6m 5.5f⁴ Nov 28] strong, compact horse: usually
takes the eye: smart performer: won listed race (by 1¼ lengths from Resplendent Cee) in
April and Victor Chandler Palace House Stakes (by length from Bahamian Pirate) in May,
both at Newmarket: easily best effort after when creditable seventh to Oasis Dream in
July Cup on same course sixth outing: left B. McMahon before final one: effective at 5f
(given bit of a test)/6f: acts on any going: usually waited with: tough and genuine. *Kathy
Walsh, USA*

NEEDWOOD BRAVE 5 b.g. Lion Cavern (USA) 117 – Woodcrest 82 (Niniski (USA) **41**
125) [2003 10.5m² 12.3m⁵ 17.2m Jun 25] rangy gelding: poor maiden handicapper: stays
10.5f: acts on good to firm going: tried blinkered. *T. J. Fitzgerald*

NEEDWOOD MERLIN 7 b.g. Sizzling Melody 117 – Enchanting Kate (Enchant- **–**
ment 115) [2003 –: 13m Jun 18] close-coupled gelding: no form since 3 yrs. *K. W. Hogg;
Isle of Man*

NEEDWOOD MYSTIC 8 b.m. Rolfe (USA) 77 – Enchanting Kate (Enchantment **75**
115) [2003 64, a53: 11.9m³ 13f* 16.5m* 14.1m 14.1f² Aug 20] smallish, workmanlike **a–**
mare: fair handicapper: better than ever at 8 yrs, winning amateur events at Hamilton in
June and Doncaster in July: effective at 1½m to 16.5f: acts on firm going, soft and polytrack: tried tongue tied. *Mrs A. J. Perrett*

Mr Michael Tabor and Mrs John Magnier's "Necklace"

NEEDWOOD SPIRIT   8 b.g. Rolfe (USA) 77 – Needwood Nymph 45 (Bold Owl   **40**
101) [2003 f14g 16.1d 17.1m 16d⁴ May 28] smallish gelding: poor handicapper: stays
2¼m: acts on good to firm and heavy going: visored once. *Mrs A. M. Naughton*

NEEDWOOD TRICKSTER (IRE)   6 gr.g. Fayruz 116 – Istaraka (IRE) (Darshaan   **–**
133) [2003 –, a42: f8s f8s f6s Feb 13] close-coupled gelding: no longer of any account:
tried blinkered/tongue tied. *R. Brotherton*

NEGWA (IRE)   2 b.f. (Mar 23) Bering 136 – Ballet 61 (Sharrood (USA) 124) [2003   **76**
6g⁴ 7.5m³ 10m³ Oct 13] 66,000Y: rather leggy, close-coupled filly: half-sister to several
winners, including 6-y-o Island Sound and useful 1¼m and 11.6f winner Serge Lifar (by
Shirley Heights): dam maiden half-sister to May Hill winner Satinette: best effort (fair
form) when third to Cohn Blue in minor event at Leicester final start, dictating pace: stays
1¼m: refused to enter stall intended second outing. *M. R. Channon*

NELLIE MELBA   4 b.f. Hurricane Sky (AUS) – Persuasion 79 (Batshoof 122) [2003   **82**
70: 8m 10g 8g⁴ 8m 8m 7m² 7m* 6.9d* 7m² 7f 7m 7g⁶ Oct 11] leggy filly: fairly useful
performer: won handicaps at Leicester and Carlisle in July: effective at 7f/1m: acts on
good to firm going, good to soft and fibresand: carries head high. *Miss I. E. Craig*

NEMINOS (IRE)   4 b.g. Lake Coniston (IRE) 131 – Bandit Girl 70 (Robellino (USA)   **–**
127) [2003 –: 8m 10s 10g 10d Jul 5] little form, including in seller at Leicester third
outing: tried tongue tied/blinkered/in cheekpieces. *Ms J. Morgan, Ireland*

NEMO FUGAT (IRE)   4 b.g. Danehill Dancer (IRE) 117 – Do The Right Thing 71   **79**
(Busted 134) [2003 93: 5f 5.1m⁵ 6g 6f 6g⁴ 6g 5s Nov 3] big, strong, lengthy gelding:
fairly useful performer at 3 yrs: just fair form in 2003: probably best at 6f/7f: acts on firm
and good to soft ground: tried blinkered: usually held up. *D. Nicholls*

NEON BLUE   2 b. or br.g. (Feb 3) Atraf 116 – Desert Lynx (IRE) 79 (Green Desert   **71**
(USA) 127) [2003 5f³ 5d³ 5f² 5d² 6g 5g⁴ 6m 6f⁴ 6g 28] 24,000F, 26,000Y, 25,000
2-y-o: smallish, compact gelding: second foal: half-brother to 3-y-o Valiant Romeo: dam,
6f winner, half-sister to smart sprinter Watching: fair maiden: second twice at Thirsk:
seemed to run very well seventh start: stays 6f: acts on firm and good to soft going.
R. M. Whitaker

NEPHETRITI WAY (IRE)   2 b.f. (Feb 5) Docksider (USA) 124 – Velvet Appeal   **92**
(IRE) 101 (Petorius 117) [2003 6.1m² 6m* 7m² Oct 17] 40,000F: rather leggy, quite
good-topped filly: third foal: half-sister to 4-y-o Craiova: dam, Irish 1m winner, sister to
smart performer up to 1m Sapieha and half-sister to smart French stayer Dajraan: won
maiden at Goodwood in September: fairly useful form when short-head second of 3 to
Mahmoom in minor event at Newmarket final start: will stay 1m: had 2 handlers in
paddock/missed break on debut. *P. R. Chamings*

NEPTUNE'S GIFT   4 b.f. Lugana Beach 116 – Not So Generous (IRE) 68 (Fayruz   **–**
116) [2003 –, a60d: f6s f6g Jan 2] modest performer: well beaten both starts at 4 yrs: tried
in cheekpieces, often visored. *I. W. McInnes*

NEQAAWI   2 br.f. (Apr 27) Alhaarth (IRE) 126 – Jinsiyah (USA) 98 (Housebuster   **60**
(USA)) [2003 6m 6m Sep 25] second foal: half-sister to 3-y-o Indian Maiden: dam, 7f
winner who stayed 8.5f, out of half-sister to Kentucky Derby winner Winning Colors:
much better effort in maidens (modest form) when slow-starting seventh of 11 at
Yarmouth on debut: should stay 1m. *B. Hanbury*

NERO'S RETURN (IRE)   2 b.c.c. (Mar 18) Mujadil (USA) 119 – Snappy Dresser   **104 p**
(Nishapour (FR) 125) [2003 6f⁴ 6m* Oct 25] IR 18,000F, 17,000Y: useful-looking colt:
brother to smart Irish 5f (at 2 yrs) to 7f winner Show Me The Money and Italian 6f winner
Mac Professore, and half-brother to winner in Italy by Jareer: dam Irish 2-y-o 5f winner:
won maiden at York by 10 lengths from Key Partners and listed race at Doncaster by short
head from Mac Love (rallied to lead again close home), both in October: will probably
stay 7f: likely to make a smart 3-y-o. *M. Johnston*

NESNAAS (USA)   2 ch.c. (Feb 4) Gulch (USA) – Sedrah (USA) 82 (Dixieland Band   **68**
(USA)) [2003 7m³ 7m 7m Sep 17] first foal: dam, lightly-raced 1½m winner, half-sister
to Poule d'Essai des Pouliches winner Ta Rib: fair form in minor event/maidens: edged
left final start: should stay 1m. *B. Hanbury*

NESSEN DORMA (IRE)   2 b.g. (Feb 22) Entrepreneur 123 – Goldilocks (IRE) (Caer-   **76**
leon (USA) 132) [2003 f6g² f6s² 7d⁵ f7g f7g⁵ f8g* f8s* Dec 27] IR 3,500F, €17,000Y:
lengthy gelding: second foal: dam, Italian 2-y-o 6f winner, half-sister to smart 1m winner
Dear Daughter: fair performer: left K. Ryan after fourth start: won maiden and nursery
at Southwell in December: should stay 1¼m: acts on fibresand, some promise on turf.
J. G. Given

NEUTRAL NIGHT (IRE)   3 b.f. Night Shift (USA) – Neutrality (IRE) (Common   **54** Grounds 118) [2003 58: f6g p6g p6g 6g 7.1g² 6.1m⁴ 6.1f 7.1m⁵ 8f 8f 6.1m⁶ 7m 7s⁶   **a46** f8.5g⁶ f7g Nov 21] modest maiden on turf, poor on all-weather: effective at 6f/7f: acts on fibresand, raced only on good ground or firmer on turf: tried visored/tongue tied. *R. Brotherton*

NEVADA DESERT (IRE)   3 b.g. Desert King (IRE) 129 – Kayanga (Green Desert   **78** (USA) 127) [2003 75: 10m 7.9g² 8g³ 8.5m* 8m³ 11m³ 9.9m⁴ 8m² 9m⁵ Aug 30] useful-looking gelding: fair handicapper: won at Beverley in June: stays 11f: acts on good to firm ground: carries head high: consistent. *R. M. Whitaker*

NEVEN   4 b.g. Casteddu 111 – Rose Burton 42 (Lucky Wednesday 124) [2003 73: f7s*   **71** f7g³ f8s 8m⁵ f8g² Nov 25] lengthy gelding: fair handicapper: won at Southwell in January: effective at 7f/1m: acts on fibresand, good to firm and good to soft going: carried head high final start. *T. D. Barron*

NEVERENDING MAGIC   2 ch.g. (Apr 1) Timeless Times (USA) 99 – Lady Magic-   **–** ian (Lord Bud 121) [2003 5m 6.1d 7m 7f Sep 2] 2,000Y: leggy gelding: second foal: dam, ran 4 times, little sign of ability: seems of little account: tried in cheekpieces/visor. *Jean-Rene Auvray*

NEVER PROMISE (FR)   5 b.m. Cadeaux Genereux 131 – Yazeanhaa (USA) 68   **40** (Zilzal (USA) 137) [2003 66d: 10.2m⁶ 10m 7f Sep 27] smallish mare: fair handicapper at best: poor form in 2003, leaving C. Roberts after second outing: visored/blinkered. *D. Loughnane, Ireland*

NEVER WILL   2 b.c. (Feb 19) Cadeaux Genereux 131 – Answered Prayer (Green   **– p** Desert (USA) 127) [2003 6f⁵ Oct 10] strong, lengthy colt: fourth foal: half-brother to 4-y-o Answered Promise and French 1m/10.5f winner Grateful Thanks (by Bering): dam, ran once in France, out of Oaks winner Jet Ski Lady: 7/1, well-beaten fifth of 9 in maiden at York, challenging briefly over 2f out and not knocked about once tiring: sure to do better. *M. Johnston*

NEVER WITHOUT ME   3 ch.g. Mark of Esteem (IRE) 137 – Festival Sister (Belmez   **56** (USA) 131) [2003 f7s⁵ p8g 8.2m f6g² f5s² Dec 31] 34,000Y: tall gelding: first foal: dam, Italian 1¼m winner, half-sister to Lancashire Oaks winner Squeak, later very smart US Grade 1 9f/1¼m winner: modest maiden: effective at 5f/6f: acts on fibresand: effective visored or not: sometimes slowly away. *P. J. McBride*

NEVICA   2 ch.f. (May 11) Prince Sabo 123 – Snow Eagle (IRE) 57 (Polar Falcon (USA)   **–** 126) [2003 5.1g 6m 6.1m⁶ Sep 19] leggy, plain filly: fourth foal: half-sister to fairly useful 2000 2-y-o 5f winner Elsie Plunkett (by Mind Games): dam, maiden who stayed 8.5f, ran only at 2 yrs: last in minor events/maiden: visored final start. *C. Smith*

NEVINSTOWN (IRE)   3 b.c. Lahib (USA) 129 – Moon Tango (IRE) 81 (Last Tycoon   **–** 131) [2003 –: p10g 9.5d 9.5m f8g Nov 25] little form, including on all-weather in Britain on reappearance and final start: tried blinkered/tongue tied. *Niall Moran, Ireland*

NEVISIAN LAD   2 b.c. (Feb 3) Royal Applause 124 – Corndavon (USA) 95 (Sheikh   **113** Albadou 128) [2003 5m* 5m³ 6m* 7d 6m Oct 3] 33,000Y: smallish, strong, lengthy colt:

TNT July Stakes, Newmarket—Nevisian Lad (right) wins going away from Cape Fear (armlets), Byron (left), Milk It Mick (second left) and Holborn (third left)

first foal: dam, 6f winner, sister to 5-y-o Injaaz: smart performer: won maiden in April and TNT July Stakes in July (took long time to find stride but burst through to beat Cape Fear by length), both at Newmarket: below form in Vintage Stakes at Goodwood and Middle Park Stakes (reportedly found to have injured a knee, and operated on) at Newmarket after: should stay 7f: acts on good to firm ground: sometimes has 2 handlers: slowly away first 2 starts. *M. L. W. Bell*

NEWCLOSE   3 b.g. Barathea (IRE) 127 – Wedgewood (USA) (Woodman (USA) 126)   **46**
[2003 8g f9.4g 8m⁵ 8g f7g Dec 16] well-made gelding: fourth foal: half-brother to 7f winner Briery (by Salse): dam unraced daughter of Cheveley Park winner/Irish 1000 Guineas second Woodstream: poor maiden: left W. Haggas after second start: stays 1m. *N. Tinkler*

NEWCORP LAD   3 b.g. Komaite (USA) – Gleam of Gold (Crested Lark 78) [2003   **78**
72: 8.2g 8.1m⁵ 8.3m* 8.3g* 8.2m² 10g⁶ Aug 1] strong gelding: fair performer: won minor events at Hamilton in June and July: acts on any going: often races up with pace: genuine: gelded after final outing. *Mrs G. S. Rees*

NEW DAY DAWNING   2 ch.f. (Feb 6) First Trump 118 – Tintinara (Selkirk (USA)   **61 ?**
129) [2003 5m 6.1m⁴ 6.1d⁶ 5m 7m Oct 1] 1,800Y: close-coupled filly: fourth foal: dam unraced: possibly flattered when fourth in maiden at Nottingham: showed little otherwise. *C. Smith*

NEW DESIGN (IRE)   3 ch.f. Bluebird (USA) 125 – Ashirah (USA) (Housebuster   **–**
(USA)) [2003 93: 6m Jul 8] lengthy filly: fairly useful for D. Wachman in Ireland at 2 yrs: well held only 3-y-o start: sold 58,000 gns in December. *M. J. Wallace*

NEW DIAMOND   4 ch.g. Bijou d'Inde 127 – Nannie Annie 60 (Persian Bold 123)   **–**
[2003 75p: p8g 12m f8g p12g Jun 28] fair winner on second of 2 outings at 3 yrs: well beaten in 2003: tried blinkered. *J. M. P. Eustace*

NEW FOUNDATION (IRE)   3 b.f. College Chapel 122 – Island Desert (IRE) 55   **78 §**
(Green Desert (USA) 127) [2003 89: 6g 6g⁵ 6m⁴ 5f⁴ 6f⁶ 6f p6g 6.1m⁶ 6.1f⁴ 7g 5.7m² 5m⁵   **a65 §**
6m⁴ 6m 6m⁵ p6g p7g f6g Nov 17] leggy filly: good mover: fair performer on turf, modest on all-weather: effective at 5f/6f: acts on polytrack, firm and good to soft going: tongue tied after second start: tried in cheekpieces/visor: sometimes slowly away/hangs: unreliable. *Mrs S. A. Liddiard*

NEW MEXICAN   2 ch.g. (Apr 15) Dr Fong (USA) 128 – Apache Star 96 (Arazi (USA)   **99**
135) [2003 6g² 7m⁴ 6m* 7d² 8m* Oct 20] 32,000Y: tall, close-coupled gelding: second living foal: half-brother to useful Irish 2001 2-y-o 6f winner (stays 1m) Sahara Desert (by Green Desert): dam, 7f (at 2 yrs) to 9f winner, from family of very smart miler Rebecca Sharp: useful performer: won maiden in July and listed event (beat Makfool by ½ length, leading over 1f out and wandering) in October, both at Pontefract: stays 1m: acts on good to firm and good to soft ground: slowly away first 3 starts (having unseated rider at start on final occasion): carries head high, and is a tricky ride. *Mrs J. R. Ramsden*

NEW MORNING (IRE)   2 b.f. (Apr 10) Sadler's Wells (USA) 132 – Hellenic 125   **73 p**
(Darshaan 133) [2003 8d⁴ Oct 14] sister to 4-y-o Islington, very smart 1¼m performer Greek Dance and smart 1¼m and 13f winner (stayed 2½m) Election Day, and half-sister to useful 7f/1m winner Desert Beauty (by Green Desert): dam won Yorkshire Oaks and second in St Leger: odds on, green when 5 lengths fourth of 10 to Mekuria in maiden at Ayr, slowly away and unable to quicken: will be well suited by 1¼m+: sure to improve. *M. A. Jarvis*

Tote International Stakes (Handicap), Ascot—those drawn low dominate in a field of twenty-two as New Seeker wins from One More Round, Danger Over and Capricho

NEW OPTIONS   6 b.g. Formidable (USA) 125 – No Comebacks 70 (Last Tycoon   –
131) [2003 75: p6g⁴ p7g² p6g² p6g³ 5.1s 5g f5g f5g⁴ Dec 16] just fair handicapper   **a74**
nowadays: stays easy 7f: acts on all-weather, little form on turf in 2003: usually blinkered
earlier in career: carries head high: has idled. *W. J. Musson*

NEW ORCHID (USA)   3 b.f. Quest For Fame 127 – Musicanti (USA) (Nijinsky   **106**
(CAN) 138) [2003 7m⁶ 10.1m* 11.9g³ 12m² 11.9m Aug 21] very big, rangy filly: third
foal: half-sister to high-class 7f (at 2 yrs, including Dewhurst Stakes) to 9f winner Distant
Music and useful 10.3f winner Fragrant View (both by Distant View): dam, French 14.5f
winner, half-sister to top-class US middle-distance performer Vanlandingham: useful
performer: won maiden at Newcastle in May: good efforts after when 5¾ lengths third to
Place Rouge in Lancashire Oaks at Haydock (struggled to handle turn) and head second
to Treble Heights in listed event at Newmarket (shade mulish to post): ran as if amiss
in listed race at York final start: stayed 1½m: raced on good/good to firm going: stud.
B. W. Hills

NEW PROSPECTIVE   5 b.g. Cadeaux Genereux 131 – Amazing Bay 100 (Mazilier   **47**
(USA) 107) [2003 a8g⁵ a6g 8.3d 10.1m 9m p10g⁶ p10g³ 9.7m 11.5s³ p10g f5s Dec 27]
poor performer: won 2 handicaps/minor event at Mijas at 4 yrs when trained by J. Brown
in Spain: left G. Bindella in Spain, after second 5-y-o start, R. C. Guest after fifth and
G. L. Moore after tenth: stays 11.5f: acts on polytrack, soft and good to firm going: tried
tongue tied/in cheekpieces: free-going sort. *D. Nicholls*

NEW SEEKER   3 b.c. Green Desert (USA) 127 – Ahbab (IRE) 81 (Ajdal (USA) 130)   **111 p**
[2003 76p: 7d³ 8.1m² 7d* 7m³ 8m* 7g* Jul 26] tall, good sort: impresses in appearance:
progressed into a smart handicapper: won at Newmarket (ducked violently left over 1f
out) in May, Royal Ascot (Britannia Stakes, beat Helm Bank by neck) in June and Ascot

Elite Racing Club's "New Seeker"

in July: beat One More Round by 1½ lengths in Tote International Stakes on last occasion, soon in front and never challenged, flashing tail: better form at 7f than 1m, and should prove effective at 6f: acts on good to firm and good to soft ground: has been taken last/ steadily to post: races prominently: reportedly sustained bruising to a sesamoid in September, but stays in training, and should win pattern races at 4 yrs. *C. G. Cox*

NEW SOUTH WALES   3 b.c. In The Wings 128 – Temora (IRE) 90 (Ela-Mana-Mou 132) [2003 104p: 10.5g⁶ 16.2f⁴ 12d 14.6d* Nov 7] good-topped, attractive colt: useful performer, lightly raced: won minor event at Doncaster in November by head from Mamcazma: good efforts when sixth to Dalakhani in Prix Lupin at Longchamp and 1¾ lengths fourth to Shanty Star in Queen's Vase at Royal Ascot: last of 20 in Deutsches Derby at Hamburg on third start: barely stays 2m: acts on firm and good to soft going: has been tongue tied. *Saeed bin Suroor*   **107**

NEWTONIAN (USA)   4 ch.g. Distant View (USA) 126 – Polly Adler (USA) (Housebuster (USA)) [2003 –: f12g² f12s³ Dec 13] well-made gelding: fair maiden, lightly raced: stays 1½m: raced only on fibresand/good to firm ground: wandered both 4-y-o starts. *J. Parkes*   **77**

NEWTON (IRE)   2 b.c. (Jan 28) Danehill (USA) 126 – Elite Guest (IRE) (Be My Guest (USA) 126) [2003 5d² 6g* 5d* 6f 7m⁵ 7s⁴ 7m² Oct 27] good-bodied, attractive colt: fifth foal: half-brother to 2 winners in France by Highest Honor, including useful 1¼m winner Hesiode: dam, French 9f winner, half-sister to smart stayer Capal Garmon out of half-sister to Sun Princess and Saddlers' Hall: useful performer: won maiden at Fairyhouse and listed race at the Curragh (by ½ length from Moon Unit) in May: good 6½ lengths third of 6 (demoted a place) to American Post in Prix Jean-Luc Lagardere at Longchamp: blinkered, respectable second of 4 to Grey Swallow in Killavullan Stakes at Leopardstown final start: stays 7f: acts on soft and good to firm ground (never going well on firm in Coventry Stakes at Royal Ascot). *A. P. O'Brien, Ireland*   **101**

NEW WISH (IRE)   3 b.g. Ali-Royal (IRE) 127 – False Spring (IRE) (Petorius 117) [2003 90: 8m⁵ 8.1m³ 9.9g 9g⁵ 10.1m 8m 7.1g 8f 8m 9m 8m 10g 10.3m Oct 24] rather leggy, quite good-topped gelding: fairly useful handicapper: below form after fourth start, leaving M. Channon 35,000 gns after seventh one: should stay 1¼m: raced only on good ground or firmer: sometimes slowly away/races freely. *M. W. Easterby*   **93 d**

NEW YORK (IRE)   2 b.f. (Mar 5) Danzero (AUS) – Council Rock 74 (General Assembly (USA)) [2003 p7g³ 7.1g² f8.5g⁴ Nov 28] leggy, attractive filly: half-sister to several winners, including smart 2000 2-y-o 5f winner Superstar Leo (by College Chapel) and useful 6f to 8.5f winner (7f winner at 2 yrs) Royal Artist (by Royal Academy): dam, maiden best at 1¼m, out of Nassau Stakes winner Dancing Rocks: best effort in maidens (fair form) when second to Disengage at Musselburgh, dictating pace: stays 7f. *W. J. Haggas*   **72**

NEXT DESERT (IRE)   4 b.c. Desert Style (IRE) 121 – Night Petticoat (GER) 116 (Petoski 135) [2003 122: 11g³ 12g² 12g⁶ Sep 7] very smart performer: impressive winner of Deutsches Derby at Hamburg in 2002 but missed remainder of year with fetlock problem: off 11 months, creditable efforts on return when 3¾ lengths third to Epalo in Grosser Mercedes-Benz-Preis at Baden-Baden and 2½ lengths second to Dai Jin in Credit-Suisse Private Banking-Pokal at Cologne: below-form sixth to Mamool in Grosser Bugatti Preis at Baden-Baden final start: stayed 1½m: acted on good to firm going, went well on softer than good: usually tracked pace: to stand at Gestut Rheinberg, Germany, fee €5,000. *A. Schutz, Germany*   **121**

NEXT FLIGHT (IRE)   4 b.g. Woodborough (USA) 112 – Sans Ceriph (IRE) 75 (Thatching 131) [2003 64: p10g f12g 10.9m 12.4g 10.1m f11g³ Dec 19] good-bodied gelding: modest maiden: left A. Jarvis after fifth start: stays 11f: acts on all-weather, yet to race on extremes of going on turf: tried visored. *R. E. Barr*   **50**

NEXT GINA (GER)   3 b.f. Perugino (USA) 84 – Night Petticoat (GER) 116 (Petoski 135) [2003 8d* 8g³ 8g 11s* 12d⁴ 10g⁴ 10s⁶ Oct 5] tall, leggy, rather plain filly: second foal: half-sister to 4-y-o Next Desert: dam won Preis der Diana and second in Deutsches St Leger: smart performer: won maiden at Mulheim in March and Buchmacher Springer - Preis der Diana (by length from White Rose) there in June: below best when fourth to Dai Jin in Deutsches Derby at Hamburg and to Ransom o'War in Grosser Dallmayr-Preis at Munich next 2 starts: ran well when 3¾ lengths sixth to Zee Zee Top in Prix de l'Opera at Longchamp final outing: stays 11f: acts on soft ground. *A. Schutz, Germany*   **112**

NIAGARA (IRE)   6 b.g. Rainbows For Life (CAN) – Highbrook (USA) 88 (Alphabatim (USA) 126) [2003 78, a63: p13g 12m⁶ May 19] stocky gelding: fair handicapper: **69**
                                                                                                                                                          a64

stays 1½m: acts on polytrack and any turf going: usually races prominently: successful over fences in September/October. *M. H. Tompkins*

NICE BALANCE (USA) 8 b.g. Shadeed (USA) 135 – Fellwaati (USA) (Alydar – §
(USA)) [2003 –§, a51?: f8g f8s f8g f6g f7g f6s f8s 13.8f May 30] big gelding: no longer
of any account: tried in headgear/tongue tie. *M. C. Chapman*

NICE COTE D'AZUR 2 ch.c. (Mar 2) Hernando (FR) 127 – Miss Beaulieu 106 **69 p**
(Northfields (USA)) [2003 7g 7m Sep 17] well-made colt: brother to useful 1m winner
Miss Riviera Golf and 4-y-o Miss Corniche, closely related to 2 winners by Niniski,
including fairly useful 1¼m and 12.5f winner Riviera Magic, and half-brother to several
winners: dam 6f (at 2 yrs) and 1¼m winner: fair form, not knocked about, in maidens at
Goodwood and Yarmouth: will stay at least 1m: open to progress. *G. Wragg*

NICHOLAS NICKELBY 3 gr.g. Fayruz 116 – Alasib 93 (Siberian Express (USA) **67**
125) [2003 f7g⁶ f7g² f9.4g² Nov 28] 14,000Y: fourth foal: brother to 5-y-o Strawberry
Dawn and half-brother to 4-y-o Salute: dam, 5f (at 2 yrs) and 6f winner, half-sister to
useful sprinter Farhana (by Fayruz): fair form in maidens: barely stays 9.4f: raced only on
fibresand. *N. P. Littmoden*

NICHOL FIFTY 9 b.g. Old Vic 136 – Jawaher (IRE) 60 (Dancing Brave (USA) 140) **46 d**
[2003 46, a52: f16g⁴ f12g f16s⁴ 16.2m 14m 13.8f⁵ 11.9m² 12.1m 16f 12f⁶ 16m 16.2m⁵ **a51 d**
11.9m Sep 4] workmanlike gelding: modest at best on all-weather, poor on turf nowadays: effective at 1½m to 17f: acts on fibresand, soft and firm going: tried in headgear/
tongue tie. *N. Wilson*

NICKEL SUNGIRL (IRE) 3 b.f. Petorius 117 – Sharp Hint 60 (Sharpo 132) [2003 **51**
49: f5s 7m 8d² 8f 7f f6g Nov 14] leggy filly: modest maiden: trained by G. M. Moore **a–**
second to fourth starts, then returned to previous trainer: stays 1m: acts on firm going,
good to soft and fibresand. *R. Hollinshead*

NICKLETTE 4 b.f. Nicolotte 118 – Cayla (Tumble Wind (USA)) [2003 66d: p5g⁶ –
p6g Mar 5] tall, workmanlike filly: fair at best: no form at 4 yrs: wore cheekpieces last 3
starts. *C. N. Allen*

NICK'S GREY (IRE) 2 gr.c. (Mar 10) Midyan (USA) 124 – Grey Goddess 117 **70**
(Godswalk (USA) 130) [2003 5.1f 6.1m⁴ 6d⁴ 6.1m² 6m p6g⁵ 7m² Oct 23] €17,000Y:
half-brother to several winners, including 7f (at 2 yrs) and 11f winner Grey Again (by
Unfuwain) and dam of very smart sprinter Pipalong: dam Irish 7f to 8.5f winner: fair
maiden: second in nurseries at Nottingham and Brighton: should stay 1m: acts on good to
firm going and polytrack: sometimes edges left: sold 18,000 gns. *R. Hannon*

NICK THE SILVER 2 gr.c. (Apr 24) Nicolotte 118 – Brillante (FR) 118 (Green **69**
Dancer (USA) 132) [2003 6m 8m³ 8g Oct 25] big colt: half-brother to several winners,
including fairly useful 9f/1¼m winner (including in Ireland) Intensity (by Bigstone):
dam, French 1m (at 2 yrs) and 11f winner, half-sister to top-class French miler Bellypha:
easily best effort in maidens (fair form) when third at Salisbury: needs to settle to stay
beyond 1m. *G. B. Balding*

NIEMBRO 3 b.g. Victory Note (USA) 120 – Diabaig 76 (Precocious 126) [2003 –: **48 ?**
9.7m⁴ 10g 11.9m 10.9m 9m 10m⁶ Aug 18] poor maiden on Flat: best effort on reappearance: stays 1¼m: raced only on good/good to firm going: tried blinkered/in cheekpieces:
won over hurdles in December for Mrs T. McInnes Skinner. *Mrs Lydia Pearce*

NIEVE LADY 4 b.f. Komaite (USA) – Nikoola Eve 69 (Roscoe Blake 120) [2003 67: **60**
p7g p8g f6s p6g 7m⁶ 7m⁴ 6.1g 6d 7m 7d⁴ 7g 8m Jun 4] leggy filly: modest handicapper:
left D. Shaw after ninth start: stayed 7f: acted on soft going, good to firm and all-weather:
dead. *C. R. Dore*

NIFTY DAN 4 b.g. Suave Dancer (USA) 136 – Nifty Fifty (IRE) 97 (Runnett 125) –
[2003 52: f7g Mar 11] good-bodied gelding: modest performer: tailed off only 4-y-o
outing. *J. M. Bradley*

NIFTY MAJOR 6 b.g. Be My Chief (USA) 122 – Nifty Fifty (IRE) 97 (Runnett 125) – §
[2003 65d: f6s f5g p6g f5g f5g f5g f5g⁶ 6.1d 7g 5.7f Jun 14] tall, workmanlike gelding: **a45 §**
poor performer: left S. R. Bowring after third start, Gay Kelleway after fifth: best at 5f:
acts on all-weather, firm and soft going: wears headgear: tried tongue tied: has twice
refused to race: untrustworthy. *Miss K. M. George*

NIGHT ARRANGEMENT 3 ch.f. Night Shift (USA) – By Arrangement (IRE) 60 –
(Bold Arrangement 127) [2003 –: 9.9m 14m 11m⁶ 10m 11f Oct 12] little form: tried
tongue tied. *S. Woodman*

NIGHT BEAUTY   3 b.f. King of Kings (IRE) 125 – Kymin (IRE) 78 (Kahyasi 130)   **70**
[2003 80: 8.1m⁶ 12.1d 10s⁴ Jun 30] big, good-topped filly: fair maiden, lightly raced:
stays 1¼m: acts on soft ground. *E. A. L. Dunlop*

NIGHT CAP (IRE)   4 ch.g. Night Shift (USA) – Classic Design (Busted 134) [2003   **57**
68: p7g p6g 6m⁵ 6m 6d p6g³ Dec 2] modest performer: effective at 6f/7f: acts on   **a68 ?**
all-weather and firm going: tried in cheekpieces: usually races prominently: none too
consistent. *T. D. McCarthy*

NIGHT DRIVER (IRE)   4 b.g. Night Shift (USA) – Highshaan (Pistolet Bleu (IRE)   **–**
133) [2003 76, a82: 8.3m Jul 7] big, strong gelding: fairly useful at best: well held only
start at 4 yrs. *P. J. Hobbs*

NIGHT FROLIC   2 b.f. (May 5) Night Shift (USA) – Miss d'Ouilly (FR) (Bikala 134)   **–**
[2003 7f 6d Nov 8] leggy filly: half-sister to several winners in France, including useful
performer up to 15f Mr Academy (by Royal Academy) and 10.5f winner Miss Caerleona
(by Caerleon), later Grade 3 9f winner in USA: dam, French 9f winner, half-sister to Prix
Jacques le Marois winner Miss Satamixa: little sign of ability in maidens at Salisbury
(slowly away) and Doncaster (tongue tied). *J. W. Hills*

NIGHT KISS (FR)   3 ch.f. Night Shift (USA) – Roxy (Rock City 120) [2003 61: p7g⁶   **71**
7m* 7g³ 8g 7g³ 7m 7m 8m² p7g² p8g Nov 12] fair performer: won handicap at Ascot in
March: stays 1m: acts on good to firm going, good to soft and polytrack: none too
consistent. *R. Hannon*

NIGHT MAIL   3 b.g. Shaamit (IRE) 127 – Penlanfeigan (Abutammam 85) [2003 –:   **42**
f7g⁶ f8g 10m 9.9m 12f⁴ 13.8m⁴ 16m 12m Oct 7] leggy gelding: poor maiden: stays
13.8f: acts on fibresand and firm ground: tried blinkered: sometimes slowly away.
M. W. Easterby

NIGHT MARKET   5 ch.g. Inchinor 119 – Night Transaction 59 (Tina's Pet 121)   **66 d**
[2003 66: f8s³ f8g f7g⁵ f8s³ f8.5s⁶ 8f³ 8.5f* 10g* 9.3g³ 9m³ 7.9m 9.9m⁴ 10s 8m 10.4m
8.5m 9.9d 10.1m⁶ 9m f9.4g Nov 1] strong gelding: fair performer: won seller at Beverley
(left B. Smart) and apprentice handicap at Pontefract in April: out of form in second half
of 2003: stays 1¼m: acts on fibresand and firm going, not on softer than good: tried
blinkered: sometimes races freely/finds little. *N. Wilson*

NIGHT MIST (IRE)   3 b.f. Alzao (USA) 117 – Night Mirage (USA) 80 (Silver Hawk   **82**
(USA) 123) [2003 80p: 8.3f² Jun 26] workmanlike filly: fairly useful performer, lightly
raced: good second to Ryme Intrinseca in minor event at Hamilton only 3-y-o start:
should be suited by 1¼m/1½m: raced only on good ground or firmer. *M. Johnston*

NIGHT PEARL (IRE)   2 b.f. (Jan 29) Night Shift (USA) – Miss Pickpocket (IRE)   **72**
64 (Petorius 117) [2003 5.1f³ 7.1m p6g⁴ 6d⁵ 6g Oct 25] leggy filly: third foal: half-sister
to 2000 2-y-o 5f winner Western Hero (by Lake Coniston), later winner in Denmark, and
4-y-o Zamyatina: dam 2-y-o 5f winner who stayed 7f: fair maiden: barely stays 7f: acts
on firm and good to soft going, probably on polytrack: blinkered (ran poorly) final start:
edgy sort. *G. A. Butler*

NIGHT PROSPECTOR   3 b.c. Night Shift (USA) – Pride of My Heart 74 (Lion   **97**
Cavern (USA) 117) [2003 86: 6m² 5m* 5m² 5m⁵ 5d* 5d 5m Sep 21] close-coupled,
good-topped colt: useful performer: won maiden at Folkestone in May and handicap at
Windsor (beat Intellibet One 2½ lengths) in August: last in listed races at Doncaster and
Milan last 2 starts: will prove best at 5f: acts on firm and good to soft going: races
prominently: tends to wander. *J. W. Payne*

NIGHT RUNNER   4 b.c. Polar Falcon (USA) 126 – Christmas Kiss 82 (Taufan   **–**
(USA) 119) [2003 88p: 5g 6d 6d 6f 7m 7m 7.5d Sep 23] leggy, unfurnished colt: fairly
useful at 3 yrs: well held in 2003: often blinkered. *T. D. Easterby*

NIGHTS CROSS (IRE)   2 b.c. (Apr 27) Cape Cross (IRE) 129 – Cathy Garcia (IRE)   **103**
(Be My Guest (USA) 126) [2003 5m⁵ 5g³ 5.7m* 6m⁶ 5m⁶ 6f⁶ 5d* 5.1m² 6m⁵ 5g² 5d³ 6d
5g³ 5m² 5m* 5g² Oct 11] IR 15,000F, 32,000Y: compact colt: fourth foal: half-brother to
6f (including at 2 yrs) winner Cantgetyourbreath (by College Chapel): dam Italian 7f
winner: useful performer: won maiden at Bath in May, minor event at Beverley in July
and listed race at Tipperary (beat Blue Crush 4½ lengths) in October: good 3½ lengths
second to Majestic Missile in Cornwallis Stakes at Ascot final start: best form at 5f: acts
on good to firm and good to soft ground: tough and reliable. *M. R. Channon*

NIGHT SHIFT BLUE'S (IRE)   4 b.g. Night Shift (USA) – Tommelise (USA)   **–**
(Dayjur (USA) 137) [2003 64, a71: f6s f5s³ f6s f6g² f6s p7g f5g³ 6.1g Mar 26] smallish,   **a68**
close-coupled gelding: fair on all-weather, well held only outing on turf in 2003: effec-

tive at 5f to 7f: acts on fibresand: wears headgear: none too consistent: sold 1,000 gns.
M. J. Polglase

NIGHT SIGHT (USA) 6 b.g. Eagle Eyed (USA) 111 – El Hamo (USA) (Search For 76
Gold (USA)) [2003 91: f8s f11g p12g⁵ 12g 12m⁴ 10.3m 11.9m⁶ 12m² 10.3f³ 12m⁵ 12d⁶
12m⁵ 11.9m 11.9m 12g 11.9f⁴ Oct 9] smallish, stocky gelding: fluent mover: fair handicapper: best at 1¼m/1½m: acts on all-weather, probably on any turf going: blinkered
once: sometimes races freely: held up: tough and consistent. *M. C. Chapman*

NIGHTSPOT 2 ch.g. (Apr 11) Night Shift (USA) – Rash Gift 78 (Cadeaux Genereux 80
131) [2003 6.1g⁵ 6m⁵ 6g* p6g⁵ Oct 27] 24,000Y: tall, quite attractive gelding: fourth
foal: half-brother to 3-y-o Allergy: dam, maiden, probably stayed 1¼m: fairly useful
performer: won maiden at Windsor in October readily by 1½ lengths from Go Yellow:
respectable effort at Lingfield final start: will probably stay 1m. *R. Charlton*

NIGHT STORM 2 b.f. (Mar 13) Night Shift (USA) – Monte Calvo 85 (Shirley Heights 67
130) [2003 6g 6m² 7g⁵ Aug 2] 19,000Y: smallish, workmanlike filly: first foal: dam 1¾m
and 17f winner: easily best effort in maidens (fair form) when second at Kempton: should
stay at least 1m: tongue tied all starts. *S. Dow*

NIGHT WARRIOR (IRE) 3 b.g. Alhaarth (IRE) 126 – Miniver (IRE) (Mujtahid 82
(USA) 118) [2003 71: p6g⁴ p7g⁶ 11.6g 10.2m⁶ p12g⁴ f16.2g 10.1g 12.1m⁵ 10.9m² f11s* a77
10f² p12g 10g p10g f11g f11g p12g⁴ Dec 17] fairly useful on turf, fair on all-weather:
won seller at Lingfield (left M. Tregoning) in May and (having left J. Best after sixth
start) handicap at Southwell in September: effective at 1¼m/1½m: acts on all-weather,
raced only on good ground or firmer on turf: tried in cheekpieces/visor: none too
consistent. *D. Flood*

NIGHTWATCHMAN (IRE) 4 b.g. Hector Protector (USA) 124 – Nightlark (IRE) 62
85 (Night Shift (USA)) [2003 62, a67: 12.3m 14.4g⁴ p16g⁵ 13.3m⁶ 14.1m⁶ 14m⁴ 16.2d³ a77
f14.8s² f16.2f* 16.4m⁴ f14.8g³ Oct 20] smallish, strong gelding: fair handicapper on
all-weather, modest on turf: won apprentice event at Wolverhampton in July: stays easy
2m: acts on all-weather, good to firm and good to soft going: sold 20,000 gns, joined
N. Henderson. *W. R. Muir*

NIGHT WOLF (IRE) 3 gr.g. Indian Ridge 123 – Nicer (IRE) 113 (Pennine Walk 78
120) [2003 –p: f8.5g³ 7.1m³ 6.1m⁴ 8.1m⁴ 8m* 8m⁵ May 31] fair handicapper: best effort
when winning at Newcastle in May by 5 lengths: stays 1m: raced only on going firmer
than good on turf. *M. R. Channon*

NIGHT WORKER 2 b.c. (Apr 10) Dracula (AUS) – Crystal Magic 92 (Mazilier 66
(USA) 107) [2003 6g⁴ 6g³ 7m 6m⁴ 6m Oct 16] 30,000Y: strong, compact colt: unimpressive mover: fourth foal: half-brother to 6f winner O B Comfort (by College Chapel) and
3-y-o I'm Magic: dam, 2-y-o 5f winner, out of sister to high-class sprinter Petong: fair
maiden: best efforts on first and final starts: should stay 7f. *R. Hannon*

NIJMAH 3 ch.f. Halling (USA) 133 – Star Ridge (USA) (Storm Bird (CAN) 134) [2003 –
71: 8g 11.5g 10m 11.1g⁶ Jun 11] small, sparely-made filly: fair maiden at 2 yrs: well held
in 2003, leaving G. Chung after reappearance. *Miss D. Mountain*

NIKAIA 2 b.f. (Feb 20) Nicolotte 118 – Noble Haven 74 (Indian King (USA) 128) [2003 –
7.1m Sep 22] 21,000F, 26,000Y: closely related to 3 winners by Night Shift, including
French/UAE 5f (at 2 yrs) to 1m winner Shoalhaven and 5f (at 2 yrs)/6f winner Night
Haven (both useful), and half-sister to winner in Italy by Faustus: dam, 2-y-o 6f winner,
half-sister to useful sprinter Night At Sea: 12/1, well held in maiden at Chepstow: sold
4,500 gns. *R. Hannon*

NIMBUS TWOTHOUSAND 3 b.f. Cloudings (IRE) 112 – Blueberry Parkes 71 48 §
(Pursuit of Love 124) [2003 –§: 7f⁴ 8.2g⁵ 10d⁶ 12.1m f11s⁵ 11g f12g f8g⁶ Nov 25] poor
maiden: stays 11f: acts on fibresand, firm and good to soft ground: blinkered last 4 starts:
wayward and not one to trust. *P. R. Wood*

NIMELLO (USA) 7 b.g. Kingmambo (USA) 125 – Zakota (IRE) (Polish Precedent ?
(USA) 131) [2003 91§: f6g⁴ f7s⁴ f8.5g³ 9m 9.2m⁴ f7s* f8.5g* 7m 8.3m⁶ f7s* f7g² f9.4s* a96 §
Dec 31] smallish, well-made gelding: useful performer on all-weather nowadays: won 2
sellers in May, claimer in September (left K. Ryan £8,000), and handicap in December,
all at Wolverhampton: effective at 7f to 9.4f: has won on firm going, goes particularly
well on softer than good and fibresand: tried blinkered, not in 2003: tends to carry head
high/find little/wander: reportedly lame fourth/eighth starts: unreliable. *A. G. Newcombe*

NINA FONTENAIL (FR) 2 gr.f. (Mar 26) Kaldounevees (FR) 118 – Ninon Fontenail –
(FR) (Turgeon (USA) 123) [2003 7.1d 6.1m⁶ Sep 22] quite good-topped filly: second

foal: half-sister to French 12.5f winner Dom Fontenail (by Tel Quel): dam ran once in France: well beaten in maidens at Sandown (slowly away) and Chepstow. *N. J. Hawke*

NINAH   2 b.f. (Apr 29) First Trump 118 – Alwal (Pharly (FR) 130) [2003 f5g^2 5m^5 f5g^4 **69** 6v^5 6g 5.1m^3 8.1g^3 7.1m 7.1g^2 7.1m^2 8.2f^4 f8s Oct 7] 1,200Y: tall, leggy filly: fifth foal: **a59** half-sister to 7-y-o Quedex and a winner in Italy by Ardkinglass: dam won in Holland, including Dutch Oaks: fair maiden on turf, modest on all-weather: second at Southwell and at Chepstow (twice): stays 1m: acts on firm ground and fibresand: often races freely/ up with pace. *J. M. Bradley*

NINEACRES   12 b.g. Sayf El Arab (USA) 127 – Mayor 86 (Laxton 105) [2003 73§,   **46 §** a85§: f5g^4 p6g^3 p6g p6g f5s^3 f6g f5g^2 f5s^5 p6g f5g^3 p6g f5g 5.1m 6f 5g 6f Aug 12]   **a56 §** angular, workmanlike gelding: useful performer in his prime, winner of 14 of his 148 races: just modest in 2003: best at 5f/6f: unraced on heavy going, acted on any other turf/ all-weather: tried visored, blinkered in recent years: reportedly broke blood vessel twelfth start: untrustworthy: reportedly retired. *J. M. Bradley*

NINE RED   2 b.f. (Apr 3) Royal Applause 124 – Sarcita 111 (Primo Dominie 121) [2003   **57** 6m^5 6m^5 5.1f^5 6g Oct 13] 40,000Y: leggy, good-topped filly: seventh foal: half-sister to smart 6f/7f winner in Britain/UAE Snow Kid (by Indian Ridge) and useful 1998 2-y-o 5f winner Sarson (by Efisio): dam won Ayr Gold Cup: modest maiden: well held in nursery final start: not sure to stay beyond 6f. *B. W. Hills*

NITEOWL DREAM   3 ch.f. Colonel Collins (USA) 122 – Nite-Owl Dancer 75   **–** (Robellino (USA) 127) [2003 59: f7g 10g May 26] tall, leggy filly: modest maiden at 2 yrs: well beaten both 3-y-o starts: tried blinkered. *J. O'Reilly*

NITEOWL EXPRESS (IRE)   2 b.f. (Mar 28) Royal Applause 124 – Nordan Raider   **–** 81 (Domynsky 110) [2003 6m Oct 17] 3,000Y: third foal: half-sister to 6-y-o Nod's Nephew: dam, 6f winner, half-sister to useful 7f/1m performer Hi Nod: 80/1 and very green, slowly away when last of 8 in maiden at Redcar. *J. O'Reilly*

NITE-OWL FIZZ   5 b.g. Efisio 120 – Nite-Owl Dancer 75 (Robellino (USA) 127)   **–** [2003 74: f8.5g f8.5g f8.5s* f8g f9.4g^5 f8s^6 f8s f8g f8.5g f8.5g^5 Nov 29] fair per-   **a69** former: won seller at Wolverhampton in March: stays 8.5f: raced almost exclusively on fibresand: inconsistent. *J. O'Reilly*

NIVERNAIS   4 b.g. Forzando 122 – Funny Wave 65 (Lugana Beach 116) [2003 83:   **92** 6m* 6f^3 5m^3 6g^6 Aug 11] smallish, lengthy gelding: fairly useful handicapper: had wind operation after final 3-y-o start: won at Salisbury (carried head awkwardly) in June: good third at Goodwood and at Sandown next 2 starts: effective at 5f to easy 7f: acts on firm and good to soft going: tried visored: tongue tied 3 of last 4 outings. *H. Candy*

NO ARGUMENT   4 b.g. Young Ern 120 – As Sharp As 64 (Handsome Sailor 125)   **–** [2003 –: f6g 9f Jun 16] maiden: no form since 2 yrs: tried blinkered. *D. W. Chapman*

NOBIGSUPRISE (IRE)   4 b.f. Courtship 88 – Pennine Sue (IRE) (Pennine Walk   **–** 120) [2003 –: f8.5s Mar 31] ex-Irish filly: first foal: dam poor Irish maiden: no form. *W. G. M. Turner*

NO BITZ (IRE)   2 ch.f. (Apr 1) Woodborough (USA) 112 – Riskie Things 62 (Risk   **54** Me (FR) 127) [2003 p5g^5 5g^4 Mar 25] 2,800Y: second foal: half-sister to 3-y-o Notty Bitz: dam 5f/6f winner, including at 2 yrs: modest form in minor event at Lingfield and maiden at Folkestone: should stay 6f. *J. S. Moore*

NOBLE CALLING (FR)   6 b.h. Caller I D (USA) – Specificity (USA) 103 (Alleged   **61** (USA) 138) [2003 59: 9.7m^3 11.9m^4 10.2m* 10m* 9f^5 10.2f^6 10m 8.1g 8m 9.9m^6 Oct 1] angular horse: modest handicapper: won amateur events at Bath in May and Newbury in June: stays easy 1½m: acts on firm and good to soft ground: often blinkered/visored earlier in career. *R. J. Hodges*

NOBLE CYRANO   8 ch.g. Generous (IRE) 139 – Miss Bergerac (Bold Lad (IRE)   **43 §** 133) [2003 55§: f12g^3 f12g^4 10.1d 12m^5 10m 10g^5 14.1m f12g 10.9m^6 12.1g 10m Aug   **a48 §** 9] tall, angular gelding: poor handicapper: won apprentice race at Southwell in March: effective at 1¼m to 14.4f: acts on any turf going and fibresand: unreliable. *Jedd O'Keeffe*

NOBLE DESERT (FR)   2 b.f. (Apr 29) Green Desert (USA) 127 – Sporades (USA)   **–** 117 (Vaguely Noble 140) [2003 p6g Dec 29] 38,000Y: half-sister to several winners abroad, including useful French 7.5f (at 2 yrs) and 8.5f winner Leave Us Leap (by Summer Squall) and French 11f winner/smart hurdler Sporazene (by Cozzene): dam, French 1m to 10.5f (Prix de Flore) winner, half-sister to Arlington Million winner Mill Native and high-class French 1m/9f performer French Stress: 33/1, well held in maiden at Lingfield, starting slowly and not knocked about. *R. Guest*

NOBLE LADY 3 ch.f. Primo Dominie 121 – Noble Destiny 89 (Dancing Brave (USA) **77**
140) [2003 65p: p5g² f6g* 5m² f7g f6s* f6s⁴ Sep 6] fair performer: won maiden at
Wolverhampton in July and minor event at Southwell in September: will prove best at 5f/
6f: raced only on all-weather and good to firm ground: blinkered last 2 starts: usually
races prominently. *Sir Mark Prescott*

NOBLE LOCKS (IRE) 5 ch.g. Night Shift (USA) – Imperial Graf (USA) (Blushing **–**
John (USA) 120) [2003 –, a69: f7s⁵ f7g⁶ f7g² f7g³ f7g² f7g² f7g⁴ f6g* f6g⁴ f8s f6s* 6g f6s **a80**
f7g⁵ f6g* Dec 26] smallish gelding: fairly useful handicapper: won at Wolverhampton in
May, September and December (amateur event): effective at 6f to 8.5f: acts on fibresand,
lightly raced and no form on turf since 3 yrs: tried blinkered/visored/tongue tied, better
form when not. *J. W. Unett*

NOBLE NICK 4 b. or br.g. Primo Dominie 121 – Pericardia 60 (Pardon 126) [2003 **81 d**
89: 6m⁴ 6d 6g 7m 7m Sep 17] useful-looking gelding: fairly useful handicapper: creditable effort at 4 yrs only on reappearance: left D. Nicholls after third start: best at 5f/6f:
acts on firm going, good to soft and fibresand: tried visored: sold 6,500 gns. *M. J. Wallace*

NOBLE PASAO (IRE) 6 b.g. Alzao (USA) 117 – Belle Passe (Be My Guest (USA) **84**
126) [2003 87, a82: 10g 9.9f⁶ 10m 9.9m 10g² Jul 22] close-coupled gelding: has a round
action: fairly useful handicapper: effective at 1¼m to 14.6f: acts on firm going, soft and
all-weather: blinkered once: usually held up. *Andrew Turnell*

NOBLE PENNY 4 b.f. Pennekamp (USA) 130 – Noble Form (Double Form 130) **64 d**
[2003 59: 7g³ 8.3g⁶ 7m 8g f8s 10.1g Oct 22] well-made filly: modest maiden: below
form last 4 starts: may prove best at 1m: raced only on good ground or firmer on turf.
Mrs K. Walton

NOBLE PHILOSOPHER 3 ch.g. Faustus (USA) 118 – Princess Lucy 42 (Local **–**
Suitor (USA) 128) [2003 10d p10g⁶ p12g Jul 23] big, angular gelding: brother to milers
Royal Philosopher (smart) and Regal Philosopher (useful), and half-brother to 6f (at 2
yrs) to 1¼m winner Roi de Danse (by Komaite): dam maiden: little form in maidens.
R. M. Beckett

NOBLE PROFILE 3 b.g. Fleetwood (IRE) 107 – Springs Welcome 86 (Blakeney 126) **–**
[2003 10.2m Apr 29] eighth foal: half-brother to several winning stayers, including fairly
useful 1½m winner who stayed 2½m and maiden (by Deploy) and 4-y-o Ziggy
Zen: dam 1¼m to 12.5f winner who stayed 2m: 16/1, tailed off in maiden at Bath: sold
£2,100 in August. *C. A. Cyzer*

NOBLE PURSUIT 6 b.g. Pursuit of Love 124 – Noble Peregrine (Lomond (USA) **82 d**
128) [2003 83: p8g³ f8.5g⁵ p8g⁶ 8.3g 10m⁶ 10m 8m 8m 8.3m⁶ 8.1g 8.3m f8g⁴ f8g⁴ f11g
Dec 16] workmanlike gelding: fairly useful handicapper: below form following reappearance, leaving N. Littmoden after third outing. P. D'Arcy after eleventh: stays 1m: acts on
all-weather, soft and firm going: tried in cheekpieces. *P. A. Blockley*

NOBLE VIEW (USA) 4 ch.f. Distant View (USA) 126 – Proud Lou (USA) (Proud **60**
Clarion) [2003 –: 8f 9m⁵ 8.2s 10.1g May 28] leggy filly: modest maiden, lightly raced:
stays 9f: acts on soft and good to firm ground. *R. Guest*

NOBRATINETTA (FR) 4 b.f. Celtic Swing 138 – Bustinetta 89 (Bustino 136) [2003 **75**
11.1d⁴ 12.1d* 16.2m Jun 5] fourth foal: sister to 5-y-o Tomasino and half-sister to 8-y-o
Bhutan: dam 11f winner out of half-sister to Terimon: fairly useful bumper winner: easily
best effort (fair form) when winning maiden at Hamilton in May: will be suited by 1¾m+.
Mrs M. Reveley

NOCATEE (IRE) 2 b.g. (Mar 24) Vettori (IRE) 119 – Rosy Sunset (IRE) (Red Sunset **45**
120) [2003 7m 8m 10m 7m⁵ f8g f8g Dec 19] 20,000F, 38,000Y: tall gelding: seventh foal:
half-brother to several winners, including useful 6f (including at 2 yrs) winner Evening
Promise (by Aragon), later Grade 3 winner in US, and 4-y-o Pagan Sky: dam lightly-
raced half-sister to 4-y-o Bandari: poor maiden: probably stays 1m. *P. C. Haslam*

NO CHANCE TO DANCE (IRE) 3 b.c. Revoque (IRE) 122 – Song of The Glens **–**
(Horage 124) [2003 8m 9.9m⁵ 11.1g Sep 27] IR 25,000Y: good-topped, lengthy colt:
half-brother to several winners, including smart 2000 2-y-o 5f/6f (Prix Morny) winner
Bad As I Wanna Be (by Common Grounds): dam, maiden, out of half-sister to 2000
Guineas winner Right Tack: well held in maidens. *H. J. Collingridge*

NO DILEMMA (USA) 2 ch.g. (Apr 26) Rahy (USA) 115 – Cascassi (USA) 91 **61**
(Nijinsky (CAN) 138) [2003 7g 8.2d Nov 6] leggy gelding: fifth living foal: closely
related to French 1999 2-y-o 1m winner Checkers Speech (by Arazi) and half-brother to
1¼m winner Gentle Dame (by Kris): dam, 1¼m and (in France at 4 yrs) 12.5f winner,

half-sister to Oaks winner Diminuendo: modest form in maidens at Newmarket and Nottingham: should stay 1¼m. *E. A. L. Dunlop*

NO DISRUPTION (IRE) 3 b.g. Lahib (USA) 129 – Angela's Venture (GER) (Simply Great (FR) 122) [2003 47: 5f 7.1f 6m f6g 5m Aug 4] well-made gelding: poor maiden: stays 7f: acts on firm going: tried in cheekpieces. *T. D. Barron* **45**

NOD'S NEPHEW 6 b.g. Efisio 120 – Nordan Raider 81 (Domynsky 110) [2003 75, a83: f8s f8s f6s 6m⁵ 8g⁴ f9.4s f6g 7g⁴ 8m 8.5g⁴ p10g 8.1m³ p10g* 10.2g* f9.4g Nov 1] lengthy gelding: modest performer: won sellers at Lingfield in July and Chepstow in August: effective at 6f to 1¼m: acts on any turf going/all-weather: often tongue tied: sometimes races freely: usually tracks pace: none too consistent. *D. E. Cantillon* **63 a55**

NOELS GANADOR (USA) 4 b.c. Our Emblem (USA) 114 – Carolita (USA) (Caro 133) [2003 a8g a8g⁶ a10.5g² 8g⁶ a8g⁶ a7g* a8g² a10g² a12g a6g⁵ a8g⁶ 8s⁶ a8g a8g a8s a8s⁴ Dec 7] fairly useful performer: successful 4 times in Spain in 2002: stiff task when sixth of 8 to Dandoun in listed race at Doncaster fourth outing: won handicap at Dos Hermanas in May: effective at 6f to 10.5f: acts on sand/fibresand, lightly raced on turf. *E. J. Creighton, Spain* **?**

NOFAN (IRE) 3 b.c. Marju (IRE) 127 – Auntie Maureen (IRE) 73 (Roi Danzig (USA)) [2003 –: f8.5g 9.7g 11.8m⁴ 10.2m⁵ Apr 29] little form: visored last 3 starts. *J. D. Czerpak* **–**

NOFA'S MAGIC (IRE) 3 b.f. Rainbow Quest (USA) 134 – Garah 107 (Ajdal (USA) 130) [2003 10m² 10m May 16] smallish filly: fifth foal: half-sister to 3 winners, including 5-y-o Olden Times and 1½m winner All Good Things (by Marju): dam, 6f winner, out of smart sprinter Abha: fair form when second to Halawanda in maiden at Newbury: ran as if amiss in listed event at same course following month: will stay 1½m. *J. L. Dunlop* **92**

NO FRONTIER (IRE) 5 ch.m. Imperial Frontier (USA) 112 – Poly Dancer (Suave Dancer (USA) 136) [2003 70: 8g 8g² 9m³ 10g⁶ 8g 7d² 7g* 9.6f 8m 7d 7g⁶ 8s⁴ 9.5g⁵ 8d³ 10g⁵ 8m⁶ 9.5d² p8g Nov 22] IR 1,000Y: first foal: dam no form: fair handicapper: won at the Curragh in August: well held on all-weather debut at Lingfield final start: effective at 7f to 1¼m: acts on firm and soft ground: usually wears tongue tie, tried in cheekpieces. *T. Hogan, Ireland* **74**

NO GROUSE 3 b.g. Pursuit of Love 124 – Lady Joyce (FR) (Galetto (FR) 118) [2003 73: f8.5g³ f9.4g² 7g⁵ 7m* 6.1m* 7m 7f 7m 6d Jul 26] strong gelding: fairly useful handicapper: left J. Hills after second start: best efforts when winning at Catterick in April and Chester in May: best at 6f/7f: acts on fibresand and good to firm ground. *E. J. Alston* **83**

NO ILLUSIONS 4 b.g. Bluegrass Prince (IRE) 110 – Dancing Years (USA) 56 (Fred Astaire (USA)) [2003 53: p12g p16g⁵ Jan 22] sparely-made gelding: poor maiden: stays easy 2m: acts on polytrack, firm and soft going: sometimes visored, tongue tied both 4-y-o starts. *R. Ingram* **46**

Tote Gold Trophy Stakes (Handicap), Goodwood—the progressive No Refuge gains his fourth success of the year; behind him come Santando (visor), Trust Rule (blaze) and Anticipating (left)

NO LOOKING BACK (IRE) 3 b.g. Revoque (IRE) 122 – Chloe (IRE) 79 (Green **47**
Desert (USA) 127) [2003 55: 12m⁶ 8m 10m 9.9m⁵ 9.3m⁶ 12d 10g 8s Jul 25] small,
angular gelding: poor maiden: stays 1¼m: acts on good to firm ground: tried blinkered.
T. D. Easterby

NO MERCY 7 ch.g. Faustus (USA) 118 – Nashville Blues (IRE) 94 (Try My Best **– §**
(USA) 130) [2003 –§, a65§: f7s⁴ p10g f8s f7g² p6g f8g f7g f8.5s⁶ f7s May 12] big, **a58 §**
lengthy gelding: modest performer: best at 7f/1m: acts on fibresand, no recent form on
turf: usually wears headgear: tried in tongue tie: unreliable. *B. A. Pearce*

NOMINATE (GER) 3 b.g. Desert King (IRE) 129 – Northern Goddess 111 (Night **67 d**
Shift (USA)) [2003 8.2g 10.9m³ 10.3m⁵ 11.7f p12g 8.1g f12g Dec 22] 110,000Y: seventh
foal: half-brother to smart 1¼m to 1½m winner in France/US Northern Quest (by
Rainbow Quest) and French 5.5f (at 2 yrs) to 10.5f winner Nortolixa (by Linamix): dam
sprinter: fair maiden: ran badly last 3 outings, leaving P. Cole before penultimate one:
stays 11f: raced only on good going or firmer on turf: tried blinkered/tongue tied: free-
going sort. *S. T. Lewis*

NON ULTRA (USA) 3 ch.f. Peintre Celebre (USA) 137 – Susun Kelapa (USA) 94 **57 §**
(St Jovite (USA) 135) [2003 63: f8.5g² p8g p8g⁴ p10g p12g 10m⁶ f9.4g 8.2d* 8d f8.5g⁶
10g⁴ Jul 5] leggy filly: modest performer: won selling handicap at Nottingham in May:
effective at 1m/1¼m: acts on all-weather, unraced on extremes of going on turf: usually
blinkered: races prominently: sometimes carries head awkwardly: unreliable: sold 9,000
gns. *B. J. Meehan*

NOORA (IRE) 2 ch.f. (Feb 2) Bahhare (USA) 122 – Esteraad (IRE) 90 (Cadeaux **59 p**
Genereux 131) [2003 6d Nov 8] good-topped filly: has scope: first foal: dam, 2-y-o 6f
winner who stayed 1¼m, half-sister to useful performer up to 1½m Vagabond Chanteuse:
8/1 and better for race, 5 lengths eighth of 14 to Miss Langkawi in maiden at Doncaster,
short of room and not knocked about: will stay at least 1m: should do better.
M. P. Tregoning

NOOSA COURT (USA) 4 b.f. Hansel (USA) – Mahmoud Dancer (USA) (Moment **–**
of Hope (USA)) [2003 55: 8m 10.9m 12f Jun 26] lightly-raced maiden: well held in
handicaps at 3 yrs. *G. A. Swinbank*

NOPEKAN (IRE) 3 b.g. Sri Pekan (USA) 117 – Giadamar (IRE) (Be My Guest (USA) **100**
126) [2003 83: 8g⁶ 9g⁵ 10d* 10.2d³ 9.5m* 10m 8.5s 10f 12d⁶ 10f 10s⁶ Sep 19] 23,000
2-y-o: leggy gelding: first foal: dam unraced half-sister to smart 1985 2-y-o Lucayan
Princess, herself dam of Luso and Warrsan: useful performer: won handicaps at the
Curragh in April and Gowran (beat Miss Odlum 2 lengths) in June: below form after,
including in listed race at Ascot sixth start: stays 1¼m: acts on firm and good to soft
going, probably on soft: tried blinkered at 2 yrs. *Patrick Mullins, Ireland*

NORDIC DANCER (IRE) 2 b.f. (Feb 27) Danehill Dancer (IRE) 117 – Nordic Abu **–**
(IRE) 60 (Nordico (USA)) [2003 f7s p7g 7d p7g Nov 18] 6,500Y: lengthy filly: sixth foal:
half-sister to winner in Italy by College Chapel: dam Irish maiden: little sign of ability in
maidens/claimer: sold 800 gns. *R. M. H. Cowell*

NOREEN 2 b.f. (Mar 3) Komaite (USA) – Fair Minded (Shareef Dancer (USA) 135) **–**
[2003 5m 6g 5.1m 8f⁵ 7m Oct 13] leggy filly: sixth foal: half-sister to winner abroad by
Keen: dam unraced: well beaten in maidens/seller: blinkered/tongue tied last 3 starts.
E. L. James

NO REFUGE (IRE) 3 ch.g. Hernando (FR) 127 – Shamarra (FR) (Zayyani 119) [2003 **112 p**
59p: f12g* 12m³ p12g* 12.1g* 12.3g² 12d* a12g³ 13d² Sep 29] rather leggy gelding:
progressed into smart performer at 3 yrs, winning handicaps at Wolverhampton,
Lingfield, Hamilton and Goodwood (Tote Gold Trophy by 1¾ lengths from Santano) in
June/July: good third to Organizer in Svenskt Derby at Jagersro next time, then excellent
neck second to Hasanpour in handicap at Hamilton (subsequently gelded): should be well
suited by 1¾m+: acts on all-weather/dirt, yet to race on extremes of going on turf: slowly
away/ran in snatches fifth outing: has idled in front: type to progress again at 4 yrs. *Sir
Mark Prescott*

NORSE DANCER (IRE) 3 b.c. Halling (USA) 133 – River Patrol 96 (Rousillon **118**
(USA) 133) [2003 101p: 8g³ 12m⁴ 10g 8d³ 10.4m⁶ 8f Sep 27]
Update: Suffragette Emily Davison's death under the King's horse in the
1913 Derby may not have been a deliberate act of protest—Davison could have
died by accident after ducking under the rail prematurely when making her way
home after a day handing out leaflets to the masses on the Downs. Update: Lord

Mr J. C. Smith's "Norse Dancer"

Derby and Lord Bunbury may not have tossed a coin to decide in whose honour the Derby would be named—the code of the day would have dictated the drawing of lots between a house full of gentlemen, who would have made sure that the draw came out in the host's favour. The Derby would be the poorer were all the myths that surround it exploded. Myth and legend are part and parcel of the romance of the Derby both on and off course. 'Had I ridden him, he would have won on the bit by many lengths,' wrote jockey Steve Donoghue of the favourite Colombo, third to Windsor Lad in 1934. At the time, debunking Donoghue's view would have required waiting for a trip to the cinema to watch British Movietone News footage when it came round. In fact, the pictures show that, though boxed in off the turn, Colombo had every chance inside the final furlong, if anything fading at the finish under his Australian-born rider Rae Johnstone, who went on to win the Derby three times, incidentally.

Bogus hard-luck stories in a modern-day Derby tend to be strangled at birth. Norse Dancer's claims to being unlucky in 2003 barely took root in print, outside the remarks attributed to his owner. 'He's a very, very good horse but he had an awful lot to do,' Jeff Smith was quoted as saying on the day. Starting at 16/1, Norse Dancer did have a lot to do off the turn in the Derby, but his problems were largely of his own making. Sluggishly away, Norse Dancer seemed not to take hold of his bit under Richard Quinn, and was niggled along up the early climb. Disputing last turning for home, he was rushed up wide in the straight and got upsides third-placed Alamshar approaching the last furlong, only to fade. At the line, Norse Dancer was beaten two and a half lengths in all, a length and a half by Alamshar for third. Norse Dancer had been supplemented for £90,000 after he had finished third in the Two Thousand Guineas on his reappearance. Only fourth in the Vintage Stakes at Goodwood and the Royal Lodge at Ascot as well as seventh in the Racing Post

Trophy at Doncaster at two, Norse Dancer started at 100/1 at Newmarket but showed he had improved considerably over the winter, staying on strongly and going down only by three quarters of a length and a head to Refuse To Bend and Zafeen.

Richard Quinn took over from Philip Robinson after Newmarket and kept the ride when Norse Dancer was supplemented again for the Eclipse at Sandown in July. With Alamshar having won the Irish Derby in the interim, Norse Dancer started third favourite behind Nayef and Islington, going off at 6/1, but he was a big disappointment, not travelling fluently again and finishing a remote twelfth. Norse Dancer was fitted with a visor for his next two starts and returned to form when beaten only a head and a short head by Reel Buddy and Statue of Liberty in the Sussex Stakes at Goodwood later in July, before running only a fair sixth for Robinson in the Juddmonte International at York, beaten over seven lengths. Norse Dancer beat only one home when seventh in the Queen Elizabeth II Stakes at Ascot on his final start, when the ride went to Martin Dwyer, Quinn having broken his collar bone in a fall at Newbury the previous week.

Norse Dancer (IRE) (b.c. 2000)	Halling (USA) (ch 1991)	Diesis (ch 1980)	Sharpen Up		
			Doubly Sure		
		Dance Machine (b 1982)	Green Dancer		
			Never A Lady		
	River Patrol (b 1988)	Rousillon (b 1981)	Riverman		
			Belle Dorine		
		Boathouse (b 1978)	Habitat		
			Ripeck		

Norse Dancer is a big, rangy sort, but he was sold at a time when his family's fortunes on the racecourse were ebbing, and he made only 26,000 guineas as a foal. His dam River Patrol represented a highly successful family when retired to stud in 1992. Her dam Boathouse finished third in the Sun Chariot Stakes, and was a half-sister to Oaks winner Bireme as well as the high-class middle-distance stayer Buoy, the smart sprinter Fluke and the smart stayer Balinger. River Patrol's first foal, the Red Ransom colt Regal Patrol, made 170,000 guineas as a yearling, but showed only fairly useful form, winning a handicap at Beverley. River Patrol, who was useful herself, making all in a maiden at Bath over a mile and a quarter for her only success, produced only two more minor winners (by Belmez and Unfuwain, both in Italy). Sent to Germany in 2000, River Patrol's 2001 produce (a filly by Ashkalani) made €180,000 as a yearling, but her 2002 produce (a filly by Winged Love) made just €26,000 as a yearling at the end of August. Halling, Norse Dancer's sire, has yet to produce a horse nearly so good as himself, but he has established himself at stud. He is joint twelfth in the table of sires with three-year-olds rated 100+ in the last four years, and sixth for two-year-olds. His three-year-olds in 2003 also included the Lingfield Derby Trial winner Franklins Gardens and the smart stayer Hilbre Island. The exploits of Halling have resulted in his being shipped to Dubai for 2004 in a bid to boost further the breeding reputation of the United Arab Emirates, which had its first pattern winner in Britain in 2003 with Cairns. As a racehorse, Halling got better with age, and showed himself top class at four and five, winning the Eclipse and the Juddmonte International twice. Norse Dancer's prospects at four are probably dependent on his temperament. The quirkiness he showed at Epsom became more pronounced as the season went on. He wandered and hung fire after hitting the front briefly in the closing stages at Goodwood and carried his head awkwardly at York, as he had on other occasions. On the bright side, he has the physical scope to train on well and has shown versatility. There is little to choose between his efforts in the Guineas and the Derby as his season's best. In addition, his only wins have been in a maiden and a minor event on his first two starts at two, so he will be unpenalised in listed and minor pattern races in 2004. A quick-actioned colt, below form so far on extremes of ground, he seems to go well fresh. *D. R. C. Elsworth*

NORTH BY NORTHEAST (IRE) 5 ch.g. Polish Precedent (USA) 131 – Catalonda **74** (African Sky 124) [2003 73: 7g 7m 8m* 7m^6 7f^6 p8g^5 8m^2 8.3d f8s Dec 27] tall, rather leggy gelding: fair handicapper: won apprentice event at Newmarket in June: stays 1m: acts on firm and good to soft going: wore cheekpieces last 8 starts. *J. W. Payne*

NORTHERN DANZIG 4 b.f. Danzig Connection (USA) – Kristiana (Kris 135) [2003 –
6m 6f Aug 27] well held in maidens, leaving B. Smart after reappearance. *G. A. Swinbank*

NORTHERN DESERT (IRE) 4 b.g. Desert Style (IRE) 121 – Rosie's Guest (IRE) –
(Be My Guest (USA) 126) [2003 103: 8g May 20] lengthy, quite good-topped gelding:
useful at 3 yrs: well held only 4-y-o outing. *P. W. Hiatt*

NORTHERN FRIEND 3 b.g. Distinctly North (USA) 115 – Pharaoh's Joy 66 (Robel- **52**
lino (USA) 127) [2003 54: 10m 8d 10m 10m⁵ 10.9f 8m³ 8m Aug 6] small, sturdy gelding:
modest maiden: stays 1¼m: acts on firm ground: often visored/blinkered: free-going sort:
sometimes finds little: sold 4,800 gns. *J. A. Glover*

NORTHERN GAMES 4 b.g. Mind Games 121 – Northern Sal 59 (Aragon 118) [2003 **68**
83: 5m 6.1d⁶ 7f⁴ 7m⁶ 7m⁴ 6.9f⁴ 8m 6.1f² 6.1m f7g⁴ Nov 1] leggy, useful-looking gelding:
fair performer: effective at 6f/7f: acts on firm going, good to soft and all-weather: wore
blinkers/cheekpieces last 3 starts too consistent. *K. A. Ryan*

NORTHERN MILL (IRE) 6 b.m. Distinctly North (USA) 115 – Aladja (Mill Reef **45**
(USA) 141) [2003 43+: p12g⁵ 13g 16d 14f Aug 15] poor handicapper: ran creditably at
Lingfield on reappearance: stays 2m: acts on polytrack and any turf going: tried blink-
ered. *Eoin Doyle, Ireland*

NORTHERN NYMPH 4 b.g. Makbul 104 – Needwood Sprite 58 (Joshua 129) **80**
[2003 87: f14g⁴ Dec 9] good-topped gelding: fairly useful handicapper: off 16 months
prior to running respectably only 4-y-o start: stays 2m: acts on fibresand, soft and good to
firm going. *R. Hollinshead*

NORTHERN SPIRIT 2 b.g. (May 2) Kadeed (IRE) – Elegant Spirit 31 (Elegant Air **58**
119) [2003 7g 7m⁵ 8m⁵ 10f Sep 30] tall gelding: first known foal: dam maiden: modest
maiden: well beaten in nursery final start: stays 1m. *K. A. Ryan*

NORTHERN SUMMIT (IRE) 2 b.g. (Feb 12) Danehill Dancer (IRE) 117 – Book –
Choice (North Summit) [2003 7m⁶ 7m 7m Oct 12] 4,000Y: workmanlike gelding:
half-brother to 3 winners, including fairly useful Irish 1¼m winner Quill Project (by
Project Manager): dam unraced: well held in maidens. *J. R. Norton*

NORTHERN SVENGALI (IRE) 7 b.g. Distinctly North (USA) 115 – Trilby's **46**
Dream (IRE) (Mansooj 118) [2003 57d: 5m 5g 5m 5g 5m 5f 10g⁵ 5m⁴ 5f 6f 6d Sep 29]
small, sturdy gelding: poor performer: effective at 5f to easy 7f: acts on any turf going/
all-weather: tried blinkered, usually tongue tied. *D. A. Nolan*

NORTH LANDING (IRE) 3 b.g. Storm Boat (CAN) 134 – Tirol Hope (IRE) 100 **63 d**
(Tirol 127) [2003 69: 8m⁶ 9.9d 8f² 8m 8m 10.1m 11g Oct 28] leggy, quite good-topped
gelding: modest maiden: left M. Johnston and no form after third start: stays 1m: acts on
firm and good to soft going: wore cheekpieces last 3 outings. *H. A. McWilliams*

NORTH LIGHT (IRE) 2 b.c. (Mar 1) Danehill (USA) 126 – Sought Out (IRE) 119 **95 P**
(Rainbow Quest (USA) 134) [2003 7.1d² 18m* Sep 24] strong, well-made colt: sixth foal:
brother to 4-y-o Researched and half-brother to 2 winners, including 6-y-o Cover Up:
dam, won Prix du Cadran, from very good family: confirmed considerable promise when
landing odds in 5-runner maiden at Goodwood by 1¾ lengths from Take A Bow, taking
good hold before asserting readily from 2f out: will stay at least 1¼m: open to good deal
of improvement, and should make his mark in stronger company at 3 yrs. *Sir Michael
Stoute*

NORTH OF KALA (IRE) 10 b.g. Distinctly North (USA) 115 – Hi Kala (Kampala **50**
120) [2003 12m⁴ Jul 12] modest handicapper: stayed 13f: acted on firm going: tried
blinkered: dead. *G. L. Moore*

NORTH POINT (IRE) 5 b.g. Definite Article 121 – Friendly Song 48 (Song 132) **65**
[2003 73: 14.1s 17.2f⁶ 16.4m⁶ 16.4m⁶ Aug 13] smallish, useful-looking gelding: fair
handicapper: stays easy 2m: acts on firm and good to soft going: tried visored. *R. Curtis*

NORTH SEA (IRE) 2 b.f. (Jan 29) Selkirk (USA) 129 – Sea Spray (IRE) 101 (Royal **– p**
Academy (USA) 130) [2003 7g Oct 25] 130,000Y: tall, quite good-topped filly: third
foal: dam, 7f (at 2 yrs)/1m winner, out of smart performer up to 1½m Sailor's Mate, a very
good family: 25/1, last of 12 in listed event at Newbury: should do better. *M. R. Channon*

NORTHSIDE LODGE (IRE) 5 b.g. Grand Lodge (USA) 125 – Alongside 58 (Slip **91**
Anchor 136) [2003 89: 10.1m⁵ 10.3m³ 10m 10f² 12f² 12m 10.3m 10g² 10m² 10.3g 10m⁴
10.4f p10g⁴ Dec 2] good-topped gelding: fairly useful handicapper: in frame 7 times in
2003: effective at 1¼m/easy 1½m: acts on polytrack, raced mainly on good going or
firmer on turf: tried blinkered at 3 yrs: usually held up: tough and consistent. *P. W. Harris*

NORTON (IRE)   6 ch.g. Barathea (IRE) 127 – Primrose Valley 99 (Mill Reef (USA)   **113**
141) [2003 109: p10g⁶ 8g³ 8g² 8m 8g 7.9m 8g Sep 13] strong, useful-looking gelding:
smart handicapper: best efforts at 6 yrs when third to Pablo in Lincoln at Doncaster and
second to Putra Pekan in Jubilee Stakes at Kempton: first home on far side when seventh
to Macadamia in Hunt Cup at Royal Ascot (won race in 2002) fourth start: effective at 7f
to 10.4f: yet to race on heavy going, acts on any other turf and polytrack: refused to enter
stall once at 5 yrs: effective held up or making running: game. *T. G. Mills*

NOSEY NATIVE   10 b.g. Cyrano de Bergerac 120 – Native Flair 87 (Be My Native   **44**
(USA) 122) [2003 –: 12g⁴ 12g 13.8f 11.6m⁶ 14.1m⁴ 14.1m Jul 2] leggy gelding: poor
performer: stays 2m: acts on any going: tried visored (early in career)/in cheekpieces:
sometimes slowly away: tends to get behind. *Mrs Lydia Pearce*

NOSSENKO (USA)   2 b.f. (Jan 27) Stravinsky (USA) 133 – Humble Fifteen (USA)   **– p**
(Feather Ridge (USA)) [2003 p6g Dec 29] €145,000Y: third foal: dam, 6f winner at 2 yrs
in USA, out of half-sister to Oaks and Irish Derby winner Balanchine: favourite but
green, struggled to handle bend when well held in maiden at Lingfield: sure to improve.
J. Noseda

NOTABLE GUEST (USA)   2 b.c. (Feb 9) Kingmambo (USA) 125 – Yenda 116   **91 p**
(Dancing Brave (USA) 140) [2003 7.1m² 8m² Oct 14] strong, useful-looking colt: fifth
foal: dam, 1½m winner (and second in Prix Vermeille), half-sister to Derby winner Quest
For Fame: fairly useful form in minor event at Sandown (beaten 1¼ lengths by Tashkil)
and maiden at Leicester (odds on, got going too late when beaten ½ length by Muhaymin): will be suited by 1¼m/1½m: open to progress, and should win races. *Sir Michael
Stoute*

NOTABLE LADY (IRE)   2 b.f. (Mar 18) Victory Note (USA) 120 – Griqualand   **95**
(Connaught 130) [2003 6m 5.3f* 6f⁵ 7m 5g⁵ Sep 13] big, good-topped filly: third foal:
half-sister to 1994 2-y-o 9.4f winner Shy Paddy (by Shy Groom) and 3-y-o Fort
McHenry: dam ran twice: useful performer: landed odds in maiden at Brighton in July:
good fifth in Phoenix Stakes at the Curragh and Flying Childers Stakes at Doncaster
(slowly away): needs to settle to stay 7f: acts on firm going: often bandaged behind.
N. A. Callaghan

NOT AMUSED (UAE)   3 ch.g. Indian Ridge 123 – Amusing Time (IRE) 104 (Sadler's   **85**
Wells (USA) 132) [2003 75p: 8g* 8.5m 10m² 10.3g² 11m⁴ 14m⁶ Oct 4] big, lengthy
gelding: fairly useful performer: won maiden at Doncaster in March: creditable efforts in
handicaps after when in frame: stays 11f: acts on soft and good to firm ground: sometimes
races freely/carries head awkwardly: sold 26,000 gns. *B. W. Hills*

NOTANOTHER   3 b.f. Inchinor 119 – Select Sale (Auction Ring (USA) 123) [2003   **67**
68: f7g² f7g³ f6s² f6s f6g³ 7d 6d 7d 6.5g* 6m³ 6m 6m⁶ 7m³ 8f Oct 18] fair handicapper:
left J. Osborne after sixth start: won at Sligo in August: stays 7f: acts on fibresand, good
to firm and good to soft going. *M. Halford, Ireland*

NOTHING DAUNTED   6 ch.g. Selkirk (USA) 129 – Khubza 86 (Green Desert (USA)   **56**
127) [2003 87: f7g p8g⁶ 7g⁶ 7.2g 7.9f Jun 15] quite attractive gelding: fluent mover: only
modest form in 2003, leaving J. Osborne after second start: best around 7f: acts on soft
and good to firm going: none too consistent. *T. A. K. Cuthbert*

NOTHING MATTERS   2 b.f. (Jan 11) Foxhound (USA) 103 – Dawn Alarm 47   **43**
(Warning 136) [2003 6g 5.7f⁵ 6f⁴ 7m 8d p8g⁵ Nov 22] rather leggy filly: first foal: dam,
ran 3 times, half-sister to useful French performer up to 1½m Rebuff out of half-sister
to champion US filly Go For Wand: poor maiden: stays 1m: acts on polytrack and firm
going. *P. R. Chamings*

NO TIME (IRE)   3 b.c. Danetime (IRE) 121 – Muckross Park 41 (Nomination 125)   **105**
[2003 102: p6g⁵ f6s p5g⁴ p5g² p7g⁴ 6g⁶ 5.5m* 5f* a6g² 5m³ 7f 6g 6d f5g p6g Dec 20]   **a96**
smallish, good-topped colt: useful performer: won handicap at Ascot (beat Rectangle ½
length) in March and listed event at Haydock (beat The Lord a head) in April: off 5
months and sweating, probably flattered when third to Colonel Cotton in listed race at
Newmarket in October (appeared to run to 115): best at 5f/6f: acts on firm going, good to
soft and dirt/polytrack: usually races prominently: has flashed tail: none too consistent.
M. J. Polglase

NOT PROVEN   4 br.g. Mark of Esteem (IRE) 137 – Free City (USA) (Danzig (USA))   **–**
[2003 –: 11.9g May 9] useful-looking gelding: modest maiden at 2 yrs: well held both
outings since. *T. J. Fitzgerald*

NOT SO DUSTY   3 b.g. Primo Dominie 121 – Ann's Pearl (IRE) 81 (Cyrano de Ber-   **93**
gerac 120) [2003 67p: f5g² p5g* 5.1m* 5f 5d 5d Sep 27] sturdy, quite attractive colt:

fairly useful performer: won maiden at Lingfield in April and handicap at Chester in May: ran poorly last 2 outings, in blinkers final one: should prove best at 5f: acts on all-weather and good to firm going. *P. J. Makin*

NOTTY BITZ (IRE)   3 b. or br.g. Darnay 117 – Riskie Things 62 (Risk Me (FR) 127)   **58**
[2003 81: 8m 7g^2 p8g 8d^3 Oct 31] lengthy gelding: just modest form in 2003: stays 1m: acts on heavy and good to firm going: wore cheekpieces at 3 yrs: tail flasher. *J. S. Moore*

NOUL (USA)   4 ch.g. Miswaki (USA) 124 – Water Course (USA) (Irish River (FR)   **74**
131) [2003 74: f8g f7s* p10g 7m 8m^6 6.9m 7d^3 f7g^6 8m f7g^4 f8.5g^2 f8g* Dec 12] sturdy   **a82**
gelding: fairly useful on all-weather, fair on turf: won handicaps at Southwell in February and December: effective at 7f/1m: acts on fibresand, soft and good to firm going: blinkered 2 of last 3 starts: held up: none too consistent. *K. A. Ryan*

NOWELL HOUSE   7 ch.g. Polar Falcon (USA) 126 – Langtry Lady 91 (Pas de Seul   **88**
133) [2003 82: 13d^5 13d* 14v^4 13.1d* f9.4g^6 f16g^5 f14.8s^3 Dec 31] smallish, lengthy   **a73**
gelding: fairly useful handicapper on turf, fair on all-weather: won at Hamilton in May and Ayr (beat Dancing Phantom ½ length) in October: stayed 14.8f: best form on good ground or softer: visored once at 5 yrs: held up. *M. W. Easterby*

NOW LOOK HERE   7 b.g. Reprimand 122 – Where's Carol 67 (Anfield 117) [2003   **89**
–: 5g 5.2m 6g 5m 5v^2 6m 5f^4 6g 5m^5 6m 5d^4 6m 5d^3 f5g^6 f5g f5g Dec 16] tall, leggy   **a79**
gelding: unimpressive mover: fairly useful handicapper on turf, fair on all-weather: effective at 5f/6f: acts on fibresand and any turf going: tried blinkered, better form without: none too consistent. *B. A. McMahon*

NOW THEN SOPHIE   3 ch.f. Keen 116 – Rachels Eden (Ring Bidder 88) [2003 49:   **54 d**
f8g^2 f8.5g^6 f8g f7s^5 6f f6g^5 8f Jun 18] modest maiden at best: stays 1m: acts on firm ground and fibresand: visored last 4 starts: none too genuine. *D. Shaw*

NOYAC (IRE)   2 b.f. (Feb 21) Bluebird (USA) 125 – Jolly Dame (USA) (Silver Hawk   **88**
(USA) 123) [2003 7m^2 6m* 6g 6.1g^6 7m Oct 18] IR 26,000F: good-bodied filly: fourth foal: dam unraced half-sister to dam of Oaks d'Italia winner Nicole Pharly from family of Law Society: fairly useful performer: won maiden at Newmarket in July: respectable seventh in Princess Margaret Stakes at Ascot next time, easily best effort after: should stay 1m: sold 31,000 gns. *R. Hannon*

NUCLEAR PROSPECT (IRE)   3 ch.g. Nucleon (USA) 94 – Carraigbyrne (IRE)   **–**
(Over The River (FR)) [2003 8g 12.4g^5 Jul 31] compact gelding: first foal: dam unraced: well held in 2 maidens, slowly away in both. *G. M. Moore*

NUGGET (IRE)   5 b.g. Goldmark (USA) 113 – Folly Vision (IRE) 58 (Vision (USA))   **–**
[2003 –: p12g 12g 15.4m Apr 15] strong, sturdy gelding: little form: tried blinkered. *P. Mitchell*

NUIT SOMBRE (IRE)   3 b.g. Night Shift (USA) – Belair Princess (USA) (Mr Pros-   **99**
pector (USA)) [2003 84: 8.5m^2 7.9m^4 9g^6 7g 10.4f^2 8m* 10g* 7.9m^2 8m 9.9g 10.5m 9.9m 8.3g^5 8g^4 8m 10g^5 8g^6 12d f8.5g Nov 17] good-topped gelding: useful handicapper on his day: won at Ripon in June and Sandown (beat Courageous Duke a head) in July: effective at 1m to 10.4f: acts on firm and good to soft going: ran poorly both starts in blinkers: often finishes weakly: inconsistent. *M. Johnston*

NUKHBAH (USA)   2 b.f. (Feb 25) Bahri (USA) 125 – El Nafis (USA) 73 (Kingmambo   **75**
(USA) 125) [2003 7m^4 9f^3 Sep 15] leggy filly: first foal: dam, 2-y-o 1m winner, out of sister to Seattle Dancer, close relative of Lomond and half-sister to Seattle Slew: fair form in maidens at York and Redcar (travelled well long way when third to Yoshka): may prove best around 1m: sold 12,000 gns. *B. W. Hills*

NULL AND VOID   4 b.g. Zamindar (USA) 116 – Nullarbor (Green Desert (USA)   **–**
127) [2003 75: f6s f8.5g f6s^6 f8s^6 f7g 7m 9m 7m 6f Aug 22] disappointing maiden: tried in cheekpieces: dead. *D. W. Chapman*

NUMITAS (GER)   3 b.c. Lomitas 129 – Narola (GER) (Nebos (GER) 129) [2003 88:   **102**
14.1f^3 12f 14g^2 13.9m 18m* 18m Oct 18] leggy, workmanlike colt: useful performer: won minor event at Pontefract in September by 1¼ lengths from Harlestone Grey: good third (promoted to second) behind disqualified Jagger in handicap at Goodwood third outing: stays 2¼m: raced only on good ground or firmer: sometimes races freely (including when mid-division in Cesarewitch at Newmarket final outing). *Sir Mark Prescott*

NUMPTY (IRE)   2 b.g. (Mar 16) Intikhab (USA) 135 – Atsuko (IRE) (Mtoto 134)
[2003 6m 8d 8m Sep 25] 22,000 2-y-o, resold 1,000 2-y-o: strong gelding: half-brother to several winners, including useful Irish 9f winner Atacat (by Catrail) and fairly useful 11f and 1¾m winner Triphenia (by Ashkalani): dam, second at 1m at 2 yrs in Ireland, closely

related to very smart French middle-distance performer Muroto: well beaten in maidens: tongue tied last 2 starts. *N. Tinkler*

NUTS FOR YOU (IRE)   2 b.f. (May 8) Sri Pekan (USA) 117 – Moon Festival 74 (Be **67** My Guest (USA) 126) [2003 7g p8g f8g² Dec 8] 27,000Y: lengthy filly: half-sister to several winners, including smart Irish 1m/1¼m winner Sita (by Indian Ridge) and 4-y-o Tikkun: dam, maiden who stayed 1¼m, half-sister to high-class middle-distance performers Sheriff's Star and Moon Madness: best effort in maidens (fair form) when 1½ lengths second to Nessen Dorma at Southwell: will probably stay 1¼m. *R. Charlton*

NUTTY (IRE)   3 b.f. Sri Pekan (USA) 117 – Mitra (IRE) 98 (Archway (IRE) 115)   **–** [2003 –: 10d 9.2m May 28] no sign of ability. *Mrs P. N. Dutfield*

NUZOOA (USA)   2 b. or br.f. (Mar 12) A P Indy (USA) 131 – Min Alhawa (USA) 108 **83 p** (Riverman (USA) 131) [2003 7f² Sep 4] fourth foal: half-sister to 4-y-o Tasneef: dam, 7f (at 2 yrs) and 1¼m winner, half-sister to 1000 Guineas winner Harayir: 14/1, 2 lengths second of 17 to Silk Fan in maiden at Salisbury, getting hang of things late on and not knocked about: will probably be suited by 1¼m/1½m: sure to do better. *M. P. Tregoning*

NUZZLE   3 b.f. Salse (USA) 128 – Lena (USA) (Woodman (USA) 126) [2003 71: p8g⁴ **70 §** f8s³ p10g⁵ p8g 8f² 10f 8.3d 8.2m³ 8m 8.1m⁶ 8.3g 8f⁵ 8m⁵ 8f 10.2f² 10.2f³ p10g³ 10.3m⁶ p10g p10g⁶ f9.4g³ f8g* Dec 15] good-topped filly: fair performer: won maiden at Southwell in December: effective at 1m/1¼m: acts on all-weather and firm going: effective visored or not: races prominently/freely: inconsistent. *M. Quinn*

NYRAMBA   2 b.f. (Mar 18) Night Shift (USA) – Maramba 97 (Rainbow Quest (USA) **107** 134) [2003 5m* 5.2m² 6f* 6.5m* 6m Oct 2] 30,000Y: quite good-topped filly: first foal: dam, 1m winner, out of high-class 6f/7f winner Gayane: useful performer: won maiden at Salisbury in May, listed race on same course (strong late run when short-heading Dowager) and Watership Down Stud Sales race at Ascot (beat Dubaian Duel by 1½ lengths), last 2 in September: found little when last of 10 in Cheveley Park Stakes at Newmarket: will stay 7f: sent to Germany. *J. H. M. Gosden*

NYSAEAN (IRE)   4 b.c. Sadler's Wells (USA) 132 – Irish Arms (FR) (Irish River (FR) **118** 131) [2003 119: 12m⁶ 10m² 10d* 10s* 9.8d Oct 4] good-topped colt: smart performer: good second to Parasol in listed event at Kempton prior to winning Golan EBF Mooresbridge Stakes (beat Mkuzi 3½ lengths) at the Curragh in April and Patrick P. O'Leary Memorial Gallinule Stakes (by 3 lengths from Handel) at same course in June, making all both times: off 4 months, below form in Prix Dollar at Longchamp final outing: barely stays 1½m: acts on soft and good to firm ground (seemed ill at ease on firm at 3 yrs). *R. Hannon*

O

OAKLEY BLUE   3 ch.g. Bluegrass Prince (IRE) 110 – Westminster Waltz (Dance In **–** Time (CAN)) [2003 8g 7m 7.6g Jul 16] half-brother to several winners, including 4-y-o Oakley Rambo and 1m to 11f winner Calldat Seventeen (by Komaite), both fairly useful: dam ran twice: well beaten in maidens. *M. Madgwick*

OAKLEY PRINCE   2 ch.g. (Feb 27) Bluegrass Prince (IRE) 110 – Susie Oakley VII **–** (Damsire Unregistered) [2003 6m 5.3m 8.3g Oct 13] non-thoroughbred gelding: third known foal: dam unraced: well held in 3 sellers. *M. Madgwick*

OAKLEY RAMBO   4 br.g. Muhtarram (USA) 125 – Westminster Waltz (Dance In **85** Time (CAN)) [2003 96, a87: p8g 8g 7g 8g 8m Jul 6] leggy colt: just fairly useful handi- **a76** capper on turf and fair on all-weather in 2003: stays 1m: acts on polytrack and any turf ground: sometimes early to post. *R. Hannon*

OASES   4 ch.g. Zilzal (USA) 137 – Markievicz (IRE) 73 (Doyoun 124) [2003 95d: p7g⁵ **68** p7g p8g⁶ p8g 6d* 6d² 6g⁶ 6m 6g 6g p6g p7g⁴ p8g p7g Nov 18] rather leggy, quite good-topped gelding: fair handicapper: won at Hamilton in May: effective at 6f/easy 7f: acts on heavy ground, good to firm and polytrack: tried blinkered/visored: sometimes starts slowly: formerly none too trustworthy. *D. Shaw*

OASIS DREAM   3 b.c. Green Desert (USA) 127 – Hope (IRE) (Dancing Brave **129** (USA) 140) [2003 122: 5f³ 6m* 5m* 6d² 8f Oct 25]

A headline in the *Thoroughbred Times* in June might well have raised a few eyebrows, but it fulfilled the genre's main requirement of getting across a clear message about the story beneath—'Make way for the Juddernaut'. The line, referring to Khalid Abdulla's Juddmonte Farms, came in the wake of classic victories for Nebraska Tornado in Europe and Empire Maker in North America. By the season's end, the 'Juddernaut' had rolled on to even greater effect, since a total of nine Juddmonte-bred horses—American Post (two), Brian Boru (one), Empire Maker (three), Etoile Montante (one), Heat Haze (two), Nebraska Tornado (two), Oasis Dream (two), Sightseek (four) and Tates Creek (two)—had won Group 1 or Grade 1 races. Three Valleys, disqualified from first in the Middle Park Stakes, and Epicentre, who suffered the same fate in the Hollywood Turf Cup, would have been two more. Nine was an improvement on the previous year's tally of seven, and confirmed Abdulla's pre-eminence as the top international breeder—he won Eclipse awards in North America as both the outstanding breeder and owner for 2003, his fourth Eclipse as breeder and his second as owner, and in the latest season he also headed the owners' lists in both Britain and France. The standard bearers for Abdulla were Empire Maker, successful in the Florida Derby, Wood Memorial Stakes and Belmont Stakes, and Oasis Dream, whose performances in the Darley July Cup and Victor Chandler Nunthorpe Stakes marked him down as a high-class sprinter.

In the first part of the season Oasis Dream's connections seemingly still harboured the hope of contesting a classic with him, even though speed had been the dominant characteristic of his juvenile campaign, highlighted by success in the Middle Park Stakes which resulted in his being the top-rated of his age. As things turned out, Oasis Dream was not ready to go for any of the mile classics, having failed to come to himself, and, despite being entered for the St James's Palace Stakes, he was aimed at the top sprints, reappearing in the King's Stand Stakes at Royal Ascot when reportedly needing the race. It was his first race at five furlongs and he was carrying a penalty too, so perhaps punters were a shade optimistic in making him favourite. He was found out by the combination of lack of fitness and a worthy opponent in the shape of Choisir, Oasis Dream chasing the leaders but failing to find any more in the closing stages, finishing two and half lengths third to Choisir without his rider being too hard on him.

Oasis Dream stripped fitter for the July Cup at Newmarket which, as befitted a race now regarded as the biggest test for a sprinter in Europe, attracted a strong field. He was third favourite behind Choisir and Airwave, first and second in the Golden Jubilee Stakes four days after the King's Stand. Next in the betting came King's Stand runner-up Acclamation, dual listed scorer Striking Ambition, Golden Jubilee fourth and fifth Zipping and Just James, as well as Jersey Stakes winner Membership; Tomahawk, the only contender from Aidan O'Brien's original entry of fourteen, was 25/1, with the first two in the 2002 renewal, Continent and Bahamian Pirate, on 40/1. The market correctly identified the first three home, but not in the correct order, as Oasis Dream, who impressed with his well-being and calmness in the preliminaries, put up a cracking performance. After slightly missing the break, Oasis Dream soon made up ground to be on the heels of front-running Choisir, challenged strongly from two furlongs out and always had the edge in the closing stages, putting a length and a half between himself and Choisir by the line. Airwave, who did not enjoy the run of the race, finished well for third, a neck away. The victory was the first in a Group 1 sprint at three by a champion two-year-old since the pattern system was introduced in 1971. Deep Diver was champion two-year-old in 1971 and won the Nunthorpe Stakes and Prix de l'Abbaye the following year, but both those events were Group 2 at the time. Marwell, champion juvenile filly in 1980 (but rated 10 lb behind the champion colt of that year, Storm Bird), won the July Cup and Prix de l'Abbaye in her second season, the latter a Group 1 by then.

The form of the July Cup was not far behind that shown by the two best recent winners of the race, Stravinsky and Mozart. Unfortunately, by the time of the Nunthorpe Stakes at York six weeks later, Choisir had been retired to stud and Airwave was under the weather, leaving Oasis Dream with an apparently straightforward task. He had the beating of four of his seven rivals—Acclamation, Bahamian Pirate, Continent and Orientor—on Newmarket form and of Dominica and The Trader on King's Stand form, while King George Stakes victor The Tatling had to improve considerably to pose a threat. Oasis Dream put on a performance that was a shade reminiscent of Dayjur's in the Nunthorpe thirteen years earlier.

Darley July Cup, Newmarket—Oasis Dream reverses King's Stand form with Choisir (rail);
Airwave finishes strongly in third, ahead of Zipping (hoops)
who runs on to pass Bahamian Pirate (on Airwave's inside)

Again looking at the peak of condition and on very good terms with himself, Oasis Dream left the stalls like lightning, clearly had the legs of the others after only two furlongs and surged clear when shaken up over a furlong out to beat The Tatling by two and a half lengths. Although not driven out fully, Oasis Dream put up a timefigure equivalent to a rating of 133, better than any sprinter had managed for over a decade, and his time of 56.20sec came within four hundredths of a second of Dayjur's course record. In fact, Oasis Dream would have broken the record but for a course alteration in the meantime which added three yards to the distance, so it was surprising that certain journalists took this particular opportunity to pooh-pooh Oasis Dream's claims to being 'the fastest horse in the world'. Comparisons with Dayjur were inevitable but, good as Oasis Dream's victory was, Dayjur's was better; he recorded a timefigure equivalent to a rating of 142, beating the very smart Statoblest by four lengths. Dayjur covered himself in glory in his remaining starts, the Haydock Sprint Cup and the Prix de l'Abbaye de Longchamp, both of which he won, and the Breeders' Cup Sprint, which he unluckily lost. The same cannot be said of Oasis Dream, but the fact that he tasted defeat in both his remaining races did little to diminish his standing.

Victor Chandler Nunthorpe Stakes, York—odds-on Oasis Dream puts up another high-class
performance, making all and easily stretching clear of The Tatling, Acclamation (right) and Dominica

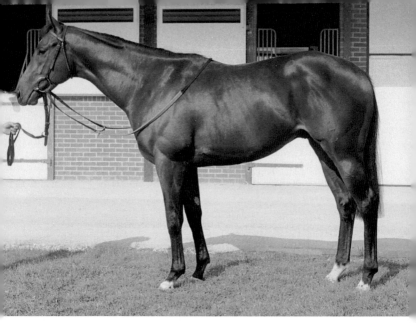

Mr K. Abdulla's "Oasis Dream"

Oasis Dream (b.c. 2000)	Green Desert (USA) (b 1983)	Danzig (b 1977)	Northern Dancer
			Pas de Nom
		Foreign Courier (b 1979)	Sir Ivor
			Courtly Dee
	Hope (IRE) (b 1991)	Dancing Brave (b 1983)	Lyphard
			Navajo Princess
		Bahamian (ch 1985)	Mill Reef
			Sorbus

In the Sprint Cup at Haydock, sponsored by Stanley Leisure, Oasis Dream was installed at 3/1-on at the five-day stage when the ground was firm, but torrential rain made it good to soft by race time, with the result that he went off at 11/8-on. Given the changed going, Richard Hughes had Oasis Dream in front but did not let him bowl along with so much abandon as at York. When shaken up over a furlong out, Oasis Dream could not draw clear and was worn down by Somnus in the last fifty yards, going down by a length and a quarter. Not a bad run by any means—Airwave was third—but not up to the standard of Oasis Dream's two previous starts, and one which suggested that six furlongs in such conditions was too far. Soft going at Longchamp led to Oasis Dream's withdrawal from the Prix de l'Abbaye, which left the Breeders' Cup at Santa Anita as one remaining target. It had always been the plan to run Oasis Dream in the Mile on turf rather than the Sprint on dirt, Gosden having won the first running of the Mile with Royal Heroine in 1984 when he trained in California. Judged on various comments in the media in the weeks leading up to the race, there was a widespread presumption that because Last Tycoon had won the Nunthorpe and the Breeders' Cup Mile, Oasis Dream ought to be able to do the same. Like many presumptions, however, it was based on a fallacy. Last Tycoon was not a strong puller and tended to be held up before producing a decisive turn of foot, whereas Oasis Dream's forte was out-and-out speed and his natural inclination was to get on with things, a trait exemplified in the

Nunthorpe and which wouldn't have been to his disadvantage in the Breeders' Cup Sprint. Starting fifth favourite at Santa Anita, he raced too freely before dropping out in the final furlong to finish tenth of thirteen behind Six Perfections. Retirement to his owner's Banstead Manor Stud at Newmarket followed, at a fee of £25,000 special live foal.

Oasis Dream's fee is only a fraction of that of his sire Green Desert, whose services now cost £85,000, having been raised by £25,000 in the autumn—he stood at £40,000 in 2002. Green Desert's sons, including first-season sire Cape Cross, Desert Prince and Desert Style, have been doing pretty well at stud and there is every reason to anticipate Oasis Dream's following suit. Like his sire, he will surely get a few good horses that stay beyond a mile. At the start of the year, the once-raced dam of Oasis Dream, Hope, was one of more than twenty Juddmonte-based mares who had foaled at least one Group 1 or Grade 1 winner. She is no longer in the list, since she died in the spring after foaling a colt by Halling, due to losing all co-ordination—she had been lightly raced owing to a severe arthritic condition. Her yearling filly by Selkirk also died during the year. The best of Hope's progeny besides Oasis Dream was Zenda, successful in the 2002 Poule d'Essai des Pouliches; Zenda won an allowance race at Saratoga in July on her only start at four before retirement due to trouble with her ankles. Oasis Dream, a strong, good-bodied, attractive colt with a great look of his sire, put up his best performances on ground firmer than good. He was tried in a crossed noseband and was once blanketed for stalls entry. *J. H. M. Gosden*

OASIS STAR (IRE) 2 b.f. (Mar 27) Desert King (IRE) 129 – Sound Tap (IRE) (Warning 136) [2003 6f* Oct 27] IR 18,000F, 12,000Y: sister to 2002 2-y-o 6f winner Princess Sabaah and half-sister to 1½m winner Playback (by Revoque), both fairly useful: dam French 6f to 1m winner: 7/1, won 9-runner maiden at Leicester comfortably by neck from Flame Queen, held up and leading final 1f: will stay at least 1m: should improve. *P. W. Harris*   **76 p**

OBAY 2 ch.c. (Jan 24) Kingmambo (USA) 125 – Parade Queen (USA) (A P Indy (USA) 131) [2003 7m Oct 3] rangy colt: second foal: dam US Grade 3 8.5f winner: 33/1 and green, 4 lengths seventh of 23 to Secret Charm in maiden at Newmarket, off bridle at halfway: will stay at least 1m: open to progress. *E. A. L. Dunlop*   **80 p**

OBE BOLD (IRE) 2 b.f. (Feb 10) Orpen (USA) 116 – Capable Kate (IRE) (Alzao (USA) 117) [2003 5f² 5m* 5m³ 5m 5d³ 5.1m 5m⁵ 6m³ 5f³ 5g⁵ 5m³ 5m³ 6m 5g 6g Oct 28] 3,000Y: small, lengthy filly: fifth living foal: half-sister to 7-y-o Golden Biff and 4-y-o Eyes To The Right: dam unraced: fair performer: won maiden at Redcar in May: third in minor events/nurseries after: barely stays 6f: acts on firm and good to soft going: sometimes hangs right. *A. Berry*   **71**

OBE ONE 3 b.g. Puissance 110 – Plum Bold 83 (Be My Guest (USA) 126) [2003 79: 5f 5m³ 5m⁴ 5m³ 5f⁶ 5f³ 5.1m 5g* 5m 5d 5g 5s Nov 3] leggy gelding: fairly useful handicapper: best effort when winning at Goodwood in August: raced mainly at 5f: acts on firm going. *A. Berry*   **87**

OBLIGE 3 b.f. Robellino (USA) 127 – Acquiesce (Generous (IRE) 139) [2003 101: 8m³ 10g³ 9.9g⁶ 8f Jun 21] strong filly: has a round action: useful performer: creditable efforts in listed events at Kempton, Newmarket (third to Hi Dubai) and Goodwood first 3 starts in 2003: needs further than 1m ideally, and should stay 1½m: raced only on good going or firmer: hung markedly right final 2-y-o start. *A. M. Balding*   **99**

OBOE 2 ch.f. (Jan 31) Piccolo 121 – Bombay (Be My Chief (USA) 122) [2003 f7s⁵ Dec 31] first foal: dam unraced half-sister to useful sprinter Boast: 10/1, well-beaten fifth of 8 in maiden at Wolverhampton. *R. Charlton*   **–**

OBRIGADO (USA) 3 b.g. Bahri (USA) 125 – Glorious Diamond (USA) (His Majesty (USA)) [2003 7.9m⁴ 8m² 8m* 8.1d⁶ Sep 27] $50,000Y: big, leggy gelding: first living foal: dam maiden in USA: progressive form: easily landed odds in maiden at Pontefract (sweating) in August: very good sixth to Desert Opal in handicap at Haydock final start: should stay 9f: has pulled hard/carried head awkwardly/wandered. *W. J. Haggas*   **89 +**

OBSCURE 3 gr.f. Salse (USA) 128 – Oscura (USA) 82 (Caro 133) [2003 10f Jun 25] sister to smart 10.5f to 1½m winner Sanmartino and half-sister to 3 winners, notably very smart 7f (at 2 yrs) to 1½m winner Urgent Request (later successful in USA, by Rainbow Quest): dam 1m winner: 20/1 and tongue tied, well held in maiden at Kempton: sold 35,000 gns in December. *J. H. M. Gosden*   **–**

OCARINA   3 ch.g. Piccolo 121 – Nanny Doon (Dominion 123) [2003 –: f8.5g 7d 7.1m – Aug 14] no form. *P. G. Murphy*

OCCAM (IRE)   9 ch.g. Sharp Victor (USA) 114 – Monterana 99 (Sallust 134) [2003 **48** 48, a45: f11g⁶ f12g* f12g f12g Feb 21] leggy gelding: poor handicapper: won selling event at Wolverhampton in January: probably stayed 15f: acted on soft going, good to firm and fibresand: tried visored: sometimes started slowly/looked none too keen: dead. *A. Bailey*

OCEAN AVENUE (IRE)   4 b.g. Dolphin Street (FR) 125 – Trinity Hall 67 (Hallgate **86** 127) [2003 76: 14g² 14f⁴ 14.4f³ 14.4m* Aug 6] fairly useful handicapper: won 4-runner event at Kempton in August: stays 14.4f: acts on firm ground: has raced freely: hung badly left penultimate start: consistent: front runner. *C. A. Horgan*

OCEAN DREAM (IRE)   2 b.f. (Mar 3) Mujadil (USA) 119 – Women In Love (IRE) **–** (Danehill (USA) 126) [2003 f5g⁶ 5.7m f7g 10d Oct 31] IR 6,000F, 3,000Y: first foal: dam Italian 1m/9f winner: well held in sellers/maidens. *A. G. Newcombe*

OCEAN ROCK   2 b.c. (Apr 7) Perugino (USA) 84 – Polistatic 53 (Free State 125) **–** [2003 7g Nov 1] strong, workmanlike colt: eighth foal: half-brother to 5-y-o Regal Gallery; dam, 11f/1½m winner, sister to Ebor winner Western Dancer: 40/1 and better for race, well held in maiden at Newmarket. *C. A. Horgan*

OCEAN SILK (USA)   3 b. or br.f. Dynaformer (USA) – Mambo Jambo (USA) (King- **119** mambo (USA) 125) [2003 83p: 10.3m* 9.9g* 12m² 12g 11.9m² 12m 12.5d³ 12f² Oct 19] quite good-topped filly: has a round action: smart performer: won maiden at Chester and listed Lupe Stakes at Goodwood (beat Mezzo Soprano 1¼ lengths) in May: good efforts after when second in Ribblesdale Stakes at Royal Ascot (beaten a head by Spanish Sun) and Yorkshire Oaks at York (beaten length by Islington): below form otherwise in Irish Oaks at the Curragh (blinkered), Prix Vermeille and Prix de Royallieu (wore cheekpieces, final outing for J. Gosden), both at Longchamp, and non-graded event at Keeneland (6¼ lengths second to Spice Island): should stay 1¾m: acts on good to firm going: has worn crossed noseband. *P. B. Byrne, USA*

Mr R. E. Sangster's "Ocean Silk"

OCEAN TIDE 6 b.g. Deploy 131 – Dancing Tide (Pharly (FR) 130) [2003 87: p16g Feb 12] angular gelding: fairly useful handicapper at 5 yrs: well held only Flat outing in 2003: stays 2m: acts on any turf going: visored. *R. Ford* —

OCEAN VICTORY 3 ch.g. Catrail (USA) 123 – Persian Victory (IRE) (Persian Bold 123) [2003 8g⁵ 10g² 7.6g* 8.5m* 8.1m² 8m* 7.9m² Aug 21] tall, leggy, unfurnished gelding: sixth living foal: half-brother to winner in Italy by Selkirk: dam unraced half-sister to smart 9f winner Big Reef: useful form: won maiden at Lingfield and handicaps at Epsom and Newmarket (made all to beat Honorine 1¼ lengths, despite hanging left) in July/August: good head second to Terfel in quite valuable handicap at York final outing: raced mainly around 1m on good/good to firm ground: races prominently: should continue to progress. *J. Noseda* **98 p**

OCOTILLO 3 b.c. Mark of Esteem (IRE) 137 – Boojum 101 (Mujtahid (USA) 118) [2003 p8g⁵ Feb 1] 110,000Y: second foal: half-brother to 4-y-o Esenin: dam 2-y-o 6f/7f winner: 3¼ lengths fifth in maiden at Lingfield, pulling hard and not given hard time: sold 4,500 gns in August. *D. R. Loder* **57**

OCTANE (USA) 7 b.g. Cryptoclearance (USA) – Something True (USA) 119 (Sir Ivor 135) [2003 87: p13g 16.2m 14f² 13d⁶ 11.9m⁵ 16.2m 11.9g⁶ 11.9g 12.4m* 14.1m² Aug 9] good-bodied gelding: fluent mover: fairly useful performer: landed odds in apprentice seller at Newcastle in August: stays 2m: acts on all-weather and firm going, seemingly on soft: tried blinkered/tongue tied: has refused to enter stall/twice failed stall tests: usually held up. *W. M. Brisbourne* **81**

OCTENNIAL 4 gr.g. Octagonal (NZ) 126 – Laune (AUS) 68 (Kenmare (FR) 125) [2003 68: 7g² f6g⁶ f6g⁵ 7m May 8] leggy gelding: modest performer: best at 6f: acts on fibresand and good to firm going: tried in visor/cheekpieces: carries head high: ungenuine. *P. A. Blockley* **60 §**

OCTOBER MIST (IRE) 9 gr.g. Roselier (FR) – Bonny Joe (Derring Rose 97) [2003 76: 12d² Nov 4] useful hurdler/fairly useful chaser at best: fair form in 2 maidens at Catterick, carrying head awkwardly in latter: will stay further than 1½m. *Mrs M. Reveley* **68**

OCTOBER MOON 3 b.f. Octagonal (NZ) 126 – Moon Carnival 94 (Be My Guest (USA) 126) [2003 –p: 7d³ 7g 6m³ 7f⁴ Aug 27] good-bodied filly: modest maiden: bred to stay at least 1m: acts on good to firm and good to soft ground: raced freely/hung final start: sold 800 gns. *W. Jarvis* **64**

ODABELLA (IRE) 3 b.f. Selkirk (USA) 129 – Circe's Isle (Be My Guest (USA) 126) [2003 8g² 8m³ 10.3m² p10g³ 10g⁴ 10m Aug 30] tall, useful-looking filly: closely related to useful 1m/1¼m winner Flint Knapper (by Kris) and half-sister to several winners, including smart 7f (at 2 yrs) and 1¼m winner Don Micheletto (by Machiavellian): dam unraced close relative of very smart 1¼m performer Sasuru: fairly useful maiden: best effort when third in handicap at Lingfield on fourth start, looking none too keen: ran poorly after: stays 10.3f: acts on polytrack, raced only on good ground or firmer on turf: sold 3,000 gns in December. *J. H. M. Gosden* **81**

ODABELLA'S CHARM 3 b.f. Cadeaux Genereux 131 – One Life (USA) (L'Emigrant (USA) 129) [2003 8.3d* 8m Aug 27] 82,000F, 4,300,000 francs Y: half-sister to several winners, including 7.5f (at 2 yrs) to 1½m winner Tenorio (by Law Society) and French 1¼m winner Healing Hands (by Zafonic), both useful: dam unraced half-sister to Miesque and to dam of Six Perfections: 9/2 and green, won maiden at Windsor in June by 1¾ lengths from Moarban: found little in minor event at Ascot next time: free-going sort, not sure to stay beyond 1m. *Sir Michael Stoute* **80 +**

ODDSMAKER (IRE) 2 b.g. (Mar 13) Barathea (IRE) 127 – Archipova (IRE) (Ela-Mana-Mou 132) [2003 5m 5.9m³ 6g 7m 8m⁴ 5.9m 7g 8.3g 8m 8m* 7f⁵ Oct 27] 8,000Y: angular gelding: second foal: half-brother to 3-y-o Autumn Glory: dam, Italian 1½m and 15f winner, sister to useful performer up to 12.5f Abyaan and half-sister to smart Irish middle-distance stayer Sadlers Wings: fair performer: left A. Berry after seventh start: won nursery at Yarmouth in October by 7 lengths, comfortably best effort: stays 1m: acts on good to firm going: wore cheekpieces/blinkers fifth to seventh starts: often slowly away/races freely/hangs: not to be trusted implicitly. *P. D. Evans* **74**

ODIHAM 2 b.g. (Feb 15) Deploy 131 – Hug Me 96 (Shareef Dancer (USA) 135) [2003 p7g 8g p8g² Nov 2] leggy gelding: half-brother to several winners, including fairly useful 1½m/1¾m winner Embracing (by Reference Point): dam 7f (at 2 yrs) and 1½m winner: fair form in maidens: staying-on second to Border Music at Lingfield: will be suited by 1¼m+: likely to progress. *H. Morrison* **77 p**

OEUF A LA NEIGE 3 b.g. Danehill (USA) 126 – Reine de Neige 96 (Kris 135) [2003 **76**
71: 8.2g⁵ 8.3g 8m⁵ 8g³ 8g Jul 5] leggy gelding: fair maiden handicapper: stays 1m: raced
only on good/good to firm going on turf: sold 17,000 gns, and gelded. *E. A. L. Dunlop*

OFARABY 3 b.g. Sheikh Albadou 128 – Maristax 74 (Reprimand 122) [2003 8g p10g* **87**
f9.4f f9.4g² f9.4g* p10g⁶ f9.4g⁴ Nov 29] 8,000Y: second foal: dam 2-y-o 7f winner: fairly
useful performer, lightly raced: won maiden at Lingfield in June and handicap at Wolverhampton (clear when tending to wander) in October: stays easy 1¼m: acts on all-weather:
raced freely third start: reliable. *M. A. Jarvis*

OFF AIR 2 b.f. (Apr 11) Robellino (USA) 127 – Sprite 71 (Fairy King (USA)) [2003 **– p**
6m Sep 23] 7,500Y: close-coupled filly: second foal: dam, maiden who stayed 8.5f,
half-sister to smart performer up to 1m (runner-up in 1000 Guineas) Niche: 12/1, eighth
of 13 in maiden at Newmarket, never a threat: should stay at least 1m: likely to do better.
C. N. Allen

OFF BEAT (USA) 2 ch.g. (Feb 22) Mister Baileys 123 – Off Off (USA) (Theatrical **78**
128) [2003 6g 7.1m 7f3 6m⁴ 6.1m⁴ 6m 7m 7m⁶ 5.7f* 6m 6g⁶ p7g* p7g Dec 29] close-
coupled gelding: second foal: dam placed in USA: fair performer: won maiden at Bath in
September and nursery at Lingfield in December: effective at 6f/7f: acts on firm going
and polytrack: blinkered last 3 starts: none too consistent. *R. F. Johnson Houghton*

OFFENBACH (USA) 2 b.c. (May 12) Danzig (USA) – Aquilegia (USA) (Alydar **88 P**
(USA)) [2003 7g* Nov 8] $2,400,000Y: fifth foal: brother to 2 winners, notably very
smart performer up to 7f Bertolini, 6f (July Stakes) winner at 2 yrs, and closely related/
half-brother to winners in USA by Dixieland Band and Deputy Minister: dam, US Grade
2 1¼m winner, half-sister to dam of Green Desert (by Danzig): 3/1, won 18-runner
maiden at Leopardstown by 2 lengths from Khulasah, leading 2f out and edging left under
pressure then staying on well: will stay 1m: probably open to good deal of improvement.
A. P. O'Brien, Ireland

OFF HIRE 7 b.g. Clantime 101 – Lady Pennington 51 (Blue Cashmere 129) [2003 69: **57**
f5s f5g 5m 5m f5g⁵ 5m⁴ 5.5m f5s Sep 2] leggy, angular gelding: modest handicapper **a49**
nowadays: best at 5f: acts on any turf going/fibresand: visored: races prominently.
C. Smith

OFFICER'S PINK 3 ch.f. Grand Lodge (USA) 125 – Arethusa 101 (Primo Dominie **79**
121) [2003 72: 7m f7g⁶ 6.1m⁶ 6m² 6m⁴ 5m* 6m³ 5g⁵ Nov 5] strong, lengthy filly: good
walker: fair performer: won maiden at Ripon in August: very good close third in handicap
at Leicester next time: effective at 5f/6f: raced only on good/good to firm ground on turf,
below form only run on fibresand: tongue tied last 3 starts. *P. F. I. Cole*

OFFTOWORKWEGO 3 b.g. Fraam 114 – Hi Hoh (IRE) (Fayruz 116) [2003 65: **–**
5m 6m 5d 8m 8g 6m 5f Jun 16] sturdy gelding: fair at 2 yrs, no form in 2003: tried
blinkered. *P. Monteith*

OFFWITHTHEFAIRIES 3 b.f. Farfelu 103 – My Ruby Ring 72 (Blushing Scribe **–**
(USA) 107) [2003 46: 6m 6m Jun 2] poor maiden, lightly raced: may prove best around
5f: very slowly away first 2 outings at 2 yrs. *W. R. Muir*

OH BOY (IRE) 3 b.c. Tagula (IRE) 116 – Pretty Sally (IRE) 51 (Polish Patriot (USA) **64**
128) [2003 –p: 6g 6.1m⁴ 7g Jul 3] good-bodied colt: best effort (modest form) in maidens
when eye-catching fourth at Nottingham: disappointed on handicap debut next time:
raced only on good/good to firm going. *R. Hannon*

OH FRIGATE 2 b.g. (Apr 23) Muhtarram (USA) 125 – Sole Control (Jupiter Island **40**
126) [2003 f7g p8g Nov 22] first foal: dam lightly raced on Flat/over hurdles: poor form
in sellers at Wolverhampton and Lingfield: should be suited by 1¼m+. *H. Candy*

OH GOLLY GOSH 2 ch.g. (Apr 22) Exit To Nowhere (USA) 122 – Guerre de Troie **67**
(Risk Me (FR) 127) [2003 p6g³ p8g Nov 2] €28,000Y: half-brother to several winners in
France, including 5-y-o French Tune: dam, French middle-distance maiden, from good
family: fair form in maidens at Lingfield: third to Sweetest Revenge: needs to settle better
to stay 1m. *N. P. Littmoden*

OH SO DUSTY 5 b.m. Piccolo 121 – Dark Eyed Lady (IRE) 82 (Exhibitioner 111) **–**
[2003 57: p10g Jan 8] smallish, sturdy mare: modest handicapper at 4 yrs: well held only
run in 2003: blinkered twice at 2 yrs. *N. P. Littmoden*

OH SO ROSIE (IRE) 3 b.f. Danehill Dancer (IRE) 117 – Shinkoh Rose (FR) 67 **69**
(Warning (USA) [2003 81: 7g 6m 7m 6g 7.1d 8m⁵ 8.3g² 9m² 8f 8f⁶ 10d⁴ 8.2d 8d² p8g Dec
2] small, angular filly: just fair performer at 3 yrs: best at 6f to 1m: acts on firm and soft
going, lightly raced on all-weather: tried visored, usually wears cheekpieces nowadays.
J. S. Moore

OH SUNNY BOY (IRE) 2 b.g. (Mar 10) Desert Sun 120 – Naivement (IRE) (Doyoun **45** 124) [2003 6m⁴ 6d 6m⁶ 6f 6m³ 7m Sep 9] IR 5,200F, €13,000Y: strong gelding: first foal: dam unraced daughter of useful middle-distance stayer Nassma: poor maiden: should stay 7f: acts on good to firm going: wore cheekpieces (ran poorly) fourth outing. *J. S. Moore*

OKOBOJI (IRE) 2 ch.c. (Apr 4) Indian Ridge 123 – Pool Party (USA) (Summer Squall **79** (USA)) [2003 7d⁴ p8g⁵ p8g Dec 10] 40,000Y: leggy, quite attractive colt: second living foal: dam unraced half-sister to Irish Derby winner Law Society: best effort in maidens (fair form) when fourth at Doncaster: slowly away/raced freely final outing: should stay 1m. *M. P. Tregoning*

OK PAL 3 b.g. Primo Dominie 121 – Sheila's Secret (IRE) 97 (Bluebird (USA) 125) **95** [2003 94p: 5.5m 5d⁴ Aug 30] lengthy gelding: useful performer, lightly raced: suffered muscle strain when virtually pulled up final 2-y-o start: better effort in 2003 when good fourth to Mornin Reserves in handicap at Sandown: subsequently gelded: will prove best at 5f/6f: acts on good to soft ground. *T. G. Mills*

OKTIS MORILIOUS (IRE) 2 b.g. (May 3) Octagonal (NZ) 126 – Nottash (IRE) – 74 (Royal Academy (USA) 130) [2003 f8g Dec 8] 6,000Y: fifth foal: half-brother to winner in Norway by Bluebird: dam, 7f winner, half-sister to top-class sprinter Lake Coniston: 16/1, green when well held in maiden at Southwell. *J. A. Osborne*

OLD BAILEY (USA) 3 gr.g. Lit de Justice (USA) 125 – Olden Lek (USA) (Cozzene **54** (USA)) [2003 63: f9.4g 7m 7f 7m 9m⁶ 8s 7g⁵ 5.9m² 6f⁶ 6m² 7m⁶ Oct 17] good-topped gelding: modest performer: stays 7f: acts on fibresand, firm and good to soft going: blinkered last 5 starts. *T. D. Barron*

OLD BLUE EYES 4 b.g. Whittingham (IRE) 104 – Special One 66 (Aragon 118) **90** [2003 6m 6g 6m⁴ 6m³ 6g Jun 28] well-made gelding: fairly useful handicapper: missed 2002: ran creditably in 2003 when in frame: will prove best at 5f/6f: raced only on good/ good to firm ground: folded in cheekpieces final start (subsequently gelded): often races prominently. *P. W. Harris*

OLD DEUTERONOMY (USA) 2 br.c. (Feb 11) Storm Cat (USA) – Jewel In The **109** Crown (USA) 81 (Seeking The Gold (USA)) [2003 6m* 5m⁴ 6g² 6f² 6s⁴ 6m⁶ Oct 3] strong, close-coupled colt: has a quick action: first foal: dam, Irish 1m winner, half-sister to useful Irish 1½m winner Alisidora out of half-sister to dam of Rainbow Quest and to outstanding broodmare Slightly Dangerous: useful performer: won maiden at Newmarket in May: in frame in Norfolk Stakes at Royal Ascot, Richmond Stakes at Goodwood (½-length second to Carrizo Creek), Phoenix Stakes at the Curragh (length second to One Cool Cat) and Prix Morny at Deauville (not at best): creditable 3½ lengths seventh (promoted to sixth) behind disqualified Three Valleys in Middle Park Stakes at Newmarket: bred to stay 1m: acts on firm going, possibly not on soft: sometimes taken steadily to post: reportedly sold privately, and joined N. O'Callaghan in USA. *A. P. O'Brien, Ireland*

OLDEN TIMES 5 b.h. Darshaan 133 – Garah 107 (Ajdal (USA) 130) [2003 120: **121** 9m* 8m³ 10m⁴ 10g⁴ 10g Aug 16]
Olden Times, who returned from injury to show himself as good as ever in the latest season, has been retired and is to take up stallion duties at the Plantation Stud, Newmarket, with his fee set at £5,000 with the October 1st concession. A very smart performer at a mile to a mile and a quarter, Olden Times has a pedigree to match his ability and is also a good-looking individual.

The winner of the Feilden Stakes at Newmarket and the Prix Jean Prat at Chantilly as a three-year-old, Olden Times finished a creditable third in the Lockinge Stakes at Newbury on his reappearance at four but then suffered a hairline fracture of the pelvis while being prepared for the Sussex Stakes. So, he was having his first race for eleven months when he returned in April for the Weatherbys Earl of Sefton Stakes at Newmarket. Looking in tremendous shape, Olden Times shared favouritism with Desert Deer in this seven-runner Group 3 contest, and the betting turned out to be a good guide to its outcome with the pair occupying the first two placings. Desert Deer helped force the pace until Olden Times moved smoothly past him over a furlong out, and, though not for the first time edging left under pressure, the latter was always in control from thereon, winning by a length and three quarters. On his next start Olden Times once again took third place in the Lockinge, though there was little merit in his performance on this occasion, as he was one of the first off the bridle and never within hailing distance of runaway

743

winner Hawk Wing. Stepped back up to a mile and a quarter, Olden Times acquitted himself much better on his next two starts, finishing fourth in both the Prince of Wales's Stakes at Royal Ascot and the Eclipse Stakes at Sandown. He was beaten four and a half lengths by Nayef in the former, though would have been a bit closer but for catching a bump off the home turn, and two and a quarter lengths by Falbrav in the latter, doing all of his best work late on. Unfortunately Olden Times's racing career ended on a low note when he finished last of thirteen in the Arlington Million, giving the impression something was wrong when dropping back quickly before the home turn.

		Shirley Heights	Mill Reef
	Darshaan	(b 1975)	Hardiemma
	(br 1981)	Delsy	Abdos
Olden Times		(br 1972)	Kelty
(b.h. 1998)		Ajdal	Northern Dancer
	Garah	(b 1984)	Native Partner
	(b 1989)	Abha	Thatching
		(b 1982)	Hardware

    Olden Times is the third foal of Garah and far and away the best of them, though she has produced a couple of other winners in Idma (by Midyan), a fair maiden in Britain who was later successful over six furlongs in the States, and the modest handicapper All Good Things (by Marju), who stays a mile and a half. Garah's fifth foal Nofa's Magic (by Rainbow Quest) showed fairly useful form when second in a mile-and-a-quarter maiden on the first of two starts for Olden Times's trainer in the latest season. Garah was unraced at two when reportedly splitting a pastern, and then won the first three of her seven starts in her three-

Prince A. A. Faisal's "Olden Times"

year-old season. Though successful only once the following year, she was rated slightly higher, and had several good placed efforts to her name, including in the Duke of York Stakes, Temple Stakes and listed Hopeful Stakes. Garah was a speedy filly, as she was bred to be. By Ajdal, she is a daughter of the smart Abha, who, like Garah, was trained by Henry Cecil. Abha was raced exclusively at five and six furlongs and only as a three-year-old, winning four races and also finishing an excellent fourth in the King's Stand Stakes. Abha is also grandam of Dandoun who has been another successful performer in pattern races at around a mile and nine furlongs for Olden Times's connections in recent seasons. Olden Times, who sometimes wore a crossed noseband, is a big, good-topped individual, and a good walker. Never raced on extremes of ground—he was withdrawn from one race at three because the going was considered too soft for him—Olden Times acted on good to firm and good to soft. *J. L. Dunlop*

OLDENWAY   4 b.g. Most Welcome 131 – Sickle Moon (Shirley Heights 130) [2003 80: 10.3g 10g* 12.1m² 11.9m⁵ 8.9f 9.9m² 10.3m f9.4g f8g Dec 12] lengthy gelding: fairly useful performer: won minor event at Nottingham in April: ran well after when second in handicaps: effective at 1¼m, barely at 1½m: acts on firm and good to soft going: races freely. *R. A. Fahey*   **90 a?**

OLD HARRY   3 b.g. Case Law 113 – Supreme Thought 68 (Emarati (USA) 74) [2003 67?: 6m 6d⁵ 6m⁴ 7.1g 6m 6f Oct 12] close-coupled gelding: just modest maiden at 3 yrs: well held last 3 starts: stays 6f: acts on good to firm ground. *L. G. Cottrell*   **62**

OLD IRISH   10 gr.g. Old Vic 136 – Dunoof 92 (Shirley Heights 130) [2003 f14.8s 10.2g Jun 13] rather leggy gelding: good mover: fairly useful performer at 3 yrs: well beaten all 3 outings since. *O. O'Neill*   **–**

OLD MALT (IRE)   2 ch.c. (Mar 14) Ashkalani (IRE) 128 – Dona Royale (IRE) 86 (Darshaan 133) [2003 6d 7m³ 7m* 7.6g² 7m* 8.5d² Oct 4] IR 36,000F, leggy, rather unfurnished colt: second foal: dam, second at 1m to 1¼m in Ireland all 3 starts, half-sister to very smart performers Foresee (suited by 1¼m to 1¾m) and Royal Touch (effective at 7f to 9f): fairly useful performer: won maiden at Brighton in August and minor event at Goodwood (by ¾ length from Vienna's Boy) in September: creditable second in minor events at Chester and Epsom: stays 8.5f: acts on good to firm and good to soft going: usually races prominently: sold 40,000 gns. *R. Hannon*   **88**

OLD TOM (IRE)   3 ch.g. Bering 136 – Lovely Lyca 76 (Night Shift (USA)) [2003 56§: f9.4g⁵ 10m⁵ 8f⁴ 7m⁵ 7f Jul 21] sturdy gelding: modest maiden: stays 1m: acts on fibresand and firm ground: often wears visor/cheekpieces: sometimes hangs left: untrustworthy: sold 4,000 gns. *R. M. H. Cowell*   **51 §**

OLIHIDER (USA)   2 gr.c. (Feb 14) Woodman (USA) 126 – Ingot's Dance Away (USA) (Gate Dancer (USA)) [2003 6m⁴ 7m⁵ 6m⁶ 7f* Sep 28] 62,000 2-y-o: smallish, rather leggy colt: third foal: half-brother to US winner by Tabasco Cat: dam, US maiden, half-sister to Breeders' Cup Classic winner Skip Away: fairly useful performer: left J. Nicol, won nursery at Ascot by neck from Zweibrucken, coming from off pace to lead near finish: will stay 1m: open to progress. *M. L. W. Bell*   **81 p**

OLIVANDER   2 b.c. (Apr 5) Danzero (AUS) – Mystic Goddess (USA) 94 (Storm Bird (CAN) 134) [2003 5m⁵ 6f² 7.1m p7g⁶ Oct 15] close-coupled, useful-looking colt: fifth foal: half-brother to high-class 1m/1¼m winner Medicean (by Machiavellian) and useful 1m winner Moon Goddess (by Rainbow Quest): dam, 2-y-o 6f/7f winner (stayed 1m), half-sister to smart 2-y-o 6f to 1m (Gran Criterium) winner Sanam: fairly useful maiden: second at York: running creditably (though had raced lazily) when saddle slipped and unseated at Musselburgh: should stay 1m. *G. A. Butler*   **83**

OLIVIA GRACE   5 ch.m. Pivotal 124 – Sheila's Secret (IRE) 97 (Bluebird (USA) 125) [2003 117: 5.1g* 5.1m³ 5f 5m 6m Oct 16] sturdy, good-quartered mare: good mover: smart performer in 2002, only useful in 2003: very much favoured by weights when beating Repertory ¾ length in minor event at Nottingham in April: left T. Mills and off 3½ months after third start, better effort subsequently when seventh to Colonel Cotton in listed race at Newmarket on penultimate start: best form at 5f: acts on good to firm, good to soft and all-weather. *L. M. Cumani*   **102**

OLIVIA ROSE (IRE)   4 b.f. Mujadil (USA) 119 – Santana Lady (IRE) 72 (Blakeney 126) [2003 71: f7s 8.2g 10g 10m⁶ 11.5g⁵ 10m³ 11.8m³ 11.9f 9f² 10.1m² 10m 9.9m⁵ 9m² 8m 10f 10.4f 9m⁴ 11g⁵ 8.2d² Nov 6] lengthy filly: fair performer: stays easy 1½m: acts on any turf ground and fibresand: usually held up: visored (ran well) final start: inconsistent. *Mrs Lydia Pearce*   **70**

O'L LUCY BROON   2 b.f. (Mar 16) Royal Applause 124 – Jay Gee Ell 78 (Vaigly   **62**
Great 127) [2003 6f⁶ 6g² 6g⁶ 5m 5f Sep 15] 15,000Y: half-sister to several winners,
including 8-y-o Friar Tuck, 3-y-o Sherwood Forest and useful 6f (at 2 yrs) to 1m (in USA)
winner Kaibo (by Safawan): dam, 2-y-o 5f/6f winner, later best at 1¼m: modest maiden:
second at Ayr, best effort: better at 6f than 5f. *J. S. Goldie*

OMAHA CITY (IRE)   9 b.g. Night Shift (USA) – Be Discreet (Junius (USA) 124)   **92**
[2003 105: 8.3d 8g 8m⁴ 7f 8.1g 8d⁵ 7m⁶ 8.9m 8g Sep 22] strong gelding: fairly useful
handicapper nowadays: mostly below form in 2003: effective at 7f/1m: has won on good
to soft ground, best form on good or firmer: visored 3 of last 4 starts: has been edgy/on
toes: usually held up. *B. Gubby*

OMAIMAH   4 b.f. Mark of Esteem (IRE) 137 – Gracious Beauty (USA) 67 (Nijinsky   **66**
(CAN) 138) [2003 68: f7s p6g² f6g⁴ f6g Feb 3] fair maiden: should stay 7f: acts on
all-weather and good to firm going. *M. R. Channon*

OMAN GULF (USA)   2 b.c. (May 1) Diesis 133 – Dabaweyaa 118 (Shareef Dancer   **84**
(USA) 135) [2003 6m* Jul 19] rather unfurnished colt: brother to 5-y-o Faithful Warrior,
closely related to fairly useful 1m winner Aneesati (by Kris) and half-brother to several
winners, including smart 1m/1¼m winner Magellan (by Hansel): dam second in 1000
Guineas: favourite, won 12-runner maiden at Newmarket by neck from Master David,
leading 1f out then edging right: took strong hold to post: suffered stress fracture of
cannon bone after: should stay 1m. *B. W. Hills*

OMAN SEA (USA)   2 b.f. (Jan 28) Rahy (USA) 115 – Ras Shaikh (USA) 105 (Sheikh   **81**
Albadou 128) [2003 5m² 6m* May 13] well-made, attractive filly: first foal: dam, 2-y-o
6f winner who stayed 1¼m, out of half-sister to smart 1m/1¼m winner Magellan: confirmed promise when winning minor event at York by ¾ length from Majestic Desert,
showing fairly useful form: suffered fracture of pastern after: should stay 7f: edgy sort,
got loose beforehand at York. *B. W. Hills*

OMEGA BAY (IRE)   2 b.g. (Feb 9) Imperial Ballet (IRE) 110 – Autumn Affair 100   **41**
(Lugana Beach 116) [2003 6f⁶ 7m 8f 8.3d⁶ Sep 29] 3,300Y: close-coupled gelding: third
foal: half-brother to 4-y-o Portacasa: dam 2-y-o 6f winner who stayed 1m: poor maiden:
visored second and third (best effort) starts. *T. D. Barron*

OMEY STRAND (IRE)   4 b.g. Desert Style (IRE) 121 – Ex-Imager (Exhibitioner 111)   **47**
[2003 54: 7g f6g 8f⁶ 8f⁵ f12s 8m Aug 6] strong gelding: poor maiden: left J. M. Bradley
after second start: stays 1m: acts on fibresand, good to firm and good to soft going: often
blinkered/visored/tongue tied: has run in snatches. *J. G. M. O'Shea*

OMNISCIENT (IRE)   4 br.f. Distinctly North (USA) 115 – Mystic Shadow (IRE) 80   **–**
(Mtoto 134) [2003 57: 7m 8g Oct 22] quite good-topped filly: modest performer at 3 yrs:
well held both starts in 2003: tried blinkered: races prominently: has looked none too
keen. *T. T. Clement*

ONCE AROUND (IRE)   2 b. or br.c. (May 19) Grand Lodge (USA) 125 – Lady   **–**
Lucre (IRE) 73 (Last Tycoon 131) [2003 f9.4g Dec 22] €27,000Y: second living foal:
half-brother to 5-y-o Prompt Payment: dam ran once: 6/1, slowly away and well held in
maiden at Wolverhampton. *T. G. Mills*

ONCE (FR)   3 gr.g. Hector Protector (USA) 124 – Moon Magic 62 (Polish Precedent   **83**
(USA) 131) [2003 78: 10m² 10m³ 12m 13.3m Jun 11] leggy, quite good-topped gelding:
fairly useful maiden handicapper: should stay 13f: raced only on good to firm ground on
turf: has been bandaged on fore joints. *M. L. W. Bell*

ONCE SEEN   3 b.g. Celtic Swing 138 – Brief Glimpse (IRE) 108 (Taufan (USA) 119)   **78**
[2003 73: 8g 8d² f8g 8g 8.2m* Oct 28] close-coupled gelding: fair performer: won maid-
en at Nottingham in October: stays 1m: unraced on extremes of going on turf: visored last
4 starts: races prominently: none too consistent: sold 18,000 gns. *R. M. Beckett*

ONE ALONE   2 b.f. (Apr 18) Atraf 116 – Songsheet 74 (Dominion 123) [2003 6m f6g   **–**
p7g f7g Dec 16] 8,000Y: third foal: half-sister to fairly useful 2002 2-y-o 5f/6f winner
Monsieur Boulanger (by Compton Place): dam best at 5f: signs of only a little ability in
maidens/nursery. *J. G. Given*

ONE COOL CAT (USA)   2 b.c. (Mar 26) Storm Cat (USA) – Tacha (USA) (Mr   **118 p**
Prospector (USA)) [2003 5d⁴ 6f* 6.3g* 6f* 7f* Sep 14]
After dominating proceedings to an unparalleled degree during the previous
four seasons—winning five of the ten European Group 1 events open to them in
1999, four in 2000, nine in 2001 and five in 2002—Aidan O'Brien's juvenile colts
had a much tougher time of it at the highest level, with twenty-two runners yielding

just two winners and four places. However, despite having two-year-olds which, as a group, couldn't live up to the astonishing standards of their predecessors, O'Brien still trains colts who are at the forefront of the betting on the Two Thousand Guineas and Derby in the shape of One Cool Cat, successful in the Phoenix Stakes and National Stakes, and once-raced Curragh maiden winner Yeats. With a profile not unlike Hawk Wing's in 2001, One Cool Cat is undoubtedly a promising colt who will improve, but to have him as short as 7/4 for the Guineas in October on the basis of what he had achieved was nonsensical. Few punters worth their salt would take 7/4 six months before a classic about a colt even making the line-up.

But to begin at the beginning. As the most expensive Coolmore purchase at the 2002 yearling sales in America, fetching 3,100,000 dollars at Keeneland in July, One Cool Cat had plenty to prove. Coolmore's most expensive purchase in Europe that year was a Sadler's Wells filly out of Sharata named Softlyisthenight, who cost 2.1 million guineas at the Houghton Sale, and was unraced as a two-year-old. However, just like another high-priced youngster in the stable, The Mighty Tiger (2,500,000 dollars), One Cool Cat did not make a winning start, finishing fourth of ten to Steel Light in a maiden at the Curragh at the end of April. It was a different story on Timeform Charity Day at York in June, when One Cool Cat showed signs of considerable inexperience in a six-runner maiden, cocking his near-side ear markedly and giving the strong impression he was idling in beating Manntab by three and a half lengths after showing a good turn of foot over a furlong out. A month later he added the Dubai Duty Free Anglesey Stakes at the Curragh to his tally. Opposed by five, including Mokabra and Leicester Square from Britain, he did not break well but gave no other hint of greenness in leading two hundred yards out and beating Leicester Square by a length and a half, idling again.

For a colt with championship aspirations, One Cool Cat had had little to beat thus far, but this seemed a certainty to change in the Independent Waterford Wedgwood Phoenix Stakes on the same course in August. The eight-length Coven-

Independent Waterford Wedgwood Phoenix Stakes, the Curragh—
One Cool Cat (dark colours) provides Aidan O'Brien with a sixth successive win in the race;
stable-companion Old Deuteronomy is second, with odds-on Three Valleys (second right) only third

Dunnes Stores National Stakes, the Curragh—One Cool Cat cements his position as Guineas favourite as he gains a fourth consecutive victory; Wathab (right) is second and Pearl of Love third

try Stakes winner Three Valleys was among his opponents, who also included One Cool Cat's stable-companions Old Deuteronomy, Born In America and Devil Moon, plus another from Britain, Notable Lady. Three Valleys started at 6/4-on and One Cool Cat at 11/8 in what was viewed as a match. With Three Valleys failing to run to his best—afterwards found to have mucus in his lungs—One Cool Cat improved easily to lead over a furlong out, after lying well off the pace, and ran on strongly despite what was by now becoming his customary idling to beat Old Deuteronomy by a length. Three Valleys finished three lengths away third. The victory was the sixth in a row in the race for O'Brien (Paddy Prendergast won seven successive Phoenix Stakes in the 'fifties), following Lavery, Fasliyev, Minardi, Johannesburg and Spartacus (only one of whom managed to win at three), but the form was far from exceptional—the best form Old Deuteronomy had achieved previously was second in the Richmond Stakes. Form considerations appeared to carry no weight with the bookmakers, however, who halved One Cool Cat's odds to as low as 4/1 for the Guineas. The fact that One Cool Cat won his next race, the Dunnes Stores National Stakes on the same course in September, merely added to the hype. One Cool Cat was odds on to defeat seven rivals headed by Pearl of Love, successful in the Chesham Stakes and Futurity Stakes, Solario Stakes winner Barbajuan, the favourite's stablemate Celtic Cat, runner-up in the Acomb Stakes, and Wathab, only sixth in the Phoenix Stakes but subsequently successful in a listed race at the Curragh. After sweating at the start and proving a little stubborn, One Cool Cat was ridden very confidently, again racing well off the pace until starting a forward move. Initially he did not obtain a clear run but, once daylight came approaching the final furlong, he quickened well. Given three sharp cracks of the whip to go about his business, One Cool Cat was always going to win thereafter, but again he idled quite noticeably in front, pricking his ears, and edged left as well. Wathab, having his tenth start, showed improved form and was beaten a length with Pearl of Love a neck away third and Barbajuan fourth. The last two named went on to finish first and third respectively in a fairly close finish for what looked an above average running of the Gran Criterium in Milan.

Beating Wathab by a length hardly amounts to Guineas-winning form but it would be dangerous to underestimate One Cool Cat. For one thing, weighing up horses with his style of racing is rarely easy; in that respect he bears a strong resemblance to a former O'Brien inmate Giant's Causeway (also by Storm Cat) in

748

having a tendency do no more than absolutely necessary in a finish. Provided this quirkiness, along with one or two other slight temperamental oddities does not become too serious, One Cool Cat will undoubtedly be a force to be reckoned with in the Guineas and other top races at up to a mile and a quarter. There are additional points in his favour besides smart form: he is a big, angular, good-topped colt with plenty of scope who should develop into a fine-looking three-year-old; he is bred in the purple; and he is trained by a master of his art. None of that, however, justifies his short odds for the Guineas. Bookmakers can hardly be blamed for taking such a view, considering O'Brien's reputation as a trainer and of his published comments on One Cool Cat from a fairly early stage of the colt's career. O'Brien's remarks make fascinating and entertaining reading. Firstly, after the Anglesey Stakes: 'He is an exciting horse and has always been a stunner in his work. He has a surge in the middle of a race that makes him very unusual. He goes from first gear to third and he still has two more gears when you want them.' After the Phoenix Stakes: 'He's a unique colt and a very relaxed one. The moves he makes in the middle of his work would knock you dead.' And after the National Stakes: 'I've never come across a horse with such a blast of speed as this fellow. Mick (Kinane) says he's dangerous.'

One Cool Cat (USA) (b.c. Mar 26, 2001)	Storm Cat (USA) (b or br 1983)	Storm Bird (b 1978)	Northern Dancer
			South Ocean
		Terlingua (ch 1976)	Secretariat
			Crimson Saint
	Tacha (USA) (b or br 1992)	Mr Prospector (b 1970)	Raise A Native
			Gold Digger
		Savannah Dancer (b or br 1982)	Northern Dancer
			Valoris

Mrs John Magnier's "One Cool Cat"

One Cool Cat, who acts on firm going, has an impressive pedigree. Storm Cat, the most expensive stallion in the world at 500,000 dollars, continues to take the bloodstock world by storm—sixteen of his offspring fetched at least a million dollars at auction during the year, including a yearling for 2,600,000 dollars, a foal for 2,400,000 and two mares for more than 3,000,000. With ninety foals born during the year, his dominance of the sales-ring looks set to continue for a while yet. Significantly, now that many of Storm Cat's best-bred progeny are coming to Europe the balance is changing a little—he had a total of three Group 1 winners in Europe in the latest season, Denebola and Nebraska Tornado being the others, but only one Grade 1 winner (Dessert in the Del Mar Oaks) in America. Few of Storm Cat's offspring stay a mile and a half and, as One Cool Cat's dam Tacha is a daughter of Mr Prospector, the colt is unlikely to get the trip even if tried, which is doubtful given the greater commercial appeal of races run over shorter distances. Tacha was a minor winner over an extended mile and has produced one other successful performer from two foals, a filly by Seattle Slew; Tacha's yearling filly by A P Indy was withdrawn from the Keeneland September Sale. Her dam Savannah Dancer was smart, successful in the Del Mar Oaks, and two of her other progeny have won stakes races. The stayer Brier Creek landed the Henri II Stakes and Sha Tha, a sister to Tacha, finished second in the Poule d'Essai des Pouliches before winning the All Along Stakes in New York. Sha Tha is the dam of a very smart colt in State Shinto, successful in the Prix Dollar. This is an excellent family, since Savannah Dancer's dam Valoris, a half-sister to Prix du Jockey Club winner Val de Loir, gained a classic success in the 1966 Oaks and foaled Val's Girl and Vincennes, second in the Oaks and Irish Oaks respectively. *A. P. O'Brien, Ireland*

ONE FOR ME   5 br.m. Tragic Role (USA) – Chantallee's Pride (Mansooj 118) [2003 48, a57: p16g 11.6m Jul 28] modest handicapper: well held on Flat in 2003, but won 4 times over hurdles: tried tongue tied: sometimes slowly away. *Jean-Rene Auvray*   **–**

ONEFORTHEBOYS (IRE)   4 b.g. Distinctly North (USA) 115 – Joyful Prospect (Hello Gorgeous (USA) 128) [2003 –: f9.4g f7g f8s 6m⁶ 6f p6g Dec 2] little form: left R. Ford after third start: tried tongue tied. *D. Flood*   **–**

ONEFOURSEVEN   10 b.g. Jumbo Hirt (USA) 90§ – Dominance (Dominion 123) [2003 54, a–: 21.6m⁶ 13.8f 17.1m³ Aug 17] angular gelding: poor handicapper nowadays: stays 21f: acts on soft going, good to firm and fibresand: tried blinkered/tongue tied: usually held up. *P. C. Haslam*   **43 a–**

ONE LAST TIME   3 b.g. Primo Dominie 121 – Leap of Faith (IRE) 65 (Northiam (USA)) [2003 93: 6m 6g 8g 8.1g⁶ 8m⁶ p8g Oct 15] good-topped gelding: has a quick action: good walker: fairly useful performer: respectable efforts at best in 2003: seems to stay 1m: yet to race on extremes of going on turf: sold 20,000 gns. *R. Hannon*   **80 ?**

ONE MORE HYMN (IRE)   3 b.g. General Monash (USA) 107 – Maz (IRE) 48 (Cyrano de Bergerac 120) [2003 59: p6g p5g⁶ f6g Jan 24] modest maiden at 2 yrs, poor in 2003: should stay 7f: acts on firm going and polytrack: has started slowly/raced freely/found little: sold only 500 gns later in January, sent to Holland. *S. L. Keightley*   **–**

ONE MORE ROUND (USA)   5 b.g. Ghazi (USA) – Life of The Party (USA) (Pleasant Colony (USA)) [2003 112: a6f² a8f 7g² 8d³ 7d² 6.3m⁵ 7g² 7d⁴ 7f² 6f 7g Oct 18] rather leggy gelding: smart performer: good efforts in 2003 when second in handicap at Nad Al Sheba, Gladness Stakes at the Curragh (beaten neck by Millennium Force), Ballycorus Stakes at Leopardstown (beaten by 1½ lengths to Abunawwas), Tote International Handicap at Ascot (beaten 1½ lengths by New Seeker) and handicap at Leopardstown (beaten ¾ length by D'Anjou): respectable seventh in Group 3 event at Caulfield final outing: stays 8.5f: acts on good to soft and dirt: found little (something possibly amiss) penultimate 4-y-o start: effective with or without blinkers: normally consistent. *D. K. Weld, Ireland*   **116**

ONE 'N' ONLY (IRE)   2 b.f. (Feb 24) Desert Story (IRE) 115 – Alpina (USA) 69 (El Prado (IRE) 119) [2003 6m 7m⁴ 7.2f⁵ 6m⁴ 7m⁵ 7m Oct 18] €6,000Y: quite good-topped filly: second living foal: dam, lightly-raced maiden, half-sister to dam of Rodrigo de Triano: modest maiden: should stay at least 1m: often slowly away. *Miss L. A. Perratt*   **54**

ONE OFF   3 b.g. Barathea (IRE) 127 – On Call 103 (Alleged (USA) 138) [2003 58: 12.1m 11.9m* f12g² 14g* 15.4m* 14.4m* 14m* 16m² Sep 18] well-made gelding: much improved in 2003, and developed into a fairly useful handicapper: completed 6-timer between June and August, at Brighton (maiden event), Wolverhampton, Haydock,   **94 p**

Folkestone, Newcastle and Sandown (by ½ length from Anak Pekan): would have been suited by stronger gallop when good ½-length second of 5 to Ravenglass at Yarmouth final start: will stay beyond 2m: acts on good to firm ground and fibresand: edgy/upset in stall on reappearance: likely to improve again at 4 yrs. *Sir Mark Prescott*

ONE UPMANSHIP   2 ch.g. (May 2) Bahamian Bounty 116 – Magnolia 52 (Petong 126) [2003 5d 5m⁶ 5g 6m⁵ 5.2m 7m² 6.1m⁴ 6m³ 6m Oct 16] 10,000Y: close-coupled gelding: third foal: dam, ran twice, sister to useful sprinter Petula: fair maiden: second in nursery at Lingfield: stays 7f: acts on good to firm ground: below form in cheekpieces fourth start, in blinkers fifth and final ones. *J. G. Portman*   **69**

ON EVERY STREET   2 b.c. (Apr 30) Singspiel (IRE) 133 – Nekhbet 74 (Artaius (USA) 129) [2003 7.9f⁵ Oct 11] 200,000Y: close-coupled, quite attractive colt: closely related to very smart 1m/1¼m performer Right Wing (by In The Wings) and half-brother to several winners, including useful 6f/7f performer Cim Bom Bom (by Dowsing): dam, maiden, half-sister to Irish St Leger winner M-Lolshan: 6/1 from 12/1, but burly, fifth of 7 in maiden at York, very green: sure to do better. *H. J. Cyzer*   **– p**

ONE WAY TICKET   3 ch.c. Pursuit of Love 124 – Prima Cominna 86 (Unfuwain (USA) 131) [2003 74p: 7m² 7m² 7m⁵ 6.1m³ 6m² 7m³ f7g⁴ 7.1m* 7m 7.1m² p7g Oct 30] lengthy, workmanlike colt: fair performer: claimed from R. Charlton on reappearance: won maiden at Warwick in August: stays 7f: acts on soft and good to firm ground: wore cheekpieces last 7 starts: looks none too resolute. *J. M. Bradley*   **74 §**

ONE WON ONE (USA)   9 b.g. Naevus (USA) – Havards Bay (Halpern Bay (USA)) [2003 111: 7g⁴ 6s² 8d 8m 8m 6f Sep 13] good-topped, attractive gelding: smart performer: creditable efforts when fourth to Millennium Force in Gladness Stakes at the Curragh and head second to Miss Emma in listed race at Naas: well below form after: effective at 6f to 1m: acts on any turf going, well beaten both starts on dirt: blinkered twice earlier in career, and has worn cheekpieces: held up. *Ms J. Morgan, Ireland*   **113 d**

ON GUARD   5 b.g. Sabrehill (USA) 120 – With Care 78 (Warning 136) [2003 67, a73: f9.4g f12g⁶ 10.9m* 10m* 10m 10g 10m f8.5s 10d f12s⁶ 10.4f⁵ 9g Oct 24] neat gelding: fair handicapper: won at Warwick and Leicester in April: best at 1m to 11f: acts on firm going, good to soft and fibresand: sometimes visored, tried in cheekpieces: tends to hang/ carry head awkwardly: held up. *P. G. Murphy*   **69 a48**

ONIZ TIPTOES (IRE)   2 ch.g. (Apr 21) Russian Revival (USA) 125 – Edionda (IRE) (Magical Strike (USA) 114) [2003 8f p7g Oct 15] IR 6,000F, €17,000Y: first foal: dam, Italian 1m (at 2 yrs) to 1½m winner, closely related to useful Irish 9f and 1½m winner Palace Royale: well held in maidens at Bath and Lingfield. *W. R. Muir*   **–**

ONLINE INVESTOR   4 b.g. Puissance 110 – Anytime Baby 56 (Bairn (USA) 126) [2003 101d: 6m 6g⁴ 6g 6g⁴ 5g 6g 5f⁶ 6f 6f 5m Oct 20] leggy, quite good-topped gelding: fairly useful performer: free-going sort, and should prove at least as effective at 5f as 6f: acts on firm going, probably good to soft: pulled too hard in blinkers once at 3 yrs: often slowly away: sold 26,000 gns, and gelded. *C. G. Cox*   **87**

ONLY FOR GOLD   8 b.g. Presidium 124 – Calvanne Miss 48 (Martinmas 128) [2003 66, a55: f9.4g f9.4g 7m⁵ 8m f7s 7.2g⁵ 8.1m 7.9f⁵ 8g 7.6m 10.9g⁶ 10g 6m Aug 8] rangy gelding: modest performer at best nowadays: effective at testing 6f to easy 8.5f: acts on heavy going, good to firm and fibresand: has worn cheekpieces: visored once at 4 yrs: broke blood vessel second start. *A. Berry*   **53 a–**

ONLY FOR SUE   4 ch.g. Pivotal 124 – Barbary Court (Grundy 137) [2003 50: f8.5g 11.6g⁶ f12g* Dec 22] rather leggy, angular gelding: modest handicapper: lightly raced: won at Wolverhampton in December: stays 1½m: acts on fibresand and soft ground. *W. S. Kittow*   **59**

ONLY IF I LAUGH   2 ch.g. (Apr 9) Piccolo 121 – Agony Aunt 81 (Formidable (USA) 125) [2003 p5g⁴ 5.1f² 5g⁶ 5f 6m³ 5.1m³ f5g* 5.1f* 5.1m⁴ 5m 5m² 6.1m⁵ 5.1m* 5m⁶ 5d⁵ 6g f6g⁴ Nov 19] 4,500Y: big, strong gelding: third foal: brother to fairly useful 6f winner Cool Tune: dam, 1¼m winner, out of half-sister to Oaks second Wind In Her Hair: fair performer: won sellers at Wolverhampton in June and Bath in July, and nursery at Chepstow in September: best at 5f: unraced on soft/heavy going, acts on any other turf and all-weather: usually blinkered/hooded: often makes running. *R. J. Meehan*   **77**

ONLY JUST IN TIME   3 ch.f. Bahamian Bounty 116 – Badger Bay (IRE) 67 (Salt Dome (USA)) [2003 –: p5g f7s Jan 14] no form in 3 starts. *D. K. Ivory*   **–**

ONLY ONE LEGEND (IRE)   5 b.g. Eagle Eyed (USA) 111 – Afifah 66 (Nashwan (USA) 135) [2003 68§, a76§: f6s f6s² f6g⁶ p6g* f6g⁶ p6g* 6.1g² p6g 6m 6f 6f⁵ 6m² 5m⁴ 6m⁶ 5f⁶ f5g⁶ f5g p6g³ Dec 6] lengthy gelding: fairly useful handicapper on all-   **77 § a82 §**

weather, fair on turf: won at Lingfield in January and March: left T. Easterby 10,000 gns after sixteenth start: best at 5f/6f: acts on firm going, good to soft and all-weather: tried in cheekpieces, usually blinkered: has found little: probably needs exaggerated waiting tactics: unreliable. *K. A. Ryan*

ONLY PENANG (IRE) 4 b.f. Perugino (USA) 84 – Unalaska (IRE) 65 (High Estate 127) [2003 87: 8g 8.3g² 7.1m 8g 9f³ 8.5m p7g 10d Oct 13] leggy filly: fairly useful handicapper: left B. R. Millman after fourth outing: below form last 3 starts: stays 9f: acts on firm and soft ground, probably on polytrack: blinkered (raced freely) once at 3 yrs: tried tongue tied: often makes running: sold 8,000 gns, sent to Sweden. *G. A. Butler* **85**

ONLYTIME WILL TELL 5 ch.g. Efisio 120 – Prejudice 83 (Young Generation 129) [2003 105, a–: 6m⁴ 7g 6g 6m² 6f 7m 6g² 6g⁵ 6m 6m Sep 20] lengthy, useful-looking gelding: useful handicapper on turf, fair when last ran on all-weather: very good efforts in 2003 when second at Epsom (beaten 1¼ lengths by Loyal Tycoon) and Ascot (beaten ½ length by Fantasy Believer) and when fifth to Patavellian in Stewards' Cup at Goodwood: best at 6f/7f: acts on fibresand/any turf going: sometimes slowly away/wanders: often races prominently. *D. Nicholls* **108 a–**

ON POINT 3 b.f. Kris 135 – Odette 72 (Pursuit of Love 124) [2003 60p: p5g* f5s p5g* p5g⁵ p5g Apr 1] fair handicapper: won at Lingfield in January (made all) and February: best at 5f: acts on polytrack: temperament under suspicion. *Sir Mark Prescott* **72**

ON PORPOISE 7 b.g. Dolphin Street (FR) 125 – Floppie (FR) (Law Society (USA) 130) [2003 –: f8.5g⁵ 11.5g Jul 3] lengthy gelding: poor performer: lightly raced nowadays. *P. W. D'Arcy* **–**

ON THE BRINK 3 b.f. Mind Games 121 – Ocean Grove (IRE) 84 (Fairy King (USA)) [2003 83: 5.5m⁴ 5f⁶ 6m 6.1d⁴ 5f 6d² 6m⁵ 6m 6m⁵ 6m⁴ 6m Oct 2] useful-looking filly: good mover: fairly useful handicapper: should stay 7f: acts on firm and good to soft ground: blinkered 4 of last 6 starts: has looked none too resolute. *T. D. Easterby* **88**

ON THE FAIRWAY (IRE) 4 b.f. Danehill Dancer (IRE) 117 – Asta Madera (IRE) 67 (Toca Madera 111) [2003 62d: p6g 7f 5g⁶ 6m Jun 20] tall filly: maiden: no form in 2003. *J. J. Bridger* **–**

ON THE LEVEL 4 ch.f. Beveled (USA) – Join The Clan 95 (Clantime 101) [2003 –: 7g 5.1m⁴ 5m 5g 5m⁴ 5m³ 6g² 6m⁵ 6m⁵ Oct 17] poor maiden: effective at 5f/6f: acts on good to firm ground: tried in cheekpieces: often races prominently. *Mrs N. Macauley* **47**

ON THE TRAIL 6 ch.g. Catrail (USA) 123 – From The Rooftops (IRE) (Thatching 131) [2003 –, a68: f6s³ f6g* p6g p6g f6s f6s f6g² 6m f6g³ f6s³ f6g² f6g³ f6s f7g f6g f6g Dec 9] strong gelding: fair performer: won handicap at Wolverhampton in January: best at 6f: acts on good to soft ground, good to firm and all-weather: has been tongue tied: usually races up with pace: often finds little. *D. W. Chapman* **65 §**

ON THE WING 2 b.f. (Jan 27) Pivotal 124 – Come Fly With Me (Bluebird (USA) 125) [2003 p7g⁵ 7m⁵ 6g⁵ 7m* 8m⁵ Oct 24] 16,000Y: tall, leggy filly: first foal: dam, once-raced half-sister to useful 7f winner Desert Alchemy, out of half-sister to smart sprinter Leap For Joy: fair performer: won maiden at Newcastle in October: creditable fifth in nursery at Doncaster final start: stays 1m: acts on good to firm going, showed promise on polytrack. *A. P. Jarvis* **78**

ONYA 3 ch.f. Unfuwain (USA) 131 – Reel Foyle (USA) 77 (Irish River (FR) 131) [2003 8.2g 10m f9.4s p12g p12g Nov 13] 17,000Y: lengthy, angular filly: eighth foal: half-sister to several winners, including 7-y-o Alastair Smellie and 9-y-o Unshaken: dam 2-y-o 5f winner: little form. *J. W. Hills* **–**

OOPSIE DAISY 4 b.f. Singspiel (IRE) 133 – Oops Pettie 93 (Machiavellian (USA) 123) [2003 81p: 10m⁶ 8g 8m* 8.3g 8m⁶ 10.1m Oct 21] angular filly: fairly useful performer, lightly raced: best effort when winning handicap at Newmarket in August: bred to stay at least 1¼m, but races freely: acts on good to firm going and polytrack: wore cheekpieces last 4 starts: carried head high fifth outing: sold 10,500 gns. *J. R. Fanshawe* **83**

OOPS (IRE) 4 b.g. In The Wings 128 – Atsuko (IRE) (Mtoto 134) [2003 79: 16.2m 16.1d 13.8f⁴ 16m² Jun 10] fair maiden handicapper: well below form after reappearance: stays 2m: acts on soft and good to firm ground: tried blinkered: has raced freely/carried head awkwardly: looks no easy ride: claimed £5,000, joined J. Coupland. *T. D. Easterby* **?**

OOS AND AHS 3 b.f. Silver Wizard (USA) 117 – Hot Feet (Marching On 101) [2003 8m Oct 6] sparely-made filly: fourth foal: dam unraced: 100/1, well held in maiden at Pontefract. *C. W. Fairhurst* **–**

OPAL'S HELMSMAN (USA) 4 b.g. Helmsman (USA) 121 – Opal's Notebook –
(USA) (Notebook (USA)) [2003 43: 12f 9.2g 15g Jul 22] poor maiden: tried visored.
B. Mactaggart

OPEN GROUND (IRE) 6 ch.g. Common Grounds 118 – Poplina (USA) (Roberto –
(USA) 131) [2003 59: p16g f16.2g Feb 3] lengthy gelding: modest handicapper: well
held in 2003: stayed 19f: acted on heavy and good to firm going: blinkered final start:
dead. *Ian Williams*

OPEN HANDED (IRE) 3 b.g. Cadeaux Genereux 131 – Peralta (IRE) (Green Desert **64 d**
(USA) 127) [2003 –: 7d 8g 7.5d* 9d 9v 7s⁶ 8m 7.5d f7s f8.5g f7g Dec 16] IR 38,000Y:
third foal: half-brother to fairly useful French 2000 2-y-o 6f winner Latina (by King's
Theatre): dam unraced half-sister to smart French 1¼m winner Caprarola: modest handicapper: won at Tipperary in April: left E. Lynam, Ireland, after sixth start: well held after:
stays 7.5f: acts on soft going: tried in cheekpieces/tongue tie: has carried head high.
B. Ellison

OPENING CEREMONY (USA) 4 br.f. Quest For Fame 127 – Gleam of Light (IRE) **80**
81 (Danehill (USA) 126) [2003 87: 7.1m⁵ 10g⁶ 12f⁶ 9f⁶ 12m 9.9m 10.1m* 9.9m³ 10.4m
10m⁵ 10.1m³ 10g* Oct 28] angular filly: fairly useful performer: won handicap at Newcastle in August and minor event at Redcar in October: probably best around 1¼m: acts
on firm and good to soft ground: sometimes edges left/carries head high: free-going sort.
R. A. Fahey

OPENING HYMN 3 b.f. Alderbrook 120 – Hymne d'Amour (USA) 58 (Dixieland **67**
Band (USA)) [2003 10m⁵ 10g⁵ Oct 25] useful-looking filly: sixth foal: half-sister to 3
winners, including smart performer up to 1¾m in Britain/USA Chelsea Barracks (by
Deploy), 1m winner at 2 yrs, and fairly useful 2001 2-y-o 1m winner Proserpine (by
Robellino): dam, lightly raced on Flat and winning hurdler, out of half-sister to Alzao:
fair form when fifth to Tanaghum in maiden at Newmarket on debut: carried head high,
disappointing in similar event at Newbury 3½ months later: not certain to stay much
beyond 1¼m: took good hold both starts. *M. P. Tregoning*

OPEN MIND 2 b.f. (Feb 1) Mind Games 121 – Primum Tempus 49 (Primo Dominie **64 d**
121) [2003 5m² 5m⁴ 5.1m 5f⁴ 6m Sep 22] rather unfurnished filly: fifth foal: half-sister to
three 5f winners (all successful at 2 yrs), including 5-y-o Time N Time Again: dam sprint
maiden: modest maiden: regressed after second at Pontefract: likely to prove best at 5f.
E. J. Alston

OPERA BABE (IRE) 2 b.f. (Mar 16) Kahyasi 130 – Fairybird (FR) 70 (Pampabird **65**
124) [2003 6m⁴ 7.1m 8.1g 8.1d⁵ Aug 29] 7,200F: good-bodied filly: fourth foal: half-
sister to 2 winners abroad by Persian Bold and Sri Pekan: dam, 5f winner, ran only at 2
yrs: fair maiden: fourth at Ascot: ran badly last 2 starts, breathing problem on first
occasion, tongue tied second: should stay at least 1m. *H. S. Howe*

OPERA COMIQUE (FR) 2 b.f. (Mar 16) Singspiel (IRE) 133 – Grace Note (FR) **100 p**
99 (Top Ville 129) [2003 9g*⁷ 7m³ Sep 21] closely related to French 11.5f winner Artist
(by In The Wings) and half-sister to several winners, notably top-class 1½m performer
Belmez (by El Gran Senor): dam 1¼m winner who stayed 1½m: won maiden at Tipperary
in September: useful form when 1¼ lengths third to Venturi in C. L. Weld Park Stakes at
the Curragh: will be well suited by 1¼m/1½m: joined Godolphin: open to progress.
J. Oxx, Ireland

OPERA GLASS 3 b.f. Barathea (IRE) 127 – Optaria 83 (Song 132) [2003 84: 8.3g² **88**
10m⁶ 8.5m* 8m 9d² 8.3d⁵ 9m Aug 24] tall, lengthy, unfurnished filly: fairly useful
performer: made all in maiden at Beverley in June: good second in handicap at Goodwood after: barely stays 1¼m: acts on good to firm and good to soft going: has been
blinkered in paddock before being mounted, but not in race: takes good hold/often edges
left. *A. M. Balding*

OPERA KNIGHT 3 ch.g. In The Wings 128 – Sans Escale (USA) (Diesis 133) [2003 **59**
74: p12g² f12g⁵ Mar 24] good-bodied gelding: fair maiden, lightly raced: unruly in
preliminaries and found little second outing: stays 1½m: acts on good to firm going,
probably on polytrack: free-going sort: sometimes looks none too keen. *M. L. W. Bell*

OPERASHAAN (IRE) 3 b.g. Darshaan 133 – Comic Opera (IRE) (Royal Academy –
(USA) 130) [2003 –: f12g⁶ 7g 9d May 18] tall gelding: well held in 4 maidens.
T. T. Clement

OPERA STAR (IRE) 2 b.f. (Feb 25) Sadler's Wells (USA) 132 – Adjalisa (IRE) 65 **– p**
(Darshaan 133) [2003 p7g Dec 17] sixth foal: half-sister to 3 winners, including smart
Irish performer up to 9f Access All Areas (by Approach The Bench), 5f/6f winner at 2

yrs: dam, Irish maiden who stayed 1m, half-sister to Irish 2000 Guineas second Adjareli: 14/1, well held in minor event at Lingfield: should do better. *B. W. Hills*

OPPORTUNE (GER) 8 br.g. Shirley Heights 130 – On The Tiles (Thatch (USA) 136) **68** [2003 11.8g 17.1m⁶ 16.2m* 18m² 16.2f* 13m⁶ 16.2d⁵ 16.1m² 16.2m³ 16.2m² 15.9m* Aug 30] deep-bodied gelding: fair handicapper: missed 2002: won at Warwick in June and July, and Chester in August: needs further than 13f, barely stays 2¼m: has form on soft ground, probably best on good or firmer (acts on firm): usually held up: consistent. *W. M. Brisbourne*

OPTIMAITE 6 b.g. Komaite (USA) – Leprechaun Lady 57 (Royal Blend 117) [2003 **76 §** 97§: 14.1g 12g 10.1m 10.3f 11m 12m⁵ 11.5g Sep 16] tall, workmanlike gelding: easy mover: just fair form in 2003: effective at 1¼m, barely at 1¾m: acts on firm and good to soft going: visored (reluctant to race) once, wore cheekpieces last 2 starts: usually tongue tied: often slowly away: sometimes hangs right/finds little: ungenuine. *B. R. Millman*

OPTIMAL (IRE) 2 gr.f. (Apr 17) Green Desert (USA) 127 – On Call 103 (Alleged **57 p** (USA) 138) [2003 8m⁴ p7g 7.5m Sep 17] lengthy, useful-looking filly: has a short, round action: second foal: half-sister to 3-y-o One Off: dam 1½m to 2m winner: modest form in maidens: will stay at least 1¼m: type to do better as 3-y-o. *Sir Mark Prescott*

OPTIMUM NIGHT 4 b.g. Superlative 118 – Black Bess (Hasty Word 84) [2003 7d **–** 10m 8m Apr 22] 2,500 3-y-o: second foal: dam unraced: well held in maidens. *P. D. Niven*

ORAKE PRINCE 4 b.g. Bluegrass Prince (IRE) 110 – Kiri Te (Liboi (USA) 76) [2003 **–** 59, a–: p10g Dec 30] maiden: well beaten only 4-y-o start: usually blinkered at 3 yrs. *W. G. M. Turner*

ORANGE TOUCH (GER) 3 b.c. Lando (GER) 128 – Orange Bowl (General Assem- **99** bly (USA)) [2003 84p: 10m⁵ 10.4m⁴ May 15] well-made colt: useful form in just 4 starts: good 3¼ lengths fifth to Shield in Classic Trial at Sandown on reappearance: again made running when well-held last of 4 to Lateen Sails in listed event at York following month: bred to stay 1½m, but tends to race freely: raced only on good to firm going. *Mrs A. J. Perrett*

ORANGINO 5 b.g. Primo Dominie 121 – Sweet Jaffa 73§ (Never So Bold 135) [2003 **50** 51: 6d 6m 8m² 10g 7d 10.9m 8m Oct 12] modest maiden: well below form after third start: stays 1m: acts on soft and good to firm going: tried blinkered. *J. S. Haldane*

ORAPA 4 b.g. Spectrum (IRE) 126 – African Dance (USA) (El Gran Senor (USA) 136) **–** [2003 –: p10g Jan 18] big, long-backed gelding: soundly beaten in 3 maidens: tried tongue tied. *Julian Poulton*

ORCADIAN 2 b.g. (Feb 12) Kirkwall 118 – Rosy Outlook (USA) 79 (Trempolino **105** (USA) 135) [2003 6m³ 6m* 7m² 6m² 6f Oct 11] close-coupled gelding: fluent mover: second foal: half-brother to 4-y-o Rapscallion: dam, 6f winner, out of half-sister to very smart French performers Squill (up to 1¼m) and Baiser Vole (up to 1m): useful perfor- mer: won maiden at Windsor in July: good second in listed race at Newbury (beaten 5 lengths by Haafhd) and minor event at Yarmouth (beaten head by Peak To Creek): ran as if amiss final start: stays 7f. *J. M. P. Eustace*

ORCHESTRA STALL 11 b.g. Old Vic 136 – Blue Brocade 91 (Reform 132) [2003 **–** 15.5g⁶ 16g Jul 31] good-topped gelding: had a splayed, round action: formerly very smart (winner of Sagaro Stakes at Ascot in 1997 and 2000), though had leg problems and lightly raced in recent years: last in Prix Vicomtesse Vigier at Longchamp and Goodwood Cup on return from 2-year absence: seemed best at 1¾m/2m: acted on soft and good to firm going: had worn bandages: retired. *J. L. Dunlop*

ORCHESTRATION (IRE) 2 ch.c. (Apr 15) Stravinsky (USA) 133 – Mora (IRE) **73** 100 (Second Set (IRE) 127) [2003 5m² 6m⁶ Aug 13] 52,000F, 60,000Y: compact colt: first foal: dam, Irish 7f/1m winner, half-sister to useful dam of smart sprinter Eastern Purple: fair form in maidens at Hamilton (second to Axis, then left J. Noseda) and Salis- bury: sold 24,000 gns. *R. Charlton*

ORIEL LADY 2 b.f. (Mar 23) Cyrano de Bergerac 120 – Hicklam Millie 49 (Absalom **40** 128) [2003 5m f5g 5g⁶ 6d 5g⁶ 7m⁶ Jun 10] 500Y: plain filly: half-sister to 3 winners abroad, including German 9f/10.5f winner One of Them (by Pharly): dam, maiden, stayed 1¼m: poor maiden: barely stays 7f. *A. Berry*

ORIENTAL MIST (IRE) 5 gr.g. Balla Cove 119 – Donna Katrina (Kings Lake **–** (USA) 133) [2003 54: 9.2g 13m 9f Jun 30] leggy gelding: no form in 2003: tried blinkered/visored. *P. Monteith*

ORIENTAL MOON (IRE) 4 ch.f. Spectrum (IRE) 126 – La Grande Cascade (USA) **– §**
(Beaudelaire (USA) 125) [2003 62§, a59§: f9.4s 9.7m 10.1m 9.7m 8.2m f8g⁶ f9.4g⁵ Dec
22] leggy filly: unreliable maiden: well held in 2003: tried blinkered/in cheekpieces.
G. C. H. Chung

ORIENTAL WARRIOR 2 b.c. (Mar 18) Alhaarth (IRE) 126 – Oriental Fashion **101 p**
(IRE) 110 (Marju (IRE) 127) [2003 6m* 7g* Oct 11] good-bodied colt: first foal: dam,
1m winner (including at 2 yrs), out of close relative to 5-y-o Nayef and half-sister to
Nashwan and Unfuwain: useful form: won maiden at Newbury in September and minor
event at Ascot (odds on, beat Primus Inter Pares comfortably by 1¼ lengths) in October:
will be suited by at least 1m: open to progress, and could well make his mark in stronger
company as 3-y-o. *M. P. Tregoning*

ORIENTOR 5 b.h. Inchinor 119 – Orient 106 (Bay Express 132) [2003 116: 6g² 6d² **112**
6m 6f 6g* 6m 6f 5m⁵ 6d 6m 6f 6g⁶ Oct 24] close-coupled horse: smart performer: won
Kronenbourg 1664 Chipchase Stakes at Newcastle in June by short head from Country
Reel: mostly at least respectable efforts otherwise in 2003, including behind Oasis Dream
in July Cup (ninth) at Newmarket and Nunthorpe Stakes (5¾ lengths fifth) at York sixth/
eighth starts: best at 6f: has form on any going, but all wins on good or softer: held up.
J. S. Goldie

ORIGINAL SIN (IRE) 3 b.g. Bluebird (USA) 125 – Majakerta (IRE) (Shernazar **64 ?**
131) [2003 7g 6.1m⁵ 7d⁶ f8g Oct 16] IR 23,000Y, 65,000 2-y-o: lengthy gelding: second
foal: dam, winning hurdler in France, half-sister to smart French miler Fine Fellow (by
Bluebird): modest maiden at best: stays 7f: unraced on extremes of going on turf: raced
freely on debut: sold 5,500 gns. *J. R. Fanshawe*

ORINOCOVSKY (IRE) 4 ch.g. Grand Lodge (USA) 125 – Brillantina (FR) (Crystal **73**
Glitters (USA) 127) [2003 77: 10m 11.9g 14d⁴ Sep 27] rangy gelding: fair handicapper:
stays 1¾m: acts on firm and good to soft going: blinkered once at 3 yrs: free-going sort.
C. R. Egerton

ORION EXPRESS 2 b.c. (Mar 14) Bahhare (USA) 122 – Kaprisky (IRE) (Red Sunset **56**
120) [2003 6m 5d 6m Jul 18] 4,000F, 12,000Y: lengthy colt: sixth foal: half-brother to 2
winners abroad, including winner up to 7.5f in Italy by First Trump: dam German 6f (at 2
yrs)/7f winner: modest form at best in maidens: needs to settle to stay 6f. *M. W. Easterby*

ORION'S BELT 3 ch.g. Compton Place 125 – Follow The Stars 86 (Sparkler 130) **–**
[2003 65: 6f Oct 12] fair maiden in 2002: below form last 2 starts that year, and well held
only outing at 3 yrs. *G. B. Balding*

ORMOLU (IRE) 3 ch.f. Perugino (USA) 84 – Gloire (Thatching 131) [2003 6g⁴ 5m **51**
5m 8m 6m⁶ 5g Oct 13] IR 10,000Y: big filly: fifth foal: half-sister to 5f (at 2 yrs) and 7f
winner Ajig Dancer (by Niniski) and 2000 2-y-o 5f winner Glory Days (by Lahib), both
fairly useful: dam unraced sister to smart sprinter Puissance: modest form: best effort on
debut: bred to prove best at 5f/6f: slowly away first 2 outings: carries head high: sold
1,500 gns, sent to Belgium. *G. A. Butler*

ORNELLAIA (IRE) 3 b.f. Mujadil (USA) 119 – Almost A Lady (IRE) 70 (Entitled **53**
126) [2003 56: 7.1m f7g⁵ p10g⁵ 10m⁵ f12g Oct 20] modest maiden: left A. Hales after
second start: stays 1¼m: acts on all-weather and good to firm ground: sold 4,000 gns.
P. M. Phelan

ORO PURO (IRE) 2 b.c. (Feb 2) Goldmark (USA) 113 – Mount Soufriere (IRE) **61**
(Maledetto (IRE) 103) [2003 6m⁶ 7.5d* 7m 8f⁵ 8.3g Oct 6] €3,000Y: smallish, sturdy
colt: first foal: dam unraced: modest performer: won seller at Beverley in July by 5
lengths: creditable effort after on penultimate start only: should stay 1¼m: acts on firm
and good to soft going. *M. G. Quinlan*

ORO VERDE 2 ch.c. (Mar 1) Compton Place 125 – Kastaway 91 (Distant Relative 128) **91**
[2003 6m⁶ 5m* 5m⁴ 5.1m² 7g 6m³ 6g⁴ 6p6g⁴ p6g⁴ p5g² Dec 10] 46,000Y: small, strong **a86**
colt: first foal: dam 2-y-o 5f winner: fairly useful performer: won maiden at Windsor in
June: in frame, running creditably, in minor events after: best at 5f/6f: acts on good to
firm going and polytrack. *R. Hannon*

ORPENBERRY (IRE) 2 b.f. (Apr 1) Orpen (USA) 116 – Forest Berries (IRE) **75**
(Thatching 131) [2003 5f³ 5m* 5.2m 6.1m Aug 18] 10,000Y: good-topped filly: seventh
foal: half-sister to 3 winners, including 6f (including at 2 yrs) and 1m winner Forest
Dancer (by Charnwood Forest) and 5f winner (including at 2 yrs) Arjan (by Paris House),
both fairly useful: dam unraced half-sister to smart middle-distance colt Pencader: fair
performer: won maiden at Musselburgh in July: good tenth of 22 in Super Sprint at
Newbury next time, much better effort after: should stay at least 6f. *K. R. Burke*

ORTHODOX 4 gr.g. Baryshnikov (AUS) – Sancta 106 (So Blessed 130) [2003 81: **89**
p13g* p12g* p13g⁶ 12g 11.6g 12g² 12m Aug 24] tall, rather leggy gelding: fairly useful
performer: won maiden and handicap at Lingfield in February: in-and-out form after:
stays 13f: acts on polytrack, raced only on good/good to firm going on turf: found little
final start. *G. L. Moore*

OSCAR MADISON (IRE) 2 b.g. (Mar 29) Petorius 117 – She's Our Lady (IRE) –
(Scenic 128) [2003 5d⁶ 6m 7.1f⁶ 6f Jul 14] 3,200Y: second foal: dam unraced: last in
maidens in Scotland. *B. Mactaggart*

OSCAR PEPPER (USA) 6 b.g. Brunswick (USA) 119 – Princess Baja (USA) (Con- **73**
quistador Cielo (USA)) [2003 78, a96: f8s² p10g f8.5s³ f8.5g² f8.5s⁵ 8m 8m² 8g³ 7.9f **a96**
7m* 8f 7.9m⁶ 7g³ 8m 8m⁵ 10.4m 10.1m⁴ 8.5m 8m⁴ Oct 1] close-coupled, useful-looking
gelding: useful on all-weather, fair on turf: won minor event at Redcar in June: placed in
minor event at Southwell and minor event/handicap at Wolverhampton earlier in season:
effective at 7f to 1¼m: acts on fibresand, firm and good to soft ground: tried visored/
blinkered, has run creditably in cheekpieces: has been slowly away. *T. D. Barron*

OSORIO (GER) 3 ch.c. Surumu (GER) – Ocotal (Vitiges (FR) 132) [2003 10d² 10m* **114**
12m* May 25] approx. 8,000Y in Germany: closely related to several winners in Germany, including 1m (at 2 yrs) to 1½m winner Olaya (by Acatenango), herself dam of
smart German stayer Olaso: dam German 6f (at 2 yrs) to 9f winner: smart performer:
raced only in Italy, winning maiden at Milan at 2 yrs, listed race there in May and Derby
Italiano at Rome later in month, last-named by 2½ lengths from Private Charter:
reportedly missed remainder of year with injury: stays 1½m well: yet to race on extremes
of ground. *U. Suter, Germany*

OSORNO 3 ch.g. Inchinor 119 – Pacifica 90 (Robellino (USA) 127) [2003 p7g p10g –
Nov 18] second foal: dam, 2-y-o 5f winner, out of half-sister to smart miler Nicolotte:
well held in maidens at Lingfield, slowly away. *C. F. Wall*

OSTERHASE (IRE) 4 b.g. Flying Spur (AUS) – Ostrusa (AUT) (Rustan (HUN)) **111**
[2003 111: 5m² 5g³ 5.3m² 5g⁶ 5g* Jul 25] smart performer: placed in listed races first 3
starts (beaten short head by Repertory at Cork on reappearance): won handicap at Cork in
July under top weight by neck from Mainly Mine: has won at 6f but best at 5f: acts on
good to firm and good to soft ground: front-runner/races prominently: blinkered.
J. E. Mulhern, Ireland

OTHER BUSINESS 2 b.f. (Apr 2) Muhtarram (USA) 125 – Carnbrea Belle (IRE) 76 –
(Kefaah (USA) 124) [2003 8m⁶ 8m Sep 9] 3,000Y: smallish, sturdy filly: third living foal:
half-sister to French 5f (at 2 yrs) to 1m winner Ginger Twist (by Most Welcome): dam,
1½m to 2m winner, half-sister to useful stayer Upper Strata, herself dam of Lord of Men:
well beaten in maidens at Yarmouth (slowly away) and Leicester. *P. L. Gilligan*

Derby Italiano, Rome—foreign raiders dominate
as German-trained Osorio beats Private Charter and Lundy's Lane (rail) from Britain

OTHER ROUTES 4 ch.g. Efisio 120 – Rainbow Fleet 66 (Nomination 125) [2003 66: **66**
p10g² 10.2f⁵ 10f 9f⁶ 8g² 8f³ 8m⁴ 8m 8m⁵ 8.5m² 8m⁵ 8.2m⁶ 9g Oct 24] fair handicapper:
probably best at 1m/1¼m: acts on firm going, good to soft and polytrack: sometimes
blinkered, usually wears cheekpieces nowadays: occasionally races freely: sold 10,000
gns. *G. L. Moore*

OTOTOTM 3 b.c. Mtoto 134 – Najmat Alshemaal (IRE) 98 (Dancing Brave (USA) **71**
140) [2003 –p: 10m⁶ 11.9m* 12.1g² 14.1d 12.4m⁴ a12f⁶ Nov 27] compact colt: fair handicapper: won at Brighton in June: left A. Stewart before final outing: should be suited by
1¾m+: acts on good to firm going: visored (ran creditably) penultimate outing: sometimes races freely: reportedly had breathing problem fourth start. *A. Smith, UAE*

OTYLIA 3 ch.f. Wolfhound (USA) 126 – Soba 127 (Most Secret 119) [2003 49: 6m 5g **57**
5.9m 6.9f 5.9f³ f6g 6m³ 6m 5m⁶ 5m⁴ 6f² 6m³ 5m⁵ 6m⁴ 6m⁴ Oct 17] smallish, strong,
lengthy filly: modest maiden: effective at 5f/6f: acts on firm ground: effective in cheekpieces. *A. Berry*

OUIJA BOARD 2 b.f. (Mar 6) Cape Cross (IRE) 129 – Selection Board 75 (Welsh **98**
Pageant 132) [2003 7m³ 7m* 8g³ Nov 1] tall, leggy filly: half-sister to several winners,
including smart 1m winner (stayed 1½m) Star Selection (by Rainbow Quest) and useful
7f winner Cruinn A Bhord (by Inchinor): dam, ran twice, sister to Teleprompter: useful
form: won 6-runner minor event at Yarmouth in October by 4 lengths from Rydal,
quickening most impressively: creditable 4 lengths third of 12 to Spotlight in listed event
at Newmarket final start, slowly away: likely to stay 1¼m. *E. A. L. Dunlop*

OUNDLE SCOUNDREL (FR) 4 b.g. Spinning World (USA) 130 – Tidal Treasure **68**
(USA) (Crafty Prospector (USA)) [2003 80d: f8g f9.4g⁵ p8g f8.5g f8g² f8g 7.1m⁵ 9s*
a7.5g³ 9d² 8g³ 8g* 8g* 8d 8s³ 10s³ 7.6g⁴ 8s Nov 29] quite good-topped gelding: just fair
performer in 2003: won claimer at Compiegne in July (claimed from P. Hiatt €13,507)
and 2 handicaps at Vichy in August: stays 1¼m: acts on firm going, soft and fibresand:
blinkered (much too free) once. *Y. Porzier, France*

OUR CHELSEA BLUE (USA) 5 ch.m. Distant View (USA) 126 – Eastern Connec- **54**
tion (USA) (Danzig Connection (USA)) [2003 73, a59: p6g⁴ p7g* p6g* p6g p7g p6g* **a66**
p6g⁵ 5g⁶ 7m p7g 6m f6g⁶ f5g⁶ f5g Dec 12] fair on all-weather, modest on turf: won
maiden handicap in January, claiming minor event in February and seller (left C. Dwyer)
in March, all at Lingfield: left Andrew Reid after eleventh start: best at 6f/easy 7f: acts on
all-weather and good to firm going: tried tongue tied: headstrong. *A. W. Carroll*

OUR DESTINY 5 b.g. Mujadil (USA) 119 – Superspring (Superlative 118) [2003 47: **58**
f9.4g* f8.5g⁴ f9.4g⁴ f8.5g* p10g f9.4g 10.2m f12g f8g f9.4g² Dec 22] big, strong, lengthy
gelding: modest performer: won amateur handicap in January and apprentice claimer in
March, both at Wolverhampton: stays 11f: acts on firm going, soft and fibresand: usually
visored: none too consistent. *D. Burchell*

OUR EMMY LOU 2 ch.f. (May 7) Mark of Esteem (IRE) 137 – Regent's Folly (IRE) **56 p**
101 (Touching Wood (USA) 127) [2003 7.1m 5.7f⁶ 8.2f⁶ Sep 30] leggy, good-topped
filly: seventh foal: half-sister to 3 winners, including fairly useful 1m (at 2 yrs) to 1½m
winner Spree Vision (by Suave Dancer) and Irish 9f winner Falcon's Fire (by Kalaglow):
dam, 2-y-o 7f winner who stayed 14.6f, out of close relative to high-class 1¼m winner
Ascot Knight: modest form in maidens: not unduly punished final start: likely to do better
at 1¼m/1½m at 3 yrs. *Sir Mark Prescott*

OUR FRED 6 ch.g. Prince Sabo 123 – Sheila's Secret (IRE) 97 (Bluebird (USA) 125) **62 §**
[2003 71§, a83§: p5g 5g 5m 5g³ 5m 5m⁶ Sep 24] lengthy gelding: fair handicapper on all- **a75 §**
weather, modest on turf: barely stays 6f: acts on soft going, good to firm and all-weather:
sometimes blinkered/visored: usually races up with pace: unreliable. *T. G. Mills*

OUR GAMBLE (IRE) 2 b.f. (Mar 26) Entrepreneur 123 – Manilia (FR) (Kris 135) **84**
[2003 5d 5g⁴ 5m* 6m Jun 7] 14,000Y: leggy filly: fluent mover: fourth foal: half-sister to
fairly useful 2002 2-y-o 6f winner Queen's Lodge (by Grand Lodge) and winner in Italy
by Salse: dam French 11f winner: fairly useful performer: won maiden at Sandown in
May: creditable seventh of 10 in listed race at Epsom final start: should stay 1m: acts on
good to firm going. *R. Hannon*

OUR GLENARD 4 b.g. Royal Applause 124 – Loucoum (FR) 93 (Iron Duke (FR) **58 §**
122) [2003 63?: p10g p10g⁴ p13g* 9.9m* 10g 8.5m⁵ f12s g12g f8g⁵ Nov 24]
smallish, sturdy gelding: modest performer: reportedly hobdayed after final 3-y-o start:
won seller at Lingfield in April and amateur handicap at Beverley in May: stays easy 13f:
acts on good to firm going and polytrack: tried tongue tied: sometimes slowly away:
untrustworthy. *S. L. Keightley*

OUR IMPERIAL BAY (USA) 4 b.g. Smart Strike (CAN) 121 – Heat Lightning   –
(USA) (Summer Squall (USA)) [2003 85: 12g 13.3m⁶ Jul 19] tall gelding: fairly useful at
3 yrs: no form in 2003, leaving Mrs A. Perrett after reappearance: sometimes blinkered:
has raced lazily/hung left. *R. M. Stronge*

OUR KID 2 ch.g. (Apr 26) Pursuit of Love 124 – Flower Princess (Slip Anchor 136)   **63**
[2003 6m⁶ 7.5m⁶ 7m⁴ 7m Aug 6] workmanlike gelding: eighth foal: half-brother to 3
winners, including 1½m winner Benjamin Frank and 1996 2-y-o 7f winner Beryllium
(both fairly useful, by Tragic Role): dam raced once out of Fillies' Mile winner Nepula:
modest maiden: should stay 1m: often slowly away. *T. D. Easterby*

OUR LADY 3 b.f. Primo Dominie 121 – Polytess (IRE) (Polish Patriot (USA) 128)   **71**
[2003 62: 7m 6g 8m* 10.1m⁴ 8f 7g³ 8m⁶ 8m 8g² 7f⁴ Oct 27] fair performer: won selling
handicap at Yarmouth in August: very best form at 1m: raced only on good ground or
firmer: unseated rider and bolted before final 2-y-o start: sold 8,500 gns. *G. G. Margarson*

OUR LODGE 2 br.c. (Mar 22) Grand Lodge (USA) 125 – Hakkaniyah 84 (Machia-   **59 ?**
vellian (USA) 123) [2003 7.1m 6m 8f⁵ Oct 12] 150,000Y: useful-looking colt: third foal:
dam, 2-y-o 6f winner, closely related to useful French performer up to 1¼m Elanaaka:
seemingly modest form at best in maidens: should stay 1¼m: tongue tied last 2 starts:
sold 1,500 gns. *B. J. Meehan*

OUR MONOGRAM 7 b.g. Deploy 131 – Darling Splodge (Elegant Air 119) [2003   **74**
61: 14.4g 16d* 17.2f* 17.2f⁵ 16.2d⁶ 16.4m² 16m⁴ 16m* Sep 5] big, strong gelding: fair
handicapper: won at Ripon in May, Bath in June and Kempton in September: stays 19f:
acts on firm and good to soft going: has wandered (including at Kempton): front runner/
races prominently. *R. M. Beckett*

OUR PADDY (IRE) 4 b.g. Ali-Royal (IRE) 127 – Lilting Air (IRE) 83 (Glenstal   **64 ?**
(USA) 118) [2003 f12s f7g p8g f9.4s 7g⁵ 9f⁵ 6m 7d³ 7g 7m f8.5g Nov 15] 8,000F, IR
7,700Y, €6,000 3-y-o: third foal: dam 6f and 9f winner in Ireland: modest maiden: left
P. D. Evans after fourth outing, W. Murphy in Ireland after tenth: stays 9f: acts on firm
and good to soft going: tried tongue tied. *Mrs L. C. Jewell*

OUR TEDDY (IRE) 3 ch.g. Grand Lodge (USA) 125 – Lady Windley (Baillamont   **103**
(USA) 124) [2003 101: p7g² 8m⁶ 8m* 10.4m 9m 8g 9.9m 8g Sep 12] lengthy gelding:
useful performer: won minor event at Doncaster in May by neck from Balin's Sword:
respectable eighth to Magistretti in Dante Stakes at York next time: below form after:
stays 1m: acts on polytrack, good to firm and good to soft going. *G. G. Margarson*

OUR WOL 4 b.g. Distant Relative 128 – Lady Highfield 62 (High Kicker (USA))   –
[2003 51: 7m May 8] modest maiden, lightly raced: has worn cheekpieces: blinkered
(well held) only run in 2003. *G. G. Margarson*

OUT AFTER DARK 2 b.c. (Mar 10) Cadeaux Genereux 131 – Midnight Shift (IRE)   **75 p**
73 (Night Shift (USA)) [2003 6g 6g⁴ 6.1d² Nov 6] 7,000Y, 13,000 2-y-o: strong, useful-
looking colt: has a quick action: third foal: brother to 3-y-o Move It and half-brother to
4-y-o Miss Anabaa: dam, 6f winner, half-sister to very smart sprinter Owington: fair form
in maidens: 5 lengths second of 16 to Malvern Light at Nottingham: will probably prove
best at 5f/6f: open to progress. *C. G. Cox*

OUTEAST (IRE) 3 b.f. Mujadil (USA) 119 – Stifen (Burslem 123) [2003 70: 5f 5m   –
5f 6d 5m 6m 6m 5m Oct 4] angular filly: fair winner at 2 yrs: no form for new trainer in
2003: tried in cheekpieces. *G. A. Harker*

OUTER HEBRIDES 2 b.g. (Apr 8) Efisio 120 – Reuval 102 (Sharpen Up 127) [2003   **86**
7m² 7m² f6g* Aug 15] 70,000Y: sturdy gelding: has round action: half-brother to several
winners, including smart 6f/7f (latter including at 2 yrs) winner Ardkinglass (by Green
Desert), 3-y-o Dubrovsky and 6-y-o Eyecatcher: dam best at 1m: fairly useful form in
maidens: runner-up at Catterick and Folkestone prior to landing odds in 13-runner event
at Wolverhampton (visored, idled): should stay 1m. *D. R. Loder*

OUT FOR A STROLL 4 b.g. Zamindar (USA) 116 – The Jotter 99 (Night Shift   **87**
(USA)) [2003 83: 8.3g 8g 7m* 8.2f* 7g Nov 1] sturdy, deep-girthed gelding: fairly useful
handicapper: won at Leicester (landed gamble) in September and Nottingham (in good
style) in October: best at 7f/1m: acts on firm going: edged left/carried head on one side
final outing. *S. C. Williams*

OUT OF MIND 2 b.c. (May 7) Mind Games 121 – Distant Isle (IRE) (Bluebird (USA)   **78**
125) [2003 5f 5.1m³ 5s 5.1m³ 5d 5f³ 5m⁵ 5m* 5g* Sep 27] 4,500Y: big, good-topped colt:
fifth living foal: half-brother to 5.7f (at 2 yrs) and 1m winner Entropy (by Brief Truce):
dam unraced: fair performer: won nurseries at Catterick and Ripon (by neck from Dispol
Katie) in September: likely to prove best at 5f on good going or firmer: usually races
prominently: game: sold 21,000 gns. *B. A. McMahon*

OUT OF MY WAY   2 ch.f. (May 3) Fraam 114 – Ming Blue 52 (Primo Dominie 121)   –
[2003 7m 6m⁴ 6m p8g Nov 22] 1,000Y: sixth foal: sister to 6-y-o Wilfram: dam poor
maiden on Flat/over hurdles: well held in maiden/sellers at Lingfield. *T. M. Jones*

OUT OF TUNE   3 ch.g. Elmaamul (USA) 125 – Strawberry Song 87 (Final Straw 127)   –
[2003 –: 8m⁵ 8f 8m Aug 18] well held in maidens/handicaps: tried blinkered. *C. Weedon*

OUTWARD (USA)   3 b.c. Gone West (USA) – Seebe (USA) 112 (Danzig (USA))   **62**
[2003 8.2f⁵ 9m⁴ Oct 25] leggy, quite attractive colt: first foal: dam, 5f (at 2 yrs) to 9f (US
Grade 3 event) winner, sister to 3-y-o Rimrod and half-sister to high-class miler Selkirk:
modest form in maidens at Nottingham (slowly away) and Musselburgh (edged left),
taking good hold both times: sold 16,000 gns. *J. H. M. Gosden*

OVERDRAWN (IRE)   2 b.g. (Apr 23) Daggers Drawn (USA) 114 – In Denial (IRE)   **96**
(Maelstrom Lake 118) [2003 5m⁴ 5g² f6s* 6m⁴ 7m* 8d² 7g³ 8s⁴ 7m* 8d⁵ Nov 7]
€16,000Y, resold 16,000Y: leggy, quite good-topped gelding: first foal: dam, ran once
in Ireland, half-sister to useful Irish/US 1m to 1¼m performer Inchacooley: useful
performer: won maiden at Wolverhampton in June and nurseries at York in September
and Doncaster (under 9-7, by neck from River Nurey) in October: rare poor effort final
start: stays 1m: acts on fibresand, good to firm and good to soft ground: usually held up.
J. A. Osborne

OVER RATING   3 ch.f. Desert King (IRE) 129 – Well Beyond (IRE) 101 (Don't   **74**
Forget Me 127) [2003 8m⁴ 8.5g² 9.9m³ 8f⁴ f8.5g² f9.4g⁶ Nov 28] half-sister to several   **a67**
winners, including 6f (at 2 yrs) to 8.5f (US Grade 3 event) winner Out of Reach and 1996
2-y-o 6f winner who stayed 7f Well Warned (both useful, by Warning): dam 5f (at 2 yrs)
to 1m winner out of sister to dam of Zafonic: fair maiden: stays 1¼m: acts on fibresand,
raced only on good ground or firmer on turf: raced freely/hung left second start: sold
24,000 gns. *J. H. M. Gosden*

OVERRIDE (IRE)   3 b.c. Peintre Celebre (USA) 137 – Catalonda (African Sky 124)   **85 d**
[2003 75: 6.1m² 6m² 7m 7g p6g⁶ p7g Dec 29] rather leggy, quite attractive colt: fairly
useful performer: below form after second start: effective at 6f/7f: raced only on good
going or firmer on turf: sometimes finds little. *J. M. P. Eustace*

OVERSTRAND (IRE)   4 b.g. In The Wings 128 – Vaison La Romaine 100 (Arctic   **86**
Tern (USA) 126) [2003 86: 13.1d 16g² Nov 5] lengthy gelding: fairly useful performer:
stays 2m: acts on firm going, good to soft and polytrack: has edged left/idled: consistent:
useful hurdler. *Mrs M. Reveley*

OVER THE RAINBOW (IRE)   2 b.c. (Mar 28) Rainbow Quest (USA) 134 – Dim-   **86**
akya (USA) 83 (Dayjur (USA) 137) [2003 7g² 8m³ 8f Sep 27] useful-looking colt: has a
quick action: fourth foal: half-brother to 3-y-o Golano and 1999 2-y-o 6f winner Tereed
Elhawa (by Cadeaux Genereux): dam, French 7.5f winner who probably stayed 1¼m, out
of smart French/US performer around 1¼m Reloy: fairly useful form when placed in
maidens at Goodwood (second to Psychiatrist) and Kempton (odds on): last of 10 in
Royal Lodge Stakes at Ascot: should be suited by 1¼m/1½m. *B. W. Hills*

OVER THE YEARS (USA)   2 b.g. (Mar 2) Silver Hawk (USA) 123 – Sporting   –
Green (USA) (Green Dancer (USA) 132) [2003 8.2d f8g Nov 24] $75,000F, €27,000Y:
very big gelding: third foal: dam 8.5f winner in USA: well held in maiden/minor event.
T. P. Tate

OVER TO YOU BERT   4 b.g. Overbury (IRE) 116 – Silvers Era 72 (Balidar 133)   **48**
[2003 p8g⁵ p8g p10g⁴ 10.9m 7m⁵ p6g 6m Jun 2] half-brother to several winners,
including 6f/7.5f winner L A Touch (by Tina's Pet): dam 2-y-o 5f winner: poor maiden:
tried in cheekpieces/visor. *Mrs P. N. Dutfield*

OVIGO (GER)   4 b.g. Monsagem (USA) 117 – Ouvea (GER) (Konigsstuhl (GER))   **74**
[2003 8d* 9.2g⁵ 5d 6d 10s f8.5g³ f8g³ f12g Dec 19] ex-German gelding: having only
second outing, won maiden at Frankfurt in May (left W. Glanz after): fair form in Britain:
stays 8.5f: acts on good to soft going and fibresand: tried blinkered. *P. A. Blockley*

OWN LINE   4 b.g. Classic Cliche (IRE) 128 – Cold Line 74 (Exdirectory 129) [2003   **53**
58: 21.6m⁴ 16.2m 16d 13.8f⁴ 17.1m 10.9m 12m* 12.1g³ 12.3m Aug 4] good-topped
gelding: modest handicapper: won at Catterick in July: effective at 1½m to 2m: acts on
firm going and fibresand: tried in cheekpieces. *J. Hetherton*

OYSTERBED (IRE)   3 b.f. Night Shift (USA) – Pearl Shell (USA) (Bering 136)   **57**
[2003 5m 6g 6m³ 5.7f 6m* Oct 17] reportedly has only one eye: third foal: sister to useful
7f winner Pearly Gates: dam, French 1½m winner, out of top-class middle-distance
performer Paulista: modest performer: won maiden at Redcar in October: should stay 7f:
reportedly had breathing problem fourth start. *J. Nicol*

P

PABLO 4 b.c. Efisio 120 – Winnebago 63 (Kris 135) [2003 112p: 8g* 9m^4 10.3m^5 8g^5 **117**
Nov 1] good-bodied colt: smart performer: better than ever when winning Freephone
Stanley Lincoln (Handicap) at Doncaster in March by 1½ lengths from Selective,
quickening in good style: respectable fourth to Olden Times in Earl of Sefton Stakes at
Newmarket (left impression ill at ease on good to firm ground) next time: below form in
listed events at Chester and Newmarket (well-backed favourite) last 2 starts 6 months
apart: stays 9f: may prove best on good ground or softer: genuine. *B. W. Hills*

PACIANO (IRE) 3 b.g. Perugino (USA) 84 – Saucy Maid (IRE) 69 (Sure Blade (USA)   **82**
130) [2003 81: 6m^2 7.5m 6.1m^3 5g^3 6g 6g^6 6m^2 7f^3 7m^4 7m^2 Oct 13] quite good-topped
gelding: fairly useful maiden handicapper: effective at 6f/7f: acts on firm and good to soft
ground: has carried head awkwardly/hung right. *C. G. Cox*

PACIFIC ALLIANCE (IRE) 7 b.g. Fayruz 116 – La Gravotte (FR) (Habitat 134)   **–**
[2003 38: 11.8m 11.6m Jul 21] one-time fairly useful performer: very much on
downgrade on Flat, but won over hurdles in Ireland in October: usually blinkered.
R. M. Stronge

PACIFIC OCEAN (ARG) 4 b.c. Fitzcarraldo (ARG) – Play Hard (ARG) (General   **56**
(FR)) [2003 –: 7g^5 8.2g^6 7.1m^6 f8.5s^6 f7s^5 f8g^3 f8g^4 Dec 15] modest maiden: should stay
1¼m: acts on fibresand, raced only on good/good to firm going on turf: tried blinkered:
tongue tied (best efforts) last 2 starts. *Mrs S. A. Liddiard*

PACKIN EM IN 5 b.h. Young Ern 120 – Wendy's Way 53 (Merdon Melody 98) [2003   **–**
–: f7g f7g f6g f7g Jun 19] modest maiden at 2 yrs: lightly raced and no form since: tried
blinkered. *J. R. Boyle*

PACWAN (IRE) 2 b.g. (May 13) Woodborough (USA) 112 – Solway Lass (IRE)   **–**
(Anita's Prince 126) [2003 6m 5m Jun 23] 500F, €1,600 2-y-o, resold 7,500 2-y-o: leggy
gelding: third foal: dam, little sign of ability, ran only at 2 yrs: ran in sellers. *D. Carroll*

PADDY MUL 6 ch.h. Democratic (USA) 101 – My Pretty Niece (Great Nephew 126)   **43**
[2003 52: 16m^4 16m^6 12.4m^2 16g^6 Aug 26] sparely-made horse: poor performer: stays
2m: acts on firm going, soft and fibresand: tried visored: tongue tied. *W. Storey*

PADDYWACK (IRE) 6 b.g. Bigstone (IRE) 126 – Millie's Return (IRE) 71 (Ballad   **86**
Rock 122) [2003 94, a88: f5s f6s f5g^2 p5g p5g 5f 5f 5g 5m 5g 6m 6m 5d^4 6g 5m 5d^2 5m*
6m 6m^4 6f 6f^3 5m^6 5s 5d^5 7d^6 f6g^6 f5s* f6g f6g Dec 26] small gelding: fairly useful
performer: won minor event at Beverley in July and handicap at Wolverhampton in
December: effective at 5f/6f: acts on firm going, good to soft and all-weather: blinkered:
saddle slipped/reportedly struck into final start: tends to get behind. *D. W. Chapman*

Freephone Stanley Lincoln (Handicap), Doncaster—
Pablo shows smart form in winning from Selective and Norton (No.5)

PADDY WINALOT (IRE) 3 ch.g. College Chapel 122 – Six Penny Express (Bay   –
Express 132) [2003 56?: 7g 9.2d 9.3f 8m⁴ Jun 20] good-topped gelding: modest maiden
at 2 yrs: well held in 2003: difficult ride: bolted before start and withdrawn second
intended 3-y-o outing. *D. Nicholls*

PAGAN CEREMONY (USA) 2 ch.g. (May 17) Rahy (USA) 115 – Delightful Linda   –
(USA) (Slew O' Gold (USA)) [2003 8m Aug 17] $95,000Y: half-brother to several minor
winners in USA: dam, US maiden, closely related to very smart US Grade 2 1m/9f winner
Old Trieste out of US Grade 1 9f winner Lovlier Linda: 16/1, last of 7 in maiden at
Kempton. *Mrs A. J. Perrett*

PAGAN DANCE (IRE) 4 b.g. Revoque (IRE) 122 – Ballade d'Ainhoa (FR) (Al Nasr   **101**
(FR) 126) [2003 93: 10d⁵ 10m² 10m* 10.1m³ 12f⁵ 9.9g 12g* 14.8m⁴ 13.3m⁴ 12m Oct 3]
strong gelding: useful performer: won minor events at Newmarket in May and August,
latter by neck from Wait For The Will: probably stays 14.8f: acts on firm and soft going:
usually wears cheekpieces: sometimes carries head awkwardly. *Mrs A. J. Perrett*

PAGAN MAGIC (USA) 2 b.c. (Feb 28) Diesis 133 – Great Lady Slew (USA) (Seattle   **68 p**
Slew (USA)) [2003 7m 8s⁵ Oct 29] $90,000Y: tall colt: fifth foal: half-brother to smart
winner up to 12.5f Slew The Red (by Red Ransom) and winner in US by Dixieland Band:
dam, winner up to 1m in USA, out of half-sister to Breeders' Cup Distaff winner Lady's
Secret: better effort in maidens (fair form) when fifth of 19 to Roehampton at Yarmouth,
not unduly punished: likely to be suited by 1¼m/1½m: should progress. *J. A. R. Toller*

PAGAN PRINCE 6 br.g. Primo Dominie 121 – Mory Kante (USA) (Icecapade (USA))   **81**
[2003 81: 8m⁶ 8f 8.1d 8.5g² 8f* 8.9f* 8m Oct 17] leggy gelding: fairly useful handicapper: won at Ascot in September and York in October: races at 1m/9f: acts on fibresand,
firm and soft going: usually waited with. *J. A. R. Toller*

The Mail On Sunday/Tote Mile Final (Handicap), Ascot—
Pagan Prince (left) gives apprentice Lisa Jones her biggest win with a neck success over Finished Article;
Ettrick Water (visor) and Krugerrand (noseband) are next

PAGAN RIVER 2 br.g. (May 25) River Falls 113 – Pagan Star (Carlitin 50) [2003 6m 6m Jun 10] leggy gelding: first foal: dam unraced: well held in maidens. *G. M. Moore* —

PAGAN SKY (IRE) 4 ch.g. Inchinor 119 – Rosy Sunset (IRE) (Red Sunset 120) [2003 87: 8g² 8.5m 10m⁵ 10.5m⁶ 10m* 10.4f⁶ 10g* Oct 25] close-coupled gelding: useful handicapper: won at Pontefract in September and Newbury (beat subsequent November Handicap winner Turbo by length, despite hanging left) in October: stays 1¼m: acts on firm going: has worn crossed noseband: has started slowly. *J. A. R. Toller* **97 +**

PAGAN STORM (USA) 3 ch.g. Tabasco Cat (USA) 126 – Melodeon (USA) (Alydar (USA)) [2003 80: 7m⁴ 7.1m 7m³ 7m⁶ 6m* 7f⁴ 5.7f⁶ Oct 12] lengthy, sparely-made gelding: fluent mover: fair performer: won maiden at Newmarket in August: effective at 6f/7f: raced on good ground or firmer: wore blinkers/cheekpieces last 3 outings: difficult ride: unreliable: sold 8,500 gns. *Mrs A. J. Perrett* **78 §**

PAGAN WOLF 3 b.g. Wolfhound (USA) 126 – Sharp Girl (FR) 114 (Sharpman) [2003 –: f7g⁵ 10m 12g Aug 2] poor maiden: best effort at 7f on fibresand. *W. Jarvis* **47**

PAGEANT 6 br.m. Inchinor 119 – Positive Attitude 82 (Red Sunset 120) [2003 54§, a39§: 9.7m 8m 8.2m 8.1m 8.1m² 8m 8.1m⁴ 8.1g⁵ 7m³ 8m 8d Oct 31] rather leggy, useful-looking mare: modest performer on turf, poor on all-weather: effective at 7f/1m: acts on fibresand and probably any turf going: often front runner: has looked none too keen: unreliable. *J. M. Bradley* **56 § a– §**

PAGE NOUVELLE (FR) 5 b.m. Spectrum (IRE) 126 – Page Bleue (Sadler's Wells (USA) 132) [2003 79: p10g 9.9m⁴ 10g* 12.3m 10.3m 10.5m 9.9m Aug 24] strong, lengthy mare: has round action: fair handicapper: won at Nottingham in April: finds 1m a minimum, barely stays 1½m: probably best on good ground or softer. *W. M. Brisbourne* **71**

PAILITAS (GER) 6 b.g. Lomitas 129 – Pradera (GER) (Abary (GER) 119) [2003 –: 8m 9.9m⁴ Oct 1] won twice in Germany in 2001: lightly raced and modest form at best since: probably stays 1¼m: has reportedly had breathing problems. *Ian Williams* **54**

PAINTBRUSH (IRE) 3 b.f. Groom Dancer (USA) 128 – Bristle 96 (Thatch (USA) 136) [2003 48: 7s³ 7f⁵ 7f⁶ p8g Dec 6] poor maiden, lightly raced: stays 1m: acts on polytrack: very slowly away second outing. *Mrs L. Stubbs* **48**

PAINTED MOON (USA) 2 ch.f. (Feb 12) Gone West (USA) – Crimson Conquest (USA) 85 (Diesis 133) [2003 7m Aug 21] eighth foal: closely related to 2 winners, notably very smart 6f (at 2 yrs) and 1¼m winner Crimplene (by Lion Cavern) and half-sister to 3 winners, including 3-y-o Dutch Gold: dam 2-y-o 6f winner who probably stayed 1¼m: 6/1, last of 8 in maiden at Folkestone. *D. R. Loder* —

PALACEGATE TOUCH 13 gr.g. Petong 126 – Dancing Chimes (London Bells (CAN) 109) [2003 62, a56: f6g⁴ f6s⁵ f7s 7g May 5] tall, good-topped gelding: fairly useful performer at his best, successful 33 times from 207 career starts: just poor form in 2003: was best at 6f/7f: acted on firm going, soft and fibresand, probably on polytrack: often blinkered/visored early in career: tended to hang left/race with head high: claimer ridden latterly: retired to Northern Racing College, Doncaster. *A. Berry* **— a40**

PALACE THEATRE (IRE) 2 b.g. (May 5) Imperial Ballet (IRE) 110 – Luminary (Kalaglow 132) [2003 6m* Jun 19] IR 9,000F, €48,000Y: third foal: half-brother to 1m/9f winner in Hong Kong by Efisio: dam unraced daughter of Cheveley Park winner/1000 Guineas second Jacinth: 10/1, won 11-runner maiden at Ripon by ½ length from Munaawashat, slowly away and leading 2f out: subsequently gelded: likely to stay 1m: should improve. *T. D. Barron* **74 p**

PALAMEDES 4 b.g. Sadler's Wells (USA) 132 – Kristal Bridge 75 (Kris 135) [2003 75: 11.6g* 14f³ 11.9m 12m 11.9g 11.6g² 12d⁵ Nov 8] compact gelding: fairly useful handicapper: won at Windsor in April: mostly creditable efforts after: effective at 11.6f to 1¾m: raced only on good going or firmer. *P. W. Harris* **88**

PALANZO (IRE) 5 b.g. Green Desert (USA) 127 – Karpacka (IRE) 99 (Rousillon (USA) 133) [2003 106§: 6m 6m 5m 6m 5.1m 6m 7.2m Sep 20] lengthy gelding: one-time useful handicapper: well held in 2003: blinkered (ran poorly) once: sometimes slowly away: ungenuine. *D. Nicholls* **– §**

PALAWAN 7 br.g. Polar Falcon (USA) 126 – Krameria 72 (Kris 135) [2003 85: p5g* p5g⁴ 5g p5g f5g⁶ 5m 5f 5g 5m* 5f* 5g 5.2g* 5f f5g² Dec 16] lengthy gelding: fairly useful performer: better than ever in 2003, winning claimer at Lingfield in January and handicaps at Folkestone in July and Salisbury (apprentices) and Yarmouth in September: **92**

best at 5f: acts on all-weather, raced mainly on good going or firmer on turf: tried visored: often makes running. *A. M. Balding*

PALVIC MOON 2 ch.f. (Apr 13) Cotation – Palvic Grey (Kampala 120) [2003 f5g **59 §** f5g 5d⁶ 5m 6.1m⁶ 6m⁶ Sep 16] workmanlike filly: sister to 5f winner Palvic Lady: dam well beaten: modest maiden: stays 6f: acts on good to firm and good to soft going: ungenuine. *C. Smith*

PANAMA (IRE) 3 b.c. Peintre Celebre (USA) 137 – Bay Queen 85 (Damister (USA) **58 ?** 123) [2003 9.2d⁵ 10g⁴ 10m p10g Jul 16] lengthy colt: fourth foal: closely related to 7-y-o Prairie Wolf and 11f/11.5f winner Dance Master (by Nureyev): dam 9f/11f winner: seemingly modest form at best: bred to be suited by 1½m: sold 1,500 gns in October. *M. L. W. Bell*

PANCAKEHILL 4 ch.f. Sabrehill (USA) 120 – Sawlah (Known Fact (USA) 135) **66** [2003 70, a72: p10g f8g² f8s³ f8g² f8s³ f7g² p7g² 7m f7g² f9.4s³ p8g⁶ f7g⁵ p7g⁵ f7g Dec 16] quite good-topped filly: fair performer: effective at 7f to 1¼m: acts on good to firm going and all-weather: tried blinkered/in cheekpieces. *D. K. Ivory*

PANCAKE ROLE 3 b.g. Tragic Role (USA) – My Foxy Lady 37 (Jalmood (USA) **–** 126) [2003 –: f9.4g⁵ f9.4g May 19] tall, rather leggy gelding: little form. *D. Haydn Jones*

PANGLOSSIAN (IRE) 3 b.f. Baratahea (IRE) 127 – Overcall (Bustino 136) [2003 **72** 65: a8.5f a8f 10m⁵ 8m 12.1d³ 12f⁶ 10m⁵ 11.1m³ Aug 19] smallish, leggy filly: fair maiden handicapper: stays 1½m: acts on good to firm and good to soft ground: races prominently. *M. Johnston*

PANGLOSS (IRE) 2 ch.g. (Mar 25) Croco Rouge (IRE) 126 – Kafayef (USA) 46 **72** (Secreto (USA) 128) [2003 7g 8m³ 8g p8g Nov 2] 110,000F, 85,000Y, 25,000 2-y-o: sturdy gelding: fifth foal: half-brother to 3 winners, including 3-y-o Almaviva: dam ran 3 times: fair maiden: third at Goodwood, easily best effort: will be suited by 1¼m+. *G. L. Moore*

PANGO 4 ch.g. Bluegrass Prince (IRE) 110 – Riverine (Risk Me (FR) 127) [2003 79: **79** 8.1d⁶ 9m² 9g⁴ 10m⁵ 9.9m² 8.5g* 10m 8.9f⁵ 9g p8g Nov 12] rather unfurnished gelding: fluent mover: fair handicapper: won at Epsom in September: effective at 1m to 11f: acts on firm going, good to soft and all-weather. *H. Morrison*

PANJANDRUM 5 b.g. Polar Falcon (USA) 126 – Rengaine (FR) (Music Boy 124) **53** [2003 –, a70: p6g³ 8.3g f6g p5g* Dec 20] lengthy, sparely-made gelding: fair handicapper **a74** on all-weather, modest on turf: left M. Hill after second start: won at Lingfield in December: best at 5f/6f: acts on all-weather and firm going: sometimes visored. *N. E. Berry*

PANSHIR (FR) 2 ch.g. (Apr 5) Unfuwain (USA) 131 – Jalcamin (IRE) (Jalmood **–** (USA) 126) [2003 7s Oct 29] €45,000Y: fifth foal: closely related to a winner in Italy by Alhaarth and half-brother to 3 winners, including fairly useful 2001 2-y-o 6f winner Takamaka (by Pennekamp): dam Italian 6f to 1m winner: 33/1, well held in maiden at Yarmouth, slowly away/pulling hard. *C. F. Wall*

PANTITA 3 b.f. Polish Precedent (USA) 131 – Dedara (Head For Heights 125) [2003 **74** 8.1m² 10m³ 10g² 12.3g⁴ 10m⁴ Sep 9] 30,000F: workmanlike filly: half-sister to several winners, including fairly useful 1997 2-y-o 1m winner Friendly Warning (by Warning): dam, French 1½m winner, half-sister to grandam of Daylami and Dalakhani: fair maiden: well below form last 2 starts: should prove effective at 1½m. *B. R. Millman*

PANTONE 3 b.f. Spectrum (IRE) 126 – Tinashaan (IRE) 100 (Darshaan 133) [2003 **92** 71: 7g* 7.5m² 8.1f* 8m⁵ 7m 12.3m² 11.8m* 10.3m³ 10f 10f Aug 27] leggy, useful-looking filly: fairly useful handicapper: won at Newmarket in May, Sandown in June and Leicester in July: stays 1½m well: acts on polytrack, firm and good to soft ground: has hung left: none too consistent. *M. Johnston*

PANTS 4 b.f. Pivotal 124 – Queenbird 90 (Warning 136) [2003 68: f7s² f7g³ f7s⁶ f7s **54** 7g² 7g 6d⁴ 6m 7m p7g³ p7g* p7g Dec 6] sparely-made filly: fair performer on all- **a65** weather, just modest on turf nowadays: won minor event at Lingfield in November: does best at 6f/7f: acts on good to soft ground, good to firm and all-weather: visored once: sometimes slowly away: usually comes from behind. *Andrew Reid*

PAOLINI (GER) 6 ch.h. Lando (GER) 128 – Prairie Darling (Stanford 121§) [2003 **121** 121: 8.9g² 10m³ 10m 10g² Aug 16] strong, good-bodied horse: carries plenty of condi- tion: very smart performer: hasn't won since 2001 but numerous good efforts in top company around the world since: placed in 2003 in Dubai Duty Free at Nad Al Sheba (3 lengths second to Ipi Tombe), Queen Elizabeth II Cup at Sha Tin (pulled hard in slowly-

763

run race, 2 lengths third to Eishin Preston) and Arlington Million: narrowly beaten after meeting trouble at Arlington for second year running final start, staying on well and promoted to equal-second having been hampered near line by demoted Storming Home: moved short to post before only eighth to Nayef in Prince of Wales's Stakes at Royal Ascot other outing: effective at 1¼m/1½m: acts on firm and good to soft going, not at best on soft: usually blinkered nowadays (not final start). *A. Wohler, Germany*

PAPEETE (GER) 2 b.f. (Mar 27) Alzao (USA) 117 – Prairie Vela (Persian Bold 123) **74**
[2003 6m³ 7m³ 7m* 8.1g 8m Sep 25] €20,000Y: leggy, close-coupled filly: half-sister to several winners in Germany, including 10.5f/11f winner Pacific River (by Law Society): dam German 8.5f/9f winner: fair performer: won maiden at Newcastle in August: well below form in nurseries last 2 starts: should be suited by 1¼m/1½m. *W. J. Haggas*

PAPPY (IRE) 2 b.f. (Mar 28) Petardia 113 – Impressive Lady 98 (Mr Fluorocarbon **63 d** 126) [2003 6m 6f 6m³ 5m⁵ 6m 6.1m Sep 19] €5,000Y: big, leggy filly: eighth foal: sister to 7-y-o Compton Arrow and half-sister to 2 winners, including 5-y-o Madeline Bassett: dam Irish 2-y-o 7f winner: modest maiden: showed little after third at Doncaster (blinkered final start): stays 6f. *J. G. Given*

PARACA (ARG) 4 b.f. Kitwood (USA) 119 – Paraguaya (ARG) (Country Doctor **?** (USA)) [2003 8g* 8g* 10.2g Oct 25] Argentinian-bred filly: dam unraced half-sister to Breeders' Cup Distaff winner Paseana: winner of 6 of her 10 starts in South Africa for G. Woodruff, including 3 Group 1 events, namely Allan Robertson Fillies Championship at Scottsville in 2002, Fancourt Majorca Stakes at Kenilworth in August and Triple Tiara 1600 at Turffontein (by 2¾ lengths from Icy Air) in March: 60/1 on debut for new connections, tailed-off last behind Fields of Omagh in Cox Plate at Moonee Valley final outing (reportedly unsuited rider on way to post): stays 1m. *A. M. Balding*

PARACHUTE 4 ch.g. Hector Protector (USA) 124 – Shortfall 103 (Last Tycoon 131) **91** [2003 58: f12s⁴ f12g* f12g* p13g* f12s³ 16g³ 14g Jul 3] big, strong, lengthy gelding: has scope: fairly useful performer: won maiden at Southwell and handicap at Wolverhampton in January and minor event at Lingfield in February: good third in handicap at Musselburgh penultimate start: stays 2m: acts on all-weather, yet to race on ground firmer than good on turf: sometimes races freely/carries head a bit awkwardly. *Sir Mark Prescott*

PARADISE BREEZE 2 b.f. (Mar 6) Perugino (USA) 84 – Paradise Forum 78 (Prince **– p** Sabo 123) [2003 6m Sep 9] seventh foal: dam 2-y-o 5f winner: 33/1, eighth of 10 in maiden at Lingfield, slowly away but some late headway: likely to do better. *C. A. Horgan*

PARADISE EVE 3 b.f. Bahamian Bounty 116 – Twilight Time (Aragon 118) [2003 46: **81** f5s² f5s* 5m* 5d* May 17] fairly useful performer: progressed to win maiden at Southwell in February and handicaps at Musselburgh and Thirsk in May: will prove best at 5f/6f: acts on fibresand, good to firm and good to soft ground: hung right only start at 2 yrs: usually makes running. *T. D. Barron*

PARADISE GARDEN (USA) 6 b.g. Septieme Ciel (USA) 123 – Water Course **–** (USA) (Irish River (FR) 131) [2003 52: 9.9m 12g 10.1m 13.8m 12m⁵ 10.5f Sep 5] tall gelding: one-time useful performer: well held in 2003: tried in headgear. *P. L. Clinton*

PARADISE ISLE 2 b.f. (Mar 8) Bahamian Bounty 116 – Merry Rous 66 (Rousillon **96** (USA) 133) [2003 6m² 6g² 6m² 5m* 6.1f* Oct 1] 17,000Y: rather sparely-made filly: half-sister to several winners, including fairly useful 1994 2-y-o 5f winner Bruton Stream (by Taufan) and 3-y-o Cheeky Girl: dam, 2-y-o 6f winner, half-sister to very smart sprinter Tina's Pet: useful performer: won maiden at Pontefract in September and minor event at Nottingham (by 2½ lengths from La Vie Est Belle, pulling hard and quickening well) in October: should prove best at 5f/6f: acts on firm going: tends to carry head high. *C. F. Wall*

PARADISE VALLEY 3 b.g. Groom Dancer (USA) 128 – Rose de Reve (IRE) (Per- **66 §** sian Heights 129) [2003 72, a64: f9.4g² f9.4g⁵ p8g³ f8g⁵ 10m 10g⁶ 10.1f³ 10.2g 10f² 11.5g⁵ 10m* f12g* p12g⁵ f14.8g² f16.2s⁵ Dec 6] good-bodied gelding: fair performer: claimed from A. Jarvis £5,000 tenth start: won seller at Leicester in October: stays 1¾m: acts on all-weather and firm ground: sometimes tongue tied/visored: has been slowly away: ungenuine. *Mrs S. A. Liddiard*

PARAGON OF VIRTUE 6 ch.g. Cadeaux Genereux 131 – Madame Dubois 121 **88** (Legend of France (USA) 124) [2003 88: p10g* p12g⁶ p10g³ p12g³ p10g* p12g Dec 17] lengthy gelding: fairly useful performer: won minor event in January and handicap (beat Mad Carew a length after 8-month break) in November, both at Lingfield: effective at 1¼m/1½m: acts on soft going, good to firm and polytrack. *P. Mitchell*

PARALLEL LINES (IRE) 2 ch.g. (Apr 30) Polish Precedent (USA) 131 – Phone **61**
Booth (USA) (Phone Trick (USA)) [2003 6d 6g 7m⁶ 5.1f² 6f² 5m 5.7f 6m Oct 2]
€15,000Y: half-brother to several minor winners in USA/Italy: dam, 2-y-o 5f winner in
USA, half-sister to grandam of Suave Dancer: modest maiden: runner-up at Bath and
Brighton: stays 6f: acts on firm and good to soft ground: blinkered (ran poorly) last 2
starts: sold 7,000 gns, and gelded. *R. F. Johnson Houghton*

PARASOL (IRE) 4 br.c. Halling (USA) 133 – Bunting 102 (Shaadi (USA) 126) [2003 **119**
105: p10g* p10g* 10m* 10.3m* 10m² 12f⁶ 10m² Jul 19] big, rangy colt: usually takes the
eye: easy mover: smart performer: trained by Saeed bin Suroor in 2002: better than ever
in 2003, winning minor event at Lingfield in February and listed events at Lingfield
(Winter Derby, by neck from Adiemus) in March, Kempton (beat Nysaean 1½ lengths) in
April and Chester (by ¾ length from Vintage Premium) in May: pulled hard and looked
none too keen but ran up to best when 1½ lengths second to Mubtaker in listed event at
Newbury final outing: stays 1¼m, not 1½m: acts on soft going, good to firm and polytrack: visored: races prominently: carries head high: has edged right. *D. R. Loder*

PARC AUX BOULES 2 b.c. (Mar 30) Royal Applause 124 – Aristocratique 71 (Cad- **– p**
eaux Genereux 131) [2003 6g Oct 24] 45,000F, 110,000Y: big, good-bodied colt: third
foal: half-brother to fair 2001 2-y-o 5f winner Noble Academy (by Royal Academy) and
3-y-o Arcalis: dam, Irish sprint maiden, half-sister to useful 6f/7f winner Royal Loft: 10/1
and backward, well held in maiden at Newbury: likely to do better. *R. Charlton*

PARDON MOI 2 ch.f. (Apr 27) First Trump 118 – Mystical Song 68 (Mystiko (USA) **52**
124) [2003 f5g 5.1m 6g 6g³ f6g⁴ 7m⁴ 6g* 6g⁵ 6m³ 6.1m 6m² 7m⁶ p6g 6.1m⁶ f7g⁵ f6g⁴
Dec 15] 1,000Y: stocky filly: second foal: dam, lightly-raced sprint maiden, half-sister to
sprinters Prince Sabo (very smart) and Millyant (smart): modest performer: won seller at
Yarmouth (edged right) in July: may prove best at 6f: acts on fibresand and good to firm
going: sometimes hangs left. *Mrs C. A. Dunnett*

PAR INDIANA (IRE) 2 b.f. (Feb 9) Indian Rocket 115 – Paryiana (IRE) (Shernazar **61 p**
131) [2003 f7g⁴ f9.4g³ Dec 22] €10,000Y: fifth living foal: half-sister to 3 winners,
including fairly useful 1999 2-y-o 5f winner Foe and 1997 2-y-o 7f winner Fayrana (later
US 1m winner), both by Fayruz: dam unraced: modest form in maidens at Wolverhampton: slowly away on debut: still green final start: likely to improve. *I. Semple*

PARIS DREAMER 2 b.f. (May 24) Paris House 123 – Stoproveritate 65 (Scorpio **–**
(FR) 127) [2003 6m 7.9f 5g 7d Nov 7] tall, leggy filly: fourth foal: dam, 7f/1m winner,
also successful over hurdles: signs of only a little ability in maidens: sometimes slowly
away. *M. W. Easterby*

PARISIAN PLAYBOY 3 gr.g. Paris House 123 – Exordium (Exorbitant 81) [2003 **59**
6m 6f 6m 7s³ Oct 29] tall gelding: fourth foal: dam unraced: modest maiden: stays 7f:
acts on soft ground. *Jedd O'Keeffe*

PARISIENNE (USA) 2 b. or br.f. (Feb 4) Good And Tough (USA) 117 – Genuine **85**
Concern (CAN) (Clever Trick (USA)) [2003 a3f* 6f 5s 8.3d 8m 8g⁴ 9m 9g⁵ 8s Nov 14]
$7,500Y: good-topped filly: fourth foal: half-sister to winner in USA by Jamiano: dam 7f/
8.5f winner in Canada: fairly useful performer: won maiden at Gulfstream in April: often
stiffish tasks after (including in Coventry Stakes at Royal Ascot), leaving F. Mourier,
USA, before recent fresh start: probably stays 9f: sometimes blinkered. *C. Ligerot, France*

PARISIEN STAR (IRE) 7 ch.g. Paris House 123 – Auction Maid (IRE) (Auction **88**
Ring (USA) 123) [2003 91: 10m 10.1m⁶ 10m 10.1m 9m* 10.2f² 9g³ 10m⁵ 10g⁶ 9m 12m
Sep 24] leggy gelding: poor mover: fairly useful performer: won handicap at Goodwood
in June for second consecutive year: effective at 1m/1¼m: possibly unsuited by heavy
going, acts on any other turf: sometimes slowly away: held up. *J. R. Boyle*

PARIS PIPER (IRE) 4 gr.g. Paris House 123 – Winter March (Ballad Rock 122) [2003 **–**
54: p7g Jan 7] workmanlike gelding: modest maiden, lightly raced: best form at 5f/6f.
D. Carroll

PARK ACCORD (IRE) 2 b. or br.f. (Feb 20) Desert Prince (IRE) 130 – Tiavanita **88**
(USA) (J O Tobin (USA) 130) [2003 7m* Sep 5] €350,000Y: sturdy, lengthy filly:
seventh foal: half-sister to 3 winners, notably 2000 Guineas winner Island Sands (by
Turtle Island), 6f winner at 2 yrs: dam French maiden half-sister to very smart middle-
distance performer Corrupt: favourite, won 7-runner minor event at Kempton by length
from Well Known, leading 1f out and idling: looked to have considerable potential, but
put down after breaking off-hind cannon bone on gallops 12 days later. *J. Noseda*

PARK AVE PRINCESS (IRE) 2 b.f. (Mar 30) Titus Livius (FR) 115 – Satinette **63**
109 (Shirley Heights 130) [2003 6m 6m³ 7.1f* 7f⁴ 7m* f7g 6.5d 7m 7f⁴ f7g⁶ p8g Dec 2]
€3,500Y: workmanlike filly: sister to 3-y-o Dusty Dazzler and half-sister to several
winners, including 1988 2-y-o 1m winner Code Satin (by Secreto): dam 2-y-o 7f/1m
(May Hill Stakes) winner: modest performer: won maiden at Musselburgh in June and
claimer at Thirsk (left I. Wood) in August: should stay 1m: acts on firm ground, probably
on good to soft. *N. P. Littmoden*

PARKER 6 b.g. Magic Ring (IRE) 115 – Miss Loving 89 (Northfields (USA)) [2003 **75**
82d: f8.5g f7g² f7g f8.5g 7m 7d³ 7.1g 7m 7m* 7m⁴ 7g f7g⁶ f6g² 6m* 7g⁵ p7g Dec 30] neat
gelding: fluent mover: fair performer: won minor event at Redcar in August: effective
at 6f to easy 1m: acts on all-weather, firm and good to soft going: tried in cheekpieces,
usually blinkered: often races prominently: sometimes looks none too keen. *B. Palling*

PARK HILL (IRE) 3 b.g. Mujadil (USA) 119 – Modest (USA) (Blushing Groom **39**
(FR) 131) [2003 8m 9.2d 8d 6.9m 7.1f⁶ Aug 21] 8,500F, IR 32,000Y, 4,200 2-y-o: close-
coupled gelding: half-brother to several winners, including 1½m winner Ghaali (by
Unfuwain), later fairly useful up to 2m in Scandinavia: dam Irish sprinter: poor maiden:
probably stays 1m. *G. A. Swinbank*

PARKLAND (USA) 3 ch.c. Distant View (USA) 126 – Victorian Style 88 (Nashwan **93 +**
(USA) 135) [2003 96: 7m² 8f⁶ Oct 1] smallish colt: fairly useful performer, lightly raced:
tongue tied, creditable 5 lengths second to Desert Destiny in minor event at Newmarket
in April: left R. Charlton and off 5½ months, 2¾ lengths sixth in allowance race at Santa
Anita only subsequent outing: probably stays 1m: raced only on good ground or firmer.
R. J. Frankel, USA

PARKNASILLA 3 b.g. Marju (IRE) 127 – Top Berry 87 (High Top 131) [2003 79: **74**
9.9d 10m⁴ 10m³ f12g⁵ 10g³ 10.1m³ f12s** 11.9f Oct 9] close-coupled gelding: fair perfor- **a78**
mer: won maiden at Southwell in September: effective at 1¼m/1½m: acts on firesand
and good to firm ground, probably on heavy: ran well only try in blinkers. *M. W. Easterby*

PARKSIDE PURSUIT 5 b.g. Pursuit of Love 124 – Ivory Bride 86 (Domynsky 110) **79**
[2003 86, a–: 5g 6.1d 6m 6g 6m⁶ 6m⁵ 6m⁴ 6m* 6d 6m² 6m⁴ 6g 7m 7m 5d² 6m 6g Oct 6]
lengthy, dipped-backed gelding: fair handicapper: won at Salisbury in July for second
year running: best at 5f/6f: acts on firm and good to soft going (below form on soft/
firesand): often held up. *J. M. Bradley*

PARK STAR 3 b.f. Gothenberg (IRE) 117 – Miriam 59 (Forzando 122) [2003 –, a61: **68**
p5g² f5s* f5g* f6g p5g⁴ p5g² f5g⁵ 5d* 5s* 5g f6g 5s f5g⁵ p6g⁶ p7g f5g p5g Dec 20] leggy, **a63**
good-topped filly: fair on turf, modest on all-weather: won 2 handicaps at Southwell in
January, and minor event at Hamilton and handicap at Windsor (made most) in May:
stays 6f: acts on all-weather and soft going: tried visored. *D. Shaw*

PARK STREET (USA) 3 b.c. Mr Prospector (USA) – Sunlit Silence (USA) (Trempo- **78**
lino (USA) 135) [2003 81p: p7g² Jan 25] fair form when placed in 2 maidens at Lingfield:
stays 7f: sent to USA. *G. A. Butler*

PARKVIEW LOVE (USA) 2 b. or br.c. (May 31) Mister Baileys 123 – Jerre Jo **103**
Glanville (USA) (Skywalker (USA)) [2003 5d* 6g² 6m* 6m⁶ 7d⁵ Jul 30] 5,000Y: leggy,
good-topped colt: sixth foal: half-brother to 3 minor winners in USA: dam US 2-y-o 6f
winner: useful performer: won maiden at Hamilton in May and listed race at Epsom (beat
Cedarberg by neck) in June: creditable sixth in July Stakes at Newmarket and fifth in
Vintage Stakes at Goodwood: stays 7f: acts on good to firm and good to soft going: races
prominently. *M. Johnston*

PARLIGHT 4 b.f. Woodborough (USA) 112 – Skedaddle 57 (Formidable (USA) 125) **–**
[2003 40: f8s f11s³ f11g f16.2g⁵ f16s* f14g 17.1m f16.2s² 16d⁶ f16.2g f14.8g⁴ f14.8g⁵ **a45**
16.5m 16g Jul 28] workmanlike filly: poor performer: won handicap at Southwell in
February: left K. Burke after eleventh start: stays 2m: acts on firesand: usually visored/
blinkered. *Mrs Lucinda Featherstone*

PARNASSIAN 3 ch.g. Sabrehill (USA) 120 – Delphic Way 63 (Warning 136) [2003 **71**
65: 7g⁴ 8m⁴ 7.1m 7d⁴ 8f³ 8f³ 8g⁴ 8.5g² 8.5m⁵ 8f 8.2d Nov 6] angular gelding: fair maiden
handicapper: should stay 1¼m: acts on firm and soft ground. *G. B. Balding*

PARNDON BELLE 4 ch.f. Clan of Roses – Joara (FR) (Radetzky 123) [2003 7.5m **–**
5d Jul 5] unfurnished filly: third reported foal: dam, lightly raced on Flat/winning hurdler,
sister to useful but ungenuine stayer Petrizzo: no sign of ability. *J. S. Wainwright*

PARTING SHOT   5 b.g. Young Ern 120 – Tribal Lady 80 (Absalom 128) [2003 83:   **76 ?**
8d 7.9m 8.5d 7.9m⁵ 8.1d 8.9f 8g Oct 28] quite good-topped gelding: fair handicapper:
stays 9f: acts on any going: usually races prominently. *T. D. Easterby*

PARTNERS IN JAZZ (USA)   2 ro.c. (Feb 19) Jambalaya Jazz (USA) 111 – Just   **88 p**
About Enough (USA) (Danzig (USA)) [2003 6g² 5f² 5m² 6d* Sep 29] $7,000Y: tall colt:
half-brother to several minor winners in USA: dam, sprint winner in USA, half-sister to
US Grade 1 1¼m winner Home At Last: runner-up in maidens before much improved to
win 17-runner nursery at Hamilton by 4 lengths, soon in front and going clear 2f out:
likely to prove best at 5f/6f: should make a useful handicapper at 3 yrs. *T. D. Barron*

PARTY PLOY   5 b.g. Deploy 131 – Party Treat (IRE) 69 (Millfontaine 114) [2003 65:   **72**
12.4m 16.2m 16d³ 14.1m⁵ 11.9f 14.1m³ 12f* 12.1g* 12.3m³ 12m 12m 11.5g⁴ 14.1m²
14.1m⁶ 12g f14.8g⁶ Nov 14] small gelding: poor mover: fair performer: won claimer at
Catterick and handicap at Hamilton in July: stays 1¾m, seemingly not 2m: acts on soft
going, firm and all-weather: tried visored at 4 yrs (often found little): tried in cheekpieces:
usually races prominently. *K. R. Burke*

PARTY PRINCESS (IRE)   2 b.f. (Mar 17) Orpen (USA) 116 – Summer Queen 80   **65**
(Robellino (USA) 127) [2003 5m² 5f5⁵ 5m³ Oct 7] €15,000Y: strong filly: second foal:
half-sister to 3-y-o Chico Guapo: dam, 7f winner, half-sister to useful 1m/9f winner Eton
Lad: fair form in maidens: second at Beverley, best effort: should stay 6f. *J. A. Glover*

PARTY TURN   3 b.f. Pivotal 124 – Third Party 63 (Terimon 124) [2003 p6g² p7g* 7g   **53**
7.1m 8m⁶ Apr 21] 10,000Y: first foal: dam, 6f winner, half-sister to formerly smart (now   **a60**
unreliable) sprinter Passion For Life: modest performer: won maiden at Lingfield in
February: stays 7f: free-going sort. *C. E. Brittain*

PASCALI   3 b.f. Compton Place 125 – Pass The Rose (IRE) (Thatching 131) [2003   **61 p**
8.1m 6m⁶ 6m⁴ Oct 13] IR 20,000Y: lengthy, quite good-topped filly: third foal: half-sister
to 1999 2-y-o 6f seller winner Methodist (by Rainbows For Life): dam unraced half-sister
to Cheveley Park winner Pass The Peace, herself dam of Cheveley Park winner Embassy:
fair form: won maiden at Windsor in September: shaped well considering lack of
experience when fourth in handicap at Leicester next time: better at 6f than 1m: should
improve further, and win more races. *H. Morrison*

PAS DE SURPRISE   5 b.g. Dancing Spree (USA) – Supreme Rose 95 (Frimley Park   **71**
109) [2003 63: p6g 7m⁶ 7m² 7g² 7.5m 9f* 7.6m 8m³ 10m 8.1g 7m* 7m 7.1g 8m³ 8.2f⁶
8f⁴ Oct 12] fair handicapper on turf, modest on all-weather: left J. Portman after fourth
start: won at Kempton (amateurs) in July and Salisbury (apprentices) in August: effective
at 7f to 9f: acts on polytrack, firm and good to soft going: tried in headgear: has raced
freely. *P. D. Evans*

PASO DOBLE   5 b.g. Dancing Spree (USA) – Delta Tempo (IRE) (Bluebird (USA)   **69**
125) [2003 67: p8g³ p7g f9.4g³ f9.4s⁵ 8.2g 11.7m f9.4g* 10m 10.2m⁴ 10m² 9.9f⁴ 12m
10m p12g Nov 18] fair performer: won claimer at Wolverhampton in May: stays 1¼m:
acts on firm going and all-weather: often races prominently. *B. R. Millman*

PASSANDO   3 b.f. Kris 135 – Iota 83 (Niniski (USA) 125) [2003 –p: 8.2g⁴ Apr 29]   **64**
7,500Y: big, strong filly: third foal: dam 14.6f to 2m winner: much better effort in
maidens (modest form) when fourth at Nottingham, only outing at 3 yrs: will be suited by
1¼m+. *A. M. Balding*

PASSERINE   5 b.m. Distant Relative 128 – Oare Sparrow 75 (Night Shift (USA))   **40**
[2003 –: 6m 6g 7m³ 7f⁵ 6m 7f Jun 27] smallish, good-topped mare: poor maiden: stays
7f: acts on firm ground, probably on soft: tried blinkered. *J. R. Weymes*

PASS GO   2 b.g. (May 11) Kris 135 – Celt Song (IRE) (Unfuwain (USA) 131) [2003   **73 p**
p5g³ Dec 10] 31,000Y: fifth foal: half-brother to smart 1000 Guineas runner-up Princess
Ellen (by Tirol), 6f/7f winner at 2 yrs: dam unraced: 4/1 and green, 1½ lengths third of 10
to Treasure Cay in minor event at Lingfield, carrying head awkwardly: will stay 1m:
should improve. *G. A. Butler*

PASSING GLANCE   4 b.c. Polar Falcon (USA) 126 – Spurned (USA) 91 (Robellino   **118**
(USA) 127) [2003 101: 8m 8.1g 8.5m* 8m² 8m* 8m² 8g* 8m⁶ 8m Dec 14] tall, rather
leggy colt: smart performer: better than ever in 2003, winning handicap at Epsom in
June, listed race at Salisbury (by short head from Priors Lodge) in August and Darley
Oettingen-Rennen at Baden-Baden (beat Bear King by 3½ lengths) in September: good
head second to Priors Lodge in Celebration Mile at Goodwood on sixth outing: below
form in Premio Vittorio di Capua at Milan and Hong Kong Mile at Sha Tin (unable to

Kingsclere Stud and Mr M. E. Wates's "Passing Glance"

lead) last 2 starts: effective at 7f, barely at 1¼m: acts on firm and soft going, well held only start on polytrack: front runner: has worn crossed noseband/carried head awkwardly: genuine. *A. M. Balding*

PASSION FOR LIFE   10 br.g. Charmer 123 – Party Game 70 (Red Alert 127) [2003 **– §**
–§: 5g 6d 7m 6d 6m 7s Oct 29] good-topped gelding: unimpressive mover: fairly useful handicaper in 2001: little worthwhile form since: tried blinkered/in cheekpieces: temperamental. *J. Akehurst*

PASSION FRUIT   2 b.f. (May 18) Pursuit of Love 124 – Reine de Thebes (FR) 67 **58**
(Darshaan 133) [2003 5f⁶ 6f 6d 7m⁶ 7m³ 7f Oct 27] seventh foal: half-sister to 5f to 7f winner (including at 2 yrs) Boldly Goes (by Bold Arrangement) and 7f (at 2 yrs) and 1½m winner King's Welcome (by Most Welcome): dam, 1m to 11f winner, half-sister to dam of Arc runner-up Egyptband: modest maiden: third in nursery at Catterick: should stay 1m: probably acts on firm going. *C. W. Fairhurst*

PASTORAL PURSUITS   2 b.c. (Apr 3) Bahamian Bounty 116 – Star 83 (Most **110 p**
Welcome 131) [2003 6m² 6.1d* 6g* 6m* Sep 6]
Hughie Morrison's most financially rewarding training performances were all achieved in the 2001/2 jumps season; with Marble Arch's win in the Ladbroke Handicap Hurdle at Ascot, the same horse's second in the Champion Hurdle and Frenchman's Creek's victory in the National Hunt Handicap Chase at the Cheltenham Festival. Morrison enjoyed his best season on the Flat in 2003 with forty-six winners, which included the Duke of Edinburgh Stakes (Handicap) at Royal Ascot with Waverley and two Group 3 events with Alcazar and Pastoral Pursuits, none of those victories coming near to matching the prize money haul from any of the aforementioned gains over the jumps. Alcazar finished first past the post in the Sagaro Stakes at Ascot in April before being disqualified and then re-instated on appeal; and Pastoral Pursuits won the Coral Sirenia Stakes at Kempton in Septem-

ber. Morrison's reputation has been earned mainly through his feats with his older horses, but he had two promising juveniles in 2003, the other being Ruby Rocket who proved useful, winning three of her five starts, including a listed race at Ayr in September. But Pastoral Pursuits was the better horse. After finishing second in a Windsor maiden on his debut in June, he trounced the opposition in a similar event at Chepstow by eight lengths. Pastoral Pursuits took on tougher opposition in a minor event at Windsor on his next start and won by the same distance as at Chepstow, a smart performance which marked him down as a colt who would be making his mark in pattern company. Pastoral Pursuits took the step up in the Sirenia, a race upgraded in 2003 from a listed event, though the first prize of £17,400 was still only around half that won by the stable in the Duke of Edinburgh Stakes. A short-priced favourite in a field of nine, Pastoral Pursuits didn't need to better the form he showed at Windsor to beat Diosypros Blue by two lengths with Cartography, who raced alone on the far rail, a further neck behind. Connections of Pastoral Pursuits were reportedly considering the Middle Park at Newmarket for his next race in preference to the Mill Reef at Newbury, but Pastoral Pursuits came back lame from an injury to his off-fore which his trainer believes was sustained halfway through the Sirenia. Pastoral Pursuits was reportedly found to have chipped a bone in his knee and was operated on soon after.

Pastoral Pursuits (b.c. Apr 3, 2001)	Bahamian Bounty (ch 1994)	Cadeaux Genereux (ch 1985)	Young Generation
			Smarten Up
		Clarentia (ch 1984)	Ballad Rock
			Laharden
	Star (b 1995)	Most Welcome (ch 1984)	Be My Guest
			Topsy
		Marista (b 1977)	Mansingh
			Evendo

The Pursuit Partnership's "Pastoral Pursuits"

Pastoral Pursuits was later said to be recovering well, and will be aimed at the Two Thousand Guineas. Whether he will run in a trial beforehand has yet to be decided, but Morrison has shown with many of his horses, including Alcazar and Tom Paddington, that he is more than capable of preparing them to do themselves justice after an absence. Pastoral Pursuits has raced only at six furlongs and, while he shapes as if he will stay seven furlongs, there are doubts about his getting the Guineas distance, judged on pedigree. His sire Bahamian Bounty, the Prix Morny and Middle Park winner, failed to stay a mile in the Poule d'Essai des Poulains, and was returned to six furlongs for his only subsequent outing. Star, the dam of Pastoral Pursuits, ran three times as a two-year-old, winning a maiden at Nottingham over five furlongs. Pastoral Pursuits, a 24,000-guinea yearling, is her third foal and the first to have won. Star should have stayed at least six furlongs and is a half-sister to Superstrike, who made a winning debut on the all-weather before being transferred to America where he won Grade 3 races, and to the useful five-furlong performer Four-Legged Friend. A well-made colt, Pastoral Pursuits acts on good to firm and good to soft going. *H. Morrison*

PATANDON GIRL (IRE)   3 b.f. Night Shift (USA) – Petite Jameel (IRE) (Ahonoora   **66** 122) [2003 6g 6m² 6m⁴ 5.1m 6m* 6m³ 7m 6f 8.1m 7.1m 6m 7f³ 6m⁶ 5.7f 5.7f⁵ 7m³ f6g 6d Oct 31] IR 16,000F, 26,000Y: small, close-coupled filly: fifth foal: half-sister to 6-y-o Mush and useful winner up to 11f in USA Ready To Roll (by Priolo): dam unraced sister to 2000 Guineas winner Don't Forget Me: modest handicapper: won at Folkestone in May: stays 7f: acts on firm ground: visored twice. *M. R. Channon*

PATAVELLIAN (IRE)   5 b.g. Machiavellian (USA) 123 – Alessia 91 (Caerleon   **124** (USA) 132) [2003 91: 6d* 6f⁵ 7m* 6g* 5s* Oct 5]

The five-year-old gelding Patavellian has made a tremendous start to fulfilling his trainer's highest hopes—that he would prove another John Cherry or Constans for the historic Beckhampton stables. Those two geldings, the first a stayer and the second a sprinter, progressed through handicaps to become high-class performers in their sphere in the 'seventies for Roger Charlton's predecessor and mentor at Beckhampton, Jeremy Tree. Charlton joined Tree as his assistant in the summer of 1978 by which time Constans had been retired and John Cherry had been sold out of the stable. Lester Piggott was associated with both horses, riding them with supreme confidence. John Cherry won eight races for the stable, including effortless victories under top weight in the Chester Cup, the Newbury Autumn Cup and the Cesarewitch as a five-year-old; Constans, gelded and hobdayed after a short three-year-old career and with a tendency to break blood vessels, won twelve races, seven of them in an unbeaten run that lasted for over a year, and was still racing at the age of nine when he completed a third successive victory in the Prix de Saint-Georges at Longchamp.

Patavellian's improvement over the course of not much more than a year was, if anything, even more spectacular than that shown in a similar period during their careers by John Cherry and Constans. Patavellian was tried over as far as ten and a half furlongs—a trip he was bred to get—as a three-year-old before being dropped back to seven furlongs. Tried in blinkers, he won his first race, at the

Vodafone Stewards' Cup (Handicap), Goodwood—the action is nearly all on the far side as Patavellian produces a most striking performance; Fire Up The Band (rail) and Colonel Cotton lead the chasing pack

Prix de l'Abbaye de Longchamp Majestic Barriere, Longchamp—
Patavellian shows further improvement on his pattern-race debut;
he's followed by, from left to right, The Trader, The Tatling, Acclamation and Porlezza

twelfth attempt, off a BHB mark of 64 at Chepstow in September 2002, then followed up in a minor event at Chepstow and a six-furlong handicap at Newmarket,
showing fairly useful form on the last occasion. The blinkers were left off when
Patavellian extended his winning sequence in a minor event at Windsor on his
reappearance at the end of April, but were refitted for the Wokingham at Royal
Ascot where, after a major ante-post gamble, he started 4/1 favourite after looking
to be in danger at one time of being ballotted out (Charlton was fined £500 after
leaving him in a race the day before as a precaution). The latest Wokingham was a
highly competitive edition run in record time, and Patavellian, receiving between
9 lb and 14 lb from the four who finished ahead of him, showed further improvement, coming second in the far-side group, beaten under four lengths by dead-
heaters Fayr Jag and Ratio after being prominent throughout. Patavellian resumed
winning ways in the seven-furlong Ladbrokes Bunbury Cup at Newmarket, again
starting favourite in a twenty-runner field. Making all the running, he was four
lengths clear inside the final two furlongs and hung on by a short head from the
previous year's winner Mine.

The Vodafone Stewards' Cup at Goodwood was the next target for Patavellian, who was again a heavily-backed 4/1-chance, just behind the 7/2 favourite
Fire Up The Band, and made light of a 5-lb penalty to put up the best performance
seen in the race for some time. With connections able to choose their draw position
through a ballot—as in the Lincoln—the highest stalls proved the most popular. A
fresh strip of ground on the far rail is used in the later part of the meeting and those
drawn high had dominated the previous day's consolation event, in which,
incidentally, David Nicholls saddled a record twelve runners only for the stable's
Zuhair to be touched off by a former inmate Undeterred. Patavellian surged clear of
the Stewards' Cup field under two furlongs out and won comfortably by three and a
half lengths and a neck from the Nicholls-trained Fire Up The Band and 16/1-shot
Colonel Cotton, the first three drawn 27, 29 and 28 respectively in the twenty-nine-
runner line-up, the previous year's winner Bond Boy being an overnight absentee,
reportedly due to a bruised foot.

Though they were among the best horses of their type around at the time,
neither Constans nor John Cherry could take part in all the championship races,
because they were geldings. The subject was one that was discussed numerous
times in these pages including in the essay on John Cherry in *Racehorses of 1977*,
which called for all the top races to be opened to the best horses, whether they were
entires or not. At the insistence of the European Pattern Committee, geldings are
still denied entry to the seven Group 1 events in Britain restricted either to two-
or three-year-old colts. The absurd ban on geldings in the Gold Cup was lifted in
1986—ten years too late for John Cherry—but the French, for example, continued
for a long time afterwards to drag their feet over the issue and have still not come
fully into line—geldings are still banned from the Arc, Jacques le Marois and
Moulin. The Prix de l'Abbaye de Longchamp's ban on geldings was still in force at
the beginning of the millennium, but the decision to open it up in 2001 enabled
Patavellian to contest the event in the latest season (Continent had become the first
gelding to win it in 2002).

771

Mr D. J. Deer's "Patavellian"

Patavellian's owners had three cracks at the Abbaye with Averti (best effort when second in 1998) and had one eye on the race for Patavellian from the time he ran in the Wokingham. The original intention had been to take in the Ayr Gold Cup but Patavellian was struck into in the Stewards' Cup, necessitating the wound being stapled, his trainer for a time seemingly considering putting him away for the season. Not only was the Abbaye the first pattern race Patavellian contested—and a Group 1 at that—but it was also his first race over five furlongs. 'All credit to the owner who insisted on running him when I told him it was impossible,' said the trainer after Patavellian recorded his seventh win in eight starts. The late defection of Oasis Dream, because of the soft ground, deprived the Abbaye of its main attraction and made the nineteen-runner contest much more open. Thirteen were trained in Britain, including the favourite the Haydock Sprint Cup winner Somnus, the Diadem winner Acclamation and the filly Airwave, back at the minimum trip for the first time since her impressive reappearance in the Temple Stakes. Another of the British challengers, the veteran Repertory, was among those who set a very strong pace—probably too strong for the conditions—but Patavellian's rider Steve Drowne had him in the lead at halfway after he had been taken off his feet a little at the start. Keeping on well, Patavellian won by a length from The Trader, who had been last until halfway, with The Tatling a neck away third, the same distance ahead of fourth-placed Acclamation, who fared best of those who raced prominently all the way and completed a clean sweep for British raiders. Somnus couldn't go the early pace and finished well for seventh, while Airwave managed only eleventh after being shuffled to the back of the field at around halfway before making late progress. Patavellian's performance showed that he was still progressing and he looks sure to go on to win more good sprint prizes in the next season. His International Classification mark of 115, which even allowing for the generally lower level of its assessments, undervalues his ability. The fact that Patavellian is equally effective at five and six furlongs (probably better at those distances than at seven), and that he has shown he is not beholden to the state of the going (acts on firm and soft) means his connections should have a wide range of options, though the Abbaye is sure to be one of his principal targets. Patavellian is usually blinkered nowadays and has run well when sweating, as he did in the Stewards' Cup. The free-going Patavellian has worn a crossed noseband.

			Raise A Native
		Mr Prospector	
	Machiavellian (USA)	(b 1970)	Gold Digger
	(b 1987)	Coup de Folie	Halo
Patavellian (IRE)		(b 1982)	Raise The Standard
(b.g. 1998)		Caerleon	Nijinsky
	Alessia	(b 1980)	Foreseer
	(b 1992)	Kiss	Habitat
		(b 1978)	Miss Petard

The pedigree of the tall, useful-looking Patavellian is of largely academic interest now. His sire Machiavellian only just stayed a mile but has sired winners over all sorts of distances, though Patavellian was the only five-furlong winner among the three-year-olds and upwards that have represented him in Britain. Patavellian is the first foal of the two-year-old seven-furlong winner Alessia, who showed fairly useful form at three at a mile and a quarter and is a sister to the Park Hill Stakes winner Casey, herself grandam of the smart three-year-old Delsarte. Patavellian's grandam Kiss was bred to stay at least a mile but was a sprinter, third in the Portland Handicap, while Patavellian's great grandam Miss Petard won the Ribblesdale. Alessia's third foal Avonbridge (by Averti) developed into a smart sprinter for Charlton in the latest season. Her second, the fair maiden Alashaan (by Darshaan), was placed twice at a mile and a half for Barry Hills before starting her stud career with a visit to Averti, who is also the sire of Alessia's once-raced two-year-old Avessia. Alessia has no yearling (died as a foal) or foal (barren), but is due to Averti again in 2004. *R. Charlton*

PATIENTES VIRTIS   4 ch.f. Lion Cavern (USA) 117 – Alzianah 102 (Alzao (USA) 117) [2003 –, a67: p7g f7g f7g f5g⁴ f5s⁵ f6g* f5s* 5d f5s⁶ f5g f6g⁶ f6g Dec 9] angular filly: modest performer: won handicap in June and seller in July, both at Wolverhampton: stays 6f: acts on all-weather, little form on turf: wore cheekpieces second start, visored after: has hinted at temperament. *Miss Gay Kelleway*   **46 a56**

PATRICIA PHILOMENA (IRE)   5 br.m. Prince of Birds (USA) 121 – Jeewan 82 (Touching Wood (USA) 127) [2003 58, a–: 13.8f 13g⁵ 14.1m* 12f⁶ 16m 14.1d* 13.8m² Aug 5] leggy, close-coupled mare: modest handicapper: won at Redcar in June and Carlisle in July: effective at 1½m to easy 2m: acts on firm and soft going: usually held up. *T. D. Barron*   **61 a–**

PATRICIA RAY   2 b.f. (Apr 24) Young Ern 120 – Lombard Ships 73 (Orchestra 118) [2003 f8s Dec 13] second foal: dam 7f/1m winner: 66/1, well beaten in maiden at Southwell. *C. Drew*   **–**

PATRICKS DAY   3 b.c. Wizard King 122 – Honour And Glory 46 (Hotfoot 126) [2003 –: 6f Apr 11] workmanlike colt: well held in maidens/claimer: tried blinkered/tongue tied: looked headstrong second 2-y-o start. *J. Balding*   **–**

PATRIXPRIAL   2 gr.c. (Feb 27) Linamix (FR) 127 – Magnificent Star (USA) 122 (Silver Hawk (USA) 123) [2003 7s Oct 29] 35,000Y: fifth living foal: half-brother to 8-y-o Profiler (formerly fairly useful 1½m winner) and 4-y-o Sir Alfred: dam won Yorkshire Oaks: 33/1, ninth of 13 in maiden at Yarmouth, not knocked about: should do better at 1¼m+. *M. H. Tompkins*   **– p**

PATRIXTOO (FR)   2 gr.c. (Mar 28) Linamix (FR) 127 – Maradadi (USA) (Shadeed (USA) 135) [2003 7m 8s Oct 29] €140,000Y: second foal: half-brother to French winner up to 1½m Maradamo (by Alamo Bay): dam French 11f winner out of Prix Royal-Oak winner Mersey: modest form in maidens at Yarmouth: will probably do better at 1¼m+. *M. H. Tompkins*   **60 p**

PAT'S MIRACLE (IRE)   3 ch.f. College Chapel 122 – Exemplaire (FR) (Polish Precedent (USA) 131) [2003 43: 8g f6g f8g Dec 19] lightly-raced maiden: no form at 3 yrs. *John Berry*   **–**

PAT'S NEMISIS (IRE) 2 b.f. (Feb 4) Sri Pekan (USA) 117 – Exemplaire (FR) –
(Polish Precedent (USA) 131) [2003 8f p5g p6g Dec 29] third foal: dam placed up to
11f in France: well held in maidens/minor event: left T. Doyle, Ireland, after debut.
B. R. Johnson

PATSY'S DOUBLE 5 b.g. Emarati (USA) 74 – Jungle Rose 90 (Shirley Heights 130) **107**
[2003 107: p7g³ 7.1d* 8.3d⁶ 7.1m² 7m 7m⁴ 7m 7m 7m Oct 18] tall, useful-looking
gelding: unimpressive mover: useful performer: won listed event at Haydock (beat Polar
Ben by ½ length) in May: ran creditably in similar events at Haydock (beaten neck by
With Reason) and York fourth/seventh starts: stiff task when tailed off in Challenge
Stakes at Newmarket final outing: effective at 6f to 7.5f: acts on firm going, soft and
polytrack: tends to sweat: races prominently. *M. Blanshard*

PATTERDALE 2 b.c. (Mar 14) Octagonal (NZ) 126 – Baize 95 (Efisio 120) [2003 **81**
5m⁵ 6m² 7m 6m Jul 17] leggy colt: third foal: half-brother to 3-y-o Masterpoint: dam,
2-y-o 5f winner (later 5f/6f winner in USA), sister to useful sprinter Bayleaf: fairly useful
maiden: second at Redcar: below form in nursery final start: stays 7f. *M. Johnston*

PATTERN MAN 2 b.c. (Apr 1) Wizard King 122 – Quick Profit 78 (Formidable (USA) –
125) [2003 8g f8.5g f8.5g Nov 17] 4,400Y: good-bodied colt: half-brother to several
winners, including 1996 2-y-o 5f winner Smokey Pete and unreliable 6f to 2m winner
Rogue Spirit (both fairly useful, by Petong): dam 7f winner: well held in maidens.
J. R. Norton

PAULA LANE 3 b.f. Factual (USA) 108 – Colfax Classic 48 (Jareer (USA) 115) **73**
[2003 54: p10g⁶ p8g⁵ f9.4g* f11s² f12g⁴ 12.6m 11.6s⁵ f12g³ f12g² f14g Dec 9] fair
performer: won maiden at Wolverhampton in February: mostly creditable efforts in
handicaps after, off over 5 months before final one: stays 1½m: acts on fibresand (some
promise on polytrack) and good to firm going, probably on soft: often races prominently.
R. Curtis

PAULA'S PRIDE 5 ch.m. Pivotal 124 – Sharp Top 62 (Sharpo 132) [2003 69, a76: **70**
p13g⁴ p12g p12g p10g 12g⁶ 9.7m² 9.7m 9.9m 10m³ May 8] strong mare: fair hand- **a74**
icapper: effective at 9.7f to 13f: acts on polytrack, firm and soft going: blinkered (ran
poorly) once: sometimes finds little: none too consistent. *J. R. Best*

PAULINES GEM (IRE) 3 b. or br.f. Petorius 117 – Clifton Lass (IRE) (Up And At **60**
'em 109) [2003 6m Jun 11] IR 3,000Y: compact filly: first foal: dam unraced granddaughter of smart sprinter Welshwyn: 16/1 and on toes, looked green and not knocked
about when seventh to Mine Behind in maiden at Newbury. *P. J. Makin*

PAULINSKI 2 b.f. (Apr 22) Suluk (USA) 72 – Tsu Hsi (Teofane) [2003 7.1m 7m Jul –
18] workmanlike filly: second foal: dam unraced: well held in maidens. *F. Jordan*

PAULS PRIDE 2 b.g. (Apr 3) Desert Sun 120 – E Sharp (USA) 49 (Diesis 133) [2003 **55**
6g 7m 8f⁶ 7m 7.1m Oct 25] 2,700Y: good-bodied gelding: third foal: half-brother to
Italian sprint winner Episkopas (by Bishop of Cashel): dam second at 7f: modest maiden:
form only at 1m: visored in seller final start: sold 1,800 gns. *M. Dods*

PAULUKE 4 b.f. Bishop of Cashel 122 – Beacon Blaze 85 (Rudimentary (USA) 118) **54**
[2003 –: 10.9m 11.7m⁶ 14.1m Oct 1] good-topped filly: modest maiden: stayed 11f: acted
on soft and good to firm going: tried blinkered: dead. *N. J. Hawke*

PAVEMENT GATES 3 b.f. Bishop of Cashel 122 – Very Bold 57 (Never So Bold **81**
135) [2003 71: 12f⁵ 11.8m⁶ 11.9m⁵ 11m 10.9m⁴ 12s⁴ 12m² 11.9m* 12.4m³ 12.1m² 12m³
Oct 7] lengthy filly: fairly useful handicapper: won 4-runner event at Haydock in August:
stays 1½m: acts on any turf ground: consistent. *W. M. Brisbourne*

PAVLA (USA) 6 ch.m. St Jovite (USA) 135 – Big E Dream (USA) (Persian Bold 123) –
[2003 58: 12.1d⁶ Sep 23] sister to Irish 1997 2-y-o 7f winner Jovine: dam, won in USA,
out of half-sister to dual Gold Cup winner Drum Taps: modest handicapper: left E. Sexton
in Ireland before well held only run in 2003: stays 13.5f: acts on firm and soft going: has
run well blinkered (not tried since 3 yrs). *N. Wilson*

PAWAN (IRE) 3 ch.g. Cadeaux Genereux 131 – Born To Glamour (Ajdal (USA) 130) **61**
[2003 80: 7g² 8m 6m² Oct 17] lengthy gelding: modest maiden, lightly raced: left
E. Dunlop after reappearance: probably better at 7f than 6f: raced only on good/good to
firm ground: hung left final start. *N. Tinkler*

PAWN BROKER 6 ch.g. Selkirk (USA) 129 – Dime Bag 87 (High Line 125) [2003 **107 +**
–§: p10g³ p10g 10m* 12m 10g⁴ 12m 10g⁶ 10m⁶ 9m 9m² 10g⁵ Oct 31] rather leggy
gelding: useful on balance of form nowadays: won minor event at Ascot in March by 3
lengths from Compton Bolter: appeared to run very well when ½-length second to Far

Lane in Darley Stakes at Newmarket penultimate start: effective at 9f to 1½m: acts on any turf going and polytrack: tried blinkered earlier in career: sometimes races freely: tends to find little. *D. R. C. Elsworth*

PAWN IN LIFE (IRE) 5 b.g. Midhish 109 – Lady-Mumtaz (Martin John) [2003 –, a62+: f8g² f8s⁴ f8g² f7s² f8s⁵ f7g f7g⁵ f7g* Dec 16] lengthy gelding: fair handicapper: won at Southwell in December: effective at 6f, barely at 1m: acts on all-weather, no form on turf: effective blinkered or not. *T. D. Barron* **– a72**

PAX 6 ch.g. Brief Truce (USA) 126 – Child's Play (USA) (Sharpen Up 127) [2003 83: 6g 6m 6m* 6m⁵ 6g 5m³ 6g 5f* 5.1m⁶ 5m⁴ 6m Sep 19] tall gelding: fairly useful handicapper: won at Newcastle in April and Carlisle in August: effective at stiff 5f/6f: acts on firm and good to soft going: often blinkered in 2001: usually waited with: consistent. *D. Nicholls* **90**

PAY ATTENTION 2 b.f. (Mar 1) Revoque (IRE) 122 – Catch Me 75 (Rudimentary (USA) 118) [2003 6m 6m⁶ 7m⁵ 7f³ 8m 8m Sep 25] quite good-topped filly: first foal: dam, 2-y-o 7f/7.5f winner, half-sister to smart performer up to 9f Missile: modest maiden: ran poorly in nurseries last 2 starts: stays 7f: acts on firm and good ground. *T. D. Easterby* **57**

PAYLANDER 7 ch.g. Karinga Bay 116 – Bichette 66 (Lidhame 109) [2003 p13g p12g Feb 25] poor maiden, very lightly raced: should stay 1¾m: acts on polytrack: possibly temperamental. *G. L. Moore* **43 ?**

PAYOLA (USA) 2 b.f. (Mar 15) Red Ransom (USA) – Bevel (USA) (Mr Prospector (USA)) [2003 7m Aug 22] rather leggy, close-coupled filly: seventh living foal: half-sister to 3-y-o Heavenly Bay and 9-y-o Bevier: dam, French 1m winner, out of close relative to Ajdal and half-sister to Formidable and to the grandam of Arazi and Noverre: 33/1, 4½ lengths last of 8 to Why Dubai in maiden at Newmarket, some late headway: will probably be suited by 1¼m/1½m: likely to improve. *C. E. Brittain* **66 p**

PAYS D'AMOUR (IRE) 6 b.g. Pursuit of Love 124 – Lady of The Land 75 (Wollow 132) [2003 84d: 7m⁵ f8g 6m* 5.9g* 7m⁴ 5.9f⁶ 7g 6f Jul 12] strong gelding: unimpressive mover: fair performer: won apprentice minor event at Catterick in April and handicap at Carlisle in May: stays 6f/easy 7f: acts on firm and soft going: held up. *D. Nicholls* **76**

PAY THE BILL (IRE) 2 b.f. (Mar 12) Lahib (USA) 129 – Jack-N-Jilly (IRE) 43 (Anita's Prince 126) [2003 5d 5d p5g 5.1f 6m Jun 16] €8,500Y: sparely-made filly: third foal: half-sister to 2001 2-y-o 5f winner Strandiam (by Darnay): dam, placed in 5f/ 6f sellers, ran only at 2 yrs: poor maiden: form only at 5f. *Mrs P. N. Dutfield* **43**

PAY THE SILVER 5 gr.g. Petong 126 – Marjorie's Memory (IRE) 76 (Fairy King (USA)) [2003 81, a64: 7m 9.7m 8m 11.9m⁵ 10d² 10.2g² 9f 10.1m* 10m 10.1m² 9m⁶ 12m⁴ 10.1g 12d² f12g³ p12g Oct 30] close-coupled, good-bodied gelding: fairly useful on turf, modest on all-weather: won handicap at Epsom (goes well there) in July: stays 1½m: acts on soft going, good to firm and polytrack (probably on firesand): tried visored, wears cheekpieces nowadays: often races freely: held up. *I. A. Wood* **82 a60**

PAY TIME 4 ch.f. Timeless Times (USA) 99 – Payvashooz 78 (Ballacashtal (CAN)) [2003 –: 6m⁶ 7g 6m 5m Aug 17] modest maiden: well held after reappearance: stays 6f: acts on good to firm ground and fibresand: tried tongue tied. *M. Brittain* **56 d**

PEACE 3 b.f. Sadler's Wells (USA) 132 – Virtuous 92 (Exit To Nowhere (USA) 122) [2003 78P: 10f² 10d* 10m⁶ 10.1s Oct 29] sturdy filly: fairly useful performer, lightly raced: won maiden at Nottingham in July: ran as if amiss in minor events at Newmarket (reportedly swallowed tongue) and Yarmouth after: should stay 1½m: acts on firm and good to soft ground. *J. R. Fanshawe* **85**

PEACE FLAG (USA) 3 ch.f. Gold Fever (USA) 119 – Fold The Flag (USA) (Raja Baba (USA)) [2003 82p: 7m 6.1m² 6m* 7m⁶ 6f⁶ a7f a6f⁴ a8.5s⁵ a5.5f² Dec 21] quite-good topped filly: fair performer: won maiden at Redcar in May: left J. Gosden after fifth outing and N. Howard after seventh: stays 7f: raced only on good going or firmer on turf: visored/blinkered last 5 outings: refused to enter stall once at 2 yrs (has been equipped with rope halter). *M. Zwiesler, USA* **78**

PEACE OFFERING (IRE) 3 b.c. Victory Note (USA) 120 – Amnesty Bay 63 (Thatching 131) [2003 105p: 7m 5g⁵ 5m 5f 6m⁶ 5.1m⁴ 5m Oct 2] good-topped colt: useful performer: best efforts at 3 yrs when fifth to Needwood Blade in Palace House Stakes at Newmarket and sixth in listed event at Newbury in July: below form last 2 starts, racing too freely in blinkers final one: will prove best at 5f/6f (pulled too hard over 7f): raced only on good ground or firmer: has been early to post: hung markedly right final 2-y-o start: sold 65,000 gns. *T. G. Mills* **105**

Redcar Two-Year-Old Trophy—one of seven victories during the year for Peak To Creek (near side) who snatches this valuable prize from Local Poet

PEACE TREATY (IRE) 2 b.f. (Apr 20) Turtle Island (IRE) 123 – Beautyofthepeace (IRE) (Exactly Sharp (USA) 121) [2003 5.1g 8.2m⁵ 6m f8g f6g Dec 19] €600Y, €11,000 2-y-o: small filly: sixth foal: half-sister to 3 winners, including 3-y-o Lakelands Lady and 7-y-o Windshift: dam unraced: little sign of ability: tried blinkered. *S. R. Bowring* –

PEAK OF PERFECTION (IRE) 2 b.g. (Mar 12) Deploy 131 – Nsx 74 (Roi Danzig (USA)) [2003 7m p8g Nov 2] good-bodied gelding: half-brother to 4-y-o Shahzan House and 6-y-o Camberley: dam 2-y-o 5f winner: well held in maidens at Newbury and Lingfield (made running). *M. A. Jarvis* –

PEAK PARK (USA) 3 b. or br.c. Dynaformer (USA) – Play Po (USA) (Play On (USA)) [2003 –: 8m 7m 11.7f 12g 16.4m³ 14.1m⁶ p16g Oct 15] strong, close-coupled colt: modest maiden handicapper: stays easy 2m: acts on firm going, yet to encounter softer than good: tends to race freely: none too consistent. *J. A. R. Toller* **56**

PEAK PRACTICE 5 b.m. Saddlers' Hall (IRE) 126 – High Habit 79 (Slip Anchor 136) [2003 –: 8f Mar 31] no form. *D. Burchell* –

PEAK TO CREEK 2 b.c. (Apr 28) Royal Applause 124 – Rivers Rhapsody 104 (Dominion 123) [2003 5m³ 5f 6m* 6g* 6.1m* 6m² 6g² 5.5d³ 6m* 6m* 6f* 7g* Oct 24] 50,000Y: smallish, quite attractive colt: half-brother to several winners, including smart 5f (at 2 yrs) to 1m winner For Your Eyes Only (by Pursuit of Love), useful 5f (including at 2 yrs) winner See You Later (by Emarati) and 4-y-o Zarzu: dam sprinter: smart performer: won maiden at Haydock, nurseries at Redcar and Chester, minor event at Yarmouth, Two-Year-Old Trophy at Redcar (by head from Local Poet), listed event at York and Vodafone Horris Hill Stakes at Newbury between July and October: beat Josephus by 3½ lengths in 9-runner event on last-named course, travelling strongly and quickening clear over 1f out: sometimes races freely, but will probably stay 1m: acts on firm and good to soft going: usually held up: tough and consistent, and a credit to his stable. *J. Noseda* **112**

PEARL DANCE (USA) 3 b.f. Nureyev (USA) 131 – Ocean Jewel (USA) (Alleged (USA) 138) [2003 102: 8m 8g May 11] sturdy filly: has a quick action: useful performer at 2 yrs: well beaten in listed race at Kempton and Poule d'Essai des Pouliches at Longchamp in 2003: stays 1m: yet to race on extremes of going: wandered penultimate 2-y-o start. *J. H. M. Gosden* –

PEARL GREY 2 gr. or ch.f. (Feb 1) Gone West (USA) – Zelanda (IRE) 108 (Night Shift (USA)) [2003 6m³ 5.1m* 6m* 6m² Jul 8] smallish, sturdy filly: second foal: closely related to 3-y-o Silver Seeker: dam, 5f/6f winner, out of smart Irish 9f and 11f winner (also third in Irish St Leger) Zafadola: useful performer: won maiden at Nottingham and **98**

776

listed race at Newmarket (beat Voile 1¾ lengths) in June: good 5 lengths second of 8 to Attraction in Cherry Hinton Stakes at Newmarket, finishing lame: should stay 7f: joined Saeed bin Suroor. *D. R. Loder*

PEARL ISLAND (USA)   2 b.c. (Feb 11) Kingmambo (USA) 125 – Mother of Pearl –
(IRE) 113 (Sadler's Wells (USA) 132) [2003 7m Aug 25] $725,000Y: sturdy colt: first foal: dam, 2-y-o 7f/1m winner (later stayed 1¼m), closely related to Irish 2000 Guineas winner Turtle Island: 9/2, last of 7 in maiden at Newcastle, slowly away. *D. R. Loder*

PEARL OF LOVE (IRE)   2 b.c. (Jan 22) Peintre Celebre (USA) 137 – Aunt   **112**
Pearl (USA) (Seattle Slew (USA)) [2003 6m² 6g* 7m* 7m* 7f³ 8m* Oct 19]
    Three other Mark Johnston-trained two-year-olds were rated higher than Pearl of Love in 2003, but Pearl of Love led the way in terms of prize money. His efforts brought in nearly £240,000, over £100,000 more than Champagne Stakes winner Lucky Story who, in turn, earned more than the other pair, Attraction and Russian Valour. Pearl of Love owed his position chiefly to success in the Gran Criterium at Milan in October on his final outing, a race Johnston had won six years earlier with Lend A Hand.
    Pearl of Love won three races and showed himself to be a smart juvenile before the Gran Criterium. A promising second of five behind the useful Botanical in a maiden at York in May on his debut, Pearl of Love won a similar event at Doncaster later that month easily by five lengths. Stepped up in class on his next outing, he took the thirteen-runner Chesham Stakes at Royal Ascot in his stride, soon putting the issue beyond doubt when quickening over a furlong out and beating Tycoon by a length and a half, with Milk It Mick a similar margin away in third. Pearl of Love provided his trainer with his third success in the last four renewals of the race. Given a two-month break, Pearl of Love then made all to win the Galileo EBF Futurity Stakes at the Curragh in August in impressive style, quickening clear approaching the final furlong and beating Tumblebrutus by three and a half lengths before going on to the National Stakes there the following month. Pearl of Love ran creditably but was no match for One Cool Cat, eventually coming home third of eight, beaten also by Wathab, but it was form good enough to give Pearl of Love a leading chance in the Gran Criterium. Starting odds on, Pearl of

Gran Criterium, Milan—an above-average renewal of Italy's top two-year-old contest goes to Pearl of Love, who beats Spirit of Desert (left)

Love beat his ten rivals after racing prominently and finding plenty when challenged, having half a length to spare over the Italian-trained Spirit of Desert in an above average renewal.

Pearl of Love (IRE) (b.c. Jan 22, 2001)	Peintre Celebre (USA) (ch 1994)	Nureyev (b 1977)	Northern Dancer / Special
		Peinture Bleue (ch 1987)	Alydar / Petroleuse
	Aunt Pearl (USA) (b 1989)	Seattle Slew (b 1974)	Bold Reasoning / My Charmer
		Mr P'S Girl (br 1978)	Mr Prospector / Native Street

The strong, good-bodied Pearl of Love, who was bought for 100,000 guineas as a yearling, is by the outstanding Arc winner Peintre Celebre, who has made a good start at stud. Besides Pearl of Love, Peintre Celebre sired the 2003 Deutsches Derby winner Dai Jin and the Prix du Jockey Club runner-up Super Celebre, as well as Fantastic Love (also trained by Johnston in 2003, but now with Godolphin), Joe Bear and the French-trained Vallee Enchantee, all at least useful. Peintre Celebre will have no European-conceived two-year-olds in 2004 as he was leased to Japan in 2001. Pearl of Love is out of Aunt Pearl, a minor six and six and a half furlong winner in the States who is herself out of a sister to the dam of both the very smart Dowsing, winner of the Haydock Sprint Cup, and Fire The Groom, winner of the 1991 Beverly D Stakes in the States and later the dam of Stravinsky. Aunt Pearl had two winners from six foals before Pearl of Love, both by Nureyev—making them close relations to Pearl of Love—and both successful as two-year-olds. The useful Kalidasa won at seven furlongs in 1998, and ran her best race the following season when third in the Free Handicap; Social Charter showed fairly useful form when successful at six and seven furlongs in 1997, before later winning a Grade 3 event in the States over nine and a half furlongs. Pearl of Love has yet to race on going softer than good and is not sure to stay much further than a mile. *M. Johnston*

PEARL OF YORK (DEN) 2 b.f. (Apr 26) Richard of York 123 – Laser Show (IRE) (Wassl 125) [2003 7m 7m p7g Oct 15] leggy filly: fourth known foal: half-sister to fairly useful 1997 2-y-o 7f winner O'Kelly (by Last Tycoon), later successful up to 11f in Denmark, and Irish 9f winner Blue Jazz (by Bluebird): dam, ran twice, from family of Salsabil and Marju: modest form in maidens: needs to settle to stay beyond 7f. *R. Guest*   **54**

PEARL PRIDE (USA) 2 ch.f. (Mar 27) Theatrical 128 – Spotlight Dance (USA) (Miswaki (USA) 124) [2003 6m⁶ 6m⁴ 7.5m² 8m Sep 25] $75,000Y: rather leggy filly: fifth living foal: sister to smart 9f/1¼m winner (latter at 2 yrs) Playapart and half-sister to 2 winners in USA: dam unraced half-sister to US Grade 1 winners Sewickley (at 7f) and Shared Interest (8.5f): fair maiden: second at Beverley: should stay 1m: raced freely last 2 starts, markedly so final one. *M. Johnston*   **71**

PEARL QUEEN (GER) 5 b.m. Lando (GER) 128 – Prime Lady (GER) (Esclavo (FR)) [2003 8m* 8.5m³ 8d³ 8g 8d Sep 28] medium-sized, good-topped mare: has a short, unimpressive action: second foal: half-sister to German winner up to 1m Power Prince (by Law Society): dam useful German 7f/1m winner: useful performer: won handicaps at Baden-Baden (2) and Mulheim in 2002: successful in minor event at Milan in May: creditable third in listed races at Epsom (to Aldora) and Ascot (behind Soldera) next 2 outings: seemed to run well when close seventh to Mary Ellen in Topkapi Trophy at Veliefendi penultimate start, but well below form final outing: stays 9f: acts on soft and good to firm going. *A. Lowe, Germany*   **100 +**

PEARLY BROOKS 5 b.m. Efisio 120 – Elkie Brooks 82 (Relkino 131) [2003 68: p7g p6g Jan 22] sturdy mare: fair performer at best: well held in 2003. *T. J. Naughton*   **–**

PEARSON GLEN (IRE) 4 ch.g. Dolphin Street (FR) 125 – Glendora (Glenstal (USA) 118) [2003 65: 8m 10m 10.1g⁵ 12g⁴ f12g⁶ Nov 10] good-topped gelding: fair handicapper: effective at 9f to 1½m: acts on good to firm and good to soft going: has drifted left. *G. A. Swinbank*   **65**

PEARTREE HOUSE (IRE) 9 b.g. Simply Majestic (USA) – Fashion Front (Habitat 134) [2003 –: f9.4s f8.5g 8.5f⁵ 8m 7m* 8m² 8.1s⁶ 8d⁴ 7.5m³ 9f² 7.9f 9.2g 7.9m 8d 8g Oct 22] rangy gelding: fair performer: won claimer at Southwell in May: effective at 7f to easy 9f: acts on firm and soft ground: tried visored: has pulled hard. *D. W. Chapman*   **66 a–**

PEDRILLO 2 b.g. (Mar 2) Singspiel (IRE) 133 – Patria (USA) 76 (Mr Prospector (USA)) [2003 6d³ 6.1m² 7m* Oct 2] quite good-topped gelding: third foal: half-brother to 2000 2-y-o 6f winner Parvenue (by Ezzoud) and 4-y-o The Player: dam, 2-y-o 7.6f winner, sister to Middle Park winner/2000 Guineas second Lycius: sweating, best effort in maidens (fairly useful form) when winning 7-runner event at Brighton easily by 4 lengths from Named At Dinner, going clear final 1f: will stay 1m, probably 1¼m: carries head awkwardly: open to progress. *Sir Mark Prescott* **91 p**

PEDRO JACK (IRE) 6 b.g. Mujadil (USA) 119 – Festival of Light (High Top 131) [2003 86, a89: p6g f7s⁶ p6g⁵ f6g f6g* 6g 6m³ 6g 6m³ 6m 6g Jun 30] tall gelding: fairly useful handicapper: won at Wolverhampton in March: best at 6f: acts on all-weather, best on good ground or firmer on turf: tried blinkered/visored/tongue tied: sometimes slowly away: virtually refused to race final 5-y-o start: none too consistent. *B. J. Meehan* **83 a92**

PEERESS 2 ch.f. (Feb 1) Pivotal 124 – Noble One 107 (Primo Dominie 121) [2003 7g³ Nov 1] rangy filly: first foal: dam 5f winner, including at 2 yrs: 12/1, 2½ lengths third of 18 to Damsel in maiden at Newmarket, waited with and staying on well under mostly hands and heels: should improve. *Sir Michael Stoute* **86 p**

PEGGY LOU 3 b.f. Washington State (USA) – Rosemary Nalden (Great Commotion (USA) 123) [2003 –: 8.2d⁴ 11m⁵ 10d⁴ 12d* 12.1m⁴ 12m³ 16.2g³ 14.1m⁶ f14.8g Nov 29] modest handicapper: won selling event at Pontefract in June: barely stays 2m: acts on good to firm and good to soft ground, well held both runs on fibresand. *B. J. Llewellyn* **56 a–**

PEGGY NAYLOR 2 ch.f. (Feb 1) Presidium 124 – Bitch 53 (Risk Me (FR) 127) [2003 5d⁶ Mar 24] leggy filly: fourth foal: dam 2-y-o 6f seller winner who stayed 1m: sixth of 9 in maiden at Newcastle: refused to enter stall in April. *James Moffatt* **–**

PEKA BOU (IRE) 2 b.c. (Feb 15) Sri Pekan (USA) 117 – Chambolle Musigny (USA) 59§ (Majestic Light (USA)) [2003 6.1g⁶ 8.3g³ Oct 13] first foal: dam, ungenuine maiden, stayed 11.5f: better effort (modest form) when third in seller at Windsor: should stay 1¼m. *D. J. Wintle* **57**

PEKAN LADY (IRE) 3 b.f. Sri Pekan (USA) 117 – Lady Dulcinea (ARG) (General (FR)) [2003 7d⁶ 8m 9.3f 9.9d 12.4m 11.9m Sep 4] IR 16,000Y: lengthy filly: half-sister to several winners, including 7-y-o It's Our Secret (by Be My Guest): dam won in Peru: poor maiden. *R. A. Fahey* **46**

PENALTA 7 ch.g. Cosmonaut – Targuette (Targowice (USA) 130) [2003 f14.8g⁵ f16.2g³ f16s⁴ f16.2g⁵ 17.1m f16.2g May 19] leggy gelding: poor handicapper: stays 2m: acts on heavy going and fibresand: tried in headgear/tongue tie: has hung. *W. M. Brisbourne* **? a46**

PENALTY CLAUSE (IRE) 3 b.g. Namaqualand (USA) – Lady Be Lucky (IRE) 57 (Taufan (USA) 119) [2003 78: f6g 7m 10m 8g 14.1m 11.5m⁶ 12d⁴ Jun 30] IR 6,000F: leggy gelding: fourth foal: half-brother to Irish 1½m/1¾m winner Jimmy Spot On (by Rainbows For Life): dam Irish 9f winner: fair maiden for G. Lyons in Ireland at 2 yrs: little form in 2003: stays 1½m: acts on soft ground, probably on good to firm: tried blinkered/tongue tied/in cheekpieces: has been slowly away. *G. Prodromou* **–**

PENDING (IRE) 2 b.g. (May 5) Pennekamp (USA) 130 – Dolcezza (FR) (Lichine (USA) 117) [2003 7m 8m⁵ Sep 5] 34,000Y: quite good-topped gelding: half-brother to several winners, including 4-y-o Martin House and German 9.5f/1¼m winner C'Est Fantastique (by Hernando): dam unraced close relation to smart French performer up to 10.5f Capparola: better effort in maidens (fair form) when fifth of 18 to Resplendent One at Kempton, travelling well before running green: will probably stay 1¼m: should progress. *J. R. Fanshawe* **78 p**

PENELEWEY 3 b.f. Groom Dancer (USA) 128 – Peryllys 67 (Warning 136) [2003 67: 7m² 6g* 7g² 7.1m 7d* 7g* Nov 1] useful performer: won maiden in May and handicap in July, both at Salisbury, and handicap at Newmarket (made all to beat Bi Polar by ½ length) in November: stays 7f: acts on good to firm and good to soft going. *H. Candy* **97**

PENEL (IRE) 2 b.g. (Mar 25) Orpen (USA) 116 – Jayess Elle 55 (Sabrehill (USA) 120) [2003 5g⁶ 5g⁵ 6.1g⁴ 5.1f Jun 14] €15,000Y: second foal: half-brother to 3-y-o Tender: dam maiden half-sister to useful 7f to 9f performer Supercal: modest maiden: made most when fourth at Chepstow: stays 6f. *B. R. Millman* **57**

PENNELESS DANCER 4 b.g. Pennekamp (USA) 130 – Villella (Sadler's Wells (USA) 132) [2003 59: 8m 8m 12f 9.9m 8.5m Aug 14] poor maiden nowadays: stays 7f: acts on fibresand, good to firm and good to soft going: blinkered final start: tends to edge left. *M. E. Sowersby* **42**

PENNY CROSS   3 b.f. Efisio 120 – Addaya (IRE) (Persian Bold 123) [2003 69p: 7g² **99**
7m³ 6f³ 7.5m* 6.9f* 8m² 8m² 8.5m* 8g³ 8m³ 8f³ Sep 27] smallish, good-topped filly:
useful performer: won maiden at Beverley and handicap at Carlisle in June, and minor
event at Beverley in August: good third after in listed race at Baden-Baden, handicap
at Musselburgh and listed rated stakes at Ascot (beaten 1¼ lengths by Tadris): stays 8.5f:
acts on firm going: races prominently: carries head awkwardly: consistent.
M. Johnston

PENNYGHAEL (UAE)   3 ch.f. Pennekamp (USA) 130 – Kerrera 115 (Diesis 133)   **81**
[2003 7g² 7m² 7f* 9d⁵ 8m⁶ Aug 17] compact filly: half-sister to several winners, including smart French miler Firth of Lorne (by Danehill): dam, second in 1000 Guineas and at
least as effective at 5f/6f, half-sister to very smart 6f to 1m performer Rock City: fairly
useful performer: won maiden at Folkestone in June: below best in handicaps last 2
starts: should stay 1m: has hung left/carried head high: sold 130,000 gns in December.
M. R. Channon

PENNY HA'PENNY   4 b.f. Bishop of Cashel 122 – Madam Millie 99 (Milford 119)   **84 d**
[2003 80: 5g² 5m⁵ 5g 5f 5m⁶ 6g 5d 6m 5g⁴ 5m³ 6g 5g Oct 22] tall, lengthy filly: fairly
useful handicapper: below form after second start: best recent form at 5f: acts on soft
and good to firm ground: sometimes wears cheekpieces: has hung left: usually races
prominently. *D. W. Barker*

PENNY PIE (IRE)   3 b.f. Spectrum (IRE) 126 – Island Lover (IRE) (Turtle Island   **67**
(IRE) 123) [2003 8.3d³ 8.1d⁵ 8m³ 10g 10g p7g Dec 6] 22,000Y: deep-girthed filly: first
foal: dam unraced half-sister to Nassau/Musidora Stakes winner Optimistic Lass, herself
dam of high-class sprinter/miler Golden Opinion: fair maiden: below form last 2 starts:
stays 1¼m. *P. W. Harris*

PENNY STALL   2 b.f. (Apr 7) Silver Patriarch (IRE) 125 – Madiyla 73 (Darshaan   **67 p**
133) [2003 7m 8m⁴ 10m⁴ Oct 22] big, good-topped filly: easy mover: half-sister to 3
winners, including smart French 1m winner Lethals Lady (by Rudimentary) and 3-y-o
Silver City: dam, 1½m winner, half-sister to National Stakes winner Manntari: fair form
in maidens: fourth at Newmarket and Nottingham (not knocked about): type to do better
as 3-y-o at 1½m+. *J. L. Dunlop*

PENNY VALENTINE   3 ch.f. My Best Valentine 122 – Precision Finish 63 (Safawan   **39**
118) [2003 52: p7g⁶ p7g 10m 8f 10f⁵ f6g Nov 24] just poor maiden at 3 yrs: left
J. Cullinan after fifth start: stays 7f: acts on all-weather. *J. R. Best*

PENRIC   3 b.g. Marju (IRE) 127 – Nafhaat (USA) 91 (Roberto (USA) 131) [2003 57?:   **53**
10f⁶ 10.2m 14.1m⁴ 11.6d⁴ 14g 16g⁵ 16.2g 16m⁶ Sep 19] neat gelding: modest maiden
handicapper: stays 2m: acts on good to firm and good to soft going. *C. G. Cox*

PENRITH (FR)   2 b.c. (Apr 16) Singspiel (IRE) 133 – Queen Mat (IRE) (Fairy King   **85 p**
(USA)) [2003 7m* Oct 14] €30,000Y: smallish, close-coupled colt: third foal: dam,
French 1m winner, half-sister to smart French performer up to 1½m Mataran: 4/1, won
9-runner maiden at Leicester comfortably by 1½ lengths from Maaloof, always close up:
will be suited by 1¼m/1½m: should improve. *M. Johnston*

PENSION FUND   9 b.g. Emperor Fountain 112 – Navarino Bay 102 (Averof 123)   **66 d**
[2003 79: 8.3d 9.9m⁵ 8.5d 7.9m⁴ 10.1m³ 10.4m 10.9m 9.9d 9.1d Oct 14] tall gelding: fair
handicapper: below form after fourth start: races at 1m/1¼m nowadays: unproven on
heavy going, acts on any other turf and fibresand: blinkered twice (including when racing
freely/finding little), below form once on cheekpieces: sometimes slowly away: no easy
ride. *M. W. Easterby*

PENTECOST   4 ch.g. Tagula (IRE) 116 – Boughtbyphone 62 (Warning 136) [2003   **108**
104: 7g 8m⁴ 8.1g⁵ 8m 8m* 7.9m³ 8.1d² 9m⁴ 9m Oct 4] sturdy, close-coupled gelding:
useful performer: won valuable handicap at Ascot (beat Green Line by ½ length) in
August: creditable efforts next 2 starts, though found little when 2½ lengths second to
Gateman in listed race at Haydock: best around 1m: yet to race on soft/heavy going, acts
on any other: tried visored: has been bandaged/worn dropped noseband: sometimes
slowly away: has raced freely. *A. M. Balding*

PENTHESILEA (USA)   2 b.f. (Apr 22) Sadler's Wells (USA) 132 – Grazia 111   **–**
(Sharpo 132) [2003 f6g Oct 16] angular filly: second foal: dam, 6f (including at 2 yrs)
winner, closely related to Halling: 14/1, green when behind in maiden at Southwell: dead.
Sir Mark Prescott

PENWELL HILL (USA)   4 b.g. Distant View (USA) 126 – Avie's Jill (USA) (Lord   **78**
Avie (USA)) [2003 –: f11g² f8s* f8g* f8s* f7s³ f7s⁴ f8g⁶ f11g⁵ Dec 15] quite good-topped
gelding: fair handicapper: won at Southwell in January (2) and February: best at 7f/1m:
acts on fibresand and good to firm going: usually makes running: game. *T. D. Barron*

PENZANCE 2 b.c. (Feb 27) Pennekamp (USA) 130 – Kalinka (IRE) 88 (Soviet Star **77**
(USA) 128) [2003 8.1f* 8.5d³ Oct 4] good-bodied colt: third foal: half-brother to 3-y-o
Soviet Song and 4-y-o Baralinka: dam 2-y-o 7f winner who probably stayed 1¼m: won
maiden at Haydock in September: similarly fair form when 6 lengths third of 5 to Prime
Powered in minor event at Epsom: not sure to stay much beyond 8.5f. *J. R. Fanshawe*

PEPE GALVEZ (SWE) 6 br.g. Mango Express 106 – Mango Sampaquita (SWE) **–**
(Colombian Friend (USA)) [2003 18.7m May 7] close-coupled gelding: lightly-raced
maiden on Flat: well held in Chester Cup only outing in 2003: likely to prove best up to
2m: yet to race on extremes of going: fairly useful hurdler. *Mrs L. C. Taylor*

PEPE (IRE) 2 b.f. (Apr 16) Bahhare (USA) 122 – Orange And Blue 50 (Prince Sabo **50**
123) [2003 6d 7d⁶ Nov 4] €8,000Y: tall filly: third foal: half-sister to winner in Sweden
by Royal Abjar: dam 2-y-o 5f winner: modest form in maidens at Thirsk and Catterick
(cheekpieces): should stay 1m. *R. Hollinshead*

PEPPER ROAD 4 ch.g. Elmaamul (USA) 125 – Floral Spark 69 (Forzando 122) **61**
[2003 58: 7m⁶ 7.1d 7g 7.9f³ 7.9m⁵ 9.2g 7.5m³ 7.9m³ 6.9m² 8m* 8.2f 8m⁶ 8d Nov 7]
modest handicapper: won at Thirsk in September, hanging markedly right: effective at 7f/
1m: acts on firm and good to soft going: taken early to post: sometimes slowly away/races
freely/wanders. *R. Bastiman*

PEPPERSHOT 3 b.g. Vettori (IRE) 119 – No Chili 86 (Glint of Gold 128) [2003 **66 d**
12.1d⁵ 11.9m⁴ p10g 16.2m 14m⁶ p12g p16g Dec 2] 6,000Y: lengthy gelding: seventh
foal: half-brother to UAE 7f/1m winner Old Kingdom (by Imp Society) and 1½m winner
Cut The Spice (by Suave Dancer): dam, 1½m winner, later successful in USA: fair form
in maidens first 2 starts, soundly beaten after, leaving A. Balding 1,000 gns following
fifth start: should be suited by 1½m+: reared as stalls opened final outing. *G. P. Enright*

PEPPIATT 9 ch.g. Efisio 120 – Fleur du Val (Valiyar 129) [2003 63: 6d 7g 6d 6d 6g **–**
Jul 31] robust gelding: no form in 2003: tried blinkered/in cheekpieces. *N. Bycroft*

PEQUENITA 3 b.f. Rudimentary (USA) 118 – Sierra Madrona (USA) (Woodman **70**
(USA) 126) [2003 –p: 7d² 7f 7m 9.3m 10g f12g⁴ f12s² 10.9d* Oct 13] leggy filly: fair
performer: won claimer at Ayr in October by 6 lengths (claimed £10,000 and joined
G. L. Moore): stays 1½m: acts on good to soft ground and fibresand: often makes running. *J. G. Given*

PER AMORE (IRE) 5 ch.g. General Monash (USA) 107 – Danny's Miracle (Super- **–**
lative 118) [2003 84: 14.8m Aug 22] fairly useful handicapper, barely held Flat start
in 2003 but was a fairly useful winner over jumps: probably stays 1½m: acts on soft and
good to firm ground: blinkered last 2 starts. *P. J. Hobbs*

PERCHANCER (IRE) 7 ch.g. Perugino (USA) 84 – Irish Hope (Nishapour (FR) **– §**
125) [2003 72§, a56§: 9.2g Jul 24] strong gelding: fair at best: well held only outing in
2003: tried visored/blinkered: often slowly away (sometimes markedly so) finds little:
one to be wary of. *P. C. Haslam*

PERCHANCE TO WIN 6 b.m. Pelder (IRE) 125 – French Plait (Thatching 131) **51**
[2003 62: p7g f8s⁴ p10g⁴ Mar 4] modest maiden handicapper: barely stays 1¼m: acts on
soft going, firm and all-weather. *R. Guest*

PERCUSSIONIST (IRE) 2 b.c. (Apr 6) Sadler's Wells (USA) 132 – Magnificent **79 p**
Style (USA) 107 (Silver Hawk (USA) 123) [2003 8.1m³ 8s² Oct 29] tall, close-coupled
colt: third foal: half-brother to 3-y-o Echoes In Eternity: dam lightly-raced 1¼m
(including Musidora Stakes) winner: fair form when placed in maidens at Sandown and
Yarmouth (staying-on second to Roehampton): will be suited by 1¼m/1½m: open to
progress. *J. H. M. Gosden*

PERCY DOUGLAS 3 b.c. Elmaamul (USA) 125 – Qualitair Dream 80 (Dreams To **77 d**
Reality (USA) 113) [2003 76: f6g³ f5s 5f 5f 5.1m 5d 6g 5m⁶ 5m⁶ 6m 6g 5m 5m 5m 6m³
f6g 5g⁶ f5s³ Dec 31] good-topped colt: fair performer: below form in second half of year:
probably best at 5f: acts on firm ground and fibresand: usually visored/wears cheekpieces: tends to edge right. *Miss A. Stokell*

PEREGIAN (IRE) 5 b.g. Eagle Eyed (USA) 111 – Mo Pheata (Petorius 117) [2003 **58**
56: p10g³ p10g⁶ p8g³ p8g² p7g 8.3g⁴ 7f 8m² 7g* 8.1m 9f 8m 9.9m 8d⁵ Oct 31] stocky
gelding: modest handicapper: won amateur event at Yarmouth in May: effective at 7f to
easy 1¼m: acts on polytrack, firm and good to soft going (below form on soft): tried
blinkered/in cheekpieces (raced freely): sometimes hangs. *J. Akehurst*

PERELANDRA (USA) 3 ch.f. Cadeaux Genereux 131 – Larentia 58 (Salse (USA) **76**
128) [2003 10g⁶ 10m⁶ 10m⁶ p12g* p12g Oct 27] 30,000Y: rather leggy, useful-looking

filly: fourth foal: half-sister to 2 winners abroad, including French 10.5f winner Lantana (by Charnwood Forest): dam lightly-raced half-sister to smart sprinter Bahamian Bounty (by Cadeaux Genereux): fair performer: won maiden at Lingfield in September: seemed as if amiss in handicap there subsequent start: stays easy 1½m: acts on polytrack, raced only on good/good to firm going on turf. *J. Noseda*

PERERIN 2 b.c. (Apr 12) Whittingham (IRE) 104 – Antithesis (IRE) 75 (Fairy King – (USA)) [2003 6m 6.1m f8s Sep 2] £1,000Y: sturdy, close-coupled colt: first living foal: dam Irish 5f winner: well held in maidens. *I. A. Wood*

PERFECT BALANCE (IRE) 2 b. or br.g. (Feb 9) Shinko Forest (IRE) – Tumble 53 (Mtoto 134) [2003 6d³ 8d 8.1d Sep 27] 21,000Y: close-coupled gelding: fourth foal: half-brother to 2000 2-y-o 7f winner Night Fall (by Night Shift) and 7f winner in Germany by Sri Pekan: dam French winner around 1m/1¼m: easily best effort in maidens (modest form) when third at Hamilton: should stay 1m. *N. Tinkler*

PERFECT DISTANCE (USA) 2 b.f. (Apr 16) Distant View (USA) 126 – Theycall- 73 mecharlie (USA) (Charlie Barley (USA)) [2003 5.1f³ 6m⁵ p5g⁵ 5m f5g⁴ 5f* 5m⁶ 5.1f⁴ Oct 12] 5,500 2-y-o: third foal: half-sister to winner in USA by Royal Academy: dam, 8.5f/1¼m winner in USA, placed in minor stakes: fair performer: won seller at Wolverhampton and nursery at Musselburgh (hung right) in August: probably best at 5f: acts on all-weather and firm going: sold 8,000 gns, sent to Hungary. *B. J. Meehan*

PERFECT ECHO 4 ch.f. Lycius (USA) 124 – Perfect Timing 107 (Comedy Star 81 (USA) 121) [2003 53: p8g* p7g² Mar 4] fairly useful performer, lightly raced: won maiden at Lingfield in February: good second in handicap there subsequent start: will prove best at 7f/1m: acts on polytrack: wore cheekpieces in 2003. *M. P. Tregoning*

PERFECT HINDSIGHT (IRE) 2 b.g. (Apr 21) Spectrum (IRE) 126 – Vinicky 68 (USA) (Kingmambo (USA) 125) [2003 5f 6.1g 5m⁵ Jul 4] €22,000Y: well-grown, quite good-topped gelding: second foal: dam, French maiden, closely related to useful UAE 9f/1¼m performer Mackook: best effort in maidens (fair form) when fifth, never placed to challenge, at Warwick: subsequently gelded: should stay at least 1m. *C. G. Cox*

PERFECT LOVE 3 b.f. Pursuit of Love 124 – Free Spirit (IRE) (Caerleon (USA) 84 132) [2003 p6g* p7g² 7d p8g p12g Dec 17] first foal: dam unraced: close relative to smart performer up to 1¼m Gold Academy: fairly useful performer: won maiden at Lingfield in January: easily best effort when second to Hoh Investor in minor event there: should stay 1m: acts on polytrack: blinkered final start. *G. A. Butler*

PERFECT NIGHT 3 b.f. Danzig Connection (USA) – Blissful Night (Cadeaux 79 Genereux 131) [2003 74: 8m 9g 8g² 8f² 8.1m 8.3g² p7g² f7g* f6g* f7s⁶ Dec 6] big, good-bodied filly: fair performer: won maiden at Wolverhampton and handicap at Southwell in November, both comfortably: effective at 6f to 1m: acts on all-weather and any turf going: hung left fourth start. *R. Charlton*

PERFECT PICTURE 4 b.g. Octagonal (NZ) 126 – Greenvera (USA) (Riverman – (USA) 131) [2003 67, a–: 10f Jun 18] leggy, lengthy gelding: fair maiden: form (fair) only on third 3-y-o start: tried tongue tied: sold 1,900 gns. *M. Johnston*

PERFECT PORTRAIT 3 ch.g. Selkirk (USA) 129 – Flawless Image (USA) 109 84 p (The Minstrel (CAN) 135) [2003 7m* Oct 13] compact gelding: half-brother to smart 7f (including at 2 yrs)/1m winner Darnay (by Darshaan) and useful Irish 7f and 8.5f winner Matangi (by Mtoto): dam Irish sprinter: 6/4, won maiden at Leicester on debut by ¾ length from Paciano, despite running green: bred to stay at least 1m: wore crossed nose-band: sure to improve. *D. R. Loder*

PERFECT PUNCH 4 b.g. Reprimand 122 – Aliuska (IRE) 70 (Fijar Tango (FR) 127) 73 [2003 62: p10g⁴ p12g* p12g 12.4g² 12g⁵ p12g⁴ 11.9d Sep 26] fair handicapper: won at a77 Lingfield in March: should stay beyond 1½m: acts on polytrack. *C. F. Wall*

PERFECT SETTING 3 b.g. Polish Precedent (USA) 131 – Diamond Park (IRE) 91 74 d (Alzao (USA) 117) [2003 85p: 5.2m⁴ 5g 5d 5d Aug 30] useful-looking gelding: fairly useful form in maiden at Sandown only 2-y-o start, wandering: regressed in 2003, looking none too keen in blinkers final start: one to treat with caution. *P. J. Makin*

PERFECT STORM 4 b.c. Vettori (IRE) 119 – Gorgeous Dancer (IRE) (Nordico 101 (USA)) [2003 102: 8m 6.1m 10.4m⁴ 10g⁶ 8m 10.3g 10.1s* 12d² Nov 8] lengthy colt: useful performer: won minor event at Yarmouth in October by 3 lengths from Ace of Hearts: good second to Turbo in November Handicap at Doncaster final start: stays 1½m: acts on firm and soft going, yet to race on heavy: blinkered (well beaten) fifth start: free-going sort. *M. Blanshard*

PERFECT TOUCH (USA) 4 b.f. Miswaki (USA) 124 – Glen Kate 118 (Glenstal **107**
(USA) 118) [2003 96: 6g⁴ 6g² 7m² 7d* 7g⁵ 7.5g² 8f² 7.5m³ 8m⁶ Oct 19] fourth foal:
half-sister to French 1997 2-y-o 9f winner Trempkate (by Trempolino) and winner in
USA by Tabasco Cat: dam 6f to 7f winner, including in USA: useful performer: second in
handicaps at Newmarket (30 ran, to Fire Up The Band) and the Curragh before improved
effort to win Irish Stallion Farms EBF Brownstown Stakes at Leopardstown in July by
3½ lengths from Irresistible: good placed efforts when neck second to eased Favourable
Terms in Matron Stakes at Leopardstown and length third to Sheppard's Watch in Concorde Stakes at Tipperary seventh/eighth starts: stays 1m: acts on firm and good to soft
going, below form on soft/heavy: blinkered (below form) final start. *D. K. Weld, Ireland*

PERFIDIOUS (USA) 5 b.g. Lear Fan (USA) 130 – Perfolia (USA) 104 (Nodouble **81**
(USA)) [2003 64, a77: p10g² f9.4g⁶ p10g² p10g² 9.7m* 9.7m² 10m 10m 10g⁶ 10.1m²
10.1g⁵ 9.9m² 10.4f 10f* Oct 17] sturdy gelding: fairly useful performer: won handicap at
Folkestone in April and 3-runner minor event at Brighton in October: best at 9f to 11f:
acts on all-weather and firm going: slowly away last 2 outings: often leads, and tends to
race moodily when unable to do so: sometimes wanders. *J. R. Boyle*

PERGOLACHA (IRE) 2 b.f. (Feb 4) Sadler's Wells (USA) 132 – Posta Vecchia **78**
(USA) (Rainbow Quest (USA) 134) [2003 8m 7s³ p8g² Nov 13] €330,000Y: strong,
rangy filly: second foal: sister to 3-y-o Top Tenor: dam, ran once at 2 yrs, out of half-sister
to very smart 1m/1¼m performer Bach: fair form in maidens: best effort final start: would
have been suited by at least 1¼m: dead. *L. M. Cumani*

PERLE D'OR (IRE) 2 b.f. (Mar 6) Entrepreneur 123 – Rose Society (Caerleon (USA) **72**
132) [2003 6f⁴ 7.1m⁵ 7m Oct 18] €60,000Y: leggy, quite attractive filly: half-sister to
several winners, including 2001 2-y-o 6f/7f winner Red Briar (by Desert King) and 1m/
1¼m winner Silverani (later won in USA, by High Estate), both useful: dam Irish maiden
who stayed 1½m: easily best effort (fair form) when fourth in maiden at York: hung left
next start: stiff task final one: should stay at least 7f. *W. J. Haggas*

PERSARIO 4 b.f. Bishop of Cashel 122 – Barford Lady 93 (Stanford 121§) [2003 82: **91 p**
7.1m⁶ 7m² 7d⁶ 7d² 7g Nov 1] lengthy filly: fairly useful performer: runner-up in handicap
at Leicester and minor event at Epsom: will be at least as effective at 6f as 7f: acts on good
to firm and good to soft ground: slowly away/hung left penultimate outing: lightly raced
and open to improvement. *J. R. Fanshawe*

PERSEPHONE HEIGHTS 3 br.f. Golden Heights 82 – Jalland (Jalmood (USA) **76 ?**
126) [2003 62: p8g⁶ p10g⁴ p10g⁴ f12g 11.7f² 12g* 12m 11m 11.9f⁶ p13g Nov 12] fair **a51**
handicapper on turf, modest on all-weather: easily best effort when winning at Newmarket in August by 8 lengths: should stay 1¾m: acts on polytrack (well beaten on
fibresand), raced only on good going or firmer on turf. *D. J. Coakley*

PERSHAAN (IRE) 3 br.f. Darshaan 133 – Persian Fantasy 94 (Persian Bold 123) **92**
[2003 74p: 10m⁴ 11.6d² 12.3d 11.9g⁵ 12m* 15.9d² 16g Oct 24] unfurnished filly: fairly
useful performer: won maiden at Catterick in September: good second in handicap at
Chester next time: stays 2m: acts on soft and good to firm ground. *J. L. Dunlop*

PERSIAN BANDIT (IRE) 5 b.g. Idris (IRE) 118 – Ce Soir (Northern Baby (CAN) **–**
127) [2003 46: 8m Jul 2] poor performer nowadays: well held only outing in 2003: tried
blinkered: looks less than keen. *J. R. Jenkins*

PERSIAN BROOK 3 b.g. Atraf 116 – Persian Role (Tragic Role (USA)) [2003 6m **–**
f7g 8m⁶ Aug 6] lengthy gelding: first foal: dam unraced: well held in maidens.
M. W. Easterby

PERSIAN DAGGER (IRE) 2 b.c. (Apr 4) Daylami (IRE) 138 – Persian Fantasy 94 **–**
(Persian Bold 123) [2003 8g Oct 25] smallish colt: sixth foal: half-brother to useful 1¾m/
2m winner Height of Fantasy (by Shirley Heights), 3-y-o Pershaan and 4-y-o Persian
Lightning: dam 1½m winner who stayed 2m: 10/1, last of 17 in maiden at Newbury.
J. L. Dunlop

PERSIAN FACT 4 b.g. Greensmith 121 – Forest Song 60 (Forzando 122) [2003 –: **–**
f8s f8.5g Jan 20] good-topped gelding: modest maiden at 2 yrs: no form since: tried
visored. *K. R. Burke*

PERSIAN GENIE (IRE) 2 br.f. (Mar 24) Grand Lodge (USA) 125 – Persia (IRE) **–**
(Persian Bold 123) [2003 6g Oct 24] 8,500Y: leggy filly: fifth foal: half-sister to 1m
winner Queen Zenobia (by Danehill): dam unraced half-sister to very smart sprinter
Sayyaf: 50/1, slowly away and always behind in maiden at Newbury. *G. B. Balding*

PERSIAN KING (IRE) 6 ch.g. Persian Bold 123 – Queen's Share (Main Reef 126) **85 ?**
[2003 98: 10.1m 12m⁵ 10m Aug 16] sturdy gelding: useful performer at 5 yrs: form in

2003 only when fifth in handicap at Epsom: probably stays 1¾m: acts on good to firm and good to soft ground: tried tongue tied (has reportedly had a wind operation): won over fences in September. *J. A. B. Old*

PERSIAN LASS (IRE) 4 ch.f. Grand Lodge (USA) 125 – Noble Tiara (USA) 110 **103** (Vaguely Noble 140) [2003 103: 10.1m⁴ 10.4m⁴ 11.9v³ 10f 10.1g³ 10g³ 10.3d⁵ p10g⁵ Nov 22] leggy filly: useful performer: mostly creditable efforts in 2003, including when in frame in handicap at Epsom (fourth to Lingo) and listed events at York and Newmarket (2¾ lengths third to Far Lane) first, second and sixth starts: best form around 1¼m: acts on soft and good to firm going, probably on firm/polytrack: usually takes strong hold/ patiently ridden. *P. W. Harris*

PERSIAN LIGHTNING (IRE) 4 b.g. Sri Pekan (USA) 117 – Persian Fantasy 94 **109** (Persian Bold 123) [2003 97: 10m⁵ 10g* 10m⁴ 10f² 10.4f³ 9.9g 10.4m⁶ 9m² 9m 10g Oct 31] strong, angular gelding: usually impresses in appearance: useful handicapper: won at Newmarket in May by 1¼ lengths from Athenian: good efforts in frame next 3 starts in Zetland Gold Cup at Redcar, listed rated stakes at Royal Ascot (neck second to In Time's Eye, wandering) and John Smith's Cup at York (third to Far Lane): best around 1¼m: raced mainly on good ground or firmer: has been early to post: sometimes races too freely: effective ridden prominently or held up: reliable. *J. L. Dunlop*

PERSIAN MAJESTY (IRE) 3 b.c. Grand Lodge (USA) 125 – Spa (Sadler's Wells **114 p** (USA) 132) [2003 94P: 10m* Jun 19] rangy, attractive colt: successful on both starts, maiden at Newmarket at 2 yrs and listed event at Royal Ascot (still green, smart form when beating Foodbroker Founder a neck despite hanging markedly right) 8 months later: had suffered bruised foot early in 2003 and after Ascot was found to have suffered hairline fracture of a knee (operated on): will stay 1½m: back in training, and is capable of better still. *P. W. Harris*

PERSIAN PEARL 4 b.f. Hurricane Sky (AUS) – Persian Fountain (IRE) 67 (Persian **72** Heights 129) [2003 –: 7m 7g² 8.1m* 7f* 8.2g⁴ /m³ 7f³ 8m⁵ 8f 10.4f 10.1m⁵ 9g Oct 24] sturdy filly: fair handicapper: won at Warwick (amateurs) in June, Kempton (apprentices) in July and Nottingham in August: best at 7f/1m: acts on firm ground: wears cheekpieces nowadays: sometimes flashes tail under pressure: held up. *H. J. Collingridge*

PERSIAN PUNCH (IRE) 10 ch.g. Persian Heights 129 – Rum Cay (USA) 75 **120** (Our Native (USA)) [2003 117: 13.3m⁴ 16.4m⁴ 20m² 16.4g* 16g* 15.9m⁴ 18d* 20s 16m* Oct 18]

Dolly the sheep, the first animal to be cloned from an adult cell, was put down in February, stuffed for posterity and put on display in an Edinburgh museum. Her cloning in 1997 was a scientific breakthrough which paved the way for genetic manipulation of other animals, and in May the first cloned foal, a draught pony named Prometea, was produced by an Italian professor. It seems only a matter of time before the same thing happens with a thoroughbred, the technology eventually opening up the prospect of cloning gelded high-class racehorses and then using the clones for conventional breeding. The International Stud Book Committee has already moved to place equine cloning and embryo transfer on the same footing as artificial insemination, which has always been banned. There seems absolutely no prospect, either, of the world's racing authorities allowing cloned thoroughbreds to race. The idea that a redoubtable gelding like Persian Punch might be able to pass

Lady O Goodwood Cup, Goodwood—a thrilling finish between the 2001 winner Persian Punch (left) and the 2002 winner Jardines Lookout; Savannah Bay is third

GNER Doncaster Cup—Persian Punch doesn't need to show his renowned battling qualities this time; Dusky Warbler (right) and Hugs Dancer are left trailing

on many of his qualities—most notably his durability and his renowned front-running battling qualities—belongs in the realms of fantasy, for the time being at least, though it might be prudent for his owner to freeze some cells just in case!

The latest season was Persian Punch's eighth on the track and he produced some of the best form of his career, winning three of the traditional Cup races, the Lady O Goodwood Cup, the GNER Doncaster Cup and the Jockey Club Cup at Newmarket. He now jointly holds the record, alongside Tedburrow, Yavana's Pace and Repertory, as the oldest horse trained in Britain to have won a pattern race. There was also a victory in the first running of a new listed race at Sandown on Eclipse day and a creditable second to Mr Dinos in the Gold Cup (Persian Punch has yet to win in ten starts at Ascot). The Jockey Club Cup provided Persian Punch with his thirteenth pattern-race victory—putting him level at the top of that list with Brigadier Gerard, Ardross and German-trained Acatenango—and it took his total earnings past the £1m mark. Persian Punch had already won more prize money than any other British-trained gelding in an admirable career that has now seen him successful in the Jockey Club Cup and the Henry II Stakes at Sandown three times and the Goodwood Cup and the Lonsdale Stakes at York twice, in addition to the Doncaster Cup, the Sagaro Stakes (when it was run at Newmarket in 1998) and the Prix Kergorlay. Persian Punch's reputation as 'the most popular horse in training' —the horse that most stirs the emotions—was cemented by his successes in Horse of the Year polls conducted by Channel 4 and by the *Racing Post*, both of which he won by a street.

Winning by a street is not a trait normally associated with Persian Punch. The sight of him doing it the hard way—snatching victory from the jaws of defeat, rallying for a narrow, hard-earned success—is much more familiar to racegoers and television viewers. His victories at Sandown, Goodwood and Newmarket in the latest season, for example, were all by a short head, after the sort of battling-back performances that have endeared him to the racing public. A slight setback in March probably affected Persian Punch's training schedule and he seemed to take more getting ready than in previous seasons, running as if in need of the race on his first two starts (though still managing to make the frame in the Henry II Stakes for the seventh time—ridden in the race by a seventh different jockey). It seemed hard to believe Persian Punch would be in the form needed to break his duck in the Gold Cup, especially at the age of ten, but, starting at 20/1, he kept on well to finish six lengths behind Mr Dinos, holding off Pole Star, Jardines Lookout and the favourite Mamool, to finish runner-up as he had to Royal Rebel in a rousing set-to in 2001 when beaten a head. The Addleshaw Goddard Stakes (Esher) on Eclipse day at Sandown featured another nail-biting finish involving Persian Punch, who, conceding 5 lb all round, got back up on the line after being headed two furlongs out by the dual Queen Alexandra Stakes winner Cover Up. Another very close call followed in the Goodwood Cup, in which, with the first and third in the Gold Cup both absent, Persian Punch fought out the finish with Jardines Lookout, the 2002 Goodwood Cup winner. Forging back into the lead well inside the final furlong, Persian Punch just held off Jardines Lookout as the latter came again in one of the most memorable finishes seen all season. The Goodwood crowd enjoyed a racing experience they are unlikely to forget in a hurry, Persian Punch's return in front of

785

*Jockey Club Cup, Newmarket—a memorable curtain-raiser to 'Champions Day'
as Persian Punch wins this event for the third time, rallying splendidly to peg back Millenary,
with Kasthari and Tholjanah (striped cap) close up*

the stands and in the winner's enclosure producing heart-stirring scenes reminiscent of those after Double Trigger's third win in the race in 1998.

A respectable fourth to Bollin Eric when attempting a third win in the Lonsdale Stakes was followed by Persian Punch's fourth appearance in the Doncaster
Cup. It wasn't a particularly strong renewal, though the field included the Gold Cup
third and sixth, Pole Star (who started favourite) and Savannah Bay (a five-length
third in the Goodwood Cup), as well as the Chester Cup winner Hugs Dancer and
Zindabad, who was being stepped up further in trip after finishing third in the
Lonsdale. Persian Punch was allowed to set up a good lead and, with his rider
getting him fully opened out earlier than usual, over a mile from home, he galloped
on to win more or less unchallenged by seven lengths and two and a half from
Dusky Warbler, who chased the winner throughout, and Hugs Dancer. Persian
Punch's main rivals may have given him too much rope, but it was a very smart
performance nonetheless, the winner's timerating of 121 a very good one for a Cup
race. A rare poor effort followed in the Prix du Cadran at Longchamp but Persian
Punch bounced back to form in the Jockey Club Cup, in which he started second
favourite to the Princess of Wales's Stakes winner Millenary. Millenary won the St
Leger in 2000 but the Jockey Club Cup was his first venture into Cup races and he
looked like making it a winning one when moving past Persian Punch on the bridle
in the Dip after the latter had raced in a clear lead for a long way. Persian Punch,
who dropped back to third place and was struck in the face by the whip of Tholjanah's rider shortly after, looked likely to be swamped, but he fought back
splendidly to thwart Millenary on the line. Gold Cup seventh Kasthari was a length
further back in third, just ahead of Tholjanah, who had to be snatched up near the
line as the runner-up edged left.

The phrase 'a credit to his stable' seems inadequate in the context of a
phenomenon like Persian Punch. His owner and trainer must have used nearly
every superlative in the dictionary in the course of interviews about him. Owner

Jeff Smith described the strapping Persian Punch—a big, strong individual with a powerful, round action—as 'a warhorse' after the Goodwood Cup. 'You could see someone in armour on top of him and charging down the opposition. We will not see his like again.' Persian Punch's trainer David Elsworth said 'He makes even a crusty old devil like me go a bit soft, he's a wonderful servant who never seems to ask anything and gives everything.' Interestingly, Elsworth also revealed during the season that he felt he might have been a little too easy on Persian Punch in recent years. 'It is only natural to want to look after a horse as special as him, but he needs his work in the mornings and I've been tougher on him this year when I think he's been better than for a long time.' The part played in Persian Punch's rejuvenation by his regular jockey of the past season or so, Martin Dwyer, should not be overlooked either. Dwyer took over in the Geoffrey Freer Stakes at Newbury in August 2002 when retirement was beckoning for Persian Punch after he had come last in the Goodwood Cup. 'Some of the boys told me to take an oxygen tank . . . he's a hard ride,' said Dwyer at the time and he has certainly earned his riding fees. Dwyer reported after the Goodwood Cup that he felt Persian Punch was 'taking the mickey'. The sight of Dwyer keeping at Persian Punch, sometimes from a fairly early stage, has become typical of the partnership. 'Clive Brittain said they should have Persian Punch before the stewards for overuse of the jockey,' said Dwyer after the Jockey Club Cup.

		Persian Bold	Bold Lad
	Persian Heights	(br 1975)	Relkarunner
	(ch 1985)	Ready And Willing	Reliance II
Persian Punch (IRE)		(b 1971)	No Saint
(ch.g. 1993)		Our Native	Exclusive Native
	Rum Cay (USA)	(b 1970)	Our Jackie
	(ch 1985)	Oraston	Morston
		(ch 1978)	Orange Cap

Mr J. C. Smith's "Persian Punch"

787

Persian Punch's pedigree is of academic interest only and has been covered in past editions of *Racehorses*, this being the fifth essay on him. The only update is that Rum Cay's eighth foal Wadmaan (by Singspiel) became her seventh winner when successful over nine furlongs in the United Arab Emirates in early-2003. Persian Punch, who is best at two miles plus and acts on any going, stays in training. The search for an elusive Group 1 victory will almost certainly see him contesting the Gold Cup for an eighth time, though, however he fares at Royal Ascot, it is already a certainty that Persian Punch will be remembered for much longer than most winners of that race. His story has been extraordinary. *D. R. C. Elsworth*

PERSIAN WATERS (IRE) 7 b.g. Persian Bold 123 – Emerald Waters (Kings Lake **81** (USA) 133) [2003 16m⁴ May 24] lengthy, quite good-topped gelding: fairly useful handicapper, lightly raced: ran creditably only Flat outing in 2003: stays 2½m: acts on soft and good to firm going: useful hurdler. *J. R. Fanshawe*

PERTEMPS BIANCA 3 b.f. Dancing Spree (USA) – Bay Bianca (IRE) (Law Society **47 ?** (USA) 130) [2003 73d: f8.5g⁵ f8g⁴ f8g 9.9m f11s⁶ Dec 13] leggy filly: poor performer: left K. Burke after fourth start: stays 8.5f: acts on soft going and fibresand: tried blinkered, usually visored. *A. D. Smith*

PERTEMPS CONECTION 3 b.f. Danzig Connection (USA) – Royal Celerity **–** (USA) (Riverman (USA) 131) [2003 8d f12s Dec 13] half-sister to 1¼m seller winner In Cahoots (by Kalaglow) and 2 winners abroad: dam Irish 1m winner: well held in claimer at Brighton (hung left) and maiden at Southwell (reportedly lost action). *A. D. Smith*

PERTEMPS MACHINE 4 b.g. Danzig Connection (USA) – Shamrock Dancer (IRE) **36** (Dance of Life (USA)) [2003 11.8m Oct 14] second foal: dam third at 8,5f: tailed off in claimer on Flat debut. *A. D. Smith*

PERTEMPS MAGUS 3 b.f. Silver Wizard (USA) 117 – Brilliant Future 58 (Welsh **71 d** Saint 126) [2003 70: 7g⁶ 8.3g 6m⁵ 5.7m 6m 6m 6g Oct 22] sparely-made filly: fair handicapper: left A. Smith after fourth start: stays 7f: acts on good to firm going, probably on soft: reportedly lost action second outing, pulled hard third. *R. A. Fahey*

PERTEMPS RED 2 ch.c. (Mar 11) Dancing Spree (USA) – Lady Lullaby (IRE) **–** (Ballad Rock 122) [2003 7m Jun 12] second foal: dam, well beaten in bumper, out of half-sister to Irish 2000 Guineas winner Northern Treasure: tailed off in seller at Yarmouth, reportedly lame. *A. D. Smith*

PERTEMPS SIA 3 b.c. Distinctly North (USA) 115 – Shamrock Dancer (IRE) 36 **40** (Dance of Life (USA)) [2003 41: f12g 10.3g⁵ 11.6g 14.1m⁶ 14.1m⁶ 14g 16.2m⁶ Jul 11] leggy, sparely-made colt: poor maiden handicapper: stays 1¾m: tried tongue tied: often slowly away. *A. D. Smith*

PERTEMPS SILENUS 5 b.g. Silca Blanka (IRE) 104 – Silvie 66 (Kind of Hush 118) **–** [2003 p13g f9.4s f12g Apr 25] second reported foal: dam 1½m winner: seemed of little account: dead. *A. D. Smith*

PERTEMPS WIZARD 3 br.g. Silver Wizard (USA) 117 – Peristyle 59 (Tolomeo **–** 127) [2003 55: f8s Feb 18] lengthy colt: signs of ability in maidens first 2 starts at 2 yrs: well held since: should stay 7f+. *F. Jordan*

PERUVIA (IRE) 3 b.f. Perugino (USA) 84 – Dane's Lane (IRE) (Danehill (USA) **86** 126) [2003 80: 8s⁴ p12g⁴ 9.2d* 10d² Oct 13] strong, workmanlike filly: fairly useful performer: won maiden at Hamilton in September: very good second in handicap at Ayr final start: will prove best short of 1½m: acts on good to firm and good to soft going: sold 13,000 gns. *H. Morrison*

PERUVIAN BREEZE (IRE) 2 b.g. (Mar 28) Foxhound (USA) 103 – Quietly **62** Impressive (IRE) 66 (Taufan (USA) 119) [2003 7m 8.3g⁶ 8m⁶ Sep 18] IR 17,000F, €40,000Y: tall, good-topped gelding: fourth foal: half-brother to 1m/1¼m winner Quiet Traveller (by Blues Traveller) and Swedish winner up to 1m by Roi Danzig: dam 1m/9f winner: best effort in maidens (modest form) when sixth of 7 at Hamilton: possibly amiss final start: not sure to stay much beyond 1m. *N. P. Littmoden*

PERUVIAN CHIEF (IRE) 6 b.g. Foxhound (USA) 103 – John's Ballad (IRE) **107** (Ballad Rock 122) [2003 99, a104: f6s f5g⁵ f6g² p5g² f6g² p5g⁴ f6s* p5g* 6g 5.2m* 6g **a113** 5m² 5m* 6g⁴ 5f 6f 5g 6.1m 6m⁶ 5.6d 6m 5f 5m 5g 5m⁵ 5m⁶ Oct 25] good-topped gelding: smart performer: won handicap at Wolverhampton (beat Massey 3 lengths), minor event at Lingfield, handicap at Newbury and listed race at Kempton (beat Vision of Night 1¾ lengths) between March and May: at least respectable efforts 3 of last 4 starts: effective at 5f to sharp 7.6f: acts on all-weather, firm and soft going: tried blinkered, usually visored nowadays: sometimes wanders. *N. P. Littmoden*

PERUVIAN STYLE (IRE)   2 b.g. (Apr 2) Desert Style (IRE) 121 – Lady's Vision   **77** (IRE) 93 (Vision (USA)) [2003 5f² 5m⁴ 6.3g 5.1g* Aug 7] €28,000Y: strong gelding: fourth foal: brother to 5f to 1m winner in Hong Kong and half-brother to winner in Holland by Alhaarth: dam, Irish 7f (at 2 yrs) to 11f winner, also won over hurdles: fair performer: won 7-runner maiden at Chepstow by neck from Phluke: likely to prove best at 5f/easy 6f: acts on firm going: wandered second start. *N. P. Littmoden*

PESSOA (GER)   4 ch.c. Platini (GER) 126 – Prairie Lila (GER) (Homing 130) [2003   **88** a9.5g* a9.5g² a10g⁴ p10g 10.5v³ May 1] approx. 9,200Y in Germany: third foal: half-brother to winner in Germany by General Assembly: dam, German winner around 1m, half-sister to Deutsches St Leger winner Prairie Neba: fairly useful performer: won 3 times in 2002 and successful in handicap at Neuss in January: not entirely discredited in listed Winter Derby at Lingfield fourth start: stays 1½m: acts on heavy going and sand: consistent. *M. Hofer, Germany*

PETANA   3 br.f. Petong 126 – Duxyana (IRE) (Cyrano de Bergerac 120) [2003 –: 6m   **49 §** 7m 5g 5m 6m⁴ 5f⁶ 5d⁶ 5g² 6m⁵ 5.9m 5m² 5m Sep 6] compact filly: poor maiden handicapper: stays 6f: acts on firm and good to soft ground: blinkered nowadays: unreliable. *M. Dods*

PETARDIAS MAGIC (IRE)   2 ch.c. (Jan 25) Petardia 113 – Alexander Confranc   **83** (IRE) 73 (Magical Wonder (USA) 125) [2003 5d⁶ 5.1m* 6g² p6g³ 6s p6g* 7.5d⁶ Dec 14] €6,500Y: first foal: dam Irish 2-y-o 7f winner: fairly useful performer: won maiden at Nottingham in June and minor event at Lingfield in November: stays 6f: acts on polytrack and good to firm ground. *E. J. O'Neill*

PETERS CHOICE   2 ch.g. (Apr 24) Wolfhound (USA) 126 – Dance of The Swans   **86 p** (IRE) 69 (Try My Best (USA)) 130 [2003 5f⁴ 5m² 6g f5g* f5g* Nov 21] 4,000Y: third foal: half-brother to 3-y-o Sandgate Cygnet: dam 2-y-o 5f winner who later stayed 7f: fairly useful performer: won maiden (by 8 lengths) and nursery (beat Blue Power comfortably by 2½ lengths) at Wolverhampton in November: will prove best at bare 5f: acts on fibresand, carried head awkwardly/hung left on turf first 3 starts: open to further improvement. *I. Semple*

PETER'S IMP (IRE)   8 b.g. Imp Society (USA) – Catherine Clare 58 (Sallust 134)   **–** [2003 51: f12g 10.5m 14.1m Aug 9] good-bodied gelding: modest at 7 yrs: well held on Flat in 2003, though won selling hurdle: has been blinkered/visored. *A. Berry*

PETER'S PUZZLE   2 gr.f. (Feb 10) Mind Games 121 – Maytong 54 (Petong 126)   **47** [2003 5m³ 6m 5m Aug 14] 500Y: second foal: dam, maiden, best at 5f or poor form in sellers (third at Catterick)/claimer: likely to prove best at 5f/6f. *R. A. Fahey*

PETER THE GREAT (IRE)   4 b.g. Hector Protector (USA) 124 – Perfect Alibi   **48** (Law Society (USA) 130) [2003 –: 12g 8m 8f⁴ 8.1m Jul 11] good-bodied gelding: fair maiden at 2 yrs, only poor form since: should stay at least 1¼m: acts on good to firm ground: tried visored, wore cheekpieces and tongue tie last 2 starts: reportedly bled final start. *R. M. Beckett*

PETIT CALVA (FR)   2 bl.f. (Mar 9) Desert King (IRE) 129 – Jimkana (FR) (Double   **100** Bed (FR) 121) [2003 5g* 5.5g⁶ 5g⁴ 6m* 6m⁵ 6d Oct 1] second foal: dam, French 1¼m winner, sister to very smart 7f to 1¼m winner Jim And Tonic: useful performer: won minor event at Longchamp in April and listed race at La Teste in August: good fifth to Pastoral Pursuits in Sirenia Stakes at Kempton: stays 6f: acts on good to firm going. *R. Gibson, France*

PETITE COLLEEN (IRE)   2 b.f. (May 7) Desert Sun 120 – Nishiki (USA) (Brogan   **69** (USA) 110) [2003 7m 8.1g² p8g³ f8.5g⁵ Nov 28] 11,000Y: leggy filly: half-sister to 3 winners by Case Law, including fairly useful 2000 2-y-o 7f winner Monte Mayor Golf and 6f (at 2 yrs) and 2m winner Cashiki: dam, lightly raced on Flat, winning hurdler: fair maiden: placed at Chepstow and Lingfield: stays 1m. *D. Haydn Jones*

PETITE FUTEE   4 b.f. Efisio 120 – Q Factor 90 (Tragic Role (USA)) [2003 67: p10g   **64** 10.9m³ 11.7m 11.6m 10.2m 9.7m⁴ 10.9m Sep 20] small, stocky filly: modest performer nowadays: below form after second start: stays 11f: acts on soft and good to firm going: often soon off bridle/flashes tail. *D. Haydn Jones*

PETITE MAC   3 b.f. Timeless Times (USA) 99 – Petite Elite 47 (Anfield 117) [2003   **59**
68, a59: f6g f6g⁴ f5s f6g 5d 5g 5m³ 6.1m⁶ 6m⁴ 5m 5g⁵ 5m* 5m 6m Sep 16] small filly:
modest performer: won selling handicap at Ripon in August: acts at 5f/6f: acts on
good to firm going, good to soft and fibresand: below form only run in cheekpieces:
usually ridden by 7-lb claimer Suzanne France. *N. Bycroft*

PETONGSKI   5 b.g. Petong 126 – Madam Petoski 61 (Petoski 135) [2003 75§, a–§:   **58 §**
6m 6m 5.9g 5m f6g 5g² 5d 6g⁵ 6m⁶ 6m⁴ 5m Sep 25] good-bodied gelding: modest
performer: left D. Barker after third start: stays 6f: acts on heavy and good to firm ground:
tried visored/blinkered: has reportedly had breathing problem: sometimes hangs right/
flashes tail. *B. Ellison*

PETROLERO (ARG)   4 gr.g. Perfect Parade (USA) – Louise (ARG) (Farnesio   **54 ?**
(ARG)) [2003 –: 7g 10d 7.1m f7s f8g⁴ f8g Dec 15] tall gelding: modest maiden: stays 1m:
acts on fibresand: tongue tied last 5 starts. *Mrs S. A. Liddiard*

PETROSA (IRE)   3 ch.f. Grand Lodge (USA) 125 – Top Brex (FR) (Top Ville 129)   **71**
[2003 9.9m³ 10m⁴ 8d 10m³ 8m² 10.2f³ Sep 15] 18,000F, 150,000Y: leggy, good-topped
filly: second foal: dam French 1½m winner: fair maiden: effective at 1m to 1¼m: acts
on good to firm ground: has been edgy/walked to post: possibly temperamental.
D. R. C. Elsworth

PETRULA   4 ch.g. Tagula (IRE) 116 – Bouffant (High Top 131) [2003 85: 8m 8g   **84**
10.3m* 11.9m⁴ 10m 10f² 11.9g 10.3m⁴ 10.3m 12.3g³ 10.3g⁴ Sep 13] good-bodied
gelding: fairly useful handicapper: won at Chester in May: best form short of 1½m: acts
on firm and soft going: tried visored: sometimes finishes weakly. *K. A. Ryan*

PETRUS (IRE)   7 b.g. Perugino (USA) 84 – Love With Honey (USA) (Full Pocket   **67 §**
(USA)) [2003 93d: p8g⁴ p7g p8g p7g⁴ p8g 7m* 8g p8g⁶ p8g p10g Jun 21] smallish,   **a82 d**
compact gelding: fairly useful at best on all-weather, just fair on turf nowadays: dead-
heated in handicap at Yarmouth in April: best at 7f: acts on all-weather and firm
ground: tried blinkered/tongue tied: sometimes wears net muzzle to post/taken down
early: unreliable: sold 5,000 gns in October. *C. E. Brittain*

PEYTO PRINCESS   5 b. or br.m. Bold Arrangement 127 – Bo' Babbity 75 (Strong   **72**
Gale 116) [2003 85: 5m³ 5m 6m 6d⁶ 5m 6m³ 6m⁴ 6m⁴ 6d 6f 6g p7g p7g⁴ p6g⁵ p7g⁶
Dec 6] strong, lengthy mare: fair handicapper: hasn't won since 2001: effective at 5f to
easy 7f: yet to race on heavy going, acts on any other turf and polytrack: sometimes wears
cheekpieces: tried visored: raced freely: tenth start: sometimes wanders: none too
consistent. *M. A. Buckley*

PHAMEDIC (IRE)   3 b.f. Imperial Ballet (IRE) 110 – Beeper The Great (USA)   **81**
(Whadjathink (USA)) [2003 62: 10m⁶ 9.9m⁶ 10m² 9.9m⁴ 12m⁴ 12f² 10m² 11.1m* 9.9m³
10m⁶ 12m⁶ Sep 6] tall, leggy filly: fairly useful performer: won maiden at Hamilton in
August: ran well in handicap at Beverley next time: barely stays 1½m: acts on firm and
good to soft ground: tried blinkered: has been slowly away: has hung/carried head
awkwardly/raced freely: sold 2,500 gns. *T. D. Easterby*

PHANTOM FLAME (USA)   3 b.g. Mt Livermore (USA) – Phantom Creek 92 (Mr   **80 d**
Prospector (USA)) [2003 p7g² f6s 7.1m² 6g⁵ 6m f9.4g 7f 8.5d 7m 8.2d f8.5g Nov 15]
leggy, quite good-topped gelding: third foal: brother to French 1m winner Dubai Spirit:
dam, UAE 6f winner, half-sister to Arazi and Noverre: fairly useful maiden: well below
form after third start: likely to prove best up to 1m: acts on good to firm and polytrack: tried visored: usually races prominently. *M. Johnston*

PHANTOM STOCK   3 b.g. Alzao (USA) 117 – Strike Alight (USA) (Gulch (USA))   **72 p**
[2003 –: f12g f12g⁶ f14.8s* Dec 31] good-bodied gelding: fair performer: easily best
effort when winning handicap at Wolverhampton in December by 8 lengths: will stay
easy 2m: raced only on fibresand/good to firm ground: should improve further. *W. Jarvis*

PHANTOM WIND (USA)   2 b.f. (Apr 12) Storm Cat (USA) – Ryafan (USA) 121   **96 p**
(Lear Fan (USA) 130) [2003 6.1f 6m* Oct 16] close-coupled filly: has a quick action:
third foal: dam, won up to 1¼m (including Nassau Stakes and 3 US Grade 1 events), Prix
Marcel Boussac winner at 2 yrs: much better effort in maidens (useful form) when
winning 12-runner event at Newmarket by 8 lengths from Great Fox, leading over 1f out
and eased close home: tongue tied, mulish to post/almost refused to race on debut: bred to
stay 1m: open to progress, temperament allowing. *J. H. M. Gosden*

PHARLY REEF   11 b.g. Pharly (FR) 130 – Hay Reef 72 (Mill Reef (USA) 141) [2003   **–**
f12g Apr 25] of little account on Flat nowadays. *D. Burchell*

PHAROAH'S GOLD (IRE) 5 b.g. Namaqualand (USA) – Queen Nefertiti (IRE) – 61 (Fairy King (USA)) [2003 69: f6s³ f7s* f7s f7s* f8.5g⁵ p8g p7g f7g f7g⁴ 7g f7s f8s³ **a72** f8g⁴ f8s² p7g f8.5g* f8g f8g f8.5g Dec 26] smallish, strong gelding: fair handicapper on all-weather: won at Southwell in January and February, and Wolverhampton in November: stays 8.5f: acts on all-weather, and on soft and good to firm going when last showed form on turf in 2002: sometimes visored: often slowly away: none too consistent. *D. Shaw*

PHECKLESS 4 ch.g. Be My Guest (USA) 126 – Phlirty (Pharly (FR) 130) [2003 69, **65** a75: p7g* f7g p8g 7d⁵ p7g⁶ p7g⁴ Dec 30] fair handicapper: won at Lingfield in February: **a78** best at 7f: acts on good to firm going, good to soft and polytrack, well below form on fibresand: sometimes slowly away: none too consistent. *R. F. Johnson Houghton*

PHI BETA KAPPA (USA) 3 ch.f. Diesis 133 – Thrilling Day 112 (Groom Dancer **74** (USA) 128) [2003 7m⁶ 8.2g² 10m 10s² 11.9f⁵ 8.1d Sep 26] small, plain filly: second foal: half-sister to fairly useful 2001 2-y-o 6f winner In Space (by Sky Classic): dam, 6f (at 2 yrs) to 8.5f (US Grade 3) winner, also won Nell Gwyn Stakes: fair maiden: below form last 2 starts: stays 1¼m: acts on soft going, probably on good to firm: reportedly found to be jarred up penultimate start: wandered and flashed tail on debut. *D. Morris*

PHILHARMONIC 2 b.g. (Mar 22) Victory Note (USA) 120 – Lambast 70 (Relkino **99 p** 131) [2003 5g² 6m* 6g* 6f⁴ Oct 11] 10,000Y: strong, lengthy gelding: fifth foal: half-brother to 1m seller winner Angie Marinie (by Sabrehill) and 4-y-o Firozi: dam, maiden who stayed 1½m, sister to useful performer up to 1½m My Lamb and half-sister to useful sprinter Bay Bay: useful performer: won maiden at York and minor event at Ripon (beat Desperate Dan comfortably by 2½ lengths) in September: gone in coat, creditable 2 lengths fourth of 8 to Peak To Creek in listed race at York: will stay 7f: should progress. *R. A. Fahey*

PHILLY DEE 2 b.f. (Mar 27) Bishop of Cashel 122 – Marbella Beach (IRE) (Bigstone **48** (IRE) 126) [2003 6g² 6g 6m⁵ 5m² 6g⁶ f5g⁶ 6m 5.3m⁴ f6g³ f5g² f6g⁵ f5s³ Dec 27] 800Y: smallish filly: poor mover: first foal: dam unraced: poor maiden: runner-up in sellers: likely to prove best at 5f/easy 6f: acts on fibresand and good to firm going: ran poorly in blinkers sixth/seventh starts: sometimes slowly away. *J. Jay*

PHILLY'S FOLLY 3 b.f. Catrail (USA) 123 – Lucie Edward (Puissance 110) [2003 – p7g 10m⁴ p10g Apr 9] first foal: dam unraced sister to very smart 5f performer Mind Games: well beaten in claimer and sellers: found little/carried head high second start. *G. C. H. Chung*

PHINDA FOREST (IRE) 4 br.f. Charnwood Forest (IRE) 125 – Shatalia (USA) – (Shahrastani (USA) 135) [2003 63: 12.3m Apr 2] tall, close-coupled filly: modest maiden at 3 yrs: well held only outing in 2003. *W. Storey*

PHLUKE 2 b.g. (May 5) Most Welcome 131 – Phlirty (Pharly (FR) 130) [2003 5m⁶ **76** 5.7m² 5.1g² 5d⁴ f7g³ p6g² Dec 29] good-bodied gelding: fifth foal: closely related to 4-y-o Pheckless and half-brother to 5f (at 2 yrs) to 1½m winner Pheisty (by Faustus) and 3-y-o Phred: dam tailed off both starts: fair maiden: stays 7f: acts on all-weather, good to firm and good to soft going: often races prominently. *R. F. Johnson Houghton*

PHNOM PENH (IRE) 4 b.g. Alhaarth (IRE) 126 – Crystal City (Kris 135) [2003 –: – f7s Jan 11] no form: has had tongue tied. *Miss J. Feilden*

PHOEBE BUFFAY (IRE) 6 b.m. Petardia 113 – Art Duo 86 (Artaius (USA) 129) **52** [2003 70d: f8s f8g² f7s f9.4g² p10g p10g f8.5g³ f9.4s* f8.5g⁵ 8.1m⁴ 9m³ 9.3f³ 11.6g Jun **a58** 30] close-coupled mare: modest handicapper: won apprentice race at Wolverhampton in May: effective at 1m/easy 1¼m: acts on good to firm going and all-weather: tried blinkered earlier in career: sometimes slowly away/finds little/carries head awkwardly: often races prominently: none too consistent: sold 3,700 gns in October. *J. W. Payne*

PHOENIX EYE 2 b.c. (Jan 30) Tragic Role (USA) – Eye Sight 67 (Roscoe Blake – 120) [2003 8.2d Nov 6] close-coupled colt: half-brother to 1994 2-y-o 7.5f seller winner Kings Vision (by Absalom) and 1½m winner The Roundsills (by Handsome Sailor): dam maiden: 66/1 and backward, well held in maiden at Nottingham. *M. Mullineaux*

PHOENIX NIGHTS (IRE) 3 b.g. General Monash (USA) 107 – Beauty Appeal **54** (USA) (Shadeed (USA) 135) [2003 –: f6g⁴ f6s 7f* 7g 8m³ 7m Oct 17] smallish, work-manlike gelding: modest performer: won maiden at Newcastle after lay-off in August: stays 1m: acts on firm ground, well beaten on fibresand. *A. Berry*

Pattison Canadian International Stakes, Woodbine—Phoenix Reach (right) reverses St Leger placings with Brian Boru (far left), Macaw (blinkered) splitting the pair

PHOENIX REACH (IRE)   3 b.c. Alhaarth (IRE) 126 – Carroll's Canyon (IRE)   **122 p**
(Hatim (USA) 121) [2003 83+: 12g* 12g* 14.6g³ 12d* Oct 19]

    The Pattison Canadian International Stakes, run at Woodbine in October, continues to be a happy hunting ground for challengers from Britain and Ireland, the victory of Phoenix Reach in the latest running following on from those of Mutafaweq, Mutamam and Ballingarry. It was a victory which set the seal on what had already been a fine first season as a trainer for Andrew Balding, who in June had won the Oaks with Casual Look. Balding surely couldn't have envisaged that another top-level success would come his way so soon after Epsom, and especially not with a colt who, when the Oaks was run, had still to make his seasonal reappearance. Indeed, Phoenix Reach's only experience of racing at that stage had come around twelve months earlier, when finishing a head second to Norse Dancer in a maiden at Salisbury. Phoenix Reach split a pastern shortly afterwards, an injury which required the insertion of three screws and a pin in his near-fore fetlock, and it was thought that his prospects of racing again were no better than fifty-fifty, making his exploits in the latest season all the more remarkable.
    After overcoming trouble in running to make a successful return to action in a maiden at Newbury in early-July, Phoenix Reach was turned out again quite quickly and stepped up markedly in class. He was one of ten who lined up for the Peugeot Gordon Stakes at Goodwood, where his rivals included the hat-trick-seeking Hawk Flyer and two horses who had distinguished themselves at Royal Ascot, the King Edward VII Stakes winner High Accolade and Salsalino, who had just failed to land a very strongly-run King George V Handicap. These four were involved in a thrilling finish to a race in which all were hampered to a degree at some stage. Phoenix Reach suffered interference in the early stages but soon recovered to travel well in mid-division, and he quickened readily when asked for his effort to take the lead just after the two-furlong marker. Strongly pressed from thereon, Phoenix Reach held the late challenge of High Accolade (who was giving away 5 lb all round) by a short head with Hawk Flyer and Salsalino breathing down their necks. Two of the race's recent winners, Nedawi and Millenary, had gone on to win the St Leger, and that was nominated as Phoenix Reach's next engagement. He failed to confirm Goodwood placings with High Accolade in finishing two and three quarter lengths third to Brian Boru at Doncaster, but did run a fine race for one still short of experience, and might well have challenged High Accolade for second had he not lost momentum when short of room around two furlongs out, going on well once in the clear.
    Phoenix Reach and Brian Boru were the only representatives from Britain and Ireland for the Grade 1 Canadian International five weeks later, when Doncaster placings were reversed over a distance almost three furlongs shorter. It was a slightly below average renewal of this well-established event, the seventh leg of the World Series, and Phoenix Reach, who wore blinkers for the first time, didn't need

to improve on his St Leger form to win it. Racing a bit freely and making the running in the early stages, Phoenix Reach tracked the leaders into the straight and was switched left to deliver his challenge shortly after, leading a furlong out and holding on by three quarters of a length from the former British-trained Macaw, with Brian Boru a head further back in third. Even if Phoenix Reach should fail to win another race, he has already achieved enough to ensure that there is a place at stud for him when the time comes, but, given how little racing he has had, there is every chance that Phoenix Reach will continue to improve and enhance his reputation still further as a four-year-old.

Phoenix Reach (IRE) (b.c. 2000)	Alhaarth (IRE) (b 1993)	Unfuwain (b 1985)	Northern Dancer
			Height of Fashion
		Irish Valley (ch 1982)	Irish River
			Green Valley
	Carroll's Canyon (IRE) (ch 1989)	Hatim (ch 1981)	Exclusive Native
			Sunday Purchase
		Tuna (ch 1969)	Silver Shark
			Vimelette

The useful-looking Phoenix Reach, an IR 16,000-guinea foal and 36,000-guinea yearling, is from the second crop of Alhaarth, the unbeaten champion two-year-old of 1995 and subsequently a very smart winner at a mile and a mile and a quarter. Alhaarth wasn't discredited on the first of two starts over a mile and a half, finishing fifth in the Derby, and he has been responsible for several other

Winterbeck Manor Stud's "Phoenix Reach"

winners at that trip and further, including Bandari, who also won the Gordon Stakes and finished third in the St Leger. Carroll's Canyon, the dam of Phoenix Reach, her seventh foal, has bred nothing remotely so good, though Arenas (by Revoque) has won at up to seven furlongs in Greece, The Director (by Prince Rupert) over a mile and a half in Ireland and the one-time fairly useful but ungenuine Capriolo (by Priolo) at up to a mile and a half in Britain. The unraced Carroll's Canyon is a half-sister to the 1989 Arc winner Carroll House. Their dam Tuna showed limited ability as a racehorse but has certainly made a name for herself at stud, producing a host of other winners besides Carroll House. The best of the rest was probably the Irish Cesarewitch winner Jean-Claude. Phoenix Reach showed in the St Leger that he stays an extended mile and three quarters, but all of his other races in 2003 were at a mile and a half and he is likely to be campaigned mainly at that distance again in 2004. He was raced only on good going in between shaping well on good to firm on his debut and winning on good to soft in Canada. *A. M. Balding*

PHOTOFIT 3 b.g. Polish Precedent (USA) 131 – Photogenic 93 (Midyan (USA) 124) **76** [2003 7.1g⁶ 8.3m² Jul 28] 320,000Y: quite attractive colt: first foal: dam, Irish 6f/7f winner (ran only at 2 yrs), out of half-sister to Bella Colora (dam of Stagecraft), Colorspin (dam of Opera House, Kayf Tara and 4-y-o Zee Zee Top) and Cezanne: better effort in maidens (fair form) when second at Windsor (swished tail and reluctant to enter stall), slowly away: stays 1m. *J. L. Dunlop*

PHRED 3 ch.g. Safawan 118 – Phlirty (Pharly (FR) 130) [2003 62: 8m⁶ 8.1m² p10g⁶ **77** 8.3g* 8d 8.1g⁶ 7.9m 8.1m* 8m p10g Oct 15] tall gelding: fair handicapper: won at Windsor in June and Chepstow in September: stays 1m: acts on heavy and good to firm going, probably on polytrack: tried blinkered: none too consistent. *R. F. Johnson Houghton*

PHRENOLOGIST 3 gr.g. Mind Games 121 – Leading Princess (IRE) 55 (Double **74** Schwartz 128) [2003 6m⁵ p7g⁶ p6g* p6g³ Dec 2] 15,000Y: first foal: dam 5f/6f winner: fair performer: won maiden at Lingfield in November: should be suited by 7f. *J. R. Fanshawe*

PHYSICAL FORCE 5 b.g. Casteddu 111 – Kaiserlinde (GER) (Frontal 122) [2003 –, **–** a68: f14g³ f16s f16.2g f16s f16.2g⁶ 12m 11.9m Sep 4] leggy gelding: poor handicapper: **a48 d** little form after reappearance: effective at 1½m to 2m: acts on all-weather, firm and soft going: tried blinkered/in cheekpieces: sometimes carries head awkwardly/flashes tail. *D. W. Chapman*

PIANO STAR 3 b.g. Darshaan 133 – De Stael (USA) 93 (Nijinsky (CAN) 138) [2003 **105** 10.3m² 11g⁴ 10f* 11.9m 12m³ Oct 3] tall, rather leggy gelding: fluent mover: closely related to fairly useful 1½m winner Fine Detail (by Shirley Heights) and half-brother to several at least useful winners, including very smart pair De Quest (1½m winner in France, by Rainbow Quest) and Wandesta (1¼m/1½m winner in Britain/USA, by Nashwan): dam, 2-y-o 6f winner, sister to Coronation Cup winner Quiet Fling: useful performer: won 2-runner maiden at Ayr in July: creditable efforts in listed races at Goodwood (fourth to High Accolade) and Newmarket (8 lengths third to Ekraar): stays 1½m: raced only on good ground or firmer. *Sir Michael Stoute*

PICATRIP 3 b.f. Piccolo 121 – Transylvania 85 (Wolfhound (USA) 126) [2003 –: p7g **–** Dec 17] little form. *P. R. Hedger*

PICCLED 5 b.g. Piccolo 121 – Creme de Menthe (IRE) (Green Desert (USA) 127) **91** [2003 80+, a97: f5s* f5g²* 5g* 5f³ 5m 5g⁶ 5m 5d⁶ 5d 5f 5s Nov 3] good-topped gelding: **a103** useful handicapper on all-weather, fairly useful on turf: won at Southwell (twice, on latter occasion beating Port St Charles ¾ length for fifth win in a row there) in January and Doncaster in March: best at 5f: acts on fibresand, firm and good to soft going: sometimes slowly away: usually tracks leaders. *E. J. Alston*

PICCLEYES 2 b.g. (Jan 25) Piccolo 121 – Dark Eyed Lady (IRE) 82 (Exhibitioner **65** 111) [2003 6g 5.7m⁵ 6d² 6m⁶ 6m 6d³ f6g⁵ f8.5g³ Nov 28] €40,000Y: fifth living foal: brother to 5-y-o Oh So Dusty and half-brother to 2001 2-y-o 5f/6.5f (in USA) winner Green Eyed Lady (by Greensmith) and 3-y-o Vision of Dreams: dam 5f/6f winner, including at 2 yrs: fair maiden: second at Leicester: stays 8.5f: acts on fibresand, good to firm and good to soft going: blinkered (ran poorly) fifth start. *R. Hannon*

PICCOLEZZA 4 b.f. Piccolo 121 – Sound Check 62 (Formidable (USA) 125) [2003 **?** –: p6g a6g* a6g⁴ a6g³ a6g² a5g⁴ a6g³ Nov 2] rather leggy filly: left D. Cantillon after reappearance: first form since 2 yrs when winning 2 minor events and handicap at

Jagersro in July/August: stays 6f: acts on dirt/fibresand, well beaten both starts on turf: tried tongue tied. *B. Hallencreutz, Sweden*

PICCOLO LADY   4 b.f. Piccolo 121 – Tonic Chord 49 (La Grange Music 111) [2003 –: 5m 6g 8m 6m Sep 2] workmanlike filly: maiden, well held since 2 yrs: tried visored/tongue tied. *M. Wigham*   **–**

PICCOLO PRINCE   2 ch.g. (Feb 9) Piccolo 121 – Aegean Flame 86 (Anshan 119) [2003 5g 6.1d 5m³ 5.1m⁵ 7m 7m Sep 9] 15,000F, 28,000Y: strong, stocky gelding: first foal: dam 2-y-o 5f winner: modest maiden: will prove best at 5f/6f: acts on good to firm going: sold 7,200 gns, and gelded. *B. W. Hills*   **56**

PICK A BERRY   2 b.f. (Feb 21) Piccolo 121 – Bonne de Berry (Habitat 134) [2003 p7g Dec 17] half-sister to several winners, including 5f winners Breakfast Boogie and Major Quality (both by Sizzling Melody, latter useful): dam French 1¼m winner: 14/1, well held in minor event at Lingfield, slowly away/pulling hard. *G. Wragg*   **–**

PICK OF THE CROP   2 ch.c. (Mar 28) Fraam 114 – Fresh Fruit Daily 92 (Reprimand 122) [2003 7m⁴ 7m p7g⁵ f6s² f6g⁵ Nov 10] tall colt: second foal: half-brother to 4-y-o Fruit of Glory: dam 9.7f to 1½m winner: fair maiden: second at Southwell: should stay 7f. *J. R. Jenkins*   **72**

PICKPOCKET   3 ch.g. Paris House 123 – Sabo Song 67 (Prince Sabo 123) [2003 48: 6m 5.9m 7f 9.3m Jun 25] workmanlike gelding: no longer of much account. *H. A. McWilliams*   **–**

PICKWICK AYR   4 b.g. Bijou d'Inde 127 – Ayr Classic 74 (Local Suitor (USA) 128) [2003 43: f8g f12s Feb 6] angular gelding: poor maiden: well held both starts in 2003: tried visored. *I. A. Wood*   **–**

PIC N MIX (IRE)   3 b.f. Piccolo 121 – Kingdom Princess 69 (Forzando 122) [2003 54: 8.2m 8m 9.3m 7.1f⁵ 7.2f⁶ Jul 14] leggy filly: poor maiden handicapper: should stay 1m: acts on firm ground: blinkered on reappearance: sent to Denmark. *C. W. Thornton*   **48**

PIC UP STICKS   4 gr.g. Piccolo 121 – Between The Sticks 83 (Pharly (FR) 130) [2003 101: 5f* 5g 5g 5m 6f 6g 6g 6m Aug 16] tall gelding: career-best effort when winning minor event at Beverley in April by 3½ lengths from Fayr Jag: well below form last 5 starts, pulled up final one: effective at 5f/6f: acts on firm and good to soft ground: often races prominently. *M. R. Channon*   **108 d**

PIE HIGH   4 ch.f. Salse (USA) 128 – Humble Pie 92 (Known Fact (USA) 135) [2003 96: 8.5d³ 9g² 8m⁵ 7f 8d⁴ 8g⁴ 9d 10f Aug 27] small, sturdy filly: fairly useful performer: below form after third start: effective at 7f, barely at 9f: acts on firm ground, good to soft and all-weather: often forces pace: sold 95,000 gns in December. *M. Johnston*   **94 d**

PIERPOINT (IRE)   8 ch.g. Archway (IRE) 115 – Lavinia (Habitat 134) [2003 54§, a41§: 8f³ 7m 8.1m Jul 4] smallish gelding: poor mover: poor nowadays: effective at 5f to easy 1m: acts on firm going, good to soft and fibresand: usually visored/blinkered: has been slowly away: usually races prominently: unreliable. *J. M. Bradley*   **47 §**

PIERRE PRECIEUSE   4 ch.f. Bijou d'Inde 127 – Time Or Never (FR) (Dowsing (USA) 124) [2003 10g⁵ 10.4f 8m⁴ Jun 19] IR 7,200F, 19,000Y: workmanlike filly: second foal: half-sister to 1½m winner Sungio (by Halling): dam French 5f (at 2 yrs) to 1¼m winner: well held in maidens/claimer: has been very slowly away. *J. S. Goldie*   **–**

PIETER BRUEGHEL (USA)   4 b.g. Citidancer (USA) – Smart Tally (USA) (Smarten (USA)) [2003 100: 7m 6m 7m³ 6f⁶ 6f 6g³ 7g 6g 6m 7g 7.6m Aug 30] neat gelding: useful handicapper: best efforts of season when third at Chester and Newcastle: probably best around 6f nowadays: acts on firm and good to soft ground (well held on heavy): often tongue tied: possibly best when able to dominate. *D. Nicholls*   **99**

PIGEON POINT (IRE)   3 b.f. Victory Note (USA) 120 – Mevlana (IRE) (Red Sunset 120) [2003 89: 7g 6m 6m 7m 6m Sep 13] leggy filly: fairly useful performer in 2002: well held in handicaps at 3 yrs: tried blinkered. *R. Hannon*   **–**

PIKESTAFF (USA)   5 ch.g. Diesis 133 – Navarene (USA) (Known Fact (USA) 135) [2003 52: 12.4m Jun 4] sturdy gelding: modest performer at 4 yrs: stiff task only Flat run in 2003: none too consistent. *M. A. Barnes*   **–**

PILGRIM GOOSE (IRE)   5 ch.g. Rainbows For Life (CAN) – Across The Ring (IRE) (Auction Ring (USA) 123) [2003 41§: f12s f11s Jan 16] poor maiden: has worn blinkers: carries head awkwardly/has found little: ungenuine. *Jedd O'Keeffe*   **– §**

PILGRIM PRINCESS (IRE)   5 b.m. Flying Spur (AUS) – Hasaid Lady (IRE) 69   **55**
(Shaadi (USA) 126) [2003 67: f6g³ f6g² f7g² f7g 6m⁴ 7m 5.5f³ 6d⁵ 6.9d⁶ 6m² 6.1m⁴
f6g⁶ Nov 25] rather angular, good-quartered mare: modest handicapper: effective at 6f/
easy 7f: acts on fibresand, firm and soft going: blinkered once as 2-y-o: often races
prominently: sometimes finds little: reportedly bled seventh start. *E. J. Alston*

PILGRIM SPIRIT (USA)   3 b. or br.f. Saint Ballado (CAN) – Oshima (USA) (Mr   **66**
Prospector (USA)) [2003 64p: 10m⁵ 11.8m⁵ 10d 14.1m² 14m Aug 8] big, rather leggy
filly: fair maiden: pulled up final start: stays 1¾m: unraced on extremes of going: tried
visored (looked reluctant early and well beaten). *J. H. M. Gosden*

PILIBERTO   3 br.g. Man of May – Briska (IRE) 69 (River Falls 113) [2003 –: f6g f7s   **–**
f12g Mar 1] probably of little account. *C. N. Kellett*

PINCHBECK   4 b.g. Petong 126 – Veuve Hoornaert (IRE) 88 (Standaan (FR) 118)   **82**
[2003 83: 6m 6m 6m⁵ 6.1m³ 6m⁴ 6d* 7d 6g³ 6m 6.1m³ Oct 28] strong, good sort: fairly useful
performer: won minor event at Leicester in July: good third in handicaps last 2 starts:
best at 6f: acts on good to firm and good to soft ground: effective blinkered or not, wore
cheekpieces last 5 starts. *M. A. Jarvis*

PINCHINCHA (FR)   9 b.g. Priolo (USA) 127 – Western Heights (Shirley Heights 130)   **88**
[2003 89: 10d 10m⁴ 10g³ 12m² 12m⁴ 10.3m* 10f 10m⁵ Sep 25] workmanlike gelding:
fairly useful handicapper: won at Doncaster in August: effective at 1¼m/1½m: acts
on fibresand and any turf going: tried visored earlier in career: tough and consistent.
D. Morris

PINES OF ROME   3 b.c. Charnwood Forest (IRE) 125 – Ninfa of Cisterna (Polish   **44**
Patriot (USA) 128) [2003 44: p8g f7s² f8g⁵ Jan 21] poor maiden: seems to stay 1m: acts
on all-weather: blinkered in 2003. *G. G. Margarson*

PININI   4 b.f. Pivotal 124 – Forget Me (IRE) (Don't Forget Me 127) [2003 63d: p10g⁶   **52**
p10g 8m 7m 6g 7m³ 6m Jun 2] modest maiden: effective at 7f, barely at 1¼m: acts
on polytrack, raced only on good going or firmer on turf: sometimes visored. *Mrs
C. A. Dunnett*

PINKERTON   3 b.c. Alzao (USA) 117 – Dina Line (USA) 60 (Diesis 133) [2003 96:   **90**
9m² 9.9g 8m³ 8m Jun 19] close-coupled, quite attractive colt: fairly useful performer:
stays 1m: acts on soft and good to firm going: sent to Hong Kong, renamed My Ego and
joined T. W. Leung. *R. Hannon*

PINK FIZZ   3 b.f. Efisio 120 – Pennine Pink (IRE) 72 (Pennine Walk 120) [2003 –:   **–**
8m f11g 8.1m Aug 7] workmanlike filly: well held in 4 claimers: tried in cheekpieces.
J. G. Portman

PINK SAPPHIRE (IRE)   2 ch.f. (Mar 19) Bluebird (USA) 125 – Highbrook (USA)   **63 +**
88 (Alphabatim (USA) 126) [2003 6g⁵ 6g* 6g Sep 12] 35,000Y: good-bodied filly: third
foal: half-sister to 6-y-o Niagara: dam 1¼m to 13f winner, also useful over hurdles:
modest form when winning maiden at Windsor in August by short head from Totally
Yours: well beaten other starts: should stay at least 7f. *D. R. C. Elsworth*

PINK SUPREME   2 ch.f. (Feb 14) Night Shift (USA) – Bright Spells 93 (Salse (USA)   **70**
128) [2003 5s² May 19] 35,000Y: good-bodied filly: fourth foal: sister to useful Irish
1997 2-y-o 7f winner Cultural Role: dam, 6f winner at 2 yrs, stayed 1¾m: fair form when
slow-starting second of 7 in maiden at Windsor: had setback after. *I. A. Wood*

PINOT NOIR   5 b.g. Saddlers' Hall (IRE) 126 – Go For Red (IRE) (Thatching 131)   **–**
[2003 80d: 10.1m May 14] rather leggy, useful-looking gelding: one-time fairly useful
performer: well held in selling handicap only run in 2003: blinkered (downed tools) once:
possibly temperamental. *G. J. Smith*

PINTLE   3 b.f. Pivotal 124 – Boozy 111 (Absalom 128) [2003 5m² 5m* 5.1m⁵ Aug 20]   **69**
20,000Y: smallish filly: eighth foal: closely related to 4-y-o Polar Impact and 6-y-o
Skylark and half-sister to 2 winners, including 5f winner (including at 2 yrs) Gwespyr (by
Sharpo): dam best at 5f: fair form: won maiden at Kempton (by 6 lengths) in August:
below form in minor event at Nottingham next time: should stay 6f. *J. L. Spearing*

PIPER   3 ch.g. Atraf 116 – Lady-H (Never So Bold 135) [2003 –: 5m 6f 5.9m 8.3m 10m   **–**
Sep 4] no form. *D. W. Barker*

PIPS MAGIC (IRE)   7 b.g. Pips Pride 117 – Kentucky Starlet (USA) 69 (Cox's Ridge   **68**
(USA)) [2003 –: 5m 6d² 6d 6g 6m* 6g 6g⁴ 6g⁴ 6m⁴ 6m 6m⁵ 6f⁶ 5m Sep 18] good-bodied
gelding: fair handicapper: won at Hamilton in June: stays 6f: acts on firm and soft going:
blinkered final start. *J. S. Goldie*

PIPSSALIO (SPA)   6 b.g. Pips Pride 117 – Tesalia (SPA) (Finissimo (SPA)) [2003   **45**
p10g p12g f9.4s 12g f11g⁴ f16g³ Dec 16] workmanlike gelding: just poor form in 2003:
stays easy 2m: acts on fibresand and heavy going: tried blinkered/tongue tied. *Jamie
Poulton*

PIPS SONG (IRE)   8 ch.g. Pips Pride 117 – Friendly Song 48 (Song 132) [2003 78,   **69 d**
a74: f7g⁴ f6g f6g f6s 6s 6m f5g² f7s⁶ f6g f6g f6g³ f6g f7s f6g Dec 19] lengthy gelding:
poor mover: fair performer: below form after seventh outing: effective at stiff 5f to 7f:
acts on all-weather, all turf wins on good ground or softer: tried blinkered/visored:
sometimes awkward leaving stall: none too consistent. *P. W. Hiatt*

PIQUET   5 br.m. Mind Games 121 – Petonellajill 73 (Petong 126) [2003 –, a52?: f8.5s   **46**
p10g⁶ p10g 8.3g 8f⁵ 9f 6f⁴ 6m⁶ 6m 6m 10f 10f⁵ 10m p10g* Dec 30] poor performer: won
seller at Lingfield in December: effective at 6f, stays easy 1¼m: acts on polytrack and
any turf going: has hung left. *J. J. Bridger*

PIRI PIRI (IRE)   3 b. or br.f. Priolo (USA) 127 – Hot Curry (USA) (Sharpen Up 127)   **75**
[2003 71: 7m⁶ 7m⁵ 7m 8g 10m⁴ 10d³ 8.3g⁵ 9.7m* 12.3m³ 10.1m⁶ 10g⁶ p12g Oct 8] rather
leggy, workmanlike filly: fair handicapper: won at Folkestone in August: probably needs
further than 1m nowadays, and stays 1½m: acts on good to firm and good to soft going,
probably on firm: has looked none too keen. *P. J. McBride*

PIRLIE HILL   3 b.f. Sea Raven (IRE) 75 – Panayr (Faraway Times (USA) 123) [2003   **43**
–: 5.9f⁴ 6m⁴ 5g⁴ 6f⁵ 5m 5g 5g Nov 5] good-bodied filly: poor maiden: stays 6f: raced only
on good ground or firmer on turf. *Miss L. A. Perratt*

PIROUETTES (IRE)   3 b.f. Royal Applause 124 – Dance Serenade (IRE) 54 (Marju   **61**
(IRE) 127) [2003 73: 6m⁴ f7s³ 6f p7g⁴ f8g³ p10g⁴ f8.5g Dec 26] big, lengthy filly: modest
maiden: left J. Gosden after third start: stays easy 1¼m: acts on good to firm ground, good
to soft and all-weather: ran badly in visor/cheekpieces. *Miss Gay Kelleway*

PISTE BLEU (FR)   3 b.f. Pistolet Bleu (IRE) 133 – Thamissia (FR) (Riverman (USA)   **65**
131) [2003 65: f7g 10f 11.6d 10g³ 9.7m 11g³ 12f* 13.8m⁶ 12.6m⁵ Sep 20] fair handicapper: left R. Beckett 3,500 gns prior to winning at Catterick in August: stays 1½m: acts
on firm ground: tried tongue tied. *R. Ford*

PIVOTAL GUEST   2 b.c. (Feb 13) Pivotal 124 – Keep Quiet 54 (Reprimand 122)   **90 d**
[2003 5.2m³ 5m* 7f³ 7s² 7d² 7.1m⁵ 7g⁴ 7d 6m⁵ 7f 7g⁵ 7m⁴ 7m 7d Nov 8] 36,000F,
140,000Y: leggy, quite attractive colt: third foal: half-brother to 1999 2-y-o 7f winner
Villa Romana (by Komaite): dam maiden who stayed 1m: fairly useful performer: won
maiden at Newcastle in April: in frame in minor events and listed race (fourth at Deauville on seventh start) after: stays 7f: unraced on heavy going, acts on any other: visored
last 5 starts, running creditably on first occasion only: sold 12,000 gns. *M. R. Channon*

PIVOTAL POINT   3 b.g. Pivotal 124 – True Precision 84 (Presidium 124) [2003 6g²   **100**
6g* 6m³ 5g⁵ 6g² Oct 31] 9,000Y: strong, close-coupled gelding: has a quick, fluent
action: fourth foal: half-brother to 3 winners, including 7-y-o Foreign Editor and 1999
2-y-o 5f winner Uncle Exact (by Distant Relative): dam 5f to 7f winner: useful performer,
lightly raced: refused to enter stall on intended debut at 2 yrs: won maiden at Windsor in
June: very good neck second to Masaader in minor event at Newmarket final outing: will
prove best at 5f/6f. *P. J. Makin*

PIZAZZ   2 ch.c. (Apr 12) Pivotal 124 – Clare Celeste 73 (Coquelin (USA) 121) [2003   **74 p**
6m Sep 19] 34,000Y: half-brother to several winners, including 1992 2-y-o 6f/7f winner
Abergele (by Absalom) and 1m/1¼m winner Sovereigns Court (by Statoblest), both
fairly useful: dam, maiden, best effort at 7f at 2 yrs: 12/1, 4½ lengths seventh of 16 to
Oriental Warrior in maiden at Newbury, green and not given hard time: will improve.
B. J. Meehan

PLACE COWBOY (IRE)   2 b.c. (Feb 26) Compton Place 125 – Paris Joelle (IRE)   **69**
(Fairy King (USA)) [2003 f6g² Jun 25] IR 34,000F, 85,000Y: fourth living foal: brother
to 3-y-o St Austell and half-brother to 4-y-o Hoh's Back: dam ran once at 2 yrs: favourite,
second of 9 in maiden at Southwell, slowly away and very green: should stay 7f.
J. A. Osborne

PLACE ROUGE (IRE)   4 b.f. Desert King (IRE) 129 – Palmeraie (USA) (Lear Fan   **112**
(USA) 130) [2003 105: 11.9g* 9.9g 10f² 12.5d 12g⁴ 10.5g⁴ Nov 11] good-topped filly:
second foal: half-sister to smart French 1m (at 2 yrs) to 15.5f winner Pushkin (by
Caerleon) and 3-y-o Policy Maker: dam, ran once, half-sister to dam of Peintre Celebre
out of half-sister to Pawneese: smart performer: won handicap at Longchamp and listed
race at Saint-Cloud in 2002, then left E. Lellouche 270,000 gns: improved form when
winning bet365 Lancashire Oaks at Haydock on reappearance in July by 5 lengths from

Mr W. S. Farish III's "Place Rouge"

Flying Wanda: creditable fourth to Imperial Dancer in St Simon Stakes at Newbury and Walkamia in Prix Fille de l'Air at Toulouse: stays 1½m: acts on heavy ground, ran respectably on firm. *J. H. M. Gosden*

PLANTERS PUNCH (IRE) 2 br.c. (Mar 6) Cape Cross (IRE) 129 – Jamaican Punch **– p** (IRE) (Shareef Dancer (USA) 135) [2003 8m 8g Oct 25] €60,000Y: strong, useful-looking colt: half-brother to several winners, including 1996 2-y-o 6f winner Close Relative (by Distant Relative) and 1m winner Mustique Dream (by Don't Forget Me), both fairly useful: dam ran twice: signs of ability in maidens at Newmarket (second favourite) and Newbury (showed up long way), slowly away both times: type to do fair bit better as 3-y-o. *R. Hannon*

PLATEAU 4 b.g. Zamindar (USA) 116 – Painted Desert 89 (Green Desert (USA) 127) **91** [2003 98: 6m 5f 5f 5f 6g 6m Sep 19] good-bodied gelding: fairly useful handicapper, lightly raced: effective at 5f/6f: acts on good to firm and good to soft ground: has been early to post: sold 30,000 gns. *D. Nicholls*

PLATINUM BOY (IRE) 3 b.g. Goldmark (USA) 113 – Brown Foam (Horage 124) **–** [2003 49, a65: p8g² f9.4g³ f8g³ f9.4g* f8.5g⁵ f9.4s 10m p10g Dec 20] compact gelding: **a61 d** modest on all-weather, poor on turf: won seller at Wolverhampton (left K. Ryan) in February: no form after: stays 9.4f: acts on all-weather and good to firm going: effective in cheekpieces/visor, below form in blinkers: sometimes edges left. *M. Wellings*

PLATINUM CHARMER (IRE) 3 b.g. Kahyasi 130 – Mystic Charm (Nashwan **76 d** (USA) 135) [2003 76, a79: p10g⁵ f8.5g⁴ f11s³ f7s 12.1m 16.1m 13.8d f11s⁴ Dec 13] compact gelding: fair performer at best: should stay at least 1½m: acts on all-weather and soft going: has wandered. *K. A. Ryan*

PLATINUM CHIEF 2 b.g. (Feb 12) Puissance 110 – Miss Beverley (Beveled (USA)) **53** [2003 5g 5m 6m³ 6g⁶ 7m 7.5m² 8g 7.1m⁴ 8.2m f8g f7g⁴ f8.5s⁵ Dec 31] 9,000Y: close-coupled gelding: second foal: closely related to 2002 2-y-o 6f winner Night Games (by Mind Games): dam unraced: modest maiden: second in selling nursery at Beverley: stays

1m: acts on good to firm going, probably on fibresand: blinkered (ran as if amiss) ninth/tenth starts. *A. Berry*

PLATINUM PIRATE 2 b.g. (Apr 17) Merdon Melody 98 – Woodland Steps 86 (Bold **49** Owl 101) [2003 6g f6s 6d 8g⁶ f8s f9.4g f9.4g Dec 22] 10,500Y: sturdy, close-coupled gelding: fifth foal: brother to 3 winners, including 5f (at 2 yrs) to 7f winner Blackpool Mamma's: dam, 2-y-o 7f winner, sister to useful sprinter Amron: poor maiden: should stay 1¼m: blinkered sixth start: sometimes races freely/carries head high. *K. R. Burke*

PLAUSABELLE 2 b.f. (May 10) Royal Applause 124 – Sipsi Fach 100 (Prince Sabo **51** 123) [2003 6m 6m 6m⁶ Sep 9] 11,000F, 15,000Y: seventh foal: half-sister to 3 winners, including smart performer up to 1¼m Supply And Demand (by Belmez) and fairly useful 1m winner Sipsi Fawr (by Selkirk): dam 6f (at 2 yrs) to 1¼m winner: modest form in maidens: likely to stay 7f: sold 1,700 gns. *T. D. Easterby*

PLAYFUL DANE (IRE) 6 b.g. Dolphin Street (FR) 125 – Omicida (IRE) (Danehill **64** (USA) 126) [2003 44: f6s⁴ f5g⁴ 6d 6m* 6.1g 7d⁴ 6m³ 6f* 6f 5g Oct 22] good-topped gelding: modest handicapper: won at Redcar (amateurs) in May and Newcastle in August: stays 6f: acts on fibresand and firm ground, probably on good to soft: has been slowly away: races prominently. *W. S. Cunningham*

PLAYFUL SPIRIT 4 b.f. Mind Games 121 – Kalimat 74 (Be My Guest (USA) 126) **56** [2003 76d: f8s³ f7s³ f6g f8g⁵ 6.1m 5.1g 7g 5m³ 6.1m f6s 7d f6g* Dec 9] leggy filly: modest performer: left S. R. Bowring prior to winning seller at Southwell in December (hung right): effective at 5f to 1m: acts on fibresand and good to firm going: sometimes visored/races freely: no easy ride. *J. Balding*

PLAY MISTY (IRE) 4 b.f. Dr Devious (IRE) 127 – Mystic Step (IRE) 90 (Fairy **–** King (USA)) [2003 51: p8g Jan 15] maiden: well held only 4-y-o start: tried blinkered. *B. R. Johnson*

PLAY THAT TUNE 3 ch.f. Zilzal (USA) 137 – Military Tune (IRE) (Nashwan (USA) **97** 135) [2003 80+: 7d³ 7m² 7g 8.1d³ 7d³ Sep 11] strong, angular filly: useful performer, lightly raced: reportedly chipped knees on second 2-y-o outing: won maiden at Newmarket in May: good third in listed races at Sandown (to Lady Bear) and Doncaster (to impressive Tantina): free-going sort, and likely to prove best at 7f/1m: has form on good to firm going, very best efforts on good to soft. *H. R. A. Cecil*

PLAY THE FLUTE 3 ch.f. Piccolo 121 – Son Et Lumiere (Rainbow Quest (USA) **–** 134) [2003 47: p12g f9.4g Mar 22] little form in 2003. *M. Blanshard*

PLAYTIME BLUE 3 b.g. Komaite (USA) – Miss Calculate 67 (Mummy's Game **69** 120) [2003 67: 7.1m 5s f5s⁴ 5m 5f* 5m 5g* 5g⁴ 5m⁴ 5d p5g f5s² Dec 31] lengthy, good-quartered gelding: fair handicapper: won at Kempton in July and Windsor in August: probably best at 5f: acts on all-weather, firm and soft ground: sometimes edges left: often makes running. *K. R. Burke*

PLEASE THE PRINCE (IRE) 3 b.g. Desert Prince (IRE) 130 – Inner Door (IRE) **68** (King of Clubs 124) [2003 –: p8g² 8m⁵ 7.5m³ 8.5m 7.5d² 10g² 10d Dec 1] fair maiden: second at Lingfield on reappearance (final start for C. Wall) and at Pisa in seller (left V. Valiani) and handicap in autumn: stays 1¼m: acts on good to firm going, good to soft and polytrack. *M. Bucci, Italy*

PLEASURE PLACE (IRE) 3 b.f. Compton Place 125 – Shifting Time 70 (Night **118** Shift (USA)) [2003 104: 5g* 6m* 5g* 6m* 5m* 5s 5m* Oct 19] 2,000Y: second foal: dam, 6f winner, half-sister to useful sprinter Poker Chip: smart performer, winner of 11 of her 15 starts: successful 5 times at 2 yrs, notably in Prix d'Arenberg at Maisons-Laffitte and 2 listed races at Rome: won all 6 races in Italy in 2003, namely 2 minor events at Rome, listed race at Milan and Premio Tudini at Rome (beat Dream Chief ½ length) in first half of year, and another listed race and Premio Omenoni (easily, by 3 lengths from Slap Shot) at Milan in autumn: well beaten in Prix de l'Abbaye at Longchamp penultimate start: effective at 5f/6f: has won on good to soft ground but seems best on good or firmer: has been tongue tied: front runner: reliable. *R. Menichetti, Italy*

PLEASURE SEEKER 2 b.f. (Mar 1) First Trump 118 – Purse 78 (Pursuit of Love **–** 124) [2003 6m 6m Oct 16] 2,500Y: leggy filly: first foal: dam, maiden who stayed 1m, out of half-sister to Grand Lodge: well held in maiden at Newbury and sales race at Newmarket (moved poorly to post). *M. D. I. Usher*

PLEASURE TIME 10 ch.g. Clantime 101 – First Experience 58 (Le Johnstan 123) **56** [2003 63: f5s⁴ f5g f5g 5m 5m f5g 5m⁵ 5.1g⁵ Aug 1] leggy, good-topped gelding: modest performer: best at 5f: acts on fibresand, best turf form on good going or firmer: has worn blinkers, visored nowadays: often a front runner. *C. Smith*

PLEINMONT POINT (IRE) 5 b.g. Tagula (IRE) 116 – Cree's Figurine 63 (Cree- **62**
town 123) [2003 62: p7g⁴ p7g p7g³ p7g p8g⁴ p8g May 28] big, workmanlike gelding:
modest maiden: stays easy 1m: acts on polytrack, heavy and good to firm ground:
blinkered last 4 starts in 2002: tried tongue tied. *P. D. Evans*

PLOUGH BOY 5 br.g. Komaite (USA) – Plough Hill (North Briton 67) [2003 f12g **–**
Feb 1] modest winner at 3 yrs: refused to settle only Flat run since. *M. J. Gingell*

PLOVERS LANE (IRE) 2 b.g. (Apr 25) Dushyantor (USA) 123 – Sweet Alma 67 **–**
(Alzao (USA) 117) [2003 8m p7g Oct 8] IR 6,500F, 16,000Y: closely related to 4-y-o
Countess Miletrian and 3-y-o Jannadav and half-brother to 3 winners: dam, Irish 1¼m
winner, half-sister to high-class 1m/1¼m performer Montekin: well held in maidens.
M. P. Tregoning

PLUM 3 br.f. Pivotal 124 – Rose Chime (IRE) 58 (Tirol 127) [2003 6m⁴ 7f⁴ 7.6g³ Jul **69**
16] 14,000Y: rather leggy filly: third foal: half-sister to 4-y-o Tiger Tops: dam 2-y-o 6f/7f
winner: best effort in maidens (fair form) when fourth to Golden Heart at Salisbury
second start: may prove best up to 7f. *A. C. Stewart*

PLUME OF FEATHERS (IRE) 3 b.f. Ali-Royal (IRE) 127 – Feather-In-Her-Cap **–**
(Primo Dominie 121) [2003 6m 8.1m Sep 8] well-made filly: seventh foal: half-sister to
several winners, including Irish 1½m winner Flame of Sion (by Be My Chief): dam
unraced half-sister to smart sprinter Governor General: well held in maidens at Kempton
and Warwick. *L. G. Cottrell*

PLUMPIE MAC (IRE) 2 b.f. (Apr 15) Key of Luck (USA) 126 – Petrine (IRE) **–**
(Petorius 117) [2003 5g 5g⁶ 6m May 22] close-coupled filly: seventh foal: half-sister to
several winners, including fairly useful 1999 2-y-o 5f winner Imperialist (by Imperial
Frontier) and 3-y-o Little Venice: dam ran 4 times in Ireland: well held in minor events/
maiden. *N. Bycroft*

PLURALIST (IRE) 7 b.g. Mujadil (USA) 119 – Encore Une Fois (IRE) 84 (Shirley **–**
Heights 130) [2003 9f 12m 16.2d⁶ 14.1m⁵ Aug 9] small, lengthy gelding: fair performer
at 4 yrs: lightly raced and well held since: tried tongue tied. *J. S. Moore*

PLUTOCRAT (USA) 6 ch.g. Silver Hawk (USA) 123 – Satin Velvet (USA) 103 (El **65**
Gran Senor (USA) 136) [2003 74: f7g⁶ 7m 7m 7f³ 7.5m 7m⁵ 7m 8g⁵ 7m* 6.9f⁵ 7m⁵ Sep
9] fair performer: won handicap at Catterick in August: effective at 7f to 9f: acts on dirt
and fibresand, raced only on good ground or firmer on turf: usually wears cheekpieces:
usually slowly away: refused to enter stall once: sold 7,000 gns. *Mrs L. Stubbs*

POACHER'S PARADISE 2 ch.g. (Mar 2) Inchinor 119 – Transylvania 85 (Wolf- **52**
hound (USA) 126) [2003 5g 5m f5s Sep 26] 5,000Y: lengthy gelding: second foal: dam
7f/1m winner: modest form in maidens: should stay at least 7f. *M. W. Easterby*

POINT CALIMERE (IRE) 2 b.g. (Feb 16) Fasliyev (USA) 120 – Mountain Ash **80**
107 (Dominion 123) [2003 f6g 6d³ 5f³ 6f Jul 12] 26,000Y: fifth foal: half-brother to
several winners, including useful 7f/1m winners Analyser and Musical Treat (both by
Royal Academy), latter also successful in Canada: dam, 7f/1m winner, out of Cheveley
Park second Red Berry: fairly useful maiden: third at Windsor and Kempton: reportedly
jarred up final start, gelded after: not sure to stay much beyond 6f. *C. R. Egerton*

POINT MAN (IRE) 3 b.g. Pivotal 124 – Pursuit of Truth (USA) 69 (Irish River (FR) **–**
131) [2003 7g 7d 6g 10m⁵ 10m Oct 13] 30,000F, 42,000Y: sturdy, quite attractive
gelding: seventh foal: half-brother to several winners, including 7-y-o Spring Pursuit and
1999 2-y-o 1m winner First Truth (also by Rudimentary), both fairly useful: dam 2-y-o 7f
winner on only start: little form. *J. W. Payne*

POINT OF DISPUTE 8 b.g. Cyrano de Bergerac 120 – Opuntia (Rousillon (USA) **88 §**
133) [2003 101: 7m 7g 7m⁵ 6m⁶ 7m³ 7.1g p7g² Oct 15] tall gelding: fairly useful performer: best at 6f/7f: acts on all-weather, firm and good to soft going: visored: sometimes
sweats: often slowly away/held up: wayward. *P. J. Makin*

POISE (IRE) 2 b.f. (Jan 30) Rainbow Quest (USA) 134 – Crepe Ginger (IRE) 67 **93 P**
(Sadler's Wells (USA) 132) [2003 7m² Sep 19] 340,000Y: rather leggy, lengthy filly:
second foal: half-sister to 3-y-o Gin 'N' Fonic: dam, ran 3 times in Ireland, half-sister to
dam of Daylami and Dalakhani: 7/2, head second of 8 to Silk Fan in minor event at
Newbury, staying on strongly after running green: will be well suited by 1¼m/1½m:
useful prospect at least, sure to win races. *Sir Michael Stoute*

POKER 2 ch.g. (Mar 16) Hector Protector (USA) 124 – Clunie 84 (Inchinor 119) [2003 **–**
f6g 6m⁶ p6g Oct 3] first foal: dam 6f winner, including at 2 yrs: signs of only a little
ability in maidens at Lingfield and Wolverhampton. *W. J. Haggas*

POLANSKI MILL　4 b.g. Polish Precedent (USA) 131 – Mill On The Floss 117 (Mill　–
Reef (USA) 141) [2003 –: 10m 13.3m 12m 16m Sep 25] lightly-raced maiden: little form.
C. A. Horgan

POLAR BEAR　3 ch.g. Polar Falcon (USA) 126 – Aim For The Top (USA) 111 (Irish　**101 p**
River (FR) 131) [2003 73p: 7g* 8m* Sep 20] rather unfurnished gelding: useful handicapper, lightly raced: successful both starts in 2003, at Newmarket in August and Ayr
(beat Nashaab comfortably by 2½ lengths despite still seeming green and carrying head
high) in September: acts on good to firm ground: reportedly had breathing
problem on debut at 2 yrs: should continue to improve and win more races. *W. J. Haggas*

POLAR BEN　4 b.g. Polar Falcon (USA) 126 – Woodbeck 90 (Terimon 124) [2003　**118**
106+: 7.1d² 7m⁶ 7g⁵ 8g³ 7d* 7s 8g Nov 1] rather leggy, useful-looking gelding: smart
performer: sweating, better than ever when winning GNER Park Stakes at Doncaster in
September by neck from With Reason: below form in Prix de la Foret at Longchamp
(checked in rear early) and listed race at Newmarket last 2 starts: effective at 7f/1m: has
won on good to firm going, but goes very well on softer than good (acts on soft).
J. R. Fanshawe

POLAR DANCER　2 b.f. (Apr 29) Polar Falcon (USA) 126 – Petonica (IRE) 77　**71**
(Petoski 135) [2003 p8g p8g⁶ p10g³ Nov 29] 28,000Y: seventh foal: closely related to
5-y-o Bourgainville and half-sister to useful 6f (at 2 yrs)/7f winner Yorkie George (by
Efisio) and 4-y-o Gig Harbor: dam second at 7f at 2 yrs: fair form in maidens at Lingfield:
best effort when third to Pukka: stays 1¼m. *Mrs A. J. Perrett*

POLAR DANCE (USA)　5 gr. or ro.g. Nureyev (USA) 131 – Arctic Swing (USA)　**– §**
(Swing Till Dawn (USA)) [2003 –, a54§: f8g f7g Mar 1] ungenuine maiden: reluctant to
race last 2 outings: visored penultimate start. *J. W. Unett*

POLAR FORCE　3 ch.g. Polar Falcon (USA) 126 – Irish Light (USA) 91 (Irish River　**82 d**
(FR) 131) [2003 105: 8g⁴ 6m⁶ 7g⁶ 5f 6m 7.1m⁶ 6m⁵ 7f p7g⁶ 5m⁵ 6g p6g 5m⁶ 6d f6g p6g³
Nov 29] neat gelding: just fairly useful at best in 2003: should stay 7f: has form on firm
going/polytrack (some promise on fibresand), best efforts on softer than good: slowly
away sixth/tenth outings. *M. R. Channon*

POLAR GALAXY　2 br.f. (Apr 10) Polar Falcon (USA) 126 – June Brilly (IRE)　**58**
(Fayruz 116) [2003 5f⁵ 5m 5m⁵ 7m⁴ 5.9m 6d Sep 26] €25,000Y: leggy filly: fourth
foal: half-sister to Italian 7.5f (including at 2 yrs) and 9f winner My Bijou (by Bijou
d'Inde): dam unraced half-sister to smart Irish performer up to 1½m/high-class hurdler
I'm Supposin: modest maiden: well beaten in nurseries last 2 starts: free-going sort,
barely stays 7f: acts on good to firm ground. *C. W. Fairhurst*

POLAR HAZE　6 ch.g. Polar Falcon (USA) 126 – Sky Music 85 (Absalom 128) [2003　**44**
55, a60: f5g² f6g 5.3m 6m 7m 7m 7.5d 7g f6g⁴ f6g* f5g f6g² Dec 19] lengthy, good-　**a60**
quartered gelding: modest on all-weather, poor on turf: left Miss S. Hall after second start:
won seller at Southwell in December: best at 5f/6f: acts on firm ground, soft and
fibresand: tried blinkered, usually visored. *Mrs Lydia Pearce*

GNER Park Stakes, Doncaster—
a cracking finish between Polar Ben (centre), With Reason (far side) and Tarjman

POLAR IMPACT   4 br.c. Polar Falcon (USA) 126 – Boozy 111 (Absalom 128) [2003   **84**
80: 7g 5g 7m 6.1m⁴ 5g² 5m³ 6g⁶ 5d 5.1m 5g 5m 5g* 6.1m a7s* a5g* Dec 14] strong,
short-backed colt: fairly useful performer: won handicap at Newcastle in October and
(after being sold 8,000 gns from A. Berry) minor events at Dos Hermanas in November/
December: stays 7f: acts on soft and good to firm going, and on sand, ran as if amiss on
firm: has been early to post. *J. H. Brown, Spain*

POLAR JEM   3 b.f. Polar Falcon (USA) 126 – Top Jem 85 (Damister (USA) 123)   **75**
[2003 8.1m⁶ 10g³ 10.1m² 10m* Oct 22] leggy filly: first foal: dam, 9f/1¼m winner,
half-sister to smart performer up to 1½m Polar Red (by Polar Falcon): fair form: won
maiden at Nottingham in October by neck from Change Partners, taking good hold and
hanging markedly right: stays 1¼m. *G. G. Margarson*

POLAR KINGDOM   5 b.g. Pivotal 124 – Scarlet Lake 60 (Reprimand 122) [2003   **80**
83: 7g² p8g f8s Dec 27] rangy gelding: fairly useful handicapper: gambled on, ran
creditably on reappearance: below form on all-weather after: effective at 6f (given test) to
7.6f: acts on soft going: tried visored/blinkered/tongue tied. *T. D. Barron*

POLAR ROCK   5 ch.m. Polar Falcon (USA) 126 – South Rock 102 (Rock City 120)   **–**
[2003 –: 11.6g Jun 30] lengthy mare: fair maiden at 3 yrs: lightly raced and well held
since: slowly away/raced freely only outing in 2003. *Jean-Rene Auvray*

POLAR TRYST   4 ch.f. Polar Falcon (USA) 126 – Lovers Tryst 91 (Castle Keep 121)   **72**
[2003 68: 14.1g 13m² 13.1m² Jun 20] leggy, lengthy, unfurnished filly: fair maiden
handicapper: stays 13f: acts on firm and good to soft ground. *Lady Herries*

POLAR WAY   4 ch.g. Polar Falcon (USA) 126 – Fetish 85 (Dancing Brave (USA) 140)   **114**
[2003 112p: 6m³ 6f⁶ 6m 6f² 6m 7m* Oct 25] angular, workmanlike gelding: unimpressive
mover in slower paces: smart performer: won minor event at Doncaster in October easily
by 1½ lengths from Digital: earlier ran well when sixth to Choisir in Golden Jubilee
Stakes at Royal Ascot and ¾-length second to Acclamation in Diadem Stakes at Ascot:
raced only at 6f/7f: successful on soft going on debut, raced only on good to firm/firm
since. *Mrs A. J. Perrett*

POLDEN CHIEF   3 br.g. Atraf 116 – Maid of Mischief (Be My Chief (USA) 122)   **61**
[2003 54: 7m* 7g 7g⁶ 8g Jul 30] modest performer: won claimer at Salisbury (left
G. Balding £7,000) on reappearance: below form last 2 starts: will probably stay 1m:
raced only on good/good to firm ground. *J. W. Mullins*

POLE STAR   5 b. or br.g. Polar Falcon (USA) 126 – Ellie Ardensky 100 (Slip Anchor   **114**
136) [2003 111: 16.2g³ 16.4m² 20m³ 15d 18d⁶ Sep 11] tall, angular gelding: smart performer: good placed efforts in 2003 in Sagaro Stakes at Ascot, Henry II Stakes at Sandown
(2½ lengths second to Mr Dinos) and Gold Cup at Royal Ascot (6¾ lengths third to Mr
Dinos): below form in Prix Kergorlay at Deauville and Doncaster Cup (favourite,
tailed-off last, reportedly found to be lame) last 2 starts: stays 2½m: acts on any going:
usually held up: reliable. *J. R. Fanshawe*

POLICASTRO   5 b.g. Anabaa (USA) 130 – Belle Arrivee 87 (Bustino 136) [2003 64:
p13g p10g f12g Feb 14] modest maiden: well below form in 2003, leaving P. Mitchell
after second start: sometimes tongue tied. *Miss K. M. George*

POLICY MAKER (IRE)   3 b.c. Sadler's Wells (USA) 132 – Palmeraie (USA) (Lear   **117**
Fan (USA) 130) [2003 10d* 10d* 12g² 12.5s* 12.5s* 12s Oct 5] tall, rather leggy colt:
third foal: half-brother to smart French 1m (at 2 yrs) to 15.5f winner Pushkin (by
Caerleon) and 4-y-o Place Rouge: dam once-raced half-sister to dam of Peintre Celebre:
smart performer: progressed well, winning newcomers race at Longchamp in April,
minor event at Saint-Cloud in May and listed race at Deauville in August: awarded Grand
Prix de Deauville Lucien Barriere later in August after being carried right final 1f and
beaten a short neck by Polish Summer: 4 lengths second of 4 to Doyen in Prix du Lys at
Longchamp third start: well held in Prix de l'Arc de Triomphe at Longchamp final outing:
stays 12.5f well: raced only on good ground or softer. *E. Lellouche, France*

POLISH CORRIDOR   4 b.g. Danzig Connection (USA) – Possibility 59 (Robellino   **93**
(USA) 127) [2003 77: 10.1d 10m³ 11m² 10m² 10.5m² 10m³ 10m³ 10.5m³ 10f⁴ 10g* 10.3g⁶
10m² Sep 25] tall, good-topped gelding: fairly useful handicapper: won at Kempton in
September: several other good efforts: probably best at 1¼m/11f: raced mostly on good
going or firmer: usually held up: genuine. *M. Dods*

POLISH EMPEROR (USA)   3 ch.g. Polish Precedent (USA) 131 – Empress Jackie   **81**
(USA) (Mount Hagen (FR) 127) [2003 82p: 6m⁴ 6f⁴ 6g 6f 7g 6g p7g f6g⁶ 5d⁴ f5g* f5g
Dec 9] lengthy gelding: fairly useful performer: reportedly suffered muscle injury after
winning maiden on only 2-y-o start, and off 1 year: won handicap at Wolverhampton in

November: best at 5f/6f: acts on all-weather, firm and soft ground: blinkered last 6 starts: races prominently. *P. W. Harris*

POLISH FLAME   5 b.g. Blushing Flame (USA) 109 – Lady Emm (Emarati (USA) 74) [2003 71p: 13d² 13d² 14d⁶ 13.1d⁶ Oct 14] fair handicapper, lightly raced: will stay beyond 17f: acts on heavy going: wore cheekpieces (ran well) final start. *Mrs M. Reveley*   **74**

POLISH MONARCH   4 b.g. Polish Precedent (USA) 131 – Chita Rivera 61 (Chief Singer 131) [2003 56: p10g⁵ 10.9m Sep 20] lightly-raced maiden, modest form at best: left R. Baker after reappearance: should stay 1½m: blinkered, refused to enter stall intended second outing in 2003. *B. R. Millman*   **52**

POLISH MONARCH   3 b.g. Mon Tresor 113 – Gentle Star 77 (Comedy Star (USA) 121) [2003 10.2g 10m Jun 16] half-brother to 8-y-o Polish Spirit and 1988 2-y-o 5f seller winner Tell Me This (by Goldhills Pride): dam 6f winner: well beaten in maidens at Chepstow and Windsor: sold £2,100. *B. R. Millman*   **–**

POLISH RHAPSODY (IRE)   2 b.f. (Feb 7) Charnwood Forest (IRE) 125 – Polish Rhythm (IRE) 77 (Polish Patriot (USA) 128) [2003 p7g Oct 30] quite good-topped filly: third foal: half-sister to fairly useful 2002 2-y-o 7f winner Stressless (by Barathea): dam, 1m winner at 4 yrs, half-sister to Cheveley Park/Moyglare Stud Stakes winner Capricciosa: 33/1 and better for race, last of 10 in maiden at Lingfield, taking good hold. *J. A. Supple*   **–**

POLISH SPIRIT   8 b.g. Emarati (USA) 74 – Gentle Star 77 (Comedy Star (USA) 121) [2003 10g⁵ Apr 1] lengthy, workmanlike gelding: fairly useful performer in 2000 (tough and genuine), well held only outing on Flat since. *B. R. Millman*   **–**

POLISH SUMMER   6 b.h. Polish Precedent (USA) 131 – Hunt The Sun (Rainbow Quest (USA) 134) [2003 120: 12g⁴ 12m⁶ 12g² 12.5s² 12f⁵ 12s* 12m² Dec 14] strong,   **118**

Mr K. Abdulla's "Polish Summer"

good sort: smart performer: first past post in Grand Prix de Deauville for second consecutive year in August (fourth start) but demoted to second after beating Policy Maker by a short neck (drifted right) and won listed race at Lyon-Parilly in November by length from Jazz d'Allier: also ran well when second in Grand Prix de Saint-Cloud (to Ange Gabriel for second year in a row, beaten 1½ lengths) and Hong Kong Vase at Sha Tin (went down by ¾ length to Vallee Enchantee): hampered 3f out when sixth to Warrsan in Coronation Cup at Epsom on second outing: probably best at 1½m to 2m: acts on soft and good to firm going: visored (ran creditably) final outing in 2002: reliable. *A. Fabre, France*

POLISH TRICK (USA) 2 b.c. (Jan 30) Clever Trick (USA) – Sunk (USA) (Polish   **80** Navy (USA)) [2003 7m⁵ 7.6m² 7g² Sep 1] $25,000F, 8,000Y, 15,000 2-y-o: fourth foal: closely related to 4-y-o Jan Brueghel: dam, winner around 1m in USA, half-sister to Rockfel Stakes winner At Risk: fairly useful form in maidens: second at Lingfield and Folkestone: will stay 1m: joined M. Dickinson in USA. *B. G. Powell*

POLKA PRINCESS 3 b.f. Makbul 104 – Liberatrice (FR) (Assert 134) [2003 72:   **–** f7g⁵ f7g 8m⁶ 10.9m 8.1m 8.5m 10.9m Aug 25] small, angular filly: fair performer at 2 yrs: little form in 2003 (claimed from I. Wood £6,000 on reappearance): seemed to run moodily final 2-y-o start. *M. Wellings*

POLLY PLUNKETT 3 b.f. Puissance 110 – Expectation (IRE) 59 (Night Shift   **88 +** (USA)) [2003 68: 8.2g² 8f³ 10.1m⁴ 8g* 8g² 10.3m⁵ 8.2m² 8.1g* 8.1m² 8m² 8.1m Aug 7] strong, angular filly: fairly useful handicapper: won at Newcastle in May and Haydock in July: good short-head second at Doncaster penultimate start: stays 1m: acts on firm and good to soft ground: often slowly away at 2 yrs, and final 3-y-o outing: races freely: reliable. *W. M. Brisbourne*

POLONIUS 2 b.g. (Mar 25) Great Dane (IRE) 122 – Bridge Pool 74 (First Trump 118)   **94 p** [2003 7.1m* 7m³ 6.1m* Oct 22] 4,500F, 6,000Y: first foal: dam, 5f winner who stayed 7f, out of half-sister to Poule d'Essai des Poulains winner Victory Note: won maiden at Chepstow in September and minor event at Nottingham (comfortably, by 3½ lengths from Bonne de Fleur) in October: likely to prove best up to 7f: useful prospect. *H. Candy*

POLYVIA 3 b.f. Polish Precedent (USA) 131 – Epagris 107 (Zalazl (USA) 120) [2003   **–** 8.1m 9.8g 9.5g⁶ 8g Oct 6] fourth foal: half-sister to 7f winner Granadilla (by Zafonic) and 1¼m winner Krantor (by Arazi), both fairly useful: dam 6f (at 2 yrs) and 7f winner who stayed 1m: well held in maidens/minor events: trained by H. Cecil on debut. *D. Sepulchre, France*

POMFRET LAD 5 b.g. Cyrano de Bergerac 120 – Lucky Flinders 77 (Free State 125)   **108** [2003 111: 6g⁶ 6m⁵ 5g 5.7f⁵ 7m* 7m 7g⁵ 7m² Sep 23] tall, good-topped gelding: useful performer: won handicap at Newbury in August by 2½ lengths from Dark Charm: good ½-length second to Three Graces in minor event at Newmarket final start, again dictating pace: effective at 6f/7f: acts on good to firm and good to soft ground: tried blinkered: inconsistent: sold 22,000 gns. *P. J. Makin*

POMPEII (IRE) 6 b.g. Salse (USA) 128 – Before Dawn (USA) (Raise A Cup (USA))   **49 ?** [2003 f8s f11g f12s 11m 12.4g⁵ 10.1m 8.9m Sep 1] rangy gelding: poor handicapper: left Ronald Thompson after sixth start: stays 1½m: acts on good to firm and heavy going: wore cheekpieces (ran creditably) fifth start: successful over hurdles in September. *A. J. Lockwood*

POMPEY BLUE 2 b.f. (Feb 10) Abou Zouz (USA) 109 – Habla Me (IRE) (Fairy   **71** King (USA)) [2003 5m² 6m³ 6m⁵ 5.2s⁵ f6g* p6g⁵ Nov 26] 6,500Y: third foal: half-sister to winner in Spain by Millkom: dam, Italian 7f winner, out of half-sister to smart performers Bog Trotter (stayed 7f) and Poteen (stayed 1m): fair performer: won maiden at Wolverhampton in November: good fifth in nursery at Lingfield final start: likely to prove best at 5f/6f: acts on all-weather and good to firm ground. *P. J. McBride*

POMPEY CHIMES 3 b.g. Forzando 122 – Silver Purse 67 (Interrex (CAN) [2003 6f⁵   **45 p** Oct 12] second foal: dam 2-y-o 5.7f winner: 20/1 and green, late headway when 9 lengths fifth of 10 to Stokesies Wish in maiden at Goodwood: should do better. *G. B. Balding*

PONDERON 3 ch.g. Hector Protector (USA) 124 – Blush Rambler (IRE) (Blushing   **102** Groom (FR) 131) [2003 –p: 10m⁴ 10d³ 10.2m³ 12f p13g* 13.1d³ 16.5d* Nov 8] lengthy gelding: useful and progressive form: won maiden at Lingfield (easily) in October and handicap at Doncaster in November by 2½ lengths from Anak Pekan: stays 2m: acts on polytrack and good to soft going, probably on firm: game. *R. F. Johnson Houghton*

PONGEE 3 b.f. Barathea (IRE) 127 – Puce 112 (Darshaan 133) [2003 72p: 10.1m*   **96** p10g* 10m* 12f* 11.9m Aug 21] quite attractive filly: useful performer: won first 4 starts in 2003, namely minor event at Yarmouth in April, handicap at Lingfield in May, apprentice minor event at Nottingham and handicap at Salisbury (idled, beat Bahrqueen by length) in June: stiff task when running respectably in listed race at York final outing: better at 1½m than shorter: acts on firm and good to soft ground: game. *L. M. Cumani*

PONT ALLAIRE (IRE) 2 b.f. (Mar 3) Rahy (USA) 115 – Leonila (IRE) 113 (Caerleon (USA) 132) [2003 7f⁴ Sep 4] second foal: half-sister to French 1m winner Quivala (by Thunder Gulch): dam, French 1½m winner, sister to Prix de Diane winner Caerlina: 8/1, 5½ lengths fourth of 17 to Silk Fan in maiden at Salisbury: will stay at least 1m: likely to improve. *H. Candy*   **72 p**

PONT NEUF (IRE) 3 b.f. Revoque (IRE) 122 – Petite Maxine 70 (Sharpo 132) [2003 67: p10g 9.1g² 10f p12g Jul 23] tall, angular filly: fair maiden: well held last 2 starts: stays 9f: acts on fibresand, firm and good to soft ground. *J. W. Hills*   **68**

POOKA'S DAUGHTER (IRE) 3 b.f. Eagle Eyed (USA) 111 – Gaelic's Fantasy (IRE) (Statoblest 120) [2003 59: f7g* f7g² f8.5g* f7s f8g⁴ f8.5g² f8g 7.1m f9.4g f7g Nov 29] modest performer: won seller and handicap at Wolverhampton in January: below form after: stays 8.5f: acts on good to soft going and fibresand: none too consistent. *J. M. Bradley*   **63 d**

POP GUN 4 ch.g. Pharly (FR) 130 – Angel Fire (Nashwan (USA) 135) [2003 56: 10.2f* 11.7m² 12g⁴ 14.1m* 16.2m³ 12m 15.9d Sep 24] fair handicapper: won at Bath in March and Nottingham in June: left B. Hills prior to well held last 2 starts: may prove best short of 2m: acts on fibresand and firm ground. *Miss K. Marks*   **69**

POP PLAY AGAIN 2 ch.c. (Mar 5) Vettori (IRE) 119 – Bellair (Beveled (USA)) [2003 7m 7.9m Sep 3] 9,000F, 11,000Y: big, plain colt: second foal: half-brother to 3-y-o Pop Up Again: dam unraced: well held in maidens at Newcastle and York. *G. A. Swinbank*   **–**

POPPYLINE 3 b.f. Averti (IRE) 117 – Shalverton (IRE) (Shalford (IRE) 124§) [2003 65: 8m² 7m 8.3g² 10f 10d 8m² 8.5g⁵ 8.5m⁵ 8f⁴ p8g⁴ 8m⁴ f8s Oct 21] close-coupled filly: fair maiden: stays 1m: acts on firm ground and polytrack. *W. R. Muir*   **69**

POPPYS FOOTPRINT (IRE) 2 ch.f. (Feb 20) Titus Livius (FR) 115 – Mica Male (ITY) (Law Society (USA) 130) [2003 6m 6m* 7g 6g* 6d⁶ 8m² 8m Oct 16] IR 4,600F: leggy, workmanlike filly: fourth foal: half-sister to Italian 2000 2-y-o 5.5f and 7.5f winner Flor de Cano (by Dancing Dissident): dam won at 7f and 11f in Italy: fairly useful performer: won maiden in July and minor event in August, both at Hamilton: good second in nursery at Ayr: effective at 6f to 1m: acts on good to firm and good to soft going: sometimes carries head high. *K. A. Ryan*   **85**

POPULAR DEB 3 b.f. Abou Zouz (USA) 109 – Pharling (Pharly (FR) 130) [2003 69: 7.5d 5s 6g 7m May 26] IR 8,000Y: first foal: dam of little account: modest maiden: blinkered (ran poorly) in seller at Redcar final start: likely to prove best at 5f/6f. *Ms J. Morgan, Ireland*   **58**

POP UP AGAIN 3 ch.f. Bahamian Bounty 116 – Bellair (Beveled (USA)) [2003 71: 6.9m² 6.9d 7f³ 7m² 7.1g 7m⁵ 7m* 7m³ Oct 17] unfurnished filly: fairly useful handicapper: won at Newcastle in October: stays 7f: acts on firm and soft ground: wandered final start. *G. A. Swinbank*   **83 +**

PORAK (IRE) 6 ch.g. Perugino (USA) 84 – Gayla Orchestra (Lord Gayle (USA) 124) [2003 84, a66: p13g³ p12g⁴ 11.9m⁶ May 3] big gelding: fair performer: effective at 1¼m to 13f: acts on heavy going, good to firm and polytrack: tried in cheekpieces: often held up. *G. L. Moore*   **67**

PORLEZZA (FR) 4 ch.f. Sicyos (USA) 126 – Pupsi (FR) (Matahawk 127) [2003 110: 5g 5m* 6d⁵ᵈ 6.5g* 5s⁵ Oct 5] strong filly: smart performer: won Prix du Gros-Chene   **117**

Prix Maurice de Gheest, Deauville—the locally-trained Porlezza (noseband) wins from Etoile Montante (right), Avonbridge (third right) and Swedish Shave (left)

at Chantilly (for second year running, by ¾ length from demoted The Trader) in June and Prix Maurice de Gheest at Deauville (by a length from Etoile Montante, ridden more patiently than usual) in August: creditable fifth to Patavellian in Prix de l'Abbaye at Longchamp final outing: stays 6.5f: acts on soft and good to firm going: injured herself after rearing in stall on last 2 seasonal reappearances. *Y. de Nicolay, France*

PORSA SYSTEM (DEN)   4 br.c. Richard of York 123 – Natalja (DEN) (Niniski   **106** (USA) 125) [2003 9s² 9g³ 9m⁶ 12g⁵ 12g⁵ 12g* 16m⁶ Oct 18] close-coupled colt: second known foal: dam second in Danish 1000 Guineas and Danish Oaks: useful performer: placed in Danish Derby and Danish/Swedish St Legers at 3 yrs: good fifth to Labirinto in Stockholm Cup at Taby before winning minor event at Copenhagen in September: tailed-off last in Jockey Club Cup at Newmarket final start: stays 1¾m: acts on soft and good to firm going. *F. Poulsen, Denmark*

PORTACASA   4 b.f. Robellino (USA) 127 – Autumn Affair 100 (Lugana Beach 116)   **70** [2003 72: 10g³ 9.9m⁵ May 10] leggy filly: fair handicapper: ran creditably in 2003: stays 10.5f: acts on good to firm and good to soft going: usually blinkered/visored (has won without). *R. A. Fahey*

PORTHCAWL   2 b.f. (Mar 22) Singspiel (IRE) 133 – Dodo (IRE) 90 (Alzao (USA)   **– p** 117) [2003 6m Oct 4] second foal: half-sister to 3-y-o Tarjman: dam, 6f winner, out of very smart but temperamental sprinter Dead Certain: 33/1, better for race and green, last of 10 in maiden at Newmarket: will probably do better. *M. L. W. Bell*

PORTICHOL PRINCESS   3 b.f. Bluegrass Prince (IRE) 110 – Barbrallen 38 (Rambo   **–** Dancer (CAN) 107) [2003 –: p10g p10g Jan 25] little sign of ability in 3 all-weather maidens. *Mrs L. C. Jewell*

PORTMANTEAU   2 b.f. (Jan 31) Barathea (IRE) 127 – Dayanata (Shirley Heights   **70 p** 130) [2003 7m Oct 13] 590,000Y: good-bodied, close-coupled filly: half-sister to several winners, including smart 1m (at 2 yrs) to 12.5f winner Courteous (by Generous) and 4-y-o Scent of Victory: dam unraced sister to Prix du Jockey Club winner Darshaan: 14/1, green and backward, ninth of 13 in maiden at Leicester, racing freely and eased once tiring: bred to be suited by 1¼m/1½m: sure to improve. *Sir Michael Stoute*

PORT MORENO (IRE)   3 b.c. Turtle Island (IRE) 123 – Infra Blue (IRE) (Bluebird   **57** (USA) 125) [2003 54: f9.4g⁴ f9.4g³ f11s⁴ f12g² 12m* f12g⁴ 10.9m 12.6f 11.5f⁶ f11g Dec   **a50** 3] rather sparely-made colt: modest handicapper: won at Southwell in March: below form after: stays 1½m: acts on firm ground and fibresand: usually visored: sometimes goes in snatches/looks none too keen. *J. G. M. O'Shea*

PORTRAIT OF A LADY (IRE)   2 ch.f. Peintre Celebre (USA) 137 –   **69** Starlight Smile (USA) (Green Dancer (USA) 132) [2003 8.2f⁵ 7m⁴ 8m Oct 24] 12,000Y: neat filly: first foal: dam unraced half-sister to useful Irish 6f/7f winner Seasonal Pickup and to dam of 2-y-o Grey Swallow: fair form in maidens: fourth at Leicester: hampered final start: should be suited by 1¼m/1½m. *H. R. A. Cecil*

PORT ST CHARLES (IRE)   6 b. or br.g. Night Shift (USA) – Safe Haven (Blakeney   **83** 126) [2003 79: p7g⁴ f6s* f5g² f6s² f6g⁴ f6s 7g 6m² 6m³ 6g f6g* Nov 28] tall gelding: fairly useful handicapper: won at Southwell in January and Wolverhampton in November: effective at 5f to easy 7f: acts on all-weather, heavy and good to firm going: free-going sort: sometimes finds little. *P. R. Chamings*

POSH SHEELAGH   2 b.f. (Apr 20) Danzero (AUS) – Button Hole Flower (IRE)   **–** (Fairy King (USA)) [2003 f7g Nov 24] 6,500Y: third foal: half-sister to Italian 2002 2-y-o 7f winner Donakety (by Millkom): dam, Italian 5f (including at 2 yrs)/6f winner, out of half-sister to Racing Post Trophy winner Be My Chief: 16/1, well held in seller at Southwell, slowly away. *J. G. Given*

POSITIVE PROFILE (IRE)   5 b.g. Definite Article 121 – Leyete Gulf (IRE) (Slip   **94** Anchor 136) [2003 87, a92: f16s* f16.2g⁴ 18g² 16m 16.1d⁴ 20m 16.1m 16.2d 21d² 13.9f* 18m Oct 18] angular gelding: fairly useful handicapper: won at Southwell in February and York in October, latter by 2½ lengths from Flotta: effective at 1¾m to 21f: acts on soft going, firm and all-weather: sometimes slowly away/flicks tail under pressure: tends to carry head high: reportedly broke blood vessel fourth start. *P. C. Haslam*

POST AND RAIL (USA)   2 b.c. (Apr 1) Silver Hawk (USA) 123 – Past The Post   **95 p** (USA) (Danzig (USA)) [2003 7.1d* Aug 29] $150,000Y: quite good-topped colt: first foal: dam, won at 8.5f in USA, sister to smart miler Emperor Jones and half-sister to William Hill Futurity winner Bakharoff: 10/1, won 14-runner maiden at Sandown by short head from North Light, disputing lead until going on over 2f out: met minor setback after: will stay 1¼m, probably 1½m: has potential to make his mark in stronger company as 3-y-o. *E. A. L. Dunlop*

POTEMKIN (IRE)   5 ch.h. Ashkalani (IRE) 128 – Ploy 87 (Posse (USA) 130) [2003   **112** 114: 9m⁵ 10g 11.6g² Jun 1] big, strong, good sort: smart performer: ran respectably on two of 3 outings in 2003, namely Earl of Sefton Stakes at Newmarket (fifth to Olden Times) and listed race at Windsor (1¾ lengths second to Leadership): effective at 1¼m/ 1½m: acts on soft and good to firm ground: often wears crossed noseband: has got worked up in preliminaries: ducked right in front/idled when winning at 4 yrs: often races up with pace: tends to hang: sold only 3,000 gns in December, sent to Qatar. *R. Hannon*

POT OF GOLD (FR)   5 gr.g. Kendor (FR) 122 – Golden Rainbow (FR) (Rainbow   **–** Quest (USA) 134) [2003 –: f11s⁶ 12.3m Apr 2] modest maiden: lightly raced and no form since 3 yrs: tried blinkered/visored/tongue tied. *T. J. Fitzgerald*

POTSDAM   5 ch.g. Rainbow Quest (USA) 134 – Danilova (USA) (Lyphard (USA)   **53** 132) [2003 56: f12g 8.5v² 7g⁴ Aug 15] modest maiden: bred to stay further than 9f, but races freely: acts on heavy ground, well beaten all starts on fibresand, including at Southwell on reappearance: sometimes tongue tied. *Niall Moran, Ireland*

POTWASH   3 b.f. Piccolo 121 – Silankka 70 (Slip Anchor 136) [2003 70: p6g* 5.5v   **73** 8g² 8g² 6g⁶ 8s³ 7d⁵ 8d³ 8d a7.5g 7s 8v a6.5g⁶ Dec 23] fair performer: won maiden at Lingfield in February: placed in several claimers in France afterwards: stays 1m: acts on polytrack, soft and good to firm going: has flashed tail. *A. Hermans, Belgium*

POULE DE LUXE (IRE)   2 b.f. (Feb 28) Cadeaux Genereux 131 – Likely Story   **60** (IRE) 94 (Night Shift (USA)) [2003 6m 6g⁴ Aug 4] 16,000Y: second foal: half-sister to 3-y-o Border Tale: dam, 6f winner (including at 2 yrs), out of half-sister to Phoenix Stakes winner Aviance, herself dam of very smart pair Chimes of Freedom (miler) and Denon (up to 1½m): better effort in maidens (modest form) when fourth at Windsor: should stay at least 7f. *J. L. Dunlop*

POWER BIRD (IRE)   3 b.f. Bluebird (USA) 125 – Polynesian Goddess (IRE) (Sal-   **88 d** mon Leap (USA) 131) [2003 8d* 8d⁶ 8d 9d 8d 7g⁵ 6g f8g p10g Dec 17] 43,000F, IR 40,000Y: seventh foal: half-sister to 3 winners, including fairly useful 1997 2-y-o 6f winner Jay Gee (by Second Set) and 1m winner Sea Squirt (by Fourstars Allstar): dam third at 7f in Ireland: fairly useful at best: won maiden at Baden-Baden in May: mostly well held after, leaving R. Suerland following fourth start and C. Von Der Recke after sixth one: stays 1m: raced only on good/good to soft going on turf: tried blinkered. *D. Flood*

POWERFUL PARRISH (USA)   2 b.f. (Apr 23) Quiet American (USA) – Parish   **92** Business (USA) (Phone Trick (USA)) [2003 5g² 8m⁵ Oct 12] $90,000Y: third foal: dam, US maiden, half-sister to US Grade 3 winner at 1m/9f Mr Sinatra: second in minor event at Salisbury: much better effort (fairly useful form) when 2¼ lengths fifth to Mamela in Premio Dormello at Milan over 5 months later: will probably stay 1¼m. *P. F. I. Cole*

POWER NAP   2 b.f. (Apr 7) Acatenango (GER) 127 – Dreams Are Free (IRE) 71   **–** (Caerleon (USA) 132) [2003 8d 8d Nov 7] 20,000Y: seventh foal: half-sister to 3 winners, including useful 7f (at 2 yrs) and 1¼m winner Bogus Dreams (by Lahib): dam 1¼m winner: well held in maidens at Ayr and Doncaster (tongue tied). *N. Tinkler*

POWERSCOURT   3 b.c. Sadler's Wells (USA) 132 – Rainbow Lake 113   **122** (Rainbow Quest (USA) 134) [2003 112p: 12m⁶ 10g* 11.9m* 14f³ Sep 13]
The close links which existed between Powerscourt and Brian Boru when they were foaled in the spring of 2000 have continued since. A pair of bay colts by Sadler's Wells out of Juddmonte mares who showed smart form at a mile and a half or more for Henry Cecil in the 'nineties, they both went into training with Aidan O'Brien and developed into very smart performers as their racing careers followed similar paths.
Powerscourt and Brian Boru have already met three times in their short careers, the first occasion at the end of their two-year-old season when Powerscourt finished second to his stable-companion in the Racing Post Trophy at Doncaster. A training setback, reportedly a pulled muscle, delayed Powerscourt's return, and he probably needed his first race for eight months when finishing sixth, two places behind Brian Boru, in the Irish Derby. It was a sharper Powerscourt who took on

Daily Telegraph Great Voltigeur Stakes, York—
Powerscourt regains the lead from stable-companion Brian Boru (left); Hawk Flyer is third

Brian Boru yet again almost two months later, having made all to land the odds in a minor event at Leopardstown in the meantime. They were among nine declared for the Daily Telegraph Great Voltigeur Stakes at York, a Group 2 event which also featured High Accolade and Hawk Flyer, who on their previous starts had finished second and third respectively behind Phoenix Reach in the Gordon Stakes at Goodwood. Despite having been beaten twice by Brian Boru, Powerscourt was the preferred mount of stable-jockey Michael Kinane and started at shorter odds. Kinane was proved right, but it was a close call. In a race run at a gallop which, until the turn, looked fair at best, Powerscourt benefited from being ridden closer to the pace than Brian Boru, the latter still a few lengths adrift when Powerscourt was sent to the front approaching the last two furlongs. A strong challenge from favourite Hawk Flyer was repelled by Powerscourt, but it was followed immediately by one from Brian Boru which probably took him into a very narrow lead close home, only for Powerscourt to fight back to regain the advantage and win by a neck. Powerscourt and Brian Boru now headed the ante-post betting on the St Leger, but in early-September the decision was made to send Powerscourt for the Irish St Leger at the Curragh on the same day, leaving Brian Boru as the stable's sole representative at Doncaster. Powerscourt, up against older horses, faced the stiffer task of the pair and acquitted himself well in finishing a length third to Vinnie Roe, who was completing a unique hat-trick in the event. Had he been sent to Doncaster in place of Brian Boru, who justified favouritism there, Powerscourt would have gone very close to winning. A Group 1 contest will surely come his way in 2004.

	Sadler's Wells (USA) (b 1981)	Northern Dancer (b 1961)	Nearctic / Natalma
Powerscourt (b.c. 2000)		Fairy Bridge (b 1975)	Bold Reason / Special
	Rainbow Lake (b 1990)	Rainbow Quest (b 1981)	Blushing Groom / I Will Follow
		Rockfest (ch 1979)	Stage Door Johnny / Rock Garden

Powerscourt's performance at the Curragh, where he was rallying towards the finish, left the firm impression that he will stay beyond a mile and three quarters. His pedigree points towards the same. Powerscourt's dam Rainbow Lake is quite stoutly bred and should certainly have stayed further than the mile and a half over which she put up her best performance, when running out a seven-length winner of the Lancashire Oaks. Rainbow Lake, a half-sister to several winners, including Best Rock and the useful performers Rock Falcon and Vertex, is a daughter of Rockfest, who won at seven furlongs and a mile as a two-year-old, and gained her highest placing at three when second in the Lingfield Oaks Trial.

Powerscourt's great grandam Rock Garden showed fairly useful form at up to a mile, gaining her sole success at that distance. Two of Rainbow Lake's five foals prior to Powerscourt were winners. Brimming (by Generous) showed smart form at around a mile and three quarters as a three-year-old, while Unaware, by the Northern Dancer stallion Unfuwain and therefore a close relative of Powerscourt, was a fairly useful winner over a mile at two, and subsequently won at up to a mile and a half in Switzerland. Rainbow Lake's seventh foal Kind (by Danehill) finished in the frame in a couple of six-furlong maidens in the latest season, and will do better when given the opportunity to tackle longer distances. Powerscourt, a good-topped colt who has worn a crossed noseband, sweated slightly and swished his tail in the paddock at York. He has shown his form on ground ranging from firm through to soft. *A. P. O'Brien, Ireland*

POWER STRIKE (USA)   2 b.c. (Feb 5) Coronado's Quest (USA) 130 – Galega   – p
(Sure Blade (USA) 130) [2003 7g Nov 1] well-made colt: sixth foal: half-brother to 2 winners, including fairly useful 1¼m winner Baringo (by Miswaki) and 8.5f to 1½m winner Burning Truth (by Known Fact), both fairly useful: dam, French 9f winner, half-sister to US Grade 3 11f winner Flaming Torch out of close relative to Coronation Cup winner Quiet Fling: 6/1, behind in maiden at Newmarket, not given hard time when tiring: bred to be suited by 1¼m/1½m: will improve. *R. Charlton*

POWER TO BURN   2 b.g. (Mar 12) Superpower 113 – Into The Fire 74 (Dominion   56
123) [2003 5g4 5m f6g6 6d p6g Nov 26] half-brother to 3 winners, including sprinter Down The Middle (by Swing Easy) and miler Cool Fire (by Colmore Row): dam, stayed 1¼m, winner in Guernsey: modest maiden: stays 6f: acts on fibresand, probably on good to firm going: tongue tied final outing. *K. Bell*

POYLE HEATHER   3 b.f. Air Express (IRE) 125 – Hithermoor Lass 75 (Red Alert   54
127) [2003 –: 7m5 8.3g 7m4 6f 7g4 6d3 6m5 7m6 Oct 14] modest maiden handicapper: effective at 6f (given a test)/7f: acts on good to firm and good to soft going: often races freely. *J. G. Portman*

POYLE JENNY   4 b.f. Piccolo 121 – Poyle Amber 55 (Sharrood (USA) 124) [2003 –:   –
8.2g 8.1m Jul 4] no sign of ability. *G. Barnett*

PRADO   4 b.g. Hernando (FR) 127 – Harefoot 92 (Rainbow Quest (USA) 134) [2003   78
83: 10m2 Jun 16] quite attractive gelding: had a round action: showed fair amount of ability both starts, length second to Trust Rule in maiden at Windsor only outing in 2003 (suffered recurrence of injury): would have been suited by 1½m: retired. *L. M. Cumani*

PRAETORIAN FORCE   4 b.g. Atraf 116 – Zaima (IRE) 92 (Green Desert (USA)   56 ?
127) [2003 56?: f8s f7g p7g6 6g 7f 6.1g 6g3 6.1m 6m Jul 19] modest maiden: mostly well held in 2003: stays 6f: acts on good to firm going and polytrack: tried in headgear. *J. M. Bradley*

PRAIRIE FALCON (IRE)   9 b.g. Alzao (USA) 117 – Sea Harrier (Grundy 137)   94
[2003 90: 16m2 16m* 13.9m4 16.2m5 16.1g6 11.9m4 14g 13.9m 14g 14.1f* 16g Oct 24] attractive gelding: good mover: fairly useful handicapper: won at Ripon (idled) in April and Redcar in September: effective at 13f to 2¼m: acts on firm and soft going: effective racing prominently or held up. *B. W. Hills*

PRAIRIE SUN (GER)   2 b.f. (Jan 12) Law Society (USA) 130 – Prairie Flame (IRE)   55
85 (Marju (IRE) 127) [2003 6m 10m 8m Oct 24] 15,000Y: quite good-topped filly: second foal: dam German 1m winner: modest form in maidens: will be suited by 1½m+. *Mrs A. Duffield*

PRAIRIE WOLF   7 ch.g. Wolfhound (USA) 126 – Bay Queen 85 (Damister (USA)   93
123) [2003 99: 10m 10.4m 10.1m 9.9g 10m3 10g2 9m3 10.4f2 10.1s Oct 29] big, strong gelding: fairly useful handicapper: creditable placed efforts sixth to eighth starts: stays 10.4f: acts on fibresand, firm and good to soft going (below form on soft/heavy): often sweating: usually tracks leaders. *M. L. W. Bell*

PRAYERFUL   4 b.f. Syrtos 106 – Pure Formality 84 (Forzando 122) [2003 47: 10g   –
Apr 1] workmanlike filly: lightly raced and poor form at best. *B. N. Doran*

PRECIOUS DAYS (USA)   3 ch.f. Deputy Minister (CAN) – Pricket (USA) 111   –
(Diesis 133) [2003 10m May 30] good-topped filly: second foal: dam, 1m (at 2 yrs)/1¼m winner and second in Oaks, sister to Diminuendo: 7/1, lethargic and backward, last of 10 in maiden at Newmarket: covered by Green Desert, sent to Australia. *Sir Michael Stoute*

PRECIOUS FREEDOM   3 b.g. Ashkalani (IRE) 128 – Prayers'n Promises (USA) **60** (Foolish Pleasure (USA)) [2003 68: 6.1m 6g⁶ 6d⁴ 6m f7s 6g f6g f7g Nov 19] sturdy **a–** gelding: modest maiden: well below form last 5 starts: will probably stay 1m: acts on soft ground, poor efforts on fibresand: wore cheekpieces last 7 starts. *J. Balding*

PRECIOUS MYSTERY (IRE)   3 ch.f. Titus Livius (FR) 115 – Ascoli (Skyliner 117) **65** [2003 –: 8.2g⁶ 8m² 8g 8m* f8.5g⁶ Oct 4] modest performer: won maiden handicap at Yarmouth in September: stays 1m: acts on good to firm going (shuffled back 3f out on fibresand): sold 16,000 gns. *J. Nicol*

PRE EMINANCE (IRE)   2 b.c. (May 11) Peintre Celebre (USA) 137 – Sorb Apple **78 p** (IRE) 79 (Kris 135) [2003 7g⁴ Nov 1] €50,000Y: useful-looking colt: fourth foal: half-brother to fairly useful Irish 1½m winner Sarayah (by Danehill): dam, Irish 1½m winner, sister to smart Irish middle-distance filly Eileen Jenny out of disqualified Irish Oaks winner Sorbus: 20/1, 2¼ lengths fourth of 13 to Hezaam in maiden at Newmarket, taking time to settle and wandering while staying on: bred to be suited by 1¼m/1½m: will improve. *C. R. Egerton*

PREGNANT PAUSE (IRE)   2 b.c. (Mar 27) General Monash (USA) 107 – Dissi- **70** dentia (IRE) (Dancing Dissident (USA) 119) [2003 6.1d 7m⁵ 5m⁴ 6.1m⁵ 5.7f³ 6m 7f p7g² p7g⁴ p5g p6g² Dec 30] €5,000Y: smallish, good-topped colt: has a quick action: second living foal: half-brother to winner in Italy by Paris House: dam 5f winner in Belgium/ France: fair maiden: should prove best at 6f/7f: acts on firm ground and polytrack: sometimes carries head awkwardly. *S. Kirk*

PRELOTTE (IRE)   4 b.g. Nicolotte 118 – Prepare (IRE) [2003 **–** 8.1d 12.6m 11.6m Jul 14] 5,000Y: fourth foal: half-brother to 5f (at 2 yrs)/6f winner Make Ready (by Beveled): dam, 7f winner, half-sister to high-class sprinter Anita's Prince: no form: hung left final start. *C. Roberts*

PREMIER CHEVAL (USA)   4 ch.g. Irish River (FR) 131 – Restikarada (FR) (Aka- **62** rad (FR) 130) [2003 p12g p12g p8g⁴ 9.7m p7g p10g p10g Dec 20] second foal: half-brother to French 9f winner Master of Dan (by Zieten): dam French 9f winner: modest maiden: probably stays 1½m. *R. Rowe*

PREMIERE'S PRIDE   3 ch.f. Young Ern 120 – Premiere Moon 80 (Bold Owl 101) **–** [2003 f7s 6m Apr 17] workmanlike filly: half-sister to winner in Italy by Executive Man: dam 7f/1m winner: well held in claimer at Southwell (slowly away) and maiden at New-market (jinked left leaving stall). *D. Morris*

PREMIER GRAND   3 ch.g. Case Law 113 – Seamill (IRE) (Lafontaine (USA) 117) **69** [2003 p6g² 6f² 6g⁴ 6d 6m³ Jun 17] 6,200Y: sturdy gelding: fourth foal: dam 1¼m/11f **a78** winner: fair maiden: should stay 7f: acts on polytrack and firm going. *P. C. Haslam*

PRENUP (IRE)   2 ch.f. (Mar 12) Diesis 133 – Mutual Consent (IRE) 107 (Reference **60 p** Point 139) [2003 6f⁵ 6.1d p6g Dec 2] lengthy, quite good-topped filly: fourth foal: dam, French 1m (at 2 yrs) and 1¼m winner who stayed 1½m, granddaughter of Poule d'Essai des Pouliches/Prix de Diane winner Madelia: modest form in maidens/minor event, not knocked about: will be suited by at least 1m: type to do better. *L. M. Cumani*

PRESENTER (IRE)   3 ch.g. Cadeaux Genereux 131 – Moviegoer 104 (Pharly (FR) **81 +** 130) [2003 76P: 8g³ May 5] big, unfurnished, rather raw-boned gelding: has plenty of scope: fairly useful form when placed both starts in maidens at Doncaster and Kempton (wore crossed noseband), still seeming green when third to Millafonic on latter course: may well be suited by further than 1m: sold 22,000 gns in October, joined D. Caro and gelded. *J. H. M. Gosden*

PRESENT 'N CORRECT   10 ch.g. Cadeaux Genereux 131 – Emerald Eagle 78 **42** (Sandy Creek 123) [2003 47, a38: f6s f5g f7g 7f 5.7f⁶ 5.1f 6.1m³ 6f 5.7f 6m⁶ Aug 20] **a–** workmanlike gelding: poor performer: effective at 5f to 7f: acts on any turf going/fibre-sand: sometimes blinkered/in cheekpieces: inconsistent. *J. M. Bradley*

PRESENT ORIENTED (USA)   2 ch.c. (Mar 7) Southern Halo (USA) – Shy Beauty **86** (CAN) (Great Gladiator (USA)) [2003 8d⁵ 8m⁶ Oct 2] $30,000Y: strong, close-coupled colt: has a fluent, round action: half-brother to several winners in North America: dam 4.5f to 6.5f winner in Canada: much better effort in maidens (fairly useful form) when fifth at Doncaster: raced freely when favourite at Newmarket: needs to settle to stay beyond 1m. *H. R. A. Cecil*

PRESIDENTS LADY   6 b.m. Superpower 113 – Flirty Lady (Never So Bold 135) **–** [2003 f8.5g f8g f8g Dec 15] lightly raced and little form. *P. W. Hiatt*

PRESTO SHINKO (IRE)   2 b. or br.c. (Feb 28) Shinko Forest (IRE) – Swift Chorus   **75**
(Music Boy 124) [2003 6m 6g³ 6g³ Oct 13] 65,000F, 50,000Y: tall colt: half-brother to
several winners, including 5-y-o Forest Tune and 1999 2-y-o 6f winner Welch's Dream
(by Brief Truce): dam Irish 2-y-o 6f winner: fair form in maidens: third twice at Windsor:
will probably stay 7f. *R. Hannon*

PRESTO TEMPO (IRE)   3 b.g. College Chapel 122 – Dance Suite (IRE) (Dancing   **65 ?**
Dissident (USA) 119) [2003 8m⁴ 8m 8.1d Sep 26] IR 10,000Y: strong gelding: first foal:
dam unraced: seemingly only form when fourth in maiden at Pontefract. *P. W. Harris*

PRESTO VENTO   3 b.f. Air Express (IRE) 125 – Placement (Kris 135) [2003 103:   **99**
7m 8g 7m* 6m⁵ 7m 7g 6m⁵ 7d 7m⁵ 6m 6m p8g³ 6d Nov 8] close-coupled filly: fluent
mover: useful performer: won listed race at Lingfield in May by ½ length from Entrap:
mostly at least respectable efforts after, third to Tadris in listed event at Lingfield on
polytrack debut penultimate start: effective at 6f to easy 1m: acts on firm and good to soft
going, probably on polytrack: has sweated/got on toes. *R. Hannon*

PRESUMPTIVE (IRE)   3 b.c. Danehill (USA) 126 – Demure (Machiavellian (USA)   **84**
123) [2003 75p: 7.1g³ Jul 3] leggy, useful-looking colt: better effort in maidens when 4¾
lengths third to Tantina at Haydock in July. *J. Noseda*

PRETENCE (IRE)   3 b.c. Danehill (USA) 126 – Narva (Nashwan (USA) 135) [2003   **99**
71p: p8g* p8g⁵ p8g* 8m⁴ 8.1g 8m Jul 19] close-coupled colt: useful performer: won
maiden in January, handicap in February and minor event in March, all at Lingfield:
creditable efforts after in handicaps when fourth of 29 to New Seeker in Britannia Stakes
at Royal Ascot and ninth in Definite Guest in quite valuable event at Newbury (hampered) final outing: will prove best at 7f/1m: acts on good to firm going and polytrack:
effective visored or not: carries head awkwardly: sent to USA. *J. Noseda*

PRETTY KOOL   3 b.f. Inchinor 119 – Carrie Kool 69 (Prince Sabo 123) [2003 –:   **–**
8.3g 10g May 24] good-topped filly: well held in 3 maidens. *S. C. Williams*

PRETTY PEKAN (IRE)   3 b.f. Sri Pekan (USA) 117 – Pretty Precedent (Polish   **47**
Precedent (USA) 131) [2003 –: 7m⁴ 10f 8m 11m³ 11.1g 8m 12d Jun 30] poor maiden: ran
badly last 3 starts: stays 11f: acts on good to firm going: edged left on reappearance: sent
to Pakistan. *G. G. Margarson*

PREVEZA   4 br.f. Presidium 124 – Ping Pong 65 (Petong 126) [2003 8.2g p7g p6g   **–**
Dec 17] sister to 7-y-o Ascari and half-sister to 1996 2-y-o 5f winner Calchou (by Barrys
Gamble): dam 2-y-o 6f winner: soundly beaten in maidens, reportedly finishing dis-
tressed on debut (only start for Miss K. Boutflower). *J. White*

PREVIEW   2 b.c. (Jan 25) Green Desert (USA) 127 – Well Warned 104 (Warning 136)   **–**
[2003 7g Jul 25] sturdy, lengthy colt: second living foal: dam, 2-y-o 6f winner, sister to
useful 7f/1m performer Out of Reach: 10/3, burly and green, possibly amiss when last of
7 in maiden at Ascot. *J. H. M. Gosden*

PRICKLY POPPY   5 b.m. Lear Fan (USA) 130 – Prickwillow (USA) 75 (Nureyev   **–**
(USA) 131) [2003 –: f9.4g 9d 6g May 16] fair maiden at 3 yrs: no form since: left
A. Newcombe after reappearance: wore cheekpieces last 2 starts. *T. T. Clement*

PRIDE (FR)   3 b.f. Peintre Celebre (USA) 137 – Specificity (USA) 103 (Alleged   **96 ?**
(USA) 138) [2003 p8g² 10g* 10.3d Nov 7] seventh foal: half-sister to several winners,
including 6-y-o Noble Calling: dam, suited by test of stamina, half-sister to St Leger
winner Touching Wood: useful form: ran once at 2 yrs for J. Hammond in France: won
maiden at Newbury in October: seemed to excel in face of stiff task when seventh to Al
Ihtithar in listed event at Doncaster subsequent start, well ridden up with pace: bred to
be suited by 1½m+: raced only on good/good to soft ground on turf, below form on
polytrack: has been early to post: raced freely on reappearance. *G. A. Butler*

PRIDE OF KINLOCH   3 ch.f. Dr Devious (IRE) 127 – Stormswept (USA) 74   **80**
(Storm Bird (CAN) 134) [2003 69: f8.5g⁶ 7g³ 7.1m⁴ 6d 8d⁵ 8m f8g f7g Dec 16]   **a–**
medium-sized, strong filly: fairly useful maiden: below form after third start: stays 7f: yet
to race on extremes of going on turf, little form on fibresand. *J. Hetherton*

PRIDE OF PERU (IRE)   6 b.m. Perugino (USA) 84 – Nation's Game 51 (Mummy's   **–**
Game 120) [2003 –: f6g Jan 28] tall mare: poor maiden in 2001: no form since: tried
blinkered. *M. Brittain*

PRIDEWAY (IRE)   7 b.m. Pips Pride 117 – Up The Gates (Captain James 123) [2003   **?**
64§, a54§: f9.4g* f8g³ f9.4g⁴ p10g f9.4g* f9.4s* f9.4g⁵ 9.7g⁶ f9.4s Dec 6] leggy, sparely-   **a71**
made mare: fair handicapper: won 3 times at Wolverhampton in January/February: stays

9.4f: acts on any turf going and fibresand (some promise on polytrack): blinkered: tried tongue tied: sometimes starts slowly: formerly moody. *W. M. Brisbourne*

PRIDEYEV (USA)   3 ch.c. Nureyev (USA) 131 – Pride of Baino (USA) (Secretariat (USA)) [2003 10g⁴ᵈ 14.1f³ 11.8m⁴ Sep 1] good-topped colt: fourth foal: dam unraced out of champion 1980 2-y-o filly in USA Heavenly Cause: modest form in maidens: stays 1¾m: sold 4,000 gns. *Mrs A. J. Perrett*   **56**

PRIMA CIELO   2 b.f. (Feb 21) Primo Dominie 121 – Song of Skye 84 (Warning 136) [2003 5g 6m⁵ 5m 7m 5m⁵ f5g⁵ Oct 4] 1,200Y, resold 1,000Y: small, close-coupled filly: first foal: dam 5f (at 2 yrs) and 7f winner: poor maiden: stays 6f: acts on good to firm going. *E. J. Alston*   **43**

PRIMA FALCON   3 b.f. Polar Falcon (USA) 126 – Prima Silk 82 (Primo Dominie 121) [2003 –: 5.1m 6.1g 5.1m 6g f6s Jun 13] leggy filly: modest maiden: clearly best effort on reappearance: tongue tied final outing. *G. G. Margarson*   **52 d**

PRIMARY CLASSIC   3 b.g. Classic Cliche (IRE) 128 – Zarzi (IRE) (Suave Dancer (USA) 136) [2003 8g a8g⁴ a12g³ a12g⁴ Nov 16] 500 2-y-o: second foal: dam unraced: sold from Miss V. Haigh 2,000 gns after debut: first form when in frame in minor events at Taby last 2 starts (demoted from second in amateur contest on first occasion): better at 1½m than 1m. *Madeleine Smith, Sweden*   **?**

PRIMA STELLA   4 br. or gr.f. Primo Dominie 121 – Raffelina (USA) (Carson City (USA)) [2003 77: f6g* f6s* p6g³ f6g² 5.7f⁴ f5s* f5g f5g² p6g Dec 6] leggy filly: fair performer: won seller at Wolverhampton in January, and claimers at Southwell (left J. Balding) in February and Wolverhampton in April: left T. Naughton after sixth start, claimed from N. Littmoden £10,000 on eighth: free-going sort, best at 5f/6f: unraced on heavy going, acts on any other turf/all-weather: sometimes slowly away: found little fourth start. *J. A. R. Toller*   **74**

PRIME ATTRACTION   6 gr.m. Primitive Rising (USA) 113 – My Friend Melody (Sizzling Melody 117) [2003 63: 10g⁶ 13.1g 12.1d² 11.8m² 13g⁶ 13.1m⁵ 12m⁶ 12m 11.9f⁴ 11.9m⁶ 15.8m³ Oct 7] lengthy mare: fair bumper winner: modest maiden on Flat: stayed 2m: acted on firm and good to soft going: dead. *W. M. Brisbourne*   **56**

PRIME POWERED (IRE)   2 b.g. (Mar 25) Barathea (IRE) 127 – Caribbean Quest 90 (Rainbow Quest (USA) 134) [2003 6d 8.5g² 8.5d* Oct 4] 16,000Y: third foal: half-brother to 4-y-o Exploring: dam, 2-y-o 1m winner, from family of high-class sprinter/miler Golden Opinion: easily best effort (fairly useful form) when winning 5-runner minor event at Epsom by 3½ lengths from Old Malt, hanging left: will probably stay 1¼m. *G. L. Moore*   **90**

PRIME RECREATION   6 b.g. Primo Dominie 121 – Night Transaction 59 (Tina's Pet 121) [2003 89d: f5s 5g* f5g f5g 5g 5f 5m 5m² 5m⁴ 5d f5g Dec 16] strong, rangy gelding: fair handicapper: won at Kempton in March: best at 5f: acts on fibresand, good to firm and heavy going: sometimes slowly away/finds little: none too reliable, and probably best when able to lead. *P. S. Felgate*   **78**

PRIMO DAWN   4 b.g. Primo Dominie 121 – Sara Sprint (Formidable (USA) 125) [2003 70: p8g f6g⁵ f6g⁴ a6.8g a6g² a6g⁶ a6g² a6g Oct 18] big, lengthy gelding: fair performer at best: below form before sold from N. Littmoden 1,400 gns after third start: second at Taby in minor event/handicap: stays 7f: acts on all-weather: free-going sort. *Annelie Larsson, Sweden*   **53**

PRIMO ROSE   3 b.f. Primo Dominie 121 – My Dear Watson (Chilibang 120) [2003 –: 6.1g 5.3m⁶ 5m⁴ 6.1m 5.1m 5.9d 7g Sep 16] sturdy filly: poor maiden: well held last 4 starts: raced mainly at 5f/6f: unraced on extremes of going: blinkered last 6 starts: sent to Belgium. *R. Guest*   **43**

PRIMO WAY   2 b.c. (Apr 30) Primo Dominie 121 – Waypoint 95 (Cadeaux Genereux 131) [2003 5m⁴ 6m³ 6g⁵ Sep 12] 70,000Y: tall, rather unfurnished colt: third foal: half-brother to useful 2002 2-y-o 5f/5.5f (Prix Robert Papin) winner Never A Doubt (by Night Shift): dam, 6f/7f winner, half-sister to 4-y-o Acclamation: fair form: in frame in maidens at Windsor: slow-starting fifth in sales race at Doncaster: not sure to stay much beyond 6f. *B. W. Hills*   **77**

PRIMROSE AND ROSE   4 b.f. Primo Dominie 121 – Cointosser (IRE) 66 (Nordico (USA)) [2003 60d: p6g p5g p8g 5.7m 5m 5g⁴ 5m 5g³ 5m 5m⁵ 6m 5g 6m 5m Sep 17] plain, sparely-made filly: poor handicapper: effective at 5f/6f: acts on soft going, good to firm and all-weather: wore cheekpieces second outing, sometimes visored. *J. J. Bridger*   **41 §**

PRIMUS INTER PARES (IRE)   2 b.c. (Apr 21) Sadler's Wells (USA) 132 – Life   **98 p**
At The Top 107 (Habitat 134) [2003 p7g³ 7m* 7g² Oct 11] 85,000F, 110,000Y: smallish,
close-coupled colt: ninth foal: half-brother to 2 winners, including smart 7f (at 2 yrs) to
9f (in Ireland) winner Tiger Shark (by Chief's Crown): dam, 2-y-o 6f/7f winner who
stayed 1¼m, also successful in USA at 4 yrs: useful form: won maiden at Newmarket in
September by 2½ lengths from Mr Tambourine Man: further improvement when 1¼
lengths second of 6 to Oriental Warrior in minor event at Ascot: should be suited by 1¼m/
1½m: races prominently: should continue to progress. *J. R. Fanshawe*

PRINCE AARON (IRE)   3 b.g. Marju (IRE) 127 – Spirito Libro (USA) 89 (Lear Fan   **60**
(USA) 130) [2003 8g⁶ 7d p10g 10m 7m 7f⁶ p6g² Dec 17] IR 37,000F: second foal: dam,
5f (at 2 yrs) to 1¼m winner, half-sister to smart Irish 6f winner Conormara: modest
maiden: best effort at 6f: acts on polytrack: slowly away third/sixth outings. *C. N. Allen*

PRINCE ADJAL (IRE)   3 b.g. Desert Prince (IRE) 130 – Adjalisa (IRE) 65 (Darshaan   –
133) [2003 –: 8m 6m Sep 16] no sign of ability on Flat: tried blinkered: won juvenile
hurdle in October. *G. M. Moore*

PRINCE ALBERT   5 ch.g. Rock City 120 – Russell Creek 80 (Sandy Creek 123) [2003   –
54: f11g p10g⁵ Mar 4] leggy, lengthy gelding: modest maiden handicapper: well held in
2003: free-going sort. *J. R. Jenkins*

PRINCE ATRAF   4 b.g. Atraf 116 – Forest Fantasy 61 (Rambo Dancer (CAN) 107)   –
[2003 86d: p13g f11g p13g Feb 12] useful-looking gelding: fairly useful at best: mostly
disappointing since 3-y-o reappearance: tried blinkered/in cheekpieces. *B. R. Millman*

PRINCE CYRANO   4 b.g. Cyrano de Bergerac 120 – Odilese 82 (Mummy's Pet 125)   **93 §**
[2003 109: 6g 5.2m⁴ 6g 6g 6g² 6f 6g Aug 2] quite good-topped gelding: just fairly useful
performer in 2003: effective at 5f/6f: acts on firm and good to soft going: blinkered on
debut (at 2 yrs): sometimes slowly away: takes strong hold: wayward. *W. J. Musson*

PRINCE DARKHAN (IRE)   7 b.g. Doyoun 124 – Sovereign Dona 117 (Sovereign   –
Path 125) [2003 14.1m Jun 21] probably of little account nowadays: tried tongue tied.
G. A. Harker

PRINCE DAYJUR (USA)   4 b. or br.g. Dayjur (USA) 137 – Distinct Beauty (USA)   **– §**
(Phone Trick) [2003 –: 5m 6d 6m 7g Jun 28] close-coupled, quite attractive gelding: useful at 2 yrs, well held since: virtually refused to race on reappearance. *D. Nicholls*

PRINCE DIMITRI   4 ch.g. Desert King (IRE) 129 – Pinta (IRE) (Ahonoora 122)   –
[2003 60: 8.1m 12.6f Jul 10] close-coupled gelding: modest handicapper at 3 yrs, no form
in 2003: visored/tongue tied (looked temperamental) final start: takes good hold/races
prominently: has hung left. *M. C. Pipe*

PRINCE DOMINO   4 b.g. Primo Dominie 121 – Danzig Harbour (USA) (Private   **66**
Account (USA)) [2003 78?: p8g 7m 7m 7m* 7m⁶ 8.5d² 7m 7f 8d⁴ p7g Dec 10] leggy,
useful-looking gelding: fair performer: won seller at Brighton in May: stays 8.5f: acts on
firm and soft going: tried in cheekpieces/blinkers: tongue tied last 7 starts: usually races
prominently. *G. L. Moore*

PRINCE DU SOLEIL (FR)   7 b.g. Cardoun (FR) 122 – Revelry (FR) (Blakeney 126)   **45 §**
[2003 58§: 8m 8.1m 8m 8.3m p16g Dec 2] quite attractive gelding: poor handicapper
nowadays: probably best around 1m: acts on heavy and good to firm going: has been
visored/tongue tied: ungenuine. *J. R. Jenkins*

PRINCE HECTOR   4 ch.g. Hector Protector (USA) 124 – Ceanothus (IRE) 61   **90**
(Bluebird (USA) 125) [2003 90: 8.3d⁶ 8.1m 7.1f⁶ 7f 7f³ 7.6m 8.1d 8m* 8f Sep 28] strong,
close-coupled gelding: fairly useful handicapper: won at Yarmouth in September: best
around 1m: acts on firm and good to soft going. *W. J. Haggas*

PRINCE HOLING   3 ch.g. Halling (USA) 133 – Ella Mon Amour 65 (Ela-Mana-Mou   **94**
132) [2003 90: 9.9m⁴ 9.9f* 11.7f² 12m² Aug 24] rangy gelding: fairly useful performer,
quite lightly raced: won maiden at Salisbury in June: good second in handicap at Goodwood final start, despite carrying head high: effective at 1¼m to 1½m: raced only on good
ground or firmer: tongue tied last 3 starts at 2 yrs: has been slowly away/raced freely: sold
26,000 gns, joined Venetia Williams. *J. H. M. Gosden*

PRINCE IVOR   3 b.g. Polar Falcon (USA) 126 – Mistook (USA) (Phone Trick (USA))   **42 §**
[2003 66: p10g f9.4g 10m 10d 10.2g⁵ 12m 8f p12g p7g Dec 17] poor maiden: left
R. Hannon after seventh start: barely stays 1¼m: acts on good to firm going: tried visored:
ungenuine. *J. C. Fox*

Daily Record Scottish Derby, Ayr—Princely Venture, under strong pressure, drifts across eventual fourth Private Charter; the pair are split by Sights On Gold (left) and Delsarte (breastgirth)

PRINCELY VENTURE (IRE) 4 ch.c. Entrepreneur 123 – Sun Princess 130 (English **118** Prince 129) [2003 98p: 12g* 10g* 12.5s Aug 31] big, strong, lengthy colt: smart form: has won 3 of 6 starts, including minor event at Goodwood in May and Daily Record Scottish Derby at Ayr (beat Sights On Gold by ¾ length, edging left) in July: disappointing last in Grand Prix de Deauville final outing: effective at 1¼m/1½m: possibly unsuited by soft going: sold 16,000 gns, sent to UAE, joined R. Bouresly. *Sir Michael Stoute*

PRINCE MILLENNIUM 5 b.g. First Trump 118 – Petit Point (IRE) 78 (Petorius **43** 117) [2003 54: 9.7m 9.9m⁴ 10.1m⁵ 12g 12.1m 9.9d Jul 5] neat gelding: poor maiden handicapper: acts on heavy and good to firm ground: usually blinkered/ visored in 2001: has carried head high. *R. A. Fahey*

PRINCE MINATA (IRE) 8 b.g. Machiavellian (USA) 123 – Aminata 98 (Glenstal **?** (USA) 118) [2003 54, a58: f8s p10g² p10g⁶ f8.5g⁶ f9.4s f8.5g* f9.4s⁵ f8g f8.5g f8.5s **a54** p10g⁶ Apr 9] sturdy gelding: modest performer: won amateur claimer at Wolverhampton in February: barely stays 1¼m: acts on all-weather, firm and soft going: tried tongue tied: has reportedly broken blood vessels: none too consistent. *P. W. Hiatt*

PRINCE NASSEEM (GER) 6 b.h. Neshad (USA) 108 – Penola (GER) (Acatenango **—** (GER) 127) [2003 f12s Jun 21] ex-German horse: second foal: half-brother to winner in Germany by Law Society: dam German 10.5f winner: successful twice at 4 yrs at Bremen in maiden/handicap: made frame most starts in 2002: well held in claimer only start in Britain: raced mainly around 1m: acts on heavy and good to firm going: formerly consistent. *A. G. Juckes*

PRINCE NUREYEV (IRE) 3 b.c. Desert King (IRE) 129 – Annaletta 89 (Belmez **102** (USA) 131) [2003 94: 10.2m⁶ 11m* 12m 12m² 10s⁴ 14.1f⁴ 12f Sep 28] angular, quite good-topped colt: has a short, choppy action: useful performer: won handicap at Newbury in May by short head from Santando: ran creditably after only when in frame in minor events, beaten neck by Hawk Flyer in 3-runner race at Ascot fourth outing: barely stays 1¾m: acts on firm and good to soft ground, probably on soft: sometimes races freely: reportedly pulled muscles when tailed off in Derby at Epsom third start. *B. R. Millman*

PRINCE OF BLUES (IRE) 5 b.g. Prince of Birds (USA) 121 – Reshift 94 (Night **84 d** Shift (USA)) [2003 96, a100: f6s p5g 6m 6g 5.1m 5.1g⁶ 5g 5f 6f 5s f6g f5g p6g⁶ f5s f6g **a89 d** Dec 26] good-topped, useful-looking gelding: poor mover: just fairly useful nowadays: below form after sixth start, left N. Littmoden after ninth: effective at 5f/6f: acts on firm going, soft and all-weather: sometimes blinkered/in cheekpieces: sometimes slowly away: usually races prominently: temperament under suspicion. *M. Mullineaux*

PRINCE OF DENMARK (IRE) 2 b.c. (Jan 8) Danetime (IRE) 121 – Villa Nova **96** (IRE) 55 (Petardia 113) [2003 5g* p5g* 5d* 5m⁴ 5m⁵ 5g² 5.2m⁴ a7f* a8f* Dec 18] 14,500Y: leggy, useful-looking colt: first foal: dam, Irish maiden, half-sister to useful Irish 1997 2-y-o 7f winner Impressionist: useful performer: successful in maiden at Folkestone in March and minor events at Lingfield in April and Windsor in May: in frame in listed races at Sandown and Super Sprint at Newbury: left R. Hannon, won minor events at Nad Al Sheba in November and December (tongue tied both times): stays 1m:

acts on polytrack/dirt, yet to race on extremes of going on turf: free-going sort: sometimes looks none too keen. *M. Al Kurdi, UAE*

PRINCE OF GOLD 3 b.c. Polar Prince (IRE) 117 – Gold Belt (IRE) 61 (Bellypha 130) [2003 77: f8.5s³ 10m⁴ 7.6m 8.5m* 8.2d* 8.1d 10.3m⁴ 8m⁵ 8.5d³ 7.5m² 10g 8m⁴ f8s* f7s³ 10.3d 8m f7g Oct 16] good-topped colt: fair performer: won handicap at Beverley and minor event at Nottingham in May and handicap at Southwell in September: stays 8.5f, probably not 1¼m: acts on firm going, good to soft and fibresand. *R. Hollinshead* **79**

PRINCE OF PERLES 2 b.c. (Jan 29) Mind Games 121 – Pearls (Mon Tresor 113) [2003 5.1m 6f 6m 5d 6m Aug 22] 13,000Y: third foal: brother to fairly useful 2001 2-y-o 6f winner Perle d'Azur and closely related to 2000 2-y-o 6f winner Wilson Blyth (by Puissance), later successful in Spain: dam unraced: poor maiden: blinkered final start: ungenuine. *A. Berry* **42 §**

PRINCE OF PERSIA 3 b.g. Turtle Island (IRE) 123 – Sianiski (Niniski (USA) 125) [2003 56: 8m 8d Oct 31] close-coupled gelding: seemingly modest form on debut at 2 yrs: well held since, leaving D. Nicholls before final one: should stay 1¼m. *R. Hannon* **–**

PRINCE OF THEBES (IRE) 2 b.c. (Apr 25) Desert Prince (IRE) 130 – Persian Walk (FR) (Persian Bold 123) [2003 6g 7m³ 7m* Jul 31] 45,000F, 50,000Y: good-topped colt: third foal: half-brother to UAE 11f winner Royal Shakespeare (by King's Theatre): dam, won both starts at 1½m in France, half-sister to smart French performers up to 1½m Walk On Mix and Walking Around: fairly useful form in maidens: made all in 7-runner event at Epsom: suffered pelvic injury after: free-going sort, but should stay 1m. *A. M. Balding* **87**

PRINCE OF THE WOOD (IRE) 3 ch.g. Woodborough (USA) 112 – Ard Dauphine (IRE) (Forest Wind (USA) 111) [2003 p6g p8g p10g⁵ f12g 11.6d² 14.1m 14m 12g 10d⁶ f16.2g⁴ Nov 10] IR 7,200F, IR 4,000Y: workmanlike gelding: first foal: dam unraced out of half-sister to Irish 2000 Guineas winner Northern Treasure: modest maiden handicapper: left D. Cosgrove after eighth start: stays 11.6f, not 2m: best efforts on good to soft ground. *A. Bailey* **56 a47**

PRINCE PROSPECT 7 b.g. Lycius (USA) 124 – Princess Dechtra (IRE) 65 (Bellypha 130) [2003 59§, a71§: f12s⁴ f12g⁶ f9.4g⁴ f11g Dec 16] sturdy gelding: unimpressive mover: modest performer: stays easy 1½m: acts on firm going, good to soft and fibresand: visored once at 2 yrs: often soon off bridle: unreliable. *Mrs L. Stubbs* **– § a54 §**

PRINCE PYRAMUS 5 b.g. Pyramus (USA) 78 – Rekindled Flame (IRE) (Kings Lake (USA) 133) [2003 65: 8m 8g 7m 8g 5g 6d 5m Jun 4] fair performer at best: well held in 2003: tried tongue tied, blinkered/in cheekpieces. *C. Grant* **–**

PRINCE RESTATE 4 ch.g. Prince of Birds (USA) 121 – Restate (IRE) 52 (Soviet Star (USA) 128) [2003 p13g 7m⁶ 7g 7g 6m 6d 5m⁶ 5m Sep 6] 800Y: second foal: dam ran twice on Flat: well held in maidens/handicaps, looking none too keen final start: tried in cheekpieces/visor. *T. T. Clement* **–**

PRINCES GRANT 2 b.g. (Apr 22) Compton Place 125 – Penny Dip 86 (Cadeaux Genereux 131) [2003 5m⁴ 7m Oct 12] 4,500Y: fifth foal: dam, 6f winner, out of smart 2-y-o 5f winner Penny Blessing: better effort in maidens (modest form) when fourth at Carlisle: raced too freely at Newcastle: bred to prove best at 5f/6f: probably open to improvement. *R. A. Fahey* **63 p**

PRINCE'S PASSION 4 b.f. Brief Truce (USA) 126 – Green Bonnet (IRE) (Green Desert (USA) 127) [2003 80: p10g p8g p10g⁵ p8g² 8f⁴ 8f⁴ 8.5m 8m⁶ Aug 14] small, good-bodied filly: fair performer: stays easy 1¼m: acts on firm going and polytrack: visored last 6 starts: unreliable: sold 12,000 gns in December. *D. J. Coakley* **68 § a75 §**

PRINCESS ALINA (IRE) 2 b.f. (Apr 19) Sadler's Wells (USA) 132 – Eilanden (IRE) (Akarad (FR) 130) [2003 8.5g⁵ p7g² Oct 30] €70,000Y: strong filly: third foal: dam unraced half-sister to smart Irish performer up to 1½m Ebaziya, herself dam of Gold Cup winner Enzeli and Irish Oaks/Prix Royal-Oak winner Ebadiyla (by Sadler's Wells): much better effort in maidens (fair form) when second to Incheni at Lingfield: will be suited by at least 1¼m. *A. M. Balding* **66**

PRINCESS ANABAA (FR) 3 b.f. Anabaa (USA) 130 – Valley Road (FR) (Noblequest (FR) 124) [2003 7.1g 7f³ 8.1d 8m* 8f Oct 17] 2,000,000 francs Y: seventh foal: half-sister to several winners in France, including useful French 5f (at 2 yrs) to 7f winner Berkoutchi (by Take Risks): dam, French maiden, best at 5f/6f at 2 yrs: easily best effort (fair form) when winning maiden at Pontefract in October: favourite, well held off seemingly lenient mark final outing: stays 1m: acts on good to firm going. *M. R. Channon* **77**

PRINCESS CLAUDIA (IRE) 5 b.m. Kahyasi 130 – Shamarra (FR) (Zayyani 119) –
[2003 18f Jul 19] small, compact mare: fluent mover: maiden handicapper at 3 yrs: well
held only start since: blinkered once: sold 3,900 gns. *M. F. Harris*

PRINCESS ERICA 3 b.f. Perpendicular 119 – Birichino (Dilum (USA) 115) [2003 63
62: 7g 6.1g³ 6.1m f6g³ 7m 6m⁵ May 26] big, good-topped filly: modest maiden: stays 6f:
acts on fibresand, heavy and good to firm ground: visored (respectable effort) final start:
slowly away third outing. *T. D. Easterby*

PRINCESS FAITH 3 b.f. Polar Prince (IRE) 117 – Crissem (IRE) 70 (Thatching 131) –
[2003 –: f8.5g f8s 11.6g Aug 4] lengthy, good-topped filly: no form: left R. Hollinshead
after second start. *A. J. Chamberlain*

PRINCESS GALADRIEL 2 b.f. (Mar 20) Magic Ring (IRE) 115 – Prim Lass 65 49
(Reprimand 122) [2003 f5s 6.1f 5m⁴ 7f Oct 27] rather leggy filly: fourth foal: half-sister
to 2001 2-y-o 5f selling winner Primarosa (by Atraf): dam, maiden, might have proved
best at 5f/6f and hinted at temperament: poor maiden: probably stays 6f. *J. R. Best*

PRINCESS GRACE 4 b.f. Inchinor 119 – Hardiprincess (Keen 116) [2003 45: f12s 45
f9.4s² f8g⁶ Dec 8] leggy, angular filly: poor maiden handicapper: barely stays 2m: acts on
fibresand. *M. L. W. Bell*

PRINCESS ISMENE 2 b.f. (Apr 25) Sri Pekan (USA) 117 – Be Practical 83 (Tragic 61
Role (USA)) [2003 6g f6g⁵ 7.5m⁴ 7.5m² f7f⁵ 7m² 7m² 7m* 8m 7m⁴ 7f 8d⁵ Oct 31]
5,500Y: small filly: second foal: dam 6f winner: modest performer: won selling nursery at
Leicester in September: stays 7.5f: acts on good to firm going, well beaten on fibresand:
blinkered 6 of last 7 starts: very slowly away tenth one. *J. Jay*

PRINCESS KAI (IRE) 2 b.f. (Apr 4) Cayman Kai (IRE) 114 – City Princess 62§ 58
(Rock City) [2003 6g 5.1f⁴ p5g⁴ 6g⁶ 5m⁴ 5m 5d³ p6g p6g³ Nov 13] €800 2-y-o: first
foal: dam temperamental 2-y-o 5f/6f seller winner: modest maiden: stays easy 6f: acts on
polytrack, firm and good to soft ground: blinkered (looked none too keen) final start.
R. Ingram

PRINCESS KIOTTO 2 b.f. (Mar 29) Desert King (IRE) 129 – Ferghana Ma 62 –
(Mtoto 134) [2003 7.5m 8g f8s Oct 7] rather leggy filly: first foal: dam, lightly-raced
maiden (should have stayed 1½m), half-sister to useful 1¼m performer Always On A
Sunday: well held in maidens. *T. D. Easterby*

PRINCESS MAGDALENA 3 ch.f. Pennekamp (USA) 130 – Reason To Dance 96 60
(Damister (USA) 123) [2003 76: 8g 7.1g 8.1m 8.3m 10.9m 10m* 11f Oct 12] leggy,
close-coupled filly: modest performer nowadays: won seller at Windsor in September:
ran as if amiss final start: stays 1¼m: raced only on good ground or firmer. *L. G. Cottrell*

PRINCESS PERFECT (IRE) 2 b.f. (Feb 16) Danehill Dancer (IRE) 117 – Resiusa –
(ITY) (Niniski (USA) 125) [2003 6m 6m Jun 22] IR 3,000F, €10,000Y: leggy, work-
manlike filly: half-sister to 3 winners, including 1996 2-y-o 5f/6f winner Robec Girl (by
Masterclass): dam Italian 7f (at 2 yrs) to 11f winner: well held in maidens at Haydock (for
K. Ryan) and Pontefract: joined H. Cecil. *A. Berry*

PRINCESS RENESIS (IRE) 2 gr.f. (Apr 29) Perugino (USA) 84 – Tajarib (IRE) 55 –
(Last Tycoon 131) [2003 5m 6.1d May 17] IR 2,000F, €17,500Y: close-coupled, quite
good-topped filly: seventh foal: half-sister to 3 winners, including fairly useful 8.5f
winner Silverado (by Indian Ridge), later successful in Hong Kong, and smart Italian/
French 5f (at 2 yrs) to 1m winner Golden Devious (by Dr Devious): dam, maiden, should
have stayed 1m: well held in maidens at Pontefract and Nottingham. *J. A. Glover*

PRINCESS ROYALE (IRE) 4 b.f. Royal Applause 124 – On The Bank (IRE) (In 63
The Wings 128) [2003 8.3m 9f⁶ p12g Jul 9] modest maiden, lightly raced: stays 9f: raced
only on good going or firmer on turf. *G. A. Butler*

PRINCESS SHOKA (IRE) 3 b.f. Definite Article 121 – Shoka (FR) 86 (Kaldoun 72
(FR) 122) [2003 72: p8g⁶ p7g² 10f⁴ p10g 10g⁵ p10g⁶ 8.1m** 10d⁵ 8m³ 10.2m 8m 8f* 9g
Oct 24] leggy filly: fair performer: won maiden claimer at Haydock in August and
handicap at Brighton in October: barely stays 8.5f: unraced on soft/heavy ground, probably
acts on any other turf/all-weather: unseated rider and bolted before start on sixth outing:
none too reliable: sold 7,500 gns. *R. Hannon*

PRINCESS SPEEDFIT (FR) 3 b.f. Desert Prince (IRE) 130 – Perfect Sister (USA) 77
(Perrault 130) [2003 72: 8.3g⁴ 9g 7d 8.3g² 8.2m⁴ 8.5g 8.3g* 9m⁴ 8m 8f⁶ Oct 27] quite
attractive filly: has a round action: fair performer: won minor event at Windsor in
August: should stay 1¼m: acts on soft and good to firm ground: none too consistent.
G. G. Margarson

PRINCESS VALENTINA   3 b.f. My Best Valentine 122 – Sandkatoon (IRE) (Arch-   –
way (IRE) 115) [2003 –: f5s p7g 6m f5g 5.7f 5f⁶ Jun 27] little form: tried tongue tied/
blinkered. *J. White*

PRINCES THEATRE   5 b.g. Prince Sabo 123 – Frisson (Slip Anchor 136) [2003 64:   74
8g³ 9f* 7.9m* 10.1m Oct 12] good-topped gelding: fair handicapper: won at Newcastle
(left G. Kelly) in August and Carlisle in September: stays 9f: acts on firm going: tried
tongue tied: very slowly away final outing: reportedly bled once at 4 yrs. *M. W. Easterby*

PRINCE TARA (IRE)   2 ch.g. (Feb 13) Docksider (USA) 124 – Bird In My Hand   78
(IRE) 57 (Bluebird (USA) 125) [2003 5f 5.1m 5m* 6g³ 6g 5f* Aug 22] IR 8,200F,
€9,000Y: good-bodied gelding: third living foal: dam, ran 3 times, half-sister to very
smart stayer Yawa: fair performer: won maiden at Pontefract in June and minor event at
Newcastle in August: raced freely when third in nursery at Pontefract: stays 6f: sold
16,000 gns, sent to USA. *J. J. Quinn*

PRINCE TULUM (USA)   4 ch.g. Bien Bien (USA) 125 – Eastsider (USA) (Diesis   69 ?
133) [2003 –, a91: f8.5g* f8.5g³ f8.5s p8g f7g⁵ f8.5s 8.1m 8.5d³ Jul 3] fairly useful   a89
handicapper on all-weather, fair on turf: won at Wolverhampton in January: best form up
to 8.5f: acts on all-weather, yet to race on extremes of going on turf: tried blinkered/in
cheekpieces: has raced freely: sold 16,000 gns. *N. P. Littmoden*

PRINCE TUM TUM (USA)   3 b.c. Capote (USA) – La Grande Epoque (USA) 120   115
(Lyphard (USA) 132) [2003 97p: 8m* Apr 19] lengthy, quite attractive colt: smart
performer: has won 3 of 5 starts: improved form when winning listed race at Kempton in
April by length from Dutch Gold, only outing at 3 yrs: stays 1m: raced only on ground
firmer than good: stays in training. *J. L. Dunlop*

Mr Robin F. Scully's "Prince Tum Tum"

PRINCE VALENTINE   2 b.g. (Mar 1) My Best Valentine 122 – Affaire de Coeur 55   **67**
(Imperial Fling (USA) 116) [2003 p8g p8g Dec 10] fifth foal: dam, 1m winner, also
successful over hurdles: better effort in maidens at Lingfield (fair form) when seventh of
12 to Jake The Snake on final start, hampered: not sure to stay beyond 1m. *D. B. Feek*

PRINCE ZAR (IRE)   3 b.g. Inzar (USA) 112 – Salonniere (FR) 88 (Bikala 134) [2003   **44**
–: f7g³ f8.5g⁵ f9.4g 8.3g f12g Jun 6] poor maiden: soundly beaten in handicaps last 3
starts: should stay beyond 8.5f: blinkered final outing. *C. G. Cox*

PRINCIPESSA   2 b.f. (Feb 14) Machiavellian (USA) 123 – Party Doll 108 (Be My   **68 p**
Guest (USA) 126) [2003 8.2d³ Nov 6] €360,000Y: leggy, close-coupled filly: sister to 3
winners, including French sprinters Titus Livius (smart) and Bahama Dream (useful), and
half-sister to 3 winners: dam French 5f (at 2 yrs) to 1m winner: 25/1, 8½ lengths third of
16 to Vaughan in maiden at Nottingham, soon prominent: not sure to stay much beyond
1m: should improve. *B. Palling*

PRINGIPESSA'S WAY   5 b.m. Machiavellian (USA) 123 – Miss Fancy That (USA)   **58 d**
99 (The Minstrel (CAN) 135) [2003 69: p8g p7g p10g f9.4g p8g 7m⁵ 6m Aug 28] close-
coupled mare: modest maiden: below form after second start: probably stays 1¼m: acts
on good to firm going and polytrack, below form on fibresand: folded only try in blinkers:
swishes tail: covered by Mark of Esteem, and sent to Greece. *P. R. Chamings*

PRINS WILLEM (IRE)   4 b.g. Alzao (USA) 117 – American Garden (USA) (Alleged   **97**
(USA) 138) [2003 84: 12g 12g* 11.9g 12d⁵ 12m² 12g⁶ 13.3m* 16g Oct 31] sturdy
gelding: useful handicapper: won at Doncaster in May and Newbury in September, best
effort when dead-heating with Starry Lodge in latter: should stay 2m: acts on good to firm
and good to soft going: has been tongue tied: raced freely third start: usually waited with.
J. R. Fanshawe

PRINTSMITH (IRE)   6 br.m. Petardia 113 – Black And Blaze (Taufan (USA) 119)   **40**
[2003 53: f8g f8s f8g 7g 6.9d⁵ Jul 30] leggy mare: poor handicapper nowadays: stays 1m:
has form on good to firm ground, but best efforts (and all wins) on good or softer: has
worn cheekpieces: inconsistent. *J. R. Norton*

PRIORS DALE   3 b.c. Lahib (USA) 129 – Mathaayl (USA) 79 (Shadeed (USA) 135)   **82**
[2003 77p: 8g 8g⁴ 10g p8g² p10g Nov 29] leggy, good-topped colt: fair maiden handicapper, lightly raced: best form at 1m: acts on polytrack, raced only on good ground or
softer on turf. *K. Bell*

PRIORS LODGE (IRE)   5 br.h. Grand Lodge (USA) 125 – Addaya (IRE) (Persian   **118**
Bold 123) [2003 113: 9m³ 8m² 8m* 9.9m⁴ Sep 13] close-coupled, quite attractive horse:
usually impresses in appearance: smart performer: trained in 2002 by R. Hannon: reportedly had his jaw broken when kicked by another horse after reappearance: better than
ever subsequently, winning Celebration Mile at Goodwood in August by head from
Passing Glance: similar form when short-head second to same rival in listed event at
Salisbury and close fourth of 5 to Leporello in Select Stakes at Goodwood: effective at 7f,
seems to stay easy 1¼m: acts on good to firm going, probably on soft: has worn crossed
noseband: usually races prominently: game and consistent. *M. P. Tregoning*

PRISSY (IRE)   3 b.f. Desert Story (IRE) 115 – Practical 95 (Ballymore 123) [2003 –:   **–**
5f 5m Jul 23] no sign of ability. *C. J. Teague*

Celebration Mile, Goodwood—Priors Lodge edges out Passing Glance (rail), with Tillerman back in third

Mr R. E. Sangster's "Private Charter"

PRIVATE BENJAMIN 3 gr.g. Ridgewood Ben 113 – Jilly Woo 60 (Environment **64** Friend 128) [2003 75: 7g 7m 7m 8m³ 8m 8m⁶ 8f⁴ 9.9m³ 10s⁶ 11.9f⁶ 11m⁴ Sep 24] angular gelding: has a round action: modest maiden handicapper nowadays: probably stays 11f: acts on firm and soft going: sometimes looks difficult ride: none too consistent: won juvenile hurdle later in September. *Jamie Poulton*

PRIVATE CHARTER 3 b.c. Singspiel (IRE) 133 – By Charter 104 (Shirley Heights **113** 130) [2003 90p: p10g* 10.3m³ 12m² 12f⁶ 10g⁴ 10f⁵ Aug 10] strong, lengthy colt: has a quick action: smart performer: won maiden at Lingfield in March: placed in Dee Stakes at Chester (5 lengths third of 4 to Kris Kin) and Derby Italiano at Rome (2½ lengths second to Osorio) next 2 outings: ran well last 2 starts when 1½ lengths fourth to Princely Venture in Scottish Derby at Ayr and 3½ lengths fifth to High Chaparral in Royal Whip Stakes at the Curragh: stays 1½m: acts on firm going and polytrack. *B. W. Hills*

PRIVATE SEAL 8 b.g. King's Signet (USA) 110 – Slender 79 (Aragon 118) [2003 **50 §** –§, a49§: p10g⁵ p10g⁵ 11.5g 11.6m p12g³ 8m⁵ p10g⁴ 11.6m⁶ 10.1f⁴ 10m 8m³ 8f 7m 10m p10g Dec 30] workmanlike gelding: modest performer: stays 11.5f: acts on firm going and polytrack: tried blinkered/in cheekpieces: usually tongue tied: has carried head awkwardly/flashed tail: one to treat with caution. *Julian Poulton*

PRIVY SEAL (IRE) 2 b.c. (May 6) Cape Cross (IRE) 129 – Lady Joshua (IRE) 88 **103** (Royal Academy (USA) 130) [2003 6g⁶ 6m* 6f³ 7m* 8m⁵ 8f⁵ Sep 27] €100,000Y: tall, quite attractive colt: has a quick action: fourth foal: half-brother to fairly useful 11.6f and 14.4f winner Lord Joshua (by King's Theatre) and winner in Australia by Alhaarth: dam, disappointing maiden who stayed 1½m, closely related to very smart performer up to 1¾m Sapience: useful performer: won maiden at Windsor in June and listed race at

819

Leopardstown (beat Wathab by length) in July: creditable efforts when third in Coventry Stakes at Royal Ascot (beaten 8¼ lengths by Three Valleys) and fifth in listed race at Goodwood and Royal Lodge Stakes at Ascot: will probably stay 1¼m: acts on firm going: sometimes bandaged fore joints. *J. H. M. Gosden*

PRIX STAR 8 ch.g. Superpower 113 – Celestine 62 (Skyliner 117) [2003 80, a–: 6d 6.1d 7f 6f 6g 6m⁴ 7m⁵ 6m 7g 6m 6.1f 7m³ Oct 18] angular gelding: just fair handicapper nowadays: effective at 6f/easy 7f: acts on fibresand and any turf going: sometimes visored, effective without. *C. W. Fairhurst* **66**

PRIZE RING 4 ch.g. Bering 136 – Spot Prize (USA) 108 (Seattle Dancer (USA) 119) [2003 79: f9.4s⁶ f12s f12g 10.1d 12m³ 10.1m 12.4g⁶ 10d 12m³ 12m⁶ 10g⁴ 10.1m* 14.1m Oct 17] tall gelding: just fair performer nowadays: won seller at Newcastle (left Mrs J. Ramsden 14,000 gns) in August: seems best at 1¼m/1½m: acts on firm ground: wore cheekpieces last 2 starts: sometimes races freely: has found less than seemed likely: held up. *G. M. Moore* **65**

PROCREATE (IRE) 3 b.g. Among Men (USA) 124 – Woodbury Princess (Never So Bold 135) [2003 f7g⁵ f6g 7m Mar 28] 1,000F, IR 3,500Y: fifth foal: half-brother to 2 winners, including Irish 1¾m winner Seomra Hocht (by Standiford): dam third at 5f/6f in Ireland: signs of a little ability in maidens. *J. A. Osborne* **–**

PROFILER (USA) 8 b.g. Capote (USA) – Magnificent Star (USA) 122 (Silver Hawk (USA) 123) [2003 f12s³ 12.3m 13f⁵ 12.1d 16m⁴ 14.1f f14.8g Nov 14] well-made gelding: modest performer at best nowadays: probably stays 2m: acts on firm ground: tried in cheekpieces. *Ferdy Murphy* **53 d**

PROFITEER (IRE) 4 b.g. Entrepreneur 123 – Champagne Girl 67 (Robellino (USA) 127) [2003 5m² 5m* 6.5m Jul 11] smallish, sturdy gelding: fairly useful form: twice raced at 2 yrs, missed 2002: landed odds in maiden at Musselburgh in June: well held in handicap at Ascot subsequent start: not sure to stay much beyond 6f: visored/blinkered since debut: ducked left when challenging on reappearance: temperamental and difficult ride (soon under pressure last 2 starts): one to treat with caution: sold 4,500 gns in October, sent to Italy. *D. R. Loder* **82 §**

PROMENADE 2 b.f. (Jan 18) Primo Dominie 121 – Hamsah (IRE) 86 (Green Desert (USA) 127) [2003 5m* 5m* 5m⁶ 5m* Jun 28] 42,000Y: smallish, sturdy filly: fifth foal: half-sister to fairly useful 1998 Irish 2-y-o 5f winner Sparkling Outlook (by College Chapel): dam, 2-y-o 5f winner, half-sister to Irish 2000 Guineas winner Wassl: fairly useful performer: won maiden at Leicester in April and minor events at Redcar in May and Doncaster in June (found to be lame behind shortly afterwards): respectable sixth to Attraction in Queen Mary Stakes at Royal Ascot (moved poorly to post) on third start: should stay 6f. *M. L. W. Bell* **87**

PROMISED (IRE) 5 b.m. Petardia 113 – Where's The Money 87 (Lochnager 132) [2003 –: f8g⁴ f7s* f8.5s p7g⁴ p10g Mar 14] short-backed, leggy mare: modest handicapper nowadays: won at Southwell in February: may prove best at 7f: acts on good to firm going, good to soft and all-weather: visored once, wore cheekpieces in 2003. *N. P. Littmoden* **58**

PROMISING (FR) 5 ch.m. Ashkalani (IRE) 128 – Sea Thunder 83 (Salse (USA) 128) [2003 56: p10g 11m 9.9d² 12f³ 10m Jun 4] strong, lengthy mare: modest maiden: probably stays 1¼m: acts on firm and good to soft going: tongue tied nowadays: often races prominently: none too consistent. *M. C. Chapman* **53**

PROMISING KING (IRE) 3 ch.c. Desert King (IRE) 129 – Bazaar Promise 58 (Native Bazaar 122) [2003 –: p8g* p8g² a7f⁴ 8f⁶ a8f Sep 1] fair performer: won on handicap debut at Lingfield in January, carrying head awkwardly: ran well next time, then left G. Butler: ran in claimers in US subsequently, well held first 2 starts, then (having left K. Mulhall) pulled up lame final outing: stays 1m: acts on polytrack: blinkered last 2 outings. *J. Bonde, USA* **66**

PROMOTE 7 gr.g. Linamix (FR) 127 – Rive (USA) (Riverman (USA) 131) [2003 –: 11.5g p13g Dec 29] one-time fairly useful 1m winner: on the downgrade: often tongue tied. *Ms A. E. Embiricos* **–**

PROMOTER 3 ch.g. Selkirk (USA) 129 – Poplina (USA) (Roberto (USA) 131) [2003 p10g⁵ 10g² 10m* 12d⁴ 13.1d 16g⁴ Oct 24] half-brother to several winners, including useful 1998 2-y-o 7f winner Come What May (by Common Grounds): dam, French 11f winner, half-sister to champion US older horse Vanlandingham and to dam of Distant Music: useful performer, lightly raced: won maiden at Newmarket in June: good efforts in handicaps after, particularly when 1½ lengths fourth to Misternando at Newbury final **100**

outing: changed ownership 100,000 gns later in October: stays 2m: acts on good to firm and good to soft going: slowly away first 2 outings: tends to carry head high. *J. Noseda*

PROMOTION 3 b.g. Sadler's Wells (USA) 132 – Tempting Prospect 95 (Shirley **90**
Heights 130) [2003 10m* 11.6m³ 12f² Aug 2] lengthy, attractive gelding: first foal: dam, 2-y-o 1m winner who stayed 1½m, half-sister to smart performer up to 13.3f Phantom Gold, herself dam of Oaks runner-up Flight of Fancy (by Sadler's Wells): fairly useful form: won maiden at Sandown on debut in May, tending to run in snatches: much better effort in minor events after when good neck second of 3 to Conquering Love at Thirsk: gelded after; will be suited by further than 1½m. *Sir Michael Stoute*

PROMPT PAYMENT (IRE) 5 b. or br.m. In The Wings 128 – Lady Lucre (IRE) 73 **104**
(Last Tycoon 131) [2003 99: 11.9v² 11.8m² 11.9g 14g³ 15.5m⁴ 14.1s⁵ 14.6d³ Nov 7] tall mare: useful performer: placed in listed races at Haydock, Leicester (¾-length second to Razkalla) and Goodwood (sweating) 3 of first 4 starts: also ran well in Prix Gladiateur at Longchamp (fourth to Darasim): below form last 2 starts, looking no easy ride final one: effective at 1¼m to 15.5f: acts on heavy and good to firm going: has been blanketed for stall entry: flashes tail, and sometimes finds little: sold 57,000 gns. *J. R. Fanshawe*

PROPRIUS 3 b.g. Perpendicular 119 – Pretty Pollyanna (General Assembly (USA)) **–**
[2003 47: f8s⁶ Feb 18] poor form at 2 yrs: well held only outing in 2003. *B. Smart*

PROSPECTOR'S COVE 10 b.g. Dowsing (USA) 124 – Pearl Cove 63 (Town And **–**
Country 124) [2003 46: f11s⁶ f9.4g f8.5g f7g f9.4s Feb 17] workmanlike gelding: one-time useful performer: well held in cheekpieces in 2003: tried visored: often slowly away. *J. M. Bradley*

PROSPECTS OF GLORY (USA) 7 b.h. Mr Prospector (USA) – Hatoof (USA) 124 **85**
(Irish River (FR) 131) [2003 89: 12.1m³ 16m⁶ 15f Jun 22] rather sparely-made horse: fairly useful performer, lightly raced: form in 2003 only on reappearance: probably stays easy 2m: acts on good to firm ground and polytrack. *E. J. O'Neill*

PROTECTION MONEY 3 ch.g. Hector Protector (USA) 124 – Three Piece (Jaaz- **–**
eiro (USA) 127) [2003 66: 12g Nov 5] form (fair) only on second of 3 starts at 2 yrs: pulled hard and carried head high only run in 2003. *Mrs M. Reveley*

PROTECTORATE 4 ch.f. Hector Protector (USA) 124 – Possessive Lady 62 (Dara **74**
Monarch 128) [2003 88: p8g⁵ 8g May 26] tall, angular filly: just fair form in 2003: needs test at 6f, and stays 1m: acts on polytrack, raced only on good ground or softer on turf: sometimes blinkered/visored at 3 yrs. *Miss Gay Kelleway*

PROTOCOL (IRE) 9 b.g. Taufan (USA) 119 – Ukraine's Affair (USA) (The Minstrel **33**
(CAN) 135) [2003 45, a–: 11.8g 10g 14.1m 16.2m 10.5f⁴ 10m Sep 18] rather leggy **a–**
gelding: poor handicapper: effective at stiff 1¼m to 17f: probably acts on any turf going and fibresand: tried visored: usually tongue tied. *Mrs S. Lamyman*

PROUD BOAST 5 b.m. Komaite (USA) – Red Rosein 97 (Red Sunset 120) [2003 **103**
104: 6.1s 5m⁴ 6m 6f⁵ 5m⁶ 5d 6.1m³ 5m 6m 5g³ 6f² 5d⁴ 5.2m 6.1d³ 5m⁶ 6m Oct 16] rather leggy, angular mare: useful performer: several creditable efforts in 2003, including when 1¼ lengths third to Resplendent Cee in listed race at Chester seventh outing: effective at 5f/6f: acts on firm and good to soft going: usually held up: sold 45,000 gns. *Mrs G. S. Rees*

PROUD NATIVE (IRE) 9 b.g. Imp Society (USA) – Karamana (Habitat 134) [2003 **90**
102: 6m 6m⁵ 5m⁴ 5f* 5g 5m* 5m 5.7m* 5.2m* 5d 5m⁵ Sep 17] sturdy gelding: poor walker/mover: fairly useful performer nowadays: won claimers at Sandown and Bath and handicaps at Newmarket and Newbury in the summer: best at 5f: acts on firm and soft ground: tried blinkered: edgy sort: usually early to post (got loose before start on reappearance): sometimes bandaged in front: usually waited with. *D. Nicholls*

PROUD TRADITION (USA) 2 b.f. (Feb 9) Seeking The Gold (USA) – Family **78 p**
Tradition (IRE) 107 (Sadler's Wells (USA) 132) [2003 8m* Sep 23] leggy, quite good-topped filly: second foal: dam, Irish 7f (at 2 yrs) and 1¾m winner, out of half-sister to outstanding broodmare Slightly Dangerous and to dam of Rainbow Quest: well-backed 9/2, won 11-runner maiden at Newmarket by 1¼ lengths from Strawberry Fair, leading over 2f out: will be suited by 1¼m/1½m: sure to progress. *J. H. M. Gosden*

PROUD VICTOR (IRE) 3 b.g. Victory Note (USA) 120 – Alberjas (IRE) (Sure **60 d**
Blade (USA) 130) [2003 64: f6g p7g p8g⁶ f8s⁴ f6g⁵ f7g⁴ p7g⁴ p7g f6g f6g 7m f5s 7g f6g f9.4g⁶ 8g f7g⁴ f8g f8s f8g⁶ Dec 19] modest performer: below form after seventh start: barely stays 1m: acts on all-weather, little form on turf: visored after third outing: has looked wayward. *D. Shaw*

PROUD WESTERN (USA)   5 b.g. Gone West (USA) – Proud Lou (USA) (Proud   **62**
Clarion) [2003 55: f8g 9.9m 7m⁴ 7.2m³ 5m² 5g 6m 6f 5m* 5m⁴ 5g Oct 22] modest on turf,
poor on all-weather: won seller at Newcastle (easily best effort in 2003) in September:
effective at 5f to 1m: acts on fibresand, good to firm and soft ground: tried blinkered/in
cheekpieces, usually tongue tied. *B. Ellison*

PROVENDER (IRE)   4 b.g. Ashkalani (IRE) 128 – Quiche 83 (Formidable (USA)   **–**
125) [2003 70, a73: p7g p10g 9.7g 8g May 19] good-topped gelding: fair maiden handicapper at 3 yrs: well held in 2003: blinkered (below form) once. *S. Dow*

PROWSE (USA)   3 b.f. King of Kings (IRE) 125 – Chelsey Dancer (USA) (Affirmed   **55**
(USA)) [2003 8.3g⁶ 10.2m⁴ 9m May 22] tall filly: half-sister to several winners in USA,
notably smart Grade 1 1¼m winner Chelsey Flower (by His Majesty): dam ran twice in
USA: no better than seventh in 3 maidens for P. Byrne in USA at 2 yrs: only modest form
in similar events in Britain. *A. M. Balding*

PROXIMA (IRE)   3 b.f. Cadeaux Genereux 131 – Alusha 88 (Soviet Star (USA) 128)   **83**
[2003 7m⁵ 8.2m* 8f Jun 20] strong, workmanlike filly: fourth foal: half-sister to useful
1¼m to 1½m winner Scheming (by Machiavellian): dam, lightly-raced 2-y-o 6f winner
who stayed 1¼m, half-sister to smart performer up to 1½m Prize Giving: fairly useful
form: won maiden at Nottingham in May: very stiff task when well-held last in Coronation Stakes at Royal Ascot final start: stays 1m. *G. Wragg*

PSALTER (IRE)   3 b.g. College Chapel 122 – Rebecca's Girl (IRE) (Nashamaa 113)   **93**
[2003 8g³ May 4] IR 17,000F, 10,000Y: half-brother to several winners, including 4-y-o
Lady of Gdansk: dam unraced: third in maiden at Newmarket: dead. *H. Candy*

PSYCHIATRIST   2 ch.g. (Apr 7) Dr Devious (IRE) 127 – Zahwa 72 (Cadeaux Gene-   **104**
reux 131) [2003 6m² 6m² 7g* 7m⁴ 8.1d* 6d² Sep 10] 19,000Y: tall, angular, useful-
looking gelding: has plenty of scope: fourth foal: half-brother to 1m winners Hero's
Journey (smart, by Halling) and 3-y-o Hawridge Prince: dam, German 7f/1m winner, out
of useful Irish 2-y-o sprinter Peace Lute: useful performer: won maiden at Goodwood
and minor event at Sandown (by 2 lengths from Saffron Fox) in August: good ¾-length
second of 22 to Cape Fear in sales race at Doncaster final start: effective at 6f to 1m: acts
on good to soft going, probably on good to firm. *R. Hannon*

PTARMIGAN   6 ch.g. Rock Hopper 124 – Tee Gee Jay 63 (Northern Tempest (USA)   **–**
120) [2003 18f Jul 19] 66/1, reportedly broke blood vessel and pulled up on Flat debut.
T. T. Clement

PTARMIGAN RIDGE   7 b.h. Sea Raven (IRE) 75 – Panayr (Faraway Times (USA)   **90**
123) [2003 93§: 5g 5g 5f⁵ 5d 5m 5d* Sep 27] quite good-topped horse: fairly useful
handicapper: won at Haydock in September by neck from Trinculo: best at 5f: acts on any
going: effective ridden prominently or held up. *Miss L. A. Perratt*

PUGIN (IRE)   5 b.h. Darshaan 133 – Gothic Dream (IRE) 113 (Nashwan (USA) 135)   **117 d**
[2003 121: 14g² 12g 13.9m 20m 15.5m⁶ 15.5s Oct 26] strong horse: has stringhalt: smart
performer at best in 2003: 1¼ lengths second to Mamool in prestige handicap at Nad Al
Sheba on reappearance but most disappointing after, including in Gold Cup at Royal
Ascot and Prix Royal Oak at Longchamp: should stay 2m: acts on good to firm going
(won on soft on debut): has been bandaged fore: often front runner: has left Godolphin.
Saeed bin Suroor

PUKKA (IRE)   2 b.c. (Apr 4) Sadler's Wells (USA) 132 – Puce 112 (Darshaan 133)   **80 p**
[2003 7m 7s⁴ p8g³ p10g* Nov 29] neat colt: third foal: closely related to 3-y-o Pongee
and half-brother to French 9f winner Platonic (by Zafonic): dam 1¼m/1½m winner who
stayed 14.6f: fairly useful performer: landed odds in maiden at Lingfield comfortably by
2 lengths from Baawrah: will be suited by 1½m+: acts on polytrack and soft going: will
progress. *L. M. Cumani*

PULAU TIOMAN   7 b.g. Robellino (USA) 127 – Ella Mon Amour 65 (Ela-Mana-   **108 ?**
Mou 132) [2003 103?: 8g 8g 8.5d* 10.1m⁶ 10s⁶ 8g⁶ 8g Nov 1] compact gelding: smart in
2001, useful nowadays: won handicap at Beverley in May by length from Tough Love:
well below form after: best form at 7f to 8.5f: acts on any going: held up: reportedly
suffered breathing problem third 6-y-o start. *M. A. Jarvis*

PULSE   5 b.g. Salse (USA) 128 – French Gift 99 (Cadeaux Genereux 131) [2003 f6g⁶   **70**
p5g³ p6g⁶ f5s² f6g³ f5g f5g* f5s f5g⁶ f5g⁴ 6m⁴ 6m⁴ 6m⁴ 5m² 5.7f² 5.3m* 5.1f* 5m² 5m⁵
5.5m⁶ Aug 25] fair performer: won seller at Wolverhampton in February and handicaps
at Brighton in June and Bath (apprentices) in July: best at 5f/6f: acts on all-weather, raced
only on good going or firmer on turf (acts on firm): wears cheekpieces nowadays.
J. M. Bradley

Sheikh Mohammed's "Punctilious"

PULVERIZE (IRE) 2 b.c. (Jan 20) Cape Cross (IRE) 129 – Grade A Star (IRE) (Alzao — (USA) 117) [2003 6m 6m p7g Oct 15] 20,000Y: fifth living foal: half-brother to useful 6f (including at 2 yrs) winner March Star (by Mac's Imp) and fairly useful 1¼m winner Jimmy Swift (by Petardia): dam Irish 2-y-o 1m winner who stayed 11f: well beaten in maidens: sold 5,500 gns. *J. Noseda*

PUNCTILIOUS 2 b.f. (May 7) Danehill (USA) 126 – Robertet (USA) 118 (Roberto **107 p** (USA) 131) [2003 7g* 8f* 8f³ Sep 27] big, good-topped filly: closely related to French 1m winner Red Star (by Lure) and half-sister to 3 winners, including smart French 10.5f and 15f winner Risk Seeker (by Elmaamul) and useful French 7f and 1¼m winner Redwood Falls (by Dancing Brave): dam, won Grand Prix de Deauville, stayed 15.5f: won maiden at Yarmouth (wandered) in July and minor event at Salisbury (beat Fantastic View 1¾ lengths) in September: favourite but on toes/free to post, best effort when 1¼ lengths third of 7 to Red Bloom in Fillies' Mile at Ascot, hanging on bend and headed over 1f out: needs to settle to stay beyond 1m: front runner: joined Godolphin: has scope to make a smart 3-y-o. *M. A. Jarvis*

PUPILLAGE (USA) 3 ch.f. Spinning World (USA) 130 – Shadowlawn (Glint of Gold — § 128) [2003 83: 7g f7g Jun 27] rather leggy filly: fairly useful performer at 2 yrs: well held in handicaps in 2003 (reared as stall opened and took virtually no part) second outing: pulled too hard/carried head high on reappearance. *M. A. Jarvis*

PUPPET KING 4 b.g. Mistertopogigo (IRE) 118 – Bold Gift 61 (Persian Bold 123) — [2003 11.9m 9m Sep 15] modest maiden at 2 yrs: tailed off on return in 2003. *A. C. Whillans*

1

PUP

PUPPET PLAY (IRE) 8 ch.m. Broken Hearted 124 – Fantoccini (Taufan (USA) 119) **60**
[2003 74: f8g f7g 6.9f³ 7g 8m 6m⁶ 8m Oct 4] workmanlike mare: modest handicapper **a56**
nowadays: effective at 6f to 1m: acts on firm going and fibresand: tried blinkered: has
idled/found little: none too trustworthy. *E. J. Alston*

PUP'S PRIDE 6 b.g. Efisio 120 – Moogie 103 (Young Generation 129) [2003 –, a70: **–**
f8g⁴ f8g⁵ f6g⁶ f7s⁶ f7g³ f7g⁴ f7s* f8.5g³ f7g⁵ f8g* f6g⁶ f7g f7s f8.5g* f8.5g* f8g f8.5g **a66**
Dec 26] good-topped gelding: fair on all-weather, poor on turf: won seller in February
and minor event in March, both at Southwell, and 2 sellers at Wolverhampton in November: effective at 7f to 9.4f: acts on fibresand and good to firm going: usually wears
headgear: sometimes slowly away/gets behind: none too consistent. *Mrs N. Macauley*

PURDEY 3 ch.f. Double Trigger (IRE) 123 – Euphorie (GER) (Feenpark (GER) 115) **–**
[2003 10.2g⁶ 10f 10f f16.2f⁴ Jul 25] first foal: dam German 7f to 1m winner (also
successful over hurdles): well held in maidens/handicap. *H. Morrison*

PURE COINCIDENCE 8 b.g. Lugana Beach 116 – Esilam 62 (Frimley Park 109) **67 d**
[2003 f5s f6g⁵ f6s f5g⁴ f5g f5g f6f May 30] rather leggy gelding: has a short action: fair
performer: below form after reappearance, reportedly finishing lame final start: probably
stays 6f: acts on firm ground, soft and all-weather: sometimes blinkered/visored. *B. Smart*

PURE ELEGANCIA 7 b.m. Lugana Beach 116 – Esilam 62 (Frimley Park 109) [2003 **–**
65, a70: p5g Jan 8] rather leggy, workmanlike mare: fair handicapper at best: well held
only once in 2003: tried visored/blinkered: none too consistent. *G. A. Butler*

PURE EMOTION 2 b.f. (Feb 17) Primo Dominie 121 – Yasalam (IRE) (Fairy King **– p**
(USA)) [2003 p8g⁵ Dec 20] first foal: dam well beaten only start (at 2 yrs): 40/1, fifth of
10 in minor event at Lingfield, slowly away and travelling comfortably long way: should
do better. *W. R. Muir*

PURE FOLLY (IRE) 2 b.f. (Feb 17) Machiavellian (USA) 123 – Spirit Willing (IRE) **54 p**
99 (Fairy King (USA)) [2003 f6g⁴ Oct 16] angular filly: first foal: dam, 2-y-o 6f winner
(only season to race), half-sister to Oaks and Irish Oaks winner Unite: 13/2, fourth of
10 in maiden at Southwell, fading: should stay at least 1m: sure to progress. *Sir Mark
Prescott*

PURE SPECULATION 3 b.f. Salse (USA) 128 – Just Speculation (IRE) 86 (Aho- **79**
noora 122) [2003 80: 9d³ 8.1m 8g 10.5d Sep 27] workmanlike filly: fair performer: below
form after reappearance: stays 9f: acts on soft and good to firm going: tends to race freely.
M. L. W. Bell

PURI 4 b.g. Mujadil (USA) 119 – Prosperous Lady (Prince Tenderfoot (USA) 126) **–**
[2003 7m May 5] tall, useful-looking gelding: half-brother to 3 winners, notably smart 7f
(including at 2 yrs)/1m winner Eurolink Thunder (by Fairy King): dam unraced: backward, well held in maiden at Doncaster. *J. G. Given*

PURR 2 b.g. (Feb 5) Pursuit of Love 124 – Catawba 98 (Mill Reef (USA) 141) [2003 8d **– p**
Nov 7] smallish, sturdy gelding: brother to 2 winners, including very smart 1½m winner
(including Yorkshire Oaks) Catchascatchcan, and half-brother to several winners, including fairly useful 1¼m/1½m winner Licorne (by Sadler's Wells): dam, 1¼m winner, out of
Ribblesdale winner Catalpa: 16/1, never a threat in maiden at Doncaster: probably
capable of better. *J. L. Dunlop*

PUTRA KUANTAN 3 b.c. Grand Lodge (USA) 125 – Fade (Persepolis (FR) 127) **100**
[2003 10m* 10.3m⁶ 12d 9.7m* 10.1m² 10m 10g Oct 11] 140,000Y: angular, quite attractive colt: half-brother to several winners, including French performer up to 13.5f Faru (by
Mtoto) and 1m and 1½m winner Birdie (by Alhaarth): dam unraced out of Cheshire/
Lancashire Oaks winner One Over Parr: reportedly had knee problem in 2002: useful
performer: won maiden at Newmarket in May and minor event at Folkestone (made all to
beat Camille Pissarro by 2½ lengths) in August: travelled strongly long way when
mid-field in handicaps at Newbury and Ascot last 2 starts: should be as effective at 1m as
1¼m: acts on good to firm ground, below form sole run on good to soft. *M. A. Jarvis*

PUTRA KU (IRE) 3 b.c. Sri Pekan (USA) 117 – London Pride (USA) 106 (Lear Fan **–**
(USA) 130) [2003 –: p10g f8s⁵ Feb 18] well held in 4 starts on all-weather. *P. F. I. Cole*

PUTRA PEKAN 5 b.h. Grand Lodge (USA) 125 – Mazarine Blue 65 (Bellypha 130) **115 §**
[2003 112: 8g* 7.9m⁶ 8.1g* 8g 7d 9m* 9m Oct 18] good-topped horse: good walker:
smart performer: won Jubilee Stakes (Handicap) at Kempton (for second successive year,
beating Norton a length) in May, Tote Scoop6 Stakes (Handicap) at Sandown (career-best
effort to beat Funfair ½ length) in July and minor event at Newbury (by head from Persian

824

Tote Scoop6 Stakes (Handicap), Sandown—Putra Pekan (blinkers) and Funfair both show smart form; Excellento (star on cap) is third and Lafi (striped cap) fourth

Lightning, despite very slow start) in September: stays easy 9f: acts on good to firm and good to soft going: often blinkered, including for all wins: free-going sort: inconsistent, and gave temperamental display fifth start. *M. A. Jarvis*

PUTRA SANDHURST (IRE) 5 b.h. Royal Academy (USA) 130 – Kharimata (IRE) **108** (Kahyasi 130) [2003 10g 12.1d 11.6g³ 12m² 12m² 13.9m 12g³ 12d⁵ Nov 8] big, lengthy, good sort: smart performer at 3 yrs: missed 2002 and just useful in 2003, best efforts when second at Newmarket on fourth/fifth starts, beaten ¾ length by Razkalla in listed race and neck by First Charter in minor event: stays 1¾m: acts on firm going, showed promise on soft: wore cheekpieces (well below form) sixth start: has been heavily bandaged in front. *M. A. Jarvis*

PUTRA SAS (IRE) 2 b.c. (Jan 21) Sri Pekan (USA) 117 – Puteri Wentworth 88 **89 p** (Sadler's Wells (USA) 132) [2003 7m² 7.9f* Oct 10] lengthy colt: has scope: first foal: dam, 1½m to 2½m winner, half-sister to smart sprinter Watching: promising second to State Dilemma in maiden at Newbury: landed odds easily in similar event at York by 2 lengths from Sun of Speed: will stay 1¼m, probably 1½m: should make a useful 3-y-o. *P. F. I. Cole*

PYRRHIC 4 b.g. Salse (USA) 128 – Bint Lariaaf (USA) (Diesis 133) [2003 83d: p7g **54** 7m⁴ 7m⁶ 7m⁶ 7m 8m 7g 9.7m 14m⁴ 11.5s⁵ 8m p10g⁵ Dec 30] smallish gelding: modest maiden: stays 1¼m: acts on good to firm and good to soft going, probably on polytrack: has worn blinkers/cheekpieces. *R. M. Flower*

Q

QAADIMM 2 b.c. (Feb 12) Rahy (USA) 115 – Zahrat Dubai 114 (Unfuwain (USA) **–** 131) [2003 7.1d 8f⁴ Sep 15] smallish colt: first foal: dam 1¼m (Musidora/Nassau Stakes) winner: little sign of ability in maidens at Sandown and Bath: sent to Spain. *M. P. Tregoning*

QABAS (USA) 3 b.c. Swain (IRE) 134 – Classical Dance (CAN) (Regal Classic **78 d** (CAN)) [2003 75p: 8m² 7.1m⁵ 10.3m⁴ 8.2d⁶ 11.7f² 10m² 10f² 9m² Oct 25] lengthy, good-topped colt: has a round action: fair maiden: runner-up 5 times in 2003, best effort on reappearance: stays 11.7f: acts on any going: thoroughly irresolute: sold 29,000 gns. *A. C. Stewart*

QANDIL (USA) 7 ch.g. Riverman (USA) 131 – Confirmed Affair (USA) (Affirmed **46 §** (USA)) [2003 f9.4g f6s³ t7g p7g 6.1m Jun 22] poor performer: stays 7f: acts on fibresand, no form on turf: tried blinkered/visored: none too reliable. *Miss J. Feilden*

QASIRAH (IRE) 2 b.f. (Feb 12) Machiavellian (USA) 123 – Altaweelah (IRE) 104 **97 p** (Fairy King (USA)) [2003 7m* 7m² 8d Sep 11] good-topped filly: second foal: dam, 10.5f/1½m winner, out of half-sister to Rothman's International winner French Glory:

won maiden at Newbury in July: useful form when 1¼ lengths second to Bay Tree in listed race at Newmarket: ran poorly when favourite in May Hill Stakes at Doncaster: should be suited by 1¼m/1½m: has scope to make a better 3-y-o. *M. A. Jarvis*

QOBTAAN (USA) 4 b.g. Capote (USA) – Queen's Gallery (USA) 98 (Forty Niner (USA)) [2003 46: f8s⁴ f8s⁵ f8.5g 8.3g f9.4s² f8.5g⁴ f7g⁶ f7s f8g⁵ f8g³ f8g⁴ Dec 19] big, strong gelding: modest maiden: barely stays 9.4f: acts on fibresand: tried blinkered/visored: comes from behind. *M. R. Bosley* **52**

QUALITAIR WINGS 4 b.g. Colonel Collins (USA) 122 – Semperflorens (Don 128) [2003 78, a73: 8m 7f² 7m 7.9m 8.5d 7.5m 8m 7.9m⁶ 8m 7.5d² 8.3d* 8m 7d² p8g⁶ Nov 12] lengthy, quite good-topped gelding: fairly useful handicapper on turf, fair on all-weather: won at Hamilton in September: stays easy 8.5f: yet to race on heavy going, acts on any other turf and polytrack: tried in cheekpieces: tends to wander. *J. Hetherton* **81 a68**

QUANTICA (IRE) 4 b.g. Sri Pekan (USA) 117 – Touche-A-Tout (IRE) (Royal Academy (USA) 130) [2003 85: 6m 5m 6m 6g 5m 5g² Oct 22] very tall, workmanlike gelding: fair handicapper: form at 4 yrs only on final start: effective at 5f/6f: best on good going or softer (acts on heavy): sometimes tongue tied. *N. Tinkler* **77**

QUANTUM LEAP 6 b.g. Efisio 120 – Prejudice 83 (Young Generation 129) [2003 81: 7d 8m 8g 8g⁴ 8m 9m² 8d 7.9m 8m⁴ 8.2f p8g p8g⁴ p10g* p10g⁵ p10g³ Dec 10] quite good-topped gelding: fair handicapper: won at Lingfield in November: stays easy 1¼m: acts on polytrack, good to firm and good to soft going: tried visored. *S. Dow* **76**

QUARRY ISLAND (IRE) 2 b.f. (Mar 23) Turtle Island (IRE) 123 – Last Quarry 52 (Handsome Sailor 125) [2003 5m⁶ f6g⁶ 6m f9.4g p8g⁴ f7g Dec 16] €8,000Y: third foal: half-sister to fairly useful 5f (at 2 yrs) to 1½m winner Bodfari Quarry (by Efisio): dam, maiden who should have stayed beyond 8.5f, half-sister to top-class 1¼m filly Cormorant Wood: poor maiden: stays 1m: acts on polytrack and good to firm going: tried visored. *P. D. Evans* **40**

QUARRYMOUNT 2 b.g. (Mar 12) Polar Falcon (USA) 126 – Quilt 53 (Terimon 124) [2003 7m 7.1m 7m Oct 14] lengthy, quite good-topped gelding: first foal: dam, maiden who stayed 1¼m, half-sister to Cambridgeshire winner Quinlan Terry and useful Irish performer up to 2m Quinze: signs of ability, slowly away and not knocked about, in maidens: will be suited by at least 1m: likely to do better as 3-y-o. *Sir Mark Prescott* **– p**

QUARTINO 2 b.c. (May 14) Dynaformer (USA) – Qirmazi (USA) 113 (Riverman (USA) 131) [2003 7m⁵ 8m² 8.2m* Sep 19] close-coupled, useful-looking colt: half-brother to several winners, including useful French 7f (at 2 yrs) to 1m winner Quarter Note (by Danehill) and 6-y-o Quito: dam, French 6f (at 2 yrs) and 9f winner, third in Prix Saint-Alary: fairly useful form: second in maiden at Kempton before landing odds in 3-runner similar event at Nottingham easily by 7 lengths from Mekuria: will probably stay 1¼m: coltish first 2 starts. *J. H. M. Gosden* **90**

QUAY WALLOPER 2 b.g. (Jan 25) In Command (IRE) 114 – Myrrh (Salse (USA) 128) [2003 7.5m 7d 8.5m 8g Sep 27] 7,500F, €9,500Y: good-bodied gelding: fourth foal: half-brother to 2 winners abroad, including French 1½m/13f winner Luarca (by Robellino): dam, lightly-raced maiden, half-sister to Gold Cup winner Celeric: no form in maidens. *J. R. Norton* **–**

QUEDEX 7 b.g. Deploy 131 – Alwal (Pharly (FR) 130) [2003 82, a–: 18g 16g⁶ Apr 1] neat gelding: has a round action: modest handicapper, lightly raced: stays 2¼m: acts on soft and good to firm going: tried in cheekpieces. *R. J. Price* **–**

QUEEN CHARLOTTE (IRE) 4 ch.f. Tagula (IRE) 116 – Tisima (FR) 61 (Selkirk (USA) 129) [2003 66: 7.9m* 8.1d Sep 26] strong filly: fair handicapper: easily best effort when winning at York in September: stays 1m: acts on fibresand and firm ground: sometimes races freely. *Mrs K. Walton* **77**

QUEEN CHIEF (IRE) 3 ch.f. Grand Lodge (USA) 125 – Granza (FR) (Saumarez 132) [2003 7d 7m³ p7g⁴ Oct 27] 85,000F, 170,000Y: big, good-bodied filly: second foal: dam, French 1½m winner, out of half-sister to smart French 2-y-o 5f winner Greenway: fair form in frame in maidens at Lingfield: will be suited by 1m+: flashed tail first 2 outings, slowly away on second, took strong hold final one: remains capable of better. *J. H. M. Gosden* **65 p**

QUEEN EXCALIBUR 4 ch.f. Sabrehill (USA) 120 – Blue Room 70 (Gorytus (USA) 132) [2003 66: 7m 8.1m² 8.2s⁶ 7g 7m 7g 8.1m 8.1m 8f 8.1g 7m⁴ 8d Oct 31] rather leggy filly: modest maiden: has form at 1½m, raced at 7f/1m at 4 yrs: acts on soft and good to firm going: tried in cheekpieces/blinkers: none too reliable. *J. M. Bradley* **69 d**

QUE

QUEEN G (USA) 4 b. or br.f. Matty G (USA) 119 – Neieb (USA) 64 (Alleged (USA) 138) [2003 –, a55: f11s* f12s³ f12g⁴ f11s Feb 4] modest performer: won apprentice maiden at Southwell in January: stays easy 1½m: form only on fibresand. *K. R. Burke* — **a57**

QUEEN LOUISA 3 b.f. Piccolo 121 – Queen of Scotland (IRE) 75 (Mujadil (USA) 119) [2003 f6g f6s Dec 6] first foal: dam 7f winner: tongue tied, well held in maiden at Southwell and claimer at Wolverhampton. *F. Watson* —

QUEEN NEFERTARI (USA) 3 b.f. King of Kings (IRE) 125 – Lyric Fantasy (IRE) 115 (Tate Gallery (USA) 117) [2003 73: p6g f5g f6g Jan 27] $210,000Y: fifth foal: half-sister to German 5.5f winner Moon God (by Thunder Gulch) and a winner in Japan by Woodman: dam, won Nunthorpe Stakes at 2 yrs and best up to 6f, closely related to Dewhurst winner In Command and half-sister to very smart sprinter Royal Applause: fair form in maidens at 2 yrs for A. O'Brien in Ireland: carried head awkwardly, just modest form at best in Britain, in blinkers final start: stays 6f: raced only on ground softer than good on turf: ungenuine: sent to Australia. *J. A. Osborne* — **54 §**

QUEEN OF ARABIA (USA) 3 b.f. Wild Again (USA) – Inca Princess (USA) (Big Spruce (USA)) [2003 9.9f⁶ 8f³ Jul 12] half-sister to several winners abroad, notably very smart German 1¼m/1½m performer Germany (by Trempolino): dam, Irish 2-y-o 6f winner, half-sister to US Grade 2 winners Hail Bold King (9f) and Exile King (11f): showed nothing in maidens at Salisbury and Ascot. *M. R. Channon* —

QUEEN OF BULGARIA (IRE) 2 b.f. (Mar 29) Imperial Ballet (IRE) 110 – Sofia Aurora (USA) (Chief Honcho (USA)) [2003 5d f5s⁴ 5m⁶ 6g* 6g⁶ 6f² 6m 6m² Oct 12] €2,800Y: small, compact filly: first foal: dam Italian 2-y-o 9f winner: modest performer: won seller at Yarmouth in July: second in claimer on same course (then left M. Bell) and selling nursery at Newcastle: stays 6f: acts on good to firm going, some promise on fibresand: races freely: none too consistent. *Mrs Lydia Pearce* — **63**

QUEEN OF NIGHT 3 b.f. Piccolo 121 – Cardinal Press (Sharrood (USA) 124) [2003 83: 6.1m 6m³ 6d 6m f6g* 7m⁵ f6g* f6s⁵ Dec 6] tall filly: fairly useful performer: won handicap at Southwell in October and claimer at Wolverhampton in November: should stay 7f: acts on fibresand, soft and good to firm going. *T. D. Barron* — **81**

QUEEN OF SCOTS (IRE) 2 b.f. (Jan 26) Dr Fong (USA) 128 – Mary Stuart (IRE) 114 (Nashwan (USA) 135) [2003 8m³ 8m⁴ Oct 24] good-topped filly: first foal: dam, 1¼m/1½m winner, half-sister to smart middle-distance stayer Bonny Scot and to dam of Golan: fair form in maidens at Yarmouth (third to Doctrine) and Doncaster (fourth to Jath, though never going well): should do better at 1¼m/1½m. *Sir Michael Stoute* — **75 p**

QUEENSBERRY 4 b.g. Up And At 'em 109 – Princess Poquito (Hard Fought 125) [2003 66: p7g f6g² f8.5g* f8.5g* p8g⁶ f8.5s² f8g f8.5f³ f9.4g f7s³ f9.4g³ f8g f12g² f12g f14.8g⁴ f8g* f11g² Dec 16] heavy-topped gelding: fair performer: left A. Jarvis after second start: won 2 claimers (latter amateur event) at Wolverhampton in February and (having left N. Littmoden after sixth outing) handicap at Southwell in December: claimed £8,000 final start: effective at 7f to easy 1½m: acts on all-weather, lightly raced and no form on turf: in cheekpieces, often visored: ungenuine. *J. O'Reilly* — **67 §**

QUEEN'S ECHO 2 b.f. (Mar 17) Wizard King 121 – Sunday News'n'echo (USA) 78 (Trempolino (USA) 135) [2003 6d⁵ Sep 26] 800Y: third living foal: dam, 1¼m/1½m winner, also successful over hurdles: 100/1, fifth of 11 in maiden at Haydock, prominent until halfway. *M. Dods* — **54**

QUEENS FANTASY 2 ch.f. (Apr 19) Grand Lodge (USA) 125 – Alcalali (USA) 96 (Septieme Ciel (USA) 123) [2003 8.2d f8g Nov 24] strong filly: second foal: dam, maiden on Flat (fourth in Ribblesdale Stakes), winning hurdler: showed little in maiden/minor event. *D. Haydn Jones* —

QUEENS JUBILEE 3 ch.f. Cayman Kai (IRE) 114 – Miss Mercy (IRE) 62 (Law Society (USA) 130) [2003 71: p7g⁶ p6g² p6g 7g 5.2m 7g Sep 16] lengthy filly: modest performer: left J. Eustace after third start: barely stays 7f: acts on polytrack and good to firm going: tried visored (including for win)/in cheekpieces: sold 1,800 gns. *P. Howling* — **a56**

QUEENSLANDER (IRE) 2 b.f. (Jan 30) Inchinor 119 – Royal Subject (USA) 53 (Kingmambo (USA) 125) [2003 6m Jun 15] €16,000Y: first foal: dam Irish maiden (stayed 8.5f): pulled up in maiden at Leicester. *J. G. Given* —

QUEENSLAND (IRE) 5 ch.m. Dr Devious (IRE) 127 – Fairy Fortune 78 (Rainbow Quest (USA) 134) [2003 –: f9.4g Jan 24] no form. *J. R. Jenkins* —

QUEEN'S PAGEANT 9 ch.m. Risk Me (FR) 127 – Mistral's Dancer (Shareef Dancer — (USA) 135) [2003 14.1g May 4] big mare: fair handicapper in 2001: banned from racing from stalls, but winning hurdler since: always behind at Salisbury (wore cheekpieces, flip start) only 9-y-o outing: tried blinkered. *J. L. Spearing*

QUEENS RHAPSODY 3 b. or br.g. Baryshnikov (AUS) – Digamist Girl (IRE) (Diga- **92** mist (USA) 110) [2003 69: f7s* f7g* p7g⁵ 6s Nov 3] fairly useful performer, lightly raced: won handicaps at Wolverhampton in January and February: better effort after when fifth to Membership in minor event at Lingfield: stays 7f: acts on all-weather, raced only on good going or softer on turf. *A. Bailey*

QUEENS SQUARE 2 b.f. (Mar 10) Forzando 122 – Queens Check 69 (Komaite **52** (USA)) [2003 5g 5m³ 5d³ 6m³ 5m⁴ 5m⁴ 6g² 5m 6m Aug 14] 1,300Y: quite good-topped filly: second foal: dam 5f winner, including at 2 yrs: modest maiden: second in claimer at Haydock: effective at 5f/6f: acts on good to firm and good to soft going. *N. Tinkler*

QUEENSTOWN (IRE) 2 b.g. (Jan 25) Desert Style (IRE) 121 – Fanciful (IRE) (Muj- **89** tahid (USA) 118) [2003 7g⁴ 7m² 7m⁶ 7.1d² 8d⁴ 8.5d⁴ 7m* f8g² p7g² Dec 17] 36,000Y: long-backed gelding: third foal: half-brother to 2000 2-y-o 7.5f winner The Fancy Man (by Definite Article) and winner in Belgium by Common Grounds: dam ran once at 2 yrs in Ireland: fairly useful performer: won 4-runner maiden at Brighton in October: good second in minor events at Southwell and Lingfield after: stays 1m: acts on all-weather, good to firm and good to soft going: blinkered last 3 starts: has ungainly action (often changes legs under pressure): races prominently. *B. J. Meehan*

QUEL FONTENAILLES (FR) 5 b.g. Tel Quel (FR) 125 – Sissi Fontenailles (FR) **72** (Pampabird 124) [2003 10g⁶ 10g 7m⁶ 10.2m² 11.9f⁴ 22.2f 16.5m⁶ Jul 10] compact gelding: first foal: dam unraced: fair performer: won maiden at Argentan at 2 yrs: left M. Rolland in France after reappearance: stays 13f: acts on any ground. *L. A. Dace*

QUERIDA ROSE (IRE) 3 b.f. Desert Story (IRE) 115 – Sanctuary Cove (Habitat **47** 134) [2003 63d: 5m 5m⁶ 8m 7f⁶ 5m 6m⁵ 5m⁴ 5f² 5g 5m⁴ 5m 5f Aug 27] small, sparely-made filly: poor maiden: best at 5f: acts on firm and good to soft going: tried visored/in cheekpieces. *B. S. Rothwell*

QUEST ON AIR 4 b.g. Star Quest 79 – Stormy Heights 62 (Golden Heights 82) **53** [2003 –: p10g p13g 9.7m⁴ 11.5m² 11.5g* 12f 11.5f³ Jul 24] modest handicapper: won at Yarmouth in May: stays 11.5f: acts on firm going. *J. R. Jenkins*

QUICK 3 b.g. Kahyasi 130 – Prompt (Old Vic 136) [2003 66: p10g Jan 4] lightly-raced — maiden: well beaten in claimer only 3-y-o outing: joined M. Pipe and gelded, won all 4 starts over hurdles. *R. M. H. Cowell*

QUICK FLIGHT 3 ch.f. Polar Falcon (USA) 126 – Constant Delight 80 (Never **70** So Bold 135) [2003 72: 7.1m⁴ 8g⁶ 8.5d 7.2f⁴ 8g 7.1m 6.9m Sep 4] sturdy filly: fair performer: barely stays 1m: acts on firm and good to soft ground: none too consistent. *J. R. Weymes*

QUICKS THE WORD 3 b.g. Sri Pekan (USA) 117 – Fast Tempo (IRE) 74 (Stato- **78** § blest 120) [2003 70: 5d² 6m 6d² 6d 5d⁵ 6g⁶ 6d 5.1m* 5d⁶ 5m 6f Oct 10] rather leggy gelding: fair performer: won minor event at Nottingham in August: effective at 5f/6f: acts on soft and good to firm going: blinkered last 4 outings: inconsistent. *C. W. Thornton*

QUICK TO MOVE (IRE) 3 b.g. Night Shift (USA) – Corynida (USA) (Alleged **37** (USA) 138) [2003 f7g f7g⁶ f9.4g⁶ f8s 12m Jul 10] IR 40,000Y: fifth foal: brother to fairly useful Irish 7f (at 2 yrs) and 1m winner Corrientes, closely related to 6-y-o Adamas and half-brother to winner in Italy by Second Set: dam unraced: poor maiden: left Mrs J. Ramsden after third start: should stay 1m: tried visored. *C. N. Kellett*

QUIDDITCH 3 b.f. Wizard King 122 – Celtic Chimes (Celtic Cone 116) [2003 8.1m — p12g f8g Dec 3] fourth foal: half-sister to 1998 2-y-o 6f seller winner Welsh Assembly (by Presidium): dam, little sign of ability on Flat, won over hurdles: soundly beaten in maidens. *P. Bowen*

QUIDNET 2 ch.f. (Feb 15) Primo Dominie 121 – Youdontsay 85 (Most Welcome 131) **50** § [2003 5m⁵ f6s³ f5g⁴ f5s 6m f5s Dec 27] 10,500Y: quite good-topped filly: second foal: dam 5f/6f winner: modest maiden: left W. Haggas and ran badly last 3 starts: stays 6f: tried in cheekpieces: ungenuine. *Paul Johnson*

QUIET ASSASSIN 3 b.g. Dashing Blade 117 – High Habit 79 (Slip Anchor 136) — [2003 p12g Feb 1] seventh foal: half-brother to fairly useful 6f winner Alegria (by Night Shift) and winner up to 13f in Scandinavia by Robellino: dam, second at 11.5f, half-sister to smart sprinter Blue Siren: 33/1, well held in maiden at Lingfield: dead. *J. M. P. Eustace*

QUIET READING (USA) 6 b.g. Northern Flagship (USA) 96 – Forlis Key (USA) – (Forli (ARG)) [2003 44, a74: f8g³ f8s f8.5g³ f8.5g³ f8s² f8.5g* f8.5s f8.5g⁶ f8g* f8g³ f7s⁴ f9.4f⁶ f8s f8.5g³ Dec 26] big, lengthy gelding: fair handicapper on all-weather, poor on turf: won at Wolverhampton in March and Southwell in June: probably best at 7f to 8.5f: acts on fibresand and any turf going: tried blinkered, usually visored: tough. *M. R. Bosley* **a76**

QUIET STORM (IRE) 3 b.f. Desert Prince (IRE) 130 – Hertford Castle (Reference Point 139) [2003 77: p7g* 8m 8.2d² 9.9m* 12m³ 9.9m² 10.1m⁴ Sep 17] smallish filly: useful performer: won handicap at Lingfield in April and minor event at Salisbury in June: improved from in listed events at Salisbury (½-length second to Hoh Buzzard) and Yarmouth (3¾ lengths fourth to Echoes In Eternity) last 2 starts: stays 1½m: acts on polytrack, good to firm and good to soft ground: consistent. *G. Wragg* **99**

QUIET TIMES (IRE) 4 ch.g. Dolphin Street (FR) 125 – Super Times (Sayf El Arab (USA) 127) [2003 67: f6s⁴ f6g² f7g f5s f6s* f5g* 6.1g³ 5m⁴ 6m 6f 5g⁶ 5m⁵ 6g⁶ 6g⁵ f6s f6g* f6g² f5g Dec 9] strong gelding: fairly useful handicapper on all-weather, fair on turf: won at Southwell in February and March and Wolverhampton in November: best at 5f/6f: acts on fibresand, soft and good to firm going: usually blinkered/visored: often slowly away: refused to race tenth outing. *K. A. Ryan* **76 a85**

QUIFF 2 b.f. (Mar 2) Sadler's Wells (USA) 132 – Wince 117 (Selkirk (USA) 129) [2003 7m⁵ Aug 22] big, strong, lengthy filly: has plenty of scope: first foal: dam, 6f (at 2 yrs) to 1m (1000 Guineas) winner, half-sister to 8-y-o Ulundi: favourite but better for race and green (unimpressive to post), 3½ lengths fifth of 8 to Why Dubai in maiden at Newmarket, slowly away and not knocked about: will stay at least 1m: type to do much better as 3-y-o, and will win races. *Sir Michael Stoute* **68 P**

QUINCANNON (USA) 2 b.g. (Jan 12) Kayrawan (USA) 91 – Sulalat 82§ (Hamas (IRE) 125§) [2003 f6g f6g⁴ Nov 17] $3,500F, 7,600Y: lengthy, good-topped gelding: first foal: dam, ungenuine 6f winner, half-sister to useful 6f to 1m winner Jila out of useful half-sister to very smart performer around 1m Gabr: green and slowly away, modest form in maidens at Southwell and Wolverhampton: likely to stay 1m: open to progress. *T. D. Barron* **57 p**

QUINN 3 ch.g. First Trump 118 – Celestine 62 (Skyliner 117) [2003 –: 8d 12.1m 17.2m⁵ 14g 13.8m⁵ 16.2m Jul 21] lengthy gelding: poor maiden: seems to stay 17f: acts on good to firm going. *C. W. Fairhurst* **44**

QUINTA SPECIAL (IRE) 4 b.f. Spectrum (IRE) 126 – Al Galop (USA) (Affirmed (USA)) [2003 63, a67: f11g Jan 21] unfurnished filly: fair performer at best: well beaten only 4-y-o outing: sent to New Zealand. *G. G. Margarson* **–**

QUINTILLION 2 gr.g. (Feb 25) Petong 126 – Lady Quinta (IRE) 59 (Gallic League 119) [2003 6m 7s Nov 3] 6,000Y: heavy-topped gelding: third foal: dam 2-y-o 5f winner: well held in maidens at Pontefract and Redcar (early speed). *T. J. Etherington* **–**

QUINTOTO 3 b.g. Mtoto 134 – Ballet 61 (Sharrood (USA) 124) [2003 70: 10f* 9m⁶ 9g 8m 7.1g 7m 8g Oct 28] smallish, stocky gelding: fairly useful handicapper: won at Brighton in April: left T. Mills 40,000 gns after second start: lost form completely after: stays 1¼m: acts on firm going. *R. A. Fahey* **82 d**

QUIRKIE (IRE) 2 b.f. (Apr 21) Revoque (IRE) 122 – Unheard Melody (Lomond (USA) 128) [2003 f7g Nov 15] 3,200F: half-sister to 3 winners, including irresolute 5f and 7f (including at 2 yrs) winner Mediate (by Thatching): dam unraced close relative to very smart French middle-distance performer Modhish, out of Irish 1000 Guineas winner Arctique Royale: 33/1, eighth of 10 in maiden at Wolverhampton, prominent long way: should do better. *K. R. Burke* **– p**

QUITE REMARKABLE 4 b.g. Danzig Connection (USA) – Kathy Fair (IRE) 46 (Nicholas Bill 125) [2003 71§, a58§: f8.5g 12g 8m 10d³ 10m May 27] workmanlike gelding: fair handicapper on turf, modest at 3 yrs on all-weather: stays 1¼m: acts on polytrack, soft and good to firm going: ungenuine. *Ian Williams* **74 § a– §**

QUITO (IRE) 6 b.r. Machiavellian (USA) 123 – Qirmazi (USA) 113 (Riverman (USA) 131) [2003 78, a91: f6s f5g f6g* f6g² f6s 7m⁶ 6m³ 7.1m* 7g⁵ 6d³ 6g² 7m* 6m 7.2f 7.1g³ 6g 6m⁴ 7d* 8f 6m 7.9m 8g³ 6m⁴ 5.6d⁴ 6m* 7f 6f 7m⁵ f5g² p7g⁶ f5g⁴ p6g⁵ Dec 20] tall, leggy rig: useful performer: improved and had very good season, winning handicap at Wolverhampton in January, minor events at Musselburgh in April and Thirsk in June, handicap at Newcastle in July and Tote Ayr Gold Cup (Handicap) in September: beat Seel **106**

Tote Ayr Gold Cup (Handicap), Ayr—
the far-side group come out on top, Quito (blinkers), Seel of Approval (left),
Fire Up The Band and Fantasy Believer (stars on sleeves) within a length of each other at the finish

of Approval a head for last-named success: effective at 6f to easy 1m: acts on all-weather, good to firm and good to soft ground, below form on firm and heavy. blinkered: tried tongue tied at 5 yrs: has been early to post: sometimes starts slowly: held up: tough and genuine. *D. W. Chapman*

QUIZZICAL LADY   5 b.m. Mind Games 121 – Salacious (Sallust 134) [2003 f6g   – §
f6g Jan 23] leggy mare: modest and inconsistent performer at 2 yrs: raced in Spain in 2001 (won 1m minor event and 6f handicap at Mijas) and 2002 for E. Creighton: well held back in Britain both 5-y-o starts: tried visored/blinkered. *T. J. Naughton*

R

RABITATIT (IRE)   2 b.f. (Apr 5) Robellino (USA) 127 – Coupled 64 (Wolfhound   **62**
(USA) 126) [2003 6m 6m 7m 7m³ 7m² 7m* 8f* 8m⁵ 7m Oct 18] €20,000Y: leggy filly: has a long stride: first foal: dam, maiden who should have stayed 1m, granddaughter of sister to Habitat: modest performer: won seller at Folkestone (hung right, then left J. Osborne) in August and nursery at Bath in September: ran as if amiss final start: stays 1m: acts on firm going. *J. G. M. O'Shea*

RACCOON (IRE)   3 b.g. Raphane (USA) 102 – Kunucu (IRE) 94 (Bluebird (USA)   **79 p**
125) [2003 6f 6m² 5g 5m* 5m* Sep 17] IR 15,500F, 26,000Y: close-coupled, good-quartered gelding: second foal: dam 5f winner, including at 2 yrs: unraced at 2 yrs: progressive form: won handicaps at Thirsk and Sandown (beat Domirati readily by ¾ length) in September: better form at 5f than 6f: raced only on good ground or firmer: tends to edge right: capable of better still. *T. D. Barron*

RACHEL   3 ch.f. Spectrum (IRE) 126 – Agnus (IRE) (In The Wings 128) [2003 –p: **94**
10f³ 10g* 10m 10.3d Nov 7] big, strong filly: fairly useful performer, lightly raced: won maiden at Windsor in August, despite edging left: very good seventh in listed event at Newmarket next time: broke down final start: would probably have stayed 1½m: acted on firm going: dead. *Mrs A. J. Perrett*

RACINGFORMCLUB BOY   4 ch.g. Blushing Flame (USA) 109 – Sonoco 61 (Song   –
132) [2003 42: 7g 8f 7f Sep 2] angular gelding: bad mover: poor maiden: no form in 2003, leaving Miss D. McHale before final start: tried in headgear. *Miss Gay Kelleway*

RACING NIGHT (USA)   3 b.g. Lear Fan (USA) 130 – Broom Dance (USA) (Dance   **80**
Spell (USA)) [2003 8m⁴ 8g⁴ 9.2m* 9f⁴ 10m⁵ 12m Sep 5] $140,000Y: heavy-topped gelding: closely related to a winner in USA by Silver Hawk and half-brother to several winners, including smart North American 6f/7f performer End Sweep (by Forty Niner):

RAG

dam US Grade 1 1¼m winner: fairly useful form: won maiden at Lingfield in May: not discredited penultimate start: should stay 1¼m: raced only on good going or firmer: sold 16,000 gns. *E. A. L. Dunlop*

RADIANT BRIDE 3 ch.f. Groom Dancer (USA) 128 – Radiancy (IRE) 77 (Mujtahid (USA) 118) [2003 61: p8g⁴ p8g⁵ 10m 13.1g 11.8m p12g² 14.1s p12g f16.2s² f11s⁵ p13g Dec 29] modest maiden: claimed from D. Arbuthnot £3,000 eighth start: stays easy 2m: acts on all-weather and good to firm ground: has worn cheekpieces: has edged left/carried head high: tail flasher: ungenuine. *K. R. Burke* **52 §**

RADIANT DAWN 2 b.f. (Apr 10) Danzero (AUS) – Indigo Dawn 78 (Rainbow Quest (USA) 134) [2003 8m⁴ Oct 14] workmanlike filly: second foal: half-sister to 3-y-o St Jerome: dam, 13f to 2m winner, half-sister to 4-y-o Fight Your Corner: 20/1, 7 lengths fourth of 11 to Muhaymin in maiden at Leicester, taking good hold and green: likely to be suited by 1¼m/1½m: should progress. *M. Johnston* **69 p**

RADIANT ENERGY (IRE) 3 b.f. Spectrum (IRE) 126 – Blaine (USA) (Lyphard's Wish (FR) 124) [2003 8.3s² 8.1m² 8s⁶ 8.1d² 8.1d* Sep 26] IR 55,000Y: angular filly: half-sister to several winners abroad, including St Blaine (by St Jovite), also 1m winner in Britain: dam, ran 4 times in North America, half-sister to dam of Croco Rouge and grandam of Taipan, Ali-Royal and Sleepytime: fair performer: won maiden at Haydock in September: raced only around 1m: acts on good to soft going: has been bandaged behind. *J. H. M. Gosden* **78**

RADISH (IRE) 2 b.f. (Mar 9) Alhaarth (IRE) 126 – Nichodoula 65 (Doulab (USA) 115) [2003 7g Nov 1] 36,000Y: tall, leggy filly: half-sister to several winners, including 5-y-o Give Back Calais and 3-y-o Ribbons And Bows: dam, 7f/1m winner, half-sister to very smart 9f to 1½m performer Terimon: 50/1, ninth of 18 to Damsel in maiden at Newmarket, held up and not unduly punished: should stay 1m: open to progress. *A. C. Stewart* **63 p**

RADLEY PARK (IRE) 4 b.g. Vettori (IRE) 119 – Livry (USA) (Lyphard (USA) 132) [2003 93?: f11s Jan 14] lightly-raced maiden: best effort (fair form) at 1¼m on debut at 3 yrs: well held subsequently: dead. *E. W. Tuer* **–**

RAFFERTY (IRE) 4 ch.c. Lion Cavern (USA) 117 – Badawi (USA) 103 (Diesis 133) [2003 93: f7g* p7g³ 8g 7.6m³ 8g⁶ 8.5m⁴ 10m⁴ 9.9g⁶ 8g⁵ 8g 9m 7m Oct 17] angular colt: useful performer: won minor event at Wolverhampton in March: several at least creditable efforts in handicaps after, including when third to Lygeton Lad at Lingfield next time, but well below form last 3 starts: very best form up to 8.5f: yet to race on soft/heavy going, acts on any other turf and all-weather: blinkered last 2 starts (raced freely on first occasion): has been early to post: goes well on sharp tracks. *C. E. Brittain* **95 a103**

RAFTERS MUSIC (IRE) 8 b.g. Thatching 131 – Princess Dixieland (USA) (Dixieland Band (USA)) [2003 83: f6s f6g* f6g⁶ f7g 6s f6g³ 6g⁵ 6g⁵ f6g² f6s² f7g⁵ f6g⁴ f6g³ f6s² f5g⁶ Dec 16] good-bodied gelding: fairly useful handicapper on all-weather, fair on turf: won at Wolverhampton in January: left B. Hills after eleventh start: effective at 5f to easy 7f: acts on all-weather and any turf going: tried blinkered/tongue tied much earlier in career: wore cheekpieces second to fifth starts: sometimes hangs: usually held up. *Julian Poulton* **74 a80**

RAGAMUFFIN 5 ch.g. Prince Sabo 123 – Valldemosa 81 (Music Boy 124) [2003 89: 5m² 6d 6m Jun 5] sturdy gelding: just fair handicapper in 2003, easily best effort on reappearance: effective at 5f/6f: acts on soft and good to firm ground: often blinkered prior to 2003: held up. *T. D. Easterby* **79**

RAGASAH 5 b.m. Glory of Dancer 121 – Slight Risk 72 (Risk Me (FR) 127) [2003 54d: f16.2g Feb 3] sparely-made mare: modest performer at best: virtually pulled up only outing in 2003. *Miss Gay Kelleway* **–**

RAGGED JACK (IRE) 2 b.g. (Mar 11) Cape Cross (IRE) 129 – Isticanna (USA) 96 (Far North (CAN) 120) [2003 7m⁵ 8g p6g p5g⁴ Dec 10] 35,000Y: leggy gelding: half-brother to several winners, including 5-y-o Chancellor and useful 6f/7f (latter including at 2 yrs) winner Purple Haze (by Spectrum): dam 2-y-o 5f/6f winner: fair form: best effort when strong-finishing fourth to Treasure Cay in minor event at Lingfield: should stay 1m: stumbled and unseated rider leaving stall third start: should do better. *G. A. Butler* **76 p**

RAGING MIND 2 b.f. (Mar 26) Mind Games 121 – Naufrage (Main Reef 126) [2003 5d⁵ 7m⁶ 7.1m Oct 25] lengthy, unfurnished filly: half-sister to 3 winners, including 3-y-o Little Louis and 5f (at 2 yrs) to 1m winner Dovebrace (by Dowsing): dam unraced: poor maiden: sent to Israel. *T. D. Easterby* **40**

RAG TOP (IRE) 3 ch.f. Barathea (IRE) 127 – Petite Epaulette 80 (Night Shift (USA)) [2003 101: 7m³ 8g 6.1s 7g 8g Aug 1] strong, useful-looking filly: has scope: poor mover: **97**

831

useful performer: creditable 2¾ lengths third to Tante Rose in Dubai Duty Free Stakes (Fred Darling) at Newbury on reappearance: below form after: stays 7f: acts on firm and soft going: races prominently. *R. Hannon*

RAHAF (USA) 3 b.g. Theatrical 128 – Gozo Baba (USA) (Raja Baba (USA)) [2003 **89** 94: p10g² a9f³ a10f 14.1d² 12f* 11.9m⁴ 12m Jun 19] leggy gelding: fairly useful performer: won maiden at Catterick in May: good fourth in handicap at Haydock penultimate start, though found little: best form around 1½m: yet to race on soft/heavy ground, probably acts on any other turf and polytrack: carries head awkwardly: sold 6,500 gns. *M. Johnston*

RAHBAR 3 b.g. Mtoto 134 – Arruhan (IRE) 87 (Mujtahid (USA) 118) [2003 10d 11.1d² **74** 12.1d³ May 16] first foal: dam 5f (at 2 yrs) and 7f winner: fair maiden: placed twice at Hamilton, finding little when odds on in latter: stays 11f: sold 12,000 gns. *L. M. Cumani*

RAHEED (IRE) 2 b.g. (Mar 3) Daggers Drawn (USA) 114 – In Due Course (USA) **63** (A P Indy (USA) 131) [2003 7.2f⁴ 8.1g⁶ Sep 11] IR 21,000F, 60,000Y: first foal: dam unraced half-sister to smart French performer up to 1½m Dark Nile out of half-sister to very smart 1¼m performer Kefaah: green, modest form in maidens at Ayr and Chepstow: shapes as if will stay 1¼m. *E. A. L. Dunlop*

RAHEEL (IRE) 3 ch.g. Barathea (IRE) 127 – Tajawuz 82 (Kris 135) [2003 –: 11.1m⁵ **66** 8g 9m 10m 9.9f⁴ 10g⁶ p12g³ 10.1m p13g p12g p12g² p16g p10g⁶ p13g Dec 29] workmanlike gelding: fair maiden handicapper: stays 1½m: acts on polytrack, raced only on good going or firmer on turf: usually tongue tied: often slowly away: has raced freely/folded tamely. *P. Mitchell*

RAHJEL SULTAN 5 b.g. Puissance 110 – Dalby Dancer 71 (Bustiki) [2003 –: f6g **–** 7.1m⁴ 7g 7g 7f⁵ 7f⁴ 7m Oct 25] big, heavy-topped gelding: little worthwhile form since 2001: tried blinkered: has raced freely. *B. A. McMahon*

RAHLEX (IRE) 5 ch.g. Rahy (USA) 115 – Lady Express (IRE) (Soviet Star (USA) **–** 128) [2003 51, a60. 8m Sep 6] lengthy, sparely-made gelding: modest performer at best: well held in stable only outing in 2003: tongue tied at 4 yrs. *Ronald Thompson*

RAHWAAN (IRE) 4 b.g. Darshaan 133 – Fawaakeh (USA) 84 (Lyphard (USA) 132) **95** [2003 100: 16m 18.7m⁴ 16.2m² 16.1g⁵ 16.2m⁵ 18.7m⁵ 16.2m 14d³ 13.9f⁴ Oct 11] lengthy gelding: useful handicapper: mostly respectable efforts in 2003: stays 18.7f: acts on firm and good to soft going, possibly not on soft: races up with pace. *C. W. Fairhurst*

RAINBOW CHASE (IRE) 5 b.g. Rainbow Quest (USA) 134 – Fayrooz (USA) 74 **53** (Gulch (USA)) [2003 –: f12g⁴ 12.1m f12s Oct 7] tall, leggy, light-bodied gelding: modest maiden, lightly raced: left S. Magnier after reappearance: stays 1½m: often blinkered. *R. A. Fahey*

RAINBOW CITY (IRE) 3 b.f. Rainbow Quest (USA) 134 – Greektown (Ela- **78** Mana-Mou 132) [2003 85p: 9.9m* May 15] quite good-topped filly: fairly useful form: favourite, made all in maiden at Salisbury in May: stayed 1¼m: stud. *Sir Michael Stoute*

RAINBOW COLOURS (IRE) 2 br.f. (Mar 16) Linamix (FR) 127 – Mill Rainbow **– p** (FR) (Rainbow Quest (USA) 134) [2003 7s⁶ Oct 29] 24,000Y: dam, French 10.5f winner, out of half-sister to Prix Jacques le Marois winner Miss Satamixa (by Linamix): 11/2, green when well-held sixth in maiden at Yarmouth, slowly away and not unduly punished: should do better at 1¼m+. *J. R. Fanshawe*

RAINBOW END 4 ch.f. Botanic (USA) – High Finish 58 (High Line 125) [2003 101: **92** 10.4m⁶ 10m 10m 8g 10.3d Nov 7] sturdy filly: just fairly useful performer in 2003: may prove best around 1¼m: acts on good to firm ground: held up. *D. R. C. Elsworth*

RAINBOW RIVER (IRE) 5 ch.g. Rainbows For Life (CAN) – Shrewd Girl (USA) **–** 79 (Sagace (FR) 135) [2003 64, a59: f12s f11g⁵ Jan 9] close-coupled gelding: shows plenty of knee action: modest handicapper in 2002: well held on Flat in 2003 but won twice over hurdles: tried visored/blinkered: sometimes races freely/hangs right: none too consistent. *M. C. Chapman*

RAINBOW SPECTRUM (FR) 4 b.f. Spectrum (IRE) 126 – Iguassu (FR) (Fabulous **57** Dancer (USA) 124) [2003 7.5m 8g⁴ 8m⁶ 10.1g 10.1g Oct 22] 480,000 francs Y: third foal: half-sister to fairly useful French 1999 2-y-o 5f/7f winner Radhwa (by Shining Steel): dam French maiden half-sister to US Grade 2 8.5f winner Shir Dar: modest maiden: stays 1m: sold 2,500 gns. *P. W. Harris*

RAINHILL (IRE) 2 b.c. (Mar 13) Fasliyev (USA) 120 – Sweet Emotion (IRE) 97 **59** (Bering 136) [2003 5m 5m 6g 6m⁶ 7f Oct 12] 135,000F, 80,000Y: first foal: dam, 1m winner, out of half-sister to very smart 6f/7f performers Lead On Time and Great Commotion: modest maiden: needs to settle to stay beyond 6f: acts on good to firm going: sent to Germany. *R. Hannon*

RAINSBOROUGH HILL   2 b.c. (Mar 22) Groom Dancer (USA) 128 – Ellebanna   –
69 (Tina's Pet 121) [2003 6m p6g p7g Oct 30] 17,000Y: rather leggy, close-coupled colt: half-brother to several winners, including useful 6.5f/7f winner (including in UAE) King Midas (by Bluebird) and 5-y-o Mine: dam, 5f (including at 2 yrs) winner, half-sister to very smart sprinter Bolshoi: signs of only a little ability in minor event/maidens. *A. King*

RAINSTORM   8 b.g. Rainbow Quest (USA) 134 – Katsina (USA) 98 (Cox's Ridge   54
(USA)) [2003 51: 10g 9.9m 10.2m 7.9f⁶ 9f 8m² 9.9m* 7.9m* 8.1g⁴ 10.9m 10m Oct 4]
stocky gelding: modest handicapper: won ladies events at Beverley in July and Carlisle in August: effective at 1m to easy 11f: acts on fibresand and firm going, probably on soft: tried visored: sometimes slowly away: used to force pace, but more patiently ridden nowadays (usually owner ridden). *W. M. Brisbourne*

RAINWASHED GOLD   3 b.c. Rainbow Quest (USA) 134 – Welsh Autumn 107   107
(Tenby 125) [2003 108: 9m* 11.8m⁶ 11.8f³ Oct 27] small, sturdy colt: useful performer, lightly raced: landed odds in 3-runner minor event at Kempton in April, beating Pinkerton easily by 11 lengths: reportedly lame on off hind after tailed off in Derby Trial at Lingfield next time: last of 3 in minor event at Leicester over 5 months later: will stay at least 1¼m: raced only on going firmer than good: effective held up or making running: sold 16,000 gns. *Mrs A. J. Perrett*

RAISE YOUR GLASS (IRE)   4 b. or br.g. Namaqualand (USA) – Toast And Honey   –
(IRE) 72 (Glow (USA)) [2003 8g 11.9m Jun 2] IR 6,400Y: smallish gelding: third foal: dam, Irish 1½m winner, also successful over hurdles: well held in 2 claimers: successful twice over hurdles in October (sold 5,400 gns in between). *C. W. Thornton*

RAJAM   5 b.g. Sadler's Wells (USA) 132 – Rafif (USA) 68 (Riverman (USA) 131)   82
[2003 –: 10.4f 10m 11.9g² 12m³ 12.3m 14.4m² 12m 16m 17.5m Sep 19] sturdy gelding: fairly useful handicapper: seems to stay 1¾m: acts on firm ground, probably on soft: tried blinkered/tongue tied in 2002: races prominently: none too consistent. *D. Nicholls*

RAJAYOGA   2 ch.c. (Feb 28) Kris 135 – Optimistic 90 (Reprimand 122) [2003 6g⁴   62
7g⁴ 6g Sep 1] first foal: dam 2-y-o 7f winner who stayed 1¼m: modest form in maidens: fourth at Lingfield and Leicester (good hold): should stay at least 1m. *M. H. Tompkins*

RAKTI   4 b.c. Polish Precedent (USA) 131 – Ragera (IRE) (Rainbow Quest   126
(USA) 134) [2003 118: 10g* 10m² 10m* 10m² Dec 14]
As summer turns to autumn, the number of meetings thins out and there is more time to savour the top fixtures—at home and abroad. Champions' Day at Newmarket, which comes sandwiched between the Arc meeting and the Breeders' Cup, is never likely to live up to its billing—racing doesn't lend itself to peaking to produce a host of definitive champions on demand—but, with six pattern events, two of them Group 1s, and the Cesarewitch, it has a good deal to offer.

The field for the Dubai Champion Stakes included several of the biggest names from the summer. Irish Derby and King George winner Alamshar started favourite at 9/4, despite defeat in the Irish Champion Stakes last time out. Russian

Premio Presidente della Repubblica, Rome—Rakti makes a successful reappearance for his new stable; next home are Tigertail, Altieri (noseband) and Sunstrach (rail)

Emirates Airline Champion Stakes, Newmarket—with the 'big names' failing to give their running, 2002 Italian Derby winner Rakti wins from Carnival Dancer, Indian Creek and Imperial Dancer (left)

Rhythm, winner of the One Thousand Guineas, the Coronation Stakes and the Nassau, was second favourite at 11/4 after her second to Falbrav in the Queen Elizabeth II Stakes at Ascot. Nayef, bidding to end his career with a second success in the race in three years, was at 5/1, with Godolphin's Vespone at 6/1. Rakti, second to Nayef in the Prince of Wales's Stakes at Royal Ascot when last seen, looked in fine shape and started at 11/1. Like nature, the form-book tends to undergo changes in the autumn and, on a crisp day at Newmarket, Rakti left his rivals scattered down the course. Soon breezing along, tracking the leaders under Philip Robinson, if anything going a bit too freely, Rakti settled the race in strides once given his head, quickening several lengths clear under two furlongs out. From the Dip, Rakti was out on his own and merely had to be kept up to his work. The 33/1-shot Carnival Dancer came out of the pack to be beaten two lengths in second, with 25/1-shot Indian Creek (third in the race for the second time in three years) a length and a half further back. The 66/1-shot Imperial Dancer took fourth after needing to be switched. The market leaders failed to show their true colours, the best of them on the day, Russian Rhythm, only fifth.

Rakti's Champion Stakes victory came exactly a year after he had refused to enter the stalls under Italian rider Mirco Demuro in the race. Trained at the time by Bruno Grizzetti, for whom he had become the first home-trained winner of the Italian Derby since Tisserand beat Carroll House in 1988, Rakti left Grizzetti after two disappointing efforts back in Italy after the Champion. Rakti was returned to Italy in May for his first outing for Michael Jarvis, winning the Group 1 Premio Presidente della Repubblica at Rome by a neck from the French-trained Tigertail. In the Prince of Wales's Stakes at Royal Ascot the following month Rakti started at 50/1 in a field of ten which included Moon Ballad, Grandera, Falbrav and Islington. With several of his rivals failing to give their running, Rakti ran the race of his life up to that point, prominent throughout and finding only Nayef too good, going down by two and a half lengths with Islington third. A small crack in his near-hind fetlock, found after Ascot, kept Rakti off the course for the rest of the summer and meant he missed a possible tilt at the Arlington Million. As a result, Rakti was still a fresh horse after Newmarket when sent to Sha Tin in December for the Hong Kong Cup. As it turned out, seizing Falbrav's mantle as the best horse to come out of Italy in many a year proved beyond Rakti, but he turned in another fine effort. A sluggish start meant Rakti had to be held up early on, but he travelled typically strongly for much of the way. He was slightly short of room as Falbrav nudged past in the straight, then failed to match the winner's turn of foot when in the clear, going down by two lengths but sticking to his task well to be a clear second.

Rakti (b.c. 1999)	Polish Precedent (USA) (b 1986)	Danzig (b 1977)	Northern Dancer / Pas de Nom
		Past Example (ch 1976)	Buckpasser / Bold Example
	Ragera (IRE) (b 1992)	Rainbow Quest (b 1981)	Blushing Groom / I Will Follow
		Smageta (b 1979)	High Top / Christine

In terms of breeding, Rakti is at least in part a product of Italy, where he was bought by owner Gary Tanaka privately from the Scuderia Il Poggio before the Italian Derby. The dam's side of his pedigree has been dominated of late by horses raced in Italy, though the cornerstone of their success, Rakti's great grandam Christine, was last of three in the Yorkshire Oaks in 1970 for Doug Smith. Among Christine's foals were Svelt, winner of the Premio Parioli (Italian Two Thousand Guineas), and Smageta, Rakti's grandam. Smageta won the Group 3 Criterium Femminile at two and a listed race at three, both over a mile. She was also placed in Group 1 company, including when third in the Premio Regina Elena (Italian One Thousand Guineas) and the Oaks² d'Italia. At stud, Smageta produced Rusoli, third in the Italian St Leger, as well as being the dam of Risiat, second in the Premio Parioli to Air Express. Ragera, Rakti's dam, a lightly-raced maiden in Italy, was placed over a mile. Ragera's first foal Riksha was a prolific winner in Italy. Riksha's sire Zilzal and Rakti's sire Polish Precedent were rivals for champion miler as three-year-olds in 1989. As a sire, Polish Precedent's most notable successes have come with offspring who have stayed a mile and a quarter or more, most importantly Pilsudski, who came early in Polish Precedent's stud career. All the same, Rakti may well prove fully effective back at a mile. He is almost certainly better at a mile and a quarter than a mile and a half, and was out on his feet at the end of the Italian Derby after cruising into the lead. Rakti's form at a mile and a quarter is high class and, all being well, he looks sure to win another good prize or two. The only shadow over him is his behaviour at the stalls. He gave trouble again in Rome and, as stated, was slowly away at Sha Tin, though his behaviour generally seems to have improved since intensive schooling from expert horse handler Steve 'Yarmy' Dyble at Newmarket. Rakti reportedly still isn't the easiest horse to handle. Perhaps, he should be played some rakti ragas, acknowledged among all Indian raga music as the best at producing a peaceful mental state. A tall, good-topped colt, Rakti has won twice on good to soft ground, but all his best form is on good or good to firm ground (he has yet to race on very firm). He takes a strong hold and is usually waited with. *M. A. Jarvis*

Mr Gary A. Tanaka's "Rakti"

RAMBLER 3 b.f. Selkirk (USA) 129 – Rahaam (USA) 91 (Secreto (USA) 128) [2003   **74**
70: f7s* 8f5 Apr 10] tall, quite good-topped filly: fair performer: won handicap at Wolverhampton in March: respectable effort in minor event at Brighton subsequent outing:
barely stays easy 1m: acts on firm going and all-weather: blinkered last 3 starts: sometimes slowly away: tends to look none too keen. *J. H. M. Gosden*

RAMPANT (IRE) 5 b.g. Pursuit of Love 124 – Flourishing (IRE) 85 (Trojan Fen 118)   **–**
[2003 –: 10d 7m 8m Jul 6] tall, useful-looking gelding: fairly useful performer at 3 yrs:
no form since. *C. J. Teague*

RANDOM QUEST 5 b.g. Rainbow Quest (USA) 134 – Anne Bonny 105 (Ajdal   **98**
(USA) 130) [2003 103: 16m 16m 16.1m2 21d3 16.2m2 14g5 18m Oct 18] leggy, useful-
looking gelding: useful handicapper: ran creditably in 2003 when placed, and when fifth
to The Persuader at Haydock: stays 21f: winner on soft ground, very best form on good/
good to firm: often races prominently: sold 15,000 gns. *P. F. I. Cole*

RANGOON (USA) 2 ch.c. (Feb 24) Distant View (USA) 126 – Rustic (IRE) 99 (Grand   **75 P**
Lodge (USA) 125) [2003 6g3 Oct 31] good-topped colt: first foal: dam, 2-y-o 6f winner
(best at 7f), half-sister to 2-y-o Grey Swallow and useful French/US performer up to 1½m
Central Lobby: 16/1, green and better for race, 4 lengths third of 11 to Caveral in maiden
at Newmarket, soon lost lot to do and running on well under tender handling: will stay 7f,
probably 1m: sure to improve good deal and win a race or 2. *Mrs A. J. Perrett*

RANI TWO 4 b.f. Wolfhound (USA) 126 – Donya 74 (Mill Reef (USA) 141) [2003   **80**
63: 10g5 p10g 10g5 10.3m* 10m2 9.2m* 10g* 11.9g 9d6 10m 10m4 10m* 10.5d Sep 27]
strong filly: fairly useful performer: won handicaps at Chester and Hamilton and minor
event at Windsor in June, and handicap at Ayr in September: stays 1¼m: acts on polytrack, firm and good to soft ground: tough. *W. M. Brisbourne*

RANNY 3 b.f. Emperor Jones (USA) 119 – Defined Feature (IRE) 91 (Nabeel Dancer   **57**
(USA) 120) [2003 7m f9.4s5 8m 8f4 8f* 8.1m 8g Oct 31] second foal: dam, 2-y-o 5f/6f
winner, should have stayed 1m: modest performer: won handicap at Brighton in September: ran poorly after: not sure to stay beyond 1m: acts on firm ground. *Dr J. D. Scargill*

RANSOM O'WAR (USA) 3 b.c. Red Ransom (USA) – Sombreffe 71 (Polish Pre-   **117**
cedent (USA) 131) [2003 86: 8.5g2 8g3 10m4 12d2 10g* 12g4 Sep 7] close-coupled, good-
topped colt: smart performer: trained by M. Johnston at 2 yrs: much improved in 2003,
successful at Munich in Grosser Muller Brot-Preis (by ½ length from Winning Dash) in
June and Grosser Dallmayr-Preis (by 1¼ lengths from dead-heaters Highdown and
Epalo) in August: in frame in pattern races other starts, including when 1¼ lengths second
of 20 to Dai Jin in Deutsches Derby at Hamburg on fourth outing and when respectable
fourth to Mamool in Grosser Bugatti Preis at Baden-Baden final one: stays 1½m: acts on
fibresand, soft and good to firm going. *Frau E. Mader, Germany*

RAOUL DUFY (USA) 3 gr.g. El Prado (IRE) 119 – Parrish Empress (USA) (His   **70**
Majesty (USA)) [2003 f9.4g2 f8.5s3 p8g 10m f8g2 8d2 10m f9.4s2 Jun 21] $30,000Y:
good-topped gelding: sixth foal: brother to winner in USA and half-brother to 3 winners,
including smart 1996 2-y-o 7.5f winner Musical Dancer (by Dixieland Band): dam, won
twice in USA, half-sister to champion older mare in USA Princess Rooney: fair maiden:
stays 9.4f: acts on fibresand and good to soft ground, below form on good to firm: tried in
cheekpieces: looks difficult ride. *P. F. I. Cole*

RAPHAEL (IRE) 4 b.f. Perugino (USA) 84 – Danny's Miracle (Superlative 118)   **88**
[2003 80: 7m2 7f 7g4 7m5 7m* 7.5m2 8.5m* 7g4 7f4 7.5m2 7d 8m6 7m6 8m5 7.1g2 7.1m2
7d3 Nov 4] leggy, quite good-topped filly: fairly useful performer: won minor events at
Redcar in May and Beverley in June: mainly at least creditable efforts in handicaps
after: stays 8.5f: acts on firm and soft ground: blinkered once at 3 yrs: tough and reliable.
T. D. Easterby

RAPHOOLA (IRE) 2 b.f. (Mar 4) Raphane (USA) 102 – Acicula (IRE) 96 (Night   **75**
Shift (USA)) [2003 5.1g 5.1m2 5m3 6.1d* p5g* 4.5g3 5d5 7g4 5.5d3 5.5d2 6d4 6g5 5d 6s
a7.5g4 a6.5g3 Dec 29] 2,500Y: good-bodied filly: first foal: dam 5f/6f winner at 2 yrs who
stayed 7f: fair performer: left N. Tinkler after third start: won sellers at Chepstow and
Lingfield for M. Johnston in May: some creditable efforts after, including in listed race/
claimers: probably stays 7.5f: acts on good to firm going, good to soft and polytrack/
all-weather at Deauville: often visored/blinkered. *A. Hermans, Belgium*

RAPID LINER 10 b.g. Skyliner 117 – Stellaris (Star Appeal 133) [2003 –: f8.5g Feb   **–**
24] of little account nowadays. *J. Gallagher*

RAPSCALLION (GER) 4 b.g. Robellino (USA) 127 – Rosy Outlook (USA) 79   **?**
(Trempolino (USA) 135) [2003 100: 7.9m 8.1m 8m 8g p10g Nov 22] leggy, unfurnished

gelding: useful performer at 2 yrs, disappointing since: stays 1m: acts on polytrack, goes well on ground softer than good: blinkered final start (raced freely): sometimes sweating: tends to edge left. *J. M. P. Eustace*

RAPT (IRE) 5 b.g. Septieme Ciel (USA) 123 – Dream Play (USA) (Blushing Groom (FR) 131) [2003 –, a72: 10.1m 8g 6d 14.1m 16m 11.9m Sep 4] leggy, useful-looking gelding: fair handicapper on all-weather at 4 yrs: little form on turf since 2001: visored (ran creditably) once at 4 yrs: tongue tied last 4 starts: successful over hurdles in October. *M. A. Barnes* –

RARE COINCIDENCE 2 ch.g. (Apr 4) Atraf 116 – Green Seed (IRE) 78 (Lead On Time (USA) 123) [2003 5m 5g⁴ 6g 5.9d 7d⁶ 8m⁵ 7.1m 8.2m⁵ f7g³ f8g² f7g Dec 16] 12,000Y: quite good-topped gelding: fifth foal: half-brother to 2 winners, including 7f to 1½m winner Take Flite (by Cadeaux Genereux): dam 2-y-o 6f winner, later stayed 1¼m: modest maiden: second in Southwell seller: stays 1m: acts on fibresand and good to firm going, probably on good to soft: wore cheekpieces last 3 starts, hanging left first 2 occasions: very slowly away seventh outing. *R. F. Fisher* 59

RARE DESTINY (IRE) 3 b.g. Mujadil (USA) 119 – Jamaican Law (IRE) (Case Law 113) [2003 –: 6g⁵ 5.9m 7f 6m⁵ f6g⁶ 5g³ 6m 5g³ 5m* 5m 5g 5m⁵ Oct 18] close-coupled gelding: fair performer: won maiden at Folkestone in August: should stay 6f: acts on good to firm ground: tried in headgear: sold 3,500 gns, sent to Macau. *A. Berry* 62

RAREFIED (IRE) 2 b.c. (Apr 22) Danehill (USA) 126 – Tenuous 111 (Generous (IRE) 139) [2003 8.2m⁶ 8.2d² Nov 6] neat colt: second living foal: dam French 1¼m (Prix de Psyche) and 1½m winner: better effort at Nottingham (fairly useful form) when 5 lengths second of 16 to Vaughan in maiden, making most: will be suited by 1¼m/1½m. *R. Charlton* 81

RARE PRESENCE (IRE) 4 b.g. Sadler's Wells (USA) 132 – Celebrity Style (USA) 96 (Seeking The Gold (USA)) [2003 78: 16m 11.6g f12s Oct 21] first foal: dam, Irish 7f/9f winner, out of close relative to US Grade 1 9f winner Chain Bracelet: fair maiden at best: left D. Weld, Ireland, 30,000 gns after 3 yrs: well held in 2003: stays 1½m: acts on soft and good to firm ground: blinkered nowadays. *C. P. Morlock* –

RASID (USA) 5 b.g. Bahri (USA) 125 – Makadir (USA) (Woodman (USA) 126) [2003 95: 10.4m 10.2g⁴ 10.3d f12g 10.1s p12g³ p10g p10g⁵ p10g³ Dec 29] rangy gelding: only fair nowadays: left E. Dunlop after second start: stays easy 1½m: acts on polytrack, soft and good to firm ground: has wandered. *C. A. Dwyer* 75 +

RAS TAILTEANN (IRE) 3 b.g. Grand Lodge (USA) 125 – Golden Mistral (Danehill (USA) 126) [2003 –: 8g 8m⁶ f8.5g Nov 15] IR 52,000Y: third foal: half-brother to winner in Italy by Rainbows For Life: dam Italian 2-y-o 5f/7f winner: lightly-raced maiden: little form, including in handicap at Wolverhampton final start. *D. Wachman, Ireland* –

RATHMULLAN 4 ch.g. Bluegrass Prince (IRE) 110 – National Time (USA) (Lord Avie (USA)) [2003 46: p8g 6m 7m 6m p7g Dec 17] workmanlike gelding: maiden: little form in 2003: tried blinkered/in cheekpieces: has looked hard ride. *E. A. Wheeler* –

RATIFIED 6 b.g. Not In Doubt (USA) 101 – Festival of Magic (USA) 73 (Clever Trick (USA)) [2003 –: f12s f8s Jan 16] good-bodied gelding: probably of little account nowadays. *M. C. Chapman* –

RATIO 5 ch.g. Pivotal 124 – Owdbetts (IRE) 69 (High Estate 127) [2003 93: 8s 6g* 6f* 7g 5.2m* 6f Sep 27] angular, good-topped gelding: smart performer: won amateur event at Chantilly in May, Wokingham Stakes (Handicap) at Royal Ascot (dead-heated with Fayr Jag) in June and Dubai International Airport World Trophy at Newbury (beat Mornin Reserves 1¼ lengths) in September: well held at Ascot in Tote International Handicap and Diadem Stakes (last of 14, reported to have had fibrillating heart) on other starts in Britain in 2003: has form up to 1m, best efforts at 5f/6f: acts on firm and soft going: blinkered/visored last 5 starts, tongue tied last 4: raced freely fourth outing. *J. E. Hammond, France* 112

RAVEL (IRE) 2 b.c. (Mar 26) Fasliyev (USA) 120 – Lili Cup (FR) (Fabulous Dancer (USA) 124) [2003 7s 7d Nov 7] €95,000Y: big, strong, good sort: half-brother to several winners, including useful Italian sprinter Uruk (by Efisio): dam unraced close relative to 4-y-o Nysaean: signs of ability in maidens at Yarmouth (slowly away) and Doncaster (badly hampered): should do better. *M. L. W. Bell* – p

RAVENGLASS (USA) 4 b.c. Miswaki (USA) 124 – Urus (USA) (Kris S (USA)) [2003 73: 10.3m³ 10.2g² 10m⁵ 11.7f* 10.2f⁴ 13g³ 12m² 14g⁶ 16m* 18m 16g Nov 5] compact colt: fairly useful performer: won maiden at Bath in June and handicap at Yarmouth 92

in September: stays easy 2m: acts on firm ground, probably on soft: has raced freely. *J. G. M. O'Shea*

RAVE REVIEWS (IRE) 2 b.f. (Mar 8) Sadler's Wells (USA) 132 – Pieds de Plume (FR) (Seattle Slew (USA)) [2003 8m⁶ 8g* Oct 25] 180,000Y: strong, lengthy filly: second foal: dam, second at 1m in France on only start, half-sister to high-class French 1¼m performer Groom Dancer: better effort in maidens (fair form) when winning 17-runner event at Newbury by head from Mission Man, staying on to lead close home: will be suited by 1¼m/1½m: open to improvement. *J. L. Dunlop* **76 p**

RAWALPINDI 2 ch.g. (Apr 9) Intikhab (USA) 135 – Just A Treat (IRE) 47 (Glenstal (USA) 118) [2003 7g Nov 1] 27,000Y: seventh foal: half-brother to 3 winners, including 1997 2-y-o 6f winner Special Treat (by Wolfhound) and 7f winner Goes A Treat (by Common Grounds): dam 2-y-o 5f winner: 50/1, possibly amiss when last of 12 in maiden at Newmarket. *J. A. R. Toller* **–**

RAWWAAH (IRE) 3 ch.c. Nashwan (USA) 135 – Muhaba (USA) 96 (Mr Prospector (USA)) [2003 –p: 10g⁴ 12.4m⁴ Apr 21] lengthy colt: fair form, lightly raced: fourth in maidens at Nottingham and Newcastle: raced only on good going or firmer. *J. L. Dunlop* **68**

RAWYAAN 4 b.c. Machiavellian (USA) 123 – Raheefa (USA) 75 (Riverman (USA) 131) [2003 117: 10m⁴ 9.9m² 12f 10.1m² 12g 10.3g* Sep 12] close-coupled, quite attractive colt: has a round action: smart performer: below form in 2003 until winning 6-runner minor event at Doncaster in September by 3 lengths from Songlark, first off bridle: should stay 1½m: yet to race on soft/heavy ground, acts on any other: usually visored, blinkered at Doncaster: has worn crossed noseband. *J. H. M. Gosden* **117**

RAYBAAN (IRE) 4 b.g. Flying Spur (AUS) – Genetta (Green Desert (USA) 127) [2003 81: 8.3g 11.6g 11.6m 12.1m² 12f² 11.6m² 11.5m 12d p12g 10m Oct 23] strong gelding: fair performer: left M. Tompkins after fifth start: stays easy 1½m: acts on firm going, good to soft and polytrack: visored (ran poorly) final 3-y-o outing: one to treat with caution: sold £1,800. *S. Dow* **69 §**

RAYIK 8 br.g. Marju (IRE) 127 – Matila (IRE) 98 (Persian Bold 123) [2003 52, a58: p16g³ Jan 22] sparely-made gelding: modest performer: stays 13f, not 2m: acts on all-weather and good to firm going: tried visored/tongue tied earlier in career: sometimes pulls hard: held up. *G. L. Moore* **50**

RAYMOND'S PRIDE 3 b.g. Mind Games 121 – Northern Sal 59 (Aragon 118) [2003 78, a71: 6.1m 5d⁴ f5s⁵ 6m 5g* 5d f5s Dec 6] tall gelding: fair handicapper: won at Ayr in October: best at 5f: acts on firm going, good to soft and fibresand: tried in cheek-pieces, blinkered last 3 starts: usually races prominently. *K. A. Ryan* **73**

RAYSOOT (IRE) 2 b.c. (Feb 17) Cape Cross (IRE) 129 – Mashkorah (USA) (Miswaki (USA) 124) [2003 7m 6g 6g Oct 24] 60,000F, 95,000Y: big, good-bodied colt: second foal: dam of no account: backward, signs of ability in maidens: type to do better as 3-y-o. *A. C. Stewart* **– p**

RAYWARE BOY (IRE) 7 b.g. Scenic 128 – Amata (USA) (Nodouble (USA)) [2003 –§: f11g⁶ f11s f12s Feb 18] leggy, short-backed gelding: temperamental performer: virtually refused to race final outing: usually blinkered/visored. *D. Shaw* **– §**

RAZKALLA (USA) 5 b.g. Caerleon (USA) 132 – Larrocha (IRE) 116 (Sadler's Wells (USA) 132) [2003 f8.5s* 12g* 13.4m³ 14m* 11.8m* 12m* 12g² 10g⁴ Aug 23] lengthy gelding: smart performer: missed 2002: won minor events at Wolverhampton in January and Doncaster in March and listed races at Leicester (beat Prompt Payment by ¾ length) and Newmarket (beat Putra Sandhurst by ¾ length) in June: very good 2 lengths second to Researched in listed Glorious Rated Stakes (Handicap) at Goodwood penultimate start: should stay 1¾m: acts on fibresand and good to firm going: genuine. *D. R. Loder* **118**

RAZOTTI (IRE) 3 b.f. Raphane (USA) 102 – Zalotti (IRE) 84 (Polish Patriot (USA) 128) [2003 62: f6g 7m 8.1m 5g 6g² 7.2f³ 5.9m Aug 4] sturdy filly: modest handicapper: stays 7.2f: raced only on good going or firmer on turf: visored last 4 starts: sold 1,400 gns, sent to Pakistan. *N. Tinkler* **54**

REALISM (FR) 3 b.g. Machiavellian (USA) 123 – Kissing Cousin (IRE) 116 (Danehill (USA) 126) [2003 8.5m f8.5g³ f8g⁵ f9.4g Nov 28] strong, good-bodied gelding: fourth foal: half-brother to Irish 1m winner Patruel (by Rainbow Quest): dam 6f (at 2 yrs) to 1m (Coronation Stakes) winner: modest form in maidens: left M. Johnston 2,500 gns and off nearly 7 months: best effort when third at Wolverhampton: stays 1m: acts on fibresand: edgy on debut: wandered third outing. *P. W. Hiatt* **60**

REAP 5 b.g. Emperor Jones (USA) 119 – Corn Futures 78 (Nomination 125) [2003 –, **79**
a75: p8g 9.7g⁴ 8m 8m 8g* f9.4f 8d* 8m* 8m* 8g² Oct 28] leggy, good-topped gelding:
fair performer: won handicaps at Ripon in July and Newmarket in August, and handicap
and minor event (flashed tail) at Newcastle in October: stays 1¼m: acts on all-weather,
good to firm and good to soft going: tried visored at 2 yrs: has wandered: often makes
running. *Mrs Lydia Pearce*

REASON (IRE) 5 b.g. Sadler's Wells (USA) 132 – Marseillaise (Artaius (USA) 129) –
[2003 f12g Aug 15] close-coupled, quite attractive gelding: useful form at best in 3 races
in 2001 for H. Cecil: tailed off in seller at Wolverhampton only run since: tried visored/
blinkered. *D. W. Chapman*

REBANNA 3 ch.f. Rock City 120 – Fuwala (Unfuwain (USA) 131) [2003 –: f7g Jun –
9] plain, lengthy filly: has a round action: well beaten in 2 maidens. *J. Balding*

REBATE 3 b.g. Pursuit of Love 124 – Aigua Blava (USA) (Solford (USA) 127) [2003 **81**
77: 8.3g³ 10d 9g 9m 7g 7.6g³ 9.9f* 10d⁴ 9g 9m 8g Sep 22] lengthy gelding: fairly useful
handicapper: won at Goodwood in June: stays 1¼m: acts on firm and good to soft going:
sometimes races freely. *R. Hannon*

REBELLE 4 b. or br.g. Reprimand 122 – Blushing Belle 74 (Local Suitor (USA) 128) **71**
[2003 71: f16.2g* f16s² f16g Dec 3] tall, close-coupled gelding: fair handicapper: won at
Wolverhampton in January: left I. Wood 4,000 gns and off 11 months before running
as if amiss final outing: stays 2m: acts on firm going and all-weather: tends to wander:
normally reliable. *P. Bowen*

REBEL ROUSER 2 b.g. (Jan 25) Kris 135 – Nanouche (Dayjur (USA) 137) [2003 –
7m p7g p7g Oct 30] 27,000Y: good-topped gelding: third foal: half-brother to 5f winner
Faiza (by Efisio): dam once-raced daughter of outstanding sprinter Habibti: 50/1, well
held in maidens at Newbury and Lingfield (2). *W. R. Muir*

Sheikh Mohammed's "Razkalla"

REBEL STAR 2 b.g. (Feb 6) Sure Blade (USA) 130 – Tamara 83 (Marju (IRE) 127) – [2003 6g 6f⁶ 7g 7m Oct 2] first foal: dam 2-y-o 5f winner: last in maidens: twice slowly away. *John Berry*

REBEL TIMES 2 ch.f. (Jan 13) Timeless Times (USA) 99 – Skiddaw Bird (Bold – Owl 101) [2003 5m 5g May 31] 900Y: good-bodied filly: sister to 5f (at 2 yrs)/6f winner Foreman: dam unraced: last in claimer/seller. *D. W. Barker*

RECADERO (GER) 7 b.h. Dashing Blade 117 – Ready Sun (GER) (Cortez (GER)) **60** [2003 7g* f6g p8g Dec 20] half-brother to 3 winners in Germany: dam German 1m winner: one-time useful performer: won claimer at Clairefontaine in August: left Frau A. Bodenhagen, well held both starts on all-weather in Britain: stays 1m: acts on heavy going and sand: tried blinkered. *T. H. Hansen, Germany*

RECALL (IRE) 3 b.f. Revoque (IRE) 122 – Toffee 66 (Midyan (USA) 124) [2003 – 8.2m f8g p10g Dec 6] workmanlike filly: second foal: half-sister to a winner abroad by So Factual: dam second at 7.5f at 2 yrs: little form: slowly away second outing. *J. G. Given*

RECKLESS MOMENT 2 b.f. (Mar 5) Victory Note (USA) 120 – Blue Indigo (FR) **49** (Pistolet Bleu (IRE) 133) [2003 p5g⁵ f5g f5s f5g Nov 14] 4,000Y: first foal: dam, French maiden, out of half-sister to Breeders' Cup Classic winner Arcangues and to smart dam of 5-y-o Aquarelliste: poor form in minor event/maidens. *W. G. M. Turner*

RECOLLECTING 2 b.f. (Mar 14) Polish Precedent (USA) 131 – Introducing 78 **58 p** (Mtoto 134) [2003 8d Nov 7] third foal: dam, 1¼m winner in France, sister to very smart performer up to 13f (also third in Derby) Presenting: 16/1 and backward, ninth of 24 to Hello It's Me in maiden at Doncaster: likely to be suited by 1¼m/1½m: will probably do better. *A. M. Balding*

RECORDING SESSION (USA) 5 ch.h. Colonial Affair (USA) 126 – Cynthia Dean – (USA) (Secretariat (USA)) [2003 10.1m³ Aug 13] $5,000Y, $15,000 2-y-o: sixth foal: half-brother to winner in France by Strike The Gold: dam, winner in USA, out of half-sister to US Grade 1 winners Image of Greatness and Buy The Firm: maiden, formerly trained by J. Smith, jnr in USA, in frame 6 times in 2002: tailed off in 3-runner event at Yarmouth on British debut: seems to stay 9f: acts on firm going and dirt. *P. J. McBride*

RECOUNT (FR) 3 b.g. Sillery (USA) 122 – Dear Countess (FR) (Fabulous Dancer **83** (USA) 124) [2003 61p: p7g⁶ 12m* 10m 11.8m* 12.3m⁴ 11g⁵ 12m May 29] good-topped gelding: fairly useful performer: won minor event at Musselburgh in March and handicap at Leicester in April: stays 1½m: raced only on good ground or firmer: signs of waywardness. *J. R. Best*

RECTANGLE (IRE) 3 ch.g. Fayruz 116 – Moona (USA) 73 (Lear Fan (USA) 130) **89** [2003 81p: 5d 5.5m² 5m⁶ 5d³ 5f Jun 17] strong gelding: fairly useful handicapper: placed at Ascot and Thirsk: loose to post before well held final start: will prove best at 5f/6f: acts on good to firm and good to soft ground: races prominently. *D. Nicholls*

RECYCLING RITA 4 ch.f. Karinga Bay 116 – Gaynor Goodman (IRE) 43 (Fayruz – 116) [2003 6g p7g Dec 17] fourth foal: dam sprint maiden: last in maiden/claimer. *P. R. Hedger*

RED ACER (IRE) 2 ch.g. (Apr 2) Shinko Forest (IRE) – Another Baileys 60 (Deploy – 131) [2003 5.1m 6g 6m f8g⁶ f8g Dec 19] IR 13,000F, 9,000Y: quite good-topped gelding: fifth foal: half-brother to 3 winners, including 5f (at 2 yrs) to 1¾m winner Irish Cream (by Petong): dam, 7f winner, ran only at 2 yrs: little form in maidens/seller: left P. McEntee after third start: usually slowly away. *P. D. Evans*

REDBANK (IRE) 2 b.g. (May 10) Night Shift (USA) – Bush Rose (Rainbow Quest **69** (USA) 134) [2003 6m⁶ 7m⁶ 7m 8d 10d⁴ f7g³ f7g³ p7g Dec 29] 7,000Y, 12,000 2-y-o: **a64** close-coupled, good-topped colt: fourth foal: dam unraced half-sister to smart 1¼m/1½m winner Young Buster: fair maiden: stays 1¼m: acts on all-weather, good to firm and good to soft going: tongue tied sixth start, blinkered last 2. *N. A. Callaghan*

RED BEAUFIGHTER 3 b.g. Sheikh Albadou 128 – Tart And A Half 83 (Distant Rel- **51 ?** ative 128) [2003 65: f8g⁴ p7g p8g 8.2g Mar 26] modest maiden: raced only at 7f/1m on all-weather/good going: blinkered (well held in handicaps) last 2 starts. *N. P. Littmoden*

RED BIRR (IRE) 2 b.g. (Mar 22) Bahhare (USA) 122 – Cappella (IRE) 75 (College **78 p** Chapel 122) [2003 7g 6m⁴ 6m³ Sep 25] €41,000Y, resold 34,000Y: leggy, quite good-topped gelding: first foal: dam 2-y-o 5f winner: fair form in maidens: in frame at Ascot (not clear run) and Pontefract: should stay 7f: type to do better in handicaps as 3-y-o. *A. M. Balding*

RED BLOODED (IRE)   6 b.g. River Falls 113 – Volkova 60 (Green Desert (USA)   –
127) [2003 –: p12g 10m Aug 6] poor maiden at 3 yrs: little form since. *Mrs L. C. Jewell*

RED BLOOM   2 b.f. (Mar 11) Selkirk (USA) 129 – Red Camellia 116 (Polar   **110 p**
Falcon (USA) 126) [2003 6m^3 7m* 8f* Sep 27]
            Wholesale defections reduced the competitiveness of some of the
championship events at Ascot's Festival of Racing at the end of September. No
fewer than twenty runners were withdrawn on the day from Saturday's programme
after the Ascot executive decided not to water overnight in view of the forecast
rainfall. With only two millimetres recorded by next morning, the going was very
firm—firmer than on the Friday—and some trainers felt there were hard patches.
After the two-year-old course record was lowered by Snow Ridge in the opening
Royal Lodge Stakes, the next race the Meon Valley Stud Fillies' Mile became the
first of the afternoon's races to be affected by withdrawals, the Irish-trained
Moyglare Stud Stakes winner Necklace and the May Hill Stakes runner-up Hathrah
being among four of the eleven declared runners taken out. The Moyglare third and
fifth, Menhoubah and River Belle, and the Prestige Stakes runner-up Ithaca were
the only Fillies' Mile runners left with pattern-race experience.
            The first two in the betting, 13/8 favourite Punctilious—recently purchased
by Sheikh Mohammed—and 3/1-shot Red Bloom, had both shaped as if they were
ready for the step up in class. Both had won in good style last time out, Punctilious
in a minor event at Salisbury and Red Bloom confirming the promise of her
debut when quickening away to beat Silk Fan by two lengths in a twelve-runner
Newmarket maiden in August. With front-running Punctilious increasing the
tempo approaching the home turn—earlier than it had been in the Royal Lodge—
the Fillies' Mile saw the two-year-old course record for Ascot's round mile broken
for the second time in under forty minutes. Red Bloom was produced with a smooth
run and deprived Punctilious of the lead after a short, sharp tussle halfway up the
straight. Despite drifting right, as she had at Newmarket, Red Bloom kept on
strongly to win by a length and a quarter and a short head from the once-raced
Sheikh Mohammed-owned maiden winner Sundrop and Punctilious, with Menhoubah fourth, River Belle sixth and Ithaca last. The form was no better than
average for a Fillies' Mile but the winner put herself very much into the classic
picture. Tall and rather leggy, Red Bloom looked anything but the finished article at
two and looks sure to progress again at three. She has the same connections as the
latest One Thousand Guineas winner Russian Rhythm and it would come as no
surprise if she went close to emulating that filly at Newmarket.
            Red Bloom's sire Selkirk, whose record includes a Guineas winner in
Wince, was a miler, but he comes up with winners over a wide variety of distances.
The notable mile-and-a-half performers Highest and Leadership were among those
to represent him in the latest season. Selkirk stands in Newmarket and has been
regularly supported by Cheveley Park Stud, who sent Red Bloom's dam Red
Camellia to him in each of her first two seasons. Red Camellia's first offspring
never reached the racecourse but the mating has paid off with Red Bloom. Red
Bloom's dam Red Camellia also contested the Fillies' Mile, starting second
favourite after winning her three previous starts (notably the Prestige Stakes very

*Meon Valley Stud Fillies' Mile, Ascot—Red Bloom puts herself very much in the Guineas picture
as Sundrop (No.10) and Punctilious battle for the minor placings*

Cheveley Park Stud's "Red Bloom"

		⎧ Sharpen Up (ch 1969)	⎧ Atan ⎩ Rocchetta
	⎧ Selkirk (USA) (ch 1988)	⎩ Annie Edge (ch 1980)	⎧ Nebbiolo ⎩ Friendly Court
Red Bloom (b.f. Mar 11, 2001)	⎨	⎧ Polar Falcon (b or br 1987)	⎧ Nureyev ⎩ Marie d'Argonne
	⎩ Red Camellia (b 1994)	⎩ Cerise Bouquet (b 1982)	⎧ Mummy's Pet ⎩ Rosia Bay

easily), but she fractured a knee when fourth to Reams of Verse and, after being operated on, ran only twice at three, finishing a good third in the Poule d'Essai des Pouliches on her reappearance. Red Camellia, by the sprinter-miler Polar Falcon, was never tried beyond a mile and her dam Cerise Bouquet was typical of the progeny of Mummy's Pet in that she won over five as a two-year-old (not raced after August and sold at the December Sales). Cerise Bouquet was, however, a half-sister to an Irish St Leger winner in Ibn Bey and a Yorkshire Oaks winner in Roseate Tern, who was also placed in the St Leger at Doncaster. Their dam the miler Rosia Bay, a half-sister to Arlington Million winner Teleprompter, produced Ibn Bey and Roseate Tern to the Derby winners Mill Reef and Blakeney. Two of Red Camellia's winning half-sisters Red Bouquet and Red Azalea were also by Derby winners, Reference Point and Shirley Heights, and won at up to thirteen furlongs and at a mile and a half respectively. Red Bouquet produced a mile-and-a-half winner by Polar Falcon in the useful Red Carnation as well as the November Handicap winner Red Wine by July Cup winner Hamas. Red Bloom should get further than a mile and, given that her pedigree is a mix of speed and stamina, it would be a mistake to dismiss her prospects of staying a mile and a half. She has a quick, rather choppy action and has so far raced only on ground firmer than good.
Sir Michael Stoute

RED CARPET 5 ch.h. Pivotal 124 – Fleur Rouge 71 (Pharly (FR) 130) [2003 109:   **108** 6g* 7m⁶ 6m⁵ 6d³ 6m Jul 19] tall, close-coupled horse: reportedly had a testicle removed: good mover: useful performer, lightly raced: won listed race at Doncaster in March by ¾ length from Orientor: respectable efforts when fifth to Twilight Blues in Duke of York Stakes at York and third to Miss Emma in Greenlands Stakes at the Curragh: best at 6f/7f: acted on firm and good to soft going: had carried head awkwardly: often made running: joined D. Nicholls: dead. *M. L. W. Bell*

RED CHIEF (IRE) 3 b.g. Lahib (USA) 129 – Karayb (IRE) 93 (Last Tycoon 131)   **73** [2003 78: 8.3g⁴ 10d 8g 8g⁶ 8m⁵ 8.5d⁴ 10g Oct 6] angular gelding: fair handicapper: stays 1m: acts on good to firm going, probably on good to soft: visored (well held) final start: sold 12,000 gns. *M. L. W. Bell*

RED CHINA 4 ch.g. Inchinor 119 – Little Tramp (Trempolino (USA) 135) [2003 68d: **44** p5g p8g⁵ p8g p6g Mar 5] poor performer nowadays: stays easy 1m: acts on good to firm going, soft and polytrack: has worn cheekpieces: sometimes slowly away. *M. Blanshard*

RED CONTACT (USA) 2 b.c. (Mar 21) Sahm (USA) 112 – Basma (USA) 104 (Grey   **72** Dawn II 132) [2003 p8g p7g p8g⁴ Dec 20] $17,000Y: closely related to 1m winner Sadaka (by Kingmambo) and half-brother to 2 winners, including useful 9f winner Dhuhook (by Dixieland Band): dam 2-y-o 6f winner and third in Cheveley Park Stakes: easily best effort at Lingfield (fair form) when 3 lengths fourth to Skidmark in minor event: stays 1m. *A. Charlton*

RED CREPE 3 b.f. Polish Precedent (USA) 131 – Red Tulle (USA) 66 (A P Indy   **76** (USA) 131) [2003 8g 10m² 10m⁵ 11.9m² 11.7f³ 11.9m² 11.9f³ Oct 17] rather leggy filly: first foal: dam, third at 1¼m on debut from 3 starts at 3 yrs, half-sister to US Grade 3 8.5f winner Namaqualand, a very good family: fair maiden: stays easy 1½m: raced only on good going or firmer: raced freely/found little fifth start: reared leaving stall final outing: sold 17,000 gns. *Mrs A. J. Perrett*

RED DAMSON (IRE) 2 b.g. (Mar 30) Croco Rouge (IRE) 126 – Damascene (IRE)   **81** (Scenic 128) [2003 6m 7m⁴ f7g 8m² 8m² 8d² Oct 14] €80,000Y: good-bodied gelding: fourth foal: half-brother to smart 1m winner Perfect Plum (by Darshaan) and 1999 Irish 2-y-o 7f winner Darbys Bridge (by Kris): dam unraced half-sister to top-class sprinter Marwell (dam of very smart miler Marling): runner-up in nurseries at Newcastle, Ripon and Ayr: will stay 1¼m: acts on good to firm and good to soft ground (tailed off on fibresand). *Sir Mark Prescott*

RED DELIRIUM 7 b.g. Robellino (USA) 127 – Made of Pearl (USA) 107 (Nureyev   **– §** (USA) 131) [2003 –, a66§: f7s* f8s* f8s³ f8.5g⁵ f7g⁵ f8.5g⁵ f8g⁴ 7g f8s f8g f7g⁶ f7g f7g   **a65 d** f12g⁴ Dec 26] small, sturdy gelding: fair on all-weather: won 2 sellers at Southwell in January: well held most starts after: stays 8.5f, not 1½m: acts on fibresand, lightly raced on turf nowadays: tried visored, blinkered nowadays: tried tongue tied: sometimes slowly away: not one to trust implicitly. *R. Brotherton*

RED FLAME (IRE) 3 ch.f. Selkirk (USA) 129 – Branston Jewel (IRE) 95 (Prince   **71** Sabo 123) [2003 7g⁶ 7d⁴ 8.1d⁴ 6g Jul 5] 50,000Y: rather sparely-made filly: third foal: half-sister to 4-y-o Falcon Hill: dam, 2-y-o 5f winner, half-sister to smart 6f/7f performer Branston Abby and 5-y-o Desert Deer: fair form: will prove best up to 1m: raced only on good/good to soft ground: raced freely penultimate start. *E. A. L. Dunlop*

RED FLYER (IRE) 4 br.g. Catrail (USA) 123 – Marostica (ITY) (Stone 124) [2003   **46** 55: f11g⁴ f8s Feb 20] close-coupled gelding: poor maiden: stays 9f: acts on all-weather and any turf going: sometimes starts slowly/carries head high. *P. C. Haslam*

RED FOREST (IRE) 4 b.g. Charnwood Forest (IRE) 125 – High Atlas 65 (Shirley   **61 d** Heights 130) [2003 63, a76: 8m 8m 10.5m⁵ 10.5m⁴ 10.9m⁵ 10.5f⁶ f12g Oct 20] medium-sized gelding: modest performer: below form last 3 starts, finding little final one: stays 10.5f: acts on soft ground, good to firm and all-weather: usually tongue tied. *J. Mackie*

RED FORT (IRE) 3 b.g. Green Desert (USA) 127 – Red Bouquet (Reference Point   **95** 139) [2003 10m 12m* 12.3m⁴ 12m Oct 3] useful-looking gelding: third foal: closely related to 4-y-o Red Wine and half-brother to Red Carnation (by Polar Falcon), both useful 1m to 1½m winners: dam, 1½m/13f winner in Germany, half-sister to smart filly up to 1m Red Camellia, herself dam of 2-y-o Red Bloom: useful form when winning maiden at Newmarket in July by 5 lengths from Harelda: possibly amiss in handicaps after: stays 1½m: raced only on good to firm ground: has been bandaged hind joints. *M. A. Jarvis*

RED FRED 3 ch.g. Case Law 113 – Mississipi Maid 47 (All Systems Go 119) [2003   **–** 51, a54: 6f 8m 10.1m⁶ Aug 6] sturdy gelding: modest performer at 2 yrs: well held in 2003: sometimes visored at 2 yrs. *P. D. Evans*

RED GALAXY (IRE)   3 b.f. Tagula (IRE) 116 – Dancing Season (Warrshan (USA)   **85**
117) [2003 91: 6g 7m 7.1g Jul 5] lengthy, well-made filly: fairly useful performer: should
stay at least 6f: raced only on good/good to firm ground: tried tongue tied: hung right on
debut. *D. W. P. Arbuthnot*

RED HALO   4 b.g. Be My Guest (USA) 126 – Pray (IRE) (Priolo (USA) 127) [2003   **58**
71: 13.1f 10g⁶ 11.8m⁶ Oct 14] close-coupled gelding: fair maiden at 3 yrs, just modest
form in 2003: probably stayed easy 2m: acted on soft going, good to firm and polytrack:
tended to race freely: sometimes found little: dead. *S. Kirk*

RED HOT POLKA (IRE)   3 b.g. Marju (IRE) 127 – Mochara (Last Fandango 125)   **60**
[2003 68: 6g p7g³ 9m p10g³ 8f⁶ 8.5g p10g p7g Oct 27] fair maiden: well below form last   **a68**
4 starts: seems to stay easy 1¼m: acts on polytrack, firm and good to soft ground: tried
visored: sold 6,000 gns. *P. Mitchell*

REDI (ITY)   2 b.c. (Apr 15) Danehill Dancer (IRE) 117 – Rossella (Shareef Dancer   **73 p**
(USA) 135) [2003 8m⁴ 8.1d 7.9f⁵ 8f⁴ Oct 17] €21,000Y: tall colt: has scope: fourth foal:
half-brother to 3 winners in Italy, including 5f (at 2 yrs) and 8.5f winner Sodoma (by Brief
Truce): dam Italian maiden: fair form in maidens: caught the eye when fifth at York: stays
1m: acts on firm ground: type to do better as 3-y-o. *L. M. Cumani*

RED LANCER   2 ch.g. (Mar 13) Deploy 131 – Miss Bussell 65 (Sabrehill (USA) 120)   **61**
[2003 6f⁶ 7d⁵ 6g⁵ 7m f7s* f7g Oct 20] 5,500Y: stocky gelding: second foal: half-brother
to 3-y-o Mannora: dam 1m winner: modest performer: won seller at Wolverhampton
in September: lost all chance with very slow start there final appearance (drifted markedly on betting exchanges): claimed £5,500 after: should stay 1m: acts on fibresand.
S. L. Keightley

RED LEICESTER   3 b.f. Magic Ring (IRE) 115 – Tonic Chord 49 (La Grange Music   **52**
111) [2003 5.1m⁴ 5m⁶ 5g 6.1m 5d Nov 4] 5,000Y: smallish filly: third foal: dam maiden
who stayed 1m: modest maiden: probably best at 5f: acts on good to firm ground: blinkered (ran badly following lay-off) final start: slowly away third outing. *J. A. Glover*

RED LION (FR)   6 ch.g. Lion Cavern (USA) 117 – Mahogany River (Irish River (FR)   **–**
131) [2003 74: 12d 12g Jul 17] big, rather angular gelding: fair handicapper in 2002, well
held in 2003 (looked difficult ride on reappearance). *N. J. Henderson*

REDMARLEY (IRE)   2 b.g. (Feb 16) Croco Rouge (IRE) 126 – Dazzling Fire (IRE)   **59**
78 (Bluebird (USA) 125) [2003 8.1d 8.2d Nov 6] €70,000Y: seventh foal: half-brother to
6f winner Mohawk (by Indian Ridge), later successful in Scandinavia, and 4-y-o Dazzling Rio: dam 1½m winner: modest form in maidens at Haydock and Nottingham
(sweating): bred to be suited by 1¼m/1½m. *J. G. Given*

RED MOOR (IRE)   3 gr.g. Eagle Eyed (USA) 111 – Faakirah (Dragonara Palace   **54**
(USA) 115) [2003 –: 7m⁶ 8.2m⁵ 8.2m 8g f9.4g f8g⁶ f11g⁵ Dec 19] leggy gelding: modest
maiden: stays 9.4f: raced only on fibresand and good/good to firm ground: wore cheekpieces last 2 starts. *R. Hollinshead*

RED MOROCCO (USA)   9 b.g. Seattle Dancer (USA) 119 – Lady's Slipper (AUS)   **–**
(Dancer's Image (USA)) [2003 p13g Feb 12] well held both outings on Flat nearly 3 years
apart: tried blinkered. *Mrs P. Townsley*

RED MOUNTAIN   2 b.c. (Mar 2) Unfuwain (USA) 131 – Red Cascade (IRE) (Danehill   **–**
(USA) 126) [2003 8d Sep 10] very big, long-backed colt: third foal: dam once-raced
half-sister to smart stayer Silence In Court: 150/1, well beaten in maiden at Doncaster.
D. W. Barker

REDOUBLE   7 b.g. First Trump 118 – Sunflower Seed 70 (Mummy's Pet 125) [2003   **–**
49+: p12g f7⁵ Jul 13] good-topped gelding: poor handicapper: well held in 2003, in
cheekpieces final start. *E. L. James*

REDOUBTABLE (USA)   12 b.h. Grey Dawn II 132 – Seattle Rockette (USA) (Seattle   **44 d**
Slew (USA)) [2003 66§, a–§: f7s f6g f7g f6g f7g 8f 7.1d⁵ 6d 5m 5m 6.9m 6g⁶ 6m⁶ 6f 6f
Aug 29] small, sturdy horse: poor handicapper nowadays: effective at 6f to easy 1m:
acts on any turf going/all-weather: occasionally blinkered (not since 2002): unreliable.
D. W. Chapman

RED POWER (IRE)   2 b.c. (Feb 5) Intikhab (USA) 135 – Sabayik (IRE) 93 (Unfuwain   **93**
(USA) 131) [2003 5g* 5.2m* 5g³ 6g⁴ Jul 17] €14,000Y: quite good-topped colt: sixth
foal: half-brother to useful 1m/1¼m winner Khibrah (by Lahib): dam 1m winner who
stayed 1½m: fairly useful performer: won minor events at Doncaster in March and
Newbury in April: in frame in minor events after (bit too free in blinkers final start):

should stay 6f: edgy sort: often troublesome in preliminaries (withdrawn as a result once): sent to Hong Kong, and joined C. S. Shum. *P. A. Blockley*

RED RACKHAM (IRE)   3 b.g. Groom Dancer (USA) 128 – Manarah 76 (Marju **76** (IRE) 127) [2003 62p: p8g⁵ Jan 7] fair form in 2 maidens at Lingfield, very slowly away on debut at 2 yrs, good late progress from poor position under hands and heels only outing in 2003: will be suited by 1¼m+: sold 2,000 gns in November. *J. Nicol*

RED RAG (USA)   2 ch.c. (Feb 14) Gold Fever (USA) 119 – Host of Angels 104 **70** (General Assembly (USA)) [2003 8m⁶ 8f⁶ 8m⁶ 10m⁴ 10m Oct 22] $14,000F, €50,000Y: quite good-topped colt: sixth foal: half-brother to French 13f winner Fruit Cup (by Strawberry Road) and winner in Hong Kong by Carson City: dam, Irish 7f and 9f winner (later won in USA), half-sister to smart Irish performer up to 1½m Phantom Breeze: fair maiden: fourth at Pontefract, best effort: should stay 1½m: sold 20,000 gns. *J. A. Osborne*

RED RENEGADE (IRE)   2 ch.c. (Mar 20) Raphane (USA) 102 – Our Duchess (IRE) **38** 67 (Mansooj 118) [2003 6m 5.1f⁶ 6f Jul 15] IR 1,000F, 4,000Y: sturdy colt: third foal: dam Irish maiden who stayed 1m: poor form in maiden/sellers. *B. R. Millman*

RED RIVER REBEL   5 b.g. Inchinor 119 – Bidweaya (USA) 45 (Lear Fan (USA) **68** 130) [2003 80: 12.3m⁵ 14.1g 12g⁶ 12m⁵ 12g⁴ 12.1m* 12.1m² 12.1m⁶ 12.6m³ 12m⁴ 13.8m Oct 18] tall, leggy gelding: fair handicapper: won at Beverley in July: barely stays 1¾m: acts on good to firm and good to soft going (no show only start on fibresand): tried visored: usually races prominently: reliable. *J. R. Norton*

RED ROCKY   2 b.f. (Mar 21) Danzero (AUS) – Post Mistress (IRE) 79 (Cyrano de **61** Bergerac 120) [2003 6m⁵ p6g⁶ f5g⁵ p6g⁵ Dec 29] 800Y: sturdy filly: seventh foal: half-sister to 5f/6f winner Polar Mist (by Polar Falcon): dam 5f winner (ran only at 2 yrs) out of half-sister to useful sprinter Case Law: modest form in maidens: stays 6f: acts on polytrack: flashed tail final start. *J. Gallagher*

RED ROMEO   2 ch.g. (Apr 20) Case Law 113 – Enchanting Eve 67 (Risk Me (FR) **73** 127) [2003 6m² 7m 7m* 8m⁶ Sep 19] 1,500Y: good-topped gelding: second foal: brother to German 7.5f winner Ross Geller: dam 5f (at 2 yrs) to 1m winner: fair performer: won maiden at Newcastle in August, making all to beat Brunel by neck: below form in nursery final start: needs to settle to stay beyond 7f: tends to hang left. *G. A. Swinbank*

RED SAHARA (IRE)   2 ch.f. (Apr 27) Desert Sun 120 – Red Reema (IRE) (Red **73 p** Sunset 120) [2003 7m f6g* Oct 4] €12,000Y, 30,000 2-y-o: third foal: dam unraced half-sister to high-class Japanese performer up to 12.5f Meisho Doto: confirmed promise when winning 12-runner maiden at Wolverhampton by neck from Lizhar, still green but getting up close home: should stay at least 7f: open to progress. *W. J. Haggas*

RED SCORPION (USA)   4 ch.g. Nureyev (USA) 131 – Pricket (USA) 111 (Diesis **79** 133) [2003 63: 8.2g 12g⁶ 12m⁴ 15f⁵ 14g 12g 11.9m 16m⁵ p16g² 16g f16.2g³ p16g⁵ Nov 26] stocky gelding: fair maiden handicapper: stays 2m: acts on all-weather and firm ground: upset in stall/slowly away on reappearance. *W. M. Brisbourne*

RED SKELTON (IRE)   2 ch.c. (Mar 10) Croco Rouge (IRE) 126 – Newala 61 (Royal **82 p** Academy (USA) 130) [2003 8m f7s* Oct 21] 10,000Y: tall colt: on weak side at 2 yrs: second foal: dam, second at 7f/1m, out of half-sister to smart Irish/US performer up to 1¼m Casey Tibbs: easily better effort in maidens (fairly useful form) when winning 13-runner event at Southwell by 1¼ lengths from Fadeela, green but strong run to lead close home: should stay at least 1¼m: will progress. *W. J. Haggas*

RED SOVEREIGN   2 b.f. (Mar 19) Danzig Connection (USA) – Ruby Princess **79** (IRE) 70 (Mac's Imp (USA) 116) [2003 6d² 6m* 6m³ p6g⁶ 5.2s⁶ Oct 29] lengthy filly: second living foal: half-sister to 4-y-o Merely A Monarch: dam second over 5f at 2 yrs on only start: fair performer: won maiden at Newcastle in August: creditable efforts in nurseries next 2 starts: likely to prove best at 5f/6f: acts on polytrack, good to firm and good to soft going: races prominently. *I. A. Wood*

RED SPELL (IRE)   2 ch.c. (Feb 22) Soviet Star (USA) 128 – A-To-Z (IRE) 101 (Aho- **77 p** noora 122) [2003 p8g* Nov 13] IR 31,000F, €40,000Y: fourth living foal: half-brother to fairly useful 1m winner Alphabet (by Saddlers' Hall): dam won Nell Gwyn Stakes: 7/1, won 11-runner maiden at Lingfield by 2 lengths from Bienvenue, going well before leading 1f out: not sure to stay much further than 1m: should progress. *R. Hannon*

REDSPIN (IRE)   3 ch.c. Spectrum (IRE) 126 – Trendy Indian (IRE) 71 (Indian Ridge **82** 123) [2003 82: 8m 10g⁴ 10g² 9.9m⁵ 11m 10f Oct 1] leggy colt: fairly useful handicapper: stays 1¼m: acts on polytrack and firm ground: visored (found little) penultimate outing: hung persistently left third start: joined J. S. Moore. *J. W. Hills*

RED STORM   4 ch.f. Dancing Spree (USA) – Dam Certain (IRE) 61 (Damister (USA)   **61**
123) [2003 57: f9.4s p10g f11g² f9.4g* 10.9m f9.4s⁵ May 12] modest handicapper: won
at Wolverhampton in March: stays 11f: acts on fibresand and any turf going: blinkered
(well held) once. *J. R. Boyle*

RED SUN   6 b.g. Foxhound (USA) 103 – Superetta 65 (Superlative 118) [2003 –, a53:   **53**
17.1m² 15m⁴ 15.9m⁴ Jul 12] modest handicapper: stays 17f: acts on fibresand and good
to firm going: fairly useful hurdler. *J. Mackie*

RED TOP (IRE)   2 b.f. (Jan 29) Fasliyev (USA) 120 – Petite Epaulette 80 (Night Shift   **76**
(USA)) [2003 6m³ May 13] 40,000F: good-topped filly: half-sister to several winners,
including 3-y-o Rag Top and fairly useful 1999 2-y-o 5f winner Lady Sarka (by Lake
Coniston): dam, 5f winner, ran only at 2 yrs: 4/1, 1¾ lengths third of 8 to Oman Sea in
minor event at York, slowly away. *R. Hannon*

RED TO VIOLET   4 b.f. Spectrum (IRE) 126 – Khalsheva 55 (Shirley Heights 130)   **83 d**
[2003 85: p8g 10.1d² 10m 10g 8g³ 10m⁶ 8.2g 8.1d p8g⁶ 10d Nov 6] good-topped filly:
fairly useful handicapper: ran creditably in 2003 only when placed: effective at 1m/1¼m:
acts on soft and good to firm going: usually wears headgear. *J. A. Glover*

RED TRANCE (IRE)   2 b.f. (Apr 8) Soviet Star (USA) 128 – Truly Bewitched (USA)   **79**
81 (Affirmed (USA)) [2003 5m 5g² 5g² 5m⁵ 5f⁴ 5m⁴ 5m³ 5g 5f² 5.1f* 5.1g³ 5d Oct 13]
sturdy, close-coupled filly: first foal: dam, 2-y-o 6f winner, granddaughter of 1000
Guineas winner Fairy Footsteps: fair performer: won maiden at Bath in August, hanging
right: creditable third in nursery at Chepstow 3 days later: should stay 6f: acts on firm
ground: blinkered (stiff task) final start, wore cheekpieces previous 2: races up with pace:
sold 11,000 gns. *A. M. Balding*

REDVIC   3 b.g. Alhaatmi – Sweet Fortune (Dubassoff (USA)) [2003 f8s f9.4g 8g f8g   **–**
May 1] third foal: dam of little account: no form in maidens/claimer. *Mrs N. Macauley*

RED WINE   4 b.g. Hamas (IRE) 125§ – Red Bouquet (Reference Point 139) [2003   **102**
101: 12.1d⁵ 12g³ 12f 16.1g⁴ 16.2f Jul 12] smallish, leggy gelding: useful performer on
Flat: ran creditably first 4 starts in 2003, including when 3½ lengths fourth to Unleash in
Northumberland Plate (Handicap) at Newcastle: effective at 1½m to 2m: acts on any turf
going/all-weather: blinkered (well beaten) once in 2002. *J. A. Osborne*

RED WIZARD   3 b.g. Wizard King 122 – Drudwen (Sayf El Arab (USA) 127) [2003   **77**
81: 7g 7g 6m 11.5m 7f Aug 26] quite good-topped gelding: just fair form in 2003: likely
to prove best at 6f/7f: acts on firm going: usually races prominently: joined Jonjo O'Neill,
and won juvenile hurdle in October. *W. A. O'Gorman*

REDWOOD ROCKS (IRE)   2 b.g. (May 5) Blush Rambler (USA) 119 – Crisp And   **82**
Cool (USA) (Ogygian (USA)) [2003 6f 6g⁴ 6m³ 6g³ 7g² 7m* 8m 7m Oct 25] €5,000Y,
13,000 2-y-o: rather leggy gelding: fluent mover: third foal: dam unraced half-sister to
dam of Gimcrack winner Chilly Billy out of US Grade 2 9f winner Sun And Snow: fairly
useful performer: landed odds in maiden at Newcastle in October: creditable seventh in
listed race next time: sweating, found little final start: barely stays 1m: acts on good to
firm going: headstrong. *B. Smart*

REDWOOD STAR   3 b.f. Piccolo 121 – Thewaari (USA) 68 (Eskimo (USA)) [2003   **60**
64: p5g⁶ 6f 5f 7g 5.2m 5m² 5m* 5m 5.3f³ 6d Oct 31] modest handicapper: won at Goodwood in September: best at 5f: raced only on good ground or firmer on turf until final start
(soundly beaten): tried tongue tied/blinkered, wore eyeshields last 6 starts. *P. L. Gilligan*

REEDSMAN (IRE)   2 ch.g. (Mar 26) Fayruz 116 – The Way She Moves (North Stoke   **44**
130) [2003 7m 7m 8m 7m p8g f7g Nov 24] IR 6,500F, €22,000Y: brother to several
winners, including fairly useful 9f winner Fayrway Rhythm, and half-brother to 3 winners, including 1988 2-y-o 7f winner Welsh Governor (by Welsh Term): dam little form:
poor maiden: blinkered other than third outing. *M. H. Tompkins*

REEDS RAINS   5 b.m. Mind Games 121 – Me Spede (Valiyar 129) [2003 –: 5g 5f 5g   **–**
Jul 24] little form since 2 yrs: tried blinkered/visored. *D. A. Nolan*

REEL BUDDY (USA)   5 ch.h. Mr Greeley (USA) 122 – Rosebud 80 (Indian   **118**
Ridge 123) [2003 116: 8g 6g 8.1g³ 8m⁵ 8.5m² 8d* 8g Sep 7]
      Eleven-times champion Pat Eddery announced his retirement from the
saddle in June, a year after passing Lester Piggott to go into second place behind Sir
Gordon Richards on the all-time jockeys' list in Britain. 'If I was close enough to
beat Sir Gordon's record in the next twelve months, then I would definitely not
be retiring,' said Eddery. After riding until the end of the season, in which he had

seventy-eight winners, Eddery was two hundred and thirty-seven behind Richards' total. 'It would take me another three years at least, but the big rides are not there for me any more, they have dried up,' he added. Eddery's riding career spanned thirty-six seasons in Britain—he reached a hundred winners a record twenty-eight times—and he won fourteen British classics, including the Derby three times. 'I can't ride winners sitting in the weighing room,' was the tireless Eddery's long-time philosophy. He followed a hectic schedule in his heyday, and when he rode two hundred and nine winners in 1990—his highest total—he became only the fourth jockey to achieve a double century in a season in Britain, and the first since Gordon Richards did it for a record twelfth time in 1952, the year Eddery was born. Eddery also rode many winners abroad and was champion in Ireland in 1982 during a period when he was first jockey at Ballydoyle; his overseas successes included eleven Irish classics, four of them in the Irish Derby, three Prix du Jockey Clubs and a joint-record four wins in the Prix de l'Arc de Triomphe, one of them on Dancing Brave, the best of the many outstanding horses he rode. A naturally gifted horseman and a fine jockey, strong and determined in a finish, the undemonstrative Eddery is to turn his attentions to syndicating horses for ownership through a new venture, Pat Eddery Racing. There were still highlights in Eddery's final season as a jockey, including his second in the Derby on The Great Gatsby, a double on Just James (Challenge Stakes) and Landing Light (Cesarewitch) on Champions' Day at Newmarket, and an emotional Group 1 victory on 20/1-shot Reel Buddy in the Sussex Stakes at Goodwood, after which Eddery received a reception which included all the jockeys not riding in the race coming out of the weighing room to greet him. Reel Buddy wasn't the final Group 1 winner of Eddery's career. After the turn of the year, Balmont was awarded the Middle Park Stakes on the disqualification of Three Valleys, bringing Eddery's final total of winners in Britain to 4,633.

Five-year-old Reel Buddy prevailed in a three-way photo finish to the Sussex Stakes, Eddery coaxing him home without recourse to the whip by a head and a short head from the three-year-olds Statue of Liberty and Norse Dancer, with Zafeen and Moon Ballad only a neck and the same further away in fourth and fifth. It was anything but a vintage renewal, the field depleted by the withdrawal on the day of Kalaman and Where Or When, but it did provide a thrilling and memorable race, Eddery switching Reel Buddy inside and bringing him with a strong run to get up near the finish after being still last of the nine runners three furlongs out. Reel Buddy had enjoyed a fine campaign as a four-year-old, winning four races, including the Hungerford Stakes at Newbury (and finishing a good third in the Sussex), but his latest season began with two very poor efforts at the opening turf meeting, in the Doncaster Mile and the Cammidge Trophy. Reunited with Eddery and tried in a crossed noseband (he had always been rather headstrong and was sometimes

Sussex Stakes, Goodwood—
Reel Buddy (far side) provides Pat Eddery with a popular Group 1 success in his last season in the saddle;
a late burst takes them past Statue of Liberty (second left), Norse Dancer (visor) and Zafeen

taken to post early), Reel Buddy ran much better when third to Desert Deer in the Sandown Mile at the end of April. Reel Buddy was never in the picture behind Hawk Wing in the Lockinge at Newbury but then finished strongly under hands and heels for second behind Gateman in the Diomed Stakes at Epsom. On his only outing after the Sussex, Reel Buddy trailed in last of fourteen in the Prix du Moulin. He may have developed a few quirks as a five-year-old—he was twice slowly away (in the Doncaster Mile and the Sandown Mile)—but he showed himself to be a smart performer in the Sussex Stakes, in which he put up the best performance of his career.

Reel Buddy (USA) (ch.h. 1998)	Mr Greeley (USA) (ch 1992)	Gone West (b 1984)	Mr Prospector
			Secrettame
		Long Legend (ch 1978)	Reviewer
			Lianga
	Rosebud (b 1992)	Indian Ridge (ch 1985)	Ahonoora
			Hillbrow
		Tiszta Sharok (b 1984)	Song
			Tin Tessa

The big, strong, close-coupled Reel Buddy is by the Kentucky-based Breeders' Cup Sprint runner-up Mr Greeley, a son of Gone West. Reel Buddy is the only significant European representative for Mr Greeley but the sire's North American progeny include several Grade 1 winners. Reel Buddy is the first foal out of the fairly useful Rosebud, a daughter of Indian Ridge who won a six-furlong maiden at Pontefract for Reel Buddy's trainer as a three-year-old before being exported to the States, where she won twice more that year, both times at around a

Speedlith Group's "Reel Buddy"

mile, and finished third in a Grade 3 event. The distaff side of Reel Buddy's pedigree is largely undistinguished, the Irish Two Thousand Guineas winner Furry Glen—a half-brother to Reel Buddy's fourth dam Gala Tess—being easily the best horse produced by the family in the last forty years or so before Reel Buddy. Consequently, Reel Buddy was sold for just 16,000 dollars as a yearling (he joined the Hannon stable for 23,000 guineas at Doncaster later the same year) but his dam's latest yearling (by Awesome Again) fetched 750,000 dollars at Keeneland in September. Reel Buddy was effective at six furlongs to eight and a half furlongs, and acted on good to firm and good to soft going. Usually held up, he has been retired to the Bearstone Stud, Shropshire at a fee of £4,500 with the October 1st concession. *R. Hannon*

REEMAAL ALSAHRA (KSA)   2 b.f. (Mar 25) Thoughtless (USA) – Nayasha (Cadeaux Genereux 131) [2003 7m 10m Oct 22] workmanlike filly: poor mover: second foal: dam unraced: better effort in maidens (modest form) when slow-starting seventh at Nottingham on final start. *C. F. Wall*   **55**

REEM AL BARARI (USA)   3 br.f. Storm Cat (USA) – Histoire (FR) (Riverman   **69** (USA) 131) [2003 6m⁴ Jun 11] useful-looking filly: half-sister to several winners, notably Derby winner Erhaab (by Chief's Crown) and smart 7f (at 2 yrs) and 1¼m winner Oumaldaaya (by Nureyev): dam French 10.5f winner: 5/1, shaped well when 3 lengths fourth to Mine Behind in maiden at Newbury, getting hang of things late on (edgy beforehand), only outing: visits Nayef. *J. L. Dunlop*

REFLECTANCE   2 b.f. (Mar 16) Sadler's Wells (USA) 132 – Spain Lane (USA) 115   **56 p** (Seeking The Gold (USA)) [2003 7g⁵ Oct 22] leggy, unfurnished filly: third living foal: sister to 6-y-o Levantine: dam, French 5f (won Prix du Gros-Chene) and 6f performer, closely related to US Grade 1 9f/1¼m winner Marquetry: 7/1 and tongue tied, green when fifth of 15 to First Candlelight in maiden at Newcastle: should do better. *Saeed bin Suroor*

REFUSE TO BEND (IRE)   3 b.c. Sadler's Wells (USA) 132 – Market Slide   **124** (USA) 94 (Gulch (USA)) [2003 110p: 8m* 8g* 12m 8f* 8g 8f Oct 25]
'There are three kinds of lies: lies, damned lies and statistics.' Mark Twain also said 'It is difference of opinion that makes horse races.' So far as race statistics go, there are plenty to choose from and difference of opinion is inevitably created by the way some of them are interpreted. Take the Two Thousand Guineas for example. Those betting on the Derby have been reluctant to heed some of the most often repeated statistics, at least where Two Thousand Guineas winners are concerned. Despite the obvious differences in the two races, a Guineas winner's lustre regularly leads to his being promoted to favouritism for the Derby almost the moment he passes the post at Newmarket. The reaction belies the history books. In the last forty years, twenty-five Two Thousand Guineas winners have tackled the Derby—thirteen as favourite or joint favourite—and only four have won, the last of them Nashwan in 1989. In the interim, Guineas winners Rodrigo de Triano, Pennekamp, Entrepreneur and Golan were all beaten favourites/joint favourites at Epsom, while Mystiko, Mister Baileys and King of Kings were also among those that failed to complete the double.
Taking another viewpoint, the case against Two Thousand Guineas winners in the race isn't quite so strong as the aforementioned statistics might suggest. Golan was a good second at Epsom after his Guineas success in 2001, while Pennekamp, Entrepreneur and King of Kings ran only one more race between them after Epsom and weren't themselves on the day (all three sustained injuries in the race). Indeed, the idea that the Two Thousand Guineas and the Derby have become races more for specialists, than in the period when Royal Palace, Sir Ivor and Nijinsky completed the double in the space of four years, possibly says more about the placing of horses than the horse population itself. Arguably, trainers have become more reluctant to run a stoutly-bred Derby prospect in the Guineas, yet looking at the statistics for the two races another way suggests they may be being over-cautious. Apart from the four to complete the double, only five other Derby winners in the last forty years took in the Guineas—three were second, one third and the other fourth. In hindsight, looking at the statistics this way, the likes of Sinndar, Galileo and High Chaparral were perhaps more of a loss to the Guineas field than widely imagined.

Sagitta 2000 Guineas Stakes, Newmarket—hard-luck stories in behind after a muddling race as Refuse To Bend wins from Zafeen (striped sleeves), Norse Dancer (No.12) and Tout Seul (rail)

Neither the Two Thousand Guineas nor the Derby took a great deal of winning by usual standards in 2003. Twenty lined up for the Sagitta Two Thousand Guineas, the last to be sponsored by that company, the favourite at 4/1 being Hold That Tiger, winner of the Grand Criterium at Longchamp and third in the Breeders' Cup Juvenile at Arlington when last seen as a two-year-old. Joint second favourite with Refuse To Bend at 9/2 was Lateen Sails, winner of a private trial in Dubai in the spring as well as his only start at Newmarket in a maiden as a two-year-old. The first two in the Dewhurst, Tout Seul and Tomahawk, were at 7/1, with Greenham winner Muqbil at 9/1, Songlark at 14/1 and Audience at 16/1. Craven winner Hurricane Alan and Free Handicap winner Indian Haven were at 20/1. Refuse To Bend came to the race unbeaten. Winner of the National Stakes at the Curragh on the second of two starts as a juvenile, he had produced a workmanlike display under his Group 1 penalty to land the odds in a field of eight for the Leopardstown 2000 Guineas Trial, a listed race over a mile in April, holding on to beat Good Day Too by half a length after quickening clear briefly. He looked fit and well and didn't blow afterwards. With connections still undecided between a crack at the Guineas and going straight to the Derby, and said to be wary of running Refuse To Bend on firm ground, it took until Guineas week when rain came for Refuse To Bend's winter odds of around 12/1 to contract significantly. With the stalls on the stand side, there was speculation that Refuse To Bend's outside draw might prove a disadvantage, but, as usual at Newmarket, the run of the race proved more significant. The field crossed to the rail and Refuse To Bend received a copybook ride under Pat Smullen from stall eighteen. Never more than three or four lengths back, he was perfectly positioned to strike as the runners were still well bunched in the Dip. Refuse To Bend missed the trouble on his inside, quickening to the front inside the final furlong and running on strongly to hold 33/1-shot Zafeen by half a length with 100/1-chance Norse Dancer a head further away, and Tout Seul a close fourth. Monsieur Bond, in sixth, and Indian Haven were among those to have poor runs. Refuse To Bend was Smullen's first British classic winner and the first for his trainer since Blue Wind won the Oaks under Lester Piggott in 1981.

With under three lengths covering the first eight home, the bare form of Refuse To Bend's Guineas looked as poor as for any running in recent memory but he was made favourite at Epsom—at as short as 5/2—immediately after winning at Newmarket. Although his odds drifted to 4/1 after he reportedly worked no more than satisfactorily in his final racecourse gallop, he was well backed on the day, going off clear market leader at 11/4. Refuse To Bend looked in perfectly good shape at Epsom, but the writing was on the wall for him when he took a strongish hold to post, setting off fifteenth in the parade but arriving at the start in the first group. Going uphill the reverse way round Tattenham Corner, it must have taken something out of him. Refuse To Bend was soon well positioned in the race, but was off the bit behind the leaders running down to the straight and soon out of contention from three furlongs out, eased in the end to finish a disappointing thirteenth. Lack of stamina alone failed to explain Refuse To Bend's performance at Epsom but he wasn't raced beyond a mile on three subsequent outings. The absence of a strong gallop in the Guineas contributed to the bunched finish and Refuse To Bend actually showed better form on his first start after the Derby. He faced no easy task conceding 8 lb to most of his six rivals in the Group 3 Desmond Stakes at Leopardstown, but, freshened up by a ten-week break, he proved well up to the job. With a pacemaker in the field, Refuse To Bend took it up going smoothly after the home turn and soon had the race sewn up, beating Latino Magic by three lengths.

The Irish Champion Stakes came under consideration next, but Refuse To Bend eventually returned to Group 1 company the same weekend, in the Prix du Moulin at Longchamp in early-September. He started second favourite (coupled with his pacemaker) but ran no sort of race, taking a strong hold up with the pace and being beaten quickly in the straight, trailing in eleventh of fourteen behind Nebraska Tornado. Refuse To Bend was purchased privately by Sheikh Mohammed after Longchamp but was leased back to his original owners to run in the Breeders' Cup Mile at Santa Anita on his final start. Once again, Refuse To Bend performed well below par, away sluggishly this time and under pressure before the straight, fading to finish eleventh of thirteen behind Six Perfections.

The modern-day reputation of milers for making the best sires is refuted somewhat by the pedigrees of the winners of the Two Thousand Guineas in recent years. Refuse To Bend was the third Guineas winner in the last ten years for Sadler's Wells, following Entrepreneur and King of Kings, and Spectrum, Darshaan and Bering have also sired winners of the race in the same period. Refuse To Bend was a first British classic winner in the colours of the Moyglare Stud operation. Owned by nonogenarian billionaire Walter Haefner since 1962, the Moyglare Stud in Ireland has a rich history, and has bred the likes of Assert, Bikala and Be My Guest, as well as a stream of pattern and graded winners on both sides of the Atlantic since. Refuse To Bend's grandam Grenzen, an 11,000-dollar yearling, was purchased by Moyglare in America after a fine racing career which included second place in the Kentucky Oaks. She has proved a major success at stud. Grenzen is the dam of Irish Edition, who produced Go And Go, winner of the Belmont Stakes for Dermot Weld in the Moyglare colours in 1990, and also of Twilight Agenda, second in the Breeders' Cup Classic. Irish Edition is also the dam of In Time's Eye, a smart performer, successful at Royal Ascot for Weld in 2003. Refuse To Bend's dam, Market Slide, another daughter of Grenzen, has more than one good horse to her name too. Her first foal was Weld's 2002 Melbourne Cup winner Media Puzzle (by Theatrical). Her only other produce before Refuse To Bend was his sister Ripple of Pride, a fairly useful winner for Weld at a mile and a half. Since Refuse To Bend, Market Slide has produced a filly by Sadler's Wells, Genuine Pride, who was

Desmond Stakes, Leopardstown—Refuse To Bend lands the odds in good style on his return to a mile; Latino Magic is second ahead of Middlemarch

Moyglare Stud Farm's "Refuse To Bend"

unraced at two in 2003, and a half-brother to Refuse To Bend by Danehill. Market Slide won a maiden from four starts in Ireland as a two-year-old and developed into a fairly useful sprinter there at three. She was then returned to America, where she won another three races and finished third in a Grade 3 handicap over six furlongs as a five-year-old.

	Sadler's Wells (USA) (b 1981)	Northern Dancer (b 1961)	Nearctic
			Natalma
Refuse To Bend (IRE) (b.c. 2000)		Fairy Bridge (b 1975)	Bold Reason
			Special
	Market Slide (USA) (ch 1991)	Gulch (b 1984)	Mr Prospector
			Jameela
		Grenzen (ch 1975)	Grenfall
			My Poly

The fact that Market Slide had produced Media Puzzle encouraged the idea that Refuse To Bend might be more likely to win the Derby than the Guineas on pedigree and after Newmarket there was even talk of the triple crown. Refuse To Bend remains in training and will almost certainly be given another chance beyond a mile—especially with Zafeen also now in the Godolphin camp—though his free-going style suggests a mile and a half may prove beyond him. Looking at the dam's side of his pedigree alone, it is possible Refuse To Bend will take well to dirt, though Sadler's Wells has few runners on it. A genuine sort, Refuse To Bend is a medium-sized, quite attractive colt with a round action. He has raced exclusively on good ground or firmer so far, though, as with many by Sadler's Wells, there has been speculation that good or softer might prove to suit him ideally. It is reported that he is likely to begin his four-year-old campaign in the Lockinge Stakes at Newbury. *D. K. Weld, Ireland*

REGAL AGENDA (IRE)   3 b.c. Ali-Royal (IRE) 127 – Hidden Agenda (FR) 55   **102**
(Machiavellian (USA) 123) [2003 93: 9m* 10m² 10g Oct 31] good-topped colt: useful
performer, lightly raced: reportedly had operation on his joints prior to landing odds
(despite saddle slipping) in maiden at Redcar in September: good 1¾ lengths second
to Counsel's Opinion in minor event at Ascot (made running), then folded tamely in
listed event at Newmarket: likely to prove best at 1m/1¼m: raced only on good/good
to firm ground: visored in 2003: mulish at stall second 2-y-o outing: sold 27,000 gns.
H. R. A. Cecil

REGAL ALI (IRE)   4 ch.g. Ali-Royal (IRE) 127 – Depeche (FR) (Kings Lake (USA)   –
133) [2003 46: f11g f12s f12g Jan 23] smallish, close-coupled gelding: poor maiden
handicapper: no form in 2003: tried blinkered. *John Berry*

REGAL FLIGHT (IRE)   2 b.c. (May 7) King's Theatre (IRE) 128 – Green Belt (FR)   **55**
(Tirol 127) [2003 6f⁵ 7g 7.1m⁵ Aug 25] 3,000Y: third foal: dam unraced daughter of very
smart winner in France and USA around 1¼m Green Reef: modest form in maidens:
needs to settle to stay beyond 7f. *I. A. Wood*

REGAL GALLERY (IRE)   5 b.m. Royal Academy (USA) 130 – Polistatic 53 (Free   **?**
State 125) [2003 55, a63: p10g⁴ p10g* Dec 17] lengthy mare: fair handicapper, lightly   **a65**
raced: won at Lingfield in December: should stay 1½m: acts on polytrack, raced only on
good/good to firm going on turf: tried tongue tied. *C. A. Horgan*

REGAL PERFORMER (IRE)   2 b.g. (Apr 3) Ali-Royal (IRE) 127 – Khatiynza   –
(Nishapour (FR) 125) [2003 7m 8g Oct 25] IR 11,000F, €52,000Y: half-brother to 1m
winner Okey Dorey (by Lake Coniston) and 1998 2-y-o 6f winner Rainbow Amethyst
(by Brief Truce), both useful in Ireland: dam second in bumpers: signs of just a little
ability in maidens at Folkestone and Newbury: sold 5,000 gns, and gelded. *S. Kirk*

REGAL RANSOM (IRE)   4 br.f. Anabaa (USA) 130 – Queen's Ransom (IRE) 70   –
(Last Tycoon 131) [2003 f8g f5s Feb 27] IR 360,000Y: third foal: half-sister to fairly
useful 5f (at 2 yrs) to 1m winner Cair Paravel (by Distant Relative) and 1m and 1¼m (in
UAE) winner Khitaam (by Charnwood Forest): dam, 2-y-o 7f winner, half-sister to smart
filly up to around 1m Circle of Gold: well held in 2 maidens at Southwell. *B. S. Rothwell*

REGAL REPOSE   3 b.f. Classic Cliche (IRE) 128 – Ideal Candidate 80 (Celestial   **52**
Storm (USA) 132) [2003 p12g 10.2m⁶ f12g* f12g p12g 16.2d² 15.8m f12g Aug 15] fifth
foal: half-sister to 2 winners, including 4-y-o Mission To Mars: dam 1¼m to 2m winner:
modest performer: won claimer at Wolverhampton in May: left C. Cyzer after sixth start:
stays 2m: acts on fibresand and good to soft ground: inconsistent. *A. J. Chamberlain*

REGAL SETTING (IRE)   2 br.g. (Feb 24) King's Theatre (IRE) 128 – Cartier   **75 p**
Bijoux 96 (Ahonoora 122) [2003 f8s² f8.5s* Sep 20] €135,000Y: half-brother to several
winners, including useful 1994 2-y-o 5f/6f winner Fallow (by Common Grounds) and
fairly useful Irish 2001 2-y-o 6f winner Hathlool (by Alhaarth): dam, 2-y-o 5f winner,
half-sister to dam of smart sprinter Central City: fair form in maidens: landed odds in
6-runner event at Wolverhampton by length from Cellarmaster, still green but leading
final 1f: will stay 1¼m: open to fair bit of progress. *Sir Mark Prescott*

REGAL SONG (IRE)   7 b.g. Anita's Prince 126 – Song Beam 84 (Song 132) [2003   **76 §**
89§, a–§: 5g 5m 5d² 5v 5g 5g⁶ 5d* 5d 5g 5s⁵ Nov 3] useful-looking gelding: fair
handicapper: won at Beverley in July: best at 5f/6f: acts on fibresand, probably on good
to firm going, but revels on softer than good: blinkered: often races prominently: has
hung right/finished weakly: unreliable. *T. J. Etherington*

REGAL VINTAGE (USA)   3 ch.g. Kingmambo (USA) 125 – Grapevine (IRE) 88   –
(Sadler's Wells (USA) 132) [2003 –p: 7m⁶ 8m 11.1g Sep 27] big, good-bodied gelding:
little solid form in 4 maidens: left B. Meehan and gelded before final start: tongue tied
first 2 starts in 2003. *C. Grant*

REGENCY MALAYA   2 b.f. (Jan 20) Sri Pekan (USA) 117 – Paola (FR) (Fabulous   **57 d**
Dancer (USA) 124) [2003 f6g 7.1m 6d 7g⁶ 7d 8d Oct 31] €6,000Y, €19,000 2-y-o: first
foal: dam ran twice in France: modest maiden: easily best effort at 7f on good to firm
going: tongue tied last 2 starts. *M. F. Harris*

REGENT'S SECRET (USA)   3 br.c. Cryptoclearance (USA) – Misty Regent (CAN)   **74**
(Vice Regent (CAN)) [2003 84: 7m³ 7.6m 9g³ 8.1d 7f³ 8m 8.3g 12m 12g⁴ 10d Oct 13]
leggy, useful-looking colt: fair maiden handicapper: left R. Hannon 18,000 gns after sixth
start: stays easy 9f: acts on polytrack, soft and good to firm going: tried in cheekpieces/
visor. *J. S. Goldie*

REGIMENTAL DANCE   3 b.f. Groom Dancer (USA) 128 – Enlisted (IRE) 83   **62**
(Sadler's Wells (USA) 132) [2003 63: f7s f8s 7f⁵ 6.9f⁶ 7.2m² 7f⁶ 7.1f⁴ 8g 7.5m 12s 12.1m

10f 7d Sep 20] quite good-topped filly: modest performer: left D. Nicholls after eleventh start: seemed to stay 1¼m: acted on firm and good to soft going: wore cheekpieces final outing: sometimes found little: dead. *C. Grant*

REGULATED (IRE) 2 b.g. (Feb 21) Alzao (USA) 117 – Royal Hostess (IRE) (Be **72** My Guest (USA) 126) [2003 7m⁵ 7m² 7d 7.6m⁴ 8g⁵ 7m Oct 23] 5,200F, 10,000Y: leggy, useful-looking gelding: good mover: third foal: half-brother to winner in Belgium by Dolphin Street: dam, ran twice in France, half-sister to Prix du Cadran winner Sought Out and to grandam of Golan: fair maiden: second at Leicester: should stay at least 1m: acts on good to firm ground: tends to look none too keen. *J. A. Osborne*

REHIA 2 b.f. (Mar 24) Desert Style (IRE) 121 – Goes A Treat (IRE) 82 (Common **61** Grounds 118) [2003 6m 5g* 5m³ 5f⁵ 5d⁵ 5m Sep 29] smallish filly: first foal: dam 2-y-o 7f winner: modest performer: won seller at Leicester in July, then left R. Hannon: creditable efforts in nurseries next 2 starts: will prove best at 5f/easy 6f: acts on firm ground: played up in preliminaries third outing. *J. W. Hills*

REIDIES CHOICE 2 b.g. (Apr 15) Royal Applause 124 – Fairy Ring (IRE) 69 (Fairy **79 §** King (USA)) [2003 5m* 5m² 6m 5d 6g 5.2s Oct 29] 37,000F, 30,000Y: lengthy, quite attractive colt: second foal: half-brother to winner in Greece by Vettori: dam, maiden, form only at 6f at 2 yrs: fair performer: won maiden at Kempton in June: below form, including in nurseries, last 3 starts: likely to prove best at 5f/6f: acts on good to firm going: wore cheekpieces last 2 outings: often slowly away/wanders/carries head high: temperamental. *J. G. Given*

REIGN OF FIRE (IRE) 2 b.f. (Apr 24) Perugino (USA) 84 – White Heat 67 (Last **69** Tycoon 131) [2003 7.9f⁴ p7g⁶ Oct 30] rather sparely-made filly: fifth foal: half-sister to useful 2000 2-y-o 5f winner Media Mogul (by First Trump), later Grade 3 1m winner in USA: dam maiden who stayed 1m: fair form in maidens at York (fourth to Putra Sas) and Lingfield: should stay 1¼m. *J. W. Hills*

REINE CLEOPATRE (IRE) 3 b.f. Danehill (USA) 126 – Nomothetis (IRE) (Law Society (USA) 130) [2003 –: 8m Apr 21] only second start when pulled up in maiden at Yarmouth: dead. *L. M. Cumani*

REINE MARIE 4 b.f. Tragic Role (USA) – Regal Salute 68 (Dara Monarch 128) – [2003 7f Sep 15] 500Y: sister to 5f (at 2 yrs) to 7f winner Patsy Culsyth and half-sister to 2 winners: dam, maiden, best at 1¼m: very green, well held in maiden at Redcar. *Don Enrico Incisa*

REJESS (IRE) 3 b.c. Septieme Ciel (USA) 123 – Vallee Dansante (USA) (Lyphard **59** (USA) 132) [2003 10.1m⁴ 10g 11.5g 12m⁶ 14.1m Jun 12] IR 52,000Y: tall, leggy colt: half-brother to several winners, including smart French performer up to 12.5f Brooklyn's Dance (by Shirley Heights) and to dam of 2000 Grand Criterium winner Okawango: dam, French 1m winner, closely related to Green Dancer: modest form on third/fourth starts. *J. D. Czerpak*

REJUVENATE (IRE) 3 ch.g. Grand Lodge (USA) 125 – Nawara 75 (Welsh Pageant **95** 132) [2003 74p: 8.2f* 9g³ p10g Dec 2] useful form from only 4 starts: won maiden at Nottingham in September: best effort when close third to Spanish Don in handicap at Newbury: should stay 1¼m: raced only on polytrack/good ground or firmer. *Mrs A. J. Perrett*

RELATIVE HERO (IRE) 3 ch.g. Entrepreneur 123 – Aunty (FR) 114 (Riverman **70** (USA) 131) [2003 –: p8g⁵ f7g⁵ 7.5f³ f9.4g⁴ p8g 8f 7m* 7d* 6.9m⁶ 7m⁵ f8g Dec 19] smallish gelding: fair performer: won seller in June and claimer in July, both at Leicester: left H. Morrison 12,000 gns before running poorly in cheekpieces final start: stays 1m: acts on firm ground, good to soft and polytrack: best efforts in blinkers. *Miss S. J. Wilton*

RELAXED GESTURE (IRE) 2 ch.c. (Mar 12) Indian Ridge 123 – Token Gesture **107** (IRE) 113 (Alzao (USA) 117) [2003 7g⁴ 7f* 8d² a8.5f Oct 25] third foal: half-brother to 4-y-o Turn of Phrase and 3-y-o Evolving Tactics: dam, Irish 7f (at 2 yrs) and 1½m winner, half-sister to US Grade 2 9f winner Wait Till Monday: useful performer: tongue tied, won maiden at Leopardstown in August: ran very well when neck second of 6 to Azamour in Beresford Stakes at the Curragh, headed close home: slowly away when only eighth in Breeders' Cup Juvenile at Santa Anita: should stay 1¼m. *D. K. Weld, Ireland*

RELAXED (USA) 2 b.f. (Jan 17) Royal Academy (USA) 130 – Sleep Easy (USA) **80 p** 116 (Seattle Slew (USA)) [2003 7m² Oct 13] lengthy filly: third foal: dam, US Grade 1 9f winner, closely related to high-class US Grade 1 1¼m winner Aptitude: weak 3/1, ½-length second of 13 to Betty Stogs in maiden at Leicester, leading 2f out until close home: should stay 1m: sure to improve. *Sir Michael Stoute*

RELLIM   4 b.f. Rudimentary (USA) 118 – Tycoon Girl (IRE) 74 (Last Tycoon 131) **56** [2003 –, a74: f5g f5s f5g^2 f5g^3 5m^6 5m^6 5m f5g^4 f5g 5.1g^6 f5g^4 5m^4 f5g^2 f5s^6 f5g^5 f5s^6 **a61** Dec 31] tall, angular filly: modest handicapper: left R. Wilman after twelfth start: best at bare 5f: acts on all-weather and good to firm ground: has run creditably in blinkers (earlier in career) and cheekpieces: has reportedly broken blood vessel: usually leads/ often finds little. *P. A. Blockley*

REMEDY   4 gr.f. Pivotal 124 – Doctor Bid (USA) (Spectacular Bid (USA)) [2003 72:   **– §** f8g^5 p10g Feb 8] tall, rather unfurnished filly: fair performer at best: looked less than keen when well held in 2003: sometimes blinkered (not in 2003): difficult ride. *Sir Mark Prescott*

REMEMBRANCE   3 b.g. Sabrehill (USA) 120 – Perfect Poppy 73 (Shareef Dancer **74 §** (USA) 135) [2003 70: 8.1f^4 11m 8.2d^5 10m p10g^2 p10g p12g^3 p12g^6 f12s^6 p10g^2 Dec 30] good-topped gelding: fair maiden: stays 1½m: acts on polytrack and firm going: tried blinkered/in cheekpieces: tongue tied last 6 starts: ungenuine. *J. M. P. Eustace*

REMINISCENT (IRE)   4 b.g. Kahyasi 130 – Eliza Orzeszkowa (IRE) 69 (Polish **62** Patriot (USA) 128) [2003 75: f14s^2 14.4d p16g 15m^5 p16g 10m^3 12.6m^4 p12g^5 p12g^3 **a75** p13g^5 f14g^2 p13g^2 Dec 29] rather leggy gelding: fair handicapper on all-weather, modest on turf: effective at 1½m to 2m: acts on all-weather and firm going: usually blinkered/ visored nowadays. *R. F. Johnson Houghton*

RENDEZVOUS POINT (USA)   2 ch.f. (Mar 10) Kingmambo (USA) 125 – Reggie **78 p** V (USA) (Vanlandingham (USA)) [2003 p8g* Nov 13] $500,000Y: sixth foal: closely related to very smart US Grade 2 6f winner Five Star Day (by Carson City) and half-sister to winner in USA by Roar: dam unraced half-sister to smart French sprinter Spain Lane and US Grade 1 9f/1¼m winner Marquetry: favourite, won 12-runner maiden at Lingfield by head from Pergolacha, soon prominent and leading close home: should stay 1¼m: will progress. *J. H. M. Gosden*

RENDORO (USA)   2 ch.c. (Apr 3) Crafty Prospector (USA) – Renge (IRE) 103 (Gen- **71** erous (IRE) 139) [2003 p8g^6 p8g^3 p8g Nov 26] $17,000Y, resold 20,000Y: second foal: half-brother to winner in Japan by Devil's Bag: dam Irish 8.5f to 11f winner: fair form in maidens at Lingfield: best effort when staying-on third to The Way We Were: ran as though amiss final start: will be suited by 1¼m/1½m. *R. Hannon*

RENO   3 ch.f. Efisio 120 – Los Alamos 73 (Keen 116) [2003 8.2g 9.2d^6 10d^4 8m f12g **59** Oct 20] small filly: third foal: dam 1¾m/15f winner: modest maiden: stays 1¼m: acts on good to soft ground: slowly away on debut. *C. W. Thornton*

RENO'S MAGIC   2 b.f. (May 11) Hello Mister 106 – Mountain Magic 58 (Magic   **–** Ring (IRE) 115) [2003 5.7m p6g Oct 3] first foal: dam, 7f winner, out of half-sister to very smart sprinter Paris House: signs of only a little ability in maidens at Bath and Lingfield (dictated pace long way). *W. G. M. Turner*

REN'S MAGIC   5 gr.g. Petong 126 – Bath 76 (Runnett 125) [2003 55: p12g^2 p13g **42** p12g 11.9m 10.2f 12.6m 11.5g^4 11.6m 14.1f^4 Aug 26] poor maiden handicapper: stays **a50** 1¾m: acts on firm going and polytrack: visored once, ran creditably in cheekpieces final start: tried tongue tied: sometimes hangs left: held up. *J. R. Jenkins*

RENZO (IRE)   10 b.g. Alzao (USA) 117 – Watership (USA) (Foolish Pleasure (USA)) **57 §** [2003 81§: f16g^3 18g Mar 21] strong gelding: has been hobdayed: just modest form in 2003: stays 2¼m: acts on any turf going: tried blinkered earlier in career: usually carries head high: held up: ungenuine. *John A. Harris*

REPEAT (IRE)   3 ch.g. Night Shift (USA) – Identical (IRE) (Machiavellian (USA) **59** 123) [2003 74, a64: f6g f7s^3 f7s^5 f6g^3 6m 6m 7m f7s^3 f7g* f8.5g^4 f7g p7g^6 f9.4g^4 Dec 22] tall, close-coupled gelding: modest performer: won seller at Southwell (left K. Ryan 3,250 gns) in November: stays 8.5f: acts on all-weather, and good to firm going: tried tongue tied: sometimes wanders. *Miss Gay Kelleway*

REPERTORY   10 b.g. Anshan 119 – Susie's Baby (Balidar 133) [2003 112: 5.1g^2 **112** 5.2m^2 5m* 5g^6 5m^2 5m^3 5.3m^6 5g^4 5m 5g* 5s Oct 5]
After Tedburrow became the first ten-year-old trained in Britain to win a pattern race in the Chipchase Stakes at Newcastle in June 2002, three others followed in his hoofprints in the space of fourteen months. Repertory became the fourth to achieve the feat (after Yavana's Pace and Persian Punch) when taking the latest running of the Group 3 Prix du Petit Couvert at Longchamp, a race he has now won in three of the last four seasons from a total of five attempts. Starting at 14.5/1 in an eleven-runner field, Repertory earned his share of the record in familiar

style, blazing the trail and driven out to hold off the outsider Traou Mad tenaciously by half a length. The victory was the thirteenth of Repertory's career, one which has so far spanned nine seasons and eighty-eight runs, in which time he has earned almost £400,000 in total prize money and become a flag-bearer for the small stable of Malcolm Saunders.

Initially trained by Mick Channon, Repertory hacked up in a maiden at Salisbury on his third start, in the May of his two-year-old season, but was sidelined with a muscular problem for the remainder of that campaign, and proved largely disappointing as a three-year-old. Gelded and sent to the Newmarket Autumn Sales, Saunders picked him up for just 8,500 guineas. The trainer, who reportedly runs a filling station and shop to subsidise his training operation in the Mendip Hills, is said to have attempted to sell on a half share in Repertory for 4,000 guineas, but was unable to find a buyer. It didn't take long for Repertory to justify his purchase, however, landing a rated stakes at Newbury on his reappearance as a four-year-old. In the next season, Repertory again showed improved form, which he has maintained admirably since, achieving ratings between 107 and 117 in each of the last six years.

Repertory's other successes in the Prix du Petit Couvert were gained in 2000 and 2001, and he also finished third in the race in 1998 and 1999. He didn't run in the race in 2002, when it was moved forward from late-October to early-September for the first time. Repertory has made a number of appearances in France, including a couple in the Prix de l'Abbaye over the same course and distance, but those, along with others at Maisons-Laffitte and Chantilly, have failed to bring him further French successes. He has also met with defeat in a couple of runs in Milan and on his only start outside Europe, in the Hong Kong Sprint at Sha Tin in 2000. But, seven outings in Ireland have yielded three victories, including two at listed level, the second gained at Cork in April. Repertory has run the odd poor race when taken on in his customary front-running role, though he can hardly be said to have had things his own way in that seven-runner event at Cork, battling with runner-up Osterhase from the word go and nosing ahead only near the line. As well as being effective on any ground, Repertory isn't beholden to any particular type of course, though he has proved particularly reliable at Epsom, where he won the same handicap in August of 1998 and 2000, and has contested the Epsom Dash in each of the last seven seasons, finishing in the frame on five occasions. Another race in which Repertory has been a regular is the Dubai International Airport World Trophy at Newbury, his highest placing in four attempts being when runner-up to Imperial Beauty in 1999. He was runner-up in the latest season in a minor event at Nottingham, a handicap at Newbury (giving plenty of weight to most of his rivals in both) and the Temple Stakes at Sandown, where he finished three lengths behind Airwave.

Prix du Petit Couvert, Longchamp—ten-year-old Repertory makes all for his third win in the race; Traou Mad, Melkior (rail) and Dobby Road (blinkers) chase him home

Mr M. S. Saunders' "Repertory"

		Persian Bold (br 1975)	Bold Lad
	Anshan (ch 1987)		Relkarunner
		Lady Zi (b 1980)	Manado
Repertory (b.g. 1993)			Exbury Grace
		Balidar (br 1966)	Will Somers
	Susie's Baby (b 1980)		Violet Bank
		Game Girl (ch 1959)	Abernant
			Game Laws

Repertory isn't a typical sprinter in appearance, being a tall, angular gelding, but he is all speed and very much a five-furlong specialist, despite running respectably at best in a few tries over further. Repertory's dam Susie's Baby, who died in May 2000, made little impact in a handful of outings at two and three, but was a half-sister to the brilliantly speedy 1972 Cornwallis Stakes winner The Go-Between. Susie's Baby failed to produce another foal as good as Repertory, though she was responsible for another four sprint winners, one of whom, Sir Tasker (by Lidhame), was more than a match for Repertory in terms of toughness, chalking up a hundred and fifty-six runs (yielding sixteen wins) until his retirement at ten. Father Time will eventually catch up with Repertory too, but there's no sign yet that his powers are in decline. *M. S. Saunders*

REPETOIRE (FR) 3 ch.f. Zafonic (USA) 130 – Lady Kate (USA) (Trempolino (USA) 135) [2003 12.1g⁴ 10f 8.3m p12g f8g Nov 25] fourth foal: dam, of little account, half-sister to top-class French 1½m performer Village Star: little solid form, trained by J. Hammond in France at 2 yrs: brought down third start. *K. O. Cunningham-Brown* –

REPLACEMENT PET (IRE) 6 b.m. Petardia 113 – Richardstown Lass (IRE) (Muscatite 122) [2003 53: 12g 11m⁶ 10.2m 10m⁵ 10.2m* 10.2m⁵ 10m 10m 10m Sep 1] angular 53 mare: modest handicapper: won at Chepstow in June: stays 1¼m: acts on all-weather and probably any turf going: blinkered/visored: has worn tongue strap: none too consistent. *H. S. Howe*

REPRISE 3 b.f. Darshaan 133 – Rapid Repeat (IRE) 95 (Exactly Sharp (USA) 121) **66** [2003 7m 10m⁴ Apr 26] good-topped filly: sister to fairly useful 1998 2-y-o 7f winner Subito and half-sister to 2 winners, including useful 1½m winner Metronome (by Salse): dam, 2-y-o 7f winner who stayed 1¾m, half-sister to smart French performer up to 1¼m Hello Soso: better effort in maidens (fair form) when fourth at Ripon: stud. *J. H. M. Gosden*

REPULSE BAY (IRE) 5 b.g. Barathea (IRE) 127 – Bourbon Topsy 108 (Ile de Bour- **67 §** bon (USA) 133) [2003 –§: f8g⁶ f8.5g⁶ f12g⁵ 8m 10.1m 8.3d 6g 8g 12m* 11.9f 12f⁴ 12m² 10.1m* 16f⁴ 12.1g 10.1m 11m³ 12.1g⁵ 10.9m 10m Oct 4] big, good-topped gelding: fair handicapper: won at Doncaster and Newcastle (amateurs) in June: stays easy 2m: acts on soft going, firm and fibresand: tried visored: has started slowly/pulled hard: carries head high: ungenuine. *J. S. Goldie*

REPUTE 5 b.g. Unfuwain (USA) 131 – Someone Special 105 (Habitat 134) [2003 **50** 12m⁴ 10.4f Jun 13] 170,000Y: big, rangy gelding: tubed: brother to 1m winner You Are The One, closely related to 7f (at 2 yrs) to 1¼m winners One So Wonderful (very smart, by Nashwan) and Alnasr Alwasheek (smart, by Sadler's Wells), and half-brother to 2 winners: dam, 7f winner who stayed 1m, half-sister to top-class miler Milligram: well held in 3 bumpers: better effort on Flat when fourth in seller at Southwell (slowly away). *G. A. Swinbank*

REQUESTOR 8 br.g. Distinctly North (USA) 115 – Bebe Altesse (GER) (Alpenkonig **–** (GER)) [2003 –: f11g f8s f8s 8g Apr 30] smallish, good-bodied gelding: fair winner in 2000: no form on Flat after: stayed 9f: probably acted on any turf going: blinkered once: had reared leaving stall: was no easy ride: dead. *T. J. Fitzgerald*

REQUITE (USA) 3 b.c. Red Ransom (USA) – Rhetorical Lass (USA) (Capote (USA)) **95** [2003 p8g² p8g* 9d⁶ p8g⁴ 10m⁵ 8f³ Jul 23] has a quick action: third foal: half-brother to fairly useful 2001 2-y-o 6f winner Ristra (by Kingmambo), later successful in USA: dam, maiden in USA, half-sister to US Grade 1 9f/1¼m winner Reloy: useful form: won maiden at Lingfield in February: creditable efforts last 3 starts, including when fourth to Buy The Sport in listed race on same course and, having left J. Noseda after penultimate start, 2 lengths third to Sweet Return in non-graded stakes at Del Mar: seems to stay easy 1¼m: acts on firm going, good to soft and polytrack. *Kathy Walsh, USA*

RESCIND (IRE) 3 b.f. Revoque (IRE) 122 – Sunlit Ride (Ahonoora 122) [2003 52: **–** 8m 7m 7g Jul 31] leggy filly: modest at 2 yrs: well held in 2003. *Jedd O'Keeffe*

RESEARCHED (IRE) 4 b.g. Danehill (USA) 126 – Sought Out (IRE) 119 (Rainbow **116** Quest (USA) 134) [2003 106: 10.4m* 12f² 10.4f 12g* 13.9m 11m² 12f⁵ Oct 24] sturdy, good sort: smart performer: won handicaps at York (idled) in May and Goodwood (beat Razkalla by 2 lengths in listed Glorious Rated Stakes) in August: also good neck second to Waverley in Duke of Edinburgh Stakes at Royal Ascot and to Compton Bolter in listed race at Newbury: respectable fifth in Grade 3 handicap at Santa Anita final outing: stays 1¾m: acts on firm going: went in snatches second 3-y-o start: sometimes looks difficult ride. *Sir Michael Stoute*

RESERVOIR (IRE) 2 b.g. (Mar 10) Green Desert (USA) 127 – Spout 115 (Salse **79** (USA) 128) [2003 7m 7s⁴ 8g³ Nov 5] 125,000Y: well-made gelding: second living foal: dam, 7f (at 2 yrs) to 1½m winner who stayed 13.5f, half-sister to smart middle-distance performers Aldwych and Dombey: fair form in maidens: third at Musselburgh: likely to stay 1¼m: acts on soft ground. *W. J. Haggas*

RESIDENTIAL 2 ch.c. (Mar 18) Zilzal (USA) 137 – House Hunting (Zafonic (USA) **75 p** 130) [2003 8g⁵ Oct 25] second foal: dam unraced out of Poule d'Essai des Pouliches winner Houseproud: co-favourite but green, 2½ lengths fifth of 17 to Rave Reviews in maiden at Newbury, late headway not knocked about: likely to stay 1¼m: sure to improve, and should win races. *Mrs A. J. Perrett*

RESILIENCE 3 b.f. Most Welcome 131 – Abstone Queen 66 (Presidium 124) [2003 **–** 51: 5d 5m 6.9f 7.2m 7.2f⁵ 5.9m 10f 9m Sep 15] angular filly: modest maiden at 2 yrs: well held in 2003: usually visored at 2 yrs, well held in cheekpieces last 3 starts: sometimes carries head awkwardly. *B. Mactaggart*

RESONANCE 2 b.f. (Feb 6) Slip Anchor 136 – Music In My Life (IRE) 59 (Law **71 p** Society (USA) 130) [2003 p7g p8g⁴ p10g³ Nov 29] useful-looking filly: closely related to 6-y-o Galleon Beach and half-sister to several winners, including 7-y-o Teyaar and

3-y-o Tuneful: dam, maiden who stayed 1m, half-sister to useful performer up to 1m Golden Nashwan: fair form in maidens: particularly eye-catching third to Keep On Movin' at Lingfield, soon travelling well in rear and finishing strongly under hands and heels: should stay at least 1½m: sold 30,000 gns: will do better. *Mrs A. J. Perrett*

RESONATE (IRE) 5 b.h. Erins Isle 121 – Petronelli (USA) (Sir Ivor 135) [2003 85: f8.5g⁶ p7g⁶ f7s f7g 7m 8m f7s 9f³ 7g* 8f⁵ 7m² 7s p8g p8g⁶ Dec 2] useful-looking horse: fairly useful handicapper on turf, fair on all-weather: won ladies event at Ascot in July: stays 9f: acts on firm and soft going, eye-catching efforts on polytrack last 2 starts. *A. G. Newcombe* — **82 a65 +**

RESOURCEFUL (IRE) 3 b.f. Entrepreneur 123 – No Reservations (IRE) 87 (Commanche Run 133) [2003 7.5m Jun 11] 7,000Y: fourth foal: half-sister to smart 6f/7f performer Hot Tin Roof (by Thatching): dam, fair (at 2 yrs)/7f winner, half-sister to smart sprinters Hanu and Sanu: 25/1 and burly, soundly beaten in maiden at Beverley: sold 5,000 gns. *T. D. Easterby* — **–**

RESPLENDENT CEE (IRE) 4 ch.c. Polar Falcon (USA) 126 – Western Friend (USA) (Gone West (USA)) [2003 112: 6g² 6d* 6g 6f³ 6g 6.1m* 7m 6f⁵ 7m³ 6m 6d Nov 8] rangy, quite attractive colt: fluent mover: just useful performer at 4 yrs: won minor event at Haydock (by 2½ lengths from Orientor) in May and listed race at Chester (beat Vita Spericolata ¾ length) in August: respectable efforts at best after: has won at 7f, may be ideally suited for 6f: acts on firm and soft going: has edged right. *P. W. Harris* — **108**

RESPLENDENT KING (USA) 2 b.g. (Mar 7) King of Kings (IRE) 125 – Sister Fromseattle (USA) (Seattle Slew (USA)) [2003 7m 7g³ 7g 8m⁴ 7m Oct 3] €60,000Y: tall, close-coupled gelding: first living foal: dam unraced half-sister to champion US 1991 2-y-o Dehere: fair maiden: in frame at Ascot and Salisbury (nursery), best efforts: stays 1m: raced too freely third outing. *T. G. Mills* — **73**

RESPLENDENTLY 3 b.c. Piccolo 121 – Llyn Gwynant 115 (Persian Bold 123) [2003 73: p8g 8.2g 8.3m Jul 7] fair form first 2 starts in 2-y-o maidens (reportedly jarred up on debut and suffered from ringworm after): well held since. *P. W. Harris* — **–**

RESPLENDENT ONE (IRE) 2 b.c. (Mar 2) Marju (IRE) 127 – Licentious 45 (Reprimand 122) [2003 p7g 8m* Sep 5] 32,000 2-y-o: close-coupled colt: fourth foal: half-brother to 1¾m winner Perestroika (by Ashkalani): dam, ran twice, half-sister to Prix Morny winner Hoh Magic: much better effort (fairly useful form, had been very slowly away on debut) when winning 18-runner maiden at Kempton by 1¼ lengths from Quartino, strong run to lead close home: will be suited by 1¼m/1½m: open to progress. *T. G. Mills* — **87 p**

RESPLENDENT STAR (IRE) 6 b.g. Northern Baby (CAN) 127 – Whitethroat (Artaius (USA) 129) [2003 p12g⁶ p13g⁵ 11.8g⁴ 16m Apr 12] sturdy, close-coupled gelding: good mover: fairly useful performer on all-weather, fair on turf: ran in UAE in 2002 (left S. Seemar after final start): stays 1½m: acts on all-weather/dirt, firm and soft going: wore cheekpieces in 2003, usually blinkered/visored previously: has found little and hung: got worked up before well held final start. *M. A. Jarvis* — **70 a91**

RESSOURCE (FR) 4 b.g. Broadway Flyer (USA) 121 – Rayonne (Sadler's Wells (USA) 132) [2003 –: p16g Oct 15] well held in France for A. Spanu, and in maiden/handicap at Lingfield. *G. L. Moore* — **–**

RESTART (IRE) 2 b.g. (Mar 11) Revoque (IRE) 122 – Stargard (Polish Precedent (USA) 131) [2003 5m⁶ 6.1m f7s³ f8s Dec 13] 12,000Y: well-made gelding: second foal: dam, French maiden, half-sister to smart stayer Give Notice: easily best effort in maidens (modest form) when third at Southwell: beaten long way in nursery final start: will be suited by 1¼m/1½m: acts on fibresand: hung left second appearance. *P. C. Haslam* — **62**

RETAIL THERAPY (IRE) 3 b.f. Bahhare (USA) 122 – Elect (USA) 113 (Vaguely Noble 140) [2003 –: 7m 11.8m 8.1m f9.4g p10g⁶ Dec 30] strong, close-coupled filly: poor maiden: should stay at least 1½m: tried visored. *M. A. Buckley* — **45**

RETIREMENT 4 b.g. Zilzal (USA) 137 – Adeptation (USA) (Exceller (USA) 129) [2003 79: 8.3d 8.3g 9m² 8.2d⁴ 9.3d² 9.1m* p10g² Nov 13] leggy gelding: unimpressive mover: fairly useful performer: won claimer at Ayr in September: ran well in apprentice handicap at Lingfield final start: effective at 1m/1¼m: acts on all-weather, soft and good to firm going: sometimes edges left. *M. H. Tompkins* — **85**

RETURNOFTHEFAIRY 3 b.f. Bluegrass Prince (IRE) 110 – Brown Fairy (USA) 73 (Northern Baby (CAN) 127) [2003 7g 9m 10f 8m Sep 16] smallish filly: first known foal: dam, 7f winner (including at 2 yrs), closely related to useful French performer up to 10.5f Amiarma: soundly beaten in maidens. *S. Woodman* — **–**

RETURN TO DUE'S 3 b.g. Revoque (IRE) 122 – High Matinee (Shirley Heights 130) –
[2003 6g Apr 30] 10,000Y: lengthy gelding: half-brother to several winners, including
fairly useful 11.6f to 2m winner Right Man (by Robellino): dam French 7.5f/1m winner:
withdrawn after unseating rider at start on intended debut: backward, well-beaten eighth
in maiden at Pontefract: dead. *Mrs J. R. Ramsden*

REVEILLEZ 4 gr.g. First Trump 118 – Amalancher (USA) 85 (Alleged (USA) 138) **100**
[2003 89: 11.9m⁴ 14m² 14m² 12m⁴ 12m² 12m⁴ 14.8m³ 11.9f⁶ 12g* 12m³ Oct 3] tall,
angular gelding: useful performer: won handicap at Newmarket (by 1¾ lengths from
Pinchincha) in June and minor event at Kempton (beat Wait For The Will 3½ lengths) in
September: effective at 1½m to 15f: acts on firm going: flashed tail sixth start: usually
held up: consistent. *J. R. Fanshawe*

REVENUE (IRE) 3 ch.c. Cadeaux Genereux 131 – Bareilly (USA) (Lyphard (USA) **100**
132) [2003 103: 6m⁴ 6m⁴ 5d 6m Sep 26] smallish, sturdy, lengthy colt: useful performer:
off 10 months (reportedly twice knocked a joint), creditable fourth in minor event at
Doncaster and listed race at Newmarket (beaten 2½ lengths by Fayr Jag): well below
form after: effective at 5f/6f: raced mainly on good going or firmer: sold 50,000 gns.
M. L. W. Bell

REVERSIONARY 2 b.c. (Apr 19) Poyle George 113 – Harold's Girl (FR) (Northfields **49**
(USA)) [2003 5f 5g⁵ 6d⁶ 6m Jun 7] 3,400Y: workmanlike colt: closely related to useful
7f/1m winner Jafn (by Sharpo) and half-brother to several winners, including 5-y-o
Deeper In Debt: dam, 2-y-o 6f winner in France, also won over jumps: poor maiden:
should stay 6f. *M. W. Easterby*

REVERSO (FR) 3 b.g. Kaldounevees (FR) 118 – Sweet Racine (FR) (Dom Racine –
(FR) 121) [2003 14f Oct 12] half-brother to French 11f to 1¾m winner Sagarade (by
Nashamaa): dam unraced: 50/1, tailed off in maiden at Goodwood. *N. J. Hawke*

REVOLVE 3 b.g. Pivotal 124 – Alpine Time (IRE) 85 (Tirol 127) [2003 8.3d⁵ 8.1m⁵ **76**
10m /g² 7.1g 7m² Oct 13] 50,000Y: second foal: dam, 2-y-o 5f/6f winner, granddaughter
of top-class French filly Luth Enchantee: fair maiden handicapper: likely to prove best at
6f/7f: acts on good to firm and good to soft ground: sold 13,000 gns. *H. Morrison*

REWAYAAT 2 b.f. (Feb 3) Bahhare (USA) 122 – Alumisiyah (USA) 93 (Danzig **80**
(USA)) [2003 5.1m⁵ 5m² 5.2f* 5.1g 5g Sep 27] strong, sturdy filly: third foal: dam, 5f (at
2 yrs) and 6f winner, closely related to useful 1997 2-y-o 5f/6f winner Asfurah: fairly
useful performer: won maiden at Yarmouth in July: respectable effort after slow start next
time, better effort in nurseries after: headstrong, and likely to prove best at 5f: acts on firm
going. *B. Hanbury*

REX ROMELIO (IRE) 4 ch.g. Priolo (USA) 127 – Romelia (USA) (Woodman –
(USA) 126) [2003 f7g Dec 22] half-brother to 6-y-o Romil Star: dam placed in Germany
around 1m/9f: won maiden at Frankfurt and handicap at Bad Doberan at 3 yrs for P. Rau
in Germany: well held in handicap on British debut: stays 9f: raced only on good going or
softer on turf. *K. R. Burke*

REYADI (IRE) 3 b.c. Peintre Celebre (USA) 137 – Valley of Hope (USA) (Riverman **91**
(USA) 131) [2003 10m² 12m⁴ 8.1m* 8m² Aug 27] IR 260,000Y: good-bodied colt: fourth
foal: half-brother to Irish 9.6f winner Nicola Bella and 7f (at 2 yrs) and 1¼m winner
Sister Bella (both useful in Ireland, by Sadler's Wells): dam unraced half-sister to Mill
Reef Stakes winner Vacarme and Prix Jacques le Marois winner Vin de France: fairly
useful form: won maiden at Haydock in August: good second in minor event at Ascot
subsequent start, again making running: will prove best at 1m/1¼m. *B. Hanbury*

REZZAGO (USA) 3 b.c. Night Shift (USA) – Western Friend (USA) (Gone West **71 p**
(USA)) [2003 63p: f7g* Nov 10] fair form: first run for 13 months and 7/4 favourite,
won maiden at Wolverhampton (beat Kingston Town by head) in November, all out after
smooth headway to lead over 1f out: stays 7f: should improve further. *P. W. Harris*

RHEINPARK 4 ch.g. Cadeaux Genereux 131 – Marina Park 112 (Local Suitor (USA) –
128) [2003 68: p8g f6g f6s Feb 13] smallish gelding: fair performer at 3 yrs: no form in
2003: blinkered last 2 starts. *J. R. Best*

RHETORICAL 2 b.g. (May 16) Unfuwain (USA) 131 – Miswaki Belle (USA) 73 **– p**
(Miswaki (USA) 124) [2003 f8s 7d⁶ 6m 7.2d Oct 13] tall, unfurnished gelding: fifth foal:
half-brother to 5-y-o Danehurst and 3-y-o Humouresque: dam, second at 7f on only start,
closely related to smart performer up to 1m Dazzle: signs of ability though well held in
maidens: slowly away final outing: should stay at least 1m: likely to do better as 3-y-o.
Sir Mark Prescott

RHETORIC (IRE) 4 b.g. Desert King (IRE) 129 – Squaw Talk (USA) (Gulch (USA)) – [2003 –: f16s p16g f14.8g⁵ Feb 1] quite attractive gelding: little form: tried blinkered/in cheekpieces. *D. G. Bridgwater*

RHINEFIELD BOY 2 ch.g. (Apr 24) Wolfhound (USA) 126 – Rhinefield Beauty – (IRE) 52 (Shalford (IRE) 124§) [2003 6m 7.2f 6m Sep 8] second foal: dam sprint maiden: well held in maidens: hung right second start. *J. S. Goldie*

RHINEFIELD LASS 3 ch.f. Bijou d'Inde 127 – Rhinefield Beauty (IRE) 52 (Shalford **41** (IRE) 124§) [2003 –: 8m 5.9m 7.2m 5m 5f³ 5m 5f Aug 21] poor maiden: should stay 6f: acts on firm going. *J. S. Goldie*

RHOSSILI (IRE) 3 b.g. Perugino (USA) 84 – Velinowski (Malinowski (USA) 123) – [2003 58: 10m Jun 4] strong gelding: seemed to show modest form on debut at 2 yrs: well beaten since. *John Allen*

RIANATTA (IRE) 4 b.f. Nicolotte 118 – Asturiana (Julio Mariner 127) [2003 53: 7g – Mar 27] maiden handicapper: well held in cheekpieces only run in 2003. *P. Butler*

RIBBONS AND BOWS (IRE) 3 gr.f. Dr Devious (IRE) 127 – Nichodoula 65 **79** (Doulab (USA) 115) [2003 91: 8.3d 10.1g⁵ 10.1m⁶ 12m p8g Nov 2] leggy, angular filly: just fair form in 2003: stays 1¼m: yet to race on extremes of going. *C. A. Cyzer*

RICH AFFAIR 3 br.f. Machiavellian (USA) 123 – Much Too Risky 87 (Bustino 136) **96** [2003 77p: 11.8m⁴ 12.1g² 11.9g 11.5f* 12m 14.1s³ Oct 29] tall, rather leggy, useful-looking filly: has scope: useful performer: landed odds in maiden at Yarmouth in August: best efforts when seventh to Place Rouge in Lancashire Oaks at Haydock and third to Marakabei in listed race at Yarmouth third/final starts: stays 1¾m: acts on soft and good to firm ground. *Sir Michael Stoute*

RICHARD 3 b.c. Distinctly North (USA) 115 – Murmuring 69 (Kind of Hush 118) – [2003 67: 6m⁵ 5d 5m 5.3f p7g Oct 27] neat colt: fair maiden at 2 yrs: well held in 2003. *P. Mitchell*

RICH DANCER 3 b.f. Halling (USA) 133 – Fairy Flight (IRE) 86 (Fairy King (USA)) **53** [2003 70p: 8.2g 10m³ 9.9d 6.9m f7g⁶ Nov 10] leggy filly: seemingly fair form only run at 2 yrs, just modest in 2003: sold 14,000 gns. *J. D. Bethell*

RICHEMAUR (IRE) 3 b.f. Alhaarth (IRE) 126 – Lady President (IRE) 72 (Dominion **85 ?** 123) [2003 89p: 9.9g 10g p8g 12d 8s Nov 29] leggy, workmanlike filly: fairly useful performer: far from discredited when seventh of 8 to Ocean Silk in listed event at Goodwood on reappearance: off 5 months, well held in handicaps/listed events after: seems to stay 1¼m: raced only on good ground or softer on turf. *M. H. Tompkins*

RICHIE BOY 2 b.c. (May 6) Dr Fong (USA) 128 – Alathezal (USA) (Zilzal (USA) **– p** 137) [2003 6g Oct 31] 16,000Y: leggy colt: fifth foal: half-brother to winners abroad by Lycius and Spectrum: dam unraced half-sister to high-class 6f/7f performers Great Commotion and Lead On Time: 20/1, well held in maiden at Newmarket, disputing early lead: will probably do better. *M. A. Jarvis*

RICHIE RICH (IRE) 8 b.g. Millfontaine 114 – Sure To Go (Camden Town 125) **61** [2003 69: 8m 7f³ 8g 9g 7f 8f p6g p7g Dec 6] modest performer: below form at Lingfield last 2 starts: stays 9f: acts on firm and good to soft going: reportedly bled when pulled up sixth outing. *Jarlath P. Fahey, Ireland*

RICHTEE (IRE) 2 ch.f. (Mar 24) Desert Sun 120 – Santarene (IRE) 46 (Scenic 128) **54** [2003 5m 5m⁶ 6m Sep 7] IR 2,000F, 7,500Y: strong filly: first foal: dam, 1¼m seller winner, half-sister to US Grade 3 1m winner Gino's Spirits: modest form at best in maidens: should stay 1m. *R. A. Fahey*

RICKY MARTAN 4 ch.c. (Apr 15) Foxhound (USA) 103 – Cyrillic 88 (Rock City **66** 120) [2003 5m 5m⁶ 6m⁴ May 30] small, close-coupled colt: fourth foal: half-brother to 5-y-o Lady Laureate and winner in Austria by Lahib: dam 2-y-o 6f winner who stayed 1m: best effort in maidens (fair form) when fourth of 5 to Carrizo Creek at Brighton: should stay 1m. *G. C. Bravery*

RIDAPOUR (IRE) 4 b.g. Kahyasi 130 – Ridiyara (IRE) 94 (Persian Bold 123) [2003 – p12g Sep 9] first foal: dam Irish 1m winner who stayed 9f: fairly useful maiden at best in France at 3 yrs for A. de Royer-Dupre: well held at Lingfield only outing in 2003: stays 15f. *D. J. Wintle*

RIDE THE TIGER (IRE) 6 ch.g. Imp Society (USA) – Krisdaline (USA) 98 (Kris S **59** (USA)) [2003 54: f12s² Jan 2] modest handicapper: stayed 1½m: acted on firm going and all-weather: difficult ride: dead. *R. Wilman*

RIDGEBACK 3 ch.g. Indian Ridge 123 – Valbra (Dancing Brave (USA) 140) [2003 **81**
–p: 6g⁶ 6.1g³ 6m* May 10] small, sturdy colt: fairly useful form in maidens, winning
at Thirsk in May: raced only at 6f: yet to race on extremes of going: carried head
awkwardly/found little on reappearance: withdrawn on veterinary advice in June: sold
12,000 gns. *B. W. Hills*

RIDGEWAY (IRE) 8 b.g. Indian Ridge 123 – Regal Promise (Pitskelly 122) [2003 **–**
81: 11.9f Jun 14] tall gelding: fairly useful handicapper at best: well held in cheekpieces/
tongue tie only outing in 2003: sometimes blinkered at 7 yrs. *M. W. Easterby*

RIDICULE 4 b.g. Piccolo 121 – Mockingbird 64 (Sharpo 132) [2003 82: 6m 6g 6m⁴ **78**
6.1m⁶ 6.1d³ 7m 6m⁵ 5m⁴ f5g Dec 16] tall, lengthy, useful-looking gelding: fair performer:
effective at 5f/6f: acts on firm and soft going: usually blinkered/visored nowadays.
J. G. Portman

RIFLEMAN (IRE) 3 ch.g. Starborough 126 – En Garde (USA) 82 (Irish River (FR) **91**
131) [2003 86p: p8g⁶ 10m³ f8.5s 8m* 8g⁴ 7.9m 7m⁴ 7g 8m 7g³ 8m³ 8m⁵ 7.9m³ 8m⁴ 10g
Sep 27] compact gelding: fairly useful handicapper: won at Ripon in May: stays 8.5f:
acts on all-weather and good to firm going: visored (ran poorly) ninth start: none too
consistent. *Mrs A. Duffield*

RIGADOON (IRE) 7 b.g. Be My Chief (USA) 122 – Loucoum (FR) 93 (Iron Duke **39**
(FR) 122) [2003 49: 16.2m 16d⁶ 17.1m Jun 1] tall gelding: poor handicapper: best at
2m+: acts on firm ground, possibly not on softer than good: blinkered. *M. W. Easterby*

RIGHT APPROACH 4 b.c. Machiavellian (USA) 123 – Abbey Strand (USA) 78 **117**
(Shadeed (USA) 135) [2003 104: 8.3d* 8f² 8f³ 10.5m⁵ 9m Oct 18] leggy, useful-looking
colt: fluent mover: smart performer: disappointing at 3 yrs (reportedly suffered hairline
fracture of vertebra): won listed race at Windsor in May by 1½ lengths from Atavus: ran
very well when 4¾ lengths third (promoted to second) behind Dubai Destination in
Queen Anne Stakes at Royal Ascot next time: below form after in Silver Trophy at Ascot
(third to Tillerman, hanging late on), Rose of Lancaster Stakes at Haydock (weakened as
if amiss) and Darley Stakes at Newmarket: likely to prove best at 1m/1¼m: acts on firm
and good to soft going: tried tongue tie: often takes strong hold: slowly away both
outings at 2 yrs: sold 65,000 gns. *Sir Michael Stoute*

RIGHTY HO 9 b.g. Reprimand 122 – Challanging 95 (Mill Reef (USA) 141) [2003 **50**
52: 12m³ 13.8f² 11.9m 12.1d Sep 23] tall, leggy gelding: modest performer: effective at
1¼m to 2m: acts on any going: often visored earlier in career: usually races prominently.
W. H. Tinning

RIGONZA 2 ch.g. (Apr 1) Vettori (IRE) 119 – Desert Nomad 56 (Green Desert (USA) **72**
127) [2003 6.1d⁵ 6g⁴ 7m³ 6g⁴ 7m³ Aug 11] 19,000Y: good-bodied gelding: seventh
foal: half-brother to 2 winners in Italy, including useful 5f winner (including at 2 yrs)
Desert Vert (by Distant Relative): dam 7f winner: fair maiden: third at Thirsk: stays 7f:
acts on good to firm going, probably on good to soft: temperament under suspicion.
T. D. Easterby

RILEY BOYS (IRE) 2 ch.g. (Apr 2) Most Welcome 131 – Scarlett Holly 81 (Red Sun- **63**
set 120) [2003 6.1d 6m³ f6g³ 6f f6f 8s Nov 3] 10,000Y: smallish, close-coupled gelding:
brother to useful 6f (at 2 yrs)/7f winner Scarlett Ribbon and half-brother to several
winners, including 4-y-o Game Guru: dam 6f (at 2 yrs)/7f winner: modest maiden: below
form in nurseries last 2 starts: stays 6f: acts on fibresand and good to firm ground: usually
races prominently. *J. G. Given*

RILEYS DREAM 4 b.f. Rudimentary (USA) 118 – Dorazine 77 (Kalaglow 132) **67 §**
[2003 75: 6.1g 6g 7m 8.3d 7d* 7f 7.1g 7.2m³ 7m 7.50d 7.1g 8.2d Nov 6] unfurnished filly:
fair handicapper: won at Brighton in May: left M. Channon after tenth start: stays 7f: acts
on good to firm and good to soft ground: inconsistent. *B. J. Llewellyn*

RILEYS ROCKET 4 b.f. Makbul 104 – Star of Flanders (Puissance 110) [2003 55, **51**
a50: f7s f9.4s³ f9.4g⁶ f9.4g 8.5m 10f 12.1d⁵ Sep 23] leggy, angular filly: modest maiden:
below form after second start: should stay 1½m: acts on good to firm going and fibresand:
sometimes slowly away. *R. Hollinshead*

RIMROD (USA) 3 b.c. Danzig (USA) – Annie Edge 118 (Nebbiolo 125) [2003 111: **116**
8m⁴ 8m³ 7g* 7m³ 7s 7m⁶ Oct 18] quite attractive colt: has a quick action: smart performer: won listed race at Epsom in June by short head from Naahy: best efforts when 2¾
lengths third to Membership in Jersey Stakes at Royal Ascot and 2 lengths sixth to Just
James in Challenge Stakes at Newmarket fourth and final starts, hampered on both
occasions: effective at 7f/1m: acts on good to firm going, probably on soft: sometimes
races freely: joined J. Sheppard in USA. *A. M. Balding*

RINGING HILL   4 b.f. Charnwood Forest (IRE) 125 – Not Before Time (IRE) (Polish   –
Precedent (USA) 131) [2003 88p: 10d May 2] lengthy filly: won last of 3 starts at 3 yrs
(fairly useful form): ran poorly only outing in 2003: should be suited by 1½m+: reportedly difficult to keep sound. *H. Candy*

RINGMOOR DOWN   4 b.f. Pivotal 124 – Floppie (FR) (Law Society (USA) 130)   **100**
[2003 74: 6d 6m* 6m³ 6m⁶ 6g* 6.5m⁶ 6m⁵ 6m 6m² 6m⁴ 6g³ Oct 24] smallish,
strong filly: useful handicapper: won at Kempton in May and Newbury (by neck from
Seel of Approval) in July: very good third to Royal Millennium at Newbury final outing:
best form at 6f: acts on good to firm going, possibly not good to soft: has been bandaged
behind: banged head and lost tooth leaving stall eighth start: usually held up.
D. W. P. Arbuthnot

RING OF DESTINY   4 b.g. Magic Ring (IRE) 115 – Canna (Caerleon (USA) 132)   **102**
[2003 98: 12m 12g 12d³ 11.9m 12m* 13.3m Sep 20] quite attractive gelding: useful
handicapper: career-best effort when winning at Thirsk in September by 1¾ lengths from
Sporting Gesture, ridden more patiently than usual: should stay 13f: acts on firm and
good to soft going: often races prominently: none too consistent. *P. W. Harris*

RINGSIDE JACK   7 b.g. Batshoof 122 – Celestine 62 (Skyliner 117) [2003 70: 13d   **54 +**
13d 14v 14.1m⁶ 13g 13m 15.9d³ 15.8m⁴ 16g⁴ Nov 5] quite good-topped gelding: modest
handicapper nowadays: appeared to run very well from out of handicap final start: stays
easy 2m: acts on any going, though all 4 wins on softer than good: effective visored or
not. *C. W. Fairhurst*

RINGSIDER (IRE)   2 ch.g. (May 26) Docksider (USA) 124 – Red Comes Up (USA)   **81 p**
(Blushing Groom (FR) 131) [2003 5m 7m* Aug 30] €65,000Y: closely related to fairly
useful 1m to 11f winner Barahin (by Diesis) and half-brother to several winners,
including 10-y-o Brilliant Red: dam, French maiden, sister to Rainbow Quest: clearly
better effort in maidens (fairly useful form) when winning 10-runner event at Chester
by ¾ length from Kibryaa, quickening to lead final 1f: will stay 1m: should progress.
G. A. Butler

RINJANI (USA)   2 b.c. (Mar 22) Gone West (USA) – Ringshaan (FR) (Darshaan 133)   **91 p**
[2003 7m⁴ 8m* Sep 18] $390,000Y: quite attractive colt: has a quick action: third foal:
dam, French 9f winner on only start, half-sister to very smart French/US 1m/9f performer
Special Ring out of half-sister to very smart French 1½m performer Poliglote: confirmed
promise of fourth in maiden at Newmarket when winning 6-runner similar event at
Yarmouth by 4 lengths from Capped For Victory, soon prominent and driven ahead 1f
out: will stay 1¼m: joined Saeed bin Suroor: useful prospect. *D. R. Loder*

RINNEEN (IRE)   2 b.f. (Feb 2) Bien Bien (USA) 125 – Sparky's Song 63 (Electric   **67 d**
126) [2003 5f 6m³ 6m p7g 8d Sep 11] 16,000Y: fourth foal: half-sister to useful 6f
(including at 2 yrs) winner Lady Links (by Bahamian Bounty): dam, 1¼m/1½m winner,
half-sister to very smart sprinter Bold Edge: fair maiden: showed little after third of 5 at
Ascot: should stay 1m. *R. Hannon*

RIO BRANCO   2 b.f. (Apr 29) Efisio 120 – Los Alamos 73 (Keen 116) [2003 6d Nov   **66 p**
8] fair sort: fourth foal: dam 1¾m/15f winner: 13/2, 4 lengths seventh of 14 to Miss
Langkawi in maiden at Doncaster, slowly away and staying on: will stay at least 1m:
should do better. *B. W. Hills*

RIO DE JUMEIRAH   2 b.f. (Apr 18) Seeking The Gold (USA) – Tegwen (USA) 79   **71**
(Nijinsky (CAN) 138) [2003 5m³ 7m 7m³ 6m⁵ Sep 1] 260,000Y: leggy filly: half-sister to
several winners, including useful 1999 2-y-o 6f and 1m (including Fillies' Mile) winner
(stayed 1½m) Teggiano (by Mujtahid) and 4-y-o Halawellfin Hala: dam 11.5f winner
who stayed 1¾m well: fair maiden: third at Leicester and Lingfield: should stay at least
1m. *C. E. Brittain*

RIO'S DIAMOND   6 b.m. Formidable (USA) 125 – Rio Piedras 86 (Kala Shikari   **46**
125) [2003 59: p10g⁴ p8g Feb 8] small mare: modest performer at best: stayed easy 1¼m:
acted on all-weather and any turf going except soft/heavy: visored twice: sometimes
idled/hung left: dead. *M. J. Ryan*

RIPCORD (IRE)   5 b.g. Diesis 133 – Native Twine 114 (Be My Native (USA) 122)   **– §**
[2003 –§: 10.9m Jun 20] big, lengthy, good-topped gelding: temperamental maiden handicapper nowadays. *Lady Herries*

RIPPLE EFFECT   3 ch.f. Elmaamul (USA) 125 – Sharp Chief 71 (Chief Singer 131)   **79**
[2003 88: p6g² f7g⁶ 7g³ 6g⁴ 5.9f* 5m⁵ 5m³ p7g p6g* p7g p6g² Dec 30] leggy filly: fair
performer: won maiden at Carlisle in June and (having left A. Balding 6,500 gns after

seventh start) minor event at Lingfield in December: effective at 5f to 7f: acts on firm ground and polytrack: tongue tied last 8 outings: usually races prominently. *C. A. Dwyer*

RIQUEWIHR 3 ch.f. Compton Place 125 – Juvenilia (IRE) 55 (Masterclass (USA) **62 +**
116) [2003 6g* 8g Nov 1] second foal: dam third at 7f both starts: reportedly broke a bone in foot in 2002: modest form when winning maiden at Yarmouth in September: well held in listed event at Newmarket subsequent start: will stay 7f. *J. A. R. Toller*

RISE 2 b.f. (Feb 1) Polar Falcon (USA) 126 – Splice 114 (Sharpo 132) [2003 5.1f⁴ 6m³ **84**
6f⁵ f6f² f7g³ p7g* p7g p7g⁴ p5g p6g Dec 30] fifth foal: closely related to 4-y-o Feet So Fast and half-sister to fairly useful 1998 2-y-o 5f winner Entwine (by Primo Dominie): dam sprinter: fairly useful performer: won nursery at Lingfield in August: subsequently left Sir Mark Prescott 26,000 gns: below form after: stays easy 7f: acts on all-weather and good to firm going: blinkered last 7 starts. *Andrew Reid*

RISING SHADOW (IRE) 2 b.g. (Feb 27) Efisio 120 – Jouet 71 (Reprimand 122) **86**
[2003 6m 6m* p6g³ 7d⁵ Nov 8] IR 34,000F, 20,000Y: compact gelding: first foal: dam, lightly-raced maiden (placed at 7f/1m), sister to useful sprinter Deep Finesse: fairly useful performer: trained on debut by T. Easterby: flashed tail when 66/1-winner of maiden at Newcastle in October: good third in minor event at Lingfield: not run of race final start: should stay 1m: slowly away last 2 outings. *R. A. Fahey*

RISKA KING 3 b.g. Forzando 122 – Artistic Licence (High Top 131) [2003 80: 7g⁴ **83**
7.5m⁴ 7d⁴ 8g⁴ 7m 8m 7.5m* 7g f8s Dec 27] smallish, good-bodied gelding: fairly useful handicapper: won at Beverley in July: acts on polytrack, heavy and good to firm ground: blinkered/visored last 4 starts at 2 yrs: none too consistent. *R. A. Fahey*

RISK FREE 6 ch.g. Risk Me (FR) 127 – Princess Lily 65 (Blakeney 126) [2003 f5g **68**
p8g f7g f6s² f7g² f7s⁶ f6g* 7f* 5.9f 6.9m⁵ 7m³ 7m 7.6m f8.5f* 10.5m 8.1m⁵ 7m³ f7s⁵ **a78**
Sep 6] lengthy gelding: fair performer, better on all-weather than turf: won handicap at Wolverhampton and minor event at Catterick in May, and claimer at Wolverhampton in July: effective at 6f to 8.5f: acts on firm going, good to soft and all-weather: usually blinkered/visored: has looked reluctant. *P. D. Evans*

RISK OF LIGHTNING 7 ch.m. Risk Me (FR) 127 – Lightning Legend 71 (Lord **–**
Gayle (USA) 124) [2003 8.3s 8.1d May 26] workmanlike mare: sister to 1994 2-y-o 6f seller winner Bitch: dam 2-y-o 7f winner: tailed off in bumper and maidens: slowly away and reluctant to race final outing. *Miss Z. C. Davison*

RISK TAKER 3 ch.c. Rainbow Quest (USA) 134 – Post Modern (USA) (Nureyev **97 d**
(USA) 131) [2003 91p: 12g* 12.3m³ 12m 10m 12d 10d Aug 30] close-coupled colt: useful performer: won 3-runner maiden at Newmarket in April on bridle by 18 lengths from Love In Seattle: well below form last 3 starts: stays 1½m: acts on good to firm going: sold 19,000 gns. *B. W. Hills*

RISQUE SERMON 5 b.g. Risk Me (FR) 127 – Sunday Sport Star 96 (Star Appeal **–**
133) [2003 68d: p6g⁶ 6m 7m p6g² 5m Jun 28] quite good-topped gelding: modest **a64**
performer: best at 5f/6f: acts on polytrack and firm going, well held on softer than good: blinkered last 2 starts: tongue tied. *Miss B. Sanders*

RISUCCHIO 4 ch.g. Thatching 131 – Skip To Somerfield 79 (Shavian 125) [2003 59: **–**
f6g Apr 4] close-coupled gelding: lightly-raced maiden: well held only start in 2003: tried visored/in cheekpieces. *A. W. Carroll*

RITA'S ROCK APE 8 b.m. Mon Tresor 113 – Failand 36 (Kala Shikari 125) [2003 **66**
82, a71: p5g f6g f5s⁴ f5s⁵ Feb 28] workmanlike mare: fair handicapper: best at 5f: acts on firm going, good to soft and fibresand: usually races up with pace: has reportedly bled. *R. Brotherton*

RIVAL (IRE) 4 b.g. Desert Style (IRE) 121 – Arab Scimetar (IRE) (Sure Blade (USA) **– §**
130) [2003 64§: 7.1g 11.7f 10.9m 8f 8.1g Sep 11] rather leggy, quite good-topped geld-ing: untrustworthy maiden: tried blinkered/in cheekpieces. *S. T. Lewis*

RIVA ROYALE 3 b.f. Royal Applause 126 – Regatta (Mtoto 134) [2003 88: 5f³ p6g **93**
6.1m² 5m 7m³ 7m⁵ 6g 7m 7s* Oct 29] close-coupled, useful-looking filly: fairly useful handicapper: won at Yarmouth in October, making all: stays 7f: acts on firm and soft going. *I. A. Wood*

RIVELLI (IRE) 4 b.f. Lure (USA) 131 – Kama Tashoof 72 (Mtoto 134) [2003 70: 8f **–**
9.7m 7.1g f12g f5g f16.2s f7g Dec 16] strong filly: maiden handicapper: well held in 2003: left P. Webber after third start: tried blinkered/tongue tied. *B. R. Foster*

RIVENDELL 7 b.m. Saddlers' Hall (IRE) 126 – Fairy Kingdom (Prince Sabo 123) **–**
[2003 f9.4s 10m Aug 6] of little account. *M. Wigham*

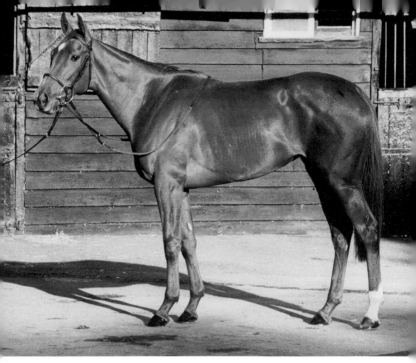

Team Valor's "River Belle"

RIVER BELLE 2 ch.f. (Mar 9) Lahib (USA) 129 – Dixie Favor (USA) 82 (Dixieland **102**
Band (USA)) [2003 6m* 6g* 7m⁵ 8f⁶ Sep 27] 14,000Y: angular, useful-looking filly:
sixth foal: half-sister to 3 winners, including 6-y-o Favorisio and useful Italian performer
up to 1m Kiralik (by Efisio): dam Irish 6f (at 2 yrs) to 1m winner: useful performer: won
maiden and Princess Margaret Stakes (by 1¼ lengths from Rosehearty) at Ascot in July,
slowly away and strong late run both times: changed ownership after: respectable fifth to
Necklace in Moyglare Stud Stakes at the Curragh and sixth to Red Bloom in Fillies' Mile
at Ascot: probably stays 1m: sent to USA. *A. P. Jarvis.*

RIVERBOAT DANCER 3 b.f. Muhtarram (USA) 125 – South Wind 62 (Tina's Pet **69**
121) [2003 72: p6g p7g 8.3g 7.1m 10f 9.9f³ 8.5m⁵ 10m Jul 18] fair handicapper: will stay
1½m: acts on firm and good to soft going: sold £1,100. *S. Dow*

RIVER CANYON (IRE) 7 b.g. College Chapel 122 – Na-Ammah (IRE) 90 **–**
(Ela-Mana-Mou 132) [2003 8.3d 8m Jul 6] workmanlike gelding: useful performer for
D. Weld in Ireland at 3/4 yrs: well held in handicaps in 2003: stays 1¼m: acts on heavy
ground: blinkered once. *W. Storey*

RIVER DAYS (IRE) 5 b.m. Tagula (IRE) 116 – Straw Boater 89 (Thatch (USA) 136) **60**
[2003 64: f5g* p5g⁴ f5s* p6g⁶ f5g f5g* f6s⁴ 5m⁴ f5g f6g Nov 17] fair performer: won **a72**
claimer in January (left I. Semple) and handicaps in February/March, all at Wolverhampton: effective at 5f/6f: acts on firm going (below form on softer than good) and all-
weather: often tongue tied, blinkered nowadays: usually races up with pace. *Miss Gay
Kelleway*

RIVER ENSIGN 10 br.m. River God (USA) 121 – Ensigns Kit (Saucy Kit 76) [2003 **40**
48: f9.4g⁴ Jan 17] small mare: has stringhalt: poor handicapper: best recent form at 8.5f

to 1¼m: acts on fibresand and heavy going (below form on good to firm): has been early to post: front runner. *W. M. Brisbourne*

RIVER FALCON   3 b.g. Pivotal 124 – Pearly River 72 (Elegant Air 119) [2003 73:   **85**
5d⁶ 6m⁴ 6d³ 6d 5m* 6f⁴ 5f² 6m 5m 6.1g 6m Sep 19] useful-looking gelding: fairly
useful handicapper: won at Redcar in May: effective at 5f/6f: acts on firm and good to
soft ground. *J. S. Goldie*

RIVER GYPSY   2 b.c. (Mar 21) In The Wings 128 – River Erne (USA) (Irish River   **72 p**
(FR) 131) [2003 p8g⁴ Nov 2] 30,000F: fifth foal: half-brother to winner abroad by
Darshaan: dam, third at 1m at 2 yrs in France, out of half-sister to Detroit, herself dam
of Carnegie (both won Arc): 33/1, fourth of 12 to King Maximus in maiden at Ling-
field, slowly away and running on well: will be suited by 1¼m+: sure to improve.
D. R. C. Elsworth

RIVER LARK (USA)   4 b.f. Miswaki (USA) 124 – Gold Blossom (USA) (Blushing   **48**
John (USA) 120) [2003 –: 6m⁵ 6m 7g 6m* 5m f5s² Dec 27] poor handicapper: won
maiden event at Thirsk in August: effective at 5f to 7f: acts on good to firm ground and
fibresand: wore cheekpieces first 3 starts. *M. A. Buckley*

RIVER LINE (USA)   2 b.g. (Feb 28) Keos (USA) 120 – Portio (USA) (Riva Ridge   **50**
(USA)) [2003 6g 6m 8g Sep 27] $5,500Y, 9,000 2-y-o: tall, lengthy, rather unfurnished
gelding: half-brother to fairly useful 1m winner Alyriva (by Alydeed) and to several
minor winners in USA: dam US 6f (including at 2 yrs) to 8.5f (minor stakes) winner:
modest form in maidens: probably stays 1m. *C. W. Fairhurst*

RIVER NUREY (IRE)   2 gr.c. (Apr 13) Fasliyev (USA) 120 – Dundel (IRE) 82   **72**
(Machiavellian (USA) 123) [2003 6g⁶ 6g 6d 6.1m⁵ 7m² Oct 25] angular, good-topped
colt: third foal: half-brother to French 1m winner Wing And Wing (by Singspiel): dam, 7f
winner, out of sister to high-class middle-distance stayer High Hawk, herself dam of In
The Wings: fair maiden: good second to Overdrawn in nursery at Doncaster: stays 7f: acts
on good to firm ground. *B. W. Hills*

RIVER OF BABYLON   2 b.f. (Apr 13) Marju (IRE) 127 – Isle of Flame (Shirley   **62**
Heights 130) [2003 8m⁵ 8s Oct 29] 50,000Y: half-sister to several winners, including
smart French 9f/1¼m winner Thattinger (by Salse) and 3-y-o Dorothy's Friend: dam
unraced out of close relation to Middle Park winner Balla Cove: modest form in maidens
at Yarmouth: went freely final start: bred to be suited by 1¼m/1½m. *M. L. W. Bell*

RIVER OF FIRE   5 ch.g. Dilum (USA) 115 – Bracey Brook (Gay Fandango (USA)   **52**
132) [2003 58: f12s³ f16.2g f12g f14.8s f14g 12m 14.1m* 16.4m* 16g 13.8m³ 14.1f⁶
p16g Oct 15] modest handicapper: left J. Eustace after reappearance: won at Folkestone
in July: barely stays 16.4f: acts on soft going, good to firm and fibresand: usually visored
prior to last 7 starts: often races up with pace. *C. N. Kellett*

RIVER TERN   10 b.g. Puissance 110 – Millaine 69 (Formidable (USA) 125) [2003   **– §**
51§: 5m 5.3m 5g Jul 17] tall gelding: has a high knee action: no longer of much account:
often starts slowly: tried in headgear. *J. M. Bradley*

RIVER TREAT (FR)   2 ch.c. (Jun 4) Irish River (FR) 131 – Dance Treat (USA) 115   **88**
(Nureyev (USA) 131) [2003 6g⁵ 6m² 6f⁴ Oct 10] angular, unfurnished colt: has a quick
action: third foal: half-brother to 3-y-o Jubilee Treat: dam, won La Coupe (1¼m) and Prix
de Flore (10.5f), out of half-sister to Derby winner Golden Fleece: fairly useful form in
maidens: neck second to Granato at Pontefract: odds on when only fourth at York: should
stay 1m. *G. Wragg*

RIYADH   5 ch.g. Caerleon (USA) 132 – Ausherra (USA) 106 (Diesis 133) [2003 103:   **92**
18.7m 14m⁴ 16.1g 16.1m⁶ 21d Jul 30] lengthy, angular gelding: poor mover: just fairly
useful handicapper for new trainer in 2003: stays 2½m: has form on good to soft going,
best efforts on good or firmer: usually blinkered/visored earlier in career: reportedly
finished distressed penultimate start: tends to hang: held up. *J. R. Fanshawe*

ROAMING VAGABOND (IRE)   2 ch.c. (Apr 13) Spectrum (IRE) 126 – Fiveofive   **– p**
(IRE) 61 (Fairy King (USA)) [2003 7m 7s Oct 29] rangy, rather unfurnished colt: sixth
foal: half-brother to 3 winners, including fairly useful 2001 2-y-o 7f winner My Only
Sunshine (by First Trump) and 3-y-o Lilli Marlane: dam 5f (at 2 yrs) and 1m winner:
signs of ability in maidens at Leicester (slowly away) and Yarmouth: likely to do better.
G. G. Margarson

ROANOKEE   3 gr.g. College Chapel 122 – Grey Again 63 (Unfuwain (USA) 131)   **–**
[2003 p6g p8g Jan 29] first foal: dam, 7f (at 2 yrs) and 11f winner, half-sister to dam of
very smart 6f performer Pipalong: well held in maidens at Lingfield. *R. Guest*

ROAN RAIDER (USA) 3 gr. or ro.g. El Prado (IRE) 119 – Flirtacious Wonder (USA) **54** (Wolf Power (SAF)) [2003 –: f8.5s 10m⁴ 10m 7m⁵ 8.5m⁴ 7m³ 8m 16g 9.9m 8.9m 8m³ **a48** f7s⁶ 6m² 6f⁴ 6d⁶ f6g f6s Dec 27] workmanlike gelding: modest maiden: left Miss V. Haigh after sixth start: effective at 6f to 8.5f: acts on fibresand and firm ground: sometimes visored/tongue tied. *M. J. Polglase*

ROAR BLIZZARD (IRE) 5 b.h. Roar (USA) 116 – Ragtime Rumble (USA) **?** (Dixieland Band (USA)) [2003 a7.5g⁵ a9.8g⁴ a9.5g⁵ a8.5g⁶ 8s² 8g⁵ 8d 9.3g 8d 8s⁵ a7.5g⁵ p8g Dec 20] second foal: half-brother to winner in Peru/USA by Unaccounted For: dam unraced close relative to smart Irish/US performer up to 1¼m Julie La Rousse: won 2 races in Germany at 3 yrs: in frame in handicaps at Dortmund and Cologne early in 2003: left Frau A. Bodenhagen, well held in minor event at Lingfield final start: stays 1¼m: acts on soft going, probably on sand: tried tongue tied. *T. H. Hansen, Germany*

ROBBIE CAN CAN 4 b.g. Robellino (USA) 127 – Can Can Lady 82 (Anshan 119) **59** [2003 71: f12s⁵ f16.2g³ 11.6g⁵ 18m³ 15.9m 12.1g² 14.1f⁶ 11.9m* Oct 2] leggy, useful-looking gelding: modest handicapper nowadays: won amateur event at Brighton in October: stays 2¼m: acts on all-weather and good to firm going (not discredited on firm): sometimes carries head high: consistent. *A. W. Carroll*

ROBE CHINOISE 4 b.f. Robellino (USA) 127 – Kiliniski 119 (Niniski (USA) 125) **91** [2003 103: 14.1g⁶ 12g⁴ 13.9f 12m⁴ 12m⁶ Oct 16] rather leggy, useful-looking filly: just fairly useful in 2003, best efforts in listed events first 2 starts: stays 1¾m: yet to race on soft/heavy going, acts on any other. *J. L. Dunlop*

ROBESPIERRE 3 b.g. Polar Falcon (USA) 126 – Go For Red (IRE) (Thatching 131) **63 §** [2003 –: 7m³ 6g 7d 8.1m 5.1m⁶ 5.9d³ 6f⁵ 6m 5.7f Oct 12] modest maiden: effective at 6f/ 7f: acts on good to firm and good to soft ground: often tongue tied: has raced freely/ carried head awkwardly: ungenuine. *H. Morrison*

ROBIN SHARP 5 ch.h. First Trump 118 – Mo Stopher 47 (Sharpo 132) [2003 –, a59: **–** f7s⁴ f7g² f7g* 7g f7g f7g f8g f7s Dec 31] strong horse: modest handicapper: won at **a64** Wolverhampton in February: ran poorly subsequently: left W. Jarvis after fifth start: stays 7f: acts on fibresand, little form on turf: usually wears cheekpieces/visor. *J. Akehurst*

ROBOCOP 2 b.g. (Mar 31) Robellino (USA) 127 – Seattle Ribbon (USA) 70 (Seattle **83** Dancer (USA) 119) [2003 5m 5.7m³ 6m⁴ 6.1g* 7m 7d⁶ 6f Oct 10] useful-looking gelding: second foal: half-brother to 3-y-o Seattle Express: dam, maiden who probably stayed 1¼m, sister to Racing Post Trophy winner Seattle Rhyme: fairly useful performer: won maiden at Nottingham in June: stiff tasks and seemed to run creditably in minor events/ nursery after: stays 7f: acts on firm and good to soft ground: sold 12,000 gns. *S. Kirk*

ROBSHAW 3 b.g. Robellino (USA) 127 – Panorama (Shirley Heights 130) [2003 6m **60 +** 7.1m⁶ 7.1g 8d Nov 7] 20,000Y: strong, deep-girthed gelding: first foal: dam, ran 3 times, half-sister to useful performer up to 1¾m Secret Archive: modest maiden: stays 7f: has been early to post: hung right third start. *T. P. Tate*

ROBWILLCALL 3 b.f. Timeless Times (USA) 99 – Lavernock Lady (Don't Forget **61** Me 127) [2003 75: 5d 6g 6s 5m⁶ 5f* f5g⁴ 5m 5f⁶ 5d⁴ 5m 5g 5g 5d Nov 4] fair performer: won minor event at Musselburgh in June: mostly below form after: barely stays 6f: acts on firm and soft ground: tried in cheekpieces/blinkers: usually races prominently. *A. Berry*

ROCHES FLEURIES (IRE) 3 b.f. Barathea (IRE) 127 – Princess Caraboo (IRE) **–** (Alzao (USA) 117) [2003 –: 9.9d 10.1m⁵ Oct 12] close-coupled filly: little sign of ability. *Andrew Turnell*

ROCINANTE (IRE) 3 b.g. Desert Story (IRE) 115 – Antapoura (IRE) 82 (Bustino **65** 136) [2003 73d: 5.1m 5.7m² 6s⁶ 8.1m³ f9.4s⁵ 8.1f⁵ 7g⁴ 5.9m⁴ 7.1m³ 6m f8.5g* f9.4g Nov 1] sturdy gelding: good walker: fair handicapper: left M. Wallace after third start: won at Wolverhampton in October: stays 8.5f: acts on fibresand and good to firm ground, probably soft: tried blinkered/visored: inconsistent. *J. J. Quinn*

ROCKABELLE 3 b.f. Bigstone (IRE) 126 – Belle de Nuit (IRE) 85 (Statoblest 120) **–** [2003 f5s 7m 6m 6g Jun 1] €2,000 2-y-o: first foal: dam, 2-y-o 6f/7f winner who stayed 1¼m, out of half-sister to very smart 1¼m performer Ruby Tiger: well held in maidens. *J. White*

ROCK CONCERT 5 b.m. Bishop of Cashel 122 – Summer Pageant 81 (Chief's **56** Crown (USA)) [2003 62, a65: f8s f8g 9.9m 9.9m 7.9m* 8m⁶ 7.9m 7.9f⁴ 8m f8s 7m 9.9d⁵ **a69** 8m³ 8.2m³ f9.4g² f8.5g² f8g* f8g³ f8g² Dec 12] deep-girthed mare: fair handicapper on all-weather, just modest on turf in 2003: left present trainer prior to winning at Carlisle (apprentices) in June: left J. Wainwright after ninth start, P. Midgley after tenth, then won at Southwell (amateurs) in November: effective at 1m/1¼m: acts on fibresand, firm and good to soft going: effective visored or not. *I. W. McInnes*

ROCKERFELLA LAD (IRE)   3 b.g. Danetime (IRE) 121 – Soucaro (Rusticaro (FR)   **75**
124) [2003 –: 8m 7.9g 8.1m 7m 8s* 7.9d² 8d⁴ 9.9m⁵ 9.1m³ 10g Sep 27] good-topped gelding: fair performer: won selling handicap at Thirsk in July: stays 9f: acts on soft and good to firm ground: sometimes visored (including for win), blinkered last 2 starts: slowly away first 2 outings at 3 yrs: awkward on bend at Beverley eighth appearance. *K. A. Ryan*

ROCKET FORCE (USA)   3 ch.c. Spinning World (USA) 130 – Pat Us (USA) (Cau-   **103**
casus (USA) 127) [2003 87p: 10.4m³ 10m² 12f Jun 20] well-made colt: useful performer: best efforts in listed events at York and Newmarket (2 lengths second to Sabre d'Argent) first 2 starts in 2003: well held in King Edward VII Stakes at Royal Ascot subsequent outing: stays 1¼m: raced only on firm/good to firm going. *E. A. L. Dunlop*

ROCKET SHIP (IRE)   3 b.c. Pennekamp (USA) 130 – Rock The Boat 52 (Slip   **96**
Anchor 136) [2003 85p: 9d⁴ 9.9g* 11m 10m² 12d 10.5d⁴ Sep 26] good-topped colt: useful performer: won handicap at Salisbury (beat Salsalino by 1¼ lengths, getting run of things up front) in May: best effort after when second of 3 to Blythe Knight in minor event at Pontefract: will prove best around 1¼m: acts on good to firm going, probably on good to soft: sold 85,000 gns, joined N. Meade in Ireland. *R. Charlton*

ROCKETS 'N ROLLERS (IRE)   3 b.c. Victory Note (USA) 120 – Holly Bird (Run-   **104**
nett 125) [2003 99: 7m⁴ 8g 8m May 24] leggy, good-topped colt: useful performer: off 11 months before good 2 lengths fourth to Muqbil in Greenham Stakes at Newbury on reappearance: pulled hard, just respectable efforts after in 2000 Guineas at Newmarket (thirteenth of 20) and listed event at Kempton (last of 7): likely to prove best short of 1m: yet to race on extremes of going: wandered both starts at 2 yrs. *R. Hannon*

ROCKFOREST   4 b.g. Superlative 118 – Rockefillee (Tycoon II) [2003 10d 12.6m 8g   **–**
8.2f 10d 7m Oct 25] leggy gelding: half-brother to 1¼m/11f winner Vanadium Ore (by Precious Metal): dam lightly-raced novice hurdler: no form: tried in cheekpieces/blinkers. *M. Mullineaux*

ROCKLEY BAY (IRE)   2 b.c. (Mar 14) Mujadil (USA) 119 – Kilkee Bay (IRE) 61   **65**
(Case Law 113) [2003 6g 6.1d⁵ p6g⁴ Nov 18] 23,000Y: lengthy, quite good-topped colt: first foal: dam, sprint maiden, half-sister to top-class sprinter Lake Coniston: fair form in maidens: fourth at Lingfield: not sure to stay much beyond 6f. *P. J. Makin*

ROCK LOBSTER   2 b.c. (Feb 2) Desert Sun 120 – Distant Music (Darshaan 133)   **76**
[2003 f8s* 8m⁴ Sep 20] 25,000Y: fourth foal: half-brother to 6-y-o Desert Island Disc: dam unraced: fair form when winning maiden at Southwell in September: well beaten in minor event at Ayr: should stay 1¼m. *J. G. Given*

ROCK'N COLD (IRE)   5 b.g. Bigstone (IRE) 126 – Unalaska (IRE) 65 (High Estate   **49**
127) [2003 p12g³ f12s p13g p13g⁵ p12g⁵ p12g⁶ Feb 25] tall, useful-looking gelding: poor maiden: should stay 1¾m: acts on soft going, good to firm and polytrack, well held on fibresand: visored/blinkered: fair hurdler, successful in March/April: subsequently sold 9,000 gns, joined J. Given. *R. M. H. Cowell*

ROCK OF CASHEL (IRE)   2 b.c. (May 26) Danehill (USA) 126 – Offshore Boom   **89**
96 (Be My Guest (USA) 126) [2003 7g³ 7s² 7f³ 7g² 8f Sep 27] quite attractive colt: brother to top-class 5f (at 2 yrs) to 1m winner Rock of Gibraltar and 3-y-o Great Pyramid, and half-brother to several winners: dam, Irish 2-y-o 6f winner, out of half-sister to Riverman: fairly useful maiden: odds on when placed first 4 starts: edgy, not discredited when eighth in Royal Lodge Stakes at Ascot: probably stays 1m: sent to Australia. *A. P. O'Brien, Ireland*

ROCKSPUR (IRE)   3 b.f. Flying Spur (AUS) – Over The Rocks (Salmon Leap   **45 §**
(USA) 131) [2003 59§: p6g f7s⁴ p7g Feb 19] poor maiden: should stay 7f: probably acts on polytrack, yet to race on extremes of going on turf: visored nowadays: usually slowly away: ungenuine. *Mrs P. N. Dutfield*

ROCKWELDA   8 b.m. Weld 122 – Hill's Rocket (Hill's Forecast 91) [2003 14m⁶ Aug   **–**
8] third foal: dam placed over hurdles: 100/1, tailed off in maiden at Lingfield on Flat debut. *M. P. Muggeridge*

ROCKY RAMBO   2 b.g. (Mar 15) Sayaarr (USA) – Kingston Girl (Formidable (USA)   **–**
125) [2003 10m Oct 22] £1,000 2-y-o: first foal: dam unraced: backward, tailed off in maiden at Nottingham. *R. D. E. Woodhouse*

ROCKY REPPIN   3 b.g. Rock City 120 – Tino Reppin 46 (Neltino 97) [2003 8.5m⁵   **57**
8g⁶ 10m⁴ 8.2m Oct 28] leggy, close-coupled gelding: half-brother to winner in Italy up to
11f by Rambo Dancer: dam best at 7f: modest maiden: stays 1¼m. *J. Balding*

ROEHAMPTON   2 b.c. (Feb 12) Machiavellian (USA) 123 – Come On Rosi 77   **83 P**
(Valiyar 129) [2003 8m 8s* Oct 29] 420,000Y: tall, angular colt: on weak side at 2 yrs:
half-brother to several at least useful winners, including very smart 7f/1m winner Bin
Rosie (by Distant Relative) and smart performers around 1¼m Generous Libra and
Generous Rosi (both by Generous): dam 6f winner: much better effort in maidens (very
green on debut) when justifying favouritism in 19-runner event at Yarmouth by 2 lengths
from Percussionist, always up with good pace: likely to be suited by 1¼m: open to good
deal of progress, and should make his mark in stronger company. *Sir Michael Stoute*

RO ERIDANI   3 b.f. Binary Star (USA) – Hat Hill (Roan Rocket 128) [2003 –: 7.1f⁶   **54**
7g 9.3m² 10m 9m 12g Nov 5] modest maiden handicapper: well below form last 3 starts:
stays 9f: raced only on good ground or firmer. *T. J. Etherington*

ROJABAA   4 b.g. Anabaa (USA) 130 – Slava (USA) (Diesis 133) [2003 45: 10.2m²   **60**
11.9m 10m⁴ 10m³ 10m 11.7f⁴ 8f⁵ 10.1m³ 11.8m⁴ 11.5m* 10m* Oct 23] lengthy gelding:
modest handicapper: won selling events at Yarmouth and Brighton within 3 days in
October: stays easy 1½m: acts on firm going: tried in cheekpieces: has taken good hold.
W. G. M. Turner

ROLEX FREE (ARG)   5 ch.g. Friul (ARG) – Karolera (ARG) (Kaljerry (ARG))   **79**
[2003 ?: f8s⁴ f16.2g Jan 18] winner at 1m and 1¼m in Argentina: fair form at best in 3
races in Britain: acts on fibresand, dirt and firm ground. *Mrs L. C. Taylor*

ROLLER   7 b.g. Bluebird (USA) 125 – Tight Spin (High Top 131) [2003 49§: f8s³ f8s⁶   **58 ?**
f8s⁴ f9.4g⁶ f8.5g³ f7s⁴ f8.5g f8.5g⁴ f9.4s⁴ f8g² Mar 13] useful-looking gelding: modest
performer: effective at 7f to easy 1¼m: acted on fibresand and probably any turf going:
sometimes went in snatches, and wasn't to be trusted implicitly: dead. *J. M. Bradley*

ROMANCERO (IRE)   2 b.c. (Mar 31) Princely Heir (IRE) 111 – Batilde (IRE) (Vic-   **101**
tory Piper (USA) 100) [2003 5g⁵ p5g⁶ 6m² 7.1m* 6f² 7.5m* 7.5m* Aug 2] IR 19,000F,
17,000Y: useful-looking colt: fourth foal: half-brother to fairly useful 7f/1m winner
Dakota Sioux (by College Chapel): dam placed in Italy: useful performer: won maiden at
Lingfield in March, minor event at Musselburgh in June and listed races at Milan in
July and Varese (best effort, by 2½ lengths from Sciur Renato) in August: stays 7.5f: acts
on good to firm ground and polytrack: sent to Hong Kong, where renamed Stay Young.
M. J. Wallace

ROMAN EMPIRE   3 b.g. Efisio 120 – Gena Ivor (USA) (Sir Ivor 135) [2003 –: p7g*   **59**
p7g⁵ 6m 8.2d f6g p7g Nov 29] lengthy, good-bodied gelding: modest handicapper: won
at Lingfield in March: likely to prove best up to 7f: acts on polytrack. *T. J. Etherington*

ROMAN MAZE   3 ch.g. Lycius (USA) 124 – Maze Garden (USA) (Riverman (USA)   **75**
131) [2003 10s p7g⁵ f9.4g⁵ f7g* f7s⁴ Dec 6] second foal: brother to 5-y-o Crossed Wire:
dam useful French 1m winner who stayed 1¼m: fair maiden: left P. Bary after only run at
2 yrs: won maiden at Wolverhampton in November, despite hanging right/flashing tail:
should be suited by further than 7f: acts on fibresand. *W. M. Brisbourne*

ROMAN MISTRESS (IRE)   3 ch.f. Titus Livius (FR) 115 – Repique (USA) 88   **79**
(Sharpen Up 127) [2003 77: 6m⁴ 5.1m³ 5m⁴ 5m* 5f 5.1m 5m 5d² 5m 6f 5m 5d Nov 7]
smallish, angular filly: fair handicapper: won at Haydock in June: below form last 4
starts: effective at 5f, barely at 7f: acts on soft and firm going: blinkered last 6 starts at 2
yrs: has been slowly away. *T. D. Easterby*

ROMAN QUINTET (IRE)   3 ch.c. Titus Livius (FR) 115 – Quintellina 83 (Robel-   **72**
lino (USA) 127) [2003 73: p5g* 5.7m 5f⁶ 6d⁴ p6g 5f³ p6g⁴ f5g⁴ p6g p5g² Dec 20] fair
performer: won maiden at Lingfield in January: tends to race freely, and may prove best
at 5f/6f: acts on all-weather, firm and good to soft going: tried in cheekpieces/tongue tie:
consistent. *D. W. P. Arbuthnot*

ROMAN THE PARK (IRE)   2 b.f. (Feb 26) Titus Livius (FR) 115 – Missfortuna 71   **–**
(Priolo (USA) 127) [2003 7m⁶ 6m 7d Nov 4] IR 1,700F, 8,500Y: leggy, quite attractive
filly: second foal: dam, 1¼m winner, out of sister to very smart 7f/1m winner Lucky
Ring: little sign of ability in maidens. *T. D. Easterby*

ROMANTIC DRAMA (IRE)   2 b.f. (Mar 8) Primo Dominie 121 – Antonia's Choice   **65**
73 (Music Boy 124) [2003 6m 6m p7g⁴ 8.3g⁶ f7g Dec 16] 68,000Y: well-made filly:
second foal: closely related to 3-y-o Ivania: dam 2-y-o 5f winner out of half-sister to very
smart sprinter Bolshoi: fair maiden: stays 1m: acts on polytrack, best turf effort on good
going: blinkered last 2 starts. *B. J. Meehan*

ROMANTIC LIASON 3 b.f. Primo Dominie 121 – My First Romance 61 (Danehill –
(USA) 126) [2003 108p: 5f 5g Jul 5] big, strong, well-made filly: useful performer,
winner of Queen Mary Stakes at Royal Ascot at 2 yrs when trained by B. Meehan: shaped
quite well in King's Stand Stakes at Royal Ascot on reappearance: collapsed in listed
race at Sandown subsequent start: would probably have proved best at 5f: raced only on
polytrack and good ground or firmer: tongue tied in 2003: dead. *Saeed bin Suroor*

ROMANY NIGHTS (IRE) 3 b.g. Night Shift (USA) – Gipsy Moth 99 (Efisio 120) **88**
[2003 80: p7g 6m⁵ 6m³ 6d⁵ 6.1m⁴ 6m* 6m 6m⁵ 6f 6.1g 6m⁵ 6m 6g² 6f⁶ 7g p6g 7d Nov 8]
strong gelding: fairly useful handicapper: left P. D. Evans after second start: won at
Newbury in May: stays 6f: acts on firm and good to soft going: tried visored. *R. Wilman*

ROMANY PRINCE 4 b.g. Robellino (USA) 127 – Vicki Romara 83 (Old Vic 136) **107**
[2003 101: 16m³ 18.7m 7.5m 14m 14g² 14m³ 14.1f³ 18m Oct 18] rangy gelding: usually
impresses in appearance: useful performer: best efforts in 2003 when 4 lengths third to
First Charter in listed race at Goodwood and 3¼ lengths third to Distinction in minor
event at Salisbury: disappointing in Cesarewitch at Newmarket final outing: should stay
beyond 2m: successful on soft ground, best efforts on good or firmer: usually waited with.
D. R. C. Elsworth

ROMARIC (USA) 2 b.c. (Apr 17) Red Ransom (USA) – Eternal Reve (USA) 116 **87**
(Diesis 133) [2003 f6g² 7m 7.5m³ Aug 14] close-coupled colt: fifth foal: closely related
to fairly useful 2000 Irish 2-y-o 6f winner Enrich (by Dynaformer) and half-brother to 2
winners, including useful 6f (at 2 yrs)/1m winner (in UAE) Infinite Spirit (by Maria's
Mon): dam, French 6f (at 2 yrs) to 1m winner, half-sister to US Grade 1 9f winner Eternity
Star out of half-sister to Miswaki: landed odds in maiden at Wolverhampton in May:
visored, best effort (fairly useful form) when third in nursery at Beverley: should stay 1m:
sometimes flashes tail. *D. R. Loder*

ROME (IRE) 4 br.g. Singspiel (IRE) 133 – Ela Romara 124 (Ela-Mana-Mou 132) **68**
[2003 10.3m⁶ p12g⁴ p12g⁵ p13g³ p16g Nov 26] 8,500 3-y-o: eighth foal: closely related
to smart French performer up to 12.5f Earlene (by In The Wings) and half-brother to 2
winners, notably smart 10.4f/1½m winner Foyer (by Sadler's Wells): dam won Lowther
and Nassau Stakes: fair bumper winner/maiden on Flat: stays 2m: acts on polytrack.
G. P. Enright

ROMEO'S DAY 2 ch.g. (Mar 28) Pursuit of Love 124 – Daarat Alayaam (IRE) –
(Reference Point 139) [2003 7g 7m 8m 8m Oct 23] 9,000F: sturdy gelding: fifth foal:
half-brother to 2000 2-y-o 7f winner Magic of You (by Magic Ring): dam unraced
half-sister to dam of Soviet Song: signs of only a little ability in minor event/maidens.
M. R. Channon

ROMEO TIAS (IRE) 2 ch.g. (Apr 12) General Monash (USA) 107 – Victim of Love –
75 (Damister (USA) 123) [2003 5f 5m 5m 5f f6s Oct 21] IR 3,000F, €7,000Y: smallish,
plain gelding: second foal: brother to 2002 2-y-o 5f seller winner G I Bride: dam 7f
winner, including at 2 yrs: no form in maidens: tried blinkered/in cheekpieces: sometimes
looks wayward. *A. Berry*

ROMIL STAR (GER) 6 b.g. Chief's Crown (USA) – Romelia (USA) (Woodman **64 ?**
(USA) 126) [2003 71: f12s⁴ f14s* f16.2g 12g 11.9f 13m⁵ 14m⁵ 14.4m⁶ 14d Sep 27] work- **a75**
manlike gelding: fair handicapper: won at Southwell in February: left R. Wylie before
below form last 2 starts: stays 1¾m: acts on heavy going and fibresand. *G. M. Moore*

RONDELET (IRE) 2 b.g. (Feb 2) Bering 136 – Triomphale (USA) (Nureyev (USA) **73**
131) [2003 6d 7.1d⁶ 7d⁴ Sep 24] 50,000Y: sturdy gelding: first living foal: dam, French
2-y-o 6f winner, sister to Full Deposit and closely related to French/US performer Tresor-
iere, both useful up to around 1¼m: fair form in maidens: fourth at Chester: should stay
1m. *R. M. Beckett*

RONDINAY (FR) 3 ch.f. Cadeaux Genereux 131 – Topline (GER) (Acatenango (GER) **74**
127) [2003 77: 9g 8d 8m 8g Nov 8] strong, close-coupled filly: fair performer: left
R. Hannon after reappearance, not discredited in blinkers final start: should stay at least
7f: acts on firm going: found little once at 2 yrs. *M. Halford, Ireland*

RONNIE FROM DONNY (IRE) 3 b.g. Eagle Eyed (USA) 111 – New Rochelle **87**
(IRE) 65 (Lafontaine (USA) 117) [2003 76, a81: f6g* f6s f6g 5d³ 5.5m³ 6m 5m⁵ 6m 5g
6f 5d f6g f5g f7g* Dec 22] sturdy, useful-looking colt: fairly useful handicapper: won at
Southwell in January and Wolverhampton in December: stays 7f: acts on firm ground,
soft and fibresand: tried in cheekpieces. *B. Ellison*

ROOD BOY (IRE) 2 b.c. (Jan 15) Great Commotion (USA) 123 – Cnocma (IRE) 58 **61**
(Tender King 123) [2003 6m p8g f8.5g⁴ f6g³ Dec 19] €7,500Y, 14,500 2-y-o: first foal:

dam Irish 1m winner: modest maiden: third in nursery at Southwell: effective at 6f to 8.5f: acts on all-weather, last only run on turf. *J. S. King*

ROOKWITH (IRE) 3 b.g. Revoque (IRE) 122 – Resume (IRE) 69 (Lahib (USA) 129) **71** [2003 60, a72: f8g² 7.5f⁵ 7.9g 8d 10m⁴ 12.3m⁴ 9m* 8d⁵ 8g⁴ 8m⁶ Oct 6] tall gelding: fair performer: won maiden at Ripon in July: below form after: stays 9f: acts on firm going, good to soft and all-weather: often blinkered, visored last 4 starts: sometimes goes in snatches: has found little: sold 12,000 gns. *J. D. Bethell*

ROOM ENOUGH 3 b.g. Muhtarram (USA) 125 – Salsita (Salse (USA) 128) [2003 **47 ?** –: 8g 8f 12m³ 16.2m 16g 16.2g⁵ 13.1f Sep 8] close-coupled gelding: poor maiden handicapper: stays 2m: acts on good to firm going: wore cheekpieces last 5 starts. *R. M. Beckett*

ROOSEVELT (IRE) 3 b.c. Danehill (USA) 126 – Star Begonia 110 (Sadler's Wells **123** (USA) 132) [2003 73p: 10g* 9.5s⁴ 12m³ 7m 12m⁴ Dec 14] first foal: dam, Irish 1½m winner (second in Ribblesdale Stakes), sister to very smart French winner up to 1½m Poliglote: won maiden at Leopardstown in March: reportedly sick when last of 4 in minor event at Gowran next time: 150/1, best effort (very smart form) when 4 lengths third to Alamshar in Irish Derby at the Curragh in June, keeping on from rear: sold out of A. O'Brien's stable and off 5 months after: respectable length fourth to Vallee Enchantee in Hong Kong Vase at Sha Tin final outing: stays 1½m: acts on good to firm going. *D. Oughton, Hong Kong*

ROOSTER JUPAGA 2 b.c. (Jan 27) Young Ern 120 – So Bold (Never So Bold 135) **–** [2003 7.1m 7m 8f 8.1g Sep 11] half-brother to useful 5f (at 2 yrs) to 8.5f winner Stoppes Brow (by Primo Dominie): dam lightly-raced maiden: well held in maidens/claimer. *I. A. Wood*

ROPPONGI DANCER 4 b.f. Mtoto 134 – Ice Chocolate (USA) 77 (Icecapade **32** (USA)) [2003 44: 16m f12g⁶ 10.1m⁴ f14.8g f16g Dec 16] small, quite good-topped filly: poor maiden: left Mrs M. Reveley after reappearance: stays 1½m: tried tongue tied/ visored: has carried head high. *Mrs N. Macauley*

ROSACARA 2 b.f. (Mar 19) Green Desert (USA) 127 – Rambling Rose 111 (Cadeaux **61** Genereux 131) [2003 6.1d⁵ 7m 7.1m⁴ Sep 8] strong, close-coupled filly: has no off-side eye: first foal: dam 1m (at 2 yrs) and listed 1½m winner: modest form in maidens: fourth at Warwick: needs to settle to stay beyond 7f. *Sir Michael Stoute*

ROSEHEARTY (USA) 2 ch.f. (Mar 21) Rahy (USA) 115 – Rosebrook (USA) (Geiger **99 §** Counter (USA)) [2003 5m² 5f² 6m* 6m 6g² 6m⁴ 6m Oct 4] $100,000Y: quite attractive filly: fluent mover: third foal: dam, 8.3f winner in USA, half-sister to dam of very smart performer up to 9f in US/Britain Jovial: useful performer: won maiden at Catterick in July: in frame in Princess Margaret Stakes at Ascot (1¼ lengths second to River Belle, best effort) and listed event at Ayr after: should stay 1m: acts on good to firm going: visored fourth/final starts: sometimes flashes tail/finds little: not to be trusted: joined Saeed bin Suroor. *D. R. Loder*

ROSE OF AMERICA 5 ch.m. Brief Truce (USA) 126 – Kilcoy (USA) (Secreto **71** (USA) 128) [2003 81: 7.1f 7.2g 7.1m 7m⁴ 8.1f⁶ Sep 5] big, strong mare: fair handicapper: best at 7f/1m: acts on firm going: free-going sort: has edged right/carried head awkwardly: reportedly lame final start: held up: sold 1,800 gns. *Miss L. A. Perratt*

ROSE OF YORK (IRE) 3 b.f. Emarati (USA) 74 – True Ring (High Top 131) [2003 **–** 12.1d 10m Jun 12] rather unfurnished filly: eighth foal: half-sister to useful 7f (at 2 yrs) to 1¼m winner Future Perfect (by Efisio) and 7f (at 2 yrs) to 1¾m winner Semi Circle (by Noble Patriarch): dam well beaten both starts at 2 yrs: soundly beaten in maidens at Chepstow and Newbury. *J. G. Portman*

ROSES OF SPRING 5 gr.m. Shareef Dancer (USA) 135 – Couleur de Rose (Kalaglow **93** 132) [2003 80: f6g² p5g* f6g p5g⁶ p5g⁶ p5g* p5g⁶ p5g 5f⁴ 5m* 5g² 5.1g* 5g 6m 5.7f² 5.1m⁶ 5m 5.7f² 5.5f 5m 6m 5.1f* 5g 5.2g Sep 16] lengthy mare: fairly useful performer: won handicaps at Wolverhampton, Lingfield (2) and Redcar and 2 minor events at Bath between January/August: well held last 2 starts, looking less than keen: best at 5f/easy 6f: acts on firm ground and all-weather: visored once, wears cheekpieces nowadays: tongue tied prior to tenth outing: sometimes slowly away, usually races prominently otherwise: has gained last 7 wins for claimer A. Quinn: tough. *R. M. H. Cowell*

ROSE TEA (IRE) 4 ro.f. Alhaarth (IRE) 126 – Shakamiyn (Nishapour (FR) 125) **–** [2003 69?: 10g 11.5g 14g 11.6m f14s Sep 2] leggy, plain filly: seemed to show fair form second start at 3 yrs: soundly beaten since: carried head high in cheekpieces third start: successful over hurdles in September/October. *N. A. Graham*

ROSE TINTED   4 b.f. Spectrum (IRE) 126 – Marie La Rose (FR) (Night Shift (USA))   **59**
[2003 8m⁵ 10.3m 8m 8m² 9.9m⁶ 10f 9.9d⁶ 15.8m 12d⁵ Nov 4] close-coupled filly:
unraced in 2002: just modest maiden nowadays: left M. Bell after third start: bred to be
suited by 1¼m/1½m: raced mainly on good ground or firmer. *M. E. Sowersby*

ROSETTA ROEBUCK   3 b.f. Fleetwood (IRE) 107 – Alwal (Pharly (FR) 130) [2003   **–**
57: f6s p10g f12g f8g Mar 13] big, workmanlike filly: modest form on debut, well held
since: tried visored. *D. Shaw*

ROSEWINGS   3 b.f. In The Wings 128 – Calvia Rose (Sharpo 132) [2003 59: 10m   **66**
14m* 14.1m⁵ 14.1m² 14.1m⁵ Jul 2] quite good-topped filly: fair performer: won minor
event at Musselburgh in May: stays 1¾m: acts on good to firm going: sold 10,000 gns in
December. *M. H. Tompkins*

ROSEY GLOW   3 b.f. Elmaamul (USA) 125 – Red Rosein 97 (Red Sunset 120) [2003   **53 §**
58: 6.1g f6g⁶ 7.9g 7m 6.1m⁵ 5.9m⁶ f6g⁶ 5.9m³ 6f 6m³ 7m Oct 17] quite good-topped filly:
modest handicapper: best at 5f/6f: acts on good to firm going: wears a hood:
sometimes gives trouble in preliminaries (withdrawn twice): usually slowly away: often
apprentice ridden: unreliable: sold 5,000 gns. *Mrs G. S. Rees*

ROSIE MALONEY (IRE)   2 b.f. (Feb 9) Docksider (USA) 124 – Magic Lady (IRE)   **–**
(Bigstone (IRE) 126) [2003 p7g f8.5g Nov 14] €20,000Y: first foal: dam unraced half-
sister to smart miler Tamburlaine: well beaten in maiden at Lingfield (for W. Muir) and
claimer at Wolverhampton. *N. P. Littmoden*

ROSIE'S RESULT   3 ch.g. Case Law 113 – Precious Girl 76 (Precious Metal 106)   **65**
[2003 73d: 5d 5f² 5m 5d⁵ 5f⁶ 5m 6m 5f 6m 5m Sep 22] sparely-made gelding: fair
performer: well held last 5 starts, reportedly losing action final one: raced mainly at 5f:
acts on firm ground: visored final 2-y-o start: none too consistent. *M. Todhunter*

ROSINA MAY (IRE)   2 ch.f. (Mar 22) Danehill Dancer (IRE) 117 – Gay Paris (IRE)   **83**
(Paris House 123) [2003 5g* 5m* 5m* May 5] €1,200Y: smallish, useful-looking filly:
first foal: dam unraced out of half-sister to very smart sprinter Cyrano de Bergerac: fairly
useful performer: won maiden at Windsor and minor events at Ripon and Doncaster in
spring: injured after: would have proved best at 5f/6f: stud. *Mrs P. N. Dutfield*

ROSKILDE (IRE)   3 br.c. Danehill (USA) 126 – Melisendra (FR) (Highest Honor   **100**
(FR) 124) [2003 98: 10m³ 10m 10m³ 10m 10g 9.2m² Jul 17] good-bodied, quite attractive
colt: useful performer: some creditable efforts in 2003, including third in listed event at
Newmarket (beaten 3 lengths by Sabre d' Argent, looking reluctant when first asked for
effort) and second in minor event at Hamilton (went down by 1¼ lengths to Gala Sunday)
third and final starts: stays 1¼m: acts on firm ground, probably on soft. *M. R. Channon*

ROSSELLINI (USA)   3 b.f. Spinning World (USA) 130 – Camilla B (USA) (Chief's   **82**
Crown (USA)) [2003 78p: 8.2g 8f³ 8m² 8m* 8.3d³ 8m⁵ Sep 6] quite good-topped filly:
fairly useful performer: made all in maiden at Pontefract in August: creditable efforts in
handicaps after: will stay 1¼m: acts on firm and good to soft going: visored last 3 starts:
edged left penultimate outing. *Sir Michael Stoute*

ROSSELLI (USA)   7 b.g. Puissance 110 – Miss Rossi (Artaius (USA) 129) [2003   **60 d**
66§: 6f⁵ 6m 6d⁶ 6d³ 6d⁶ 6d 6f 6g 5.9f 6g 6g³ 6m 6f 6m 5m 6f³ 8m⁶ 5d 6d 6m⁴ 7f⁴ Oct 27]
tall, good-topped gelding: modest at best nowadays: stays 7f: acts on any ground: tried
in headgear/tongue tie: sometimes early to post: usually races prominently: unreliable.
A. Berry

ROSSIYA (FR)   3 gr.f. Machiavellian (USA) 123 – Russian Royal (USA) 108 (Nureyev   **78**
(USA) 131) [2003 8f 8.1m* 10m 8m Sep 16] sister to useful French 1m (including
at 2 yrs) winner Queen Catherine, closely related to 5-y-o Nautical and half-sister to 2
winners, including useful 1996 2-y-o 7f winner Gretel (by Hansel): dam 6f (at 2 yrs) and
7f winner: fair performer: won maiden at Sandown in August, dictating pace: pulled hard/
slowly away when below form after: should stay 1¼m. *M. P. Tregoning*

ROSTI   3 b.g. Whittingham (IRE) 104 – Uae Flame (IRE) (Polish Precedent (USA)   **55 +**
131) [2003 f7s f5s⁵ 7g 6m 5.9m f8g⁵ f7g⁴ Dec 16] 13,000F, 16,000Y: big, workmanlike
gelding: fourth foal: brother to 4-y-o Devon Flame and 5-y-o Flambe: dam unraced out of
smart 1¼m performer On The Staff: modest maiden: barely stays 1m: acts on fibresand,
best turf effort on good ground. *P. C. Haslam*

ROTHERAM (USA)   3 b.g. Dynaformer (USA) – Out of Taxes (USA) (Out of Place   **79 +**
(USA)) [2003 69: f12g* 12m³ 14.1f² 15g³ 14g 14.4g Sep 6] tall, useful-looking gelding:
fair performer: won maiden at Wolverhampton in March: will be suited by 2m+: acts on
firm ground, good to soft and fibresand: tongue tied (tailed off) final outing: sold 3,000
gns. *P. F. I. Cole*

ROTUMA (IRE) 4 b.g. Tagula (IRE) 116 – Cross Question (USA) 84 (Alleged (USA) **74**
138) [2003 58: 8.3d* 10d 10.1m⁴ 13m⁴ 12f⁵ 12.1g⁶ 10m³ 10.1m² 10f² 10.5f² 8.3d⁴ 10d*
10s 10d⁴ Nov 6] smallish, useful-looking gelding: fair handicapper: won at Hamilton
(NH jockeys event) in May and Ayr in October: has form at 1½m, at least as effective
around 1¼m: acts on any going: blinkered: carries head awkwardly. *M. Dods*

ROUGE BLANC (USA) 3 b.f. King of Kings (IRE) 125 – Style N' Elegance (USA) **65**
(Alysheba (USA)) [2003 10m 10m p12g⁵ 16g³ 16.4m⁴ 14.1f² 14.1m⁴ 16m² 17.1m³ 18m*
Oct 20] IR 14,500Y: tall, leggy filly: fourth foal: dam, placed in USA, half-sister to Irish
1000 Guineas winner Trusted Partner: fair handicapper: left D. Bridgwater after third
start: won at Pontefract in October: stays 2¼m: raced only on good going or firmer on
turf: visored on debut. *P. J. McBride*

ROUSING THUNDER 6 b.g. Theatrical 128 – Moss (USA) (Woodman (USA) 126) **49**
[2003 52: 14.1m 9f⁵ 12m² 11.9m⁶ 12m* 16.2m⁶ 12.1m 14.1m⁵ 14m⁴ 12m⁴ 15.8d⁶ 12m³
Oct 18] leggy gelding: poor performer: won selling handicap at Musselburgh in July:
best short of 2m: acts on firm going, possibly not on softer than good: wears headgear:
reportedly had breathing problem final 5-y-o start, usually tongue tied since: often races
freely. *W. Storey*

ROUTE BARREE (FR) 5 ch.g. Exit To Nowhere (USA) 122 – Star Des Evees (FR) **59**
(Moulin 103) [2003 78d: 12g 11.7m 11.9m² 12g p12g³ p12g⁴ p12g² f14.8s 12m p12g⁶
p12g Nov 13] quite attractive gelding: modest performer: stays 2m: acts on polytrack,
best turf efforts on good going or firmer: tried visored at 3 yrs: carries head awkwardly/
sometimes wanders. *S. Dow*

ROUTE SIXTY SIX (IRE) 7 b.m. Brief Truce (USA) 126 – Lyphards Goddess **55**
(IRE) (Lyphard's Special (USA) 122) [2003 63: 7.9m 8m 10m 9.1g³ 10m⁵ 10f f8g Dec
19] strong, close-coupled mare: modest handicapper: stays 1¼m: acts on any going:
blinkered once in 2000: waited with. *Jedd O'Keeffe*

ROVELLA 2 b.f. (Apr 22) Robellino (USA) 127 – Spring Flyer (IRE) 66 (Waajib 121) **–**
[2003 6.1m 6.1d 6m Sep 1] leggy filly: sixth foal: dam, 7f (at 2 yrs) to 9.4f winner, half-
sister to smart sprinter A Prayer For Wings: well held in maidens. *Mrs H. Dalton*

ROVING VIXEN (IRE) 2 b.f. (Apr 12) Foxhound (USA) 103 – Rend Rover (FR) **–**
(Monseigneur (USA) 127) [2003 f6g f8g Dec 19] €2,500Y: half-sister to 3 winners,
including 7f and 8.5f winner Rendita (by Waajib): dam Italian 8.5f to 11f winner: well
held in maidens. *J. L. Spearing*

ROWAN APPLAUSE 2 b.f. (Mar 19) Royal Applause 124 – Chatterberry 67 (Aragon **56**
118) [2003 5m⁴ 5.7f² Sep 29] 24,000Y: rather leggy filly: sixth foal: half-sister to 3
winners, including 3-y-o Candelabra: dam, 2-y-o 5f winner, sister to smart sprinter
Argentum: modest form in maidens at Beverley and Bath: dead. *W. J. Haggas*

ROWAN EXPRESS 3 b.f. Air Express (IRE) 125 – Nordico Princess 71 (Nordico **70 §**
(USA)) [2003 72§, a78§: p6g⁵ 6.1g a6f a6.5f⁵ 6.5f² 6.5f⁵ 5.5f⁶ Nov 14] close-coupled
filly: fair performer: left M. Tompkins after second outing and claimed for $62,500 on
final start: stays 6.5f: acts on all-weather, firm and soft going: usually blinkered/visored
(not last 3 starts): ungenuine. *B. D. A. Cecil, USA*

ROWAN LAKE (IRE) 3 b.f. Lake Coniston (IRE) 131 – Kind of Cute 52 (Prince **–**
Sabo 123) [2003 56: p6g f7s⁶ 6g 6m⁶ 7m 5g Jul 9] smallish filly: modest maiden at 2 yrs,
well held in 2003: stays 6f: acts on polytrack: tried blinkered. *Andrew Reid*

ROWAN PURSUIT 2 b.f. (Apr 13) Pursuit of Love 124 – Golden Seattle (IRE) **63**
(Seattle Dancer (USA) 119) [2003 6.1m 6.1d⁴ 7.6m 7g⁴ 8.3g f8g 7.1m* p7g³ p8g* Nov
22] small filly: first foal: dam Italian 2-y-o 5f/6f winner: modest performer: won sellers
at Musselburgh in October and Lingfield in November: stays easy 1m: acts on good to
firm going, good to soft and polytrack (showed little on fibresand): blinkered last 3 starts:
joined J. Akehurst. *M. H. Tompkins*

ROXANNE MILL 5 b.m. Cyrano de Bergerac 120 – It Must Be Millie 66 (Reprimand **86**
122) [2003 93, a–: f5g f5f³ 5f⁶ 5g 5.1m 5d 5m² 5.1m 5.2g⁴ 5d 5g 5m² f5g Nov 15] sturdy **a61**
mare: fairly useful handicapper on turf, modest on all-weather: left M. Usher 11,000 gns
before final start: best at 5f: acts on firm ground, soft and fibresand: blinkered: swerves
away: often claimer ridden: races prominently/travels strongly. *J. M. Bradley*

ROYAL ADVOCATE 3 b.g. Royal Applause 124 – Kept Waiting 75 (Tanfirion 110) **63**
[2003 8g 7d 6g⁶ 6f⁵ 8m⁴ Jul 10] 4,500F, 30,000Y: lengthy gelding: half-brother to winner
abroad by Daring March: dam sprinting half-sister to smart performer up to 9f Cloud
of Dust and useful 5f performer Crowded Avenue: modest maiden: stays 1m: acts on

good to firm ground: reluctant at stall penultimate outing: gelded after final appearance. *J. W. Hills*

ROYAL APPROACH 2 b.f. (Feb 10) Royal Applause 124 – Passionelle 56 (Nashwan **61** (USA) 135) [2003 8.3g⁶ 8m Sep 9] 18,000Y: rather leggy filly: second foal: dam, ran twice, closely related to 4-y-o Treble Heights: much better effort in maidens (modest form) when sixth at Windsor: started slowly and possibly amiss at Leicester. *M. Blanshard*

ROYAL APPROVAL 4 b.c. Royal Applause 124 – Inimitable 66 (Polish Precedent **76** (USA) 131) [2003 78: 10m⁵ 10d⁴ 10mᵈ 10.1m⁶ 10f⁴ 12m³ 11.7f Oct 12] rather leggy, quite attractive colt: fair handicapper: stays 1½m: acts on firm going, yet to race on soft/heavy: sold 6,500 gns. *J. L. Dunlop*

ROYAL AWAKENING (IRE) 2 b.g. (Mar 12) Ali-Royal (IRE) 127 – Morning Sur- **61** prise 58 (Tragic Role (USA)) [2003 5f³ f6g Nov 17] second foal: half-brother to 5f seller winner Blue Eyes (by Imp Society): dam 2-y-o 5f seller winner: favourite but green, much better effort in maidens (modest form) when third of 6 at Catterick: should stay 6f. *A. P. Jarvis*

ROYAL AXMINSTER 8 b.g. Alzao (USA) 117 – Number One Spot 71 (Reference **52** Point 139) [2003 45, a48: f16s³ p12g² 10.2m 12m³ 12m* 12.1d⁶ 12m f14.8g⁵ Nov 14] **a48** useful-looking gelding: modest handicapper: won amateur race at Salisbury in July, wandering: stays 1½m: acts on all-weather, firm and good to soft going: blinkered (well held) once: consistent. *Mrs P. N. Dutfield*

ROYAL BATHWICK (IRE) 3 b.f. King's Theatre (IRE) 128 – Ring of Light **83** (Auction Ring (USA) 123) [2003 8f⁵ 8.1m* 9.9g 9m⁴ 8f 10.9f* 11.7f 10f⁶ Oct 1] IR 15,000Y: small filly: fifth foal: half-sister to winners up to 1¼m in Italy by Indian Ridge and Royal Academy: dam Irish 2-y-o 5f/6f winner: fairly useful performer: won maiden in May and handicap in July, both at Warwick: below form after: should stay 1½m: raced only on good going or firmer: sometimes slowly away. *B. R. Millman*

ROYAL BEACON 3 b.c. Royal Applause 124 – Tenderetta (Tender King 123) [2003 **103** 97: 5m⁵ 7g 6m 6m² 6m* 6m⁵ 6m 6m Sep 26] tall, strong colt: useful performer: neck second to Move It in Shergar Cup Sprint at Ascot prior to winning 5-runner handicap at Newmarket in August by neck from Dazzling Bay: respectable efforts at best after: stays 6f: acts on firm going: has been early to post: usually races up with pace: sometimes wanders: sold 48,000 gns, sent to UAE. *M. Johnston*

ROYAL BLAZER (IRE) 3 b.g. Barathea (IRE) 127 – Royale (IRE) 102 (Royal **–** Academy (USA) 130) [2003 f7g 12g 12.4g Oct 22] IR 95,000Y: second foal: half-brother to fairly useful 1¼m winner Love Appeal (by Singspiel): dam Irish 7f/1m winner: well held in maidens, leaving Mrs J. Ramsden after debut. *C. Grant*

ROYAL CASCADE (IRE) 9 b.g. River Falls 113 – Relative Stranger (Cragador 110) **50** [2003 58, a63: f8.5g f8.5g⁵ f8.5s f8.5s⁴ Mar 31] lengthy gelding: modest handicapper: effective at 7f to 9.4f: raced mainly on fibresand, acts on soft and good to firm going on turf: sometimes blinkered/visored. *B. A. McMahon*

ROYAL CASTLE (IRE) 9 b.g. Caerleon (USA) 132 – Sun Princess 130 (English **60** Prince 129) [2003 62, a66: f16s 16g* f14.8g⁴ 17.1m 15.9m 15.8d³ 16m Oct 28] sturdy, lengthy gelding: good mover: modest handicapper: won at Nottingham in April: stays 18.7f: acts on fibresand, firm and good to soft ground: tried visored. *Mrs K. Walton*

ROYAL CAVALIER 6 b.g. Prince of Birds (USA) 121 – Gold Belt (IRE) 61 (Bellypha **107** 130) [2003 97, a–: 14f⁵ 18.7m 12m⁴ 14g⁴ 12g² 12m 12m² 12d f12g⁶ Dec 19] sturdy **a–** gelding: useful handicapper: twice runner-up at Doncaster in autumn, career-best effort when beaten 1½ lengths by Wunderwood on second occasion: effective at 1½m/1¾m (well held over 18.7f): acts on fibresand (though no form on it last 3 seasons) and any turf going: usually waited with. *R. Hollinshead*

ROYAL CHALLENGE 2 b.c. (Feb 5) Royal Applause 124 – Anotheranniversary **61 p** 95 (Emarati (USA) 74) [2003 6d Nov 8] 54,000F, 70,000Y: well-made colt: second foal: dam 2-y-o 5f winner: 10/1, tenth of 14 in maiden at Doncaster, green and not knocked about: should do better. *G. A. Butler*

ROYAL DIGNITARY (USA) 3 b. or br.g. Saint Ballado (CAN) – Star Actress (USA) **111** (Star de Naskra (USA)) [2003 89: 8f* 8g³ 8m⁴ 7g⁵ 8.1g 8g Aug 2] useful-looking gelding: smart performer: won listed race at Thirsk in April by 1¼ lengths from Salcombe: ran well when in frame in Premio Parioli at Rome (3¼ lengths third to Le Vie Dei Colori) and listed event at Kempton (fourth to Kalaman) next 2 starts: well below form after: stays 1m: raced only on good going or firmer: visored final 2-y-o start. *D. R. Loder*

ROYAL DISTANT (USA)   2 ch.f. (Mar 31) Distant View (USA) 126 – Encorenous   **81**
(USA) (Diesis 133) [2003 6m⁶ 7.6m³ 8.1g* 8m² 8d⁴ Oct 14] 65,000Y: workmanlike filly:
fourth foal: closely related to useful 2002 2-y-o 1m winner Love You Always (by Woodman) and half-sister to 1¼m winner in Sweden by Lear Fan: dam unraced half-sister to
very smart German 7f/1m performer Royal Abjar: fairly useful performer: won maiden at
Chepstow in September: good efforts in nurseries at Pontefract and Ayr after: will be
suited by at least 1¼m: acts on good to firm and good to soft ground: sold 26,000 gns.
J. H. M. Gosden

ROYAL ENCLOSURE (IRE)   5 b.g. Royal Academy (USA) 130 – Hi Bettina 96   **– §**
(Henbit (USA) 130) [2003 50§: f12g f9.4s Feb 28] close-coupled gelding: modest handicapper: well held in 2003: often blinkered/visored (not in 2003): usually tongue tied:
often goes in snatches. *Mrs S. M. Johnson*

ROYALE PEARL   3 gr.f. Cloudings (IRE) 112 – Ivy Edith (Blakeney 126) [2003 6g   **–**
8f 8.3m 10m³ 12m⁴ 8.3g Oct 13] 3,000F, 8,000 2-y-o: second foal: dam fairly useful 2m
hurdler: signs of some ability. *R. Ingram*

ROYAL FASHION (IRE)   3 b.f. Ali-Royal (IRE) 127 – Fun Fashion (IRE) 64 (Polish   **68**
Patriot (USA) 128) [2003 62: 6g³ 6m p6g² p7g p7g⁶ Dec 30] neat filly: fair performer:
stays easy 7f: acts on firm going and all-weather: sometimes led to post/slowly away.
Miss S. West

ROYAL FLIGHT   2 b.c. (Feb 1) Royal Applause 124 – Duende 75 (High Top 131)   **– p**
[2003 7g⁵ Nov 1] €85,000Y: big, strong, lengthy colt: half-brother to several winners,
including 1993 2-y-o 1m winner The Deep (by Shernazar) and 10.4f to 1½m winner
Jalousie (by Barathea), both useful: dam 2-y-o 6f winner who stayed 1m: 20/1 and better
for race, well-beaten fifth of 13 in maiden at Newmarket, hampered early: should do
better. *D. J. Daly*

ROYAL GRAND   3 ch.c. Prince Sabo 123 – Hemline 77 (Sharpo 132) [2003 71: f6g⁴   **72**
f6g³ f7g⁵ f6g³ f6s* 6m² Jun 4] small, leggy colt: fair performer: won claimer at Wolverhampton in March: should stay 7f: acts on fibresand, raced only on good to firm going on
turf. *T. D. Barron*

ROYAL HECTOR (GER)   4 b.g. Hector Protector (USA) 124 – Rudolfina (CAN)   **–**
(Pleasant Colony (USA)) [2003 p12g Oct 8] first foal: dam German 9.5f/10.5f winner:
fairly useful performer at best: trained by C. Von Der Recke in Germany at 3 yrs, winning
maiden at Mannheim and ladies handicap at Cologne: well held at Lingfield only outing
2003: raced only at 9f/1¼m until reappearance: acts on soft and good to firm ground:
tried blinkered. *A. G. Hobbs*

ROYAL INDULGENCE   3 b.g. Royal Applause 124 – Silent Indulgence (USA)   **53 §**
(Woodman (USA) 126) [2003 75: 5d 7.1m 6g 8m 7f 7f 7.1f⁶ 7.5m⁶ 8s 6.9m⁵ 7g 7m Sep
22] sturdy gelding: just modest form at 3 yrs: best at 6f/7f: acts on firm ground: tried in
cheekpieces, blinkered last 8 starts: sold 1,000 gns. *M. Dods*

ROYAL MELBOURNE (IRE)   3 ch.g. Among Men (USA) 124 – Calachuchi 74   **–**
(Martinmas 128) [2003 f7g 7m 7.5d f12g Jun 30] lengthy, workmanlike gelding: sixth
foal: half-brother to 3 winners, including 1½m and 2m winner Quezon City (by Keen):
dam prolific winner from 7.5f to 12.4f: little form. *Miss J. A. Camacho*

ROYAL MILLENNIUM (IRE)   5 b.g. Royal Academy (USA) 130 – Galatrix   **118**
72 (Be My Guest (USA) 126) [2003 111: 7m⁴ 6g³ 6m⁴ 6f 7g 7d 6m⁵ 7f 7s² 6m² 6g*
6s⁴ 6d² 6d⁵ Nov 16]
     The essay on Fayr Jag points out the strength in depth of the field for the
latest renewal of the Wokingham Stakes at Royal Ascot. Back in sixteenth place
in the twenty-nine-runner line-up came the heavily-backed second favourite
Royal Millennium. Unlike the first six in the Wokingham, he ended the season
without a pattern win to his name, though that looked all set to change when, as the
54/1-outsider, he surged a couple of lengths clear over a furlong out in the Group 1
Prix de la Foret at Longchamp in early-October. Etoile Montante overhauled
Royal Millennium to win by a length and a half, third-placed Saratan heading the
remainder a similar distance back, with the other British raiders, Mount Abu,
Rimrod, Polar Ben, Blaise Castle and Capricho filling the last five places. Royal
Millennium had the widest draw and left the impression he might have gone closer
still waited with a little longer.
     As it was, Royal Millennium had to wait until later in October to gain his
only victory of the season, back in handicap company. That performance, in

Q Associates Rated Stakes (Handicap), Newbury—Royal Millennium gains a richly deserved win; behind him are Royal Storm, Ringmoor Down (No.14) and Najeebon (striped sleeves)

overcoming fifteen rivals off a BHB mark of 100 at Newbury, was almost as meritorious, in terms of form, as his Foret effort. He travelled supremely well, held up as usual, and cruised to the front entering the final furlong before, not for the first time, giving the impression he was idling as he held off Royal Storm by half a length. Royal Millennium's only other victories have been in a maiden at Salisbury as a three-year-old and in a minor event at Goodwood the following season, but he is more reliable than is suggested by his record of three wins from thirty-eight starts and a below-form effort in the Wokingham. He has had more than his share of bad luck too. Within the space of eight days in September, for example, he finished first home on the stand side in both the Ayr Gold Cup and the Tote Trifecta Stakes at Ascot, coming only fifth and seventh overall respectively. Other good efforts by Royal Millennium in 2003 included, only five days after the Foret, a second in the Bentinck Stakes at Newmarket, beaten half a length by Ashdown Express. After that win at Newbury, Royal Millennium appeared on three further occasions, when a respectable fourth to Soave in the Prix de Seine-et-Oise at Maisons-Laffitte and when second to Steenberg in a listed race at Doncaster, possibly finding himself in front too soon in the latter, and then, on his final outing of the year, coming a below-par fifth in the Premio Umbria in Rome. Royal Millennium will start the next season without a pattern-race penalty and is clearly capable of winning a good prize outside handicaps.

		Nijinsky (b 1967)	Northern Dancer
	Royal Academy (USA) (b 1987)		Flaming Page
		Crimson Saint (ch 1969)	Crimson Satan
Royal Millennium (IRE) (b.g. 1998)			Bolero Rose
		Be My Guest (ch 1974)	Northern Dancer
	Galatrix (b 1986)		What A Treat
		Alligatrix (b 1980)	Alleged
			Shore

Royal Millennium's dam Galatrix raced only as a three-year-old, winning a mile maiden on fibresand at Southwell less than a month after the first all-weather meeting at the track. Her only other winning foal is Dramatic Entry (by Persian Bold), a fair maiden in Britain as a two-year-old who later won in Sweden. Galatrix is a half-sister to the high-class French middle-distance colt Croco Rouge and the remarkable broodmare Alidiva, whose first three foals were the very smart middle-distance horse Taipan, Sussex Stakes winner Ali-Royal and One Thousand Guineas winner Sleepytime, the last two by Royal Millennium's sire Royal Academy. The lengthy, angular Royal Millennium, who, like his dam, failed to make the race-course as a juvenile, has been tried at as far as nine furlongs but has shown his best form at six and seven. He has yet to race on heavy going but, though an unimpressive mover, is equally effective on firm ground as on soft. *M. R. Channon*

ROYAL NITE OWL 2 b.g. (Mar 29) Royal Applause 124 – Nite-Owl Dancer 75   –
(Robellino (USA) 127) [2003 8.2m 7s Nov 3] leggy, rather unfurnished gelding: fourth
foal: half-brother to 6f winner Nite-Owl Mate (by Komaite) and 5-y-o Nite-Owl Fizz:
dam 5f winner: well held in maidens. *J. O'Reilly*

ROYAL OVATION 4 b.g. Royal Applause 124 – Thevetia 65 (Mummy's Pet 125)   –
[2003 61: 5f 6g 9m 9g f6g Dec 9] 30,000F, IR 20,000Y, 16,000 2-y-o: half-brother to
several winners, including useful 7f/1m (including at 2 yrs) winner In Like Flynn (by
Handsome Sailor): dam, maiden, should have stayed 7f: modest maiden at best: no form
in 2003, leaving D. O'Connell in Ireland after penultimate start: stays 1m: acts on soft
going: tried blinkered. *N. P. Littmoden*

ROYAL PARTNERSHIP (IRE) 7 b.g. Royal Academy (USA) 130 – Go Honey   –
Go (General Assembly (USA)) [2003 –, a53: f12g f11g f12g Jan 23] tall, angular gelding:
no form in 2003: visored. *D. L. Williams*

ROYAL PAVILLION (IRE) 2 b.c. (Mar 21) Cape Cross (IRE) 129 – Regal Scintilla   **61 p**
103 (King of Spain 121) [2003 6m Oct 16] 32,000Y: strong, well-made colt: fourth foal:
dam, 5f winner (including at 2 yrs), half-sister to useful sprinter Rivers Rhapsody: 16/1,
better for race and green, eighth of 12 in maiden at Newmarket, not knocked about:
should do better. *W. J. Musson*

ROYAL PORTRAIT 3 b.f. Perugino (USA) 84 – Kaguyahime (Distant Relative   **67**
128) [2003 –p: 8.2m 10m⁶ 10d 10f* 10m² 10m⁴ 12.6m² 10m³ Oct 20] sturdy filly: fair
handicapper: won at Brighton in July: stays 12.6f: acts on firm ground: sold 8,000 gns.
J. L. Dunlop

ROYAL PRINCE 2 gr.c. (Mar 12) Royal Applause 124 – Onefortheditch (USA) 79   **78 p**
(With Approval (CAN)) [2003 p6g³ 7m⁴ Sep 17] 31,000F, 54,000Y: second foal: half-
brother to 3-y-o Morning After: dam 1m/1¼m winner: fair form in maidens at Lingfield
and Yarmouth (good late headway when fourth to Eden Rock): likely to stay 1m: should
progress. *J. R. Fanshawe*

ROYAL PRODIGY (USA) 4 ch.g. Royal Academy (USA) 130 – Prospector's   **78**
Queen (USA) (Mr Prospector (USA)) [2003 77: p8g⁵ f12s* p12g³ 11.6g f12s* f12g³
f12g* p13g*] Dec 29] close-coupled gelding: fair performer: won sellers at Southwell and
Wolverhampton (2, left M. Pipe prior to latter) and handicap at Lingfield: stays 13f: acts
on all-weather and good to soft going: visored (well held) once. *R. J. Hodges*

ROYAL RACER (FR) 5 b.g. Danehill (USA) 126 – Green Rosy (USA) (Green Dan-   –
cer (USA) 132) [2003 78d: p12g Oct 8] rangy gelding: one-time fairly useful performer:
on downgrade. *J. R. Best*

ROYAL ROBE (IRE) 3 gr.g. King of Kings (IRE) 125 – Sallanches (USA) (Gone   **91 ?**
West (USA)) [2003 80: p7g* p7g⁴ f7g³ p6g² 5.5f* 5.5f² 8f a6.5f⁴ 6.5f⁶ 5.5f⁴ 5.5f² Dec 20]
close-coupled gelding: fluent mover: fairly useful performer: won maiden at Lingfield
in January: creditable efforts in handicaps third/fourth (blinkered, unlucky) starts: left
B. Meehan prior to winning allowance race at Hollywood in May: stays 7f: acts on firm
going and on all-weather: tends to race freely. *P. G. Aguirre, USA*

ROYAL ROMEO 6 ch.g. Timeless Times (USA) 99 – Farinara (Dragonara Palace   –
(USA) 115) [2003 –: 10.1m 12.4m Jun 4] good-bodied gelding: unimpressive mover: fair
5f/6f winner at best: well held since 2001: sometimes blinkered. *I. Semple*

ROYAL SATIN (IRE) 5 b.g. Royal Academy (USA) 130 – Satinette 109 (Shirley   – §
Heights 130) [2003 16m 12g⁶ 12.4g Oct 22] big, rangy gelding: little form: tried blinkered: looks wayward. *B. Mactaggart*

ROYAL SPIN 4 b.g. Prince Sabo 123 – Cabaret Artiste (Shareef Dancer (USA) 135)   **72**
[2003 68?: f9.4s² f7s* p7g f8.5g² Mar 3] fair performer: reportedly lame only 3-y-o start:
won maiden at Southwell in February: stays easy 9.4f: acts on all-weather. *J. A. Osborne*

ROYAL STAMP (USA) 4 br.c. With Approval (CAN) – Louis d'Or (USA) (Mr Pros-   **112**
pector (USA)) [2003 105: 10g² 10g⁶ Jul 21] tall, leggy, quite attractive colt: smart form in
only 4 starts (unraced at 2 yrs): good 6 lengths second to Ikhtyar in listed race at Sandown:
reportedly finished lame when below best in Scottish Derby at Ayr later in July: should
stay 1½m: raced only on good/good to firm ground: held up: joined R. Frankel in
USA. *J. H. M. Gosden*

ROYAL STARLET 2 b.f. (Feb 19) Royal Applause 124 – Legend 74 (Belmez (USA)   –
131) [2003 7g 6m 6m Sep 5] 26,000F, €50,000Y: well-made filly: first foal: dam, maiden
who stayed 1½m, half-sister to smart performer up to 2m Arabian Story: signs of only a
little ability in maidens. *Mrs A. J. Perrett*

ROYAL STORM (IRE) 4 b.c. Royal Applause 124 – Wakayi 87 (Persian Bold 123) **102** [2003 92: p7g³ p7g³ 7d⁶ 8m 7.1m² 7m* 7m⁵ 7m⁵ 7.1m² 7f 7d 7.1m⁵ 7m² 7m² p7g 7f⁵ 7m³ **a90** 7f² 7m* 6g² p7g⁶ Oct 30] tall, lengthy colt: useful handicapper on turf, fairly useful on all-weather: won at Lingfield in May and Newmarket (beat Uraib by length) in October: good second to Royal Millennium at Newbury next time: effective at 6f/7f: acts on poly-track, best turf form on good or firmer: usually races prominently: tough and consistent. *Mrs A. J. Perrett*

ROYAL SUPREMACY (IRE) 2 ch.f. (Apr 27) Desert Prince (IRE) 130 – Saucy **55** Maid (IRE) 69 (Sure Blade (USA) 130) [2003 5.1m⁵ 5.7m 5f³ 5m 5f 5.1m³ Sep 22] €50,000Y: fifth foal: half-sister to 3 winners, including fairly useful 2001 2-y-o 6f winner Sophorific (by Danehill) and 11f winner La Mondotte (by Alzao): dam, maiden who stayed 1¼m, half-sister to dam of Pilsudski: modest maiden: third at Sandown and Chep-stow (nursery): will stay at least 6f: sometimes looks no easy ride. *C. G. Cox*

ROYAL TIME 3 b.f. Emperor Jones (USA) 119 – Anytime Baby 56 (Bairn (USA) **44** 126) [2003 –p: f5g f5g⁶ Mar 8] good-topped filly: poor maiden, lightly raced: may prove best at 5f/6f. *T. D. Barron*

ROYAL TRIGGER 3 b.c. Double Trigger (IRE) 123 – Jeronime (USA) 81 (Sauce **84** Boat (USA)) [2003 67: p10g* 9.9g⁶ 11m 12m² 12m Aug 6] leggy, lightly-made colt: fairly useful performer: won maiden at Lingfield in January: good second in handicap at Kempton in June: stays 1½m: acts on polytrack and good to firm going, some promise on soft at 2 yrs. *B. W. Hills*

ROYAL TWIST (USA) 3 ch.g. Royal Academy (USA) 130 – Musical Twist (USA) **63** 97 (Woodman (USA) 126) [2003 63: 7m³ 8.2g⁵ 6d⁵ 7.5m⁵ 8.3m³ 10m 6m 6m 7m Sep 9] big, strong gelding: modest maiden handicapper: poor efforts last 4 starts: may prove best short of 1m: acts on good to firm and good to soft going: tried blinkered: sold 1,800 gns. *T. P. Tate*

ROYAL UPSTART 2 b.g. (Apr 11) Up And At 'em 109 – Tycoon Tina 61 (Tina's Pet **54** 121) [2003 f6g 6m³ 6m⁵ 7m 8f 8.2m Oct 28] 500Y: quite good-topped gelding: first foal: dam 1m to 1½m winner: modest maiden: below form after third in seller at Haydock: should stay 1m: possibly temperamental. *W. M. Brisbourne*

ROYAL WARRANT 2 b.c. (Apr 14) Royal Applause 124 – Brand (Shareef Dancer **81** (USA) 135) [2003 6d⁴ 6g³ 6m* 7.1m Sep 20] quite good-topped colt: seventh foal: half-brother to fairly useful 6f to 1m winner Double Brandy (by Elmaamul) and 3-y-o Captain Ginger: dam unraced half-sister to useful performer up to 1½m Clever Cliche, from family of Unfuwain, Nashwan and 5-y-o Nayef: fairly useful performer: favourite, won maiden at Thirsk in August: failed to handle bend in nursery at Warwick final start: should stay at least 7f: acts on good to firm going. *A. M. Balding*

ROYAL WINDMILL (IRE) 4 b.g. Ali-Royal (IRE) 127 – Salarya (FR) (Darshaan **57** 133) [2003 51: f8s f7g³ f7g f7g⁴ 7m³ 6m⁵ 7.1d⁶ f7s 7.1f⁶ 8f³ 8m* 7m² 8s³ 8m² 8m 8m⁶ Sep 18] leggy gelding: modest performer: won seller at Musselburgh in July: stays 1m: acts on fibresand, firm and soft going: wore cheekpieces last 8 starts: sometimes slowly away/races freely. *M. D. Hammond*

ROYAL ZEPHYR (USA) 2 b.f. (Feb 15) Royal Academy (USA) 130 – Cassation **62** (USA) (Lear Fan (USA) 130) [2003 6g³ 6m⁶ 7m Oct 4] $67,000Y: leggy, unfurnished filly: first foal: dam unraced sister to very smart performer up to 10.5f Ryafan: modest form in maidens: third at Epsom: should stay 1m. *Sir Mark Prescott*

ROY MCAVOY (IRE) 5 b.g. Danehill (USA) 126 – Decadence (Vaigly Great 127) **77 d** [2003 68: p7g² p6g* p7g* p6g⁶ p7g⁵ p8g 7d 8.1g⁶ 7m p7g p7g p8g p7g Dec 6] fair handicapper: won twice at Lingfield within 4 days in January: below form after fifth outing: left C. Cyzer 13,500 gns before final one: best at 6f/7f: acts on all-weather, lightly raced on turf: sometimes slowly away. *Mrs G. Harvey*

ROZANEE 3 ch.f. Nashwan (USA) 135 – Belle Genius (USA) 111 (Beau Genius **64** (CAN)) [2003 9.2d³ 10.1m³ p10g³ Nov 18] 32,000 3-y-o: big, lengthy filly: has scope: third foal: half-sister to useful 6f/7f winner Birjand (by Green Desert) and Irish 1½m winner Battish (by Pennekamp): dam won Moyglare Stud Stakes: modest form in maidens: should be as effective at 1m as 1¼m: acts on polytrack and good to firm going. *J. W. Payne*

RUBAIYAT (IRE) 2 b.g. (Apr 28) Desert Story (IRE) 115 – Lovers' Parlour 83 (Bel- **– p** dale Flutter (USA) 130) [2003 6m 7s⁶ Oct 29] €20,000Y: fifth living foal: half-brother to 3 winners, including 3-y-o Grand Passion and 7f (at 2 yrs) to 1¾m (in Jersey) winner Out On A Promise (by Night Shift): dam lightly-raced half-sister to high-class 1m/1¼m performer Persian Heights: signs of ability in maidens at Yarmouth: slowly away/took good hold on debut: likely to do better. *G. Wragg*

RUBY ANNIVERSARY   3 b.f. Catrail (USA) 123 – River of Fortune (IRE) 68 (Lahib (USA) 129) [2003 8m 7f⁴ 8.2g 7m f7g f8g f11g Dec 19] 8,500Y: second foal: dam 2-y-o 7f seller winner out of useful 11f/1½m winner: poor maiden: should stay 1m: no form on fibresand. *J. Balding*   **45 ?**

RUBY LEGEND   5 b.g. Perpendicular 119 – Singing High 87 (Julio Mariner 127) [2003 62: 7.9f 8m⁴ 10.5m² 10.1m⁴ 9f² 10.1m* 8m² 10.4f 10.1m* 10s Nov 3] leggy gelding: fair handicapper: won at Newcastle in September and October: stays 10.5f: acts on firm and good to soft going: probably best in blinkers: reliable. *Mrs M. Reveley*   **78**

RUBY ROCKET (IRE)   2 b.f. (Mar 2) Indian Rocket 115 – Geht Schnell (Fairy King (USA)) [2003 6m* 6m* 6f³ 6m* 6m⁴ Oct 2] €40,000Y: good-bodied filly: half-sister to several winners, including fairly useful German 6f (at 2 yrs) to 1m winner Inzar's Best (by Inzar): dam Irish sprint maiden out of half-sister to high-class sprinter Anita's Prince: useful performer: won maiden at Kempton in July, minor event at Haydock in August and listed race at Ayr (beat Unshooda 1¼ lengths, leading well over 1f out) in September: no extra late on when 3 lengths fourth of 10 to Carry On Katie in Cheveley Park Stakes at Newmarket: likely to prove best at 5f/6f. *H. Morrison*   **100**

RUDDINGTON GRANGE   3 gr.f. Bahamian Bounty 116 – Rain Splash 74 (Petong 126) [2003 45: 6m f7g Jun 9] leggy filly: poor maiden at 2 yrs: well held in 2003: tried blinkered. *J. Balding*   **–**

RUDETSKI   6 b.g. Rudimentary (USA) 118 – Butosky 71 (Busted 134) [2003 48: f11g² f11s f9.4s f12s³ f11g⁴ 16.1d⁴ 11.9m³ Jun 2] big, lengthy gelding: modest performer at best: stays 1½m: acts on any turf going and fibresand: tongue tied last 4 starts, wore cheekpieces last 2: has been early to post/taken fierce hold: sold 5,000 gns. *M. Dods*   **54 d**

RUDIK (USA)   6 b. or br.g. Nureyev (USA) 131 – Nervous Baba (USA) (Raja Baba (USA)) [2003 92d: f6g f7s³ f6g² p6g⁴ f7s² f7g⁵ f6s² Feb 13] compact gelding: just fair performer nowadays: last won in 1999: stays 7f: acts on heavy going, good to firm and all-weather: often tongue tied: has been visored: untrustworthy. *D. Nicholls*   **74 §**

RUDI'S PET (IRE)   9 ch.g. Don't Forget Me 127 – Pink Fondant (Northfields (USA)) [2003 113: 5m⁵ 6g 5m 5m 5m⁴ 6m 5d³ 5.6d 5m* 5d⁴ 5d Oct 4] strong gelding: just useful at best in 2003, running to form only in listed event at Kempton on reappearance and when third to Mornin Reserves in handicap at Sandown seventh start: below earlier form when winning claimer at latter course in September: best at 5f: acts on firm and good to soft going: usually blinkered/visored, but effective when not: has been early to post/bandaged in front: sometimes slowly away/hangs left: usually races prominently. *D. Nicholls*   **98**

RUDOOD (USA)   3 b.g. Theatrical 128 – Kardashina (FR) (Darshaan 133) [2003 86p: 8.1m⁴ 10m* 11m Sep 24] smallish, rather leggy gelding: fair performer, lightly raced: landed odds in 4-runner maiden at Leicester in September: ran poorly in handicap at Goodwood after: should stay 1½m: unraced on extremes of going: hung left on reappearance (reportedly returned home injured and off 5 months): sold 9,000 gns in October, then gelded. *A. C. Stewart*   **78**

RUE DE PARIS   3 br.g. Paris House 123 – Innocent Abroad (DEN) 53 (Viking (USA)) [2003 57: 5m 6m⁴ 6m f6f³ 5f 6m 6m 7.5m 5m 7m Sep 9] leggy, good-topped gelding: modest maiden: well beaten last 6 starts: best at 5f/6f: acts on firm and soft going: tried in tongue tie/eyeshields: sometimes gives trouble in preliminaries (withdrawn once): inconsistent. *N. Bycroft*   **57 d**

RUE DE VERTBOIS (USA)   2 ch.f. (Mar 4) King of Kings (IRE) 125 – Tea Cozzy (USA) (Irish River (FR) 131) [2003 6m 6d 6d 8m p6g Dec 20] 40,000Y: third foal: dam unraced half-sister to US Grade 2 9f winner Mugatea: signs of only a little ability: left R. Hannon prior to final start. *J. C. Fox*   **–**

RULE BRITANNIA   4 b.f. Night Shift (USA) – Broken Wave 103 (Bustino 136) [2003 79p: 10m 12f* 11m 12d 13.3m⁵ 10g² 10.1m Sep 17] quite good-topped filly: fairly useful handicapper, lightly raced: won at Kempton in June: also ran well when second on same course: stays 1½m: acts on firm ground, probably on good to soft: sometimes races freely. *J. R. Fanshawe*   **89**

RULE OF LAW (USA)   2 b.c. (Mar 6) Kingmambo (USA) 125 – Crystal Crossing (IRE) 99 (Royal Academy (USA) 130) [2003 7.1f³ 7m* 7m* 8f³ Sep 27] leggy, attractive colt: has a quick action: third foal: dam, 2-y-o 6f winner, sister to smart performer up to 9f Circle of Gold: useful performer: won maiden (by 7 lengths) in July and listed race (beat Celtic Cat by neck) in August, both at York: some further improvement when   **109**

¾-length third of 10 to Snow Ridge in Royal Lodge Stakes at Ascot: stays 1m: acts on firm going: visored last 3 starts: front runner: joined Saeed bin Suroor. *D. R. Loder*

RULES FOR JOKERS (IRE)   2 b.g. (Apr 15) Mujadil (USA) 119 – Exciting (Mill **80**
Reef (USA) 141) [2003 6f⁴ 6g³ f5g⁵ 7.1d 7m³ 6.1m³ 6d* 6m* 6f Oct 10] €20,000Y: rather
leggy, useful-looking gelding: brother to useful 2000 2-y-o 1m winner Tudor Reef and
half-brother to several winners, notably very smart 6f (at 2 yrs) to 1m winner Almushtarak (by Fairy King) and 3-y-o Tiber: dam ran once: fairly useful performer: won
nurseries at Haydock in September and Pontefract (beat Garrigon 3 lengths) in October:
below form turned out quickly final start: should stay 7f: acts on firm and good to soft
ground: races up with pace. *J. A. Osborne*

RUMBLING BRIDGE   2 ch.g. (Mar 20) Air Express (IRE) 125 – Rushing River **56**
(USA) (Irish River (FR) 131) [2003 7g⁵ 7m⁴ 7.1m⁶ Sep 20] 15,000Y: fourth foal: dam
unraced: modest form in maidens: should stay 1m. *J. L. Dunlop*

RUM DESTINY (IRE)   4 b.g. Mujadil (USA) 119 – Ruby River (Red God 128§) **65**
[2003 –: 5g 5m 5m⁴ 5m 5m* 5m 5m 5m 5m 5m 5d Nov 4] small gelding: unimpressive
mover: just fair handicapper nowadays: won at Catterick in July: best at 5f: acts on firm
and good to soft going: often blinkered/visored, tried tongue tied/in cheekpieces.
J. S. Wainwright

RUMOUR   3 b.f. Lion Cavern (USA) 117 – Thea (USA) 95 (Marju (IRE) 127) [2003 **65**
8.2g³ Aug 1] third foal: half-sister to fairly useful 2001 2-y-o 1m winner Zone (by Zilzal):
dam 7f winner: 7/1, 6¼ lengths third to stable-companion Ice Palace in maiden at
Nottingham, green then staying on not knocked about. *J. R. Fanshawe*

RUMOUR MILL (IRE)   2 b.c. (May 9) Entrepreneur 123 – Pursuit of Truth (USA) **67 ?**
69 (Irish River (FR) 131) [2003 f5g p6g p7g p8g Dec 2] €58,000Y: half-brother to several
winners, including fairly useful 1999 2-y-o 1m winner First Truth (by Rudimentary) and
7-y-o Spring Pursuit: dam, 2-y-o 7f winner on only start, out of half-sister to Saddlers'
Hall and Sun Princess: seemingly fair form in maiden at Lingfield third start (left Sir
Mark Prescott after): showed nothing, including in nursery, otherwise: should stay at least
1m. *N. E. Berry*

RUM SHOT   2 b.c. (Mar 31) Efisio 120 – Glass (Bering 136) [2003 6m⁶ 6g* 6m* Oct **104 p**
21] 22,000F, 36,000Y: sturdy, close-coupled colt: first foal: dam, ran twice in France,
half-sister to useful French miler Gallipoli (by Efisio): won maiden at Windsor (by 5
lengths from Cyfrwys) and minor event at Yarmouth (by 1¼ lengths from Swinbrook) in
October, travelling strongly and quickening impressively both times: has plenty of speed
but will probably stay 7f: potentially smart, and should win more races. *H. Candy*

RUNAWAY STAR   6 ch.m. Superlative 118 – My Greatest Star 93 (Great Nephew **57**
126) [2003 55: p10g 12g* p12g² 12m⁴ 11.8g⁵ 14.8m⁴ 11.6g⁵ 14.1f⁴ 16.2m⁶ Aug 25] **a63**
workmanlike mare: modest handicapper: won at Newmarket (amateurs) in May: best at
1½m to 2m: acts on good to firm going, good to soft and polytrack: raced too freely 3 of
last 4 starts. *W. J. Musson*

RUNNING TIMES (USA)   6 b.g. Brocco (USA) 124 – Concert Peace (USA) (Hold **–**
Your Peace (USA)) [2003 12.1d Jul 25] good-topped gelding: unimpressive mover:
winning hurdler: well held only start on Flat since 2001: tried blinkered/visored.
H. J. Manners

RUN ON   5 b.h. Runnett 125 – Polar Storm (IRE) 76 (Law Society (USA) 130) [2003 **58**
53: 5.3f⁴ 6m 5.3m² 6m 5.3m⁴ 5.3m⁶ 6m⁵ 5.1g³ 5.3f⁴ 5.3f⁶ 5.1g⁶ Sep 11] robust horse:
modest performer: stays 6f: acts on fibresand, firm and good to soft going: tried tongue
tied: sometimes slowly away: none too consistent. *D. G. Bridgwater*

RUPERT BROOKE   4 b.g. Polar Falcon (USA) 126 – Vayavaig 78 (Damister (USA) **61**
123) [2003 8m⁴ 10g Jul 8] 16,000Y: big, leggy, lengthy gelding: fifth foal: closely related
to fairly useful 6f (at 2 yrs) and 1m (in USA) winner Wolfhunt (by Wolfhound) and half-
brother to 3 winners, including useful 6f (at 2 yrs)/8.5f winner Sweet Prospect (by
Shareef Dancer): dam 2-y-o 6f winner: better effort in maidens (modest form) when
fourth at Newcastle. *P. W. Harris*

RUPESH (IRE)   3 ch.f. Fayruz 116 – Maricica (Ahonoora 122) [2003 57: f9.4g 8.5g **–**
Jul 17] modest maiden at 2 yrs: raced freely and well held in 2003: wore cheekpieces final
start. *D. W. P. Arbuthnot*

RUSHCUTTER BAY   10 br.g. Mon Tresor 113 – Llwy Bren (Lidhame 109) [2003 **100 §**
101§: 5g 5m⁵ 6m 5m Oct 16] close-coupled gelding: impresses in appearance: just useful
nowadays: best effort in 2003 when fifth to The Trader in minor event at Newmarket,
slowly away: effective at 5f/6f: acts on firm and soft going: effective visored or not: has
twice reportedly bled: tends to wander/look none too keen: unreliable. *P. L. Gilligan*

RUSSALKA   2 b.f. (Feb 2) Opening Verse (USA) 126 – Philarmonique (FR) (Trem-   **65**
polino (USA) 135) [2003 8m^4 8f^6 7d f8.5g^2 f9.4g^2 Dec 22] workmanlike filly: second
foal: half-sister to 7.5f to 1¼m winner in Italy by Shaamit: dam French 1¼m winner out
of half-sister to top-class French performer up to 1½m Luth Enchantee: fair form in
maidens: second twice at Wolverhampton: will stay at least 1¼m: acts on fibresand, good
to firm and good to soft going: rather headstrong early starts. *Julian Poulton*

RUSSIAN COMRADE (IRE)   7 b.g. Polish Patriot (USA) 128 – Tikarna (FR)   **71 §**
(Targowice (USA) 130) [2003 72d: 12m 10d* 8.3g Aug 4] half-brother to several
winners, including Irish 7.8f winner Tikashar (by Doyoun) and 1½m performer Timour-
tash (by Riverman), both useful: dam French 1m winner: fair performer: successful 5
times in Ireland, including in apprentice event at Navan in June: left W. Fitzpatrick in
Ireland, looked reluctant when well held on British debut: stays 1½m: acts on firm and
soft going: tried blinkered: refused to race twice in 2000: one to treat with caution.
J. C. Tuck

RUSSIAN DANCE (USA)   2 br.f. (Mar 5) Nureyev (USA) 131 – Population   **93**
(General Assembly (USA)) [2003 6m^2 6m* 7m^4 8d Sep 11] $600,000Y: sturdy, attractive
filly: sister to French 11.5f winner Popolaccio, closely related to Racing Post Trophy/
Dante Stakes winner Saratoga Springs (by El Gran Senor), and half-sister to 3 winners:
dam, Irish maiden, half-sister to Washington International winner Providential and Prix
Marcel Boussac winner Play It Safe: fairly useful performer: landed odds in minor event
at Windsor in July: good 3½ lengths fourth of 6, taking time to find stride, to Gracefully
in Prestige Stakes at Goodwood, much better effort after: should stay 1m: acts on good to
firm going. *Sir Michael Stoute*

RUSSIAN DOLL (CZE)   2 b.f. (Mar 21) Beccari (USA) 112 – Russian Olive 70   **–**
(Primo Dominie 121) [2003 5m Apr 24] compact filly: first reported foal: dam 1m/9f
winner in Czech Republic: 100/1, showed nothing in claimer at Beverley. *R. Bastiman*

RUSSIAN ICON   2 b.f. (Apr 18) Wace (USA) 82 – Lady Millennium (IRE) (Prince   **–**
Rupert (FR) 121) [2003 p7g 10d Oct 31] second foal: dam unraced: tailed off in maidens
at Lingfield (very slowly away) and Brighton. *L. A. Dace*

RUSSIAN PRINCESS (IRE)   3 b.f. Mujadil (USA) 119 – Romanovna (Mummy's   **73**
Pet 125) [2003 74: 7m^4 7g^4 7m 7m^5 8.1g 8.5g Jul 17] small filly: fair maiden handicapper:
stays 7f: acts on good to firm ground: has been slowly away: sold 1,000 gns, sent to
Holland. *P. W. Harris*

RUSSIAN RHYTHM (USA)   3 ch.f. Kingmambo (USA) 125 – Balistroika   **123**
(USA) (Nijinsky (CAN) 138) [2003 113p: 8g* 8f* 9.9g* 8f^2 10m^5 Oct 18]
Until a lacklustre run in the Champion Stakes, Russian Rhythm—who stays
in training—hardly put a foot wrong, contesting four Group 1 races and being
beaten only by Falbrav. No Houdini acts, such as that achieved when landing the
Lowther Stakes as a two-year-old, were required as she used her redoubtable turn
of foot to land the Sagitta One Thousand Guineas, Coronation Stakes and Vodafone
Nassau Stakes, a treble last achieved by Happy Laughter in 1953.
With an increasing number of Two Thousand Guineas and One Thousand
Guineas runners making their seasonal debuts in Europe in the classics—fifty of
the one hundred and eleven runners in the last three seasons have been in this

Sagitta 1000 Guineas Stakes, Newmarket—
a good renewal and Russian Rhythm puts reports of some disappointing home work firmly behind her;
unlucky Six Perfections (far left) has been taken right to the outside after encountering trouble,
while Intercontinental (right) is third and Soviet Song (light jacket, dark cap) fourth

position, with five of them winning—the betting market on these races in the spring relies heavily on reports of home work unseen by the general public. Such reports from Newmarket are prolific but virtually non-existent from Lambourn, Middleham and Ballydoyle, and, in terms of providing precise knowledge, their reliability is dubious anyway. The trainer's expression and/or enthusiasm after a horse works is often taken as the best guide to what has happened, in the absence of anything more concrete such as the evidence of weights carried or time clocked, but trainers are under no obligation to give anything away. A home gallop is also not necessarily an accurate guide to what is going to happen on the racecourse. Some horses are lazy and do little at home, only to excel on the track, while others, the 'morning glories', reverse the process. After her Lowther victory, Russian Rhythm had been as low as 5/2 for the Guineas, but defeat when in season in the Cheveley Park Stakes saw her pushed out to 5/1. On Guineas day, in the wake of a string of reports that her work had been anything but sparkling, that the race would almost certainly come too soon for her and that she had not come in her coat, plus even a hint that she might be withdrawn late on, Russian Rhythm started at 12/1. That put her behind favourite Six Perfections, Soviet Song, Intercontinental and Mezzo Soprano, and not far ahead of Tante Rose (Fred Darling Stakes, 14/1) and Khulood (Nell Gwyn Stakes, 16/1); Ballydoyle's first string Yesterday went off at 20/1. For all the supposed doubts, Russian Rhythm, who was bandaged on her near-hind, impressed with her appearance—a big, good-topped filly with plenty of scope and a powerful, round action, she had obviously done well physically over the winter. She was soon going well, held up towards the rail, where the whole field of nineteen converged, and she obtained a perfect run through from two furlongs out, sweeping past the leaders in the final furlong and running on strongly to hold Six Perfections by a length and a half. Intercontinental was third and Soviet Song fourth. The runner-up was still last approaching the final furlong and, encountering all sorts of trouble in running, has to be regarded as unlucky. But it would be foolish to remember the race exclusively as one the French filly lost rather than one Russian Rhythm won. The first two did not meet again, but, on their best form, there was precious little between them.

Six Perfections was not seen in Britain again and, in her absence, Russian Rhythm started at odds on for the Coronation Stakes at Royal Ascot. Soviet Song reopposed her, with two-year-old Group 1 winner Mail The Desert, making her reappearance, also among the nine runners. The race concerned only the two principals. Looking magnificent again, and wearing a crossed noseband, as she had at Newmarket, Russian Rhythm was kept close to the leaders this time, took over in front early in the straight and, despite idling a little, kept on strongly for firmish handling to defeat Soviet Song by a length and a half. Her timefigure, equivalent to a rating of 122, was excellent and, given her superiority among the British-trained fillies and the absence of any subsequent Group 1 races over a mile restricted to her sex, there must have been a strong temptation to run Russian Rhythm in the Sussex Stakes at Goodwood. At first Sir Michael Stoute seemed to favour this option

Coronation Stakes, Royal Ascot—Soviet Song is the only one to give odds-on Russian Rhythm a race; Mail The Desert takes third

*Vodafone Nassau Stakes, Goodwood—Russian Rhythm, after being short of room
and having to be switched, finally pegs back Ana Marie (noseband);
Zee Zee Top battles back to take third off Hi Dubai (partly hidden by runner-up), with Macadamia fifth*

but, in the event, Russian Rhythm was aimed at another fillies' race, stepped up in distance, in the Nassau Stakes. After rain had turned the going good, she took her chance only after Stoute had walked the course. She started at odds on in a field of eight, in which Lancashire Oaks winner Place Rouge and Godolphin's Hi Dubai were the only ones near her in the betting. The Group 1 treble was duly completed, but not so easily as expected by most people since Russian Rhythm, who sweated, raced freely in the early stages and was short of room on the rails halfway up the straight. Once switched outside, she had all of four lengths to make up on the leader, French four-year-old Ana Marie, but Russian Rhythm kept on gamely and led close home to score by a neck, the first two clear of Russian Rhythm's stable-companion Zee Zee Top. Having proved that a mile and a quarter was within her capabilities, Russian Rhythm's connections had a wider range of races to aim at, with the Prix de l'Opera initially mentioned. However, they plumped for a crack at the colts in the Queen Elizabeth II Stakes at Ascot in September. Second favourite to the supplemented Falbrav, Russian Rhythm did herself proud, unable to match Falbrav's sparkling turn of foot in the straight but chasing him gamely and going down by two lengths, putting up marginally her best performance of the season and confirming form with Soviet Song in fourth. It was a different story in the Champion Stakes at Newmarket, where, despite travelling well for a long way, Russian Rhythm failed to respond to pressure from two furlongs out, finishing fifth to Rakti. Perhaps a strongly-run mile and a quarter had proved too much for her; perhaps she was over the top—she certainly looked edgy. Either way, she can be forgiven the lapse.

So what prospects does Russian Rhythm have as a four-year-old? She has the make and shape of a filly who will train on, and it is to her advantage—and that of Six Perfections and Nebraska Tornado—that there will be more Group 1 races available to older fillies and mares than previously. In the autumn a radical overhaul of the pattern system relating to fillies was announced, more discussion of which can be found in the essays on Buy The Sport, Dimitrova and Macadamia. The idea behind the move, according to the British Horseracing Board, is to encourage owners and breeders to keep their fillies and mares in training in Europe after the age of three rather than retire them to stud or transfer them to America, where there are more opportunities. Well and good, but the changes may prove a mixed blessing. Elevating the status of a race in the expectation of raising the standard of its runners, instead of doing so to reflect the quality already there, is no guarantee of success and will most likely result in unwarranted kudos attaching to some winners. The average annual rating of the twenty-five winners of the Falmouth, Prix d'Astarte, Matron, Pretty Polly and Sun Chariot, all to be Group 1 in 2004, over the last five years is around 114, with only two rated 120 or over—Bright Sky and Dress to Thrill (the latter winning two of the races), neither of whom had to run

Cheveley Park Stud's "Russian Rhythm"

to her best to win. This leaves room for improvement if the races mentioned are to become genuine Group 1s, but exactly where is the improvement to come from? During the same five-year period there was an average of eighteen fillies per year trained in Europe rated 115 or more, compared to around seventy colts and geldings, which means the quality from which to draw runners for the new Group 1 races is in short supply. For what it is worth, there has been no great shortage of top three-year-old fillies kept in training in Europe lately anyway, notable examples being Aquarelliste, Banks Hill, Bright Sky, Ela Athena and Islington, and the plan to continue with Russian Rhythm originated before the announcement about the upgrades was made. Moreover, the system in the States, where there is a full Grade 1 season for four-year-old fillies and mares on both turf and dirt, is not necessarily one worth mimicking wholesale. With so many options, the fillies there tend not to take on the colts at all. Clashes between top fillies and top colts always provide added interest to the races involved. The position in Europe could end up being more problematical since all the new Group 1 races will be open to three-year-olds as well. Three- and four-year-old fillies have consistently added to the competitiveness of open races for almost as long as racing has been going. In the latest season, Bright Sky, Etoile Montante, Islington, Nebraska Tornado, Russian Rhythm and Six Perfections did so to great effect, just as Aquarelliste, Banks Hill and Rebelline had the previous year. To create conditions where this might no longer happen is a retrograde step, but at least some top owners are likely to continue running their fillies in open Group 1s. It has to be more satisfying to take on the opposite sex and beat them than to compete solely in restricted events. It will take a good miler, male or female, to beat Russian Rhythm and she should have another successful season.

Russian Rhythm (USA) (ch.f. 2000)	Kingmambo (USA) (b 1990)	Mr Prospector (b 1970)	Raise A Native
			Gold Digger
		Miesque (b 1984)	Nureyev
			Pasadoble
	Balistroika (USA) (ch 1988)	Nijinsky (b 1967)	Northern Dancer
			Flaming Page
		Balidaress (gr 1973)	Balidar
			Innocence

Whatever Russian Rhythm achieves at four, she is already worth much more than the 440,000 guineas she cost her owners as yearling, and when she comes to be retired her pedigree as well as her looks should stand her in good stead. As mentioned in last year's Annual, she hails from an exceptional family that has been producing Group 1 winners with abandon for the last twenty years or so—on the December Sales catalogue page for Russian Rhythm's four-year-old half-sister Balade Russe there were seven horses of that ilk displayed. Balade Russe fetched 525,000 guineas, making her the second-highest priced progeny of unraced Balistroika sold during the year. The yearling colt by Rahy was bought on behalf of Sheikh Mohammed for 1,100,000 dollars at Keeneland in September. Marisa, Russian Rhythm's two-year-old half-sister by Swain, is also in training with Stoute but in different ownership and has yet to run. Russian Rhythm has raced only on good going or firmer and, given her trainer's doubts after the rain at Goodwood, it seems unlikely that she will be tried on soft. Usually waited with, she tends to race freely and has taken a good hold going to post. *Sir Michael Stoute*

RUSSIAN RUBY (FR) 2 b.f. (Feb 23) Vettori (IRE) 119 – Pink Sovietstaia (FR) **85** (Soviet Star (USA) 128) [2003 5g 6g² 6m 6.1m* 6g 7g 6m⁴ 7m⁵ 6m* 7m* 6g⁶ Oct 31] 17,000F: good-bodied filly: first living foal: dam awarded 9f event in France: fairly useful performer: won maiden at Nottingham in July and nurseries at Newmarket and Brighton (by 1½ lengths from Nick's Grey) in October: below form in listed event at Newmarket final start: stays 7f: acts on good to firm going: refused to enter stall intended third outing: held up. *N. A. Callaghan*

RUSSIAN SOCIETY 3 b.f. Darshaan 133 – Russian Snows (IRE) 113 (Sadler's **103** Wells (USA) 132) [2003 82p: 10.1m* 10.3d² Nov 7] leggy, good-topped filly: useful form, lightly raced: off 13 months, landed odds in maiden at Newcastle in October: very good head second to Al Ihtithar in listed race at Doncaster, allowing winner first run and quickening well once switched: fully effective at 1¼m, bred to stay further: acts on good to firm and good to soft ground: tongue tied in 2003: has worn crossed noseband/had 2 handlers. *Saeed bin Suroor*

RUSSIAN SYMPHONY (USA) 2 ch.c. (Feb 8) Stravinsky (USA) 133 – Backwoods **71 p** Teacher (USA) (Woodman (USA) 126) [2003 6m 6m⁵ Aug 20] $145,000F, €260,000Y: first foal: dam unraced half-sister to smart Irish performer up to 9f Savoureux: better effort in maidens (fair form) when fifth of 12 at Kempton, slowly away: needs to settle to stay beyond 6f: open to progress. *C. R. Egerton*

RUSSIAN VALOUR (IRE) 2 b.c. (Apr 1) Fasliyev (USA) 120 – Vert Val (USA) **115** 103 (Septieme Ciel (USA) 123) [2003 5m³ 5g* 5s² 5m* 5m* Jun 19]
Like father, like son. Russian Valour's two-year-old career echoed that of his sire Fasliyev in that it was curtailed by injury after only five starts. Russian Valour, whose victories included a decisive success in the Norfolk Stakes, did not achieve the same level of form as Fasliyev, but high ratings by two-year-olds are very rarely achieved until after Royal Ascot because of the relatively uncompetitive nature of two-year-old racing in the early part of the season. The general trend among leading trainers nowadays—Aidan O'Brien and Russian Valour's trainer Mark Johnston being notable exceptions—is to introduce their better two-year-olds, especially the well-bred ones, in the second half of the year, giving them time to mature, and training them for the more valuable two-year-old pattern events in late-summer and autumn. Fasliyev's final outing, and his best effort, came in the 1999 Prix Morny at the end of August, over two months later in the year than

Russian Valour's final appearance. It is not inconceivable that, but for injury intervening, Russian Valour could have gone close to equalling Fasliyev's rating of 120 and, in turn, establishing himself among the leading two-year-olds of 2003. He progressed really well, winning three of his starts, and looked all set to improve further still after his Norfolk Stakes success. Fasliyev was retired after his serious injury, but Russian Valour, who had arthroscopic surgery to remove bone chips from his knees, will hopefully get the chance to fulfil his promise as a three-year-old. He is reportedly to be aimed initially at the Two Thousand Guineas, with the strong possibility of taking in a trial beforehand to see whether he stays a mile.

Third in a maiden at Newcastle in April on his debut, Russian Valour won a similar seven runner event at Pontefract later that month before going down narrowly, hanging left under pressure and collared close home by Crafty Fancy, in an eight-runner minor event at Windsor. Russian Valour again showed a tendency to hang—this time to the right—when stepped up to listed company in the betfair.com National Stakes at Sandown next time, but on this occasion it did not stop him from winning. He never looked like being caught, despite twice colliding with the rail, when beating Incise by a length and a half. Then came the Norfolk. Facing seven rivals, including the odds-on Kheleyf who had made an excellent impression when winning on his debut, Russian Valour was quickly sent across from his wide draw to race against the stand rail and, showing no wayward tendencies this time, travelled strongly in the lead and found plenty when challenged to beat Kheleyf by a length and three quarters with subsequent July Stakes winner Nevisian Lad in third.

Russian Valour (IRE) (b.c. Apr 1, 2001)	Fasliyev (USA) (b 1997)	Nureyev (b 1977)	Northern Dancer / Special
		Mr P'S Princess (b 1993)	Mr Prospector / Anne Campbell
	Vert Val (USA) (b 1994)	Septieme Ciel (b 1987)	Seattle Slew / Maximova
		Valthea (ch 1989)	Antheus / Green Valley

The excellent start made by Fasliyev at stud is detailed thoroughly in the essay on Carry On Katie. Russian Valour's dam Vert Val was a useful performer and is a very well-bred mare. She won five times at two and three in France, gaining her first success over nine furlongs on her debut before being dropped back down to six and seven furlongs in her remaining races. Vert Val is out of a half-sister to both the Poule d'Essai des Poulains and Prix Lupin winner Green Dancer and to the dam of champion 1995 two-year-old Alhaarth, and she has had one other winner from two foals prior to Russian Valour, the 2003 three-year-old Come Away With Me, who won a seven-furlong maiden at Thirsk. Russian Valour is not the best of movers in his slower paces but is a grand physical specimen with the scope to train on. A big, good-bodied colt, Russian Valour is reportedly the biggest horse of any age in the Johnston yard, reportedly weighing more than the big, strong—and three years older—Desert Deer at the time of the Norfolk Stakes. Russian Valour was raced only at five furlongs at two, but should stay at least six. Whether he will get much further remains to be seen. Russian Valour's wayward tendencies were probably the result of immaturity, but, if they were taken as indicative of a head-strong nature, Russian Valour could well turn out purely and simply a sprinter. Russian Valour has form on soft going, though his two best efforts—his last two—came on good to firm. *M. Johnston*

RUST EN VREDE   4 b.g. Royal Applause 124 – Souveniers (Relko 136) [2003 57: p10g p7g 10.3g 9m 10.3m 7.9m³ 7f⁶ 6.1g 7m Jul 23] tall gelding: modest maiden handicapper: stays 1m: acts on good to firm going. *D. Carroll*   **51**

RUSTIC CHARM (IRE)   3 b.f. Charnwood Forest (IRE) 125 – Kabayil 75 (Dancing Brave (USA) 140) [2003 8.2g³ 8.1d³ 8.1d⁴ 10d Nov 6] tall, good-topped filly: fourth foal: half-sister to useful 7f to 2m winner Dancing Bay (by Suave Dancer) and 4-y-o Kasamba: dam 1¼m winner and fairly useful hurdler: fair maiden: reportedly suffered infected foot after debut: probably stays 1¼m (raced freely at trip). *C. G. Cox*   **72**

RUSTLE IN THE WIND   3 b.f. Barathea (IRE) 127 – Night Owl 73 (Night Shift (USA)) [2003 70p: 8m 8.2m 7g 7m Oct 10] close-coupled, quite good-topped filly: fair form only 2-y-o start: well held in 2003, leaving M. Channon 3,800 gns after second start. *Joseph Quinn, Ireland*   **–**

RUSTY BOY   2 b.g. (Mar 3) Defacto (USA) – Berl's Gift 44 (Prince Sabo 123) [2003 9f⁶ 7.2d Oct 13] first foal: dam, maiden who stayed 1m, out of half-sister to 9-y-o Indian Spark: last in maidens at Redcar and Ayr. *A. Crook*   **–**

RUTHIE   2 ch.f. (Apr 18) Pursuit of Love 124 – Moogie 103 (Young Generation 129) [2003 7.5m³ 7.5m* 7m Sep 7] lengthy, workmanlike filly: has scope: half-sister to several winners, including 2-y-o 7f winners Catwalk (in 1996, by Shirley Heights) and Mr Pitz (in 2001, by Hector Protector): dam, 2-y-o 6f winner, later best at 9f: fair form: won maiden at Beverley in August: well beaten in nursery final start: should stay 1m. *T. D. Easterby*   **72**

RUTLAND CHANTRY (USA)   9 b.g. Dixieland Band (USA) – Christchurch (FR) 88 (So Blessed 130) [2003 74: 9.9m 12.3g 12m 10g Oct 28] robust gelding: fair handi-capper in 2002: well held at 9 yrs: blinkered once. *S. Gollings*   **–**

RUTTERS REBEL (IRE)   2 b.g. (Feb 2) Entrepreneur 123 – No Quest (IRE) (Rainbow Quest (USA) 134) [2003 5.9m⁴ 7m 7m 8m* 8g² 8d⁶ Oct 14] €58,000Y: quite good-topped gelding: fourth foal: half-brother to useful 1m/1¼m winner (now smart up to 1½m in North America) Macaw (by Bluebird) and French 9f/1¼m winner Nakos (by Turtle Island): dam, French maiden, half-sister to very smart French performer up to 1¼m No Pass No Sale: fair performer: won nursery at Musselburgh in September: creditable efforts in similar events after: should stay 1¼m: acts on good to firm and good to soft ground: sometimes slowly away/carries head high/hangs left. *G. A. Swinbank*   **75**

RYAN'S ACADEMY (IRE)   3 b.c. Ali-Royal (IRE) 127 – Bradwell (IRE) 76 (Taufan (USA) 119) [2003 90: 7.5d³ 7g⁵ 6d⁶ 5m⁵ 8m 8g³ 7d Aug 3] strong, workmanlike colt: fifth foal: half-brother to winners in Spain and Italy by Bobs Return and Fayruz: dam 5f winner who probably stayed 7f: fairly useful performer: won maiden at Tipperary at 2 yrs: below form in minor event at Newmarket second start: stays 1m: acts on soft ground: often blinkered in 2003. *G. T. Lynch, Ireland*   **93**

RYAN'S BLISS (IRE)   3 b.f. Danetime (IRE) 121 – Raja Moulana 75 (Raja Baba (USA)) [2003 69: 6m 6m 6m 8m Sep 12] fair maiden at 2 yrs: well held in handicaps in 2003: stays 7f. *T. D. McCarthy*   **–**

RYAN'S FUTURE (IRE)   3 b.c. Danetime (IRE) 121 – Era 70 (Dalsaan 125) [2003 6g 6m* 6m³ 7g⁴ 8.1d 7m⁵ 8.2m* p10g⁴ p10g* p10g⁵ Dec 29] IR 8,000Y: leggy, useful-looking colt: half-brother to several winners, including fairly useful 1992 2-y-o 6f/7f winner After The Last (by Infantry) and 1m to 1¼m winner in Italy by Petardia: dam second at 5f at 2 yrs: fairly useful performer: won maiden at Catterick in July, apprentice handicap at Nottingham in October and (having left A. Stewart 21,000 gns) handicap at Lingfield in December: stays 1¼m: acts on good to firm going and polytrack, well below form only run on good to soft. *J. Akehurst*   **88**

RYAN'S GOLD (IRE)   5 b.g. Distant View (USA) 126 – Kathleen's Dream (USA) (Last Tycoon 131) [2003 –: 6g 6g 9.2g Jul 24] close-coupled gelding: fair maiden at best: little form since 3 yrs: tried blinkered/in cheekpieces. *B. Mactaggart*   **–**

RYANS MISTAKE (IRE)   3 ch.g. Dr Devious (IRE) 127 – Jane Heller (USA) (Halo (USA)) [2003 8m 11.1d 9.3f⁶ 12.1g² 13.8m³ 10.9d Oct 13] IR 10,000Y, 8,800 2-y-o: smallish gelding: fourth foal: half-brother to 2 winners abroad, including French 1m and (at 2 yrs) 1¼m winner Saint Andrew (by St Jovite): dam unraced: fair maiden: broke   **69**

down final outing: probably stayed 13.8f: acted on good to firm going: dead. *G. A. Swinbank*

RYAN'S QUEST (IRE)   4 b.f. Mukaddamah (USA) 125 – Preponderance (IRE) 85   **57**
(Cyrano de Bergerac 120) [2003 58: p6g p5g³ p5g 5.3m 5.3m 5g⁴ 5m⁴ 5g 5m⁵ Aug 21]
neat filly: modest maiden handicapper: left K. Burke after reappearance: best at 5f: acts
on firm ground and polytrack: none too resolute. *T. D. McCarthy*

RYDAL (USA)   2 ch.c. (Feb 16) Gilded Time (USA) – Tennis Partner (USA) (Northern   **88**
Dancer) [2003 6d⁴ 6m² p7g² 7m² 8g* Nov 5] good-topped colt: has scope: half-brother to
several winners, including 1½m/1¾m winner Disputed Call (by Alleged): dam unraced
sister to top-class sprinter Ajdal: fairly useful performer: favourite and blinkered, won
6-runner maiden at Musselburgh comfortably by 3 lengths from Hathlen, making most:
stays 1m: acts on polytrack and good to firm ground. *G. A. Butler*

RYEFIELD   8 b.g. Petong 126 – Octavia (Sallust 134) [2003 7m 5.9g 7.1m 7.2g 7m   **68 §**
7.1f 7.2g 7d* 7.2g Aug 1] small gelding: fair performer: missed 2002: won amateur
claimer at Newcastle in July: effective at 6f to 1m: acts on any going: refused/reluctant
to race third/fourth outings: races freely, and held up: has carried head high: unreliable.
Miss L. A. Perratt

RYE (IRE)   2 b.f. (Apr 11) Charnwood Forest (IRE) 125 – Silver Hut (USA) 80 (Silver   **75 p**
Hawk (USA) 123) [2003 7f⁵ Jul 9] 26,000Y: fourth foal: sister to useful 2000 2-y-o 6f/7f
winner Forwood and half-sister to 2 winners by Barathea, including useful 1m winner
Barrister (later successful in USA): dam 1m winner from 3 starts at 2 yrs: 50/1, fifth of 10
in maiden at Kempton, not given hard time: reportedly treated for a small chip in a knee
after: will stay 1m: should improve. *J. A. Osborne*

RYELAND   7 b.m. Presidium 124 – Ewe Lamb 86 (Free State 125) [2003 f8g Mar 13]   **–**
angular mare: little form. *Mrs P. Sly*

RYE N DRY (IRE)   3 ch.f. Timeless Times (USA) 99 – Inonder 31 (Belfort (FR) 89)   **–**
[2003 –: f7g Jan 9] workmanlike filly: well held in maidens/seller. *A. Berry*

RYME INTRINSECA   4 ch.f. Hector Protector (USA) 124 – Star And Garter 75   **91**
(Soviet Star (USA) 128) [2003 88: 7.1m 8m³ 8m 8.3f* 8.1g Jul 5] workmanlike filly:
fairly useful performer: won 5-runner minor event at Hamilton in June: free-going sort,
not sure to stay beyond 1m: acts on firm and good to soft going: reportedly in foal to
Singspiel. *M. R. Channon*

RYMER'S RASCAL   11 b.g. Rymer 121 – City Sound 63 (On Your Mark 125) [2003   **54 §**
66§, a–§: 8.5f⁶ 8g⁶ 8g⁴ 9.2g 8g 8d³ 8.3m 8m² Sep 18] sturdy gelding: modest performer   **a– §**
nowadays: best at 7f/1m: acts on any going: takes good hold/sometimes finds little, and
usually held up: unreliable. *E. J. Alston*

S

SAADA ONE (IRE)   3 b. or br.f. Polish Precedent (USA) 131 – Donya 74 (Mill Reef   **66**
(USA) 141) [2003 8.3g⁴ 8.2m³ p10g⁴ Nov 18] leggy filly: closely related to 7-y-o Invader
and half-sister to several winners, including useful 10.5f/1½m winner Altaweelah
(by Fairy King): dam twice-raced half-sister to Rothman's International winner French
Glory out of Prix de Diane winner Dunette: fair maiden: best effort on debut: stays 1m.
L. M. Cumani

SAAFEND ROCKET (IRE)   5 b.g. Distinctly North (USA) 115 – Simple Annie   **–**
(Simply Great (FR) 122) [2003 53, a67: f9.4g Mar 24] fair performer at best: well beaten
only start on Flat in 2003, but subsequently won 3 times over hurdles for H. Daly: tried
visored/blinkered. *R. Lee*

SAAMEQ (IRE)   2 b.g. (Feb 4) Bahhare (USA) 122 – Tajawuz 82 (Kris 135) [2003   **–**
8.2m Oct 28] strong colt: second foal: dam 1¼m winner from family of Rainbow Quest:
8/1 and very green, well held in maiden at Nottingham, slowly away/racing freely: sold
6,500 gns. *E. A. L. Dunlop*

SABALARA (IRE)   3 b.f. Mujadil (USA) 119 – Sabaniya (FR) (Lashkari 128) [2003   **61**
6m⁵ 6g⁶ 6d² 6g Sep 27] IR 52,000Y: sturdy filly: third foal: sister to fairly useful 2000
2-y-o 5f winner (stayed 1m) Chaguaramas: dam, Irish bumper winner, half-sister to grandam of Sinndar: modest maiden: will stay 7f: unraced on extremes of going. *P. W. Harris*

SABANA (IRE)   5 b.g. Sri Pekan (USA) 117 – Atyaaf (USA) 48 (Irish River (FR) 131)   **58**
[2003 69, a60: 6d 6f 6m³ 6m 7.1g f5g Nov 28] quite attractive gelding: modest handi-

capper: stays 6f: acts on firm going, good to soft and fibresand: blinkered twice: sometimes wanders: none too reliable. *J. M. Bradley*

SABBEEH (USA)   2 b.c. (Jan 28) Red Ransom (USA) – Capistrano Day (USA) 110   **107** (Diesis 133) [2003 6d* 6f 7d* 7g⁶ Oct 24] well-made, quite attractive colt: first foal: dam, 7f winner (including at 2 yrs) and fourth in 1000 Guineas, out of smart 1¼m performer Alcando: useful performer: won maiden at Ripon (by 13 lengths) in May and minor event at Doncaster (beat New Mexican by 2½ lengths) in September: well below form on other starts, in Coventry Stakes at Royal Ascot (favourite, returned with sore shins on firm ground) and Horris Hill Stakes at Newbury (faded tamely): bred to stay 1m: acts on good to soft going: free-going sort, and has been taken steadily to post: races prominently: joined Godolphin. *M. A. Jarvis*

SABIANGO (GER)   5 ch.h. Acatenango (GER) 127 – Spirit of Eagles (USA) (Beau's   **116** Eagle (USA)) [2003 11g³ 12d* 12g⁴ 12f⁴ 12d⁵ 12m Dec 14] very smart performer in 2001: well below form both 4-y-o outings: returned to near best in 2003, winning 4-finisher WestLB-Deutschland-Preis at Dusseldorf in July by 3½ lengths from Storm Trooper: ran well when 4 lengths fourth to Sulamani in Turf Classic at Belmont fourth start and respectable fifth to Phoenix Reach in Canadian International at Woodbine next time: stays 1½m: acts on firm and good to soft going: blinkered twice, including when last in Hong Kong Vase at Sha Tin final outing. *A. Wohler, Germany*

SABIYAH   3 b.f. Machiavellian (USA) 123 – Waqood (USA) 75 (Riverman (USA)   **74** 131) [2003 8.2g⁴ 8.1s² 8g² 8g* 7d 10.3d Nov 7] compact filly: fourth foal: sister to fairly useful UAE 5f/6f winner Rezif and half-sister to 2 winners, including 5-y-o Mutawaqed: dam, maiden who should have stayed 1½m, half-sister to 1000 Guineas winner Harayir: fair performer: landed odds in maiden at Ayr in August: out of depth in listed company last 2 starts: should stay beyond 1m: raced only on good ground or softer: sold 46,000 gns. *N. A. Graham*

Sheikh Ahmed Al Maktoum's "Sabbeeh"

SABLE 'N SILK   2 b.f. (Feb 1) Prince Sabo 123 – Sibilant (Selkirk (USA) 129) [2003   **57**
f6g⁶ f6g* p7g Dec 29] second foal: dam, ran 3 times in France, out of half-sister to very
smart 7f to 1¼m performer in Britain/USA Tinners Way: easily best effort (modest form)
when winning maiden at Wolverhampton in November by short head from Anisette:
pulled hard in nursery at Lingfield final start: should stay 7f. *D. Haydn Jones*

SABRE D'ARGENT (USA)   3 b. or br.c. Kris S (USA) – Sterling Pound (USA)   **119**
(Seeking The Gold (USA)) [2003 10g* 12g³ 10m* 10.5m* Aug 9] $1,000,000Y: rather
leggy, quite good-topped colt: third foal: half-brother to US Grade 2 7f winner Exchange
Rate (by Danzig): dam US Grade 3 8.5f winner from family of Ajdal: smart performer:
won maiden at Newmarket in April, listed race on same course (pulled hard and drifted
right) in May and Petros Rose of Lancaster Stakes at Haydock in August: best effort when
beating Far Lane by ½ length in last-named, getting on top final 1f: should stay 1½m:
raced only on good/good to firm ground: visored last 2 starts: wears crossed noseband:
joined Saeed bin Suroor. *D. R. Loder*

SABRELINE   4 ch.f. Sabrehill (USA) 120 – Story Line 98 (In The Wings 128) [2003   **53**
64, a57: f12s⁴ f9.4s⁴ 8m 10m 9.7g³ 10m f12g⁵ f12s⁵ f16g Dec 16] sturdy filly: modest
maiden handicapper: left D. Arbuthnot 2,200 gns after sixth start: stays 1½m: acts on
fibresand, unraced on extremes of going on turf: usually races prominently. *B. R. Foster*

SABRE'S EDGE (IRE)   2 b.c. (Apr 13) Sadler's Wells (USA) 132 – Brave Kris (IRE)   **81**
104 (Kris 135) [2003 7s 7d² Nov 7] quite good-topped colt: second foal: half-brother to
3-y-o Little Good Bay: dam, 1m winner, out of half-sister to Lowther winner Kingscote:
much better effort in maidens (fairly useful form) when 2½ lengths second of 17 to Spring
Surprise at Doncaster: pulled hard/carried head high both outings: needs to settle to stay
beyond 7f. *J. H. M. Gosden*

Godolphin's "Sabre d'Argent"

SABRINA BROWN 2 br.f. (Mar 10) Polar Falcon (USA) 126 – So True 116 (So **56**
Blessed 130) [2003 6.1d p6g p7g⁶ Dec 17] good-topped filly: has scope: sister to smart
1m winner Bomb Alaska and half-sister to 2 winners, including 1m/9f winner Keep Your
Word (by Castle Keep): dam, 5f (at 2 yrs) and 1m winner, best at 1½m: modest form in
maidens/minor event: will stay 1m. *G. B. Balding*

SACCHARINE 2 b.f. (May 8) Whittingham (IRE) 104 – Sweet And Lucky (Lucky –
Wednesday 124) [2003 6m 6m Sep 23] 1,500Y: sixth foal: half-sister to 3 winners, including 6f (at 2 yrs) to 1m winner Komlucky (by Komaite) and 7-y-o Sounds Lucky: dam
unraced: last in maidens at Brighton (put head in air) and Newmarket. *N. P. Littmoden*

SACHIN 2 b.g. (Mar 2) Bijou d'Inde 127 – Dark Kristal (IRE) 66 (Gorytus (USA) 132) **72**
[2003 6m p6g⁴ 6m³ 7d⁴ p8g Nov 18] 5,000F, 12,000Y: good-bodied gelding: seventh
foal: brother to fairly useful 2001 2-y-o 6f winner Saphir Indien and half-brother to
ungenuine 1999 2-y-o 6f winner Risky Gem (by Risk Me): dam, 6f winner, half-sister to
dam of Queen Mary/Molecomb winner Risky: fair maiden: third at Pontefract, best
effort: should stay 7f: acts on good to firm going, probably on good to soft and polytrack:
blinkered final start: sold £6,200, then gelded. *G. A. Butler*

SACRED LOVE (IRE) 3 ch.f. Barathea (IRE) 127 – Abstraction (Rainbow Quest **63**
(USA) 134) [2003 69p: 8.3d⁴ 10d 12g Oct 31] close-coupled, angular filly: modest
maiden, lightly raced: should stay at least 1¼m, but races freely: raced only on good
ground or softer: very slowly away second outing: sold 42,000 gns. *E. A. L. Dunlop*

SACSAYHUAMAN 4 b.f. Halling (USA) 133 – La Dolce Vita 76 (Mazilier (USA) –
107) [2003 69: p10g 10m 8m Jun 10] lengthy filly: fair maiden at best: well held in 2003:
tried in cheekpieces final start. *R. M. Beckett*

SADDAD (USA) 4 ch.c. Gone West (USA) – Lite Light (USA) (Majestic Light (USA)) **109 ?**
[2003 112: 5m⁵ 5f 6g⁵ 6m⁴ a5f⁵ a6f⁵ Nov 28] strong, lengthy, attractive colt: reportedly
injured a sesamoid in 2002: just useful form at 4 yrs, best effort when 1¾ lengths fourth
to Somnus in listed race at Newbury on fourth start (final one for Sir Michael Stoute): off
3½ months, tongue tied when well below form in minor events in UAE last 2 outings:
effective at 5f/6f: raced only on good or firmer going on turf: edgy sort: wore crossed
noseband/started slowly last two 2-y-o outings. *D. Watson, UAE*

SADDLER'S QUEST 6 b.g. Saddlers' Hall (IRE) 126 – Seren Quest 90 (Rainbow **67**
Quest (USA) 134) [2003 11.6m* 12f f14.8g⁶ 11.8m⁵ 11.6m Jul 28] rather leggy gelding:
fair performer: won claimer at Windsor (claimed from C. Morlock) in June: stays 1½m:
best efforts on soft/heavy ground: has been very slowly away: none too reliable. *J. White*

SADIE JANE 3 b.f. Zahran (IRE) 77 – So We Know (Daring March 116) [2003 5.7f⁵ –
7g f7g Nov 10] third foal: dam of little account: no form. *J. M. Bradley*

SADIKA (IRE) 3 b.f. Bahhare (USA) 122 – Nordica 99 (Northfields (USA)) [2003 55: –
8g 8.3d 8.3g Aug 10] tongue tied, little form at 3 yrs: has carried head high. *A. M. Balding*

SADLER'S COVE (FR) 5 b.g. King's Theatre (IRE) 128 – Mine d'Or (FR) (Posse **64**
(USA) 130) [2003 11.6m⁴ p12g* 16.4m 14.1d* 12g 12m⁶ p16g Sep 3] 130,000 francs Y,
resold 30,000Y, 1,700 3-y-o: half-brother to several winners, including French winner up
to 1½m Minandaya (by Fabulous Dancer): dam French maiden half-sister to Prix Royal-
Oak winner Mersey and Prix Saint-Alary winner Muncie: modest performer: won seller
at Lingfield in June and handicap at Salisbury in July: stays 2m: acts on good to soft
going, good to firm and polytrack: tongue tied: sometimes slowly away. *Mrs L. C. Jewell*

SADLER'S PRIDE (IRE) 3 b.c. Sadler's Wells (USA) 132 – Gentle Thoughts 73 **58 ?**
(Darshaan 133) [2003 12.3g³ 11.1g Sep 27] 80,000Y: heavy-topped gelding: first foal:
dam, lightly raced in Ireland, sister to useful 1½m winner Firecrest: better effort (seemed
to show modest form) on debut. *Andrew Turnell*

SADLERS SWING (USA) 7 b.g. Red Ransom (USA) – Noblissima (IRE) 77 –
(Sadler's Wells (USA) 132) [2003 f8.5s⁶ 10m f9.4g⁵ Aug 15] leggy gelding: maiden
handicapper, lightly raced: well held in 2003. *J. J. Sheehan*

SADLERS WINGS (IRE) 5 b.g. In The Wings 128 – Anna Comnena (IRE) 71 **106**
(Shareef Dancer (USA) 135) [2003 105: 14g⁴ 14d³ 13.9m 16f Sep 14] useful performer:
best 5-y-o efforts when in frame in listed event at Leopardstown (1¾ lengths fourth to
Blue Corrig) and handicap at Galway (2½ lengths third to Holy Orders): best at 1½m/
1¾m: acts on soft going, below form on firmer than good (including in Ebor at York third
start): tried blinkered/tongue tied: impressive winner on hurdling debut in December.
W. P. Mullins, Ireland

SAFFRON FOX   2 ch.f. (Feb 24) Safawan 118 – Fox Oa (FR) (French Friend (USA)   **89**
125) [2003 7m⁴ 7m 8d* 8.1d² 8g Nov 1] sturdy, workmanlike filly: sister to a winner in
Turkey and half-sister to 3 winners abroad, including French 1m winner Fox Croft (by
Bustino): dam French 1m/9f winner: fairly useful performer: won maiden at Newmarket
in August: creditable efforts in minor event at Sandown (second to Psychiatrist) and
listed race at Newmarket after: will be suited by 1¼m/1½m: acts on good to soft going.
J. G. Portman

SAFFRON RIVER   2 b.c. (Apr 26) Polar Prince (IRE) 117 – Cloudy Reef 57 (Cragador   **57**
110) [2003 f5g⁴ f5g.³ f6g f6g⁴ Dec 12] sixth foal: brother to 3-y-o Gilded Cove and half-
brother to 2 winners, including 4-y-o Vermilion Creek: dam, maiden, raced only around
5f: modest maiden: stays 6f. *R. Hollinshead*

SAFRANINE (IRE)   6 b.m. Dolphin Street (FR) 125 – Webbiana (African Sky 124)   **83**
[2003 61: f5g f5s f6g f5g³ f5g⁵ 5m⁶ 5m 5m² 5d 5d 5m⁶ 5f³ 5.5f* 5.1m⁵ 5.5f* 5.2m 5g   **a54**
6m* 6m 5.2g 6d 6m⁶ 6f 7g 7g 5s f6g f5g Dec 12] rather leggy mare: fairly useful handicapper on turf, modest on all-weather: improved in 2003, winning at Warwick (2) in July
and Redcar in September: effective at 5f/6f: acts on fibresand, firm and soft ground:
tried blinkered/visored, wears cheekpieces nowadays: sometimes slowly away: none too
consistent. *Miss A. Stokell*

SAGES END (IRE)   3 b.c. College Chapel 122 – Celtic Guest (IRE) (Be My Guest   **–**
(USA) 126) [2003 56: 6f Apr 11] twice raced at 2 yrs, showing modest form on debut:
well beaten only start in 2003. *T. D. Easterby*

SAGITTATE   3 ch.c. Grand Lodge (USA) 125 – Pretty Sharp 64 (Interrex (CAN)   **62**
[2003 7g⁵ f6g⁵ Jun 27] 170,000Y: second foal: half-brother to 4-y-o Twilight Blues: dam
maiden at 2 yrs (best form at 7f) who became temperamental: reportedly split a pastern in
2002: modest form in maidens, looking ungenuine second start (blinkered). *D. R. Loder*

SAHAAT   5 b. or br.g. Machiavellian (USA) 123 – Tawaaded (IRE) 91 (Nashwan (USA)   **106 d**
135) [2003 109: p10g f8.5s² 8g 8m⁵ 8g⁶ 7 9m⁴ 10g⁵ 10.1m 8m 10.1ₛ p10g p8g Dec 20]
leggy gelding: first foal: dam, 7f winner who stayed 1m, from family of Singspiel: useful
performer: trained before 2003 by J. Hammond in France: best 5-y-o effort when second
to Razkalla in minor event at Wolverhampton on second start: well below form last 6
starts, folding final one: effective at 1m/1¼m: acts on fibresand, good to firm and heavy
ground: usually waited with. *J. A. Osborne*

SAHARAN SONG (IRE)   2 ch.f. (Apr 16) Singspiel (IRE) 133 – Sahara Baladee   **64 p**
(USA) 79 (Shadeed (USA) 135) [2003 p7g⁴ Oct 8] €29,000Y, resold €22,000Y: half-
sister to several winners, including 1m/1¼m winner Bint Baladee (by Nashwan) and
1¼m winner Shanaladee (by Darshaan), both useful: dam, maiden who stayed 1m,
half-sister to top-class French/US performer up to 9f Thrill Show: 9/1, slow-starting 4
lengths fourth of 15 to Celtic Heroine in maiden at Lingfield: bred to be suited by at least
1m: should improve. *B. W. Hills*

SAHARA SCIROCCO (IRE)   2 b.c. (Apr 29) Spectrum (IRE) 126 – St Bride's Bay   **62 ?**
(Caerleon (USA) 132) [2003 5.1g 5.1m⁵ 6g 8f⁴ 8.2m Oct 28] 20,000Y: leggy colt: second
foal: dam unraced half-sister to useful performers up to 1m Sweet Robin and (in France)
Love And Adventure: modest maiden: blinkered, fourth at Bath, seemingly best effort
(clear leader long way): well beaten in seller final start: stays 1m. *I. A. Wood*

SAHARA SHADE (USA)   3 ch.f. Shadeed (USA) 135 – Tadwin 109 (Never So Bold   **–**
135) [2003 79: 6g Mar 22] good-topped filly: fair winner in 2002 for T. D. Barron:
blinkered, tailed off (reportedly lost both front shoes) only 3-y-o start. *S. L. Keightley*

SAHARA SILK (IRE)   2 b.f. (Mar 23) Desert Style (IRE) 121 – Buddy And Soda   **61**
(IRE) 75 (Imperial Frontier (USA) 112) [2003 p5g 5m 5m² f5g* 5s 5m² f5s* 5g 6m⁵ 5g   **a71**
f5s Oct 7] 10,000Y: well-made filly: second foal: half-sister to 3-y-o Dunn Deal: dam
Irish 7f winner: fair on all-weather, modest on turf: won maiden in May and nursery
(made all) in September, both at Southwell: stays 6f: acts on fibresand and good to firm
ground: visored after second start: sometimes looks none too keen. *D. Shaw*

SAHARA SPIRIT (IRE)   6 b.g. College Chapel 122 – Desert Palace (Green Desert   **–**
(USA) 127) [2003 p10g 8m May 6] smallish, quite attractive gelding: fairly useful
performer at 3 yrs for E. Dunlop: well beaten both Flat outings since. *R. J. Baker*

SAHARA STORM (IRE)   2 b.f. (Mar 17) Desert Prince (IRE) 130 – Deluge (Rainbow   **73**
Quest (USA) 134) [2003 6m³ 7m³ 8m⁴ 7f Oct 27] 55,000Y: strong, well-made filly: has a
quick action: first foal: dam unraced sister to smart 1¾m winner Tuning: fair maiden:
third at Newbury and Newmarket: below form in nursery final start: barely stays 1m:
usually races close up. *L. M. Cumani*

SAHEM (IRE) 6 b.g. Sadler's Wells (USA) 132 – Sumava (IRE) (Sure Blade (USA) **89**
130) [2003 12.4m² 10.1m³ 9.2d* 12m³ 13.9f³ 16.1g Jun 28] 400,000Y: well-made gelding: bumper winner: fairly useful performer on Flat: won maiden at Hamilton in May:
probably stays 1¾m: acts on firm and good to soft going. *D. Eddy*

SAHNOUR 3 ch.c. Singspiel (IRE) 133 – Carmita (Caerleon (USA) 132) [2003 10m⁵ **70 d**
11.1m² 10.3m 11.8m 14m⁵ 11.9m⁴ 16m* 17.2f³ 14m⁴ 14.4m⁵ 17.1m 16m⁶ 12m⁵ 14.4g⁶
17.1m⁶ 11.9f Oct 17] neat colt: seventh foal: closely related to 4-y-o Chai Walla and
half-brother to 2 winners, including useful 7.5f (in UAE)/1m winner Claranet (by Arazi):
dam French 1½m listed winner: fair handicapper: won at Redcar in July: below form after
next outing: stays 17f: raced only on good ground or firmer: visored 4 of last 5 starts: has
raced freely: none too genuine: sold 6,000 gns. *M. R. Channon*

SAHOOL 2 b.f. (Mar 3) Unfuwain (USA) 131 – Mathaayl (USA) 79 (Shadeed (USA) **84 p**
135) [2003 7g⁶ 8.2d* Nov 6] IR 78,000F, 180,000Y: tall, good-topped filly: has plenty of
scope: has a quick action: fifth living foal: closely related to useful Irish 9f winner Nasanice (by Nashwan) and half-sister to fairly useful 1m winner Alikhlas (by Lahib): dam 6f
and 1¼m winner: confirmed promise when winning 17-runner maiden at Nottingham by
3½ lengths from Song of Vala, ridden to lead over 1f out and drifting left: will be suited
by 1¼m/1½m: type to train on well as 3-y-o, and potentially useful. *M. P. Tregoning*

SAIDA LENASERA (FR) 2 b.f. (Apr 13) Fasliyev (USA) 120 – Lanasara (Generous **76**
(IRE) 139) [2003 7f⁴ 7m³ 7m* 8m⁴ 8m Sep 19] 140,000 francs Y: tall, leggy filly: third
foal: half-sister to useful Azkaban (by Ashkalani), 1m winner in USA: dam unraced daughter of Yorkshire Oaks/Prix Vermeille winner Bint Pasha: fair performer: won
maiden at Catterick in August: creditable fourth at Ripon, much better effort in nurseries
after: stays 1m: races prominently: sold 12,000 gns. *M. R. Channon*

SAILING THROUGH 3 b.g. Bahhare (USA) 122 – Hopesay 84 (Warning 136) [2003 **101**
65p: p10g² 10.1m³ p10g³ 11.8m 10m⁵ 8.5g* 10m* 10g* 10m* 10.1g⁴ 10g Oct 11] rangy
gelding: has scope: useful performer: won handicaps at Epsom (maiden event), Windsor
(2) and Newbury (beat Not Amused by 5 lengths) in July/August: effective at 1m/1¼m:
acts on polytrack, yet to race on extremes of going on turf: free-going sort: has been
mulish in preliminaries/slowly away, and refused to enter stall intended twelfth outing:
has hung right: sold 52,000 gns. *T. G. Mills*

SAILMAKER (IRE) 2 ch.g. (Apr 8) Peintre Celebre (USA) 137 – Princess Amalie **66 p**
(USA) (Rahy (USA) 115) [2003 8.2d⁶ Nov 6] 85,000Y: quite good-topped gelding:
second foal: dam, lightly raced in USA, half-sister to William Hill Futurity winner Al
Hareb: 16/1 and better for race, sixth of 17 to Sahool in maiden at Nottingham, slowly
away and not knocked about: will stay at least 1¼m: should improve. *R. Charlton*

SAINT ALEBE 4 b.g. Bishop of Cashel 122 – Soba Up 74 (Persian Heights 129) [2003 **106**
79: 12g* 12g⁶ 12m² 14g⁵ 16.2f⁶ 13.9m* Aug 20] heavy-topped gelding: poor mover:
useful handicapper: progressed steadily in 2003, winning at Newmarket in May and York
(22-runner Tote Ebor) in August: 20/1, beat Sun Bird by ½ length at York, coming with

*Tote Ebor (Handicap), York—Europe's most valuable handicap; Saint Alebe (left) comes from last place
to collar Sun Bird; the favourite Salsalino also finishes strongly in third, while Unleash (right) is fourth*

storming run down outside to lead close home having been last entering straight: stays 2m: acts on firm and soft ground: sweated at Newmarket and York: usually held up. *D. R. C. Elsworth*

SAINT JOHANN (IRE) 4 b.g. Ali-Royal (IRE) 127 – Up To You (Sallust 134) [2003 7.1g 5f 5.7f Jul 13] lightly-raced maiden: little form. *L. G. Cottrell*   **–**

SAINT LAZARE (IRE) 2 b.c. (Apr 16) Peintre Celebre (USA) 137 – Height of Passion (Shirley Heights 130) [2003 8.1d⁶ 8s Oct 29] 30,000Y: big, quite good-topped colt: half-brother to several winners, including 6f (at 2 yrs) and 1¼m winner Precede (by Polish Precedent) and 1½m to 2m winner Warm Feeling (by Kalaglow), both smart, and 4-y-o Treble Heights: dam ran 3 times: better effort in maidens (modest form) when sixth at Haydock: not knocked about at Yarmouth: should do better at 1¼m+. *J. G. Given*   **61 p**

SAINTLY PLACE 2 ch.g. (Mar 4) Compton Place 125 – Always On A Sunday 101 (Star Appeal 133) [2003 5g 7m⁶ 6d Jul 25] 19,000F, 16,000Y, 38,000 2-y-o: eighth foal: half-brother to fairly useful 1m (at 2 yrs)/1¼m winner No Cliches (by Risk Me): dam 1¼m winner: modest form in maidens: possibly amiss final start, and subsequently gelded: not sure to stay beyond 7f. *M. R. Channon*   **57**

SAINTLY THOUGHTS (USA) 8 b. or br.g. St Jovite (USA) 135 – Free Thinker (USA) 100 (Shadeed (USA) 135) [2003 16.2d* f14.8g³ 16.2m² 16.2m³ f14.8s² 16f 16m Oct 28] good-bodied gelding: fair performer: won claimer at Chepstow (first Flat run since 2000) in July: stays 17.4f: acts on good to firm ground, good to soft and fibresand: ran poorly in blinkers at 3 yrs: wore cheekpieces/visor in 2003. *B. J. Llewellyn*   **67**

SAIPAN (FR) 2 b.c. (Feb 16) Alhaarth (IRE) 126 – Ishtiyak 80 (Green Desert (USA) 127) [2003 7m 7m 7.1g 8.3g Oct 13] €70,000Y: good-bodied colt: has scope: half-brother to 3-y-o Arzoo and winner in Greece by Persian Bold: dam 5f (at 2 yrs)/6f winner: modest maiden: below form in nursery final start. *R. Hannon*   **62**

SAKHYA (IRE) 2 b.f. (Mar 8) Barathea (IRE) 127 – Um Lardaff (Mill Reef (USA) 141) [2003 8g Oct 25] leggy filly: half-sister to several winners, including useful 1997 2-y-o 7f winner Fantasy Island (later winner in UAE) and 4-y-o Mr Sandancer: dam, French 11f/1½m winner, sister to Shirley Heights: 33/1, well held in maiden at Newbury, slowly away and not knocked about: will be suited by 1¼m+: should do better. *M. R. Channon*   **– p**

SALAGAMA (IRE) 3 br.f. Alzao (USA) 117 – Waffle On 89 (Chief Singer 131) [2003 7m* Apr 11] sturdy, angular filly: fourth foal: half-sister to French 9.5f winner La Frou Frou (by Night Shift), later successful in USA and 7f winner Desert Alchemy (by Green Desert), both useful: dam, 2-y-o 6f winner, out of half-sister to high-class sprinter College Chapel: 10/1, won newcomers race at Newbury by 2 lengths from Dawnus, always prominent: looked sure to improve. *P. F. I. Cole*   **89**

SALAMBA 2 ch.c. (Mar 5) Indian Ridge 123 – Towaahi (IRE) (Caerleon (USA) 132) [2003 7m⁵ 7.2d³ Oct 13] 42,000Y: good-bodied colt: second foal: half-brother to 3-y-o Kristoffersen: dam unraced out of Yorkshire Oaks winner Untold: fair form in maidens at York and Ayr (third to Makfool): will stay 1m. *M. H. Tompkins*   **75**

SALCOMBE 3 ch.c. Elmaamul (USA) 125 – West Devon (USA) (Gone West (USA)) [2003 100: 8f² 7g³ 8g² 10.5m 10g⁴ Oct 25] well-made colt: smart performer: 1¼ lengths second to Royal Dignitary in listed race at Thirsk on reappearance: best effort when fourth to Pagan Sky in handicap at Newbury final start: stays 1¼m: raced only on good ground or firmer: sold 170,000 gns, sent to USA. *B. W. Hills*   **111**

SALERNO 4 ch.g. Mark of Esteem (IRE) 137 – Shamwari (USA) 63 (Shahrastani (USA) 135) [2003 47+: f5g* p6g f5g f5s 6m f5g⁴ f5s f5g f6s f5s Dec 31] rather un-furnished gelding: reportedly had wind operation at 2 yrs: fair performer: won maiden at Wolverhampton in January: below form after: best at 5f: acts on fibresand and any turf going: usually wears headgear: tried tongue tied: races up with pace: tail flasher. *Miss Gay Kelleway*   **66 d**

SALFORD CITY (IRE) 2 b.c. (Apr 20) Desert Sun 120 – Summer Fashion 84 (Moorestyle 137) [2003 8g* Oct 25] IR 48,000F, €115,000Y: tall, useful-looking colt: has scope: half-brother to several winners, notably very smart 7f (at 2 yrs) and 1¼m winner (also second in Irish Derby) Definite Article (by Indian Ridge), smart 1¼m (Dante)/11f winner Salford Express (by Be My Guest) and 5-y-o Sun Bird: dam 1m/1¼m winner: 12/1 and green, won 17-runner maiden at Newbury most impressively by 7 lengths from Mountain Meadow, slowly away and soon off bridle in rear, but leading 1f out and sprinting clear: will be well suited by 1¼m/1½m: exciting prospect, should make his mark in good races as 3-y-o. *D. R. C. Elsworth*   **100 P**

SALFORD LASS   4 b.f. Mtoto 134 – Heresheis 69 (Free State 125) [2003 f12g Feb 24]   –
seventh foal: half-sister to several winning stayers, including useful Athenry (by Siberian
Express): dam 1½m to 2m winner: 25/1, well beaten in maiden at Wolverhampton. *Mrs
Lydia Pearce*

SALFORD ROCKET   3 b.g. Slip Anchor 136 – Mysterious Maid (USA) 76 (L'Emi-   –
grant (USA) 129) [2003 10m Oct 22] second foal: dam 1¼m to 1¾m winner: 100/1, very
slowly away when tailed off in maiden at Nottingham. *G. C. H. Chung*

SALIERI   3 b.f. Silver Wizard (USA) 117 – Queen of Tides (IRE) 62 (Soviet Star (USA)   –
128) [2003 51: p8g⁶ p7g p10g Jun 28] little form at 3 yrs. *S. Dow*

SALIM   6 b.g. Salse (USA) 128 – Moviegoer 104 (Pharly (FR) 130) [2003 –§: f9.4g*   **39 §**
f9.4g⁶ 9.7m 9.7m⁶ 10.2m⁶ May 30] useful-looking gelding: modest handicapper on all-   **a55 §**
weather, poor on turf: won at Wolverhampton in March: left J. Long after third start: stays
easy 1¼m: acts on fibresand, good to firm and good to soft going: tried blinkered/visored:
free-going sort: ungenuine. *G. L. Moore*

SALIM TOTO   5 b.m. Mtoto 134 – Villasanta (Corvaro (USA) 124) [2003 107: 12m⁴   **103**
10f 11.9g Jul 5] quite good-topped mare: useful performer: creditable fourth to Gallery
God in handicap at Epsom on reappearance: well held after: effective at 1¼m/1½m: unraced on heavy going, acts on any other: front runner. *H. Morrison*

SALINOR   3 ch.g. Inchinor 119 – Salanka (IRE) 68 (Persian Heights 129) [2003 61:   **85 p**
8g³ f9.4s⁴ 8.5m* 8m³ 8.1m² 8.1f³ Sep 5] sturdy gelding: fairly useful handicapper: won
apprentice event at Beverley in July: unlucky fast-finishing second to Borrego at Haydock fifth start: stays 1m: acts on firm and soft ground: upset in stall and slowly away on
reappearance: should do better still at 4 yrs. *A. C. Stewart*

SALISBURY PLAIN   2 b.c. (Apr 13) Mark of Esteem (IRE) 137 – Wild Pavane   **73 p**
(Dancing Brave (USA) 140) [2003 6m⁴ 7m* Jul 6] 140,000Y: half-brother to several
winners, including useful 7f to 9f winner Apache Star (by Arazi): dam unraced half-sister
to dam of Coronation Stakes winner Rebecca Sharp: fair form in maidens: landed odds
comfortably at Redcar: will stay 1m: open to progress. *D. R. Loder*

SALLY TRAFFIC   4 b.f. River Falls 113 – Yankeedoodledancer (Mashhor Dancer   –
(USA)) [2003 57: 5m 5m 5m 5m 5m 8d 6.1m f7g Nov 19] small, sturdy filly: modest
handicapper at 3 yrs: showed little in 2003: tried in cheekpieces. *R. M. Whitaker*

SALONIKA SKY   2 ch.f. (Apr 16) Pursuit of Love 124 – Willisa 67 (Polar Falcon   **40**
(USA) 126) [2003 5g 5m⁵ 6m f5g 6m Oct 12] 1,600Y: workmanlike filly: third foal: half-
sister to 5-y-o Waterpark: dam 7f winner: poor maiden: left J. Weymes before final start:
stays 6f: acts on good to firm going. *C. W. Thornton*

SALON PRIVE   3 b.g. Green Desert (USA) 127 – Shot At Love (IRE) 79 (Last Tycoon   **73**
131) [2003 7m 6f² p7g³ p6g² Nov 13] fourth foal: brother to 7f winner (including at 2 yrs)
Silence And Rage: dam 1m winner: fair maiden: effective at 6f/7f: raced only on poly-
track/ground firmer than good. *C. A. Cyzer*

SALSALINO   3 ch.c. Salse (USA) 128 – Alicedale (USA) (Trempolino (USA)   **115 p**
135) [2003 95: p7g 9m⁴ 9.9g² 10.2m⁴ 11.9m³ 12m² 12g⁴ 13.9m³ Aug 20]
      The prestigious staying handicaps on the Flat are being won more regularly
by horses from leading jumping stables. In 2003, for example, Fortune Island gave
Martin Pipe his third success in the last five years in the Queen's Prize at Kempton
and Sindapour became his fifth winner of the Ascot Stakes; Philip Hobbs landed
the Northumberland Plate with Unleash; and Nicky Henderson's Landing Light
provided Pat Eddery with his first Cesarewitch winner at the final attempt. Clearly
the facilities at the disposal of the best jumping trainers nowadays make them a
match for their counterparts on the Flat, and it seems only a matter of time before
some of them start to make a regular impact in staying pattern races too. One trainer
who could start the ball rolling is Alan King with the smart Salsalino, provided the
colt recovers from the shoulder injury which caused his eleventh-hour withdrawal
from the St Leger. Salsalino was quoted as short as 8/1 on the morning of the race.
      Salsalino, along with Howle Hill and Trouble At Bay, formed their trainer's
first team of two-year-olds in 2002, with juvenile hurdling apparently the long-term
aim, King reportedly considering three-year-olds bought out of Flat stables for the
same purpose offer poor value for money. Whatever the trio could achieve on the
Flat would seemingly be considered a bonus. Some bonus! Howle Hill and Trouble
At Bay have proved smart and useful respectively (both duly made fine starts to

their hurdling careers in the autumn) and Salsalino did so well that plans to send him over timber had reportedly been postponed even before injury intervened. A 25,000-guinea two-year-old, Salsalino made the track three times in his first season, landing a six-furlong Salisbury maiden on his second start and going on to finish sixth to Foss Way in the Solario Stakes at Sandown. Subsequent July Cup and Nunthorpe winner Oasis Dream was among those behind Salsalino at Salisbury, but it soon became clear that stamina would be Salsalino's forte when he embarked on his three-year-old campaign (he held a Two Thousand Guineas entry until after his second outing). Gradually stepped up in trip on his first five starts, but found out each time by the lack of a true pace, Salsalino finally showed his true colours at Royal Ascot.

Racing from a BHB mark of 95 in the King George V Stakes, Salsalino got the end-to-end gallop his earlier efforts had suggested he needed and put up a smart performance, improving to be in the firing line all the way up the straight and answering his rider's every call as Fantastic Love came at him. The pair looked inseparable as they flashed past the post, but the photo went in Fantastic Love's favour. Salsalino appeared the following month in the Gordon Stakes at Goodwood, his Royal Ascot form looking just about the best on offer. Salsalino was again unlucky, finishing around a length fourth to Phoenix Reach in yet another race which wasn't truly run, staying on well after having his ground taken around

Mr Nigel Bunter's "Salsalino"

three furlongs out. Salsalino enjoyed a rare piece of fortune when making the cut for the Ebor, some others who had been well backed ante-post being eliminated, and he went into the race with a similar profile to 2000 winner Give The Slip (who had won the King George V and finished fourth in the Gordon Stakes). Sent off favourite at 4/1, Salsalino came third, two and a quarter lengths behind Saint Alebe, leaving the impression he'd have gone even closer ridden more in touch. Salsalino was held up in rear after being hampered slightly leaving the stalls and got into top gear only after the winner had asserted, meeting slight interference twice as he stayed on best of all. Salsalino remains unexposed, at least over a minimum of a mile and three quarters. He would have needed to improve only a little to make the frame in the St Leger and could emerge as a leading contender for the Cup races in 2004.

		Topsider	Northern Dancer
	Salse (USA)	(b 1974)	Drumtop
	(b 1985)	Carnival Princess	Prince John
Salsalino		(ch 1974)	Carnival Queen
(ch.c. 2000)		Trempolino	Sharpen Up
	Alicedale (USA)	(ch 1984)	Trephine
	(ch 1992)	Alice En Ballade	Tap On Wood
		(b or br 1985)	Donna Cressida

On what he has shown on the racecourse, it looks a near-certainty that Salsalino will stay at least two miles, some encouragement for which can also be derived from elements of his pedigree. His sire, the splendidly consistent Salse, who died in 2001, was unraced beyond a mile and his most notable successes as a racehorse came in the Challenge Stakes and the Prix de la Foret. However, Salse's sire Topsider was out of Drumtop, winner of the thirteen-furlong Canadian International Championship, and Salse soon established himself as capable of siring good stayers, Gold Cup winner Classic Cliche the most notable. Salsalino's dam Alicedale, who was placed at up to eleven furlongs in France, has had only one other winner, her first foal Ocean Rain, who scored over six furlongs as a two-year-old, like Salsalino, but was a lazy sort who later proved himself at up to ten and a half furlongs, despite being by the sprinter Lake Coniston. Grandam Alice En Ballade, a winner over a mile in France and a half-sister to the dam of One Thousand Guineas winner Las Meninas, was sent to Saudi Arabia in 2001, while great grandam Donna Cressida was also the dam of Persian War Novices' Hurdle winner High Alltitude, useful over hurdles at up to two and three quarter miles in the early-'nineties, before turning into a moody customer when sent over fences. Physically, there isn't a lot of substance to Salsalino, who is a rather leggy, quite attractive sort. Apart from when reappearing over an inadequate trip on polytrack, he has raced only on good and good to firm ground. His trainer had reportedly thought about equipping him with some form of headgear in the St Leger, though, unlike some members of his family on his dam's side, Salsalino hasn't struck us as being lazy or quirky so far (though he was accompanied by two handlers at Haydock on his fifth start and got decidedly on edge prior to the Ebor). Salsalino might not have managed a win in the latest season but he is both game and consistent. *A. King*

SALSELON 4 b.c. Salse (USA) 128 – Heady (Rousillon (USA) 133) [2003 113: 8g* **118** 8m² 10m² 8m³ 7s* 8d Nov 16] 33,000Y: third foal: half-brother to fairly useful 8.5f to 1½m winner Tipsy (by Kris) and French 1¼m winner Tipsy Topsy (by Ashkalani): dam unraced half-sister to top-class miler Markofdistinction: smart performer: won Prix Edmond Blanc at Saint-Cloud (by nose from Almond Mousse) in March and gained third successive victory in Premio Chiusura at Milan (by ¾ length from Glad To Be Fast) in November, coming from last place both times: placed at Milan all starts in between, running well when neck second of 5 to Walzerkoenigin in Premio Emilio Turati second outing (lost 2 shoes before/during race): ran poorly final start: best at 7f/1m: acts on soft and good to firm ground: has been blinkered (not in 2003): held up: to join L. Cumani. *M. Ciciarelli, Italy*

SAL'S GAL 5 b.m. Efisio 120 – Ann's Pearl (IRE) 81 (Cyrano de Bergerac 120) [2003 **59** 67: f6g⁶ f7g⁶ f6s⁶ f8.5g² p7g f7g³ 7g² f7s⁴ f7g⁵ Jun 19] small, workmanlike mare: modest performer: left N. Littmoden after eighth start: barely stayed 8.5f: acted on good to firm going, good to soft and fibresand: often wore cheekpieces/blinkers: dead. *D. G. Bridgwater*

SALT LAKE CITY (USA) 3 b. or br.c. Danzig (USA) – Good Example (FR) 110 **88** (Crystal Glitters (USA) 127) [2003 94p: 8d 7m Jun 18] smallish, good-bodied colt: sixth foal: half-brother to 3 winners, including 1¼m winner Heartwood (by Woodman) and 1999 US 2-y-o 6f minor stakes winner Mycatcandance (by Storm Cat): dam, French 1m (at 2 yrs) and 10.5f winner, later successful in USA: fairly useful form: won maiden at Leopardstown at 2 yrs: stiff tasks when behind in Irish 2000 Guineas at the Curragh and Jersey Stakes at Royal Ascot in 2003: should stay 1m: acts on heavy ground: sent to Australia. *A. P. O'Brien, Ireland*

SALTRIO 5 b.g. Slip Anchor 136 – Hills' Presidium (Presidium 124) [2003 109: 13d⁵ **104 ?** 18m Oct 18] tall, angular, attractive gelding: useful handicapper, lightly raced: seemingly creditable effort when fifth to Hasanpour in handicap at Hamilton: well held in Cesarewitch at Newmarket only other start in 2003: stays 15.5f: acts on soft and good to firm ground: none too consistent. *W. M. Brisbourne*

SALUTE (IRE) 4 b.g. Muhtarram (USA) 125 – Alasib 93 (Siberian Express (USA) **100** 125) [2003 99: 10m³ 10.4m² 10m⁶ 10f 12g⁶ 12m Sep 5] lengthy, quite attractive gelding: useful handicapper: good placed efforts at Kempton and York (1¼ lengths second to Researched) first 2 starts: well below form last 3 outings: best form at 9f/1¼m: acts on firm and soft going: effective visored or not: edgy sort (troublesome to post final appearance): sold 30,000 gns. *J. M. P. Eustace*

SALUT SAINT CLOUD 2 b.c. (Mar 4) Primo Dominie 121 – Tiriana (Common **62 d** Grounds 118) [2003 6m⁶ 6m⁴ 6m⁶ 7m 6f 6g⁶ 6m⁵ 6m 8.2m 7s f7g⁴ f8g⁵ Dec 8] 20,000F, 53,000Y: close-coupled colt: second foal: half-brother to 3-y-o Madamoiselle Jones: dam, third at 1m in France, half-sister to useful 1996 2-y-o 5f winner Head Over Heels: modest maiden: below form after third start: left G. Bravery after fifth: should stay 7f: acts on good to firm ground: tried blinkered/visored/in cheekpieces. *Miss V. Haigh*

SALVIATI (USA) 6 b.g. Lahib (USA) 129 – Mother Courage 67 (Busted 134) [2003 **100** 100: 5v 5g² 5f⁴ 6m 5f³ 5f 5m* 5d* 5m 6m 5d 6g⁴ 5f² 5g 5m⁵ Oct 25] sturdy gelding: useful handicapper: won at Catterick and Ascot in July, latter by ¾ length from Beyond The Clouds: heavily bandaged in front, creditable second to Baltic King at Ascot after: best at 5f: acts on firm and good to soft ground: sometimes slowly away: travels strongly, and usually held up. *J. M. Bradley*

SAMARA SOUND 2 b.c. (Apr 20) Savahra Sound 111 – Hosting (Thatching 131) – [2003 6m 6m 8s Oct 29] smallish, close-coupled colt: brother to fairly useful 7f/1m winner Samara Song: dam unraced: well held in maidens. *A. G. Newcombe*

SAMARQAND 4 b.f. Selkirk (USA) 129 – Sit Alkul (USA) 73 (Mr Prospector (USA)) **59 d** [2003 56: 10.2m f9.4g³ f8s f12s p12g f9.4g³ f8.5g⁶ f12g⁵ f11s³ Dec 13] leggy, quite good-topped filly: modest maiden at best: effective at 1¼m/1½m: acts on fibresand, firm and good to soft ground: tried in cheekpieces: none too consistent. *Julian Poulton*

SAMBA BEAT 4 ch.f. Efisio 120 – Special Beat 65 (Bustino 136) [2003 –, a66d: f8s – f11g⁵ f12s Jan 11] fair handicapper at best at 3 yrs: well below form in 2003: tried blinkered. *R. F. Marvin*

SAMBAMAN 3 b.g. Groom Dancer (USA) 128 – Guest of Anchor (Slip Anchor 136) **67** [2003 66: 12m 14.1m f12g² f12g* f12g² f16.2g* Jul 11] fair handicapper: won at Southwell (fortunate, beat eased Claptrap by short head) in June and Wolverhampton (by 8 lengths) in July: stays 2m: acts on fibresand and good to soft going: usually races prominently. *W. R. Muir*

SAMBUCAN DAZE (IRE) 3 b.c. Mujadil (USA) 119 – Non Dimenticar Me (IRE) **67 d** 63 (Don't Forget Me 127) [2003 –p: a8g² 7s⁵ 8m 8.1m f8s Oct 21] rather leggy colt: modest maiden: best effort when second in minor event at Cagnes-sur-Mer on reappearance: well below form back in Britain: tried blinkered. *J. D. Bethell*

SAMHARI (USA) 4 ch.c. Indian Ridge 123 – Cambara 97 (Dancing Brave (USA) 140) **113** [2003 107: 10f⁴ 10g⁴ 10.5m 10.4m⁴ Aug 20] strong, close-coupled colt: smart handicapper: returned to former trainer in 2003, good efforts when fourth to Nuit Sombre at Sandown second start and to Akshar at York on final one: stays 1¼m: acts on good to firm and heavy going: tongue tied at 3 yrs, visored in 2003: has started slowly/wandered: sent to UAE, joined A. Smith. *D. R. Loder*

SAMMIE DUROSE (IRE) 6 b.g. Forest Wind (USA) 111 – La Calera (Corvaro – (USA) 124) [2003 10.1m 12f⁵ 12.4m⁵ 13g 10.9m⁶ 12.1m⁵ 12f Jul 16] deep-girthed gelding: poor maiden: missed 2001/2: little form in 2003: tried in headgear: dead. *Ronald Thompson*

SAMMY'S SHUFFLE   8 b.g. Touch of Grey 90 – Cabinet Shuffle (Thatching 131)   **60 ?**
[2003 68: p10g⁶ p10g p10g⁵ Dec 20] modest handicapper: effective at 1¼m/easy 1½m: acts on firm going, soft and polytrack: usually blinkered: held up. *Jamie Poulton*

SAMMY'S SISTER   4 gr.f. Touch of Grey 90 – Northwold Star (USA) 71 (Monteverdi   **–**
129) [2003 –: p8g p7g Mar 5] well held in maidens: dead. *Jamie Poulton*

SAMOLIS (IRE)   2 b.g. (Apr 24) College Chapel 122 – Joyful Music (IRE) 62 (Accor-   **–**
dion) [2003 6.1m f6g 8d f8s Dec 13] second foal: dam Irish 9f winner: no sign of ability in maidens/nursery: tried blinkered. *R. Curtis*

SAM THE SORCERER   2 b.c. (Feb 24) Wizard King 122 – Awham (USA) (Lear   **–**
Fan (USA) 130) [2003 6m 7m f6g Oct 16] 2,500Y: quite good-topped colt: seventh foal: half-brother to 1997 2-y-o 7f winner Suggest (by Midyan): dam unraced: well beaten in maidens. *J. R. Norton*

SAMUEL CHARLES   5 b.g. Green Desert (USA) 127 – Hejraan (USA) 73 (Alydar   **64 ?**
(USA)) [2003 8.1m⁴ 6.9m⁴ 8m 8.1m 10f Sep 30] 2,000 3-y-o, 20,000 4-y-o: third foal: closely related to 6f winner Haajra (by Polish Precedent) and half-brother to useful 1½m winner Helvetius (by In The Wings): dam lightly raced: ran in bumpers/novice hurdles for Venetia Williams: modest maiden at best on Flat: stays 1m: tried visored/in cheek-pieces: has carried head awkwardly: sold 3,500 gns. *Mrs A. L. M. King*

SAN ANTONIO   3 b.g. Efisio 120 – Winnebago 63 (Kris 135) [2003 7g p7g 7m* 8g*   **90**
8m² 7g² 7d 8.1d 7g Oct 28] strong, well-made gelding: has a round action: second foal: brother to 4-y-o Pablo: dam, 13f winner, half-sister to very smart middle-distance colt Apache: fairly useful performer: much improved to win maiden at Doncaster and handicap at Pontefract in May: good second in handicaps at Newmarket and Goodwood, then well below form after: effective at 7f/1m: acts on good to firm ground: races prominently. *B. W. Hills*

SANBONAH (USA)   2 b.f. (Jan 23) King of Kings (IRE) 125 – Oh Nellie (USA) 113   **75**
(Tilt The Stars (CAN)) [2003 7m 6f 6m 7g* 8m² 8m⁵ Oct 21] big, good sort: first foal: dam 5.5f (at 2 yrs) to 1m (Grade 3 event) winner in USA and second in 1000 Guineas: fair performer: won nursery at Yarmouth in September: made most when good second at Newmarket, much better effort in similar events after: stays 1m: probably acts on firm going. *N. A. Callaghan*

SANDABAR   10 b.g. Green Desert (USA) 127 – Children's Corner (FR) 106 (Top Ville   **– §**
129) [2003 14.1m Oct 4] strong gelding: fair performer at best: well held on first run on Flat for 3 years: usually tongue tied: not one to trust. *G. A. Swinbank*

SAND AND STARS (IRE)   2 ch.f. (Mar 7) Dr Devious (IRE) 127 – Charm The Stars   **68**
(Roi Danzig (USA)) [2003 7m⁵ 8m⁴ 8d Oct 14] €16,000Y: sturdy filly: third foal: half-sister to 4-y-o Astrocharm: dam, ran twice, out of half-sister to Breeders' Cup Turf winner Northern Spur and high-class stayer Kneller: best effort in maidens (fair form) when fourth at Newmarket: should stay at least 1¼m: blinkered last 2 starts: hung left on debut: flashed tail next time. *M. H. Tompkins*

SANDENISTA   3 b.f. Diesis 133 – Santi Sana 80 (Formidable (USA) 125) [2003 8g⁴   **76**
8m* 8f³ p8g Nov 22] big filly: fifth foal: half-sister to 1998 2-y-o 7f winner Minnesota (by Danehill): dam, 7f winner, sister to very smart 7f/1m winner Efisio: fair performer: won maiden at Newcastle in August: stays 1¼m: acts on polytrack, raced only on good ground or firmer on turf: sold 14,000 gns. *L. M. Cumani*

SANDERSTEAD   4 b.g. So Factual (USA) 120 – Charnwood Queen 61 (Cadeaux   **–**
Genereux 131) [2003 44: f8.5g Jan 20] close-coupled gelding: poor maiden: well beaten only 4-y-o start: tried in blinkers/cheekpieces/tongue tie. *K. G. Wingrove*

SANDGATE CYGNET   3 ch.f. Fleetwood (IRE) 107 – Dance of The Swans (IRE)   **69**
69 (Try My Best (USA) 130) [2003 66: 6g⁵ 6d 5m 5m 5g² f5g⁶ f5g⁴ f5s* Dec 31] work-manlike filly: fair handicapper: won at Wolverhampton in December: effective at 5f/6f: acts on fibresand, heavy and good to firm ground: wore cheekpieces 3 of last 4 starts. *I. Semple*

SANDLES   5 b.g. Komaite (USA) – Miss Calculate 67 (Mummy's Game 120) [2003   **–**
66: 12.1g f12s⁶ Sep 6] tall, useful-looking gelding: fair handicapper at best: well held in 2003: has worn tongue strap. *Miss K. M. George*

SANDORRA   5 b.m. Emperor Jones (USA) 119 – Oribi 59 (Top Ville 129) [2003 –:   **54**
7d⁵ 9.9m 8g 6.9d Jul 30] big, leggy mare: modest maiden: barely stays 1¼m: acts on firm
and soft going. *M. Brittain*

SANDRONE (IRE)   3 b.f. In Command (IRE) 114 – Florinda (CAN) (Vice Regent   **–**
(CAN)) [2003 64, a73: 6m 10.2g p7g Nov 29] good-topped filly: fair maiden at best at 2
yrs: well beaten in 2003: tried blinkered/tongue tied. *P. M. Phelan*

SANDS ISLAND (IRE)   3 b.g. Spectrum (IRE) 126 – Dazzling Fire (IRE) 78 (Blue-   **–**
bird (USA) 125) [2003 9.3f 8g⁵ 10g Jul 8] IR 11,000Y: workmanlike gelding: sixth foal:
half-brother to 6f winner Mohawk (by Indian Ridge, later winner in Scandinavia) and
4-y-o Dazzling Rio: dam 1½m winner: well held in maidens. *G. A. Swinbank*

SANDY BAY (IRE)   4 b.g. Spectrum (IRE) 126 – Karinski (USA) (Palace Music   **–**
(USA) 129) [2003 69: 10d 7f 10m 9.9m 10g Jul 8] rather leggy, useful-looking gelding:
fair maiden at 3 yrs: well held in 2003: tried blinkered. *M. W. Easterby*

SANDY LADY (IRE)   4 b.f. Desert King (IRE) 129 – Mamma's Too 104 (Skyliner   **90**
117) [2003 91: 8.3g² 8.1g 7.6g² 7.1m⁶ 8m 8g 7m³ 7d 7g Oct 11] leggy, close-coupled
filly: fairly useful performer: stays 1m: acts on soft going, firm and polytrack: sold 15,000
gns. *R. Hannon*

SANGIOVESE   4 b.g. Piccolo 121 – Kaprisky (IRE) (Red Sunset 120) [2003 69: f8s³   **91**
p7g f8s* Dec 13] fairly useful handicapper: off 16 months before reappearance: much
improved when winning at Southwell in December by 13 lengths: best form around 1m:
raced only on all-weather and good/good to firm ground: tends to race freely. *H. Morrison*

SAN HERNANDO   3 b.g. Hernando (FR) 127 – Sandrella (IRE) (Darshaan 133) [2003   **79**
69p: 10.3m⁵ 11.5m² 12f* 11.9m⁶ 13.1m 16f⁶ 16g Oct 24] leggy, workmanlike gelding:
shows knee action: fair performer: won maiden at Doncaster in June: respectable efforts
in handicaps next 3 starts: effective at 1½m to 2m: acts on firm ground: wore visor/
cheekpieces last 2 outings: has been slowly away/carried head high: sold 25,000 gns.
E. A. L. Dunlop

SAN JUAN MATIA   3 br.f. Makbul 104 – The Lady Vanishes (Robin Des Pins (USA)   **§§**
119) [2003 65?: 14.1m 14.1d Jul 25] fair maiden: refused to enter stall intended third
2-y-o outing and served ban from racing afterwards: tailed off in 2003. *Dr J. R. J. Naylor*

SAN MARCO (IRE)   5 b.g. Brief Truce (USA) 126 – Nuit Des Temps (Sadler's Wells   **54**
(USA) 132) [2003 80, a74: p12g* f12s p13g 10.5m 12.1m⁴ 11.8m 16.2m⁴ Aug 14]
modest performer: won maiden at Lingfield in January: probably best short of 2m: acts
on firm going, good to soft and polytrack: tried blinkered, wore cheekpieces all 5-y-o
starts. *Mrs P. Sly*

SAN REMY (IRE)   2 b.g. (Mar 2) Danehill (USA) 126 – Gazette (Zafonic (USA) 130)   **71**
[2003 6m 6m* 7m³ Aug 8] €180,000Y: leggy, useful-looking gelding: first foal: dam,
placed up to 11f in France, half-sister to smart French miler Battle Dore out of very smart
French 1m/1¼m performer Nashmeel: fair form: landed odds in 7-runner maiden at
Catterick in July: sweating profusely/on toes, creditable third in nursery at Newmarket,
hanging left: stays 7f: sold 10,000 gns, gelded and sent to Italy. *J. Noseda*

SANTA CATALINA (IRE)   4 br.f. Tagula (IRE) 116 – Bui-Doi (IRE) 58 (Dance of   **–**
Life (USA)) [2003 55: p7g 10m 10.1g⁶ 10m f8g³ Dec 15] modest maiden: left J. Matthias   **a53**
after fourth start: stays 1m: acts on all-weather, little form on turf since 2 yrs: has worn
cheekpieces/visor/tongue tie. *Miss Gay Kelleway*

SANTA CATERINA (IRE)   2 b.f. (Mar 8) Daylami (IRE) 138 – Samara (IRE) 108   **64 p**
(Polish Patriot (USA) 128) [2003 7m 8m 8m Oct 24] angular, quite good-topped filly:
third foal: half-sister to 3-y-o Santa Sophia: dam, miler, half-sister to smart middle-
distance stayer Lille Hammer: modest form in maidens: not at all knocked about second
start: likely to do better in handicaps at 1¼m+. *J. L. Dunlop*

SANTANDO   3 b.c. Hernando (FR) 127 – Santarem (USA) 71 (El Gran Senor (USA)   **107**
136) [2003 p8g⁶ p10g⁴ f12s² p12g* 10.3g* 10m³ 12.3m* 11m² 16.2f 14.8m⁴ 12d²
13.3m⁵ 11.9m 14.6g⁶ Sep 13] 5,500Y: tall, useful-looking colt: sixth foal: half-brother to
fairly useful 1¼m/1½m winner Imani (by Danehill): dam, lightly-raced staying maiden,
half-sister to smart stayer Al Maheb: useful performer: won maiden at Lingfield and
handicaps at Doncaster in March and at Chester in May: good 1¾ lengths second to No
Refuge in Tote Gold Trophy (Handicap) at Goodwood eleventh start: sweating, ran well
when 12¼ lengths sixth to Brian Boru in St Leger at Doncaster final one: should stay
2m (lacklustre effort when tried): acts on all-weather, good to firm and good to soft
going: wore cheekpieces/visor 4 of last 5 starts: often soon off bridle: held up: tough.
C. E. Brittain

SANTA SOPHIA (IRE) 3 gr.f. Linamix (FR) 127 – Samara (IRE) 108 (Polish Patriot **106** (USA) 128) [2003 79: 10g* 11.8m* 12g 11.9g⁵ 10m Oct 16] leggy, useful-looking filly: good walker: useful performer: won maiden at Windsor in April and listed race at Lingfield (beat Midsummer by 1¼ lengths) in May: good 5 lengths seventh to Casual Look in Oaks at Epsom next time: disappointing in Lancashire Oaks at Haydock and listed race at Newmarket (raced freely) last 2 starts: stayed 1½m: raced only on good/good to firm going: often raced prominently: stud. *J. L. Dunlop*

SANTIBURI LAD (IRE) 6 b.g. Namaqualand (USA) – Suggia (Alzao (USA) 117) **64** [2003 66: 7.9m 10m* 9f³ 9.9m 8.5m⁴ 9f⁶ 10.4m Sep 3] leggy gelding: modest performer: won claimer at Redcar in June: stays 1¼m: acts on fibresand and any turf going. *N. Tinkler*

SANTISIMA TRINIDAD (IRE) 5 b.m. Definite Article 121 – Brazilia 63 (For- **94 §** zando 122) [2003 92: 7g 7.6m² 7m 7f 7.1g⁶ 8f⁴ 7d⁵ 7.6m* 7.6m³ 7d⁶ 7.2m 7m 7f Oct 9] lengthy, useful-looking mare: fairly useful handicapper: won at Chester in August: best around 7f: acts on any going: sometimes slowly away: unreliable. *T. D. Easterby*

SAPHILA (IRE) 3 b.f. Sadler's Wells (USA) 132 – Fanny Cerrito (USA) (Gulch **72** (USA)) [2003 –p: 8.2m 10.5v⁶ 10m 11.9m² 11.6m 14.1m³ 14.1f 14.1m⁵ Sep 2] small, leggy filly: fair maiden handicapper: effective at 1½m/1¾m: acts on good to firm ground: often races prominently. *L. M. Cumani*

SAPONI (IRE) 5 b.g. Indian Ridge 123 – Taking Liberties (IRE) 57 (Royal Academy **89** (USA) 130) [2003 58p: f7g³ f8g* f8s* 10.3m⁶ May 5] fairly useful performer: won maiden in January and handicap in February, both at Southwell: stayed 1m: acted on fibresand, suffered pastern injury only run on turf: dead. *W. J. Haggas*

SAPPERDOT 6 b.g. St Ninian 104 – Beau Gem (Kalaglow 132) [2003 –: 12.4m 10.1m **–** f14.8g Jun 6] well held in maidens/claimer. *F. Watson*

SAPPHIRE ALLISE 3 b.f. Royal Applause 124 – Paradise News 51 (Sure Blade **–** (USA) 130) [2003 55: p6g f5g Jan 18] modest maiden: well held in 2003: blinkered final start. *D. K. Ivory*

SARATOGA SPLENDOUR (USA) 2 b.f. (Mar 23) Diesis 133 – Saratoga One **–** (USA) (Saratoga Six (USA)) [2003 7g 7s Nov 3] 26,000Y: quite good-topped filly: fifth foal: half-sister to 3 winners in USA/Brazil: dam, won in USA, daughter of US Grade 1 9f winner Inca Queen: well held in maidens. *Jedd O'Keeffe*

SAREE 2 b.f. (Feb 18) Barathea (IRE) 127 – Shouk 94 (Shirley Heights 130) [2003 **95** 7m* 8f² 9f⁶ Oct 26] 17,000Y: second foal: half-sister to 3-y-o Grand Wizard: dam, 10.5f winner, closely related to smart performer up to 14.6f Puce: won maiden at Lingfield in July: left M. Quinlan and useful form when head second to Pink Champagne in Grade 3 at Woodbine: respectable sixth in non-graded stakes at Belmont: should stay at least 1¼m. *M. E. Casse, Canada*

SARENA PRIDE (IRE) 6 b.m. Persian Bold 123 – Avidal Park 68 (Horage 124) **–** [2003 68, a73: f9.4g Jan 17] leggy mare: fair handicapper at 5 yrs: well held only start on Flat in 2003: usually blinkered: tends to be slowly away/race freely. *R. J. O'Sullivan*

SARENA SPECIAL 6 b.g. Lucky Guest 109 – Lariston Gale 81 (Pas de Seul 133) **–** [2003 54: f8.5s Feb 28] angular gelding: fair at best: well held only outing in 2003: usually blinkered earlier in career. *J. D. Frost*

SARGENTS DREAM 3 b.f. Regal Embers (IRE) – Dance Lady (Cosmonaut) [2003 **–** p6g f12s p7g Dec 17] first foal: dam last on only outing: no form. *J. A. Gilbert*

SARIBA 4 b.f. Persian Bold 123 – En Vacances (IRE) 90 (Old Vic 136) [2003 –: p12g **51** 13.1g⁴ 18m⁴ 17.2f* p16g Sep 3] modest handicapper: won at Bath in July: stays 2¼m: acts on firm ground: races up with pace. *A. Charlton*

SARIN 5 b.g. Deploy 131 – Secretilla (USA) 61 (Secreto (USA) 128) [2003 88: 10g **88** 11.9m 12m⁴ Sep 15] good-bodied gelding: fairly useful handicapper: off 9 months before reappearance: ran creditably final start: will stay 1¾m: acts on soft and good to firm ground: usually held up. *L. M. Cumani*

SARISTAR 2 b.f. (Mar 8) Starborough 126 – Sari 83 (Faustus (USA) 118) [2003 5.1g⁵ **82** 5.1m* 6.1g f5s* 5m Oct 18] close-coupled, useful-looking filly: first foal: dam 7f winner (including at 2 yrs): fairly useful performer: won maiden at Chepstow in August and minor event at Southwell (beat Shank On Fourteen by length) in October: well below form final start: should stay 6f: acts on fibresand and good to firm going: seemed unsuited by course at Chester on third outing. *P. F. I. Cole*

SARN 4 b.g. Atraf 116 – Covent Garden Girl 67 (Sizzling Melody 117) [2003 59, a–: **63** 8g⁵ 8.3d² 7.2g 7.6m 7.2g* 7.2g* 9.1m⁴ 10.3d 8.3d 8m f8g Dec 8] smallish gelding: **a–** modest performer: won seller and claimer at Ayr in July/August: effective at 7f to easy 9f: acts on any going, well beaten on fibresand: none too consistent. *A. Bailey*

SAROS (IRE) 2 b. or br.c. (Apr 20) Desert Sun 120 – Fight Right (FR) (Crystal Glitters **51** (USA) 127) [2003 5f 7.5m 8.5m⁶ 8m f8s⁶ Oct 7] 18,000Y: smallish, workmanlike colt: half-brother to several winners, including 2001 2-y-o 6f winner Brigadier Jones (by Emperor Jones) and 3-y-o Trouble At Bay: dam French 2-y-o 1m winner: modest maiden: form only on third start: needs to settle to stay beyond 8.5f: sometimes carries head awkwardly/edges right. *B. Smart*

SARRAAF (IRE) 7 ch.g. Perugino (USA) 84 – Blue Vista (IRE) (Pennine Walk 120) **82 §** [2003 89§, a78§: f8g⁴ f7s³ f7g* 8g 8g 7.1m⁴ 8d 8g³ 8.3g⁴ 9.1f³ 7.9m 9f* 7.9m 9.2m³ 5.9d **a78 §** 7.1m 8.1m³ 9.2g² 7.5m 8.1f 8m³ 8.1d* 10m 10.4f⁴ 7m² Oct 18] smallish, strong gelding: fair performer: won minor event at Wolverhampton (left P. Johnson to rejoin former stable) in February, claimer at Musselburgh in June and handicap at Haydock in September: effective at 7f to 1¼m: acts on any going and fibresand: tried blinkered/visored: effective ridden prominently or held up: usually finds little, and is unreliable. *J. Semple*

SARREGO 4 b.g. Makbul 104 – Simmie's Special 75 (Precocious 126) [2003 78: 6m **66** 5s⁶ 6m Jun 5] close-coupled gelding: fair handicapper, lightly raced: below form in 2003: best at 5f: acted on good to firm going: dead. *R. Hollinshead*

SARTORIAL (IRE) 7 b.g. Elbio 125 – Madam Slaney 92 (Prince Tenderfoot (USA) **105 d** 126) [2003 114: 6g⁴ 6m 6d 6g Oct 24] big, strong gelding: reportedly difficult to train: just useful form when fourth to Somnus in minor event at Haydock: stays 6f: acts on fibresand, firm and good to soft going: visored (well held) once: free-going sort: none too consistent: sold only 4,000 gns. *P. J. Makin*

SASHAY 5 b.m. Bishop of Cashel 122 – St James's Antigua (IRE) 79 (Law Society **55** (USA) 130) [2003 62, a67: f16.2g⁴ p16g¹ p16g f16s p16g p16g⁴ 17.2f 17.2f⁴ 16.2f f16.2g⁶ **a72** f14.8s* f16.2g⁴ f16.2s³ f14.8s⁴ Dec 31] close-coupled mare: fair performer on all-weather, modest on turf: won handicap at Wolverhampton in January and (having left C. Cox after ninth outing) minor event there in September: stays 17f: acts on all-weather and good to firm ground: usually waited with. *R. Hollinshead*

SATELCOM (USA) 3 b.c. Alhaarth (IRE) 126 – Tommelise (USA) (Dayjur (USA) **87** 137) [2003 75p: p8g* p7g² p7g³ p8g⁴ 6m³ 8m² 8g p7g Oct 3] rather leggy, unfurnished colt: fairly useful handicapper: won at Lingfield in January: creditable efforts next 5 starts: stayed 1m: acted on polytrack and good to firm going: was sometimes slowly away: dead. *Noel T. Chance*

SATSU (IRE) 2 ch.f. (Apr 6) Shinko Forest (IRE) – Cap And Gown (IRE) 81 (Royal **53** Academy (USA) 130) [2003 6m 7m 6g⁵ Jul 22] €14,000Y: well-grown, useful-looking filly: second foal: half-sister to sprint winner abroad by Charnwood Forest: dam, 1m winner, half-sister to smart performer up to 1½m Papering: modest form in maidens: shapes as if will prove best at 5f/6f. *J. G. Given*

SATTAM 4 b.g. Danehill (USA) 126 – Mayaasa (USA) 70 (Lyphard (USA) 132) [2003 **86** –: 8.5m² 7m⁴ 8m⁵ 9g⁵ 7.1m³ 7m² 7m* 7m Oct 17] smallish, stocky gelding: fairly useful handicapper, lightly raced: won at Salisbury in September: effective at 7f to 8.5f: acts on good to firm going: blinkered/visored last 3 starts: tends to hang/has raced freely. *M. P. Tregoning*

SATURNALIA 3 ch.f. Cadeaux Genereux 131 – Treasure Trove (USA) 62 (The **–** Minstrel (CAN) 135) [2003 7m 7m⁵ 7d 6g 7f⁶ Jun 16] 40,000F, 29,000Y: strong, work-manlike filly: fifth foal: sister to smart German 6f/7f winner Toylsome and half-sister to 5-y-o Zhitomir: dam, maiden who stayed 7f, half-sister to useful 5f (Queen Mary Stakes) to 1m (US Grade 2 event) winner Dance Parade: little form: tried blinkered. *B. J. Meehan*

SATURN (IRE) 3 b.g. Marju (IRE) 127 – Delphinus (Soviet Star (USA) 128) [2003 **112** 111p: 8m⁴ 8g⁵ 8d⁴ 7m 10d² 5m Dec 20] good-topped gelding: smart performer: good efforts when 2¾ lengths fifth to Refuse To Bend in 2000 Guineas at Newmarket second start and short-headed by Kalabar in Prix Guillaume d'Ornano at Deauville (made most) fifth one: respectable fourth to Indian Haven in Irish 2000 Guineas at the Curragh in between: reportedly sold, and left M. Bell before final outing: races freely, but stays 1¼m: unraced on extremes of going: bandaged in front on reappearance: moved poorly to post/found little fourth start. *I. W. Allan, Hong Kong*

SATYR 5 b.g. Pursuit of Love 124 – Sardonic 105 (Kris 135) [2003 73: 8.2g 8g⁶ 8.1m⁵ **72** 8m 10m 10m 10m* 10m² 10.1m² Aug 13] quite good-topped gelding: fair handicapper:

won amateur event at Newmarket in July: stays easy 11f: acts on polytrack, firm and good to soft going: has awkward head carriage: usually held up: sold 14,000 gns. *W. J. Musson*

SAUCY   2 b.f. (Feb 10) Muhtarram (USA) 125 – So Saucy 59 (Teenoso (USA) 135) – [2003 6m Jul 21] sixth foal: half-sister to 3 winners, including 7-y-o Most-Saucy and 4-y-o Tidal: dam 1¼m and 17f winner: 33/1, eleventh of 15 in maiden at Windsor, not knocked about. *B. J. Meehan*

SAUCY PICKLE   2 b.f. (Feb 18) Makbul 104 – Bewails (IRE) 53 (Caerleon (USA) – 132) [2003 p7g Dec 17] sixth foal: dam, ran twice, granddaughter of Yorkshire Oaks and Park Hill winner Attica Meli: 66/1, well held in minor event at Lingfield. *Miss Z. C. Davison*

SAUCY SHIP (IRE)   2 b.c. (Apr 28) Blue Ocean (USA) 87 – Cyrano's Song (IRE) – (Cyrano de Bergerac 120) [2003 6m 6m Sep 9] IR 1,000F, €1,000Y, 10,000 2-y-o: first foal: dam ran once in Ireland: little encouragement in maidens at Newmarket and Lingfield (slowly away). *D. J. Daly*

SAVANNAH BAY   4 ch.g. In The Wings 128 – High Savannah 77 (Rousillon (USA)   **113** 133) [2003 109: 16.2g^2 20m^6 16g^3 18d^5 16m^5 Oct 18] good-topped gelding: smart performer: best efforts when neck second to Alcazar in Sagaro Stakes at Ascot (originally awarded race, placings reinstated on appeal), 7½ lengths sixth to Mr Dinos in Gold Cup at Royal Ascot and 5 lengths third to Persian Punch in Goodwood Cup: lacklustre efforts last 2 starts: stays 2½m: acts on firm going: tried blinkered/tongue tied: has worn crossed noseband: carries head awkwardly: usually waited with. *B. J. Meehan*

Mr Joe L. Allbritton's "Savannah Bay"

SAVANNAH RIVER (IRE) 2 b.f. (Apr 5) Desert King (IRE) 129 – Hayward 81 **47**
(Indian Ridge 123) [2003 6m 7.5m 6g Jul 3] 5,000Y: good-topped filly: second foal: dam
Irish 9.6f winner: poor form in maidens/claimer: will stay at least 1m. *C. W. Thornton*

SAVANNAH SUE 2 b.f. (Feb 18) Emarati (USA) 74 – Bidweaya (USA) 45 (Lear Fan **–**
(USA) 130) [2003 5d May 28] fifth foal: half-sister to 5-y-o Red River Rebel: dam, 1m
winner at 5/6 yrs, half-sister to Gimcrack winner Chilly Billy: tailed off in Ripon maiden.
J. R. Norton

SAVERNAKE BRAVE (IRE) 2 b.g. (Apr 14) Charnwood Forest (IRE) 125 – **55 §**
Jordinda (IRE) 64 (Indian Ridge 123) [2003 5.7m 6m 5.3f² 5m⁶ 5m⁶ 5.7f⁵ 7f f7g Dec
16] 2,500Y: compact gelding: second foal: half-brother to fairly useful Irish 5f winner
(including at 2 yrs) Fly Haia (by Flying Spur): dam Irish maiden who stayed 1m: modest
maiden: stays 6f: acts on firm going: often slowly away, and reluctant to race final outing.
K. R. Burke

SAVILE'S DELIGHT (IRE) 4 b.g. Cadeaux Genereux 131 – Across The Ice (USA) **72**
(General Holme (USA) 128) [2003 94: 6f 5m 6g 6.1m⁴ 6f* 7g 7m² 7g 7.1m³ f6s 6.1m² **a62**
f7g f6g p7g⁴ Dec 17] 80,000Y: fifth living foal: half-brother to 3 winners, including
smart Irish 5f/6f winner Timote (by Indian Ridge) and French 1¼m winner Glissando (by
In The Wings): dam French 6.5f winner: fairly useful at best at 2/3 yrs for D. Weld in
Ireland: just fair in 2003: won seller at Catterick (left M. Easterby) in July: effective at 6f/
7f: acts on polytrack, firm and soft ground: tried blinkered/tongue tied/in cheekpieces:
none too consistent. *R. Brotherton*

SAVIOURS SPIRIT 2 ch.g. (Apr 1) Komaite (USA) – Greenway Lady (Prince Daniel **70**
(USA)) [2003 6d 6m 6g⁵ p6g³ Dec 29] 32,000Y: second foal: brother to 5-y-o Nearly A
Fool: dam, lightly raced on Flat, won selling hurdle: fair maiden: third at Lingfield:
should stay at least 7f: acts on polytrack, probably on good to firm and good to soft going.
T. G. Mills

SAVITSKY (USA) 2 ch.c. (Mar 23) Stravinsky (USA) 133 – Odori (USA) (The **83**
Minstrel (CAN) 135) [2003 5g³ 5g² 6m⁵ 5d⁵ 6d* 6m³ 5.1g⁴ 6d⁴ Sep 26] 150,000Y: good-
topped colt: fifth foal: half-brother to 3 winners, including fairly useful 2-y-o winners
Georgette (at 6f in 1998, by Geiger Counter) and Iyavaya (at 5f in 1999, by Valiant
Nature): dam lightly raced in USA: fairly useful performer: won maiden at Leicester in
July: creditable efforts in nurseries on next and final starts: likely to prove best at 5f/6f:
acts on good to firm and good to soft ground: blinkered fifth to seventh outings:
sometimes slowly away/finds little. *N. A. Callaghan*

SAWAH 3 br.g. Linamix (FR) 127 – Tarhhib 95 (Danzig (USA)) [2003 p10g f8g f8g **–**
f6g⁶ Dec 26] 9,000 3-y-o: fourth foal: dam, 7f winner, half-sister to high-class French
1¼m/1½m performer Dancehall: poor maiden: form only at 6f. *D. Shaw*

SAWWAAH (IRE) 6 ch.g. Marju (IRE) 127 – Just A Mirage 76 (Green Desert (USA) **93**
127) [2003 91: 8g⁶ 10g⁴ 8.3g³ 8m⁶ 9.2m* 8g 8g² 10m 8.5m⁵ 10m 8f* 8d 8d³ 9g Aug 2]
big, useful-looking gelding: fairly useful performer: won claimer at Hamilton in April
and handicap at Goodwood (by neck from Finished Article) in June: best around 1m: acts
on firm and soft ground: tends to hang/find little: usually held up. *D. Nicholls*

SAXE-COBURG (IRE) 6 b.g. Warning 136 – Saxon Maid 108 (Sadler's Wells (USA) **66**
132) [2003 74d: p10g f9.4g f7s³ f7g f8.5g⁵ 8.1m 11.6m* 11.6m 11.6g² 10d² 12.6m⁶ 10m³
12m⁵ 11.7f⁴ f12g Oct 20] modest performer: trained by Mrs L. Stubbs on reappearance: won selling handicap at Windsor in July: stays 1½m: acts on firm and good to soft
going, dirt and all-weather: tried blinkered/visored: free-going sort: often slowly away.
G. A. Ham

SAYADAW (FR) 3 b.c. Darshaan 133 – Vingt Et Une (FR) (Sadler's Wells (USA) **103**
132) [2003 12g² 11.8m* Jun 2] good-bodied, imposing colt: third foal: brother to useful
1½m winner Year Two Thousand: dam, French 1¼m winner, sister to very smart 1m to
1½m performer Johann Quatz and half-sister to Hernando: useful form: favourite but
still green, confirmed debut promise when winning maiden at Leicester in June by 1½
lengths from Clever Clogs, hanging right when leading 2f out: will stay at least 1¾m.
H. R. A. Cecil

SAY WHAT YOU SEE (IRE) 3 b.c. Charnwood Forest (IRE) 125 – Aster Aweke **77**
(IRE) 87 (Alzao (USA) 117) [2003 58: 9m 8.3d 10.2m* 10.4f⁴ 9m⁶ 10m³ 10m² 8.9m 10g
Oct 6] workmanlike colt: fair performer: won maiden at Bath in May: stays 10.4f: acts on
firm going: visored last 7 outings: often makes running. *J. W. Hills*

SCALADO (USA) 4 ch.c. Mister Baileys 123 – Lady di Pomadora (USA) (Danzig **67**
Connection (USA)) [2003 81: p10g p8g 12s 10g 10g 16m⁶ Aug 30] smallish, strong colt:

fairly useful at 3 yrs: just fair form at best in 2003 (ran at Lingfield first 2 outings): should stay at least 1¼m: acts on good to firm going, good to soft and polytrack: tried blinkered. *R. J. Osborne, Ireland*

SCALLOWAY (IRE) 3 b.g. Marju (IRE) 127 – Zany (Junius (USA) 124) [2003 68: 10.2f* 11.9m⁴ 10.9f⁴ Jul 19] strong, compact gelding: fair handicapper: won at Bath in June: stays easy 1¼m: acts on firm ground: effective blinkered or not. *J. A. Osborne* **74**

SCARLET EMPRESS 2 b.f. (Apr 20) Second Empire (IRE) 124 – Daltak (Night Shift (USA)) [2003 6m 6m⁴ 7m 6g 6.1m 6m⁶ 6.5m p6g* p6g⁴ p7g Nov 12] 19,000Y: strong filly: third foal: dam unraced close relation to smart sprinter Ya Malak out of half-sister to Cadeaux Genereux: fair performer: won nursery at Lingfield in October: possibly amiss final start: should stay 7f: acts on polytrack: blinkered last 4 outings. *R. Hannon* **79**

SCARLET FANTASY 3 b.g. Rudimentary (USA) 118 – Katie Scarlett 70 (Lochnager 132) [2003 –: p8g p6g 6g 5.2m f6g 6d⁵ 8m 5.7f Oct 12] modest maiden: should stay 7f: acts on good to soft going: tried blinkered. *E. A. Wheeler* **52**

SCARLET SECRET 3 ch.f. Piccolo 121 – Rise 'n Shine 67 (Night Shift (USA)) [2003 53: p7g p7g p6g* p6g³ p6g³ p5g 6g³ f6s⁵ 5m³ f6g⁴ 6m f6s* f7s⁵ p6g 11f 8g⁴ 6s⁴ a7g* Nov 23] fair performer: won seller at Lingfield in January, handicap at Wolverhampton in April, claimer at Wolverhampton in June and (after sold 10,500 gns from C. Cyzer following fifteenth start) minor event at Gran Canaria in November: effective at 6f/7f: acts on all-weather/sand and good to firm ground: blinkered (below form) once: usually held up. *F. Miranda, Spain* **66**

SCARLETT BREEZE 2 b.f. (Mar 8) Shinko Forest (IRE) – La Suquet 72 (Puissance 110) [2003 5m⁴ 5m 6m p6g⁶ 5.1d⁵ Nov 6] 20,000Y: leggy filly: fourth foal: half-sister to 2002 2-y-o 6f winner Cotton Kid (later won in Norway, by Lake Coniston) and 5f to 7f (latter seller at 2 yrs) winner Castle Sempill (by Presidium): dam 5f winner: modest maiden: stays easy 6f: acts on polytrack, good to firm and good to soft going. *J. W. Hills* **55**

SCARLETTI (GER) 6 ch.g. Master Willie 129 – Solidago (USA) (Decies 129) [2003 –: 12g³ 12m⁵ 13.1m 8.3d⁶ 10d Oct 13] angular gelding: fair handicapper: left Jonjo O'Neill after second start: stays 1½m: acts on soft ground: tried visored/tongue tied. *I. Semple* **72**

SCARLETT ROSE 2 b.f. (Feb 27) Royal Applause 124 – Billie Blue 63 (Ballad Rock 122) [2003 6m³ 7g⁶ p7g Nov 29] neat filly: half-sister to several winners, notably smart 5f and 7f (including at 2 yrs) winner Tumbleweed Ridge (by Indian Ridge): dam second at 7f only start: fair form in maidens at Newmarket first 2 starts, third to Mahmoom: well held in minor event at Lingfield: needs to settle to stay beyond 7f. *Dr J. D. Scargill* **72**

SCARPIA 3 ch.g. Rudimentary (USA) 118 – Floria Tosca § (Petong 126) [2003 55: 5g 5.1m 5m 8.1g Sep 11] modest maiden at 2 yrs: no form in 2003, starting very slowly on reappearance. *E. L. James* **–**

SCARRABUS (IRE) 2 b.c. (Mar 1) Charnwood Forest (IRE) 125 – Errazuriz (IRE) 94 (Classic Music (USA)) [2003 8m⁵ 7g⁶ 7.1m Sep 22] IR 8,200F, 23,000Y: angular, good-topped colt: third foal: half-brother to Italian 7.5f (at 2 yrs) to 1¼m winner Erina (by Mukaddamah) and 3-y-o Evangelist: dam Irish 2-y-o 1m winner: seemingly fair form in slowly-run maiden/minor event first 2 starts: stays 1m. *B. G. Powell* **66 ?**

SCARROTTOO 5 ch.g. Zilzal (USA) 137 – Bold And Beautiful 105 (Bold Lad (IRE) 133) [2003 81: 7m 6g 8g 8m 6m⁶ 7f⁶ 7m⁴ 7f⁵ 7m³ 7m⁴ 7m Aug 28] strong gelding: modest handicapper: stays 7f: acts on firm ground and fibresand: tried tongue tied/in cheekpieces: usually waited with. *S. C. Williams* **64**

SCARTO 2 b.g. (Apr 25) First Trump 118 – Lawn Order 51 (Efisio 120) [2003 5f 7m 5m Oct 7] third foal: dam 1½m winner: no form, including in seller: tried in cheekpieces. *G. M. Moore* **–**

SCARY NIGHT (IRE) 3 b.g. Night Shift (USA) – Private Bucks (USA) (Spend A Buck (USA)) [2003 67: f6g* f5s² f6g² f5s³ 6d f6s Jun 13] tall, good-topped gelding: fair handicapper: won at Southwell in January: effective at 5f to easy 7f: acts on fibresand, modest at best on turf: wore cheekpieces in 2003: often races prominently. *J. Balding* **75**

SCENIC FLIGHT 2 b.f. (Apr 30) Distant View (USA) 126 – Bird of Time (IRE) 75 (Persian Bold 123) [2003 5.1f 6m⁴ 7m 6f 7m Sep 9] 22,000Y: fifth foal: half-sister to winner in USA by Conte di Savoya: dam, 7f/1m winner, half-sister to smart Italian 1¼m/1½m winner Redipuglia out of half-sister to Champagne Stakes winner Unblest: modest maiden: went wrong way after second start: should stay at least 7f: sold 2,500 gns. *Mrs A. J. Perrett* **57 d**

SCENIC LADY (IRE) 7 b.m. Scenic 128 – Tu Tu Maori (IRE) (Kings Lake (USA) **68**
133) [2003 63: 9.7m 11.5m* 11.9m 11.5g 10.1g 10m⁵ 12m⁶ 9f⁵ 10f⁵ 11.9f² Jul 21]
smallish mare: fair handicapper: won at Yarmouth in April: effective at 9f to 1½m: acts
on firm and soft going: blinkered twice as 4-y-o: tried in cheekpieces: sometimes slowly
away: none too reliable. *L. A. Dace*

SCENT AHEAD 4 b.g. Foxhound (USA) 103 – Sonseri 95 (Prince Tenderfoot **44**
(USA) 126) [2003 –: f5g f5g⁵ Jun 6] poor maiden: best form at 5f: acts on fibresand and
firm going: tried blinkered/tongue tied/in cheekpieces. *Mrs G. S. Rees*

SCENTED AIR 6 b.m. Lion Cavern (USA) 117 – Jungle Rose 90 (Shirley Heights **65**
130) [2003 58: f9.4g* f9.4g* f9.4s⁶ f9.4g⁵ f9.4g 10.9m* 9d 10.3m 11.8g May 26] leggy, **a57**
plain mare: fair handicapper on turf, modest on all-weather: won at Wolverhampton (2)
in January and, having left P. Hiatt after fifth start, at Warwick in April: stays 11f: acts on
fibresand, firm and soft going: visored once: sometimes slowly away/looks difficult ride.
J. D. Czerpak

SCENT OF VICTORY (IRE) 4 b. or br.g. Polish Precedent (USA) 131 – Dayanata **92**
(Shirley Heights 130) [2003 94: 12g 10m⁶ 10m³ 12d³ 10.3m² 10f 12m² Oct 17] big,
lengthy gelding: fairly useful performer: possibly better around 1¼m than 1½m nowadays: acts on firm going, good to soft and all-weather: sold 23,000 gns. *P. F. I. Cole*

SCHAPIRO (USA) 2 b.g. (Feb 17) Nureyev (USA) 131 – Konvincha (USA) (Cor- **77**
morant (USA)) [2003 7m 7m⁴ 7.2d⁵ Oct 13] $110,000Y: strong, good sort: fifth foal:
closely related to 5-y-o Askham: dam, won up to 9f in USA, half-sister to US Grade 2 7f
winner Lottsa Talc: fair form in maidens: fourth at Leicester: will probably stay 1m:
below form on good to soft going. *J. H. M. Gosden*

SCHINKEN OTTO (IRE) 2 ch.c. (Apr 2) Shinko Forest (IRE) – Athassel Rose (IRE) **–**
(Reasonable (FR) 119) [2003 6g 5m⁶ 6m Aug 30] €5,000Y, 17,000 2-y-o: strong colt:
fourth living foal: dam Italian 7f winner, half-sister to Prix Robert Papin winner Maelstrom Lake: signs of only a little ability in maidens. *J. M. Jefferson*

SCHOLARSHIP (IRE) 2 b.g. (Mar 6) College Chapel 122 – Royal Bracelet (IRE) **85 §**
(Night Shift (USA)) [2003 6g³ 6g³ f6g⁴ 6g 6.1d⁴ 8.1d⁵ 7g Oct 24] €12,500Y: compact
gelding: first foal: dam unraced out of half-sister to dam of smart 6f/7f performer Danehill Dancer: fairly useful maiden: best effort on debut: will prove best at 6f/7f: blinkered
3 of last 4 starts: ungenuine. *B. J. Meehan*

SCHOOL DAYS 4 b.f. Slip Anchor 136 – Cradle of Love (USA) 87 (Roberto (USA) **–**
131) [2003 76: f9.4s Mar 31] angular filly: fair handicapper: pulled up early (bled) only
4-y-o start: visored (stirrup leather broke) once. *P. A. Blockley*

SCHOONER (GER) 3 b.g. Slip Anchor 136 – Sweet Enough 79 (Caerleon (USA) **74 p**
132) [2003 p12g⁶ p12g⁵ p12g³ Nov 29] half-brother to several winners, including useful
German 5f (at 2 yrs) to 7.5f winner Stolzing (by Pivotal): dam 1½m to 17f winner: best
effort in maidens at Lingfield (fair form) when eye-catching third to Sea Holly, finishing
strongly from poor position: should stay at least 1¾m: raced only on polytrack: slowly
away first 2 outings: capable of better still. *Lady Herries*

SCIENCE ACADEMY (USA) 2 ch.f. (Feb 3) Silver Hawk (USA) 123 – Dance **62**
Design (IRE) 119 (Sadler's Wells (USA) 132) [2003 7g⁵ p7g p6g Nov 18] smallish filly:
second foal: half-sister to 3-y-o Sindy: dam Irish 7f (at 2 yrs) to 1½m (Irish Oaks) winner:
modest form in maidens: best effort on debut: should be suited by 1¼m/1½m: broke out
of stall and withdrawn third outing. *P. F. I. Cole*

SCIENTIST 2 ch.c. (Feb 3) Dr Fong (USA) 128 – Green Bonnet (IRE) (Green Desert **85 p**
(USA) 127) [2003 6g⁶ 6m⁵ Jun 12] 135,000Y: well-made colt: second foal: half-brother
to 4-y-o Prince's Passion: dam, French maiden, sister to useful 7f/1m performer Mauri
Moon: better effort in maidens (fairly useful form) when fifth to Gwaihir at Newbury,
taking time to settle but going on strongly, not knocked about: bred to stay 1m: should
progress. *J. H. M. Gosden*

SCIPPIT 4 ch.g. Unfuwain (USA) 131 – Scierpan (USA) 86 (Sharpen Up 127) [2003 **–**
–: f6g 6m May 12] close-coupled gelding: maiden: little form since 2 yrs: tried visored.
F. Watson

SCONCED (USA) 8 ch.g. Affirmed (USA) – Quaff (USA) 115 (Raise A Cup (USA)) **51 §**
[2003 –, a52: f16s f14g 16.1d* f14.8s 17.1m 16d* 14.1s 14m 16d 14.1f⁴ 19.1m³ 16m⁵
16.2m Jul 19] leggy gelding: modest performer: won handicap at Newcastle in March and
claimer at Musselburgh in May: stays 19f: acts on fibresand and any turf going: usually
visored/blinkered: tends to run in snatches: unreliable. *M. J. Polglase*

SCOOBY DOOBY DO   2 b.f. (May 18) Atraf 116 – Redgrave Design 77 (Nebbiolo   **62**
125) [2003 6m⁶ 5g Oct 28] 4,000Y: lengthy filly: closely related to 2 winners by Clantime, including useful 5f (including at 2 yrs) to 1m winner Saint Express, and half-sister
to several winners: dam 2-y-o 5f winner: better effort in maidens (modest form) when
sixth at Newcastle: looked very wayward next time. *R. M. Whitaker*

SCORCH   2 b.c. (Apr 23) Mark of Esteem (IRE) 137 – Red Hot Dancer (USA) (Seattle   **62**
Dancer (USA) 119) [2003 6g⁵ 5m⁶ Jul 18] 14,000F, 18,000Y: fifth foal: half-brother to
winner in USA by Technology: dam, placed in USA, half-sister to dam of Poule d'Essai
des Pouliches winner Ta Rib: better effort in maidens (modest form) when fifth at Salisbury: raced freely at Hamilton: sold 7,200 gns. *M. R. Channon*

SCORCHING   2 b.c. (Feb 19) Efisio 120 – Catch The Flame (USA) (Storm Bird (CAN)   **68**
134) [2003 5.1m⁴ 5m⁴ 6g 6m 7f Oct 12] 16,000F, €50,000Y: compact colt: third foal:
half-brother to 3-y-o Spark Up and winner in Turkey by Bishop of Cashel: dam unraced:
fair maiden: below form in nurseries last 2 starts: stays 6f: acts on good to firm going:
tongue tied after debut: blinkered penultimate start. *R. F. Johnson Houghton*

SCORCHIO (IRE)   2 b.c. (May 5) Desert Sun 120 – White-Wash 94 (Final Straw 127)   **45**
[2003 7.1f⁶ 7.5m 7f6g f8s 6m⁶ Oct 20] IR 4,600F, €7,000Y, 10,500 2-y-o: seventh foal:
half-brother to several winners, including 2m winner Maknaas (by Wolfhound) and Irish
6f (at 2 yrs) and 1m winner Soranna (by Compton Place), both fairly useful: dam, best at
1¼m, half-sister to smart but temperamental 1¼m/1½m winner Torchon: poor maiden:
seems to stay 7.5f. *M. F. Harris*

SCOTCH N' DRY   2 ch.g. (Apr 11) Piccolo 121 – Magical Dancer (IRE) 53 (Magical   **87**
Wonder (USA) 125) [2003 5.1m³ 6g³ 7g² 7g* 6f⁴ 6g² 6g² 7m⁶ 6.1m³ 6m 6m 6m⁵ Oct 21]
leggy, close-coupled gelding: second foal: dam, 1m winner, half-sister to smart sprinter
Don't Worry Me: fairly useful performer: won nursery at Salisbury in July: creditable
efforts in frame in minor events/nurseries after: effective at 6f/7f: acts on firm going:
often races prominently: sold 10,000 gns. *M. R. Channon*

SCOTISH LAW (IRE)   5 ch.g. Case Law 113 – Scotia Rose (Tap On Wood 130)   **62**
[2003 65: 10f² 9.9m³ Aug 13] close-coupled gelding: modest handicapper: visored,
creditable efforts in 2003: effective at 1m/1¼m: acts on firm going, possibly not on soft.
P. R. Chamings

SCOTLAND THE BRAVE   3 ch.f. Zilzal (USA) 137 – Hunters of Brora (IRE) 102   **75**
(Sharpo 132) [2003 7m* 7m⁴ 7g 8m⁵ 8.1m Sep 17] leggy, lengthy filly: first foal: dam 7f
to 8.5f winner: fair performer: won maiden at Redcar in May: ran creditably penultimate
start: raced only at 7f/1m on good/good to firm ground. *J. D. Bethell*

SCOTS GUARD (IRE)   2 b.g. (Mar 30) Selkirk (USA) 129 – Island Race 93 (Com-   **–**
mon Grounds 118) [2003 7s Nov 3] neat gelding: second foal: half-brother to smart
German 7.5f (at 2 yrs) to 8.5f winner Soldier Hollow (by In The Wings): dam 6f winner:
14/1 and green, well beaten in maiden at Redcar, slowly away. *J. G. Given*

SCOTTISH EXILE (IRE)   2 b.f. (Mar 28) Ashkalani (IRE) 128 – Royal Jade 82 (Last   **63**
Tycoon 131) [2003 5d⁴ 5m 6m⁴ 5m⁴ 6m f5g² p5g³ f5g* Dec 15] 13,000Y: strong, angular   **a73**
filly: fourth foal: sister to 4-y-o Million Percent and half-sister to 3-y-o Mullion and
5-y-o Xaloc Bay: dam, 7f winner, half-sister to smart sprinter Averti: fair on all-weather,
modest on turf: visored, won maiden at Southwell by 5 lengths, soon leading: should
prove best at 5f/6f: acts on all-weather, best turf effort on good to soft going. *K. R. Burke*

SCOTTISH RIVER (USA)   4 b.g. Thunder Gulch (USA) 129 – Overbrook 95 (Storm   **74**
Cat (USA)) [2003 99: a9f a9f a7f⁶ a6f 7.1g 8.9m⁵ 10m⁵ p8g 11.9m f8.5g p8g p10g³ Dec
20] strong gelding: useful at 2/3 yrs: gelded and reportedly had soft palate operation
before reappearance: just fair form in 2003: left K. McLaughlin in UAE after fourth start:
stays 1¼m: acts on soft and good to firm going, below form on dirt/all-weather: tried
visored: often races up with pace: very slowly away final outing. *M. D. I. Usher*

SCOTTISH SONG   10 b.g. Niniski (USA) 125 – Miss Saint-Cloud 102 (Nonoalco   **–**
(USA) 131) [2003 16.1d Mar 24] no form on Flat after 1999: dead. *Mrs M. Reveley*

SCOTT'S VIEW   4 b.g. Selkirk (USA) 129 – Milly of The Vally 93 (Caerleon (USA)   **116**
132) [2003 121: 12m⁴ 14m² 14.1f² 10.9m³ 12f⁴ 12d² 12g 16g² 12d* Nov 8] small, rather
leggy gelding: smart performer: off 10 months before reappearance: runner-up in listed
races at Goodwood, the Curragh (beaten 2½ lengths by L'Ancresse) and Musselburgh
(went down by ¾ length to Misternando) on second/sixth and eighth starts: won similar
event at Doncaster in November by 3½ lengths from The Whistling Teal: probably best at

CIU Serlby Stakes, Doncaster—Scott's View dictates to win from The Whistling Teal and Gamut (rail), the last-named providing the retiring Pat Eddery with his final ride in Britain

11f to 1¾m: acts on polytrack, firm and good to soft going: sweated first 2 starts in 2003: has been early to post: sometimes idles: tough. *M. Johnston*

SCOTTY'S FUTURE (IRE)   5 b.g. Namaqualand (USA) – Persian Empress (IRE)   **94**
51 (Persian Bold 123) [2003 105: 8g 7g 8g 10.4m⁵ 10m 12f 10f 8m Sep 20] close-coupled, quite good-topped gelding: just a fairly useful handicapper in 2003: probably best at 7f (given a test)/1m: acts on firm and soft going: edgy sort: slowly away/looked reluctant final 4-y-o outing: held up: joined D. Loder. *D. Nicholls*

SCRAGGLES   2 b.f. (Mar 24) Young Ern 120 – Georgia Stephens (USA) 64 (The Minstrel (CAN) 135) [2003 5m 5m Apr 24] 500Y, resold 1,500Y: smallish, leggy filly: half-sister to 3 winners, including French 9f (at 2 yrs)/10.5f winner Sir Hamelin (by Hernando) and UAE 7f winner Heartbreak House (by Shavian): dam maiden: little sign of ability in maiden/claimer. *J. J. Quinn*

SCRAMBLE (USA)   5 ch.g. Gulch (USA) – Syzygy (ARG) (Big Play (USA)) [2003   **60**
56, a61: f8g⁶ 8m 7g 7.9m 10.1m 8g² 8.5m⁶ 7.9m⁶ 8.5m⁴ 8m⁴ 8g* f8g³ f8g⁴ f7s⁶
f8.5g⁴ Dec 26] long-backed gelding: modest handicapper: won at Newcastle in October: effective at 1m to 1¼m: acts on firm going and fibresand: tried blinkered: often tongue tied/wears cheekpieces: races prominently. *B. Ellison*

SCRAPPY DOO   3 b.g. Petong 126 – Maziere 45 (Mazilier (USA) 107) [2003 45§:   **– §**
p10g 10m f9.4g 7m f8g Nov 25] temperamental maiden: tried blinkered/visored. *Miss V. Haigh*

SCRAPS   3 b.g. Wolfhound (USA) 126 – Jamarj 113 (Tyrnavos 129) [2003 62: 7.9g 6d   **61**
7f³ 7f³ 7.1f³ 7f² 8s 8m 7.5m⁵ Aug 24] quite good-topped gelding: poor mover: modest maiden: stays 7.5f: best on good ground or firmer (acts on firm). *T. D. Easterby*

SCREAMING SHAMAL (USA)   2 gr.f. (Jan 16) Tabasco Cat (USA) 126 – Carefree   **– p**
Cheetah (USA) 66 (Trempolino (USA) 135) [2003 7m 7m Sep 22] $72,000Y: rangy filly: first foal: dam, maiden (ran 3 times at 1¼m), sister to very smart 6f to 1m performer Arkadian Hero: signs of ability in maidens at Salisbury and Kempton: sent to UAE, joined D. Watson: will probably do better. *R. Hannon*

SCREENPLAY   2 ch.g. (Jan 26) In The Wings 128 – Erudite 114 (Generous (IRE) 139)   **76**
[2003 7m 8m⁴ 7m⁴ Oct 24] smallish, sturdy gelding: has a rather round action: first foal: dam, French 11f/1½m winner who stayed 15.5f, half-sister to dam of 3-y-o Trade Fair and granddaughter of 1000 Guineas and Champion Stakes winner Cairn Rouge: fair form in maidens: fourth to Art Trader at Newmarket and Alekhine at Doncaster (swished tail paddock): will be suited by 1¼m/1½m. *Sir Michael Stoute*

SCRIPTORIUM   2 b.c. (May 29) Singspiel (IRE) 133 – Annie Albright (USA) (Ver-   **– p**
batim (USA)) [2003 7s Oct 29] half-brother to useful 5f (at 2 yrs) and 6f winner Shamanic (by Fairy King) and French 11.5f winner Belmontee (by Belmez): dam, Irish sprint maiden, half-sister to smart performer up to 1m Crystal Gazing: 25/1, seventh of 13 in maiden at Yarmouth, slowly away and never dangerous: likely to do better. *L. M. Cumani*

SCURRA   4 b.g. Spectrum (IRE) 126 – Tamnia 106 (Green Desert (USA) 127) [2003   **52 §**
72d: 9m 6m 10.9m⁴ 10.1m 9.2g³ 11g² f8g Nov 24] leggy gelding: modest maiden: stays 11f: acts on good to firm and heavy ground, below form on fibresand: unreliable. *A. C. Whillans*

908

SCYTHIAN   3 b.g. Selkirk (USA) 129 – Sarmatia (USA) (Danzig (USA)) [2003 81:   **72**
6m 6m⁵ 6m⁶ 6d 6g 7.1m 6g Oct 13] fair performer: effective at 5f/6f: acts on good to firm
ground: sold 7,000 gns. *R. Hannon*

SEA COVE   3 b.f. Terimon 124 – Regal Pursuit (IRE) 61 (Roi Danzig (USA)) [2003   **–**
12.4g⁶ 9.9m⁵ 10m 10m Sep 25] 1,500Y: workmanlike filly: first foal: dam, maiden who
stayed 13f, successful over hurdles: no sign of ability. *J. M. Jefferson*

SEA FERN   2 b.g. (Apr 16) Petong 126 – Duxyana (IRE) (Cyrano de Bergerac 120)   **55**
[2003 5d 5d 6g Jul 31] 6,200Y, 16,000 2-y-o: small, good-bodied gelding: seventh foal:
brother to fairly useful 6f winner Vista Alegre and half-brother to 4-y-o Kelsey Rose:
dam unraced: modest form in maidens: will prove best at 5f/6f. *D. Eddy*

SEAFIELD TOWERS   3 ch.g. Compton Place 125 – Midnight Spell 79 (Night Shift   **82**
(USA)) [2003 72: 8m 5m 6d 6d 5m² 6g 5f³ 5f² 6g² 6g* 6d³ 5m* 6.1g⁶ 6m Sep 19] good-
bodied gelding: fairly useful handicapper: won at Ripon in July and York (beat Ikan a
neck) in August: effective at 5f/6f: acts on firm and good to soft ground: usually wears
cheekpieces: front runner: consistent. *Miss L. A. Perratt*

SEAGOLD   2 b.f. (Apr 7) Shahrastani (USA) 135 – Raeleen (Jupiter Island 126) [2003   **–**
7s Oct 29] first foal: dam ungenuine maiden: 25/1, slowly away when well held in maiden
at Yarmouth. *C. F. Wall*

SEA HOLLY (IRE)   3 b.g. Barathea (IRE) 127 – Mountain Holly 69 (Shirley Heights   **82**
130) [2003 –p: 10g² 10g³ 11m 11m⁶ 10m f12g² p12g* p13g⁴ f12g Dec 19] big gelding:
has a round action: fairly useful performer: won maiden at Lingfield in November: stays
13f: acts on all-weather, best turf efforts on good ground: has started slowly: sometimes
looks none too keen. *G. G. Margarson*

SEAHORSE BOY (IRE)   6 b.g. Petardia 113 – Million At Dawn (IRE) 63 (Fayruz   **–**
116) [2003 –: f8g f12g Jun 27] no longer of any account: tried visored/blinkered.
Mrs A. C. Tate

SEA JADE (IRE)   4 b.f. Mujadil (USA) 119 – Mirabiliary (USA) 74 (Crow (FR) 134)   **51**
[2003 56: 9m 7d 7g² 7m⁶ 8m⁴ 7f⁶ 7d Sep 20] workmanlike filly: modest maiden handicapper: effective at 7f to 8.5f: acts on firm and soft going: sometimes flashes tail: often
races prominently. *J. W. Payne*

SEALILY (IRE)   2 gr.f. (Mar 13) Docksider (USA) 124 – Hariyana (IRE) 66 (Kahyasi   **67**
130) [2003 6f 6d³ 6g⁵ Jul 31] €14,000Y: first foal: dam lightly-raced half-sister to smart
Irish/US performer up to 9f Harghar: fair form in maidens: third at Thirsk: will probably
stay 7f: acts on good to soft going. *Mrs A. Duffield*

SEAL OF OFFICE   4 ch.g. Mark of Esteem (IRE) 137 – Minskip (USA) 64 (The   **82 ?**
Minstrel (CAN) 135) [2003 94²: p8g p8g⁶ p10g³ 10m⁶ 8.1g 10m⁶ 9.9f 10.1g Sep 11]
workmanlike gelding: fairly useful performer: stays easy 1¼m: acts on polytrack and
good to firm going: free-going sort: none too consistent. *J. Cullinan*

SEAN'S MEMORY (USA)   3 b.g. Theatrical 128 – Memories (IRE) 95 (Don't Forget   **–**
Me 127) [2003 f12s Dec 19] 1,500 3-y-o: third foal: dam Irish 6f (at 2 yrs)/9f winner and
US Grade 2 1½m winner, half-sister to smart 1¼m/1½m performers Garuda and Danish
Rhapsody: 20/1, always behind in maiden at Southwell. *Mrs C. A. Dunnett*

SEA OF HAPPINESS   3 b.g. Pivotal 124 – Ella Lamees 61 (Statoblest 120) [2003   **33**
9.7m 8m⁴ 8m 13.8d⁴ Sep 20] 12,000F, 70,000Y: first foal: dam, 6f winner, half-sister to
smart performer who stayed 11f Francesco Guardi: poor form: left M. Channon 10,000
gns after second start. *C. Grant*

SEA PLUME   4 b.f. Slip Anchor 136 – Fine Quill (Unfuwain (USA) 131) [2003 70:   **80**
10g⁴ 13.3m³ 14g 16g² p13g p16g f14g Dec 9] leggy filly: fairly useful maiden handi-   **a64**
capper on turf, modest on all-weather: stays 2m: acts on good to firm ground (probably
on soft), best all-weather run on polytrack: sometimes edgy/flashes tail: has hung left/
carried head high: often races prominently: inconsistent. *Lady Herries*

SEARCH MISSION (USA)   2 b.f. (Feb 28) Red Ransom (USA) – Skimble (USA)   **82**
116 (Lyphard (USA) 132) [2003 6m⁵ 7m* 7g² Sep 1] well-made filly: has scope: sixth
foal: half-sister to very smart 8.5f to 1¼m winner in Britain/US Skimming (by Nureyev)
and fairly useful 1¼m winner Cloud Hopping (by Mr Prospector): dam, 6f (at 2 yrs) and
10.4f winner (later graded stakes winner around 1m in USA), sister to dam of 1000
Guineas winner Wince: made most when winning maiden at Folkestone in August: best
effort (fairly useful form) when second of 6 in nursery there, flicking tail and headed
close home: will probably stay 1m. *Mrs A. J. Perrett*

SEA RIDGE   3 b.f. Slip Anchor 136 – Beveridge (USA) 86 (Spectacular Bid (USA))   **65 §**
[2003 9.7g² 12m⁵ 12m⁶ Aug 15] closely related to 3 winners, including useful stayer
Stelvio and useful performer up to 1½m Safa (both by Shirley Heights), and half-sister
to 2 winners: dam 2-y-o 7f winner: fair maiden: looked wayward at Catterick final start,
pulling hard, trying to run out then finding little: may prove better around 1¼m than
further: one to treat with caution. *J. L. Dunlop*

SEA SKATE (USA)   3 b.f. Gilded Time (USA) – Sea of Serenity (USA) (Conquistador   **80**
Cielo (USA)) [2003 f8.5g⁴ p7g f9.4g⁴ 8g⁴ 7f⁵ 8.5s² 8.5d² 9.6f² 10m⁴ 10m² 11f³ 10m 10s
Sep 19] €1,500 2-y-o: third foal: half-sister to fairly useful 2001 Irish 2-y-o 7f winner
Serene Princess (by Louis Quatorze): dam 1m/8.5f winner in USA: fairly useful maiden:
trained by John A. Quinn (showing just modest form on all-weather in Britain) first 3
starts: mostly good efforts after: stays 11f: acts on firm and soft going. *R. Donohoe,
Ireland*

SEA STORM (IRE)   5 b.g. Dolphin Street (FR) 125 – Prime Interest (IRE) (Kings   **96**
Lake (USA) 133) [2003 94, a102: p8g 7g 7.1m³ 7m⁵ 7.2f 7.2g* 7.1g⁴ 7f 7.1f* 7.6m⁶ 7m 7d   **a?**
8m² 7.2m 7m⁵ Oct 1] big, strong gelding: useful performer: won handicap at Newcastle
in June and minor event at Warwick in July: better form at 7f than 1m: acts on polytrack
and firm ground: often wears cheekpieces: blinkered (forced strong pace and below form)
final start: has been early to post: usually races prominently: sometimes wanders: joined
D. MacLeod. *R. F. Fisher*

SEA SWALLOW   4 b.f. Sea Raven (IRE) 75 – Denby Wood (Lord Bud 121) [2003   **–**
10.1m Oct 12] compact filly: fourth foal: dam unraced: 100/1, well beaten in maiden at
Newcastle. *J. S. Wainwright*

SEA TERN   3 b.f. Emarati (USA) 74 – Great Tern 59 (Simply Great (FR) 122) [2003 –:   **–**
7g 6m Aug 28] leggy filly: no sign of ability. *N. M. Babbage*

SEA THE WORLD (IRE)   3 b.g. Inzar (USA) 112 – Annie's Travels (IRE) (Mac's
Imp (USA) 116) [2003 71: f5s⁴ f5s⁵ 5d f5g 6d⁴ 8d p6g f5g³ f5g f5g f5g Dec 16] tall, leggy   **a71**
gelding: fair performer: won maiden at Southwell in February: well held in handicaps
after: should stay 6f: form only on fibresand: tried visored: tends to hang. *D. Shaw*

SEATTLE EXPRESS   3 b.g. Salse (USA) 128 – Seattle Ribbon (USA) 70 (Seattle   **79 d**
Dancer (USA) 119) [2003 p7g* 8.3g 8.1m⁵ 11g 9.9f⁵ 8m⁴ 10m³ 10.1m* 11.5g³ 10m⁴ 10m
Sep 29] small, quite attractive gelding: first foal: dam, maiden who probably stayed 1¼m,
sister to Racing Post Trophy winner Seattle Rhyme: fair performer: won maiden at Lingfield in March and claimer at Yarmouth (claimed from D. Elsworth £10,000) in August:
stays 1¼m: acts on polytrack, raced only on good going or firmer on turf: blinkered/
visored last 5 starts: ungenuine: sold 3,200 gns. *M. A. Buckley*

SEATTLE PRINCE (USA)   5 gr.g. Cozzene (USA) – Chicken Slew (USA) (Seattle   **58**
Slew (USA)) [2003 63: 14.1g 12m 16m⁴ Apr 22] strong, quite attractive gelding: modest
handicapper: stays 2m: acts on firm and soft going: tried visored/blinkered at 3 yrs: has
carried head awkwardly/drifted left. *S. Gollings*

SEA VICTOR   11 b.g. Slip Anchor 136 – Victoriana (USA) (Storm Bird (CAN) 134)   **–**
[2003 14.1s May 17] sturdy, good-topped gelding: off over 2 years before tailed off only
11-y-o start: tried visored. *John A. Harris*

SEA YA MAITE   9 b.g. Komaite (USA) – Marina Plata (Julio Mariner 127) [2003 –,   **?**
a58§: f8.5g f8.5g f8s f8.5g f9.4s⁶ f9.4g f8g 10.1m³ f11g 8f 8.5m Aug 13] tall, rangy
gelding: poor mover: modest at best nowadays: appeared to run to 60 on eighth outing but
well held otherwise in 2003: stays 1¼m: acts on fibresand and firm going: tried blinkered,
usually tongue tied: sometimes slowly away. *S. R. Bowring*

SEBRING   4 ch.g. Hurricane Sky (AUS) – Carmenoura (IRE) (Carmelite House (USA)   **75 d**
118) [2003 68: 8m 10.2m⁶ 11.9m* 10.1m 8.5d 12g 9f 12g⁶ 12g Oct 7] close-coupled
gelding: fair handicapper: won at Brighton in July: left G. Butler after fourth start: below
form subsequently: stays 1½m: acts on polytrack and firm going: blinkered (below best)
fourth to sixth 3-y-o starts: usually tongue tied. *A. J. Martin, Ireland*

SECLUDED   3 b.g. Compton Place 125 – Secret Dance (Sadler's Wells (USA) 132)   **72 p**
[2003 f8.5s⁴ f9.4s³ p12g⁵ 8m⁵ Sep 12] 25,000F, 66,000Y: sixth foal: half-brother to 6f to
10.5f winner Silver Secret (by Absalom) and a winner in Greece by Mind Games: dam
unraced half-sister to July Stakes winner Royal Harmony: fair form: improved with each
run, never-nearer fifth to Ice Cracker in handicap at Goodwood final start: stays 1½m:
raced only on all-weather/good to firm ground: very slowly away and carried head high
on debut: should do better still at 4 yrs. *A. C. Stewart*

SECOND GENERATION (IRE)   6 ch.g. Cadeaux Genereux 131 – Title Roll (IRE)   –
107 (Tate Gallery (USA) 117) [2003 f6g Dec 9] poor maiden at 3 yrs, well held both
outings since: tried blinkered. *R. J. Hodges*

SECOND MINISTER   4 ch.g. Lion Cavern (USA) 117 – Crime of Passion 115   –
(Dragonara Palace (USA) 115) [2003 66d: f5g 5g 6m f6g³ p6g² Dec 2] big, leggy gelding: **a72**
fair maiden: left T. D. Barron after third start: effective at 5f/6f: acts on polytrack and
good to firm ground: blinkered last 2 starts: often races prominently. *D. Flood*

SECOND OF MAY   3 ch.f. Lion Cavern (USA) 117 – Giant Nipper (Nashwan (USA)   **72**
135) [2003 8.3m⁶ 8.1m⁶ 8.1m² 8m* 8m⁵ p7g⁴ f8g² Nov 19] 10,000Y: sturdy filly: second
foal: half-sister to 5-y-o Sharpinch: dam ran once: fair performer: won minor event at
Brighton in October: will stay 1¼m: acts on all-weather, raced only on good to firm
ground on turf: carried head awkwardly and flashed tail fifth start. *P. R. Chamings*

SECOND PAIGE (IRE)   6 b.g. Nicolotte 118 – My First Paige (IRE) 53 (Runnett 125)   **56**
[2003 66d: p16g⁸ f16.2g⁶ p16g 14.4d⁴ 17.1m⁵ 14.1m Apr 21] tall gelding: modest
performer: won seller at Lingfield in January: stays 2m: acts on polytrack, good to
firm and good to soft ground: usually blinkered: sometimes finds little: fair hurdler.
N. A. Graham

SECOND TO GO (USA)   3 b. or br.f. El Prado (IRE) 119 – Sharp Tradition (USA)   **81**
65 (Sharpen Up 127) [2003 75: p10g 7m* 7g 7m³ 7m⁵ Oct 24] smallish, useful-looking
filly: fairly useful handicapper: won at Kempton in June: good third at Goodwood: should
stay 1m: raced only on good going or firmer on turf: none too consistent. *E. A. L. Dunlop*

SECOND VENTURE (IRE)   5 b.g. Petardia 113 – Hilton Gateway (Hello Gorgeous   **55 d**
(USA) 128) [2003 66, a52: f7s 6d 7g⁴ 8g⁵ 7.2g 5.9d 7.2g 8m 8.2m⁵ 7m f8.5g⁴ Nov 17]   **a41**
good-topped gelding: modest performer: stays 8.5f: acts on soft and good to firm going:
sometimes visored/wears cheekpieces: none too consistent: sold 3,000 gns. *J. R. Weymes*

SECOND WARNING   2 ch.c. (Mar 1) Piccolo 121 – St Helena (Monsanto (FR) 121)   **59**
[2003 6m 6d p7g Oct 15] 15,000Y: tall, workmanlike colt: half-brother to several
winners, including 5f (including at 2 yrs)/6f winner Swino (by Forzando), fairly useful at
best, became untrustworthy: dam Italian 5f and 6.5f winner: modest form in maidens:
trained by D. Cosgrove first 2 starts: not sure to stay beyond 7f. *D. J. Daly*

SECOND WIND   8 ch.g. Kris 135 – Rimosa's Pet 109 (Petingo 135) [2003 67§, a60§:   **§§**
7.1m 6m 7.1d 6d⁶ 8.3d 8g 9.2g 6f 7.1f 6g 10.9m Sep 20] lengthy, workmanlike gelding:
fair performer in 2002, well held in 2003: tongue tied: sometimes refuses to race: one to
avoid. *D. A. Nolan*

SECRETARY GENERAL (IRE)   2 b.c. (Feb 28) Fasliyev (USA) 120 – Katie   **88 p**
McLain (USA) 85 (Java Gold (USA)) [2003 7m² 7g⁴ 7m* Sep 3] €70,000Y: big, good-
topped colt: has a quick action: fifth foal: half-brother to 3 winners, including Irish 7f
winner Fair McLain (by Fairy King) and fairly useful Irish 9.5f to 1¾m winner Catherina
(by Sadler's Wells): dam Irish 7f and 1¼m winner: fairly useful form in maidens: landed
odds in 8-runner event at York by 1¼ lengths from West Country, always prominent and
quickening on 2f out: will stay 1m: open to progress. *P. F. I. Cole*

SECRET BLOOM   2 b.g. (Apr 28) My Best Valentine 122 – Rose Elegance 83 (Bairn   –
(USA) 126) [2003 7m f8s f7g⁵ f7g Nov 24] 3,500Y: sturdy gelding: half-brother to 2000
2-y-o 6f winner Myhat (by Factual): dam 1m/1¼m winner: little sign of ability, including
in sellers: twice slowly away. *J. R. Norton*

SECRET CHARM (IRE)   2 b.f. (Apr 18) Green Desert (USA) 127 – Viz (USA)   **105 p**
(Kris S (USA)) [2003 7m* 7g* Oct 25] strong, useful-looking filly: fourth living foal:
half-sister to smart 2000 2-y-o 7f winner Relish The Thought (by Sadler's Wells), also
third in Oaks, and fairly useful 1½m winner Valiant Effort (by In The Wings): dam,
US 2-y-o 1m winner and third in Grade 1 1m event, out of half-sister to Breeders' Cup
Juvenile winner Brocco: won maiden at Newmarket and listed event at Newbury (by 1¾
lengths from Hathrah in 12-runner race, quickening well to lead over 1f out), both in
October: should stay 1m: likely to make a smart 3-y-o. *B. W. Hills*

SECRET CONQUEST   6 b.m. Secret Appeal – Mohibbah (USA) 86 (Conquistador   **47**
Cielo (USA)) [2003 56: f8s 8m 7m⁴ 8m⁵ 8m 8g 7m 7d Jul 26] strong mare: poor handicapper nowadays: left G. M. Moore after fifth start: barely stays 1m: has won on good to
soft going, best efforts on good or firmer: tried in headgear/tongue tie. *A. Crook*

SECRET FLAME   2 b.f. (Apr 22) Machiavellian (USA) 123 – Secret Obsession (USA)   **74 p**
89 (Secretariat (USA)) [2003 7g⁵ Nov 1] leggy, rather unfurnished filly: sister to winner
around 1m (including at 2 yrs) Secret Agent, closely related to 2 winners, including 1995
2-y-o 6f winner Obsessive (by Seeking The Gold), and half-sister to several winners,

including 1m/9f winner It's A Secret (by Polish Precedent), all useful: dam, 1¼m winner, half-sister to smart 1½m performer Beyton: 12/1, 3½ lengths fifth of 17 to Si Si Amiga in maiden at Newmarket, travelling strongly behind leaders long way: will stay at least 1m: sure to improve. *W. J. Haggas*

SECRET FORMULA 3 b.f. So Factual (USA) 120 – Ancient Secret (Warrshan (USA) 117) [2003 85: 6g³ 7g² 8f⁴ 7m 7f 8f³ 9g Oct 25] tall filly: fairly useful handicapper: placed at Salisbury, Newmarket and Goodwood: stays 1m (raced freely at 9f): acts on firm going, showed promise on good to soft. *S. Kirk*   **92**

SECRET JEWEL (FR) 3 b.f. Hernando (FR) 127 – Opalette 75 (Sharrood (USA) 124) [2003 51p: 10g Apr 7] better effort in maidens (fair form) when seventh at Windsor only 3-y-o start, again slowly away: should be suited by 1½m+. *Lady Herries*   **66**

SECRET PLACE 2 ch.g. (Mar 17) Compton Place 125 – Secret Circle (Magic Ring (IRE) 115) [2003 p8g p8g² Dec 10] 31,000F, 62,000Y: second foal: dam unraced half-sister to high-class 1m/1¼m performer Bijou d'Inde: clearly better effort in maidens at Lingfield (fair form) when 3 lengths second of 12 to Jake The Snake: not sure to stay much beyond 1m: should progress. *E. A. L. Dunlop*   **71 p**

SECRET PRIDE 3 b.f. Green Desert (USA) 127 – Talented 112 (Bustino 136) [2003 89: 5f 6m 6.1g³ 6g⁵ 7m 6s Nov 3] leggy filly: fairly useful handicapper: creditable efforts at Chester and Kempton third/fourth starts: stays 6f: acts on good to firm ground: sold 50,000 gns. *B. W. Hills*   **85**

SECRET SPELL 3 b.f. Wizard King 122 – Clonavon Girl (IRE) 44 (Be My Guest (USA) 126) [2003 8.1m 9.9d May 20] 500Y: lengthy filly: second foal: half-sister to 2000 2-y-o 5f winner London Eye (by Distinctly North): dam maiden who stayed 7.5f: well beaten in maidens: dead. *J. W. Unett*   **–**

SECRET SPOOF 4 b.g. Mind Games 121 – Silver Blessings (Statoblest 120) [2003 83: 6m 6m 5d 5s 5f 5f 6m 7m⁶ 6.9m Jul 18] sturdy gelding: fairly useful handicapper at 3 yrs: only fair form in 2003: stays 6f: acts on soft and good to firm going: blinkered last 5 starts: has been very slowly away: sold 1,200 gns. *T. D. Easterby*   **70**

SECRET VISION (USA) 2 ch.f. (May 10) Distant View (USA) 126 – Secret Angel (Halo (USA)) [2003 7m² Aug 28] seventh living foal: half-sister to US 5f (at 2 yrs) to 8.5f winner Satisfy (by Known Fact) and French 9f winner Far Post (by Defensive Play): dam, 1m winner in USA, out of US Grade 1 9f/1¼m winner Ack's Secret: 8/1, head second of 13 to Mango Mischief in maiden at Salisbury, leading over 1f out until close home: will probably stay 1m: should improve and win a race or 2. *Mrs A. J. Perrett*   **83 p**

SEEJAY 3 b.f. Bahamian Bounty 116 – Grand Splendour 79 (Shirley Heights 130) [2003 8.1m p12g p10g Nov 18] second foal: sister to 4-y-o Smith N Allan Oils: dam 1¼m winner at 4 yrs: well held in maidens. *M. A. Allen*   **–**

SEEKING ANSWERS (IRE) 2 b.c. (Mar 23) Shinko Forest (IRE) – Lady At War (Warning 136) [2003 6m³ 6m* 6g 8m⁶ 8.3g 7g⁶ Oct 24] 36,000Y: good-bodied colt: second foal: half-brother to 4-y-o Sir Northerndancer: dam unraced sister to useful performer up to 2m Weet For Me: fairly useful performer: won maiden at Haydock in August: respectable efforts after only when sixth in nurseries: probably stays 1m: acts on good to firm going: sometimes slowly away/races lazily: sold 23,000 gns, sent to USA. *A. C. Stewart*   **80**

SEEKING A WAY (USA) 2 b.f. (Apr 15) Seeking The Gold (USA) – Seattle Way (USA) (Seattle Slew (USA)) [2003 8.2f² 7m* Oct 17] big, good-bodied filly: has a quick action: sister to a winner in USA, closely related to fairly useful Irish 2002 2-y-o 1m winner Russia (by Kingmambo) and half-sister to 3 winners, including useful French 1999 2-y-o 7.5f winner Seattle Bay (by Opening Verse): dam, ran 3 times in US, out of US Grade 1 winner up to 1½m Waya: fair form: on toes and green, 6 lengths second to Deraasaat in maiden at Nottingham: beat Bubbling Fun 14 lengths in 2-runner Newmarket Challenge Whip: should stay 1¼m: likely to progress. *J. H. M. Gosden*   **78 p**

SEEKING THE SUN (IRE) 4 b. or br.g. Petardia 113 – Femme Savante 89 (Glenstal (USA) 118) [2003 77: 8.3g 8g 7m⁵ 7m 7g⁵ 7g Jul 28] useful-looking gelding: fair handicapper: pulled up lame final start: stays 7f: best efforts on good/good to soft going. *C. F. Wall*   **74**

SEEL OF APPROVAL 4 br.g. Polar Falcon (USA) 126 – Petit Point (IRE) 78 (Petorius 117) [2003 85: 6m 6m* 6m⁵ 6g² 6.5m⁴ 6m* 6m⁶ 6m* 6f* 6m² Sep 20] strong gelding: smart performer: had a good season, winning handicap at Kempton in April, minor event at Haydock in August and handicap at York (by 1¾ lengths from Smart Predator) and minor event at Haydock (by 1½ lengths from Proud Boast) in September: best effort when   **113**

T Mobile Rated Stakes (Handicap), York—the progressive Seel of Approval wins in good style from the grey Smart Predator and Simianna (right)

head second of 26 to Quito in Ayr Gold Cup (Handicap) final start: stays 6f: acts on firm ground: reliable. *R. Charlton*

SEEMS SO EASY (USA) 4 b.f. Palmister (USA) – I'm An Issue (USA) (Cox's Ridge (USA)) [2003 51?: p8g May 17] smallish, strong filly: maiden: well held only 4-y-o start: tried blinkered/tongue tied. *J. Jay* —

SEEYAAJ 3 b.g. Darshaan 133 – Subya 107 (Night Shift (USA)) [2003 8m 10g* 12f³ 10f 10.3m Oct 24] 270,000Y: good-bodied gelding: fourth foal: half-brother to smart 1¼m/1½m winner Villa Carlotta (by Rainbow Quest): dam 5f (at 2 yrs) to 1¼m winner: fairly useful performer: won maiden at Pontefract in July by 3½ lengths from Dawaarr: disappointing after, racing freely final start: should stay 1½m: raced only on good ground or firmer: edgy (ran poorly) fourth outing: has worn blanket for stall entry: sold 16,000 gns, joined Jonjo O'Neill. *A. C. Stewart* **90**

SEE YOU HARRY 3 b.g. Polar Prince (IRE) 117 – Etma Rose (IRE) (Fairy King (USA)) [2003 8.2m Oct 28] 6,000F: compact gelding: first foal: dam of little account: 50/1 and backward, always behind in maiden at Nottingham. *R. Hollinshead* —

SEFTON BLAKE 9 b.g. Roscoe Blake 120 – Rainbow Lady 65 (Jaazeiro (USA) 127) [2003 f12g Apr 4] lightly-raced maiden: off over 3 years before well beaten only 9-y-o start: visored once: dead. *R. D. Wylie* —

SEFTON LODGE 4 b.g. Barathea (IRE) 127 – Pine Needle 89 (Kris 135) [2003 45: f7s⁴ p6g² f6g 6g p6g⁶ 8.1m Jul 4] sturdy gelding: modest maiden: left M. Ryan after reappearance, C. Allen after second start: should stay 7f: acts on all-weather and soft going: tried tongue tied: wore cheekpieces last 5 outings. *Andrew Reid* **51**

SEGRETEZZA (IRE) 3 b.f. Perugino (USA) 84 – Secrets of Honour (Belmez (USA) 131) [2003 f7g 6g f7g³ 8.3m⁵ 7m f7s Oct 21] IR 5,500Y: fourth foal: half-sister to 4-y-o Double Ransom and 5-y-o Another Secret: dam unraced half-sister to high-class sprinter Mr Brooks: poor maiden: stays 1m: raced only on fibresand and good/good to firm ground: tried blinkered. *D. Haydn Jones* **48**

SEGUIDILLA (IRE) 2 b.f. (Mar 28) Mujadil (USA) 119 – Alzeam (IRE) 61 (Alzao (USA) 117) [2003 5.1f² 5m 5m⁴ Jul 7] €62,000Y: rather leggy, quite attractive filly: fifth foal: sister to useful 2001 2-y-o 5f/6f winner Leggy Lou and fairly useful 1999 2-y-o 6f winner Dashing Duke and half-sister to winner in Italy by Case Law: dam Irish maiden **82**

who stayed 1½m: second in maiden at Bath: best effort (fairly useful form) when seventh in Queen Mary Stakes at Royal Ascot: should stay 6f. *G. C. Bravery*

SEIFI 4 b.g. Hector Protector (USA) 124 – Garconniere (Gay Mecene (USA) 128) [2003 81: 13d 12.4m 12m⁶ 14g⁵ f14.8s Jul 14] 16,000F, 55,000Y: ex-Irish gelding: half-brother to several winners, including Italian 7f (at 2 yrs, including listed race) and 1m winner Giselle Penn (by Cozzene): dam ran twice in France: fairly useful at 3 yrs for K. Prendergast, winning maiden at Clonmel: mostly well held in Britain: stays 1¾m: acts on heavy ground: tried blinkered. *B. Ellison* –

SELEBELA 2 ch.f. (Feb 7) Grand Lodge (USA) 125 – Risarshana (FR) (Darshaan 133) [2003 8m³ 8.1d⁶ 8m 7d⁵ Nov 4] 20,000Y: heavy-bodied filly: first foal: dam, ran once in France, granddaughter of smart French performer up to 10.5f Restiver, herself half-sister to Prix de Diane winner Resless Kara: modest form in maidens: third at Milan: likely to do better at 1¼m+. *L. M. Cumani* **63 p**

SELECTIVE 4 b.g. Selkirk (USA) 129 – Portelet 91 (Night Shift (USA)) [2003 101: 8g² 7m² 7g² 7.1m³ 8m Jun 18] good-bodied gelding: smart performer: second in competitive handicaps at Doncaster (Lincoln, beaten 1½ lengths by Pablo), Newmarket (to Attache) and Ascot (best effort, beaten ¾ length by Camp Commander in Victoria Cup) first 3 starts: not discredited when never-nearer ninth of 32 in Hunt Cup at Royal Ascot (injured) final outing: subsequently gelded: effective at 7f/1m: acts on good to firm and good to soft ground (yet to race on soft/heavy): tends to carry head awkwardly: has run creditably when sweating: waited with: consistent. *A. C. Stewart* **116**

SELF BELIEF 2 b.f. (May 2) Easycall 115 – Princess of Spain (King of Spain 121) [2003 5.1f⁴ 5m³ 5m⁴ 6g Aug 11] 5,000Y: half-sister to several winners abroad, including useful German 7.5f/1m winner Peace Time (by Surumu): dam German 2-y-o 5f winner: fair maiden: third at Windsor: ran poorly in nursery final start: should stay 6f. *D. E. Cantillon* **67**

SELF EVIDENT (USA) 3 b. or br.c. Known Fact (USA) 135 – Palisade (USA) 87 (Gone West (USA)) [2003 87p: 8m 7.5m* 8g* 8m 8m³ 8m² 8m Oct 17] compact colt: useful performer: won handicaps at Beverley in April and Newmarket in May, beating Arakan by ½ length in latter: ran creditably when placed in minor events at Salisbury (1¾ lengths third to Three Graces) and Newmarket (½-length second to King's County): free-going sort, best at 7f/1m: raced only on good ground or firmer: often races prominently: sold 65,000 gns, and joined G. Butler. *Mrs A. J. Perrett* **103**

SELF RAZIN (IRE) 2 b.f. (Apr 27) Inzar (USA) 112 – Abbessingh (Mansingh (USA) 120) [2003 p8g Nov 26] half-sister to several winners, including 1993 French 2-y-o 7f winner Fasil (by Diamond Prospect): dam French maiden half-sister to useful sprinter Roaring Riva: 100/1, well held in maiden at Lingfield. *Mrs S. A. Liddiard* –

SEMAH'S PARC 5 b.g. Pure Melody (USA) 77 – Semah's Dream 39 (Gunner B 126) [2003 –: 14.1m May 26] little form. *Mrs A. M. Naughton* –

SEMELLE DE VENT (USA) 2 b.f. (Mar 3) Sadler's Wells (USA) 132 – Heeremandi (IRE) 105 (Royal Academy (USA) 130) [2003 8.2f p7g⁵ p10g⁶ Nov 29] strong, useful-looking filly: second foal: half-sister to fairly useful 2002 2-y-o 5f winner Chateau Beach (by Danehill): dam, 2-y-o 6f winner in Ireland, closely related to dam of high-class US filly Flawlessly: modest form in maidens at Nottingham and Lingfield (2): probably stays 1¼m: type to do better in handicaps as 3-y-o. *J. H. M. Gosden* **64 p**

SEMENOVSKII 3 b.g. Fraam 114 – Country Spirit (Sayf El Arab (USA) 127) [2003 82: 6g 6m 6.1m 6f* 6d² 5m² 6m⁴ 6m* 6m⁶ 6m 7d 6m 6g⁶ 5d f6g Nov 17] strong gelding: fairly useful handicapper: won at Catterick (final start for D. Nicholls) in May and Brighton in August: well held last 6 starts: best at 5f/easy 6f: acts on firm and good to soft going: usually races prominently. *P. W. D'Arcy* **84**

SEMPERGREEN 3 ch.f. Hector Protector (USA) 124 – Star Tulip 99 (Night Shift (USA)) [2003 65p: 7m Sep 9] fair form only 2-y-o start: off 15 months (reportedly suffered minor injury) and weak favourite, well held in maiden at Lingfield: sold 1,300 gns in December, sent to Germany. *J. L. Dunlop* –

SEMPER PARATUS (USA) 4 b.g. Foxhound (USA) 103 – Bletcha Lass (AUS) 67 § (Bletchingly (AUS)) [2003 80: f6g 6m f5g⁵ f6g⁶ 6f f6g⁵ f6g 6g 7m p7g f7g* f6g⁴ p7g Dec 6] close-coupled gelding: unimpressive mover: fair handicapper: left J. Balding after seventh start: won at Wolverhampton in November: stays 7f: acts on fibresand, soft and firm going: tried in headgear: unreliable. *H. J. Collingridge*

SEMPRE SORRISO 3 b.f. Fleetwood (IRE) 107 – Ever Genial 117 (Brigadier Gerard **52**
144) [2003 –: 8.2g 7g 7m⁶ 8.3m 8.1m 8f Sep 2] leggy filly: modest maiden: should stay
9f: raced mainly on good ground or firmer: none too consistent. *A. Charlton*

SENDINTANK 3 ch.g. Halling (USA) 133 – Colleville 97 (Pharly (FR) 130) [2003 55: **– p**
8d⁶ f8g 8.5g Jul 17] maiden handicapper: will be suited by 1¼m+. *S. C. Williams*

SENESCHAL 2 b.c. (Jan 30) Polar Falcon (USA) 126 – Broughton Singer (IRE) 61 **97 p**
(Common Grounds 118) [2003 5m² 5g* Apr 14] 22,000F, 60,000Y: fourth foal: half-
brother to fairly useful 8.5f (at 2 yrs) and 9.7f winner Keltic Bard (by Emperor Jones):
dam 9f winner: promising debut, then useful form when winning 6-runner maiden at
Windsor by 6 lengths from Bachelor of Arts, making all: will probably stay 1m: well
regarded, and reportedly given time to mature. *M. R. Channon*

SENIOR MINISTER 5 b.g. Lion Cavern (USA) 117 – Crime Ofthecentury 80 (Pharly **68 §**
(FR) 130) [2003 –: 6.1d⁵ 6m 5m 6m³ 7g 6m 5m Aug 17] good-topped gelding: fair
handicapper: best at 5f/6f: acts on firm ground: tried blinkered: unreliable. *P. W. Hiatt*

SENNA (IRE) 3 b.g. Petardia 113 – Saborinie 56 (Prince Sabo 123) [2003 p8g p8g **–**
p8g 10g Oct 6] leggy gelding: third foal: dam lightly-raced Irish maiden: well held in
maidens. *P. D. Cundell*

SENNEN COVE 4 ch.g. Bering 136 – Dame Laura (IRE) 100 (Royal Academy (USA) **54 d**
130) [2003 67: p7g f7g⁶ 9m² 9m⁵ 8.5f 10.1m 8g⁶ 7f 8f 8m⁴ 7f⁵ 7m 8m f8g Dec 19] close-
coupled gelding: modest maiden handicapper: left H. Morrison after reappearance,
I. Semple after ninth start: stays 9f: acts on firm and good to soft going: tried blinkered/in
cheekpieces: tongue tied last 5 starts: unreliable. *R. Bastiman*

SENOR BOND (USA) 2 ch.g. (Jan 29) Hennessy (USA) 122 – Troppa Freska (USA) **79**
(Silver Hawk (USA) 123) [2003 5m 7m 6g⁴ 6m 5.9m* 6g 6m 7m⁴ 7m 7d Nov 8]
$25,000F, 54,000Y: smallish, good-bodied gelding: first foal: dam fairly useful Italian
7f/1m winner (including at 2 yrs) who stayed 11f: fair performer: won nursery at Carlisle
in September: ran badly in similar events last 2 starts: probably stays 7f: acts on good to
firm going: sometimes reluctant to post. *B. Smart*

SENOR EDUARDO 6 gr.g. Terimon 124 – Jasmin Path (Warpath 113) [2003 7.5m **63**
10.3m 12g 10m⁴ 7.5m³ 7m f8s⁵ Oct 7] good-topped gelding: modest maiden: will stay
1m: raced only on good going or firmer on turf: none too consistent. *S. Gollings*

SENORITA (IRE) 3 b.f. Spectrum (IRE) 126 – Princess Natalie 78 (Rudimentary **–**
(USA) 118) [2003 –: 7m 7g 5d May 22] lengthy filly: no form: sent to Israel.
T. D. Easterby

SENOR MANX TOUCH 4 b.g. Magic Ring (IRE) 115 – Inveraven 53 (Alias Smith **–**
(USA)) [2003 f7g Feb 7] smallish, good-bodied gelding: of little account. *B. D. Leavy*

SENOR MIRO 5 b.g. Be My Guest (USA) 126 – Classic Moonlight (IRE) (Machia- **59**
vellian (USA) 123) [2003 60: f7g 7g 7m⁴ p8g³ p7g³ Dec 10] leggy, useful-looking
gelding: modest maiden: effective at 7f/1m: acts on polytrack, yet to race on extremes of
going on turf: tried tongue tied: sometimes races freely. *J. Akehurst*

SENOR PEDRO 3 b.g. Piccolo 121 – Stride Home 78 (Absalom 128) [2003 60: **62**
p10g² p8g* p8g f9.4g f8.5g³ f8g 11.8m f8.5g Jun 6] modest performer: left M. Channon
after winning seller at Lingfield in January: below form after: stays 1¼m: acts on
all-weather and firm going: has been tongue tied/worn cheekpieces: sent to Sweden. *Miss
Gay Kelleway*

SENOR SOL (USA) 3 b.g. El Prado (IRE) 119 – One Moment In Time (USA) **85**
(Magesterial (USA) 116) [2003 89: 10.5f⁴ 11m 10.9f³ 12s⁵ 10g Oct 6] big, good-bodied
gelding: type to carry condition: fairly useful handicapper: should stay 1½m: acts on
firm and good to soft ground: usually races prominently: sold 37,000 gns, and gelded.
P. F. I. Cole

SENOR TORAN (USA) 3 b.g. Barathea (IRE) 127 – Applaud (USA) 105 (Rahy **–**
(USA) 115) [2003 75p: f9.4g⁵ f12g⁵ f12g⁵ f12g p8g Dec 6] big, strong gelding: disappointing
maiden: well held on all-weather in 2003: left P. Cole after third start: tried blinkered.
P. Burgoyne

SENSATIONAL MOVER (USA) 3 ch.f. Theatrical 128 – Blushing Heiress (USA) **68**
(Blushing John (USA) 120) [2003 f12g² f12g³ f8.5s⁴ Apr 12] lengthy, well-made filly:
second foal: half-sister to a winner in USA by Deputy Minister: dam US Grade 2 8.5f
winner: withdrawn on intended debut in October 2002 on veterinary advice: fair maiden:
best effort on debut: raced only on fibresand: sold 3,500 gns, sent to Sweden. *P. F. I. Cole*

SENSIBLE (FR)   5 b.h. Sadler's Wells (USA) 132 – Raisonnable 105 (Common **107**
Grounds 118) [2003 115: 9.5g 10g² 10.5d³ 10s 10d* 10d⁶ 8s Nov 21] strong, good-topped
horse: first foal: dam, French miler, half-sister to smart US Grade 1 1¼m winner Aube
Indienne: smart performer at best: won minor event and listed race at Longchamp at 3
yrs: in frame in several pattern races in 2002, including Prix Ganay and La Coupe, both at
Longchamp: just useful form in 2003, winning minor event at Deauville in July by neck
from Secret Singer: 1¾ lengths second to Carnival Dancer in similar event at Newmarket
second start: best around 1¼m: acts on heavy ground: blinkered last 3 starts in 2002: has
found less than expected. *P. Bary, France*

SENTINEL   4 ch.g. Hector Protector (USA) 124 – Soolaimon (IRE) 71 (Shareef Dancer **98 +**
(USA) 135) [2003 100: 12m 16.1g² 16g 13.9m 14.6g Sep 12] well-made colt: useful
performer: good ½-length second to Unleash in Northumberland Plate at Newcastle:
probably flattered when seventh to Persian Punch in Goodwood Cup next time, hanging
markedly right: well held in handicaps after: will stay beyond 2m: acts on soft going,
good to firm and all-weather: tried blinkered/tongue tied: held up: has carried head
awkwardly: races lazily. *G. A. Butler*

SENTRY (IRE)   3 b.c. In Command (IRE) 114 – Keep Bobbin Up (IRE) 76 (Bob Back **88**
(USA) 124) [2003 79p: 11m² 10s³ p12g* Nov 12] strong, lengthy colt: has a quick action:
fairly useful form in maidens: best effort when 3 lengths second to Westmoreland Road
at Newbury on reappearance (off nearly 7 months after): won at Lingfield in November:
should stay 1¾m: acts on polytrack, soft and good to firm ground. *J. H. M. Gosden*

SENZA SCRUPOLI   3 ch.g. Inchinor 119 – Gravette 79 (Kris 135) [2003 –p: 8m 7m **61 ?**
8g⁵ f12s Dec 13] good-bodied gelding: modest maiden: best effort on third outing,
though possibly flattered: left L. Cumani and off 5 months after: should be suited by
1¼m+. *M. D. Hammond*

SEPARATED (USA)   2 b.f. (Feb 24) Unbridled (USA) 128 – Lemhi Go (USA) (Lemhi **52 p**
Gold (USA) 123) [2003 p8g f9.4g⁵ Dec 24] seventh foal: sister to fairly useful 1¼m
winner Abscond and half-sister to 2 winners, including 4-y-o Unleash: dam won 12
times in USA, including Grade 2 1½m event: modest form in maidens at Lingfield and
Wolverhampton: will stay at least 1¼m: should do better. *E. A. L. Dunlop*

SEQUENTIAL   4 b.g. Rainbow Quest (USA) 134 – Dance Sequence (USA) 105 (Mr   **–**
Prospector (USA)) [2003 98: 11.9f 12m Aug 25] tall, quite attractive gelding: useful
performer at 3 yrs: tailed off for new stable in 2003. *S. Gollings*

SEQUESTRO (USA)   2 b. or br.c. (May 21) Red Ransom (USA) – Sha Tha (USA) **100 p**
118 (Mr Prospector (USA)) [2003 6d³ 8m* Sep 16] half-brother to several winners,
notably very smart 1m (including at 2 yrs) to 10.5f winner State Shinto (by Pleasant
Colony): dam, French/US 1m/9f performer, sister to dam of 2-y-o One Cool Cat: third of
6 to Ximb in newcomers race at Deauville: won minor event at Maisons-Laffitte by ¾
length from Graphic Design: will stay 1¼m: joined Godolphin: useful already, and likely
to improve. *A. Fabre, France*

SEQUIN SLIPPERS (IRE)   3 b.f. Revoque (IRE) 122 – Strutting (IRE) 95 (Ela-   **–**
Mana-Mou 132) [2003 74d: f7g⁴ Jan 3] 8f Nov 3] IR 35,000Y: fourth foal: half-sister to smart Irish
7f/1¼m winner Chiming (by Danehill): dam 7f (at 2 yrs) and 1¼m winner: fair maiden:
left K. Prendergast in Ireland cheaply prior to showing little only 3-y-o start. *K. A. Ryan*

SERAPH   3 ch.g. Vettori (IRE) 119 – Dahlawise (IRE) 76 (Caerleon (USA) 132) [2003 **48**
–: 8.3g⁵ 10m 8m³ 7m 7g 8f Oct 17] leggy, workmanlike gelding: poor maiden: left
I. Wood after fifth start: stays 1m: acts on good to firm going: tried in cheekpieces, usually
blinkered. *John A. Harris*

SERBELLONI   3 b.g. Spectrum (IRE) 126 – Rose Vibert (Caerleon (USA) 132) [2003 **74**
73p: 7.9f⁴ 8.3d⁶ 10m⁶ 10.3d Sep 24] lengthy, useful-looking gelding: fair maiden: stays
1¼m: acts on firm and good to soft ground. *P. W. Harris*

SERGEANT CECIL   4 ch.g. King's Signet (USA) 110 – Jadidh 64 (Touching Wood **95**
(USA) 127) [2003 82: 11.6g² 12m 14m* 14f² 14g** 16.2f 12m² 14g Sep 6] workmanlike
gelding: useful handicapper: better than ever in 2003, winning at Sandown in May and
July, latter by ¾ length from Mr Ed: creditable second to Capitano Corelli at Ascot
seventh start: reportedly lost action final outing: effective at 1½m: barely stays 2m: acts
on firm ground, good to soft and probably on polytrack: wore cheekpieces (well held)
second start: has raced freely/carried head awkwardly. *B. R. Millman*

SERGEANT SLIPPER   6 ch.g. Never So Bold 135 – Pretty Scarce (Handsome Sailor   **– §**
125) [2003 53§: f6g⁴ f6s⁶ f6g⁵ f5s² f5g f5g* f5g f5s 6.1m 6m f5g⁵ Dec 12] workmanlike **a51 §**

gelding: modest performer: ended long losing run in handicap at Southwell in April: raced only at 5f/6f: acts on fibresand, good to firm and heavy going: tried blinkered, usually visored: usually slowly away: untrustworthy. *C. Smith*

SERIEUX   4 b.c. Cadeaux Genereux 131 – Seranda (IRE) (Petoski 135) [2003 109: 7.1m³ 8g* 8.3d⁵ 8m 8m⁴ 10s³ 10.4m 10.1g Sep 10] strong, lengthy, useful-looking colt: useful performer: won minor event at Ascot in April by ½ length from With Reason: ran creditably after only on fifth/sixth outings: best form up to 1m: acts on good to firm and soft going: free-going sort: effective making running or held up: wandered seventh start: inconsistent. *Mrs A. J. Perrett*   **106 §**

SERRAFINA   3 ch.f. Bluegrass Prince (IRE) 110 – Josifina (Master Willie 129) [2003 –: 8g 8m⁶ 10m 8.1f⁴ 10.2g⁶ 11m 8g Oct 31] leggy filly: modest maiden handicapper: bred to be suited by further than 1m, but races freely: raced only on good ground or firmer: tongue tied (folded tamely) final start. *B. De Haan*   **60**

SERRAMANNA   2 ch.f. (Feb 13) Grand Lodge (USA) 125 – Spry 84 (Suave Dancer (USA) 136) [2003 7g⁶ 8.1g² Aug 25] first foal: dam, 1½m winner from 2 starts, half-sister to very smart 1½m performer Sandmason (by Grand Lodge) out of Lancashire Oaks winner Sandy Island, herself close relation to Slip Anchor: much better effort in maidens (fairly useful form) when clear second to Coventina at Chepstow: will be suited by 1¼m+: open to progress, and should win a race or 2. *H. R. A. Cecil*   **85 p**

SERVICE   3 ch.f. College Chapel 122 – Centre Court 74 (Second Set (IRE) 127) [2003 65§: p5g⁶ p5g⁵ f5g⁶ p6g⁴ p5g⁵ Feb 25] sparely-made filly: poor performer: effective at 5f/6f: acts on firm ground and all-weather: tried in blinkers/cheekpieces: sometimes slowly away: tail flasher. *J. Akehurst*   **49**

SESSAY   2 b.g. (Jan 31) Cyrano de Bergerac 120 – Green Supreme (Primo Dominie 121) [2003 5g³ 5d² Sep 12] 40,000Y: sturdy, useful-looking gelding: fifth foal: brother to smart 5f to 7f (latter at 2 yrs) winner Sampower Star and half-brother to 6-y-o Absent Friends and 4-y-o Fire Up The Band: dam unraced: fair form in maidens at Pontefract and Hamilton: possibly amiss after 4-month absence final start: likely to prove best at 5f/6f. *D. Nicholls*   **67**

SESTINA (FR)   3 ch.f. Bering 136 – Secrecy (USA) (Halo (USA)) [2003 8g³ 7g⁴ 6g 5.5g p7g p7g Nov 13] 350,000 francs Y: sister to French 7f winner Sky Secret, closely related to French 1997 2-y-o 1m/1¼m winner Secretern (by Arctic Tern) and half-sister to a winner in France by Jeune Homme: dam unraced daughter of Prix de l'Opera winner Secret Form: best effort (fairly useful form) when fourth to Man O Desert in minor event at Longchamp second start: well below form after, leaving R. Gibson in France after fourth outing: stays 7f: raced only on polytrack and good ground. *S. Dow*   **86 ?**

SET THE STYLE (IRE)   4 b.f. Desert Style (IRE) 121 – Penka (IRE) 85 (Don't Forget Me 127) [2003 91: 8m 7g 5.8s 7d 7d 7d 8g⁴ 8.5m 8m⁵ 8.3m p12g Oct 8] second foal: sister to useful Irish 7f (at 2 yrs)/1m winner Galanta: dam Irish 2-y-o 6f winner: fair performer: won nursery at Fairyhouse at 2 yrs and handicap at Leopardstown at 3 yrs: left J. Bolger in Ireland 11,000 gns, well held in handicaps last 4 starts: was best at 1m: acted on heavy and good to firm going: tried in cheekpieces, often blinkered: dead. *R. Ingram*   **79**

SETTLEMENT CRAIC (IRE)   2 b.c. (Feb 16) Ela-Mana-Mou 132 – Medway (IRE) 60 (Shernazar 131) [2003 7m² Sep 16] €50,000Y: tall, leggy colt: fourth foal: half-brother to fairly useful 15f winner Missouri (by Charnwood Forest): dam, 1½m winner, half-sister to very smart Hong Kong 1¼m/1½m performer Indigenous: 33/1 and green, 9 lengths second of 15 to Brunel in maiden at Salisbury, staying on: will be well suited by 1¼m+: should improve. *T. G. Mills*   **79 p**

SEVEN NO TRUMPS   6 ch.g. Pips Pride 117 – Classic Ring (IRE) 50 (Auction Ring (USA) 123) [2003 108d: 5g 7m 7g 5v³ 6g 6g 5d Sep 27] rangy, good-topped gelding: fairly useful handicapper: ran poorly last 3 starts: effective at 5f/6f: acts on any going: blinkered once at 3 yrs, wore cheekpieces fourth/fifth outings: edgy sort: tends to carry head high: sold 17,000 gns. *B. W. Hills*   **88**

SEVEN SHIRT   2 b.g. (Mar 5) Great Dane (IRE) 122 – Bride's Answer 81 (Anshan 119) [2003 6m 7g⁵ 6g⁴ 8.3g 8.2m Oct 28] tall gelding: first foal: dam, 1m winner, half-sister to 4-y-o Funfair Wane: fair maiden: ran badly in seller final start: probably stays 1m: form only on good going: tends to carry head awkwardly. *M. R. Channon*   **65**

SEVEN SPRINGS (IRE)   7 b.g. Unblest 117 – Zaydeen (Sassafras (FR) 135) [2003 –, a49: p7g⁶ f8s f5g 7m 6m 5.1f⁴ 5m 5.5m Aug 25] tall, workmanlike gelding: poor handi-   **39**

capper: best at 5f (given test)/6f: acts on fibresand and any turf going: wore cheekpieces/
visor last 3 starts. *R. Hollinshead*

SEVEN YEAR ITCH (IRE)   3 b.c. Danehill (USA) 126 – Itching (IRE) (Thatching   **75 p**
131) [2003 p10g² Nov 18] brother to very smart 1m to 1¼m winner Great Dane and
half-brother to 2 winners, including fairly useful 1996 2-y-o 6f winner (later stayed 1m)
Witching Hour (by Alzao): dam unraced half-sister to Croco Rouge and to dam of Ali-
Royal, Sleepytime and Taipan: favourite, head second to Tetou in maiden at Lingfield,
leading 1f out but running green (flashed tail) and caught final strides: should improve.
M. P. Tregoning

SEVICHE (IRE)   5 ch.m. College Chapel 122 – Smeraldina (USA) (Night Shift (USA))   **–**
[2003 f12g f8.5g⁶ f8.5g⁵ Mar 3] IR 6,500Y: first foal: dam unraced: fair winner at 2 yrs
for T. Stack in Ireland: well held in 2003: usually blinkered. *F. Jordan*

SEVILLANO   2 b.g. (Apr 23) Nicolotte 118 – Nashville Blues (IRE) 94 (Try My Best   **95**
(USA) 130) [2003 p5g² 6m* 7d³ 6g² Aug 23] 4,000Y, resold 11,000Y: big, lengthy gelding: half-brother to several winners, including fairly useful 7f/1m winner Rhythm of Life
(by Dr Devious) and 5-y-o Urban Myth: dam, 7f/1m winner, not one to trust implicitly:
useful performer: won maiden at Epsom in July: placed in minor events at Ascot and
Windsor (sweating, very good 1½ lengths second to Azarole) after: free-running sort, but
probably stays 7f. *P. D. Cundell*

SEWMORE CHARACTER   3 b.c. Hector Protector (USA) 124 – Kyle Rhea 104   **84**
(In The Wings 128) [2003 83: 8.2g⁴ 7.1m 8.1s⁴ 8.1d⁶ p8g² Dec 2] angular colt: fairly
useful maiden: best effort when beaten head by Lobos in handicap at Lingfield final
start: should stay 1¼m: acts on heavy ground and polytrack: possibly none too resolute.
M. Blanshard

SEWMUCH CHARACTER   4 b.g. Magic Ring (IRE) 115 – Diplomatist 69 (Domin-   **82**
ion 123) [2003 76: 7m² 7m 6m* 7.6g⁴ 6g⁶ 6m 6d⁵ 5m 6m³ 6f 6g⁴ Oct 6] big, good-topped
gelding: fairly useful handicapper: won at Pontefract in June: best at 6f/7f: acts on soft
and good to firm going: usually races prominently: has looked none too keen/edged right:
none too reliable. *M. Blanshard*

SEW'N'SO CHARACTER (IRE)   2 b.c. (Mar 2) Imperial Ballet (IRE) 110 – Hope   **97**
And Glory (USA) 87 (Well Decorated (USA)) [2003 6m⁴ 6d² 6g* 7m³ 7m² 7m⁶ 7g² 7.6d²
8m⁵ Oct 20] 15,500F: good-topped colt: closely related to 2 winners by Saddlers' Hall,
including fairly useful 1¼m winner Saddlers' Hope, and half-brother to several winners,
including 3-y-o Doris Souter: dam 2-y-o 6f winner: useful performer: won maiden at
Haydock in July: mostly good efforts after, placed in minor events/nursery: stays 7.5f:
acts on good to firm and good to soft going. *M. Blanshard*

SFORZANDO   2 b.f. (Mar 1) Robellino (USA) 127 – Mory Kante (USA) (Icecapade   **68**
(USA)) [2003 6.1m⁶ 6m⁵ 6m 7m Oct 4] 13,500Y: well-made filly: eighth foal: sister to a
winner in Italy and half-sister to 3 winners, including 6-y-o Pagan Prince: dam German
7f/1m winner: fair maiden: fifth at Ascot, best effort: not clear run last 2 starts: needs to
settle to stay 7f. *J. A. R. Toller*

SGT PEPPER (IRE)   2 b.c. (Apr 22) Fasliyev (USA) 120 – Amandine (IRE) (Dar-   **100**
shaan 133) [2003 6m³ 7m* 8m* 7g⁴ 10d Nov 8] 60,000 2-y-o: compact colt: fifth foal:
half-brother to 3 winners, including 1m winner Waabl and 1¼m winner Duchcov (both
useful, by Caerleon): dam, French 1m winner, out of smart French performer up to 1¼m
Libertine: useful performer: won maiden in July and listed race in August (got run of
things up front when beating America America by 3 lengths), both at Salisbury: respectable fourth to Peak To Creek in Horris Hill Stakes at Newbury, better effort after: stays
1m: acts on good to firm going. *R. Hannon*

SHAAMIT'S ALL OVER   4 b.f. Shaamit (IRE) 127 – First Time Over (Derrylin   **–**
115) [2003 p13g p10g⁶ p10g p10g Dec 29] sister to a winner in Italy and half-sister to
1991 2-y-o 6f winner Gabes (by Aragon): dam, second at 1m, half-sister to smart but
temperamental middle-distance performer Out of Shot: little form in maidens/handicap
at Lingfield. *B. A. Pearce*

SHAANDAR (IRE)   5 br.h. Darshaan 133 – Moon Parade 73 (Welsh Pageant 132)   **–**
[2003 8m Sep 6] tall, useful-looking, rather sparely-made horse: very lightly raced: useful
form in 2001, broke down final start: pulled up only 5-y-o outing. *D. W. Chapman*

SHABERNAK (IRE)   4 gr.g. Akarad (FR) 130 – Salinova (FR) (Linamix (FR) 127)   **114**
[2003 89: 14.1g 12g² 12f 11.9g⁵ 14g³ 16.2m* 14.6g* 18m Oct 18] smallish, lengthy gelding: smart handicapper: improved form when winning at Ascot (5 lengths from Random

Tote Exacta Mallard Stakes (Handicap), Doncaster—
Shabernak (right) and Itemise finish eight lengths clear of the remainder

Quest) in August and Doncaster (Tote Exacta Mallard Stakes, beat Itemise by ¾ length) in September: raced freely over longer trip when mid-field in Cesarewitch at Newmarket final outing: effective at 1½m to 2m: acts on firm ground. *M. L. W. Bell*

SHADES OF THE WEST   3 b.f. The West (USA) 107 – Spanish Luck 47 (Mazilier (USA) 107) [2003 7m May 15] first foal: dam 2-y-o 7f winner: 100/1, well beaten in claimer at Salisbury. *G. A. Ham*   –

SHADOW CAPTAIN   3 gr.g. Compton Place 125 – Magnolia 52 (Petong 126) [2003 –: 5f⁶ 6m⁵ 7g⁶ 6m 7m 7m 5g Oct 13] leggy gelding: poor maiden: stays 6f: acts on firm ground: tried visored: sold 800 gns. *E. J. Alston*   45

SHADOWFAX   3 b.g. Anabaa (USA) 130 – Prends Ca (IRE) 98 (Reprimand 122) [2003 74, a77: f6g⁶ f6s² Dec 27] useful-looking gelding: modest maiden: stays 7f: acts on fibresand, firm and soft ground: tried tongue tied. *Miss Gay Kelleway*   60

SHADOWLAND (USA)   2 ch.c. (Apr 6) Distant View (USA) 126 – Fire And Shade (USA) 91 (Shadeed (USA) 135) [2003 6f* a8f* Dec 7] $130,000Y: closely related to fairly useful 7f winner Miss Shema (by Gulch) and half-brother to 2 winners, including useful 1¼m winner Freedom Flame (by Darshaan): dam, 2-y-o 6f winner, out of Musidora winner Fatah Flare: won 11-runner maiden at Thirsk in June (then left A. Balding) and allowance race at Turfway Park in December: stays 1m: open to further progress. *D. L. Romans, USA*   ?

SHADOWY   2 b.f. (Mar 14) Unfuwain (USA) 131 – Shady Leaf (IRE) 56 (Glint of Gold 128) [2003 6d⁶ 8d⁶ 10m Oct 22] leggy, quite good-topped filly: seventh foal: closely related to Irish 2m winner Academy House (by Sadler's Wells) and half-sister to 7f winner Fig Leaf (by Distant Relative), both fairly useful: dam, maiden who stayed 1½m, half-sister to Princess Royal Stakes winner Dancing Bloom and to dams of Spectrum and 6-y-o Millenary: best effort in maidens (modest form) when sixth at Ayr: should be suited by 1¼m+: edgy sort: sold 1,800 gns. *R. F. Johnson Houghton*   62

SHADY DEAL   7 b.g. No Big Deal – Taskalady 47 (Touching Wood (USA) 127) [2003 62, a–: 5g⁴ 5m 5.7f⁵ 5m² 6.1g⁴ 5m⁶ 5m⁶ 5.1d² 5m³ 5g⁵ Aug 4] angular gelding: modest performer: best at 5f/6f: acts on firm and soft ground: tried blinkered: usually races prominently. *J. M. Bradley*   60

SHADY LITES (FR)   3 ch.f. Definite Article 121 – Shade (Contract Law (USA) 108) [2003 68: 8.2g 7.1m f8.5s³ 11.8m 8.5g³ 9g Oct 24] modest maiden: stays 8.5f: acts on fibresand, raced only on good/good to firm going on turf: sold 5,000 gns. *C. G. Cox*   60

SHADY REFLECTION (USA)   2 b.f. (Mar 2) Sultry Song (USA) – Woodland Melody (USA) 108 (Woodman (USA) 126) [2003 7m⁵ 8m 8.3d* Sep 29] rangy filly: second foal: dam, 2-y-o 6f/7f (Prix du Calvados) winner, out of useful 5f performer   74 p

Eloquent Minister: favourite, easily best effort in maidens (fair form) when making all in 7-runner event at Hamilton: stays 1m: should progress. *J. H. M. Gosden*

SHAHM (IRE)   4 b.g. Marju (IRE) 127 – Istibshar (USA) 78 (Mr Prospector (USA))   **60**
[2003 –: f8.5s⁵ f7g* Dec 16] good-topped gelding: modest handicapper: off 10 months, won at Southwell in December: stays 1m: acts on fibresand, good to firm and good to soft going: sometimes tongue tied: tried visored/blinkered, not in 2003: sometimes carries head high. *B. J. Curley*

SHAHZAN HOUSE (IRE)   4 b.c. Sri Pekan (USA) 117 – Nsx 74 (Roi Danzig (USA))   **98**
[2003 97: 12g⁶ 10.4f 10d⁴ 10.1g* 10g Oct 25] sturdy colt: fluent mover: useful performer: mostly creditable efforts in 2003, and won minor event at Epsom in September by neck from Wing Commander: best around 1¼m: acts on good to firm and good to soft going. *M. A. Jarvis*

SHALAMAK   2 b.f. (Feb 27) Makbul 104 – Shalateeno 80 (Teenoso (USA) 135) [2003   **–**
5m⁵ 6m⁶ 6g f8.5g Nov 17] £4,000Y: well-made filly: has scope: first foal: dam 1¼m/1½m winner who stayed 2m: little sign of ability: free-going sort: broke out of stall and withdrawn once. *B. R. Millman*

SHALAYA (IRE)   2 b.f. (Apr 22) Marju (IRE) 127 – Shalama (IRE) 91 (Kahyasi 130)   **87 p**
[2003 8m* 8g⁶ Nov 1] smallish, close-coupled filly: first living foal: dam, runner-up on all 3 starts (9f/1¼m), half-sister to Derby and Irish Derby winner Shahrastani: won maiden at Leicester in September: better effort (fairly useful form) when sixth of 12 to Spotlight in listed event at Newmarket, racing freely and well there until over 1f out: bred to be well suited by 1¼m/1½m: open to progress. *Sir Michael Stoute*

SHALBEBLUE (IRE)   6 b.g. Shalford (IRE) 124§ – Alberjas (IRE) (Sure Blade   **59**
(USA) 130) [2003 –, a58: f11g f12g⁴ f11s⁴ 12.3m² 12m* 12f⁴ 10g² 10g⁵ 9.9m 12m³ 11.9m² 10.9m⁵ Sep 18] smallish gelding: modest handicapper: won at Musselburgh (amateurs) in June: effective at 1¼m/1½m: acts on soft going, firm and fibresand: wears headgear: often races prominently: tends to hang. *B. Ellison*

SHAMAN   6 b.g. Fraam 114 – Magic Maggie 38 (Beveled (USA)) [2003 62: p10g* p10g   **64**
9.7m⁶ 10m⁶ 10d 9f Jun 29] modest handicapper: below form after winning at Lingfield   **a54**
in January: probably stays 1½m: acts on any turf going and all-weather: inconsistent.
G. L. Moore

SHAMARA (IRE)   3 b.f. Spectrum (IRE) 126 – Hamara (FR) (Akarad (FR) 130) [2003   **85 +**
10g⁴ 10m³ 9.9m* 10.5d³ 12g* 12v Nov 19] 27,000F: smallish filly: first foal: dam unraced daughter of French listed 1¼m winner Hamaliya: fairly useful performer: won maiden at Goodwood in September and handicap at Newmarket in October, beating In Love by ½ length in latter: stays 1½m: acts on good to firm and good to soft going (stiff task on heavy final one). *C. F. Wall*

SHAMI   4 ch.c. Rainbow Quest (USA) 134 – Bosra Sham (USA) 132 (Woodman   **105**
(USA) 126) [2003 87: p10g⁵ p12g f8.5g p10g* p10g 12m² 10g May 3] lengthy colt: useful handicapper: won at Lingfield in March by neck from Perfidious: good second to Chai Walla at Newmarket sixth outing: effective at 1¼m/1½m: acts on polytrack, soft and good to firm going: tried tongue tied: effective visored or not. *D. R. Loder*

SHAMONE   2 ch.c. (Feb 20) Case Law 113 – Seek The Jade (USA) (Jade Hunter   **–**
(USA)) [2003 6d 5m 5f 5g f5g f5s Dec 27] 1,100Y: compact colt: first foal: dam unraced: probably of little account. *H. A. McWilliams*

SHAMROCK CITY (IRE)   6 b.g. Rock City 120 – Actualite (Polish Precedent   **95**
(USA) 131) [2003 –: 10d 8g² 10m⁴ 7.9m 8g Sep 13] rather leggy, workmanlike gelding: smart at 3 yrs, lightly raced since: useful form when short-head second to Duck Row and last of 4 to Bonecrusher in minor events at Newmarket: well held in handicaps after: effective at 1m/1¼m: acts on firm ground: has been early to post: sometimes sweats: often makes running. *P. Howling*

SHAMROCK TEA   2 b.c. (Feb 16) Imperial Ballet (IRE) 110 – Yellow Ribbon (IRE)   **77 d**
72 (Hamas (IRE) 125§) [2003 5.2m 5m⁵ 6d* 6g⁵ 5m⁵ 5m 6d f6g Nov 19] 2,500Y: small colt: first foal: dam 7f winner: fair performer: won seller at Ripon in May by 7 lengths, then left D. Cosgrove: well below form last 4 starts: should stay 7f: acts on good to soft ground. *M. E. Sowersby*

SHAMS WA MATAR   2 ch.f. (Feb 26) Polish Precedent (USA) 131 – Rain And Shine   **–**
(FR) 78 (Rainbow Quest (USA) 134) [2003 f5g⁵ May 8] third foal: closely related to 4-y-o Jadeeron: dam, Irish 1½m winner who stayed 2m, closely related to smart 1m/1¼m performer Kabool and granddaughter of outstanding broodmare Fall Aspen: well held in maiden at Southwell, slowly away: sold 6,000 gns. *B. Hanbury*

SHAMWARI FIRE (IRE) 3 ch.g. Idris (IRE) 118 – Bobby's Dream 53 (Reference **65** Point 139) [2003 62: 7g³ 9.3m⁴ 8.5m 7g 8m f8.5g⁵ 8m² 8.2m⁴ f7g⁴ f8g f7g Dec 8] fair **a49** maiden: left M. Tompkins after second outing: well below form last 3 starts: effective at 7f/1m: acts on fibresand (probably on polytrack), good to firm and good to soft ground. *I. W. McInnes*

SHANGHAI SURPRISE 2 b.c. (Mar 7) Komaite (USA) – Shanghai Lil 57 (Petong **49** 126) [2003 7g⁴ f8.5s⁶ 8.3m 8.3g f7g Oct 20] compact colt: first foal: dam, 6f to 1½m winner, half-sister to useful French performer up to 1½m Tocabelle: poor maiden: stays 1m: ran badly in blinkers final start. *I. A. Wood*

SHANK 4 b.c. Lahib (USA) 129 – Mixwayda (FR) (Linamix (FR) 127) [2003 55: f11g **55** f12g⁴ f16s⁶ Feb 13] modest maiden: stayed 1½m: raced only on all-weather: blinkered last 2 starts: dead. *Sir Mark Prescott*

SHANK ON FOURTEEN (IRE) 2 b.g. (Apr 8) Fayruz 116 – Hever Rosina 63 **90** (Efisio 120) [2003 5m² 5m* 5g* 5s⁵ 5f 5.1m⁴ 5g³ 5f⁴ 5.1g⁴ 5m f5s² 5m⁶ Oct 18] IR 1,000F, 6,500Y: small, good-bodied gelding: first foal: dam 6f winner: fairly useful performer: won maiden at Ripon in April and minor event at Thirsk in May: mostly creditable efforts after, in frame in minor events/nurseries: slowly away when running poorly final start: likely to prove best at 5f: unraced on heavy going, acts on any other turf and on fibresand. *K. R. Burke*

SHANOOK 4 ch.g. Rainbow Quest (USA) 134 – Twafeaj (USA) 110 (Topsider (USA)) **88** [2003 86: 7m* 7g 7.1m May 19] tall, angular gelding: fairly useful performer, lightly raced: won handicap at Catterick in March: well below form after: likely to prove best at 7f/1m: acts on good to firm and heavy ground: usually races prominently: carries head awkwardly: sold 11,000 gns. *M. Johnston*

SHANTY STAR (IRE) 3 gr.c. Hector Protector (USA) 124 – Shawanni 105 (Shareef **109** Dancer (USA) 135) [2003 86p: 12m* 11.8m³ 16.2f* Jun 20] big, lengthy, good-bodied colt: useful performer: won minor event at Catterick in April and Queen's Vase at Royal Ascot, in latter beating Singleton by ¾ length in thoroughly game fashion: 11½ lengths

Queen's Vase, Royal Ascot—Shanty Star proves suited by the step up in trip;
Singleton, Cruzspiel (blinkers) and New South Wales (left) come next

third to Franklins Gardens in Derby Trial at Lingfield in between: will stay beyond 2m: acts on firm going: looked open to further improvement. *M. Johnston*

SHAPE UP (IRE)   3 b.g. Octagonal (NZ) 126 – Bint Kaldoun (IRE) 82 (Kaldoun (FR)   **71**
122) [2003 p12g² f12g⁴ 11m⁵ 11.8m⁴ 12.3m 11m⁵ 10.5m⁶ 11.6d p12g³ 11.9m⁴ 12s² 12g⁶ 12.1m⁴ 14.1m Aug 24] 5,500 2-y-o: close-coupled, quite good-topped gelding: first foal: dam, maiden effective at 1m to 1½m, sister to dam of Zafeen out of half-sister to very smart 6f/7f performer Diffident: fair maiden handicapper: stays 1½m: acts on polytrack, soft and good to firm ground: blinkered last 4 outings: held up. *T. Keddy*

SHARAAB (USA)   2 b. or br.c. (Jan 27) Erhaab (USA) 127 – Ghashtah (USA) (Nijin-   **72**
sky (CAN) 138) [2003 8m³ 8.1d Sep 27] leggy colt: seventh foal: half-brother to 1998 2-y-o 1m winner El Nafis (by Kingmambo): dam unraced sister to Seattle Dancer, close relative of Lomond and half-sister to Seattle Slew: much better effort in maidens (fair form) when third at Newmarket, despite not clear run: tongue tied both starts: should be suited by 1¼m+. *B. Hanbury*

SHARAKKA (IRE)   2 b.f. (Feb 27) Daylami (IRE) 138 – Mafaatin (IRE) (Royal   **73**
Academy (USA) 130) [2003 7m³ 7m Oct 4] close-coupled filly: first foal: dam unraced granddaughter of Arc winner All Along: easily better effort in maidens (fair form) when third at Kempton: will be suited by 1¼m/1½m: sold 11,000 gns. *E. A. L. Dunlop*

SHARARAH   4 br.f. Machiavellian (USA) 123 – Raknah (IRE) 91 (Night Shift (USA))   **–**
[2003 87: 5m Oct 2] leggy filly: fairly useful performer at 3 yrs: well beaten for new stable only 4-y-o start: tried tongue tied. *S. C. Williams*

SHARDDA   3 b.f. Barathea (IRE) 127 – Kronengold (USA) (Golden Act (USA)) [2003   **70 ?**
8f⁴ 9.2f³ 9.2d Sep 29] fifth foal: half-sister to German 10.5f winner Aneefah (by Unfuwain): dam, German 9f to 11f winner (placed in 1½m Group 3 event), half-sister to smart middle-distance performer Komtur: fair maiden: left M. Channon 9,500 gns before running poorly final start: should stay 1¼m: acts on firm ground. *F. Watson*

SHARES (IRE)   3 b.g. Turtle Island (IRE) 123 – Glendora (Glenstal (USA) 118) [2003   **60**
67: 7.1m 7.9f³ 10.9m³ p10g Jul 16] good-bodied gelding: modest maiden: should stay 1½m: acts on firm and good to soft going: tried tongue tied: blinkered (found little) final start: very slowly away on reappearance. *G. A. Butler*

SHARMA   3 b.f. Bijou d'Inde 127 – Star of Jupiter (Jupiter Island 126) [2003 53: 8m   **51**
6.1m 5g⁶ 7m³ 7.1m 7m 8m Sep 24] close-coupled, quite good-topped filly: modest maid-en: should stay 1m: acts on good to firm ground: has looked difficult ride. *J. L. Spearing*

SHARMY (IRE)   7 b.g. Caerleon (USA) 132 – Petticoat Lane (Ela-Mana-Mou 132)   **–**
[2003 99, a104: p12g* p12g* p10g p10g Mar 15] close-coupled, quite attractive gelding: **a109**
has a short, unimpressive action: useful performer: won handicaps at Lingfield in January and February, latter by 1½ lengths from Nawamees: below form there after, including in listed race final start: effective at 1¼m/1½m: acts on polytrack and probably any turf going: sometimes slowly away: won over fences in December. *Ian Williams*

SHAROURA   7 ch.m. Inchinor 119 – Kinkajoo 53 (Precocious 126) [2003 61: f6g p5g   **70**
p6g f6g f5s 7.1f⁴ 7.1f² 6g* 7m³ 6d* 6g² 6m³ 6f³ 6m⁵ 6m f6g⁵ Nov 24] angular mare: poor   **a59**
mover: fair handicapper on turf, modest on all-weather: left J. M. Bradley after fifth start: won at Hamilton (apprentices) and Thirsk in July: effective at 6f/7f: acts on firm going, soft and all-weather: tried visored/tongue tied/in cheekpieces: has raced freely/hung/ carried head high. *R. A. Fahey*

SHARP AS CROESUS   3 b.f. Sesaro (USA) 81 – Chushan Venture (Pursuit of Love   **–**
124) [2003 55: 14.1m 8g Oct 31] modest at 2 yrs: refused to enter stall in April and subsequently banned from racing from stalls for 6 months: no show in handicaps at Salis-bury (flip start) and Newmarket after: should stay at least 1m: acts on polytrack. *J. R. Best*

SHARP BREEZE (USA)   3 b. or br.g. Mr Prospector (USA) – Windy Mindy (USA)   **91**
(Honey Jay (USA)) [2003 76p: f9.4g³ p8g* f9.4g³ f8g f8.5g* 7.9m Sep 7] angular gelding: fairly useful performer: won maiden in February and handicap at Wolverhampton in August: ran as though amiss final start: stay 8.5f: acts on all-weather, some promise only outing on turf at 2 yrs: wore blinkers/cheekpieces last 4 appearances: races prominently: sold 14,000 gns, sent to USA, joined M. Puhich. *D. R. Loder*

SHARP GOSSIP (IRE)   7 b.g. College Chapel 122 – Idle Gossip (Runnett 125) [2003   **61 §**
66, a–: f7s f8g⁶ f7s* f7g⁵ f8g f7g f7g³ f7s f7g 7m f8g 6m³ 7m 7g 7.1f f7g Jun 19] sparely-   **a54 §**
made gelding: modest performer: won handicap at Southwell in January: effective at 6f/ 7f: acts on fibresand and any turf going: wears headgear: unreliable. *J. R. Weymes*

SHARP HAT 9 ch.g. Shavian 125 – Madam Trilby (Grundy 137) [2003 87, a81: p5g **83** f6s f5g⁵ f5g f5g f6g* f5s 6.1d 5m* 6f* 6g f7s* 5f⁶ 5d³ 5m² 5f⁴ 5m² 6m² 5m 5m 5m⁶ 7m **a76** 5m 5m 5d* f5g* f6s³ f6g⁵ Dec 26] leggy, angular gelding: fair performer: won amateur claimer at Southwell, seller at Musselburgh, claimer at Catterick and amateur handicap at Wolverhampton between April and June, and claimers at Catterick and Wolverhampton (left D. Chapman £8,000) in November: claimed back £10,000 after penultimate start (only run for D. Nicholls): effective at 5f to easy 7f: acts on any turf going/all-weather: well held in blinkers: sometimes goes freely, including to post: often races handily: very tough. *D. W. Chapman*

SHARPINCH 5 b.g. Beveled (USA) – Giant Nipper (Nashwan (USA) 135) [2003 –: **80 d** f7g⁴ f7g p6g p7g Nov 18] fairly useful handicapper: well held in 2003 after reappearance: effective at 7f/1m: acts on fibresand, soft and good to firm going: free-going sort: inconsistent. *P. R. Chamings*

SHARPLAW DESTINY (IRE) 2 br.f. (Apr 10) Petardia 113 – Coolrain Lady (IRE) **55 p** 74 (Common Grounds 118) [2003 p6g 7.1m f6g⁴ Oct 16] IR 15,500F, 37,000Y: close-coupled, unfurnished filly: sister to 2001 2-y-o 7f winner Princess Petardia and half-sister to 3 useful or better 2-y-o winners, including 5f/6f winner Bella Tusa (in 2002, by Sri Pekan): dam placed at 1m/1¼m in Ireland: best effort in maidens (modest form) when fourth at Southwell, late headway not knocked about: will stay 7f, probably 1m: open to progress. *W. J. Haggas*

SHARPLAW VENTURE 3 b.f. Polar Falcon (USA) 126 – Breakaway 98 (Song 132) **95** [2003 94: 7m⁵ 8f² 8g³ 8d Jul 25] lengthy, angular filly: useful performer: creditable placed efforts in listed rated stakes at Royal Ascot (5 lengths second to Hold To Ransom) and minor event at Salisbury (came from poor position when third to Mubeen): stays 1m: acts on firm going: on toes/wore net muzzle when below form on reappearance. *W. J. Haggas*

SHARP RIGGING (IRE) 3 b.g. Son of Sharp Shot (IRE) 105 – In The Rigging **67** (USA) 78 (Topsider (USA)) [2003 59: 8.2g⁴ 10m³ 8.5g⁴ 8.3m Sep 29] leggy gelding: fair maiden: stays 1¼m: raced on good/good to firm going: sold 7,500 gns. *E. A. L. Dunlop*

SHARP SECRET (IRE) 5 b.m. College Chapel 122 – State Treasure (USA) (Secret- **65** ariat (USA)) [2003 64: 8g 7m 8m² 7m³ 8g⁴ 8f* 8m³ 8.2m⁴ 8m² 8m⁶ 8.2d⁵ Nov 6] leggy mare: fair handicapper: won at Yarmouth in July: stays 1m: acts on firm and soft going: sometimes carries head high/edges left. *J. A. R. Toller*

SHARP SPICE 7 b.m. Lugana Beach 116 – Ewar Empress (IRE) 57 (Persian Bold 123) **–** [2003 67d, a59d: p10g⁵ f11s³ p12g⁵ p12g p12g⁵ 12g 10m⁶ 11.5s⁶ 11.7f Oct 12] angular **a50** mare: poor handicapper: best around 1½m: acts on any turf going and all-weather: usually visored: sometimes slowly away: has carried head awkwardly/found little: held up. *D. J. Coakley*

SHARPSPORT (FR) 4 b.g. Charnwood Forest (IRE) 125 – Wild Sable (IRE) 88 (Kris **39** 135) [2003 52: f9.4g f9.4s⁴ Apr 12] quite good-topped gelding: poor performer: stays 8.5f: acts on fibresand, best turf efforts on good going: has worn cheekpieces/blinkers. *I. Semple*

SHARP STEEL 8 ch.g. Beveled (USA) – Shift Over (USA) 62 (Night Shift (USA)) **–** [2003 –, a55: f8s Jan 10] leggy, workmanlike gelding: modest performer: well held only 8-y-o start: tried visored/in cheekpieces: won over fences in July: dead. *Miss S. J. Wilton*

SHASTA 4 b.f. Shareef Dancer (USA) 135 – Themeda 69 (Sure Blade (USA) 130) [2003 **74** 81: 13.1g 12f 11.6g 10m⁵ 10m² 10m* 10d* 10m⁵ 10m* Sep 19] angular filly: fair performer: won minor events at Windsor in August and Nottingham in September: best recent form around 1¼m: acts on soft and good to firm going: has taken keen hold: usually races up with pace. *R. M. Beckett*

SHATIN HERO 3 ch.c. Lion Cavern (USA) 117 – Moogie 103 (Young Generation **65** 129) [2003 50: 7.1f 5d 8m⁴ 8g 9.2g 8.3m⁵ 10g 9.2g⁶ 10.9g 8f⁵ 8m³ 9.2d⁴ 9.1d* 10.1g⁴ 8.2d⁴ f8.5g² f7g f8g⁵ f8g³ Dec 12] fair performer: won seller at Ayr in October: left Miss L. Perratt after sixteenth start: stays 9f: acts on fibresand, firm and good to soft going: usually wears cheekpieces: sometimes slowly away: has hung left/carried head high/given trouble at start. *G. C. H. Chung*

SHATIN SPECIAL 3 ch.f. Titus Livius (FR) 115 – Lawn Order 51 (Efisio 120) [2003 **57 d** 50: 8m 9.2d 8g² 7.2m⁵ 9.1g 8m⁵ 9.2d 9.1d⁴ 8g 12d⁴ f12g f12g² Dec 26] modest maiden: left Miss L. Perratt after tenth start: stays easy 1½m: acts on fibresand, heavy and good to firm ground: sometimes wears cheekpieces: inconsistent. *G. C. H. Chung*

SHAVA 3 b.g. Atraf 116 – Anita Marie (IRE) (Anita's Prince 126) [2003 52: 7m* 8g 7g⁶ **58**
6g 6m⁵ Aug 7] modest handicapper: won at Newcastle in May: ran as though amiss final
start: stays 7f: acts on good to firm going: tried blinkered/in cheekpieces: sold 3,200 gns.
W. J. Haggas

SHAWNEE WARRIOR (IRE) 2 b.c. (Feb 27) So Factual (USA) 120 – It's So Easy **–**
63 (Shaadi (USA) 126) [2003 5.1m 6g 6m f5g Jul 19] 13,000Y: good-bodied colt: third
foal: half-brother to 5-y-o Gemtastic: dam 7f winner: little sign of ability in maidens.
M. Mullineaux

SHAYADI (IRE) 6 b.g. Kahyasi 130 – Shayrdia (IRE) 57 (Storm Bird (CAN) 134) **86**
[2003 97: p12g 16m⁶ 12g 12.1g⁴ 10f⁶ 11.9f 10g* 10g Aug 26] leggy gelding: fairly useful
handicapper nowadays: won at Ayr in July: folded tamely final outing: effective at 1¼m
(ridden positively) to 2m: acts on firm and soft going: blinkered last 5 starts: sold 5,500
gns, joined B. Ellison and won twice over hurdles in December. *M. Johnston*

SHAYDEYLAYDEH (IRE) 4 b.f. Shaddad (USA) 75 – Spirito Libro (USA) 89 (Lear **–**
Fan (USA) 130) [2003 53, a–: 17.1m p12g Jun 21] unfurnished filly: modest maiden at 3
yrs: well beaten in 2003: wore cheekpieces last 4 outings. *C. N. Allen*

SHAYMEE'S GIRL 2 b.f. (Apr 29) Wizard King 122 – Mouchez Le Nez (IRE) 41 **–**
(Cyrano de Bergerac 120) [2003 f6g Nov 29] €5,000Y: fifth foal: half-sister to fairly
useful 1m and 11f winner Kilmeny (by Royal Abjar) and 1m winner in Belgium by
Case Law: dam lightly-raced maiden: 66/1, well held in maiden at Wolverhampton.
Ms Deborah J. Evans

SHEAPYS LASS 2 b.f. (Feb 3) Perugino (USA) 84 – Nilu (IRE) 58 (Ballad Rock **50**
122) [2003 5f⁶ 5g⁵ 5.1m² 5m⁶ Jul 18] 7,000Y, 8,000 2-y-o: good-bodied filly: sixth foal:
half-sister to 5f (including at 2 yrs)/6f winner Moocha Cha Man (by Sizzling Melody)
and winner in Austria by Clantime: dam 2-y-o 6f winner: modest maiden: second of 3 at
Chester: should stay 6f. *A. Crook*

SHEARWATER 6 b.m. Shareef Dancer (USA) 135 – Sea Ballad (USA) (Bering 136) **–**
[2003 –: f14.8g Nov 29] well held in varied company. *A. Senior*

SHEBAAN 2 b.f. (Mar 8) Compton Place 125 – Chairmans Daughter 68 (Unfuwain **59**
(USA) 131) [2003 6g 7m² 7m 8m 8m⁵ 7m Oct 4] 1,300Y: leggy, unfurnished filly: fourth
foal: half-sister to winners abroad by Danzig Connection and Bin Ajwaad: dam 1m (at 2
yrs) and 2m winner: modest maiden: second in seller at Newmarket, only form: stays 7f:
possibly none too genuine. *P. S. McEntee*

SHEBEEN 3 ch.f. Aragon 118 – Sheesha (USA) (Shadeed (USA) 135) [2003 70p: 6m² **82**
6f² 6f² 7.1m* Jul 5] angular filly: fairly useful performer: landed odds in maiden at
Chepstow in July: stays 7f: acts on firm and good to soft going: very edgy (below form)
second start: sold 10,000 gns, sent to USA. *H. Candy*

SHEER FOCUS (IRE) 5 b.g. Eagle Eyed (USA) 111 – Persian Danser (IRE) 69 **57**
(Persian Bold 123) [2003 70: 8m 9.3g 9m 9f⁵ 8.1g⁶ 8m 8.1m⁴ 9f³ 8f f9.4g³ Nov 1] leggy,
angular gelding: modest handicapper nowadays: stays 1¼m: acts on fibresand, soft and
firm going: tried tongue tied: tends to race freely. *E. J. Alston*

SHEER GUTS (IRE) 4 b.g. Hamas (IRE) 125§ – Balakera (FR) (Lashkari 128) [2003 **–**
69: 10.1m⁵ 10.4m f12g 14.1s⁶ Oct 29] fair performer in 2002: well beaten on Flat at 4 yrs,
but won over hurdles: tried blinkered/tongue tied/in cheekpieces. *John A. Harris*

SHEIK'N SWING 4 b.f. Celtic Swing 138 – Elegantissima 57 (Polish Precedent **67 d**
(USA) 131) [2003 73: 7m⁴ 7f 7m 8m 8g 7.6m Jul 12] fair handicapper: below form after
reappearance: stays 7f: acts on firm and good to soft ground, well held on fibresand.
W. G. M. Turner

SHE LEGGED IT (IRE) 2 b.f. (Feb 11) Cape Cross (IRE) 129 – Mrs Siddons (IRE) **51**
82 (Royal Academy (USA) 130) [2003 6d 5.7m 5m 8.3g⁴ Oct 13] €19,000Y: first
foal: dam, easily best effort (from 4 starts) on debut at 7f at 2 yrs, half-sister to smart
1¼m to 2¼m performer Lear White: modest maiden: fourth in Windsor seller: stays 1m.
R. Hannon

SHELIAK 2 b.f. (Apr 5) Binary Star (USA) – Flo's Choice (IRE) 35 (Dancing Dissident **–**
(USA) 119) [2003 8m⁵ 7s Nov 3] quite good-topped filly: second foal: dam sprint
maiden: last in minor event/maiden. *B. S. Rothwell*

SHELINI 3 b.f. Robellino (USA) 127 – Agama (USA) 44 (Nureyev (USA) 131) [2003 **80**
91: 8g 9f⁴ 8.1g Jul 4] leggy, quite good-topped filly: fairly useful handicapper: favourite,
reportedly banged head in stall when well beaten final start: should stay at least 1¼m: acts
on any going. *M. A. Jarvis*

SHELL GARLAND (USA)   3 b.f. Sadler's Wells (USA) 132 – Shell Ginger (IRE)   –
110 (Woodman (USA) 126) [2003 80: 9.9d³ 10.1g⁶ Jul 17] lengthy filly: fairly useful
form in maidens at 2 yrs: disappointing in 2003 (wandered/carried head high on reappearance). *Sir Michael Stoute*

SHENLEY CHARM   3 b.c. First Trump 118 – Glimpse 77 (Night Shift (USA)) [2003   **91**
83: 8m³ 8m⁴ 8d p7g⁶ 8m² 10g Oct 13] sturdy colt: fairly useful performer: best effort
when second in handicap at Pontefract: stayed 1m: acted on soft going, good to firm and
fibresand: often front runner: dead. *H. Morrison*

SHEPPARD'S WATCH   5 b.m. Night Shift (USA) – Sheppard's Cross 88 (Soviet Star   **105 ?**
(USA) 128) [2003 8f⁵ 7g 8f² 7d⁴ 7m⁵ 7.5m* Oct 5] attractive, good-topped mare: useful
performer: trained by M. Tregoning most of 2001: sent to USA, ran only once in 2002
and left C. Clement after reappearance: apparently back to near best to win Coolmore
Stud Home of Champions Concorde Stakes at Tipperary in October by neck from Latino
Magic, coming from last to lead close home: stays 9f: acts on firm going. *G. Wragg*

SHERAZADE   4 ch.f. Beveled (USA) – Miss Ritz 65 (Robellino (USA) 127) [2003   –
55, a49: f5g Jan 18] modest maiden at best: well beaten only 4-y-o start. *C. N. Kellett*

SHERIFF'S DEPUTY   3 b.g. Atraf 116 – Forest Fantasy 61 (Rambo Dancer (CAN)   **81**
107) [2003 70: 7.1m² 7.1m⁵ 8m² 8.1f² 8g² 8d² 8.1m* 8.1m 10f⁴ f9.4g² Oct 20] strong
gelding: fairly useful performer: won maiden at Warwick in September: will probably
stay 1¼m: acts on fibresand, firm and good to soft ground: consistent. *J. W. Unett*

SHERWOOD FOREST   3 ch.g. Fleetwood (IRE) 107 – Jay Gee Ell 78 (Vaigly Great   **56**
127) [2003 –: 9.2d 9.2d⁵ 8m 8m³ 8m³ 10.9g⁴ 10.9g* 12.1g⁴ 12.1m 12.1g⁶ 10.9m 10.9m⁵
12m 10.9d Oct 13] strong gelding: modest handicapper: won at Ayr in August: probably
stays 1½m: acts on good to firm ground: usually wears headgear: none too consistent.
Miss L. A. Perratt

SHERZABAD (IRE)   6 b. or br.g. Doyoun 124 – Sheriya (USA) (Green Dancer (USA)   **52**
132) [2003 51: p12g 11.5g⁶ 16.5m⁴ 14.1d⁶ 11.5m* 12m 10.9m 12d Oct 4] sturdy, lengthy
gelding: modest handicapper: won at Lingfield in August: effective at 1½m/1¾m: acts on
good to firm going, lightly raced and little form on all-weather: usually visored: tried
tongue tied: best held up. *H. J. Collingridge*

SHE'S A DIAMOND   6 b.m. Mystiko (USA) 124 – Fairy Kingdom (Prince Sabo   –
123) [2003 –: 6s 6g 6m Oct 17] little sign of ability. *T. T. Clement*

SHE'S A FOX   2 b.f. (Mar 3) Wizard King 122 – Foxie Lady 77 (Wolfhound (USA)   –
126) [2003 6f Oct 27] 1,000Y: first foal: dam, maiden who stayed 7.5f, out of half-sister
to Middle Park Stakes winner Creag-An-Sgor: 66/1, slowly away when tailed off in
maiden at Leicester. *S. T. Lewis*

SHE'S A GEM   8 b.m. Robellino (USA) 127 – Rose Gem (IRE) 62 (Taufan (USA)   –
119) [2003 –: f14g Mar 11] smallish mare: modest performer at 4 yrs: lightly raced and
no form since: tried visored/blinkered. *T. T. Clement*

SHE'S FLASH (IRE)   4 b.f. Woodborough (USA) 112 – Beechwood Quest (IRE) 65   –
(River Falls 113) [2003 –: f7g 7g 10m Apr 26] maiden: no form since 2 yrs: left F. Murphy
after reappearance. *J. A. Supple*

SHE'S MY VALENTINE   3 b.f. My Best Valentine 122 – Hong Kong Girl 94 (Petong   **53**
126) [2003 –: 7.1m³ 6d 7.1m 7.1m³ 5.7f³ 7m Sep 22] poor maiden: stays 7f: acts on firm
and good to soft ground. *B. R. Millman*

SHE'S OUR LASS (IRE)   2 b.f. (Feb 6) Orpen (USA) 116 – Sharadja (IRE) (Doyoun   **57**
124) [2003 5f² p6g⁵ f8.5s⁵ f8s⁴ f7s² Oct 21] €4,000Y: sturdy filly: first foal: dam unraced
granddaughter of Prix Vermeille winner Sharaya: modest maiden: second at Catterick
and Southwell: stays 7f, possibly not quite 1m: best effort on fibresand. *D. Carroll*

SHE WHO DARES WINS   3 b.f. Atraf 116 – Mirani (IRE) 55 (Danehill (USA) 126)   **54 ?**
[2003 56: 5f⁴ f5g 6d 5m Aug 17] smallish, workmanlike filly: modest maiden: well held
after reappearance: raced mainly at 5f: acts on firm ground. *L. R. James*

SHIBUMI   2 ch.f. (Apr 1) Cigar 68 – Hurricane Rose (Windjammer (USA)) [2003 7m   **– p**
Oct 13] tall, rather unfurnished filly: sister to Italian sprint winner Leccino: dam poor
maiden: 25/1 and green, eighth of 13 in maiden at Leicester, prominent until 2f out:
should do better. *H. Morrison*

SHIELALIGH   2 ch.f. (Apr 22) Aragon 118 – Sheesha (USA) (Shadeed (USA) 135)   **83**
[2003 6d* 6m² 6g⁴ 6.1m³ Sep 8] 1,000Y: leggy, close-coupled filly: fifth foal: sister to
3-y-o Shebeen: dam, ran once, closely related to smart stayer Samraan: fairly useful

performer: won maiden at Windsor in June: creditable efforts in minor event/nurseries: free-going sort, but will probably stay 7f: acts on good to firm and good to soft ground: sold 6,500 gns. *H. Candy*

SHIELD   3 b.c. Barathea (IRE) 127 – Shesadelight 67 (Shirley Heights 130) [2003 97p: 10m* 12m Jun 7] strong, rangy, good sort: useful performer: won Bonusprint.com Classic Trial at Sandown (beat Inch Again by ½ length, leading close home) in April: never-nearer tenth of 20 to Kris Kin in Derby at Epsom only subsequent outing: should have proved suited by 1½m+: acted on polytrack and good to firm going: wore crossed noseband/had 2 handlers: reported in July to have been put down after fracturing a pastern. *G. A. Butler*   **107**

SHIFTY   4 b.g. Night Shift (USA) – Crodelle (IRE) (Formidable (USA) 125) [2003 73: 6m 9m 7m 7.5m 7m* 6.9m 7m 7m 8m 7m4 8.5m 8f6 8m5 9m f8g4 f8g2 f9.4s3 f6g4 f7g2 f8s6 Dec 27] well-made gelding: has a round action: fair handicapper: won at Thirsk in June: stays 1m: acts on firm going and fibresand: effective blinkered or not: has given trouble in preliminaries, unseating rider and bolting before thirteenth start. *D. Nicholls*   **66**

SHIFTY NIGHT (IRE)   2 b.f. (May 9) Night Shift (USA) – Bean Island (USA) (Afleet (CAN)) [2003 6m 7.5m Jun 24] €6,000Y: workmanlike filly: third foal: dam, 1m winner in USA, half-sister to dam of smart 1¼m performer Johan Cruyff: backward, well held in maidens at Newmarket and Beverley (sweating/edgy). *Mrs C. A. Dunnett*   **–**

SHINGALANA   6 ch.m. Lion Cavern (USA) 117 – Zealous Kitten (USA) 58 (The Minstrel (CAN) 135) [2003 f12g Jan 21] second foal: dam, stayer, also successful over hurdles: 100/1, tailed off in maiden at Southwell. *Miss D. A. McHale*   **–**

SHINGLES (IRE)   3 ch.c. Desert Prince (IRE) 130 – Nibbs Point (IRE) 107 (Sure Blade (USA) 130) [2003 71: p10g5 p12g f11s* f9.4g* f12g* 12.3m May 7] smallish, useful-looking colt: fairly useful performer: won claimer at Southwell in February and handicaps at Wolverhampton in February and March: stayed 1½m: acted on fibresand, firm and soft going: was reliable: dead. *N. P. Littmoden*   **84**

SHINING WHITE   4 b.f. Zafonic (USA) 130 – White Shadow (IRE) 87 (Last Tycoon 131) [2003 84: p5g5 p6g6 6m 6m Apr 14] fair performer, lightly raced: should stay 7f: acts on polytrack, raced only on good/good to firm ground on turf: sold 1,500 gns in December. *J. M. P. Eustace*   **77 d**

SHINKO FEMME (IRE)   2 b.f. (Feb 25) Shinko Forest (IRE) – Kilshanny 70 (Groom Dancer (USA) 128) [2003 6.1g6 6.1m 6.1m 6.1d6 6f2 6f4 7f6 6m3 6d Nov 4] 12,000Y: third foal: half-sister to 3-y-o Leitrim Rock and Italian 2001 2-y-o 7f winner Golden Gables (both by Barathea): dam, 1½m winner, out of smart 1½m performer Kiliniski: modest maiden: second at Brighton: left W. Muir before final start: needs to settle to stay 7f: acts on firm ground: often slowly away. *N. Tinkler*   **60**

SHIN PARADISE   3 b.g. Night Shift (USA) – Silent Love (USA) (Hansel (USA)) [2003 f7g f8g4 f7s6 8m* 8g 7.9d 10.1m 8.5d 8m Oct 6] 30,000DM, 600,000 francs Y: second foal: half-brother to fairly useful 2001 2-y-o 1m winner Diamond Lover (by Alhaarth): dam placed at 5f/6f in Germany at 2 yrs: modest performer: won maiden handicap at Musselburgh in March: stays 1m: acts on good to firm ground and fibresand: blinkered (found nothing) eighth outing: inconsistent: sold 1,000 gns, sent to Belgium. *T. D. Easterby*   **59**

SHINY   4 b.f. Shambo 113 – Abuzz 101 (Absalom 128) [2003 98: 6g5 p7g 7.1m4 8.5m4 7.1f 7m 7.1f3 7g6 Jul 31] tall filly: fairly useful performer: creditable efforts in listed events at Doncaster (fifth to Red Carpet) and Epsom (fourth to Aldora) on first/fourth starts, and when third in minor event at Warwick: effective at 6f to 8.5f: acts on firm and good to soft ground: tried blinkered: usually races prominently: in foal to Diktat. *C. E. Brittain*   **93**

SHIRAZI   5 b.g. Mtoto 134 – Al Shadeedah (USA) 86 (Nureyev (USA) 131) [2003 81: p10g5 p10g* p10g3 12g6 Jul 17] strong gelding: fairly useful handicapper: won at Lingfield in January: left J. Hills and off 5 months before final start: successful over hurdles in between: stays 1¼m: acts on polytrack, soft and firm ground: has been tongue tied: held up. *D. R. Gandolfo*   **82**

SHIRLEY COLLINS   4 b.f. Robellino (USA) 127 – Kisumu (Damister (USA) 123) [2003 76, a69: 10g6 8.2s 9.2m4 8g 8g4 Jul 26] smallish, good-topped filly: fair maiden handicapper: best around 1¼m: acts on good to firm going and fibresand, below form both starts on turf: tried visored and in cheekpieces: none too reliable. *Lady Herries*   **73 a–**

SHIRLEY NOT   7 gr.g. Paris House 123 – Hollia 72 (Touch Boy 109) [2003 66: 7m 7g 5f f5s 5m 5m Oct 4] big, lengthy gelding: fair performer at best: showed little in 2003:   **–**

left S. Gollings after second start: often blinkered/visored earlier in career: held up. *D. Nicholls*

SHIRLEY OAKS (IRE) 5 b.m. Sri Pekan (USA) 117 – Duly Elected (Persian Bold **40** 123) [2003 51: f6g 7g 8f⁴ 7f 7f⁴ 8m 7f 8m Oct 23] small, sparely-made mare: poor performer: left Gay Kelleway after reappearance: stays easy 1m: acts on good to soft going, good to firm, dirt and polytrack: has been blinkered/visored/tongue tied: sometimes slowly away. *Miss Z. C. Davison*

SHIRLEYS QUEST 4 b.f. Bin Ajwaad (IRE) 119 – Mainly Me 76 (Huntingdale 132) **–** [2003 –: 10g 11.8m 14.1m 9m 7f Oct 27] leggy filly: little form: left G. Wragg after second outing. *G. C. H. Chung*

SHOCK AND AWE 2 b.f. (Mar 4) Danzig Connection (USA) – No Comebacks 70 **–** (Last Tycoon 131) [2003 6g 7.1m Jul 31] 12,000Y: workmanlike filly: fifth foal: sister to 4-y-o Steely Dan and half-sister to 6-y-o New Options: dam, 1m to 1½m winner, out of half-sister to Irish 1000 Guineas winner Katies: pulled hard when well beaten in maidens at Newcastle and Musselburgh (slowly away). *K. A. Ryan*

SHOESHINE BOY (IRE) 5 b. or br.g. Prince Sabo 123 – Susie Sunshine (IRE) 81 **86 §** (Waajib 121) [2003 94: 5g 5f 5.5f 5d 5f³ 5.3f³ 5f 5m 5d⁴ Oct 4] smallish, strong gelding: fairly useful handicapper: stays 5.6f: acts on any turf going: blinkered once in 2000: played up badly in preliminaries seventh outing: often races prominently: unreliable: sold 12,000 gns, sent to Belgium. *B. J. Meehan*

SHOLAY (IRE) 4 b.g. Bluebird (USA) 125 – Splicing 82 (Sharpo 132) [2003 85: **65** p10g p10g⁵ p8g 7m⁶ 7g 10.5g⁶ 12g⁵ 12g⁴ 10.5g 10.5s Nov 1] lightly-made gelding: fair performer: left G. Butler after reappearance, P. Mitchell after fourth start: stays 1½m: acts on good to firm and good to soft going, probably on polytrack: tried visored/blinkered: joined N. Twiston-Davies. *E. Danel, France*

SHOLOKHOV (IRE) 4 b.c. Sadler's Wells (USA) 132 – La Meilleure 86 (Lord Gayle (USA) 124) [2003 121: 10g Apr 26] sturdy colt: very smart performer on his day, runner-up in Irish Derby at the Curragh and Eclipse Stakes at Sandown at 3 yrs for A. O'Brien in Ireland: tailed off in Gordon Richards Stakes at Sandown on only outing of 2003 (reportedly underwent soft palate operation after): better at 1¼m/1½m than shorter: acted on soft and good to firm going: wore crossed noseband: had 2 handlers: often made running (acted as pacemaker on 2 occasions in 2002): carried head awkwardly: inconsistent: to stand at Gestut Etzean, Germany, fee €5,000, Oct 1st. *M. A. Jarvis*

SHOLTO 5 b.g. Tragic Role (USA) – Rose Mill (Puissance 110) [2003 62: 5m* 6m⁴ **71** 5m 5m* 5m 5m⁶ 5m⁶ 5m 5m 5g Oct 22] close-coupled gelding: fair performer: won handicap at Warwick in April and minor event at Pontefract in June: best at 5f: acts on soft and good to firm ground: usually blinkered: tried tongue tied: often hangs. *J. O'Reilly*

SHOOT 3 b.f. Barathea (IRE) 127 – Prophecy (IRE) 109 (Warning 136) [2003 7f² 7m* **82 +** 7m³ Aug 15] fifth foal: half-sister to useful 6f winner Arabesque (by Zafonic) and 7-y-o Threat: dam, 2-y-o 5f/6f (latter including Cheveley Park Stakes) winner who stayed 1m, out of Lancashire Oaks winner Andaleeb: fairly useful form: won maiden at Newmarket in July: good second (caused interference, demoted) in handicap there final start: should stay 1m: raced only on ground firmer than good: joined R. Frankel in USA. *J. H. M. Gosden*

SHOOTING LODGE (IRE) 2 b.f. (Mar 10) Grand Lodge (USA) 125 – Sidama **– p** (FR) (Top Ville 129) [2003 7.1m Sep 8] 200,000F, 360,000Y: rangy filly: has scope: half-sister to several winners, including fairly useful Irish 1½m winner Sincere (by Bahhare) and Irish 1¼m and (including listed race) 2m winner Sinntara (by Lashkari), herself dam of Sinndar (by Grand Lodge): dam French 1¼m/1½m winner: 11/1, well held in maiden at Warwick, slowly away, very green and not knocked about: will be well suited by 1¼m+: sure to do better. *Sir Michael Stoute*

SHORELINE SUITE (IRE) 2 ch.f. (Apr 25) Woodborough (USA) 112 – Hyannis **33** (FR) (Esprit du Nord (USA) 126) [2003 5f 5m 5m⁶ 5d May 20] 1,100Y: small filly: half-sister to 3 winners, including 7f winner Hyperactive (by Perugino): dam unraced: poor maiden: tends to start slowly. *M. E. Sowersby*

SHORE VISION 5 b.g. Efisio 120 – South Shore 102 (Caerleon (USA) 132) [2003 **74** 73: f8s⁴ f8g⁴ p8g² p8g² f8g⁴ 8.3d⁴ 10d 8.1m f8g⁴ 8.3m² 8f 10m⁴ 8g Jul 30] strong, good-bodied gelding: fair handicapper: best form around 1m: acts on good to firm going, good to soft and all-weather: wore cheekpieces last 4 starts: often races prominently. *P. W. Harris*

SHORT CHANGE (IRE) 4 b.g. Revoque (IRE) 122 – Maafi Esm (Polish Precedent **63**
(USA) 131) [2003 64: 11.7m 10d 10m 10f 10m² 10m³ 11.6g³ 11.6g* 10d⁴ 11.9m 11.5g³
9.9d² 11.7f² 11.9m² Oct 23] big, lengthy gelding: modest handicapper: won at Windsor in
August: effective at 1m to 1½m: acts on firm and good to soft ground: tried blinkered/in
cheekpieces: often races prominently: won over hurdles in November. *A. W. Carroll*

SHORT CHORUS 2 ch.f. (May 3) Inchinor 119 – Strawberry Song 87 (Final Straw **52**
127) [2003 5f⁵ 5m* f5s 6.1m 6.5m Sep 26] 5,500Y: small filly: half-sister to 3 winning
sprinters, including fairly useful 1999 2-y-o 5f/6f winner Ebba (by Elmaamul): dam 1¼m
winner: modest performer: won claimer at Beverley in June, then left J. Portman: stiff
tasks in nurseries/sales race after: should stay 7f: acts on good to firm going. *J. Balding*

SHORT PAUSE 4 b.c. Sadler's Wells (USA) 132 – Interval 122 (Habitat 134) [2003 **119**
8.5g³ 10d⁴ 10d* 10m⁴ 9.8d² Oct 4] half-brother to several winners, notably useful French
1m and (at 2 yrs) 9f winner Cheyenne Dream (by Dancing Brave): dam 5f (at 2 yrs) to
1m winner: smart performer: improved in 2003, winning listed race at Longchamp in
September by length from Secret Singer: best effort when 2 lengths second to Weightless
in Prix Dollar there final start, finishing strongly having been detached last home turn:
stays 1¼m: acts on good to firm and good to soft ground, probably on heavy. *A. Fabre,
France*

SHORT RESPITE 4 b.f. Brief Truce (USA) 126 – Kingdom Princess 69 (Forzando **53 §**
122) [2003 78: 10g 10g 10g 9.2g 10.5g 10.9g² 9.2g⁴ 8.5m 9.1d Oct 14] leggy filly: modest
performer: left K. Burke after fifth start: stays 11f: acts on soft and good to firm going:
tried visored/in cheekpieces: sometimes slowly away/flashes tail/hangs: untrustworthy:
sold 1,200 gns. *K. A. Ryan*

SHOTACROSS THE BOW (IRE) 6 b.g. Warning 136 – Nordica 99 (Northfields **50**
(USA)) [2003 63, a84: f8.5g 11.7m 10d⁵ 10.2f⁶ 8.1m⁶ 10.3g⁴ 8f 10f 10m² 10.2g⁶ 9.7g **a72**
8m f9.4g⁴ f8g* f8.5g⁴ f8g Nov 25] tall, angular gelding: fair performer on all-weather,
modest on turf: won minor event at Southwell in October: best at 1m/1¼m: acts on fibresand, good to firm and good to soft going: tried blinkered: held up. *M. Blanshard*

SHOTLEY DANCER 4 ch.f. Danehill Dancer (IRE) 117 – Hayhurst (Sandhurst **53**
Prince 128) [2003 57: 9.9d⁵ 7.5m⁶ 10.9m 8g 8g³ 8.1m² 7.9f⁵ 9.9m 7f⁶ 10m Sep 25] leggy
filly: fluent mover: modest maiden: stays 1m: acts on firm and soft ground: tried blinkered. *N. Bycroft*

SHOTSTOPPA (IRE) 5 ch.g. Beveled (USA) – From The Rooftops (IRE) (Thatch- **–**
ing 131) [2003 45: f7g Jan 28] strong gelding: poor maiden. *M. Dods*

SHOT TO FAME (USA) 4 b.g. Quest For Fame 127 – Exocet (USA) (Deposit Ticket **104**
(USA)) [2003 112: 8.1m⁶ 8m 10g 8m⁵ 10d⁶ 8m³ 9m 8g Nov 1] angular, lightly-made
gelding: useful handicapper: creditable third to Irony at Kempton sixth start: best at 1m/
9f: yet to race on firm going, probably acts on any other: sweated (below form in Cambridgeshire) seventh outing. *P. W. Harris*

SHOUETTE (IRE) 3 b.f. Sadler's Wells (USA) 132 – Sumava (IRE) (Sure Blade **76 +**
(USA) 130) [2003 68p: 10.5d² 9.2d³ 10d* Oct 14] angular filly: fair performer: off 5
months, won maiden at Ayr in October by 2 lengths from Allied Victory: will stay 1½m:
raced only on good to soft going: sold 11,000 gns. *B. W. Hills*

SHOUTING THE ODDS (IRE) 3 br.f. Victory Note (USA) 120 – Spout House **89 d**
(IRE) 55 (Flash of Steel 120) [2003 91: 6m 5d² 5f 5.1m 5g 5d 5s Nov 3] leggy filly: fairly
useful handicapper: below form after second outing: best at 5f/6f: acts on firm and good
to soft ground. *J. G. Given*

SHOW ME THE LOLLY (FR) 3 b.f. Sri Pekan (USA) 117 – Sugar Lolly (USA) **57**
(Irish River (FR) 131) [2003 8.2f 8.2m⁵ f2g f12g Dec 3] 5,500F: leggy filly: second foal:
dam ran once in Italy: modest maiden: tailed off on fibresand last 2 starts: stays 1m: raced
only on ground firmer than good on turf. *P. J. McBride*

SHOW ME THE ROSES (USA) 2 b.f. (Feb 24) Storm Cat (USA) – Myth (USA) **91**
(Ogygian (USA)) [2003 5m³ 5m 6g² 7m⁶ 6d Oct 12] leggy filly: second living foal:
closely related to top 2001 2-y-o Johannesburg (by Hennessy), 5f to 8.5f (Breeders' Cup
Juvenile) winner: dam, sprint winner in USA, half-sister to US Grade 2 7f winner Tale of
The Cat (by Storm Cat) and 2000 Middle Park Stakes winner Minardi: fairly useful
maiden: placed at Sandown and Listowel: best effort when sixth of 10 to Venturi in
C. L. Weld Park Stakes at the Curragh: stays 7f: sent to USA. *A. P. O'Brien, Ireland*

SHOW NO FEAR 2 b.c. (Feb 14) Groom Dancer (USA) 128 – La Piaf (FR) (Fabulous **69**
Dancer (USA) 124) [2003 6g³ 6m 6m f8s⁵ 10m⁵ 8.2m² Oct 28] 10,000F, 26,000Y: good-

topped colt: sixth foal: half-brother to 3 winners, including 3-y-o Merlin's Dancer and 5-y-o Gilded Dancer: dam, French 2-y-o 7.5f winner (later winner in USA), half-sister to very smart US 9f/1¼m performer Golden Apples: fair maiden: left N. Callaghan after fourth start: visored/edgy, second to Border Castle at Nottingham, clear leader long way: stays 1¼m: acts on good to firm going, some promise on fibresand. *H. J. Cyzer*

SHOWTIME ANNIE   2 b.f. (Jan 20) Wizard King 122 – Rebel County (IRE) 97 **63** (Maelstrom Lake 118) [2003 5d 5.1m 6g⁵ 6m⁴ 7.5m 7m 8m³ 8.1d³ 7m 8d Oct 14] good-bodied filly: first foal: dam 6f (at 2 yrs) to 1¼m winner: modest maiden: third at Ayr (nursery) and Haydock (probably flattered): stays 1m: acts on good to firm and good to soft going: often races up with pace. *A. Bailey*

SHREDDED (USA)   3 b.c. Diesis 133 – Shiitake (USA) (Green Dancer (USA) 132) **73 +** [2003 81p: 9m⁵ 10d⁴ Oct 14] fair maiden: stays 1¼m: acts on good to soft ground: carried head awkwardly final start. *J. H. M. Gosden*

SHRIEK   3 gr.f. Sheikh Albadou 128 – Normanby Lass 100 (Bustino 136) [2003 –: p6g **53** p5g⁴ p5g 6.1m Jul 5] modest maiden: should stay 7f: acts on polytrack. *J. A. Osborne*

SHRINK   2 b.f. (Mar 4) Mind Games 121 – Miss Mercy (IRE) 62 (Law Society (USA) **71** 130) [2003 5.1m² 5f² Aug 22] fourth foal: sister to useful 2001 2-y-o 5f winner Pachara (later successful in USA) and half-sister to 6f winner That's Jazz (by Cool Jazz) and 3-y-o Queens Jubilee: dam 2-y-o 6f winner: fair form when runner-up in maiden at Chepstow (missed break) and minor event at Newcastle (made most): will prove best at 5f/6f. *M. L. W. Bell*

SHUDDER   8 b.g. Distant Relative 128 – Oublier L'Ennui (FR) 79 (Bellman (FR) 123) **55** [2003 7d5d: 6d 6s⁵ f6g 6m Aug 20] just modest at best in 2003: effective at 5.7f to 7f: acts on heavy and good to firm going: often visored: inconsistent. *R. J. Hodges*

SHUHOOD (USA)   3 b.g. Kingmambo (USA) 125 – Nifty (USA) (Roberto (USA) **91** 131) [2003 81p: 10m³ 9.9m² 10m⁵ Jun 27] tall, quite attractive gelding: fairly useful performer, lightly raced: creditable efforts when second in minor event at Salisbury and fifth in handicap at Newmarket (visored and sweating): should stay 1½m: raced only on good to firm ground: sold 30,000 gns in October. *E. A. L. Dunlop*

SHUSH   5 b.g. Shambo 113 – Abuzz 101 (Absalom 128) [2003 74, a69: p10g⁶ p10g⁴ **70** f12g² p13g³ p12g* 12m 14.1s 12d⁴ 11.5f⁴ 10.2g* 11m² 9.9m Oct 1] quite attractive gelding: fair handicapper: won at Lingfield in March and Chepstow in August: stays easy 13f: acts on any turf going/all-weather: occasionally blinkered: often races prominently/makes running. *C. E. Brittain*

SICILY (USA)   3 b.f. Kris S (USA) – Najecam (USA) (Trempolino (USA) 135) [2003 **74 §** 10m 9.9m² 11.9m³ 14.1m* 12m⁵ Aug 13] $150,000Y: big, plain filly: second foal: sister to 2003 Breeders' Cup Juvenile winner Action This Day: dam, 6f (at 2 yrs) to 8.5f winner in USA, placed in Grade 2 events: fair performer: odds on, far from keen to go past runner-up when winning 3-runner maiden at Redcar in June: stays 1¾m: raced only on good to firm going: visored/blinkered last 2 outings: ungenuine. *J. H. M. Gosden*

SIEGFRIEDS NIGHT (IRE)   2 ch.g. (Mar 10) Night Shift (USA) – Shelbiana **68 §** (USA) (Chieftain) [2003 6m 7f⁴ 6g 7m⁶ 7m⁵ 7m⁵ 5.2f¹⁴ 5m 5m 5.1d f5g f5g³ f5s⁵ Dec 27] good-topped gelding: brother to fairly useful 1996 French 2-y-o 6f winner Elle Est Revenue and UAE 5f/6f winner Moonlight Acre, and half-brother to 2 winners, including useful Irish 1m winner Alluring (by Lure): dam won up to 9f in USA at 2 yrs, including minor stakes: fair maiden: left M. Channon after sixth start: well below form after next outing: stays 7f: acts on firm ground: ungenuine. *M. C. Chapman*

SIENA STAR (IRE)   5 b.g. Brief Truce (USA) 126 – Gooseberry Pie 63 (Green **88** Desert (USA) 127) [2003 78, a84: p10g² p12g² p10g⁴ p10g 10.2m² 10.2f³ 10.1g⁵ 10.3m⁶ 10g* 10g 10.4f² 12m⁵ p12g Nov 22] close-coupled gelding: has a quick action: fairly useful performer: won handicap at Leicester in August: stays easy 1½m: acts on firm ground, soft and polytrack, probably on fibresand: held up: consistent. *P. F. I. Cole*

SIENNA SUNSET (IRE)   4 ch.f. Spectrum (IRE) 126 – Wasabi (IRE) (Polar Falcon **68** (USA) 126) [2003 66: 10f⁴ 9.7f² 11.6g 8f² 8g 10m Sep 1] tall filly: fair handicapper: stays 1¼m: acts on firm ground, soft and polytrack. *Mrs H. Dalton*

SIERRA   2 ch.f. (Apr 3) Dr Fong (USA) 128 – Warning Belle (Warning 136) [2003 8m **–** Sep 23] 18,000Y: tall, quite good-topped filly: third foal: half-sister to useful 2001 2-y-o 7f winner Desert Warning (by Mark of Esteem): dam unraced half-sister to high-class 1¼m performer Stagecraft from excellent family of Opera House and Kayf Tara: 12/1, last of 11 in maiden at Newmarket. *C. E. Brittain*

SIERRA NEVADA (GER) 3 ch.f. Lake Coniston (IRE) 131 – Spirit Lake (GER) –
(Surumu (GER)) [2003 f6g Nov 19] first living foal: dam, ran once in Germany, closely
related to 5-y-o Sabiango and half-sister to high-class German 1¼m/1½m performer
Silvano: 6/1, well beaten in maiden at Southwell. *M. A. Magnusson*

SIERRA VISTA 3 ch.f. Atraf 116 – Park Vista (Taufan (USA) 119) [2003 95: 6m⁴ **91**
5.1m⁵ 6.1d³ 5m⁵ 6f 5d 5f³ 5g⁴ 5m⁵ 6.1g 5d³ 5d⁶ 5g 5m⁴ Oct 20] leggy filly: fairly useful
handicapper: failed to win in 2003, but mostly creditable efforts: best at 5f: acts on firm
and good to soft going. *D. W. Barker*

SIGHT SCREEN 3 b.f. Eagle Eyed (USA) 111 – Krisia (Kris 135) [2003 72: 10g⁶ 8m –
Jul 18] small, close-coupled filly: fair form on second 2-y-o start: well held in 2003,
sweating and heavily bandaged final outing: sold 14,000 gns in December. *B. W. Hills*

SIGHTS ON GOLD (IRE) 4 ch.c. Indian Ridge 123 – Summer Trysting (USA) 83 **119**
(Alleged (USA) 138) [2003 116: 8.9g² 8.9g⁶ 10m* 10g² Jul 21] strong, angular colt:
smart performer: trained by D. Weld in Ireland at 3 yrs: won betfair.com Brigadier Gerard
Stakes at Sandown in May by ½ length from Parasol: creditable efforts when runner-up,
beaten 3¾ lengths by Ipi Tombe in Jebel Hatta at Nad Al Sheba on reappearance and ¾
length by Princely Venture in Scottish Derby at Ayr (suffered injury): effective at 9f to
1½m: acts on soft and good to firm going: tongue tied last 2 starts: has been bandaged in
front: reliable: stays in training. *Saeed bin Suroor*

SIGNORA PANETTIERA (FR) 2 ch.f. (Mar 10) Lord of Men 116 – Karaferya **54**
(USA) 101 (Green Dancer (USA) 132) [2003 7f⁶ 8.1g⁴ 8m Sep 9] leggy filly: half-sister
to several winners, including Irish 2m winner Karakam (by Rainbow Quest): dam, best at
1¼m, sister to dam of Kalanisi and 3-y-o Kalaman: modest form in maidens: should be
suited by 1¼m/1½m. *M. R. Channon*

SIGNOR PANETTIERE 2 b.c. (Mar 7) Night Shift (USA) – Christmas Kiss 82 (Tau- **76 §**
fan (USA) 119) [2003 5g* 5g⁴ 5.1m⁴ 6g⁴ 5m 5f 6g 5m 6g⁵ Oct 25] 42,000Y: well-made
colt: reportedly had wind operation: fourth foal: half-brother to 4-y-o Night Runner and
5-y-o Festive Affair: dam 5f/6f winner: fair performer: made all in maiden at Kempton in
March: mostly disappointing, including in nurseries, after: headstrong, and will prove
best at 5f/easy 6f: acts on good to firm going: hard ride: untrustworthy. *R. Hannon*

SIGWELLS CLUB BOY 3 b.g. Fayruz 116 – Run With Pride (Mandrake Major –
122) [2003 66: f6s 7f 5.7m 6m 7.1g Jun 13] good-bodied gelding: fair performer: well
held in 2003: tried visored. *W. G. M. Turner*

SILCA BOO 3 b.f. Efisio 120 – Bunty Boo 110 (Noalto 120) [2003 99: 6g 6v 7g 5m 6m **74**
7m 6f 7g 5d Nov 7] smallish, workmanlike filly: useful at 2 yrs, only fair in 2003: stays
6f, not testing 7f: acts on firm and soft ground: edgy sort: sold 42,000 gns. *M. R. Channon*

SILCA'S GIFT 2 b.f. (Feb 21) Cadeaux Genereux 131 – Odette 72 (Pursuit of Love **104**
124) [2003 5s* 6f* 6m 6.5m 6m Oct 4] 40,000Y: rangy filly: has scope: second foal: half-
sister to 3-y-o On Point: dam, 5f/5.7f winner, half-sister to useful 6f/7f winner Caballero
(by Cadeaux Genereux) out of Queen Mary winner On Tiptoes: useful performer: won
maiden at Windsor in May and listed event at Royal Ascot (by 3 lengths from Tolzey) in
June: well below form in Lowther Stakes at York (favourite), sales race at Ascot and Two-
Year-Old Trophy at Redcar: should stay 7f: unraced on heavy going, probably acts on any
other. *M. R. Channon*

SILENCE IS GOLDEN 4 ch.f. Danehill Dancer (IRE) 117 – Silent Girl 75 (Krayyan **103**
117) [2003 97: 10.3m³ 12m² 10.1m⁴ 12f 10d² 10.5m² 10.4m³ 10.1m² 10m⁵ Oct 16] rather
leggy, angular filly: useful performer: good efforts when placed in handicaps at Ascot and
York fifth/seventh starts, and when 1¼ lengths second to Echoes In Eternity in listed race
at Yarmouth on eighth: best form around 1¼m: acts on firm and soft going: blinkered
once at 2 yrs: usually waited with: tends to wander. *B. J. Meehan*

SILENT ANGEL 3 b.f. Petong 126 – Valls d'Andorra 75 (Free State 125) [2003 8m –
8m 8m Sep 16] 2,000Y: smallish, compact filly: fifth foal: half-sister to a winner in
Holland by Mujadil: dam 1¼m to 2m winner: well beaten in maidens. *Mrs Lucinda
Featherstone*

SILENT COMFORT 3 b.f. Cadeaux Genereux 131 – Siwaayib 97 (Green Desert **52**
(USA) 127) [2003 p7g³ p7g 10.2m⁵ 10s Nov 3] leggy, lengthy filly: fifth foal: half-sister
to smart 1½m/1¾m winner Rainbow Ways and 1½m winner Storm Seeker (both by Rainbow Quest): dam 6f (including at 2 yrs) winner: best effort in maidens (modest form)
when third at Lingfield on debut: should be suited by 1m+: acts on polytrack: sold 6,500
gns. *B. W. Hills*

SILENTE TRIBUTE (USA)   3 gr.g. Distant View (USA) 126 – Homestead West   –
(USA) (Gone West (USA)) [2003 7m Sep 1] approx. 33,000Y in Italy, 6,000 3-y-o: fifth
foal: half-brother to winners in USA and Panama: dam unraced: tailed off in claimer at
Leicester. *D. Carroll*

SILENT HAWK (IRE)   2 b.c. (Apr 4) Halling (USA) 133 – Nightbird (IRE) 108   **86 p**
(Night Shift (USA)) [2003 7g² Nov 1] good-topped colt: third foal: half-brother to 6f
winner in Sweden by Cadeaux Genereux: dam, 5f to 7f winner (latter at 2 yrs), out of half-
sister to smart 11.4f winner Rockerlong and to dam of smart 2000 2-y-o 5f performer
Superstar Leo: 6/1, neck second of 12 to Golden Grace in maiden at Newmarket, soon in
touch and running on well: should stay 1m: likely to improve. *Saeed bin Suroor*

SILENT HEIR (AUS)   4 br.f. Sunday Silence (USA) – Park Heiress (IRE) (Sadler's   **82**
Wells (USA) 132) [2003 10m* 10m⁶ 10m Oct 16] leggy, attractive filly: half-sister to
Irish 17f winner Birth Rite (by Mujtahid): dam unraced half-sister to Japanese Group 1 6f
winner Shinko Forest and smart Irish 1m/1¼m performer Dazzling Park out of Phoenix
Champion Stakes winner Park Express: fairly useful form when winning maiden at
Redcar in May on debut, easily best effort: off 4 months before final start: raced only at
1¼m on good to firm ground. *J. Noseda*

SILENT MEMORY (IRE)   4 b.f. Danehill (USA) 126 – All Hush (IRE) (Highest   **55**
Honor (FR) 124) [2003 55: 11.9f* 12.4m⁵ 12.1m 10.2f 12.3m⁴ 16m⁵ 14.1m 11.9f³ 10f³
f12s 14.1m Oct 17] big, lengthy filly: modest handicapper: won at Brighton (ladies event)
in April: claimed from P. Blockley £6,000 after ninth start: stays 1½m: acts on fibresand,
firm and good to soft ground: tried blinkered/tongue tied/in cheekpieces: free-going sort:
sometimes finds little: none too reliable. *G. M. Moore*

SILENT REVENGE (IRE)   2 b.f. (Feb 19) Daggers Drawn (USA) 114 – Tread Softly   **61**
(IRE) 70 (Roi Danzig (USA)) [2003 5m⁶ 5m⁶ f5s* 7g f7g⁵ 7.5m³ 7m³ Oct 17] €15,000Y:
small, close-coupled filly: first foal: dam 2-y-o 6f winner: modest performer: won maiden
at Wolverhampton in May: creditable third in selling nursery/claimer: barely stays 7.5f:
acts on fibresand and good to firm going: sent to France. *R. Hannon*

SILENT THUNDER   3 ch.c. Cadeaux Genereux 131 – Silent Tribute (IRE) 104   **71**
(Lion Cavern (USA) 117) [2003 8.1d⁴ 10d⁵ Oct 14] 50,000Y: first foal: dam, 2-y-o 6f/1m
winner, out of useful half-sister to Middle Park winner Balla Cove: better effort in
maidens (fair form) when fifth at Ayr: stays 1¼m: sold 18,000 gns. *J. Noseda*

SILENT WATERS   3 gr.f. Polish Precedent (USA) 131 – Gleaming Water 81 (Kala-   –
glow 132) [2003 –: 9m 10m 11m⁴ Jun 27] leggy, close-coupled filly: little form.
A. P. Jarvis

SILENT WITNESS (AUS)   4 b.g. El Moxie (USA) – Jade Tiara (AUS) (Bureaucracy   **126**
(NZ)) [2003 6m* 5m* 6g* 5d* 5g* 5m* 5m* Dec 14] first foal: dam Australian 5f/6f
winner: high-class performer: unbeaten in 8 races, all at Sha Tin, including handicaps in
January/February/March, Group 2/3 handicaps in June/October, Group 2 International
Sprint Trial (by 2½ lengths from Cheerful Fortune) in November and Hong Kong Sprint
in December: proved himself one of the best horses trained in Hong Kong for some
time when beating South African challenger National Currency by a length in last-named
event, tracking leader and asserting final 150 yards (British-trained Acclamation, The
Trader and The Tatling beaten 4 lengths and more): stays 6f: acts on good to firm and
good to soft going. *A. S. Cruz, Hong Kong*

SILISTRA   4 gr.g. Sadler's Wells (USA) 132 – Dundel (IRE) 82 (Machiavellian (USA)   – §
123) [2003 77§: p12g p10g p10g p7g Dec 29] big, good-topped gelding: fair maiden
at best: no form on all-weather in 2003: wears headgear nowadays: temperamental.
Mrs L. C. Jewell

SILK CRAVAT (IRE)   2 ch.c. (Apr 8) Dr Devious (IRE) 127 – Dances With Dreams   – p
109 (Be My Chief (USA) 122) [2003 7m Sep 23] close-coupled, good-bodied colt:
second living foal: dam, 2-y-o 6f winner who stayed 1¼m, half-sister to very smart
performer in France/USA up to 1½m Dark Moondancer: 33/1, very green and always rear
in maiden at Newmarket: should be suited by 1¼m/1½m: likely to do better. *G. Wragg*

SILKEN BRIEF (IRE)   4 b.f. Ali-Royal (IRE) 127 – Tiffany's Case (IRE) 65 (Thatch-   **81**
ing 131) [2003 86: 7m 9g⁴ p8g³ Dec 30] sturdy filly: fairly useful performer, lightly
raced: left Sir Michael Stoute after second outing: stays 1m: acts on polytrack, good to
firm and good to soft ground: tried tongue tied: has carried head high. *D. J. Daly*

SILK FAN (IRE)   2 b.f. (Feb 19) Unfuwain (USA) 131 – Alikhlas 81 (Lahib (USA)   **98 p**
129) [2003 6m² 7m² 7f* 7m* Sep 19] 32,000Y: good-bodied filly: has quick action:
second foal: half-sister to 7f winner Anne Tudor (by Anabaa): dam, 1m winner, out of

half-sister to dam of smart US 6f/7f performer Istintaj: useful performer: made running when winning 17-runner maiden at Salisbury and 8-runner minor event at Newbury (by head from Poise), both in September: should stay 1m: open to progress. *P. W. Harris*

SILK ON SONG (USA)   5 b.g. Hazaam (USA) 113 – Wazeerah (USA) (The Minstrel   **– §**
(CAN) 135) [2003 –§, a44§: f12g 13.8f May 30] no longer of much account: tried
blinkered/tongue tied. *W. M. Brisbourne*

SILK SCREEN (IRE)   3 b.c. Barathea (IRE) 127 – Sun Screen (Caerleon (USA) 132)   **84**
[2003 91: 12m 12g⁶ 10s Sep 19] IR 32,000Y: good-topped colt: fourth reported foal:
half-brother to fairly useful Irish 7f and 1¼m winner Hill Society (by Law Society): dam
maiden half-sister to 1000 Guineas and Oaks winner Mysterious: fairly useful performer:
won maiden at Leopardstown at 2 yrs: easily best effort in handicaps in 2003 (well held
in King George V Stakes at Royal Ascot on reappearance) when sixth to Englishtown at
the Curragh: stays 1½m: acts on heavy ground. *W. P. Mullins, Ireland*

SILK ST BRIDGET   6 b.m. Rock Hopper 124 – Silk St James (Pas de Seul 133)   **36**
[2003 –: 10.1m² 8.1m f7g 7.2m⁴ 8m 6m Aug 28] workmanlike mare: poor maiden: stays
1¼m: acts on good to firm going and fibresand: tried blinkered: none too reliable.
W. M. Brisbourne

SILK ST JOHN   9 b.g. Damister (USA) 123 – Silk St James (Pas de Seul 133) [2003   **–**
–: 8.3d 10m May 8] close-coupled gelding: no longer of much account. *W. M. Brisbourne*

SILVALINE   4 gr.g. Linamix (FR) 127 – Upend 120 (Main Reef 126) [2003 70: f12g³   **83**
p12g² p12g 11.6g³ 12m⁵ 12.3m⁶ 10.3m⁵ 10g² 9g³ 8s 8m 8m³ 9.9m* 10d* 10.3g 10m³
p12g³ Oct 8] close-coupled gelding: fairly useful handicapper: won at Goodwood and
Sandown in August: has form at 1½m, at least as effective at 9f/1¼m: acts on polytrack,
good to firm and good to soft going: usually races prominently. *T. Keddy*

SILVER CALLING (USA)   2 b.f. (Apr 23) Silver Deputy (CAN) – Glorious Calling   **75**
(USA) (Nijinsky (CAN) 138) [2003 6m⁴ 6m* 8d 8f Nov 22] leggy filly: half-sister to
several winners, including 3-y-o Crafty Calling and US Grade 2 11f winner Mr Bluebird
(by Crafty Prospector): dam, won up to 9f in USA, out of half-sister to Japan Cup winner
Mairzy Doates: fair form when winning minor event at Pontefract in June: left P. Cole,
below form in allowance races at Churchill Downs after (blinkered final outing): should
stay at least 7f. *A. M. Stall jnr, USA*

SILVER CHARTER (USA)   4 b.g. Silver Hawk (USA) 123 – Pride of Darby (USA)   **–**
(Danzig (USA)) [2003 82: p10g p12g Jan 29] deep-girthed gelding: fairly useful performer at 3 yrs: well held in 2003: tried visored. *G. B. Balding*

SILVER CHEVALIER (IRE)   5 gr.g. Petong 126 – Princess Eurolink (Be My Guest   **–**
(USA) 126) [2003 11.7f⁵ f12g⁵ Jun 27] leggy, close-coupled gelding: little form: tried
visored/blinkered. *D. Burchell*

SILVER CHIME   3 gr.f. Robellino (USA) 127 – Silver Charm (Dashing Blade 117)   **74**
[2003 74p: 6m² 6m³ 6g* 6m p6g⁵ f7g Oct 16] rather leggy filly: fair handicapper: below
form after winning at Leicester in July: should stay 7f: acts on polytrack, raced only on
good/good to firm ground on turf: sold 11,000 gns. *J. M. P. Eustace*

SILVER CITY   3 ro.g. Unfuwain (USA) 131 – Madiyla 73 (Darshaan 133) [2003 79:   **85**
11.1m³ 12g² 11g⁶ 12.1m* 10g Oct 13] big gelding: fairly useful performer: landed odds
in maiden at Beverley in June: free-going sort, but should stay 1¾m: acts on firm and soft
ground: tends to carry head awkwardly: front runner. *Mrs A. J. Perrett*

SILVER COIN (IRE)   3 gr.g. Night Shift (USA) – Eurythmic 58 (Pharly (FR) 130)   **66**
[2003 –: f8g f7s⁵ 10m 6g 8m f12g³ f12g 12.3m⁵ 16d 12.4m³ 9.9m 12f² 13.8m*
14.1m⁴ 14.1m² Oct 17] leggy, good-topped gelding: fair handicapper: won at Catterick in
September: should stay 2m: acts on fibresand and firm going: effective with or without
blinkers. *T. D. Easterby*

SILVER CRYSTAL (IRE)   3 b.f. Among Men (USA) 124 – Silver Moon (Environ-   **53**
ment Friend 128) [2003 p8g⁶ 8f⁵ 8f 8.1m 8d 8.1m³ 8f 8.2m⁶ f8g⁴ f9.4g⁵ f8g Dec 9] IR
900Y: lengthy filly: second foal: half-sister to 4-y-o Sorbiesharry: dam, little sign of
ability: modest maiden: left B. R. Millman after seventh start: stays 9.4f: acts on all-
weather and firm going: tried in cheekpieces. *Mrs N. Macauley*

SILVERDALE LADY (IRE)   4 b.f. Great Commotion (USA) 123 – Holme Sound   **–**
(Fools Holme (USA)) [2003 7m 8.1d 7.1m f9.4g Jul 19] small, strong filly: fourth foal:
half-sister to winner in Spain by Colonel Collins: dam tailed off only start: no form in
maidens/seller: trained by M. McElhone in Ireland only outing at 2 yrs. *B. A. McMahon*

SILVER ELITE   4 gr.f. Forzando 122 – Final Call 79 (Town Crier 119) [2003 62: 6g⁵   **62**
5g f6g* f6s f6g⁴ f5g* 6m f6s f6g Nov 1] fair performer on all-weather, modest on turf: **a67**
won maiden at Southwell in June and handicap at Wolverhampton in August: effective at
5f/6f: acts on good to firm ground, soft and fibresand: tried in headgear/tongue tie. *Miss
Gay Kelleway*

SILVER GILT   3 b.c. Silver Hawk (USA) 123 – Memory's Gold (USA) 68 (Java Gold   **104**
(USA)) [2003 102: 10.1m³ 12d⁴ May 8] strong, lengthy, slightly dipped-backed colt:
useful performer: creditable efforts in minor event at Epsom (3 lengths third of 4 to
Franklins Gardens) and Prix Hocquart at Longchamp (3¼ lengths fourth to Coroner):
stays 1½m: yet to race on extremes of ground: flashes tail: front runner. *J. H. M. Gosden*

SILVERHAY   2 b.g. (Apr 21) Inchinor 119 – Moon Spin 83 (Night Shift (USA)) [2003   **73**
5m⁵ 7m² 7d³ Nov 4] 13,500Y: neat gelding: sixth foal: half-brother to 3 winners, including useful 1m (at 2 yrs) and 1¼m winner Golden Sparrow (by Elmaamul) and fairly
useful 1¾m to 2¼m winner Rosa Canina (by Bustino): dam 1m to 1½m winner: fair
form in maidens: placed at Newcastle (led stand side) and Catterick: will stay at least 1m.
T. D. Barron

SILVERINE (USA)   2 b. or br.f. (May 8) Silver Deputy (CAN) – Special Broad (USA)   **– p**
115 (Broad Brush (USA)) [2003 6g Oct 24] $45,000Y: fourth foal: half-sister to winner
in USA by Cryptoclearance: dam US Grade 3 2-y-o 1m winner: 33/1 and better for race,
well beaten in maiden at Newbury, not knocked about: should do better. *L. M. Cumani*

SILVER ISLAND   2 ch.c. (Feb 10) Silver Patriarch (IRE) 125 – Island Maid (Forzando   **–**
122) [2003 7d p8g Nov 26] sturdy, compact colt: first foal: dam unraced: well held in
maidens. *G. A. Butler*

SILVER KRIS (USA)   3 gr.f. Diesis 133 – P J'S Affair (USA) (Black Tie Affair 128)   **–**
[2003 51: f8.5g f8s 10m Aug 30] lengthy, angular filly: modest maiden at 2 yrs: well
beaten in 2003. *M. Johnston*

SILVER LOUIE (IRE)   3 gr.f. Titus Livius (FR) 115 – Shakamiyn (Nishapour (FR)   **§§**
125) [2003 –: 8.2g⁵ 11.6d 7m 10d 10m 10m 8d 8.3g Aug 10] leggy filly: modest maiden:
well beaten in 2003 after reappearance: stays 1m: unraced on extremes of going: tried
visored: refused to race last 2 starts: best left alone. *G. B. Balding*

SILVER MASCOT   4 gr.g. Mukaddamah (USA) 125 – Always Lucky 71 (Absalom   **48 §**
128) [2003 73§, a65§: f6g 6m⁶ f5s f6g Dec 9] sturdy, good-quartered gelding: fair
performer at best, just poor form in 2003: best at 5f/6f: acts on fibresand and any turf
going: tends to sweat: none too consistent. *R. Hollinshead*

SILVER MODE (USA)   4 ch.g. Silver Deputy (CAN) – A La Mode (USA) 77 (Known   **62**
Fact (USA) 135) [2003 p8g⁴ p6g p8g p10g⁴ 10.1g 8.3m Jun 16] 3,500 3-y-o: second foal:
half-brother to fairly useful 7f winner More Modern (by Mt Livermore): dam, 9f winner
in USA at 5 yrs, half-sister to Oaks winner Reams of Verse and Eclipse winner Elmaamul:
modest maiden: stayed 1¼m: acted on polytrack: dead. *G. L. Moore*

SILVER PRELUDE   2 b.c. (Feb 8) Prince Sabo 123 – Silver Blessings (Statoblest 120)   **95**
[2003 5.2m 5.1m² 5m² 5m* 5.2m⁵ 5f² 5m⁵ 5g Sep 13] 900Y, resold 10,000Y: good-
bodied colt: fifth foal: half-brother to 4-y-o Secret Spoof and 3-y-o Glistening Silver:
dam unraced half-sister to smart 5f/6f performer Sylvan Barbarosa: useful performer:
won maiden at Windsor in July: creditable efforts next 3 starts, particularly in listed race
at York on last of them: veered left start when below form final outing: will prove best at
bare 5f: acts on firm going: races prominently. *D. K. Ivory*

SILVER PROPHET (IRE)   4 gr.g. Idris (IRE) 118 – Silver Heart (Yankee Gold 115)   **84**
[2003 90: f11s 10m 11m⁴ 10d³ 10.1g p12g f12g Dec 3] rather leggy gelding: fairly useful   **a70**
handicapper on turf, fair on all-weather: stays 11f: acts on polytrack, soft and good to firm
going: tried visored, not in 2003: sometimes slowly away. *M. R. Bosley*

SILVER RHYTHM   2 ch.f. (Mar 15) Silver Patriarch (IRE) 125 – Party Treat (IRE)   **– p**
69 (Millfontaine 114) [2003 7m Oct 4] strong filly: third reported foal: half-sister to 5-y-o
Party Ploy: dam, ungenuine maiden, placed at 5f: 100/1, tenth of 12 in maiden at Redcar,
always rear: likely to do better at 1¼m+. *K. R. Burke*

SILVER SEEKER (USA)   3 gr. or ro.g. Seeking The Gold (USA) – Zelanda (IRE)   **74 +**
108 (Night Shift (USA)) [2003 90: 6m Apr 3] smallish, good-bodied colt: fairly useful at
2 yrs: visored, found little only 3-y-o start: stays 7f: raced only on good/good to firm
going: sold 6,000 gns in October. *D. R. Loder*

SILVER SHOES 4 b.f. Woodborough (USA) 112 – Emerald Dream (IRE) 47 (Vision **35** (USA)) [2003 –: f11s f16g f14.8g⁶ f8g 12.3m⁵ 10m⁵ Apr 26] small, good-topped filly: poor maiden: stays 1½m: acts on firm going, good to soft and fibresand: tried visored/blinkered: inconsistent. *J. Parkes*

SILVERTOWN 8 b.g. Danehill (USA) 126 – Docklands (USA) (Theatrical 128) [2003 **81** 69: 12m* 11.9f* Jun 26] lengthy gelding: has reportedly had wind operation: fairly useful handicapper: completed hat-trick over hurdles prior to winning at Musselburgh in May and Carlisle in June: stays 1½m: acts on all-weather, firm and good to soft going: front runner: tail flasher. *L. Lungo*

SILVER WOOD 3 b.f. Silver Wizard (USA) 117 – Eastwood Heiress (Known Fact **–** (USA) 135) [2003 –: 6g May 4] little form. *J. C. Fox*

SIMIANNA 4 b.f. Bluegrass Prince (IRE) 110 – Lowrianna (IRE) 50 (Cyrano de **99** Bergerac 120) [2003 99: p5g⁴ 5f 6d³ 6d³ 6m⁴ 6m 6f⁴ 6m⁵ 6m* 6m⁵ 6m⁶ 6g⁶ 6m 6m⁴ 6m³ 5.6d⁶ 6m³ 6.1d 7g Oct 11] tall filly: useful performer: won minor event at Newmarket in June: one of several other good efforts when narrowly-beaten third of 26 to Native Title in handicap at Ayr seventeenth start: effective at 5f/6f: acts on any turf going and poly-track: tried blinkered at 2 yrs, wore cheekpieces fifth/sixth starts: sometimes slowly away: tough and consistent. *A. Berry*

SIMIOLA 4 b.f. Shaamit (IRE) 127 – Brave Vanessa (USA) 62 (Private Account **–** (USA)) [2003 55, a61: f12g Jan 17] modest performer: well beaten only 4-y-o start. *S. T. Lewis*

SIMLET 8 b.g. Forzando 122 – Besito 79 (Wassl 125) [2003 16d⁵ 16g Aug 26] angular **42** gelding: winning hurdler: poor handicapper on Flat nowadays: stays 2m: acts on fibre-sand, firm and soft going: has flashed tail/wandered: often blinkered/visored earlier in career. *E. W. Tuer*

SIMONOVSKI (USA) 2 b.c. (Mar 4) Miswaki (USA) 124 – Earthra (USA) (Rahy **69** (USA) 115) [2003 p7g⁵ p8g⁵ Nov 2] $55,000F, €50,000Y: third foal: dam unraced: fair form in maidens at Lingfield, green and slowly away: not sure to stay much beyond 1m. *J. A. Osborne*

SIMON'S SEAT (USA) 4 ch.g. Woodman (USA) 126 – Spire (USA) (Topsider **75** (USA)) [2003 75: 10m 10m 12g⁶ 16.1m⁵ 14.8m 16.2f³ 16g Oct 24] leggy, useful-looking gelding: fair maiden handicapper: stays 2m: acts on firm ground: sometimes slowly away/looks none too keen: sold 13,000 gns. *J. A. R. Toller*

SIMONS WOOD 2 b.g. (Mar 22) Up And At 'em 109 – Roleover Mania (Tragic Role **52** (USA)) [2003 5d⁶ 5m 7m 5f³ 5.9m³ 7.5m 7m³ Oct 18] 500Y: close-coupled, quite good-topped gelding: second foal: dam unraced: modest maiden: stays 7f: acts on firm and good to soft going: blinkered (below form) fifth/sixth starts: wore cheekpieces (seemed to run well) final one: sent to Sweden. *G. M. Moore*

SIMON THE POACHER 4 br.g. Chaddleworth (IRE) 103 – Lady Crusty (Golden **–** Dipper 119) [2003 –: 10m 8.1d 10.2g 11.6g 8.2d f12s f12s Dec 13] small, sturdy gelding: little form. *L. P. Grassick*

SIMPLE IDEALS (USA) 9 b. or br.g. Woodman (USA) 126 – Comfort And Style **44** 95 (Be My Guest (USA) 126) [2003 56, a–: 11.9g 14.1s 14.1m 14g 14.1m⁵ 15g⁵ 14.1d⁶ **a–** 14.4m⁵ 14.1m 14.1m f14g⁴ f14g Dec 9] smallish, workmanlike gelding: has a round action: poor handicapper: races mainly at 1¾m/2m: acts on any going, well held on all-weather: tried blinkered: sometimes races freely/carries head high: usually held up. *Don Enrico Incisa*

SIMPLE SONG 3 ch.f. Simply Great (FR) 122 – Cumbrian Rhapsody 79 (Sharrood **–** (USA) 124) [2003 –: 12d Jun 30] no form. *T. D. Easterby*

SIMPLEX (FR) 2 b.c. (Apr 17) Rainbow Quest (USA) 134 – Russyskia (USA) (Green **110** Dancer (USA) 132) [2003 8g² 8s* 10d² Nov 8] second foal: dam, French 1¼m winner, half-sister to Prix Royal-Oak winner Top Sunrise out of half-sister to Prix Morny winner Sakura Reiko: smart form: won minor event at Longchamp in October by 2 lengths from Ange Gardien: improved again when 1½ lengths second of 10 to Voix du Nord in Criter-ium de Saint-Cloud, leading briefly final 1f: will stay at least 1½m. *C. Laffon-Parias, France*

SIMPLY RED 2 ch.g. (Apr 14) Vettori (IRE) 119 – Amidst 86 (Midyan (USA) 124) **–** [2003 7.1f 5.1m 5.7f⁴ Aug 22] 800Y: fourth foal: half-brother to fairly useful 7f winner Aploy (by Deploy) and 1m winner Ago (later successful at 9f in Spain, by Rudimentary): dam 6f (at 2 yrs) and 1m winner: no sign of ability, including in seller. *R. Brotherton*

Ascot Stakes (Handicap), Royal Ascot—the cannily-campaigned Sindapour (preceded by the riderless Jasmick) continues Martin Pipe's good recent record in prestigious long-distance handicaps on the Flat; the Nicky Henderson-trained Landing Light completes a 1,2 for top jumping yards

SIMPLY REMY 5 ch.g. Chaddleworth (IRE) 103 – Exemplaire (FR) (Polish Precedent (USA) 131) [2003 52: 12m Apr 8] lengthy gelding: maiden handicapper: well beaten only 5-y-o start. *John Berry* —

SIMPLY SID 2 b.g. (May 3) Presidium 124 – Chadwick's Ginger (Crofthall 110) [2003 6m 6m 7.5d Jul 5] leggy, angular gelding: first foal: dam, maiden on Flat, unreliable winning hurdler/chaser: well beaten in maidens/seller. *W. H. Tinning* —

SIMPLY THE GUEST (IRE) 4 b.g. Mujadil (USA) 119 – Ned's Contessa (IRE) 48 (Persian Heights 129) [2003 52: f6g f7s f7s f8.5g f8g f6g 5.9d f8g Nov 25] lengthy gelding: poor performer: left N. Tinkler after fifth start: barely stays 1m: acts on firm ground and fibresand: tried visored/tongue tied. *Don Enrico Incisa* **44**

SIMPSONS SUPREME 3 ch.g. Abou Zouz (USA) 109 – Conwy (Rock City 120) [2003 7g 7d p10g⁵ 12g Aug 2] third foal: dam of little account: little form. *R. M. Flower* —

SINAMATELLA 4 ch.f. Lion Cavern (USA) 117 – Regent's Folly (IRE) 101 (Touching Wood (USA) 127) [2003 71: 8.1g 8.2s 7m 7f 7m Aug 8] sturdy, good-bodied filly: disappointing maiden: sold 3,000 gns. *C. G. Cox* —

SINDAPOUR (IRE) 5 b.g. Priolo (USA) 127 – Sinntara (IRE) (Lashkari 128) [2003 8f⁴ 10m⁶ 6g 8.2s³ 10.2m 14f* 20m* 16.2d² 18m Oct 18] good-bodied gelding: fourth foal: half-brother to 3 winners, notably Derby, Irish Derby and Arc winner Sinndar (by Grand Lodge): dam Irish 1½m/2m winner: fairly useful performer: trained in Ireland by J. Oxx at 2 yrs, missed next 2 seasons: won handicaps at Sandown and Royal Ascot (27-runner Ascot Stakes by 3 lengths from Landing Light) in June: good second to Kahyasi Princess at Ascot: well held in Cesarewitch at Newmarket final outing (raced alone long way): stays 2½m: acts on firm and soft going. *M. C. Pipe* **90**

SINDY (USA) 3 b.f. A P Indy (USA) 131 – Dance Design (IRE) 119 (Sadler's Wells (USA) 132) [2003 81p: 10d 11.9m* 12.5g 12g Oct 11] lengthy filly: fairly useful performer: won maiden at Brighton in August: appeared to run well when seventh of 8 in Prix Minerve at Deauville next time: stays 1½m: acts on soft and good to firm ground: withdrawn twice at start (got down in stall first occasion, refused to enter on second): possibly temperamental. *P. F. I. Cole* **91 ?**

SINGING POET (IRE) 2 b.c. (Apr 4) Singspiel (IRE) 133 – Bright Finish (USA) 108 (Zilzal (USA) 137) [2003 7s* Oct 29] second foal: dam, French 5f/5.5f winner, half-sister to very smart North American performer up to 1¼m Alydeed: 13/2, won 13-runner maiden at Yarmouth by neck from Heart's Desire, ridden to lead 1f out: should stay 1m: likely to improve. *Saeed bin Suroor* **85 p**

SINGLET 2 ch.c. (Apr 5) Singspiel (IRE) 133 – Ball Gown 98 (Jalmood (USA) 126) [2003 7g Nov 1] leggy colt: second foal: half-brother to 3-y-o Leoballero: dam 1m to 1½m winner: 66/1, ninth of 12 in maiden at Newmarket. *H. J. Collingridge* —

Mr K. Abdulla's "Singleton"

SINGLETON   3 b.f. Singspiel (IRE) 133 – Rive (USA) (Riverman (USA) 131) [2003   **105**
10m² 12m* 16.2f² 11.9m³ 14.6d³ 14m² 12g⁵ Oct 11] tall, good-topped filly: unimpressive
mover in slower paces: fifth foal: half-sister to 3 winners, including 2001 2-y-o 1m
winner Revealing (by Halling) and 8-y-o Brevity, both useful: dam, French 2-y-o 1¼m
winner, half-sister to dam of very smart performer up to 1¾m Mons: useful performer:
won maiden at Newmarket in May: placed after in Queen's Vase at Royal Ascot (beaten
¾ length by Shanty Star), listed race at York (third to Mezzo Soprano), Park Hill Stakes
at Doncaster (9 lengths third behind Discreet Brief) and listed race at Newmarket (went
down by 3½ lengths to Hilbre Island): stayed 2m: acted on firm and good to soft going:
had worn crossed noseband: stud. *H. R. A. Cecil*

SINGLE TRACK MIND   5 b.g. Mind Games 121 – Compact Disc (IRE) 48 (Royal   **–**
Academy (USA) 130) [2003 57d: 6m 6m Jul 2] neat, quite attractive gelding: little form
since second 4-y-o outing: tried visored/tongue tied. *J. R. Boyle*

SINGLE TRIGGER (IRE)   5 ch.m. Ela-Mana-Mou 132 – Tycoon Aly (IRE) 70 (Last   **57 ?**
Tycoon 131) [2003 10.9m⁵ p12g 10g⁵ 12.6m Sep 20] 8,000Y: second foal: half-sister to
11.5f winner Chez Bonito (by Persian Bold) and 3-y-o King Revo: dam third over 1m in
Ireland on only start: poor form in bumpers: seemed to show modest form on Flat debut:
visored/blinkered after. *H. E. Haynes*

SINGULARITY   3 b.g. Rudimentary (USA) 118 – Lyrical Bid (USA) 77 (Lyphard   **63 d**
(USA) 132) [2003 59: f6g p5g 6g⁴ 7f³ 6m⁶ 5g³ 6g 5m 10f³ 7g 10.1m⁵ 8f⁵ Oct 17] angular
gelding: modest maiden: well below form last 6 starts: stays easy 7f: acts on fibresand
and firm ground: below form in blinkers/cheekpieces: often races prominently: none too
consistent: sold 6,000 gns, resold £5,200. *W. R. Muir*

SINJAREE   5 b.g. Mark of Esteem (IRE) 137 – Forthwith 104 (Midyan (USA) 124)   **68 d**
[2003 f11s f8.5g⁴ f8.5s⁵ f8.5g³ f8.5g 10m 10m⁴ 10d² 12g 9.9m 8m 8m 10.4m f8s 8.2d f8g
f11g Dec 15] leggy, unfurnished gelding: fair handicapper: trained in 2002 by J. Pubben

in Holland, winning 6 times, including 4 in Germany: well below form last 6 starts in 2003, including in cheekpieces/visor: stays 1¼m: acts on heavy going, good to firm and fibresand. *Mrs S. Lamyman*

SINORA WOOD (IRE) 2 b.f. (Apr 28) Shinko Forest (IRE) – Moira My Girl **70** (Henbit (USA) 130) [2003 5m⁶ 6.1m 5.1f² 5m⁴ 6g⁵ 5.7m 6m⁴ 6.1m⁶ 7.1m² 7m 7m Oct 23] €7,000Y: good-bodied filly: half-sister to numerous winners, notably useful 1998 2-y-o 6f/7f winner Smittenby (by Tenby): dam third at 1¼m in Ireland: fair maiden: second at Bath and Warwick (nursery): stays 7f: acts on firm going: wore cheekpieces (below form) sixth start. *Mrs P. N. Dutfield*

SION HILL (IRE) 2 b.g. (Feb 8) Desert Prince (IRE) 130 – Mobilia 67 (Last Tycoon **75** 131) [2003 5.1m² 6m 6g² Oct 13] 240,000F, 375,000Y: first foal: dam, Irish maiden (best efforts at 9f/1¼m), half-sister to very smart 6f/7f performer Desert Style, the family of Barathea and Gossamer: fair form in maidens: second at Chester and Windsor (made most): needs to settle to stay beyond 6f: slowly away on debut: played up in preliminaries next time. *Sir Michael Stoute*

SIOUX RIVER 2 ch.f. (Mar 27) Indian Ridge 123 – Washm (USA) (Diesis 133) [2003 **75** 6m 7m⁵ 7g* 8.1g⁵ 7m⁴ 7m 6m Oct 4] lengthy filly: third living foal: dam, ran twice at 2 yrs, out of half-sister to Irish 1000 Guineas winner Ensconse: fair performer: won maiden at Kempton in July: seemingly creditable efforts next 2 starts: free-going sort, barely stays 1m: carries head high: sold 25,000 gns. *B. J. Meehan*

SIOUX RYDER (IRE) 2 gr.f. (Apr 18) Intikhab (USA) 135 – Street Lina (FR) **68** (Linamix (FR) 127) [2003 5m² May 15] €14,000Y: sturdy filly: second foal: dam, useful French 1¼m winner (also won in USA), half-sister to smart French stayers Street Shaana and Stretarez: backward, second of 6 in maiden at York: bred to stay at least 1m. *R. A. Fahey*

SIPOWITZ 9 b.g. Warrshan (USA) 117 – Springs Welcome 86 (Blakeney 126) [2003 **–** 14.1d Jul 26] poor performer: well beaten only Flat outing since 2000. *J. Mackie*

SIRAJ 4 b.g. Piccolo 121 – Masuri Kabisa (USA) 48 (Ascot Knight (CAN) 130) [2003 **72** 69: 6m f6g⁴ 6m* 6g p7g p6g² p5g⁵ Dec 20] good-bodied gelding: fair performer: won minor event at Pontefract in July: stays 6f: acts on all-weather, yet to race on extremes of going on turf: tried blinkered. *N. A. Graham*

SIR ALFRED 4 b.g. Royal Academy (USA) 130 – Magnificent Star (USA) 122 (Silver **74 §** Hawk (USA) 123) [2003 77: 10d 10d⁶ 10.2f² 10.2m 10g 14.1d⁶ 13.1f³ 16m Sep 5] fair handicapper: barely stays 13f: acts on firm and good to soft ground: edgy sort, has been mounted on track/early to post: tends to hang/flash tail: unreliable. *A. King*

SIR BOND (IRE) 2 ch.g. (Apr 3) Desert Sun 120 – In Tranquility (IRE) (Shalford **–** (IRE) 124§) [2003 8g Sep 27] 10,000Y: heavy-bodied gelding: third foal: dam unraced half-sister to smart 6f (including Prix Morny at 2 yrs)/7f winner Tagula: 16/1 and backward, slowly away and always rear in maiden at Ripon. *B. Smart*

SIR BRASTIAS 4 b.g. Shaamit (IRE) 127 – Premier Night 102 (Old Vic 136) [2003 **88** 88: p13g 12m³ 14m 13.9f 12f⁵ Jun 25] leggy, angular gelding: fairly useful handicapper: stays 13f: acts on soft ground, good to firm and polytrack. *S. Dow*

SIR DESMOND 5 gr.g. Petong 126 – I'm Your Lady 77 (Risk Me (FR) 127) [2003 **89** 88: f5s f6s⁶ 6g 6d⁴ 6m 5g* 6g⁴ 5d f6g p6g³ p6g⁴ Dec 6] workmanlike gelding: fairly useful handicapper: won at Hamilton in July: effective at 5f/6f: acts on all-weather and any turf going: blinkered (ran poorly) once: usually wears cheekpieces: often held up: tends to edge left. *R. Guest*

SIR DON (IRE) 4 b.g. Lake Coniston (IRE) 131 – New Sensitive (Wattlefield 117) **77** [2003 65: f6g f8s⁵ p6g p7g⁵ 6m⁴ 8f* 8m³ 7m 6m 7f 7m² 7.5m 7m² 6f* 6m⁵ 6g³ 6m Aug 14] sparely-made gelding: fair handicapper: won at Thirsk in April and York in July: effective at 6f (very best form) to easy 1m: acts on polytrack, raced only on good going or firmer on turf: usually visored: often races prominently. *D. Nicholls*

SIR EDWIN LANDSEER (USA) 3 gr.c. Lit de Justice (USA) 125 – Wildcat Blue **107 d** (USA) (Cure The Blues (USA)) [2003 102: 7m⁴ 6m 7m³ 7m⁵ 6m⁵ 7.6g⁵ 7m⁶ 7m 6m Oct 23] good-quartered colt: useful performer: disappointing after fourth to Indian Haven in listed Free Handicap at Newmarket on reappearance: stays 7f: yet to race on soft/heavy going, acts on any other: tried blinkered: has edged left: sold 23,000 gns, sent to UAE. *P. F. I. Cole*

SIR ERNEST (IRE) 2 b.g. (Jan 9) Daggers Drawn (USA) 114 – Kyra Crown (IRE) **84** (Astronef 116) [2003 p5g² f5g² 5f⁶ 5f* 5f 5.1m* 5.2m 5.2g⁴ 5m 6m 5m Sep 15] €27,000Y: rather leggy gelding: third foal: half-brother to 2 winners in France, including

10.5f winner Croga Crown (by Mukaddamah): dam French 2-y-o 7f winner: fairly useful performer: made most to win minor events at Catterick and Chester in June: mostly below form after: likely to prove best at 5f/easy 6f: acts on firm going, probably on all-weather. *M. J. Polglase*

SIR FRANCIS (IRE)   5 b.g. Common Grounds 118 – Red Note (Rusticaro (FR) 124) **84** [2003 88: p6g p7g⁵ p7g⁵ 6g 7g⁴ 7m 7d⁶ p7g Aug 28] useful-looking gelding: has a round action: fairly useful handicapper: stays easy 7f: acts on polytrack and soft ground: visored (tailed off) once at 2 yrs: has wandered: none too consistent. *J. Noseda*

SIR FRANK GIBSON   2 b.g. (Apr 24) Primo Dominie 121 – Serotina (IRE) 73 (Mtoto **52** 134) [2003 6m 6m 6m³ 6g 8g⁴ f7g Dec 8] 32,000Y: half-brother to several winners, including fairly useful 1997 2-y-o 6f/7f winner Alconleigh (by Pursuit of Love) and useful 1¼m winner Serotonin (by Barathea): dam, 9f winner, half-sister to dam of top-class French miler Keltos: modest maiden: third at Hamilton: barely stays 1m: acts on good to firm going. *M. Johnston*

SIR GALAHAD   2 ch.g. (Apr 25) Hector Protector (USA) 124 – Sharpening 72 (Sharpo **59 p** 132) [2003 7m⁶ Aug 22] 20,000F, 20,000Y: sixth foal: half-brother to 3 winners, including 3-y-o Langford: dam 6f (at 2 yrs)/7f winner: 25/1 and better for race, sixth of 11 in maiden at Thirsk, slowly away and not knocked about: should stay at least 1m: open to progress. *T. D. Easterby*

SIR HAYDN   3 ch.g. Definite Article 121 – Snowscape (Niniski (USA) 125) [2003 **78** 85p: 9m⁴ 11.6s 10m⁶ 12m 8m³ 10m³ Jul 1] big, leggy gelding: fair performer: stays 1¼m: acts on good to firm and good to soft ground: blinkered last 4 starts: gelded after. *N. P. Littmoden*

SIRIUS LADY   3 b.f. Sir Harry Lewis (USA) 127 – Intrepida (Fair Season 120) [2003 **–** –: 10g Jun 2] well held in maidens. *A. M. Balding*

SIR JASPER (IRE)   2 b.g. (Mar 22) Sri Pekan (USA) 117 – Ashover Amber 81 (Green **58** Desert (USA) 127) [2003 f6g⁵ f6s⁵ f6g⁶ f7g⁵ Dec 16] 10,000Y: workmanlike gelding: first foal: dam, 5f/6f winner, out of useful 7f/1m winner Zafaaf: modest performer: won seller at Southwell: stays 7f: visored last 2 starts. *T. D. Barron*

SIR LAUGHALOT   3 b.c. Alzao (USA) 117 – Funny Hilarious (USA) 76 (Sir Ivor **77** 135) [2003 –: 8m 9g 7d p7g² p7g Dec 10] strong colt: fair maiden handicapper: should stay at least 1m: acts on polytrack. *Miss E. C. Lavelle*

SIR LOIN   2 ch.g. (Feb 18) Compton Place 125 – Charnwood Queen 61 (Cadeaux **63** Genereux 131) [2003 5g² 5m 5m⁶ 5m 5g Sep 28] 7,500F, 8,200Y: leggy gelding: fourth foal: half-brother to 5-y-o Greenwood and 3-y-o Educating Rita: dam, 6f winner, half-sister to smart 7f/1m performer Sunstreak: modest maiden: second at Newcastle: ran badly final start: should stay 6f. *N. Tinkler*

SIR NIGHT (IRE)   3 b.g. Night Shift (USA) – Highly Respected (IRE) 57 (High **67** Estate 127) [2003 61: f8g⁴ f7s⁶ f7s² f7s⁶ f7g* 8.2g 8.2m² 9.9m* 9.9d³ 10m² 10g² 10.3m⁴ 9.9m³ 10g⁴ 9.9d 10.1m 10.1g Oct 22] quite good-topped gelding: fair performer: won sellers at Southwell in March and Beverley in May: well held last 3 starts, racing freely in cheekpieces on second of them: stays 1¼m: acts on fibresand, good to firm and good to soft going: tried visored/blinkered: sold 15,000 gns, then gelded. *J. D. Bethell*

SIR NINJA (IRE)   6 b.g. Turtle Island (IRE) 123 – The Poachers Lady (IRE) (Salmon **–** Leap (USA) 131) [2003 89: p10g⁴ Dec 30] heavy-bodied gelding: fairly useful handicapper at best: off 13 months, well held in seller only run in 2003: visored once in 2000: difficult ride: none too consistent. *S. Kirk*

SIR NORTHERNDANCER (IRE)   4 b.c. Danehill Dancer (IRE) 117 – Lady At **79** War (Warning 136) [2003 83: f7g² f6s f6s* f6g⁵ f6g⁶ 7m 7.1m⁶ 6m 5.9g⁶ 6.1d² 6m 6f Jun 14] workmanlike colt: fair performer: won handicap at Southwell in February: effective at 6f/7f: acts on good to firm going, heavy and all-weather: usually wears blinkers/cheekpieces: races prominently. *B. Ellison*

SIR SANDROVITCH (IRE)   7 b.g. Polish Patriot (USA) 128 – Old Downie (Be **78** My Guest (USA) 126) [2003 80, a76: 5m 5g 5d⁵ 5g² 5m² 5m* 5f* 5.1m* 5d 5m⁴ 5f 5d 5m 5m⁶ 5m⁶ 5f 5m 5g Nov 5] tall gelding: fair handicapper: won at Beverley (apprentices), Thirsk and Chester in space of 5 days in June: best at 5f: acts on firm going, good to soft and fibresand: tried blinkered, usually wore cheekpieces in 2003: sometimes early to post/slowly away: tends to pull hard, and best covered up. *R. A. Fahey*

SIR SIDNEY   3 b.g. Shareef Dancer (USA) 135 – Hattaafeh (IRE) 79 (Mtoto 134) [2003 **87** 90: p8g³ 10g² 11.9m² 12m⁴ 12f² 10.4m³ 11m² 14m⁴ Oct 4] smallish, lengthy gelding: fairly useful maiden: in frame all starts at 3 yrs: stays 1¾m: acts on heavy and good to firm ground: tried in cheekpieces/blinkers: sometimes finds little. *D. Morris*

SI SI AMIGA (IRE)   2 b.f. (Apr 21) Desert Style (IRE) 121 – No Hard Feelings (IRE)   **79 p**
86 (Alzao (USA) 117) [2003 7g* Nov 1] €80,000Y: neat filly: half-sister to several
winners, including 1998 2-y-o 5f winner Inca Tern (by Polar Falcon), later 1m winner in
USA, and 1½m winner Athletic Sam (by Definite Article), both fairly useful: dam 5f (at
2 yrs) to 1½m winner: 16/1, won 17-runner maiden at Newmarket by length from Maid
To Treasure, racing in touch and ridden to lead final 1f: will stay 1m: open to improvement. *B. W. Hills*

SISSY SLEW (USA)   3 b.f. Unbridled's Song (USA) 125 – Missy Slew (USA) (Seattle   **95**
Slew (USA)) [2003 7.5d* 7d³ 8d⁴ 8f 10g⁶ 7.5g⁶ 9m* 9.5m Oct 11] $180,000Y: tall, leggy
filly: half-sister to 3 minor winners in USA: dam, won 8.5f minor stakes in USA, half-
sister to Breeders' Cup Distaff winner Lady's Secret: useful performer: won maiden at
Tipperary in April and handicap at Navan (by neck from Emmas Princess) in October:
stays 9f: acts on good to firm and good to soft going, below form on firm in listed rated
stakes at Royal Ascot. *D. K. Weld, Ireland*

SISTER BLUEBIRD   3 b.f. Bluebird (USA) 125 – Pain Perdu (IRE) (Waajib 121)   **93 ?**
[2003 94: 7g⁶ 7d 6g⁴ 8f⁵ 7m Jul 8] close-coupled filly: fairly useful performer: stays 7f:
acts on good to firm and good to soft going: usually blinkered: usually races prominently.
B. J. Meehan

SISTER IN LAW (FR)   4 b.f. Distant Relative 128 – Despina (Waajib 121) [2003 95:   **–**
5g May 31] tall, quite good-topped filly: useful 5f handicapper at 3 yrs, well held only
start in 2003: reportedly had haematoma on quarters earlier in year. *H. Candy*

SISTER SOPHIA (USA)   3 b. or br.f. Deputy Commander (USA) 124 – Sophia's   **71**
Choice (USA) (Clev Er Tell (USA)) [2003 79p: 7m³ 7m² 9m 7m 6m⁶ p10g Jul 19]
lengthy, attractive filly: fair maiden: free-going sort, not sure to stay beyond 7f: raced
only on polytrack and good to firm ground: has worn cheekpieces: sold 2,500 gns in
December. *G. Wragg*

SIX PACK (IRE)   5 ch.g. Royal Abjar (USA) 121 – Regal Entrance (Be My Guest   **42**
(USA) 126) [2003 60d: f7g 10.1m f8g 8m 8s 8.1m⁶ 10m Aug 18] tall, good-topped
gelding: poor handicapper nowadays: stays 1m: acts on fibresand, firm and soft ground:
tried blinkered: sometimes slowly away. *Andrew Turnell*

SIX PERFECTIONS (FR)   3 br. or bl.f. Celtic Swing 138 – Yogya (USA)   **124**
(Riverman (USA) 131) [2003 120p: 7g* 8g² 8d² 8d² 8d* 8f* Oct 25]
        'The whistle please Gennaro—attention, three, two, one!' From the
perspective of jockey Thierry Thulliez, television's popular 'seventies game show
'Jeux Sans Frontieres' might have made a more appropriate setting than the
racecourse for his performance in the One Thousand Guineas. Given the plight of
Thulliez on his mount Six Perfections, the familiar bellowing, infectious laughter
of commentator Stuart Hall that used to accompany some of the hapless contestants
as they blundered their way down the course might have made a more suitable
backdrop than the roar of the Newmarket crowd. Unfortunately for Thulliez,
the consequences of his performance were a bit more serious, his excruciating
misfortune in defeat on the favourite resulting in his losing the ride in the Irish One
Thousand Guineas. Though he had regained it by the time of Six Perfections' most
important success on home soil in the Prix Jacques le Marois, he was left counting
the cost again as an American rider replaced him for what turned out to be the filly's
finest hour in the Breeders' Cup Mile at Santa Anita in October.
        Horses for courses is a well-worn adage and jockeys for courses is catching
on too; or at least jockeys for countries appears to be. Every racing nation has
its peculiarities in its tracks, or sometimes in the way races are run, and it is easy
for a rider unfamiliar with them to be caught out. Of course, like the game show
contestants dressed in oversized costumes, to an extent Thulliez was dressed up
to look more ridiculous than he actually was at Newmarket. Despite the width
of the course, fields in mile races at Newmarket regularly gravitate to the earliest
opportunity to the rail nearest where the stalls are placed. With the stalls on the
stand side in the Guineas, the chance of Six Perfections becoming pocketed on the
rail from stall one was even greater than Thulliez probably imagined. In a field of
nineteen, Kieren Fallon was drawn next to him in stall two, but, with the advantage
of considerable experience of Newmarket, Fallon was almost certainly more aware
of the likely crucial stage of the race. The stiffness of the Rowley Mile encourages
riders to conserve their mounts longer than they might on other courses, the

downhill stretch into the Dip often a pivotal spot. Over two furlongs out in the Guineas, the runners were still very tightly packed. Around this point, Thulliez actually had Fallon boxed in on his inside, both their mounts still full of running, but, as Fallon waited for the gaps to appear, Thulliez angled right, cannoning into horses and having to snatch up sharply. Knocked back to last just as the pace was quickening in earnest, Thulliez then switched right again as the field entered the Dip over a furlong out, eventually ending up widest of all. Six Perfections still had three to four lengths to make up on Russian Rhythm inside the last furlong and, though she produced a storming finish, she was still a length and a half down at the line.

Inevitably, criticism of Thulliez was stinging, as it tends to be in the media throughout the world when foreign-based jockeys are considered to have erred. Thulliez wasn't the first to suffer a similar fate in the One Thousand Guineas, however, Steve Cauthen getting out too late when beaten a head by Hatoof on Marling in 1992 for instance. After the controversy over the Two Thousand Guineas in 2002, when the field split into three groups, Newmarket narrowed the course in 2003 to discourage a repeat. The outcome of the One Thousand Guineas brought calls for the stalls to be placed in the centre in future, but tactics are always likely to play a part at Newmarket, where the pitfalls for riders are many and varied. Moving the stalls simply creates a different set of problems. A more satisfactory solution might have to wait until the day when guidelines are extended to keep horses straight from the start for longer. Encouraging such a practice for at least the first two furlongs, for example, might go against the grain with those riders looking to settle their mounts by covering them up in the pack—one of the root causes of trouble—but it would make bunching less likely in the closing stages, as well as improving safety.

Although trainer Pascal Bary himself took defeat at Newmarket reasonably philosophically, judged by his comments afterwards, connections recruited Johnny Murtagh for Six Perfections in the Irish One Thousand Guineas at the Curragh

Prix du Haras de Fresnay-Le-Buffard Jacques le Marois, Deauville—
Six Perfections, making up for a couple of unlucky runs earlier in the season,
holds off stable-companion Domedriver (left), giving the sponsors their eighth victory in the race;
Japanese raider Telegnosis is third, with Special Kaldoun (far side),
Dubai Destination (dark colours) and Nebraska Tornado next

later in the month. Home advantage proved of no obvious benefit for Murtagh, who arguably had far fewer excuses in the face of a more straightforward task than Thulliez had at Newmarket, yet criticism of Murtagh was minimal in comparison. After starting at 7/4 at Newmarket, Six Perfections went off at 100/30-on in a field of eight at the Curragh, the smallest since 1939. Her closest market rival at 11/2 was Yesterday, who had been eighth at Newmarket. Classic success again eluded Six Perfections in frustrating circumstances for connections. She travelled very strongly held up, but her rider courted trouble by going up the far rail from the turn and had to sit and suffer as Six Perfections became pocketed until a furlong out. Once extricated, Six Perfections still had a good two lengths to make up on Yesterday and she failed by a short head.

Six Perfections was certainly not ridden to perfection in the classics, but, with luck, her three-year-old season would have come close to being perfect, just as her two-year-old season had almost been. Unbeaten in three starts after finishing second on her debut at two, including when looking an outstanding classic prospect in the Prix Marcel Boussac, Six Perfections started her three-year-old campaign with a comfortable win in the Prix Imprudence at Maisons-Laffitte in April. Her only defeat after the classics came in the Prix d'Astarte at Deauville in early-August but, instead of signalling the end of her progress, it proved to be a springboard to her finally fulfilling her potential. In hindsight, she might have needed the run in the d'Astarte, in which she went down by a neck to the four-year-old Bright Sky after racing closer to the pace than in the classics. Connections had toyed with running Six Perfections in the Prix de Diane after the Curragh, but had opted instead to give her a break. As a result, Six Perfections had been off for over two months before Deauville and, with the run behind her, she showed herself better than ever in the Prix Jacques le Marois at the same course later in the month.

Not unusually, the Prix du Haras de Fresnay-Le-Buffard Jacques le Marois proved a triumph for the Niarchos family, whose French stud sponsors the race. In the betting Six Perfections was coupled with her stable-companions Domedriver, winner of the Breeders' Cup Mile in the same colours the previous season, and Fomalhaut. In a strong international field, only the coupled pairing of Dubai Destination and Blatant started at shorter odds, the former having been a convincing winner of the Queen Anne at Royal Ascot, while the home challenge included the Poule d'Essai des Poulains winner Clodovil and the Prix de Diane winner Nebraska Tornado. In the event, none of those gave their running as Six Perfections and Domedriver finished first and second. The field spread across the centre of the track with a couple of the pacemakers to take them along, including Fomalhaut. Six Perfections tended to race freely and was still going strongly when switched to the stand side to make her move, quickening to lead around a furlong out and holding her older stable-companion by a short neck. The Japanese-trained Telegnosis was a length further away in third with Special Kaldoun fourth. Remarkably, Six Perfections was the sponsors' eighth success in the race since the legendary Miesque started the ball rolling as a three-year-old in 1987, though it was also their first since Spinning World won for a second time in 1997.

Connections refused to allow Six Perfections' overdue first Group 1 win of the season to go to their heads. Thulliez lost the mount to Jerry Bailey in the Breeders' Cup Mile, despite having ridden a faultless race to defeat Rock of Gibraltar on Domedriver at Arlington the previous year. Connections stated that Thulliez would have had a better chance of retaining the ride on Six Perfections had the race been over a one-turn mile. Six Perfections' wide draw in thirteen of thirteen over Santa Anita's two-turn mile raised some concern, but, in a field lacking a top-class performer, she started joint third favourite all the same at 53/10. Heading the market at 31/10 was Peace Rules, third in the Kentucky Derby, but having his first turf race of the season; Eddie Read Handicap winner Special Ring was second favourite, while another American-trained runner Designed For Luck was at the same odds as Six Perfections. Among those at longer odds were the other European challengers, Oasis Dream and Refuse To Bend, both of whom failed to do themselves justice. Six Perfections looked as if she might do likewise, becoming so upset at the start she had to be put in the stalls without her jockey. To the relief of her supporters, she proved straightforward in the race. Given a fine ride, soon in mid-division as the low-drawn runners took the early initiative, Bailey used her

NetJets Breeders' Cup Mile, Santa Anita—Six Perfections is given an excellent ride by Jerry Bailey to overcome a wide draw, and quickens in good style to beat Touch of The Blues and Century City

turn of foot to good effect as Six Perfections weaved through in the short straight, leading inside the final furlong. Once in front, she held on well without drawing away, beating the formerly European-trained pair Touch of The Blues and Century City by three quarters of a length and a neck. Peace Rules finished last. Six Perfections was her trainer's third Breeders' Cup success, following Miss Alleged in the Turf in 1991 and Domedriver. She was the sixth French-trained winner of the Mile and a fourteenth winner at the fixture for Bailey, the leading rider in the twenty years of the Breeders' Cup.

Despite her misfortunes, Six Perfections ranks close to some of the best miling fillies since the 'eighties. Among those from the 'nineties, she is rated significantly behind only Bosra Sham, who put up her best performance at the trip in defeat when second to Mark of Esteem in the Queen Elizabeth II Stakes at Ascot. Six Perfections ranks alongside Sussex Stakes winners Marling and Sayyedati, Moulin winner All At Sea, Ridgewood Pearl, another winner of the Breeders' Cup Mile, and Cape Verdi, the best Guineas winner of that decade with the exception of Bosra Sham. Six Perfections is also of similar standard to another French-trained filly of the new millennium, Banks Hill, a high-class winner of the Jacques le Marois at four, among other races. It says a lot for the achievements of her owner's brilliant filly Miesque that Six Perfections still has a way to go to rival her. Miesque enjoyed better fortune in the classics, winning the One Thousand Guineas at Newmarket and Longchamp, and went on to show herself among the very best fillies since *Racehorses* began, winning a total of ten Group 1 or Grade 1 races in three seasons, all but one of them at a mile. Several of Miesque's most important wins were gained in brilliant style, her two in the Breeders' Cup Mile coming by an aggregate of seven and a half lengths. As a result of her tendency to race freely, Six Perfections was usually covered up until late as a three-year-old, though her three juvenile successes were gained by an aggregate of twelve lengths, food for thought for those who put her narrow victories in 2003 down to idling. Despite all the furore, Six Perfections would probably have won the Guineas at Newmarket narrowly too, even with a clear run, and, on the balance of her form, she is probably only marginally a better filly than Russian Rhythm. Arguments over their respective merits might be resolved in 2004, when the upgraded catalogue of Group 1 races for fillies and mares would benefit from having two such horses in opposition, though it is probably only in open competition that Six Perfections and Russian Rhythm will have a realistic opportunity to perform nearer to Miesque's standard.

So far, Six Perfections is the shining light of Celtic Swing's stallion career; the Racing Post Trophy and Prix du Jockey Club winner has had only a handful of other smart performers in Europe, including Celtic Silence and Tomasino. Celtic Swing, now at the Irish National Stud, spent part of his stud career in France, where he covered Six Perfections' unraced dam Yogya, who has produced only one other recorded foal (a filly by Ocean of Wisdom in 2003), despite reaching the age of ten.

Yogya is a half-sister to Miesque, no less. Miesque has done particularly well at stud, producing among others Kingmambo and East of The Moon, the latter another winner of the Jacques le Marois in the Niarchos colours. Her three-year-old Mingun made into a smart colt with Aidan O'Brien in the latest season, while another of her sons, Miesque's Son, was responsible for the latest Prix Morny winner Whipper. Miesque, Kingmambo and East of The Moon were all trained by Francois Boutin, for whom, after a stint with Sir Mark Prescott, Pascal Bary worked as assistant prior to taking out a licence in 1981. Bary now handles over a hundred horses at Chantilly, from where he has trained four Prix du Jockey Club winners. He has yet to have a winner in Britain from very few runners. Only time will tell whether British racegoers will have further opportunities to see Six Perfections. Miesque was given a light season at four in preparation for her second Breeders' Cup and

		Celtic Swing (br 1992)	Damister (b 1982)	Mr Prospector Batucada
Six Perfections (FR) (br. or bl.f. 2000)			Celtic Ring (b 1984)	Welsh Pageant Pencuik Jewel
		Yogya (USA) (ch 1993)	Riverman (b 1969)	Never Bend River Lady
			Pasadoble (b 1979)	Prove Out Santa Quilla

Niarchos Family's "Six Perfections"

skipped the Queen Elizabeth II Stakes, in which she had suffered a rare defeat at a mile as a three-year-old. Miesque's only other reverse at three was inflicted by another outstanding filly in Indian Skimmer, who beat her by four lengths in the Prix de Diane. On the balance of her pedigree, there are good reasons to think that Six Perfections will stay a mile and a quarter. Her second dam Pasadoble, however, was bred to stay a mile and a half but did her winning at a mile, showing smart form. Six Perfections gives the impression she has much more speed than stamina and may well prove less than fully effective beyond a mile.

Six Perfections so far has the edge over Miesque in one minor respect, in that she has yet to be out of the first two in ten races, Miesque suffering that fate once when third in the Prix Morny as a two-year-old. A close-coupled filly, Six Perfections is a less imposing individual at present than was Miesque, but her trainer, who has handled her with great skill and no little dignity, is reportedly hopeful she will thrive physically from three to four. Miesque wore blinkers at two, when reportedly of a nervous disposition, but she grew out of that. Hopefully, the signs of temperament in Six Perfections at Santa Anita won't become any more manifest. She has shown herself genuine, as well as most consistent, once under way. Raced only at seven furlongs and a mile since her debut, she has yet to encounter heavy ground but seems to act on any other. All being well, Six Perfections will add a great deal to the next season, just as she did to 2003. *P. Bary, France*

SIX STAR 3 b.f. Desert Story (IRE) 115 – Adriya 94 (Vayrann 133) [2003 58: 6g 7.1m 6m 5.3m 6m Aug 28] disappointing maiden. *B. W. Duke* —

SIXTILSIX (IRE) 2 ch.c. (Apr 23) Night Shift (USA) – Assafiyah (IRE) 62 (Kris 135) [2003 5d⁶ 5s 5m 6g 5.1m Oct 28] €30,000Y: sturdy colt: second foal: half-brother to Italian 2002 2-y-o 1m winner by Salse: dam, lightly-raced maiden (stayed 1½m), out of half-sister to Prix de Diane winner Rafha: well held in maidens: left Ms J. Morgan in Ireland after second start: edgy sort. *J. C. Fox*

SKARA BRAE 3 b.f. Inchinor 119 – Tahilla 112 (Moorestyle 137) [2003 49: f7g Jan 23] poor maiden: well beaten only 3-y-o start. *G. G. Margarson* —

SKATER BOY 2 b.g. (Mar 28) Wizard King 122 – Makalu 79 (Godswalk (USA) 130) [2003 6.1m 8.2m p8g Dec 10] €8,000Y: small gelding: brother to 8.5f winner in Italy and half-brother to 2 winners, including early useful 5f to 1m winner Mr Bergerac (by Cyrano de Bergerac): dam maiden who stayed 1¼m: well held in maidens. *Miss S. West* —

SKEHANA (IRE) 3 b.f. Mukaddamah (USA) 125 – Lominda (IRE) 80 (Lomond (USA) 128) [2003 69: 7m 10.1m⁶ 10d Nov 6] leggy, lengthy filly: fair performer: stays 1¼m: acts on good to firm and good to soft ground. *J. Nicol* — 67

SKELLIGS ROCK (IRE) 3 b.c. Key of Luck (USA) 126 – Drew (IRE) (Double Schwartz 128) [2003 70: 10f² 12g Jul 3] fair maiden: should stay 1½m (faded when tried): raced only on good ground or firmer. *B. W. Duke* — 74

SKELTHWAITE 2 b.g. (Apr 19) Desert Story (IRE) 115 – Skip To Somerfield 79 (Shavian 125) [2003 p8g p7g f8g Nov 25] fourth foal: dam 2-y-o 6f winner: soon behind in maiden/claimers. *M. H. Tompkins* —

SKETCH (IRE) 2 ch.f. (Mar 26) Perugino (USA) 84 – Skew (Niniski (USA) 125) [2003 6m⁵ 7f* Jun 27] second foal: dam unraced half-sister to smart performer up to 13.5f Spout: fair form in maidens: won at Folkestone, taking good hold and leading 2f out: should stay 1m: open to progress. *R. Charlton* — 72 p

SKIBEREEN (IRE) 3 b.g. Ashkalani (IRE) 128 – Your Village (IRE) 64 (Be My Guest (USA) 126) [2003 80p: 10d² 12.1d⁴ p10g² p12g³ 12.1m² Aug 14] fairly useful maiden: stays 1½m: unraced on extremes of going on turf, just fair form on polytrack: tried tongue tied/blinkered: has raced freely: none too genuine: sold 10,000 gns, joined I. McInnes. *J. H. M. Gosden* — 80 a70

SKIDDAW JONES 3 b.g. Emperor Jones (USA) 119 – Woodrising 64 (Nomination 125) [2003 –: 9.1m* 9m 9.1g² 10.5m⁵ 8f⁴ 10.1m 10m 10d Oct 13] good-topped gelding: fair handicapper: 50/1-winner at Ayr in June: effective at 1m/1¼m: acts on firm ground: often slowly away. *Miss L. A. Perratt* — 67

SKIDMARK 2 b.c. (Feb 12) Pennekamp (USA) 130 – Flourishing (IRE) 85 (Trojan Fen 118) [2003 p7g³ p8g* Dec 20] 22,000Y: half-brother to several winners, including 1998 2-y-o 5f winner Kastaway (by Distant Relative) and 1m/1½m winner Rampant (by Pursuit of Love), both fairly useful: dam 2-y-o 7f winner: confirmed considerable promise and showed fair form when winning minor event at Lingfield by 1¼ lengths from — 79 P

Anuvasteel, slowly away again but strong late run: should stay 1¼m: open to good deal of improvement, and should win more races. *D. R. C. Elsworth*

SKIFF 3 b.f. Fleetwood (IRE) 107 – Dame Helene (USA) (Sir Ivor 135) [2003 8.3g   **55**
10.2m² 10.1d⁴ 12.1m² 11.7m⁶ Aug 5] 4,500Y: poor mover: sixth foal: half-sister to fairly
useful 1998 2-y-o 7f winner Autocrat (by Polar Falcon), later winner in Austria: dam, no
form, out of half-sister to high-class 7f to 9f performer Indian Lodge: modest maiden:
stays easy 1½m: unraced on extremes of going. *D. J. Coakley*

SKI JUMP (USA) 3 gr.g. El Prado (IRE) 119 – Skiable (IRE) (Niniski (USA) 125)   **85**
[2003 *77*: 10m* 12.3m⁶ 11.6s 10.2f* Jul 7] good-bodied gelding: fairly useful handicapper: won at Leicester in April and, having disappointed in between, Bath (blinkered)
in July (subsequently gelded): better form at 1¼m than 1½m: acts on firm going: ran
poorly in cheekpieces: races prominently. *R. Charlton*

SKIRT AROUND 5 b.m. Deploy 131 – Fairy Feet 78 (Sadler's Wells (USA) 132)   **57**
[2003 69, a–: f12g⁵ f12g Feb 1] tall, leggy mare: just modest form at best in 2003: stays
13f: acts on soft ground and fibresand. *W. J. Musson*

SKY COVE 2 b.g. (Mar 25) Spectrum (IRE) 126 – Aurora Bay (IRE) (Night Shift   **–**
(USA)) [2003 7.9f f6s f9.4g Dec 22] leggy gelding: third foal: half-brother to 3-y-o
Acomb: dam, no form, out of useful half-sister to high-class 1¼m performer Shady
Heights: well held in maidens. *M. W. Easterby*

SKY DOME (IRE) 10 ch.g. Bluebird (USA) 125 – God Speed Her (Pas de Seul 133)   **73 +**
[2003 74: p10g⁶ p10g³ 9.7g² f9.4s 9.3g⁶ 8g 7.6m 8g 8f⁴ f7s f8g⁵ f8g³ Nov 24]
lengthy, leggy gelding: poor mover: fair handicapper: won at Southwell in November:
stays easy 1¼m: acts on soft going, firm and all-weather: often blinkered/visored: sometimes carries head awkwardly/finds little. *M. H. Tompkins*

SKYERS A KITE 8 b.m. Deploy 131 – Milady Jade (IRE) (Drumalis 125) [2003 –:   **–**
f12s f12g Mar 20] small, good-topped mare: poor performer: well held in 2003. *Ronald
Thompson*

SKYE'S FOLLY (USA) 3 b.g. Kris S (USA) – Bittersweet Hour (USA) (Seattle Slew   **86**
(USA)) [2003 p8g⁴ 10g⁵ 10d 11.7f* 14.4g⁵ 16f* 16f⁵ Oct 12] good-topped gelding: sixth
foal: half-brother to 3 winners in USA, including minor stakes winner by Kingmambo:
dam, ran once in US, half-sister to US 2-y-o Grade 1 8.5f winners Success Express and
Greenwood Lake: fairly useful performer: won maiden at Bath in August and handicap at
Nottingham (beat Faraway Lady by neck) in September: stays 2m: acts on firm ground:
sold 28,000 gns. *Mrs A. J. Perrett*

SKY GALAXY (USA) 2 ch.f. (Feb 12) Sky Classic (CAN) – Fly To The Moon (USA)   **84**
90 (Blushing Groom (FR) 131) [2003 6m² 6m* 7m⁵ 6.5d 6m 6g Oct 13] stocky filly: type
to carry plenty of condition: seventh foal: closely related to useful 1996 2-y-o 5f winner
Moonshine Girl (by Shadeed) and half-sister to UAE 5f to 1m winner Tala Ya (by Storm
Bird): dam, 1m winner (later successful in USA), sister to smart 1987 2-y-o sprinter
Digamist: fairly useful performer: won maiden at Redcar in June: ran creditably in listed
race/nursery next 2 starts, poorly last 2: barely stays 7f: acts on good to firm and good to
soft going. *E. A. L. Dunlop*

SKYHARBOR 2 b.g. (Mar 26) Cyrano de Bergerac 120 – Pea Green 98 (Try My Best   **87**
(USA) 130) [2003 5.1m⁴ 6d* 6g³ 5f* 5f 6d Sep 10] 15,000Y: leggy, quite good-topped
gelding: half-brother to several winners, including fairly useful 1m to 1½m performer
The Green Grey (by Environment Friend) and 6-y-o Sussex Lad and to dam of smart
sprinters Sampower Star (by Cyrano de Bergerac) and 4-y-o Fire Up The Band: dam
2-y-o 5f winner who probably stayed 1m: fairly useful performer: won maiden at
Hamilton in May and minor event at Carlisle in June: long way below form last 2 starts:
barely stays 6f: acts on firm and good to soft ground. *D. Nicholls*

SKYLARK 6 ch.m. Polar Falcon (USA) 126 – Boozy 111 (Absalom 128) [2003 77:   **65**
6m 6f 7m 7.2g 6m 6m³ 6m⁶ 6.1m² 6g 8m⁴ Oct 12] leggy mare: fair handicapper: stays
easy 7f: acts on firm and good to soft going: often slowly away/looks hard ride. *Don
Enrico Incisa*

SKYLARKER (USA) 5 b.g. Sky Classic (CAN) – O My Darling (USA) 76 (Mr   **83**
Prospector (USA)) [2003 92: p10g⁶ f9.4s² 8.3g³ 10m⁶ 11.9m 10g⁴ 12m³ 14g p8g⁴ Dec
30] tall, rather leggy gelding: fairly useful handicapper: best at 1¼m/1½m: acts on good
to firm going, good to soft and all-weather: tried in cheekpieces: has been early to post:
consistent. *W. S. Kittow*

SKYMAITE 3 b.f. Komaite (USA) – Sky Fighter 43 (Hard Fought 125) [2003 63:   **–**
f6g 7.9g 6.9f f6g Jun 27] modest maiden at 2 yrs: well held in 2003: tried blinkered/in
cheekpieces. *Mrs G. S. Rees*

Bubwith Rated Stakes (Handicap), Doncaster—sixth win of the year for Smart Hostess,
who beats her half-brother and stable-companion the lighter grey Smart Predator

SKY QUEST (IRE) 5 b.g. Spectrum (IRE) 126 – Rose Vibert (Caerleon (USA) 132) **94**
[2003 77: p12g³ p10g² p10g⁵ 12.3m² 11.5m 10m² 10.2f* 10m² 10d² 10.5m⁶ 10g 10m²
10.1m* Oct 21] smallish, quite good-topped gelding: fairly useful handicapper: won
at Bath in June and Yarmouth in October, better than ever when beating Clarisse by 1½
lengths in latter: effective at 1¼m/easy 1½m: acts on firm going, good to soft and polytrack: usually wears tongue tie/cheekpieces: suited by waiting tactics. *P. W. Harris*

SLALOM (IRE) 3 b.g. Royal Applause 124 – Skisette (Malinowski (USA) 123) [2003 **78**
8.2m⁵ 8.1d³ Sep 26] 38,000F, 29,000Y: well-made gelding: half-brother to several
winners, notably Italian 5f performer Late Parade (by Astronef) and winner in Italy and
USA (including Grade 2 events at 1m/9f) Sweet Ludy (by Be My Guest), both smart:
dam, French maiden, out of half-sister to Great Voltigeur winner Nisnas: better effort in
maidens (fair form) when narrowly beaten at Haydock, again slowly away: should stay
beyond 1m. *Miss Gay Kelleway*

SLAP SHOT (IRE) 4 ch.f. Lycius (USA) 124 – Katanning (Green Desert (USA) 127) **108**
[2003 115: 5m* 5m* 5g³ 5m 5m² 6d⁶ Nov 16] lengthy filly: career-best effort when
second in Prix de l'Abbaye at Longchamp in 2002: just useful form at 4 yrs, successful at
Naples in minor event and Premio Citta di Napoli (beat Sopran Foldan 1½ lengths) on
return in summer: creditable efforts when ¾-length third to The Tatling in King George
Stakes at Goodwood and 3 lengths second to easy winner Pleasure Place in Premio
Omenoni at Milan: won at 6f, very best form at 5f: acted on soft and good to firm ground:
visits Singspiel. *L. Riccardi, Italy*

SLAVONIC (USA) 2 ch.c. (Feb 15) Royal Academy (USA) 130 – Cyrillic (USA) 106 **80 p**
(Irish River (FR) 131) [2003 7m⁵ 8m⁵ 8s⁴ Oct 29] strong, close-coupled colt: first foal:
dam, 1m to 1½m winner in France/USA, out of smart French/US performer up to 1¼m
Polemic: fairly useful form in maidens: fourth of 19 to Roehampton at Yarmouth, travelling well long way: stays 1m: type to make a better 3-y-o. *J. H. M. Gosden*

SLINK ALONG (USA) 3 b.c. Gone West (USA) – Kool Kat Katie (IRE) 120 (Fairy **–**
King (USA)) [2003 8.1m 10m 9m⁶ 16.2g Aug 25] tall, quite good-topped colt: first
foal: dam, 7f (at 2 yrs in Britain) to 1¼m (in North America) winner, sister to smart
performer up to 1½m Kalypso Katie: well held in maidens/handicap: sold 4,000 gns.
J. H. M. Gosden

SLIP KILLICK 6 b.m. Cosmonaut – Killick 69 (Slip Anchor 136) [2003 –§: 10.3m **– §**
6d 10g 10.5m 12.3m f8g Jun 25] tall mare: temperamental and seems of little account
nowadays: tried in headgear. *M. Mullineaux*

SLIPPY HITHERAO 3 b.f. First Trump 118 – Child Star (FR) 58 (Bellypha 130) **48**
[2003 7m p12g³ 10g 8.1m p12g p12g 10.2f⁴ 10m⁵ 10m⁶ Oct 23] 10,000Y: fourth foal:
half-sister to 3 winners, including 4-y-o Vandenberghe and 5-y-o Animal Cracker: dam
14.6f/2m winner on Flat and winning hurdler: poor maiden: claimed from J. Osborne
after second start: stays easy 1½m: acts on polytrack, raced only on good ground or firmer
on turf: tried in cheekpieces. *B. R. Johnson*

SLOE GIN 4 b.f. A P Indy (USA) 131 – Rose Bourbon (USA) (Woodman (USA) 126) **70**
[2003 81: 11.7m 10m 10.3m May 28] lengthy, angular filly: fairly useful maiden at 3 yrs:
just fair form at best in 2003: stays 1½m: acts on firm and good to soft going: tried
blinkered. *J. L. Dunlop*

SMART BOY PRINCE (IRE) 2 b.g. (Apr 21) Princely Heir (IRE) 111 – Miss Mulaz **61**
(FR) 114 (Luthier 126) [2003 6g 7.6m 6m 10m⁵ f7g f8g⁴ f8s⁶ f7s⁶ Dec 31] €11,000Y:
workmanlike gelding: half-brother to numerous winners abroad, including US Grade 2
11f winner My Style (by Kings Lake) and smart French performer around 1¼m Rhenium
(by Rainbows For Life): dam French 1½m winner: modest maiden: left I. Wood after
debut, J. Harris after fourth start: stays 1m: acts on fibresand, some promise on turf.
P. A. Blockley

SMART DANNY 2 gr.g. (Apr 28) Danzero (AUS) – She's Smart 88 (Absalom 128) **– p**
[2003 7m⁴ 7s Nov 3] good-topped gelding: seventh foal: half-brother to 3 winners,
including 7-y-o Smart Predator and 4-y-o Smart Hostess: dam sprinter: signs of ability in
maidens at Catterick and Redcar (raced freely): type to do better as 3-y-o. *J. J. Quinn*

SMARTER CHARTER 10 br.g. Master Willie 129 – Irene's Charter 72 (Persian Bold **–**
123) [2003 54: 12g 12m 12.4m 14f Jun 14] leggy, lengthy gelding: modest handicapper:
well beaten in 2003. *Mrs L. Stubbs*

SMART HOSTESS 4 gr.f. Most Welcome 131 – She's Smart 88 (Absalom 128) [2003 **101 +**
77: f6s⁴ f6g* f6s* 7m 6m⁵ 6m⁰ 7g 8.3d⁵ 6g* 5m* 5g 5m* 5m* Oct 25] heavy-bodied filly:
made into a useful performer in 2003: won handicaps at Wolverhampton and Southwell in
February: much improved after 4½-month break, winning handicap at Ripon, minor
event at Redcar and handicaps at Pontefract and Doncaster (beat Smart Predator by ¾
length) in September/October: best at 5f/6f: acts on soft going, good to firm and
fibresand: has been bandaged in front: usually waited with: tough. *J. J. Quinn*

SMART JOHN 3 b.g. Bin Ajwaad (IRE) 119 – Katy-Q (IRE) 58 (Taufan (USA) 119) **68**
[2003 65p: 8.2g 8d³ 8.1m 10.9m⁵ 10d Jul 26] good-topped gelding: fair maiden handicapper: stays 10.9f: acts on good to firm and good to soft ground. *B. P. J. Baugh*

SMART MINISTER 3 gr.g. Muhtarram (USA) 125 – She's Smart 88 (Absalom 128) **63**
[2003 –p: 7m 8d 7.5m 7.9f³ 7m⁶ f8.5s⁴ 8.5d² f8s Oct 21] workmanlike gelding: modest
maiden handicapper: stays 8.5f: acts on firm and good to soft ground: usually races
prominently. *J. J. Quinn*

SMART PREDATOR 7 gr.g. Polar Falcon (USA) 126 – She's Smart 88 (Absalom **107**
128) [2003 102: 6m 6m 5g 5m 6g 7m² 7m⁶ 6m* 6g² 6f⁴ 5m 6g³ 6m* 6m* 6m² 5.6d 5d*
6f 5m* 5m² Oct 25] big, lengthy, good-quartered gelding: useful performer: had a good
season, winning handicaps at Redcar, Newmarket and York, minor event at Beverley

Royal & SunAlliance Handicap, York—
the grey Smart Predator gains one of his five victories during the year;
Smirfys Systems is a good second ahead of Najeebon (No.13) and Undeterred (diamond on cap)

and handicap at Newmarket between June and October: good ¾-length second to Smart Hostess in handicap at Doncaster final start: best at 5f/6f: acts on any ground: tried visored: has worn blanket for stall entry: usually races prominently: tough. *J. J. Quinn*

SMART SCOT　4 ch.g. Selkirk (USA) 129 – Amazing Bay 100 (Mazilier (USA) 107)　**41**
[2003 –: 10g 11.5g 8f 10.9m 10m f9.4g⁶ 7g Aug 10] poor maiden: tried in cheekpieces. *B. P. J. Baugh*

SMART SQUALL (USA)　8 b.h. Summer Squall (USA) – Greek Wedding (USA)　**–**
(Blushing Groom (FR) 131) [2003 14.1g May 4] formerly useful up to 1¾m: seems of little account nowadays. *A. J. Lidderdale*

SMART STARPRINCESS (IRE)　2 b.f. (Feb 23) Soviet Star (USA) 128 – Takeshi　**56**
(IRE) 67 (Cadeaux Genereux 131) [2003 p5g³ p5g² p5g² 6m 5f f5s⁵ f5s³ 5.3m³ 5m⁵ f5g⁴　**a69**
f5g⁴ f5g* f5s* Dec 27] €6,000Y: fifth foal: dam, maiden who stayed 1m, half-sister to dam of very smart Irish 7f to 1¼m performer Rebelline: fair on all-weather, modest on turf: left P. McEntee after third start: won maiden and seller at Southwell in December, making all each time: best at 5f: acts on all-weather and good to firm going: blinkered last 9 outings: races prominently: sometimes hangs. *P. A. Blockley*

SMASHING TIME (USA)　5 b.m. Smart Strike (CAN) 121 – Broken Peace (USA)　**–**
(Devil's Bag (USA)) [2003 49: f11g f12s 8d 10d Aug 18] good-topped mare: maiden: well held in 2003. *M. C. Chapman*

SMIRFYS DANCE HALL (IRE)　3 b.f. Halling (USA) 133 – Bigger Dances (USA)　**–**
(Moscow Ballet (USA)) [2003 8g 12f⁶ Apr 11] tall, leggy filly: third foal: dam ran once in USA: little form. *W. M. Brisbourne*

SMIRFYS LINCLON　4 b.g. Never So Bold 135 – Party Scenes (Most Welcome　**–**
131) [2003 –: p8g 6m Sep 6] of no account. *W. M. Brisbourne*

SMIRFYS PARTY　5 ch.g. Clantime 101 – Party Scenes (Most Welcome 131) [2003　**65**
79: 5g 7.6m 6.1d 7m 7m 7m 7m 6m* 5m Aug 6] rather leggy gelding: fair handicapper: best effort in 2003 when 50/1-winner at Redcar in August: effective at 6f, probably at 1m: acts on fibresand, firm and good to soft going: visored last 5 starts: races prominently. *D. Nicholls*

SMIRFYS SYSTEMS　4 b.g. Safawan 118 – Saint Systems 68 (Uncle Pokey 116)　**94**
[2003 79: 7m⁵ 7.2f 7f 6m* 6m² Aug 19] close-coupled, workmanlike gelding: fairly useful handicapper: 66/1-winner at Thirsk (wandered) in August: good ½-length second to Smart Predator at York next time: free-going sort, and should be as effective at 5f as 6f: acts on firm and good to soft going. *W. M. Brisbourne*

SMIRK　5 ch.h. Selkirk (USA) 129 – Elfin Laughter 76 (Alzao (USA) 117) [2003 117:　**114**
8g 8g³ 8.1g² 8.5m 8g Aug 1] tall, lengthy horse: usually takes eye: smart performer: best effort in 2003 when 2½ lengths second to Desert Deer in attheraces Mile at Sandown third start: subsequently well held in Diomed Stakes at Epsom and William Hill Mile (Handicap) at Goodwood: best at 1m/9f: acts on any going: sold 40,000 gns, sent to USA. *D. R. C. Elsworth*

SMITH N ALLAN OILS　4 b.g. Bahamian Bounty 116 – Grand Splendour 79　**68**
(Shirley Heights 130) [2003 70: 6m 7.1d 5.9g 7f⁶ 6m 7m⁴ 6.9m⁵ 8.2g 7g² 7m² 7.5m² 6.9m 7m 8m 7m⁵ 7f² p7g³ p7g p8g* f7g p7g* Dec 30] sparely-made gelding: fair performer: won claimer and handicap at Lingfield in December: stays 1m: acts on polytrack, firm and good to soft ground: tried blinkered, usually wears cheekpieces: sometimes slowly away. *M. Dods*

SMITHY　4 ch.f. Greensmith 121 – Biscay 67 (Unfuwain (USA) 131) [2003 56: f7g f7s　**44**
f7g⁵ f6g⁵ f8s Feb 20] sturdy filly: poor maiden: headstrong, but stays 8.5f: acts on fibresand, raced only on good/good to firm going on turf: tried in headgear: sometimes finds little: none too consistent. *Mrs N. Macauley*

SMOCKINGTON HOLLOW　2 b.f. (May 11) Makbul 104 – Indian Flower 87　**–**
(Mansingh (USA) 120) [2003 6.1g Jun 23] twelfth known foal: dam, 5f winner, also successful in USA: 66/1 and green, tailed off in maiden at Nottingham. *J. A. Pickering*

SMOKIN BEAU　6 b.g. Cigar 68 – Beau Dada (IRE) 66 (Pine Circle (USA)) [2003 116:　**112**
6g³ 6g 5g³ 6m 5m⁶ 5g 5d⁵ 6m⁴ 6m 5m Oct 2] smallish, robust gelding: smart performer: less consistent than usual at 6 yrs, best effort when third to Needwood Blade in Palace House Stakes at Newmarket on third start: effective at 5f/6f: acts on fibresand and any turf going: visored twice at 3 yrs, wore cheekpieces final outing: sometimes gets upset in stall/starts slowly/edges right: moved poorly to post and reportedly finished lame second start: reportedly broke blood vessel fourth outing: often forces pace. *N. P. Littmoden*

SMOKING BARRELS 3 ch.c. Desert Prince (IRE) 130 – Scandalette (Niniski (USA) – 125) [2003 78: 9m 10g 7d Oct 31] big, good-topped colt: fair form in maidens at 2 yrs: well beaten in handicaps in 2003, sold from J. Gosden 11,000 gns after reappearance. *P. J. Flynn, Ireland*

SMOKIN JOE 2 b.c. (Apr 4) Cigar 68 – Beau Dada (IRE) 66 (Pine Circle (USA)) **74** [2003 5m p6g⁶ 6.1d⁶ f6g² p5g² p6g* p6g⁶ Dec 30] small, quite attractive colt: brother to 6-y-o Smokin Beau and half-brother to winner in Sweden by Kylian: dam 6f (at 2 yrs) to 1m winner: fair performer: left J. Cullinan after second start: won maiden at Lingfield: sixth in nursery there following day: likely to stay 7f: acts on all-weather, probably on good to soft going. *J. R. Best*

SMOOTHIE (IRE) 5 gr.g. Definite Article 121 – Limpopo 49 (Green Desert (USA) **67** 127) [2003 77: p12g⁴ p10g p10g p10g⁴ 9m 9.7m 10d 10g* f14.8g⁶ 10d⁶ f12g* f12g **a72** f11g⁴ Dec 15] close-coupled gelding: unimpressive mover: fair performer: won seller at Leicester (sold from P. Cole 8,500 gns) in May and minor event at Wolverhampton in November: stays 1½m: acts on all-weather, firm and soft ground: tried blinkered: has found little: none too consistent. *Ian Williams*

SMOOTHLY DOES IT 2 b.g. (Mar 11) Efisio 120 – Exotic Forest 66 (Dominion 123) **69** [2003 5d⁵ 6g⁵ f6g⁵ 6.1d³ 7m 7.1m 8.3g² 8m Oct 20] 30,000F, 12,000Y: leggy gelding: fifth foal: half-brother to useful 2000 2-y-o 5f winner Threezedzz and 5f/6f winner Zoena (both by Emarati): dam 1m winner: fair maiden: second in nursery at Windsor: never placed to challenge final start: stays 1m: acts on good to soft going, well below form on good to firm and fibresand. *Mrs A. J. Bowlby*

SMOOTH PASSAGE 4 b.g. Suave Dancer (USA) 136 – Flagship 84 (Rainbow Quest – (USA) 134) [2003 –: p10g 10m 10.3g 10.2g Aug 7] little form: usually blinkered. *J. Gallagher*

SMYSLOV 5 b.g. Rainbow Quest (USA) 134 – Vlaanderen (IRE) 77 (In The Wings **72 ?** 128) [2003 10m 9.9f⁵ 14g 12g⁵ Jul 17] strong, lengthy gelding: fairly useful performer in 2001: missed 2002: fair at best in handicaps in 2003: stays 1½m: acts on soft and good to firm going: visored last 3 starts: sold 5,500 gns in August. *P. R. Webber*

SNINFIA (IRE) 3 b.f. Hector Protector (USA) 124 – Christmas Kiss 82 (Taufan (USA) **78** 119) [2003 10m 10g 8m⁴ 8.3d 10g² 10.4m 11.7f Oct 12] 35,000Y: rangy, unfurnished filly: third foal: half-sister to 4-y-o Night Runner and 5-y-o Festive Affair: dam 5f/6f winner: stays 1¼m: acts on good to firm going: slowly away fourth outing: sold 20,000 gns. *L. M. Cumani*

SNIPPETS (IRE) 3 b.f. Be My Guest (USA) 126 – Sniffle (IRE) 60 (Shernazar 131) **105** [2003 95: 10m⁴ 11.4m³ 12f* 10m² 12g 8f⁵ Oct 11] sturdy, good-bodied filly: second foal: dam lightly-raced half-sister to Prix Vermeille winner Pearly Shells and smart performer up to 1½m in Europe/USA Frenchpark: useful performer: third to Hammiya in listed race at Chester before winning similar event at Naas in June by ¾ length from Juliette: good 1¼ lengths third (promoted to second) to Hanami in Pretty Polly Stakes at the Curragh after: well below form last 2 starts: stays 1½m: acts on any going. *J. S. Bolger, Ireland*

SNIP SNAP 4 b.f. Revoque (IRE) 122 – Snap Crackle Pop (IRE) 87 (Statoblest 120) – [2003 –: 6d 5g 5g 6m 5m Sep 17] fair performer at 2 yrs for Sir Mark Prescott: no form since: tried visored. *L. Montague Hall*

SNOOKER AT RAY'S 2 ch.c. (Mar 11) Komaite (USA) – Hollia 72 (Touch Boy – 109) [2003 5g 6m Sep 7] 5,400Y, resold 7,800Y: lengthy colt: half-brother to several winners, including fairly useful 1996 2-y-o 5f winner Fredrik The Fierce (by Puissance) and 4-y-o Weet A Round: dam 2-y-o 5f winner: well held in maidens at Ripon and York. *M. W. Easterby*

SNOOTY ROMANCE (IRE) 3 br.f. Grand Lodge (USA) 125 – Easy Romance – (Northern Jove (CAN)) [2003 60: 7m⁶ 7f⁶ 8.3m f12g 7f Sep 14] IR 30,000Y: seventh foal: half-sister to several winners, including Irish 1998 2-y-o 6f/7f winner Storm Cove (by Catrail) and 1m winner Northern Fan (by Lear Fan), both fairly useful: dam won up to 7f in USA: modest form on first 2 starts at 2 yrs for D. Wachman in Ireland: little form in 2003, leaving W. Jarvis after fourth start: tried tongue tied/blinkered. *M. P. Sunderland, Ireland*

SNOW BUNTING 5 ch.g. Polar Falcon (USA) 126 – Marl 94 (Lycius (USA) 124) **70** [2003 69: 6m 6m 7m² 6m⁴ 6m 7m⁴ 6m 6m⁶ 6f⁵ 7m⁶ 7m Oct 13] leggy gelding: fair handicapper: effective at 6f/7f: acts on firm going and polytrack (well held on heavy/fibresand): has raced freely: suited by waiting tactics. *Jedd O'Keeffe*

SNOW CHANCE (IRE) 2 ch.f. (Apr 29) Compton Place 125 – Snowscape (Niniski **43**
(USA) 125) [2003 6m 7m 8m⁴ f8s Oct 7] IR 6,500F, €7,000Y, resold 3,200Y: workmanlike filly: third foal: half-sister to 3-y-o Sir Haydn: dam ran 3 times in Ireland: poor
maiden: fourth in Ayr seller, only form: stays 1m: sold 600 gns. *K. R. Burke*

SNOWDROP (IRE) 3 ch.f. Petardia 113 – Richardstown Lass (IRE) (Muscatite 122) **–**
[2003 63: p6g f6g p6g Feb 5] disappointing maiden. *J. W. Hills*

SNOWED UNDER 2 gr.g. (Mar 9) Most Welcome 131 – Snowy Mantle 54 (Siberian **–**
Express (USA) 125) [2003 8d Nov 7] good-topped gelding: first foal: dam, 1m winner,
not one to trust: 50/1 and backward, always behind in maiden at Doncaster. *J. D. Bethell*

SNOW GOOSE 2 b.f. (Feb 7) Polar Falcon (USA) 126 – Bronzewing 103 (Beldale **102 p**
Flutter (USA) 130) [2003 6m⁴ 6d* 7m* 7m* 7m² Oct 18] unfurnished filly: has a quick,
fluent action: sister to smart 7f (at 2 yrs) and 1¼m winner Merry Merlin and half-sister
to several winners, including 4-y-o Dusky Warbler: dam 6f and 1m winner: useful
performer: won maiden at Leicester in July, minor event at Redcar in August and nursery
at Newmarket (beat Why Dubai by length in 18-runner event) in October: good 1½
lengths second to Cairns in Rockfel Stakes at Newmarket: will stay at least 1m: acts on
good to firm and good to soft going: often races up with pace: sometimes wanders: open
to progress. *J. L. Dunlop*

SNOW JOKE (IRE) 2 b.f. (Mar 23) Desert Sun 120 – Snowcap (IRE) (Snow Chief **57**
(USA)) [2003 5m 6g 6g Jul 4] €12,000Y: sturdy filly: third foal: dam lightly-raced
daughter of Breeders' Cup Sprint winner Very Subtle: modest form in maidens/minor
event: shapes as if will stay 7f. *Mrs P. N. Dutfield*

SNOW LEOPARD (IRE) 4 gr.g. Highest Honor (FR) 124 – Leopardess (IRE) 79 **–**
(Ela-Mana-Mou 132) [2003 95: 10g 10m May 24] leggy, lengthy gelding: useful handicapper: disappointing since reportedly sustaining stress fracture to near-hind splint bone
second 3-y-o outing: tried blinkered. *J. L. Dunlop*

SNOW RIDGE (IRE) 2 b.c. (Apr 9) Indian Ridge 123 – Snow Princess (IRE) **111 p**
111 (Ela-Mana-Mou 132) [2003 7g* 8f* 7m Oct 18]
Snow Ridge's unbeaten record went west in the Dewhurst Stakes at Newmarket, where, as second favourite, he finished ninth of twelve, albeit beaten only
around four lengths by Milk It Mick, racing freely in touch but proving unable to

Hackney Empire Royal Lodge Stakes, Ascot—
Snow Ridge finds his stride for an impressive victory from Moscow Ballet (centre)
and the Sheikh Mohammed trio Rule of Law (visor), Leicester Square and Privy Seal

Exors of the late Lord Weinstock's "Snow Ridge"

respond when the tempo quickened and having quite a hard race into the bargain. On the face of it, this was not a particularly encouraging performance with Snow Ridge's three-year-old career in mind. However, in Snow Ridge's defence, lack of experience—he had made only two previous appearances—and a drop back in trip from a mile to seven furlongs were not in his favour, coupled with the fact that the Dewhurst had seemingly come as something of an afterthought for his connections. On the basis of his victory in the Hackney Empire Royal Lodge Stakes at Ascot three weeks previously, and of his looks—he is a big, lengthy colt with a fluent, easy action—Snow Ridge remains a promising colt likely to add to his reputation as a three-year-old for Godolphin, who purchased him from the Weinstock family after the end of the season.

Snow Ridge arrived at Ascot the winner of a seven-runner minor event at Kempton early in September, when he drifted in the betting but was fit enough to do himself justice. Pushed ahead of odds-on Iqte Saab, successful in a Salisbury maiden, two furlongs out, Snow Ridge showed a good turn of foot and was impressive in asserting himself, winning by three and half lengths. Snow Ridge started favourite for the ten-runner Royal Lodge ahead of Rule of Law, successful in a listed event at York, Tipperary winner Moscow Ballet, one of two in the field representing Ballydoyle, and easy Leicester winner Almuraad. Full of himself in the paddock, swishing his tail and so much on his toes that two handlers were required, Snow Ridge looked anything but the likely winner early in the straight.

As the leaders quickened, Snow Ridge was last, not really having found his stride and carrying his head a shade awkwardly. Once his jockey got him opened out, however, after switching him outside, Snow Ridge ate up the ground, catching Moscow Ballet and the front-running Rule of Law well inside the final furlong to win with something in hand by three quarters of a length. The time was a course record on the round course for a two-year-old, though nothing too significant should be read into that—Red Bloom lowered it again in the next race.

		Indian Ridge (ch 1985)	Ahoonora (ch 1975)	Lorenzaccio
				Helen Nichols
			Hillbrow (ch 1975)	Swing Easy
Snow Ridge (IRE)				Golden City
(b.c. Apr 9, 2001)		Snow Princess (IRE) (b 1992)	Ela-Mana-Mou (b 1976)	Pitcairn
				Rose Bertin
			Karelia (b 1977)	Sir Ivor
				Karelina

A mile obviously suited Snow Ridge and, in the event, the Racing Post Trophy might have proved a more suitable race for him than the Dewhurst. Snow Ridge's sire Indian Ridge was a sprinter sired by another sprinter and the majority of his offspring prove best at up to a mile, with only a small percentage of his successful progeny aged three and upwards, notably High Pitched and Indian Creek, winning over further than a mile and a quarter. The distaff side of Snow Ridge's pedigree is certainly not short of stamina. His dam Snow Princess, also responsible for the Irish mile-and-a-half winner White Queen (by Spectrum), was a tough racemare, running nineteen times for six successes, including the November Handicap at three and a listed race in Milan at four. She stayed long distances, finishing second in the Northumberland Plate and the Prix Royal-Oak, and was out of a mare who won at a mile and stayed a mile and a half well, finishing third in the Prix de Royallieu. On balance, Snow Ridge, who acts on firm going, is more likely to stay a mile and a half than not. *M. P. Tregoning*

SNOW'S RIDE   3 gr.c. Hernando (FR) 127 – Crodelle (IRE) (Formidable (USA) 125)   **103**
[2003 71: 11m⁶ 9g 11.8m 12.1m² 11.6d⁵ 14.1m³ 14m⁶ 14m⁵ p16g² 15.9d* 16.1m⁵ 16g f16.2g* f16g* Dec 3] leggy, good-topped colt: useful handicapper: improved steadily in 2003, winning at Chester in September, Wolverhampton in November and Southwell (beat Bid For Fame a neck) in December: stays 2m: acts on all-weather, yet to race on extremes of going on turf: has started slowly/raced freely. *W. R. Muir*

SNOW WOLF   2 ch.c. (Mar 7) Wolfhound (USA) 126 – Christmas Rose (Absalom   **80**
128) [2003 5.7m 5.1f² 6g³ Oct 22] smallish, quite attractive colt: first foal: dam twice-raced half-sister to Gimcrack Stakes winner Bannister out of half-sister to very smart sprinter Dead Certain: fairly useful form in maidens: second of 5 at Nottingham: stays 6f: acts on firm going: sold 21,000 gns. *M. P. Tregoning*

SNUKI   4 b.g. Pivotal 124 – Kennedys Prima 65 (Primo Dominie 121) [2003 65, a75:   **–**
p10g p10g⁶ p10g² p8g 8g p10g p8g p10g Dec 29] fair handicapper: below form after   **a77**
third start: stays 1¼m: acts on polytrack, yet to race on extremes of going on turf: tried blinkered. *G. L. Moore*

SOAKED   10 b.g. Dowsing (USA) 124 – Water Well 96 (Sadler's Wells (USA) 132)   **70 §**
[2003 78§: f5g⁶ f5g⁶ f5s⁴ f5g f5g 5m 5g³ 5s³ 5g 5g* 5m⁵ 5g⁵ 5g f5g² 5m⁶ 5m⁴ 5m² 6m⁵   **a62 §**
5m 5m f5g³ 5g⁵ f5g Dec 12] workmanlike gelding: fair handicapper: won at Musselburgh in May: best at 5f: acts on fibresand, firm and soft ground: visored once, usually blinkered nowadays: sometimes early/led to post: has reportedly bled/finished lame: front runner: unreliable. *D. W. Chapman*

SOAP STONE   8 b.m. Gunner B 126 – Tzarina (USA) (Gallant Romeo (USA)) [2003   **–**
11.9f Apr 10] temperamental hurdler: of little account on Flat. *Miss A. M. Newton-Smith*

SOAP WATCHER (IRE)   2 b.g. (Apr 27) Revoque (IRE) 122 – Princess of Zurich   **58**
(IRE) (Law Society (USA) 130) [2003 6m 7.5m⁴ 6m 8d Oct 14] 23,000Y: heavy-topped, plain gelding: has a markedly round action: seventh living foal: half-brother to 3 winners, including 4-y-o Dawn Invasion and fairly useful 5f (at 2 yrs)/6f winner Princely Dream (by Night Shift): dam, Irish 7f winner, half-sister to smart 6f/7f winner Prince Echo: modest maiden: form only at 7.5f: signs of waywardness: sold 1,800 gns, sent to Sweden. *R. A. Fahey*

SOL

SOBA JONES   6 b.g. Emperor Jones (USA) 119 – Soba 127 (Most Secret 119) [2003   **83**
81: f6g f6s* f5s⁵ f6g⁴ 6g⁴ 5m 6m 6g⁵ 6m 6g 5m 5f f6s⁵ 5s² Nov 3] tall gelding: fairly
useful handicapper: won at Southwell in February: best at 5f/6f: acts on any turf going/
fibresand: effective blinkered or not, tried in cheekpieces: has reared leaving stall: usually
races prominently. *J. Balding*

SOCIAL CONTRACT   6 b.g. Emarati (USA) 74 – Just Buy Baileys 69 (Formidable   **68 §**
(USA) 125) [2003 73§, a82§: f6s⁶ p7g f7s⁵ f6s* f6s³ 7m² 7m 6d 7m³ 7f⁵ 6m 7m 6.1g
6.1m 7m² 8m⁶ 6m⁶ 7f 7g² 7m 8m p7g⁶ Dec 6] strong, useful-looking gelding: fair
performer: won claimer at Southwell in February: left D. Shaw after fourteenth outing:
effective at 6f to easy 1m: acts on firm going, soft and fibresand: often wears headgear:
tried tongue tied: unreliable. *S. Dow*

SOCIALISE   3 b.f. Groom Dancer (USA) 128 – Society Rose 88 (Saddlers' Hall (IRE)   **–**
126) [2003 69p: 7f⁵ Jul 16] well-made filly: fair form in 2 races in 2002: well below form
only 3-y-o start: should stay at least 1m. *W. J. Haggas*

SOCIETY PET   4 b.f. Runnett 125 – Polar Storm (IRE) 76 (Law Society (USA) 130)   **– §**
[2003 50§: f9.4s Jan 31] ungenuine maiden. *D. G. Bridgwater*

SO DETERMINED (IRE)   2 b.g. (Mar 25) Soviet Star (USA) 128 – Memory Green   **–**
(USA) (Green Forest (USA) 134) [2003 7m p8g Nov 2] well-grown gelding: fourth foal:
half-brother to useful 1m (at 2 yrs) to 1¼m winner Dr Greenfield (by Dr Devious) and to
fairly useful 13f/1¾m winner Forum Chris (by Trempolino): dam, won around 1¼m on
turf in USA, out of sister to Glint of Gold and Diamond Shoal: signs of only a little ability
in maidens at Leicester (tongue tied) and Lingfield. *G. A. Butler*

SOLANZA   4 ch.f. Bahamian Bounty 116 – Son Et Lumiere (Rainbow Quest (USA)   **–**
134) [2003 f9.4g 7g⁵ 8f Jun 4] little form. *Noel T. Chance*

SOLAR POWER (IRE)   2 b.f. (Mar 30) Marju (IRE) 127 – Next Round (IRE) 83   **77 p**
(Common Grounds 118) [2003 7m* Sep 22] smallish, compact filly: second foal: half-
sister to 3-y-o Treaty of Utrecht: dam, 2-y-o 7f winner, half-sister to smart US Grade 1 9f
winner Caffe Latte: 5/1 and green, won 10-runner maiden at Kempton by ¾ length from
Garryurra, racing freely and idling after leading 1f out: should stay 1m: will improve.
J. R. Fanshawe

SOLAR PRINCE (IRE)   2 b.g. (Feb 11) Desert Prince (IRE) 130 – Quiche 83 (Form-   **57 d**
idable (USA) 125) [2003 5d 5d⁴ 5s 5m 6m 7m Oct 2] €26,000Y: lengthy gelding:
half-brother to several winners, including smart 6f performer Lionhearted (by Catrail)
and useful 5f to 7f performer (in Ireland/France) Symboli Kildare (by Kaldoun): dam 6f
winner: modest maiden: below form after second start, leaving Ms J. Morgan in Ireland
after fourth, Mrs A. M. Naughton after fifth: best efforts at 5f: acts on good to soft going:
tongue tied third and fourth (also blinkered/slowly away) appearances. *J. C. Fox*

SOLDERA (USA)   3 b.f. Polish Numbers (USA) – La Pepite (USA) (Mr Prospector   **107**
(USA)) [2003 95p: 8.1g⁴ 8d* 8f⁴ 8m Oct 4] lengthy filly: fluent mover: useful performer,
lightly raced: won listed race at Ascot in July by ½ length from Miss Ivanhoe: close fourth
to Favourable Terms in Matron Stakes at Leopardstown third start: just respectable eighth
behind Echoes In Eternity in Sun Chariot Stakes at Newmarket final outing: should stay
1¼m: acts on firm and good to soft going. *J. R. Fanshawe*

SOLDIER ON (IRE)   5 b.g. General Monash (USA) 107 – Golden Form (Formidable   **–**
(USA) 125) [2003 –: 8g f6g May 23] tall, useful-looking gelding: fairly useful at 2 yrs:
lightly raced and no form since. *M. J. Wallace*

SOLEIL D'HIVER   2 b.f. (Feb 4) Bahamian Bounty 116 – Catriona 75 (Bustino 136)   **43**
[2003 5g 7m⁴ 6f 7m⁴ 6m f7g Nov 24] 3,500F, 4,000Y: sturdy, lengthy filly: first foal:
dam, 7f winner, out of sister to top Irish 1982 2-y-o Danzatore: poor maiden: stays 7f:
best efforts on good to firm going. *P. C. Haslam*

SOLINIKI   2 b.g. (Feb 12) Danzero (AUS) – Pride of My Heart 74 (Lion Cavern (USA)   **84 p**
117) [2003 6m* Aug 27] 10,500F, 20,000Y: second foal: half-brother to 3-y-o Night
Prospector: dam, 7f winner, half-sister to smart sprinter Northern Goddess: 16/1, won
16-runner maiden at Ascot comfortably by 1¼ lengths from Magic Amigo, always close
up (flashed tail): will probably stay 7f: sure to improve. *J. A. Osborne*

SOLLER BAY   6 b.g. Contract Law (USA) 108 – Bichette 66 (Lidhame 109) [2003 78d,   **86**
a82d: 8.2g 8.3d* 8.1m 8.1s* 8.3g 7.1g 8d 7.6m⁴ 7.6m⁶ 8.1d⁶ Sep 26] quite good-topped   **a–**
gelding: fairly useful handicapper: won at Windsor in April and Haydock in May,
dictating pace both times: stays 1m: acts on heavy going, good to firm and fibresand:
races freely/up with pace. *K. R. Burke*

SOLO FLIGHT   6 gr.g. Mtoto 134 – Silver Singer 65 (Pharly (FR) 130) [2003 104:   **97**
10m 10g 10m 12f 10.3f⁶ 9.9g 10.5m⁶ 11.9m 10.3d² 10m 12m⁶ Oct 3] angular gelding:
useful performer: mostly just respectable efforts in 2003: neck second to Marinas Charm
in minor event at Doncaster on only outing outside handicaps in last 3 seasons: effective
at 1¼m/1½m: acts on firm and good to soft going, possibly not on soft/heavy: has worn
crossed noseband/net muzzle: edgy sort: best held up in truly-run race: sometimes finds little. *B. W. Hills*

SOLOMON'S MINE (USA)   4 b.g. Rahy (USA) 115 – Shes A Sheba (USA)   **81**
(Alysheba (USA)) [2003 84: f11s f14s⁵ f16s⁵ 18g* 16m² 16.2m³ Mar 29] strong gelding:
poor mover: fairly useful handicapper: won at Doncaster in March: good third to
Flownaway at Ascot final outing: stays 2¼m: acts on fibresand and any turf going: has
won in blinkers, not tried in 2003: races up with pace: tough. *M. J. Polglase*

SOLO SOLE (ITY)   2 b.c. (Feb 17) Grand Lodge (USA) 125 – Storm Flash 65 (Green   **72**
Desert (USA) 127) [2003 8s⁶ p8g p6g p7g³ Dec 17] €34,000Y: third foal: half-brother to
winner in Italy by Shantou: dam lightly-raced daughter of smart sprinter Storm Warning:
fair maiden: clearly best effort when third in minor event at Lingfield: should stay at least
1m. *L. M. Cumani*

SOLO SOLERO (IRE)   4 b.f. Bigstone (IRE) 126 – Dreaming Spires 64 (Sadler's   **51**
Wells (USA) 132) [2003 67d: 5.8s 5.7g 5f⁴ 5g 5m* 5f 5f⁵ 5m Oct 1] IR 1,400F, IR
1,600Y: half-sister to winners in Italy by River Falls and Spectrum: dam soundly beaten
after debut: just modest handicapper in 2003: below form at Bath second outing: won at
Bellewstown in July: races mainly around 5f: acts on firm and soft ground: often
blinkered, including for win. *Bernard Lawlor, Ireland*

SOMAYDA (IRE)   8 b.g. Last Tycoon 131 – Flame of Tara 124 (Artaius (USA) 129)   **59**
[2003 –: 8.3g⁶ 9.7m 9m 8.3m⁴ 10m⁴ 8g² 8m⁵ 7m 8.1g 8.3m Sep 29] modest handicapper
nowadays: stays easy 1½m: acts on heavy and good to firm going: tried blinkered/
visored. *Miss Jacqueline S. Doyle*

SOMEONE'S ANGEL (USA)   2 gr.f. (Apr 10) Runaway Groom (CAN) –   **– p**
Yazeanhaa (USA) 68 (Zilzal (USA) 137) [2003 8m 8m Oct 24] leggy filly: on weak side
at 2 yrs: fourth living foal: closely related to fairly useful 1998 2-y-o 1m winner Fancy
My Chance (by Rainbow Quest) and half-sister to 5-y-o Never Promise: dam once-raced
half-sister to very smart sprinter Nabeel Dancer: signs of ability in maidens at Newmarket
and Doncaster: likely to do better. *E. A. L. Dunlop*

SOMERSET WEST (IRE)   3 b.g. Catrail (USA) 123 – Pizzazz 47 (Unfuwain   **64**
(USA) 131) [2003 74: p5g⁵ p6g p5g⁵ p5g⁴ 8m 6d 5.7f* Sep 8] workmanlike gelding:
modest performer: won maiden at Bath in September, dictating pace: stays 6f: acts on
polytrack and firm going: sometimes tongue tied: sold 3,000 gns. *B. R. Millman*

SOMETHINGABOUTHER   3 b.f. Whittingham (IRE) 104 – Paula's Joy 75   **64**
(Danehill (USA) 126) [2003 63: 5.1m 5m³ 5.3d² 5f³ 5.3m 5g⁵ 5m 5m² 5m f5g f6g⁵ f5g   **a40**
f6s Dec 27] smallish, sturdy filly: modest maiden handicapper: left D. Ivory after tenth
start: best form at 5f: acts on firm and good to soft ground: poor form on all-weather: none
too consistent. *P. W. Hiatt*

SOMEWHERE MY LOVE   2 br.f. (Jan 29) Pursuit of Love 124 – Grand Coronet   **63**
66 (Grand Lodge (USA) 125) [2003 7m⁵ 7m Oct 4] useful-looking filly: first foal: dam 7f
winner: modest form in maidens at Kempton (shaped well after slow start) and Redcar:
should stay 1m. *T. G. Mills*

SOMNUS   3 b.g. Pivotal 124 – Midnight's Reward 84 (Night Shift (USA)) [2003   **125**
117: 6g⁵ 7m 6g* 6m* 6m⁴ 6m² 6d* 5s Oct 5]
Three years after Pipalong provided Tim Easterby with his first Group 1
winner when successful in the Stanley Leisure Sprint Cup at Haydock, Somnus
repeated the feat for the stable in the latest renewal. The high-class Somnus, who
lowered the colours of the champion sprinter Oasis Dream at Haydock, is
Easterby's third Group 1 winner since he took over at Habton Grange in 1996,
following also the 2002 St Leger winner Bollin Eric. Somnus and Bollin Eric are
the best horses that Easterby has trained so far and they helped his stable to pass the
£1m mark in first-three prize money for the second successive season. Easterby
will not have Bollin Eric in 2004 as he has been retired to stud, but the gelding
Somnus should be around for a while yet.

Somnus recorded lacklustre efforts on his first two starts as a three-year-old when fifth in a listed event at Ascot in April and only eighth in the seven-furlong Jersey Stakes at the Royal meeting two months later, running well below the smart form he had produced at two, when four wins included the valuable St Leger Yearling Stakes at Doncaster and the Two-Year-Old Trophy at Redcar, where he beat the subsequent Dewhurst winner Tout Seul narrowly. Somnus got his three-year-old career back on track in an eleven-runner minor event at Haydock in July. Back at six furlongs, he beat Maltese Falcon comfortably by two and a half lengths and followed up later in the month in a listed event at Newbury, where he responded gamely to get the better of Ashdown Express by a neck. Returned to Ascot for the Shergar Cup Sprint, Somnus was an unlucky fourth to Move It in a blanket finish, failing to obtain a clear run, but for which he would have won. Another defeat followed in a six-runner listed race at Newmarket, where a muddling pace was against Somnus, who, on unfavourable weight-for-age terms with the winner, stormed home late and just failed to peg back stable-companion Fayr Jag. Somnus was in good heart but looked to have plenty on in the Sprint Cup against odds-on Oasis Dream, who had won the July Cup and the Nunthorpe, while July Cup third Airwave, who went off second favourite, was also in the line-up. Somnus shares his name with the Roman god of sleep and the weather on Sprint Cup day brought to mind another Roman god, Jupiter, as the heavens opened. A heavy downpour, following watering the previous evening, changed the going overnight from firm to good to soft. The change turned out to suit Somnus, who, racing on going softer than good for the first time, followed Oasis Dream and Airwave through the field from two furlongs out before responding really well to pressure to go clear in the last fifty yards or so, beating Oasis Dream by a length and a quarter with Airwave a further three quarters of a length back in third. It was a first Group 1 winner in Britain for jockey Ted Durcan, who had been out of action on two occasions in the latest season, having broken a leg in Dubai in February and a wrist at Carlisle in June. Somnus completed his campaign in the Prix de l'Abbaye but ran as if unsuited by the drop to five furlongs (his first attempt at the trip), even on soft ground. He was doing all his best work at the finish when seventh behind Patavellian.

Somnus (b.g. 2000)	Pivotal (ch 1993)	Polar Falcon (b or br 1987)	Nureyev
			Marie d'Argonne
		Fearless Revival (ch 1987)	Cozzene
			Stufida
	Midnight's Reward (b 1986)	Night Shift (b 1980)	Northern Dancer
			Ciboulette
		Margaret's Ruby (b 1968)	Tesco Boy
			Pixie Jet

Stanley Leisure Sprint Cup, Haydock—
Somnus (right) gives jockey Ted Durcan a memorable winner in an injury-hit season
as the conditions contribute to favourite Oasis Dream's defeat in second, while Airwave is third

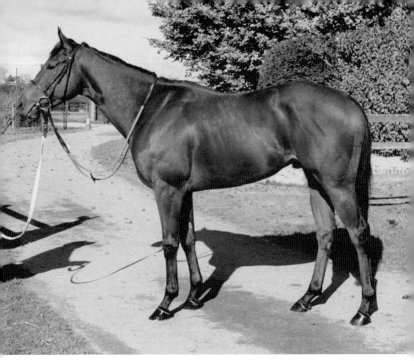

Legard Sidebottom & Sykes's "Somnus"

The good-topped Somnus had his pedigree detailed fully in *Racehorses of 2002*, and there is nothing new to add. A genuine sort, who is usually held up, he has shown his best form at six furlongs and acts on good to firm and good to soft going. *T. D. Easterby*

SONDERBORG 2 b.f. (Mar 14) Great Dane (IRE) 122 – Nordico Princess 71 (Nordico (USA)) [2003 6d⁶ 7.1f³ 8.3g 6m f7g⁶ Dec 16] 3,500Y, resold 8,000Y: workmanlike filly: fourth foal: half-sister to 3 winners, including 3-y-o Rowan Express and ungenuine 1999 2-y-o 5f/6f winner City Princess (by Rock City): dam 5f/6f winner: modest maiden: left H. Candy 6,500 gns before final start: stays 7f, possibly not 1m: acts on firm and good to soft going: wore cheekpieces (ran respectably fourth outing. *G. L. Moore* **55**

SONGINO (IRE) 7 ch.g. Perugino (USA) 84 – Sonbere 68 (Electric 126) [2003 14m 16g 12.1m f14s Sep 2] no form, leaving J. Clements (Ireland) after second outing: tried blinkered/in cheekpieces. *J. Parkes* **–**

SONG KOI 2 b.f. (Feb 18) Sri Pekan (USA) 117 – Eastern Lyric 93 (Petong 126) [2003 5m⁴ 5g⁴ May 3] lengthy filly: first foal: dam 5f winner, including at 2 yrs: green, modest form in maiden at Warwick and minor event at Thirsk: should stay 6f. *J. G. Given* **57**

SONGLARK 3 br.c. Singspiel (IRE) 133 – Negligent 118 (Ahonoora 122) [2003 107: a10f² 8g 10.4m⁴ 12m⁵ 10.3g² Sep 12] lengthy colt: smart performer: ran well when ½-length second to Victory Moon in UAE Derby at Nad Al Sheba in March: respectable 2¼ lengths fourth to Magistretti in Dante Stakes at York and 3 lengths second to Rawyaan in minor event at Doncaster (off 3½ months before): below form in 2000 Guineas at **111 a115**

956

Newmarket and Derby Italiano at Rome on other starts: stays 10.4f: acts on dirt and good to firm going (pulled too hard on heavy): tongue tied in 2003. *Saeed bin Suroor*

SONG OF THE SEA   2 ch.f. (May 3) Bering 136 – Calypso Run (Lycius (USA) 124)   **– p** [2003 p7g Sep 9] fourth foal: half-sister to French 1½m winner Newtown (by Darshaan): dam, ran once, from very good middle-distance family: 25/1, seventh of 11 in maiden at Lingfield, racing freely and late headway not knocked about: will be suited by 1¼m/ 1½m: should do better. *J. W. Hills*

SONG OF VALA   2 ch.g. (Mar 10) Peintre Celebre (USA) 137 – Yanka (USA) (Blush-   **82** ing John (USA) 120) [2003 8d 8g⁴ 8.2d² Nov 6] good-topped gelding: third foal: dam, US 1½m winner, out of close relative to July Cup winner Ajdal: fairly useful form in maidens: better for race first 2 starts: 3½ lengths second of 17 to Sahool at Nottingham: will be suited by 1¼m/1½m. *R. Charlton*

SONNE DE LOUP   2 ch.f. (May 12) Wolfhound (USA) 126 – Son Et Lumiere (Rain-   **40 §** bow Quest (USA) 134) [2003 6.1d f6g p7g f8g Dec 8] workmanlike filly: half-sister to several winners, including useful miler Sonatina (by Distant Relative), 6f winner at 2 yrs: dam, maiden, out of smart miler Soprano: poor maiden: ran out at Southwell final start. *Mrs S. A. Liddiard*

SONO   6 b.g. Robellino (USA) 127 – Sweet Holland (USA) (Alydar (USA)) [2003 10d   **85** 12m² 12.1g 11.9g 10m 13.1d Oct 14] close-coupled gelding: fairly useful performer: winner of 7 races in Germany from 1m (including at 2 yrs) to 1¼m, including minor event at Hamburg and handicaps at Cologne and Baden-Baden for H. Groeschel in 2002: best effort in Britain when second in handicap at Pontefract: stays 1½m: acts on soft and good to firm ground: usually held up. *P. D. Niven*

SON OF A GUN   9 b.g. Gunner B 126 – Sola Mia 78 (Tolomeo 127) [2003 75, a–:   **56** f16g⁵ f16s 16g Jul 28] workmanlike gelding: modest maiden nowadays: stays 2¼m: acts on fibresand, firm and soft going. *M. J. Polglase*

SON OF FLIGHTY   5 b.g. Then Again 126 – Record Flight (Record Token 128)   **–** [2003 –: 10m f14.8g 10m Oct 14] of no account. *R. J. Hodges*

SON OF GREEK MYTH (USA)   2 b.c. (Jan 8) Silver Hawk (USA) 123 – Greek   **84** Myth (IRE) 58 (Sadler's Wells (USA) 132) [2003 8m² 8f³ 8.1d⁴ Sep 27] $250,000F, $260,000Y: sturdy, quite attractive colt: first foal: dam twice-raced half-sister to smart performer up to 13f Multicoloured and 4-y-o Gamut: fairly useful form: placed in maiden at Newmarket and minor event at Salisbury: found little final start: should be well suited by 1¼m/1½m: acts on firm going: sent to Germany. *J. H. M. Gosden*

SON OF HALLING   3 ch.c. Halling (USA) 133 – La Sorrela (IRE) (Cadeaux Gene-   **76** reux 131) [2003 7.1g² 8m³ 8m* 8m Oct 6] lengthy, sturdy colt: third foal: half-brother to 4-y-o Colisay: dam unraced half-sister to smart sprinter Central City: fair performer: landed odds in maiden at Thirsk in September: tailed off in handicap final start: stays 1m: raced only on good/good to firm ground. *D. J. Daly*

SON OF REMBRANDT (IRE)   2 b.g. (Apr 27) Titus Livius (FR) 115 – Avidal Park   **66** 68 (Horage 124) [2003 5m⁶ 5m 5.1g⁵ 6g 5.1m⁶ 5m³ Oct 3] 2,500F: smallish gelding: half-brother to several winners, including 6f (at 2 yrs) to 1¼m winner Sarena Pride (by Persian Bold): dam 2-y-o 5f winner: fair maiden: third at Lingfield: stays 6f: acts on good to firm going. *D. K. Ivory*

SON OF THUNDER (IRE)   2 ch.g. (Apr 18) Dr Fong (USA) 128 – Sakura Queen   **–** (IRE) 52 (Woodman (USA) 126) [2003 6m 7.2d Oct 13] leggy, close-coupled gelding: half-brother to several winners, including 1999 2-y-o 7f winner Seeking Utopia (by Wolf- hound) and 1½m winner Reine Cerise (by Shareef Dancer): dam, maiden who stayed 1¼m, half-sister to dam of Rock of Gibraltar: well held in maidens at Pontefract and Ayr (went freely up with pace). *M. Dods*

SONOMA (IRE)   3 ch.f. Dr Devious (IRE) 127 – Mazarine Blue (USA) (Chief's   **78** Crown (USA)) [2003 11.5g⁶ 11.8m 13.8m* 14.1m² 16.4m² 16f⁵ Sep 30] IR 8,000Y: sturdy filly: fourth foal: half-sister to fairly useful performer 1997 2-y-o 6f winner Poly Blue (by Thatching) and 1½m winner Irish Dancer (by Lahib): dam, ran twice in France, half-sister to dual Gold Cup winner Sadeem: fair performer: won maiden at Catterick in July: creditable efforts in handicaps after: stays 2m: raced only on good ground or firmer: front runner: sold 18,000 gns. *M. L. W. Bell*

SOONEST (IRE)   2 br.c. (Mar 1) Intikhab (USA) 135 – Oklahoma (Shareef Dancer   **97** (USA) 135) [2003 5m² 5.1m* 5s³ 5m 5.1m* 5g 6.1m* 7g³ Oct 11] IR 64,000F, 38,000Y: compact colt: first foal: dam unraced daughter of Sun Chariot Stakes winner Ranimer:

useful performer: won maiden at Bath in April and minor events at Chepstow in July and Chester (beat Desert Dreamer by 2 lengths) in August: ran creditably in minor event at Ascot final start: barely stays 7f: acts on good to firm going, probably on soft: sold 80,000 gns, sent to USA. *R. Hannon*

SOPHIE EM 3 ch.f. High Kicker (USA) – Golden Target (USA) (Gold Crest (USA) – 120) [2003 7m 7m Jun 26] second foal: dam well beaten on Flat/over hurdles: well held in maiden/seller. *D. Shaw*

SOPHIES SYMPHONY 4 b.f. Merdon Melody 98 – Gracious Imp (USA) (Imp **57** Society (USA)) [2003 61: f7s⁶ f6g 7m⁵ 7m⁶ 7m 7.1f 5m⁵ 7f⁴ 6d³ 6f³ 6m 6m Aug 20] **a–** workmanlike filly: modest performer: effective at 6f/7f: acts on fibresand, firm and good to soft going: tried visored and in cheekpieces: tends to carry head high. *K. R. Burke*

SOPHOMORE 9 b.g. Sanglamore (USA) 126 – Livry (USA) (Lyphard (USA) 132) – [2003 –: 7m Oct 13] workmanlike gelding: no form since 6 yrs. *John A. Harris*

SOPHRANO (IRE) 3 b.g. Spectrum (IRE) 126 – Sophrana (IRE) (Polar Falcon **68** (USA) 126) [2003 78: 8g⁶ 10m 8g p10g⁶ f8g² p10g Dec 10] leggy, angular gelding: fair maiden: should stay 1½m: acts on good to soft ground and polytrack: visored (ran poorly) final start: has carried head awkwardly. *P. W. Harris*

SO PRECIOUS (IRE) 6 b.m. Batshoof 122 – Golden Form (Formidable (USA) 125) **62 d** [2003 63: f12g⁶ f12s² f11s* f12g f11s⁵ f12s² f12s⁴ p12g f12s⁴ f14g⁴ Mar 11] good-topped mare: modest performer at best: won seller at Southwell in January: stays 1¾m: acts on fibresand: tried visored/blinkered. *D. K. Ivory*

SORBIESHARRY (IRE) 4 gr.g. Sorbie Tower (IRE) 120 – Silver Moon (Environ- – ment Friend 128) [2003 55, a62: f8s² f8s f8g* f8s⁵ p10g p10g f8g f9.4f f8s f12s³ f12s⁵ **a64** f9.4g f12g⁴ f8g² f8g² Dec 19] leggy gelding: poor mover: modest handicapper: won at Southwell in January: best at 1m/1¼m: acts on all-weather, raced only on good going or firmer on turf: visored (below form) final 3-y-o start: usually wears cheekpieces: some- times slowly away. *Mrs N. Macauley*

SO SOBER (IRE) 5 b.g. Common Grounds 118 – Femme Savante 89 (Glenstal (USA) **47** 118) [2003 58, a64: f6g f5g⁴ f5s⁶ f5g² f5g³ f5s f5g² 5m f5g 5f f5g f5s Dec 31] compact **a53** gelding: modest performer on all-weather, poor on turf: effective at 5f/6f: acts on all- weather, soft and firm going. *D. Shaw*

SO SURE (IRE) 3 b.g. Definite Article 121 – Zorilla (Belmez (USA) 131) [2003 66d: **67** f8g⁵ 9.3m* 10g 10f* Oct 1] sparely-made gelding: fair performer: won seller at Carlisle **a–** in June and selling handicap at Nottingham in October: stays 1¼m: raced only on good going or firmer on turf, below form in 3 runs on fibresand: won juvenile hurdle in October, then joined J. O'Shea. *P. C. Haslam*

SO TEMPTED 4 br.f. So Factual (USA) 120 – Bystrouska (Gorytus (USA) 132) – [2003 9.9m 9.3m⁶ 10m⁵ Sep 18] 6,000F, 4,800Y: sixth foal: half-sister to fairly useful 6f (including at 2 yrs) and 7f winner Charlie Sillett (by Handsome Sailor) and winner in Belgium by Green Ruby: dam ran once: well beaten in maidens. *N. Wilson*

SOTONIAN (HOL) 10 br.g. Statoblest 120 – Visage 75 (Vision (USA)) [2003 65§: **48 §** p5g⁶ f5s f5s 5m 5.1s⁵ 5m 5m⁵ 5m 5.5m 5m Sep 1] rather sparely-made gelding: modest **a53 §** handicapper on all-weather, poor on turf: best at 5f/easy 6f: acts on firm ground, soft and all-weather: tried blinkered in 1996: unreliable. *P. S. Felgate*

SOULACROIX 2 b.c. (Feb 19) Kylian (USA) – California Dreamin (Slip Anchor **87 p** 136) [2003 7.1m² 7.1m² 8.3m² 10d* Oct 31] 21,000Y: sturdy colt: fourth foal: dam, of little account, closely related to useful performer up to 14.6f Misbelief: fairly useful performer: landed odds in 11-runner maiden at Brighton by 6 lengths from Bold Joe: will stay at least 1½m: acts on good to firm and good to soft going: tends to carry head high: should progress. *Mrs A. J. Perrett*

SOUL PROVIDER (IRE) 2 ch.f. (May 9) Danehill Dancer (IRE) 117 – Wing And **62** A Prayer (IRE) 63 (Shalford (IRE) 124§) [2003 5m⁵ f5s⁵ 6.1g⁵ Jun 5] €12,000Y: leggy filly: second foal: half-sister to fairly useful Irish 7f winner Sophister (by College Chapel): dam, ran 3 times, out of half-sister to smart middle-distance performer Noble Patriarch: modest form: second in claimer at Wolverhampton: slowly away final outing: should stay 6f. *I. A. Wood*

SOUND BLASTER (IRE) 2 ch.g. (Apr 4) Zafonic (USA) 130 – Blasted Heath 105 **74 p** (Thatching 131) [2003 6m 8.1g⁴ 8f* Sep 15] 26,000F: tall gelding: has scope: half- brother to 3 winners, including fairly useful 1¼m/11f winner Hamlet (by Danehill): dam,

Irish 5f (at 2 yrs) and 1m winner, half-sister to Middle Park winner Balla Cove: fair form in maidens: won 7-runner event at Bath by short head, making most despite handling turn poorly: needs to settle to stay beyond 1m: open to progress. *A. M. Balding*

SOUND LEADER (USA) 3 ch.c. Diesis 133 – Colledge Leader (USA) (Sheikh **40** Albadou 128) [2003 8g 8g 10g 11.6m⁴ p10g 10m 10f Oct 1] 21,000F, 28,000Y: good-bodied colt: second foal: dam, ran once in USA, half-sister to very smart 1¼m to 1¾m performer Red Bishop: poor maiden: stays 11.6f: raced only on good ground or firmer on turf: blinkered last 3 starts. *J. W. Hills*

SOUND OF FLEET (USA) 2 ch.c. (Feb 11) Cozzene (USA) – Tempo (USA) (Gone **82 p** West (USA)) [2003 7m² Jul 11] $37,000Y: big, angular, good-bodied colt: has plenty of scope: third foal: half-brother to 2 winners in USA by Rahy: dam, 6f winner in USA, granddaughter of 1000 Guineas winner Glad Rags: 9/2 and green, 7 lengths second of 11 to Rule of Law in maiden at York: should stay at least 1m: likely to improve. *P. F. I. Cole*

SOUNDS LUCKY 7 b.g. Savahra Sound 111 – Sweet And Lucky (Lucky Wednesday **51** 124) [2003 61, a71: p6g* p6g* p6g⁴ p7g p5g f6g p6g 6.1g p6g² 6d⁵ p6g⁴ f8.5g Jun 27] **a76** leggy gelding: has a round action: modest on turf: won claimer and handicap at Lingfield in January, both amateur events: best at 6f: acts on all-weather and good to firm going: wears headgear: sometimes slowly away/swishes tail/edges left. *N. P. Littmoden*

SOUTHAMPTON JOE (USA) 3 ch.g. Just A Cat (USA) – Maple Hill Jill (USA) **–** (Executive Pride 127) [2003 76: p7g 7g 6g 6m 8g 7g f8.5g Oct 4] quite good-topped gelding: fair winner at 2 yrs: well beaten in 2003: stays 7f: acts on soft and good to firm going: tried in cheekpieces: sold 3,000 gns. *A. M. Balding*

SOUTH ATLANTIC 3 b.c. Sadler's Wells (USA) 132 – Shimmering Sea 89 (Slip **105** Anchor 136) [2003 85: 6m² 8g* 7.1g⁶ 8m* 7m Oct 3] good-topped colt: useful performer: won maiden at Musselburgh in May and handicap at Newmarket in June, beating Inverness by head in latter: off 2½ months, well below form final start: stays 1m: raced only on good going or firmer: sold 32,000 gns. *Sir Michael Stoute*

SOUTHERN BAZAAR (USA) 2 ch.c. (May 2) Southern Halo (USA) – Sunday **78 p** Bazaar (USA) (Nureyev (USA) 131) [2003 7m⁵ Aug 22] good-bodied colt: fluent mover: half-brother to several winners, notably very smart 1½m winner Perfect Sunday (by Quest For Fame) and 3-y-o Gala Majesty: dam, French 1½m winner, half-sister to US Grade 1 winners Bates Motel (at 1m/1¼m) and Hatim (at 9f): 4/1, 5¾ lengths fifth of 15 to Torinmoor in maiden at Newmarket, green before rallying: should stay 1¼m, probably 1½m: sure to do better. *B. W. Hills*

SOUTHERN BOUND (IRE) 2 b.f. (Mar 21) Fasliyev (USA) 120 – Headrest (Habitat **94** 134) [2003 5s* 6g⁶ 7f 6m⁶ 6m⁴ 6m⁵ Sep 20] leggy filly: has a quick action: half-sister to 3 winners, including useful Irish 7f (including at 2 yrs) and 1¼m winner Polaire (by Polish Patriot) and 1¼m winner Lurdi (by Lure): dam lightly-raced sister to Princess Royal winner One Way Street: fairly useful performer: won maiden at the Curragh in June and nursery at Fairyhouse in August: respectable efforts in listed races at the Curragh and Ayr last 2 starts: should stay 7f: acts on good to firm and soft going. *James G. Burns, Ireland*

SOUTHERN HAZE (USA) 2 ch.c. (Feb 16) Southern Halo (USA) – Hollow Haze **–** (USA) 90 (Woodman (USA) 126) [2003 8f Oct 12] second foal: half-brother to Italian 10.5f winner by Singspiel: dam, 8.5f winner, from family of Generous and Imagine: last of 7 in maiden at Bath, slowly away: sent to Germany. *J. S. Moore*

SOU'WESTER 3 b.g. Fleetwood (IRE) 107 – Mayfair 82 (Green Desert (USA) 127) **–** [2003 69: 9m 10d Nov 6] angular gelding: fair maiden: well held in 2003, leaving M. Tregoning after reappearance. *B. J. Llewellyn*

SOVEREIGN DREAMER (USA) 3 b.c. Kingmambo (USA) 125 – Spend A Dream **90** (USA) (Spend A Buck (USA)) [2003 73: 12.3m* 11.8m³ 14.6m³ 11g 12.3m³ 11m 12s⁶ 12.3m* 12.4m* 11.9m Sep 3] tall colt: fairly useful handicapper: won at Ripon in April and at Ripon and Newcastle in August: should stay 1¾m (below form when tried): acts on soft and good to firm going: tried blinkered: tongue tied last 3 starts: races prominently. *P. F. I. Cole*

SOVEREIGN SEAL 3 b.f. Royal Applause 124 – Downeaster Alexa (USA) (Red **– §** Ryder (USA)) [2003 64§: p7g Jan 8] good-topped filly: modest form second outing at 2 yrs: well held since: tried blinkered/visored: looks ungenuine. *M. Johnston*

SOVIET SCEPTRE (IRE) 2 ch.c. (Feb 17) Soviet Star (USA) 128 – Princess Sceptre **75**
(Cadeaux Genereux 131) [2003 7g⁵ p8g⁶ Nov 26] 36,000F, 58,000Y: leggy colt: first foal:
dam, showed signs of ability, half-sister to useful performer up to 1½m Humourless:
much better effort in maidens (fair form) when fifth to Psychiatrist at Goodwood: subsequently off almost 4 months: should stay at least 1m. *G. A. Butler*

SOVIET SONG (IRE) 3 b.f. Marju (IRE) 127 – Kalinka (IRE) 88 (Soviet Star (USA) **118**
128) [2003 115p: 8g⁴ 8f² 8g⁴ 8f⁵ Sep 27] sturdy, lengthy filly: smart performer: unbeaten
in 3 starts at 2 yrs, including Fillies' Mile at Ascot: in frame in 2003 in 1000 Guineas at
Newmarket (4¼ lengths fourth to Russian Rhythm), Coronation Stakes at Royal Ascot
(1½ lengths second to Russian Rhythm, edging right) and Prix du Moulin de Longchamp
(3 lengths fourth to Nebraska Tornado): just respectable fifth to Falbrav in Queen
Elizabeth II Stakes at Ascot final start: stays 1m: acts on firm and soft going: usually
waited with: missed Irish 1000 Guineas on intended second outing after scoping
unsatisfactorily: stays in training. *J. R. Fanshawe*

SO VITAL 3 b.c. Pivotal 124 – Sumoto 101 (Mtoto 134) [2003 10s⁶ p12g² Nov 29] **74**
fifth foal: half-brother to very smart 7f (at 2 yrs) to 1¼m winner Compton Admiral (by
Suave Dancer) and smart 1m (including at 2 yrs)/1¼m winner Summoner (by Inchinor):
dam 6f (at 2 yrs)/7f winner: fair form in maidens in November, ¾-length second to Sea
Holly at Lingfield: stays 1½m. *Mrs Lydia Pearce*

SO WILL I 2 ch.c. (Feb 19) Inchinor 119 – Fur Will Fly 66 (Petong 126) [2003 6m⁴ **95 p**
6g* Oct 24] 27,000Y: sturdy colt: first living foal: dam, second at 6f from 4 starts, out
of useful sprinter Bumpkin: confirmed promise and showed useful form when winning
19-runner maiden at Newbury by 1½ lengths from Coming Again, leading final 1f:
should stay 7f: changed ownership 160,000 gns: open to progress. *M. P. Tregoning*

SOYUZ (IRE) 3 ch.g. Cadeaux Genereux 131 – Welsh Mist 102 (Damister (USA) **92**
123) [2003 92p: 6m³ 8.1v² 7g³ 7g 7d p7g Oct 3] angular, quite good-topped gelding:
fairly useful handicapper: good efforts at Haydock (6 lengths second to Jazz Messenger
in Silver Bowl) and Epsom (third to Tarjman) second/third starts: disappointing after,
including in blinkers final outing: probably best at 6f/7f: acts on heavy and good to firm
going: has been bandaged behind. *M. A. Jarvis*

SPACE COWBOY (IRE) 3 b.c. Anabaa (USA) 130 – Lady Moranbon (USA) **84**
(Trempolino (USA) 135) [2003 9.7m³ p12g⁴ 9.9m* Sep 25] 27,000Y: half-brother to
several winners, including French 11.5f winner Anchorage (by Slip Anchor): dam French
9f/1¼m winner: fairly useful form in maidens: won 3-runner event at Goodwood in
September by neck: stays 1¼m: acts on good to firm ground: sold 35,000 gns, joined
G. L. Moore. *Mrs A. J. Perrett*

SPACE STAR 3 b.g. Cosmonaut – Sophiesue (Balidar 133) [2003 –: 8m⁶ 10g⁴ 11.9m **65**
10m Jun 9] lengthy gelding: fair maiden: stays 1¼m. *J. G. Given*

SPAINKRIS 4 b.g. Kris 135 – Pennycairn 84 (Last Tycoon 131) [2003 16g Nov 5] **–**
22,000Y: second foal: dam, 1m winner, half-sister to very smart performers Invermark
(stayed 2½m) and Craigsteel (best at 1½m/1¾m): useful performer at best (stayed 15f)
when trained in France by X. Nakkachdji: won newcomers race at Deauville at 2 yrs:
winning hurdler for current stable, but tailed off in handicap on return to Flat. *A. Crook*

SPA LANE 10 ch.g. Presidium 124 – Sleekit 78 (Blakeney 126) [2003 60: 16g 17.1m* **68**
16m* 16.2m³ 16.1d² 17.1m⁶ 16m⁵ 16.2m⁵ 16g⁵ f14s⁴ 18m⁵ 17.1m⁵ 18m⁶ 16m* f16g **a57**
f14.8g⁶ Nov 29] leggy gelding: fair handicapper: better than ever at 10 yrs, winning at
Pontefract and Southwell in April and Nottingham in October: best around 2m: acts on
firm ground, soft and fibresand: has reportedly had breathing problem: has found little:
held up: tough. *J. F. Coupland*

SPANIOLA (IRE) 3 ch.f. Desert King (IRE) 129 – Baddi Baddi (USA) (Sharpen Up **–**
127) [2003 f7g Jan 17] 160,000 francs Y, €1,500 2-y-o: half-sister to several winners in
France, including 9f/1¼m winner Baddi Heights (by Shirley Heights): dam French 2-y-o
1m winner: well held in maiden at Wolverhampton. *D. Haydn Jones*

SPANISH ACE 2 b.c. (May 16) First Trump 118 – Spanish Heart 86 (King of Spain **99**
121) [2003 5m² 5g* 6f⁶ 6m² 7m⁶ 7d Jul 30] rather leggy, close-coupled colt: half-brother
to several winners, including useful 7f/1m winner Bold King (by Anshan) and 3-y-o
Spanish Gold: dam, effective at 7f to 9f, half-sister to smart sprinter Northern Goddess:
useful performer: won minor event at Ascot in April: quite highly tried after, ½-length
second of 7 to Antonius Pius in Railway Stakes at the Curragh, best effort: should stay 7f:
acts on good to firm going: moved poorly to post penultimate start. *A. M. Balding*

SPANISH DON   5 b.g. Zafonic (USA) 130 – Spanish Wells (IRE) (Sadler's Wells   **100** (USA) 132) [2003 106d: 8.3d 12m 10g⁶ 8.3m* 8.9f⁴ 9g* Oct 25] tall gelding: useful handicapper: left P. Mitchell after third start: revitalized for new stable, winning at Windsor in September and Newbury (beat Alrafid by neck) in October: saddle slipped in between: best at 1m/9f: acts on firm and good to soft going: blinkered (well held) once: usually waited with. *D. R. C. Elsworth*

SPANISH GOLD   3 b.f. Vettori (IRE) 119 – Spanish Heart 86 (King of Spain 121)   **82** [2003 –p: f8.5g² f8.5s* 8m⁶ p7g Dec 10] big, useful-looking filly: has a quick action: fairly useful performer: won maiden at Wolverhampton in March by 8 lengths: left P. Makin and off 5½ months before well held final start: stays 8.5f: acts on fibresand, probably on good to soft going in firm ground. *A. M. Balding*

SPANISH JOHN (USA)   4 b. or br.g. Dynaformer (USA) – Esprit d'Escalier (USA)   **98 +** (Diesis 133) [2003 113: 16.2g⁵ 13.4m⁴ 13.3m 13.9f⁶ 13.9m 12g⁶ 11.8f² Oct 27] good-topped gelding: carries condition: smart performer at 3 yrs: respectable efforts in Sagaro Stakes at Ascot and Ormonde Stakes at Chester first 2 starts in 2003: well below form after: stays 2m: acts on firm going, well held only run on soft: races prominently: sold 38,000 gns. *P. F. I. Cole*

SPANISH STAR   6 b.g. Hernando (FR) 127 – Desert Girl (Green Desert (USA) 127)   **–** [2003 42, a58: f11g⁵ f9.4g⁵ f9.4g² f11s² f9.4g³ f9.4s⁶ f12s⁵ f9.4s³ f12g⁴ f9.4g f9.4s   **a58** f8g f11g⁴ f11g* Dec 15] compact gelding: modest handicapper on all-weather, poor (unraced in 2003) on turf: won at Southwell in December: effective at 9.4f to 1½m: acts on fibresand and soft going: twice visored in 2001: usually held up. *Mrs N. Macauley*

SPANISH SUN (USA)   3 b.f. El Prado (IRE) 119 – Shining Bright 98 (Rainbow Quest   **119** (USA) 134) [2003 84p: 12m⁵ 12g⁶ Jul 13] angular, quite good-topped filly: smart form: having only second outing (still green) when winning Ribblesdale Stakes at Royal Ascot by head from Ocean Silk, held up after another slow start but staying on to lead inside final 1f: second favourite, never-dangerous sixth to Vintage Tipple in Irish Oaks at the Curragh in July: raced freely, but stayed 1½m: raced only on good/good to firm going: stud. *Sir Michael Stoute*

SPARKLING CLEAR   2 b.f. (Apr 21) Efisio 120 – Shoot Clear 111 (Bay Express   **48** 132) [2003 6f⁵ p7g f6g⁶ f6g⁶ Nov 19] small filly: half-sister to several winners, including 3-y-o Famous Grouse and useful 1½m winner Shoot Ahead (by Shirley Heights): dam, 5f to 7f winner at 2 yrs and fourth in 1000 Guineas, half-sister to Yorkshire Oaks winners Untold and Sally Brown: poor maiden: tried in cheekpieces/visor. *R. M. H. Cowell*

SPARKLING JEWEL   3 b.f. Bijou d'Inde 127 – Jobiska (Dunbeath (USA) 127) [2003   **75** 75: p6g³ 5.2m* May 28] good-topped filly: fair form: won maiden at Newbury in May by head from Best Before: should prove best at 5f/6f: raced only on polytrack/good to firm ground. *R. Hannon*

SPARKLING WATER (USA)   4 br. or b.c. Woodman (USA) 126 – Shirley Valentine   **– §** 104 (Shirley Heights 130) [2003 106§: 22.2f 10g 10.1m⁵ 12.3m Aug 3] quite attractive colt: useful but unreliable performer at 3 yrs: well held in 2003. *D. L. Williams*

Ribblesdale Stakes, Royal Ascot—Spanish Sun (No.7), making a belated reappearance,
just holds off Ocean Silk; Mezzo Soprano (right) and Sun On The Sea are next

SPARK OF LIFE   6 b.m. Rainbows For Life (CAN) – Sparkly Girl (IRE) 79 (Danehill   **53 §**
(USA) 126) [2003 60§: p12g² Feb 15] small mare: modest handicapper: stays 13f: acts
on polytrack and firm going: often blinkered: often slowly away/hangs: untrustworthy.
T. D. McCarthy

SPARK UP   3 b.f. Lahib (USA) 129 – Catch The Flame (USA) (Storm Bird (CAN)   **71**
134) [2003 81: 6.1m 6s 6.1m 7m⁴ 6g f7s⁶ f7g* f8.5g² f7g⁶ f7s⁶ Dec 31] smallish, quite
attractive filly: fair performer: left T. Easterby after fifth start: won handicap at Wolverhampton in October: likely to prove best short of 8.5f: acts on fibresand, good to firm and
good to soft ground: blinkered last 5 starts. *J. W. Unett*

SPARKY'S MATE   3 b.g. Vettori (IRE) 119 – Nikiya (IRE) (Lead On Time (USA)   **90**
123) [2003 78: p7g⁵ f8.5s² 10m* 10.4m³ 7m Nov 22] leggy, lengthy gelding: fairly useful   **a72 +**
performer on turf, fair on all-weather: made all in maiden at Brighton in May: good third
to Etesaal in handicap at York next time: left M. Tompkins before final outing: stays
10.4f: yet to race on extremes of going on turf: races prominently: consistent. *C. S. Shum,
Hong Kong*

SPARTACUS (IRE)   3 b.c. Danehill (USA) 126 – Teslemi (USA) 73 (Ogygian (USA))   **–**
[2003 107: 10g 8d Jul 30] strong, close-coupled colt: had a markedly round action: useful
performer: won Phoenix Stakes at the Curragh and Gran Criterium at Milan at 2 yrs: last
in Grand Prix de Paris at Longchamp and Sussex Stakes at Goodwood (acted as
pacemaker) in 2003: stayed 1m: raced only on good going or softer: to stand at Coolmore,
Co Tipperary, Ireland, fee €7,500, Oct 1st. *A. P. O'Brien, Ireland*

SPARTAN ODYSSEY   2 b.g. (Feb 5) Overbury (IRE) 116 – Spartan Native (Native   **–**
Bazaar 122) [2003 f5g 5m Aug 8] close-coupled, plain gelding: eighth foal: dam poor
maiden hurdler/chaser: showed nothing in maidens. *A. Senior*

SPARTAN PRINCIPLE   3 b.f. Spartan Monarch – Altar Point (Persian Bold 123)   **–**
[2003 10g Jun 2] second reported foal: dam poor maiden: well held in maiden at Windsor.
R. Guest

SPARTAN SPEAR   2 b.g. (Mar 22) Sure Blade (USA) 130 – Confection (Formidable   **74**
(USA) 125) [2003 8s 7d⁴ Nov 7] strong, lengthy gelding: half-brother to several winners,
including useful 1995 2-y-o 5f/6f winner (stayed 1¼m) Anthelia and 4-y-o Athenian:
dam ran twice: much better effort in maidens (fair form) when fourth of 18 to Divine Gift
at Doncaster: should stay 1m. *D. Morris*

SPEARIOUS (IRE)   2 b.c. (Feb 1) Tagula (IRE) 116 – Gloria Crown (IRE) (Waajib   **74**
121) [2003 6g 6d⁶ 6m f5s² 5m² Sep 29] €21,000Y: strong colt: second foal: half-brother
to Italian 7f (at 2 yrs)/8.5f winner Axamuk (by Mukaddamah): dam French 7f/1m
winner: fair maiden: second in nurseries at Southwell (slowly away) and Windsor (made
running): will prove best at 5f/easy 6f: acts on fibresand, good to firm and good to soft
going. *B. R. Millman*

SPECIAL BRANCH   3 ch.g. Woodborough (USA) 112 – Sixslip (USA) 94 (Diesis   **66**
133) [2003 74: f12g⁵ 11.9g⁶ 12.1d 12.4m² 14f 12.1g³ f12g⁴ f14.8g⁵ Aug 8] fair maiden
handicapper: below form last 4 starts: stays 1½m: acts on soft and good to firm ground:
usually races prominently: free-going sort. *Jedd O'Keeffe*

SPECIAL ELLIE (FR)   3 b.f. Celtic Swing 138 – Recherchee (Rainbow Quest (USA)   **55**
134) [2003 p10g⁴ 10m Apr 26] 13,000Y: leggy, quite good-topped filly: seventh foal:
sister to 5-y-o Celtic Star and half-sister to useful 5f (at 2 yrs) to 1m (in France) winner
Recondite and 1¼m/1½m winner Freedom Quest (both by Polish Patriot): dam unraced:
better efforts in maidens (modest form) when fourth at Lingfield. *I. A. Wood*

SPECIALI (IRE)   4 b.g. Bluebird (USA) 125 – Fille Dansante (IRE) (Dancing Dissi-   **66 +**
dent (USA) 119) [2003 –: 7g 8.2g³ Jun 23] good-bodied, quite attractive gelding: has a
quick action: thrice-raced maiden: form only when third at Nottingham: should stay
1¼m. *J. H. M. Gosden*

SPECIALISM   5 ch.g. Spectrum (IRE) 126 – Waft (USA) 67 (Topsider (USA)) [2003   **–**
–: f12s f16.2g Jan 18] little form: tried in cheekpieces. *M. J. Gingell*

SPECIALITY (IRE)   3 ch.f. Entrepreneur 123 – Park Special (Relkino 131) [2003   **–**
10m Jul 8] 220,000Y: ninth foal: closely related to very smart 6f (at 2 yrs) to 1½m winner
who stayed 2m Central Park and smart 1¼m/1½m (Lancashire Oaks) winner Mellow
Park (both by In The Wings), and half-sister to 3 winners, including useful 6f (at 2 yrs)/
1¼m winner Velvet Moon (by Shaadi), herself dam of Moon Ballad: dam Irish 1¼m
winner: ran as if amiss in maiden at Newmarket: refused to enter stall next intended
outing in October. *R. Charlton*

SPECIAL KALDOUN (IRE) 4 b.c. Alzao (USA) 117 – Special Lady (FR) **124**
(Kaldoun (FR) 122) [2003 112+: 8g⁵ 8g 8g² 8g* 8d⁴ 8g 8d* 8f 8m Dec 14]

Special Kaldoun emerged in the latest season as the main challenger to
Domedriver among France's best older milers. His three-year-old season had been
interrupted by a life-threatening bout of colic, but an unlucky third place in the Prix
Quincey at Deauville, and then a win in the Prix Perth at Saint-Cloud that autumn,
showed that he had made a full recovery and was well up to holding his own in
pattern company. In the latest season, the majority of Special Kaldoun's
performances in France's top mile races suggested he was no more than a smart
colt, but there were two occasions when everything fell right for him and he showed
himself a good deal better than that.

The highlight of his campaign was an authoritative win in the Prix Daniel
Wildenstein Casino Barriere de La Rochelle at Longchamp in October. Special
Kaldoun had finished only ninth behind Domedriver in the Group 2 event twelve
months earlier and, whilst Domedriver was now retired, the placed horses from the
year before, Suggestive and Gateman, were in the line-up again. That pair were just
two among an eight-strong Anglo-Irish contingent in the field of ten, leaving the
progressive Prix Quincey winner My Risk as the only other French-trained horse in
the field. The presence of so many overseas runners in the race ensured it was run at
a truer pace than many French contests, Gateman setting off in front pursued by the
Sussex Stakes runner-up Statue of Liberty and his intended pacemaker Carpanetto.
Special Kaldoun was asked to bide his time, along with My Risk, but began to make
steady progress from the rear early in the straight, quickening ahead as the leader
gave way over a furlong out. Special Kaldoun forged clear, Dominique Boeuf
looking round and realising the race was in safe keeping and having the luxury of
being able to pat his partner down the neck as they crossed the line four lengths
clear of My Risk. Gateman fared best of the visitors to take third for the second
year, a length further back, with Duck Row, Suggestive and Tout Seul completing
the first six home. It was probably no coincidence that the only time Special
Kaldoun had shown a similar level of form earlier in the season was when getting
the same combination of a well-run race and ground softer than good. That had
been in the Prix Jacques le Marois at Deauville in August, when he had finished a
never-nearer fourth behind Six Perfections, beaten just over two lengths.

Special Kaldoun ran creditably on most of his starts prior to the Jacques le
Marois without suggesting he was quite up to troubling the best milers in Europe.
He finished close up when fifth in the Prix Edmond Blanc at Saint-Cloud on his
reappearance and when fourth, promoted to second, behind Tripat in the Prix du
Chemin de Fer du Nord at Chantilly in June. Between those runs, he ran into trouble
on the rails early in the straight when finishing down the field behind Dandoun and
Domedriver in the Prix du Muguet at Saint-Cloud. Special Kaldoun booked his
place in the Jacques le Marois when coming out on top in a tight finish to the Prix
Messidor over the same course and distance a month beforehand. That was a much
more muddling affair, but Special Kaldoun got a clearer run from a slightly more
prominent position than the favourite Domedriver (who finished fifth) to win by a
short neck from the only three-year-old in the field Tashkandi. Special Kaldoun
contested two Group 1 events in the Far East on his last two starts but was below
form both times under firmer conditions than he was used to. He finished ninth of

*Prix Daniel Wildenstein Casino Barriere de La Rochelle, Longchamp—Special Kaldoun is a clear-cut
winner from My Risk, Gateman (armlets), Duck Row (right) and Suggestive (rail)*

the eighteen runners in the Mile Championship at Kyoto but was beaten little more than three lengths behind the winner Durandal and fared better than both Telegnosis (a place in front of him in the Jacques le Marois) and the other European challenger Tout Seul. In the Hong Kong Mile, Special Kaldoun came ninth of the thirteen finishers behind Lucky Owners; Lohengrin and Telegnosis were also among those to finish ahead of him.

Special Kaldoun was bought for 340,000 francs at Deauville as a yearling. He is the second living foal, and first winner, out of his dam Special Lady, who was also trained by David Smaga but ran just once, finishing fourth over seven furlongs as a two-year-old. Special Lady was by the very smart miler Kaldoun, who was also responsible for the best member of this family before Special Kaldoun came along. La Koumia, a half-sister to Special Kaldoun's grandam Macedoine, was a cheaply-bought yearling who started out in the Provinces but was much improved at three, when her wins included the Prix de Psyche at Deauville, by which time she had been purchased by Robert Sangster. She fared better still as a four-year-old in the United States, gaining a Grade 1 success in the Gamely Handicap at Hollywood for John Gosden. Macedoine's only win came in the humbler surroundings of Seiches-sur-Loir in the French Provinces over a mile and a quarter, and she was out of a half-sister to the smart French stayer Silver Green.

		Lyphard (b 1969)	Northern Dancer
	Alzao (USA)		Goofed
	(b 1980)	Lady Rebecca	Sir Ivor
Special Kaldoun (IRE)		(b 1971)	Pocahontas II
(b.c. 1999)		Kaldoun (gr 1975)	Caro
	Special Lady (FR)		Katana
	(gr 1992)	Macedoine	King of Macedon
		(b 1983)	Sainte Colere

Special Kaldoun had shown useful form as early as his two-year-old days when sixth in the Criterium de Saint-Cloud over a mile and a quarter, but he has raced exclusively at a mile since then, a trip that clearly suits him well. He acts on heavy ground, and is best held up in a truly-run race. Given the right conditions, he is capable of winning another pattern race or two in 2004. *D. Smaga, France*

SPECIAL THREAD (IRE) 2 b.c. (Apr 6) Ela-Mana-Mou 132 – Treadmill (IRE) 51 – (High Estate 127) [2003 f5g⁵ 6m⁶ Jul 23] €8,000Y: good-bodied colt: third foal: half-brother to winner in Italy by Mujtahid: dam ran 3 times at 2 yrs in Ireland: well held in maidens at Southwell and Catterick. *Mrs A. Duffield*

SPECOTIA 2 ch.c. (Apr 5) Spectrum (IRE) 126 – Clan Scotia 47 (Clantime 101) [2003 62 6.1g⁵ 6.1m⁵ 5m Jul 14] 5,000Y: fifth foal: dam 2-y-o 5f winner: modest form in maidens: will probably stay 7f. *M. C. Pipe*

SPECTACULAR HOPE 3 b.f. Marju (IRE) 127 – Distant Music (Darshaan 133) 55 [2003 8g 10g⁵ 12f 11.7m⁵ 10m⁵ 8m² 8m 7f Oct 27] 12,500Y: third foal: half-sister to 6-y-o Desert Island Disc: dam unraced: modest maiden: should stay 1¼m: raced only on good ground or firmer: sold 7,500 gns. *R. M. Beckett*

SPECTESTED (IRE) 2 ch.g. (Mar 26) Spectrum (IRE) 126 – Nisibis (In The Wings 52 128) [2003 7m⁵ f8s⁵ p8g Oct 27] IR 10,000F, 10,000Y: first foal: dam, well beaten in 3 starts, half-sister to smart performer up to 9f Nijo: modest form in minor event/maidens: will probably stay 1¼m: blinkered final start: looks bit wayward. *B. J. Meehan*

SPECTROMETER 6 ch.g. Rainbow Quest (USA) 134 – Selection Board 75 (Welsh 93 Pageant 132) [2003 89: 13.9m 14m³ 13g* 11.9m 14g³ 14.6g Sep 12] close-coupled, leggy gelding: fairly useful performer: won minor event at Hamilton in August on first start after leaving P. Hobbs: good third to The Persuader in handicap at Haydock fifth start: stays 1¾m: acts on good to firm and good to soft going: races prominently. *M. Johnston*

SPECTROSCOPE (IRE) 4 b.g. Spectrum (IRE) 126 – Paloma Bay (IRE) 92 (Alzao 70 (USA) 117) [2003 74: 11.9m 14d 13.9f⁵ Oct 11] compact, quite attractive gelding: useful hurdler, winner of Triumph Hurdle in March: fair handicapper on Flat: probably stays 1¾m: acts on firm ground. *Jonjo O'Neill*

SPECTRUM STAR 3 b.g. Spectrum (IRE) 126 – Persia (IRE) (Persian Bold 123) – [2003 –: f8g May 1] quite good-topped gelding: little form: tried blinkered. *D. K. Ivory*

964

ladbrokes.com Handicap, Ascot—the genuine and consistent Speed Cop shares the spoils with Halmahera (far side); Budelli is third

SPEEDBIRD (USA) 2 ch.f. (Mar 2) Sky Classic (CAN) – Egoli (USA) 93 (Seeking The Gold (USA)) [2003 6g² 7g Nov 1] strong filly: first foal: dam, 7f (at 2 yrs) and 9f (in USA) winner, half-sister to Poule d'Essai des Pouliches winner Rose Gypsy: better effort in maidens (fair form) when staying-on second to Fiddle Me Blue at Windsor: favourite when only seventh at Newmarket: should stay at least 1m. *G. Wragg* **76**

SPEED COP 3 ch.f. Cadeaux Genereux 131 – Blue Siren 113 (Bluebird (USA) 125) [2003 99: 5.1m⁴ 5m⁶ 5m⁴ 5f⁴ 5g* 5m Oct 16] rather leggy, useful-looking filly: has a quick action: useful performer: best effort when dead-heating with Halmahera in 20-runner handicap at Ascot in October, edging right: best at 5f: acts on firm and good to soft ground: sometimes bandaged behind: races prominently: genuine and consistent. *A. M. Balding* **104**

SPEEDFIT FREE (IRE) 6 b.g. Night Shift (USA) – Dedicated Lady (IRE) 101 (Pennine Walk 120) [2003 53§, a56§: f6g f5g³ f6g⁶ f7s f6g f6s* f7g⁶ 6d⁶ f6s 6d 5m⁴ 6f* 6g 7.2g 7.2g³ f6g⁵ 5m 6f* 6g f7g⁵ f6s⁴ Dec 6] smallish, well-made gelding: fair performer on turf, modest on all-weather: won seller at Wolverhampton in February and handicaps at Hamilton in June and Ayr in August: best at 6f to easy 1m: acts on any turf going and fibresand: usually wears headgear: usually waited with: unreliable. *I. Semple* **68 § a58 §**

SPEED ON 10 b.g. Sharpo 132 – Pretty Poppy 67 (Song 132) [2003 65§: 5.7g⁶ 5m 6m⁶ Sep 18] small, strong gelding: modest handicapper: barely stays 6f: acts on polytrack, firm and soft going: tried visored: often ridden by inexperienced apprentice nowadays: unreliable. *H. Candy* **51 §**

SPEED RACER 2 b.f. (Mar 29) Zieten (USA) 118 – Sharenara (USA) (Vaguely Noble 140) [2003 6.1m³ 7m 5.7f⁵ Sep 15] €110,000Y: half-sister to several winners, including useful French 1½m winner Vampress (by Marju) and fairly useful 1¼m winner Sharera (by Kahyasi): dam, ran twice, half-sister to Shahrastani: modest form in maidens: third at Nottingham: should stay 7f: sold 5,500 gns. *M. R. Channon* **62**

SPEEDWELL 4 b.f. Spectrum (IRE) 126 – Missed Again 84 (High Top 131) [2003 p10g⁶ p10g 8.1d f12s Jun 21] 1,300Y: sixth foal: half-sister to 3 winners, including 5-y-o Canterloupe and 10-y-o Failed To Hit: dam, 1¼m winner, half-sister to smart performers Desert Shot (up to 1½m) and Mojave (up to 7f): well held in maidens/claimer. *P. J. Makin*

SPEEDY GEE (IRE) 5 b.g. Petardia 113 – Champagne Girl 67 (Robellino (USA) –
127) [2003 72d: f6s f5g⁵ f6g f5g⁶ Feb 14] strong, good-quartered gelding: fair performer
at 4 yrs, well held in 2003: tried visored/tongue tied: sometimes slowly away/carries head
awkwardly. *D. Nicholls*

SPEEDY JAMES (IRE) 7 ch.g. Fayruz 116 – Haraabah (USA) 99 (Topsider (USA)) –
[2003 –: f6s Jan 1] strong gelding: good mover: one-time useful performer: no form since
2001: visored once at 2 yrs: sold 3,000 gns. *D. Nicholls*

SPENCERS WOOD (IRE) 6 b.g. Pips Pride 117 – Ascoli (Skyliner 117) [2003 102: **90**
7g⁴ 7m Oct 17] strong, close-coupled gelding: just fairly useful performer in 2003: best at
6f/7f: acts on good to firm and good to soft going: tried visored: sometimes sweats:
reluctant to post on reappearance: takes strong hold: often races prominently: sold 6,000
gns. *P. J. Makin*

SPHINX (FR) 5 b.g. Snurge 130 – Egyptale (Crystal Glitters (USA) 127) [2003 90: **86**
p12g p12g p12g 20m 14g⁴ 14.8m³ Jul 27] smallish, workmanlike gelding: fairly useful
handicapper: left N. Littmoden after third outing: stays 1¾m: acts on polytrack, heavy
and good to firm going. *Jamie Poulton*

SPIDER MCCOY (USA) 3 ch.g. Irish River (FR) 131 – Indy's Princess (USA) (A P
Indy (USA) 131) [2003 80: 10.3g 12f 9.9m⁵ 14.6m⁴ 14.1m f12g⁶ 12d 11g⁶ 10f Aug 27]
well-made gelding: disappointing maiden at 3 yrs: left N. Tinkler after eighth start: tried
tongue tied/in cheekpieces: usually soon off bridle. *Miss B. Sanders*

SPINDOR (USA) 4 ch.g. Spinning World (USA) 130 – Doree (USA) 110 (Stop The **73**
Music (USA)) [2003 f7g⁴ f6g* f8g 7f f6g 7m 6m* 7g 5.7f 6g f7g⁵ p7g Dec 6] second **a62**
foal: dam, French 2-y-o 5f/6f winner, half-sister to dam of very smart 1m/1¼m performer
Ryafan: fair performer on turf, modest on all-weather: trained at 3 yrs by Mme C. Head-
Maarek in France: won maiden at Wolverhampton in February and selling handicap at
Lingfield in August: best form at 6f: acts on fibresand, good to firm and good to soft
ground: often blinkered, and has worn cheekpieces: none too reliable. *J. A. Osborne*

SPINETAIL RUFOUS (IRE) 5 b.g. Prince of Birds (USA) 121 – Miss Kinabalu 50 **55 §**
(Shirley Heights 130) [2003 –§, a69§: p6g p6g p5g Jan 29] modest performer: best at 5f/
6f: acts on all-weather: tried in blinkers/cheekpieces: sometimes tongue tied: untrustworthy. *D. W. P. Arbuthnot*

SPIN KING (IRE) 2 b.c. (Apr 8) Intikhab (USA) 135 – Special Dissident (Dancing **79**
Dissident (USA) 119) [2003 6g⁵ 6m⁶ 7m* 7d³ Aug 1] €50,000Y: lengthy colt: fourth
foal: half-brother to Italian winner up to 8.5f by Spectrum: dam, 5f/6f winner in Italy,
half-sister to smart 1996 2-y-o 6f winner (also second in Dewhurst) Musical Pursuit: fair
performer: won 17-runner maiden at Leicester in July: respectable third of 5 in minor
event at Newmarket, no extra late on: not sure to stay much beyond 7f. *M. L. W. Bell*

SPINNAKER 3 b.f. Nashwan (USA) 135 – Throw Away Line (USA) (Assert 134) –
[2003 10m Jun 12] sturdy filly: half-sister to several winners, including useful 1½m
winner in France Rebuff and fairly useful 7.5f (at 2 yrs in Britain) and 1¼m (in France)
winner Wavey (both by Kris): dam, minor winner at 4 yrs in USA, half-sister to champion
US filly Go For Wand: well held in maiden at Newbury. *G. A. Butler*

SPINNING DOVE 3 ch.f. Vettori (IRE) 119 – Northern Bird 86 (Interrex (CAN)) **68**
[2003 70: p8g⁴ 8m⁶ 7g⁴ 7g² 7m³ Jun 28] big, workmanlike filly: fair maiden: probably
better at 7f than 1m: yet to race on extremes of going: tried in cheekpieces. *N. A. Graham*

SPINNING JENNI 3 b.f. Mind Games 121 – Giddy 60 (Polar Falcon (USA) 126) –
[2003 71: p6g p6g 6g 7m 8.5d Jul 3] close-coupled filly: fair performer at 2 yrs: well held
in 2003: tried visored. *S. Dow*

SPINOLA (FR) 3 b.f. Spinning World (USA) 130 – Exocet (USA) (Deposit Ticket **100**
(USA)) [2003 103: 8g 7d 8m⁶ 8d 7d 7m⁴ Sep 19] close-coupled, quite attractive filly:
useful performer: won Cherry Hinton Stakes at Newmarket at 2 yrs: best efforts in 2003
when sixth in Falmouth Stakes on same course and fourth (of 5 to Trade Fair) in listed
race at Newbury on final one: barely stays 1m: yet to race on extremes of going: has raced
freely/found little: sold 140,000 gns, reportedly to stud. *P. W. Harris*

SPINSKY (USA) 3 b.f. Spinning World (USA) 130 – Walewskaia (IRE) (Slip Anchor –
136) [2003 73: 11.6s 10.3m 8m Jul 23] neat filly: fair performer at 2 yrs: last all starts in
2003, including in seller: sold 4,000 gns. *P. F. I. Cole*

SPIRIT OF DESERT (IRE) 2 b.c. (Mar 9) Desert Prince (IRE) 130 – Nomothetis **111**
(IRE) (IRE) (Law Society (USA) 130) [2003 7m* 7.5m* 8g* 8s* 8m² Oct 19] €80,000Y:
second foal: dam once-raced half-sister to very smart 1½m performer Posidonas: smart

performer: won newcomers event in June and listed race in July at Naples and minor event in September and listed race in October at Rome: best effort when keeping-on ½-length second to Pearl of Love in Gran Criterium at Milan: will stay 1¼m: acts on good to firm and soft ground: has had tongue tied. *L. Brogi, Italy*

SPIRIT OF GOLD (USA) 3 ch.c. Silver Hawk (USA) 123 – Gazayil (USA) 80 (Irish River (FR) 131) [2003 10.5v a11g Dec 18] $82,000Y: heavy-topped colt: brother to 6-y-o Mubtaker and half-brother to several winners, including Irish 1998 2-y-o 7f winner Crystal Downs (by Alleged): dam, 2-y-o 7f winner (later successful in Australia), half-sister to smart Husyan: soundly beaten in maiden at Haydock (tongue tied, for E. Dunlop) and amateur seller at Rome. *M. R. Salvioni, Italy* —

SPIRIT'S AWAKENING 4 b.g. Danzig Connection (USA) – Mo Stopher 47 (Sharpo 132) [2003 62: 8.1m 8f⁶ 8.3m 8.5g⁴ 8.3m² 9g² Oct 24] fair handicapper: stays 9f: acts on any ground: sometimes races freely: none too consistent. *J. Akehurst* **69**

SPIRITUAL AIR 3 b.f. Royal Applause 124 – Samsung Spirit 79 (Statoblest 120) [2003 93: 8f⁴ 8d² 8g³ 8f⁶ 10g 8.1d⁵ 9s Oct 26] lengthy filly: fairly useful performer: best 3-y-o efforts first 3 starts: stays 1m: acts on firm and good to soft ground: front runner. *J. R. Weymes* **90**

SPIRITUS 2 ch.g. (Mar 7) Double Trigger (IRE) 123 – Nafla (FR) (Arctic Tern (USA) 126) [2003 8g 7d Nov 4] 3,500Y: lengthy, good-bodied gelding: half-brother to 1993 2-y-o 5f and 7f winner Lambent (by Rambo Dancer), later successful in USA: dam French 7f (at 2 yrs) and 1¼m winner: pulled up (ran wide)/last in maidens. *C. N. Kellett* —

SPITFIRE BOB (USA) 4 b.g. Mister Baileys 123 – Gulf Cyclone (USA) (Sheikh Albadou 128) [2003 67, a75: f9.4g* f12g⁵ 10.1d f9.4s⁴ 8m 7.9m 10.1m² 12.1g 9.9m² 10m* 10.1m 10m Sep 18] sturdy gelding: fair handicapper: won at Wolverhampton in January and Pontefract in August: best around 1¼m: acts on firm going and fibresand (below form on polytrack): has been slowly away: usually races prominently. *T. D. Barron* **71 a76**

SPITTING IMAGE (IRE) 3 ch.f. Spectrum (IRE) 126 – Decrescendo (IRE) (Polish Precedent (USA) 131) [2003 68: 12m² 12.1f⁴ 11.9g² 12m 11.8m² 13.8d⁴ f16.2g Nov 10] close-coupled, quite attractive filly: fair maiden handicapper: stays 1¾m: acts on firm and good to soft going, ran poorly on soft and fibresand. *Mrs M. Reveley* **68**

SPLASH OUT AGAIN 5 b.g. River Falls 113 – Kajetana (FR) (Caro 133) [2003 73: 10.9m⁵ 11.7m* 14m⁴ 17.2f 14m³ 16m⁴ Sep 25] big gelding: fair handicapper: won at Bath in May: barely stays 2m: acts on good to firm and good to soft going: tried blinkered: usually waited with. *H. Morrison* **69**

SPLENDID ERA (UAE) 3 b.c. Green Desert (USA) 127 – Valley of Gold (FR) 117 (Shirley Heights 130) [2003 105p: 8m³ 10d³ 10.3g³ 8m* Oct 3] tall, good-topped, attractive colt: smart performer: off 4½ months and 25/1, won 4-runner Shadwell Stud Joel Stakes at Newmarket in October by 1¼ lengths from Kalaman, dictating steady pace: had finished third at Newmarket on first 2 starts in Craven Stakes (to Hurricane Alan) and listed race (behind Delsarte): probably better at 1m than 1¼m: acts on polytrack, good to firm and good to soft going: hard ride (has twice looked ill at ease on left-handed bend) and possibly none too genuine. *B. W. Hills* **110 ?**

SPLENDID TOUCH 3 b.f. Distinctly North (USA) 115 – Soft Touch (GER) (Horst-Herbert) [2003 8v⁵ 8d⁴ 10.3g 7d 8d 9.3g p12g Nov 29] second foal: dam German 7f/7.5f winner: well beaten in maidens in Germany (for T. Gibson) and at Lingfield on British Flat debut: tried blinkered. *J. R. Jenkins* —

SPLIFF 2 b.c. (Mar 14) Royal Applause 124 – Snipe Hall 93 (Crofthall 110) [2003 5m 5m² 5m* Oct 18] 20,000Y: leggy, useful-looking colt: third foal: dam, 2-y-o 5f/6f winner, half-sister to dam of smart sprinter Atraf: off 5 months and still green, best effort when winning 8-runner minor event at Catterick comfortably by ½ length from Handsome Cross, leading over 1f out and edging left: will prove best at 5f/6f: should make a useful 3-y-o. *H. Candy* **89 p**

SPLODGER MAC (IRE) 4 b.g. Lahib (USA) 129 – Little Love (Warrshan (USA) 117) [2003 46: 5m 7m⁴ 8.5m⁷ 9f 7m⁶ Sep 9] sturdy gelding: poor maiden handicapper: stays 8.5f: acts on good to firm ground: free-going sort. *N. Bycroft* **47**

SPORTING AFFAIR (IRE) 3 ch.f. Ashkalani (IRE) 128 – The Multiyorker (IRE) 72 (Digamist (USA) 110) [2003 59: p7g f7g p8g p6g Feb 12] maiden: well held in 2003, including in blinkers (looked reluctant). *N. P. Littmoden* — §

Queen Mother's Cup (Ladies) Handicap, York—
just a short head separates Sporting Gesture (rail) and Kylkenny; Kuster is third

SPORTING GESTURE   6 ch.g. Safawan 118 – Polly Packer 81 (Reform 132) [2003   **86**
70: 10g⁴ 10m* 11m⁴ 12.3m² 11.9m² 12m⁴ 11.9f* 11.9f² 15.9m 11.9m⁶ 11.9m* 12m²
11.9f 12m 12d Nov 8] rather leggy, close-coupled gelding: has a round action: fairly
useful handicapper: better than ever in 2003, winning at Pontefract in April and York in
June (ladies event) and September: stays 1½m: acts on firm and good to soft going: tried
blinkered, not in 2003: waited with: reliable. *M. W. Easterby*

SPORTING GRAND (USA)   2 b.g. (Mar 28) Southern Halo (USA) – Al Yazi (USA)   **–**
(Danzig (USA)) [2003 5f f6g 6f 7.5d 6m Jul 19] $13,000Y, resold 3,000Y: big, strong
gelding: sixth foal: half-brother to winners abroad by Woodman and Machiavellian: dam
ran twice in Ireland: well held in maidens/sellers: wore cheekpieces third start, then left
T. D. Barron: sent to Spain. *J. R. Weymes*

SPORTS EXPRESS   5 ch.m. Then Again 126 – Lady St Lawrence (USA) 65 (Bering   **58**
136) [2003 58: f14g² 14g⁴ 14.1d³ Jul 30] workmanlike mare: modest maiden handicapper, lightly raced: stays 2m: acts on fibresand, firm and good to soft ground: raced
prominently in 2003. *G. A. Swinbank*

SPORTSMAN (IRE)   4 b.g. Sri Pekan (USA) 117 – Ardent Range (IRE) (Archway   **44**
(IRE) 115) [2003 –: f12g³ Jan 2] poor maiden: stays 1½m: acts on fibresand: blinkered
(best effort) only 4-y-o start: sometimes slowly away. *M. W. Easterby*

SPORTULA   2 b.f. (Mar 19) Silver Patriarch (IRE) 125 – Portent (Most Welcome 131)   **–**
[2003 7m 8s p10g Nov 29] well-made filly: second foal: dam, ran twice at 3 yrs, out of
half-sister to Derby Italiano winner My Top: well beaten in maidens. *Mrs A. J. Perrett*

SPOTLIGHT   2 ch.f. (Apr 23) Dr Fong (USA) 128 – Dust Dancer 116 (Suave Dancer   **104 p**
(USA) 136) [2003 7m³ 7.1m* 7m² 8g* Nov 1] rather leggy, quite good-topped filly: third
foal: half-sister to fairly useful 2003 2-y-o 7f winner Dusty Answer (by Zafonic) and
3-y-o Tyranny: dam, 7f to 1½m winner (including 1¼m Prix de la Nonette), half-sister to
very smart performer up to 1½m Zimzalabim: useful performer: won maiden at Warwick
in September and listed event at Newmarket (gone in coat, beat St Francis Wood 4 lengths
in 12-runner event, making running and quickening 2f out) in November: should be
suited by at least 1¼m: open to progress. *J. L. Dunlop*

SPRING ADIEU   2 b.f. (Apr 26) Green Desert (USA) 127 – Nanda 83 (Nashwan   **60**
(USA) 135) [2003 8m 7d Nov 7] 75,000Y: third foal: dam, 1¼m winner who stayed 1½m,
sister to Nell Gwyn Stakes winner Myself and half-sister to very smart performer up to 7f
Bluebook: modest form in maidens at Doncaster. *Mrs A. J. Perrett*

SPRINGALONG (USA)   3 ch.g. Gone West (USA) – Seven Springs (USA) 114 (Irish   **75 d**
River (FR) 131) [2003 8m⁴ 9.2m³ 7.1m³ 8.1d p10g⁴ Dec 30] smallish, sturdy gelding:
closely related to 3 winners, notably high-class miler Distant View (by Mr Prospector),
and half-brother to 3 winners abroad: dam, won Prix Robert Papin and Prix Morny, later
stayed 1m: fair maiden: well below form after second start, leaving H. Cecil 19,000 gns,
gelded and off 3 months before final one: likely to prove best at 7f/1m: unraced on
extremes of going on turf. *P. D. Evans*

968

SPRING BREEZE 2 ch.g. (May 5) Dr Fong (USA) 128 – Trading Aces 71 (Be My **55**
Chief (USA) 122) [2003 6.1g 6g⁴ 7m 8f³ 10f Sep 30] workmanlike gelding: third foal:
dam, 6f (at 2 yrs) and 7f winner, half-sister to useful performer up to 1m Crazee Mental:
modest maiden: third in claimer at Newcastle, then left M. Channon: should stay 1¼m:
acts on firm going. *M. Dods*

SPRING DANCER 2 b.f. (Mar 3) Imperial Ballet (IRE) 110 – Roxy Music (IRE) 63 **78 d**
(Song 132) [2003 6g² 6m* 6m³ 6f² 6m 7m⁶ 7g⁶ 6m 6f Oct 10] 4,000Y: quite good-topped
filly: eighth foal: half-sister to 3 winners, including fairly useful 5f (at 2 yrs) to 8.5f
winner Foot Battalion (by Batshoof): dam 2-y-o 7f winner: fair performer: won maiden
at Pontefract in June: ran badly in nurseries last 3 starts: probably stays 7f: acts on firm
going: wore visor/cheekpieces last 2 appearances: unreliable. *A. P. Jarvis*

SPRING GODDESS (IRE) 2 b.f. (Mar 22) Daggers Drawn (USA) 114 – Easter Girl **82**
(Efisio 120) [2003 6m 7m³ 7.5m* 7m⁶ 8m Oct 20] 29,000Y: good-topped filly: second
foal: half-sister to 4-y-o Eastborough: dam unraced half-sister to smart 6f/7f performer
Bollin Knight: fairly useful performer: won maiden at Beverley in September: creditable
sixth in nursery at Newmarket: stiff task final start: stays 7.5f. *A. P. Jarvis*

SPRING JIM 2 b.g. (Apr 28) First Trump 118 – Spring Sixpence 60 (Dowsing (USA) **71**
124) [2003 6.1m⁴ 6m⁵ 6m Oct 24] 7,000Y: close-coupled gelding: fourth foal: brother to
5-y-o Torosay Spring and half-brother to winner in Germany by Sabrehill: dam 7f and
1½m winner: fair form in maidens/sales race: slowly away final outing: will probably
stay 7f. *J. R. Fanshawe*

SPRING PURSUIT 7 b.g. Rudimentary (USA) 118 – Pursuit of Truth (USA) 69 (Irish **–**
River (FR) 131) [2003 74d: 10d 12m f12g Nov 21] close-coupled gelding: fairly useful
handicapper at best: well held in 2003: blinkered once at 2 yrs: usually held up. *R. J. Price*

SPRING SURPRISE 2 b.f. (Mar 31) Hector Protector (USA) 124 – Tender Moment **82 p**
(IRE) 78 (Caerleon (USA) 132) [2003 6g 7d* Nov 7] lengthy filly: sister to 4-y-o Marlo
and half-sister to several winners, including 7-y-o Summer Bounty: dam 7f winner: much
better effort in maidens (fairly useful form) when winning 17-runner event at Doncaster
by 2½ lengths from Sabre's Edge, leading over 1f out: will probably stay 1m: should
progress. *B. W. Hills*

SPRING WHISPER (IRE) 2 b.f. (Apr 3) Halling (USA) 133 – Light Fresh Air **49**
(USA) (Rahy (USA) 115) [2003 7d p10g f8g Dec 8] sixth foal: half-sister to fairly useful
1½m winner Almost Free (by Darshaan): dam French 1m winner, including at 2 yrs: poor
form in maidens: best effort when visored at 1¼m: hung right final start. *E. A. L. Dunlop*

SPURADICH (IRE) 3 b.c. Barathea (IRE) 127 – Svanzega (USA) (Sharpen Up 127) **106 +**
[2003 –p: 10g³ 10g⁵ 8m* 8m 9.1g* 9.9m* 10m Sep 20] strong colt: useful performer:
successful in maiden at Milan in May, then progressed well to win handicaps at Ayr and
Beverley (quite valuable event by 3½ lengths from Tug of Love) in August: well-backed
favourite, reportedly lame when well held in Courage Best Handicap at Newbury final
start: stays 1¼m: raced mainly on good/good to firm ground on turf: tends to race freely/
carry head high. *L. M. Cumani*

SPY GUN (USA) 3 ch.g. Mt Livermore (USA) – Takeover Target (USA) (Nodouble **68**
(USA)) [2003 76p: 8m 10m f8g f8g* f7g⁴ Dec 16] angular, useful-looking gelding: fair
performer: sold out of E. Dunlop's stable 8,000 gns after second start: 25/1-winner of
handicap at Southwell in December, idling: effective at 7f/1m: acts on fibresand. *T. Wall*

SPY MASTER 5 b.g. Green Desert (USA) 127 – Obsessive (USA) 102 (Seeking The **–**
Gold (USA)) [2003 –: f8s f8g 6d 5.9d 6m Aug 19] small, strong gelding: well held since
2 yrs: usually visored/blinkered: sometimes tongue tied. *J. Parkes*

SQUARE DANCER 7 b.g. Then Again 126 – Cubist (IRE) 71 (Tate Gallery (USA) **–**
117) [2003 51: 9m 7.1d 7.1f Jun 16] tall, good-bodied gelding: fair performer at best: well
held in 2003: tried visored: tongue tied. *D. A. Nolan*

SQUEAKY 6 ch.m. Infantry 122 – Steady Saunter VII (Damsire Unregistered) [2003 **72**
71: 10m² 11.6g² 10m 13.8d p10g Nov 26] lengthy mare: fair handicapper: well below
form after second start: effective at 1¼m to 12.6f: acts on firm and soft going, well held
on all-weather. *Miss K. M. George*

SQUIRE MICHAEL (USA) 3 b.c. Affirmed (USA) – Elle Meme (USA) (Zilzal **61**
(USA) 137) [2003 67: 10f 10.9m⁶ 10m⁴ May 9] rather leggy colt: modest maiden: stays
1¼m: acts on fibresand and firm going: ran creditably when tried in blinkers/cheekpieces.
P. F. I. Cole

SQUIRTLE TURTLE 3 ch.g. Peintre Celebre (USA) 137 – Hatton Gardens 96 **79**
(Auction Ring (USA) 123) [2003 10.3g 12g 7.1g³ 10.2g⁵ 8m 11f³ Oct 12] 100,000Y: tall,
quite good-topped gelding: half-brother to several winners, including smart Irish 7f (at
2 yrs) and 12.5f (Prix Minerve) winner Lime Gardens (by Sadler's Wells) and useful 7f
(at 2 yrs) to 10.4f winner Ludgate (by Lyphard): dam, Irish 6f to 1m winner, half-sister to
high-class 1m/1¼m filly Kooyonga: fair maiden: stiff task, improved form when close
third in claimer at Goodwood final start, despite handling turns none too well: stays 11f:
raced only on good ground or firmer: blinkered twice, including at Goodwood: refused to
enter stall third intended outing: has been slowly away/hung left. *P. F. I. Cole*

SRI ANGKASA (IRE) 3 ch.g. Night Shift (USA) – Miss Kelly (Pitskelly 122) [2003 **93**
8.3d 8.1m² 8m³ Jul 18] 20,000F, IR 75,000Y: big, good-topped gelding: closely related to
1m/1¼m winner Total Rach (by Nordico) and half-brother to Irish 2001 2-y-o 1m/8.5f
winner Arkaga (by Key of Luck) and 1¼m/1½m winner Frankie Ferrari (by Common
Grounds), both fairly useful: dam Irish maiden: fairly useful maiden: placed at Warwick
and Newmarket: gelded after: should be at least as effective at 7f as 1m: acts on good to
firm ground. *M. A. Jarvis*

SRI DIAMOND 3 b.g. Sri Pekan (USA) 117 – Hana Marie 101§ (Formidable (USA) **92**
125) [2003 89p: 10.3d p7g³ 8f Oct 12] good-topped colt: fairly useful performer: best
effort when third in handicap at Lingfield: stays 7f: acts on polytrack and good to firm
ground. *S. Kirk*

SRI (IRE) 4 b.f. Sri Pekan (USA) 117 – Verify (IRE) (Polish Precedent (USA) 131) **–**
[2003 78: p7g p7g p7g 6g p8g 10g 9.2g 9.1d Oct 14] IR 1,000Y: first foal: dam Italian
maiden: fair performer at 2/3 yrs for J. Burns in Ireland, winning maiden and minor event
at Sligo in 2001: well held in 2003, leaving S. Dow after sixth start: stays 1m: raced only
on good ground or softer on turf. *P. Monteith*

STAFF NURSE (IRE) 3 b.f. Night Shift (USA) – Akebia (USA) (Trempolino (USA) **53**
135) [2003 71: 8.2g 7.5f 8.2g 9.2d⁶ 10.1g 12.4m⁵ 10m³ 13.8d² 10f³ 10.9d⁵ 11.5m³ Oct
21] well-made filly: modest handicapper: stays 1¾m: yet to race on heavy going, acts on
any other: visored (ran poorly) once. *N. Tinkler*

STAGE BY STAGE (USA) 4 ch.g. In The Wings 128 – Lady Thynn (FR) (Crystal **–**
Glitters (USA) 127) [2003 100: 10.4m 12f 14g Sep 6] workmanlike gelding: lightly
raced: useful at 2/3 yrs, well held in 2003. *C. R. Egerton*

STAGECOACH REVIVAL (IRE) 3 ch.c. Nashwan (USA) 135 – Hill of Snow 80 **59**
(Reference Point 139) [2003 11.1d⁵ May 4] IR 16,000Y: fourth foal: half-brother to 3
winners, including Irish 7f (Moyglare Stud Stakes)/1m winner Preseli (by Caerleon) who
stayed 1¼m, and 1000 Guineas runner-up Snowfire (by Machiavellian), 7f winner at 2
yrs, both smart: dam Irish 1¼m winner: very green when fifth in maiden at Hamilton,
slowly away: dead. *M. Johnston*

STAGECOACH RUBY 2 b.f. (Mar 27) Bijou d'Inde 127 – Forum Girl (USA) 79 **58 d**
(Sheikh Albadou 128) [2003 5f 5.1m 6v 6m 7m* 7m* 6m³ 6g⁶ 7m 7m⁶ 7m⁵ 8m Sep 13]
tall, plain filly: first foal: dam 7f winner: modest performer: won seller at Redcar and
claimer at Brighton (then left M. Johnston) in June: only poor form after next start:
effective at 6f/7f: acts on good to firm ground: often wears eyeshields (has only one eye).
J. R. Best

STAGE DIRECTION (USA) 6 b.g. Theatrical 128 – Carya (USA) (Northern Dan- **–**
cer) [2003 55: 16m Apr 22] modest performer at 5 yrs: well beaten only start in 2003:
tried tongue tied. *B. J. Llewellyn*

STAGE SHY (USA) 3 ch.f. Theatrical 128 – Garimpeiro (USA) (Mr Prospector **90 ?**
(USA)) [2003 69p: 10g* 10m 12m Aug 3] fairly useful performer: won maiden at Sandown in June: seemed to run well when seventh of 8 to Hanami in Pretty Polly Stakes at
the Curragh next time, still prominent when bumped under 2f out: ran as though amiss
final outing: should stay 1½m: raced only on good or firmer going: sent to USA, joined
N. Drysdale. *J. H. M. Gosden*

STAGNITE 3 ch.g. Compton Place 125 – Superspring (Superlative 118) [2003 70: f6g **65**
p6g p7g⁵ p7g⁴ p7g⁴ 6m 7m 7m 6m² 6.1g² 6f² 6f² 6.1m² 6f 5m 6m² 6m 5.7f Oct 12] fair
maiden: runner-up 6 times in 2003, including in 5 handicaps: effective at 6f/easy 7f: acts
on firm ground and polytrack: often races prominently. *K. R. Burke*

STAKHANOVITE (IRE) 3 b.c. Darshaan 133 – Homage (Ajdal (USA) 130) [2003 **84**
8.1m³ Apr 9] rather leggy colt: sixth living foal: brother to outstanding miler Mark of
Esteem and half-brother to useful 1m winner Earl of March (by Caerleon): dam unraced
half-sister to high-class 2-y-o Local Suitor and very smart French winner of Prix Jean

STA

Prat Local Talent: 11/2, third in maiden at Warwick: struck into on a hind leg and not seen out after. *D. R. Loder*

STALLONE   6 ch.g. Brief Truce (USA) 126 – Bering Honneur (USA) (Bering 136)   **79**
[2003 –§: f8g 8.5f² 8g³ 10.1m* 10.1m* 9.9m³ 9m³ 10m⁵ 10.1m⁵ 12.1m² 10.4m³ 12m*
11.9f Oct 9] good-bodied gelding: fair handicapper: won at Newcastle in May (selling
event) and June and at Thirsk in September: stays 1½m: acts on soft and firm ground:
tends to start slowly: usually held up: refused to race once at 5 yrs, but game and reliable
in 2003. *N. Wilson*

STAMFORD BLUE   2 b.c. (Apr 7) Bluegrass Prince (IRE) 110 – Fayre Holly (IRE) 57   **58**
(Fayruz 116) [2003 5.1m⁶ 5g* 5m f6s 5.1d p6g f8g p6g³ f6g⁵ Dec 26] fourth foal: brother
to 3-y-o Docduckout and half-brother to 2 winners, including 4-y-o Hollybell: dam,
maiden, might have proved best at 5f/6f: modest performer: best effort when winning
seller at Windsor in August: stays 6f: acts on polytrack (no form on fibresand), unraced
on extremes of going on turf: wore blinkers/cheekpieces 4 of last 5 starts. *J. S. Moore*

STANCE   4 b.g. Salse (USA) 128 – De Stael (USA) 93 (Nijinsky (CAN) 138) [2003 98:   **?**
14f 13d a12g a12g⁵ a10.5g a12s² a12g³ Dec 14] strong, well-made, attractive gelding:
type to carry condition: has a quick, fluent action: useful at 3 yrs: mostly disappointing
since, leaving R. C. Guest after second outing and G. Bindella after fifth: placed in
handicap/minor event at Dos Hermanas last 2 starts: stays 1¾m: acts on good to firm and
good to soft going, and on sand. *J. H. Brown, Spain*

STAND BY   6 b.m. Missed Flight 123 – Ma Rivale (Last Tycoon 131) [2003 51, a64:   **–**
f6g² p6g p5g² f6g⁴ p6g f6g⁶ f5g² f5g² 5g⁵ 7g 5m f5g f8g Nov 24] modest performer: **a58**
claimed from B. Pearce £4,000 after tenth start: best at 5f/6f: acts on all-weather and
good to firm going: tried visored and in cheekpieces: sometimes slowly away: none too
consistent. *T. D. McCarthy*

STANDIFORD GIRL (IRE)   6 b.m. Standiford (USA) – Pennine Girl (IRE) (Pennine   **–**
Walk 120) [2003 –: f16s f8.5g⁶ f16.2g Mar 3] sparely-made mare: no form since 2000.
L. A. Dace

STANHOPE FORBES (IRE)   2 b.c. (Feb 2) Danehill Dancer (IRE) 117 – Hinari   **66**
Disk Deck 75 (Indian King (USA) 128) [2003 5d 7m⁶ 7.1f³ 8m⁵ 8s p8g⁶ f7g p6g² p6g⁵   **a54**
Dec 30] IR 4,500F, 30,000Y: sturdy colt: eighth foal: half-brother to winner in Holland
by Common Grounds: dam, 2-y-o 5f winner, half-sister to dam of July Cup winner
Compton Place: fair maiden on turf, modest on all-weather: best effort when third
in minor event at Warwick: will probably prove best at 6f/7f: acts on firm ground and
polytrack: tried in cheekpieces. *N. P. Littmoden*

STANLEY CRANE (USA)   2 b.rg. (Feb 13) Bahri (USA) 125 – Grey Starling 70   **79**
(Pharly (FR) 130) [2003 6m⁴ p7g³ 7m⁵ Oct 21] 30,000Y: good-topped gelding: sixth foal:
half-brother to winners abroad by Spectacular Bid and Local Talent: dam, maiden in
Britain (best at 1¼m), later 4.5f winner in Canada: fair form: third in maiden at Lingfield:
took good hold final start: needs to settle to stay 1m: wears tongue tie. *B. Hanbury*

STAR APPLAUSE   3 b.f. Royal Applause 124 – Cominna (Dominion 123) [2003 53:   **54 d**
f5g* f5g⁵ 5m² 5d 5f⁶ f5s 5m f5g Dec 12] good-topped filly: modest performer: won seller
at Wolverhampton in February: below form in handicaps last 5 starts: raced only at 5f:
acts on fibresand and good to firm ground: tried in cheekpieces: usually races up with
pace. *J. Balding*

STARBECK (IRE)   5 b.m. Spectrum (IRE) 126 – Tide of Fortune (Soviet Star (USA)   **94**
128) [2003 84, a73: f8g 7d 7m⁴ 6m 6m³ 7m 7m⁶ 6.1m 7m⁵ 7m⁵ 7g² 7m Oct 17] lengthy   **a?**
mare: fairly useful performer: left J. Bethell 3,500 gns after reappearance: easily best
efforts of season tenth and eleventh starts, 2 lengths equal-second to Chic in listed event
at Ascot on latter occasion: stays 7f: acts on fibresand, soft and good to firm ground: tried
tongue tied: on a long losing run, and none too reliable. *P. S. McEntee*

STARBRIGHT   2 b.g. (Apr 15) Polar Falcon (USA) 126 – Treasure Hunt (Hadeer   **–**
118) [2003 6m Sep 9] 2,200Y: third foal: dam unraced half-sister to useful sprinter Lago
di Varano: 66/1, last of 7 in maiden at Catterick. *Miss S. E. Hall*

STAR CROSS (IRE)   4 b.g. Ashkalani (IRE) 128 – Solar Star (USA) 93 (Lear Fan   **87**
(USA) 130) [2003 –: 10g 12g 12m 14.8m² 14d Sep 27] big, rangy gelding: fairly useful
performer, lightly raced: best effort when second in handicap at Newmarket, making
running: stays 14.8f: acts on soft and good to firm going: sold 6,000 gns. *J. L. Dunlop*

STARCROSS VENTURE   2 b.f. (Feb 16) Orpen (USA) 116 – Maculatus (USA)   **63**
(Sharpen Up 127) [2003 p6g³ Dec 6] 4,000Y: seventh foal: half-sister to 3 winners,
including 7f winner Nordic Doll (by Royal Academy) and useful 1998 2-y-o 5f winner

971

Chomper (by Mujtahid), later successful in USA: dam ran twice: 100/1, never-nearer length third of 14 to La Landonne in maiden at Lingfield: should stay 7f. *R. A. Fahey*

STAR FERN 2 br.g. (Apr 22) Young Ern 120 – Christening (IRE) (Lahib (USA) 129) **63 p** [2003 p7g⁴ Dec 17] fourth foal: dam, unraced, out of half-sister to smart middle-distance stayers Bright Finish and Shining Finish: 33/1, 2 lengths fourth to Whitgift Rock in minor event at Lingfield, slowly away and never nearer: should improve. *J. Akehurst*

STARGEM 2 b.f. (Mar 5) Compton Place 125 – Holy Smoke 83 (Statoblest 120) [2003 **81** 6m 6m² Oct 4] rather leggy filly: first foal: dam 1m/1¼m winner: much better effort in maidens at Newmarket (fairly useful form) when second to Valjarv, disputing lead long way: will probably stay 7f. *Mrs Lydia Pearce*

STAR LAD (IRE) 3 ch.g. Lake Coniston (IRE) 131 – Simply Special (IRE) (Petit **62** Loup (USA) 123) [2003 55, a63: f5s⁵ f5g⁴ f6g³ f6g⁵ 5.1m⁵ 6m² 5.3m² 5.7m 6f⁶ f6g f6g f6g f5g⁶ f5g f6g⁶ Dec 19] modest handicapper: best at 5f/easy 6f: acts on fibresand and good to firm going: blinkered/visored: usually races up with pace. *R. Brotherton*

STARLIGHT NIGHT (USA) 4 ch.f. Distant View (USA) 126 – Diese (USA) 111 **63** (Diesis 133) [2003 71: p10g⁴ Feb 8] lightly-raced maiden, fair form at best: respectable effort only outing in 2003: raced only at 1¼m on polytrack and firm ground. *Mrs A. J. Perrett*

STAR MEMBER (IRE) 4 b.g. Hernando (FR) 127 – Constellation (IRE) (Kaldoun **87** (FR) 122) [2003 85: f11g 14.4f⁶ 14.4m³ 14g² 14.6g 16.2f⁵ 16g Oct 24] leggy, quite good-topped gelding: fairly useful handicapper: sometimes races freely, but stays 2m: acts on all-weather, raced only on good ground or firmer on turf. *A. P. Jarvis*

STARMINDA 3 b.f. Zamindar (USA) 116 – Starfida (Soviet Star (USA) 128) [2003 **–** 50: 7g Jul 9] quite good-topped filly: modest maiden in 2002: well beaten only 3-y-o start: tried visored. *Mrs C. A. Dunnett*

STAR OF ARABIA (IRE) 4 b.f. Hamas (IRE) 125§ – Thank One's Stars (Alzao **64** (USA) 117) [2003 67: 5m 5g 5g 7m⁴ 6m* 5.7f 5m 6m* p6g p7g Nov 2] small, sturdy filly: modest handicapper: won at Salisbury in August and Leicester in October: stays 6f: acts on firm ground, good to soft and polytrack. *N. A. Gaselee*

STAR OF GERMANY (IRE) 3 b.g. Germany (USA) 124 – Twinkle Bright (USA) **–** 40 (Star de Naskra (USA)) [2003 –: f8g⁵ f11s⁴ Feb 20] little sign of ability. *T. P. Tate*

STAR OF LIGHT 2 b.g. (Mar 26) Mtoto 134 – Star Entry 67 (In The Wings 128) **77** [2003 7m p7g⁶ p7g² p7g* Nov 18] good-bodied gelding: third foal: dam 9.7f winner: fair performer: won claimer at Lingfield by ¾ length from Stonor Lady: should be suited by at least 1¼m: acts on polytrack, little promise on turf. *B. J. Meehan*

STAR OF NORMANDIE (USA) 4 b.f. Gulch (USA) – Depaze (USA) (Deputy **91** Minister (CAN)) [2003 83: 10m⁴ 8g⁶ 8.3g p8g 8g³ 10d* f9.4g² p8g* p10g* p8g² Dec 30] tall filly: fairly useful handicapper: won at Nottingham and Lingfield in November and at Lingfield again in December: effective at 1m/1¼m: acts on all-weather, firm and soft going: tried in blinkers/cheekpieces, better form without: usually waited with. *G. G. Margarson*

STAR OVATION (IRE) 6 ch.g. Fourstars Allstar (USA) 122 – Standing Ovation **65 ?** (Godswalk (USA) 130) [2003 73: 9m⁶ 7m 6.1g⁶ 8.3m⁴ Jul 17] good-bodied gelding: modest maiden, lightly raced: stays 1m: unraced on extremes of going. *Mrs A. M. Naughton*

STAR PETE 2 b.g. (Mar 31) Fraam 114 – Stride Home 78 (Absalom 128) [2003 8.1g⁵ **64** Sep 11] seventh foal: brother to fairly useful 1¼m/1½m winner Pedro Pete and half-brother to 2 winners, including 3-y-o Senor Pedro: dam 5f (at 2 yrs) to 1¼m winner: fifth of 12 in maiden at Chepstow: dead. *M. R. Channon*

STAR PRINCESS 6 b.m. Up And At 'em 109 – Princess Sharpenup 63 (Lochnager **–** 132) [2003 –: p6g f8s* f8g f8g⁴ f8.5g f8g⁶ f7g 8m Jun 22] workmanlike mare: modest **a50** performer: 100/1-winner of maiden at Southwell in January: stays 1m: acts on fibresand, no form on turf since 2001. *J. Gallagher*

STAR PUPIL 2 ch.c. (Jan 13) Selkirk (USA) 129 – Lochangel 119 (Night Shift **86 p** (USA)) [2003 7m 7g² Nov 1] strong, good-topped colt: first foal: dam, 5f/6f (latter at 2 yrs) winner, half-sister to Lochsong: much better effort in maidens at Newmarket (fairly useful form) when head second of 13 to Hezaam, briefly clear over 1f out but hanging right and headed close home: needs to settle to stay beyond 7f: open to progress, and should win a race or 2. *A. M. Balding*

STARRY LODGE (IRE) 3 b.c. Grand Lodge (USA) 125 – Stara (Star Appeal 133) **104**
[2003 64: 10.9m* 11m* 11.9m^3 10.9g* 12f^6 11m^4 11.9m* 11.9m^2 13.3m* Sep 20] useful-looking colt: progressed with every run in 2003, winning at Warwick in April, Redcar and Ayr in May, Carlisle in August and Newbury (dead-heated with Prins Willem) in September: stays 13.3f: acts on firm going and polytrack: usually waited with: reliable. *L. M. Cumani*

STARRY MARY 5 b.m. Deploy 131 – Darling Splodge (Elegant Air 119) [2003 63, **64**
a50: 12m^3 11.7m^5 13.1g^2 12.1d 14d p12g p16g p13g^6 Dec 29] close-coupled mare: mod- **a50**
est handicapper, better on turf than all-weather: barely stays 14.8f: acts on all-weather, heavy and good to firm going: sometimes slowly away: usually held up. *E. L. James*

STARS AT MIDNIGHT 3 b.f. Magic Ring (IRE) 115 – Boughtbyphone 62 (Warning **54 +**
136) [2003 –: 8g^4 6m 8.1m 8.3m* 8m 7.9m Aug 4] modest handicapper: won at Windsor in July: well held after, spoiling chance with very slow start final outing: stays 1m: unraced on extremes of going. *I. A. Wood*

STAR SENSATION (IRE) 3 b. or br.f. Sri Pekan (USA) 117 – Dancing Sensation **98**
(USA) 72 (Faliraki 125) [2003 85: 8m^6 8.2d^4 8m^2 8f^6 8m* 8m 8.1m^4 8.3d^2 8.1d^5 8m^4 8.1d 7.9f Oct 10] smallish, good-topped filly: useful handicapper: won at Leicester in June: stays 1m: acts on good to firm and good to soft going: has worn cheekpieces/been bandaged near-hind joint. *P. W. Harris*

STAR SEVENTEEN 5 ch.m. Rock City 120 – Westminster Waltz (Dance In Time **–**
(CAN)) [2003 78: f12g Jan 24] angular mare: fair handicapper: well held only 5-y-o start. *T. H. Caldwell*

STAR SOUND 3 br.g. Millkom 124 – Tarnside Rosal 68 (Mummy's Game 120) [2003 **–**
50: f8g f7g Jan 23] modest maiden at 2 yrs: well held in 2003, including in seller. *T. D. Barron*

STARTLED 4 ch.f. Zilzal (USA) 137 – Zelda (USA) (Sharpen Up 127) [2003 43: **–**
f8.5g 8d Oct 31] poor maiden: well held in 2003, leaving D. Cosgrove after reappearance. *J. Jay*

START OVER (IRE) 4 b.c. Barathea (IRE) 127 – Carnelly (IRE) 101 (Priolo (USA) **84**
127) [2003 84: p8g^3 10.1d p8g^2 10g^5 8.1m^5 8f 8.2m^3 9.2m* 8.2d* 10g^6 9.2g^2 8m 8m^2 8g^2 8.9f Oct 11] sturdy, close-coupled colt: fairly useful performer: won minor events at Hamilton and Nottingham in July, dictating pace each time: best at 1m/9f: acts on polytrack and any turf going: sold 25,000 gns. *E. J. O'Neill*

STAR WELCOME 2 ch.f. (Mar 19) Most Welcome 131 – My Greatest Star 93 (Great **– p**
Nephew 126) [2003 6m Oct 16] rather leggy, close-coupled filly: eighth foal: half-sister to 3 winners, including fairly useful 2002 2-y-o 7f winner Star Vega (by Blue Ocean) and 6-y-o Runaway Star: dam maiden (barely stayed 1¼m) half-sister to Galtres Stakes winner Startino: 100/1 and backward, slowly away and never on terms in maiden at Newmarket: should do better. *W. J. Musson*

STAR WONDER 3 b.f. Syrtos 106 – Galava (CAN) (Graustark) [2003 10d 7.1g 7m^4 **–**
7.1m Sep 20] lengthy, workmanlike filly: half-sister to 3 winners, including fairly useful 1997 2-y-o 1m winner Merciless (by Last Tycoon) and 1¾m winner Grey Galava (by Generous): dam placed at 7f/1m in France: no form. *B. N. Doran*

STATE CITY (USA) 4 ch.c. Carson City (USA) – Wajna (USA) 108 (Nureyev (USA) **117**
131) [2003 113: 6g a5f* a6f^6 a6f^5 a6s^5 a7f^3 a6s^5 a7f^5 Oct 25] half-brother to 1998 2-y-o 1m winner Mount Irish (by Irish River): dam, 7f (at 2 yrs) and 1¼m winner, half-sister to US Grade 1 1½m winner Navarone: smart performer: won 6 of his 11 starts in UAE, including listed race at Jebel Ali in February and Dubai Golden Shaheen at Nad Al Sheba in March: beat Avanzado by ¾ length on latter course: left P. Rudkin, below form afterwards in Grade 2/3 handicaps at Belmont (3) and Saratoga (trained by Saeed bin Suroor for fifth outing only): has won at 1m, but probably best at 5f/6f: acts on dirt (below form in sloppy conditions), well held only outing on turf: has rejoined Saeed bin Suroor. *T. Albertrani, USA*

STATE DILEMMA (IRE) 2 b.c. (Mar 29) Green Desert (USA) 127 – Nuriva (USA) **91 p**
100 (Woodman (USA) 126) [2003 7m^3 7m^3 7m* 8m^4 Oct 16] good-bodied colt: has a quick, fluent action: fourth living foal: closely related to 5-y-o Brave Dane: dam 2-y-o 6f winner and third in Cork And Orrery, sister to smart 1990 2-y-o Mujtahid: made all in maiden at Newbury in September, beating Putra Sas by head: creditable fourth to Top Spec in nursery at Newmarket, no extra late on: barely stays 1m: type to make a useful handicapper at 3 yrs. *B. W. Hills*

STATEMENT (IRE) 3 b.c. Singspiel (IRE) 133 – Last Spin 77 (Unfuwain (USA) **96**
131) [2003 90p: 12f² 10.4f⁴ 11g* 10f⁴ Dec 3] tall, good-topped colt: useful performer:
good fourth to Black Falcon on handicap debut at York in June, then left Sir Michael
Stoute: won maiden at Belmont in September: creditable fourth in optional claimer at
Hollywood final outing: stays 1½m: raced only on good ground or firmer: free-going sort.
C. Clement, USA

STATE OF BALANCE 5 ch.m. Mizoram (USA) 105 – Equilibrium 67 (Statoblest **65**
120) [2003 f7s p8g p10g⁴ p10g Dec 17] 500Y: second foal: dam 2-y-o 6f winner: well
held in bumpers: fair maiden: stays 1¼m: raced only on all-weather. *K. Bell*

STATEROOM (USA) 5 ch.g. Affirmed (USA) – Sleet (USA) (Summer Squall (USA)) **83**
[2003 92: 6m 7.1m⁵ 10.2f⁵ 10.3m 9.9m 8m* p8g⁵ 8f⁴ Oct 27] close-coupled gelding:
fairly useful performer: won minor event at Leicester in September: best at 7f/1m: acts on
firm going and polytrack: blinkered last 3 outings: sometimes tongue tied. *J. A. R. Toller*

STATOYORK 10 b.g. Statoblest 120 – Ultimate Dream 74 (Kafu 120) [2003 59: p5g⁴ **55**
f5s f5g⁵ 5m 5m⁴ 5.1f 5m 6f Aug 2] strong gelding: modest handicapper: best at 5f: acts
on firm and soft going, probably on polytrack: tried visored/blinkered: usually slowly
away: best produced late: has reportedly bled on several occasions. *D. Shaw*

STATUE OF LIBERTY (USA) 3 b. or br.c. Storm Cat (USA) – Charming Lassie **115**
(USA) (Seattle Slew (USA)) [2003 109p: 8f 8d² 8g 8d a8.5f Oct 25] strong, heavy-bodied
colt: carried plenty of condition: smart performer, lightly raced: won Coventry Stakes at
Royal Ascot at 2 yrs: reportedly damaged muscle in shoulder after, and off a year: best
effort in 2003 when head second to Reel Buddy in Sussex Stakes at Goodwood in July,
switched and running on: respectable ninth in Prix du Moulin de Longchamp next
time, but well held last 2 starts in Prix Daniel Wildenstein at Longchamp and non-graded
handicap at Santa Anita (only outing on dirt, stumbled coming out of stall): stayed 1m:
acted on good to soft going (won on soft on debut at 2 yrs): blinkered/visored last 2 starts:
had worn crossed noseband/gone steadily to post/become stirred up in preliminaries: to
stand at Coolmore, Co Tipperary, Ireland, fee €12,000. *A. P. O'Brien, Ireland*

ST AUSTELL 3 b.g. Compton Place 125 – Paris Joelle (IRE) (Fairy King (USA)) **76**
[2003 –: 5.2m³ 5.1m² 6f 5f² 5g* Jul 9] sturdy gelding: fair performer: landed odds in
maiden at Lingfield in July: probably best at 5f: raced only on good ground or firmer: has
carried head high. *J. A. R. Toller*

STAVROS (IRE) 3 b.c. General Monash (USA) 107 – Rivers Rainbow (Primo **49**
Dominie 121) [2003 63: 6g 6f 6g 5m 5.9m⁵ 7m 5m 5f³ 6m 5m⁶ 5m 5m 6m 6m⁶ Oct 17]
rather leggy, lengthy colt: poor maiden nowadays: effective at 5f/6f: acts on firm going:
tried in headgear: sometimes slowly away: none too consistent. *J. S. Wainwright*

ST CASSIEN (IRE) 3 b.g. Goldmark (USA) 113 – Moonlight Partner (IRE) 81 (Red **–**
Sunset 120) [2003 –: 7m f6g p10g Dec 30] seems of little account: tried visored.
T. M. Jones

STEALING BEAUTY (IRE) 3 b.f. Sadler's Wells (USA) 132 – Imitation **80 p**
(Darshaan 133) [2003 69p: 10m 11.9f* Oct 17] leggy filly: off 5 months, best effort in
maidens (fairly useful form) when winning 3-runner event at Brighton by 1¾ lengths
from Wasted Talent: almost certainly better at 1½m than shorter: remains capable of
better. *L. M. Cumani*

STEALTHELIMELIGHT (IRE) 2 b.c. (Feb 28) Royal Applause 124 – Scylla 50 **86**
(Rock City 120) [2003 5m³ 5.1m⁴ 5.3m* 6.1d⁵ 5.1m² 5m⁴ 5m³ 6.1m⁵ 6m* 7g* 7d 6m
Oct 17] 8,000F, 30,000Y: sturdy, lengthy colt: third foal: dam maiden half-sister to smart
sprinter Northern Goddess: fairly useful performer: won maiden at Brighton in May and
nursery at Catterick and claimer at Chester in August: below form in nurseries last 2
starts: stays easy 7f: acts on good to firm going: blinkered third/fourth starts: sometimes
races freely/edges left: sold 21,000 gns, sent to USA. *N. A. Callaghan*

ST EDITH (IRE) 3 ch.f. Desert King (IRE) 129 – Carnelly (IRE) 101 (Priolo (USA) **–**
127) [2003 58: 7m⁶ 10.1g 10d Aug 18] close-coupled filly: modest maiden at 2 yrs: well
held in 2003. *C. F. Wall*

STEEL BLUE 3 b.g. Atraf 116 – Something Blue (Petong 126) [2003 94: a7.5f⁵ a6f⁶ **91**
6g 6d⁴ 6g 5d⁵ 6f 5m 6s² 5d² f5g p6g Nov 26] leggy, quite good-topped gelding: fairly **a83**
useful handicapper: ran in UAE first 2 outings: good efforts when runner-up at Redcar
and Doncaster: effective at 5f/6f: acts on dirt, soft and good to firm going: wore
cheekpieces last 3 starts *R. M. Whitaker*

STEEL CAT (USA) 3 b.c. Sir Cat (USA) 118 – Daisy Daisy (IRE) 67 (Dance of Life **96**
(USA)) [2003 74p: 7g³ f7g* 9.9f* 10m⁶ 12d 9.2g⁴ Aug 13] rangy, good-bodied colt:

useful performer: won maiden at Wolverhampton (edged right and unseated rider after line) in April and minor event at Salisbury in June: eye-catching sixth to Leporello in handicap at Newmarket fourth outing: disappointing last 2 starts, finding little in visor final one: stays 1¼m: acts on fibresand and firm going. *L. M. Cumani*

STEELY DAN 4 b.g. Danzig Connection (USA) – No Comebacks 70 (Last Tycoon 131) [2003 68, a82: f7g p8g 10m 9.7m 8.1g 6m⁵ Aug 14] strong gelding: fairly useful handicapper at 3 yrs, well held in 2003: sometimes carries head high/hangs right. *J. R. Best* –

STEENBERG (IRE) 4 ch.g. Flying Spur (AUS) – Kip's Sister (Cawston's Clown 113) [2003 109: 6m⁶ 6g⁵ 6f 6m 9m⁴ 8m⁴ 7m³ 6d⁴ 6f 6d* Nov 8] big, lengthy gelding: smart performer: good never-nearer 3¾ lengths fourth to Somnus in Stanley Leisure Sprint Cup at Haydock eighth start: won 21-runner listed race at Doncaster on final outing by ½ length from Royal Millennium: probably best at 6f/7f: acts on firm and good to soft going: blinkered (well below form) twice: tends to carry head awkwardly/hang right: usually held up. *M. H. Tompkins* **111**

STELLA MARAIS (IRE) 2 b.f. (May 15) Second Empire (IRE) 124 – Karakapa (FR) (Subotica (FR) 131) [2003 7.1m⁴ 6g 7g Nov 1] rather sparely-made filly: first foal: dam unraced out of unraced Irish 1¼m/1½m winner Karikata: modest form in maidens: should stay 1m. *P. R. Chamings* **63**

STELLITE 3 ch.g. Pivotal 124 – Donation (Generous (IRE) 139) [2003 6g 8m 9.2d⁵ 10d Oct 14] 9,000F, 15,000Y: workmanlike gelding: first foal: dam unraced close relative to smart performer up to around 9f in Britain/USA Hal's Pal: poor maiden: likely to prove best short of 1¼m: unraced on extremes of going. *J. S. Goldie* –

STEMAGNUM 4 ch.c. Beveled (USA) – Stemegna (Dance In Time (CAN)) [2003 61: 7g 6d 6f Oct 12] modest maiden: well held in 2003, including when tongue tied. *H. Morrison* –

STEPALONG 2 b.f. (May 3) Piccolo 121 – Saunders Lass 68 (Hillandale 125) [2003 5.1m 6.1d⁶ May 26] eighth foal: sister to 2000 2-y-o 5f winner Piccolo Rose and half-sister to 2 winners, including 1996 2-y-o 5f winner Saunders Wren (by Handsome Sailor): dam selling winner at 6f at 2 yrs and over hurdles: no form in sellers. *Mrs P. N. Dutfield* –

STEPASTRAY 6 gr.g. Alhijaz 122 – Wandering Stranger 69 (Petong 126) [2003 54: f11s² f12s⁶ f12g⁵ 12.4m⁶ 8m⁶ 8g⁴ f8g 10.1m 16m 8m³ 10m* 11m 10.1m 9.9d 10m Oct 4] tall gelding: modest handicapper: won maiden at Redcar in August: effective at 1m to 1½m: acts on fibresand and firm ground, probably on soft: tried in headgear. *R. E. Barr* **56**

STEPHANO 2 ch.c. (Feb 4) Efisio 120 – Polo 83 (Warning 136) [2003 6m⁵ 7m Aug 5] workmanlike colt: first foal: dam, 1¼m winner, out of sister to Prix du Jockey Club winner Polytain: much better effort (fair form) when fifth to Fokine in minor event at Newmarket: odds on for maiden at Catterick month later: suffered sore shins after: should stay at least 1m. *B. W. Hills* **79**

STEPPENWOLF 2 gr.c. (May 6) Sesaro (USA) 81 – Lozzie (Siberian Express (USA) 125) [2003 6m 6f 8g 10d Oct 31] 1,000Y: close-coupled colt: second foal: dam unraced half-sister to high-class middle-distance colt Raami: well beaten in maidens. *W. de Best-Turner* –

STEP PERFECT (USA) 2 b.g. (May 21) Royal Academy (USA) 130 – Gossiping (USA) (Chati (USA)) [2003 8m⁶ 10.2f⁶ 8.2m⁵ Oct 28] rangy, angular gelding: brother to 3-y-o Wondrous Story, closely related to a winner in USA, and half-brother to several winners, including 1991 2-y-o 6f/7f winner and Fred Darling Stakes winner Musicale (by The Minstrel) and smart 1½m performer Theatre Script (by Theatrical): dam, 6f winner in USA, half-sister to high-class sprinter Committed: green, modest form in maidens: seems to stay 1¼m. *M. Johnston* **57**

STERLING GUARANTEE (USA) 5 b.g. Silver Hawk (USA) 123 – Sterling Pound (USA) (Seeking The Gold (USA)) [2003 7m 8.5m⁶ 12g³ 12d Oct 4] close-coupled gelding: lightly raced: just fair form second and third outings in 2003: barely stays 1½m: unraced on extremes of going. *D. Nicholls* **65**

STEVEDORE (IRE) 2 ch.c. (Apr 6) Docksider (USA) 124 – La Belle Katherine (USA) (Lyphard (USA) 132) [2003 6m 6m² 7g* 7f⁴ Oct 12] 16,000F, 30,000Y: good-topped colt: fourth foal: half-brother to 3-y-o Aventura and 6f winner Criss Cross (by Lahib): dam ran twice in France: fairly useful performer: won maiden at Folkestone in September: creditable fourth in nursery at Goodwood: will probably stay 1m: races up with pace. *B. J. Meehan* **80**

ST FRANCIS WOOD (USA) 2 ch.f. (Feb 23) Irish River (FR) 131 – Francisco **95 p**
Road (USA) (Strawberry Road (AUS) 128) [2003 8g² Nov 1] leggy filly: on weak side at
2 yrs: third foal: sister to 6f winner Abbey Bridge, later successful in USA: dam minor
winner in USA around 1m: 7/1, 4 lengths second of 12 to Spotlight in listed event at
Newmarket, slowly away but running on well despite looking green: will probably stay
1¼m: open to progress, and should win races. *J. Noseda*

ST GEORGE'S GIRL 2 b.f. (Apr 23) Muthahb (IRE) – Nickelodeon (Nickel King **–**
116) [2003 7m 6f f6s Oct 7] big, leggy filly: first foal: dam unraced: well held in seller/
claimers. *J. R. Jenkins*

STILA (IRE) 4 b.f. Desert Style (IRE) 121 – Noorajo (IRE) (Ahonoora 122) [2003 50: **–**
p7g p10g Feb 1] fifth foal (all others by Erins Isle): half-sister to Irish 1½m to 2m winner
Traditionalist: dam placed at 1m in Ireland: lightly-raced maiden: left J. Bolger in Ireland
after final 3-y-o start: well held in 2003. *B. W. Duke*

STILETTO LADY (IRE) 2 b.f. (Apr 16) Daggers Drawn (USA) 114 – Nordic Pride **64**
(Horage 124) [2003 7m 7g⁴ 7s Nov 3] IR 8,500F: lengthy filly: half-sister to 3 winners in
Ireland, including useful 7f (at 2 yrs) to 1¼m winner Identify (by Persian Bold): dam
Irish 2-y-o 6f winner: modest form in maidens: fourth at Epsom: will probably stay 1m.
J. G. Given

STILL SPEEDY (IRE) 6 b.g. Toulon 125 – Gorge (Mount Hagen (FR) 127) [2003 **–**
18f⁶ Jul 19] modest form in bumpers: raced freely and carried head high when well held
in maiden at Warwick. *Noel T. Chance*

STING LIKE A BEE (IRE) 4 b.g. Ali-Royal (IRE) 127 – Hidden Agenda (FR) 55 **63**
(Machiavellian (USA) 123) [2003 70: f9.4g² f9.4g 12g⁵ 10.1m⁵ 12g⁶ 12.1g 12m⁶ 10.1g
Oct 22] rather unfurnished gelding: modest maiden handicapper: barely stays 1½m: acts
on fibresand, good to firm and heavy going: tried tongue tied: won selling hurdle in
November. *J. S. Goldie*

STITCH IN TIME 7 ch.g. Inchinor 119 – Late Matinee 84 (Red Sunset 120) [2003 –, **–**
a69d: f11g p13g f12s⁶ f16.2g Mar 3] big, leggy gelding: fair handicapper at best: soundly
beaten in 2003: tried visored/tongue tied. *G. C. Bravery*

ST IVIAN 3 b.g. Inchinor 119 – Lamarita 92§ (Emarati (USA) 74) [2003 70§, a65§: **77 §**
f6g³ p6g⁶ f6g* 7g f5g 6.1m f5g⁵ 5s² 6.1m³ 5f⁵ 6g⁴ 5m³ 5d⁶ 7f 5m⁶ 5f f6g f6g f5g⁵ f6g*
Dec 26] leggy gelding: fair handicapper: won at Southwell in March and Wolverhampton
(amateur event) in December: stays 6f: acts on fibresand, soft and good to firm going:
usually wears headgear: sometimes slowly away: tends to hang (looked set to win when
swerving violently right and unseating rider fifth start): untrustworthy. *Mrs N. Macauley*

ST JEROME 3 ch.g. Danzig Connection (USA) – Indigo Dawn 78 (Rainbow Quest **63**
(USA) 134) [2003 –: 12.6m³ 18m 13.8m* 16g 14.1f⁵ Aug 20] big, rather angular gelding:
modest performer: won maiden at Catterick in July: stays 1¾m: acts on firm ground.
N. P. Littmoden

ST JUDE 3 b.c. Deploy 131 – Little Nutmeg 38 (Gabitat 119) [2003 6m 8.2m Oct 28] **–**
small colt: third foal: dam lightly-raced sprint maiden: well beaten in maidens. *K. A. Ryan*

STOIC LEADER (IRE) 3 b.g. Danehill Dancer (IRE) 117 – Starlust 79 (Sallust 134) **76**
[2003 57: f6g⁵ 6m³ 5m³ 6m* 5d* 5f² 6m⁴ 5g 6g⁴ f6g 6m⁶ 6g 6m 5f 5.5m⁴ 6f² 5m 5g
6g 6.1m Oct 28] sturdy gelding: fair handicapper: won at Southwell and Hamilton on
consecutive days in May: best at 5f/6f: acts on firm and good to soft ground, well below
form on fibresand. *R. F. Fisher*

STOKESIES BOY 3 b.c. Key of Luck (USA) 126 – Lesley's Fashion 67 (Dominion **–**
123) [2003 8.3m f7g⁵ 7m⁶ 5.7f⁴ Sep 8] fourth foal: half-brother to fairly useful Irish 2000
2-y-o 5f winner Stokesie (by Fumo di Londra): dam 1¼m winner: little form: reluctant to
enter stall second outing, hung left under pressure final one. *J. L. Spearing*

STOKESIES WISH 3 ch.f. Fumo di Londra (IRE) 108 – Jess Rebec 63 (Kala Shikari **67**
125) [2003 57: 5m 6.1m 5.1m 5g³ 5.7f 5.5m³ 5m 5.1g 5m³ 6m³ 5m 6f* 6.1m 6d² Oct 31]
fair performer: won maiden at Goodwood in October: ran well in handicap final outing:
effective at 5f/6f: acts on firm and soft ground: usually races up with pace. *J. L. Spearing*

STOLEN HOURS (USA) 3 b. or br.c. Silver Deputy (CAN) – Fasta (USA) (Seattle **74**
Song (USA) 130) [2003 10m⁴ 11.1g⁶ 10g⁴ 14f³ 12.4g⁴ Oct 22] $90,000Y: good-topped
colt: second foal: half-brother to 4-y-o Theatre: dam, US 1m/9f winner (second in Grade
3 8.5f event), sister to Prix Lupin winner Cudas: fair maiden: should stay 2m: raced only
on good ground or firmer: visored (carried head awkwardly) final start: sold 26,000 gns.
E. A. L. Dunlop

STOLEN SONG   3 b.g. Sheikh Albadou 128 – Sparky's Song 63 (Electric 126) [2003 **67**
73, a62: 7d 7.1m 7f⁴ 10m 10m³ p10g³ 10m⁵ f12s² Oct 21] good-topped gelding: fair **a64**
maiden: stays 1½m: acts on all-weather and firm ground, showed promise on soft: tried
in headgear. *M. J. Ryan*

STONEGRAVE   4 ch.f. Selkirk (USA) 129 – Queen Midas 119 (Glint of Gold 128) **52**
[2003 57: 11.9m⁵ 17.5m⁶ 14.1m Oct 4] modest maiden handicapper: may prove best at
1½m: acts on soft and good to firm going: blinkered (ran poorly) final start.
M. W. Easterby

STONOR LADY (USA)   2 b. or br.f. (Feb 19) French Deputy (USA) 118 – Blush **57**
With Love (USA) (Mt Livermore (USA)) [2003 6g p7g² p7g f8s⁶ Dec 27] $12,000F,
32,000Y: smallish filly: first foal: dam, ran twice in USA, half-sister to smart French 1¼m
performer Tuesday's Special: modest maiden: left B. Meehan after second in claimer at
Lingfield, best effort: slowly away final start: should stay 1m. *P. W. D'Arcy*

STOOP TO CONQUER   3 b.g. Polar Falcon (USA) 126 – Princess Genista 108 (Ile **78**
de Bourbon (USA) 133) [2003 10m 10.1d⁵ 12g³ 16g⁵ 16.5d⁶ Nov 8] leggy, lengthy
gelding: closely related to 7f/1m winner Sovinista and 1995 2-y-o 7f winner Tsarnista
(both useful, by Soviet Star) and half-brother to 3 winners, including smart 1¾m to 2½m
winner Give Notice (by Warning): dam, 1m (including at 2 yrs) winner, stayed 15f: fairly
useful maiden, lightly raced: off 3½ months, best effort when fifth to Misternando in
handicap at Newbury fourth start: slowly away final outing: stays 2m. *J. L. Dunlop*

STOP THE NONSENSE (IRE)   2 b.c. (Apr 30) Orpen (USA) 116 – Skip The Non-   **–**
sense (IRE) (Astronef 116) [2003 8m 8.1g 8m Oct 1] IR 7,000F, €4,500Y: leggy colt:
sixth foal: half-brother to winners in Italy by Taufan and Sri Pekan: dam unraced: signs of
only a little ability in maidens. *E. J. O'Neill*

STOPWATCH (IRE)   8 b.g. Lead On Time (USA) 123 – Rose Bonbon (FR) (High Top   **–**
131) [2003 –, a41: 11.9f Apr 10] poor performer: well beaten only 8-y-o start.
Mrs L. C. Jewell

STORM CLEAR (IRE)   4 b.c. Mujadil (USA) 119 – Escape Path (Wolver Hollow **61**
126) [2003 78: 8.2g⁴ 8.5m⁶ 8m 7.1g 8.3m 8f⁵ 8m Aug 18] tall, good sort: modest maiden
handicapper: stays 1m: acts on firm and good to soft going: sometimes finds little: often
makes running. *R. Hannon*

STORM CLOUDS   2 gr.c. (Apr 11) Cloudings (IRE) 112 – Khalsheva 55 (Shirley   **–**
Heights 130) [2003 7m 9f⁵ Sep 15] fourth foal: brother to 3-y-o Grey Clouds and half-
brother to 5-y-o Moyeala and 4-y-o Red To Violet: dam lightly-raced maiden who should
have stayed well: soundly beaten in maidens at Chester and Redcar. *T. D. Easterby*

STORMING HOME   5 b.h. Machiavellian (USA) 123 – Try To Catch Me (USA) **125**
(Shareef Dancer (USA) 135) [2003 125: 12f⁵ 10f* 10g4 10f* 12f Oct 25] leggy, close-
coupled horse: had a fluent, round action: high-class performer: won Champion Stakes at
Newmarket for B. Hills at 4 yrs: first past post in 2003 in very valuable non-graded event
(by 2 lengths from Denon) and Charles Whittingham Handicap (beat Mister Acpen by ¾
length), both at Hollywood, Arlington Million (demoted to fourth after beating Sulamani
by ½ length, ducking badly right near finish and unseating rider after line) and Clement
L. Hirsch Memorial Turf Championship at Santa Anita (by ½ length from Johar):
below-form seventh to High Chaparral and Johar in Breeders' Cup Turf at Santa Anita
final outing (reportedly injured heel): was effective at 1¼m/1½m: acted on firm and soft
going: wore cheekpieces/blinkers last 8 outings: held up: to stand at Nunnery Stud,
Thetford, Norfolk, fee £10,000, special live foal. *N. D. Drysdale, USA*

STORMING STAR (ITY)   3 b.f. Shantung (USA) 125 – Somalia (FR) (Formidable   **?**
(USA) 125) [2003 78p: 10m⁶ 10g 8m⁵ 7.5m* 9d⁴ 7.5d⁵ a9.8g⁵ Dec 8] workmanlike filly:
has a round action: fair performer: tailed off in minor event at Newbury on reappearance
on only outing in Britain: left C. Wall after next start: won minor event at Florence in
October: stays 1¼m: acts on soft and good to firm ground. *V. Valiani, Italy*

STORMONT (IRE)   3 gr.c. Marju (IRE) 127 – Legal Steps (IRE) (Law Society (USA) **116**
130) [2003 93p: 6m 6m 6f² 6m 6m⁶ 6m³ 6m* 6m Oct 17] leggy, good-topped colt: smart
performer: reportedly had chip removed from joint during winter: much improved form
to win Fahrhof Goldene Peitsche at Baden-Baden in September by 1½ lengths from
Soave, leading 2f out: dictated pace when creditable 4 lengths seventh to Ashdown
Express in Bentinck Stakes at Newmarket final start: should be just as effective at 5f as
6f: acts on polytrack and firm going, probably on good to soft. *H. J. Collingridge*

STORM SHOWER (IRE)   5 b.g. Catrail (USA) 123 – Crimson Shower 61 (Dowsing   **– §**
(USA) 124) [2003 –§, a56§: 7s⁶ f7s f8.5g² f7s⁵ f8.5s f8g⁶ f7s f7g³ f8.5g f8g Nov 24] **a51 §**

good-topped gelding: modest handicapper: stays 9.4f: acts on fibresand, little form on turf: usually visored: sometimes starts slowly/pulls hard: ungenuine. *Mrs N. Macauley*

STORMVILLE (IRE) 6 b.g. Catrail (USA) 123 – Haut Volee (Top Ville 129) [2003 70, a?: 7m Apr 21] sparely-made gelding: fair handicapper in 2002: well held only 6-y-o start. *M. Brittain* —

STORM WIZARD (IRE) 6 b.g. Catrail (USA) 123 – Society Ball 72 (Law Society (USA) 130) [2003 f16.2s Apr 12] workmanlike gelding: fairly useful maiden at best at 3 yrs: blinkered, pulled up on first Flat outing since: has reportedly bled. *D. G. Bridgwater* —

STORMY DAY 3 b.f. Rainbow Quest (USA) 134 – Broken Peace (USA) (Devil's Bag (USA)) [2003 8m⁶ 8s Jul 27] tall, good-topped filly: fifth foal: half-sister to 3 winners abroad, including useful French miler Riverse Angle (by Spinning World): dam French 1m winner (including at 2 yrs): poor form in maidens at Newmarket and Ascot. *M. A. Jarvis* —

STORMY NATURE (IRE) 2 b. or br.f. (Apr 29) Mujadil (USA) 119 – Ossana (USA) (Tejano (USA)) [2003 6m⁴ 5d² 6g Jul 31] €28,000Y: rather leggy, lengthy filly: third foal: sister to fairly useful 2001 2-y-o 6f winner Ocean Sound (later showed smart form in USA at 9f): dam 2-y-o 5f winner in Germany and winning jumper in France: fair form in maidens: strong-finishing second at Pontefract: hampered final start: will prove better at 6f than 5f. *P. W. Harris* 74

STORMY RAINBOW 6 b.g. Red Rainbow 105 – Stormy Heights 62 (Golden Heights 82) [2003 –: p10g 8.1m 10d 10m 11.6g p12g 9.9m 10.9m Sep 8] little form since 2001. *M. Blanshard* —

STORMY SKYE (IRE) 7 b.g. Bluebird (USA) 125 – Canna (Caerleon (USA) 132) [2003 16m Sep 25] angular gelding: fair performer in 2001: unraced on Flat in 2002, and tailed off only 7-y-o start: usually blinkered/tongue tied. *G. L. Moore* – §

ST PANCRAS (IRE) 3 b.c. Danehill Dancer (IRE) 117 – Lauretta Blue (IRE) (Bluebird (USA) 125) [2003 104p: 7g⁵ 9.2m⁴ 6m⁵ 7m⁶ Sep 25] big, good-topped colt: useful performer at 2 yrs: little solid form in minor events/Group 3 contest in 2003. *N. A. Callaghan* —

ST PETERSBURG 3 ch.g. Polar Falcon (USA) 126 – First Law 57 (Primo Dominie 121) [2003 79: 7d 7g p7g* p7g p7g f7g³ 8g* p7g⁵ Oct 30] strong, lengthy gelding: useful handicapper: won at Lingfield in September and Redcar (best effort, beat Reap by 5 lengths) in October: stays 1m: acts on all-weather, raced only on good ground or softer on turf. *M. H. Tompkins* 96

STRACOMER THALIA (IRE) 5 b.m. Mujadil (USA) 119 – Peach Melba 96 (So Blessed 130) [2003 –: f8g f7s p12g Feb 15] IR 9,000Y: half-sister to several winners, including useful winner up to 9.4f Reported (by Heraldiste): dam 2-y-o 5f winner: little form: left R. McGlinchey in Ireland before reappearance. *Ian Williams* —

STRACOMER URANIA (IRE) 5 gr.m. Paris House 123 – Pheopotstown (Henbit (USA) 130) [2003 –: f12g f12g Jan 27] little form: tried blinkered. *Ian Williams* —

STRAIGHT EIGHT 4 b.g. Octagonal (NZ) 126 – Kalymnia (GER) (Mondrian (GER) 125) [2003 –: a12g⁵ a9.5g 9g 7s 12d Nov 4] big, lengthy gelding: little form: trained by R. Pritchard-Gordon in France first four 4-y-o starts: dead. *T. D. Easterby* —

STRAIGHTEN UP (IRE) 2 b.f. (Mar 8) Nashwan (USA) 135 – Alignment (IRE) 98 (Alzao (USA) 117) [2003 7g Nov 1] second foal: dam, headstrong maiden (fourth in Musidora Stakes), half-sister to smart performer up to 14.6f Bonny Scot and to dam of Golan, out of half-sister to Prix du Cadran winner Sought Out: 11/1, very green when well held in maiden at Newmarket: will do better at 1¼m+. *Sir Michael Stoute* – p

STRANGE (IRE) 5 b.g. Alzao (USA) 117 – Partie de Dames (USA) (Bering 136) [2003 46: f12s Jan 14] poor maiden: well beaten only 5-y-o start: tongue tied: dead. *E. J. O'Neill* —

STRANGELY BROWN (IRE) 2 b.g. (Mar 3) Second Empire (IRE) 124 – Damerela (IRE) (Alzao (USA) 117) [2003 6g 5.1m Oct 28] 13,000Y: sturdy gelding: fourth foal: half-brother to 3 winners, including 4-y-o Gallant Boy and fairly useful Irish 1½m to 2m winner Cincuenta (by Bob Back): dam, French maiden, half-sister to dam of Daylami and 3-y-o Dalakhani: signs of a little ability in maidens at Windsor (slowly away) and Nottingham: bred to stay at least 1m: will probably do better. *S. C. Williams* – p

STRATEGY 3 br.f. Machiavellian (USA) 123 – Island Story 88 (Shirley Heights 130) [2003 10g³ 11.8m⁴ 10.9m* 10.3m⁶ 10g* 10m² 10m³ Aug 27] quite good-topped filly: 92

first foal: dam, 1¼m winner who stayed 2m, half-sister to smart winner up to 1½m Arabian Story, out of sister to smart 1¼m performer Starlet: fairly useful performer: won maiden at Warwick in June and handicap at Nottingham in August: good efforts in handicaps at Sandown and Ascot (third to Weecandoo) last 2 starts: stays 1¼m (raced freely over 1½m): raced only on good/good to firm ground: sold 35,000 gns in December. *Sir Michael Stoute*

STRATHCLYDE (IRE)   4 b.g. Petong 126 – It's Academic 73 (Royal Academy   **91** (USA) 130) [2003 87: 6m² 6m 6g³ 5g 6f 5f* 5.2m 5.2m⁵ 6m 6m 6m 5f 5g Oct 11] good-topped gelding: fairly useful handicapper: won at Ascot in July by short head from Connect: best at 5f: acts on firm ground, good to soft and polytrack: free-going sort: usually races prominently: joined J. Best. *J. Cullinan*

STRATH FILLAN   5 b.m. Dolphin Street (FR) 125 – Adarama (IRE) (Persian Bold   **–** 123) [2003 49: 11.9m 19.1m 9f Jul 2] small mare: poor performer: well held in 2003. *H. J. Collingridge*

STRATHSPEY   4 ch.f. Dancing Spree (USA) – Diebiedale 58 (Dominion 123) [2003   **76** 75: 8g⁵ 9f³ 9f⁴ 9.9m² 10f³ 8m⁴ Sep 22] sturdy filly: fair handicapper: barely stays 1¼m: acts on firm going: gave trouble to post/behind stall fifth outing: consistent. *C. F. Wall*

STRAVMOUR   7 ch.h. Seymour Hicks (FR) 125 – La Stravaganza 74 (Slip Anchor   **54** 136) [2003 10g⁵ 10m f12s f12s⁶ 10.1g f11g⁴ f14g³ f12s* Dec 27] big, lengthy horse: third foal: half-brother to 7f/1m winner Stravsea (by Handsome Sailor): dam, maiden, stayed 1¼m: well held in bumpers: modest handicapper on Flat: won at Southwell in December: stays 1¾m: raced only on fibresand and good/good to firm ground. *R. Hollinshead*

STRAW BEAR (USA)   2 ch.c. (Mar 14) Diesis 133 – Highland Ceilidh (IRE) 100   **83** (Scottish Reel 123) [2003 f6g⁵ f6s² 7.5m⁷ f8.5s* Sep 6] 25,000Y: brother to 1½m winner Carioca Dream and half-brother to 3 winners, including fairly useful 2002 2-y-o 7.5f/1m winner Cranshaws (by Green Dancer): dam, 1m (at 2 yrs)/1¼m winner, from family of Halling (by Diesis): fairly useful performer: won minor event at Wolverhampton by short head from Countrywide Flyer: likely to stay 1¼m. *Sir Mark Prescott*

STRAWBERRY DAWN   5 gr.m. Fayruz 116 – Alasib 93 (Siberian Express (USA)   **54** 125) [2003 –: f5g² f5s⁵ p5g* f5s f5s* f5g 5g² f5g⁵ f5g 5.7m May 6] modest performer: won maiden at Lingfield and handicap at Southwell in February: raced mainly at 5f: acts on all-weather and firm ground: usually races prominently. *J. R. Boyle*

STRAWBERRY FAIR   2 b.f. (Feb 24) Kingmambo (USA) 125 – Storm Song (USA)   **75 p** 123 (Summer Squall (USA)) [2003 8m² Sep 23] compact, attractive filly: third foal: closely related to US 2001 2-y-o winner by Gone West: dam won Breeders' Cup Juvenile Fillies: favourite, 1¼ lengths second of 11 to Proud Tradition in maiden at Newmarket, green under strong pressure: joined Saeed bin Suroor: will probably improve. *D. R. Loder*

STRAWBERRY PATCH (IRE)   4 b.g. Woodborough (USA) 112 – Okino (USA)   **71** (Strawberry Road (AUS) 128) [2003 63: 6g 6m 5g⁶ 6f 5g Jul 1] strong, good-topped gelding: fair handicapper: effective at 5f/6f: acts on firm and good to soft going: wore cheekpieces last 3 starts. *Miss L. A. Perratt*

STRAW BOSS (IRE)   3 b.g. Darshaan 133 – Ezana (Ela-Mana-Mou 132) [2003 p12g³   **74** 14f⁴ Oct 12] 125,000F, 2,100,000 francs Y, 75,000 2-y-o: brother to smart Irish 7f (at 2 yrs) to 1½m winner Ebaziya (dam of 3 Group 1 winners, including Gold Cup winner Enzeli) and half-brother to 3 winners, including fairly useful Irish 1½m winner Erzadjan (by Kahyasi): dam French 11.5f winner: fair form in maidens at Lingfield and Goodwood (hung left and found little). *Mrs A. J. Perrett*

STRAW POLL (USA)   2 ch.c. (Apr 29) Dixieland Band (USA) – Golden Opinion   **84** (USA) 127 (Slew O' Gold (USA)) [2003 5d* 6.1g³ 5.1m² 5.1m³ Jul 11] leggy colt: closely related to useful 7f winner Meiosis (by Danzig) and 2 winners by Sadler's Wells and half-brother to 2 winners by Rahy, including 3-y-o Excellento: dam won Coronation Stakes and second in July Cup: fairly useful performer: won maiden at Newcastle in March: stays 6f: acts on good to firm and good to soft ground: sold 20,000 gns, sent to USA. *M. R. Channon*

STREAKY (IRE)   3 b.f. Danetime (IRE) 121 – Solo Symphony (IRE) 67 (Fayruz 116)   **–** [2003 63: 5.7g 5.7f 5g Jun 21] smallish, sturdy filly: modest performer at 2 yrs: well held in 2003. *Mrs P. N. Dutfield*

STREET GAMES   4 b.g. Mind Games 121 – Pusey Street 96 (Native Bazaar 122)   **–** [2003 –: 7.1m 8.2g Jun 23] no form: tried tongue tied. *J. Gallagher*

STREET LIFE (IRE)   5 ch.g. Dolphin Street (FR) 125 – Wolf Cleugh (IRE) 65 (Last   **76**
Tycoon 131) [2003 85: p12g⁶ p12g³ p12g p10g 10g 10m p10g⁶ Dec 10] tall gelding: fair
handicapper: stays easy 1½m: acts on polytrack, best turf form on good going or softer:
usually held up: sometimes edges left. *W. J. Musson*

ST REGS (IRE)   2 b.c. (May 13) Sri Pekan (USA) 117 – Young Isabel (IRE) (Last   **82**
Tycoon 131) [2003 6d⁴ 6m² 5m² 5d⁶ 6.1m* Sep 8] €6,000Y, 18,000 2-y-o: good-topped
colt: fourth foal: half-brother to 7f/1m winner (including at 2 yrs) Church Farm Flyer (by
College Chapel): dam placed in Italy: fairly useful performer: won nursery at Warwick
by short head, rallying to lead again close home: should stay 7f, probably 1m: acts on
good to firm ground: sold 44,000 gns, sent to USA. *R. Hannon*

STRENGTH 'N HONOUR   3 b.g. Hernando (FR) 127 – Seasonal Splendour (IRE)   **104**
95 (Prince Rupert (FR) 121) [2003 85: p12g* 10m* 10m³ 12m 12f⁵ 14.8m Jul 9] strong,
workmanlike gelding: useful performer: won maiden at Lingfield in March and minor
event at Newbury (beat Hilbre Island by 1¼ lengths) in April: creditable efforts after
when 1¼ lengths third to Shield in Classic Trial at Sandown and 6 lengths fifth to High
Accolade in King Edward VII Stakes at Royal Ascot (wore crossed noseband): well held
in Derby at Epsom in between: bred to be suited by 1¾m+ (pulled hard when tried): acts
on polytrack, raced only on firm/good to firm going on turf: gelded after final outing.
C. A. Cyzer

STRENSALL   6 b.g. Beveled (USA) – Payvashooz 78 (Ballacashtal (CAN)) [2003 71,   **86**
a60+: f5s⁶ f5g 5m² 5f² 5m 5g⁴ 5m 5d³ 5g³ 5m³ 5f² 5m 5m³ 5m 5m³ 5d* 5.1m² 5g 5d⁶ 5d   **a67**
5f 5m* 5s⁴ f5g² f5g Dec 12] leggy gelding: fairly useful handicapper on turf, fair on
all-weather: won at Newcastle in July and Catterick in October: best at 5f: acts on firm
ground, soft and fibresand: sometimes slowly away: often races prominently: tough.
R. E. Barr

STRETTON (IRE)   5 br.g. Doyoun 124 – Awayil (USA) 82 (Woodman (USA) 126)   **88**
[2003 93: a10g 8.9f⁶ 10.1m⁴ 7.9m⁴ 10.3m 9.9m³ 9m³ 10.4f* 9g Oct 25] leggy,
close-coupled gelding: fairly useful handicapper: consistent in 2003, won at York
in October: effective at 1m to 10.4f: unraced on heavy going, acts on any other turf
(below form both outings on fibresand): has run respectably when sweating: held up.
J. D. Bethell

STREYZA (IRE)   6 b.m. Shernazar 131 – Millzao (Alzao (USA) 117) [2003 32: 9.7g   **–**
8m 10m May 14] fifth foal: dam well beaten in Ireland: modest performer: won maiden at
Tralee on debut at 3 yrs: left F. Keogh in Ireland, no form in Britain in 2003. *J. R. Jenkins*

STRICTLY SPEAKING (IRE)   6 b.g. Sri Pekan (USA) 117 – Gaijin 97 (Caerleon   **–**
(USA) 132) [2003 55, a63: f16.2g f11g³ f12g³ p12g f14.8g² Jun 30] tall gelding: modest   **a61**
performer: stays 14.8f: acts on fibresand, firm and soft going: effective blinkered or not:
sometimes goes in snatches/finds little: none too consistent. *P. F. I. Cole*

STRIDENT (USA)   2 ch.c. (Feb 6) Deputy Commander (USA) 124 – Regrets Only   **56**
(USA) (Black Tie Affair 128) [2003 5m⁶ May 26] $105,000Y: second foal: dam, 2-y-o
sprint winner in USA, half-sister to US Grade 1 winner Lemhi Go: sixth of 10 in
maiden at Leicester, slowly away. *G. A. Butler*

STRIDER   2 ch.c. (Feb 9) Pivotal 124 – Sahara Belle (USA) (Sanglamore (USA) 126)   **70 p**
[2003 7m 7m Oct 24] 32,000F, 170,000Y: good-topped colt: second foal: dam, 1m/11.5f
winner in Norway, half-sister to very smart 1½m winner Perfect Sunday out of half-sister
to US Grade 1 winners Bates Motel (at 1m to 1¼m) and Hatim (at 9f): better effort in
maidens (fair form) when seventh of 16 to Alekhine at Doncaster, still backward but some
late headway: will stay 1m: open to progress. *Sir Michael Stoute*

STRIKE LUCKY   3 ch.g. Millkom 124 – Lucky Flinders 77 (Free State 125) [2003   **64 ?**
7m⁴ 9m p7g Dec 29] 13,500Y: good-topped gelding: eighth foal: closely related to 5-y-o
Pomfret Lad and half-brother to 2 winners: dam, 1m winner, sister to smart Italian winner
up to 1m Melbury Lad: seemingly modest form when fourth in maiden at Newmarket:
well beaten in similar events after. *P. J. Makin*

STRIKING AMBITION   3 b. or br.c. Makbul 104 – Lady Roxanne 65 (Cyrano de   **114**
Bergerac 120) [2003 105p: p8g³ 6g* 6m* 6m 6s 5s Oct 5] rather unfurnished, useful-
looking colt: smart performer: beat Avonbridge when winning listed races at Ascot (by
length) in April and Newbury (by head, rallying splendidly) in May: well held after in
July Cup at Newmarket, Prix de Meautry at Deauville and Prix de l'Abbaye at Longchamp: will prove best at 6f/7f: acts on heavy and good to firm going: usually races
prominently. *G. C. Bravery*

STRIPTEASE 2 b.f. (May 7) Mind Games 121 – Kalymnia (GER) (Mondrian (GER) 125) [2003 5m⁴ 6f Jun 13] fourth foal: half-sister to winner abroad by Highest Honor: dam, German 1½m winner, half-sister to Derby Italiano winner Kallisto: well held in maiden at Leicester and seller at York. *T. D. Easterby* –

STRONG HAND 3 b.f. First Trump 118 – Better Still (IRE) (Glenstal (USA) 118) [2003 78: 8m f6g⁵ 7.5m³ 8.3g* 8.5d³ 8.5m³ f7g⁵ f9.4g* f9.4g* f9.4s Dec 31] big, lengthy, heavy-topped filly: useful handicapper on all-weather, fairly useful on turf: won at Hamilton in June and twice at Wolverhampton in November, best effort when beating Mi Odds by ½ length for final success: stays 9.4f: acts on fibresand, yet to race on extremes of going on turf. *M. W. Easterby* **85 a99**

STRONG WILL 3 b.g. Primo Dominie 121 – Reine de Thebes (FR) 67 (Darshaan 133) [2003 63: 8m⁵ 7m 7m 10m 12.1m³ 16.2m Aug 14] leggy gelding: shows knee action: modest maiden handicapper: stays 1½m: acts on firm ground. *C. W. Fairhurst* **53**

ST SAVARIN (FR) 2 ch.g. (Mar 17) Highest Honor (FR) 124 – Sacara (GER) (Monsagem (USA) 117) [2003 5.1m⁵ 5m 5g 5m 6m p6g² 6m⁶ 7d* p8g f8s⁵ p7g* Dec 29] €16,000Y, resold 15,000Y, 21,000 2-y-o: workmanlike gelding: first foal: dam useful German 7.5f/1m winner: fair performer: won maiden at Catterick in November and nursery at Lingfield in December: stays 7f: acts on polytrack, good to firm and good to soft ground: reared as stall opened fourth/fifth outings. *J. R. Best* **72**

ST TROPEZ (IRE) 2 b.f. (Mar 13) Revoque (IRE) 122 – Kaziranga (USA) 69 (Lear Fan (USA) 130) [2003 p7g 8.2f Sep 30] €10,000Y: sturdy filly: second foal: dam, maiden who should have stayed 1¼m, out of German 1000 Guineas winner Kazoo: last in maidens at Lingfield and Nottingham (strong hold). *B. G. Powell* –

Mr Peter Webb's "Striking Ambition"

STUDMASTER   3 ch.g. Snurge 130 – Danlu (USA) (Danzig (USA)) [2003 10d 12.1d   **72**
11.8m⁶ f12g 18m⁵ 16m Sep 5] strong, good-bodied gelding: half-brother to several
winners, notably very smart middle-distance stayer Strategic Choice (by Alleged) and
useful 1m/1¼m winner Sure Dancer (by Affirmed): dam, probably stayed 1¼m in
Ireland, sister to smart 6f/7f performer Nicholas: fair maiden: stays 2¼m: acts on good to
firm ground: sold 7,500 gns. *P. F. I. Cole*

STUNNING FORCE (IRE)   4 b.c. Ezzoud (IRE) 126 – New Wind (GER) (Wind-   **98**
wurf (GER)) [2003 11.6g 12m* 11.9m* 12.1d⁴ 12g⁴ May 24] good-bodied colt: useful
performer: won handicaps at Catterick in April and Brighton in May: creditable fourth in
listed rated stakes at Hamilton and minor event at Newmarket last 2 starts: will stay 1¾m:
acts on good to firm and good to soft ground: tends to wander: sold only 4,500 gns.
M. Johnston

STUNNING MAGIC   3 b.g. Magic Ring (IRE) 115 – Absolutelystunning 63 (Aragon   **–**
118) [2003 –: 8.2g f7s Sep 26] well beaten in maidens. *Mrs Barbara Waring*

STUTTER   5 ch.h. Polish Precedent (USA) 131 – Bright Spells 93 (Salse (USA) 128)   **–**
[2003 56: 8m Sep 18] good-topped horse: modest maiden: lightly raced: well held in
seller only 5-y-o start. *J. G. Carr, Ireland*

STYLE DANCER (IRE)   9 b.g. Dancing Dissident (USA) 119 – Showing Style (Pas   **72**
de Seul 133) [2003 84, a72: 8.1m⁶ 7.9m 8f 7.9m 8d 9g 9.9m⁴ 9f⁴ 10.4m⁶ 10.9m 10m Oct
4] good-topped gelding: good mover: fair handicapper: stays 10.4f: acts on all-weather,
possibly best on good ground or firmer on turf: tried in headgear: free-going sort: usually
held up. *T. D. Easterby*

STYLISH PRINCE   3 b.g. Polar Prince (IRE) 117 – Simply Style (Bairn (USA) 126)   **–**
[2003 56: 8.1m 12.1d Jul 25] modest performer at 2 yrs: well beaten in 2003: tried
visored. *J. G. M. O'Shea*

STYLISH SUNRISE (IRE)   2 b.g. (Mar 8) Desert Style (IRE) 121 – Anita At Dawn   **76**
(IRE) 77 (Anita's Prince 126) [2003 8m 7.9f³ 8.2d⁶ Nov 6] IR 26,000F, 55,000Y: lengthy
gelding: first foal: dam, 6f (at 2 yrs)/7f winner, half-sister to dam of smart miler Bachir
(by Desert Style): best effort in maidens (fair form) when third to Putra Sas at York: not
sure to stay much beyond 1m: raced prominently last 2 starts. *M. L. W. Bell*

SUALDA (IRE)   4 b.g. Idris (IRE) 118 – Winning Heart 98 (Horage 124) [2003 78:   **75**
8m 9.3g 9m⁴ 9.9m 10m 12g* 12.1m⁵ 11.9f 12.3m⁵ 11.9m 11.9f Oct 9] unfurnished
gelding: fair handicapper: won at Doncaster in July: races freely, but stays 1½m: best
form on good going or firmer: tried in blinkers/cheekpieces/tongue tie: usually held up.
R. A. Fahey

SUAVE PERFORMER   6 b.g. Suave Dancer (USA) 136 – Francia 59 (Legend of   **52**
France (USA) 124) [2003 59, a50: 10m 10.1g⁵ 9m 9.9m 9g Jul 3] neat gelding: modest   **a–**
handicapper: effective at 9f/1¼m: has form on fibresand and good to firm going, goes
well on softer than good: sometimes races freely, and best patiently ridden. *S. C. Williams*

SUAVE QUARTET (USA)   2 b.g. (Mar 7) Slew City Slew (USA) – Leallah M (USA)   **75**
(Big Spruce (USA)) [2003 7m⁶ p8g² p8g² Nov 26] $4,500Y, 24,000 2-y-o: attractive colt:
seventh foal: half-brother to 3 winners in USA: dam ran twice in USA: fair form in
maidens: second twice at Lingfield: will probably stay 1¼m. *G. A. Butler*

SUBADAR MAJOR   6 b.g. Komaite (USA) – Rather Gorgeous 37§ (Billion (USA)   **–**
120) [2003 35, a–: 12f 14.1m 12.1m 12.3g Aug 29] big gelding: no longer of any account.
Mrs G. S. Rees

SUBLIMITY (FR)   3 b.c. Selkirk (USA) 129 – Fig Tree Drive (USA) 94 (Miswaki   **109 p**
(USA) 124) [2003 7g⁴ 7.9m* 8m* 10m⁴ 8g⁴ Nov 1] 210,000Y: big, strong, lengthy colt:
second foal: dam, 2-y-o 6f winner (her only start), out of sister to US Grade 1 winners De
La Rose (9f) and Upper Nile (1¼m): useful form, lightly raced: won maiden at York and
minor event at Newmarket (beat Adekshan a length, idling) in May: best effort when 3¼
lengths fourth to Persian Majesty in listed event at Royal Ascot next time: off 4½ months
before below-form fourth to Babodana in similar race at Newmarket final outing: effective at 1m/1¼m: raced only on good/good to firm ground: has worn crossed noseband:
tongue tied after debut (hung badly left/reportedly coughed): has plenty of scope, and
remains the type to improve further at 4 yrs. *Sir Michael Stoute*

SUBTLE MOVE (USA)   3 b.f. Known Fact (USA) 135 – Substance (USA) (Diesis   **60 d**
133) [2003 8g⁴ 7.1m 6d³ 6d 7m 6m 8g f6g f8g f8g p7g f6s Dec 27] angular, quite
good-topped filly: fourth living foal: half-sister to 5-y-o Demonstrate and fairly useful 9f/
1¼m winner Moratorium (by El Gran Senor): dam unraced half-sister to Ribblesdale

Stakes winner Ballinderry, herself dam of Sanglamore: modest maiden: left J. Gosden 23,000 gns after third start: no form for new stable: should be suited by 7f+: yet to race on extremes of going: tried visored. *D. Shaw*

SUCHWOT (IRE)   2 b.g. (Apr 29) Intikhab (USA) 135 – Fairy Water 88 (Warning 136) [2003 6d⁶ 6f 7.1m Sep 20] €17,000Y, 16,000 2-y-o: workmanlike gelding: fourth foal: dam Irish 1m winner: best effort in maidens (modest form) when sixth at Leicester: should stay 1m. *F. Jordan*   **56**

SUDDEN FLIGHT (IRE)   6 b.g. In The Wings 128 – Ma Petite Cherie (USA) 93 (Caro 133) [2003 80: p12g f11s* p12g³ f11g² f14s p13g 12.3m 14m⁶ 14g⁶ 12d 11.6g 11.9d* f14g Dec 9] close-coupled gelding: unimpressive mover: fairly useful handicapper: won at Southwell in January and Haydock in September: stays 1¾m: acts on any turf ground and all-weather: tried visored, not in 2003: tends to wander/carry head awkwardly: often makes running. *R. Ingram*   **78 + a87**

SUDRA   6 b.g. Indian Ridge 123 – Bunting 102 (Shaadi (USA) 126) [2003 –, a61: f8s* p8g f8s p8g³ p8g⁵ p10g f8g⁶ f7s² f8.5g² f7g⁴ f7g⁴ f8.5g* f8.5s² f8.5g f8s⁵ 8.5m f9.4g f8s f7g f8g Dec 19] smallish gelding: fair on all-weather, poor on turf: won seller at Southwell in January and (having left C. Dwyer after seventh start) handicap at Wolverhampton in June: stays 8.5f: acts on all-weather and firm going: usually wears cheekpieces: has high head carriage: none too reliable. *J. O'Reilly*   **– a72**

SUE ALLEN (IRE)   3 b.f. Pennekamp (USA) 130 – Jambo Jambo (IRE) (Kafu 120) [2003 37: f6g 6d 5f⁵ f5s 5m 6m⁵ Oct 7] lengthy, quite attractive filly: poor maiden: stays 6f: acts on firm ground and fibresand: tried in cheekpieces: has carried head awkwardly. *R. F. Fisher*   **39**

SUERTE   3 b.f. Halling (USA) 133 – Play With Me (IRE) 73 (Alzao (USA) 117) [2003 –: 10s f9.4g⁴ p10g Dec 17] rather leggy filly: modest maiden, lightly raced: stays 1¼m: acts on soft ground and fibresand. *J. G. Given*   **55**

SUGARBABE   2 b.f. (Feb 15) Kirkwall 118 – Lightning Legacy (USA) 78 (Super Concorde (USA) 128) [2003 6g 7m 7m³ 7m f8g Nov 25] 2,000Y: sturdy, close-coupled filly: half-sister to several winners, including useful performer up to 1½m Black Monday (by Busted) and fairly useful 5f (at 2 yrs)/6f winner Mrs Malaprop (by Night Shift): dam, maiden, stayed 1m: poor maiden: stays 7f. *M. Blanshard*   **47**

SUGAR CUBE TREAT   7 b.m. Lugana Beach 116 – Fair Eleanor (Saritamer (USA) 130) [2003 f7g f6g f8g Dec 8] small, close-coupled mare: poor performer: well beaten in 2003. *M. Mullineaux*   **–**

SUGAR SNAP   3 b.f. Sesaro (USA) 81 – Cuddle Bunny (IRE) (Statoblest 120) [2003 62: 7m 6.1m 6m Aug 13] modest maiden at 2 yrs: well held in 2003: tried blinkered. *C. Drew*   **–**

SUGGESTIVE   5 b.g. Reprimand 122 – Pleasuring 68 (Good Times (ITY)) [2003 118: 6m⁴ 7g² 7g⁴ 7g⁴ 8m* 8d⁵ Oct 4] big, good sort: smart performer: creditable fourth to Nayyir in Lennox Stakes at Goodwood fourth start: simple task when winning minor event at Musselburgh in September: respectable fifth to Special Kaldoun in Prix Daniel Wildenstein at Longchamp final outing, racing freely: effective at 6f to easy 1m: acts on soft and good to firm going: visored/blinkered: tends to carry head high: best waited with: consistent. *W. J. Haggas*   **114**

SUITCASE MURPHY (IRE)   2 b.g. (Mar 26) Petardia 113 – Noble Rocket (Reprimand 122) [2003 6m 6d f5s 5g f5g⁴ Dec 22] tall gelding: fourth foal: half-brother to 4-y-o Dragon Flyer: dam unraced: poor maiden: likely to prove best at 5f/6f. *Ms Deborah J. Evans*   **49**

SUJOSISE   2 b.c. (Apr 4) Prince Sabo 123 – Statuette 57 (Statoblest 120) [2003 5g 7m 8g Sep 27] 4,000Y: well-grown colt: third foal: dam, 5f winner, ran only at 2 yrs: poor form in maidens: likely to prove best at 5f/6f. *J. J. Quinn*   **48**

SULAMANI (IRE)   4 b.c. Hernando (FR) 127 – Soul Dream (USA) 78 (Alleged (USA) 138) [2003 130: 12g* 12g⁴ 12d² 10g* 12f* 12f⁵ Oct 25]   **128**

If Godolphin's season started with a flourish thanks to Moon Ballad and Sulamani winning the Dubai World Cup and Dubai Sheema Classic, it ended in something of a damp squib with no runners on Arc day, two on Champions Day, two on Breeders' Cup day and only one at the big Hong Kong meeting in December. None of Godolphin's contenders in these events made the frame and, adding injury to insult, Mamool fractured a fetlock when finishing last in the

Melbourne Cup in November. In between, the organisation eventually notched its one hundredth Group 1 or Grade 1 winner, through Sulamani in the Arlington Million in mid-August, though the tally of nine such events for the year, with only one in Britain and one in France, was Godolphin's lowest since 1997. Among the older horses, Grandera and Moon Ballad, who both failed to reach the frame in a total of seven starts after the World Cup, were packed off to stud in Japan in mid-October and Leadership wasn't seen out after July. Sulamani was widely viewed as Godolphin's main hope for races over a mile and a half after being purchased for an undisclosed sum from the Niarchos family in the wake of victory in the Prix du Jockey Club and an unlucky second in the Prix de l'Arc de Triomphe. Sulamani did not quite manage to reproduce his best three-year-old form but he was still Godolphin's most successful performer, also winning the Turf Classic Invitational, and he looks set to continue to be a leading contender for the top prizes as a five-year-old.

Predictably, given his form as well as the expectations attached to him, Sulamani started a warm favourite for the Sheema Classic at Nad Al Sheba in March—chosen in preference to the World Cup—ahead of Ange Gabriel, Califet, Highest, Zindabad, Polish Summer and Boreal. Sulamani won in good style, making ground in the straight after being held up and quickening to lead inside the final furlong, accounting for Ange Gabriel by three quarters of a length, the pair clear of Ekraar and Polish Summer; Highest and Zindabad both suffered interference. By the time Sulamani next appeared, after some unspecified problems, in the Grand Prix de Saint-Cloud at the end of June, Godolphin had reached the ninety-nine mark in Group/Grade 1s through Dubai Destination in the Queen Anne Stakes and Leadership in the Gran Premio di Milano. Reopposed by Ange Gabriel and Polish Summer, Sulamani started at odds on, coupled with Millstreet as pacemaker, but showed no sparkle (and no acceleration) when fifth past the post behind Ange Gabriel, with Polish Summer second and the subsequently demoted Millstreet third. Despite this performance, Sulamani still started third favourite behind Nayef and Kris Kin for the King George VI and Queen Elizabeth Stakes at Ascot four weeks later and bounced back to something like his best, going down by three and a half lengths to Alamshar after moving through early in the straight and being hard driven to try to close on the winner. Sulamani's performance wasn't all praiseworthy: he did not take the eye beforehand, looking lean, and in the race he hung badly right over a furlong out, forcing his jockey almost to stop riding him. Sulamani had hung in the Arc as well.

The decision to bring Sulamani back in distance for the Arlington Million was bold, as he had not been raced over a mile and a quarter since his racecourse debut and had looked for all the world like a colt who required a mile and a half to bring out the best in him. Connections had the additional worry of his bruising a foot in the run-up to the race but Sulamani did them proud, even though—in the

Dubai Sheema Classic, Nad Al Sheba—Sulamani makes a successful start for new connections, beating Ange Gabriel (rail), Ekraar and Polish Summer (almost hidden by runner-up)

Arlington Million Stakes—Sulamani (left) provides Godolphin with its 100th Group/Grade 1 success after first-past-the-post Storming Home's demotion for veering sharply near the finish; Kaieteur (No.9) and Paolini (No.3) have to settle for a share of the minor honours

end—he was a decidedly fortunate winner. A large European-trained contingent of eight for the Arlington Million also included Kaieteur, Olden Times, Paolini and Vangelis, none of them with form on a par with Sulamani's best. The five-strong home defence was headed by ex-British five-year-old Storming Home, winner of the Champion Stakes at four and the Grade 1 Charles Whittingham Handicap on his most recent start, plus The Tin Man, runner-up in the United Nations Handicap, and Perfect Drift, a Grade 1 winner from Mineshaft but seemingly better on dirt than turf. Storming Home started favourite ahead of Sulamani and he should have won. Sulamani finished best of all, after losing his place and coming off the bridle five furlongs out and then racing very wide into the straight, but was clearly held when Storming Home spooked at something a few yards from the winning post, impeding the third-placed dead-heaters Kaieteur and Paolini. Sulamani finished half a length behind Storming Home but was awarded the race. The Godolphin camp was clearly relieved at reaching the century of Group/Grade 1 winners, which had taken just over nine years and included successes in eleven countries. Sheikh Mohammed went so far as to say: 'The result of a hundred Group 1s has come from the three Ps: planning, preparation and patience. A hundred Group 1s is a step forward and we must now look for the next hundred in less time.' Hope springs eternal, but an average of twelve victories a year looks a tall order, especially as the operation seems more heavily dependent on its older horses nowadays. Godolphin has been short in recent years of younger horses making the grade. Only one three-year-old, Mezzo Soprano in the Prix Vermeille, won a Group 1 in the latest season, and of the thirty-one victories by horses of that age in the first hundred, twenty-one came in the period 1994 to 1999. The twenty-one victories came from sixteen horses; the ten since 2000 have come from only six. Furthermore, there have been only three

*Turf Classic Invitational Stakes, Belmont—Sulamani overcomes a bad stumble
on the home turn before quickening clear of Deeliteful Irving (rail) and Balto Star*

Group 1 successes by Godolphin two-year-olds, and none in Europe since Aljabr in
the 1998 Prix de la Salamandre. It has been no better for Sheikh Mohammed,
himself, as he has not had a juvenile Group 1 winner in his own colours since 1998.
Moreover, two-year-olds trained by David Loder in Europe and Eoin Harty in the
States that would formerly have carried the Godolphin colours have been running
more recently for Sheikh Mohammed or his Darley stable, which must count
against Godolphin's being able to meet Sheikh Mohammed's target.

The Arlington Million indicated that a mile and a quarter was indeed on
the sharp side for Sulamani, who reverted to a mile and a half for his remaining
races, starting not with the Arc, which he bypassed, but with the Turf Classic at
Belmont Park at the end of September. Odds on in a below-par renewal, there was a
moment's worry when he clipped another runner's heels and stumbled when
making smooth headway on the home turn. But he swiftly recovered and quickened
impressively to win by two and three quarter lengths from Deeliteful Irving. The
opposition in the Breeders' Cup Turf at Santa Anita was altogether stronger,
including High Chaparral, Falbrav and Bright Sky from Europe and Storming
Home. Second favourite behind the last-named, Sulamani was hampered and lost
his place on the turn after passing the winning post for the first time and never got

into the race thereafter, finishing fifth to dead-heaters High Chaparral and Johar. An indifferent end to a season that had promised so much.

Sulamani (IRE) (b.c. 1999)	Hernando (FR) (b 1990)	Niniski (b 1976)	Nijinsky Virginia Hills
		Whakilyric (b 1984)	Miswaki Lyrism
	Soul Dream (USA) (br 1990)	Alleged (b 1974)	Hoist The Flag Princess Pout
		Normia (gr 1981)	Northfields Mia Pola

Sulamani is testament to the effectiveness of the Niarchos family's breeding methods, since not only did they breed Sulamani, but they also bred his sire Hernando, whose best runner he is, and his dam Soul Dream. Hernando won the Prix du Jockey Club as did another of his sons, Holding Court, and he is a pretty strong influence for stamina. With the dam an eleven-furlong winner at Claire-fontaine, it is hardly surprising that Sulamani is suited by a mile and a half, as was his Sadler's Wells half-brother Dream Well, who landed the Prix du Jockey Club and Irish Derby in the Niarchos colours. Soul Dream's three foals after Sulamani are Awakened (by Sadler's Wells), who failed to reach the frame in three starts in France in the latest season, and two colts by Machiavellian. Sulamani, a close-coupled, attractive colt with a short, unimpressive action, acts on firm and good to soft going; he has yet to encounter really testing conditions. His best form has come on galloping tracks and if he is to be campaigned at a mile and a quarter he is likely to need a pacemaker to ensure an end-to-end gallop. Whatever the trip, it would be no surprise to see him ridden more prominently than has been the custom. He did not idle once in front in the Turf Classic and allowing him to use his turn of foot earlier would help him to secure a position against a rail, thereby helping his jockey to prevent the tendency to hang that has been shown on occasions. *Saeed bin Suroor*

SULLIVAN'S GOLD 3 ch.f. Bedford (USA) 109 – Lady Millennium (IRE) (Prince Rupert (FR) 121) [2003 –: 8m 11.6m 14.1d Jul 26] no form. *L. A. Dace* —

SULLYS HOPE 6 b.g. Rock Hopper 124 – Super Sally 108 (Superlative 118) [2003 p12g Jan 7] fair winning hurdler: well held only Flat outing: dead. *Nick Williams* —

SUMMER BOUNTY 7 b.g. Lugana Beach 116 – Tender Moment (IRE) 78 (Caerleon (USA) 132) [2003 69, a57: f12g⁶ f9.4g⁴ 11.8g² 10m² 10.9m² 12.3m⁴ 10m⁵ 10f Sep 30] leggy, close-coupled gelding: fair handicapper on turf, poor on all-weather: effective at 1m to 1½m: acts on soft going, firm and fibresand: tried blinkered at 4 yrs: sometimes starts slowly (has virtually refused to race): none too genuine: won over hurdles in October. *F. Jordan* **73 a48**

SUMMER CHERRY (USA) 6 b.g. Summer Squall (USA) – Cherryrob (USA) (Roberto (USA) 131) [2003 58: f8.5g⁵ p12g p12g³ Feb 25] leggy gelding: modest handicapper: effective at 1¼m/easy 1½m: acts on polytrack, firm and soft going: blinkered twice (raced freely on first occasion): usually tongue tied: sometimes slowly away: carried head high/found little final start: held up. *Jamie Poulton* **54**

SUMMERISE 2 b.f. (Apr 6) Atraf 116 – Summerhill Special (IRE) 80 (Roi Danzig (USA)) [2003 7m 7m⁶ 7m* f6s Oct 7] 2,000Y: second foal: dam, 1½m/13f winner, also won over hurdles: modest performer: made all in seller at Thirsk in August: slowly away and showed little other starts: will probably stay 1m. *D. W. Barker* **55**

SUMMERLAND (IRE) 3 b.g. Danehill (USA) 126 – Summerosa (USA) 78 (Woodman (USA) 126) [2003 110: 10m⁶ 12.3m² 12m 12f³ 11.9m² 7m Nov 30] tall, good sort: has high knee action: useful performer: creditable efforts in Chester Vase (6 lengths second of 4 to Dutch Gold), King Edward VII Stakes at Royal Ascot (3 lengths third to High Accolade) and listed race at Haydock (2½ lengths second of 3 to Yawmi): sold privately, left J. Gosden and off 4½ months before final outing: stays 1½m: has form on any going, though may not stand repeated racing on firm: blinkered fourth/fifth starts: has worn near-side pricker: often races freely. *I. W. Allan, Hong Kong* **108**

SUMMER LIGHTNING (IRE) 3 b.f. Tamure (IRE) 125 – Papita (IRE) 77 (Law Society (USA) 130) [2003 80: 6.1d 6m⁵ 5f* 5.1m 5m⁴ 5g 5d 5d 5d⁶ Nov 7] smallish filly: fairly useful handicapper: won at Ayr in June: effective at 5f to 6.5f: acts on firm and soft going, yet to race on heavy: none too consistent. *R. M. Beckett* **81**

SUMMER MAGIC (IRE) 2 ch.f. (Mar 28) Desert Sun 120 – Cimeterre (IRE) 49 **78** (Arazi (USA) 135) [2003 7m⁴ 6d* 6.1m⁶ 5m² 5f Sep 15] 14,000Y: strong, lengthy filly: first foal: dam Irish maiden out of smart performer up to 1¼m Scimitarra, herself half-sister to top-class sprinter Double Form: fair performer: won maiden at Thirsk in July: good second at Catterick, easily best effort in nurseries after: likely to prove best at 5f/6f: acts on good to firm and good to soft ground: usually makes running. *T. D. Barron*

SUMMER RECLUSE (USA) 4 gr.g. Cozzene (USA) – Summer Retreat (USA) 78 **87 +** (Gone West (USA)) [2003 70: p7g⁴ p7g² p7g* 7d p8g* 8g³ May 21] fairly useful performer, lightly raced: won maiden at Lingfield in March and handicap there in May: stays 1m: acts on polytrack: free-going sort: reportedly lame when below form fourth start. *B. R. Johnson*

SUMMER SHADES 5 b.m. Green Desert (USA) 127 – Sally Slade 80 (Dowsing **79** (USA) 124) [2003 69, a72: f8.5g³ 7f² 8f² 8m² 8m² 8m* 9f² 8.3m* 8.3m⁶ 8g² 8m Aug 9] small mare: fair handicapper: won at Pontefract in June and Windsor in July: effective at 7f, barely stays 9.4f: acts on firm going and fibresand: sometimes blinkered at 3 yrs. *W. M. Brisbourne*

SUMMERSON 4 b.g. Whittingham (IRE) 104 – Summer Sky 75 (Skyliner 117) – [2003 66: 6m 5.9g 7g 6g Oct 14] rather leggy gelding: fair handicapper at 3 yrs: well held in 2003: tried visored. *M. R. Channon*

SUMMER SPECIAL 3 b.g. Mind Games 121 – Summerhill Special (IRE) 80 (Roi **70 d** Danzig (USA)) [2003 73: 6m² 6f⁵ 7m³ 6g³ 6d² 6m 7g 6m 6m 6m³ 6g 6g Oct 14] close-coupled gelding: fair maiden handicapper: well below form after fifth start: effective at 6f/7f: unraced on heavy going, acts on any other turf: often wears cheekpieces: usually races prominently: often looks less than keen: sold 4,500 gns. *D. W. Barker*

SUMMER SPICE (IRE) 3 b. or br.f. Key of Luck (USA) 126 – Summer Fashion 84 **79** (Mooresyle 137) [2003 88: 8m 8g⁴ 7m 7f Sep 4] leggy filly: fair performer, lightly raced: respectable efforts in listed races at Kempton and Ascot (dictated pace/found little) first 2 starts in 2003, well beaten in handicaps after (blinkered final outing): stays 1m: raced only on good going or firmer: sold 55,000 gns. *R. Hannon*

SUMMER STOCK (USA) 5 b.g. Theatrical 128 – Lake Placid (IRE) (Royal **64** Academy (USA) 130) [2003 69, a63: p10g 10.3g 10.9m⁴ 11.5m 10m 10d May 23] modest **a59 +** maiden handicapper: left F. Murphy after reappearance: stays 11f: acts on firm going, good to soft and fibresand: sometimes blinkered: tongue tied: none too consistent. *J. A. Supple*

SUMMER VIEW (USA) 6 ch.g. Distant View (USA) 126 – Miss Summer (Luthier **99** 126) [2003 98: 8g 8f⁴ 8m 8.1f² 8m Sep 20] tall, good-topped gelding: just useful handicapper nowadays: found guilty under non-triers rule at Goodwood on reappearance: best effort in 2003 when second to Camelot at Haydock: stays 9f: acts on firm and good to soft going: tongue tied: has been bandaged in front: effective held up or making running. *R. Charlton*

SUMMER WINE 4 b.f. Desert King (IRE) 129 – Generous Lady 98 (Generous (IRE) – 139) [2003 82: 12g 10.5d 14.1s Oct 29] good-topped filly: fairly useful performer at 3 yrs: well held in 2003. *C. F. Wall*

SUMMERY (IRE) 4 b.f. Indian Ridge 123 – Please Believe Me 93 (Try My Best **59** (USA) 130) [2003 52: p8g³ f7g 7m Aug 8] lengthy filly: modest form: likely to prove best up to 1m: blinkered (well held) final start. *B. J. Meehan*

SUMMITVILLE 3 b.f. Grand Lodge (USA) 125 – Tina Heights 79 (Shirley Heights **114** 130) [2003 105: 8g 10g 12g³ 12m⁵ 11.9m³ 14.6g 12g² Oct 11] tall, close-coupled, quite attractive filly: smart performer: seventh to Russian Rhythm in 1000 Guineas at Newmarket on reappearance: good efforts after when ¾-length third to Casual Look in Oaks at Epsom (hampered turn) in June, 4 lengths third to Islington in Yorkshire Oaks at York and length second to Itnab in Princess Royal Stakes at Ascot (wore crossed noseband) in October: stays 1½m (raced too freely in St Leger penultimate start): acts on soft and good to firm going: takes strong hold. *J. G. Given*

SUMUT 4 b.g. Hamas (IRE) 125§ – Simaat (USA) 72 (Mr Prospector (USA)) [2003 7d – f12g 8m 10g 9.9m Jul 29] 3,800 3-y-o: lengthy, workmanlike gelding: fifth foal: closely related to useful 7f winner Al Ihsas and fairly useful 1998 2-y-o 7.5f winner Samut (both by Danehill) and half-brother to winner in Spain by Last Tycoon: dam 1m winner: well held in maidens/handicaps. *G. A. Swinbank*

SUN BIRD (IRE) 5 ch.g. Prince of Birds (USA) 121 – Summer Fashion 84 (Moore- **112** style 137) [2003 91: 12.1m⁵ 16g* 15f* 16.1g 11.9g 18.7m* 13.9m² 13.4m⁵ 13d 18m² Oct

18] well-made gelding: smart handicapper, better than ever in 2003: won at Musselburgh in May, Ayr in June and Chester in August: excellent second in Ebor at York (beaten ½ length by Saint Alebe) in August and Cesarewitch at Newmarket (raced freely, beaten 2½ lengths by Landing Light) in October: effective at 1½m to 18.7f: acts on any turf going: ran well in blinkers/visor earlier in career: sometimes races freely/wanders: ran as if amiss penultimate start: effective making running or held up: genuine. *R. Allan*

SUN CAT (IRE) 3 br.g. Catrail (USA) 123 – Susie Sunshine (IRE) 81 (Waajib 121) **47 +**
[2003 f7g⁶ f5s⁵ f6g³ f8g f6g 12m³ 12m⁴ 12g f12g May 1] IR 6,000Y: tall gelding: fifth foal: half-brother to 5-y-o Shoeshine Boy and 7f winner Haymaker (by Thatching): dam Irish 2-y-o 9f winner who stayed 1½m: poor maiden: seems to stay 1½m: acts on fibresand and good to firm going. *M. J. Polglase*

SUNDARI (IRE) 4 b.f. Danehill (USA) 126 – My Ballerina (USA) 94 (Sir Ivor 135) **103**
[2003 8m⁶ 10d 10d 8f⁵ Sep 27] strong, short-backed filly: useful performer: missed 2002: seemingly as good as ever in 2003, 2 lengths seventh to Tadris in listed race at Longchamp and fifth (second home on stand side) to Mer de Corail in listed rated stakes at Ascot last 2 starts: stays 1¼m: acts on firm and good to soft going. *J. H. M. Gosden*

SUNDAY GOLD 3 b.f. Lion Cavern (USA) 117 – Sunday Night (GER) 51 (Bakharoff (USA) 130) [2003 –: 8.1d Aug 30] 50/1, well held in maidens at Windsor and Sandown a year apart. *H. S. Howe* **–**

SUNDAY'S WELL (IRE) 4 b.f. Sadler's Wells (USA) 132 – Marie de Beaujeu (FR) **65**
108 (Kenmare (FR) 125) [2003 80: 11.6g 10g 10d 11.9d Sep 26] leggy, useful-looking filly: maiden: just fair form for new trainer in 2003 (reportedly struck into on reappearance): stays 1½m: acts on good to firm and good to soft going. *N. A. Gaselee*

Mountain High Partnership's "Summitville"

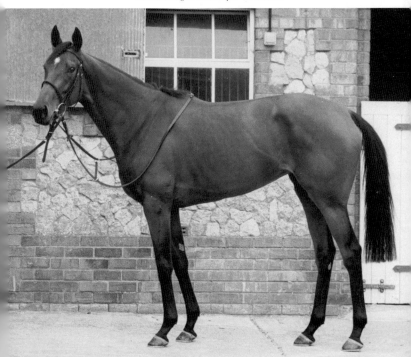

Sheikh Mohammed's "Sundrop"

SUNDIAL 4 ch.f. Cadeaux Genereux 131 – Ruby Setting 91 (Gorytus (USA) 132) –
[2003 –: f6g 7m 6m Aug 11] tall, lengthy filly: little form: left B. Hills 2,100 gns after
reappearance: tried in cheekpieces: headstrong. *A. E. Jones*

SUNDRIED TOMATO 4 b.g. Lugana Beach 116 – Little Scarlett 54 (Mazilier **88**
(USA) 107) [2003 85, a96: f5s⁴ f6s⁵ f5g⁶ f6g³ f6s² f7s* f6g⁶ f6s³ p7g 6m* 6d 6d² 6g 6d **a99**
5.1d⁶ 5d 6s f5g f5g p6g p7g Dec 29] good-topped gelding: useful handicapper on
all-weather, fairly useful on turf: won at Southwell in February and Ripon in April:
effective at 5f to easy 7f: acts on all-weather, heavy and good to firm going: often races
prominently: very tough. *P. W. Hiatt*

SUNDROP (JPN) 2 b.f. (Mar 16) Sunday Silence (USA) – Oenothera (IRE) 106 **107 p**
(Night Shift (USA)) [2003 p7g* 8f² Sep 27] neat, strong filly: third known foal: half-
sister to winners in Japan by Machiavellian and Brian's Time: dam 1¼m/11f winner
in Ireland/Germany, closely related to Breeders' Cup Turf winner Northern Spur and
high-class stayer Kneller: landed odds in maiden at Lingfield in September by head from
Grandalea: much improved (useful form) when 1¼ lengths second of 7 to Red Bloom in
Fillies' Mile at Ascot, staying on having been switched 1f out: should be suited by 1¼m/
1½m: joined Saeed bin Suroor: open to progress. *D. R. Loder*

SUNGIO 5 b.g. Halling (USA) 133 – Time Or Never (FR) (Dowsing (USA) 124) [2003 **59**
67: p10g p13g⁵ Dec 29] just modest handicapper in 2003: stays 1½m: acts on polytrack,
soft and good to firm going: tried blinkered/visored: sometimes hangs/finds little.
B. G. Powell

SUN HILL 3 b.g. Robellino (USA) 127 – Manhattan Sunset (USA) 76 (El Gran Senor (USA) 136) [2003 59: 8.1m 11.8m 8.2d Nov 6] sturdy, close-coupled gelding: modest maiden: should stay 1m: acts on soft going. *M. Blanshard* –

SUNISA (IRE) 2 b.f. (Apr 29) Daggers Drawn (USA) 114 – Winged Victory (IRE) 93 (Dancing Brave (USA) 140) [2003 6m6 6m2 6m4 Sep 9] IR 5,000F, €15,000Y: robust, close-coupled filly: fifth foal: half-sister to 3 winners, including 1998 2-y-o 7f winner Miss Dragonfly (by Brief Truce) and Irish 1m/9f winner Victory Flight (by Distinctly North): dam 7f winner: best effort in maidens (fair form) when second at Leicester: never going well final start: should stay 7f. *B. W. Hills* 73

SUN KING 6 ch.g. Zilzal (USA) 137 – Opus One 63 (Slip Anchor 136) [2003 12m4 14.1f4 9m4 15.8d2 16g6 Sep 28] second foal: dam 1¾m winner: fair maiden on Flat: should be suited by 2m+: acts on good to soft going. *Mrs M. Reveley* 69

SUNNY GLENN 5 ch.h. Rock Hopper 124 – La Ballerine 62 (Lafontaine (USA) 117) [2003 –: 10d2 12s5 11.5d 10g p10g Nov 22] lengthy horse: unimpressive mover: smart performer at 3 yrs for N. Littmoden: just fair form since, including when second in amateur event at Fontainebleau on 5-y-o reappearance: left J. Pease in France, soundly beaten in 2 listed events back in Britain: stays 1½m: acts on firm and soft going. *Mrs P. N. Dutfield* 71 +

SUNNY LADY (FR) 2 ch.f. (Apr 6) Nashwan (USA) 135 – Like The Sun (USA) 74 (Woodman (USA) 126) [2003 p8g6 f8s Dec 13] fifth live foal: dam, maiden who stayed 1¼m, sister to Preakness/Belmont Stakes winner Hansel: better effort in maidens (modest form) when sixth at Lingfield: will stay 1¼m. *E. A. L. Dunlop* 56

SUNNYSIDE ROYALE (IRE) 4 b.g. Ali-Royal (IRE) 127 – Kuwah (IRE) 77 (Be My Guest (USA) 126) [2003 52: 14.1m3 14f4 14.1m6 Jun 21] leggy gelding: modest maiden handicapper: stays 1¾m: raced mainly on good going or firmer: tried blinkered/tongue tied. *M. W. Easterby* 56

SUN OF SPEED (IRE) 2 b.c. (Mar 29) Desert Sun 120 – Spout House (IRE) 55 (Flash of Steel 120) [2003 7g 8.5m2 7.9f2 8f Oct 17] IR 28,000F, €80,000Y: useful-looking colt: fifth foal: half-brother to 3 winners, including 4-y-o Lady Dominatrix and 3-y-o Shouting The Odds: dam maiden who stayed 1½m: fairly useful maiden: second at Beverley and York: fell and died at Brighton: stayed 1m. *Mrs A. J. Perrett* 81

SUN ON THE SEA (IRE) 3 ch.f. Bering 136 – Shimmer (FR) (Green Dancer (USA) 132) [2003 7m4 8m4 10m* 12m4 10g6 Jul 14] 17,000F: good-bodied filly: sixth foal: sister to French winner up to 15f Strathtay and half-sister to 2 winners, including useful French/US performer up to 1¾m Beau Temps (by Mtoto): dam French 10.5f/11.5f winner: useful performer: won listed event at Newbury in May by 3½ lengths from Waldmark, making all: good 2¾ lengths fourth to Spanish Sun in Ribblesdale Stakes at Royal Ascot next time: last in Prix Eugene Adam at Maisons-Laffitte final outing: free-going front runner, barely stays 1½m: raced only on good/good to firm going: sold 250,000 gns in December. *B. J. Meehan* 109

SUNRIDGE FAIRY (IRE) 4 b.f. Definite Article 121 – Foxy Fairy (IRE) (Fairy King (USA)) [2003 –, a58: f12g Jan 2] smallish, lengthy filly: modest at best: well held only outing in 2003. *Ronald Thompson* –

SUNSET KING (USA) 3 b.c. King of Kings (IRE) 125 – Sunset River (USA) (Northern Flagship (USA) 96) [2003 10.2g 10m 8.1m 7.1m 8f2 7f2 7.1g 9.9m p7g Nov 29] $22,000Y, 38,000 2-y-o: close-coupled colt: fourth foal: dam unraced out of half-sister to Arazi and Noverre: fair maiden: left S. Kirk after sixth start: below form after: effective at 7f/1m: raced only on good ground or firmer on turf: blinkered (not at best) first 3 outings. *J. C. Fox* 66

SUNSET MIRAGE (USA) 2 br.f. (May 3) Swain (IRE) 134 – Yafill (USA) 80 (Nureyev (USA) 131) [2003 8m Sep 23] compact filly: half-sister to several winners, including useful French 2002 2-y-o 6f and 1m winner Loving Pride (by Quiet American) and 7-y-o Ipledgeallegiance: dam 2-y-o 6f winner (only season to race) out of half-sister to Zilzal: 16/1, eighth of 11 in maiden at Newmarket, green and not knocked about: should progress. *E. A. L. Dunlop* 63 p

SUN SLASH (IRE) 3 b.f. Entrepreneur 123 – Charmed Lady (Rainbow Quest (USA) 134) [2003 102: 5.3m3 5.1m6 6m4 6f2 7.5g5 5m6 6f 7.5m 6d Oct 12] IR 2,700Y: second foal: dam, French 11f winner only start, granddaughter of US Grade 1 9f winner Sharp Belle: useful performer: creditable efforts when third to Deportivo in listed race at the Curragh and 1½ lengths second to Bonus in Phoenix Sprint Stakes there on first/fourth 97

SUN

starts: just respectable efforts at best otherwise in 2003: stays 6f: acts on firm going: slowly away from wide draw at Chester second outing. *Ms J. Morgan, Ireland*

SUNSTRACH (IRE) 5 b.h. Polar Falcon (USA) 126 – Lorne Lady (Local Suitor **119** (USA) 128) [2003 120: 10g² 10g⁴ 10d³ 10m* 9.8d 10d³ Nov 16] smart performer: won well-contested minor event at Milan (only outing for R. Pinzauti) in September by 1½ lengths from Salselon: ran poorly in Prix Dollar at Longchamp next time, but at least respectable efforts all other starts, including when 3¼ lengths third to Imperial Dancer when seeking repeat win in Premio Roma final outing: best at 1¼m: acts on soft and good to firm ground: has had tongue tied: to join L. Cumani. *E. Borromeo, Italy*

SUNTAGONAL (AUS) 4 b.g. Octagonal (NZ) 126 – Urge To Merge (AUS) (Last – Tycoon 131) [2003 6m 6g 6.1m Jul 11] A$80,000Y: good-topped gelding: second foal: half-brother to winning sprinter in Australia by Woodman: dam, 6.5f winner in Australia, sister to South African Group 1 5f/6f winner Tracy's Element and half-sister to Australian Group 1 7f winner Danasinga out of smart Irish sprinter Princess Tracy: formerly trained in South Africa by D. Ferraris: won 3 times there in 2002, notably Group 2 Protea Stakes at Turffontein and Group 1 Premier's Champion Stakes (from Fort Danzig) at Greyville: last all 3 starts in Britain in 2003, racing too freely final outing: stays 7f: acts on soft ground: races prominently. *W. J. Haggas*

SUPERAPPAROS 9 b.g. Superpower 113 – Ayodessa 78 (Lochnager 132) [2003 –, **60** a53: f6g³ f6s³ f6s² f6s³ f6s f6g² 6m f6g f5g⁵ f6g⁶ f6g Jun 30] strong gelding: modest maiden: effective at 5f to 7f: form only on fibresand and good to firm going: blinkered: usually races up with pace. *S. R. Bowring*

SUPER CANNES 3 b.c. Alzao (USA) 117 – Miss Riviera 103 (Kris 135) [2003 12d³ **79 §** 12m³ 12m² 12f⁴ 12g* 14g 12d⁶ 10.1m Oct 21] good-bodied colt: second foal: dam, 2-y-o 6f winner (later best at 7f/1m), half-sister to useful winners Miss Riviera Golf (at 1m) and Miss Corniche (up to 1¼m): fair performer: landed odds in 3-runner maiden at Doncaster in July: poor efforts in handicaps after, weakening tamely in blinkers final outing: stays 1½m: acts on firm and good to soft ground: races prominently: sold 18,000 gns: one to treat with caution. *G. Wragg*

SUPER CANYON 5 ch.g. Gulch (USA) – Marina Park 112 (Local Suitor (USA) 128) **73** [2003 66: 6m 6.1g³ 6m³ 6m⁴ f6g* f6s⁵ 6g⁵ f6s³ f6g² Nov 1] fair handicapper: won at Wolverhampton in August: stays 6f: acts on firm ground and fibresand: visored once at 4 yrs (won), and on last 3 starts, also tongue tied last 2: sometimes drifts right: sold 12,000 gns. *P. W. Harris*

SUPER CELEBRE (FR) 3 b.c. Peintre Celebre (USA) 137 – Supergirl (USA) **121** (Woodman (USA) 126) [2003 11g* 10.5g² 12m² Jun 1]

The fact that Dalakhani will not be around in 2004 will be a cause for regret in most quarters, but perhaps less so among the connections of Super Celebre. The two colts were arch rivals in France through the first half of the season, and whilst Super Celebre proved himself better than all the other colts he encountered, Dalakhani was the one rival he could not beat. Super Celebre made a good impression when comfortably winning one of the earliest trials for the Prix du Jockey Club, the Prix Noailles at Longchamp on his reappearance in April, by two and a half lengths from Coroner. Dalakhani had much the better form of the pair as a two-year-old and also made a successful return, in the Prix Greffulhe, but, on the evidence of his reappearance, Super Celebre was improving fast, and three days after Coroner had franked the Noailles form by winning the Prix Hocquart, Super Celebre lined up as second favourite to Dalakhani in the Prix Lupin at Longchamp. In finishing a length second to the odds-on Dalakhani, who won readily, Super Celebre ran a sound trial for the Prix du Jockey Club, held up and quickening well from further back than the favourite to mount his challenge inside the final furlong, though never looking like getting past him. Super Celebre looked to have further improvement in him, particularly over the extra furlong and a half at Chantilly but, unfortunately for him, those same comments applied just as well to Dalakhani, who was headed for the same race.

Like Dalakhani (by the 1984 winner Darshaan), Super Celebre was attempting to emulate his sire at Chantilly, Peintre Celebre having won the Prix du Jockey Club in 1997. Dominique Boeuf on Super Celebre kept Dalakhani closer in his sights than in the Lupin, tracking him throughout as the pair were both held up and following his move when Soumillon asked Dalakhani to take up the running in the

992

straight. However, Super Celebre's challenge proved only short-lived, and, whilst he confirmed earlier form with Coroner, who finished three lengths behind him in third, Super Celebre was very much second-best to Dalakhani for a second time, beaten two lengths and unable to respond to Soumillon's 'hurry-up' gestures on the winner. The remainder of Super Celebre's season was to have focused on the Prix de l'Arc de Triomphe, though had those plans come to fruition, that would have meant running into Dalakhani again. Super Celebre's best chance of winning a good race looked to depend on avoiding him but, as it turned out, injury prevented Super Celebre being seen out at all after the Prix du Jockey Club. It was announced in September that Super Celebre had suffered a cut to a foreleg in the Prix Lupin; although it had not affected his participation at Chantilly, the wound had opened again on the firm ground during the summer and Super Celebre was to be put aside for a four-year-old campaign to allow the injury to heal properly.

It had been the intention for Super Celebre's sire to race on as a four-year-old after his brilliant Prix de l'Arc de Triomphe success but an injury sustained just twenty-four hours before his intended reappearance in the Prix Ganay brought an end to Peintre Celebre's racing career. Super Celebre comes from his first crop, which also includes stable-companion Vallee Enchantee, winner of the Prix de Pomone, Prix du Conseil de Paris and Hong Kong Vase, and the Deutsches Derby winner Dai Jin. Super Celebre is his dam's second foal after the Bigstone colt Superman, who is a useful winner up to around thirteen furlongs in France. His two-year-old half-sister Super Lina (by Linamix) has made a good start and won over nine furlongs at Maisons-Laffitte in November—Super Celebre had won the corresponding race for colts on the same card twelve months earlier. This family first became associated with the Wildenstein colours in the late-'sixties when

Ecurie Wildenstein's "Super Celebre"

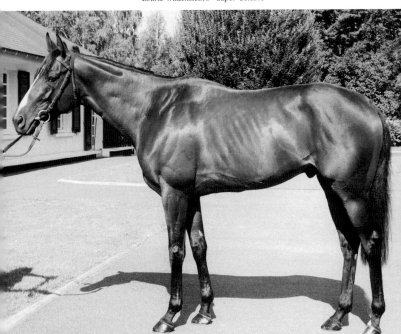

Daniel Wildenstein acquired the German filly Schonbrunn. She had already won both fillies' classics in her native country and the following season won the Grand Prix de Deauville for her new owner. It was at stud that she proved herself a really shrewd purchase, however. One of her daughters, Seneca, produced the Arc winner Sagace, the Prix Royal-Oak winner Star Lift, and the Dante winner Simply Great, while her other, the useful stayer Southern Seas, is dam of the Breeders' Cup Mile and Arlington Million winner Steinlen and the smart French mile-and-a-half winner Seurat, as well as Super Celebre's unraced dam Supergirl. One of Supergirl's half-sisters, the French listed winner Sophonisbe, is dam of Allen Paulson's Irish Derby winner Zagreb.

		Nureyev	Northern Dancer
	Peintre Celebre (USA)	(b 1977)	Special
	(ch 1994)	Peinture Bleue	Alydar
Super Celebre (FR)		(ch 1987)	Petroleuse
(b.c. 2000)		Woodman	Mr Prospector
	Supergirl (USA)	(ch 1983)	Playmate
	(b 1994)	Southern Seas	Jim French
		(b or br 1975)	Schonbrunn

Super Celebre stays a mile and a half and acts on good to firm ground; he clearly also handled heavy going well as a two-year-old, winning that Maisons-Laffitte race by six lengths. His injury was not serious, and his trainer predicted he would return in 2004 stronger than ever. With just five races behind him, Super Celebre may improve further and could emerge from Dalakhani's shadow as a four-year-old. *E. Lellouche, France*

SUPERCHIEF 8 b.g. Precocious 126 – Rome Express (Siberian Express (USA) 125) [2003 –, a77: p7g³ p7g⁴ p7g p7g² p8g p10g p8g p8g p7g² Dec 30] smallish, sturdy gelding: fair handicapper on all-weather: best form at 7f/1m: acts on good to firm going and polytrack: has been visored, blinkered/tongue tied nowadays. *Miss B. Sanders* — **a74**

SUPERCLEAN 3 ch.f. Environment Friend 128 – Star Mover 48 (Move Off 112) [2003 8.2g 11.9s⁵ 12.1g⁵ Jun 13] leggy, plain filly: first foal: dam, ran 3 times on Flat, winning hurdler: last in maidens. *A. W. Carroll* —

SUPER DOLPHIN 4 ch.g. Dolphin Street (FR) 125 – Supergreen (Superlative 118) [2003 55: 12.3m Apr 2] big, lengthy gelding: modest maiden: refused to race only outing in 2003: stays 7f: acts on good to firm going: needs treating with caution. *T. P. Tate* — §

SUPER DOMINION 6 ch.g. Superpower 113 – Smartie Lee 66 (Dominion 123) [2003 65: f8s f8.5g f9.4s 8m 8g 8m³ 8g Jul 30] sturdy gelding: formerly fair 6f to 9.4f winner: just modest in 2003: acts on fibresand, good to firm and soft ground: tried in cheekpieces, wears tongue tie. *R. Hollinshead* — **58**

SUPERFRILLS 10 b.m. Superpower 113 – Pod's Daughter (IRE) 43 (Tender King 123) [2003 49§, a54§: f6s f6s f6s⁵ f6g f6s⁴ f6s⁵ 6d 5.1g Aug 1] small mare: poor handicapper: effective at 5f/6f: acts on fibresand and any turf going: unreliable. *Miss L. C. Siddall* — **49 §**

SUPER KING 2 b.g. (Apr 17) Kingsinger (IRE) 94 – Super Sisters (AUS) (Call Report (USA)) [2003 7m² Oct 12] leggy gelding: half-brother to several winners, including 8-y-o Guilsborough and 6-y-o Castlebridge: dam Australian 7f winner: better effort in maidens (fair form) when length second of 12 to On The Wing at Newcastle: should stay 1m. *N. Bycroft* — **76**

SUPERPRIDETWO 3 b.g. Superpower 113 – Lindrake's Pride (Mandrake Major 122) [2003 –: 5.9m 7m 6f 5.9f⁵ 8m 7.1f 7d⁵ Sep 20] lengthy gelding: poor maiden: left Mrs M. Reveley after fourth start: seems to stay 7f: visored/blinkered last 3 outings. *P. D. Niven* —

SUPER SONG 3 b.g. Desert Prince (IRE) 130 – Highland Rhapsody (IRE) 78 (Kris 135) [2003 75p: 7m² 7.1m 7m* Aug 20] quite good-topped gelding: fairly useful form from 5 starts: won maiden at Lingfield in August easily by 4 lengths from Mutamared, slowly away: raced only at 7f: unraced on extremes of going on turf: raced freely second start: sold only 9,000 gns, and gelded. *Sir Michael Stoute* — **85**

SUPREMACY 4 ch.g. Vettori (IRE) 119 – High Tern 93 (High Line 125) [2003 111: 16.1g 13.9f 13.4m² 16.2f* Sep 28] sturdy gelding: smart performer: unraced at 2 yrs: won 4-runner listed race at Ascot in September by length from Manama Rose: good 1½ lengths second to Compton Bolter in handicap at Chester previous month: should be fully — **110**

effective at 1¾m+: raced only on good ground or firmer: ran as though amiss first 2 starts at 4 yrs. *Sir Michael Stoute*

SUPREME SALUTATION   7 ch.g. Most Welcome 131 – Cardinal Press (Sharrood (USA) 124) [2003 78: f8.5g f9.4g⁴ f9.4g² f8.5g⁵ f8g³ f6g 8m³ 7.1d² 9.3g* 8.2d³ 7m 7m* 8.2m⁶ 10m p7g 8.3d 8g 7d⁵ f8g⁶ f7s Dec 13] leggy, sparely-made gelding: fairly useful handicapper on turf, fair on all-weather: won at Carlisle in May and Catterick in July: effective at 7f to 11f: acts on all-weather, firm and soft going: tried blinkered earlier in career: sometimes slowly away/carries head awkwardly: usually races prominently: unreliable. *D. W. Chapman*   **81 §** **a72 §**

SUPREME SILENCE (IRE)   6 b.g. Bluebird (USA) 125 – Why So Silent (Mill Reef (USA) 141) [2003 43, a54: f16s f16.2g f16.2g f14g 21.6m Apr 14] lengthy gelding: modest handicapper at 5 yrs: well held in 2003: has worn cheekpieces/tongue tie: looked less than keen on reappearance. *Jedd O'Keeffe*   **–**

SURDOUE   3 b.g. Bishop of Cashel 122 – Chatter's Princess (Cadeaux Genereux 131) [2003 66, a85: 7g 8g 8g⁵ f7g 8g f8.5g f11g f8s f12s⁵ Dec 27] leggy gelding: fair handicapper: left G. Margarson after fifth outing: barely stays 1½m: acts on fibresand and good to firm ground. *P. Howling*   **75**

SURE QUEST   8 b.m. Sure Blade (USA) 130 – Eagle's Quest 62 (Legal Eagle 126) [2003 66: f12g⁶ Jan 17] close-coupled mare: just modest form only start in 2003 (wore cheekpieces): stays 2m: acts on all-weather and any turf going: visored once in 1999: sold 6,000 gns. *D. W. P. Arbuthnot*   **59**

SURE SIGN   3 ch.g. Selkirk (USA) 129 – Beyond Doubt 87 (Belmez (USA) 131) [2003 73: 8m 8.2d³ f8.5g f8s 10.3g p8g 13.1d Oct 14] good-topped gelding: fair maiden handicapper: left R. Charlton following reappearance: well held last 5 starts: should stay at least 1¼m: acts on good to soft ground, no form on all-weather: visored penultimate start. *D. Shaw*   **72** **a–**

SURF THE NET   2 b.f. (Apr 3) Cape Cross (IRE) 129 – On The Tide 72 (Slip Anchor 136) [2003 6m* 7m⁶ Oct 18] rather leggy filly: fourth foal: half-sister to 3 winners, including 1m/1¼m winner (stayed 1½m) Tier Worker (by Tenby) and fairly useful 1¼m winner Mingling (by Wolfhound): dam, 1m winner, half-sister to very smart winner up to 1m Rock City: won maiden at Newmarket in June: fairly useful form when sixth of 10 to Cairns in Rockfel Stakes at same track, soon chased along: will stay 1m: slowly away both starts: probably open to further progress. *R. Hannon*   **91 p**

SURPRISE ENCOUNTER   7 ch.g. Cadeaux Genereux 131 – Scandalette (Niniski (USA) 125) [2003 111: 8.1m³ 7.1m 8m 7.9m³ 8m³ Aug 9] quite good-topped gelding: smart handicapper at best: won Hunt Cup at Royal Ascot in 2001: useful form in 2003, running creditably when third at Sandown, York and Ascot (beaten 3 lengths by Pentecost): effective at 7f/1m: easily best form on good going or firmer: tried visored: was often early to post: was usually held up: sometimes raced freely/found little: retired. *E. A. L. Dunlop*   **109**

SURVAL (IRE)   3 b.f. Sadler's Wells (USA) 132 – Courtesane (USA) (Majestic Light (USA)) [2003 89: 10g⁶ 10.5v* 12m Sep 26] tall, leggy filly: fairly useful form: won maiden at Haydock in May by 5 lengths: well held in listed race at Ascot subsequent start, seeming to lose action on bend and carrying head high under pressure: should be suited by 1½m+: acts on heavy going: hung left second start, has been mounted on track and walked to post: free-going sort. *L. M. Cumani*   **91**

SUSAN'S DOWRY   7 b.m. Efisio 120 – Adjusting (IRE) (Busted 134) [2003 –, a74: f11g⁴ p10g⁴ Jan 18] leggy, angular mare: has a round action: fair handicapper: effective at 1¼m/1½m: acts on heavy going and all-weather: has been slowly away: best waited with. *Andrew Turnell*   **–** **a70**

SUSIEDIL (IRE)   2 b.f. (Apr 9) Mujadil (USA) 119 – Don't Take Me (IRE) (Don't Forget Me 127) [2003 6.1d 7m 7f* 7.1m⁴ 8.3g Oct 6] IR 4,000F, 8,000Y: sturdy filly: fourth foal: sister to 2 winners in Italy: dam 1¼m/11f winner in Belgium: fair performer: won maiden at Brighton in September, hanging left: creditable fourth in nursery at Warwick, better effort after: should stay 1m: acts on firm ground. *P. W. Harris*   **65**

SUSSEX   2 b.c. (Mar 12) Danehill (USA) 126 – Oh So Sharp 131 (Kris 135) [2003 7m² Aug 22] big, angular, heavy-topped colt: has plenty of scope: half-brother to numerous winners, including 1¼m winner (stayed 13f) Savoire Vivre and 1¼m winner (stayed 1¾m) Sacho (both by Sadler's Wells) and French 1¼m winner Rosefinch (by Blushing Groom), all smart: dam won 1000 Guineas, Oaks and St Leger: 4/1, head second of 15 to Torinmoor in maiden at Newmarket, leading briefly final 1f: had minor setback after: will   **93 p**

be suited by at least 1m: joined Saeed bin Suroor: sure to improve and win a race or 2. *D. R. Loder*

SUSSEX LAD   6 b.g. Prince Sabo 123 – Pea Green 98 (Try My Best (USA) 130) [2003   **64**
75, a71: p7g⁵ p6g p5g p6g 6g⁵ 6m 7f⁶ 7m⁵ 7m² 5f⁴ 6f³ 6m⁵ 8m⁵ 7f⁴ 6m² 7m³ Aug 28]
strong gelding: just modest performer in 2003: claimed from P. Chamings after ninth
start, from J. Best after eleventh: effective at 6f/easy 7f: has form on soft going, better
efforts on firmer than good, and acts on all-weather: has worn cheekpieces: usually held
up: on long losing run, and probably not one to trust implicitly. *Mrs A. J. Perrett*

SUSSEX STYLE (IRE)   2 b.g. (Apr 1) Desert Style (IRE) 121 – Anita's Love (IRE)   **–**
53 (Anita's Prince 126) [2003 p6g Dec 29] IR 5,000F, €8,000Y: sixth foal: half-brother to
1998 2-y-o 5f winner Thornaby Girl (by Fayruz) and 3-y-o Monte Verde: dam sprint
maiden: 50/1, well held in maiden at Lingfield. *R. M. Flower*

SUTTER'S FORT (IRE)   2 b. or br.c. (Apr 24) Seeking The Gold (USA) – Mayenne   **97**
(USA) (Nureyev (USA) 131) [2003 5f² 5.9m² 7m* 7m³ 6.3m* 6f⁵ Oct 11] €375,000Y:
leggy, close-coupled colt: third foal: half-brother to 1m winner Menaggio (by Danehill)
and 3-y-o My Renee: dam unraced close relative to Carnegie out of Detroit, both winners
of Arc: useful performer: won maiden at Carlisle in June, nursery at Newmarket in
August and Irish Breeders Foal Levy Stakes at the Curragh (by ¾ length from Favourite
Nation) in September: respectable fifth of 8 in listed race at York: not sure to stay beyond
7f: reportedly had stall test after second outing and sometimes blanketed for stall entry:
joined Saeed bin Suroor. *D. R. Loder*

SUZUKA (USA)   3 br.c. A P Indy (USA) 131 – Sha Tha (USA) 118 (Mr Prospector   **79**
(USA)) [2003 10m² 10g 12.3f² 11m 12s* 14g 12.1g³ 16m 15.9m 15m² Sep 18] tall,
good-topped colt: has scope: fifth foal: half-brother to 3 winners, notably very smart 1m
(including at 2 yrs) to 10.5f winner State Shinto (by Pleasant Colony): dam, French/US
1m/9f performer, sister to dam of One Cool Cat: fair handicapper: won at Thirsk in July:
in-and-out form after: likely to prove best short of 15f: acts on firm and soft ground: tried
blinkered: very slowly away seventh outing: sold 22,000 gns. *M. Johnston*

SVENSON   2 ch.c. (Apr 29) Dancing Spree (USA) – Bella Bambola (IRE) 42 (Tate   **–**
Gallery (USA) 117) [2003 7m Aug 22] workmanlike colt: fifth foal: dam sprint maiden:
100/1, last of 15 in maiden at Newmarket, leading early. *J. J. Matthias*

Irish Breeders Foal Levy Stakes, the Curragh—British-trained Sutter's Fort takes this valuable event, which is restricted to horses foaled in Ireland; Favourite Nation (rail) is second

SWAGGER STICK (USA) 2 gr. or ro.c. (Apr 5) Cozzene (USA) – Regal State **73** (USA) 122 (Affirmed (USA)) [2003 6d 6g 7.1d 8m* 10f⁴ Sep 30] tall, leggy colt: half-brother to several winners, including Breeders' Cup Classic winner Pleasantly Perfect (by Pleasant Colony) and useful 1996 2-y-o 6f/6.5f winner Hurricane State (by Miswaki): dam, won Prix Morny, half-sister to dam of high-class miler Distant View: fair performer: won nursery at Yarmouth in September: respectable fourth of 16 in similar event at Nottingham, slowly away and never on terms: likely to stay at least 1½m: acts on firm ground: sometimes edges left. *J. L. Dunlop*

SWAHILI (IRE) 2 br. or gr.f. (Mar 7) Kendor (FR) 122 – Irish Celebrity (USA) (Irish **76** River (FR) 131) [2003 6m² May 22] IR 5,500F, 30,000Y: tall filly: first foal: dam unraced out of close relation to smart 1985 2-y-o Truly Nureyev: fair form when second of 8 in maiden at Goodwood, taking good hold. *R. Hannon*

SWAIN DAVIS 3 b.f. Swain (IRE) 134 – Exclusive Davis (USA) (Our Native (USA)) **72** [2003 –: 10g 10.3m 10.2m⁶ 12m⁵ p12g f16.2g* Aug 15] tall, leggy, quite good-topped filly: fair performer: won handicap at Wolverhampton in August by 12 lengths: stays 2m: acts on fibresand, raced only on good going or firmer on turf. *D. J. S. ffrench Davis*

SWANKY LAD (IRE) 2 b.g. (Apr 21) Atraf 116 – Sweet As A Nut (IRE) 75 (Pips **51** Pride 117) [2003 5f⁶ 5f⁵ 5g³ 7m 6m 6m Oct 12] €6,000Y, 10,000 2-y-o: smallish, close-coupled gelding: first foal: dam 2-y-o 5f winner: modest maiden: showed little in nurseries last 3 starts: will prove best at 5f/6f. *A. Crook*

SWEDISH SHAVE (FR) 5 ch.h. Midyan (USA) 124 – Shavya (Shavian 125) [2003 **116** 116: 5.5s* 5.5g* 5.5g* 5m 6d* 6.5g⁴ 6d 6f 6s⁶ Oct 31] 200,000 francs Y: rangy horse: second foal: brother to fairly useful French 1999 2-y-o 5.5f/7.5f winner Psycadelic: dam unraced: smart performer: successful in Grosser Preis von Berlin at Hoppegarten at 3 yrs and listed race at Chantilly on 4-y-o reappearance: comfortable winner of first 3 starts (minor event and 2 listed races) at Maisons-Laffitte in spring and successful in Prix de Ris-Orangis at Deauville in July by short head from Vasywait: creditable 1½ lengths fourth to Porlezza in Prix Maurice de Gheest at Deauville next outing: respectable efforts last 2 starts when eighth to Acclamation in Diadem Stakes at Ascot and sixth to Soave in Prix de Seine-et-Oise at Maisons-Laffitte: has won at 7f, best at shorter: has form on firm going, though best efforts on good ground or softer (acts on heavy). *R. Gibson, France*

SWEEP THE BOARD (IRE) 2 b.c. (May 11) Fasliyev (USA) 120 – Fun Board **–** (FR) (Saumarez 132) [2003 6g Jun 11] IR 28,000F, 14,000Y: third foal: half-brother to 3-y-o Glenviews Polly: dam placed up to 12.5f in France: 9/2, last of 11 in maiden at Hamilton. *A. P. Jarvis*

SWEET AROMA 4 b.f. Bedford (USA) 109 – Tango Country (Town And Country **–** 124) [2003 –: f5g f7s f12g Nov 24] quite good-topped filly: little sign of ability. *Mrs N. Macauley*

SWEET AZ 3 b.f. Averti (IRE) 117 – Yen Haven (USA) (Lear Fan (USA) 130) [2003 **–** 54: p10g 10d 7g 8m 9.3m 8f 7.1g⁵ 8f 7.1m Sep 22] modest maiden at 2 yrs: little solid form in 2003, leaving A. Jones after sixth start: tried visored. *S. C. Burrough*

SWEET BRIAR 4 b.f. Common Grounds 118 – Pervenche (Latest Model 115) [2003 **–** –: p8g Jan 15] lightly-raced maiden, poor form at 2 yrs. *H. Candy*

SWEET BROOMSTICK 2 b.f. (Jan 2) Wizard King 122 – Sweet Compliance 71 **–** (Safawan 118) [2003 6d 7m⁶ 8f Aug 22] 2,600Y: first foal: dam, 2-y-o 7f winner, half-sister to useful performer up to 11f Sick As A Parrot: well beaten in maidens/claimer. *C. Grant*

SWEET CANDO (IRE) 2 b. or br.f. (Mar 30) Royal Applause 124 – Fizzygig 71 **66** (Efisio 120) [2003 5m³ 6g³ 5m⁶ 5m* 5g 6g³ 6g³ f7g⁴ Nov 28] 3,000Y, 19,000 2-y-o: first foal: dam 7f winner: fair performer: won maiden at Musselburgh in September: in frame in nurseries last 3 starts: stays 6f: acts on good to firm going, probably on fibresand: sometimes early/led to post. *Miss L. A. Perratt*

SWEET CORAL (FR) 3 b.f. Pennekamp (USA) 130 – Sweet Contralto 89 (Danehill **–** (USA) 126) [2003 8m⁵ 8.2f 6m f6g Nov 24] 6,000Y, 1,500 3-y-o: good-topped filly: second foal: half-sister to 2001 2-y-o 7f winner Sweet Singer (by Hector Protector), later successful in Spain: dam, 7f/9f winner, sister to smart 1¼m/1½m performer Alriffa: little form. *S. Rothwell*

SWEETEST REVENGE (IRE) 2 ch.f. (Mar 26) Daggers Drawn (USA) 114 – Joza **69** 90 (Marju (IRE) 127) [2003 5m 5f³ p6g² 5g p6g* 6m p5g⁴ p6g² p5g⁵ p6g⁴ Dec 30] **a78** 10,000Y: leggy filly: second foal: dam, 5f winner (ran 3 times only at 2 yrs), out of half-sister to 2000 Guineas winner Don't Forget Me: fair performer: won maiden at Lingfield in October: creditable efforts in nurseries there last 2 starts: will prove best at 5f/6f: acts on polytrack and firm going: usually races up with pace. *M. D. I. Usher*

SWEET FINESSE (IRE)   3 b.f. Revoque (IRE) 122 – Moira My Girl (Henbit (USA)   **53**
130) [2003 –: 13.1g⁻ 11.8m 10m⁶ 10d 11.7f⁶ 10m⁴ 10m⁶ 10m⁵ 10m Oct 23] big,
workmanlike filly: modest maiden handicapper: stays 1¼m: acts on firm and good to soft
ground, unraced on softer: has been slowly away/raced freely. *Mrs P. N. Dutfield*

SWEET FURY (IRE)   2 b.c. (Feb 10) Imperial Ballet (IRE) 110 – Muneera (USA) 67   **70 ?**
(Green Dancer (USA) 132) [2003 7m 8m 8m f9.4g Nov 15] IR 21,000F, 40,000Y: lengthy
colt: first foal: dam twice-raced sister to useful German miler Huambo out of half-sister
to Irish St Leger winner Mashaallah: easily best effort in maidens (fair form) when
seventh at Leicester third start, possibly flattered in slowly-run race: should stay 1¼m:
sold 6,000 gns. *E. A. L. Dunlop*

SWEET HARRIET   3 ch.f. Hector Protector (USA) 124 – Swame (USA) (Jade   **–**
Hunter (USA)) [2003 10m p12g Jul 23] fourth foal: half-sister to 3 winners, including
useful 1¼m/1½m winner Algunnaas (by Red Ransom) and fairly useful 1½m/1¾m
winner Shadowblaster (by Wolfhound): dam, won up to 9f in USA, granddaughter of top-
class 1m/1¼m performer Rose Bowl: well held in maidens at Newmarket and Lingfield.
M. P. Tregoning

SWEET INDULGENCE (IRE)   2 ch.c. (Mar 15) Inchinor 119 – Silent Indulgence   **84 p**
(USA) (Woodman (USA) 126) [2003 7m⁷ 7m³ Aug 23] 50,000Y: strong, lengthy colt:
has scope: fourth foal: half-brother to 2000 2-y-o 6f winner In The Woods (by You And
I), later useful in Scandinavia, and useful 6f/7f winner Tudor Wood (by Royal Applause):
dam placed in USA: green and better for race, won 18-runner maiden at Newmarket in
August by short head from Master David: similar form (fairly useful) when 2½ lengths
third of 4 to Snow Goose in minor event at Redcar, no extra late on: not sure to stay much
beyond 7f: should progress. *B. Hanbury*

SWEET MILITARY MAN (USA)   2 b.c. (Feb 7) Allied Forces (USA) 123 –   **59**
Brown Sugar (VEN) (Imperial Ballet (IRE) 110) [2003 5g 5d⁶ f6g⁴ Jun 25] $8,000F,
15,000Y: leggy colt: first foal: dam unraced: modest form in minor event/maidens: should
stay 7f. *D. Shaw*

SWEET PICKLE   2 b.f. (Apr 11) Piccolo 121 – Sweet Wilhelmina 87 (Indian Ridge   **75**
123) [2003 5.7f³ 6d 6m* 6g Oct 25] leggy filly: second foal: dam 7f (at 2 yrs)/1m winner:
fair performer: easily best effort when winning maiden at Lingfield in September by 4
lengths from Mikati Maid: last in nursery final start: will probably stay 7f. *D. J. Coakley*

SWEET PORTIA (IRE)   3 ch.f. Pennekamp (USA) 130 – My Mariam 79 (Salse   **59 §**
(USA) 128) [2003 61: 7g 6.1d 6g 8d⁴ f8.5s 8.2d Nov 6] strong filly: modest maiden:
dived left and unseated rider leaving stall first 2 outings in 2003, then left A. Balding:
stays 1m: acts on good to firm and good to soft going: tried tongue tied, wore cheekpieces
last 4 starts: temperamental. *R. T. Phillips*

SWEET REFLECTION (IRE)   3 b.f. Victory Note (USA) 120 – Shining Creek   **–**
(CAN) (Bering 136) [2003 7d 8.3d 8.3m 10m Aug 6] IR 8,000Y: rather unfurnished filly:
second foal: dam, Italian winner around 7f (including at 2 yrs), half-sister to dam of smart
French performer up to 15f Russian Hope: well held in maidens/handicap: slowly away
third outing. *W. J. Musson*

SWEET REPLY   2 ch.f. (Mar 24) Opening Verse (USA) 126 – Sweet Revival 41   **84**
(Claude Monet (USA) 121) [2003 7.1m 6m⁴ 6m⁵ 6m* 7m 6g⁴ Sep 27] tall, angular filly:
half-sister to 3 winners, including 2002 2-y-o 7.5f winner (later smart Grade 1 winner
in USA) Sweet Return (by Elmaamul) and fairly useful but ungenuine 6f (at 2 yrs) to
1¼m winner Sweet Reward (by Beveled): dam 1¼m winner: fairly useful performer:
won maiden at Redcar in August: respectable fourth of 6 in minor event at Ripon, better
effort after: will stay 7f. *I. A. Wood*

SWEET REPOSE (USA)   2 b.f. (Apr 10) Gulch (USA) – Bint Baladee 101 (Nashwan   **– p**
(USA) 135) [2003 7s⁵ Oct 29] third foal: dam, 1m/1¼m winner, out of half-sister to
top-class French/US 1m/9f performer Thrill Show: 20/1, well-held fifth of 14 in maiden
at Yarmouth, not knocked about: should stay 1m: will probably do better. *E. A. L. Dunlop*

SWEETSTOCK   5 b.m. Anshan 119 – Stockline (Capricorn Line 111) [2003 49: 13m   **–**
f12g 12.4g f16g Nov 19] poor maiden: little form in 2003, leaving R. Ford after second
start. *Mrs G. S. Rees*

SWEET TALKING GIRL   3 b.f. Bin Ajwaad (IRE) 119 – Arabellajill 97 (Aragon   **–**
118) [2003 6g⁶ 7.1m⁵ f7g Nov 10] 1,400F: fifth foal: half-sister to 3 winners, including

6-y-o Bond Boy and 5-y-o Bond Mirage: dam 5f (at 2 yrs) and 6f winner: well held in maidens. *J. M. Bradley*

SWELL (IRE)   3 b.c. Sadler's Wells (USA) 132 – Lydara (USA) (Alydar (USA)) [2003   **61** 10g⁴ 11.1m⁶ 10d Apr 28] fifth foal: closely related to 2 winners around 7f by Danzig, including useful Sporting Lad: dam winning sprinter in USA: fair form when fourth to Briareus in maiden at Windsor on debut (slowly away): well held after, needing early reminders/running in snatches final outing: should stay 11f. *P. F. I. Cole*

SWIFT ALCHEMIST   3 b.f. Fleetwood (IRE) 107 – Pure Gold 88 (Dilum (USA)   **78** 115) [2003 76: 8m* 8g² 8.2m⁴ 9f 8.1g⁵ p7g² p7g p7g f8.5g Nov 10] tall, rather angular filly: fair performer: won maiden at Newcastle (dead-heated) in April: stays 1m: acts on polytrack, soft and good to firm ground: sometimes looks difficult ride. *K. R. Burke*

SWIFT APPRAISAL   4 gr.g. Slip Anchor 136 – Minsden's Image 78 (Dancer's   **–** Image (USA)) [2003 –: 14.1g 11.5m Apr 21] lightly-raced maiden: signs of just a little ability: bred to be well suited by 1m+: has been slowly away. *S. C. Williams*

SWIFTMIX   3 gr.f. Linamix (FR) 127 – Swift Spring (FR) 56 (Bluebird (USA) 125)   **65 d** [2003 73: 9.7g 12m² 12.6m 14m 11.6d f12g Jul 19] leggy filly: fair maiden: virtually refused to race on reappearance: ran as though amiss last 4 starts: stays 1½m: acts on good to firm ground: tongue tied (ran poorly) final 2-y-o start: sold 11,000 gns. *P. F. I. Cole*

SWIFT SAILING (USA)   2 b.c. (Mar 31) Storm Cat (USA) – Saytarra (USA) 111   **84** (Seeking The Gold (USA)) [2003 6m 6d* 7m⁵ Aug 21] rather leggy, attractive colt: first foal: dam, 2-y-o 7f/1m (Prix d'Aumale) winner, her only starts, half-sister to Lammtarra out of Oaks winner Snow Bride: fairly useful form: won maiden at Salisbury in July: respectable fifth of 7 in nursery at York: will stay 7f, probably 1m: acts on good to soft going. *B. W. Hills*

SWIFT TANGO (IRE)   3 b.g. Desert Prince (IRE) 130 – Ballet Society (FR) (Sadler's   **94** Wells (USA) 132) [2003 70§: 7g 8.5m³ 8.3m* 8.5m² 10.3m³ 8.5m² 8.1g² 8.5m² 9m* 8m⁶ 8.5d² 10m³ Oct 22] good-topped gelding: fairly useful performer: won minor event at Windsor in June and handicap at Ripon in August: barely stays 1¼m: acts on firm and soft going, below form on polytrack: has worn cheekpieces/visor last 6 starts: carries head high: reliable. *E. A. L. Dunlop*

SWINBROOK (USA)   2 ch.g. (Apr 8) Stravinsky (USA) 133 – Dance Diane (USA)   **88 p** (Affirmed (USA)) [2003 6m⁵ 6m² Oct 21] $50,000Y: first foal: dam Canadian 2-y-o 1m stakes winner: much better effort in minor events (fairly useful form, had been gelded since debut) when 1¼ lengths second of 6 to Rum Shot at Yarmouth: will stay 7f: open to progress, and should win a race or 2. *J. A. R. Toller*

SWING WING   4 b.g. In The Wings 128 – Swift Spring (FR) 56 (Bluebird (USA) 125)   **113** [2003 110: 13.3m³ 15.5g* 16g⁵ 15d³ 14.5s³ Nov 2] good-topped gelding: has a quick, fluent action: smart performer: won listed event at Longchamp in June by neck from Blue Inside, making all but needing several reminders throughout: also ran well when third in listed race at Newbury (to Gamut) and Prix Kergorlay at Deauville (3 lengths behind Darasim) first/fourth starts: stays 15.5f: acts on heavy and good to firm going, probably on fibresand: blinkered (respectable fifth in Goodwood Cup) third start. *P. F. I. Cole*

SWORN TO SECRECY   2 ch.f. (Apr 27) Prince Sabo 123 – Polly's Teahouse 68   **62** (Shack (USA) 118) [2003 6m 6m⁴ 6g³ 5.1m⁵ Aug 14] half-sister to several winners by Weldnaas, including fairly useful 5f (including at 2 yrs) winner Polly Golightly and temperamental 7f winner Tea For Texas: dam sprint maiden: modest maiden: third at Windsor: probably better at 6f than 5f. *S. Kirk*

SWYNFORD ELEGANCE   6 ch.m. Charmer 123 – Qualitairess 49 (Kampala 120)   **47 §** [2003 51: 7.1d 9f 8m² 7m 8m 8f³ 8.1g 8.5m 10f³ Aug 27] quite good-topped mare: just a poor handicapper nowadays: left J. Hetherton after sixth start: effective at 7f to 1¼m: acts on any ground: tried in cheekpieces/tongue tie: unreliable. *I. A. Wood*

SWYNFORD PLEASURE   7 b.m. Reprimand 122 – Pleasuring 68 (Good Times   **68** (ITY)) [2003 70, a–: 10m⁴ 12.4m 10g 10.1g² 12m* 12m 12m³ 10m 12.1d⁴ 12m⁴ 11.9f⁴   **a–** 12.1m* 12.3m* 12d 12m 11.9f 14.1m⁵ 12g Nov 5] strong mare: fair handicapper: won at Pontefract, Beverley and Ripon in the summer: has form at 8.5f, but races mostly at 1½m/ 1¾m nowadays: acts on firm and soft going: tried blinkered (not since 1999): refused to enter stall intended fourteenth outing, also mulish before fifteenth: often held up: tough. *J. Hetherton*

SWYNFORD WELCOME   7 b.m. Most Welcome 131 – Qualitair Dream 80   **68 d** (Dreams To Reality (USA) 113) [2003 74§, a60§: 7m 6m 7d 5g 7.1g³ 7m 8f 7m 10g 7d*   **a– §** 8m 6m 7f 8.5m 6.9m 5m 7m 6m 7f 7m 7g 7d 8.2f 6m 10d f8.5g⁴ f7g Nov 19] good-topped mare: fair handicapper: won at Epsom in July: stayed 7f: acted on polytrack, firm and soft going: tried in blinkers/cheekpieces: reared start and unseated rider ninth outing: effective held up or ridden prominently: unreliable: dead. *I. A. Wood*

SYDNEY STAR 2 b.f. (Mar 17) Machiavellian (USA) 123 – Sena Desert 89 (Green Desert (USA) 127) [2003 7g² Nov 1] neat filly: first foal: dam, 1¼m winner, half-sister to very smart 1¼m performer Best of The Bests (by Machiavellian): 5/1, ½-length second of 18 to Damsel in maiden at Newmarket, leading briefly over 1f out: will be suited by 1m/1¼m: useful prospect, should win races. *B. W. Hills* — **91 p**

SYLVA BOUNTY 4 br.g. Bahamian Bounty 116 – Spriolo (Priolo (USA) 127) [2003 –: f8s f12g 10m Apr 26] compact gelding: little sign of ability: tried visored/tongue tied. *B. P. J. Baugh* — **–**

SYLVAN TWISTER 4 br.c. First Trump 118 – Storm Party (IRE) (Bluebird (USA) 125) [2003 –: p12g p16g Mar 5] well held in maidens/handicap. *P. Mitchell* — **–**

SYLVA STORM (USA) 5 ch.g. Miswaki (USA) 124 – Sudden Storm Bird (USA) (Storm Bird (CAN) 134) [2003 72, a85: 9g⁶ Jul 16] close-coupled gelding: fairly useful on all-weather in 2002, fair on turf: respectable effort only run in 2003: stays easy 1¾m: acts on all-weather and firm going: sometimes blinkered: reportedly had breathing problem second 4-y-o start: has looked less than keen: none too trustworthy: sold 3,200 gns in October, resold £300 in December. *C. E. Brittain* — **66 ?**

SYMBOLI KRIS S (USA) 4 b.c. Kris S (USA) – Tee Kay (USA) (Gold Meridian (USA) 112) [2003 125: 11f⁵ 10f* 12d³ 12.5f* Dec 28] second foal: half-brother to winner in USA by Gone West: dam US Grade 3 8.5f winner: top-class performer: Horse of The Year in Japan in 2002 and 2003: off 4 months after reappearance at 4 yrs, then successful in Tenno Sho (Autumn) at Tokyo (beat Tsurumaru Boy 1½ lengths) in November and Arima Kinen at Nakayama in December, both for second year in a row: best effort in latter, beating Lincoln by 9 lengths: 9¾ lengths third to all-the-way winner Tap Dance City in muddling Japan Cup at Tokyo on penultimate start, staying on well: effective at 1¼m/1½m: acted on firm going, probably on soft: to stand at Shadai Stallion Station, Japan. *K. Fujisawa, Japan* — **132**

SYRIAN FLUTIST 5 ch.m. Shaamit (IRE) 127 – Brave Vanessa (USA) 62 (Private Account (USA)) [2003 59: f12s² Jan 10] modest maiden: stays 1½m: acts on good to firm going, soft and fibresand: has had tongue tied: ran creditably in cheekpieces only outing in 2003. *D. E. Cantillon* — **59**

SYSTEMATIC 4 b.c. Rainbow Quest (USA) 134 – Sensation 114 (Soviet Star (USA) 128) [2003 121: 13.3m² 12g⁵ 11m⁵ Sep 20] good-topped colt: very smart and thoroughly genuine performer at 3 yrs, winning 7 races: suffered injury to near-fore cannon bone in early-April: creditable 3½ lengths second of 5 to Mubtaker in Geoffrey Freer Stakes at Newbury on reappearance: respectable fifth to Mamool in Grosser Bugatti Preis at Baden-Baden then well below form in listed event at Newbury (visored, dropped away tamely): will stay 1¾m: acts on soft and good to firm going: has edged right/been difficult at start: often makes running. *M. Johnston* — **118**

T

TAAQAAH 2 ch.c. (Apr 15) Grand Lodge (USA) 125 – Belle Ile (USA) 67 (Diesis 133) [2003 7g⁶ 8.3g² Sep 1] 80,000F, 68,000Y: sturdy colt: has a quick action: sixth foal: half-brother to 2 winners abroad, including French 10.5f winner Enchanted Isle (by Mujtahid): dam, 1m winner, out of smart performer up to 1¾m Bonne Ile: fair form in maidens at Goodwood and Hamilton (second to Woody Valentine, dictating pace): should be suited by 1¼m/1½m. *M. P. Tregoning* — **72**

TABADUL (IRE) 2 b.c. (Feb 4) Cadeaux Genereux 131 – Amaniy (USA) 96 (Dayjur (USA) 137) [2003 7.2d* Oct 13] fourth foal: half-brother to 6f winner Ikbal (by Indian Ridge): dam, 2-y-o 5f/6f winner, half-sister to smart UAE 7f winner Kayrawan: 12/1, won 10-runner maiden at Ayr by 1½ lengths from Divine Gift, getting up final 100 yds: should stay 1m: open to improvement. *E. A. L. Dunlop* — **92 p**

TABARKA (GER) 2 b.f. (Apr 10) Big Shuffle (USA) 122 – Tirana (GER) (Esclavo (FR)) [2003 5.2f⁴ 5.2f⁵ 5m³ 6m Sep 22] €4,500Y: sister to 2 winners in Germany, including 6f (at 2 yrs) to 9f winner Ticiano and half-sister to several winners in Germany: dam — **61**

German 1m (at 2 yrs) and 11f winner: modest maiden: third at Musselburgh: likely to prove best at 5f: blinkered final start. *P. A. Blockley*

TABINDA 3 b.g. Wizard King 122 – Mouchez Le Nez (IRE) 41 (Cyrano de Bergerac 120) [2003 54: p10g 8m Sep 18] modest form in 2-y-o maidens: well held in handicaps in 2003. *N. P. Littmoden* —

TABLEAU (USA) 2 ch.c. (Apr 19) Marquetry (USA) 121 – Model Bride (USA) (Blushing Groom (FR) 131) [2003 7d⁵ Nov 7] half-brother to 3 winners, including useful 1m winners Arabride (by Unfuwain) and Mediterraneo (by Be My Guest): dam unraced half-sister to smart miler Zaizafon (dam of Zafonic) and to dam of Reams of Verse and Elmaamul: 8/1 and green, 8¼ lengths fifth of 17 to Spring Surprise in maiden at Doncaster, hampered 2f out and staying on: will stay at least 1m: should improve. *B. W. Hills* **68 p**

TABOOR (IRE) 5 b.g. Mujadil (USA) 119 – Christoph's Girl 50 (Efisio 120) [2003 69, a78: p5g⁴ p5g³ p6g⁵ p5g 5g 5m⁴ 5g* 5m 5m 5m Jul 23] heavy-topped gelding: fair performer: won minor event at Carlisle in May: probably best at 5f: acts on good to soft ground, firm and all-weather: blinkered nowadays, and usually wears hood: very slowly away final outing. *J. W. Payne* **65 a76**

TACITUS (IRE) 3 ch.c. Titus Livius (FR) 115 – Idara 109 (Top Ville 129) [2003 105: 8g* 10m 8g⁴ 8s Oct 12] well-made, attractive colt: useful performer: bit below 2-y-o form in 2003, though still won minor event at Doncaster in March: not discredited last 2 starts in minor event at Doncaster and listed race at Longchamp: stays 1m: acts on soft going: sold 72,000 gns. *R. Hannon* **97**

TACTILE 2 b.f. (Feb 13) Groom Dancer (USA) 128 – Trinity Reef 80 (Bustino 136) [2003 8.2f Sep 30] 75,000Y: unfurnished filly: second foal: dam, 1½m winner, sister to smart 1¼m/1½m performer Talented and half-sister to dam of 6-y-o Three Points: 9/2 and unimpressive in appearance, well held in maiden at Nottingham. *Sir Michael Stoute* —

TADEO 10 ch.g. Primo Dominie 121 – Royal Passion 78 (Ahonoora 122) [2003 83d: 6g Sep 27] small, strong gelding: one-time smart performer: on downgrade. *I. A. Wood* —

TADRIS (USA) 3 b.f. Red Ransom (USA) – Manwah (USA) 72 (Lyphard (USA) 132) [2003 77p: 10m² 8s* 8f³ 8.1d⁴ 8f* 10m² p8g* p10g Nov 22] tall, leggy filly: useful performer: won maiden in July and listed rated stakes in September (beat Convent Girl ¾ length), both at Ascot, and listed race at Lingfield (by 1¼ lengths from Zietory) in November: also good head second to Al Ihtithar in listed race at Newmarket (free to post) **106**

Kotex Rosemary Rated Stakes (Handicap), Ascot—
from right to left, Tadris, Convent Girl and Penny Cross

sixth start: stayed 1¼m: won on soft going, better form on firm going and polytrack: sometimes reluctant at stall/on toes: tended to flick tail under pressure: found little fourth/ final starts: visits Montjeu. *M. P. Tregoning*

TADSBII 2 ch.g. (Jan 25) Entrepreneur 123 – Intervene (Zafonic (USA) 130) [2003 8.1d — 7.9f 7m Oct 17] 19,000Y: quite good-topped gelding: first foal: dam unraced half-sister to dam of July Cup winner Continent: well beaten in maidens/claimer: blinkered second start: tends to be slowly away. *T. D. Easterby*

TADZIO 4 bl.g. Mtoto 134 – Fresher 113 (Fabulous Dancer (USA) 124) [2003 f12g — f8.5g Nov 29] no form over hurdles: well held in maiden and seller (visored). *M. J. Gingell*

TAFAAHUM (USA) 2 b.c. (Mar 10) Erhaab (USA) 127 – Makadir (USA) (Woodman **88** (USA) 126) [2003 7.1m⁶ 7.2m* 8m Oct 20] good-bodied colt: poor mover: fifth foal: half-brother to 5-y-o Rasid and 7f/1m winner in USA by Holy Bull: dam, 1m/9f winner in USA, third in 2-y-o Grade 3 event: fairly useful form when winning 12-runner maiden at Ayr in September by 4 lengths from Universal King, leading 2f out: well held in listed event at Pontefract final start: should stay at least 1m. *M. Johnston*

TAFFRAIL 5 b.g. Slip Anchor 136 – Tizona (Pharly (FR) 130) [2003 105: 16m 16.2g⁶ — 16.4m 22.2f 16.4g⁵ 16.2m 16m⁵ Sep 18] lengthy, good sort: useful performer at best: well held in 2003: tried in cheekpieces: usually bandaged fore joints: sold 11,000 gns. *J. L. Dunlop*

TAFFS WELL 10 b.g. Dowsing (USA) 124 – Zahiah 90 (So Blessed 130) [2003 71: — 8m Oct 1] small gelding: fair in 2002: well held only appearance in 2003: blinkered (pulled too hard) final 9-y-o outing: held up. *B. Ellison*

TAFFY DANCER 5 b.g. Emperor Jones (USA) 119 – Ballerina Bay 75 (Myjinski **62** (USA)) [2003 59: 13.3m 10.2g⁴ 11.9m³ 12m³ 12.1d⁴ f16.2g⁴ f14s² 18m² Oct 20] rangy gelding: modest handicapper: stays 2¼m: acts on fibresand, good to firm and good to soft ground: has carried head high: races prominently. *H. Morrison*

TAGGERTY (IRE) 5 b.m. Definite Article 121 – Kewaashi (USA) 69 (Storm Bird **53** (CAN) 134) [2003 60, a52: f7s f7s⁶ p7g³ p7g p7g p7g 6m⁵ 7d 7m² 7f² 6.1g 7.1m² 6.1m² 7m⁵ 7.2g 5m² 5.3m³ 6f 6m⁵ 7f³ 6.1m 6m⁴ 6f⁶ Oct 12] leggy, sparely-made mare: modest maiden: effective at 6f to 1m: unraced on heavy going, acts on any other turf/all-weather: sometimes wears blinkers/cheekpieces: has carried head high: none too resolute: sold 2,700 gns, sent to Holland. *M. J. Polglase*

TAG TEAM (IRE) 2 ch.c. (Apr 11) Tagula (IRE) 116 – Okay Baby (IRE) 67 (Treasure **– p** Kay 114) [2003 6m Sep 16] €19,000Y: lengthy, quite good-topped colt: second foal: half-brother to 6f winner Classy Lassie (by Goldmark): dam 1m winner: 10/1, eighth of 11 in maiden at Salisbury, green and not knocked about: should do better. *A. M. Balding*

TAGULA BLUE (IRE) 3 b.g. Tagula (IRE) 116 – Palace Blue (IRE) (Dara Monarch **94** 128) [2003 63: 7m 8d* 8.1m⁴ 9.1m⁶ 8.2g² 8.2d* 8m 8.1d 8.2m⁶ Oct 28] good-bodied gelding: has a round action: fairly useful handicapper: won at Thirsk in May and Nottingham in July: below form after: stays 1m: acts on good to soft ground: usually tongue tied: sometimes slowly away: has raced freely. *J. A. Glover*

TAHIRAH 3 b.f. Green Desert (USA) 127 – Kismah 111 (Machiavellian (USA) 123) **99** [2003 7.1m² 8m* 8.1m 7m⁴ 7f 7m* 7d⁷ 7s Nov 14] smallish, close-coupled filly: first foal: dam, 1m winner on both starts, out of half-sister to top-class US filly Glorious Song (dam of Singspiel and Rahy) and champion 1983 US 2-y-o Devil's Bag: useful performer: won maiden at Brighton in June and apprentice handicaps at Doncaster in October and (having left A. Stewart 29,000 gns) November (beat Golden Chalice by 1¾ lengths): well held in listed race at Maisons-Laffitte after: stays 1m: acts on good to firm and good to soft ground: reluctant at stall/slowly away third outing. *R. Guest*

TAHREEB (FR) 2 ch.c. (May 17) Indian Ridge 123 – Native Twine 114 (Be My Native **108** (USA) 122) [2003 6m² 6f² 6d⁶ 6m³ 5g⁴ 8m⁴ Oct 25] 85,000Y: compact, attractive colt: half-brother to several winners, including useful 7f (at 2 yrs) to 1½m winner Ihtiyati (by Chief's Crown), later successful in Australia: dam, 7f (at 2 yrs) to 1¼m winner, half-sister to Alderbrook: useful performer: made all in maiden at Goodwood in July: in frame in Mill Reef Stakes at Newbury (good length third to Byron), Cornwallis Stakes at Ascot and Racing Post Trophy at Doncaster (close to form when last of 4 to American Post) after: probably stays 1m: acts on good to soft ground, probably on firm. *M. P. Tregoning*

TAI LASS 3 b. or br.f. Taipan (IRE) 124 – Kerry's Oats (Derrylin 115) [2003 14f⁶ — Oct 12] first foal: dam winning hurdler: 50/1, always behind in maiden at Goodwood. *P. R. Hedger*

TAILI 2 b.f. (Apr 16) Taipan (IRE) 124 – Doubtfire 71 (Jalmood (USA) 126) [2003 6g –
7.1m 8.3g Aug 13] 1,000Y: fifth reported foal: dam, 2-y-o 6f seller winner, probably
stayed 1¼m: well beaten in minor event/maidens. *D. A. Nolan*

TAIPAN LAD (IRE) 3 b.g. Taipan (IRE) 124 – Newgate Lady (IRE) (Whistling Deer –
117) [2003 –: 7.9g 8d 12d Jun 30] leggy gelding: little form: tried in cheekpieces.
G. M. Moore

TAIPO PRINCE (IRE) 3 b.g. Entrepreneur 123 – Dedicated Lady (IRE) 101 (Pennine 55
Walk 120) [2003 10.1m 8g 7m 8m 10g f9.4g² Jul 11] IR 12,000Y: lengthy, good-topped
gelding: seventh foal: half-brother to 3 winners, notably 7f (at 2 yrs) to 12.5f (Prix de
Royallieu) winner Fairy Queen (by Fairy King) and 6f (at 2 yrs) to 1m (Falmouth Stakes)
winner Tashawak (by Night Shift), both smart: dam Irish 2-y-o 5f/6f winner: modest
maiden: likely to prove best short of 9.4f: acts on fibresand, raced only on good ground or
firmer on turf: visored (ran well) final start: sold 7,200 gns. *A. P. Jarvis*

TAIYO 3 b.f. Tagula (IRE) 116 – Tharwa (IRE) 63 (Last Tycoon 131) [2003 61p: 6m⁵ 59
6.1g 6g⁵ p7g⁶ p7g Dec 6] well-made filly: modest maiden, lightly raced: stays 7f: raced
only on polytrack and good/good to firm ground. *J. W. Payne*

TAJAR (USA) 11 b.g. Slew O'Gold (USA) – Mashaarif (USA) (Mr Prospector (USA)) – §
[2003 33§: 12m Apr 8] strong, angular gelding: poor handicapper: well held only outing
in 2003: tried blinkered/tongue tied: irresolute. *T. Keddy*

TAKE A BOW 2 b.c. (Mar 23) Royal Applause 124 – Giant Nipper (Nashwan (USA) 83
135) [2003 7.1m 8m² Sep 24] 24,000Y: rather leggy, lengthy colt: third foal: half-brother
to 5-y-o Sharpinch and 3-y-o Second of May: dam ran once: better effort in maidens
(fairly useful form) when 1¾ lengths second of 5 to North Light at Goodwood, dictating
pace: withdrawn after breaking out of stall in October: not sure to stay much beyond 1m.
P. R. Chamings

TAKE GOOD TIME (IRE) 3 ch.g. Among Men (USA) 124 – Bold Motion (Anshan 46
119) [2003 6f⁶ Oct 12] IR 2,500Y: second foal: dam, third in 7f seller at 2 yrs, half-sister
to high-class middle-distance performer Raami: 25/1 and green, 8½ lengths sixth to
Gallery Breeze in maiden at Goodwood: should be suited by 7f+. *John Berry*

TAKES TUTU (USA) 4 b.g. Afternoon Deelites (USA) 122 – Lady Affirmed (USA) 94 §
(Affirmed (USA)) [2003 99: a8f a7f a8f* a7.5f a8f³ a7f 8m 8.5m 7f⁴ 8.1g 7m 9.9g 8g⁶
9.2g⁵ Aug 13] tall, useful-looking gelding: fairly useful handicapper: won at Jebel Ali in
February: in-and-out form after: effective at 7f to easy 10.5f: acts on all-weather and firm
going, possibly not on softer than good: blinkered/visored: has raced freely/idled: sold
18,000 gns: quirky. *M. Johnston*

TALBOT AVENUE 5 b.g. Puissance 110 – Dancing Daughter 79 (Dance In Time 99
(CAN)) [2003 94: 5.1m⁴ 5m 5f 5g³ 5m* 5.1m⁴ 6m 6m 5f 5d 6f 5m Oct 25] compact
gelding: useful performer: won handicap at York in July: ran well in listed event at
Chester 24 hrs later: below par after: likely to prove best at 5f: best form on good/good to
firm going: has been bandaged fore/hind joints: sometimes wanders. *M. Mullineaux*

TALENT STAR 6 b.g. Mizoram (USA) 105 – Bells of Longwick 92 (Myjinski –
(USA)) [2003 –: f9.4s Jan 31] modest maiden at 4 yrs: lightly raced and well held since.
A. W. Carroll

TALE OF THE TIGER 2 ch.c. (Mar 16) Bijou d'Inde 127 – La Belle Dominique 76 –
(Dominion 123) [2003 5.1m Apr 21] second foal: dam 5f winner: last of 13 in maiden at
Nottingham (reportedly lame). *Julian Poulton*

TALKING CHALK 2 ch.c. (Apr 9) Docksider (USA) 124 – Zoom Lens (IRE) 65 41
(Caerleon (USA) 132) [2003 5g 5g⁴ 6m 6g⁵ 7m 7m⁵ f6g Oct 4] 22,000Y: half-brother to
several winners, including smart 7f/1m winner (including at 2 yrs) Atlantis Prince (by
Tagula) and 3-y-o Zeis: dam in frame up to 1½m: poor maiden: stays 7f: tongue tied last
3 starts. *W. R. Muir*

TALLASSEE 3 ch.f. Indian Ridge 123 – Red Rose Garden 87 (Electric 126) [2003 60
6.1g 9.2d 7f 10.9g³ Aug 1] IR 48,000Y: sturdy filly: sister to very smart 7f (at 2 yrs) to
1¼m winner Handsome Ridge and half-sister to 2 winners, including fairly useful 1m (at
2 yrs) and 1¾m winner Red Bustaan (by Aragon): dam Irish 1½m winner: modest
maiden: stays 10.8f: acts on firm ground: blinkered (ran well) final start. *G. A. Butler*

TALLDARK'N'ANDSOME 4 b.g. Efisio 120 – Fleur du Val (Valiyar 129) [2003 84
91: p12g p10g 10.3m 10m 10m⁴ 9.9m 10.5g⁵ 10m² 10d 10.1g⁶ 10.3d⁶ 10s* Nov 3] workmanlike gelding: fairly useful handicapper: won at Redcar in November: should stay

beyond 1¼m: acts on polytrack, soft and good to firm ground: blinkered last 3 starts. *N. P. Littmoden*

TALLY (IRE) 3 ch.g. Tagula (IRE) 116 – Sally Chase 101 (Sallust 134) [2003 59, a65: f6g f6g³ f6g³ p6g* p6g* f6g⁴ 7m 6f 6m² 5.9m* 6g 6m⁶ 7.1f⁴ 6g⁶ Aug 25] close-coupled gelding: fair performer: won maiden and handicap at Lingfield in February, and handicap at Carlisle in June: barely stays easy 7f: acts on all-weather and firm going, probably on good to soft: hung right twelfth start: effective making running or held up. *A. Berry*   **68**

TAMARELLA (IRE) 3 b.f. Tamarisk (IRE) 127 – Miss Siham (IRE) 59 (Green Forest (USA) 134) [2003 66: 6.1g 6.1m³ 5.1m* 6.1m³ 5s 5.7m⁴ f5s 5f⁴ 5.7f⁵ 6.1m 5m 6g 6.1m⁵ f6g p6g Nov 29] smallish, well-made filly: fair handicapper: won at Bath in April: below form after next start: effective at 5f/6f: acts on good to firm going, showed little on fibresand. *G. G. Margarson*   **75 d a–**

TAMARILLO 2 gr.f. (Jan 28) Daylami (IRE) 138 – Up And About 77 (Barathea (IRE) 127) [2003 7f² 7f² 8.2m* 8d⁵ Sep 11] 40,000Y: compact filly: first foal: dam 15f winner out of very smart 1¼m/1½m winner Upend, herself half-sister to dam of high-class stayer/Champion Hurdle winner Royal Gait: useful performer: landed odds in maiden at Nottingham in August by 2½ lengths from Doctrine, dictating pace: travelled well long way when respectable fifth to Kinnaird in May Hill Stakes at Doncaster: bred to be suited by 1¼m+: acts on firm going: sent to UAE, joined M. Al Kurdi. *M. L. W. Bell*   **98**

TAMARINA (IRE) 2 ch.f. (Mar 11) Foxhound (USA) 103 – Tamasriya (IRE) (Doyoun 124) [2003 8g⁵ f8g f8g f9.4g⁴ Dec 22] IR 5,200F, 8,000Y: leggy, angular filly: third foal: half-sister to 4-y-o Ulysees: dam French 9.5f winner: left M. Tregoning after debut: seemingly best effort (modest form) when fourth to Bill Bennett in maiden at Wolverhampton: stays easy 9.4f. *N. E. Berry*   **56**

TAMESIS (IRE) 2 b.f. (May 9) Fasliyev (USA) 120 – Cocktail Party (USA) (Arctic Tern (USA) 126) [2003 5f³ 5m³ 6m⁴ 5m⁴ 5m⁴ 6g⁴ 5m⁴ 5m⁶ 5m Oct 25] IR 34,000F, €25,000Y: smallish filly: second living foal: dam, 8.5f winner in USA, sister to US Grade 3 9f winner Freewheel: modest maiden: probably stays 6f: acts on firm going: consistent. *T. D. Easterby*   **55**

TAMIAMI TRAIL (IRE) 5 ch.g. Indian Ridge 123 – Eurobird 118 (Ela-Mana-Mou 132) [2003 105: 10m⁶ 22.2f² 16.4g⁴ 18.7m⁶ Aug 3] sturdy, close-coupled gelding: useful performer: reportedly suffered setback after final 3-y-o start, and ran only twice in 2002: creditable efforts in 2003 when 1¼ lengths second to Cover Up in Queen Alexandra Stakes at Royal Ascot and 3 lengths fourth to Persian Punch in listed race at Sandown: stays 2¾m: acts on firm and soft ground. *B. J. Meehan*   **106**

TAMINOULA (IRE) 2 b.f. (Jan 24) Tagula (IRE) 116 – Taormina (IRE) (Ela-Mana-Mou 132) [2003 6g 7m³ 7f* 7f* Oct 12] 35,000F, €45,000Y: first foal: dam unraced sister to useful performers up to 1½m Mayshiel (in France) and O'Connor (in Germany): fairly useful performer: won maiden at Brighton in August and nursery at Goodwood (raced freely, got up near finish) in October: should stay 1m: acts on firm going. *Mrs A. J. Perrett*   **82**

TAMWEEL (USA) 3 b.f. Gulch (USA) – Naazeq 80 (Nashwan (USA) 135) [2003 7m 7.1m² 8m* 7m* Aug 24] medium-sized, workmanlike filly: third foal: sister to 4-y-o Thunder Canyon and closely related to 5-y-o Mostarsil (by Kingmambo): dam, 10.5f winner, sister to smart performer up to 2½m Shaya: fairly useful performer: won maiden at Thirsk and 5-runner handicap at Yarmouth, both in August: free-going sort, better form at 7f than 1m: sold 47,000 gns, sent to USA. *A. C. Stewart*   **85**

TANAFFUS 3 ch.g. Cadeaux Genereux 131 – El Rabab (USA) 70 (Roberto (USA) 131) [2003 75: 7m⁵ 6m⁶ Aug 9] strong, well-made gelding: easy mover: maiden: fair form in 2 races at 2 yrs: found little/left impression something amiss in 2003: sold 10,500 gns, and gelded. *B. W. Hills*   **–**

TANAGHUM 3 b.f. Darshaan 133 – Mehthaaf (USA) 121 (Nureyev (USA) 131) [2003 10m* 9.9m⁴ 12m² 12g⁴ 10.3d Nov 7] rather leggy, quite attractive filly: fluent mover: fifth foal: half-sister to several winners by Nashwan, including smart 1¼m winner Najah and fairly useful 1½m winner Raaqi: dam, 6f (at 2 yrs) and 1m (Irish 1000 Guineas) winner, closely related to high-class sprinter Elnadim and granddaughter of outstanding broodmare Fall Aspen: useful performer, lightly raced: won maiden at Newmarket in July: easily best effort when 1½ lengths second to My Renee in listed race at Ascot in September: stayed 1½m: acted on good to firm going: visits Sakhee. *J. L. Dunlop*   **104**

TANAJI 4 b.f. Marju (IRE) 127 – Hamsaat (IRE) 80 (Sadler's Wells (USA) 132) [2003 78: 12m 10.3m⁶ May 28] strong, lengthy filly: fair performer: may prove best at 1m/1¼m: acts on good to firm and good to soft going: effective blinkered or not. *P. R. Webber*   **76**

TANARA   2 ch.f. (Jan 22) Bianconi (USA) 123 – Tryarra (IRE) 99 (Persian Heights   **49 §**
129) [2003 5m⁵ 5f⁴ 5m⁴ f6g⁶ 6m 6g⁶ f5g² 5m f5g Aug 7] angular filly: sixth foal:
half-sister to untrustworthy 7f winner Little Pixie (by Woodman): dam Irish 8.5f to 1¼m
winner: poor maiden: left J. Given after third start: second in seller at Wolverhampton:
best form at 5f: acts on firm going and fibresand: untrustworthy. *R. Brotherton*

TANCRED ARMS   7 b.m. Clantime 101 – Mischievous Miss 73 (Niniski (USA) 125)   **51 §**
[2003 61, a40: 7m 6m⁶ 7m 7m 6f⁵ f7g 7.2m* 7.6m 7d⁶ 6.9d Jul 30] lengthy mare: modest   **a– §**
handicapper on turf, poor on all-weather: won at Ayr in June: best around 7f: acts on
fibresand and probably on any turf going: often visored (not at Ayr): inconsistent.
D. W. Barker

TANCRED IMP   2 b.f. (Mar 25) Atraf 116 – Tancred Mischief 44 (Northern State   **49**
(USA) 91) [2003 7m 7m 8m³ Sep 18] 2,000Y: sturdy filly: second foal: dam, 2m/2¼m
winner, also successful over hurdles: poor form: third in seller at Ayr: stays 1m.
D. W. Barker

TANCRED MISS   4 b.f. Presidium 124 – Mischievous Miss 73 (Niniski (USA) 125)   **50 d**
[2003 64, a51: f6g⁴ f7s f7s f6g 7m 7m 6.9m 7d Sep 20] smallish, leggy filly: modest
handicapper: well held after reappearance: seems best at 6f/7f: acts on fibresand, firm and
good to soft going: usually races prominently. *D. W. Barker*

TANCRED TIMES   8 ch.m. Clantime 101 – Mischievous Miss 73 (Niniski (USA)   **70**
125) [2003 68, a64: f5g 5m 6m 5m⁵ 6m* 5d 6f² 5m 5f² 5g⁴ 6d 6m³ 5m* 6m 5m 6m Sep 8]
small mare: fair performer: won handicap at Thirsk in May and minor event at Hamilton
(hung right) in August: best at 5f/easy 6f: acts on firm going, soft and fibresand: tried
blinkered: usually races prominently. *D. W. Barker*

TANCRED TYKE   3 b.f. Atraf 116 – Tancred Mischief 44 (Northern State (USA) 91)   **–**
[2003 –: 8m 7m Sep 9] small filly: well held in maidens. *D. W. Barker*

TANCRED WALK   5 b.m. Clantime 101 – Mischievous Miss 73 (Niniski (USA) 125)   **–**
[2003 44+: f5g f6g Jan 21] smallish mare: poor maiden: no form in 2003. *D. W. Barker*

TANDAVA (IRE)   5 ch.g. Indian Ridge 123 – Kashka (USA) (The Minstrel (CAN) 135)   **84**
[2003 90: 12.1g 15f² 11.9g 13g² 16m 17.5m⁴ 13.1d 16.5d Nov 10] lengthy gelding: fairly
useful performer: stays 17f: acts on firm and soft going, yet to race on heavy: visored last
2 starts: sometimes slowly away: has taken good hold: reportedly pulled a muscle third
start. *I. Semple*

TANGA DANCER   3 ch.f. Blue Ocean (USA) 87 – Tangalooma 56 (Hotfoot 126)   **53**
[2003 57d: 8.5m 8s⁴ 7.9d⁶ 8.3m* f9.4g f8g Dec 8] modest performer: won seller at
Hamilton in August: stays 1m: acts on soft and good to firm ground, tailed off on all-
weather: none too consistent. *B. Smart*

TANGO CAT (USA)   3 b. or br.f. Tale of The Cat (USA) 113 – Rutledge Place (USA)   **81**
(Caro 133) [2003 88p: 10m⁴ 10.1m² 10m² 12.3f* 11.8g 12m Aug 6] $250,000Y: big,
good-topped filly: half-sister to several winners, including smart 6f (at 2 yrs)/7f winner
Firm Pledge (by Affirmed), later Grade 3 winner in USA: dam unraced half-sister to very
smart French sprinter Gem Diamond: fairly useful performer: once-raced at 2 yrs for
A. O'Brien: won 4-runner maiden at Ripon in June: well held in handicaps after: likely to
prove best short of 1½m: raced only on good ground or firmer: sent to Australia. *W. Jarvis*

TANGO STEP (IRE)   3 b.g. Sesaro (USA) 81 – Leitrim Lodge (IRE) 64 (Classic   **57**
Music (USA)) [2003 59: 5.8s 8d 6.5f² 6g 8f⁴ 8.5d 7f⁶ 8d f7g Nov 21] IR 5,600F, IR
5,200Y: third foal: half-brother to winners abroad by Royal Abjar and Danehill Dancer:
dam 2-y-o 5f seller winner, half-sister to useful Irish performer up to 7f Fairy Fable:
modest maiden handicapper: well held on all-weather debut at Wolverhampton final
start: stays 1m: acts on firm and soft going: blinkered penultimate 2-y-o outing. *Bernard
Lawlor, Ireland*

TANGO TANGO   2 ch.f. (Mar 16) Rudimentary (USA) 118 – Lady Mabel 34 (Inchinor   **56**
119) [2003 5m⁴ 5.1f⁶ 5m⁶ 5.3f⁴ 5.1f⁵ f6g 6m Oct 24] 800Y: second foal: dam, maiden,
stayed 1m: modest maiden: should stay 6f: acts on firm going. *P. A. Blockley*

TANNOOR (USA)   2 b.c. (Feb 2) Miswaki (USA) 124 – Iolani 59 (Alzao (USA) 117)   **79 p**
[2003 7m 7m³ 7s³ Oct 20] 160,000Y: well-made colt: fourth foal: dam, maiden, out of
Galtres Stakes winner Sans Blague: favourite, fair form in maidens: third at York and Yarmouth (to Singing Poet, led until final 1f): will probably stay 1m: open to improvement.
M. A. Jarvis

TANSHAN   8 ch.g. Anshan 119 – Nafla (FR) (Arctic Tern (USA) 126) [2003 p12g Feb   **–**
5] good-bodied gelding: modest maiden: well held only outing in 2003. *R. Rowe*

Mr Wafic Said's "Tante Rose"

TANTE ROSE (IRE)   3 b.f. Barathea (IRE) 127 – My Branch 111 (Distant Relative   **111**
128) [2003 91p: 7m* 8g 7m⁶ 6m 7g³ 6.5g 7d⁴ 7m Oct 18] big, good-bodied filly: type to
carry plenty of condition: smart performer: won Dubai Duty Free Stakes (Fred Darling)
at Newbury in April by 1¼ lengths from Crystal Star: best efforts when close third to
Nayyir in Lennox Stakes at Goodwood and 2½ lengths seventh to Just James in Challenge
Stakes at Newmarket final one: best at 6f/7f (failed to stay 1m in 1000 Guineas): unraced
on extremes of going: tends to be on toes: sometimes slowly away: sold 350,000 gns.
B. W. Hills

TANTINA (USA)   3 ch.f. Distant View (USA) 126 – Didina 115 (Nashwan (USA) 135)   **115**
[2003 7.1g* 7f* 7g* 7d* 7m³ Sep 25] strong, well-made filly: second foal: closely related
to fairly useful 1¼m winner Trekking (by Gone West): dam, 6f (at 2 yrs) to 8.5f (US
Grade 2 event) winner, out of half-sister to Xaar: quickly improved into a smart
performer: won maiden at Haydock and minor event at Yarmouth in July and listed
races at Goodwood (by 1½ lengths from Gonfilia) in August and Doncaster (beat Chic
impressively by 5 lengths, again making all) in September: reportedly returned lame
when below-form third behind With Reason in Supreme Stakes at Goodwood (odds on,
refused to settle) final outing: raced only at 7f: acted on firm and good to soft going: stud.
B. W. Hills

TANTRIC   4 br.g. Greensmith 121 – Petunia (GER) (Chief Singer 131) [2003 70, a77:   **75**
f9.4g f8.5g⁶ f6g f7g⁶ f7g f7g 8m 7f f7g³ 8g⁴ f9.4f 6.9m* 6.9f* 7m 7.5d 7m Oct 18] quite

attractive gelding: fair performer: won 2 minor events at Carlisle in August: effective at 7f to 9.4f: acts on fibresand and firm going: blinkered (below form) fifth/sixth starts: has raced freely/found little: usually races prominently. *J. O'Reilly*

TAP 6 b.g. Emarati (USA) 74 – Pubby 73 (Doctor Wall 107) [2003 41: f5g⁶ f8s² f8s⁵ f8g³ f7s 7m⁴ 7.1d² 7.2g² f8g 8.2m⁵ f7g* 7.5d* 6m⁴ 7.2g² f8s f7g f8g Dec 12] angular gelding: modest handicapper: won selling events at Southwell (apprentices) in June and Beverley in July: left D. Nicholls after fifteenth start: best around 7f nowadays: acts on fibresand, soft and good to firm ground: tried blinkered/visored/tongue tied: unseated rider and bolted before eighth outing. *Ian Emmerson* **63**

TAPAU (IRE) 5 b.m. Nicolotte 118 – Urtica (IRE) (Cyrano de Bergerac 120) [2003 78: 6.1d⁴ f6g 7f³ 6m² 7f* 6g³ 6m Oct 1] lengthy mare: fairly useful handicapper: won at Kempton in June: best at 6f/7f: acts on firm and good to soft ground: races freely. *I. A. Wood* **82**

TAPLEON 2 br.f. (Apr 1) Danzig Connection (USA) – Reem El Fala (FR) (Fabulous Dancer (USA) 124) [2003 8g 7m 7d Nov 1] 500Y: sturdy filly: seventh foal: sister to winner in Greece: dam French 7.6f/11f winner: well beaten in maidens. *C. J. Teague* **–**

TAPPIT (IRE) 4 b.g. Mujadil (USA) 119 – Green Life 63 (Green Desert (USA) 127) [2003 74, a69: 7d² 7.1g 7.1g⁴ 6m² 6m 5.7f* 5.5f³ 5d 5.2m 5.2m 5.1m Aug 30] neat gelding: fair handicapper: won at Bath in July: effective at 5f to 7f: yet to race on heavy going, acts on any other turf and fibresand. *J. M. Bradley* **79**

TARAFAH 4 ch.g. Machiavellian (USA) 123 – Elfaslah (IRE) 107 (Green Desert (USA) 127) [2003 82: 8.1m⁵ 11.8g³ 9.9m⁶ p13g Oct 3] good-bodied gelding: fair maiden: left M. Tregoning after third start, well held in cheekpieces subsequent outing: stays 1½m: acts on good to firm ground: sold 7,000 gns. *Ian Williams* **74**

Mr K. Abdulla's "Tantina"

Sheikh Ahmed Al Maktoum's "Tarjman"

TARANAI (IRE) 2 ch.f. (Mar 29) Russian Revival (USA) 125 – Miss Flite (IRE) **55**
(Law Society (USA) 130) [2003 6m 6m⁶ 6m 6m 5.7f p7g p6g⁶ Nov 26] close-coupled
filly: sixth foal: half-sister to 3 winners, including 3-y-o Coppington Flyer: dam unraced:
modest maiden: ran creditably in nursery final start: should stay 7f. *B. W. Duke*

TARANAKI 5 b.h. Delta Dancer – Miss Ticklepenny (Distant Relative 128) [2003 86, **89**
a?: p7g³ p7g⁴ 7m⁴ 7m³ 6m³ 7g³ 7m³ 7m² 7m 7f 7m* 7g⁵ 7m 7m⁶ 6m* 7m p6g* Dec 2]
rather leggy horse: fairly useful performer: won handicaps at Newbury in July and Salisbury in October and minor event at Lingfield in December: has won at 1m, probably best
at 6f/7f: acts on all-weather, firm and good to soft going: blinkered (raced freely) once:
tends to edge right: tough and consistent. *P. D. Cundell*

TARANDOT (IRE) 2 b.f. (Mar 12) Singspiel (IRE) 133 – Rifada 103 (Ela-Mana-Mou **–**
132) [2003 8m Sep 2] 36,000Y: seventh foal: half-sister to 3 winners, including smart
French 10.5f/1½m winner Rifapour (by Shahrastani) and useful French 1m (at 2 yrs) to
1½m winner Tiger Groom (by Arazi): dam, 1½m winner, would have stayed further:
25/1, last of 7 in maiden at Yarmouth, slowly away and flashing tail. *G. G. Margarson*

TARAS EMPEROR (IRE) 5 b.g. Common Grounds 118 – Strike It Rich (FR) 88 **–**
(Rheingold 137) [2003 86: f6s 7m Mar 26] close-coupled, workmanlike gelding: fairly
useful handicapper at best: looked temperamental in 2003, unseating rider leaving stall
final outing: dead. *J. J. Quinn*

TARA'S FLAME 3 ch.g. Blushing Flame (USA) 109 – Lady Emm (Emarati (USA) **63**
74) [2003 –p: 7.1f 9d⁴ 14.1m f12g 13.1d Oct 14] tall, leggy gelding: modest maiden: left
J. Given after fourth outing: should be suited by 1½m+: acts on good to soft ground.
Mrs M. Reveley

TARASHANI (IRE) 5 ch.g. Primo Dominie 121 – Tarakana (USA) 101 (Shahrastani **–**
(USA) 135) [2003 f8g 9.2d 12f⁶ 11m Aug 23] sturdy gelding: little sign of ability on Flat:
tried in headgear. *B. Ellison*

TARAWAN 7 ch.g. Nashwan (USA) 135 – Soluce 98 (Junius (USA) 124) [2003 67: **80**
p10g³ p16g p12g p10g² p10g* 10.3g* 10g* p10g⁵ 10m p10g⁴ 10.1m 10.1g³ 9.9m⁶ 11.7f **a74**
Aug 17] strong, long-backed gelding: fairly useful on turf, fair on all-weather: won handicaps at Lingfield, Doncaster and Leicester in March: best at 1m to 10.5f: acts on firm
going, soft and polytrack: tried blinkered, usually visored: often slowly away/sometimes
races lazily: held up: usually amateur/apprentice ridden. *A. M. Balding*

TARBIYAH 3 br.f. Singspiel (IRE) 133 – Amanah (USA) 100 (Mr Prospector (USA)) **89**
[2003 8f* Jun 15] fourth foal: half-sister to 1000 Guineas winner Lahan (by Unfuwain),
7f (including Rockfel Stakes) winner at 2 yrs: dam 1m winner out of US Grade 1 1m/8.5f
winner Cheval Volant: landed odds in maiden at Salisbury by length from Beneventa,
flashing tail once: visits Anabaa. *Saeed bin Suroor*

TARDIS 2 ch.f. (Feb 23) Vettori (IRE) 119 – Time Lapse 62 (The Noble Player (USA) **63**
126) [2003 6g⁵ 7g⁶ 7m⁶ 7.1m* 6.1m⁵ 8m² 8m⁴ Sep 25] 5,000Y: smallish, angular filly:
second foal: dam, 2-y-o 6f winner (later won in Jersey), out of sister to Park Hill winner
Quay Line: modest performer: won maiden at Musselburgh in July: good efforts in frame
in nurseries: will stay at least 1¼m: tends to wander. *M. L. W. Bell*

TARGA 3 b.g. Royal Applause 124 – Tintinara (Selkirk (USA) 129) [2003 12m⁴ 12g **?**
f9.4g 16.2m Aug 25] unfurnished gelding: third foal: dam unraced: seemingly fair form
(appeared to run to 77) when fourth of 5 in maiden at Newmarket on debut: well held
after, leaving Lady Herries following second appearance: gave trouble at start and very
slowly away second outing, blinkered since: probably ungenuine. *J. W. Unett*

TARJMAN 3 b.c. Cadeaux Genereux 131 – Dodo (IRE) 90 (Alzao (USA) 117) [2003 **118**
86p: 6m* 7g* 7g* 7m² 7d³ 8m⁴ Oct 3] neat colt: smart performer: won handicaps at
Newmarket in April and Epsom in June and minor event at Yarmouth (beat Suggestive a
neck) in July: good efforts when length second to With Reason in Hungerford Stakes at
Newbury and close third to Polar Ben in Park Stakes at Doncaster next 2 starts: ran as
though amiss in Joel Stakes at Newmarket final outing: will prove at least as effective at
1m as 7f: yet to race on extremes of going: carries head awkwardly: held up, and has fine
turn of foot. *A. C. Stewart*

TARKWA 4 gr.f. Doyoun 124 – Shining Fire (Kalaglow 132) [2003 56: 9.7f⁴ 9.7m **51**
11.9f⁵ 10m³ 10m² 11.9f⁶ f12g Nov 21] strong, sturdy filly: modest handicapper: stays
1½m: acts on firm going: none too consistent. *R. M. H. Cowell*

TARNATION (IRE) 3 ch.g. Tagula (IRE) 116 – Steal 'em 66 (Efisio 120) [2003 –: **–**
8m f12g Jun 19] angular gelding: well held in 4 starts. *J. R. Weymes*

TAROT CARD 2 b.f. (May 15) Fasliyev (USA) 120 – Well Beyond (IRE) 101 (Don't **100**
Forget Me 127) [2003 6d* 8f⁵ 7m Oct 18] lengthy filly: half-sister to several winners,
including 6f (at 2 yrs) to 8.5f (US Grade 3 event) winner Out of Reach and 1996 2-y-o 6f
winner Well Warned (both useful, by Warning): dam, 5f (at 2 yrs) to 1m winner, out of
sister to dam of Zafonic: won maiden at Goodwood in July, slowly away: useful form
when 4½ lengths fifth of 7 to Red Bloom in Fillies' Mile at Ascot (wrong in coat):
possibly amiss final start: not sure to stay beyond 1m. *B. W. Hills*

TARSKI 9 ch.g. Polish Precedent (USA) 131 – Illusory 81 (Kings Lake (USA) 133) **48 ?**
[2003 50: 10.2f 16.2d⁴ Jul 25] sturdy gelding: poor handicapper: stays 1½m: acts on good
to firm and good to soft going: tried blinkered/visored: held up. *W. S. Kittow*

TARTIRUGA (IRE) 2 b.g. (Mar 27) Turtle Island (IRE) 123 – Palio Flyer (Slip **–**
Anchor 136) [2003 6m 6m Jul 28] 3,000F, 5,000Y: workmanlike gelding: fourth foal:
half-brother to fairly useful 2000 2-y-o 7f winner Matlock (by Barathea), later successful
in USA: dam unraced out of half-sister to dam of Oaks winner Lady Carla: well held in
maidens at Salisbury and Windsor. *L. G. Cottrell*

TARUSKIN (IRE) 2 b.g. (Mar 1) Danehill Dancer (IRE) 117 – Jungle Jezebel 107 **85**
(Thatching 131) [2003 7.1m³ 7g² 6d³ 6f* Aug 7] IR 60,000F, €150,000Y: tall, useful-
looking gelding: brother to 4-y-o Lady Lindsay and half-brother to 3 winners, including
fairly useful 1¼m winner Bluebell Wood (by Bluebird): dam 2-y-o 7f winner: fairly
useful performer: landed odds in maiden at Brighton by 5 lengths: stays 7f: acts on firm
and good to soft ground: wandered at Epsom second outing. *N. A. Callaghan*

TARWIJ (USA) 3 br.f. Diesis 133 – Roseate Tern 123 (Blakeney 126) [2003 10m³ **77**
10m Oct 22] lengthy filly: seventh foal: sister to useful 7f (at 2 yrs) and 1¼m winner
Esloob and half-sister to useful 1¼m winner Siyadah (by Mr Prospector) and fairly useful
1997 2-y-o 7f winner who stayed 1½m Fakhr (by Riverman): dam, won Yorkshire Oaks
and placed in Oaks/St Leger, half-sister to high-class performer up to 1¾m Ibn Bey: fair
form when 4 lengths third to Urowells in maiden at Newbury on debut, edging left: off 5

months and blinkered, started slowly/dropped out tamely in similar event at Nottingham only subsequent outing: raced freely both starts: visits Alhaarth. *M. P. Tregoning*

TASHKANDI (IRE) 3 gr.c. Polish Precedent (USA) 131 – Tashiriya (IRE) 106 (Kenmare (FR) 125) [2003 8.5g* 8d* 9m³ 8g² Jul 13] first foal: dam, French 1m winner who stayed 1¼m, out of Princess Royal winner Tashtiya: smart performer: won minor event at Longchamp and 4-runner listed race at Chantilly (made all, quickened clear to beat King's Drama 3 lengths) in May: ran well last 2 starts, 3¼ lengths third to Vespone in Prix Jean Prat at Chantilly and short-neck second to Special Kaldoun in Prix Messidor at Deauville: stays 9f: acts on good to firm and good to soft going: joined Godolphin. *A. de Royer Dupre, France* **115**

TASHKIL (IRE) 2 b.c. (Feb 26) Royal Applause 124 – Surprise Visitor (IRE) (Be My Guest (USA) 126) [2003 7m⁴ 7m* 7m³ 7m Oct 18] IR 200,000F, 180,000Y: lengthy, good-topped colt: has scope: third foal: half-brother to useful French 4.5f (at 2 yrs)/5f winner Ziria (by Danehill Dancer) and 5f (at 2 yrs) and 7f winner Densim Blue (by Lake Coniston): dam, lightly-raced French maiden, half-sister to dam of very smart miler Swallow Flight: useful performer: hung right when winning maiden at Doncaster in August and minor event at Sandown (by 1¼ lengths from Notable Guest) in September: raced freely, bumped and eased when last of 12 in Dewhurst Stakes at Newmarket: needs to settle to stay beyond 7f: has had 2 handlers. *J. H. M. Gosden* **104**

TASK TRUMP 2 ch.f. (May 30) First Trump 118 – Taskone (Be My Chief (USA) 122) [2003 5.1f f7f Jul 25] first foal: dam little form: last in sellers. *J. A. Osborne* **–**

TASNEEF (USA) 4 b.g. Gulch (USA) – Min Alhawa (USA) 108 (Riverman (USA) 131) [2003 92: 11.6g 14.4g 11.6g⁵ 14f 12f² 11.5m⁶ 12m* 12g⁴ 11.7f Oct 12] lengthy, workmanlike gelding: fair handicapper nowadays: won at Folkestone in August: stays 1¾m: acts on firm and good to soft ground: tried blinkered: races up with pace. *T. D. McCarthy* **72**

TASS HEEL (IRE) 4 b.g. Danehill (USA) 126 – Mamouna (USA) 113 (Vaguely Noble 140) [2003 62: f14g* f14s³ f14.8g² p16g⁶ 14.1m⁵ 16.2m⁸ 14m² 16g 14f⁵ 16g² 16.4m 15.4m 17.1m 16m* 15.8m* 16f 14.1m 13.8m* Oct 18] strong, lengthy gelding: fair performer: won handicaps at Southwell in January, Beverley in May, Musselburgh in September and twice at Catterick in October, latter in minor event: stays 2m: acts on all-weather, raced mainly on good going or firmer on turf (acts on firm): effective making running/held up: sold 42,000 gns. *M. R. Channon* **72**

TATA NAKA 3 ch.f. Nashwan (USA) 135 – Overcast (IRE) 72 (Caerleon (USA) 132) [2003 p8g 10m⁶ p10g⁵ f9.4g Nov 28] 4,500 3-y-o: fifth foal: half-sister to 3 winners by Zafonic, including 7f to 1¼m winner Thunder Sky: dam, Irish 1m winner, closely related to smart Irish middle-distance performer Phantom Breeze: modest maiden: stays 1¼m. *Mrs C. A. Dunnett* **54 ?**

TATWEER (IRE) 3 b.g. Among Men (USA) 124 – Sandystones 60 (Selkirk (USA) 129) [2003 71p: p7g 6d p6g⁵ f6g⁵ f6g⁵ p7g p6g f5g Dec 22] good-bodied gelding: has a round action: modest maiden: well held last 3 starts: stays 7f: acts on all-weather: visored. *D. Shaw* **63 d**

TAWADDOD (IRE) 4 b.f. Alhaarth (IRE) 126 – Gloire (Thatching 131) [2003 7.5m 8.2g 6m⁶ Oct 17] 22,000F, IR 95,000Y, 1,200 3-y-o: fourth foal: half-sister to 5f (at 2 yrs) and 7f winner Ajig Dancer (by Niniski) and 5f (at 2 yrs)/6f winner Glory Days (by Lahib), both fairly useful: dam unraced sister to smart sprinter Puissance: well beaten in maidens, leaving J. Wainwright after second start. *P. T. Midgley* **–**

TAWNY WAY 3 b.f. Polar Falcon (USA) 126 – Ma Petite Anglaise 81 (Reprimand 122) [2003 7m⁴ 9m 7.1m⁴ 9f 9f* 10m² 10.1d² 9.9g Aug 1] quite good-topped filly: fourth foal: half-sister to winner in Denmark by Magic Ring: dam 7f/1m winner: fairly useful performer: won handicap at Kempton in July: good second next 2 starts: stays easy 1¼m: acts on firm and good to soft ground. *W. Jarvis* **92 +**

TAW PARK 9 b.g. Inca Chief (USA) – Parklands Belle 73 (Stanford 121§) [2003 10.9m Jul 4] workmanlike gelding: maiden handicapper: lightly raced and little form on Flat since first start in 2001: won over hurdles in August. *R. J. Baker* **–**

TAYASH 3 b.g. Fleetwood (IRE) 107 – Wassl's Sister (Troy 137) [2003 –: 10.9m 11.6s p12g⁵ 16.2g Aug 25] neat gelding: no form: tried tongue tied, visored (slipped up) final start. *A. W. Carroll* **–**

TAYIF 7 gr.g. Taufan (USA) 119 – Rich Lass (Broxted 120) [2003 90: f5s f5s p6g p7g f7g⁶ f6s⁴ 6m 6m³ 6m² 6s 6f⁶ 5m 6g 5d⁶ f7g p6g³ Dec 30] quite good-topped gelding: fairly useful performer: reportedly underwent operation on joints after final 5-y-o outing: **80**

generally disappointing in 2003, leaving D. Nicholls after penultimate start: effective at 6f, barely at testing 7f: acts on soft and good to firm going, probably on polytrack: usually tongue tied: often slowly away. *Andrew Reid*

TBM CAN 4 b.g. Rock City 120 – Fire Sprite 83 (Mummy's Game 120) [2003 –: 11m^5 12f* 13m* 12f* 12f^3 13g^4 12.6f* 12.1g^3 12g^3 12.1m* 12.1m^5 11.9f 11.9f^6 Oct 9] quite good-topped gelding: fair performer: much improved and had good season, winning handicaps at Musselburgh, Hamilton (apprentices), Folkestone and Warwick (apprentices) and minor event at Beverley, all in summer: should stay 1¾m: acts on firm going: held up: genuine. *W. M. Brisbourne* **74**

T C FLYER 3 b.f. Wizard King 122 – Kaleidophone 73 (Kalaglow 132) [2003 54§: 7m 7f^6 Jun 6] tall, leggy filly: poor maiden: stays easy 7f: acts on firm ground: tried blinkered: headstrong and not one to trust. *P. D. Evans* **42 §**

TEAM-MATE (IRE) 5 b.g. Nashwan (USA) 135 – Ustka 60 (Lomond (USA) 128) [2003 92: 14.1g 12g^6 11.9m 12m 12m^6 11.8g* 12m^5 12m^4 11.6g Oct 6] leggy gelding: fairly useful performer: won minor event at Leicester in August: should stay 1¾m: acts on firm going, probably on soft: tried tongue tied at 3 yrs: below form in cheekpieces fifth start: occasionally slowly away: has hinted at temperament. *Miss J. Feilden* **84**

TEASE (IRE) 3 b.f. Green Desert (USA) 127 – Mockery (Nashwan (USA) 135) [2003 81: p7g p7g 7g* 6.1m 7m^3 7g 8.2m 7g^3 7m^6 6m 7g 8m^3 Oct 2] fair performer: won maiden at Leicester in March: barely stays 1m: raced mainly on good/good to firm going on turf, below form both starts on polytrack: none too consistent: sold 10,000 gns, joined R. Gibson in France. *R. Hannon* **73**

TEA'S MAID 3 b.f. Wizard King 122 – Come To Tea (IRE) (Be My Guest (USA) 126) [2003 –: 9.3m^5 10f^6 14.1s^5 Oct 29] well held in maidens/seller. *J. G. Given* **–**

TECHNICIAN (IRE) 8 ch.g. Archway (IRE) 115 – How It Works (Commanche Run 133) [2003 78d: 7f^2 7m^5 6m 7.9f^4 7.9m 7.6m 7.9m 8m^5 7m Oct 13] good-bodied gelding: poor mover: fair handicapper at best nowadays: below form after reappearance: best at 6f/7f: possibly unsuited by heavy going, acts on any other turf and fibresand: wears headgear: sold £1,000. *E. J. Alston* **69 d**

TEDBURROW 11 b.g. Dowsing (USA) 124 – Gwiffina 87 (Welsh Saint 126) [2003 116: 6g^5 6g 7.1m^6 6g 6.1m^5 Aug 3] sturdy, workmanlike gelding: reportedly had joint problem and not seen in second half of 2002: just useful performer in 2003: respectable fifth to Needwood Blade in listed event at Newmarket on reappearance: below form after: effective at 5f/6f: acts on firm and soft going, probably not on heavy: has won when sweating. *E. J. Alston* **105 d**

TEDESKA (IRE) 3 b.f. Up And At 'em 109 – Tropicana (IRE) (Imperial Frontier (USA) 112) [2003 6m^6 5.9f^2 6g^5 6.9m^2 7m* Jul 23] IR 14,000Y: second foal: dam unraced half-sister to useful sprinter Harvest Girl: fair form: won handicap at Leicester in July: stayed 7f: raced only on good going or firmer: dead. *M. Johnston* **72**

TEDSDALE MAC 4 ch.g. Presidium 124 – Stilvella (Camden Town 125) [2003 64: 6m^4 5g^2 7m 5m^6 6.1g^5 5m 7m^5 8.5m 8m^6 8.5m^4 7m^3 8g^3 7f 8d^4 Nov 7] close-coupled, quite good-topped gelding: fair performer: effective at 5f to 8.5f: acts on firm and soft going, yet to race on heavy: tried blinkered at 3 yrs, often wears cheekpieces: often takes strong hold. *N. Bycroft* **68**

TEDSTALE (USA) 5 ch.g. Irish River (FR) 131 – Carefree Kate (USA) (Lyphard (USA) 132) [2003 94: 8m* 8g^4 8.1s 8m^2 8.9f^2 10m^6 7.9m 9m^4 Aug 30] smallish, sturdy, close-coupled gelding: unimpressive mover: fairly useful handicapper: won at Newcastle in April: creditable efforts when in frame subsequently: best around 1m/9f: acts on firm and good to soft going: sometimes slowly away: usually waited with: sometimes finds little. *T. D. Easterby* **94**

TEDZAR (IRE) 3 b.g. Inzar (USA) 112 – Chesham Lady (IRE) (Fayruz 116) [2003 44: 7.1g 10m p10g f8.5g Nov 17] little form: claimed from M. Tompkins after second start: tried blinkered. *B. R. Johnson* **–**

TEEHEE (IRE) 5 b.g. Anita's Prince 126 – Regal Charmer (Royal And Regal (USA)) [2003 69: f7s^2 7g f7g^3 7g^2 7g f7s^3 7f g^4 7g f7g^5 f6s 7s^2 f6s f7g* 7s^5 f7s Dec 31] tall, useful-looking gelding: fair handicapper: won at Wolverhampton in November: races mainly at 7f nowadays: acts on fibresand, lightly raced recently on turf but seems best on going softer than good: visored/blinkered: free-going sort: sometimes carries head awkwardly/finds little. *B. Palling* **a76**

TEE JAY KASSIDY 3 b.g. Petong 126 – Priceless Fantasy (Dunbeath (USA) 127) [2003 7m 7g 10m⁵ f6g 7m 7f⁴ Jul 24] smallish, workmanlike gelding: no solid form: tried blinkered/visored. *Julian Poulton* —

TEES COMPONENTS 8 b.g. Risk Me (FR) 127 – Lady Warninglid (Ela-Mana-Mou 132) [2003 107: 12g⁶ Mar 22] tall, well-made gelding: lightly raced: useful in 2002: tongue tied, well held only outing on Flat in 2003 (useful winner over hurdles in May). *Mrs M. Reveley* —

TEFI 5 ch.g. Efisio 120 – Masuri Kabisa (USA) 48 (Ascot Knight (CAN) 130) [2003 50, a56: f6g f7s³ f6g f12g f8s* p7g f8g f8g² f7g⁶ f8g f7g⁶ f6g Dec 9] smallish gelding: has a round action: modest performer: won apprentice maiden handicap at Southwell in February: left S. R. Bowring, and off nearly 6 months before final outing: very best form at 6f to 1m: acts on firm going and all-weather: visored once, usually blinkered: often tongue tied: usually races up with pace: inconsistent. *J. Balding* — / a50

TEG 5 b.m. Petong 126 – Felinwen (White Mill 76) [2003 –: 7g 11.6m Jun 9] no form: tried visored. *I. A. Wood* —

TELEFONICA (USA) 2 b.f. (Jan 30) Distant View (USA) 126 – Call Account (USA) (Private Account (USA)) [2003 7m⁴ 7g² Oct 22] tall filly: second foal: sister to 3-y-o Dialing Tone: dam, 7f to 8.5f winner in USA and third in Grade 2 7f event, half-sister to useful 1m/1¼m performer Keyboogie: fair form in maidens at Kempton and Newcastle (second to First Candlelight): will stay at least 1m: should progress. *Sir Michael Stoute* — 74 p

TELEGNOSIS (JPN) 4 b.c. Tony Bin 134 – Make A Wish (JPN) (Northern Taste (CAN) 129) [2003 116: 9d 8d⁶ 7f* 8f 8d³ 8g 8f 8m Dec 14] Japanese-bred colt: high-class performer: won twice at Tokyo in first half of 2002, notably NHK Mile Cup by 1¾ lengths from Agnes Sonic: best effort in Japan in 2003 when winning Group 2 Keio Hai Spring Cup at Tokyo in May by 1¼ lengths from Kiss Me Tender: excellent effort on European debut when 1¼ lengths third to Six Perfections in Prix Jacques le Marois at Deauville fifth start: below form after in Prix du Moulin de Longchamp, Mile Championship at Kyoto and Hong Kong Mile at Sha Tin (3¼ lengths seventh to Lucky Owners): best at 7f/1m: acts on firm and good to soft going: held up. *H. Sugiura, Japan* — 125

TELEGRAM GIRL 4 b.f. Magic Ring (IRE) 115 – Lucky Message (USA) 71 (Phone Trick (USA)) [2003 –, a68d: f7g⁶ f9.4g⁴ Jan 17] close-coupled filly: just poor form in 2003: barely stays 8.5f: acts on all-weather, little form on turf: usually blinkered/visored prior to 2003. *D. Haydn Jones* — 46

TELEMACHUS 3 b.g. Bishop of Cashel 122 – Indian Imp (Indian Ridge 123) [2003 83: 8m³ f8.5g* 10.4m⁴ 12m 10.3m* 10m³ 9.9g⁵ 9.9m⁵ 10.1s³ 12d Nov 8] workmanlike gelding: useful performer: won maiden at Wolverhampton in April and handicap at Chester (made all, beat Downtime by 6 lengths) in July: should stay 1½m (raced up with strong gallop at Royal Ascot when tried): acts on soft ground, good to firm and fibresand: reliable. *J. G. Given* — 97

TELEPATHIC (IRE) 3 b.g. Mind Games 121 – Madrina 70 (Waajib 121) [2003 85: 5f 5.1m 5d⁶ 6m 5m² 5f⁵ 5m⁵ 5.1m⁵ 6.1f⁶ 6m 5m 5.1m 5m p6g Dec 6] big, good-bodied gelding: fairly useful handicapper: below form after eighth start: effective at 5f/6f: acts on firm and good to soft ground: sometimes awkward leaving stall. *A. Berry* — 82

TELEPHONE SAL (IRE) 5 b.m. Namaqualand (USA) – Lyphard's Lady (Lyphard's Special (USA) 122) [2003 75, a?: p10g 12m 16g⁵ 12g⁶ 14f⁶ Aug 18] fourth foal: sister to Irish 9f to 13f winner Breffni Flyer and half-sister to 2 winners in Ireland, including useful 8.5f to 11f winner Renge (by Generous): dam Irish 7f winner: fair maiden handicapper at best: just modest form in 2003, including at Lingfield on reappearance: stays 12.5f: acts on firm and soft going: tried blinkered/in cheekpieces. *Eoin Doyle, Ireland* — 56 ?

TELL HER OFF 3 b.f. Reprimand 122 – My Valentina 84 (Royal Academy (USA) 130) [2003 –: p10g 8g 8.2m 7d 7g 8m 10m⁴ Oct 13] leggy filly: has a markedly round action: little form: has looked difficult ride. *Mrs C. A. Dunnett* —

TELL NOTHING (IRE) 7 b.m. Classic Secret (USA) 91 – Derbouka (FR) (Shernazar 131) [2003 11.9m⁵ 16m⁶ 17.2m³ 16f* f16.2g 16m Jul 31] ex-Irish mare: poor handicapper: won amateur event at Musselburgh in June: stays 17f: acts on firm going, well beaten on fibresand: usually races prominently. *K. R. Burke* — 47

TELL THE TREES 2 br.f. (Mar 28) Tamure (IRE) 125 – Bluebell Copse (Formidable (USA) 125) [2003 6m 7m 8.3g Oct 13] close-coupled, quite good-topped filly: half-sister to 1997 2-y-o 5f seller winner Sage (by Greensmith), later 5f/6f winner in Sweden, and to winner in Italy by Faustus: dam, winner in Jersey, half-sister to very smart middle-distance stayer Sapience: little sign of ability in maidens/seller. *R. M. Beckett* —

TELORI 5 ch.m. Muhtarram (USA) 125 – Elita (Sharpo 132) [2003 72, a65: p6g p7g³ **61**
p7g f6g 7m 6.1m 6m 7m⁶ 7m 6f 7m 7.1g⁴ 7d⁴ f7s⁵ Sep 26] lengthy mare: modest
handicapper nowadays: stays 7f: acts on all-weather, best turf form on good ground or
firmer: has run well in cheekpieces: edgy sort: has dropped away tamely. *I. A. Wood*

TEMPER TANTRUM 5 b.g. Pursuit of Love 124 – Queenbird 90 (Warning 136) **71**
[2003 59, a64: f8s⁶ p8g² p7g* p7g 7m⁵ 7m* 8m p8g 8.3m 7d³ 7f* 7m⁶ 7f* 7g⁶ 8.1m*
8m³ p7g p7g⁵ p7g p7g² p7g³ Dec 30] fair performer: won minor event at Lingfield, and
handicaps at Brighton (3) and Warwick between March/September: effective at 7f/1m:
acts on all-weather, firm and good to soft ground: wears headgear: tried tongue tied: held
up: tough. *Andrew Reid*

TEMPLE OF ARTEMIS 4 b.c. Spinning World (USA) 130 – Casessa (USA) (Caro –
133) [2003 –: 16m 8.5d 12m f12g p12g f16g Dec 16] good-topped colt: has a round
action: fairly useful 7f winner at 2 yrs: well beaten since, leaving A. O'Brien after final
3-y-o start. *P. A. Blockley*

TEMPLE PLACE (IRE) 2 b.c. (Mar 1) Sadler's Wells (USA) 132 – Puzzled Look **97 p**
(USA) (Gulch (USA)) [2003 8m⁵ 8.3m* 8g³ Oct 11] €430,000Y: good-topped, attractive
colt: third foal: brother to fairly useful 2001 2-y-o 7f winner Ballet Score: dam, minor
stakes sprint winner in USA, half-sister to smart performer in Britain and USA up to 1½m
Winged Victory: won maiden at Windsor in September, hanging left: sweating, useful
form when 6½ lengths third of 5 to Fantastic View in Autumn Stakes at Ascot: should be
suited by at least 1¼m: open to progress. *M. L. W. Bell*

TEMPLET (USA) 3 b.c. Souvenir Copy (USA) 113 – Two Step Trudy (USA) (Capote **70 p**
(USA)) [2003 10g⁴ Oct 25] $70,000Y: quite good-topped colt: first foal: dam, maiden in
USA, half-sister to useful 1991 2-y-o 7f/1m winner Ninja Dancer out of half-sister to dam
of Poule d'Essai des Poulains winner L'Emigrant: 15/2 and green, 8½ lengths fourth to
Pride in maiden at Newbury, starting slowly and not knocked about when tiring: on toes/
had 2 handlers: sold 45,000 gns: should improve. *J. H. M. Gosden*

TEMPSFORD (USA) 3 b.c. Bering 136 – Nadra (IRE) 61 (Sadler's Wells (USA) 132) **98**
[2003 –p: f12g* p12g* 14.1d³ 14.1m* 14.1m⁵ 12d* f12g* Oct 4] useful handicapper:
won at Wolverhampton and Lingfield in July, Nottingham in August, Catterick in September and Wolverhampton (beat Eoz by 1¼ lengths, ran bit in snatches) in October: stays
1¾m: acts on all-weather, good to firm and good to soft going. *Sir Mark Prescott*

TEMPTING TILLY (IRE) 4 b.f. Namaqualand (USA) – Go Tally-Ho 66 (Gorytus –
(USA) 132) [2003 –: f8g Mar 13] little form: tried blinkered. *C. J. Teague*

TEN CARAT 3 b.c. Grand Lodge (USA) 125 – Emerald (USA) (El Gran Senor (USA) **106**
136) [2003 –p: 12g⁴ 14.1d* 16.2m* 14m* 18m Oct 18] big, strong colt: useful form: won
maiden at Nottingham in May, and handicaps at Beverley in August and Newmarket (beat
Alkaased by a length, again making running) in October: disappointing in Cesarewitch at
Newmarket final outing: effective at 1¾m/2m: acts on good to firm ground: lightly raced.
Mrs A. J. Perrett

TENDER FALCON 3 br.g. Polar Falcon (USA) 126 – Tendresse (IRE) 60 (Tender **73**
King 123) [2003 62: 8.2g 10.9m⁵ 10m* 10.2f³ 11.6d³ 10g³ 10d² 10m* 9.7m⁴ Aug 21]
tall, good-topped gelding: has scope: fair handicapper: won at Nottingham in May and
Sandown in August: effective at 1¼m/1½m: acts on firm and good to soft going.
R. J. Hodges

TENDER (IRE) 3 b.f. Zieten (USA) 118 – Jayess Elle 55 (Sabrehill (USA) 120) [2003 **71**
76, a71: p5g 6m 5.1m⁶ 5s⁴ 6m³ 5m⁶ 5f⁶ 5m⁴ 5.1m 6g p7g⁶ p7g Nov 29] angular filly: fair **a66**
handicapper: left D. Cosgrove after ninth start: probably stays easy 7f: acts on polytrack,
firm and soft going. *D. J. Daly*

TENNY'S GOLD (IRE) 2 b.f. (Apr 15) Marju (IRE) 127 – Itatinga (USA) 66 (River- **74 p**
man (USA) 131) [2003 6m 7s² Nov 3] €80,000Y: rather leggy filly: first foal: dam 1¾m
winner: better effort in maidens (fair form) when ½-length second of 14 to Zeitgeist at
Redcar, edging left: should be suited by 1¼m/1½m: open to progress. *B. W. Hills*

TEN PAST SIX 11 ch.g. Kris 135 – Tashinsky (USA) (Nijinsky (CAN) 138) [2003 ?: –
f12s f12s 12.4m 8.9m Sep 7] lengthy, good-quartered gelding: no longer of much
account: usually blinkered/visored. *H. A. McWilliams*

TENTATIVE (USA) 2 ch.f. (Mar 16) Distant View (USA) 126 – Danzante (USA) 107 **93**
(Danzig (USA)) [2003 5m³ 5.1f* 5.1f² 5m* 5g* 5.2m 6m³ Sep 20] sturdy, quite attractive
filly: closely related to several winners, including useful French 1996 2-y-o 7f winner
Alpha Plus (by Mr Prospector) and fairly useful 1998 2-y-o 5f winner Forante (by Forty
Niner): dam, won up to 8.5f in France/USA, half-sister to Breeders' Cup Classic winner

Skywalker: fairly useful performer: won maiden at Bath in June and minor event and nursery at Doncaster in July: good 2½ lengths third of 6 to Ruby Rocket in listed event at Ayr final start, racing freely: barely stays 6f: acts on firm going: usually races prominently. *R. Charlton*

TEORBAN (POL) 4 b.g. Don Corleone 115 – Tabaka (POL) (Pyjama Hunt 126) [2003 f14.8s² f16.2s* 14.1g f16.2g* 16d May 28] Polish-bred gelding: winner of 2 of his 14 starts in native country: fair form when winning handicaps at Wolverhampton in April and May: stays 2m: acts on fibresand. *M. Pitman* **?** **a76**

TE QUIERO 5 gr.g. Bering 136 – Ma Lumiere (FR) (Niniski (USA) 125) [2003 –, a91: f9.4g² p10g f8.5s* 10.1s f8.5g⁵ f8g² f12g³ f9.4s Dec 31] useful on all-weather, fair on turf: won valuable handicap at Wolverhampton (successful on 4 of 7 starts there) in March gamely by 1¾ lengths from Creskeld: good second to Cardinal Venture at Southwell after: stays 9.4f, probably not 1½m: acts on fibresand (below form both runs on polytrack), yet to race on extremes of going on turf: tongue tied: reportedly lame second start: front runner. *Miss Gay Kelleway* **?** **a101**

TERESA 3 b.f. Darshaan 133 – Morina (USA) (Lyphard (USA) 132) [2003 8m 10m 12f³ 12s³ 14m* 12m³ 16g³ Oct 31] 120,000Y: leggy filly: fifth foal: closely related to very smart 6f (at 2 yrs) to 1½m winner Mons and smart 1¼m winner Inforapenny (both by Deploy): dam, French 11f winner, out of US Grade 1 2-y-o 8.5f winner Arewehavingfunyet: fairly useful performer: landed odds in maiden at Lingfield in August by 8 lengths: good close third in handicap at Newmarket final outing: stays 2m: unraced on heavy going, acts on any other turf. *J. L. Dunlop* **85**

TERFEL 4 ch.g. Lion Cavern (USA) 117 – Montserrat 81 (Aragon 118) [2003 97: 8g 8.3d² 7.1m² 7.1g 8g⁵ 7.9m* 8g 7m³ 7.9f³ 8g Nov 1] quite attractive gelding: useful performer: won handicap at York in August by head from Ocean Victory: creditable efforts subsequently when third in minor event at Newmarket and another handicap at York: effective at 7f/1m: acts on soft and firm going: races prominently. *M. L. W. Bell* **103**

TERIMON'S DREAM 6 gr.g. Terimon 124 – I Have A Dream (SWE) (Mango Express 106) [2003 –: f7g p7g Jan 29] tall, workmanlike gelding: little form. *A. W. Carroll* **–**

TERMONFECKIN 5 b.g. Runnett 125 – Crimson Sol (Crimson Beau 124) [2003 14.1d³ 11.5g⁴ 12g⁶ f14.8g Aug 8] sixth foal: dam poor maiden hurdler: modest maiden: reluctant stall and went too freely final start: stays 1½m. *P. W. Hiatt* **57**

Arriva Trains Rated Stakes (Handicap), York—a race formerly known as the Bradford & Bingley; 33/1-shot Terfel edges out the favourite Ocean Victory (quartered cap), with Pentecost (rail) taking third ahead of Blue Spinnaker (left)

TERN INTERN (IRE) 4 b. or br.g. Dr Devious (IRE) 127 – Arctic Bird (USA) (Storm –
Bird (CAN) 134) [2003 –: f7s f9.4g 12g May 24] workmanlike gelding: modest maiden
at 2 yrs, little form since: tried blinkered/in cheekpieces. *Miss J. Feilden*

TERRAQUIN (IRE) 3 b.c. Turtle Island (IRE) 123 – Play The Queen (IRE) (King of 84
Clubs 124) [2003 76: 7m* 7.1m⁴ 8.1f⁶ 8g⁴ 7g* 7m⁶ Aug 16] good-bodied colt: fairly
useful performer: won maiden at Southwell in May and handicap at Kempton in July:
stays 1m: acts on good to firm going: sold 11,000 gns, joined J. Bridger. *J. A. R. Toller*

TERTULLIAN (IRE) 4 b.g. Petorius 117 – Fiddes (IRE) 52 (Alzao (USA) 117) [2003 –
92: p10g p10g p10g Jan 22] sturdy, good-bodied gelding: fairly useful handicapper at best:
stayed 1¼m: acted on good to firm and good to soft going, well held on heavy/polytrack:
dead. *S. Dow*

TESIO 5 b.g. Danehill (USA) 126 – Pale Grey (Linamix (FR) 127) [2003 92, a105: 5g 96
5m 7m* 7g 5d 6m Oct 1] good-topped gelding: useful handicapper: easily best effort of a?
2003 when dead-heating with Flint River at Brighton in May: stays 7f: acts on soft
ground, firm and fibresand: has flashed tail/looked less than keen. *P. J. Hobbs*

TEST THE WATER (IRE) 9 ch.g. Maelstrom Lake 118 – Baliana (CAN) (Riverman – §
(USA) 131) [2003 50§, a–§: 9.7m Apr 15] dipped-backed gelding: poor walker/mover:
one-time fairly useful performer: well held only start in 2003: tried visored, usually
blinkered: ungenuine. *Dr J. R. J. Naylor*

TETOU (IRE) 3 ch.f. Peintre Celebre (USA) 137 – Place of Honour (Be My Guest 70
(USA) 126) [2003 8.2m³ 10m p10g* Nov 18] 200,000F, 180,000Y: lengthy filly: half-
sister to several winners, notably smart German miler Sinyar (by Machiavellian): dam
Irish 1¼m winner out of Coronation Stakes winner Sutton Place: fair form: easily best
effort when winning maiden at Lingfield in November by head from Seven Year Itch:
stays 1¼m. *B. J. Meehan*

TETRAGON (IRE) 3 b.g. Octagonal (NZ) 126 – Viva Verdi (IRE) 70 (Green Desert 77
(USA) 127) [2003 60d: f8s³ f8.5s² f9.4g³ f12g² f12g³ 9.2d* 11.1g* Jun 11] good-topped
gelding: fair performer: dictated pace when winning claimers at Hamilton in May
and June (claimed £12,000, joined Lucinda Russell): barely stays 1½m: yet to race on
extremes of turf going, acts on fibresand: has run well in visor, blinkered last 2 starts:
raced freely/wandered fifth start: probably best ridden up with pace. *K. R. Burke*

TEUTONIC (IRE) 2 b.f. (Apr 11) Revoque (IRE) 122 – Classic Ring (IRE) 50 –
(Auction Ring (USA) 123) [2003 5d 5m⁶ May 2] €34,000Y: tall, quite good-topped filly:
eighth foal: half-sister to 3 winners, including 4-y-o Waterside and 6-y-o Seven No
Trumps: dam 2-y-o 7f winner: last in maidens at Newcastle and Musselburgh. *R. F. Fisher*

TEXAS GOLD 5 ch.g. Cadeaux Genereux 131 – Star Tulip 99 (Night Shift (USA)) 99
[2003 83: p5g² 5m⁵ 6m⁵ 5g 5.7f* 6f* 6m³ 6m⁶ 5.2m⁶ 5m* 6m² 6m 5.2g⁵ 5f³ 6m⁶ 5g p6g*
p6g* p6g³ Dec 20] sturdy, close-coupled gelding: useful performer: improved again in
2003 and had good season: won handicaps at Bath and Goodwood in June, minor event at
Kempton (wandered) in August and handicap and minor event (beat Law Breaker by ¾
length) at Lingfield in November: effective at 5f/easy 6f: acts on polytrack (well beaten
on fibresand), firm and good to soft going: usually waited with: tough and consistent.
W. R. Muir

TEXT 2 b.g. (Mar 30) Atraf 116 – Idle Chat (USA) 93 (Assert 134) [2003 5.1m⁶ p5g³ 61
6f² p7g Aug 28] 15,000F, 9,000Y, 6,000 2-y-o: sixth living foal: half-brother to 7.5f
winner Atlantic Prince (by Fairy King) and 7.5f to 11f winner Central Committee (by
Royal Academy), both fairly useful: dam 2-y-o 1m winner who stayed 11.5f (later
successful in Australia): modest maiden: placed at Lingfield (best effort) and Brighton:
stays 6f: ran poorly in blinkers final start. *J. White*

TEYAAR 7 b.g. Polar Falcon (USA) 126 – Music In My Life (IRE) 59 (Law Society –
(USA) 130) [2003 62, a80: f6s p5g² p6g⁵ p5g f6g f6g f7g⁵ f5g p8g f6g f5g⁴ f6s f7s f6s³ a79
f5g⁵ p6g* p7g p6g p5g³ Dec 20] strong gelding: fair handicapper: left D. Shaw after
thirteenth start: won at Lingfield in October: best at 5f/6f: acts on all-weather, best turf
form on good going or softer (acts on heavy): tried blinkered earlier in career, good effort
in visor final start: sometimes hangs: none too reliable. *Mrs N. Macauley*

THAAYER 8 b.g. Wolfhound (USA) 126 – Hamaya (USA) 60 (Mr Prospector (USA)) –
[2003 54, a81d: f6g f7g f6g f7s f8.5g f8.5g f7g f8g Dec 19] fairly useful at best: little form
in 2003: blinkered (no show) once. *I. A. Wood*

THADEA (IRE) 2 b. or br.f. (May 15) Grand Lodge (USA) 125 – Kama Tashoof 62 64
(Mtoto 134) [2003 5.1m³ 6.1m 7.5d³ 7g 8.3g³ Oct 6] 20,000Y: close-coupled filly: fifth
foal: half-sister to useful 7f/1m winner Judicious (by Fairy King) and 3-y-o Alchemystic:

dam maiden who stayed 1½m: modest maiden: good third in Windsor nursery final start: should stay 1¼m: acts on good to firm and good to soft going. *J. G. Given*

THAI HI (IRE) 3 b.f. Perugino (USA) 84 – Fancy Boots (IRE) 62 (Salt Dome (USA)) [2003 81p: 7d⁶ 6g⁴ 7m⁶ 7g 7m p7g p6g Dec 30] IR 5,200Y: third foal: half-sister to 5-y-o After Shock: dam, Irish maiden, half-sister to dams of dual Breeders' Cup Mile winner Da Hoss and Prix Morny winner Tagula: modest maiden: left M. Halford in Ireland after fifth start: raced only at 6f/7f: yet to race on extremes of going on turf, below form on polytrack. *S. Kirk* — **62**

THAJJA (IRE) 2 b.c. (Mar 15) Daylami (IRE) 138 – Jawlaat (USA) 91 (Dayjur (USA) 137) [2003 7m* Jul 27] third foal: half-brother to useful 2000 2-y-o 6f winner Khulan (by Bahri): dam, 6f winner (including at 2 yrs), closely related to July Cup winner Elnadim and half-sister to Irish 1000 Guineas winner Mehthaaf, an outstanding family: 5/2-on, won 5-runner maiden at Newmarket comfortably by 5 lengths from Vamose, bit slowly away but leading over 1f out and pushed clear: sustained injury after: should stay 1m: potentially useful if all is well. *J. L. Dunlop* — **80 p**

THAMINAH (USA) 2 b.f. (Jan 19) Danzig (USA) – Bashayer (USA) 103 (Mr Prospector (USA)) [2003 8m 6d* Nov 8] sturdy filly: fourth foal: half-sister to 3 winners, including useful 1m winner Mosayter (by Storm Cat): dam, 1m winner (including at 2 yrs) who stayed 11.4f, closely related to 5-y-o Nayef and half-sister to Nashwan and Unfuwain: much better effort in maidens (had raced freely on debut) when justifying favouritism in 13-runner event at Doncaster by 2½ lengths from Naomi, quickening on over 1f out: likely to prove best up to 7f: useful prospect. *M. P. Tregoning* — **84 p**

THANKS MAX (IRE) 5 b.g. Goldmark (USA) 113 – Almost A Lady (IRE) 70 (Entitled 126) [2003 65d: 8m 7m 6d 9.2g 9f 8m⁵ 11.1m Jul 17] strong gelding: poor performer nowadays: stays easy 1m: acts on fibresand, firm and soft going (seemingly not on heavy): sometimes blinkered/visored: ungenuine. *Miss L. A. Perratt* — **36 §**

THARA'A (IRE) 2 b.f. (Feb 5) Desert Prince (IRE) 130 – Tycoon's Drama (IRE) (Last Tycoon 131) [2003 f8s Dec 13] 160,000Y: closely related to useful French 5f to 6.5f (at 2 yrs) winner Desert Drama (by Green Desert), and half-sister to 3 (including 2 useful) winners in France/US, including 6f (at 2 yrs) to 1m winner Tycoon's Dolce (by Rainbows For Life): dam, 6f (in France) to 8.5f (in US) winner, ran only at 2 yrs: 20/1 and green, well beaten in maiden at Southwell, starting slowly. *E. A. L. Dunlop* — **–**

THAT MAN AGAIN 11 ch.g. Prince Sabo 123 – Milne's Way 83 (The Noble Player (USA) 126) [2003 –§: 6f 5m Jul 28] robust gelding: one-time useful sprinter: blinkered/visored: best left alone nowadays. *S. C. Williams* — **– §**

THATS ALL JAZZ 5 b.m. Prince Sabo 123 – Gate of Heaven 43 (Starry Night (USA)) [2003 52§, a49§: f7s f8g f6g f7s p7g p7g 7m 7f 10m 8.5g⁶ 8.1m 7m 8.2m 8f Oct 27] workmanlike mare: poor handicapper: on long losing run: effective at 6f to easy 1m: acts on soft going, good to firm and polytrack (possibly not fibresand): tried visored: unreliable. *C. R. Dore* — **46 §** **a– §**

THATS ENOUGH 3 b.g. Robellino (USA) 127 – Sea Fairy 64 (Wollow 132) [2003 72: 6d⁶ 5m⁵ 6m 8m Oct 23] modest maiden nowadays: below form after reappearance: stays 6f: acts on soft and good to firm going, well held on polytrack: has carried head awkwardly. *S. C. Williams* — **59 ?**

THAT'S RACING 3 ch.g. Classic Cliche (IRE) 128 – All On 68 (Dunbeath (USA) 127) [2003 12.1m⁶ 11.1d⁴ 10.1d⁶ 12.1m 12.1m 14g 13.8m 15.8d Sep 20] rather lengthy, good-topped gelding: second foal: dam, successful at 1½m to 21.5f, also won over hurdles: disappointing maiden: bred to be suited by at least 1¾m. *J. Hetherton* — **62 d**

THAW 4 ch.f. Cadeaux Genereux 131 – Ice House 89 (Northfields (USA)) [2003 69: 6.1g⁴ Jun 13] angular filly: fair maiden handicapper: lightly raced: good effort (went left at start) only outing in 2003: races freely, but should stay 1m: acts on soft going. *R. Charlton* — **74**

THE ANGEL GABRIEL 8 ch.g. My Generation 111 – Minsk 36 (Kabour 80) [2003 –: 5g 6m⁶ Jul 18] no form. *D. A. Nolan* — **–**

THEATRE BELLE 2 b.f. (Feb 15) King's Theatre (IRE) 128 – Cumbrian Rhapsody 79 (Sharrood (USA) 124) [2003 f8s 8.1d Sep 27] rather leggy filly: third foal: dam, 1½m winner, also successful over hurdles: better effort in maidens (modest form) when seventh of 14 at Haydock on final start: should be suited by 1½m+. *T. D. Easterby* — **57**

THEATRE LADY (IRE) 5 b.m. King's Theatre (IRE) 128 – Littlepace (Indian King (USA) 128) [2003 50, a–: f8.5g 8.3g 8f⁶ 8.1m⁴ 9f 8g³ 9.7m² 9g⁵ 8m⁶ 9.7m⁴ 8g³ 8.1g² — **59** **a–**

10f^2 8.1m* 8.2m^3 8f 9m Oct 17] sturdy mare: modest handicapper: won at Chepstow in August: stays 1¼m: acts on any turf ground, no form on fibresand: tried visored: usually held up: tough. *P. D. Evans*

THEATRE TIME (USA) 3 b.c. Theatrical 128 – Kyka (USA) (Blushing John (USA) **82** 120) [2003 85: 10m* 10m May 27] lengthy, well-made colt: fairly useful performer, lightly raced: straightforward task when winning 4-runner maiden at Redcar: last in handicap at Sandown later in May: stays 1¼m: acts on firm and good to soft ground: raced freely at 2 yrs: sold 5,000 gns in October. *B. W. Hills*

THEATRE TINKA (IRE) 4 b.g. King's Theatre (IRE) 128 – Orange Grouse (IRE) **69** 105 (Taufan (USA) 119) [2003 84: 12.3m 12g 10m^5 10f 9.9d 12f^3 12d^2 13.8d f11s* Dec 13] close-coupled gelding: fair performer nowadays: easily best effort in 2003 when winning claimer at Southwell in December: stays 1½m: acts on good to soft ground and fibresand: wore cheekpieces last 4 starts: inconsistent. *R. Hollinshead*

THEATRE (USA) 4 b.g. Theatrical 128 – Fasta (USA) (Seattle Song (USA) 130) **91** [2003 82: p12g^3 p12g^4 p16g 14.4d^3 16m* 14m^2 13.9f^4 16.2f 14g 16g 16g^4 Oct 31] close-coupled gelding: fairly useful handicapper: won at Newbury in April: ran creditably when in frame subsequently: stays 2m: acts on firm going, good to soft and polytrack: blinkered (ran to form) twice at 3 yrs: usually waited with. *Jamie Poulton*

THE BARONESS (IRE) 3 b.f. Blues Traveller (IRE) 119 – Wicken Wonder (IRE) **65** 71 (Distant Relative 128) [2003 –: p5g* p6g^2 p5g^4 f5g^4 5m* f7g 6.1m^2 5m 6m^5 5m^4 5.3f^5 **a57** Sep 2] fair performer on turf, modest on all-weather: won seller at Lingfield in January and (having left S. Williams after second start) claimer at Folkestone in April: best at 5f/ 6f: acts on all-weather and good to firm ground: sold 3,000 gns. *J. R. Best*

THE BEDUTH NAVI 3 b.g. Forzando 122 – Sweets (IRE) (Persian Heights 129) **–** [2003 –: 8.1m 8.2g 11.8m Sep 1] angular, heavy-topped gelding: well beaten in maidens: looked ungenuine in blinkers on reappearance. *D. G. Bridgwater*

THE BEST YET 5 ch.h. King's Signet (USA) 110 – Miss Klew (Never So Bold 135) **84** [2003 67: f6s^6 p6g* p6g^2 6m 5.7f* 5.7f^2 6g^4 p7g^6 5.7f^3 7m p7g^2 p7g^2 Dec 29] fairly useful performer: won apprentice handicap at Lingfield in February and minor event at Bath in June: good second in handicaps at Lingfield last 2 starts: stays easy 7f: acts on all-weather and firm ground: has been slowly away/raced freely/wandered: held up. *A. G. Newcombe*

THE BOLTER 4 b.g. Puissance 110 – Miami Dolphin 85 (Derrylin 115) [2003 61: **–** 9.3g 8.3d May 16] lengthy gelding: poor mover: maiden handicapper: tailed off both starts in 2003 (visored final one). *James Moffatt*

THE BONUS KING 3 b.g. Royal Applause 124 – Selvi (Mummy's Pet 125) [2003 **94 ?** 106: 5f 6m 7g^6 7m 7m^6 7.1m Oct 25] strong, angular, good-topped gelding: has a fluent action: useful performer at 2 yrs: reportedly very sick at end of 2002, and below best in 2003: stays 6f: acts on good to firm and good to soft going: blinkered final outing (well held). *M. Johnston*

THE BUTTERFLY BOY 2 ch.c. (Feb 13) Inchinor 119 – Crime of Passion 115 **67 p** (Dragonara Palace (USA) 115) [2003 6g^6 Aug 11] half-brother to several winners, including 5f/6f winner Master of Passion (by Primo Dominie), useful at 2 yrs, and fairly useful 5f winner Licence To Thrill (by Wolfhound): dam: won Cherry Hinton Stakes at 2 yrs, didn't train on: 50/1, sixth of 16 in maiden at Windsor, not knocked about: should do better. *P. F. I. Cole*

THE BUTTERWICK KID 10 ch.g. Interrex (CAN) – Ville Air 85 (Town Crier 119) **–** [2003 80: 12g May 24] workmanlike gelding: fairly useful handicapper at best: won hunter chase prior to well beaten only Flat outing in 2003: usually blinkered/visored: best held up. *T. P. Tate*

THE CHOCOLATIER (IRE) 5 b.m. Inzar (USA) 112 – Clover Honey (King of **–** Clubs 124) [2003 –: 10m Oct 23] close-coupled mare: fair performer at 3 yrs, well held since. *Mrs Lydia Pearce*

THE COPT 4 b.g. Charmer 123 – Coptic Dancer (Sayf El Arab (USA) 127) [2003 **–** 63: 7.9m 10m f7g Jun 25] leggy gelding: maiden handicapper: no form in 2003. *Mrs S. Lamyman*

THE CUTE WON (USA) 5 b.g. Defensive Play (USA) 118 – Alzabella (IRE) 98 **56** (Top Command (USA)) [2003 85: 11m 10.1m^6 12g 10.1m 7m 8m^6 Jul 6] fairly useful performer in Ireland for V. Bowens, winning maiden at Downpatrick in 2002: only modest in 2003: needs further than 1m, stays 1½m: acts on good to soft going: wore cheekpieces last 2 starts. *Mrs A. M. Naughton*

THE DIDDY MAN (IRE) 3 b.c. Night Shift (USA) – March Star (IRE) 109 (Mac's Imp (USA) 116) [2003 45: f6g f8.5g Mar 8] smallish, heavy-topped colt: poor walker/mover: poor maiden: no form in 2003. *A. Berry* —

THE FAIRY FLAG (IRE) 5 ch.m. Inchinor 119 – Good Reference (IRE) 84 (Reference Point 139) [2003 10g⁵ 13.8f⁶ 9.2m³ 10.9m² 12f 11.9g* 10g 10g³ 9.1g⁴ 12.3m 10.5m² 10m² 9.9m⁶ 12.3g* 10.5f 10.9m³ 10m⁴ 10.3d³ 10.5d⁶ Sep 27] angular mare: fair handicapper: missed 2002: won at Haydock in July and Chester (amateurs event) in August: stays 1½m: acts on any turf going and fibresand: usually wears cheekpieces: often front runner. *A. Bailey* 70

THE FISIO 3 b.g. Efisio 120 – Misellina (FR) 57 (Polish Precedent (USA) 131) [2003 81, a90: p5g 5d 5d 5s 5d p6g Dec 6] smallish, strong gelding: fairly useful performer: well held last 4 starts: will prove best at 5f/easy 6f: acts on all-weather, good to firm and good to soft going: occasionally visored (below form). *A. M. Balding* 80

THE FOOTBALLRESULT 2 b.f. (Apr 1) The West (USA) 107 – Bunny Gee (Last Tycoon 131) [2003 7m 7m⁶ 7m Sep 16] rather leggy filly: fifth foal: half-sister to 1½m seller winner Bee Gee (by Beveled) and winner in Sweden by Forzando: dam no form: modest form in maidens: needs to settle to stay beyond 7f. *Mrs G. Harvey* 59

THE FUN MERCHANT 2 b.g. (Apr 30) Mind Games 121 – Sinking (Midyan (USA) 124) [2003 6m⁶ 6m Jun 26] 28,000Y: close-coupled, workmanlike gelding: has markedly round action: seventh foal: half-brother to French 5.5f (at 2 yrs) to 1¼m winner Zilzoom (by Zilzal), 5f (at 2 yrs)/6f winner Molly Brown (by Rudimentary) and Italian 7f/1m performer Stato King (by Statoblest), all useful: dam unraced: modest form in maidens at Doncaster and Leicester: subsequently gelded. *W. Jarvis* 55

THE GAIKWAR (IRE) 4 b.c. Indian Ridge 123 – Broadmara (IRE) 91 (Thatching 131) [2003 94: 8m 8m 9g p10g f9.4g p7g⁴ f7g p7g⁴ Dec 30] lengthy colt: fair nowadays: left Mrs A. Perrett 6,000 gns after third start: not sure to stay further than 1m: acts on firm ground and polytrack: sometimes blinkered: has raced freely/started slowly. *N. E. Berry* 76

THE GAMBLER 3 ch.g. First Trump 118 – Future Options 71 (Lomond (USA) 128) [2003 66: 6m³ 6m² 6m* 6d 6f² 5f 7m³ 5f⁶ 8.3m² 7f 7m 7.5m⁵ 6.9m f8g Nov 24] good-bodied gelding: fair performer: left Mrs A. Duffield £8,000 after winning claimer at Redcar in May: very best form at 6f/7f: acts on firm and good to soft ground: often wears cheekpieces nowadays: often races prominently: none too consistent. *Paul Johnson* 71

THE GAY FOX 9 gr.g. Never So Bold 135 – School Concert 80 (Music Boy 124) [2003 58, a64: p6g p6g⁶ p7g f6s p8g⁵ p7g p6g⁵ p7g² 7f³ 6m 7m 7m 7g 7m⁶ 7f⁵ 6m³ f8g p6g⁵ f6g p7g f6g⁵ Dec 26] good-topped gelding: unimpressive mover: modest performer: stays 7f, not 1m: acts on all-weather/any turf going: wears headgear/tongue tie: often slowly away. *B. G. Powell* 56 d

THE GLEN 5 gr.g. Mtoto 134 – Silver Singer 65 (Pharly (FR) 130) [2003 90§: p10g p10g 8g 10.1m³ 10.3m 10m 10.4f³ 10.3m² 10.3m* 10m³ 10m² 9m³ 10.3d⁴ 10g Oct 13] leggy gelding: unimpressive mover: fairly useful performer: won minor event at Chester in July: mostly creditable efforts after: best efforts at 9f to 11f: acts on firm going, good to soft and polytrack: sometimes edges left/finds little: usually front runner: sold 25,000 gns, joined R. Lee. *M. H. Tompkins* 90

THE GREAT GATSBY (IRE) 3 b.c. Sadler's Wells (USA) 132 – Ionian Sea (Slip Anchor 136) [2003 105: 10g² 12m² 12m² 12m⁵ Jun 29] 120

Racing is unlikely to remember Aidan O'Brien and Pat Eddery as 'nearly-men' but on Derby Day 2003 that is what they were briefly. Aidan O'Brien came close to an unprecedented hat-trick of wins in the big race as a trainer when The Great Gatsby was second under Eddery, who was bidding for his fourth Derby success on what turned out to be his final mount in the race before retirement. Following Galileo and High Chaparral, O'Brien was the first trainer to be in the position in the Derby since Dick Hern won with Troy and Henbit over twenty years earlier—Hern's representative in his attempt for a hat-trick in 1981 was Church Parade, who finished fifth behind Shergar. Originally booked for the Terry Mills-trained Let Me Try Again, Eddery, successful in the Derby on Grundy, Golden Fleece and Quest For Fame, opted for a rare association with O'Brien. Winner of a maiden at Galway over an extended mile from five starts at two, The Great Gatsby had split Alamshar and Brian Boru in the Derrinstown Stud Derby Trial at

Vodafone Derby Stakes, Epsom—
approaching the final furlong and eventual runner-up The Great Gatsby is still out in front

Leopardstown on his reappearance in May, making most before going down by a head. Nevertheless, he was ostensibly only third best among his stable's four runners in the Derby and started at 20/1.

Ride of the season awards rarely go to jockeys on beaten horses, but Eddery's effort on The Great Gatsby was a strong contender all the same. In a maximum field of twenty, Eddery took the initiative from the start. When Philip Robinson joined him in the lead on Dutch Gold, Eddery eased The Great Gatsby to prevent his getting involved in a battle too early. Waiting until turning out of Tattenham Corner before asking The Great Gatsby to quicken, still hugging the rail as he did so, Eddery sent his mount into a definite lead under three furlongs out, in the process stealing a good four lengths on Kris Kin, who was still several horses back. Inside the final furlong, The Great Gatsby briefly looked the winner, but he had no answer once Kris Kin found his stride, going down by a length under strong pressure, keeping on to hold Alamshar's challenge for second by a short head. It was the sixth time Eddery had finished second in the race.

Surprisingly, Eddery's master-class round the difficult Derby course came in for criticism in some quarters, one 'time expert' insisting Eddery had gone too fast, judged on the writer's interpretation of his own sectional times logged over the last thirty years or so. Timeform's timefigure for the race as a whole was highly respectable for the standard of Derby it was, a timerating for The Great Gatsby of 117 suggesting Eddery set something very close to a true pace, arguably getting it just about right on a horse that had looked a relatively one-paced performer without appearing simply to be an out-and-out stayer. Of course, the distilling of overall times into timefigures is about split seconds and sectional times can work to finer margins still. Credible study of sectional times is still in its youth, in Europe at least, and calculations from which meaningful conclusions can be drawn are a good deal more difficult than some might believe. The attraction of sectional time analysis is that it can reach conclusions that are unique, though it is often prudent to balance them against other factors known about the horses involved. The Great Gatsby ran his best race at Epsom—running about a stone above the form he had shown previously—and he was by no means out on his feet at the end. Alamshar's part in the race hardly suggested the gallop had been too strong either; if anything, he ran as though an even stronger pace would have suited him, finishing well. Norse Dancer was beaten only two and a half lengths by the winner in fourth, yet showed equally good form at a mile. The 66/1-shot Balestrini, who kept closest to The Great Gatsby of those to finish in the first five, was beaten little over three lengths—hardly suggesting he had been drained by an overly-strong pace.

The Derby was The Great Gatsby's first race on ground firmer than good and, as well as he ran, it possibly left a mark. His short, choppy action raised doubts beforehand as to how he might handle the ground on the course, and The Great Gatsby ran below his Derby form on his only run afterwards, also on good to firm going. He started the shortest priced of his stable's six runners in a field of nine for the Irish Derby but managed only fifth, dropped out this time, never a threat and beaten nearly ten lengths.

		Sadler's Wells (USA) (b 1981)	Northern Dancer (b 1961)	Nearctic / Natalma
The Great Gatsby (IRE) (b.c. 2000)			Fairy Bridge (b 1975)	Bold Reason / Special
		Ionian Sea (b 1989)	Slip Anchor (b 1982)	Shirley Heights / Sayonara
			Snow Day (b 1978)	Reliance II / Vindaria

Fuller details of The Great Gatsby's pedigree are given in the essay on his brother Magritte, a promising two-year-old in 2003, who may well line up in the Derby himself. The Great Gatsby, incidentally, completed an Epsom classic double of sorts for his sire Sadler's Wells, who was also responsible for Oaks runner-up Yesterday. Sadler's Wells, who also sired the Two Thousand Guineas and St Leger winners in 2003, is also the sire of another Derby runner-up in Blue Stag, a son of The Great Gatsby's grandam Snow Day. A compact, quite attractive colt, The Great Gatsby has yet to tackle very firm ground. *A. P. O'Brien, Ireland*

THE GUINEA STAMP 4 b.g. Overbury (IRE) 116 – Gagajulu 75 (Al Hareb (USA) 123) [2003 8.5f f12g 7m May 10] second foal: dam 2-y-o 5f winner: no sign of ability. *A. Berry* —

THE JOB 2 ch.c. (Feb 20) Dancing Spree (USA) – Bay Bianca (IRE) (Law Society (USA) 130) [2003 5g 5m⁴ 6g 8d p8g* f8s⁴ Dec 13] £4,000Y: workmanlike colt: fifth foal: brother to 3-y-o Pertemps Bianca and half-brother to winner in Greece by Lead On Time: dam German 6f winner: modest performer: won seller at Lingfield in November: stays 1m: acts on good to firm ground and polytrack, probably on fibresand. *A. D. Smith* 61

THE JOBBER (IRE) 2 b.g. (Apr 15) Foxhound (USA) 103 – Clairification (IRE) 57 (Shernazar 131) [2003 6m 6m² 6d* Sep 26] IR 27,000F, 30,000Y: strong gelding: fifth foal: closely related to 2 winners by Hamas, including fairly useful 6f (including at 2 yrs) winner Central Coast, and half-brother to fairly useful Irish 1m winner Flying Knight (by Flying Spur): dam 7f/1m winner: fair form in maidens: won 13-runner event at Haydock by short head from Tropical Storm, leading over 1f out and not hard ridden: not sure to stay much beyond 6f. *M. Blanshard* 70

THE JUDGE 5 b.g. Polish Precedent (USA) 131 – Just Speculation (IRE) 86 (Aho-noora 122) [2003 90: 8.3g⁴ 8.1g 8g 8.1d⁵ 10m² 9.9m* 10m 10.3m* 9.9g 9.2g* Sep 1] lengthy gelding: useful performer: reportedly broke pelvis only 2-y-o start: won handicap at Beverley and claimer at Chester in June, and claimer at Hamilton (claimed £31,000) in September: was effective at 1m/1¼m: acted on good to firm and good to soft going (possibly not on soft): sometimes raced freely: dead. *P. F. I. Cole* 96

THE KIDDYKID (IRE) 3 b.g. Danetime (IRE) 121 – Mezzanine (Sadler's Wells (USA) 132) [2003 91: 7m³ 6g² 6.1d* 6v* 6f⁵ 6m³ 6.1m⁶ 6m⁵ Aug 9] tall, lengthy gelding: smart performer: won minor event at Nottingham and listed rated stakes at Haydock (made all to beat Coconut Penang by ½ length) in May: below form in handicaps next 2 starts, particularly when 1¼ lengths third to Move It at Newmarket: below form in listed race at Chester and Shergar Cup Sprint at Ascot last 2 outings: best at 6f: acts on any turf going: drifted right sixth start: usually races up with pace: reliable. *P. D. Evans* 111

THE KING OF ROCK 2 b.c. (Apr 23) Nicolotte 118 – Lv Girl (IRE) 67 (Mukad-damah (USA) 125) [2003 5.1m 5f⁵ 5.1g 7m⁴ 7g² f8s 8f8g f7g Dec 8] rather leggy colt: first foal: dam maiden who stayed 1m: modest maiden: visored, second in claimer at Chester, then left G. Balding: stays 7f: well held on fibresand. *A. G. Newcombe* 61

THE LADY WOULD (IRE) 4 ch.f. Woodborough (USA) 112 – Kealbra Lady (Petong 126) [2003 51, a–: f6g⁵ f6g 10.2m 6.1m 6m Sep 29] poor maiden: stays 6f: sometimes wears cheekpieces. *D. G. Bridgwater* 40

THE LAST MOHICAN 4 b.g. Common Grounds 118 – Arndilly 75 (Robellino (USA) 127) [2003 44: f16.2g⁵ f14.8s Jul 14] small, workmanlike gelding: bad mover: poor maiden: stays 1½m: acts on firm going. *P. Howling* 40

THE LAVERTON LAD　2 ch.g. (Apr 1) Keen 116 – Wyse Folly (Colmore Row 111)　**41**
[2003 5m 6d 7m f8g Dec 8] smallish gelding: second reported foal: dam ran twice: poor
form, including in sellers. *C. W. Thornton*

THE LEATHER WEDGE (IRE)　4 b.c. Hamas (IRE) 125§ – Wallflower (Polar　**46**
Falcon (USA) 126) [2003 74d: f5g⁶ 5g 5m 5m 5f f5s³ 5m f5g 5f 5f⁴ f5s f5g² f5s Dec 31]　**a57**
tall, quite good-topped colt: modest on all-weather, poor on turf: best at 5f: acts on firm
going, good to soft and fibresand: tried in cheekpieces: folded third/fourth starts: usually
races prominently: inconsistent. *A. Berry*

THE LOCAL　3 b.g. Selkirk (USA) 129 – Finger of Light 89 (Green Desert (USA)　**75 d**
127) [2003 78: 11.6g⁴ 11.6s³ 10m⁵ 12m p12g 10s³ 14.4g 10.2g f12s f12s Oct 21] fair
handicapper: below form last 4 starts: stays 11.6f: acts on soft and good to firm ground,
below form on all-weather: usually races prominently: sold £13,000. *M. Blanshard*

THE LOOSE SCREW (IRE)　5 b.g. Bigstone (IRE) 126 – Princess of Dance (IRE)　**53**
(Dancing Dissident (USA) 119) [2003 –: 7m 5m 10.1m⁶ 10.1m² 8m f8g Nov 19] good-
bodied gelding: modest maiden handicapper: left Miss A. Naughton after second start:
stays 1¼m: acts on heavy and good to firm going: tried blinkered. *G. M. Moore*

THE LORD　3 b.g. Averti (IRE) 117 – Lady Longmead (Crimson Beau 124) [2003　**97 d**
104: 5g 5f² 6g 6m⁶ 5m 5f 5g Aug 2] close-coupled, quite good-topped gelding: has a
quick action: useful performer: ran creditably in 2003 only when head second to No Time
in listed event at Haydock in April, edging left: effective at 5f/6f: acts on firm and soft
ground: often races prominently: inconsistent: gelded after final start. *W. G. M. Turner*

THEME PARK　3 b.g. Classic Cliche (IRE) 128 – Arcady 69 (Slip Anchor 136) [2003　**–**
77: f12g 14.6m p12g⁶ 11.7m Aug 5] fair maiden at 2 yrs: tongue tied
last 2 starts: pulled up amiss second outing. *H. Morrison*

THEMESOFGREEN　2 ch.g. (Jun 4) Botanic (USA) – Harmonia (Glint of Gold 128)　**–**
[2003 7m Oct 1] fourth reported foal: brother to 3-y-o Kew The Music and half-brother to
2 winners, including useful 1998 2-y-o 7f winner Thank Heavens (by Theatrical Charmer), later 6f/7f performer in Hong Kong: dam unraced: 66/1 and very green, showed little
in minor event at Salisbury, slowly away. *M. R. Channon*

THE MIGHTY TIGER (USA)　2 ch.c. (Feb 27) Storm Cat (USA) – Clear Mandate　**108**
(USA) 117 (Deputy Minister (CAN)) [2003 6m³ 6m* 7d² 7m³ Aug 23] $2,500,000Y:
strong, angular colt: third foal: brother to useful Irish 2002 2-y-o 6f winner Newfound-
land, later winner in USA, and half-brother to a winner in USA by A P Indy: dam US
Grade 1 1m/1¼m winner: useful performer: won maiden at the Curragh in June, making
most: good 1¼ lengths second to Lucky Story in Vintage Stakes at Goodwood: respectable third to Pearl of Love in Futurity Stakes at the Curragh final start: will stay 1m: best
effort on good to soft going. *A. P. O'Brien, Ireland*

THE MOG　4 b.g. Atraf 116 – Safe Secret 50 (Seclude (USA)) [2003 49§, a56§: f7s f6g　**– §**
f7s⁵ f7s³ Feb 18] close-coupled gelding: poor performer: effective at 6f/7f: acts on fibre-　**a47 §**
sand and firm going: sometimes tongue tied: has been blinkered (including for only win):
ungenuine. *S. R. Bowring*

THE NAMES BOND　5 b.g. Tragic Role (USA) – Artistic Licence (High Top 131)　**–**
[2003 12.3m Apr 2] tall, leggy gelding: modest handicapper at 3 yrs: well held only Flat
start since. *Andrew Turnell*

THE NUMBER　2 gr.g. (Mar 18) Silver Wizard (USA) 117 – Elite Number (USA) 56　**70**
(Elmaamul (USA) 125) [2003 7.2g⁵ 7m⁶ Aug 25] rather leggy gelding: first foal: dam,
maiden, should have stayed beyond 1m: better effort in maidens (fair form) when fifth at
Ayr: still backward final start: should stay 1m. *I. Semple*

THE OLD SOLDIER　5 b.g. Magic Ring (IRE) 115 – Grecian Belle 53 (Ilium 121)　**64**
[2003 58: 5m³ 5m* 6m³ 5m 5f⁵ 6m² 7m 5g Oct 22] tall gelding: modest handicapper: won
at Catterick in August: best at 5f/6f: acts on firm going. *A. Dickman*

THEORIST　3 b.g. Machiavellian (USA) 123 – Clerio 108 (Soviet Star (USA) 128)　**76 d**
[2003 62: 8.5m* 8.5m⁴ 10g 10g⁶ 9.9m⁵ 9g 10g 10.3m f8.5g Nov 15] strong gelding: fair
performer: won maiden at Epsom in April: disappointing following next start, leaving
M. Johnston 20,000 gns after sixth one: should stay 1¼m: raced only on good/good to
firm ground on turf: tried blinkered/in cheekpieces: has looked less than keen/difficult
ride: needs treating with caution. *J. L. Spearing*

THE PERSUADER (IRE)　3 b.g. Sadler's Wells (USA) 132 – Sister Dot (USA)　**88 +**
(Secretariat (USA)) [2003 –: p12g⁶ 14.1m* 11.9m* 12.1d* 11.8g² 14g* 13.1d Oct 14]

good-topped, quite attractive gelding: fairly useful handicapper: won at Nottingham, York and Beverley in May and valuable event at Haydock (despite veering markedly left and idling) in September: effective at 1½m/1¾m: acts on good to firm and good to soft going, probably on polytrack: also hung left final start. *M. Johnston*

THE PLAYER   4 b.g. Octagonal (NZ) 126 – Patria (USA) 76 (Mr Prospector (USA)) [2003 68p: 8.3g⁴ f7s* Sep 26] angular gelding: fairly useful form: unraced at 2 yrs, ran once at 3 (for J. Gosden): impressive when winning maiden at Southwell in September by 2 lengths (rated value much more) from Malak Al Moulouk: probably stays 1m: should improve further. *A. M. Balding*   **82 p**

THE PRINCE   9 b.g. Machiavellian (USA) 123 – Mohican Girl 112 (Dancing Brave (USA) 140) [2003 p8g² 8.5d* 7.9m 8.3g³ 9m* Sep 15] well-made gelding: has a quick action: fairly useful performer: won claimers at Galway (easily) in August and Musselburgh (made hard work of simple task) in September: good efforts in handicaps other starts in 2003: best around 1m: acts on good to soft going and all-weather, probably on firm: tried visored/blinkered: usually tongue tied: sometimes slowly away: needs exaggerated waiting tactics. *Ian Williams*   **93**

THE PRIVATEER   3 b.g. Bahamian Bounty 116 – Petriece 64 (Mummy's Pet 125) [2003 80: 6g⁴ 7g⁵ 6.1m 6m⁵ 7g 5m 7m Sep 25] tall, leggy gelding: has scope: fairly useful performer: won maiden at Doncaster in March despite carrying head awkwardly: best effort in handicap next time: ran poorly last 3 starts, finding nothing final one: stays 7f: acts on good to firm and good to soft going, below form on firm: tends to wander: none too reliable: sold 11,000 gns. *R. Hannon*   **91**

THE RECRUITER   3 gr.g. Danzig Connection (USA) – Tabeeba (Diesis 133) [2003 42: p10g f8g⁵ 10.2g f9.4s 11.7f 10.9g 10.2m Aug 14] little form at 3 yrs, leaving R. Beckett after second start: should stay 1¼m: visored (ran poorly) final outing. *J. G. M. O'Shea*   **–**

THE RING (IRE)   3 b.g. Definite Article 121 – Renata's Ring (IRE) (Auction Ring (USA) 123) [2003 72p: 11.8m⁵ 11.9m⁶ 12m 11.6d³ 14g⁴ 12s⁴ 10.9g⁴ 12.1m³ 16.1m* Oct 1] big, rangy gelding: has plenty of scope: fair handicapper: mostly creditable efforts in 2003, leaving M. Channon prior to winning at Newcastle in October: stays 2m: acts on heavy ground, good to firm and fibresand. *Mrs M. Reveley*   **79**

THE RIP   2 ch.c. (Jan 22) Definite Article 121 – Polgwynne 48 (Forzando 122) [2003 6m 7d 7m⁴ Aug 5] 10,000Y: strong colt: third foal: dam 7f winner: easily best effort in maidens (fair form) when eye-catching fourth at Catterick, never nearer and not at all knocked about: will stay at least 1m: should progress. *T. D. Easterby*   **68 p**

THE RISEN LARK (IRE)   3 b.f. Celtic Swing 138 – May Hills Legacy (IRE) 68 (Be My Guest (USA) 126) [2003 63: 10m 11.7f³ 10.2m 12m Aug 11] big, good-topped filly: modest maiden handicapper: will stay 1¾m: acts on polytrack and firm going: wore cheekpieces (tailed off having run wide first bend) final outing. *D. W. P. Arbuthnot*   **64**

THE RISK OF REFORM   3 b.f. Petorius 117 – Bedtime Model (Double Bed (FR) 121) [2003 39: 5m 5g 7m Oct 25] compact filly: little form. *E. J. Alston*   **–**

THESAURUS   4 gr.g. Most Welcome 131 – Red Embers 64 (Saddlers' Hall (IRE) 126) [2003 81: 10m 8.1d 8.3g 8.1m 9f* 8.5m⁴ 8d 8m 8g³ 10m⁵ 8f 10m 12g f8g⁵ Nov 19] tall gelding: fairly useful handicapper: won amateur event at Goodwood in June despite hanging left: below form last 8 starts, claimed from I. Wood £10,000 after third of them: stays 9f, possibly not 1¼m: acts on firm and good to soft going, well held on soft/heavy. *A. Crook*   **82 d**

THE SCAFFOLDER   5 b.g. Tachyon Park 87 – Fallal (IRE) 47 (Fayruz 116) [2003 56§: f8s f8.5g f6g Apr 4] workmanlike gelding: modest and unreliable at 4 yrs: no form in 2003: sometimes blinkered/visored. *Mrs N. Macauley*   **– §**

THE SINGING BUTLER   3 ch.f. Primo Dominie 121 – Funny Choice (IRE) 68 (Commanche Run 133) [2003 8.3m Jul 7] fourth foal: sister to 5-y-o Tickle and half-sister to 1m winner Ronni Pancake (by Mujadil): dam 6.5f (at 2 yrs) to 15f winner: 16/1, fell in maiden at Windsor: dead. *B. Hanbury*   **–**

THE SPOOK   3 b.g. Bin Ajwaad (IRE) 119 – Rose Mill (Puissance 110) [2003 –: 8m 9m 5m⁵ 5d³ 6m 5g Oct 13] poor maiden: should stay 6f: acts on good to soft going: starts slowly: has raced freely/looked difficult ride for inexperienced claimer. *J. S. Goldie*   **41**

THE STAFFORD (IRE)   2 b.g. (Feb 17) Selkirk (USA) 129 – Bint Zamayem (IRE) 95 (Rainbow Quest (USA) 134) [2003 p8g Dec 20] fifth foal: half-brother to useful Irish   **–**

6f (at 2 yrs)/7f winner Sweet Deimos (by Green Desert) and fairly useful 7.6f winner Queenie (by Indian Ridge): dam, 1¼m winner, half-sister to smart French miler Rouquette: 33/1, always rear in minor event at Lingfield. *L. Wells*

THE STICK   2 b.f. (May 11) Singspiel (IRE) 133 – Fatah Flare (USA) 121 (Alydar (USA)) [2003 7m⁶ 8m⁵ 8m⁶ Oct 25] 24,000Y: sister to 3-y-o Compton Eclipse and half-sister to several winners, including 6f (at 2 yrs)/7f winner Flavian (by Catrail) and 1¼m winner Refugio (by Reference Point), both fairly useful: dam 6f (at 2 yrs) and 10.5f (Musidora Stakes) winner: modest form in minor event/maidens: stays 1m. *M. R. Channon*   **61**

THE TATLING (IRE)   6 b.g. Perugino (USA) 84 – Aunty Eileen (Ahonoora 122) [2003 113: 6m² 6g² 6m² 5g⁴ 6f³ 5m⁶ 5g* 6m³ 5g* 5m² 6d⁶ 5.2m⁵ 6f⁵ 5s³ 6m⁴ 5m Dec 14]   **120**

Milton Bradley started as a lithographer in Springfield, Massachusetts in 1860 and got his first big commission when the Republican National Convention suggested he produce a print of their candidate Abraham Lincoln. Bradley pressed thousands of the pictures but, by the time Lincoln had won the election months later, he had grown a beard, rendering Bradley's print out of date. Sales of the beardless lithography dropped away and instead Bradley began producing a board-game called *The Checkered Game of Life*, the object of which was to reach happy old age by avoiding financial ruin, based on making correct moral decisions. The game was spectacularly successful and MB Games went on to become one of the largest makers of games in the world. Over the years, the object of the *The Game of Life*—as it is now known—shifted and, in the modern version, the person who retires with the biggest fortune wins.

(John) Milton Bradley took somewhat longer than his nineteenth century namesake to make his mark. He first took out a permit to train jumpers in 1968/9 and has held a full licence since 1971/2, enjoying success with the prolific winners Mighty Marine, Grey Dolphin and Yangtse-Kiang. The most wins over jumps achieved by Bradley in a campaign is just twenty (in 1983/4) and seasonal totals have regularly been in single figures. According to Bradley, the limiting factor is the high rate of injuries sustained by jumpers and, by the mid-'nineties, he had switched his attention to the Flat, and more specifically to sprinters. 'I like speed horses more than I do stayers, primarily because they are cheaper to buy, and once you have them up and ready you can run them again and again,' Bradley reasoned. Bradley had only eleven Flat winners in the 'eighties and reached double figures for the first time in 1995, soon becoming one of the most prolific trainers of sprint winners in Britain, with a reputation for rejuvenating horses acquired from other yards. Bradley's number of wins in a season peaked at sixty-two in 2001, even though his team, assembled on a shoestring, lacked quality and most of his successes came in ordinary races.

Bradley pushed the boat out in July 2002, going to £15,000 to buy The Tatling after he had won a Catterick claimer for David Nicholls. Useful in his younger days, The Tatling had finished second in the Cornwallis Stakes as a two-year-old, but then had problems with his knees, being restricted to just seven outings in total in the following couple of seasons, leaving Michael Bell after his

King George Stakes, Goodwood—The Tatling (check sleeves) and Dragon Flyer are wide apart; Italian-trained Slap Shot (next to winner), Repertory (spots on cap) and Bishops Court (noseband) come next

reappearance as a four-year-old. An operation in April 2002 left The Tatling with knees 'full of nuts and bolts' and he made little impact in handicaps for Nicholls before being claimed by Bradley. Later that year The Tatling went on to win handicaps at Sandown and York (the Coral Eurobet Sprint Trophy) and finish second in the Ayr Gold Cup. The Tatling showed even better form in the latest season, no horse having done more to advertise Bradley's skills. For the first time, the trainer found himself with a sprinter with whom he could chase big prizes outside handicaps and, when The Tatling was promoted from the reserve list for the Hong Kong Sprint at Sha Tin in December, sixty-eight-year-old Bradley boarded a plane for the first time in his life and travelled six thousand miles to saddle the gelding in the richest five-furlong race ever run. Unfortunately, 100/1-shot The Tatling didn't get in the money, failing to travel with his usual fluency after being a shade slow out of his stall and unable to get into the race behind Silent Witness.

The Tatling stood up well to a busy campaign in 2003 and provided Bradley with several good pay days, finishing first past the post on three of his sixteen starts, and reaching the frame on eight other occasions. The Tatling short-headed Capricho in a handicap at Newmarket in May, but edged across his rival near the finish, resulting in the placings being reversed. The Tatling then got a dream run through and caused no such interference when beating stable-companion Bali Royal by a head in a listed race at Sandown in July, the pair finishing three lengths clear. Bradley twice saddled first, second and third in a race in 2003, but being denied victory by one from the same stable evidently didn't please the owner of Bali Royal, who promptly removed the horse from Bradley's Chepstow yard. The Tatling became Bradley's first runner in a pattern race in the King George Stakes at Goodwood later in the month, and didn't need to be at his best to beat Dragon Flyer by a neck. Stepped up to Group 1 company in the Nunthorpe Stakes at York in August, The Tatling acquitted himself with plenty of credit to finish second, beaten two and a half lengths, racing more prominently than usual and being the only one to keep tabs on all-the-way winner Oasis Dream. Bradley does much of his own horsebox driving and set foot on foreign soil for the first time when The Tatling lined up for the Prix de l'Abbaye de Longchamp in October. Bradley clearly wasn't worried by the prospect of a drive to Paris, saying before his departure 'There'll be lots of boxes going over so we'll tag on behind someone else who knows the way.' The Tatling ran another sound race to finish third to Patavellian, beaten a length and a neck. Another notable performance came in the Bentinck Stakes at Newmarket later in October when, beaten around a length into fourth by Ashdown Express, The Tatling came out the best horse at the weights, carrying 4 lb more than the trio who beat him.

			Danzig	Northern Dancer
The Tatling (IRE) (b.g. 1997)	Perugino (USA) (b 1991)		(b 1977)	Pas de Nom
			Fairy Bridge (b 1975)	Bold Reason
				Special
	Aunty Eileen (b 1983)		Ahonoora (ch 1975)	Lorenzaccio
				Helen Nichols
			Safe Haven (b 1974)	Blakeney
				Amazer

The Tatling's sire Perugino, a six-furlong maiden winner on his only start as a two-year-old for Vincent O'Brien, could hardly be better bred, being by Danzig out of Fairy Bridge and therefore a close relative of Sadler's Wells and Fairy King. He has not had the same degree of success as that pair but, exported to Germany in 2001, has been responsible for the 2003 Preis der Diana winner Next Gina. The Tatling's dam Aunty Eileen has produced six other winners, four of whom were successful at five or six furlongs at two, including useful 1998 juvenile Amazing Dream (by Thatching). Aunty Eileen was an unraced half-sister to the smart 1990 Duke of York Stakes winner Lugana Beach, while The Tatling's grandam Safe Haven was a French maiden half-sister to Mtoto. A lengthy sort in appearance, The Tatling is as effective at six furlongs as at five. He was tailed off on his only run on heavy going but acts on any other. Tried tongue tied a couple of times in previous seasons, he sometimes makes a tardy start but travels strongly waited with, occasionally a little too strongly for his own good. The Tatling, a tough and consistent gelding, should continue to give a good account in top sprints in 2004, making another healthy contribution towards Bradley's retirement fund, not that the trainer has given any hint that he is ready to call it a day just yet. *J. M. Bradley*

THE TOFF   4 b.f. Overbury (IRE) 116 – Fenian Court (IRE) (John French 123) [2003 –
p10g Jan 18] first foal: dam poor 2m hurdler: 100/1 and blinkered, well beaten in claimer at Lingfield. *P. D. Evans*

THE TRADER (IRE)   5 ch.g. Selkirk (USA) 129 – Snowing 88 (Tate Gallery (USA)   **120**
117) [2003 115: 5m³ 5f⁵ 5g⁵ 5m* 6m⁶ 5m⁶ 5m* 5.2m² 5s² 5m⁶ Dec 14] sturdy, close-coupled gelding: usually impresses in appearance: poor mover: very smart performer: won minor events at Newmarket (by 3½ lengths from Bali Boyal) in July and Leicester (beat Manaar ½ length) in September: seemed to run very well when length second to Patavellian in Prix de l'Abbaye de Longchamp penultimate outing, last early following slow start but finishing strongly: only sixth to Silent Witness in Hong Kong Sprint at Sha Tin final appearance: best at 5f: acts on firm and soft going: blinkered: also slowly away sixth outing: usually travels strongly. *M. Blanshard*

THE VARLET   3 b.g. Groom Dancer (USA) 128 – Valagalore 91 (Generous (IRE) 139)   **74**
[2003 61: 12.1m³ 13.3m⁴ 14m² 16.2f⁶ 11.9m² 12.4m⁶ p13g 12.4g⁵ Oct 22] leggy gelding: fair maiden handicapper: poor efforts last 3 starts, reportedly having breathing problem on first occasion: should stay 2m: acts on good to firm ground: effective visored or not: tongue tied (looked none too keen) final outing. *M. P. Tregoning*

THEVENIS   2 ch.c. (Feb 27) Dr Fong (USA) 128 – Pigeon Hole (Green Desert (USA)   **60**
127) [2003 5.1g 5.1f⁵ 6m 7.1g 8.3g f8g⁵ f8g Dec 19] 8,000Y, 9,500 2-y-o: sturdy colt: fourth foal: dam lightly-raced half-sister to 1000 Guineas runner-up Niche: modest maiden: stays 1m: acts on fibresand and firm going. *J. S. King*

THE VIOLIN PLAYER (USA)   2 b.g. (Mar 26) King of Kings (IRE) 125 – Silk   **81**
Masque (USA) 91 (Woodman (USA) 126) [2003 6m 6f³ 7.1g* 7m³ Oct 14] $35,000Y, 65,000 2-y-o: stocky gelding: fourth foal: half-brother to 8.5f (at 2 yrs) and 1½m winner Forum Finale (by Silver Hawk) and 2 minor stakes winners in USA: dam, 2-y-o 6f winner, later won in USA, out of Fillies' Mile winner Silk Slippers: fairly useful performer: won maiden at Chepstow in September: creditable third of 4 to Jedburgh in minor event at Leicester final start, racing freely: stays 7f: acts on firm going. *W. Jarvis*

THE WARLEY WARRIOR   2 b.g. (Jan 13) Primo Dominie 121 – Brief Glimpse   **54**
(IRE) 108 (Taufan (USA) 119) [2003 6d⁵ May 18] quite good-topped gelding: second foal: half-brother to fairly useful 1m winner Once Seen (by Celtic Swing): dam 5f (at 2 yrs) to 7f winner: backward, fifth of 12 in maiden at Ripon: withdrawn having proved troublesome more than once after. *M. W. Easterby*

THE WAY WE WERE   2 ch.c. (Feb 2) Vettori (IRE) 119 – Pandrop (Sharrood (USA)   **74 P**
124) [2003 7m³ p8g* Oct 27] 11,000Y: second foal: half-brother to 2001 2-y-o 6f winner Diana Panagaea (by Polar Falcon): dam, ran once, half-sister to Ribblesdale/Geoffrey Freer winner Phantom Gold, herself dam of Oaks runner-up Flight of Fancy: much better effort in maidens (fair form) when winning 11-runner event at Lingfield by head from Elusive Kitty, travelling strongly and merely nudged out: should be suited by 1¼m/1½m: type to do good deal better as 3-y-o, and potentially useful. *T. G. Mills*

THEWHIRLINGDERVISH (IRE)   5 ch.g. Definite Article 121 – Nomadic Dancer   **87**
(IRE) 52 (Nabeel Dancer (USA) 120) [2003 93: 16m⁵ 16m³ 16g⁴ 20m 16.2f² 16.1m 14g 16.2f Sep 27] leggy, lengthy gelding: fairly useful handicapper: one of several creditable efforts when second to Mana d'Argent at Ascot: well below form after: stays 2¼m (though probably not 2½m): possibly best on good going or firmer: sometimes finds little. *T. D. Easterby*

THE WHISTLING TEAL   7 b.g. Rudimentary (USA) 118 – Lonely Shore (Blakeney   **110**
126) [2003 120: 12g⁴ 12m⁴ 12g⁵ 12d² Nov 8] strong gelding: carries condition: very smart performer at 6 yrs: just respectable efforts at best in 2003, 6¾ lengths fifth to Imperial Dancer in St Simon Stakes at Newbury (had won the race in 2002) and 3½ lengths second to Scott's View in listed event at Doncaster last 2 outings: should stay 1¾m: acts on fibresand, firm and soft going: held up: genuine. *G. Wragg*

THE WIZARD MUL   3 br.g. Wizard King 122 – Longden Pride (Superpower 113)   **74**
[2003 60: 8m 8g 6d* 6m 7g* 6g 8g⁴ Oct 28] leggy gelding: fair handicapper: won at Ripon in May and Newcastle in July: stays 7f: acts on good to firm and good to soft going: none too consistent. *W. Storey*

Mr Nick Fuller's "Thingmebob"

THIHN (IRE) 8 ch.g. Machiavellian (USA) 123 – Hasana (USA) (Private Account **101**
(USA)) [2003 98: 8g⁵ 8g 8g 8.3g² 8.5m 7d⁶ 10g 7g* 8g* Nov 1] sturdy gelding: useful
handicapper: won at Redcar (beat Polar Kingdom 3 lengths) in October and Newmarket
(beat King's County a head) in November: best at 7f/1m: acts on any going: sometimes
starts slowly/hangs right: free-going sort, and usually travels strongly: normally held up:
tough. *J. L. Spearing*

THINGMEBOB 3 b.f. Bob Back (USA) 124 – Kip's Sister (Cawston's Clown 113) **106**
[2003 81p: 8d* 10.3m⁴ 12g 11.9f* 12m³ 11.9m² 14.6d Sep 10] leggy, rather unfurnished
filly: useful performer: won Newmarket Challenge Whip in May and maiden at York (by
8 lengths) in July: ran well when 5¼ lengths eighth to Casual Look in Oaks at Epsom on
third start and when second in listed race at York (beaten a neck by Mezzo Soprano):
should stay 1¾m (last in Park Hill Stakes when tried): acts on firm going. *M. H. Tompkins*

THINK QUICK (IRE) 3 b.f. Goldmark (USA) 113 – Crimson Ring (Persian Bold **50**
123) [2003 f6g⁶ f12g³ 8d⁵ f12g⁴ 10m 12d³ 10g² 7.9d 10m 10m 10f⁴ f12g Dec 26]
workmanlike filly: half-sister to 3 winners, including 1m winner Fistful of Bucks (by
Lochnager): dam lightly-raced maiden: modest maiden handicapper: stays 1½m: acts on
fibresand and good to soft going, probably on firm: tried tongue tied: refused to enter stall
intended second outing, mulish at start next time: has raced freely. *R. Hollinshead*

THINK TANK 2 b.c. (Mar 27) Robellino (USA) 127 – Lucca (Sure Blade (USA) 130) **94 p**
[2003 6m³ 6g* 7f* 7m³ Aug 9] 25,000Y: fifth foal: half-brother to winner in Japan by
Keen: dam, behind in bumper, sister to smart 1m to 1½m performer Needle Gun and
half-sister to Luso and Warrsan: won maiden at Ayr in May and minor event at Catterick
in July: best effort (fairly useful form) when third to Kinnaird in minor event at Ascot

1026

final start, tending to wander: bred to be suited by 1¼m/1½m: sold to race in USA: open to progress. *M. Johnston*

THIRD EMPIRE 2 b.g. (Jan 21) Second Empire (IRE) 124 – Tahnee (Cadeaux Gene- **61**
reux 131) [2003 5d⁴ 5m 10m⁵ 8m Oct 21] 22,000Y: robust gelding: has a round action:
fifth foal: dam unraced half-sister to Phoenix Stakes winner Princely Heir out of very
smart miler Meis El-Reem: modest maiden: soundly beaten in nursery final start: stays
1¼m. *C. Grant*

THIRN 4 b.g. Piccolo 121 – Midnight Owl (FR) (Ardross 134) [2003 65: p7g p7g f7s **–**
Feb 6] strong gelding: fair maiden on turf: no form on all-weather, including all 3 starts in
2003: sometimes swishes tongue/tied: sometimes races freely. *D. Carroll*

THIRTEEN TRICKS (USA) 2 b.f. (Mar 26) Grand Slam (USA) 120 – Talltalelady **76**
(USA) (Naskra (USA)) [2003 7m 7m³ p8g⁴ Nov 2] $100,000Y: strong, lengthy filly:
half-sister to several minor winners in USA: dam, Canadian 5.5f (at 2 yrs) to 9f winner
and US 2-y-o Grade 2 8.5f runner-up, half-sister to Breeders' Cup Sprint runner-up Mr
Greeley: fair form in maidens: in frame at Leicester and Lingfield: barely stays 1m.
Mrs A. J. Perrett

THOLJANAH (IRE) 4 b.g. Darshaan 133 – Alkaffeyeh (IRE) (Sadler's Wells **113**
(USA) 132) [2003 109: 20m 11m⁴ 16m⁴ Oct 18] leggy, angular gelding: smart performer,
lightly raced: best effort when 1½ lengths fourth of 6 to Persian Punch in Jockey Club
Cup at Newmarket final outing, forced to snatch up close home: stays 2m: acts on soft
and firm ground: tried blinkered/visored (not at Newmarket): usually on toes and often
sweats. *M. P. Tregoning*

THOMAS LAWRENCE (USA) 2 ch.c. (May 7) Horse Chestnut (SAF) 119 – **94**
Olatha (USA) (Miswaki (USA) 124) [2003 5m⁴ 7f³ 6m² Jul 13] 52,000 2-y-o: well-made
colt: has scope: half-brother to several winners, including smart 1996 2-y-o 7f winner
Putra (by Dixie Brass) and fairly useful 1993 2-y-o 6f winner who stayed 1¼m Amber
Valley (by Bering): dam sprint winner in USA: best effort in maidens (fairly useful form)
when second to Peak To Creek at Haydock: should stay 7f: carried head high second start.
P. F. I. Cole

THOMAS PAINE 4 b.g. Green Desert (USA) 127 – Glorious (Nashwan (USA) 135) **–**
[2003 –: 10m 10.3m 8m 10.1f⁶ Jul 24] close-coupled gelding: little sign of ability: tried
visored. *P. W. D'Arcy*

THORNABY GREEN 2 ch.c. (Feb 25) Whittingham (IRE) 104 – Dona Filipa 51 **67**
(Precocious 126) [2003 5m⁵ 5m⁴ 5g* 5.1g⁵ 5m⁶ 5g 6g Oct 28] 1,000Y, resold 6,200Y:
tall, quite good-topped colt: first foal: dam 5f/6f winner: fair performer: won seller at
Musselburgh in May, making all: creditable effort in nurseries after next start only:
should prove best at 5f/easy 6f: best efforts on good going. *T. D. Barron*

THORNTOUN GOLD (IRE) 7 ch.m. Lycius (USA) 124 – Gold Braisim (IRE) 77 **58**
(Jareer (USA) 115) [2003 64, a–: 11m⁴ 13.1g⁴ 11.6g 11.6m³ 8f 12.6m⁶ 11.6g⁵ 10.2m³ **a–**
12.1m² 11.6m 11.9F⁴ 11.9m³ 10.9m Sep 20] workmanlike mare: modest handicapper on
turf: claimed from I. Wood fourth start, from P. D. Evans after tenth: effective at 1¼m to
13f: acts on firm and good to soft going, little form in 3 runs on fibresand: tried visored/
blinkered: effective racing prominently or held up. *I. A. Wood*

THREAT 7 br.g. Zafonic (USA) 130 – Prophecy (IRE) 109 (Warning 136) [2003 65, **57**
a54: 6g f6g 7f 6m 7g 5m³ 6m² 5.7f⁴ 5m³ 5.1f² 6.1m 5g 5.1m f8.5g Nov 17] well-made **a–**
gelding: modest performer: effective at 5f to easy 7f: acts on any turf going and fibresand:
tried in headgear/tongue tie: sometimes slowly away. *J. M. Bradley*

THREE DAYS IN MAY 4 b.f. Cadeaux Genereux 131 – Corn Futures 78 (Nomina- **65**
tion 125) [2003 70: p7g⁶ p6g² 6.1g f6g 5.3m⁶ 6.1g 6f 6m 7.1g³ 7m³ 6.1m 6m 7m f7g
Nov 21] lengthy filly: fair handicapper: left H. Cyzer after fourth start/B. Johnson after
seventh: effective at stiff 5f to easy 7f: acts on good to firm going, good to soft and
polytrack: tried blinkered/visored. *M. R. Channon*

THREE DIMENSIONS (IRE) 3 b.f. Sadler's Wells (USA) 132 – Bequest (USA) **72**
108 (Sharpen Up 127) [2003 10m 10m³ 10m³ Aug 30] good-bodied filly: fourth reported
foal: half-sister to winner in USA by Lion Cavern: dam, 6f winner in Britain, later US
Grade 1 1¼m winner: fair maiden: best effort when third at Ripon final outing: stays
1¼m. *L. M. Cumani*

THREE GRACES (GER) 3 ch.c. Peintre Celebre (USA) 137 – Trefoil 111 (Kris **109**
135) [2003 8m* 10.1d 8.2d² 8.1m* 9m² 8m* 8.1d⁵ 7m* 7m² Oct 4] good-bodied colt:
fifth foal: half-brother to useful French 1¼m (at 2 yrs) to 1½m winner Trefula (by Rainbow Quest): dam, French 10.5f and 11f winner, half-sister to very smart middle-distance

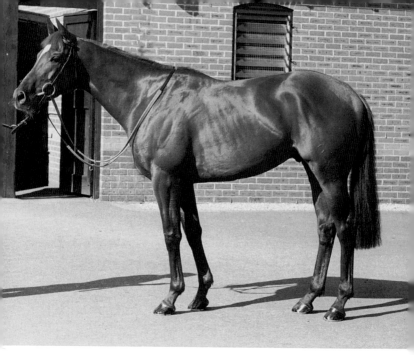

Sheikh Mohammed's "Three Graces"

performers Maysoon, Richard of York and Three Tails: useful performer: won maiden at Goodwood in June, handicap at Haydock and minor event at Salisbury in August and minor event at Newmarket (beat Pomfret Lad by ½ length) in September: good length second to Membership in listed race at Redcar final outing: races freely, and better at 7f/1m than further: best efforts on good to firm going: visored (below form) third start: joined Godolphin. *M. P. Tregoning*

THREE POINTS   6 b.h. Bering 136 – Trazl (IRE) 88 (Zalazl (USA) 120) [2003 114:   **101** 6f 6m Aug 2] leggy, close-coupled horse: smart performer at best: just useful form when tenth in Golden Jubilee Stakes at Royal Ascot: found little in minor event at Doncaster next time: best at 6f/7f: acts on firm and good to soft going, below form on dirt, not well drawn only run on soft: tongue tied nowadays: has been bandaged in front: usually races up with pace: left Godolphin in November. *Saeed bin Suroor*

THREE SECRETS (IRE)   2 b.f. (May 10) Danehill (USA) 126 – Castilian Queen   **82** (USA) 82 (Diesis 133) [2003 6g² 6m Aug 21] 90,000Y: close-coupled, workmanlike filly: fifth foal: half-sister to 2 winners, notably very smart 5f winner (including at 2 yrs) Carmine Lake (by Royal Academy): dam, 2-y-o 6f winner, out of Breeders' Cup Mile winner Royal Heroine: fairly useful form in maiden at Ascot (beaten 12 lengths) and Lowther Stakes at York (never-dangerous seventh of 9), both won by Carry On Katie: will probably stay 7f. *G. G. Margarson*

THREE SHIPS   2 ch.c. (Jun 7) Dr Fong (USA) 128 – River Lullaby (USA) (Riverman   **67 p** (USA) 131) [2003 7m Oct 24] half-brother to several winners, including very smart 1m winner Wixim (by Diesis) and smart 1m/1¼m winner Run Softly (by Deputy Minister): dam, Irish 2-y-o 6f winner, third in 1¼m listed race at 3 yrs: 9/1, ninth of 16 to Alekhine in maiden at Doncaster (early to post), not knocked about when unable to quicken: will stay at least 1m: should improve. *B. W. Hills*

1028

THREE VALLEYS (USA)   2 ch.c. (Feb 19) Diesis 133 – Skiable (IRE) (Niniski **119** (USA) 125) [2003 6.1d* 6f* 6f³ 6m*ᵈⁱˢ 7m² Oct 18]

'And it's the fair-haired, slightly-balding Charlton to kick off.' If not exactly 'sir' joining in a games lesson at school, how much are leading two-year-olds the equivalent of relatively mature pupils outmuscling their less precocious classmates? Like actor Brian Glover, as the teacher imagining himself as Bobby Charlton in a game of football with pupils in the film *Kes*, jockey Richard Hughes could have allowed himself the luxury of doing a commentary as he steered his mount Three Valleys to a runaway victory in the Coventry Stakes at Royal Ascot, the like of which is seen rarely in a six-furlong pattern race in any age group. The Coventry provided Three Valleys with a strikingly one-sided victory, suggesting he would prove the pick of his crop, but domination of the two-year-old scene as a whole proved beyond him. Though he was first past the post in the Middle Park at Newmarket, he was nowhere near so superior as at Royal Ascot and was then beaten on merit in the Dewhurst on his final start.

A comfortable winner of a minor event over six furlongs at Nottingham on his debut in May, Three Valleys started at 7/1 in the Coventry, only fourth favourite behind another once-raced unbeaten colt Sabbeeh in a field of thirteen. As the eight-length winning margin suggests, Three Valleys outclassed his rivals from start to finish, still on the bridle when leading over two furlongs out and quickening clear to record the widest margin of victory in the race since Mill Reef beat four rivals by the same distance in 1970, the only disconcerting aspect of the performance being that Three Valleys drifted markedly right on the very firm ground late on, ending up in the centre of the course. Three Valleys would have had more to do had the likes of Russian Valour and Pearl of Love tackled the Coventry instead of other races at the meeting, but the placed horses Botanical and Privy Seal were still useful rivals to have beaten so convincingly, and the timefigure for Three Valleys, equivalent to a timerating of 124, was clearly the best by a two-year-old all season. A strong, close-coupled colt, Three Valleys was younger than some of his opponents in the Coventry, but, for the record, he was the eighth winner of the race in the last ten years to be foaled before the end of February. Interestingly, relatively early foals also have a good record in the Two Thousand Guineas, the last ten winners all foaled before the end of March.

Three Valleys was made the early favourite at 12/1 for the Two Thousand Guineas after Royal Ascot, his trainer describing him as 'certainly the best juvenile I have trained'. For a two-year-old of comparable ability in the history of the yard, Roger Charlton harked back to the days of Jeremy Tree, his predecessor at Beckhampton. The Tree-trained Double Jump topped the Free Handicap in 1964 after going unbeaten through five races, including the Prix Robert Papin and the Gimcrack, before breaking a blood vessel severely in the Middle Park on his final start. Charlton's comments came on the eve of Three Valleys' next appearance in

Coventry Stakes, Royal Ascot—a scintillating display from Three Valleys, who wins by eight lengths from the Sheikh Mohammed pair Botanical (star on cap) and Privy Seal

the Group 1 Phoenix Stakes at the Curragh in August. Although a shade on his toes and notably free to post, Three Valleys looked in good shape at the Curragh, where he went off at 6/4-on to beat Aidan O'Brien's Anglesey Stakes winner One Cool Cat. The much anticipated showdown did not materialise, Three Valleys failing to run to within a stone of his Ascot form and soon being in trouble after leading briefly over two furlongs out. He finished four lengths third to One Cool Cat, clearly not himself and reportedly returning with mucus in his lungs.

Three Valleys recovered well enough after treatment to run in the Middle Park in early-October, though he reportedly returned to full training only two weeks beforehand. In a field of twelve, Three Valleys started favourite at 2/1 ahead of One Cool Cat's stable-companion Grand Reward. Another O'Brien-trained colt Old Deuteronomy, who had been three lengths ahead of Three Valleys when second at the Curragh, was among the relative outsiders at 14/1. Looking in fine shape, despite his problems, and more tractable on the way to post this time, Three Valleys went a long way to restoring his reputation with a convincing display. He travelled strongly, racing closer to the Ballydoyle pacemakers than most, and quickened readily to lead over a furlong out, holding Balmont by three quarters of a length up the hill. Guineas quotes for Three Valleys afterwards varied between 7/2 and 8/1.

Three Valleys' performance in the Middle Park was far less spectacular than his Coventry Stakes success, but there was little to choose between the two runs in terms of form. Gimcrack winner Balmont, who held Holborn by half a length for second at Newmarket, had shown smart form previously, as had Auditorium and Whipper, who were close up in fourth and fifth. Timeform's weight-for-age scale

Mr K. Abdulla's "Three Valleys"

suggests a two-year-old should mature by 7 lb between mid-June and early-October at six furlongs in order to keep pace with its contemporaries. On the balance of the Coventry and Middle Park form, Three Valleys was doing at least that, though whether he was no more mature than the 'average' two-year-old at the time of Royal Ascot is highly debatable, particularly in view of the superiority of his Coventry Stakes timefigure by comparison (timefigure calculations allow him the full weight-for-age allowance appropriate at the time).

Three Valleys started favourite again for the Dewhurst back at Newmarket two weeks after the Middle Park. Again in a field of twelve, he went off at 11/4, preferred to Royal Lodge winner Snow Ridge, who was at 7/2. Stepping up to seven furlongs for the first time, Three Valleys tracked the pace from his wide draw and briefly looked sure to win when improving smoothly in the Dip, only to find Milk It Mick a little too strong on his outside, going down by a head. Three Valleys was pushed out to as much as 14/1 for the Guineas afterwards, though it was another good effort all the same, and he saw the trip out well, rallying when passed and finishing just over a length ahead of third-placed Haafhd.

There was a sting in the tail to Three Valleys' two-year-old campaign when it was announced in November that he had failed a routine dope test after the Middle Park, testing positive for clenbuterol, a drug used in the treatment of respiratory infections. According to the stable's records, the drug had not been administered to Three Valleys for nine days before the Middle Park. The manufacturer's guidelines recommend that a horse usually needs only six and a half days for the drug to clear its system, but when Three Valleys' 'B' sample also proved positive, his disqualification became a near-formality, and he forfeited the race at a subsequent hearing. He was the first horse to lose a Group 1 in Britain through failing a dope test since the Aga Khan's Aliysa was stripped of the 1989 Oaks and the first at a similar level in Europe since Noverre was disqualified in the Poule d'Essai des Poulains in 2001. It was the second such setback for Juddmonte Farms in Britain in 2003, following the disqualification of the Amanda Perrett-trained Tillerman from second place in the Queen Anne also after testing positive for clenbuterol, a drug which is said to be used fairly routinely for treating horses with congested lungs. By all accounts, Three Valleys continued to have similar treatment between the Middle Park and the Dewhurst, but another routine test after the Dewhurst proved negative.

Three Valleys (USA) (ch.c. Feb 19, 2001)	Diesis (ch 1980)	Sharpen Up (ch 1969)	Atan
			Rocchetta
		Doubly Sure (or b 1971)	Reliance II
			Soft Angels
	Skiable (IRE) (ch 1990)	Niniski (or b 1976)	Nijinsky
			Virginia Hills
		Kerali (ch 1984)	High Line
			Sookera

The dam of Three Valleys, Skiable, was being very much overshadowed at stud by her half-sister Hasili until Three Valleys arrived, though the same goes for many others in the highly-successful band of Juddmonte broodmares. Hasili is very much a 'queen bee', having produced the high-class pair Dansili and Banks Hill, the latter successful in the Breeders' Cup Filly & Mare Turf and the Prix Jacques le Marois. Hasili's reputation was boosted further in 2003 when Intercontinental finished third in the One Thousand Guineas and another of her produce Heat Haze showed much improved form as a four-year-old in America, where she won two Grade 1 races, the Beverly D Stakes at Arlington and the Matriarch Stakes at Hollywood. Skiable and Hasili are out of the lightly-raced seven-furlong winner Kerali and are bred along similar lines, the pair descended on their sire's side from Nijinsky. Skiable also ended up in America after a successful start to her racing career in France, winning four races all told at up to nine furlongs on both sides of the Atlantic. Three Valleys is Skiable's fifth foal. The first four were also winners, though the best of them, Ski Jump (by El Prado), has shown only fairly useful form, winning twice at around a mile and a quarter in the latest season. The better horses in Three Valleys' family have all had at least as much speed as stamina—his third dam the Cheveley Park Stakes winner Sookera produced Cork And Orrery and Nunthorpe winner So Factual among others—and Three Valleys shaped for much of the season as though he was likely to prove best at six or seven furlongs. Judged by the way he ran in the Dewhurst, Three Valleys will probably stay a mile after all. Also encouraging is that he behaved in more sober manner as the year went on and took the preliminaries in his stride on Dewhurst day. Diesis, the sire of Three Valleys, has an average winning distance for three-year-olds of nine furlongs, and, despite his own precocity (he won the Middle Park and Dewhurst), some of his best performers, such as Halling, Sabrehill and Keen Hunter, came into their own as they got older. A powerful mover with a fluent action, Three Valleys often impresses to post and has raced only on firm and good to firm ground since his debut. Given his form, it would be wrong to rule him out of the Two Thousand Guineas picture. *R. Charlton*

THREE WELSHMEN 2 b.c. (Apr 15) Muhtarram (USA) 125 – Merch Rhyd-Y-Grug (Sabrehill (USA) 120) [2003 p5g² p5g² 5f 6m 7g 6m⁵ 6g Jul 30] £2,800Y: unfurnished colt: second foal: dam no form: modest maiden: second twice at Lingfield (including in minor event): possibly amiss fourth start and below form in nurseries after: needs to settle to stay beyond 5f: acts on polytrack. *B. R. Millman* — **64 d**

THROUGH THE RYE 7 ch.g. Sabrehill (USA) 120 – Baharlilys 67 (Green Dancer (USA) 132) [2003 52: 13.8d Nov 4] rangy gelding: good mover: modest performer nowadays: stays 1½m: acts on fibresand and good to firm going, probably on heavy: has had tongue tied. *G. A. Swinbank* — **52**

THUMAMAH (IRE) 4 b.f. Charnwood Forest (IRE) 125 – Anam 79 (Persian Bold 123) [2003 76: f6g 7f 7m⁶ 7m 7m Jun 17] lengthy filly: has a short action: just modest handicapper in 2003: stays 1m: acts on firm and good to soft going: tongue tied. *B. P. J. Baugh* — **64**

THUMPER (IRE) 5 b.g. Grand Lodge (USA) 125 – Parkeen Princess (He Loves Me 120) [2003 75, a69: 11.8g⁶ 10.5m⁵ Aug 7] angular gelding: fair handicapper: left J. Mackie after reappearance, well held subsequent start: stays 1¼m: acts on good to firm going, good to soft and polytrack: races prominently: blinkered last 5 starts in 2002, visored on reappearance. *Jonjo O'Neill* — **65 a?**

THUNDER CANYON (USA) 4 b. or br.g. Gulch (USA) – Naazeq 80 (Nashwan (USA) 135) [2003 81: 12f 14.1f⁶ Jun 15] close-coupled gelding: fairly useful performer in 2002: well held for new trainer in 2003 (reportedly jarred up latter start): blinkered once at 3 yrs: sold 6,000 gns. *P. A. Blockley* — **–**

THUNDERCLAP 4 b. or br.c. Royal Applause 124 – Gloriana 78 (Formidable (USA) 125) [2003 75: p10g p10g f8g³ 8.2g⁶ 8.1g² 8m 8f³ 8m² 8f 8f 8f⁴ 8m⁴ 9m 9g Oct 24] quite good-topped colt: fair handicapper: best at 7f/1m: acts on firm going, good to soft and polytrack: tried visored, blinkered nowadays: often slowly away: usually held up: sold 15,000 gns. *J. W. Hills* — **67**

THUNDERED (USA) 5 gr.g. Thunder Gulch (USA) 129 – Lady Lianga (USA) 81 (Secretariat (USA)) [2003 54, a39: p8g³ Jan 8] workmanlike gelding: modest performer: probably best at 7f/1m: possibly needs good going or firmer on turf and acts on polytrack (little show both starts on fibresand): tried blinkered in 2001. *G. A. Swinbank* — **50**

THUNDERING BAH BOU 3 ch.f. Bahamian Bounty 116 – Thunder Bug (USA) 66 (Secreto (USA) 128) [2003 10d 11.5g 10g Jun 2] fifth foal: half-sister to useful 1¼m/1½m winner Thundering Surf (by Lugana Beach): dam 1¼m winner: tailed off in 3 maidens. *J. R. Jenkins* — **–**

THURLESTONE ROCK 3 ch.g. Sheikh Albadou 128 – Don't Smile 76 (Sizzling Melody 117) [2003 82: p6g⁶ 6m 5.1m⁴ 6.1m 6m² 6m* 6m 7m 6g* Sep 22] compact gelding: fairly useful handicapper: won at Lingfield in August and Kempton in September: stays 6f: acts on all-weather, raced only on good/good to firm going on turf: effective blinkered or not: often hangs left. *B. J. Meehan* — **83**

THYOLO (IRE) 2 ch.c. (Mar 6) Bering 136 – Topline (GER) (Acatenango (GER) 127) [2003 7g⁴ 8m* 8m* Oct 24] €26,000Y: big, useful-looking colt: sixth foal: half-brother to 3 winners, including 3-y-o Rondinay and French/German 1¼m/1½m winner Titus Manius (by Be My Guest): dam, German 1¼m/1½m winner, half-sister to German performers Turfkonig (very smart up to 1½m) and Tryphosa (smart at 1m/1¼m): won maiden at Goodwood in September and nursery at Doncaster (by neck from Wavertree Dream) in October: should be suited by 1¼m/1½m: type to train on well and make a useful 3-y-o. *C. G. Cox* — **91 p**

TIBER (IRE) 3 b.c. Titus Livius (FR) 115 – Exciting (Mill Reef (USA) 141) [2003 **113 +**
89: 10.5f² 9.9g⁴ 10m² 10.1m² 10m² 9.9g* 7m² Dec 14] quite good-topped colt: smart
handicapper: runner-up 4 of first 5 starts in 2003, veering left away from whip when
beaten short head by Leporello in quite valuable event at Newmarket fifth start: further
improvement when winning at Goodwood in August by ½ length from Famous Grouse:
reportedly sold out of J. Gosden's stable before runner-up at Sha Tin final outing: likely
to prove best at 1m/1¼m: raced only on good going or firmer: usually blinkered: tongue
tied last 4 outings: has good turn of foot, but tends to wander/idle in front. *J. Moore,
Hong Kong*

TIBER TIGER (IRE) 3 b.g. Titus Livius (FR) 115 – Genetta (Green Desert (USA) **86**
127) [2003 75: 7g 7.1m⁵ 8d⁴ 7.5m* 7m² 7m* 7m² 8m⁶ 8m 8m 7m⁵ 8m 8m Oct 6] rather
angular gelding: fairly useful handicapper: won at Beverley and Redcar (hung left) in
June, then at Newmarket in July: below form last 5 starts: effective at 7f/1m: acts on good
to firm and good to soft going, well held on fibresand: usually blinkered, tried visored.
N. P. Littmoden

TICERO 2 ch.c. (Apr 18) First Trump 118 – Lucky Flinders 77 (Free State 125) [2003 **79 p**
5g 7m⁴ Oct 21] 25,000Y: close-coupled colt: half-brother to 3 winners, notably 5-y-o
Pomfret Lad: dam, 1m winner, sister to smart Italian winner up to 1m Melbury Lad: much
better effort in minor events 7 months apart (fair form) when fourth of 6 to Ouija Board at
Yarmouth, not unduly knocked about: likely to stay 1m: should do better. *C. E. Brittain*

TICKER TAPE 2 b.f. (Jan 26) Royal Applause 124 – Argent du Bois (USA) (Silver **96**
Hawk (USA) 123) [2003 6g² 7.1f* 7g 6.5d* 7m⁴ 6m² 7g³ 8f² Nov 28] 20,000Y: smallish,
well-made filly: first foal: dam, French maiden who stayed 1m, half-sister to useful
French performer up to 1½m On Reflection: useful performer: won maiden at Warwick
in July and nursery at Doncaster in September: placed last 3 starts in sales race at Newmarket, listed contest at Newbury (good 3 lengths third to Secret Charm, sold out of
J. Osborne's stable 100,000 gns after) and Grade 3 Miesque Stakes at Hollywood (1½
lengths second to Mambo Slew): stays 1m: acts on firm and good to soft going: sweated/
hung right third outing. *J. M. Cassidy, USA*

TICKLE 5 b.m. Primo Dominie 121 – Funny Choice (IRE) 68 (Commanche Run 133) **67**
[2003 64: 5g² 6g f6g 5.7m⁵ p7g p6g⁶ p6g Dec 30] good-topped mare: fair handicapper:
best up to 7f: acts on polytrack, raced mainly on good or softer ground on turf: tried
visored/tongue tied: inconsistent. *P. J. Makin*

TICKLEPENNY LOCK (IRE) 2 b.c. (May 30) Mujadil (USA) 119 – Barncogue
(Monseigneur (USA) 127) [2003 5m⁶ 5.6f 7.5m⁶ 7.5m⁶ 7m f5s f6g Dec 15] €5,000Y,
resold 1,500Y: smallish, compact colt: sixth foal: half-brother to 3 winners, including
1m winner Doodies Pool (by Mazaad) and Irish 1¼m winner Natalie Know's (by Polish
Patriot): dam unraced: signs of only a little ability, including in selling nursery. *C. Smith*

TICK TOCK 6 ch.m. Timeless Times (USA) 99 – Aquiletta 67 (Bairn (USA) 126) **–**
[2003 62: f6d 5g 5m 5g 5m 5.1d 6m 5s Nov 3] small mare: modest handicapper at 5 yrs:
showed little in 2003: visored (not for wins in 2001) earlier in career, tried blinkered in
2003. *M. Mullineaux*

TICTACTOE 2 b.f. (Feb 21) Komaite (USA) – White Valley (IRE) 54 (Tirol 127) **64**
[2003 5.1f 5m⁴ f5g⁴ 6m² 7m⁵ 6m 6g⁴ 5.3m⁵ f6g³ f8g⁶ f6g* Dec 26] first foal: dam, lightly-
raced maiden who stayed 7f, half-sister to 5-y-o Chookie Heiton: modest performer: left
S. Dow after eighth start: won claimer at Wolverhampton: stays 6f, not 1m: acts on
fibresand and good to firm going: tends to start slowly. *D. J. Daly*

TIDAL 4 br.f. Bin Ajwaad (IRE) 119 – So Saucy 59 (Teenoso (USA) 135) [2003 82: **–**
14.1g 10m 10g 10d⁶ 10m 12.1d⁶ 10f f8s 10.1g Oct 22] lengthy, angular filly: fairly useful
performer at 3 yrs: well held in 2003, leaving B. Meehan after sixth start: should stay
1½m: acts on firm going, probably on good to soft: tried blinkered: often races prominently. *P. Howling*

TIDY (IRE) 3 b.c. Mujadil (USA) 119 – Neat Shilling (IRE) (Bob Back (USA) 124) **80**
[2003 73: 6d* 7g³ 7.1m f7g⁶ 8g Jul 3] fairly useful performer: won handicap at Haydock
in May: below form last 2 starts: stays 7f: acts on fibresand and good to soft ground: races
prominently: has drifted left: sold 8,000 gns. *J. A. Osborne*

TIFFANY'S QUEST 4 b.f. Atraf 116 – Pleasure Quest (Efisio 120) [2003 65, a47: f7g **–**
6g 6m May 14] fair form when second in maiden at 3 yrs, but has shown little otherwise.
D. W. P. Arbuthnot

TIGER BABY 3 b.c. Averti (IRE) 117 – Risky Baby 62 (Risk Me (FR) 127) [2003 7f⁶ **–**
7m⁵ Aug 14] sturdy colt: first foal: dam, lightly raced, second at 6f only 2-y-o start: well
beaten in maidens. *W. S. Kittow*

TIGERETTE (USA)   3 b.f. Swain (IRE) 134 – Hot Thong (BRZ) (Jarraar (USA) 78)   –
[2003 66p: p7g f9.4g Apr 25] small, sparely-made filly: lightly raced: fair form when
third in maiden at Brighton at 2 yrs: no form in 2003: should stay at least 1m. *R. Guest*

TIGERTAIL (FR)   4 b.f. Priolo (USA) 127 – Tiger Stripes (Prince Rupert (FR) 121)   **112**
[2003 112: 10g⁵ 10g² 12g 11.9m⁴ 10s² 11f³ 12d⁶ 10m Dec 14] 180,000 francs Y: close-
coupled filly: second foal: sister to French/Belgian 1m to 11f winner Tigerstop: dam
useful French 5f (at 2 yrs) to 11f winner: smart performer: won minor event at Maisons-
Laffitte and Prix Minerve at Deauville in 2002: creditable efforts at 4 yrs when in frame
in Premio Presidente della Repubblica at Rome (neck second to Rakti), Yorkshire Oaks at
York (5¾ lengths fourth to Islington), E. P. Taylor Stakes at Woodbine (went down by a
head to Volga, switched and finishing strongly) and Queen Elizabeth II Commemorative
Cup at Kyoto (1½ lengths third to Admire Groove): not discredited when sixth to Tap
Dance City in Japan Cup at Tokyo penultimate start, no threat in Hong Kong Cup at Sha
Tin final outing: stays 12.5f: acts on firm and soft going: held up: consistent. *Rodolphe
Collet, France*

TIGER TIGER (FR)   2 b.c. (Mar 24) Tiger Hill (IRE) 127 – Adorable Emilie (FR)   –
(Iron Duke (FR) 122) [2003 p8g Nov 2] €13,000Y, €11,000 2-y-o: fourth foal: half-
brother to French 13.5f winner Petite Emilie (by Mtoto): dam French 7.5f (including at 2
yrs) to 11f winner: 33/1, slowly away and always behind in maiden at
Lingfield. *Jamie Poulton*

TIGER TOPS   4 ch.g. Sabrehill (USA) 120 – Rose Chime (IRE) 58 (Tirol 127) [2003   **71**
69: p10g³ p10g³ p8g* p8g 8.3d³ p8g 8m 8.1m² 8m⁵ 8d 8.5g³ 8g 8.9f 9g⁶ Oct 24] good-   **a77**
topped gelding: fair handicapper: won at Lingfield (apprentices) in March: left C. Wall
after twelfth start: has form at 1¼m, seems best at 1m: acts on good to firm going, good to
soft and polytrack: respectable effort in cheekpieces final outing: free-going sort.
J. A. Supple

TIGHT SQUEEZE   6 br.m. Petoski 135 – Snowline (Bay Express 132) [2003 86, a55:   **85 +**
f11s² f11g⁶ f9.4s⁶ p10g* f9.4g² p10g² p10g* p10g⁴ 10d⁵ 10m⁵ 10m³ 9.9m⁵ 11.6g⁴
10.2m⁴ 10m⁶ 10.3m 10f⁶ 9.9m* 10.4m⁵ 10m⁵ 10.3d 10m* p12g⁶ Dec 17] big, plain mare:
fairly useful handicapper: won at Lingfield (3, including apprentice event), Beverley and
Redcar in 2003: effective at 1¼m/easy 1½m: acts on firm going, good to soft and all-
weather: usually waited with: game and reliable. *P. W. Hiatt*

TIGRESS (IRE)   4 b.f. Desert Style (IRE) 121 – Ervedya (IRE) (Doyoun 124) [2003   –
–, a57: f6g⁶ f5g* f5s* f5g³ f5s² f5g⁶ f5g⁶ f5s Dec 6] tall filly: fair performer: 6 of 7 wins   **a72**
at Wolverhampton, including in claimer and handicap in January: off over 8 months
before final start: best at 5f/easy 6f: acts on soft ground and fibresand: tried visored,
blinkered nowadays: sometimes slowly away/wanders. *J. W. Unett*

TIKITANO (IRE)   2 b.f. (Feb 12) Dr Fong (USA) 128 – Asterita 103 (Rainbow Quest   **55**
(USA) 134) [2003 5d⁶ Apr 28] 6,500Y: fourth foal: half-sister to 2000 2-y-o 7f winner
(later winner in USA) Gulchie (by Thunder Gulch) and 3-y-o Californian: dam, 11.5f
winner who stayed 2m, half-sister to dam of top-class miler Keltos: 50/1, sixth of 19 in
maiden at Windsor: bred to stay at least 1m. *D. K. Ivory*

TIKKUN (IRE)   4 gr.g. Grand Lodge (USA) 125 – Moon Festival 74 (Be My Guest   –
(USA) 126) [2003 111: 10m 8g 8.5f 6.5g Dec 27] rangy gelding: smart performer at
3 yrs: looked temperamental, and well held all starts in 2003: left R. Charlton and off
nearly 7 months before penultimate one. *B. D. A. Cecil, USA*

TIKRAM   6 ch.g. Lycius (USA) 124 – Black Fighter (USA) 79 (Secretariat (USA))   **81**
[2003 83: 18m Oct 18] tall, close-coupled gelding: fairly useful handicapper, lightly
raced: respectable twelfth in Cesarewitch at Newmarket only Flat outing in 2003: will
stay 1¾m: raced mainly on going softer than good (acts on heavy): useful hurdler.
G. L. Moore

TILLA   3 b.f. Bin Ajwaad (IRE) 119 – Tosca (Be My Guest (USA) 126) [2003 –p: 10d   **78**
9.9m p12g⁶ 12g² 12m* 16m³ 13.8d* Nov 4] workmanlike filly: fair handicapper: won at
Pontefract in October and Catterick in November: effective at 1½m to 2m: unraced on
extremes of going. *H. Morrison*

TILLERMAN   7 b.h. In The Wings 128 – Autumn Tint (USA) (Roberto (USA) 131)   **122**
[2003 123: 7m⁵ 8m⁶ 8f²ᵈ 8f* 7g 8m³ 8f³ 7m Oct 18] big, strong, good sort: impresses in
appearance: very smart performer: won Tom Fruit Leicestershire Stakes at Leicester (by
short head from Gateman) in April and Michael Page International Silver Trophy Stakes
at Ascot (beat Beauchamp Pilot ¾ length) in July: good efforts when 4 lengths second to
Dubai Destination in Queen Anne Stakes at Royal Ascot (disqualified after failing dope

Michael Page International Silver Trophy Stakes, Ascot—the first running of the race as a Group 3 attracts a small field; Tillerman comfortably accounts for Beauchamp Pilot, Right Approach (dark cap), Duck Row and Lips Lion (right)

test), and when 3¼ lengths third to Falbrav in Queen Elizabeth II Stakes at Ascot on seventh start: unsuited by steady pace in Challenge Stakes at Newmarket final outing: best at 7f/1m: best efforts on good going or firmer: usually taken steadily to post: sometimes slowly away: wears crossed noseband: held up: stays in training. *Mrs A. J. Perrett*

TIMBER ICE (USA) 3 b.f. Woodman (USA) 126 – Salchow (USA) (Nijinsky (CAN) 138) [2003 –p: 11.5g⁴ 11.8m³ Jun 2] big, good-topped filly: has scope: fair form in maidens: third to Sayadaw at Leicester final outing: will stay 1½m. *H. R. A. Cecil* **76**

TIMBUKTU 2 b.c. (Apr 13) Efisio 120 – Sirene Bleu Marine (USA) (Secreto (USA) 128) [2003 6.1d f8g f9.4g⁶ Dec 22] stocky colt: brother to useful 1¼m to 13f winner Flossy and half-brother to 3-y-o Down Memory Lane and 6f (at 2 yrs) to 1¼m winner Society Girl (by Shavian): dam unraced: well beaten in maidens: twice slowly away. *C. W. Thornton* **–**

TIME AHEAD 3 b.f. Spectrum (IRE) 126 – Not Before Time (IRE) (Polish Precedent (USA) 131) [2003 70p: 8g² 10g* 10.5g² 11.9g⁶ 10d Aug 24] sturdy filly: smart performer: won maiden at Newmarket in May impressively by 6 lengths: marked improvement when ¾-length second to Nebraska Tornado in Prix de Diane at Chantilly following month: well below that form after in Lancashire Oaks at Haydock (seemed not to stay) **112**

1035

Mr R. Barnett's "Time Ahead"

and Prix de la Nonette at Deauville: stayed easy 10.5f: raced only on good/good to soft going: reared and unseated rider before being loaded at Chantilly: stud. *J. L. Dunlop*

TIME BOMB 6 b.m. Great Commotion (USA) 123 – Play For Time (Comedy Star – §
(USA) 121) [2003 58§: 5.7m 6m 6m 6m 7.1m Sep 22] angular mare: unreliable handicapper at 5 yrs: well held in 2003: has given trouble at stall: free-going sort. *Simon Earle*

TIME CAN TELL 9 ch.g. Sylvan Express 117 – Stellaris (Star Appeal 133) [2003 –: –
f16g f14.8g Jan 17] big gelding: modest handicapper at 7 yrs: lightly raced and little form since: tried in headgear. *A. G. Juckes*

TIME CRYSTAL (IRE) 3 b.f. Sadler's Wells (USA) 132 – State Crystal (IRE) 114 **83**
(High Estate 127) [2003 10g 11.9f⁴ 12m* 11.9f⁴ Oct 9] good-topped filly: has a short, unimpressive action: fourth living foal: sister to fairly useful 1¼m winner True Crystal: dam, 7f (at 2 yrs) and 1½m (Lancashire Oaks) winner, half-sister to middle-distance stayer Tchaikovsky (by Sadler's Wells) and Fillies' Mile winner Crystal Music, both smart: fairly useful form: won maiden at Doncaster in August by neck from Heavenly Bay: well beaten in minor event at York final outing: should stay 1¾m+. *H. R. A. Cecil*

TIME FLYER 3 b.c. My Best Valentine 122 – Sally's Trust (IRE) 51 (Classic Secret –
(USA) 91) [2003 5m 8m 6.1m 6g Oct 24] sturdy, close-coupled colt: half-brother to 7f winner Beltane (by Magic Ring) and 1m winner in Sweden by Forzando: dam maiden who stayed 1m: well held all starts. *W. de Best-Turner*

TIME FOR FAME (USA) 6 b.g. Quest For Fame 127 – Intimate (USA) (Topsider –
(USA)) [2003 –: f9.4g Jan 17] lightly-raced maiden: well beaten both starts in Britain.
W. J. Musson

TIME FOR MUSIC (IRE) 6 b.g. Mukaddamah (USA) 125 – Shrewd Girl (USA) –
79 (Sagace (FR) 135) [2003 75, a67: p7g Jan 7] lengthy, quite attractive gelding: fair and
consistent handicapper at best: probably best at 7f: acted on firm ground and polytrack:
blinkered once: dead. *T. G. Mills*

TIMELY TWIST 2 b.f. (Feb 1) Kirkwall 118 – Timely Raise (USA) (Raise A Man 54
(USA)) [2003 7m 7f⁴ 6m⁶ 6m 8.3g⁵ f7g³ p6g Dec 20] lengthy filly: half-sister to several
winners, including 9f/1¼m winner Double Bluff (by Sharrood) and 5f (at 2 yrs)/6f winner
Poker Chip (by Bluebird), both useful: dam, miler in North America, sister to smart
middle-distance stayer Primitive Rising: modest maiden: third in seller at Wolverhampton: probably stays 1m: acts on fibresand and firm going. *S. Kirk*

TIME MARCHES ON 5 b.g. Timeless Times (USA) 99 – Tees Gazette Girl 42 (Kala- 42
glow 132) [2003 46: 12.3m² 10f Sep 15] leggy gelding: poor handicapper: stays 1½m:
acts on firm and soft going, probably on fibresand: sometimes looks none too keen.
Mrs M. Reveley

TIME N TIME AGAIN 5 b.g. Timeless Times (USA) 99 – Primum Tempus 49 76
(Primo Dominie 121) [2003 82: 5m 5g 5.1m³ 5g³ 5m 5m³ 5m⁶ 5f⁵ 6f³ 5.1m* 5g 5.1d³ 5m⁴
5m f6g⁵ f5g⁴ f5s² Dec 6] leggy, useful-looking gelding: fair handicapper: won at Chester
in August: best at 5f: acts on fibresand, firm and good to soft going: tried blinkered:
usually races up with pace. *E. J. Alston*

TIMES OF TIMES (IRE) 10 b.m. Distinctly North (USA) 115 – Lady Fandet (Gay a–
Fandango (USA) 132) [2003 6m 6.1m Sep 19] rather leggy mare: fair performer at 3 yrs:
very lightly raced and little form since: tried blinkered/visored. *Andrew Reid*

TIME SPIN 3 b.g. Robellino (USA) 127 – Chiltern Court (USA) (Topsider (USA)) 62
[2003 66: 10m³ 12d Nov 4] modest maiden, lightly raced: shaped as though amiss final
outing: probably stays 1¼m. *C. Grant*

TIMES REVIEW (USA) 2 b.c. (May 12) Crafty Prospector (USA) – Previewed 81
(USA) (Ogygian (USA)) [2003 5m⁵ f6g² 5m* 6d³ 5f² 5f⁵ 6m 8.1g Sep 6] $37,000Y: quite
good-topped colt: eighth foal: brother to winner and half-brother to winner by Dehere,
both in USA: dam ran once (at 2 yrs) in USA: fairly useful performer: won maiden at
Newcastle in June: creditable efforts in minor event/nurseries next 3 starts: effective at 5f/
6f: acts on firm and good to soft going, probably on fibresand: usually races prominently.
T. D. Easterby

TIME'S THE MASTER (IRE) 2 b.g. (Apr 22) Danetime (IRE) 121 – Travel Tricks 40
(IRE) (Presidium 124) [2003 5m 5m⁶ f5g 5m⁴ 6m⁵ f5g f6g Nov 1] €2,000Y, 10,000
2-y-o: leggy gelding: first foal: dam last in Irish listed race only outing: poor maiden:
will prove best at 5f/6f: below form on fibresand: proved almost unrideable on debut.
M. F. Harris

TIMETOBENICE (IRE) 3 b.f. Danetime (IRE) 121 – Woodenitbenice (USA) (Nasty –
And Bold (USA)) [2003 39: 7.1g 7m Jul 10] maiden: no form in 2003, including in
cheekpieces. *J. L. Spearing*

TIME TO REGRET 3 b.g. Presidium 124 – Scoffera 63 (Scottish Reel 123) [2003 57
59: f6g 7m⁶ 8g 6m 7f² 8f⁴ 9.3m² 8.5m² 9.3m⁵ Jul 18] tall gelding: modest maiden: stays
9.3f: acts on any going: raced too freely final start. *J. J. Quinn*

TIME TO RELAX (IRE) 2 b.f. (Apr 8) Orpen (USA) 116 – Lassalia (Sallust 134) 63
[2003 6m⁴ 7m³ 7.9m⁶ 8m 7d Nov 8] IR 8,200F, 9,000Y: smallish, sturdy filly: half-sister
to numerous winners, notably smart 1991 2-y-o 7f winner Free Flyer (by Bluebird),
stayed 1¼m and later successful in USA: dam placed from 6f to 9.5f in Ireland: modest
maiden: third at Newcastle: ran poorly in nurseries last 2 starts: stays 1m: wandered third
start. *J. J. Quinn*

TIME TO REMEMBER (IRE) 5 b.g. Pennekamp (USA) 130 – Bequeath (USA) 82
(Lyphard (USA) 132) [2003 86: 7m 7.6m⁶ 6m 6f* 6g 6f 6g 6m 6m 7m Oct 18] big
gelding: fluent mover: fairly useful handicapper: won at York in June: below form
otherwise: best form at 6f to 7.6f: acts on firm going: usually wears crossed noseband/
early to post: has got upset in stall (had to pass stall test after reappearance, still had
blindfold on after stall opened and took no part final outing): often races freely: has hung
left. *D. Nicholls*

TIME TO SHINE   4 b.f. Pivotal 124 – Sweet Jaffa 73§ (Never So Bold 135) [2003   **69**
69: p16g⁴ p13g⁶ f12g p12g p13g² 12g³ 11.9f 14.1g Apr 29] fair handicapper: effective at
1½m to 2m: acts on polytrack, best turf effort on good going: blinkered third start:
winning hurdler. *B. R. Johnson*

TIMING   4 b.f. Alhaarth (IRE) 126 – Pretty Davis (USA) (Trempolino (USA) 135)   **90**
[2003 92, a–: 14f⁴ 13.9m⁶ 16.2m⁴ 15f⁴ 16.1g 16.2m⁴ 14g Jul 29] rather leggy, angular   **a–**
filly: fairly useful handicapper: below form last 3 starts: will stay beyond 2m: acts on firm
and good to soft going, possibly not on soft (modest form at 2 yrs on fibresand): tends to
be slowly away (has twice failed stall test, and refused to enter stall intended final outing):
held up. *T. D. Easterby*

TINAS PRINCE (IRE)   3 b.c. Desert Prince (IRE) 130 – Bold Tina (IRE) 72 (Persian   **–**
Bold 123) [2003 –: 7m 5.9m Jun 2] well held in maidens: tried blinkered. *J. S. Wainwright*

TING (IRE)   6 b.g. Magical Wonder (USA) 125 – Rozmiyn (Caerleon (USA) 132) [2003   **–**
–: f8g Jan 9] leggy, quite good-topped gelding: fair performer at 4 yrs, well held since:
tried blinkered. *M. J. Polglase*

TINIAN   5 b.g. Mtoto 134 – Housefull 81 (Habitat 134) [2003 7d* 7g³ 8g 8g* 7.5g*   **55**
7.5g⁶ 8g* f7g⁵ f9.4g³ p10g Dec 30] short-backed gelding: fair maiden for I. Balding in
2001: has since won 6 times in Germany, including handicaps at Hoppegarten, Bremen
(2) and Dresden in 2003: left W. Giedt in Germany, modest form in Britain last 3 starts:
has form at 1¼m, should prove best at 7f/1m nowadays: acts on heavy ground and fibresand: tried visored. *K. R. Burke*

TINK'S MAN   4 b.g. Puissance 110 – Expectation (IRE) 59 (Night Shift (USA)) [2003   **–**
53: f6g Jan 2] strong gelding: maiden: well held in claimer only run in 2003: stays 6f: acts
on fibresand: tried tongue tied. *Mrs A. Duffield*

TINTAWN GOLD (IRE)   3 b.f. Rudimentary (USA) 118 – Clear Ahead (Primo   **62**
Dominie 121) [2003 56: 7.1m⁶ 9m 8.3g⁴ 8f⁴ 10d⁵ 10m² 10d 9.7g² 8f⁵ 8f 10d Oct 31]
sturdy filly: modest maiden handicapper: left Mrs P. N. Dutfield after sixth start: stays
1¼m: acts on firm and good to soft going, unraced on soft/heavy. *S. Woodman*

TIOGA GOLD (IRE)   4 b.g. Goldmark (USA) 113 – Coffee Bean (Doulab (USA)   **58**
115) [2003 57: f14s⁵ f12s⁴ f12g⁴ f14.8g f12s Oct 7] leggy gelding: modest performer:
well below form last 3 starts: stays 1½m: acts on fibresand and good to firm going:
blinkered (well held) once. *L. R. James*

TIOMAN (IRE)   4 b. or br.g. Dr Devious (IRE) 127 – Tochar Ban (USA) 83 (Assert   **88**
134) [2003 87: f12g⁴ 16m⁵ 11.9f Jun 14] tall, good sort: fairly useful form, lightly raced:
won maiden at Southwell in April: good fifth in handicap at Kempton following month:
stays 2m: found little final 3-y-o outing: sold 6,000 gns. *M. A. Jarvis*

TIP THE DIP (USA)   3 ch.c. Benny The Dip (USA) 127 – Senora Tippy (USA) (El   **90 p**
Gran Senor (USA) 136) [2003 8.3g² 10m* 12m³ 12m* Sep 24] sturdy, compact colt: sixth
foal: half-brother to 3 winners in USA, including Grade 3 8.5f winner Tippity Witch (by
Affirmed): dam, French 9f listed winner, later successful in USA: fairly useful form: won
maiden at Nottingham in August and minor event at Goodwood (comfortably by 1¼
lengths from Wasted Talent, still bit green and taking while to respond) in September:
third in handicap at Thirsk in between: stays 1½m: should do better still. *J. H. M. Gosden*

TIPU SULTAN   3 ch.c. Kris 135 – Eye Witness (IRE) 72 (Don't Forget Me 127) [2003   **63**
90p: 8m² 8.1d⁵ Sep 26] big, angular colt: has a markedly round action: fairly useful form
when third in maiden at Newmarket at 2 yrs: just modest form in similar events on belated
return: raced only around 1m: has been bandaged in front/behind: sold 13,500 gns, sent to
Spain. *E. A. L. Dunlop*

TIRAILLEUR (IRE)   3 b.f. Eagle Eyed (USA) 111 – Tiralle (IRE) 71 (Tirol 127)   **56**
[2003 66: p7g p6g p5g³ 5.1f³ 5m 8m⁵ 8m³ 7g 8m* 7d 10.2m* 8f 11.5g⁶ Sep 16] sturdy
filly: modest performer: won seller at Leicester in July and apprentice handicap at
Chepstow in August: best up to 1¼m: acts on all-weather, good to firm and good to soft
going: sometimes blinkered: looked ungenuine earlier in career. *J. White*

TIRANA (IRE)   5 b.g. Brief Truce (USA) 126 – Cloche du Roi (FR) (Fairy King   **–**
(USA)) [2003 55: f9.4g f8g Mar 13] angular, workmanlike gelding: modest handicapper
at best: well held in 2003: tried visored: usually tongue tied. *D. Burchell*

TIRARI (IRE)   4 b.f. Charnwood Forest (IRE) 125 – Desert Victory (Green Desert   **–**
(USA) 127) [2003 45, a55: f8s⁶ f11s⁵ p16g 12.3m Apr 2] smallish, useful-looking filly:
has a short, round action: showed little in 2003: tried visored: often slowly away.
C. R. Dore

TISHOMINGO 4 ch.g. Alhijaz 122 – Enchanted Guest (IRE) 74 (Be My Guest (USA) **– §**
126) [2003 55§: f12s f11s Jan 16] strong, close-coupled gelding: unreliable performer:
well held in 2003: tongue tied. *Ronald Thompson*

TITIAN FLAME (IRE) 3 ch.f. Titus Livius (FR) 115 – Golden Choice (Midyan **69**
(USA) 124) [2003 69: 10m 12.6m⁴ 11.6d³ 11.8m⁶ 11.6d⁴ 10g Jun 30] unfurnished filly:
fair handicapper: stays 1½m: acts on good to firm and good to soft going. *Mrs
P. N. Dutfield*

TITIAN LASS 4 ch.f. Bijou d'Inde 127 – Liebside Lass (IRE) (Be My Guest (USA) **58**
126) [2003 69: p7g f7s⁵ 8m f8.5g² 7m 8f 7g 8m 8f 7m² 7m 8.2m² f8g p7g Dec 30] quite
attractive filly: modest handicapper: stays 1¼m: acts on fibresand, raced mainly on good/
good to firm going on turf: blinkered. *C. E. Brittain*

TITINIUS (IRE) 3 ch.c. Titus Livius (FR) 115 – Maiyria (IRE) 68 (Shernazar 131) **83 +**
[2003 79: 6.1m* 6m 6m² Jun 28] good-bodied colt: has scope: fairly useful form: won
maiden at Nottingham in May: very unlucky runner-up to Merlin's Dancer in handicap
at Newmarket final outing, quickening well once finally clear: reportedly suffered from
cracked cannon bone after: stays 6f: acts on soft and good to firm going, probably on
heavy. *L. M. Cumani*

TITUREL 3 b.g. Amfortas (IRE) 115 – Musetta (IRE) 107 (Cadeaux Genereux 131) **100**
[2003 84: 8g³ 10m⁴ 10m⁴ 11.8m⁴ 12g 14.6g Sep 13] big, lengthy gelding: useful maiden:
good efforts in minor event at Newbury and Classic Trial at Sandown (2¾ lengths
fourth to Shield) in spring: well beaten in Gordon Stakes at Goodwood and St Leger at
Doncaster last 2 starts: should stay 1½m: acts on good to firm ground, shaped well on
soft: edged right final 2-y-o start. *C. E. Brittain*

TITUS SALT (USA) 2 ch.g. (Apr 15) Gentlemen (ARG) 136 – Farewell Partner **80**
(USA) (Northern Dancer) [2003 5m⁴ 8m⁴ f7g² f7g* Dec 12] $2,000F, $12,000Y: sturdy
gelding: half-brother to several winners in USA, including smart US Grade 3 1½m
winner Lakeshore Road (by Alleged): dam unraced sister to Ajdal and half-sister to
Formidable: fairly useful performer: blinkered, best effort when winning maiden at
Southwell by 3½ lengths from Kingsmaite, making all: should stay 1m: acts on fibresand:
raced freely second start. *T. D. Barron*

TIYOUN (IRE) 5 b.g. Kahyasi 130 – Taysala (IRE) (Akarad (FR) 130) [2003 88: f11s **82**
12g 10m⁶ 12m³ 12m⁵ 12.3m³ 12m⁴ 16m² 14g 14.1f² 16g⁵ Sep 28] leggy, lengthy gelding:
fairly useful handicapper nowadays: left D. Barker after fifth start: creditable efforts in
frame after: stays 2m: acts on firm and soft going: tried visored. *Jedd O'Keeffe*

TIZI OUZOU (IRE) 2 ch.f. (Apr 23) Desert Prince (IRE) 130 – Tresor (USA) **–**
(Pleasant Tap (USA)) [2003 7m 8m Oct 24] good-bodied filly: second foal: closely
related to French 9f/1¼m winner Tresor Secret (by Green Desert): dam, French maiden,
half-sister to Prix Saint-Alary winner Treble and to dam of high-class sprinter Tamarisk
out of half-sister to Triptych: jinked and unseated rider in minor event at Newbury: last of
22 in maiden at Doncaster. *J. L. Dunlop*

TIZ MOLLY (IRE) 2 ch.f. (Apr 29) Definite Article 121 – Almadaniyah (Dunbeath **54**
(USA) 127) [2003 8g 8.2d Nov 6] angular filly: half-sister to 5f winner Last But Not
Least (by Dominion) and to winner in Italy by Midyan: dam unraced: modest form in
maidens at Newbury and Nottingham. *M. R. Channon*

TIZ WIZ 2 b.f. (Mar 16) Wizard King 122 – Dannistar 57 (Puissance 110) [2003 7m **44**
5g⁶ 7g Oct 22] 500Y: second foal: dam 9.4f winner: poor form in maidens: should stay 7f.
W. Storey

TIZZY MAY (FR) 3 ch.c. Highest Honor (FR) 124 – Forentia 89 (Formidable (USA) **106**
125) [2003 99: 7m⁵ 8g 8d⁴ 8.1v 7.1g² 9m⁴ 9m² 10.5d² 10m³ 10m² 10g⁴ p10g Nov 22]
close-coupled colt: has a quick action: useful performer: good efforts last 5 starts on turf,
including when short-headed by Tusk in handicap at Newmarket and 4 lengths fourth to
Far Lane in listed event at Newmarket tenth/eleventh outings: raced too freely on all-
weather debut final appearance: stays 10.5f: acts on soft and good to firm going: waited
with: consistent. *R. Hannon*

TIZZY'S LAW 2 b.f. (Apr 14) Case Law 113 – Bo' Babbity 75 (Strong Gale 116) **– p**
[2003 6m Sep 23] 20,000Y: sturdy filly: half-sister to several winners, including useful
sprinters 7-y-o Abbajabba and Blue Iris (by Petong): dam, 2-y-o 5f winner, half-sister
to high-class sprinter Anita's Prince: 20/1 and in need of race, tenth of 13 in maiden at
Newmarket: bred to prove best at 5f/6f: will probably do better. *M. A. Buckley*

T K O GYM   4 b.g. Atraf 116 – Pearl Pet 56 (Mummy's Pet 125) [2003 53: f7s⁵ 10.9m **46**
7m 10m³ 9.9m⁶ 10f² f12g Nov 24] smallish, close-coupled gelding: poor maiden in 2003:
stays 1¼m: acts on firm ground and fibresand. *D. Nicholls*

TOBEROE COMMOTION (IRE)   5 b.g. Great Commotion (USA) 123 – Fionn **57**
Varragh (IRE) (Tender King 123) [2003 63: p10g³ f12s 12f⁴ 12.6f 9.7m 10m 12g⁶ Sep 1] **a62**
modest maiden handicapper: probably best at 1¼m/1½m: acts on polytrack and firm
going: tried blinkered: sold 4,500 gns. *W. R. Muir*

TOCCATA ARIA   5 b.m. Unfuwain (USA) 131 – Distant Music (Darshaan 133) [2003 **51**
–: 10g 9.9m 8.1d³ 10.2m 10.9m 8.2f⁶ Sep 30] big mare: modest maiden, lightly raced:
stays 1m: acts on firm and good to soft ground. *J. M. Bradley*

TODDEANO   7 b.g. Perpendicular 119 – Phisus 48 (Henbit (USA) 130) [2003 10.2m   –
f7s Sep 6] no form. *G. Fierro*

TODLEA (IRE)   3 b.g. Desert Prince (IRE) 130 – Imelda (USA) (Manila (USA)) [2003 **81**
7.1m⁴ 8g* 10.1m 12m f9.4g p10g Dec 10] IR 70,000Y: smallish, quite good-topped **a72**
gelding: second foal: half-brother to fairly useful 2001 2-y-o 6f winner Rapadash (by
Boundary), later successful in USA: dam once-raced half-sister to very smart French
miler Shaanxi: fairly useful form: won maiden at Goodwood in May by ½ length from
Kawagino: off 5 months, well held last 2 starts: will probably stay 1¼m: tongue tied
second to fourth starts. *J. A. Osborne*

TOEJAM   10 ch.g. Move Off 112 – Cheeky Pigeon (Brave Invader (USA)) [2003 56:   –
f8s f8s Jan 14] angular gelding: modest in 2002: no form in 2003: tried visored: sometimes slowly away. *R. E. Barr*

TOJONESKI   4 b.g. Emperor Jones (USA) 119 – Sampower Lady 55 (Rock City 120) **67 d**
[2003 78§: p10g f9.4s f6g 7m 10.5m f12s 11.6m³ 10.1f⁵ 12.4m³ f12s Sep 6] one-time
fairly useful performer: on downgrade, leaving P. Makin after reappearance: wore cheekpieces last 5 starts. *K. A. Morgan*

TOKEWANNA   3 b.f. Danehill (USA) 126 – High Atlas 65 (Shirley Heights 130) [2003 **63**
64: 5f 6g⁴ 6g⁶ 7m⁴ 5m 6m⁴ 6m Oct 13] good-bodied filly: modest maiden handicapper:
seems best around 7f: acts on firm ground: tried visored/in cheekpieces: tail flasher:
found little final 2-y-o start. *C. E. Brittain*

TOLDYA   6 b.m. Beveled (USA) – Run Amber Run (Run The Gantlet (USA)) [2003 93: **87**
f6g f6s 6g 5m 5m 6d² 6m 6m 6f 6g⁵ 5f 6m⁵ 6m 6m Aug 23] smallish mare: fairly useful
handicapper: effective at 5f to easy 7f: acts on any turf going/all-weather: tried blinkered,
wore cheekpieces/visor in 2003: sometimes slowly away: inconsistent. *A. P. Jarvis*

TOLEDO SUN   3 b.g. Zamindar (USA) 116 – Shafir (IRE) 68 (Shaadi (USA) 126) **62**
[2003 53+: p7g 8.2g 8.1m 7g 7m p10g³ p12g p12g p10g p10g Dec 20] compact gelding:
modest maiden: left S. Keightley after sixth start: stays easy 1½m: acts on polytrack: tried
visored/blinkered. *H. J. Collingridge*

TOLZEY (USA)   2 ch.f. (Apr 23) Rahy (USA) 115 – Legal Opinion (IRE) (Polish **94**
Precedent (USA) 131) [2003 5d² 6v³ 5m² 6f² 6m⁵ 6.1d* 7m⁶ 6m⁵ Aug 21] strong filly:
third foal: sister to useful French 2002 2-y-o 4.5f to 7f winner Inner Temple and half-
sister to UAE 1m winner Fight (by Darshaan): dam twice-raced daughter of high-class
sprinter/miler Golden Opinion: fairly useful performer: second in listed races at Beverley
and Ascot third and fourth starts: landed odds in maiden at Nottingham in July: creditable
fifth in Lowther Stakes at York final appearance: doesn't quite stay 7f: acts on firm and
good to soft ground, probably not heavy. *M. R. Channon*

TOMAHAWK (USA)   3 b.c. Seattle Slew (USA) – Statuette (USA) (Pancho Villa **111**
(USA)) [2003 118: 7d* 8d⁴ 8g 8d 6m Jul 10] big, well-made colt: smart performer:
runner-up in Middle Park Stakes and Dewhurst Stakes (wandered) at Newmarket at 2 yrs:
won listed race at the Curragh in March: unlucky in running in Prix de Fontainebleau at
Longchamp (close fourth to Clodovil, not clear run then finished strongly) and 2000
Guineas at Newmarket (2¾ lengths eighth to Refuse To Bend, might have been upsides
placed horses with clearer run): well held in Irish 2000 Guineas at the Curragh and July
Cup at Newmarket (visored) last 2 starts: stays 1m: acts on firm and soft going: sweating
and very much on edge twice in 2003: sent to USA, joined T. Pletcher. *A. P. O'Brien,
Ireland*

TOMASINO   5 br.h. Celtic Swing 138 – Bustinetta 89 (Bustino 136) [2003 104: 12.1d⁶   –
12m⁶ Jul 10] good-topped horse: one-time smart performer: reportedly had small fracture
of off-fore cannon bone at 3 yrs: lightly raced and below form since, well held both starts
in 2003 (virtually pulled up last time, had fibrillating heart): should stay 1¾m: acts on any
going. *M. Johnston*

TOM BELL (IRE)   3 b.g. King's Theatre (IRE) 128 – Nordic Display (IRE) 77   –
(Nordico (USA)) [2003 –: 10.2m f12g 10.2f 13.8m⁵ Oct 18] little form: tried visored
(raced freely). *J. G. M. O'Shea*

TOM FROM BOUNTY   3 ch.g. Opera Ghost 91 – Tempus Fugit 85 (Timeless Times   –
(USA) 99) [2003 69?: 6g 7m 8f 8.1m 6m 8.3g 7f Oct 27] little form at 3 yrs: tried tongue
tied. *B. R. Millman*

TOMILLIE   4 ch.g. Ventiquattrofogli (IRE) 118 – Royal Comedian 58 (Jester 119)   –
[2003 49: f5g Apr 25] good-topped gelding: poor maiden nowadays: well held only
outing in 2003: tried blinkered. *A. Berry*

TOMINA   3 b.g. Deploy 131 – Cavina 64 (Ardross 134) [2003 67: p8g⁶ 12.6m* 12m⁴   **82**
14m³ Jul 24] workmanlike gelding: fairly useful handicapper: won at Warwick in May: at
least creditable efforts next 2 starts: probably stays 1¾m: acts on good to firm ground and
polytrack. *N. A. Graham*

TOMMY CARSON   8 b.g. Last Tycoon 131 – Ivory Palm (USA) 93 (Sir Ivor 135)   –
[2003 44: p16g⁵ Dec 2] sturdy gelding: poor maiden: off 20 months, never dangerous
only start in 2003: usually blinkered earlier in career. *Jamie Poulton*

TOMMY NUTTER (IRE)   3 b.g. Desert Style (IRE) 121 – Ahakista (IRE) (Persian   **51 §**
Bold 123) [2003 65§: p6g⁶ p6g⁵ p5g f5g⁵ 5.7m⁵ 5.1m⁶ 7m 6.1m Jul 5] modest maiden: **a47 §**
best at 5f: acts on all-weather and good to firm ground: tried in headgear: has carried head
awkwardly/edged left: unreliable. *R. Brotherton*

TOMMY SMITH   5 ch.g. Timeless Times (USA) 99 – Superstream (Superpower 113)   **90 §**
[2003 92§: 5g 5f 5g6 5m² 5g 5f³ 5f 5m 5d⁶ 5m⁵ 5m² 5m⁶ 5f³ 5g Sep 12] smallish, sturdy
gelding: fairly useful handicapper: has won at 6f, best form at 5f: goes well on going
firmer than good: visored/blinkered: often starts slowly/hangs: reared and unseated rider
in stall eighth 4-y-o outing: front runner: can't be trusted. *J. S. Wainwright*

TOMMY TWO HAIRS (IRE)   2 b.f. (Mar 31) Mujadil (USA) 119 – Grosvenor Miss   **52**
(IRE) (Tirol 127) [2003 5g 5.1f⁶ f5g⁶ 5.1m Apr 21] IR 3,000F, 4,000Y: small, leggy filly:
third foal: half-sister to winner in Spain by Idris: dam maiden: modest maiden: should
stay at least 6f: best effort on fibresand. *P. S. McEntee*

TOMOKIM (IRE)   2 b.c. (Feb 19) Mujadil (USA) 119 – Snowtop (Thatching 131)   –
[2003 6d p6g p6g Dec 29] 14,000F, 21,000Y: good-bodied colt: half-brother to several
winners, including fairly useful 7f/1m winner Tiptronic (by Woodborough): dam Irish
sprinter: well beaten in maidens at Haydock and Lingfield (2). *M. Quinn*

TOM PADDINGTON   8 b.g. Rock Hopper 124 – Mayfair Minx (St Columbus 98)   **95**
[2003 81: 12g⁴ 14g² 16.2d³ 14.6g 18m⁵ 16g⁵ Oct 31] good-bodied gelding: useful handicapper: good fifth last 2 starts, behind Landing Light in Cesarewitch at Newmarket
on first occasion: stays 2¼m: acts on soft and good to firm going: usually held up.
H. Morrison

TOM'S CRUISING   4 b.g. Fraam 114 – Fading (Pharly (FR) 130) [2003 98: 8.1g 7g   –
8g⁶ 8g⁶ p7g Aug 28] tall, leggy, close-coupled gelding: fairly useful performer at 3 yrs:
showed little in 2003, leaving J. Fanshawe after second outing: not sure to stay further
than 1m: acts on good to firm and good to soft ground: tried tongue tied: sold 1,000 gns.
H. J. Cyzer

TOMSK (IRE)   3 b.g. Definite Article 121 – Merry Twinkle (Martinmas 128) [2003 –:   –
7.1m 7.2m⁴ Jun 20] no sign of ability in maidens. *A. Berry*

TOMTHEVIC   5 ch.g. Emarati (USA) 74 – Madame Bovary 82 (Ile de Bourbon   **67**
(USA) 133) [2003 67: f5g 5g 5.3f 5m 5g² 5m⁵ 5m³ 5m* 5m⁵ 5m⁵ 5.2m 5f² 5m² 5f Sep 4]
strong-quartered gelding: fair handicapper: won at Windsor in July: probably best at 5f
on good going or firmer: tried tongue tied/visored earlier in career: sometimes slowly
away: usually races prominently: consistent: sold 6,500 gns. *P. R. Chamings*

TOM TUN   8 b.g. Bold Arrangement 127 – B Grade 59 (Lucky Wednesday 124) [2003   **103**
106: p7g 6g 6g 6g 7d 6d* 6d Nov 8] workmanlike gelding: has a round action: useful
performer: won minor event at Hamilton in September by neck from Bond Boy: races
mainly at 6f nowadays, stays easy 7f: acts on all-weather, clearly best efforts on ground
softer than good (acts on heavy): blinkered last 2 starts: tried tongue tied earlier in career:
tends to be soon off bridle. *J. G. Given*

TON-CHEE   4 b.g. Vettori (IRE) 119 – Najariya (Northfields (USA)) [2003 –: 17.2m   **31 +**
14.1d 12.4m⁴ 16d³ Aug 11] poor performer: stays 2m: acts on good to soft ground.
K. W. Hogg, Isle of Man

TONG ICE   4 gr.g. Petong 126 – Efficacious (IRE) 49 (Efisio 120) [2003 –, a47: 5m   –
Apr 15] poor maiden: showed nothing only outing in 2003: usually visored/blinkered:
sometimes carries head awkwardly. *B. A. Pearce*

TONI ALCALA   4 b.g. Ezzoud (IRE) 126 – Etourdie (USA) (Arctic Tern (USA) 126)   **75**
[2003 71: f12g³ f12s⁴ f12g² 16.1d² 16m³ f14g⁶ f14.8s 17.1m⁵ 13m³ 18m⁶ 16f 13g³ 12.6f
15g³ 13.8m* 17.1m 14f² 16.2m 15.9d⁴ f16.2g Nov 17] close-coupled gelding: fair
handicapper: won at Catterick in August: stays 17f: acts on firm going, good to soft and
fibresand: sometimes slowly away/races freely: edgy sort: held up: none too consistent.
R. F. Fisher

TONI'S PET   3 b.g. Wizard King 122 – Dannistar 57 (Puissance 110) [2003 f9.4g⁶ f8s   –
7m⁵ 5.7f 11.5m Oct 21] 1,100Y: first foal: dam 9.4f winner: little form: left R. Wilman
after second start, P. Blockley after third. *B. N. Pollock*

TONTO (FR)   2 gr.g. (Feb 16) Second Empire (IRE) 124 – Malabarista (FR) (Assert   **82 §**
134) [2003 5.7m² 5f 6m³ 7m⁴ 6.1m³ 6m 5.7f² p6g Dec 29] 15,000Y: leggy gelding: fifth
foal: half-brother to 3 winners, including 3-y-o Capulette: dam French 12.5f winner:
fairly useful maiden: second twice at Bath: left P. Webber before final start: stays 7f: acts
on good to firm going: visored (ran creditably)/wore cheekpieces once each: tends to
carry head high/find little: not to be trusted. *Miss D. Mountain*

TONY THE TAP   2 b.g. (Apr 28) Most Welcome 131 – Laleston 73 (Junius (USA)   **69 p**
124) [2003 p6g⁴ Dec 29] half-brother to several 5f winners, including 1998 2-y-o winner
Ewenny (by Warrshan): dam 5f winner: 25/1 and green, 2 lengths fourth of 10 to Smokin
Joe in maiden at Lingfield, starting slowly and finishing strongly under hands and heels:
should stay 7f: will improve. *N. A. Callaghan*

TONY TIE   7 b.g. Ardkinglass 114 – Queen of The Quorn 53 (Governor General 116)   **84**
[2003 95: 8g 8m 10m 8g 10g 8.3g 7.9m 9.2g² 9.2g⁵ 8m 8.5m* 10m⁴ 9.2g³ 9.2m 7.6m 8m⁶
10d Oct 13] leggy, angular gelding: unimpressive mover: fairly useful handicapper: won
at Beverley in July: probably needs test at 7f nowadays, and stays easy 1¼m: acts on any
going: tried in cheekpieces/visor: has idled in front: tough. *J. S. Goldie*

TOOTIN MAC   2 b.f. (Jan 30) Piccolo 121 – Bangles 83 (Chilibang 120) [2003 5m⁶   **38**
5m 6f 5d 7.5m⁶ 7m 7m Oct 17] 3,500Y: good-bodied filly: fourth foal: half-sister to 6f
winner Bangled (by Beveled): dam 5f winner, including at 2 yrs: poor maiden: stays 7.5f:
acts on good to firm ground: blinkered third/fourth starts. *N. Bycroft*

TOP ACHIEVER (IRE)   2 ch.c. (Feb 19) Intikhab (USA) 135 – Nancy Maloney   –
(IRE) 53 (Persian Bold 123) [2003 5m⁵ Jul 18] 34,000F, €60,000Y, 18,000 2-y-o: second
foal: dam, lightly-raced maiden (should have stayed further than 1m), half-sister to
Cherry Hinton winner Torgau: 66/1 and green, slowly away when fifth of 8 in maiden at
Hamilton. *Mrs L. Stubbs*

TOPARUDI   2 b.g. (Apr 7) Rudimentary (USA) 118 – Topatori (IRE) 89 (Topanoora   **72**
118) [2003 6f 6g⁵ 6m³ 7d³ 8d³ 7d Nov 8] big, good-topped gelding: first foal: dam 7f to
10.5f winner: fair maiden: third 3 times, including in nurseries: will stay at least 1¼m:
acts on good to firm and good to soft ground. *M. H. Tompkins*

TOP DIRHAM   5 ch.g. Night Shift (USA) – Miller's Melody 86 (Chief Singer 131)   **82**
[2003 –: 7f 8.3d 8m* 7.9m* 7.9m⁵ 8m 8.1d 8m 8.9f 8g Oct 28] good-topped gelding:
fairly useful handicapper: won at Thirsk and Carlisle in June: stays 1m: acts on good to
firm ground: tried tongue tied. *M. W. Easterby*

TOP HAT   2 b.c. (Mar 16) Easycall 115 – Whispering Sea 52 (Bustino 136) [2003 5f   **44**
5m 5m 6f 6f Jun 13] 1,500Y: leggy colt: seventh foal: dam ran twice: poor maiden: best
form at 5f. *M. W. Easterby*

TOPKAMP   3 b.f. Pennekamp (USA) 130 – Victoria Regia (IRE) 90 (Lomond (USA)   **104**
128) [2003 96: 5f 6g* 6m* 7.1m³ 6m⁴ 6.5g² 7g³ 6.5s⁵ Oct 12] small, strong, lengthy filly:
useful performer: won minor event at Kempton in May and listed race at Haydock (beat
Valiantly 1¼ lengths) in June: ran creditably when 3 lengths second to Fiepes Shuffle in
Grosser Preis von Berlin at Hoppegarten and 3½ lengths third to Monsieur Bond in listed
race at Epsom (edged left) sixth/seventh starts: effective at 6f/easy 7f: acts on firm going,
probably on soft: sometimes starts slowly. *M. L. W. Bell*

TOP LINE DANCER (IRE)   2 b.c. (Mar 11) Fasliyev (USA) 120 – Twafeaj (USA)   **72**
110 (Topsider (USA)) [2003 6g⁵ 6m⁴ Aug 22] 12,000 2-y-o: well-made colt: seventh
foal: half-brother to 4-y-o Shanook and 1½m winner Inthaar (by Nashwan): dam, won
Moyglare Stud Stakes, best around 6f: easily better effort (fair form) when fourth in
maiden at Thirsk, tending to wander: will probably stay 7f. *M. Johnston*

TOP OF THE CLASS (IRE)   6 b.m. Rudimentary (USA) 118 – School Mum (Reprimand 122) [2003 54§, a41§: f8s⁶ f9.4g⁶ f9.4g⁶ f9.4g⁴ f9.4g f9.4s f9.4s 9.2m⁵ 10.5m* 9.2m 9.9m³ 9.2g⁴ 11.9g p10g⁶ 10m⁶ 10.2m* 9.9m 9.2m 10m³ 10f² 10m⁴ 10.9m 9.1m⁶ 10.3d* 11.7f⁵ 10d⁴ 10m f9.4g⁵ f8g Nov 24] fair handicapper on turf, modest on all-weather: won at Haydock (ladies event) in June, Bath in July and Chester in September: stays easy 11.7f: acts on any turf going and all-weather: tried blinkered, visored nowadays: sometimes slowly away/pulls hard/finds little. *P. D. Evans*   **66 a53**

TOP PLACE   2 b.f. (Apr 11) Compton Place 125 – Double Top (IRE) (Thatching 131) [2003 5g Apr 7] 3,000Y: third foal: half-sister to winners abroad by Hamas and Perugino: dam unraced: behind in maiden at Windsor: gave birth unexpectedly in July. *C. A. Dwyer*   **47**

TOPPLING   5 b.g. Cadeaux Genereux 131 – Topicality (USA) (Topsider (USA)) [2003 73d: 7m 7m⁴ 7.1g² 6m* 6.1g* 6m⁵ 6m² 5.7f 5.3f f6s 6g p7g f6g Nov 17] smallish, good-bodied gelding: fair handicapper nowadays: won at Yarmouth and Nottingham in June: free-going sort, and probably best at 6f/7f: acts on good to firm going. *J. M. Bradley*   **71 a–**

TOP ROMANCE (IRE)   2 ch.f. (Mar 15) Entrepreneur 123 – Heart's Harmony (Blushing Groom (FR) 131) [2003 7m* 7m* Oct 4] small, close-coupled filly: half-sister to several winners, including smart 1¼m winner National Anthem (by Royal Academy) and 3-y-o Tug of Love: dam won at 1m from 2 starts in France: won maiden at Yarmouth in September and listed event at Newmarket (beat Spotlight by neck in 9-runner race, rallying having been headed over 1f out) in October: will be suited by at least 1m: potentially smart, and should win more races. *Sir Michael Stoute*   **105 p**

TOP SEED (IRE)   2 b.c. (Apr 27) Cadeaux Genereux 131 – Midnight Heights 104 (Persian Heights 129) [2003 7g² 7m³ 7.5m* 7m⁴ 7.1d⁵ 8m³ 8f 9m³ 8m⁶ 8s² 10d⁴ Nov 8] €130,000Y: quite good-topped colt: third foal: dam, 1m to 1½m winner (latter in Italy), half-sister to smart performer up to 1¼m Galitzin: useful performer: won minor event at Beverley in July: placed in listed events at Goodwood and Milan and Criterium International at Saint-Cloud (best effort when 6 lengths second to Bago) after: had too much use made of him (still clear over 1f out) when fourth in Criterium de Saint-Cloud final start: should stay 1¼m: acts on good to firm and soft going: sometimes edgy. *M. R. Channon*   **109**

TOP SON   4 b.c. Komaite (USA) – Top Yard (Teekay) [2003 7m p7g p12g f14g Dec 12] seventh foal: dam unraced: well held in claimers/handicap. *A. P. Jones*   **–**

TOP SPEC (IRE)   2 b.g. (Apr 14) Spectrum (IRE) 126 – Pearl Marine (IRE) (Bluebird (USA) 125) [2003 5m⁴ 5g³ 7d³ 7m² 7m² 8m* 8.1g⁶ 8m* Oct 16] IR 30,000F, 25,000Y: leggy, close-coupled gelding: has a quick action: seventh foal: brother to Mark of Excellence, winner around 1m in Hong Kong, and half-brother to winners abroad by Bigstone and Night Shift: dam lightly-raced maiden in France: fairly useful performer: won nurseries at Newmarket in August and October (beat Sanbonah short head, leading close home): will stay at least 1¼m: acts on good to firm going: often slowly away. *R. Hannon*   **88**

TOP SPOT   3 b.f. Cadeaux Genereux 131 – Number One Spot 71 (Reference Point 139) [2003 8.1m 7f² 8m⁵ 7m⁵ Oct 21] small, leggy filly: fifth foal: half-sister to 6-y-o Desert Fury and 8-y-o Royal Axminster: dam, 7f winner, closely related to top-class miler Milligram out of 1000 Guineas winner One In A Million: fair form in maidens: stays 7f: raced only on ground firmer than good. *C. E. Brittain*   **76**

TOP TENOR (IRE)   3 b.c. Sadler's Wells (USA) 132 – Posta Vecchia (USA) (Rainbow Quest (USA) 134) [2003 65: 11.8m 14.1m⁴ 14.1m* 14.1m² 16f³ Sep 30] strong, compact colt: fairly useful handicapper: won at Salisbury in August: stays 2m: raced only on good ground or firmer: has shown reluctance at stall. *J. L. Dunlop*   **80**

TOPTON (IRE)   9 b.g. Royal Academy (USA) 130 – Circo 77 (High Top 131) [2003 85, a–: p8g p10g f8s⁴ f8s p8g 8.3g⁶ 8g 8g 8m² 7m 8m* 8f 8m⁴ 8g* 8d⁶ 8.1m⁴ 9m⁴ 8m 8.1f⁵ 9g 7g⁶ 7d p8g* Dec 2] tall, angular gelding: fairly useful handicapper on turf, fair on all-weather: won at Newbury in June, Doncaster in July and Lingfield in December: best form at 7f/1m: acts on firm going, soft and all-weather/dirt: has won in visor, blinkered nowadays: has run well sweating: usually held up: tough, but quirky. *P. Howling*   **89 a78**

TOP TREES   5 b.g. Charnwood Forest (IRE) 125 – Low Line 66 (High Line 125) [2003 69§: f12s⁵ f12g 12.1g 13.1f* f12g Nov 21] modest nowadays: won maiden handicap at Bath in September: stays 13f: acts on fibresand and firm ground: has been slowly away/reluctant to race. *W. S. Kittow*   **52 §**

TOP TUNE   3 b.f. Victory Note (USA) 120 – Topwinder (USA) (Topsider (USA)) [2003 f9.4g⁵ f8.5s 11.8m⁵ 12.1d May 20] sixth living foal: half-sister to 3 winners, including 5f   **–**

TOR

winner Piper's Clan (by Aragon) and fairly useful 1¼m winner (stayed 1¾m) Master George (by Mtoto): dam ran twice in France: little form in maidens/handicap. *A. Bailey*

TORA BORA 3 ch.f. Grand Lodge (USA) 125 – Brilliance 74 (Cadeaux Genereux 131) **101**
[2003 67: 6.1g⁴ 8d⁴ 7m* 7.1m* 7g³ 7m 7d 6m Sep 26] lengthy filly: useful performer: won handicap at Leicester and listed event (beat Littleton Arwen by short head) at Warwick in June: good efforts next 2 starts, 3¼ lengths third to Tantina in listed race at Goodwood then seventh to With Reason in Hungerford Stakes at Newbury: best form at 7f: acts on good to firm ground, possibly unsuited by going softer than good. *P. W. D'Arcy*

TORCHLIGHT (USA) 3 b. or br.f. Seeking The Gold (USA) – Cap Beino (USA) **66**
(Lyphard (USA) 132) [2003 7m⁵ Jun 12] close-coupled, useful-looking filly: third foal: half-sister to US winner by Trempolino: dam US 8.5f (including minor stakes)/1¼m winner: 6/1, 3¼ lengths fifth to Tree Peony in maiden at Newbury, running on not knocked about. *J. H. M. Gosden*

TORCROSS 2 b.f. (May 4) Vettori (IRE) 119 – Sheppard's Cross 88 (Soviet Star **96 p**
(USA) 128) [2003 7m* 7g⁴ Oct 25] lengthy, attractive filly: fifth foal: half-sister to 5-y-o Sheppard's Watch and 3-y-o Fovant: dam, 7f winner, out of smart sprinter Cutlers Corner: won maiden at Leicester in October by short head from Vas Y Carla: improved (useful form) when 3 lengths fourth of 12 to Secret Charm in listed event at Newbury, taking time to respond: will stay at least 1m: open to progress. *M. P. Tregoning*

TORINMOOR (USA) 2 ch.c. (May 4) Intikhab (USA) 135 – Tochar Ban (USA) **93 p**
83 (Assert 134) [2003 7g³ 7m* 8m⁶ Sep 12] 70,000 2-y-o: good-bodied colt: sixth foal: half-brother to French 1999 2-y-o 1m winner Uncharted Haven (by Turtle Island), later US Grade 2 1m/9f winner, and to 3-y-o Albany: dam 1¼m winner: confirmed promise when winning 15-runner maiden at Newmarket in August by head from Sussex: forced wide throughout when respectable sixth of 8 in listed race at Goodwood: probably stays 1m: potentially useful as 3-y-o. *Mrs A. J. Perrett*

TORO BRAVO (IRE) 3 b.g. Alhaarth (IRE) 126 – Set Trail (IRE) 76 (Second Set –
(IRE) 127) [2003 74: 10g 9.9d p12g 10d p10g f11g f11s p10g Dec 30] small, lengthy gelding: fair winner at 2 yrs: well held in 2003: tried tongue tied/in blinkers/cheekpieces. *R. M. Beckett*

TORONTO HEIGHTS (USA) 2 ch.g. (Feb 5) King of Kings (IRE) 125 – Revol- **81**
tosa (IRE) (Catrail (USA) 123) [2003 5g² 5m⁴ 5d³ 6g 7g³ 6.1m² 6m f5s⁶ Oct 7] 65,000F, 70,000Y: smallish, compact gelding: has a quick action: first foal: dam, French 5f winner, half-sister to smart sprinter Polar Bird: fairly useful maiden: second at Kempton and Warwick (nursery): barely stays 7f: acts on good to firm going, probably on good to soft: blinkered final start, wore cheekpieces previous 2: sold 21,000 gns, gelded and joined P. Chapple-Hyam. *B. W. Hills*

TOROSAY SPRING 5 ch.m. First Trump 118 – Spring Sixpence 60 (Dowsing **116**
(USA) 124) [2003 106: 6g³ 6f⁶ 6m* 6m 6m² 6f 5m⁴ Oct 2] sturdy, lengthy mare: smart performer, lightly raced: better than ever in 2003: won Cuisine de France Summer Stakes at York in July by 2 lengths from Khulood: best effort when head second of 5 to Acclamation in listed race at Goodwood: creditable fourth (would have gone close with clear run) to Colonel Cotton in similar event at Newmarket: effective at 5f/6f: raced only on good going or firmer (acts on firm): usually waited with. *J. R. Fanshawe*

TORQUEMADA (IRE) 2 ch.c. (Feb 7) Desert Sun 120 – Gaelic's Fantasy (IRE) **68**
(Statoblest 120) [2003 6m⁶ 6m Sep 23] 35,000F, 26,000Y: compact colt: second foal: half-brother to 3-y-o Pooka's Daughter: dam, Italian 1m winner, half-sister to smart miler Bachir: fair form in maidens at Goodwood and Newmarket: should stay 1m. *W. Jarvis*

TORRENT 8 ch.g. Prince Sabo 123 – Maiden Pool 85 (Sharpen Up 127) [2003 –§, **62 §**
a57§: f5g⁵ p6g f6g⁵ f6g f6g⁵ f5g p7g⁵ f6g⁴ f5g 5g⁴ 5m⁵ 5m* 5m 5m³ 5d 5m⁶ 5g 6f⁶ 5m⁵ **a49 §**
6m⁵ 5m² 5f 5f⁶ 6g Oct 14] strong, lengthy gelding: modest handicapper: left P. McEntee £1,600 and rejoined former stable after eighth outing: won at Ripon in June: best at 5f/6f: acts on any turf going/all-weather: wears headgear: tried tongue tied: has broken blood vessels, and reportedly can't be subjected to strong pressure: carries head high: one to treat with caution. *D. W. Chapman*

TORRID KENTAVR (USA) 6 b.g. Trempolino (USA) 135 – Torrid Tango (USA) **73**
(Green Dancer (USA) 132) [2003 89d: 9.3g 8.1m³ 7.9m⁴ 8.5d² 10g³ 9g 7.9m⁵ Sep 4] close-coupled gelding: fair handicapper nowadays: effective at 1m/1¼m: acts on firm going, soft and fibresand: tried blinkered (not since 2000): free-going sort, usually held up: has hung: winning hurdler/chaser. *B. Ellison*

1044

TORTUETTE 2 b.f. (Apr 18) Turtle Island (IRE) 123 – Allmosa 66 (Alleging (USA) 120) [2003 6m 7.5m³ p7g 10m 8d Oct 31] smallish filly: first foal: dam 1½m to 2¼m winner: little form, including in nursery. *Jean-Rene Auvray* —

TORTUGA DREAM (IRE) 4 b.g. Turtle Island (IRE) 123 – Tycoon's Catch (IRE) (Thatching 131) [2003 –: 8.1d⁵ 10.2g f12s p12g Sep 3] good-bodied gelding: lightly-raced maiden: little form. *A. Charlton* —

TORZAL 3 br.g. Hector Protector (USA) 124 – Alathezal (USA) (Zilzal (USA) 137) [2003 –: f6g 7g f8g f8g Dec 9] tall, leggy gelding: little sign of ability. *R. F. Marvin* —

TOTAL DEVOTION 3 b.f. Desert Prince (IRE) 130 – Totality 103 (Dancing Brave (USA) 140) [2003 10f⁴ 10m* 10g Sep 27] strong, deep-girthed filly: type to carry plenty of condition: third foal: half-sister to fairly useful 1½m winner Total Care (by Caerleon): dam, 1¾m winner, sister to Derby winner Commander In Chief and half-sister to Warning, an excellent family: fairly useful form: won maiden at Ripon in August comfortably by 1¾ lengths from Glamorous Girl: ran as if amiss in handicap there final start: would have been suited by at least 1½m: stud. *H. R. A. Cecil* 78 +

TOTAL FORCE (IRE) 2 b.c. (Apr 9) Night Shift (USA) – Capegulch (USA) (Gulch (USA)) [2003 7.1m 7m⁵ Oct 2] 10,000Y: tall colt: fourth foal: dam, sprint winner in USA, out of half-sister to Blushing Groom: better effort in maidens (modest form) when fifth at Brighton: slowly away/failed to handle turn at Warwick: will probably stay 1m. *R. Hannon* 59

TOTALLY SCOTTISH 7 b.g. Mtoto 134 – Glenfinlass (Lomond (USA) 128) [2003 51: 17.1m⁴ 13g² Jun 12] smallish, quite attractive gelding: modest maiden handicapper: finds 13f a minimum, and stays 2m well: acts on good to firm and good to soft going: tried blinkered/tongue tied: held up: fair but moody hurdler. *Mrs M. Reveley* 51

TOTALLY YOURS (IRE) 2 b.f. (Feb 16) Desert Sun 120 – Total Aloof 72 (Groom Dancer (USA) 128) [2003 6m 6g² 6m² 6g* 6m Oct 2] €40,000Y: tall filly: half-sister to 3-y-o Tout Seul and 2001 Irish 2-y-o 6f winner Soaring Eagle (by Eagle Eyed): dam, 5f winner, granddaughter of Yorkshire Oaks winner Condessa: fairly useful performer: landed odds in maiden at Epsom in September: good second in sales race at the Curragh and seventh in Cheveley Park Stakes at Newmarket starts either side: will stay 7f: tends to flash tail. *W. R. Muir* 90

TOTAL PACKAGE 3 b.f. Fraam 114 – Sunley Solaire (Aragon 118) [2003 –: f7g f8g⁶ p7g⁶ 8f⁵ 7g⁵ 8f 8f Jun 25] poor maiden: seems to stay 1m: acts on polytrack and probably on firm going. *M. S. Saunders* 48 ?

TO THE WOODS (IRE) 4 ch.f. Woodborough (USA) 112 – Iktidar 80 (Green Desert (USA) 127) [2003 86d: p7g Jan 18] smallish filly: fairly useful at best: on downgrade. *N. P. Littmoden* —

TOUCH DOWN (GER) 5 b.h. Dashing Blade 117 – Time To Run (GER) (Sicyos (USA) 126) [2003 116: 8g⁵ 8d 7m 8g 8g⁶ Aug 3] approx. 20,600Y in Germany: sturdy horse: second foal: brother to German winner up to 11.5f Time To Love: dam, German 1m winner, half-sister to useful German miler Tropical King: smart performer at best: successful in 2002 in listed race at Milan and Badener Meile at Baden-Baden: just useful form at 5 yrs, sixth to Scapolo in Otto Wolff-Meile at Cologne final start: raced mainly at 1m (behind over 7f in Criterion Stakes at Newmarket third start): acts on heavy and good to firm going. *D. Richardson, Germany* 103

TOUCH OF EBONY (IRE) 4 b.c. Darshaan 133 – Cormorant Wood 130 (Home Guard (USA) 129) [2003 66: 12m⁴ 15.4m 11.5g 11.8g 14.1m 12d² Jul 31] sparely-made colt: fair maiden handicapper: left C. Roberts after fifth start: stays 1¾m, possibly not 15f: acts on fibresand (some promise on polytrack), soft and good to firm going: blinkered (well beaten) fifth start: sometimes slowly away: held up. *D. Loughnane, Ireland* 66 ?

TOUCH OF FAIRY (IRE) 7 b.g. Fairy King (USA) – Decadence (Vaigly Great 127) [2003 65: 6m 6.1m³ 6m 6.1g Jun 13] strong, lengthy gelding: modest maiden handicapper: effective at 5f/6f: acts on heavy and good to firm going: usually blinkered nowadays: tried tongue tied: edged markedly left second start: slowly away/found little final outing: needs treating with caution. *J. M. Bradley* 58 §

TOUCH OF GOLD 3 b.c. Robellino (USA) 127 – Nanouche (Dayjur (USA) 137) [2003 73: 8g 6d 6g 8.3m⁶ 8.5g³ 6g 8m f8.5s 6.1f Sep 30] sturdy, lengthy, slightly hollow-backed colt: fair maiden handicapper: left W. Muir after reappearance: below form last 4 starts: stayed 1m: acted on good to firm going, soft and polytrack (looked reluctant on fibresand): carried head awkwardly: ungenuine: dead. *R. Hannon* 67 §

TOUGH LEADER   9 b.g. Lead On Time (USA) 123 – Al Guswa 98 (Shernazar 131)   –
[2003 89: 10g Jun 2] robust gelding: fairly useful handicapper at best: pulled up
(reportedly lost action) only outing in 2003: tried blinkered/tongue tied earlier in career.
M. C. Pipe

TOUGH LOVE   4 ch.g. Pursuit of Love 124 – Food of Love 109 (Music Boy 124)   **102**
[2003 81: 8m* 8g³ 8.5d² 8g² 8.1m* 8m³ 7m³ 7g Jul 26] strong, lengthy gelding: useful
handicapper: won at Pontefract in April and Haydock (by 4 lengths from Atlantic Quest)
in June: very good third in Hunt Cup at Royal Ascot (beaten 3½ lengths by Macadamia)
and Bunbury Cup at Newmarket (beaten 1¼ lengths by Patavellian) next 2 starts: effective at 7f to 8.5f: acts on firm and soft ground: wears crossed noseband: on edge (rare
poor effort) final outing: carries head awkwardly: usually waited with. *T. D. Easterby*

TOUGH NUT (IRE)   3 b.g. Sri Pekan (USA) 117 – Dancing At Lunasa (IRE) 70   **63**
(Dancing Dissident (USA) 119) [2003 61: p6g f7g* f6g⁵ f7s f7s⁵ p7g⁶ p7g³ f7g⁵ Mar 13]
modest performer: won apprentice handicap at Wolverhampton in January: better at 7f
than 6f: acts on good to firm going, good to soft and all-weather: wore cheekpieces
last 3 starts: has been awkward leaving stall: hung right penultimate start: inconsistent.
J. A. Osborne

TOUMAI   3 b.f. Mind Games 121 – Flower Princess (Slip Anchor 136) [2003 –: 7m 6m   **51 ?**
7.5d⁴ 7f 8.3m 12.1m⁶ 12m a8g a8g a12g a9s a10g⁵ a10.5s a10s Dec 7] modest maiden:
sold from Mrs A. Duffield 2,000 gns after seventh start: stays 7f: best effort on good to
soft ground: tried visored/tongue tied. *M. Lundgren, Spain*

TOUR DE FORCE   4 b.g. Saddlers' Hall (IRE) 126 – Rensaler (USA) (Stop The   **88**
Music (USA)) [2003 8.2g* 10d⁶ 10m 8g* 8m Oct 17] good-topped gelding: brother to
useful 1¼m winner Silence Reigns, closely related to 2 winners by Sadler's Wells,
including fairly useful 1¾m winner Sadler's Realm, and half-brother to several winners,
notably very smart winner up to 1¼m in USA Jovial (by Northern Jove), 6f winner in
Britain at 2 yrs: dam won around 1m in USA: fairly useful form: made most when
winning maiden at Nottingham in March and minor event at Musselburgh (rallied to beat
Start Over a neck) in September: likely to prove best around 1m: sold 23,000 gns, joined
E. Griffin in Ireland. *W. J. Haggas*

TOURMALET   3 b.f. Night Shift (USA) – Robsart (IRE) 91 (Robellino (USA) 127)   **84**
[2003 88: 7.6m 7m 7.1m 7m⁴ 8.1g⁴ 7m² 7m² 8d³ p7g⁵ 6g p6g⁶ f7g² 7s p8g² Dec 2] strong,
close-coupled filly: fairly useful handicapper: left A. Berry 14,000 gns after penultimate
start: stays 1m: acts on all-weather, good to firm and good to soft going: tried tongue tied/
blinkered (ran poorly): tends to hang/flash tail. *M. R. Channon*

TOUT LES SOUS   2 ch.g. (Apr 10) Tout Ensemble – Suzie Sue (IRE) (Ore 116) [2003   –
8.2d Nov 6] first known foal: dam no form: 100/1, last of 16 in maiden at Nottingham.
Jean-Rene Auvray

TOUT SEUL (IRE)   3 b.c. Ali-Royal (IRE) 127 – Total Aloof 72 (Groom Dancer   **115**
(USA) 126) [2003 121: 8g⁴ 8d³ 8f 8d⁶ 8f 8d⁵ Nov 30] smallish, leggy, quite good-topped
colt: smart performer: won Dewhurst Stakes at Newmarket at 2 yrs: creditable 1½ lengths
fourth of 20 to Refuse To Bend in 2000 Guineas at Newmarket on reappearance: bit
below that form after, including in Irish equivalent at the Curragh (3½ lengths third to
Indian Haven), St James's Palace Stakes at Royal Ascot (seventh to Zafeen on third
outing, reportedly returned lame behind, off 3½ months after) and in 2 races in Japan last
2 starts: stays 1m: acts on heavy and good to firm going: blinkered final outing: hung
markedly right fourth 2-y-o start. *R. F. Johnson Houghton*

TO WIT TO WOO   3 b.g. Efisio 120 – Sioux 76 (Kris 135) [2003 6g 7m⁴ 6g f8.5g   **70**
f9.4g* f12g⁴ Nov 21] good-bodied gelding: second foal: dam 1½m winner: best effort
(fair form) when winning maiden easily at Wolverhampton in November: stays 1½m:
acts on fibresand, raced only on good/good to firm ground on turf. *B. W. Hills*

TOWN CALLED MALICE (USA)   3 b.g. Mister Baileys 123 – Dubiously (USA)   **?**
(Jolie Jo (USA)) [2003 67, a77: p10g⁵ f8g² a8g⁵ a8g⁵ a12g² a8g a10.5g² a8g⁶ a10.5s*   **a77**
a10g⁴ Nov 30] quite good-topped gelding: fair performer: claimed from N. Littmoden
£11,000 after second in claimer at Southwell second start: won minor event at Mijas in
October by 6¼ lengths from Mejhar: seems to stay 1½m: acts on all-weather, sand, firm
and good to soft going. *C. Bjorling, Spain*

TOY SHOW (IRE)   3 b.f. Danehill (USA) 126 – March Hare 60 (Groom Dancer   **86 +**
(USA) 128) [2003 73: 9g 10f* 10g⁶ 10g⁵ 10m² 10s* 10m⁵ 9.5m Oct 11] small filly: useful
performer: won handicaps at Sandown in June and Lingfield (beat Dancing Forest a

length) in August: probably flattered when fifth of 7 to Napper Tandy in listed race at the Curragh next time: stays 1¼m: yet to race on heavy going, acts on any other. *R. Hannon*

TRACE CLIP   5 b.g. Zafonic (USA) 130 – Illusory 81 (Kings Lake (USA) 133) [2003   –
103: 5m 6g 6g 5d 5.2g 5d Nov 7] neat, quite attractive gelding: useful handicapper at 4 yrs: slowly away and always behind in 2003: tongue tied all starts at 3/4 yrs, and on penultimate outing: headstrong: has found little. *W. J. Musson*

TRADE FAIR   3 b.c. Zafonic (USA) 130 – Danefair 109 (Danehill (USA) 126)   **124**
[2003 114p: 7m* 7m* 8d⁶ 7m* 7m⁵ Oct 18]
‘Frustrating’ is not a word that often springs to mind to describe a very smart racehorse who won three of his five starts in his most recent campaign, but its use can be justified with Trade Fair. Trade Fair has raced in higher than Group 3 company three times—in the Dewhurst as a two-year-old, and at three in the Sussex Stakes at Goodwood and the Challenge Stakes at Newmarket—and each time he has started favourite and let his supporters down. Before the Dewhurst, Trade Fair won a maiden at Newbury in most striking style, shaping with a great deal of promise, while the form he showed as a three-year-old when winning the Betfair Criterion Stakes at Newmarket in June and the listed Dubai Duty Free Cup at Newbury in September was good enough to make him the form choice in both the Sussex and the Challenge. Heavily backed for the Two Thousand Guineas over the winter (he was as short as 6/1 second favourite in mid-April), Trade Fair didn’t give ante-post punters even a run for their money, forced to miss the race after returning from a piece of work with a broken blood vessel. While there is a strong suspicion that Trade Fair’s somewhat highly-strung nature may have played a part in his defeats, it is possible to advance plausible reasons as to why he was beaten. In the Dewhurst, Trade Fair might have lacked experience as much as anything, while at Goodwood he clearly failed to stay a mile on rain-softened ground, coming home a well-held sixth behind Reel Buddy. An explanation is not so readily available for Trade Fair’s effort in the Challenge Stakes, in which, after racing freely, he finished fifth to Just James, beaten just over a length and a half and not knocked about in the closing stages. Trade Fair’s performances in victory in the most recent season were in sharp contrast. After a comfortable success from Membership in the listed Cheveley Park Stud King Charles II Stakes at Newmarket in May on his reappearance, Trade Fair won the Criterion Stakes readily by four lengths from Just James. Trade Fair’s final listed success, when he beat Lago d’Orta by three lengths, was achieved just as comfortably, Trade Fair quickening right away when challenged and able to be eased close home.

		Zafonic (USA) (b 1990)	Gone West (b 1984)	Mr Prospector Secrettame
Trade Fair (b.c. 2000)			Zaizafon (ch 1982)	The Minstrel Mofida
		Danefair (b 1992)	Danehill (b 1986)	Danzig Razyana
			Roupala (b 1986)	Vaguely Noble Cairn Rouge

Trade Fair’s pedigree was detailed extensively in *Racehorses of 2002*, and there is little to add other than to note that his year-younger half-sister Well Known (by Sadler’s Wells) made a very promising debut to finish second in a Kempton minor event. Also, it is interesting to note that Trade Fair’s sire Zafonic (who

Betfair Criterion Stakes, Newmarket—
Trade Fair already has it well sewn up as Just James finishes with a flourish to take second

incidentally also suffered from broken blood vessels) has had his share of runners who have appeared less than straightforward. One notable example is Killer Instinct, a frustrating three-year-old in 1999 who was never able to live up to his exalted home reputation on the track. Trade Fair has demonstrated on the racecourse that he is a colt with plenty of ability, one certainly capable of winning a good race, but he will start his four-year-old campaign with something to prove. It may well be that the strong, good-bodied, attractive Trade Fair, whose best form is on going firmer than good (he was withdrawn from Doncaster's Park Stakes in September an hour before the start due to the softish ground), will benefit from a drop in trip. An edgy sort (he reportedly works alone at home) who has been last or early to post, Trade Fair has long shaped as if he will prove at least as effective at six furlongs as he is at seven. *R. Charlton*

TRAINED BYTHE BEST   5 b.m. Alderbrook 120 – Princess Moodyshoe 72 (Jalmood (USA) 126) [2003 86: 14m² 16.1m 15.9d 18m Oct 18] fairly useful handicapper: tailed off after reappearance: better at 2m/2¼m than shorter: acts on firm and good to soft going: visored/tongue tied nowadays: carries head high: held up: ungenuine. *M. C. Pipe*   **87 §**

TRANCE (IRE)   3 ch.g. Bahhare (USA) 128 – Lady of Dreams (IRE) 84 (Prince Rupert (FR) 121) [2003 70: 8d 8d² 8d 12g f8g* Dec 3] IR 37,000Y: fourth living foal: half-brother to 3 winners, including fairly useful Irish 2-y-o winners Huangdi (at 1m in 1999, by Catrail) and Urban Legend (at 7f in 2000, by Be My Guest): dam, 1¼m winner, out of half-sister to very smart miler Pennine Walk: fairly useful performer: left D. Weld in Ireland 8,500 gns/off 5 months, won maiden at Southwell in December by 6 lengths: stays 1m: acts on fibresand, raced only on good ground or softer on turf: blinkered (well beaten) third/fourth starts. *T. D. Barron*   **82**

TRANQUIL SKY   2 b.f. (Jan 31) Intikhab (USA) 135 – Tranquillity 70 (Night Shift (USA)) [2003 6m⁶ 6g³ 6m* 6f³ 7f* 7g Aug 2] 19,000Y: strong, lengthy filly: fourth foal: half-sister to 2-y-o 5f winners The Bull Macabe (in 1999, by Efisio, later sprint winner in Norway) and Quiescent (in 2000, by Primo Dominie), latter fairly useful winner: dam, 1m winner, out of half-sister to smart performers Lemon Souffle (up to 1m) and Caramba (up to 1¼m): fairly useful performer: won minor event at Goodwood in June and nursery at Brighton in July: edgy, not clear run final start: stays 7f: acts on firm going. *N. A. Callaghan*   **87**

TRANSCENDANTALE (FR)   5 b. or br.m. Apple Tree (FR) 126 – Kataba (FR) (Shardari 134) [2003 60: f8g f12s f8g f9.4s⁵ f8.5g⁶ 10g 9.9m² 10g 8m⁴ 8m⁵ 9f 12m 10.1g 10m Sep 9] smallish mare: modest handicapper on turf, poor on all-weather: stays 1¼m: acts on firm going, soft and fibresand: none too consistent. *Mrs S. Lamyman*   **54 a37**

TRANSIT   4 b.c. Lion Cavern (USA) 117 – Black Fighter (USA) 79 (Secretariat (USA)) [2003 82: f8g f9.4g 12.4m³ 9m Jul 6] tall, leggy colt: has a fluent, round action: fair maiden: seems to stay 1½m: acts on good to firm and heavy going: ran poorly in cheekpieces final start. *B. Ellison*   **72**

TRAVELLERS JOY   3 b.f. The West (USA) 107 – Persian Fortune 53 (Forzando 122) [2003 –: 5.7m³ 5.3d 5.1m² 5.7f 8f 6.1m 5.1m⁵ 5.1m⁶ 6f⁶ 6m Aug 20] modest maiden: best at 5f/6f (raced too freely at 1m): acts on firm ground. *R. J. Hodges*   **53**

TRAVELLER'S TALE   4 b.g. Selkirk (USA) 129 – Chere Amie (USA) 75 (Mr Prospector (USA)) [2003 79: 10m⁴ 10m³ 10m 10s³ f9.4g⁴ Dec 26] leggy, useful-looking gelding: fair handicapper: left P. Harris 10,000 gns then below form on all-weather debut: best form around 1¼m: acts on firm and soft going: sometimes hangs left: usually waited with. *P. G. Murphy*   **79**

TRAVELLING BAND (IRE)   5 b.g. Blues Traveller (IRE) 119 – Kind of Cute 52 (Prince Sabo 123) [2003 92: f8.5g 8g 10d² 10.1d⁴ Jul 3] leggy, quite attractive gelding: fairly useful performer, lightly raced: stays 1¼m: raced mainly on good going or softer (acts on heavy), well held on fibresand. *A. M. Balding*   **85**

TRAVELLING TIMES   4 ch.g. Timeless Times (USA) 99 – Bollin Sophie (Efisio 120) [2003 82: 6g 7f 6d 5m 7g 6m 5.9f 6g⁴ 6m² 7m f6s⁵ 6m 6g f6g⁴ f7g³ f6g² f6g f7g Dec 16] strong, lengthy gelding: modest nowadays: seems best at 6f: acts on fibresand and firm going, possibly not on softer than good: best form when blinkered/visored: none too consistent. *J. S. Wainwright*   **63**

TRAVEL TARDIA (IRE)   5 br.h. Petardia 113 – Annie's Travels (IRE) (Mac's Imp (USA) 116) [2003 –, a88d: 7m p7g p10g Dec 20] sturdy horse: fairly useful performer: on downgrade since 4-y-o reappearance. *I. A. Wood*   **–**

TRAWLERS 3 b.f. Polish Precedent (USA) 131 – My Preference (Reference Point – 139) [2003 10g⁶ 8f 7.1m Jun 21] 1,200Y: third foal: dam unraced half-sister to very smart 1989 2-y-o Be My Chief: well held in maidens, leaving E. O'Neill £1,000 after debut. *A. J. Chamberlain*

TRAYTONIC 2 b.c. (Mar 20) Botanic (USA) – Lady Parker (IRE) (Nordico (USA)) **101** [2003 5g* 6m³ 5.2g* 5m² 5m⁴ 7.1d 6m⁴ 6f* 6m Oct 25] leggy colt: third foal: dam unraced: useful performer: won seller at Doncaster (sold from W. Turner 17,000 gns) in March, minor event at Yarmouth in July and nursery at York (beat Jazz Scene by length) in October: well held in listed event final start, racing freely: effective at 5f/6f: acts on firm ground. *H. J. Cyzer*

TREASON TRIAL 2 b.g. (Feb 22) Peintre Celebre (USA) 137 – Pampabella (IRE) **70 p** (High Estate 127) [2003 7m⁴ 8s Oct 29] 25,000F, €75,000Y: second foal: dam, German 1¼m winner, half-sister to smart performer up to 1½m Noble Patriarch: better effort in maidens (fair form) when never-nearer fourth at Doncaster: still in need of race and went freely at Yarmouth: should be suited by 1¼m/1½m: open to progress. *J. R. Fanshawe*

TREASURE CAY 2 ch.c. (Apr 10) Bahamian Bounty 116 – Madame Sisu 47 (Emarati **78 p** (USA) 74) [2003 p5g* Dec 10] 6,000Y, resold 12,000Y: first foal: dam, ran twice, out of half-sister to high-class 1m to 1¼m performer Bijou d'Inde: 20/1 and wearing eyeshields, won minor event at Lingfield cosily by ½ length from Oro Verde, quickening well to lead final 1f: open to improvement. *P. W. D'Arcy*

TREASURE HOUSE (IRE) 2 b.c. (Jan 19) Grand Lodge (USA) 125 – Royal Wolff **100** (Prince Tenderfoot (USA) 126) [2003 6g⁴ 6m² 6m² 6f* 6m Sep 19] IR 28,000F, €150,000Y: well-made colt: half-brother to numerous winners, including 5-y-o Chookie Heiton and useful 1998 2-y-o 5.7f winner She-Wolff (by Pips Pride): dam Irish sprinter: won 4-runner maiden at Brighton in August: easily best effort (useful form) when nearly 4 lengths seventh of 10 to Byron in Mill Reef Stakes at Newbury, weakening late on: shapes as if will prove best at 5f/6f: races prominently. *B. J. Meehan*

TREASURE TRAIL 4 b.g. Millkom 124 – Forever Shineing 62 (Glint of Gold 128) **85** [2003 91: 11.9m 13.3m³ 12d² 14g 13.3m⁶ 13.9m 14d p13g Dec 29] good-bodied gelding: fairly useful handicapper: below form after fourth start: effective at 1½m/2m: acts on good to firm and good to soft going. *S. Kirk*

TREATY OF UTRECHT (IRE) 3 b.g. College Chapel 122 – Next Round (IRE) – 83 (Common Grounds 118) [2003 80, a71: 6d 8d 7f 5m 5.9m Jun 25] fair at best at 2 yrs: well beaten in 2003: wore cheekpieces penultimate start: has raced freely/hung right. *I. Semple*

TREBLE HEIGHTS (IRE) 4 b.f. Unfuwain (USA) 131 – Height of Passion (Shirley **106** Heights 130) [2003 107p: 11.9g⁴ 12m* 13.5g² 14.6d⁵ Sep 10] lengthy, attractive filly: useful performer: won listed event at Newmarket in July by head from New Orchid: creditable 6 lengths second to Vallee Enchantee in Prix de Pomone at Deauville next time, making most: stays 1¾m: acts on good to firm ground, below form on good to soft final outing. *J. H. M. Gosden*

TREBLE TRIGGER 3 ch.f. Double Trigger (IRE) 123 – Fresh Lady (IRE) (Fresh – Breeze (USA) 80) [2003 8g 10g p12g Jun 21] second foal: dam poor maiden over jumps: soundly beaten in maiden/sellers. *W. G. M. Turner*

TRE COLLINE 4 b.g. Efisio 120 – Triple Joy 104 (Most Welcome 131) [2003 76: 6g **82** 7g 7m* 7m⁶ 7m³ 6g² 6g Jul 31] robust gelding: fairly useful performer: won handicap at Doncaster in June: good placed efforts on same course: effective at 6f/7f: acts on good to firm ground and fibresand: sold 10,500 gns. *C. F. Wall*

TRECULIAR (USA) 3 b.c. Trempolino (USA) 135 – Lady Peculiar (CAN) (Sunshine **91** Forever (USA)) [2003 80p: 10m 10g⁴ 12.6m² 14g 10m³ 12.6m³ 12g² 14m* 16g* 12m⁵ Oct 16] good-topped colt: fairly useful handicapper: won twice at Musselburgh in September: stays easy 2m: acts on polytrack, raced only on good/good to firm ground on turf: tried in headgear: usually held up: sold 50,000 gns. *G. A. Butler*

TREE CHOPPER (USA) 2 ch.f. (Mar 21) Woodman (USA) 126 – Gazayil (USA) **79 p** 80 (Irish River (FR) 131) [2003 8f* Oct 12] half-sister to several winners, including 6-y-o Mubtaker and useful Irish 1998 2-y-o 7f winner Crystal Downs (by Alleged): dam, 2-y-o 7f winner (later successful in Australia), half-sister to smart 1¼m winner Husyan: 3/1 and tongue tied, won 7-runner maiden at Bath by 2 lengths from Kabis Booie, quickening readily over 1f out: should stay 1¼m: will improve. *M. P. Tregoning*

TREE PEONY 3 ch.f. Woodman (USA) 126 – Pivoine (USA) (Nureyev (USA) 131) **79** [2003 63p: 7m³ 8.1g⁶ 8g⁶ Jul 24] rangy, rather unfurnished filly: has scope: fair performer: won maiden at Newbury in June: good sixth in handicap at Haydock next time: below form/tended to hang final outing: stays 1m: raced only on good/good to firm ground: carries head high. *R. Charlton*

TREE ROOFER 4 b.g. King's Signet (USA) 110 – Armaiti 78 (Sayf El Arab (USA) 127) [2003 51, a57: f5g⁴ p6g f5g² f6g p6g⁵ f5g³ f5s⁵ 6f 6m⁴ 5f Aug 27] modest maiden: left J. S. Moore after second outing: best at 5f/6f: acts on all-weather and good to firm ground: sometimes wears headgear. *N. P. Littmoden* **50 a57**

TREETOPS HOTEL (IRE) 4 ch.g. Grand Lodge (USA) 125 – Rousinette (Rousillon (USA) 133) [2003 90: p7g p8g p8g 8.3g 6m 7g 8.3m 11.6g p7g Dec 30] quite attractive gelding: fairly useful handicapper at 3 yrs: well held after leaving Mrs A. Perrett 24,000 gns second start in 2003: tried in cheekpieces. *B. R. Johnson* **86 d**

TREGARRON 2 br.c. (Apr 17) Efisio 120 – Language of Love 63 (Rock City 120) [2003 5.2m 5m⁴ 5m 5m² 6m⁴ 6d² 6d⁶ 5d 6g f6g Nov 10] leggy colt: first foal: dam, lightly-raced maiden, sister to smart 6f/7f performer Tomba and half-sister to Prix du Jockey Club winner Holding Court: fair maiden: second twice at Haydock, seeming to run very well on second occasion: below form in nurseries after: stays 6f: acts on good to firm and good to soft going: often slowly away. *R. Hannon* **68**

TRENCH COAT (USA) 2 ch.c. (Mar 19) Gulch (USA) – Glamor Queen (USA) (Prized (USA)) [2003 5.7f² 6d⁵ p7g³ Oct 15] workmanlike colt: first foal: dam, runner-up in USA at 2 yrs only start, half-sister to US Grade 2 9f winner Class Kris: fair form in maidens: second (in match) at Bath and third at Lingfield (best effort): stays 7f. *A. M. Balding* **72**

TREVIAN 2 ch.g. (Mar 18) Atraf 116 – Ascend (IRE) (Glint of Gold 128) [2003 6m 6m⁵ 6m⁶ Sep 23] 2,500Y: big gelding: fifth living foal: half-brother to 1¼m/1½m winner Elms Schoolgirl (by Emarati): dam unraced: fair form in maidens: strong-finishing sixth at Newmarket: should stay at least 1m: type to do better as 3-y-o. *S. C. Williams* **70 p**

TREVORS SPREE 4 ch.g. Dancing Spree (USA) – Trevorsninepoints 71 (Jester 119) [2003 53: 6m 7m f7g 6m 8.1m 8.1m Jul 11] leggy, workmanlike gelding: maiden: well held in 2003: tried visored/in cheekpieces. *Mrs Lydia Pearce* **–**

TRIBALINNA (IRE) 2 b.f. (Apr 30) Indian Rocket 115 – Cappuchino (IRE) 59 (Roi Danzig (USA)) [2003 5f 5m⁵ 6m 5g Oct 28] 6,000 2-y-o: stocky filly: sixth foal: half-sister to useful 1999 2-y-o 7f winner Blue Bolivar (by Blues Traveller) and 5f winner Cayman Expresso (by Fayruz): dam 7f winner: well held in maidens. *I. Semple* **–**

TRIBAL PRINCE 6 b.g. Prince Sabo 123 – Tshusick 81 (Dancing Brave (USA) 140) [2003 86: 7m⁴ 8m 7m 7m 7.6g⁵ 7g³ 7m³ 7m³ 7m* 7m⁵ 7m Oct 12] sturdy gelding: fairly useful handicapper: won at Kempton in August: was effective at 7f to 8.5f: acted on polytrack, best turf form on good going or firmer: visored once at 2 yrs, sometimes wore cheekpieces: sometimes started slowly/looked tricky ride: dead. *P. W. Harris* **82**

TRIBUTE (IRE) 2 b.g. (Jan 26) Green Desert (USA) 127 – Zooming (IRE) (Indian Ridge 123) [2003 5m⁶ 6m³ 6g² 6g⁶ 5m* Aug 20] 380,000Y: quite attractive gelding: first foal: dam, maiden, half-sister to 4-y-o Zipping out of half-sister to top-class sprinter/miler Last Tycoon: fairly useful performer: good second in maiden at Lingfield: landed odds in similar event there by 2 lengths from Green Manalishi: free-going sort, and will probably prove best at 5f/6f: sometimes early to post. *D. R. Loder* **87**

TRICK CYCLIST 2 b.c. (May 4) Mind Games 121 – Sabonis (USA) 68 (The Minstrel (CAN) 135) [2003 5.1m³ 5m² 5.1g* 5f 5.2m 6d 6m² 6d p6g Oct 8] 8,000Y: leggy colt: half-brother to 1997 2-y-o 1m winner Premium Quest (by Forzando) and fairly useful 2000 2-y-o 5f winner Stregone (by Namaqualand): dam 2-y-o 6f winner: fairly useful performer: won minor event at Bath in May: second in nursery at Ayr in September: ran poorly last 2 starts: stays 6f: acts on good to firm and good to soft going: visored (slowly away but ran creditably) fifth outing. *A. M. Balding* **81**

TRICKY LADY (IRE) 4 b.f. Persian Bold 123 – Tropicana (IRE) (Imperial Frontier (USA) 112) [2003 51: p10g f8.5g⁵ p7g 7f f8.5g May 19] smallish, leggy filly: maiden: little form in 2003, leaving J. S. Moore after fourth start: tried blinkered/tongue tied. *Miss K. M. George* **–**

TRICKY VENTURE 3 gr.g. Linamix (FR) 127 – Ukraine Venture 96 (Slip Anchor 136) [2003 p10g⁵ f9.4s⁴ 7m 8m⁴ f8.5g⁵ 9.9m² Aug 24] leggy gelding: second foal: half-brother to 4-y-o Indian Steppes: dam, 1¼m winner, granddaughter of Poule d'Essai des Pouliches winner Ukraine Girl: fair maiden: left R. Charlton after third start: clearly best effort when second at Beverley final outing: will stay 1½m: raced solely on good to firm ground on turf. *P. W. Hiatt* **71**

TRIGGER MEAD 3 b.f. Double Trigger (IRE) 123 – Normead Lass 36 (Norwick **50** (USA) 125) [2003 10m 13.8m⁴ 10.5m³ 9.9m Aug 23] workmanlike filly: second foal: dam maiden, including over jumps: only form (modest) when third in maiden at Haydock: will be suited by return to further than 1¼m: raced only on good to firm ground. *M. Johnston*

TRILEMMA 2 b.f. (May 26) Slip Anchor 136 – Thracian 92 (Green Desert (USA) **59 p** 127) [2003 f8s 8.1g 7.1m 7.2d⁶ Oct 13] 50,000Y: fourth foal: half-sister to fairly useful 2001 2-y-o 7f winner Thrasher (by Hector Protector) and a winner in Japan by Zafonic: dam, 2-y-o 6f/7f winner, half-sister to Ribblesdale winner Third Watch (by Slip Anchor): modest form in maidens: should do better as 3-y-o at 1¼m+. *Sir Mark Prescott*

TRINAREE (IRE) 2 b.g. (Mar 23) Revoque (IRE) 122 – Ball Cat (FR) (Cricket Ball **–** (USA) 124) [2003 7s Oct 29] €600Y: fourth foal: half-brother to 2 winners abroad, including French 1½m winner Aldiruos (by Bigstone): dam winner in Belgium: 66/1, led long way when tailed off in maiden at Yarmouth. *S. Gollings*

TRINCULO (IRE) 6 b.g. Anita's Prince 126 – Fandangerina (USA) (Grey Dawn II **99** 132) [2003 6m 6m 5g 5.1m 5m 6m⁶ 5.7m⁶ 6g³ 5d² 5d 5m 5m f5g* f5g⁶ p6g Dec 20] tall, rather leggy gelding: has a long, round action: useful handicapper: raced in Hong Kong under name of Cliffhanger in 2001/2: won at Southwell in November by head from Quito: effective at 5f/6f: acts on fibresand, firm and soft going: tried in blinkers/cheekpieces: has had 2 handlers/been early to post: often forces pace. *N. P. Littmoden*

TRINITY (IRE) 7 b.h. College Chapel 122 – Kaskazi (Dancing Brave (USA) 140) **57** [2003 –: 6m 5.9g 5g 6d⁴ 6g Oct 14] close-coupled horse: modest handicapper nowadays: effective at 5f/6f: acts on firm and good to soft going: has worn tongue tie: sometimes finds little: none too consistent. *M. Brittain*

TRIPLE ACT (USA) 3 b.f. Theatrical 128 – Multiply (USA) (Easy Goer (USA)) **66 +** [2003 7m Apr 11] $2,200,000Y: leggy, quite attractive filly: fourth foal: half-sister to smart US Grade 2 1m winner Desert Hero (by Sea Hero): dam unraced out of half-sister to Grand Criterium winner Jade Robbery: 7/2, 6 lengths seventh of 15 to Salagama in newcomers race at Newbury, not punished after travelling well 4f: on toes and swished tail in paddock: sent to Ireland, joined E. Harty. *D. R. Loder*

TRIPLE JUMP 2 ch.g. (Mar 1) Inchinor 119 – Meteoric 102 (High Line 125) [2003 **–** 7f⁴ Oct 9] 44,000Y: angular, useful-looking gelding: half-brother to several winners, including 1¼m/1½m winner Meteor Strike (by Lomond) and to dam of smart 1998 2-y-o 7f winner Auction House: dam, 6f winner, including at 2 yrs: 9/2, tongue tied and green, tailed off in minor event at York. *M. P. Tregoning*

TRIPLEMOON (USA) 4 ch.f. Trempolino (USA) 135 – Placer Queen (Habitat 134) **68** [2003 77: 12m⁴ 14.1g⁶ 14m 13.3m⁵ 16g³ 14.4f⁵ 16g⁶ 14.1m⁴ 14.1m* 14.1m* 14.1m* 16m Oct 28] rather leggy filly: fair handicapper: completed hat-trick at Redcar in September/October: will probably stay 2m: acts on firm and soft going: usually tracks leaders: sold 6,500 gns. *P. W. Harris*

TRIPLE PLAY (IRE) 4 br.g. Tagula (IRE) 116 – Shiyra (Darshaan 133) [2003 –: 8m **–** 8g 8f 8.5d 8g 7m 8m 8.5m 8.1m 8g⁶ Aug 26] rather leggy gelding: little form since 2 yrs: tried blinkered/visored. *Don Enrico Incisa*

TRIPTI (IRE) 3 b.f. Sesaro (USA) 81 – Chatelsong (USA) (Seattle Song (USA) 130) **72 d** [2003 67: p5g⁶ 5f³ 5.3m* 5.3d⁶ 5.1g⁵ 5m³ 6g 5.1m 5m⁶ 5f 5m⁶ 6g 5.7f⁴ p6g p6g⁶ Dec 30] angular filly: fair performer: won handicap at Brighton in May: below form after sixth start, leaving D. Arbuthnot 5,000 gns before penultimate one: best at 5f: acts on polytrack and firm going: tried in cheekpieces/blinkers. *J. J. Bridger*

TRISHAY 2 gr.f. (Feb 13) Petong 126 – Marjorie's Memory (IRE) 76 (Fairy King **56** (USA)) [2003 6d 6m⁴ f5g² 6m⁶ 5.1f⁵ Sep 8] 13,000Y: fourth foal: sister to 3 winners, including fairly useful 2001 2-y-o 5f winner Keep The Silver and 5-y-o Pay The Silver: dam 5f winner, including at 2 yrs: modest maiden: effective at 5f/6f: acts on good to firm going and fibresand: sometimes starts slowly/carries head high. *A. P. Jarvis*

TRIUMPH OF DUBAI (IRE) 3 b.g. Eagle Eyed (USA) 111 – Jack-N-Jilly (IRE) **59 d** 43 (Anita's Prince 126) [2003 49: p7g 7m³ 10.2m 6f 7.1m 8.2m Oct 22] modest maiden: disappointing after reappearance: stays easy 7f: acts on polytrack, soft and good to firm going: tried in cheekpieces. *J. S. Moore*

TRIWAN 3 b.g. Nashwan (USA) 135 – Triple Joy 104 (Most Welcome 131) [2003 60: **58** f7g⁵ Jan 13] good-topped, quite attractive gelding: modest maiden: best efforts at 7f: acted on fibresand: dead. *Sir Mark Prescott*

TROFANA FALCON 3 b.g. Polar Falcon (USA) 126 – Silk St James (Pas de Seul –
133) [2003 f8g f8g Dec 9] half-brother to several winners, including useful miler Silk St
John (by Damister) and fairly useful 1m to 1¼m winner Lady Rockstar (by Rock
Hopper): dam unraced: well held in maidens at Southwell. *H. J. Collingridge*

TROIS ETOILES (IRE) 2 ch.f. (Apr 1) Grand Lodge (USA) 125 – Stardance –
(USA) (Rahy (USA) 115) [2003 p7g 7g Nov 1] workmanlike filly: first foal: dam unraced
half-sister to smart French performers around 1m/1¼m Drapeau Tricolore and Dam-
pierre: green, well held in maidens at Lingfield and Newmarket. *J. W. Hills*

TROJAN FLIGHT 2 b.g. (Mar 8) Hector Protector (USA) 124 – Fairywings 85 **70**
(Kris 135) [2003 5d 5m 6g Jul 31] good-topped gelding: second foal: dam 1¼m winner:
best effort in maidens (fair form) when seventh at Newcastle final start, first home stand
side: should stay at least 1m. *Mrs J. R. Ramsden*

TROJAN (IRE) 4 ch.g. Up And At 'em 109 – Fantasise (FR) (General Assembly –
(USA)) [2003 72: 8.3g Jun 11] lightly-raced maiden: well held only outing in 2003
(blinkered): has flashed tail/carried head high/hung right. *J. G. Given*

TROJAN WOLF 8 ch.g. Wolfhound (USA) 126 – Trojan Lady (USA) (Irish River – §
(FR) 131) [2003 –§, a65¾: f8s f11s² f9.4g f12s⁴ f12s p12g f12g f11g Jun 19] strong **a56 d**
gelding: modest performer: ran creditably in 2003 only on fourth start: best at 1m to 1½m:
acts on firm going, soft and fibresand: tried visored/tongue tied earlier in career: usually
races up with pace: moody and unreliable. *P. Howling*

TROMPE L'OEIL (IRE) 2 b.f. (Feb 25) Distant View (USA) 126 – Milly Ha Ha **63**
106 (Dancing Brave (USA) 140) [2003 6m⁴ 6d 7f⁵ 8m p10g² f8g⁴ f8g Dec 19] leggy filly:
sixth foal: closely related to fairly useful 1¼m winner Laughing Girl (by Woodman) and
half-sister to useful 11f winner Jolly Sharp (by Diesis): dam, 1¼m winner who stayed
1¾m, half-sister to 5-y-o Bosham Mill: modest maiden: second at Lingfield: should
stay 1½m: acts on all-weather, probably on good to firm going: often races prominently.
E. A. L. Dunlop

TROODOS JET 2 b.g. (Apr 30) Atraf 116 – Costa Verde 77 (King of Spain 121) **64**
[2003 5s² 5m⁴ 6m⁶ 6.1d⁴ Nov 6] 10,000 2-y-o: big, good-topped gelding: fourth foal:
half-brother to useful 2002 2-y-o 5f winner Tilak (by Tagula) and 1998 2-y-o 6f winner
Isle of Sodor (by Cyrano de Bergerac): dam 2-y-o 7.5f winner: modest maiden: second at
Haydock: swerved leaving stall next 2 starts: stays 6f: best efforts on going softer than
good. *A. Berry*

TROPICAL CORAL (IRE) 3 ch.f. Pennekamp (USA) 130 – Tropical Dance **82**
(USA) 93 (Thorn Dance (USA) 107) [2003 74: f9.4g* 8f* 8m* 8g 9f⁵ 10m⁵ 8.5m 9m*
8m⁴ 10g⁵ p10g p8g⁴ f8s⁵ p10g² Dec 29] sturdy filly: fairly useful performer: won maiden
at Wolverhampton in January and handicaps at Bath (hung left) in March, Leicester in
April and Kempton in August: left A. Lidderdale after eleventh start: stays 1¼m: acts on
all-weather and firm going: sometimes races freely. *C. Tinkler*

TROPICAL SON 4 b.g. Distant Relative 128 – Douce Maison (IRE) 67 (Fools **52**
Holme (USA)) [2003 68: f14.8s 10m 14.1m 9.2g f12g 8m p10g² 12g f8.5s³ 8m f7s 10d
f8s f8g Dec 19] well-made gelding: just modest maiden nowadays: best at 1¼m/1½m:
acts on all-weather, little form on turf in 2003: visored. *D. Shaw*

TROPICAL STORM (IRE) 2 ch.g. (Apr 11) Alhaarth (IRE) 126 – Rainstone 57 **70**
(Rainbow Quest (USA) 134) [2003 6d² 6g⁴ Oct 22] £180,000Y: rather leggy gelding:
half-brother to several winners, including useful 1998 2-y-o 5f/6f winner Gipsy Rose
Lee (by Marju) and 1m winner Yajtahed (by Mujtahid): dam, placed both starts at 2 yrs
(later won in Belgium), half-sister to smart 1991 2-y-o sprinter Magic Ring: fair form in
maidens at Haydock (short-headed by The Jobber after slow start) and Newcastle (carried
head awkwardly): should stay at least 7f. *J. Noseda*

TROTTERS BOTTOM 2 b.g. (May 5) Mind Games 121 – Fleeting Affair 98 **82**
(Hotfoot 126) [2003 5d 7g 5m³ 6g* 6g 6m² 6m p6g⁶ 6.1m³ p5g² p5g⁶ Dec 10] 4,500Y:
quite good-topped gelding: half-brother to numerous winners, including useful 1¼m/
1½m winner Infatuation (by Music Boy): dam, 1¼m/1½m winner, stayed 2m: fairly
useful performer: made all in maiden at Lingfield in July: second in nursery/minor event
after: best at 5f/6f: acts on polytrack and good to firm going: often bandaged: unruly at
start/withdrawn second intended outing. *Andrew Reid*

TROUBADOUR (IRE) 2 b.c. (May 3) Danehill (USA) 126 – Taking Liberties (IRE) **114**
57 (Royal Academy (USA) 130) [2003 6f* 6m³ 7m⁵ Oct 18] big, rangy colt: has badly
scarred near hip/quarter/knee: fourth foal: half-brother to 3 winners, including 5-y-o
Saponi and fairly useful French 7f/1m (latter at 2 yrs) winner Tosca's Impulse (both by

Indian Ridge): dam, ran once, sister to smart 1996 2-y-o 7f/1m winner Equal Rights out of Australian Group 1 1½m winner Lady Liberty: won maiden at the Curragh in August: third to Wathab in listed race on same course: 40/1 and gone in coat, smart form when 2 lengths fifth of 12 to Milk It Mick in Dewhurst Stakes at Newmarket, helping make running: should be suited by 1m. *A. P. O'Brien, Ireland*

TROUBLE AT BAY (IRE)   3 b.g. Slip Anchor 136 – Fight Right (FR) (Crystal   **98** Glitters (USA) 127) [2003 74: 10m² 10.2m 12m² 12m* 12f³ 14g 12m* 12g⁴ Sep 13] quite good-topped gelding: useful handicapper: won at Newbury in June and Ascot (beat Briareus 2 lengths) in August: probably better at 1½m than 1¾m: acts on polytrack and firm ground: usually held up: reliable: useful juvenile hurdler. *A. King*

TROUBLEINPARADISE (IRE)   2 b.f. (Jan 31) Pursuit of Love 124 – Sweet   **59** Holland (USA) (Alydar (USA)) [2003 6g 7m³ 7.1m⁵ Jul 31] €21,000Y: fifth foal: sister to French 1m winner Aventurine and half-sister to 3 winners, including 1¼m/1½m winner Chalcedony (by Highest Honor) and useful German performer up to 1¼m Calcio (by Polar Falcon): dam ran 3 times in France: best effort in maidens (modest form) when third at Redcar: will stay 1m. *J. G. Given*

TROUBLE MOUNTAIN (USA)   6 br.g. Mt Livermore (USA) – Trouble Free   **80** (USA) (Nodouble (USA)) [2003 83: 10.1d 9.9f* 12g² 11.9m 12m⁵ 9.9d 10.4f 9.9m³ 10.3m 10.5m 11.9m 10.3d⁵ 10.4f⁴ 12m⁴ f11g f11g² f12s³ Dec 27] small, sparely-made gelding: good mover: has a quick action: fairly useful handicapper: won at Beverley in April: effective at 1¼m/1½m: acts on fibresand, firm and good to soft going: blinkered occasionally: has worn stick-on shoes in front: consistent. *M. W. Easterby*

TROUSERS   4 b.g. Pivotal 124 – Palo Blanco 82 (Precocious 126) [2003 –: 7m p8g³   **81** 9g² p8g* p7g³ p8g⁶ Dec 2] fairly useful performer: won maiden at Lingfield in October: at least as effective at 7f as 1m: acts on polytrack. *Andrew Reid*

TRUE COMPANION   4 b.g. Brief Truce (USA) 126 – Comanche Companion 88   **72** (Commanche Run 133) [2003 74, a67: p10g⁵ p8g⁵ 11.9m 10.1m 10.1m⁴ 12.1m⁶ 9g* 10s⁵ p10g³ p10g³ Dec 10] fair handicapper: won at Newbury (apprentices) in October: stays 1¼m: acts on polytrack, soft and good to firm going: free-going sort: has idled/wandered markedly under pressure. *N. P. Littmoden*

TRUE HOLLY   3 b.f. Bishop of Cashel 122 – Polly's Teahouse 68 (Shack (USA) 118)   **–** [2003 44: 5.9m 5m 7m 6.1m Sep 19] good-topped filly: little form at 3 yrs: blinkered last 2 starts. *J. D. Bethell*

TRUE (IRE)   2 ch.f. (Mar 29) Barathea (IRE) 127 – Bibliotheque (USA) 79 (Woodman   **72** (USA) 126) [2003 6m⁴ 7m³ Aug 9] lengthy filly: third foal: sister to 3-y-o McQueen: dam, 1m winner, out of half-sister to very smart 6f to 1m performer Lycius: fair form in maidens at Newmarket (raced freely) and Redcar: should stay 1m. *Sir Michael Stoute*

TRUE MAGIC   2 b.f. (Apr 19) Magic Ring (IRE) 115 – True Precision 84 (Presidium   **59** 124) [2003 5g³ 6m³ 6.5m 5g⁶ Oct 28] 4,800Y: compact filly: fifth foal: sister to 7-y-o Foreign Editor and half-sister to 3 winners, including 3-y-o Pivotal Point: dam 5f to 7f winner: modest maiden: third at Ripon and Catterick: should stay 7f. *J. D. Bethell*

TRUE NIGHT   6 b.g. Night Shift (USA) – Dead Certain 123§ (Absalom 128) [2003   **93** 93: 6g 6d 7g 7f 7m 6f 6m³ 8m 7f 7.2g⁶ 8d³ 8d⁴ 7.6m² 7.6m* 8m⁵ Sep 20] smallish, attractive gelding: fairly useful handicapper: won at Chester (for second successive year) in August: effective at 6f to 1m: acts on firm and good to soft going: sometimes races freely: tough. *D. Nicholls*

TRUENO (IRE)   4 b.g. Desert King (IRE) 129 – Stitching (IRE) 50 (High Estate 127)   **89** [2003 12m² 12d⁵ 14.8m² 13.9m⁴ Sep 7] 54,000F: leggy, quite good-topped gelding: first living foal: dam, Irish maiden, half-sister to very smart 1m/1¼m performer Great Dane from family of Sleepytime and Croco Rouge: fairly useful performer: won minor event for C. Laffon-Parrias at Aix-Les-Bains in France in 2002: best effort in 2003 when second in handicap at Newmarket penultimate start: stays 15f: acts on good to firm and good to soft going: races prominently (too free final outing). *L. M. Cumani*

TRUE PATRIOT   2 b.c. (Feb 28) Rainbow Quest (USA) 134 – High Standard 83   **–** (Kris 135) [2003 7m 7m 8m Sep 25] lengthy, good-topped colt: fifth foal: brother to smart 1½m winner Al Moulatham, closely related to 3-y-o Clever Clogs and half-brother to fairly useful 7f (at 2 yrs) to 1½m winner Summer Song (by Green Desert): dam, 2-y-o 1m winner who stayed 1½m, out of close relative to Nureyev and half-sister to dam of Sadler's Wells: well beaten in maidens: awkward stall first 2 starts, visored second one: sold 10,000 gns. *E. A. L. Dunlop*

TRUE THUNDER   6 b.g. Bigstone (IRE) 126 – Puget Dancer (USA) 62 (Seattle **76** Dancer (USA) 119) [2003 92: p10g f8.5g 11.6g 10d⁶ 10d⁶ 10.3m 9.9m⁴ 10.1m 10.3m 10m Aug 9] leggy gelding: fair handicapper: should stay 1½m: acts on firm and good to soft ground: tongue tied last 2 starts: reared up as stall opened sixth outing, finished lame on eighth. *Julian Poulton*

TRUE TO YOURSELF (USA)   2 b.g. (Apr 18) Royal Academy (USA) 130 –   **–** Romilly (Machiavellian (USA) 123) [2003 f7s Oct 21] $6,000Y, 3,000 2-y-o: well-grown, useful-looking gelding: second foal: dam unraced half-sister to smart French 1¼m to 13f winner Lycitus from excellent family: well held in maidens: left M. Chapman after debut. *J. G. Given*

TRULLITTI (IRE)   2 b.f. (May 24) Bahri (USA) 125 – Penza 79 (Soviet Star (USA) **71 p** 128) [2003 7f⁶ 7m⁵ Oct 4] quite attractive filly: second known foal: dam, ran twice, half-sister to high-class performer up to 1½m White Muzzle and useful dam of very smart 1¼m performer Almutawakel: fair form in maidens at Salisbury (shaped well) and Redcar (fifth to Antediluvian): will be suited by at least 1m: should do better. *J. L. Dunlop*

TRULY WONDERFUL (IRE)   2 ch.f. (Apr 17) Highest Honor (FR) 124 – Ahliyat **76** (USA) 55 (Irish River (FR) 131) [2003 7f⁶ 5m² 5m* 7g 6g⁵ 6.1m³ 5.9m⁴ 6.1m⁴ 5.7f² 6.1m² 6m⁴ p6g⁵ 7f Oct 12] €35,000Y: tall filly: third foal: half-sister to fairly useful Irish 1½m winner Allude (by Darshaan): dam, 8.5f winner, half-sister to smart 1½m/1¾m winner Artillery out of half-sister to disqualified Oaks winner Aliysa: fair performer: won maiden at Sandown in July: mostly creditable efforts in nurseries after: fell early at Goodwood final start: stays 7f: acts on polytrack and firm ground. *M. R. Channon*

TRUMAN   2 b.c. (Apr 30) Entrepreneur 123 – Sabria (USA) (Miswaki (USA) 124)   **– p** [2003 6m⁵ Sep 18] fifth foal: half-brother to 4 winners, notably high-class 6f (at 2 yrs) to 1m (including Poule d'Essai des Poulains) winner Landseer (by Danehill) and 3-y-o Ikhtyar: dam unraced half-sister to smart middle-distance performer King Sound: 20/1, fifth of 6 to Peak To Creek in minor event at Yarmouth, soon outpaced and not knocked about: should stay at least 1m: likely to do better. *J. A. R. Toller*

TRUSTED MOLE (IRE)   5 b.g. Eagle Eyed (USA) 111 – Orient Air 74 (Prince Sabo **61** 123) [2003 57§: 12.3m³ 10m⁵ 12m⁵ 14m³ 12f⁵ 12.6m³ Jun 22] deep-girthed gelding: modest handicapper: won at Ripon in April: stays easy 1¾m: acts on firm going, good to soft and polytrack (no form on fibresand): often blinkered prior to 2003: formerly unreliable. *W. M. Brisbourne*

TRUST RULE   3 b.c. Selkirk (USA) 129 – Hagwah (USA) 109 (Dancing Brave **108 p** (USA) 140) [2003 65p: p10g² 10.3g² 12.3m³ 11.9m² 10m* 10m 12d³ 11.9m² 11.9m* 12f 12m² Oct 16] big, quite good-topped colt: useful form: won maiden at Windsor in June and handicap at York (beat Starry Lodge 3 lengths) in September: didn't get clear run next time, then good 1½ lengths second to Dawn Invasion in handicap at Newmarket final outing: stays 1½m: acts on good to firm and good to soft ground: has carried head high/wandered: held up: reliable: looks the type to make an even better 4-y-o. *B. W. Hills*

TRYFAN   4 b.g. Distant Relative 128 – Sister Sal 74 (Bairn (USA) 126) [2003 –: f8.5g   **–** f7g⁶ Feb 14] little solid form: tried blinkered. *A. Bailey*

TRY THE AIR (IRE)   2 ch.f. (Apr 20) Foxhound (USA) 103 – Try To Catch Me   **–** (USA) (Shareef Dancer (USA) 135) [2003 6m 7.1m 7m f8s Dec 13] smallish, close-coupled filly: half-sister to several winners, notably 5-y-o Storming Home: dam, French 1m winner, out of champion US 2-y-o filly who stayed 1¼m It's In The Air: signs of only a little ability in maidens/nursery: left A. Lidderdale after third start. *C. Tinkler*

TSARBUCK   2 b.c. (Apr 28) Perugino (USA) 84 – Form At Last (Formidable (USA)   **–** 125) [2003 7g Sep 1] second foal: dam, no form in France, out of sister to US Grade 2 9f winner Colway Rally: 50/1, last of 8 in maiden at Folkestone. *R. M. H. Cowell*

TSHUKUDU   2 ch.f. (Feb 27) Fleetwood (IRE) 107 – Pab's Choice 61 (Telsmoss 91) **46** [2003 6m 6g⁵ 7.6m 6m p6g Oct 27] third foal: dam 6f/7f winner who stayed 8.5f: poor maiden: should stay at least 1m. *T. D. McCarthy*

TUAREG (IRE)   2 b.c. (Apr 16) Ashkalani (IRE) 128 – Shining Fire (Kalaglow 132)   **–** [2003 7g 7.9f⁶ Oct 11] second foal: half-brother to 4-y-o Tarkwa: dam unraced: behind in maidens at Epsom (slowly away) and York. *R. M. H. Cowell*

TUCKER FENCE   4 br.g. So Factual (USA) 120 – Daisy Topper (Top Ville 129) [2003   **–** 57, a–: f9.4g 8.5f Apr 16] sturdy gelding: modest performer at 3 yrs: well held in 2003: tried blinkered/visored. *Ian Emmerson*

TUDOR BELL (IRE)   2 b.c. (Mar 1) Definite Article 121 – Late Night Lady (IRE)   **65 p**
65 (Mujadil (USA) 119) [2003 7.1g⁴ Nov 5] €16,000Y, 23,000 2-y-o: first foal: dam
2-y-o 5f winner: 100/1, 5½ lengths fourth of 10 to Disengage in maiden at Musselburgh,
hampered start and late headway: will stay at least 1m: should improve. *J. G. M. O'Shea*

TUG OF LOVE (IRE)   3 ch.c. Halling (USA) 133 – Heart's Harmony (Blushing   **105**
Groom (FR) 131) [2003 87p: 7d³ 9g⁴ 8m 10m⁴ 9.9m² 10.3g* 9m Oct 4] good-topped colt:
useful handicapper: won at Doncaster in September by short head from Arcalis: below
form in Cambridgeshire at Newmarket subsequent outing: stays 1¼m: acts on firm and
good to soft ground: sold 150,000 gns, joined D. Oughton in Hong Kong and renamed
Connoisseur's Love. *Sir Michael Stoute*

TUMBLEBRUTUS (USA)   2 br.c. (Mar 27) Storm Cat (USA) – Mariah's Storm   **102**
(USA) 116 (Rahy (USA) 115) [2003 7.1f⁶ 6d² 6d* 7m² a8f⁶ Sep 14] fifth foal: brother to
3 winners, notably top-class 6f (at 2 yrs) to 1¼m winner Giant's Causeway: dam, won
several Grade 2/3 events at 1m/9f in USA, closely related to very smart French middle-
distance performer Panoramic: useful performer: won maiden at Naas in July: good 3½
lengths second of 8 to Pearl of Love in Futurity Stakes at the Curragh next time: last in
Futurity Stakes at Belmont (played up in preliminaries/slowly away) final start: should
stay 1m: acts on good to firm and good to soft going. *A. P. O'Brien, Ireland*

TUMBLEWEED QUARTET (USA)   7 b.g. Manila (USA) – Peggy's String (USA)   **– §**
(Highland Park (USA)) [2003 –§: f8.5g p10g p12g Oct 3] strong, rangy gelding: fairly
useful performer in 2000: well beaten all 4 runs since: tried in headgear: often tongue
tied: not to be trusted. *Jean-Rene Auvray*

TUMBLEWEED TENOR (IRE)   5 b.g. Mujadil (USA) 119 – Princess Carmen   **57**
(IRE) 61 (Arokar (FR) 124) [2003 –: p10g 7g 11.9m³ 10g⁶ f14.8g p12g² p12g⁵ p10g³
11.6m Jul 21] angular gelding: modest performer: pulled up, reportedly lame, final
outing: stays 1½m: acts on firm ground and fibresand: tried blinkered, sometimes tongue
tied: has been slowly away, sometimes markedly so. *J. White*

TUMBLING SAND (IRE)   3 b.f. Desert Prince (IRE) 130 – Velvet Morning (IRE)   **–**
(Machiavellian (USA) 123) [2003 58: 8.2g 12.1f 10m⁶ Apr 26] leggy filly: modest
maiden at 2 yrs: well held in 2003: folded tamely final start. *T. D. Easterby*

TUNEFUL   3 b.f. Pivotal 124 – Music In My Life (IRE) 59 (Law Society (USA) 130)   **89 ?**
[2003 82p: 8m⁶ 10m 8m Jul 27] well-made filly: fairly useful performer, lightly raced:
seemed to run well in listed races at Kempton (sixth to Nasij) and Newbury (ninth to
Sun On The Sea) first 2 starts: below form in handicap final outing: seems to stay 1¼m:
yet to race on ground softer than good: tends to get upset in stall: sold 14,000 gns.
Mrs A. J. Perrett

TUNGSTEN STRIKE (USA)   2 ch.g. (Feb 1) Smart Strike (CAN) 121 – Bathilde   **70 ?**
(IRE) 102 (Generous (IRE) 139) [2003 8m⁴ 8m 8m Sep 13] 52,000Y: good-bodied
gelding: third foal: half-brother to fairly useful 2000 2-y-o 7f winner Baillieston (by
Indian Ridge): dam, 10.4f winner, half-sister to smart performer up to 2m Crimson Quest:
best effort in maidens (seemingly fair form) when fourth in slowly-run race at
Newmarket: will stay at least 1¼m. *Mrs A. J. Perrett*

TUNING FORK   3 b.c. Alzao (USA) 117 – Tuning 114 (Rainbow Quest (USA) 134)   **113 d**
[2003 10.5d* 10.4m² 10m⁶ 10m⁶ 10.3g⁵ 9m Oct 18] strong, lengthy, attractive colt: first
foal: dam, 1¾m winner (including Ebor), out of half-sister to smart Phoenix Stakes
winner Digamist: reportedly had a cyst on a pedal bone and couldn't be trained at 2 yrs:
smart performer at best: won maiden at Haydock in May: much improved when ½-length
second to Magistretti in Dante Stakes at York later in month, worn down close home:
disappointing after in 2 listed races, minor event and Darley Stakes, last-named at Newmarket (tailed off in visor): bred to stay at least 1½m: gives impression may not stand
repeated racing on ground firmer than good: has raced freely/hung left/found little:
temperament under suspicion: sold 150,000 gns. *H. R. A. Cecil*

TUPPENCE HA'PENNY   4 gr.f. Never So Bold 135 – Mummy's Chick 77   **–**
(Mummy's Pet 125) [2003 64?: p8g 6.1g Apr 29] unfurnished filly: lighly-raced maiden,
well held in 2003: tried in cheekpieces. *G. G. Margarson*

TUPPENNY   4 b.f. Salse (USA) 128 – Dazzling Heights 99 (Shirley Heights 130)   **57**
[2003 f12g² f12g⁵ Mar 3] seventh foal: half-sister to several winners, including French
performer around 1¼m All Glory (by Alzao) and 6f (at 2 yrs) to 1m winner Mauri Moon
(by Green Desert), both useful: dam 7f (at 2 yrs) and 11f (in France) winner: modest
maiden: sold from J. Pease in France 10,000 gns after final 3-y-o start: better effort at
Wolverhampton on reappearance: stays 1½m. *J. Noseda*

Enter The £1 Million Tote Ten To Follow November Stakes (Handicap), Doncaster—
as usual nowadays, the last big race of the turf season staged as second last on the card,
takes place in poor light; Turbo has charged through from last to first, with Perfect Storm (No.6),
Gold Ring and Wunderwood next to finish

TUPPENNY BLUE   3 ch.f. Pennekamp (USA) 130 – Seal Indigo (IRE) 93 (Glenstal   **49**
(USA) 118) [2003 p7g⁴ 7g Mar 27] 12,000Y, 3,500 2-y-o: seventh foal: half-sister to
several winners, including useful 2001 2-y-o 6f winner Prism (by Spectrum) and fairly
useful 6f winner Cielito Lindo (by Pursuit of Love): dam, 10.5f/1½m winner, out of half-
sister to Irish Oaks winner Give Thanks: modest form in maidens at Lingfield (slowly
away) and Leicester. *R. Hannon*

TURBO (IRE)   4 b.g. Piccolo 121 – By Arrangement (IRE) 60 (Bold Arrangement   **103**
127) [2003 94: 8m⁶ 10d 10m 9m 10g² 12d* Nov 8] close-coupled gelding: useful
handicapper: better than ever on last 2 starts: 25/1, won November Handicap at Doncaster
by 1½ lengths from Perfect Storm, waited with and making up great deal of ground in
straight: effective at 1¼m/1½m: acts on firm and soft going: tried visored, wore cheekpieces last 5 starts. *G. B. Balding*

TURF PRINCESS   2 b.f. (Jan 25) Wizard King 122 – Turf Moor (IRE) 53 (Mac's Imp   **60**
(USA) 116) [2003 5m 5f³ 5m⁵ 6s* 6m 7.1m² f8g² f8s⁶ Dec 13] first foal: dam maiden
who stayed 7f: modest performer: won claimer at Southwell (left R. Fahey) in October:
left J. Best after good second penultimate start: barely stays 1m: acts on fibresand and
firm going. *Ian Emmerson*

TURFTANZER (GER)   4 b.g. Lomitas 129 – Tower Bridge (GER) (Big Shuffle   **–**
(USA) 122) [2003 12m f11g⁵ f11s Dec 13] first foal: dam 6f/7.5f winner in Germany:
won handicap at Turin in 2002: left A. & G. Botti in Italy after final 3-y-o outing: well
held in claimers in Britain: stays 1¼m: raced only on good going or softer prior to British
debut: tried tongue tied. *Don Enrico Incisa*

TURIBIUS   4 b.g. Puissance 110 – Compact Disc (IRE) 48 (Royal Academy (USA)   **83**
130) [2003 73: p5g⁶ p6g³ p5g⁵ p6g 5m³ 6m⁴ 5.3m³ 5.3m⁴ 5m* 5.3f³ 6m⁴ 5d 6m²
5m* Sep 22] leggy gelding: fairly useful handicapper: won at Sandown in July and
Leicester in September: effective at 5f/easy 6f: acts on polytrack and firm ground, below
form on good to soft: sometimes visored, not after fourth start in 2003: sometimes slowly
away: effective held up or ridden up with pace. *T. E. Powell*

TURKISH DELIGHT   2 b.f. (Mar 31) Prince Sabo 123 – Delicious 51 (Dominion   **67**
123) [2003 6m⁴ 6d⁴ 6m⁴ f6g³ p7g Dec 10] 4,000Y: fourth foal: half-sister to 5-y-o Fantasy
Believer: dam lightly-raced maiden: fair maiden: likely to prove best at 5f/6f: acts on
fibresand, good to firm and good to soft going. *D. Morris*

TURKS AND CAICOS (IRE)   2 b. or br.g. (Mar 19) Turtle Island (IRE) 123 – Need   **60**
You Badly 59 (Robellino (USA) 127) [2003 6g f8.5g⁴ f8g Dec 8] €10,000Y: second
living foal: dam 5f winner out of half-sister to Lake Coniston: best effort (modest form)
when fourth in claimer at Wolverhampton: likely to stay at least 1¼m. *P. C. Haslam*

TURKU   5 b.g. Polar Falcon (USA) 126 – Princess Zepoli 61 (Persepolis (FR) 127) [2003   **60**
–, a73: f8s 7m 8.3g f8.5f⁶ f7g p10g⁵ f7g Nov 19] lengthy gelding: modest performer: left
Mrs L. Pearce after reappearance, J. Cullinan after penultimate start: effective at 7f/1m:
acts on all-weather, soft and good to firm going: tried cheekpieces/visor: sold £900.
D. Shaw

TURN AROUND 3 b.g. Pivotal 124 – Bemuse 89 (Forzando 122) [2003 86?: 6g 5d –
f6g p6g Dec 6] well-made gelding: fairly useful at best at 2 yrs: well beaten in handicaps
(reportedly lame on reappearance) in 2003: should stay 7f: acts on good to soft going:
slowly away first 2 outings at 2 yrs. *B. W. Hills*

TURN BACK 4 b.f. Pivotal 124 – Trachelium 65 (Formidable (USA) 125) [2003 73: –
f11g 9.9m 12g 17.1m Jun 1] tall filly: has a markedly round action: fair performer at 3
yrs: well held in 2003. *Miss S. E. Hall*

TURNBERRY (IRE) 2 b.c. (Apr 10) Petardia 113 – Sunrise (IRE) 58 (Sri Pekan **60**
(USA) 117) [2003 6m 7m p7g 7m p8g p7g⁴ Dec 29] 10,000Y: first foal: dam, maiden
(best effort at 5f at 2 yrs), half-sister to useful sprinter March Star: modest maiden: best
efforts at 7f on polytrack: blinkered last 2 starts. *J. W. Hills*

TURNER 2 gr.c. (Feb 22) El Prado (IRE) 119 – Gaily Royal (IRE) (Royal Academy **73 §**
(USA) 130) [2003 8.1m³ 8m⁶ p8g Oct 15] 120,000Y: second foal: dam, Japanese 1m/9f
winner, half-sister to smart French winner up to 15f New Frontier: best effort in maidens
(fair form) when third at Sandown: should stay 1¼m: hung left first 2 starts: found little
final one: untrustworthy: sold 12,500 gns. *J. H. M. Gosden*

TURNING THE TIDE 4 b.g. Lugana Beach 116 – Robert's Daughter (Robellino –
(USA) 127) [2003 –: 13.8m⁵ f16.2g 13.1f Sep 8] maiden handicapper: little form: tried
visored/blinkered: sometimes slowly away. *I. A. Wood*

TURN 'N BURN 2 b.c. (Apr 17) Unfuwain (USA) 131 – Seasonal Splendour (IRE) **69 p**
95 (Prince Rupert (FR) 121) [2003 p8g⁵ p8g³ Oct 27] £9,000Y: third living foal: half-
brother to smart 1¾m winner When In Rome (by Saddlers' Hall) and 3-y-o Strength 'n
Honour: dam 1½m winner who stayed 2m: fair form in maidens at Lingfield: took
good hold when third to Cracking Rosie: bred to be suited by 1½m+: open to progress.
C. A. Cyzer

TURN OF PHRASE (IRE) 4 b.g. Cadeaux Genereux 131 – Token Gesture (IRE) **70**
113 (Alzao (USA) 117) [2003 67, a?: f8s⁵ p10g² 12.4m* 13g³ Jun 12] first foal: dam, Irish
7f (at 2 yrs) and 1½m winner, half-sister to US Grade 2 9f winner Wait Till Monday: fair
performer: trained by D. Weld at 2/3 yrs: won apprentice minor event at Newcastle in
June: stays 13f: acts on firm ground, probably on polytrack: usually blinkered: winning
hurdler. *R. A. Fahey*

TURNSTILE 2 gr.c. (Apr 2) Linamix (FR) 127 – Kissing Gate (USA) 62 (Easy Goer **73 p**
(USA)) [2003 8.2d⁴ Nov 6] tall, good-topped colt: third foal: half-brother to winner up
to 1½m in Sweden by Green Desert: dam, 2-y-o 8.5f winner, half-sister to very smart
sprinter Keen Hunter and smart performers up to 1¼m Altibr and Marnor: 12/1, burly and
green, 8½ lengths fourth of 16 to Vaughan in maiden at Nottingham, slowly away and late
headway: will be suited by 1¼m/1½m: sure to do better. *R. Hannon*

TURTLE LOVE (IRE) 4 b.f. Turtle Island (IRE) 123 – A Little Loving (He Loves **49**
Me 120) [2003 58, a52: 16.5m 11.8m² 14.1d⁴ Jul 26] good-topped filly: poor performer:
left K. Morgan and returned to a former trainer after reappearance: stays 1¾m: acts on
soft going, good to firm and fibresand: usually blinkered before 2003: has worn cheekpieces. *Miss V. Haigh*

TURTLE PATRIARCH (IRE) 2 b.c. (Mar 10) Turtle Island (IRE) 123 – La **62 +**
Doyenne (IRE) 65 (Masterclass (USA) 116) [2003 6m⁶ 6g Jul 9] 5,000Y: angular, quite
good-topped colt: first foal: dam 5f to 7f winner: better effort in maidens (modest form)
when slow-starting sixth at Salisbury: beaten long way when favourite at Lingfield:
should stay at least 7f. *Mrs A. J. Perrett*

TURTLE VALLEY (IRE) 7 b.g. Turtle Island (IRE) 123 – Primrose Valley 99 (Mill **75**
Reef (USA) 141) [2003 96, a–: f12s p16g 14.4d⁶ 14.1g 14.1s³ 14v* 14d Sep 27] small, **a–**
strong gelding: unimpressive mover: only fair handicapper nowadays: won at Haydock
in May: ran as if something amiss subsequent start: stays 2m: has form on firm going,
very best efforts on good or softer: blinkered once at 2 yrs: sometimes hangs left. *S. Dow*

TUSCAN DREAM 8 b.g. Clantime 101 – Excavator Lady 65 (Most Secret 119) **47**
[2003 67: f5g⁶ f5g² f5g f5s³ f5g f5s⁶ f5g f5s⁶ f5s Dec 27] smallish, sturdy gelding: poor
performer: best at bare 5f: acts on all-weather, raced mainly on good ground or firmer on
turf: below form in blinkers: has bolted to post: sometimes rears as stall opens: usually
races prominently. *A. Berry*

TUSCAN FLYER 5 b.g. Clantime 101 – Excavator Lady 65 (Most Secret 119) [2003 **73**
67: 5f 6d 5g 5.9f 5m² 5.3f⁴ 5f* 5f 5.3f* 6m⁴ 6m² Sep 18] deep-bodied gelding: fair performer: won apprentice handicap at Musselburgh in August and minor event at Brighton

TUS

in September: effective at 5f/6f: acts on polytrack, firm and good to soft going: often blinkered, including last 7 starts: races up with pace. *R. Bastiman*

TUSCAN SKY (USA) 3 b.f. Gulch (USA) – Search Committee (USA) (Roberto (USA) 131) [2003 77: 7.9m 7g 7m Jun 15] good-bodied filly: fair performer at 2 yrs: well held in handicaps in 2003: sent to Australia. *B. W. Hills* —

TUSCAN TREATY 3 b.f. Brief Truce (USA) 126 – Fiorenz (USA) (Chromite (USA)) [2003 50: f8.5g³ f12g 7g⁵ 7m* 7m² 7m 7g 7m 6f* 7m 6m 6d p7g p7g Nov 29] quite good-topped filly: fair handicapper: won at Folkestone (seller) in April and Brighton in June: below form after: effective at 6f/7f: acts on firm going, some promise on fibresand: has been slowly away. *T. T. Clement* 60

TUSCARORA (IRE) 4 b.f. Revoque (IRE) 122 – Fresh Look (IRE) 64 (Alzao (USA) 117) [2003 69: p6g* p6g⁴ f6s p7g⁶ p7g* p7g⁵ 8m² 8g² 8f* 8f⁶ 8m⁴ 8f⁶ 7m⁴ 7g 7.5d⁶ Sep 23] smallish filly: fair performer: won claimer in January (left P. Haslam after next start) and handicap in April, both at Lingfield, and seller at Brighton in June: effective at 7f/1m: acts on firm going and polytrack: often slowly away: sometimes races freely. *A. W. Carroll* 71

TUSK 3 ch.g. Fleetwood (IRE) 107 – Farmer's Pet 90 (Sharrood (USA) 124) [2003 77: 8.3g⁶ 10.2m* 10.4m 12f 11m⁵ 8m² 8g* 8.1g⁴ 10m* 11.9m 10.1m⁴ 10m* Oct 4] big gelding: type to carry condition: useful performer: won handicaps at Bath in April and Doncaster in July, and minor event in August and handicap (beat Tizzy May by short head) in October, both at Newmarket: effective at 1m to 11f: acts on good to firm going: usually makes running: sold 55,000 gns, joined Miss H. Knight. *M. R. Channon* 96

TUTUM (IRE) 2 b.g. (Mar 29) Revoque (IRE) 122 – Dieci Anno (IRE) 72 (Classic Music (USA)) [2003 f6g⁵ 5g⁵ 7g Jun 21] 7,000Y: third foal: half-brother to fairly useful 2001 2-y-o 5f winner Anima Mundi (by Namaqualand), later successful in USA: dam Irish 5f winner: modest form in seller/minor event/maiden: likely to prove best at 5f/6f. *T. P. McGovern* 51

TWEED 6 ch.g. Barathea (IRE) 127 – In Perpetuity 90 (Great Nephew 126) [2003 69, a90?: f16s⁴ 18g 16m 16d f14.8g² Jun 6] good-bodied gelding: type to carry condition: modest performer: left J. Best after reappearance: stays 2m: acts on fibresand, firm and soft ground: tried in headgear: sold 1,000 gns. *B. Ellison* 55 a63

TWEEDSMUIR 4 b.g. Zilzal (USA) 137 – Sakura Queen (IRE) 52 (Woodman (USA) 126) [2003 73: f12g⁶ 14.1g 12.4m⁴ 11.5g 12m 11.8m Jul 17] rangy, angular gelding: lightly-raced maiden, just modest form in 2003: stays 1½m: acts on soft and good to firm ground: has carried head awkwardly. *P. W. Harris* 64

TWENTYTWOSILVER (IRE) 3 ro.g. Emarati (USA) 74 – St Louis Lady 71 (Absalom 128) [2003 80: 6g 6m⁵ 7.1m 6m 7g⁶ 7g 7m 6g Oct 13] fair performer: below form after second start: free-going sort, likely to prove best up to 7f: acts on all-weather and good to firm ground: blinkered (raced too freely) penultimate outing: usually races prominently. *J. A. Osborne* 73 d

TWICE UPON A TIME 4 ch.f. Primo Dominie 121 – Opuntia (Rousillon (USA) 133) [2003 76: 5f 5m 5.1m* 5g 5m 5m 5m² 5f* 5m Oct 18] good-topped filly: has a quick action: fair handicapper: won at Nottingham in July and York in October: best at 5f/6f: acts on firm and soft ground: often rears as stall opens/slowly away. *B. Smart* 79

TWILIGHT BLUES (IRE) 4 ch.c. Bluebird (USA) 125 – Pretty Sharp 64 (Interrex (CAN)) [2003 111: 7m⁴ 6m* 6f 6m 6d 7m Oct 18] good-topped colt: smart performer: better than ever when winning Duke of York Hearthstead Homes Stakes at York in May by ½ length from Just James, getting first run: failed to run up to that form subsequently, including in Golden Jubilee Stakes at Royal Ascot (mulish stall), July Cup at Newmarket and Sprint Cup at Haydock: probably best at 6f/7f: acts on firm and soft going: missed break when well held twice at 3 yrs. *B. J. Meehan* 118

TWILIGHT HAZE 5 b.g. Darshaan 133 – Hiwaayati (Shadeed (USA) 135) [2003 90§, a85§: f14.8g³ f14s³ f16s⁶ f12s* f11g² 14.4d Mar 22] lengthy, good-topped gelding: fairly useful performer: won minor event at Wolverhampton in February: probably best at 1½m/1¾m: acts on fibresand, heavy and good to firm going: tongue tied: usually makes running: formerly unreliable. *Miss Gay Kelleway* 80

TWILIGHT MISTRESS 5 b.m. Bin Ajwaad (IRE) 119 – By Candlelight (IRE) 84 (Roi Danzig (USA)) [2003 81: 5f³ 5m² 6m 6m⁵ 5.1m⁴ 5.2m⁶ 5m² 7f 5.7f* Sep 8] leggy, good-topped mare: fairly useful handicapper: won at Bath in September: winner at 7f, best recent form at 5f/6f: acts on firm going, good to soft and all-weather: wore cheek- 84

1058

pieces sixth start: sometimes starts slowly/races freely: reportedly in foal to Bold Edge. *D. W. P. Arbuthnot*

TWO JACKS (IRE)   6 b.g. Fayruz 116 – Kaya (GER) (Young Generation 129) [2003   –
41, a51: f8s f8g Mar 13] workmanlike gelding: maiden: well held in 2003: tried tongue
tied. *W. S. Cunningham*

TWO OF A KIND (IRE)   3 ch.g. Ashkalani (IRE) 128 – Dulcinea 73 (Selkirk (USA)   58
129) [2003 p8g 10m⁵ p12g⁵ 14f⁵ p13g⁵ f14.8g⁵ Nov 29] second foal: half-brother to
useful 7f winner Hideaway Heroine (by Hernando): dam, 7f/1m winner: out of smart
winner up to 10.5f Ahohoney: modest maiden: stays 13f: carries head high: sometimes
slowly away/races freely. *J. W. Hills*

TWO OF CLUBS   2 b.g. (Feb 18) First Trump 118 – Sulaka (Owington 123) [2003   71
5d⁴ 6g³ 6m⁴ 6g⁵ f7g⁴ Nov 14] 9,000Y: lengthy, good-topped gelding: first foal:
dam unraced: fair maiden: third at Newcastle: probably stays 7f. *P. C. Haslam*

TWO STEP KID (USA)   2 ch.c. (Feb 3) Gone West (USA) – Marsha's Dancer (USA)   94 p
(Northern Dancer) [2003 p6g* Oct 27] seventh foal: closely related/half-brother to 3
winners in USA: dam, 1m/8.5f winner in USA (third in Grade 2 9f event) out of half-sister
to Japan Cup winner Mairzy Doates: favourite, made all in 7-runner minor event at Lingfield, travelling strongly and quickening clear to beat Big Bradford 3½ lengths: likely to
prove best at 5f/6f: open to progress, and should win more races. *J. Noseda*

TWO STEPS TO GO (USA)   4 b.g. Rhythm (USA) – Lyonushka (CAN) (Private   44 §
Account (USA)) [2003 57, a88: f8s f11s⁴ f12s⁵ 10.1m f12g f9.4g⁴ 14.1m 11.9m⁴ f11s Dec
13] smallish, sturdy gelding: just poor performer in 2003: left T. D. Barron after third
start: seems to stay 11f: acts on fibresand and good to firm going, probably on good to
soft: sometimes blinkered/visored: temperamental. *Ian Emmerson*

Mrs Susan Roy's "Twilight Blues"

TYC

TYCHY 4 ch.f. Suave Dancer (USA) 136 – Touch of White 77 (Song 132) [2003 73: 6.1g³ 5.9g⁵ 5g* 6m* 6m 7f⁵ 6.5m² 7g* 6m* 7f Sep 27] good-topped filly: useful performer: won handicaps at Lingfield and Newbury, minor event at Epsom and handicap at Pontefract (best effort, beat Yomalo 2½ lengths) between May and September: better form at 6f/7f than 5f: yet to race on heavy going, acts on any other: usually races prominently. *S. C. Williams* **97**

TYCOON 2 b.c. (Mar 21) Sadler's Wells (USA) 132 – Fleeting Glimpse 109 (Rainbow Quest (USA) 134) [2003 7m³ 7m² 7f* 7s⁵ Oct 5] small, sturdy colt: second foal: half-brother to useful 7f/1m winner (including at 2 yrs) who stayed 1¼m Half Glance (by Danehill); dam, French 1¼m winner and second in Prix Saint-Alary on only starts, sister to 8-y-o Ulundi and half-sister to 1000 Guineas winner Wince: useful performer: landed odds in maiden at Leopardstown in September: good second to Pearl of Love in listed race at Royal Ascot and fourth (demoted) to American Post in Prix Jean-Luc Lagardere at Longchamp (mulish paddock/sweating): will stay at least 1m. *A. P. O'Brien, Ireland* **101**

TYCOON HALL (IRE) 3 ch.c. Halling (USA) 133 – Tycooness (IRE) 80§ (Last Tycoon 131) [2003 96: 8g⁵ 10s⁵ 7m Aug 23] good-topped colt: useful performer: ran creditably when fifth to Mubeen in minor event at Salisbury on reappearance: folded tamely both starts after, flashing tail final one: should stay 1¼m: acts on good to firm and good to soft ground. *R. Hannon* **96**

TYKEYVOR (IRE) 13 b.g. Last Tycoon 131 – Ivoronica 89 (Targowice (USA) 130) [2003 p12g Oct 30] lengthy, good-topped gelding: one-time fairly useful handicapper: well held only run since 1998: tried visored/blinkered. *Lady Herries* **–**

TYNE 2 b.c. (Jan 28) Komaite (USA) – High Typha 61 (Dowsing (USA) 124) [2003 5m² 5m* 5f⁶ Jul 12] 11,500F, 10,000Y, 16,000 2-y-o: tall, quite good-topped colt: second foal: dam 7f winner: fairly useful form: landed odds in 4-runner maiden at Redcar in June: failed to take eye in paddock/on way to post and ran poorly in nursery final start: will prove best at 5f/6f. *T. D. Barron* **88**

TYNEHAM 3 b.c. Robellino (USA) 127 – Diamond Wedding (USA) 65 (Diamond Shoal 130) [2003 74: f9.4f 8s 11.8g Nov 7] well-made colt: fair maiden at 2 yrs: well held in 2003, leaving G. Bravery after reappearance. *M. Pimbonnet, France* **–**

TYPE ONE (IRE) 5 b.g. Bigstone (IRE) 126 – Isca 66 (Caerleon (USA) 132) [2003 84§: p6g* 5f² 5d* 5f⁴ 5m³ 6g² p6g* Dec 30] well-made gelding: fairly useful performer: won claimers at Lingfield in May and December, and handicap at Sandown in between: best at 5f/6f: acts on polytrack, firm and good to soft going: visored (below form) once at 4 yrs: formerly unreliable, but did nothing wrong in 2003. *T. G. Mills* **87**

TYPHONIC (IRE) 2 ch.c. (Apr 21) Efisio 120 – Blown-Over 41 (Ron's Victory (USA) 129) [2003 p6g² 6g Oct 13] 54,000Y: fourth foal: half-brother to 3-y-o Mezereon and a winner in Italy by Charnwood Forest: dam, lightly-raced maiden, half-sister to very smart sprinter Piccolo: fair form in maidens at Lingfield (second to Sweetest Revenge) and Windsor: will probably stay 7f: sold 27,000 gns. *R. Charlton* **69**

TYPHOON TILLY 6 b.g. Hernando (FR) 127 – Meavy 86 (Kalaglow 132) [2003 79: 13.11f* 13.9m³ 13.3m³ 16.2f 13.9f³ p12g³ Nov 22] quite good-topped gelding: fairly useful handicapper: won at Bath in August: mostly creditable efforts after: effective at 1½m to 2½m: acts on polytrack, best turf efforts on good ground or firmer: blinkered twice at 4 yrs: races freely: consistent, but sometimes finds little. *C. R. Egerton* **87**

TYPHOON TODD (IRE) 4 ch.g. Entrepreneur 123 – Petite Liqueurelle (IRE) (Shernazar 131) [2003 75: f12s* f12g Jan 24] fair performer: won maiden at Southwell in January: stayed 1½m: acted on good to firm going, good to soft and all-weather: visored last 3 outings: sometimes wandered/carried head awkwardly: dead. *P. G. Murphy* **69**

TYRANNY 3 b.f. Machiavellian (USA) 123 – Dust Dancer 116 (Suave Dancer (USA) 136) [2003 88: 8.3g⁴ 7g* 6m⁴ 7m* 7g⁵ 8d 7d Sep 11] tall, leggy filly: useful performer: won maiden in May and handicap in June, both at Lingfield: good fifth to Tantina in listed event at Goodwood on fifth start: races freely and best at 7f: acts on firm and soft ground: wandered and found little as 2-y-o start. *J. L. Dunlop* **97**

TYTHEKNOT 2 b.c. (Feb 5) Pursuit of Love 124 – Bundled Up (USA) (Sharpen Up 127) [2003 7.2d 8m² Oct 25] 14,000Y: half-brother to several winners, including 5f to 7f winner Rififi (by Aragon), fairly useful at best but became temperamental: dam French 2-y-o 9.7f winner: better effort in maidens (fair form) when 3 lengths second of 13 to Mr Tambourine Man at Musselburgh: will stay 1¼m. *Jedd O'Keeffe* **76**

TYUP POMPEY (IRE) 2 ch.g. (Apr 28) Docksider (USA) 124 – Cindy's Baby 36 (Bairn (USA) 126) [2003 7.5m³ Sep 17] strong, close-coupled gelding: sixth foal: half- **58 p**

1060

brother to 7f (at 2 yrs) and 1¼m winner Karakul (by Persian Bold) and winners in Italy by Priolo and Paris House: dam, maiden, half-sister to smart sprinter Two Clubs: 20/1, 5 lengths third of 10 to Kythia in maiden at Beverley, slowly away and getting hang of things gradually: should stay at least 1m: will do better. *B. Smart*

TYZACK (IRE)   2 b.c. (Mar 17) Fasliyev (USA) 120 – Rabea (USA) 61 (Devil's Bag (USA)) [2003 7.2f² 6m⁵ 8m² 7m⁴ 7d Nov 4] IR 40,000F, 22,000Y: good-topped colt: second foal: dam won at 12.5f in Germany: fair maiden: second at Ayr and Newcastle: barely stays 1m: acts on good to firm ground: sometimes troublesome at post: tends to find little/hang: not to be trusted. *J. G. Given*   **79 §**

TZAR   4 b.g. Makbul 104 – Tzarina (USA) (Gallant Romeo (USA)) [2003 –, a69d: p10g p6g p8g 8.1m Jul 4] smallish gelding: fair performer at best: well held in 2003: was probably best at 6f/7f: acted on firm going, soft and all-weather: blinkered last 2 outings: fell heavily final start: dead. *J. R. Best*   **–**

U

UGIE GIRL   4 gr.f. Passing Point (IRE) – Nawtinookey (Uncle Pokey 116) [2003 9m Apr 10] first foal: dam, bad novice hurdler/chaser, stayed 2½m: tailed off in bumper/maiden: troublesome to post. *A. C. Whillans*   **–**

UHOOMAGOO   5 b.g. Namaqualand (USA) – Point of Law (Law Society (USA) 130) [2003 95: f7s f8s⁶ 8g 8m f7g* 7.6m 7m 7.2f³ 7g 7f⁵ 7.2g* 7.6m³ 7m⁴ 8g⁴ 7.6m 7d³ 7.2m³ 7m⁴ 7m³ 7g Oct 28] leggy gelding: fairly useful on turf, fair on all-weather: won minor event at Wolverhampton in April and handicap at Ayr in July: effective at 7f/1m: acts on all-weather/any turf going: usually wears headgear: often slowly away/takes long time to warm up: held up: tends to wander. *K. A. Ryan*   **90 a77**

UHURU DAWN (IRE)   3 b.c. Fayruz 116 – Come Dancing 48 (Suave Dancer (USA) 136) [2003 76, a61: p5g⁴ 5.5v⁶ 6g³ 8s 7d 7d 5.5g⁵ 6g⁴ 6s 6s a6.5g Dec 9] well-grown colt: modest performer: fourth in seller at Lingfield on reappearance: also made frame in 20-runner handicaps at Maisons-Laffitte in March and Deauville in October: stays 7f: acts on good to soft ground (probably on heavy) and polytrack: often blinkered nowadays. *A. Hermans, Belgium*   **64**

ULSHAW   6 ch.g. Salse (USA) 128 – Kintail 76 (Kris 135) [2003 51: f16.2g² f16.2g³ f16.2g* f16.2g³ f16.2g f16.2s³ 18g* 19.1m² 15.9m² 21d f16.2g f16.2g Nov 17] quite good-topped gelding: modest handicapper: won at Wolverhampton in February and Chepstow in June: stays 21f: acts on any turf going/fibresand: visored last 3 starts at 3 yrs: usually held up. *B. J. Llewellyn*   **63 a59**

ULSTER PRINCE   2 b.g. (Feb 20) Prince Sabo 123 – Tonic Chord 49 (La Grange Music 111) [2003 5g⁶ f5g f5s Oct 7] 800F, 7,000Y: lengthy gelding: fourth foal: dam maiden who stayed 1m: well beaten in maidens/minor event: sent to Italy. *D. Carroll*   **–**

ULTIMATA   3 ch.f. Unfuwain (USA) 131 – Last Look (Rainbow Quest (USA) 134) [2003 8g* May 26] second foal: half-sister to 4-y-o Littlemissattitude: dam unraced out of half-sister to very smart sprinter/miler Pursuit of Love: joint favourite, won maiden at Leicester on debut by 1½ lengths from Leoballero, eased (injured off-hind): will stay 1¼m. *J. R. Fanshawe*   **81**

ULTRA MARINE (IRE)   3 b.c. Blues Traveller (IRE) 119 – The Aspecto Girl (IRE) 53 (Alzao (USA) 117) [2003 64: 8.5m 8d f12g 9m⁵ 9m 8m⁴ 9.9m⁵ 10m⁶ 9.9d 10.4f 11g 12d⁴ Nov 4] leggy, useful-looking colt: modest maiden: seemingly stays 1½m: acts on good to firm and good to soft going: tried in cheekpieces, blinkered (seemed to run very well) final start. *J. S. Wainwright*   **56**

ULUNDI   8 b.g. Rainbow Quest (USA) 134 – Flit (USA) 72 (Lyphard (USA) 132) [2003 122: 10m 12m 10g Jul 4] rangy gelding: useful hurdler: very smart performer in 2002, well below form in 2003: has reportedly undergone a third wind operation: effective at 1¼m/easy 1½m: acts on firm and good to soft going, possibly not on soft: has been bandaged in front: waited with. *P. R. Webber*   **99**

ULYSEES (IRE)   4 b.g. Turtle Island (IRE) 123 – Tamasriya (IRE) (Doyoun 124) [2003 92: 6g 9s⁵ 6d 6d 8.5d 8s 9.5g⁶ f8.5g⁶ f8g f7s Dec 6] IR 10,000F, IR 8,500Y: first foal: dam French 9.5f winner: fairly useful handicapper: below form after second start, leaving P. Mullins in Ireland €8,000 after seventh: best form at 6f/7f: raced mainly on good going or softer on turf. *I. Semple*   **83 d**

UMISTA (IRE)   4 b.f. Tagula (IRE) 116 – Nishiki (USA) (Brogan (USA) 110) [2003   –
–: f7g³ f8.5g f6g 8f Jun 4] rather leggy filly: little form: tried visored. *M. Quinn*

UMOJA (FR)   3 b. or br.f. Anabaa (USA) 130 – Frustration 108 (Salse (USA) 128)   **76**
[2003 78p: 10m⁵ 10m³ 10g⁶ p12g⁵ Jul 23] well-made filly: fair maiden, lightly raced:
effective at 1m to 1¼m, possibly not 1½m: acts on soft and good to firm going: sold 3,500
gns in December. *C. F. Wall*

UN AUTRE ESPERE   4 b.g. Golden Heights 82 – Drummer's Dream (IRE) 48   –
(Drumalis 125) [2003 –: 10.5m³ 12.6f 10.5m⁵ 10m 13.1f Aug 22] leggy gelding: no form:
tried in cheekpieces/blinkers. *T. Wall*

UNAVAILABLE (IRE)   2 b.f. (Feb 19) Alzao (USA) 117 – Maid of Killeen (IRE) 97   **94 p**
(Darshaan 133) [2003 6m* 7m⁶ 7.9f* Oct 9] 80,000Y: sturdy filly: first foal: dam, Irish
2-y-o 9f winner who stayed 1½m, out of half-sister to very smart performers Royal Touch
(at 7f to 9f) and Foresee (middle-distance stayer): won maiden at Goodwood (hung right)
in August and nursery at York (beat Weet A Head by length) in October: should be suited
by 1¼m/1½m: has had 2 handlers: should make a useful 3-y-o. *M. A. Magnusson*

UNCLE BERNON   4 ch.g. Pivotal 124 – Magical Veil 73 (Majestic Light (USA))   **77**
[2003 83: 6g 7m p6g Dec 10] angular, good-topped gelding: lightly-raced gelding:
just fair performer in 2003: bred to stay 7f: acts on polytrack, unraced on extremes of
going on turf. *G. B. Balding*

UNCLE CENT (IRE)   2 ch.c. (Apr 19) Peintre Celebre (USA) 137 – Butter Knife   **95**
(IRE) (Sure Blade (USA) 130) [2003 7m⁵ 8m³ 7.9m³ 10m* Oct 22] 17,000 2-y-o: small,
close-coupled colt: has a quick action: fourth foal: dam unraced half-sister to very smart
performer up to 1¼m Hawkeye: useful performer: much improved in maidens when
winning 12-runner event at Nottingham by 8 lengths from Heir To The Throne, leading
over 2f out and edging left: will stay at least 1½m: sent to USA. *E. J. O'Neill*

UNCLE JOHN   2 b.c. (Apr 30) Atraf 116 – Bit O' May 71 (Mummy's Pet 125) [2003   **67**
8.3g 8.1m f8.5g* p8g f8s⁵ Dec 13] 4,000Y: half-brother to 3 winners, including 6f winner
Summer Express (by Bay Express): dam maiden: fair performer: won maiden at Wolverhampton in November: below form after: stays 8.5f: acts on fibresand, some promise on
turf. *S. Kirk*

UNCLE MAX (IRE)   3 b.g. Victory Note (USA) 120 – Sunset Park (IRE) 61 (Red   **70**
Sunset 120) [2003 p8g³ f8s² p7g³ p10g³ 10.2m 8g 10s⁵ 11.9f⁴ 12g Sep 10] IR 9,500F, IR
15,000Y: second foal: half-brother to a winner abroad by College Chapel: dam, lightly
raced in Ireland, out of half-sister to Arc winner Rheingold: fair maiden handicapper:
probably stays easy 1½m: acts on all-weather, firm and soft going: tried blinkered: raced
freely seventh outing: failed to handle bend at Epsom final start: races prominently:
joined N. Twiston-Davies, won juvenile hurdle in November. *J. A. Osborne*

UNCOMPREHENDABLE (USA)   3 ch.f. Loup Sauvage (USA) 125 – Benguela   –
(USA) 76 (Little Current (USA)) [2003 9m⁶ Jul 19] half-sister to several winners,
including 1m winner Naif (by Storm Bird) and 1½m winner Lady Angola (by Lord At
War), both fairly useful: dam winner in USA at 4 yrs (stayed 11.7f): 7/1, tailed-off last in
maiden at Ripon on debut (said to have had breathing problem). *B. Hanbury*

UNDER MY SPELL   2 b.f. (Apr 6) Wizard King 122 – Gagajulu 75 (Al Hareb (USA)   **80**
123) [2003 5.1m* 5.1m³ 5s⁴ 5m³ 5m 5m³ 6f³ 6d⁵ 6.1m⁵ 6m⁵ Aug 27] £4,000Y: leggy
filly: fourth foal: dam 2-y-o 5f winner: fairly useful performer: won seller at Nottingham
in April: third in minor events and listed race (behind Russian Valour at Sandown) on
fourth start: should prove best at 5f/6f: acts on good to firm ground. *P. D. Evans*

UNDERWRITER (USA)   3 b.c. With Approval (CAN) – Night Risk (USA) (Wild   –
Again (USA)) [2003 8.2m Sep 19] 900,000 francs Y: useful-looking colt: second foal:
half-brother to winner in USA by Private Terms: dam, won in USA, out of smart French
performer around 1m Be Exclusive: 10/3 and poorly to post, well held in maiden at
Nottingham: sold 13,000 gns. *J. H. M. Gosden*

UNDETERRED   7 ch.g. Zafonic (USA) 130 – Mint Crisp (IRE) 108 (Green Desert   **90**
(USA) 127) [2003 88§: 6m³ 6d 6m⁶ 6f² 6m² 6g* 6m² 6m⁴ 6m 6m 6f Oct 10] lengthy,
deep-girthed gelding: has a quick action: fairly useful handicapper: won at Goodwood in
August: ran well at Ripon (second to Hidden Dragon) and York (fourth to Smart Predator)
next 2 starts: probably best at 6f: acts on firm going, probably on soft: has been blinkered,
sometimes visored: edgy sort: sometimes early/reluctant to post, and withdrawn having
bolted under apprentice once at 6 yrs: sometimes slowly away. *T. D. Barron*

UNHOLY ALLIANCE (IRE)   2 ch.g. (Mar 29) General Monash (USA) 107 – Holy   –
Water (Monseigneur (USA) 127) [2003 p7g p7g Oct 15] €4,000Y: half-brother to 3

winners, including fairly useful 5f to 7f (including 6f at 2 yrs) winner Broadstairs Beauty (by Dominion Royale) and 1m (at 2 yrs) to 1½m winner Drinks Party (by Camden Town): dam unraced: last in maidens at Lingfield. *R. M. Flower*

UNICORN REWARD (IRE)   3 b.c. Turtle Island (IRE) 123 – Kingdom Pearl 57 (Statoblest 120) [2003 78: 8g 7m³ 8m⁵ 8.3g* 8g* 8.1m* 8.1g* 8g⁵ 8f Sep 28] neat colt: fairly useful handicapper: improved in 2003, winning at Windsor in June, Leicester and Chepstow in July and Chepstow in August: stays 1m: acts on polytrack and good to firm going, ran badly on firm final outing: usually races prominently: joined M. Hammond. *R. Hannon* — **91**

UNIGOLD (USA)   3 ch.g. Silver Deputy (CAN) – Desert Queen (USA) (Wavering Monarch (USA)) [2003 95p: 10g* 11g² 12m 10.5m³ 12g 10.1m³ 12g Sep 13] angular, good-topped gelding: smart performer: landed odds in maiden at Nottingham in March: excellent 1½ lengths second to High Accolade in listed race at Goodwood next time: below form after (including in Derby): should stay 1½m: raced only on good/good to firm ground: wore cheekpieces penultimate outing: sent to USA. *E. A. L. Dunlop* — **110 d**

UNINTENTIONAL   2 b.f. (Mar 5) Dr Devious (IRE) 127 – Tamnia 106 (Green Desert (USA) 127) [2003 6.1f 6.1d⁶ f7g⁵ f9.4g² Dec 22] strong, sturdy filly: fourth foal: half-sister to smart French 10.5f and 1½m winner Coroner (by Mtoto): dam, 2-y-o 6f/ 7f winner, half-sister to smart middle-distance stayers Azzilfi and Khamaseen: modest maiden: left J. Dunlop 22,000 gns after debut: best effort when second at Wolverhampton: will stay 1½m: acts on fibresand. *R. Brotherton* — **60**

UNITED SPIRIT (IRE)   2 b.f. (Mar 22) Fasliyev (USA) 120 – Atlantic Desire (IRE) 100 (Ela-Mana-Mou 132) [2003 6m⁵ 6d f6g⁴ Nov 29] €80,000Y, 80,000 2-y-o: rather leggy, lengthy filly: second foal: half-sister to 3-y-o Jack Durrance: dam 1m/1¼m winner: modest form in maidens: fourth at Wolverhampton: likely to stay 1m: should progress. *M. A. Magnusson* — **55 p**

UNITED UNION (IRE)   2 b. or br.g. (Apr 8) Imperial Ballet (IRE) 110 – Madagascar 43 (Puissance 110) [2003 f6s 6d³ p6g 6d Sep 26] €10,000Y: leggy, quite good-topped gelding: first foal: dam, maiden (form only at 1m), half-sister to smart 1m/1¼m winner Cap Juluca: modest maiden: third at Leicester, best effort: likely to stay 7f: acts on good to soft ground. *D. Haydn Jones* — **62**

UNIVERSAL KING (USA)   2 b.c. (Mar 5) El Prado (IRE) 119 – Arjunand (USA) (Diesis 133) [2003 5f⁵ 5.2f⁵ 5m² 7.2m² Sep 19] $25,000Y: compact colt: fluent mover: sixth foal: half-brother to useful US 1m/8.5f winner Boyum (by Valiant Nature): dam unraced sister to useful 1m/9f performer Badawi: fair maiden: second at Haydock and Ayr: should stay 1m: edgy sort: sent to Macau. *Mrs L. Stubbs* — **78**

UNLEADED   3 ch.f. Danzig Connection (USA) – Mo Stopher 47 (Sharpo 132) [2003 –: 7g 10m 12d f14g Dec 12] small, stocky filly: well held in maidens/handicaps. *J. Akehurst* — **–**

UNLEASH (USA)   4 ch.g. Benny The Dip (USA) 127 – Lemhi Go (USA) (Lemhi Gold (USA) 123) [2003 102: 16.1g* 16.2m⁴ 13.9m⁴ 18m Oct 18] strong, close-coupled gelding: useful handicapper: won John Smith's Northumberland Plate at Newcastle in — **105**

John Smith's Northumberland Plate (Handicap), Newcastle—Unleash makes a successful return to the Flat following a hat-trick of wins over hurdles; Sentinel (No.14) and Zibeline fill the minor placings

June by ½ length from Sentinel: good fourth at Ascot and York (Ebor, rallied in good style behind Saint Alebe) next 2 starts: presumably amiss when well held in Cesarewitch: should prove ideally suited by 2m+: acts on firesand, firm and soft ground: blinkered (raced freely, found nothing) final 3-y-o start: has idled: useful hurdler. *P. J. Hobbs*

UNO MENTE   4 b.f. Mind Games 121 – One Half Silver (CAN) (Plugged Nickle **70** (USA)) [2003 73: p8g³ p8g⁴ p10g⁵ f8g 10m³ 9.7m 8.3g* 8m³ 8.3g⁵ 8m Sep 24] sturdy filly: fair handicapper: won at Windsor in August: best form around 1m: acts on poly-track, form on turf only on good going or firmer: has worn cheekpieces: sold 3,400 gns. *Mrs P. N. Dutfield*

UNPERTURBED   3 ch.f. Unfuwain (USA) 131 – Mudflap 82 (Slip Anchor 136) [2003   – f8g 7m May 8] 10,000Y: second foal: dam 2-y-o 7f winner: 100/1, well held in claimer/maiden at Southwell. *J. Balding*

UNPRECEDENTED (IRE)   2 br.g. (Mar 12) Primo Dominie 121 – Misellina (FR)   – 57 (Polish Precedent (USA) 131) [2003 5g⁶ 6g 6m Sep 16] 51,000Y: quite good-topped gelding: third foal: half-brother to 3-y-o The Fisio and 4-y-o Cast Iron: dam, tempera-mental maiden, stayed 1m: signs of only a little ability in maidens: blinkered final start: sold 800 gns. *R. Hannon*

UNRIVALLED   2 b.c. (Feb 18) Unfuwain (USA) 131 – No Sugar Baby (FR) (Crystal   **88** Glitters (USA) 127) [2003 6m² 7m p7g³ 6f* Oct 27] 95,000F: sturdy colt: fluent mover: brother to 2 winners, including useful 1½m to 2m winner Sweetness Herself, and half-brother to 3 winners, including useful French winner around 7f (including at 2 yrs) Texas Tornado (by Last Tycoon): dam French maiden: fairly useful performer: landed odds in 6-runner maiden at Leicester easily by 2½ lengths from Intikraft: bred to stay at least 7f: acts on firm going, showed promise on polytrack: front runner: sold 62,000 gns, sent to USA. *J. H. M. Gosden*

UNSCRUPULOUS   4 ch.g. Machiavellian (USA) 123 – Footlight Fantasy (USA) 68   **91 p** (Nureyev (USA) 131) [2003 76: 7m 7m³ 7m² 8m* Jul 2] angular gelding: fairly useful form: won handicap at Yarmouth in July by length from Ballare: stays 1m: raced only on good ground or firmer: has given trouble in preliminaries: should improve further. *J. R. Fanshawe*

UNSHAKABLE (IRE)   4 b.g. Eagle Eyed (USA) 111 – Pepper And Salt (IRE)   **106** (Double Schwartz 128) [2003 110: 7.9m 8m⁶ 8m² 8g 7.9m 7f 8g Nov 1] good-bodied gelding: useful handicapper, lightly raced: creditable head second to Definite Guest in quite valuable event at Newbury: below form after: effective at 7f to 9f: acts on soft and good to firm ground: sometimes bandaged behind: sometimes races freely. *Bob Jones*

UNSHAKEN   9 b.h. Environment Friend 128 – Reel Foyle (USA) 77 (Irish River (FR)   **65** 131) [2003 72d, a62d: 8g 7m⁴ 8m³ 8.1g³ 8m⁴ 10.4f³ 9.1d Oct 14] strong, sturdy horse: **a–** fair performer: effective at 1m/10.4f: acts on any turf going and fibresand: tried blink-ered/visored earlier in career: held up: sold 800 gns. *E. J. Alston*

UNSHOODA   2 ch.f. (Feb 10) Machiavellian (USA) 123 – Rawaabe (USA) 87 (Nure-   **96** yev (USA) 131) [2003 6m² 6m* 6m² 7m⁶ Oct 4] lengthy, angular filly: has a quick action: sister to smart 6f (at 2 yrs) to 1m (in UAE) winner Assal, and half-sister to several winners, including 10-y-o Afaan and useful 1997 2-y-o 6f/7f winner La-Faah (by Lahib): dam, 5f winner, closely related to smart sprinter Doulab: useful performer: won maiden at Kempton in September: good 1¼ lengths second of 6 to Ruby Rocket in listed event at Ayr next time: raced too freely final start: needs to settle to stay beyond 6f. *B. W. Hills*

UNSIGNED (USA)   5 b. or br.g. Cozzene (USA) – Striata (USA) (Gone West (USA))   – [2003 65: p16g Jan 4] close-coupled, good-bodied gelding: fair handicapper at 4 yrs: well held only outing on Flat in 2003: won over hurdles in June. *R. H. Buckler*

UNSUITED   4 b.f. Revoque (IRE) 122 – Nagnagnag (IRE) 103 (Red Sunset 120) [2003   – 56: 6d 5m⁶ 7.1m⁵ p7g p7g Dec 29] lightly-raced maiden: showed little in 2003. *J. E. Long*

UNTIDY DAUGHTER   4 b.f. Sabrehill (USA) 120 – Branitska (Mummy's Pet 125)   – [2003 69: f8g 10.1g Oct 22] lightly-raced maiden on Flat: well held in handicaps in 2003: wore cheekpieces final outing: winning hurdler. *B. Ellison*

UP FRONT (IRE)   4 b.f. Up And At 'em 109 – Sable Lake (Thatching 131) [2003 48:   – f8s f8s f8s⁵ f9.4g⁵ f9.4g f8g 10m Apr 26] close-coupled filly: no form in 2003: has worn cheekpieces. *A. Berry*

UP IN FLAMES (IRE)   12 br.g. Nashamaa 113 – Bella Lucia (Camden Town 125)   – [2003 46: f12g Apr 28] leggy gelding: poor performer in 2002: tailed off only run in 2003: tried blinkered: tongue tied: usually held up (sometimes slowly away). *Mrs G. S. Rees*

UP TEMPO (IRE) 5 b.g. Flying Spur (AUS) – Musical Essence 65 (Song 132) [2003 **76** 82: f7s f8s⁴ 7m 5.9g³ 6d⁴ 7g 7m 6m² 6g³ 7f 6d 7m 7g⁶ 6f⁴ 6g Sep 27] useful-looking gelding: fair handicapper nowadays: effective at 6f to 1m: acts on any turf going/all-weather: effective with or without headgear. *T. D. Easterby*

UPTHEDALE (IRE) 2 b.g. (Mar 13) General Monash (USA) 107 – Pimpinella (IRE) **49** (Reprimand 122) [2003 5g 5g⁵ f6g 7d Nov 4] 800F, 4,200Y: sturdy gelding: first foal: dam little form: poor maiden: form only on second start: wore cheekpieces/carried head high final one. *J. R. Weymes*

URAIB (IRE) 3 b. or br.f. Mark of Esteem (IRE) 137 – Hamsaat (IRE) 80 (Sadler's **94** Wells (USA) 132) [2003 10f* 8d 9.7m⁴ 8m 8.5d³ 7m² 8m³ 7g Nov 1] big, leggy, quite good-topped filly: fourth foal: half-sister to useful 1999 2-y-o 7f winner Jalad and 1¼m winner Tanaji (both by Marju): dam, 1m winner on stiff start (would have stayed further), sister to very smart 1¼m performer Batshoof: fairly useful performer: won maiden at Kempton in June: good efforts in handicaps at Newmarket and Musselburgh sixth/seventh starts: effective at 7f to 1¼m: acts on firm and good to soft ground. *B. Hanbury*

URBAN KNIGHT 2 br.g. (Mar 22) Dracula (AUS) – Anhaar (Ela-Mana-Mou 132) **40** [2003 5.1m⁶ 5.1m 7m Jul 6] €15,000Y, 20,000 2-y-o: half-brother to 3 winners, including 3-y-o Half Inch: dam bad maiden: poor form in maidens: started very slowly in visor final start. *J. W. Unett*

URBAN MYTH 5 b.g. Shaamit (IRE) 127 – Nashville Blues (IRE) 94 (Try My Best **79** (USA) 130) [2003 49: f9.4g⁴ f9.4g³ f8.5g* f8.5g² f7g f8.5g f8.5f Jul 25] fair handicapper: won at Wolverhampton in February: stays 8.5f: acts on good to firm going and fibresand: tongue tied: races up with pace. *J. W. Unett*

URBAN ROSE 2 b.f. (Apr 30) Piccolo 121 – Blue Lamp (USA) 68 (Shadeed (USA) **69** 135) [2003 6m 6.1m* 6m 6.1f⁴ 6.1m⁴ Oct 22] 4,000Y, 17,000 2-y-o: leggy, close-coupled filly: third foal: half-sister to fairly useful 2001 2-y-o 1m winner More Specific (by Definite Article): dam maiden who stayed 1¼m: fair performer: won maiden at Warwick in September: respectable fourth in minor event at Nottingham penultimate start, best effort after: should stay 7f. *J. W. Unett*

URGENT SWIFT 10 ch.g. Beveled (USA) – Good Natured § (Troy 137) [2003 45, **–** a55: f16.2g⁴ f12g⁴ f14g⁵ Mar 11] rangy gelding: poor performer nowadays: best at 1½m **a48** to 2m: possibly unsuited by soft/heavy going, acts on any other turf/all-weather: blinkered once as 5-y-o: sometimes slowly away: usually held up. *A. P. Jarvis*

UROWELLS (IRE) 3 b.g. Sadler's Wells (USA) 132 – Highest Accolade 71 (Shirley **94 +** Heights 130) [2003 76p: 10.5d⁴ 10m* May 16] small, good-bodied gelding: reportedly injured after only 2-y-o start: fairly useful form when winning maiden at Newbury in May by ½ length from Singleton, edging left (subsequently gelded and also met minor setback): should be suited by 1½m+. *E. A. L. Dunlop*

UVANI 3 ch.f. Classic Cliche (IRE) 128 – Spirit of The Wind (USA) (Little Current **56 ?** (USA)) [2003 p12g⁴ f12s 10g Oct 25] 7,500Y: tall filly: half-sister to useful 11f winner North Wind (by Lomond) and fairly useful 1m winner Moon Mistress (by Storm Cat): dam unraced: seemingly only form (modest) when fourth in maiden at Lingfield on debut. *J. A. R. Toller*

V

VADEMECUM 2 br.g. (Mar 14) Shinko Forest (IRE) – Sunshine Coast 86 (Posse **83** (USA) 130) [2003 7m 8.3d⁴ 7m* 8.2m³ Oct 22] 20,000Y: good-topped gelding: half-brother to several winners, including 5-y-o Inchdura and 6-y-o Cote Soleil: dam best at 7f: fairly useful performer: won maiden at Newcastle in October: creditable 9 lengths third of 8 to Carini in minor event at Nottingham: barely stays 1m: acts on good to firm going. *B. Smart*

VALANCE (IRE) 3 br.g. Bahhare (USA) 122 – Glowlamp (IRE) 93 (Glow (USA)) **89** [2003 76: 8.1m 9.7m⁴ p12g* 12m 14m³ Oct 4] lengthy gelding: fairly useful performer: won maiden at Lingfield in September: good third to Ten Carat in handicap at Newmarket final start: stays 1¾m: acts on polytrack, raced only on ground firmer than good on turf: won juvenile hurdle in November. *C. R. Egerton*

VALAZAR (USA) 4 b.g. Nicholas (USA) 111 – Valor's Minion (USA) (Turkey Shoot **63** (USA)) [2003 64: f6g⁵ f5s² f5g⁴ f5g f6s f6g Dec 19] sturdy gelding: modest performer:

VAL

left T. D. Barron 2,100 gns after third start: effective at 5f/6f: acts on fibresand, raced only on going firmer than good on turf. *D. W. Chapman*

VALDASHO   4 b.f. Classic Cliche (IRE) 128 – Ma Rivale (Last Tycoon 131) [2003 47:   –
6m 6m Jun 15] sturdy filly: poor performer at 3 yrs: well held in 2003. *J. D. Bethell*

VAL DE FLEURIE (GER)   8 b.m. Mondrian (GER) 125 – Valbonne (Master Willie   64
129) [2003 11.7m 10.2f 10.2g 12f³ 12m 12.1m* 12.6m⁴ Sep 20] first foal: dam German
2-y-o 6f/6.7f winner: won 6 times in Germany up to 1¼m for W. Haustein, including 5
times in 1999: lightly raced and modest form on Flat since, winning apprentice handicap
at Chepstow in July: stays 1½m: acts on firm ground: often races prominently: successful
5 times over hurdles between July and October. *J. G. M. O'Shea*

VAL DE MAAL (IRE)   3 ch.c. Eagle Eyed (USA) 111 – Miss Bojangles (Gay Fan-   79
dango (USA) 132) [2003 74: 6g 6.1m 8.3d 7g 7s* 7m³ 7s f7g³ 6m³ 6m* 5m⁵ 6m² 6g⁴
6m Oct 1] quite good-topped colt: fair performer: won handicap at Wolverhampton in
June and minor event at Pontefract in August: effective at 6f/7f: acts on fibresand and
good to firm going: effective visored or not: usually races up with pace. *G. C. H. Chung*

VALENTIA (IRE)   2 b.f. (Feb 24) Perugino (USA) 84 – Teide (Sabrehill (USA) 120)   61
[2003 5d 6m⁵ Aug 6] €25,000Y: first foal: dam unraced half-sister to useful 1½m
performer Port Helene, herself dam of smart French middle-distance stayer Helen of
Spain: modest form in maidens at Windsor and Newcastle: should stay at least 1m.
M. H. Tompkins

VALENTINE'S DREAM   2 b.f. (Feb 14) Mind Games 121 – I'm Playing (Primo   65
Dominie 121) [2003 7g⁴ 6g⁴ 7d³ 6s a6g⁶ 6m Oct 24] 1,000Y: third foal: dam, sprint bred,
no form: fair maiden: in frame at Cologne, Krefeld and Mulheim: not discredited when
equal-seventh in sales race at Doncaster final start, slowly away: stays 7f: acts on good to
firm and good to soft going. *B. Hellier, Germany*

VALERIAN (IRE)   3 b.g. Perugino (USA) 84 – Liberty Song (IRE) (Last Tycoon 131)   78
[2003 77: 7d 10d 10g⁵ f9.4g* Nov 28] fourth foal: half-brother to 3 winners, including
useful Irish 7f (at 2 yrs) to 1½m winner Smuggler's Song (by Dr Devious): dam, French
1m and 11f winner, granddaughter of Lupe: fair performer: won maiden at Wolverhampton in November by 2½ lengths from Nicholas Nickelby, idling: stays 9.4f: acts on
fibresand and good to firm ground. *Charles O'Brien, Ireland*

VALERIE ANN BURTON (IRE)   3 br.f. Charnwood Forest (IRE) 125 – Ezilana   –
(IRE) (Shardari 134) [2003 –: 9.7m p12g May 24] no form in maidens/seller: tried in
cheekpieces. *M. R. Hoad*

VALEUREUX   5 ch.g. Cadeaux Genereux 131 – La Strada (Niniski (USA) 125) [2003   64
63: 8.3d⁴ 12g³ 13.1g³ 7.9f 9.9d 10.9m² Sep 18] big gelding: modest performer: stays
1½m: acts on good to firm and heavy ground: tried visored/in cheekpieces: none too
reliable: won over hurdles in October. *J. Hetherton*

VALIANT AIR (IRE)   2 b.c. (Jan 13) Spectrum (IRE) 126 – Shining Desert (IRE) 82   –
(Green Desert (USA) 127) [2003 7.2g 8m⁴ 8g Sep 27] 25,000F, 10,000Y: good-bodied
colt: first foal: dam, 2-y-o 5f winner, might not have been altogether genuine: signs of
only a little ability in maidens. *J. R. Weymes*

VALIANTLY   4 b.f. Anabaa (USA) 130 – Valbra (Dancing Brave (USA) 140) [2003   103
6m² 6m⁴ 6d 6v Nov 19] compact filly: fifth foal: half-sister to 9.7f winner Valfonic (by
Zafonic): dam twice-raced half-sister to dam of very smart sprinter Continent: useful
performer: won minor event at Deauville at 3 yrs: sold from P. Bary 35,000 gns afterwards: easily best effort when 1¼ lengths second to Topkamp in listed race at Haydock on
reappearance: left J. Noseda after third start: should stay 7f: acts on good to firm ground.
N. Clement, France

VALIANT ROMEO   3 b.c. Primo Dominie 121 – Desert Lynx (IRE) 79 (Green   –
Desert (USA) 127) [2003 89: 5.1m 5d 5m 5g 5f 5m 5f Oct 10] sturdy colt: fairly useful
for M. Channon at 2 yrs: showed little in 2003: often visored. *R. Bastiman*

VALJARV (IRE)   2 b.f. (Mar 28) Bluebird (USA) 125 – Iktidar 80 (Green Desert   94
(USA) 127) [2003 5.1m² 6m² 6m³ 6m⁴ 6d⁴ 6.3m 6.5m³ 6m* Oct 4] IR 14,800F, 30,000Y:
sturdy filly: half-sister to 3-y-o Ikan and 4-y-o To The Woods: dam, maiden, out of half-
sister to Sheikh Albadou: fairly useful performer: third in listed race at Newmarket and
fourth in Lowther Stakes at York (beaten 5 lengths by Carry On Katie) on third and fourth
starts: won 10-runner maiden at Newmarket by 2½ lengths from Stargem: will probably
stay 7f: acts on good to firm and good to soft going: tough and reliable. *N. P. Littmoden*

Hong Kong Vase, Sha Tin—The French again provide the 1,2 as Vallee Enchantee beats Polish Summer; Warrsan and the ex-Irish Roosevelt are close behind

VALLEE ENCHANTEE (IRE) 3 b.f. Peintre Celebre (USA) 137 – Verveine (USA) 120 (Lear Fan (USA) 130) [2003 104p: 10.5g⁶ 10.5g³ 10.5g 13.5g* 12m⁴ 12g* 12m* Dec 14] leggy, sparely-made filly: smart performer: bit disappointing first 3 starts in 2003 (including in Prix de Diane at Chantilly third occasion), but successful after in Prix de Pomone at Deauville (by 6 lengths from Treble Heights) in August, Prix du Conseil de Paris at Longchamp (by ½ length from Kalabar) in October and Hong Kong Vase at Sha Tin (beat Polish Summer ¾ length) in December: respectable 3¼ lengths fourth to Mezzo Soprano in Prix Vermeille at Longchamp fifth outing: better suited by 1½m/13f than shorter: acts on heavy and good to firm going: wears special noseband: held up. *E. Lellouche, France* **115**

VALUABLE GIFT 6 ch.g. Cadeaux Genereux 131 – Valbra (Dancing Brave (USA) 140) [2003 65: f6g⁴ f7s⁶ f6g³ f6g² 6f f6g f6g f6s Dec 6] strong gelding: modest maiden: left I. Semple and below form after fourth start: effective at 5f/6f: acts on fibresand and good to soft going: wears headgear: tried tongue tied: sometimes finds little. *R. C. Guest* **59 d**

VALUABLE (IRE) 6 b.m. Jurado (USA) – Can't Afford It (IRE) 44 (Glow (USA)) [2003 f9.4s Apr 12] first foal: dam ran twice in Ireland: no sign of ability, including in seller at Wolverhampton. *Mrs A. Duffield* **–**

VALUE ADDED 3 b.f. Petoski 135 – Valiancy 87 (Grundy 137) [2003 p10g⁶ f9.4g⁴ p12g⁶ 12m⁴ Mar 27] 16,500F: closely related to German Derby runner-up Calcavecchia (by Niniski), and half-sister to several winners, including 5-y-o Basinet: dam 1¼m winner out of Oaks second Val's Girl: modest maiden: should stay 1½m. *M. A. Jarvis* **62 ?**

VAMOSE (IRE) 2 ro.c. (Feb 28) Victory Note (USA) 120 – Narrow Band (IRE) (Standaan (FR) 118) [2003 7g 7m² 8d³ 7m Aug 9] 11,500Y: workmanlike colt: fifth foal: half-brother to fairly useful 2002 2-y-o 6f winner Xhosa (by Ali-Royal) and winner in Italy by Colonel Collins: dam unraced: fair maiden: placed twice at Newmarket: not sure to stay beyond 1m. *Miss Gay Kelleway* **69 +**

VAMPIRE QUEEN (IRE) 2 b.f. (May 5) General Monash (USA) 107 – Taniokey (Grundy 137) [2003 7m f7g⁶ f7g f7g Dec 12] sister to useful 2000 2-y-o 5f/6f winner Bram Stoker (later successful in Italy) and half-sister to several winners, including fairly useful 1¼m/1½m winner Wafir (by Scenic): dam Irish 1m winner: modest maiden: trained on debut by J. Harley in Ireland: best effort when sixth at Wolverhampton: not sure to stay beyond 7f. *R. P. Elliott* **54**

VANBRUGH (FR) 3 ch.g. Starborough 126 – Renovate (Generous (IRE) 139) [2003 56: f8g* p10g² 10.3m 7g 10s 10m f12g p10g⁶ p12g⁶ f11g f14g² f16g² f14.8s⁶ Dec 31] fair handicapper: won at Southwell in January: left Gay Kelleway after second start, A. Bailey after third: stays 2m: acts on all-weather, no solid form on turf: often tongue tied: wore cheekpieces/visor last 6 starts: usually races prominently. *Miss D. A. McHale* **? a74**

VANDAL 3 b.c. Entrepreneur 123 – Vax Star 96 (Petong 126) [2003 7g⁶ 7m² 7f³ 7g p7g* p7g 8m Sep 17] sturdy, attractive colt: second foal: half-brother to fairly useful 2001 2-y-o 6f winner Negligee (by Night Shift): dam, 2-y-o 5f winner, became one to treat with caution: fair performer: best effort when winning handicap at Lingfield in August: should stay 1m: acts on polytrack and firm going: sold 12,000 gns. *J. A. R. Toller* **77**

VANDENBERGHE 4 b.g. Millkom 124 – Child Star (FR) 58 (Bellypha 130) [2003 65: 14.1m p12g f9.4g⁶ f12g³ f16g⁵ Dec 16] deep-girthed gelding: modest handicapper: barely stays 2m: acts on all-weather and firm going. *J. A. Osborne* **57**

VANDERLIN 4 ch.g. Halling (USA) 133 – Massorah (FR) 108 (Habitat 134) [2003 109: 6g³ 6f 7g 6g 7m* 7g² 7g² 6m 7.5m⁴ 6m Oct 17] strong gelding: usually takes the eye: smart performer: won listed event at York in August by short head from Monsieur Bond: good second in handicap at Chester (beaten 1½ lengths by Little Good Bay) and listed event at Epsom (beaten 2 lengths by Monsieur Bond): stays easy 7f: acts on good to firm and good to soft going: tried visored: tended to hang/carry head awkwardly earlier in career. *A. M. Balding* **114**

VANGELIS (USA) 4 gr.c. Highest Honor (FR) 124 – Capades Dancer (USA) (Gate Dancer (USA)) [2003 8.5g* 9.5d 8g⁵ 10d* 10g 9.8d 12g³ 10d Nov 16] third foal: brother to smart French performer up to 1½m Marichal and half-brother to a winner in USA by Chimes Band: dam, won in USA, half-sister to US Grade 1 2-y-o 8.5f winner Capades: smart performer: won minor event at Longchamp in April and Grand Prix de Vichy (by 2 lengths from Labirinto) in July: creditable efforts when seventh to demoted Storming Home in Arlington Million next time, staying on well, and 1¼ lengths third to Vallee Enchantee in Prix du Conseil de Paris at Longchamp: stays 1½m: raced only on good going or softer. *A. de Royer Dupre, France* **116**

VANILLA MOON 3 b.f. Emperor Jones (USA) 119 – Daarat Alayaam (IRE) (Reference Point 139) [2003 58: p7g 11.6g 10m⁴ 10m 11.8m f12g p12g⁴ 8.3m 11f⁵ Oct 12] tall, leggy filly: modest maiden: stays easy 11f: acts on polytrack and firm ground: blinkered/visored last 4 starts. *J. R. Jenkins* **61**

VANISHED (IRE) 3 b.f. Fayruz 116 – Where's The Money 87 (Lochnager 132) [2003 77, a59: 5d f6g⁴ 6s f5g² f6g⁴ 5m⁴ f5g Aug 8] modest performer: will prove best at 5f/easy 6f: acts on fibresand, good to firm and good to soft ground: wore cheekpieces last 2 starts. *K. A. Ryan* **62**

VANISHING DANCER (SWI) 6 ch.g. Llandaff (USA) – Vanishing Prairie (USA) 93 (Alysheba (USA)) [2003 16m⁴ 14m 14.1m⁶ 14.1f³ Aug 20] fair handicapper: left T. Etherington after second start: stays easy 2m: acts on all-weather and firm going, not on soft: tried visored (pulled too hard)/tongue tied. *B. Ellison* **65**

VANTAGE (IRE) 2 b.g. (Feb 21) Marju (IRE) 127 – Anna Comnena (IRE) 71 (Shareef Dancer (USA) 135) [2003 6m 7m³ 8.2m³ 8d Sep 11] 22,000Y: big, lengthy gelding: brother to 1999 2-y-o 5f winner Gipsy Anna and half-brother to several winners, including 5-y-o Sadlers Wings and useful 1¼m winner (stayed 12.5f) Abyaan (by Ela-Mana-Mou): dam maiden who stayed 1½m: fair maiden: third at Newmarket and Nottingham (4-runner minor event): possibly amiss final start: should be suited by 1¼m/1½m. *N. P. Littmoden* **79**

VA PENSIRO 3 b.g. Lugana Beach 116 – Hopperetta 45 (Rock Hopper 124) [2003 –: f6g Jan 24] well held in maidens/claimer at Wolverhampton. *D. Haydn Jones* **—**

VARIETY CLUB 2 b.c. (Mar 24) Royal Applause 124 – Starfida (Soviet Star (USA) 128) [2003 7m 8.3g 8m Aug 23] 10,000Y: leggy colt: fourth foal: dam, ran once, half-sister to dam of very smart sprinter Pivotal: best effort in maidens (modest form) when seventh at Windsor on second start: sweating/coltish final one: not sure to stay beyond 1m. *A. M. Balding* **63**

VARNAY 2 b.f. (Feb 7) Machiavellian (USA) 123 – Valleria 76 (Sadler's Wells (USA) 132) [2003 6m⁵ 5m* 6m² 6.5d⁶ 7m³ Oct 4] quite attractive filly: first foal: dam, Irish maiden who stayed 1¼m, sister to smart 1¼m winner (including in UAE) Musha Merr: fairly useful performer: won maiden at Beverley in August: good efforts in nurseries at Ascot, Doncaster and Newmarket (late headway after slow start when third to Snow **91**

Goose) after: will stay 1m: acts on good to firm and good to soft ground: visored last 4 outings. *D. R. Loder*

VARUNI (IRE)   2 b.f. (Feb 12) Ali-Royal (IRE) 127 – Sauvignon (IRE) 63 (Alzao   –
(USA) 117) [2003 6m Aug 3] 4,000Y: sixth foal: half-sister to 6-y-o Lordofenchantment
and winner in Sweden by Polish Patriot: dam 7f winner: 66/1, slowly away and always
behind in maiden at Newbury. *J. G. Portman*

VAS Y CARLA (USA)   2 ch.f. (Feb 21) Gone West (USA) – Lady Carla 122 (Caerleon   **80**
(USA) 132) [2003 7m⁶ 7m² 7g⁶ Nov 1] close-coupled filly: third foal: dam 1m (at 2 yrs)
to 1½m (Oaks) winner: best effort in maidens (fairly useful form) when short-headed
by Torcross at Leicester: favourite, hampered when respectable sixth to Damsel at
Newmarket final start: likely to be suited by 1¼m/1½m: sold 180,000 gns. *J. L. Dunlop*

VAUDEVIRE   2 b.c. (Mar 30) Dancing Spree (USA) – Approved Quality (IRE) 66   –
(Persian Heights 129) [2003 5m⁶ Apr 17] tall, close-coupled colt: first foal: dam maiden
who barely stayed 1½m: tailed off in maiden at Ripon, reportedly lame. *A. Berry*

VAUGHAN   2 b.c. (Feb 4) Machiavellian (USA) 123 – Labibeh (USA) 109 (Lyphard   **94 p**
(USA) 132) [2003 8g 8.2d* Nov 6] 42,000Y: big, good-topped colt: third foal: dam,
winner around 1½m, out of sister to very smart French performer up to 10.5f Smuggly:
much better effort in maidens when winning 16-runner event at Nottingham by 5 lengths
from Rarefied, still green but asserting quickly final 1f and eased close home: will be
suited by 1¼m/1½m: should make a useful 3-y-o at least. *Mrs A. J. Perrett*

VEINTE SIETE (USA)   3 ch.g. Trempolino (USA) 135 – Satz (USA) 50 (The Min-   **57 §**
strel (CAN) 135) [2003 –: 7g 7m⁵ 8m⁶ 8f³ 10m 9.7g Sep 1] strong, close-coupled gelding:
modest maiden: refused to race penultimate outing, tailed off in blinkers final one: should
stay 1¼m: raced only on good ground or firmer: one to avoid. *J. A. R. Toller*

VELOCITAS   2 b.g. (Feb 19) Magic Ring (IRE) 115 – Folly Finnesse 80 (Joligeneration   –
111) [2003 p7g Oct 15] 12,500Y: fourth foal: half-brother to 2000 2-y-o 5f/6f winner
Quantum Lady (by Mujadil) and a winner in Switzerland by Bigstone: dam, 6f (at 2 yrs)
to 11f winner, half-sister to useful sprinter Westcourt Magic: 50/1, well beaten in maiden
at Lingfield. *H. J. Collingridge*

VELOCITY BELLE   2 b.f. (Apr 7) Groom Dancer (USA) 128 – Rapid Repeat (IRE)   **62**
95 (Exactly Sharp (USA) 121) [2003 7f⁵ 7m 8m⁴ 10f³ 8d Oct 14] 10,000Y: seventh foal:
half-sister to 3 winners, including useful 1½m winner Metronome (by Salse) and fairly
useful 1998 2-y-o 7f winner Subito (by Darshaan): dam 2-y-o 7f winner who stayed 1¾m:
modest maiden: third in nursery at Nottingham: stayed 1¼m: acted on firm going: dead.
M. L. W. Bell

VELOCITYS IMAGE (IRE)   3 b.f. Tagula (IRE) 116 – Pike Creek (USA) 86   –
(Alwasmi (USA) 115) [2003 8.1m 6f⁶ 8m Oct 6] IR 1,700Y: lengthy filly: first foal: dam,
1½m winner who stayed 15f, closely related to useful 7f/1m performer Moccasin Run:
little form in maidens. *E. J. Alston*

VELVET RHYTHM   3 b.f. Forzando 122 – Bold Gayle 57 (Never So Bold 135)   –
[2003 f11g Dec 19] first foal: dam, maiden, likely to have proved best at 5f: 25/1, soundly
beaten in maiden at Southwell. *K. R. Burke*

VELVET TOUCH   2 b.f. (Feb 8) Danzig Connection (USA) – Soft Touch (GER)   **66**
(Horst-Herbert) [2003 6.1d³ p6g f5g² f5g² Dec 19] 500Y: workmanlike filly: third foal:
dam German 7f/7.5f winner: fair maiden: placed at Nottingham and Southwell (twice):
will probably prove best at 5f/6f. *J. R. Jenkins*

VELVET WATERS   2 b.f. (Apr 5) Unfuwain (USA) 131 – Gleaming Water 81 (Kala-   **60**
glow 132) [2003 6d⁶ 7m 8m Sep 9] leggy filly: half-sister to several winners, including
1995 2-y-o 6f winner (probably stayed 1½m) Faraway Waters (by Pharly) and 1m/1¼m
winner Prince of Denial (by Soviet Star), both useful: dam, 2-y-o 6f winner, sister to
smart stayer Shining Water, herself dam of Tenby: modest form in maidens: likely to be
suited by 1¼m/1½m. *R. F. Johnson Houghton*

VENABLES (USA)   2 ch.c. (Feb 5) Stravinsky (USA) 133 – Hope For A Breeze   **100**
(CAN) (Briartic (CAN)) [2003 6m⁶ 6f* 6m* 6g⁴ 6m Aug 20] $190,000F, 175,000Y:
rangy colt: on weak side at 2 yrs: fourth foal: half-brother to winner in Canada by Dehere:
dam, champion filly in Canada, won at 8.5f/9f: useful performer: won minor event at
Kempton and listed race at Newbury (beat America America by ¾ length) in July: good
fourth, beaten just over a length by Carrizo Creek, in Richmond Stakes at Goodwood:
respectable eighth of 9 in Gimcrack Stakes at York: should stay 7f: acts on firm going.
R. Hannon

VENDOME (IRE) 5 b.g. General Monash (USA) 107 – Kealbra Lady (Petong 126) –
[2003 61d: f5s Jan 31] strong gelding: poor mover: just modest at best in 2002, and well
held only 5-y-o start. *J. A. Osborne*

VENDORS MISTAKE (IRE) 2 b.f. (Jan 14) Danehill (USA) 126 – Sunspangled **61 ?**
(IRE) 111 (Caerleon (USA) 132) [2003 p7g⁶ p6g p8g Dec 20] 18,000Y: first foal: dam,
Irish 2-y-o 7f/1m (Fillies' Mile) winner and second in Irish Oaks, out of very smart
performer up to 1½m Filia Ardross: modest maiden: best effort on debut, though hung
right/flashed tail: seems not to stay 1m. *Andrew Reid*

VENERDI TREDICI (IRE) 2 b.f. (Apr 12) Desert Style (IRE) 121 – Stifen (Burslem **55**
123) [2003 f5g 6m 6f³ 6m Oct 2] rather leggy filly: half-sister to numerous winners,
including 5f (at 2 yrs)/6f winner Ruzen (by Fayruz) and 2000 2-y-o 6f winner Where's
Jasper (by Common Grounds), both fairly useful: dam unraced: modest maiden: third
of 4 at Brighton: well held in nursery final start: not sure to stay much beyond 6f.
P. A. Blockley

VENETIAN PRIDE (USA) 2 b.f. (Mar 25) Gone West (USA) – Via Borghese (USA) **89**
116 (Seattle Dancer (USA) 119) [2003 6g* 6m⁶ 6g³ 6m 6d Sep 29] leggy filly: sixth foal:
sister to fairly useful 7f winner Pietro Siena and closely related to 2 winners abroad by
Seeking The Gold, including 2-y-o winner in USA: dam, Irish 1m winner, later US Grade
2 9f winner: fairly useful performer: won maiden at Hamilton in June: creditable third in
nursery at Goodwood, best effort after (twice highly tried): should stay 7f. *M. Johnston*

VENETIAN ROMANCE (IRE) 2 ch.f. (Feb 2) Desert Story (IRE) 115 – Cipriani **54**
102 (Habitat 134) [2003 5.2m 6m 6m 7d³ 8g 8m⁵ Oct 17] 7,000 2-y-o: smallish filly:
half-sister to 3 winners, including fairly useful 6f winner Hoh Returns (by Fairy King)
and 1996 2-y-o 5f winner Seaside (by Salt Dome): dam, best at 7f/1m in Ireland, out of
champion New Zealand mare La Mer: modest maiden: third in nursery at Catterick:
probably stays 1m: acts on good to soft ground. *A. P. Jones*

VENEZIANA 2 ch.f. (Apr 21) Vettori (IRE) 119 – Fairy Story (IRE) 80 (Persian Bold **67**
123) [2003 7m p7g³ p7g Oct 30] tall, leggy filly: fifth foal: half-sister to 3-y-o Zietory
and useful 7f (at 2 yrs)/1m winner (later winner in Hong Kong) Welenska (by Danzig
Connection): dam, 7f winner (including at 2 yrs), out of half-sister to dam of Shaamit:
best effort in maidens (fair form) when strong-finishing third at Lingfield: apparently
amiss final start: should stay at least 1m. *P. F. I. Cole*

VENGEANCE 3 b.c. Fleetwood (IRE) 107 – Lady Isabell 62 (Rambo Dancer (CAN) **95**
107) [2003 10g² 9.7m* 12m* 12m² 11.6m* 12d 12m⁵ Aug 27] tall colt: first foal: dam
maiden who should have been suited by 1m+, half-sister to useful 7f performer Hand
Chime: useful performer: won maiden at Folkestone and handicap at Goodwood in May
then handicap at Windsor in July: good fifth to Trouble At Bay in handicap at Ascot final
start: stays 1½m: acts on good to firm ground. *Mrs A. J. Perrett*

VENGEROV 2 b.c. (Feb 7) Piccolo 73 (Indian Ridge 123) [2003 **64**
6m⁵ 6m 7g³ 7.1m⁴ 7.9f Oct 9] useful-looking colt: second foal: half-brother to 3-y-o
Dmitri: dam 6f winner: modest maiden: third at Folkestone: ran creditably in nursery
final start: stays 1m: acts on firm going. *M. L. W. Bell*

VENTURI 2 b.f. (Feb 7) Danehill Dancer (IRE) 117 – Zagreb Flyer (Old Vic 136) **103 p**
[2003 5s⁶ 6m* 7m* Sep 21] 4,000F, 32,000Y: fourth foal: dam unraced out of half-sister
to 2000 Guineas winner To-Agori-Mou: useful form: won maiden at the Curragh in
August by 9 lengths from Ocean Bounty: progressed again to win 10-runner C. L. Weld
Park Stakes there in September by ¾ length from Misty Heights, coming from last to lead
final 1f: will stay 1m: sent to USA: open to further improvement. *D. Wachman, Ireland*

VERASI 2 b.g. (Mar 9) Kahyasi 130 – Fair Verona (USA) (Alleged (USA) 138) [2003 –
8g 7s f9.4g Nov 15] leggy, quite good-topped gelding: first foal: dam, ran twice, out of
half-sister to US Grade 1 winners Tis Juliet and Stella Madrid: signs of ability in maidens:
will be suited by 1¼m+. *R. Charlton*

VERKHOTINA 2 b.f. (Apr 21) Barathea (IRE) 127 – Alusha 88 (Soviet Star (USA) **75**
128) [2003 6g⁵ 6m⁵ Sep 30] close-coupled, good-topped filly: fourth foal: half-sister to
useful 1¼m/1½m winner Scheming (by Machiavellian) and 3-y-o Proxima: dam,
lightly-raced 2-y-o 6f winner who stayed 1¼m, half-sister to smart performer up to 1½m
Prize Giving: best effort in maidens (fair form) when fifth to Oriental Warrior at Newbury
second start: possibly amiss final one: will stay at least 1m. *R. Charlton*

VERMILION CREEK 4 b.f. Makbul 104 – Cloudy Reef 57 (Cragador 110) [2003 **68**
56: f12g² f8.5g⁴ f9.4s³ f12g⁶ 8m 8f* 10.2m⁶ 10m* 8.2f⁴ f9.4g 8.2d f9.4g f8g f8g f9.4g⁶ **a54**
Dec 22] close-coupled filly: fair on turf, modest on all-weather: won apprentice events at

Ripon (seller) in June and Nottingham (handicap) in August: effective at 1m to 1½m: acts on all-weather, firm and good to soft going: none too consistent. *R. Hollinshead*

VERMILLIANN (IRE) 2 b.f. (Mar 4) Mujadil (USA) 119 – Refined (IRE) 95 (Stato-blest 120) [2003 5m* 5g* 5g⁶ Oct 11] €50,000Y: angular filly: first foal: dam, 2-y-o 5f winner, half-sister to smart 7f/1m performer Pipe Major: useful form: won maiden at Newmarket in April and minor event at Salisbury (beat Powerful Parrish 2 lengths) in May: shaped well when 7 lengths sixth of 11 to Majestic Missile in Cornwallis Stakes at Ascot, slowly away but travelling strongly long way: likely to prove best at 5f. *R. Hannon* **98**

VERTEDANZ (IRE) 3 b.f. Sesaro (USA) 81 – Blade of Grass 78 (Kris 135) [2003 61: p8g⁵ p10g⁶ p8g 8d 10m Jun 2] IR 23,000F, 15,000Y: good-topped filly: half-sister to 3 winners, including sprinter Warning Star (by Warning) and French 1m/1¼m winner Brindle (by Polar Falcon), both useful: dam 7f winner: modest maiden handicapper: left F. Ennis in Ireland, after third start: stays easy 1¼m: acts on good to soft going and polytrack: tried visored/tongue tied. *Miss I. E. Craig* **57**

VERTICAL 3 ch.g. Ashkalani (IRE) 128 – Waft (USA) 67 (Topsider (USA)) [2003 –: 7f⁴ 9.7m 10m³ 10.2m 10m³ Oct 2] modest maiden: stays 1¼m: raced only on going firmer than good on turf. *P. R. Chamings* **60**

VERY EXCLUSIVE (USA) 4 b.g. Royal Academy (USA) 130 – Exclusive Davis (USA) (Our Native (USA)) [2003 –: 11.5g 11.5g⁵ 10m 10.9m 10f⁴ 12m³ 11.9m p13g Dec 29] poor maiden: left R. Cowell after fourth start: stays easy 1½m: raced only on good going or firmer on turf: sometimes tongue tied (has reportedly had breathing problems when not): tried in cheekpieces: free-going sort. *G. L. Moore* **46**

VESPONE (IRE) 3 ch.c. Llandaff (USA) – Vanishing Prairie (USA) 93 (Alysheba (USA)) [2003 8g* 7g² 10s* 9m* 10g* 10m Oct 18] **125**

Godolphin usually bolsters its squad with summer and autumn signings and 2003 proved no exception. Among those due to carry the royal blue silks for the first time during the next season are Refuse To Bend, Zafeen and Snow Ridge, successful in 2003 in the Two Thousand Guineas, St James's Palace Stakes and Royal Lodge Stakes respectively, while the Cheveley Park winner Carry On Katie has also joined Godolphin, having been purchased by an associate of Sheikh Mohammed on his advice after her wide-margin debut success in July. Another high-profile acquisition was the dual Group 1 winner Vespone, winner of four of his six starts, for trainer Nicolas Clement, at the time of the purchase in July, including the Prix Jean Prat at Chantilly and the Juddmonte Grand Prix de Paris at Longchamp, both in June. Vespone has already raced for his new owners—finishing tailed-off last in the Champion Stakes at Newmarket on his final outing—but is reportedly set to follow in the hoofprints of so many other Godolphin horses and be campaigned internationally as a four-year-old. Vespone's first intended race at four, the J & B Met at Kenilworth in South Africa, would have made him the first major foreign contender for a race in that country, but an outbreak of equine flu has led to the race being postponed from January to April, resulting in plans for Vespone reportedly being shelved.

Vespone ran only once at two, runner-up in a newcomers event at Maisons-Laffitte, and made a successful reappearance in a minor event at Saint-Cloud in March. Unsuited by the drop to seven furlongs when a length-and-a-half second to

Juddmonte Grand Prix de Paris, Longchamp—a second Group 1 success for Vespone, who dictates the pace and keeps on too well for, from right to left, Magistretti, Look Honey and Lateen Sails (No.6)

Mister Charm in the Prix Djebel at Maisons-Laffitte the following month, Vespone was then tried at a mile and a quarter in the five-runner Prix La Force at Saint-Cloud in May. Though he refused to settle, Vespone beat Vadalix readily by two lengths before progressing again in the Prix Jean Prat. Facing seven rivals, Vespone was allowed to dictate matters and ran out a convincing winner, beating Prince Kirk by three lengths with Tashkandi, another Godolphin acquisition at the end of the season, a short neck away in third. Then came the eleven-runner Grand Prix de Paris three weeks later when Vespone started favourite. Again he was allowed the run of things up front, but he was always travelling well and responded once challenged, coming home a length and a half ahead of British-trained Magistretti who had won the Dante at York and was to finish a good second to Falbrav in the International Stakes at York on his next outing. Third and fourth in the Grand Prix de Paris were Look Honey and the Godolphin-owned Lateen Sails, both of whom won pattern races in France on their next starts. Vespone was off the course for four months afterwards, completing the switch to Godolphin in the interim before shaping as if something had gone amiss in the Champion, making the early running, racing apart from the main group, and weakening tamely in the final three furlongs.

Vespone (IRE) (ch.c. 2000)	Llandaff (USA) (ch 1990)	Lyphard (b 1969)	Northern Dancer Goofed
		Dahlia (ch 1970)	Vaguely Noble Charming Alibi
	Vanishing Prairie (USA) (ch 1990)	Alysheba (b 1984)	Alydar Belsheba
		Venise (ch 1985)	Nureyev Virunga

Godolphin's "Vespone"

Amazingly, at the time of Vespone's Group 1 win, the advertised fee of his sire Llandaff was reportedly the equivalent of less than £100. Now standing in Poland, where that fee is sure to be higher in 2004, Llandaff was resident at the Gestut Sohrenhof in Switzerland at the time of Vespone's conception. The very well bred Llandaff was owned by Sheikh Mohammed throughout his racing career and won the Jersey Derby, a Grade 2 event on turf in the States over eight and a half furlongs. He is a brother to the Prix Lupin winner Dahar, who was later successful in Grade 1 company in North America and a half-brother to the North American Grade 1 winners Rivlia, Delegant and Dahlia's Dreamer. All are out of Dahlia, whose Group 2-winning daughter Wajd in turn produced St Leger winner Nedawi. Dahlia was an extraordinary racemare, twice winner of the King George and successful in five different countries, and her career at stud turned out to be equally as extraordinary. Her tally of four Group/Grade 1 winners has been matched in recent times only by Fall Aspen (Northern Aspen, Timber Country, Fort Wood and Hamas) and by Toussaud (Chester House, Honest Lady, Chiselling and Empire Maker). Vespone's dam Vanishing Prairie showed fairly useful form when winning over a mile and a quarter and a mile and a half in Ireland. She is a half-sister to the very smart French performers Vetheuil, who was best at a mile, and Verveine (also dam of Vallee Enchantee and the latest E.P. Taylor Stakes winner Volga), who stayed a mile and a half. Vespone is Vanishing Prairie's sixth foal, and he is a brother to two winners, including the mile-and-a-half winner and winning hurdler Vanishing Dancer, and a half-brother to three winners in France, notably the smart Prix Penelope winner La Sylphide (by Barathea). Vespone, who went through the sales ring for 450,000 francs as a yearling, acts on soft and good to firm ground. Though his biggest wins have come at nine furlongs and a mile and a quarter, he races freely and should prove as effective at a mile. *Saeed bin Suroor*

VESTA FLAME 2 b.f. (Apr 25) Vettori (IRE) 119 – Ciel de Feu (USA) (Blushing – John (USA) 120) [2003 8d f8.5g f9.4g Dec 22] rather sparely-made filly: fourth foal: half-sister to 1m/9f winner in Spain/France by Primo Dominie: dam, French 9f winner, out of top-class Prix de Diane/Prix Vermeille winner Northern Trick: well beaten in maidens. *M. Johnston*

VEVERKA 2 b.f. (Mar 12) King's Theatre (IRE) 128 – Once Smitten (IRE) 58 (Caer- **74** leon (USA) 132) [2003 6g 7m² 7m⁶ 8m² 8m³ 7m Oct 1] 2,500Y: small filly: first foal: dam, ran 3 times in Ireland, out of half-sister to dam of Vintage Crop: fair maiden: second at Lingfield and Leicester: should stay 1¼m: seemed not to handle track at Brighton third outing: races prominently. *W. S. Kittow*

VEVINA (USA) 2 b.f. (Apr 9) Rahy (USA) 115 – Lovely Keri (USA) (Eastern Echo – p (USA)) [2003 6m p7g 7m Oct 13] $500,000Y: rangy filly: second foal: dam unraced half-sister to champion US filly Serena's Song (by Rahy), herself dam of Coronation Stakes winner Sophisticat and 2-y-o Grand Reward: backward, well beaten in maidens: type to do better as 3-y-o. *Sir Mark Prescott*

VIBURNUM 9 b.m. Old Vic 136 – Burning Desire (Kalaglow 132) [2003 –: f9.4g Jan – 17] lightly-raced maiden: cheekpieces, well beaten only 9-y-o outing. *M. Wellings*

VICARIO 2 gr.c. (Mar 15) Vettori (IRE) 119 – Arantxa 77§ (Sharpo 132) [2003 8s 8.2d – Nov 6] 8,000Y: close-coupled colt: second foal: half-brother to 2002 2-y-o 6f winner Vilas (by Inchinor): dam, unreliable 6f winner (including at 2 yrs), half-sister to useful Irish performer up to 1¾m Damancher: tailed off in maidens at Yarmouth and Notting-ham. *M. L. W. Bell*

VICARS DESTINY 5 b.m. Sir Harry Lewis (USA) 127 – Church Leap (Pollerton **73** 115) [2003 11.9m⁶ 12m⁵ 8m⁶ 15.9m² 18m⁶ Sep 18] leggy mare: fourth foal: dam winning 3m hurdler: fair maiden on Flat: will probably prove best around 2m: raced only on good to firm ground: winning hurdler. *Mrs S. Lamyman*

VICEREINE 3 b.f. Zamindar (USA) 116 – Victoriana (USA) (Storm Bird (CAN) 134) **94** [2003 9m⁵ 8f* 10m⁵ 10.1m⁵ 8m² Oct 14] compact, quite attractive filly: sister to smart French 1m/1¼m performer Victorian Order and half-sister to 3 winners, including fairly useful miler around 1m Victorian Style (by Nashwan): dam, French 5f winner, half-sister to Xaar from family of El Gran Senor and Try My Best: fairly useful performer: won maiden at Bath in June: best efforts when fifth in listed events at Newbury (to Approach) and Yarmouth (to Echoes In Eternity): stays 1¼m: raced only on going firmer than good: sold 240,000 gns. *J. H. M. Gosden*

UAE Derby, Nad Al Sheba—
*Victory Moon adds to his previous month's win in the UAE 2000 Guineas;
the Godolphin pair Songlark (rail) and Inamorato (left, noseband) are placed*

VICIOUS KNIGHT   5 b.g. Night Shift (USA) – Myth 89 (Troy 137) [2003 112§: **106 §**
7.1m* 8g⁵ May 5] robust, good sort: good walker: just useful performer in 2003: won
minor event at Warwick (edged left) in April by length from Granny's Pet: creditable fifth
to Putra Pekan in handicap at Kempton following month: subsequently reported to have
been injured: best at 7f/1m: raced mainly on good going or firmer: sometimes finds little:
unreliable. *L. M. Cumani*

VICIOUS LADY   3 b.f. Vettori (IRE) 119 – Ling Lane (Slip Anchor 136) [2003 –: 10s   **–**
10g 12.1d 10f Oct 1] good-bodied filly: little form. *R. M. Whitaker*

VICIOUS PRINCE (IRE)   4 b.g. Sadler's Wells (USA) 132 – Sunny Flower (FR)   **–**
(Dom Racine (FR) 121) [2003 100: a12f 12m 13.9m 13.1m 13d 13.1d Oct 14] strong,
lengthy gelding: has a fluent, round action: useful handicapper at 3 yrs: well held in 2003.
R. M. Whitaker

VICIOUS WARRIOR   4 b.g. Elmaamul (USA) 125 – Ling Lane (Slip Anchor 136)   **93**
[2003 97: a10f⁴ a9f a9f a8f 10.3m² 10.1d 10.3g 8m⁴ 10.4f 8m² f8.5g Nov 17] good sort: **a83**
fairly useful handicapper: best 4-y-o effort when second to Millagros at Musselburgh
tenth start: probably better at 1m than 1¼m: acts on good to firm ground, probably on dirt
(well held on fibresand): free-going sort. *R. M. Whitaker*

VICTORIAN DANCER (IRE)   2 b.f. (Mar 6) Groom Dancer (USA) 128 – Victoria   **60**
Regia (IRE) 90 (Lomond (USA) 128) [2003 6d 6m⁴ f6g 7m 7m⁴ Sep 4] smallish filly:
second foal: half-sister to 3-y-o Topkamp: dam 2-y-o 6f winner (later 1m winner in USA)
out of half-sister to Prix Vermeille winner Walensee: modest maiden: barely stays 7f: acts
on good to firm going (hampered on fibresand). *K. A. Ryan*

VICTORIA PARK (IRE)   3 b.f. Victory Note (USA) 120 – Break For Tee (IRE) 62   **61**
(Executive Perk 120) [2003 f7s f6g 6m⁶ 5m² 6m⁴ 5m* 5f² 5m⁵ 5m 6d 5m Aug 4]
€3,000Y: third foal: half-sister to useful Irish 9f/1¼m winner Distinguished Cove (by
Distinctly North): dam, third at 1½m in Ireland, half-sister to dam of high-class performer
up to 1½m River Keen: modest handicapper: won at Carlisle in June: will prove best at
5f/6f: acts on firm ground: very slowly away last 2 outings: refused to enter stall final
intended appearance: sold 600 gns in November. *D. Nicholls*

VICTOR VALENTINE (IRE)   4 ch.g. Ridgewood Ben 113 – Tarliya (IRE) 73   –
(Doyoun 124) [2003 –, a64: 7f 6g Jun 11] lengthy gelding: poor mover: lightly-raced
maiden: well held at 4 yrs. *M. D. Hammond*

VICTORY FLIP (IRE)   3 b.f. Victory Note (USA) 120 – Two Magpies 43 (Doulab   **58**
(USA) 115) [2003 67, a–: f7g² f7s⁵ f6g f7s⁶ f6g² 6.1d f8.5g² f8.5g 8.1m f8.5g f7g³ f7g⁶
f8g⁴ f5g⁶ f6s Dec 27] lengthy filly: modest maiden: stays 8.5f: acts on fibresand, unraced
on extremes of going on turf: usually wears cheekpieces: sometimes slowly away: has
hung left: none too reliable. *R. Hollinshead*

VICTORY LAP (GER)   2 ch.f. (May 1) Grand Lodge (USA) 125 – Vicenca (USA)   **67 p**
(Sky Classic (CAN)) [2003 f8s³ Dec 13] €30,000Y, resold 19,000Y: second foal:
half-sister to German 1m winner Victory's Pleasure (by Desert King): dam, French 11f to
12.5f winner, closely related to Racing Post Trophy winner Seattle Rhyme: 20/1 and
green, 5 lengths third of 16 to Bethanys Boy in maiden at Southwell, starting slowly: will
stay at least 1¼m: sure to do better. *M. R. Channon*

VICTORY MOON (SAF)   4 b.c. Al Mufti (USA) 112 – Dancing Flower (SAF)   **120**
(Dancing Champ (USA)) [2003 107: a8f* a9f² a10f* 8f 10g⁵ 12d Jul 26] tall, rather leggy
South African-bred colt: has won 5 of his 9 starts, namely maiden at Scottsville, minor
event at Jebel Ali and prestige race at Nad Al Sheba in 2002, then UAE 2000 Guineas
(beat Western Diplomat by ½ length) in February and UAE Derby (by ½ length from
Songlark) in March, both at Nad Al Sheba: best effort in Britain when 2¾ lengths fifth to
Falbrav in Eclipse Stakes at Sandown, keeping on well having been shuffled back 2f out:
well held in King George VI and Queen Elizabeth Diamond Stakes at Ascot final outing:

MAD Syndicate's "Victory Moon"

stays 1¼m: acts on dirt, best turf run on good going: sweating last 2 starts: free-going sort. *M. de Kock, South Africa*

VICTORY QUEST (IRE) 3 b.g. Victory Note (USA) 120 – Marade (USA) (Dahar (USA) 125) [2003 8g 10d 12.1d 14m* 12.3m² 14.1m⁵ f14g² f14g* f12s² Dec 27] IR 8,500F, 25,000Y: fourth foal: half-brother to winners in Italy and Greece by Paris House and Distinctly North: dam, ran twice in Ireland, out of half-sister to dam of high-class 1m/9f performer Priolo: fairly useful handicapper: won at Goodwood in June and (having left J. Hills after fifth start) Southwell in December: stays 1¾m: acts on fibresand, unraced on extremes of going on turf: visored last 6 starts. *Mrs S. Lamyman* — **82**

VICTORY ROLL 7 b.g. In The Wings 128 – Persian Victory (IRE) (Persian Bold 123) [2003 p16g⁶ May 17] tall, lengthy gelding: modest maiden on Flat: stays easy 2m: acts on heavy going and polytrack: winning hurdler. *Miss E. C. Lavelle* — **64**

VICTORY SIGN (IRE) 3 b.g. Forzando 122 – Mo Ceri 63 (Kampala 120) [2003 63: 10m⁶ 11.6g⁵ 10m² 11.6d⁴ 12.1m³ 12.1m⁶ 12.1g⁵ 12.1m* 11.5s⁴ Aug 28] big, useful-looking gelding: fair performer: won selling handicap at Beverley in July: claimed £6,000 final start: stays 1½m: has form on good to soft going, but best efforts on ground firmer than good (acts on firm): tried visored. *K. R. Burke* — **68**

VICTORY VEE 3 ch.g. Vettori (IRE) 119 – Aldevonie 75 (Green Desert (USA) 127) [2003 57: f7s f6g² f6s⁴ f6g⁶ f6g² 6m 6s f8.5g² f6g f8.5g⁴ f7g* f7g³ p7g f7g f7g³ Nov 21] well-made gelding: fair performer: won maiden at Wolverhampton in August: effective at 7f to 8.5f: acts on good to firm going and fibresand: none too consistent. *M. Blanshard* — **a66**

VICTORY VENTURE (IRE) 3 b.g. Victory Note (USA) 120 – Shirley Venture 74 (Be My Chief (USA) 122) [2003 8g² 12m* 12.3m 11.5g 10g³ 10d Oct 13] leggy, quite good-topped gelding: first foal: dam, placed up to 2m on Flat, successful over hurdles: fairly useful performer: won maiden at Catterick in August: easily best effort when third in handicap at Windsor: will stay 1¾m: acts on good to firm ground. *M. Johnston* — **87**

VIENNA'S BOY (IRE) 2 b.c. (Apr 27) Victory Note (USA) 120 – Shinkoh Rose (FR) 67 (Warning 136) [2003 5m* 5m⁶ 5f² 5g* 5g³ 7m⁴ 5d² 6m 7m² 6m Oct 4] €8,000Y, 18,000 2-y-o: tall, leggy colt: fourth foal: half-brother to 3-y-o Oh So Rosie and winner abroad by Danehill: dam third at 9f in Ireland: fairly useful performer: won maiden at Folkestone in May and minor event at Windsor in June: placed in listed races at Sandown and Deauville (second to Black Escort) and minor contest at Goodwood after: probably stays easy 7f: acts on firm and good to soft ground: tends to hang. *R. Hannon* — **93**

VI ET VIRTITE 4 b.f. Dancing Spree (USA) – Princess Scully (Weld 122) [2003 p12g f12s Sep 26] 3,000 2-y-o: first foal: dam unraced: well beaten in maidens at Lingfield and Southwell (cheekpieces). *Mrs A. Dobloug Talbot, Norway* — **–**

VIEWFORTH 5 b.g. Emarati (USA) 74 – Miriam 59 (Forzando 122) [2003 70: 5m 6m 6d 6d² 5g² 5g² 5m 5d⁵ 6m* 5m* 5d² 6m⁵ 5d⁴ 5g⁶ 7.1m 6s Nov 3] good-bodied gelding: fairly useful handicapper: left Miss L. Perratt after seventh start: much improved at Haydock, winning at Beverley in August then good second to Blackheath on former course: best at 5f/6f: acts on any going: blinkered. *I. Semple* — **91**

VIEW THE FACTS 4 b.f. So Factual (USA) 120 – Scenic View (IRE) (Scenic 128) [2003 –: f8.5g p7g Oct 27] little form. *P. L. Gilligan* — **–**

VIGOROUS (IRE) 3 b.f. Danetime (IRE) 121 – Merrily 73 (Sharrood (USA) 124) [2003 62p: 6m* 5m* 6m 6m 5f 5m⁴ 5f⁴ 5m Oct 20] leggy, quite good-topped filly: fairly useful performer: won 4-runner events at Folkestone (maiden) and Hamilton (minor event) in April: ran creditably last 3 outings: may prove best at 5f: raced only on going firmer than good: has run well when sweating: often slowly away: sold 27,000 gns. *M. R. Channon* — **82**

VIGOUREUX (FR) 4 b.g. Villez (USA) – Rouge Folie (FR) (Agent Bleu (FR) 118) [2003 12d⁶ Nov 4] ex-French gelding: first foal: dam ran once in France: won juvenile hurdle in France for M. Rolland in 2002: seemingly modest form when sixth in maiden at Catterick on Flat debut, racing freely. *S. Gollings* — **54 ?**

VIJAY (IRE) 4 ch.g. Eagle Eyed (USA) 111 – Foolish Fun (Fools Holme (USA)) [2003 59: 5d⁴ 6m* 7d a6g² 5f* 5m⁵ 5g⁴ 5f⁵ 6m⁴ 5g³ 6g⁴ 5m³ 5f⁶ f7g Nov 21] IR 9,000Y: fourth foal: half-brother to useful 1998 2-y-o 6f winner Hunan (by College Chapel): dam lightly raced in Ireland: fair performer: won handicaps at Cork in April and Down Royal in June: left J. Gorman in Ireland/off 2 months, well held on British/all-weather debut final start: effective at 5f to 7f: acts on firm and good to soft going: tried blinkered, including last 3 outings. *I. Semple* — **65**

VIKINGS BAY   2 b.c. (Apr 17) Intikhab (USA) 135 – Night At Sea 107 (Night Shift **96**
(USA)) [2003 6g⁵ f5s* 6g* 8f² Dec 29] 14,000Y: strong, good-bodied colt: half-brother
to several winners, including 7f to 13f winner Muhandis (by Persian Bold) and 7f/1m
winner Nautical Warning (by Warning), both fairly useful: dam sprinter: useful performer: won maiden at Southwell in September and nursery at Ayr (18-runner contest) in
October: sold out of J. Gosden's stable 160,000 gns before good 4 lengths second to
Greek Sun in non-graded event at Santa Anita: stays 1m: acts on firm going and fibresand. *M. Puhich, USA*

VILAMOURA   2 b.g. (Mar 30) Forzando 122 – Alpi Dora (Valiyar 129) [2003 p6g²   **82 p**
f6g* Oct 16] 15,500Y: lengthy, angular gelding: half-brother to 17f winner Windmill
Lane (by Saddlers' Hall) and 2 winners in Italy: dam Italian 7.5f (at 2 yrs) and 8.5f
winner: fairly useful form in maidens at Lingfield and Southwell, getting up close home
to land odds on latter course by short head from College Time: will stay 7f: sold 26,000
gns, sent to USA: should progress. *W. J. Haggas*

VILLA DEL SOL   4 br.f. Tagula (IRE) 116 – Admonish 57 (Warning 136) [2003 –,   **–**
a51: f7s f8g⁴ f7s⁵ f7g⁴ Feb 7] leggy, plain filly: poor handicapper: effective at 6f/7f: acts   **a46**
on fibresand, good to firm and soft going. *B. Smart*

VINANDO   2 ch.c. (Mar 28) Hernando (FR) 127 – Sirena (GER) (Tejano (USA)) [2003   **76 p**
7g⁵ Nov 1] 160,000Y: tall, close-coupled colt: first foal: dam, German 1m to 9.5f winner,
half-sister to high-class German 1¼m/1½m performer Silvano and 5-y-o Sabiango:
50/1, 4½ lengths fifth of 12 to Golden Grace in maiden at Newmarket, slowly away,
unbalanced Dip and best work finish: will be suited by 1¼m/1½m: sure to improve.
C. R. Egerton

VINCENT   8 b.g. Anshan 119 – Top-Anna (IRE) 71 (Ela-Mana-Mou 132) [2003 –,   **54**
a51: f14g f14.8g⁶ f16.2g² f16.2g⁴ 14.1d⁵ 16m 15.8m⁶ f14g* f16g* Dec 16] tall gelding:
modest handicapper: won twice at Southwell in December: stays 17f: acts on any turf
going and fibresand: tried visored/blinkered, not in 2003: carries head high: held up.
John A. Harris

VINCENTIA   5 ch.m. Komaite (USA) – Vatersay (USA) (Far North (CAN) 120) [2003   **60**
69: 6.1g⁶ 5g⁶ 6g f5s³ Sep 2] sparely-made mare: poor mover: modest performer: effective
at 5f to 7f: acts on fibresand, good to firm and heavy going: usually races prominently:
none too consistent. *C. Smith*

VINDICATION   3 ch.g. Compton Place 125 – Prince's Feather (IRE) 77 (Cadeaux   **102**
Genereux 131) [2003 80: 7m 7g* 7m² 6.5m⁵ 7g 7g⁶ p7g⁵ 7m* 7m* p7g Oct 30] well-
made gelding: useful handicapper: won at Lingfield in June, Goodwood in September
and Newmarket (beat Master Robbie a head) in October: stays 7f: acts on polytrack and
good to firm going, probably on soft: visored (slowly away) sixth start: usually tongue
tied. *J. R. Fanshawe*

VIN DU PAYS   3 b.g. Alzao (USA) 117 – Royale Rose (FR) 75 (Bering 136) [2003 78:   **54 +**
p10g⁶ 11.6d 8.3d 10m 10m 12m p16g f8.5s⁵ 10.1d⁵ f12g* f16.2g* f14g⁶ Nov 24] fair on   **a78**
all-weather, modest on turf: won minor event (by 11 lengths) in October and handicap in
November, both at Wolverhampton: stays 2m: acts on all-weather and good to soft
ground: none too reliable. *M. Blanshard*

VINNIE ROE (IRE)   5 b.h. Definite Article 121 – Kayu (Tap On Wood 130)   **125**
[2003 126: 12f* 14f* 12s⁵ 15.5s⁴ Oct 26]
    Vinnie Roe did not make his reappearance as a five-year-old until August,
but he added two more wins to an already admirable record, most importantly
becoming the first horse to win the Irish St Leger three times. Vinnie Roe had
purposely been given plenty of time to recover from his exertions in the Melbourne
Cup on his final start in 2002, when he had finished a highly creditable fourth under
top weight behind stable-companion Media Puzzle on very firm going. That run
capped a fine four-year-old campaign, Vinnie Roe having already won the Irish
St Leger, two listed events and finished a good second in the Gold Cup at Royal
Ascot. Vinnie Roe's six victories as a two- and three-year-old included his first
Irish St Leger and the Prix Royal-Oak. Vinnie Roe did well to make a winning
reappearance in 2003 in the listed Ballyroan Stakes over a mile and a half at Leopardstown—a race he had also won in 2002—looking in trouble halfway up the
straight but staying on gamely once getting a gap to beat Carpanetto by a head,
before running in the six-runner Irish Field St Leger at the Curragh in September.
Despite both his record in the race and the fact that his campaign had been geared

Ballyroan Stakes, Leopardstown—Vinnie Roe (noseband) makes a successful return in a race he also won in 2002; he stays on gamely to reel in Carpanetto (No.4)

towards the contest, 2/1-shot Vinnie Roe did not start favourite. Heading the betting at 15/8 was Bollin Eric, the 2002 St Leger winner fresh from a comfortable victory in the Lonsdale Stakes at York on his previous outing. Also in the line-up was 11/4-shot Powerscourt, who had also won at York on his previous outing, beating Brian Boru by a neck in the Great Voltigeur. Brian Boru, incidentally, was favourite for the St Leger at Doncaster, timed to go off only twenty minutes after the Irish version. The other principal candidate was the progressive British-trained four-year-old Gamut, who started at 8/1, tackling a mile and three quarters for the first time. Gamut set the pace until Vinnie Roe took the lead over a furlong out. Keeping on well, Vinnie Roe had a length to spare over Gamut, with Powerscourt a very

Irish Field St Leger, the Curragh—Vinnie Roe completes a unique hat-trick in this event; Gamut (behind winner), Powerscourt and Bollin Eric make him pull out all the stops

close, fast-finishing third. Three quarters of a length behind Powerscourt was a below-par Bollin Eric in fourth, well clear of the rank outsiders Queens Wharf and Rayshan. Vinnie Roe was sent for the Arc at Longchamp in October on his next outing, when the soft ground was expected to bring his stamina into play, and he was far from discredited in finishing fifth behind Dalakhani, beaten just under nine lengths. Vinnie Roe started favourite but managed only fourth to Westerner when bidding for a second success in the Prix Royal-Oak three weeks later, possibly feeling the effects of his race in the Arc.

Vinnie Roe (IRE) (b.h. 1998)	Definite Article (b 1992)	Indian Ridge (ch 1985)	Ahonoora Hillbrow
		Summer Fashion (b 1985)	Moorestyle My Candy
	Kayu (ch 1985)	Tap On Wood (ch 1976)	Sallust Cat O'Mountaine
		Ladytown (ch 1980)	English Prince Supreme Lady

    The pedigree of the leggy, useful-looking Vinnie Roe has been detailed in previous editions of *Racehorses*. He stays two and a half miles and is to have the Gold Cup as his first major target as a six-year-old. A clash between Vinnie Roe and the 2003 Gold Cup winner Mr Dinos would be a race to savour. Slightly further down the road, Vinnie Roe is likely to make a fourth appearance in the Irish St Leger, though another tilt at the Melbourne Cup looks less likely given his trainer's critical remarks about the firmness of the going sometimes at Flemington in November. Usually blinkered nowadays, though not in the most recent season on either his reappearance (for the second year in a row) or on his final outing, the game, genuine and consistent Vinnie Roe acts on any going. *D. K. Weld, Ireland*

VINTAGE PREMIUM 6 b.g. Forzando 122 – Julia Domna (Dominion 123) [2003 **104** 114: 10g⁶ 10.3m² 9.9m⁴ 10m³ 10.3f² 11.9g Jul 5] tall, leggy gelding: just useful performer in 2003, best efforts when ¾-length second to Parasol in listed event at Chester and when beaten 1½ lengths by Leo's Luckyman in 2-runner minor event at Doncaster: stays 11f: acts on any turf going and fibresand: visored once: usually races prominently. *R. A. Fahey*

VINTAGE STYLE 4 ch.g. Piccolo 121 – Gibaltarik (IRE) 68 (Jareer (USA) 115) **61** [2003 71: 5.9f 6g³ 6m 6g 6m 6f⁴ 7g 6m⁴ 8m f7g⁵ f6g Nov 25] lengthy gelding: just modest **a49 +** performer on turf, poor on all-weather in 2003: stays 7f: acts on all-weather, firm and soft going: often wears cheekpieces/blinkers: none too reliable. *H. A. McWilliams*

VINTAGE TIPPLE (IRE) 3 b.f. Entrepreneur 123 – Overruled (IRE) 91 (Last **117** Tycoon 131) [2003 98p: 7d² 12g* 10f 12d⁶ Oct 12]
    The talk after Vintage Tipple's success in the Darley Irish Oaks at the Curragh in July was as much about her trainer as of the filly herself. Not only had Paddy Mullins trained his first classic winner, but at the ripe old age of eighty-four he had become the oldest trainer to do so in living memory. Mullins was, however, certainly no stranger to big-race successes. In a career spanning half a century he had hit the heights under both codes. He trained the mare Dawn Run, who, in the 'eighties, became the first and thus far only jumper to win both the Champion Hurdle and the Cheltenham Gold Cup, while on the Flat he had charge of the high-class Hurry Harriet, third in the Irish Oaks in 1973 before going on to win the Champion Stakes at Newmarket from Allez France later that season.
    Vintage Tipple had long been compared favourably to Hurry Harriet by Mullins, though the form she had shown in three outings before the Irish Oaks had fallen well short of the standard required for the race. Vintage Tipple won a maiden over a mile at Tralee and a minor event at the Curragh over seven furlongs as a two-year-old, and finished two lengths second of eight to Walayef in the Athasi Stakes at the Curragh in April on her reappearance, also over seven furlongs, an effort that represented only useful form. Vintage Tipple was found to have suffered a hairline fracture to a hind cannon bone after the Athasi Stakes and her consequent absence made victory in the Irish Oaks look a tall order. But Vintage Tipple justified Mullins' faith in her, running by far her best race stepped up to a mile and a half. She faced ten rivals, including the Irish One Thousand Guineas winner Yesterday (who started favourite), the filly who beat Yesterday in the Oaks, Casual Look, and

the first two in the Ribblesdale at Royal Ascot, Spanish Sun and Ocean Silk. In a strongly-run race, Dettori held up Vintage Tipple some way off the pace set by Yesterday's stable-companion L'Ancresse and, turning for home, still had quite a bit to do. Vintage Tipple stayed on strongly, however, getting on top well inside the final furlong as L'Ancresse tired late in the race. Vintage Tipple passed the post with a length and a half to spare, L'Ancresse holding off third-placed Casual Look by a head. Yesterday, set even more to do than the winner, came a further two lengths back in fourth; Spanish Sun and Ocean Silk were sixth and seventh. Being relatively unexposed, high hopes were understandably entertained for Vintage Tipple after the Irish Oaks, including an ambitious tilt at the Arc, but she disappointed in her next two races. She was tailed off in the Irish Champion Stakes at Leopardstown (reportedly her blood wasn't right for a few days afterwards), and then managed only sixth in a listed event at the Curragh on her final start, behind L'Ancresse.

Vintage Tipple was retired at the end of the season and is due to visit Dubai Destination, the winner of the Queen Anne Stakes in 2003. Vintage Tipple's Irish Oaks win came too late for her sire Entrepreneur, who is now in Japan. Entrepreneur was also represented in 2003 by the smart Scottish Derby winner Princely Venture, but, given the opportunities he received, his overall record at stud is disappointing. Entrepreneur's progeny have tended to stay well, though, and there is also plenty of stamina on the distaff side of Vintage Tipple's pedigree. Her

Darley Irish Oaks, the Curragh—Vintage Tipple (hooped sleeves) proves well suited by the marked step up in trip and provides a popular win for her veteran trainer; she stays on strongly to overhaul L'Ancresse (left) and Casual Look

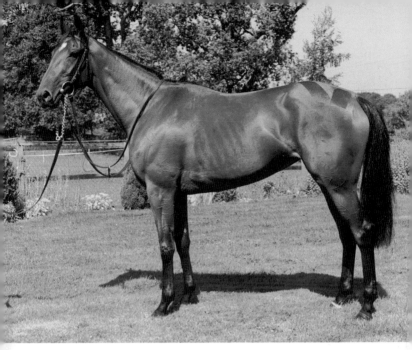

Mr Patrick J. O'Donovan's "Vintage Tipple"

Vintage Tipple (IRE) (b.f. 2000)	Entrepreneur (b 1994)	Sadler's Wells (b 1981)	Northern Dancer
			Fairy Bridge
		Exclusive Order (ch 1979)	Exclusive Native
			Bonavista
	Overruled (IRE) (b 1993)	Last Tycoon (b 1983)	Try My Best
			Mill Princess
		Overcall (b 1984)	Bustino
			Melodramatic

dam Overruled was a fairly useful performer for David Loder, winning over a mile as a two-year-old then over a mile and a quarter at three and showing her form at up to a mile and three quarters. Like Vintage Tipple, however, she ran only six times. Vintage Tipple is her dam's second foal to race after the Spectrum colt Spettro, a winner up to a mile and a half in Italy who showed useful form for Paul Cole as a two-year-old. Overruled's two-year-old colt Vintage Fizz (by Ashkalani), also with the Mullins stable, finished in mid-division in a maiden at the Curragh on his only start in the autumn. Overruled is a half-sister to the smart Overbury, winner of the Grade 2 American Derby and second in the Derby Italiano and Deutsches Derby in 1994 before winning the very valuable Queen Elizabeth II Cup at Sha Tin the following year, and is out of a sister to the dam of high-class Melbourne Cup and dual Irish St Leger winner Vintage Crop. For her part, Vintage Tipple would probably have stayed a mile and three quarters, and she acted on good to firm and good to soft going. Incidentally, Vintage Tipple can be counted among the biggest bargains of recent years; bought for only €16,500 early as a two-year-old, Vintage Tipple won over €270,000 on the racecourse and is now worth a good deal more than that as a broodmare. *Patrick Mullins, Ireland*

VIOLA DA BRACCIO (IRE) 2 ch.f. (Apr 21) Vettori (IRE) 119 – Push A Button – (Bold Lad (IRE) 133) [2003 8m Oct 17] lengthy, quite good-topped filly: half-sister to several winners, including 8-y-o Wuxi Venture and 6-y-o Winning Venture and to dam of Rock of Gibraltar: dam, Irish 2-y-o 6f winner, half-sister to Riverman: 33/1, in rear in maiden at Newmarket, racing freely up with pace early. *D. J. Daly*

VIOLENT 5 b.m. Deploy 131 – Gentle Irony 65 (Mazilier (USA) 107) [2003 51d: – 10.2m 11.9m May 14] small mare: no longer of any account: tried visored/blinkered/tongue tied. *Jamie Poulton*

VIOLET AVENUE 2 ch.f. (Apr 26) Muhtarram (USA) 125 – Ivoronica 89 (Targowice **61** (USA) 130) [2003 6g² 6d 6m⁴ Aug 23] half-sister to several winners, including sprinters Lochonica (by Lochnager) and Diamond Appeal (by Star Appeal) and 8.5f and 1¼m winner Putuna (by Generous), all useful: dam 2-y-o 5f winner: best effort in maidens (modest form) when second at Ayr: needs to settle to stay beyond 6f. *J. G. Given*

VIPASSANA 3 b.f. Sadler's Wells (USA) 132 – Reef Squaw (Darshaan 133) [2003 –p: **98** 10m³ 12m² 14.1f* 12g⁴ 12d⁶ 12s⁴ 12v⁶ Nov 19] big, quite attractive filly: useful performer: made all in maiden at Carlisle in August on final start for Sir Michael Stoute: much better form all 4 starts in listed races in France afterwards: will probably stay 2m: best form on good ground or softer (acts on heavy). *D. Sepulchre, France*

VIRGIN SOLDIER (IRE) 7 ch.g. Waajib 121 – Never Been Chaste (Posse (USA) **86** 130) [2003 90: 13.8m 16m³ 16g⁶ May 31] angular gelding: fairly useful handicapper: stays 2¼m: acts on fibresand, good to firm and good to soft going: well held blinkered/visored: none too consistent: won 4 times over fences between July and October. *G. A. Swinbank*

VIRTUOSO 9 b.g. Suave Dancer (USA) 136 – Creake 80 (Derring-Do 131) [2003 – p12g Feb 1] fairly useful maiden for C. O'Brien in Ireland at 3 yrs: well held only outing on Flat since: one-time useful hurdler/fairly useful chaser. *B. G. Powell*

VIRTUS 3 ch.c. Machiavellian (USA) 123 – Exclusive Virtue (USA) 94 (Shadeed **60** (USA) 135) [2003 8.1m⁴ Jun 6] lengthy colt: closely related to useful 1½m winner Exclusion Zone and fairly useful performer up to 11.5f Virtuous, 1m winner at 2 yrs (both by Exit To Nowhere), and half-brother to winner in Germany by Polar Falcon: dam, 2-y-o 7f winner who stayed 1½m, half-sister to 2000 Guineas winner Entrepreneur and Coronation Stakes winner Exclusive: 5/1 and green, fourth to Low Cloud in maiden at Haydock, slowly away: sold 18,000 gns. *J. R. Fanshawe*

VISION OF DREAMS 3 b.f. Efisio 120 – Dark Eyed Lady (IRE) 82 (Exhibitioner **91 d** 111) [2003 93: 6m⁵ 6g⁶ 5.2m 6.1g 5d 5m f5g Nov 21] fairly useful performer: long way below form last 4 starts: stays 6f: acts on fibresand, yet to race on extremes of going on turf: tried blinkered/hooded: sold 7,500 gns. *B. J. Meehan*

VISION OF NIGHT 7 b.h. Night Shift (USA) – Dreamawhile 85 (Known Fact **108** (USA) 135) [2003 115: 6g⁶ 6m 5m² 6m* 5g³ 6m 6m² 6m* 6m³ 5m 6m⁶ Oct 17] smallish, strong horse: smart performer at best: just useful in 2003, winning minor events at Yarmouth in June and August: tenth career success when beating Budelli 1½ lengths in latter: placed otherwise in listed races at Kempton, Sandown and Goodwood (short of room when third to Acclamation), and minor event at Yarmouth (second to Ashdown Express) on seventh outing: effective at 5f/6f: unraced on heavy going, acted on any other: blinkered last 9 starts: often hung left: waited with: to stand at Bracklyn Stud, nr Mullingar, Co Westmeath, Ireland. *J. L. Dunlop*

VITA SPERICOLATA (IRE) 6 b.m. Prince Sabo 123 – Ahonita 90 (Ahonoora **100** 122) [2003 101: 5m 5m 5.1m⁵ 6.1m² 6m⁴ 6m³ 5g 5.2m 6.1d 5g Oct 11] lengthy, rather plain mare: useful performer: creditable efforts at 6 yrs only when placed in listed events at Chester (second to Resplendent Cee) and Pontefract (third to Lochridge): best at 5f/6f: acts on any going: tried blinkered, sometimes visored: has edged left: often makes running. *J. S. Wainwright*

VITELUCY 4 b.f. Vettori (IRE) 119 – Classic Line 71 (Last Tycoon 131) [2003 62: **54** p13g² p13g* 12m f14.8s Jul 14] lengthy filly: modest performer: won claimer at Lingfield (left A. Balding) in February: should stay 1¾m: acts on polytrack, probably on heavy and good to firm going: won over hurdles in August. *Miss S. J. Wilton*

VITTORIOSO (IRE) 2 b.g. (Apr 1) Victory Note (USA) 120 – Miss Anita (IRE) 70 **55** (Anita's Prince 126) [2003 f6g f6g⁵ f7g Dec 12] €2,000Y, 12,000 2-y-o: third foal: dam, Irish 5f winner, later successful in Belgium: best effort in maidens (modest form) when fifth at Wolverhampton: should stay 7f: wore cheekpieces all starts. *Miss Gay Kelleway*

VIVA ATLAS ESPANA 3 b.f. Piccolo 121 – Bay Risk (Risk Me (FR) 127) [2003 –: 6g 7g 8.5g⁶ 8.5m Jul 31] poor maiden: stays 8.5f: often slowly away. *Miss B. Sanders* **39**

VIZULIZE 4 b.f. Robellino (USA) 127 – Euridice (IRE) 66 (Woodman (USA) 126) [2003 70: 12m⁴ 11.7m 12m³ 10.3m⁵ 10.2m⁴ 9f 10.2m⁵ 8f⁴ 8.1g Sep 11] good-topped filly: fair maiden: stays easy 1½m: acts on firm ground: tried blinkered: free-going sort. *B. R. Millman* **66**

VLASTA WEINER 3 b.g. Magic Ring (IRE) 115 – Armaiti 78 (Sayf El Arab (USA) 127) [2003 65d: 6g 5.1m 7m 5.1g 6.1m 7.1m 7g⁶ Sep 16] poor maiden: stays 7f: acts on good to firm going: tried blinkered. *J. M. Bradley* **–**

VODKA QUEEN (IRE) 4 b.f. Ali-Royal (IRE) 127 – Gentle Guest (IRE) (Be My Guest (USA) 126) [2003 36: f12s⁴ f11s Jan 16] bad maiden: tried visored/blinkered: sold 500 gns. *K. R. Burke* **27**

VOICE MAIL 4 b.g. So Factual (USA) 120 – Wizardry 83 (Shirley Heights 130) [2003 78: p7g³ p7g³ p8g³ p8g⁶ p8g⁴ p8g⁴ 8.1g⁵ 8m⁶ 8.3m 8m 8f* 9f² 8.5m³ 8f³ 9g⁴ 8m⁴ 8f⁵ 8.5g⁵ 8m Sep 16] useful-looking gelding: fairly useful handicapper: won at Bath in June: effective at 7f to 9f: acts on polytrack and firm going, probably on soft: effective visored or not: held up: consistent. *A. M. Balding* **81**

VOILE (IRE) 2 b.f. (Apr 28) Barathea (IRE) 127 – Samriah (IRE) (Wassl 125) [2003 6m* 6m² 6g⁴ 6g³ 7m⁴ 6m⁵ Oct 2] 32,000Y: quite good-topped filly: half-sister to several winners, including fairly useful 1997 2-y-o 5f winner Baby Grand (by Mukaddamah) and 6-y-o Cedar Master: dam unraced: useful performer: won maiden at Newbury in June: placed in listed race at Newmarket and Princess Margaret Stakes at Ascot (third to River Belle): good fifth, beaten nearly 3 lengths by Carry On Katie, in Cheveley Park Stakes at Newmarket, getting going too late: free-going sort, but will probably stay 1m: handled turns poorly at Leopardstown third. *R. Hannon* **100**

VOIX DU NORD (FR) 2 b.c. (Feb 27) Valanour (IRE) 125 – Dame Edith (FR) (Top Ville 129) [2003 7d² 7.5g* 8d² 8g⁴ 9g² 10d* Nov 8] second foal: dam, lightly raced in France, half-sister to smart French performers Varxi (up to 1¼m) and Snow Cap (up to 1½m): smart performer: won minor event at Deauville in August and Criterium de Saint-Cloud in November, latter in workmanlike style by 1½ lengths from Simplex: in frame in between in valuable listed race at Deauville (1½ lengths second to Gwaihir), Prix des Chenes at Longchamp (3¾ lengths fourth to Bago) and Prix de Conde at Longchamp (½-length second to Latice): should stay 1½m. *D. Smaga, France* **113**

VOLATICUS (IRE) 2 b.c. (May 2) Desert Story (IRE) 115 – Haysel (IRE) (Petorius 117) [2003 6m Sep 18] €3,800Y, 50,000 2-y-o: second foal: dam unraced: 33/1 and green, well held in maiden at Ayr. *D. Nicholls* **–**

VOLCANIC 4 b.g. Zafonic (USA) 130 – Ryafan (USA) 121 (Lear Fan (USA) 130) [2003 63: p7g p10g 7m 6m Aug 1] leggy, good-topped gelding: modest maiden at 3 yrs, well held in 2003: tried visored, usually tongue tied: sometimes slowly away. *P. D. Evans* **–**

VOLUPTUOUS 3 b.f. Polish Precedent (USA) 131 – Alzianah 102 (Alzao (USA) 117) [2003 65: f6g* p7g f7s³ f7g² f7s³ f6g 7m 8.1m f6g Oct 16] fair performer: won maiden at Southwell in January: well below form last 4 starts, leaving J. Osborne after seventh: should stay 1m: acts on fibresand: reared as stall opened sixth outing: tried in cheekpieces. *T. H. Caldwell* **72 d**

Criterium de Saint-Cloud, Saint-Cloud—Voix du Nord (quartered cap) and Simplex fight it out

VONADAISY   2 b.f. (Apr 21) Averti (IRE) 117 – Vavona 60 (Ballad Rock 122) [2003   **72**
6m⁶ 6m 6m³ 6.5d⁴ 8g⁴ Sep 27] 800F, 15,000Y: rather leggy filly: third foal: sister to
3-y-o Aversham and half-sister to 10.5f winner in Italy by Dolphin Street: dam maiden
half-sister to smart 6f/7f performer Savahra Sound: fair maiden: third at Ascot: stays 6.5f:
acts on good to firm and good to soft going. *W. J. Haggas*

VORTEX   4 b.c. Danehill (USA) 126 – Roupala (USA) 75 (Vaguely Noble 140) [2003   **82**
76: 7m² 8m⁶ 7g²ᵈ 8.2m* f7g* 8d⁶ 7m Aug 24] big, good-bodied colt: fairly useful   **a88**
performer: won minor events at Nottingham and Wolverhampton (best effort) in July,
idling both times: effective at 7f/1m: acts on all-weather and good to firm going: tongue
tied: visored (raced freely) final start: has been heavily bandaged in front: held up. *Miss
Gay Kelleway*

VOYAGER (IRE)   3 b.c. Green Desert (USA) 127 – Rafha 123 (Kris 135) [2003 –p: **–**
8.2g Mar 26] leggy, quite good-topped colt: well held in maidens/handicap. *J. L. Dunlop*

VRISAKI (IRE)   2 b.c. (Feb 19) Docksider (USA) 124 – Kingdom Queen (IRE) 65   **61**
(Night Shift (USA)) [2003 6m p6g Dec 6] 13,000Y: second foal: half-brother to 3-y-o
Janes Gem: dam, 1¼m winner, stayed 15f: off 6 months, better effort in maidens (modest
form) when seventh at Lingfield: should stay 1m. *Miss D. Mountain*

VRUBEL (IRE)   4 ch.g. Entrepreneur 123 – Renzola (Dragonara Palace (USA) 115)   **53**
[2003 66, a66: p10g p10g 9.9m³ 9f 9f Jul 2] well-made gelding: modest performer: won
in Jersey in August: stays 1¼m: acts on firm going, soft and all-weather: wore cheekpieces last 3 starts: none too consistent. *H. J. Collingridge*

W

WAAEDAH (USA)   2 ch.f. (Apr 13) Halling (USA) 133 – Agama (USA) 44 (Nureyev   **81**
(USA) 131) [2003 5.1f 7g* 7m⁶ 7m² 7m Sep 7] rangy, rather unfurnished filly: fifth foal:
sister to UAE 1½m winner Saihook and half-sister to 3 winners, including useful 1997
2-y-o 7f/1m winner Setteen (by Robellino) and 3-y-o Shelini: dam, poor form both starts
in Britain, 13.5f winner in France: fairly useful performer: won maiden at Epsom in
July: form in nurseries after only when good second of 5 on same track: will stay 1m.
M. R. Channon

WADUD   3 b.f. Nashwan (USA) 135 – The Perfect Life (IRE) 106 (Try My Best (USA)   **59**
130) [2003 10m 11.8m 12f⁴ 16.2m Jul 21] rather leggy filly: sixth foal: sister to 3 winners,
including smart 7f (at 2 yrs) to 1½m (Gordon Stakes) winner Rabah and useful 1m/
1¼m winner Muhtafel and half-sister to fairly useful 2001 2-y-o 7f winner Nayyel (by
Zafonic): dam, French 5f (at 2 yrs) and 7f winner, sister to Last Tycoon: modest maiden:
reportedly had breathing problem when tailed off final start: stays 1½m: tail swisher.
J. L. Dunlop

WAFANI   4 b.g. Mtoto 134 – Wafa (IRE) (Kefaah (USA) 124) [2003 –: 10.4f Jun 13]   **–**
leggy gelding: no sign of ability: tried blinkered. *W. J. Musson*

WAGES   3 b.g. Lake Coniston (IRE) 131 – Green Divot (Green Desert (USA) 127)   **–**
[2003 83: p7g 6m 7d p7g 10.4f 9g Oct 24] leggy gelding: fairly useful in 2002: well held
at 3 yrs, leaving A. Hales after third start: stays 7f: acts on polytrack: sometimes races
freely, including when tried blinkered. *P. M. Phelan*

WAHCHI (IRE)   4 ch.c. Nashwan (USA) 135 – Nafhaat (USA) 91 (Roberto (USA)   **–**
131) [2003 105: 12m⁴ 12g Aug 1] strong, lengthy colt: lightly-raced colt, useful form at
best: reportedly returned distressed after latter 3-y-o start, then later fractured cannon
bone: well-beaten last both outings at 4 yrs: sold 12,000 gns. *E. A. L. Dunlop*

WAHJ (IRE)   8 ch.g. Indian Ridge 123 – Sabaah (USA) 65 (Nureyev (USA) 131)   **57**
[2003 98: 7.1m 7g 7g³ 7m f8.5g Jun 27] sturdy gelding: formerly useful, only modest
nowadays: at least as effective at 7f as 8.5f: acts on firm going, soft and fibresand: tried
tongue tied/in cheekpieces: often makes running: carries head high: one to treat with
some caution. *C. A. Dwyer*

WAHOO SAM (USA)   3 ch.g. Sandpit (BRZ) 129 – Good Reputation (USA) (Gran   **–**
Zar (MEX)) [2003 87: f10g 6m 10.3m 8g 7g Jul 26] good-topped gelding: fairly useful
winner at 2 yrs: stumbled and unseated rider leaving stall on reappearance: no form after,
twice shaping as if amiss. *T. D. Barron*

WAHSHEEQ   3 b.c. Green Desert (USA) 127 – Moss (USA) (Woodman (USA) 126)   **99**
[2003 99: 6f 7m Jul 10] lengthy, quite good-topped colt: useful performer, lightly raced:

much better effort in valuable handicaps at 3 yrs when seventh to Dazzling Bay at York on reappearance: stays 7f: raced only on good ground or firmer: sent to UAE, joined E. Charpy. *E. A. L. Dunlop*

WAINAK (USA) 5 b.g. Silver Hawk (USA) 123 – Cask 99 (Be My Chief (USA) 122) **– §** [2003 –§: 14m Apr 10] tall, good-topped gelding: temperamental maiden: tried in headgear. *Miss Lucinda V. Russell*

WAINWRIGHT (IRE) 3 b.g. Victory Note (USA) 120 – Double Opus (IRE) (Petorius **69** 117) [2003 77: 6g² 7m² 8m⁴ 7d² f7s f6g⁵ f6g² 6d³ f7g⁵ f6g³ f5g³ f6s* Dec 27] IR 66,000F, IR 280,000Y: quite attractive gelding: first foal: dam unraced half-sister to dam of 7-y-o Damalis: fair performer: trained in Ireland by A. O'Brien at 2 yrs: won maiden at Southwell in December: effective at 5f to easy 7f: acts on good to firm ground, soft and fibresand: tried tongue tied/blinkered/in cheekpieces: consistent. *P. A. Blockley*

WAIT FOR THE WILL (USA) 7 ch.g. Seeking The Gold (USA) – You'd Be Sur- **97** prised (USA) 117 (Blushing Groom (FR) 131) [2003 97: p13g⁴ 12m 14.1g³ 14m⁵ 12m* 12m⁵ 14g 12g² 11.6g⁴ 12g² 12f⁶ Sep 28] tall gelding: useful performer: won handicap at Goodwood in June: several creditable efforts otherwise at 7 yrs, including when second to Pagan Dance in minor event at Newmarket eighth start: effective at 11.6f to 1¾m: acts on polytrack, firm and good to soft going: tried tongue tied/visored, usually blinkered: held up: sometimes finds little, but is consistent. *G. L. Moore*

WAKE UP HENRY 2 ch.g. (Mar 5) Nashwan (USA) 135 – River Saint (USA) 73§ **56 p** (Irish River (FR) 131) [2003 8d p8g f8g⁶ Nov 24] 60,000Y: good-bodied gelding: first foal, unreliable maiden who should have stayed 1m, half-sister to champion US filly Serena's Song (best up to 9f), herself dam of Coronation Stakes winner Sophisticat and 2-y-o Grand Reward: modest form in maidens/minor event (travelled comfortably long way): will stay 1¼m: open to improvement. *R. Charlton*

WALDMARK (GER) 3 ch.f. Mark of Esteem (IRE) 137 – Wurftaube (GER) 119 **106** (Acatenango (GER) 127) [2003 83P: 10m² 12g 8m² 8d⁴ 10g 8f Sep 27] big, quite good-topped filly: useful performer: runner-up in listed race at Newbury (to Sun On The Sea) and Falmouth Stakes at Newmarket (unlucky, beaten a length by Macadamia): just respectable efforts after: races freely, and may prove best around 1m: acts on good to firm going, probably on good to soft: wears crossed noseband. *Sir Michael Stoute*

WALKER BAY (IRE) 5 ch.m. Efisio 120 – Lalandria (FR) (Highest Honor (FR) **57** 124) [2003 a7f 6m² 6f⁴ 6g² p6g p7g p7g Dec 17] IR 22,000Y: first foal: dam French 11f **a–** to 13.5f winner: modest maiden: left P. Rudkin in UAE after reappearance, R. Hannon after third start: stays 6f: acts on good to firm ground, little form on dirt/polytrack: tried blinkered. *J. C. Fox*

WALL STREET RUNNER 2 ch.f. (Apr 6) Kirkwall 118 – Running Tycoon (IRE) **64** 62 (Last Tycoon 131) [2003 6g⁶ 6m 5f⁵ Jun 25] fourth foal: half-sister to 3 winners, including 2-y-o 6f winners Dillionaire (in 1998, by Dilum) and Tycando (in 1999, by Forzando), successful later in USA/Denmark respectively: dam, ran only at 2 yrs, best effort at 7f: modest form in minor event/maidens: should stay 7f: sold 3,500 gns in October, sent to Spain. *D. R. C. Elsworth*

WALTON MANOR BOY (IRE) 2 b.c. (Apr 3) Titus Livius (FR) 115 – Burren **–** Breeze (IRE) (Mazaad 106) [2003 5m f5g 6m Jun 2] €11,000Y, 8,600 2-y-o: fourth foal: half-brother to 1¼m winner in Sweden by Petardia: dam unraced: last in maidens. *C. N. Kellett*

WALTZING BEAU 2 ch.g. (Apr 16) Dancing Spree (USA) – Blushing Belle 74 (Local **– p** Suitor (USA) 128) [2003 p8g Dec 20] £400Y: fifth foal: half-brother to 4-y-o Rebelle and 3-y-o Bluegrass Beau: dam, 10.6f seller winner at 2 yrs, also won over hurdles: 25/1, well held in minor event at Lingfield, slowly away and travelling well long way: will probably do better. *I. A. Wood*

WALTZING WIZARD 4 b.g. Magic Ring (IRE) 115 – Legendary Dancer 90 **60** (Shareef Dancer (USA) 135) [2003 78: 7.6m 7m 8g 6g⁶ 8d p7g⁵ f7g² Dec 16] tall, leggy gelding: modest handicapper: stays 7f: acts on all-weather/any turf going: tried tongue tied. *A. Berry*

WALZERKOENIGIN (USA) 4 b.f. Kingmambo (USA) 125 – Great Revival (IRE) **116** (Keen 116) [2003 111: 8m* 8m³ 9.5g⁴ 10f² 10s⁵ Oct 19] $275,000Y: rangy filly: second foal: dam, ran 3 times in Ireland, half-sister to Washington International winner Providential and Prix Marcel Boussac winner Play It Safe: smart performer: won 3 times at 3 yrs, notably Prix Chloe at Chantilly and Ernst & Young Euro-Cup at Frankfurt: improved in 2003, and won Premio Emilio Turati at Milan in May by neck from Salselon: good length second to Dimitrova in Flower Bowl Invitational at Belmont on penultimate start, then unlucky fifth to Volga in E. P. Taylor Stakes at Woodbine final outing, unable to find a way through when going well: respectable third to Macadamia in Falmouth Stakes at Newmarket on second outing: stayed 1¼m: acted on firm and soft going: had worn crossed noseband: stud. *P. Schiergen, Germany*

WANCHAI LAD 2 b.c. (Mar 31) Danzero (AUS) – Frisson (Slip Anchor 136) [2003 **89** 5g* 5m* 6m⁶ 6m Oct 4] 14,000Y: good-topped colt: has scope: third foal: half-brother to 5-y-o Princes Theatre: dam unraced out of useful 7f to 9f winner Comic Talent: fairly useful performer: won maiden at Ripon in August and minor event at Redcar (landed odds by head from Handsome Cross) in September: well held after, though showed up well long way final start: will prove best at 5f. *A. P. Jarvis*

WANNABE AROUND 5 b.g. Primo Dominie 121 – Noble Peregrine (Lomond **94 ?** (USA) 128) [2003 109: p7g 8g⁵ 7m 7f 7.1g 8g 8m⁶ 10.4m 9m Sep 12] tall gelding: just fairly useful form for new trainer in 2003: best at 1m/9f: acts on any going: tried visored: reportedly struck into penultimate start: sent to Singapore. *D. Nicholls*

WANNA SHOUT 5 b.m. Missed Flight 123 – Lulu (Polar Falcon (USA) 126) [2003 **48 §** 52: 9.9m⁶ 11.8g 10.2f⁴ 12.6m 10m 8.1m 10.2g⁴ Aug 25] poor handicapper: stays 1¼m: below form on heavy going, acts on any other turf and fibresand: tried tongue tied/blinkered/visored at 3 yrs: often slowly away: inconsistent. *R. Dickin*

WANT (USA) 2 ch.c. (Mar 15) Miswaki (USA) 124 – Substance (USA) (Diesis 133) **67 p** [2003 6g⁶ Oct 24] fifth living foal: half-brother to 5-y-o Demonstrate and fairly useful 9f/1¼m winner Moratorium (by El Gran Senor): dam unraced half-sister to Ribblesdale winner Ballinderry, herself dam of Sanglamore: 14/1, 9 lengths sixth of 19 to So Will I in maiden at Newbury, starting very slowly: likely to stay 1m: sure to improve. *J. H. M. Gosden*

WARAQA (USA) 4 b.f. Red Ransom (USA) – Jafn 104 (Sharpo 132) [2003 69: 6m **–** f7g 7m 6m⁶ Jun 27] smallish, good-topped filly: fair performer in 2002: well held at 4 yrs: tried blinkered/tongue tied. *J. A. Osborne*

WARDEN COMPLEX 2 b.g. (Feb 24) Compton Place 125 – Miss Rimex (IRE) 84 **75 p** (Ezzoud (IRE) 126) [2003 7m³ Sep 1] smallish, quite good-topped gelding: first foal: dam 6f (at 2 yrs) and 1m winner: 25/1, 3 lengths third of 13 to Almuraad in maiden at Leicester, late headway under hands and heels: will probably stay 1m: open to progress. *J. R. Fanshawe*

WARDEN WARREN 5 b.g. Petong 126 – Silver Spell 54 (Aragon 118) [2003 76§: **81 §** f7s* f7s⁵ f7g⁴ 6.1g⁶ 7f 7m 7m 7m* 7f³ 7g 7m 7m* 6f 7m 7m 7s 7d p7g f6g f7s f7s² f7s* Dec 31] sparely-made gelding: fairly useful handicapper: won at Southwell in January, Doncaster in July, Yarmouth in August and Wolverhampton in December: best around 7f: acts on all-weather, firm and soft ground: wears headgear: usually races prominently: often races alone (reportedly unsuited by being crowded): unreliable. *Mrs C. A. Dunnett*

WARED (USA) 2 gr.c. (Feb 14) El Prado (IRE) 119 – My Shafy 92 (Rousillon (USA) **–** 133) [2003 6d Nov 8] good-bodied colt: half-brother to several winners, including smart 7f/1m (including at 2 yrs) winner Ramooz (by Rambo Dancer) and useful 7f (at 2 yrs)/1m winner My Hansel (by Hansel): dam 1m winner out of smart French middle-distance performer Lys River: 7/1 but in need of run, last of 14 in maiden at Doncaster, possibly amiss. *B. W. Hills*

WAREED (IRE) 5 b.h. Sadler's Wells (USA) 132 – Truly Special 116 (Caerleon **110** (USA) 132) [2003 123: 12g² 15.5s Oct 26] big, rangy horse: has a round action: very smart performer for Saeed bin Suroor in 2001/2: returned to former trainer, better effort in 2003 when 2½ lengths second to Dubai Success in listed race at Doncaster in September: stays 2½m: acts on soft and good to firm going: visored at 3/4 yrs: has been bandaged behind. *D. R. Loder*

WARES HOME (IRE) 2 b.c. (Mar 15) Indian Rocket 115 – Pepilin (Coquelin (USA) **78** 121) [2003 5d² 5m³ 6m² 6g* 6.1m 6d f6g p8g⁶ Dec 2] 6,500Y: sturdy, close-coupled colt: ninth foal: half-brother to 2 winners abroad, including UAE 6f winner Adrien de Vries (by Thatching): dam Irish 2-y-o 6f winner: fair performer: raced alone when making all in minor event at Hamilton in July: well held after: likely to prove best at 5f/6f: acts on good to firm going. *K. R. Burke*

WARIF (USA) 2 ch.c. (Feb 18) Diesis 133 – Alshoowg (USA) (Riverman (USA) 131) **59 ?** [2003 7m 7m p10g Nov 29] compact colt: second foal: dam unraced out of close relative to 2000 Guineas winner Lomond and half-sister to Seattle Slew: modest form at best in maidens: left J. Dunlop 6,500 gns after second start. *E. J. O'Neill*

WARLINGHAM (IRE) 5 b.g. Catrail (USA) 123 – Tadjnama (USA) (Exceller (USA) 129) [2003 73, a76: p7g f6g p7g p7g² p7g* p7g p7g Dec 30] modest performer: won claimer at Lingfield (left M. Pitman £7,000) in December: best at 6f/7f: acts on firm going, good to soft and all-weather: blinkered once: tends to carry head awkwardly. *P. Howling* **? a60**

WARM HILL 2 b.c. (Feb 18) Great Dane (IRE) 122 – Ballet Rambert 69 (Rambo Dancer (CAN) 107) [2003 6m⁴ 6d⁵ 6d³ 7m p6g Oct 8] second foal: dam, 2 y-o 5f winner, didn't train on: fair maiden: stayed 6f, probably not 7f: dead. *A. King* **70**

WAR OWL (USA) 6 gr.g. Linamix (FR) 127 – Ganasheba (USA) (Alysheba (USA)) [2003 70: 8.2d p10g⁴ Dec 10] lengthy gelding: modest handicapper: stays 1¼m: acts on heavy going and all-weather: often tongue tied at 5 yrs. *Ian Williams* **59**

WARRAD (USA) 2 b.c. (Feb 6) Kingmambo (USA) 125 – Shalimar Garden (IRE) 89 (Caerleon (USA) 132) [2003 6g* Oct 24] 48,000 2-y-o: rather leggy colt: second foal: dam, maiden who stayed 1½m, sister to Bach out of top-class Prix de la Foret/Prix de l'Opera winner Producer: favourite, won 18-runner maiden at Newbury by length from Zonus, tracking pace and leading final 1f: should stay 1m: open to progress. *G. A. Butler* **90 p**

WARREN PLACE 3 ch.g. Presidium 124 – Coney Hills 35 (Beverley Boy 99) [2003 64: 6g 6g 7m 6m 5.9m 6m 5d 8.1m Aug 7] leggy, sparely-made gelding: little form in 2003: usually blinkered/visored. *N. Bycroft* **–**

WARRSAN (IRE) 5 b.h. Caerleon (USA) 132 – Lucayan Princess 111 (High Line 125) [2003 119: 12m* 12d* 13.9m² 12m* 12f² 12d⁶ 12g³ 12m³ 12m³ Dec 14] **121**
    'This old b*****d is going under' is reportedly the conclusion Clive Brittain thought some would have jumped to, seeing him shuffling around in agony during a disappointing 2002 for his stable. However, a hip replacement in February allowed Brittain to return to a more hands-on approach at his Carlburg stables, and he answered would-be critics in the best possible way—with a season which yielded the yard's highest domestic prize money total since 1992. The horse who did most to put him back on the map was Coronation Cup winner Warrsan, the only horse during 2003 to win pattern races in Britain at Group 1, 2 and 3 level.
    Warrsan's dam Lucayan Princess has been responsible for three other horses who won pattern races for Brittain, the 1998 Nell Gwyn winner Cloud Castle (by In The Wings) and the much travelled middle-distance pair Needle Gun (by Sure Blade) and Luso (by Salse). It took Warrsan some time to become a fourth. Originally with Saeed bin Suroor, Warrsan was reportedly weak, backward and reluctant to exert himself when he first went into training. He was unraced when

Vodafone Coronation Cup, Epsom—Warrsan is as resolute as ever
as he gets the better of Highest (centre) and Black Sam Bellamy (blaze); Bandari is fourth

joining Brittain towards the end of his two-year-old season. Warrsan showed fairly useful form at best in six runs at three, but did better as a four-year-old, progressing from finishing seventh from a BHB mark of 84 on his reappearance to making the frame in the Irish St Leger, Cumberland Lodge Stakes and St Simon Stakes on his last three outings.

The Group 3 Dubai Irish Village Stakes (John Porter) at Newbury in April on his reappearance was the first leg of Warrsan's British pattern-race treble and he owed it partly to a really shrewd ride, his jockey dictating the pace and Warrsan then finding plenty under pressure to hold off the favourite Asian Heights by a short head. The Group 2 Sagitta Jockey Club Stakes at Newmarket in May was the next port of call. Warrsan started joint outsider in the six-runner field at 12/1 and stayed on in most determined fashion to beat 2001 winner Millenary by a length and a half, with Highest, the only one of Warrsan's opponents not making his reappearance, four lengths back in third. The following month's Vodafone Coronation Cup drew a field of nine—the biggest since 1994—and, though not a vintage renewal, it was certainly competitive. Warrsan had run creditably to finish second to Mamool in the Yorkshire Cup after his Newmarket success and started second favourite at Epsom behind the eight-length Tattersalls Gold Cup winner Black Sam Bellamy. Held up, Warrsan came out best in a rousing finish, running on resolutely to lead well inside the final furlong and beat Highest by half a length, with Black Sam Bellamy a short head back in third. Warrsan showed himself in the Coronation Cup to be a better horse than his siblings Cloud Castle and Needle Gun (both rated 119 at best),

Mr Saeed Manana's "Warrsan"

but he couldn't go on to match the best form shown by Luso, who was rated 124 at his peak. Warrsan held his form well enough though, despite failing to win in five subsequent outings, including in the Credit Suisse Private Banking-Pokal at Cologne, which Luso had won in 1996 and 1998 (when it was held at Gelsenkirchen) and in the Hong Kong Vase, which Luso had won in 1996 and 1997 (Needle Gun, who never won a Group 1, was beaten a neck in the race in 1995). Warrsan ran respectably to finish third in both, making the running and earning Philip Robinson a fine for excessive use of the whip behind Dai Jin and Next Desert in the former, and always close up in a steadily-run race when beaten less than a length by Vallee Enchantee in the latter. Warrsan was 5/1-on when beaten by Leadership in the Gran Premio di Milano, after which Brittain blamed the defeat on mosquitoes swarming round Warrsan in the stalls. Luso had been runner-up in the race in 1996 and 1997, Brittain interestingly putting forward a similar excuse on the first occasion. Warrsan was also beaten on his return to Milan later in the season, finishing third to Ekraar in the Gran Premio del Jockey Club. He was out of the first three just once all season, when a respectable sixth in the King George VI and Queen Elizabeth Stakes at Ascot in July.

			Nijinsky	Northern Dancer
		Caerleon (USA)	(b 1967)	Flaming Page
		(b 1980)	Foreseer	Round Table
Warrsan (IRE)			(b or br 1969)	Regal Gleam
(b.h. 1998)			High Line	High Cat
		Lucayan Princess	(ch 1966)	Time Call
		(b 1983)	Gay France	Sir Gaylord
			(b 1976)	Sweet And Lovely II

Warrsan is from the last crop of the Prix du Jockey Club winner Caerleon. The distaff side of Warrsan's pedigree was covered in three essays on Luso in the 'nineties. Apart from those already mentioned, Lucayan Princess has produced two other winners, the modest mile winner Celia Brady (by Last Tycoon) and the useful sprinter Luana (by Shaadi), while another of Lucayan Princess' foals, Lunda (by Soviet Star), is the dam of the useful three-year-old Lundy's Lane. The smart Lucayan Princess ran three times as a two-year-old, gaining the second of her two wins in the Sweet Solera Stakes, and finished third in the Cheshire Oaks on her only outing at three years. The grandam Gay France won over six furlongs as a two-year-old and is one of eleven winners produced by Sweet And Lovely II, among the others being Sweetly, the grandam of Kris Kin. Warrsan, a neat sort in appearance, seemed to run creditably when eighth in the Gold Cup at Ascot in 2002, though he was never in the hunt in a race run at a steady early pace, and he has shown his very best form at a mile and a half and a mile and three quarters. Yet to race on heavy ground, he acts on any other going on turf and is effective waited with or ridden prominently. He unseated his rider on the way to post once at four but is splendidly tough, game and reliable. He reportedly stays in training.
C. E. Brittain

WAR VALOR (USA) 4 b.g. Royal Academy (USA) 130 – Western Music (USA) **74** (Lord At War (ARG)) [2003 78: p8g 7g 6f⁴ 6m⁴ 6d² 6m² 6m a7f* 8f* 8f² Nov 30] rather leggy, useful-looking gelding: fair performer: good second in handicaps at Newmarket before winning maiden claimer at Keeneland and allowance race at Churchill Downs, both in October: left J. Nicol before final outing: effective at 6f to 1m: acts on any turf going and on dirt: often wears headgear. *T. M. Amoss, USA*

WASEYLA (IRE) 6 b.m. Sri Pekan (USA) 117 – Lady Windley (Baillamont (USA) **– §** 124) [2003 –§: f11g Jan 4] modest and unreliable in 2001: no form since: tried in headgear. *Julian Poulton*

WASHBROOK 2 b.c. (Mar 7) Royal Applause 124 – Alacrity 62 (Alzao (USA) 117) **64** [2003 5m 6g 5m⁶ 7m⁴ 8d Oct 14] 35,000F, 50,000Y: good-topped colt: has scope: sixth foal: half-brother to French 7f and (including at 2 yrs) 1m winner Fast Trick (by First Trump): dam 11f winner out of sister to smart 1¼m performer Perpendicular: modest maiden: fourth at Newcastle, best effort: stays 7f: acts on good to firm ground: sometimes troublesome start/slowly away, including final outing. *Andrew Turnell*

WASHINGTON PINK (IRE) 4 b.g. Tagula (IRE) 116 – Little Red Rose (Precocious **–** 126) [2003 71: 11g Oct 28] strong, close-coupled gelding: has quick action: fair performer at 2/3 yrs: tailed off in claimer only 4-y-o start. *C. Grant*

WASTED TALENT (IRE) 3 b.f. Sesaro (USA) 81 – Miss Garuda 94 (Persian Bold **81** 123) [2003 74: f12g³ 12m² 12.1f³ 11.9m⁴ 10m² 10f⁶ 11.9m² 10g² 10m⁴ 10m⁴ 12m² 11.6g⁶ **a66** 11.9f² p10g⁵ f12g³ f11g* Dec 19] angular filly: fairly useful on turf, fair on all-weather: won maiden at Southwell in December: effective at 1¼m/1½m: acts on firm going and all-weather: wore cheekpieces after sixth start: front runner: consistent. *J. G. Portman*

WATAMU (IRE) 2 b.c. (Mar 9) Groom Dancer (USA) 128 – Miss Golden Sands 80 **84 p** (Kris 135) [2003 7m 7g* Sep 11] 28,000F, 30,000Y: strong, lengthy colt: second living foal: half-brother to German 9.5f winner Lips Love (by Hernando): dam, lightly-raced maiden (stayed 1m), half-sister to dam of 5-y-o Asian Heights: easily better effort in maidens (fairly useful form) when winning 11-runner event at Epsom readily by 1½ lengths from Makfool, leading 1f out: should stay 1m: open to progress. *P. J. Makin*

WATCHING 6 ch.g. Indian Ridge 123 – Sweeping 104 (Indian King (USA) 128) **101 d** [2003 104: p5g 5g³ 6g 5.1m 7g⁶ 6m⁴ 6f 5.6d 6d 6s⁴ 7d Nov 8] neat gelding: useful handicapper: mainly well below form after creditable third at Doncaster in March: best at 5f/6f: acts on heavy and good to firm going: tried in cheekpieces/visor: often races prominently: none too consistent. *D. Nicholls*

WATCHWORD 4 ch.f. Polish Precedent (USA) 131 – Step Aloft 87 (Shirley Heights **45 §** 130) [2003 65, a60: f7s f8g p7g f6g⁵ f7g p12g 6g May 16] poor maiden handicapper: left C. Dore after sixth start: stays 1m: acts on all-weather and good to firm ground: sometimes blinkered: tail swisher: unreliable. *Mrs C. A. Dunnett*

WATERFALL ONE 3 ch.f. Nashwan (USA) 135 – Spout 115 (Salse (USA) 128) **–** [2003 62p: 12.1f Apr 16] well-made filly: modest form in maidens in 2002: tailed off only 3-y-o outing. *R. Charlton*

WATERFORD SPIRIT (IRE) 7 ch.g. Shalford (IRE) 124§ – Rebecca's Girl (IRE) **– §** (Nashamaa 113) [2003 55§: f5g Jan 4] big, good-topped gelding: modest performer in 2002: ran as if amiss only 7-y-o outing: tried blinkered/tongue tied at 4 yrs: unreliable. *G. J. Smith*

WATER KING (USA) 4 b.g. Irish River (FR) 131 – Brookshield Baby (IRE) (Sadler's **–** Wells (USA) 132) [2003 83: f9.4s 10d May 12] fairly useful maiden in 2002: well held at 4 yrs: gelded after. *G. Brown*

WATERLINE BLUE (IRE) 2 b.g. (Apr 24) Mujadil (USA) 119 – Blues Queen 85 **86** (Lahib (USA) 129) [2003 5f⁵ 6f 6m* 6g³ 7d² 7.1m⁶ 5.7f² 6.1m⁴ 6m⁶ 6m⁶ Oct 21] 10,000Y: workmanlike gelding: third foal: half-brother to 6f seller winner Speed Queen (by Goldmark): dam 2-y-o 6f winner: fairly useful performer: won maiden at Leicester in June: placed in minor events after: stays 7f: acts on firm and good to soft going: visored (below best) eighth start. *P. D. Evans*

WATERLINE DANCER (IRE) 3 b. or br.f. Danehill Dancer (IRE) 117 – Thrill **59** Seeker (IRE) (Treasure Kay 114) [2003 69, a62: p8g⁴ p8g p7g 6.1m 8g p6g 6g³ 6.1m 6g⁴ 7m 7.1m 6m f7g Dec 8] leggy filly: modest performer: effective at 6f to easy 1m: acts on firm going, good to soft and polytrack: usually tongue tied: visored last 2 starts: none too consistent. *P. D. Evans*

WATERLINE QUEEN 3 b.f. Wizard King 122 – Miss Waterline 77 (Rock City 120) **–** [2003 –: 8.3g 6g 5.1m 7.1g Jun 13] well held in maidens/claimers. *P. D. Evans*

WATERLINE SPIRIT 3 b.g. Piccolo 121 – Gina of Hithermoor (Reprimand 122) **§§** [2003 48§: 8.2d 8m f8g Nov 24] thoroughly ungenuine maiden: tried visored. *P. D. Evans*

WATER MELODY (IRE) 2 gr.f. (Mar 19) Lake Coniston (IRE) 131 – Cantata (IRE) **–** (Saddlers' Hall (IRE) 126) [2003 6m 8m⁵ 7m⁶ Aug 21] €2,800Y: third foal: half-sister to 3-y-o Canatrice and winner in Spain by Danehill Dancer: dam ran twice in France: little form in maidens/seller. *B. R. Johnson*

WATERMOUSE 3 b.g. Alhaarth (IRE) 126 – Heavenly Waters 64 (Celestial Storm **–** (USA) 132) [2003 44: 11m May 29] poor maiden: well held only 3-y-o start. *R. Dickin*

WATER NYMPH (IRE) 3 ch.f. Be My Guest (USA) 126 – Justitia (Dunbeath **–** (USA) 127) [2003 7m 10.5v May 24] 24,000Y: sturdy filly: half-sister to several winners, including fairly useful 5f (at 2 yrs)/6f winner Shatin Venture (by Lake Coniston) and top-class chaser Bacchanal (by Bob Back): dam won in Belgium: well held in maidens. *B. A. McMahon*

WATER OF LIFE (IRE) 4 b.f. Dr Devious (IRE) 127 – Simulcast (Generous (IRE) **63 d** 139) [2003 81: f7g* p7g² 7m 8.5m f7g 8f 8.3g 6m 8g 10.1m p12g⁵ p12g³ Nov 26] well-made filly: good mover: modest performer: won maiden at Wolverhampton in February: left J. Hills after second outing, below form after third: effective at 7f to easy 1½m: acts on soft going, good to firm and all-weather: tried tongue tied: sometimes finds little. *J. R. Boyle*

WATERPARK 5 b.m. Namaqualand (USA) – Willisa 67 (Polar Falcon (USA) 126) [2003 45: f8g f8g* 7.1d³ 7m* May 12] leggy mare: modest handicapper: won at Southwell (apprentices) in March and Redcar in May: effective at 7f/1m: acts on firm going, good to soft and fibresand: tried visored: races prominently. *R. Craggs* **54**

WATERSHIP CRYSTAL (IRE) 2 b.f. (Apr 12) Sadler's Wells (USA) 132 – Crystal Spray 75 (Beldale Flutter (USA) 130) [2003 7g Nov 1] leggy, useful-looking filly: sister to smart 7f (at 2 yrs) and 1¼m winner Tchaikovsky and 3-y-o Dubai Success, closely related to smart 2000 2-y-o 7f/1m (Fillies' Mile) winner Crystal Music, and half-sister to 3 winners, 2 of them smart: dam Irish 1¾m winner from good family: 10/1, green when well held in maiden at Newmarket: will be suited by 1¼m/1½m: sure to do better. *J. H. M. Gosden* **– p**

WATERSIDE (IRE) 4 b.g. Lake Coniston (IRE) 131 – Classic Ring (IRE) 50 (Auction Ring (USA) 123) [2003 90: 7m 7.6g 7m p7g² p7g⁶ 7.5d³ 6g* p7g⁴ p7g p6g⁴ Dec 20] strong gelding: has a round action: fairly useful handicapper on all-weather, fair on turf: won at Windsor in October: best at 6f/7f: acts on polytrack, soft and good to firm going: tried tongue tied: sometimes slowly away: held up: consistent. *J. W. Hills* **79 + a92**

WATERSTONE 2 b.c. (Apr 20) Cape Cross (IRE) 129 – Aquaba (USA) (Damascus (USA)) [2003 5d² 5d* 5f Jun 21] close-coupled, quite attractive colt: half-brother to several winners, including sprinter Millstream (by Dayjur) and 1995 2-y-o 6f winner Polska (by Danzig), both useful: dam, 7f (including at 2 yrs) to 9f winner in USA, including Grade 3 8.5f event: fairly useful form: won maiden at Ripon in May: only eighth in minor event at Royal Ascot: should stay at least 6f. *M. Johnston* **84**

WATHAB (IRE) 2 b.c. (Feb 2) Cadeaux Genereux 131 – Bally Souza (IRE) 87 (Alzao (USA) 117) [2003 5d² 5s² 6d* 6d³ 6m 7m² 6f⁶ 7m⁴ 6m* 7f² Sep 14] 60,000Y: well-made colt: second foal: dam, 11f/1½m winner, half-sister to useful miler A La Carte: smart performer: made all in maiden at the Curragh in May and listed race there (beat Simple Exchange ½ length) in August: improved when length second of 8 to One Cool Cat in National Stakes at same course final start: will stay 1m: acts on firm going, probably on soft: joined D. Weld. *K. Prendergast, Ireland* **113**

WAVERLEY (IRE) 4 b.c. Catrail (USA) 123 – Marble Halls (IRE) (Ballad Rock 122) [2003 101: 10.4m 10m⁵ 12f* 11.9g² Jul 5] tall, leggy colt: useful handicapper: won Duke of Edinburgh Stakes at Royal Ascot in June by neck from Researched, edging left: career-best effort when ½-length second to Collier Hill in Old Newton Cup at Haydock final start: suffered injury after: effective at 9f to 1½m: acts on firm and good to soft going: usually races prominently: game and reliable. *H. Morrison* **106**

WAVERLEY ROAD 6 ch.g. Pelder (IRE) 125 – Lillicara (FR) (Caracolero (USA) 131) [2003 79, a67: p13g p12g 14.1m 12d⁶ 10.9m 16m⁵ p16g* p13g Dec 29] leggy gelding: modest handicapper: left A. Jarvis, won at Lingfield in December: stays easy 2m: acts on good to firm going, soft and polytrack: tried visored: usually races prominently. *M. Madgwick* **55 a53**

Duke of Edinburgh Stakes (Handicap), Royal Ascot—Waverley (check cap) has a neck to spare over Researched, the pair tracked by third-placed Hambleden; Canada (noseband) is fourth

WAVERTREE BOY (IRE)   3 ch.g. Hector Protector (USA) 124 – Lust (Pursuit of   **109**
Love 124) [2003 91: 10m⁵ 12.3m 11g* 14.1f* 16.2f 14.8m³ 12g 13.9m³ 14.6g 16.2f⁴ Sep
28] rather leggy, good-topped gelding: useful performer: won handicaps at Goodwood in
May and Salisbury in June: best efforts when third to Gold Medallist (beaten 2¾ lengths)
in listed race at Newmarket and to Jagger in Melrose Rated Stakes (Handicap) at York:
not discredited when ninth to Brian Boru in St Leger at Doncaster penultimate outing:
should stay 2m: acts on firm and soft going: held up. *D. R. C. Elsworth*

WAVERTREE DREAM   2 b.g. (Feb 4) Dushyantor (USA) 123 – Dream On Deya   **88**
(IRE) (Dolphin Street (FR) 125) [2003 5.2m 5m² 5m 7m² 7m* 6m⁶ 8m² 8d p7g Nov 12]
8,500Y: rather leggy, useful-looking gelding: first foal: dam, tailed off only start, half-
sister to smart sprinter Proud Native: useful performer: won nursery at Newmarket
in July: good second in similar event at Doncaster, clearly best effort after: stays 1m: acts
on good to firm ground. *N. P. Littmoden*

WAVERTREE GIRL (IRE)   2 b.f. (Apr 4) Marju (IRE) 127 – Lust (Pursuit of Love   **93**
124) [2003 6m³ 6g⁴ 6.1m 6.1g⁴ Aug 28] 15,000Y: tall, leggy filly: fourth foal: half-sister
to 3-y-o Wavertree Boy: dam unraced half-sister to Classic Cliche (won St Leger and
Gold Cup) and My Emma (by Marju, won Prix Vermeille and Yorkshire Oaks): fairly
useful form when 3½ lengths fourth to River Belle in Princess Margaret Stakes at Ascot
second start: fair at best otherwise: bred to be suited by at least 1¼m. *N. P. Littmoden*

WAVERTREE SPIRIT   2 ch.c. (Mar 30) Hector Protector (USA) 124 – Miss Clarinet   **– p**
(Pharly (FR) 130) [2003 7m⁶ Sep 3] 17,000Y: compact colt: fourth foal, well beaten
only start (at 2 yrs), half-sister to very smart sprinter Piccolo: 25/1 and green, sixth of 8 in
maiden at York, which sways away: will probably do better. *N. P. Littmoden*

WAVET   3 b.f. Pursuit of Love 124 – Ballerina Bay 75 (Myjinski (USA)) [2003 64p: **53**
12g⁶ p10g p10g p13g Dec 29] lengthy filly: modest maiden, lightly raced: should be
suited by at least 1½m: raced freely last 2 starts. *Mrs Lydia Pearce*

WAXWING   4 b.f. Efisio 120 – Mountain Bluebird (USA) 79 (Clever Trick (USA))   **71 d**
[2003 71: f7s f6s³ f7s² f7g² f5g⁴ 7m 6.1g 7m f7g³ f7g* f6g 7f 8m 6m f7s⁴ f6s⁶ f8s⁶ Oct
21] lengthy filly: unimpressive mover: fair performer: won claimer at Southwell (left
P. Murphy) in June: below form after: barely stays 1m: acts on firm going and fibresand,
probably on polytrack: usually visored: often tongue tied. *A. W. Carroll*

WAYWARD MELODY   3 b.f. Merdon Melody 98 – Dubitable 59 (Formidable   **–**
(USA) 125) [2003 51: p10g 14.1m 14.1m 10m Jun 12] modest maiden at 2 yrs: well held
on Flat in 2003: tried visored: won juvenile hurdle in September. *S. Dow*

WAZIRI (IRE)   2 b.g. (Feb 13) Mtoto 134 – Euphorie (GER) (Feenpark (GER) 115)   **71**
[2003 p8g⁴ p8g⁶ p8g⁴ Nov 13] second foal: dam German 7f/1m winner (also successful
over hurdles): fair form in maidens at Lingfield: should be suited by 1½m+. *H. Morrison*

WEAKEST LINK   2 b.g. (Mar 30) Mind Games 121 – Sky Music 85 (Absalom 128)   **– p**
[2003 6d Nov 8] 1,600Y: lengthy, useful-looking gelding: fifth foal: half-brother to 6-y-o
Polar Haze: dam 6f/7f winner: unruly and withdrawn in September: 100/1, tenth of 13 in
maiden at Doncaster, travelling comfortably long way: should do better. *Miss S. E. Hall*

WEAVER OF DREAMS (IRE)   3 b.g. Victory Note (USA) 120 – Daziyra (IRE)   **–**
(Doyoun 124) [2003 –: 10g 9.2d 10d⁵ 9m⁵ 14.1m Jul 12] good-topped gelding: little form.
G. A. Swinbank

WEAVER SPELL   2 b.g. (May 20) Wizard King 122 – Impy Fox (IRE) 53 (Imp Society   **37**
(USA)) [2003 6d 6m f7g 6g⁶ Jul 3] 1,800Y: leggy gelding: second foal: dam 2-y-o 6f
seller winner: poor maiden: should stay 7f. *J. R. Norton*

WEAVERS PRIDE (FR)   3 ch.c. Barathea (IRE) 127 – Creese (USA) (Diesis 133)   **105**
[2003 97: 7g* 10m 7.6m³ 8.1v 8m 8m⁵ Jul 10] quite attractive colt: has scope: useful
performer: won maiden at Doncaster in March: best efforts in handicaps at Chester (third
to Lago d'Orta) and Newmarket (fifth to South Atlantic): likely to prove best at 7f/1m:
acts on good to firm going: has raced freely: sent to Hong Kong, where renamed
Dendranthema Love. *B. W. Hills*

WEBBINGTON LASS (IRE)   2 b.f. (May 4) Petardia 113 – Richardstown Lass   **–**
(IRE) (Muscatite 122) [2003 6g 5.7f 7m 6g Oct 6] 4,000 2-y-o: lengthy filly: sixth living
foal: sister to 2 winners, including 6-y-o Replacement Pet, and half-sister to 2 winners,
including 5-y-o Music Maid: dam unraced: well held in maidens. *Dr J. R. J. Naylor*

WEB PERCEPTIONS (USA)   3 ch.c. Distant View (USA) 126 – Squaw Time (USA)   **89**
(Lord At War (ARG)) [2003 81p: 8.3g 9m 10.2m² 11.9m 9.9f³ 11m* 14g⁶ 12.1g* 13.9m
10d* 12m* Sep 16] sturdy colt: fairly useful performer: won handicaps at Redcar and

Hamilton and claimers at Sandown and Salisbury (3 ran, claimed £40,000) in second half of 2003: effective at 1¼m to 1¾m: acts on fibresand, firm and good to soft going: blinkered third/last 4 starts: usually goes in snatches: fairly useful juvenile hurdler for M. Harris. *P. F. I. Cole*

WEDDING   3 ch.f. Groom Dancer (USA) 128 – Champagne 'n Roses 63 (Chief Singer   **66**
131) [2003 8m⁵ 10m⁶ 7g⁶ 8m Jun 11] big, strong filly: half-sister to 2000 2-y-o 7f winner Up On Points (by Royal Academy) and 3 winners abroad: dam, Irish 7f winner, half-sister to Nell Gwyn winner Thrilling Day: fair maiden: stays 1m: raced only on good/good to firm going: sent to New Zealand. *J. G. Given*

WEDGEWOOD STAR   3 b.f. Bishop of Cashel 122 – Away To Me (Exit To Nowhere   **–**
(USA) 122) [2003 74: 7.1m 7g 6m May 28] fair maiden at 2 yrs: well held in 2003 (hung badly left final start): will prove best at 6f/7f: yet to race on extremes of going. *R. Hannon*

WEECANDOO (IRE)   5 b.m. Turtle Island (IRE) 123 – Romantic Air 62 (He Loves   **97 ?**
Me 120) [2003 72: p10g* p10g³ p10g³ p10g⁴ p10g² 8.3d 10f* 10g³ 10m³ 10m* 9.9m⁵   **a72**
10m⁴ Oct 16] workmanlike mare: useful on turf, fair on all-weather: won maiden at Lingfield in January and handicaps at Sandown in June and Ascot (by ¾ length from Kelpie) in August: apparently further improvement when fourth to Al Ihtithar in listed event at Newmarket final start: best at 1¼m: acts on all-weather and firm going: tough and genuine. *C. N. Allen*

WEE DINNS (IRE)   2 b.f. (Apr 21) Marju (IRE) 127 – Tir-An-Oir (IRE) (Law   **67**
Society (USA) 130) [2003 7m 7.1d 8g Oct 25] close-coupled filly: half-sister to several winners, including useful Irish 1¼m/1½m winner Dragon Triumph (by Alzao): dam unraced: fair form in maidens: not knocked about when ninth of 17 at Newbury final start: should stay 1¼m. *S. Kirk*

WEET A HEAD (IRE)   2 b.c. (Jan 23) Foxhound (USA) 103 – Morale (Bluebird   **87**
(USA) 125) [2003 6.1g* 6m⁴ 6d³ 7.9f² 8m⁶ f8g³ Nov 24] 21,000F, 24,000 2-y-o: quite good-topped colt: second foal: dam, lightly-raced French maiden, half-sister to useful 1m/1¼m performer Sheba Spring: fairly useful performer: won maiden at Chepstow in June: creditable efforts in nurseries/minor event last 4 starts: stays 1m: acts on fibresand, firm and good to soft ground. *R. Hollinshead*

WEET A MO (IRE)   3 b.g. Sri Pekan (USA) 117 – Ozwood (IRE) (Royal Academy   **66**
(USA) 130) [2003 67: 8.2g³ 8m³ 7.9g⁶ 7.5d² f9.4s 8.1m 7m 8m 8.1m⁴ 7g⁵ 7.5m³ 7m Sep 1] rather leggy gelding: fair maiden: broke leg at Leicester final start: stayed 1m: acted on good to firm and good to soft going: tried in cheekpieces/blinkers: dead. *R. Hollinshead*

WEET AN HAUL   2 b.g. (May 9) Danzero (AUS) – Island Ruler 79 (Ile de Bourbon   **58**
(USA) 133) [2003 5d f6s⁶ 5.9d 8g f7s f7g* f7g² f8s Dec 27] 13,000Y: sturdy gelding: half-brother to several winners, including fairly useful 1995 2-y-o 7f winner who stayed 1¼m Cebwob (by Rock City): dam French 1½m winner: modest performer: left J. Bethell after fifth start: best effort when winning nursery at Southwell (flashed tail/carried head awkwardly) in December: stays 7f: acts on fibresand, well beaten on turf. *P. A. Blockley*

WEET AN STORE (IRE)   2 gr.c. (Apr 20) Spectrum (IRE) 126 – Karmisymixa (FR)   **–**
(Linamix (FR) 127) [2003 f8.5g f8.5g Nov 17] 7,500F, €10,000Y: fifth foal: dam unraced sister to useful Kalimisik and half-sister to smart Karmiska, both 1¼m performers in France: soundly beaten in maidens: tried tongue tied. *R. Hollinshead*

WEET A ROUND   4 ch.g. Whittingham (IRE) 104 – Hollia 72 (Touch Boy 109) [2003   **71**
75: 6.1g⁵ 7f 7m 6d⁵ 6m 6g⁴ f7g f6s Sep 2] big, good-topped gelding: fair performer: won amateur minor event at Hamilton in May: stays 7f: acts on any turf going and all-weather: usually blinkered/tongue tied: sold 2,600 gns, sent to Spain. *P. A. Blockley*

WEETMAN'S WEIGH (IRE)   10 b.h. Archway (IRE) 115 – Indian Sand (Indian   **–**
King (USA) 128) [2003 56, a65: f8s* f8s⁶ f7g² f7s⁴ f8g 8g 7g May 5] useful-looking   **a52**
horse: had stringhalt: useful performer at best, winner of 20 of his 132 starts: just modest in recent years: won seller at Southwell in January: effective at 7f to 9.4f: acted on fibresand, firm and good to soft going: wore cheekpieces last 11 starts: tried tongue tied: sometimes hung left: to stand at Oakham Stud, Rutland. *R. Hollinshead*

WEET WATCHERS   3 b.g. Polar Prince (IRE) 117 – Weet Ees Girl (IRE) 75   **75**
(Common Grounds 118) [2003 75: f7g² 8g 6s³ 6.1m f8.5g 7f Dec 22] rather leggy, workmanlike gelding: fair performer: won maiden at Wolverhampton in January: stays 7f: acts on fibresand and soft going: broke blood vessel fifth start. *R. Hollinshead*

WEIGHTLESS 3 ch.g. In The Wings 128 – Orford Ness 107 (Selkirk (USA) 129) [2003   **120**
8d² 10.5d* 10d* 10g² 10g* 9.8d* 10m Dec 14] first foal: dam, won Prix de Sandringham, also 1m winner at 2 yrs: very smart performer: won minor events at Longchamp in June

and Deauville in August, Prix du Prince d'Orange at Longchamp (beat strong-finishing Shakis ¾ length) in September and Prix Dollar Fouquet's Barriere at Longchamp (improved again, beat Short Pause 2 lengths) in October: well held in Hong Kong Cup at Sha Tin final outing: stays 10.5f: acts on good to soft ground: front runner. *P. Bary, France*

WELCOME BACK 6 ch.g. Most Welcome 131 – Villavina 59 (Top Ville 129) [2003 **38** 41: f12g² f16.2s Dec 6] leggy gelding: poor handicapper, lightly raced: stays 2m: acts on fibresand, firm and good to soft going. *K. A. Ryan*

WELCOME ON LINE 4 ch.g. Most Welcome 131 – Pegs 60 (Mandrake Major 122) **–** [2003 12.6m Jun 16] 2,200F, IR 20,000Y: third foal: dam, third at 1m on 2-y-o debut, well beaten after: 50/1, no show in maiden at Warwick. *F. Jordan*

WELCOME SIGNAL 3 ch.g. Most Welcome 131 – Glenfinlass (Lomond (USA) **72 +** 128) [2003 –p: p8g³ 7m³ p8g 10m³ 10m⁵ Jul 28] fair maiden, lightly raced: should stay 1½m: acts on good to firm ground and polytrack. *J. R. Fanshawe*

WELCOME STRANGER 3 b.g. Most Welcome 131 – Just Julia (Natroun (FR) **86** 128) [2003 69: p8g* p10g 8m* 8m* 8m 8m⁴ Oct 6] leggy gelding: fairly useful performer: won minor event at Lingfield in May then similar contest at Newbury and handicap at Newcastle in June: stays 1m: acts on good to firm ground and polytrack: fractious in stall/slowly away (ran well) penultimate outing. *J. M. P. Eustace*

WELCOME SUN (IRE) 2 ch.g. (Mar 16) Desert Sun 120 – Ever Welcome 58 (Be **–** My Guest (USA) 126) [2003 7m 8.1g Sep 11] 10,000Y, 4,000 2-y-o: big, good-topped gelding: half-brother to several winners, including useful 7f winner Toffee Nosed (by Selkirk) and 6f to 8.5f winner Tame Deer (by Hadeer): dam 1¼m winner at 4 yrs: well held, though not knocked about, in claimer at Salisbury and maiden at Chepstow. *J. S. Moore*

WELCOME TO UNOS 6 ch.g. Exit To Nowhere (USA) 122 – Royal Loft 105 **54** (Homing 130) [2003 59: 13.8m Mar 26] close-coupled gelding: modest maiden handicapper: stays 1¾m: best efforts on good ground: held up: joined M. Pipe, won over hurdles in October/December. *Mrs M. Reveley*

WELL CHOSEN 4 b.c. Sadler's Wells (USA) 132 – Hawajiss 114 (Kris 135) [2003 **84** 83: 14v² 17.1m⁴ 12f³ Jun 25] good-topped, angular colt: fairly useful handicapper, lightly raced: good efforts all starts at 4 yrs: effective at 1½m, barely at 17f: acts on polytrack and any turf going. *E. A. L. Dunlop*

WELL CONNECTED (IRE) 3 b.g. Among Men (USA) 124 – Wire To Wire (Welsh **57** Saint 126) [2003 50: 7.9g³ 9.1m 8.5d 7f⁶ 8m 8.5d³ 10m Oct 20] tall gelding: modest maiden: stays 8.5f: acts on firm and good to soft ground: usually races prominently: headstrong. *B. Smart*

WELLINGTON HALL (GER) 5 b.g. Halling (USA) 133 – Wells Whisper (FR) 71 **55** (Sadler's Wells (USA) 132) [2003 98?: p12g p13g 14.1g 20m 14.1d⁵ 12d p10g Nov 26] just a modest handicapper in 2003: stays 1¾m: raced mostly on good going or softer on turf: usually wears headgear. *A. Charlton*

WELL KNOWN 2 b.f. (Jan 25) Sadler's Wells (USA) 132 – Danefair 109 (Danehill **86 P** (USA) 126) [2003 7m² Sep 5] compact, quite attractive filly: fourth foal: half-sister to 3-y-o Trade Fair: dam, French 1¼m/1½m (Prix Minerve) winner, half-sister to smart French performer up to 2m Erudite: 6/1, free to post and better for race, length second of 7 to Park Accord in minor event at Kempton, taking good hold and leading briefly 2f out: should be suited by 1¼m/1½m: likely to improve considerably, and will win races. *R. Charlton*

WE'LL MAKE IT (IRE) 5 b.g. Spectrum (IRE) 126 – Walliser (Niniski (USA) 125) **68** [2003 70: 14m⁵ 14g³ 14f Jun 14] fair maiden handicapper: stays 1¾m: acts on polytrack, good to firm and good to soft going: usually blinkered: carries head high: none too genuine. *G. L. Moore*

WE'LL MEET AGAIN 3 ch.g. Bin Ajwaad (IRE) 119 – Tantalizing Song (CAN) **61** (The Minstrel (CAN) 135) [2003 66d: f12g 8m³ 7f* 9m 8d⁶ 8.5d⁵ Sep 23] well-grown gelding: has round action: modest handicapper: won at Thirsk in June: best at 7f: acts on firm and good to soft ground. *M. W. Easterby*

WELL RED (IRE) 3 ch.c. Prince of Birds (USA) 121 – Fairy Domino 66 (Primo **58 §** Dominie 121) [2003 66: p5g p5g f5s a6s² a5g⁶ a6.8g a6.8g² a6g* a6f² a8f Dec 14] modest performer: sold from C. Cox 1,400 gns after third start: won maiden at Taby in November: stays 6f: acts on dirt: tried blinkered/visored: untrustworthy. *T. Persson, Sweden*

WELSH AND WYLDE (IRE) 3 b.g. Anita's Prince 126 – Waikiki (GER) (Zampano **56**
(GER)) [2003 75d: f7g⁵ f8.5g² 7g 8d⁶ f8s 10m Oct 13] modest maiden: stays easy 8.5f:
acts on good to firm going and fibresand: tried blinkered/in cheekpieces: none too
reliable. *B. Palling*

WELSH BORDER 5 ch.g. Zafonic (USA) 130 – Welsh Daylight (Welsh Pageant 132) **–**
[2003 97: p10g Dec 10] rangy gelding: useful performer at best in 2002: winning (but
untrustworthy) hurdler: soundly beaten on return to Flat. *C. R. Dore*

WELSH DIVA 4 b.f. Selkirk (USA) 129 – Khubza 86 (Green Desert (USA) 127) **104**
[2003 112: 8.1g 9d 8m² 8m 8m Oct 4] big, good-bodied filly: useful performer: form at 4
yrs only when second to Aldora in listed race at Goodwood: ran as if amiss in Sun Chariot
Stakes at Newmarket final start: stays 1m: acts on soft and good to firm going: has been
bandaged hind joints: wore cheekpieces last 3 starts: carries head high. *Mrs A. J. Perrett*

WELSH EMPEROR (IRE) 4 b.g. Emperor Jones (USA) 119 – Simply Times (USA) **113**
64 (Dodge (USA)) [2003 103: p7g 7.1d³ 5v⁴ 6s² 6d⁴ 6s² 6v⁶ Nov 19] tall gelding: smart
performer: runner-up in Holsten-Trophy (promoted after finishing length third to
Capricho) at Hamburg in July and Prix de Seine-et-Oise at Maisons-Laffitte (best effort,
beaten ½ length by Soave) in October: best at 6f: goes well on ground softer than good
(acts on heavy): blinkered: races prominently. *T. P. Tate*

WELSH EMPRESS 2 b.f. (Mar 18) Bahamian Bounty 116 – Azola (IRE) 63 (Alzao **53**
(USA) 117) [2003 6m 7g⁶ 7d 7.6m⁶ 6.1m⁶ 6m 8.2m³ Oct 28] 3,500Y: rather sparely-made
filly: fifth foal: half-sister to 5f to 1¼m winner City Reach (by Petong): dam, 1m winner,
half-sister to very smart miler Sarab: modest maiden: third in seller at Nottingham, best
effort: stays 1m. *P. L. Gilligan*

WELSH HOLLY (IRE) 4 br.f. Idris (IRE) 118 – Jane Avril (IRE) 66 (Danehill **57**
(USA) 126) [2003 60d: 6g 6s 6m May 27] leggy, workmanlike filly: modest maiden: tried
tongue tied. *Miss Gay Kelleway*

WELSH WHISPER 4 b.f. Overbury (IRE) 116 – Grugiar (Red Sunset 120) [2003 **–**
f9.4g Nov 1] half-sister to 1½m/1¾m winner Barti-Ddu (by Mister Majestic) and 7f
winner Croeso Adref (by Most Welcome): dam ran 3 times at 2 yrs: collapsed in bumper
on debut: well held in maiden at Wolverhampton 2 months later. *S. A. Brookshaw*

WELSH WIND (IRE) 7 b.g. Tenby 125 – Bavaria 80 (Top Ville 129) [2003 86d: **82 d**
p7g⁶ p8g⁵ 8g² 8g 8.3m² 8.5m³ 8.3g⁴ 7.9m 8d 8m³ 8g p10g⁴ p10g² Dec 20] strong, lengthy
gelding: fairly useful handicapper: below form after runner-up to Everest at Ascot third
start: best at 1m/easy 1¼m: acts on firm going, soft and polytrack: tried tongue tied:
sometimes slowly away/gets behind: none too reliable. *M. Wigham*

WEND'S DAY (IRE) 8 br.g. Brief Truce (USA) 126 – Iswara (USA) (Alleged (USA) **–**
138) [2003 54: f11g Jan 4] lightly-raced maiden handicapper: well held only 8-y-o start:
tongue tied: sold 2,500 gns. *A. M. Hales*

WENDYLYNNE 3 b.f. Weldnaas (USA) 112 – Dusty's Darling (Doyoun 124) [2003 **–**
–: 8.2f 10m Oct 13] no form. *J. G. Given*

WENDY'S GIRL (IRE) 2 b.f. (Mar 30) Ashkalani (IRE) 128 – Mrs Evans (IRE) 97 **64**
(College Chapel 122) [2003 f5g³ 5m³ 5m³ 6m⁵ f5g⁵ 6g 5.1m⁴ 5m⁶ 7g⁵ 5m³ 6m³ 6d Sep
29] €11,000Y: strong, compact filly: first foal: dam Irish 7f winner (including at 2 yrs):
modest maiden: left Mrs A. Duffield after third outing: third 5 times, including in nursery:
effective at 5f/6f: acts on good to firm going and fibresand: blinkered (ran creditably
tenth start: often races prominently. *R. P. Elliott*

WENSLEY BLUE (IRE) 4 b.g. Blues Traveller (IRE) 119 – Almasa 83 (Faustus **46**
(USA) 118) [2003 48: f11g³ f12s⁵ f16.2g⁵ Feb 3] tall, rather unfurnished gelding: poor
maiden handicapper on Flat: stays 11f: acts on good to firm going, good to soft and
fibresand: wore blinkers/cheekpieces at 4 yrs: won selling hurdle in April. *P. C. Haslam*

WENSLEYDALE LAD (USA) 3 ch.g. Is It True (USA) – Miss Tarheel (USA) (Fit **?**
To Fight (USA)) [2003 53: f6g⁵ f6g⁴ f6g⁴ f8s³ f7s* f8g⁴ 8g f8.5g⁴ May 23] rangy gelding: **a60**
modest performer: won seller at Southwell in February: should stay 1m: acts on
fibresand: blinkered once: sold 3,600 gns, sent to Sweden. *T. D. Barron*

WENTBRIDGE BOY 3 gr.g. Keen 116 – Wentbridge Girl 52 (Petong 126) [2003 **–**
8.2m 10s f6s Dec 27] quite good-topped gelding: third reported foal: dam sprint maiden:
well beaten in maidens. *J. O'Reilly*

WEQAAR (USA) 3 br.f. Red Ransom (USA) – Thawakib (IRE) 108 (Sadler's Wells **83**
(USA) 132) [2003 83: 10.2m* 10.3m² 12.3m 10m 10.5d 10.3m⁵ Oct 24] leggy, close-
coupled filly: fairly useful performer: won maiden at Bath in April: best effort when

second to Moonsprite in minor event at Chester: stayed 1¼m: acted on good to firm going, probably on soft: free-going sort: visits Nayef. *J. L. Dunlop*

WE'RE NOT JOKEN 6 b.m. Foxhound (USA) 103 – We're Joken 62 (Statoblest 120) – [2003 –: f7g f5g Feb 14] of little account nowadays: tried visored/blinkered. *R. Wilman*

WESSEX (USA) 3 ch.c. Gone West (USA) – Satin Velvet (USA) 103 (El Gran Senor 90 (USA) 136) [2003 10d 7.9f* 8f Jun 25] big, rather leggy, useful-looking colt: fourth foal: closely related to French 2001 2-y-o 5f winner On Velvet (by Woodman) and half-brother to useful Irish 6f winner Scarlet Velvet (by Red Ransom) and 6-y-o Plutocrat: dam, 7f winner, half-sister to smart performer up to 9f Satin Flower, herself dam of Middle Park winner Lujain: reportedly fractured pelvis on gallops at 2 yrs: fairly useful form when making all in maiden at York in June, beating Hawk Flyer 2½ lengths: edged left/reportedly made a noise when tailed off in handicap at Salisbury later in month: stays 1m: acts on firm ground: sold only 5,000 gns, joined James Moffatt. *M. Johnston*

WESTBOROUGH (IRE) 2 ch.g. (Apr 29) Woodborough (USA) 112 – Filey Brigg 59 80 (Weldnaas (USA) 112) [2003 5d 5m 5m 5m4 6.1m 5f2 5g 5g5 Oct 28] 9,000Y: good-topped gelding: first foal: dam 2-y-o 5f winner: modest maiden: second in nursery at Redcar: should stay 6f: acts on firm ground. *N. Tinkler*

WESTBOUND ROAD (USA) 6 b.g. Gone West (USA) – Jood (USA) 87 (Nijinsky 94 (CAN) 138) [2003 f8.5s6 p12g2 p13g 12m Oct 3] big, leggy gelding: fairly useful handicapper, lightly raced: good second at Lingfield in February: stays 1½m: acts on polytrack and soft ground: sold 15,000 gns, joined USA. *D. R. Loder*

WEST COUNTRY (UAE) 2 br.c. (Feb 26) Gone West (USA) – Crystal Gazing 85 (USA) 114 (El Gran Senor (USA) 136) [2003 7m2 7m3 7m2 Oct 24] leggy, close-coupled colt: seventh foal: brother to smart UAE 5f/6f winner Conroy, closely related to Irish 1¼m winner Dark Veil (by Gulch) and half-brother to winner in USA by Pleasant Colony: dam won Nell Gwyn and third in 1000 Guineas: fairly useful form in maidens: second to Secretary General at York and Alekhine at Doncaster (wandered): should stay 1m: races prominently. *M. Johnston*

WESTCOURT DREAM 3 ch.f. Bal Harbour 113 – Katie's Kitty 42 (Noble Patriarch 53 115) [2003 8.5m 7m3 7f3 7d3 Sep 20] 5,000Y: workmanlike filly: first foal: dam, maiden, stayed 7f: modest maiden: should stay 1m: acts on firm and good to soft going. *M. W. Easterby*

WESTERLY AIR (USA) 3 b.f. Gone West (USA) – Midnight Air (USA) 111 (Green 80 Dancer (USA) 132) [2003 10d p10g3 f9.4s* 10m Aug 3] 375,000Y: fifth living foal: sister to fairly useful 1¼m winner L'Amour and half-sister to 2 winners, including smart 7f (at 2 yrs) to 1½m winner Midnight Line (by Kris S): dam won May Hill Stakes and first past post in Fillies' Mile: fairly useful form: won maiden at Wolverhampton in June: should stay 1½m: acts on all-weather. *Sir Michael Stoute*

WESTERN APPLAUSE 4 b.f. Royal Applause 124 – Western Sal 75 (Salse (USA) 128) [2003 61: 7m 7m 9f Aug 22] leggy filly: lightly-raced maiden: well held at 4 yrs. *Jedd O'Keeffe*

WESTERN BELLE 4 b.f. Magic Ring (IRE) 115 – Western Horizon (USA) 58 (Gone West (USA)) [2003 –: f6s Feb 4] poor maiden: tailed off only 4-y-o start. *Mrs Lucinda Featherstone*

WESTERN COMMAND (GER) 7 b.g. Saddlers' Hall (IRE) 126 – Western Friend – (USA) (Gone West (USA)) [2003 –, a70d: f11g f9.4g f9.4g5 f11s f9.4g f12s6 f9.4s f12g a33 f14g5 f16.2s5 f14.8g5 f14s Sep 2] quite good-topped gelding: poor performer nowadays: stays 1¾m: raced mainly on fibresand: tried in headgear. *Mrs N. Macauley*

WESTERN DIPLOMAT (USA) 3 b. or br.c. Gone West (USA) – Dabaweyaa 118 107 (Shareef Dancer (USA) 135) [2003 93P: a8f2 Feb 13] won maiden at Ayr for M. Johnston only 2-y-o start: tongue tied, useful form when ½-length second to Victory Moon in UAE 2000 Guineas at Nad Al Sheba only outing in 2003, clear over 1f out: stays 1m: stays in training. *Saeed bin Suroor*

WESTERNER 4 b.c. Danehill (USA) 126 – Walensee 126 (Troy 137) [2003 105: 121 8d 12d* 12g5 14g2 15d2 15.5m2 20s* 15.5s* Oct 26]
   The death of seventeen-year-old Danehill as a result of breaking a leg in a paddock at Coolmore in mid-May removed an exceptional sire and an exceptional source of revenue, since the highest in a wide range of reported sums for the insurance claim filed by his owners with Lloyd's of London—55m dollars—approximated to around two years' work for the stallion, based on his standing at IR

£200,000 (officially private) in 2002 and getting at least one hundred foals a year. In fact, in thirteen full seasons at stud in the northern and southern hemispheres he covered more than 3,000 mares and sired more than 2,200 foals, around ten per cent of whom have won stakes races. He has been champion sire seven times in Australia and twice in France, and runner-up to Sadler's Wells four times in the British and Irish list. Danehill's twenty Group 1 scorers in the northern hemisphere—he has had more than thirty further south—are headed by Rock of Gibraltar, Mozart and Desert King. The two latest additions to the list are not in the same league as that trio. Clodovil was successful in the Poule d'Essai des Poulains and Westerner proved himself the best French stayer in training with emphatic victories in the Prix du Cadran and Prix Royal-Oak. Equally, Westerner may have a little improvement in him since, for most of his career, he has raced over inadequate trips. Remarkably, he is suited by a thorough test of stamina, a rare but not unheard of profile for a runner by Danehill, who is one of only three sires in modern times—the others being Warning and Machiavellian—to get Group 1 winners aged three and up over five furlongs (Mozart) and two and a half miles, as well as at virtually all distances in between. If any single statement sums up Danehill's contribution to the sport, that does.

As a three-year-old, Westerner raced seven times and showed useful form, starting off at a mile and a quarter and spending the rest of his time at a mile. He did pretty well considering, finishing a close second in listed events at Chantilly and Deauville and fourth of five, beaten less than four lengths, in the Prix de la Jonchere. Westerner recommenced operations as a four-year-old over a mile again, at Saint-Cloud in March, but thereafter he raced exclusively over a mile and a half and more, his trainer evidently having concluded that something different needed to be tried. It did not take long for the new policy to bear fruit since Westerner made much of the running to land a listed event at Longchamp in May. Upped to a mile and three quarters two starts later, he finished second to Martaline, beaten three quarters of a length, in the Prix Maurice de Nieuil at Maisons-Laffitte, a position he also occupied over a slightly longer trip when chasing home all-the-way British-trained winner Darasim in the Prix Kergorlay at Deauville (beaten three lengths) and in the Prix Gladiateur at Longchamp (beaten two lengths, on terms 4 lb better). Clearly stamina was Westerner's strong suit—he plugged on willingly both times—and given soft going and two and a half miles he proved a revelation in the Prix du Cadran Casinos Barriere at Longchamp on Arc day.

Starting at just over 10/1 in a Cadran market headed by Gold Cup winner Mr Dinos (odds on), Darasim and Persian Punch, Westerner travelled well from the outset as Germinis set a strong pace. Switched to the outside on the home turn, Westerner stayed on to lead two furlongs out and forged clear, despite wandering a little, to win by five lengths from the 2001 winner Germinis. The remainder, led by Darasim, were well strung out. Even though none of the British challengers ran up to their best—Mr Dinos came sixth and Persian Punch eighth—this was still an

Prix du Cadran Casinos Barriere, Longchamp—of Westerner's nine rivals,
only the 2001 winner Germinis and the visored Darasim manage to get in the picture

impressive staying performance. Another in the Prix Royal-Oak at Longchamp later in the month confirmed Westerner's status as the top stayer in France. Germinis and Darasim took him on again and new rivals included Behkara (Prix Hubert de Chaudenay), Moon Search (Prix de Royallieu) and the favourite Vinnie Roe, successful in the race in 2001 and in good form in the current season with yet another win in the Irish St Leger and fifth place in the Arc. Never far away, Westerner tracked the leaders into the straight, led a furlong out and ran on strongly to beat another British-trained runner Alcazar by two and a half lengths, with Behkara third and Vinnie Roe below his best in fourth; Darasim finished last. This was the first time the Cadran and Royal-Oak double had been achieved since the former was switched from its spring slot in 1991. Judged on his form in the autumn, Westerner must be regarded as a leading Gold Cup candidate. The race has been announced as an intended target. The trip will not trouble Westerner and the state of the ground is unlikely to pose too many problems either—his very best performances have come on soft going but he also has form on good to firm.

As a point of interest, Westerner wears ear plugs, often used to keep horses calm but also used for another purpose—releasing them two furlongs or so from the finish supposedly galvanises a horse to greater efforts. In the Cadran they were left flapping about the face of Westerner, which possibly explains why he wandered. Made of cork or cotton wool, ear plugs are used on many French trotters and were also used on the best Scandinavian horse of the mid-'nineties, Songline, as well as the Arthur Stephenson-trained chaser of the late-'eighties and early-'nineties Irish Red. On the face of it, suddenly meeting a wall of noise in the closing stages of a race would seem as likely to put a horse off as to spur it on, though, given the sparse crowds at all but the major meetings, that would be an unlikely occurrence in France. One thing is certain—Westerner's rider will not be faced with the problem when he runs in Britain. Instruction H3 of the *Rules of Racing* states: 'When any horse runs in a race with ear plugs of any type, such plugs must not be removed during the course of the race.' Apparently the plugs were used initially on Westerner on the recommendation of his jockey Dominique Boeuf in the hope of making him pull less, so he should not suffer any disadvantage in the Gold Cup.

		⎧ Danzig	⎧ Northern Dancer
	⎧ Danehill (USA)	⎨ (b 1977)	⎨ Pas de Nom
	⎪ (b 1986)	⎩ Razyana	⎩ His Majesty
Westerner	⎨	(b 1981)	Spring Adieu
(b.c. 1999)	⎪	⎧ Troy	⎧ Petingo
	⎩ Walensee	⎨ (b 1976)	⎨ La Milo
	(b 1982)	⎩ Warsaw	⎩ Bon Mot
		(b 1972)	War Path

Westerner clearly gets his stamina from his dam Walensee, a lightly-raced, high-class filly who won three of her five starts as a three-year-old, culminating in success in the Prix Vermeille, before training off at four. Better at a mile and a half than shorter, she would have stayed further and the best of her three winners on the Flat before Westerner, the useful War Game (by Caerleon), won the Prix Maurice de Nieuil over twelve and a half furlongs. Walensee's dam Warsaw won both her starts, including a thirteen-furlong listed race by eight lengths and foaled five other winners on the Flat plus top-class jumper World Citizen, successful in the Grande

Prix Royal-Oak, Longchamp—Westerner completes a rare double;
Alcazar (right) stays on well to take second ahead of Behkara and Vinnie Roe (left)

Ecurie Wildenstein's "Westerner"

Course de Haies d'Auteuil. Warsaw's descendants had a particularly fruitful season in 2003, as apart from Westerner, they included two more French pattern winners, Voix du Nord and Walkamia, plus the listed winner in Britain Topkamp. Two of Warsaw's half-sisters won Grade 1 events over middle distances in North America, notably Waya, who notched five including the Man o'War Stakes and collected an Eclipse award as top mare in 1979. *E. Lellouche, France*

WESTERN (IRE)   3 ch.g. Gone West (USA) – Madame Est Sortie (FR) (Longleat **80** (USA) 109) [2003 –: 10g⁴ 11.8m 10f 10.1g 11.9m⁵ 11.9m⁶ p12g⁴ p13g* Dec 6] close-coupled, attractive gelding: fairly useful handicapper: left Mrs A. Perrett after third start: won at Lingfield in December: stays easy 13f: acts on good to firm ground and polytrack: wore cheekpieces third/fourth starts. *J. Akehurst*

WESTERN RIDGE (FR)   6 b.g. Darshaan 133 – Helvellyn (USA) 83 (Gone West **–** (USA)) [2003 68: f12s 11.8g Mar 27] close-coupled gelding: fair handicapper: well held on Flat in 2003, but won 3 times over hurdles subsequently: tried in cheekpieces. *B. J. Llewellyn*

WESTERN ROOTS   2 ch.g. (Mar 9) Dr Fong (USA) 128 – Chrysalis 66 (Soviet Star **81** (USA) 128) [2003 p5g* p6g⁴ p7g Dec 10] second foal: half-brother to 3-y-o Just Fly: dam, maiden who stayed 1m, out of half-sister to Arc winner Saumarez: fairly useful form: won minor race at Lingfield in March: gelded and off 8 months, best effort when fourth of 6 to Petardias Magic in minor event there: virtually pulled up final start: should stay at least 7f. *P. F. I. Cole*

WESTFIELD STAR (IRE) 6 b.g. Fourstars Allstar (USA) 122 – Mokaite 55 **94 §**
(Komaite (USA)) [2003 89: 8d 10g³ 7g⁵ 10.3m 8g 7d⁶ 8m 7.5m² 7d⁶ 7f* 7f⁴ 8s 6m 12m
8g Nov 8] lengthy gelding: fairly useful handicapper: won at Leopardstown (beat Hadath
a neck) in August: below form at Chester fourth start: effective at 7f, barely at 1¼m: acts
on any turf going and fibresand: tried blinkered/in cheekpieces: inconsistent. *T. Cooper,
Ireland*

WESTGATE RUN 6 b.m. Emperor Jones (USA) 119 – Glowing Reference (Reference **–**
Point 139) [2003 63: f12s 10g⁶ 10.1g 12.3m Aug 14] close-coupled, sparely-made mare:
modest handicapper at 5 yrs: well held in 2003: tried visored/in cheekpieces: sold 9,000
gns. *R. A. Fahey*

WEST HIGHLAND WAY (IRE) 2 b.g. (Mar 5) Foxhound (USA) 103 – Gilding **80**
The Lily (IRE) 58 (High Estate 127) [2003 6g 7.2f⁴ 7m 6g² 6m² 6d⁵ 6m 7g² Oct 28]
€16,000Y: good-bodied gelding: second foal: half-brother to Italian 1m (at 2 yrs) and
10.5f winner Samui (by Among Men): dam, lightly-raced maiden (placed at 6f at 2 yrs),
out of smart Cheveley Park and Irish 1000 Guineas runner-up Millingdale Lillie: fairly
useful maiden: second 3 times, running well in minor event won by La Coruna at Redcar
on final start: should stay 1m: acts on good to firm ground. *I. Semple*

WEST HILL DANCER 3 b.f. Man Among Men (IRE) – My Poppet (Midyan (USA) **–**
124) [2003 –: 5m 7m Sep 1] no sign of ability. *Mrs P. N. Dutfield*

WESTMEAD ETOILE 3 b.f. Unfuwain (USA) 131 – Glossary (Reference Point **53**
139) [2003 –: 8.3g⁶ 10m⁴ 11.5m 10d 8.5m 8d³ 7f 7g Sep 1] leggy filly: modest maiden
handicapper: stays 1m: acts on good to firm and good to soft going: none too consistent.
J. R. Jenkins

WESTMEAD TANGO 3 b.f. Pursuit of Love 124 – Tango Teaser (Shareef Dancer **57**
(USA) 135) [2003 59d: f5g p5g* 6m² f6g p7g Dec 6] modest performer: won seller at
Lingfield in February: well below form last 2 starts, carrying head high on final one:
effective at 5f/easy 6f: acts on polytrack, yet to race on extremes of going on turf: sometimes visored: has given plenty of trouble at start, and was banned from racing from stalls
for 6 months after second outing. *J. R. Jenkins*

WESTMORELAND ROAD (USA) 3 b.c. Diesis 133 – Tia Gigi (USA) (Assert **117**
134) [2003 78p: 11m* 12g* 11g³ 12m* 14.6g Sep 13] rangy, good-topped colt: smart
performer: won maiden at Newbury in April and 4-runner minor events at Newmarket in
May (beat Calibre 7 lengths) and August (best effort, beat Foreign Affairs a neck, edging
left): 3 lengths third to High Accolade in listed race at Goodwood on third start (off 3
mnths after): ran poorly in St Leger at Doncaster final start: should stay 1¾m: raced only
on good going or firmer. *Mrs A. J. Perrett*

WESTWOOD LADY (IRE) 2 b.f. (May 8) Fayruz 116 – Payne's Grey (Godswalk **38**
(USA) 130) [2003 5g⁶ f5g 5.1f⁵ 5.1m⁵ p5g⁵ May 28] €1,200Y: half-sister to 5f winner El
Dolor (by Elbio) and winner in Italy by Woods of Windsor: dam unraced: poor maiden:
should prove best at 5f/6f. *J. S. Moore*

WETHAAB (USA) 6 b.g. Pleasant Colony (USA) – Binntastic (USA) (Lyphard's **a45**
Wish (FR) 124) [2003 45: f12g f14g³ f12g⁴ f12g 14m 13.8f May 30] sturdy, well-made
gelding: poor mover: poor performer: stays 1¾m: acts on good to firm going, soft and
fibresand: usually wears headgear: tried tongue tied: travels strongly. *Miss A. Stokell*

WHALEEF 5 b.g. Darshaan 133 – Wilayif (USA) 75 (Danzig (USA)) [2003 102: 10m **80**
10f⁵ 8m* 9.2m² Jul 17] fairly useful performer, lightly raced: won claimer at Yarmouth
(slowly away) in July: effective at 1m to 1½m: acts on firm ground and polytrack: won 3
races over hurdles between August and October. *P. R. Webber*

WHAT-A-DANCER (IRE) 6 b.g. Dancing Dissident (USA) 119 – Cool Gales 85 **93**
(Lord Gayle (USA) 124) [2003 91: 7g 7g 7f⁶ 6.9m² 7g³ 8m 7m³ 7.1m² 7m* p7g⁵ 7.1g⁴
p7g p7g* Dec 10] sparely-made gelding: fairly useful performer: won minor event at
Goodwood in August and handicap at Lingfield (beat Incline 1½ lengths) in December:
best at 7f: acts on polytrack and firm going: usually held up: sometimes finds little.
G. A. Swinbank

WHAT A SPREE 2 ch.f. (Feb 26) Dancing Spree (USA) – Saint Navarro 77 (Raga **–**
Navarro (ITY) 119) [2003 f8.5g Nov 28] seventh foal: dam best at 5f: 66/1, soundly
beaten in maiden at Wolverhampton. *W. R. Muir*

WHERE OR WHEN (IRE) 4 ch.c. Danehill Dancer (IRE) 117 – Future Past (USA) **118**
(Super Concorde (USA) 128) [2003 124: 8m² 8f³ 8m⁴ 8g⁶ 8f⁶ Sep 27] lengthy, workmanlike colt: showed plenty of knee action: very smart performer at 3 yrs, winning twice,
including Queen Elizabeth II Stakes at Ascot: not quite so good in 2003, in frame in

Lockinge Stakes at Newbury (11 lengths second to Hawk Wing), Queen Anne Stakes at Royal Ascot (fourth, promoted to third, found to be dehydrated after) and Celebration Mile at Goodwood (2½ lengths fourth to Priors Lodge): again came from poor position when respectable sixth to Nebraska Tornado in Prix du Moulin de Longchamp: well held in Queen Elizabeth II Stakes at Ascot final outing: was best around 1m: unraced on soft/heavy going, acted on any other: sometimes wore crossed noseband/raced freely: held up: to stand at Cheveley Park Stud, Newmarket, fee £6,000, Oct 1st. *T. G. Mills*

WHICH WITCH (IRE)   5 b.m. Alzao (USA) 117 – First Fastnet 64 (Ahonoora 122)   –
[2003 9.2d 5m 5g Jul 11] no form. *P. Monteith*

WHINHILL HOUSE   3 ch.g. Paris House 123 – Darussalam 78 (Tina's Pet 121)   **56**
[2003 53: f6g f5g³ f5s* 5d 5m⁶ 5d³ 5f Aug 27] strong gelding: modest handicapper: won at Southwell in February: will prove best at 5f: acts on fibresand, good to firm and good to soft ground: tried in cheekpieces: usually races prominently. *D. W. Barker*

WHIPLASH (IRE)   2 b.c. (Feb 9) Orpen (USA) 116 – La Colombari (ITY) (Lomond   **54**
(USA) 128) [2003 5g 5.3m² 7g 8m 8.3g Oct 6] IR 6,200F, 4,000Y: lengthy colt: first foal: dam, winner in Italy (including at 2 yrs), from family of 4-y-o Islington and Greek Dance: modest maiden: second at Brighton: well beaten in nurseries last 2 starts: should stay at least 7f. *R. Hannon*

WHIPPASNAPPER   3 b.g. Cayman Kai (IRE) 114 – Give Us A Treat (Cree Song 99)   **68 d**
[2003 76: p7g* p6g³ p6g 5.5m 6m 7.5m 6.1m 7d⁶ 7g 6m f6g f8g Dec 12] leggy gelding: **a74**
fair handicapper: won at Lingfield in January: effective at 6f/7f: acts on polytrack, soft and good to firm going. *J. R. Best*

Miss Belinda Bauer's "Westmoreland Road"

*Prix Morny Casinos Barriere, Deauville—Whipper is too good for the
stable companions Much Faster and Denebola (rail); Irish challenger Old Deuteronomy is fourth*

WHIPPER (USA)   2 b.c. (Mar 13) Miesque's Son (USA) 117 – Myth To Reality   **118**
(FR) (Sadler's Wells (USA) 132) [2003 5d⁵ 5g³ 6d⁴ 5.5d* 6s* 6m⁴ 6s* Oct 31]
    The match was the foundation of racing, and what takes place for the most
part nowadays is merely a more complex form. The modern-day horserace is
potentially more difficult to understand, but it need not be. Breaking down a field
into smaller parts, if not pairs of horses, gives a powerful insight into how a race has
been run. With two pacemakers in the field, the Middle Park Stakes at Newmarket
in October, viewed as a whole, had the look of a strongly-run race. To some extent
it was, but most of the riders would have been aware of the role the two leaders
were likely to play, and none gave genuine chase early on, which left the three at the
head of the main pack to fill the first three places once the pacemakers dropped
away. Nothing got into the race from well back and Whipper, who finished strongly
into fifth, after being dropped out nearly last of the twelve runners, shaped better
than the bare result, still only tenth in the Dip. He was promoted to fourth on the
eventual disqualification of the winner Three Valleys.
    Whipper was one of two leading French-trained sprinting two-year-olds
who failed to do themselves justice on their only outing in Britain. Beaten only two
lengths, Whipper gave more like his running in the Middle Park than his compatriot
Much Faster had done in the Cheveley Park Stakes on the course the previous day,
but he showed better form at home, winning pattern events either side of Newmarket. Whipper began his career in a pattern race, the Prix du Bois at Deauville in
July, finishing fifth of eight long behind Much Faster. He reached the frame in a decent
minor event at Vichy and the Group 3 Prix de Cabourg at Deauville again before
breaking his duck in a minor event at Chateaubriant in August. The first of
Whipper's pattern successes came back at Deauville later in the month in the
Group 1 Prix Morny Casinos Barriere. In an eight-runner field in which Much
Faster started odds on, Whipper was also up against Denebola, who had won the
Cabourg, as well as the Aidan O'Brien-trained trio, Colossus, Haydn and Old
Deuteronomy. Another foreign challenger Carrizo Creek, winner of the Richmond
Stakes at Goodwood on his previous start, also took his chance. Whipper was the
complete outsider at over 25/1, but he revelled in the soft ground and showed vastly
improved form, wandering a bit before leading inside the final furlong. He beat the
fading Much Faster by two lengths with the never-nearer Denebola a further short
head away in third. Whipper's second pattern success came in the Group 2
Criterium de Maisons-Laffitte on the last day of October. Without a penalty for his
Group 1 win, Whipper was a short-priced favourite (coupled with his stable-
companion Le Boss) in a largely home-based field of ten. He won accordingly, in
similar conditions to Deauville but ridden a lot more prominently than previously.
He led two furlongs out, beating Chineur by two and a half lengths.

Whipper has proved a rare bargain since being bought as a foal in America for only 4,000 dollars. His success has already had a wider impact, with his sire Miesque's Son being sold since to continue his stallion career in France. Miesque's Son was nowhere near so good a racehorse as his dam, the brilliant Miesque, but, as a brother to her first foal Kingmambo, he was sold at the end of his racing days reputedly for around eight million dollars. He stood at Three Chimneys Farm, Kentucky initially before modest success with his stock saw him arrive in California in 2003 to stand at only a fraction of his original fee of 20,000 dollars. Whipper is comfortably the best produce of his dam, Myth To Reality, though all seven of her previous offspring have been winners, the majority at a mile and a quarter and up, including the useful pair Indigo Myth (by Kingmambo) and Assos (by Alleged). They also include the dam of the latest season's Yorkshire Oaks runner-up Ocean Silk. Myth To Reality, who is out of a sister to Shirley Heights, was a successful middle-distance performer in France.

Whipper (USA) (b.c. Mar 13, 2001)	Miesque's Son (USA) (b or br 1992)	Mr Prospector (b 1970)	Raise A Native
			Gold Digger
		Miesque (b 1984)	Nureyev
			Pasadoble
	Myth To Reality (FR) (b 1986)	Sadler's Wells (b 1981)	Northern Dancer
			Fairy Bridge
		Millieme (b 1977)	Mill Reef
			Hardiemma

Mr R. C. Strauss's "Whipper"

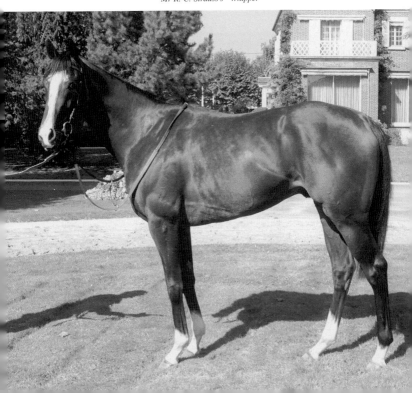

In three seasons, Miesque's Son raced only at up to a mile, gaining his one success in the Group 3 Prix de Ris-Orangis at Evry over six furlongs as a four-year-old. Miesque's Son was second in the Prix de la Foret over seven furlongs and, on balance, it will be surprising if Whipper fails to prove at least as good at seven furlongs and a mile as shorter, though his run in the Middle Park wasn't a case of his lacking in speed under the conditions. A tall, leggy colt with a round action, Whipper has yet to race on firm ground and clearly goes well on soft. He will reportedly head back to Maisons-Laffitte to tackle the Prix Djebel before returning to Newmarket for the Guineas, in which Zipping was fourth in 2002 for trainer Robert Collet and Whipper's owner, who purchased Whipper privately after the Morny. Whipper's winter odds of 33/1 overestimate the amount of improvement he has to find to make a bold showing at Newmarket. *R. Collet, France*

WHISPERED PROMISES (USA) 2 b.c. (Mar 21) Real Quiet (USA) 131 – Anna's **83**
Honor (USA) (Alleged (USA) 138) [2003 6g⁴ 7m² 7m* 7.5m* Aug 14] $8,000Y, resold $50,000Y: strong colt: sixth foal: half-brother to 3-y-o Kentucky King and to winner in USA by Phone Trick: dam, French 7f (at 2 yrs) to 1½m (listed race) winner: fairly useful performer: won maiden at Catterick in July and nursery at Beverley (beat Major Danger by neck) in August: will stay at least 1m: races prominently. *M. Johnston*

WHISPERING VALLEY 3 ch.f. The West (USA) 107 – Taciturn (USA) 32 (Tasso **–**
(USA)) [2003 10f Jul 9] half-sister to winner abroad by Law Society: dam bad maiden: 20/1, well beaten in maiden at Kempton. *Mrs A. J. Perrett*

WHISPER TO ME (IRE) 3 b.f. Brief Truce (USA) 126 – Watch Me (IRE) 106 **–**
(Green Desert (USA) 127) [2003 6g Jul 4] second foal: half-sister to fairly useful Irish 2001 2-y-o 5f winner Church Cross (by Cadeaux Genereux), later successful in USA: dam, 6f winner, out of smart 5f to 7f winner (also later successful in USA) Fenny Rough: 16/1, well beaten in maiden at Salisbury: sold 3,500 gns. *M. R. Channon*

WHIST DRIVE 3 ch.g. First Trump 118 – Fine Quill (Unfuwain (USA) 131) [2003 –: **65**
10g⁵ 14.1m 14m Jun 13] big, lengthy gelding: fair maiden: stays easy 1¾m: acts on good to firm ground: tried blinkered: joined Mrs N. Smith. *J. L. Dunlop*

WHISTFUL (IRE) 2 b.f. (Feb 10) First Trump 118 – Atmospheric Blues (IRE) 91 **68**
(Double Schwartz 128) [2003 6m 7m⁵ 7m⁴ 6m² Oct 20] €5,500Y: quite good-topped filly: fifth foal: half-sister to 3-y-o Isolde's Idol and Irish 7f winner Bear Camp (by Charnwood Forest): dam, 2-y-o 5f winner, later 1m winner in Italy: fair maiden: staying-on second to Attacca at Pontefract, best effort: should stay 7f. *C. F. Wall*

WHISTLER 6 ch.g. Selkirk (USA) 129 – French Gift 99 (Cadeaux Genereux 131) **88**
[2003 86: 5g 5g⁶ 5.1s* 5s² 5g⁵ 5g⁴ 5.3m* 5m³ 5.5f 5m² 5d⁶ 5.2m² 5m* 5.2m⁴ 5m⁵ 5d 5.2g Sep 16] angular, workmanlike gelding: has a quick action: fairly useful handicapper: won at Nottingham in May, Brighton (blinkered) in July and Haydock (beat Dabaian Gift a neck) in August: best at 5f: acts on any going: tried blinkered, wore cheekpieces at 6 yrs: travels very strongly, and best covered up: tends to hang left under pressure: consistent. *J. M. Bradley*

WHISTLING DIXIE (IRE) 7 ch.g. Forest Wind (USA) 111 – Camden's Gift **68**
(Camden Town 125) [2003 74: 16m⁵ Mar 27] workmanlike gelding: fair handicapper: stays 2m: acts on any turf going and fibresand: blinkered (below form) 3 times: held up: useful hurdler. *Mrs M. Reveley*

WHITBARROW (IRE) 4 b.g. Royal Abjar (USA) 121 – Danccini (IRE) 78 (Dancing **90 ?**
Dissident (USA) 119) [2003 108: p5g 7.1g⁵ 5m⁶ Sep 9] strong, good sort: fairly useful performer: form at 4 yrs only when fifth to Attache in minor event at Chepstow: probably best at 5f/6f: acts on firm and good to soft ground: effective blinkered or not: races up with pace. *B. R. Millman*

WHITE EMIR 10 b.g. Emarati (USA) 74 – White African (Carwhite 127) [2003 74: **60**
10.2m 8g⁵ 7m 8.1m p10g² p10g⁵ f8.5g⁴ p10g³ 8m p8g⁵ Oct 8] good-quartered gelding: modest performer: stays easy 1¼m: acts on any turf going and all-weather: won in blinkers earlier in career: best with strong handling/waiting tactics. *L. G. Cottrell*

WHITE HAWK 2 b.c. (Jan 26) Silver Hawk (USA) 123 – Polska (USA) 103 (Danzig **98**
(USA)) [2003 7.1m* 7m² f7g* f7g⁴ Aug 15] sturdy colt: fourth foal: half-brother to 2001 2-y-o 5f/6f winner Grizel (by Lion Cavern): dam, 2-y-o 6f winner, closely related to useful 5f performer Millstream: useful performer: won maiden at Warwick in June and nursery at Wolverhampton (by 4 lengths) in August: respectable effort final start: not sure to stay beyond 7f: races prominently. *D. R. Loder*

WHITE LEDGER (IRE) 4 ch.g. Ali-Royal (IRE) 127 – Boranwood (IRE) (Exhibi- –
tioner 111) [2003 71, a74: 5.3f 6d 5g 6m f7s Jul 14] useful-looking gelding: fair
handicapper at 3 yrs: sometimes visored. *I. A. Wood*

WHITE O' MORN 4 gr.f. Petong 126 – I'm Your Lady 77 (Risk Me (FR) 127) [2003 –
f6g f5g Dec 22] 8,000Y: second foal: sister to 5-y-o Sir Desmond: dam 6f/7f winner: well
held in maidens. *B. A. McMahon*

WHITE PARK BAY (IRE) 3 b.f. Blues Traveller (IRE) 119 – Valiant Friend (USA) **62**
(Shahrastani (USA) 135) [2003 53: 10m 7g⁴ 7.2m³ 8.5g³ f8.5g² 7.9d⁴ 8.1m f8.5s³ 8.5g **a72**
f8g³ f12s³ p13g Dec 29] quite good-topped filly: fair maiden on all-weather, modest on
turf: left J. Quinn after eighth start: stays easy 1½m: acts on fibresand, good to firm and
good to soft ground. *J. Gallagher*

WHITE PLAINS (IRE) 10 b.g. Nordico (USA) – Flying Diva 100 (Chief Singer **37**
131) [2003 –, a69: f16g² f11s³ f14.8g⁴ f12s³ f12g²* f12s⁴ f14g* p13g f12g* f14.8s⁶ **a59**
11.9m⁴ f12s² 11.9f f14s Sep 12] good-bodied gelding: modest on all-weather, poor on turf:
won claimers at Wolverhampton and Southwell (left T. D. Barron) and apprentice seller
at Wolverhampton between February/April: effective at 1½m, barely at 2m: acts on all-
weather, firm and good to soft going: usually tongue tied: sometimes slowly away: none
too consistent. *A. G. Newcombe*

WHITE ROSE (GER) 3 br.f. Platini (GER) 126 – Wild Romance (GER) 111 (Alkalde **105**
(GER)) [2003 103: 8g⁶ 8g² 11s² 11g 10.5d⁵ 10.3d⁶ Nov 7] ex-German filly: closely
related to smart German performer up to 1¾m (German St Leger winner) Win For Us (by
Surumu) and half-sister to useful German 1½m performer Wild Side (by Sternkoenig):
dam, German 1m winner (including at 2 yrs), half-sister to useful German stayer Win's
Fiction: useful performer: won Prix Miesque at Maisons-Laffitte at 2 yrs: runner-up in
Henkel-Rennen at Dusseldorf (beaten 1¼ lengths by Diacada) and Preis der Diana at
Mulheim (went down by a length to Next Gina) second/third starts: left A. Trybuhl after
fourth outing: creditable 3½ lengths fifth to Visorama in Prix de Flore at Saint-Cloud, but
bit below form in listed race at Doncaster last 2 starts: effective at 1m to 11f: raced only
on good going or softer. *M. A. Jarvis*

WHITE STAR PRINCE 2 b.g. (Feb 25) Whittingham (IRE) 104 – Logarithm (King –
of Spain 121) [2003 7m 7m 6m⁵ 6m 7m⁶ Jul 23] 3,000Y: quite good-topped gelding:
sixth foal: half-brother to 2 winners, including 7f winner (including at 2 yrs) Alabama
Wurley (by Environment Friend): dam poor maiden half-sister to smart sprinter Northern
Goddess: of little account: tried blinkered: sent to Spain. *J. R. Weymes*

WHITGIFT ROCK 2 b.c. (Apr 24) Piccolo 121 – Fly South (Polar Falcon (USA) **72**
126) [2003 6m⁵ 5.1f 6f⁴ 6g 6m⁵ 6m⁶ 7g³ p7g²* Dec 17] 17,000Y: good-topped colt: third
foal: dam unraced: fair performer: won minor event at Lingfield: stays 7f: acts on firm
going and polytrack. *S. Dow*

WHITKIRK STAR (IRE) 2 b.g. (Apr 20) Alhaarth (IRE) 126 – Three Stars 93 (Star –
Appeal 133) [2003 7m Oct 1] 9,000Y: close-coupled gelding: closely related to 3 winners
by Unfuwain, notably Irish Oaks winner Bolas, and half-brother to 3 winners: dam 1½m
winner from staying family: 66/1, soon tailed off in maiden at Newcastle. *S. P. Griffiths*

WHITSBURY CROSS 2 b.c. (May 5) Cape Cross (IRE) 129 – Vallauris 94 (Faustus –
(USA) 118) [2003 7g Nov 1] 22,000Y: sturdy colt: seventh living foal: half-brother
to 3 winners, including 3-y-o Burley Firebrand and 7f/1m winner Mystic Ridge (by
Mystiko): dam 1¼m winner: 16/1, very green when well held in maiden at Newmarket.
D. R. C. Elsworth

WHITTINGHAMVILLAGE 2 b.f. (May 22) Whittingham (IRE) 104 – Shaa Spin **58**
63 (Shaadi (USA) 126) [2003 6d 5f⁴ 6m³ f5g⁶ 5d⁵ 6m³ 5.9d³ 5m³ 6m⁶ 5f⁴ 5m⁴ 6m⁶ 5g
f6g⁴ f6g Dec 15] 2,000Y: leggy, workmanlike filly: third living foal: dam, maiden best at
2 yrs (probably stayed 7f), half-sister to Ebor winner Vicious Circle: modest maiden:
stays 6f: acts on firm and good to soft going (only a little promise on fibresand): usually
races prominently. *A. Berry*

WHITTLE WARRIOR 3 b.g. Averti (IRE) 117 – Polish Descent (IRE) (Danehill **58**
(USA) 126) [2003 73: 8m 7g 8.1d Sep 26] leggy gelding: modest handicapper: stays 1m:
acts on good to firm and good to soft going: tried blinkered: carries head awkwardly:
free-going front runner: none too consistent. *C. W. Fairhurst*

WHIZZ KID 9 b.m. Puissance 110 – Panienka (POL) 70 (Dom Racine (FR) 121) **37 §**
[2003 62§, a–§: p6g f5g⁵ f5s Jan 31] tall mare: just poor form in 2003: effective at 5f/
easy 6f: probably best on good ground or softer on turf and acts on fibresand: tried

blinkered/in cheekpieces: has been reluctant to post: sometimes slowly away: unreliable. *J. M. Bradley*

WHO CARES WINS   7 ch.g. Kris 135 – Anne Bonny 105 (Ajdal (USA) 130) [2003   –
p16g p16g Jan 25] rather leggy, quite good-topped gelding: one-time fairly useful handicapper: tailed off both 7-y-o starts: tried visored/blinkered at 4 yrs. *J. R. Jenkins*

WHOLE GRAIN   2 b.f. (May 29) Polish Precedent (USA) 131 – Mill Line 71 (Mill   – p
Reef (USA) 141) [2003 7m Oct 13] rangy filly: sister to several winners, notably Irish/ Yorkshire Oaks winner Pure Grain, 7f winner at 2 yrs, and half-sister to 1½m/1¾m winner Serious Trust (by Alzao): dam, 14.6f winner, out of Park Hill winner Quay Line: weak 13/2-shot and very green, tenth of 13 in maiden at Leicester, slowly away: will be suited by 1¼m/1½m: sure to do better. *Sir Michael Stoute*

WHO'S WINNING (IRE)   2 ch.g. (Apr 21) Docksider (USA) 124 – Quintellina 83   75
(Robellino (USA) 127) [2003 5m* 5.1m⁵ 6.1d⁶ 6m⁴ 6g 5m⁴ 6f³ 5.7f⁶ Sep 15] 16,500F, €23,000Y: sturdy gelding: third foal: half-brother to fairly useful Irish 7f (at 2 yrs)/1m winner Nutley King (by Night Shift) and 3-y-o Roman Quintet: dam 2-y-o 7f winner: fair performer: won maiden at Folkestone in April: creditable third in nursery at Newmarket, best effort in second half of year: stays 6f: acts on firm ground: wore cheekpieces fifth start: free-going sort. *C. A. Dwyer*

WHY DUBAI (USA)   2 br.f. (Apr 22) Kris S (USA) – Highest Goal (USA) (Slew O'   93
Gold (USA)) [2003 6m 7m* 6f 7m² Oct 4] $75,000Y: quite good-topped filly: has a fluent, quick action: first foal: dam, ran 3 times in USA, sister to US Grade 1 9f/9.5f winner Awe Inspiring: fairly useful performer: won maiden at Newmarket in August: very good length second of 18 to Snow Goose in nursery on same course, always to fore: will stay 1m. *R. Hannon*

WICKED UNCLE   4 b.g. Distant Relative 128 – The Kings Daughter 79 (Indian King   82
(USA) 128) [2003 87: 6g 5m 5.1m 5g 5m² 5f³ 5g² 5d Nov 7] smallish, sturdy gelding: impresses in appearance: fairly useful handicapper: left D. Nicholls after fourth start: good efforts after when runner-up at Newcastle and Musselburgh: best at 5f: acts on firm going: often visored/blinkered. *S. Gollings*

WIGGY SMITH   4 ch.g. Master Willie 129 – Monsoon 66 (Royal Palace 131) [2003   88 p
80: 11.9g⁴ 11m* Jul 18] angular gelding: fairly useful handicapper: career-best effort when winning at Newbury in July by 2½ lengths from Hoh Viss: stays 1½m: acts on soft and good to firm going: lightly raced, and open to further improvement. *H. Candy*

WIGMO PRINCESS   4 ch.f. Factual (USA) 108 – Queen of Shannon (IRE) 76   50 d
(Nordico (USA)) [2003 56, a45: f7s³ f8g⁴ 8.3g 9.7m⁴ 7g f7g p10g 10m 8f Sep 8] modest handicapper: below form after fourth start: stays easy 9.7f: acts on all-weather, good to firm and good to soft going: often slowly away: sold £2,100. *A. W. Carroll*

WILDERBROOK LAHRI   4 b.g. Lahib (USA) 129 – Wilsonic 78 (Damister (USA)   56
123) [2003 –: 9m⁴ 7.9m² 8m 9f 8.2f 8g⁵ f8g Nov 19] modest maiden handicapper: stays 9f: acts on good to firm going: wore cheekpieces/blinkers last 4 starts. *B. Smart*

WILD OVATION   3 b.c. Royal Applause 124 – Daring Ditty (Daring March 116)   68
[2003 77: 7g⁵ 6m 5.7m May 30] leggy colt: fair maiden, lightly raced: may prove best at 5f/6f: raced only on good/good to firm going. *R. Hannon*

WILD PITCH   2 ch.g. (Apr 13) Piccolo 121 – Western Horizon (USA) 58 (Gone West   –
(USA)) [2003 6m⁶ May 24] 6,000Y: fourth foal: dam, maiden who stayed 1¾m, out of sister to Ribblesdale winner Nanticious and Stewards' Cup winner Repetitious, latter dam of high-class 7f to 9f winner Indian Lodge: sixth of 7 in minor event at Kempton: subsequently gelded. *P. Mitchell*

WILFRAM   6 b.g. Fraam 114 – Ming Blue 52 (Primo Dominie 121) [2003 61§, a46§:   – §
f8.5g f8.5g Feb 7] modest and inconsistent handicapper in 2002: no form at 6 yrs: blinkered. *J. M. Bradley*

WILFRED (IRE)   2 b.g. (Apr 29) Desert King (IRE) 129 – Kharaliya (FR) (Doyoun   70
124) [2003 6m 7m⁶ 8.1g³ 8.3g Oct 6] €36,000Y, 25,000 2-y-o: tall gelding: third foal: half-brother to German 1m winner Adecco (by Eagle Eyed): dam, French maiden, closely related to smart French stayer Kharizmi: fair maiden: third at Chepstow: ran poorly in nursery final start: should be suited by 1¼m/1½m. *Jonjo O'Neill*

WILFUL   3 ch.c. Bering 136 – Prickwillow (USA) 75 (Nureyev (USA) 131) [2003   107
100p: 10d² 10.3g² May 24] good-bodied colt: useful performer, lightly raced: best effort when 5 lengths second of 4 to Delsarte in listed race at Newmarket in May: found nothing

and well below best in minor event at Doncaster later in month: stays 1¼m: raced only on good/good to soft ground: sent to UAE, joined I. Mohammed. *Saeed bin Suroor*

WILHEHECKASLIKE 2 b.g. (Apr 7) Wizard King 122 – La Ciotat (IRE) 40 **51** (Gallic League 119) [2003 6d 5m 5f 5m² 5m 5m Oct 25] 1,000Y: rather unfurnished gelding: fifth foal: half-brother to 6f (at 2 yrs) to 9f winner in Italy by Noble Patriarch: dam lightly-raced maiden: modest maiden: form only when front-running second in seller at Musselburgh: will prove best at 5f/6f: blinkered/visored last 3 starts. *W. Storey*

WILKIE 4 br.g. Mistertopogigo (IRE) 118 – Titian Girl (Faustus (USA) 118) [2003 –: **–** f6g Jan 2] no sign of ability. *Miss L. C. Siddall*

WILLHECONQUERTOO 3 ch.g. Primo Dominie 121 – Sure Care 62 (Caerleon **87** (USA) 132) [2003 83: 6m 6.1m⁵ 5m 7m* 7d 8.3g 7g⁶ 7m² 7g² 7g 7g p7g⁵ 7g⁶ 7.1m⁵ p7g p8g Oct 27] sturdy gelding: fairly useful performer: won minor event at Brighton in May: stays easy 7f: acts on polytrack and firm going: tried in cheekpieces, usually tongue tied: often slowly away: goes well on left-handed turning tracks: held up: none too consistent. *Andrew Reid*

WILLHEFLY 2 b.g. (Feb 25) Most Welcome 131 – Leave It To Lib 66 (Tender King **47** 123) [2003 5.1g 6.1d 6g f6g² f5g⁴ Jun 30] workmanlike gelding: fourth foal: half-brother to 3-y-o Willhewiz: dam 7f/1m winner: poor maiden: in frame in sellers at Wolverhampton: stays 6f: form only on fibresand: looked ungenuine when visored third outing. *C. A. Dwyer*

WILLHEGO 2 ch.g. (Apr 9) Pivotal 124 – Woodrising 64 (Nomination 125) [2003 **53** 6m 7s 6.1d Nov 6] 15,000Y: plain gelding: third foal: half-brother to 3-y-o Skiddaw Jones: dam, 1¼m winner, also successful over hurdles: modest form at best in maidens: should stay 7f: refused to enter stall second intended outing. *J. R. Best*

WILL HE WISH 7 b.g. Winning Gallery 94 – More To Life (Northern Tempest **103** (USA) 120) [2003 8g 7.5m 6m* 6m* 7m 7g* 7m⁵ 6d³ 7m⁴ 6m⁵ 7d* 7.2m² 7f⁶ 7f* Oct 27] good-bodied gelding: first foal: dam no sign of ability over hurdles (refused to race once): no form in bumper/over hurdles: progressed into useful performer on Flat, winning maiden at Redcar in June, handicaps at Yarmouth and Kempton in July and Doncaster in September, and minor event at Leicester (4 ran, beat Aversham ¾ length) in October: effective at 6f/7f: acts on firm and good to soft going: blinkered since debut: has raced freely: tough and consistent. *S. Gollings*

WILLHEWIZ 3 b.c. Wizard King 122 – Leave It To Lib 66 (Tender King 123) [2003 **100** 97: 5.5m⁶ 5f 6.1d² 6m⁴ 5f 6g⁵ 6.1f* 5m 6m* Sep 2] good-topped colt: useful performer: won claimers at Warwick in July and Yarmouth (claimed 32,000 gns) in September: best 3-y-o efforts when runner-up in minor event at Nottingham (beaten ½ length by The Kiddykid) and fourth in handicap at Newmarket (behind Dazzling Bay) third/fourth starts: effective at 5f/6f: acts on firm going, good to soft and fibresand: visored last 7 starts: front runner: sold 18,000 gns in November. *C. A. Dwyer*

WILLIAM'S WELL 9 ch.g. Superpower 113 – Catherines Well 99 (Junius (USA) **69** 124) [2003 69: 7f³ 7m* 7.5m⁵ 7m 7.5m 7.5m⁶ 6g³ 6.9m⁴ 6m* 6m² 7m 6g² 6g Oct 22] useful-looking gelding: fair handicapper: won at Newcastle in April and August: effective at 6f to 7.5f: acts on firm and soft ground: blinkered: consistent. *M. W. Easterby*

WILLJOJO 2 b.f. (Mar 15) Mind Games 121 – Millie's Lady (IRE) (Common Grounds **55** 118) [2003 f6s³ 6m² 5d³ 5.9m⁵ 6d 6m³ Oct 12] 10,000Y: quite good-topped filly: sister to 2 winners, including 2000 2-y-o 5f winner Milly's Lass: dam unraced: modest maiden: left K. Ryan after second in seller at Thirsk: visored, ran creditably in selling nursery at Newcastle final start: should stay 7f: acts on fibresand, good to firm and good to soft going: reportedly finished lame fourth outing. *R. A. Fahey*

WILLOFCOURSE 2 b.g. (Apr 11) Aragon 118 – Willyet (Nicholas Bill 125) [2003 **85** 6m⁶ 6.1m² Jul 5] 1,800Y: fourth foal: brother to 5f winner Yetti: dam unraced out of half-sister to useful sprinter Up And At 'em: better effort in maidens (fairly useful form) when second of 10 to Cedarberg at Chepstow, seen off only late on: likely to prove best at 5f/6f. *H. Candy*

WILLOUGHBY'S BOY (IRE) 6 b.g. Night Shift (USA) – Andbell (Trojan Fen **75 §** 118) [2003 77§: p10g⁴ p10g p10g 10d 10m⁴ 10.2g* p10g p8g 11m⁶ 7g 10f² 10.1m 10.4m 10f Sep 30] smallish, sturdy gelding: usually takes the eye: fair handicapper: won at Chepstow in June: barely stays 11f: acts on firm going, good to soft and polytrack: tried blinkered/tongue tied/in cheekpieces: ungenuine. *B. Hanbury*

WILOM (GER) 5 ch.g. Lomitas 129 – Whispering Willows (Mansingh (USA) 120) **48**
[2003 53: p10g p10g 9g 7m 10m⁵ 10m³ p10g⁴ 10m p10g³ Dec 30] poor performer: stays
10.5f: acts on heavy going, good to firm and polytrack. *M. R. Hoad*

WILSON BLUEBOTTLE (IRE) 4 ch.g. Priolo (USA) 127 – Mauras Pride (IRE) **52**
(Cadeaux Genereux 131) [2003 –: 7f 8m* 9.2g⁴ 8m 7.9m 11m Aug 23] smallish, strong,
lengthy gelding: modest handicapper: won ladies maiden event at Redcar in June:
stays 9f: acts on good to firm ground: blinkered last 5 starts: often makes running.
M. W. Easterby

WIMPLE (USA) 3 b.f. Kingmambo (USA) 125 – Tunicle (USA) (Dixieland Band **96 d**
(USA)) [2003 101: p8g² 7m 8g 7g 6m 7.1m⁵ 6m 7m 7f⁶ 6.1d p7g⁴ Oct 3] smallish,
sturdy filly: useful performer: best 3-y-o effort when runner-up to Pretence in minor event
at Lingfield on reappearance: best at 7f/1m: yet to race on heavy going, acts on any other
turf and polytrack: tried blinkered/tongue tied. *C. E. Brittain*

WIN ALOT 5 b.g. Aragon 118 – Having Fun (Hard Fought 125) [2003 –: f12s f14g⁴ **52**
f12s³ f12g f12g f9.4g⁴ f12g⁴ 10s* 12m 9.9m Jul 29] sturdy gelding: modest handicapper:
left S. R. Bowring after seventh start: won apprentice event at Pontefract in June: stays
easy 1½m: acts on fibresand, firm and soft ground: tried blinkered/tongue tied.
M. C. Chapman

WIND CHIME (IRE) 6 ch.h. Arazi (USA) 135 – Shamisen 86 (Diesis 133) [2003 **76**
70, a51: p8g² p10g p10g⁴ 8.1m⁵ 9m* 8.1m⁵ 8f⁴ 10.2f 7.5m 8f Aug 17] smallish horse: **a58**
fair handicapper on turf, modest on all-weather: back to best at 6 yrs, winning at Kempton
(apprentices) and Warwick in June: stays easy 9f: acts on firm going, good to soft and
all-weather. *A. G. Newcombe*

WINDERMERE (IRE) 4 b.c. Lear Fan (USA) 130 – Madame L'Enjoleur (USA) **113**
(L'Enjoleur (CAN)) [2003 112: 12.3m* 13.3m⁵ 15m² Jun 1] tall, lengthy, good sort: smart
performer: won minor event at Ripon in April by neck from Bangalore: good short-head
second to Barathea Blazer in listed race at Chantilly final start: will stay 2m: acts on firm
and good to soft going: often makes running: sold 27,000 gns. *J. H. M. Gosden*

WINDSHIFT (IRE) 7 b.g. Forest Wind (USA) 111 – Beautyofthepeace (IRE) (Exactly **53 §**
Sharp (USA) 121) [2003 –§: f8g f11g f8s³ f8g f11s⁵ f12s³ f9.4s* f12g³ f12g² f14.8s* **a72 §**
14.1m 16.1d⁵ 16d May 28] leggy, workmanlike gelding: fair handicapper on all-weather,
modest on turf: won at Wolverhampton in February (amateurs) and March: effective at
9.4f to 2m: acts on fibresand, soft and good to firm going: usually blinkered, often visored
earlier in career: unreliable. *S. R. Bowring*

WINDY BREEZE (IRE) 3 b.f. Mujadil (USA) 119 – Bosa (Kris 135) [2003 –: p5g **–**
f6g Jan 20] little form. *M. R. Channon*

WINDY BRITAIN 4 b.f. Mark of Esteem (IRE) 137 – For My Love (Kahyasi 130) **100**
[2003 59+: p10g² 9.9m* 11.9g* 10g* 11.1g³ 9.9m³ 10m* 10m³ 10m* p10g³ p10g* Dec
10] compact filly: progressed into useful performer at 4 yrs and had very good season,
winning handicap at Beverley in April, minor event at Carlisle and handicap at Pontefract in
May, handicaps at Leicester in September (apprentices) and Pontefract and minor event
at Lingfield in December: best effort when 1½ lengths third to Compton Bolter in listed
race at Lingfield penultimate start: effective at 1¼m/1½m: acts on polytrack and good to
firm going: waited with: tends to idle in front: tough and consistent. *L. M. Cumani*

WING COLLAR 2 b.c. (Mar 28) In The Wings 128 – Riyoom (USA) 83 (Vaguely **66**
Noble 140) [2003 7.5d⁴ 7.5m⁴ 8.3g⁴ 7.9f Oct 9] 25,000Y: quite good-topped colt: sixth
foal: half-brother to fairly useful 1998 2-y-o 5f winner Shining Desert (by Green Desert)
and winner up to 10.5f in France/Italy by Alzao: dam, Irish 2-y-o 1m winner, half-sister
to US Grade 3 8.5f/9f winner Lt Lao: fair maiden: last in nursery final start: should stay
1¼m: acts on good to soft ground. *T. D. Easterby*

WING COMMANDER 4 b.g. Royal Applause 124 – Southern Psychic (USA) **98**
(Alwasmi (USA) 115) [2003 102: 7.9m⁵ 8.1m⁴ 8m 10.1g² 12g³ 10g³ Oct 11] strong,
lengthy gelding: useful performer: several creditable efforts, including when third to
Counsel's Opinion in handicap at Ascot final outing: probably best at 1m/1¼m: raced
only on good going or firmer: tried visored at 3 yrs: reportedly finished lame third start:
has been bandaged. *M. L. W. Bell*

WINGS OF LOVE 3 b.f. Groom Dancer (USA) 128 – Dance To The Top 107 (Sadler's **61**
Wells (USA) 132) [2003 10d 9.2m⁴ May 28] fifth foal: half-sister to several winners,
including fairly useful 1m winner Dress Rehearsal (by Machiavellian) and smart French
1m to 10.5f winner Cheshire (by Warning): dam 2-y-o 7f winner (second in Fillies' Mile)

who stayed 10.4f: better effort in maidens (modest form) when fourth at Lingfield: should stay 1¼m. *J. R. Fanshawe*

WINGS OF MORNING (IRE)   2 ch.g. (Feb 3) Fumo di Londra (IRE) 108 – Hay Knot (Main Reef 126) [2003 7g 7m p10g f7g² Dec 16] €12,000Y: half-brother to 3 winners, including 6f/7f winner Walnut Burl (by Taufan) and useful 7f (at 2 yrs)/1m winner Cazzuto (by Kefaah): dam unraced half-sister to dam of high-class miler Wassl: modest maiden: trained in Ireland by K. Prendergast first 2 starts: ridden by claimer, short-headed in seller at Southwell, then joined P. Blockley: should stay 1m. *N. A. Callaghan*   **58 +**

WINGS TO SOAR (USA)   3 b.f. Woodman (USA) 126 – Only Royale (IRE) 121 (Caerleon (USA) 132) [2003 63p: 8.2m 10m 10m⁴ Jul 1] smallish filly: fair maiden: should stay 1½m: raced only on good to firm ground: raced freely final start. *R. Hannon*   **67**

WING WEST   3 ch.g. The West (USA) 107 – Ballet On Ice (FR) 46 (Fijar Tango (FR) 127) [2003 –: 7m 7.6g⁶ Jul 16] well beaten in maidens/seller: tried blinkered. *J. Gallagher*   **–**

WINNERS DELIGHT   2 ch.g. (Feb 15) First Trump 118 – Real Popcorn (IRE) 52 (Jareer (USA) 115) [2003 6g⁶ 7g* 7f⁶ 7m⁵ Jul 25] 11,000Y: fourth foal: half-brother to 4-y-o Game Time and a winner abroad by Clantime: dam 1½m winner: fairly useful performer: won maiden at Lingfield in June: below form in nursery final start: gelded after: should stay 1m. *A. P. Jarvis*   **82**

WINNING NOTE (IRE)   3 b.f. Victory Note (USA) 120 – Ruby Affair (IRE) 68 (Night Shift (USA)) [2003 64: 7m² 7g Jun 3] fair maiden: should stay 1m: unraced on extremes of going: sold 3,000 gns in October. *J. L. Dunlop*   **66**

WINNING PLEASURE (IRE)   5 b.g. Ashkalani (IRE) 128 – Karamana (Habitat 134) [2003 –, a88: f5g f6s⁶ 6m 6m 6m 6.1m f6g f7s⁵ f6g² Dec 15] leggy, sparely-made gelding: fairly useful handicapper on all-weather, fair on turf: reportedly chipped knee after second 4-y-o start: probably best at 6f: acts on fibresand and good to firm ground: usually wears headgear: sometimes carries head high. *J. Balding*   **68 a82**

WINNING VENTURE   6 b.g. Owington 123 – Push A Button (Bold Lad (IRE) 133) [2003 101: 8.3d⁴ 7m⁴ 8m 7.9m⁴ 8g⁴ 7m⁶ 7m³ 6m 7.2m⁵ Sep 20] lengthy, good-topped gelding: unimpressive mover: useful handicapper: mostly creditable efforts at 6 yrs, including when fourth when fourth to Lady Bear in William Hill Mile at Goodwood fifth start: effective at 6f to 1m: yet to race on heavy going, acts on any other: blinkered once: often tongue tied at 4 yrs: usually races prominently. *D. Nicholls*   **97**

WINSLOW BOY (USA)   2 b. or br.g. (Jan 19) Expelled (USA) 116 – Acusteal (USA) (Acaroid (USA)) [2003 6g 8s f8.5g Nov 17] 9,000Y: fourth foal: half-brother to 2 winners in USA, including minor stakes winner by Dixie Brass: dam won at 6f to 9f in US: best effort in maidens (modest form) when eighth of 19 to Roehampton at Yarmouth on second start, fading: not sure to stay much beyond 1m. *C. F. Wall*   **55**

WINTHORPE (IRE)   3 b.g. Tagula (IRE) 116 – Zazu 58 (Cure The Blues (USA)) [2003 69: f6s³ f6g 6f⁴ 6g 6d² 6.1m⁵ 6f² 6m² 5g* 5.1m* 5m* 5m 5d Aug 30] leggy, unfurnished gelding: fairly useful performer: won maiden at Hamilton and handicap at Bath in July and handicap at Doncaster in August: well below form last 2 starts, reportedly finished lame penultimate one: effective at 5f/6f: acts on fibresand, firm and good to soft going: sometimes carries head high. *J. J. Quinn*   **85**

WISDOM PENANG (IRE)   3 b.f. Hamas (IRE) 125§ – Firey Encounter (IRE) (Kris 135) [2003 6.1g 5m May 14] IR 5,000F, IR 7,500Y: well-made filly: fourth foal: half-sister to 5-y-o Ball King: dam unraced: refused to race and unseated rider in maiden at Nottingham in April: tongue tied, very slowly away when last in similar event at Newcastle. *G. A. Butler*   **– §**

WISEGUY (IRE)   4 b.g. Darshaan 133 – Bibliotheque (USA) 79 (Woodman (USA) 126) [2003 90: 12g 9g⁵ 9m² 10m³ 9g Oct 25] lengthy, good-topped gelding: fairly useful maiden handicapper: best efforts at 4 yrs when placed at Ripon and Sandown (carried head awkwardly/wandered): stays 1½m: acts on good to firm and good to soft ground: sold 75,000 gns, joined J. Howard Johnson. *M. P. Tregoning*   **87**

WISE PETORIUS (IRE)   3 b.g. Petorius 117 – Wise Wish (Baragoi 115) [2003 71§: p5g 7m 8.2m 8.2d 10g May 26] smallish gelding: ungenuine maiden: wore cheekpieces last 3 starts. *Mrs N. Macauley*   **– §**

WISE TALE   4 b.g. Nashwan (USA) 135 – Wilayif (USA) 75 (Danzig (USA)) [2003 78: 14.1f² 18m 15.8m⁵ 14.4m⁴ Aug 6] well-made gelding: fair maiden handicapper: stays   **73**

1¾m: acts on polytrack and firm going: tried visored/in cheekpieces: none too consistent. *P. D. Niven*

WITH DISTINCTION   3 br.f. Zafonic (USA) 130 – Air of Distinction (IRE) 99   **59**
(Distinctly North (USA) 115) [2003 7m 8.2g 10m 10.9m⁵ 12m³ 11.9f⁵ 10m⁶ Oct 2] leggy
filly: third foal: half-sister to fairly useful 2001 2-y-o 1m winner Him of Distinction (by
Rainbow Quest) and useful 6f (at 2 yrs) and 1m winner Man of Distinction (by Spectrum): dam Irish 6f winner, including Anglesey Stakes at 2 yrs: modest maiden: barely
stays 1½m: raced only on good ground or firmer: blinkered (well held) final start.
J. L. Dunlop

WITHORWITHOUTYOU (IRE)   2 b.f. (Mar 29) Danehill (USA) 126 – Morning-   **91**
surprice (USA) (Future Storm (USA)) [2003 5m² 5.1f² 7.1m 7.1m* 7m 7m⁵ 6g⁴ Oct 31]
€75,000Y: tall, good-topped filly: third foal: dam unraced half-sister to dam of Oaks/Irish
Derby winner Balanchine: fairly useful performer: won nursery at Warwick in September: creditable efforts in listed races and Rockfel Stakes (fifth to Cairns) at Newmarket
after: free-going sort, but stays 7f: acts on good to firm going. *B. A. McMahon*

WITHOUT WORDS   5 ch.m. Lion Cavern (USA) 117 – Sans Escale (USA) (Diesis   **?**
133) [2003 55, a49: f9.4s² f8g⁶ 9m 9.2m Jun 18] good-topped mare: modest maiden   **a50**
handicapper: barely stays 1¼m: acts on good to firm going, good to soft and fibresand:
tried blinkered/in cheekpieces: sometimes finds little: sold 1,000 gns in November.
W. M. Brisbourne

WITH REASON (USA)   5 ch.g. Nashwan (USA) 135 – Just Cause (Law Society   **117**
(USA) 130) [2003 f9.4s* p10g⁵ 8g² 9m 8g² 7.9m² 7.1m* 7g⁶ 7m* 7d² 7m* Sep 25]
sturdy, lengthy gelding: seventh foal: half-brother to several winners, including useful
performer up to 11f Jural (by Kris), 7f/1m winner at 2 yrs: dam unraced daughter of Prix
Saint-Alary winner Tootens, herself half-sister to 1000 Guineas winner Nocturnal Spree:
progressed into smart performer, winning maiden at Wolverhampton in January, listed

Sheikh Mohammed's "With Reason"

event at Haydock in June, Stan James Online Hungerford Stakes at Newbury (beat Tarjman by length) in August and Charlton Hunt Supreme Stakes at Goodwood (by length from Monsieur Bond) in September: neck second to Polar Ben in Park Stakes at Doncaster penultimate start: probably best at 7f/1m: acts on good to firm going, good to soft and all-weather: wears crossed noseband: usually races prominently: tough and reliable: joined Saeed bin Suroor. *D. R. Loder*

WITNESS   4 b.f. Efisio 120 – Actualite (Polish Precedent (USA) 131) [2003 68: f7s⁴   **71** f6g⁴ f7g* Feb 7] good topped filly: fair handicapper: won at Wolverhampton in February: effective at 7f/1m: acts on all-weather, good to firm and good to soft ground. *B. W. Hills*

WITTICISM   3 b.f. Barathea (IRE) 127 – Applecross 117 (Glint of Gold 128) [2003   **74** 10f 12m³ p12g² 11.1g³ a11.5g 11.8g Nov 7] quite good-topped filly: half-sister to several winners, notably stayer Invermark (by Machiavellian) and 1½m/1¾m performer Craigsteel (by Suave Dancer), both very smart: dam, 1¼m to 13.3f winner, second in Park Hill Stakes: fair maiden: left H. Cecil after fourth start: will be suited by 1¾m: acts on polytrack/all-weather at Deauville and good to firm ground. *N. Clement, France*

WITTILY   3 ch.f. Whittingham (IRE) 104 – Lucky Dip 68 (Tirol 127) [2003 69d: f5g   **48** p6g 5d⁴ 5d⁶ 5.1m⁴ 5m 5f 6m 5f 5m 6f⁵ 5m² 5m Aug 22] strong, lengthy filly: poor performer: best at 5f: acts on polytrack, firm and good to soft going: tried in cheekpieces/blinkers: none too reliable: sold 3,800 gns. *A. Berry*

WIZARD LOOKING   2 b.g. (Apr 14) Wizard King 122 – High Stepping (IRE)   **73** (Taufan (USA) 119) [2003 7g⁶ 7.1f 7m⁵ 6m² p8g⁶ Nov 18] 10,000Y: tall gelding: fifth foal: half-brother to 7f to 9f winner Bint Habibi (by Bin Ajwaad) and 3-y-o Looking Down: dam unraced: fair maiden: second at Pontefract: stays 7f: acts on good going: tried tongue tied. *R. Hannon*

WIZARD OF EDGE   3 b.g. Wizard King 122 – Forever Shineing 62 (Glint of Gold   **66 +** 128) [2003 69p: 8m³ Aug 28] fair maiden, lightly raced: should stay 1¼m: acts on good to firm ground, soft and fibresand. *G. B. Balding*

WIZARD OF NOZ   3 b.g. Inchinor 119 – Winning Girl (Green Desert (USA) 127)   **111** [2003 104: 7m⁴ 7g Jul 26] workmanlike gelding: smart performer, lightly raced: sweating profusely and unimpressive to post, best effort when 2¾ lengths fourth to Membership in Jersey Stakes at Royal Ascot: mid-division in Tote International Stakes (Handicap) on same course following month: likely to stay 1m: acts on soft and good to firm ground. *J. Noseda*

WIZARD OF THE WEST   3 b.g. Wizard King 122 – Rose Burton 42 (Lucky   **?** Wednesday 124) [2003 71: p10g f9.4g³ f9.4g⁶ 9.7g 11.6g Apr 14] fair maiden: stays 9.4f: **a65** acts on fibresand: sometimes slowly away: tried blinkered. *Miss S. West*

WIZARD OF US   3 b.g. Wizard King 122 – Sian's Girl (Mystiko (USA) 124) [2003   **–** 49: 8g May 5] smallish, workmanlike gelding: poor maiden: well held only 3-y-o start. *B. Smart*

WODHILL BE   3 b.f. Danzig Connection (USA) – Muarij (Star Appeal 133) [2003   **–** p6g Dec 17] fifth reported foal: half-sister to 6-y-o Wodhill Folly: dam no form: 40/1, well held in maiden at Lingfield. *D. Morris*

WODHILL FOLLY   6 ch.m. Faustus (USA) 118 – Muarij (Star Appeal 133) [2003   **52** 52: f8s⁶ p10g⁵ f8.5g⁴ f8.5g³ f9.4g⁴ 10.1g* 10m⁵ 10m 10m Oct 20] angular, workmanlike mare: modest handicapper: won at Yarmouth in July: stays easy 1½m: acts on all-weather and good to firm going: often visored. *D. Morris*

WOLFE TONE (IRE)   2 b.c. (May 24) Sadler's Wells (USA) 132 – Angelic Song   **95 p** (CAN) (Halo (USA)) [2003 8.5d* Aug 2] brother to very smart 1m (at 2 yrs in Ireland) to 1½m (in USA) winner Sligo Bay, and half-brother to winners in Japan (by Unbridled) and USA (by Gone West): dam unraced sister to US champions Glorious Song (dam of Singspiel) and Devil's Bag (at 2 yrs): 11/4-on, won 7-runner maiden at Galway by 4½ lengths from German Malt, tracking pace and staying on to lead final 1f: will be well suited by 1¼m/1½m: sure to improve. *A. P. O'Brien, Ireland*

WOLVERENE   2 b.g. (Mar 14) Wolfhound (USA) 126 – Blushing Victoria 74 (Weld-   **–** naas (USA) 112) [2003 5d 5m Jul 15] 3,000Y: close-coupled gelding: first foal: dam 2-y-o 5f winner: well beaten in maidens at Beverley: very slowly away on debut. *K. A. Ryan*

WONDERFUL MAN   7 ch.g. Magical Wonder (USA) 125 – Gleeful 72 (Sayf El   **– §** Arab (USA) 127) [2003 44§, a60§: f8g³ f7s f8s 12f Jul 16] compact gelding: modest   **a58 §**

handicapper on all-weather, poor on turf: effective at 1m to 1½m: acts on good to firm ground and fibresand: unreliable. *R. D. E. Woodhouse*

WONDER WOLF   2 b.f. (Feb 13) Wolfhound (USA) 126 – Wrangbrook (Shirley   – Heights 130) [2003 6.1m Aug 18] 2,400Y, resold 4,500Y: half-sister to 3 winners, including useful 1990 2-y-o 6f/7f winner Punch N'Run (by Forzando), later winner in Italy: dam third at 1½m: 100/1, well held in maiden at Nottingham. *R. A. Fahey*

WONDROUS JOY   3 b.f. Machiavellian (USA) 123 – Girl From Ipanema 106 (Salse   **98** (USA) 128) [2003 73: 8m* 8.2m⁶ 10.2m* 10m⁵ 10.2g* 10m⁶ 10.3d Nov 7] leggy, useful-looking filly: useful performer: won maiden at Thirsk in May and handicaps in July and September (beat Freeloader 1½ lengths), both at Chepstow: creditable 2½ lengths sixth to Al Ihtithar at Newmarket, better effort in listed races after: should stay 1½m: acts on good to firm ground (ran as if amiss on good to soft). *E. A. L. Dunlop*

WONDROUS STORY (USA)   3 ch.f. Royal Academy (USA) 130 – Gossiping   **91** (USA) (Chati (USA)) [2003 79p: 8.5m⁵ 8f Jun 21] rangy filly: fairly useful performer, lightly raced: best effort when fifth to Aldora in listed race at Epsom in June: hung right when last in listed rated stakes at Ascot later in month: barely stayed 8.5f: raced only on going firmer than good: stud. *J. H. M. Gosden*

WONKY DONKEY   2 b.g. (Mar 1) Piccolo 121 – Salinas 65 (Bay Express 132) [2003   – 5m May 26] 14,000 2-y-o: tenth foal: dam maiden who stayed 6f: last of 10 in maiden at Leicester, slowly away. *S. C. Williams*

WOOD BE KING   4 b.c. Prince Sabo 123 – Sylvan Dancer (IRE) 64 (Dancing   – Dissident (USA) 119) [2003 –: 10m Apr 14] smallish colt: of no account. *A. P. James*

WOODBORO KAT (IRE)   4 b.g. Woodborough (USA) 112 – Kitty Kildare (USA)   – 68 (Seattle Dancer (USA) 119) [2003 51, a68: f11g⁶ 10g 12g 10.9m Jun 16] lengthy,   **a60** quite attractive gelding: fair handicapper at best at 3 yrs: modest form on fibresand on reappearance, well held on turf subsequently: stays 1½m: acts on all-weather and firm going. *M. Blanshard*

WOODBURY   4 b.f. Woodborough (USA) 112 – Jeewan 82 (Touching Wood (USA)   **70** 127) [2003 82: p6g p6g 6g 5.7f² 6g 5.7m 5.7g 5.7f⁶ 6m³ 6.1g 6f⁵ 6m² 6f² 6m⁵ 6m 6m² 6.1m⁶ p6g Nov 29] small filly: fair handicapper: should prove at least as effective at 5f as 6f: acts on firm ground, well held on polytrack: often races prominently. *K. R. Burke*

WOODCRACKER   2 ch.g. (Feb 8) Docksider (USA) 124 – Hen Harrier 94 (Polar   **69 p** Falcon (USA) 126) [2003 8m Oct 17] lengthy, good-topped gelding: third foal: half-brother to 4-y-o King Eider: dam, 7f (at 2 yrs) to 1¼m winner, granddaughter of Oaks winner Circus Plume: 40/1 and green, eleventh of 20 to Lunar Exit in maiden at Newmarket, slowly away: will stay at least 1¼m: should do better. *M. L. W. Bell*

WOOD DALLING (USA)   5 b.g. Woodman (USA) 126 – Cloelia (USA) (Lyphard   **78 d** (USA) 132) [2003 94: p7g⁶ p10g p7g⁴ 8.3g 8.5f⁴ 7m³ 8m f8.5f⁵ Jul 25] small, sturdy gelding: fairly useful form at 4 yrs for H. Cecil: disappointing in 2003: best form around 1m: acts on good to firm going and all-weather: tried in visor/cheekpieces: ungenuine. *C. A. Dwyer*

WOOD FERN (UAE)   3 b.c. Green Desert (USA) 127 – Woodsia 97 (Woodman   **80** (USA) 126) [2003 8m³ 7.9m³ p10g p12g p7g* Dec 29] strong, close-coupled colt: second foal: half-brother to useful 2001 2-y-o 1m winner Lahooq (by Indian Ridge): dam, Irish 1m/1¼m winner, half-sister to useful 5f performer Millstream: fairly useful performer: won maiden at Lingfield in December: stays 1m: has raced freely. *M. R. Channon*

WOODIE (IRE)   3 ch.g. Woodborough (USA) 112 – Better Goods (IRE) (Glow   – (USA)) [2003 53: f6g f6g⁶ f5g Jan 28] lengthy gelding: modest maiden at 2 yrs: well held in 2003: often visored. *D. Nicholls*

WOODLAND BLAZE (IRE)   4 b.g. Woodborough (USA) 112 – Alpine Sunset   **64** (Auction Ring (USA) 123) [2003 76: f5s* 5g f6s f5g² f5g* 5s 5g f5g* f5g Dec 9] fairly   **a83** useful handicapper on all-weather, fair on turf: won at Wolverhampton in February, Southwell in May and Wolverhampton in November: best at 5f/6f: acts on soft ground and fibresand: tried blinkered: sometimes slowly away: goes well fresh. *P. R. Chamings*

WOODLAND RIVER (USA)   6 ch.g. Irish River (FR) 131 – Wiener Wald (USA)   – (Woodman (USA) 126) [2003 –: 7m 7.6m Jul 12] strong gelding: fairly useful at 3 yrs: no form since: has reportedly had breathing problem (often tongue tied). *M. W. Easterby*

WOODLAND SPIRIT   4 b.g. Charnwood Forest (IRE) 125 – Fantastic Charm   **77** (USA) (Seattle Dancer (USA) 119) [2003 66: p8g⁵ p8g* p8g³ 10d 8.1m² 8m⁵ 8.1m⁵ 9g 8m⁴ 8f 8g Sep 22] good-topped gelding: fair performer: won maiden at Lingfield in

March: stays 9f: acts on good to firm going, heavy and polytrack: blinkered (ran poorly) last 2 starts. *D. R. C. Elsworth*

WOODSMOKE (IRE) 4 b.g. Woodborough (USA) 112 – Ma Bella Luna 76 (Jalmood (USA) 126) [2003 –, a57: 6m Apr 15] strong gelding: modest handicapper at 3 yrs: well held only 4-y-o start. *J. S. Moore* –

WOODSTOCK EXPRESS 3 b.g. Alflora (IRE) 120 – Young Tess 56 (Teenoso (USA) 135) [2003 8m 12.1g⁶ 14f Oct 12] third foal: dam 1½m winner: tailed off in maidens. *P. Bowen* –

WOOD STREET (IRE) 4 b.g. Eagle Eyed (USA) 111 – San-Catrinia (IRE) (Knesset (USA) 105) [2003 70: p10g 8.2g 8.2m Jun 14] big, strong gelding: just modest handicapper in 2003: stays 8.5f: acts on polytrack and good to firm going: has given trouble at start: free-going sort: sold £5,600. *Mrs A. J. Bowlby* 59

WOODYATES 6 b.m. Naheez (USA) 126 – Night Mission (IRE) (Night Shift (USA)) [2003 70, a66: 11.8g 14.1m³ 16.2m 14.1s² 13.3m 17.1m 14.1m² 14.1m⁶ 14.1m² Aug 24] tall mare: fair handicapper: stays 2m: acts on heavy going, good to firm and polytrack: tried tongue tied: none too consistent. *W. J. Musson* 66

WOODYBETHEONE 3 b.g. Wolfhound (USA) 126 – Princesse Zelda (FR) 45 (Defensive Play (USA) 118) [2003 67?: 8.3g 14m Jun 13] good-topped gelding: maiden: well held since debut at 2 yrs. *R. Hannon* –

WOODY VALENTINE (USA) 2 ch.g. (Feb 14) Woodman (USA) 126 – Mudslinger (USA) (El Gran Senor (USA) 136) [2003 7m³ 8.1m² 8.3g* 8m⁴ 8.3g 8m Oct 24] $40,000Y: rather leggy gelding: has a round action: first foal: dam minor US stakes winner around 8.5f/9f, including at 2 yrs: fair performer: won maiden at Hamilton in September: creditable fourth at Ayr, best effort in nurseries after: stays 1m: sometimes on toes/races freely. *M. Johnston* 79

WOOLFE 6 ch.m. Wolfhound (USA) 126 – Brosna (USA) (Irish River (FR) 131) [2003 44: 7.1m 11.1d 8.3d May 17] strong, lengthy mare: maiden: no form in 2003: tried visored/blinkered. *D. A. Nolan* –

WOOLLOOMOOLOO BAY 3 br.f. Bin Ajwaad (IRE) 119 – Marton Maid 74 (Silly Season 127) [2003 –: 9.3m³ 7.9f 9.3m 8m⁶ 9.9m Aug 13] poor maiden: stayed 9.3f: acted on good to firm going: tried blinkered: dead. *Mrs G. S. Rees* 49

WORCESTER LODGE 2 ch.c. (Mar 16) Grand Lodge (USA) 125 – Borgia 91 (Machiavellian (USA) 123) [2003 p8g 8.2m⁴ 8.2d Nov 6] strong, good sort: first foal: dam 1½m/1¾m winner: modest form in maidens: tenderly handled final start: will be suited by 1¼m+: type to do better in handicaps as 3-y-o. *R. Charlton* 58 p

WORDS AND DEEDS (USA) 4 ch.g. Shadeed (USA) 135 – Millfit (USA) 62 (Blushing Groom (FR) 131) [2003 68: 8m 10.1m 12.4g⁴ 10.1m Jun 4] strong gelding: modest maiden handicapper: stays 12.4f: raced mainly on good ground or firmer: tried in cheekpieces. *R. A. Fahey* 60

WORLABY DALE 7 b.g. Terimon 124 – Restandbethankful (Random Shot 116) [2003 12g 14.1d⁶ 12f⁴ 12m 16g² 16g³ 16.1m³ 18m³ 16m⁴ f16.2g Nov 10] workmanlike gelding: fair form at best in bumpers in 2000/1: modest maiden on Flat: stays 2¼m: acts on good to firm going: sometimes slowly away/races freely. *Mrs S. Lamyman* 55

WOTAN (FR) 4 ch.g. Beaudelaire (USA) 125 – Woglinde (USA) (Sunny's Halo (CAN)) [2003 11g 12m Jun 1] first foal: dam French maiden: little form: left C. Wroe in UAE after reappearance. *Miss I. E. Craig* –

WOTAN (IRE) 5 ch.g. Wolfhound (USA) 126 – Triple Tricks (IRE) 70 (Royal Academy (USA) 130) [2003 –: f14.8g⁶ p13g⁶ p12g⁴ Feb 25] strong gelding: poor maiden: stays 13f: acts on polytrack: tried blinkered. *R. Curtis* 48

WOU OODD 2 ch.f. (Feb 9) Barathea (IRE) 127 – Abyaan (IRE) 106 (Ela-Mana-Mou 132) [2003 7m Aug 16] tall filly: weak at 2 yrs: first foal: dam, 1¼m winner who stayed 12.5f, half-sister to 5-y-o Sadlers Wings from family of very smart performers Annus Mirabilis (9f to 1½m) and Annaba (1½m): 25/1, behind in maiden at Newmarket, not knocked about: likely to do better. *M. R. Channon* – p

WOZZECK 3 b.g. Groom Dancer (USA) 128 – Opera Lover (IRE) 97 (Sadler's Wells (USA) 132) [2003 77p: 10d⁶ 10m⁶ 12.3g⁶ 10m⁴ p16g Sep 3] lengthy, angular gelding: fair maiden: stays 1¼m: acts on soft and good to firm ground: visored last 2 starts: sometimes races freely: sold 20,000 gns. *J. R. Fanshawe* 69

WRENLANE 2 ch.g. (Apr 17) Fraam 114 – Hi Hoh (IRE) (Fayruz 116) [2003 5g³ 6m **67**
Aug 6] 7,000Y: third foal: brother to 4-y-o Zinging and 3-y-o Offtoworkwego: dam
seemed of little account: much better effort in maidens (fair form) when third of 5 to
Ballykeating at Redcar: should stay 6f. *R. A. Fahey*

WROOT DANIELLE (IRE) 3 b.g. Fayruz 116 – Pounding Beat (Ya Zaman (USA) **64**
122) [2003 62: f7g 7.5f 6.1m 6.1g 7.5d 7.5m* 7g 8m 7.5m² 8.5m Sep 17] leggy gelding:
modest performer: won claimer at Beverley in July: stays 7.5f: acts on good to firm
ground: wore cheekpieces last 2 starts: none too consistent. *Ronald Thompson*

WUB CUB 3 b.f. Averti (IRE) 117 – Ray of Hope 53 (Rainbow Quest (USA) 134) **53 ?**
[2003 6m f6g 7f⁴ 5f 5m Sep 6] 900Y: sturdy filly: fourth foal: half-sister to 5f/6f winner
Al's Me Trainer (by Emarati): dam lightly raced: modest maiden: stays easy 7f: raced
only on ground firmer than good on turf. *A. Dickman*

WUN CHAI (IRE) 4 b.g. King's Theatre (IRE) 128 – Flower From Heaven (Baptism **–**
119) [2003 –: p10g f11g Jan 21] close-coupled gelding: little form. *F. Jordan*

WUNDERS DREAM (IRE) 3 b.f. Averti (IRE) 117 – Pizzicato 64 (Statoblest 120) **95**
[2003 107: 5g 6.1s 5f 5g 5m Aug 20] small, quite good-topped filly: useful performer:
won Molecomb Stakes at Goodwood and Flying Childers Stakes at Doncaster at 2 yrs:
below that form in 2003: was best at 5f: unraced on heavy going, probably acted on any
other: often forced pace: stud. *J. G. Given*

WUNDERWOOD (USA) 4 b.g. Faltaat (USA) – Jasoorah (IRE) 98 (Sadler's Wells **100**
(USA) 132) [2003 p10g* 10m* 10m² 10g² 12m² 12f 12m* 12d⁴ Nov 8] 12,000 3-y-o:
well-made gelding: sixth foal: half-brother to useful German 9f to 1¾m winner Aljaarif
and UAE 7.5f/1m winner Iljasoor (both by Rainbow Quest): dam 1m (at 2 yrs) and 1½m
winner: sixth in bumper in December 2002: progressed into useful performer on Flat,
winning maiden at Lingfield in January, then maiden at Nottingham in May and handicap
at Doncaster (beat Royal Cavalier 1½ lengths) in October: good fourth to Turbo in
November Handicap at Doncaster final start: stays 1½m: acts on polytrack, good to firm
and good to soft going: consistent. *Lady Herries*

WUXI VENTURE 8 b.g. Wolfhound (USA) 126 – Push A Button (Bold Lad (IRE) **73**
133) [2003 9.2g² 9.2m* 9m⁶ 8.3d Sep 29] sturdy gelding: has a fluent, round action: fair
handicapper: unraced on Flat in 2001/2002: won at Hamilton in August, idling: best at
1m/9f: acts on heavy and good to firm going: tried blinkered/visored at 2 yrs: often held
up: former hurdler/chaser. *R. A. Fahey*

WYATT EARP (IRE) 2 b.g. (Feb 26) Piccolo 121 – Tribal Lady 80 (Absalom 128) **75**
[2003 6m 6m⁴ 6g⁶ Oct 31] 20,000F, 46,000Y: sturdy gelding: brother to fairly useful 1m
winner (including in Hong Kong) Triccolo and half-brother to 2 winners, including 5-y-o
Parting Shot: dam, 2-y-o 5f/6f winner, out of sister to high-class sprinter Runnett: fair
form in maidens at Newmarket: best effort when fourth to Phantom Wind: should stay 7f.
J. A. R. Toller

WYCHBURY (USA) 2 ch.c. (May 9) Swain (IRE) 134 – Garden Rose (IRE) 115 **79**
(Caerleon (USA) 132) [2003 8d⁵ 6m³ 5.2f² Aug 26] $20,000Y, 60,000 2-y-o: well-made
colt: fourth foal: brother to French 7f winner Giardino (by Rahy): dam, French 1m
(including at 2 yrs)/9f winner, sister to Queen Mary winner Gloriella: fair form in
maidens: placed at Kempton and Yarmouth (possibly ill at ease on firm going): bred to
stay at least 1m. *M. J. Wallace*

WYOMING 2 ch.f. (Mar 28) Inchinor 119 – Shoshone (Be My Chief (USA) 122) **–**
[2003 7m p7g Oct 15] smallish filly: third foal: sister to useful 2001 2-y-o 6f winner
(stayed 1m) Asheer: dam, maiden who shaped like a stayer, half-sister to very smart
7f to 1¼m performer Lockton: well held in maidens at Newmarket and Lingfield.
J. A. R. Toller

X

XALOC BAY (IRE) 5 br.g. Charnwood Forest (IRE) 125 – Royal Jade 82 (Last **61**
Tycoon 131) [2003 –, a75: 7m a6f f6g⁴ f7g f6g² f6g 6d⁵ 6f f6g 8.3m⁴ 8m³ 8.1g² p8g³ 8m⁶ **a65**
f6g Nov 25] sturdy gelding: poor mover: fair performer on turf, modest on all-weather
nowadays: sold 5,800 gns and left K. Burke after fourteenth start: stays 1m: acts on
all-weather, soft and good to firm ground: usually wears headgear: none too consistent.
B. P. J. Baugh

XANADU   7 ch.g. Casteddu 111 – Bellatrix 45 (Persian Bold 123) [2003 65: 5m 6m 5g   **59 §**
6f 5.9f 5m 6m⁵ 6m 6m* 5f² 6f 6m 6f 5g Oct 22] big, strong gelding: modest handicapper:
won at Hamilton (for sixth time, made all) in August: effective at 5f/6f: best on good
going or firmer: wore cheekpieces last 6 starts: sometimes slowly away but usually races
prominently: carries head awkwardly: none too consistent. *Miss L. A. Perratt*

XCESS BAGGAGE   3 b.g. Air Express (IRE) 125 – Abundance 62 (Cadeaux Gene-   **–**
reux 131) [2003 77: 8m p7g 7g 7m Sep 22] workmanlike gelding: easy mover: fair
performer at 2 yrs: well held in 2003, including in blinkers/visor. *W. J. Haggas*

XIBALBA   6 b.g. Zafonic (USA) 130 – Satanic Dance (FR) 80 (Shareef Dancer (USA)   **–**
135) [2003 54: f9.4g Jan 17] leggy, angular gelding: modest performer in 2002: well
beaten only 6-y-o start: tried visored/blinkered. *Mrs M. Reveley*

XIXITA   3 ch.f. Fleetwood (IRE) 107 – Conquista 87 (Aragon 118) [2003 f7g⁴ f9.4s   **42**
f9.4g⁴ f12s⁵ f11s Sep 26] 800Y: fifth foal: half-sister to fairly useful 1997 2-y-o 6f winner
Cumbrian Caruso (by Primo Dominie): dam 1m winner: poor maiden: raced only on
fibresand. *Dr J. D. Scargill*

XPRES DIGITAL   2 b.c. (Feb 28) Komaite (USA) – Kustom Kit Xpres 69 (Absalom   **77**
128) [2003 5d⁶ f6g* 5m⁴ 6g 6m² 6g³ 5m⁴ 7m⁵ 6m⁶ 6g* 7d Nov 8] good-topped colt: third
foal: closely related to winner in Greece by Samim: dam maiden, form only at 2 yrs (best
effort at 6f): fair performer: won maiden at Southwell in June and nursery at Redcar in
October: not run of race final start: stays 7f: acts on good to firm going and fibresand:
tongue tied fourth to sixth starts: often races prominently. *S. R. Bowring*

XPRESSIONS   2 b.g. (Apr 15) Turtle Island (IRE) 123 – Make Ready 76 (Beveled   **58**
(USA)) [2003 7m⁴ 7m 8m* 10f⁵ Sep 30] 5,000Y: close-coupled gelding: has round
action: first foal: dam, 5f (at 2 yrs)/6f winner, out of half-sister to high-class sprinter
Anita's Prince: modest performer: won seller at Ayr in September: respectable fifth in
nursery at Nottingham: shapes as if will stay 1¼m. *R. A. Fahey*

XSYNNA   7 b.g. Cyrano de Bergerac 120 – Rose Ciel (IRE) 80 (Red Sunset 120) [2003   **55 §**
58§: f7s f5g 7g f7g 7g 6.1m 7.1m³ 8m 7m p7g p7g Dec 17] tall gelding: unimpressive
mover: modest handicapper: left M. Polglase after reappearance, M. Wigham after sixth
start and M. Polglase again after ninth: stays 7f: acts on firm going, good to soft and
fibresand: sometimes wears blinkers: has reportedly bled: unreliable. *P. S. McEntee*

Y

YAFOUL (USA)   3 b.f. Torrential (USA) 117 – My Shafy 92 (Rousillon (USA) 133)   **95 ?**
[2003 76p: 8m 6g⁴ 7.6g² 7m 7m Sep 20] sturdy, lengthy filly: useful performer: best effort
when fourth to Bollin Janet in handicap at Haydock: ran poorly last 2 starts, blinkered on
final one: best form at 6f: raced only on good ground or firmer. *B. W. Hills*

YAHESKA (IRE)   6 b.m. Prince of Birds (USA) 121 – How Ya Been (IRE) (Last   **45**
Tycoon 131) [2003 13.8f⁶ 17.2f* 19.1m⁴ 16f 16g³ 17.1m⁶ Aug 17] sparely-made mare:
poor handicapper: 50/1-winner at Bath in June: stays 19f: acts on firm going: tried
blinkered. *I. A. Wood*

YAKIMOV (USA)   4 ch.g. Affirmed (USA) – Ballet Troupe (USA) (Nureyev (USA)   **102**
131) [2003 88: 8g⁴ 8m f8.5g* 8g 8.1s² 8.3g³ 8.5d* 8g³ 8g* 8m 8g² 8.9m³ Sep 7] strong,
lengthy gelding: useful performer: won handicaps at Wolverhampton in April, Beverley
in July and Leicester (beat Border Edge by 5 lengths) in August: effective at 1m to 9.7f:
acts on fibresand, best recent turf efforts on good ground or softer (acts on soft): often
races prominently: sold 42,000 gns, joined D. Wintle. *P. F. I. Cole*

YALLA (IRE)   3 b.g. Groom Dancer (USA) 128 – Creeking 65 (Persian Bold 123)   **57**
[2003 –: f8s* f8.5g* 9.2d⁶ 10m⁶ f8.5g⁵ 10m⁴ f8g Oct 16] good-topped gelding: has a   **a66**
round action: fair all-weather, modest on turf: won handicap at Southwell (by 10
lengths) in February and minor event at Wolverhampton (odds on) in March: below form
after: stays 8.5f: acts on fibresand and good to firm ground: sold 16,000 gns. *W. J. Haggas*

YALLA LARA   4 b.f. Marju (IRE) 127 – Versami (Riverman (USA) 131)   **82 §**
[2003 78: p7g* p8g p7g p7g⁵ p8g⁵ p7g³ 10g Apr 29] good-topped filly: fairly useful
handicapper: won at Lingfield in January: effective at 7f/1m: acts on polytrack, probably
on fibresand, raced only on good going on turf: tried visored: unreliable: sold 11,000 gns.
A. M. Balding

YAMATO PINK   2 ch.f. (May 9) Bijou d'Inde 127 – Time Or Never (FR) (Dowsing **51**
(USA) 124) [2003 5.3f⁵ 5.7m 5.1f⁴ 6f⁶ f8.5g⁶ f7g Nov 24] 1,700Y: fourth foal: half-sister
to 5-y-o Sungio: dam French 5f (at 2 yrs) to 1¼m winner: modest maiden: should stay
1m. *K. R. Burke*

YANKEEDOODLEDANDY (IRE)   2 b.g. (Mar 8) Orpen (USA) 116 – Laura **43**
Margaret (Persian Bold 123) [2003 5g 6d⁴ f6s 8m f8s⁴ Dec 13] 13,000F, 6,000Y: compact
gelding: half-brother to several winners abroad, including useful Scandinavian winner up
to 2m Account Express (by Roi Danzig): dam Italian 2-y-o 9.5f winner: poor maiden:
should stay 1¼m: acts on fibresand and good to soft. *P. C. Haslam*

YARN SPINNER (IRE)   2 b.g. (Mar 6) Turtle Island (IRE) 123 – Pam Story (Sallust **60**
134) [2003 5f 6m⁴ 5m 7.2f⁶ 7m⁵ 7m* 8m 7m f7s² 6m Oct 12] IR 7,600F, 7,000Y: sturdy
gelding: half-brother to several winners, including 1992 2-y-o 6f winner Stroika (by Shy
Groom) and 1989 2-y-o 5f winner Midsummer Breeze (by Tumble Wind): dam placed in
Ireland/France: modest performer: won seller at Catterick in August: good second in
similar event at Wolverhampton, only form after: should stay 1m: acts on good to firm
going and fibresand: wore cheekpieces last 5 starts: sometimes finds little: none too
consistent: sold 5,500 gns, sent to Macau. *Mrs J. R. Ramsden*

YARRITA   3 b.f. Tragic Role (USA) – Yanomami (USA) 71 (Slew O' Gold (USA)) –
[2003 67, a77: f8.5s⁵ f8g 7.5f f7g 10m 7d 8.5d Sep 23] leggy, close-coupled filly: fair at 2
yrs: showed little in handicaps in 2003: tried in cheekpieces: very slowly away sixth
outing. *K. A. Ryan*

YASHIN (IRE)   2 b.g. (Apr 1) Soviet Star (USA) 128 – My Mariam 79 (Salse (USA) **62**
128) [2003 6m 7g⁵ 7m Aug 8] 15,500Y: sturdy gelding: fourth foal: half-brother to minor
winner in USA by Revoque: dam, 6f winner at 2 yrs, sister to Moyglare Stud Stakes
winner Bianca Nera: modest form in maidens: pulled too hard to post final start
(subsequently gelded): not sure to stay much beyond 7f. *M. H. Tompkins*

YAVARI (IRE)   4 b.f. Alzao (USA) 117 – Twin Island (IRE) (Standaan (FR) 118) **79**
[2003 66: f8s² f8g* f8g* a9.5g p10g Mar 14] strong, close-coupled filly: fair performer:
won 2 handicaps at Southwell in January: well held after, in listed race at Neuss fourth
start: stays 1m: acts on good to soft going and fibresand: blinkered (raced freely) once:
waited with. *B. J. Meehan*

YAWMI   3 ch.c. Zafonic (USA) 130 – Reine Wells (IRE) 107 (Sadler's Wells (USA) **109**
132) [2003 10.3m* 11.9m² 11.9m Aug 19] 5,000,000 francs Y: angular, good-topped
colt: second foal: brother to Italian 7f/1m winner Rentless: dam, French 1½m winner who
probably stayed 13.5f, half-sister to smart but untrustworthy French stayer Rachmaninov:
useful performer: won maiden at Chester (by 10 lengths) in June and 3-runner listed event
at Haydock (by 2½ lengths from Summerland, wandering) in July: well held in Great
Voltigeur Stakes at York only subsequent start: stays 1½m: raced only on good to firm
ground. *B. W. Hills*

YEATS (IRE)   2 b.c. (Apr 23) Sadler's Wells (USA) 132 – Lyndonville (IRE) **95 P**
(Top Ville 129) [2003 8m* Sep 21]
  What's in a name? Well, more than meets the eye, apparently, in the case of
the two colts known as Yeats that have raced in Ireland during the past twenty-five
years, with the first one named after the Irish poet and dramatist William Butler
Yeats and the second in recognition of his brother Jack Butler Yeats, the most
distinguished Irish painter of the twentieth century. Vincent O'Brien trained the
Yeats who raced at the end of the 'seventies. A beautifully-bred individual by
Nijinsky out of the Coronation Stakes winner Lisadell (Lissadell, with the extra 's',
is the name of the house in Sligo with which W. B. Yeats had close associations),
Yeats was a smart six-furlong performer who won all three of his starts as a
three-year-old and went on to become a successful sire in Australia. The latest Yeats
has a very different profile. A two-year-old trained by Aidan O'Brien, he created
such a favourable impression when winning on his only appearance to date, that he
was installed as favourite for the 2004 Derby.
  The race in which Yeats made his debut was a maiden run over a mile at the
Curragh in September. It attracted fifteen runners of which only six had had
previous experience, the pick of this sextet seemingly the once-raced Straycat Strut,
who had finished fourth of seventeen in a similar event won by Yeats's stable-
companion Tycoon. Straycat Strut was fourth again, neither he nor any of the others
able to trouble Yeats in the slightest. Yeats took up the running three furlongs out,

travelling extremely well, and quickly drew clear when shaken up shortly after. Merely nudged along by Michael Kinane, he galloped on strongly to win by four lengths from Haratila, one of two Aga Khan newcomers. On her next start Haratila justified favouritism easily in a maiden at Tipperary. Aidan O'Brien was as glowing in his praise for Yeats as he had been about Galileo after the 2001 Derby winner had made an even more impressive debut as a two-year-old. 'A proper horse all along' is how O'Brien described Yeats after his victory, going on to say that the colt would follow the Galileo route to Epsom—the Ballysax Stakes and Derrinstown Stud Derby Trial Stakes, both of which are run at Leopardstown. We will know a good deal more about Yeats after those races. All that can be said at this juncture is that he looks a most exciting prospect.

	Sadler's Wells (USA) (b 1981)	Northern Dancer (b 1961)	Nearctic
Yeats (IRE)			Natalma
(b.c. Apr 23, 2001)		Fairy Bridge (b 1975)	Bold Reason
			Special
	Lyndonville (IRE) (b 1988)	Top Ville (b 1976)	High Top
			Sega Ville
		Diamond Land (br 1978)	Sparkler
			Canaan

Yeats certainly won't be troubled by the distance of the Derby. Indeed, he will prove very well suited by the step up to a mile and a half, and should stay even further. By Galileo's sire Sadler's Wells, Yeats is the seventh living foal of Lyndonville, who won a mile-and-three-quarter maiden at Galway on the second of her three starts. Lyndonville's only other winning produce to date is her first foal

Mrs John Magnier's "Yeats"

Tsukuba Symphony (by Danehill), a smart performer at up to a mile and a half in Japan, where he was successful in the Group 3 Epsom Cup. Yeats's year older half-brother by Danehill, named Solskjaer, was also in the O'Brien stable in the latest season, finishing down the field in the Irish Two Thousand Guineas on his only outing. Lyndonville is one of five winners produced by Diamond Land, which include the 1992 Fillies' Mile winner Ivanka, the useful seven-furlong and mile-and-a-quarter winner Pretoria and the fairly useful Irish five-furlong to seven-furlong winner Keen Cut, later successful at around a mile in the States. Diamond Land, a winner over thirteen and a half furlongs in Ireland, is out of an unraced half-sister to the St Leger winner Cantelo. This is a very stout family, and it is worth underlining just how much Yeats is going to improve when he gets the opportunity to tackle distances that are more in keeping with his pedigree. *A. P. O'Brien, Ireland*

YELLOW RIVER (IRE) 3 b.g. Sesaro (USA) 81 – Amtico (Bairn (USA) 126) [2003 66: p7g f7g² f7s² p7g⁶ 7m 6m 6d 10.2g p10g Dec 20] strong gelding: fair handicapper: left B. Meehan following fourth start: long way below form after: stays 7f: acts on all-weather, no form on turf: usually tongue tied (reportedly had breathing problem eighth start): races prominently. *R. Curtis* — **a68**

YENALED 6 gr.g. Rambo Dancer (CAN) 107 – Fancy Flight (FR) 74 (Arctic Tern (USA) 126) [2003 68, a82: f8s³ f9.4g⁶ f8.5g⁵ f9.4s⁵ f8.5g 9m³ 7.1m⁵ 8m⁴ 10.3m² 8.3m⁵ 9m⁴ f9.4s⁵ Dec 6] leggy, sparely-made gelding: fair handicapper: left I. Semple after eleventh start: effective at 1m to 1¼m: acts on fibresand and any turf going: tried visored/in cheekpieces: best held up. *K. A. Ryan* **74 a78**

YEOMAN LAD 3 b.g. Groom Dancer (USA) 128 – First Amendment (IRE) 78 (Caerleon (USA) 132) [2003 84: 7g⁶ 8.1m⁴ 8.2d³ 8m 10.3m 8g 9g Oct 25] angular gelding: fairly useful handicapper: should be suited by 1¼m+ (below form when tried): acts on firm and good to soft ground: has hung left. *A. M. Balding* **86**

YERTLE (IRE) 6 b.g. Turtle Island (IRE) 123 – Minatina (IRE) 78 (Ela-Mana-Mou 132) [2003 69: p16g² 17.2f² 18m³ Jun 22] smallish gelding: fair handicapper: stays 2¼m: acts on polytrack, firm and good to soft ground: sometimes slowly away, and refused to race in net muzzle once at 4 yrs: consistent. *J. A. R. Toller* **72**

YESTERDAY (IRE) 3 b.f. Sadler's Wells (USA) 132 – Jude 53 (Darshaan 133) [2003 106p: 8g 8d* 12g² 12g⁴ 12m² 10s² 10f³ Oct 25] **119**

Leaving the song-title connection to one side, there are more meaningful comparisons to be made between the racehorses Yesterday and Imagine. Not only did they share an illustrious sire and trainer, and carried the famous dark blue colours of Sue Magnier, but both were winners of the Irish One Thousand Guineas who ended their three-year-old careers with identical Timeform ratings. Similarities would have been closer still had Yesterday managed to emulate Imagine's feat in 2001 of also winning the Oaks at Epsom. Luck was not on Yesterday's side that day, though she had enjoyed a huge slice of it when successful at the Curragh.

Twice a winner as a two-year-old, including in a nine-furlong listed event, Yesterday looked the type to benefit from the step up to middle distances at three, a view seemingly borne out by a one-paced eighth behind Russian Rhythm in the One Thousand Guineas at Newmarket on her reappearance. Yesterday was kept to a mile, however, for the Irish equivalent at the Curragh later in the month, when the seven in opposition included the long odds-on Six Perfections, a most unlucky second at Newmarket. Johnny Murtagh replaced Thierry Thulliez at the Curragh, but Six Perfections endured another nightmare run—and Yesterday took full advantage. Settled near the rail, with Six Perfections squeezed in tightly behind her, Yesterday wasn't asked to make her move until approaching the final furlong and she stayed on strongly to lead near the finish; Six Perfections, trapped with nowhere to go until Yesterday quickened, stormed home once in the clear, but Yesterday held on by a short head. Three quarters of a length back in third was Dimitrova, with a further two and a half lengths to L'Ancresse, who finished clear of the rest after making most of the running. It was the turn of Yesterday to meet more than her share of trouble in running when attempting to follow up in the fifteen-runner Oaks at Epsom. Yesterday, who went off favourite, just couldn't obtain a clear passage the way things unfolded in the straight, pocketed and forced to be checked before finally being switched left to make a vain and all-too-late

Entenmann's Irish 1000 Guineas, the Curragh—Yesterday (No.8) gets first run on Six Perfections;
Dimitrova (noseband) is third ahead of L'Ancresse

challenge well inside the final furlong. Failing by a neck to catch the resolute Casual Look, Yesterday would have won had she enjoyed an untroubled run like the winner. She was a never-nearer fourth of eleven to Vintage Tipple in the Irish Oaks at the Curragh in July next time out, when set too much to do, as well as reportedly being slightly jarred up afterwards. Yesterday concluded her campaign with good efforts in her three remaining races. She twice went down by a head in eleven-runner Group 1 events at Longchamp, beaten firstly by Mezzo Soprano in the Prix Vermeille in September (when Yesterday was again set a fair bit more to do than the winner) and then by Zee Zee Top in the Prix de l'Opera in October, before going on to finish third of twelve, running very close to her best, a neck and two and a half lengths behind Islington and L'Ancresse in the Breeders' Cup Filly & Mare Turf at Santa Anita in October.

		Northern Dancer	Nearctic
	Sadler's Wells (USA)	(b 1961)	Natalma
	(b 1981)	Fairy Bridge	Bold Reason
Yesterday (IRE)		(b 1975)	Special
(b.f. 2000)		Darshaan	Shirley Heights
	Jude	(br 1981)	Delsy
	(b 1994)	Alruccaba	Crystal Palace
		(gr 1983)	Allara

Yesterday was the twelfth Aidan O'Brien-trained classic winner ridden by Michael Kinane, whose highly successful stint with the stable came to an end in 2003. Kinane's retainer has been taken by Jamie Spencer, who won his first classic for Ballydoyle when partnering Brian Boru in the St Leger. Kinane has taken over from Johnny Murtagh at another powerful Irish yard, that of John Oxx. While Yesterday will not go down as one of the best classic winners Kinane has ridden, she is certainly a filly whose value as a broodmare looks incalculable. Yesterday's dam Jude was just a modest maiden, but she is a sister to the unlucky Irish Oaks third Arrikala and a half-sister to the Nassau Stakes and Sun Chariot winner Last Second; another full sister, the useful Alouette, became the dam of the Nassau Stakes and dual Champion Stakes winner Alborada. Yesterday is Jude's second foal and she went one better, by winning a classic, than her sister Quarter Moon. Quarter Moon won the Moyglare Stud Stakes in 2001, but failed to win at all as a three-year-old the following year, though was runner-up in the Irish One Thousand Guineas and in the Oaks at both Epsom and the Curragh. Yesterday's year-younger sister, the unraced Because, is also in training at Ballydoyle. Incidentally, Yesterday shares her fourth dam, Nucciolina, with another Irish classic winner from the latest season, Alamshar. Yesterday's maternal grandsire Darshaan has had a number of

1119

Mrs John Magnier & Mrs Richard Henry's "Yesterday"

mares who have met with notable success mated with Sadler's Wells: Yesterday follows in the hoofprints of other similarly-bred Group 1 winners in Ebadiyla, Greek Dance, High Chaparral, Islington and Milan. Yesterday, who was held up in all her races after the Irish Guineas, is a good-topped filly with a short, choppy action. Effective at a mile to a mile and a half, and on any going, Yesterday's resolution was called into question once or twice (including after she nosed ahead briefly in the Prix Vermeille), though not by us. She performed with credit throughout the year, never out of Group 1 company. At the time of writing it seems that Yesterday is likely to be kept in training as a four-year-old, with the newly-elevated Group 1, the Pretty Polly Stakes at the Curragh, likely to be one of her first targets. *A. P. O'Brien, Ireland*

YMLAEN (IRE)   3 b.f. Desert Prince (IRE) 130 – Dathuil (IRE) 97 (Royal Academy (USA) 130) [2003 84: 7g 6m⁶ 7g⁶ p7g f7g f8.5g Nov 10] leggy, quite good-topped filly: fair performer: stays 7f: acts on polytrack, unraced on extremes of going on turf: sweated and reportedly lost action on reappearance: none too reliable. *B. Palling*   **79 ?**

YNYS   2 b.c. (Mar 14) Turtle Island (IRE) 123 – Kiss Me Goodknight 86 (First Trump 118) [2003 f6g 6.1d⁵ f6g⁵ f8s p8g f8g Dec 8] 5,000Y: first foal: dam, 2-y-o 6f winner, half-sister to smart sprinter Atraf: poor maiden: blinkered on debut. *B. Palling*   **39**

YNYSMON   5 b.g. Mind Games 121 – Florentynna Bay 61 (Aragon 118) [2003 64§, a71§: f6s f5g f7g 6m f6g 6m² 6m² 7.5m⁶ f7g Jun 19] lengthy gelding: modest performer: was best at 5f/6f: acted on firm going, good to soft and fibresand: tried blinkered: often tongue tied: was sometimes slowly away: was ungenuine: dead. *S. R. Bowring*   **58 §**

YOB (IRE) 4 b.c. Common Grounds 118 – First Veil 94 (Primo Dominie 121) [2003 –
44: f7s f6g 5m 5.1f f6g f6g Dec 26] poor maiden handicapper: tried visored: usually
tongue tied. *P. D. Evans*

YOCKLETON 3 b.g. Wizard King 122 – Awham (USA) (Lear Fan (USA) 130) [2003 –
40: f8.5g⁶ f7s Feb 20] poor maiden at 2 yrs: well held in 2003. *N. P. Littmoden*

YOMALO (IRE) 3 ch.f. Woodborough (USA) 112 – Alkariyh (USA) 79 (Alydar 77
(USA)) [2003 6.1m⁶ 6f f7g² 6m⁴ 5m* 6m⁴ 6m² 6g Oct 22] IR 5,000Y: angular filly:
half-sister to several winners, notably smart 6f (at 2 yrs) to 1¼m (in France) winner Jarn
(by Green Desert): dam 2-y-o 6f winner out of half-sister to high-class 2-y-o up to 1m
Dunbeath: fair performer: won maiden at Beverley in August and handicap at Lingfield
in September: good efforts after when second in handicaps: should stay 7f: raced only on
good going or firmer on turf: has been slowly away. *R. Guest*

YORK CLIFF 5 b.g. Marju (IRE) 127 – Azm (Unfuwain (USA) 131) [2003 8g² 8d 91
8.1d² 8g 10g Oct 13] good-bodied, quite attractive gelding: fairly useful handicapper,
lightly raced: missed 2002: best effort when neck second to African Sahara at Sandown
third start: ran as though amiss next time: stays 1m: raced mainly on good going or softer
(acts on heavy): sold only 2,000 gns, joined M. Brisbourne. *J. H. M. Gosden*

YORKER (USA) 5 b.g. Boundary (USA) 117 – Shallows (USA) (Cox's Ridge (USA)) 77
[2003 71, a78: f9.4g² f8.5g² f8s⁶ f8.5g³ f8.5g* 8.3g⁵ 8m⁴ 8d 8f⁶ 8f⁵ 8.1m³ 8.3m p7g 8d*
f8.5g f11g f7g² f8.5g Dec 26] strong, lengthy gelding: fair performer: won handicap at
Wolverhampton in March and claimer at Brighton (left J. Eustace £8,000) in October:
effective at 7f to 9.4f: acts on all-weather, soft and firm ground: free-going sort, races up
with pace. *Ms Deborah J. Evans*

YORKE'S FOLLY (USA) 2 b.f. (May 24) Stravinsky (USA) 133 – Tommelise 50
(USA) (Dayjur (USA) 137) [2003 5f⁵ f5s Sep 26] 6,000Y: third foal: half-sister to 3-y-o
Satelcom and 4-y-o Night Shift Blue's: dam, French 6f winner, closely related to US
Grade 2 1½m winner Ampulla: better effort (modest form) when seventh in maiden at
Southwell: should stay at least 6f. *C. W. Fairhurst*

YORKIE 4 b.g. Aragon 118 – Light The Way 72 (Nicholas Bill 125) [2003 80: 5g 6m 71
5m 6d⁵ 5s 5m 7m 7.5m⁴ 7.9m 7.1f⁶ 8m² 7.5m 7.5m Aug 23] tall, quite good-topped
gelding: fair handicapper: effective at 5f to 1m: acts on polytrack, soft and good to firm
ground: tried blinkered: usually tongue tied: races freely. *D. Carroll*

YORKIES BOY 8 gr.g. Clantime 101 – Slipperose 72 (Persepolis (FR) 127) [2003 78 d
96§: 6m 5g⁵ 6m 6m 6m⁵ 5m³ 5f⁵ 6.1m⁶ 6g 5.1d 6m⁴ 7m 7m Aug 28] good-bodied
gelding: just fair handicapper nowadays: ideally suited by further than 5f, and stays 7f:
acts on firm and good going: tried blinkered earlier in career, wore cheekpieces most starts
in 2003: none too reliable. *J. M. Bradley*

YORKSHIRE BLUE 4 b.g. Atraf 116 – Something Blue (Petong 126) [2003 –, a72: 64 d
8.5f 7m* 8m 7.5m⁴ 8f⁶ 7.9m 8.1m 8m 9.1d f8g Oct 16] close-coupled gelding: modest
performer: won seller at Redcar in May: well below form last 3 starts: stays 1m: acts
on fibresand and firm ground: blinkered (below form) last 2 starts: sold 2,200 gns.
R. M. Whitaker

YORKSHIRE SPIRIT 2 b.g. (Feb 25) Imperial Ballet (IRE) 110 – Barnacla (IRE) –
83 (Bluebird (USA) 125) [2003 6m Sep 7] 7,200F, 11,500Y: first foal: dam 6f winner:
50/1, tongue tied and better for race, very slowly away and always behind in maiden at
York. *N. Tinkler*

YOSHKA 2 ch.c. (Feb 9) Grand Lodge (USA) 125 – Greenvera (USA) (Riverman 78 p
(USA) 131) [2003 9f* Sep 15] 40,000Y: seventh foal: half-brother to dual Gold Cup
winner Royal Rebel (by Robellino): dam, maiden in France, half-sister to useful French
winner up to 7f Way West: 4/1 and green, won 6-runner maiden at Redcar by ½ length
from Hathlen, making all: will stay at least 1½m: should improve. *M. Johnston*

YOU JUST KNOW 3 b.g. Forzando 122 – Petindia 65 (Petong 126) [2003 f7g Jan –
13] 4,000F, 8,000 2-y-o: third foal: dam 2-y-o 7f seller winner: 33/1, well held in maiden
at Wolverhampton. *P. C. Haslam*

YOU NEVER NO (IRE) 3 b.c. Eagle Eyed (USA) 111 – Nordic Doll (IRE) 71 (Royal 75
Academy (USA) 130) [2003 72: 11.1d³ 10.9g² 8.5m⁴ 7g⁶ 7.5m⁴ Jul 15] close-coupled,
quite good-topped colt: fair maiden: stays 8.5f: acts on good to firm going: blinkered
(below form) final start: free-going sort. *E. J. O'Neill*

YOUNG ALEX (IRE) 5 ch.g. Midhish 109 – Snipe Hunt (IRE) (Stalker 121) [2003 80
82, a90: f7s 6d⁶ 7m⁴ 7m⁴ 7.1g² 7.2f⁶ 7.1f⁴ 7m⁵ 7.5m⁶ 7m³ 7m⁴ 8m³ Sep 22] leggy, work- a?

manlike gelding: fairly useful handicapper: best at 6f to easy 1m: better form on polytrack than fibresand, and acts on firm going: tried in cheekpieces: sometimes carries head awkwardly: held up. *K. R. Burke*

YOUNG BUTT   10 ch.g. Bold Owl 101 – Cymbal 80 (Ribero 126) [2003 f8.5g Feb – 24] leggy gelding: of no account. *L. A. Dace*

YOUNG COLLIER   4 b.g. Vettori (IRE) 119 – Cockatoo Island 99 (High Top 131)   72 [2003 –: f12g² f16s* f14.8g* f16g² f16s* f16.2g³ Feb 15] fair handicapper: won at Southwell (2) and Wolverhampton in January/February: found little final start: will stay beyond 2m: raced only on fibresand: joined J. Old. *Sir Mark Prescott*

YOUNG JACKART   2 b.g. (Apr 15) Compton Place 125 – Princesse Lyphard 36 – (Keen 116) [2003 7m Jul 12] second foal: dam third at 7f: 100/1, last of 10 in maiden at Salisbury. *J. W. Mullins*

YOUNG LOVE   2 ch.f. (Mar 18) Pursuit of Love 124 – Polar Fair 62 (Polar Falcon – (USA) 126) [2003 p7g f7s Oct 21] lengthy filly: first foal: dam 8.5f winner: burly, well held in maidens at Lingfield and Southwell. *Miss E. C. Lavelle*

YOUNG MR GRACE (IRE)   3 b.c. Danetime (IRE) 121 – Maid of Mourne (Fairy   86 King (USA)) [2003 79: 6m² 7m 7.5m⁴ 8m⁶ f7g Oct 16] quite good-topped colt: fairly useful performer: below form last 2 starts: effective at 6f to easy 1m: acts on firm and good to soft ground, well held on heavy/fibresand: usually races prominently. *T. D. Easterby*

YOUNG MYSTERY   2 b.g. (Apr 20) Young Ern 120 – Court Mystery (Mystiko – (USA) 124) [2003 6m⁶ Jun 27] first foal: dam unraced: last in seller at Newcastle. *C. Grant*

YOUNG OWEN   5 b.g. Balnibarbi 95 – Polly Potter (Pollerton 115) [2003 9m⁵ 9m⁴   69 11.1d² 13d 11.9m Jun 2] fair form: easily best effort when second in maiden at Hamilton: should stay 1½m: raced freely fourth start, saddle slipped next time. *R. A. Fahey*

YOUNG PATRIARCH   2 b.c. (May 19) Silver Patriarch (IRE) 125 – Mortify (Prince   61 Sabo 123) [2003 7m⁴ 8.1f⁴ Sep 5] 14,000Y: well-made colt: third foal: half-brother to 4-y-o Monksford: dam unraced: modest form in maidens at Salisbury (shaped well after slow start) and Haydock (odds on): will be suited by about 1¼m. *J. L. Dunlop*

YOUNG ROONEY   3 b.c. Danzig Connection (USA) – Lady Broker 54 (Petorius   74 117) [2003 –: f8.5s⁴ f8.5s² f9.4g² 7.6m 10.3g⁴ 9.1g³ 9.1m² 10.3m⁴ Jun 28] fair maiden: in frame most starts, including in handicaps: stays 10.3f: acts on good to firm going and fibresand: usually makes running. *M. Mullineaux*

YOUNG SAFAWAN   3 ch.g. Safawan 118 – Madame Bovary 82 (Ile de Bourbon   72 (USA) 133) [2003 8g⁶ 8f⁴ 8.3d 10m⁶ 10m* 10.1m 10m⁵ 10.2g 10g 10m Oct 20] 2,000Y: sturdy gelding: half-brother to 3 winners, including 5-y-o Tomthevic and fairly useful 1994 2-y-o 7f winner La Contessa (by Robellino), later successful in USA: dam 1m/1¼m winner: fair handicapper: won at Newmarket in July: well below form after: stays 1¼m: acts on firm going: tried tongue tied: has carried head awkwardly: sold 3,000 gns, sent to Macau. *P. W. Harris*

YOUNGS FORTH   3 b.f. Most Welcome 131 – Pegs 60 (Mandrake Major 122) [2003   50 57: f5s 6.1g⁵ f6g⁵ 6.1m 8.1m Aug 14] close-coupled filly: modest maiden handicapper: should stay 1m: acts on soft going: sometimes slowly away. *A. W. Carroll*

YOUNG TERN   5 b.g. Young Ern 120 – Turnaway 79 (Runnett 125) [2003 43, a60: – f11g f9.4s⁵ f9.4g⁶ May 19] smallish gelding: modest performer at 4 yrs: well held in 2003: usually blinkered. *B. J. Llewellyn*

YOUR JUST LOVELY (IRE)   2 b.f. (Jan 23) Second Empire (IRE) 124 – Nawaji   61 (USA) 45 (Trempolino (USA) 135) [2003 p6g 6g⁶ p5g Nov 12] €35,000Y: third foal: dam, maiden who stayed 13f, sister to smart 9f to 1½m performer Triarius: modest form in maidens: needs to settle to stay beyond 6f. *A. M. Balding*

Z

ZABADOU   2 b.g. (Mar 21) Abou Zouz (USA) 109 – Strapped 57 (Reprimand 122)   – [2003 8d 8d Nov 7] 2,000Y: fourth foal: half-brother to 1998 2-y-o 6f seller winner Banningham Breeze (by Cyrano de Bergerac): dam, 6f winner, ran only at 2 yrs: well beaten in maidens at Doncaster. *C. B. B. Booth*

ZABAGLIONE 3 ch.g. Zilzal (USA) 137 – Satin Bell 99 (Midyan (USA) 124) [2003 **107**
95: 8m⁴ 7g⁴ 8.1v 8m 10m⁵ 9.9g³ 9m* 10m² 9m Oct 4] close-coupled gelding: useful
handicapper: won at Goodwood in August by 1½ lengths from Tizzy May: best effort
when 1¼ lengths second to Navado in Courage Best Stakes at Newbury: respectable ninth
in Cambridgeshire at Newmarket final outing: stays 1¼m: acts on heavy and good to firm
going: visored last 3 starts: waited with: sold 160,000 gns, joined G. Lane in Hong Kong
and renamed Bear Dominance. *R. Charlton*

ZADOK THE PRIEST (IRE) 3 b. or br.g. Zafonic (USA) 130 – Valency (IRE) **60 §**
(Sadler's Wells (USA) 132) [2003 65?: 10.2m 14.1d 11.8m⁵ 11.9m p12g⁶ 18m² 18f⁴
16.2g⁴ 14.1m³ 13.1f 16m³ 17.1m 18m Oct 20] modest maiden handicapper: stays 2¼m:
acts on firm going, below form on good to soft: usually wears blinkers/cheekpieces:
sometimes slowly away: ungenuine. *J. W. Hills*

ZAFARSHAH (IRE) 4 b.g. Danehill (USA) 126 – Zafarana (FR) (Shernazar 131) **70**
[2003 71: p8g* f8.5g p10g p7g³ f9.4g p10g 10.3g 8f² 8g 8m³ 8.1m* 7.1g⁵ 8.3m⁵ 8.1m³ 8f
8f 7.9m 8g³ 8.1d 8.2m 8f⁵ 8d Nov 7] good-bodied gelding: fair performer: won maiden at
Lingfield in January and handicap at Sandown in May: effective at 7f to 8.5f: yet to race
on heavy going, acts on any other turf/all-weather: tried visored/tongue tied. *P. D. Evans*

ZAFEEN (FR) 3 b.c. Zafonic (USA) 130 – Shy Lady (FR) 91 (Kaldoun (FR) **123**
122) [2003 111: 7m² 8g² 8d 8f* 8d⁴ Jul 30]
The summer sale of Zafeen to Godolphin was a blow to trainer Mick
Channon but, in contrast to Godolphin's trainer Saeed bin Suroor, Channon had his
best season in 2003, sending out 144 winners in Britain and amassing £1,855,922
in first three prize money. The next milestone in the former footballer's training
career would be a classic success. Channon has been unlucky in that respect, with
both Bint Allayl (in 1999) and Queen's Logic (in 2002) failing to make the line-up
after being ante-post favourites for the One Thousand Guineas over the winter, the
former having to be put down after fracturing a shoulder on the gallops and a bout
of coughing putting paid to Queen's Logic's bid on the eve of the race. Zafeen went
closest to classic success for Channon in the latest season, going down by three
quarters of a length to Refuse To Bend in the Two Thousand Guineas after coming
second to Muqbil in the Greenham at Newbury on his reappearance. Zafeen had
also appeared to have his classic limitations exposed in the Middle Park and
Dewhurst as a two-year-old and he started at 33/1 for the Guineas. He showed
improved form and was arguably unlucky not to have got closer to the winner,
finishing strongly after being short of room in the Dip. Zafeen was one of five
Guineas runners who contested the Irish equivalent later in the month, but he ran
poorly, the good to soft going blamed for his performance. Back on a firm surface
in the St James's Palace Stakes at Royal Ascot, Zafeen put up his best effort to win
his first race since the Mill Reef Stakes at Newbury as a two-year-old. The winning

St James's Palace Stakes, Royal Ascot—Zafeen holds off the unlucky-in-running Kalaman;
the grey Clodovil is only fifth

margin was a length, but he was lucky to beat the favourite and strong-finishing runner-up Kalaman, who endured a troubled passage in the straight. The pair were clear of the Mehl-Mulhens-Rennen winner Martillo, Hold That Tiger and Clodovil, the last-named having been successful in the Poule d'Essai des Poulains. At his owner's request, Zafeen's regular rider Steve Drowne had been replaced by Darryll Holland at Royal Ascot but Drowne was aboard Channon's other Royal Ascot winners Silca's Gift and Holborn. Zafeen's only start after Royal Ascot came in the Sussex Stakes at Goodwood. In a substandard renewal Zafeen again showed he is not at his best on going softer than good, though he was beaten only a head, a short head and a neck into fourth by Reel Buddy after leading narrowly inside the final two furlongs. Before his sale, connections had been aiming him at the Jacques le Marois at Deauville in August but Godolphin relied on Dubai Destination in that contest. Dubai Destination's win in the Queen Anne Stakes was Godolphin's only domestic Group 1 success and he enhanced an excellent record in the Queen Anne, Godolphin having won five of the last eight runnings. Zafeen looks to have decent prospects of adding to that record in 2004. He has shown his best form on going firmer than good and is likely to be trained with a summer campaign in mind.

Zafeen (FR) (b.c. 2000)	Zafonic (USA) (b 1990)	Gone West (b 1984)	Mr Prospector Secrettame
		Zaizafon (ch 1982)	The Minstrel Mofida
	Shy Lady (FR) (b 1994)	Kaldoun (gr 1975)	Caro Katana
		Shy Danceuse (ch 1989)	Groom Dancer Shy Princess

Mr Jaber Abdullah's "Zafeen"

Zafeen's sire the 1993 Two Thousand Guineas winner Zafonic died in a freak paddock accident in Australia in 2002. As well as Zafeen, he was represented notably by Trade Fair and Zee Zee Top in 2003. Zafeen is the second foal of Shy Lady. The first Ya Hajar, also owned by Jaber Abdullah and trained by Channon, was useful as a two-year-old, winning a maiden at Ascot over six furlongs and the seven-furlong Prix du Calvados at Deauville. She was well beaten on both starts at three, in the Nell Gwyn Stakes and the One Thousand Guineas. Shy Lady herself was a fairly useful performer in Germany for Bruno Schutz, winning at five and six furlongs as a two-year-old. Zafeen's grandam Shy Danceuse was a winner at a mile in France for Criquette Head-Maarek and is a half-sister to the very smart performer at up to a mile Diffident, who was transferred to Godolphin after being trained by Andre Fabre at two and three. Shy Danceuse is a daughter of the Prix Morny runner-up Shy Princess. A tall, rather leggy colt, Zafeen is far from certain to stay beyond a mile. *M. R. Channon*

ZAFFRANI (IRE) 4 b. or br.f. Danehill (USA) 126 – Zariysha (IRE) (Darshaan 133) – [2003 8d Jul 25] smallish, angular, workmanlike filly: useful performer at 2 yrs: ran 5 times for N. O'Callaghan in US in 2002, best effort when second in allowance race at Churchill Downs: rejoined former stable and sweating, last in listed race at Ascot only 4-y-o start: stays 1m: acts on firm and soft going: tried blinkered. *D. Wachman, Ireland*

ZAGALA 3 b.f. Polar Falcon (USA) 126 – Whittle Woods Girl 80 (Emarati (USA) 74) **70** [2003 58: p6g⁶ p8g³ f6s f7s f7g² f7g* p7g³ Nov 29] fair performer: suspended for 40 days under non-triers rule on reappearance: won handicap at Wolverhampton in November, despite hanging left: stays 7f: raced only on all-weather: tongue tied last 3 starts. *S. L. Keightley*

ZAHUNDA (IRE) 4 b.f. Spectrum (IRE) 126 – Gift of Glory (FR) (Niniski (USA) **55 §** 125) [2003 73: 12g 9.2m 10.9m 15m f8.5g* f8.5s f8.5g f8s f9.4g f7g f8g Dec 19] fifth foal: half-sister to 3 winners, including French 11.5f winner Seixo Branco (by Saddlers' Hall): dam, French maiden, closely related to smart French 1m/1¼m performer Garden Rose: modest handicapper: trained in 2002 by K. Prendergast in Ireland: easily best 4-y-o effort when winning at Wolverhampton in July: finished lame next start: effective at 8.5f, seems to stay 1½m: acts on heavy going and fibresand: blinkered once at 3 yrs: unreliable. *W. M. Brisbourne*

ZAIBAS (USA) 3 b.g. Tabasco Cat (USA) 126 – Sudden Sun (USA) (Danzig (USA)) – [2003 –: 7m⁶ 8.2g 7s Jul 25] big, good-bodied gelding: no form in maidens: tried blinkered. *A. Dickman*

ZAK FACTA (IRE) 3 b.g. Danetime (IRE) 121 – Alexander Goddess (IRE) (Alzao **72 d** (USA) 117) [2003 78: 5s 6m³ 6d 6m⁵ 5m⁶ f6f³ 6f² 5m 8.5d f8.5g⁴ f7s² p7g⁵ f8g⁴ p7g f7g Dec 16] leggy gelding: fair maiden: below form following second start, leaving N. Littmoden after sixth outing, J. Given after eleventh: effective at 6f to 8.5f: acts on all-weather and firm ground: blinkered/visored after fourth appearance. *Miss D. A. McHale*

ZAKFREE (IRE) 2 b.g. (Feb 25) Danetime (IRE) 121 – Clipper Queen 66 (Balidar **67** 133) [2003 6.1m 8m³ 8m 8.3g⁴ 8m 8s³ 7d Nov 8] 7,500Y: rather leggy gelding: half-brother to fairly useful Irish 6f to 9f winner Short Shift (by Mac's Imp) and 8-y-o Near Dunleer: dam 6f winner: fair maiden: third at Thirsk and Redcar (nursery): stays 1m: acts on good to firm and soft going: blinkered last 4 starts. *N. P. Littmoden*

ZAKTOO (IRE) 2 b.c. (Apr 14) Sri Pekan (USA) 117 – Alpine Symphony (Northern – Dancer) [2003 7.1f 8.1d Sep 27] IR 6,500F, 7,000Y: half-brother to 3 winners, including smart 1m to 1½m winner High Baroque and fairly useful 1¼m winner Dancing Heights (both by High Estate): dam unraced half-sister to Irish 2000 Guineas winner Nikoli: well held in maidens at Sandown and Haydock: sold 1,400 gns. *N. P. Littmoden*

ZALDA 2 ch.f. (Mar 29) Zilzal (USA) 137 – Gold Luck (USA) (Slew O' Gold (USA)) **59 p** [2003 8.2f p7g 8m⁶ Oct 23] big, close-coupled filly: fifth foal: half-sister to 1999 2-y-o 1m winner Top Hand (by First Trump) and 7f/1m winner in Scandinavia by Averti: dam unraced half-sister to dam of Melbourne Cup winner Makybe Diva: modest form in maidens: not knocked about when sixth at Brighton: will probably stay 1¼m: slowly away first 2 outings: type to do better as 3-y-o. *R. Charlton*

ZALKANI (IRE) 3 ch.g. Cadeaux Genereux 131 – Zallaka (IRE) (Shardari 134) – [2003 9.2m⁶ 10f 8.3d Jun 23] fifth foal: half-brother to 7-y-o Linning Wine and useful 1¼m/1½m winner Zalal (by Darshaan): dam French 11f winner: well held in maidens. *B. G. Powell*

ZAMAT   7 b.g. Slip Anchor 136 – Khandjar 77 (Kris 135) [2003 74: 13d⁴ 11.9d Sep 26]   **67**
fair performer: probably stays 13f: acts on soft and good to firm going. *P. Monteith*

ZAMEEL (IRE)   2 b.c. (Mar 28) Marju (IRE) 127 – Impatiente (USA) (Vaguely Noble   **–**
140) [2003 8m 8d Nov 7] 16,000Y: quite good-topped colt: half-brother to several
winners, including useful stayers Busy Lizzie and Eminence Grise (both by Sadler's
Wells): dam, French maiden, out of US Grade 1 9f/1¼m winner Sangue: well held in
maidens at Musselburgh and Doncaster. *Jedd O'Keeffe*

ZAMIR   4 ch.g. Zamindar (USA) 116 – Fairy Flax (IRE) 97 (Dancing Brave (USA)   **–**
140) [2003 –: f12s f12g Jan 24] sturdy gelding: no sign of ability. *A. Crook*

ZAMORIN   4 b.g. Zafonic (USA) 130 – Armeria (USA) 79 (Northern Dancer) [2003   **–**
64: f16g f12s Jan 14] modest performer at 3 yrs: no form in 2003: tried visored: dead.
P. S. McEntee

ZAMYATINA (IRE)   4 br.f. Danehill Dancer (IRE) 117 – Miss Pickpocket (IRE) 64   **64**
(Petorius 117) [2003 46: 6m 6m 8g 7m* 7.6m 7m⁶ 8g⁴ 7m 7m 7.1g Sep 11] angular filly:
modest performer: 66/1-winner of minor event at Catterick in July: stays easy 7f: acts on
polytrack, soft and good to firm ground. *P. L. Clinton*

ZANAY   7 b.g. Forzando 122 – Nineteenth of May 86 (Homing 130) [2003 –: 8.3g 10d   **–**
8.3g 8m Aug 27] tall gelding: reportedly had knee chips removed at 4 yrs: formerly smart
1m/1¼m all-weather performer: no form since 2001: has worn blinkers/tongue tie/
cheekpieces. *Miss Jacqueline S. Doyle*

ZANJEER   3 b.g. Averti (IRE) 117 – Cloudslea (USA) (Chief's Crown (USA)) [2003   **–**
66: 10g⁴ 7f Sep 15] fair maiden at 2 yrs: well held in 2003. *D. Nicholls*

ZANOG   4 b.g. Forzando 122 – Logarithm (King of Spain 121) [2003 –: p6g 7g 5m Jun   **–**
9] little form: usually blinkered. *Miss Jacqueline S. Doyle*

ZAP ATTACK   3 b.g. Zafonic (USA) 130 – Rappa Tap Tap (FR) 111 (Tap On Wood   **74**
130) [2003 79: 8m p10g 9m 7m³ 7m³ 6.1m* 7.5m 6g² 7m 7.5d Sep 23] close-coupled
gelding: fair handicapper: won maiden event at Chepstow in July: left M. Channon
13,000 gns after: stays 7f: acts on firm ground: swerved violently left leaving stall seventh
outing. *J. Parkes*

ZAQRAH (USA)   2 b.f. (Mar 21) Silver Hawk (USA) 123 – Istiqlal (USA) (Diesis   **80 p**
133) [2003 7m⁴ Jul 8] tall, useful-looking filly: third living foal: half-sister to 3-y-o
Muqbil and fairly useful 1m winner Hureya (by Woodman): dam unraced half-sister to
Bahri and Bahhare: 10/1 and green, 1½ lengths fourth of 13 to Josephus in maiden at
Newmarket, running on well having taken good hold/been checked: sustained injury after
but reported to have recovered fully: will stay at least 1m: sure to do better if all remains
well. *J. L. Dunlop*

ZARA LOUISE   3 b.f. Mistertopogigo (IRE) 118 – Petonica (IRE) 77 (Petoski 135)   **52 d**
[2003 64d: f6g 6.1g² 7m 8.2d³ 8m 6.1m 5.9m 8.1m 7m⁶ Sep 22] leggy filly: modest
maiden handicapper on turf, poor on all-weather: left A. Bailey after fifth start: stays easy
1m: acts on good to firm and good to soft ground: tried visored. *R. P. Elliott*

ZARGUS   4 b.g. Zamindar (USA) 116 – My First Romance 61 (Danehill (USA) 126)   **83**
[2003 95: 6g 5g 5m 5m 6g 5.1f⁴ 5g Sep 12] stocky, quite attractive gelding: just fairly
useful handicapper at best in 2003: effective at 5f/6f: acts on firm going, and has won on
good to soft: tried in cheekpieces. *W. R. Muir*

ZARIANO   3 b.c. Emperor Jones (USA) 119 – Douce Maison (IRE) 67 (Fools Holme   **87**
(USA)) [2003 82: p7g 8g² 9m⁵ 8m* 6m⁶ 8g Sep 12] fairly useful performer: best effort
when second to Tacitus in minor event at Doncaster in March: odds on, simple task when
winning maiden at Ayr in June by 13 lengths: ran poorly after: bred to stay beyond 1m,
but races freely: unraced on extremes of going on turf: often early to post. *S. L. Keightley*

ZARIN (IRE)   5 b.g. Inzar (USA) 112 – Non Dimenticar Me (IRE) 63 (Don't Forget   **91 d**
Me 127) [2003 104: f8s⁵ p8g² 8g 7.1f³ 7.2g 8.5m f7g⁶ f8.5g f7s² f8s³ Dec 13] tall, leggy
gelding: useful at 4 yrs: mostly well below form in 2003, leaving T. J. Naughton 15,000
gns after third start: best efforts around 1m: acts on soft going and all-weather: reportedly
lame sixth outing: none too consistent. *D. W. Chapman*

ZARNEETA   2 b.f. (Jan 20) Tragic Role (USA) – Compton Amber 78 (Puissance 110)   **63 d**
[2003 6m³ 7m⁵ 6m⁵ 7m 7.5m f8g Oct 16] 600Y: smallish, leggy filly: first foal: dam,
temperamental maiden (placed at 2 yrs at 5f to 7f), half-sister to 3-y-o Golden Nun:
modest maiden: lost form after second start: blinkered in seller final one: barely stays 7f.
I. A. Wood

ZARZA BAY (IRE)   4 b.g. Hamas (IRE) 125§ – Frill (Henbit (USA) 130) [2003 64§,   **59 §**
a70§: p12g p13g^4 p13g^3 p16g 16.1d^5 13.8m^3 14m 14.1m f12g^5 Apr 28] strong gelding: **a64 §**
modest performer: stays 1¾m: acts on all-weather, best turf form on good/good to firm
going: twice visored as 3-y-o: ungenuine. *K. R. Burke*

ZARZU   4 b.g. Magic Ring (IRE) 115 – Rivers Rhapsody 104 (Dominion 123) [2003   **81**
88: f5s^2 f6s^3 f5g f6g^5 p5g^3 f6g f6s^5 p7g^5 7m^5 7.1m 6d 7.6m 5f^3 7.1f^5 6.9m 5m* 7d 5m^3 **a92**
5.1m^3 5m 6m^3 5m^6 f7g* p7g 5d^2 f5g^5 p6g^4 f5g* Dec 9] close-coupled, good-topped
gelding: fairly useful performer: won claimers at Catterick in July and Wolverhampton
in October and (having been claimed from K. Burke £12,000 after twenty-fifth start)
handicap at Southwell in December: effective at 5f to easy 7f: acts on all-weather, firm
and good to soft ground: tried in visor/cheekpieces: sometimes races freely: tough.
C. R. Dore

ZAWRAK (IRE)   4 ch.g. Zafonic (USA) 130 – Gharam (USA) 108 (Green Dancer   **69**
(USA) 132) [2003 95: 8g 10m 10.5f^6 10.3m 10m 12.1m 11.5g 15.9d p10g^3 Dec 20] tall,
close-coupled gelding: useful performer at 3 yrs, only fair in 2003: stays 1¼m: acts on
firm ground and polytrack: inconsistent. *I. W. McInnes*

ZAYNAAT   3 b.f. Unfuwain (USA) 131 – Walesiana (GER) (Star Appeal 133) [2003   **67**
71: 10.3g 10g 8d^5 8g 8f Jun 15] workmanlike filly: fair maiden: stays 1m: acts on good to
firm ground, well held on soft: hung left on reappearance. *M. R. Channon*

ZAZOUS   2 b.c. (Apr 25) Zafonic (USA) 130 – Confidentiality (USA) (Lyphard (USA)   **73**
132) [2003 6m 6g^3 Jul 4] 35,000Y: well-made colt: seventh foal: half-brother to 3 winners
in USA, including Grade 3 1m winner Confidential Talk (by Damascus): dam, 2-y-o 6f
winner in USA, half-sister to US Grade 1 1¼m winner Private Account: fair form in
maidens at Newbury (shaped well) and Salisbury (favourite when third): will probably
stay 7f. *A. King*

ZEE ZEE TOP   4 b.f. Zafonic (USA) 130 – Colorspin (FR) 118 (High Top 131)   **116**
[2003 104p: 10.4m* 10m^3 9.9g^3 11.9m^6 10s* Oct 5]
     Success in top pattern company is the goal of owner-breeders like Meon
Valley Stud, and Sir Michael Stoute achieved that for them again in the latest season
with Zee Zee Top. Stoute has trained many of Zee Zee Top's relatives and had sent
out her dam Colorspin to win the Irish Oaks and grandam Reprocolor to win the
Oaks Trial at Lingfield and the Lancashire Oaks. Zee Zee Top's pattern win came
on her fourth attempt in such company, in the Prix de l'Opera Casino Barriere
d'Enghien-Les-Bains at Longchamp, and it proved her last, an announcement being
made after the race that she was to be retired. The latest Prix de l'Opera was an
average renewal, but Zee Zee Top still had to show improved form to come out on
top in a blanket finish under a typically strong ride from Kieren Fallon, beating
Yesterday a head, with the previous year's winner and odds-on favourite Bright Sky
and Trumbaka a neck and a head respectively further behind in third and fourth. It
was the first time Zee Zee Top had encountered going softer than good; Colorspin's
Irish Oaks victory came on her only outing on going softer than good.
     Zee Zee Top didn't make her racecourse debut until October as a three-year-
old. Racing in the famous colours of Helena Springfield Ltd, as do all the horses
retained by Meon Valley Stud, Zee Zee Top landed the odds from a modest bunch
in a maiden at Pontefract and was stepped up to listed company at Newmarket later

*Prix de l'Opera Casino Barriere d'Enghien-Les-Bains, Longchamp—a very close shave for Zee Zee Top
(No.3); Yesterday (far side), Bright Sky (noseband) and Trumbaka (No.5) contribute to a thrilling finish*

in the month, running an excellent race for one so inexperienced when second to Salim Toto. Zee Zee Top looked a smart performer in the making and confirmed that impression on her reappearance in a listed race at York in May, beating subsequent dual Group 3 winner Chorist by a length. Zee Zee Top was campaigned solely in pattern company afterwards, finishing second past the post to Hanami, beaten a neck, in the Pretty Polly Stakes at the Curragh (subsequently demoted to third for barging her way out) and third to her stable-companion Russian Rhythm in the Nassau Stakes at Goodwood. Zee Zee Top again finished behind a more illustrious stable-companion when a keeping-on sixth to Islington in the Yorkshire Oaks, below her best but shaping as though the longer trip was not a problem on her only outing at a mile and a half.

Zee Zee Top (b.f. 1999)	Zafonic (USA) (b 1990)	Gone West (b 1984)	Mr Prospector
			Secrettame
		Zaizafon (ch 1982)	The Minstrel
			Mofida
	Colorspin (FR) (b 1983)	High Top (b 1969)	Derring-Do
			Camenae
		Reprocolor (ch 1976)	Jimmy Reppin
			Blue Queen

Zee Zee Top has the look of Colorspin, being a big, lengthy filly, and is an exciting addition to the broodmare ranks at Meon Valley. She comes along at a good time for the stud as Reprocolor was retired from stud duties in 2000 having had eighteen foals. Reprocolor was purchased as a yearling for 25,000 guineas in 1977 and, along with Odeon and One In A Million, who were bought for 38,000 guineas and 18,500 guineas respectively, became a foundation mare at the stud. All three have played their part in Meon Valley's becoming one of the leading commercial

Helena Springfield Ltd's "Zee Zee Top"

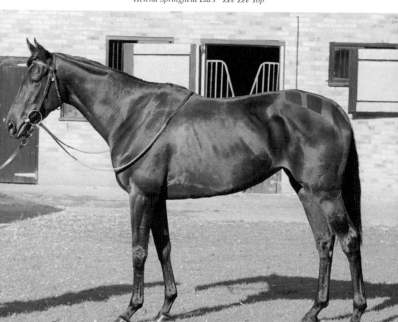

breeders in Britain, though Reprocolor's influence has been pre-eminent. This says a lot for Reprocolor, seeing that Odeon is the grandam of an Oaks winner in Lady Carla and One In A Million is the dam of a top-class miler in Milligram and grandam of the Juddmonte International winner One So Wonderful. Colorspin is just one of several of Reprocolor's daughters that have done at least as well at stud as they did on the racecourse, if they raced at all. The most notable among the others is One Thousand Guineas third Bella Colora, who, like Zee Zee Top, won the Prix de l'Opera and is the dam of the high-class mile-and-a-quarter performer Stagecraft. Colorspin's highest-rated progeny have been the top-class pair Opera House and Kayf Tara, both owned by Sheikh Mohammed. Opera House, trained by Stoute, won the Eclipse and the King George, while Kayf Tara won eight times in pattern company for Godolphin, including two Gold Cups at Royal Ascot. In the latest season the family was also represented by the Aidan O'Brien two-year-old Necklace, who won twice in pattern company, including the Moyglare Stud Stakes at the Curragh. Her dam Spinning The Yarn is a half-sister to Zee Zee Top. Interestingly, Kayf Tara, Opera House and Stagecraft are all by Sadler's Wells, but Zee Zee Top's sire Zafonic was one of the many alternatives Meon Valley used after ending an association with Coolmore in the late-'nineties. However, the policy of not using Coolmore stallions seems to be less rigid now, Colorspin having been barren to Sadler's Wells' son Galileo in 2003. Zee Zee Top begins her stud career with a visit to the same stallion, while the latest Houghton sales-topper for Meon Valley in 2003 was also by a Coolmore stallion, Giant's Causeway. *Sir Michael Stoute*

ZEIS (IRE)   3 ch.g. Bahhare (USA) 122 – Zoom Lens (IRE) 65 (Caerleon (USA) 132)   –
[2003 87p: 10.1s 8.2d Nov 6] sturdy, good-bodied gelding: fairly useful form when winning maiden at Newbury only 2-y-o start: well held in minor events in autumn 2003, leaving H. Cecil 26,000 gns after reappearance: should stay at least 1¼m. *H. Morrison*

ZEITGEIST (IRE)   2 b.c. (Feb 23) Singspiel (IRE) 133 – Diamond Quest (Rainbow   **80 p**
Quest (USA) 134) [2003 7m 7s* Nov 3] €95,000Y: useful-looking colt: second foal: half-brother to Irish 7f winner Kloonlara (by Green Desert): dam unraced out of useful Irish 6f to 1m winner Hatton Gardens, herself half-sister to Kooyonga: much better effort in maidens (fairly useful form) when winning 14-runner contest at Redcar by ½ length from Tenny's Gold, still green but getting up close home: will stay at least 1m: open to progress. *L. M. Cumani*

ZEITLOS   4 b.g. Timeless Times (USA) 99 – Petitesse 55 (Petong 126) [2003 57, a51:   **44**
p7g⁵ p6g f6s⁵ f6g⁴ f5s³ f5s 6g f5g 6m 5m 6f 5m 5m 5.3f Oct 17] small gelding: modest   **a50**
handicapper on all-weather, just poor on turf: effective at 5f/6f: acts on good to firm going, soft and all-weather: blinkered. *R. M. Flower*

ZERLINA (USA)   2 b.f. (Feb 5) Singspiel (IRE) 133 – Tass (Soviet Star (USA) 128)   **92 p**
[2003 7m² 6.5m p7g* Oct 30] smallish filly: fifth foal: sister to useful 1½m winner Blagovest and half-sister to 2000 2-y-o 5f seller winner Syringa (by Lure): dam unraced half-sister to good-class middle-distance colts Nomrood, Monastery and Alleging, and to dam of Racing Post Trophy/Dante winner Dilshaan: second in maiden at Leicester: won 9-runner similar event at Lingfield comfortably by 6 lengths from Clog Dance, leading over 1f out: quite free-going sort, but likely to stay at least 1m: useful prospect. *R. Hannon*

ZERO GRAVITY   6 b.g. Cosmonaut – Comfort (Chief Singer 131) [2003 57§: 11.6g   **– §**
Aug 11] big, leggy gelding: modest and untrustworthy maiden handicapper: well beaten only 6-y-o start: dead. *M. Madgwick*

ZERO TOLERANCE (IRE)   3 ch.g. Nashwan (USA) 135 – Place de L'Opera 98   **94 p**
(Sadler's Wells (USA) 132) [2003 55p: f8g² f8s* 10d 9.9d* 10m³ 12m 10.3m⁴ Oct 24] leggy, workmanlike gelding: fairly useful form: won maiden at Southwell in February and handicap at Beverley in May: off 4 months, travelled strongly long way when fourth to Bravo Dancer in handicap at Doncaster final start: stays 1¼m: acts on fibresand, yet to race on extremes of going on turf: free-going sort: lightly raced, and type to do better still at 4 yrs. *T. D. Barron*

ZERYAAB (IRE)   3 b.c. Barathea (IRE) 127 – Safa 109 (Shirley Heights 130) [2003   **76**
10d³ Apr 28] fifth living foal: closely related to smart 1m to 10.5f winner Saafeya (by Sadler's Wells) and half-brother to 8.5f winner Bayt Alasad (by Lion Cavern): dam, 2-y-o 6f winner who stayed 1½m, sister to Queen's Vase winner Stelvio: 10/3, close third of 20

to Desert Quest in maiden at Windsor, leading 3f out: sent to UAE, joined A. Smith. *M. A. Jarvis*

ZEUSS 3 b.c. Zamindar (USA) 116 – Shallop 55 (Salse (USA) 128) [2003 82: p7g* 8d **85** 8m² p7g 8m Sep 17] workmanlike colt: fairly useful performer: landed odds in maiden at Lingfield in January: good second in handicap at Bath after: stays 1m: acts on polytrack and good to firm going: sold 4,500 gns, sent to Italy. *B. W. Hills*

ZHITOMIR 5 ch.g. Lion Cavern (USA) 117 – Treasure Trove (USA) 62 (The Minstrel **67 d** (CAN) 135) [2003 77, a70: 7m⁶ 8m 6d 6d 7m f8g p8g Dec 6] strong gelding: fair handicapper: well below form after reappearance: best form at 7f: acts on soft and good to firm going: has run well when sweating: sometimes slowly away. *M. Dods*

ZIBELINE (IRE) 6 b.g. Cadeaux Genereux 131 – Zia (USA) 88 (Shareef Dancer **97** (USA) 135) [2003 96: 12g 12m² 16.1g³ 16.2f 13.9m 13.1m² 18m Oct 18] tall gelding: useful handicapper: good efforts when third to Unleash in Northumberland Plate at Newcastle (left B. R. Millman after next start), and when second to Late Claim at Ayr on sixth outing: effective at 1½m to 2¼m: acts on firm going, probably not on softer than good: tried blinkered and in cheekpieces: sometimes pulls hard, and is held up. *B. Ellison*

ZIET D'ALSACE (FR) 3 b.f. Zieten (USA) 118 – Providenc Mill (FR) (French **64** Stress (USA) 125) [2003 f8g⁶ f8s⁶ p6g⁴ p5g⁶ p5g⁶ 6g⁶ 6m f7g 7m* 7g³ 8.3m² 7m³ 8f 7f 7g* 8.1m p8g 8f⁵ 7m⁴ Oct 24] first foal: dam unraced half-sister to smart US Grade 1 9f winner Sicy d'Alsace: modest performer: won sellers at Yarmouth in July and September, sold from G. Bravery 7,200 gns after latter: effective at 7f/1m: acts on polytrack and firm ground, unraced on softer than good: has raced freely. *A. W. Carroll*

ZIETORY 3 b.f. Zieten (USA) 118 – Fairy Story (IRE) 80 (Persian Bold 123) [2003 **107** 76p: 7g* 7g⁶ 7m² 8d* 8g² 8m⁴ p8g² Nov 2] angular, workmanlike filly: useful performer: won handicap at Newbury in May and listed race at Deauville (got up on line to beat Gonfilia short head) in August: in frame after in listed race at Saint-Cloud (½-length second to Mystic Melody), Premio Sergio Cumani at Milan (1¾ lengths fourth to Marbye) and listed race at Lingfield (went down by 1¼ lengths to Tadris): stays 1m: acts on polytrack, good to firm and good to soft ground, successful on soft at 2 yrs. *P. F. I. Cole*

ZIETZIG (IRE) 6 b.g. Zieten (USA) 118 – Missing You 89 (Ahonoora 122) [2003 **62 §** 67d: f8s 7m* 7g 6f 5.9f⁴ 7m² 7.6m³ 7m 7m⁶ Aug 15] shallow-girthed gelding: modest **a– §** performer: made all in seller at Catterick in March: best at 6f/7f: acts on firm and soft going: free-going sort: usually races prominently: unreliable. *H. A. McWilliams*

ZIGALI 4 b.g. Zilzal (USA) 137 – Alilisa (USA) (Alydar (USA)) [2003 –: 11.8m⁵ 16m **49** Oct 28] leggy gelding: poor maiden: stays 1½m: unraced on extremes of going. *John A. Harris*

ZIGGY DAN 3 b.g. Slip Anchor 136 – Nikatino 63 (Bustino 136) [2003 f9.4g f9.4g **—** f8.5g Dec 26] 8,200Y: half-brother to 2 winning sprinters, including 1996 2-y-o 6f winner Perfect Bliss (by Superlative): dam won around 1½m: no sign of ability. *Ms Deborah J. Evans*

ZIGGY ZEN 4 b.g. Muhtarram (USA) 125 – Springs Welcome 86 (Blakeney 126) **75** [2003 69: p10g p13g f16.2g² 15m* 16.2m⁵ May 10] fair handicapper: won at Warwick in April, rallying: stays 2m: acts on good to firm going and all-weather: carried head high on reappearance: sold 12,000 gns in July and joined C. Mann. *C. A. Cyzer*

ZILCH 5 ch.g. Zilzal (USA) 137 – Bunty Boo 110 (Noalto 120) [2003 90: 6g 7g f8.5g **85** p7g³ Dec 10] leggy, close-coupled gelding: fairly useful performer: stays 7f: acts on polytrack, soft and good to firm ground: tried blinkered: has folded/edged right: held up: none too consistent. *M. L. W. Bell*

ZILMAID DANCER 4 b.f. Zilzal (USA) 137 – Briggsmaid 70 (Elegant Air 119) **69** [2003 68: p7g 7d³ 7m 7g 10f Sep 30] good-topped filly: fair maiden handicapper: only form at 4 yrs when third at Salisbury: will stay 1m: acts on firm and good to soft going, probably on polytrack: tongue tied: none too reliable. *P. W. Harris*

ZILZALAHA (IRE) 2 b.f. (Mar 28) Zilzal (USA) 137 – Fear Not (IRE) 64 (Alzao **65** (USA) 117) [2003 7m 8m 6d⁵ Nov 8] 8,000Y: quite good-topped filly: second foal: dam, 7f winner, half-sister to useful performer up to 1m Himiko: easily best effort in maidens (fair form) when fifth to Miss Langkawi at Doncaster: should stay 7f. *C. B. B. Booth*

ZINDABAD (FR) 7 b.h. Shirley Heights 130 – Miznah (IRE) 102 (Sadler's Wells **114** (USA) 132) [2003 126: 12g 13.9m⁴ 12m⁵ 12f³ 12m⁵ 14g⁴ 15.9m³ 18d⁴ Sep 11] quite good-topped horse: fluent mover: high-class performer at 6 yrs, just smart in 2003: respectable efforts third to seventh starts, finishing fifth to Warrsan in Coronation Cup at

Epsom, third to Indian Creek in Hardwicke Stakes (won race in 2002) at Royal Ascot, fifth to Millenary in Princess of Wales's Stakes at Newmarket, fourth to Martaline in Prix Maurice de Nieuil at Maisons-Laffitte and third to Bollin Eric in Lonsdale Stakes at York: effective at 1½m to 2m: acted on firm and soft going: visored last 2 outings: raced prominently: to stand at Wood Farm Stud, Telford, Shropshire, fee £1,750, Oct 1st. *M. Johnston*

ZINGARI 3 ch.f. Groom Dancer (USA) 128 – Antigua (Selkirk (USA) 129) [2003 88: **90** 8f* 8m² 8d 7m Oct 1] well-made filly: fairly useful performer: won minor event at Ayr in July: good second in similar race at Thirsk next time: tailed-off both starts after, including in blinkers: effective at 7f/1m: acts on firm and good to soft going: flashed tail at 2 yrs: usually races prominently. *Sir Mark Prescott*

ZINGING 4 b.g. Fraam 114 – Hi Hoh (IRE) (Fayruz 116) [2003 70§, a61§: p7g f8.5s² **58 §** p10g³ p7g* p6g 7m 7m 9f 8m 10m 7f 7m 8m p8g³ p7g* p7g Dec 30] small, compact gelding: modest performer: won handicap at Lingfield in March and claimer there in December: effective at 7f to easy 1¼m: acts on firm going, soft and all-weather: tried visored/blinkered: sometimes races freely/finds little: unreliable. *J. J. Bridger*

ZIPPING (IRE) 4 b.c. Zafonic (USA) 130 – Zelda (IRE) (Caerleon (USA) 132) [2003 **119** 119: 5g2 5m² 6f⁴ 6m⁴ 6.5g Aug 10] leggy, quite attractive colt: smart performer: runner-up in Prix de Saint-Georges at Longchamp and Prix du Gros-Chene at Chantilly (not best of runs, promoted after third past post behind Porlezza) first 2 starts: good fourth next 2 outings behind Choisir in Golden Jubilee Stakes at Royal Ascot and Oasis Dream in July Cup at Newmarket: took heavy fall after breaking blood vessel in Prix Maurice de Gheest at Deauville final outing (soon recovered but rested for remainder of year): has form at 1m (fourth in 2000 Guineas), but best at 5f/6f: acts on soft and firm ground: best held up: consistent. *R. Collet, France*

ZITHER 3 b.f. Zafonic (USA) 130 – Rose Noble (USA) 62 (Vaguely Noble 140) [2003 **93** 84: 8g 7m* 8m² 7m⁵ 7f³ 8.1d 7g⁵ p8g⁶ p8g Nov 22] close-coupled filly: fairly useful performer: won minor event at Leicester in June: effective at 7f/1m: acts on firm ground and polytrack. *R. Hannon*

ZOEANNA (IRE) 3 b.f. Danetime (IRE) 121 – Age of Elegance (Troy 137) [2003 **49** p8g 7m 8.1m 14.1m⁵ f12g 12.1g⁶ p13g f7g Nov 19] 10,000Y: angular filly: half-sister to several winners, including useful 6f (at 2 yrs) to 1¼m (in Italy) winner Sheer Precocity (by Precocious) and 1¼m to 1¾m winner Netta Rufina (by Night Shift): dam French 1½m winner: modest maiden: stays 1¾m: raced only on good ground or firmer on turf, well beaten on fibresand. *R. Guest*

ZOLUBE (IRE) 3 b.f. Titus Livius (FR) 115 – Seattle Siren (USA) 101 (Seattle Slew **57** (USA)) [2003 5f⁵ 6g 5g⁶ f5g Jun 25] 7,500Y: workmanlike filly: half-sister to numerous winners, including 6f winner Focused Attraction (by Eagle Eyed) and stayer Il Principe (by Ela-Mana-Mou), both fairly useful: dam French 2-y-o 6f winner: modest maiden: should stay 6f: well held on fibresand final outing. *John Berry*

ZOLUSHKA (IRE) 2 ch.f. (Mar 13) Russian Revival (USA) 125 – Persian Myth **–** (Persian Bold 123) [2003 7.1m 7m 7f f7g Dec 8] smallish filly: half-sister to several winners, including Irish 2m winner Takeamemo (by Don't Forget Me) and 5f winner Millesime (by Glow): dam, ran once, sister to dam of Lake Coniston: no form in maidens/nursery: tends to be slowly away. *B. W. Duke*

ZONERGEM 5 ch.g. Zafonic (USA) 130 – Anasazi (IRE) (Sadler's Wells (USA) 132) **102** [2003 105: 8m⁶ 8g⁴ 8g 8m 8m³ 10g⁶ 8g p10g³ Dec 2] good-topped gelding: useful handicapper: best 5-y-o efforts in competitive events at Newbury (behind Mystic Man) and Kempton (behind Putra Pekan) first 2 starts: stays easy 1¼m: acts on polytrack and firm going, possibly not heavy: often wears blinkers/cheekpieces: has been slowly away/carried head high: held up: withdrawn after getting upset in stall intended fifth outing: quirky. *Lady Herries*

ZONIC BOOM (FR) 3 ch.g. Zafonic (USA) 130 – Rosi Zambotti (IRE) 104 (Law **61** Society (USA) 130) [2003 8m 8.1m Jul 24] 800,000 francs F, IR 66,000Y: second foal: half-brother to a 9f winner in Italy by Rainbow Quest: dam, Italian 7.5f (at 2 yrs) to 1½m winner, out of half-sister to very smart 1m/1¼m performer Vertige: modest form in maidens at Kempton and Sandown: gelded after: should stay 1¼m. *J. R. Fanshawe*

ZONNEBEKE 2 b.f. (Apr 30) Orpen (USA) 116 – Canlubang (Mujtahid (USA) 118) **64** [2003 7m⁴ f8.5g f7g Nov 15] smallish filly: fourth foal: half-sister to Swedish winner up to 1¼m Clear Ambition (by Definite Article): dam ran 3 times at 2 yrs: best effort in maidens (modest form) when fourth at Newcastle: found little next time: should stay 1m. *K. R. Burke*

ZONUS 2 b.c. (Apr 20) Pivotal 124 – Jade Mistress 51 (Damister (USA) 123) [2003 6g² Oct 24] 15,000F, 60,000Y: tall colt: weak at 2 yrs: fifth foal: half-brother to 1¼m/ 1½m winner Dion Dee (by Anshan) and a winner in Italy by Sheikh Albadou: dam, maiden who stayed 1½m, half-sister to smart performers Just A Flutter (miler) and Slicious (Italian 1¼m/1½m performer): 7/1 and green, length second of 18 to Warrad in maiden at Newbury, held up and running on strongly for hands and heels: should stay 1m: open to good deal of improvement, and will win races. *B. W. Hills* · **87 P**

ZOOT 3 br.g. Zafonic (USA) 130 – Bint Zamayem (IRE) 95 (Rainbow Quest (USA) 134) [2003 70p: 8g May 5] lengthy, useful-looking gelding: fair form in 2-y-o maidens: tailed off only outing in 2003: dead. *Mrs A. J. Perrett* · –

ZORN 4 br.c. Dilum (USA) 115 – Very Good (Noalto 120) [2003 –: p12g⁵ p12g p13g p12g p10g Mar 26] little form. *P. Howling* · –

ZOROASTER 3 gr.c. Linamix (FR) 127 – Persian Walk (FR) (Persian Bold 123) [2003 78p: 8m⁴ Apr 12] leggy, unfurnished colt: fair maiden: fourth to Kalaman at Newbury, only outing at 3 yrs: should be suited by 1¼m+: raced only on good to firm ground. *J. H. M. Gosden* · **76**

ZOTA (IRE) 4 b.f. Barathea (IRE) 127 – Afisiak 60 (Efisio 120) [2003 27: 6.1g Jun 23] first foal: dam 2-y-o 5f winner: trained by C. Collins in Ireland at 3 yrs: little form. *J. G. Given* · –

ZOUAVE (IRE) 2 b.c. (May 15) Spectrum (IRE) 126 – Lady Windley (Baillamont (USA) 124) [2003 8m* 8m 8m³ Sep 19] IR 6,000F, 32,000Y: sturdy, angular colt: sixth foal: half-brother to 3 winners, including 3-y-o Our Teddy and 6-y-o Waseyla: dam, French 11f winner, out of top-class French middle-distance performer Northern Trick: fairly useful form: won maiden at Kempton in August: seemingly creditable efforts when last of 8 in listed race at Goodwood and third of 5 (beaten 5 lengths by Elshadi) in minor event at Newbury: will be suited by at least 1¼m. *B. J. Meehan* · **91**

ZOUCHE 3 b.g. Zamindar (USA) 116 – Al Corniche (IRE) 62 (Bluebird (USA) 125) [2003 83p: 6g p7g⁶ f8.5g 7m³ 6.1g 7.1m⁶ 6.1g f8.5s⁶ f9.4g⁵ Oct 20] close-coupled gelding: disappointing maiden, claimed from B. Meehan £3,000 fourth outing, sold out of Mrs S. Liddiard's stable £3,000 after seventh: stays 7f: acts on all-weather and good to firm ground: tried blinkered/in cheekpieces: ungenuine. *W. M. Brisbourne* · **65 d**

ZUCCHERO 7 br.g. Dilum (USA) 115 – Legal Sound 85 (Legal Eagle 126) [2003 104: 7g 8m 8m 8g 9m 8g Nov 1] big, lengthy gelding: type to carry condition: useful handicapper at best: little impact in competitive events in 2003: often blinkered/visored earlier in career: slowly away third/fourth outings. *D. W. P. Arbuthnot* · –

ZUHAIR 10 ch.g. Mujtahid (USA) 118 – Ghzaalh (USA) 87 (Northern Dancer) [2003 90: 5m³ 5d 5g 6m 6m⁶ 6f⁴ 5m 5d 6g² 5m² 6m 6m Aug 23] strong gelding: fairly useful handicapper: short-headed by Undeterred at Goodwood (goes well there) ninth start: effective at 5f/6f: unsuited by soft/heavy going, acts on any other: well beaten both runs in blinkers: wears bandages: tends to sweat: usually held up. *D. Nicholls* · **87**

ZULETA 2 ch.f. (Mar 24) Vettori (IRE) 119 – Victoria (Old Vic 136) [2003 6g 7g 7.1m 8m f7s⁴ f8.5g⁴ Nov 1] angular filly: fifth foal: half-sister to winners abroad by Rudimentary and Forzando: dam, ran twice, half-sister to smart sprinter Cragside: modest maiden: will stay at least 1¼m: best efforts on fibresand. *M. Blanshard* · **57**

ZUMA (IRE) 2 b.c. (May 10) Grand Lodge (USA) 125 – Paradise Waters 73 (Celestial Storm (USA) 132) [2003 7.1d 7m Sep 16] 54,000 2-y-o: good-bodied colt: fourth foal: brother to a winner in Japan and half-brother to 4-y-o Lord of Methley: dam, 7f (at 2 yrs) to 13f winner, half-sister to useful performer up to 1½m Prince of Denial: modest form in maidens at Sandown and Salisbury (slowly away): should be suited by 1¼m/1½m. *R. Hannon* · **63**

ZURS (IRE) 10 b.g. Tirol 127 – Needy (High Top 131) [2003 –§: f16s p12g 12g⁵ 11.9m May 14] sturdy gelding: poor and ungenuine handicapper: tried blinkered/visored: often slowly away. *H. J. Collingridge* · **41 §**

ZWADI (IRE) 2 b.f. (Mar 9) Docksider (USA) 124 – Local Custom (IRE) (Be My Native (USA) 122) [2003 f6g³ 6m⁴ 6m³ 7m² p7g⁴ Sep 9] 26,000F, 65,000Y: leggy filly: half-sister to several winners, including useful 1m winner Lady Miletrian (by Barathea) and 3-y-o Duty Paid: dam, Irish maiden, half-sister to Middle Park winner Balla Cove: · **74**

fair maiden: second at Folkestone: free-going sort, but stays 7f: acts on good to firm ground, some promise on all-weather. *B. W. Hills*

ZWEIBRUCKEN (IRE) 2 b.f. (May 19) Alhaarth (IRE) 126 – Solar Attraction **83** (IRE) 60 (Salt Dome (USA)) [2003 6g 6m³ 7m² 7.1d* 7f² 7g Oct 25] leggy filly: fifth foal: half-sister to 3 winners, including 4-y-o Neckar Valley and 3-y-o Heidelburg: dam third at 5f in Ireland at 2 yrs: fairly useful performer: won nursery at Sandown in August: good second in similar event at Ascot next time: stiff task final start: will stay 1m: unraced on soft/heavy going, acts on any other. *S. Kirk*

ZYGOMATIC 5 ch.g. Risk Me (FR) 127 – Give Me A Day (Lucky Wednesday 124) **–** [2003 16d May 2] fair form in bumpers: wearing cheekpieces and tongue strap, well beaten in claimer at Musselburgh: winning hurdler. *R. F. Fisher*

ZYZANIA 4 b.f. Zafonic (USA) 130 – Moneefa 73 (Darshaan 133) [2003 68: f8g³ **96** f9.4g* 6.9d² 8.1m* 8f⁴ 8.1d² 7d Sep 11] angular filly: useful performer, lightly raced: much improved for new stable in 2003, winning maiden at Wolverhampton (edged right) in February and handicap at Haydock in August: good efforts in listed races fifth/sixth starts, length second to Lady Bear at Sandown: effective at 7f to 9.4f: acts on fibresand, firm and good to soft ground: reportedly covered by Agnes World after second outing. *H. Morrison*

The following unraced horses appeared in ante-post lists for 2004 classics or had a Group 1 entry at two years, and are included for information purposes.

ALL TOO BEAUTIFUL (IRE) 2 b.f. (Apr 30) Sadler's Wells (USA) 132 – Urban Sea (USA) 126 (Miswaki (USA) 124) 1,100,000F: sister to top-class 1m (at 2 yrs) to 1½m (including Derby) winner Galileo and 4-y-o Black Sam Bellamy, and half-sister to 1¼m winner Melikah (by Lammtarra) and 1m (at 2 yrs) to 1½m winner Urban Ocean (by Bering), both smart: dam 1m (at 2 yrs) to 1½m (Arc) winner, closely related to 2000 Guineas winner King's Best and half-sister to dam of Prix du Jockey Club winner Anabaa Blue. *A. P. O'Brien, Ireland*

ALQWAH (IRE) 2 b.f. (Feb 11) Danehill (USA) 126 – Delage (Bellypha 130) €90,000Y: fourth foal: half-sister to 2 winners, including 4-y-o Mystic Mile: dam unraced half-sister to very smart performer up to 7f College Chapel. *Saeed bin Suroor*

AUSTRIA (IRE) 2 b.c. (Feb 1) Sadler's Wells (USA) 132 – Desert Bluebell 83 (Kalaglow 132) 240,000Y: brother to a winner in USA, closely related to 2 winners, including useful 6f (in USA) and 1m winner Roses In The Snow (by Be My Guest), and half-brother to 2 winners by Caerleon, including useful performer up to 1½m Desert Mirage: dam, maiden who probably stayed 13.6f, sister to dam of Tenby. *A. P. O'Brien, Ireland*

BACKGAMMON 2 b.c. (Feb 14) Sadler's Wells (USA) 132 – Game Plan 118 (Darshaan 133) closely related to fairly useful 1m/1¼m winner Night Vigil (by Night Shift), and half-brother to several winners, including very smart Irish 1m (at 2 yrs)/1¼m winner Strategic (by Caerleon) and smart French 1¼m winner Sobieski (by Polish Precedent): dam, 1¼m winner and second in Oaks, half-sister to Oaks winner Shahtoush. *D. R. Loder*

BALIMAYA (IRE) 2 b.f. (Mar 6) Barathea (IRE) 127 – Banque Privee (USA) 78 (Private Account (USA)) sister to smart French/US performer around 1¼m Blue Steller and half-sister to 3 winners in Ireland around 1½m, including fairly useful Banariya (by Lear Fan): dam, 1½m winner, half-sister to Rothmans International winner River Memories. *J. Noseda*

BECAUSE (IRE) 2 b.f. (Mar 27) Sadler's Wells (USA) 132 – Jude 53 (Darshaan 133) third foal: sister to 3-y-o Yesterday and 2001 Moyglare Stud Stakes winner/Oaks second Quarter Moon: dam lightly-raced sister to smart Irish performer up to 1¾m Arrikala and half-sister to very smart 1¼m performer Last Second. *A. P. O'Brien, Ireland*

BOOK OF KINGS (USA) 2 b.c. (Mar 12) Kingmambo (USA) 125 – Honfleur (IRE) 100 (Sadler's Wells (USA) 132) $450,000Y: fourth foal: closely related to useful Irish 2001 2-y-o 7f winner Creekview (by Gone West) and fairly useful 1m winner Argentan (by Gulch) and half-brother to a winner in USA by Thunder Gulch: dam, 1¼m and 13.5f winner, sister to Carnegie out of Detroit, both Arc winners. *A. P. O'Brien, Ireland*

BOSTON IVY (USA) 2 b.f. (Feb 12) Mark of Esteem (IRE) 137 – Hedera (USA) 90 (Woodman (USA) 126) third foal: closely related to 3-y-o Heisse and half-sister to useful French performer up to 11.5f winner Ivy League (by Doyoun): dam, 2-y-o 7f winner (stayed 1m), out of Ribblesdale runner-up Ivrea. *D. R. Loder*

BOUNDARY 2 b.c. (May 19) Grand Lodge (USA) 125 – Persian Song 45 (Persian Bold 123) 200,000Y: brother to 3-y-o Barney McAll and half-brother to several winners, including smart 7f (at 2 yrs) to 1¼m winner Mountain Song (by Tirol): dam, ran 3 times at 2 yrs, sister to high-class performer up to 1¼m Bold Arrangement. *A. P. O'Brien, Ireland*

BYWAYOFTHESTARS 2 b.f. (Jan 31) Danehill (USA) 126 – Solo de Lune (IRE) (Law Society (USA) 130) 475,000Y: half-sister to several winners, notably French 1m (including at 2 yrs) and 1¼m (Prix Saint-Alary) winner Cerulean Sky and 1¼m winner Qaatef (both smart and by Darshaan) and 3-y-o L'Ancresse: dam, French 11f winner, half-sister to very smart stayer Wareed, a good family. *A. P. O'Brien, Ireland*

CERTAIN FACT (USA) 2 b.c. (Mar 15) Sir Cat (USA) 118 – Pure Misk 55 (Rainbow Quest (USA) 134) $32,000F, $52,000F: fourth living foal: half-brother to 5-y-o Certain Justice and useful 7f (at 2 yrs) to 10.5f winner Shfoug (by Sheikh Albadou): dam twice-raced half-sister to useful 1993 2-y-o 6f winner Fast Eddy. *P. F. I. Cole*

COOL CLEAR WATER (USA) 2 b.f. (Mar 27) Seeking The Gold (USA) – Miznah (IRE) 102 (Sadler's Wells (USA) 132) half-sister to several winners, notably 7-y-o Zindabad and 4-y-o Navado: dam, Irish 2-y-o 6f winner, closely related to dam of US champion turf mare Flawlessly . *B. J. Meehan*

DAY OF RECKONING 2 b.f. (Feb 14) Daylami (IRE) 138 – Trying For Gold (USA) 103 (Northern Baby (CAN) 127) half-sister to 3 at least useful winners, including smart 1m (at 2 yrs) to 13f winner Phantom Gold (by Machiavellian), now dam of Oaks runner-up Flight of Fancy: dam, 1½m winner, out of Ribblesdale winner Expansive. *Sir Michael Stoute*

DIAMOND LODGE 2 ch.f. (Mar 17) Grand Lodge (USA) 125 – Movieland (USA) 109 (Nureyev (USA) 131) 47,000Y, 58,000 2-y-o: half-sister to 2 winners, including 1¼m winner Monsieur Rick (by Sillery): dam, French 2-y-o 1m (Prix des Reservoirs) winner, sister to smart miler Only Star. *J. Noseda*

EBAZIYAN (IRE) 2 gr.c. (May 7) Daylami (IRE) 138 – Ebadiyla (IRE) 132 (Sadler's Wells (USA) 132) second foal: dam, won Irish Oaks and Prix Royal-Oak, half-sister to Gold Cup winner Enzeli. *J. Oxx, Ireland*

GLENCALVIE (IRE) 2 ch.c. (Mar 13) Grand Lodge (USA) 125 – Top of The Form (IRE) 79 (Masterclass (USA) 116) 75,000F, 225,000Y: second foal: dam, 5f (at 2 yrs)/6f winner, half-sister to useful 5f performers Double Quick and Speedy James. *J. Noseda*

GO SUPERSONIC 2 b.f. (Jan 30) Zafonic (USA) 130 – Shirley Superstar 94 (Shirley Heights 130) half-sister to very smart 1m (at 2 yrs) to 1½m (Oaks) winner Lady Carla (by Caerleon) and 9f winner Azores (by Polish Precedent): dam, lightly-raced 7f winner (at 2 yrs), out of smart performer up to 1¾m Odeon. *Sir Michael Stoute*

INSTANT RECALL (IRE) 2 ch.c. (Apr 10) Indian Ridge 123 – Happy Memories (IRE) (Thatching 131) 140,000Y: second foal: dam unraced half-sister to smart Irish 1¼m/1½m performer Topanoora. *B. J. Meehan*

KATAVI (USA) 2 b.f. (Mar 3) Stravinsky (USA) 133 – Halholah (USA) 65 (Secreto (USA) 128) $160,000F, $230,000Y: half-sister to several winners, including smart 6f (at 2 yrs) to 10.5f winner Murajja and fairly useful 1m and 15f winner Yanabi (both by Silver Hawk): dam maiden who stayed 1¼m. *J. Noseda*

KNOCKNACREA 2 b.f. (Apr 18) Green Desert (USA) 127 – Criquette 104 (Shirley Heights 130) fourth living foal: half-sister to useful 2000 2-y-o 1m winner Candice (by Caerleon) and fairly useful French 7f/1m winner Open Offer (by Cadeaux Genereux): dam, 2-y-o 7f winner and later 9f winner in UAE (refused to enter stall both intended 3-y-o starts), half-sister to top-class miler Markofdistinction. *J. H. M. Gosden*

LAKE CHARLOTTE (USA) 2 b.f. (Apr 16) Danzig (USA) – Quinpool (USA) (Alydar (USA)) fourth foal: dam US 8.5f/9f winner and third in 9f Kentucky Oaks. *D. R. Loder*

LANDERNEAU (IRE) 2 b.f. (Mar 15) Desert Prince (IRE) 130 – Pont-Aven 113 (Try My Best (USA) 130) half-sister to several winners, notably French 5f performer Sainte Marine (by Kenmare) and 6f (Gimcrack Stakes)/7f winner Josr Algarhoud (by Darshaan), both smart: dam, second in Poule d'Essai des Pouliches, probably best at 5f/6f. *R. Collet, France*

LANE COUNTY (USA) 2 ch.f. (Apr 28) Rahy (USA) 115 – Link River (USA) 83 (Gone West (USA)) fourth foal: half-sister to useful Irish 7f (including at 2 yrs) and 1m winner Egyptian (by Green Desert): dam, 1m winner in Britain who later won 9f Grade 1 event in US, granddaughter of close relation to high-class sprinter Ajdal. *D. R. Loder*

MADID (IRE) 2 br.c. (Feb 3) Cape Cross (IRE) 129 – Waffle On 89 (Chief Singer 131) 150,000Y: fifth foal: closely related to useful 7f winner Desert Alchemy (by Green Desert) and half-brother to 2 winners, including useful French 9.5f winner La Frou Frou (by Night Shift, later successful in USA): dam, 2-y-o 6f winner, out of half-sister to very smart performer up to 7f College Chapel. *J. H. M. Gosden*

MAJORS CAST (IRE) 2 b.c. (Feb 1) Victory Note (USA) 120 – Ziffany 68 (Taufan (USA) 119) IR 38,000Y, 190,000Y: third foal: half-brother to smart 5f/6f winner Jessica's Dream (by Desert Style): dam, 7f seller winner, ran only at 2 yrs. *Sir Michael Stoute*

MASNOOD 2 b.c. (Mar 29) Selkirk (USA) 129 – Alruccaba 83 (Crystal Palace (FR) 132) €350,000Y: half-brother to numerous winners, including very smart 1¼m performer Last Second (by Alzao), 6f/7f winner at 2 yrs, smart stayer Alleluia (by Caerleon) and to dams of Alborada, Quarter Moon and 3-y-o Yesterday: dam 2-y-o 6f winner. *M. P. Tregoning*

MULLINS BAY 2 b.c. (Apr 3) Machiavellian (USA) 123 – Bella Colora 119 (Bellypha 130) 525,000Y: half-brother to several winners, notably high-class 1¼m performer Stagecraft (by Sadler's Wells) and smart 1m winner Hyabella (by Shirley Heights): dam, 6f (at 2 yrs) to 1¼m winner, half-sister to Irish Oaks winner Colorspin, herself dam of Opera House, Kayf Tara and 4-y-o Zee Zee Top. *A. P. O'Brien, Ireland*

NAPOLEON (IRE) 2 b.c. (Feb 14) Sadler's Wells (USA) 132 – Love For Ever (IRE) (Darshaan 133) second foal: brother to 3-y-o Albanov: dam, French 1m and 9.5f winner, out of smart performer up to 1½m Fleur d'Oranger. *A. P. O'Brien, Ireland*

NASSIRIA 2 b.f. (Apr 17) Singspiel (IRE) 133 – Naskhi 102 (Nashwan (USA) 135) second foal: half-sister to 1m winner in Italy by Machiavellian: dam, 1m (at 2 yrs) and 1¼m winner. *C. E. Brittain*

PINCHING (IRE) 2 ch.f. (Jan 29) Inchinor 119 – Input – (Primo Dominie 121) 55,000Y: first foal: dam, ran once at 2 yrs, out of half-sister to 1m/9f performer Danceabout and French sprinter Pole Position, both smart. *H. R. A. Cecil*

QUEEN (IRE) 2 gr.f. (May 6) Sadler's Wells (USA) 132 – Infamy 123 (Shirley Heights 130) sister to 3 winners, notably Irish 1½m/1¾m winner Rostropovich and French/US winner up to 12.5f Moon Queen (both smart), closely related to useful 1998 2-y-o 7f/1m winner Barafamy (by Barathea) and half-sister to several winners: dam 1¼m/1½m performer from family of In The Wings (by Sadler's Wells) and High-Rise. *A. P. O'Brien, Ireland*

QUEEN OF STARS (USA) 2 b.f. (Mar 22) Green Desert (USA) 127 – Queen Catherine (Machiavellian (USA) 123) second foal: half-sister to 3-y-o Lady Catherine: dam useful French 1m winner, including at 2 yrs. *D. R. Loder*

SABANDER BAY (USA) 2 b.f. (Mar 7) Lear Fan (USA) 130 – Sambac (USA) 96 (Mr Prospector (USA)) second foal: half-sister to fairly useful French 2002 2-y-o 6f winner Spinning Globe (by Spinning World): dam, 2-y-o 6f winner, closely related to smart 6f/7f performer Welcome Friend and half-sister to Poule d'Essai des Poulains second Rainbow Corner. *J. H. M. Gosden*

SAINTLY SCHOLAR (USA) 2 b.f. (Feb 24) Danzig (USA) – Tres Facile (USA) (Easy Goer (USA)) $260,000Y: second foal: dam, ran twice, half-sister to Grand Criterium winner Treizieme and Gold Cup runner-up Eastern Mystic. *E. A. L. Dunlop*

SEATTLE (IRE) 2 b.c. (Mar 28) Fasliyev (USA) 120 – Litani River (USA) (Irish River (FR) 131) eighth foal: half-brother to smart 1m and (in USA) 8.5f winner who stayed 11f The Editor (by Alzao): dam, French maiden, sister to useful dam of Irish 2000 Guineas winner Saffron Walden and high-class sprinter/miler Dolphin Street. *A. P. O'Brien, Ireland*

SERENGETI SKY (USA) 2 br.c. (May 15) Southern Halo (USA) – Genovefa (USA) 107 (Woodman (USA) 126) fifth foal: half-brother to 3 winners, including 4-y-o Mamool and useful French 1999 2-y-o 1m winner Ejlaal (by Caerleon): dam, won 1¼m Prix de Royaumont, closely related to smart French 1m/1¼m winner Grafin. *D. R. Loder*

SPARKLE OF STONES (FR) 2 b.f. (Feb 10) Sadler's Wells (USA) 132 – Gwydion (USA) 118 (Raise A Cup (USA)) sister to useful French 1m and 11f winner Synergetic, closely related to 2 winners, including very smart 7f winner (including at 2 yrs, also second in 2000 Guineas) Enrique (by Barathea), and half-sister to 3 winners, including smart French 6f and 1m winner Piperi (by Machiavellian): dam sprinter. *H. R. A. Cecil*

THREE COUNTIES (IRE) 2 b.c. (Mar 3) Danehill (USA) 126 – Royal Show (IRE) 63 (Sadler's Wells (USA) 132) 360,000Y: first foal: dam, third at 1¼m on only start, sister to King George VI & Queen Elizabeth Diamond Stakes winner King's Theatre and half-sister to high-class 1988 2-y-o High Estate. *D. R. Loder*

TUSSAH 2 b.f. (Apr 1) Daylami (IRE) 138 – Bombazine (IRE) 97 (Generous (IRE) 139) third foal: half-sister to 4-y-o Camelot and fairly useful French 12.5f winner Affirmative Action (by Rainbow Quest): dam, 1¼m winner who stayed 1½m, half-sister to Barathea and Gossamer. *L. M. Cumani*

WEDDING CAKE (IRE) 2 ch.f. (Mar 26) Groom Dancer (USA) 128 – Greektown (Ela-Mana-Mou 132) sister to useful 7f (at 2 yrs) and 1¼m winner Athens Belle, closely related to 2 winners by Rainbow Quest, notably smart 1¼m and 13f winner Multi-coloured, and half-sister to 4-y-o Gamut: dam, French 1¼m/1½m winner, half-sister to Prix du Cadran winner Sought Out and to grandam of Golan. *Sir Michael Stoute*

ERRATA & ADDENDA

'Racehorses of 1962'

La Sega	the photographs on pages 433 and 435 have been transposed
Shandon Belle	in the photograph on page 710, Tender Annie is the horse on the left

'Racehorses of 1962' and 'Racehorses of 1963'

Hula Dancer The errata & addenda on p838 in 'Racehorses of 1963' concerning photographs on p373 & p374 of 'Racehorses of 1962' was incorrect. The photo at the top of p373 in 'Racehorses of 1962' is of the Prix de la Salamandre, that at the bottom of p373 is of the Grand Criterium and that at the top of p374 is of the Prix Yacowlef. The person responsible has left the company!

'Racehorses of 2000'

Dajam Vu dam 9.7f to 2m winner, **out of half-sister** to smart French miler King James

'Racehorses of 2001'

Anne's Birthday	dam won in Norway
Dawn Invasion	half-brother to fairly useful **5f (at 2 yrs)/6f winner** Princely Dream

'Racehorses of 2002'

Azreme	disqualified from second place at Sandown after failing dope test
Bollin Eric	p140 line 2 should read Marion **Morrison**
Bond Playboy	disqualified from win at Southwell after failing dope test; race awarded to Tidy
Burning Sun	p170 lines 7,8 and 9 should read **Media Nox**, not Sky Love
Ela-Aristokratissa	comment should read:

ELA-ARISTOKRATISSA 4 b.f. Danehill (USA) 126 – June Brilly (IRE) (Fayruz **49** 116) [2002 8.1m⁵ 7m 6d 12g Aug 21] 25,000F: lengthy filly: first foal: dam unraced half-sister to smart Irish winner up to 1½m/high-class hurdler I'm Supposin: best effort in maidens when fifth at Warwick reportedly lost action next time, then left P. D'Arcy. *D. O'Connell, Ireland*

Excelsius	was not gelded
Rock of Gibraltar	p830, 4 lines from the end of the essay—it is now understood that Sir Alex Ferguson paid nothing for his share

PROMISING HORSES

Selected British-trained horses (plus those trained by Aidan O'Brien and Dermot Weld) with either a p or P in *Racehorses of 2003* are listed under the trainer for whom they had their final start.

C. N. ALLEN
Jake The Snake (IRE) 2 ch.c   93p

D. W. P. ARBUTHNOT
Bravo Maestro (USA) 2 b.c   95p

A. M. BALDING
Border Music 2 b.g   83p
Indiana Blues 2 ch.f   90p
Mr Lambros 2 ch.c   78p
Red Birr (IRE) 2 b.g   78p
Sound Blaster (IRE) 2 ch.g   74p
Star Pupil 2 ch.c   86p
Phoenix Reach (IRE) 3 b.c   122p
The Player 4 b.g   82p

G. B. BALDING
King's Caprice 2 ch.c   91p

T. D. BARRON
Palace Theatre (IRE) 2 b.g   74p
Partners In Jazz (USA) 2 ro.c   88p
Raccoon (IRE) 3 b.g   79p
Zero Tolerance (IRE) 3 ch.g   94p

M. L. W. BELL
Ganymede 2 gr.c   77p
Olihider (USA) 2 gr.c   81p
Temple Place (IRE) 2 b.c   97p

P. A. BLOCKLEY
Key Partners (IRE) 2 b.g   74p

C. E. BRITTAIN
Bahiano (IRE) 2 ch.c   73p
Ticero 2 b.c   79p
Borrego (IRE) 3 b.c   85p

G. A. BUTLER
Disengage (USA) 2 gr.c   78p
Donna Vita 2 b.f   78p
Dvinsky (USA) 2 b.c   92p
Pass Go 2 b.g   73p
Ragged Jack (IRE) 2 b.g   76p
Ringsider (IRE) 2 ch.g   81p
Warrad (USA) 2 b.c   90p
Jagger 3 gr.c   109p

H. CANDY
Adaptable 2 b.f   75p
Carini 2 b.f   97p
Classical Dancer 2 ch.f   86p
Polonius 2 b.g   94p
Pont Allaire (IRE) 2 b.f   72p
Rum Shot 2 b.c   104p
Spliff 2 b.c   89p
Wiggy Smith 4 ch.g   88p

D. CARROLL
Kings Empire 2 b.g   86p

H. R. A. CECIL
Akimbo (USA) 2 b.c   96p
Muscida (USA) 2 b.f   89p
Serramanna 2 ch.f   85p
Fine Palette 3 ch.c   79p

M. R. CHANNON
Gatwick (IRE) 2 b.c   71p
Hana Dee 2 b.f   72p
Hoxne Star (IRE) 2 b.g   74p
Jazz Scene (IRE) 2 b.c   91p
Seneschal 2 b.c   97p

R. CHARLTON
Alderney Race (USA) 2 ch.c   89p
Blue Monday 2 b.c   100p
Colour Wheel 2 ch.c   89p
Extra Cover (IRE) 2 b.g   74p
Hatch 2 ch.c   86p
Josephus (IRE) 2 ch.c   103p
Kali 2 gr.f   71p
Kind (IRE) 2 b.f   77p
La Coruna 2 b.f   92p
Messe de Minuit (IRE) 2 ch.c   76p
Sketch (IRE) 2 ch.f   72p
Well Known 2 b.f   86P
Dorothy's Friend 3 b.g   90p

P. F. I. COLE
Bukit Fraser (IRE) 2 b.c   79p
Dr Thong 2 ch.c   74P
Girl Warrior (USA) 2 ch.f   76p
Impartial 2 b.c   72p
Putra Sas (IRE) 2 b.c   89p
Secretary General (IRE) 2 b.c   88p
Sound of Fleet (USA) 2 ch.c   82p

H. J. COLLINGRIDGE
Hello It's Me 2 ch.g   78p

L. G. COTTRELL
Hawridge Prince 3 b.g   84p

C. G. COX
Thyolo (IRE) 2 ch.c   91p
New Seeker 3 b.c   111p

L. M. CUMANI
Aesculus (USA) 2 b.f   71p
Pukka (IRE) 2 b.c   80p
Zeitgeist (IRE) 2 b.c   80p
Jubilee Time 3 b.c   78p
Stealing Beauty (IRE) 3 b.f   80p

P. W. D'ARCY
Treasure Cay 2 ch.c   78p

E. A. L. DUNLOP
Deraasaat 2 ch.f   92p
Golden Empire (USA) 2 br.c   78p

Golden Grace 2 b.c 87p
Mutassem (FR) 2 b.c 73p
Obay 2 ch.c 80p
Post And Rail (USA) 2 b.c 95p
Secret Place 2 ch.g 71p
Tabadul (IRE) 2 b.c 92p

J. L. DUNLOP
Ashwaaq (USA) 2 b.f 81p
Chanterelle (IRE) 2 ch.f 86p
Goodwood Finesse (IRE) 2 b.f 70p
Hathran (IRE) 2 gr.f 101p
Hezaam (USA) 2 b.c 84p
Iqte Saab (USA) 2 b.c 96p
Jedburgh 2 b.c 93p
Karamea (SWI) 2 gr.f 76p
Kodiac 2 b.c 82p
Kristal's Dream (IRE) 2 b.f 77p
Let The Lion Roar 2 b.c 97p
Maid To Treasure (IRE) 2 b.f 77p
Malin (IRE) 2 b.c 99p
Mango Mischief (IRE) 2 ch.f 84p
Muhaymin (USA) 2 ch.c 89p
Mukafeh (USA) 2 b.c 96p
Rave Reviews (IRE) 2 b.f 76p
Snow Goose 2 b.f 102p
Spotlight 2 ch.f 104p
Thajja (IRE) 2 b.c 80p
Zaqrah (USA) 2 b.f 80p

C. R. EGERTON
Pre Eminance (IRE) 2 b.c 78p
Vinando 2 ch.c 76p

D. R. C. ELSWORTH
River Gypsy 2 b.c 72p
Salford City (IRE) 2 b.c 100P
Skidmark 2 b.c 79P

T. J. ETHERINGTON
Celtic Thunder 2 b.g 86p

R. A. FAHEY
Philharmonic 2 b.g 99p

J. R. FANSHAWE
Baboosh (IRE) 2 b.f 78p
High Reserve 2 b.f 71p
Pending (IRE) 2 b.g 78p
Primus Inter Pares (IRE) 2 b.c 98p
Royal Prince 2 gr.c 78p
Solar Power (IRE) 2 b.f 77p
Warden Complex 2 b.g 75p
Able Baker Charlie (IRE) 4 b.g 100p
Frizzante 4 b.f 106p
Persario 4 b.f 91p
Unscrupulous 4 ch.g 91p

J. G. GIVEN
Antediluvian 2 b.f 91p
Dakota Blackhills 2 b.c 88p
First Candlelight 2 b.f 82p
Cadeaux Des Mages 3 b.g 93p

J. H. M. GOSDEN
Cape Vincent 2 b.c 92p
Courtyard 2 b.f 70p
Damsel 2 b.f 92p
Danclare (USA) 2 ch.f 82p
Dumfries 2 ch.g 82p

Latif (USA) 2 b.c 82p
Majorca 2 b.c 73p
Maraakeb (FR) 2 gr.c 84P
Percussionist (IRE) 2 b.c 79p
Phantom Wind (USA) 2 b.f 96p
Proud Tradition (USA) 2 b.f 78p
Rendezvous Point (USA) 2 ch.f 78p
Scientist 2 ch.c 85p
Seeking A Way (USA) 2 b.f 78p
Shady Reflection (USA) 2 b.f 74p
Slavonic (USA) 2 ch.c 80p
Tip The Dip (USA) 3 ch.c 90p

W. J. HAGGAS
Ace Club 2 ch.g 74p
Aperitif 2 ch.g 74p
Arkholme 2 b.g 81p
Bygone Days 2 ch.g 74p
Fyodor (IRE) 2 b.c 86p
Majestic Missile (IRE) 2 b.c 116p
Malvern Light 2 b.f 87p
Red Sahara (IRE) 2 ch.f 73p
Red Skelton (IRE) 2 ch.c 82p
Secret Flame 2 b.f 74p
Escayola (IRE) 3 b.g 99p
Flowerdrum (USA) 3 b.f 90p
Polar Bear 3 ch.g 101p
Alnaja (USA) 4 b.g 82p

B. HANBURY
Sweet Indulgence (IRE) 2 ch.c 84p

R. HANNON
Boogie Street 2 b.c 108p
Caveral 2 ch.f 82p
I Won't Dance (IRE) 2 b.c 84p
Red Spell (IRE) 2 ch.c 77p
Surf The Net 2 b.f 91p
Turnstile 2 gr.c 73p
Zerlina (USA) 2 b.f 92p

P. W. HARRIS
Alekhine (IRE) 2 b.g 86p
Christina's Dream 2 b.f 74p
Halicardia 2 br.f 94p
Hills Spitfire (IRE) 2 b.c 95p
Oasis Star (IRE) 2 b.f 76p
Silk Fan (IRE) 2 b.f 98p
Baltic Blazer 3 b.g 78p
Best Be Going (IRE) 3 b.g 88p
Grooms Affection 3 b.c 80p
Leporello (IRE) 3 b.c 118p
Persian Majesty (IRE) 3 b.c 114p
Rezzago (USA) 3 b.c 71p

P. C. HASLAM
Kinnaird (IRE) 2 ch.f 105p

LADY HERRIES
Lunar Exit (IRE) 2 gr.g 95p
Schooner (GER) 3 b.g 74p

B. W. HILLS
Alfonso 2 ch.c 71p
Aqualung 2 b.c 78p
Brindisi 2 b.f 75p
City Palace 2 ch.c 74p
Coming Again (IRE) 2 b.c 91p
Crystal Curling (IRE) 2 ch.f 88p

Daytime Girl (IRE) 2 gr.f   77p
Exclusive Danielle 2 ch.f   73p
Flamboyant Lad 2 ch.c   86p
Four Pence (IRE) 2 b.c   71p
Galvanise (USA) 2 b.c   78p
Heart's Desire (IRE) 2 b.f   79p
Honest Injun 2 b.c   77p
Mutawassel (USA) 2 b.c   97p
Secret Charm (IRE) 2 b.f   105p
Si Si Amiga (IRE) 2 b.f   79p
Southern Bazaar (USA) 2 ch.c   78p
Spring Surprise 2 b.f   82p
State Dilemma (IRE) 2 b.c   91p
Sydney Star 2 b.f   91p
Tenny's Gold (IRE) 2 b.f   74p
Zonus 2 b.c   87P
Best Flight 3 gr.g   78p
Trust Rule 3 b.c   108p

P. HOWLING
Nadir 2 b.c   81p

M. A. JARVIS
Autumn Pearl 2 b.f   82p
Divine Gift 2 b.c   89p
Iffraaj 2 b.c   88p
Maganda (IRE) 2 b.f   84p
New Morning (IRE) 2 b.f   73p
Qasirah (IRE) 2 b.f   97p
Tannoor (USA) 2 b.c   79p
Anak Pekan 3 ch.g   94p

W. JARVIS
La Persiana 2 gr.f   73p
Phantom Stock 3 b.g   72p

M. JOHNSTON
Asiatic 2 ch.c   81p
Awesome Love (USA) 2 br.c   75p
Caracara (IRE) 2 ch.f   88p
Etmaam 2 b.c   74P
Go Padero (IRE) 2 ch.c   82p
Just A Fluke (IRE) 2 b.c   78P
King of Dreams (IRE) 2 b.c   79p
Lucky Story (USA) 2 br.c   119p
Man of Letters (UAE) 2 b.c   66p
Mekuria (JPN) 2 b.f   84p
Mister Monet (IRE) 2 b.c   92p
Nero's Return (IRE) 2 b.c   104p
Penrith (FR) 2 b.c   85p
Think Tank 2 b.c   94p
Yoshka 2 ch.c   78p
Morson Boy (USA) 3 b.g   110p

A. KING
Salsalino 3 ch.c   115p

N. P. LITTMODEN
Benny The Ball (USA) 2 b.c   86p
Chauvinist (IRE) 2 b.g   92p

D. R. LODER
Andean 2 b.c   82p
Salisbury Plain 2 b.c   73p
Anglo Saxon (USA) 3 br.c   89p
Perfect Portrait 3 ch.g   84p

J. MACKIE
Foursquare (IRE) 2 b.c   86p

M. A. MAGNUSSON
Unavailable (IRE) 2 b.f   94p

P. J. MAKIN
Watamu (IRE) 2 b.c   84p

T. D. MCCARTHY
Jimmy Ryan (IRE) 2 b.c   85p

B. A. MCMAHON
Fictional 2 b.c   80p

B. J. MEEHAN
Crystal (IRE) 2 b.f   85p
Gjovic 2 br.c   73p
Innclassic (IRE) 2 b.f   72p
Pizazz 2 ch.c   74p

T. G. MILLS
Resplendent One (IRE) 2 b.c   87p
Settlement Craic (IRE) 2 b.c   79p
The Way We Were 2 ch.c   74P

P. MITCHELL
Joe Bear (IRE) 3 ch.c   109p

K. A. MORGAN
Kingkohler (IRE) 4 b.g   82p

H. MORRISON
Fiddle Me Blue 2 ch.f   77p
Killinallan 2 b.f   70p
Little Ridge (IRE) 2 b.g   84p
Odiham 2 b.g   77p
Pastoral Pursuits 2 b.c   110p
Cape St Vincent 3 gr.c   78p

J. NOSEDA
Burning Moon 2 b.c   75p
St Francis Wood (USA) 2 ch.f   95p
Two Step Kid (USA) 2 ch.c   94p
Ocean Victory 3 ch.g   98p

A. P. O'BRIEN, IRELAND
Cobra (IRE) 2 b.c   104p
Magritte (IRE) 2 b.c   112p
Mikado 2 b.c   106p
Necklace 2 b.f   105p
Offenbach (USA) 2 b.c   88P
One Cool Cat (USA) 2 b.c   118p
Wolfe Tone (IRE) 2 b.c   95p
Yeats (IRE) 2 b.c   95P

J. A. OSBORNE
Desperate Dan 2 b.c   92p
Laawaris (USA) 2 b.c   78p
Rye (IRE) 2 b.f   75p
Soliniki 2 b.g   84p

MRS A. J. PERRETT
Art Trader (USA) 2 b.c   95p
Bread of Heaven 2 b.f   79p
Corsican Native (USA) 2 b.c   79p
Enrapture (USA) 2 b.f   80p
Exterior (USA) 2 ch.c   75p
King Maximus (USA) 2 b.g   79p
Mountain Meadow 2 ch.g   83p
Rangoon (USA) 2 ch.c   75P
Residential 2 ch.c   75p

Secret Vision (USA) 2 ch.f   83p
Soulacroix 2 b.c   87p
Torinmoor (USA) 2 ch.c   93p
Vaughan 2 b.c   94p

JULIAN POULTON
Jath 2 b.f   84p

SIR MARK PRESCOTT
Pedrillo 2 b.g   91p
Regal Setting (IRE) 2 br.g   75p
Coat of Honour (USA) 3 gr.g   101p
Fall In Line 3 gr.g   66p
No Refuge (IRE) 3 ch.g   112p
One Off 3 b.g   94p

J. J. QUINN
Coxmoore (IRE) 2 b.g   84p

MRS J. R. RAMSDEN
Arcalis 3 gr.g   100p

I. SEMPLE
Peters Choice 2 ch.g   86p

A. C. STEWART
Asaleeb 2 b.f   79p
Cellarmaster (IRE) 2 ch.g   73p
Day To Remember 2 gr.c   77p
Granato (GER) 2 b.c   89p
Maren (USA) 2 b.c   88p
Radish (IRE) 2 b.f   63p
Salinor 3 ch.g   85p
Secluded 3 b.g   72p
Lafi (IRE) 4 ch.g   106p

SIR MICHAEL STOUTE
Admiral (IRE) 2 b.c   77p
Almuraad (IRE) 2 b.c   100p
Always First 2 b.c   102P
Border Castle 2 b.c   82p
Coy (IRE) 2 b.f   88p
Daring Aim 2 b.f   80P
Desert Diplomat (IRE) 2 br.g   71p
Eden Rock (IRE) 2 b.c   84P
Esteemed Lady (IRE) 2 b.f   96p
Fort Dignity (USA) 2 b.c   93p
Garryurra 2 gr.f   75p
Imperial Stride 2 b.c   113p
Kingsword (USA) 2 bl.c   89p
Liberty 2 b.f   71p
Lord Mayor 2 b.c   92p
Maclean 2 b.g   80p
Magnetic Pole 2 b.c   88P
Major Effort (USA) 2 b.c   79p
Maraahel (IRE) 2 b.c   87p
Menokee (USA) 2 b.c   102p
North Light (IRE) 2 b.c   95P
Notable Guest (USA) 2 b.c   91p
Peeress 2 ch.f   86p
Poise (IRE) 2 b.f   93P
Portmanteau 2 b.f   70p
Queen of Scots (IRE) 2 b.f   75p
Quiff 2 b.f   68P
Red Bloom 2 b.f   110p
Relaxed (USA) 2 b.f   80p
Roehampton 2 b.c   83P
Shalaya (IRE) 2 b.f   87p
Strider 2 ch.c   70p

Telefonica (USA) 2 b.f   74p
Top Romance (IRE) 2 ch.f   105p
Argonaut 3 ch.g   86p
Fremen (USA) 3 ch.c   102p
Hasanpour 3 b.g   103p
Sublimity (FR) 3 b.c   109p

SAEED BIN SUROOR
Al Sifaat 2 ch.f   88p
Dawn Surprise (USA) 2 b.f   78p
Golden Sahara (IRE) 2 b.c   101p
Silent Hawk (IRE) 2 b.c   86p
Singing Poet (IRE) 2 b.c   85p
Murashah (USA) 3 ch.c   82p

J. A. R. TOLLER
Bachelor Duke (USA) 2 b.c   115p
Swinbrook (USA) 2 ch.g   88p

M. P. TREGONING
Laabbij (USA) 2 ch.c   71p
Manyana (IRE) 2 b.c   97p
Meneef (USA) 2 b.c   82p
Mudawin (IRE) 2 b.g   73P
Nuzooa (USA) 2 b.f   83p
Oriental Warrior 2 b.c   101p
Sahool 2 b.f   84p
So Will I 2 ch.c   95p
Thaminah (USA) 2 b.f   84p
Torcross 2 b.f   96p
Tree Chopper (USA) 2 ch.f   79p
Alkaadhem 3 b.c   106p
Janayen (USA) 3 b.f   97p
Seven Year Itch (IRE) 3 b.c   75p

C. F. WALL
Cimyla (IRE) 2 b.c   78p
Fanny's Fancy 3 b.f   99p

D. K. WELD, IRELAND
Grey Swallow (IRE) 2 gr.c   116p

S. C. WILLIAMS
Dont Call Me Derek 2 b.g   74p
Trevian 2 ch.g   70p
Individual Talents (USA) 3 ch.f   77p

G. WRAGG
Coqueteria (USA) 2 b.f   83p
Graham Island 2 b.c   74p
Incheni (IRE) 2 b.f   71p
Larkwing (IRE) 2 b.c   70p
Lochbuie (IRE) 2 b.c   73p
Miss Langkawi 2 gr.f   76p

SELECTED BIG RACES 2003

Prize money for racing abroad has been converted to £ sterling at the exchange rate current at the time of the race. The figures are correct to the nearest £. The Timeform ratings (TR) recorded by the principals in each race appear on the last line.

NAD AL SHEBA Saturday, Mar 29   Turf course: GOOD, Dirt track: FAST

1   Dubai Sheema Classic (Gr 1) (4yo+) £769,599   1½m (Turf)

SULAMANI (IRE) *SaeedbinSuroor,UAE* 4-8-11 LDettori	6/4f		1
ANGE GABRIEL (FR) *ELibaud,France* 5-8-11 TJarnet	4/1	¾	2
EKRAAR (USA) *MPTregoning,GB* 6-8-11 RHills	25/1	3¼	3
Polish Summer *AFabre,France* 6-8-11 RHughes	14/1	1¼	4
Grand Ekinoks (TUR) *ADeMieulle,Turkey* 5-8-11 (b) HKaratas	28/1	1	5
Nowrass *KPMcLaughlin,UAE* 7-8-11 WSupple	50/1	3¼	6
Highest (IRE) *SaeedbinSuroor,UAE* 4-8-11 JPSpencer	8/1	nk	7
Celtic Silence *JWickham,UAE* 5-8-11 (t) JCarroll	50/1	1¼	8
Pugin (IRE) *SaeedbinSuroor,UAE* 5-8-11 KMcEvoy	25/1	4	9
Dano-Mast *FPoulsen,Denmark* 7-8-11 OPeslier	25/1	2	10
Morshdi *ASmith,UAE* 5-8-11 GHind	40/1	1½	11
Well Made (GER) *HBlume,Germany* 6-8-11 AStarke	33/1	8½	12
Perfect Sunday (USA) *KMcAuliffe,SaudiArabia* 5-8-11 SMadrid	66/1	3¼	13
Zindabad (FR) *MJohnston,GB* 7-8-11 KDarley	9/1	½	14
Califet (FR) *SaeedbinSuroor,UAE* 5-8-11 (t) JVelazquez	8/1	14	15
Boreal (GER) *PSchiergen,Germany* 5-8-11 KFallon	16/1	¾	16

Godolphin 16ran 2m27.67   127+/124/118/115/114

2   Dubai World Cup (Gr 1) (4yo+) £2,308,798   1¼m (Dirt)

MOON BALLAD (IRE) *SaeedbinSuroor,UAE* 4-9-0 (t) LDettori (11)	11/4		1
HARLAN'S HOLIDAY (USA) *TAPletcher,USA* 4-9-0 (t) JVelazquez (10)	11/2	5	2
NAYEF (USA) *MPTregoning,GB* 5-9-0 RHills (7)	11/8f	1	3
Grandera (IRE) *SaeedbinSuroor,UAE* 5-9-0 JPSpencer (9)	5/1	sh	4
State Shinto (USA) *JDSadler,UAE* 5-9-0 (b) JMurtagh (2)	100/1	3	5
Grundlefoot (USA) *KMcAuliffe,SaudiArabia* 6-9-0 SMadrid (6)	20/1	nk	6
Blue Burner (USA) *WIMott,USA* 4-9-0 (b) KDesormeaux (5)	66/1	6¾	7
Sei Mi (ARG) *JBarton,SaudiArabia* 7-9-0 JVelez (3)	50/1	½	8
Aquarelliste (FR) *ELellouche,France* 5-8-10 (ec) DBoeuf (1)	15/2	2¾	9
Crimson Quest (IRE) *JBarton,SaudiArabia* 6-9-0 (t) ASolis (8)	100/1	7¾	10
Hans Anderson (USA) *AMishreff,SaudiArabia* 5-9-0 (t) WRamos (4)	66/1	½	11

Godolphin 11ran 2m00.48   131/123/120/120/114/114

NEWBURY Saturday, Apr 12   GOOD to FIRM

3   Dubai Irish Village Stks (John Porter) (Gr 3) (4yo+) £29,000   1½m5y

WARRSAN (IRE) *CEBrittain,GB* 5-8-12 PRobinson (1)	5/1		1
ASIAN HEIGHTS *GWragg,GB* 5-9-1 DHolland (7)	7/4f	sh	2
COMPTON BOLTER (IRE) *GAButler,GB* 6-8-12 KFallon (9)	20/1	3	3
Bollin Eric *TDEasterby,GB* 4-9-4 KDarley (8)	7/2	sh	4
Imperial Dancer *MRChannon,GB* 5-9-1 CCatlin (2)	25/1	2	5
Nysaean (IRE) *RHannon,GB* 4-8-11 JFortune (6)	11/1	1	6
Barathea Blazer *PWHarris,GB* 4-8-11 JMurtagh (3)	14/1	4	7
Marble Arch *HMorrison,GB* 7-8-12 SDrowne (5)	33/1	4	8
Pawn Broker *DRCElsworth,GB* 6-8-12 DaneO'Neill (4)	11/1	1	9

Mr Saeed Manana 9ran 2m32.32   120/123/114/122

LONGCHAMP Sunday, Apr 27   GOOD to SOFT

4   Prix Ganay (Gr 1) (4yo+) £59,111   1¼m110y

FAIR MIX (IRE) *MRolland,France* 5-9-2 OPeslier	41/10		1
EXECUTE (FR) *JEHammond,France* 6-9-2 TGillet	35/1	2½	2
FALBRAV (IRE) *LMCumani,GB* 5-9-2 KFallon	37/10	sh	3
Chancellor (IRE) *BWHills,GB* 5-9-2 MHills	29/1	1½	4
Valentino (IRE) *AdeRoyerDupre,France* 4-9-2 TJarnet	106/10	nk	5
Ana Marie (FR) *PHDemercastel,France* 4-8-13 CSoumillon	22/10f	dh	5
Secret Singer (FR) *FHead,France* 4-9-2 BDonilla	92/10	1	7
Kaieteur (USA) *BJMeehan,GB* 4-9-2 PatEddery	30/1	2	8
Black Sam Bellamy (IRE) *APO'Brien,Ireland* 4-9-2 MJKinane	36/10	6	9

Ecurie Week-End 9ran 2m13.00   123/118+/118/114/115/112

NEWMARKET Saturday, May 3   GOOD (Rowley Mile Course)

5   Sagitta 2000 Guineas Stks (Gr 1) (3yo c+f) £185,600   1m

REFUSE TO BEND (IRE) *DKWeld,Ireland* 3-9-0 PJSmullen (18)	9/2		1

ZAFEEN (FR) *MRChannon* 3-9-0 SDrowne (4).. 33/1 ¾ 2
NORSE DANCER (IRE) *DRCElsworth* 3-9-0 PRobinson (8) .... 100/1 hd 3
Tout Seul (IRE) *RFJohnsonHoughton* 3-9-0 SCarson (17)..................... 7/1 ½ 4
Saturn (IRE) *MLWBell* 3-9-0 RHughes (6).. 50/1 1¼ 5
Monsieur Bond (IRE) *BSmart* 3-9-0 PJScallan (3) .... 100/1 sh 6
Hurricane Alan (IRE) *RHannon* 3-9-0 JFortune (9)................................ 20/1 sh 7
Tomahawk (IRE) *APO'Brien,Ireland* 3-9-0 JMurtagh (2).................... 7/1 hd 8
Jay Gee's Choice *MRChannon* 3-9-0 GCarter (12)................................ 200/1 3 9
Songlark *SaeedbinSuroor* 3-9-0 (t) JPSpencer (10)............................... 14/1 ½ 10
Mister Links (IRE) *RHannon* 3-9-0 PatEddery (7) .... 66/1 hd 11
Muqbil (USA) *JLDunlop* 3-9-0 WSupple (11)....................................... 9/1 nk 12
Rockets 'n Rollers (IRE) *RHannon* 3-9-0 DaneO'Neill (19)............... 100/1 sh 13
Indian Haven *PWD'Arcy* 3-9-0 JFEgan (1).. 20/1 ¾ 14
Audience *WJHaggas* 3-9-0 KFallon (5) 16/1 1½ 15
Checkit (IRE) *MRChannon* 3-9-0 CCatlin (15)...................................... 100/1 nk 16
Hold That Tiger (USA) *APO'Brien,Ireland* 3-9-0 MJKinane (16)...... 4/1f ¾ 17
Tizzy May (FR) *RHannon* 3-9-0 SSanders (13)...................................... 200/1 nk 18
Lundy's Lane (IRE) *CEBrittain* 3-9-0 OPeslier (14) .... 66/1 ½ 19
Lateen Sails *SaeedbinSuroor* 3-9-0 LDettori (20).................................. 9/2 ½ 20
Moyglare Stud Farms Ltd 20ran 1m37.98   118+/116+/116/115/112/111+

NEWMARKET Sunday, May 4   GOOD (Rowley Mile Course)

6   Sagitta 1000 Guineas Stks (Gr 1) (3yo f) £185,600   1m

RUSSIAN RHYTHM (USA) *SirMichaelStoute* 3-9-0 KFallon (2).............. 12/1 1
SIX PERFECTIONS (FR) *PBary,France* 3-9-0 TThulliez (1) 7/4f 1½ 2
INTERCONTINENTAL *AFabre,France* 3-9-0 CSoumillon (9)................. 5/1 1¼ 3
Soviet Song (IRE) *JRFanshawe* 3-9-0 OUrbina (11)............................... 4/1 1½ 4
Hanami *JARToller* 3-9-0 DHolland (4).. 50/1 nk 5
Casual Look (USA) *AMBalding* 3-9-0 MartinDwyer (5)........................ 50/1 hd 6
Summitville *JGGiven* 3-9-0 MFenton (13)... 66/1 1¼ 7
Yesterday (IRE) *APO'Brien,Ireland* 3-9-0 MJKinane (21)................... 20/1 1 8
Presto Vento *RHannon* 3-9-0 PatEddery (20)... 150/1 nk 9
Duty Paid (IRE) *DRCElsworth* 3-9-0 TQuinn (10)................................ 50/1 2 10
Look Here's Carol (IRE) *BAMcMahon* 3-9-0 GGibbons (3) 150/1 5 11
Gonfilia (GER) *SaeedbinSuroor* 3-9-0 JPSpencer (18)........................... 20/1 ½ 12
Spinola (FR) *PWHarris* 3-9-0 EAhern (7)... 100/1 5 13
Mezzo Soprano (USA) *SaeedbinSuroor* 3-9-0 LDettori (19)................... 7/1 hd 14
L'Ancresse (IRE) *APO'Brien,Ireland* 3-9-0 KDarley (17).................... 50/1 ¾ 15
Tante Rose (IRE) *BWHills* 3-9-0 MHills (12) 14/1 1¼ 16
Wimple (USA) *CEBrittain* 3-9-0 PRobinson (16)................................... 200/1 7 17
Hector's Girl *SirMichaelStoute* 3-9-0 JFortune (8)................................ 16/1 ½ 18
Khulood (USA) *JLDunlop* 3-9-0 WSupple (14)..................................... 16/1 3½ 19
Cheveley Park Stud 19ran 1m38.43   117+/113+/110/106+/106+/105

CHESTER Thursday, May 8   GOOD to FIRM

7   Philip Leverhulme Dee Stks (Gr 3) (3yo c+g) £43,400   1¼m75y

KRIS KIN (USA) *SirMichaelStoute* 3-8-8 FLynch (3) 20/1 1
BIG BAD BOB (IRE) *JLDunlop* 3-8-8 KFallon (2)................................. 4/9f 2 2
PRIVATE CHARTER *BWHills* 3-8-8 MHills (4)....................................... 5/1 3 3
Always Esteemed (IRE) *GWragg* 3-8-8 DHolland (1)............................ 11/2 4 4
Mr Saeed Suhail 4ran 2m10.01   122+/118/111+/103

LONGCHAMP Sunday, May 11   GOOD

8   Prix Lupin (Gr 1) (3yo c+f) £59,937   1¼m110y

DALAKHANI (IRE) *AdeRoyerDupre,France* 3-9-2 CSoumillon (2) 8/11f 1
SUPER CELEBRE (FR) *ELellouche,France* 3-9-2 DBoeuf (3)............... 3/1 1 2
ALBERTO GIACOMETTI (IRE) *APO'Brien,Ireland* 3-9-2 MJKinane (1).. 15/2 ¾ 3
Balestrini (IRE) *APO'Brien,Ireland* 3-9-2 KFallon (4)......................... 16/1 2½ 4
Snipewalk (USA) *MmeCHead-Maarek,France* 3-9-2 OPeslier (5) .... 20/1 sn 5
New South Wales *SaeedbinSuroor,GB* 3-9-2 LDettori (6) 8/1 2½ 6
Diyapour (FR) *AdeRoyerDupre,France* 3-9-2 TJarnet (7) 66/1 2½ 7
H.H. Aga Khan 7ran 2m09.40   120+/118+/116/111/110

9   Gainsborough Poule d'Essai des Poulains (Gr 1) (3yo c) £139,853   1m

CLODOVIL (FR) *AFabre,France* 3-9-2 CSoumillon (3)........................... 9/4f 1
CATCHER IN THE RYE (IRE) *APO'Brien,Ireland* 3-9-2 KFallon (8).......... 9/1 1 2
KRATAIOS (FR) *CLaffon-Parias,France* 3-9-2 OPeslier (4)................. 12/1 1½ 3
France *APO'Brien,Ireland* 3-9-2 (b) MJKinane (6) .... 13/2 ¾ 4
Desert Destiny *DRLoder,GB* 3-9-2 JPSpencer (7)................................... 11/2 sn 5
Sign of The Wolf *FRohaut,France* 3-9-2 TJarnet (5) .... 7/1 ¾ 6
Zanyboy (FR) *RCollet,France* 3-9-2 DBonilla (9).................................. 50/1 nk 7

1143

Bourbonnais (IRE) *SaeedbinSuroor,GB* 3-9-2 LDettori (1) 5/1 1½ 8
Elusive City (USA) *GAButler,GB* 3-9-2 EAhern (2) 8/1 1½ 9
Dalcassian (IRE) *APO'Brien,Ireland* 3-9-2 TPQueally (10) 40/1 ¾ 10
Famille Lagardere 10ran 1m36.40 116/113+/110/108+/107+/106

10 **Gainsborough Poule d'Essai des Pouliches (Gr 1) (3yo f)** £139,853 1m

MUSICAL CHIMES (USA) *AFabre,France* 3-9-0 CSoumillon (2) 12/1 1
MAIDEN TOWER *H-APantall,France* 3-9-0 C-PLemaire (12) 9/2 1 2
ETOILE MONTANTE (USA) *MmeCHead-Maarek,France* 3-9-0 RHughes (3) 9/4f sn 3
Welcome Millenium (FR) *J-CRouget,France* 3-9-0 (b) IMendizabal (5) 12/1 1½ 4
Garlinote (FR) *MmeCBarbe,France* 3-9-0 VVion (1) 33/1 1½ 5
Acago (USA) *MmeCHead-Maarek,France* 3-9-0 OPeslier (8) 14/1 sn 6
Mes Bleus Yeux (FR) *H-APantall,France* 3-9-0 TJarnet (11) 25/1 sn 7
Anyaas (IRE) *SaeedbinSuroor,GB* 3-9-0 LDettori (7) 14/1 2½ 8
Crystal Star *SirMichaelStoute,GB* 3-9-0 KFallon (6) 5/1 3 9
Fidelio's Miracle (USA) *H-APantall,France* 3-9-0 TThulliez (4) 10/1 2½ 10
Pearl Dance (USA) *JHMGosden,GB* 3-9-0 JFortune (10) 14/1 11
Londonnetdotcom (IRE) *MRChannon,GB* 3-9-0 SDrowne (9) 14/1 12
Maktoum Al Maktoum 12ran 1m36.00 117/114/114/110/106/106+/106

YORK Thursday, May 15 GOOD to FIRM

11 **Emirates Airline Yorkshire Cup (Gr 2) (4yo+)** £81,200 1m5f197y

MAMOOL (IRE) *SaeedbinSuroor* 4-8-9 LDettori (2) 11/2 1
3 WARRSAN (IRE) *CEBrittain* 5-8-13 PRobinson (4) 4/1 ½ 2
3 BOLLIN ERIC *TDEasterby* 4-9-0 KDarley (8) 2/1f 4 3
1 Zindabad (FR) *MJohnston* 7-8-13 DHolland (6) 4/1 5 4
Gulf (IRE) *DRCElsworth* 4-8-9 KFallon (3) 20/1 1¼ 5
Jardines Lookout (IRE) *APJarvis* 6-8-13 MJKinane (1) 14/1 ½ 6
Balakheri (IRE) *SirMichaelStoute* 4-8-12 (v) JMurtagh (5) 14/1 2 7
1 Pugin (IRE) *SaeedbinSuroor* 5-8-10 JPSpencer (7) 12/1 1¾ 8
Godolphin 8ran 2m52.54 120+/121/118/108/104/105

NEWBURY Saturday, May 17 GOOD to FIRM

12 **Juddmonte Lockinge Stks (Gr 1) (4yo+)** £116,000 1m

HAWK WING (USA) *APO'Brien,Ireland* 4-9-0 MJKinane (4) 2/1f 1
WHERE OR WHEN (IRE) *TGMills* 4-9-0 KDarley (6) 7/2 11 2
OLDEN TIMES *JLDunlop* 5-9-0 KFallon (7) 10/1 8 3
Domedriver (IRE) *PBary,France* 5-9-0 TThulliez (1) 9/4 1 4
Reel Buddy (USA) *RHannon* 5-9-0 PatEddery (5) 50/1 ¾ 5
Tillerman *MrsAJPerrett* 7-9-0 RHughes (3) 16/1 3½ 6
Mrs John Magnier 6ran 1m36.78 136/111/91/89/87

LONGCHAMP Sunday, May 18 GOOD

13 **Prix d'Ispahan (Gr 1) (4yo+)** £61,662 1m1f55y

4 FALBRAV (IRE) *LMCumani,GB* 5-9-2 KFallon (7) 32/10 1
BRIGHT SKY (IRE) *ELellouche,France* 4-8-13 DBoeuf (2) 14/10cpf 1½ 2
CARNIVAL DANCER *MrsAJPerrett,GB* 5-9-2 PatEddery (3) 36/1 3 3
Bernebeau (FR) *AFabre,France* 4-9-2 CSoumillon (4) 105/10 ½ 4
4 Execute (FR) *JEHammond,France* 6-9-2 TGillet (1) 59/10 2 5
Imtiyaz (USA) *SaeedbinSuroor,GB* 4-9-2 LDettori (6) 56/10 ¾ 6
Dandoun *JLDunlop,GB* 5-9-2 OPeslier (8) 53/10 2½ 7
Poussin (IRE) *ELellouche,France* 5-9-2 SCoffigny (5) 14/10cpf 10 8
Scuderia Rencati Srl 8ran 1m51.00 126+/120/116/115/111/110

CURRAGH Saturday, May 24 GOOD to SOFT

14 **Entenmann's Irish 2000 Guineas (Gr 1) (3yo c+f)** £159,716 1m

5 INDIAN HAVEN *PWD'Arcy,GB* 3-9-0 JFEgan (3) 8/1 1
9 FRANCE *APO'Brien* 3-9-0 (b) JAHeffernan (9) 14/1 1 2
5 TOUT SEUL (IRE) *RFJohnsonHoughton,GB* 3-9-0 SCarson (14) 5/1 2½ 3
5 Saturn (IRE) *MLWBell,GB* 3-9-0 JMurtagh (7) 10/1 ½ 4
Great Pyramid (IRE) *APO'Brien* 3-9-0 TPQueally (13) 33/1 hd 5
Napper Tandy (IRE) *JSBolger* 3-9-0 KJManning (10) 16/1 3 6
Abunawwas (IRE) *KPrendergast* 3-9-0 DPMcDonogh (8) 20/1 ¾ 7
Makhlab (USA) *BWHills,GB* 3-9-0 WSupple (6) 16/1 hd 8
Evolving Tactics (IRE) *DKWeld* 3-9-0 PJSmullen (2) 16/1 hd 9
9 Desert Destiny *DRLoder,GB* 3-9-0 LDettori (5) 9/1 1 10
5 Tomahawk (USA) *APO'Brien* 3-9-0 MJKinane (16) 10/3f hd 11
Dolmur (IRE) *AnthonyMullins* 3-9-0 FMBerry (15) 20/1 hd 12
Solskjaer (IRE) *APO'Brien* 3-9-0 CO'Donoghue (11) 25/1 ½ 13
5 Zafeen (FR) *MRChannon,GB* 3-9-0 SJDrowne (12) 11/2 ¾ 14

Salt Lake City (USA) *APO'Brien* 3-9-0 PCosgrave (4)................................. 33/1   3½ 15
Chappel Cresent (IRE) *GKeane* 3-9-0 KDarley (1) 50/1   2 16
P. Gleeson, J. Smith, L. Conway 16ran 1m41.50   117+/115/109+/108/107/101+

CURRAGH Sunday, May 25   GOOD to SOFT

15   **Entenmann's Irish 1000 Guineas (Gr 1) (3yo f) £159,716**   1m

  6   YESTERDAY (IRE) *APO'Brien* 3-9-0 MJKinane (8) 11/2   1
  6   SIX PERFECTIONS (FR) *PBary,France* 3-9-0 JMurtagh (6)...................... 3/10f   sh 2
     DIMITROVA (USA) *DKWeld* 3-9-0 PJSmullen (5)...................................... 16/1   ¾ 3
  6   L'Ancresse (IRE) *APO'Brien* 3-9-0 JAHeffernan (4) 20/1   2½ 4
     Plume Rouge *KPrendergast* 3-9-0 WJSmith (1).. 50/1   5 5
     Cat Belling (IRE) *KPrendergast* 3-9-0 EAhern (2)................................... 50/1   1½ 6
     Luminata (IRE) *JSBolger* 3-9-0 KJManning (3) .... 16/1   ¾ 7
     Walayef (USA) *KPrendergast* 3-9-0 DPMcDonogh (7)............................ 9/1   2½ 8
Mrs John Magnier 8ran 1m40.80   117/117+/115/109/98/94

SANDOWN Monday, May 26   GOOD to FIRM

16   **Bonusprint Henry II Stks (Gr 2) (4yo+) £58,000**   2m78y

     MR DINOS (IRE) *PFICole* 4-9-3 LDettori (4)... 6/1   1
     POLE STAR *JRFanshawe* 5-9-0 PatEddery (8) 8/1   2½ 2
     KASTHARI (IRE) *SirMichaelStoute* 4-8-12 JMurtagh (1)...................... 9/1   nk 3
     Persian Punch (IRE) *DRCElsworth* 10-9-0 MartinDwyer (7)..................... 8/1   3 4
     Boreas *LMCumani* 8-9-0 KFallon (5) .... 15/8f   nk 5
  3   Compton Bolter (IRE) *GAButler* 6-9-0 EAhern (3) 12/1   8 6
     Darasim (IRE) *MJohnston* 5-9-0 (v) KDarley (2) 11/1   1 7
     Hugs Dancer (FR) *JGGiven* 6-9-0 DeanMcKeown (9)............................ 9/1   ½ 8
     Bangalore *MrsAJPerrett* 7-9-0 SSanders (6) 12/1   1 9
     Taffrail *JLDunlop* 5-9-0 MJKinane (10)... 33/1   16 10
Mr C. Shiacolas 10ran 3m30.50   122/+113/113/109/109

CHANTILLY Sunday, Jun 1   GOOD to FIRM

17   **Prix Jean Prat (Gr 1) (3yo c+f) £61,662**   1m1f

     VESPONE (IRE) *NClement,France* 3-9-2 C-PLemaire (4) 28/10   1
     PRINCE KIRK (ITY) *EBorromeo,Italy* 3-9-2 LDettori (1) 66/10   3 2
     TASHKANDI (IRE) *AdeRoyerDupre,France* 3-9-2 CSoumillon (2) .... 17/10f   sn 3
     Art Moderne (USA) *ELellouche,France* 3-9-2 DBoeuf (3) .... 64/10   ns 4
     Marshall (FR) *CLaffon-Parias,France* 3-9-2 TThulliez (1) .... 47/10   nk 5
     Vadalix (FR) *AFabre,France* 3-9-2 OPlacais (6)...................................... 128/10   2½ 6
  5   Audience *WJHaggas,GB* 3-9-2 ESaint-Martin (8) 182/10   2½ 7
     Our Teddy (IRE) *GGMargarson,GB* 3-9-2 OPeslier (5) 41/1   3 8
Ecurie Mister Ess A.S. 8ran 1m47.10   122+/115/115/115/114/108

18   **Prix du Jockey Club (Gr 1) (3yo c+f) £395,683**   1½m

  8   DALAKHANI (IRE) *AdeRoyerDupre,France* 3-9-2 CSoumillon (4) 2/5cpf   1
  8   SUPER CELEBRE (FR) *ELellouche,France* 3-9-2 DBoeuf (3).................. 33/10   2 2
     CORONER (IRE) *J-CRouget,France* 3-9-2 SPasquier (5) 21/1   3 3
     Touch of Land (FR) *H-APantall,France* 3-9-2 OPeslier (2) 142/10   3 4
     Papineau *AFabre,France* 3-9-2 LDettori (1) 48/10   6 5
     Victory Taita (FR) *XThomasDemeaulte,France* 3-9-2 ESaint-Martin (7)...... 57/1   2½ 6
  8   Diyapour (FR) *AdeRoyerDupre,France* 3-9-2 TJarnet (6) 2/5cpf   20 7
H.H. Aga Khan 7ran 2m26.70   125+/121/115/111

EPSOM DOWNS Friday, Jun 6   Race 19: GOOD to FIRM, Race 20: GOOD

19   **Vodafone Coronation Cup (Gr 1) (4yo+) £174,000**   1½m10y

 11   WARRSAN (IRE) *CEBrittain* 5-9-0 PRobinson (4) 9/2   1
  1   HIGHEST (IRE) *SaeedbinSuroor* 4-9-0 LDettori (8)................................. 6/1   ½ 2
  4   BLACK SAM BELLAMY (IRE) *APO'Brien,Ireland* 4-9-0 MJKinane (7)... 4/1f   sh 3
     Bandari (IRE) *MJohnston* 4-9-0 RHills (9) 5/1   1¾ 4
 11   Zindabad (FR) *MJohnston* 7-9-0 KDarley (5)... 12/1   2 5
  1   Polish Summer *AFabre,France* 6-9-0 CSoumillon (10)........................... 6/1   sh 6
     Albanova *SirMarkPrescott* 4-8-11 GDuffield (1) 11/2   3½ 7
  3   Pawn Broker *DRCElsworth* 6-9-0 DaneO'Neill (3) 33/1   2 8
     Ulundi *PRWebber* 8-9-0 RHughes (6).. 20/1   dist 9
Mr Saeed Manana 9ran 2m35.68   121/121/121/118/114/114+

20   **Vodafone Oaks (Gr 1) (3yo f) £240,700**   1½m10y

  6   CASUAL LOOK (USA) *AMBalding* 3-9-0 MartinDwyer (7) 10/1   1
 15   YESTERDAY (IRE) *APO'Brien,Ireland* 3-9-0 MJKinane (11).................. 10/3f   nk 2
  6   SUMMITVILLE *JGGiven* 3-9-0 MFenton (9).. 25/1   ½ 3
     Inchberry *GAButler* 3-9-0 EAhern (14) 100/1   1¾ 4
     Hi Dubai *SaeedbinSuroor* 3-9-0 LDettori (3) .... 7/2   ¾ 5

```
    6  Hanami JARToller 3-9-0 DHolland (12)..................................................  7/1      1 6
       Santa Sophia (IRE) JLDunlop 3-9-0 PatEddery (2) ..............................  16/1     ¾ 7
       Thingmebob MHTompkins 3-9-0 TEDurcan (10) .................................  100/1    hd 8
       Geminiani (IRE) BWHills 3-9-0 MHills (5) .........................................  16/1     3 9
       Hearts 'n Minds CACyzer 3-9-0 PJSmullen (13) ...............................  100/1    6 10
       Hammiya (IRE) MPTregoning 3-9-0 RHills (6)....................................  7/1      2 11
       High Praise (USA) JHMGosden 3-9-0 RHughes (15) ...........................  16/1    19 12
       Waldmark (GER) SirMichaelStoute 3-9-0 KFallon (1).........................  14/1     8 13
       Halawanda (IRE) SirMichaelStoute 3-9-0 KMurtagh (8).....................  25/1    2½ 14
   15  L'Ancresse (IRE) APO'Brien,Ireland 3-9-0 KDarley (4)......................  16/1      pu

       Mr W. S. Farish III 15ran 2m38.07                114/114+/113/110/109/107/106/106

       EPSOM DOWNS Saturday, Jun 7   GOOD to FIRM
   21  Vodafone Derby Stks (Gr 1) (3yo c+f) £852,600                              1½m10y
    7  KRIS KIN (USA) SirMichaelStoute 3-9-0 KFallon (4) ........................  6/1      1
       THE GREAT GATSBY (IRE) APO'Brien,Ireland 3-9-0 PatEddery (16) .....  20/1     1 2
       ALAMSHAR (IRE) JOxx,Ireland 3-9-0 JMurtagh (8)............................  4/1     sh 3
    5  Norse Dancer (IRE) DRCElsworth 3-9-0 TQuinn (14)..........................  16/1    1½ 4
    8  Balestrini (IRE) APO'Brien,Ireland 3-9-0 JPSpencer (20) ..................  66/1     ¾ 5
       Dutch Gold (USA) CEBrittain 3-9-0 PRobinson (18) ..........................  20/1     4 6
       Let Me Try Again (IRE) TGMills 3-9-0 DHolland (1) .........................  50/1     4 7
       Graikos SaeedbinSuroor 3-9-0 (t) LDettori (12) ...............................  25/1    1¼ 8
       Magistretti (USA) NACallaghan 3-9-0 KDarley (7) ...........................  20/1    hd 9
       Shield GAButler 3-9-0 EAhern (10) .................................................  20/1    1 10
       Summerland (IRE) JHMGosden 3-9-0 JFortune (5) ..........................  100/1    ½ 11
    8  Alberto Giacometti (IRE) APO'Brien,Ireland 3-9-0 CSoumillon (9)..........  12/1   1¼ 12
    5  Refuse To Bend (IRE) DKWeld,Ireland 3-9-0 PJSmullen (6)................  11/4f    ½ 13
       Franklins Gardens MHTompkins 3-9-0 TEDurcan (19)......................  25/1    hd 14
       Dunhill Star (IRE) BWHills 3-9-0 MHills (12) ..................................  50/1   2½ 15
       Brian Boru APO'Brien,Ireland 3-9-0 MJKinane (2) ..........................  9/2     2 16
       Strength 'n Honour CACyzer 3-9-0 RHughes (15)............................  100/1   nk 17
       Unigold (USA) EALDunlop 3-9-0 SSanders (3) ................................  50/1    3 18
    5  Lundy's Lane (IRE) CEBrittain 3-9-0 BDoyle (17)............................  20/1     4 19
       Prince Nureyev (IRE) BRMillman 3-9-0 SDrowne (11).....................  150/1    7 20

       Mr Saeed Suhail 20ran 2m33.35                            122+/120/120/118/117/111

       CHANTILLY Sunday, Jun 8   GOOD
   22  Grand Prix de Chantilly (Gr 2) (4yo+) £38,957                              1½m
    1  ANGE GABRIEL (FR) ELibaud,France 5-9-4 TJarnet...........................  3/5f     1
       MARTALINE AFabre,France 4-8-11 RHughes......................................  186/10   1½ 2
   11  BALAKHERI (IRE) SirMichaelStoute,GB 4-8-11 JMurtagh......................  7/1    2½ 3
    4  Ana Marie (FR) PHDemercastel,France 4-8-12 SPasquier ....................  76/10   nk 4
       Westerner ELellouche,France 4-8-11 DBoeuf ...................................  117/10    2 5
       Sangreal (NZ) AFabre,France 5-8-11 OPlacais ................................  55/1     8 6
       Morozov (USA) AFabre,France 4-9-2 LDettori ..................................  36/10    ur

       Mme H. Devin 7ran 2m27.40                             124/115/111/111/107
   23  Prix de Diane Hermes (Gr 1) (3yo f) £205,540                              1¼m110y
       NEBRASKA TORNADO (USA) AFabre,France 3-9-0 RHughes (10)....  106/10     1
       TIME AHEAD JLDunlop,GB 3-9-0 KFallon (9)....................................  166/10    ¾ 2
   10  MUSICAL CHIMES (USA) AFabre,France 3-9-0 CSoumillon (5) ...........  33/10    1 3
       Baie (FR) FRohaut,France 3-9-0 TJarnet (7).....................................  154/10   nk 4
       Cassis (USA) JNoseda,GB 3-9-0 PatEddery (8)................................  117/10    1 5
       Commercante (FR) J-MBeguigne,France 3-9-0 (ec) IMendizabal (3)..........  40/1     1 6
       Vallee Enchantee (IRE) ELellouche,France 3-9-0 DBoeuf (1)..................  13/2    sn 7
       Fidelite (IRE) MmeCHead-Maarek,France 3-9-0 OPeslier (4).................  13/10f   1½ 8
       Arvada RPritchard-Gordon,France 3-9-0 TGillet (6) ..........................  24/1     3 9
       Campsie Fells (UAE) H-APantall,France 3-9-0 LDettori (2)................  126/10   2½ 10

       Mr K. Abdulla 10ran 2m08.10                            114/112/110/109/106+/104

       ASCOT Tuesday, Jun 17   FIRM
   24  Coventry Stks (Gr 3) (2yo) £37,700                                         6f
       THREE VALLEYS (USA) RCharlton 2-8-12 RHughes (7) ....................  7/1      1
       BOTANICAL (USA) DRLoder 2-8-12 LDettori (11) ...........................  7/2     8 2
       PRIVY SEAL (IRE) JHMGosden 2-8-12 JFortune (9) .......................  20/1    nk 3
       Barbajuan (IRE) NACallaghan 2-8-12 CSoumillon (5) ......................  16/1     ¾ 4
       Fancy Foxtrot BJMeehan 2-8-12 KFallon (9) ..................................  20/1    hd 5
       Spanish Ace AMBalding 2-8-12 MartinDwyer (10)...........................  14/1     3 6
       Sabbeeh (USA) MAJarvis 2-8-12 PRobinson (1)..............................  3/1f     ½ 7
       Waterline Blue (IRE) PDEvans 2-8-12 JFEgan (3)...........................  150/1    1 8
       Newton (IRE) APO'Brien,Ireland 2-8-12 MJKinane (15) ..................  9/2     2 9
```

Carlburg (IRE) *CEBrittain* 2-8-12 DHolland (8).. 66/1   5 10
Parisienne (IRE) *FMourier,USA* 4-9-2 KDarley (6) 66/1   8 11
Docklands Brian *PSMcEntee* 2-8-12 KDalgleish (12) 150/1   1¼ 12
Dellagio (IRE) *DNicholls* 2-8-12 ANicholls (2)... 16/1   9 13

Mr K. Abdulla 13ran 1m13.62   119/97/96/94+/94

25   **King's Stand Stks (Gr 2) (3yo+)** £81,200   5f

     CHOISIR (AUS) *PaulPerry,Australia* 4-9-7 (es) JMurtagh (8).................... 25/1   1
     ACCLAMATION *LGCottrell* 4-9-2 PatEddery (7) 16/1   1 2
     OASIS DREAM *JHMGosden* 3-9-1 RHughes (10) 6/1f   1½ 3
     Dominica *MPTregoning* 4-8-13 MartinDwyer (1)....................................... 10/1   1½ 4
     The Trader (IRE) *MBlanshard* 5-9-2 (b) DSweeney (19) .... 16/1   ¾ 5
   9   Elusive City (USA) *GAButler* 3-8-10 (t) GaryStevens (9)........................... 11/1   ¾ 6
     Captain Rio *DNicholls* 4-9-2 KFallon (5)... 10/1   hd 7
     Bahamian Pirate (USA) *DNicholls* 8-9-2 OPeslier (18).............................. 33/1   1¼ 8
     Firebolt (IRE) *IWAllan,HongKong* 5-9-2 (b) WCMarwing (2)..................... 12/1   1 9
     Olivia Grace *TGMills* 5-8-13 KDarley (6)... 9/1   hd 10
     Romantic Liason *SaeedbinSuroor* 3-8-7 (t) LDettori (21) 11/1   1 11
     Saddad (USA) *SirMichaelStoute* 4-9-2 RHills (11)..................................... 14/1   ½ 12
     Peace Offering (IRE) *TGMills* 3-8-10 AClark (13).................................... 66/1   sh 13
     Indian Spark *JSGoldie* 9-9-2 AClhane (14)... 50/1   ½ 14
     Continent *DNicholls* 6-9-7 (t) DHolland (3)... 10/1   sh 15
     Peruvian Chief (IRE) *NPLittmoden* 6-9-2 (v) AHern (17) 25/1   2½ 16
     Wunders Dream (IRE) *JGGiven* 3-8-10 MFenton (20)................................ 33/1   1¾ 17
     Talbot Avenue *MMullineaux* 5-9-2 ANicholls (15)..................................... 100/1   hd 18
     Boleyn Castle (USA) *TGMills* 6-9-2 RMiles (4) 20/1   4 19
     Lady Dominatrix (IRE) *MrsPNDutfield* 4-8-13 PDoe (12)......................... 40/1   ½ 20

Mr T. W. Wallace & Partners 20ran 59.68secs   126/118/115/105/106+/101

26   **St James's Palace Stks (Gr 1) (3yo c)** £156,600   1m (Rnd)

  14   ZAFEEN (FR) *MRChannon* 3-9-0 DHolland (5) 8/1   1
     KALAMAN (IRE) *SirMichaelStoute* 3-9-0 JMurtagh (7)............................ 5/2f   1 2
     MARTILLO (GER) *RSuerland,Germany* 3-9-0 WMongil (2)..................... 12/1   3 3
   5   Hold That Tiger (USA) *APO'Brien,Ireland* 3-9-0 KFallon (11)................... 9/1   ½ 4
   9   Clodovil (IRE) *AFabre,France* 3-9-0 CSoumillon (9) .... 10/3   sh 5
   5   Hurricane Alan (IRE) *RHannon* 3-9-0 JFortune (4).................................... 50/1   1 6
  14   Tout Seul (IRE) *RFJohnsonHoughton* 3-9-0 SCarson (4)........................... 16/1   hd 7
     Statue of Liberty (USA) *APO'Brien,Ireland* 3-9-0 JPSpencer (1)................ 16/1   1¼ 8
  14   France *APO'Brien,Ireland* 3-9-0 (v) MJKinane (6) 20/1   1¾ 9
   5   Monsieur Bond (IRE) *BSmart* 3-9-0 PJScallan (3) .... 20/1   nk 10
  14   Indian Haven *PWD'Arcy* 3-9-0 JFEgan (10)... 6/1   16 11

Mr Jaber Abdullah 11ran 1m39.91   123/121+/113+/112+/112/110

27   **Queen Anne Stks (Gr 1) (4yo+)** £145,000   1m (Str.)

     Order as they passed the post: Tillerman failed a dope test and was disqualified

     DUBAI DESTINATION (USA) *SaeedbinSuroor* 4-9-0 (t) LDettori (10) 9/2   1
  12   TILLERMAN *MrsAJPerrett* 7-9-0 RHughes (3).. 16/1   4 2
     RIGHT APPROACH *SirMichaelStoute* 4-9-0 KFallon (9)........................... 20/1   ¾ 3
  12   Where Or When (IRE) *TGMills* 4-9-0 KDarley (2) 8/1   3½ 4
     Gateman *MJohnston* 4-9-0 KDalgleish (1).. 50/1   hd 5
     Blatant *SaeedbinSuroor* 4-9-0 (v+t) RHills (5)... 100/1   2 6
  12   Hawk Wing (USA) *APO'Brien,Ireland* 4-9-0 MJKinane (4)...................... 8/13f   nk 7
     Victory Moon (SAF) *MdeKock,SouthAfrica* 4-8-12 JMurtagh (6)............... 33/1   3 8
     Beauchamp Pilot *GAButler* 5-9-0 EAhern (7)... 50/1   7 9
     Desert Deer *MJohnston* 5-9-0 DHolland (11).. 20/1   1¾ 10

Godolphin 10ran 1m38.56   127/118+/117/109/109/104

ASCOT Wednesday, Jun 18   GOOD to FIRM

28   **Prince of Wales's Stks (Gr 1) (4yo+)** £203,000   1¼m

   2   NAYEF (USA) *MPTregoning* 5-9-0 RHills (6) 5/1   1
     RAKTI *MAJarvis* 4-9-0 PRobinson (9) 50/1   2½ 2
     ISLINGTON (IRE) *SirMichaelStoute* 4-8-11 KFallon (10) 7/1   1 3
  12   Olden Times *JLDunlop* 5-9-0 OPeslier (2).. 33/1   1 4
  13   Falbrav (IRE) *LMCumani* 5-9-0 MDemuro (3)... 9/2   3 5
   4   Kaieteur (USA) *BJMeehan* 4-9-0 PatEddery (4).. 66/1   3½ 6
   2   Grandera (IRE) *SaeedbinSuroor* 5-9-0 JPSpencer (8)................................ 4/1   1 7
     Paolini (GER) *AWohler,Germany* 6-9-0 (b) EPedroza (1)........................... 25/1   ¾ 8
   2   Moon Ballad (IRE) *SaeedbinSuroor* 4-9-0 (t) LDettori (7) 2/1f   1½ 9
   1   Ekraar (USA) *MPTregoning* 6-9-0 (v) WSupple (11) 33/1   6 10

Mr Hamdan Al Maktoum 10ran 2m05.30   128/122/117/118+/111+

ASCOT Thursday, Jun 19   GOOD to FIRM

29   Gold Cup (Gr 1) (4yo+) £145,000   2½m

16	MR DINOS (IRE) *PFICole* 4-9-0 KFallon (6)	3/1			1
16	PERSIAN PUNCH (IRE) *DRCElsworth* 10-9-2 MartinDwyer (5)	20/1		6	2
16	POLE STAR *JRFanshawe* 5-9-2 PatEddery (11)	12/1		¾	3
11	Jardines Lookout (IRE) *APJarvis* 6-9-2 DHolland (3)	16/1		nk	4
11	Mamool (IRE) *SaeedbinSuroor* 4-9-0 LDettori (2)	5/2f		½	5
	Savannah Bay *BJMeehan* 4-9-0 PJSmullen (13)	20/1		sh	6
16	Kasthari (IRE) *SirMichaelStoute* 4-9-0 JMurtagh (12)	12/1		2½	7
19	Black Sam Bellamy (IRE) *APO'Brien,Ireland* 4-9-0 MJKinane (4)	10/1		¾	8
	Tholjanah (IRE) *MPTregoning* 4-9-0 (b) RHills (10)	16/1		14	9
11	Pugin (IRE) *SaeedbinSuroor* 5-9-2 KDarley (7)	25/1		1½	10
	Fight Your Corner *SaeedbinSuroor* 4-9-0 JPSpencer (8)	8/1		15	11
	Alcazar (IRE) *HMorrison* 8-9-2 MFenton (9)	25/1		11	12

Mr C. Shiacolas 12ran 4m20.15   123+/115/114/114/115/113

ASCOT Friday, Jun 20   FIRM

30   Coronation Stks (Gr 1) (3yo f) £156,600   1m (Rnd)

6	RUSSIAN RHYTHM (USA) *SirMichaelStoute* 3-9-0 KFallon (11)	4/7f			1
6	SOVIET SONG (IRE) *JRFanshawe* 3-9-0 OUrbina (6)	9/2		1½	2
	MAIL THE DESERT (IRE) *MRChannon* 3-9-0 SDrowne (8)	14/1		3	3
23	Cassis (USA) *JNoseda* 3-9-0 PatEddery (4)	10/1		4	4
	Fantasize *SirMichaelStoute* 3-9-0 GaryStevens (5)	16/1		1	5
6	Duty Paid (IRE) *DRCElsworth* 3-9-0 TQuinn (1)	16/1		sh	6
	Blaise Castle (USA) *GABulter* 3-9-0 EAhern (10)	50/1		4	7
	Diacada (GER) *HBlume,Germany* 3-9-0 AStarke (7)	14/1		½	8
	Proxima (IRE) *GWragg* 3-9-0 DHolland (9)	16/1		1	9

Cheveley Park Stud 9ran 1m38.51   121+/117/+/110/101/98/98

ASCOT Saturday, Jun 21   FIRM

31   Hardwicke Stks (Gr 2) (4yo+) £87,000   1½m

	INDIAN CREEK *DRCElsworth* 5-8-9 TQuinn (3)	14/1			1
11	BOLLIN ERIC *TDEasterby* 4-9-0 KDarley (9)	4/1		nk	2
19	ZINDABAD (FR) *MJohnston* 7-8-9 DHolland (6)	9/2		3	3
19	Bandari (IRE) *MJohnston* 4-8-9 RHills (2)	11/2		1	4
19	Highest (IRE) *SaeedbinSuroor* 4-8-9 (v) LDettori (4)	5/2f		1	5
	Parasol (IRE) *DRLoder* 4-8-9 (v) JPSpencer (10)	9/1		4	6
	Rawyaan *JHMGosden* 4-8-9 (v) WSupple (7)	16/1		3½	7
22	Balakheri (IRE) *SirMichaelStoute* 4-8-11 JMurtagh (1)	14/1		3	8
16	Compton Bolter (IRE) *GABulter* 6-8-9 EAhern (8)	25/1		nk	9

Mr Seymour Cohn 9ran 2m27.24   119/123/112/112/110/103

32   Golden Jubilee Stks (Gr 1) (3yo+) £145,000   6f

25	CHOISIR (AUS) *PaulPerry,Australia* 4-9-4 (es) JMurtagh (20)	13/2			1
	AIRWAVE *HCandy* 3-8-8 DaneO'Neill (4)	11/8f		½	2
	BARON'S PIT *RHannon* 3-8-11 JFortune (9)	50/1		1	3
	Zipping (IRE) *RCollet,France* 4-9-4 DBonilla (22)	20/1		1¼	4
	Just James *JNoseda* 4-9-4 OPeslier (5)	10/1		nk	5
	Polar Way *MrsAJPerrett* 4-9-4 RHughes (13)	20/1		1	6
	Malhub (USA) *JHMGosden* 5-9-4 RHills (2)	13/2		nk	7
	Twilight Blues (IRE) *BJMeehan* 4-9-4 MJKinane (19)	25/1		1¼	8
6	Khulood (USA) *JLDunlop* 3-8-8 WSupple (10)	20/1		2½	9
	Three Points *SaeedbinSuroor* 6-9-4 (t) JPSpencer (7)	14/1		¾	10
	Firebreak *SaeedbinSuroor* 4-9-4 LDettori (16)	14/1		hd	11
	Orientor *JSGoldie* 5-9-4 KFallon (14)	33/1		1	12
	Needwood Blade *BAMcMahon* 5-9-4 TQuinn (6)	33/1		2½	13
	Steenberg (IRE) *MHTompkins* 4-9-4 (b) TEDurcan (1)	33/1		9	14
	Belle du Jour (AUS) *DKWeld,Ireland* 6-9-1 (b) PJSmullen (21)	16/1		nk	15
25	Continent *DNicholls* 6-9-4 (t) DHolland (3)	25/1		1½	16
	Morluc (USA) *RLMorse,USA* 7-9-4 (t) GaryStevens (1)	14/1		8	17

Mr T. W. Wallace & Partners 17ran 1m12.23   126/120/119/118/117+/114

LONGCHAMP Sunday, Jun 22   GOOD

33   Juddmonte Grand Prix de Paris (Gr 1) (3yo c+f) £202,624   1¼m

17	VESPONE (IRE) *NClement,France* 3-9-2 C-PLemaire (2)	17/10f			1
21	MAGISTRETTI (USA) *NACallaghan,GB* 3-9-2 CSoumillon (8)	19/2		1½	2
	LOOK HONEY (USA) *CLerner,France* 3-9-2 YLerner (11)	22/1		½	3
5	Lateen Sails *SaeedbinSuroor,GB* 3-9-2 LDettori (5)	31/10		¾	4
	Jipapibaquigrafo (USA) *MmeCHead-Maarek,France* 3-9-2 TGillet (3)	17/1		hd	5
21	Alberto Giacometti (IRE) *APO'Brien,Ireland* 3-9-2 MJKinane (10)	68/10cp		2½	6
	Maxwell (FR) *MmeCHead-Maarek,France* 3-9-2 OPeslier (7)	62/10		sn	7

1148

	Illustrator *SirMichaelStoute,GB* 3-9-2 RHughes (4)	15/1	nk 8
9	Sign of The Wolf *FRohaut,France* 3-9-2 TJarnet (6)	19/1	5 9
	Rios (FR) *GBrillet,France* 3-9-2 PBruneau (9)	115/1	nk 10
	Spartacus (IRE) *APO'Brien,Ireland* 3-9-2 CO'Donoghue (1)	68/10cp	11
	Ecurie Mister Ess A.S. 11ran 2m01.10		120+/117/116/114/114/108

MILAN Sunday, Jun 22 FIRM

34 Gran Premio di Milano (Gr 1) (3yo+) £169,401 — 1½m

	LEADERSHIP *SaeedbinSuroor,GB* 4-9-6 RHills	41/10	1
19	WARRSAN (IRE) *CEBrittain,GB* 5-9-6 PRobinson	1/5f	1¾ 2
	MAKTUB (ITY) *BGrizzetti,Italy* 4-9-6 MDemuro	9/1	9 3
	Rainer (FR) *JBUdaondo,Italy* 4-9-6 CColombi	89/10	4 4
	Levirat (GER) *MHofer,Germany* 4-9-6 JPalik	25/1	1¼ 5
	Olaso (GER) *PVovcenko,Germany* 4-9-6 EPedroza	126/10	19 6
	Godolphin 6ran 2m28.30		124/120/105

NEWMARKET Saturday, Jun 28 GOOD to FIRM (July Course)

35 Betfair Criterion Stks (Gr 3) (3yo+) £29,000 — 7f

	TRADE FAIR *RCharlton* 3-8-7 RHughes (9)	10/11f	1
32	JUST JAMES *JNoseda* 4-9-2 DaneO'Neill (3)	9/2	4 2
	KING OF HAPPINESS (USA) *SirMichaelStoute* 4-9-2 (t) KDalgleish (6)	10/1	3 3
	Meshaheer (USA) *SaeedbinSuroor* 4-9-2 (t) LDettori (1)	6/1	2½ 4
	Atavus *GGMargarson* 6-9-2 JMackay (2)	25/1	1¼ 5
	Polar Ben *JRFanshawe* 4-9-2 MFenton (5)	20/1	hd 6
	Monkston Point (IRE) *DWPArbuthnot* 7-9-2 (v) SWhitworth (7)	100/1	nk 7
	Shiny *CEBrittain* 4-8-13 PRobinson (11)	66/1	2 8
	Touch Down (GER) *DRichardson,Germany* 5-9-2 JQuinn (8)	50/1	1½ 9
	Battle Chant (USA) *EALDunlop* 3-8-7 (t) SDrowne (10)	20/1	sh 10
	Patsy's Double *MBlanshard* 5-9-2 SSanders (4)	25/1	¾ 11
	Mr K. Abdulla 11ran 1m23.84		124/116+/108+/101/98/98

CURRAGH Sunday, Jun 29 GOOD to FIRM

36 Budweiser Irish Derby (Gr 1) (3yo c+f) £515,105 — 1½m

21	ALAMSHAR (IRE) *JOxx* 3-9-0 JMurtagh (2)	4/1	1
18	DALAKHANI (IRE) *AdeRoyerDupre,France* 3-9-0 CSoumillon (9)	4/7f	½ 2
	ROOSEVELT (IRE) *APO'Brien* 3-9-0 CO'Donoghue (3)	150/1	3½ 3
21	Brian Boru *APO'Brien* 3-9-0 (t) JPSpencer (10)	12/1	2½ 4
21	The Great Gatsby (IRE) *APO'Brien* 3-9-0 MJKinane (5)	6/1	3 5
	Powerscourt *APO'Brien* 3-9-0 JAHeffernan (7)	12/1	¾ 6
14	Napper Tandy (IRE) *JSBolger* 3-9-0 (t) KJManning (1)	40/1	2 7
	Handel (IRE) *APO'Brien* 3-9-0 PCosgrave (4)	25/1	5 8
	High Country (IRE) *APO'Brien* 3-9-0 TPQueally (6)	150/1	20 9
	H. H. Aga Khan 9ran 2m28.20		130+/129+/123/119/112/111/108

SAINT-CLOUD Sunday, Jun 29 GOOD

37 Grand Prix de Saint-Cloud (Gr 1) (3yo+) £139,853 — 1½m

Order as they passed the post: Millstreet was demoted to sixth for causing interference

22	ANGE GABRIEL (FR) *ELibaud,France* 5-9-8 TJarnet (5)	2/1	1
19	POLISH SUMMER *AFabre,France* 6-9-8 RHughes (3)	149/10	1½ 2
	MILLSTREET *SaeedbinSuroor,GB* 4-9-8 RHills (9)	7/10cpf	nk 3
	Loxias (FR) *CLaffon-Parias,France* 4-9-8 (b) TThulliez (2)	99/10	½ 4
1	Sulamani (IRE) *SaeedbinSuroor,GB* 4-9-8 LDettori (7)	7/10cpf	2 5
22	Ana Marie (FR) *PHDemercastel,France* 4-9-5 SPasquier (1)	23/1	sh 6
	Trumbaka (IRE) *MmeCHead-Maarek,France* 4-9-5 OPeslier (6)	149/10	hd 7
	Labirinto (USA) *RodolpheCollet,France* 5-9-8 FSpanu (8)	40/1	2 8
	Tigertail (FR) *RodolpheCollet,France* 4-9-5 TGillet (10)	42/1	¾ 9
	Dance Routine *AFabre,France* 4-9-5 MSautjeau (4)	149/10	3 10
	Mme H. Devin 10ran 2m30.90		121/118/119?/118/115/112+/112

SANDOWN Friday, Jul 4 GOOD

38 Gala Stks (L) (3yo+) £18,560 — 1¼m7y

	IKHTYAR (IRE) *JHMGosden* 3-8-8 RHills (5)	5/2f	1
	ROYAL STAMP (USA) *JHMGosden* 4-9-5 RHughes (7)	16/1	6 2
	NAHEEF (IRE) *SaeedbinSuroor* 4-9-8 LDettori (2)	13/2	½ 3
	Island House (IRE) *GWragg* 7-9-8 DHolland (4)	8/1	nk 4
	Burning Sun (USA) *HRACecil* 4-9-5 TQuinn (13)	9/2	2 5
19	Pawn Broker *DRCElsworth* 6-9-5 DaneO'Neill (11)	28/1	¾ 6
	Leo's Luckyman (USA) *MJohnston* 4-9-5 JFanning (8)	16/1	nk 7
21	Lundy's Lane (IRE) *CEBrittain* 3-8-8 SSanders (6)	14/1	1¾ 8
	Imoya (IRE) *BJMeehan* 4-9-0 PatEddery (12)	66/1	2½ 9

19 Ulundi *PRWebber* 8-9-5 MJKinane (10) 16/1 ¾ 10
Artistic Lad *SirMichaelStoute* 3-8-8 KFallon (9) 5/1 5 11
Foodbroker Founder *DRCElsworth* 3-8-8 MartinDwyer (1) 16/1 ¾ 12
Mr Hamdan Al Maktoum 12ran 2m06.35 124/112+/114/114/106/105

SANDOWN Saturday, Jul 5 GOOD

39 Coral-Eclipse Stks (Gr 1) (3yo+) £214,600 1¼m7y

28 FALBRAV (IRE) *LMCumani* 5-9-7 DHolland (14) 8/1 1
28 NAYEF (USA) *MPTregoning* 5-9-7 RHills (5) 6/4f ¾ 2
28 KAIETEUR (USA) *BJMeehan* 4-9-7 EAhern (11) 100/1 1½ 3
28 Olden Times *JLDunlop* 5-9-7 GMosse (12) 20/1 sh 4
27 Victory Moon (SAF) *MdeKock,SouthAfrica* 4-9-4 WayneSmith (13) 66/1 ½ 5
28 Islington (IRE) *SirMichaelStoute* 4-9-4 KFallon (7) 9/2 nk 6
Comfy (USA) *SirMichaelStoute* 4-9-7 RHughes (4) 50/1 1¼ 7
28 Grandera (IRE) *SaeedbinSuroor* 5-9-7 LDettori (15) 9/1 1½ 8
26 Hold That Tiger (USA) *APO'Brien,Ireland* 3-8-10 MJKinane (6) 10/1 ½ 9
21 Balestrini (IRE) *APO'Brien,Ireland* 3-8-10 GDuffield (8) 20/1 1½ 10
21 Dutch Gold (USA) *CEBrittain* 3-8-10 PRobinson (9) 28/1 4 11
21 Norse Dancer (IRE) *DRCElsworth* 3-8-10 TQuinn (10) 6/1 5 12
Delsarte (USA) *MJohnston* 3-8-10 KDalgleish (1) 14/1 5 13
Izdiham (IRE) *MPTregoning* 4-9-7 (b) WSupple (2) 100/1 3 14
Narrative (IRE) *SaeedbinSuroor* 5-9-7 (t) JPSpencer (3) 100/1 13 15
Scuderia Rencati Srl 15ran 2m05.59 126+/124+/121/121/117+/116/116

NEWMARKET Tuesday, Jul 8 GOOD to FIRM (July Course)

40 Chippenham Lodge Stud Cherry Hinton Stks (Gr 2) (2yo f) £40,600 6f

ATTRACTION *MJohnston* 2-8-12 KDarley (3) 4/7f 1
PEARL GREY *DRLoder* 2-8-9 LDettori (8) 11/2 5 2
BIRTHDAY SUIT (IRE) *TDEasterby* 2-8-9 KFallon (1) 7/1 1 3
Menhoubah (USA) *CEBrittain* 2-8-9 DHolland (6) 14/1 nk 4
Tolzey (USA) *MRChannon* 2-8-9 SDrowne (7) 16/1 ½ 5
Crafty Fancy (IRE) *DJSffrenchDavis* 2-8-9 JFEgan (4) 33/1 ½ 6
Rosehearty (USA) *DRLoder* 2-8-9 (v) JPSpencer (5) 20/1 ½ 7
Glebe Garden *MLWBell* 2-8-9 MFenton (2) 33/1 4 8
Duke of Roxburghe 8ran 1m11.10 114+/96+/94/93/91/90

41 Princess of Wales's UAE Equestrian and Racing Federation Stks (Gr 2) (3yo+) £58,000 1½m

MILLENARY *JLDunlop* 6-9-2 (b) PatEddery (2) 5/1 1
31 BANDARI (IRE) *MJohnston* 4-9-2 RHills (4) 15/2 1½ 2
GAMUT (IRE) *SirMichaelStoute* 4-9-2 (t) KFallon (1) 5/1 1 3
31 Bollin Eric *TDEasterby* 4-9-7 KDarley (5) 2/1f 1½ 4
31 Zindabad (FR) *MJohnston* 7-9-2 DHolland (6) 8/1 nk 5
High Accolade *MPTregoning* 3-8-6 MartinDwyer (3) 7/2 1¼ 6
Mr L. Neil Jones 6ran 2m27.60 121/118/116+/119/113/113

NEWMARKET Thursday, Jul 10 GOOD to FIRM (July Course)

42 Darley July Cup (Gr 1) (3yo+) £145,000 6f

25 OASIS DREAM *JHMGosden* 3-8-13 RHughes (11) 9/2 1
32 CHOISIR (AUS) *PaulPerry,Australia* 4-9-5 (es) JMurtagh (1) 9/4f 1½ 2
32 AIRWAVE *HCandy* 3-8-10 KFallon (9) 11/4 nk 3
32 Zipping (IRE) *RCollet,France* 4-9-5 DBonilla (12) 16/1 2 4
25 Bahamian Pirate (USA) *DNicholls* 8-9-5 CSoumillon (2) 40/1 nk 5
32 Continent *DNicholls* 6-9-5 (t) OPeslier (16) 40/1 1 6
32 Needwood Blade *BAMcMahon* 5-9-5 WSupple (6) 50/1 ½ 7
6 Tante Rose (IRE) *BWHills* 3-8-10 MHills (15) 66/1 1¼ 8
32 Orientor *JSGoldie* 5-9-5 JPSpencer (7) 33/1 nk 9
32 Twilight Blues (IRE) *BJMeehan* 4-9-5 EAhern (3) 25/1 nk 10
25 Acclamation *LGCottrell* 4-9-5 PatEddery (18) 14/1 1¾ 11
35 Just James *JNoseda* 4-9-5 DHolland (13) 16/1 1¼ 12
Membership (USA) *CEBrittain* 3-8-13 LDettori (10) 16/1 ½ 13
Striking Ambition *GCBravery* 3-8-13 GCarter (5) 16/1 2 14
14 Tomahawk (USA) *APO'Brien,Ireland* 3-8-13 (v) MJKinane (14) 25/1 2½ 15
32 Steenberg (IRE) *MHTompkins* 4-9-5 (b) PRobinson (17) 100/1 6 16
Mr K. Abdulla 16ran 1m09.94 128/126/120/119/118?/115

CURRAGH Sunday, Jul 13 GOOD

43 Darley Irish Oaks (Gr 1) (3yo f) £155,310 1½m

VINTAGE TIPPLE (IRE) *PatrickMullins* 3-9-0 LDettori (8) 12/1 1
20 L'ANCRESSE (IRE) *APO'Brien* 3-9-0 JAHeffernan (10) 33/1 1½ 2
20 CASUAL LOOK (USA) *AMBalding,GB* 3-9-0 MDwyer (2) 7/1 hd 3

Yesterday (IRE) *APO'Brien* 3-9-0 MJKinane (6).. 11/8f   2 4
     Juliette (IRE) *JOxx* 3-9-0 (t) JMurtagh (7) 33/1   2 5
     Spanish Sun (USA) *SirMichaelStoute,GB* 3-9-0 RHughes (11)....................... 9/2 1½ 6
     Ocean Silk (USA) *JHMGosden,GB* 3-9-0 (b) KDarley (4)............................. 11/2 ½ 7
     Snippets (IRE) *JSBolger* 3-9-0 KJManning (5)... 11/1 1 8
     Jakarta Jade (IRE) *KPrendergast* 3-9-0 DPMcDonogh (3)........................ 100/1 ¾ 9
     Miss Nashwan (IRE) *DKWeld* 3-9-0 (b) PJSmullen (1)............................... 100/1 9 10

20 Hanami *JARToller,GB* 3-9-0 KFallon (9).. 12/1 4½ 11
     Mr Patrick J. O'Donovan 11ran 2m28.30   117/114/114/111+/107/105

ASCOT Saturday, Jul 26   GOOD to SOFT

44   **King George VI and Queen Elizabeth Diamond Stks (Gr 1) (3yo+) £435,000**   1½m

36 ALAMSHAR (IRE) *JOxx,Ireland* 3-8-9 JMurtagh (5).................................... 13/2   1
37 SULAMANI (IRE) *SaeedbinSuroor* 4-9-7 LDettori (6).................................. 9/2 3½ 2
21 KRIS KIN (USA) *SirMichaelStoute* 3-8-9 KFallon (3) 7/2   2 3
41 Bollin Eric *TDEasterby* 4-9-7 KDarley (7) .... 16/1 ½ 4
39 Falbrav (IRE) *LMCumani* 5-9-7 DHolland (1)... 12/1 3 5
34 Warrsan (IRE) *CEBrittain* 5-9-7 PRobinson (14).. 14/1 ½ 6
39 Nayef (USA) *MPTregoning* 5-9-7 RHills (4) 3/1f 1½ 7
41 Millenary *JLDunlop* 6-9-7 (b) PatEddery (10) 16/1 2 8
39 Izdiham (IRE) *MPTregoning* 4-9-7 WSupple (12) 200/1 4 9
39 Victory Moon (SAF) *MdeKock,SouthAfrica* 4-9-2 WSmith (13)................ 12/1 hd 10
39 Grandera (IRE) *SaeedbinSuroor* 5-9-7 (s) MJKinane (2)............................. 33/1 11 11
34 Leadership *SaeedbinSuroor* 4-9-7 JPSpencer (8) 25/1 6 12
     H.H. Aga Khan 12ran 2m33.26   133/128+/124+/123+/119/118

GOODWOOD Wednesday, Jul 30   GOOD to SOFT

45   **Sussex Stks (Gr 1) (3yo+) £165,300**   1m

12 REEL BUDDY (USA) *RHannon* 5-9-7 PatEddery (7) 20/1   1
26 STATUE OF LIBERTY (USA) *APO'Brien,Ireland* 3-8-13 MJKinane (9)...... 6/1 hd 2
39 NORSE DANCER (IRE) *DRCElsworth* 3-8-13 (v) TQuinn (8)..................... 8/1 sh 3
26 Zafeen (FR) *MRChannon* 3-8-13 DHolland (6) .... 11/2 nk 4
28 Moon Ballad (IRE) *SaeedbinSuroor* 4-9-7 (t) LDettori (4).......................... 11/4 nk 5
35 Trade Fair *RCharlton* 3-8-13 RHughes (3)... 9/4f 6 6
27 Blatant *SaeedbinSuroor* 3-8-13 (v+t) JPSpencer (4) .... 50/1 nk 7
     Eventuail (ARG) *WJHaggas* 5-9-7 KFallon (11) 16/1 1¾ 8
33 Spartacus (IRE) *APO'Brien,Ireland* 3-8-13 WSupple (10) 20/1 1 9
     Speedlith Group 9ran 1m40.00   118/115/115/114+/116

CURRAGH Sunday, Aug 10   FIRM

46   **Royal Whip Stks (Gr 2) (3yo+) £54,545**   1¼m

     HIGH CHAPARRAL (IRE) *APO'Brien* 4-9-13 MJKinane (4) 9/10f   1
3 IMPERIAL DANCER (IRE) *MRChannon,GB* 5-9-6 RHughes (1) .... 11/2 ¾ 2
     IN TIME'S EYE *DKWeld* 4-9-6 (b) PJSmullen (2) .... 3/1 nk 3
     Mkuzi (USA) *JOxx* 4-9-6 JMurtagh (6) 8/1 2 4
7 Private Charter *BWHills,GB* 3-8-11 MHills (5) .... 9/1 ½ 5
15 Cat Belling (IRE) *KPrendergast* 3-8-8 PShanahan (3)................................... 20/1 1½ 6
     Mr Michael Tabor 6ran 2m04.92   126+/117+/117/113/111/105?

47   **Independent Waterford Wedgwood Phoenix Stks (Gr 1) (2yo c+f) £117,902**   6f

     ONE COOL CAT (USA) *APO'Brien* 2-9-0 MJKinane (2).............................. 11/8   1
     OLD DEUTERONOMY (USA) *APO'Brien* 2-9-0 JAHeffernan (5)............. 12/1 1 2
24 THREE VALLEYS (USA) *RCharlton,GB* 2-9-0 RHughes (4)...................... 4/6f 3 3
     Devil Moon (IRE) *APO'Brien* 2-9-0 CO'Donoghue (3)............................... 33/1 ¾ 4
     Notable Lady (IRE) *NACallaghan,GB* 2-8-11 JPSpencer (6) .... 50/1 nk 5
     Wathab (IRE) *KPrendergast* 2-9-0 DPMcDonogh (7).................................. 20/1 2 6
     Born In America (USA) *APO'Brien* 2-9-0 TPQueally (1).............................. 33/1 14 7
     Mrs John Magnier 7ran 1m11.35   112+/109/101/98/95/92+

NEWBURY Saturday, Aug 16   GOOD to FIRM

48   **Stan James Geoffrey Freer Stks (Gr 2) (3yo+) £59,500**   1m5f61y

     MUBTAKER (USA) *MPTregoning* 6-9-3 RHills (3).................................... 4/6f   1
     SYSTEMATIC *MJohnston* 4-9-3 KDarley (5) 10/3 3½ 2
29 MAMOOL (IRE) *SaeedbinSuroor* 4-9-6 (b) LDettori (1).............................. 4/1 3 3
21 Let Me Try Again (IRE) *TGMills* 3-8-6 (v) DHolland (4) 16/1 1¾ 4
     Santando *CEBrittain* 3-8-6 (v) JFortune (2) 50/1 10 5
     Mr Hamdan Al Maktoum 5ran 2m47.76   124/118+/115/110

ARLINGTON Saturday, Aug 16   GOOD

49   **Arlington Million Stks (Gr 1) (3yo+) £372,671**   1¼m

     Order as they passed the post: Storming Home was demoted to fourth place for causing
     interference to the dead-heaters

STORMING HOME *NDDrysdale,USA* 5-9-0 (b) GaryStevens.................. 24/10f 1
44 SULAMANI (IRE) *SaeedbinSuroor,GB* 4-9-0 DFlores .... 28/10 ½ 2
28 PAOLINI (GER) *AWohler,Germany* 6-9-0 ASuborics............................... 175/10 hd 3
39 KAIETEUR (USA) *BJMeehan,GB* 4-9-0 RDouglas .... 37/1 dh 3
   Perfect Soul (IRE) *RLAttfield,Canada* 5-9-0 (b) CNakatani .... 166/10 nk 5
   The Tin Man (USA) *REMandella,USA* 5-9-0 MESmith 59/10 1¾ 6
   Vangelis (USA) *AdeRoyerDupre,France* 4-9-0 CSoumillon .... 54/1 nk 7
   Perfect Drift (USA) *MWJohnson,USA* 4-9-0 PDay .... 38/10 ½ 8
   Honor In War (USA) *PJMcGee,USA* 5-9-0 JValdivia .... 137/10 nk 9
   Tripat (IRE) *RGibson,France* 4-9-0 MJKinane 100/1 3½ 10
18 Touch of Land (FR) *H-APantall,France* 3-8-8 PJSmullen......................... 70/1 3 11
27 Beauchamp Pilot *GAButler,GB* 5-9-0 EAhern 89/1 2 12
39 Olden Times *JLDunlop,GB* 5-9-0 KDesormeaux 21/1 15 13

   Godolphin 13ran 2m02.29   122+/121+/121/121/120/117/116

   LEOPARDSTOWN Sunday, Aug 17 FIRM

50 Desmond Stks (Gr 3) (3yo+) £32,042   1m
21 REFUSE TO BEND (IRE) *DKWeld* 3-9-8 PJSmullen (2) 8/11f 1
   LATINO MAGIC (IRE) *RJOsborne* 3-9-0 RMBurke (1) 10/1 3 2
   MIDDLEMARCH (IRE) *APO'Brien* 3-9-0 MJKinane (3) 10/1 2 3
   Sea Dart (USA) *JOxx* 3-9-6 FMBerry (4) 3/1 3 4
36 Napper Tandy (IRE) *JSBolger* 3-9-0 KJManning (5)............................... 10/1 nk 5
   Livadiya (IRE) *HRogers* 7-9-3 DPMcDonogh (7) 10/1 1 6
   Military Option (USA) *DKWeld* 3-9-0 (t) NGMcCullagh (6) 33/1 13 7

   Moyglare Stud Farm 7ran 1m37.30   124/108/103/101/94/90

   COLOGNE Sunday, Aug 17 GOOD

51 Credit Suisse Private Banking-Pokal (Gr 1) (3yo+) £83,098   1½m
   DAI JIN *ASchutz,Germany* 3-8-8 OPeslier.. 11/10f 1
   NEXT DESERT (IRE) *ASchutz,Germany* 4-9-6 AStarke 42/10 2½ 2
44 WARRSAN (IRE) *CEBrittain,GB* 5-9-6 PRobinson 27/10 2 3
   Sabiango (GER) *AWohler,Germany* 4-9-6 EPedroza 22/10 4½ 4
   Sagittarius *RHaugen,Norway* 7-9-6 FDiaz... 20/1 9 5

   W. H. Sport International 5ran 2m28.53   123/121/117/109

   DEAUVILLE Sunday, Aug 17 GOOD to SOFT

52 Prix du Haras de Fresnay-Le-Buffard Jacques le Marois (Gr 1) (3yo+)   1m
   £201,197
15 SIX PERFECTIONS (FR) *PBary,France* 3-8-9 TThulliez (5) 28/10cp 1
12 DOMEDRIVER (IRE) *PBary,France* 5-9-4 KFallon (3)............................. 28/10cp sn 2
   TELEGNOSIS (JPN) *HSugiura,Japan* 4-9-4 MKatsuura (8) 86/10cp 1 3
   Special Kaldoun (IRE) *DSmaga,France* 4-9-4 DBoeuf (10) 126/10 1 4
27 Dubai Destination (USA) *SaeedbinSuroor,GB* 4-9-4 LDettori (6).......... 14/10cpf 2½ 5
23 Nebraska Tornado (USA) *AFabre,France* 3-8-9 RHughes (2) 68/10 1½ 6
26 Martillo (GER) *RSuerland,Germany* 3-8-13 WMongil (12) 94/10 3 7
26 Clodovil (IRE) *AFabre,France* 3-8-13 IMendizabal (9) 59/10cp 6 8
   Vahorimix (FR) *AFabre,France* 5-9-4 CSoumillon (1) .... 59/10cp ¾ 9
   Lohengrin (JPN) *MIto,Japan* 4-9-4 HGoto (11)................................... 86/10cp ¾ 10
   Fomalhaut (USA) *PBary,France* 4-9-4 C-PLemaire (4) 59/10cp 11
45 Blatant *SaeedbinSuroor,GB* 4-9-4 (v+t) JPSpencer (13) 14/10cpf 12

   Niarchos Family 12ran 1m38.30   124/128/125/123/116/109

   YORK Tuesday, Aug 19 GOOD to FIRM

53 Weatherbys Insurance Lonsdale Stks (Gr 3) (3yo+) £58,000   1m7f198y
44 BOLLIN ERIC *TDEasterby* 4-9-6 KDarley (2) 7/4f 1
   COVER UP (IRE) *SirMichaelStoute* 6-9-1 KFallon (4) 15/2 2 2
41 ZINDABAD (FR) *MJohnston* 7-9-1 (v) KDalgleish (5).......................... 11/1 sh 3
29 Persian Punch (IRE) *DRCElsworth* 10-9-4 MartinDwyer (1)................ 11/2 1½ 4
29 Jardines Lookout (IRE) *APJarvis* 6-9-1 DHolland (3)........................... 5/1 ½ 5
16 Boreas *LMCumani* 8-9-1 LDettori (6) 4/1 1½ 6

   Sir Neil Westbrook 6ran 3m23.25   123/114/114/115/111/109

54 Juddmonte International Stks (Gr 1) (3yo+) £266,800   1¼m88y
44 FALBRAV (IRE) *LMCumani* 5-9-5 DHolland (2) 5/2 1
33 MAGISTRETTI (USA) *NACallaghan* 3-8-11 KFallon (9)........................... 16/1 2 2
44 NAYEF (USA) *MPTregoning* 5-9-5 RHills (6) 11/4 1¾ 3
   Mingun (USA) *APO'Brien,Ireland* 3-8-11 MJKinane (7).......................... 12/1 1½ 4
31 Indian Creek *DRCElsworth* 5-9-5 TQuinn (8).................................... 20/1 nk 5
45 Norse Dancer (IRE) *DRCElsworth* 3-8-11 (v) PRobinson (5) 20/1 2 6
26 Kalaman (IRE) *SirMichaelStoute* 3-8-11 CSoumillon (3)...................... 15/8f 1¾ 7

1152

44 Izdiham (IRE) *MPTregoning* 4-9-5 (v) WSupple (4) 150/1   22 8
      Scuderia Rencati Srl 8ran 2m06.84   129+/124/121/117/117/112

55 **Daily Telegraph Great Voltigeur Stks (Gr 2) (3yo c+g)** £87,000   1m3f198y

36 POWERSCOURT *APO'Brien,Ireland* 3-8-9 MJKinane (7).............................. 5/1   1
36 BRIAN BORU *APO'Brien,Ireland* 3-8-9 (t) JPSpencer (1) .... 8/1   nk 2
      HAWK FLYER (USA) *SirMichaelStoute* 3-8-9 KFallon (2) 3/1f   2½ 3
39 Delsarte (USA) *MJohnston* 3-8-9 KDalgleish (10) 5/1   4 4
      Dubai Success *BWHills* 3-8-9 MHills (4).. 50/1   1¼ 5
41 High Accolade *MPTregoning* 3-8-12 (b) MartinDwyer (5) 4/1   1½ 6
39 Dutch Gold (USA) *CEBrittain* 3-8-9 (t) PRobinson (9).......................... 10/1   1 7
      Yawmi *BWHills* 3-8-9 RHills (8) 12/1   3 8
      Piano Star *SirMichaelStoute* 3-8-9 RHughes (3)................................... 14/1   7 9
      Mrs John Magnier 9ran 2m27.81   122/121+/117/109/107/107

      YORK Wednesday, Aug 20   GOOD to FIRM

56 **Aston Upthorpe Yorkshire Oaks (Gr 1) (3yo+ f+m)** £145,000   1m3f198y

39 ISLINGTON (IRE) *SirMichaelStoute* 4-9-4 KFallon (5)........................... 8/11f   1
43 OCEAN SILK (USA) *JHMGosden* 3-8-8 JFortune (3) 18/1   1 2
20 SUMMITVILLE *JGGiven* 3-8-8 MFenton (4)... 25/1   3 3
37 Tigertail (IRE) *RodolpheCollet,France* 4-9-4 LDettori (1) 16/1   1¾ 4
43 L'Ancresse (IRE) *APO'Brien,Ireland* 3-8-8 MJKinane (8)........................ 7/1   ½ 5
      Zee Zee Top *SirMichaelStoute* 4-9-4 PatEddery (2) .... 10/1   hd 6
43 Casual Look (USA) *AMBalding* 3-8-8 MartinDwyer (6)............................ 8/1   2 7
      Chorist *WJHaggas* 4-9-4 DHolland (7) 14/1   9 8
      Exors of the late Lord Weinstock 8ran 2m27.44   121/119/114/111/110/110

      YORK Thursday, Aug 21   GOOD to FIRM

57 **Victor Chandler Nunthorpe Stks (Gr 1) (2yo+)** £116,000   5f3y

42 OASIS DREAM *JHMGosden* 3-9-9 RHughes (2) 4/9f   1
      THE TATLING (IRE) *JMBradley* 6-9-11 DHolland (3) 9/1   2½ 2
42 ACCLAMATION *LGCottrell* 4-9-11 KDarley (1) 9/1   1¼ 3
25 Dominica *MPTregoning* 4-9-8 MartinDwyer (6) 8/1   1 4
42 Orientor *JSGoldie* 5-9-11 KFallon (8) 40/1   1 5
25 The Trader (IRE) *MBlanshard* 5-9-11 (b) JQuinn (10) .... 20/1   ¾ 6
42 Bahamian Pirate (USA) *DNicholls* 8-9-11 MHills (9) 50/1   3½ 7
42 Continent *DNicholls* 6-9-11 (t) LDettori (5)... 14/1   6 8
      Mr K. Abdulla 8ran 56.20secs   129/120/116/109/109/106

      DEAUVILLE Sunday, Aug 31   SOFT

58 **Prix Morny Casinos Barriere (Gr 1) (2yo c+f)** £98,517   6f

      WHIPPER (USA) *RCollet,France* 2-9-0 SMaillot (3) 258/10   1
      MUCH FASTER (IRE) *PBary,France* 2-8-11 TThulliez (5) 9/10f   2 2
      DENEBOLA (USA) *PBary,France* 2-8-11 C-PLemaire (1) .... 91/10   sh 3
47 Old Deuteronomy (USA) *APO'Brien,Ireland* 2-9-0 JPSpencer (2) 32/10cp   5 4
      Carrizo Creek (IRE) *BJMeehan,GB* 2-9-0 DHolland (6) 39/10   4 5
      Haskilclara (FR) *YdeNicolay,France* 2-8-11 OPeslier (7).......................... 72/10   1 6
      Colossus (IRE) *APO'Brien,Ireland* 2-9-0 KFallon (4)........................... 32/10cp   2½ 7
      Haydn (USA) *APO'Brien,Ireland* 2-9-0 CO'Donoghue (8).................... 32/10cp   6 8
      Mr Elias Zaccour 8ran 1m14.00   118/110+/109+/99

      HAYDOCK Saturday, Sep 6   GOOD to SOFT

59 **Stanley Leisure Sprint Cup (Gr 1) (3yo+)** £130,500   6f

      SOMNUS *TDEasterby* 3-8-12 TEDurcan (7)... 12/1   1
57 OASIS DREAM *JHMGosden* 3-8-12 RHughes (5) 8/11f   1¼ 2
42 AIRWAVE *HCandy* 3-8-9 DaneO'Neill (9)... 10/3   ¾ 3
42 Steenberg (IRE) *MHTompkins* 4-9-0 SSanders (10)............................. 100/1   1¾ 4
      Fayr Jag *TDEasterby* 4-9-0 WSupple (6) 25/1   1¾ 5
57 The Tatling (IRE) *JMBradley* 6-9-0 KDarley (2)................................... 16/1   nk 6
42 Twilight Blues (IRE) *BJMeehan* 4-9-0 EAhern (4)................................. 50/1   1¾ 7
57 Orientor *JSGoldie* 5-9-0 PHanagan (1).. 25/1   ¾ 8
      Swedish Shave (FR) *RGibson,France* 5-9-0 TJarnet (3)......................... 25/1   2½ 9
57 Continent *DNicholls* 6-9-0 (v) KDalgleish (8) 25/1   27 10
      Legard Sidebottom & Sykes 10ran 1m13.49   125/122/117+/115?/110/109

      KEMPTON Saturday, Sep 6   GOOD

60 **Coral September Stks (Gr 3) (3yo+)** £20,825   1½m

48 MUBTAKER (USA) *MPTregoning* 6-9-8 RHills (1)................................... 8/13f   1
      FIRST CHARTER *SirMichaelStoute* 4-9-3 PatEddery (2) 13/2   5 2
54 INDIAN CREEK *DRCElsworth* 5-9-8 TQuinn (4).................................... 4/1   1½ 3
      The Whistling Teal *GWragg* 7-9-3 JFEgan (5)...................................... 8/1   ¾ 4

Nadour Al Bahr (IRE) *TGMills* 8-9-3 RMiles (3).. 25/1   hd 5
Mr Hamdan Al Maktoum 5ran 2m31.72   127/114+/116/110/110

LEOPARDSTOWN Saturday, Sep 6   FIRM

61   Ireland The Food Island Champion Stks (Gr 1) (3yo+) £395,139   1¼m

46 HIGH CHAPARRAL (IRE) *APO'Brien* 4-9-4 MJKinane (6) 4/1   1
54 FALBRAV (IRE) *LMCumani,GB* 5-9-4 DHolland (5)...................................... 11/4   nk 2
56 ISLINGTON (IRE) *SirMichaelStoute,GB* 4-9-1 KFallon (2)........................... 16/1   hd 3
44 Alamshar (IRE) *JOxx* 3-8-11 JMurtagh (1) 5/4f   1½ 4
45 Moon Ballad (IRE) *SaeedbinSuroor,GB* 4-9-4 (v+t) LDettori (4) .... 12/1   hd 5
26 France *APO'Brien* 3-8-11 JAHeffernan (7) 100/1   25 6
43 Vintage Tipple (IRE) *PatrickMullins* 3-8-8 PJSmullen (3) 10/1   6 7
Mr Michael Tabor 7ran 2m03.30   128+/127+/124/124/124

BADEN-BADEN Sunday, Sep 7   GOOD

62   Grosser Bugatti Preis (Gr 1) (3yo+) £347,222   1½m

48 MAMOOL (IRE) *SaeedbinSuroor,GB* 4-9-6 LDettori 54/10   1
29 BLACK SAM BELLAMY (IRE) *APO'Brien,Ireland* 4-9-6 MJKinane....... 25/2   ½ 2
1   DANO-MAST *FPoulsen,Denmark* 7-9-6 THellier................................. 29/2   2 3
    Ransom O'War (USA) *FrauEMader,Germany* 3-8-9 SKMChin 3/1   2½ 4
48 Systematic *MJohnston,GB* 4-9-6 DHolland .... 42/10   ½ 5
51 Next Desert (IRE) *ASchutz,Germany* 4-9-6 AStarke.............................. 22/10f 1¼ 6
    Storm Trooper (GER) *ASchutz,Germany* 3-8-9 ASuborics .... 21/2   nk 7
37 Loxias (FR) *CLaffon-Parias,France* 4-9-6 (b) C-PLemaire.......................... 5/1   nk 8
Godolphin 8ran 2m32.75   122/121/118/112/113/111

LONGCHAMP Sunday, Sep 7   GOOD

63   NetJets Prix du Moulin de Longchamp (Gr 1) (3yo+ c+f) £119,042   1m

52 NEBRASKA TORNADO (USA) *AFabre,France* 3-8-8 RHughes (7)...... 146/10   1
52 LOHENGRIN (JPN) *MIto,Japan* 4-9-2 HGoto (14) .... 13/1cp   ½ 2
13 BRIGHT SKY (IRE) *ELellouche,France* 4-8-13 DBoeuf (1)................... 2/1f   1 3
30 Soviet Song (IRE) *JRFanshawe,GB* 3-8-11 OUrbina (5) 164/10   1½ 4
52 Clodovil (IRE) *AFabre,France* 3-8-11 CSoumillon (4) 81/10   1½ 5
27 Where Or When (IRE) *TGMills,GB* 4-9-2 KDarley (8) .... 29/1   ½ 6
52 Domedriver (IRE) *PBary,France* 5-9-2 TThulliez (3) .... 49/10   nk 7
52 Special Kaldoun (IRE) *DSmaga,France* 4-9-2 TGillet (9) .... 138/10   ¾ 8
45 Statue of Liberty (USA) *APO'Brien,Ireland* 3-8-11 JPSpencer (6).............. 34/1   sh 9
13 Dandoun *JLDunlop,GB* 5-9-2 TJarnet (11).. 46/1   2 10
50 Refuse To Bend (IRE) *DKWeld,Ireland* 3-8-11 PJSmullen (10)............... 39/10cp hd 11
50 Military Option (USA) *DKWeld,Ireland* 3-8-11 PShanahan (2)................ 39/10cp nk 12
52 Telegnosis (JPN) *HSugiura,Japan* 4-9-2 MKatsuura (13)....................... 13/1cp sh 13
45 Reel Buddy (USA) *RHannon,GB* 5-9-2 PatEddery (12) 186/10   1 14
Mr K. Abdulla 14ran 1m38.70   123/125/120/116+/115/114+

DONCASTER Friday, Sep 12   GOOD

64   Champagne Stks (Gr 2) (2yo c+g) £79,200   7f

    LUCKY STORY (USA) *MJohnston* 2-9-0 DHolland (2) 2/1   1
    AUDITORIUM *SirMichaelStoute* 2-8-10 KFallon (4) .... 8/1   nk 2
    HAAFHD *BWHills* 2-8-10 RHills (1)... 10/11f   2 3
    Azarole (IRE) *JRFanshawe* 2-8-10 JPSpencer (5)................................. 20/1   hd 4
    Milk It Mick *JAOsborne* 2-8-10 TQuinn (3) 20/1   3 5
    Leitrim House *BJMeehan* 2-8-10 LDettori (6) 25/1   4 6
Mr Abdulla BuHaleeba 6ran 1m27.92   119/114/109/109/102/92

DONCASTER Saturday, Sep 13   GOOD

65   Seabiscuit St Leger Stks (Gr 1) (3yo c+f) £240,000   1¾m132y

55 BRIAN BORU *APO'Brien,Ireland* 3-9-0 (t) JPSpencer (9) 5/4f   1
55 HIGH ACCOLADE *MPTregoning* 3-9-0 MartinDwyer (8)...................... 8/1   1¼ 2
    PHOENIX REACH (IRE) *AMBalding* 3-9-0 DHolland (5)...................... 8/1   1½ 3
    Maharib (IRE) *DKWeld,Ireland* 3-9-0 RHills (2) 9/1   2 4
    Moments of Joy *RGuest* 3-8-11 SSanders (4)....................................... 7/1   1½ 5
48 Santando *CEBrittain* 3-9-0 (v) PRobinson (13).................................... 200/1   6 6
48 Let Me Try Again (IRE) *TGMills* 3-9-0 (v) LDettori (6) 20/1   1½ 7
    Gold Medallist *DRCElsworth* 3-9-0 DaneO'Neill (10) 66/1   3½ 8
    Wavertree Boy (IRE) *DRCElsworth* 3-9-0 TQuinn (9) .... 66/1   sh 9
    Westmoreland Road (USA) *MrsAJPerrett* 3-9-0 PatEddery (7) 13/2   4 10
56 Summitville *JJGiven* 3-8-11 MFenton (12)... 16/1   3½ 11
    Titurel *CEBrittain* 3-9-0 BDoyle (11).. 200/1   16 12
Mrs John Magnier 12ran 3m04.64   124/122/120+/117/112+/107

1154

CURRAGH Saturday, Sep 13   FIRM

66   Irish Field St Leger (Gr 1) (3yo+) £119,167   1¾m

	VINNIE ROE (IRE) *DKWeld* 5-9-9 (b) PJSmullen (4)	2/1		1
41	GAMUT (IRE) *SirMichaelStoute,GB* 4-9-9 (t) KFallon (5)	8/1	1	2
55	POWERSCOURT *APO'Brien* 3-8-12 MJKinane (1)	11/4	sh	3
53	Bollin Eric *TDEasterby,GB* 4-9-9 KDarley (9)	15/8f	¾	4
	Queens Wharf (IRE) *MHalford* 5-9-6 TPO'Shea (2)	66/1	8	5
	Rayshan (IRE) *JOxx* 3-8-12 JMurtagh (6)	50/1	4½	6

Mr Seamus Sheridan 6ran 2m58.90   122+/121/121/119

CURRAGH Sunday, Sep 14   FIRM

67   Dunnes Stores National Stks (Gr 1) (2yo) £116,944   7f

47	ONE COOL CAT (USA) *APO'Brien* 2-9-0 MJKinane (2)	4/6f		1
47	WATHAB (IRE) *KPrendergast* 2-9-0 DPMcDonogh (3)	20/1	1	2
	PEARL OF LOVE (IRE) *MJohnston,GB* 2-9-0 DHolland (8)	13/8	nk	3
24	Barbajuan (IRE) *NACallaghan,GB* 2-9-0 JMurtagh (6)	16/1	2	4
	Simple Exchange (IRE) *DKWeld* 2-9-0 PJSmullen (7)	20/1	1½	5
	Celtic Cat (IRE) *APO'Brien* 2-9-0 JAHeffernan (5)	12/1	¾	6
	Groom Raider *MJGrassick* 2-9-0 NGMcCullagh (9)	33/1	2	7
58	Haydn (USA) *APO'Brien* 2-9-0 TPQueally (4)	33/1	13	8

Mrs John Magnier 8ran 1m23.10   116+/113/112/107/103/101

LONGCHAMP Sunday, Sep 14   GOOD to FIRM

68   Prix Niel Casino Barriere d'Enghien-Les-Bains (Gr 2) (3yo c+f) £43,541   1½m

36	DALAKHANI (IRE) *AdeRoyerDupre,France* 3-9-2 CSoumillon (2)	7/10cpf		1
	DOYEN (IRE) *AFabre,France* 3-9-2 LDettori (8)	26/10	1½	2
44	KRIS KIN (USA) *SirMichaelStoute,GB* 3-9-2 KFallon (3)	25/10	2½	3
	Rhythm Mad (FR) *AFabre,France* 3-9-2 OPeslier (1)	30/1	nk	4
33	Look Honey (IRE) *CLerner,France* 3-9-2 YLerner (4)	152/10	5	5
	High Action (USA) *SirMichaelStoute,GB* 3-9-2 JPSpencer (6)	62/1	2	6
18	Diyapour (FR) *AdeRoyerDupre,France* 3-9-2 TJarnet (7)	7/10cpf	10	7

H.H. Aga Khan 7ran 2m27.60   121+/118+/114/114/105/102

69   Prix Vermeille Fouquet's Barriere (Gr 1) (3yo f) £99,202   1½m

6	MEZZO SOPRANO (USA) *SaeedbinSuroor,GB* 3-9-0 LDettori (2)	94/10		1
43	YESTERDAY (IRE) *APO'Brien,Ireland* 3-9-0 JPSpencer (10)	61/10cp	hd	2
23	FIDELITE (IRE) *MmeCHead-Maarek,France* 3-9-0 OPeslier (5)	82/10	3	3
23	Vallee Enchantee (IRE) *ELellouche,France* 3-9-0 DBoeuf (4)	19/10f	sn	4
	Whortleberry (FR) *FRohaut,France* 3-9-0 TJarnet (8)	149/10	nk	5
	Mandela (GER) *RSuerland,Germany* 3-9-0 TThulliez (4)	44/1	1½	6
56	Ocean Silk (USA) *JHMGosden,GB* 3-9-0 KDarley (7)	6/1	1½	7
56	Casual Look (USA) *AMBalding,GB* 3-9-0 MDwyer (9)	187/10	3	8
23	Commercante (FR) *J-MBeguigne,France* 3-9-0 (ec) IMendizabal (1)	87/10	4	9
	Butterfly Blue (IRE) *APO'Brien,Ireland* 3-9-0 CO'Donoghue (11)	61/10cp	20	10
	State of Art (FR) *DSmaga,France* 3-9-0 CSoumillon (3)	62/10		pu

Godolphin 11ran 2m26.10   117/117+/112/112/111/108

ASCOT Saturday, Sep 27   FIRM

70   Queen Elizabeth II Stks (Sponsored By NetJets) (Gr 1) (3yo+) £188,500   1m (Rnd)

61	FALBRAV (IRE) *LMCumani* 5-9-1 DHolland (4)	6/4f		1
30	RUSSIAN RHYTHM (USA) *SirMichaelStoute* 3-8-8 KFallon (9)	3/1	2	2
27	TILLERMAN *MrsAJPerrett* 7-9-1 RHughes (6)	22/1	1¼	3
52	Blatant *SaeedbinSuroor* 4-9-1 (v+t) RHills (7)	100/1	2½	4
63	Soviet Song (IRE) *JRFanshawe* 3-8-8 JPSpencer (13)	8/1	½	5
63	Where Or When (IRE) *TGMills* 4-9-1 KDarley (1)	16/1	1½	6
54	Norse Dancer (IRE) *DRCElsworth* 3-8-11 MartinDwyer (2)	33/1	hd	7
52	Dubai Destination (USA) *SaeedbinSuroor* 4-9-1 (t) LDettori (8)	7/2	1½	8

Scuderia Rencati Srl 8ran 1m38.99   131+/123/121+/114/110/109

BELMONT PARK Saturday, Sep 27   FIRM

71   Turf Classic Invitational Stks (Gr 1) (3yo+) £276,073   1½m

49	SULAMANI (IRE) *SaeedbinSuroor,GB* 4-9-0 JBailey	75/100f		1
	DEELITEFUL IRVING (USA) *MWDickinson,USA* 5-9-0 JBravo	65/10	2¾	2
	BALTO STAR (USA) *TAPletcher,USA* 5-9-0 EPrado	65/10	¾	3
51	Sabiango (GER) *AWohler,Germany* 5-9-0 DFlores	202/10	½	4
37	Polish Summer *AFabre,France* 6-9-0 JVelazquez	61/10	1½	5
	Slew Valley (USA) *GSciacca,USA* 6-9-0 JCastellano	142/10	2	6
	Lunar Sovereign (USA) *KPMcLaughlin,UAE* 4-9-0 RMigliore	36/10	19	7

Godolphin 7ran 2m27.51   123+/118/117/116/114/111

1155

72   Tommy's (The Baby Charity) Cumberland Lodge Stks (Gr 3) (3yo+) £29,750   1½m

65	HIGH ACCOLADE *MPTregoning* 3-8-11 MartinDwyer (3)	9/4f	1
31	COMPTON BOLTER (IRE) *GAButler* 6-9-0 EAhern (5)	4/1	3 2
60	INDIAN CREEK *DRCElsworth* 5-9-5 DaneO'Neill (6)	11/4	hd 3
22	Martaline *AFabre,France* 4-9-5 RHughes (1)	3/1	2½ 4
60	Nadour Al Bahr (IRE) *TGMills* 8-9-0 RMiles (2)	16/1	2 5

Lady Tennant 5ran 2m35.59   122/111/116/112/103

73   Sky Bet Cheveley Park Stks (Gr 1) (2yo f) £98,600   6f

	CARRY ON KATIE (USA) *JNoseda* 2-8-11 LDettori (4)	13/8f	1
	MAJESTIC DESERT *MRChannon* 2-8-11 KFallon (2)	16/1	sh 2
	BADMINTON *CEBrittain* 2-8-11 DHolland (6)	12/1	1¾ 3
	Ruby Rocket (IRE) *HMorrison* 2-8-11 KDarley (8)	10/1	1 4
	Voile (IRE) *RHannon* 2-8-11 PatEddery (5)	25/1	sh 5
	China Eyes (IRE) *BWHills* 2-8-11 MHills (11)	16/1	3 6
	Totally Yours (IRE) *WRMuir* 2-8-11 RMullen (7)	100/1	½ 7
	Indiana Blues *AMBalding* 2-8-11 MartinDwyer (9)	100/1	hd 8
58	Much Faster (IRE) *PBary,France* 2-8-11 TThulliez (3)	3/1	2 9
	Nyramba *JHMGosden* 2-8-11 RHughes (1)	5/1	¾ 10

Mr Mohammed Rashid 10ran 1m13.03   108+/108/103/100/100/92

74   Shadwell Stud Middle Park Stks (Gr 1) (2yo c) £105,560   6f

Order as they passed the post: Three Valleys failed a dope test and was disqualified at a Jockey Club inquiry in January 2004

47	THREE VALLEYS (USA) *RCharlton* 2-8-11 RHughes (10)	2/1f	1
	BALMONT (USA) *JNoseda* 2-8-11 PatEddery (4)	8/1	¾ 2
	HOLBORN (UAE) *MRChannon* 2-8-11 DHolland (7)	50/1	½ 3
64	Auditorium *SirMichaelStoute* 2-8-11 KFallon (9)	8/1	nk 4
58	Whipper (USA) *RCollet,France* 2-8-11 CSoumillon (3)	16/1	½ 5
	Grand Reward *APO'Brien,Ireland* 2-8-11 MJKinane (12)	4/1	nk 6
58	Old Deuteronomy (USA) *APO'Brien,Ireland* 2-8-11 JPSpencer (6)	14/1	1 7
	Fokine *BWHills* 2-8-11 MHills (5)	16/1	½ 8
58	Colossus (IRE) *APO'Brien,Ireland* 2-8-11 JAHeffernan (2)	100/1	nk 9
	Kheleyf (USA) *DRLoder* 2-8-11 LDettori (8)	5/1	1¼ 10
	Nevisian Lad *MLWBell* 2-8-11 TEDurcan (4)	25/1	1 11
47	Born In America (USA) *APO'Brien,Ireland* 2-8-11 CO'Donoghue (1)	150/1	24 12

Mr Sanford R. Robertson 12ran 1m10.68   119/117/115/114/113+/112

75   Prix Daniel Wildenstein Casino Barriere de La Rochelle (Gr 2) (3yo+)   1m
£43,241

63	SPECIAL KALDOUN (IRE) *DSmaga,France* 4-9-1 DBoeuf (5)	28/10f	1
	MY RISK (FR) *J-MBeguigne,France* 4-9-1 CSoumillon (9)	11/2	4 2
27	GATEMAN *MJohnston,GB* 6-9-1 KDalgleish (6)	7/2	1 3
	Duck Row (USA) *JARToller,GB* 8-9-1 SWhitworth (7)	47/1	2 4
	Suggestive *WJHaggas,GB* 5-9-1 (v) DBonilla (3)	86/10	¾ 5
26	Tout Seul (IRE) *RFJohnsonHoughton,GB* 3-8-11 SCarson (10)	8/1	½ 6
63	Statue of Liberty (USA) *APO'Brien,Ireland* 3-8-11 (v) MJKinane (1)	41/10	3 7
63	Dandoun *JLDunlop,GB* 5-9-3 OPeslier (2)	17/1	5 8
50	Sea Dart (IRE) *JOxx,Ireland* 3-9-0 FMBerry (4)	106/10	2½ 9
	Carpanetto (IRE) *APO'Brien,Ireland* 3-8-11 CO'Donoghue (8)	41/10	6 10

Ecurie Chalhoub 10ran 1m42.40   124/116+/114/110/108/107

76   Prix du Cadran Casinos Barriere (Gr 1) (4yo+) £78,814   2½m

22	WESTERNER *ELellouche,France* 4-9-2 DBoeuf (8)	104/10	1
	GERMINIS (FR) *PChevillard,France* 9-9-2 RJanneau (9)	25/1	5 2
16	DARASIM (IRE) *MJohnston,GB* 5-9-2 (v) JFanning (2)	53/10	6 3
	Terrazzo (USA) *NBranchu,France* 8-9-2 OPlacais (4)	78/1	10 4
	Clety (FR) *FDoumen,France* 7-9-2 TThulliez (1)	30/1	2 5
29	Mr Dinos (IRE) *PFICole,GB* 4-9-2 KFallon (7)	1/2f	5 6
	Cut Quartz (FR) *RGibson,France* 6-9-2 TJarnet (5)	167/10	hd 7
53	Persian Punch (IRE) *DRCElsworth,GB* 10-9-2 MartinDwyer (6)	67/10	20 8
	Soreze (FR) *DSepulchre,France* 5-9-2 IMendizabal (3)	57/1	8 9
	Illumbe (FR) *RMartin-Sanchez,Spain* 5-9-2 (b) DBonilla (10)	78/1	dist 10

Ecurie Wildenstein 10ran 4m37.50   120/115/109

77 Prix de l'Abbaye de Longchamp Majestic Barriere (Gr 1) (2yo+) £78,814 — 5f

	PATAVELLIAN (IRE) *RCharlton,GB* 5-9-11 (b) SDrowne (7)	205/10	1
57	THE TRADER (IRE) *MBlanshard,GB* 5-9-11 (b) KFallon (1)	36/1	1 2
59	THE TATLING (IRE) *JMBradley,GB* 6-9-11 RLMoore (14)	35/1	nk 3
57	Acclamation *LGCottrell,GB* 4-9-11 LDettori (12)	43/10	nk 4
	Porlezza (FR) *YdeNicolay,France* 4-9-8 CSoumillon (3)	108/10	nk 5
57	Bahamian Pirate (USA) *DNicholls,GB* 8-9-11 JPSpencer (17)	45/1	1½ 6
59	Somnus *TDEasterby,GB* 3-9-11 TEDurcan (4)	28/10f	1 7
	Lochridge *AMBalding,GB* 4-9-8 KDarley (10)	44/1	2 8
	Dobby Road (FR) *MlleVDissaux,France* 4-9-11 (b) IMendizabal (11)	20/1	nk 9
	Dragon Flyer (IRE) *MQuinn,GB* 4-9-8 MJKinane (2)	60/1	sn 10
59	Airwave *HCandy,GB* 3-9-8 DaneO'Neill (5)	6/1	¾ 11
	Traou Mad (IRE) *RCollet,France* 3-9-8 DBoeuf (6)	29/1	1 12
	Danehurst *SirMarkPrescott,GB* 5-9-8 (b) SSanders (16)	86/10	1½ 13
	Repertory *MSSaunders,GB* 10-9-11 TGMcLaughlin (8)	46/1	sh 14
	Victorieux (FR) *MmeCHead-Maarek,France* 3-9-11 OPeslier (9)	135/10	sh 15
42	Striking Ambition *GCBravery,GB* 3-9-11 DHolland (20)	71/1	½ 16
	Pleasure Place (IRE) *RMenichetti,Italy* 3-9-8 DVargiu (13)	16/1	hd 17
57	Dominica *MPTregoning,GB* 4-9-8 (v) MartinDwyer (18)	22/1	3 18
	Best Walking (GER) *WHefter,Germany* 4-9-8 (b) TJarnet (19)	73/1	5 19

Mr D. J. Deer 19ran 59.30secs — 124/120/119/118/114/113+

78 Prix Marcel Boussac-Criterium des Pouliches Royal Barriere Deauville (Gr 1) (2yo f) £98,517 — 1m

58	DENEBOLA (USA) *PBary,France* 2-8-11 C-PLemaire (14)	91/10	1
	GREEN NOON (FR) *CLerner,France* 2-8-11 YLerner (3)	31/10	sn 2
	TULIPE ROYALE (FR) *MmeNRossio,France* 2-8-11 SPasquier (12)	62/1	2 3
	Green Swallow (FR) *PHDemercastel,France* 2-8-11 TGillet (10)	28/1	½ 4
	Grandes Illusions (FR) *DSmaga,France* 2-8-11 DBoeuf (9)	25/1	1½ 5
	Bright Abundance (USA) *CLaffon-Parias,France* 2-8-11 CSoumillon (1)	81/10	1 6
	Roseanna (FR) *MmeCHead-Maarek,France* 2-8-11 KFallon (15)	29/1	1 7
	Leila (FR) *MmeCBarbe,France* 2-8-11 TJarnet (11)	23/1	sh 8
	Bay Tree (IRE) *BWHills,GB* 2-8-11 MHills (8)	119/10	2 9
	Necklace *APO'Brien,Ireland* 2-8-11 MJKinane (6)	19/10cpf	1 10
	Malaica (FR) *RPritchard-Gordon,France* 2-8-11 OPeslier (2)	52/1	¾ 11
	Red Feather (IRE) *EdwardLynam,Ireland* 2-8-11 NGMcCullagh (7)	31/1	1 12
	Anabaa Republic (FR) *FDoumen,France* 2-8-11 TThulliez (4)	33/1	¾ 13
	Donna Vita *GAButler,GB* 2-8-11 EAhern (13)	40/1	3 14
	Danclare (USA) *JHMGosden,GB* 2-8-11 LDettori (5)	137/10	15 15
	Oh So Precious (IRE) *APO'Brien,Ireland* 2-8-11 TPQueally (16)	19/10cpf	4 16

Niarchos Family 16ran 1m40.90 — 112+/112/107/106/103/100

79 Prix Jean-Luc Lagardere (Grand Criterium) (Gr 1) (2yo c+f) £137,924 — 7f

Order as they passed the post: Newton and Tycoon were demoted to fourth and fifth places respectively after stablemate Acropolis caused interference to Ximb

	AMERICAN POST *MmeCHead-Maarek,France* 2-9-0 RHughes (3)	7/2	1
	CHARMING PRINCE (IRE) *AFabre,France* 2-9-0 OPeslier (4)	14/10f	4 2
24	NEWTON (IRE) *APO'Brien,Ireland* 2-9-0 JPSpencer (2)	21/10	2½ 3
	Tycoon *APO'Brien,Ireland* 2-9-0 MJKinane (1)	21/10	sh 4
	Ximb (FR) *J-CRouget,France* 2-9-0 IMendizabal (7)	5/2	½ 5
	Acropolis (IRE) *APO'Brien,Ireland* 2-9-0 KFallon (6)	21/10	sh 6

Mr K. Abdulla 6ran 1m24.50 — 118/108/101/101/99+/99+

80 Prix de l'Arc de Triomphe Lucien Barriere (Gr 1) (3yo+ c+f) £630,510 — 1½m

68	DALAKHANI (IRE) *AdeRoyerDupre,France* 3-8-11 CSoumillon (14)	14/10cpf	1
60	MUBTAKER (USA) *MPTregoning,GB* 6-9-5 RHills (10)	33/1	¾ 2
61	HIGH CHAPARRAL (IRE) *APO'Brien,Ireland* 4-9-5 MJKinane (1)	26/10cp	5 3
68	Doyen (IRE) *AFabre,France* 3-8-11 LDettori (4)	71/10	1½ 4
66	Vinnie Roe (IRE) *DKWeld,Ireland* 5-9-5 (b) PJSmullen (13)	15/1	1½ 5
62	Black Sam Bellamy (IRE) *APO'Brien,Ireland* 4-9-5 JPSpencer (6)	26/10cp	1½ 6
51	Dai Jin *ASchutz,Germany* 3-8-11 OPeslier (5)	16/1	nk 7
66	Bollin Eric *TDEasterby,GB* 4-9-5 KDarley (9)	63/1	3 8
37	Ange Gabriel (FR) *ELibaud,France* 5-9-5 TJarnet (7)	71/10	3 9
	Policy Maker (IRE) *ELellouche,France* 3-8-11 DBoeuf (8)	34/1	8 10
68	Kris Kin (USA) *SirMichaelStoute,GB* 3-8-11 KFallon (2)	138/10cp	20 11
60	First Charter *SirMichaelStoute,GB* 4-9-5 BDoyle (12)	138/10cp	1 12
68	Diyapour (FR) *AdeRoyerDupre,France* 3-8-11 TGillet (3)	14/10cpf	20 13

H.H. Aga Khan 13ran 2m32.30 — 133/132/124/122/119/117

NEWMARKET Saturday, Oct 18 GOOD to FIRM (Rowley Mile Course)

81 Jockey Club Cup (Gr 3) (3yo+) £23,200 — 2m

76	PERSIAN PUNCH (IRE) *DRCElsworth* 10-9-5 MartinDwyer (6)	5/2	1

44	MILLENARY *JLDunlop* 6-9-5 PatEddery (3)	15/8f	sh	2
29	KASTHARI (IRE) *SirMichaelStoute* 4-9-0 JMurtagh (5)	7/2	1	3
29	Tholjanah (IRE) *MPTregoning* 4-9-0 RHills (4)	10/1	nk	4
29	Savannah Bay *BJMeehan* 4-9-0 PJSmullen (1)	8/1	4	5
	Porsa System (DEN) *FPoulsen,Denmark* 4-9-0 RHughes (2)	50/1	23	6
	Mr J. C. Smith 6ran 3m26.92	120/120+/113/112+/107		

82 Victor Chandler Challenge Stks (Gr 2) (3yo+) £46,400 7f

42	JUST JAMES *JNoseda* 4-9-0 PatEddery (10)	16/1		1
	NAYYIR *GAButler* 5-9-4 JPSpencer (2)	11/2	½	2
	ARAKAN (USA) *SirMichaelStoute* 3-8-12 KFallon (5)	8/1	nk	3
42	Membership (USA) *CEBrittain* 3-8-12 PRobinson (3)	20/1	½	4
45	Trade Fair *RCharlton* 3-8-12 RHughes (7)	10/11f	½	5
	Rimrod (USA) *AMBalding* 3-8-12 MartinDwyer (8)	33/1	nk	6
42	Tante Rose (IRE) *BWHills* 3-8-9 MHills (4)	25/1	½	7
32	Baron's Pit *RHannon* 3-8-12 LDettori (9)	40/1	2	8
70	Tillerman *MrsAJPerrett* 7-9-0 MJKinane (1)	6/1	½	9
59	Twilight Blues (IRE) *BJMeehan* 4-9-4 PJSmullen (11)	25/1	1	10
35	Patsy's Double *MBlanshard* 5-9-0 FNorton (6)	100/1	14	11
	Lucayan Stud 11ran 1m24.68	120/123+/118+/117+/116/115+		

83 Darley Dewhurst Stks (Gr 1) (2yo c+f) £142,100 7f

64	MILK IT MICK *JAOsborne* 2-9-0 DHolland (11)	33/1		1
74	THREE VALLEYS (USA) *RCharlton* 2-9-0 RHughes (12)	11/4f	hd	2
64	HAAFHD *BWHills* 2-9-0 RHills (6)	7/1	1¼	3
	Bachelor Duke (USA) *JARToller* 2-9-0 SSanders (4)	25/1	hd	4
	Troubadour (IRE) *APO'Brien,Ireland* 2-9-0 JPSpencer (7)	40/1	½	5
	Imperial Stride *SirMichaelStoute* 2-9-0 KFallon (3)	14/1	nk	6
74	Balmont (USA) *JNoseda* 2-9-0 PatEddery (10)	10/1	nk	7
	Cape Fear *BJMeehan* 2-9-0 PJSmullen (5)	25/1	1	8
	Snow Ridge (IRE) *MPTregoning* 2-9-0 MartinDwyer (8)	7/2	nk	9
	Duke of Venice (USA) *MJohnston* 2-9-0 LDettori (9)	13/2	1¾	10
	Antonius Pius (USA) *APO'Brien,Ireland* 2-9-0 MJKinane (1)	10/1	½	11
	Tashkil (IRE) *JHMGosden* 2-9-0 WSupple (2)	25/1	3	12
	Mr Paul J. Dixon 12ran 1m25.22	119+/119/115/115/114/113/112/110		

84 Emirates Airline Champion Stks (Gr 1) (3yo+) £232,000 1¼m

28	RAKTI *MAJarvis* 4-9-2 PRobinson (3)	11/1		1
13	CARNIVAL DANCER *MrsAJPerrett* 5-9-2 DHolland (10)	33/1	2	2
72	INDIAN CREEK *DRCElsworth* 5-9-2 DaneO'Neill (11)	25/1	1½	3
46	Imperial Dancer *MRChannon* 5-9-2 TEDurcan (4)	66/1	¾	4
70	Russian Rhythm (USA) *SirMichaelStoute* 3-8-8 KFallon (7)	11/4	2	5
61	Alamshar (IRE) *JOxx,Ireland* 3-8-11 JMurtagh (1)	9/4f	½	6
49	Kaieteur (USA) *BJMeehan* 4-9-2 PatEddery (6)	14/1	sh	7
54	Nayef (USA) *MPTregoning* 5-9-2 RHills (12)	5/1	2½	8
50	Middlemarch (IRE) *APO'Brien,Ireland* 3-8-11 (v) MJKinane (2)	50/1	hd	9
62	Dano-Mast *FPoulsen,Denmark* 7-9-2 JPSpencer (9)	50/1	sh	10
26	Indian Haven *PWD'Arcy* 3-8-11 JFEgan (5)	33/1	7	11
33	Vespone (IRE) *SaeedbinSuroor* 3-8-11 LDettori (8)	6/1	9	12
	Mr Gary A. Tanaka 12ran 2m03.34	126/121/118/117+/110/112/112+		

WOODBINE Sunday, Oct 19 GOOD to SOFT

85 Pattison Canadian International Stks (Gr 1) (3yo) £538,922 1½m

65	PHOENIX REACH (IRE) *AMBalding,GB* 3-8-7 (b) MartinDwyer	54/10		1
	MACAW (IRE) *BTagg,USA* 4-9-0 (b) SBridgmohan	1225/100f	¾	2
65	BRIAN BORU *APO'Brien,Ireland* 3-8-7 JPSpencer	125/100f	hd	3
	Bowman Mill (USA) *MWDickinson,USA* 5-9-0 BBlanc	14/1	1	4
71	Sabiango (GER) *AWohler,Germany* 5-9-0 EPedroza	625/100	4	5
71	Lunar Sovereign (USA) *KPMcLaughlin,UAE* 4-9-0 RMigliore	56/10	1¾	6
	Gruntled *JEHammond,France* 4-9-0 LDettori	20/1	1½	7
	Shoal Water (USA) *MRFrostad,Canada* 3-8-7 TKabel	18/1	1½	8
	Art Variety (BRZ) *KGMcPeek,USA* 5-9-0 (b) EPrado	16/1	2	9
	Portcullis (CAN) *MRFrostad,Canada* 4-9-0 SCallaghan	41/1	2½	10
	Winterbeck Manor Stud 10ran 2m33.62	120/119/119/117/110/108		

DONCASTER Saturday, Oct 25 GOOD to FIRM

86 Racing Post Trophy (Gr 1) (2yo c+f) £151,500 1m (Str.)

79	AMERICAN POST *MmeCHead-Maarek,France* 2-9-0 CSoumillon (4)	5/6f		1
	FANTASTIC VIEW (USA) *RHannon* 2-9-0 PDobbs (3)	7/2	1¾	2
	MAGRITTE (IRE) *APO'Brien,Ireland* 2-9-0 JPSpencer (2)	11/4	1¼	3
	Tahreeb (FR) *MPTregoning* 2-9-0 GDuffield (6)	16/1	2	4
	Mr K. Abdulla 4ran 1m39.57	117+/113/110+/105		

NEWBURY Saturday, Oct 25 GOOD

87 Tote St Simon Stks (Gr 3) (3yo+) £17,400 1½m5y

84 IMPERIAL DANCER *MRChannon* 5-9-0 TEDurcan (6) 4/1 1
72 HIGH ACCOLADE *MPTregoning* 3-8-13 MartinDwyer (5) 13/8f 3 2
55 DUBAI SUCCESS *BWHills* 3-8-7 MHills (2) 7/1 1 3
Place Rouge (IRE) *JHMGosden* 4-9-0 DaneO'Neill (4) 33/1 1½ 4
60 The Whistling Teal *GWragg* 7-9-0 SSanders (9) 16/1 1¼ 5
Eastern Breeze (IRE) *PWD'Arcy* 5-9-0 (es) JFEgan (1) 33/1 ½ 6
72 Compton Bolter (IRE) *GAButler* 6-9-0 EAhern (7) 7/1 3½ 7
Hilbre Island *BJMeehan* 3-8-7 PatEddery (8) 6/1 9 8
Scott's View *MJohnston* 4-9-0 JFanning (3) 14/1 6 9
Imperial Racing 9ran 2m35.20 121+/122/114/111/109/108?

SANTA ANITA Saturday, Oct 25 Turf course: FIRM, Dirt track: FAST

88 NetJets Breeders' Cup Mile (Gr 1) (3yo+) £467,066 1m (Turf)

52 SIX PERFECTIONS (FR) *PBary,France* 3-8-7 JBailey (13) 53/10 1
TOUCH OF THE BLUES (FR) *NDDrysdale,USA* 6-9-0 KDesormeaux (9) 119/10 ¾ 2
CENTURY CITY (IRE) *CBGreely,USA* 4-9-0 (b) JValdivia (8) 39/1 nk 3
Irish Warrior (USA) *WDollase,USA* 5-9-0 ASolis (11) 33/1 1¼ 4
Soaring Free (CAN) *MRFrostad,Canada* 4-9-0 JVelazquez (4) 22/1 1 5
Freefourinternet (USA) *JoanScott,USA* 5-9-0 JLEspinoza (7) 57/1 hd 6
Designed For Luck (USA) *VCerin,USA* 6-9-0 (b) PValenzuela (3) 53/10 1½ 7
Special Ring (USA) *JCCanani,USA* 6-9-0 (b) DFlores (6) 51/10 nk 8
49 Perfect Soul (IRE) *RLAttfield,Canada* 5-9-0 (b) JSantos (14) 16/1 1 9
59 Oasis Dream *JHMGosden,GB* 3-8-10 RHughes (10) 87/10 1½ 10
63 Refuse To Bend (IRE) *DKWeld,Ireland* 3-8-10 PJSmullen (5) 97/10 1 11
Decarchy (USA) *DO'Neill,USA* 6-9-0 MESmith (12) 52/1 2½ 12
Peace Rules (USA) *RJFrankel,USA* 3-8-10 EPrado (1) 31/10f 4½ 13
Niarchos Family 13ran 1m33.86 123+/125/124/121/118/117

89 Breeders' Cup Filly & Mare Turf (Gr 1) (3yo+ f+m) £330,060 1¼m (Turf)

61 ISLINGTON (IRE) *SirMichaelStoute,GB* 4-8-11 KFallon (4) 29/10f 1
56 L'ANCRESSE (IRE) *APO'Brien,Ireland* 3-8-6 EPrado (11) 465/10 nk 2
69 YESTERDAY (IRE) *APO'Brien,Ireland* 3-8-6 MJKinane (2) 147/10 2½ 3
Heat Haze *RJFrankel,USA* 4-8-11 JBailey (3) 7/1 ns 4
Megahertz *RJFrankel,USA* 4-8-11 ASolis (9) 16/1 ¾ 5
Riskaverse (USA) *PJKelly,USA* 4-8-11 JVelasquez (8) 46/1 1½ 6
Voodoo Dancer (USA) *CClement,USA* 5-8-11 CNakatani (7) 89/10 hd 7
Tates Creek (USA) *RJFrankel,USA* 5-8-11 PValenzuela (1) 47/10 1 8
Bien Nicole (USA) *DKvonHemel,USA* 5-8-11 DPettinger (12) 16/1 ½ 9
69 Mezzo Soprano (USA) *SaeedbinSuroor,GB* 3-8-6 LDettori (5) 18/1 ns 10
23 Musical Chimes (USA) *NDDrysdale,USA* 3-8-6 (b) GaryStevens (6) 46/10 15 11
15 Dimitrova (USA) *DKWeld,Ireland* 3-8-6 PJSmullen (10) 117/10 4½ 12
Exors of the late Lord Weinstock 12ran 1m59.13 124/123/118/118/116/112

90 John Deere Breeders' Cup Turf (Gr 1) (3yo+) £457,006 1½m (Turf)

80 HIGH CHAPARRAL (IRE) *APO'Brien,Ireland* 4-9-0 MJKinane (3) 49/10 1
JOHAR (USA) *REMandella,USA* 4-9-0 ASolis (9) 142/10 dh 1
70 FALBRAV (IRE) *LMCumani,GB* 5-9-0 DHolland (8) 36/10 hd 3
49 The Tin Man (USA) *REMandella,USA* 5-9-0 MESmith (7) 14/1 5½ 4
71 Sulamani (IRE) *SaeedbinSuroor,GB* 4-9-0 LDettori (4) 31/10 ¾ 5
63 Bright Sky (IRE) *ELellouche,France* 4-8-11 DBoeuf (2) 23/1 1¾ 6
49 Storming Home *NDDrysdale,USA* 5-9-0 (b) GaryStevens (5) 2/1f 1 7
Toccet (USA) *JFScanlan,USA* 3-8-9 (b) RBaze (1) 47/1 14 8
71 Balto Star (USA) *TAPletcher,USA* 5-9-0 JVelasquez (6) 24/1 1½ 9
Mr M. Tabor & Mrs John Magnier
The Thoroughbred Corporation 9ran 2m24.24 130/130/130/120/119/112

91 Breeders' Cup Classic Powered By Dodge (Gr 1) (3yo+) £1,245,509 1¼m (Dirt)

PLEASANTLY PERFECT (USA) *REMandella,USA* 5-9-0 (b) ASolis (2) 142/10 1
MEDAGLIA D'ORO (USA) *RJFrankel,USA* 4-9-0 JBailey (8) 26/10f 1½ 2
DYNEVER (USA) *CClement,USA* 3-8-9 CNakatani (6) 152/10 ¾ 3
Congaree (USA) *RBaffert,USA* 5-9-0 PValenzuela (9) 63/10 nk 4
39 Hold That Tiger (USA) *APO'Brien,Ireland* 3-8-9 EPrado (5) 85/10 5 5
49 Perfect Drift (USA) *MWJohnson,USA* 4-9-0 GaryStevens (7) 57/10 2¼ 6
Evening Attire (USA) *PJKelly,USA* 5-9-0 (b) JVelazquez (1) 25/1 2 7
Ten Most Wanted (USA) *WDollase,USA* 3-8-9 (b) PDay (10) 41/10 2½ 8
Funny Cide (USA) *BTagg,USA* 3-8-9 JulieKrone (4) 87/10 ½ 9
Volponi (USA) *PGJohnson,USA* 5-9-0 (b) JSantos (3) 17/1 5 10
Diamond A Racing Corporation 10ran 1m59.88 126/124/123/122/113/110

LONGCHAMP Sunday, Oct 26 SOFT

92 **Prix Royal-Oak (Gr 1) (3yo+)** £59,521 1m7f110y

76	WESTERNER *ELellouche,France* 4-9-4 DBoeuf (5)	31/10	1
29	ALCAZAR (IRE) *HMorrison,GB* 8-9-4 MFenton (12)	39/1	2½ 2
	BEHKARA (IRE) *AdeRoyerDupre,France* 3-8-6 CSoumillon (14)	9/2	1 3
80	Vinnie Roe (IRE) *DKWeld,Ireland* 5-9-4 PJSmullen (13)	21/10f	1 4
	Moon Search *AFabre,France* 4-9-1 ACarre (6)	171/10	5 5
19	Albanova *SirMarkPrescott,GB* 4-9-1 (b) GDuffield (10)	39/1	2½ 6
76	Germinis (FR) *PChevillard,France* 9-9-4 RJanneau (4)	7/1	2 7
	Craig's Falcon (FR) *JdeRoualle,France* 4-9-4 (b) SPasquier (1)	49/1	¾ 8
29	Pugin (IRE) *SaeedbinSuroor,GB* 5-9-4 JPSpencer (11)	47/1	1½ 9
	Risk Seeker *ELellouche,France* 3-8-9 TThulliez (8)	31/10	sn 10
76	Cut Quartz (FR) *RGibson,France* 6-9-4 C-PLemaire (9)	43/1	3 11
	Wareed (IRE) *DRLoder,GB* 5-9-4 RHills (7)	111/10	2 12
	Grey Glitters (FR) *PHDemercastel,France* 3-8-9 RMarchelli (2)	43/1	6 13
76	Darasim (IRE) *MJohnston,GB* 5-9-4 (v) JFanning (3)	142/10	15 14

Ecurie Wildenstein 14ran 3m31.20 120+/117/115/114/106/104

MAISONS-LAFFITTE Friday, Oct 31 SOFT

93 **Criterium de Maisons-Laffitte (Gr 2) (2yo)** £75,208 6f

74	WHIPPER (USA) *RCollet,France* 2-9-0 CSoumillon	13/10cpf	1
	CHINEUR (FR) *MDelzangles,France* 2-9-0 SPasquier	6/1	2½ 2
	BLACK ESCORT (USA) *CLaffon-Parias,France* 2-8-11 DBonilla	213/10	2½ 3
	Raffelberger (GER) *MHofer,Germany* 2-9-0 ASuborics	178/10	nk 4
	Mokabra (IRE) *MRChannon,GB* 2-9-0 TEDurcan	122/10	1½ 5
	Villadolide (FR) *MmeCHead-Maarek,France* 2-8-11 TGillet	78/10	¾ 6
	Le Boss (FR) *RCollet,France* 2-9-0 SMaillot	13/10cpf	6 7
79	Ximb (FR) *J-CRouget,France* 2-9-0 IMendizabal	23/10	2½ 8
	Sister Moonshine (FR) *RPritchard-Gordon,France* 2-8-11 TJarnet	31/1	3 9
	Petardias Magic (IRE) *EJO'Neill,GB* 2-9-0 KDarley	59/1	½ 10

Mr R. C. Strauss 10ran 1m14.70 117+/110+/101/103/99/94

SAINT-CLOUD Saturday, Nov 1 SOFT

94 **Criterium International (Gr 1) (2yo c+f)** £99,201 1m

	BAGO (FR) *JEPease,France* 2-9-0 TGillet (1)	2/5cpf	1
	TOP SEED (IRE) *MRChannon,GB* 2-9-0 ACulhane (6)	35/1	6 2
79	ACROPOLIS (IRE) *APO'Brien,Ireland* 2-9-0 MJKinane (7)	73/10	4 3
	Marabout Directa (GER) *ALowe,Germany* 2-9-0 SPasquier (5)	179/10	3 4
	Joursanvault (FR) *AdeRoyerDupre,France* 2-9-0 CSoumillon (2)	28/10	6 5
	Alnitak (USA) *JEPease,France* 2-9-0 (b) C-PLemaire (4)	2/5cpf	3 6
	Brief Floyed (IRE) *AUSerikov,Russia* 2-9-0 ELegrix (3)	28/1	15 7

Niarchos Family 7ran 1m46.82 121/109/101/95

FLEMINGTON Tuesday, Nov 4 GOOD

95 **Tooheys New Melbourne Cup (Hcap) (Gr 1) (3yo+)** £1,171,548 2m

	MAKYBE DIVA *DHall,Australia* 5-8-0 GBoss (15)	7/1	1
	SHE'S ARCHIE (AUS) *DWeir,Australia* 5-7-12 (b) SSeamer (9)	40/1	1¼ 2
53	JARDINES LOOKOUT (IRE) *APJarvis,GB* 6-8-10 DHolland (12)	40/1	3 3
	Pentastic (AUS) *DHall,Australia* 5-8-6 (b) SArnold (1)	10/1	sh 4
	Zagalia (NZ) *CConners,Australia* 4-7-12 (b) CMunce (24)	12/1	hd 5
	Grey Song (AUS) *THughes,Australia* 5-8-0 SRKing (20)	9/1	1 6
	Distinctly Secret (NZ) *MWalker,NewZealand* 5-8-4 (b) KMcEvoy (19)	14/1	sh 7
	Yakama (AUS) *BLaming,Australia* 6-7-10 MRodd (2)	50/1	½ 8
16	Hugs Dancer (FR) *JGGiven,GB* 6-8-3 DeanMcKeown (14)	15/1	2½ 9
	Big Pat (AUS) *RGriffiths,Australia* 6-7-11 PMertens (18)	30/1	½ 10
	Frightening (AUS) *BCummings,Australia* 4-7-12 SDye (4)	8/1	¾ 11
	Mr Prudent (AUS) *GHanlon,Australia* 9-8-5 (b) DMOliver (7)	25/1	sn 12
	Ain't Seen Nothin' (AUS) *BarbaraJoseph,Australia* 4-7-11 (b) CNewitt (16)	30/1	2 13
	Tumeric (AUS) *DLFreedman,Australia* 7-8-0 BPrebble (17)	20/1	1½ 14
	County Tyrone (AUS) *KLees,Australia* 5-8-5 (b) JCassidy (13)	40/1	1¼ 15
	Bold Bard (AUS) *BStanaway,Australia* 7-7-12 RWheeler (6)	400/1	¾ 16
	Holy Orders (IRE) *WPMullins,Ireland* 6-8-5 (b) DJCondon (21)	30/1	¾ 17
	Fawaz (AUS) *GARogerson,Australia* 4-7-10 SBaster (3)	60/1	2¼ 18
	Debben (AUS) *LMacdonald,Australia* 4-7-10 (b) ClareLindop (5)	200/1	¾ 19
	Piachay (NZ) *DHall,Australia* 6-8-0 MPumpa (22)	150/1	nk 20
37	Millstreet *SaeedbinSuroor,GB* 4-8-8 PPayne (23)	30/1	3 21
	Schumpeter (AUS) *PGMoody,Australia* 4-7-13 CBrown (8)	200/1	¾ 22
62	Mamool (IRE) *SaeedbinSuroor,GB* 4-8-10 LDettori (11)	11/2f	12 23

Emily Krstina (Aus) Pty Ltd Syndicate 23ran 3m19.90 114/110/119/115/107/107

ROME Sunday, Nov 16   GOOD to SOFT

96 **Premio Roma SIS (Gr 1) (3yo+) £97,241**   1¼m

87	IMPERIAL DANCER *MRChannon,GB* 5-9-2 TEDurcan	53/10	1
	ALTIERI *VCaruso,Italy* 5-9-2 MEsposito	77/10	3 2
	SUNSTRACH (IRE) *EBorromeo,Italy* 5-9-2 (t) LDettori	48/10	sn 3
37	Trumbaka (IRE) *MmeCHead-Maarek,France* 4-8-13 TJarnet	33/10	¾ 4
4	Fair Mix (IRE) *MRolland,France* 5-9-2 SPasquier	11/4f	hd 5
13	Execute (FR) *JEHammond,France* 6-9-2 DBoeuf	9/2	1½ 6
	Quel Del Giaz (IRE) *FCamici,Italy* 4-9-2 DPorcu	56/1	2 7
	Blu For Life (IRE) *RMimmocchi,Italy* 6-9-2 MMimmocchi	45/1	1 8
34	Maktub (ITY) *BGrizzetti,Italy* 4-9-2 (t) MDemuro	52/10	3½ 9
49	Vangelis (USA) *AdeRoyerDupre,France* 4-9-2 FBlondel	20/1	2½ 10

Imperial Racing 10ran 2m01.60   123/117/116/112/114/111

TOKYO Sunday, Nov 30   GOOD to SOFT

97 **Japan Cup (Gr 1) (3yo+) £1,365,002**   1½m

	TAP DANCE CITY (USA) *SSasaki,Japan* 6-9-0 TSato (1)	138/10	1
	THAT'S THE PLENTY (JPN) *KHashiguchi,Japan* 3-8-10 KAndo (10)	14/1	9 2
	SYMBOLI KRIS S (USA) *KFujisawa,Japan* 4-9-0 OPeslier (5)	19/10f	¾ 3
	Neo Universe (JPN) *TSetoguchi,Japan* 3-8-10 MDemuro (8)	7/1	hd 4
	Active Bio (JPN) *HSakiyama,Japan* 6-9-0 KTake (11)	124/1	1¼ 5
56	Tigertail (FR) *RodolpheCollet,France* 4-8-10 TGillet (17)	111/1	nk 6
80	Ange Gabriel (FR) *ELibaud,France* 5-9-0 TJarnet (9)	12/1	½ 7
	Denon (USA) *RJFrankel,USA* 5-9-0 CNakatani (2)	20/1	½ 8
89	Islington (IRE) *SirMichaelStoute,GB* 4-8-10 KFallon (14)	20/1	1¼ 9
	Derby Regno (JPN) *STakahashi,Japan* 5-9-0 HMiyuki (12)	143/1	1½ 10
	Sunrise Pegasus (JPN) *SIshizaka,Japan* 5-9-0 YShibata (18)	52/1	½ 11
37	Ana Marie (FR) *PHDemercastel,France* 4-8-10 C-PLemaire (6)	141/1	nk 12
71	Slew Valley (USA) *GSciacca,USA* 6-9-0 JChavez (15)	135/1	ns 13
	Sakura President (JPN) *FKojima,Japan* 3-8-10 (b) YTake (3)	21/1	½ 14
	Tsurumaru Boy (JPN) *KHashiguchi,Japan* 5-9-0 NYokoyama (7)	21/1	3 15
90	Johar (USA) *REMandella,USA* 4-9-0 ASolis (13)	16/1	dist 16
	Sarafan (USA) *NDDrysdale,USA* 4-9-0 VEspinoza (16)	55/1	2 17
	Fields of Omagh (AUS) *TMcEvoy,Australia* 6-9-0 (b) SRKing (4)	39/1	dist 18

Yushun Horse Club Co. 18ran 2m28.70   125/115+/112+/114+/110+/105+

SHA TIN Sunday, Dec 14   GOOD to FIRM

98 **Hong Kong Sprint (Gr 1) (3yo+) £425,373**   5f

	SILENT WITNESS (AUS) *ASCruz,HongKong* 4-9-0 FCoetzee (11)	3/10f	1
	NATIONAL CURRENCY (SAF) *MAzzie,SouthAfrica* 4-9-0 WCMarwing (6)	6/1	1 2
	CAPE OF GOOD HOPE *DOughton,HongKong* 5-9-0 (v+t) MJKinane (14)	64/1	½ 3
25	Firebolt (IRE) *IWAllan,HongKong* 5-9-0 (b) AMarcus (2)	27/1	1¼ 4
77	Acclamation *LGCottrell,GB* 4-9-0 LDettori (3)	45/1	1¼ 5
77	The Trader (IRE) *MBlanshard,GB* 5-9-0 (b) KFallon (13)	49/1	¾ 6
77	The Tatling (IRE) *JMBradley,GB* 6-9-0 RMoore (12)	100/1	¾ 7
	Cheerful Fortune (NZ) *TWLeung,HongKong* 4-9-0 CWilliams (10)	24/1	½ 8
	Into The Night (AUS) *KDryden,Australia* 5-9-0 DBeadman (4)	13/1	1¼ 9
	All Thrills Too (AUS) *DAHayes,HongKong* 6-9-0 (b) GMosse (5)	55/1	hd 10
	Grand Delight (AUS) *JSize,HongKong* 6-9-0 (b) SDye (7)	32/1	sh 11
	Dantana (AUS) *RHore-Lacy,Australia* 4-9-0 (b) DMOliver (1)	29/1	ns 12
	Bomber Bill (AUS) *RSmerdon,Australia* 8-9-0 (b+t) SArnold (8)	100/1	hd 13
	Deportivo *RCharlton,GB* 3-9-0 RHughes (9)	73/1	5¼ 14

Mr A. A. Da Silva 14ran 56.50secs   126/123/121/117/113/111

99 **Hong Kong Mile (Gr 1) (3yo+) £597,015**   1m

	LUCKY OWNERS (NZ) *ASCruz,HongKong* 4-9-0 FCoetzee (7)	54/10	1
	BOWMAN'S CROSSING (IRE) *DOughton,HongKong* 4-9-0 MJKinane (13)	35/1	½ 2
63	LOHENGRIN (JPN) *MIto,Japan* 4-9-0 KDesormeaux (12)	9/10f	½ 3
	Admire Max (JPN) *MHashida,Japan* 4-9-0 YFukunaga (14)	57/10	½ 4
32	Firebreak *SaeedbinSuroor,GB* 4-9-0 LDettori (10)	48/1	sh 5
	Meridian Star (AUS) *DAHayes,HongKong* 7-9-0 (b) GMosse (6)	68/1	1¾ 6
63	Telegnosis (JPN) *HSugiura,Japan* 4-9-0 MKatsuura (2)	22/1	sh 7
	Ho Choi *IWAllan,HongKong* 4-9-0 (b) CSoumillon (8)	11/1	nk 8
75	Special Kaldoun (IRE) *DSmaga,France* 4-9-0 DBoeuf (4)	28/1	4¼ 9
	Mister Acpen (CHI) *KMulhall,USA* 5-9-0 (b+t) DFlores (9)	55/1	2½ 10
	Passing Glance *AMBalding,GB* 5-9-0 MartinDwyer (11)	100/1	¾ 11
	Citizen Kane (ARG) *ASCruz,HongKong* 7-9-0 RFradd (5)	47/1	2¼ 12
	Ninetyfive Emperor (AUS) *CLeck,Singapore* 4-9-0 (s) JSaimee (3)	34/1	8½ 13
	Olympic Express *IWAllan,HongKong* 5-9-0 DJWhyte (1)	9/1	pu

Mr & Mrs Leung Kai Fai 14ran 1m34.30   122/121/119/118/118/114

1161

100 Hong Kong Cup (Gr 1) (3yo+) £761,194 1¼m

90	FALBRAV (IRE) *LMCumani,GB* 5-9-0 LDettori (5)	7/10f		1
84	RAKTI *MAJarvis,GB* 4-9-0 PRobinson (4)	54/10	2	2
	ELEGANT FASHION (AUS) *DAHayes,HongKong* 5-8-10 GMosse (7)	54/10	1¼	3
90	Bright Sky (IRE) *ELellouche,France* 4-8-10 DBoeuf (2)	28/1	½	4
	Self Flit (NZ) *IWAllan,HongKong* 5-9-0 (b) WCMarwing (12)	50/1	3¼	5
	Dr More (AUS) *JSize,HongKong* 6-9-0 SDye (1)	48/1	½	6
	Eishin Preston (USA) *SKitahashi,Japan* 6-9-0 (h+t) YFukunaga (13)	83/10	nk	7
	Blue Stitch *ATMillard,HongKong* 4-9-0 (b+t) DJWhyte (10)	64/1	4¼	8
97	Tigertail (FR) *RodolpheCollet,France* 4-8-10 TGillet (6)	100/1	hd	9
	Precision (FR) *DOughton,HongKong* 5-9-0 MJKinane (8)	25/1	1¼	10
97	Denon (USA) *RJFrankel,USA* 5-9-0 CNakatani (9)	38/1	nk	11
	Weightless *PBary,France* 3-8-11 TThulliez (3)	33/1	1¼	12
	Magnaten (USA) *KFujisawa,Japan* 7-9-0 KDesormeaux (14)	65/1	1¼	13
84	Dano-Mast *FPoulsen,Denmark* 7-9-0 CSoumillon (11)	96/1	¾	14

Scuderia Rencati Srl 14ran 2m00.90   130+/126/119/118/115/114

INDEX TO SELECTED BIG RACES

1162

Debben (AUS) 95
Decarchy (USA) 88
Deeliteful Irving (USA) 71[2]
Dellagio (IRE) 24
Delsarte (USA) 39, 55[4]
Denebola (USA) 58[3], 78*
Denon (USA) 97, 100
Deportivo 98
Derby Regno (JPN) 97
Desert Deer 27
Desert Destiny 95[5], 14
Designed For Luck (USA) 88
Devil Moon (IRE) 47[4]
Diacada (GER) 30
Dimitrova (USA) 15[3], 89
Distinctly Secret (NZ) 95
Diyapour (FR) 8, 18, 68, 80
Dobby Road (FR) 77
Docklands Brian 24
Dolmur (IRE) 14
Domedriver (IRE) 12[4], 52[2], 63
Dominica 25[4], 57[4], 77
Donna Vita 78
Doyen (IRE) 68[2], 80[4]
Dragon Flyer (IRE) 77
Dr More (AUS) 100[6]
Dubai Destination (USA) 27*, 52[5], 70
Dubai Success 55[5], 87[3]
Duck Row (USA) 75[4]
Duke of Venice (USA) 83
Dunhill Star (IRE) 21
Dutch Gold (USA) 21[6], 39, 55
Duty Paid (IRE) 6, 30[6]
Dynever (USA) a91[3]

Eastern Breeze (IRE) 87[6]
Eishin Preston (USA) 100
Ekraar (USA) 1[3], 28
Elegant Fashion (AUS) 100[3]
Elusive City (USA) 9, 25[6]
Etoile Montante (USA) 10[3]
Evening Attire (USA) a91
Eventuail (ARG) 45
Evolving Tactics (IRE) 14
Execute (FR) 4[2], 13[5], 96[6]

Fair Mix (IRE) 4*, 96[5]
Falbrav (IRE) 4[3], 13*, 28[5], 39*, 44[5], 54*, 61[2], 70*, 90[3], 100*
Fancy Foxtrot 24[5]
Fantasize 30[5]
Fantastic View (USA) 86[2]
Fawaz (AUS) 95
Fayr Jag (IRE) 59[5]
Fidelio's Miracle (USA) 10
Fidelite (IRE) 23, 69[3]
Fields of Omagh (AUS) 97
Fight Your Corner 29
Firebolt (IRE) 25, 98[4]
Firebreak 32, 99[5]
First Charter 60[2], 80
Fokine (USA) 74
Fomalhaut (USA) 52
Foodbroker Founder 38
France 9[4], 14[2], 26, 61[6]
Franklins Gardens 21
Freefourinternet (USA) 88[6]
Frightening (AUS) 95
Funny Cide (USA) a91

Gamut (IRE) 41[3], 66[2]

Garlinote (FR) 10[5]
Gateman 27[4], 75[3]
Geminiani (IRE) 20
Germinis (FR) 76[2], 92
Glebe Garden 40
Gold Medallist 65
Gonfilia (GER) 6
Graikos 21
Grand Delight (AUS) 98
Grand Ekinoks (TUR) 1[5]
Grandera (IRE) a24, 28, 39, 44
Grandes Illusions (FR) 78[5]
Grand Reward (USA) 74[5]
Great Pyramid (IRE) 14[5]
Green Noon (FR) 78[2]
Green Swallow (FR) 78[4]
Grey Glitters (FR) 92
Grey Song (USA) 95[6]
Groom Raider 67
Grundlefoot (USA) a2[6]
Gruntled 85
Gulf (IRE) 11[5]

Haafhd 64[3], 83[3]
Halawanda (IRE) 20
Hammiya (IRE) 20
Hanami 6[5], 20[6], 43
Handel (IRE) 36
Hans Anderson (USA) a2
Harlan's Holiday (USA) a2[2]
Haskilclara (FR) 58[6]
Hawk Flyer (USA) 55[3]
Hawk Wing (USA) 12*, 27[6]
Haydn (USA) 58, 67
Hearts 'n Minds 20
Heat Haze 89[4]
Hector's Girl 6
Hi Dubai 20[5]
High Accolade 41[6], 55[6], 65[2], 72*, 87[2]
High Action (USA) 68[6]
High Chaparral (IRE) 46*, 61*, 80[3], 90*
High Country (IRE) 36
Highest (IRE) 1, 19[2], 31[5]
High Praise (USA) 20
Hilbre Island 87
Ho Choi 99
Holborn (UAE) 74[2]
Hold That Tiger (USA) 5, 26[4], 39, a91[5]
Holy Orders (IRE) 95
Honor In War (USA) 49
Hugs Dancer (FR) 16, 95
Hurricane Alan (IRE) 5, 26[6]

Ikhtyar (IRE) 38*
Illumbe (FR) 76
Illustrator 33
Imoya (IRE) 38
Imperial Dancer 3[5], 46[2], 84[4], 87*, 96*
Imperial Stride 83[6]
Imtiyaz (USA) 13[6]
Inchberry 20[4]
Indiana Blues 73
Indian Creek 31*, 54[5], 60[3], 72[3], 84[3]
Indian Haven 5, 14*, 26, 84
Indian Spark 25
Intercontinental 6[3]
In Time's Eye 46[3]

Into The Night (AUS) 98
Irish Warrior (USA) 88[4]
Island House (IRE) 38[4]
Islington (IRE) 28[3], 39[6], 56*, 61[3], 89*, 97
Izdiham (IRE) 39, 44, 54

Jakarta Jade (IRE) 43
Jardines Lookout (IRE) 11[6], 29[4], 53[5], 95[3]
Jay Gee's Choice 5
Jipapibaquigrafo (USA) 33[5]
Johar (USA) 90*, 97
Joursanvault (FR) 94[5]
Juliette (FR) 43[5]
Just James 32[5], 35[2], 42, 82*

Kaieteur (USA) 4, 28[6], 39[3], 49[2], 84
Kalaman (IRE) 26[2], 54
Kasthari (IRE) 16[3], 29, 81[3]
Kheleyf (USA) 74
Khulood (USA) 6, 32
King of Happiness (USA) 35[3]
Krataios (FR) 9[3]
Kris Kin (USA) 7*, 21*, 44[3], 68[3], 80

Labirinto (USA) 37
Lady Dominatrix (IRE) 25
L'Ancresse (IRE) 6, 15[4], 20, 43[2], 56[5], 89[2]
Lateen Sails 5, 33[4]
Latino Magic (IRE) 50[2]
Leadership 34*, 44
Le Boss (FR) 93
Leila (FR) 78
Leitrim House 64[6]
Leo's Luckyman (USA) 38
Let Me Try Again (IRE) 21, 48[4], 65
Levirat (GER) 34[5]
Livadiya (IRE) 50[6]
Lochridge 77
Lohengrin (JPN) 52, 63[2], 99[3]
Londonnetdotcom (IRE) 10
Look Here's Carol (IRE) 6
Look Honey (USA) 33[3], 68[5]
Loxias (FR) 37[3], 62
Lucky Owners (NZ) 99*
Lucky Story (USA) 64*
Luminata (IRE) 15
Lunar Sovereign (USA) 71, 85[6]
Lundy's Lane (IRE) 5, 21, 38

Macaw (IRE) 85[2]
Magistretti (USA) 21, 33[2], 54[2]
Magnaten (USA) 100
Magritte (IRE) 86[3]
Maharib (IRE) 65[4]
Maiden Tower 10[2]
Mail The Desert (IRE) 30[3]
Majestic Desert 73[2]
Makhlab (USA) 14
Maktub (ITY) 34[3], 96
Makybe Diva 95*
Malaica (FR) 78
Malhub (USA) 32
Mamool (IRE) 11*, 29[5], 48[3], 62*, 95
Mandela (GER) 69[6]

THE TIMEFORM 'TOP HORSES ABROAD'

This review of the year covers the major racing countries outside Britain. It includes Timeform Ratings for the top two-year-olds, three-year-olds and older horses. Horses not rated highly enough to be included in the main lists but which finished in the first three in a European pattern race or, in the sections on Japan and North America, won a Grade 1 during the season are included below the cut-off line. Fillies and mares are denoted by (f); * denotes the horse was trained for only a part of the season in the country concerned. Overseas customers wishing to keep in touch with Timeform's coverage of racing through the year can subscribe to Computer Timeform, Timeform Perspective or our internet site (http://www.timeform.com) for reports on all the important races. It is now possible to obtain up-to-date Timeform commentaries (including many not published in the weekly Timeform Black Book), undertake progeny research and access daily form guides on the internet site. Race Cards for all Group 1 races in France and Ireland, plus major races in several other countries, are also available.

IRELAND   To some he was a tip-top miler, to others he was vastly overrated. Few horses in recent times have generated such fierce debate as **Hawk Wing**. Though Irish trained, Hawk Wing did not run in Ireland in 2003, but his spectacular eleven-length win in the Lockinge Stakes at Newbury in May meant that, for the second year in succession, Ballydoyle housed the horse with the highest Timeform rating in Europe, following Rock of Gibraltar in 2002.

Like Hawk Wing, Ballydoyle's dual Derby winner **High Chaparral** vindicated the decision to keep him in training by winning two more Group/Grade 1 events: the Irish Champion Stakes, in which he survived an objection, a stewards' inquiry and an appeal to the Irish Turf Club, and the Breeders' Cup Turf, in which he dead-heated in a thrilling finish. **Black Sam Bellamy** provided trainer Aidan O'Brien with a third Group 1-winning older horse when running away with the Tattersalls Gold Cup. Both High Chaparral and Black Sam Bellamy played a significant part in making O'Brien champion trainer again in front of John Oxx and Dermot Weld. Weld's grand campaigner **Vinnie Roe** became the first horse to win the Irish St Leger three times, and all being well he should be bidding for number four in 2004. Only two other Irish older horses won pattern races. **Avorado** was better than ever at the age of five and gained the last of three wins in the Minstrel Stakes (beating **D'Anjou** into second), while **Perfect Touch** won the Brownstown Stakes. **In Time's Eye**, **One More Round**, **Holy Orders** and **Osterhase** all showed their very best form in handicaps and/or listed races, while **Mkuzi** produced a good weight-carrying performance to win a handicap at Cork before repeating that form when fourth behind High Chaparral in the Royal Whip Stakes. Special mention should be made of **Livadiya**, who ran fourteen times and won five races, including the Irish Lincolnshire on her reappearance, showing herself better than ever at the age of seven.

2003 was a particularly good year for the classic generation. Leading the way was the Oxx-trained **Alamshar**, who inflicted his only defeat on Dalakhani when winning the Irish Derby. Alamshar followed that with a top-class effort to win the King George VI and Queen Elizabeth Stakes. Irish Derby fifth **The Great Gatsby** had earlier split Alamshar and Brian Boru in the Derrinstown Stud Derby Trial at Leopardstown and been a gallant second in the Derby at Epsom, in which Alamshar came third and the Ballysax Stakes winner **Balestrini** fifth. The 150/1-shot **Roosevelt** came out best of the Ballydoyle runners in the Irish Derby, one place ahead of subsequent St Leger winner **Brian Boru**. Brian Boru was ridden by Jamie Spencer at Doncaster, and he is set to take over as retained jockey at Ballydoyle in 2004, replacing Michael Kinane who rode twelve classic winners for O'Brien during his highly successful time with the yard. Kinane has moved to another powerful Irish yard, that of Oxx. Brian Boru was the second British classic winner for Irish trainers, **Refuse To Bend** having won the Two Thousand Guineas for Weld. The latter was also successful in the Desmond Stakes before being bought by Godolphin. Among the fillies, **Vintage Tipple** made Paddy Mullins the oldest trainer of a classic winner in living memory when she won the Irish Oaks, in which **Yesterday** gave her only below-par performance of the year, having already won the Irish One Thousand Guineas and finished an unlucky second in the Oaks at Epsom. **Dimitrova** and **L'Ancresse**, who finished third and fourth respectively in the Irish One Thousand Guineas, both progressed well. Dimitrova gained her biggest wins across the Atlantic in the American Oaks and the Flower Bowl Invitational—Weld also saddled **Evolving Tactics** to win the Grade 2 American Derby—while L'Ancresse excelled herself when second in the Breeders' Cup Filly & Mare Turf, having finished second in the Irish Oaks and won a listed race previously. Others placed in a classic were **Catcher In The Rye**, second in the Poule d'Essai des Poulains before suffering an injury, **France**, runner-up in the Irish Two Thousand Guineas, and **Powerscourt**, third in the Irish St Leger having beaten Brian Boru in the Great Voltigeur Stakes at York on his previous start. Three other three-year-olds who ran with credit in top company were: the Curragh Cup winner **Maharib**, fourth in the St Leger at Doncaster; the Meld Stakes winner **Mingun**, fourth in the Juddmonte International; and **Statue of Liberty**, second in the Sussex Stakes. **Miss Emma** failed to repeat the form of her four-length success in the Greenlands Stakes, while **Abunawwas**'s effort when winning the Ballycorus Stakes was by some way his best of the year. The Goffs International Stakes was the weakest Group 2 event of the year, the form shown by the winner **Sea Dart** being inferior to that shown by most Group 3 winners. Two colts who didn't win in Ireland in 2003, but nevertheless showed smart form, were **Alberto Giacometti**, third in the Ballysax Stakes and the Prix Lupin, and **Marino Marini**. Both were transferred to the States, the latter showing plenty of improvement on his Irish form when beaten a head in the Grade 1 Malibu Stakes on dirt at Santa Anita.

There is plenty to look forward to with the crop of Irish two-year-olds. O'Brien's **One Cool Cat** won four races, including the Phoenix Stakes from **Old Deuteronomy**, and the National Stakes, in which he beat **Wathab**. One Cool Cat went into the winter at the head of the Two Thousand Guineas ante-post market, with stable-companion **Yeats** also to the forefront in the Derby market. Yeats was very impressive when winning a maiden on his only start and is reportedly set to follow the same Ballysax Stakes/Derrinstown Stud Derby Trial route to the Derby as the stable's Derby winners in 2001 and 2002, Galileo and High Chaparral. **Grey Swallow** also made a big impression on both his starts, including in the Killavullan Stakes, and looks sure to make a very smart three-year-old at the very least. Another unbeaten colt is **Azamour**, who gave the Oxx stable a second consecutive success in the Beresford Stakes, following Alamshar in 2002. **Necklace** had a good campaign, her two wins coming in the Debutante Stakes and the Moyglare Stud Stakes, while **Antonius Pius** won the Railway Stakes and **Venturi** was successful in the C. L. Weld Park Stakes. **Colossus** was highly tried in some of his races, but gave 18 lb and more away when winning a nursery at Naas. **Magritte**, **Moscow Ballet** and **Troubadour** all showed at least useful form in pattern races in Britain without winning. A few maiden winners well worth looking out for in 2004 are **Opera Comique** (who has since joined Godolphin), **Wolfe Tone** and **Cobra**. Cobra in particular recorded a good time when gaining his success, and he seems sure to go on to better things.

Two-Year-Olds

118p	One Cool Cat	103p	Venturi (f)	99	Alexander Duchess (f)
116p	Grey Swallow	103	Mustameet	98p	Five Dynasties
114	Colossus	103	Simple Exchange	98	Maroochydore (f)
114	Troubadour	102	King Hesperus	97	Mahogany
113	Wathab	102	Red Feather (f)	96p	Meath
112p	Magritte	102	Tumblebrutus	96	Acciacatura (f)
109	Moscow Ballet	101	Acropolis	96	Groom Raider
109	Old Deuteronomy	101	Blue Crush (f)	96	Jemmy's Brother
108p	Azamour	101	*Castledale	96	Moon Unit
108	The Mighty Tiger	101	Devil Moon	96?	Haydn
107	Relaxed Gesture	101	Misty Heights (f)	95P	Yeats
106p	Mikado	101	Newton	95p	Wolfe Tone
106	Celtic Cat	101	Tycoon	95+	Favourite Nation
105p	Necklace (f)	100p	Opera Comique (f)	95	Chestnut Gallinule
105	Antonius Pius	100	Alexander Goldrun (f)	95	Il Pirata
104p	Cobra	100	Steel Light	95	Liss Ard
		100	Tarakala (f)		

95	Miss Childrey (f)	104	Walayef (f)	114	Avorado
88	Takrice (f)	103	Dossier (f)	114	Holy Orders
		103	Jakarta Jade (f)	113	D'Anjou
		103	Mombassa	113	Mkuzi

Three-Year-Olds

133	Alamshar	103	Sea Dart	113d	One Won One
124	Brian Boru	102	Definate Spectacle	112	*Belle du Jour (f)
124	Refuse To Bend	102	Englishtown	111	Livadiya (f)
123	L'Ancresse (f)	101	Hazelhatch	111	Osterhase
123	*Roosevelt	101	Zimbabwe	110d	Final Exam
122	Powerscourt	100	Behrasia (f)	109	Mr Houdini
120	The Great Gatsby	100	Dalcassian	109	Tiger Royal
119	Dimitrova (f)	100	Elasouna (f)	107	Mutakarrim
119	Yesterday (f)	100	*European	107	Perfect Touch (f)
117	Balestrini	100	Hymn of Love (f)	107	Timawari
117	Hold That Tiger	100	Jade Quest	106	Sadlers Wings
117	Maharib	100	Nopekan	105	Chartres (f)
117	Mingun	99	Dramadoir	104	Aqualina (f)
117	Vintage Tipple (f)	99	Kiteflyer (f)	104	Desert Fantasy
116	*Alberto Giacometti	98	Conspiring (f)	104	Queens Wharf (f)
116	*Marino Marini	98	Delacroix	104	Tarry Flynn
115	Catcher In The Rye	98	Pepperwood	104d	Minashki
115	France	98	Royal Fortune	103	Golly Gosh (f)
115	Statue of Liberty	97	Anna Frid (f)	103	Miss Honorine (f)
114	*Middlemarch	97	Gianfanti	103	Wrong Key (f)
113	Miss Emma (f)	97	Ivowen (f)	102	Atlantic Rhapsody
111	Hanabad	97	*Miss Nashwan (f)	102	Bowmore
111	Tomahawk	97	Miss Trish (f)	102	Cool Cousin (f)
110	Abunawwas	97	Sun Slash (f)	102	Jacks Estate
110	Arundel	97d	Shangri La (f)	102	Moonbi Ridge (f)
108	Latino Magic	96	Bon Expresso (f)	101	Crimphill (f)
108	Multazem	96	Dixie Evans (f)	101	Glocca Morra
108	Napper Tandy	96	Luminata (f)	101	Green Castle (f)
107	Blue Corrig	96	Military Option	101	Mobasher
107	Dolmur	96	Pantarez	101	Quality Team
107	Eklim	96	Roisin's Star (f)	100	Almost Famous
107	Evolving Tactics	95p	Excalibur	100	Fearn Royal (f)
107	Good Day Too	95	Akash	100	Senators Alibi
107	Handel	95	Amid The Chaos	99d	Calorando
107	Juliette (f)	95	Faadhil	98	Carallia (f)
107	My Renee (f)	95	Sissy Slew (f)	98	Direct Bearing
107	Queen Astrid (f)	95	Sophister	98	Frosty Wind
107	Rayshan	95	*Tajseed	97?	Really (f)
107	Spartacus	95	Uncle Tiny	97	Bragadino
107d	Great Pyramid			97	Ridakiya (f)
106	Cruzspiel	94	Cat Belling (f)	97	Twiggy's Sister (f)
106	Shizao (f)	94	Flamelet (f)	96	Cache Creek (f)
106	Tipperary All Star			96	Desert Hill
105	Carpanetto	**Older Horses**		96	La Pieta (f)
105	Legacy	136	Hawk Wing	95	King Carew
105	Snippets (f)	132	High Chapparal	95	Love Token (f)
104	Daganya (f)	125	Vinnie Roe	95	Lupine (f)
104	Icklingham	121	Black Sam Bellamy	95	Quest For A Star
104	Plume Rouge (f)	119	In Time's Eye	95	She's Our Girl (f)
		116	One More Round		

FRANCE   Already established as the best two-year-old colt in France, **Dalakhani** looked set to progress further over longer distances at three and did not disappoint, retiring to stud after a top-class win over older rivals in the Prix de l'Arc de Triomphe, and with just one defeat in his nine-race record. That defeat had come at the Curragh at the hands of his owner's other top-class three-year-old Alamshar, but on French soil Dalakhani reigned supreme, winning the Prix Greffulhe, Prix Lupin, Prix du Jockey Club and Prix Niel en route to the Arc. Now that Dalakhani has been retired to stud, a couple of his chief rivals will have the chance to emerge from his shadow in 2004. **Super Celebre** missed the second half of the season but was the colt who tested Dalakhani most earlier on, finishing second to him in both the Prix Lupin and Prix du Jockey Club. On his reappearance Super Celebre had defeated **Coroner** (later winner of the Prix Hocquart and third at Chantilly) in the Prix Noailles. The later-developing **Doyen** emerged as a promising colt in the autumn, chasing home Dalakhani in the Niel and finishing fourth in the Arc, having easily won the Prix du Lys at Longchamp in June. Doyen looks sure to progress again and win good races for Godolphin as a four-year-old.

Godolphin also acquired another of the leading French three-year-olds, **Vespone**. He did not show what he is capable of on his first start for his new owners in the Champion Stakes, but had put up good front-running displays to win both the Prix Jean Prat and the Grand Prix de Paris in the summer. Another front runner to do well was the gelding **Weightless**. He made rapid progress at Longchamp in the autumn, following up a win in the Prix du Prince d'Orange with a defeat of older rivals in the Prix Dollar. The same connections (Khalid Abdulla/Pascal Bary) were represented by another progressive type in **Kalabar**. He won the Prix Guillaume d'Ornano at Deauville between second places in the Prix Eugene Adam (won by the Grand Prix de Paris third **Look Honey**) and the Prix du Conseil de Paris. With Super Celebre sidelined, **Policy Maker** carried the Wildenstein colours in the Arc, and, whilst he was well held there and had been no match for Doyen in the Prix du Lys, he was in good form at Deauville in August, winning a listed race and being awarded the Grand Prix there.

Over shorter trips there was less strength in depth among the three-year-old colts. **Clodovil** was still unbeaten when winning a substandard Poule d'Essai des Poulains but he struggled in top mile company subsequently. **Star Valley** and **Tashkandi** (another Godolphin recruit) finished second against older milers at Deauville in the Prix Quincey and Prix Messidor respectively, and the latter also ran well when holding off **Art Moderne** and **Marshall** narrowly for third place behind Vespone in the Prix Jean Prat.

In contrast to the colts, the strength among the three-year-old fillies lay with the milers rather than the middle-distance performers. **Six Perfections** had been the outstanding two-year-old filly of 2002 and, like Dalakhani, maintained her position as the best of her age and sex in France after another season's racing. Her Guineas sorties will be remembered for her luckless second places at both Newmarket and the Curragh, but she more than atoned for those defeats when maintaining the Niarchos colours' excellent record in both the Prix Jacques le Marois and the Breeders' Cup Mile. **Nebraska Tornado** was a later-developing filly altogether, though made rapid improvement once she reached the track. She won the Prix de Diane barely a month after her debut and, and, back at a mile, took the Prix du Moulin after suffering her only defeat in the Jacques le Marois. Both Six Perfections and Nebraska Tornado stay in training.

Musical Chimes completed a French Guineas double (initiated by Clodovil) for Andre Fabre and Christophe Soumillon when winning the Poule d'Essai des Pouliches from **Maiden Tower** and **Etoile Montante**. All three fillies had joined American stables by the end of the year and Musical Chimes again emerged best, finishing second, when the trio re-opposed in the Matriarch Stakes at Hollywood in November. By then, Maiden Tower had gained a win over **Acago** (also in the Pouliches and Matriarch fields) and the One Thousand Guineas third **Intercontinental** in the Prix de Sandringham at Chantilly, while Etoile Montante had put up marginally the best effort of the trio to land the Prix de la Foret at Longchamp.

The lack of a good French filly over middle distances was one reason for there being no fillies at all in the Arc line-up. **Vallee Enchantee** was noted in the 2002 review as a good prospect and, after taking a while to fulfil her promise, gained Group 2 victories in the Prix de Pomone and Prix du Conseil de Paris, and then a top-level success in the Hong Kong Vase. In between, she had finished a place behind the Prix Saint-Alary winner **Fidelite** when fourth in the Prix Vermeille. Similar form was shown by the Andre Fabre stable-companions **Visorama** and **Walkamia** when they won the Prix de Flore and Prix Fille de l'Air respectively. The Aga Khan's filly **Behkara** emerged as the best three-year-old stayer, beating the colt **Risk Seeker** in the Prix Hubert de Chaudenay before finishing a good third to older rivals in the Prix Royal-Oak.

The previous season's Breeders' Cup Mile winner **Domedriver** was the best older horse in France. He made a promising return when second to the British-trained Dandoun in the Prix du Muguet at Saint-Cloud but failed to add to his successes of the previous campaign, running his best race when beaten narrowly by stable-companion Six Perfections in the Prix Jacques le Marois. Domedriver has been retired to stud, but a couple of good older milers who could make more of a name for themselves in 2004 are **Special Kaldoun** and **My Risk**, the pair who took the first two places in the Prix Daniel Wildenstein at the Arc meeting. Special Kaldoun had also won the Prix Messidor at Deauville before finishing a good fourth in the Jacques le Marois, while the much improved My Risk's five wins included the Prix Quincey at Deauville and a defeat of the Ganay runner-up **Execute** in the Prix Perth at Saint-Cloud.

Ange Gabriel's five-year-old season proved more rewarding than Domedriver's, and he collected another three pattern wins, notably recording a second successive victory from **Polish Summer** in the Grand Prix de Saint-Cloud. Either side of that success, Ange Gabriel defeated Polish Summer's stable-companion **Martaline** in both the Grand Prix de Chantilly and the Prix Foy. Ange Gabriel was below form in the Arc and Japan Cup on his last two starts before retirement, but he had run well on his reappearance when second in the Dubai Sheema Classic. Polish Summer finished just behind him in fourth in Dubai, and performed consistently for the remainder of the year, ending with second place in the Hong Kong Vase, though he lost what would have been his second successive Grand Prix de Deauville in the stewards' room. The improved Martaline had better luck, winning the Prix d'Hedouville at Longchamp and the Prix Maurice de Nieuil at Maisons-Laffitte. The Hedouville runner-up **Loxias** benefited from stewards' decisions on his next two outings, awarded the Prix Jean de Chaudenay on Millenary's demotion, and then promoted to third in the Grand Prix de Saint-Cloud. Former claiming winner **Fair Mix** reached new heights when winning the Prix Ganay in April but he underwent surgery for an injury subsequently and ran just respectably on his return in the autumn. **Short Pause** improved with each run as a four-year-old and caught the eye on his final outing when coming from last place to take second, ahead of Execute, in the Prix Dollar.

Some good older fillies remained in training. **Bright Sky** reappeared with a good second to Falbrav in the Prix d'Ispahan but gained her only win of the year when dropped back to a mile for the Prix d'Astarte at Deauville. She ran creditably kept to a mile to finish third in the Prix du Moulin, and then filled the same position when attempting a repeat win in the Prix de l'Opera. Bright Sky's year-older stable-companion **Aquarelliste** warmed up for the Dubai World Cup with an impressive win in the Prix Exbury, though finished well held in Dubai before retiring to stud. **Ana Marie** also made a winning reappearance, taking the Prix d'Harcourt ahead of Fair Mix, but put up her best effort when running Russian Rhythm to a neck in the Nassau Stakes at Goodwood. **Tigertail** was another older filly to run some good races abroad, reaching the frame in the Premio Presidente della Repubblica at Rome, the Yorkshire Oaks, the E. P. Taylor Stakes in Canada and a Group 1 event in Japan. She had Ana Marie behind her in the last-named race, and again in the Japan Cup, in which she fared best of the European contingent in sixth place.

Top French sprinter **Zipping** maintained his good record in Britain when finishing fourth in both the Golden Jubilee Stakes and the July Cup. His season ended prematurely when he took a heavy fall in the Prix Maurice de Gheest as a consequence of breaking a blood vessel. That race went to the filly **Porlezza**, who had previously seemed best at five furlongs. Her other win came at that trip when she won the Prix du Gros-Chene at Chantilly for the second year running, with Zipping promoted to second. Porlezza fared best of the French runners when fifth in the Prix de l'Abbaye, which was, as usual, dominated by British-trained sprinters. Few other French-trained sprinters made their mark in pattern company. **Swedish Shave** rattled off an early-season hat-trick at Maisons-Laffitte, and, though he later won a substandard Prix de Ris-Orangis at Deauville, he was mostly found wanting in pattern company. The formerly British-trained **Ratio** maintained John Hammond's good record with sprinters—and with his runners in Britain—when dead-heating in the Wokingham at Royal Ascot and winning the Dubai International Airport World Trophy at Newbury.

Westerner, having spent much of his career campaigned at a mile, improved markedly when given a thorough test of stamina and ended the season as France's top stayer. He was a convincing winner of the Prix du Cadran from the 2001 winner **Germinis** and British raider Darasim, to whom he had earlier finished second in both the Prix Kergorlay and Prix Gladiateur, and then went on to become the first horse to complete the Cadran/ Royal-Oak double in the same year since Royal Gait in 1987 when the races were five months apart. Westerner could be a Gold Cup contender in 2004. **Morozov** returned in good form at Longchamp in the spring, winning the Prix de Barbeville, but his last two performances were less than satisfactory and he was sold in the autumn to race in Britain with Conrad Allen.

The latest crop of French two-year-olds featured several promising individuals, particularly among the colts, none more so than the unbeaten **Bago**. The winner of his four starts, Bago followed in Dalakhani's footsteps by winning the Prix des Chenes and the Criterium International, his impressive six-length victory at Saint-Cloud the best performance put up by a two-year-old in Europe all year. **Diamond Green** also looked a colt with a big future when going through his season unbeaten, the last of his three successes coming in the Prix La Rochette at Longchamp, where he beat stable-companion **Charming Prince** in good style. Soft ground prevented Diamond Green running in the Prix Jean-Luc Lagardere, formerly the Grand Criterium, the race having been renamed in honour of his late owner/breeder, who died in the spring. The race went to **American Post**, who followed up a decisive win over Charming Prince with victory in the Racing Post Trophy at Doncaster. Another leading French two-year-old seen out in Britain was **Whipper**. His fifth past the post in the Middle Park Stakes did not do him full justice, however, and he was better judged on wins in the Prix Morny and Criterium de Maisons-Laffitte. The runner-up in the latter race, **Chineur**, boosted the form with a listed win at Saint-Cloud next time and is himself a smart colt. **Apsis** looked a colt to follow when registering a smooth win in the Prix Thomas Bryon at Saint-Cloud in October. He'd made a winning debut with a defeat of **Simplex**, who went on to chase home **Voix du Nord** in the Criterium de Saint-Cloud.

The Pascal Bary-trained pair **Much Faster** and **Denebola** had the best form among the two-year-old fillies. Much Faster was indeed the speedier of the two, winning her first four starts, notably the Prix Robert Papin, before finishing second to Whipper in the Prix Morny and then disappointing under firmer conditions in the Cheveley Park Stakes. Denebola, a half-sister to the dam of Bago, looks the better three-year-old prospect. She finished third in the Morny before stepping up in trip to inflict her first defeat on the Prix d'Aumale winner **Green Noon** in the Prix Marcel Boussac. Denebola earlier had three future pattern winners behind her when winning the Prix de Cabourg at Deauville from **Bonaire** (Prix Eclipse) and **Via Milano** (Prix des Reservoirs), with Whipper back in fourth. **Latice** ended the year with two wins from two starts when beating Voix du Nord half a length in the Prix de Conde at Longchamp in October.

Two-Year-Olds

121p	Bago
118p	American Post
118	Whipper
115p	Diamond Green (Fr)
113p	Denebola (f)
113	Much Faster (f)
113	Voix du Nord
112	Green Noon (f)
111p	Apsis
111	Chineur
110p	Latice (f)
110	Simplex
108	Charming Prince
108	Villadolide (f)
107	Green Swallow (f)
107	Tulipe Royale (f)
107	Valixir
107	Ximb
106	Bonaire (f)
106	Via Milano (f)
105p	Dalna (f)
105	Chopoulou
105	Quel Fou
104	Day Or Night
104	Dolma (f)
104	Prospect Park
103P	Malevitch

103	Grandes Illusions (f)
103	Malaica (f)
102p	Millemix
102p	Miss Alabama (f)
102	Ange Gardien
102	*King of Cry
101	Always King
101	Black Escort (f)
101	Charmo
101	*Dealer Choice
100p	Bright Abundance (f)
100p	Sequestro
100	Agata (f)
100	Colony Band (f)
100	Ershaad
100	Fabulous Groom
100	Haskilclara (f)
100	Islero Noir
100	Leila (f)
100	Petit Calva (f)
100	Tigron
98	Anabaa Republic (f)
97	Sister Moonshine (f)
94	Kate Winslet (f)

Three-Year-Olds

133	Dalakhani
125	Vespone

124	Six Perfections (f)
123	Nebraska Tornado (f)
122p	Doyen
121	Super Celebre
120	Weightless
119	Etoile Montante (f)
117	*Fairly Ransom
117	Kalabar
117	*Musical Chimes (f)
117	Policy Maker
116	Clodovil
116	Look Honey
116	*Maiden Tower (f)
115	*Acago (f)
115	Art Moderne
115	Behkara (f)
115	Coroner
115	*Golden Devious
115	Marshall
115	Star Valley
115	Tashkandi
115	Vallee Enchantee (f)
114	Jipapibaquigrafo
114	Rhythm Mad
114	Walkamia (f)
113	Fidelite (f)
113	*Sign of The Wolf
113	Visorama (f)

112p	Ancient World	105	Forestier	112	Victorian Order
112+	Shakis	105	Gatewick	111	Bezrin
112	Commercante (f)	105	Gript	111	Le Carre
112	Victorieux	105	Precious Pearl (f)	111	Mer de Corail (f)
111	*Campsie Fells (f)	105	Private War	110	Aravis
111	*Mille Millions	105	Puppeteer	110	Blanche (f)
111	Risk Seeker	105	Sweet Stream (f)	110	Charming Groom
111	Touch of Land			110	Clety
111	Whortleberry (f)	104	Aynthia (f)	110	Massigann
110	Intercontinental (f)	104	Grey Glitters	110	Miraculous
110	King's Drama	104	Mosogno	110	Moon Search (f)
110	Krataios	103	*Liska (f)	110	Nashwan Rose (f)
110	Paraiyor	103	Sovana (f)	110	Vasywait
110	Snipewalk	102	Streamix	109	Almond Mousse (f)
110	*Welcome Millenium (f)	102	Suborneuse (f)	109	Cielago
109	Actrice (f)			109	Melkior
109	*Baie (f)	**Older Horses**		109	Soreze
109	Mister Charm	128	Domedriver	108	Great Pretender
109	Samando (f)	124	Ange Gabriel	108	Le Fou
109	Shuttle Diplomacy	124	Special Kaldoun	108	Petite Speciale (f)
109	Sweet Folly (f)	123	Fair Mix	108	*Tau Ceti
109	Underwater (f)	121	Aquarelliste (f)	107	Allez Olive
109	Vadalix	121	Westerner	107	Cherbon
108+	Fidelio's Miracle (f)	120	Bright Sky (f)	107	Crystal Castle
108	Maxwell	120	My Risk	107	Go Got
108	Mystic Melody (f)	119	Short Pause	107	Mont Rocher
108	Peinture Rose (f)	119	Zipping	107	*On Reflection
108	State of Art (f)	118	Ana Marie (f)	107	Pinkhair
108	Zinziberine (f)	118	Execute	107	Sarrasin
107	Clear Thinking	118	Loxias	107	Sensible
107	Diasilixa (f)	118	Martaline	107§	Terrazzo
107	Kindjhal	118	Polish Summer	106	Dexterity
107	Maredsous (f)	117	Porlezza (f)	106	Dobby Road
107	Messager du Roi	116	Swedish Shave	106	Maximum Security
107	Millenium Mambo	116	Vangelis	106	Minds Locked
107	Monetary (f)	115	Bernebeau	106	Snow Cap
107	Papineau	115	Germinis	106	Tsigane
107	Ridaar	115	Gruntled	106	Turbo Jet
107	Traou Mad (f)	115	Morozov	106	Whim (f)
106	Affirmative Action	115	Trumbaka (f)	105	Amathia (f)
106	Astronomic	115	Valentino (Fr)	105	Bonne Gargotte (f)
106	Bailador	114	Saratan	105	L'Impatient
106	*Derrianne (f)	114	Without Connexion	105	Lugny
106	Ela Merici (f)	113	Caesarion	105	Notre Dauphine (f)
106	French Polo	113	Craig's Falcon	105	Rashbag
106	Garlinote (f)	113	Cut Quartz	105	Spray Gun
106	Mes Bleus Yeux (f)	113	Secret Singer	105	Tustarta (f)
105	Alnamara (f)	113	*Tripat	105?	*Lord Protector
105	Amazon Beauty (f)	112	Labirinto		
105	Arvada (f)	112	Ratio	103	Handria (f)
		112	Tigertail (f)		
		112	Vahorimix		

GERMANY   Financial problems in German racing continue to be a factor in forcing some connections to look beyond their own borders to campaign their horses. One of Germany's top older horses, **Paolini**, for example, has not raced in his own country for the last two seasons. As in 2002, he failed to win on his travels in the latest season but picked up place money in valuable events, finishing second in the Dubai Duty Free, third in the Queen Elizabeth II Cup in Hong Kong and promoted to equal-second in the Arlington Million. **Osorio** is a German-trained three-year-old but has never raced there, his five career starts all coming in Italy, where his wins in the latest season included the Derby Italiano (worth around £180,000 more than the Deutsches Derby) on his final start. Another good horse campaigned exclusively abroad was the four-year-old filly **Walzerkoenigin**. She won the Premio Emilio Turati at Milan on her reappearance, finished third in the Falmouth Stakes at Newmarket on her next start and ran some good races in North America, making the frame in both the Beverly D Stakes and the Flower Bowl

1172

Mehl-Mulhens-Rennen, Cologne—
the German equivalent of the 2000 Guineas is won in fine style by Martillo

Invitational. German-trained horses compete regularly in France nowadays, and increasingly in Britain, and not just in listed or pattern races. Also, German bloodstock is becoming increasingly attractive abroad, and is finding demand growing from British jumps trainers. In the latest season **Simoun** followed the likes of other former smart German pattern winners, including Subiaco, Tareno and Limerick Boy, in continuing his career over jumps in Britain.

Three-year-old **Dai Jin** was Germany's best horse, making into a very smart colt once stepped up to a mile and a half. He was seemingly the least-fancied among the Schutz stable's three runners when winning one of the main German Derby trials, the Oppenheim-Union-Rennen at Cologne. **Storm Trooper** started odds on at Cologne, but Dai Jin confirmed himself the stable's number one when following up in the Deutsches Derby with Storm Trooper back in third. Incidentally, Andreas Schutz saddled four of the first five home in the Deutsches Derby after fielding the first three in both 2000 and 2002. Dai Jin went on to beat another stable-companion, the previous year's Derby winner **Next Desert**, in the Credit Suisse Private Banking-Pokal at Cologne but suffered a career-ending injury when finishing a respectable seventh in the Arc.

Ransom o'War was the colt who prevented a clean sweep for the Schutz stable at Hamburg by finishing second. He had given little indication that he was a smart colt in the making when trained by Mark Johnston in Britain as a two-year-old but made into a leading three-year-old in Germany, winning the other main German Derby trial, the Grosser Muller Brot-Preis at Munich, and later the Grosser Dallmayr-Preis at the same course against older rivals. The other three-year-old colt of note was the miler **Martillo**. His six-length victory in the Mehl-Mulhens-Rennen made him an above-average German Guineas winner (Ransom o'War was third), and he also won the Group 2 Grosser Porsche Preis at Hoppegarten in July after finishing third in the St James's Palace Stakes at Royal Ascot. **Fruhlingssturm** put up one of the best performances by a three-year-old in the autumn when beating Godolphin's challenger Naheef in the Ernst & Young Euro-Cup over a mile and a quarter at Frankfurt.

Dai Jin's stable-companion **Next Gina** was the best three-year-old filly. She emulated her dam, Night Petticoat, by winning the Preis der Diana (Oaks), but was unable to match

Grosser Dallmayr-Preis, Munich—Deutsches Derby runner-up Ransom o'War takes on older horses
for the first time; Godolphin challenger Highdown (visor) finishes well to dead-heat with Epalo for second

the exploits of her half-brother Next Desert, finishing fourth in the Deutsches Derby. Her season ended with a good sixth in the Prix de l'Opera at Longchamp. **Meridiana** won the Oaks d'Italia and stable-companion **Diacada** the Henkel-Rennen (1000 Guineas), but neither met with success subsequently.

With Paolini campaigned abroad, Next Desert was Germany's best older horse on home turf and the only older German horse to contest the Grosser Bugatti Preis, the newly-sponsored Grosser Preis von Baden. He was below form at Baden-Baden on what turned out to be his final start and his best effort in a three-race campaign was that second place to Dai Jin at Cologne. **Salve Regina** (the previous season's Oaks winner and Derby second) and Next Desert were both upstaged on their reappearance in the Group 2 Grosser Mercedes-Benz-Preis at Baden-Baden by a third stable-companion, **Epalo**, who went on to finish second in his three remaining starts, including when dead-heating for second behind Ransom o'War in the Grosser Dallmayr-Preis. Yet another four-year-old to do well for the Schutz stable was **Aolus**. Unbeaten in three starts at three, he completed a hat-trick in pattern company in the latest season, winning twice at Cologne before taking the Group 2 Hansa-Preis at Hamburg from Epalo and **Sabiango**. Aolus was pulled up lame on his final outing, but with six wins from his seven completed starts, he could well be a force again in good races in 2004. Sabiango had been a leading three-year-old in 2001 and was back to near his best, winning the Deutschland-Preis from Storm Trooper and finishing a good fourth in the Turf Classic at Belmont. Stable-companion **Terre de L'Home** maintained his fine track record at Hoppegarten when winning the Group 3 Preis der Deutschen Einheit in October for the second year running, but **Well Made**'s bid to win a second successive Preis von Europa came unstuck when he finished only third to Godolphin's Mamool, who had also won the Grosser Bugatti Preis at Baden-Baden.

There was little to choose between the leading older milers. **Zarewitsch** put up one of the best performances among them to win the Badener Meile in May, showing a similar level of form to the aforementioned Walzerkoenigin. There was a notable family double in the Grosse Europa Meile at Cologne in September when **Peppercorn** got the better of his younger brother **Peppershot** by half a length. The leading sprinters also took turns beating each other. **Ingolf** won the Benazet-Rennen at Baden-Baden and three-year-old **Fiepes Shuffle** the Grosser Preis von Berlin, while mudlark **Soave** hit top form in the autumn when the Prix de Seine-et-Oise at Maisons-Laffitte formed part of his end-of-season hat-trick.

Germany's top two-year-old contest, the Preis der Winterfavoriten, was fought out by the Uwe Ostmann-trained colts **Glad Lion** and **Pepperstorm** (a brother to Peppercorn and Peppershot), though the form did not work out that well and neither is bred to stay the Derby trip at three. The fillies' equivalent, the Preis der Winterkonigin, went to **Night Lagoon**, with third-placed **La Ina** going on to fill the same position in the Prix Miesque at Maisons-Laffitte. Others who ran well in France were **Joyce**, who won a listed race at Deauville, and **Raffelberger**, who finished fourth in the Criterium de Maisons-Laffitte and second in a listed race at Saint-Cloud. In Italy, the fillies **Mamela** and **Saldentigerin** took the first two places in the Premio Dormello.

Two-Year-Olds		Three-Year-Olds			
105p	Glad Lion			109	Glad Hunter
104p	Joyce (f)	95	Sagarmatha	109	Meridiana (f)
103	Pepperstorm			109	Silver Spur
103	Raffelberger	123	Dai Jin	108	Corriolanus
102	Er	119	Martillo	108	Diacada (f)
102	Night Lagoon (f)	117	Ransom o'War	108	Mandela (f)
101	Slawomira (f)	116	Fruhlingssturm	108	Royal Dubai (f)
100	La Ina (f)	115	Fiepes Shuffle	108	Royal Fantasy (f)
100	Vallera (f)	114	Medici	108	*Royal Price
98	Egerton	114	Osorio	108?	Forever Free
97p	Apeiron	113	Storm Trooper	108?	Western Devil
97p	Mamela (f)	112	Next Gina (f)	107	Arlecchina (f)
97	Marabout Directa	112	Senex	107	North Lodge
97	Saldentigerin (f)	111	Glad To Be First	107	Wild Passion
96p	Attilia (f)	111	Soldier Hollow	106	Anzasca (f)
96	Nocino	111	Winning Dash	106	Aubonne (f)
		110	Flambo	106	Furioso Directa

106	North America (f)	116?	King of Boxmeer	109	*Chan Chan
105	Anna Conda (f)	115	Liquido	109	El Dessert
105	Avenir Rubra (f)	115	Soave	109	Syrakus
105	Key To Pleasure	114	Ingolf	108	Ammonias
105	Lysuna (f)	114	Olaso	108	Areias
105	Nureus	114	War Blade	108	Lindholm
105	Prima (f)	113	Salve Regina (f)	108	Longridge
105	Rajpute	113	Simoun	108	Pappus
105	*White Rose (f)	113	Up And Away	108	Saldenschwinge (f)
105	Winterthur (f)	112	Bear King	108	Tempelwachter
		112	Desirao	107	Anthurium (f)
103	Perima (f)	112	Horeion Directa	107	Auenteufel
102	Caluna (f)	112	Konig Shuffle	107	Berber
102	Finora (f)	112	Peppercorn	107	Capital Secret
102	Lomicelli	112	Scapolo	107	Fleurie Domaine (f)
102	Palmridge	111	Diamante	107	Kaka
101	Minley	111	Meliksah	107	Ryono
		111	Peppershot (Ger)	106	Madresal
Older Horses		111	Sambaprinz	106d	Molly Mello (f)
121	Next Desert	111	Toylsome	105	Dark Marble
121	Paolini	110	Best Walking (f)	105	Mister Big
118	Aolus	110	Call Me Big		
117	Epalo	110	Fruhtau	104	Blueberry Forest
117	Terre de L'Home	110	Gold Type	104	Serenus
116	Sabiango	110	Levirat	104	Templerin (f)
116	Walzerkoenigin (f)	110	Near Honor	104	Tomster
116	Well Made	110	Picotee	103	Larana (f)
116	Zarewitsch	110	Sacho	103	Luttje Lage (f)
		110	Simonas		

ITALY   Italy lost two of its best horses to Newmarket stables at the end of 2002, and both Falbrav and Rakti thrived in no uncertain terms for their respective yards. They were a hard act to follow, and even though all but one of Italy's Group 1 races went abroad, there were still some smart performers around over a range of distances. Former Italian St Leger winner **Maktub** added six further wins to his record in 2003, including

Premio Vittorio di Capua, Milan—
Le Vie dei Colori records his tenth success from twelve starts, winning from Godolphin hope Blatant

pattern victories in the Premio Carlo d'Alessio at Rome in May and the Premio Federico Tesio at Milan in October. He was also placed twice in Group 1 company at Milan, running particularly well when second to Ekraar in the Gran Premio del Jockey Club. **Sunstrach** gained his only win in a well-contested minor event (from Salselon), but showed he was still a smart ten-furlong performer, finishing third to Imperial Dancer when attempting a repeat win in the Premio Roma. **Altieri** was second in the Premio Roma, though has mostly been campaigned at a mile of late and put up a good performance when winning a listed race over that trip in April. **Salselon** was again a leading miler, and won the Prix Edmond Blanc at Saint-Cloud before being placed in the Premio Emilio Turati and Premio Vittorio di Capua at Milan, and gained his third successive win in the seven-furlong Premio Chiusura there in November. He disappointed on his final start in the Premio Ribot at Rome, a race which went instead to long-shot **Duca d'Atri** on his pattern-race debut. Unfortunately for Italian racing, the subsequent success of Falbrav and Rakti with British yards seems to have started a trend; of the leading older horses mentioned above, Maktub (Michael Jarvis), Sunstrach and Salselon (both Luca Cumani) are all to be trained in Britain in 2004.

Italy's top two-year-old colt and filly of 2002, **Le Vie dei Colori** and **Pleasure Place**, both trained on well. Le Vie dei Colori won an above-average Premio Parioli (2000 Guineas) at Rome in April from the subsequent Prix Jean Prat runner-up **Prince Kirk** and gained his other big win in the Premio Vittorio di Capua at Milan in October, becoming the first Italian-trained winner of the race since Jurado won the first running as a Group 1 contest in 1988. Le Vie dei Colori has now won ten of his twelve starts. Sprinting filly Pleasure Place also has an impressive ratio of wins to runs. Her only defeat of the year came in the Prix de l'Abbaye at Longchamp, but she was unbeaten in six outings on home turf, her best effort coming when beating older filly **Slap Shot** easily in the Premio Omenoni at Milan. **Golden Nepi** kept the Premio Regina Elena (1000 Guineas) at home but she died following surgery later in the year after joining an American stable. **Marbye** missed the Regina Elena but ran well over a mile later on, beating a big field in the Premio Sergio Cumani at Milan before finishing third in the Premio Ribot. She had also run a good race at Deauville when third behind Bright Sky and Six Perfections in the Prix d'Astarte. Incidentally, as part of the upgrading of European pattern races for fillies, Milan's Premio Lydia Tesio returns to Group 1 status in 2004, a label it last carried in 1987, though it looks a good candidate to be the weakest of the newly-promoted Group 1 contests. As well as Le Vie dei Colori, a couple more three-year-old colts who had smart form over a mile were **Golden Devious**, who won listed races at Milan and Deauville, and **Romaldo** who was second in the Premio Ribot.

Italy looks to have a potential successor to Le Vie dei Colori in the form of two-year-old colt **Spirit of Desert**, who ran an excellent second to the British-trained Pearl of Love in an above-average renewal of the Gran Criterium. The son of Desert Prince had been unbeaten in four previous starts, including listed races at Naples and Rome. The Gran Criterium fourth **Whilly** had the next-best form among the two-year-olds, while **Groom Tesse**, winner of the Premio Guido Berardelli, was the only pattern-race winner among them.

Two-Year-Olds		Three-Year-Olds		Older Horses	
111	Spirit of Desert	119	Le Vie dei Colori	119	Sunstrach
106	Whilly	118	Pleasure Place (f)	118	Maktub
101p	Cromo	115	*Golden Devious	118	Salselon
100	Miss Vegas (f)	115	Prince Kirk	117	Altieri
99	Groom Tesse	114	Romaldo	112	Duca d'Atri
99	Mister Strong	111	*Golden Nepi (f)	111	Giovane Imperatore
97	Golden Pivotal	111	Marbye (f)	111?	Golden Cavern
96	Distant Way	108	Sammiyo	110	Arabian Pivot
96	Vol de Nuit	106	*Mac Monarch	110	Quel del Giaz
95	Boysun	105	Nonno Carlo	110	Rainer
95	Good Chocolate (f)	105	T E Lawrence	109	Caluki
				109	Frottola (f)
91	Noble Stella (f)	103	Vale Mantovani (f)	108	Slap Shot (f)
90	Flint Fly	100	*Kiralik (f)	107	Dream Chief
				107	Hopes Are High
				106	Darrel

106	Long Goodbye	105	Golden Honor	105	Rosso India
106	Sopran Foldan	105	Mystery Golden (f)	105	Sunsu Desura
105	Blu For Life	105	Nordhal		
				104	Fairy Beauty
				104	Regina Saura (f)

SCANDINAVIA   **Dano-Mast** was again Scandinavia's best horse, and with a wider margin of superiority in 2003. Already established as an international performer, he made his first appearance in Britain in the autumn, but the Champion Stakes saw him some way below his best, as did the Hong Kong Cup. His third place in the Grosser Bugatti Preis at Baden-Baden was much closer to his real form and he had been as good as ever when winning the Scandinavian Open Championship back home in Copenhagen from the nine-year-old **Parthe**. His old rival Valley Chapel, winner of the Scandinavian Open in the two previous seasons, was not around to attempt the hat-trick after sadly breaking a leg in Germany earlier in the year. With Dano-Mast running at Baden-Baden instead, Scandinavia's other Group 3 race over a mile and a half, the Stockholm Cup, went to the French-trained Labirinto ahead of the veteran **Albaran**. Remarkably, the ten-year-old contested both the Scandinavian Open (finishing fifth) and the Stockholm Cup for the seventh consecutive year. Albaran had earlier finished second to the lightly-raced **Sagittarius** in the listed Oslo Cup in June.

All the horses mentioned so far are aged seven or more, which suggests there's an opportunity for younger rivals to make a breakthrough in coming seasons. The Chilean-bred four-year-old **Mandrake El Mago** is one who could do so. He finished third in the Stockholm Cup but is a versatile type who also showed his form at a mile and won listed races on both dirt and turf earlier in the year. Similar comments apply to **Hovman**, a listed winner over a mile on turf at Taby and over a mile and a half on dirt (by eight lengths) at Jagersro. Another four-year-old, **Royal Experiment**, made the frame in both the Scandinavian Open (finishing third) and the Stockholm Cup (fourth) and gained a Group 3 win in between in the nine-furlong Marit Sveaas Minnelop at Ovrevoll. A couple of the best performances over a mile came from **Memorion** and **Hanzano**, first and second in a listed race on dirt at Taby in September, when Hovman was third.

Scandinavia's two Group 3 sprints, the Polar Cup at Ovrevoll in July over an extended six furlongs and the Taby Open Sprint Championship over a furlong shorter in September, were competitive affairs, though the form of the former race was turned round in the latter. **Aramus** was only sixth at Ovrevoll but went one better than in the two previous seasons when winning at Taby, where he had three former winners of the Sprint Championship behind him. **Musadif** improved a good deal on his Polar Cup run to finish a close second, with **Shawdon** putting up his best effort all year in third, ahead of the 2002 winner **Pistachio**. Fifth and sixth were **Waquaas** and **King Quantas** who had been the first two, but in reverse order, in the Polar Cup. Aramus had begun his campaign with fourth place in the Palace House Stakes at Newmarket and he was also first past the post in listed races on turf at Taby (from Pistachio) and on dirt at Jagersro (from Waquaas).

Three-Year-Old		112	Sagittarius	108	Exbourne's Wish
105	Rue La Fayette (f)	111	Albaran	107	Alpino Chileno
		111	Hanzano	106	Harrier
Older Horses		111	Hovman	106	Honeysuckle Player
120	Dano-Mast	111	Mandrake El Mago	106	Magic Fact
114	Aramus	111	Pistachio	106	Porsa System
114	Musadif	111	Royal Experiment	106	Rocket (Swe)
113	King Quantas	110	Bellamont Forest	106	Sankodar
113	Shawdon	110	Ecology	105	Apple Green
113	Waquaas	110	Martellian	105	Hide And Seek
112	Barros Luco	110	Tesorero	105	Nicki Hill
112	Buffalo Boy	109	El Gran Lode	105	Royal Gold
112	Memorion	109	Terroir		
112	Parthe	108	Blue Mountain		

UNITED ARAB EMIRATES   Dubai is a city that barely sits still. The racing in the Emirates very much mirrors that and Sheikh Mohammed has gone to great lengths to ensure it gets better with each year. The international racing barn was set up in 2001 and the following year saw an increased number of trainers sending their horses to winter in Dubai. The concept really took off in 2003. Mark Johnston sent a team of ten horses, and, although he had only limited success, he vowed to be back with new methods. One man who did make a huge success of it was South African Mike de Kock, who took home two big prizes on Dubai World Cup night courtesy of **Ipi Tombe** and **Victory Moon**. 2004 sees the birth of the Dubai International Racing Carnival, nine weeks of racing, with a big meeting each week, attracting horses from around the world competing for generous prize money. The Carnival will build up to the Dubai World Cup in which Godolphin maintained their excellent recent record with the victory in 2003 of **Moon Ballad**, who beat the American-trained Harlan's Holiday impressively by five lengths, after being prominent throughout under Frankie Dettori and being sent for home as they entered the straight. In a well-contested renewal Nayef was below his best in third place on his first outing on dirt, a short head in front of **Grandera**. Grandera had earlier won Round 3 of the Maktoum Challenge from the Saudi-trained **Grundlefoot** and, like Moon Ballad, was retired to stud in Japan after failing to recapture his best form. Godolphin chose the Dubai Sheema Classic for **Sulamani**'s debut in their colours, having purchased him following his second in the Arc the previous year. He showed fine acceleration to collar Ange Gabriel well inside the final furlong. Godolphin and Frankie Dettori had initiated a hat-trick of victories on the night with **Firebreak**, who beat the previous year's American-trained winner Grey Memo in the Godolphin Mile. The much improved **Estimraar** was third, having previously won Round 1 of the Maktoum Challenge, in which he beat **State Shinto** and **Conflict**.

Victory Moon emulated Essence of Dubai by winning both the UAE 2000 Guineas and the UAE Derby. Having beaten **Western Diplomat** and **Bourbonnais** in the Guineas at Nad Al Sheba, the South Hemisphere-bred Victory Moon went down by six lengths to **Inamorato** in a prestige race on the same course, before reversing that form in the Derby. Both Victory Moon and Inamorato (who finished third) suffered interference in the Derby, the winner doing particularly well to catch **Songlark**, a stable companion of Inamorato.

Dubai Duty Free, Nad Al Sheba—
South African mare Ipi Tombe justifies favouritism in good style from Germany's Paolini (blinkers)

South Africa's other victory on World Cup night came when champion mare Ipi Tombe landed the Dubai Duty Free in fine style by three lengths from Paolini with **Royal Tryst** and **Eventuail** coming next. Ipi Tombe had been even more impressive on her two previous starts in Dubai, winning a listed race and the Group 3 Jebel Hatta, the latter by nearly four lengths from **Sights On Gold**. The Golden Shaheen had been farmed by the Americans in recent years, but local trainer Paddy Rudkin kept the prize at home with **State City**. The horse's chance wasn't obvious going into the race following a poor run in the Group 3 Mahab Al Shimaal behind **Conroy** on his previous start and he failed to make much of an impact in the States afterwards.

   Highest joined Godolphin after finishing second in the 2002 St Leger and paid an instant return on his purchase price when taking the Group 3 Dubai City of Gold on his first start for new connections, beating the Turkish horse **Grand Ekinoks** by three quarters of a length, before running below form in the Sheema Classic. The ex-Willie Musson trained **Feet So Fast** returned to form to win two listed races narrowly from Royal Tryst and Firebreak respectively. Of the three-year-old fillies in the Emirates, **Danuta** emerged as one of the best, taking both the Moonshell Mile and UAE Oaks by clear margins, though both races were uncompetitive and she was twice beaten in the States afterwards. The first two in the UAE 1000 Guineas, Mezzo Soprano and Gonfilia, went on to show better form in Europe.

   The performances reviewed here are those that took place in the calendar year 2003. Horses which were trained and raced in the UAE but showed significantly better form elsewhere are not included in the list below.

Three-Year-Olds					
115	*Inamorato	116	*Naheef	108	*Dancal (f)
115	*Songlark	116	Royal Tryst	108	*Go Underground
108	*Danuta (f)	115	*Cayoke	108	Marhoob
107	*Bourbonnais	115	Estimraar	108	*Mr John
107	Western Diplomat	115	*Grand Ekinoks	108	*Nowrass
105	Dublin	115	Proven	108	Proud Irishman
		114	*State Shinto	107	Chaplinesque
		114	St Expedit	107	Divine Task
		113	Conflict	107	Orchestrated
Older Horses		113	*Eventuail	106	Baaridd
131	*Moon Ballad	112	Celtic Silence	106	Dubai Honor
128	*Sulamani	112	*Trademark	106	Essence of Dubai
126	*Ipi Tombe (f)	111	*Equerry	106	Meadaaar
121	*Highest	111	Masterful	106	Simeon
120	*Grandera	111	*Northern Rock	106	Yajree
120	*Victory Moon	110	Al Maali	106§	Clodion
119	*Grundlefoot	110	Curule	105	Kundooz
119	*Sights On Gold	110	Elghani	105	Muthaaber
118	*Firebreak	109	*Bonecrusher	105	Persuasivo Fitz
117	*Feet So Fast	109	*Calcutta	105	Walmooh
117	*State City	109	*Narrative	105d	Mahfooth
117d	*Pugin	109	*Raheibb		
116	*Imtiyaz	108	*Conroy (USA)	101	Seeking The Prize

NORTH AMERICA   The American Triple Crown, last won in 1978 by Affirmed, remains as elusive as ever. For the fifth time in the last seven years, the Kentucky Derby winner also won the Preakness Stakes but failed in the final leg at Belmont. Two horses dominated the American classics in 2003, at one time or another during the spring, first **Empire Maker** and then **Funny Cide** raised hopes that the twenty-five year wait for a Triple Crown winner would be over. Always well regarded, and out of a mare who had already produced three Grade 1 winners, Empire Maker shot to favouritism for the Kentucky Derby with a near ten-length defeat of the Fountain of Youth winner **Trust N Luck** in the Florida Derby, and he remained the one to beat at Churchill Downs after a half-length defeat of the then-unheralded Funny Cide in the Wood Memorial Stakes at Aqueduct.

   However, those who had seen Empire Maker as a potential Triple Crown winner were soon disappointed when Funny Cide turned the tables in the Kentucky Derby, becoming the first gelding to win the 'Run for the Roses' since 1929. When Funny Cide followed

Belmont Stakes, Belmont Park—Kentucky Derby runner-up Empire Maker ends the Triple Crown bid by Funny Cide (right); Ten Most Wanted (left) takes second

up with a near ten-length victory in the Preakness Stakes, Triple Crown expectations were now on him instead, and he started at even money at Belmont. Ironically, it was Empire Maker, who had bypassed the Preakness, who won the final leg, with Funny Cide only third, giving trainer Bobby Frankel his first win in a classic. Coincidentally, the two horses are related, both sharing the same fifth dam. Neither three-year-old made much of an impact after the Belmont. Funny Cide ran a sluggish third in the Haskell Invitational (he was found to have had a fever) before beating only one home in the Breeders' Cup Classic, while Empire Maker made only one more appearance, going down to **Strong Hope** (later a remote third in the Travers) in the Grade 2 Jim Dandy Stakes at Saratoga. A cough kept Empire Maker out of the Travers Stakes, and a bruised foot forced him to miss the Jockey Club Gold Cup, and he was retired to stud before the Breeders' Cup.

The first two in the Travers Stakes, **Ten Most Wanted** and Empire Maker's stable-companion **Peace Rules**, had played supporting roles in the Triple Crown races. Ten Most Wanted hurt his back in the Kentucky Derby but fared much better when a staying-on second in the Belmont. He also won the Grade 2 Super Derby from **Soto**, but proved a disappointing second favourite for the Breeders' Cup Classic. Granted a strong pace to bring his stamina into play, there are more good races for him as a four-year-old. The front-running Peace Rules ran a close third in the Kentucky Derby after winning his trial, the Blue Grass Stakes at Keeneland. Only fourth in the Preakness, Peace Rules bounced back with a defeat of the previous season's unbeaten two-year-old Sky Mesa (rated 116) in the Haskell Invitational, the pair clear of Funny Cide. Peace Rules had recorded his three wins at two on turf, and he ended the year back on grass, finishing last when favourite in the Breeders' Cup Mile.

Dynever fared best of the three-year-olds who made it to the Breeders' Cup Classic, staying on well for third. He had finished a well-held fourth in the Belmont, but twice ran well in defeat in between, and he should do well again in 2004. Inevitably, some of the leading three-year-olds showed their best form before the Triple Crown races. **Buddy Gil** gained a narrow win over **Indian Express** in the Santa Anita Derby, but it was Santa

Anita fourth **Atswhatimtalknbout** who fared best of the three when a strong-finishing fourth in the Kentucky Derby.

Away from the classics, the three-year-old males included a couple of leading performers over shorter trips. The lightly-raced **Ghoztzapper** found the post coming too soon when a close third to **Valid Video** in the King's Bishop Stakes, but he turned the Vosburgh Stakes at Belmont into a rout, winning by six and a half lengths. He bypassed the Breeders' Cup Sprint, but looks an exciting prospect for 2004 when the Carter Handicap and Metropolitan Mile could be on his agenda. **Cajun Beat** proved a progressive gelding, and overcame both a wide draw and racing up with a furious pace to win the Breeders' Cup Sprint, which for the second year running lacked a European challenger. He too should go on again in 2004.

European visitor **Phoenix Reach** put up the best performance by a three-year-old colt on turf in North America when winning the Canadian International, with his St Leger conqueror Brian Boru a below-par third. Among the American horses, the former Solario Stakes runner-up **Sweet Return** benefited from a fine tactical ride to beat his unlucky stable-companion, the ex-French Del Mar Derby winner **Fairly Ransom**, in a blanket finish to the Hollywood Derby, with the Secretariat Stakes winner **Kicken Kris** a close third. **Stroll** has yet to contest a Grade 1 event, but he looks well up to the task, having won his last five races, including a defeat of Kicken Kris in the Grade 2 Jamaica Handicap at Belmont. Canada's first Triple Crown winner for ten years, Wando (116), finished a creditable fourth when favourite for the Atto Mile at Woodbine.

Honours were spread fairly evenly among the leading three-year-old fillies on dirt. **Lady Tak** put up the division's best performance to win the seven-furlong Test Stakes at Saratoga by four and a half lengths in near course-record time. She also looked a different class to her rivals for most of the way in the Gazelle Handicap at Belmont over nine furlongs next time, but weakened dramatically in the closing stages to be beaten half a length by the British-trained longshot **Buy The Sport**, who received 8 lb. The same trip in both the Kentucky Oaks and Breeders' Cup Distaff proved beyond Lady Tak, but at around a mile earlier in the year she had finished second in both the Ashland Stakes and the Acorn Stakes. The Test Stakes runner-up **Bird Town** had won both her earlier meetings with Lady Tak, firstly showing improved form to land the Kentucky Oaks and then pipping her in the Acorn at Belmont. Bird Town finished her career with a good second in the Beldame Stakes in October, faring best of the three-year-olds in the race.

Both **Island Fashion** and **Spoken Fur** ran on turf late in the year, but both had been among the best fillies around on dirt. Island Fashion ran out a six-length winner of the Alabama Stakes at Saratoga, when helped by the poor showing of both Spoken Fur and Bird Town, and returned to form to win the La Brea Stakes by a similar margin in December. Spoken Fur had earlier won the first two legs of New York's Triple Tiara, showing improvement on her first start for Bobby Frankel when beating the Kentucky Oaks third Yell (112) over five lengths in the Mother Goose Stakes, and then landing the odds easily in a weak Coaching Club American Oaks over a mile and a half. Spoken Fur ran well on her final start on dirt when a close third in the Gazelle Handicap.

The previous year's Breeders' Cup Juvenile Fillies winner Storm Flag Flying failed to show her form in two races, missing the second half of the year due to injury, but the runner-up in that contest, **Composure**, made a promising return at three with Grade 1 wins early on in the Las Virgenes Stakes and the Santa Anita Oaks. Unfortunately, she was unable to race again after sustaining a fractured sesamoid in the latter race. Composure was sold in foal to A P Indy for $3.6m at Keeneland in November, purchased by Sheikh Mohammed's Darley Stud. The genuine and consistent **Elloluv** finished second to Composure in both those races at Santa Anita before an all-the-way win over Lady Tak in the Ashland Stakes at Keeneland in April. After a fourth place in the Kentucky Oaks, she was back in the autumn, finishing a creditable second in the Breeders' Cup Distaff.

European fillies, or those formerly trained in Europe, dominated the turf scene among the three-year-old fillies. **Dimitrova** did well in a four-race American campaign for Dermot Weld, winning both the valuable non-graded American Oaks (which receives Grade 1 status in 2004) and the Flower Bowl Invitational Stakes. In between, she was a good second to **Indy Five Hundred** in the Garden City Breeders' Cup Handicap, giving the winner plenty of weight. Both Dimitrova and the Poule d'Essai des Pouliches winner

Woodward Stakes, Belmont Park—Horse of The Year Mineshaft
cruises up on the outside of Hold That Tiger and the blinkered Puzzlement

Musical Chimes ran poorly in the Breeders' Cup Filly & Mare Turf, but the French filly was a good second against older fillies either side of that run in both the Yellow Ribbon Stakes and the Matriarch Stakes. Like Dimitrova and Musical Chimes, the Pouliches runner-up Maiden Tower had joined an American stable by the end of the year, having been beaten a nose by **Film Maker** in the Queen Elizabeth II Challenge Cup at Keeneland.

Not for the first time, the Breeders' Cup Classic was notable for some important absentees. Empire Maker's absence has already been mentioned, and neither of the top two older horses on dirt, **Candy Ride** and **Mineshaft**, was in the field at Santa Anita. Candy Ride was being rested for the following season, while Mineshaft had succumbed to injury. Mineshaft, voted Horse of The Year, had the harder campaign of the pair, winning seven of his nine starts, including all but one of his five outings in Grade 1 company. He had shown just useful form on turf in Britain for John Gosden but improved out of all recognition once switched to dirt. Mineshaft's best effort actually came in his only defeat in a Grade 1 when failing by a head to give 8 lb to **Perfect Drift** (who later beat Congaree in a Grade 2 at Turfway Park) in the Stephen Foster Handicap at Churchill Downs in June, the pair drawing right away in a thrilling finish. A month earlier, Mineshaft won the Pimlico Special Handicap, and after the Stephen Foster he completed a Grade 1 hat-trick at Belmont in the Suburban Handicap, the Woodward Stakes and the Jockey Club Gold Cup, winning impressively each time.

In contrast, the Argentinian-bred Candy Ride has had only six races in his life and remains unbeaten. He won all three of his races in his native country by wide margins in 2002, and put up a top-class effort on his North American Grade 1 debut when breaking the track record in the Pacific Classic at Del Mar. Although Candy Ride had just three rivals, he beat a stronger field than any Mineshaft had faced, with **Medaglia d'Oro** over three lengths behind in second. That was Medaglia d'Oro's first defeat of the year after winning two Grade 2 events, and then the Whitney Handicap at Saratoga. The Whitney saw Medaglia d'Oro turn the tables on **Volponi**, who had beaten him into second in the previous year's Breeders' Cup Classic. At the time, Volponi's Breeders' Cup win was some way in advance of anything he had achieved previously, and he never came close to repeating that form in the latest season. Although Volponi also finished second to Mineshaft in the Suburban Handicap, he failed to win in 2003 and was retired to stud after trailing home in the latest Breeders' Cup Classic. Medaglia d'Oro, on the other hand, managed to repeat his placing of the year before in the Classic, though his involvement in a duel for the lead set things up for **Pleasantly Perfect** to record a length-and-a-half victory. Pleasantly Perfect had had to miss the race the year before and minor injuries had restricted him to just three prior outings in the latest season, though they included a defeat of the subsequent Japan Cup Dirt winner **Fleetstreet Dancer** (also third to Candy Ride in the Pacific Classic) in the Grade 2 Goodwood Breeders' Cup Handicap at Santa Anita. Pleasantly Perfect completed a remarkable day for trainer Richard Mandella, who was responsible for a record four winners on the Breeders' Cup card.

The Breeders' Cup Classic fourth **Congaree**, who had taken on Medaglia d'Oro for the lead, may have been a bit behind the very best dirt performers, but he lacked nothing in toughness and versatility. After losing out in a thrilling duel with the previous year's winner **Milwaukee Brew** for the Santa Anita Handicap, Congaree dropped back three furlongs for an easy success in the seven-furlong Carter Handicap at Aqueduct in April. Back at a mile and a quarter, he gained an authoritative win over **Harlan's Holiday** in the Hollywood Gold Cup in July, and, after the Breeders' Cup, Congaree rounded off a fine year with a second successive victory in the Cigar Mile Handicap at Aqueduct. Congaree could take his chance in the Dubai World Cup, and with Medaglia d'Oro another possible for the race in 2004, the American challenge could be a particularly strong one. Harlan's Holiday finished second in the latest renewal of the world's richest race after a successful prep in the Donn Handicap, but was forced into retirement in August after sustaining an injury.

Congaree's claims to being the best seven-furlong/mile performer on dirt were seriously challenged by the formerly British-trained horse **Aldebaran**. He shook off his 'nearly-horse' tag (he was runner-up four times in Grade 1 company in 2002) with three successes at the top level in 2003. After winning the San Carlos Handicap at Santa Anita and finishing runner-up to Congaree in the Carter, Aldebaran won the Metropolitan Handicap at Belmont (where Congaree paid for chasing a strong pace) and the Forego Handicap at Saratoga. He started favourite for the Breeders' Cup Sprint on his final start but lacked the pace to figure in the six-furlong contest, staying on well for sixth. The tough geldings **Bluesthestandard** and **Shake You Down**, both of them formerly campaigned in claiming company, fared best of the older brigade to fill the places in the Sprint. Shake You Down went on to finish second in the Frank J. de Francis Memorial Dash at Laurel behind **A Huevo**. The seven-year-old winner was another testament to the training skills

Breeders' Cup Classic Powered by Dodge, Santa Anita—
Pleasantly Perfect (left) stays on well to catch Medaglia d'Oro (rail) and eventual fourth Congaree

of Michael Dickinson, who had brought the gelding back in the summer after nearly four years off the track.

Another big name missing from the Breeders' Cup meeting was that of the 2002 Horse of the Year and champion filly **Azeri**. Her top-class performance in the previous year's Breeders' Cup Distaff whetted the appetite for a clash with male rivals in 2003 but it never took place, and her latest campaign, although remunerative for connections, told us little new about her. She landed the odds in the Apple Blossom, Milady Breeders' Cup, and Vanity Handicaps, all Grade 1 races that she had also won in 2002, though the weight concession to her rivals was not enough to make the last two races competitive. A defeat of the subsequent Breeders' Cup Distaff third **Got Koko** in a Grade 2 at Del Mar took Azeri's winning streak to eleven, but she was beaten into third (promoted to second) by the same rival in a similar event at Santa Anita in September on what turned out to be her final start. Azeri was found to be suffering from a viral infection after that run, but it was tendon trouble which caused her to miss defending her Distaff title at the Breeders' Cup. Transferred from Laura de Seroux to Wayne Lukas amid controversial circumstances, she'll reportedly be back in 2004.

With Azeri out of the way, the Distaff looked at the mercy of **Sightseek**, who progressed very well during the season and emerged as Azeri's chief rival among the older fillies. She went to Santa Anita after completing a four-timer in Grade 1 company, winning the Humana Distaff Handicap at Churchill Downs, the Ogden Phipps Handicap at Belmont, the Go For Wand Stakes by over eleven lengths at Saratoga, and the Beldame Stakes against five other Grade 1 winners at Belmont. However, Sightseek ran her only poor race of the year when finishing a well-held fourth to rank outsider **Adoration** in the Distaff. Adoration had been only fourth past the post in the race that had seen Azeri's defeat at Santa Anita in September, and was beaten in Grade 2 company after the Distaff.

With Azeri and Sightseek dominating the division, few others got the chance of Grade 1 success. **Starrer** returned better than ever to win the Santa Maria and Santa Margarita Handicaps at Santa Anita early in the year, giving weight to Sightseek in the latter event, but she was subsequently retired. The genuine and consistent **Take Charge Lady** came up against both the big two, going down narrowly to Azeri in the Apple Blossom and finishing second to Sightseek in the Ogden Phipps before maintaining her unbeaten course record at Keeneland with a second successive defeat of **You** in the Spinster Stakes. However, as in the two previous seasons, the Breeders' Cup meeting did not see Take Charge Lady at her best and she finished only sixth of seven in the Distaff.

The Chilean-bred **Wild Spirit** was not entered for the Breeders' Cup but she stays in training in 2004 and put herself in line for more good prizes after winning three of her four starts for Bobby Frankel. They included a defeat of You and **Passing Shot** in the Ruffian Handicap after the latter had beaten Wild Spirit a nose in the Personal Ensign Handicap. Over shorter trips, the six-year-old mare **Shine Again** failed by just a nose to

Breeders' Cup Distaff Presented by Nextel, Santa Anita—Adoration causes an upset, winning from Elloluv

complete a hat-trick of wins in the seven-furlong Ballerina Handicap at Saratoga, a race which went to **Harmony Lodge**. **Xtra Heat** gained a remarkable twenty-fifth stakes win (a record for a filly or mare) in a Grade 2 event at Laurel in February but was retired to stud after injuring herself in Dubai, where she had been due to contest the Golden Shaheen.

Racing on turf featured a couple of the most dramatic Grade 1 contests of recent years. The Breeders' Cup Turf resulted in the first dead-heat in the meeting's history, with **High Chaparral** catching Falbrav on the post to win the race for the second year running, though having to share the spoils with the late-finishing **Johar**. Another of Richard Mandella's quartet of winners, Johar showed plenty of improvement for the step up in trip, and had missed most of the year with a shoulder injury. **Sulamani** and **Storming Home** (who had beaten Johar in the Clement L. Hirsch Memorial Turf Championship over a mile and a quarter the time before) weren't involved in the finish at Santa Anita, but they had earlier been the main protagonists in an equally dramatic Arlington Million. Storming Home was first past the post at Arlington, but ducked right just yards from the line and unseated Gary Stevens shortly afterwards, hampering the European challengers **Paolini** and **Kaieteur**, who dead-heated for third. Sulamani missed the worst of the trouble to snatch second and was awarded the race, thereby becoming Godolphin's one hundredth Group/Grade 1 winner. Sulamani again took advantage of the lack of good turf horses over middle distances in America when winning the Turf Classic Invitational easily, providing rider Jerry Bailey with one of a record twenty-six Grade 1 victories for the year, in which he also broke his own prize money record, winning more than twenty-three million dollars. The former Champion Stakes winner Storming Home, who has returned to Britain to start a stud career, had earlier made a good start in the States, beating **Denon** impressively in a very valuable event at Hollywood before a Grade 1 success there in the Charlie Whittingham Handicap.

Denon went on to run with credit in most of the big turf races. He won the Manhattan Handicap at Belmont before carrying top weight into a close fifth behind **Balto Star** in the United Nations Handicap and when fourth to **Whitmore's Conn** in the Sword Dancer Invitational Handicap. However, he was unable to take advantage of level terms in the Man o'War Stakes, finishing third to **Lunar Sovereign** and Slew Valley (116), that pair having finished third in the United Nations and Sword Dancer respectively. **The Tin Man** was a creditable fourth in the Breeders' Cup Turf for the second year running after a close second in the United Nations Handicap earlier in the year, while **Macaw**, a useful handicapper when trained in Britain by Jim Goldie, developed into a smart performer with second places in the Sword Dancer and the Canadian International. **Continuously**, another formerly trained in Britain, was not among the best of Bobby Frankel's stars in a team which had formidable strength (including the likes of Empire Maker, Medaglia d'Oro, Sightseek, Ghostzapper and Aldebaran to name just a few), but he benefited from the disqualification of stable-companion **Epicentre** in the Hollywood Turf Cup in November. Despite saddling four beaten favourites in the Breeders' Cup, Frankel's prize money total for the season of over nineteen million dollars broke the record set by Wayne Lukas in 1988.

French filly **Six Perfections** might have beaten the best North American milers in the Breeders' Cup Mile, but there was more strength in depth among the turf performers at that trip than over further. **Touch of The Blues** improved again at the age of six and chased home Six Perfections at Santa Anita. He had earlier beaten Canada's top milers **Soaring Free** and **Perfect Soul** in the Atto Mile at Woodbine. Soaring Free fared the better of that pair when fifth at the Breeders' Cup, but Perfect Soul had **Honor In War** (the Woodford Reserve Turf Classic winner), Touch of The Blues and Soaring Free in the frame behind him when winning Keeneland's Shadwell Turf Mile three weeks before the Breeders' Cup. Perfect Soul had done most of his racing over longer trips and was a close fifth in the Arlington Million.

Outsiders **Century City** and **Irish Warrior** completed the frame at Santa Anita in the Mile. **Special Ring** was among the leading contenders but met with trouble in the Breeders' Cup Mile and had good form earlier on, breaking the nine-furlong track record with a five-length win in the Eddie Read Handicap at Del Mar. **Designed For Luck** was another who was not at his best in the Breeders' Cup Mile, but he had some of the best form after his Grade 2 success over the same course and distance three weeks earlier, finishing ahead of **Sarafan**, Century City and Special Ring. **Redattore** was the main name missing from the Breeders' Cup Mile field: like most South American-bred horses (Candy Ride and Wild Spirit were others), he was not nominated to the Breeders' Cup. He was better than ever at the age of eight though, his victories including three successes in Grade 2 company, the first of which was gained from **Good Journey** (who himself put up a high-class effort giving the winner weight) at Santa Anita in March, and a defeat of both Special Ring and Touch of The Blues in the Grade 1 Shoemaker Breeders' Cup Mile at Hollywood in May. Bill Shoemaker, after whom that race was named, died in October. He amassed what was then a record 8,833 victories as a jockey, including four in the Kentucky Derby. 2003 also saw the death of John Longden, the jockey whose record Shoemaker broke. Another legendary rider, Laffit Pincay Jr, announced his retirement following a bad fall in March, having taken the record to a new mark of 9,530 wins, while Chris McCarron, the all-time leading jockey by earnings (he won the Breeders' Cup Classic five times), was another record-breaking rider to retire.

The older fillies on turf were not a strong group and **Heat Haze**'s fourth place was the best they could manage behind **Islington** (the first British-trained winner of a Breeders' Cup race in six meetings at a Californian track) and the Aidan O'Brien three-year-olds **L'Ancresse** and **Yesterday** in the Breeders' Cup Filly & Mare Turf. A close relative to the 2001 winner of the race Banks Hill, Heat Haze ran well in all her Grade 1 races, which included a narrow defeat by **Voodoo Dancer** in the Diana Handicap and wins in the Beverly D Stakes at Arlington from **Bien Nicole** and the Matriarch Stakes at Hollywood, in which she provided Bobby Frankel with a twenty-fifth Grade 1 success of the year, two more than Aidan O'Brien's previous record haul of Group/Grade 1 winners in 2001. Former Prix de la Foret winner **Dedication** fared best of the other older fillies in the Matriarch (run over a mile for the first time in 2003), finishing a close third. As well as Heat Haze, Frankel and Juddmonte Farms had another leading older female on turf in the form of Sightseek's elder half-sister **Tates Creek**. Like that filly, the normally consistent Tates Creek did not give her running at the Breeders' Cup, but had earlier gained Grade 1 wins in the Gamely Handicap at Hollywood (over Dublino (116) and **Megahertz**) and the Yellow Ribbon Stakes at Santa Anita. Between those wins, Tates Creek had been involved in one of the tightest finishes to a Grade 1 all year when sharing a triple dead-heat for second with Dublino and **Golden Apples**, half a length behind Megahertz (also trained by Frankel) in the John C. Mabee Handicap at Del Mar.

The Juvenile was another Breeders' Cup race with a list of notable absentees, and just two of the field had contested a Grade 1 previously. In a race run at an overly-strong pace, the Mandella stable-companions **Action This Day** and **Minister Eric** drew five lengths clear of the remainder, and both will be suited by a mile and a quarter at three. Third-placed **Chapel Royal**, one of the pace-setters, had earlier finished second behind Breeders' Cup absentees **Silver Wagon** in the Hopeful Stakes and Bird Town's half-brother **Birdstone** in the Champagne Stakes. Silver Wagon won the Hopeful Stakes in fine style but was subsequently beaten in non-graded company behind **Second of June**. **Ruler's Court** also missed the Breeders' Cup, having by then joined Godolphin after his fourteen-length victory in the Grade 2 Norfolk Stakes at Santa Anita. However, a knee injury sustained in Dubai has ruled him out of the Kentucky Derby. **Cuvee** lined up as the only Grade 1 winner in the Breeders' Cup Juvenile field but finished last at Santa Anita from

Bessemer Trust Breeders' Cup Juvenile, Santa Anita—Action This Day is one of four winners on the card for trainer Richard Mandella; Minister Eric makes it a 1,2 for the stable

Breeders' Cup Juvenile Fillies, Santa Anita—Julie Krone becomes the first female jockey to win a Breeders' Cup race; Halfbridled is chased home by Ashado (left) and Victory U.S.A.

the worst of the draw. He had been an impressive winner of the Futurity Stakes at Belmont in September, though he is not certain to stay so well as some of the other leading colts. Birdstone's stable-companion **Eurosilver** side-stepped the Breeders' Cup, though an impressive and near five-length defeat of the subsequent Juvenile fourth **Tiger Hunt** in the Grade 2 Lane's End Breeders' Futurity at Keeneland suggests he would have been thereabouts at Santa Anita. Along with Eurosilver and Birdstone, a third classic prospect emerged for the Nick Zito stable when **The Cliff's Edge**, who had finished sixth behind Eurosilver at Keeneland, won the Grade 2 Kentucky Jockey Club Stakes at Churchill Downs in November. Other promising winners late in the year were the unbeaten Hollywood Futurity winner **Lion Heart**, Grade 2 Remsen Stakes winner **Read The Footnotes** (who beat the Brian Meehan-trained Master David) and Michael Dickinson's Grade 3 Laurel Futurity winner **Tapit**.

The Breeders' Cup Juvenile Fillies was a better-contested race than the colts' equivalent. **Halfbridled**, ridden by Julie Krone, initiated a double for the Mandella stable in the Juvenile events. Krone, who made a comeback from retirement late in 2002, became the first female rider to win a Breeders' Cup race, and earlier in the year she had also been the first female jockey to win a million-dollar race when partnering Candy Ride in the Pacific Classic. The unbeaten Halfbridled looks a really good prospect, overcoming a wide draw to beat a couple of fillies, **Ashado** and **Victory U.S.A.**, who also already had Grade 1 form to their names, the first three finishing well clear. Ashado (the winner of the Spinaway Stakes at Saratoga) and Victory U.S.A. had also been placed (in reverse order) in the Frizette Stakes at Belmont behind **Society Selection**, who was to disappoint at Santa Anita. Both Ashado and Victory U.S.A. were successful after the Juvenile Fillies, Ashado's win coming in the Grade 2 Demoiselle Stakes at Aqueduct over nine furlongs, a race in which she beat **La Reina** by a nose. Victory U.S.A., however, could finish only fourth on her final outing behind Breeders' Cup Juvenile Fillies fourth **Hollywood Story** in the Hollywood Starlet Stakes. **Tizdubai**, a sister to the dual Breeders' Cup Classic winner Tiznow, looked an interesting prospect after winning both her starts in the summer (including the Grade 2 Sorrento Stakes at Del Mar), but, like her stable-companion Ruler's Court, she picked up a leg injury.

European-trained horses who showed or reproduced their best form in North America are included in this list	**Two-Year-Olds**	
	121 Action This Day	117 Minister Eric
	121p Halfbridled (f)	116p Lion Heart
	119 Cuvee	116 Ashado (f)
	118p Eurosilver	116 Victory U.S.A. (f)
† commentary in *Racehorses of 2003*	118 Ruler's Court	115p Birdstone
	118 Silver Wagon	115 La Reina (f)
	118 Society Selection (f)	114p Read The Footnotes
	117 Hollywood Story (f)	114 Tizdubai (f)
		113 Class Above (f)

113p The Cliff's Edge
112   Be Gentle (f)
112   Lokoya (f)
112   Marylebone (f)
112   Perfect Moon
112   Rahy Dolly (f)
111   Feline Story (f)
111   Siphonizer
111   Whoopi Cat (f)
111   Zosima (f)
110p Tapit
110   Chapel Royal
110   Maple Syrple (f)
110   Mr Jester
110   Salty Romance (f)
109   Cactus Ridge
109   Dirty Diana (f)
109   Fire Slam
109   Heckle
109   Limehouse
109   Paddington
109   Spectacular Moon (f)
109   St Averil
109   Tiger Hunt
109   Wacky Patty (f)
108p Second of June
108   Dr Kathy (f)
108   Pomeroy
108   Smokey Glacken (f)
108   Tarlow (f)
108   That's An Outrage
108   Unbridled Beauty (f)

DIRT

Three-Year-Olds
129   Empire Maker
128   Funny Cide
128   Ten Most Wanted
126   Ghostzapper
124   Lady Tak (f)
123   Cajun Beat
123   Dynever
122   Atswhatimtalknbout
122   Peace Rules
121   Island Fashion (f)
121   Spoken Fur (f)
120   Bird Town (f)
120   Buddy Gil
120   Composure (f)
120   Indian Express
120   Strong Hope
119   Elloluv (f)
118   Midas Eyes
118   Soto
118   Trust N Luck
118   Valid Video
117   Eye of The Tiger
117   †Hold That Tiger

117   Nacheezmo
117   Randaroo (f)
117   Sir Cherokee

116   House Party (f)
116   Southern Image
114   †Buy The Sport (f)

Older Horses
133   †Candy Ride
132   †Mineshaft
129   Azeri (f)
128   Medaglia d'Oro
127   Congaree
126   Aldebaran
126   Pleasantly Perfect
126   Sightseek (f)
125   Perfect Drift
125   Starrer (f)
124   Adoration (f)
124   Harlan's Holiday
123   Take Charge Lady (f)
122   Milwaukee Brew
122   Wild Spirit (f)
121   Xtra Heat (f)
120   Bluesthestandard
120   Shine Again (f)
120   Volponi
119   A Huevo
119   Got Koko (f)
119   Joey Franco
119   Kudos
119   Quest
119   Shake You Down
118   Affluent (f)
118   Allamerican Bertie (f)
118   Avanzado
118   Beau's Town
118   You (f)
117   Bowman's Band
117   Carson Hollow (f)
117   Gold Mover (f)
117   Grey Memo
117   Iron Deputy
117   Piensa Sonando
117   Publication
117   Summer Colony (f)
117   Total Impact

116   Fleetstreet Dancer
115   Harmony Lodge (f)
114   Passing Shot (f)

TURF

Three-Year-Olds
124   †Six Perfections (f)
123   †L'Ancresse (f)

122p †Phoenix Reach
119p Stroll
119   †Dimitrova (f)
119   †Yesterday (f)
117   *Fairly Ransom
117   †Musical Chimes (f)
117   Indy Five Hundred (f)

116   Film Maker (f)
116   Kicken Kris
116   Sweet Return
109   Dessert (f)

Older Horses
132   †High Chaparral
130   Johar
128   †Sulamani
126   Good Journey
125   †Storming Home
125   Touch of The Blues
124   Century City
124   †Islington (f)
124   Redatorre
122   Designed For Luck
122   Perfect Soul
122   Soaring Free
122   Special Ring
121   Denon
121   Irish Warrior
121   †Kaieteur
121   *Lunar Sovereign
121   †Paolini
121   Sarafan
121   The Tin Man
121   Voodoo Dancer (f)
120   Heat Haze (f)
120   Honor In War
119   Balto Star
119   Deeliteful Irving
119   Macaw
119   Strut The Stage
118   Bowman Mill
118   Continously
118   Dedication (f)
118   Della Francesca
118   Epicentre
118   Grammarian
118   Man From Wicklow
118   Proud Man
118   Tates Creek (f)
117   Bien Nicole (f)
117   Freefourinternet
117   Golden Apples (f)
117   Rouvres
117   Runaway Dancer
117   Whitmore's Conn

116   Megahertz (f)
114   Volga (f)
112   Passinetti

JAPAN For the second year running, Horse of The Year honours went to the top-class colt **Symboli Kris S**. He became only the fourth horse in the history of the Japan Racing Association to win two such titles, and the first since Symboli Rudolf in 1984/1985. Symboli Kris S repeated his Group 1 successes of the year before in both the Tenno Sho (Autumn), beating **Tsurumaru Boy** and **Tenzan Seiza**, and the Arima Kinen. He rounded off his career by winning the latter by nine lengths under his by-then regular partner

Olivier Peslier, before being syndicated with a stud value of fifteen million dollars. Symboli Kris S retired as one of the best Japanese middle-distance horses of recent years never to win the Japan Cup. Favourite for the race for the second time, he once again had to settle for third place, this time behind the wide-margin winner **Tap Dance City**. Allowed a clear lead from an early stage on unusually rain-softened ground, Tap Dance City's nine-length victory flattered him somewhat, and he finished well held in the Arima Kinen on his next outing. **Hishi Miracle**, the previous season's St Leger winner, had to miss the big autumn races with a leg injury, but had returned earlier in the year with Group 1 successes in the two-mile Tenno Sho (Spring) and the Takarazuka Kinen over eleven furlongs. He beat a strong field in the latter event, with Tsurumaru Boy and Tap Dance City filling the places and Symboli Kris S (making his reappearance) only fifth.

Over shorter trips, milers **Lohengrin** and **Telegnosis** put up a couple of the best performances, finishing placed in the Prix du Moulin and Prix Jacques le Marois respectively on their joint visit to France. Both colts won in Group 2 company at home, with Lohengrin also finishing third in the Yasuda Kinen, behind **Agnes Digital** and **Admire Max**, and in the Hong Kong Mile in which Admire Max finished fourth. Agnes Digital's Yasuda Kinen victory made 2003 the fourth year in succession that he had scored in Group 1 company. There was no Japanese success at the Hong Kong International meeting, but **Eishin Preston** maintained his good record at Sha Tin when registering a second successive win in the Queen Elizabeth II Cup in April, and was then fourth in the Tenno Sho (Autumn). The mare **Believe** failed by a nose to complete a double in Japan's Group 1 sprints, taking the Takamatsunomiya Kinen in the spring before being touched off by **Durandal** (Admire Max third) when seeking a second successive win in the Sprinters Stakes in the autumn. Durandal went on to further Group 1 success in the Mile Championship over a field which included Tout Seul from Britain and Special Kaldoun from France.

Unlike its British counterpart, Japan's St Leger, the Kikuka Sho (over a full fifteen furlongs) at Kyoto, isn't shunned by the connections of the leading three-year-old colts. In the latest running, four of the top colts of the classic generation took the first four places, with victory going to the subsequent Japan Cup runner-up **That's The Plenty**. **Neo Universe** started favourite for the Kikuka Sho after winning the first two colts' classics, the Satsuki Sho (2000 Guineas) and Tokyo Yushun (Derby) but could finish only third in the St Leger and fourth against older horses in both the Takarazuka Kinen and the Japan Cup. Like Symboli Kris S, he was the regular mount of a European rider, Italian Mirco Demuro becoming the first foreign jockey to win the Japanese Derby. **Lincoln** took second place in the St Leger and filled the same spot in the Arima Kinen at the end of the year ahead of the Derby runner-up and St Leger fourth **Zenno Rob Roy**, who had beaten all the aforementioned colts in a Group 2 at Hanshin in between the Derby and St Leger. **Gallant Arrow** put up the best effort by a three-year-old against older horses over shorter trips when third in the Mile Championship.

Neo Universe, Lincoln and Zenno Rob Roy are all by the outstanding sire Sunday Silence, who died in 2002, and he was also responsible for the top two three-year-old fillies, **Still In Love** and **Admire Groove**. Still In Love won the Oka Sho (1000 Guineas) and Yushun Himba (Oaks) before completing the fillies' triple crown with victory over

Japan Cup, Tokyo—Tap Dance City's clear lead is maintained to the line; the first five are all home-trained

Guineas third Admire Groove in the Shuka Sho over a mile and a quarter in the autumn. However when the pair met again, this time against older fillies (French-trained Tigertail was third) in the Queen Elizabeth II Commemorative Cup, Admire Groove turned the tables to win by a nose.

Three-year-olds		125	Telegnosis	116	Agnes Sonic
119	That's The Plenty	122	Durandal	116	Balance of Game
118	Lincoln	122	Eishin Preston	116	Dantsu Flame
118	Neo Universe	122	Hishi Miracle	116	Dantsu Running
117	Admire Groove (f)	121	Tsurumaru Boy	116	Fast Tateyama
117	Gallant Arrow	120	Agnes Digital	116	Fine Motion (f)
117	Still In Love (f)	119	Admire Max	116	Precise Machine
117	Zenno Rob Roy	118	Believe (f)	115	Admire Don
116	Sakura President	118	Gold Allure	115	Biwa Shinseiki
114	Win Kluger	118	Tenzan Seiza	115	Camphor Best
		117	Air Eminem	115	Ingrandire
Older Horses		117	Daitaku Bertram	115	Millennium Bio
132	Symboli Kris S	117	Eagle Cafe	115	No Reason
125	Lohengrin	117	Shonan Kampf	115	Sunningdale
125	Tap Dance City	117	Sunrise Jaeger	115	Toshi The V

HONG KONG   Three locally-trained Group 1 winners on the International card in December 2002 had seen the number of horses in Hong Kong with a rating of 115 or more rise to fourteen. 2003 saw the figure rise to twenty-one as the quality of racing in Hong Kong continues to improve. With most of the runners being geldings, and the races richly endowed compared to most other countries, there is little incentive for them to compete abroad. However, ex-British **Firebolt** took up the challenge to run in the King's Stand Stakes at Royal Ascot in 2003, but finished ninth, the only time he was out of the frame in seven starts during the year.

The main star in 2003 was sprinter **Silent Witness**, who progressed rapidly, extending his unbeaten record to eight when landing the odds in the Hong Kong Sprint by a length from the South African-trained National Currency, with **Cape of Good Hope** (without a win in 2003) third and Firebolt fourth. Further down the field were four British-trained horses and the 2002 winner All Thrills Too, who was a shadow of his former self in 2003 after finishing third in the Bauhinia Sprint Trophy and Centenary Sprint Cup early in the year. Both those races were won by **Grand Delight**, who added the Chairman's Sprint Prize (from Cape of Good Hope) to complete the Sprint Triple Crown before his form tailed off late in the year, finishing down the field in the Hong Kong Sprint. Grand Delight's trainer, John Size, won the trainers' premiership for the second time in two years since his move from Australia.

The winners of the Hong Kong Mile and Hong Kong Cup in 2002, **Olympic Express** and **Precision**, failed to make an impact in the same races in the latest season, the former being pulled up, but both had recorded major wins earlier in the year. Precision won the Hong Kong Champions & Chater Cup in June from ex-Australian filly **Elegant Fashion**, and Olympic Express took the Hong Kong Gold Cup in February from **Dr More** with Elegant Fashion third. Afterwards, Elegant Fashion beat the Classic Mile winner **Self Flit**

Hong Kong Sprint, Sha Tin—
the current star of Hong Kong racing Silent Witness takes his unbeaten run to eight;
South African-trained National Currency is second

comfortably to land the Hong Kong Derby with other notable runners such as **River Dancer** (formerly known as Diaghilev in Ireland) in fifth and **Bowman's Crossing** in tenth. Elegant Fashion was also second to the Japanese-trained Eishin Preston in the Audemars Piguet Queen Elizabeth II Cup and a good third to Falbrav and Rakti in the Hong Kong Cup.

The Hong Kong Mile went the way of local runner **Lucky Owners**, who, like Silent Witness, had progressed through the ranks on the way to Group 1 glory. He beat Bowman's Crossing by half a length to take his record to seven wins from eleven starts. His task in the Mile was made considerably easier by the absence through injury to **Electronic Unicorn** which, at the time of writing, is still threatening to curtail his career. Electronic Unicorn was unlucky in the 2002 renewal of the Hong Kong Mile but was unbeaten in three races in 2003, winning the Stewards' Cup (by nearly four lengths from Dr More), the Group 2 Chairman's Trophy (from **Goggles**) and the Champions Mile by two and a quarter lengths from **Meridian Star**.

Hong Kong's representatives at the International meeting usually face their stiffest task in the Hong Kong Vase and things were no different in 2003. The best of the locally-trained horses was Roosevelt, who finished a respectable fourth to Vallee Enchantee without being able to reproduce the form of his third in the Irish Derby when in the care of Aidan O'Brien.

126	Silent Witness	119	Goggles	117	Red Pepper
125	Electronic Unicorn	118	Citizen Kane	116	Self Flit
122	Lucky Owners	118	Grand Delight	115	Cheerful Fortune
121	Bowman's Crossing	118	Precision	115	Meridian Star
121	Cape of Good Hope	118	River Dancer	115	Red Sun
121	Olympic Express	117	Firebolt		
120	Dr More	117	Ho Choi		
119	Elegant Fashion (f)	117	Housemaster		

AUSTRALIA AND NEW ZEALAND   2003 was a significant year for the Australasian racing industry mainly through the European deeds of the high-class sprinter **Choisir**. Choisir caused an upset when leading throughout in the King's Stand Stakes at Royal Ascot to become the first Australian-trained horse to win in Britain, and then repeated the performance in the Golden Jubilee Stakes four days later. In his final run in Britain, Choisir was beaten by the champion sprinter Oasis Dream in the July Cup at Newmarket. Choisir had taken time to mature as a sprinter in Australia, his waywardness early in his career hindering his progress until his true worth became evident after a dazzling win in the Group 1 Lightning Stakes over the straight five furlongs at Flemington. Choisir was purchased after the July Cup by Coolmore and will operate in Australia and Ireland as a shuttle stallion.

Australasian racing witnessed a change at the top following a career-threatening injury to champion **Northerly**. The dual Cox Plate winner was in excellent form early in the year, winning the Australian Cup (ten furlongs) at Flemington for the second time, having already scored in 2001 and finished runner-up in 2002. Following that win, Northerly was taken to Sydney but failed to reproduce his best on the right-handed tracks. His three runs in Sydney resulted in two Group 1 seconds, in the Ranvet Stakes (ten furlongs) and the BMW (twelve furlongs), and one unplaced run. Northerly then suffered a leg injury while being prepared for a defence of the Cox Plate, though a return to the track has not been ruled out. Northerly is the winner of nine Group 1 races and AU $9,340,950.

With the departure of Northerly, the way was clear for **Lonhro** to assert his superiority. He had an exceptional year, winning at Group 1 level five times from seven and a half to ten furlongs; victories in the Chipping Norton Stakes, George Main Stakes, George Ryder Stakes, Queen Elizabeth Stakes and Caulfield Stakes earned him the highest rating for 2003. However, Lonhro couldn't win the Cox Plate, finishing a close third, below his best in the wet conditions and on a slippery surface. The year also saw the loss of the very smart **Shogun Lodge** who suffered a heart attack while running in the Emirates Stakes at Flemington on the last day of the Melbourne Cup carnival. Shogun Lodge, who made a winning reappearance in the listed Tattersalls Lightning Handicap over five furlongs at

Randwick, raced 58 times for 13 wins, including three at Group 1 level plus a further 12 placings at that level and AU$4,652,224 in earnings.

Spinning Hill was the top sprinting mare in Australia, just ahead of New Zealand mare **Our Egyptian Raine**, the former's best performances including finishing runner-up to Choisir in the Lightning Stakes and winning the Manikato Stakes at Moonee Valley and the Group 2 T J Smith at Randwick. Our Egyptian Raine started the year in dazzling style, winning the Group 1 Railway Stakes and being runner-up in the Group 1 Telegraph Stakes in New Zealand. However, it was not until late in the year in Melbourne that we saw the best of her again. She recorded impressive wins in the Group 2 A J Moir Stakes at Moonee Valley (from Spinning Hill) and the Emirates Classic down the Flemington straight.

Australasia's weight-for-age championship, the W S Cox Plate at Moonee Valley, was won by **Fields of Omagh**, who landed the event after just two runs back from a long spell off the course following injury. In 2002, Fields of Omagh was overshadowed by champion Northerly but the 2003 Cox Plate provided the son of Rubiton with a richly deserved victory, as well as being a splendid advertisement for his trainer Tony McEvoy. Other older horses worthy of mention include Freemason, Grand Armee and Defier. **Freemason** has been a consistent performer in weight-for-age events for a number of years and he gained his most important win narrowly from Northerly in the BMW at Rosehill in April, setting a strong pace from the outset. In one of the most exciting races seen in Sydney for a long time, Freemason and Northerly went neck and neck in the lead for the last four furlongs of the race, setting a new course record. Champion trainer Gai Waterhouse produced **Grand Armee** to win the AJC Doncaster Handicap over a mile at Randwick in April with a career-best effort, giving Waterhouse her sixth win in the event. **Defier**, who promised so much coming into 2003, was plagued by niggling injuries, but he did run Fields of Omagh to a neck in the Cox Plate, finishing runner-up for the second successive year.

While Choisir held the top spot among those of his own age, he was pushed by other good horses in a year when there was strength in depth in this group. As well as Choisir, the sprinters included Bel Esprit, Yell and the leading older mares Spinning Hill and Our Egyptian Raine. **Bel Esprit** gained a high-class win in the Doomben 10000 over just short of seven furlongs. Bel Esprit was retired to stud after finishing unplaced in the Stradbroke Handicap next time. **Yell** completed a hat-trick of Group 1 wins in the William Reid Stakes (six furlongs) at Moonee Valley, becoming the first horse since Vo Rogue (1988) to win the William Reid Stakes, Futurity Stakes and C. F. Orr Stakes in successive starts, the last two contests over seven furlongs. Others to have achieved this feat were Crewman (1970) and the champion sprinter Manikato, three times (1979, 1980, 1981).

Group 1 AJC Derby (twelve furlongs) and AJC Epsom Handicap (mile) winner **Clangalang** achieved high ratings all year. He atoned for an unlucky effort in the Rosehill Guineas by winning a strong AJC Derby with subsequent Caulfield Cup winner Mummify third. Also in the field was VRC Derby/Rosehill Guineas winner **Helenus**, VRC Derby runner-up Hydrometer and AJC Oaks winner Sunday Joy. Clangalang had a set-back when being prepared for the Caulfield and Melbourne Cups but made a better than expected recovery and was aimed at the Group 1 Epsom. Despite a month's break from racing, starting from stall 17 and carrying 8-11, he caught the AJC Doncaster winner Grand Armee in the shadow of the post to become the first horse in history to achieve the AJC Derby/Epsom double. **Mummify** enjoyed an excellent autumn campaign which saw him capture the Underwood Stakes (nine furlongs) at Caulfield and the Caulfield Cup (twelve furlongs), as well as push Lonhro when runner-up in the Caulfield Stakes. Mummify was being aimed at the Melbourne Cup but was a race morning scratching when running a high temperature. The highest-rated four-year-old filly was the lightly-raced **Private Steer** who defeated a strong field in the Stradbroke Handicap (seven furlongs) at Eagle Farm which included **Into The Night**, **Falvelon** and Bel Esprit.

Overall, the standard of the three-year-old category was slightly lower than in 2002. **Exceed And Excel** topped the ratings in this age-group following some blistering displays late in the year, his best performance coming in the Dubai Racing Club Cup (seven furlongs) at Caulfield, where he beat a quality field of sprinters in track record time. The win gave young Sydney-based trainer Tim Martin his first Group 1 success and the stable is considering an overseas campaign in 2004 similar to that followed by Choisir. Fillies figured prominently among the three-year-olds. **Haliberry** showed considerable promise early in the year, when she was runner-up in the Blue Diamond Stakes, but her best effort came in the Group 2 Schillaci Stakes at Caulfield, where she led throughout to defeat a good field of sprinters. **Special Harmony** scored two Group 1 victories, the Thousand Guineas at Caulfield and the VRC Oaks at Flemington. The ease of her VRC Oaks win over an extended twelve furlongs suggests she has the makings of a good stayer in 2004.

Queensland-trained filly **Regimental Gal** burst to prominence by winning the Magic Millions (six furlongs) on the Gold Coast in January. When she returned after a break in the San Domenico Stakes (five furlongs) at Randwick she beat a good field which included **Spark of Life**, **Handsome Ransome**, **How Funny** and Exceed And Excel. Golden Slipper Stakes (six furlongs) winner **Polar Success** recorded a workmanlike win in the world's richest juvenile race at Rosehill, but her form tapered off late in the year. A similar fate befell **Hasna**, who ran well in the juvenile Triple Crown earlier in the year, winning both the AJC Sires' Produce Stakes (seven furlongs) and AJC Champagne Stakes (mile) at Randwick after a luckless third in the Golden Slipper Stakes.

The pick of a limited number of two-year-olds making their debut in 2003 was **Not A Single Doubt**, unbeaten in three runs which included the Strawberry Hill Slipper at Wyong and the Canonbury Stakes at Randwick, both over five furlongs. He is an exciting colt who has yet to be tested. The filly **Alinghi** impressed on her only run when winning the Debutante Stakes (extended four furlongs) while Breeders' Stakes (five furlongs) winner **Charge Forward** is also among the leading two-year-olds.

The Melbourne Cup held at Flemington again featured several European raiders in the twenty-three runner field, Jardines Lookout faring best of them in third. However it was the local David Hall-trained mare **Makybe Diva** who prevailed after being settled back in the field early on before producing her customary acceleration to run out a fairly comfortable winner by just over a length. An overseas campaign is being planned for her in 2004. Choisir's European successes were in stark contrast to the efforts of Australia's overseas raiders to Japan and Hong Kong late in 2003. Fields of Omagh failed to handle the rain-softened ground in the Japan Cup and then failed to make much impression in the Hong Kong Vase. Sprinters Into The Night, **Bomber Bill** and **Dantana** were outclassed in the Hong Kong Sprint.

Tooheys New Melbourne Cup, Flemington—Makybe Diva comes from well off the pace

Ratings and text for
Australia and New
Zealand are supplied
courtesy of Gary Crispe
(www.aapracingandsports.com.au).
The ages listed below are
as at 31st December 2003.

Two-Year-Olds
123 Not A Single Doubt
121 Dance Hero
118? Oratorio
115p Alinghi (f)
115p Charge Forward
115 Econsul
114p Crimson Reign (f)
114 Segments (f)
114 Subreilly
112 Collate
112 Deafen
112 Jolie (f)
112 Kapsdan (f)
112 One World (f)
112 Picket Fence
112 Rich Megadale (f)
112 Sanziro
112 Squad
112 Successor
112 The General
112 Wenceslas Square
111 Covertly (f)
111 Jade Diva (f)
111 More Than Hugs (f)

Three-Year-Olds
125 Exceed And Excel
122 Halibery (f)
122 Regimental Gal (f)
122 Special Harmony (f)
122 Untouchable
121p Niello
121 Hasna (f)
121 Polar Success (f)
120 Allgunadoit
120 Ambulance
119p Lago Delight
119 Abdullah
119 Classy Dane (f)
119 Elvstroem
119 In Top Swing
119 Mufti
119 Murphy's Blu Boy
119 Scaredee Cat
118 Face Value
118 Handsome Ransom
118 Legally Bay (f)
118 Shamekha (f)
118 Unearthly (f)
117 Casual Pass
117 Delzao
117 Dorky (f)
117 Gilded Youth
117 Great Is Great
117 King's Chapel
117 November Dreaming
117 Secret Land (f)
117 Snip Attack

117 Tsuimai
116p Dante's Paradiso
116 Hammerbeam
116 How Funny (f)
116 Sir Dex
116 Winestock
115 Danbird
115 Kempinsky
115 Kusi
115 Red Hot Pepper
115 Spark of Life
115 Spurcent (f)
115 Spur Me On
115 Ultimate Fever (f)

Four-Year-Olds
126 Choisir
125 Bel Esprit
125 Clangalang
122 Yell
122 Mummify
122 Thorn Park
121 Private Steer (f)
120 Delago Brom
120 Platinum Scissors
120 Snowland
120 Star of Florida
119 Dantana
118 Half Hennessy
118 Lovely Jubly (f)
118 Sportsman
117 Strasbourg
117 True Glo
116 Force Apollo
116 La Bella Dame (f)
116 Maskerado
116 Planchet
115 Bollinger (f)
115 Helenus
115 Innovation Girl (f)
115 Natural Blitz
115 So Assertive
115 Titanic Jack
115 Tycoon Ruler

Older Horses
128 Lonhro
126 Northerly
122 Defier
122 Freemason
121 Dash For Cash
121 Fields of Omagh
121 Grand Armee
121 Make Mine Magic
120 Shogun Lodge
120 Spinning Hill (f)
119 Into The Night
119 Pentastic
118 Bomber Bill
118 Chong Tong
118 Dress Circle
118 Excellerator
118 Falvelon
118 Fouardee
118 Our Egyptian Raine (f)
117 Arlington Road
117 Gordo

117 Le Zagaletta
117 Lord Essex
117 Makybe Diva (f)
117 Mistegic
116 Bush Padre
116 Distinctly Secret
116 Grey Song
116 Mr Murphy
116 Pembleton
116 Patezza
116 Scenic Peak
115 Carael Boy
115 Carnegie Express
115 Crawl
115 Hail
115 Super Elegant
115 This Manshood
115 Tit For Taat

The following horses trained
elsewhere also figured in
races outside their own
country:

Three-Year-Old
109 Benvenuto (Holland)

Older Horses
123 National Currency
     (South Africa)
113 Lucky Strike
     (Holland)

INDEX TO PHOTOGRAPHS

PORTRAITS & SNAPSHOTS

Humouresque	3 b.f Pivotal – Miswaki Belle	*John Crofts*	472
Hurricane Alan	3 b.c Mukaddamah – Bint Al Balad	*Clare Williams*	473
Ikhtyar	3 b.c Unfuwain – Sabria	*John Crofts*	477
Indian Creek	5 br.h Indian Ridge – Blue Water	*John Crofts*	487
Indian Haven	3 ch.c Indian Ridge – Madame Dubois	*Clare Williams*	490
Intercontinental	3 b.f Danehill – Hasili	*John Crofts*	494
Jardines Lookout	6 b.g Fourstars Allstar – Foolish Flight	*Clare Williams*	511
Kaieteur	4 b.c Marlin – Strong Embrace	*Clare Williams*	523
Kalaman	3 b.c Desert Prince – Kalamba	*John Crofts*	525
Kheleyf	2 br.c Green Desert – Society Lady	*Clare Williams*	534
Kris Kin	3 ch.c Kris S – Angel In My Heart	*John Crofts*	552
Lateen Sails	3 ch.c Elmaamul – Felucca	*John Crofts*	568
Leporello	3 b.c Danehill – Why So Silent	*Clare Williams*	575
Macadamia	4 b.f Classic Cliche – Cashew	*Clare Williams*	604
Magistretti	3 b.c Diesis – Ms Strike Zone	*Clare Williams*	612
Maiden Tower	3 b.f Groom Dancer – Sawara	*John Crofts*	613
Majestic Missile	2 b.c Royal Applause – Tshusick	*Clare Williams*	617
Mamool	4 b.c In The Wings – Genovefa	*John Crofts*	624
Membership	3 ch.c Belong To Me – Shamisen	*John Crofts*	641
Mezzo Soprano	3 b.f Darshaan – Morn of Song	*John Crofts*	645
Milk It Mick	2 b.c Millkom – Lunar Music	*John Crofts*	651
Moon Ballad	4 ch.c Singspiel – Velvet Moon	*John Crofts*	672
Mubtaker	6 ch.h Silver Hawk – Gazayil	*John Crofts*	687
Much Faster	2 b.f Fasliyev – Interruption	*John Crofts*	689
Muqbil	3 ch.c Swain – Istiqlal	*John Crofts*	693
Musical Chimes	3 b.f In Excess – Note Musicale	*Bertrand*	695
Naheef	4 b.c Marju – Golden Digger	*John Crofts*	705
Nayef	5 b.h Gulch – Height of Fashion	*John Crofts*	710
Nebraska Tornado	3 br.f Storm Cat – Media Nox	*John Crofts*	715
Necklace	2 b.f Darshaan – Spinning The Yarn	*Caroline Norris*	717
New Seeker	3 b.c Green Desert – Ahbab	*Clare Williams*	721
Norse Dancer	3 b.c Halling – River Patrol	*John Crofts*	730
Oasis Dream	3 b.c Green Desert – Hope	*John Crofts*	738
Ocean Silk	3 b.f Dynaformer – Mambo Jambo	*John Crofts*	740
Olden Times	5 b.h Darshaan – Garah	*John Crofts*	744
One Cool Cat	2 b.c Storm Cat – Tacha	*Caroline Norris*	749
Passing Glance	4 b.c Polar Falcon – Spurned	*John Crofts*	768
Pastoral Pursuits	2 b.c Bahamian Bounty – Star	*Clare Williams*	769
Patavellian	5 b.g Machiavellian – Alessia	*John Crofts*	772
Persian Punch	10 ch.g Persian Heights – Rum Cay	*John Crofts*	787
Phoenix Reach	3 b.c Alhaarth – Carroll's Canyon	*John Crofts*	793
Place Rouge	4 b.f Desert King – Palmeraie	*John Crofts*	798
Polish Summer	6 b.h Polish Precedent – Hunt The Sun	*John Crofts*	803
Prince Tum Tum	3 b.c Capote – La Grande Epoque	*John Crofts*	817
Private Charter	3 b.c Singspiel – By Charter	*John Crofts*	819
Punctilious	2 b.f Danehill – Robertet	*John Crofts*	823
Rakti	4 b.c Polish Precedent – Ragera	*John Crofts*	835
Razkalla	5 b.g Caerleon – Larrocha	*Clare Williams*	839
Red Bloom	2 b.f Selkirk – Red Camellia	*John Crofts*	842
Reel Buddy	5 ch.h Mr Greeley – Rosebud	*Clare Williams*	848
Refuse To Bend	3 b.c Sadler's Wells – Market Slide	*Peter Mooney*	852
Repertory	10 b.g Anshan – Susie's Baby	*Bill Selwyn*	857
River Belle	2 ch.f Lahib – Dixie Favor	*Clare Williams*	865
Russian Rhythm	3 ch.f Kingmambo – Balistroika	*John Crofts*	884
Sabbeeh	2 b.c Red Ransom – Capistrano Day	*John Crofts*	889
Sabre d'Argent	3 b.c Kris S – Sterling Pound	*Clare Williams*	890
Salsalino	3 ch.c Salse – Alicedale	*Clare Williams*	896
Savannah Bay	4 ch.g In The Wings – High Savannah	*John Crofts*	903
Singleton	3 b.f Singspiel – Rive	*Clare Williams*	936
Six Perfections	3 br.f Celtic Swing – Yogya	*Bertrand*	943
Snow Ridge	2 b.c Indian Ridge – Snow Princess	*John Crofts*	951
Somnus	3 b.g Pivotal – Midnight's Reward	*Alec Russell*	956
Striking Ambition	3 b.c Makbul – Lady Roxanne	*Clare Williams*	981
Summitville	3 b.f Grand Lodge – Tina Heights	*Clare Williams*	989
Sundrop	2 b.f Sunday Silence – Oenothera	*Clare Williams*	990
Super Celebre	3 b.c Peintre Celebre – Supergirl	*Bertrand*	993
Tante Rose	3 b.f Barathea – My Branch	*Clare Williams*	1006

RACE PHOTOGRAPHS

Desmond Stakes (Leopardstown)	*Peter Mooney*	851
Dubai Duty Free Mill Reef Stakes (Newbury)	*John Crofts*	170
Dubai Sheema Classic (Nad Al Sheba)	*Frank Sorge*	984
Dubai World Cup (Nad Al Sheba)	*George Selwyn*	671
Duke of Edinburgh Stakes (Handicap) (Royal Ascot)	*John Crofts*	1091
Dunnes Stores National Stakes (the Curragh)	*Peter Mooney*	748
Emirates Airline Champion Stakes (Newmarket)	*Alec Russell*	834
Emirates Airline Yorkshire Cup (York)	*John Crofts*	623
Entenmann's Irish 1000 Guineas (the Curragh)	*John Crofts*	1119
Entenmann's Irish 2000 Guineas (the Curragh)	*John Crofts*	489
Enter The £1 Million Tote Ten To Follow November Stakes (Handicap) (Doncaster)	*Alec Russell*	1056
Flower Bowl Invitational Stakes (Belmont)	*International Racing Photos*	290
Four Star Sales Richmond Stakes (Goodwood)	*Bill Selwyn*	188
Freephone Stanley Lincoln (Handicap) (Doncaster)	*Alec Russell*	760
Freephone Stanley Zetland Gold Cup (Handicap) (Redcar)	*Alec Russell*	443
Gainsborough Poule d'Essai des Poulains (Longchamp)	*Ed Byrne*	222
Gainsborough Poule d'Essai des Pouliches (Longchamp)	*Ed Byrne*	694
Gazelle Handicap (Belmont Park)	*International Racing Photos*	169
GNER Doncaster Cup (Doncaster)	*Alec Russell*	785
GNER Park Stakes (Doncaster)	*Alec Russell*	801
Godolphin Mile (Nad Al Sheba)	*Frank Sorge*	368
Gold Cup (Royal Ascot)	*John Crofts*	681
Golden Jubilee Stakes (Royal Ascot)	*Ed Byrne*	214
Gran Criterium (Milan)	*Enzo De Nardin*	777
Grand Prix de Saint-Cloud (Saint-Cloud)	*John Crofts*	65
Gran Premio del Jockey Club (Milan)	*Enzo De Nardin*	323
Gran Premio di Milano (Milan)	*Enzo De Nardin*	571
Grosser Bugatti Preis (Baden-Baden)	*Frank Nolting*	623
Hackney Empire Royal Lodge Stakes (Ascot)	*W. Everitt*	950
Hardwicke Stakes (Royal Ascot)	*John Crofts*	486
Hong Kong Cup (Sha Tin)	*George Selwyn*	351
Hong Kong Vase (Sha Tin)	*George Selwyn*	1067
Hopeful Stakes (Newmarket)	*John Crofts*	361
Independent Waterford Wedgwood Phoenix Stakes (the Curragh)	*Caroline Norris*	747
Ireland The Food Island Champion Stakes (Leopardstown)	*Peter Mooney*	454
Irish Breeders Foal Levy Stakes (the Curragh)	*Caroline Norris*	996
Irish Field St Leger (the Curragh)	*Peter Mooney*	1078
Iveco Daily Solario Stakes (Sandown)	*W. Everitt*	109
Jersey Stakes (Royal Ascot)	*Alec Russell*	640
Jockey Club Cup (Newmarket)	*John Crofts*	786
John Deere Breeders' Cup Turf (Santa Anita)	*Bill Selwyn*	455
John Roarty Memorial Scurry Handicap (the Curragh)	*Caroline Norris*	91
John Smith's Cup (Handicap) (York)	*Alec Russell*	357
John Smith's Northumberland Plate (Handicap) (Newcastle)	*Alec Russell*	1063
Juddmonte Beresford Stakes (the Curragh)	*Peter Mooney*	92
Juddmonte Grand Prix de Paris (Longchamp)	*John Crofts*	1071
Juddmonte International Stakes (York)	*Ed Byrne*	349
Juddmonte Lockinge Stakes (Newbury)	*John Crofts*	438
King Edward VII Stakes (Royal Ascot)	*John Crofts*	450
King George Stakes (Goodwood)	*John Crofts*	1023
King George V Stakes (Handicap) (Royal Ascot)	*John Crofts*	354
King George VI and Queen Elizabeth Diamond Stakes (Ascot)	*John Crofts*	41
King's Stand Stakes (Royal Ascot)	*Ed Byrne*	212
Kotex Rosemary Rated Stakes (Handicap) (Ascot)	*George Selwyn*	1001
ladbrokes.com Handicap (Ascot)	*George Selwyn*	965
ladbrokes.com Prestige Stakes (Handicap) (Goodwood)	*John Crofts*	265
Ladbrokes Handicap (Newmarket)	*Ed Byrne*	370
Lady O Goodwood Cup (Goodwood)	*John Crofts*	784
Lennox Stakes (Goodwood)	*John Crofts*	712
March Stakes (Goodwood)	*Ed Byrne*	371
Melrose Rated Stakes (Handicap) (York)	*John Crofts*	508
Meon Valley Stud Fillies' Mile (Ascot)	*John Crofts*	841
Michael Page International Silver Trophy Stakes (Ascot)	*W. Everitt*	1035
Millennium & Copthorne Hotels Diadem Stakes (Ascot)	*Ed Byrne*	27

Moyglare Stud Stakes (the Curragh)	*Peter Mooney*	716
NetJets Breeders' Cup Mile (Santa Anita)	*George Selwyn*	942
NetJets Prix du Moulin de Longchamp (Longchamp)	*Bertrand*	714
Norfolk Stakes (Royal Ascot)	*John Crofts*	886
Owen Brown Rockfel Stakes (Newmarket)	*Alec Russell*	173
Pattison Canadian International Stakes (Woodbine)	*Bill Selwyn*	792
Peugeot Lowther Stakes (York)	*John Crofts*	190
Peugeot Sun Chariot Stakes (Newmarket)	*Ed Byrne*	320
Philip Leverhulme Dee Stakes (Chester)	*Bill Selwyn*	545
Polypipe Flying Childers Stakes (Doncaster)	*John Crofts*	468
Premio Presidente della Repubblica (Rome)	*Garofalo Corrado*	833
Premio Roma SIS (Rome)	*Garofalo Corrado*	480
Prince of Wales's Stakes (Royal Ascot)	*Alec Russell*	709
Princess Elizabeth Stakes (sponsored by Vodafone) (Epsom)	*John Crofts*	47
Princess of Wales's UAE Equestrian and Racing Federation Stakes (Newmarket)	*John Crofts*	653
Princess Royal Willmott Dixon Stakes (Ascot)	*John Crofts*	504
Prix Daniel Wildenstein Casino Barriere de La Rochelle (Longchamp)	*John Crofts*	963
Prix d'Astarte (Deauville)	*John Crofts*	160
Prix d'Aumale Casino Barriere de Biarritz (Longchamp)	*John Crofts*	420
Prix de Diane Hermes (Chantilly)	*Bertrand*	714
Prix de l'Abbaye de Longchamp Majestic Barriere (Longchamp)	*George Selwyn*	771
Prix de la Foret (Longchamp)	*John Crofts*	334
Prix de l'Arc de Triomphe Lucien Barriere (Longchamp)	*John Crofts*	256
Prix de l'Opera Casino Barriere d'Enghien-Les-Bains (Longchamp)	*John Crofts*	1127
Prix d'Ispahan (Longchamp)	*Bertrand*	347
Prix du Cadran Casinos Barriere (Longchamp)	*John Crofts*	1097
Prix du Haras de Fresnay-Le-Buffard Jacques le Marois (Deauville)	*Bertrand*	940
Prix du Jockey Club (Chantilly)	*Ed Byrne*	254
Prix du Petit Couvert (Longchamp)	*Bertrand*	856
Prix Ganay (Longchamp)	*Bertrand*	343
Prix Gladiateur Royal Thalasso Barriere (Longchamp)	*Ed Byrne*	266
Prix Gontaut-Biron (Deauville)	*Bertrand*	186
Prix Jean-Luc Lagardere (Grand Criterium) (Longchamp)	*John Crofts*	59
Prix La Rochette (Longchamp)	*Bertrand*	286
Prix Lupin (Longchamp)	*John Crofts*	253
Prix Marcel Boussac–Criterium des Pouliches Royal Barriere Deauville (Longchamp)	*John Crofts*	276
Prix Maurice de Gheest (Deauville)	*John Crofts*	805
Prix Morny Casinos Barriere (Deauville)	*Bertrand*	1102
Prix Niel Casino Barriere d'Enghien-Les-Bains (Longchamp)	*John Crofts*	255
Prix Robert Papin (Maisons-Laffitte)	*John Crofts*	688
Prix Royal-Oak (Longchamp)	*Bertrand*	1098
Prix Saint-Alary (Longchamp)	*Bertrand*	364
Prix Thomas Bryon (Saint-Cloud)	*Bertrand*	71
Prix Vermeille Fouquet's Barriere (Longchamp)	*John Crofts*	644
Q Associates Rated Stakes (Handicap) (Newbury)	*John Crofts*	876
Queen Alexandra Stakes (Royal Ascot)	*Ed Byrne*	242
Queen Anne Stakes (Royal Ascot)	*John Crofts*	310
Queen Elizabeth II Stakes (sponsored by NetJets) (Ascot)	*John Crofts*	350
Queen Mary Stakes (Royal Ascot)	*John Crofts*	86
Queen Mother's Cup (Ladies) Handicap (York)	*Alec Russell*	968
Queen's Vase (Royal Ascot)	*Alec Russell*	921
Racing Post Trophy (Doncaster)	*John Crofts*	59
Rathbarry Stud's Barathea Finale Stakes (the Curragh)	*Peter Mooney*	563
Redcar Two-Year-Old Trophy (Redcar)	*Alec Russell*	776
Ribblesdale Stakes (Royal Ascot)	*Alec Russell*	961
R. L. Davison Pretty Polly Stakes (Newmarket)	*John Crofts*	449
Rogerthorpe Manor Hotel Handicap (Pontefract)	*Fotosport*	452
Royal & SunAlliance Handicap (York)	*Bill Selwyn*	947
Royal Hunt Cup (Handicap) (Royal Ascot)	*Alec Russell*	603
Royal Whip Stakes (the Curragh)	*Peter Mooney*	453
Sagitta 1000 Guineas Stakes (Newmarket)	*Ed Byrne*	881
Sagitta 2000 Guineas Stakes (Newmarket)	*Ed Byrne*	850

Sandringham Rated Stakes (Handicap) (Royal Ascot)	John Crofts	465
Scottish Equitable Gimcrack Stakes (York)	Ed Byrne	104
Seabiscuit St Leger Stakes (Doncaster)	Ed Byrne	155
Shadwell Stud Middle Park Stakes (Newmarket)	Ed Byrne	105
Sky Bet Cheveley Park Stakes (Newmarket)	John Crofts	190
skybet.com Stakes (Aston Park) (Newbury)	John Crofts	395
Slatch Farm Stud Flying Fillies' Stakes (Pontefract)	Alec Russell	586
Stan James Falmouth Stakes (Newmarket)	John Crofts	603
Stan James Geoffrey Freer Stakes (Newbury)	John Crofts	686
Stan James Now Online Winter Hill Stakes (Windsor)	John Crofts	574
Stanley Leisure Sprint Cup (Haydock)	Alec Russell	955
St James's Palace Stakes (Royal Ascot)	Alec Russell	1123
Sussex Stakes (Goodwood)	John Crofts	847
Tattersalls Breeders Stakes (the Curragh)	Peter Mooney	616
Tattersalls Gold Cup (the Curragh)	John Crofts	131
The Mail On Sunday/Tote Mile Final (Handicap) (Ascot)	George Selwyn	761
T Mobile Rated Stakes (Handicap) (York)	Alec Russell	913
TNT July Stakes (Newmarket)	John Crofts	719
Tote Ayr Gold Cup (Handicap) (Ayr)	Alec Russell	830
Tote Cambridgeshire (Handicap) (Newmarket)	Ed Byrne	211
Tote Cesarewitch (Handicap) (Newmarket)	George Selwyn	564
Tote Chester Cup (Handicap) (Chester)	Ed Byrne	470
Tote Dante Stakes (York)	John Crofts	611
Tote Ebor (Handicap) (York)	Alec Russell	893
Tote Exacta Mallard Stakes (Handicap) (Doncaster)	John Crofts	919
Tote Exacta Rated Stakes (Handicap) (Newmarket)	Ed Byrne	679
Tote Gold Trophy Stakes (Handicap) (Goodwood)	Ed Byrne	728
Tote International Stakes (Handicap) (Ascot)	Alec Russell	720
Tote Scoop6 Sprint (Handicap) (Lingfield)	W. Everitt	146
Tote Scoop6 Stakes (Handicap) (Sandown)	John Crofts	825
Tote Trifecta Portland (Handicap) (Doncaster)	Alec Russell	430
Tote Trifecta Stakes (Handicap) (Ascot)	John Crofts	635
Tote Trifecta Stakes (Handicap) (Goodwood)	W. Everitt	210
Tripleprint Temple Stakes (Sandown)	George Selwyn	35
Turf Classic Invitational Stakes (Belmont)	International Racing Photos	986
£200000 St Leger Yearling Stakes (Doncaster)	Alec Russell	180
UAE Derby (Nad Al Sheba)	Bill Selwyn	1074
Veuve Clicquot Vintage Stakes (Goodwood)	John Crofts	598
Victor Chandler Challenge Stakes (Newmarket)	Ed Byrne	521
Victor Chandler Nunthorpe Stakes (York)	Alec Russell	737
Vodafone Coronation Cup (Epsom)	John Crofts	1087
Vodafone 'Dash' Rated Stakes (Handicap) (Epsom)	John Crofts	84
Vodafone Derby Stakes (Epsom)	George Selwyn	547
Vodafone Derby Stakes (Epsom)	Ed Byrne	1019
Vodafone Derby Stakes (Epsom)	John Crofts	548
Vodafone Diomed Stakes (Epsom)	George Selwyn	397
Vodafone Group Handicap (Newbury)	John Crofts	663
Vodafone Live! Handicap (Epsom)	W. Everitt	513
Vodafone Nassau Stakes (Goodwood)	Ed Byrne	883
Vodafone Newbury Handicap (Epsom)	Ed Byrne	37
Vodafone Oaks (Epsom)	John Crofts	195
Vodafone Stewards' Cup (Handicap) (Goodwood)	John Crofts	770
Weatherbys Insurance Lonsdale Stakes (York)	Alec Russell	142
Weatherbys Super Sprint (Newbury)	George Selwyn	476
William Hill Great St Wilfrid Stakes (Handicap) (Ripon)	Alec Russell	448
William Hill Mile (Handicap) (Goodwood)	John Crofts	556
William Hill Trophy (Handicap) (York)	Alec Russell	271
Willie Park Trophy Stakes (Musselburgh)	John Grossick	664
Willmott Dixon Cornwallis Stakes (Ascot)	John Crofts	617
Wokingham Stakes (Handicap) (Royal Ascot)	Alec Russell	361
Wolferton Rated Stakes (Handicap) (Royal Ascot)	John Crofts	495

ACT ONE

grey 1999 by IN THE WINGS - SUMMER SONNET by Baillamont

GROUP 1 WINNER AT 2 AND 3

RACE RECORD

At 2 years, 2001, ran 3, won 3:

WON	Criterium International **Gr.1**, Saint-Cloud, 8f
	by ¼l from LANDSEER (subsequent Classic winner)
WON	Prix Thomas Bryon **Gr.3**, Saint-Cloud, 8f
WON	Prix du Val Profond, Chantilly, 8f

At 3 years, 2002, ran 3, won 2; placed 1:

WON	Prix Lupin **Gr.1**, Longchamp,10½f
WON	Prix Greffulhe **Gr.2**, Longchamp, 10½f
2nd	Prix du Jockey Club **Gr.1**, Chantilly, 12f, beaten 1½l
	by SULAMANI, and 5l clear of the third

Highest Rated French-trained Two Year Old   **Timeform: 124**

COMPTON PLACE

chesnut 1994 by INDIAN RIDGE - NOSEY by Nebbiolo

CHAMPION EUROPEAN
3-Y-O SPRINTER

CHAMPION 2nd SEASON SIRE
IN EUROPE IN 2003
(Races won)

Standing at:
Whitsbury Manor Stud
Fee: £5,000 October 1st
Limited to 100 Mares

C. Oakshott,
Whitsbury Manor Stud,
Fordingbridge, SP6 3QP
Telephone: 01725 - 518254
Fax: 01725 - 518503

Enquiries to:
LONDON THOROUGHBRED
SERVICES LTD.,
Biddlesgate Farm, Nr Cranborne,
Dorset BH21 5RS.
Telephone: 01725 - 517711.
Fax: 01725 - 517833.
email: lts@lts-uk.com
Website: www.lts-uk.com

LTS

NB ONLY BRITISH-BASED STALLIONS' PROGENY CAN BE ELIGIBLE FOR BHB OWNERS' PRIZES

GENEROUS

chesnut 1988 by Caerleon - Doff The Derby by Master Derby

TIMEFORM's EUROPEAN
CHAMPION OF THE DECADE - Rated **139**
Group 1 Winner at 2 - European Champion at 3

From his first 4 European crops sire of:-

◆ **27** Black Type Winners inc. **15** Group Winners
◆ **14%** Black Type Winners to Foals
◆ **19%** Black Type Performers to Foals

Broodmare Sire of GOLAN (Gr.1), **HIGH ACCOLADE** (Gr.2)

*His first Plantation-conceived foals <u>averaged</u>
£60,765 at Tattersalls and Goffs in 2003*

OLDEN TIMES

bay 1998 by DARSHAAN - GARAH by Ajdal

GR.1 WINNING SON OF DARSHAAN

defeated **3 Classic Winners** and
13 other Gr.1 Winners

Performed consistently at the highest level from **8F - 10F**

Timeform Racehorses of 2002 - Rated **121**

A SPEEDY SON OF DARSHAAN
FOR YOUR NORTHERN DANCER LINE MARES

PURSUIT OF LOVE

bay 1989 by GROOM DANCER - DANCE QUEST by Green Dancer

DUAL CHAMPION 2YO
AND GROUP 1 SIRE

21 Black Type performers including
CATCHASCATCHCAN (Gr.1)

Sire of the winners of **515 races** and **over £5.6 million**

In 2003 sire of the winners of 75 races
63% Winners to runners (first 7 crops)

ROBELLINO

bay 1979 by ROBERTO - ISOBELLINE by Pronto

PROVEN CLASSIC SIRE

CLASSIC PARK	Airlie/Coolmore Irish 1000 Gns **Gr.1**
MISTER BAILEYS	2000 Gns **Gr.1**
ROBERTICO	Deutsches Derby **Gr.1**
REBELLINE	Tattersalls Gold Cup **Gr.1**
ROYAL REBEL	Ascot Gold Cup **Gr.1** (twice)

From the family of **JOHANNESBURG**, **MINARDI**, **TALE OF THE CAT** and **PULPIT**

EXCELLENT FERTILITY

SELKIRK LANWADES

chesnut 1988 by SHARPEN UP - ANNIE EDGE by Nebbiolo

DUAL EUROPEAN CHAMPION MILER AND CLASSIC SIRE

WINCE	1000 Guineas **Gr.1**
RED BLOOM	Meon Valley Stud Fillies Mile **Gr.1 at 2 in 2003**
LEADERSHIP	Gran Premio di Milano **Gr.1 in 2003**
SULK	Prix Marcel Boussac **Gr.1 at 2**
FIELD OF HOPE	Prix de la Foret **Gr.1**
SQUEAK	Beverly Hills H'cap **Gr.1,** Matriarch Stakes **Gr.1**
INDEPENDENCE	Sun Chariot Stakes **Gr.2**
FAVOURABLE TERMS	Matron Stakes **Gr.2 in 2003**
HIGHDOWN	Prix Guillaume d'Ornano **Gr.2**

THE CHAMPION BRITISH-BASED SIRE IN EUROPE IN 2003

Standing at: **Lanwades Stud**
Fee: **£30,000 October 1st**

Kirsten Rausing,
Lanwades Stud, Moulton,
Suffolk, CB8 8QS.
Telephone: 01638 - 750222.
Fax: 01638 - 751186.
email: lanwades@msn.com
Website: www.lanwades.com

Enquiries to:
**LONDON THOROUGHBRED
SERVICES LTD.,**
Biddlesgate Farm,
Nr Cranborne, Dorset BH21 5RS.
Telephone: 01725 - 517711.
Fax: 01725 - 517833.
email: lts@lts-uk.com
Website: www.lts-uk.com

LTS

NB ONLY BRITISH-BASED STALLIONS' PROGENY CAN BE ELIGIBLE FOR BHB OWNERS' PRIZES

SUPERIOR PREMIUM

brown 1994 by FORZANDO - DEVIL'S DIRGE by Song

ROYAL ASCOT GR.2 WINNING SPRINTER

By **FORZANDO** - Prolific Sire of winners including
**EASYCALL (Sire), GREAT DEEDS, HIGH PREMIUM,
MISTERIOSO, PHILIDOR (Sire), POOL MUSIC,
PUNCH N'RUN, UP AND AT 'EM (Sire),
VINTAGE PREMIUM, ZANAY**

GROUP WINNING SON OF A
LEADING 2-Y-O SIRE

A Tradition of Excellence...

Over the years, **Airlie Stud** has built up an enviable reputation as a leading thoroughbred nursery. In fact, the stud has produced the winners of **11 Group 1** races in recent years, a record which must rank it amongst the top breeders in the world.

Airlie also has a reputation for standing commercial stallions at competitive fees, and, in **DOCKSIDER**, the tradition continues. A multiple Group winner by Diesis (*sire of Three Valleys in 2003*), **Docksider** was one of the best international milers of his generation, winning in the UK, Germany and Hong Kong, and just getting touched off in the **Gr.1 Breeders' Cup Mile** in the USA.

Being from the family of Champion sires **Sadler's Wells**, **Nureyev** and **Fairy King**, he certainly has the pedigree to succeed, and had already sired **12 individual winners** from his first crop by the end of January. He represents tremendous value at his 2004 fee of €6,000 (1st Oct).

Finally, just a reminder that **Airlie** can offer breeders high quality boarding facilities for mares, and sales preparation for yearlings.

Airlie

AIRLIE STUD, Grangewilliam, Maynooth, Co Kildare.
Contact: Anthony Rogers. Tel: +353 (0)1 6286336 or 6286038 (yard).
Mobile: 087 2450438. Fax: +353 (0)1 6286674.
e-mail: info@airlie-stud.com web site: www.airlie-stud.com

THE CHAMPIONS

Timeform's 'Racehorses' series stretches back to 1948 when the first prototype Annual—the 'Timeform Supplement'—was produced covering the 1947 season. The selecting of a 'horse of the year' began in the 'sixties.

Horse of the Year

The title has usually been awarded to the highest rated horse, except in 1969 (when Habitat was rated higher at 134), 1984 (El Gran Senor 136), 1985 (Slip Anchor 136) and 2003 (Hawk Wing 136).

1960	Charlottesville	**135**
	Floribunda	**135**
1961	Molvedo	**137**
1962	Match	**135**
1963	Exbury	**138**
1964	Relko	**136**
1965	Sea Bird	**145**
1966	Danseur	**134**
1967	Petingo	**135**
1968	Vaguely Noble	**140**
1969	Levmoss	**133**
1970	Nijinsky	**138**
1971	Brigadier Gerard	**141**
	Mill Reef	**141**
1972	Brigadier Gerard	**144**
1973	Apalachee	**137**
	Rheingold	**137**
1974	Allez France	**136**
1975	Grundy	**137**
1976	Youth	**135**
1977	Alleged	**137**
1978	Alleged	**138**
1979	Troy	**137**
1980	Moorestyle	**137**
1981	Shergar	**140**
1982	Ardross	**134**
1983	Habibti	**136**

1984	Provideo	**112**
1985	Pebbles	**135**
1986	Dancing Brave	**140**
1987	Reference Point	**139**
1988	Warning	**136**
1989	Zilzal	**137**
1990	Dayjur	**137**
1991	Generous	**139**
1992	St Jovite	**135**
1993	Opera House	**131**
1994	Celtic Swing	**138**
1995	Lammtarra	**134**
1996	Mark of Esteem	**137**
1997	Peintre Celebre	**137**
1998	Intikhab	**135**
1999	Daylami	**138**
2000	Dubai Millennium	**140**
2001	Sakhee	**136**
2002	Rock of Gibraltar	**133**
2003	Falbrav	**133**

Best Two-Year-Old Colt

1960	Floribunda	**135**	1981	Wind And Wuthering	**132**
1961	Abdos	**134 p**	1982	Diesis	**133**
1962	Le Mesnil	**131 ?**	1983	El Gran Senor	**131**
1963	Santa Claus	**133 +**	1984	Kala Dancer	**129**
	Showdown	**133**	1985	Huntingdale	**132**
1964	Grey Dawn	**132**	1986	Reference Point	**132**
1965	Soleil	**133**	1987	Warning	**127 p**
	Young Emperor	**133**	1988	Prince of Dance	**128**
1966	Bold Lad (Ire)	**133**		Scenic	**128**
1967	Petingo	**135**	1989	Be My Chief	**123 p**
1968	Ribofilio	**130**	1990	Hector Protector	**122 p**
	Yelapa	**130**	1991	Arazi	**135**
1969	Nijinsky	**131**	1992	Armiger	**131 p**
1970	My Swallow	**134**	1993	Grand Lodge	**120 p**
1971	Deep Diver	**134**	1994	Celtic Swing	**138**
1972	Simbir	**130**	1995	Alhaarth	**126 p**
	Targowice	**130**	1996	Bahhare	**122 p**
1973	Apalachee	**137**		Revoque	**122 p**
1974	Grundy	**134**	1997	Xaar	**132**
1975	Manado	**130**	1998	Mujahid	**125 p**
1976	Blushing Groom	**131**	1999	Distant Music	**121 p**
1977	Try My Best	**130 p**	2000	Nayef	**123 p**
1978	Tromos	**134**	2001	Johannesburg	**127**
1979	Monteverdi	**129**	2002	Oasis Dream	**122**
1980	Storm Bird	**134**	2003	Bago	**121 p**

Best Two-Year-Old Filly

Year	Horse	Rating	Year	Horse	Rating
1960	Kathy Too	131	1983	Treizieme	121
1961	La Tendresse	135	1984	Triptych	125
1962	Hula Dancer	133	1985	Femme Elite	124
1963	Texanita	128	1986	Forest Flower	127
1964	Fall In Love	126	1987	Ravinella	121 p
1965	Soft Angels	124	1988	Pass The Peace	116 p
1966	Silver Cloud	125		Tessla	116 p
1967	Sovereign	129	1989	Negligent	118 p
1968	Saraca	125	1990	Shadayid	117 p
1969	Mange Tout	125	1991	Midnight Air	111 p
1970	Cawston's Pride	131	1992	Sayyedati	116 p
1971	First Bloom	129	1993	Lemon Souffle	115
1972	Jacinth	133	1994	Gay Gallanta	112
1973	Hippodamia	130	1995	Blue Duster	116 p
1974	Broadway Dancer	131	1996	Dazzle	116 d
1975	Theia	128		Red Camellia	116
1976	Cloonlara	130	1997	Embassy	114
1977	Cherry Hinton	125	1998	Bint Allayl	114 p
1978	Sigy	132	1999	Morning Pride	113 p
1979	Aryenne	120	2000	Superstar Leo	114
1980	Marwell	124	2001	Queen's Logic	125
1981	Circus Ring	122	2002	Six Perfections	120 p
1982	Ma Biche	123	2003	Attraction	118

Best Sprinter

Year	Horse	Rating	Year	Horse	Rating
1960	Bleep Bleep	134	1980	Moorestyle	137
1961	Floribunda	136	1981	Marwell	133
1962	Gay Mairi	131	1982	Sharpo	130
	Secret Step	131	1983	Habibti	136
1963	Matatina	132	1984	Chief Singer	131
1964	Althrey Don	130	1985	Never So Bold	135
1965	Majority Blue	126	1986	Last Tycoon	131
	Port Merion	126	1987	Ajdal	130
1966	Caterina	124	1988	Soviet Star	128
1967	Be Friendly	126	1989	Cadeaux Genereux	131
1968	Be Friendly	130	1990	Dayjur	137
	So Blessed	130	1991	Polish Patriot	128
1969	Song	132	1992	Sheikh Albadou	128
1970	Amber Rama	133	1993	Lochsong	129
	Balidar	133	1994	Lochsong	129
	Huntercombe	133	1995	Lake Coniston	131
1971	Joshua	129	1996	Anabaa	130
1972	Deep Diver	134	1997	Elnadim	126 p
1973	Sandford Lad	133	1998	Elnadim	128
1974	Saritamer	130	1999	Stravinsky	133
1975	Flirting Around	134	2000	Namid	128
1976	Lochnager	132	2001	Mozart	131
1977	Gentilhombre	131	2002	Kyllachy	129
1978	Solinus	130	2003	Oasis Dream	129
1979	Thatching	131			

Best Miler

Year	Horse	Rating	Year	Horse	Rating
1960	Martial	131	1971	Brigadier Gerard	141
1961	Petite Etoile	131	1972	Brigadier Gerard	144
1962	Romulus	129	1973	Thatch	136
1963	Hula Dancer	133	1974	Nonoalco	131
1964	Baldric	131	1975	Bolkonski	134
1965	Carlemont	132	1976	Wollow	132
1966	Silver Shark	129	1977	Blushing Groom	131
1967	Reform	132	1978	Homing	130
1968	Sir Ivor	135	1979	Kris	135
1969	Habitat	134	1980	Known Fact	135
1970	Nijinsky	138	1981	Northjet	136

1982	Green Forest	134	1993	Zafonic	130
1983	Luth Enchantee	130	1994	Barathea	127
1984	El Gran Senor	136	1995	Pennekamp	130
1985	Shadeed	135	1996	Mark of Esteem	137
1986	Dancing Brave	140	1997	Spinning World	130
1987	Miesque	131	1998	Intikhab	135
1988	Warning	136	1999	Dubai Millennium	132
1989	Zilzal	137	2000	King's Best	132
1990	Markofdistinction	130	2001	Medicean	128
	Royal Academy	130		Slickly	128
1991	Selkirk	129	2002	Rock of Gibraltar	133
1992	Lahib	129	2003	Hawk Wing	136
	Selkirk	129			

Best Middle-Distance Horse

1960	Charlottesville	135	1984	Sagace	135
1961	Molvedo	137		Teenoso	135
1962	Match	135	1985	Slip Anchor	136
1963	Exbury	138	1986	Dancing Brave	140
1964	Relko	136	1987	Reference Point	139
1965	Sea Bird	145	1988	Mtoto	134
1966	Nelcius	133		Tony Bin	134
1967	Busted	134	1989	Old Vic	136
1968	Vaguely Noble	140	1990	Saumarez	132
1969	Levmoss	133	1991	Generous	139
1970	Nijinsky	138	1992	St Jovite	135
1971	Mill Reef	141	1993	Opera House	131
1972	Mill Reef	141	1994	Balanchine	131
1973	Rheingold	137	1995	Lammtarra	134
1974	Allez France	136	1996	Helissio	136
1975	Grundy	137	1997	Peintre Celebre	137
1976	Youth	135	1998	Swain	132
1977	Alleged	137	1999	Daylami	138
1978	Alleged	138	2000	Dubai Millennium	140
1979	Troy	137	2001	Sakhee	136
1980	Argument	133	2002	High Chaparral	130
1981	Shergar	140		Sulamani	130
1982	Ardross	134	2003	Alamshar	133
	Assert	134		Dalakhani	133
1983	Shareef Dancer	135		Falbrav	133

Best Stayer/Best Performance In A Staying Race

1960	Charlottesville	135		Le Moss	131
1961	Pandofell	132	1980	Le Moss	135
	St Paddy	132	1981	Ardross	131
1962	Hethersett	134	1982	Ardross	134
1963	Ragusa	137	1983	Little Wolf	127
1964	Prince Royal	134	1984	Commanche Run	129
1965	Reliance	137	1985	Lanfranco	123
1966	Danseur	134		Phardante	123
1967	Ribocco	129	1986	Moon Madness	128
1968	Dhaudevi	127	1987	Reference Point	139
	Samos	127	1988	Minster Son	130
1969	Levmoss	133	1989	Michelozzo	127 p
1970	Hallez	130	1990	Snurge	130
	Roll of Honour	130	1991	Toulon	125
1971	Ramsin	130	1992	Mashaallah	123
1972	Rock Roi	127	1993	Vintage Crop	125
1973	Parnell	130	1994	Moonax	121
1974	Sagaro	131		Vintage Crop	121
1975	Bruni	132	1995	Double Trigger	122
1976	Crow	131 *		Moonax	122
1977	Alleged	135 *		Strategic Choice	122
1978	Buckskin	133	1996	Classic Cliche	124 *
1979	Buckskin	131		Oscar Schindler	124 *

	Shantou	124		2000	Kayf Tara	130
1997	Classic Cliche	126		2001	Milan	129
1998	Kayf Tara	126		2002	Vinnie Roe	126
1999	Kayf Tara	130		2003	Vinnie Roe	125

achieved higher rating at middle distances

Best Three-Year-Old Colt

1960	Charlottesville	135		1981	Shergar	140
1961	Molvedo	137		1982	Assert	134
1962	Arctic Storm	134			Green Forest	134
	Hethersett	134		1983	Shareef Dancer	135
1963	Ragusa	137		1984	El Gran Senor	136
1964	Prince Royal	134		1985	Slip Anchor	136
1965	Sea Bird	145		1986	Dancing Brave	140
1966	Danseur	134		1987	Reference Point	139
1967	Reform	132		1988	Warning	136
1968	Vaguely Noble	140		1989	Zilzal	137
1969	Habitat	134		1990	Dayjur	137
1970	Nijinsky	138		1991	Generous	139
1971	Brigadier Gerard	141		1992	St Jovite	135
	Mill Reef	141		1993	Zafonic	130
1972	Deep Diver	134		1994	Tikkanen	130
	Sallust	134		1995	Lammtarra	134
1973	Thatch	136		1996	Mark of Esteem	137
1974	Caracolero	131		1997	Peintre Celebre	137
	Dankaro	131		1998	Desert Prince	130
	Nonoalco	131			High-Rise	130
	Sagaro	131		1999	Montjeu	137
1975	Grundy	137		2000	Sinndar	134
1976	Youth	135		2001	Galileo	134
1977	Alleged	137		2002	Rock of Gibraltar	133
1978	Ile de Bourbon	133		2003	Alamshar	133
1979	Troy	137			Dalakhani	133
1980	Moorestyle	137				

Best Three-Year-Old Filly

1960	Marguerite Vernaut	129			Time Charter	131
1961	Crisper	127		1983	Habibti	136
	Sweet Solera	127		1984	Northern Trick	131
1962	Gay Mairi	131		1985	Oh So Sharp	131
	Secret Step	131		1986	Darara	129
1963	Hula Dancer	133			Sonic Lady	129
	Noblesse	133		1987	Indian Skimmer	132
1964	La Bamba	129		1988	Diminuendo	126
1965	Aunt Edith	128		1989	Behera	129
1966	Caterina	124			Sierra Roberta	129
1967	Casaque Grise	126		1990	Salsabil	130
1968	Roseliere	127		1991	Magic Night	128
1969	Flossy	129		1992	User Friendly	128
1970	Highest Hopes	129		1993	Intrepidity	124
	Miss Dan	129		1994	Balanchine	131
1971	Pistol Packer	133		1995	Ridgewood Pearl	125
1972	San San	133		1996	Bosra Sham	132
1973	Allez France	132		1997	Borgia	124
	Dahlia	132		1998	Cape Verdi	126
1974	Comtesse de Loir	131		1999	Ramruma	123
1975	Rose Bowl	133		2000	Egyptband	128
1976	Pawneese	131		2001	Banks Hill	128
1977	Dunfermline	133		2002	Bright Sky	124
1978	Swiss Maid	129		2003	Six Perfections	124
1979	Three Troikas	133				
1980	Detroit	131				
1981	Marwell	133				
1982	Akiyda	131				

Best Older Male

Year	Horse	Rating	Year	Horse	Rating
1960	Bleep-Bleep	134	1983	Diamond Shoal	130
1961	Pandofell	132	1984	Sagace	134
	St Paddy	132		Teenoso	134
1962	Match	135	1985	Rainbow Quest	134
1963	Exbury	138		Sagace	134
1964	Relko	136	1986	Shardari	134
1965	Free Ride	129	1987	Mtoto	134
	Indiana	129	1988	Mtoto	134
1966	Diatome	132		Tony Bin	134
1967	Busted	134	1989	Carroll House	132
1968	Royal Palace	131	1990	Markofdistinction	130
1969	Levmoss	133		Old Vic	130
1970	Balidar	133	1991	Epervier Bleu	129
1971	Caro	133	1992	Pistolet Bleu	133
1972	Brigadier Gerard	144	1993	Opera House	131
1973	Rheingold	137	1994	Barathea	127
1974	Admetus	133		Hernando	127
	Margouillat	133	1995	Freedom Cry	132
1975	Bustino	136	1996	Halling	133
1976	Trepan	133 ?	1997	Pilsudski	134
	Lochnager	132		Swain	134
1977	Balmerino	133	1998	Intikhab	135
	Sagaro	133	1999	Daylami	138
1978	Alleged	138	2000	Dubai Millennium	140
1979	Ile de Bourbon	133	2001	Sakhee	136
1980	Le Moss	135	2002	Keltos	132
1981	Northjet	136	2003	Hawk Wing	136
1982	Ardross	134			

Best Older Female

Year	Horse	Rating	Year	Horse	Rating
1960	Petite Etoile	134	1988	Indian Skimmer	133
1961	Petite Etoile	131		Miesque	133
1962	Crisper	126	1989	Gabina	121
1963	Secret Step	128		Indian Skimmer	121
1964	Matatina	124		Royal Touch	121
1965	Astaria	123	1990	Lady Winner	121
1966	Aunt Edith	126		Ode	121
1967	Parthian Glance	119	1991	Miss Alleged	125
1968	Bamboozle	114	1992	Kooyonga	125
	Park Top	114	1993	Lochsong	129
	Secret Ray	114	1994	Lochsong	129
1969	Park Top	131	1995	Hever Golf Rose	123
1970	Park Top	129	1996	Timarida	125
1971	Miss Dan	124	1997	Bosra Sham	130
1972	Abergwaun	128	1998	One So Wonderful	121
1973	Attica Meli	125		Seeking The Pearl	121
1974	Allez France	136	1999	Alborada	122
1975	Lianga	133		Susu	122
1976	Ivanjica	132	2000	Shiva	127
1977	Flying Water	132	2001	Pipalong	121
1978	Sanedtki	129	2002	Banks Hill	126
	Trillion	129	2003	Islington	124
1979	Trillion	124			
1980	Three Troikas	128			
1981	Gold River	132			
1982	April Run	130			
1983	All Along	134			
1984	Cormorant Wood	130			
1985	Pebbles	135			
1986	Triptych	132			
1987	Triptych	133			